CHILTON®

FORD
SERVICE MANUAL
2008 EDITION
VOLUME II

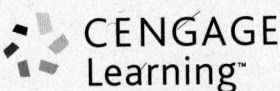

CENGAGE
Learning™

Australia • Brazil • Japan • Korea • Mexico • Singapore • Spain • United Kingdom • United States

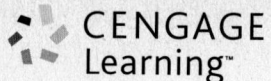
CENGAGE
Learning™

CHILTON®
Ford Service Manual
2008 Edition
Volume II

Vice President,
Technology Professional Business Unit:
Gregory L. Clayton

Publisher,
Technology Professional Business Unit:
David Koontz

Director of Marketing:
Beth A. Lutz

Production Director:
Patty Stephan

Editorial Assistant:
Jason Yager

Production Manager:
Andrew Crouth

Marketing Specialist:
Jennifer Stall

Marketing Assistant:
Rachael Conover

Publishing Coordinator:
Paula Baillie

Sr. Content Project Manager:
Elizabeth C. Hough

Managing Editor:
Terry L. Blomquist

Editors:
Dennis Bailley
Tim Crain
Scott Critchfield
Eugene F. Hannon Jr.
Tom Mellon
Kyla Nyjordet
Christine Sheeky

Graphical Designer:
Melinda Possinger

For more information contact:
Cengage Learning
Executive Woods
5 Maxwell Drive, PO Box 8007,
Clifton Park, NY 12065-8007
Visit us at **www.chiltononline.com**
For more learning solutions, visit **www.cengage.com**
For permission to use material from
the text or product, contact us by
Tel. (800) 730-2214
Fax (800) 730-2215
www.cengage.com/permissions

Cengage Learning products are represented in Canada by Nelson Education, Ltd.

ISBN-13 : 978-1-4283-2210-3
ISBN-10 : 1-4283-2210-8
ISSN: 1939-621X

NOTICE TO THE READER

Publisher does not warrant or guarantee any of the products described herein or perform any independent analysis in connection with any of the product information contained herein. Publisher does not assume, and expressly disclaims, any obligation to obtain and include information other than that provided to it by the manufacturer.

The reader is expressly warned to consider and adopt all safety precautions that might be indicated by the activities herein and to avoid all potential hazards. By following the instructions contained herein, the reader willingly assumes all risks in connection with such instructions.

The publisher makes no representation or warranties of any kind, including but not limited to, the warranties of fitness for particular purpose or merchantability, nor are any such representations implied with respect to the material set forth herein, and the publisher takes no responsibility with respect to such material. The publisher shall not be liable for any special, consequential, or exemplary damages resulting, in whole or part, from the readers' use of, or reliance upon, this material.

Printed in the United States of America
1 2 3 4 5 xx12 11 10 09 08 07

Table of Contents

Model Index

USING THIS INFORMATION

Organization

To find where a particular model section or procedure is located, look in the Table of Contents. Main topics are listed with the page number on which they may be found. Following the main topics is an alphabetical listing of all of the procedures within the section and their page numbers.

Manufacturer and Model Coverage

This product covers 2005–2008 Ford Motor Company models that are produced in sufficient quantities to warrant coverage, and which have technical content available from the vehicle manufacturers before our publication date. Although this information is as complete as possible at the time of publication, some manufacturers may make changes which cannot be included here. While striving for total accuracy, the publisher cannot assume responsibility for any errors, changes, or omissions that may occur in the compilation of this data.

Part Numbers & Special Tools

Part numbers and special tools are recommended by the publisher and vehicle manufacturer to perform specific jobs. Before substituting any part or tool for the one recommended, you must be completely satisfied that neither your personal safety, nor the performance of the vehicle will be endangered.

ACKNOWLEDGEMENT

This product contains material that is reproduced and distributed under license from Ford Motor Company. No further reproduction or distribution of the Ford Motor Company material is allowed without express written permission from Ford Motor Company.

PRECAUTIONS

Before servicing any vehicle, please be sure to read all of the following precautions, which deal with personal safety, prevention of component damage, and important points to take into consideration when servicing a motor vehicle:

- Always wear safety glasses or goggles when drilling, cutting, grinding or prying.
- Steel-toed work shoes should be worn when working with heavy parts. Pockets should not be used for carrying tools. A slip or fall can drive a screwdriver into your body.
- Work surfaces, including tools and the floor should be kept clean of grease, oil or other slippery material.
- When working around moving parts, don't wear loose clothing. Long hair should be tied back under a hat or cap, or in a hair net.
- Always use tools only for the purpose for which they were designed. Never pry with a screwdriver.
- Keep a fire extinguisher and first aid kit handy.
- Always properly support the vehicle with approved stands or lift.
- Always have adequate ventilation when working with chemicals or hazardous material.
- Carbon monoxide is colorless, odorless and dangerous. If it is necessary to operate the engine with vehicle in a closed area such as a garage, always use an exhaust collector to vent the exhaust gases outside the closed area.
- When draining coolant, keep in mind that small children and some pets are attracted by ethylene glycol antifreeze, and are quite likely to drink any left in an open container, or in puddles on the ground. This will prove fatal in sufficient quantity. Always drain the coolant into a sealable container.
- To avoid personal injury, do not remove the coolant pressure relief cap while the engine is operating or hot. The cooling system is under pressure; steam and hot liquid can come out forcefully when the cap is loosened slightly. Failure to follow these instructions may result in personal injury. The coolant must be recovered in a suitable, clean container for reuse. If the coolant is contaminated it must be recycled or disposed of correctly.
- When carrying out maintenance on the starting system be aware that heavy gauge leads are connected directly to the battery. Make sure the protective caps are in place when maintenance is completed. Failure to follow these instructions may result in personal injury.
- Do not remove any part of the engine emission control system. Operating the engine without the engine emission control system will reduce fuel economy and engine ventilation. This will weaken engine performance and shorten engine life. It is also a violation of Federal law.
- Due to environmental concerns, when the air conditioning system is drained, the refrigerant must be collected using refrigerant recovery/recycling equipment. Federal law requires that refrigerant be recovered into appropriate recovery equipment and the process be conducted by qualified technicians who have been certified by an approved organization, such as MACS, ASI, etc. Use of a recovery machine dedicated to the appropriate refrigerant is necessary to reduce the possibility of oil and refrigerant incompatibility concerns. Refer to the instructions provided by the equipment manufacturer when removing refrigerant from or charging the air conditioning system.
- Always disconnect the battery ground when working on or around the electrical system.
- Batteries contain sulfuric acid. Avoid contact with skin, eyes, or clothing. Also, shield your eyes when working near batteries to protect against possible splashing of the acid solution. In case of acid contact with skin or eyes, flush immediately with water for a minimum of 15 minutes and get prompt medical attention. If acid is swallowed, call a physician immediately. Failure to follow these instructions may result in personal injury.
- Batteries normally produce explosive gases. Therefore, do not allow flames, sparks or lighted substances to come near the battery. When charging or working near a battery, always shield your face and protect your eyes. Always provide ventilation. Failure to follow these instructions may result in personal injury.
- When lifting a battery, excessive pressure on the end walls could cause acid to spew through the vent caps, resulting in personal injury, damage to the vehicle or battery. Lift with a battery carrier or with your hands on opposite corners. Failure to follow these instructions may result in personal injury.
- Observe all applicable safety precautions when working around fuel. Whenever

servicing the fuel system, always work in a well-ventilated area. Do not allow fuel spray or vapors to come in contact with a spark, open flame, or excessive heat (a hot drop light, for example). Keep a dry chemical fire extinguisher near the work area. Always keep fuel in a container specifically designed for fuel storage; also, always properly seal fuel containers to avoid the possibility of fire or explosion. Do not smoke or carry lighted tobacco or open flame of any type when working on or near any fuel-related components.

• Fuel injection systems often remain pressurized, even after the engine has been turned OFF. The fuel system pressure must be relieved before disconnecting any fuel lines. Failure to do so may result in fire and/or personal injury.

• The evaporative emissions system contains fuel vapor and condensed fuel vapor. Although not present in large quantities, it still presents the danger of explosion or fire. Disconnect the battery ground cable from the battery to minimize the possibility of an electrical spark occurring, possibly causing a fire or explosion if fuel vapor or liquid fuel is present in the area. Failure to follow these instructions can result in personal injury.

• The EPA warns that prolonged contact with used engine oil may cause a number of skin disorders, including cancer! You should make every effort to minimize your exposure to used engine oil. Protective gloves should be worn when changing oil. Wash your hands and any other exposed skin areas as soon as possible after exposure to used engine oil. Soap and water, or waterless hand cleaner should be used.

• Some vehicles are equipped with an air bag system, often referred to as a Supple-mental Restraint System (SRS) or Supplemental Inflatable Restraint (SIR) system. The system must be disabled before performing service on or around system components, steering column, instrument panel components, wiring and sensors. Failure to follow safety and disabling procedures could result in accidental air bag deployment, possible personal injury and unnecessary system repairs.

• Always wear safety goggles when working with, or around, the air bag system. When carrying a non-deployed air bag, be sure the bag and trim cover are pointed away from your body. When placing a non-deployed air bag on a work surface, always face the bag and trim cover upward, away from the surface. This will reduce the motion of the module if it is accidentally deployed.

• Electronic modules are sensitive to electrical charges. The ABS module can be damaged if exposed to these charges.

• Brake pads and shoes may contain asbestos, which has been determined to be a cancer-causing agent. Never clean brake surfaces with compressed air. Avoid inhaling brake dust. Clean all brake surfaces with a commercially available brake cleaning fluid.

• When replacing brake pads, shoes, discs or drums, replace them as complete axle sets.

• When servicing drum brakes, disassemble and assemble one side at a time, leaving the remaining side intact for reference.

• Brake fluid often contains polyglycol ethers and polyglycols. Avoid contact with the eyes and wash your hands thoroughly after handling brake fluid. If you do get brake fluid in your eyes, flush your eyes with clean, running water for 15 minutes. If eye irritation persists, or if you have taken brake fluid internally, immediately seek medical assistance.

• Clean, high quality brake fluid from a sealed container is essential to the safe and proper operation of the brake system. You should always buy the correct type of brake fluid for your vehicle. If the brake fluid becomes contaminated, completely flush the system with new fluid. Never reuse any brake fluid. Any brake fluid that is removed from the system should be discarded. Also, do not allow any brake fluid to come in contact with a painted or plastic surface; it will damage the paint.

• Never operate the engine without the proper amount and type of engine oil; doing so will result in severe engine damage.

• Timing belt maintenance is extremely important! Many models utilize an interference-type, non-freewheeling engine. If the timing belt breaks, the valves in the cylinder head may strike the pistons, causing potentially serious (also time-consuming and expensive) engine damage.

• Disconnecting the negative battery cable on some vehicles may interfere with the functions of the on-board computer system (s) and may require the computer to undergo a relearning process once the negative battery cable is reconnected.

• Steering and suspension fasteners are critical parts because they affect performance of vital components and systems and their failure can result in major service expense. They must be replaced with the same grade or part number or an equivalent part if replacement is necessary. Do not use a replacement part of lesser quality or substitute design. Torque values must be used as specified during reassembly to ensure proper retention of these parts.

FORD AND LINCOLN

Excursion • Expedition • Navigator

SPECIFICATIONS AND MAINTENANCE CHARTS

ENGINE AND VEHICLE IDENTIFICATION

		Engine							Model Year	
Code ①	Liters (cc)	Cu. In.	Cyl.	Fuel Sys.	Type	Eng. Mfg.		Code ②	Year	
S	6.8 (6802)	415	10	MFI	SOHC	Ford		5	2005	
L	5.4 (5409)	330	8	EFI	SOHC	Ford		6	2006	
P	6.0 (5999)	365	8	DI ③	SOHC	Ford		7	2007	
5	5.4 (5409)	330	8	EFI	SOHC	Ford				

EFI: Electronic Fuel Injection

SOHC: Single Overhead Camshaft

① 8th digit of the Vehicle Identification Number (VIN)

② 10th digit of the Vehicle Identification Number (VIN)

③ Turbo

22086_EXPD_C0001

GENERAL ENGINE SPECIFICATIONS

Year	Model	Engine Displacement Liters (VIN)	Net Horsepower @ rpm	Net Torque @ rpm (ft. lbs.)	Bore x Stroke (in.)	Compression Ratio	Oil Pressure @ rpm
2005	Excursion	5.4 (L)	235@4250	330@3000	3.55X4.17	9.0:1	40-75@2000
		6.8 (S)	265@4250	410@2750	4.09X4.17	9.0:1	40-75@2000
		6.0 (P)	325@3300	560@2000	3.74x4.13	18.0:1	24@1200
	Expedition	5.4 (5)	300@5000	365@3750	3.55X4.17	9.8:1	75@2000
	Navigator	5.4 (5)	300@5000	365@3750	3.55X4.17	9.8:1	75@2000
2006	Expedition	5.4 (5)	300@5000	365@3750	3.55X4.17	9.8:1	75@2000
	Navigator	5.4 (5)	300@5000	365@3750	3.55X4.17	9.8:1	75@2000
2007	Expedition	5.4 (5)	300@5000	365@3750	3.55X4.17	9.8:1	75@2000
	Navigator	5.4 (5)	300@5000	365@3750	3.55X4.17	9.8:1	75@2000

22086_EXPD_C0002

GASOLINE ENGINE TUNE-UP SPECIFICATIONS

Year	Engine Displacement Liters	Engine ID/VIN	Spark Plug Gap (in.)	Ignition Timing (deg.) ① MT	Ignition Timing (deg.) ① AT	Fuel Pump (psi) ①	Idle Speed (rpm) MT	Idle Speed (rpm) AT	Valve Clearance In.	Valve Clearance Ex.
2005	5.4	L	0.052-0.056	—	10B	28-45	—	②	HYD	HYD
	5.4	5	0.040-0.050	—	10B	28-45	—	②	HYD	HYD
	6.8	S	0.052-0.055	—	10B	28-45	—	②	HYD	HYD
2006	5.4	5	0.040-0.050	—	10B	28-45	—	②	HYD	HYD
2007	5.4	5	0.040-0.050	—	10B	62-69	—	②	HYD	HYD

NOTE: The Vehicle Emission Control Information label often reflects specification changes changes made during production. The label figures must be used if they differ from those in this chart.

B: Before top dead center

HYD: Hydraulic

NA: Not Available

① With engine running

② Idle speed and timing are electronically controlled and cannot be adjusted

22086_EXPD_C0003

DIESEL ENGINE TUNE-UP SPECIFICATIONS

Year	Engine Displacement Liters (VIN)	Valve Clearance Intake (in.)	Exhaust (in.)	Intake Valve Opens (deg.)	Injection Pump Setting (deg.)	Injection Nozzle Pressure (psi) New	Used	Idle Speed (rpm)	Cranking Compression Pressure (psi)
2005	6.0 (P)	HYD	HYD	—	①	NA	NA	②	NA

NOTE: The Vehicle Emission Control Information label often reflects specification changes made during production. The label figures must be used if they differ from those in this chart.

HYD: Hydraulic

B: Before top dead center

NA: Not Available

① PCM controlled

② See underhood emission label

22086_EXPD_C0004

CAPACITIES

Year	Model	Engine Displacement Liters (VIN)	Engine Oil with Filter (qts.)	Transmission (pts.) 5-Spd	Auto.	Transfer Case (pts.)	Drive Axle Front (pts.)	Rear (pts.)	Fuel Tank (gal.)	Cooling System (qts.)
2005	Excursion	5.4 (L)	6.0	—	①	4.2	6.0	6.0	44.0	19.8
	Excursion	6.8 (S)	7.0	—	①	4.2	6.0 ②	6.0 ②	44.0	23.0
	Excursion	6.0 (P)	15.0	11.6	③	4.2	6.0 ②	6.0 ②	44.0	27.5
	Expedition	5.4 (5)	7.0	—	①	4.0	3.7	④	28.0	⑤
	Navigator	5.4 (5)	7.0	—	①	4.0	3.7	④	28.0	⑤
2006	Expedition	5.4 (5)	7.0	—	①	3.5	3.6	④	28.0	⑤
	Navigator	5.4 (5)	7.0	—	①	3.5	3.6	④	28.0	⑤
2007	Expedition	5.4 (5)	7.0	—	⑥	3.5	3.6	④	28.0	⑤
	Navigator	5.4 (5)	7.0	—	⑥	3.5	3.6	④	28.0	⑤

NOTE: All capacities are approximate. Add fluid gradually and check to be sure a proper fluid level is obtained.

① With 4R70W: 28 pts.
  With 4R100: 32.0 pts.
  With E40D: 32.0 pts.
  2005 Expedition with 4R70/75: 28 pts.
  2005 Navigator : 32 pts.

② Heavy duty: 7.5 pts.

③ 4R100: 34.2 pts.
  TorqShift: 38.4 pts.

④ 8.8 inch coventional axle: 4.0 pts.
  9.75 inch coventional axle: 4.5 pts.
  8.8 inch limited slip axle: 3.75 pts.
  9.75 inch limited slip axle: 4.25 pts.

⑤ Base radiator without aux rear heat: 19.4
  Heavy duty radiator without aux rear heat: 19.4
  Base radiator with aux rear heat: 20.7
  Heavy duty radiator with aux rear heat: 20.9

⑥ With 4R75E: 28 pts
  With ZF6HP26: 17 pts
  With 6R75: 21pts

22086_EXPD_C0005

FLUID SPECIFICATIONS

Year	Model	Engine Displacement Liters	Engine ID/VIN	Engine Oil	Auto. Trans.④	Drive Axle②③	Power Steering Fluid	Brake Master Cylinder
2005	Excursion	5.4	L	5W-20	Mercon®①	75W-140	Mercon®	DOT 3
		6.0	P	15W-40	Mercon®①	75W-140	Mercon®	DOT 3
		6.8	S	5W-20	Mercon®①	75W-140	Mercon®	DOT 3
	Expedition	5.4	5	5W-20	Mercon®①	75W-140	Mercon®	DOT 3
	Navigator	5.4	5	5W-20	Mercon®①	75W-140	Mercon®	DOT 3
2006	Expedition	5.4	5	5W-20	Mercon® SP	75W-140	Mercon®	DOT 3
	Navigator	5.4	5	5W-20	Mercon® SP	75W-140	Mercon®	DOT 3
2007	Expedition	5.4	5	5W-20	Mercon® SP	75W-140	Mercon®	DOT 3
	Navigator	5.4	5	5W-20	Mercon® SP	75W-140	Mercon®	DOT 3

DOT: Department Of Transpotation

① TorqueShift,6HP26 transmissions Mercon® SP transmission fluid

② Front axles 80W-90

③ On Traction-Lok® axles always install friction modifier

④ Mercon® V is recommended for 4R70E/4R75E transmissions

22086_EXPD_C0012

VALVE SPECIFICATIONS

Year	Engine Displacement Liters (VIN)	Seat Angle (deg.)	Face Angle (deg.)	Spring Test Pressure (lbs. @ in.)	Spring Installed Height (in.)	Stem-to-Guide Clearance (in.) Intake	Stem-to-Guide Clearance (in.) Exhaust	Stem Diameter (in.) Intake	Stem Diameter (in.) Exhaust
2005	5.4 (L)	45.0-44.50	45.75-45.25	150@1.10	1.689 1.665	0.0008-0.0027	0.0018-0.0037	0.2754-0.2746	0.274-0.2736
	5.4 (5)	44.5-45.0	45.5	79@1.66	1.660	0.0010-0.0020	0.0030-0.0040	0.2350-0.2360	0.2340-0.2350
	6.0 (P)	①	①	191@1.51	1.820	0.0055 max.	0.0055 max.	0.2720-0.2735	0.2720-0.2735
	6.8 (S)	44.50-45.00	45.25-45.75	150@1.10	1.570	0.0008-0.0027	0.0018-0.0037	0.275-0.2746	0.274-0.2735
2006	5.4 (5)	44.5-45.0	45.5	79@1.66	1.660	0.0010-0.0020	0.0030-0.0040	0.2350-0.2360	0.2340-0.2350
2007	5.4 (5)	44.5-45.0	45.5	79@1.66	1.660	0.0010-0.0020	0.0030-0.0040	0.2350-0.2360	0.2340-0.2350

① Intake: 30 degrees

  Exhaust: 37.5 degrees

22086_EXPD_C0006

CAMSHAFT AND BEARING SPECIFICATIONS CHART

All measurements are given in inches.

Year	Engine Displ. Liters	Engine ID/VIN	Journal Dia.	Brg. Oil Clearance	Shaft End-play	Runout	Journal Bore	Lobe Height Intake	Lobe Height Exhaust
2005	5.4L	L	1.0615-1.0605	0.0030-0.0010	0.0011-0.0075	0.001	1.0635-1.0625	0.2799	0.2952
	6.0L	P	2.440-2.441	0.0015-0.0060	0.002-0.008	NA	2.443-2.446	0.2261	0.2296
	6.8L	S	1.0615-1.0605	0.076-0.025	0.0011-0.0075	0.001	1.0635-1.0625	0.2799	0.2952
	5.4L	5	1.126-1.127	0.001-0.003	0.003-0.007	0.001	1.128-1.129-	0.2170	0.2170
2006	5.4L	5	1.126-1.127	0.001-0.003	0.003-0.007	0.001	1.128-1.129-	0.2170	0.2170
2007	5.4L	5	1.126-1.127	0.001-0.003	0.003-0.007	0.001	1.128-1.129-	0.2170	0.2170

① Intake: 30 degrees
Exhaust: 37.5 degrees

22086_EXPD_C0007

CRANKSHAFT AND CONNECTING ROD SPECIFICATIONS

All measurements are given in inches.

Year	Engine Displacement Liters (VIN)	Crankshaft Main Brg. Journal Dia.	Crankshaft Main Brg. Oil Clearance	Crankshaft Shaft End-play	Crankshaft Thrust on No.	Connecting Rod Journal Diameter	Connecting Rod Oil Clearance	Connecting Rod Side Clearance
2005	5.4 (L)	2.6568-2.6576	0.0009-0.0019	0.0051-0.0120	5	2.0859-2.0867	0.0010-0.0025	0.0006-0.0177
	5.4 (5)	2.6567-2.6576	NA	0.0030-0.0148	5	2.0885-2.0877	NA	0.0187-0.0049
	6.0 (P)	3.1500-3.1880	NA	0.0087	NA	2.7160-2.7170	NA	0.012-0.0240
	6.8 (S)	2.6568-2.6576	0.0009-0.0019	0.0015-0.0030	5	2.0859-2.0867	0.0010-0.0025	0.0006-0.0177
2006	5.4 (5)	2.6567-2.6576	NA	0.0030-0.0148	5	2.0885-2.0877	0.0010-0.0025	0.0187-0.0049
2007	5.4 (5)	2.6567-2.6576	NA	0.0030-0.0148	5	2.0885-2.0877	0.0010-0.0025	0.0187-0.0049

NA: Not Available

22086_EXPD_C0009

PISTON AND RING SPECIFICATIONS

All measurements are given in inches.

Year	Engine Displacement Liters (VIN)	Piston Clearance	Ring Gap			Ring Side Clearance		
			Top Compression	Bottom Compression	Oil Control	Top Compression	Bottom Compression	Oil Control
2005	5.4 (L)	0.0002-0.0010	0.006-0.015	0.0098-0.0197	0.0059-0.0256	0.0002-0.0013	0.0012-0.0031	NA
	5.4 (5)	0.0010-0.0018	0.006-0.012	0.0098-0.0197	0.0059-0.0256	0.0008-0.0031	0.0012-0.0028	NA
	6.0 (P)	0.0017-0.0036	0.011-0.0210	0.055-0.0650	0.009-0.0190	NA	NA	NA
	6.8 (S)	0.0002-0.0010	0.005-0.011	0.010-0.016	0.006-0.026	0.0012-0.0037	0.0012-0.0037	NA
2006	5.4 (5)	0.0010-0.0018	0.006-0.012	0.0098-0.0197	0.0059-0.0256	0.0008-0.0031	0.0012-0.0028	NA
2007	5.4 (5)	0.0010-0.0018	0.006-0.012	0.0098-0.0197	0.0059-0.0256	0.0008-0.0031	0.0012-0.0028	NA

NA: Not Available

22086_EXPD_C0008

TORQUE SPECIFICATIONS

All readings in ft. lbs.

	Engine Displacement Liters (VIN)	Cylinder Head Bolts	Main Bearing Bolts	Rod Bearing Bolts	Crankshaft Damper Bolts	Flywheel Bolts	Manifold		Spark Plugs	Oil Pan Drain Plug
							Intake *	Exhaust		
2005	5.4 (L)	①	②	③	④	54-64	⑤	18-25	8	10
	5.4 (5)	①	⑥	⑦	④	59	⑧	18	25	10
	6.0 (P)	⑨	⑩	⑪	⑫	69	8	28 ⑬	—	18
	6.8 (S)	①	⑭	⑮	④	54-64	⑯	18-25	11	11
2006	5.4 (5)	①	⑥	⑦	④	59	⑧	18	25	10
2007	5.4 (5)	①	⑥	⑦	④	59	⑧	18	25	10

① Step 1: 30 ft. lbs.

Step 2: Plus 90 degrees

Step 3: Plus 90 degrees

② Cast Aluminum Block:

Vertical mounted bolts:

Step 1: 89 inch lbs.

Step 2: 18 ft. lbs.

Step 3: 30 ft. lbs.

Step 4: plus an additional 90 degrees

Side Bolts:

Step 1: 30 ft. lbs.

Step 2: plus 90 degrees

Cast Iron Block:

Step 1: 30 ft. lbs.

Step 2: Plus 90 degrees

Side Bolts:

Step 1: 44 ft. lbs.

Step 2: 89 inch lbs.

③ Step 1: 32 ft. lbs.

Step 2: Plus 90-120 degrees

④ Step 1: 66 ft. lbs.

Step 2: Loosen bolt

Step 3: 37 ft. lbs.

Step 4: Plus 90 degrees

⑤ Step 1: 18 inch lbs.

Step 2: 18 ft. lbs.

⑥ Vertical mounted bolts:

Step 1: 30 ft. lbs.

Step 2: Plus 90 degrees

Side Bolts:

Step 1: 22 ft. lbs.

Step 2: plus 90 degrees

⑦ Step 1: 32 ft. lbs.

Step 2: Plus 105 degrees

⑧ Step 1: 18 inch lbs.

Step 2: 18 ft. lbs.

⑨ Tighten bolts 1-10

Step 1: 65 ft. lbs.

Step 2: 85 ft. lbs.

Step 3: Plus 90 degrees

Step 4: An additional 90 degrees

Tighten bolts 11-15

Step 1: 18 ft. lbs.

Step 1: 23 ft. lbs.

⑩ Vertical mounted bolts:

Step 1: 110 ft. lbs.

Step 2: 130 ft. lbs.

Step 3: 170 ft. lbs.

Side Bolts:

Step 1: 18 ft. lbs.

⑪ Step 1: 33 ft. lbs.

Step 2: 50 ft. lbs.

⑫ Step 1: 50 ft. lbs.

Step 2: Plus 90 degrees

⑬ Apply high temp nickel anti-seize to the threads

⑭ Vertical mounted bolts:

Step 1: 30 ft. lbs.

Step 2: Plus 90 degrees

Side Bolts:

Step 1: 22 ft. lbs.

Step 2: Plus 90 degrees

⑮ Step 1: 32 ft. lbs.

Step 2: Plus 105 degrees

⑯ Lower manofold:

Step 1: 18 inch lbs.

Step 2: 89 inch lbs.

Upper Manifold:

Step 1: 18 inch lbs.

Step 2: 18 ft. lbs.

22086_EXPD_C0010

WHEEL ALIGNMENT

Year	Model		Caster		Camber		Toe-in (in.)
			Range (+/-Deg.)	Preferred Setting (Deg.)	Range (+/-Deg.)	Preferred Setting (Deg.)	
2005	Excursion	2WD	1.00	+0.62	+4.40	1.00	0.10+/-0.25
		4WD	1.00	+0.25	+3.63	+0.20	0.01+/-0.25
	Expedition	Coil spring	1.00	+5.3	0.75	-0.30	0.14+/-0.20
	Navigator	Air	1.00	+5.5	0.75	-0.60/-0.30	0.14+/-0.20
2006	Expedition	Coil spring	1.00	+5.3	0.75	-0.30	0.14+/-0.20
	Navigator	Air	1.00	+5.5	0.75	-0.60/-0.30	0.14+/-0.20
2007	Expedition	Coil spring	1.00	+4.3①	0.75	-0.30	0.14+/-0.20
	Navigator	Air	1.00	+4.3①	0.75	-0.30	0.14+/-0.20

22086_EXPD_C0011

TIRE, WHEEL AND BALL JOINT SPECIFICATIONS

Year	Model	OEM Tires		Tire Pressures (psi)		Wheel Size	Ball Joint Inspection	Lug Nut (ft. lbs.)
		Standard	Optional	Front	Rear			
2005	Excursion	LT265/75R16	LT275/65R18	45	55	7K/8K	0.030 in. ①	165
	Expedition	P265/70R17		35	35	7-JJ	0.030 in. ①	②
	Navigator	P255/70R18	P275/65R18	35	35	8J	0.030 in. ①	②
2006	Expedition							
	Eddie Bauer 4x2	P265/70R17	—	35	35	7.5J	0.030 in. ①	②
	Eddie Bauer 4x4	P265/70R17	—	35	35	7.5J	0.030 in. ①	②
	King Ranch 4x2	P265/70R17	—	35	35	7.5J	0.030 in. ①	②
	King Ranch 4x4	P265/70R17	—	35	35	7.5J	0.030 in. ①	②
	Limited & EL	P265/70R17	—	35	35	7.5J	0.030 in. ①	②
	SSV	P265/70R17	—	35	35	7.5J	0.030 in. ①	②
	XLT	P265/70R17	—	35	35	7.5J	0.030 in. ①	②
	XLS	P265/70R17	—	35	35	7.5J	0.030 in. ①	②
	Navigator	P255/70R18	—	35	35	8J	0.030 in. ①	②
2007	Expedition							
	Eddie Bauer 4x2	P265/70R17	P255/70R18	35	35	8J/8.5J	0.030 in. ①	②
	Eddie Bauer 4x4	P265/70R17	P255/70R18	35	35	8J/8.5J	0.030 in. ①	②
	20" Tire Option	P275/55R20		35	35	8.5J	0.030 in. ①	②
	Eddie Bauer EL	P255/70R18	P275/55R20	35	35	8.5J	0.030 in. ①	②
	Limited	P255/70R18	P275/55R20	35	35	8.5J	0.030 in. ①	②
	Limited EL	P255/70R18	P275/55R20	35	35	8.5J	0.030 in. ①	②
	SSV	P265/70R17	—	35	35	8.5J	0.030 in. ①	②
	XLT	P265/70R17	P255/70R18	35	35	8.5J	0.030 in. ①	②
	Navigator	P255/70R18	—	35	35	8.5J	0.030 in. ①	②
	20" Tire Option	P275/55R20	—	35	35	8.5J	0.030 in. ①	②

OEM: Original Equipment Manufacturer

PSI: Pounds Per Square Inch

STD: Standard

OPT: Optional

① Both upper and lower

② 12mm nuts 100 ft. lbs.

14mm nuts 150 ft. lbs.

22086_EXPD_C0013

BRAKE SPECIFICATIONS
All measurements in inches unless noted

Year	Model		Brake Disc Original Thickness	Brake Disc Minimum Thickness	Brake Disc Maximum Runout	Brake Drum Diameter Original Inside Diameter	Max. Wear Limit	Max. Machine Diameter	Minimum Lining Thickness	Brake Caliper Bracket Bolts (ft. lbs.)	Brake Caliper Mounting Bolts (ft. lbs.)
2005	Expedition	F	1.023	0.106	0.0025	—	—	—	0.118	148	41
		R	0.700	0.074	0.0250	—	—	—	0.039	140	20
	Navigator	F	1.023	0.106	0.0025	—	—	—	0.118	148	41
		R	0.700	0.074	0.0250	—	—	—	0.039	140	20
	Excursion	F	1.023	1.140	0.0025	—	—	—	0.118	166	42
		R	0.700	1.10	0.0250	—	—	—	0.118	150	27
2006	Expedition	F	1.023	0.106	0.0025	—	—	—	0.118	148	41
		R	0.700	0.074	0.0250	—	—	—	0.039	140	20
	Navigator	F	1.023	0.106	0.0025	—	—	—	0.118	148	41
		R	0.700	0.074	0.0250	—	—	—	0.039	140	20
2007	Expedition	F	1.023	0.106	0.0025	—	—	—	0.118	148	41
		R	0.700	0.075	0.0250	—	—	—	0.039	140	20
	Navigator	F	1.023	0.106	0.0025	—	—	—	0.118	148	41
		R	0.700	0.075	0.0250	—	—	—	0.039	140	20

NOTE: Due to changes made during production, refer to manufacturer's specifications if they differ from those in this chart

F: Front

R: Rear

22086_EXPD_C0014

SCHEDULED MAINTENANCE INTERVALS
2005-07 FORD—EXPEDITION & LINCOLN—NAVIGATOR

TO BE SERVICED	TYPE OF SERVICE	VEHICLE MILEAGE INTERVAL (x1000)												
		5	10	15	20	25	30	35	40	45	50	55	60	65
Engine oil & filter	R	✓	✓	✓	✓	✓	✓	✓	✓	✓	✓	✓	✓	✓
Tires	Rotate	✓	✓	✓	✓	✓	✓	✓	✓	✓	✓	✓	✓	✓
Wheels	I ①	✓	✓	✓	✓	✓	✓	✓	✓	✓	✓	✓	✓	✓
Auto trans. fluid	I			✓			✓			✓			✓	
Brake pads/shoes	I			✓			✓			✓			✓	
Coolant hoses	S/I			✓			✓			✓			✓	
Steering linkage	I			✓			✓			✓			✓	
(Navigator) seat cushion filters (if equipped)	R						✓						✓	
Cabin air filter	R			✓			✓				✓		✓	
Ball joints (2wd)	L			✓			✓			✓			✓	
Exhaust system	I						✓						✓	
Engine air filter	R						✓						✓	
Fuel filter	R						✓						✓	
Auto trans fluid ②	R						✓						✓	
Front wheel bearings (2wd)	R	at 150,000 miles, if not previously done so												
Spark plugs	R	every 100,000 miles												
PCV valve	R	every 120,000 miles												
Spark plugs	R	every 100,000 miles												
PCV valve	R	every 120,000 miles												
Premium Gold coolant	R	every 5 years or 100,000 miles												
Auto trans fluid (all exc. 4R100)	R	every 150,000 miles												
Differential fluid	R	every 150,000 miles												
Transfer case fluid	R	every 150,000 miles												
Accessory drive belts	R	every 150,000 miles, if not previously done so												

R: Replace   S: Service   I: Inspect   L: Lubricate

① Inspect for end play and noise

② Change transmission fluid on 4R100 and Torqshift transmissions. Replace in-linr filters if equipped.

Special Operating Condition Requirements

When towing a trailer or using a camper or car-top carrier:

Change engine oil and install a new oil filter every 4,800 km (3,000 miles), 3 months or 200 hours of engine operation (whichever occurs first).

Change transfer case fluid every 96,000 km (60,000 miles).

Change manual transmission fluid as required.

Inspect and lubricate U-joints as required.

During extensive idling and/or low speed driving for long distances, as in heavy commercial use such as delivery, taxi, patrol car or livery:

Change engine oil and install a new oil filter every 4,800 km (3,000 miles), 3 months or 200 hours of engine operation (whichever occurs first).

Lube front lower control arm and steering linkage ball joints with zerk fittings (if equipped) every 4,800 km (3,000 miles) or 3 months.

Inspect brake system and check battery electrolyte level (Patrol cars) every 8,000 km (5,000 miles).

Install a new fuel filter every 24,000 km (15,000 miles).

Change automatic transmission fluid, lubricate 4x2 wheel bearings, install new grease seals and adjust bearings every 48,000 km (30,000 miles). If equipped, change the in-line service installed transmission fluid filter.

Install new spark plugs and change transfer case fluid every 96,000 km (60,000 miles).

Install a new cabin air filter as required.

SCHEDULED MAINTENANCE INTERVALS
2005-07 FORD—EXPEDITION & LINCOLN—NAVIGATOR
Footnotes Continued

When operating in dusty conditions such as unpaved or dusty roads:

Change engine oil and install a new oil filter every 4,800 km (3,000 miles) or 3 months.

Install a new fuel filter every 24,000 km (15,000 miles).

Change automatic transmission fluid every 48,000 km (30,000 miles). If equipped, change the in-line service installed transmission fluid filter.

Change transfer case fluid every 96,000 km (60,000 miles).

Install a new engine air filter as required.

Install a new cabin air filter as required.

When operating in off-road conditions:

Change automatic transmission fluid every 48,000 km (30,000 miles). If equipped, change the in-line service installed transmission fluid filter.

Change transfer case fluid every 96,000 km (60,000 miles).

Install a new cabin air filter as required.

Inspect and lubricate U-joints.

Inspect and lubricate steering linkage ball joints with zerk fittings.

22086_EXPD_C0016

SCHEDULED MAINTENANCE INTERVALS
2005 Excursion With Gasoline Engines

TO BE SERVICED	TYPE OF SERVICE	VEHICLE MILEAGE INTERVAL (x1000)												
		5	10	15	20	25	30	35	40	45	50	55	60	65
Engine oil & filter	R	✓	✓	✓	✓	✓	✓	✓	✓	✓	✓	✓	✓	✓
Tires	Rotate	✓	✓	✓	✓	✓	✓	✓	✓	✓	✓	✓	✓	✓
Wheels	I ①	✓	✓	✓	✓	✓	✓	✓	✓	✓	✓	✓	✓	✓
Auto trans. fluid	I			✓			✓			✓			✓	
Brake pads, hoses, etc.	I			✓			✓			✓			✓	
Coolant hoses	I			✓			✓			✓			✓	
Steering linkage	I/L			✓			✓			✓			✓	
Cabin air filter	R			✓			✓			✓			✓	
Ball joints (2wd)	L			✓			✓			✓			✓	
Driveshaft	I			✓			✓			✓			✓	
4x4 front axle U-joints	L			✓			✓			✓			✓	
Exhaust system	I						✓						✓	
Engine air filter	R						✓						✓	
Fuel filter	R						✓						✓	
Auto trans fluid (4R100)	R						✓							
4x2 front wheel bearings	Adj.												✓	
4x2 front wheel bearing grease seals	R												✓	
Accessory drive belts	I	Every 100,000 miles												
Front wheel bearings (2wd)	R	at 150,000 miles, if not previously done so												
4x4 front hub needle bearings	L	every 120,000 miles												
Spark plugs	R	every 100,000 miles												
PCV valve	R	every 120,000 miles												
Manual trans. Fluid	R	every 120,000 miles												
Premium Gold coolant	R	every 3 years or 100,000 miles and every 50,000 miles thereafter												
Coolant (exc. Premium Gold)	R	every 135,000 miles												
Auto trans fluid (exc. 4R100)	R	every 150,000 miles												
Differential fluid	R	at 150,000 miles then every 50,000 thereafter												
Transfer case fluid	R	every 150,000 miles												
Accessory drive belts	R	every 150,000 miles, if not previously done so												

R: Replace   S: Service   I: Inspect   L: Lubricate   Adj: adjust

① Inspect for end play and noise

Special Operating Condition Requirements

When towing a trailer or using a camper or car-top carrier:

Change engine oil and install a new oil filter every 4,800 km (3,000 miles), 3 months or 200 hours of engine operation (whichever occurs first).

Change transfer case fluid every 96,000 km (60,000 miles).

Change manual transmission fluid as required.

Inspect and lubricate U-joints as required.

During extensive idling and/or low speed driving for long distances, as in heavy commercial use such as delivery, taxi, patrol car or livery:

Change engine oil and install a new oil filter every 4,800 km (3,000 miles), 3 months or 200 hours of engine operation (whichever occurs first).

Lube front lower control arm and steering linkage ball joints with zerk fittings (if equipped) every 4,800 km (3,000 miles) or 3 months.

Inspect brake system and check battery electrolyte level (Patrol cars) every 8,000 km (5,000 miles).

Install a new fuel filter every 24,000 km (15,000 miles).

Change automatic transmission fluid, lubricate 4x2 wheel bearings, install new grease seals and adjust bearings every 48,000 km (30,000 miles). If equipped, change the in-line service installed transmission fluid filter.

Install new spark plugs and change transfer case fluid every 96,000 km (60,000 miles).

Install a new cabin air filter as required.

SCHEDULED MAINTENANCE INTERVALS
2005 Excursion With Gasoline Engines
Footnotes Continued

When operating in dusty conditions such as unpaved or dusty roads:

Change engine oil and install a new oil filter every 4,800 km (3,000 miles) or 3 months.

Install a new fuel filter every 24,000 km (15,000 miles).

Change automatic transmission fluid every 48,000 km (30,000 miles). If equipped, change the in-line service installed transmission fluid filter.

Change transfer case fluid every 96,000 km (60,000 miles).

Install a new engine air filter as required.

Install a new cabin air filter as required.

When operating in off-road conditions:

Change automatic transmission fluid every 48,000 km (30,000 miles). If equipped, change the in-line service installed transmission fluid filter.

Change transfer case fluid every 96,000 km (60,000 miles).

Install a new cabin air filter as required.

Inspect and lubricate U-joints.

Inspect and lubricate steering linkage ball joints with zerk fittings.

22086_EXPD_C0018

SCHEDULED MAINTENANCE INTERVALS
2005 Excursion with 6.0L Diesel Engine

TO BE SERVICED	TYPE OF SERVICE	VEHICLE MILEAGE INTERVAL (x1000)												
		7.5	15	22.5	30	37.5	45	52.5	60	67.5	75	82.5	90	97.5
Engine oil & filter	R	✓	✓	✓	✓	✓	✓	✓	✓	✓	✓	✓	✓	✓
Tires	Rotate	✓	✓	✓	✓	✓	✓	✓	✓	✓	✓	✓	✓	✓
Air filter minder	I ①	✓	✓	✓	✓	✓	✓	✓	✓	✓	✓	✓	✓	✓
Wheels	I ②	✓	✓	✓	✓	✓	✓	✓	✓	✓	✓	✓	✓	✓
Brake pads, hoses, etc.	I		✓		✓		✓		✓		✓		✓	
Coolant hoses	I		✓		✓		✓		✓		✓		✓	
Steering linkage and suspension	I/L		✓		✓		✓		✓		✓		✓	
Cabin air filter	R		✓		✓		✓		✓		✓		✓	
Ball joints (2wd)	L		✓		✓		✓		✓		✓		✓	
Driveshaft	I/L		✓		✓		✓		✓		✓		✓	
4x4 front axle U-joints	L		✓		✓		✓		✓		✓		✓	
Exhaust system and heat shields	I		✓		✓		✓		✓		✓		✓	
Engine air filter	R				✓				✓				✓	
Fuel filters ③	R		✓		✓		✓		✓		✓		✓	
Auto trans fluid ④	R				✓				✓				✓	
4x2 front wheel bearings	L								✓					
4x2 front wheel bearing grease seals	R								✓					
Accessory drive belts	I													✓
4x4 front hub needle bearings	L								✓					
Manual trans. Fluid	R								✓					
Coolant	R										✓			✓
Rear differential fluid ⑤	R													✓
Transfer case fluid	R	every 150,000 miles												
4x2 front wheel bearings	R	every 150,000 miles												
Accessory drive belts	R	every 150,000 miles, if not previously done so												

R: Replace   S: Service   I: Inspect   L: Lubricate   Adj: adjust

① Reset after new filter is installed

② Inspect for end play and noise

③ Frame-mounted and engine

④ Including external and in-line filters

⑤ Dana axles using non-synthetic fluid only

Special Operating Condition Requirements

When towing a trailer or using a camper or car-top carrier:

Change engine oil and install a new oil filter every 4,800 km (3,000 miles), 3 months or 200 hours of engine operation (whichever occurs first).

Change transfer case fluid every 96,000 km (60,000 miles).

Change manual transmission fluid as required.

Inspect and lubricate U-joints as required.

22086_EXPD_C0019

SCHEDULED MAINTENANCE INTERVALS
2005 Excursion with 6.0L Diesel Engine
Footnotes Continued

During extensive idling and/or low speed driving for long distances, as in heavy commercial use such as delivery, taxi, patrol car or livery:

Change engine oil and install a new oil filter every 4,800 km (3,000 miles), 3 months or 200 hours of engine operation (whichever occurs first).

Lube front lower control arm and steering linkage ball joints with zerk fittings (if equipped) every 4,800 km (3,000 miles) or 3 months.

Inspect brake system and check battery electrolyte level (Patrol cars) every 8,000 km (5,000 miles).

Install a new fuel filter every 24,000 km (15,000 miles).

Change automatic transmission fluid, lubricate 4x2 wheel bearings, install new grease seals and adjust bearings every 48,000 km (30,000 miles). If equipped, change the in-line service installed transmission fluid filter.

Change transfer case fluid every 96,000 km (60,000 miles).

Install a new cabin air filter as required.

When operating in dusty conditions such as unpaved or dusty roads:

Change engine oil and install a new oil filter every 4,800 km (3,000 miles) or 3 months.

Install a new fuel filter every 24,000 km (15,000 miles).

Change automatic transmission fluid every 48,000 km (30,000 miles). If equipped, change the in-line service installed transmission fluid filter.

Change transfer case fluid every 96,000 km (60,000 miles).

Install a new engine air filter as required.

Install a new cabin air filter as required.

When operating in off-road conditions:

Change automatic transmission fluid every 48,000 km (30,000 miles). If equipped, change the in-line service installed transmission fluid filter.

Change transfer case fluid every 96,000 km (60,000 miles).

Install a new cabin air filter as required.

Inspect and lubricate U-joints.

Inspect and lubricate steering linkage ball joints with zerk fittings.

22086_EXPD_C0020

PRECAUTIONS

Before servicing any vehicle, please be sure to read all of the following precautions, which deal with personal safety, prevention of component damage, and important points to take into consideration when servicing a motor vehicle:

• Never open, service or drain the radiator or cooling system when the engine is hot; serious burns can occur from the steam and hot coolant.

• Observe all applicable safety precautions when working around fuel. Whenever servicing the fuel system, always work in a well-ventilated area. Do not allow fuel spray or vapors to come in contact with a spark, open flame, or excessive heat (a hot drop light, for example). Keep a dry chemical fire extinguisher near the work area. Always keep fuel in a container specifically designed for fuel storage; also, always properly seal fuel containers to avoid the possibility of fire or explosion. Refer to the additional fuel system precautions later in this section.

• Fuel injection systems often remain pressurized, even after the engine has been turned **OFF**. The fuel system pressure must be relieved before disconnecting any fuel lines. Failure to do so may result in fire and/or personal injury.

• Brake fluid often contains polyglycol ethers and polyglycols. Avoid contact with the eyes and wash your hands thoroughly after handling brake fluid. If you do get brake fluid in your eyes, flush your eyes with clean, running water for 15 minutes. If eye irritation persists, or if you have taken brake fluid internally, IMMEDIATELY seek medical assistance.

• The EPA warns that prolonged contact with used engine oil may cause a number of skin disorders, including cancer. You should make every effort to minimize your exposure to used engine oil. Protective gloves should be worn when changing oil. Wash your hands and any other exposed skin areas as soon as possible after exposure to used engine oil. Soap and water, or waterless hand cleaner should be used.

• All new vehicles are now equipped with an air bag system, often referred to as a Supplemental Restraint System (SRS) or Supplemental Inflatable Restraint (SIR) system. The system must be disabled before performing service on or around system components, steering column, instrument panel components, wiring and sensors. Failure to follow safety and disabling procedures could result in accidental air bag deployment, possible personal injury and unnecessary system repairs.

• Always wear safety goggles when working with, or around, the air bag system. When carrying a non-deployed air bag, be sure the bag and trim cover are pointed away from your body. When placing a non-deployed air bag on a work surface, always face the bag and trim cover upward, away from the surface. This will reduce the motion of the module if it is accidentally deployed. Refer to the additional air bag system precautions later in this section.

• Clean, high quality brake fluid from a sealed container is essential to the safe and proper operation of the brake system. You should always buy the correct type of brake fluid for your vehicle. If the brake fluid becomes contaminated, completely flush the system with new fluid. Never reuse any brake fluid. Any brake fluid that is removed from the system should be discarded. Also, do not allow any brake fluid to come in contact with a painted surface; it will damage the paint.

• Never operate the engine without the proper amount and type of engine oil; doing so WILL result in severe engine damage.

• Timing belt maintenance is extremely important. Many models utilize an interference-type, non-freewheeling engine. If the timing belt breaks, the valves in the cylinder head may strike the pistons, causing potentially serious (also time-consuming and expensive) engine damage. Refer to the maintenance interval charts for the recommended replacement interval for the timing belt, and to the timing belt section for belt replacement and inspection.

• Disconnecting the negative battery cable on some vehicles may interfere with the functions of the on-board computer system(s) and may require the computer to undergo a relearning process once the negative battery cable is reconnected.

• When servicing drum brakes, only disassemble and assemble one side at a time, leaving the remaining side intact for reference.

• Only an MVAC-trained, EPA-certified automotive technician should service the air conditioning system or its components.

BRAKES

GENERAL INFORMATION

The 4-wheel, 4-channel Anti-lock Brake System (ABS) consists of the following components:

• ABS module
• Front wheel speed sensor
• Front wheel speed sensor ring (integral to the front wheel bearing)
• Hydraulic control unit (HCU)
• Rear wheel speed sensor
• Rear wheel speed sensor ring (integral to the rear halfshaft)
• Yellow ABS warning indicator

The front wheel speed sensor rings are integral to the front hub and bearing assemblies.

The rear wheel speed sensor rings are integral to the rear halfshaft.

The Anti-lock Brake System (ABS) with stability assist consists of the following components:

• Active brake booster with integral solenoid
• Brake booster release switch
• Stability assist event indicator
• Steering wheel position sensor
• 2 brake pressure sensors
• Stability assist switch
• Lateral accelerometer (part of stability control sensor cluster)
• Longitudinal accelerometer (part of stability control sensor cluster)
• Roll rate sensor (part of stability control sensor cluster)
• Yaw rate sensor (part of stability control sensor cluster)

ANTI-LOCK BRAKE SYSTEM (ABS)

SPEED SENSORS

REMOVAL & INSTALLATION

Excursion

Front Speed Sensor—2WD Models

1. Before servicing the vehicle, refer to the precautions section.
2. Raise and safely support the vehicle.
3. Disconnect the front wheel speed sensor electrical connector.
4. Separate the sensor cable from the brake hose clips.
5. Remove the sensor cable bolt.
6. Remove the bolt and the sensor.
7. To install, reverse the removal procedure. Tighten the speed sensor bolt to 9 ft. lbs. (12 Nm) and the speed sensor cable bolt to 11 ft. lbs. (15 Nm).

Front Speed Sensor—4WD Models

1. Before servicing the vehicle, refer to the precautions section.
2. Disconnect the front wheel speed sensor electrical connector.
3. Remove the front disc brake rotor shield.
4. Remove the front wheel speed sensor bolts and the front wheel speed sensor.
5. Installation is the reverse of the removal procedure. Tighten the speed sensor bolt to 71 inch lbs. (8 Nm).

Rear Speed Sensor

1. Before servicing the vehicle, refer to the precautions section.
2. Disconnect the battery.
3. Raise and support the vehicle.

> ❈❈ **WARNING**
> **Clean off dirt and debris that may have collected around the rear axle speed sensor before removal to prevent fluid contamination.**

4. Remove the rear axle speed sensor:
   a. Disconnect the electrical connector.
   b. Remove the bolt.
   c. Remove the rear axle speed sensor.

To install:

> ❈❈ **WARNING**
> **Use care not to get dirt in the rear axle housing.**

5. Clean and inspect the rear axle speed sensor:
   a. Clean the axle mounting surface.
   b. Inspect and clean the magnetized rear axle speed sensor pole piece.
   c. Inspect the rear axle speed sensor O-ring for damage. Install new if necessary.
   d. Lightly lubricate the rear axle speed sensor O-ring with rear axle lubricant.
6. Install the rear axle speed sensor:

➡ **Do not apply force to the plastic rear axle speed sensor connector.**

   e. Position the rear axle speed sensor and install the rear axle speed sensor bolt. Tighten to 27 ft. lbs. (37 Nm).
7. Connect the electrical connector.

➡ **When the battery is disconnected and reconnected, some abnormal drive symptoms may occur while the vehicle relearns its adaptive strategy. The vehicle may need to be driven 16 km (10 mi) or more to relearn the strategy.**

8. Connect the battery.

Expedition & Navigator

Front Speed Sensor

See Figure 1.

1. Before servicing the vehicle, refer to the precautions section.

➡ **If equipped, turn the air suspension switch to the OFF position.**

2. With the vehicle in NEUTRAL, position it on a hoist.
3. Disconnect the wheel speed sensor electrical connector.
4. Remove the wheel speed sensor harness retainer bolt and the retainers.

> ❈❈ **WARNING**
> **Do not allow the caliper to hang from the brake hose or damage to the hose can result.**

5. Remove the bolts and position the caliper, pads and anchor plate aside.
6. Remove the brake disc.
7. Remove the bolt and the front wheel speed sensor.
8. Installation is the reverse of the removal procedure. Please note the following tightening specifications:
   a. Front wheel speed sensor bolt: 13 ft. lbs. (18 Nm).
   b. Caliper anchor plate mounting bolts: 148 ft. lbs. (200 Nm).

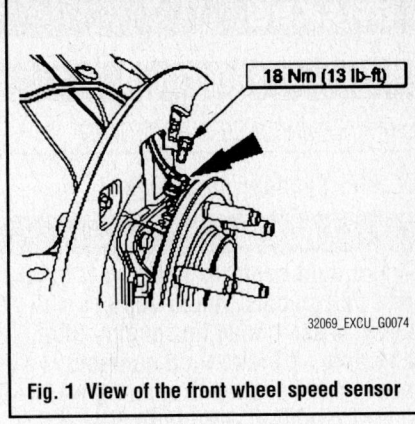

18 Nm (13 lb-ft)

32069_EXCU_G0074

Fig. 1 View of the front wheel speed sensor

   c. Wheel speed sensor harness retainer: 9 ft. lbs. (12 Nm).

Rear Speed Sensor

See Figure 2.

1. Before servicing the vehicle, refer to the precautions section.
2. Remove the parking brake shoes, as outlined in this section.
3. Disconnect the wheel speed sensor wire from the retaining clips.
4. Remove the bolt and the rear wheel speed sensor.
5. Installation is the reverse of the removal procedure. Tighten the rear wheel speed sensor retaining bolt to 13 ft. lbs. (18 Nm).

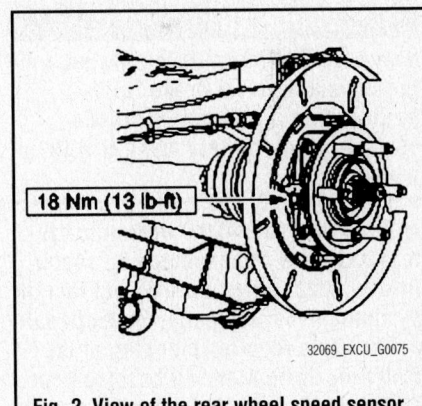

18 Nm (13 lb-ft)

32069_EXCU_G0075

Fig. 2 View of the rear wheel speed sensor

BRAKES **BLEEDING THE BRAKE SYSTEM**

BLEEDING PROCEDURE

MASTER CYLINDER BLEEDING

Master Cylinder, In Vehicle

> **✳✳ CAUTION**
>
> Brake fluid contains polyglycol ethers and polyglycols. Avoid contact with eyes. Wash hands thoroughly after handling. If brake fluid contacts eyes, flush eyes with running water for 15 minutes. Get medical attention if irritation persists. If taken internally, drink water and induce vomiting. Get medical attention immediately. Failure to follow these instructions may result in personal injury.

> **✳ WARNING**
>
> Do not allow the brake master cylinder reservoir to run dry during the bleeding operation. Keep the brake master cylinder reservoir filled with the specified brake fluid. Never reuse the brake fluid that has been drained from the hydraulic system.

> **✳ WARNING**
>
> Brake fluid is harmful to painted and plastic surfaces. If brake fluid is spilled onto a painted or plastic surface, immediately wash it with water.

➡ When any part of the hydraulic system has been disconnected for repair or new installation, air may get into the system and cause spongy brake pedal action. This requires bleeding of the hydraulic system after it has been correctly connected. The hydraulic system can be bled manually or with pressure bleeding equipment.

➡ When a new brake master cylinder has been installed or the system has been emptied, or partially emptied, it should be primed to prevent air from getting into the system.

1. Disconnect the brake master cylinder outlet tubes.
2. Install short brake tubes with ends submerged in the brake master cylinder reservoir and fill the brake master cylinder reservoir with brake fluid.

3. Have an assistant pump the brake pedal until clear fluid flows from both brake tubes without air bubbles.
4. Remove the short brake tubes and install the brake outlet tubes.
5. Bleed each brake tube at the brake master cylinder as follows:
   a. Have an assistant pump the brake pedal and then hold firm pressure on the brake pedal.
   b. Loosen the rearmost brake tube fittings until a stream of brake fluid comes out. Have an assistant maintain pressure on the brake pedal while tightening the brake tube fitting.
   c. Repeat this operation until clear, bubble-free fluid comes out.
   d. Refill the brake master cylinder reservoir as necessary. Repeat the bleeding operation at the front brake tube.
6. While the assistant maintains pressure on the brake pedal, tighten the brake tubes to 18 ft. lbs. (25 Nm).

Master Cylinder, Bench Bleeding

> **✳✳ CAUTION**
>
> Brake fluid contains polyglycol ethers and polyglycols. Avoid contact with eyes. Wash hands thoroughly after handling. If brake fluid contacts eyes, flush eyes with running water for 15 minutes. Get medical attention if irritation persists. If taken internally, drink water and induce vomiting. Get medical attention immediately. Failure to follow these instructions may result in personal injury.

> **✳✳ WARNING**
>
> Do not allow the brake master cylinder reservoir to run dry during the bleeding operation. Keep the brake master cylinder reservoir filled with the specified brake fluid. Never reuse the brake fluid that has been drained from the hydraulic system.

> **✳✳ WARNING**
>
> Brake fluid is harmful to painted and plastic surfaces. If brake fluid is spilled onto a painted or plastic surface, immediately wash it with water.

➡ When any part of the hydraulic system has been disconnected for repair or new installation, air may get into the

system and cause spongy brake pedal action. This requires bleeding of the hydraulic system after it has been correctly connected. The hydraulic system can be bled manually or with pressure bleeding equipment.

1. Support the brake master cylinder body in a vise and fill the brake master cylinder reservoir with specified brake fluid. Make sure to use clean brake fluid.
2. Install short brake tubes with the ends submerged in the brake master cylinder reservoir.
3. Slowly depress the primary piston until clear fluid flows from both brake tubes, without air bubbles. Remove the short brake tubes.

BRAKE LINE BLEEDING

Gravity Bleeding

> **✳✳ CAUTION**
>
> Brake fluid contains polyglycol ethers and polyglycols. Avoid contact with eyes. Wash hands thoroughly after handling. If brake fluid contacts eyes, flush eyes with running water for 15 minutes. Get medical attention if irritation persists. If taken internally, drink water and induce vomiting. Get medical attention immediately. Failure to follow these instructions may result in personal injury.

> **✳✳ WARNING**
>
> Do not allow the brake master cylinder reservoir to run dry during the bleeding operation. Keep the brake master cylinder reservoir filled with the specified brake fluid. Never reuse the brake fluid that has been drained from the hydraulic system.

> **✳✳ WARNING**
>
> Brake fluid is harmful to painted and plastic surfaces. If brake fluid is spilled onto a painted or plastic surface, immediately wash it with water.

➡ When any part of the hydraulic system has been disconnected for repair or new installation, air may get into the system and cause spongy brake pedal action. This requires bleeding of the hydraulic system after it has been correctly connected. The hydraulic system can be bled manually or with pressure bleeding equipment.

➡When a new brake master cylinder has been installed or the system has been emptied, or partially emptied, it should be primed to prevent air from getting into the system.

1. Fill the brake master cylinder reservoir with brake fluid.

2. Bleed the rear disc brake calipers.

   a. Place a box end wrench on the RH rear disc brake caliper bleeder screw.

   b. Attach a rubber drain tube to the RH rear disc brake caliper bleeder screw and submerge the free end of the tube in a container partially filled with clean brake fluid.

   c. Open the bleeder screw and leave open until clear bubble-free brake fluid flows.

   d. Repeat for LH rear disc brake caliper.

3. Tighten the rear disc brake caliper bleeder screws to 11 ft. lbs. (15 Nm).

4. Bleed the front disc brake calipers.

   a. Place a box end wrench on the RH front disc brake caliper bleeder screw.

   b. Attach a rubber drain tube to the RH front disc brake caliper bleeder screw and submerge the free end of the tube in a container partially filled with clean brake fluid.

   c. Open the bleeder screw and leave open until clear bubble-free brake fluid flows.

   d. Repeat for LH front disc brake caliper.

5. Tighten the front disc brake caliper bleeder screws to 11 ft. lbs. (15 Nm).

Manual Bleeding

✳✳ CAUTION

Brake fluid contains polyglycol ethers and polyglycols. Avoid contact with eyes. Wash hands thoroughly after handling. If brake fluid contacts eyes, flush eyes with running water for 15 minutes. Get medical attention if irritation persists. If taken internally, drink water and induce vomiting. Get medical attention immediately. Failure to follow these instructions may result in personal injury.

✳✳ WARNING

Do not allow the brake master cylinder reservoir to run dry during the bleeding operation. Keep the brake

master cylinder reservoir filled with the specified brake fluid. Never reuse the brake fluid that has been drained from the hydraulic system.

✳✳ WARNING

Brake fluid is harmful to painted and plastic surfaces. If brake fluid is spilled onto a painted or plastic surface, immediately wash it with water.

➡When any part of the hydraulic system has been disconnected for repair or new installation, air may get into the system and cause spongy brake pedal action. This requires bleeding of the hydraulic system after it has been correctly connected. The hydraulic system can be bled manually or with pressure bleeding equipment.

1. Place a box end wrench on the RH rear disc brake caliper bleeder screw. Attach a rubber drain tube to the RH rear disc brake caliper bleeder screw and submerge the free end of the tube in a container partially filled with clean brake fluid.

2. Have an assistant pump the brake pedal and then hold firm pressure on the brake pedal.

3. Loosen the RH rear disc brake caliper bleeder screw until a stream of brake fluid comes out. Have an assistant maintain pressure on the brake pedal while tightening the RH rear disc brake caliper bleeder screw.

   a. Repeat until clear, bubble-free fluid comes out.

   b. Refill the brake master cylinder reservoir as necessary.

4. Tighten the RH rear disc brake caliper bleeder screw to 11 ft. lbs. (15 Nm).

5. Repeat Steps 1, 2, 3, and 4 for the LH rear disc brake caliper.

6. Place a box end wrench on the RH front disc brake caliper bleeder screw. Attach a rubber drain tube to the RH front disc brake caliper bleeder screw and submerge the free end of the tube in a container partially filled with clean brake fluid.

7. Have an assistant pump the brake pedal and then hold firm pressure on the brake pedal.

8. Loosen the RH front disc brake caliper bleeder screw until a stream of brake fluid comes out. Have an assistant maintain pressure on the brake pedal while tightening the RH front disc brake caliper bleeder screw.

   a. Repeat until clear, bubble-free fluid comes out.

   b. Refill the brake master cylinder reservoir as necessary.

9. Tighten the RH front disc brake caliper bleeder screw to 11 ft. lbs. (15 Nm).

10. Repeat Steps 6, 7, 8, and 9 for the LH front disc brake caliper bleeder screw.

11. If necessary, bleed the brake master cylinder.

Pressure Bleeding

✳✳ CAUTION

Brake fluid contains polyglycol ethers and polyglycols. Avoid contact with eyes. Wash hands thoroughly after handling. If brake fluid contacts eyes, flush eyes with running water for 15 minutes. Get medical attention if irritation persists. If taken internally, drink water and induce vomiting. Get medical attention immediately. Failure to follow these instructions may result in personal injury.

✳✳ WARNING

Do not allow the brake master cylinder reservoir to run dry during the bleeding operation. Keep the brake master cylinder reservoir filled with the specified brake fluid. Never reuse the brake fluid that has been drained from the hydraulic system.

✳✳ WARNING

Brake fluid is harmful to painted and plastic surfaces. If brake fluid is spilled onto a painted or plastic surface, immediately wash it with water.

➡When any part of the hydraulic system has been disconnected for repair or new installation, air may get into the system and cause spongy brake pedal action. This requires bleeding of the hydraulic system after it has been correctly connected. The hydraulic system can be bled manually or with pressure bleeding equipment.

➡Bleed the longest line first. Be sure the bleeder tank contains enough specified brake fluid to complete the bleeding operation.

1. Clean all dirt from and remove the brake master cylinder filler cap and fill the brake master cylinder reservoir with the specified brake fluid.

➡ Master cylinder pressure bleeder adapter tools are available from various manufacturers of pressure bleeding equipment. Follow the instructions of the manufacturer when installing the adapter.

2. Install the bleeder adapter to the brake master cylinder reservoir and attach the bleeder tank hose to the fitting on the adapter.

3. Place a box end wrench on the RH rear disc brake caliper bleeder screw. Attach a rubber drain tube to the RH rear disc brake caliper bleeder screw and submerge the free end of the tube in a container partially filled with clean brake fluid.

4. Open the valve on the bleeder tank.

5. Loosen the rear disc brake caliper bleeder screw. Leave open until clear, bubble-free brake fluid flows, then tighten rear disc brake caliper bleeder screw to 11 ft. lbs. (15 Nm) and remove the rubber hose.

6. Continue bleeding the rest of the system, going in order from the LH rear disc brake caliper to the RH front disc brake caliper ending with the LH front disc brake caliper.

7. Close the bleeder tank valve and remove the tank hose from the adapter and remove the adapter.

8. Fill the brake master cylinder reservoir and install the brake master cylinder filler cap.

BLEEDING THE ABS SYSTEM

❋❋ CAUTION

Brake fluid contains polyglycol ethers and polyglycols. Avoid contact with eyes. Wash hands thoroughly after handling. If brake fluid contacts eyes, flush eyes with running water for 15 minutes. Get medical attention if irritation persists. If taken internally, drink water and induce vomiting. Get medical attention immediately. Failure to follow these instructions may result in personal injury.

❋❋ WARNING

Do not allow the brake master cylinder reservoir to run dry during the bleeding operation. Keep the brake master cylinder reservoir filled with the specified brake fluid. Never reuse the brake fluid that has been drained from the hydraulic system.

❋❋ WARNING

Brake fluid is harmful to painted and plastic surfaces. If brake fluid is spilled onto a painted or plastic surface, immediately wash it with water.

➡ When any part of the hydraulic system has been disconnected for repair or new installation, air may get into the system and cause spongy brake pedal action. This requires bleeding of the hydraulic system after it has been correctly connected. The hydraulic system can be bled manually or with pressure bleeding equipment.

➡ This procedure must be performed if the 4 wheel anti-lock brake (4WABS) hydraulic control unit (HCU) has been installed new.

➡ One conventional pressure bleed cycle consists of advancing the brake pedal to its depressed position, opening the disc brake caliper bleeder screw, allowing fluid to be released into the waste container, closing the disc brake caliper bleeder screw and releasing the brake pedal.

➡ Performing the diagnostic program routine drives entrapped air from the otherwise inaccessible lower section of the 4WABS valve into the upper sections (accessible by bleeding the brakes). Subsequent bleedings remove the air from the system.

➡ Add recommended brake fluid as necessary throughout the procedure.

1. Connect a clear waste line to the RH rear disc brake caliper bleeder screw and the other end in a container partially filled with recommended brake fluid.

2. Have an assistant pump the brake pedal and then hold firm pressure on the brake pedal.

3. Loosen the RH rear disc brake caliper bleeder screw until a stream of brake fluid comes out. Have an assistant maintain pressure on the brake pedal while tightening the RH rear disc brake caliper bleeder screw.

   a. Repeat until clear, bubble-free fluid comes out.

   b. Refill the brake master cylinder reservoir as necessary.

4. Tighten the RH rear disc brake caliper bleeder screw to 11 ft. lbs. (15 Nm).

5. Repeat Steps 1, 2, 3, and 4 for the LH rear disc brake caliper bleeder screw, RH front disc brake caliper bleeder screw, and the LH front disc brake caliper bleeder screw. Tighten to 11 ft. lbs. (15 Nm).

➡ Go to the Help menu in the diagnostic tool.

6. Connect the diagnostic tool DCL cable adapter into the vehicle data link connector (DLC) under the dash and follow the diagnostic tool instructions.

7. Repeat the conventional bleed procedure as outlined in Steps 1 through 5.

8. If the brake pedal feels spongy, repeat the diagnostic tool service bleed procedure.

BRAKES   **FRONT DISC BRAKES**

✳✳ CAUTION

Dust and dirt accumulating on brake parts during normal use may contain asbestos fibers from production or aftermarket brake linings. Breathing excessive concentrations of asbestos fibers can cause serious bodily harm. Exercise care when servicing brake parts. Do not sand or grind brake lining unless equipment used is designed to contain the dust residue. Do not clean brake parts with compressed air or by dry brushing. Cleaning should be done by dampening the brake components with a fine mist of water, then wiping the brake components clean with a dampened cloth. Dispose of cloth and all residue containing asbestos fibers in an impermeable container with the appropriate label. Follow practices prescribed by the Occupational Safety and Health Administration (OSHA) and the Environmental Protection Agency (EPA) for the handling, processing, and disposing of dust or debris that may contain asbestos fibers.

BRAKE CALIPER

REMOVAL & INSTALLATION

Excursion

1. Before servicing the vehicle, refer to the precautions section.
2. Raise and support the vehicle.
3. Remove the wheel and tire assembly.
4. Remove the brake hose bolt.
5. Disconnect the brake hose.
6. Remove and discard the copper washers. Plug the brake hose.
7. Remove the disc brake caliper pin bolts.
8. Lift the disc brake caliper from the disc brake caliper anchor plate.
9. Inspect the disc brake caliper for leaks.
10. If leaks are found, disassembly is required to repair. Or replace the caliper.

To install:

11. Install the disc brake caliper.
12. Install the disc brake caliper pin bolts and tighten to 42 ft. lbs. (56 Nm).
13. Use new copper washers. Connect the brake hose.
14. Install the brake hose bolt and tighten to 26 ft. lbs. (35 Nm).

15. Bleed the brake system.
16. Install the wheel and tire assembly.
17. Fill the brake master cylinder reservoir with clean DOT 3 motor vehicle brake fluid. Install the brake master cylinder filler cap.
18. Inspect the brake system operation.

Expedition & Navigator

✳✳ WARNING

The electrical power to the air suspension system must be shut off prior to hoisting, jacking or towing an air suspension vehicle. Failure to shut the system off may lead to an unexpected inflation or deflation of the air springs, which may result in a shift of the vehicle.

1. Before servicing the vehicle, refer to the precautions section.
2. Remove or disconnect the following:
   • Wheels
   • Brake pads
   • Front brake hose bolt and the copper washers and plug the front brake hose
   • 2 front disc brake caliper bolts, then lift the caliper off of the front caliper anchor plate

To install:

3. Install or connect the following:
   • 2 front disc brake caliper bolts, tighten the bolts to 41 ft. lbs. (55 Nm).
   • Front brake hose to the brake caliper, using new copper washers. Tighten the retaining bolt to 26 ft. lbs. (35 Nm).
   • Brake pads
   • Wheels

DISC BRAKE PADS

REMOVAL & INSTALLATION

Excursion

✳✳ WARNING

The electrical power to the air suspension system must be shut off prior to hoisting, jacking or towing an air suspension vehicle. Failure to shut the system off may lead to an unexpected inflation or deflation of the air springs, which may result in a shift of the vehicle.

1. Before servicing the vehicle, refer to the precautions section.

2. Using a suitable suction device, remove the brake fluid in the master cylinder reservoir until it is half filled.
3. Remove the wheels.
4. Remove the disc brake caliper.
5. Remove the V-springs.
6. Remove the pads and rail clips.

✳✳ CAUTION

Do not allow grease, oil, brake fluid or other contaminants to contact the pad lining material. Do not install contaminated pads.

To install:

7. Install the pads.
8. Install the disc brake caliper anchor plate stainless steel rail clips.
9. If necessary, install the V-springs.
10. Compress the caliper pistons.

✳✳ CAUTION

Use care not to damage the bleeder screw or front disc brake rotor shield.

11. Install the disc brake caliper.
12. Install the wheel and tire assembly.
13. Fill the brake master cylinder reservoir with DOT 3 motor vehicle brake fluid. Install the brake master cylinder filler cap.
14. Inspect brake operation.

Expedition & Navigator

✳✳ WARNING

The electrical power to the air suspension system must be shut off prior to hoisting, jacking or towing an air suspension vehicle. Failure to shut the system off may lead to an unexpected inflation or deflation of the air springs, which may result in a shift of the vehicle.

1. Before servicing the vehicle, refer to the precautions section.
2. Using a suitable suction device, remove the brake fluid in the master cylinder reservoir until it is half filled.
3. Remove or disconnect the following:
   • Wheels
   • Anchor housing spring.

➡Ensure the anchor housing spring has one end with two tabs. If yes, the Left Hand (left hand) side anchor housing spring must be installed with the two-tabbed end in the upper brake caliper cavity.

4. On the left hand brake caliper, release the lower portion of the anchor housing spring as follows:

a. Apply force at the center of the anchor housing spring and pull outward at the bottom of the anchor housing spring to remove it from the lower brake caliper cavity.

b. Rotate the spring upward then remove it from the brake caliper.

➡ **On the Right Hand (RH) side, the anchor housing spring must be installed with the two-tabbed end in the lower brake caliper cavity.**

5. For the RH brake caliper, release the upper portion of the anchor housing spring as follows:

a. Apply force at the center of the anchor housing spring and pull outward at the top of the anchor housing spring to remove it from the upper brake caliper cavity.

b. Rotate the spring downward then remove it from the brake caliper.

➡ **Never allow the brake caliper to hang from the brake hose.**

6. Remove the brake caliper as follows:

a. Remove the zero-drag spring.

b. Remove and discard the brake caliper-to-anchor plate bolts, guide pins and boots.

7. Remove the brake pads from the brake caliper.

8. Compress the brake caliper pistons using a C-clamp or other suitable tool.

To install:

9. Clean the inner surfaces of the brake caliper where the brake pads attach.

10. Install new brake hardware as follows:

a. Install the guide pin bushings into the caliper bores.

b. Apply grease to the inside of the guide pin bushing. Do not apply grease to the guide pin threads.

c. Push the guide pins into the bushing.

11. Install or connect the following:

- Inboard brake pad into the brake caliper.
- Outboard brake pad into the brake caliper
- Brake caliper on the brake disc. Tighten the guide pins and install the dust caps.
- Zero-drag spring

➡ **If present, the 2-tabbed end of the anchor housing spring must be installed first.**

12. Install the anchor housing spring as follows:

a. Insert tab of the anchor housing spring into the brake caliper cavity.

b. Twist tab into the brake caliper cavity (left hand side-upper brake caliper cavity/RH side-lower brake caliper cavity).

c. Rotate the anchor housing spring and position the upper portion onto the anchor plate.

d. Position the other anchor housing spring portion onto the brake caliper anchor plate.

e. Push down and inward until the upper and lower ends of the anchor housing spring are latched and seated in the brake caliper cavities.

13. Verify that the anchor housing spring is correctly latched.

14. Bleed the brake system, filling the brake master cylinder reservoir as required.

15. Install the wheels.

16. Make sure that the brakes are operating correctly.

BRAKES

❋❋ CAUTION

Dust and dirt accumulating on brake parts during normal use may contain asbestos fibers from production or aftermarket brake linings. Breathing excessive concentrations of asbestos fibers can cause serious bodily harm. Exercise care when servicing brake parts. Do not sand or grind brake lining unless equipment used is designed to contain the dust residue. Do not clean brake parts with compressed air or by dry brushing. Cleaning should be done by dampening the brake components with a fine mist of water, then wiping the brake components clean with a dampened cloth. Dispose of cloth and all residue containing asbestos fibers in an impermeable container with the appropriate label. Follow practices prescribed by the Occupational Safety and Health Administration (OSHA) and the Environmental Protection Agency (EPA) for the handling, processing, and disposing of dust or debris that may contain asbestos fibers.

BRAKE CALIPER

REMOVAL & INSTALLATION

Excursion

❋❋ WARNING

The electrical power to the air suspension system must be shut off prior to hoisting, jacking or towing an air suspension vehicle. Failure to shut the system off may lead to an unexpected inflation or deflation of the air springs, which may result in a shift of the vehicle.

1. Before servicing the vehicle, refer to the precautions section.

2. Before servicing the vehicle, refer to the precautions section.

3. Remove enough brake fluid from the brake master cylinder reservoir until it is ½ full.

4. Remove or disconnect the following:

- Wheels
- Stone shield
- 2 brake caliper slide pins and lift the caliper off the anchor plate

REAR DISC BRAKES

- Banjo bolt connecting the brake hose to the disc brake caliper and plug the brake hose. Discard 2 copper sealing washers.

To install:

5. Retract the disc brake caliper pistons fully in the piston bores using an old brake pad or block of wood and a C-clamp or equivalent.

6. Install or connect the following:

- Disc brake caliper above the rotor and install it with a rotating motion. Make sure the inner and outer pads are properly positioned and the anti-rattle clips are correctly installed. The brake caliper bleed screw should be positioned on top of the caliper when assembled on the vehicle.
- Brake hose to the disc brake caliper using 2 new copper sealing washers. Tighten the banjo bolt to 37 ft. lbs. (50 Nm).

7. Lubricate the locating pins and the inside of the insulators with silicone grease.

- Locating pins through the caliper insulators and hand-start the threads into the steering knuckle attaching holes. Tighten the locating pins to 27–41 ft. lbs. (36–55 Nm).

8. Bleed the brake system, filling the brake master cylinder reservoir as required.

- Wheels

9. Lower the vehicle.

10. Pump the brake pedal several times to position the brake pads prior to moving the vehicle.

11. Road-test the vehicle and check for proper brake system operation.

Expedition & Navigator

> ✳✳ **WARNING**
>
> **The electrical power to the air suspension system must be shut off prior to hoisting, jacking or towing an air suspension vehicle. Failure to shut the system off may lead to an unexpected inflation or deflation of the air springs, which may result in a shift of the vehicle.**

1. Before servicing the vehicle, refer to the precautions section.

2. Remove or disconnect the following:

- Wheels
- 2 rear disc brake caliper bolts and caps, then lift the caliper off of the front caliper anchor plate
- Rear brake hose bolt and the copper washers and plug the front brake hose

To install:

3. Install or connect the following:

- 2 rear disc brake caliper bolts and caps. Tighten the bolts to 26 ft. lbs. (35 Nm).
- Rear brake hose to the brake caliper, using new copper washers. Tighten the retaining bolts to 26 ft. lbs. (35 Nm).
- Brake pads
- Wheels

4. Bleed the brake system, filling the brake master cylinder reservoir as required.

5. Road-test the vehicle and check for proper brake system operation.

DISC BRAKE PADS

REMOVAL & INSTALLATION

Excursion

> ✳✳ **WARNING**
>
> **The electrical power to the air suspension system must be shut off prior to hoisting, jacking or towing an air suspension vehicle. Failure to shut the system off may lead to an unexpected inflation or deflation of the air springs, which may result in a shift of the vehicle.**

1. Before servicing the vehicle, refer to the precautions section.

2. Remove the brake master cylinder filler cap. Check brake fluid level in brake master cylinder reservoir. Remove fluid until brake master cylinder reservoir is half full.

3. Remove the wheel assembly.

4. Inspect the brake pads for wear or contamination.

5. Remove the nuts and the stone shield.

6. Remove the caliper pin bolts.

> ✳✳ **CAUTION**
>
> **Never allow the rear disc brake caliper to hang from the brake hose. Provide suitable support.**

7. Remove the rear disc brake caliper and support with mechanics wire.

8. Remove the brake pads and rail clips.

To install:

9. Install new pads and clips.

10. Install the caliper and tighten the pin bolts to 27 ft. lbs. (36 Nm).

11. Install the stone shield and tighten to 46 ft. lbs. (62 Nm).

12. Bleed the brake system, filling the brake master cylinder reservoir as required.

13. Install the wheel assembly.

14. Make sure that the brakes are operating correctly.

Expedition & Navigator

> ✳✳ **WARNING**
>
> **The electrical power to the air suspension system must be shut off prior to hoisting, jacking or towing an air suspension vehicle. Failure to shut the system off may lead to an unexpected inflation or deflation of the air springs, which may result in a shift of the vehicle.**

1. Before servicing the vehicle, refer to the precautions section.

2. Remove enough brake fluid from the brake master cylinder reservoir until it is ½ full.

3. Remove or disconnect the following:

- Wheels
- Anchor housing spring by squeezing at the center of the spring until it unlatches from the brake caliper at both ends, then rotate the spring to remove it from the caliper housing
- Caps and brake caliper bolts
- Brake caliper without disconnecting the brake hose
- Brake pads

4. Thoroughly clean the areas of the caliper and caliper support assembly which contact each other during the sliding action of the caliper.

To install:

5. Compress the caliper piston using a C–clamp or other suitable tool.

6. Install or connect the following:

- Brake shoes on the disc brake caliper support bracket
- Anchor housing spring by placing the upper anchor housing spring end into the brake caliper cavity, then rotate the anchor housing spring and position the lower arm onto the anchor plate
- Upper arm onto the anchor plate, then press down and inward until it is correctly seated and latched into the brake caliper cavities
- Rear disc brake caliper onto the rear support bracket
- Brake caliper caps and bolts, tighten pin bolts to 26 ft. lbs. (35 Nm).

7. Bleed the brake system, filling the brake master cylinder reservoir as required.

- Front wheels

8. Make sure that the brakes are operating correctly.

BRAKES

PARKING BRAKE

PARKING BRAKE CABLES

REMOVAL & INSTALLATION

2005–06 Expedition & Navigator

Front Cable

❊❊ WARNING

The electrical power to the air suspension system must be shut off prior to hoisting, jacking or towing an air suspension vehicle. This can be accomplished by turning off the air suspension switch located near the jack storage area in the rear of the passenger compartment. Failure to do so may result in unexpected inflation or deflation of the air springs which may result in shifting of the vehicle during these operations. Failure to follow these instructions may result in personal injury.

1. Before servicing the vehicle, refer to the precautions section.
2. Remove the parking brake control.
3. If equipped, turn the air suspension switch to the OFF position.
4. With the vehicle in NEUTRAL, position it on a hoist.
5. Remove the front park brake cable P-clip-to-frame bolt.
6. Pry the rubber seal from the front floor pan.
7. Compress the retainer and release the conduit from the bracket.
8. Remove the front cable and conduit from the cable union.
9. To install, reverse the removal procedure and tighten the P-clip-to-frame bolt to 11 ft. lbs. (15 Nm).

Right Rear Cable

❊❊ WARNING

The electrical power to the air suspension system must be shut off prior to hoisting, jacking or towing an air suspension vehicle. This can be accomplished by turning off the air suspension switch located near the jack storage area in the rear of the passenger compartment. Failure to do so may result in unexpected inflation or deflation of the air springs which may result in shifting of the vehicle during these operations. Failure to follow these instructions may result in personal injury.

1. Before servicing the vehicle, refer to the precautions section.
2. Verify that the parking brake control is fully released.

➡This step will require the aid of an assistant.

3. Relieve the tension on the parking brake cable system:
   • Pull down on the front parking brake cable at the connector clip.
   • Insert a 4 mm (5/32 inch) pin into the parking brake lever lockout hole
4. With the vehicle in NEUTRAL, position it on a hoist.
5. Remove the RH rear cable from the cable union.
6. Compress the cable clip and release the conduit from the equalizer.
7. Remove the RH rear cable from the retaining clip.
8. Remove the bolt and the wireform bracket from the upper control arm.
9. Remove the rear park brake cable P-clip-to-frame bolt from the crossmember.
10. Compress the retainer and release the conduit, then unclip the cable end fitting from the brake caliper lever.
11. To install, reverse the removal procedure and note the following:
   a. Tighten the wireform bracket bolt to 26 ft. lbs. (35 Nm).
   b. Tighten the P-clip-to-frame bolt to 80 inch. lbs. (90 Nm).

Left Rear Cable

❊❊ WARNING

The electrical power to the air suspension system must be shut off prior to hoisting, jacking or towing an air suspension vehicle. This can be accomplished by turning off the air suspension switch located near the jack storage area in the rear of the passenger compartment. Failure to do so may result in unexpected inflation or deflation of the air springs which may result in shifting of the vehicle during these operations. Failure to follow these instructions may result in personal injury.

1. Before servicing the vehicle, refer to the precautions section.
2. Verify that the parking brake control is fully released.

➡This step will require the aid of an assistant.

3. Relieve the tension on the parking brake cable system:
   • Pull down on the front parking brake cable at the connector clip.
   • Insert a 4 mm (5/32 inch) pin into the parking brake lever lockout hole
4. With the vehicle in NEUTRAL, position it on a hoist.
5. Compress the retainer
6. Remove the conduit from the bracket.

➡Be sure to correctly install the park brake cable retainer spring during installation or the park brake system will not operate correctly.

7. Remove the LH rear cable from the retaining clip.
8. Disconnect the park brake cable retainer spring.
9. Disconnect the ABS sensor wire from the retaining clip.
10. Remove the wireform bracket retaining screw and the bracket.
11. Compress the retainer and release the conduit, then unclip the cable end fitting from the brake caliper lever.
12. To install, reverse the removal procedure and tighten the wireform bracket bolt to 26 ft. lbs. (35 Nm).

2007 Expedition & Navigator

Front Cable

1. Before servicing the vehicle, refer to the precautions section.
2. Remove the parking brake control.
3. If equipped, turn the air suspension switch to the OFF position.
4. With the vehicle in NEUTRAL, position it on a hoist.
5. Remove the front park brake cable P-clip-to-frame bolt.
6. Pry the rubber seal from the front floor pan.
7. Compress the retainer and release the conduit from the bracket.
8. Remove the front cable and conduit from the cable union.
9. To install, reverse the removal procedure and tighten the P-clip-to-frame bolt to 13 ft. lbs. (18 Nm).

Right Rear Cable

1. Before servicing the vehicle, refer to the precautions section.

2. Relieve the tension on the parking brake cable system.

3. With the vehicle in NEUTRAL, position it on a hoist.

4. Disconnect the RH rear cable from the cable union.

5. Compress the 2 tabs and release the conduit from the equalizer.

6. Remove the RH rear cable from the retaining clip.

7. Remove the bolt and the wire form bracket from the LH side of the vehicle.

8. Remove the rear park brake cable-to-crossmember bolt.

9. Remove the bolt and the wire form bracket from the RH side of the vehicle.

10. Compress the 2 tabs and release the conduit, then unclip the cable end fitting from the parking brake shoe lever.

To install, reverse the removal procedure and note the following:

c. Tighten the left wire form bracket bolt to 13 ft. lbs. (18 Nm).

d. Tighten the rear park brake cable-to-crossmember bolt to 80 inch. lbs. (90 Nm).

e. Tighten the right wire form bracket bolt to 13 ft. lbs. (18 Nm).

Left Rear Cable

1. Before servicing the vehicle, refer to the precautions section.

2. Relieve the tension on the parking brake cable system.

3. With the vehicle in NEUTRAL, position it on a hoist.

4. Separate the LH rear cable from the equalizer.

5. Compress the 2 tabs.

6. Remove the conduit from the bracket.

➡ **Be sure to correctly install the park brake cable retainer spring and route cables between suspension links.**

7. Remove the LH rear cable from the retaining clip.

8. Disconnect the park brake cable retainer spring.

9. If equipped, disconnect the anti-lock brake system (ABS) sensor wire from the retaining clip.

10. Remove the wireform bracket retaining bolt and the bracket.

11. Compress the retainer and release the conduit, then unclip the cable end fitting from the parking brake shoe lever.

12. To install, reverse the removal procedure and note the following:

a. Tighten the wire form bracket bolt to 13 ft. lbs. (18 Nm).

PARKING BRAKE CABLE TENSION RELEASE

See Figure 3.

1. Remove the LH cowl side trim panel.

2. With the help of an assistant, release the parking brake cable tension by pulling down on the intermediate cable at the cable-to-cable connector clip until the parking brake control sector rotates to its stop and a 4 mm (0.15 in) x 150 mm (5.9 in) retainer pin can be inserted.

3. Disconnect the cable-to-cable connector clip.

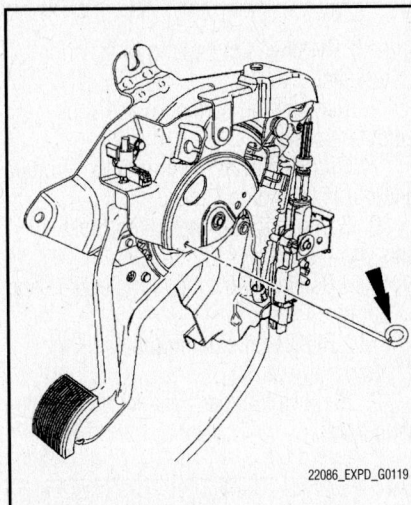

22086_EXPD_G0119

Fig. 3 Insert the retainer pin as shown

4. To reload the tension on the parking brake cable, follow the release procedure in reverse.

5. Make sure the cable-to-cable connector clip is connected to the front and rear cable before removing the brake control retaining pin, and the cable tension is reloaded slowly.

PARKING BRAKE SHOES

REMOVAL & INSTALLATION

Excursion

✳ CAUTION

Asbestos fiber dust can be present on brake and clutch assemblies and is hazardous if inhaled. Brake and clutch assemblies must be cleaned using a vacuum cleaner recommended for use with asbestos fibers such as a brake/clutch/service vacuum. The bag must be labeled per OSHA instruction, sealed, and the trash hauler notified as to the bag's contents. If a vacuum suitable for

asbestos is not available, cleaning must be done wet. If dust generation is still possible, you must wear government-approved toxic dust purifying respirators.

1. Before servicing the vehicle, refer to the precautions section.

2. Remove the rear disc brake rotor.

3. Disconnect the rear parking brake cable at the parking brake intermediate cable.

4. Disconnect the parking brake cable at the parking brake lever.

5. Remove the outboard brake shoe retracting spring.

6. Remove the brake shoe adjusting screw spring.

7. Remove the brake shoe hold-down springs.

8. Remove the brake adjuster screw.

9. Remove the parking brake shoe and linings along with the inboard brake shoe retracting spring.

10. Inspect the components for excessive wear or damage and install new as required.

To install:

➡ **Make sure the inboard brake shoe retracting spring is attached to the parking brake shoe.**

11. Install the LH parking brake shoe and brake shoe hold-down spring, along with the inboard brake shoe retracting spring.

12. Connect the inboard brake shoe retracting spring to the RH parking brake shoe, and install the RH parking brake shoe and the brake shoe hold-down spring.

13. Install the brake adjuster screw.

14. Install the brake shoe adjusting screw spring.

➡ **The outboard brake shoe retracting spring mounts above the inboard brake shoe retracting spring.**

15. Install the outboard brake shoe retracting spring.

16. Connect the parking brake cable at the parking brake lever.

17. Connect the rear parking brake cable at the parking brake intermediate cable.

18. Install the rear disc brake rotor.

19. Use the Brake Adjusting Gauge 206-D002 (D81L-1103-A) or equivalent special tool to set the rear brake shoe and lining diameter to 0.030 in. (0.76mm) less than the inside diameter of the drum portion of the rear disc brake rotor.

20. Burnish the parking brake shoe and linings, as follows:

   a. Accelerate the vehicle to 25 mph (40 km/h).

   b. Shift the transmission to NEUTRAL.

   c. Slowly apply the parking brake control to approximately one-half to three-quarters of its travel.

   d. Allow the vehicle to come to a complete stop.

   e. Release the parking brake.

Expedition & Navigator

See Figures 4 through 11.

1. Before servicing the vehicle, refer to the precautions section.

➡**Verify that the parking brake control is fully released.**

➡**This step will require the aid of an assistant.**

2. Relieve the tension on the parking brake cable system:

   a. Pull down on the front parking brake cable at the coupler.

   b. Insert a $\frac{5}{32}$ in. (4mm) pin into the parking brake lever.

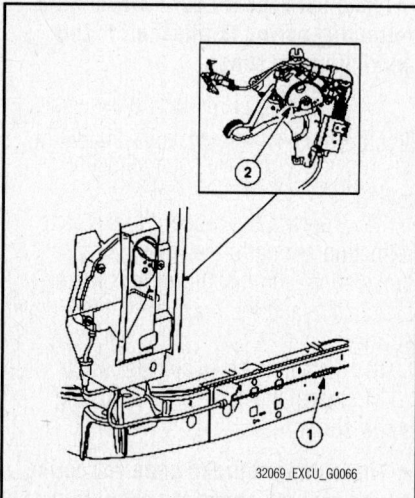

Fig. 4 Pull down on the front parking brake cable at the coupler (1), then insert a $\frac{5}{32}$ in. (4mm) pin into the parking brake lever (2)

3. Remove the brake disc.

➡**The hub has been removed for clarity.**

4. Remove the front parking brake shoe retaining clip and pin.

5. Remove the parking brake shoe adjuster, as follows:

   a. Using a suitable tool, spread the bottom of the parking brake shoes apart.

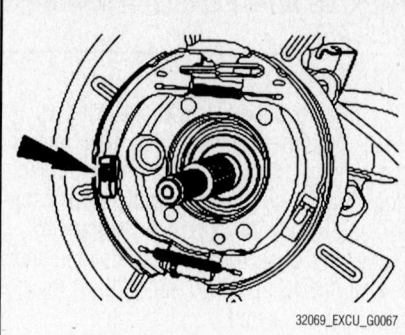

Fig. 5 Remove the front parking brake shoe retaining clip and pin

   b. Remove the parking brake shoe adjuster.

6. Remove the parking brake shoe adjuster spring.

7. Slide the front parking brake shoe up and out of the guide flange.

8. Remove the front parking brake shoe, as follows:

   a. Rotate the front parking brake shoe outward.

   b. Remove the parking brake shoe return spring.

9. Remove the rear parking brake shoe, as follows:

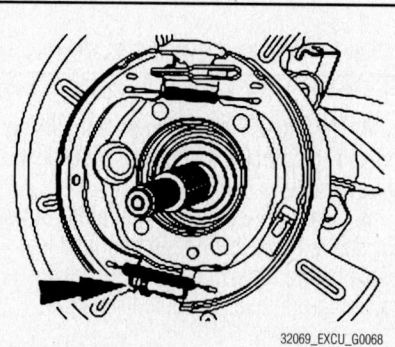

Fig. 6 Remove the parking brake shoe adjuster

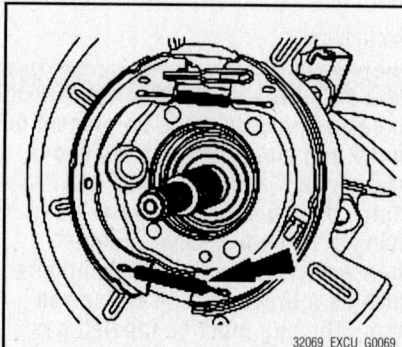

Fig. 7 Remove the parking brake shoe adjuster spring

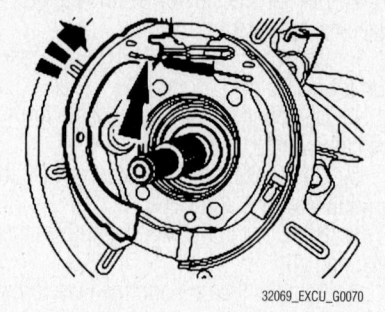

Fig. 8 Rotate the front parking brake shoe outward, then remove the parking brake shoe return spring

   a. Remove the retaining clip and pin.

   b. Remove the rear parking brake shoe.

10. Inspect the components for excessive wear or damage and install new parts as required.

To install:

➡**Before installation, lubricate the parking brake shoe contact points using silicone brake caliper grease.**

11. Install the rear parking brake shoe, as follows:

   a. Hold the rear parking brake shoe in position.

   b. Install the retaining pin and clip.

12. Install the front parking brake shoe, as follows:

   a. Install the parking brake shoe return spring to the rear parking brake shoe and to the front parking brake shoe.

   b. Rotate the front parking brake shoe into the guide flange.

13. Slide the front parking brake shoe down into position on the flange.

14. Install the front parking brake shoe retaining pin and clip.

15. Install the parking brake shoe adjuster spring.

16. Install the parking brake shoe adjuster, as follows:

   a. Using a suitable tool, spread the bottom of the parking brake shoes apart.

   b. Install the parking brake shoe adjuster.

17. Using the Brake Adjusting Gauge 206-D002 (D81L-1103-A) or equivalent special tool, measure the inside diameter of the drum portion of the rear brake disc. Record the measurement.

➡**Make sure that the parking brake shoes are correctly centered. Take the measurement at the widest point across the center of the parking brake shoes.**

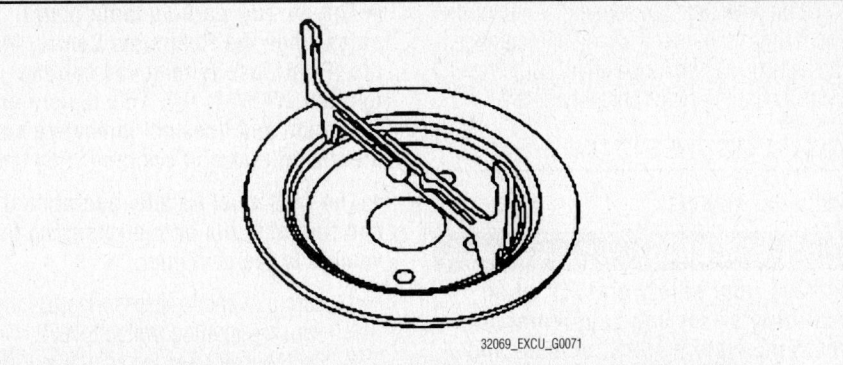

Fig. 9 Use the special tool to measure the inside diameter of the drum portion of the rear brake disc

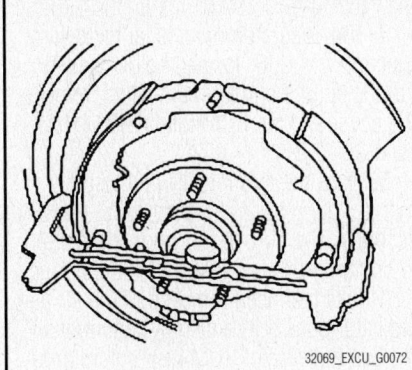

Fig. 10 Using the special tool, measure the parking brake shoe diameter. Rotate the adjuster to set the parking brake shoe diameter to 0.02 inch (0.5mm) less than the recorded inside diameter of the drum portion of the rear brake disc

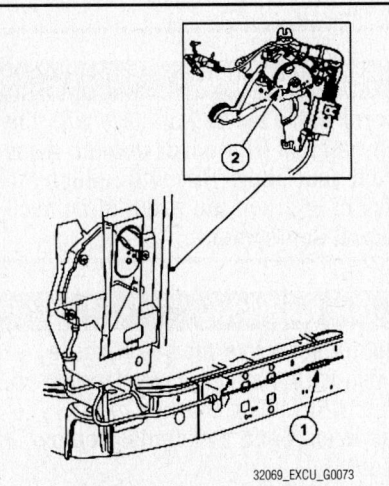

Fig. 11 Pull down on the front parking brake cable at the coupler (1), then remove the retaining pin from the parking brake lever (2)

18. Using the special tool, measure the parking brake shoe diameter. Rotate the adjuster to set the parking brake shoe diameter to 0.02 inch (0.5mm) less than the recorded inside diameter of the drum portion of the rear brake disc.

19. Install the brake disc.

➡ **This step will require the aid of an assistant.**

20. Enable the parking brake cable system, as follows:
   a. Pull down on the front parking brake cable at the coupler.
   b. Remove the retaining pin from the parking brake lever.

21. Check the operation of the parking brake.

ADJUSTMENT

Excursion

1. Raise and support the vehicle.
2. Remove the wheel and tire assembly.
3. Remove the brake adjusting hole cover from the backing plate.
4. Turn the brake adjuster screw to expand the parking brake shoe and linings until they drag against the drum-in-hat rotor.
5. Back off the brake adjuster screw until no drag is evident.

Expedition & Navigator

Refer to the Parking Brake Shoes Removal & Installation procedure.

CHASSIS ELECTRICAL — AIR BAG (SUPPLEMENTAL RESTRAINT SYSTEM)

GENERAL INFORMATION

✳✳ CAUTION

These vehicles are equipped with an air bag system. The system must be disarmed before performing service on, or around, system components, the steering column, instrument panel components, wiring and sensors. Failure to follow the safety precautions and the disarming procedure could result in accidental air bag deployment, possible injury and unnecessary system repairs.

SERVICE PRECAUTIONS

Disconnect and isolate the battery negative cable before beginning any airbag system component diagnosis, testing, removal, or installation procedures. Allow system capacitor to discharge for two minutes before beginning any component service. This will disable the airbag system. Failure to disable the airbag system may result in accidental airbag deployment, personal injury, or death.

Do not place an intact undeployed airbag face down on a solid surface. The airbag will propel into the air if accidentally deployed and may result in personal injury or death.

When carrying or handling an undeployed airbag, the trim side (face) of the airbag should be pointing towards the body to minimize possibility of injury if accidental deployment occurs. Failure to do this may result in personal injury or death.

Replace airbag system components with OEM replacement parts. Substitute parts may appear interchangeable, but internal differences may result in inferior occupant protection. Failure to do so may result in occupant personal injury or death.

Wear safety glasses, rubber gloves, and long sleeved clothing when cleaning powder residue from vehicle after an airbag deployment. Powder residue emitted from a deployed airbag can cause skin irritation. Flush affected area with cool water if irritation is experienced. If nasal or throat irritation is experienced, exit the vehicle for fresh air until the irritation ceases. If irritation continues, see a physician.

Do not use a replacement airbag that is not in the original packaging. This may result in improper deployment, personal injury, or death.

The factory installed fasteners, screws and bolts used to fasten airbag components have a special coating and are specifically designed for the airbag system. Do not use substitute fasteners. Use only original equipment fasteners listed in the parts catalog when fastener replacement is required.

During, and following, any child restraint anchor service, due to impact event or vehicle repair, carefully inspect all mounting hardware, tether straps, and anchors for proper installation, operation, or damage. If a child restraint anchor is found damaged in any way, the anchor must be replaced. Failure to do this may result in personal injury or death.

Deployed and non-deployed airbags may or may not have live pyrotechnic material within the airbag inflator.

Do not dispose of driver/passenger/curtain airbags or seat belt tensioners unless you are sure of complete deployment. Refer to the Hazardous Substance Control System for proper disposal.

Dispose of deployed airbags and tensioners consistent with state, provincial, local, and federal regulations.

After any airbag component testing or service, do not connect the battery negative cable. Personal injury or death may result if the system test is not performed first.

If the vehicle is equipped with the Occupant Classification System (OCS), do not connect the battery negative cable before performing the OCS Verification Test using the scan tool and the appropriate diagnostic information. Personal injury or death may result if the system test is not performed properly.

Never replace both the Occupant Restraint Controller (ORC) and the Occupant Classification Module (OCM) at the same time. If both require replacement, replace one, then perform the Airbag System test before replacing the other.

Both the ORC and the OCM store Occupant Classification System (OCS) calibration data, which they transfer to one another when one of them is replaced. If both are replaced at the same time, an irreversible fault will be set in both modules and the OCS may malfunction and cause personal injury or death.

If equipped with OCS, the Seat Weight Sensor is a sensitive, calibrated unit and must be handled carefully. Do not drop or handle roughly. If dropped or damaged, replace with another sensor. Failure to do so may result in occupant injury or death.

If equipped with OCS, the front passenger seat must be handled carefully as well. When removing the seat, be careful when setting on floor not to drop. If dropped, the sensor may be inoperative, could result in occupant injury, or possibly death.

If equipped with OCS, when the passenger front seat is on the floor, no one should sit in the front passenger seat. This uneven force may damage the sensing ability of the seat weight sensors. If sat on and damaged, the sensor may be inoperative, could result in occupant injury, or possibly death.

DISARMING THE SYSTEM

2005–06 Models

✳✳ WARNING

Always wear safety glasses when repairing an air bag supplemental restraint system (SRS) vehicle and when handling an air bag module. This will reduce the risk of injury in the event of an accidental deployment.

✳✳ WARNING

Carry a live air bag module with the air bag and trim cover pointed away from your body. This will reduce the risk of injury in the event of an accidental deployment.

✳✳ WARNING

Do not set a live air bag module down with the trim cover face down. This will reduce the risk of injury in the event of an accidental deployment.

✳✳ WARNING

After deployment, the air bag surface can contain deposits of sodium hydroxide, a product of the gas generant combustion that is irritating to the skin. Wash your hands with soap and water afterwards.

✳✳ WARNING

Never probe the connectors on the air bag module. Doing so can result in air bag deployment, which can result in personal injury.

✳✳ WARNING

Never probe the connectors on the safety canopy module. Doing so can result in safety canopy module deployment.

✳✳ WARNING

To reduce the risk of personal injury, do not use any memory saver devices.

➡**The air bag warning lamp illuminates when the Restraints Control Module (RCM) fuse is removed and the ignition switch is ON. This is normal operation and does not indicate a supplemental restraint system (SRS) fault.**

➡**The SRS must be fully operational and free of faults before releasing the vehicle to the customer.**

1. Turn all vehicle accessories OFF.
2. Turn the ignition switch to OFF.
3. On Navigator and Expedition models, at the Central Junction Box (CJB), located below the right hand side of the instrument panel, open the kick panel cover and remove the RCM fuse F1.19 (10A) from the CJB.
4. On Excursion models, at the central junction box CJB, located below the left hand side of the instrument panel, remove the cover and the RCM fuse F2.26 (10A) from the CJB.
5. Turn the ignition ON and visually monitor the air bag indicator for at least 30 seconds. The air bag indicator will remain lit continuously (no flashing) if the correct RCM fuse has been removed. If the air bag indicator does not remain lit continuously, remove the correct RCM fuse before proceeding.
6. Turn the ignition OFF.

✳✳ WARNING

To avoid accidental deployment and possible personal injury, the backup power supply must be depleted before repairing or replacing any front or side air bag Supplemental Restraint System (SRS) components and before servicing, replacing, adjusting or striking components near the front or side air bag sensors or RCM, such as doors, instrument panel, console, door latches, strikers, seats and hood latches.

7. To deplete the backup power supply energy, disconnect the battery ground cable and wait at least one minute. Be sure to disconnect auxiliary batteries and power supplies (if equipped).

2007 Models

✳✳ WARNING

Always wear safety glasses when repairing an air bag supplemental restraint system (SRS) vehicle and when handling an air bag module. This will reduce the risk of injury in the event of an accidental deployment.

❈❈ WARNING

Never probe the connectors on the air bag module. Doing so can result in air bag deployment, which can result in personal injury.

❈❈ WARNING

To reduce the risk of personal injury, do not use any memory saver devices.

➡ The air bag warning lamp illuminates when the restraints control module (RCM) fuse is removed and the ignition switch is ON. This is normal operation and does not indicate a supplemental restraint system (SRS) fault.

➡ The SRS must be fully operational and free of faults before releasing the vehicle to the customer.

1. Turn all vehicle accessories OFF.
2. Turn the ignition switch to OFF.
3. At the smart power distribution junction box (SPDJB), located in the RH lower kick panel, remove the cover and the restraints control module (RCM) fuse 32 (10A) from the SPDJB.
4. Turn the ignition ON and visually monitor the air bag warning indicator for at least 30 seconds. The air bag warning indicator will remain lit continuously (no flashing) if the correct RCM fuse has been removed. If the air bag warning indicator does not remain lit continuously, remove the correct RCM fuse before proceeding.
5. Turn the ignition switch to OFF.

❈❈ CAUTION

To avoid accidental deployment and possible personal injury, the backup power supply must be depleted before repairing or replacing any front or side air bag supplemental restraint system (SRS) components and before servicing, replacing, adjusting or striking components near the front or side air bag sensors, such as doors, instrument panel, console, door latches, strikers, seats and hood latches.

➡ The front impact severity sensor is located on the bottom of the radiator support bracket.

➡ The front door side impact sensors (if equipped) are located in the first row doors, behind the door trim panel.

➡ The C-pillar side impact sensors (if equipped) are located on the C-pillar.

➡ To deplete the backup power supply energy, disconnect the battery ground cable and wait at least one minute. Be sure to disconnect auxiliary batteries and power supplies (if equipped). Failure to follow these instructions may increase the risk of personal injury or death in a crash.

6. Disconnect the battery ground cable and wait at least one minute.

ARMING THE SYSTEM

2005–06 Models

❈❈ WARNING

The restraint system diagnostic tool is for restraint system service only. Remove from vehicle prior to road use. Failure to remove could result in injury and possible violation of vehicle safety standards.

1. Make sure all restraint system diagnostic tool(s) that may have been installed during the repair have been removed from the vehicle and all SRS components are connected.
2. Turn the ignition switch from OFF to ON.
3. Install the RCM fuse to the CJB and close the cover.

❈❈ WARNING

Be sure that nobody is in the vehicle and that there is nothing blocking or set in front of any air bag module when the battery ground cable is connected.

4. Connect the battery ground cable.
5. Prove out the SRS as follows:
   a. Turn the ignition key from ON to OFF. Wait 10 seconds, then turn the key back to ON and visually monitor the air bag indicator with the air bag modules installed. The air bag indicator will light continuously for approximately six seconds and then turn off. If an air bag supplemental restraint system (SRS) fault is present, the air bag indicator will either, fail to light, remain lit continuously or flash.
   b. The flashing might not occur until approximately 30 seconds after the ignition switch has been turned from the OFF to the ON position. This is the time required for the RCM to complete the testing of the SRS.
   c. If the air bag indicator is inoperative and a SRS fault exists, a chime will sound in a pattern of five sets of five beeps. If this occurs, the air bag indicator

and any SRS fault discovered must be diagnosed and repaired.
   d. Clear all continuous DTCs from the restraints control module using a scan tool.

2007 Models

1. Make sure that all supplemental restraint system (SRS) components are connected.
2. Turn the ignition switch from OFF to ON.
3. Install restraints control module (RCM) fuse 32 (10A) to the SPDJB and close the cover.

❈❈ CAUTION

Be sure that nobody is in the vehicle and that there is nothing blocking or set in front of any air bag module when the battery ground cable is connected. Failure to follow these instructions may increase the risk of personal injury or death in a crash.

4. Connect the battery ground cable.
5. Prove out the SRS as follows:
6. Turn the ignition key from ON to OFF. Wait 10 seconds, then turn the key back to ON and visually monitor the air bag warning indicator with the air bag modules installed. The air bag warning indicator will light continuously for approximately 6 seconds and then turn off. If an air bag SRS fault is present, the air bag warning indicator will either:
   a. Fail to light.
   b. Remain lit continuously.
   c. Flash.
   d. The air bag warning indicator may not illuminate until approximately 30 seconds after the ignition switch has been turned from the OFF to the ON position. This is the time required for the RCM to complete the testing of the SRS. If the air bag warning indicator is inoperative and an SRS fault exists, a chime will sound in a pattern of 5 sets of 5 beeps. If this occurs, the air bag warning indicator will need to be repaired before diagnosis can continue.

   Clear all continuous memory DTCs from the restraints control module using a scan tool.

CLOCKSPRING CENTERING

❈❈ WARNING

Overturning will destroy the clockspring. The internal ribbon wire acts as the stop and can be broken from its internal connection. Make sure the road wheels are in the straight-ahead position.

1. Centralize the clockspring.
2. Hold the clockspring outer housing stationary.
3. While holding the clockspring locking tab in the released position, turn the rotor

counterclockwise, carefully feeling for the ribbon wire to run out of length and a slight resistance to be felt. Stop turning at this point.
4. While holding the clockspring locking tab in the released position, turn the

clockspring clockwise approximately 2.25 turns. This is the center point of the clockspring.
5. Do not allow the rotor to turn from this position.

DRIVETRAIN

AUTOMATIC TRANSMISSION ASSEMBLY

REMOVAL & INSTALLATION

4R100 Transmission

2005 Excursion

1. Before servicing the vehicle, refer to the precautions in the beginning of this section.
2. With the vehicle in NEUTRAL position it on a hoist.

➡When the battery has been disconnected and reconnected, some abnormal drive symptoms can occur while the vehicle relearns its adaptive strategy. The vehicle owner should to be notified that they may experience slightly different upshifts (either soft or firm) and that this is a temporary condition that will return to normal operating condition.

3. Disconnect the negative battery cable.
4. On 4WD models, remove the transfer case assembly.
5. On 2WD models, remove the rear driveshaft.
6. Drain the transmission fluid.
CAUTION: Mixing the 2WD and the 4WD style transmission fluid filters and transmission pan assembly components can cause transmission damage.

Install the correct pan with gasket for this application. Alternately tighten the bolts.

✶✶ CAUTION

Make sure securing straps or the transmission jack adapter do not touch the Cooler Bypass Valve (CBV). Do not use the CBV as a handle as damage to the CBV can cause a leak.

7. Install a suitable transmission jack and support the transmission.
8. On 4WD models, remove the jack stand after installing a suitable transmission jack.
9. On 2WD models, perform the following:
   a. Disconnect the wire loom from the crossmember.
   b. Remove the crossmember bolts.

   c. Remove the crossmember bolts.
   d. Remove the transmission mount nuts and the crossmember.
10. On 2WD models, perform the following:
   a. Remove the right hand crossmember nuts.
   b. Remove the left hand crossmember nuts.
   c. Remove the nuts and the crossmember.
   d. Remove the transmission mount.
11. On models equipped with a transmission-mounted parking brake, perform the following:
   a. Disconnect the parking brake lever return spring from the parking brake lever.
   b. Apply penetrating oil to the adjusting clevis, jam nut and the threads on the front parking brake cable and conduit.
   c. Disconnect the front parking brake cable and conduit.
   d. Loosen the jam nut.
   e. Remove the clevis locking pin.
   f. Remove the clevis pin.
   g. Remove the adjusting clevis from the parking brake lever.
   h. Compress the retainer, and remove the front parking brake cable and conduit from the cable bracket.

➡If the vehicle is equipped with a Power Take-Off (PTO) unit, all or part of the PTO unit will need to be removed.

12. Disconnect the shift cable from the transmission.
13. Disconnect the shift cable from the manual lever.
14. Remove the shift cable bracket from the transmission and position aside.
15. Disconnect the digital Transmission Range (TR) sensor connector and the wire loom from the shift cable bracket.
16. Disconnect the solenoid body connector.
17. Disconnect the Turbine Shaft Speed (TSS) sensor and the Output Shaft Speed (OSS) sensor.
18. Remove the wiring harness from the transmission and position aside.
19. Remove the flexplate inspection cover.
20. Remove the bolts.
21. Remove the inspection plate.
22. Remove the starter motor.

23. Remove the cylinder block opening cover.
24. Remove and discard the torque converter-to-flexplate nuts.
25. Position a suitable drain pan and disconnect the transmission fluid cooler tubes from the cooler bypass valve.
26. Remove the transmission.
27. Remove the seven transmission-to-engine mounting bolts and gently rock the transmission side-to-side to disengage it from the locator dowels.
28. Move the transmission and the transmission jack rearward to clear the engine flexplate.

✶✶ WARNING

The torque converter is heavy and can result in injury if it falls out of the transmission. Secure the torque converter in the transmission. If the torque converter is dropped, a new one must be installed.

29. Use tool 307-346 to hold the torque converter in place.

✶✶ CAUTION

Use care while removing the transmission to avoid obstructions.

30. Lower the transmission out of the vehicle.
31. On models equipped with a transmission-mounted parking brake, perform the following:
   a. Remove the transmission-mounted parking brake.
   b. Keep the parking brake vent in the upward position to prevent contamination of the brake shoes and linings.
   c. Remove the six bolts, parking brake assembly and the gasket from the extension housing.
   d. Discard the bolts and the gasket.
   e. Clean the mating surfaces.

To install:

✶✶ CAUTION

Prior to the installation of the transmission, the fluid, cooler lines and the cooler bypass valve must be cleaned. A new transmission

Oil-To-Air (OTA) cooler must be installed if the transmission was overhauled or exchanged due to a failure of the transmission. Transmission failure can occur if these procedures are not followed.

32. Inspect the wiring harness and the connectors for damage, terminal condition, corrosion and seal integrity. Repair or install new as required.

33. On models equipped with a transmission-mounted parking brake, perform the following:

    a. Install the parking brake, if removed.

    b. Position the parking brake assembly with a new gasket on the transmission extension housing.

    c. Install six new bolts and tighten to 41 ft. lbs. (55 Nm).

✳✳ CAUTION

Prior to the installation of the transmission, the torque converter pilot hub must be lubricated or damage to the torque converter or the engine crankshaft can occur.

34. Lubricate the torque converter pilot hub with multi-purpose grease.

35. Raise the transmission into position.

✳✳ CAUTION

Do not use the CBV as a handle. Damage to the CBV assembly can occur or damage to the case can result. Be careful not to raise the transmission up too far. The sensors can make contact with the underbody of the vehicle and cause damage to the sensors. Sensor failure or leakage can occur.

➡**While raising the transmission up into the engine compartment, make sure to align the fluid filler tube with the stub tube on the transmission, using the dipstick as a guide.**

36. Position the transmission.

37. Remove tool 307-346.

✳✳ CAUTION

Do not allow the torque converter drive flats to disengage from the pump gear. Use care not to damage the flexplate and the converter pilot. The torque converter must rest squarely against the flexplate, indicating the converter pilot is not binding in the crankshaft.

38. While installing the transmission to the engine, align the torque converter studs with the mounting holes in the flexplate.

39. Install the transmission-to-engine bolts and tighten to 35 ft. lbs. (47 Nm).

40. Install the new torque converter-to-flexplate nuts and tighten to 26 ft. lbs. (35 Nm).

41. Install the cylinder block opening cover.

42. Install the flexplate inspection cover and bolts and tighten to 25 ft. lbs. (34 Nm).

43. Install the starter motor.

44. Connect the solenoid pack electrical connector.

45. Connect the digital TR sensor connector.

46. Connect the TSS and the OSS sensors.

➡**If the vehicle is equipped with a PTO unit, all or part of the PTO unit will need to be installed.**

47. Connect the shift cable.

48. Install the cable housing bracket.

49. Install the shift cable to the manual lever and tighten to 18 ft. lbs. (25 Nm).

50. Install the transmission fluid cooler tubes to the cooler bypass valve and tighten to 20 ft. lbs. (27 Nm).

51. On models equipped with a transmission-mounted parking brake perform the following:

    a. Position the front parking brake cable and conduit, and press the retainer into the cable bracket until it snaps into place.

    b. Set the adjusting clevis.

    c. Loosen the jam nut several turns.

    d. Position the parking brake lever in the applied position.

    e. Tighten or loosen the adjusting clevis until the adjusting clevis hole lines up with the parking brake lever hole, then loosen the adjusting clevis to 0.5 inch (13mm).

    f. Install the pins, and tighten the jam nut.

    g. Install the clevis pin through the adjusting clevis and the parking brake lever.

    h. Install the locking pin in the clevis pin. Tighten the jam nut to 17 ft. lbs. (23 Nm).

    i. Install the parking brake lever return spring.

52. On 4WD models, perform the following:

    a. Support the extension housing with a jack stand and remove the transmission jack.

    b. Install the transfer case.

53. On 2WD models, perform the following:

    a. Install the transmission mount and tighten to 70 ft. lbs. (95 Nm).

    b. Position the crossmember to the transmission mount and loosely install the nuts.

    c. Install the crossmember bolts and tighten to 60 ft. lbs. (81 Nm).

    d. Reconnect the wire harness to the frame.

54. On 2WD models, remove the transmission jack and tighten the crossmember to the transmission mount nuts 69 ft. lbs. (94 Nm).

55. Install the rear driveshaft.

56. If the transmission was overhauled and the vehicle was equipped with an in-line fluid filter, install a new in-line fluid filter.

57. If the transmission was overhauled and the vehicle was not equipped with an in-line fluid filter, install a new in-line fluid filter kit.

58. If the transmission is being installed for a non-internal repair, do not install an in-line filter or filter kit.

59. If installing a new or a Ford-authorized remanufactured transmission, install the in-line transmission fluid filter that is supplied.

60. Prior to lowering the vehicle, install a new in-line transmission filter or a filter kit.

61. Connect the negative battery cable.

62. Refill all transmissions with the correct amount of automatic transmission fluid.

Torqshift Transmission

2005 Excursion

1. Before servicing the vehicle, refer to the precautions section.

2. On 4WD vehicles, remove the transfer case assembly.

3. On 2WD vehicles, remove the driveshaft.

4. If transmission disassembly is required, drain the transmission fluid. Remove the drain plug and allow the fluid to drain.

5. Install the drain plug. Tighten to 18 ft. lbs. (25 Nm).

6. Install a suitable high-lift transmission jack.

7. on 4WD vehicles, install a suitable jack under the transmission and remove the jack stand from under the extension housing.

8. On 2WD vehicles, remove the wire harness from the rear crossmember.

9. Disconnect the shift cable from the manual lever.

10. Remove the bolts and position the shift cable and bracket out of the way.

11. Loosen the bolt and disconnect the solenoid body electrical connector.

12. Disconnect the Output Shaft Speed (OSS) sensor electrical connector.

13. Disconnect the turbine shaft and intermediate shaft combination speed sensor electrical connector.

14. Disconnect the right hand and left hand wire harness from the side of the transmission.

15. On 2WD vehicles perform the following:

   a. Remove the left hand crossmember bolts.

   b. Remove the right hand crossmember bolts.

   c. Remove the transmission mount nuts and the crossmember.

   d. Remove the rear transmission mount from the extension housing.

16. Remove the cylinder block opening cover in order to gain access to the torque converter nuts.

➡**Using a suitable strap wrench, rotate the crankshaft pulley to gain access to the torque converter nuts.**

17. Remove and discard the six torque nuts.

18. While holding the case fitting, disconnect the front and rear fluid cooler tube nuts and tubes.

19. Secure the transmission to a suitable transmission jack.

20. Remove the nine transmission-to-engine mounting bolts.

21. Slide the transmission back enough to install torque converter holding tool 307-346.

22. Remove the transmission.

To install:

※ CAUTION

Prior to the installation of the transmission, the fluid cooler lines must be cleaned. Otherwise transmission failure can occur.

23. Clean the fluid cooler lines.

※ CAUTION

Prior to the installation of the transmission, a new transmission fluid cooler remote filter must be installed. Otherwise transmission failure can occur.

24. Install a new transmission fluid cooler remote filter.

※ CAUTION

Prior to the installation of the assembly, the torque converter pilot hub must be correctly lubricated or damage to the torque converter or the engine crankshaft can occur.

25. Lubricate the torque converter pilot hub with multi-purpose grease.

➡**Rotate the torque converter so the orange or green paint daubs are in the 12 o'clock position.**

26. If the torque converter holding tool 307-346 has not been installed during the assembly of the transmission, install the tool to hold the torque converter in place while moving and positioning the transmission in place. Once the transmission is in place and before bolting it to the engine remove the tool.

27. Position the transmission in place. While raising the transmission into the engine compartment, align the fluid filler tube with the stub tube on the transmission using the fluid level indicator as a guide.

28. While installing the transmission to the engine, align the torque converter studs with the mounting holes in the flexplate.

29. Install nine transmission-to-engine bolts. Tighten to 35 ft. lbs. (47 Nm).

➡**Using a suitable strap wrench, rotate the crankshaft pulley to gain access to the torque converter nuts.**

30. Install six new torque converter-to-flexplate nuts. Tighten to 35 Nm (26 lb-ft).

31. Install the cylinder block opening cover.

32. Install the front transmission fluid cooler tube. Tighten to 30 ft. lbs. (40 Nm).

33. Install the rear transmission fluid cooler tube. Tighten to 30 ft. lbs. (40 Nm).

34. On 4WD models, support the extension housing with a jack stand and remove the transmission jack.

35. On 2WD models, install the transmission mount. Tighten to 94 Nm (69 lb-ft).

36. Position the crossmember to the transmission mount and loosely install the nut.

37. Install the crossmember bolts. Tighten to 81 Nm (60 lb-ft).

38. Tighten the rear insulator nuts. Tighten to 94 Nm (69 lb-ft).

39. Connect the right hand and left hand wiring harness to the side of the transmission.

40. Connect the OSS sensor electrical connector.

41. Connect the intermediate shaft and turbine shaft combination speed sensor electrical connector.

42. Connect the solenoid body electrical connector.

43. Install the cable housing bracket.

44. Install the shift cable to the manual lever. Tighten to 18 ft. lbs. (25 Nm).

45. On 2WD models, reconnect the wire harness to the frame.

46. On 4WD models, if equipped, install the transfer case.

47. On 2WD models, install the rear driveshaft.

48. Adjust the shift linkage. Verify that the vehicle starts in PARK and NEUTRAL and the REVERSE lamps illuminate in REVERSE as follows:

   a. Remove the upper instrument panel steering column cover.

   b. Place the gearshift lever in the (D) position.

   c. Rotate the gearshift lever clockwise until it bottoms out (first gear), then rotate the lever three indents counterclockwise (D).

   d. Hang an three pound weight on the gearshift lever.

   e. Center the pointer in the middle of the (D) position.

   f. Rotate the thumbwheel located on the bottom of the steering column to adjust the pointer.

   g. Remove the three pound weight.

   h. Carefully move the gearshift lever from detent to detent and compare with transmission settings and readjust if necessary.

   i. Install the upper instrument panel steering column cover.

49. With the engine running and the transmission at normal operating temperature 66–77°C (150–170°F), check and adjust the transmission fluid level, and check for any leaks. If fluid is needed, add fluid in increments of 0.24-liter (0.5-pint) until the correct level is achieved (fluid should be in the cross-hatched area of the fluid level indicator).

50. Use the following guidelines for the in-line transmission fluid filter:

   a. If the transmission was overhauled and the vehicle was equipped with an in-line fluid filter, install a new in-line fluid filter.

   b. If the transmission was overhauled and the vehicle was not equipped with an in-line fluid filter, install a new in-line fluid filter kit.

   c. If the transmission is being installed for non-internal repair, do not install an in-line filter or filter kit.

d. If installing a new or a Ford-authorized remanufactured transmission, install the in-line transmission fluid filter that is supplied.

e. Prior to lowering the vehicle, install a new in-line transmission filter or a filter kit.

Expedition & Navigator 6HP26 Transmission

4WD Models

1. Before servicing the vehicle, refer to the precautions section.
2. Disconnect the negative battery cable.
3. Remove the transfer case.

➡If transmission disassembly or installation of a new transmission is necessary, the transmission fluid will need to be drained.

4. Remove the transmission fluid pan drain plug and allow the fluid to drain.
5. Install the transmission fluid pan drain plug and tighten to 8 Nm (71 lb-in).
6. Remove the fuel line bracket bolt from the bracket. Position the bracket and lines aside.
7. Disconnect the shift cable end and remove the shift cable bracket bolts. Position the cable and bracket aside.
8. Remove the flexplate inspection cover bolts and the inspection cover.
9. Remove the bolts and the left hand engine-to-transmission support bracket.
10. Remove the rubber torque converter nut access plug.
11. Remove and discard the four flexplate-to-torque converter nuts.
12. Remove the bolts and the right hand engine-to-transmission support bracket.
13. Remove the plastic starter motor electrical connector cap.
14. Remove the starter motor electrical connectors.
15. Remove the ground wire from the stud.
16. Remove the three bolts and the starter motor.

➡Note the band seals and backer rings may stick into the case. Remove the band seals and backer rings if still in the case.

17. Remove the transmission cooler tube bracket bolt and the cooler tubes.
18. Remove one transmission retaining bolt and position the transmission fluid cooler tube retainer aside.
19. Disconnect the engine oil level sensor connector.

20. Disconnect the fluid cooler tube.
21. Remove the transmission fluid cooler tube bracket nut and position the bracket and lines aside.
22. Remove the right hand exhaust shield bolt.
23. Remove the left hand exhaust shield bolt.

❊❊ CAUTION

This new style pan is designed with the two outside ribs of the pan taller than the rest for side-to-side support. The transmission can be supported on the fluid pan as long as it is resting on the two outer ribs, if not, damage to the fluid pan will occur.

➡Make sure that the transmission jack makes contact on the outer ribs of the fluid pan. Make sure that the transmission is securely fastened to the transmission jack.

24. Position a suitable high-lift transmission jack under the transmission.
25. Remove the four rear crossmember bolts.
26. Remove the two rear transmission nuts and the crossmember.
27. Remove the left hand exhaust hanger bolt.
28. Remove the right hand bolt for the rear transmission support.
29. Remove the left hand bolt for the rear transmission support.
30. Remove the rear transmission support.
31. Disconnect the left and right hand Heated Oxygen (HO2S) sensor connector from the side of the transmission.
32. Disconnect the wire harness from the top of the transmission.

❊❊ CAUTION

Do not pull on the wire harness to disconnect the connector or damage to the connector will occur.

33. Disconnect the main transmission electrical harness by twisting the outer shell and pulling back on the connector. Disconnect the wire harness retainer from the top of the transmission.
34. Remove the four nuts for the front sway bar U-shaped brackets and position the sway bar aside.

➡Note the length and the location of the bolts during removal.

35. Remove the seven transmission-to-engine retaining bolts.

36. Slide the transmission back enough to install the torque converter retaining tool 307-346.
37. Remove the transmission from the vehicle.

To install:

38. Install the torque converter retaining tool.

❊❊ CAUTION

The converter housing is piloted into position by dowels in the rear of the engine block. The torque converter must rest squarely against the flexplate. This indicates that the converter pilot is not binding in the engine crankshaft.

39. Position and secure the transmission on the high-lift transmission jack. Raise and position the transmission into the vehicle.

➡Make sure the torque converter is fully seated in the transmission before aligning the transmission to the engine.

40. With the transmission in a horizontal position move it toward the engine. Align the orange balancing marks between the torque converter studs and the flexplate bolt holes.

➡Install the transmission bolts in their correct locations noted during removal.

41. Install the seven transmission-to-engine bolts and tighten to 35 ft. lbs. (48 Nm).
42. Install the front sway bar U-brackets and install the bolts. Tighten to 75 ft. lbs. (102 Nm).
43. Connect the wire harness retainer to the top of the transmission and connect the main transmission electrical harness by pushing it in and twisting the outer shell to lock it in place.
44. Connect the wire harness to the top of the transmission.
45. Connect the HO2S connectors to the side of the transmission.
46. Install the rear transmission mount. Install the left hand bolt for the rear transmission support. Tighten the bolt to 59 ft. lbs. (80 Nm).
47. Install the right hand bolt for the rear transmission support. Tighten the bolt to 59 ft. lbs. (80 Nm).
48. Install the exhaust hanger. Tighten the bolt to 30 ft. lbs. (40 Nm).
49. Position the rear crossmember in place and loosely install the transmission retaining nuts.

50. Install the bolts for the rear cross-member. Tighten the bolt to 66 ft. lbs. (90 Nm).

51. Tighten the two rear transmission nuts to 76 ft. lbs. (103 Nm).

52. Install the right hand exhaust heat shield bolt.

53. Install the left hand exhaust heat shield bolt.

54. Connect the transmission fluid cooler tubes.

55. Install the transmission fluid cooler tube bracket and the nut.

56. Connect the engine oil level sensor electrical connector.

57. Install the transmission fluid cooler tube retainer and the bolt. Tighten the bolt to 35 ft. lbs. (48 Nm).

➡Inspect the case to make sure that the old band seals and backer rings are not stuck in the case.

➡Install new band seals and backer rings on the ends of the cooler tubes prior to installing.

58. Install new seals on the transmission fluid cooler tubes.

➡Inspect the case to make sure that the old band seals and backer rings are not stuck in the case.

➡Install new band seals and backer rings on the ends of the cooler tubes prior to installing.

59. Position the fluid cooler tubes into the transmission, then install the bolt for the transmission cooler tube retainer. Tighten the bolt to 17 ft. lbs. (23 Nm).

60. Install the starter motor.

61. Install four new torque converter nuts.

62. Rotate the crankshaft to access all the torque converter nuts. Tighten the bolts to 26 ft. lbs. (35 Nm).

63. Install the rubber access plug.

64. Install the flexplate inspection cover. Tighten the bolts to 26 ft. lbs. (35 Nm).

65. Install the right hand engine-to-transmission support bracket and the bolts. Tighten the bolts to 35 ft. lbs. (48 Nm).

66. Install the left hand engine-to-transmission support bracket and the bolts. Tighten the bolts to 35 ft. lbs. (48 Nm).

67. Install the shift cable bracket bolts and connect the shift cable end. Tighten the bolts to 35 ft. lbs. (48 Nm).

68. Install the transfer case.

69. Install the fuel line bracket and the bolt.

70. Connect the negative battery cable.

71. Remove the fluid fill plug. The fill plug is located on the right hand rear side of the case near the transmission electrical connector.

✳✳ CAUTION

The use of any other transmission fluid than specified, can result in the transmission failing to operate correctly or transmission failure.

72. Fill the transmission. Add 4.7 liters (5 quarts) of clean automatic transmission fluid to the transmission through the fluid fill hole. Stop when the fluid runs out of the bottom of the hole.

73. Install the fluid fill plug. Tighten the bolts to 26 ft. lbs. (35 Nm).

74. Verify that the shift cable is correctly adjusted for column mounted shifters as follows:

   a. Place the gearshift lever in the (D) position.

   b. Place a three pound weight on the gearshift lever.

   c. With the vehicle in NEUTRAL, position it on a hoist.

   d. Disconnect the transmission shift cable from the manual control lever.

➡Make sure the cable moves freely.

   e. Unlock the lock tab on the transmission shift cable.

   f. Place the manual control lever in the (D) position.

   g. Place the manual control lever in the first gear position.

   h. Move the manual control lever two detents to the (D) position.

   i. Connect the transmission shift cable to the manual control lever.

   j. Lock the transmission shift cable lock tab.

   k. Remove the three pound weight.

   l. Carefully move the manual control lever from detent to detent and compare with transmission settings. Verify that the vehicle will start in PARK or NEUTRAL and backup lamps illuminate in REVERSE. If not, the adjustment steps must be repeated.

75. Verify that the shift cable is correctly adjusted for floor mounted shifters as follows:

   a. Place the gearshift lever in the (D) position.

   b. With the vehicle in NEUTRAL, position the vehicle on a hoist.

   c. Disconnect the transmission shift cable from the manual control lever.

➡Make sure the cable moves freely.

   d. Unlock the lock tab on the transmission shift cable.

   e. Place the manual control lever in the (D) position.

   f. Place the manual control lever in the first gear position.

   g. Move the manual control lever three detents to the (D) position.

   h. Connect the transmission shift cable to the manual control lever.

   i. Lock the transmission shift cable lock tab.

   j. Carefully move the manual control lever from detent to detent and compare with transmission settings. Verify that the vehicle will start in PARK or NEUTRAL and backup lamps illuminate in REVERSE. If not, the adjustment steps must be repeated.

76. Re-flash the transmission control module (TCM) to the latest level of software.

77. Start the engine. Move the transmission range selector lever through all the gear ranges, checking for engagements.

78. With the engine idling (600–750 rpm) in PARK and the transmission temperature at 30°C–50°C (86°F–122°F), check and adjust the transmission fluid level.

79. With the engine still running in PARK, check the fluid level. If more fluid is needed, remove the fluid fill plug on the side of the case and fill with clean automatic transmission fluid until the fluid runs out of the bottom of the hole.

80. Install the fluid fill plug. Tighten to 25 ft. lbs. (35 Nm).

2WD Models

1. Before servicing the vehicle, refer to the precautions section.

2. Disconnect the negative battery cable.

➡If transmission disassembly or installation of a new transmission is necessary, the transmission fluid will need to be drained.

3. Remove the transmission fluid pan drain plug and allow the fluid to drain.

4. Install the transmission fluid pan drain plug. Tighten to 8 Nm (71 lb-in).

5. Mark the driveshaft flange with the insulator flange and the output shaft flange for correct alignment during installation.

6. Remove the three bolts and nuts and position the driveshaft aside.

7. Remove the fuel line bracket bolt from the bracket. Position the bracket and lines aside.

8. Disconnect the shift cable end and remove the shift cable bracket bolts. Position the cable and bracket aside.

9. Remove the flexplate inspection cover bolts and remove the inspection cover.

10. Remove the rubber torque converter nut access plug.

11. Remove and discard the four flexplate-to-torque converter nuts.

12. Remove the plastic starter motor electrical connector cap.

13. Remove the starter motor.

➡**Note the band seals and backer rings may stick into the case. Remove the band seals and backer rings if still in the case.**

14. Remove the transmission cooler tube bracket bolt and the cooler tubes.

15. Remove one transmission retaining bolt and position the transmission fluid cooler tube retainer aside.

16. Disconnect the engine oil level sensor electrical connector.

17. Disconnect the fluid cooler tube.

18. Remove the transmission fluid cooler tube bracket nut and position the bracket and lines aside.

19. Remove the right hand exhaust shield bolt.

20. Remove the left hand exhaust shield bolt.

➡**This new style pan is designed with the two outside ribs of the pan taller than the rest for side-to-side support. The transmission can be supported on the fluid pan as long as it is resting on the two outer ribs, if not, damage to the fluid pan will occur.**

➡**Make sure that the transmission jack makes contact on the outer ribs of the fluid pan. Make sure that the transmission is securely fastened to the transmission jack.**

21. Position a suitable high-lift transmission jack under the transmission.

22. Remove the four rear crossmember bolts.

23. Remove the two rear transmission nuts and the crossmember.

24. Remove the left hand exhaust hanger bolt.

25. Remove the right hand bolt for the rear transmission support.

26. Remove the left hand bolt for the rear transmission support. Remove the rear transmission support.

27. Disconnect the left and right hand Heated Oxygen (HO2S) sensor connector from the side of the transmission.

28. Disconnect the wire harness from the top of the transmission.

✳✳ CAUTION

Do not pull on the wire harness to disconnect the connector or damage to the connector will occur.

29. Disconnect the main transmission electrical harness by twisting the outer shell and pulling back on the connector. Disconnect the wire harness retainer from the top of the transmission.

30. Remove the four nuts for the front sway bar U-shaped brackets. Position the sway bar aside.

➡**Note the length and the location of the bolts during removal.**

31. Remove the seven transmission-to-engine retaining bolts.

32. Slide the transmission back enough to install the torque converter retaining tool 307-346.

33. Remove the transmission from the vehicle.

To install:

34. Install the torque converter retaining tool.

✳✳ CAUTION

The converter housing is piloted into position by dowels in the rear of the engine block. The torque converter must rest squarely against the flexplate. This indicates that the converter pilot is not binding in the engine crankshaft.

35. Position and secure the transmission on the high-lift transmission jack. Raise and position the transmission into the vehicle.

➡**Make sure the torque converter is fully seated in the transmission before aligning the transmission to the engine.**

36. With the transmission in a horizontal position move it toward the engine. Align the orange balancing marks between the torque converter studs and the flexplate bolt holes.

➡**Install the transmission bolts in their correct locations noted during removal.**

37. Install the seven transmission-to-engine bolts and tighten to 35 ft. lbs. (48 Nm).

38. Install the front sway bar U-brackets and install the bolts. Tighten to 75 ft. lbs. (102 Nm).

39. Connect the wire harness retainer to the top of the transmission and connect the main transmission electrical harness by pushing it in and twisting the outer shell to lock it in place.

40. Connect the wire harness to the top of the transmission.

41. Connect the HO2S connectors to the side of the transmission.

42. Install the rear transmission mount. Install the left hand bolt for the rear transmission support. Tighten the bolt to 59 ft. lbs. (80 Nm).

43. Install the right hand bolt for the rear transmission support. Tighten the bolt to 59 ft. lbs. (80 Nm).

44. Install the exhaust hanger. Tighten the bolt to 30 ft. lbs. (40 Nm).

45. Position the rear crossmember in place and loosely install the transmission nuts.

46. Install the bolts for the rear crossmember. Tighten the bolt to 66 ft. lbs. (90 Nm).

47. Tighten the two rear transmission nuts to 76 ft. lbs. (103 Nm).

48. Install the right hand exhaust heat shield bolt.

49. Install the left hand exhaust heat shield bolt.

50. Connect the transmission fluid cooler tubes.

51. Install the transmission fluid cooler tube bracket and install the nut.

52. Connect the engine oil level sensor electrical connector.

53. Install the transmission fluid cooler tube retainer and install the bolt. Tighten the bolt to 35 ft. lbs. (48 Nm).

➡**Inspect the case to make sure that the old band seals and backer rings are not stuck in the case.**

➡**Install new band seals and backer rings on the ends of the cooler tubes prior to installing.**

54. Install new seals on the transmission fluid cooler tubes.

➡**Inspect the case to make sure that the old band seals and backer rings are not stuck in the case.**

➡**Install new band seals and backer rings on the ends of the cooler tubes prior to installing.**

55. Position the fluid cooler tubes into the transmission, then install the bolt for the transmission cooler tube retainer.

56. Install the starter motor.

57. Install four new torque converter nuts. Rotate the crankshaft to access all the torque converter nuts. Tighten the bolt to 26 ft. lbs. (35 Nm).

58. Install the rubber access plug.

59. Install the flexplate inspection cover. Tighten the bolts to 26 ft. lbs. (35 Nm).

60. Install the shift cable bracket bolts and connect the shift cable end. Tighten the bolt to 35 ft. lbs. (48 Nm).

61. Install the fuel line bracket and install the bolt.

➡**To maintain initial driveshaft balance, align the index marks made during removal.**

62. Install the rear driveshaft. Tighten the bolt to 81 Nm (60 ft. lbs.)

63. Connect the negative battery cable.

64. Remove the fluid fill plug. The fill plug is located on the right hand rear side of the case near the transmission electrical connector.

✳✳ CAUTION

The use of any other transmission fluid than specified, can result in the transmission failing to operate in a normal manner or transmission failure.

65. Fill the transmission. Add 4.7 liters (5 quarts) of clean automatic transmission fluid to the transmission through the fluid fill hole. Stop when the fluid runs out of the bottom of the hole.

66. Install the fluid fill plug. Tighten to 25 ft. lbs. (35 Nm).

67. Verify that the shift cable is correctly adjusted for column mounted shifters as follows:

   a. Place the gearshift lever in the (D) position.

   b. Place a three pound weight on the gearshift lever.

   c. With the vehicle in NEUTRAL, position it on a hoist.

   d. Disconnect the transmission shift cable from the manual control lever.

➡**Make sure the cable moves freely.**

   e. Unlock the lock tab on the transmission shift cable.

   f. Place the manual control lever in the (D) position.

   g. Place the manual control lever in the first gear position.

   h. Move the manual control lever two detents to the (D) position.

   i. Connect the transmission shift cable to the manual control lever.

   j. Lock the transmission shift cable lock tab.

   k. Remove the three pound weight.

   l. Carefully move the manual control lever from detent to detent and compare with transmission settings. Verify that the vehicle will start in PARK or NEUTRAL and backup lamps illuminate in REVERSE. If not, the adjustment steps must be repeated.

68. Verify that the shift cable is correctly adjusted for floor mounted shifters as follows:

   a. Place the gearshift lever in the (D) position.

   b. With the vehicle in NEUTRAL, position the vehicle on a hoist.

   c. Disconnect the transmission shift cable from the manual control lever.

➡**Make sure the cable moves freely.**

   d. Unlock the lock tab on the transmission shift cable.

   e. Place the manual control lever in the (D) position.

   f. Place the manual control lever in the first gear position.

   g. Move the manual control lever three detents to the (D) position.

   h. Connect the transmission shift cable to the manual control lever.

   i. Lock the transmission shift cable lock tab.

   j. Carefully move the manual control lever from detent to detent and compare with transmission settings. Verify that the vehicle will start in PARK or NEUTRAL and backup lamps illuminate in REVERSE. If not, the adjustment steps must be repeated.

69. Re-flash the transmission control module (TCM) to the latest level of software.

70. Start the engine. Move the transmission range selector lever through all the gear ranges, checking for engagements.

71. With the engine idling (600-750 rpm) in PARK and the transmission temperature at 30°C–50°C (86°F–122°F), check and adjust the transmission fluid level.

72. With the engine still running in PARK, check the fluid level. If more fluid is needed, remove the fluid fill plug on the side of the case and fill with clean automatic transmission fluid until the fluid runs out of the bottom of the hole.

73. Install the fluid fill plug. Tighten to 25 ft. lbs. (35 Nm).

2005–07 Expedition & Navigator 4R70E/4R75E Transmissions

4WD Models

1. Before servicing the vehicle, refer to the precautions section.

2. Disconnect the negative battery cable.

3. Remove the transfer case.

➡**Drain the transmission fluid if the transmission is disassembled, or installation of a new transmission is necessary.**

4. Loosen the transmission fluid pan bolts and allow the fluid to drain.

5. After the fluid has drained, remove the transmission fluid pan and drain the remaining fluid from the pan.

➡**It is not necessary to torque the transmission fluid pan bolts in this step.**

6. Install the transmission fluid pan.

7. Disconnect the shift cable end and remove the shift cable bracket.

8. Remove the flexplate inspection cover.

9. Remove the rubber access plug.

10. Remove and discard the 4 flexplate-to-torque converter nuts.

11. Remove the starter motor.

12. Disconnect the transmission cooler lines and position them aside.

13. Remove the bolt from the right hand cylinder head for the transmission filler tube and position the filler tube aside.

14. Remove the 2 bolts for the exhaust hanger.

15. Remove the right hand exhaust shield bolt.

16. Remove the left hand exhaust shield bolt.

➡**Make sure that the transmission is securely fastened to the transmission jack.**

17. Position a suitable high-lift transmission jack under the transmission.

18. Remove the rear crossmember bolts.

19. Remove the rear transmission retainer nuts and remove the crossmember.

20. Remove the rear transmission support.

21. Disconnect the transmission electrical connectors.

22. Disconnect the solenoid body assembly electrical connector.

➡**Note the length and the location of the bolts during removal.**

23. Remove the seven transmission-to-engine bolts.

➡**The torque converter is heavy and can result in injury if it falls out of the transmission. Secure the torque converter in the transmission.**

24. Leaving the transmission in a horizontal position, slide it back far enough to install the torque converter holding tool 307-346.

✳✳ CAUTION

To remove the transmission from the vehicle, it will be necessary to put the transmission into a nose-down position to clear the flexplate and the exhaust system.

25. Make sure that the torque converter holding tool 307-346 is in place and the transmission is securely fastened to the transmission jack before tilting the transmission.

26. Lower the transmission from the vehicle.

To install:

27. Install the torque converter holding tool 307-346 if not already done.

28. Position the vent tube on the top of the transmission.

✳✳ CAUTION

To position the transmission in the vehicle, put the transmission into a nose-down position to get the tail shaft over the exhaust system. The converter housing is piloted into position by dowels in the rear of the engine block. The torque converter must rest squarely against the flexplate. This indicates that the converter pilot is not binding in the engine crankshaft.

29. Position and secure the transmission on the high-lift transmission jack. Raise and position the transmission into the vehicle. Once the transmission is in position, place the transmission in a horizontal position.

➡**Do not remove the torque converter holding tool 307-346 until the transmission is in a horizontal position.**

30. Remove the torque converter holding tool 307-346.

➡**Make sure that the torque converter is fully seated in the transmission before aligning the transmission to the engine.**

31. With the transmission in a horizontal position move it toward the engine. Align the orange balancing marks between the torque converter and the flexplate bolt holes.

➡**Install the transmission retaining bolts in their correct locations made during removal. Tighten to 35 ft. lbs. (48 Nm).**

32. Install the shift cable bracket and the left hand transmission retaining bolts. Tighten to 35 ft. lbs. (48 Nm).

➡**Install the transmission retaining bolts in their correct locations made during removal.**

33. Position the vent tube in its correct location and install the right hand transmission retaining bolts. Tighten to 35 ft. lbs. (48 Nm).

➡**It may be necessary to disconnect the rubber vent hose in order to route the wire harness under the vent hose.**

34. Route the harness under the vent hose, connect the solenoid body connector and connect the harness retainer to the transmission.

35. Connect the transmission electrical connectors.

36. Install the rear transmission support. Tighten to 59 ft. lbs. (80 Nm).

37. Position the rear crossmember in place and install the nuts. Tighten to 76 ft. lbs. (103 Nm).

38. Position the rear crossmember in place and install the bolts and nuts. Tighten to 66 ft. lbs. (90 Nm).

39. Install the right hand exhaust bolts.

40. Install the left hand exhaust bolts.

41. Install the bolts retaining the exhaust hanger to the crossmember. Tighten to 30 ft. lbs. (40 Nm).

42. Position the transmission fluid fill tube into the transmission and install the retaining bolt on the right hand cylinder head.

43. Connect the transmission fluid cooler tubes.

44. Install the starter motor.

45. Install the 4 torque converter nuts. Tighten to 27 ft. lbs. (36 Nm).

46. Install the rubber access plug.

47. Install the flexplate inspection cover. Tighten to 25 ft. lbs. (34 Nm).

48. Install the shift cable end and the bracket. Tighten to 18 ft. lbs. (25 Nm).

49. Install the transfer case.

50. Use the following guidelines for the in-line transmission fluid filter:

   a. If the transmission was overhauled and the vehicle was equipped with an in-line fluid filter, install a new in-line fluid filter.

   b. If the transmission was overhauled and the vehicle was not equipped with an in-line fluid filter, install a new in-line fluid filter kit.

   c. If the transmission is being installed for a non-internal repair, do not install an in-line filter or filter kit.

   d. If installing a Ford-authorized remanufactured transmission, install the in-line transmission fluid filter that is supplied.

   e. Prior to lowering the vehicle, install a new in-line transmission filter or a filter kit.

51. Fill to correct level with clean automatic transmission fluid.

52. Connect the negative battery cable.

2WD Models

1. Before servicing the vehicle, refer to the precautions section.

2. Disconnect the negative battery cable.

➡**Drain the transmission fluid if the transmission is disassembled, or installation of a new transmission is required.**

3. Loosen the transmission fluid pan bolts and allow the fluid to drain.

4. After the fluid has drained, remove the transmission fluid pan and drain the remaining fluid from the pan.

➡**It is not necessary to torque the transmission fluid pan bolts in this step.**

5. Install the transmission fluid pan.

6. Mark the driveshaft flange and rear axle pinion flange for correct alignment during installation.

7. Remove the rear driveshaft bolts and driveshaft.

8. Remove the fuel line bracket from the extension bolt.

9. Disconnect the shift cable end and remove the shift cable bracket.

10. Remove the flexplate inspection cover.

11. Remove the rubber access plug.

12. Remove and discard the 4 flexplate-to-torque converter nuts.

13. Remove the starter motor.

14. Disconnect the transmission cooler lines and position them aside.

15. Remove the bolt from the right hand cylinder head for the transmission filler tube and position the filler tube aside.

16. Remove the 2 bolts for the exhaust hanger.

17. Remove the right hand exhaust shield bolt.

18. Remove the left hand exhaust shield bolt.

➡**Make sure that the transmission is securely fastened to the transmission jack.**

19. Position a suitable high-lift transmission jack under the transmission.

20. Remove the rear crossmember bolts.

21. Remove the rear transmission retainer nuts and remove the crossmember.

22. Remove the rear transmission support.

23. Disconnect the transmission electrical connectors.

24. Disconnect the solenoid body assembly electrical connector.

➡️**If the transmission fluid has not been drained, position a drain pan and install a suitable plug into the transmission.**

➡️**Note the length and the location of the bolts during removal.**

25. Remove the seven transmission-to-engine bolts.

❊❊ CAUTION

The torque converter is heavy and can result in injury if it falls out of the transmission. Secure the torque converter in the transmission.

26. Leaving the transmission in a horizontal position, slide it back far enough to install the torque converter holding tool 307-346.

❊ CAUTION

To remove the transmission from the vehicle, it will be necessary to put the transmission into a nose-down position to clear the flexplate and the exhaust system.

27. Make sure that the torque converter holding tool 307-346 is in place and the transmission is securely fastened to the transmission jack before tilting the transmission.

28. Lower the transmission from the vehicle.

To install:

29. Install the torque converter holding tool 307-346 if not already done.

30. Position the vent tube on the top of the transmission.

❊ CAUTION

To position the transmission in the vehicle, put the transmission into a nose-down position to get the tail shaft over the exhaust system. The converter housing is piloted into position by dowels in the rear of the engine block. The torque converter must rest squarely against the flexplate. This indicates that the converter pilot is not binding in the engine crankshaft.

31. Position and secure the transmission on the high-lift transmission jack. Raise and position the transmission into the vehicle. Once the transmission is in position, place the transmission in a horizontal position.

➡️**Do not remove the torque converter holding tool 307-346 until the transmission is in a horizontal position.**

32. Remove the torque converter holding tool 307-346.

➡️**Make sure that the torque converter is fully seated in the transmission before aligning the transmission to the engine.**

33. With the transmission in a horizontal position move it toward the engine. Align the orange balancing marks between the torque converter and the flexplate bolt holes.

➡️**Install the transmission retaining bolts in their correct locations made during removal. Tighten to 35 ft. lbs. (48 Nm).**

34. Install the shift cable bracket and the left hand transmission retaining bolts. Tighten to 35 ft. lbs. (48 Nm).

➡️**It may be necessary to disconnect the rubber vent hose in order to route the wire harness under the vent hose.**

35. Route the harness under the vent hose, connect the solenoid body connector and connect the harness retainer to the transmission.

36. Connect the transmission electrical connectors.

37. Install the rear transmission support. Tighten to 59 ft. lbs. (80 Nm).

38. Position the rear crossmember in place and install the nuts. Tighten to 76 ft. lbs. (103 Nm).

39. Position the rear crossmember in place and install the bolts and nuts. Tighten to 66 ft. lbs. (90 Nm).

40. Remove the transmission jack.

41. Install the right hand exhaust bolts.

42. Install the left hand exhaust bolts.

43. Install the bolts retaining the exhaust hanger to the crossmember. Tighten to 30 ft. lbs. (40 Nm).

44. Position the transmission fluid fill tube into the transmission and install the retaining bolt on the right hand cylinder head.

45. Connect the transmission fluid cooler tubes.

46. Install the starter motor.

47. Install the 4 torque converter nuts. Rotate the crankshaft to access all the torque converter nuts. Tighten to 27 ft. lbs. (36 Nm).

48. Install the rubber access plug.

49. Install the flexplate inspection cover. Tighten to 25 ft. lbs. (34 Nm).

50. Install the shift cable end and the bracket. Tighten to 18 ft. lbs. (25 Nm).

51. Install the fuel line bracket. Tighten to 18 ft. lbs. (25 Nm).

➡️**The output shaft and the driveshaft are a balanced assembly.**

52. Install the driveshaft. Align the yellow dots and position the driveshaft on the transmission.

53. Position the driveshaft to the rear differential.

➡️**To maintain initial driveshaft balance, align the index marks made during removal.**

54. Install the rear driveshaft. Tighten the bolts to 76 ft. lbs. (103 Nm).

55. Use the following guidelines for the in-line transmission fluid filter:

   a. If the transmission was overhauled and the vehicle was equipped with an in-line fluid filter, install a new in-line fluid filter.

   b. If the transmission was overhauled and the vehicle was not equipped with an in-line fluid filter, install a new in-line fluid filter kit.

   c. If the transmission is being installed for a non-internal repair, do not install an in-line filter or filter kit.

   d. If installing a Ford authorized remanufactured transmission, install the in-line transmission fluid filter that is supplied.

   e. Prior to lowering the vehicle, install a new in-line transmission filter or a filter kit.

56. Connect the negative battery cable.

57. Fill the transmission with clean automatic transmission fluid and inspect for correct operation.

2007 Expedition & Navigator 6R75 Transmission

4WD Models

1. Before servicing the vehicle, refer to the precautions section.

2. Disconnect the battery ground cable.

3. With the vehicle in NEUTRAL, position it on a hoist.

4. Remove the fluid fill plug fluid level indicator assembly located on the passenger side front portion of the transmission case. Removal of the plug will relieve any vacuum that might have built up in the transmission. This will aid in allowing the

fluid pan to be easily removed when the bolts are removed.

➡**If transmission disassembly or installation of a new transmission is necessary, the transmission fluid will need to be drained.**

5. Remove the transmission fluid pan and allow the fluid to drain.

6. Install the fluid pan and tighten the bolts in a crisscross pattern.

7. Remove the transfer case.

8. Remove the fuel line bracket bolt and position the bracket and lines aside.

9. If equipped, remove the heat shield.

10. Move the locking tab up and disconnect the selector lever cable from the manual lever ball stud.

11. Remove the selector lever bracket bolts and remove the bracket.

12. Remove the flexplate inspection cover bolts and the inspection cover.

13. Remove the rubber torque converter nut access plug.

14. Remove and discard the 4 flexplate-to-torque converter nuts.

15. Remove the transmission cooler tube bracket bolt.

16. Remove the transmission case bolt.

17. Remove the transmission fluid cooler tube bracket nut and position the bracket and tubes.

18. Remove the plastic starter motor electrical connector cap.

19. Remove the starter motor electrical connectors.

20. Remove the ground wire from the stud.

21. Remove the 3 starter motor bolts and the starter motor.

22. Disconnect the wiring harness from the top of the transmission.

23. Disconnect the main transmission electrical harness by twisting the outer shell and pulling back on the connector.

➡**The top 2 transmission-to-engine bolts need to be removed prior to removing the rest of the bolts. The top left bolt secures the fuel line bracket to the transmission case.**

24. Remove the 6 remaining transmission case bolts.

25. Leaving the transmission in a horizontal position, slide it back far enough to install the torque converter holding tool 307-346.

26. Make sure that the torque converter holding tool 307-346 is in place and the transmission is securely fastened to the transmission jack before tilting the transmission.

27. Remove the transmission from the vehicle.

To install:

☀☀ WARNING

The converter housing is piloted into position by dowels in the rear of the engine block. The torque converter must rest squarely against the flexplate. This indicates that the converter pilot is not binding in the engine crankshaft.

28. Position and secure the transmission on the high-lift transmission jack. Raise and position the transmission into the vehicle.

29. Remove the torque converter retainer tool 307-346.

➡**Make sure the torque converter is fully seated in the transmission before aligning the transmission to the engine.**

30. With the transmission in a horizontal position, move it toward the engine. Align the orange balancing marks between the torque converter studs and the flexplate bolt holes.

31. Install the transmission case bolts in their correct locations noted during removal.

➡**The top 2 transmission case bolts need to be installed prior to installing the rest of the bolts. The top left bolt is inserted through the fuel line bracket first, then through the transmission case.**

32. Install 6 of the 7 transmission case bolts and tighten to 35 ft. lbs. (48 Nm).

33. Connect the main transmission electrical harness by pushing it in and twisting the outer shell to lock it in place.

34. Connect the wire harness to the top of the transmission.

35. Position the starter motor in place, install and tighten the 3 starter motor bolts to 19 ft. lbs. (26 Nm).

36. Install the ground wire on the stud, install and tighten the ground wire nut to 17 ft. lbs. (23 Nm).

37. Install the starter motor electrical connectors. Tighten main power cable to 9 ft. lbs. (15 Nm).

38. Tighten the smaller solenoid feed wire to 53 inch. (6 Nm).

39. Install the plastic starter motor electrical connector cap.

40. Position the transmission cooler tubes in place, install and tighten the bracket nut to 20 ft. lbs. (27 Nm).

41. Align the bracket and install the remaining transmission case bolt. Tighten to 35 ft. lbs. (48 Nm).

➡**Inspect the case to make sure that the old O-rings are not stuck in the case. Install new O-rings on the ends of the cooler lines prior to installing.**

42. Install new O-rings on the transmission fluid cooler tubes.

43. Install the transmission cooler tubes and tighten the bracket bolt to 17 ft. lbs. (23 Nm).

44. Install 4 new flexplate-to-torque converter nuts. Tighten the nuts to 26 ft. lbs. (35 Nm).

45. Install the rubber access plug.

46. Install the flexplate inspection cover and tighten the inspection cover bolts to 26 ft. lbs. (35 Nm).

47. Install the selector lever bracket and tighten the bolts to 35 ft. lbs. (48 Nm).

➡**When installing the selector lever cable, make sure that the selector lever cable locking tabs are locked in place and the cable end is snapped onto the ball stud. Press the selector lever cable into the bracket and listen for the cable to click into place. Pull back on the selector lever cable to make sure that it is locked into the bracket. Also, make sure that the selector lever cable end is correctly installed onto the ball stud. Pull back on the selector lever cable to make sure that the cable end is correctly installed.**

48. With the manual lever in NEUTRAL, connect the selector lever cable onto the manual lever ball stud and move the locking tab down. Listen for the audible click.

49. Pull back on the selector lever cable to make sure that it is correctly installed.

50. If equipped, install the heat shield.

51. Install the fuel line bracket and tighten the mounting bolt to 18 ft. lbs. (25 Nm).

52. Install the transfer case.

53. Connect the battery ground cable.

54. Verify that the selector lever cable is correctly adjusted.

55. Reflash the transmission control module (TCM) to the latest level of software.

56. Fill the transmission with clean automatic transmission fluid.

57. Test drive and check for leaks.

2WD Models

1. Before servicing the vehicle, refer to the precautions section.

2. Disconnect the battery ground cable.

3. Remove the driveshaft.

4. Remove the fluid fill plug fluid level indicator assembly located on the passenger side front portion of the transmission case. Removal of the plug will relieve any vacuum that might have built up in the transmission. This will aid in allowing the fluid pan to be easily removed when the bolts are removed.

➡ **If transmission disassembly or installation of a new transmission is necessary, the transmission fluid will need to be drained.**

5. Remove the transmission fluid pan and allow the fluid to drain.

6. Install the fluid pan and tighten the bolts in a crisscross pattern.

7. If equipped, remove the heat shield.

8. Move the locking tab up and disconnect the selector lever cable from the manual lever ball stud.

9. Remove the selector lever bracket bolts and remove the bracket.

10. Remove the flexplate inspection cover bolts and the inspection cover.

11. Remove the rubber torque converter nut access plug.

12. Remove and discard the 4 flexplate-to-torque converter nuts.

13. Remove the transmission cooler tube bracket bolt.

14. Remove the transmission case bolt.

15. Remove the transmission fluid cooler tube bracket nut and position the bracket and tubes aside.

16. Remove the plastic starter motor electrical connector cap.

17. Remove the starter motor electrical connectors.

18. Remove the ground wire from the stud.

19. Remove the starter motor bolts and the starter motor.

20. Remove the RH exhaust heat shield bolt.

21. Remove the LH exhaust heat shield and evaporative emissions canister assembly bolts.

22. Disconnect the RH and LH heated oxygen sensors (HO2S) and the catalyst monitor sensor (CMS) electrical connectors.

23. Remove the fuel line bracket bolt and position the bracket and lines aside.

➡ **Make sure that the transmission jack makes contact on the outer ribs of the fluid pan. And that the transmission is securely fastened to the transmission jack.**

24. Position a suitable high-lift transmission jack under the transmission.

25. Remove the 2 rear crossmember nuts.

26. Remove the 4 crossmember bolts and nuts.

27. Remove the rear crossmember.

28. Remove the 3 bolts and remove the insulator

29. Remove the RH and LH exhaust flange nuts.

30. Remove the 2 dual converter Y-pipe bolts and the dual converter Y-pipe.

31. Disconnect the wire harness from the top of the transmission.

32. Disconnect the main transmission electrical harness by twisting the outer shell and pulling back on the connector.

➡ **The top 2 transmission-to-engine bolts need to be removed prior to removing the rest of the bolts. The top left bolt secures the fuel line bracket to the transmission case.**

33. Remove the 6 remaining transmission case bolts.

34. Slide the transmission back far enough to install the torque converter retainer tool 307-346. This holds the torque converter in place.

35. Remove the transmission from the vehicle.

※※ WARNING

If the transmission is to be overhauled or if installing a new transmission, carry out transmission fluid cooler back flushing and cleaning. Make sure the cooler is not restricted. If you have poor cooler flow replace with a new transmission cooler.

To install:

※※ WARNING

The converter housing is piloted into position by dowels in the rear of the engine block. The torque converter must rest squarely against the flexplate. This indicates that the converter pilot is not binding in the engine crankshaft.

36. Position and secure the transmission on the high-lift transmission jack. Raise and position the transmission into the vehicle.

37. Remove the torque converter retainer tool 307-346.

➡ **Make sure the torque converter is fully seated in the transmission before aligning the transmission to the engine.**

38. With the transmission in a horizontal position, move it toward the engine. Align the orange balancing marks between the torque converter studs and the flexplate bolt holes.

39. Install the transmission case bolts in their correct locations noted during removal.

➡ **The top 2 transmission case bolts need to be installed prior to installing the rest of the bolts. The top left bolt is inserted through the fuel line bracket first, then through the transmission case.**

40. Install 6 of the 7 transmission case bolts and tighten to 35 ft. lbs. (48 Nm).

41. Connect the main transmission electrical harness by pushing it in and twisting the outer shell to lock it in place.

42. Connect the wire harness to the top of the transmission.

43. Position the dual converter Y-pipe in place. Install and tighten the 2 dual converter Y-pipe to 30 ft. lbs. (40 Nm).

44. Install the LH and RH exhaust flange nuts and tighten to 30 ft. lbs. (40 Nm).

45. Install the 3 bolts and the insulator, tighten to 66 ft. lbs. (90 Nm).

46. Position the rear crossmember in place and loosely install the transmission insulator nuts.

47. Install the crossmember.

48. Install the 4 crossmember bolts and nuts and tighten to 66 ft. lbs. (90 Nm).

49. Tighten the transmission insulator nuts to 76 ft. lbs. (103 Nm).

50. Install the fuel line bracket tighten the mounting bolt to 18 ft. lbs. (25 Nm).

51. Connect the RH and LH heated oxygen sensors (HO2S) electrical connectors and the CMS electrical connectors.

52. Install the LH exhaust heat shield and evaporative emissions canister assembly bolts. Tighten the bolts to 11 ft. lbs.(15 Nm).

53. Install the RH exhaust heat shield bolt and tighten to 11 ft. lbs.(15 Nm).

54. Position the starter motor in place, install and tighten the 3 starter motor bolts to 19 ft. lbs. (26 Nm).

55. Install the ground wire on the stud, install and tighten the ground wire nut to 17 ft. lbs. 23 (Nm).

56. Install the starter motor electrical connectors. Tighten main power cable to 9 ft. lbs. (15 Nm).

57. Tighten the smaller solenoid feed wire to 53 inch. (6 Nm).

58. Install the plastic starter motor electrical connector cap.

59. Position the transmission cooler tubes in place, install and tighten the bracket nut to 20 ft. lbs. (27 Nm).

60. Align the bracket and install the

remaining transmission case bolt. Tighten to 35 ft. lbs. (48 Nm).

➡**Inspect the case to make sure that the old O-rings are not stuck in the case. Install new O-rings on the ends of the cooler lines prior to installing.**

61. Install new O-rings on the transmission fluid cooler tubes.

62. Install the transmission cooler tubes and tighten the bracket bolt to 17 ft. lbs. (23 Nm).

63. Install 4 new flexplate-to-torque converter nuts. Tighten the nuts to 26 ft. lbs. (35 Nm).

64. Install the rubber access plug.

65. Install the flexplate inspection cover and tighten the flexplate inspection cover bolts to 26 ft. lbs. (35 Nm).

66. Install the selector lever bracket and tighten the bolts to 35 ft. lbs. (48 Nm).

➡**When installing the selector lever cable, make sure that the selector lever cable locking tabs are locked in place and the cable end is snapped onto the ball stud. Press the selector lever cable into the bracket and listen for the cable to click into place. Pull back on the selector lever cable to make sure that it is locked into the bracket. Also, make sure that the selector lever cable end is correctly installed onto the ball stud. Pull back on the selector lever cable to make sure that the cable end is correctly installed.**

67. With the manual lever in NEUTRAL, connect the selector lever cable onto the manual lever ball stud and move the locking tab down. Listen for the audible click.

68. Pull back on the selector lever cable to make sure that it is correctly installed.

69. If equipped, install the heat shield.

70. Install the driveshaft.

71. Connect the battery ground cable.

72. Verify that the selector lever cable is correctly adjusted.

73. Reflash the transmission control module (TCM) to the latest level of software.

74. Fill the transmission with clean automatic transmission fluid.

75. Test drive and check for leaks.

TRANSFER CASE ASSEMBLY

REMOVAL & INSTALLATION

Excursion

1. Before servicing the vehicle, refer to the precautions in the beginning of this section.

2. Shift the transfer case to the 2W HI position.

3. Remove the four bolts and the skid plate, if equipped.

4. Match mark the driveshaft to maintain driveline balance.

5. Remove the rear driveshaft.

6. Match mark the front driveshaft to the transfer case flange.

7. Support the front driveshaft with wire or a strap.

8. Remove and discard the four bolts and position the front driveshaft aside.

9. On models with a manual shift transfer case, perform the following:

a. Remove the manual shift linkage, if equipped.

b. Disconnect the switch electrical connector. Position the wire harness aside.

10. On models equipped with an electric shift transfer case, perform the following:

a. Disconnect the gear motor encoder assembly electrical connector and the gear motor electrical connector.

b. Position the wire harness aside.

c. Disconnect the transfer case vent hose.

11. Drain the fluid into a suitable container. Install the plug when finished.

12. Position a suitable high-lift jack under the transfer case and secure it with safety straps.

13. Detach the wire harness from the crossmember.

14. Remove the crossmember-to-frame bolts.

15. Remove the nuts and the crossmember.

16. Remove the transmission mount.

17. Position a suitable jack stand under the extension housing.

18. Remove the transfer case-to-transmission bolts.

19. Separate the transfer case from the extension housing. Pull the transfer case rearward, then lower the transfer case from the vehicle.

❋❋ CAUTION

Carefully clean the gasket surfaces as nicks and gouges can cause fluid leaks.

20. Remove the transfer case-to-transmission gasket. Clean the mating surfaces, using metal surface cleaner.

To install:

21. Install a new mounting gasket.

22. Secure the transfer case to the high-lift jack using a safety strap.

23. Raise the transfer case into position.

24. Install the bolts retaining the transfer case to the extension housing and tighten to 37 ft. lbs. (50 Nm).

25. Remove the jack stand from the extension housing.

26. Install the transmission mount and tighten to 70 ft. lbs. (95 Nm).

27. Position the crossmember and loosely install the two nuts.

28. Install the crossmember bolts and tighten to 60 ft. lbs. (81 Nm).

29. Attach the wire harness to the crossmember.

30. Remove the high-lift jack.

31. Tighten the transmission mount-to-crossmember nuts to 69 ft. lbs. (94 Nm).

32. On models with an electric shift transfer case, perform the following:

a. Connect the vent hose.

b. Connect the two gear motor encoder assembly electrical connectors.

33. On models with a manual shift transfer case, perform the following:

a. Connect the 3-position mode switch harness connector.

b. Connect the manual shift linkage.

34. Connect the front driveshaft to the transfer case, aligning the match marks made prior to removal and install the four new bolts. Tighten to 82 ft. lbs. (111 Nm).

35. Install the rear driveshaft.

36. Install the skid plate and the four bolts and tighten to 18 ft. lbs. (25 Nm).

• Fill the transfer case.

2005–06 Expedition & Navigator

1. Before servicing the vehicle, refer to the precautions in the beginning of this section.

2. Drain the fluid if the transfer case is to be disassembled.

3. Install the drain plug when finished draining.

4. Remove the transfer case–to–transmission brace.

5. Remove the bolts from the transmission.

6. Remove the nuts from the transfer case.

7. Remove the two nuts and the front driveshaft shield.

➡**Index-mark the driveshaft(s) to maintain initial driveshaft balance during installation.**

8. Remove the front driveshaft.

9. Remove the rear driveshaft.

10. Disconnect the electrical connector.

11. Disconnect the vent hose.

→One transfer case–to–brace nut is located at the top of the transfer case input flange.

12. Remove the three transfer case–to–brace nuts.

13. Remove the stud.

14. Remove the transmission–to–brace nuts.

❊ CAUTION

Never support the transmission from the bottom of the transmission pan.

15. Using a suitable jack stand, support the transmission.

❊ CAUTION

Secure the transfer case to the jack with a safety strap.

16. Using a suitable transmission jack, support the transfer case.

17. Remove the two exhaust heat shield–to–crossmember bolts.

18. Remove the bolt and the exhaust hanger bracket.

19. Position a suitable drain pan below the transmission extension housing.

20. Remove the six transfer case–to–transmission extension housing bolts.

→Watch for obstructions.

21. Separate the transfer case from the transmission extension housing, move the transfer case rearward off the output shaft, then lower the transfer case from the vehicle.

❊ CAUTION

Carefully clean the gasket surfaces. Nicks and gouges cause fluid leaks.

22. Remove the transfer case–to–transmission gasket and clean the mating surfaces.

To install:

23. Installation is the reverse of removal, please note the following torque specifications:

a. Tighten the six transfer case–to–transmission extension housing bolts in a star pattern to 30 ft. lbs. (41 Nm).

b. Tighten the bolt retaining the exhaust hanger bracket to 30 ft. lbs. (41 Nm).

c. Tighten the transmission-to-brace nuts to 35 ft. lbs. (48 Nm).

d. Tighten the three transfer case-to-brace nuts to 52 ft. lbs. (70 Nm).

e. Tighten the two nuts retaining the front driveshaft shield to 13 ft. lbs. (18 Nm).

f. Tighten the transfer case-to-transmission brace bolts to 22 ft. lbs. (30 Nm) and the nuts to 21 ft. lbs. (28 Nm).

24. Fill the transfer case.

2007 Expedition & Navigator

1. Before servicing the vehicle, refer to the precautions in the beginning of this section.

2. With the vehicle in NEUTRAL, position it on a hoist.

3. Drain the fluid if the transfer case is to be disassembled. Install the drain plug when finished draining.

4. Remove the 2 nuts and the front driveshaft shield.

→Index-mark Both of the driveshaft's to maintain initial driveshaft balance during installation.

5. Remove the front driveshaft.

6. Remove the rear driveshaft.

7. Disconnect the electrical connector.

8. Disconnect the vent hose.

9. Using a suitable transmission jack, support the transfer case.

10. For Navigator model remove the 2 exhaust heat shield-to-crossmember bolts.

11. For Navigator model remove the bolt and the exhaust hanger bracket.

❊ WARNING

Secure the transfer case to the jack with a safety strap.

→Position a suitable drain pan below the transmission extension housing.

12. Remove the 6 transfer case-to-transmission extension housing bolts.

13. Separate the transfer case from the transmission extension housing, move the transfer case rearward off the output shaft, then lower the transfer case from the vehicle.

14. Remove the transfer case-to-transmission gasket and clean the mating surfaces.

To install:

15. To install, reverse the removal procedure and note the following:

g. Tighten the transfer case-to-transmission bolts evenly in a star pattern.

h. Tighten the transfer case-to-transmission bolts to 35 ft. lbs. (47 Nm).

i. Navigator model tighten the transfer case-to-transmission bolts to 30 ft. lbs. (40 Nm).

j. Navigator model tighten the 2 exhaust heat shield-to-crossmember bolts to 30 ft. lbs. (40 Nm).

k. Navigator model tighten the exhaust hanger bracket to 30 ft. lbs. (40 Nm).

l. Tighten the front drive shaft shield nuts to 13 ft. lbs. (18 Nm).

m. Install a new transfer case-to-transmission gasket.

n. Adjust the transmission selector lever cable.

o. Fill the transfer case if previously drained. Refer to Specifications in this section for the correct type and quantity of fluid.

p. Tighten drain plug to 11 ft. lbs. (15 Nm).

FRONT AUTOMATIC LOCKING HUBS

REMOVAL & INSTALLATION

Excursion

See Figure 12.

1. Before servicing the vehicle, refer to the precautions section.

2. Raise and safely support the vehicle.

3. Remove or disconnect the following:
   - Tire
   - 3 screws and separate the cap from the body
   - Lockring seated in the groove of the hub assembly
   - Body assembly from the brake rotor/hub
   - Snapring from the groove in the stub-shaft
   - 3 thrust washers from the stub-shaft

4. Pull the cam assembly to remove it.

To install:

5. Align the fixed cam retaining key on the cam assembly with the keyway on the spindle. Firmly push the cam assembly on the wheel retaining nut.

6. Install or connect the following:
   - Metal, plastic, then the splined washers on the stub-shaft
   - Snapring in the groove of the stub-shaft. It may be necessary to push the stub-shaft outward from the back of the knuckle assembly.

❊ WARNING

Do not pack the hub assembly with grease. Too much grease will damage the hub assembly.

7. Rotate the moving cam assembly to the 1 o'clock position in relation to the fixed cam retaining key. Use any 1 of the 3 stops.
   - Body assembly onto the hub by lining up the 3 legs with the 3 pockets in the cam assembly. Be sure the

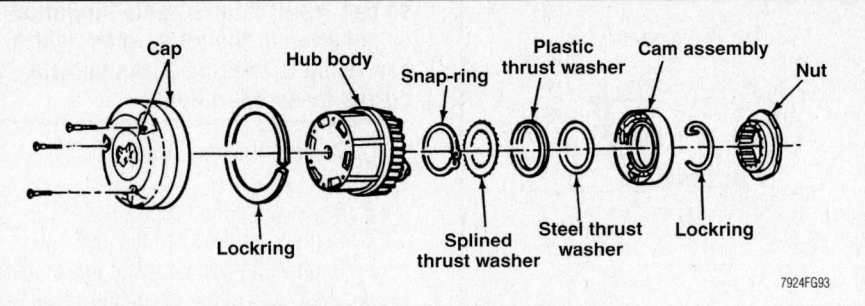

Fig. 12 Exploded view of the typical automatic locking hub assembly

22086_EXPD_G0068

Fig. 13 Four crossmember bolts shown

assembly is in far enough to see the groove in the hub.

- Large lockring in the groove on the hub. Ensure the lockring is seated completely.
- Cap using the 3 screws. Tighten the screws to 35–53 inch lbs. (4–6 Nm).
- Tire and lower the vehicle to the floor

FRONT AXLE HOUSING

REMOVAL & INSTALLATION

Excursion Dana 50

1. Before servicing the vehicle, refer to the precautions section.
2. Remove the disc brake calipers.
3. Remove the disc brake pads.
4. Disconnect the power vacuum hub hose from the knuckle, then disconnect the ABS sensor.
5. Remove the front stabilizer bar-to-axle retaining bolts.
6. If equipped, disconnect the steering damper at the axle.
7. Disconnect the steering linkage at the steering knuckles and position it aside.

❋❋ CAUTION

Index-mark the driveshaft to the companion flange to maintain proper driveline balance.

8. Disconnect the driveshaft at the front axle and position it aside. Wrap electrical tape around the bearing cups.
9. Disconnect the vent tube and plug the fitting.

➡**It is necessary to load the suspension to remove the track bar. Load the springs by allowing most of the front vehicle weight to rest on the axle.**

10. Support the axle with a suitable jack and lower the vehicle enough to relieve the tension on the track bar. Then, disconnect the track bar at the axle and position it aside.
11. Relieve the load on the suspension after disconnecting the track bar.

12. Leave the jack supporting the axle for removal from the vehicle.
13. Remove the U-bolts securing the axle to the springs.
14. Lower and remove the axle.

To install:

15. Installation is the reverse of removal. Note the following torque specifications:
    a. Tighten the U-bolts to 99 ft. lbs. (133 Nm).
    b. Tighten the track bar to axle bolts to 129 ft. lbs. (174 Nm).
    c. Tighten the stabilizer bar-to-axle retaining bolts to 35 ft. lbs. (47 Nm).

Expedition & Navigator

See Figure 13.

1. Before servicing the vehicle, refer to the precautions section.

❋❋ WARNING

The electrical power to the air suspension system must be shut off prior to hoisting, jacking or towing an air suspension vehicle. This can be accomplished by turning off the air suspension switch located in the LH rear quarter trim panel area. Failure to do so can result in unexpected inflation or deflation of the air springs, which can result in shifting of the vehicle during these operations.

2. With the transmission in NEUTRAL, raise and support the vehicle.
3. Index-mark the front driveshaft to the universal joint drive pinion flange.
4. Disconnect and support the front driveshaft.

➡**Do not allow the driveshaft to hang unsupported.**

5. Remove the bolts, and disconnect both front drive halfshafts from the front axle shaft.
6. Remove the 4 crossmember bolts and the crossmember.

7. For 2007 models Remove the bolt from the lower steering shaft-to-steering gear and disconnect the coupler from the rack.
8. Use a high-lift jack to support the axle assembly.
9. Remove the axle housing isolator nut and bolts.
10. Carefully lower the front drive axle assembly.
11. Disconnect the vent hose from the axle vent barbed fitting.

To install:

12. To install, reverse the removal procedure and not the following:
    a. Tighten axle housing isolator bolts and nut to 85 ft. lbs. (115 Nm).
    b. For 2007 models tighten housing isolator bolts and nut to 111 ft. lbs. (150 Nm).
    c. Tighten crossmember bolts to 66 ft. lbs. (90 Nm).
    d. Tighten halfshaft mounting bolts to 60 ft. lbs. (82 Nm).
    e. Tighten front drive shaft mounting bolts to 83 ft. lbs. (112 Nm).
    f. For 2007 models tighten the bolt from the lower steering shaft-to-steering gear to 22 ft. lbs. (22 Nm).

FRONT AXLE SHAFT, BEARING & SEAL

REMOVAL & INSTALLATION

Excursion Dana 50

See Figures 14 and 15.

1. Before servicing the vehicle, refer to the precautions section.
2. Position the vehicle on a hoist.
3. Remove the front wheel and tire assemblies.
4. Remove the differential housing cover and drain the lubricant.
5. Clean the gasket material from the differential housing and the differential housing cover.
6. Remove front brake calipers.
7. Remove the front brake discs.

8. Remove the wheel hubs and bearings.

9. If equipped, disconnect the pulse vacuum hub (PVH) hoses.

10. Using a drift, drive the axle shaft main seal out of the wheel knuckle.

11. Remove the axle shafts and main seals.

➡Inspect axle shafts for bearing wear from inner hub bearing. Inspect hub bearing.

12. Remove the differential bearing caps.

➡Prior to removal, note the stamped mating letters positioning on the bearing caps and the differential housing for correct reassembly.

13. Using the special tools100-D002 and 205-001, spread the differential housing.

✷✷ WARNING

Do not spread the differential housing more than specified, 0.015 inch. (0.38mm)

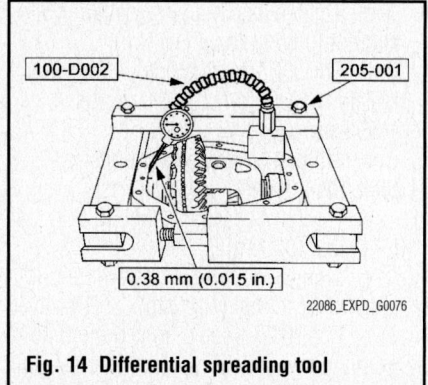

Fig. 14 Differential spreading tool

14. Using two pry bars, remove the differential with the bearing cups.

➡Mark the bearing shims for proper installation of the carrier.

15. Drive the inner axle shaft oil seals out of the differential housing through the axle tubes. Discard the seals.

To install:

➡To ease installation, coat the seal axle tube mating surfaces with lubricant.

16. Using the special tools 205-428 and 205-424,205-425, install the axle shaft oil seals.

17. Place the axle shaft oil seals onto the tool and position the assembly into the differential housing. Lengthen the tool as necessary until both seals start evenly in the

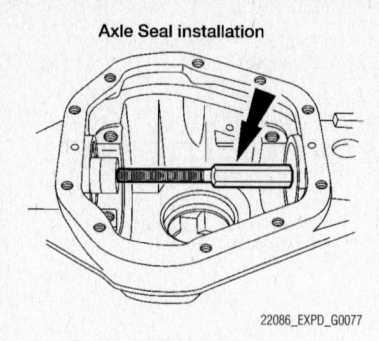

Fig. 15 Axle seal installation and tools shown

axle tubes. Continue to lengthen the tool until both step plates bottom out against the housing.

18. Install carrier, shims and bearing caps.

19. Tighten bearing caps to 80 ft. lbs. (109 Nm).

20. Apply 1/8-1/4 inch. (3.2-6 mm) bead of silicone rubber sealer on differential housing cover.

21. Install the differential housing cover and tighten to 35 ft. lbs. (47 Nm).

➡Allow one hour curing time before filling the axle with lubricant.

22. Install axle shafts and main seals.

23. Reconnect the pulse vacuum hub (PVH) hoses if removed.

24. Install the wheel hubs and bearings tighten mounting nuts to 133 ft. lbs. (180 Nm).

25. Install the front brake discs.

26. Install front brake calipers and tighten mounting bolts to 42 ft. lbs. (56 Nm).

27. Install the front wheel and tire assemblies.

28. Fill the axle with the specified type and quantity of lubricant.

FRONT HALFSHAFT

REMOVAL & INSTALLATION

2005-06 Expedition & Navigator

1. Before servicing the vehicle, refer to the precautions section.

✷✷ WARNING

The electrical power to the air suspension system must be shut off prior to hoisting, jacking or towing an air suspension vehicle. This can be accomplished by turning off the air suspension switch located in the left rear quarter trim panel. Failure to do

so can result in unexpected inflation or deflation of the air springs, which can result in shifting of the vehicle during these operations.

2. Remove the front wheel and tire assembly.

3. Remove the dust cap.

4. Remove and discard the axle nut.

5. Remove the vacuum/vent line at the vacuum/vent port of the integrated wheel end disconnect.

6. Remove the three bolts retaining the integrated wheel end disconnect to the steering knuckle.

7. Remove and discard the tie rod end nut. Disconnect the tie rod end from the steering knuckle.

8. Remove and discard the upper ball joint nut. Disconnect the upper ball joint from the steering knuckle.

9. Remove the front stabilizer bar brackets and allow the bar to hang from the stabilizer bar links.

✷✷ WARNING

Do not damage the hub seal.

➡Allow the steering knuckle to swing outboard while keeping the constant velocity shaft pushed inboard.

10. Once clearance is available, remove the constant velocity shaft joint outboard end and integrated wheel end disconnect from the steering knuckle hub bearing.

11. Remove the integrated wheel end disconnect from the outboard constant velocity joint housing.

12. Remove the six bolts retaining the halfshaft to the axle.

13. Separate the halfshaft from the axle and the hub, and remove the assembly from the vehicle.

✷✷ WARNING

Verify the spline engagement by checking for spline lash before installing the halfshaft nut.

To install:

14. Installation is the reverse of removal, please note the following torque specifications:

a. Tighten the six bolts retaining the halfshaft to the axle to 60 ft. lbs. (82 Nm).

b. Install the ball joint and use a new nut. Tighten the nut to 111 ft. lbs. (150 Nm).

c. Install the tie rod and use a new nut. Tighten the nut to 111 ft. lbs. (150 Nm).

d. Install the three bolts retaining the integrated wheel and tighten to 11 ft. lbs. (15 Nm).

e. Install a new axle nut and tighten to 20 ft. lbs. (27 Nm).

f. Install and tighten the sway bar bracket bolts to 41 ft lbs. (55 Nm).

2007 Expedition & Navigator

See Figure 16.

1. Before servicing the vehicle, refer to the precautions section.

➡**Whenever a halfshaft is removed, a new circlip and stub shaft pilot bearing seal must be installed.**

2. With the vehicle in NEUTRAL, position it on a hoist.

3. Disable the air suspension system.

4. Remove the dust cap.

5. Remove and discard the axle nut.

6. Remove the vacuum/vent line at the vacuum/vent port of the Integrated Wheel End (IWE) disconnect.

7. Remove the 3 IWE retaining bolts to the steering knuckle.

8. Disconnect the tie-rod end from the steering knuckle.

9. Discard the tie-rod end nut.

10. Disconnect the upper ball joint from the steering knuckle.

11. Discard the upper ball joint nut.

✳✳ WARNING

Do not damage the hub seal.

➡**Allow the steering knuckle to swing outboard while keeping the constant velocity (CV) shaft pushed inboard.**

12. Once clearance is available, remove the CV shaft joint outboard end and IWE disconnect from the steering knuckle hub bearing.

13. Remove the IWE disconnect from the outboard CV joint housing.

14. Using special tools 205-832 and 100-001, remove the halfshaft from the differential and the intermediate shaft.

15. Remove and discard the circlip and the stub shaft seal.

✳✳ WARNING

Verify the spline engagement by checking for spline lash before installing the halfshaft nut.

To install:

16. To install, reverse the removal procedure.

a. Install a new axle nut, tie-rod end nut and an upper ball joint nut.

b. Install the tie rod and use a new nut. Tighten the nut to 111 ft. lbs. (150 Nm).

c. Install the ball joint and use a new nut. Tighten the nut to 111 ft. lbs. (150 Nm).

d. Tighten the 3 IWE retaining bolts to 9 ft. lbs. (12 Nm).

e. Install a new axle nut and tighten to 20 ft. lbs. (27 Nm).

CV-JOINTS OVERHAUL

➡**Before continuing with this procedure, make sure to have available a new CV-joint boot kit, for each CV-joint being serviced. The outer CV-joint cannot be disassembled, only the boot can be replaced.**

Inner CV-Joint And Boot

1. Before servicing the vehicle, refer to the precautions section.

2. Remove the halfshaft assembly from the vehicle.

3. Clamp the halfshaft in a vise equipped with jaw caps to prevent damage to machined surfaces. Do not allow the vise jaws to contact the boot or its clamp.

4. Slide 2 inboard clamp protectors off the boot clamps.

5. Carefully remove 2 boot clamps, and slide the boot off the inner CV-joint and housing.

6. Remove the CV-joint retaining ring and remove the housing.

7. Mark the inner race and the ball cage for assembly.

8. Remove 6 cage balls.

9. Remove the snapring.

10. Remove the inner race and ball cage.

11. Clean all parts in suitable parts cleaning solvent and inspect for wear.

To install:

12. Place the boot and the small boot clamp and protector on the shaft.

13. Place the ball cage on the shaft with the tapered end toward the outer CV-joint.

➡**Line up the marks made at disassembly.**

14. Position the inner race on the driveshaft in the position marked on disassembly.

15. Install the snapring.

16. Lubricate and position 6 balls with suitable CV-joint grease.

17. Place the boot protector and boot clamp on the CV-joint housing. Fill the housing with 8.29 ounces of suitable CV-joint grease.

18. Place the housing to the cage and bearings and install the retaining ring.

19. Remove any excess grease from the mating surface and position the boot and clamp.

20. Adjust the CV-joint to boot spacing to 16.43 in. (417.25mm).

21. After adjusting the CV-joint to boot spacing, insert a dull bladed screwdriver blade to relieve built up air pressure in the boot.

22. Use CV Boot Clamp Installer T95P-3514-A or equivalent, to install the boot clamps.

23. Place the clamp protectors over the boot clamps.

24. Install the halfshaft into the vehicle.

25. Road test the vehicle and check for proper operation.

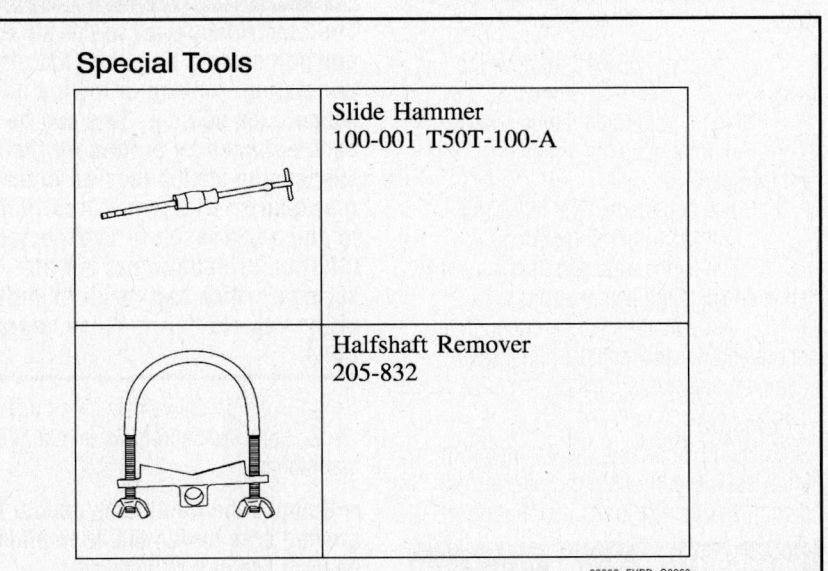

Special Tools	
	Slide Hammer 100-001 T50T-100-A
	Halfshaft Remover 205-832

22086_EXPD_G0069

Fig. 16 Special tools, slide hammer and halfshaft remover

Outer Boot

See Figures 17 and 18.

1. Remove the inner CV-joint and housing from the halfshaft.
2. Remove the inner boot from the half-shaft.
3. Remove the outer boot clamp protectors and carefully remove the boot clamps.
4. Remove the outer boot from the half-shaft and inspect the grease for contamination.
5. If the grease is contaminated, clean and inspect the joint for wear. Replace the joint and shaft if worn or damaged.

To install:

6. Place the new CV-joint boot on the shaft.
7. Using 5.82 ounces (165 grams) of suitable CV-joint grease, pack the outer CV-joint with grease, then spread the remaining grease inside the boot.
8. Clean the boot mounting surface and position the boot in the joint grooves.
9. Place the clamps in position and use CV Boot Clamp Installer T95P-3514-A or equivalent, to install the boot clamps.
10. Place the clamp protectors over the boot clamps.
11. Install the inner boot on the halfshaft.
12. Install the inner CV-joint and housing on the halfshaft.
13. If equipped, compress the Integrated Wheel End (IWE) disconnect on the bench to collapse the vacuum chamber.
14. While the IWE disconnect is collapsed, install a vacuum cap on the vacuum port.
15. Install the IWE disconnect on the outer CV joint housing.

> ⁂ **WARNING**
>
> Do not install the integrated wheel end disconnect in the knuckle. It must be installed on the outer constant velocity joint housing.

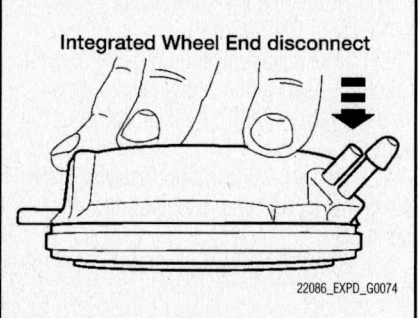

Fig. 17 Integrated Wheel End collapsed and vacuum cap installed

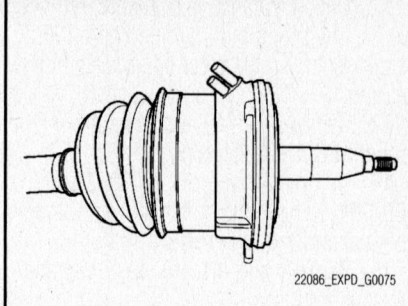

Fig. 18 Integrated Wheel End disconnect Correctly installed on axle

16. Install the halfshaft in the vehicle.
17. Road test the vehicle and check for proper operation.

FRONT PINION SEAL

REMOVAL & INSTALLATION

Excursion Dana 50 Front Axle

1. Before servicing the vehicle, refer to the precautions section.
2. Index-mark the front driveshaft and the front axle flange to maintain driveline balance.
3. Disconnect the front driveshaft from the front axle flange and position it aside.
4. Measure the pinion bearing torque preload. Record the reading.
5. Rotate the pinion with a Nm (inch-pound) torque wrench. Record the torque necessary to maintain rotation of the pinion through several revolutions.
6. Using tool 205-012, remove and discard the nut and washer.

→ **Index-mark the flange and the pinion shaft.**

7. Using tool 205-018, remove the flange.
8. Using a puller and flange removal tool 205-018, remove the pinion seal. Discard the seal.
9. Clean and inspect the following:
   a. The seal mounting surface.
   b. The flange lugs and the flange end that contacts the bearing cone.
   c. Verify that the flange nut counterbore and the seal contact surfaces are smooth and free of nicks.

To install:

10. Using a suitable driver, install the pinion seal. Lightly coat the pinion seal lip with lubricant prior to installation.

> ⁂ **CAUTION**
>
> Never use a metal hammer on the pinion flange or install the flange with power tools. If necessary, use a plastic hammer to tap on a tight fitting flange.

→ **Align the index marks.**

11. Lightly coat the flange splines and seal mating area with lubricant, then install the flange with a new washer and nut.

> ⁂ **CAUTION**
>
> Never back off the pinion nut to reduce preload. If preload reduction is necessary, install a new collapsible spacer and pinion nut.

12. Tighten the nut as follows:
   a. Use tool 205-011 to prevent the flange from turning while tightening the nut.
   b. Remove the special tool when taking pinion bearing torque preload readings.
   c. Take frequent pinion bearing torque preload readings.
   d. The final reading must be 5 inch lbs. (0.56 Nm) more than the initial reading taken during removal.
13. If installing a new nut on the pinion shaft and tighten it to 250–300 ft. lbs. (339–407 Nm).
14. Connect the front driveshaft to the front axle flange. Install the two new retainers and four new bolts and tighten to 26 ft. lbs. (35 Nm).
15. Check and, if necessary, fill the axle with the specified lubricant.

2005–06 Expedition & Navigator

See Figure 19.

> ⁂ **WARNING**
>
> The electrical power to the air suspension system must be shut off prior to hoisting, jacking or towing an air suspension vehicle. This can be accomplished by turning off the air suspension switch located in the LH rear quarter trim panel area. Failure to do so can result in unexpected inflation or deflation of the air springs, which can result in shifting of the vehicle during these operations.

1. Position the vehicle on a hoist.
2. Remove the front wheel and tire assemblies.

→ **Remove the front brake caliper to prevent drag during the drive pinion bearing preload adjustment.**

3. Remove the front brake calipers. Wire the caliper aside.

Special Tool(s)

	2-Jaw Puller 205-D072 (D97L-4221-A) or equivalent
	Holding Fixture, Drive Pinion Flange 205-126 (T78P-4851-A)
	Installer, Drive Pinion Flange 205-002 (TOOL-4858-E)

22086_EXPD_G0071

Fig. 19 Special tools

4. Index-mark the front driveshaft to the axle universal joint flange.

5. Remove the 4 bolts.

6. Carefully disconnect and support the front driveshaft.

7. Using a (Nm) inch./pound torque wrench, measure the torque necessary to maintain pinion rotation. Record the measurement for reference during installation.

8. Install the special holding tool 205-126 and remove the pinion nut.

➡**After removing the pinion nut, discard it. Use a new pinion nut for installation.**

9. Index-mark the axle universal joint flange to the pinion stem.

10. Using special tool 205-D072, separate the axle universal joint flange from the pinion gear.

11. Remove the flange.

12. Force up on the metal flange of the rear axle drive pinion seal. Install gripping pliers and strike with a hammer to remove the pinion seal.

13. Inspect the axle universal joint flange for burrs, the nut counterbore and the seal contact surface for nicks, and the bearing cone contact area for damage. Install a new flange if necessary.

14. Check the pinion stem splines for burrs. If burrs are evident, remove them with a fine crocus cloth.

To install:

15. Clean the pinion seal bore and use an oil seal installer to install the pinion seal.

16. Lubricate the axle universal joint flange splines and the pinion seal.

17. Align the index-marks and position the axle universal joint flange on the pinion shaft.

➡**Rotate the pinion gear occasionally to make sure the pinion bearings seat correctly.**

18. Using the special tool 205-002, install the axle universal joint flange.

19. Install the special tool, and tighten the pinion nut.

   a. Rotate the pinion gear occasionally to make sure the pinion bearings are seating correctly.

   b. Take frequent pinion bearing torque preload readings by rotating the pinion gear with a (Nm)inch/pound torque wrench.

   c. If the preload recorded prior to disassembly is lower than the specification for used bearings, then tighten the pinion

nut to the specification 29 inch. lbs. (1.8–3.3 Nm).

   d. If the preload recorded prior to disassembly is higher than the specification for used bearings, then tighten the pinion nut to the original reading as recorded.

20. Align the index-marks then attach the front driveshaft and tighten to 26 ft. lbs. (35 Nm).

21. Inspect and, if necessary, fill the differential.

22. Lower the vehicle.

23. If equipped with air suspension, reactivate the system by turning on the air suspension switch.

2007 Expedition & Navigator

See Figures 20 and 21.

1. Before servicing the vehicle, refer to the precautions section.

2. Position the vehicle on a hoist.

➡**Remove the front brake caliper to prevent drag during the drive pinion bearing preload adjustment.**

3. Remove the front brake calipers. Wire the caliper aside.

4. Index-mark the front driveshaft to the axle universal joint flange.

5. Remove and discard the 6 bolts and 3 washers.

6. Carefully disconnect and support the front driveshaft.

7. Using a Nm (inch/pound) torque wrench, measure the torque necessary to maintain pinion rotation. Record the measurement for reference during installation.

8. Install special tool 205-126 and remove the pinion nut.

9. Index-mark the axle universal joint flange to the pinion stem.

10. Using special tool 205-D072, separate the axle universal joint flange from the pinion gear.

11. Remove the flange.

12. Inspect the axle universal joint flange

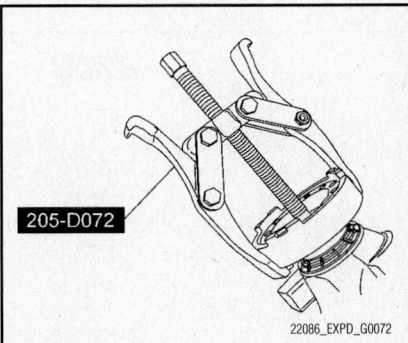

205-D072

22086_EXPD_G0072

Fig. 20 Flange removal with special tool 205-D072

for burrs, the nut counterbore and the seal contact surface for nicks, and the bearing cone contact area for damage. Install a new flange if necessary.

13. Check the pinion stem splines for burrs. If burrs are evident, remove them with a fine crocus cloth.

To install:

14. Clean the pinion seal bore and use an oil seal installer to install the pinion seal.

15. Lubricate the axle universal joint flange splines and the pinion seal.

➡**Disregard the scribe marks if installing a new flange.**

16. Align the index marks and position the axle universal joint flange on the pinion shaft.

➡**Rotate the pinion gear occasionally to make sure the pinion bearings seat correctly.**

17. Using special tool 205-002, install the axle universal joint flange.

18. Install the special tool, and tighten the pinion nut.

a. Rotate the pinion gear occasionally to make sure the pinion bearings are seating correctly.

b. Take frequent pinion bearing torque preload readings by rotating the pinion gear with a (Nm)inch/pound torque wrench.

c. If the preload recorded prior to dis-assembly is lower than the specification for used bearings, then tighten the pinion nut to the specification 29 inch. lbs. (1.8-3.3 Nm).

d. If the preload recorded prior to dis-assembly is higher than the specification for used bearings, then tighten the pinion nut to the original reading as recorded.

19. Align the index-marks then attach the front driveshaft and tighten the 6 flange bolts to 41 ft. lbs. (55 Nm).

20. Inspect and, if necessary, fill the differential.

21. Lower the vehicle.

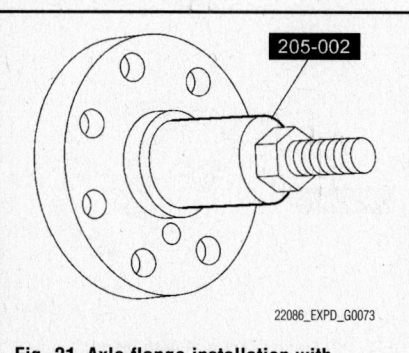

Fig. 21 Axle flange installation with special tool 205-002

FRONT STUB SHAFT, PILOT BEARING & SEAL

REMOVAL & INSTALLATION

2005–06 Expedition & Navigator

See Figures 22 and 23.

1. Before servicing the vehicle, refer to the precautions section.

2. Position the vehicle on a hoist.

3. Remove the halfshafts.

4. Remove the lower shock absorber and spring assembly nut and bolt.

5. Position the shock absorber and spring assembly aside.

6. Using a suitable axle shaft remover, remove the axle shafts.

7. Remove and discard the axle shaft circlips.

8. Using a suitable seal remover, remove the stub shaft oil seals.

9. Using special tool 307-318 and a slide hammer, remove the stub shaft pilot bearings or bushings, as equipped.

10. Clean the bearing and seal surfaces of any foreign material.

To install:

11. Using a suitable driver, install the stub shaft pilot bearing or bushing, as equipped.

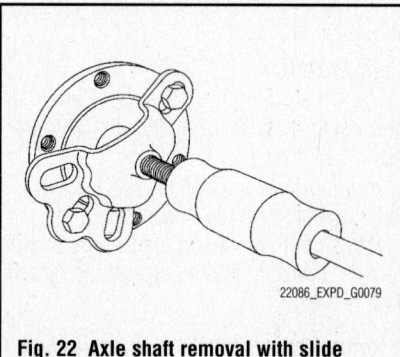

Fig. 22 Axle shaft removal with slide hammer

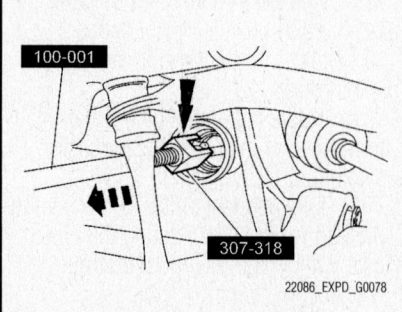

Fig. 23 Slide hammer and bearing removal tool shown

12. Using a suitable driver, install the stub shaft oil seals.

13. Install new axle shaft circlips.

➡**Care should be taken not to damage the axle seal surface.**

14. Install the axle shafts making sure the circlips are engaged in the side gears.

15. Refill the front drive axle to the correct level with lubricant.

16. Install the lower shock absorber and spring assembly bolt and nut. Tighten to 295 ft. lbs. (475 Nm).

17. Install the halfshafts.

2007 Expedition & Navigator

See Figures 24 and 25.

➡**Install a new stub shaft seal whenever a halfshaft is removed.**

1. Remove the front drive halfshafts.

2. Using special tools 307-397 and slide hammer 100-001, remove the intermediate shaft.

3. Remove and discard the intermediate shaft circlip and O-ring.

4. Using a suitable seal remover, remove and discard the stub shaft pilot bearing oil seal.

5. Using the special tools 308-047 and slide hammer 100-001, remove and discard the stub shaft pilot bearing.

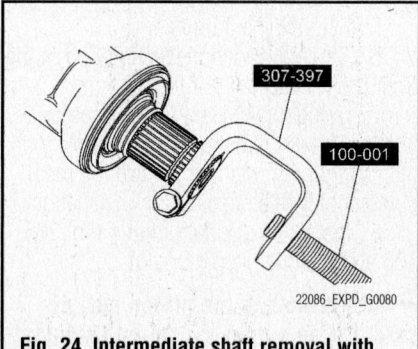

Fig. 24 Intermediate shaft removal with special tools

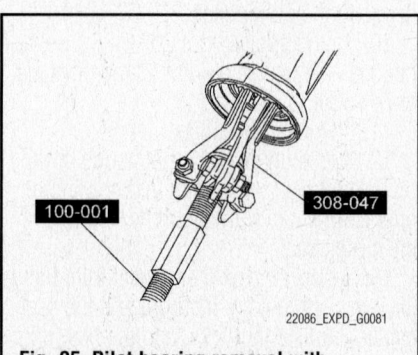

Fig. 25 Pilot bearing removal with special tools

To install:

6. Position the stub shaft pilot bearing in the axle tube or differential housing bore and using a bearing install tool install the bearing.

7. Carefully align the stub shaft pilot bearing oil seal with the housing bore and install the stub shaft bearing oil seal flush in the housing using a seal driver.

8. Install a new O-ring and new circlips on the intermediate shaft ends.

9. Insert the intermediate shaft and engage the circlip with the differential side gear.

10. Install the front drive halfshafts.

REAR AXLE HOUSING

REMOVAL & INSTALLATION

Excursion

See Figure 26.

1. Before servicing the vehicle, refer to the precautions section.

2. Remove the driveshaft.

3. Remove the rear wheels and tires.

4. Disconnect the rear anti-lock brake sensor.

5. Remove the nuts and the stone shield.

6. Remove the caliper pin bolts.

7. Remove the rear disc brake caliper.

➡ **Make sure the parking brake control is fully released.**

8. Release the tension on the parking brake system:
- Have an assistant pull the front parking brake cable and conduit to its full range.
- Insert a suitable retainer.

9. Disconnect the parking brake cable at the parking brake lever.

10. Remove the cable clamp bolt.

11. Unclip the brake line and remove the retainer from the parking brake cable bracket and position the cable aside.

12. Remove the bolts from the brake hose brackets.

13. Remove the vent hose at the brake hose junction block.

14. Remove the brake junction block from the rear axle housing and let it hang.

15. Remove the brake lines from the rear axle housing tie strap (but not from the disc brake calipers) and let the tubing hang.

❊❊ WARNING

Strap the axle securely to the jack.

16. Use a suitable transmission jack to support the axle.

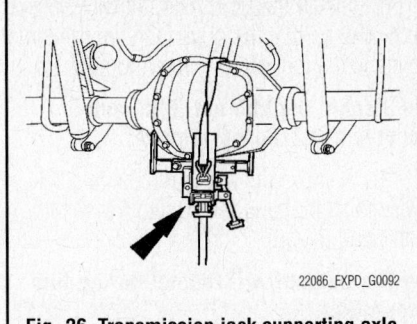

Fig. 26 Transmission jack supporting axle

17. Remove the lower shock absorber nuts and bolts.

18. Loosen the nuts from both lower ends of the stabilizer bar links.

➡ **When lowering or raising the differential housing, position the sway bar forward to clear the front of the differential housing.**

19. Remove the nuts from both stabilizer bar retainer-to-axle brackets and remove the stabilizer bar retainers, stabilizer bar mounting brackets and U-bolts. Let the stabilizer bar hang from the links.

➡ **Once the rear spring plate nuts and bolts are removed, new nuts and bolts must be installed.**

20. Remove the rear spring plate U-bolts and nuts.

21. Lower the axle from the vehicle.

22. To install, reverse the removal procedure:

   a. Tighten stone shields to 46 ft. lbs. (63 Nm).

   b. Tighten caliper pin bolts to 27 ft. lbs. (36 Nm).

   c. Tighten cable clamp bolt to 15 ft. lbs.(20 Nm).

   d. Tighten brake line retainer to 13 ft. lbs. (18 Nm).

   e. Tighten brake hose brackets to 62 inch. lbs. (7 Nm).

   f. Tighten the brake junction block to 13 ft. lbs. (18 Nm).

   g. Tighten shock mounting bolts to 46 ft. lbs. (63 Nm).

   h. Tighten stabilizer link nuts to 46 ft. lbs. (63 Nm).

   i. Tighten the rear spring plate U-bolt nuts to185 ft. lbs. (251 Nm).

   j. Bleed and adjust brake system.

   k. Check rear axle lubricant 75W-140 recommended.

Expedition & Navigator

Rear Air Suspension

See Figure 27.

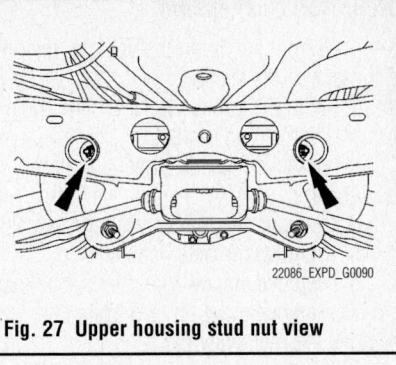

Fig. 27 Upper housing stud nut view

1. Before servicing the vehicle, refer to the precautions section.

2. Deflate the rear air springs.:
- Make sure that the air suspension switch is in the ON position.
- Make sure that a battery voltage of at least 11 volts is maintained while carrying out this procedure.
- Turn the ignition switch to the ON position.
- Connect the diagnostic tool to the Data Link Connector (DLC).
- Select Air Suspension Control Module under Active Command Mode.
- Follow the diagnostic tool directions to lift or vent the rear suspension.

3. With the vehicle in NEUTRAL, position the vehicle on a hoist.

4. Remove the rear wheel and tire assemblies.

5. Remove the rear driveshaft assembly.

6. Remove the axle halfshafts.

7. Remove the lower rear sway bar links.

8. Remove the 4 bracket bolts and remove the rear sway bar.

9. Using a suitable jack, support the axle housing.

10. Remove the upper axle housing stud nuts.

11. Remove the front torque arm bolt.

➡ **Move the axle housing forward to clear the rear mounting studs from the bushings.**

12. Lower the axle housing from the vehicle.

13. To install, reverse the removal procedure and note the following:

   a. Tighten the lower rear sway bar link nuts to 66 ft. lbs. (90 Nm).

   b. Tighten the 4 bracket bolts to 30 ft. lbs. (40 Nm).

   c. Tighten the upper axle housing stud nuts to 100 ft. lbs. (135 Nm).

   d. Tighten the front torque arm bolt to 100 ft. lbs. (135 Nm).

   e. Reactivate rear air suspension.

Rear Coil Suspension

1. Before servicing the vehicle, refer to the precautions section.
2. With the vehicle in NEUTRAL, position the vehicle on a hoist.
3. Remove the rear wheel and tire assemblies.
4. Remove the rear driveshaft assembly.
5. Remove the axle halfshafts.
6. Remove the lower rear sway bar links.
7. Remove the 4 bracket bolts and remove the rear sway bar.
8. Using a suitable jack, support the axle housing.
9. Remove the upper axle housing stud nuts.
10. Remove the front torque arm bolt.

➡**Move the axle housing forward to clear the rear mounting studs from the bushings.**

11. Lower the axle housing from the vehicle.
12. To install, reverse the removal procedure and note the following:
   a. Tighten the lower rear sway bar link nuts to 66 ft. lbs. (90 Nm).
   b. Tighten the 4 bracket bolts to 30 ft. lbs. (40 Nm).
   c. Tighten the upper axle housing stud nuts to 100 ft. lbs. (135 Nm).
   d. Tighten the front torque arm bolt to 100 ft. lbs. (135 Nm).

REAR AXLE SHAFT, BEARING & SEAL

REMOVAL & INSTALLATION

Excursion

See Figure 28.

1. Before servicing the vehicle, refer to the precautions section.
2. Set the parking brake.
3. Loosen the axle shaft retaining bolts.
4. Raise the vehicle to the desired working height, keeping the axle parallel with the floor.
5. Release the parking brake.
6. Remove the wheel(s).
7. Remove the brake caliper and brake disc on the single rear wheel axle.
8. Remove the retaining bolts and axle shaft.

✳✳ **WARNING**

The hub nuts are right-hand thread (right hub) and left-hand thread (left hub). Each hub nut is stamped RH or LH.

9. Install the Ford Axle Locknut Socket 205-448 so that the drive tangs of the tool engage the four slots in the hub nut.

➡**Discard the hub nut if the hub nut comes apart during removal.**

10. Remove the hub nut (counterclockwise for right-hand thread; clockwise for left-hand thread).

➡**The hub nut will ratchet during this operation.**

11. Install the Step Plate.
12. Install the 2-Jaw Puller and loosen the rear hub to the point of removal.
13. Remove the rear hub assembly.

➡**Do not drop the outer hub bearing when removing the hub.**

✳✳ **WARNING**

Install a new hub seal each time the hub assembly is removed.

14. Pack each bearing and install new hub seals.
15. If after hub removal, the hub seal or seal inner sleeve remains on the spindle, remove it using the Step Plate and the 2-Jaw Puller.
16. Inspect the seal surface and inner shoulder for scratches and damage.
17. Remove all scratches, gouges or galling damage with No. 600 or finer crocus cloth.

To install:

18. Coat the spindle with axle lubricant.

➡**The hub bearings must be prelubed prior to installation.**

19. Fill the hub cavity with 29.6 ml (1 oz) of axle lubricant.

➡**Use extreme care not to damage the hub seal by allowing it to contact the spindle during installation.**

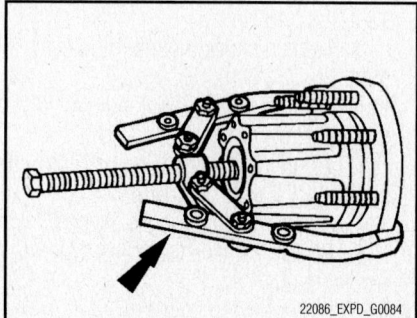

22086_EXPD_G0084

Fig. 28 Rear hub removal using step plate and jaw puller

20. Coat the spindle and hub seal inside diameter with axle lubricant.
21. Push the rear hub and outer bearing onto the spindle as an assembly. Hold the outer bearing seated and use the bearing as a pilot.

✳✳ **WARNING**

Make sure the hub nut tab is located in the keyway prior to thread engagement.

22. Install the hub nut on the spindle.
23. Turn the hub nut clockwise for right-hand thread or counterclockwise for left-hand thread.
24. Position the Ford Axle Locknut Socket on the hub nut.

➡**The hub nut will ratchet as torque is applied.**

25. Tighten the hub nut, rotating the rear hub occasionally while tightening.
26. Adjust hub nuts as follows:
   • For new bearings, ratchet back five teeth or notches (1/8 turn) on the hub nut. Five notches must be felt during this operation in order to have carried it out correctly.
   • For used bearings, ratchet back seven teeth or notches (1/6 turn) on the hub nut. Seven notches must be felt during this operation to have carried it out correctly.
27. Inspect the axle shaft O-ring seal for cracks, nicks or wear and replace it if required.
28. Lubricate the O-ring seal with lubricant prior to installation of axle shaft.
29. Install the axle shaft and tighten bolts until they seat.
30. Install the brake disc and caliper on the single rear wheel axles.
31. Install the wheels and tires but do not tighten the wheel nuts to specification at this time.
32. Check the axle lubricant level and add if needed.
33. Lower the vehicle.
34. Tighten the wheel nuts.
35. Tighten the axle shaft retaining bolts to 80 ft. lbs. (109 Nm).

REAR HALFSHAFT

REMOVAL & INSTALLATION

2005–06 Expedition & Navigator

See Figures 29 and 30.

✳✳ **WARNING**

Do not loosen the rear axle wheel hub retainer until after the wheel and

Special Tool(s)

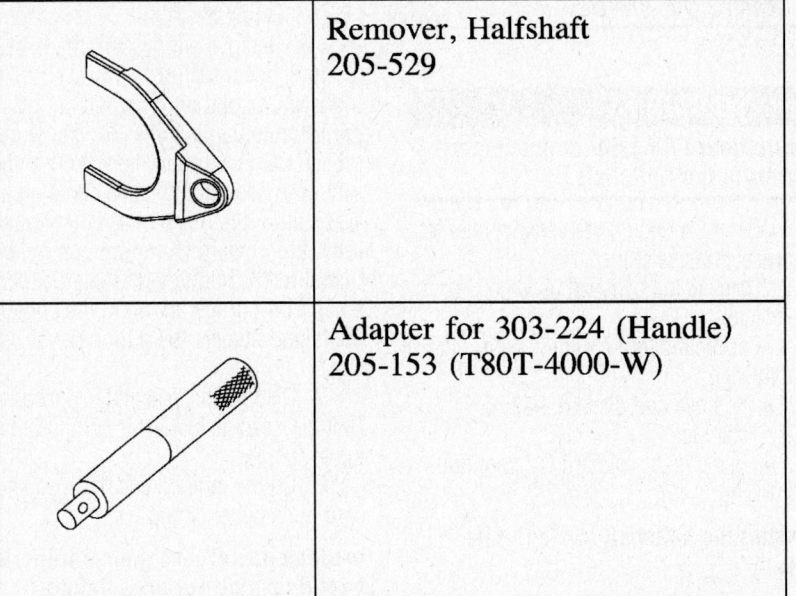	Remover, Halfshaft 205-529
	Adapter for 303-224 (Handle) 205-153 (T80T-4000-W)

22086_EXPD_G0085

Fig. 29 Special tools

tire assembly is removed from the vehicle. Wheel bearing damage will occur if the wheel bearing is unloaded with the weight of the vehicle applied.

1. Before servicing the vehicle, refer to the precautions section.

2. With the vehicle in NEUTRAL, raise and support the vehicle.

3. Remove the rear wheel and tire assembly.

➡**Have an assistant press the brake pedal to keep the axle from rotating.**

4. Remove and discard the rear axle wheel hub retainer and the washer.

5. Using a suitable hub puller, separate the halfshaft from the knuckle.

6. Disconnect the toe link from the rear knuckle.

7. Remove the bolt retaining the knuckle to the lower control arm.

8. Pivot the rear knuckle on the upper control arm bolts and support the knuckle in a raised position.

⁂ **WARNING**

Do not damage the axle shaft oil seal or the machined sealing surface on the inboard CV joint housing.

➡**A circlip retains the inboard CV joint housing to the differential side gear in the axle.**

9. Using the special tool 205-529 and 205-153, disengage the inboard CV joint housing from the differential side gear.

10. Remove the halfshaft assembly from the vehicle.

11. Remove and discard the halfshaft retainer circlip.

12. Remove and discard the halfshaft excluder seal, if equipped.

⁂ **WARNING**

Always install a new differential stub shaft seal, halfshaft retainer circlip and a new rear axle wheel hub retainer.

13. To install, reverse the removal procedure and note the following:

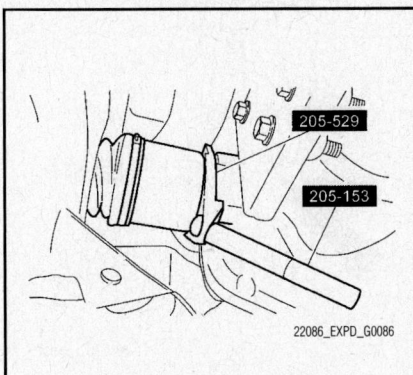

22086_EXPD_G0086

Fig. 30 Axle removal from differential side gear using special tools

a. Tighten the bolt retaining the knuckle to the lower control arm to 295 ft. lbs. (400 Nm).

b. Tighten the toe link to the rear knuckle to 41 ft. lbs.(45 Nm).

c. Tighten the rear axle wheel hub retainer nut to 254 ft. lbs. (345 Nm).

d. Check fluid level and add if needed.

⁂ **WARNING**

Never use power tools to tighten the rear axle wheel hub retainer.

2007 Expedition & Navigator
See Figures 31 and 32.

⁂ **WARNING**

Do not loosen the rear axle wheel hub retainer until after the wheel and tire assembly is removed from the vehicle. Wheel bearing damage will occur if the wheel bearing is unloaded with the weight of the vehicle applied.

1. Before servicing the vehicle, refer to the precautions section.

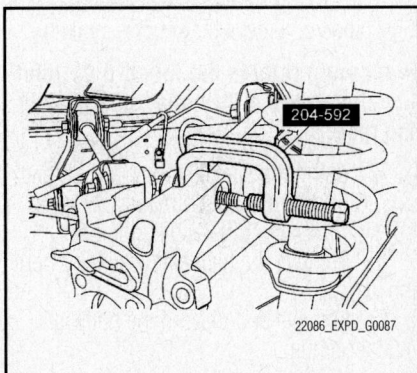

22086_EXPD_G0087

Fig. 31 Separating the upper arm from the wheel knuckle using the special tools

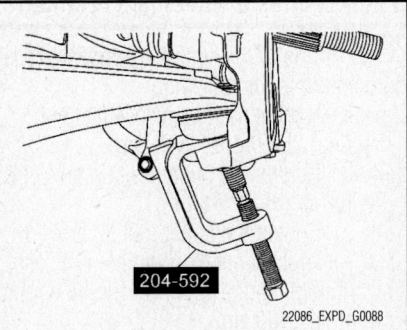

22086_EXPD_G0088

Fig. 32 Separating the lower ball joint from the wheel knuckle using the special tools

2. With the vehicle in NEUTRAL, raise and support the vehicle.

➡ **Have an assistant press the brake pedal to keep the axle from rotating.**

3. Remove and discard the rear axle wheel hub retainer and the washer.

4. Using a suitable hub puller, separate the halfshaft from the knuckle.

5. Remove the brake disc rotor.

6. Remove the upper trailing arm bolt.

7. Remove the upper trailing arm-to-wheel knuckle nut.

8. Using the special tool 204-592, separate the upper arm from the wheel knuckle.

9. Remove the stabilizer bar link.

10. Remove the toe link-to-knuckle bolt.

11. Disconnect the anti-lock brake sensor at the connector and open the wire retaining clips.

12. Compress the spring, depress the retaining tabs and detach the parking brake cable from the wheel knuckle.

13. Remove the 2 lower trailing arm-to-wheel knuckle bolts.

14. Remove the lower ball joint nut.

15. Using the special tool 204-592, separate the lower ball joint from the wheel knuckle.

16. Rotating the top of the knuckle assembly outboard, remove the knuckle assembly.

➡ **A circlip retains the inboard CV joint housing to the differential side gear in the axle.**

17. Using the special tool 205-529 and 205-123, disengage the inboard CV joint housing from the differential side gear.

18. Remove the halfshaft assembly from the vehicle.

19. Remove and discard the halfshaft retainer circlip.

❋❋ **WARNING**

Always install a new differential stub shaft seal, a new retainer circlip and a new rear axle wheel hub retainer.

20. To install, reverse the removal procedure and note the following:

a. Tighten the rear axle wheel hub retainer 254 ft. lbs. (345 Nm).

b. Tighten the upper trailing arm bolt to 184 ft. lbs. (250 Nm).

c. Tighten the upper trailing arm-to-wheel knuckle nut to 76 ft. lbs. (103 Nm).

d. Tighten the stabilizer bar link nut to 46 ft. lbs. (63 Nm).

e. Tighten the toe link-to-knuckle bolt to 166 ft. lbs. (225 Nm).

f. Tighten the 2 lower trailing arm-to-wheel knuckle bolts to 76 ft. lbs. (103 Nm).

g. Tighten the lower ball joint nut to 111 ft. lbs. (150 Nm).

CV-JOINTS OVERHAUL

See Figure 33.

❋❋ **WARNING**

The outboard CV joint is not removable from the halfshaft.

1. Before servicing the vehicle, refer to the precautions section.

2. Remove the halfshaft assembly from the vehicle.

3. For the inboard CV joint, carry out the following:

- Remove and discard the boot clamps.
- Remove the inboard CV joint housing.

➡ **Install the halfshaft in a soft-jaw vise.**

4. For the inboard CV joint, carry out the following:

- Remove and discard the retainer circlip.
- Slide the boot away from the CV joint.

5. Using a suitable 3-jaw puller, remove the CV joint.

6. Remove and discard the tri-lobe insert and the boot.

❋❋ **WARNING**

The outboard CV joint is not removable from the halfshaft. The boot must be removed or installed from the inboard CV joint side of the shaft.

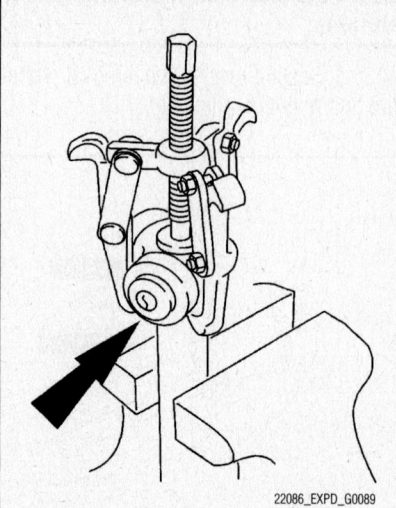

22086_EXPD_G0089

Fig. 33 Removal of inner CV joint with 3-jaw puller

7. For the outboard CV joint, carry out the following:

- Remove and discard the boot clamps.
- Remove and discard the boot.

8. Inspect the grease, packed in the inboard CV joint and the outboard CV joint, for contamination. Rub some of the grease from each joint between 2 fingers. Any gritty feeling indicates contamination. Wash all of the grease from the inboard CV joint, the inboard CV joint housing, the outboard CV joint and the interconnecting shaft. Thoroughly dry all of the components and inspect them for wear or damage.

9. Discard the assembly, if necessary. Only proceed as follows if not discarding the assembly.

10. On the inboard end, remove and discard the retainer circlip.

➡ **Clean any excess grease from the boot mounting surfaces before installing the boot.**

11. For the outboard CV joint, carry out the following:

- Slide the boot on the interconnecting shaft.
- Pack the outboard CV joint with 275 grams (9.7 ounces) of grease.
- Spread any remaining grease evenly inside the boot.
- Install the boot by seating it in the groove in the CV joint housing.

12. Using the special tool 205-343 or equivalent, install both boot clamps.

➡ **The lip on the end of the tri-lobe insert must seat against the end of the boot.**

13. For the inboard CV joint, carry out the following:

- Position the clamp on the interconnecting shaft.
- Position the boot on the interconnecting shaft.
- Install the tri-lobe insert.

➡ **One side of the inboard CV joint has a chamfer cut in the edge of joint at the inner diameter near the splines. Install the inboard CV joint so that the chamfer faces the outboard end of the halfshaft.**

14. Install the CV joint with tool 205-133 or equivalent.

15. Install the retainer circlip.

➡ **Clean any excess grease from the boot mounting surfaces before installing the boot.**

16. For the inboard CV joint, carry out the following:

- Pack the inboard CV joint housing with 325 grams (11.5 ounces) of grease.
- Spread any remaining grease evenly inside the boot and on the CV joint.
- Install the inboard CV joint housing, seating the boot in the groove in the housing.

17. Set the halfshaft assembled length. For LH set to 39.29 inch. (997.8 mm) and for the RH 37.65 inch. (956.3 mm).

- Measure the entire assembly length.
- Push in or pull out on the inner joint as necessary to adjust the halfshaft assembled length to specification.
- Hold the inner joint to prevent the assembled length from changing, and insert a small flat-blade screwdriver between the boot and the joint to equalize the pressure.

18. Using the special tool, install both boot clamps.

19. Install a new retainer circlip.

✳✳ WARNING

Do not over expand or twist the circlip during installation.

20. Install the halfshaft assembly in the vehicle.

REAR PINION SEAL

REMOVAL & INSTALLATION

Excursion 10.50 Inch Ring Gear

➡ **The rear wheels and brake calipers must be removed to prevent brake drag during drive pinion bearing preload adjustment.**

1. Remove the rear brake calipers.
2. Remove the driveshaft.
3. Install a Nm torque wrench on the pinion nut and record the rotational torque required to maintain rotation of the pinion through several revolutions.

➡ **After removal of the pinion nut, discard it. A new nut must be used for installation.**

4. Using the tool 205-126, hold the pinion flange while removing the pinion nut.
5. Mark the pinion flange in relation to the drive pinion stem to make sure alignment is correct during installation.
6. Using puller tool 205-D072, remove the pinion flange.

7. Force up on the metal flange of the rear axle drive pinion seal. Install gripping pliers to the seal flange and strike with a hammer until the rear axle drive pinion seal is removed.

To install:

8. Lubricate the new pinion seal with clean premium long-life grease.

✳✳ WARNING

If the rear axle drive pinion seal becomes misaligned during installation, remove the rear axle drive pinion seal and replace it with a new seal.

9. Using seal installer tool 205-208, install a new rear axle drive pinion seal.
10. Lubricate the pinion flange splines with clean synthetic rear axle lubricant.

➡ **Disregard the scribe marks if a new pinion flange is being installed.**

11. Align the pinion flange with the drive pinion shaft.
12. With the pinion flange in place in the rear axle housing, use tool 205-233 to install the pinion flange.
13. Position the new pinion nut.

✳✳ WARNING

Under no circumstances is the pinion nut to be backed off to reduce preload. If reduced preload is required, a new collapsible spacer and pinion nut must be installed.

14. Use holding tool 205-126 to hold the pinion flange while tightening the pinion nut.
15. Tighten the pinion nut, rotating the pinion occasionally to make sure the cone and roller bearings are seating correctly. Take frequent cone and roller bearing torque preload readings until the original recorded preload reading is obtained by rotating the pinion with a Nm torque wrench.
16. Install the driveshaft.
17. Install the brake calipers.

Expedition & Navigator 9.75 Inch Ring Gear

See Figures 34 and 35.

1. Before servicing the vehicle, refer to the precautions section.

➡ **If equipped, turn the air suspension switch to the OFF position.**

➡ **The rear wheels and brake calipers must be removed to prevent brake drag during drive pinion bearing preload adjustment.**

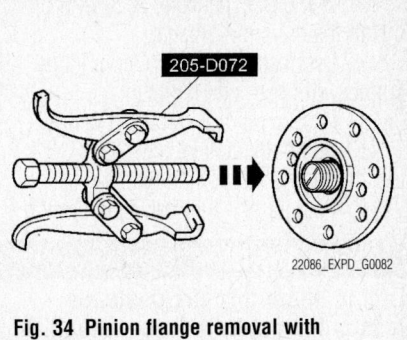

Fig. 34 Pinion flange removal with jaw puller

2. With the vehicle in NEUTRAL, position the vehicle on a hoist.
3. Remove the rear wheel and tire assemblies.
4. Remove the rear brake calipers and the brake discs.
5. Remove the rear driveshaft assembly.
6. Install a Nm (lb-in) torque wrench on the nut and record the torque necessary to maintain rotation of the drive pinion gear through several revolutions.

✳✳ WARNING

After removing the pinion nut, discard it. Use a new nut for installation.

7. Use the special tool to hold the pinion flange while removing the pinion nut.
8. Index-mark the drive pinion flange and the drive pinion gear stem to maintain initial balance during installation.
9. Using the special tool 205-D072, remove the drive pinion flange.
10. Force up on the metal flange of the drive pinion seal. Install gripping pliers and strike with a hammer until the pinion seal is removed.

To install:

11. Lubricate the lips of the new drive pinion seal with grease.

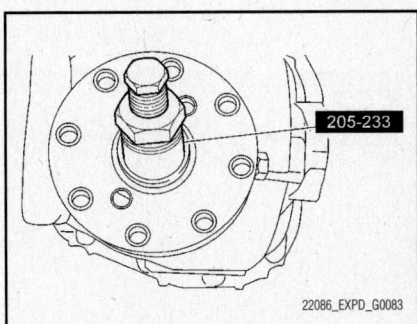

Fig. 35 Drive pinion flange installation with special tool

12. Using the special tool 205-208, install the drive pinion seal.

13. Lubricate the drive pinion flange splines with rear axle lubricant.

14. Position the drive pinion flange.

15. Using the special tool 205-233, install the drive pinion flange.

16. Position the new drive pinion nut.

✳✳ WARNING

Do not under any circumstance loosen the nut to reduce preload. If it is necessary to reduce preload, install a new drive pinion collapsible spacer and nut.

17. Use the special tool 205-126 to hold the pinion flange while tightening the nut.

- Rotate the pinion occasionally to make sure the pinion bearings seat correctly. Take frequent pinion bearing torque preload readings by rotating the drive pinion gear with a Nm (lb-in) torque wrench.
- If the preload recorded prior to disassembly is lower than the specification for used bearings, tighten the nut to 16-29 inch. lbs. (1.8-3.3 mm).
- If the preload recorded prior to disassembly is higher than the specification for used bearings, tighten the nut to the original reading as recorded.

➡**Install the driveshaft with new bolts. If new bolts are not available, apply sealer to the threads of the original bolts.**

18. Align the index marks.

➡**The driveshaft flange yoke fits tightly on the pinion flange pilot. To make sure that the yoke seats squarely on the flange, tighten the bolts evenly in a cross pattern as shown.**

19. Install the rear driveshaft.

20. Install the rear brake discs and the brake calipers.

21. Check fluid level and add if needed.

22. Install the rear wheel and tire assemblies.

23. Lower the vehicle.

24. If equipped with air suspension, reactivate the system.

REAR STUB SHAFT, PILOT BEARING & SEAL

REMOVAL & INSTALLATION

Expedition & Navigator

See Figure 36.

1. Before servicing the vehicle, refer to the precautions section.

2. Remove the halfshaft assembly.

3. Using the special tools 100-001 slide hammer and 308-047, remove and discard the stub shaft pilot bearing and the stub shaft pilot bearing oil seal.

- Firmly engage the tangs of the special tool on the stub shaft pilot bearing.
- Remove and discard the bearing and the stub shaft pilot bearing oil seal.

➡**If removing the stub shaft pilot bearing oil seal only, engage the tangs of**

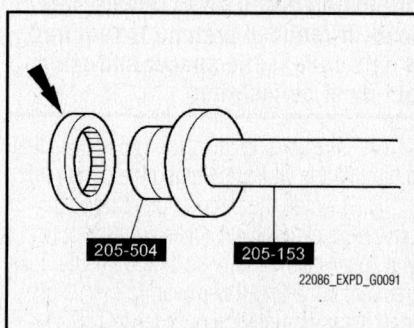

205-504   205-153

22086_EXPD_G0091

Fig. 36 Pilot bearing and special tools

the special tool on the stub shaft pilot bearing oil seal.

4. Inspect the seal journal for rust, nicks and scratches. Polish the seal journal surface with fine crocus cloth, if necessary.

5. Lubricate the new stub shaft pilot bearing with axle lubricant.

✳✳ WARNING

Installation of the stub shaft pilot bearing or stub shaft oil seal without the correct tools can result in early bearing or seal failure. If the stub shaft pilot bearing becomes cocked in the bore during installation, remove it and install a new one.

6. Place the stub shaft pilot bearing onto the special tools.

7. Install the stub shaft pilot bearing into the rear axle housing bore.

➡**Do not disassemble the new oil seal. Use a tool like the Lisle LIS17850 to avoid interference with the suspension components.**

8. Install the new seal onto a suitable installer.

9. Carefully align the stub shaft pilot bearing seal with the housing bore and install the stub shaft pilot bearing seal flush in the differential housing. Strike only the handle. Directly striking the installer tool will damage the seal.

➡**Make sure the stub shaft oil seal is correctly seated in the differential housing. If a feeler gauge of 0.010 inch. (0.025 mm) can be inserted between the stub shaft oil seal and the differential housing, the stub shaft seal is not seated correctly. Remove the stub shaft oil seal and install a new stub shaft oil seal.**

10. Install the halfshaft.

ENGINE COOLING

ENGINE FAN

REMOVAL & INSTALLATION

Excursion

5.4L & 6.8L Engines

1. Before servicing the vehicle, refer to the precautions section.
2. Drain the cooling system.
3. Remove the three bolts and position the degas bottle out of the way.
4. Squeeze the clamp, pull the hose off and position the upper radiator hose out of the way.

❄ WARNING

The large clutch assembly nut has a right-hand thread and must be rotated counterclockwise to remove it.

5. On 6.8L Engines:
   a. Using Fan Pulley Holding Wrench Special Tool 303-478 (T94T-6312-AH), or equivalent, hold the coolant pump pulley steady.
   b. Using the Fan Clutch Nut Wrench Special tool 303-214- (T83T-6312-B), or equivalent, remove the cooling fan assembly locknut.
6. On 5.4L engines:
   a. Using Fan Pulley Holding Wrench Special Tool 303-239 (T84T-6312-C), or equivalent, hold the coolant pump pulley steady.
   b. Using the Fan Clutch Nut Wrench Special tool 303-240- (T84T-6312-D), or equivalent, remove the cooling fan assembly locknut.
7. Remove the fan and fan clutch from the coolant pump pulley.
8. Carefully position the fan and the fan clutch into the shroud.
9. Remove the bolts, the shroud, fan and clutch.
10. To install, reverse the removal procedure. Observe the following tightening specifications:
    a. Upper shroud retainers: 80 inch lbs. (9 Nm)
    b. Fan clutch nut: 98 ft. lbs. (133 Nm).

6.0L Diesel Engine

1. Before servicing the vehicle, refer to the precautions section.
2. Remove the radiator assembly, as outlined in this section.
3. Disconnect the cooling fan clutch electrical connector. Unclip and position the fan wiring aside.

➡**Use a hole in the fan hub to prevent the fan from turning.**

4. Using Fan Clutch Nut Special Tool no. 303-591, remove the cooling fan and clutch.
5. Remove the cooling fan and clutch assembly.
6. If necessary, remove the bolts and separate the cooling fan and the clutch.
7. To install, reverse the removal procedure. Observe the following tightening specifications:
   a. Cooling fan-to-clutch bolts: 13 ft. lbs. (17 Nm).
8. Cooling fan and clutch assembly-to-engine bolt: 98 ft. lbs. (133 Nm).

2005–06 Expedition & Navigator

See Figures 37 and 38.

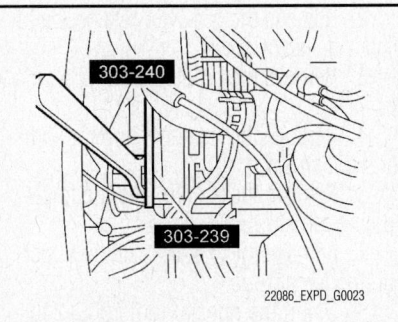

Fig. 37 Cooling fan removal tools 303-240 & 303-239 shown

1. Remove the pin-type retainers and the air deflector cover.
2. Remove the air cleaner inlet pipe and resonator.
3. Remove the retainers and the radiator sight shield.
4. Remove the 2 bolts and the lower cooling fan shroud.
5. Remove the 2 bolts and the upper cooling fan shroud.
6. Using the special tools 303-240 and 303-239, remove the cooling fan assembly.
7. To install, reverse the removal procedure. Observe the following tightening specifications:
   a. Tighten fan assembly to 41 ft. lbs. (55 Nm).
   b. Tighten cooling fan shroud mounting bolts to 27 inch. lbs. (3 Nm).

2007 Expedition & Navigator

1. With the vehicle in NEUTRAL, position it on a hoist.
2. Disconnect the cooling fan electronic clutch electrical connector.
3. Remove the nut and the cooling fan electronic clutch harness support bracket from the stud bolt.
4. Release the cooling fan shroud position tab and rotate the shroud upwards until the lower tab locks into position.
5. Using the special tools 303-214 and 303-239, remove the cooling fan assembly.

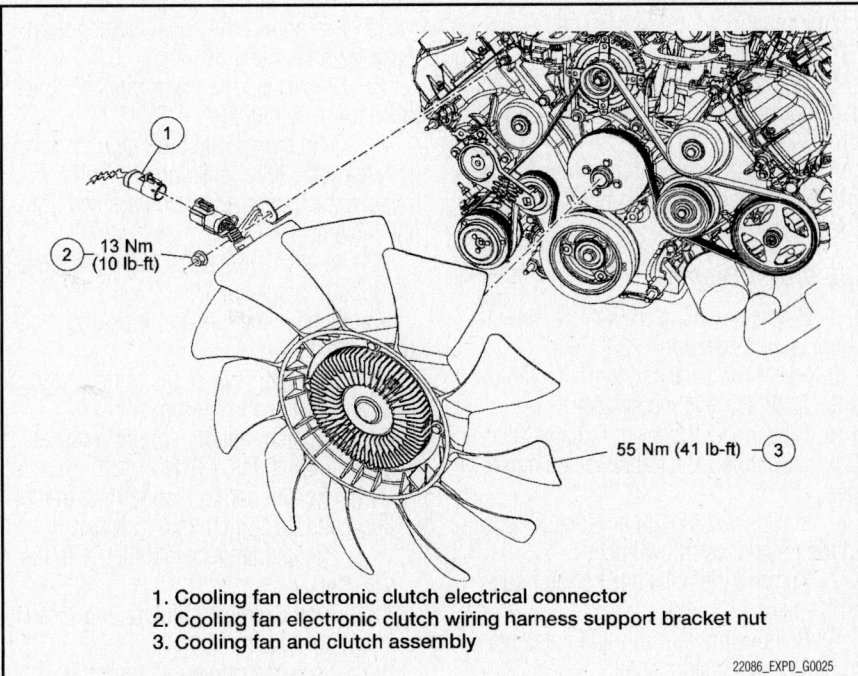

1. Cooling fan electronic clutch electrical connector
2. Cooling fan electronic clutch wiring harness support bracket nut
3. Cooling fan and clutch assembly

Fig. 38 2005 Cooling fan and clutch assembly 5.4L engine

6. To install, reverse the removal procedure and note the following:

a. Tighten the cooling fan electronic clutch harness support bracket nut to 10 ft. lbs. (13 Nm).

b. Tighten fan assembly to 41 ft. lbs. (55 Nm).

RADIATOR

REMOVAL & INSTALLATION

Excursion

5.4L & 6.8L Engines

1. Before servicing the vehicle, refer to the precautions section.

2. Drain the cooling system.

3. Remove the transmission oil cooler tubes from the radiator.

4. Remove the fan blade, clutch and shroud.

5. Raise the vehicle.

6. Remove the degas drain hose and the lower radiator hose from the radiator.

7. Lower the vehicle.

8. Remove the upper hose from the radiator.

9. Remove the plastic pin-type retainers and position the radiator sight shield out of the way.

10. Remove the bolts and the right upper radiator support.

11. Remove the insulator.

12. Remove the vent hose from the radiator.

13. Remove the bolts and the left side radiator support.

14. Remove the insulator.

15. Remove the radiator and the lower insulators from the radiator or frame extension.

16. To install, reverse the removal procedure. Tighten the radiator support bolts to 22 ft. lbs. (30 Nm).

6.0L Diesel Engine

1. Before servicing the vehicle, refer to the precautions section.

2. Raise and safely support the vehicle.

3. Drain the cooling system.

4. Disconnect the lower radiator hose.

5. Disconnect the transmission cooler tubes.

6. Disconnect the upper radiator hose and the radiator overflow hose.

7. Remove the bolts and radiator support brackets.

8. Remove the four pin-type retainers and pull back the sight shield.

9. Disconnect the three pin-type retainers and two wiring retainers. Position the

cable so that the radiator can be moved forward.

10. Remove the radiator assembly.

11. Remove the bolts and the cooling fan shroud, if necessary.

To install:

12. To install, reverse the removal procedure. Observe the following tightening specifications:

a. Radiator support bracket bolts: 9 ft. lbs (12 Nm).

b. 1/2 inch transmission cooler tube: 30 ft. lbs. (40 Nm).

c. 3/8 inch transmission cooler tube: 20 ft. lbs. (27 Nm).

13. Check and top off the transmission fluid level.

2005–06 Expedition & Navigator

See Figures 37 and 38.

1. Drain the engine cooling system.

2. Remove the pin-type retainers and the air deflector cover.

3. Remove the air cleaner inlet pipe and resonator.

4. Remove the retainers and the radiator sight shield.

5. Remove the 2 bolts and the lower cooling fan shroud.

6. Remove the 2 bolts and the upper cooling fan shroud.

7. Using the special tools 303-240 and 303-239, remove the cooling fan assembly.

8. Disconnect the upper radiator coolant hose from the radiator.

9. Disconnect the degas bottle return hose from the radiator.

10. Disconnect the lower radiator coolant hose from the radiator.

11. Push the special tool into the fitting to release the tube retaining clip and remove the transmission cooler lines from the radiator.

12. Remove the 2 bolts and the 2 radiator support brackets.

13. Remove the radiator and the 4 radiator insulators.

14. To install, reverse the removal procedure and note the following:

a. Tighten radiator support bracket bolts to 22 ft. lbs. (30 Nm).

b. Tighten cooling fan shroud mounting bolts to 27 inch. lbs. (3 Nm).

c. Tighten fan assembly to 41 ft. lbs. (55 Nm).

15. Install Correct antifreeze and bleed the cooling system.

16. Check trans fluid and top off if needed.

2007 Expedition & Navigator

1. Before servicing the vehicle, refer to the precautions section.

2. With the vehicle in NEUTRAL, position it on a hoist.

3. Remove the RH and LH headlamp assemblies.

4. Remove the cooling fan shroud.

5. Remove the 2 radiator-to-radiator support bolts.

6. Remove the 2 bolts and position the degas bottle aside.

7. Disconnect the electrical connector and remove the bolt and the horn assembly.

8. Remove the 6 LH and RH air deflector-to-condenser core pin-type retainers.

9. Disconnect the 2 transmission fluid cooler-to-radiator hoses.

➡**The cooling module must be positioned rearward to raise and detach the 4 condenser mounts from the radiator.**

10. Depress the retaining tabs on the 2 lower condenser mounting brackets and raise the condenser assembly until the 4 condenser mounting brackets detach from the radiator.

11. Remove the radiator.

12. To install, reverse the removal procedure and note the following:

a. Tighten radiator-to-radiator support bolts to 11 ft. lbs.(15 Nm).

b. Tighten degas bottle mounting bolts to 11 ft. lbs.(15 Nm).

c. Tighten horn assembly mounting bolt to 89 inch. lbs. (10 Nm).

THERMOSTAT

REMOVAL & INSTALLATION

Excursion

5.4L & 6.8L Engines

See Figures 39 and 40.

1. Before servicing the vehicle, refer to the precautions section.

2. Partially drain the cooling system to a level below the thermostat.

3. Disconnect the upper radiator hose.

4. Remove the coolant outlet connection, as follows:

a. Remove the bolts.

b. Remove the coolant outlet connection.

5. Remove the (A) coolant thermostat and the (B) O-ring seal.

6. Discard the (B) O-ring seal.

To install:

➡**Thermostat must be installed as illustrated.**

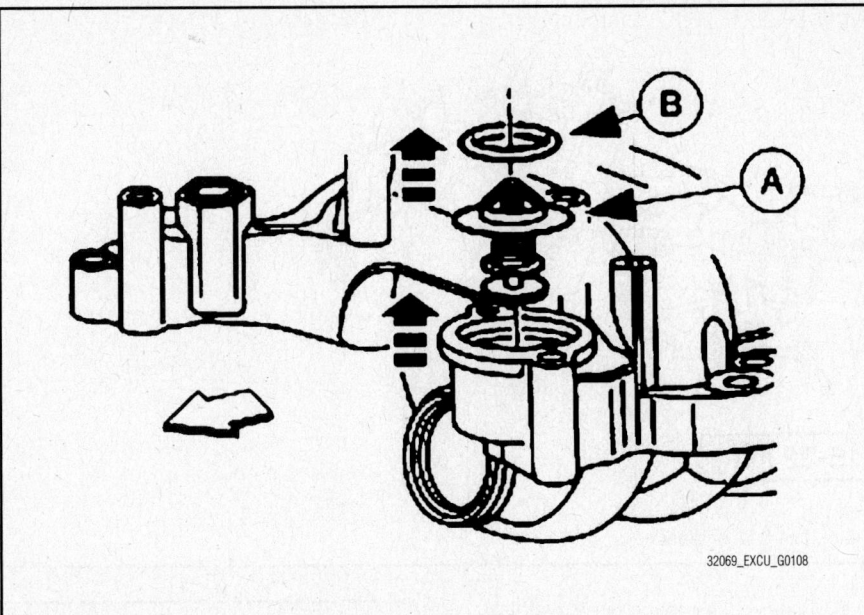

Fig. 39 Remove the (A) coolant thermostat and the (B) O-ring seal

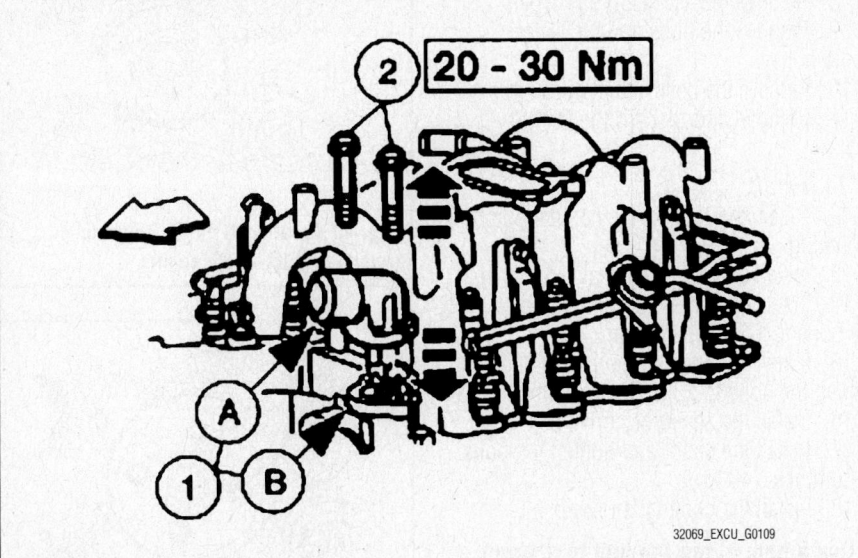

Fig. 40 Use a new (A) O-ring seal to position the (B) coolant thermostat in the upper intake manifold

7. Use a new (A) O-ring seal to position the (B) coolant thermostat in the (C) upper intake manifold.

8. Install the coolant outlet connection, as follows:

    a. Position the coolant outlet connection on the upper intake manifold.

    b. Install the bolts and tighten to 15–22 ft. lbs. (20–30 Nm).

9. Connect the upper radiator hose.

10. Fill the cooling system.

6.0L Diesel Engine

1. Before servicing the vehicle, refer to the precautions section.

2. Drain the engine cooling system.

3. Remove the air cleaner assembly.

4. Loosen the clamps and remove the charge air cooler duct.

5. Disconnect and position the upper radiator hose aside.

6. On early build vehicles:

    a. Disconnect the exhaust backpressure sensor electrical connector and retaining clip.

    b. Disconnect the exhaust backpressure tube at the exhaust manifold.

    c. Remove the retaining nuts and exhaust backpressure assembly.

7. Remove the stud bolts and thermostat assembly.

8. To install, reverse the removal procedure and note the following:

    a. If removed tighten the backpressure tube retaining nut to 22 ft. lbs. (30 Nm).

    b. Tighten stud bolts to 17 ft. lbs. (27 Nm).

    c. If removed tighten the backpressure tube bracket retaining nuts to 23 ft. lbs. (31 Nm).

    d. Tighten charge air cooler duct to 9 inch. lbs. (12 Nm).

Expedition & Navigator

1. Before servicing the vehicle, refer to the precautions section.

2. Drain the engine cooling system.

3. If replacing the thermostat housing, disconnect the upper radiator hose from the thermostat.

4. Remove the 2 bolts, the thermostat housing and the thermostat. Discard the O-ring seal.

5. Inspect the mating surfaces. Clean the sealing surfaces with metal surface prep.

6. Install a new O-ring seal.

7. To install, reverse the removal procedure and note the following:

    a. Tighten thermostat housing bolts to 89 inch. lbs. (10 Nm).

WATER PUMP

REMOVAL & INSTALLATION

Excursion

5.4L & 6.8L Engines

See Figure 41.

1. Before servicing the vehicle, refer to the precautions section.

2. Remove or disconnect the following:

- Negative battery cable
- Radiator, fan blade assembly and fan shroud
- Accessory drive belt
- Water pump pulley
- Heater hose from the water pump
- Water pump bolts and nuts. Note the locations of the bolts if different lengths.
- Water pump stud bolt, the water pump and the water pump housing gasket. Discard the water pump housing gasket.

To install:

3. Before installing the water pump, be sure to completely clean the water pump mounting surfaces of all dirt, grime and old gasket material.

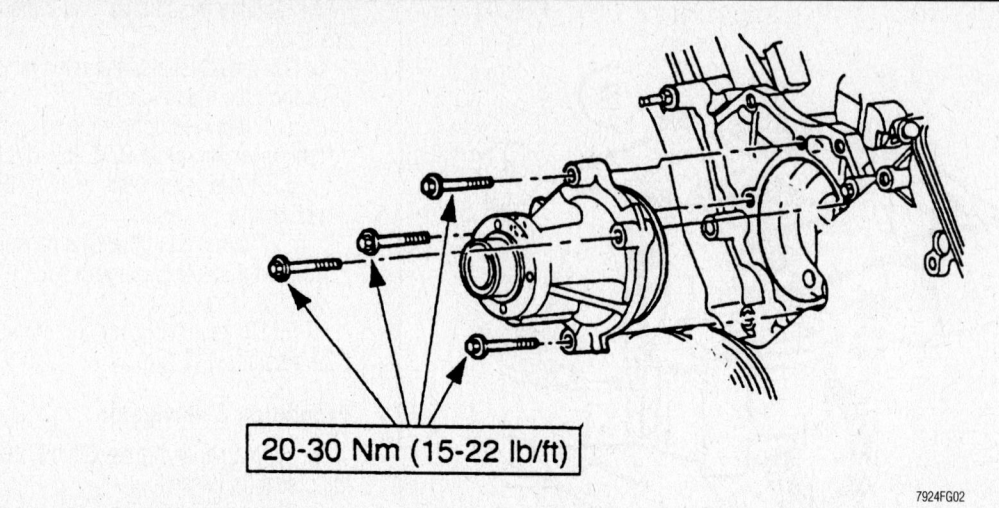

20-30 Nm (15-22 lb/ft)

7924FG02

Fig. 41 Exploded view of the water pump mounting—5.4L and 6.8L engines

➡**All water pump housing bolts, nuts and studs are tightened to 15–22 ft. lbs. (20–30 Nm).**

4. Install or connect the following:
- Water pump onto the engine with a new gasket. Install the water pump stud bolt temporarily finger-tight.
- Water pump mounting nuts and bolts temporarily finger-tight, then tighten all water pump housing fasteners to 15–22 ft. lbs. (20–30 Nm).
- Water outlet tube for the heater, if equipped
- Water pump pulley and accessory drive belt
- Fan shroud, fan blade assembly and the radiator
- Coolant
- Negative battery cable

5. Start the engine and check for any fluid leaks.

6. If necessary, bleed the cooling system.

6.0L Diesel Engine

See Figures 42 through 45.

1. Before servicing the vehicle, refer to the precautions in the beginning of this section.

2. With the vehicle in NEUTRAL, position it on a hoist.

3. Remove the radiator and shroud assembly.

4. Disconnect the cooling fan electrical connector. Unclip and position the fan wiring aside.

➡**Use a hole in the fan hub to prevent the fan from turning.**

5. Using the special tool 303-591, loosen the cooling fan and clutch.

6. Remove the cooling fan assembly.

7. Remove the stator bolts and the stator.

8. Remove the accessory drive belt.

9. Remove the bolts and the water pump pulley.

10. Remove the bolts and the water pump.

11. Remove and discard the O-ring seal.

To install:

12. Clean and inspect the coolant pump mounting.

13. Install a new O-ring seal.

14. Install the water pump and tighten the bolts to 17 ft. lbs. (23 Nm).

15. Install the water pump pulley and tighten the bolts to 23 ft. lbs. (31 Nm).

16. Install the accessory drive belt.

17. Install the stator and tighten the bolts to 30 ft. lbs. (40 Nm).

18. Install the cooling fan assembly.

➡**Use a hole in the fan hub to prevent the fan from turning.**

19. Using the special tool 303-591, tighten the cooling fan and clutch to 98 ft. lbs. (133 Nm).

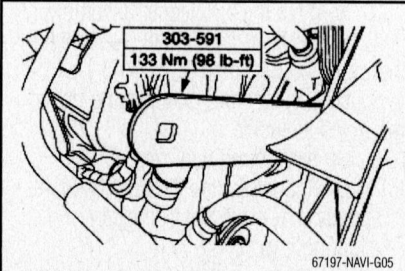

303-591
133 Nm (98 lb-ft)

67197-NAVI-G05

Fig. 42 Using the special tool 303-591, loosen the cooling fan and clutch—6.0L engine

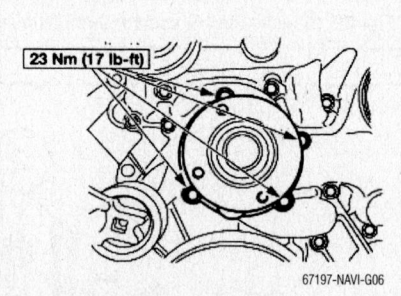

23 Nm (17 lb-ft)

67197-NAVI-G06

Fig. 43 Location of the water pump retaining bolts—6.0L engine

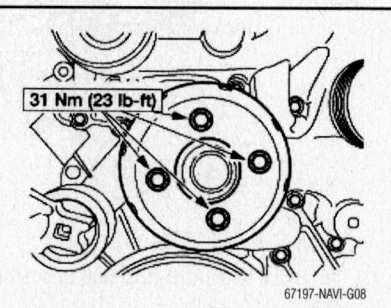

31 Nm (23 lb-ft)

67197-NAVI-G08

Fig. 44 Location of the water pump pulley retaining bolts—6.0L engine

40 Nm (30 lb-ft)

67197-NAVI-G07

Fig. 45 Location of the stator retaining bolts—6.0L engine

20. Connect the cooling fan electrical connector.

21. Install the radiator and shroud assembly.

Expedition & Navigator

See Figure 46.

1. Before servicing the vehicle, refer to the precautions section.
2. Drain the engine cooling system.
3. Remove the cooling fan.
4. Loosen the 4 coolant pump pulley bolts.

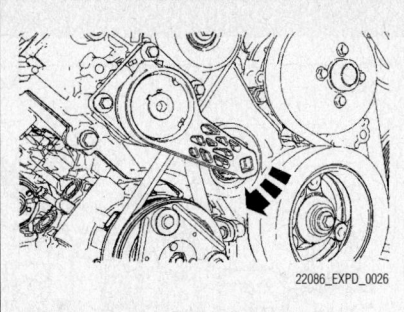

22086_EXPD_0026

Fig. 46 Belt tensioner rotation— Expedition & Navigator

5. Rotate the belt tensioner clockwise and disconnect the accessory drive belt from the coolant pump pulley.
6. Remove the 4 bolts and the coolant pump pulley.
7. Remove the 4 bolts and the coolant pump. Discard the O-ring seal.
8. To install, reverse the removal procedure and note the following:
   a. Tighten water pump pulley bolts and water pump mounting bolts to 18 ft. lbs. (25 Nm).

ENGINE ELECTRICAL

CHARGING SYSTEM

ALTERNATOR

REMOVAL & INSTALLATION

Excursion

5.4L & 6.8L Engines

1. Before servicing the vehicle, refer to the precautions section.
2. Remove or disconnect the following:
   - Negative battery cable
   - Air cleaner assembly, if necessary
   - Alternator bracket bolts, if necessary
   - Drive belt from the alternator pulley
   - Electrical harness connectors at the alternator assembly
   - Positive battery cable, the nut and washer
   - 2 front alternator bolts
   - Rear alternator support bracket retaining bolts and the support bracket
   - Alternator from the vehicle

To install:

3. Install or connect the following:
   - Alternator in position
   - 2 front alternator retaining bolts, loosely
   - Alternator bracket and 3 alternator bracket bolts. Tighten to 84 inch lbs. (10 Nm).
   - Tighten 2 front alternator retaining bolts to 19 ft. lbs. (26 Nm)
   - 2 electrical harness connectors to the alternator assembly
   - Positive battery cable, the nut and washer. Tighten the nut to 72 inch lbs. (8 Nm).
   - Drive belt on the alternator pulley
   - Alternator bracket bolts, if removed
   - Air cleaner assembly, if removed
   - Negative battery cable
4. Start the engine and check for proper charging system operation.

6.0L Diesel Engine—Single Alternator

1. Before servicing the vehicle, refer to the precautions in the beginning of this section.
2. Disconnect the negative battery cable.
3. Remove the cooling fan.
4. Remove the accessory drive belt.
5. Disconnect the alternator electrical connectors.
6. Remove the bolts and the alternator.

To install:

7. Before servicing the vehicle, refer to the precautions in the beginning of this section.
8. Install the alternator and tighten the bolts to 35 ft. lbs. (47 Nm).
9. Connect the alternator electrical connectors.
10. Install the accessory drive belt.
11. Install the cooling fan.
12. Connect the negative battery cable.

6.0L Diesel Engine—Dual Alternator

1. Before servicing the vehicle, refer to the precautions in the beginning of this section.
2. Disconnect the negative battery cable.
3. Remove the cooling fan.
4. Remove the accessory drive belt.
5. Remove the nut and position the generator B+ cable aside.
6. Loosen the 2 clamps and remove the turbo-to-air cooler pipe.
7. Disconnect the alternator electrical connectors.
8. Remove the bolts and the alternator.

To install:

9. Before servicing the vehicle, refer to the precautions in the beginning of this section.

10. Install the alternator and tighten the bolts to 35 ft. lbs. (47 Nm).
11. Connect the alternator electrical connectors.
12. Install the turbo-to-air cooler pipe and tighten the 2 clamps to 9 ft. lbs. (12 Nm).
13. Connect the generator B+ cable.
14. Install the accessory drive belt.
15. Install the cooling fan.
16. Connect the negative battery cable.

Expedition & Navigator

1. Disconnect the negative battery cable.
2. For Navigator, release the 2 retainers and remove the engine cover.
3. Remove the air cleaner intake pipe.
4. Rotate the front end accessory drive belt tensioner counterclockwise and position the accessory drive belt aside.
5. Remove the harness locator from the alternator bracket.
6. Remove the 4 bolts and the alternator bracket.
7. Remove the 2 bolts and position the alternator aside.
8. Disconnect the alternator electrical connector.
9. Position the alternator B+ protective cover aside, remove and discard the nut, then position the generator B+ terminal aside.
10. Remove the alternator.
11. To install, reverse the removal procedure and note the following:
   - Alternator bracket bolts 89 inch. lbs. (10 Nm).
   - Alternator mounting bolts 18 ft. lbs. (25 Nm).
   - Install a new B+ terminal nut; tighten to 71 inch. lbs. (8 Nm).

ENGINE ELECTRICAL

IGNITION SYSTEM

FIRING ORDER

79243G58

Fig. 47 5.4L Engines
Firing order: 1–3–7–2–6–5–4–8
Distributorless ignition system
(one coil on each cylinder)

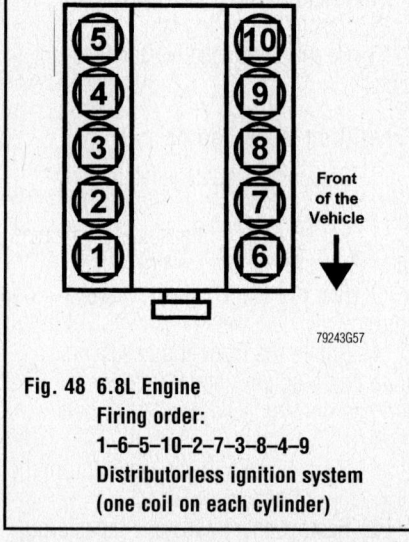

Front
of the
Vehicle

79243G57

Fig. 48 6.8L Engine
Firing order:
1–6–5–10–2–7–3–8–4–9
Distributorless ignition system
(one coil on each cylinder)

IGNITION COIL MODULE

REMOVAL & INSTALLATION

Excursion

5.4L & 6.8L Engines

See Figure 49.

1. Disconnect the Coil On Plug (COP) electrical connectors.
2. Remove the bolts.
3. Remove the coil on plugs.

To install:

➡Apply silicone brake caliper grease and dielectric compound to the inside of the coil boots.

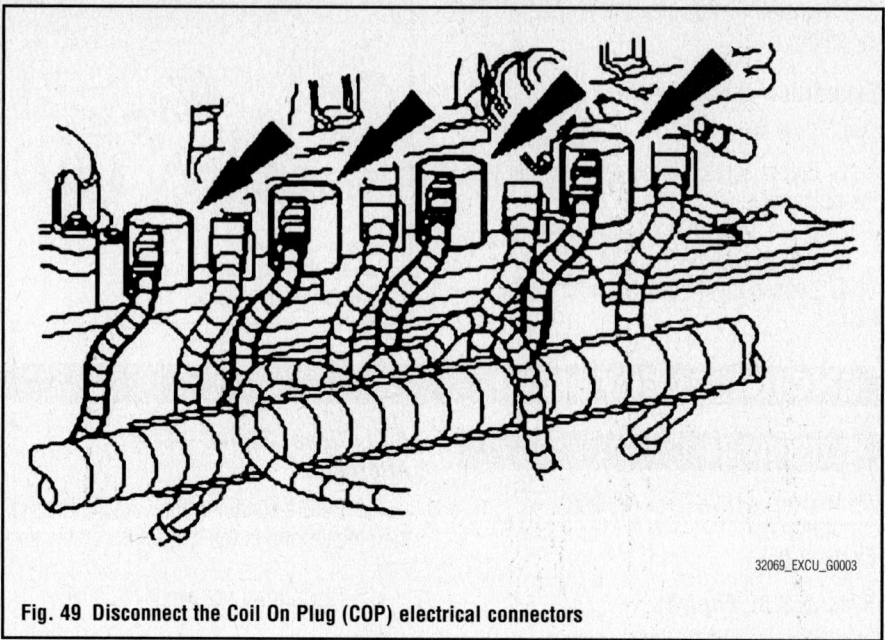

32069_EXCU_G0003

Fig. 49 Disconnect the Coil On Plug (COP) electrical connectors

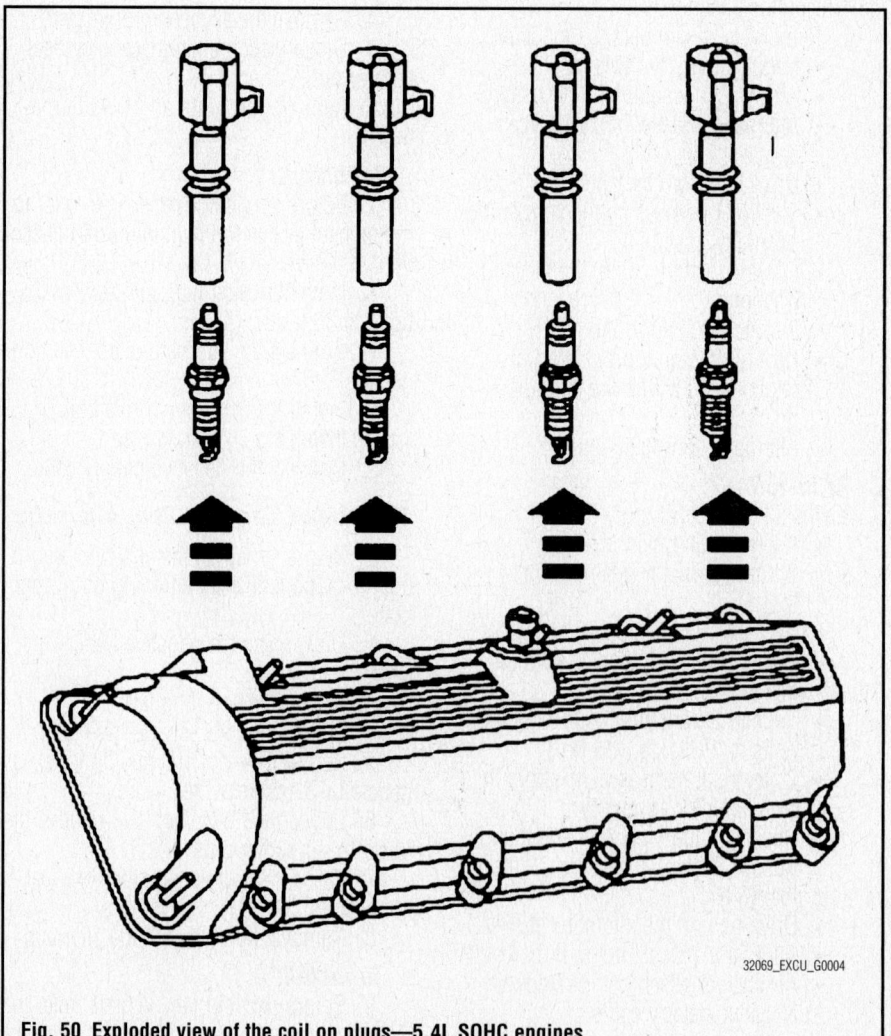

32069_EXCU_G0004

Fig. 50 Exploded view of the coil on plugs—5.4L SOHC engines

4. Install the coil on plugs.
5. Secure with the retaining bolts and tighten to 44–62 inch lbs. (5–7 Nm).
6. Attach the coil on plug electrical connectors.

Expedition & Navigator

1. Disconnect the negative battery cable.
2. Remove the bolts and the ignition coil cover.
3. Disconnect the electrical connector from the ignition coil.
4. Remove the ignition coils.
5. Installation is the reverse of the removal procedure. Tighten the ignition coil cover bolts to 9 ft. lbs. (12 Nm).

IGNITION TIMING

ADJUSTMENT

Base timing for distributorless ignition engines is set at the factory at 10 degrees Before Top Dead Center (BTDC) and is not adjustable.

SPARK PLUGS

REMOVAL & INSTALLATION

5.4L & 6.8L Engines
See Figure 50.

1. Disconnect the negative battery cable.
2. Remove the coil on plugs as outlined under Ignition Coil in this section.

➥Remove any foreign material from the spark plug wells with compressed air before removing the spark plugs.

3. Remove the spark plugs.
4. Inspect the spark plugs.
5. Adjust the spark plug gap as necessary. Proper gap is 0.52–0.56 in. (1.32–1.42mm).

To install:

6. Install the spark plugs and tighten them to 13 ft. lbs. (18 Nm) for 5.4L SOHC engines. For 5.4L DOHC and 6.8L engines, tighten the spark plugs to 15 ft. lbs. (20 Nm).
7. For 2005–5,4L engines tighten to 25 ft. lbs. (34 Nm).
8. Install the coil on plugs.
9. Connect the negative battery cable.

ENGINE ELECTRICAL
STARTING SYSTEM

STARTER

REMOVAL & INSTALLATION

Excursion

5.4L & 6.8L Engines

1. Before servicing the vehicle, refer to the precautions section.
2. Disconnect the negative battery cable.
3. Raise and safely support the vehicle.
4. Remove or disconnect the following:
   - Starter terminal cover
   - Terminal nut and separate the battery starter cable from the starter motor
   - Solenoid **S** terminal connector, if equipped with a starter mounted solenoid

➥To disconnect the hard-shell connector from the solenoid S terminal, grasp the plastic shell and pull off; do not pull on the wire. Pull straight off to prevent damage to the connector and S terminal.

5. Remove or disconnect the following:
   - Starter motor retaining bolts
   - Starter motor from the vehicle

To install:
6. Install or connect the following:
   - Starter motor and retaining bolts.

Tighten the bolts to 15–20 ft. lbs. (20–27 Nm).
   - Battery starter cable and a terminal nut to the starter motor. Tighten the terminal nuts to 79 inch lbs. (9 Nm).
   - Solenoid**S** terminal connector, if equipped with a starter mounted solenoid
   - Starter solenoid safety cap, if equipped
7. Lower the vehicle.
8. Connect the negative battery cable.
9. Start the engine several times to check starter motor operation.

6.0L Diesel Engine

1. Before servicing the vehicle, refer to the precautions section.
2. Disconnect the battery ground cable.
3. Remove starter solenoid protective cap.
4. Disconnect the starter motor electrical connections.
5. Remove the bolts and the starter.

To install:
6. Installation is the reverse of the removal procedure. Tighten the starter bolts to 18 ft. lbs. (25 Nm).

Expedition & Navigator

1. With the vehicle in NEUTRAL, position it on a hoist.

2. Disconnect the negative battery cable.
3. Remove the starter terminal cover and remove the nut and the solenoid S-terminal electrical connection.
4. Remove the nut and the solenoid B-terminal electrical connection.
5. Remove the nut and the starter battery ground cable from the stud.
6. Remove the 2 bolts, the stud bolt and the starter motor.

To install:
7. Position the starter and install the 2 bolts and the stud bolt in 3 stages.
   - Stage 1: Install the 2 starter bolts and the stud bolt finger tight.
   - Stage 2: Tighten the upper bolt to 18 ft. lbs. (25 Nm).
   - Tighten the lower bolt and stud bolt to 18 ft. lbs. (25 Nm).
8. Position the starter battery ground cable onto the stud and install the nut. Tighten to 18 ft. lbs. (25 Nm).
9. Connect the solenoid B-terminal electrical connection and install the nut. Tighten to 9 ft. lbs. (12 Nm).
10. Connect the solenoid S-terminal electrical connection and install the nut and the starter terminal cover. Tighten to 56 inch. lbs. (6 Nm).
11. Connect the negative battery cable.

ENGINE MECHANICAL

➡Disconnecting the negative battery cable may interfere with the functions of the on board computer systems and may require the computer to undergo a relearning process, once the negative battery cable is reconnected.

ACCESSORY DRIVE BELTS

ACCESSORY BELT ROUTING

See Figures 51 through 55.

INSPECTION

❊❊ WARNING

Under no circumstances should the accessory drive belt, tensioner or pulleys be lubricated as potential damage to the belt material and tensioner damping mechanism will occur. Do not apply any fluids or belt dressing to the accessory drive belt or pulleys.

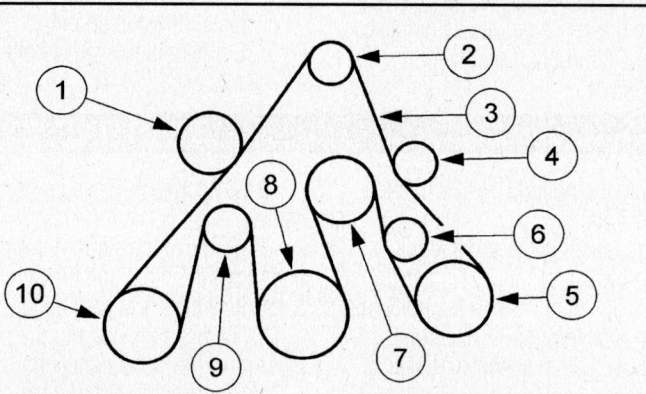

1. Belt idler pulley
2. Generator pulley
3. Drive belt
4. Belt idler pulley
5. Power steering pump pulley
6. Belt idler pulley
7. Coolant pump pulley
8. Crankshaft pulley
9. Drive belt tensioner pulley
10. A/C compressor pulley

22086_EXPD_G0008

Fig. 51 Accessory serpentine belt routing—2005–07 Expedition / Navigator 5.4L, engines with A/C

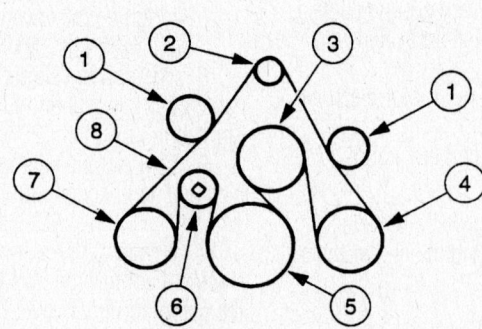

1. Idler
2. Alternator
3. Water Pump
4. Power Steering
5. Crankshaft
6. Drive Belt Tensioner
7. A/C Pulley
8. Drive Belt

79244G86

Fig. 52 Accessory serpentine belt routing—Ford 5.4L, and 6.8L engines with A/C

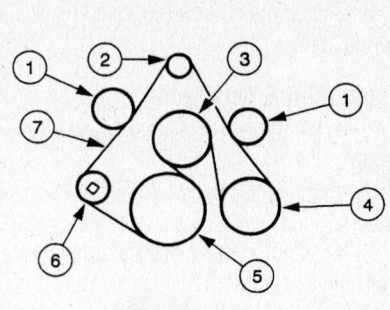

1. Idler
2. Alternator
3. Water Pump
4. Power Steering
5. Crankshaft
6. Drive Belt Tensioner
7. Drive Belt

79244G87

Fig. 53 Accessory serpentine belt routing—Ford 5.4L, and 6.8L engines without A/C

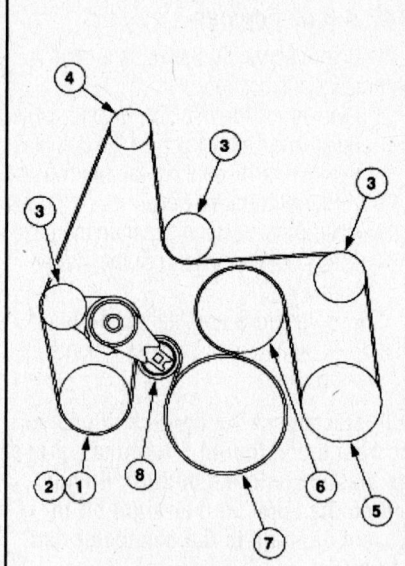

1 A/C clutch pulley
2 Idler pulley (without A/C)
3 Belt idler pulley
4 Generator pulley
5 Power steering pump pulley
6 Water pump pulley
7 Crankshaft pulley
8 Drive belt tensioner

67197-NAVI-G21

Fig. 54 Accessory drive belt routing—6.0L diesel engine with single alternator

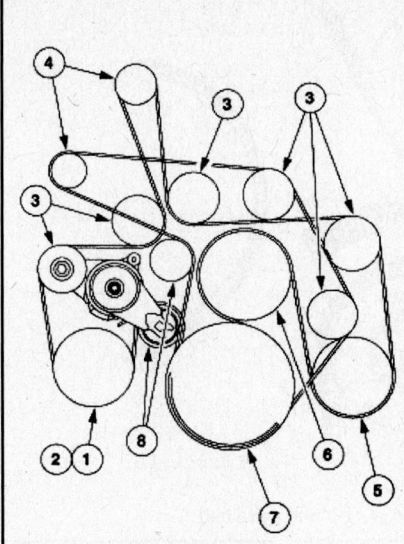

1 A/C clutch pulley
2 Idler pulley (without A/C)
3 Belt idler pulley
4 Generator pulley
5 Power steering pump pulley
6 Water pump pulley
7 Crankshaft pulley
8 Drive belt tensioner

67197-NAVI-G22

**Fig. 55 Accessory drive belt routing—
6.0L diesel engine with dual alternator**

Visual Inspection

Visually inspect the belt for obvious signs of mechanical damage:
- Drive belt cracking/chunking/wear
- Belt/pulley contamination
- Incorrectly routed belt
- Pulley misalignment or excessive pulley runout
- Loose or mislocated hardware
- Incorrectly routed power steering tubes (rubbing)

Eliminate all other non-belt related noises that could cause belt misdiagnosis, such as A/C compressor engagement chirp, power steering cavitations at low temperatures, variable camshaft timing (VCT) tick or generator whine.

If a concern is found, correct the condition before proceeding to the next section.

V-Ribbed Serpentine Drive Belt With Cracks Across Ribs

See Figure 56.

➡Up to 15 cracks in a rib over a distance of 4 inches (100mm) can be considered acceptable. If damage exceeds the acceptable limit or any chunks are

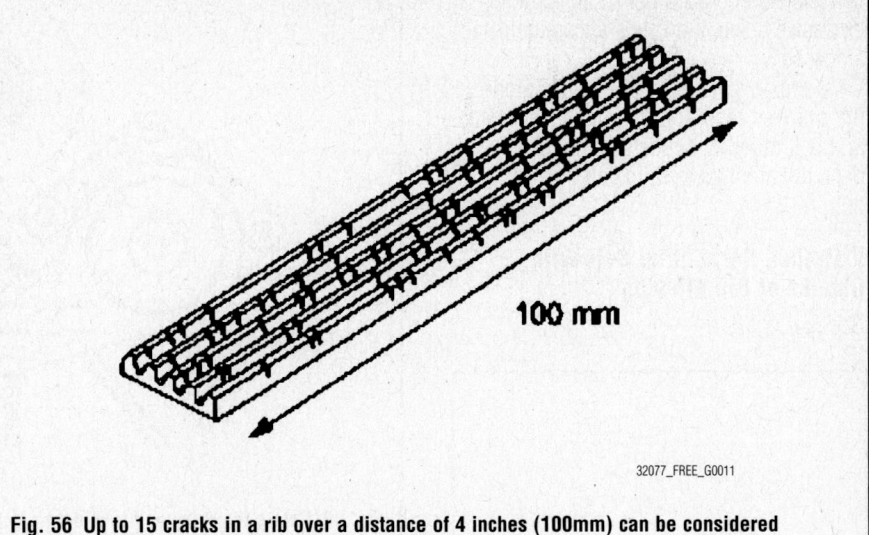

32077_FREE_G0011

Fig. 56 Up to 15 cracks in a rib over a distance of 4 inches (100mm) can be considered acceptable. If cracks exceed this standard, install a new belt

found to be missing from the ribs, a new belt must be installed.

1. Check the belt for cracks. Up to 15 cracks in a rib over a distance of 4 inches (100mm) can be considered acceptable. If cracks exceed this standard, install a new belt.

V-Ribbed Serpentine Belt With Piling

See Figure 57.

➡Piling is an excessive buildup in the V-grooves of the belt.

The condition of the V-ribbed drive belt should be compared against the illustration and appropriate action taken.

1. Small scattered deposits of rubber material. This is not a concern, therefore, installation of a new belt is not required.

2. Longer deposit areas building up to 50 percent of the rib height. This is not

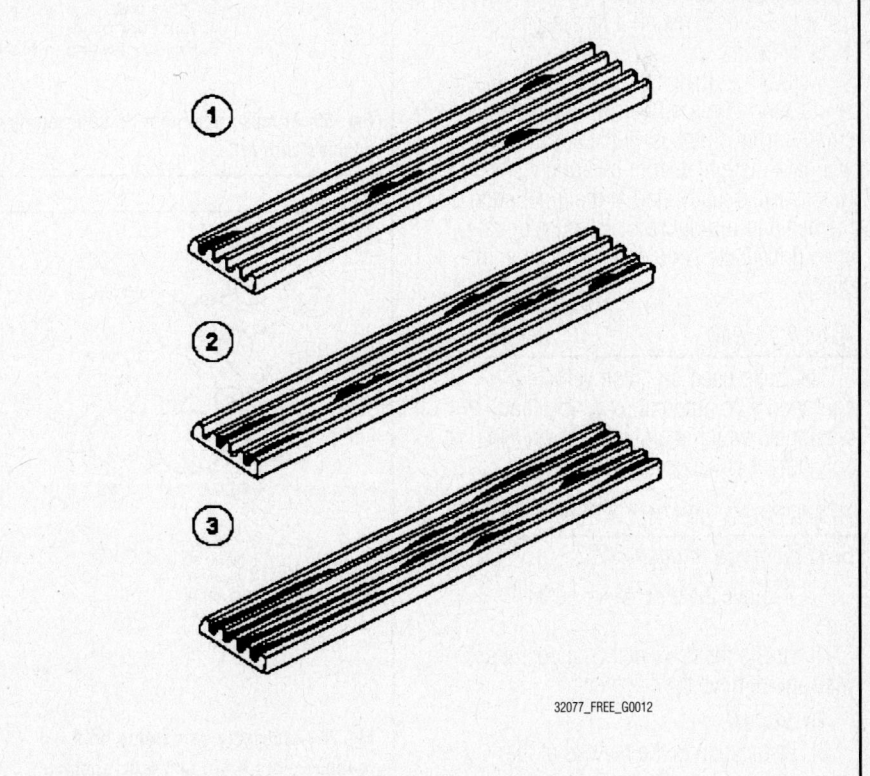

32077_FREE_G0012

Fig. 57 Compare the condition of the belt with the accompanying text

considered a concern but it can result in excessive noise. If noise is apparent, install a new belt.

3. Heavy deposits building up along the grooves resulting in a possible noise and belt stability concern. If heavy deposits are apparent, install a new belt.

V-Ribbed Serpentine Belt With Chunks of Rib Missing

See Figure 58.

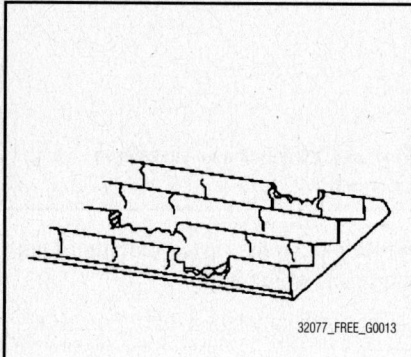

Fig. 58 Replace the belt if missing chunks are found during inspection

There should be no chunks missing from the belt ribs. If the belt shows any evidence of this, install a new accessory drive belt.

Inspect the drive belt for signs of glazing or cracking. A glazed belt will be perfectly smooth from slippage, while a good belt will have a slight texture of fabric visible. Cracks will usually start at the inner edge of the belt and run outward. All worn or damaged drive belts should be replaced immediately.

ADJUSTMENT

The belts used on these vehicle are equipped with automatic (spring load) tensioners which maintain tension. No adjustment is necessary or possible.

REMOVAL & INSTALLATION

See Figures 59 through 64.

1. Remove the air cleaner outlet pipe.

2. Rotate the drive belt tensioner clockwise and remove the drive belt.

To install:

3. Installation is the reverse of the removal procedure. Make sure the belt is routed properly.

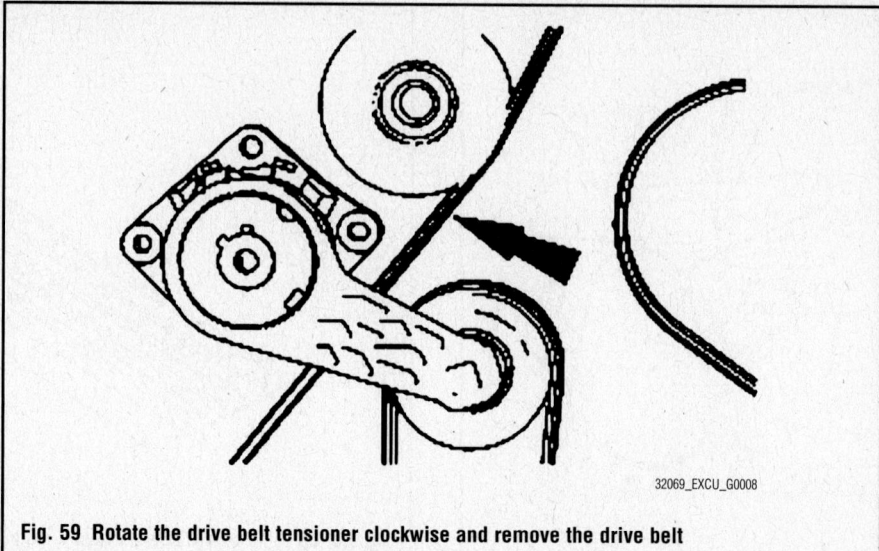

Fig. 59 Rotate the drive belt tensioner clockwise and remove the drive belt

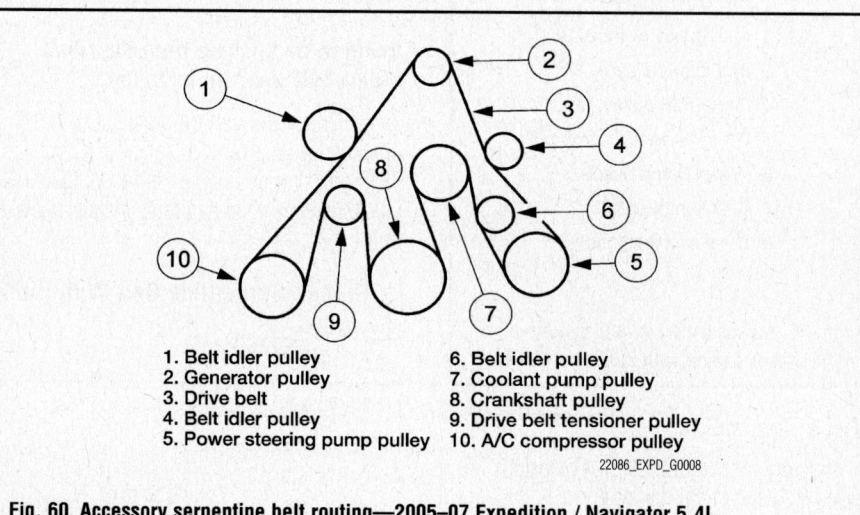

1. Belt idler pulley
2. Generator pulley
3. Drive belt
4. Belt idler pulley
5. Power steering pump pulley
6. Belt idler pulley
7. Coolant pump pulley
8. Crankshaft pulley
9. Drive belt tensioner pulley
10. A/C compressor pulley

Fig. 60 Accessory serpentine belt routing—2005–07 Expedition / Navigator 5.4L, engines with A/C

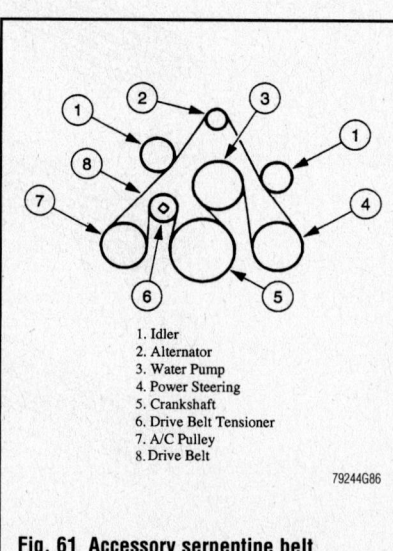

1. Idler
2. Alternator
3. Water Pump
4. Power Steering
5. Crankshaft
6. Drive Belt Tensioner
7. A/C Pulley
8. Drive Belt

Fig. 61 Accessory serpentine belt routing—Ford 5.4L, and 6.8L engines with A/C

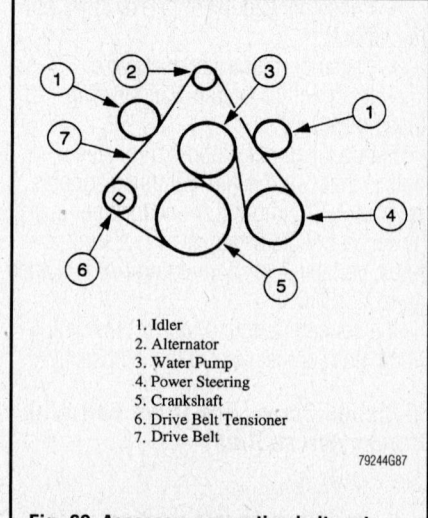

1. Idler
2. Alternator
3. Water Pump
4. Power Steering
5. Crankshaft
6. Drive Belt Tensioner
7. Drive Belt

Fig. 62 Accessory serpentine belt routing—Ford 5.4L, and 6.8L engines without A/C

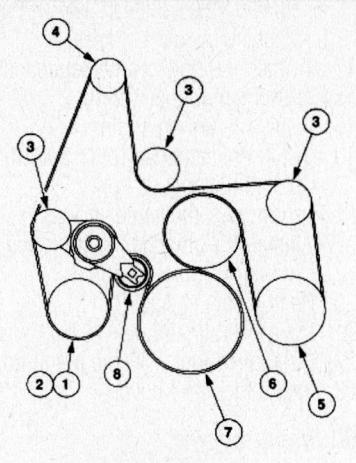

1 A/C clutch pulley
2 Idler pulley (without A/C)
3 Belt idler pulley
4 Generator pulley
5 Power steering pump pulley
6 Water pump pulley
7 Crankshaft pulley
8 Drive belt tensioner

67197-NAVI-G21

Fig. 63 Accessory drive belt routing—6.0L diesel engine with single alternator

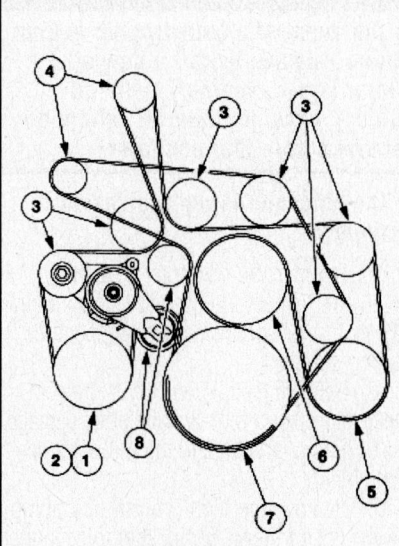

1 A/C clutch pulley
2 Idler pulley (without A/C)
3 Belt idler pulley
4 Generator pulley
5 Power steering pump pulley
6 Water pump pulley
7 Crankshaft pulley
8 Drive belt tensioner

67197-NAVI-G22

Fig. 64 Accessory drive belt routing—6.0L diesel engine with dual alternator

CAMSHAFT AND VALVE LIFTERS

INSPECTION

Camshaft Runout

See Figure 65.

➡ **Camshaft journals must be within specifications before checking runout.**

1. Use a Dial Indicator Gauge with Holding Fixture to measure the camshaft runout.
   - Rotate the camshaft and subtract the lowest indicator reading from the highest indicator reading.
   - For additional information, refer to the specification chart in the appropriate engine section.
   - If out of specification, install new components as necessary.

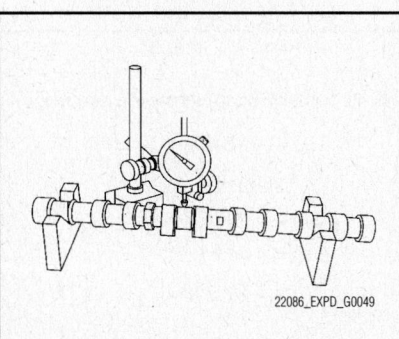

22086_EXPD_G0049

Fig. 65 Dial Indicator Gauge with Holding Fixture

Camshaft End Play

See Figure 66.

1. Use a Dial Indicator Gauge with Holding Fixture to measure camshaft end play.
2. Position the camshaft to the rear of the cylinder head.
3. Zero the indicator.
4. Move the camshaft to the front of cylinder head. Note and record the camshaft end play.

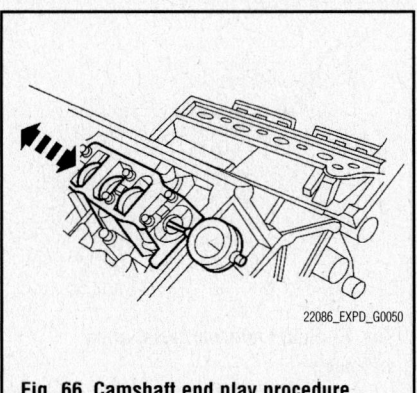

22086_EXPD_G0050

Fig. 66 Camshaft end play procedure

- If camshaft end play exceeds specifications, install new camshaft and recheck end play.
- If camshaft end play exceeds specification after camshaft installation, install a new cylinder head.
- Refer to the specification chart in the appropriate engine section.

Valve Lash Adjusters

See Figure 67.

1. Inspect the hydraulic lash adjuster and roller follower for damage. If any damage is found, inspect the camshaft lobes and valves for damage.

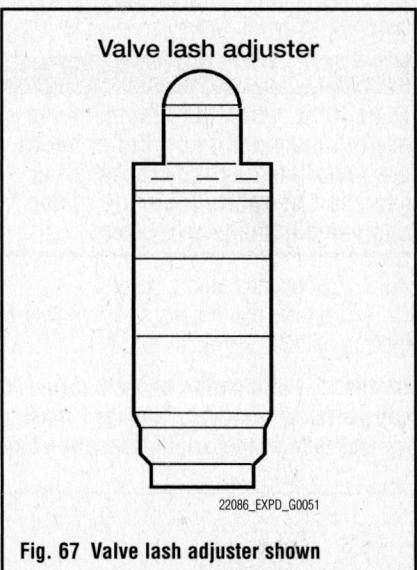

Valve lash adjuster

22086_EXPD_G0051

Fig. 67 Valve lash adjuster shown

REMOVAL & INSTALLATION

Excursion

5.4L & 6.8L Engines

See Figures 68 through 72.

1. Remove intake manifold for 6.8L engines.
2. Disconnect the negative battery cable.
3. Remove the valve cover.
4. Remove the cooling fan for 5.4L engines.
5. Position the piston of the cylinder being repaired at the bottom of the stroke.
6. Install the special tool 303-382 between the valve spring coils to prevent valve stem seal damage.

➡ **The camshaft roller followers must be installed in their original locations. Record the camshaft roller follower locations.**

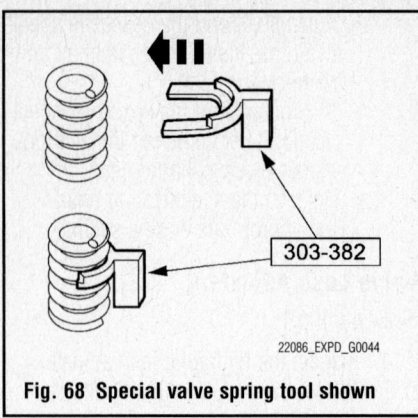

Fig. 68 Special valve spring tool shown

7. Use the special tool 303-567 to compress the valve springs and remove the camshaft roller followers.

⁂ WARNING

At no time, when the timing chains are removed and the cylinder heads are installed may the crankshaft or camshaft be rotated. Severe piston and valve damage will occur.

8. Remove the timing chains.
9. Remove the thirteen camshaft bearing cap bolts.

➡ **Identify the location of the bearing caps prior to removal. The caps must be installed in the original location and**

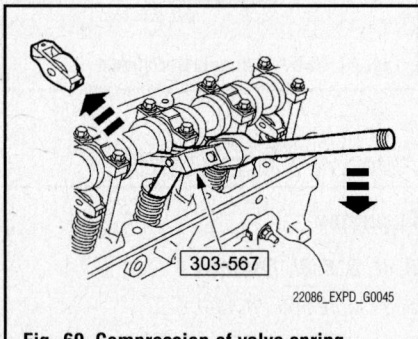

Fig. 69 Compression of valve spring using tool

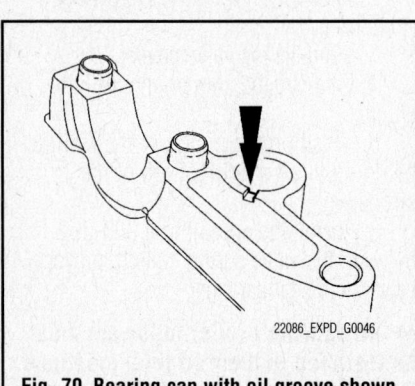

Fig. 70 Bearing cap with oil groove shown

orientation or engine damage can occur.

10. Remove the camshaft bearing caps.
11. Clean and inspect the camshaft bearing caps.

- One of the bearing caps contains an oil flow restriction groove. Make sure the groove is free of foreign material.

12. Remove the camshaft from the cylinder head.

To install:

13. Lubricate the camshaft journals with clean engine oil.
14. Install the camshaft onto the cylinder head.
15. Lubricate the camshaft bearing caps with clean engine oil.
16. Install the camshaft bearing caps in their original locations.

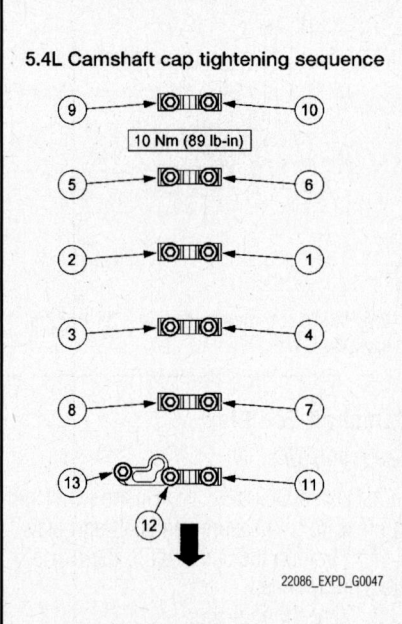

Fig. 71 Camshaft caps tightening sequence 5.4L engine

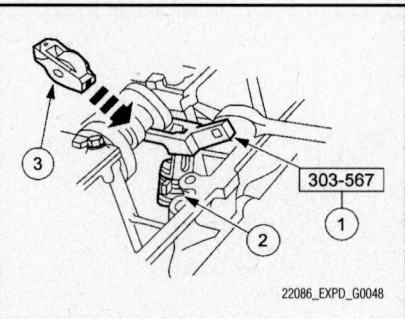

Fig. 72 Roller follower installation with tools

a. Position the camshaft bearing caps.
b. Loosely install the bolts.
17. Tighten the bolts in the sequence shown to 89 inch. lbs. (10 Nm).
18. Install the timing chains.
19. Install the camshaft roller followers.
- Install the special tool.
- Compress the valve springs.
- Install the camshaft roller followers in their original locations.
20. Remove the special tool.
21. If removed install the cooling fan.
22. If removed install intake manifold.
23. Install the valve covers.

6.0L Diesel Engine

1. Before servicing the vehicle, refer to the precautions section.
2. Mount the engine on an engine stand.
3. Remove the serpentine belt idler.
4. Remove the serpentine belt tensioner.
5. Remove and discard the O-rings from the oil filter base.
6. Remove the Exhaust Gas Recirculation (EGR) cooler coolant supply port cover. Clean and inspect the gaskets. Install new gaskets if necessary. Clean and inspect the sealing surfaces.

⁂ WARNING

In the event of a catastrophic engine failure, always install a new oil cooler cover assembly (with oil cooler). Foreign material cannot be removed from the oil cooler.

➡ **The oil cooler is replaced as an assembly.**

7. Remove the oil cooler assembly. Clean and inspect the gaskets. Install a new gasket if necessary. Clean and inspect the sealing surfaces.
8. Remove the oil pump inlet strainer. Clean and inspect for tears and other damage.
9. Remove bolts and the turbocharger heat shield.
10. Remove the high-pressure oil pump cover. Use a thin gasket scraper to separate the cover from the crankcase. Clean and inspect the gaskets. Install a new gasket if necessary. Clean and inspect the sealing surfaces.
11. Remove the bolts from the high-pressure oil pump discharge pipe.
12. Disconnect and remove the high-pressure oil pump discharge pipe.
13. Remove and discard the D-ring seal.
14. Remove and discard the high-pressure pump O-ring seal.
15. Remove the bolts and the high-pressure oil pump.

16. Remove and discard the lower O-ring seal.

17. Remove the glow plug buss bar.

18. Remove the eight glow plugs.

➡**Mark the location of the stud bolts.**

19. Remove the valve covers. Clean and inspect the gaskets. Install a new gasket if necessary. Clean and inspect the sealing surfaces.

20. Remove the bolts and the coolant pump pulley.

21. Remove the coolant pump.

22. If equipped, remove the bolts and the dual generator pulley.

23. Prior to removing the crankshaft damper, check the crankshaft vibration damper runout.

➡**Pry the crankshaft forward at the same point to eliminate possible error caused by crankshaft end play.**

24. Rotate the crankshaft 90 degrees. Pry the crankshaft forward. Record the measurement. Repeat every 90 degrees. If the runout exceeds specification, install a new crankshaft vibration damper.

※ **WARNING**

To prevent engine damage, you must always replace all four bolts when installing the vibration damper.

※ **CAUTION**

To avoid personal injury, support the vibration damper during mounting bolt removal. The damper can slide off the nose of the crankshaft very easily.

25. Remove the bolts and the crankcase vibration damper. Discard the bolts.

26. Punch two holes in the seal. Remove the crankshaft seal with a slide hammer.

➡**Production engine will not have a wear sleeve. If equipped, remove the crankshaft damper wear sleeve.**

27. Remove the oil pump body. Remove and discard the O-ring seal.

➡**Mark the front of each drive rotor for correct reassembly orientation.**

28. Remove the inner and outer oil pump drive rotors.

29. Remove the engine front cover. Clean and inspect the gaskets. Install new gaskets if necessary. Clean and inspect the sealing surfaces.

30. Using a quick-disconnect tool, disconnect the high-pressure oil rail supply line at the high-pressure oil rail.

31. Remove the bolts and the high pressure oil rail. Disconnect and remove the high-pressure oil supply line.

※ **WARNING**

Do not attempt to put battery voltage to the fuel injector or damage to the fuel injector will occur.

32. Using a 19 mm socket, push the fuel injector electrical connector out of the rocker arm carrier.

※ **WARNING**

To prevent engine damage, do not use air tools to remove the fuel injectors. The clip that extracts the injector can dislodge and fall into the oil drain hole.

➡**If engine oil is found in the engine coolant or engine coolant is found in the combustion chambers, new injector sleeve may need to be installed.**

33. Remove the bolt, the fuel injector hold down and the fuel injector.

34. Remove and discard the crankcase-to-head tube assembly.

35. Remove the inner head bolts from both cylinder heads.

36. Remove the 16 bolts and the rocker arm assemblies.

37. Remove the rocker arm carrier from the cylinder head. Clean and inspect the gaskets. Install new gaskets if necessary. Clean and inspect the sealing surfaces.

➡**Mark the location of the valve bridges before removing.**

38. Remove the 16 valve bridges.

※ **WARNING**

To prevent engine damage, keep the push rods in the order in which they were removed. Install all push rods back in their original positions.

39. Mark the location and remove the 16 push rods.

40. Remove the 10 outer head bolts.

41. Remove the cylinder heads.

42. Remove and discard the cylinder head gasket.

43. Remove and discard the four cylinder head dowel sleeves.

44. Remove the bolts from the rear engine tube assembly.

45. Remove the bolt and the rear engine tube assembly.

※ **WARNING**

To prevent engine damage, keep the cam followers in the order in which they were removed. Install all cam followers back in their original positions.

46. Remove the bolts and the roller follower guides. Remove the hydraulic cam followers.

47. Install the special tool and measure the camshaft gear backlash. Install a new camshaft gear if backlash is not within specification.

48. Install the special tool and measure the camshaft end play. Install a new camshaft thrust plate if end play is not within specification.

49. Remove the bolt and the camshaft position (CMP) sensor.

※ **WARNING**

Do not knick or scratch the camshaft bearings with the camshaft lobes or engine damage will occur.

50. Remove the thrust plate mounting bolts and remove the camshaft and gear.

To install:

➡**Check alignment of the oil holes after installing the bearings.**

51. If removed, install the camshaft bearings.

※ **WARNING**

Do not nick or scratch the camshaft bearings with the camshaft lobes or engine damage can occur.

➡**Apply clean engine oil to the camshaft prior to installing.**

52. Using camshaft alignment tool 303-772, install the camshaft and gear assembly. Aligning it with the crankshaft. Install the thrust plate mounting bolts.

53. The remainder of installation is the reverse of removal.

Expedition & Navigator

See Figures 73 through 83.

1. Before servicing the vehicle, refer to the precautions section.

※ **WARNING**

The camshaft procedure must be followed exactly or damage to the valves and pistons will result.

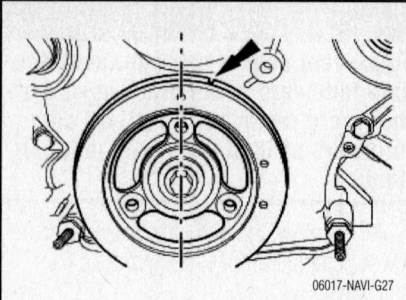

Fig. 73 Position the crankshaft damper spoke at the 12 o'clock position and the timing mark indentation at the 1 o'clock position—2005 Expedition and Navigator models

➡If removing both camshafts, you must remove the right hand camshaft first.

2. Position the crankshaft damper spoke at the 12 o'clock position and the timing mark indentation at the 1 o'clock position.

3. For the right hand camshaft:
   a. Remove the right hand valve cover.

✳✳ CAUTION

Damage to the camshaft phaser sprocket assembly will occur if mishandled or used as a lifting or leveraging device.

   b. Loosen and back off the right hand camshaft phaser bolt 1 full turn.
   c. Disconnect the right hand Camshaft Position (CMP) sensor connector.
   d. Remove the bolt and the right hand CMP sensor.

➡If the camshaft lobes are not exactly positioned as shown, the crankshaft

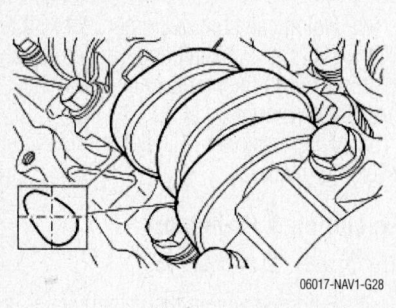

Fig. 74 The number 1 cylinder camshaft exhaust lobe must be coming up on the exhaust stroke. Verify by noting the position of the 2 intake camshaft lobes and the exhaust lobe on the number 1 cylinder—2005 Expedition and Navigator models

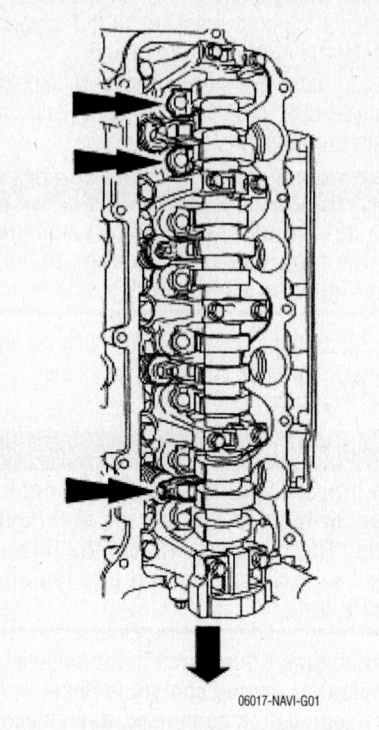

Fig. 75 Remove only the 3 roller followers shown from the right hand cylinder head—2005 Expedition and Navigator models

will require 1 full additional rotation to 12 o'clock.

   e. The number 1 cylinder camshaft exhaust lobe must be coming up on the exhaust stroke. Verify by noting the position of the 2 intake camshaft lobes and the exhaust lobe on the number 1 cylinder.

4. Remove only the 3 roller followers shown in the illustration.

Fig. 76 Using the tool illustrated, remove the 3 designated roller followers—2005 Expedition and Navigator models

✳✳ WARNING

Do not allow the valve keepers to fall off the valve or the valve may drop into the cylinder.

➡The camshaft roller followers must be installed in their original locations. Record camshaft roller follower locations. It may be necessary to push the valve down while compressing the spring.

   f. Using the tool illustrated, remove the 3 designated roller followers in the previous step from the right hand cylinder head.
5. For the left hand camshaft:
   a. Remove the left hand valve cover.

✳✳ WARNING

Damage to the camshaft phaser sprocket assembly will occur if mishandled or used as a lifting or leveraging device.

   b. Loosen and back off the left hand camshaft phaser bolt 1 full turn.
   c. Disconnect the left hand Camshaft Position (CMP) sensor connector.
   d. Remove the left hand CMP sensor and the bolt.

➡If servicing both camshafts, do not rotate the crankshaft. As camshaft position has been established.

➡If the camshaft lobes are not exactly positioned as shown, the crankshaft keyway will require one full additional rotation to 12 o'clock.

   e. The number 5 cylinder camshaft lobe must be coming up on the exhaust stroke. Verify by noting the position of

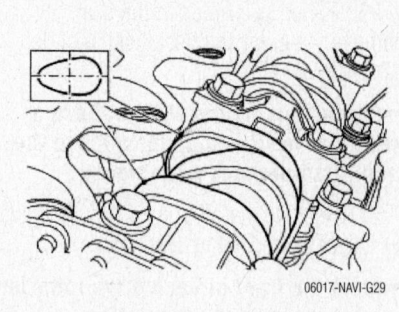

Fig. 77 The number 5 cylinder camshaft lobe must be coming up on the exhaust stroke. Verify by noting the position of the 2 intake camshaft lobes and the exhaust lobe on the number 5 cylinder—2005 Expedition and Navigator models

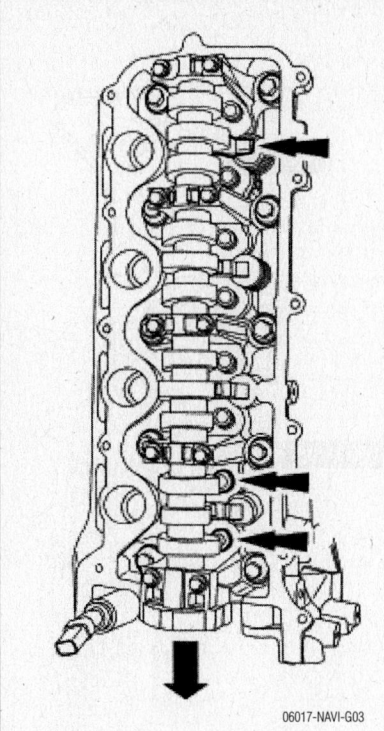

06017-NAVI-G03

Fig. 78 Remove only the 3 roller followers shown from the left hand cylinder head—2005 Expedition and Navigator models

the 2 intake camshaft lobes and the exhaust lobe on the number 5 cylinder.

f. Remove only the 3 roller followers shown in the illustration from the left hand cylinder head.

➡ **The camshaft roller followers must be installed in their original locations. Record camshaft roller follower locations.**

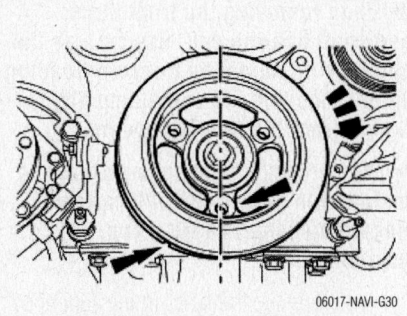

06017-NAVI-G30

Fig. 79 Rotate the crankshaft clockwise, as viewed from the front, positioning the crankshaft damper spoke at the 6 o'clock position and the timing mark indentation at the 7 o'clock position—2005 Expedition and Navigator models

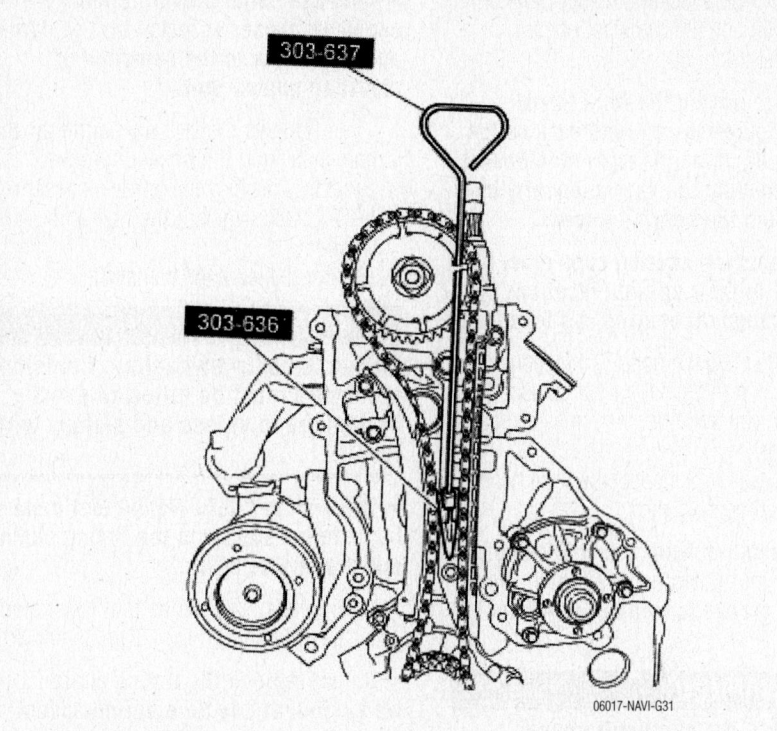

06017-NAVI-G31

Fig. 80 Install the wedge tool illustrated in the right hand timing chain—2005 Expedition and Navigator models

➡ **It may be necessary to push the valve down while compressing the spring.**

g. Using the tool illustrated, remove the 3 designated roller followers in the previous step from the left hand cylinder head.

➡ **The crankshaft cannot be moved past the 6 o'clock position once set.**

6. Rotate the crankshaft clockwise, as viewed from the front, positioning the

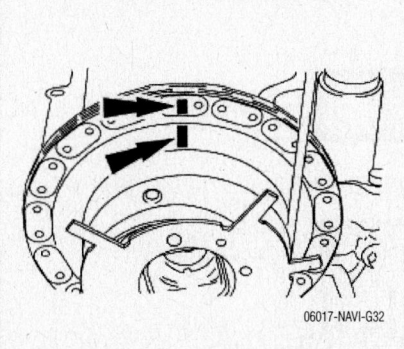

06017-NAVI-G32

Fig. 81 Scribe a location mark on the timing chain and the camshaft phaser sprocket assembly, right side shown, left side similar—2005 Expedition and Navigator models

crankshaft damper spoke at the 6 o'clock position and the timing mark indentation at the 7 o'clock position.

7. For the right hand camshaft:

※ **CAUTION**

Engine is not freewheeling. Camshaft procedure must be followed exactly or damage to valves and pistons will result.

※ **CAUTION**

The Timing Chain Wedge tool must be installed square to the timing chain and the engine block.

h. Install the wedge tool illustrated in the right hand timing chain as shown.

➡ **Do not remove the timing chain wedge tool at any time during assembly. If the tool is removed or out of placement, the engine front cover must be removed and the engine must be retimed.**

※ **WARNING**

The timing chain must be installed in its original position onto the camshaft phaser sprocket using the scribed marks, or damage to valves and pistons will result.

i. Scribe a location mark on the timing chain and the camshaft phaser sprocket assembly.

➡ When removing the front thrust camshaft bearing cap, use care as the cap may be damaged from sideloading when removing the cam unequally in height from the bearing towers.

➡ The camshaft bearing caps must be installed in their original locations. Record camshaft bearing cap locations.

j. Remove the bolts in the sequence shown and remove the front camshaft bearing cap and then the remaining bearing caps.

k. Clean and inspect the right hand camshaft bearing caps.

➡ The camshaft front thrust bearing cap contains an oil metering groove. Make sure the groove is free of foreign material.

✳✳ WARNING

Damage to the camshaft phaser sprocket assembly will occur if mishandled or used as a lifting or leveraging device.

➡ Only use hand tools to remove the camshaft phaser sprocket bolt or damage may occur to the camshaft or camshaft phaser unit.

l. Remove the bolt and withdraw the camshaft from the phaser sprocket assembly leaving the sprocket assembly in place. Discard the bolt and washer.

8. For the left hand camshaft:

✳✳ WARNING

Engine is not freewheeling. Camshaft procedure must be followed exactly or damage to valves and pistons will result.

➡ The Timing Chain Wedge tool must be installed square to the timing chain and the engine block.

m. Install the wedge tool illustrated in the left hand timing chain as shown.

➡ Do not remove the timing chain wedge tool at any time during assembly. If the special tool is removed or out of placement, the engine front cover must be removed and the engine must be retimed.

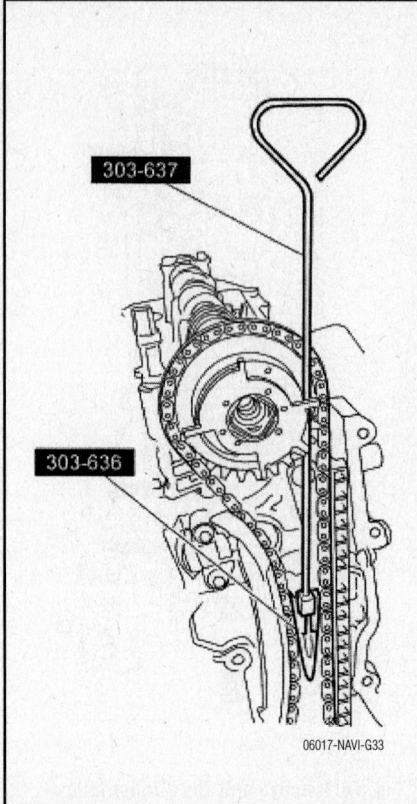

Fig. 83 Install the wedge tool illustrated in the left hand timing chain—2005 Expedition and Navigator models

✳✳ WARNING

The timing chain must be installed in its original position onto the camshaft phaser sprocket using the scribed marks, or damage to valves and pistons will result.

n. Scribe a location mark on the timing chain and the camshaft phaser sprocket assembly.

➡ When removing the front thrust camshaft bearing cap, use care as the cap may be damaged from sideloading when removing the cam unequally in height from the bearing towers.

➡ The camshaft bearing caps must be installed in their original locations. Record camshaft bearing cap locations.

o. Remove the bolts in the sequence shown and remove the front camshaft bearing cap and then the remaining bearing caps.

p. Clean and inspect the left hand camshaft bearing caps.

➡ The camshaft front thrust bearing cap contains an oil metering groove. Make

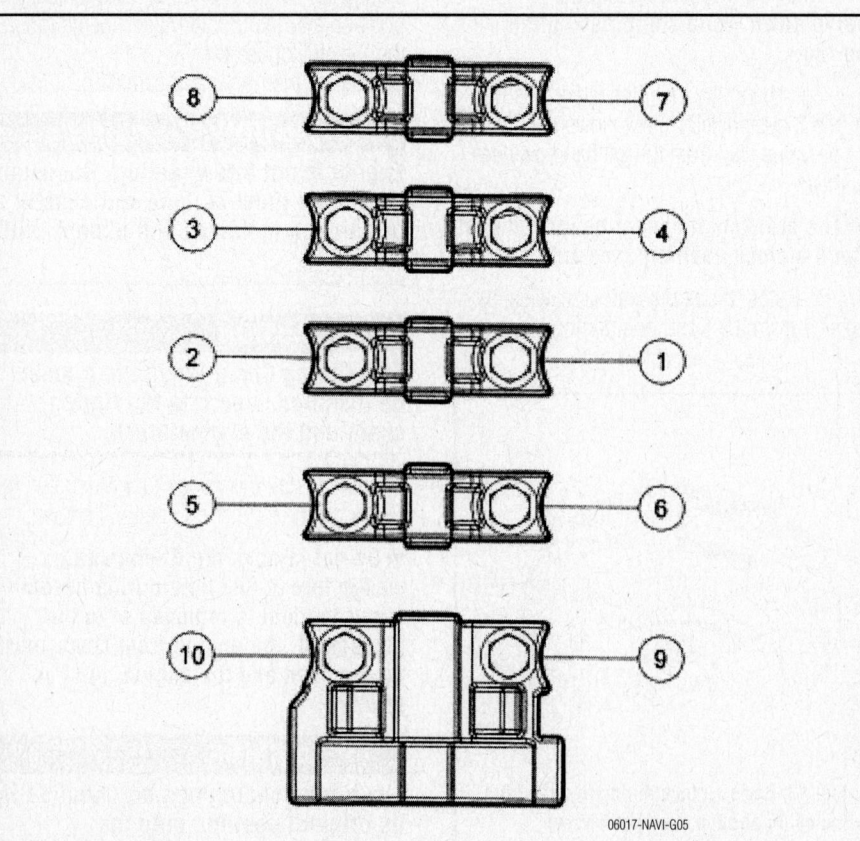

Fig. 82 Right side bearing cap removal and tightening sequence, left side similar—2005 Expedition and Navigator models

sure the groove is free of foreign material.

❋ WARNING

Damage to the camshaft phaser sprocket assembly will occur if mishandled or used as a lifting or leveraging device.

➡ Only use hand tools to remove the camshaft phaser sprocket bolt or damage may occur to the camshaft or camshaft phaser unit.

❋ WARNING

Do not remove the timing chain wedge tool at any time during assembly. If the special tool is removed or out of placement, the engine front cover must be removed and the engine must be retimed.

q. Remove the bolt and withdraw the camshaft from the phaser sprocket assembly leaving the sprocket assembly in place. Discard the bolt and washer.

To install:

9. Lubricate the camshaft and camshaft journals with clean engine oil.
10. For the right hand camshaft:

➡ Damage to the camshaft phaser sprocket assembly will occur if mishandled or used as a lifting or leveraging device.

➡ Do not allow the roller followers to move out of position when installing the camshaft.

r. Install the camshaft into the camshaft phaser sprocket assembly and onto the head. Install a new camshaft phaser bolt finger tight.

❋ WARNING

Do not remove the timing chain wedge tool at any time during assembly. If the special tool is removed or out of placement, the engine front cover must be removed and the engine must be retimed.

❋ WARNING

The timing chain must be installed in its original position onto the camshaft phaser sprocket using the scribed marks, or damage to valves and pistons will result.

s. Verify the camshaft phaser sprocket and timing chain scribe marks are still in alignment.

❋ CAUTION

Do not allow the roller followers to move out of position when installing the camshaft.

t. Lubricate the camshaft bearing caps with clean engine oil.
u. Install the camshaft bearing caps in their original locations.
v. Install the bolts loosely, then tighten the bolts in the sequence illustrated to 89 inch lbs. (10 Nm).
w. Remove the wedge tools.
11. For the left hand camshaft:

➡ Damage to the camshaft phaser sprocket assembly will occur if mishandled or used as a lifting or leveraging device.

➡ Do not allow the roller followers to move out of position when installing the camshaft.

x. Install the camshaft into the camshaft phaser sprocket assembly and onto the head. Install a new camshaft phaser bolt finger tight.

❋ WARNING

Do not remove the timing chain wedge tool at any time during assembly. If the special tool is removed or out of placement, the engine front cover must be removed and the engine must be retimed.

❋ WARNING

The timing chain must be installed in its original position onto the camshaft phaser sprocket using the scribed marks, or damage to valves and pistons will result.

y. Verify the camshaft phaser sprocket and timing chain scribe marks are still in alignment.

➡ Do not allow the roller followers to move out of position when installing the camshaft.

z. Lubricate the camshaft bearing caps with clean engine oil.
aa. Install the camshaft bearing caps in their original locations. Install the bolts loosely.
bb. Tighten the bolts in the sequence illustrated to89 inch lbs. (10 Nm).
cc. Remove the wedge tools.
dd. Rotate the crankshaft a half turn counterclockwise and position the crank-

shaft damper spoke at the 12 o'clock position and the timing mark indentation at the 1 o'clock position.
12. For the right hand camshaft:
a. Verify correct cam position by noting the position of the number 1 cylinder intake and exhaust camshaft lobes.
b. Using the tool 303-1039, install the 3 originally removed roller followers.
c. Install the CMP sensor and the bolt.
d. Connect the CMP connector.

❋ WARNING

Only use hand tools to install the camshaft phaser sprocket assembly or damage may occur to the camshaft or camshaft phaser unit.

➡ Damage to the camshaft phaser sprocket assembly will occur if mishandled or used as a lifting or leveraging device.

e. Tighten the camshaft phaser bolt in 2 steps: Tighten to 30 ft. lbs. (40 Nm), then tighten an additional 90 degrees.
f. Install the right hand valve cover.
13. For the left hand camshaft:
a. Verify correct cam position by noting the position of the number 5 cylinder intake and exhaust camshaft lobes.
b. Using the tool 303-1039, install the 3 originally removed roller followers.
c. Install the CMP sensor and the bolt.
d. Connect the CMP connector.

❋ WARNING

Damage to the camshaft phaser sprocket assembly will occur if mishandled or used as a lifting or leveraging device.

e. Tighten the camshaft phaser bolt in 2 steps. Tighten to 30 ft. lbs. (40 Nm), then tighten an additional 90 degrees.
f. Install the left hand valve cover.

CRANKSHAFT FRONT SEAL

REMOVAL & INSTALLATION

All Gasoline Engines

See Figures 84 and 85.

1. Remove the crankshaft pulley.
2. Using the special tool 303-107, remove the crankshaft front seal.

To install:

3. Lubricate the engine front cover and the crankshaft front seal inner lip with clean engine oil.

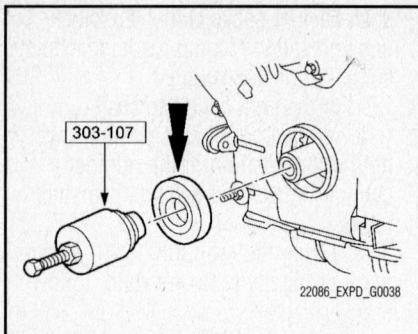

Fig. 84 Front crank seal removal with special tool

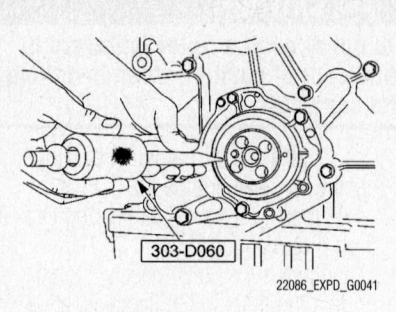

Fig. 87 Slide hammer shown removing seal

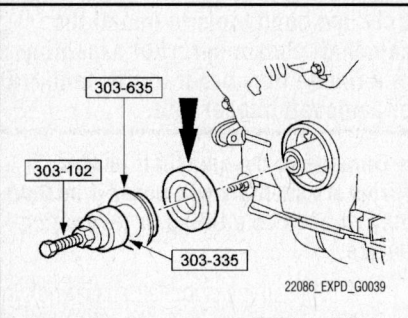

Fig. 85 Front crank seal installation with special tools

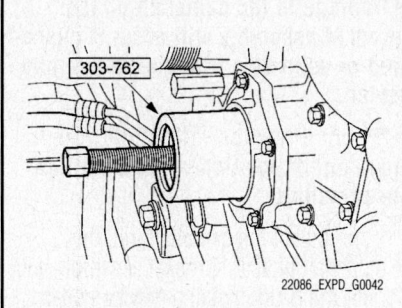

Fig. 88 Crankshaft front wear sleeve removal with tool

4. Using the special tools, install the crankshaft front seal into the engine front cover.

5. Install the crankshaft pulley.

6.0L Diesel Engine

See Figures 86 through 89.

1. Remove the crankshaft vibration damper as outlined in this section.

2. Punch 2 holes in the seal.

3. Using the special tool 303-D060, remove the crankshaft seal.

➡**Production engines will not have a wear sleeve.**

4. If equipped, remove the crankshaft damper wear sleeve.

To install:

5. Thoroughly clean the crankshaft front seal mounting surface.

6. Apply Threadlock 262 to the outer circumference of the leading edge of the crankshaft.

➡**New seal and wear sleeve must not be separated.**

7. Using the special tool 303-761, install the oil seal and wear sleeve assembly.

8. Install the crankshaft damper.

CYLINDER HEAD

REMOVAL & INSTALLATION

Excursion

5.4L & 6.8L Engines

See Figures 90 through 97.

1. Before servicing the vehicle, refer to the precautions section.

2. Remove the engine.

3. Remove the bolts and the flexplate.

☀ CAUTION

To prevent damage to the oil pan, use care when lowering the engine.

4. Lower the engine onto wooden blocks.

5. Remove the engine support tool.

6. Install the tools 303-D087 and 303-D088 onto the cylinder heads where illustrated.

7. Mount the engine on a suitable work stand.

8. Remove tools 303-D087 and 303-D088.

9. Remove the right hand engine mount.

10. Remove the cylinder block drain plugs, and drain the coolant in a suitable container.

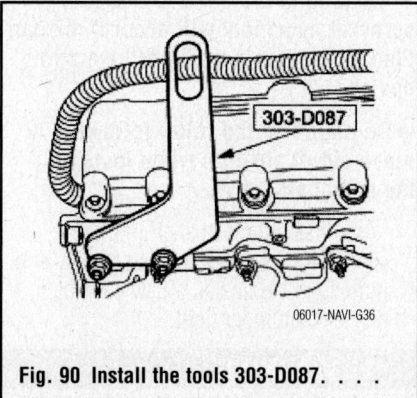

Fig. 90 Install the tools 303-D087. . . .

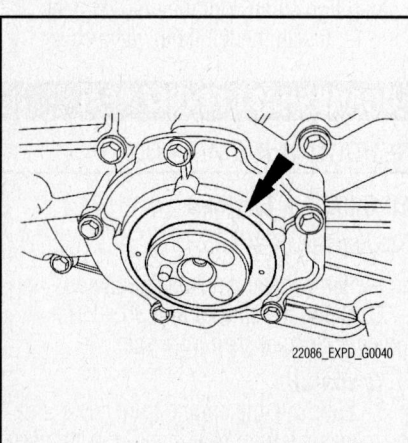

Fig. 86 Front seal shown with holes

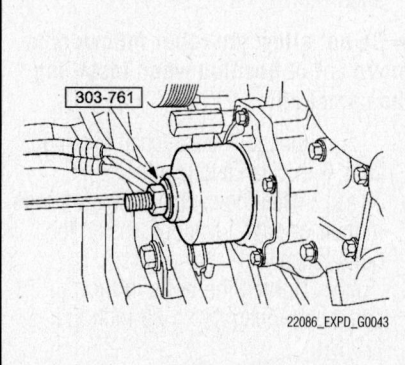

Fig. 89 Crankshaft seal and wear sleeve assembly installation with tool

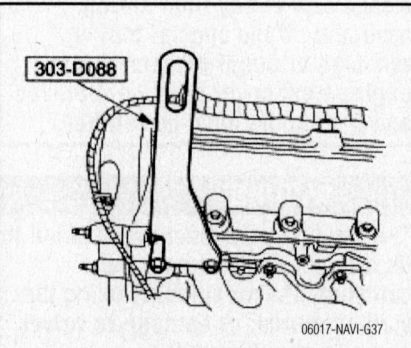

Fig. 91 Install the tools 303-D088 onto the cylinder heads—2005 Excursion models

11. Disconnect the left hand radio frequency interference capacitor and Cylinder Head Temperature (CHT) sensor connectors.

12. Disconnect the Camshaft Position (CMP) sensor connector.

13. Disconnect the right hand radio frequency interference capacitor connector.

14. Disconnect the knock sensor connector.

15. On vehicles without A/C, disconnect the Crankshaft Position (CKP) sensor connector.

16. Disconnect the oil pressure switch connector.

17. Remove the nuts and position the wiring harness bracket aside.

18. Disconnect all of the harness routing clips and connector retainers. Remove the engine control sensor wiring harness.

19. Remove the nuts and the two radio interference capacitors.

20. Remove the crankcase ventilation tube from the left hand valve cover.

21. Remove the Positive Crankcase Ventilation (PCV) hose from the right hand valve cover.

✲✲ CAUTION

Do not use metal scrapers, wire brushes, power abrasive discs or other abrasive means to clean the sealing surfaces. These tools cause scratches and gouges which make leak paths. Use a plastic scraping tool to remove all traces of old sealant.

➡The bolts are part of the valve cover and should not be removed.

22. Remove the valve covers.

23. Remove the bolt and the belt idler pulley.

24. Remove the coolant pump pulley.

25. Remove and discard the crankshaft pulley bolt.

26. Use tool 303-009 to remove the crankshaft pulley.

27. Use tool 303-107 to remove the crankshaft front oil seal.

28. Remove the front oil pan bolts.

➡Correct fastener location is essential for front cover assembly procedure. Record fastener location.

29. Remove the front cover fasteners.

30. Remove the engine front cover from the cylinder block.

31. Remove the crankshaft sensor ring from the crankshaft.

✲✲ CAUTION

Use care when removing the spark plugs.

➡Use compressed air to remove any foreign material from the spark plug well before removing the spark plugs.

32. Remove the eight spark plugs.

33. Install tool 303-382 between the valve spring coils to prevent valve stem seal damage.

➡The camshaft roller followers must be reinstalled in their original locations. Record the camshaft roller follower locations.

➡Position the cam lobe away from the camshaft roller follower prior to removing each camshaft roller follower.

34. Use tool 303-567 to compress the valve springs, and remove the camshaft roller followers.

35. Remove tool 303-382.

36. Position the crankshaft with the keyway at the 12 o'clock position.

✲✲ CAUTION

If one or both of the tensioner mounting bolts are loosened or removed, the tensioner-sealing bead must be inspected for seal integrity. If cracks, tears, separation from the tensioner body or permanent compression of the seal bead is observed, install a new tensioner.

37. Remove both timing chains and guide components.

38. Remove the nuts, exhaust manifolds and gaskets. Discard the gaskets.

39. Remove the bolt and the oil level indicator tube.

40. Install cylinder head removal/installation tools 303-572 on both ends of the cylinder head.

➡The hydraulic lash adjusters must be reinstalled in their original locations. Record the hydraulic lash adjuster locations.

41. Remove the hydraulic lash adjusters.

✲✲ CAUTION

The cylinder head must be cool before removing it from the engine. Cylinder head warpage can result if a warm or hot cylinder head is removed. Place clean shop towels over exposed engine cavities. Carefully remove the towels so foreign material is not dropped into the engine.

✲✲ CAUTION

The cylinder head bolts must be discarded and new bolts installed. They are tighten-to-yield designed and cannot be reused.

✲✲ CAUTION

Do not use metal scrapers, wire brushes, power abrasive discs or other abrasive means to clean the sealing surfaces. These tools cause scratches and gouges that make leak paths. Use a plastic scraping tool to remove all traces of the head gasket. Aluminum surfaces are soft and can be scratched easily. Never place the cylinder head gasket surface, unprotected, on a bench surface.

42. Remove the bolts and the cylinder heads. Discard the cylinder head gasket and bolts.

To install:

✲✲ CAUTION

The gasket sealing surfaces on the cylinder head and cylinder block must be clean. The use of sealing aids (aviation cement, copper spray, and glue) is not permitted. The gasket must be installed dry. The new gasket has a film coating which is crucial to the gasket's ability to seal correctly. Do not scratch the gasket.

43. Install the head gasket over the dowel pins.

➡The new cylinder head bolts must be lightly oiled with a rag, and allowed to drain for a few minutes prior to installation.

44. Install the cylinder head on the dowels and the head gasket. Loosely install new bolts.

➡Make sure to tighten the bolts in sequence in three stages.

45. Tighten the bolts in the sequence shown:

a. Step 1: Tighten to 30 ft. lbs. (40 Nm).

b. Step 2: Tighten an additional 90 degrees.

c. Step 3: Tighten an additional 90 degrees.

46. Remove tools 303-572 from both ends of the cylinder head.

➡**Lubricate the hydraulic lash adjusters with clean engine oil.**

47. Install the hydraulic lash adjusters in their original locations.

48. Install the exhaust manifold gaskets and the exhaust manifold.

➡**Lubricate the O-ring seal with clean engine oil.**

49. Install the oil level indicator tube using a new O-ring seal on the oil level indicator tube.

❖ CAUTION

Timing chain procedures must be followed exactly or damage to valves and pistons will result.

50. Install the timing chain assemblies.
51. Install tool 303-382 between the valve spring coils to prevent valve stem seal damage.

➡**Lubricate the camshaft roller followers using clean engine oil. Position the cam lobe away from the camshaft roller follower location prior to installing each camshaft roller follower.**

52. Install the camshaft roller followers in their original locations. Use tool 303-567 to compress the valve spring.
53. Remove tool 303-382.

❖ CAUTION

When installing the spark plugs, use care not to exceed the recommended torque.

54. Install the eight spark plugs. Tighten the spark plugs to 13 ft. lbs. (18 Nm).
55. Install the crankshaft sensor ring on the crankshaft.
56. Install a new engine front cover gasket on the engine front cover.
57. Install the engine front cover. Install the fasteners finger-tight.
58. Loosely install the front oil bolts, then tighten the bolts in two stages, in the sequence shown:
   a. Step 1: Tighten to 15 ft. lbs. (20 Nm).
   b. Step 2: Tighten an additional 60 degrees.
59. Position the belt idler pulley and install the bolt. Tighten to 25 Nm (18 ft-lbs.).
60. Lubricate the engine front cover and the crankshaft front seal inner lip with clean engine oil.

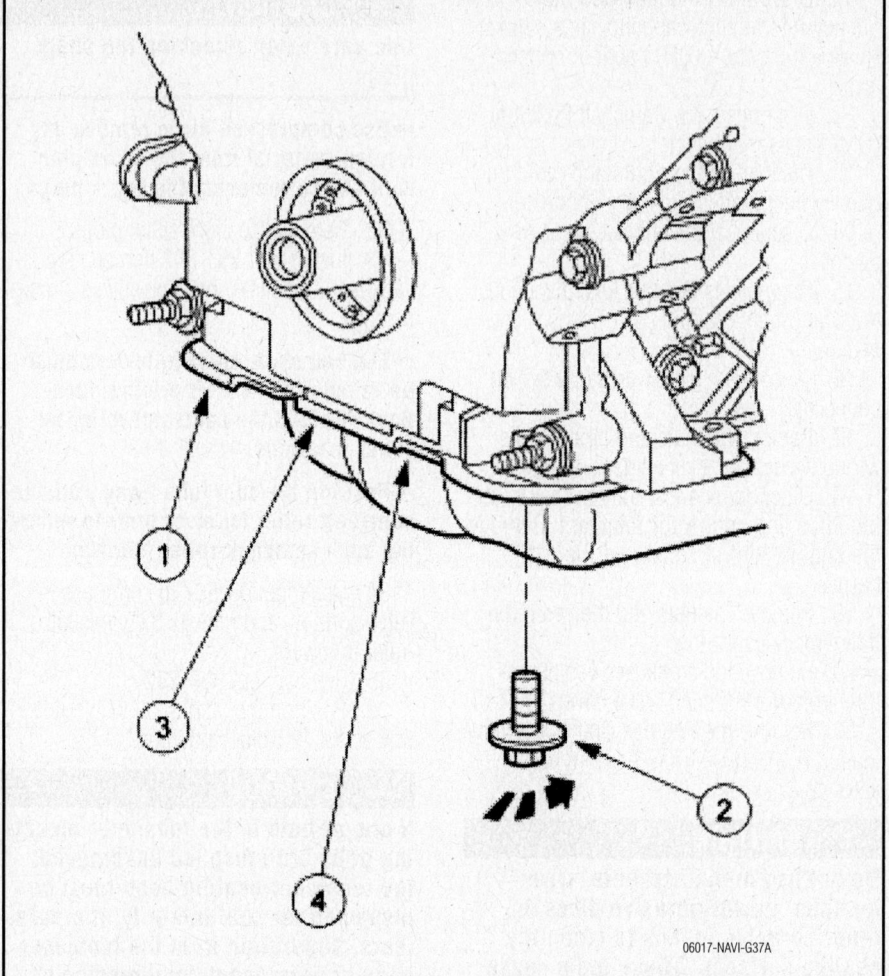

Fig. 92 Install the front oil pan bolts using this sequence—2005 Excursion models

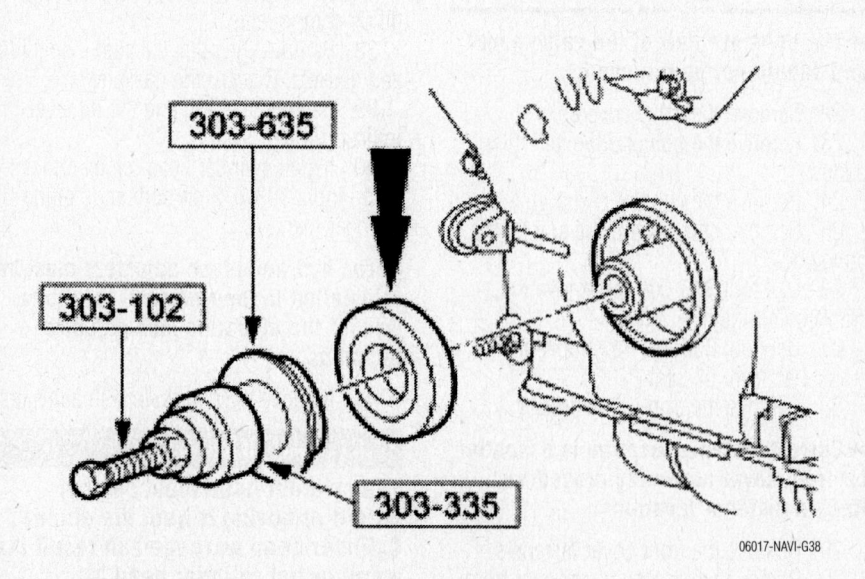

Fig. 93 Use the tools illustrated to install the crankshaft front seal into the engine front cover—2005 Excursion models

61. Use the tools illustrated to install the crankshaft front seal into the engine front cover.

➡ **If not secured within four minutes, the sealant must be removed and the sealing area cleaned. To clean the sealing area, use silicone gasket remover and metal surface prep. Follow the directions on the packaging. Failure to follow this procedure can cause future oil leakage.**

62. Apply a 0.32 in. (8mm) bead of silicone gasket and sealant to the Woodruff key slot on the crankshaft pulley.

63. Use tool 303-102 to install the crankshaft pulley.

➡ **Use a suitable strap wrench (303-D055) to hold the pulley while tightening the bolt.**

64. Tighten the new crankshaft pulley bolt in four steps:
　a. Step 1: Tighten to 66 ft. lbs. (90 Nm).
　b. Step 2: Loosen 360 degrees.
　c. Step 3: Tighten to 37 ft. lbs. (50 Nm).
　d. Step 4: Tighten an additional 90 degrees.

65. Position the coolant pump pulley on the coolant pump and install the bolts.

66. If a new gasket is being installed, apply instant gel adhesive completely around the gasket groove in the left hand valve cover. Install the new valve cover gasket.

➡ **If not secured within four minutes, the sealant must be removed and the sealing area cleaned. To clean the sealing area, use silicone gasket remover and metal surface prep.**

67. Apply silicone gasket and sealant in two places where the engine front cover meets the left cylinder head.

68. Position the left hand valve cover and gasket on the cylinder head and install the bolts loosely.

69. Tighten the bolts in the sequence shown.

70. If a new gasket is being installed, apply instant gel adhesive completely around the gasket groove in the right hand valve cover. Install the new valve cover gasket.

➡ **If not secured within four minutes, the sealant must be removed and the sealing area cleaned. To clean the sealing area, use silicone gasket remover and metal surface prep.**

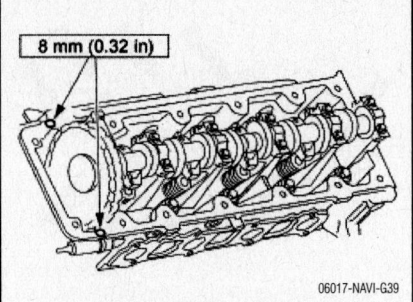

06017-NAVI-G39

Fig. 94 Apply silicone gasket and sealant in two places where the engine front cover meets the left cylinder head—2005 Excursion models

71. Apply silicone gasket and sealant in two places where the engine front cover meets the cylinder head.

72. Position the right hand valve cover and gasket on the cylinder head and install the bolts loosely. Tighten the bolts in the sequence shown.

73. Install the crankcase ventilation tube on the left hand valve cover.

74. Install the PCV hose on the right hand valve cover.

75. Install the radio frequency interference capacitors.

76. Roughly position the engine control sensor wiring harness and mount it on the valve cover studs. Install the bracket and tighten to 22 ft. lbs. (30 Nm).

77. On vehicles without A/C, connect the CKP sensor connector.

78. Connect the oil pressure switch connector.

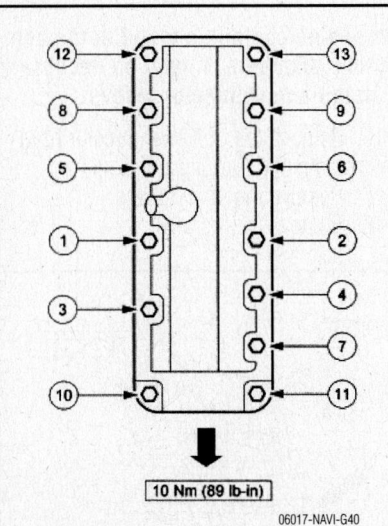

10 Nm (89 lb-in)

06017-NAVI-G40

Fig. 95 Tighten the left hand valve cover bolts in this sequence to the torque value shown—2005 Excursion models

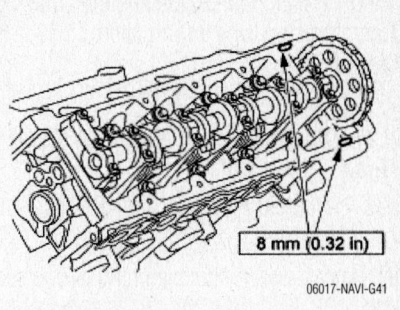

8 mm (0.32 in)

06017-NAVI-G41

Fig. 96 Apply silicone gasket and sealant in two places where the engine front cover meets the right cylinder head—2005 Excursion models

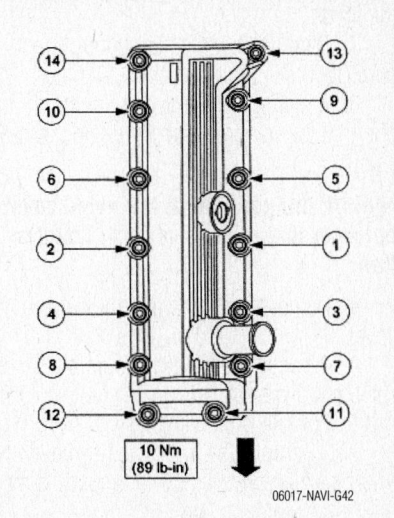

10 Nm (89 lb-in)

06017-NAVI-G42

Fig. 97 Tighten the right hand valve cover bolts in this sequence to the torque value shown—2005 Excursion models

79. Connect the knock sensor connector.

80. Connect the right hand radio frequency interference capacitor connector.

81. Connect the CMP sensor connector.

82. Connect the left hand radio frequency interference capacitor and CHT sensor connectors.

83. Install the cylinder block drain plugs. Tighten to 18 ft. lbs. (24 Nm).

84. Install the right hand engine mount. Tighten the bolts to 46 ft. lbs. (63 Nm).

85. Install tools 303-D087 and 303-D088.

86. Install a hoist and attach to tools 303-D087 and 303-D088 and remove the engine from the work stand.

87. Lower the engine onto wooden blocks.

88. Remove the tools 303-D087 and 303-D088.

89. Install engine support tool 303-F047and raise the engine.

90. Install the flexplate and the bolts. Tighten the bolts in a star pattern to 59 ft. lbs. (80 Nm).

91. Install the engine.

6.0L Diesel Engine—Right Cylinder Head

See Figures 98 through 103.

1. Before servicing the vehicle, refer to the precautions in the beginning of this section.

2. With the vehicle in NEUTRAL, position it on a hoist.

3. Drain the engine oil.

4. Remove the intake manifold.

5. Remove the evaporator core housing.

6. Disconnect the wiring retainers from the studs.

7. Remove the injection control pressure (ICP) sensor

8. If equipped, remove the nut and position the transmission fluid and indicator aside.

➡ Mark the position of the valve cover bolts for the valve cover bolt installation.

9. Remove the bolts and the valve cover.

10. Remove the high-pressure oil rail-to-valve cover gasket.

11. For late build vehicles:
   a. Remove the crankcase-to-head tube assembly. Remove and discard the D-ring seals.

✳ WARNING

Do not remove the oil rail end plugs or acoustic wave attenuator port fitting. Service parts are not available to support the components.

12. Remove the bolts and the high-pressure oil rail.

13. For early build vehicles:

➡ The rings on the crankcase-to-head tube must be used to pry the tube assembly from the branch tube assembly or the oil rail assembly.

   b. Remove the crankcase-to-head tube.
   c. Remove and discard the D-ring seals.

14. For late build vehicles:

✳ WARNING

Use care not to deform the lower crankcase-to-head tube during removal. If the tube is damaged, a new tube must be installed.

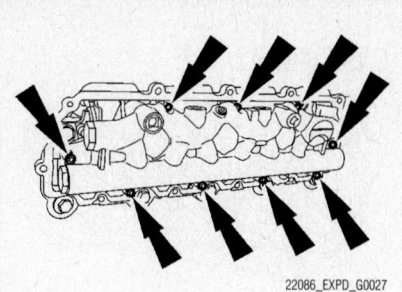

Fig. 98 High pressure oil rail and bolts shown

➡ Use a shop towel and metal brake parts cleaner to remove the oil residue prior to removing.

➡ If the crankcase-to-head tube separated, using a pair of soft-jawed pliers, remove the lower crankcase-to-head tube.

   d. Remove and discard the D-ring seal.

15. Using the special tool, push the fuel injector electrical connector out of the rocker arm carrier.

➡ Prior to removing the fuel injector assembly, insert clean shop towels in the oil drain holes adjacent to each glow plug.

✳ WARNING

Failure to account for all snap rings or pieces prior to placing the vehicle back into service can cause engine damage. A missing snap ring can be ingested into the lube oil system and cause severe engine damage.

➡ If engine coolant is found in the combustion chambers, it may be necessary to install a new injector sleeve.

16. Remove the bolt, fuel injector hold-down clamp and fuel injector.

17. Remove the shop towels.

18. Remove the starter.

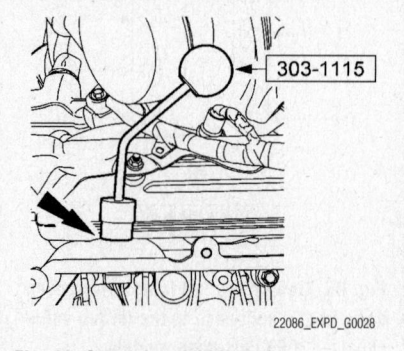

303-1115

Fig. 99 Special tool 303-1115

19. Remove the cylinder block coolant drain plug.

20. Remove the nuts and bolts from the turbocharger adapter pipe.

21. For early build vehicles:
   a. Remove the turbocharger adapter pipe.

22. For late build vehicles:
   a. Position the turbocharger adapter pipe to gain access to the adapter pipe joint. Remove the bolts, separate the adapter pipe joint and remove the gasket. Remove the 2 parts of the turbocharger adapter pipe.

23. Using the special tool 303-1114, remove the glow plug harness. Position the wiring harness aside.

24. Remove the 4 glow plugs.

25. Remove and discard the 10 inner cylinder head bolts.

26. Remove the 8 bolts and the rocker arm assemblies.

27. Mark the 8 valve bridges with a permanent marker and remove.

✳ WARNING

To prevent engine damage, keep the push rods in the order in which they were removed. Install all push rods back in their original positions.

28. Mark the location and remove the 8 push rods.

29. Remove the outer cylinder head bolts.

30. Install the special tool 303-759 and a lifting crane. With the help of an assistant, remove the cylinder head from the vehicle.

31. Check for cylinder head distortion.

32. Remove and discard the cylinder head gasket and dowels.

33. Clean and inspect the gasket sealing surfaces.

To install:

✳ WARNING

Install new D-ring seals on the crankcase-to-head tube. It requires

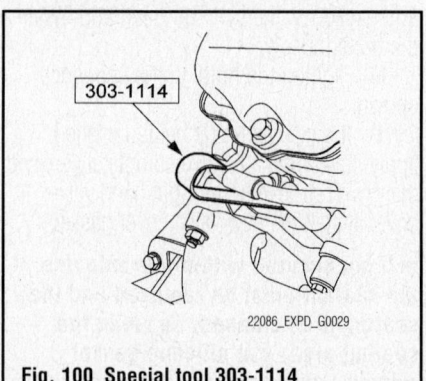

303-1114

Fig. 100 Special tool 303-1114

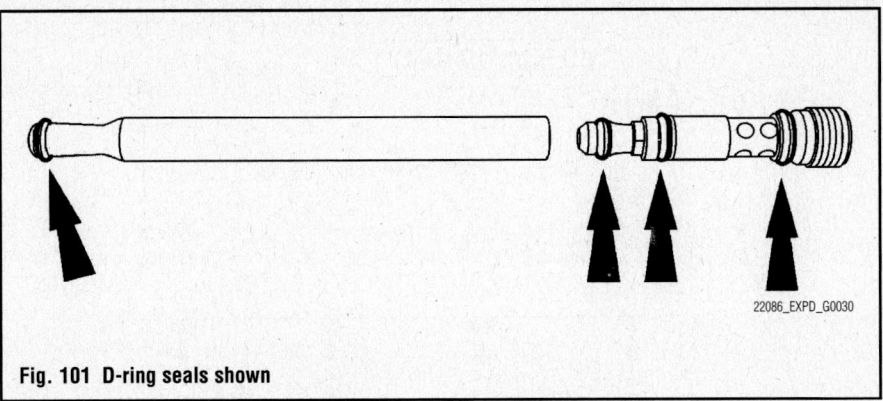

Fig. 101 D-ring seals shown

several hours after installation for the D-ring seals to relax back to their original size. If the tube assembly is installed before the D-ring seals have relaxed, damage to the D-ring seals can occur.

34. Install new D-ring seals on the crankcase to head tube assemblies.

➡Use care to avoid scratching the blue compound on the cylinder head gasket. Install a new cylinder head gasket with the part number facing up and verify the top 5 holes and the head gasket push rod holes line up.

35. Install the dowels and the cylinder head gasket.

36. Using the special tool 303-759 and a lifting crane. With the help of an assistant, install the cylinder head on the engine. Remove the special tools.

37. Install the outer cylinder head bolts finger-tight.

➡To prevent engine damage, keep the push rods in the order in which they were removed. Install all push rods back in their original positions. Higher mileage engines require push rods to be cleaned so the copper-colored end of the push rod can be identified.

38. Apply clean engine oil to each end of the push rods. Insert them into their respective positions with the copper-colored end up.

39. Install the 8 valve bridges.

➡Coat the end of each valve stem with clean engine oil. Coat top of valve bridge with engine oil.

✳✳ WARNING

Rotate the crankshaft until the damper locating dowel notch is in the 6 o'clock position or engine damage can occur.

40. Install the rocker arm assemblies and 8 bolts.

✳✳ WARNING

Using too much engine oil on the threads of the cylinder head bolts can cause damage to the threads and poor sealing. Using anti-seize compounds, grease or any other lubricants other than engine oil on the cylinder head bolt threads can affect the true torque value of the bolts.

41. Lightly lubricate the new cylinder head bolt threads and flanges with clean engine oil.

42. Install the 10 inner cylinder head retaining bolts finger-tight.

43. Tighten the head bolts in the following sequence.

 a. Tighten bolts 1 through 10 to 65 ft. lbs. (88 Nm).

 b. Tighten bolts 1 through 10 to 85 ft. lbs. (115 Nm).

 c. Tighten bolts in sequence 1 through 10, clockwise 90 degrees.

 d. Tighten bolts in sequence 1 through 10, a second time, clockwise 90 degrees.

 e. Tighten bolts in sequence 1 through 10, a third time, clockwise 90 degrees.

 f. Tighten bolts 11 through 15 to 18 ft lbs. (24 Nm).

 g. Tighten bolts 11 through 15 to 23 ft lbs. (31 Nm).

44. Install the 4 glow plugs and tighten to 14 ft. lbs. (19 Nm).

➡Clean and apply clean engine oil to the O-ring seals.

45. Using the special tool 303-1114, install the glow plug harness.

46. For early build vehicles, position the turbocharger adapter pipe.

47. For late build vehicles, position the 2 parts of the turbocharger adapter pipe into the vehicle. Install the gasket, connect the adapter pipe joint and install the bolts. Position the turbocharger adapter pipe on the exhaust manifolds. Tighten the nuts to 20 ft. lbs. (27 Nm).

➡Apply anti-seize lubricants to the bolt threads prior to installing the bolts. Do not tighten until after the turbocharger is installed.

48. Install the nuts and bolts in the adapter pipe and tighten to 20 ft. lbs. (27 Nm).

49. Install the cylinder block coolant drain plug and oil to the O-ring seal prior to installing.

50. Tighten the cylinder block plug to 15 ft. lbs. (20 Nm).

51. Install the starter.

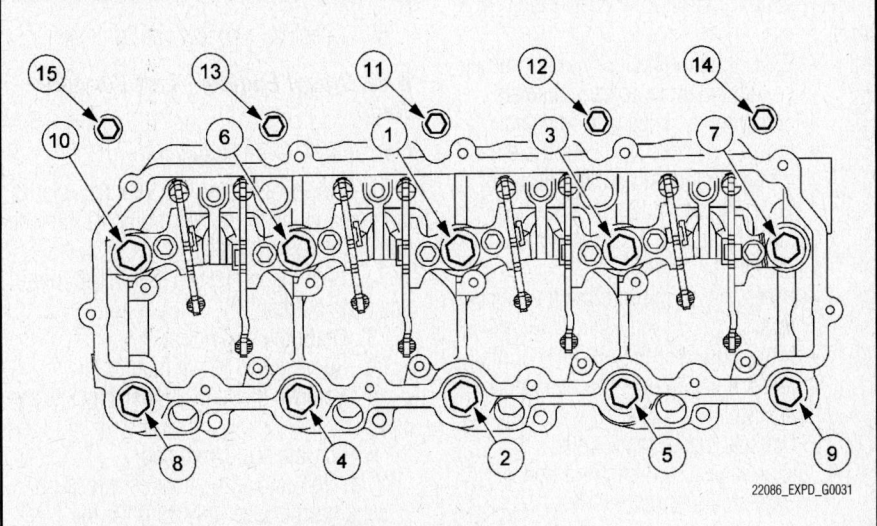

Fig. 102 RH 6.0L diesel engine tightening sequence

52. Install new O-ring seals and copper washer on the fuel injector. Lubricate the fuel injector and O-ring seals liberally with clean engine oil.

> ❈❈ **WARNING**
>
> **To prevent engine damage, do not use air tools to install the fuel injectors. The snap ring that extracts the injector can dislodge and fall into the oil drain hole. Failure to tighten the injector properly can lead to engine failure.**

53. Install the fuel injector, fuel injector hold-down clamp and tighten bolt to 24 ft. lbs. (33 Nm).

➡ **Make sure the injector wiring is clear of all moving parts or engine damage can occur.**

54. Install the fuel injector electrical connector into the rocker arm carrier.

55. Apply engine oil to the top fuel injector O-ring seals.

56. For early build vehicles: apply clean engine oil on the crankcase-to-head tube D-ring seals and install the tube.

> ❈❈ **WARNING**
>
> **To prevent engine damage, check that the crankcase-to-head tube assembly bottoms out in the branch tube assembly. The oil rail, crankcase-to-head tube and fuel injectors will not function correctly if the tubes are not bottomed out.**

➡ **Apply clean engine oil on the tubes prior to installing the high-pressure oil rail.**

57. Position the oil rail on the fuel injectors.

- Place the oil rail on top of the carrier so that the 4 single ball tubes are engaging the injector lead angle.
- Insert 3 guide bolts, 2 on the ends of the straight side of the oil rail and 1 in the middle of the wavy side of the rail. Install the guide studs 6 to 7 turns.
- Press the oil rail into the fuel injectors.
- Make sure that the oil rail mounting feet are flat against the mounting surface.
- Loosely install the 6 bolts.

58. Install the oil rail retaining bolts.

- Remove the 3 guide bolts.
- Loosely install the 3 remaining bolts.

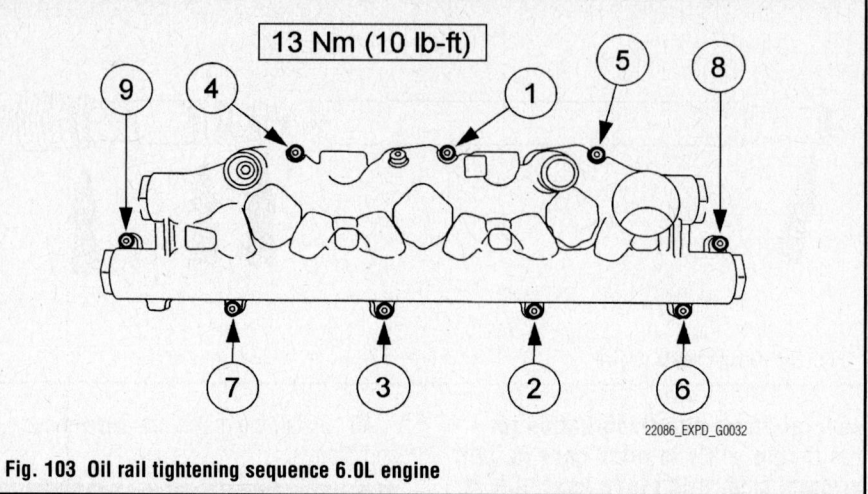

13 Nm (10 lb-ft)

22086_EXPD_G0032

Fig. 103 Oil rail tightening sequence 6.0L engine

- Tighten the bolts in the sequence shown to 10 ft. lbs. (13 Nm).

59. For late build vehicles, install the crankcase-to-head tube assembly. Apply clean engine oil to the crankcase-to-head tube prior to installing. Tighten to 60 ft. lbs. (82 Nm).

60. Install the high-pressure oil rail-to-valve cover gasket.

61. Position the valve cover gasket. Install the valve cover and tighten bolts to 80 inch. lbs. (9 Nm).

62. If equipped, position back the transmission fluid indicator and tube. Install the retaining nut.

63. Install the ICP sensor.

64. Connect the wiring retainers to the studs.

65. Install the evaporator core housing.

66. Install the intake manifold.

67. Install a new oil filter and fill crankcase with oil.

68. Install required antifreeze mixture and type.

69. Check all connections for leaks.

6.0L Diesel Engine—Left Cylinder Head

See Figures 104 through 106.

1. Before servicing the vehicle, refer to the precautions in the beginning of this section.

2. With the vehicle in NEUTRAL, position it on a hoist.

3. Drain the engine oil.

4. Remove the intake manifold.

5. Remove the left cylinder block drain plug.

6. For late build vehicles:

   a. To remove the exhaust pressure sensor tube assembly, remove the exhaust pressure sensor tube retaining nut and disconnect the exhaust pressure sensor tube fitting at the exhaust manifold.

7. Remove the fuel injector control module mounting bracket.

8. Disconnect the wire retainer. Remove the nut and position the oil level indicator and tube aside.

➡ **Mark the position of the valve cover bolts for valve cover bolt installation.**

9. Remove the 11 bolts and the valve cover.

10. Clean and inspect the valve cover gasket. Install a new gasket if necessary.

11. For late build vehicles:

   a. Remove the crankcase-to-head tube assembly. Remove and discard the D-ring seals.

➡ **Do not remove the oil rail end plugs or acoustic wave attenuator port fitting. Service parts are not available to support the components.**

12. Remove the bolts and the high-pressure oil rail.

13. For early build vehicles:

   a. Remove the crankcase-to-head tube assembly. Remove and discard the D-ring seals

14. For late build vehicles:

➡ **Use a shop towel and metal brake parts cleaner to remove the oil residue prior to removing.**

➡ **If the crankcase-to-head tube separated, using a pair of soft-jawed pliers, remove the lower crankcase-to-head tube.**

   b. Remove and discard the D-ring seal

15. Using the special tool 303-1115, push the fuel injector electrical connector out of the rocker arm carrier.

16. Prior to removing the injector assembly, insert clean shop towels in the oil drain holes adjacent to each glow plug.

17. Remove the bolt, fuel injector hold-down and fuel injector.

✳✳ WARNING

Do not pull on the glow plug wire or damage may occur.

18. Using the special tool 303-1114, remove the glow plug harness. Position the wiring harness aside.

19. Remove the 4 glow plugs.

20. Remove the nuts and bolts from the turbocharger adapter pipe.

21. For early build vehicles:

   a. Remove the turbocharger adapter pipe.

22. For late build vehicles:

   a. Position the turbocharger adapter pipe to gain access to the adapter pipe joint. Remove the bolts, separate the adapter pipe joint and remove the gasket. Remove the 2 parts of the turbocharger adapter.

23. Remove the oil level indicator and tube.

24. Remove the bolts and turbocharger heat shield.

25. For early build vehicles:

   a. Disconnect the exhaust pressure tube at the exhaust manifold.

   b. Remove the retaining nuts. Remove the exhaust pressure bracket assembly.

26. Remove the retaining bolt from the fuel line bracket and position the fuel lines aside.

27. Remove the bolt and the idler pulley.

28. Disconnect the heater hose from the front cover and position aside.

29. Remove the banjo fitting and the fuel line.

✳✳ WARNING

Make sure the insulation blanket is not damaged (torn, cracked or fabric separated from the metallic skin) when removing the lower rear cylinder head bolt. If the insulation blanket is damaged, the entire blanket must be replaced.

➡**It may be necessary to slightly compress or deform the insulation blanket to gain tool clearance to remove the lower rear cylinder head bolt. The back 2 cylinder head bolts cannot be removed from the head in vehicle. Raise these bolts and secure them in position, so they will clear the cylinder block deck as the head is removed.**

30. Remove and discard the inner cylinder head bolts.

31. Remove the 8 bolts and the rocker arm assemblies.

32. Mark the 8 valve bridges with a permanent marker and remove.

33. Mark the location and remove the 8 push rods.

✳✳ WARNING

To prevent engine damage, keep the push rods in the order in which they were removed. Install all push rods back in their original positions.

34. Mark the location and remove the 8 push rods.

35. Remove the outer cylinder head bolts.

36. Install the special tool 303-759 and the lifting crane. With the help of an assistant, remove the cylinder from the vehicle.

37. Check for cylinder head distortion.

38. Remove and discard the cylinder head gasket and dowels.

39. Clean and inspect the gasket sealing surfaces.

To install:

✳✳ WARNING

Install new D-ring seals on the crankcase-to-head tube. It requires several hours after installation for the D-ring seals to relax back to their original size. If the tube assembly is installed before the D-ring seals have relaxed, damage to the D-ring seals can occur.

40. Install new D-ring seals on the crankcase-to-head tube assemblies.

➡**Use care to avoid scratching the blue compound on the cylinder head gasket. Install the gasket with the part number facing upward and verify the 5 top holes and head gasket push rod holes line up.**

41. Install the dowels and the cylinder head gasket.

➡**The back two cylinder head bolts cannot be installed into the head in vehicle. Lightly lubricate the threads of 2 new cylinder head bolts with clean engine oil. Position these bolts in the head and secure them in position, so they will clear the cylinder block deck as the head is installed.**

➡**Position the fuel lines in place before the cylinder head is installed.**

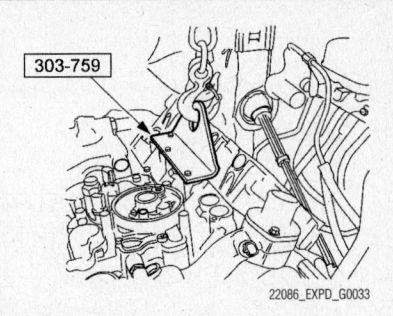

303-759

22086_EXPD_G0033

Fig. 104 Cylinder head installation tool 303-759 shown

42. Using the special tools and with the help of an assistant, install the cylinder head on the engine. Remove the special tools

43. Install the outer cylinder head bolts finger-tight.

➡**If a push rod has been replaced, it may not have a copper-colored end and can be installed with either end up.**

44. Apply clean engine oil to each end of the push rods. Insert them into their respective positions with the copper-colored end up.

45. Coat the end of each valve stem with clean engine oil.

46. Install the 8 valve bridges.

✳✳ WARNING

Rotate the crankshaft until the damper locating dowel notch is in the 6 o'clock position or engine damage can occur.

47. Apply clean engine oil to the top center of each valve bridge.

48. Install the rocker arm assemblies and tighten bolts to 23 ft. lbs. (33 Nm).

➡**It may be necessary to slightly compress or deform the insulation blanket to gain tool clearance to install the lower rear cylinder head bolt.**

49. Lightly lubricate the new cylinder head bolt threads and flanges with clean engine oil.

50. Install the 10 cylinder head retaining bolts finger-tight.

51. Tighten the head bolts in the following sequence.

   a. Tighten bolts 1 through 10 to 65 ft. lbs. (88 Nm).

   b. Tighten bolts 1 through 10 to 85 ft. lbs. (115 Nm).

   c. Tighten bolts in sequence 1 through 10, clockwise 90 degrees.

   d. Tighten bolts in sequence 1 through 10, a second time, clockwise 90 degrees

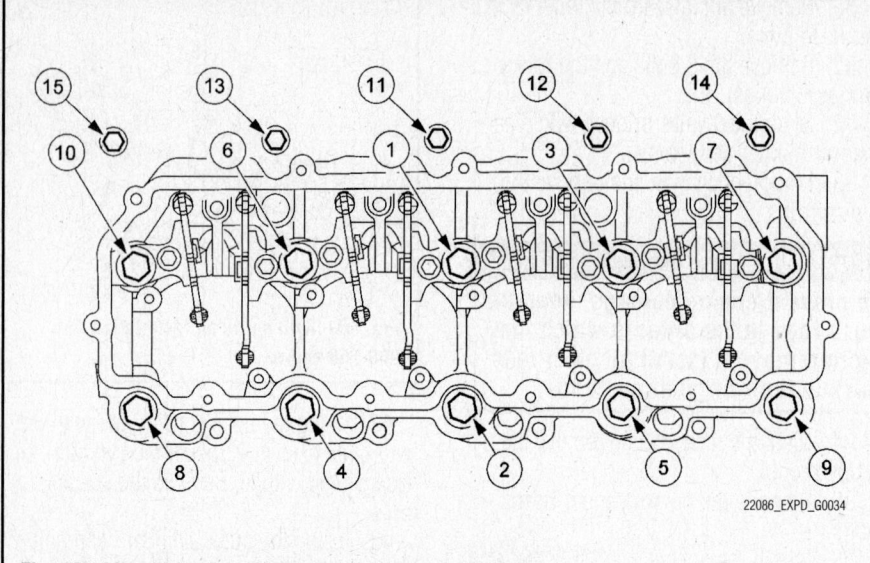

Fig. 105 LH cylinder head tightening sequence 6.0L engine

e. Tighten bolts in sequence 1 through 10, a third time, clockwise 90 degrees.

f. Tighten bolts 11 through 15 to 18 ft lbs. (24 Nm).

g. Tighten bolts 11 through 15 to 23 ft lbs. (31 Nm).

➡Install new sealing washers.

52. Install the fuel line and the banjo fitting and tighten to 28 ft. lbs. (38 Nm).

53. Position and connect the heater hose.

54. Install the idler pulley and tighten bolt to 35 ft. lbs. (37 Nm).

Early build vehicles

55. Position the exhaust pressure bracket assembly and install and tighten the retaining nuts to 23 ft. lbs. (33 Nm).

56. Tighten the exhaust pressure tube fitting at the exhaust manifold to 22 ft. lbs. (30 Nm).

All vehicles

57. Position the fuel lines and install and tighten the fuel line bracket retaining bolt to 10 ft. lbs. (13 Nm).

58. Install the oil level indicator and tube.

59. Install the turbocharger heat shield and bolts.

60. For late build vehicles, position the 2 parts of the turbocharger adapter pipe into the vehicle. Install the gasket, connect the adapter pipe joint and install the bolts. Position the turbocharger adapter pipe on the exhaust manifolds. Tighten the nuts to 20 ft. lbs. (27 Nm).

61. For early build vehicles:

a. Position the turbocharger adapter pipe.

➡Apply anti-seize lubricants to the bolt threads prior to installing the bolts.

➡Do not tighten until after the turbocharger is installed.

b. Install the nuts and bolts in the adapter pipe and tighten to 20 ft. lbs. (27 Nm).

c. Install the 4 glow plugs and tighten to 14 ft. lbs. (19 Nm).

d. Using the special tool 303-1114, install the glow plug harness.

✳✳ WARNING

If the fuel injector oil inlet D-shaped O-ring seal is damaged, a new fuel injector must be installed.

e. Install new O-ring seals and copper washer on the fuel injector. Lubricate the fuel injector and O-rings liberally with clean engine oil.

62. Install the fuel injector, fuel injector hold-down and bolt. Tighten bolt to 24 ft. lbs. (33 Nm).

✳✳ WARNING

Failure to tighten the injector properly can lead to engine failure.

➡Make sure the injector wiring is clear of all moving parts or engine damage can occur.

f. Install the fuel injector electrical connector into the rocker carrier.

g. Apply engine oil to the top fuel injector O-ring seals.

63. For early build vehicles:

a. Apply clean engine oil and install the crankcase-to-head tube assembly.

✳✳ WARNING

To prevent engine damage, check that the crankcase-to-head tube assemblies bottom out in the branch tube assembly. The oil rail, crankcase-to-head tube and the fuel injectors will not function correctly if the tube is not bottomed out.

b. Apply clean engine oil and install the crankcase-to-head tube assembly.

➡Apply clean engine oil on the tubes prior to installing the high-pressure oil rail.

64. Position the oil rail on the fuel injectors:

a. Place the oil rail on top of the carrier so that the 4 single ball tubes are engaging the injector lead angle.

b. Insert 3 guide bolts, 2 on the ends of the straight side of the oil rail and 1 in the middle of the wavy side of the rail. Install the guide studs 6 to 7 turns.

c. Press the oil rail into the fuel injectors.

d. Make sure that the oil rail mounting feet are flat against the mounting surface.

e. Loosely install the 6 bolts.

65. Install the oil rail retaining bolts:

a. Remove the 3 guide bolts.

b. Loosely install the 3 remaining bolts.

c. Tighten the bolts in the sequence shown to 10 ft. lbs. (13 Nm).

66. For late build vehicles:

a. Apply clean engine oil to the crankcase-to-head tube prior to installing.

b. Install the crankcase-to-head tube assembly and tighten to 60 ft. lbs. (82 Nm).

67. Position the valve cover gasket. Install the valve cover and 11 bolts. Tighten bolts to 80 inch. lbs. (9 Nm).

68. Position back the oil level indicator and install the nut. Connect the wire retainer.

69. Install the fuel injector control module mounting bracket.

70. For late build vehicles:

a. Connect the exhaust pressure sensor tube fitting to the exhaust manifold and tighten to 22 ft. lbs. (30 Nm). Install the exhaust pressure sensor retaining nut and tighten to 10 ft. lbs. (13 Nm).

71. Install a new oil filter and refill crank case with oil.

72. Install the cylinder block coolant drain plug.

73. Install the intake manifold.

74. Refill engine coolant and check for leaks.

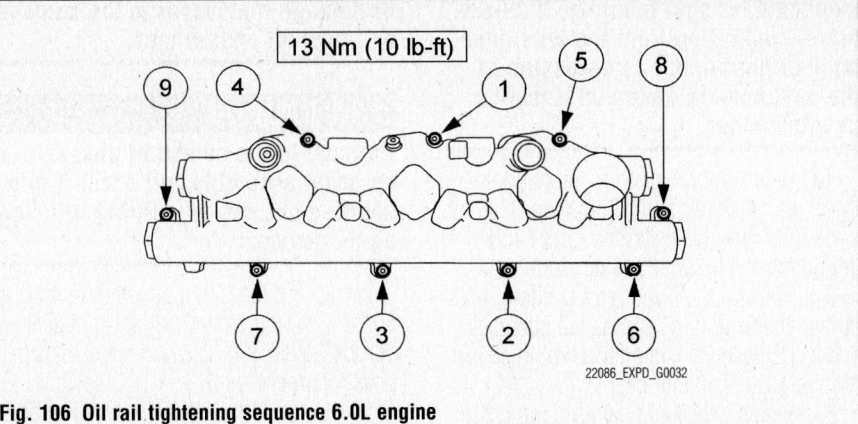

13 Nm (10 lb-ft)

9 4 1 5 8

7 3 2 6

22086_EXPD_G0032

Fig. 106 Oil rail tightening sequence 6.0L engine

Expedition & Navigator

See Figures 107 through 129.

➡To correctly tighten the cylinder head bolts, an angle torque wrench is needed.

1. Before servicing the vehicle, refer to the precautions section.
2. Remove the engine.
3. Remove the bolts and the flexplate.
4. Install the engine onto a suitable engine stand.
5. Disconnect the right hand Camshaft Position (CMP) sensor connector.
6. Remove the stud bolt and the right hand radio ignition interference capacitor.
7. Disconnect the right hand Variable Camshaft Timing (VCT) solenoid connector.
8. Disconnect the 2 engine wiring harness retainers from the right hand valve cover studs.
9. Disconnect the connector retainer from the coolant tube.
10. Disconnect the 4 right hand ignition coil connectors.
11. Disconnect the Cylinder Head Temperature (CHT) sensor connector.
12. Disconnect the 2 engine wiring harness retainers from the left hand valve cover studs.
13. Disconnect the left hand VCT solenoid connector.
14. Disconnect the oil pressure sensor connector.

15. Disconnect the left hand CMP sensor connector.
16. Remove the stud bolt and the left hand radio ignition interference capacitor.
17. Disconnect the 4 left hand ignition coil connectors.
18. Remove the 8 bolts and the 8 ignition coils.
19. Disconnect the Crankshaft Position (CKP) sensor connector.
20. Remove the engine wiring harness from the engine assembly.
21. Remove the bolt and the oil level indicator tube and discard the O-ring seal.
22. Remove the bolt and the right hand CMP sensor.
23. Remove the bolt and the left hand CMP sensor.
24. Remove the bolt and the CKP sensor.

⁕⁕ **CAUTION**

Do not use metal scrapers, wire brushes, power abrasive discs or other abrasive means to clean the sealing surfaces. These tools cause scratches and gouges which make leak paths. Use a plastic scraping tool to remove all traces of old sealant.

⁕⁕ **CAUTION**

When removing the valve cover, make sure to avoid damaging the variable camshaft timing (VCT) solenoid.

➡The bolts are part of the valve cover and should not be removed.

25. Remove the bolts and the valve covers.
26. Clean the valve cover mating surface of the cylinder head with silicone gasket remover and metal surface prep.

27. Inspect the valve cover gasket. If the gasket is damaged, remove and discard the gasket. Clean the valve cover gasket groove with soap and water or a suitable solvent.
28. Remove the bolts, the coolant pump pulley and the 3 accessory drive belt idler pulleys.
29. Remove the bolts and the accessory drive belt tensioner.
30. Remove and discard the crankshaft pulley bolt. Using tool 303-009, remove the crankshaft pulley.
31. Using the tool 303-107, remove the crankshaft seal.
32. Remove the front 4 oil pan bolts.

➡Correct fastener location is essential for assembly procedure. Record fastener location.

33. Remove the engine front cover fasteners and the cover.
34. Remove the crankshaft sensor ring from the crankshaft.
35. Position the crankshaft keyway at the 12 o'clock position.

➡If the camshaft lobes are not exactly positioned at the 12 o'clock position, the crankshaft will require one full additional rotation to 12 o'clock. The number 1 cylinder camshaft exhaust lobe must be coming up on the exhaust stroke. Verify by noting the position of the 2 intake camshaft lobes and the exhaust lobe on the number 1 cylinder.

➡If the components are to be reinstalled, they must be installed in the same positions. Mark the components for installation into the original locations.

36. Remove only the 3 roller followers shown in the illustration from the right hand cylinder head.

⁕⁕ **CAUTION**

Do not allow the valve keepers to fall off the valve or the valve may drop into the cylinder.

➡It may be necessary to push the valve down while compressing the spring.

37. Using the tool illustrated, remove the 3 designated roller followers in the previous step from the right hand cylinder head.
38. Remove only the 3 roller followers shown in the illustration from the left hand cylinder head.
39. Using the tool 303-1039, remove the

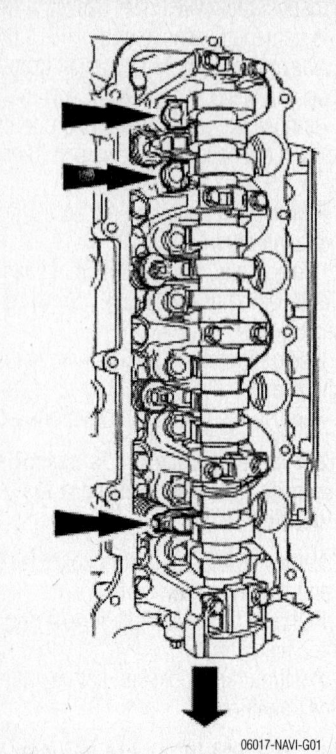

06017-NAVI-G01

Fig. 107 Remove only the 3 roller followers shown from the right hand cylinder head—2005–07 Expedition and Navigator models

3 designated roller followers in the previous step from the left hand cylinder head.

40. The crankshaft cannot be moved past the 6 o'clock position once set.

41. Rotate the crankshaft clockwise and position the crankshaft keyway at the 6 o'clock position.

✳✳ CAUTION

If one or both of the tensioner mounting bolts are loosened or removed, the tensioner-sealing bead must be

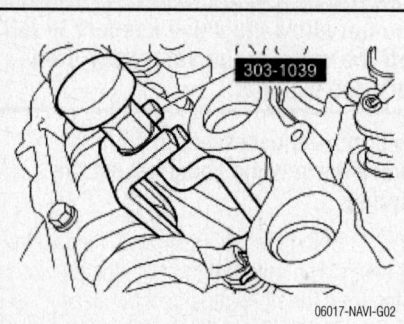

06017-NAVI-G02

Fig. 108 Using the tool illustrated, remove the 3 designated roller followers—2005–07 Expedition and Navigator models

inspected for seal integrity. If cracks, tears, separation from the tensioner body or permanent compression of the seal bead is observed, install a new tensioner.

42. Remove the bolts, the left hand timing chain tensioner and tensioner arm.

43. Remove the bolts, the right hand timing chain tensioner and tensioner arm.

44. Remove the right hand and left hand timing chains and the crankshaft sprocket.

45. Remove the right hand timing chain from the camshaft sprocket.

46. Remove the right hand timing chain from the crankshaft sprocket.

47. Remove the left hand timing chain from the camshaft sprocket.

48. Remove the left hand timing chain and crankshaft sprocket.

49. Remove the left hand and right hand timing chain guides.

✳✳ CAUTION

Damage to the camshaft phaser sprocket assembly will occur if mishandled or used as a lifting or leveraging device.

✳✳ CAUTION

Only use hand tools to remove the camshaft phaser sprocket assembly

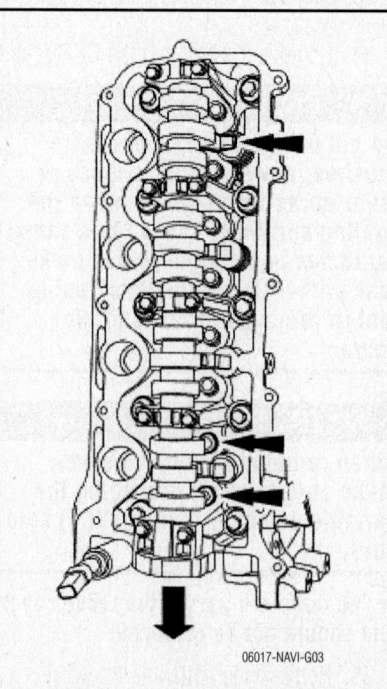

06017-NAVI-G03

Fig. 109 Remove only the 3 roller followers shown from the left hand cylinder head—2005–07 Expedition and Navigator models

or damage may occur to the camshaft or camshaft phaser unit.

✳✳ CAUTION

Damage to the camshaft phaser sprocket assembly will occur if mishandled or used as a lifting or leveraging device.

50. Using the tool illustrated, remove the bolt and the right hand camshaft phaser sprocket assembly. Discard the camshaft phaser sprocket bolt.

51. Using tool 303-1046, remove the bolt and the left hand camshaft phaser sprocket assembly. Discard the camshaft phaser sprocket bolt.

✳✳ CAUTION

When removing the front thrust camshaft bearing cap, use care as the cap may be damaged from side loading when removing the cam unequally in height from the bearing towers.

➡ The camshaft bearing caps must be installed in their original locations. Record camshaft bearing cap locations.

52. Remove the bolts in the sequence shown and remove the right hand cylinder head front camshaft bearing cap and then the remaining bearing caps.

53. Clean and inspect the right hand camshaft bearing caps.

54. The camshaft front thrust bearing cap contains an oil metering groove. Make sure the groove is free of foreign material.

55. Remove the right hand camshaft.

56. Remove the bolts in the sequence shown and remove the left hand cylinder head front camshaft bearing cap and then the remaining bearing caps.

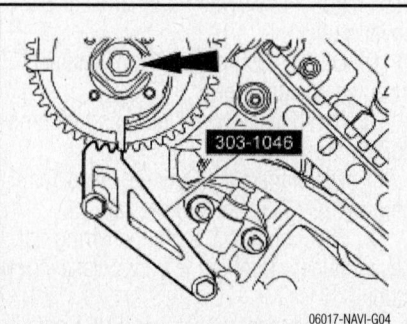

06017-NAVI-G04

Fig. 110 Remove the bolt and the right hand camshaft phaser sprocket assembly—2005–07 Expedition and Navigator models

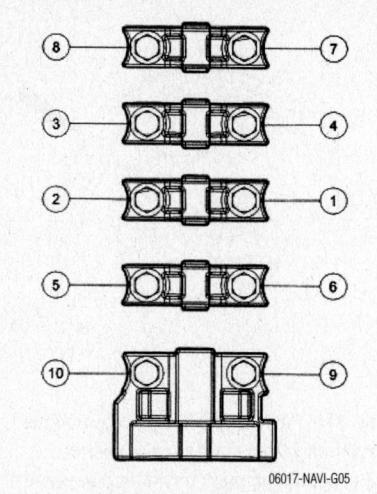

Fig. 111 Right side bearing cap removal and tightening sequence, left side similar—2005–07 Expedition and Navigator models

57. Clean and inspect the left hand camshaft bearing caps.

58. The camshaft front thrust bearing cap contains an oil metering groove. Make sure the groove is free of foreign material.

59. Remove the left hand camshaft.

✳✳ CAUTION

If the components are to be reinstalled, they must be installed in the same positions. Mark the components for installation into the original locations.

60. Remove the all of the remaining roller followers from the cylinder heads.

61. Remove the hydraulic lash adjusters from the cylinder heads.

62. Install the tool illustrated onto the cylinder head.

63. Remove the exhaust manifold. Discard the gasket.

64. Remove the stud bolt and the coolant tube. Discard the O-ring seals.

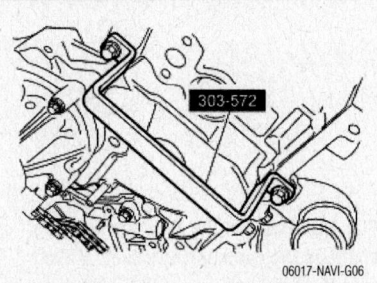

Fig. 112 Install the tool illustrated onto the left or right hand cylinder head—2005–07 Expedition and Navigator models

✳✳ CAUTION

The cylinder head must be cool before removing it from the engine. Cylinder head warpage can result if a warm or hot cylinder head is removed.

✳✳ CAUTION

Place clean shop towels over exposed engine cavities. Carefully remove the towels so foreign material is not dropped into the engine.

✳✳ CAUTION

The cylinder head bolts must be discarded and new bolts must be installed. They are tighten-to-yield designed and cannot be reused.

✳✳ CAUTION

Do not use metal scrapers, wire brushes, power abrasive discs or other abrasive means to clean the sealing surfaces. These tools cause scratches and gouges that make leak paths. Use a plastic scraping tool to remove all traces of the head gasket.

✳✳ CAUTION

Aluminum surfaces are soft and can be scratched easily. Never place the cylinder head gasket surface, unprotected, on a bench surface.

65. Remove the bolts and the cylinder head.

66. Discard the cylinder head gasket and bolts.

To install:

✳✳ CAUTION

Make sure all coolant residue and foreign material are cleaned from the block surface and cylinder bore.

✳✳ CAUTION

The use of sealing aids (aviation cement, copper spray, and glue) is not permitted. The gasket must be installed dry.

➡Do not turn the crankshaft until instructed to do so.

67. Position the cylinder head gaskets and cylinder heads over the dowels and install the cylinder head bolts loosely.

68. Tighten the bolts in three steps, in the sequence shown as follows:
   a. Step 1: Tighten to 30 ft. lbs. (40 Nm).
   b. Step 2: Tighten an additional 90 degrees.
   c. Step 3: Tighten an additional 90 degrees.

69. Remove the tool from the left hand cylinder head.

70. Lubricate the hydraulic lash adjusters with clean engine oil prior to installation.

71. Install the hydraulic lash adjusters into the left hand cylinder head.

72. Using a new gasket, install the exhaust manifold.

73. Install the coolant tube and the stud bolt.

74. Lubricate the camshaft and camshaft journals with clean engine oil prior to installation.

75. Install the left hand and right hand camshafts.

76. Install the left hand and right hand camshaft bearing caps in their original locations.

77. Lubricate the camshaft bearing caps with clean engine oil.

78. Install the camshaft bearing cap. Position the remaining camshaft bearing caps. Install the bolts loosely, then tighten to 89 inch lbs. (10 Nm).

✳✳ CAUTION

Damage to the camshaft phaser sprocket assembly will occur if mishandled or used as a lifting or leveraging device.

79. Install the camshaft phaser sprockets and new camshaft phaser bolts finger tight.

✳✳ CAUTION

Only use hand tools to remove the camshaft phaser sprocket assembly or damage may occur to the camshaft or camshaft phaser unit.

80. Using tool 303-1046, tighten the left hand and right hand camshaft phaser sprocket bolts in 2 steps:
   a. Step 1: Tighten to 30 ft. lbs. (40 Nm).
   b. Step 2: Tighten an additional 90 degrees.

✳✳ CAUTION

Timing chain procedures must be followed exactly or damage to valves and pistons will result.

❋❋ CAUTION

Prior to installation, inspect the tensioner-sealing bead for seal integrity. If cracks, tears, separation from the tensioner body or permanent compression of the seal bead is observed, install a new tensioner.

81. Compress the tensioner plunger, using a vise.

82. Install a retaining clip on the tensioner to hold the plunger in during installation.

83. Remove the tensioner from the vise.

84. If the copper links are not visible, mark two links on one end and one link on the other end, and use as timing marks.

85. Install the crankshaft sprocket, making sure the flange faces forward.

86. Install the 4 bolts and the left hand and right hand timing chain guides. Tighten to 89 inch lbs. (10 Nm).

87. Position the lower end of the left hand (inner) timing chain on the crankshaft sprocket, aligning the timing mark on the outer flange of the crankshaft sprocket with the single copper (marked) link on the chain.

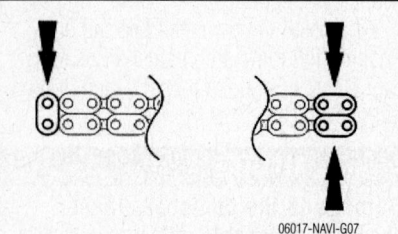

Fig. 113 If the copper links are not visible, mark two links on one end and one link on the other end, and use as timing marks—2005–07 Expedition and Navigator models

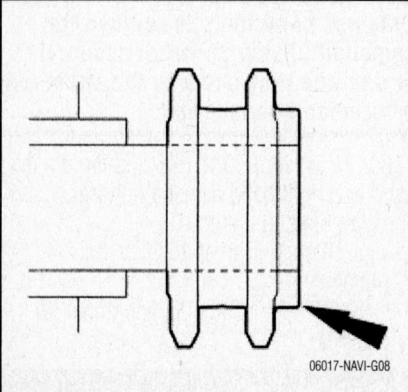

Fig. 114 Install the crankshaft sprocket, making sure the flange faces forward—2005–07 Expedition and Navigator models

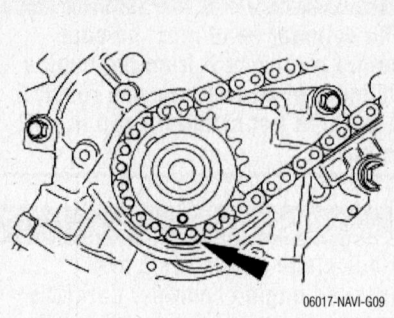

Fig. 115 Position the lower end of the left hand (inner) timing chain on the crankshaft sprocket, aligning the timing mark on the outer flange of the crankshaft sprocket with the single copper (marked) link on the chain—2005–07 Expedition and Navigator models

➡ **Make sure the upper half of the timing chain is below the tensioner arm dowel.**

88. Position the timing chain on the camshaft sprocket with the camshaft sprocket timing mark positioned between the two copper (marked) chain links.

➡ **The left hand timing chain tensioner arm has a bump near the dowel hole for identification.**

89. Position the left hand timing chain tensioner arm on the dowel pin and install the left hand timing chain tensioner and bolts. Tighten the bolts to 18 ft. lbs. (25 Nm).

90. Remove the retaining clip from the left hand timing chain tensioner.

91. Position the lower end of the right hand (outer) timing chain on the crankshaft sprocket, aligning the timing mark on the sprocket with the single copper (marked) chain link.

➡ **The lower half of the timing chain must be positioned above the tensioner arm dowel.**

92. Position the right hand timing chain on the camshaft sprocket. Make sure the camshaft sprocket timing mark is positioned between the two copper (marked) chain links.

93. Position the right hand timing chain tensioner arm on the dowel pin and install the right hand timing chain tensioner and bolts. Tighten the bolts to 18 ft. lbs. (25 Nm).

94. Remove the retaining clip from the right hand timing chain tensioner.

95. As a final-check, verify correct alignment of all timing marks.

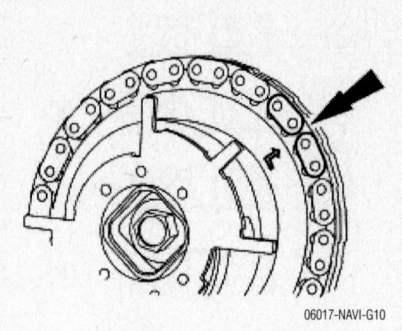

Fig. 116 Position the timing chain on the camshaft sprocket with the camshaft sprocket timing mark positioned between the two copper (marked) chain links—2005–07 Expedition and Navigator models

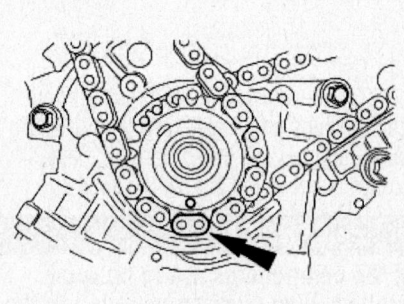

Fig. 117 Position the lower end of the right hand (outer) timing chain on the crankshaft sprocket, aligning the timing mark on the sprocket with the single copper (marked) chain link—2005–07 Expedition and Navigator models

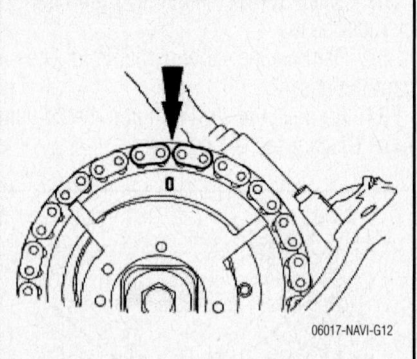

Fig. 118 Position the right hand timing chain on the camshaft sprocket. Make sure the camshaft sprocket timing mark is positioned between the two copper (marked) chain links—2005–07 Expedition and Navigator models

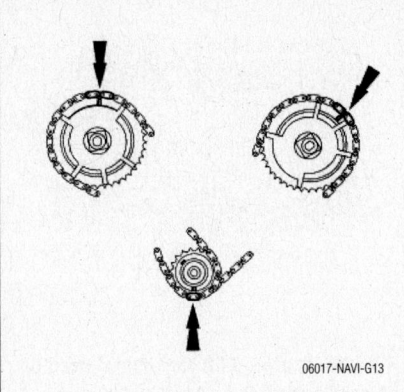

Fig. 119 Verify correct alignment of all timing marks—2005–07 Expedition and Navigator models

96. Install the crankshaft sensor ring on the crankshaft.

97. Lubricate the roller followers with clean engine oil prior to installation.

98. Using tool 303-1039, install all of the camshaft roller followers.

✳✳ CAUTION

Do not use metal scrapers, wire brushes, power abrasive discs or other abrasive means to clean the sealing surfaces. These tools cause scratches and gouges which make leak paths. Use a plastic scraping tool to remove all traces of old sealant.

➡If the engine front cover is not secured within 4 minutes, the sealant must be removed and the sealing area cleaned. To clean the sealing area, use silicone gasket remover and metal surface prep. Failure to follow this procedure can cause future oil leakage.

➡Make sure that the engine front cover gasket is in place on the engine front cover before installation.

99. Apply a bead of silicone gasket and sealant along the cylinder head-to-cylinder block surface and the oil pan-to-cylinder block surface, at the locations illustrated.

100. Install a new engine front cover gasket on the engine front cover. Position the engine front cover onto the dowels. Install the fasteners finger-tight.

101. Tighten the engine front cover fasteners in sequence in 2 steps:

   a. Step 1: Tighten fasteners 1 through 15 to 18 ft. lbs. (25 Nm).

   b. Step 2: Tighten fasteners 6 and 7 to 35 ft. lbs. (48 Nm).

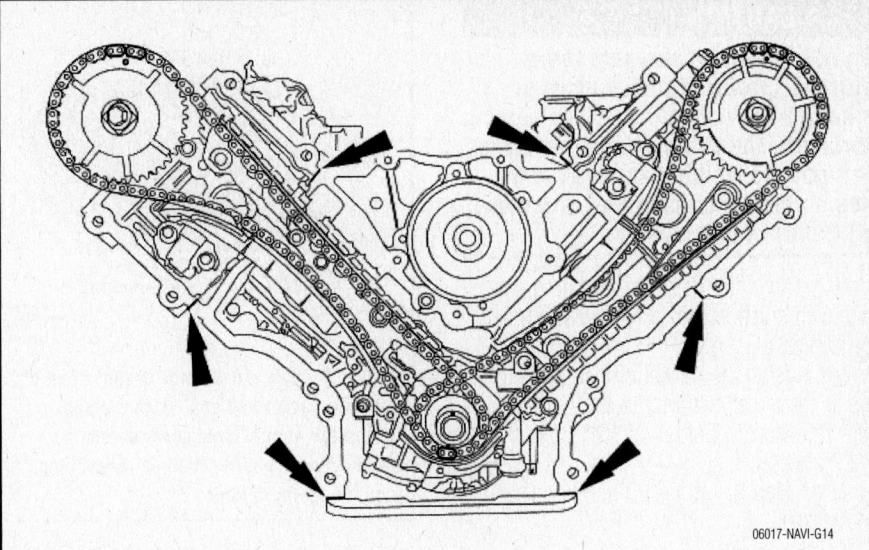

Fig. 120 Apply a bead of silicone gasket and sealant along the cylinder head-to-cylinder block surface and the oil pan-to-cylinder block surface, at the locations shown—2005–07 Expedition and Navigator models

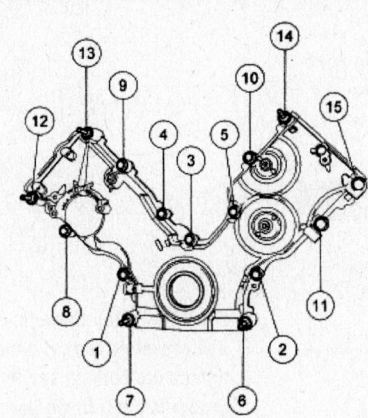

1	Bolt, Hex Flange Head Pilot, M8 x 1.25 x 50
2	Bolt, Hex Flange Head Pilot, M8 x 1.25 x 50
3	Bolt, Hex Flange Head Pilot, M8 x 1.25 x 50
4	Bolt, Hex Flange Head Pilot, M8 x 1.25 x 50
5	Bolts, Hex Flange Head Pilot, M8 x 1.25 x 50
6	Stud, Hex Head Pilot, M10 x 1.5 x 1.5 x 103
7	Stud, Hex Head Pilot, M10 x 1.5 x 1.5 x 103
8	Bolt, Hex Flange Head Pilot, M8 x 1.25 x 50
9	Bolt, Hex Flange Head Pilot, M8 x 1.25 x 50
10	Bolt, Hex Flange Head Pilot, M8 x 1.25 x 50
11	Bolt, Hex Flange Head Pilot, M8 x 1.25 x 50
12	Stud and Washer, Hex Head Pilot, M8 x 1.25 x 1.25 x 94
13	Stud and Washer, Hex Head Pilot, M8 x 1.25 x 1.25 x 94
14	Stud and Washer, Hex Head Pilot, M8 x 1.25 x 1.25 x 94
15	Bolt, Hex Head Pilot, M8 x 1.25 x 56

Fig. 121 Engine front cover fastener location and torque sequence—2005–07 Expedition and Navigator models

✳✳ CAUTION

Do not use metal scrapers, wire brushes, power abrasive discs or other abrasive means to clean sealing surfaces. These tools cause scratches and gouges which make leak paths. Use a plastic scraping tool to remove all traces of old sealant.

102. Clean the valve cover mating surface with silicone gasket remover and metal surface prep.

103. Install the 4 front oil pan bolts in the sequence shown in 2 steps.

    a. Step 1: Tighten to 15 ft. lbs. (20 Nm).

    b. Step 2: Tighten an additional 60 degrees.

➡If not secured within 4 minutes, the sealant must be removed and the sealing area cleaned. To clean the sealing area, use silicone gasket remover and metal surface prep. Failure to follow this procedure can cause future oil leakage.

104. Apply a 0.32 inch (8mm) bead of silicone gasket and sealant in 2 places where the engine front cover meets the cylinder head.

✳✳ CAUTION

When installing the valve cover, make sure to avoid damaging the Variable Camshaft Timing (VCT) solenoid.

105. Install the right hand valve cover and gasket on the cylinder head and tighten the bolts in the sequence shown and tighten to 89 inch lbs. (10 Nm).

➡If not secured within 4 minutes, the sealant must be removed and the sealing area cleaned. To clean the sealing

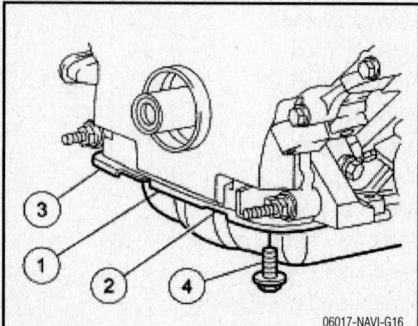

Fig. 122 Front oil pan bolts torque sequence—2005–07 Expedition and Navigator models

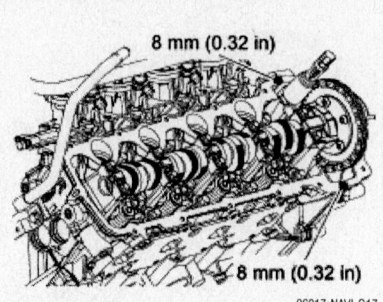

Fig. 123 Apply a 0.32 inch (8mm) bead of silicone gasket and sealant in 2 places where the engine front cover meets the right cylinder head—2005–07 Expedition and Navigator models

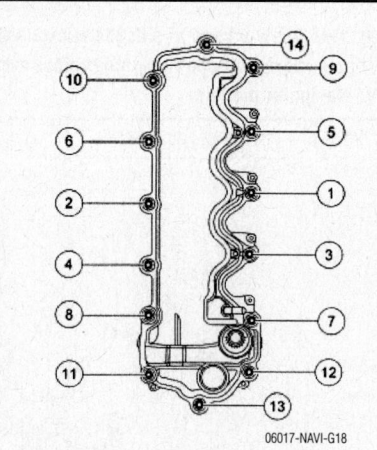

Fig. 124 Install the right hand valve cover and gasket on the cylinder head and tighten the bolts in sequence—2005–07 Expedition and Navigator models

area, use silicone gasket remover and metal surface prep. Failure to follow this procedure can cause future oil leakage.

106. Apply a 0.32 inch (8mm) bead of silicone gasket and sealant in 2 places where the engine front cover meets the left cylinder head.

107. Install the left hand valve cover and gasket on the cylinder head and tighten the bolts in the sequence shown and tighten to 89 inch lbs. (10 Nm).

108. Lubricate the engine front cover and the crankshaft seal inner lip with clean engine oil.

109. Use the tools illustrated to install the crankshaft seal into the engine front cover.

➡If not secured within 4 minutes, the sealant must be removed and the sealing area cleaned. To clean the sealing

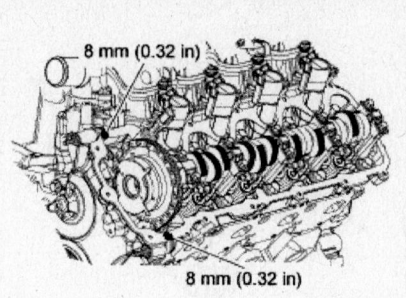

Fig. 125 Apply a 0.32 inch (8mm) bead of silicone gasket and sealant in 2 places where the engine front cover meets the left cylinder head—2005–07 Expedition and Navigator models

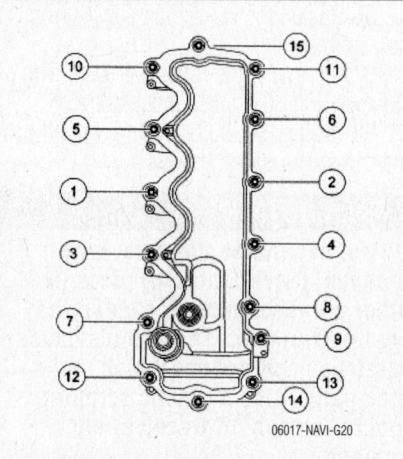

Fig. 126 Install the left hand valve cover and gasket on the cylinder head and tighten the bolts in sequence—2005–07 Expedition and Navigator models

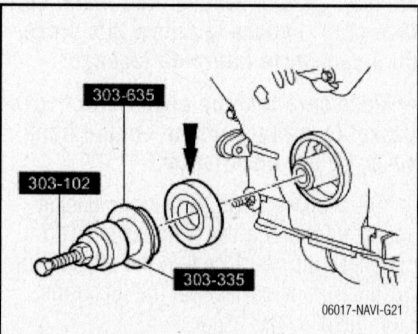

Fig. 127 Install the crankshaft seal into the engine front cover—2005–07 Expedition and Navigator models

area, use silicone gasket remover and metal surface prep. Failure to follow this procedure can cause future oil leakage.

110. Apply a 0.32 inch (8mm) bead of silicone gasket and sealant to the Woodruff key slot on the crankshaft pulley.

111. Use the tool illustrated to install the crankshaft pulley.

112. Tighten the new crankshaft pulley bolt in 4 steps

    a. Step 1: Tighten to 66 ft. lbs. (90 Nm).

    b. Step 2: Loosen 360 degrees.

    c. Step 3: Tighten to 37 ft. lbs. (50 Nm).

    d. Step 4: Tighten an additional 90 degrees.

➡**Lubricate the new O-ring seal with clean engine oil prior to installation.**

113. Install the left hand CMP sensor and the bolt.

➡**Lubricate the new O-ring seal with clean engine oil prior to installation.**

114. Install the right hand CMP sensor and the bolt.

115. Install the CKP sensor and the bolt.

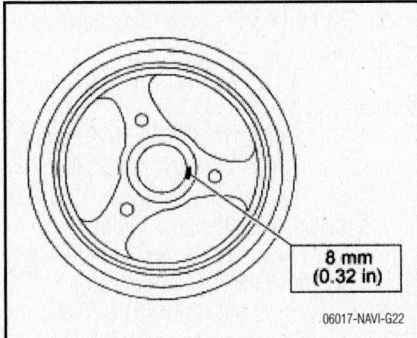

06017-NAVI-G22

Fig. 128 Apply a 0.32 inch (8mm) bead of silicone gasket and sealant to the Woodruff key slot on the crankshaft pulley—2005–07 Expedition and Navigator models

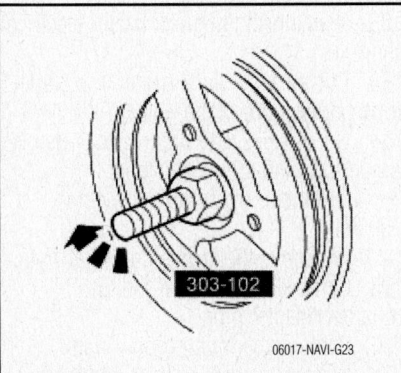

06017-NAVI-G23

Fig. 129 Install the crankshaft pulley—2005–07 Expedition and Navigator models

116. Install the accessory drive belt tensioner and install the 3 bolts. Tighten the bolts to 18 ft. lbs. (25 Nm).

117. Install the 3 accessory drive belt idler pulleys, the coolant pump pulley and the 7 bolts. Tighten the bolts to 18 ft. lbs. (25 Nm).

118. Position the electrical harness on the engine assembly and connect the engine wiring harness retainers to the valve cover studs.

119. Connect the CKP sensor connector.

120. Install the 8 ignition coils and the 8 bolts.

121. Connect the 4 left hand ignition coil connectors.

122. Install the left hand radio ignition interference capacitor and the stud bolt. Tighten the bolt to 18 ft. lbs. (25 Nm).

123. Connect the left hand CMP sensor connector.

124. Connect the engine oil pressure sensor connector.

125. Connect the left hand VCT solenoid connector.

126. Connect the 2 engine wiring harness retainers to the left hand valve cover studs.

127. Connect the CHT sensor connector.

128. Connect the 4 right hand ignition coil connectors.

129. Connect the connector retainer to the coolant tube.

130. Connect the 2 engine wiring harness retainers to the right hand valve cover studs.

131. Connect the right hand VCT solenoid connector.

132. Install the right hand radio ignition interference capacitor and the stud bolt. Tighten the bolt to 18 ft. lbs. (25 Nm).

133. Connect the right hand CMP sensor connector.

134. Using a suitable floor crane, remove the engine from the engine stand.

135. Install the flexplate and the 8 bolts in a star pattern. Tighten the bolts to 59 ft. lbs. (80 Nm).

136. Install the engine.

ENGINE ASSEMBLY

REMOVAL & INSTALLATION

Excursion

5.4L & 6.8L Engines

1. Before servicing the vehicle, refer to the precautions section.

2. Disconnect the negative battery cable.

3. Remove the hood.

4. Drain the cooling system.

5. Remove the radiator grille supports.

6. Remove the radiator.

7. Recover the A/C system refrigerant.

8. Remove the condenser.

9. Disconnect the two 42 pin and 16 ping connectors.

10. Remove the intake manifold.

11. Remove the lower radiator hose from the oil water cooler outlet.

12. Remove the power steering pump and set aside.

13. Disconnect the A/C cycling switch.

14. Disconnect the A/C compressor electrical connector.

15. Disconnect the suction hose at the accumulator.

16. Disconnect the heater hoses at the heater core.

17. Disconnect the Heated Oxygen Sensor (HO2S) electrical connectors.

18. Remove the bolts and position the A/C compressor aside.

19. Remove the exhaust pipe.

20. Remove the transmission and clutch, if equipped with a manual transmission.

21. Drain the oil and remove the bypass filter.

22. Loosen the threaded shaft and position the oil cooler aside.

23. Remove the starter, if equipped with an automatic transmission.

24. Remove the transmission cooler hoses from the block bracket, if equipped with an automatic transmission.

25. Remove the stud bolt and position the ground strap aside.

26. Remove the nut and position the wiring bracket aside.

27. Remove the flywheel inspection cover, if equipped with an automatic transmission.

28. Remove the access plug, if equipped with an automatic transmission.

29. Remove the torque converter nuts, if equipped with an automatic transmission.

30. Support the transmission, using a block of wood and a floor jack, if equipped with an automatic transmission.

31. Remove the four lower transmission-to-engine bolts, if equipped with an automatic transmission.

32. Remove the nut retaining the ground strap, and on automatic transmission equipped vehicles remove the transmission oil filler tube.

33. Remove the two studs and the heater water tube.

34. Remove the three upper transmission to engine bolts, if equipped with an automatic transmission.

35. Install modular engine lifting bar 303-F047 tool.

36. Remove the engine support insulator nuts.

37. Support the transmission using a transmission jack, if equipped with an automatic transmission.

38. Remove the engine from the vehicle.

To install:

39. Install the engine in the vehicle.

40. Install the engine support insulator nuts and tighten to 66 ft. lbs. (90 Nm).

41. Remove modular engine lifting bar 303-F047 tool.

42. Install the transmission oil level tube, and the ground strap on all vehicles equipped with an automatic transmission.

43. Install the heater water tube and the two studs and tighten to 30 ft. lbs. (40 Nm) on 5.4L and 2005 6.8L engines and 15–22 ft. lbs. (20–30 Nm) on 2001–04 6.8L engines.

44. Align the transmission to the engine and install the five lower transmission-to-engine bolts. Tighten to 35 ft. lbs. (48 Nm), if equipped with an automatic transmission.

45. Install and tighten the four new nuts retaining the torque converter to 26 ft. lbs. (35 Nm) , if equipped with an automatic transmission.

46. Install the access plug, if equipped with an automatic transmission.

47. Install the flywheel inspection cover, if equipped with an automatic transmission.

48. Install the wiring bracket and tighten to 18 ft. lbs. (25 Nm).

49. Install the starter motor, if equipped with an automatic transmission.

✳✳ CAUTION

A new oil cooler must be installed or severe damage to the engine can occur.

50. Install the oil cooler to the oil filter adapter and install the oil bypass filter. Tighten to 43 ft. lbs. (58 Nm).

51. Install the clutch and transmission, if equipped with a manual transmission.

52. Tighten the exhaust pipe nuts to 30 ft. lbs. (40 Nm).

53. Install the A/C compressor.

54. Install the ground strap.

55. Install the transmission cooler line bracket, if equipped with an automatic transmission and tighten to 18 ft. lbs. (25 Nm).

56. Install the remaining transmission-to-engine bolts, tighten to 35 ft. lbs. (48 Nm), if equipped with an automatic transmission.

57. Install the fuel line bracket.

58. Connect the transmission wiring harness

59. Connect the HO2S electrical connectors.

60. Connect the heater hose.

61. Install the suction line to the accumulator.

62. Connect the A/C cycling switch.

63. Connect the A/C compressor clutch connector.

64. Connect the lower radiator hose to the oil cooler inlet.

65. Install the power steering pump and tighten to 18 ft. lbs. (25 Nm).

66. Install the intake manifold.

67. Connect the 42-pin and 16-pin connectors.

68. Install the condenser.

69. Install the radiator and engine cooling fan.

70. Install the radiator grille supports.

71. Install the engine air cleaner.

72. Fill the engine with clean engine oil.

✳✳ CAUTION

The oil pump must be primed prior to starting the engine.

73. Connect the negative battery cable.

74. Fill the engine cooling system.

75. Fill the power steering system.

76. Recharge the A/C system.

77. Install the hood.

6.0L Diesel Engine

1. Before servicing the vehicle, refer to the precautions in the beginning of this section.

2. With the vehicle in NEUTRAL, position it on a hoist.

3. Disconnect the left hand and right hand battery ground cables.

4. On vehicles with manual transmission perform the following steps:

➡**On vehicles equipped with manual transmissions, the transmission must be removed before the engine can be removed.**

  e. Remove the transmission.
  f. Remove the clutch.

5. Remove the air cleaner assembly.

6. Remove the radiator.

7. Remove the charge air cooler.

8. Remove the A/C condenser assembly.

9. Remove the parking lamp and the headlamp assemblies.

10. Remove the radiator grille, the radiator grille opening panel, and the upper radiator core supports.

11. Remove the front bumper.

12. Disconnect the transmission cooler hoses.

13. Remove the bolts and the transmission oil cooler.

14. Remove the bolts and position the power steering cooler out of the way.

15. Remove the intake manifold.

16. Disconnect the heater hose at the coolant pump.

17. Remove the battery cable cover.

18. Remove the nut and position the cable out of the way.

19. Remove the clips and disconnect the fuel lines.

20. Remove the lower radiator hose clamp and the hose.

21. Remove the power steering upper mounting bolts.

➡**The power steering bolts must be removed evenly.**

22. Remove the bolts and position the power steering pump out of the way.

23. Remove the bolt and the left side ground cable.

24. Remove the nut and the battery cable bracket.

25. Remove the ground stud and the ground cable.

26. Disconnect the glow plug electrical connectors.

27. On vehicles with A/C perform the following steps:

  a. Disconnect the A/C high pressure switch and the A/C clutch electrical connectors.

  b. Disconnect the air conditioning manifold lines from the A/C compressor.

  c. Remove the A/C compressor.

28. Disconnect the Crankshaft Position (CKP) sensor electrical connector.

29. On vehicles with automatic transmission, remove the automatic transmission fluid indicator and tube.

30. Remove the ground strap at the back of the right head.

31. Remove the solenoid cap and disconnect the starter wiring.

32. Disconnect the block heater electrical connector.

33. Position the block heater and starter wiring harness out of the way.

34. On vehicles with automatic transmission perform the following steps:

  a. Remove the torque converter cover.

  b. Remove the torque converter nuts.

35. Remove the bolts for the turbocharger adapter pipe.

36. Remove the motor mount nuts.

37. Loosen the nuts at the turbocharger adapter pipe flange.

38. On vehicles with automatic transmission, remove the nine bell housing bolts.

39. Remove the turbocharger adapter pipe.

40. Remove the fuel injection control module mounting bolts for access to the module electrical connectors.

41. Disconnect the electrical connectors and remove the fuel injection control module.

42. Remove the nuts and the fuel injection control module bracket.

43. Remove the left rear valve cover stud.

44. Remove the transmission cooler line bracket.

45. Secure the turbocharger outlet pipe.

46. Remove the manufacturer's lifting eye.

47. Install the engine lifting eye 303-D043-02 on the right hand cylinder head.

48. Install the front lifting brackets 303-D043-01.

49. On vehicles with automatic transmission, position a suitable jack under the transmission.

50. Install the Heavy Duty Floor Crane and Diesel Engine Lifting Bracket on the engine.

51. Raise the engine high enough to clear the No. 1 crossmember and pull the engine forward and clear of the vehicle.

To install:

52. With the vehicle in NEUTRAL, position it on a hoist.

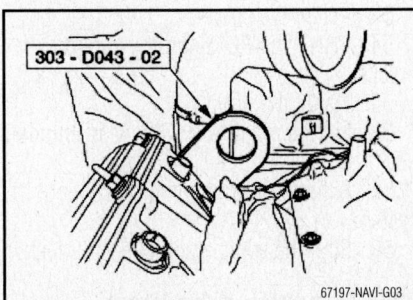

Fig. 130 Install the engine lifting eye 303-D043-02 on the right hand cylinder head—6.0L engine

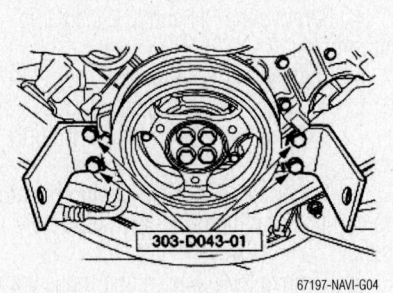

Fig. 131 Install the front lifting brackets 303-D043-01—6.0L engine

53. Raise the engine high enough to clear the No. 1 crossmember, then position the engine into the vehicle.

54. On vehicles with automatic transmission, align the torque converter studs with the holes in the engine flywheel, then lower the engine onto the engine mount towers.

55. On vehicles with manual transmission, lower the engine onto the engine mount towers.

56. Remove the Heavy Duty Floor Crane and the Diesel Engine Lifting Bracket.

57. On vehicles with automatic transmission perform the following steps:

a. Remove the transmission jack.

b. Install the transmission-to-engine mounting bolts and tighten to 35 ft. lbs. (47 Nm).

c. Install the torque converter-to-flywheel retaining nuts and tighten to 26 ft. lbs. (35 Nm).

d. Install the flywheel housing cover.

58. Install the left hand and right hand side engine mount retaining nuts and tighten to 76 ft. lbs. (103 Nm).

59. Remove the engine lifting eye from the right side cylinder head.

60. Install the manufacturer's lifting bracket.

61. Remove the two engine lift adapters.

62. Position the turbocharger outlet pipe.

63. Install the transmission cooler tube bracket and nut and tighten to 89 inch lbs. (10 Nm).

64. Install the left rear valve cover stud and tighten to 71 inch lbs. (8 Nm).

65. Install the fuel injection control module bracket and nuts and tighten to 71 inch lbs. (8 Nm).

66. Connect the fuel injection control module electrical connectors and position the module on the bracket.

67. Install the fuel injection control module bolts and nuts and tighten to 10 ft. lbs. (13 Nm).

68. Position the turbocharger adapter pipe.

69. Install the bolts for the turbocharger adapter pipe but do not tighten bolts at this time.

70. Position back the block heater and starter wiring.

71. Connect the block heater electrical connector.

72. Connect the starter wiring and install the solenoid cap.

73. Connect the ground strap on the right head and install the bolt and tighten to 89 inch lbs. (10 Nm).

74. On vehicles with automatic transmission, install the automatic transmission

fluid indicator and tube and tighten to 71 inch lbs. (8 Nm).

75. Connect the CKP sensor electrical connector.

76. On vehicles with A/C perform the following steps:

a. Install the A/C compressor and tighten the bolts to 18 ft. lbs. (25 Nm).

b. Position the A/C compressor manifold and install the bolt and tighten to 15 ft. lbs. (21 Nm).

c. Connect the A/C high pressure switch and the clutch electrical connectors.

77. Connect the glow plug module electrical connectors.

78. Connect the ground cable and the ground stud and tighten to 35 ft. lbs. (47 Nm).

79. Install the battery cable bracket and the nut and tighten to 35 ft. lbs. (47 Nm).

80. Install the ground cable and bolt onto the left side of the engine block and tighten to 35 ft. lbs. (47 Nm).

81. Position the power steering pump and install the lower bolts and tighten to 18 ft. lbs. (25 Nm).

➡ **The lower bolts need to be installed evenly.**

82. Install the power steering pump upper bolts and tighten to 18 ft. lbs. (25 Nm).

83. Install the lower radiator hose and clamp.

84. Connect the fuel lines and install the clips.

85. Connect the battery crossover cable and tighten to 9 ft. lbs. (12 Nm).

86. Install the battery cable cover.

87. Connect the heater hose at the coolant pump.

88. Install the intake manifold.

89. Tighten the turbocharger adapter pipe at the flanges to 20 ft. lbs. (27 Nm).

90. Install the power steering cooler and bolts and tighten to 8 ft. lbs. (11 Nm).

91. Install the transmission oil cooler and tighten to 71 inch lbs. (8 Nm).

92. Connect the transmission cooler hoses.

93. Install the bumper.

94. Install the upper radiator core support, radiator grill opening panel and the radiator grill.

95. Install the headlamp and the parking lamp assemblies.

96. On vehicles with A/C, install the A/C condenser assembly.

97. Install the charge air cooler.

98. Install the radiator.

99. Install the air cleaner assembly.

100. On vehicles with manual transmission perform the following steps:

   a. Install the clutch assembly.

   b. Install the transmission.

101. Fill the cooling system.

102. Fill the motor with clean engine oil.

103. Connect the left and right hand battery cables.

104. Check and fill the automatic transmission, if equipped.

2005–06 Expedition & Navigator

1. Before servicing the vehicle, refer to the precautions section.

2. Disconnect the negative battery cable.

3. Remove the radiator.

4. Remove the intake manifold.

5. Remove the accessory drive belt.

6. Remove the Powertrain Control Module (PCM) and the support bracket.

7. Remove the starter.

8. Remove the hood.

9. Disconnect the heater hose.

10. Disconnect the degas bottle coolant hose.

11. If equipped, disconnect the block heater electrical connector.

12. Remove the power steering reservoir and support bracket lower bolt.

13. Remove the nut and position the power steering reservoir and support bracket aside.

14. Remove the bolts and position the power steering pump aside.

15. Disconnect the A/C compressor electrical connector.

16. Remove the bolts and position the A/C compressor aside.

17. Remove the nut and the transmission cooler tube support bracket.

18. Remove the nut and the power steering pressure hose support bracket.

19. Remove the bolt and the starter electrical harness support bracket.

20. Remove the bolts and the flexplate inspection cover.

21. Remove the cylinder block opening cover.

22. Remove the torque converter-to-flexplate nuts and discard the nuts.

➡**The upper 2 transmission-to-engine bolts will be removed later.**

23. Remove the lower 5 transmission-to-engine bolts.

24. Disconnect the Heated Oxygen (HO2S) sensor connectors.

25. Remove the 4 exhaust manifold flange nuts.

✳✳ CAUTION

Only use hand tools when removing the engine mount nut or damage to the engine mount can occur.

26. Remove the right hand engine mount nut.

➡**If the left hand engine mount through bolt nut is missing or damaged install a new nut using service part number W709375. If the left hand engine mount through bolt nut cage is damaged or missing, remove the cage and install a new nut using service part number W520516-S301.**

27. Remove the left hand engine mount through bolt.

28. Remove the upper 2 transmission-to-engine bolts and install the engine support tool 303-F047.

29. Using a suitable floor crane, remove the engine assembly from the vehicle.

To install:

30. Using a suitable floor crane, position the engine assembly into the vehicle.

31. Remove the engine support tool 303-F047.

✳✳ CAUTION

Only use hand tools when installing the left hand engine mount through bolt or damage to the cage nut can occur.

➡**If the left hand engine mount through bolt nut is missing or damaged install a new nut using service part number W709375. If the left hand engine mount through bolt nut cage is damaged or missing, remove the cage and install a new nut using service part number W520516-S301.**

32. Install and the left and right hand engine mount through bolts and tighten to 129 ft. lbs. (175 Nm).

➡**Align the engine-to-transmission dowels before installing the engine-to-transmission bolts.**

33. Install the lower 5 transmission-to-engine bolts and tighten to 35 ft. lbs. (48 Nm).

34. Install the 4 exhaust manifold-to-catalytic converter nuts and tighten to 30 ft. lbs. (40 Nm).

35. Connect the HO2S connectors.

36. Install the torque converter-to-nuts and tighten to 26 ft. lbs. (35 Nm).

37. Install the cylinder block opening cover.

38. Install the flexplate inspection cover and the 2 bolts and tighten to 26 ft. lbs. (35 Nm).

39. Install the starter wiring harness support bracket and bolt.

40. Install the upper two transmission-to-engine bolt and tighten to 35 ft. lbs. (48 Nm).

41. Install the transmission cooler tube support bracket and the nut.

42. Position the power steering pump and install the 3 bolts and tighten to 18 ft. lbs. (25 Nm).

43. Install the power steering pump support bracket and the nut.

44. Install the power steering reservoir and support bracket and install the bolt. Tighten to 18 ft. lbs. (25 Nm).

45. Install the power steering reservoir and support bracket nut. Tighten to 18 ft. lbs. (25 Nm).

46. Install the A/C compressor and install the 3 bolts. Tighten to 18 ft. lbs. (25 Nm).

47. Connect the A/C compressor electrical connector.

48. Connect the degas bottle coolant hose.

49. If equipped, connect the block heater electrical connector.

50. Connect the heater coolant hose.

51. Install the intake manifold.

52. Install the radiator.

53. Install the starter.

54. Install the PCM and the support bracket.

55. Install the hood.

56. Fill the crankcase with clean engine oil.

57. Fill and bleed the engine cooling system.

58. Start the vehicle and check for leaks.

2007 Expedition & Navigator

See Figure 132.

1. Disconnect the negative battery cable.

2. Drain and the engine coolant.

3. Recover A/C system refrigerant.

4. Remove the RH and LH headlamp assemblies.

5. Remove the front fascia.

6. Remove the cooling fan shroud.

7. Remove the 2 hood latch assembly bolts.

8. Disconnect the cable position retainers and position the hood latch assembly aside.

9. Remove the pushpin and move the air deflector aside.

10. Remove the transmission cooler tube secondary latches.

11. Using the quick disconnect tool 307-309, disconnect the transmission fluid cooler tubes from the transmission fluid cooler hoses.

12. Remove the 2 condenser inlet fitting nuts and disconnect the 2 fittings.

Expedition vehicles

13. Disconnect the horn electrical connector.

Navigator vehicles

14. Disconnect the electrical connector and remove the bolt and the horn assembly

All vehicles

15. Disconnect the ambient temperature sensor electrical connector.

16. Remove the 6 radiator support bolts and remove the cooling module from the vehicle.

17. Remove the bypass tube.

18. If servicing the engine on a four wheel drive (4WD) vehicle, remove the front drive shaft.

19. Remove the starter.

20. Remove the accessory drive belt.

21. Remove the nut and the ground cable and disconnect the wiring harness retainer.

22. Disconnect the Powertrain Control Module (PCM) electrical connector.

23. Remove the bolt and the ground cable.

24. If equipped, disconnect the 2 auxiliary heat coolant hose quick connect couplings.

25. Disconnect the heater coolant hose quick connect coupling.

26. Disconnect and remove the 2 heater coolant hose quick connect couplings.

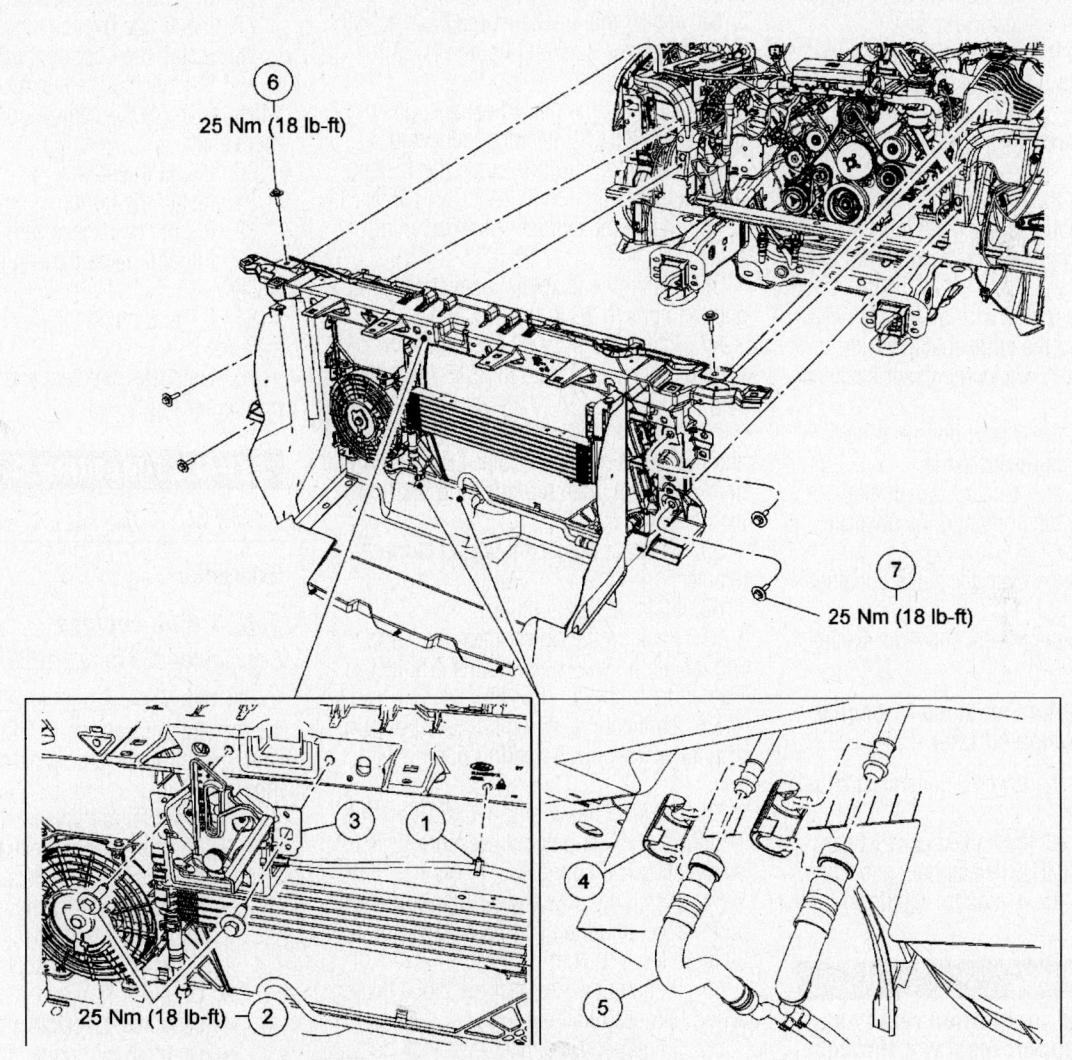

1. Hood latch assembly cable retainer
2. Hood latch assembly bolts (2 required)
3. Hood latch assembly
4. Transmission fluid cooler tube secondary latches (2 required)
5. Transmission fluid cooler tube (2 required)
6. Cooling module upper bolt (2 required)
7. Cooling module front bolt (4 required)

22086_EXPD_G0009

Fig. 132 Expedition & Navigator Cooling Module and related parts

27. Remove the clip and disconnect the degas bottle coolant outlet hose quick connect coupling.

28. If equipped, disconnect the block heater electrical connector.

29. If equipped, disconnect the block heater wiring harness retainers.

30. Disconnect the wiring harness position retainer from the power steering pump stud bolt.

31. Disconnect the wiring harness position retainer and the engine oil pressure (EOP) switch electrical connector and position the wiring harness aside.

32. Remove the nut and the power steering pressure tube support bracket.

33. Remove the 2 bolts, the stud bolt and position the power steering pump aside.

34. Disconnect the starter wiring harness retainer.

35. Remove the nut and remove the starter wiring harness and transmission fluid cooler tube support brackets from the nut.

36. Disconnect the wiring harness position retainer and the crankshaft position (CKP) sensor and A/C compressor electrical connectors.

37. Remove the 3 stud bolts and position the A/C compressor aside.

38. Remove and discard the oil filter.

39. Remove the bolts and the flexplate inspection cover.

40. Remove the cylinder block opening cover.

41. Remove the torque converter-to-flexplate nuts.

➡**The upper 2 transmission-to-engine bolts will be removed later.**

42. Remove the lower 5 transmission-to-engine bolts.

43. Disconnect the heated exhaust gas oxygen sensor (HO$_2$S) electrical connectors.

44. Remove the 4 exhaust manifold flange nuts.

❄❄ WARNING

Only use hand tools when removing the engine support insulator through bolts or damage to the engine support insulator-to-cylinder block bracket can occur.

45. Remove the RH and LH engine support insulator through bolts.

46. Remove the upper 2 transmission-to-engine bolts and install the special tool.

47. Using a suitable floor crane, remove the engine assembly from the vehicle.

To install:

48. Using a suitable floor crane, position the engine assembly into the vehicle.

49. Install the LH and RH engine support insulator bolts.

50. Apply Threadlock 262 to the bolt threads prior to installation and tighten to 258 ft. lbs. (350 Nm).

➡**Align the engine-to-transmission dowels before installing the engine-to-transmission bolts.**

51. Install the lower 5 transmission-to-engine bolts and tighten to 35 ft. lbs. (48 Nm).

52. Install the 4 exhaust manifold-to-catalytic converter nuts and tighten to 30 ft. lbs. (40 Nm).

53. Connect the heated exhaust gas oxygen sensor (HO$_2$S) electrical connectors.

54. Install new torque converter-to-flexplate nuts and tighten to 26 ft. lbs. (35 Nm).

55. Install the cylinder block opening cover.

56. Install the flexplate inspection cover and the bolts to 26 ft. lbs. (35 Nm).

57. Install the upper 2 transmission-to-engine bolts and tighten to 35 ft. lbs. (48 Nm).

58. Position the starter wiring harness and transmission fluid cooler tube support brackets and tighten the retaining nut to 89 inch. lbs. (10 Nm).

59. Connect the starter wiring harness retainer.

60. Install a new oil filter.

61. Position the power steering pump and install the stud bolt and the 2 bolts. Tighten to 18 ft. lbs. (25 Nm).

62. Connect the wiring harness position retainer to the power steering pump stud bolt.

63. Connect the wiring harness position retainer and the engine oil pressure (EOP) switch electrical connector.

64. Install the power steering pump support bracket and the nut. Tighten the nut to 89 inch. lbs. (10 Nm).

65. If equipped, connect the block heater wiring harness retainers.

66. If equipped, connect the block heater electrical connector.

67. Position the A/C compressor and install the 3 stud bolts. Tighten to 18 ft. lbs. (25 Nm).

68. Connect the wiring harness position retainer and the crankshaft position (CKP) sensor and A/C compressor electrical connectors.

69. Install the clip and connect the degas bottle coolant outlet hose quick connect coupling.

70. Position the ground cable and install the bolt. Tighten to 89 inch. lbs. (10 Nm).

71. Position the 2 heater coolant hoses and connect the quick connect couplings.

72. Connect the heater coolant hose quick connect coupling.

73. If equipped, connect the 2 auxiliary heat coolant hose quick connect couplings.

74. Connect the Powertrain Control Module (PCM) electrical connector.

75. Connect the wiring harness retainer and ground cable and install the nut. Tighten to 89 inch. lbs. (10 Nm).

76. Install the accessory drive belt.

77. Install the bypass tube.

78. Install the cooling module.

79. If servicing the engine on a four wheel drive (4WD) vehicle, install the front drive shaft.

80. Install the starter.

81. Install the hood.

82. Fill the crankcase with oil.

83. Fill and bleed the engine cooling system.

84. Fill and bleed the power steering system.

85. Evacuate, leak test and charge the refrigerant system.

EXHAUST MANIFOLD

REMOVAL & INSTALLATION

Excursion

5.4L & 6.8L Engines
See Figures 133 through 136.

1. Before servicing the vehicle, refer to the precautions section.

2. Remove or disconnect the following:

- Front fender splash shield
- For the left-hand exhaust manifold: the Exhaust Gas Recirculation (EGR) valve-to-exhaust manifold tube and if equipped, the DPFE gas recirculation transducer hoses.
- On the 5.4L engines: the catalytic converter-to-exhaust manifold bolts
- On the 6.8L engine: the front exhaust pipe from the manifold
- The exhaust manifold mounting nuts, then remove the exhaust manifold itself. Remove and discard the old gasket.

3. Clean and inspect the exhaust manifold for damage.

To install:

4. Position a new gasket and the exhaust manifold onto the engine block.

5. Install the mounting nuts and tighten following the sequence shown.
   • 18 ft. lbs. (25 Nm)
6. On the 6.8L engine, tighten the exhaust manifold-to-front pipe fasteners to 27–34 ft. lbs. (34–46 Nm).
7. On the 5.4L engines, attach the catalytic converter to the exhaust manifold, install the catalytic converter-to-exhaust manifold bolts and tighten to 25–34 ft. lbs. (34–46 Nm)
8. For the left-hand exhaust manifold, install the DPFE transducer hoses if

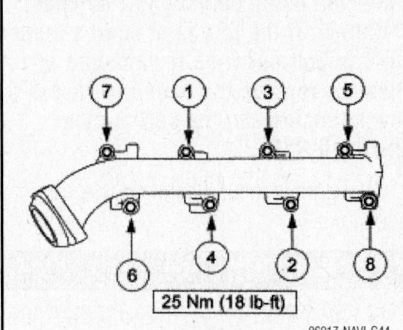

Fig. 133 Tighten the right side exhaust manifold bolts in the sequence shown

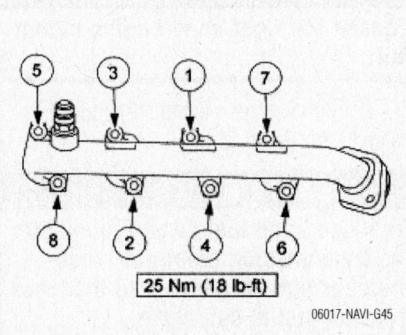

Fig. 134 Tighten the left side exhaust manifold bolts in the sequence shown

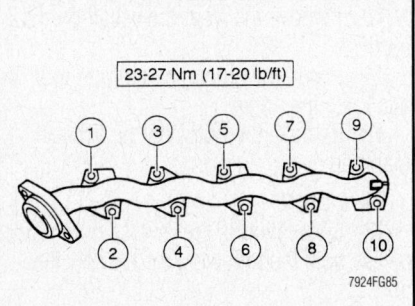

Fig. 135 Tighten the exhaust manifold bolts in the sequence shown—right side of 6.8L engine shown

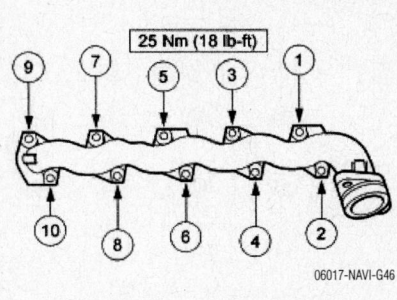

Fig. 136 Tighten the exhaust manifold bolts in the sequence shown—left side of 6.8L engine shown

equipped, and the EGR valve-to-exhaust manifold tube. Tighten the upper and lower fittings to 26–33 ft. lbs. (35–45 Nm).
9. Install the front fender splash shield.
10. Lower the vehicle to the ground.

6.0L Diesel Engine—Left Side

See Figures 137 and 138.

1. Before servicing the vehicle, refer to the precautions in the beginning of this section.
2. If equipped, remove the exhaust manifold to Exhaust Gas Recirculation (EGR) valve tube.
3. On 4WD vehicles, remove the front wheel opening molding.
4. Remove the front fender splash shield.
5. Remove the pipe-to-manifold nuts.
6. Remove the nuts and the exhaust manifold.
7. Remove the exhaust manifold gasket.
8. Clean and inspect the exhaust manifold.

To install:

9. Installation is the reverse of removal. Tighten the manifold retainers in the sequence illustrated to 18 ft. lbs. (25 Nm). If equipped, install the exhaust manifold to EGR valve tube and tighten the fasteners as shown

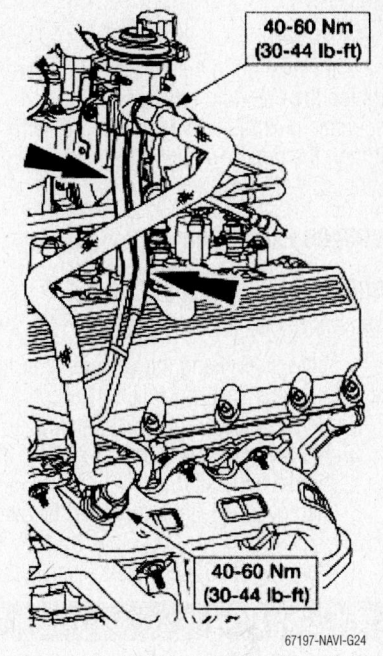

Fig. 138 If equipped, install the exhaust manifold to EGR valve tube and tighten the fasteners as specified in this illustration—6.0L engine

in the illustration. Tighten the pipe-to-manifold bolts to 27–24 ft. lbs. (34–46 Nm).

6.0L Diesel Engine—Right Side

See Figure 139.

1. Before servicing the vehicle, refer to the precautions in the beginning of this section.
2. Disconnect the battery ground cable.
3. Remove the pipe-to-manifold nuts.
4. Remove the right front wheel.
5. Remove the right front inner fender well.
6. Remove the nuts, the exhaust manifold and the gasket. Discard the gasket.

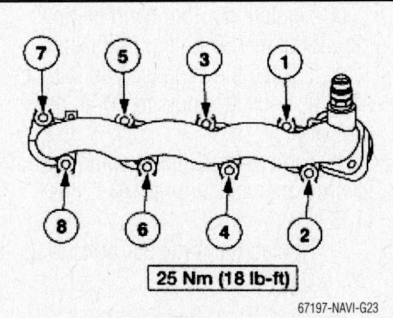

Fig. 137 Tighten the left side exhaust manifold retainers in the sequence illustrated—6.0L engine

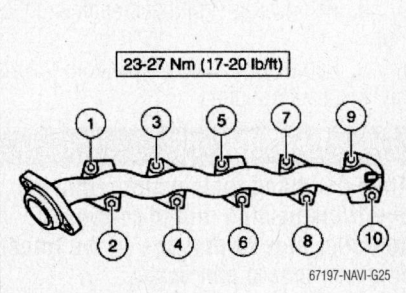

Fig. 139 Tighten the right side exhaust manifold retainers in the sequence illustrated—6.0L engine

7. Clean and inspect the exhaust manifold.

To install:

8. Installation is the reverse of removal. Tighten the manifold retainers in the sequence illustrated to 18 ft. lbs. (25 Nm). Tighten the pipe-to-manifold bolts to 27–24 ft. lbs. (34–46 Nm).

2005–06 Expedition & Navigator

Right Side

See Figure 140.

1. Before servicing the vehicle, refer to the precautions section.
2. Remove the air cleaner housing.
3. Remove the alternator.
4. Remove the starter.
5. Remove the right hand inner fender well.
6. Remove the upper radiator shroud.

> **⌷ CAUTION**
>
> **Only use hand tools when loosening the left hand engine mount through bolt or damage to the cage nut can occur.**

NOTE: If the left hand engine mount through bolt nut is missing or damaged install a new nut using service part number W709375. If the left hand engine mount through bolt nut cage is damaged or missing, remove the cage and install a new nut using service part number W520516-S301.

7. Loosen the left hand engine support insulator bolt.

> **⌷ CAUTION**
>
> **Only use hand tools when removing the right hand engine mount nut or damage to the engine mount can occur.**

8. Remove the right hand engine mount nut.
9. Remove the exhaust manifold-to-catalytic converter nuts.

> **✳✳ CAUTION**
>
> **Only use hand tools when removing the transmission mount-to-crossmember nuts or damage to the transmission mount can occur.**

10. Loosen the transmission mount-to-crossmember nuts.
11. Remove the bolts and position the sway bar down.

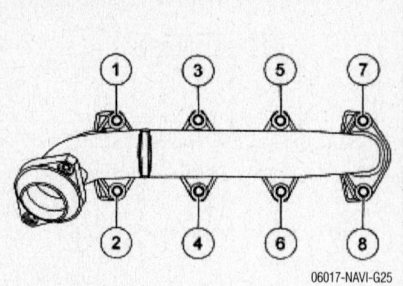

Fig. 140 Tighten the right side exhaust manifold bolts in the sequence shown—2005 Expedition and Navigator models

12. Install the and engine support tool and raise the engine.
13. Remove the nuts and the exhaust manifold.

> **✳✳ CAUTION**
>
> **Do not use metal scrapers, wire brushes, power abrasive discs, or other abrasive means to clean the sealing surfaces. These may cause scratches and gouges resulting in leak paths. Use a plastic scraper to clean the sealing surfaces.**

➡ Clean the sealing surfaces with metal surface prep. Remove and discard the exhaust manifold gaskets. Clean the sealing surfaces with metal surface prep. To install, reverse the removal procedure.

To install:

14. Installation is the reverse of removal, please note the following torque specifications:

  a. Tighten the manifold bolts in the sequence illustrated to 18 ft. lbs. (25 Nm).

  b. Tighten the left hand engine support insulator bolt to 129 ft. lbs. (175 Nm).

  c. Tighten the right hand engine mount nut to 129 ft. lbs. (175 Nm).

  d. Tighten the exhaust manifold-to-catalytic converter nuts to 30 ft. lbs. (40 Nm).

  e. Tighten the transmission mount-to-crossmember nuts to 76 ft. lbs. (103 Nm).

  f. Tighten the sway bar bolts to 22 ft. lbs. (30 Nm).

Left Side

See Figure 141.

1. Before servicing the vehicle, refer to the precautions section.

2. Remove the air cleaner housing.
3. Remove the alternator.
4. Remove the left hand inner fender well.
5. Remove the upper radiator shroud.

> **✳✳ CAUTION**
>
> **Only use hand tools when removing the left hand engine mount through bolt or damage to the cage nut can occur.**

➡ If the left hand engine mount through bolt nut is missing or damaged install a new nut using service part number W709375. If the left hand engine mount through bolt nut cage is damaged or missing, remove the cage and install a new nut using service part number W520516-S301.

6. Remove the left hand engine support insulator bolt.

> **✳✳ CAUTION**
>
> **Only use hand tools when loosening the right hand engine mount nut or damage to the engine mount can occur.**

> **✳✳ CAUTION**
>
> **Loosen the right hand engine mount nut.**

7. Remove the 4 exhaust manifold-to-catalytic converter nuts.

> **✳✳ CAUTION**
>
> **Only use hand tools when removing the transmission mount-to-crossmember nuts or damage to the transmission mount can occur.**

8. Loosen the transmission mount-to-crossmember nuts.
9. Remove the bolts and the exhaust manifold heat shield.
10. Remove the front driveshaft on 4WD models.
11. Install the an engine support tool and raise the engine.
12. Remove the nuts and the exhaust manifold.

To install:

13. Installation is the reverse of removal, please note the following torque specifications:

  a. Tighten the manifold bolts in the sequence illustrated to 18 ft. lbs. (25 Nm).

  b. Tighten the left hand engine support insulator bolt to 129 ft. lbs. (175 Nm).

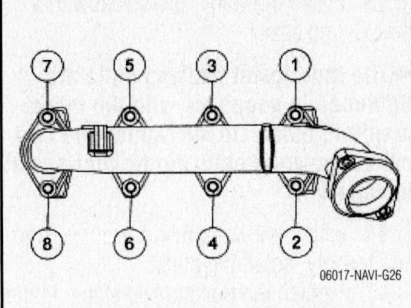

Fig. 141 Tighten the left side exhaust manifold bolts in the sequence shown— 2005 Expedition and Navigator models

c. Tighten the right hand engine mount nut to 129 ft. lbs. (175 Nm).

d. Tighten the exhaust manifold-to-catalytic converter nuts to 30 ft. lbs. (40 Nm).

e. Tighten the transmission mount-to-crossmember nuts to 76 ft. lbs. (103 Nm).

2007 Expedition & Navigator

Right Side

See Figure 142.

1. Before servicing the vehicle, refer to the precautions section.

2. With the vehicle in NEUTRAL, position it on a hoist.

3. Remove the RH inner fender well.

4. Remove the RH engine support insulator.

5. Remove the 2 bolts and the exhaust manifold heat shield.

6. Remove the 8 exhaust manifold nuts, studs and the exhaust manifold. Discard the exhaust manifold nuts and studs.

7. Remove and discard the exhaust manifold gaskets. Clean the sealing surfaces with metal surface prep.

8. Inspect the exhaust manifold.

To install:

9. Using new exhaust manifold gaskets and studs, position the 2 gaskets and exhaust manifold and install the 8 studs. Tighten the studs to 9 ft. lbs. (12 Nm).

10. Using new exhaust manifold nuts, install the 8 nuts and tighten in sequence shown to 18 ft. lbs. (25 Nm).

11. Position the exhaust manifold heat shield and install the 2 bolts. Tighten to 89 inch. lbs. (10 Nm).

12. Install the RH engine support insulator and tighten the 2 stud bolts to 11 ft. lbs. (15 Nm).

13. Tighten the RH insulator bracket bolts to 46 ft. lbs. (63 Nm).

14. Install the RH inner fender well.

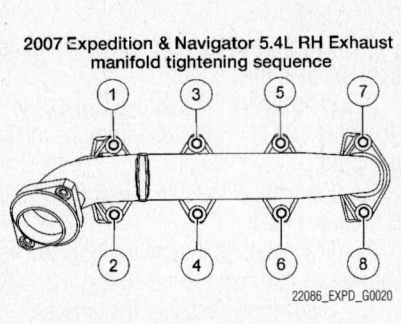

Fig. 142 RH exhaust manifold tightening sequence 2007 5.4L Engine

Left Side

See Figures 143 and 144.

1. Before servicing the vehicle, refer to the precautions section.

2. With the vehicle in NEUTRAL, position it on a hoist.

3. Remove the air cleaner outlet tube.

4. Remove the degas bottle.

☀ WARNING

Do not allow the steering column shaft to rotate while the intermediate shaft is disconnected or damage to the clock spring can result. If there is evidence that the shaft has rotated, the clockspring must be removed and recentered.

5. Remove the bolt and disconnect the steering shaft and position aside.

6. Remove the 4 (2 LH and 2 RH) exhaust manifold-to-catalytic converter nuts.

7. Remove the 3 bolts and the exhaust manifold heat shield.

8. For Four Wheel Drive (4WD) models, remove the front driveshaft.

9. Remove the 8 exhaust manifold nuts, studs and the exhaust manifold.

10. Remove and discard the exhaust manifold gaskets. Clean the sealing surfaces with metal surface prep.

11. Inspect the exhaust manifold.

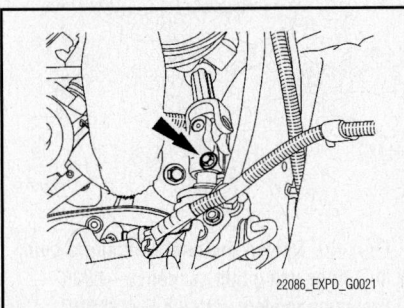

Fig. 143 Steering shaft and bolt view

To install:

12. Using new exhaust manifold gaskets and studs, position the 2 gaskets and exhaust manifold and install the 8 studs. Tighten the studs to 9 ft. lbs. (12 Nm).

13. Using new exhaust manifold nuts, install the 8 nuts and tighten in sequence shown to 18 ft. lbs. (25 Nm).

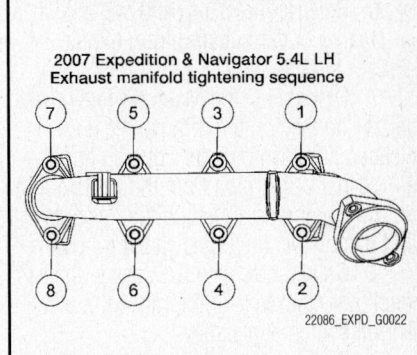

Fig. 144 LH exhaust manifold tightening sequence 2007 5.4L Engine

14. For 4WD models, install the front driveshaft.

15. Connect the steering shaft, install and tighten bolt to 22 ft. lbs. (30 Nm).

16. Install the 4 exhaust manifold-to-catalytic converter nuts.

17. Position the exhaust manifold heat shield and install the 2 bolts. Tighten to 89 inch. lbs. (10 Nm).

18. Install the degas bottle.

19. Install the air cleaner outlet tube.

INTAKE MANIFOLD

REMOVAL & INSTALLATION

Excursion

5.4L Engine

See Figure 145.

☀ CAUTION

Fuel injection systems remain under pressure, even after the engine has been turned OFF. The fuel system pressure must be relieved before disconnecting any fuel lines. Failure to do so may result in fire and/or personal injury.

➡ When the battery is disconnected and reconnected, some abnormal drive symptoms may occur while the vehicle relearns its adaptive strategy. The vehicle may need to be driven 10 miles (16 km) or more to relearn the strategy.

1. Before servicing the vehicle, refer to the precautions section.
2. Disconnect the negative battery cable.
3. Drain and recycle the engine coolant.
4. Disconnect the Idle Air Control (IAC) fresh air tube and crankcase ventilation tube from the air cleaner outlet pipe.
5. Loosen the clamp and disconnect the air cleaner outlet pipe from the throttle body.
6. Release the clamp and separate the air cleaner outlet housing from the air cleaner inlet housing.
7. Disconnect the Mass Air Flow (MAF) sensor connector and remove the air cleaner, air cleaner outlet housing and the air cleaner outlet pipe from the vehicle.
8. Compress and slide the hose clamp and disconnect the upper radiator hose.
9. On vehicles with A/C, rotate the belt tensioner clockwise and remove the belt from the alternator pulley.
10. On vehicles without A/C, rotate the belt tensioner counterclockwise and remove the belt from the alternator pulley.
11. Remove the harness routing clips from the alternator stud and the engine front cover.
12. Remove the alternator upper mounting bracket stud and bolt.
13. Remove the alternator lower mounting bolts and position the alternator aside.
14. Remove the accelerator control splash shield.
15. Disconnect the throttle body cam.
16. Disconnect the accelerator cable.
17. If equipped, disconnect the speed control cable.
18. Remove the throttle return spring.
19. Remove accelerator cable bracket the bolts and position the bracket aside.
20. Disconnect the Throttle Position (TP) sensor connector.
21. Release the IAC fresh air tube from the routing clip and remove it from the vehicle.
22. Disconnect the Evaporative Emission (EVAP) canister purge valve vacuum hose from the throttle body adapter.
23. Disconnect the brake booster vacuum hose and main vacuum harness from the throttle body adapter.
24. Disconnect the IAC connector.
25. On vehicles with an Exhaust Gas Recirculation (EGR) system, position the exhaust manifold to EGR valve tube aside.
26. Position the differential pressure feedback EGR system bracket aside.
27. Disconnect the EGR vacuum regulator solenoid connections.
28. Disconnect the EGR valve vacuum hose.
29. Remove the throttle body adapter.
30. Remove and discard the throttle body gasket.
31. Disconnect the spring lock couplings from the fuel lines.
32. Disconnect the Positive Crankcase Ventilation (PCV) valve tube from the intake manifold.
33. Disconnect the fuel pressure regulator vacuum hose.
34. Disconnect the eight ignition coil connectors and remove the coils.
35. Disconnect the eight fuel injector connectors.
36. Disconnect the hose clamp and remove the heater water hose.
37. Remove the bolts, water thermostat housing, O-ring seal and the water thermostat. Discard the O-ring seal.
38. Remove the intake manifold bolts.
39. Remove the intake manifold.
40. Remove and discard the intake manifold gaskets.

⁂ CAUTION

Do not use metal scrapers, wire brushes, power abrasive discs or other abrasive means to clean the sealing surfaces. These tools cause scratches and gouges that make leak paths.

41. Clean all mating surfaces.

To install:

42. Install the intake manifold with new gaskets. Loosely install the bolts.

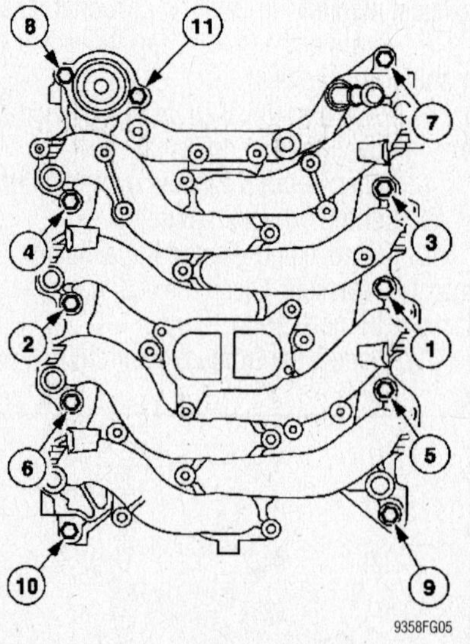

Fig. 145 Tighten the intake manifold bolts in 2 steps using this sequence—2005 Excursion models with the 5.4L SOHC engine

43. Install the water thermostat with a new O-ring seal.

➡The thermostat housing bolts are tightened in sequence with the intake manifold bolts. Do not tighten the thermostat housing bolts during thermostat installation.

44. Install the water thermostat housing and loosely install the bolts.
45. Tighten the bolts in two steps, in the sequence shown:
   a. Step 1: Tighten to 2 Nm (18 lb-in).
   b. Step 2: Tighten to 18 ft. lbs. (25 Nm).
46. Install the heater water hose and position the clamp.
47. Connect the eight fuel injector connectors.
48. Install the eight ignition coils.
49. Connect the eight ignition coil connectors.
50. Position the vacuum harness and connect the fuel pressure regulator vacuum hose.
51. Connect the PCV valve tube to the intake manifold.
52. Connect the spring lock couplings.
53. Install a new throttle body adapter gasket.
54. Install the throttle body adapter. Install the four bolts.
55. Connect the EGR valve vacuum hose.
56. Connect the EGR vacuum regulator solenoid connections.
57. Install the differential pressure feedback EGR system bracket.
58. Connect the exhaust manifold to EGR valve tube upper fitting. Tighten both fittings starting at the top in three steps: First, hand-tighten, then tighten the upper fitting to 37 ft. lbs. (50 Nm) and tighten the lower fitting to 37 ft. lbs. (50 Nm).
59. Connect the IAC connector.
60. Connect the brake booster vacuum hose and main vacuum harness to the throttle body adapter.
61. Connect the evaporative emission canister purge valve vacuum hose to the throttle body adapter.
62. Install the IAC fresh air tube and insert it in the routing clip.
63. Connect the TP sensor connector.
64. Install the accelerator cable bracket.
65. Connect the throttle body cam.
66. Connect the accelerator cable.
67. If equipped, connect speed control cable. Install the return spring.
68. Install the accelerator control splash shield.
69. Install the alternator.

70. Rotate the belt tensioner counter-clockwise and install the belt on the alternator pulley, on models without A/C.

71. Rotate the belt tensioner clockwise and install the belt on the alternator pulley, on models with A/C.

72. Install the upper radiator hose and reposition the clamp.

73. Position the air cleaner, air cleaner outlet housing and the air cleaner outlet pipe in the vehicle and connect the MAF sensor connector.

74. Join the air cleaner outlet housing to the air cleaner inlet housing and secure the clamp.

75. Connect the air cleaner outlet pipe to the throttle body and tighten the clamp.

76. Connect the IAC fresh air tube and crankcase ventilation tube to the air cleaner outlet pipe.

77. Fill the cooling system.

78. Connect the negative battery cable.

6.0L Diesel Engine

See Figures 146 and 147.

1. Before servicing the vehicle, refer to the precautions in the beginning of this section.

2. Remove the auxiliary battery.

3. Remove the air cleaner assembly.

4. Remove the cooling fan-blade, clutch and shroud.

5. Remove the coolant reservoir.

6. Remove the upper radiator hose.

7. Remove the turbocharger-to-charge air cooler tube.

8. Remove the charge air cooler-to-engine tube.

9. on vehicles with dual alternators, perform the following steps:

    a. Remove the accessory drive belt.

    b. Remove the bolt and the accessory drive belt tensioner.

    c. Remove the accessory drive belt.

    d. Remove the bolts, bracket and accessory drive belt idler pulley.

    e. Remove the bolts and the accessory drive belt tensioner.

    f. Disconnect the wire retainer, generator electrical connector and B+ wire.

    g. Remove the bolts and the generator with mounting bracket.

10. On vehicles with single alternator, perform the following steps:

    a. Remove the accessory drive belt.

    b. Disconnect the generator B+ wire and electrical connector.

    c. Remove the three bolts and the alternator.

    d. Remove the turbocharger and the turbocharger pedestal.

11. Remove the bolts and position the heater hose tube aside.

12. Remove and discard the O-ring.

13. Disconnect the Manifold Absolute Pressure (MAP) sensor hose.

14. Disconnect the engine coolant vent hose.

15. Remove the fuel injector control module.

16. Disconnect the wiring retainer, injector pressure regulator and Injector Control Pressure (ICP) sensor electrical connector.

17. Disconnect the Exhaust Gas Recirculation (EGR) valve electrical connector.

18. Disconnect the oil pressure sensor electrical connector.

19. Disconnect the oil temperature sensor electrical connector.

20. Disconnect the Throttle Position (TP) control module electrical connector.

21. Disconnect the TP sensor electrical connector.

22. Disconnect the pin-type retainer and water temperature sensor.

23. Disconnect the Intake Air Temperature (IAT) sensor electrical connector and wiring connector.

24. Disconnect the exhaust backpressure sensor and retaining clip.

25. Disconnect the eight fuel injectors. Remove the nut and the fuel injector wiring harness.

26. Disconnect the fuel line fittings.

➡ **It is necessary to remove the filter and drain the housing.**

27. Remove the four bolts and the oil filter housing.

28. Remove the bolt and the oil filter return tube.

29. Remove the fuel line.

30. Remove the bolt, and the banjo fitting from the fuel line.

31. Discard the sealing washers and remove the fuel line.

32. Remove the nuts and the turbocharger heat shield.

➡ **Align the flat edge with the index feature located on the coolant supply port.**

33. Pull the EGR cooler clamp forward, twist and then slide the EGR cooler hose rearward to remove.

34. Remove the EGR cooler V-clamp and gasket.

35. Remove the bolts and the intake manifold.

36. Remove the intake manifold gaskets.

37. Clean and inspect the gaskets. Install new gaskets if necessary.

38. Clean and inspect the sealing surfaces.

To install:

➡ **Locating tabs on the gaskets must be up and toward the center of the engine, or a leak will occur.**

39. Install the intake manifold gaskets.

40. Install the intake manifold and bolts and tighten in the following sequence:

    a. Loosely install the bolts 1-8.

    b. Tighten bolts 9-16 to 8 ft. lbs. (11 Nm).

    Tighten all bolts to 11 Nm (8 ft. lbs.) in the sequence shown.

41. Install the gasket and the EGR cooler V-clamp and tighten to 53 inch lbs. (8 Nm).

42. Slide the EGR cooler hose forward and rotate flat to lock.

43. Install the turbocharger heat shield and the nuts and tighten to 8 ft. lbs. (11 Nm).

44. Install the fuel line.

45. Install new sealing washers.

46. Install the fuel line.

47. Install the banjo fitting and the bolt. Tighten the upper bolt to 10 ft. lbs. (13 Nm) and the lower bolt to 28 ft. lbs. (38 Nm).

48. Install the oil filter return tube and bolt as follows:

    a. On new oil filter return tubes, tighten to 53 inch lbs. (6 Nm).

    b. On used oil filter return tubes, tighten to 27 inch lbs. (3 Nm).

49. Install the oil filter and the four bolts and tighten to 11 ft. lbs. (15 Nm).

50. Connect the fuel line fittings. Tighten the upper fitting to 19 ff. lbs. (26 Nm) and the lower fitting to 32 ft. lbs. (43 Nm).

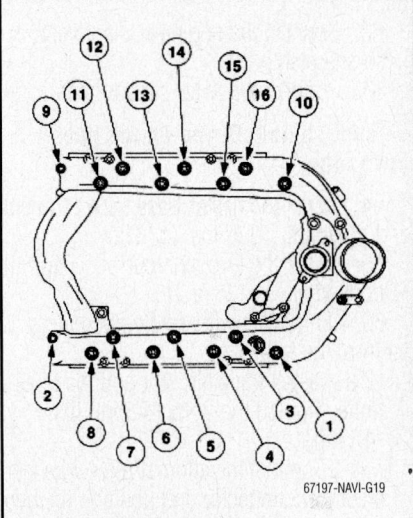

67197-NAVI-G19

Fig. 146 Intake manifold torque sequence—6.0L engine

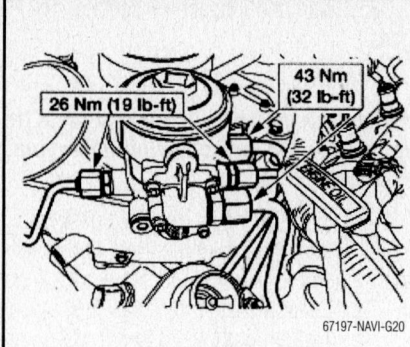

67197-NAVI-G20

Fig. 147 Connect the fuel line fittings— 6.0L engine

51. Position the fuel injector harness and install the retaining nut and tighten to 8 ft. lbs. (11 Nm). Connect the eight fuel injector's electrical connectors.

52. Connect the retaining clip and exhaust backpressure sensor electrical connector.

53. Connect the wiring retainer and the IAT sensor electrical connector.

54. Connect the water temperature sensor and the pin-type retainer.

55. Connect the TP sensor electrical connector.

56. Connect the TP control module electrical connector.

57. Connect the oil temperature sensor electrical connector.

58. Connect the oil pressure sensor electrical connector.

59. Connect the EGR valve electrical connector.

60. Connect the wiring retainer, injector pressure regulator and ICP sensor electrical connectors.

61. Install the fuel injector control module.

62. Connect the engine coolant vent hose and clamp.

63. Connect the MAP sensor hose.

➡**Install a new O-ring on the heater hose tube.**

64. Install the heater hose tube and bolts and tighten to 10 ft. lbs. (13 Nm).

65. Install the turbocharger pedestal and turbocharger.

66. On models with single alternators perform the following:

  a. Install the alternator and the three bolts. Tighten the bolts to 35 ft. lbs. (47 Nm).

  b. Connect the alternator B+ wire land electrical connector and position the boot back.

  c. Install the accessory drive belt.

67. On vehicles with dual alternators:

  a. Install the alternator with mounting bracket and bolts. Tighten the bolts to 35 ft. lbs. (47 Nm).

  b. Connect the B+ wire, alternator electrical connector and wire retainer.

  c. Install the accessory drive belt tensioner and bolts. Tighten the bolts to 18 ft. lbs. (25 Nm).

  d. Position the accessory drive belt idler pulley. Install the bracket and bolts and tighten to 18 ft. lbs. (25 Nm).

  e. Install the accessory drive belt tensioner and bolt and tighten to 18 ft. lbs. (25 Nm).

  f. Install the accessory drive belt.

68. Install the charge air cooler-to-engine tube and tighten the retainers to 9 ft. lbs. (12 Nm).

69. Install the turbocharger-to-charge air cooler tube and tighten the retainers to 9 ft. lbs. (12 Nm).

70. Install the upper radiator hose.

71. Install the coolant reservoir.

72. Install the auxiliary battery.

73. Install the air cleaner assembly.

74. Install the cooling fan blade, clutch and shroud.

6.8L Engine
See Figure 148.

☀ CAUTION

Fuel injection systems remain under pressure, even after the engine has been turned OFF. The fuel system pressure must be relieved before disconnecting any fuel lines. Failure to do so may result in fire and/or personal injury.

➡**When the battery is disconnected and reconnected, some abnormal drive symptoms may occur while the vehicle relearns its adaptive strategy. The vehicle may need to be driven 10 miles (16 km) or more to relearn the strategy.**

1. Before servicing the vehicle, refer to the precautions section.

2. Properly relieve the fuel system pressure.

3. Disconnect the negative battery cable.

4. Drain and recycle the engine coolant.

5. Remove the air cleaner outlet tube.

6. Remove the alternator.

7. Disconnect the fuel tube spring lock couplings.

8. Compress and slide the hose clamp and disconnect the coolant outlet hose.

9. Remove the accelerator cable splash shield.

10. Disconnect the accelerator and speed control cables and remove the return spring.

11. Position the accelerator cable bracket aside.

12. Disconnect the Positive Crankcase Valve (PCV) tube and the vacuum tubes.

13. Disconnect the heated PCV coolant hose.

14. Disconnect the vacuum tube.

15. Disconnect the five right hand fuel injector connectors and five ignition coil connectors.

16. Disconnect the Idle Air Control (IAC) motor connector and the bypass hose.

17. Disconnect the heater hose.

18. Disconnect the five left hand fuel injector Throttle Position (TP) sensor connectors and ignition coil connectors.

19. Remove the ignition coils.

20. Disconnect the vacuum connector from the fuel pressure regulator.

21. Remove the bolts and the thermostat and housing.

22. Remove the bolts, the upper intake manifold and the intake manifold gaskets. Discard the intake manifold gaskets.

☀ CAUTION

Do not use metal scrapers, wire brushes, power abrasive discs or other abrasive means to clean the aluminum retainer plate. These tools cause scratches and gouges, which make leak paths.

23. Clean all mating surfaces. Clean the intake manifold mating surface of the cylinder heads with silicone gasket remover and metal surface prep. Follow the directions on the packaging.

To install:
24. Position the thermostat and housing and loosely install the bolts.

25. Install the upper intake manifold. Position the upper intake manifold gaskets and the intake manifold, and loosely install the bolts.

26. Tighten the bolts in two steps, in the sequence shown:

  a. Step 1: Tighten to 2 Nm (18 lb-in).

  b. Step 2: Tighten to 18 ft. lbs. (25 Nm).

27. Connect the fuel tube spring lock couplings .

28. Connect the vacuum tube to the fuel injection supply manifold.

29. Install the ignition coils.

30. Connect the five left hand fuel injector, TP sensor connectors and five left hand ignition coil connectors.

31. Connect the coolant hose.

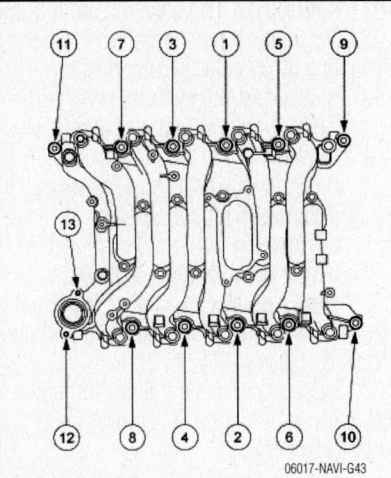

Fig. 148 Tighten the intake manifold bolts in this sequence—2005 Excursion models with the 6.8L engine

32. Connect the IAC motor bypass hose and connector.

33. Connect the five right hand fuel injector connectors and five right hand ignition coil connectors.

34. Connect the vacuum tube.

35. Connect the PCV tube and the vacuum tubes.

36. Connect the heated PCV coolant hose.

37. Install the accelerator bracket.

38. Connect the accelerator and speed control cables and the return spring.

39. Install the accelerator cable splash shield.

40. Connect the engine coolant outlet hose and position the hose clamp.

41. Install the alternator.

42. Install the air cleaner outlet tube.

43. Connect the negative battery cable.

44. Fill and bleed the cooling system.

Expedition & Navigator

2005–06 Models

See Figure 149.

❊❊ CAUTION

Fuel injection systems remain under pressure, even after the engine has been turned OFF. The fuel system pressure must be relieved before disconnecting any fuel lines. Failure to do so may result in fire and/or personal injury.

➡ **When the battery is disconnected and reconnected, some abnormal drive symptoms may occur while the vehicle relearns its adaptive strategy. The vehicle may need to be driven 10 miles (16 km) or more to relearn the strategy.**

1. Disconnect the fuel supply spring lock coupling from the fuel rail.

2. Drain the cooling system.

3. Remove the generator.

4. Remove the air cleaner.

5. Disconnect the upper radiator hose from the thermostat housing.

6. Disconnect the heater coolant hose from the coolant bypass tube.

7. Disconnect the evaporative emissions system (EVAP) tube quick connect coupling from the intake manifold.

8. Disconnect the quick connect couplings and remove the positive crankcase ventilation (PCV) tube.

9. Disconnect the fuel rail pressure and temperature sensor electrical connector and vacuum connector.

10. Disconnect the 8 fuel injector electrical connectors.

11. Disconnect the 4 LH ignition coil electrical connectors.

12. Disconnect the throttle position (TP) sensor and electronic acceleration control electrical connectors.

13. Disconnect the LH radio ignition interference capacitor electrical connector.

14. Disconnect the camshaft position (CMP) sensor electrical connector.

15. Disconnect the variable camshaft timing (VCT) solenoid electrical connector.

16. Disconnect the engine oil pressure (EOP) sensor electrical connector.

17. Disconnect the LH heated exhaust gas oxygen sensor (HO2S) electrical connector and detach the electrical connector retainer.

18. Disconnect the heated PCV intake fitting electrical connector.

19. Disconnect the brake booster vacuum hose from the intake manifold vacuum tube.

20. Disconnect the LH engine wiring harness retainers from the LH valve cover studs and position aside.

21. Remove the 10 intake manifold bolts.

❊❊ WARNING

Do not use metal scrapers, wire brushes, power abrasive discs or other abrasive means to clean the sealing surfaces. These tools cause scratches and gouges which make leak paths. Use a plastic scraping tool to remove all traces of old sealant.

22. Remove the 3 bolts, the coolant bypass tube and discard the gaskets.

23. Clean and inspect the sealing surfaces with silicone gasket remover and metal surface prep.

24. Position the intake manifold assembly forward to gain access to the remaining electrical connectors.

25. Disconnect the charge motion control valve (CMCV) electrical connector.

26. Disconnect the manifold vacuum tube from the valve cover stud and the support bracket.

27. Disconnect the cylinder head temperature (CHT) sensor jumper harness electrical connector.

28. Disconnect the LH and RH knock sensor (KS) electrical connectors.

29. Remove the nut and disconnect the engine wiring harness retainer from the CMCV stud.

30. Remove the intake manifold and discard the gaskets.

31. Inspect and clean the sealing surfaces with silicone gasket remover and metal surface prep.

To install:

➡ **Electrical and vacuum harnesses must not restrict movement of the CMCV control rods at rear of the intake manifold. Use extreme care on installation of the intake manifold to prevent any pinching of electrical and vacuum harnesses.**

32. Using new intake manifold gaskets, position the intake manifold.

33. Using new gaskets, position the coolant crossover and install the 3 bolts. Tighten to 89 inch. lbs. (10 Nm).

34. Install the intake manifold bolts and tighten in 2 stages, in the sequence shown.

    a. Stage 1: Tighten to 18 inch. lbs. (2 Nm).

    b. Stage 2: Tighten to 89 inch. lbs. (10 Nm).

35. Connect the engine wiring harness retainer to the CMCV stud and install the nut. Tighten nut to 89 inch. lbs. (10 Nm).

36. Connect the CMCV electrical connector.

37. Connect the CHT sensor jumper harness electrical connector.

38. Connect the LH and RH KS electrical connectors.

39. Connect the manifold vacuum tube to the support bracket and the valve cover stud.

40. Connect the brake booster vacuum hose to the intake manifold vacuum tube

41. Connect the heated PCV intake fitting electrical connector.

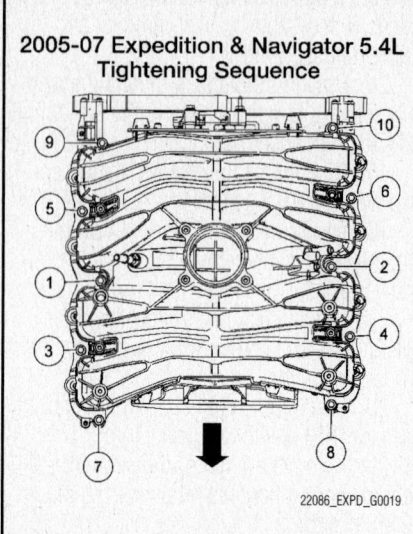

2005-07 Expedition & Navigator 5.4L Tightening Sequence

22086_EXPD_G0019

Fig. 149 Intake manifold tightening sequence—5.4L Expedition & Navigator 2005–06

42. Connect the LH HO2S electrical connector and attach the wiring harness retainer.

43. Connect the EOP sensor electrical connector.

44. Connect the VCT solenoid electrical connector.

45. Connector the CMP sensor electrical connector.

46. Connect the LH radio ignition capacitor electrical connector.

47. Connect the TP sensor and electronic acceleration control electrical connectors.

48. Connect the 8 fuel injector electrical connectors.

49. Connect the 4 LH ignition coil electrical connectors.

50. Connect the fuel rail pressure and temperature sensor electrical connector and vacuum connector.

51. Connect the fuel supply spring lock coupling to the fuel rail.

52. Position the PCV tube and connect the quick connect couplings.

53. Position the EVAP tube and connect the quick connect coupling to the intake manifold.

54. Connect the heater coolant hose to the coolant bypass.

55. Connect the upper radiator hose to the thermostat housing.

56. Install the generator.

57. Install the air cleaner.

58. Fill and bleed the engine cooling system.

59. Check all connections for leaks.

2007 Models

See Figure 150.

※ CAUTION

Fuel injection systems remain under pressure, even after the engine has been turned OFF. The fuel system pressure must be relieved before disconnecting any fuel lines. Failure to do so may result in fire and/or personal injury.

➡**When the battery is disconnected and reconnected, some abnormal drive symptoms may occur while the vehicle relearns its adaptive strategy. The vehicle may need to be driven 10 miles (16 km) or more to relearn the strategy.**

1. Before servicing the vehicle, refer to the precautions section.

2. Properly relieve the fuel system pressure.

3. Drain the cooling system.

4. Disconnect the battery ground cable.

5. Disconnect the fuel supply hose spring lock coupling from the fuel rail.

6. Remove the generator.

7. Remove the air cleaner outlet pipe.

8. Disconnect the crankcase ventilation tube quick connect coupling from the intake manifold.

9. Disconnect the quick connect coupling and remove the evaporative emissions system (EVAP) hose from the intake manifold.

10. Disconnect the EVAP hose position retainer from the intake manifold.

11. Remove the 4 bolts and the air cleaner outlet pipe-to-TB adapter.

12. Disconnect the heater coolant hose from the coolant bypass tube.

13. Disconnect the quick connect couplings and remove the positive crankcase ventilation (PCV) tube. For additional information.

14. Disconnect the 8 fuel injector electrical connectors.

15. Disconnect the 8 ignition coil electrical connectors.

16. Disconnect the throttle position (TP) sensor and electronic acceleration control electrical connectors.

17. Disconnect the heated PCV intake fitting electrical connector.

18. Remove the intake manifold vacuum tube support bracket bolt and disconnect the intake manifold vacuum tube-to-intake manifold hose.

19. Disconnect the brake booster vacuum hose from the intake manifold vacuum tube.

20. Disconnect the intake manifold vacuum tube support retainer from the valve cover and position the intake manifold vacuum tube aside.

---

21. Remove the 10 intake manifold bolts.

22. Disconnect the charge motion control valve (CMCV) electrical connector.

23. Disconnect the cylinder head temperature (CHT) sensor jumper harness electrical connector.

24. Disconnect the LH and RH knock sensor (KS) electrical connectors.

25. Remove the nut and disconnect the engine wiring harness retainer from the CMCV stud.

26. Remove the intake manifold and discard the gaskets.

27. Inspect and clean the sealing surfaces with silicone gasket remover and metal surface prep.

To install:

➡**Electrical and vacuum harnesses must not restrict movement of the CMCV control rods at rear of the intake manifold. Use extreme care on installation of the intake manifold to prevent any pinching of electrical and vacuum harnesses.**

28. Using new intake manifold gaskets, position the intake manifold.

29. Connect the engine wiring harness retainer to the CMCV stud and install the nut. Tighten nut to 89 inch. lbs. (10 Nm).

30. Connect the CMCV electrical connector.

31. Connect the CHT sensor jumper harness electrical connector.

32. Connect the LH and RH KS electrical connectors.

33. Install the intake manifold bolts and tighten in 2 stages, in the sequence shown.

 a. Stage 1: Tighten to 18 inch. lbs. (2 Nm).

 b. Stage 2: Tighten to 89 inch. lbs. (10 Nm).

34. Install the intake manifold vacuum tube support bracket bolt and connect the intake manifold vacuum tube-to-intake manifold hose. Tighten to 89 inch. lbs. (10 Nm).

35. Connect the intake manifold vacuum tube support retainer to the valve cover and position the intake manifold vacuum tube aside.

36. Connect the brake booster vacuum hose to the intake manifold vacuum tube.

37. Connect the heated PCV intake fitting electrical connector.

38. Connect the TP sensor and electronic acceleration control electrical connectors.

39. Connect the 8 fuel injector electrical connectors.

40. Connect the 8 ignition coil electrical connectors.

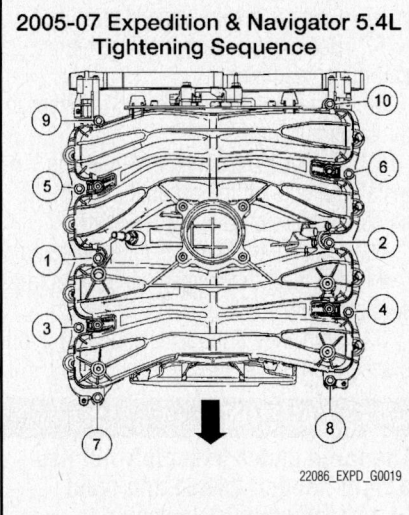

Fig. 150 2007 Intake manifold tightening sequence—5.4L Expedition & Navigator

41. Position the air cleaner outlet pipe-to-TB adapter and install the 4 bolts. Tighten to 89 inch. lbs. (10 Nm).

42. Connect the crankcase ventilation tube quick connect coupling to the intake manifold.

43. Position the EVAP hose and connect the quick connect coupling to the intake manifold.

44. Connect the EVAP hose position retainer to the intake manifold.

45. Position the PCV tube and connect the quick connect couplings.

46. Connect the heater coolant hose to the coolant bypass.

47. Connect the fuel supply spring lock coupling to the fuel rail.

48. Install the generator.

49. Install the air cleaner outlet pipe.

50. Connect the battery ground cable.

51. Fill and bleed the engine cooling system.

OIL PAN

REMOVAL & INSTALLATION

Excursion

5.4L Engine

See Figures 151 through 154.

1. Before servicing the vehicle, refer to the precautions section.

2. Disconnect the negative battery cable.

3. Remove the air cleaner outlet pipe.

4. Remove the accelerator cable snow shield.

5. Disconnect the throttle body cam.

6. Disconnect the accelerator cable.

7. If equipped, disconnect the speed control cable.

8. Remove the throttle return spring.

9. Position the accelerator cable bracket aside.

10. Release the Idle Air Control (IAC) fresh air tube from the routing clip and remove it from the vehicle.

11. Disconnect the IAC electrical connector.

12. If equipped, disconnect the differential pressure feedback Exhaust Gas Recirculation (EGR) system electrical connector.

13. Disconnect the Throttle Position (TP) sensor electrical connector.

14. If equipped, disconnect the differential pressure feedback EGR system vacuum hoses.

15. If equipped, disconnect the exhaust manifold to EGR valve tube fittings and remove the tube.

16. If equipped, remove the differential pressure feedback EGR system bracket.

17. If equipped, disconnect the EGR valve vacuum hose.

18. If equipped, disconnect the EGR vacuum regulator solenoid electrical and vacuum connections.

19. Position aside the throttle body adapter. Discard the throttle body adapter gasket.

20. Remove the alternator.

> ※※ **CAUTION**
>
> **The large clutch assembly nut has a right-handed thread and must be rotated counterclockwise to remove it.**

21. Using tools shown, remove the fan and fan clutch from the coolant pump pulley.

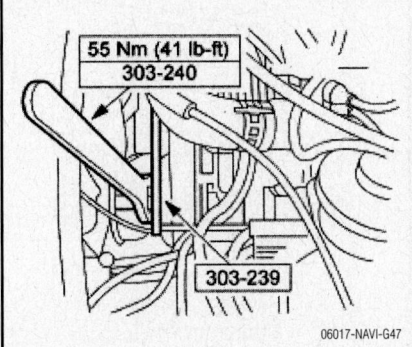

Fig. 151 Using tools shown, remove the fan and fan clutch from the coolant pump pulley—2005 Excursion models with the 5.4L engine

22. Install the modular engine support bracket on the engine using the alternator mounting holes.

23. Remove the engine mount nuts.

> ※※ **CAUTION**
>
> **Damage to the Turbine Shaft Speed/Output Shaft Speed (TSS/OSS) sensors may occur and cause the transmission or torque converter operational concerns if the transmission is raised prior to removing TSS/OSS.**

> ※※ **CAUTION**
>
> **Sensor bosses must be cleaned prior to removal and then plugged to prevent contamination from damaging internal components.**

24. Remove the TSS or the OSS sensor and install plugs in the transmission.

25. Loosely install the transmission mount nuts and the crossmember.

26. Loosely install the crossmember bolts.

27. Loosely install the crossmember bolts.

28. Remove the jack from under the transmission and lower the vehicle.

29. Raise the engine using the a heavy duty engine support.

30. Drain the engine oil and remove the oil bypass filter.

31. Disconnect the Heated Oxygen (HO2S) sensor connectors.

32. Remove the nuts and the exhaust Y-pipe.

33. Remove the flywheel inspection plate.

> ※※ **CAUTION**
>
> **Support the transmission on the oil pan rails only or internal transmission damage can occur.**

34. Support the transmission with a transmission jack.

35. Remove the transmission mount nuts.

36. Raise the transmission.

37. Remove the bolts and partially lower the oil pan.

38. Remove the bolts from the oil pump screen and pickup tube and let them drop into the oil pan.

39. Remove the rear bolt and the oil pump screen and pickup tube and let them drop into the oil pan.

40. Remove the oil pan and the oil pan gasket from the rear of the engine.

41. Clean the oil pan thoroughly and inspect the oil pan gasket.

❋❋ CAUTION

Do not use metal scrapers, wire brushes, power abrasive discs or other abrasive means to clean the sealing surface. These tools cause scratches and gouges, which make leak paths. Use a plastic scraping tool to remove all traces of sealant.

42. Clean the mating surfaces for the oil pan with silicone gasket remover and metal surface prep.

To install:

➡ The oil pump screen and pickup tube must be in the oil pan when the oil pan is positioned in the vehicle.

43. Position the oil pan gasket and the oil pan in the vehicle from the rear of the engine.

❋ CAUTION

Make sure the O-ring is in place and not damaged. A missing or damaged O-ring can cause foam in the lubrication system, low oil pressure and severe engine damage.

➡ Clean and inspect the mating surfaces and install a new O-ring. Lubricate with clean engine oil.

44. Install the oil pump screen and pickup tube.

➡ If not secure within four minutes, the sealant must be removed and the sealing area cleaned.

45. Apply a bead of silicone gasket and sealant at the crankshaft rear seal retainer-to-cylinder block surface, at the locations shown.

➡ If not secure within four minutes, the sealant must be removed and the sealing area cleaned.

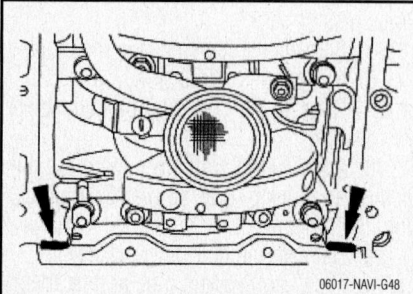

Fig. 152 Apply a bead of silicone gasket and sealant at the crankshaft rear seal retainer-to-cylinder block surface—2005 Excursion models with the 5.4L engine

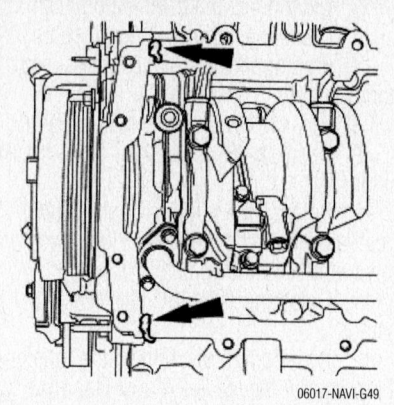

Fig. 153 Apply a bead of silicone gasket and sealant at the engine front cover-to-cylinder block surface—2005 Excursion models with the 5.4L engine

46. Apply a bead of silicone gasket and sealant at the engine front cover-to-cylinder block surface, at the locations shown.

➡ Be sure to tighten the bolts in two stages.

47. Tighten the bolts in the sequence shown:

  a. Step 1: Tighten to 15 ft. lbs. (20 Nm).

  b. Step 2: Tighten an additional 90 degrees.

48. Lower the transmission.
49. Remove the transmission jack.
50. Install the flywheel inspection plate. Tighten to 25 ft. lbs. (34 Nm).
51. Install the oil bypass filter.
52. Align the engine mount studs and lower the engine, using the engine support.
53. Remove the engine support.
54. Install the engine mount nuts. Tighten to 66 ft. lbs. (99 Nm).

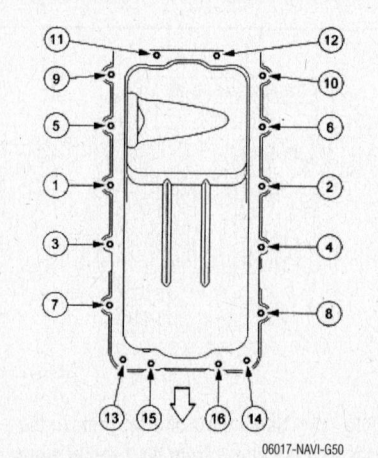

Fig. 154 Oil pan torque sequence—2005 Excursion models with the 5.4L engine

55. Install a suitable transmission jack and support the transmission.
56. Remove the crossmember bolts.
57. Remove the transmission mount nuts and the crossmember.
58. Install the TSS or the OSS sensor in the transmission.
59. Position the exhaust Y-pipe and install the nuts on the exhaust manifold studs. Tighten to 30 ft. lbs. (40 Nm).
60. Install the exhaust Y-pipe flange nuts.
61. Connect the oxygen sensor electrical connectors.
62. Remove the modular engine support bracket from the engine.

❋❋ CAUTION

The large clutch assembly nut has a right-handed thread and must be rotated counterclockwise to remove it.

63. Using the tools used for removal, install the fan and fan clutch to the coolant pump pulley. Tighten to 41 ft. lbs. (55 Nm).
64. Install the alternator.
65. Install the throttle body adapter using a new throttle body adapter gasket.
66. If equipped, connect the EGR vacuum regulator solenoid electrical and vacuum connections.
67. If equipped, connect the EGR valve vacuum hose.
68. If equipped, install the differential pressure feedback EGR system bracket.
69. If equipped, install the exhaust manifold to EGR valve tube as follows:

  a. Step 1: Hand-tighten the fittings.

  b. Step 2: Tighten the upper fitting to 37 ft. lbs. (50 Nm).

  c. Step 3: Tighten the lower fitting to 37 ft. lbs. (50 Nm).

70. If equipped, connect the differential pressure feedback EGR system vacuum lines.
71. If equipped, connect the differential pressure feedback EGR system electrical connector.
72. Connect the TP sensor electrical connector.
73. Connect the IAC electrical connector.
74. Install the IAC fresh air tube and insert it in the routing clip.
75. Install the accelerator cable bracket.
76. Position the bracket and cables.
77. Connect the throttle body cam.
78. Connect the accelerator cable.
79. If equipped, connect the speed control cable.
80. Install the throttle return spring.
81. Install the accelerator cable snow shield.

82. Install the air cleaner outlet pipe.
83. Connect the negative battery cable.

✳✳ CAUTION

The oil pump must be primed prior to starting the engine.

84. Fill the engine with clean engine oil.

6.8L Engine

See Figures 155 and 156.

1. Before servicing the vehicle, refer to the precautions section.
2. Disconnect the negative battery cable.
3. Remove the air cleaner outlet tube.
4. Remove the accelerator cable splash shield.
5. Disconnect the accelerator and speed control cables and return spring.
6. Position the accelerator cable bracket aside.
7. Disconnect the Positive Crankcase Ventilation (PCV) tube and the vacuum hoses.
8. Disconnect the vacuum hose.
9. Disconnect the Throttle Position (TP) sensor electrical connector.
10. Disconnect the Idle Air Control (IAC) motor electrical connector and the bypass hose.
11. Remove the bypass hose routing clip.
12. Position aside the throttle body adapter. Discard the throttle body adapter gasket.

✳✳ CAUTION

The large clutch assembly nut has a right-hand thread and must be rotated counterclockwise to remove it.

13. Using the tools shown, remove the fan and fan clutch from the coolant pump pulley.

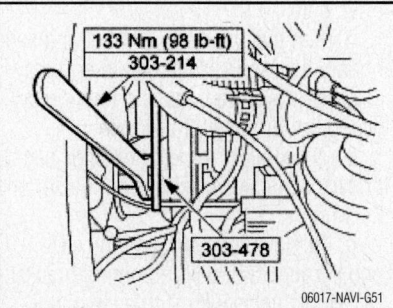

133 Nm (98 lb-ft)
303-214
303-478
06017-NAVI-G51

Fig. 155 Using tools shown, remove the fan and fan clutch from the coolant pump pulley—2005 Excursion models with the 6.8L engine

14. Remove the alternator.
15. Install the tool 303-639 on the engine, using the alternator mounting holes.
16. Remove the engine mount nuts.

✳✳ CAUTION

Damage to the TSS/OSS may occur and cause the transmission or torque converter operational concerns if the transmission is raised prior to removing TSS/OSS.

✳✳ CAUTION

Sensor bosses must be cleaned prior to removal and then plugged to prevent contamination from damaging internal components.

17. Remove the Turbine Shaft Speed (TSS) or Output Shaft Sensors (OSS), and install plugs in the transmission.
18. Loosely install the transmission mount nuts and the crossmember.
19. Loosely install the crossmember bolts.
20. Loosely install the crossmember bolts.
21. Remove the jack assembly supporting the transmission.
22. Raise the engine, using support tool 303-F070.
23. Drain the engine oil and remove the oil bypass filter.
24. Remove the threaded insert and position the oil cooler aside.
25. Disconnect the Heated Oxygen (HO2S) sensor electrical connectors.
26. Remove the exhaust Y-pipe flange nuts.
27. Remove the nuts and the exhaust Y-pipe.
28. Remove the flywheel inspection plate.

✳✳ CAUTION

Support the transmission on the oil pan rails only or internal transmission damage can occur.

29. Support the transmission with a transmission jack.
30. Remove the transmission mount nuts.
31. Using the transmission jack, raise the transmission.
32. Remove the nut and detach the transmission cooling tube bracket.
33. Remove the bolts and partially lower the oil pan.
34. Remove the bolts retaining the oil pump screen cover and pickup tube.
35. Remove the pickup tube and spacer and let them drop into the oil pan

36. Remove the oil pan and the oil pan gasket from the rear of the engine.

✳✳ CAUTION

Do not use metal scrapers, wire brushes, power abrasive discs or other abrasive means to clean the sealing surface. These tools cause scratches and gouges, which make leak paths. Use a plastic scraping tool to remove all traces of sealant.

37. Clean the mating surfaces and thoroughly clean the oil pan.

To install:

38. Clean and inspect the oil pump screen cover and tube mating surfaces and install a new O-ring. Lubricate the O-ring with clean engine oil.

➡**The oil pump screen and pickup tube must be in the oil pan when the oil pan is positioned in the vehicle.**

39. Position the oil pan gasket and the oil pan in the vehicle from the rear of the engine.
40. Install the oil pump screen and pickup tube.

➡**If not secure within four minutes, the sealant must be removed and the sealing area cleaned.**

41. Apply a bead of silicone gasket and sealant where the front cover and rear crankshaft seal retainer fit to the engine block.

➡**Be sure to tighten the bolts in two stages.**

42. Tighten the oil pan bolts in the sequence shown:
   a. Step 1: Tighten to 15 ft. lbs. (20 Nm).
   b. Step 2: Tighten an additional 90 degrees.

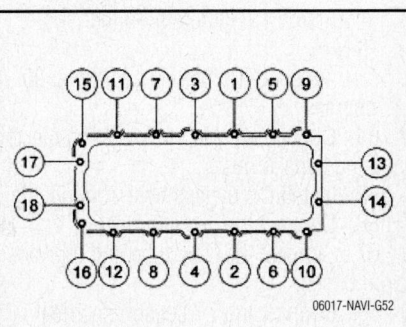

06017-NAVI-G52

Fig. 156 Oil pan bolt torque sequence—2005 Excursion models with the 6.8L engine

43. Attach the transmission cooling tube bracket and install the nut. Tighten to 18 ft. lbs. (25 Nm).

44. Lower the transmission.

45. Loosely install the transmission mount nuts.

46. Install the flywheel inspection plate. Tighten to 25 ft. lbs. (34 Nm).

47. Position the engine oil cooler adapter and install the threaded insert. Tighten to 43 ft. lbs. (58 Nm).

48. Install the oil bypass filter.

49. Align the engine mount studs and lower the engine.

50. Remove the engine support.

51. Install the engine mount nuts. Tighten to 66 ft. lbs. (90 Nm).

52. Install a suitable transmission jack and support the transmission.

53. Remove the crossmember bolts.

54. Remove the crossmember bolts.

55. Remove the transmission mount nuts and the crossmember.

56. Install the TSS or turbine/OSS sensors in the transmission.

57. Position the exhaust Y-pipe and install the nuts on the exhaust manifold studs. Tighten to 30 ft. lbs. (40 Nm).

58. Install the exhaust Y-pipe flange nuts.

59. Connect the oxygen sensor electrical connectors.

✳✳ CAUTION

The large clutch assembly nut has a right-hand thread and must be rotated clockwise to install it.

60. Using the tools used during removal, install the fan and fan clutch to the coolant pump pulley. Tighten to 98 ft. lbs. (133 Nm).

61. Install the alternator.

62. Position the throttle body adapter with a new gasket.

63. Install the four bolts and tighten in two steps.:
   a. Step 1: Tighten to 80 inch lbs. (9 Nm).
   b. Step 2: Tighten an additional 90 degrees.

64. Connect the IAC electrical connector and the bypass hose.

65. Install the bypass hose routing clip.

66. Connect the vacuum hose.

67. Connect the PCV tube and the vacuum hoses.

68. Connect the TP sensor electrical connector.

69. Install the accelerator cable bracket.

70. Position the bracket and cables.

71. Connect the accelerator and speed control cables and return spring.

72. Install the accelerator cable splash shield.

73. Install the air cleaner outlet tube.

74. Connect the negative battery cable.

✳✳ CAUTION

The oil pump must be primed prior to starting the engine.

75. Fill the engine with clean engine oil.

6.0L Diesel Engine
See Figure 157.

1. Before servicing the vehicle, refer to the precautions section.

2. With the vehicle in NEUTRAL, position it on a hoist.

3. Disconnect the negative battery cable.

✳✳ WARNING

Never remove the pressure relief cap while the engine is operating or when the cooling system is hot. Failure to follow these instructions can result in damage to the cooling system or engine or result in personal injury. To avoid having scalding hot coolant or steam blow out of the degas bottle when removing the pressure relief cap, wait until the engine has cooled then wrap a thick cloth around the pressure relief cap and turn it slowly. Step back while the pressure is released from the cooling system. When certain all the pressure has been released, (still with a cloth) turn and remove the pressure relief cap. Failure to follow these instructions can result in personal injury.

✳✳ CAUTION

The coolant must be removed in a suitable, clean container for reuse. If the coolant is contaminated, it must be recycled or disposed of correctly and the system filled with new coolant.

➡ **Less than 80% of coolant capacity can be recovered with the engine in the vehicle. Dirty, rusty, or contaminated coolant requires replacement.**

4. Place a suitable container below the radiator draincock. If equipped, disconnect the coolant return hose at the fluid cooler.

5. Remove the fill cap from the degas bottle.

6. Remove the oil pan drain plug and drain the engine oil.

7. Loosen the exhaust pipe retaining nuts.

8. Remove the motor mount retaining nuts.

9. Open the radiator draincock.

10. Disconnect the lower radiator hose.

11. Disconnect the transmission cooler tubes.

12. Remove the air cleaner assembly.

13. On vehicles with metal ducts, remove the charge air cooler duct.

➡ **Charge air cooler side shown, engine side similar.**

14. On vehicles with blow molded ducts, loosen the clamps and remove the charge air cooler duct.

15. Remove the radiator support brackets.

16. Remove the 4 pin-type retainers and pull back the sight shield.

17. With the sight shield pulled back, remove the 3 pin-type retainers and the 2 wiring retainers and position the harness rearward out of the way.

18. Disconnect the upper radiator hose and the radiator overflow hose.

19. Remove the radiator and shroud as an assembly.

20. Disconnect the cooling fan electrical connector. Unclip and position the fan and wiring aside.

➡ **Use a hole in the fan hub to prevent the fan from turning.**

21. Using the special tool 303-591, loosen the fan clutch. Remove the cooling fan.

22. Remove the bolts from the stator, remove the stator.

23. On vehicles with dual alternator perform the following:
   a. Remove the secondary accessory drive belt.
   b. Remove the bolt and the secondary accessory drive belt tensioner.
   c. Remove the primary accessory drive belt.
   d. Remove the bolts, bracket and secondary accessory drive belt idler pulley.
   e. Remove the bolts and the primary accessory drive belt tensioner.
   f. Disconnect the wire retainer, secondary generator electrical connector and B+ wire.
   g. Remove the bolts and the secondary generator with mounting bracket.

24. On vehicles with single alternator, remove the primary accessory drive belt.

25. Remove the bolts and position the alternator back.

26. Support the hood and disconnect the hood lift assemblies.

27. Install two lifting eyes 303-D030 on the right hand cylinder head.

28. Remove the retaining bolt for the fuel lines.

29. Disconnect the heater hose at the coolant pump.

30. Remove the fan shroud mounting stud.

31. Install one lifting eye 303-D030 on the left hand cylinder head.

✳✳ CAUTION

Do not use the special tool to raise the engine. Damage to the special tool or vehicle may occur.

➡️**The ball studs may have to be removed.**

➡️**This procedure requires a second bolt hook assembly. The tools are available through Rotunda tools with the following numbers: bolt hook 303-F070-6, handle 303-F070-8, bracket 303-F070-7 and washer 303-F070-12004.**

32. Install the special tool.

➡️**The engine must be raised evenly.**

33. Using a lifting crane, raise the engine until the turbo charger is about to touch the cowl. Secure the engine with the special tool.

34. Remove the transmission cooler line bracket.

35. Remove the bolts and position back the oil pan until the oil pick-up tube bolts are accessible.

36. Remove the bolts and let the oil pick-up tube go into the oil pan. Remove the oil pan.

37. Remove the press-in-place gasket and discard.

38. Clean and inspect the sealing surfaces.

39. Remove and discard the oil pick-up tube O-ring.

To install:

40. Install a new O-ring on the oil pick-up tube and position the oil pick-up tube in the oil pan.

41. Install a new press-in-place gasket into the upper oil pan.

42. Position the oil pan in the vehicle.

43. Install the oil pick-up tube and bolts. Tighten to 10 ft. lbs. (13 Nm).

44. Position the oil pan and install the bolts. Tighten to 10 ft. lbs. (13 Nm).

45. Install the transmission cooler tube bracket and nut. Tighten to 18 inch lbs. (10 Nm).

46. Using the special tool 303-F070, lower the engine.

47. Remove the lifting eyes 303-D030 and the special tool.

48. Install the fan shroud mounting stud. Tighten to 30 ft. lbs. (40 Nm).

49. Connect the heater hose at the coolant pump.

50. Install the retaining bolt for the fuel lines. Tighten to 10 ft. lbs. (10 Nm).

51. If removed, install the ball studs.

52. Connect the hood lifts and remove the hood support.

53. Position the primary alternator and install the bolts.

54. On a vehicle with a single alternator, install the primary accessory drive belt.

55. On vehicles with dual alternators, perform the following:

   a. Install the secondary alternator with mounting bracket and bolts. Tighten to 35 ft. lbs. (47 Nm).

   b. Connect the B+ wire, secondary generator electrical connector and wire retainer.

   c. Install the primary accessory drive belt tensioner and bolts. Tighten to 18 ft. lbs. (25 Nm).

   d. Position the secondary accessory drive belt idler pulley. Install the bracket and bolts. Tighten to 18 ft. lbs. (25 Nm).

   e. Install the primary accessory drive belt.

   f. Install the secondary accessory drive belt tensioner and bolt. Tighten to 18 ft. lbs. (25 Nm).

   g. Install the secondary accessory drive belt.

56. Install the stator and stator bolts. Tighten to 30 ft. lbs. (40 Nm).

57. Install the cooling fan clutch. Use the special tool 303-591 to tighten the cooling fan clutch. Tighten to 98 ft. lbs. (133 Nm).

58. Position and clip the cooling fan wiring. Connect the cooling fan electrical connector.

59. Install the radiator and shroud as an assembly.

60. Connect the upper radiator hose and the radiator overflow hose.

61. Position the harness wiring, install the 2 wiring retainers and 3 pin-type retainers.

62. Position the sight shield and install the 4 pin-type retainers.

63. Install the radiator support brackets. Tighten to 22 ft. lbs. (30 Nm).

64. On vehicles with metal ducts, install the charge air cooler duct and tighten the clamps.

65. On vehicles with blow molded ducts, install the charge air cooler duct and tighten the clamps.

66. Install the air cleaner assembly.

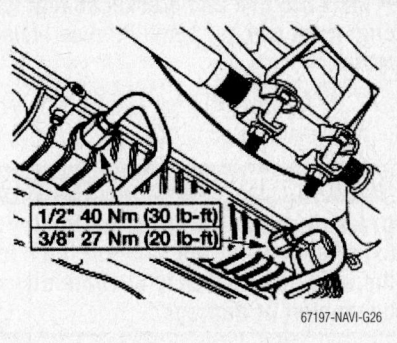

```
1/2" 40 Nm (30 lb-ft)
3/8" 27 Nm (20 lb-ft)
```
67197-NAVI-G26

Fig. 157 Connect the transmission cooler tubes. Tighten to the specifications illustrated—6.0L engine

67. Connect the transmission cooler tubes. Tighten to the specifications illustrated.

68. Close the radiator draincock. Connect the lower radiator hose.

69. Install the motor mount retaining nuts. Tighten to 76 ft. lbs. (103 Nm).

70. Tighten the exhaust pipe retaining nuts to 35 ft. lbs. (47 Nm).

71. Clean and inspect the oil pan drain plug and gasket, install new if necessary.

72. Install the oil pan drain plug and tighten to 18 ft. lbs. (25 Nm).

73. Connect the negative battery cables.

74. Fill the engine with clean engine oil.

75. Fill the coolant system.

76. Run the engine and check for leaks.

Expedition & Navigator

See Figure 158.

1. Before servicing the vehicle, refer to the precautions section.

2. Drain the engine oil.

3. Remove the bolts and the frame crossmember.

4. Remove the nut and remove the starter wiring harness and transmission fluid cooler tube support brackets from the stud bolt.

5. Remove the bolt and detach the wire harness bracket.

6. On 4WD models:

   a. Support the front axle housing with a jack stand.

➡️**Mark the bolt and bracket so that alignment can be maintained on installation.**

   b. Remove the front axle housing right hand mounting bolt.

➡️**Mark the bolt and bracket so that alignment can be maintained on installation.**

   c. Remove the front axle housing left hand front mounting bolt.

➥Mark the bolt and bracket so that alignment can be maintained on installation.

d. Remove the front axle housing left hand rear mounting bolt.

❊ CAUTION

Use care when lowering the front axle housing, or the vacuum lines to the axle solenoid may become disconnected or damaged.

e. Lower the axle to allow clearance for the oil pan to be removed.

➥**Be careful when removing the oil pan gasket. It is reusable.**

7. Remove the 16 bolts, the oil pan and the gaskets. Inspect the oil pan gasket for damage.

8. If damaged, discard the oil pan gasket and the oil pan-to-oil pump gaskets.

To install:

❊ CAUTION

Do not use metal scrapers, wire brushes, power abrasive discs or other abrasive means to clean the sealing surfaces. These tools cause scratches and gouges, which make leak paths. Use a plastic scraping tool to remove all traces of old sealant.

9. Inspect the oil pan. Clean the mating surface for the oil pan with silicone gasket remover and metal surface prep.

➥**If not secured within four minutes, the sealant must be removed and the sealing area cleaned. To clean the sealing area, use silicone gasket remover and metal surface prep. Follow the directions on the packaging. Failure to follow this procedure can cause future oil leakage.**

10. Apply silicone gasket and sealant at the crankshaft rear seal retainer plate-to-cylinder block sealing surface.

11. Apply silicone gasket and sealant at the engine front cover-to-cylinder block sealing surface.

12. Install the oil pan gasket and the oil pan and loosely install the 16 bolts.

13. Tighten the bolts in 3 steps, in the sequence illustrated.

a. Step 1: Tighten to 2 Nm (18 lb-in).

b. Step 2: Tighten to 15 ft. lbs. (20 Nm).

c. Step 3: Tighten an additional 60 degrees.

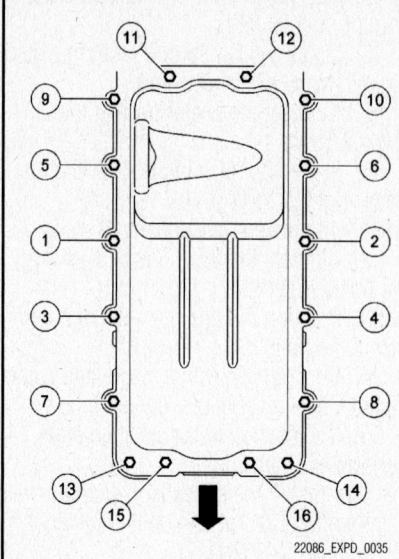

Fig. 158 Oil pan tightening sequence 5.4L engine

14. On 4WD models:

❊❊ CAUTION

Use care when positioning the front axle housing, or the vacuum lines to the axle solenoid may become disconnected or damaged.

d. Position the front axle housing and loosely install the three bolts, aligning the bolt location marks made during removal.

e. Install the front axle housing right hand mounting bolt. Tighten to 89 Nm (66 ft. lbs.).

f. Install the front axle housing left hand front mounting bolt. Tighten to 89 Nm (66 ft. lbs.).

g. Install the front axle housing left hand rear mounting bolt. Tighten to 89 Nm (66 ft. lbs.).

15. Position the frame crossmember and the 4 bolts. Tighten to 75 ft. lbs. (102 Nm).

16. Install the wire harness bracket and the bolt. Tighten to 89 inch lbs. (10 Nm).

17. Fill the crankcase with clean engine oil.

OIL PUMP

REMOVAL & INSTALLATION

Excursion

5.4L Engine

See Figure 159.

1. Before servicing the vehicle, refer to the precautions section.

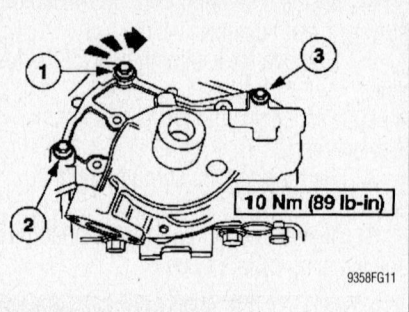

Fig. 159 Tighten the oil pump mounting bolts in the sequence shown

2. Disconnect the negative battery cable.

3. Remove or disconnect the following:
- Timing chains and the LH timing chain guide
- Oil pan
- Bolts and the oil pump

To install:

4. Clean and inspect the mating surfaces.

5. Install or connect the following:
- Oil pump, and the bolts loosely. Tighten the bolts in the sequence illustrated to 89 inch lbs. (10 Nm).
- Oil pan
- LH timing chain guide and the timing chains

6.8L Engine

See Figure 159.

1. Before servicing the vehicle, refer to the precautions section.

2. Disconnect the negative battery cable.

3. Remove the timing drive components.

4. Drain the engine oil.

5. Remove the oil pan.

6. Remove the 3 oil pump mounting bolts, then remove the oil pump from the engine.

To install:

7. Clean and inspect the mating surfaces.

8. Install the oil pump and loosely install the oil pump mounting bolts. Tighten the bolts in the sequence illustrated to 89 inch lbs. (10 Nm).

9. Install the oil pan.

10. Install the timing drive components.

11. Install the front cover.

12. Refill the engine oil with the recommended engine oil and amount.

13. Install the negative battery cable.

6.0L Diesel Engine

See Figures 160 through 163.

1. Before servicing the vehicle, refer to the precautions in the beginning of this section.

2. With the vehicle in NEUTRAL, position it on a hoist.

3. Disconnect the battery ground cable(s).

4. Remove the cooling fan.

5. On vehicles with dual alternator, perform the following:

   a. Remove the dual generator accessory drive belt.

   b. Remove the bolts and the dual generator pulley.

6. Remove the accessory drive belt.

7. Check the crankshaft vibration damper runout.

8. Remove the paint from the face of the crankshaft vibration damper at four points 90 degrees apart. Attach dial indicator 100-002 to the cylinder block. Position the tool on one of the unpainted surfaces. Using a suitable tool, pry the crankshaft forward. Zero the dial indicator.

➡ **Pry the crankshaft forward only to eliminate possible error caused by crankshaft end play. Rotate the crankshaft 90 degrees. Pry the crankshaft forward. Record the measurement. Repeat at each unpainted surface.**

9. If the runout exceeds specification, install a new crankshaft vibration damper.

✳✳ CAUTION

To avoid personal injury, support the vibration damper during mounting bolt removal. The damper can slide off the nose of the crankshaft very easily.

10. Remove the bolts and the crankshaft vibration damper.

11. Discard the bolts.

12. Punch two holes in the seal.

13. Using the special tool 303-D060, remove the crankshaft seal.

➡ **Production engine will not have a wear sleeve.**

14. If equipped, remove the crankshaft damper wear sleeve using tool 303-762.

15. Remove the bolts and the gerotor cover. Remove and discard the O-ring seal.

➡ **Mark the front of the inner and outer gerotor for correct reassembly.**

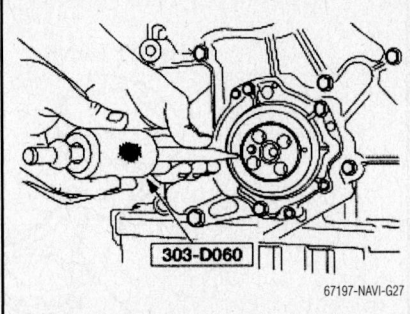

Fig. 160 Using the special tool 303-D060, remove the crankshaft seal—6.0L engine

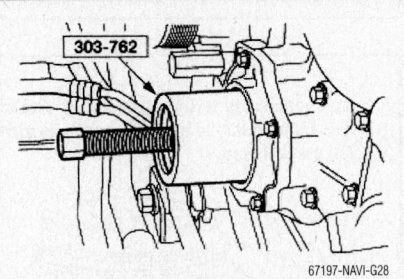

Fig. 161 Remove the crankshaft damper wear sleeve using tool 303-762, if equipped—6.0L engine

16. Remove the inner and outer gerotors.

17. Inspect the oil pump components and replace as necessary.

18. Inspect the oil pump for excessive metal particles.

19. Inspect the oil pump for gouging, cracks or deep scratches.

20. Inspect the oil pump inner and outer gear rotors for damage or excessive wear.

To install:

➡ **Install the gears with marks pointing outward.**

21. Lubricate the inner gear with lithium assembly grease and install onto the crankshaft. Lubricate the outer gear with lithium assembly grease and mesh with the inner gear rotor in the oil pump housing. Wipe off the excess assembly grease.

22. Install a new O-ring seal.

23. Install the gerotor cover and bolts. Tighten to 71 inch lbs. (8 Nm).

24. Thoroughly clean the crankshaft front seal mounting surface.

25. Apply Threadlock 262® to the outer circumference of the leading edge of the crankshaft.

➡ **New seal and wear sleeve must not be separated.**

26. Using the special tool 303-361, install the oil seal and wear sleeve assembly.

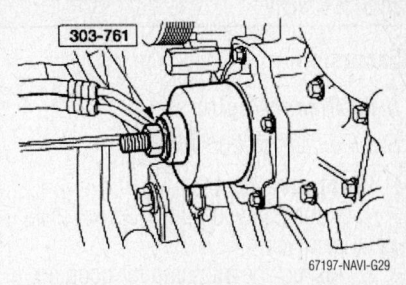

Fig. 162 Use tool 303-361 to install the oil seal and wear sleeve assembly—6.0L engine

✳✳ CAUTION

To prevent engine damage, you must always install four new bolts when installing the vibration damper.

➡ **Do not use anti-seize compounds, grease or any lubricants. Lubricants have an adverse effect on the torque results.**

27. Install the crankshaft vibration damper and bolts.

28. Tighten the bolts in the sequence illustrated as follows:

   a. Tighten the bolts to 50 ft. lbs. (68 Nm).

   b. Tighten the bolts an additional 90 degrees.

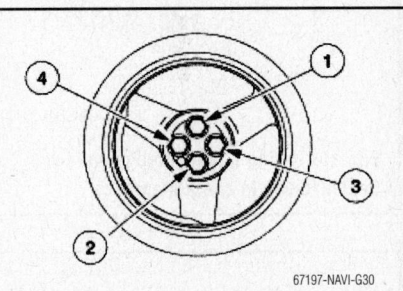

Fig. 163 Tighten the crankshaft vibration damper bolts in this sequence—6.0L engine

29. Install the accessory drive belt.

30. On vehicles with dual alternator, perform the following:

   a. Install the dual alternator pulley and bolts. Tighten to 35 ft. lbs. (47 Nm).

   b. Install the dual generator accessory drive belt.

31. Install the cooling fan stator

32. Connect the battery ground cables.

INSPECTION

Excursion

6.0L Diesel Engine

See Figures 164 and 165.

Clearance Test

1. Inspect the oil pump for excessive metal particles.

2. Inspect the oil pump for gouging, cracks or deep scratches.

3. Inspect the oil pump inner and outer gear rotors for damage or excessive wear.

4. Using a straightedge and the Feeler Gauge, measure the height clearance between the oil pump housing and the inner and outer rotors. If the measurement does not meet specifications, 0.001–0.004 inch. (0.025–0.095 mm) install new gerotors as a set.

5. Using the Feeler Gauge, measure the clearance between the outer rotor and the oil pump housing. If the measurement does not meet specifications 0.007–0.012 inch. (0.17–0.295 mm), install new gerotors as a set.

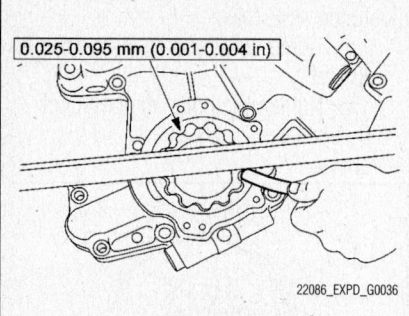

Fig. 164 Using a straightedge and the Feeler Gauge to check clearance

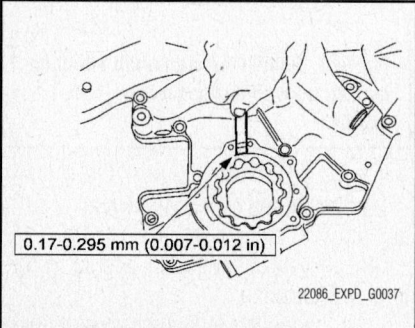

Fig. 165 Using the Feeler Gauge, measure the clearance

PISTON AND RING

POSITIONING

See Figures 166 and 167.

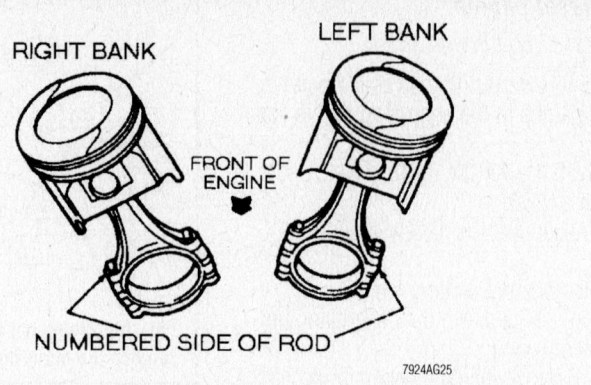

Fig. 166 5.4L, and 6.8L engines—piston and connecting rod assembly positioning

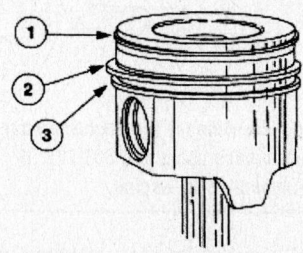

1. Top compression ring is identified with one indentation mark and a 15 degree keystone profile.
2. The intermediate compression ring is identified with two indentation marks and a square profile.
3. Oil control ring.

Fig. 167 6.0L Diesel engines—piston ring locations

REAR MAIN SEAL

REMOVAL & INSTALLATION

All Gasoline Engines

See Figures 168 through 172.

1. Before servicing the vehicle, refer to the precautions section.

2. Disconnect the negative battery cable.

3. Remove the transmission.

4. Remove the 8 bolts and the flexplate.

5. Using the special tools 303-514 and 100-001, remove the crankshaft oil slinger.

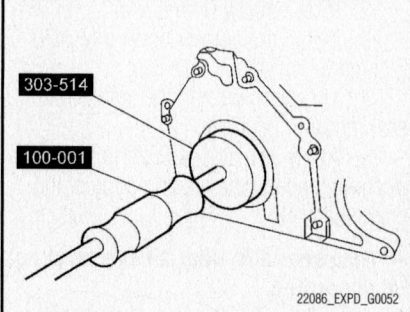

Fig. 168 Rear crankshaft oil slinger removal

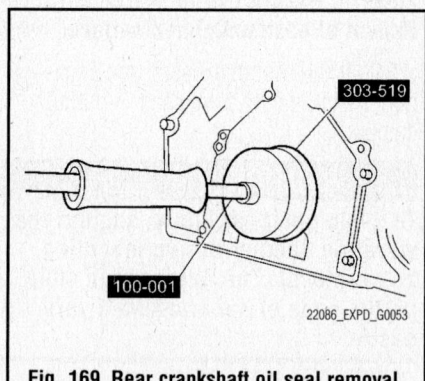

Fig. 169 Rear crankshaft oil seal removal

6. Using the special tools 303-519 and 100-001, remove the crankshaft rear seal.

To install:

7. Lubricate the inner lip of the crankshaft rear seal with clean engine oil.

8. Using the special tools 303-516 and 303-518, install a new crankshaft rear seal.

9. Using the special tools 303-516, 303-517 and 303-518, install a new crankshaft rear oil slinger.

10. Install the flexplate and tighten the 8 bolts in the sequence shown to 59 ft. lbs. (80 Nm).

11. Install the transmission.

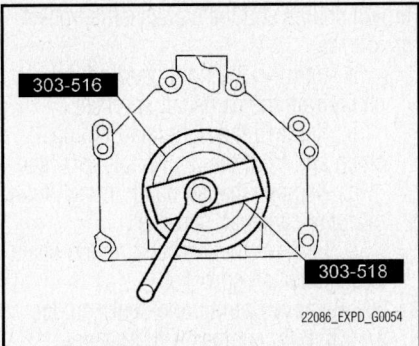

Fig. 170 Rear crankshaft seal installation

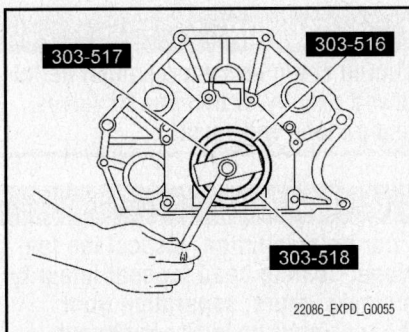

Fig. 171 Rear crankshaft oil slinger installation

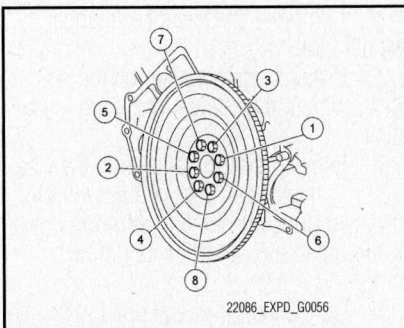

Fig. 172 Flexplate tightening sequence 5.4L–6.8L engines

6.0L Diesel Engine

See Figures 173 through 175.

1. Before servicing the vehicle, refer to the precautions section.
2. Remove the transmission.
3. Remove the bolts.
4. Remove the flexplate or flywheel.

➡**Use extreme care when removing the flywheel front adapter to prevent damage to the alignment dowel pin.**

5. Remove the flywheel front adapter.

⁕⁕ CAUTION

To prevent engine damage, do not remove the rear primary crankshaft flange bolts under any circumstances. If the flange is removed and reinstalled, it will result in engine vibration and premature transmission component wear.

6. Punch two holes in the rear main seal, across from each other.
7. Using the puller tool 100-001, remove the rear main seal.

➡**Production engines will not have a wear sleeve.**

8. If equipped with a crankshaft wear sleeve, use the tool 303-771 to remove the crankshaft rear wear sleeve.

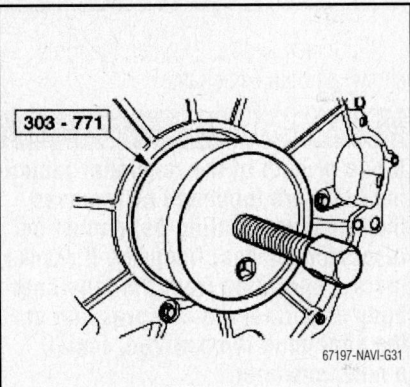

Fig. 173 If equipped with a crankshaft wear sleeve, use tool 303-771 to remove the crankshaft rear wear sleeve—6.0L engine

9. Clean and inspect the crankshaft sealing surface.

To install:

➡**The crankshaft rear oil seal and wear sleeve are installed as an assembly.**

➡ **Lubricate the outer diameter of the rubber seal with a solution of dish soap and water (approximately 50/50 mix) prior to assembly. Do not use any other type of lubricant.**

10. Apply a bead of Threadlock 262® around the circumference of the outer rear edge of the secondary crankshaft flange.
11. Using tool 303-770, install the crankshaft rear oil seal.
12. Install the flywheel front adapter.
13. Install the flexplate or flywheel.
14. Install the bolts. Snug all bolts to 44 inch lbs. (5 Nm), then tighten all bolts to 69 ft. lbs. (94 Nm) in the sequence illustrated.
15. Install the transmission.

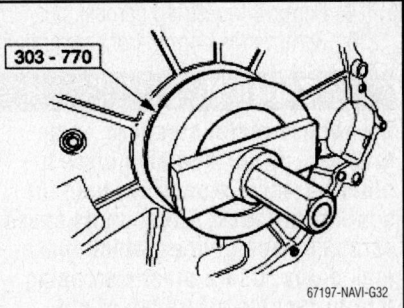

Fig. 174 Use tool 303-770 to install the crankshaft rear oil seal—6.0L engine

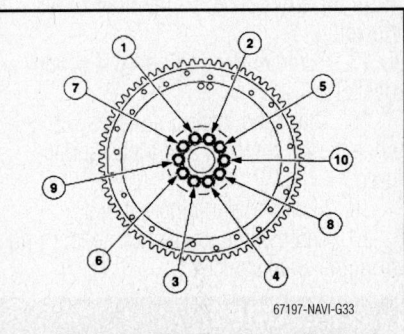

Fig. 175 Tighten the flexplate or flywheel bolts in this sequence—6.0L engine

TIMING CHAIN, SPROCKETS AND FRONT COVER

REMOVAL & INSTALLATION

Excursion

5.4L & 6.8L Engines
See Figures 176 through 194.

1. Disconnect the negative battery cable.
2. Remove both valve covers.
3. Remove the radiator.
4. Remove the water pump.
5. Remove the top bolts and the lower bolt and position the power steering pump aside.
6. Disconnect the Crankshaft Position (CKP) sensor electrical connector.
7. Remove the drain plug and drain the engine oil.
8. Remove the four front oil pan bolts.
9. Remove the crankshaft front seal.
10. Disconnect the Camshaft Position (CMP) sensor electrical connection.
11. Remove the nuts and position the radio interference capacitors aside.
12. Remove the bolt and the belt idler pulley.
13. Remove the nuts and position the wiring harness bracket aside.

14. Remove the wiring harness nut.
15. Remove the engine front cover bolts.

❋ CAUTION

Do not use metal scrapers, wire brushes, power abrasive discs or other abrasive means to clean the sealing surfaces. These tools cause scratches and gouges which make leak paths. Use a plastic scraping tool to remove all traces of old sealant.

16. Remove the engine front cover from the front cover to cylinder block dowel.
17. Remove the engine front cover gasket.
18. Clean the mating surfaces with silicone gasket remover and metal surface prep.
19. Inspect the mating surfaces.
20. Remove the crankshaft sensor ring from the crankshaft.

❋ CAUTION

Unless otherwise instructed, at no time when the timing chains are removed and the cylinder heads are installed is the crankshaft or camshaft to be rotated. Severe piston and valve damage will occur.

❋❋ CAUTION

The caps must be marked for installation in their original location or damage to the engine can occur.

21. On 6.8L engines, remove the six bolts and remove the balance shaft bearing caps and the balance shaft.
22. Position the crankshaft with the keyway at the 12 o'clock position.

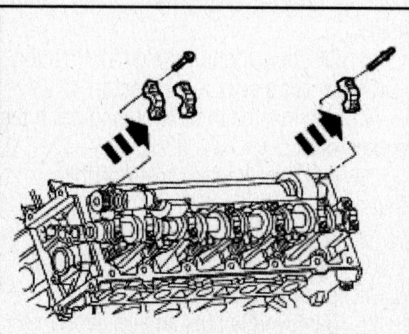

Fig. 176 Remove the six bolts and remove the balance shaft bearing caps and the balance shaft—2005 Excursion models with 6.8L engine

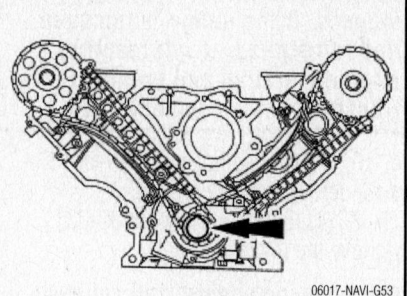

Fig. 177 Position the crankshaft with the keyway at the 12 o'clock position—2005 Excursion models with 5.4L and 6.8L engines

23. Install and fully tighten the tools shown on both camshafts.

❋❋ CAUTION

If one or both of the tensioner mounting bolts are loosened or removed, the tensioner-sealing bead must be inspected for seal integrity. If cracks, tears, separation from the tensioner body or permanent compression of the seal bead is observed, install a new tensioner.

24. Remove the timing chain tensioning system from both timing chains.

❋❋ CAUTION

Unless otherwise instructed, at no time when the timing chains are removed and the cylinders heads are installed is the crankshaft or camshaft to be rotated. Severe piston and valve damage will occur.

25. Remove the right hand and left hand

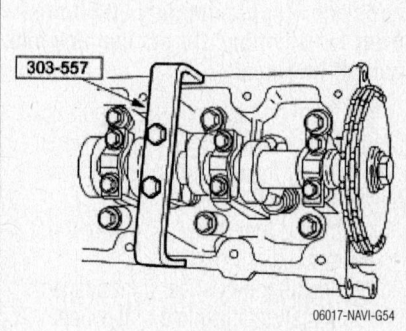

Fig. 178 Install the tools shown on the camshafts—2005 Excursion models with 5.4L and 6.8L engines

timing chains and the crankshaft sprocket as follows:

   a. Remove the right hand timing chain from the camshaft sprocket.
   b. Remove the right hand timing chain and from the crankshaft sprocket.
   c. Remove the left hand timing chain from the camshaft sprocket.
   d. Remove the left hand timing chain and crankshaft sprocket.
26. Remove both timing chain guides.
27. On 6.8L engines with bolt-on sprockets, remove the camshaft sprocket.

To install:

❋❋ CAUTION

Timing chain procedures must be followed exactly or damage to valves and pistons will result.

❋❋ CAUTION

Prior to installation, inspect the tensioner-sealing bead for seal integrity. If cracks, tears, separation from the tensioner body or permanent compression of the seal bead is observed, install a new tensioner.

28. Compress the tensioner plunger, using a vise.
29. Install a retaining clip on the tensioner to hold the plunger in during installation.
30. Remove the tensioner from the vise.
31. If the copper links are not visible, mark two links on one end and one link on the other end, and use as timing marks.
32. On 6.8L engines equipped with bolt-on sprockets, install the camshaft sprocket as follows:

   a. Tighten the M10 bolt in two steps, first to 30 ft. lbs. (40 Nm). Then tighten an additional 90 degrees.
   b. Tighten the M12 bolt to 120 Nm (90 lb
33. Install the timing chain guides.

❋❋ CAUTION

Do not turn the engine over with the camshaft positioning tool or damage to the camshaft sprocket or the bolt can occur.

34. Install the camshaft positioning tool.

➡Slightly loosen the camshaft position aligner to allow slight camshaft movement.

35. Pre-position the camshafts as follows:

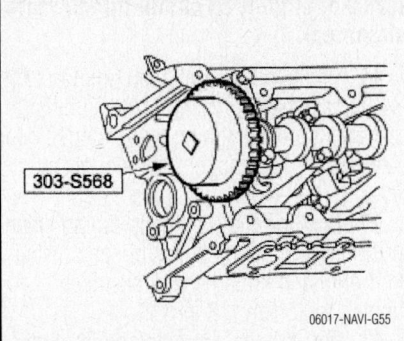

Fig. 179 Install the camshaft positioning tool—2005 Excursion models with 5.4L and 6.8L engines

a. Rotate the left hand camshaft with the camshaft position aligner until the timing mark is approximately at 12 o'clock.

b. Rotate the right hand camshaft with the camshaft position aligner until the timing mark is approximately at 11 o'clock.

c. Tighten the camshaft position aligner to maintain camshaft pre-positioning.

※※ CAUTION

Unless otherwise instructed, at no time when the timing chains are removed and the cylinder heads are installed is the crankshaft or camshaft to be rotated. Severe piston and valve damage will occur.

※※ CAUTION

Rotate the crankshaft counterclockwise only. Do not rotate past position shown or severe piston and valve damage can occur.

➡The number one cylinder is at Top Dead Center (TDC) when the stud on

the engine block fits into the slot in the handle of the special tool.

36. Position the crankshaft so the number one cylinder is at TDC with the tool shown.

37. Remove the crankshaft position aligner.

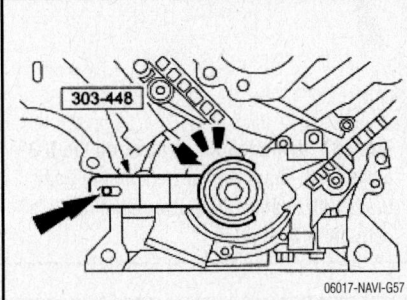

Fig. 181 Position the crankshaft so the number one cylinder is at TDC—2005 Excursion models with 5.4L and 6.8L engines

38. Install the crankshaft sprocket, make sure the flange faces forward.

39. Position the lower end of the left hand (inner) timing chain on the crankshaft sprocket, aligning the timing mark on the outer flange of the crankshaft sprocket with the single copper (marked) link on the chain.

➡Make sure the upper half of the timing chain is below the tensioner arm dowel.

➡If necessary, use the camshaft position aligner to adjust the camshaft sprocket slightly to obtain timing mark alignment.

40. Position the timing chain on the camshaft sprocket with the camshaft sprocket timing mark positioned between the two copper (marked) chain links.

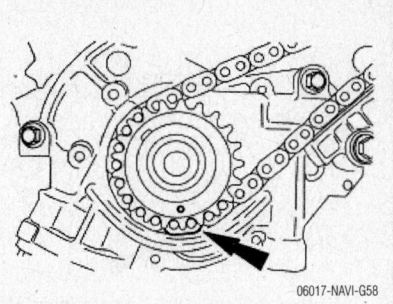

Fig. 182 Position the lower end of the left hand (inner) timing chain on the crankshaft sprocket, aligning the timing mark on the outer flange of the crankshaft sprocket with the single copper (marked) link on the chain—2005 Excursion models with 5.4L and 6.8L engines

➡The left hand timing chain tensioner arm has a bump near the dowel hole, for identification.

41. Position the left hand timing chain tensioner arm on the dowel pin and install the left hand timing chain tensioner. Tighten to 25 Nm (18 lb-ft.).

42. Remove the retaining clip from the left hand timing chain tensioner.

➡The lower half of the timing chain must be positioned above the tensioner arm dowel.

43. Position the lower end of the right hand (outer) timing chain on the crankshaft sprocket, aligning the timing mark on the sprocket with the single copper (marked) link on the timing chain.

➡If necessary, use the camshaft position aligner to adjust the camshaft

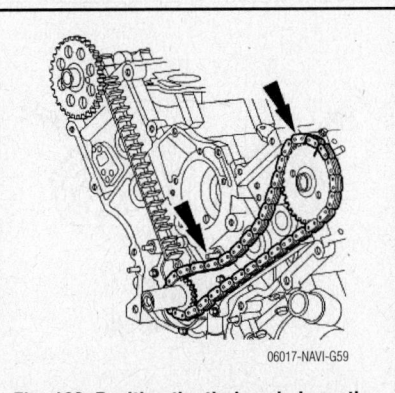

Fig. 183 Position the timing chain on the camshaft sprocket with the camshaft sprocket timing mark positioned between the two copper (marked) chain links—2005 Excursion models with 5.4L and 6.8L engines

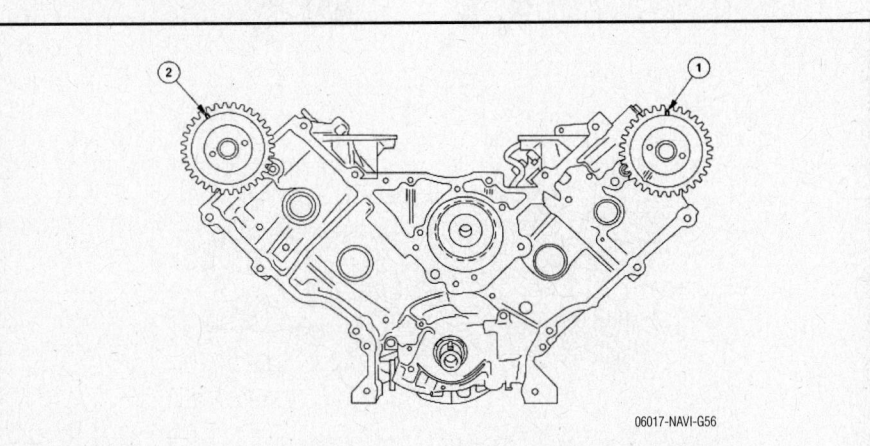

Fig. 180 Pre-position the camshafts as shown—2005 Excursion models with 5.4L and 6.8L engines

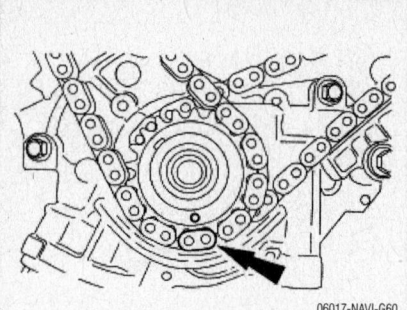

06017-NAVI-G60

Fig. 184 Position the lower end of the right hand (outer) timing chain on the crankshaft sprocket, aligning the timing mark on the sprocket with the single copper (marked) link on the timing chain—2005 Excursion models with 5.4L and 6.8L engines

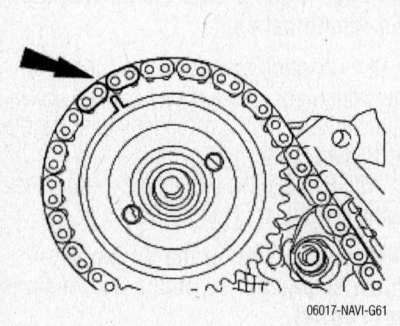

06017-NAVI-G61

Fig. 185 Position the right hand timing chain on the camshaft sprocket. Make sure the camshaft sprocket timing mark is positioned between the two copper (marked) chain links—2005 Excursion models with 5.4L and 6.8L engines

06017-NAVI-G62

Fig. 186 As a post-check, verify correct alignment of all timing marks—2005 Excursion models with 5.4L and 6.8L engines

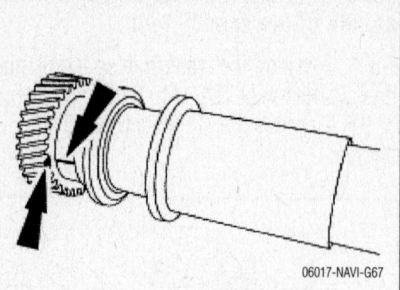

06017-NAVI-G67

Fig. 187 Using the index mark on the balance shaft, mark the corresponding gear tooth with chalk—2005 Excursion models with the 6.8L engine

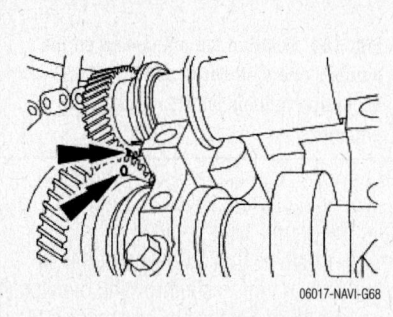

06017-NAVI-G68

Fig. 188 Align the chalk mark on the balance shaft with the camshaft timing mark as shown—2005 Excursion models with the 6.8L engine

sprocket slightly to obtain timing mark alignment.

44. Position the right hand timing chain on the camshaft sprocket. Make sure the camshaft sprocket timing mark is positioned between the two copper (marked) chain links.

45. Position the right hand timing chain tensioner arm on the dowel pin and install the right hand timing chain tensioner. Tighten to 25 Nm (18 lb-ft.).

46. Remove the retaining clip from the right hand timing chain tensioner.

47. As a post-check, verify correct alignment of all timing marks.

48. Remove the camshaft holding tool.

49. Position the crankshaft sensor ring on the crankshaft.

50. On 6.8L engines perform the following:

    a. Lubricate the balance shaft journals with clean engine oil.

    b. Using the index mark on the balance shaft, mark the corresponding gear tooth with chalk.

    c. Position the balance shaft on the journals.

➡ **It may be necessary to use an inspection mirror to see the marks.**

    d. Align the chalk mark on the balance shaft with the camshaft timing mark as shown.

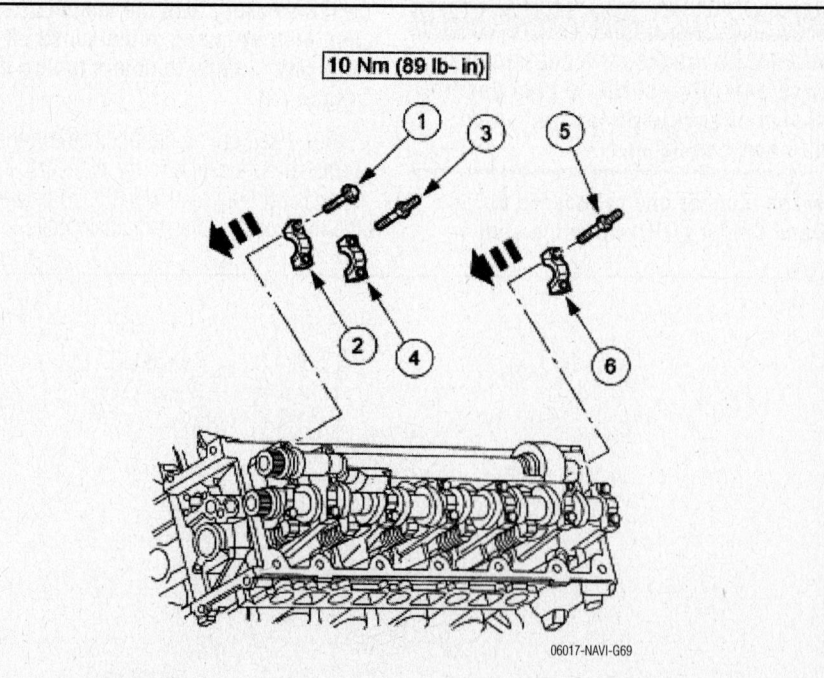

10 Nm (89 lb- in)

06017-NAVI-G69

Fig. 189 Install the bearing caps in their original locations. Install the bolts and tighten the bolts in the sequence shown—2005 Excursion models with the 6.8L engine

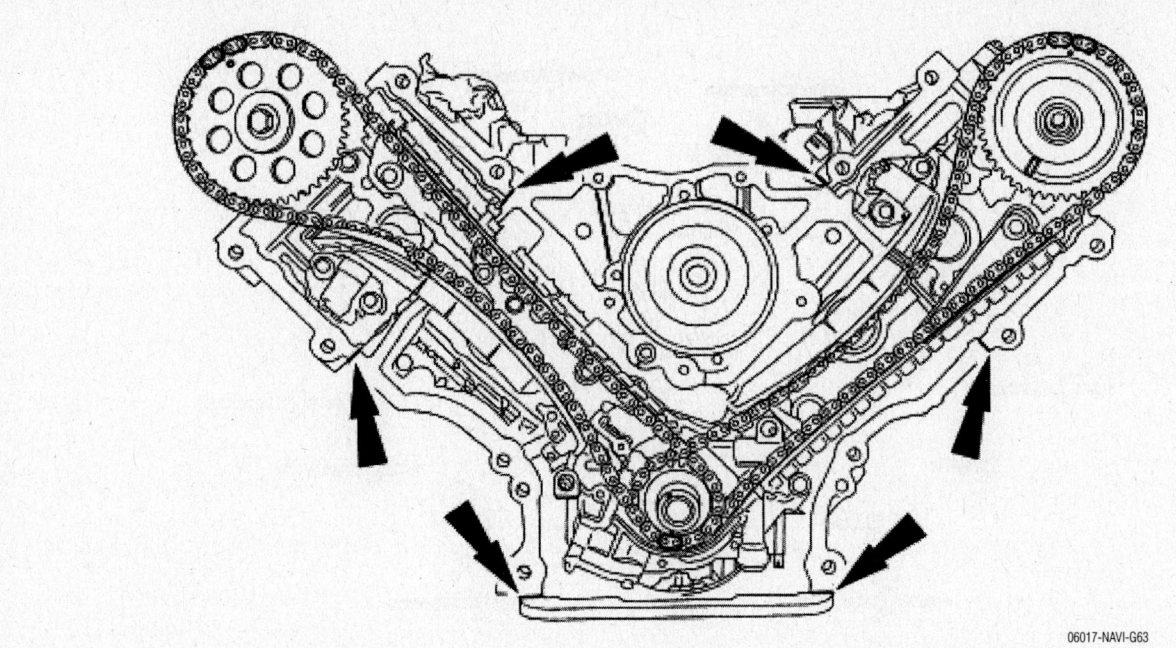

Fig. 190 Apply a bead of silicone gasket and sealant along the cylinder head-to-cylinder block surface and the oil pan-to-cylinder block surface—2005 Excursion models with the 5.4L engine

e. Install the bearing caps in their original locations. Install the bolts and tighten the bolts in the sequence shown.

✳✳ CAUTION

Do not use metal scrapers, wire brushes, power abrasive discs or other abrasive means to clean the sealing surfaces. These tools cause scratches and gouges which make leak paths. Use a plastic scraping tool to remove all traces of old sealant.

➡ **If the engine front cover is not secured within four minutes, the sealant must be removed and the sealing area cleaned.**

➡ **Make sure that the engine front cover gasket is in place on the engine front cover before installation.**

51. Apply a bead of silicone gasket and sealant along the cylinder head-to-cylinder block surface and the oil pan-to-cylinder block surface, at the locations shown.

52. Install the engine front cover with engine front cover gasket on the front cover to cylinder block dowel and loosely install the bolts.

53. On 5.4L engines, tighten the engine front cover fasteners in sequence in three steps.

a. Step 1: Tighten fasteners 1 through 7 to 18 ft. lbs. (25 Nm).

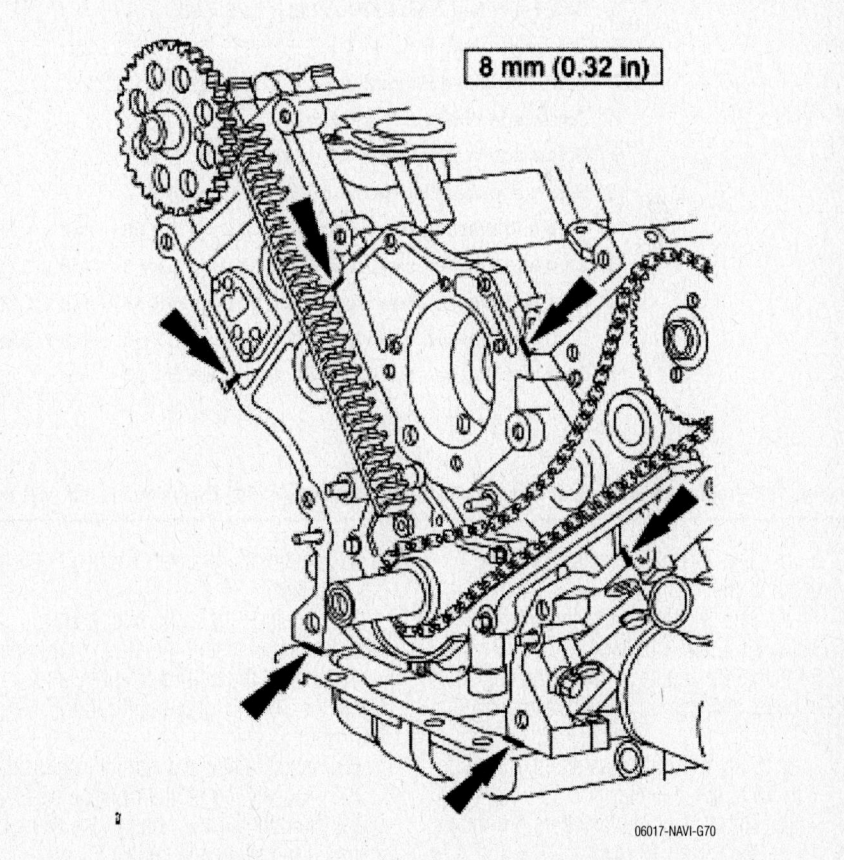

Fig. 191 Apply a bead of silicone gasket and sealant along the cylinder head-to-cylinder block surface and the oil pan-to-cylinder block surface—2005 Excursion models with the 6.8L engine

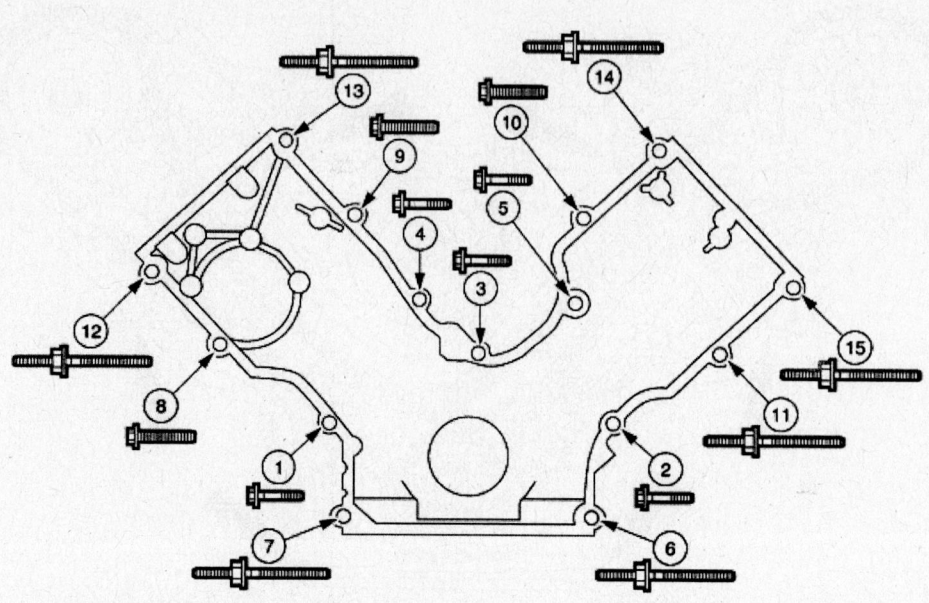

1 Bolt, Hex Flange Head Pilot, M8 x 1.25 x 53

2 Bolt, Hex Flange Head Pilot, M8 x 1.25 x 53

3 Bolt, Hex Flange Head Pilot, M8 x 1.25 x 53

4 Bolt, Hex Flange Head Pilot, M8 x 1.25 x 53

5 Bolt, Hex Flange Head Pilot, M8 x 1.25 x 53

6 Stud, Hex Head Pilot, M10 x 1.5 x 59 — M10 x 1.5 x 30

7 Stud, Hex Head Pilot, M10 x 1.5 x 59 — M10 x 1.5 x 30

8 Screw and Washer, Hex Pilot, M10 x 1.5 x 57.5

9 Screw and Washer, Hex Pilot, M10 x 1.5 x 57.5

10 Screw and Washer, Hex Pilot, M10 x 1.5 x 57.5

11 Stud and Washer, Hex Head Pilot, M10 x 1.5 x 68 — M8 x 1.25 x 27

12 Stud and Washer, Hex Head Pilot, M10 x 1.5 x 68 — M8 x 1.25 x 27

13 Stud and Washer, Hex Head Pilot, M10 x 1.5 x 68 — M8 x 1.25 x 27

14 Stud and Washer, Hex Head Pilot, M10 x 1.5 x 68 — M8 x 1.25 x 27

15 Stud and Washer, Hex Head Pilot, M10 x 1.5 x 68 — M8 x 1.25 x 27

06017-NAVI-G64

Fig. 192 Front cover bolts size, location and torque sequence—2005 Excursion models with the 5.4L engine

b. Step 2: Tighten fasteners 6 and 7 to 35 ft. lbs. (48 Nm).

c. Step 3: Tighten fasteners 8 through 15 to 35 ft. lbs. (48 Nm).

54. On 6.8L engines, tighten the engine front cover fasteners in sequence in two steps.

a. Step 1: Tighten fasteners 1 through 7 to 18 ft. lbs. (25 Nm).

b. Step 2: Tighten fasteners 6 through 15 to 35 ft. lbs. (48 Nm).

55. Connect the CMP electrical connection.

56. Install the bracket and the nut. Tighten to 18 ft. lbs. (25 Nm).

57. Install the bracket. Tighten to 22 ft. lbs. (30 Nm).

58. Position the radio interference capacitors and install the nuts, if equipped.

59. Install the belt idler pulley and tighten the bolt. Tighten to 18 ft. lbs. (25 Nm).

60. Install a new crankshaft front seal.

61. Loosely install the front oil pan bolts, then tighten the bolts in the two steps, in the sequence shown.

a. Step 1: Tighten to 15 ft. lbs. (20 Nm).

b. Step 2: Tighten an additional 60 degrees.

62. Connect the CKP sensor electrical connector.

➡ **The front lower hole in the power steering pump is not used.**

63. Position the power steering pump and install the bolts. Tighten to 18 ft. lbs. (25 Nm).

64. Install the drain plug. Tighten to 17 ft. lbs. (23 Nm).

65. Install the valve covers.

66. Fill the engine with clean engine oil.

67. Install the water pump.

68. Install the radiator.

69. Connect the negative battery cable.

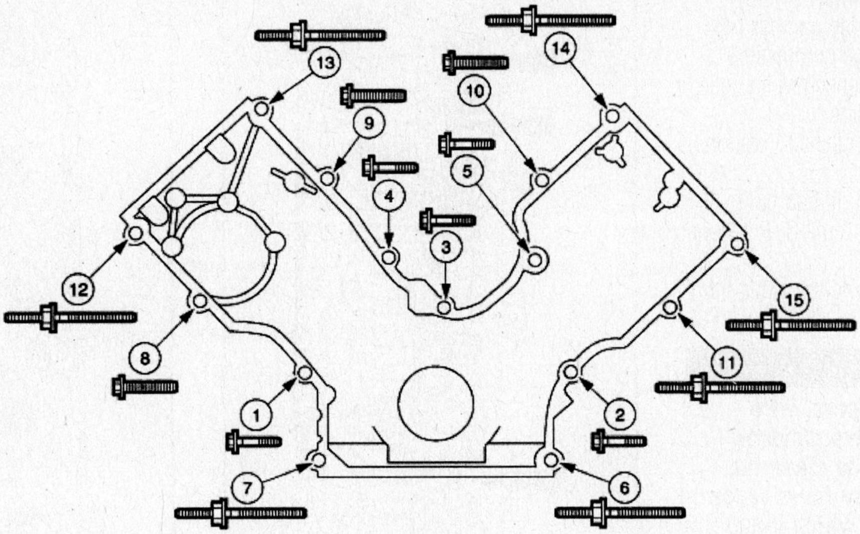

1	Bolt, Hex Flange Head Pilot, M8 x 1.25 x 50
2	Bolt, Hex Flange Head Pilot, M8 x 1.25 x 50
3	Bolt, Hex Flange Head Pilot, M8 x 1.25 x 50
4	Bolt, Hex Flange Head Pilot, M8 x 1.25 x 50
5	Bolts, Hex Flange Head Pilot, M8 x 1.25 x 50
6	Stud, Hex-Head Pilot, M10 x 1.5 x 59 - M10 x 1.5 x 30
7	Stud, Hex-Head Pilot, M10 x 1.5 x 59 - M10 x 1.5 x 30
8	Screw and Washer, Hex Pilot, M10 x 1.5 x 54
9	Screw and Washer, Hex Pilot, M10 x 1.5 x 54
10	Screw and Washer, Hex Pilot, M10 x 1.5 x 54
11	Stud and Washer, Hex Head Pilot, M10 x 1.5 x 68 - M8 x 1.25 x 27
12	Stud and Washer, Hex Head Pilot, M10 x 1.5 x 68 - M8 x 1.25 x 27
13	Stud and Washer, Hex Head Pilot, M10 x 1.5 x 68 - M8 x 1.25 x 27
14	Stud and Washer, Hex Head Pilot, M10 x 1.5 x 68 - M8 x 1.25 x 27
15	Stud and Washer, Hex Head Pilot, M10 x 1.5 x 68 - M8 x 1.25 x 27

06017-NAVI-G71

Fig. 193 Front cover bolts size, location and torque sequence—2005 Excursion models with the 6.8L engine

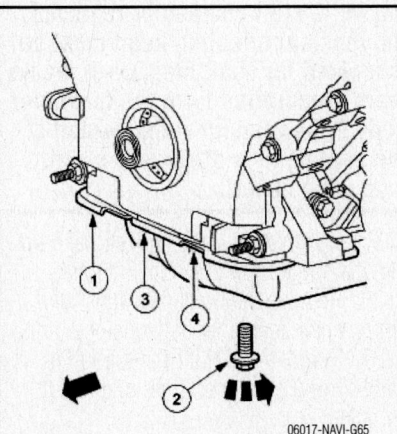

06017-NAVI-G65

Fig. 194 Front oil pan bolt torque sequence—2005 Excursion models with 5.4L and 6.8L engines

Expedition & Navigator

See Figures 195 through 214.

1. Before servicing the vehicle, refer to the precautions section.

2. Drain the engine oil.

3. Remove the engine cooling fan.

4. Remove the valve covers.

5. Remove the accessory drive belt.

6. Remove the nut and the power steering pressure hose support bracket.

7. Remove the nut and the transmission cooler tube support bracket.

8. Remove the crankshaft pulley bolt and washer. Discard the crankshaft pulley bolt.

9. Using the tool 303-009, remove the crankshaft pulley.

10. Using the tool 303-107, remove the crankshaft front seal.

11. Remove the bolts and the accessory drive idler pulleys.

12. Remove the bolts and the coolant pump pulley.

13. Remove the bolts and the accessory drive belt tensioner.

14. Disconnect the right hand Camshaft Position (CMP) sensor. Discard the O-ring seal.

15. Disconnect the A/C compressor electrical connector.

16. Disconnect the radio ignition interference capacitor electrical connectors.

17. Remove the nut and the right hand radio ignition interference capacitor.

18. Disconnect the left CMP sensor. Discard the O-ring seal.

19. Remove the nut and the left hand radio ignition interference capacitor.

20. Remove the bolts and position the power steering pump assembly aside.

21. Disconnect the wiring harness position retainer and the engine oil pressure (EOP) switch electrical connector and position the wiring harness aside.

22. Disconnect the Crankshaft Position (CKP) sensor connector.

23. Remove the 4 front oil pan bolts.

24. Remove the bolt and the CKP sensor. Discard the O-ring seal.

25. Remove the bolts and the studs from the front cover.

✲✲ CAUTION

Do not use metal scrapers, wire brushes, power abrasive discs or other abrasive means to clean the sealing surfaces. These tools cause scratches and gouges which make leak paths. Use a plastic scraping tool to remove all traces of old sealant.

26. Remove the engine front cover from the front cover to cylinder block dowel.

27. Remove the engine front cover gaskets.

28. Clean the mating surfaces with silicone gasket remover and metal surface prep. Follow the directions on the packaging.

29. Inspect the mating surfaces.

30. Remove the crankshaft sensor ring from the crankshaft.

31. Position the crankshaft keyway at the 12 o'clock position.

➡️ **If the camshaft lobes are not exactly positioned at the 12 o'clock position, the crankshaft will require one full additional rotation to 12 o'clock. The number 1 cylinder camshaft exhaust lobe must be coming up on the exhaust stroke. Verify by noting the position of the 2 intake camshaft lobes and the exhaust lobe on the number 1 cylinder.**

➡️ **If the components are to be reinstalled, they must be installed in the same positions. Mark the components for installation into the original locations.**

32. Remove only the 3 roller followers shown in the illustration from the right hand cylinder head.

✲✲ CAUTION

Do not allow the valve keepers to fall off the valve or the valve may drop into the cylinder.

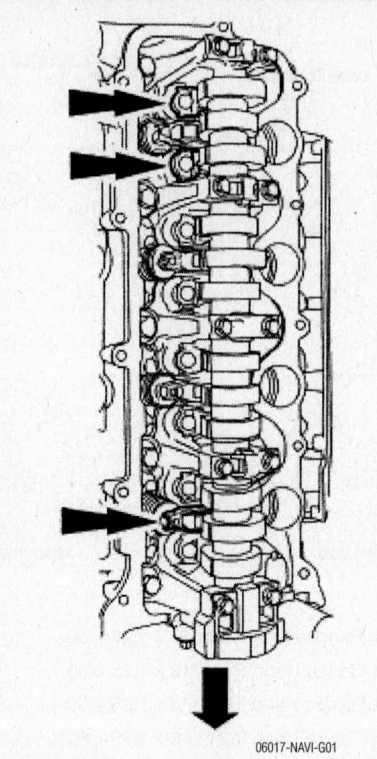

Fig. 195 Remove only the 3 roller followers shown from the right hand cylinder head—2005–07 Expedition and Navigator models

06017-NAVI-G01

➡️ **It may be necessary to push the valve down while compressing the spring.**

33. Using the tool illustrated, remove the 3 designated roller followers in the previous step from the right hand cylinder head.

34. Remove only the 3 roller followers shown in the illustration from the left hand cylinder head.

35. Using the tool 303-1039, remove the 3 designated roller followers in the previous step from the left hand cylinder head.

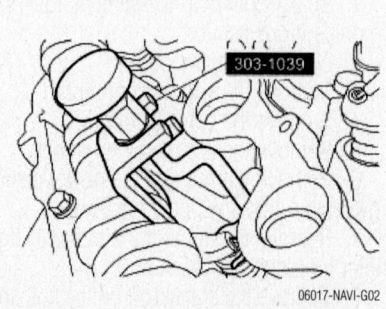

Fig. 196 Remove the 3 designated roller followers from the right hand cylinder head—2005–07 Expedition and Navigator models

06017-NAVI-G02

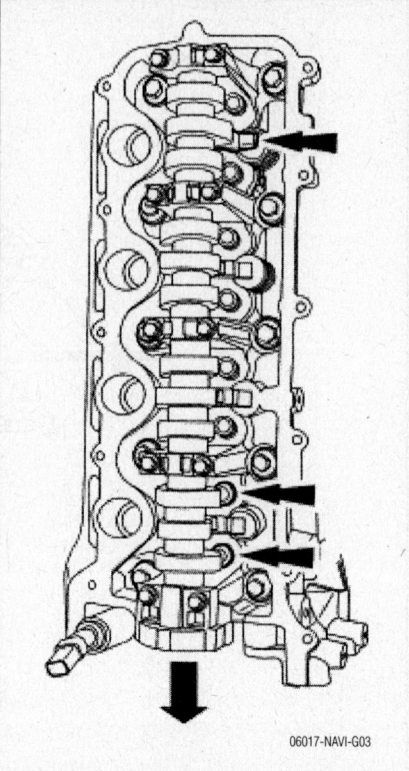

Fig. 197 Remove only the 3 roller followers shown from the left hand cylinder head—2005–07 Expedition and Navigator models

06017-NAVI-G03

✲✲ WARNING

The crankshaft cannot be moved past the 6 o'clock position once set.

36. Rotate the crankshaft clockwise and position the crankshaft keyway at the 6 o'clock position.

✲✲ CAUTION

If one or both of the tensioner mounting bolts are loosened or removed, the tensioner-sealing bead must be inspected for seal integrity. If cracks, tears, separation from the tensioner body or permanent compression of the seal bead is observed, install a new tensioner.

37. Remove the bolts, the left hand timing chain tensioner and tensioner arm.

38. Remove the bolts, the right hand timing chain tensioner and tensioner arm.

39. Remove the right hand and left hand timing chains and the crankshaft sprocket.

40. Remove the right hand timing chain from the camshaft sprocket.

41. Remove the right hand timing chain from the crankshaft sprocket.

42. Remove the left hand timing chain from the camshaft sprocket.

43. Remove the left hand timing chain and crankshaft sprocket.

44. Remove the left hand and right hand timing chain guides.

To install:

> ❊❊ **CAUTION**
>
> **Timing chain procedures must be followed exactly or damage to valves and pistons will result.**

> ❊❊ **CAUTION**
>
> **Prior to installation, inspect the tensioner-sealing bead for seal integrity. If cracks, tears, separation from the tensioner body or permanent compression of the seal bead is observed, install a new tensioner.**

45. Compress the tensioner plunger, using a vise.

46. Install a retaining clip on the tensioner to hold the plunger in during installation.

47. Remove the tensioner from the vise.

48. If the copper links are not visible, mark two links on one end and one link on the other end, and use as timing marks.

49. Install the crankshaft sprocket, making sure the flange faces forward.

50. Install the 4 bolts and the left hand and right hand timing chain guides. Tighten to 89 inch lbs. (10 Nm).

51. Position the lower end of the left hand (inner) timing chain on the crankshaft sprocket, aligning the timing mark on the outer flange of the crankshaft sprocket with the single copper (marked) link on the chain.

➡Make sure the upper half of the timing chain is below the tensioner arm dowel.

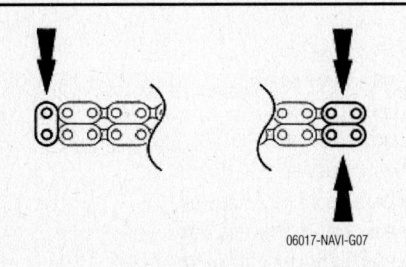

Fig. 198 If the copper links are not visible, mark two links on one end and one link on the other end, and use as timing marks—2005–07 Expedition and Navigator models

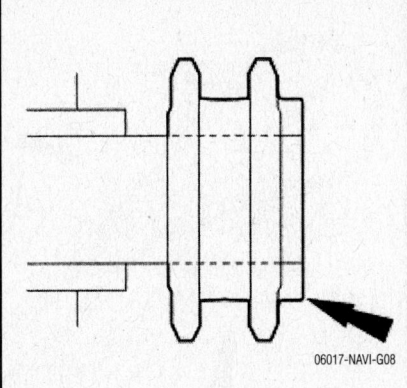

Fig. 199 Install the crankshaft sprocket, making sure the flange faces forward—2005–07 Expedition and Navigator models

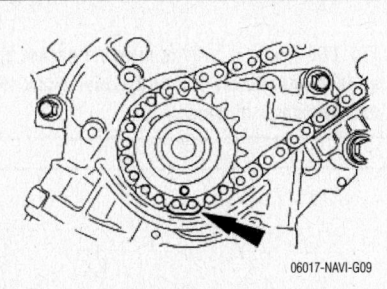

Fig. 200 Position the lower end of the left hand (inner) timing chain on the crankshaft sprocket, aligning the timing mark on the outer flange of the crankshaft sprocket with the single copper (marked) link on the chain—2005–07 Expedition and Navigator models

52. Position the timing chain on the camshaft sprocket with the camshaft sprocket timing mark positioned between the two copper (marked) chain links.

➡The left hand timing chain tensioner arm has a bump near the dowel hole for identification.

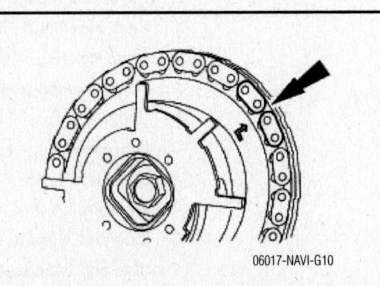

Fig. 201 Position the timing chain on the camshaft sprocket with the camshaft sprocket timing mark positioned between the two copper (marked) chain links—2005–07 Expedition and Navigator models

53. Position the left hand timing chain tensioner arm on the dowel pin and install the left hand timing chain tensioner and bolts. Tighten the bolts to 18 ft. lbs. (25 Nm).

54. Remove the retaining clip from the left hand timing chain tensioner.

55. Position the lower end of the right hand (outer) timing chain on the crankshaft sprocket, aligning the timing mark on the sprocket with the single copper (marked) chain link.

➡The lower half of the timing chain must be positioned above the tensioner arm dowel.

56. Position the right hand timing chain on the camshaft sprocket. Make sure the camshaft sprocket timing mark is positioned between the two copper (marked) chain links.

57. Position the right hand timing chain tensioner arm on the dowel pin and install the right hand timing chain tensioner and bolts. Tighten the bolts to 18 ft. lbs. (25 Nm).

58. Remove the retaining clip from the right hand timing chain tensioner.

59. As a final-check, verify correct alignment of all timing marks.

60. Install the crankshaft sensor ring on the crankshaft.

61. Lubricate the roller followers with clean engine oil prior to installation.

62. Using tool 303-1039, install all of the camshaft roller followers.

> ❊❊ **CAUTION**
>
> **Do not use metal scrapers, wire brushes, power abrasive discs or other abrasive means to clean the sealing surfaces. These tools cause scratches and gouges which make leak paths. Use a plastic scraping tool to remove all traces of old sealant.**

➡If the engine front cover is not secured within 4 minutes, the sealant must be removed and the sealing area cleaned. To clean the sealing area, use silicone gasket remover and metal surface prep. Failure to follow this procedure can cause future oil leakage.

➡Make sure that the engine front cover gasket is in place on the engine front cover before installation.

63. Apply a bead of silicone gasket and sealant along the cylinder head-to-cylinder block surface and the oil pan-to-cylinder block surface, at the locations illustrated.

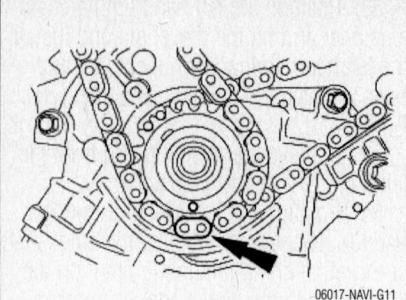

06017-NAVI-G11

Fig. 202 Position the lower end of the right hand (outer) timing chain on the crankshaft sprocket, aligning the timing mark on the sprocket with the single copper (marked) chain link—2005–07 Expedition and Navigator models

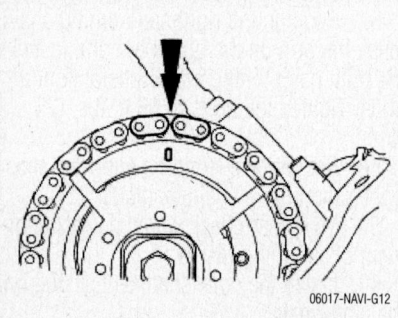

06017-NAVI-G12

Fig. 203 Position the right hand timing chain on the camshaft sprocket. Make sure the camshaft sprocket timing mark is positioned between the two copper (marked) chain links—2005–07 Expedition and Navigator models

64. Install a new engine front cover gasket on the engine front cover. Position the engine front cover onto the dowels. Install the fasteners finger-tight.

65. Tighten the engine front cover fasteners in sequence in 2 steps:

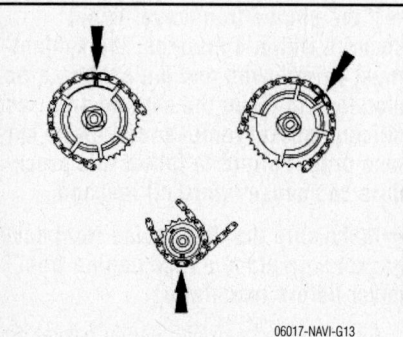

06017-NAVI-G13

Fig. 204 Verify correct alignment of all timing marks—2005–07 Expedition and Navigator models

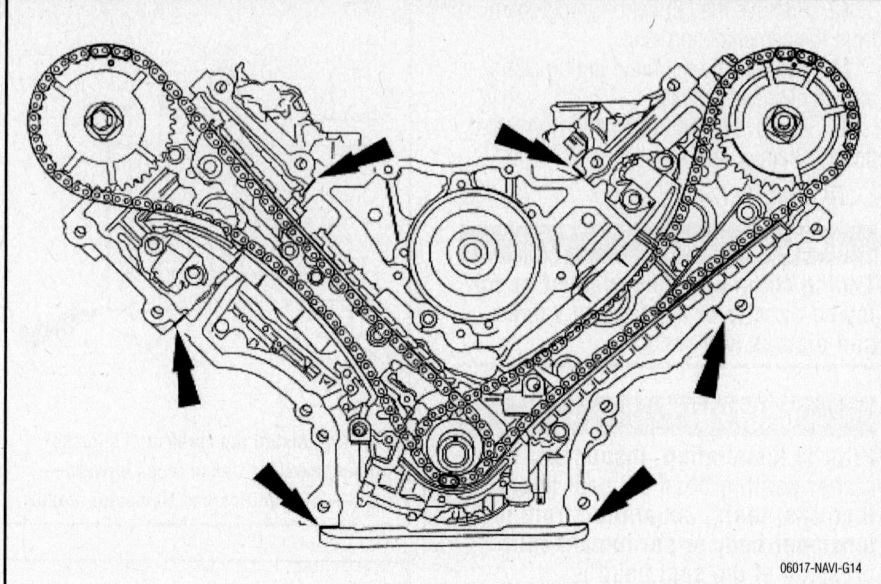

06017-NAVI-G14

Fig. 205 Apply a bead of silicone gasket and sealant along the cylinder head-to-cylinder block surface and the oil pan-to-cylinder block surface, at the locations shown—2005–07 Expedition and Navigator models

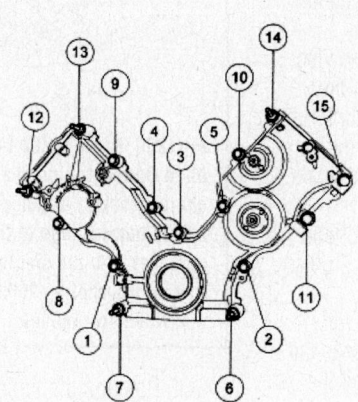

1	Bolt, Hex Flange Head Pilot, M8 x 1.25 x 50
2	Bolt, Hex Flange Head Pilot, M8 x 1.25 x 50
3	Bolt, Hex Flange Head Pilot, M8 x 1.25 x 50
4	Bolt, Hex Flange Head Pilot, M8 x 1.25 x 50
5	Bolts, Hex Flange Head Pilot, M8 x 1.25 x 50
6	Stud, Hex Head Pilot, M10 x 1.5 x 1.5 x 103
7	Stud, Hex Head Pilot, M10 x 1.5 x 1.5 x 103
8	Bolt, Hex Flange Head Pilot, M8 x 1.25 x 50
9	Bolt, Hex Flange Head Pilot, M8 x 1.25 x 50
10	Bolt, Hex Flange Head Pilot, M8 x 1.25 x 50
11	Bolt, Hex Flange Head Pilot, M8 x 1.25 x 50
12	Stud and Washer, Hex Head Pilot, M8 x 1.25 x 1.25 x 94
13	Stud and Washer, Hex Head Pilot, M8 x 1.25 x 1.25 x 94
14	Stud and Washer, Hex Head Pilot, M8 x 1.25 x 1.25 x 94
15	Bolt, Hex Head Pilot, M8 x 1.25 x 56

06017-NAVI-G15

Fig. 206 Engine front cover fastener location and torque sequence—2005–07 Expedition and Navigator models

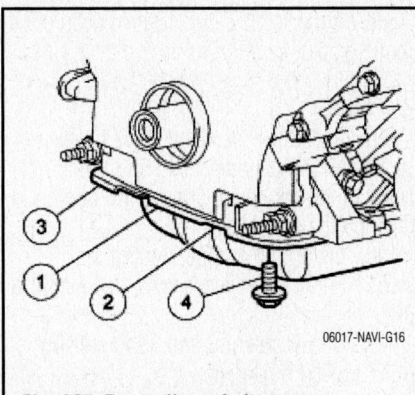

Fig. 207 Front oil pan bolts torque sequence—2005–07 Expedition and Navigator models

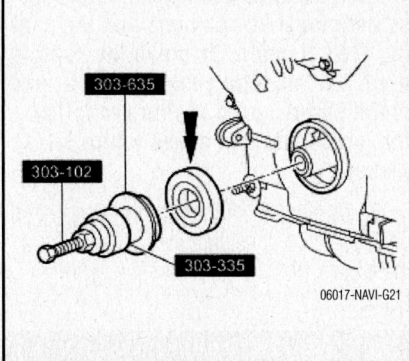

Fig. 208 Install the crankshaft seal into the engine front cover—2005–07 Expedition and Navigator models

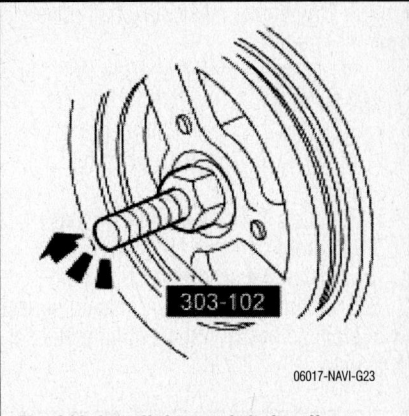

Fig. 210 Install the crankshaft pulley—2005–07 Expedition and Navigator models

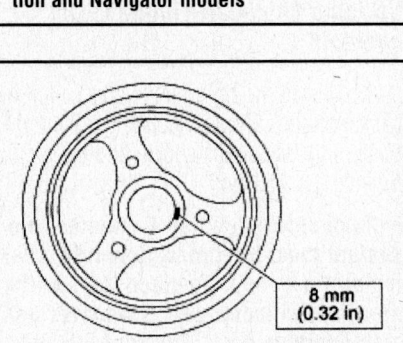

Fig. 209 Apply a 0.32 inch (8mm) bead of silicone gasket and sealant to the Woodruff key slot on the crankshaft pulley—2005–07 Expedition and Navigator models

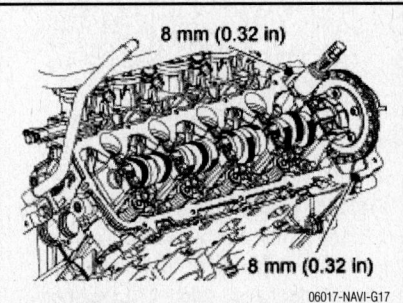

Fig. 211 Apply a 0.32 inch (8mm) bead of silicone gasket and sealant in 2 places where the engine front cover meets the right cylinder head—2005–07 Expedition and Navigator models

a. Step 1: Tighten fasteners 1 through 15 to 18 ft. lbs. (25 Nm).

b. Step 2: Tighten fasteners 6 and 7 to 35 ft. lbs. (48 Nm).

66. Install the 4 front oil pan bolts in the sequence shown in 2 steps.

a. Step 1: Tighten to 15 ft. lbs. (20 Nm).

b. Step 2: Tighten an additional 60 degrees.

✳✳ CAUTION

Do not use metal scrapers, wire brushes, power abrasive discs or other abrasive means to clean sealing surfaces. These tools cause scratches and gouges which make leak paths. Use a plastic scraping tool to remove all traces of old sealant.

67. Connect the CKP sensor electrical connector.

68. Position the power steering pump assembly and install the bolts. Tighten to 18 ft. lbs. (25 Nm).

69. Position the power steering pressure hose support bracket and install the nut.

70. Position the transmission cooler tube support bracket and install the nut.

➡**Lubricate the O-ring seal with clean engine oil prior to installation.**

71. Using a new O-ring seal, install the right hand CMP sensor and the bolt.

72. Connect the right hand CMP sensor electrical connector.

73. Install the left hand radio ignition interference capacitor and the nut.

➡**Lubricate the O-ring seal with clean engine oil prior to installation.**

74. Using a new O-ring seal, install the left hand CMP sensor and the bolt.

75. Connect the left hand CMP sensor electrical connector.

76. Install the right hand radio ignition interference capacitor and the nut.

77. Connect the radio ignition interference capacitor electrical connectors.

78. Install the 3 accessory drive belt idler pulleys, the coolant pump pulley and the 7 bolts. Tighten the bolts to 18 ft. lbs. (25 Nm).

79. Lubricate the engine front cover and the crankshaft seal inner lip with clean engine oil.

80. Use the tools illustrated to install the crankshaft seal into the engine front cover.

➡**If not secured within 4 minutes, the sealant must be removed and the sealing area cleaned. To clean the sealing area, use silicone gasket remover and metal surface prep. Failure to follow this procedure can cause future oil leakage.**

81. Apply a 0.32 inch (8mm) bead of silicone gasket and sealant to the Woodruff key slot on the crankshaft pulley.

82. Use the tool illustrated to install the crankshaft pulley.

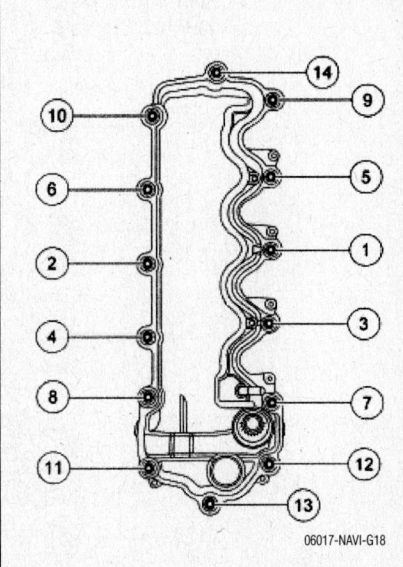

Fig. 212 Install the right hand valve cover and gasket on the cylinder head and tighten the bolts in sequence—2005–07 Expedition and Navigator models

83. Tighten the new crankshaft pulley bolt in 4 steps:

    a. Step 1: Tighten to 66 ft. lbs. (90 Nm).

    b. Step 2: Loosen 360 degrees.

    c. Step 3: Tighten to 37 ft. lbs. (50 Nm).

    d. Step 4: Tighten an additional 90 degrees.

84. Install the accessory drive belt.

85. Clean the valve cover mating surface with silicone gasket remover and metal surface prep.

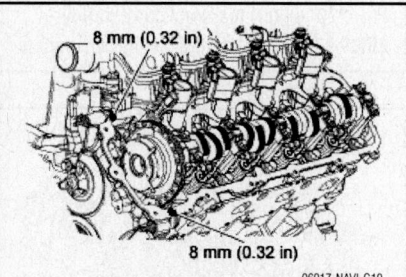

Fig. 213 Apply a 0.32 inch (8mm) bead of silicone gasket and sealant in 2 places where the engine front cover meets the left cylinder head—2005–07 Expedition and Navigator models

➡If not secured within 4 minutes, the sealant must be removed and the sealing area cleaned. To clean the sealing area, use silicone gasket remover and metal surface prep. Failure to follow this procedure can cause future oil leakage.

86. Apply a 0.32 inch (8mm) bead of silicone gasket and sealant in 2 places where the engine front cover meets the cylinder head.

❄ CAUTION

When installing the valve cover, make sure to avoid damaging the Variable Camshaft Timing (VCT) solenoid.

87. Install the right hand valve cover and gasket on the cylinder head and tighten the bolts in the sequence shown and tighten to 89 inch lbs. (10 Nm).

➡If not secured within 4 minutes, the sealant must be removed and the sealing area cleaned. To clean the sealing area, use silicone gasket remover and metal surface prep. Failure to follow this procedure can cause future oil leakage.

88. Apply a 0.32 inch (8mm) bead of silicone gasket and sealant in 2 places where the engine front cover meets the left cylinder head.

89. Install the left hand valve cover and gasket on the cylinder head and tighten the bolts in the sequence shown and tighten to 89 inch lbs. (10 Nm).

90. Install the engine cooling fan.

91. Fill the crankcase with clean engine oil.

92. Check steering and transmission fluid, top off if needed.

93. Check all connections for leaks.

TIMING GEARS, FRONT COVER AND SEAL

REMOVAL & INSTALLATION

Excursion 6.0L Diesel Engine

1. Before servicing the vehicle, refer to the precautions section.

2. Remove the intake manifold.

3. Disconnect the exhaust pressure tube at the exhaust.

4. Remove the nuts and the exhaust pressure bracket assembly.

➡Remove the thermostat housing only if a new front cover is being installed.

5. Remove the stud bolts and the thermostat housing.

6. Remove and discard the O-ring.

7. Disconnect the engine coolant fill hose.

8. Disconnect the lower radiator hose.

9. Remove the stator stand-off bolt.

10. Remove the four bolts and position aside the power steering pump.

11. Remove the bolts and the accessory drive belt tensioner.

12. Remove the bolts and the accessory drive idler pulleys.

➡Remove the coolant pump pulley only if a new front cover is being installed.

13. Remove the coolant pump pulley.

➡Remove the coolant pump only if a new front cover is being installed.

14. Remove the bolts and the coolant pump.

15. Remove and discard the O-ring.

16. Remove the nut and the battery cable bracket.

17. Remove the oil pump.

18. Check the crankshaft vibration damper runout.

Fig. 214 Install the left hand valve cover and gasket on the cylinder head and tighten the bolts in sequence—2005–07 Expedition and Navigator models

19. Remove the paint from the face of the crankshaft vibration damper at four points 90 degrees apart.

20. Attach the special tool to the cylinder block. Position the special tool on one of the unpainted surfaces.

21. Using a suitable tool, pry the crankshaft forward. Zero the dial indicator.

➡**Pry the crankshaft forward at the same point to eliminate possible error caused by crankshaft end play.**

22. Rotate the crankshaft 90 degrees. Pry the crankshaft forward. Record the measurement. Repeat at each unpainted surface. If the runout exceeds specification, install a new crankshaft vibration damper.

❄❄ WARNING

To prevent engine damage, you must always install four new bolts when installing the vibration damper.

❄❄ WARNING

To avoid personal injury, support the vibration damper during mounting bolt removal. The damper can slide off the nose of the crankshaft very easily.

23. Remove the bolts and the crankcase vibration damper.
24. Discard the bolts.
25. Remove the bolts and the front cover.

❄❄ WARNING

Sealant is used where the crankcase and lower crankcase meet. Failure to cut the sealant could result in pulling the lower crankcase seal out while removing the front cover gasket.

26. Use a thin blade scraper to cut the sealant where the crankcase and the lower crankcase meet. Remove and discard the front cover gasket.

27. Clean and inspect the sealing surfaces.

28. Punch two holes in the seal.

29. Using the special tool, remove the crankshaft seal.

➡**Production engine will not have a wear sleeve.**

30. If equipped, remove the crankshaft damper wear sleeve.

31. Remove the thrust plate mounting bolts and remove the camshaft and gear.

➡**To Remove camshaft and gear upper valve components must first be removed. Refer to camshaft removal in this section.**

To install:

32. Install the camshaft and gear assembly. Using the special tool, align the camshaft timing mark as shown. Install the thrust plate mounting bolts.

33. Thoroughly clean the crankshaft front seal mounting surface.

34. Apply Threadlock 262® to the outer circumference of the leading edge of the crankshaft.

➡**New seal and wear sleeve must not be separated.**

35. Using the special tool, install the oil seal and wear sleeve assembly.

36. If removed, install the front cover crankcase dowels into the cylinder block.

➡**Use guide studs to aid in installation. Studs must be fabricated locally.**

37. Install the guide studs.

38. Apply a bead of sealant at the seam where the crankcase and the lower crankcase meet.

39. Install a new engine front cover gasket.

40. Install the engine front cover and bolts.

❄❄ WARNING

To prevent engine damage, you must always install four new bolts when installing the vibration damper.

➡**Do not use anti-seize compounds, grease or any lubricants. Lubricants have an adverse effect on the torque results.**

41. Install the crankshaft vibration damper and bolts.

42. Tighten the bolts in the sequence shown.

   a. Tighten the bolts to 68 Nm (50 ft. lbs.).

   b. Tighten the bolts an additional 90 degrees.

43. Install the oil pump.

44. Install the battery cable bracket and nut.

➡**Install a new O-ring on the coolant pump pulley.**

45. If removed, install the coolant pump and bolts.

46. If removed, install the coolant pump pulley and bolts.

47. Install the accessory drive idler pulleys and bolts.

48. Install the accessory drive belt tensioner and bolts.

49. Position back the power steering pump and install the bolts.

50. Install the stator stand-off bolt.

51. Connect the lower radiator coolant hose.

52. Connect the engine coolant hose.

➡**Install a new O-ring.**

53. If removed, install the thermostat housing and stud bolts.

54. Install the exhaust pressure bracket assembly and retaining nuts.

55. Connect the exhaust pressure tube fitting at the exhaust manifold.

56. Install the intake manifold.

TURBOCHARGER

REMOVAL & INSTALLATION

Excursion 6.0L Diesel Engine

1. Before servicing the vehicle, refer to the precautions in the beginning of this section. Remove the air cleaner assembly.

❄❄ CAUTION

Never remove the pressure relief cap while the engine is operating or when the cooling system is hot. Failure to follow these instructions can result in damage to the cooling system or engine or result in personal injury. To avoid having scalding hot coolant or steam blow out of the degas bottle when removing the pressure relief cap, wait until the engine has cooled, then wrap a thick cloth around the pressure relief cap and turn it slowly. Step back while the pressure is released from the cooling system. When certain all the pressure has been released, (still with a cloth) turn and remove the pressure relief cap. Failure to follow these instructions can result in personal injury.

❄❄ CAUTION

The coolant must be recovered in a suitable, clean container for reuse. If the coolant is contaminated, it must be recycled or disposed of correctly and the system filled with new coolant.

❋❋ CAUTION

Always fill the cooling system with the same type of coolant that was drained from the system. Do not mix coolant types. Do not add orange-colored Motorcraft Specialty Orange Engine Coolant VC-2, or equivalent meeting WSS-M97B44-D. Mixing coolants may degrade the coolant's corrosion protection. Do not add alcohol, methanol, brine, or any engine coolants mixed with alcohol or methanol antifreeze. These can cause engine damage from overheating or freezing.

2. Disconnect and plug the engine vent and radiator vent hoses.

3. Remove the bolts and position the degas bottle aside.

4. Loosen the clamp at the turbocharger.

5. Remove the bolts and remove the turbocharger intake tube.

6. Disconnect the charge air cooler inlet pipe.

7. Remove the push pins.

8. Disconnect the two wiring harness push pins and position out of the way.

9. Disconnect the turbocharger variable hydraulic control valve electrical connector.

10. Remove the bolts for the oil supply tube.

11. Remove and discard the gasket.

12. Remove the bolt and the wire retainer.

13. Using the special tool 303-755, remove the oil feed tube.

14. Remove the marmon clamp from the turbocharger outlet.

15. Remove the marmon clamp from the turbocharger inlet.

16. Remove the rear turbocharger mounting bolt.

17. Remove the front mounting bolts.

18. Position the turbocharger and remove the turbocharger drain tube.

19. Remove and discard the drain tube O-rings.

20. Remove the turbocharger.

To install:

21. Position the turbocharger on the turbocharger pedestal.

➡**Install new O-rings and apply clean engine oil.**

22. Position the turbocharger and install the turbocharger drain tube.

23. Install the turbocharger and the rear mounting bolt and tighten to 28 ft. lbs. (38 Nm).

24. Install the turbocharger front mounting bolts and tighten to 28 ft. lbs. (38 Nm).

25. Install the turbocharger inlet marmon clamp and tighten to 9 ft. lbs. (12 Nm).

26. Install the turbocharger exhaust marmon clamp and tighten to 89 inch lbs. (10 Nm).

27. Install the oil feed tube.

28. Position the wire retainer and install the bolt.

29. Pre-lubricate the oil inlet hole of the turbocharger assembly with clean engine oil and spin the compressor wheel several times to coat the bearing with oil.

30. Position the oil feed tube and install the bolts and tighten to 18 ft. lbs. (25 Nm).

31. Install a new gasket.

32. Connect the turbocharger variable vane hydraulic control valve electrical connector.

33. Position the wiring harness and connect the push pins.

34. Install the push pins.

35. Connect the charge air cooler inlet pipe and tighten to 9 ft. lbs. (12 Nm).

36. Install the turbocharger intake tube.

VALVE LASH

ADJUSTMENT

These engines do not require valve lash adjusting, because they utilize hydraulic lash components in their valve actuation systems.

ENGINE PERFORMANCE & EMISSION CONTROL   COMPONENTS & SYSTEMS

MALFUNCTION INDICATOR LIGHT (MIL) RESET PROCEDURES

A diagnostic scan tool must be connected to the data link connector (DLC) for communication with the vehicle.

1. The required diagnostic tool functions are described below:

- Diagnostic test modes; self-test, clear diagnostic trouble codes (DTCs)
- Resetting keep alive memory (KAM)
- On-board system readiness (OBD monitor completion status)
- Diagnostic monitoring test results (mode 6) for on-board diagnostic (OBD) on-board monitors
- Output test mode
- Monitor, record, and playback of parameter identification (PIDs)
- Freeze frame PID data

COMPONENT LOCATIONS

See Figures 215 through 221.

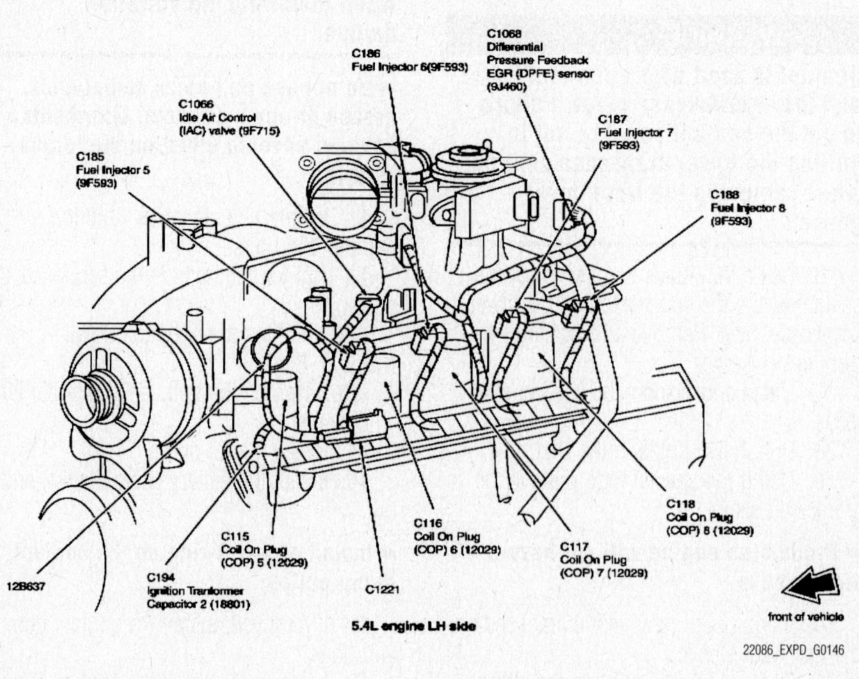

Fig. 215 5.4L Engine LH side view

22086_EXPD_G0146

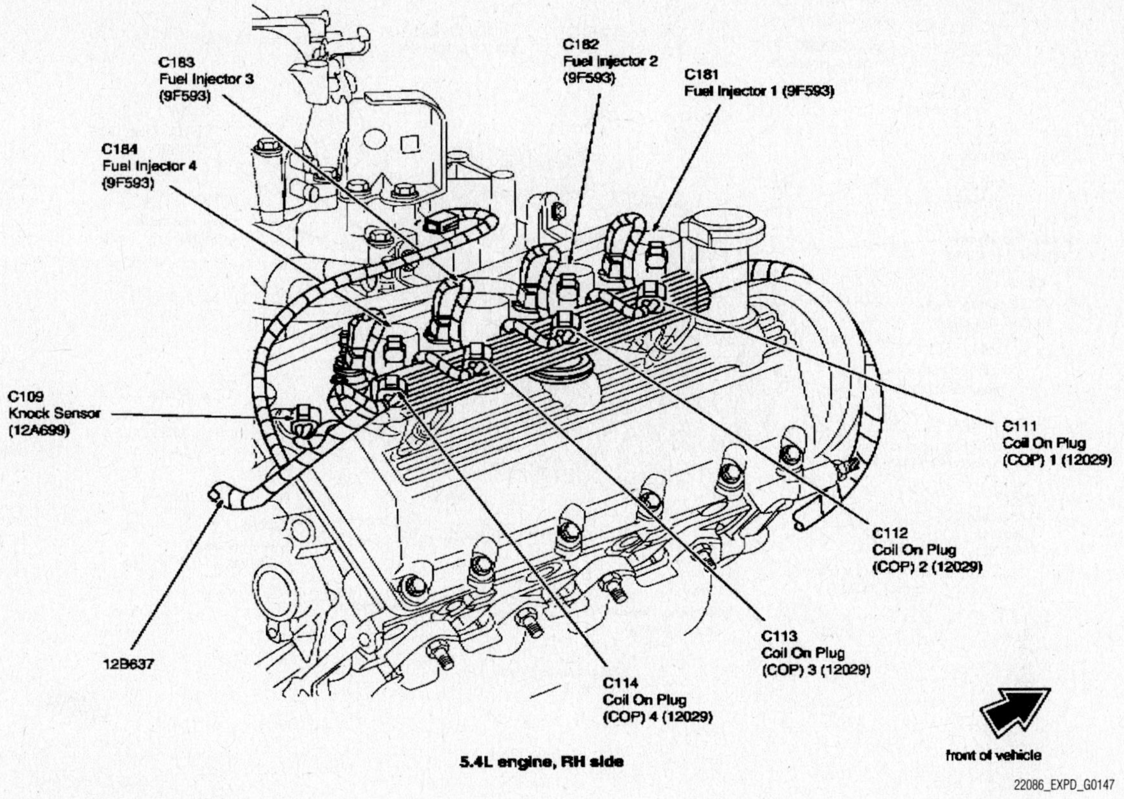

C183
Fuel Injector 3
(9F593)

C182
Fuel Injector 2
(9F593)

C181
Fuel Injector 1 (9F593)

C184
Fuel Injector 4
(9F593)

C109
Knock Sensor
(12A699)

C111
Coil On Plug
(COP) 1 (12029)

C112
Coil On Plug
(COP) 2 (12029)

C113
Coil On Plug
(COP) 3 (12029)

12B637

C114
Coil On Plug
(COP) 4 (12029)

5.4L engine, RH side

front of vehicle

22086_EXPD_G0147

Fig. 216 5.4L Engine RH side view

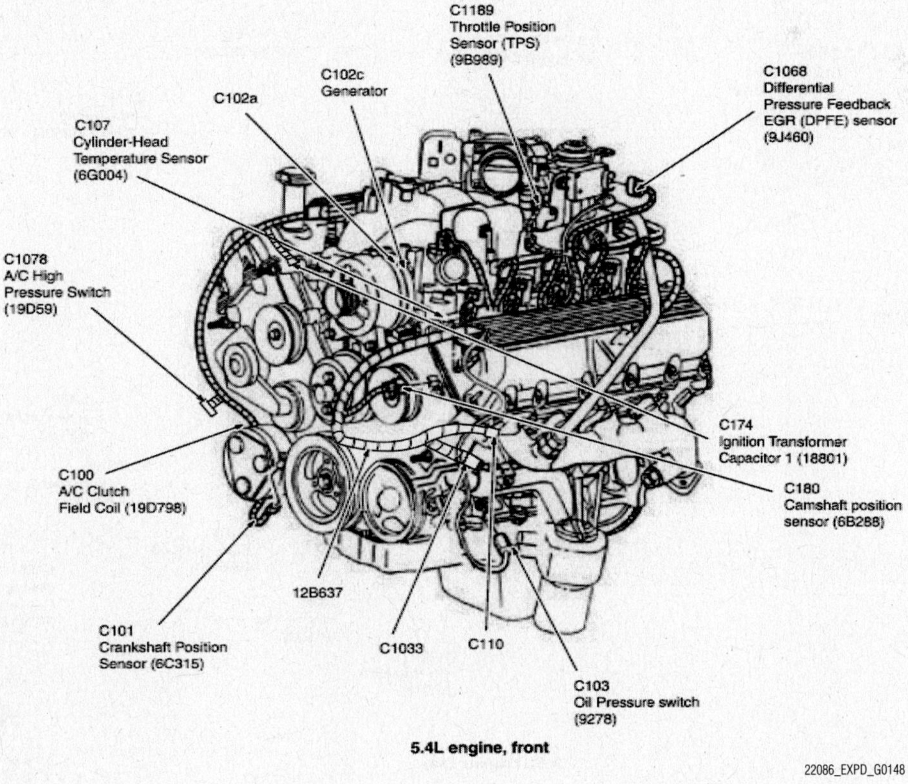

C1189
Throttle Position
Sensor (TPS)
(9B989)

C102c
Generator

C102a

C1068
Differential
Pressure Feedback
EGR (DPFE) sensor
(9J460)

C107
Cylinder-Head
Temperature Sensor
(6G004)

C1078
A/C High
Pressure Switch
(19D59)

C100
A/C Clutch
Field Coil (19D798)

C174
Ignition Transformer
Capacitor 1 (18801)

C180
Camshaft position
sensor (6B288)

C101
Crankshaft Position
Sensor (6C315)

12B637

C1033

C110

C103
Oil Pressure switch
(9278)

5.4L engine, front

22086_EXPD_G0148

Fig. 217 5.4L Engine front view

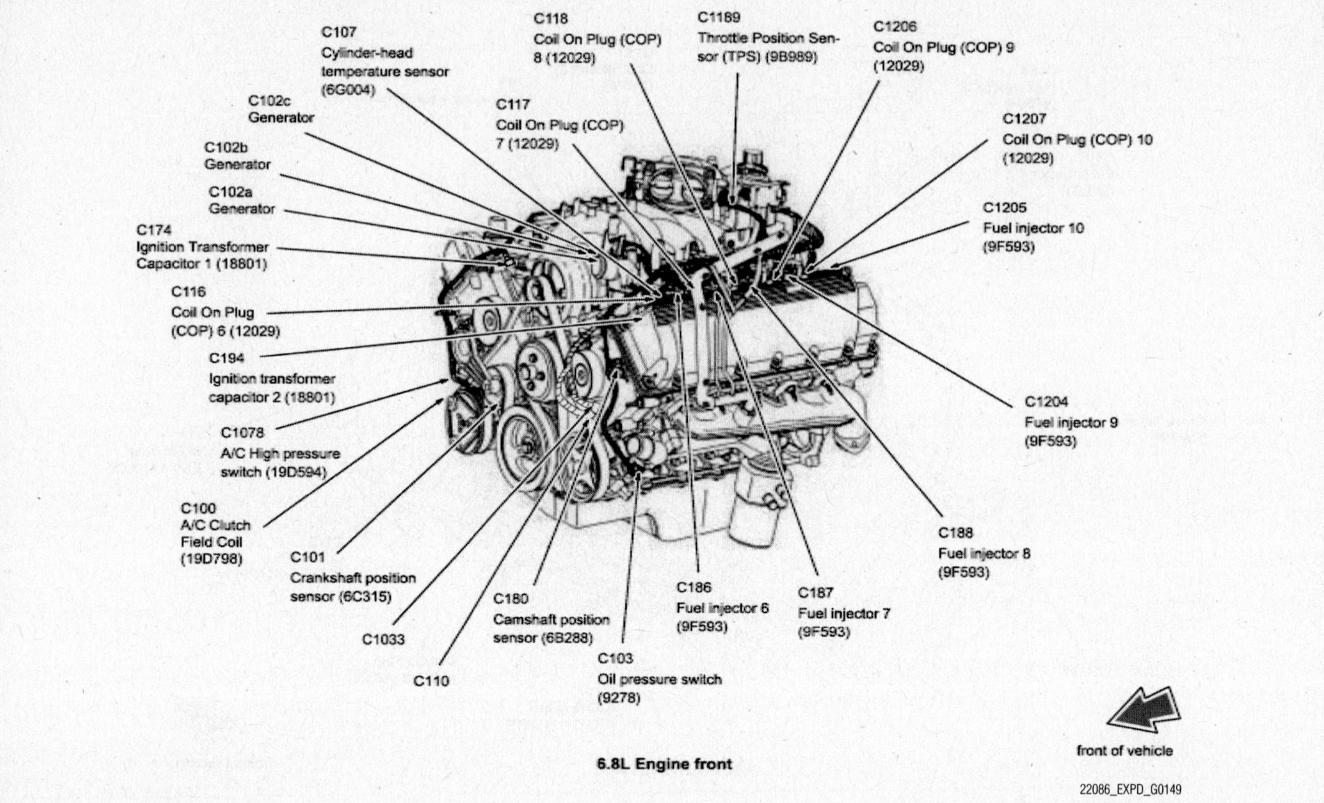

C107
Cylinder-head
temperature sensor
(6G004)

C118
Coil On Plug (COP)
8 (12029)

C1189
Throttle Position Sensor (TPS) (9B989)

C1206
Coil On Plug (COP) 9
(12029)

C102c
Generator

C117
Coil On Plug (COP)
7 (12029)

C1207
Coil On Plug (COP) 10
(12029)

C102b
Generator

C102a
Generator

C1205
Fuel injector 10
(9F593)

C174
Ignition Transformer
Capacitor 1 (18801)

C116
Coil On Plug
(COP) 6 (12029)

C194
Ignition transformer
capacitor 2 (18801)

C1204
Fuel injector 9
(9F593)

C1078
A/C High pressure
switch (19D594)

C100
A/C Clutch
Field Coil
(19D798)

C188
Fuel injector 8
(9F593)

C101
Crankshaft position
sensor (6C315)

C180
Camshaft position
sensor (6B288)

C186
Fuel injector 6
(9F593)

C187
Fuel injector 7
(9F593)

C1033

C110

C103
Oil pressure switch
(9278)

6.8L Engine front

front of vehicle

22086_EXPD_G0149

Fig. 218 6.8L Engine front view

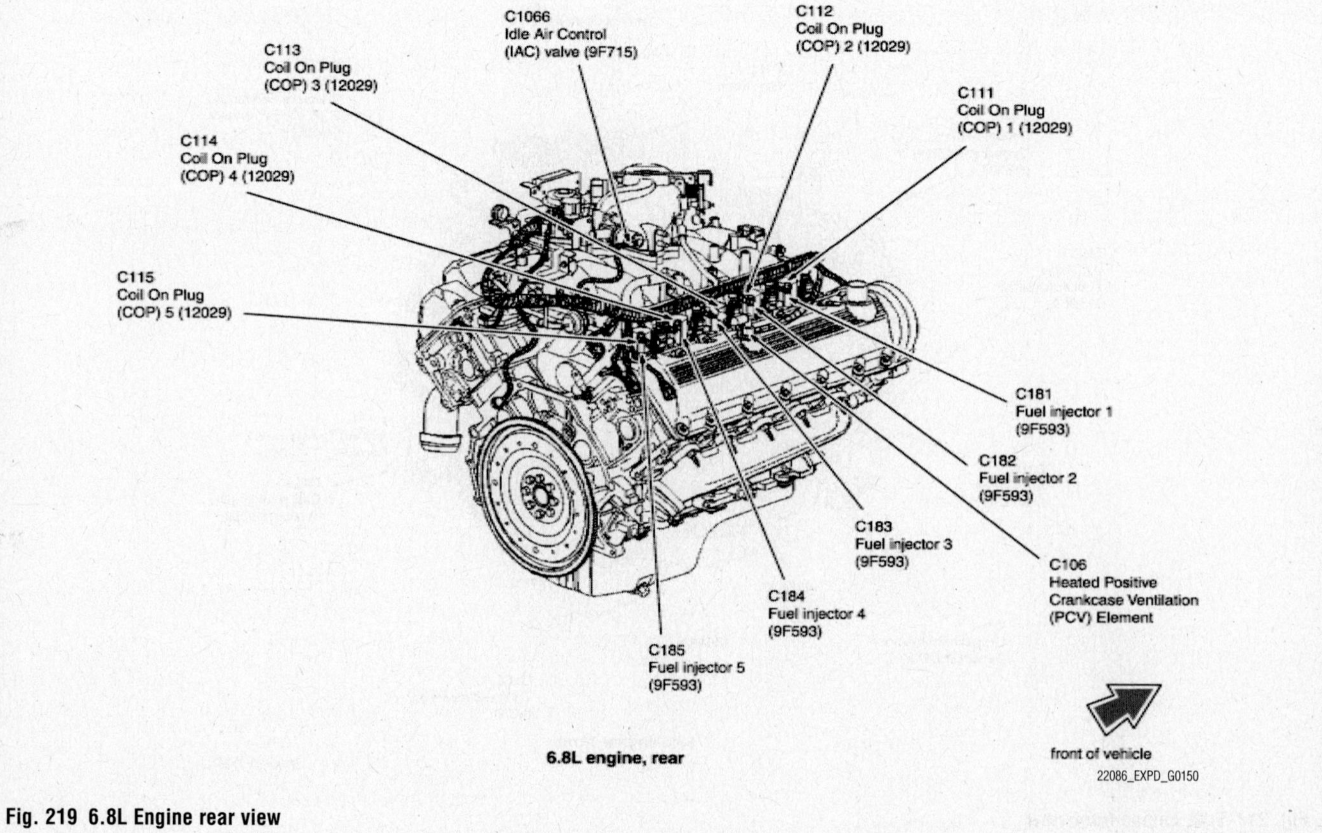

C1066
Idle Air Control
(IAC) valve (9F715)

C112
Coil On Plug
(COP) 2 (12029)

C113
Coil On Plug
(COP) 3 (12029)

C111
Coil On Plug
(COP) 1 (12029)

C114
Coil On Plug
(COP) 4 (12029)

C115
Coil On Plug
(COP) 5 (12029)

C181
Fuel injector 1
(9F593)

C182
Fuel injector 2
(9F593)

C183
Fuel injector 3
(9F593)

C184
Fuel injector 4
(9F593)

C106
Heated Positive
Crankcase Ventilation
(PCV) Element

C185
Fuel injector 5
(9F593)

6.8L engine, rear

front of vehicle

22086_EXPD_G0150

Fig. 219 6.8L Engine rear view

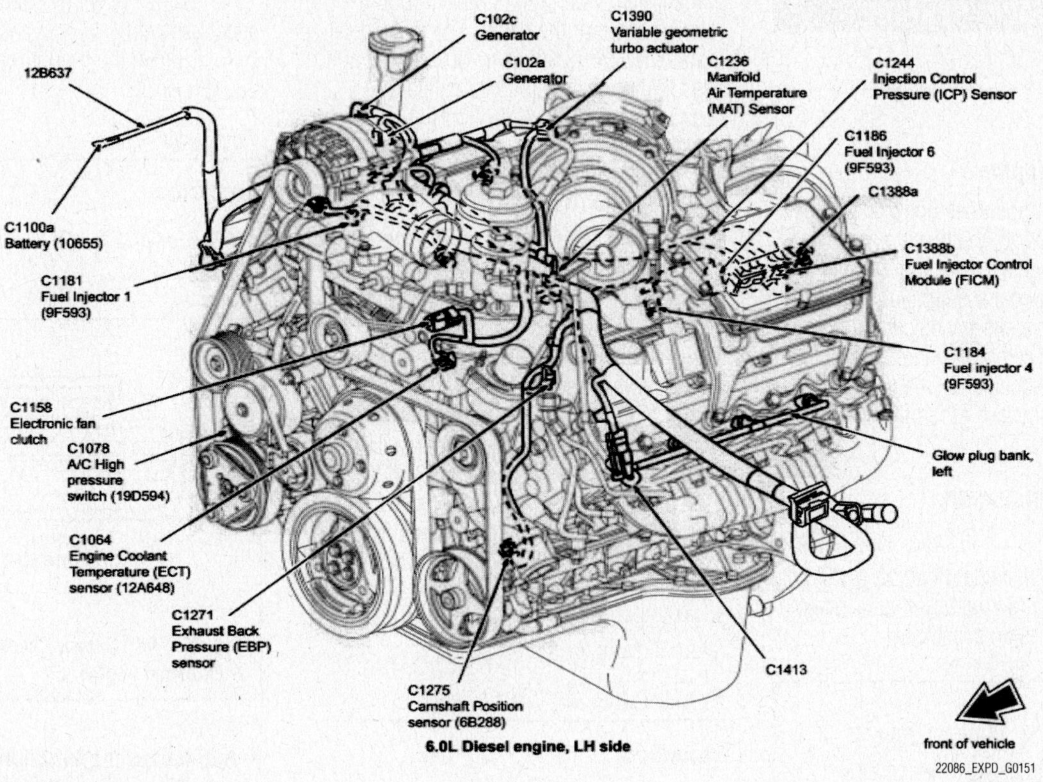

12B637

C102c
Generator

C102a
Generator

C1390
Variable geometric
turbo actuator

C1236
Manifold
Air Temperature
(MAT) Sensor

C1244
Injection Control
Pressure (ICP) Sensor

C1186
Fuel Injector 6
(9F593)

C1388a

C1100a
Battery (10655)

C1388b
Fuel Injector Control
Module (FICM)

C1181
Fuel Injector 1
(9F593)

C1184
Fuel injector 4
(9F593)

C1158
Electronic fan
clutch

C1078
A/C High
pressure
switch (19D594)

Glow plug bank,
left

C1064
Engine Coolant
Temperature (ECT)
sensor (12A648)

C1271
Exhaust Back
Pressure (EBP)
sensor

C1413

C1275
Camshaft Position
sensor (6B288)

6.0L Diesel engine, LH side

front of vehicle

22086_EXPD_G0151

Fig. 220 6.0L Diesel Engine LH side view

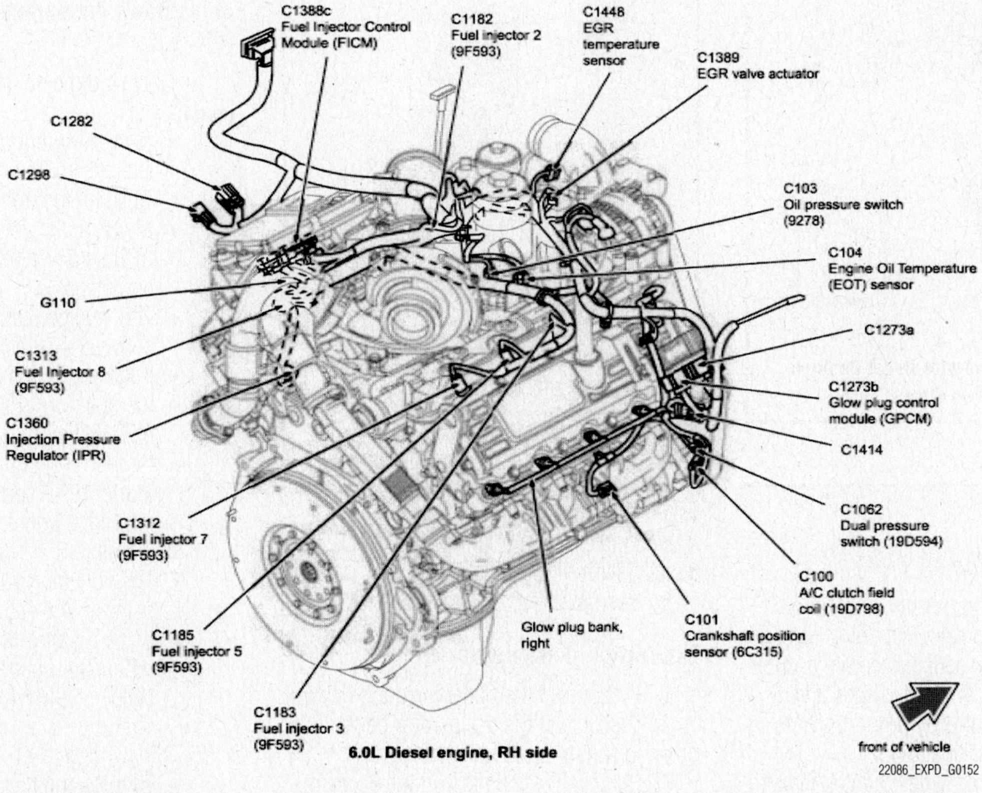

C1388c
Fuel Injector Control
Module (FICM)

C1182
Fuel injector 2
(9F593)

C1448
EGR
temperature
sensor

C1389
EGR valve actuator

C1282

C103
Oil pressure switch
(9278)

C1298

C104
Engine Oil Temperature
(EOT) sensor

C1273a

G110

C1313
Fuel Injector 8
(9F593)

C1273b
Glow plug control
module (GPCM)

C1360
Injection Pressure
Regulator (IPR)

C1414

C1062
Dual pressure
switch (19D594)

C1312
Fuel injector 7
(9F593)

C100
A/C clutch field
coil (19D798)

C1185
Fuel injector 5
(9F593)

Glow plug bank,
right

C101
Crankshaft position
sensor (6C315)

C1183
Fuel injector 3
(9F593)

6.0L Diesel engine, RH side

front of vehicle

22086_EXPD_G0152

Fig. 221 6.0L Diesel Engine RH side view

ACCELERATOR PEDAL POSITION (APP) SENSOR

LOCATION

Excursion

6.0L Diesel Engine

The diesel engine does not use an accelerator cable. Instead, the diesel engine uses an accelerator sensor assembly located on the accelerator pedal assembly. This drive-by-wire system is entirely electronic and, except for the accelerator pedal assembly, does not use mechanically moving parts. The accelerator sensor assembly is not adjustable.

Expedition & Navigator

See Figure 222.

The Accelerator Pedal Position (APP) Sensor is located on the accelerator pedal and is serviced as an assembly.

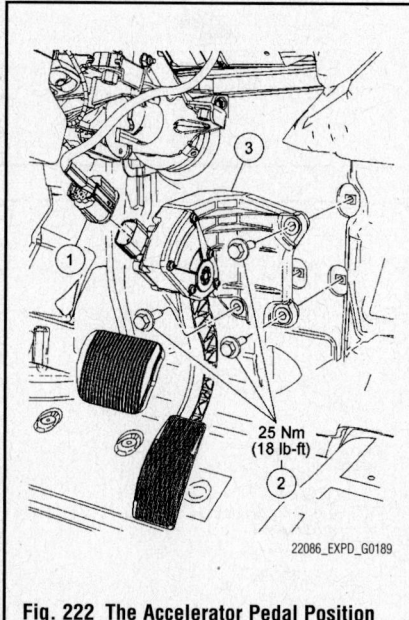

Fig. 222 The Accelerator Pedal Position (APP) Sensor location view

OPERATION

Excursion

6.0L Diesel Engine

The APP sensor is a 3-track potentiometer that is used to calculate driver demand for fuel quantity. The sensor receives a VREF voltage from the PCM and provides a variable voltage signal directly proportional to the accelerator pedal position.

The APP sensor provides 3 independent input signals to the Powertrain Control Module (PCM) indicating the driver's demand for power and is based upon the rotation angle of the pedal. The PCM determines the APP position by processing and uses the input signals to calculate the desired fuel quantity, injection timing, and the correct injection control pressure.

Expedition & Navigator

The APP sensor is an input to the Powertrain Control Module (PCM) and is used to determine the torque demand. There are 3 pedal position signals in the sensor. Signal 1, APPS1, has a negative slope (increasing angle, decreasing voltage) and signals 2 and 3, APPS2 and APPS3, both have a positive slope (increasing angle, increasing voltage). During normal operation APPS1 is used as the indication of pedal position by the strategy. The 3 pedal position signals make sure the PCM receives a correct input even if 1 signal has a concern. There are 2 reference voltage circuits and 2 signal return circuits for the sensor.

REMOVAL & INSTALLATION

Excursion

6.0L Diesel Engine

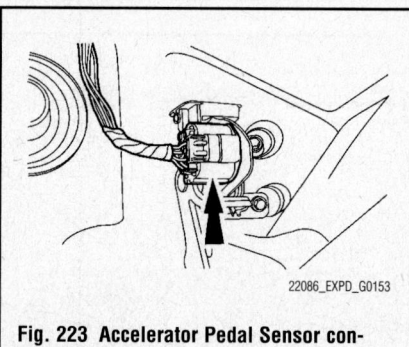

Fig. 223 Accelerator Pedal Sensor connector view

1. Disconnect the electrical connector.
2. Remove the bolts and remove the accelerator pedal and sensor assembly.

To install:

3. Install the accelerator pedal sensor assembly and mounting bolts.
4. Tighten the mounting bolts to 18 ft. lbs. (25 Nm).
5. Reconnect the electrical connector.

Expedition & Navigator

1. Disconnect the battery ground cable.
2. Disconnect the accelerator pedal position sensor electrical connector.
3. Remove the 3 bolts and the accelerator pedal assembly.

To install:

4. Install the 3 bolts and the accelerator pedal assembly.
5. Tighten the mounting bolts to 18 ft. lbs. (25 Nm).

TESTING

Excursion

6.0L Diesel Engine

See Figure 224.

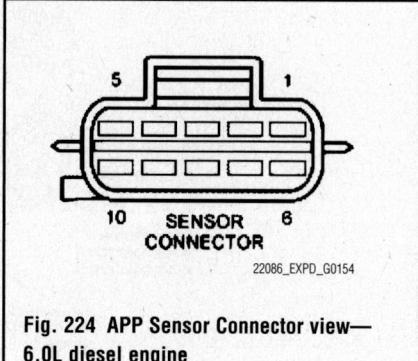

Fig. 224 APP Sensor Connector view— 6.0L diesel engine

➡ A detected malfunction of the APP sensor illuminates the electronic throttle control (wrench) indicator. A PCM detected fault on one of the 3 sensor signals permits normal engine operation. A fault with 2 sensor signals only allows the engine to operate at idle.

1. Checking the voltage reference circuits:
   - Turn the ignition off.
   - Disconnect the APP sensor.
   - Turn the ignition on.
   - Measure the voltage between the APP sensor pins 4 and 9, on the harness side.
   - The voltage reading should be between 4.5—5.5 volts.
   - If the reading is not as stated repair the open on VREF or SIGNAL RETURN circuits.
   - Repeat procedure checking pins 5 and 10 of secondary voltage reference and signal return circuits.
   - The voltage reading should be between 4.5—5.5 volts.
   - If the reading is not as stated repair the open on secondary VREF or SIGNAL RETURN circuits.
2. Checking the APP Sensor:
   - Turn the ignition off.
   - Disconnect the APP sensor.

- Measure the resistance between the APP sensor pin 2, component side and the APP sensor pin 8, component side.
- The resistance reading should be between 2,700—6,500 ohms.
- If the reading is not as stated replace the APP sensor.

5.4L Expedition & Navigator

See Figures 225 and 226.

1. Checking the VREF voltage to the Accelerator Pedal Sensor
   - Turn the ignition switch to the off position.
   - Disconnect the Accelerator Pedal sensor connector.
   - Measure the voltage between pin 6, 7 (ETCREF+) and 1, 3 (ETCRTN-).
   - The voltage should read between 4—6 volts, If not repair circuits in question.
2. Checking the Functionality of the APP sensor.
   - Turn the ignition off.
   - Disconnect the Accelerator Pedal sensor connector.
   - Refer to Resistance Chart:

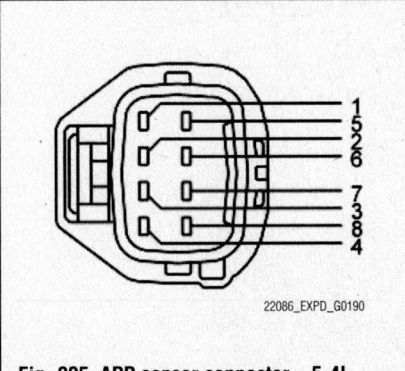

Fig. 225 APP sensor connector—5.4L engine

BAROMETRIC PRESSURE (BARO) SENSOR

LOCATION

6.0L Diesel Engine

The Barometric Pressure Sensor (BARO) is located inside the cab of the vehicle. It is mounted behind the instrument panel steering column cover.

OPERATION

6.0L Diesel Engine

The BARO sensor is a cab-mounted variable capacitance sensor used to determine altitude. The BARO signal affects injection timing and fuel quantity to optimize engine operation and control smoke throughout all altitude conditions. The BARO signal is one of the variables used to calculate glow plug on time. At higher altitudes, glow plug on time is increased to reduce start-up smoke.

REMOVAL & INSTALLATION

6.0L Diesel Engine

See Figure 227.

> ❊❊ **WARNING**
>
> **Make sure the ignition switch is in the OFF position prior to working on the electronic engine controls.**

1. Turn the ignition switch to the OFF position.

> ❊❊ **WARNING**
>
> **Use care when removing the instrument panel steering column cover or damage to the cover locating tab can occur.**

2. Unlock the retainers and remove the instrument panel steering column cover.

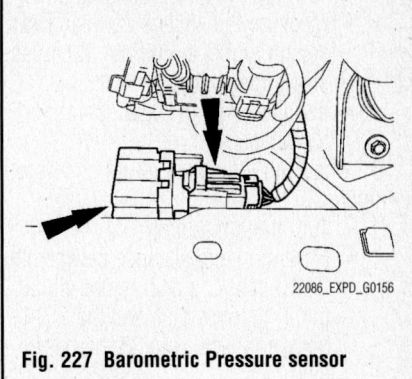

Fig. 227 Barometric Pressure sensor and connector

3. Disconnect the BARO sensor electrical connector.
4. Release the clip and remove the BARO sensor.
5. To install, reverse the removal procedure.

TESTING

6.0L Diesel Engine

See Figure 228.

1. Checking the voltage reference circuit:
   - Turn the ignition off.
   - Disconnect the BARO sensor.
   - Turn the ignition on engine off.
   - Measure the voltage between the BARO sensor reference voltage circuit pin 2, harness side and the BARO sensor signal return circuit pin 1, harness side.
   - Voltage reading should be between 4.5—5.5 volts.
   - If reading is not as stated repair an open or short in the reference voltage or signal return circuit.
2. Checking the Signal circuit for a short to voltage
   - Turn the ignition off.
   - Disconnect the PCM body connector.

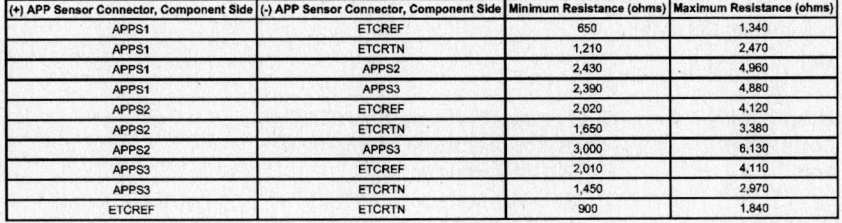

(+) APP Sensor Connector, Component Side	(-) APP Sensor Connector, Component Side	Minimum Resistance (ohms)	Maximum Resistance (ohms)
APPS1	ETCREF	650	1,340
APPS1	ETCRTN	1,210	2,470
APPS1	APPS2	2,430	4,960
APPS1	APPS3	2,390	4,880
APPS2	ETCREF	2,020	4,120
APPS2	ETCRTN	1,650	3,380
APPS2	APPS3	3,000	6,130
APPS3	ETCREF	2,010	4,110
APPS3	ETCRTN	1,450	2,970
ETCREF	ETCRTN	900	1,840

Fig. 226 APP Diagnostic resistance chart

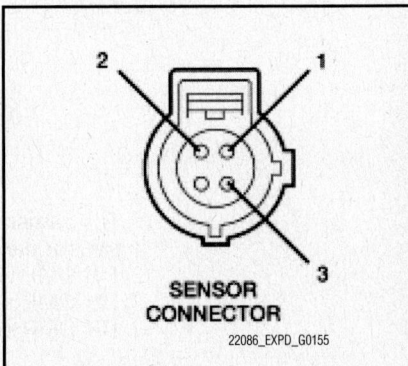

SENSOR CONNECTOR

Fig. 228 Barometric Pressure Sensor Connector view

- Turn the ignition on engine off.
- Measure the voltage between BARO sensor signal circuit pin 3, harness side and ground.
- If voltage is indicated repair short to voltage.
3. Checking the signal return circuit for an open:
  - Turn the ignition off.
  - Measure the resistance between the BARO sensor signal return circuit pin 1, harness side and the PCM body connector pin 33, harness side.
  - If the resistance is less than 5 ohms suspect PCM, if not repair the open circuit.

CAMSHAFT POSITION (CMP) SENSOR

LOCATION

5.4L & 6.8L Gasoline Engines
See Figure 229.

The Camshaft Position (CMP) Sensors are located on front of the engine. Just below valve covers.

6.0L Diesel Engine

The Camshaft Position (CMP) Sensor is located behind the power steering pump.

OPERATION

6.0L Diesel Engine

The CMP sensor is a variable reluctance sensor, which responds to a rotating trigger protruding from the camshaft. The trigger is a single 0.375 inch. (9.525 mm) diameter peg approximately 18 degrees wide, projecting 0.12 - 0.20 inch. (3-5 mm) from the camshaft. The sensor produces a sine wave in response to the peg as it passes the sensor. The sensor output is required to determine the camshaft position.

5.4L & 6.8L Gasoline Engines

The CMP sensor detects the position of the camshaft. The CMP sensor identifies when piston No. 1 is on its compression stroke. A signal is then sent to the PCM and used for synchronizing the sequential firing of the fuel injectors. Coil-on-plug (COP) ignition applications use the CMP signal to select the proper ignition coil to fire.

The input circuit to the PCM is referred to as the CMP input or circuit.

REMOVAL & INSTALLATION

Excursion

5.4L & 6.8L Engines

1. Disconnect the battery ground cable.
2. Disconnect the camshaft position (CMP) sensor electrical connector.
3. Remove the bolt and remove the CMP sensor.

To install:
4. To install, reverse the removal procedure and note the following:
   a. Tighten the CMP sensor mounting bolt to 89 inch. lbs. (10 Nm).

6.0L Diesel Engine

✳✳ WARNING

Make sure the ignition switch is in the OFF position prior to working on the electronic engine controls.

1. Turn the ignition switch to the OFF position.

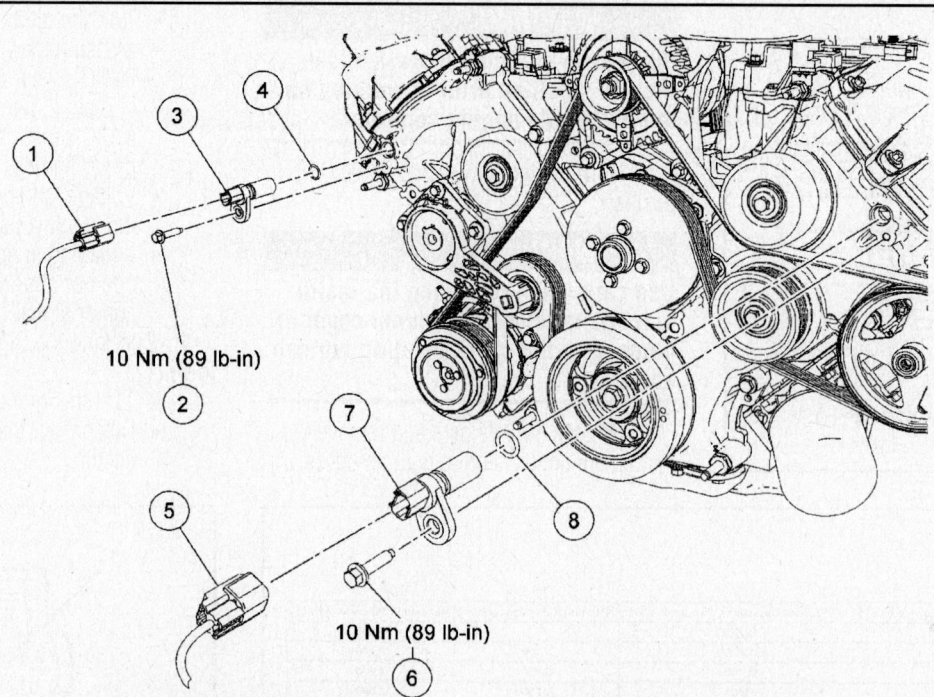

1. RH camshaft position (CMP) sensor electrical connector
2. RH CMP sensor bolt
3. RH CMP sensor
4. RH CMP sensor O-ring seal
5. LH camshaft position (CMP) sensor electrical connector
6. LH CMP sensor bolt
7. LH CMP sensor
8. LH CMP sensor O-ring seal

22086_EXPD_G0179

Fig. 229 Camshaft location view 2007 Expedition shown

➡The CMP sensor is located behind the power steering pump.

2. Disconnect the Camshaft Position (CMP) Sensor electrical connector.
3. Remove the bolt and the CMP sensor.
4. Apply clean engine oil to the O-ring before installation.
5. To install, reverse the removal procedure and tighten the CMP sensor mounting bolt to 10 ft. lbs. (13 Nm).

2005—07 Expedition & Navigator

1. Disconnect the negative battery cable.
2. Disconnect the Camshaft Position (CMP) sensor electrical connector.
3. For the left CMP sensor, remove the air cleaner inlet tube.
4. Remove the bolt and the CMP sensor.

To install:

5. To install, reverse the removal procedure and note the following:
 a. Tighten the CMP sensor mounting bolt to 89 inch. lbs. (10 Nm).

TESTING

5.4L & 6.8L Gasoline Engines

See Figure 230.

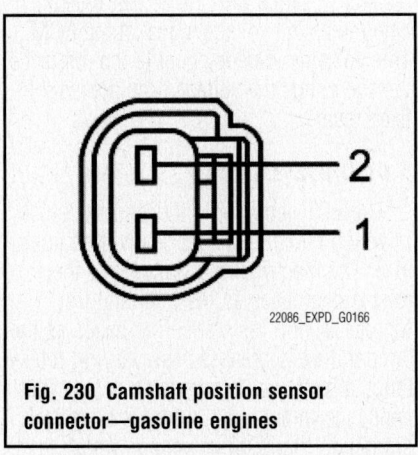

Fig. 230 Camshaft position sensor connector—gasoline engines

1. Checking the CMP sensor resistance:
 • Turn the ignition off.
 • Disconnect the CMP electrical connector.
 • Measure the resistance between Pin 1 (SIGRTN) and Pin 2 (CMP).
 • The resistance reading should be between 250—1,000 ohms.
 • If the resistance reading is not as stated, install a new CMP sensor.

6.0L Diesel Engine

See Figure 231.

1. Checking the resistance CMP sensor:

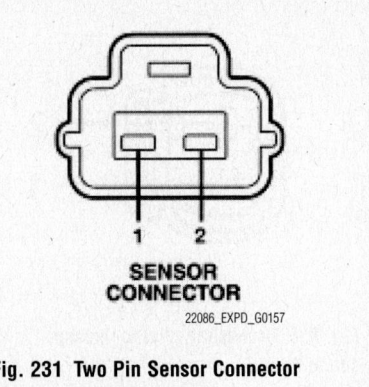

Fig. 231 Two Pin Sensor Connector view—6.0L diesel engine

• Turn the ignition off.
• Disconnect the CMP sensor connector.
• Measure the resistance between sensor pin 1 and 2 component side.
• If the resistance value is not 800—1,000 ohms, suspect bad CMP sensor.
2. Checking the CMP sensor:
 • Inspect the CMP sensor for misalignment and improper installation.
 • Remove the CMP sensor.
 • Inspect the CMP sensor for damage.
 • Repair as necessary.

CRANKSHAFT POSITION (CKP) SENSOR

LOCATION

5.4L & 6.8L Gasoline Engines

See Figure 232.

The Crankshaft Position (CKP) Sensor is located to the left of the balancer pulley and behind the air conditioning compressor.

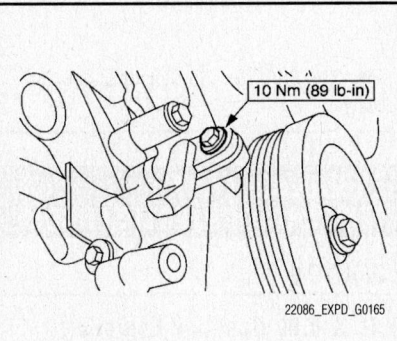

Fig. 232 Crankshaft Position Sensor view gas engines

6.0L Diesel Engine

The Crankshaft Position (CKP) Sensor is located underneath the air conditioning compressor.

OPERATION

5.4L & 6.8L Gasoline Engines

The CKP sensor is a magnetic transducer mounted on the engine block or timing cover and is adjacent to a pulse wheel located on the crankshaft. By monitoring the crankshaft mounted pulse wheel, the CKP is the primary sensor for ignition information to the PCM. The trigger wheel has a total of 35 teeth spaced 10 degrees apart with one empty space for a missing tooth. The 6.8L 10-cylinder pulse wheel has 39 teeth spaced 9 degrees apart and one 9 degree empty space for a missing tooth. By monitoring the trigger wheel, the CKP indicates crankshaft position and speed information to the PCM. By monitoring the missing tooth, the PCM uses the CKP signal to synchronize the ignition system and track the rotation of the crankshaft.

6.0L Diesel Engine

The CKP sensor is a variable reluctance sensor which responds to a rotating actuator positioned on the crankshaft. The actuator is a 60-2 tooth steel disk with 58 evenly spaced teeth and a minus 2 tooth slot. The sensor produces a sine wave for each tooth edge of the actuator. The sensor output is required to determine crankshaft speed, position, and acceleration.

The Powertrain Control Module (PCM) uses the CKP and camshaft position (CMP) signals to calculate the engine speed and piston position. The CKP creates a signal used by the PCM to indicate cylinder identification in a particular bank. The CKP contains a permanent magnet that creates a magnetic field. The signal is created when the target wheel rotates and breaks the magnetic field created by the sensor. The engine will not operate without a CKP signal.

REMOVAL & INSTALLATION

5.4L & 6.8L Gasoline Engines

1. Disconnect the battery ground cable.
2. Remove the accessory drive belt from the A/C compressor pulley.
3. Raise and support the vehicle.
4. Disconnect the wiring harness connector from the crankshaft position sensor.
5. Disconnect the A/C compressor field coil electrical connector.

➡It is not necessary to remove the A/C compressor bolts

6. Loosen the bolts enough for the compressor to slide down one inch, allowing access for crankshaft position (CKP) sensor removal.

7. For 2007 models remove the compressor and position aside.

8. Remove the bolt and the CKP sensor.

To install:

9. To install, reverse the removal procedure and note the following:

a. Tighten the CKP sensor mounting bolt to 89 inch. lbs. (10 Nm).

b. Tighten A/C mounting bolts to 18 ft. lbs. (25 Nm).

6.0L Diesel Engine

✻✻✻ WARNING

Make sure the ignition switch is in the OFF position prior to working on the electronic engine controls.

1. Turn the ignition switch to the OFF position.

➡The crankshaft position (CKP) sensor is located underneath the air conditioning compressor.

2. Remove the nut and position the positive battery cable and bracket aside.

3. Remove the bolt and position the battery negative cable aside.

4. Disconnect the CKP sensor electrical connector.

5. Remove the bolt and the CKP sensor.

To install:

6. To install, reverse the removal procedure and note the following:

a. Apply clean engine oil to the O-ring before installation.

b. Tighten the CKP sensor mounting bolt to 10 ft. lbs. (13 Nm).

c. Tighten the battery negative cable to 35 ft. lbs. (47 Nm).

d. Tighten the battery positive cable to 22 ft. lbs. (30 Nm).

TESTING

5.4L & 6.8L Gasoline Engines

See Figure 233.

1. Checking the CKP sensor resistance:
- Turn ignition switch off.
- Disconnect the CKP sensor electrical connector.
- Measure the resistance between Pin 1 (CKP +) and Pin 2 (CKP -).
- The resistance reading should be between 250—1,000 ohms.

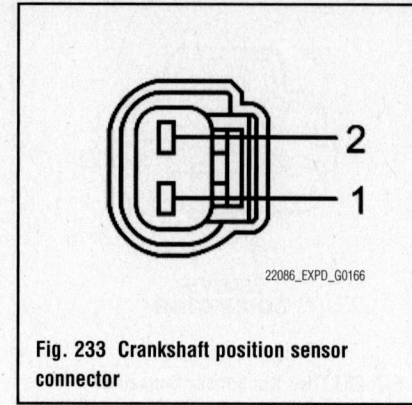

Fig. 233 Crankshaft position sensor connector

- If the resistance reading is not as stated, install a new CKP sensor.

6.0L Diesel Engine

See Figure 234.

1. Measuring the voltage between CKP sensor terminals:
- Backprobe the sensor connector or purchase test harness:
- Check the voltage reading with engine running it should be more than 0.1 volt.
- If the reading is not as stated suspect faulty CKP sensor.
2. Inspecting the CKP sensor:
- Remove the CKP sensor.
- Check for misalignment and improper installation.
- Inspect the CKP sensor for damage.
- Repair as necessary.

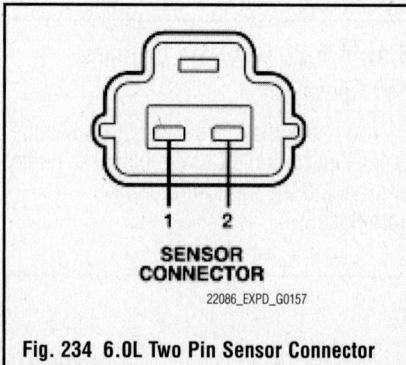

Fig. 234 6.0L Two Pin Sensor Connector view

ENGINE COOLANT TEMPERATURE (ECT) SENSOR

LOCATION

5.4L & 6.8L Gasoline Engines

➡On these engines, the sensor is referred to as a Cylinder Head Temperature (CHT) sensor.

The Cylinder Head Temperature (CHT) sensor is located under the intake manifold, and to the front of the left cylinder head.

6.0L Diesel Engine

The Engine Coolant Temperature (ECT) sensor is located just below thermostat housing.

OPERATION

5.4L & 6.8L Gasoline Engines

The CHT sensor is a thermistor device in which resistance changes with temperature. The electrical resistance of a thermistor decreases as temperature increases, and the resistance increases as the temperature decreases. The varying resistance affects the voltage drop across the sensor terminals and provides electrical signals to the PCM corresponding to temperature.

Thermistor-type sensors are considered passive sensors. A passive sensor is connected to a voltage divider network so that varying the resistance of the passive sensor causes a variation in total current flow.

Voltage that is dropped across a fixed resistor in series with the sensor resistor determines the voltage signal at the PCM. This voltage signal is equal to the reference voltage minus the voltage drop across the fixed resistor.

6.0L Diesel Engine

The ECT sensor is a thermistor device in which resistance changes with temperature. The electrical resistance of a thermistor decreases as the temperature increases, and resistance increases as the temperature decreases. The varying resistance affects the voltage drop across the sensor terminals and provides electrical signals to the PCM corresponding to temperature.

REMOVAL & INSTALLATION

5.4L & 6.8L Gasoline Engines

1. Remove the upper intake manifold.
2. Disconnect the electrical connector.
3. Remove the Cylinder Head Temperature (CHT) sensor.

To install:

4. To install, reverse the removal procedure and note the following:

a. Tighten the CHT sensor to 18 ft. lbs. (25 Nm).

b. For 2007 models tighten the CHT sensor to 89 inch. lbs. (10 Nm).

6.0L Diesel Engine

> **☀☀ WARNING**
>
> **Make sure the ignition switch is in the OFF position prior to working on the electronic engine controls.**

1. Turn the ignition switch to the OFF position.
2. Drain the cooling system.
3. Disconnect the cooling fan electrical connector.
4. Disconnect the engine coolant temperature (ECT) electrical connector.
5. Remove the ECT sensor.

To install:

6. To install, reverse the removal procedure and note the following:
   a. Apply clean engine oil to the O-ring before installation.
   b. For early build vehicles, tighten to 9 ft. lbs. (12 Nm).
   c. For late build vehicles, tighten to 13 ft. lbs. (18 Nm).
   d. Fill and bleed the engine cooling system.

TESTING

5.4L & 6.8L Gasoline Engines

See Figures 235 through 237.

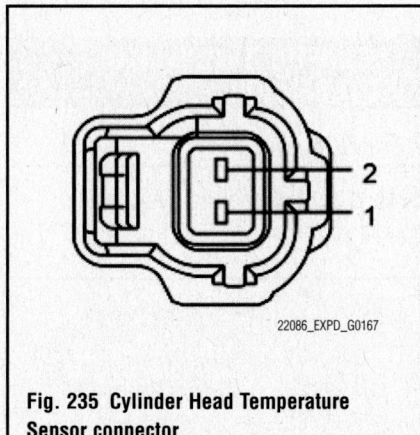

22086_EXPD_G0167

Fig. 235 Cylinder Head Temperature Sensor connector

1. Checking the resistance of the CHT sensor:
- The vehicle must be at normal operating temperature.
- Turn the ignition switch off.
- Disconnect the CHT sensor electrical connector.
- Measure the resistance between Pin 1 (CHT+) and Pin 2 (SIGRTN -) on component side.
- Refer to the chart at the beginning of this test for resistance specifications.

Cylinder Head Temperature Sensor Expected Values

Temperature		CHT Sensor Values		
°C	°F	Cold End (volts)	Hot End (volts)	Resistance (K ohms)
-40	-40	4.89	-	965.808
-30	-22	4.81	-	513.019
-20	-4	4.67	-	283.664
-10	14	4.45	-	162.584
0	32	4.14	-	96.255
10	50	3.73	-	59.175
20	68	3.26	-	37.387
30	86	2.74	-	24.215
40	104	2.23	-	16.043
50	122	1.76	-	10.85
60	140	1.36	-	7.487
70	158	1.04	-	5.268
80	176	0.79	3.99	3.775
85	185	0.69	3.86	3.215
90	194	0.60	3.71	2.75
95	203	0.53	3.56	2.361
100	212	0.46	3.41	2.034
110	230	-	3.07	1.523
120	248	-	2.74	1.155
130	266	-	2.41	0.8866
140	284	-	2.10	0.6891
150	302	-	1.81	0.5417
160	320	-	1.55	0.4301
170	338	-	1.33	0.3449
180	356	-	1.13	0.2791
190	374	-	0.96	0.2278
200	392	-	0.82	0.1875
210	410	-	0.70	0.155
220	428	-	0.60	0.130
230	446	-	0.51	0.109
240	464	-	0.44	0.092
250	482		0.35	0.078
260	500		0.33	0.067

22086_EXPD_G0168

Fig. 236 CHT Resistance Values Chart

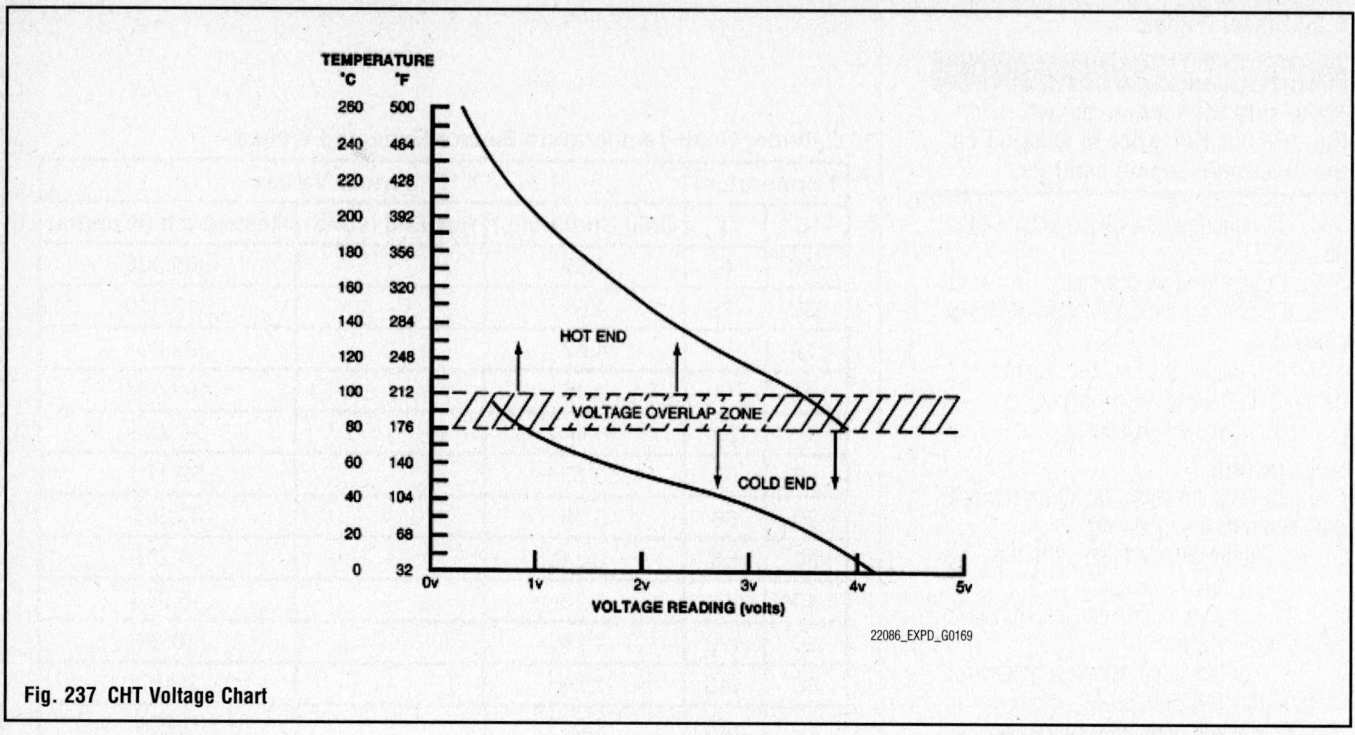

Fig. 237 CHT Voltage Chart

6.0L Diesel Engine

See Figures 238 and 239.

➡ **If the PCM receives a high engine temperature signal from the ECT, it adjusts fueling rates to protect the engine from damage due to overheating.**

1. Checking the ECT sensor voltage versus resistance:

- Disconnect the ECT sensor connector.
- Connect an ohmmeter between the ECT sensor terminals.
- With a cold engine measure and note the ECT sensor resistance.
- Reconnect the ECT sensor electrical connector.
- Start and run the engine to reach proper operating temperature.
- Turn off engine and disconnect ECT sensor electrical connector.

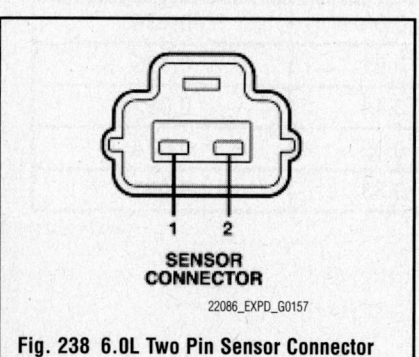

SENSOR CONNECTOR

22086_EXPD_G0157

Fig. 238 6.0L Two Pin Sensor Connector view

Temperature VS. Resistance Values Chart (Approximate)		
°C	°F	Ohms
100	212	2,080
90	194	2,803
80	176	3,836
70	158	5,337
60	140	7,556
50	122	10,908
45	113	13,216
40	104	16,092
35	95	19,696
30	86	24,329
25	77	30,000
20	68	37,352
15	59	46,797
10	50	59,016
5	41	79,940
0	32	95,851
-5	23	124,485
-10	14	160,313
-15	5	209,816
-20	-4	276,959
-30	-22	496,051
-40	-40	925,021

22086_EXPD_G0158

Fig. 239 Excursion Temperature Versus Resistance Chart

- Measure and note the reading.
- Compare both readings to the temperature —resistance chart.
- If the readings do not approximate those in the chart suspect a faulty ECT sensor.

ENGINE OIL TEMPERATURE (EOT) SENSOR

LOCATION

5.4L & 6.8L Gasoline Engines

See Figure 240.

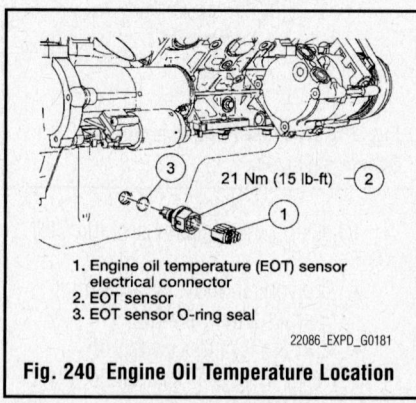

1. Engine oil temperature (EOT) sensor electrical connector
2. EOT sensor
3. EOT sensor O-ring seal

22086_EXPD_G0181

Fig. 240 Engine Oil Temperature Location

The Engine Oil Temperature (EOT) Sensor is located in the side of the oil pan below the starter motor.

6.0L Diesel Engine

See Figure 241.

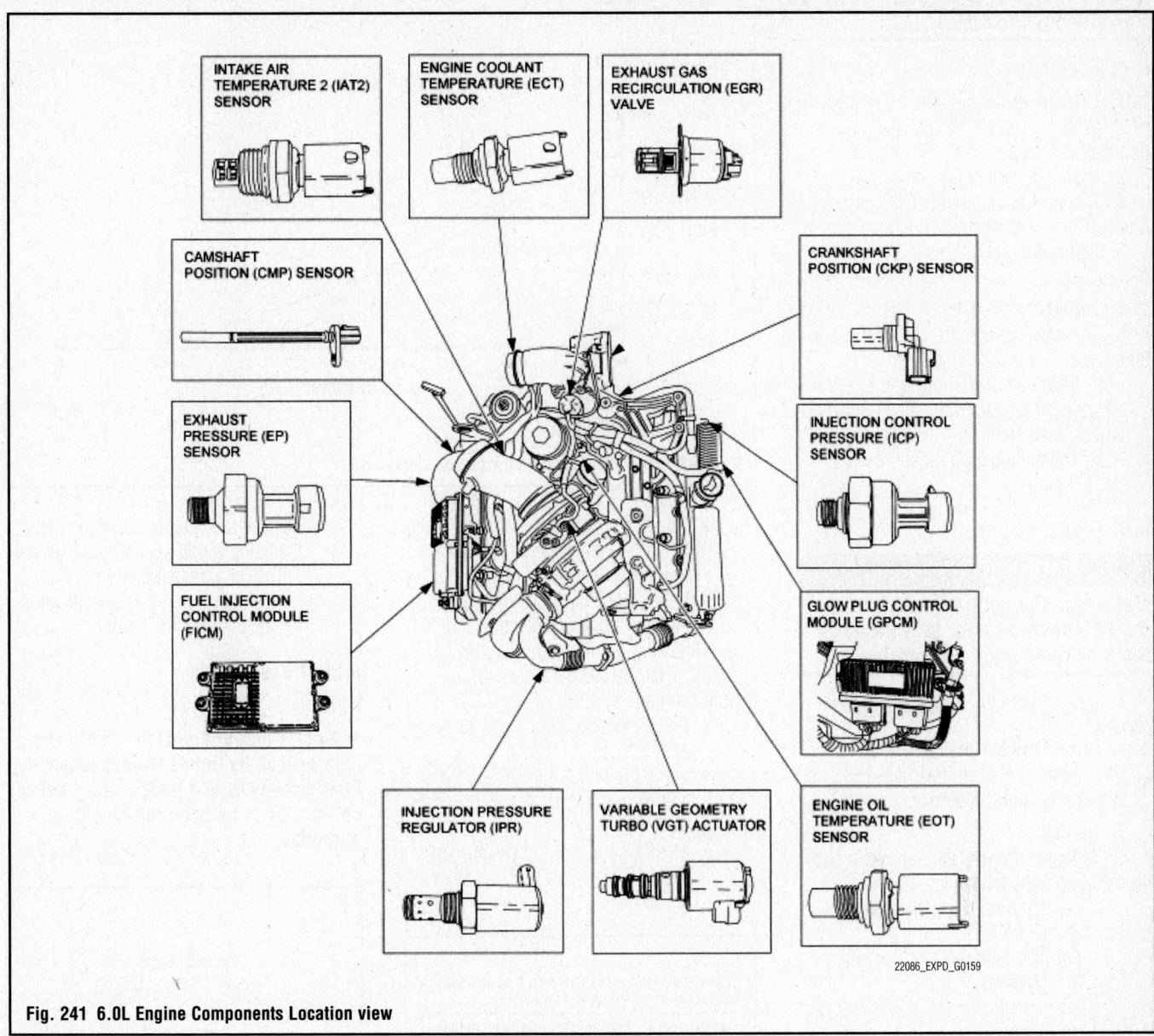

Fig. 241 6.0L Engine Components Location view

Refer to the accompanying illustration for Engine Oil Temperature (EOT) sensor location.

OPERATION

All Gasoline Engines

The EOT sensor is a thermistor device in which resistance changes with temperature. The electrical resistance of a thermistor decreases as the temperature increases and the resistance increases as the temperature decreases. The varying resistance affects the voltage drop across the sensor terminals and provides electrical signals to the PCM corresponding to temperature.

Thermistor-type sensors are considered passive sensors. A passive sensor is connected to a voltage divider network so that varying the resistance of the passive sensor causes a variation in total current flow. Voltage that is dropped across a fixed resistor in a series with the sensor resistor determines the voltage signal at the PCM. This voltage signal is equal to the reference voltage minus the voltage drop across the fixed resistor.

The EOT sensor measures the temperature of the engine oil. The sensor is typically threaded into the engine oil lubrication system. The PCM can use the EOT sensor input to determine the following:

• On variable camshaft timing (VCT) applications the EOT input is used to adjust the VCT control gains and logic for camshaft timing.

• The PCM can use EOT sensor input in conjunction with other PCM inputs to determine oil degradation.

• The PCM can use EOT sensor input to initiate a soft engine shutdown. To prevent engine damage from occurring as a result of high oil temperatures, the PCM has the ability to initiate a soft engine shutdown. Whenever engine RPM exceeds a calibrated level for a certain period of time, the PCM begins reducing power by disabling engine cylinders.

6.0L Diesel Engine

The EOT sensor is a thermistor whose resistance decreases as engine oil temperature increases. The EOT signal is used by the PCM to calculate fuel quantity, injection timing, and glow plug operation. At low ambient air temperatures and an oil temperature of less than 70°C (158°F), low idle is increased to maintain stable idle quality. Fuel quantity and timing is controlled throughout the total operating range to provide adequate torque and power.

REMOVAL & INSTALLATION

5.4L Engine

1. Disconnect the negative battery cable.
2. With the vehicle in NEUTRAL, position it on a hoist.
3. Drain the engine oil.
4. Disconnect the Engine Oil Temperature (EOT) sensor electrical connector.
5. Remove the EOT sensor. Discard the O-ring seal.

To install:

6. To install, reverse the removal procedure and note the following:

a. Install a new O-ring seal. Lubricate the new O-ring seal with clean engine oil prior to installation.

b. Tighten the EOT sensor to 15 ft. lbs. (21 Nm).

6.0L Diesel Engine

❊❊ WARNING

Make sure the ignition switch is in the OFF position prior to working on the electronic engine controls.

1. Turn the ignition switch to the OFF position.
2. Disconnect the engine oil temperature (EOT) sensor.
3. Remove the EOT sensor.

To install:

4. To install, reverse the removal procedure and note the following:

a. For early build vehicles, tighten to 9 ft. lbs. (12 Nm).

b. For late build vehicles, tighten to 13 ft. lbs. (18 Nm).

TESTING

5.4L Engine

See Figures 242 through 244.

1. Checking the resistance of the Engine Oil Temperature sensor with the engine off:

- Disconnect the Engine Oil Temperature sensor connector.
- Measure the resistance between Pin 1 (EOT+) and Pin 2 (SIGRTN-).

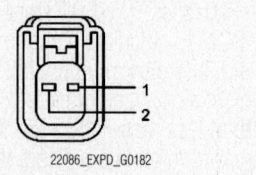

Fig. 242 Engine Oil Temperature sensor connector

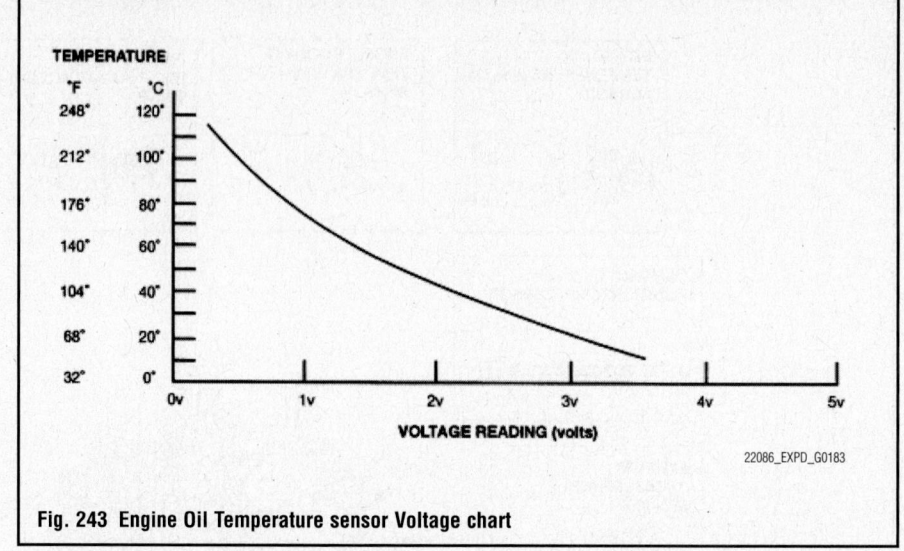

Fig. 243 Engine Oil Temperature sensor Voltage chart

- Check the chart to see if the resistance is within specification for the given engine temperature.
- If resistance is not in specification, suspect faulty EOT sensor.

2. Checking the resistance of the Engine Oil Temperature sensor with the engine running:

- Disconnect the Engine Oil Temperature sensor connector.
- Verify the radiator hoses are hot and the cooling system is pressurized.
- Measure the resistance between Pin 1 (EOT+) and Pin 2 (SIGRTN-).

Temperature		Temperature Sensor Values	
°C	°F	Voltage	Resistance (K ohms)
120	248	0.28	1.18
110	230	0.36	1.55
100	212	0.47	2.07
90	194	0.61	2.80
80	176	0.80	3.84
70	158	1.05	5.37
60	140	1.37	7.70
50	122	1.77	10.97
40	104	2.23	16.15
30	86	2.74	24.27
20	68	3.26	37.30
10	50	3.73	58.75
0	32	4.14	95.85
-10	14	4.45	160.31

TEMPERATURE SENSOR VOLTAGE AND RESISTANCE SPECIFICATIONS

Fig. 244 Engine Oil Temperature sensor Voltage and Resistance Specification chart

- Check the chart to see if the resistance is within specification for the given engine temperature.
- If resistance is not in specification, suspect faulty EOT sensor.

6.0L Diesel Engine

See Figures 245 and 246.

➡ An EOT signal detected out of range, high or low, by the PCM causes the PCM to substitute a temperature based on the ECT to be used for operating purposes.

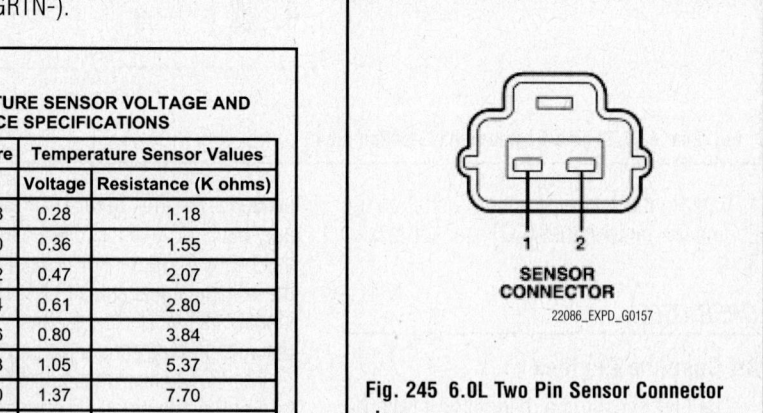

Fig. 245 6.0L Two Pin Sensor Connector view

1. Checking the EOT sensor voltage versus resistance:

- Disconnect the EOT sensor connector.
- Connect an ohmmeter between the EOT sensor terminals.
- With a cold engine measure and note the EOT sensor resistance.
- Reconnect the EOT sensor electrical connector.

- Start and run the engine to reach proper operating temperature.
- Turn off engine and disconnect EOT sensor electrical connector.
- Measure and note the reading.
- Compare both readings to the temperature—resistance chart.

Temperature VS. Resistance Values Chart (Approximate)

°C	°F	Ohms
100	212	2,080
90	194	2,803
80	176	3,836
70	158	5,337
60	140	7,556
50	122	10,908
45	113	13,216
40	104	16,092
35	95	19,696
30	86	24,329
25	77	30,000
20	68	37,352
15	59	46,797
10	50	59,016
5	41	79,940
0	32	95,851
-5	23	124,485
-10	14	160,313
-15	5	209,816
-20	-4	276,959
-30	-22	496,051
-40	-40	925,021

22086_EXPD_G0158

Fig. 246 Excursion Temperature Versus Resistance Chart

- If the readings do not approximate those in the chart suspect a faulty EOT sensor.
2. Checking the EOT Sensor
- Make sure the engine is at operating temperature.
- Turn the ignition switch on engine off.
- Install scanner and access the EOT PID.
- Monitor EOT PID while tapping on sensor.
- If the EOT fluctuates or decreases more than 68°F—20°C (3.82 volts).
- Replace EOT sensor.

→Check the cooling system for proper operation.

EXHAUST BACKPRESSURE SENSOR

LOCATION

6.0L Diesel Engine

The Exhaust Pressure Sensor in mounted in the tube coming from right exhaust manifold.

OPERATION

6.0L Diesel Engine

The EP sensor is a variable capacitor sensor that is supplied a 5-volt reference signal by the PCM and returns a linear analog voltage signal that indicates pressure. The EP sensor measures the pressure in the LH exhaust manifold. The sensor feedback signal is used for variable geometry turbo (VGT) and exhaust gas recirculation (EGR) valve control.

REMOVAL & INSTALLATION

6.0L Diesel Engine

Early Build Models

❄❄ WARNING

Make sure the ignition switch is in the OFF position prior to working on the electronic engine controls.

1. Turn the ignition switch to the OFF position.
2. Disconnect the electrical harness clip and disconnect the exhaust pressure sensor electrical connector.
3. Remove the exhaust pressure sensor.

To install:

4. To install, reverse the removal procedure and note the following:

a. Tighten the exhaust pressure sensor to 89 inch. lbs. (10 Nm).

❄❄ WARNING

Make sure the ignition switch is in the OFF position prior to working on the electronic engine controls.

Late Build Models

1. Turn the ignition switch to the OFF position.
2. Disconnect the exhaust pressure sensor electrical connector.
3. Using a backup wrench, remove the exhaust pressure sensor.

To install:

4. To install, reverse the removal procedure and note the following:

a. Tighten the exhaust pressure sensor to 15 ft. lbs. (20 Nm).

TESTING

6.0L Diesel Engine

See Figure 247.

→**An open or short in the EP sensor wiring results in an out-of-range low voltage at the PCM.**

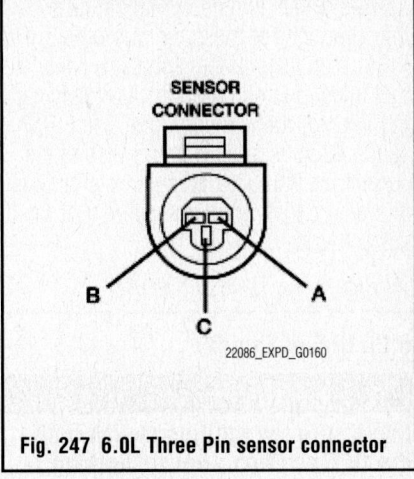

22086_EXPD_G0160

Fig. 247 6.0L Three Pin sensor connector

1. Preliminary Checks:
- Check for contamination, restrictions or carbon build-up in the EP sensor port, mounting bracket or tube.
- Check for moisture in the EP sensor port. If moisture is present, use 10 psi (69 kPa) regulated air pressure to remove the moisture.
- Inspect the turbo pipe and exhaust manifolds for leaks.
2. Checking the EP sensor:
- Disconnect the EP sensor.

- Install the ICP/EBC Adapter Cable D94T-50-A or equivalent between the EP sensor and the vehicle harness.
- Key ON, engine running
- Measure the voltage between the EP signal circuit and ground on the ICP/EBC Adapter Cable D94T-50-A.
- Accelerate the engine to wide open throttle (WOT) several times.
- The voltage should be greater than 1.35 volts during acceleration, if not suspect a faulty EP sensor.

FUEL INJECTOR CONTROL MODULE

LOCATION

6.0L Diesel Engine

The Fuel Injector Control Module is located on right side of the engine.

OPERATION

6.0L Diesel Engine

The FICM receives information from the PCM, including the volume of fuel desired, RPM, engine oil temperature, injection control pressure, and others. The FICM then uses those signals to calculate fuel injection and duration. After calculating injector fuel delivery time, the FICM sends 48 volts at a 20-amp pulse to the correct injector so that the correct amount of fuel is delivered to the cylinder at the correct time.

REMOVAL & INSTALLATION

6.0L Diesel Engine

> ✳✳ **WARNING**
>
> **Make sure the ignition switch is in the OFF position prior to working on the electronic engine controls.**

1. Turn the ignition switch to the OFF position.
2. Relieve the cooling system pressure. Disconnect and plug or cap the engine vent hose and radiator vent hose.

> ✳✳ **CAUTION**
>
> **Never remove the pressure relief cap while the engine is operating or when the cooling system is hot. Failure to follow these instructions can result in damage to the cooling**

system or engine or result in personal injury. To avoid having scalding hot coolant or steam blow out of the degas bottle when removing the pressure relief cap, wait until the engine has cooled, then wrap a thick cloth around the pressure relief cap and turn it slowly. Step back while the pressure is released from the cooling system. When certain all the pressure has been released, (still with a cloth) turn and remove the pressure relief cap. Failure to follow these instructions can result in personal injury.

3. Remove the bolts and position the degas bottle aside.
4. For late build vehicles:
   a. Disconnect the two exhaust pressure (EP) sensor harness pin-type retainers.
   b. Disconnect the two exhaust pressure (EP) sensor harness pin-type retainers.
5. Remove the two bolts, two nuts and turbocharger intake tube bracket.
6. Remove the fuel injector control module (FICM) bolts.

> ✳✳ **WARNING**
>
> **Make sure both latches are released before removing the electrical connectors or connector damage can occur.**

7. Position out the FICM and disconnect the electrical connectors. Remove the FICM.

> ✳✳ **WARNING**
>
> **With the engine cold, fill vehicles without a yellow fill level decal on the degas bottle only to the MIN line. The correct fill level on these vehicles is between the MIN line and 15 mm (0.59 in) below the MIN line. Fill vehicles with a yellow fill level decal to within the yellow cold fill range shown on the decal. These fill levels will allow for coolant expansion. Overfilling the degas bottle may result in damage to the pressure cap, which can cause the engine to overheat.**

To install:

8. To install, reverse the removal procedure and note the following:
   a. Tighten the fuel injector control module bolts to 10 ft. lbs. (13 Nm).

b. Tighten the turbocharger intake tube bracket nuts to 10 ft. lbs. (13 Nm).
   c. Tighten the degas bottle bolts to 89 inch. lbs. (10 Nm).

TESTING

6.0L Diesel Engine

See Figure 248.

1. Checking the ignition power circuit for voltage:
   - Turn ignition switch off.
   - Disconnect the FICM C connector.
   - Turn ignition switch on engine off.
   - Measure the voltage between the FICM ignition power circuit pin 7, harness side and ground.
   - The voltage reading should be higher than 10 volts.
   - If the voltage is not as stated repair power circuit.
2. Checking the FICM ground circuits for an open condition:
   - Check Pin 1 and ground
   - Check Pin 2 and ground
   - Check Pin 3 and ground
   - Check Pin 22 and ground
   - Check Pin 26 and ground
   - The resistances readings should be less than 5 ohms, if not repair the circuit in question.

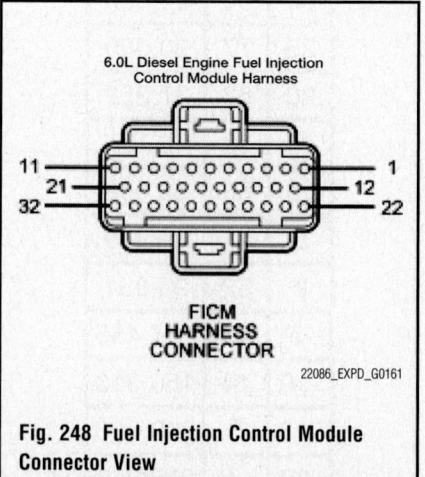

Fig. 248 Fuel Injection Control Module Connector View

HEATED OXYGEN (HO2S) SENSOR

LOCATION

5.4L & 6.8L Engines

The HO2S sensors are located at the top of front pipe near exhaust manifolds.

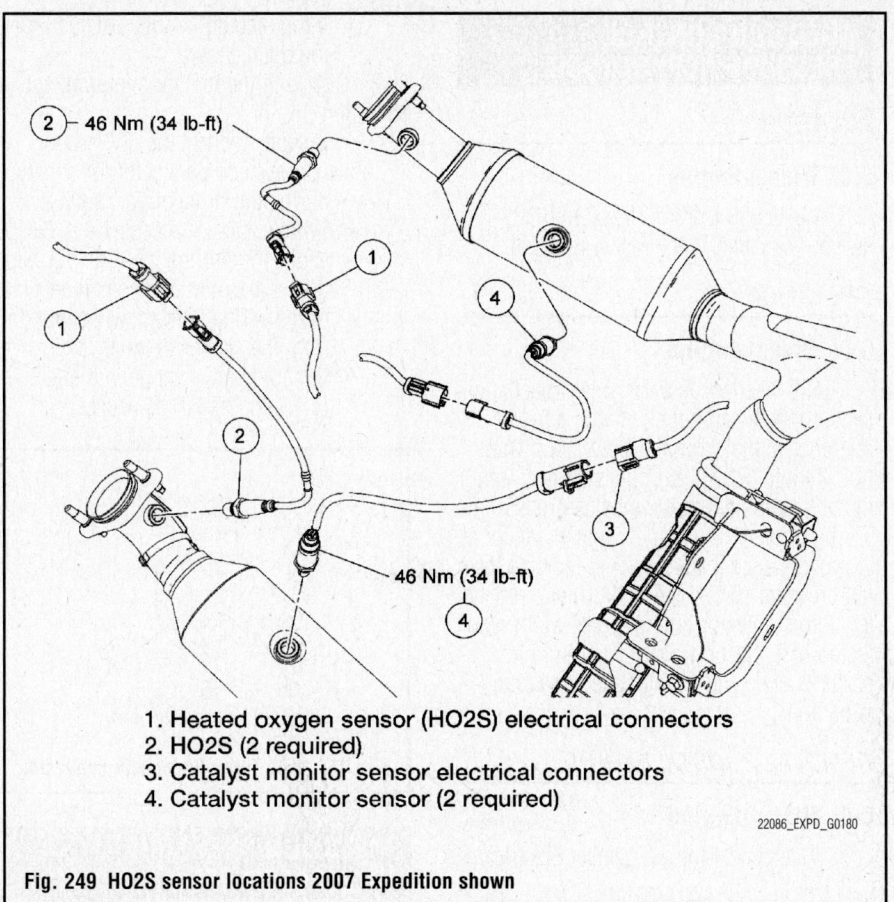

1. Heated oxygen sensor (HO2S) electrical connectors
2. HO2S (2 required)
3. Catalyst monitor sensor electrical connectors
4. Catalyst monitor sensor (2 required)

22086_EXPD_G0180

Fig. 249 HO2S sensor locations 2007 Expedition shown

OPERATION

5.4L & 6.8L Engines

The HO2S detects the presence of oxygen in the exhaust and produces a variable voltage according to the amount of oxygen detected. A high concentration of oxygen (lean air/fuel ratio) in the exhaust produces a voltage signal less than 0.4 volt. A low concentration of oxygen (rich air/fuel ratio) produces a voltage signal greater than 0.6 volt. The HO2S provides feedback to the PCM indicating air/fuel ratio in order to achieve a near stoichiometric air/fuel ratio of 14.7:1 during closed loop engine operation. The HO2S generates a voltage between 0.0 and 1.1 volts.

Embedded with the sensing element is the HO2S heater. The heating element heats the sensor to a temperature of 800°C (1400°F). At approximately 300°C (600°F) the engine can enter closed loop operation. The VPWR circuit supplies voltage to the heater. The PCM will turn on the heater by providing the ground when the proper conditions occur. The heater allows the engine to enter closed loop operation sooner. The use of this heater requires the HO2S heater control to be duty cycled, to prevent damage to the heater.

REMOVAL & INSTALLATION

5.4L & 6.8L Engines

1. Disconnect the battery ground cable.
2. Disconnect the Heated Oxygen Sensor (HO2S) electrical connector.

➡**If removing the HO2S on a 6.8L engine, raise and support the vehicle.**

3. Using a HO2S socket tool 303-476, remove the HO2S.

➡**If necessary, lubricate the HO2S with penetrating and lock lubricant to aid in removal.**

To install:
4. To install, reverse the removal procedure and note the following:
   a. Tighten the HO2S sensor to 34 ft. lbs. (46 Nm).

➡**Apply a light coat of nickel anti-seize lubricant to the threads of the HO2S.**

TESTING

5.4L & 6.8L Engines

1. Checking the internal resistance of the HO2S sensor heater:
   • Turn the ignition switch off.

• Disconnect the HO2S electrical connector.
• Measure the resistance between Pin 1 (HO2S Heater+) and Pin 2 (VPWR-) on component side.
• If the resistance is not between 3—30 ohms, replace HO2S sensor.

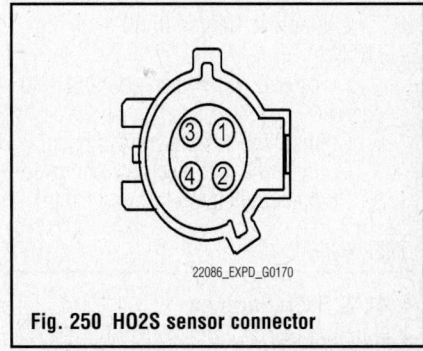

22086_EXPD_G0170

Fig. 250 HO2S sensor connector

IDLE AIR CONTROL (IAC) VALVE

LOCATION

5.4L & 6.8L Engines

The Idle Air Control Valve is mounted on the intake manifold, just behind the throttle body.

OPERATION

5.4L & 6.8L Engines

The IAC valve assembly controls the engine idle speed and provides a dashpot function. The IAC valve assembly meters intake air around the throttle plate through a bypass within the IAC valve assembly and throttle body. The PCM determines the desired idle speed or bypass air and signals the IAC valve assembly through a specified duty cycle. The IAC valve responds by positioning the IAC valve to control the amount of bypassed air. The PCM monitors engine RPM and increases or decreases the IAC duty cycle in order to achieve the desired RPM.

1. The PCM uses the IAC valve assembly to control:
   • No touch start.
   • Cold engine fast idle for rapid warm-up.
   • Idle (corrects for engine load).
   • Stumble or stalling on deceleration (provides a dashpot function).
   • Over-temperature idle boost.

REMOVAL & INSTALLATION

5.4L & 6.8L Engines

1. Disconnect the battery ground cable.

2. Disconnect the idle air control (IAC) valve electrical connector.

3. Disconnect the throttle bypass hose.

4. Remove the two bolts and the IAC valve.

To install:

5. Install the IAC valve and tighten the bolts in two stages:

a. Stage 1: Tighten to 89 inch. lbs. (10 Nm).

b. Stage 2: Tighten an additional 90 degrees.

6. Connect the throttle bypass hose.

7. Connect the IAC electrical connector.

8. Connect the battery ground cable.

TESTING

5.4L & 6.8L Engines

See Figure 251.

➡**The IAC valve assembly is NOT ADJUSTABLE and CANNOT BE CLEANED, also some IAC valves are normally open and others are normally closed. Some IAC valves require engine vacuum to operate.**

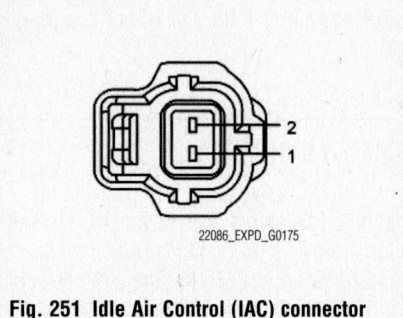

Fig. 251 Idle Air Control (IAC) connector

22086_EXPD_G0175

1. Checking the voltage to the Idle Air Control (IAC) Solenoid:

• Disconnect the Idle Air Control electrical connector.

• Turn the ignition switch on.

• Measure the voltage between Pin 1 (PWR+) connector side and Negative battery terminal.

• If the voltage reading is not 10.5 volts or greater repair the open circuit.

2. Checking the resistance of the Idle Air Control (IAC) Solenoid:

• Disconnect the Idle Air Control electrical connector.

• Measure the resistance between Pin 1 (PWR+) and Pin 2 (IAC-) component side.

• If the reading is not between 6—15 ohms, install a new IAC solenoid.

INJECTION CONTROL PRESSURE (ICP) SENSOR

LOCATION

6.0L Diesel Engine

The Injection Control Pressure (ICP) sensor is located in the RH valve cover.

OPERATION

6.0L Diesel Engine

The ICP sensor is a variable capacitance sensor that, when supplied with a 5-volt reference signal from the Powertrain Control Module (PCM), produces a linear analog voltage signal that indicates pressure.

The primary function of the ICP sensor is to provide a feedback signal to indicate the rail pressure so that the PCM can command the correct injector timing, pulse width, and the correct injection control pressure for proper fuel delivery at all speed and load conditions.

REMOVAL & INSTALLATION

6.0L Diesel Engine

1. Disconnect the ICP sensor electrical connector.

2. Remove the ICP sensor.

To install:

3. To install, reverse the removal procedure and note the following:

a. Verify the sensor O-ring seal is in place.

b. Tighten the ICP sensor to 9 ft. lbs. (12 Nm).

TESTING

6.0L Diesel Engine

See Figure 252.

➡**If the PCM detects an out of range high or low ICP sensor, the malfunction indicator lamp (MIL) is illuminated and the PCM functions from an estimated injection control pressure (open loop control of injection control pressure).**

1. Checking voltage reference to ICP sensor:

• Turn the ignition switch off.

• Disconnect the ICP sensor.

• Turn the Ignition switch on engine off.

• Measure the voltage between the ICP sensor VREF circuit pin B, harness side and ground.

• The voltage reading should be between 4.5—5.5 volts.

• If the reading is not as stated repair the open circuit.

2. Checking the ICP for a intermittent condition.

• Visually inspect the ICP sensor harness and connector for damage, corrosion, or incorrect routing.

• With a scanner access the ICP PID.

• While monitoring the ICP PID, wiggle, shake, and bend small sections of the wiring harness while working from the sensor to the PCM.

• If there is any change in the ICP PID value, repair as necessary.

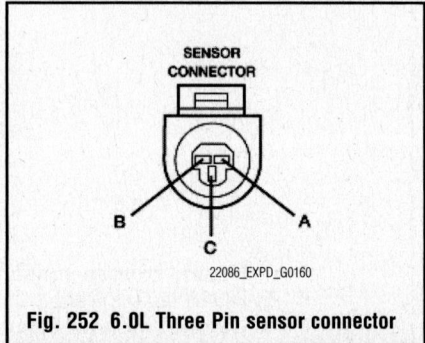

Fig. 252 6.0L Three Pin sensor connector

SENSOR CONNECTOR

B   A

C

22086_EXPD_G0160

INJECTION PRESSURE REGULATOR (IPR)

LOCATION

6.0L Diesel Engine

The Injection Pressure Regulator (IPR) valve is located in the high-pressure pump cover.

OPERATION

6.0L Diesel Engine

The IPR controls the injection oil pressure. An electrical signal to a solenoid creates a magnetic field which applies a variable force on a valve servo to the control the pressure. The quantity of fuel delivered to the combustion chamber is proportional to the injection control pressure.

REMOVAL & INSTALLATION

6.0L Diesel Engine

Early Build Models

1. With the vehicle in NEUTRAL, position it on a hoist.

2. Remove the fluid level indicator.

3. Remove the transmission fluid fill tube nut.

4. Position aside the transmission fluid filler tube.

5. Remove the turbocharger heat shield.

➡ **It will be necessary to position aside or remove the heat insulating wrap.**

6. Disconnect the injector pressure regulator (IPR) valve electrical connector.

➡ **Use a 1-3/8 inch 12-point deep flare nut crowfoot wrench, such as a Snap-on® AN850882B or equivalent, to remove the valve.**

7. Remove the IPR valve.
8. To install, reverse the removal procedure and note the following:

    a. Apply clean engine oil to the IPR valve prior to installing it.

    b. Tighten the IPR valve to 37 inch lbs. (50 Nm).

Late Build Models

1. Remove the turbocharger intake tube.
2. Remove the fuel injector control module (FICM).
3. Remove the retaining nuts and the rear FICM bracket.
4. Remove the retaining nuts from the heat shield bracket.
5. Disconnect the wiring retainer from the back of the heat shield bracket.
6. Remove the bolts and the heat shield bracket.
7. Remove the intake manifold stud.
8. Position back the injection pressure regulator (IPR) valve electrical connector heat insulating wrap.
9. Disconnect the IPR valve electrical connector.
10. Disconnect the snap and remove the heat insulating wrap.
11. Using the special socket 303-1112, remove the IPR valve.

➡ **It is necessary to re-install the heat insulating wrap on the IPR valve.**

To install:

12. To install, reverse the removal procedure and note the following:

    a. Apply clean engine oil to the IPR valve prior to installing.

    b. Tighten IPR valve with special socket 303-1112 and tighten to 37 inch. lbs. (50 Nm).

    c. Tighten the intake manifold stud to 8 ft. lbs. (11 Nm).

    d. Tighten the retaining nuts to the rear FICM bracket to 71 inch. lbs. (8 Nm).

TESTING

6.0L Diesel Engine

See Figure 253.

➡ **An open circuit results in minimal oil pressure and a no-start situation. A short to ground in a circuit results in maximum oil pressure, limited by a mechanical pop-off valve to 27,580 kPa (4,000 psi).**

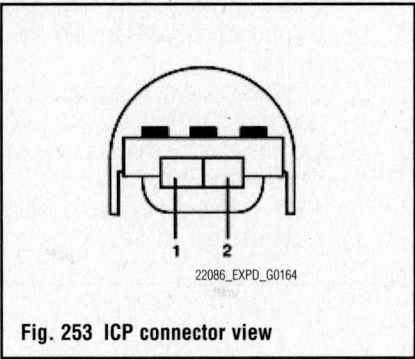

Fig. 253 ICP connector view

1. Checking the IPR solenoid resistance:
   - Turn ignition switch off.
   - Disconnect the IPR electrical connector.
   - Measure the resistance between the IPR solenoid pin 1, component side and the IPR solenoid pin 2, component side.
   - The resistance reading should be between 3.0—15.0 ohms.
   - If the reading is not as stated replace the IPR solenoid.

INTAKE AIR TEMPERATURE (IAT) SENSOR

LOCATION

6.0L Diesel Engine

The Intake Air Temperature (IAT) sensor is located in the air inlet tube before the turbo charger.

OPERATION

6.0L Diesel Engine

The IAT2 or manifold air temperature (MAT) sensor is a thermistor device. The electrical resistance of a thermistor decreases as the temperature increases, and resistance increases as the temperature decreases. The varying resistance affects the voltage drop across the sensor providing a signal corresponding to temperature. The IAT2 sensor is located in the intake manifold. The sensor provides a manifold air temperature signal to the PCM. The PCM uses the IAT2 signal to control timing and fuel rate during cold starts and provide an input to the cold idle kicker.

REMOVAL & INSTALLATION

6.0L Diesel Engine

❄❄ WARNING

Make sure the ignition switch is in the OFF position prior to working on the electronic engine controls.

1. Turn the ignition switch to the OFF position.
2. Disconnect the intake air temperature 2 (IAT2) electrical connector and wiring harness retainer.
3. Remove the IAT2 sensor.

To install:

4. To install, reverse the removal procedure and note the following:

    a. Tighten air intake temperature sensor to 13 ft. lbs. (18 Nm).

TESTING

6.0L Diesel Engine

See Figure 254.

1. Checking the signal circuit for an open condition.
   - Turn ignition switch off.
   - Disconnect the PCM engine harness connector.
   - Measure the resistance between the PCM engine connector pin 45, harness side and the IAT2 sensor signal circuit pin 2, harness side.
   - If the resistance is not less than 5 ohms, repair the open in the IAT2 signal circuit.

2. Checking the signal return circuit for an open condition:
   - Turn ignition switch off.
   - Measure the resistance between the IAT2 sensor signal return circuit pin 1, harness side and the PCM engine connector pin 25, harness side.
   - If the resistance is not less than 5 ohms, repair the open in the IAT2 signal return circuit.

3. Checking the IAT2 sensor operation:
   - Install a scanner.
   - Clear any of the continuous DTCs.
   - Turn the ignition on engine off.
   - Access and monitor the IAT2 and EOT PIDs.
   - Record the IAT2 PID value.
   - Drive the vehicle while monitoring the IAT2 sensor PID.
   - Operate the vehicle until the EOT PID is greater than 176°F (80°C)
   - Idle the engine for 10 minutes.
   - If the IAT2 PID value did not change from the initial recorded value, install a new IAT2 sensor.

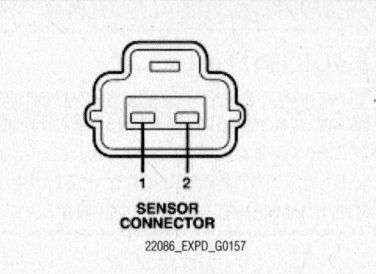

Fig. 254 6.0L Two Pin Sensor Connector view

KNOCK SENSOR (KS)

LOCATION

5.4L & 6.8L Engines

See Figure 255.

1. The Knock Sensor (KS) is located under the intake manifold just about in the center.

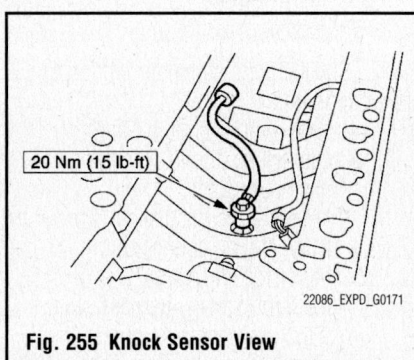

Fig. 255 Knock Sensor View

OPERATION

The Knock sensor is a tuned accelerometer on the engine which converts engine vibration to an electrical signal. The PCM uses this signal to determine the presence of engine knock and to retard spark timing.

REMOVAL & INSTALLATION

5.4L & 6.8L Gasoline Engines

1. Disconnect the negative battery cable.
2. Remove the upper intake manifold.
3. Disconnect the knock sensor (KS) electrical connector.
4. Remove the bolt and the KS.

➡**Make sure the black tapered side is facing up.**

To install:

5. To install, reverse the removal procedure and note the following:
    a. Tighten the KS to 15 ft. lbs. (20 Nm).

TESTING

See Figure 256.

1. Checking the resistance of the Knock Sensor (KS).
- Disconnect the knock sensor electrical connector.
- Check the connector for any signs of corrosion or damaged pin connectors.
- On the component side measure the resistance between Pin 2 (KS+) and Pin 1 (KS-) of the sensor connector.
- If the reading is not between 4.39—5.35m ohms suspect faulty knock sensor.

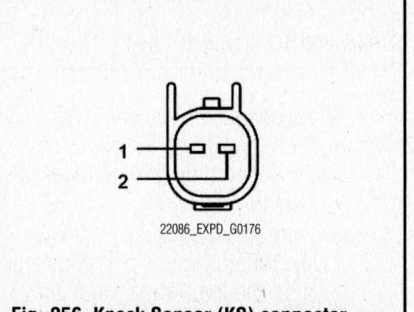

Fig. 256 Knock Sensor (KS) connector

MASS AIR FLOW (MAF) SENSOR

LOCATION

See Figures 257 and 258.

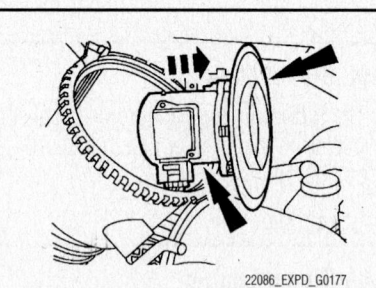

Fig. 257 Excursion Mass Air Flow sensor location view

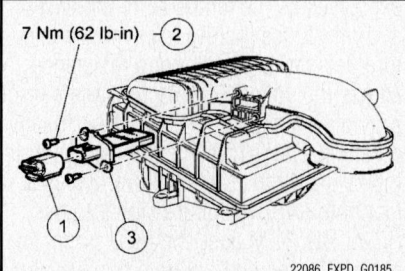

Fig. 258 Expedition & Navigator Mass Air Flow sensor location view

The Mass Air Flow (MAF) is located between the air cleaner and the throttle body or inside the air cleaner assembly.

OPERATION

The MAF sensor uses a hot wire sensing element to measure the amount of air entering the engine. Air passing over the hot wire causes it to cool. This hot wire is maintained at 200°C (392°F) above the ambient temperature as measured by a constant cold wire. If the hot wire electronic sensing element must be replaced, then the entire assembly must be replaced. Replacing only the element may change the air flow calibration.

The current required to maintain the temperature of the hot wire is proportional to the mass air flow. The MAF sensor then outputs an analog voltage signal to the PCM proportional to the intake air mass. The PCM calculates the required fuel injector pulse width in order to provide the desired air/fuel ratio. This input is also used in determining transmission electronic pressure control (EPC), shift and torque converter clutch scheduling.

Most MAF sensors have integrated bypass technology (IBT) with an integrated intake air temperature (IAT) sensor.

REMOVAL & INSTALLATION

Excursion

5.4L & 6.8L Engines

1. Disconnect the negative battery cable.

➤❋❋ WARNING

Do not tamper with the mass air flow (MAF) sensing elements located in the airflow meter. Tampering may result in unit failure.

➡ **The MAF sensor and body are calibrated and repaired as an assembly.**

2. Open the engine air cleaner.
    a. Disconnect the MAF sensor electrical connector.
    b. Release the air cleaner clamp.
    c. Separate the inlet side from the outlet side of the air cleaner.
3. Remove the MAF assembly.
4. Disconnect the MAF sensor electrical connector.
5. Remove the nuts and separate the MAF sensor from the MAF sensor plate.

To install:

❋❋ WARNING

The grommet used to seal the engine air cleaner housing at the extension

harness must be fully seated. Failure to do so will result in unmetered air entering the engine.

➡ **Use the alignment notch to properly align the inlet side and the outlet side of the engine air cleaner.**

➡ **When reinstalling the Mass Air Flow (MAF) sensor, make sure wires are not trapped behind MAF. Make sure electrical connector is pointing up on installation.**

6. To install, reverse the removal procedure and note the following:

a. Tighten the (MAF) sensor mounting nuts to 89 inch. lbs. (10 Nm).

Expedition & Navigator

1. Disconnect the negative battery cable.
2. Disconnect the mass air flow (MAF) sensor electrical connector.
3. Remove the 2 bolts and the MAF sensor.

To install:

4. To install, reverse the removal procedure and note the following:

a. Tighten the MAF sensor mounting bolts to 62 inch. lbs. (7 Nm).

TESTING

See Figure 259.

1. Checking the VPWR To the Mass Air Flow (MAF) sensor:
   - Disconnect the MAF sensor connector.
   - Turn the ignition switch on engine off.
   - Measure the voltage between Pin 6 (VPWR+) and the negative battery terminal.
   - The voltage reading should be greater than 10.5 volts, if not repair the circuit.
2. Checking the PWRGND circuit to the Mass Air Flow sensor:
   - Disconnect the MAF sensor connector.

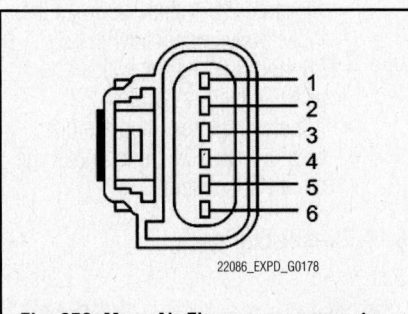

Fig. 259 Mass Air Flow sensor connector

- Turn the ignition switch on engine off.
- Measure the voltage between the positive battery terminal and Pin 5 (PWRGND-)
- The voltage reading should be greater than 10.5 volts, if not repair the circuit.

MANIFOLD ABSOLUTE PRESSURE (MAP) SENSOR

LOCATION

The MAP sensor is located in engine compartment close to the oil fill.

OPERATION

6.0L Diesel Engine

The MAP sensor is a variable capacitor sensor that is supplied a 5-volt reference signal by the PCM and returns a voltage signal to the PCM relative to the intake manifold pressure. The sensor voltage increases as the pressure increases. The MAP sensor allows the PCM to determine the engine boost to calculate fuel quantity. In addition, the MAP signal is used to control smoke by limiting fuel quantity during acceleration until a specified boost pressure is obtained, and is used by the PCM for EGR system calculations and control.

REMOVAL & INSTALLATION

6.0L Diesel Engine

❊❊ WARNING

Make sure the ignition switch is in the OFF position prior to working on the electronic engine controls.

1. Turn the ignition switch to the OFF position.
2. Disconnect the electrical connector.
3. Disconnect the pressure hose.
4. Remove the mounting screws and the MAP sensor.
5. To install, reverse the removal procedure.

TESTING

6.0L Diesel Engine

See Figure 260.

➡ **A MAP signal fault detected by the PCM causes the PCM to calculate an estimated manifold pressure based on known engine conditions.**

1. Checking the Map sensor voltage:

- Disconnect the pressure hose from the MAP sensor.
- Turn the ignition on engine off.
- Using the Pressure Adapter Kit 014-00761, or equivalent (gauge bar), apply 10 psi (69 kPa) of pressure to the MAP sensor.
- Measure the voltage between the MAP sensor signal pin 2, harness side and ground.
- The voltage reading should be 2.8 volts ± 0.3 volts, if not install a new map sensor.

2. Checking the voltage reference:
- Turn the ignition switch off.
- Disconnect the MAP sensor.
- Turn ignition switch on engine off.
- Measure the voltage between the MAP sensor VREF circuit pin 1, harness side and the MAP sensor signal return circuit pin 3, harness side.
- The voltage should be between 4.5 and 5.5 volts, if not repair an open in the VREF or signal return circuit.

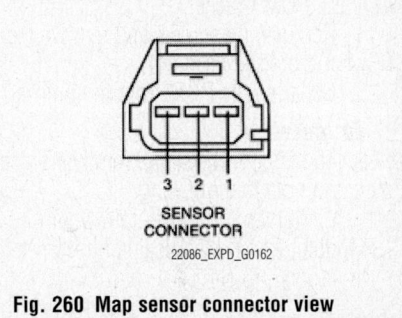

Fig. 260 Map sensor connector view

POWERTRAIN CONTROL MODULE (PCM)

LOCATION

6.0L Diesel Engine

The PCM is located on the left side of engine compartment.

5.4L & 6.8L Excursion Gasoline Engines

The PCM is located at the lower dash panel on the driver side.

5.4L Expedition & Navigator

The PCM Is located on the left side of engine Compartment.

OPERATION

The center of the EEC system is the PCM. The PCM contains both engine and transmission microprocessors. Operating information, as well as fault information, is communicated between the 2 processors through controller area network (CAN) communications. Both can be programmed individually, however, the PCM is replaced as an assembly. The PCM has 3 electrical connectors (122 pins total). The PCM receives input from sensors and other electronic components (switches and relays) and places this information into random access memory (RAM) or keep alive memory (KAM). Based on information programmed into its read-only memory (ROM), the PCM generates output signals to control various relays, solenoids, and actuators. For vehicles equipped with manual transmissions, only 2 electrical connectors are used.

REMOVAL & INSTALLATION

5.4L & 6.8L Excursion Gas Engines

1. Disconnect the negative battery cable.
2. Loosen the bolt and disconnect the Powertrain Control Module (PCM) electrical connector.
3. Release the two harness retainers from the PCM bracket.
4. Remove the screws and remove the PCM and bracket assembly.
5. Separate the PCM from the bracket.

To install:

6. To install, reverse the removal procedure and note the following:
    a. Tighten the Powertrain Control Module (PCM) electrical connector bolt to 44 inch. (5 Nm).

5.4L Expedition & Navigator

➡**Any Powertrain Control Module (PCM) replacement will require that ALL customer keys are available to be programmed at the time of installation. PCM replacement DOES NOT require new keys.**

1. Retrieve the module configuration. Carry out the module configuration retrieval steps of the Programmable Module Installation procedure.
2. Disconnect the PCM connectors.
3. Remove the 4 bolts and the PCM.
4. If necessary, remove the 3 bolts and the PCM bracket.

To install:

5. If removed, install the PCM bracket and 3 bolts and tighten to 89 inch. lbs. (10 Nm).
6. Install the PCM and 4 bolts and tighten to 62 inch. lbs. (7 Nm).
7. Connect the PCM electrical connectors.
8. Restore the module configuration. Carry out the module configuration restore

steps of the Programmable Module Installation procedure.
9. Reprogram the passive anti-theft system (PATS). Carry out the Key Programming Using Two Programmed Keys procedure.

6.0L Diesel Engine

> ❋❋ **WARNING**
>
> **Make sure the ignition switch is in the OFF position prior to working on the electronic engine controls.**

1. Disconnect the battery ground cable.
2. Disconnect the auxiliary battery positive cable (LH side of the engine compartment).
3. Remove the auxiliary battery cover.
4. Unlatch and disconnect the Powertrain Control Module (PCM) electrical connectors.
5. Remove the bolts and PCM.

To install:

6. To install, reverse the removal procedure and note the following:
7. Tighten PCM mounting bolts to 62 inch. lbs. (7 Nm).

TESTING

5.4L & 6.8L Excursion Gas Engines

1. Checking the vehicle battery power circuits:
   - Turn the ignition switch off.
   - Disconnect the PCM body harness connector.
   - Turn the ignition switch on.
   - Measure the voltage between the PCM body connector Pin 71 and Pin 97, harness side and ground.
   - Check for loose connections. Check for damaged pins or corrosion. Wiggle the harness while taking measurements.
   - If the voltage readings are not greater than 10.5 volts, repair the circuit in question.
2. Checking the PWRGND circuits:
   - Turn the ignition switch off.
   - Disconnect the PCM body harness connector.
   - Measure the voltage between the PCM body connector Pins 3, 24, 51, 76, 77 and 103 harness side and positive battery terminal.
   - If the voltage readings are not greater than 10.5 volts, repair the circuit in question.

5.4L Expedition & Navigator 2005—06

1. Checking the vehicle battery power circuits:

   - Turn the ignition switch off.
   - Disconnect the PCM body harness connector.
   - Turn the ignition switch on.
   - Measure the voltage between the PCM body connector Pin B 51, B52 and B 53, harness side and ground.
   - Check for loose connections. Check for damaged Pins or corrosion. Wiggle the harness while taking measurements.
   - If the voltage readings are not greater than 10.5 volts, repair the circuit in question.
2. Checking the PWRGND circuits:
   - Turn the ignition switch off.
   - Disconnect the PCM body harness connector.
   - Measure the voltage between the PCM body connector Pins B 67, B 68, B 69, and B 70 harness side and positive battery terminal.
   - If the voltage readings are not greater than 10.5 volts, repair the circuit in question.

5.4L Expedition & Navigator 2007

1. Checking the vehicle battery power circuits:
   - Turn the ignition switch off.
   - Disconnect the PCM body harness connector.
   - Turn the ignition switch on.
   - Measure the voltage between the PCM body connector Pin B 51, and B 52 harness side and ground.
   - Check for loose connections. Check for damaged Pins or corrosion. Wiggle the harness while taking measurements.
   - If the voltage readings are not greater than 10.5 volts, repair the circuit in question.
2. Checking the PWRGND circuits:
   - Turn the ignition switch off.
   - Disconnect the PCM body harness connector.
   - Measure the voltage between the PCM body connector Pins B 67, B 68, and B 69 harness side and positive battery terminal.
   - If the voltage readings are not greater than 10.5 volts, repair the circuit in question.

6.0L Diesel Engine

See Figure 261.

1. Checking the vehicle battery power circuits:

- Turn the ignition switch off.
- Disconnect the PCM body harness connector.
- Turn the ignition switch on.
- Measure the voltage between the PCM body connector Pins 34 and 36, harness side and ground.
- Check for loose connections. Check for damaged pins or corrosion. Wiggle the harness while taking measurements.
- If the voltage readings are not greater than 10.5 volts, repair the circuit in question.

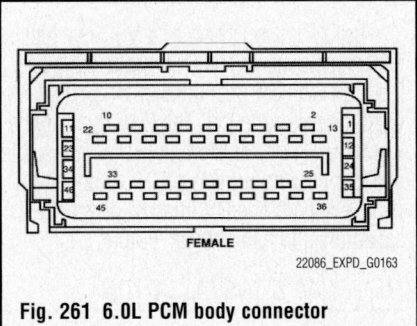

Fig. 261 6.0L PCM body connector

THROTTLE POSITION SENSOR (TPS)

LOCATION

The Throttle Position Sensor is located on the left side of throttle body.

OPERATION

The TP sensor is a rotary potentiometer sensor that provides a signal to the PCM that is linearly proportional to the throttle plate/shaft position. The sensor housing has a 3-blade electrical connector that may be gold plated. The gold plating increases corrosion resistance on terminals and increases connector durability. The TP sensor is mounted on the throttle body. As the TP sensor is rotated by the throttle shaft, 4 operating conditions are determined by the PCM from the TP. Those conditions are closed throttle (includes idle or deceleration), part throttle (includes cruise or moderate acceleration), wide open throttle (includes maximum acceleration or de-choke on crank), and throttle angle rate.

REMOVAL & INSTALLATION

Excursion Gas Engines

1. Disconnect the battery ground cable.
2. Loosen the clamp and position the air cleaner outlet tube aside.

3. Remove the accelerator cable snow shield.
4. To remove the throttle position (TP) sensor.
   a. Disconnect the electrical connector.
   b. Remove the screws.
   c. Remove the TP sensor.
5. To install, reverse the removal procedure.

Expedition & Navigator

1. Remove the throttle body (TB).

✷✷ WARNING

Failure to remove the TP sensor screws in the following manner will result in damage to the screws. First loosen the screws 1—2 full turns using a hand tool and then use a suitable high speed driver to complete the removal.

2. Remove and discard the screws and the TP sensor.

✷✷ WARNING

Do not reuse the TP sensor and screws. A new TP sensor and screws must be installed.

➡ When installing the new TP sensor, make sure that the radial locator tab on the TP sensor is aligned with the radial locator hole on the throttle body.

3. To install, reverse the removal procedure and note the following:
   a. Tighten the new sensor screws to 27 inch. lbs. (3 Nm).

TESTING

Excursion, Expedition & Navigator Gas Engines

See Figure 262.

1. Checking the Throttle Position sensor for mechanical operation:
- Turn the ignition switch to the on position.
- Install a scanner.
- Slowly move the throttle from the closed throttle position to the wide open throttle position and observe the TP V PID.
- Access the PCM and monitor the TP V PID.
- If the voltage is not between 0.49—4.65 V, suspect a faulty TP sensor.

2. Checking the voltage between the VREF and SIGRTN circuits at the TP sensor harness connector.

- Disconnect the Throttle Position sensor connector.
- Turn the ignition switch to the on position.
- Measure the voltage between Pin 1 (VREF+) and Pin 3 (SIGRTN-)
- If the voltage reading is between 4.5—5.5 the circuits are okay.
- Visually inspect the throttle linkage and throttle plate for binding or sticking.

➡ Verify the throttle plate and linkage is at closed throttle position.

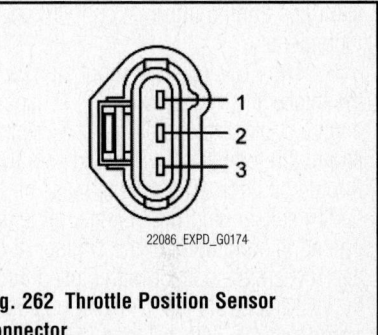

Fig. 262 Throttle Position Sensor connector

VARIABLE CAMSHAFT TIMING OIL CONTROL SOLENOID

LOCATION

See Figure 263.

The Variable Camshaft Timing Oil Control Solenoid (VCT) is located under the valve cover.

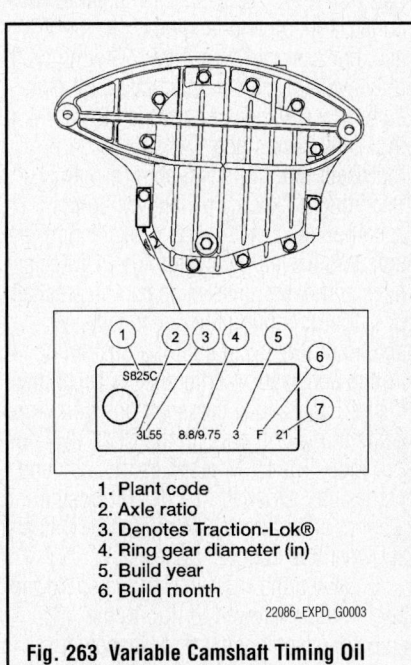

1. Plant code
2. Axle ratio
3. Denotes Traction-Lok®
4. Ring gear diameter (in)
5. Build year
6. Build month

Fig. 263 Variable Camshaft Timing Oil Control Solenoid (VCT) view

OPERATION

The VCT system consists of an electric hydraulic positioning control solenoid, a camshaft position (CMP) sensor, and a trigger wheel. The CMP trigger wheel has a number of equally spaced teeth equal to the number (n) of cylinders on a bank plus one extra tooth (n+1). Four cylinder and V8 engines use a CMP 4+1 tooth trigger wheel. V6 engines use a CMP 3+1 tooth trigger wheel. The extra tooth placed between the equally spaced teeth represents the CMP signal for that bank. A crankshaft position sensor (CKP) provides the PCM with crankshaft positioning information in 10 degree increments.

1. The PCM receives input signals from the intake air temperature (IAT) sensor, engine coolant temperature (ECT) sensor, engine oil temperature (EOT) sensor, CMP, throttle position (TP) sensor, mass air flow (MAF) sensor, and CKP to determine the operating conditions of the engine. At idle and low engine speeds with closed throttle, the PCM controls the camshaft position based on ECT, EOT, IAT, and MAF. During part and wide open throttle, the camshaft position is determined by engine RPM, load and throttle position. The VCT system does not operate until the engine is at normal operating temperature.

2. The VCT system is enabled by the PCM when the correct conditions are met.

3. The CKP signal is used as a reference for CMP positioning.

4. The VCT solenoid valve is an integral part of the VCT system. The solenoid valve controls the flow of engine oil in the VCT actuator assembly. As the PCM controls the duty cycle of the solenoid valve, oil pressure/flow advances or retards the cam timing. Duty cycles near 0% or 100% represent rapid movement of the camshaft. Retaining a fixed camshaft position is accomplished by dithering (oscillating) the solenoid valve duty cycle. The PCM calculates and determines the desired camshaft position. It continually updates the VCT solenoid duty cycle until the desired position is achieved. A difference between the desired and actual camshaft position represents a position error in the PCM VCT control loop. The PCM disables the VCT and places the camshaft in a default position if a concern is detected. A related DTC is also set when the concern is detected.

5. When the VCT solenoid is energized, engine oil is allowed to flow to the VCT actuator assembly which advances or retards the camshaft timing. One half of the VCT actuator is coupled to the camshaft and the other half is connected to the timing chain. Oil chambers between the 2 halves couple the camshaft to the timing chain. When the flow of oil is shifted from one side of the chamber to the other, the differential change in oil pressure forces the camshaft to rotate in either an advance or retard position depending on the oil flow.

REMOVAL & INSTALLATION

1. Remove the valve cover. Refer to valve cover removal in this section.
2. Remove the bolt and the variable camshaft timing (VCT) oil control solenoid.

To install:

3. To install, reverse the removal procedure and note the following:
   a. Tighten the VCT to 44 inch. lbs. (5 Nm).

TESTING

2005—07 Expedition & Navigator

See Figure 264.

1. Checking the Variable Camshaft Timing (VCT) solenoid resistance:
- Turn the ignition switch to the off position.
- Disconnect the VCT solenoid connector.
- Measure the resistance between Pin1 (VPWR-) and Pin 2 (VCT1+ or VCT2+) component side.
- The resistance reading should be between 5—14 ohms, if not suspect faulty VCT solenoid.

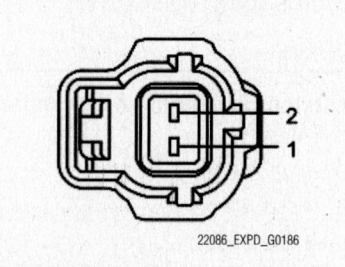

Fig. 264 Variable Camshaft Timing Oil Control connector

VEHICLE SPEED SENSOR (VSS)

LOCATION

5.4L & 6.8L Excursion Gasoline Engines

See Figure 265.

The transmission output shaft speed (OSS) sensor is located on the extension housing.

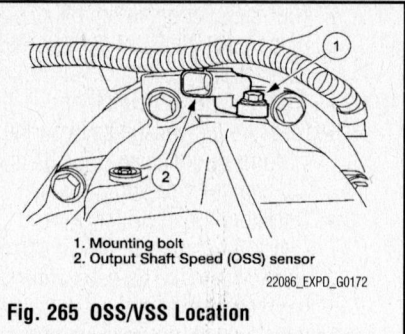

1. Mounting bolt
2. Output Shaft Speed (OSS) sensor

22086_EXPD_G0172

Fig. 265 OSS/VSS Location

OPERATION

5.4L & 6.8L Excursion Gas Engines

The OSS also known as a VSS is a hall effect type sensor. The OSS reads the gear teeth on the park gear, different than the teeth used for park function. The OSS input to the Powertrain Control Module (PCM) is used for shift scheduling, timing and TCC operation vehicle speed. The OSS has bi-directional capability and has a digital output.

REMOVAL & INSTALLATION

5.4L & 6.8L Excursion Gas Engines

1. With the vehicle in NEUTRAL, position it on a hoist.
2. Disconnect the output shaft speed (OSS) sensor electrical connector.

➥**Prior to removing the speed sensor, make sure that the area around the sensor is free of foreign material to prevent contamination of the transmission.**

3. Remove the output shaft speed (OSS) sensor bolt.
4. Remove the output shaft speed (OSS) sensor.

To install:

5. Lubricate the O-ring and install the output shaft speed (OSS) sensor.
6. Install the bolt.
7. Connect the output shaft speed (OSS) sensor electrical connector.
8. Tighten the bolt to 80 inch. lbs. (9 Nm).

TESTING

Excursion, Expedition & Navigator

See Figure 266.

1. Visual Inspection:
- Disconnect the Output Shaft Speed sensor.
- Inspect the OSS harness for damage.
- Inspect the OSS vehicle harness connector for damage and proper seating.

- If possible, carry out a wiggle test.
- Repair as necessary.
2. Checking the resistance of the OSS sensor:
   - Disconnect the Output Shaft Speed sensor.
   - Measure the voltage between Pin 1 (SIGRTN) and Pin 2 (OSS).

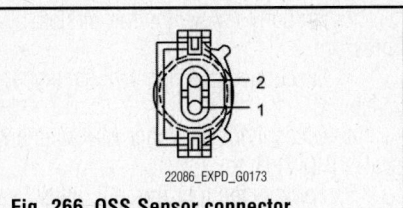

22086_EXPD_G0173

Fig. 266 OSS Sensor connector

- If the resistance is not between 400—1.25K ohms for OSS, and 170—270 ohms, for VSS suspect faulty OSS/VSS sensor.

➡**Remove the OSS sensor and inspect the target wheel. Repair as necessary.**

FUEL · GASOLINE FUEL INJECTION SYSTEM

FUEL SYSTEM SERVICE PRECAUTIONS

Safety is the most important factor when performing not only fuel system maintenance but any type of maintenance. Failure to conduct maintenance and repairs in a safe manner may result in serious personal injury or death. Maintenance and testing of the vehicle's fuel system components can be accomplished safely and effectively by adhering to the following rules and guidelines.

- To avoid the possibility of fire and personal injury, always disconnect the negative battery cable unless the repair or test procedure requires that battery voltage be applied.
- Always relieve the fuel system pressure prior to disconnecting any fuel system component (injector, fuel rail, pressure regulator, etc.), fitting or fuel line connection. Exercise extreme caution whenever relieving fuel system pressure to avoid exposing skin, face and eyes to fuel spray. Please be advised that fuel under pressure may penetrate the skin or any part of the body that it contacts.
- Always place a shop towel or cloth around the fitting or connection prior to loosening to absorb any excess fuel due to spillage. Ensure that all fuel spillage (should it occur) is quickly removed from engine surfaces. Ensure that all fuel soaked cloths or towels are deposited into a suitable waste container.
- Always keep a dry chemical (Class B) fire extinguisher near the work area.
- Do not allow fuel spray or fuel vapors to come into contact with a spark or open flame.
- Always use a back-up wrench when loosening and tightening fuel line connection fittings. This will prevent unnecessary stress and torsion to fuel line piping.
- Always replace worn fuel fitting O-rings with new Do not substitute fuel hose or equivalent where fuel pipe is installed.

Before servicing the vehicle, make sure to also refer to the precautions in the beginning of this section as well.

RELIEVING FUEL SYSTEM PRESSURE

RELIEVING

Excursion

➡**A fuel pressure gauge is needed to correctly perform this procedure.**

⁂ **CAUTION**

Fuel injection systems remain under pressure, even after the engine has been turned OFF. The fuel system pressure must be relieved before disconnecting any fuel lines. Failure to do so may result in fire and/or personal injury.

1. Before servicing the vehicle, refer to the precautions section.
2. Disconnect the negative battery cable and remove the fuel filler cap.
3. Remove the cap from the pressure relief valve on the fuel supply manifold. Install a fuel pressure gauge to the pressure relief valve.
4. Direct the gauge drain hose into a suitable container and depress the pressure relief button.
5. Remove the gauge and replace the cap on the pressure relief valve.

➡**As an alternate method, disconnect the inertia switch and crank the engine for 15–20 seconds until the pressure is relieved.**

Expedition & Navigator

➡**The electrical connector is located on the left hand frame rail under the driver side door.**

1. Disconnect the electrical connector.
2. Start the engine and allow it to idle until it stalls.
3. After the engine stalls, crank the engine for approximately 5 seconds to make sure the fuel rail pressure has been released.
4. Turn the ignition switch to the OFF position.

5. When fuel system service is complete, connect the electrical connector.

➡**It may take more than one key cycle to pressurize the fuel system.**

6. Cycle the ignition key and wait three seconds to pressurize the fuel system. Check for leaks before starting the engine.
7. Install the diagnostic tool. Turn the key ON with the engine OFF. Cycle the key OFF, then ON. Select the appropriate vehicle and engine qualifier. Clear all diagnostic trouble codes (DTCs) and carry out a PCM reset.
8. Start the vehicle and check the fuel system for leaks

FUEL FILTER

REMOVAL & INSTALLATION

➡**A fuel line disconnect tool is needed for this procedure.**

⁂ **CAUTION**

Fuel injection systems remain under pressure, even after the engine has been turned OFF. The fuel system pressure must be relieved before disconnecting any fuel lines. Failure to do so may result in fire and/or personal injury.

1. Before servicing the vehicle, refer to the precautions section.
2. Remove or disconnect the following:
   - Negative battery cable.
3. Relieve the fuel system pressure.
   - Fuel lines from the fuel filter. Have a drain pan handy to catch any residual fuel once the lines are separated.
4. On newer models, disconnect the fuel lines from the filter as follows:
   - Safety clip from the male hose.
   - Install and push the fuel line disconnect tool into the female fitting.
5. Remove or disconnect the following:
   - Male and female fittings from the filter.

➡**Inspect the fuel lines for any damage after the fuel is finished draining.**

- Fuel filter from the bracket and the retainer, if equipped. Note the direction of the flow arrow so the replacement filter can be installed correctly.

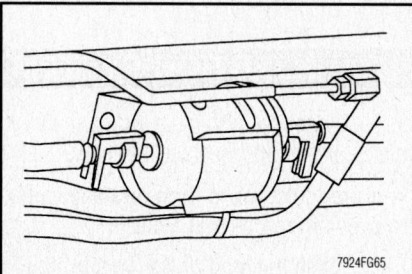

7924FG65

Fig. 267 Typical fuel filter mounting along an under-vehicle frame rail

To install:

6. Install or connect the following:
   - Fuel filter into the mounting bracket with the flow arrow pointing in the correct direction.
   - Fuel lines to the fuel filter. Align and push the male tube into the female fitting until a click is heard. Pull on the fitting to ensure that it is fully engaged, then install the safety clip.
7. Lower the vehicle to the ground.

➡**When the battery has been disconnected and reconnected, some abnormal drive symptoms may occur while the Powertrain Control Module (PCM) relearns its adaptive strategy. The vehicle may need to be driven 10 miles (16 km) or more to relearn the strategy.**

8. Connect the negative battery cable.

FUEL INJECTORS

REMOVAL & INSTALLATION

Excursion

5.4L Engine

> ✳✳ **CAUTION**
>
> **Fuel injection systems remain under pressure, even after the engine has been turned OFF. The fuel system pressure must be relieved before disconnecting any fuel lines. Failure to do so may result in fire and/or personal injury.**

1. Before servicing the vehicle, refer to the precautions section.

2. Properly relieve the fuel system pressure.
3. Disconnect the negative battery cable.
4. Disconnect the Vapor Management Valve (VMV) hose.
5. Remove the four fuel rail bolts.
6. Remove the fuel injectors.
7. Remove and discard the two O-ring seals from the fuel injectors.
8. Shift and remove the fuel injection supply manifold.

> ✳✳ **CAUTION**
>
> **Check for fuel leakage after installation is complete.**

To install:

➡**Make sure the fuel injectors and the fuel rail are fully seated.**

9. Install new O-ring seals and lubricate them with clean engine oil.
10. Attach the injector to the fuel rail.
11. Install the fuel rail and tighten the retainers to 89 inch lbs. (10 Nm).
12. Install the remaining components in the reverse of removal.
13. If equipped, connect the upper fitting to the exhaust manifold-to-EGR valve tube. Tighten the fittings to 37 ft. lbs. (50 Nm).

6.8L Engine

> ✳✳ **CAUTION**
>
> **Fuel injection systems remain under pressure, even after the engine has been turned OFF. The fuel system pressure must be relieved before disconnecting any fuel lines. Failure to do so may result in fire and/or personal injury.**

1. Before servicing the vehicle, refer to the precautions section.
2. Properly relieve the fuel system pressure.
3. Disconnect the negative battery cable.
4. Remove the throttle body spacer.
5. Disconnect the right hand radio ignition capacitor electrical connector.
6. Disconnect the fuel pressure regulator vacuum hose.
7. Remove the fuel line tether clamps.
8. Disconnect the fuel lines.
9. Remove and discard the fuel line O-ring seals.
10. Disconnect the fuel injector electrical connectors.
11. Remove the crankcase vent connector and hose.

12. Remove the four bolts, the fuel injection supply manifold assembly and fuel injectors.
13. Discard the fuel injector O-ring seals.

To install:

14. Installation is the reverse of removal, please note the
   a. Lubricate the new fuel injector O-ring seals with clean engine oil prior to installation.
   b. Be sure fuel injectors and fuel injection supply manifold are fully seated.
   c. Lubricate the new fuel line O-ring seals with clean engine oil prior to installation.
   d. Tighten the fuel rail retainers to 89 inch lbs. (10 Nm).

> ✳✳ **CAUTION**
>
> **Check for fuel leakage after installation is complete.**

Expedition & Navigator

> ✳✳ **CAUTION**
>
> **Fuel injection systems remain under pressure, even after the engine has been turned OFF. The fuel system pressure must be relieved before disconnecting any fuel lines. Failure to do so may result in fire and/or personal injury.**

1. Before servicing the vehicle, refer to the precautions section.
2. Properly relieve the fuel system pressure.
3. Disconnect the negative battery cable.
4. Disconnect the fuel supply tube spring lock coupling.
5. Remove the air cleaner outlet pipe.
6. Disconnect the quick connect couplings and remove the crankcase vent tube.
7. Disconnect the generator wiring harness retainer from the air cleaner outlet pipe-to-throttle body (TB) adapter.
8. Remove the 4 bolts and the air cleaner outlet pipe-to-TB adapter.
9. Disconnect the quick connect couplings and remove the positive crankcase ventilation (PCV) tube.
10. Disconnect the electronic throttle control electrical connector.
11. Disconnect the throttle position (TP) sensor electrical connector.
12. Disconnect the heated PCV intake fitting electrical connector.

13. Disconnect the 8 fuel injector electrical connectors.

14. Remove the 4 fuel rail bolts.

15. Remove the fuel rail and fuel injectors as an assembly.

16. Separate the fuel injectors from the fuel rail.

❋❋ WARNING

Use O-ring seals that are made of special fuel-resistant material. Use of ordinary O-rings can cause the fuel system to leak. Do not reuse the O-ring seals. Lubricate the O-ring seals with clean engine oil prior to installation.

17. To install, reverse the removal procedure and note the following:

- Lubricate the air cleaner outlet pipe-to-TB adapter seal with clean engine coolant prior to installation.
- Tighten the fuel rail retainers to 89 inch lbs. (10 Nm).
- Tighten the 4 bolts to the air cleaner outlet pipe-to-TB adapter, to 89 inch lbs. (10 Nm).

FUEL PUMP

REMOVAL & INSTALLATION

Excursion

❋❋ CAUTION

Fuel injection systems remain under pressure, even after the engine has been turned OFF. The fuel system pressure must be relieved before disconnecting any fuel lines. Failure to do so may result in fire and/or personal injury.

1. Before servicing the vehicle, refer to the precautions section.

2. Remove or disconnect the following:
- Negative battery cable
- Fuel pressure
- Fuel tank
- Retaining ring
- Fuel pump assembly

3. Squeeze the locking tabs while pushing down.
- Fuel pump mounting gasket.

To install:

4. Install or connect the following:
- Fuel pump mounting gasket.
- Fuel pump assembly
- Tighten retaining ring to 60 ft. lbs. (82 Nm).
- Fuel tank
- Negative battery cable

Expedition & Navigator

❋❋ CAUTION

Fuel injection systems remain under pressure, even after the engine has been turned OFF. The fuel system pressure must be relieved before disconnecting any fuel lines. Failure to do so may result in fire and/or personal injury.

1. Before servicing the vehicle, refer to the precautions section.

2. Release the fuel system pressure.

3. Drain the fuel tank.

4. If equipped, remove the four nuts and the fuel tank skid plate.

5. Disconnect the two vapor tubes at the rear of the fuel tank.

6. Disconnect the vapor tube and the fuel filter outlet tube forward of the fuel tank.

7. Disconnect the vapor tube from the Evaporative Emissions (EVAP) system dust separator.

❋❋ CAUTION

Do not support the fuel tank directly beneath the fuel pump mounting area. Damage to the fuel pump assembly can occur.

8. Position a suitable jack under the fuel tank.

➡ The location of the fuel vent hose is critical to fuel system operation. Note the routing of the fuel vent hose at this time.

9. Remove the two bolts and the fuel tank front and rear support straps. Lower the front of the fuel tank approximately 25 mm (1 in).

10. Disconnect the vent tube from the fuel pump module.

11. Disconnect the fuel pump module and fuel pressure transducer electrical connectors.

12. Remove the fuel tank from the vehicle.

13. Disconnect the fuel and vapor tubes from the fuel pump module.

14. Using the lock ring removal tool 310-123, remove the fuel pump lock ring.

❋❋ CAUTION

Note the location of the fuel pump alignment tabs.

❋❋ CAUTION

Carefully remove the fuel pump assembly to avoid damaging the fuel level sensor.

15. Remove the fuel pump module assembly. Discard the O-ring seal

To install:

16. Installation is the reverse of removal. Note the following torque specifications:
   a. Fuel tank front and rear support straps bolts to 35 ft. lbs. (47 Nm).
   b. If equipped, fuel tank skid plate nuts to 15 ft. lbs. (20 Nm).

FUEL TANK

REMOVAL & INSTALLATION

Excursion

❋❋ CAUTION

Do not smoke or carry lighted tobacco or open flame of any type when working on or near any fuel-related components. Highly flammable mixtures are always present and may be ignited. Failure to follow these instructions may result in personal injury.

❋❋ CAUTION

Fuel in the fuel system remains under high pressure even when the engine is not running. Before working on or disconnecting any of the fuel lines or fuel system components, the fuel system pressure must be relieved. Failure to follow these instructions may result in personal injury.

1. Before servicing the vehicle, refer to the precautions section.

2. Disconnect the battery ground cable.

3. Relieve the fuel pressure.

4. Drain the fuel from the fuel tank.

5. Raise and support the vehicle.

6. Disconnect the fuel tank filler pipe hose and the filler pipe vent tube from the fuel tank.

7. Position a jack under the fuel tank.

8. Remove the four fuel tank cover strap bolts.

9. Partially lower the fuel tank.

10. Disconnect the fuel lines from the fuel pump.

11. Disconnect the fuel pump electrical connector.

12. On gasoline fuel tanks, disconnect the hose(s) from the evaporative emission valve.

13. Lower the fuel tank.

14. If a new fuel tank is being installed, transfer the necessary components to the new fuel tank.

15. To install, reverse the removal procedure and note the following:

16. Tighten the fuel tank strap bolts to 98 ft. lbs. (133 Nm).

Expedition & Navigator

2005–06 Models

※※ CAUTION

Do not smoke or carry lighted tobacco or open flame of any type when working on or near any fuel-related components. Highly flammable mixtures are always present and may be ignited. Failure to follow these instructions may result in personal injury.

※※ CAUTION

Fuel in the fuel system remains under high pressure even when the engine is not running. Before working on or disconnecting any of the fuel lines or fuel system components, the fuel system pressure must be relieved. Failure to follow these instructions may result in personal injury.

※※ WARNING

Fuel injection equipment is manufactured to very precise tolerances and fine clearances. It is therefore essential that absolute cleanliness is observed when working with these components. Always install blanking plugs to any open orifices or tubes.

1. Before servicing the vehicle, refer to the precautions section.

2. With the vehicle in NEUTRAL, position it on a hoist.

3. Release the fuel system pressure.

4. Drain the fuel tank.

5. If equipped, remove the four nuts and the fuel tank skid plate.

6. Disconnect the two vapor tubes at the rear of the fuel tank.

7. Disconnect the vapor tube and the fuel filter outlet tube forward of the fuel tank.

➡**Do not support the fuel tank directly beneath the fuel pump mounting area. Damage to the fuel pump assembly can occur.**

8. Position a suitable jack under the fuel tank.

➡**The location of the fuel vent hose is critical to fuel system operation. Note the routing of the fuel vent hose at this time.**

9. Remove the two bolts and the fuel tank front and rear support straps. Lower the front of the fuel tank approximately 1 inch. (25 mm).

10. Disconnect the vent tube from the fuel pump module.

11. Disconnect the fuel pump module and fuel pressure transducer electrical connectors.

12. Remove the fuel tank from the vehicle.

13. To install, reverse the removal procedure and note the following:

14. For 2005 models if removed, tighten the fuel tank skid plate bolts to 15 ft. lbs. (20 Nm). For 2006 models 22 ft. lbs. (30 Nm).

15. For 2005 models tighten fuel tank strap bolts to 35 ft. lbs. (47 Nm). For 2006 models tighten strap bolts to 30 ft. lbs. (40 Nm).

2007 Models

See Figure 268.

※※ CAUTION

Do not smoke or carry lighted tobacco or open flame of any type when working on or near any fuel-related components. Highly flammable mixtures are always present and may be ignited. Failure to follow these instructions may result in personal injury.

※※ CAUTION

Fuel in the fuel system remains under high pressure even when the engine is not running. Before working on or disconnecting any of the fuel lines or fuel system components, the fuel system pressure must be relieved. Failure to follow these instructions may result in personal injury.

※※ WARNING

Fuel injection equipment is manufactured to very precise tolerances and fine clearances. It is therefore essential that absolute cleanliness is observed when working with these components. Always install blanking plugs to any open orifices or tubes.

1. Before servicing the vehicle, refer to the precautions section.

2. With the vehicle in NEUTRAL, position it on a hoist.

3. Release the fuel system pressure.

4. Drain the fuel tank.

5. If equipped with a 28 gal. (106 L) fuel tank, remove the 4 nuts and the fuel tank skid plate.

6. If equipped with a 33.5 gal. (127 L) fuel tank, remove the 5 nuts and the fuel tank skid plate.

7. Disconnect the fuel tank filler pipe vapor tube from the evaporative emissions (EVAP) canister fresh air tube, and the fuel tank filler pipe vent tube-to-fuel tank pressure sensor and vapor tube assembly quick connect coupling in the rear of the fuel tank.

8. Disconnect the fuel filter outlet tube-to-fuel tube spring lock coupling, EVAP canister fresh air tube-to-dust separator quick connect coupling and the fuel tank pressure sensor and vapor tube assembly-to-EVAP canister quick connect coupling in the front of the fuel tank.

9. Remove the sway bar bracket nuts and let the sway bar hang down.

10. Position a suitable jack under the fuel tank.

➡**Do not support the fuel tank directly beneath the fuel pump mounting area. Damage to the fuel pump assembly can occur.**

11. If equipped with a 33.5 gal. (127 L) fuel tank, remove the center fuel tank support strap bolt.

12. Remove the 2 bolts from the front and rear fuel tank support straps.

13. Remove the front fuel tank support strap.

14. If equipped with a 28 gal. (106 L) fuel tank, lower the fuel tank slightly and rotate the center fuel tank support strap aside.

➡**To assist in removing the center fuel tank support strap, you may have to push up slightly on the front of the tank to get the center fuel tank support strap to clear the fuel tank.**

15. Rotate the rear fuel tank support strap aside.

16. Lower the fuel tank slightly. Disconnect the fuel pump module and fuel tank pressure sensor electrical connectors.

17. Remove the fuel tank from the vehicle.

18. If equipped with a 33.5 gal. (127 L) fuel tank, if installing a new center fuel tank support strap, remove the center fuel tank support strap from the vehicle.

※※ WARNING

When installing a new fuel supply tube, fuel return tube or a fuel tank, it is essential that a new mastic

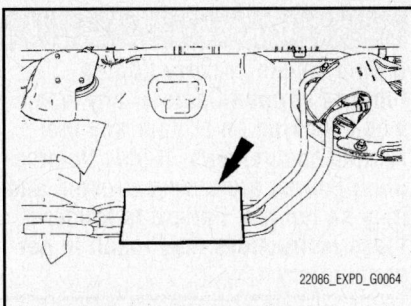

Fig. 268 Mastic patch location

patch be installed over both fuel tubes. If a new mastic patch is not installed correctly, fuel tube damage will occur.

➡Clean the fuel supply tube, fuel return tube and the fuel tank of any dirt and foreign material before installing the new mastic patch.

➡If installing a new fuel supply tube, fuel return tube or a fuel tank, install a new mastic patch over both fuel tubes. Position the mastic patch over the fuel tubes as shown. If the patch is installed too far inboard, it can interfere with installation of the fuel tank.

19. If installing a new rear fuel tank support strap, remove the rear fuel tank support strap from the vehicle.
20. To install, reverse the removal procedure and note the following:
21. Tighten fuel tank support strap bolt to 30 ft. lbs. (40 Nm).
22. Tighten sway bar bracket nuts to 35 ft. lbs. (48 Nm).
23. If removed, tighten the fuel tank skid plate nuts to 15 ft. lbs. (20 Nm).

IDLE SPEED

ADJUSTMENT

Idle speed is maintained by the Powertrain Control Module (PCM). No adjustment is necessary or possible.

THROTTLE BODY

REMOVAL & INSTALLATION

Excursion

5.4L Engine
See Figures 269 and 270.

※※ CAUTION

Do not smoke or carry lighted tobacco or open flame of any type when working on or near any fuel-

related components. Highly flammable mixtures are always present and can be ignited. Failure to follow these instructions can result in personal injury.

1. Before servicing the vehicle, refer to the precautions section.

※※ WARNING

Throttle body bore and plate area have a special coating and cannot be cleaned.

2. Disconnect the negative battery cable.
3. Remove the air cleaner outlet pipe.
4. Disconnect the Throttle Position (TP) sensor electrical connector.
5. Disconnect the accelerator controls:
a. Disconnect the accelerator cable.
b. Disconnect the speed control cable.
c. Disconnect the return spring.

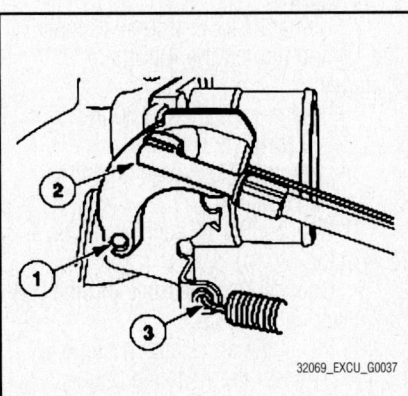

Fig. 269 Disconnect the accelerator cable (1), speed control cable (2) and return spring (3)

➡Discard the throttle body gasket.

6. Remove the bolts, the throttle body and the throttle body gasket.

To install:
7. Position a new gasket and the throttle body. Install the bolts in two stages.
a. Stage 1: Tighten the bolts to 80 inch lbs. (9 Nm).
b. Stage 2: Tighten an additional 90 degrees.
8. Connect the TP sensor electrical connector.
9. Connect the throttle body cam.
a. Connect the accelerator cable.
b. Connect the speed control actuator cable.
c. Install the accelerator return spring.

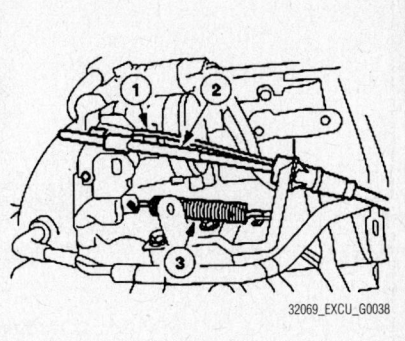

Fig. 270 Connect the accelerator cable (1), speed control actuator cable (2) and accelerator return spring (3)

10. Connect the air cleaner outlet pipe.
11. Connect the negative battery cable.

6.8L Engine
See Figure 271.

※※ CAUTION

Do not smoke or carry lighted tobacco or open flame of any type when working on or near any fuel-related components. Highly flammable mixtures are always present and may be ignited. Failure to follow these instructions may result in personal injury.

1. Before servicing the vehicle, refer to the precautions section.
2. Disconnect the negative battery cable.
3. Remove the air cleaner outlet tube and the accelerator cable splash shield.
4. Disconnect the accelerator cable.
• Disconnect the speed control actuator.
• Disconnect the accelerator cable.
• Remove the acceleration control return spring.
5. Remove the accelerator cable bracket.
• Remove the bolts.
• Remove the accelerator cable bracket.
6. Disconnect the throttle position (TP) sensor electrical connector.
7. Remove the throttle body (TB).
• Remove the four bolts.
• Remove the TB.
• Remove and discard the TB gasket.

To install:
8. Install a new TB gasket.
9. Position the TB.

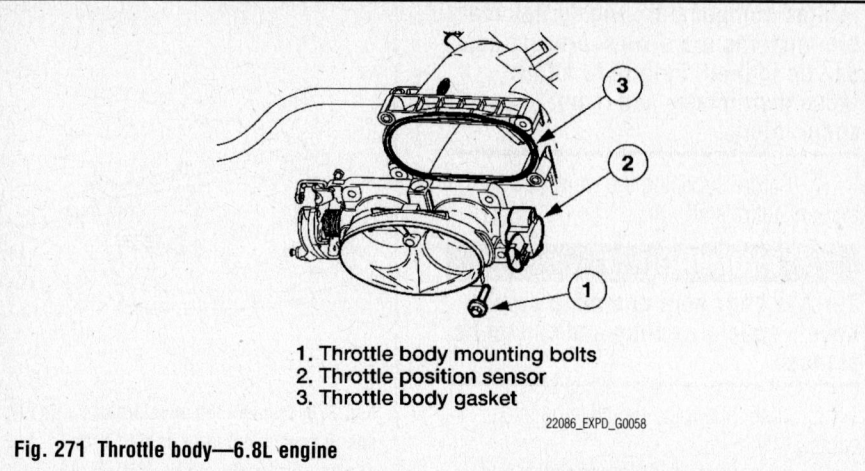

1. Throttle body mounting bolts
2. Throttle position sensor
3. Throttle body gasket

22086_EXPD_G0058

Fig. 271 Throttle body—6.8L engine

10. Install the four bolts in two stages:
- Stage 1: Tighten the bolts to 80 inch. lbs. (9 Nm).
- Stage 2: Tighten an additional 90 degrees.

11. Connect the TP sensor electrical connector.

12. Install the accelerator cable bracket.
- Position the accelerator cable bracket.
- Install the bolts and tighten to 80 inch. lbs. (9 Nm).

13. Connect the accelerator cable.
- Connect the speed control actuator.
- Connect the accelerator cable.
- Install the acceleration control return spring.

14. Install the air cleaner outlet tube and the accelerator cable splash shield.

15. Connect the negative battery cable.

Expedition & Navigator

2005–06 Models

> **❊❊ CAUTION**
>
> **Do not smoke or carry lighted tobacco or open flame of any type when working on or near any fuel-related components. Highly flammable mixtures are always present and may be ignited. Failure to follow these instructions may result in personal injury.**

1. Before servicing the vehicle, refer to the precautions section.
2. Disconnect the negative battery cable.
3. Remove the air cleaner assembly.

4. Disconnect the electronic throttle control electrical connector.
5. Disconnect the throttle position (TP) sensor electrical connector.
6. Remove the 4 bolts and the throttle body (TB) assembly.

To install:

7. Using a new O-ring seal, install the TB and tighten the 4 bolts in 2 stages.
- Stage 1: Tighten to 80 inch. lbs. (9 Nm).
- Stage 2: Tighten an additional 90 degrees.

8. Connect the TP sensor electrical connector.
9. Connect the electronic throttle control electrical connector.
10. Install the air cleaner assembly.
11. Connect the negative battery cable.

2007 Models

See Figures 272 and 273.

> **❊❊ CAUTION**
>
> **Do not smoke or carry lighted tobacco or open flame of any type when working on or near any fuel-related components. Highly flammable mixtures are always present and may be ignited. Failure to follow these instructions may result in personal injury.**

1. Before servicing the vehicle, refer to the precautions section.
2. Disconnect the negative battery cable.
3. Remove the air cleaner outlet pipe.
4. Disconnect the quick connect couplings and remove the crankcase vent tube.
5. Disconnect the generator wiring harness retainer from the air cleaner outlet pipe-to-throttle body (TB) adapter.
6. Remove the 4 bolts and position aside the air cleaner outlet tube-to-TB adapter.
7. Disconnect the electronic throttle control electrical connector
8. Disconnect the throttle position (TP) sensor electrical connector.
9. Remove the 4 bolts and the vibration damper.
10. Remove the TB assembly.

To install:

11. Using a new O-ring seal, position the TB and vibration damper and tighten the 4 bolts in 2 stages.
- Stage 1: Tighten to 80 inch. lbs. (9 Nm).
- Stage 2: Tighten an additional 90 degrees.

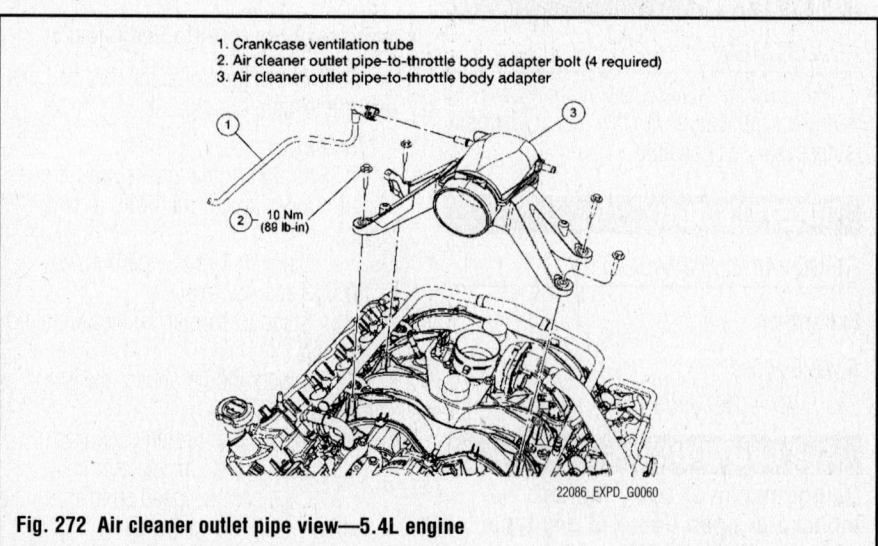

1. Crankcase ventilation tube
2. Air cleaner outlet pipe-to-throttle body adapter bolt (4 required)
3. Air cleaner outlet pipe-to-throttle body adapter

10 Nm
(89 lb-in)

22086_EXPD_G0060

Fig. 272 Air cleaner outlet pipe view—5.4L engine

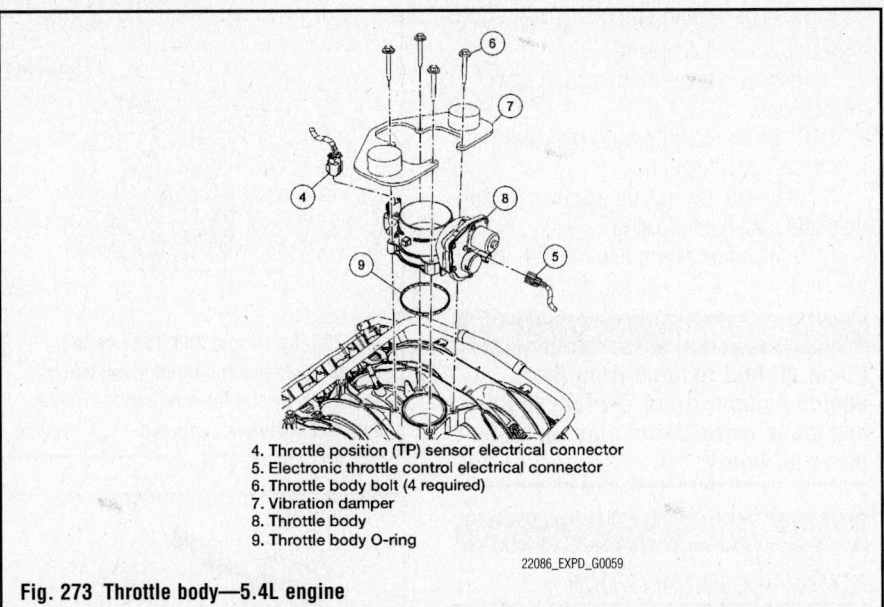

4. Throttle position (TP) sensor electrical connector
5. Electronic throttle control electrical connector
6. Throttle body bolt (4 required)
7. Vibration damper
8. Throttle body
9. Throttle body O-ring

22086_EXPD_G0059

Fig. 273 Throttle body—5.4L engine

12. Connect the TP sensor electrical connector.

13. Connect the electronic throttle control electrical connector.

14. Lubricate the air cleaner outlet pipe-to-TB adapter seal with clean engine coolant prior to installation.

15. Position the air cleaner outlet pipe-to-TB adapter and install the 4 bolts.

16. Tighten bolts to 80 inch. lbs. (9 Nm).

17. Connect the generator wiring harness retainer to the air cleaner outlet tube-to-TB adapter.

18. Position the crankcase vent tube and connect the quick connect couplings.

19. Install the air cleaner outlet pipe.

20. Connect the negative battery cable.

FUEL

DIESEL FUEL INJECTION SYSTEM

FUEL SYSTEM SERVICE PRECAUTIONS

Safety is the most important factor when performing not only fuel system maintenance but any type of maintenance. Failure to conduct maintenance and repairs in a safe manner may result in serious personal injury or death. Maintenance and testing of the vehicle's fuel system components can be accomplished safely and effectively by adhering to the following rules and guidelines.

• To avoid the possibility of fire and personal injury, always disconnect the negative battery cable unless the repair or test procedure requires that battery voltage be applied.

• Always relieve the fuel system pressure prior to disconnecting any fuel system component (injector, fuel rail, pressure regulator, etc.), fitting or fuel line connection. Exercise extreme caution whenever relieving fuel system pressure to avoid exposing skin, face and eyes to fuel spray. Please be advised that fuel under pressure may penetrate the skin or any part of the body that it contacts.

• Always place a shop towel or cloth around the fitting or connection prior to loosening to absorb any excess fuel due to spillage. Ensure that all fuel spillage (should it occur) is quickly removed from engine surfaces. Ensure that all fuel soaked cloths or towels are deposited into a suitable waste container.

• Always keep a dry chemical (Class B) fire extinguisher near the work area.

• Do not allow fuel spray or fuel vapors to come into contact with a spark or open flame.

• Always use a back-up wrench when loosening and tightening fuel line connection fittings. This will prevent unnecessary stress and torsion to fuel line piping.

• Always replace worn fuel fitting O-rings with new. Do not substitute fuel hose or equivalent where fuel pipe is installed.

Before servicing the vehicle, make sure to also refer to the precautions in the beginning of this section as well.

RELIEVING FUEL SYSTEM PRESSURE

RELIEVING

6.0L Engine

1. Before servicing the vehicle, refer to the precautions in the beginning of this section.

2. Remove the Schrader valve cap and install the fuel pressure gauge 310-012.

3. Open the manual valve slowly on the fuel pressure gauge 310-012 and relieve the fuel pressure. This will drain some fuel out of the system; place the fuel in a suitable container.

FUEL CONDITIONING MODULE

The Fuel Condition Module contains the fuel pump and water separator.

DRAINING WATER FROM THE SYSTEM

6.0L Diesel Engine

> ✳✳ **CAUTION**
>
> **Smoking or open flame of any type must not be present when working near fuel or fuel vapor.**

1. Disconnect both battery ground cables.
2. Raise and support the vehicle.
3. Open the fuel/water separator drain valve to release the fuel pressure.

REMOVAL & INSTALLATION

6.0L Diesel Engine

1. Before servicing the vehicle, refer to the precautions in the beginning of this section.

> ✳✳ **CAUTION**
>
> **Smoking or open flame of any type must not be present when working near fuel or fuel vapor.**

2. Disconnect both battery ground cables.
3. Raise and support the vehicle.
4. Open the fuel/water separator drain valve to release the fuel pressure.

5. Disconnect the electrical connectors.

6. Disconnect the fuel pump electrical connector.

7. Disconnect the fuel warmer electrical connector.

8. Disconnect the water-in-fuel electrical connector.

9. Disconnect the fuel hoses.

10. Remove the fuel hose retaining clips and discard. Disconnect the fuel hoses from the fuel pump.

11. Press in the retaining clips and release the fuel hoses.

12. Remove the mounting nuts and the fuel conditioning module.

13. To install, reverse the removal procedure.

FUEL FILTER

REMOVAL & INSTALLATION

The fuel filter for the 6.0L engine is located inside the fuel conditioning module.

FUEL PRESSURE REGULATOR

REMOVAL & INSTALLATION

✳✳ CAUTION

Fuel in the fuel system remains under high pressure even when the engine is not running. Before working on or disconnecting any of the fuel lines or fuel system components, the fuel system pressure must be relieved. Failure to follow these instructions may result in personal injury.

1. Before servicing the vehicle, refer to the precautions section.

2. Remove the secondary fuel filter and remove all fuel from the fuel filter housing.

3. Remove the screws and the fuel pressure regulator cover.

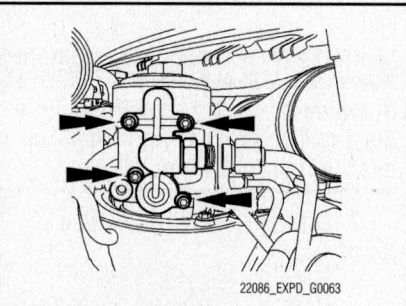

Fig. 274 Fuel regulator cover screws shown 6.0L diesel engine.

4. Remove and discard the fuel pressure regulator cover O-ring seal.

5. Remove the restrictor, spring and poppet valve.

6. Clean the fuel pressure regulator bore in the fuel filter housing.

7. To install, reverse the removal procedure and note the following:

8. Tighten fuel return line to 32 ft. lbs (43 Nm).

✳✳ WARNING

Clean all fuel residue from the engine compartment. Failure to follow these instructions may result in personal injury.

GLOW PLUGS

REMOVAL & INSTALLATION

6.0L Engine

1. Before servicing the vehicle, refer to the precautions in the beginning of this section.

2. If servicing the right hand glow plugs, remove the evaporator core housing.

3. Disconnect the glow plug electrical connector.

4. Remove the glow plug buss bar.

5. Remove the glow plug.

➡**To install new glow plug sleeves, the cylinder heads must be removed from the vehicle.**

6. If required, remove the cylinder heads from the engine.

➡**The glow plug sleeve is made of stainless steel. Lubrication of the glow plug sleeve removal tap is necessary, or damage to the tap and excessive force will be needed to get the tap started.**

7. Thread the glow plug sleeve removal tap 303-764 into the glow plug sleeve.

8. Install the glow plug sleeve removal tool 303-764 into the threaded sleeve and tighten. Use a wrench to thread the tool into the sleeve until the sleeve is extracted.

9. Clean the glow plug bore with a stiff wire brush. Use filtered compressed air to remove the debris from the glow plug recess.

To install:

10. Verify the glow plug bore is completely clean and dry.

11. Apply Threadlock 262 sealant to the glow plug sleeve in the two places illustrated.

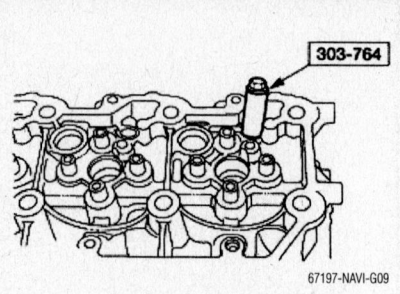

Fig. 275 Insert tool 303-764 into the threaded sleeve and tighten and use a wrench to thread the tool into the sleeve until the sleeve is extracted—6.0L engine

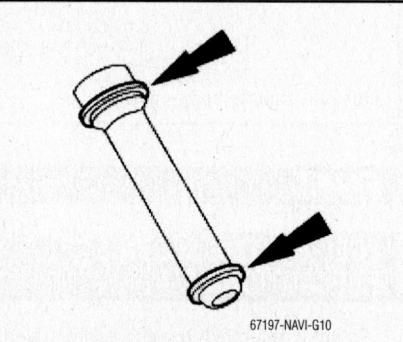

Fig. 276 Apply Threadlock 262 sealant to the glow plug sleeve in the two places shown—6.0L engine

12. Install the glow plug sleeve 303-763 into the glow plug bore until it bottoms.

13. Clean the glow plug sleeve after installation with a nylon brush and solvent. Make sure Threadlock 262 sealant is cleaned out before it hardens.

14. Install the cylinder heads.

15. Install the glow plug and tighten to 14 ft. lbs. (19 Nm).

16. Inspect and install new the O-rings as necessary.

17. Install the glow plug buss bar.

18. Connect the glow plug electrical connector.

19. If removed, install the evaporator core housing.

HIGH PRESSURE OIL PUMP

REMOVAL & INSTALLATION

6.0L Engine

Early Build Models

1. Before servicing the vehicle, refer to the precautions in the beginning of this section.

2. Remove the intake manifold.

3. Remove the turbocharger heat shield.

4. Remove the bolts and the high-pressure oil pump cover.

5. Use a thin gasket scraper to separate the cover from the crankcase.

6. Remove and discard the press-in-place gasket.

7. Position the dial indicator with bracketry onto the oil pump drive and check the oil pump drive gear backlash. The reading should be 0.007–0.0124 inch (0.179–0.315mm).

8. Remove the bolts from the high-pressure oil pump discharge pipe.

9. Using the tool 303-755, disconnect and remove the high-pressure oil pump discharge pipe.

10. Remove and discard the D-shaped O-ring seal.

11. Remove and discard the high-pressure pump O-ring seal.

12. Remove the bolts and the high-pressure oil pump.

13. Remove and discard the lower O-ring seal.

To install:

14. Install a new lower O-ring seal.

15. Install the high-pressure oil pump and bolts. Tighten to 18 ft. lbs. (25 Nm).

16. Install the high-pressure pump O-ring seal.

17. Install the oil pump discharge pipe.

18. Install the bolts for the oil discharge pipe. Tighten to 71 inch lbs. (8 Nm).

19. Position the dial indicator with bracketry onto the oil pump drive and check the oil pump drive gear backlash. The reading should be 0.007–0.0124 inch (0.179–0.315mm).

20. Install a new D-ring seal on the high-pressure discharge pipe.

21. Install a new press-in-place gasket in the high-pressure pump cover.

22. Clean the cover mounting surface and apply sealer at the seams.

23. Install the high-pressure pump cover and bolts. Tighten to 8 ft. lbs. (11 Nm).

24. Install the turbocharger heat shield.

25. Install the intake manifold

Late Build Models

1. Before servicing the vehicle, refer to the precautions in the beginning of this section.

2. Remove the intake manifold.

3. Remove the turbocharger heat shield.

4. Remove the bolts and the high-pressure oil pump cover.

5. Use a thin gasket scraper to separate the cover from the crankcase.

6. Remove and discard the press-in-place gasket.

7. Position the dial indicator with bracketry onto the oil pump drive and check the oil pump drive gear backlash. The reading should be 0.007–0.0124 inch (0.179–0.315mm).

8. Remove the bolts from the high-pressure oil pump discharge pipe. Position the high-pressure discharge pipe aside.

9. Remove and discard the high-pressure pump O-ring seal.

10. Remove the bolts and the high-pressure oil pump.

11. Remove and discard the lower O-ring seal.

To install:

12. Install a new lower O-ring seal.

13. Install the high-pressure oil pump and bolts. Tighten to 18 ft. lbs. (25 Nm).

14. Install the high-pressure pump O-ring seal.

15. Position back the high-pressure discharge tube and install the bolts. Tighten to 71 inch lbs. (8 Nm).

16. Position the dial indicator with bracketry onto the oil pump drive and check the oil pump drive gear backlash. The reading should be 0.007–0.0124 inch (0.179–0.315mm).

17. Install a new D-ring seal on the high-pressure discharge pipe.

18. Install a new press-in-place gasket in the high-pressure pump cover.

19. Clean the cover mounting surface and apply sealer at the seams.

20. Install the high-pressure pump cover and bolts. Tighten to 8 ft. lbs. (11 Nm).

21. Install the turbocharger heat shield.

22. Install the intake manifold.

IDLE SPEED

ADJUSTMENT

See Figure 277.

1. Before servicing the vehicle, refer to the precautions section.

2. Place the transmission in **P**.

3. Bring the engine up to normal operating temperature.

➡**Idle speed is measured with the transmission in D.**

4. Ensure that the curb idle adjusting screw is against the stop. If not, correct the vehicle linkage.

5. Check curb idle speed. Curb idle speed is specified on the Vehicle Emissions Control Information (VECI) decal on the underside of the vehicle's hood. Adjust the idle speed to specification using the idle speed adjusting screw.

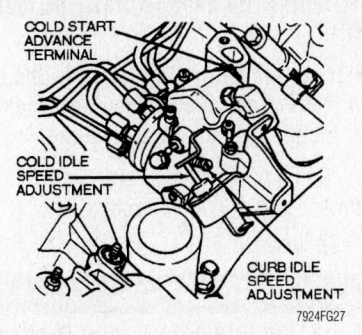

Fig. 277 Raise or lower the curb idle speed by turning the curb idle speed adjusting screw—diesel engines

6. Place the transmission in **P**. Rev the engine momentarily, then place the transmission in the specified gear and recheck the idle speed. Adjust again if necessary.

7. Remove the tachometer and close the hood.

INJECTORS

REMOVAL & INSTALLATION

6.0L Engine

Early Build Models

1. Before servicing the vehicle, refer to the precautions in the beginning of this section.

2. If removing the right hand fuel injectors, remove the evaporator case.

3. Remove the valve cover.

4. Disconnect the fuel injector electrical connector.

5. Disconnect the high-pressure oil rail supply line at the high-pressure oil rail.

6. Remove the bolts and the high-pressure oil rail.

7. Disconnect and remove the high-pressure oil supply line.

❉❉ CAUTION

Do not attempt to apply battery voltage to the fuel injector or damage to the fuel injector will occur.

8. Using a 19 mm socket, push the fuel injector electrical connector out of the rocker arm carrier.

❉❉ CAUTION

To prevent engine damage, do not use air tools to remove/install the fuel injectors. The clip that extracts the injector can dislodge and fall into the oil drain hole.

➡There is no need to drain the fuel rail.

➡If engine coolant is found in the combustion chambers, It may be necessary to install a new injector sleeve.

9. Remove the bolt, fuel injector hold-down clamp and fuel injector.

To install:

> ✳✳ CAUTION
>
> **If the fuel injector oil inlet D-shaped O-ring is damaged, a new fuel injector must be installed.**

10. Install new O-ring seals and copper washer on the fuel injector. Lubricate the fuel injector and O-ring seals liberally with clean engine oil.

11. Install the fuel injector, fuel injector hold-down clamp and bolt. Tighten to 24 ft. lbs. (33 Nm).

12. Install the fuel injector electrical connector into the rocker carrier.

13. Apply engine oil to the top fuel injector O-ring seals.

14. Install the high-pressure oil rail and bolts.

15. Install the high-pressure oil rail.

16. Install the bolts finger tight. Tighten the bolts in the sequence shown to 8 ft. lbs. (11 Nm).

17. Install the high-pressure oil line.

18. Connect the fuel injector electrical connector.

19. Install the valve covers.

Fig. 278 On early build models, tighten the high-pressure oil rail bolts in the sequence shown—6.0L engine—right side shown, left side similar

20. If removed, install the evaporator case.

Late Build Models

1. Before servicing the vehicle, refer to the precautions in the beginning of this section.

2. If removing the right hand fuel injectors, remove the evaporator case.

3. Remove the valve cover.

4. Disconnect the fuel injector electrical connector.

5. Remove the bolts and the high-pressure oil rail.

> ✳✳ CAUTION
>
> **Do not attempt to apply battery voltage to the fuel injector or damage to the fuel injector will occur.**

6. Using a 19 mm socket, push the fuel injector electrical connector out of the rocker arm carrier.

> ✳✳ CAUTION
>
> **To prevent engine damage, do not use air tools to remove/install the fuel injectors. The clip that extracts the injector can dislodge and fall into the oil drain hole.**

➡There is no need to drain the fuel rail.

➡If engine coolant is found in the combustion chambers, it may be necessary to install a new injector sleeve.

7. Remove the bolt, fuel injector hold-down clamp and fuel injector.

To install:

> ✳✳ CAUTION
>
> **If the fuel injector oil inlet D-shaped O-ring is damaged, a new fuel injector must be installed. Install new O-ring seals and copper washer on the fuel injector. Lubricate the fuel injector and O-ring seals liberally with clean engine oil.**

8. Install the fuel injector, fuel injector hold-down clamp and bolt. Tighten to 24 ft. lbs. (33 Nm).

9. Install the fuel injector electrical connector into the rocker carrier.

10. Apply engine oil to the top fuel injector O-ring seals.

11. Apply clean engine oil on the crankcase-to-head tube O-ring seal.

➡Apply clean engine oil on the tubes prior to installing the oil manifold.

12. Position the oil rail on the fuel injectors as follows:

a. Place the oil rail on top of the carrier so that the four single ball tubes are engaging the injector lead angle.

b. Insert three bolts, two on the ends of the straight side of the oil rail and one in the middle of the wavy side of the rail. Install the guide studs six to seven turns.

c. Press the oil rail into the fuel injectors.

d. Make sure that the oil rail mounting feet are flat against the mounting surface.

e. Loosely install the six bolts.

13. Install the oil rail retaining bolts.

14. Remove the three guide bolts.

15. Install the bolts finger tight. Tighten the bolts in the sequence shown to 10 ft. lbs. (14 Nm).

16. Connect the fuel injector electrical connector.

17. Install the valve covers.

18. If removed, install the evaporator case.

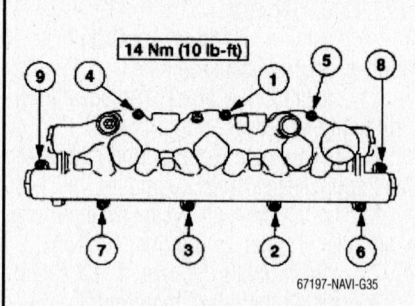

Fig. 279 On late build models, tighten the high-pressure oil rail bolts in the sequence shown—6.0L engine—right side shown, left side similar

HEATING & AIR CONDITIONING SYSTEM

BLOWER MOTOR

REMOVAL & INSTALLATION

Excursion

1. Before servicing the vehicle, refer to the precautions section.
2. On 5.4L and 6.8L engines, perform the following:
    a. Disconnect the speed control servo connector.
    b. Remove the bolts and remove the speed control servo.
3. Disconnect the connector.
4. Remove the blower motor ventilation tube.

> ❊❊ **WARNING**
>
> **Carefully remove the blower motor so as not to damage the wheel.**

5. Remove the screws and remove the blower motor.

> ❊❊ **WARNING**
>
> **If the wheel is to be reused, clean the corrosion from the shaft end prior to removing the wheel.**

6. Remove the wheel from the blower motor.
7. Remove the push clip.
8. Remove the wheel from the blower motor.
9. Installation is the reverse of the removal procedure. Tighten the blower motor screws to 18–31 inch lbs.

Expedition & Navigator

2005–06 Models

See Figure 280.

1. Before servicing the vehicle, refer to the precautions section.
2. Remove the RH lower instrument panel insulator.
3. For Navigator, remove the RH scuff plate.
4. For Expedition models:
    a. Remove the RH scuff plate.
    b. Remove the RH lower A-pillar trim panel.
5. Position the carpet aside.
6. Remove the blower motor, as follows:
    a. Disconnect the electrical connector and position the wire harness aside.
    b. Remove the screws, then remove the blower motor.

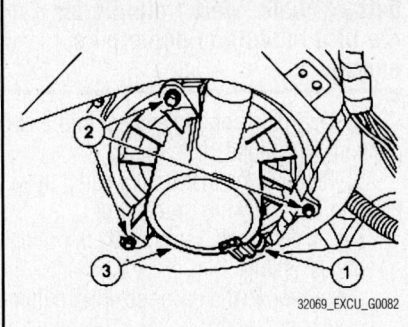

Fig. 280 Detach the electrical connector (1), remove the screws (2) and remove the blower motor (3)

7. Installation is the reverse of the removal procedure.

2007 Models

See Figure 281.

1. Before servicing the vehicle, refer to the precautions section.

➥**The blower motor vent tube must be completely removed from the blower motor before it can be rotated and disengaged from the heater core and evaporator core housing.**

2. Remove the RH lower instrument panel insulator (if equipped).

3. Remove the RH lower A-pillar junction box cover.
4. Position the carpet below the blower motor aside.
5. Release the 2 blower motor vent tube clips and remove the blower motor vent tube.
6. Disconnect the blower motor electrical connector.

➥**The blower motor will have to be carefully manipulated along the dash panel insulator, and the dash panel insulator will have to be slightly deflected to allow the blower motor to clear the heater core and evaporator core housing.**

7. Rotate the blower motor counterclockwise to disengage it from the housing and remove the blower motor.
8. To install, reverse the removal procedure.

HEATER CORE

REMOVAL & INSTALLATION

Excursion

1. Before servicing the vehicle, refer to the precautions in the beginning of this section.
2. Drain and recycle the engine coolant.

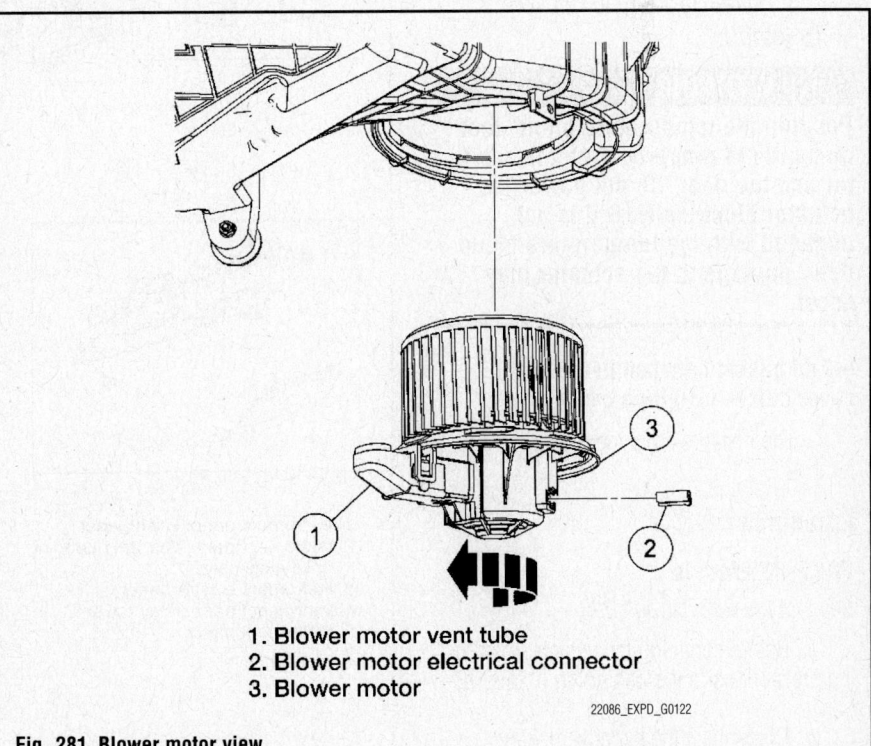

1. Blower motor vent tube
2. Blower motor electrical connector
3. Blower motor

Fig. 281 Blower motor view

※※ **CAUTION**

Never open, service or drain the radiator or cooling system when hot; serious burns can occur from the steam and hot coolant. Also, when draining engine coolant, keep in mind that cats and dogs are attracted to ethylene glycol antifreeze and could drink any that is left in an uncovered container or in puddles on the ground. This will prove fatal in sufficient quantities. Always drain coolant into a sealable container. Coolant should be reused unless it is contaminated or is several years old.

3. Remove or disconnect the following:

- Heater water hoses from the heater core.
- Stops and lower the glove compartment door.
- Electronic blend door actuator and bracket assembly.

※※ **WARNING**

The heater core cover must be raised vertically before removal to avoid damage to the heater core housing.

- Heater core cover screws and the cover
- Heater core from the housing

To install:

※※ **WARNING**

Position the temperature blend door manually to properly align the actuator and the door. Do not power the actuator electrically. If it is not engaged with the temperature blend door, damage to the actuator may occur.

➡ Add gasket between housing and cover before installing cover.

4. The installation is the reverse of the removal.

Expedition

2005–06 Models

See Figures 282 through 296.

1. Before servicing the vehicle, refer to the precautions in the beginning of this section.

2. Disconnect the negative battery cable.

※※ **CAUTION**

After disconnecting the negative battery cable, wait 1 minute for the SRS module to deplete its energy.

3. Drain the cooling system into a clean container for reuse.

4. Remove the instrument panel by performing the following procedure:

c. If equipped, remove the floor console assembly.

d. Remove the lower steering column cover bolts and the cover.

e. Remove both front door scuff plates.

f. Remove both side cowl trim panels.

g. Disconnect the electrical connector from the Brake Pedal Position (BPP) switch.

h. Remove the radio ground and the GEM/CTM ground bolts.

i. Disconnect the left side instrument panel main wiring harness connector.

j. In the engine compartment, remove the bulkhead wiring harness connector bolts and disconnect the wiring connectors.

k. In the driver's compartment, release the 6 locking tabs and remove the bulkhead electrical connector from the instrument panel.

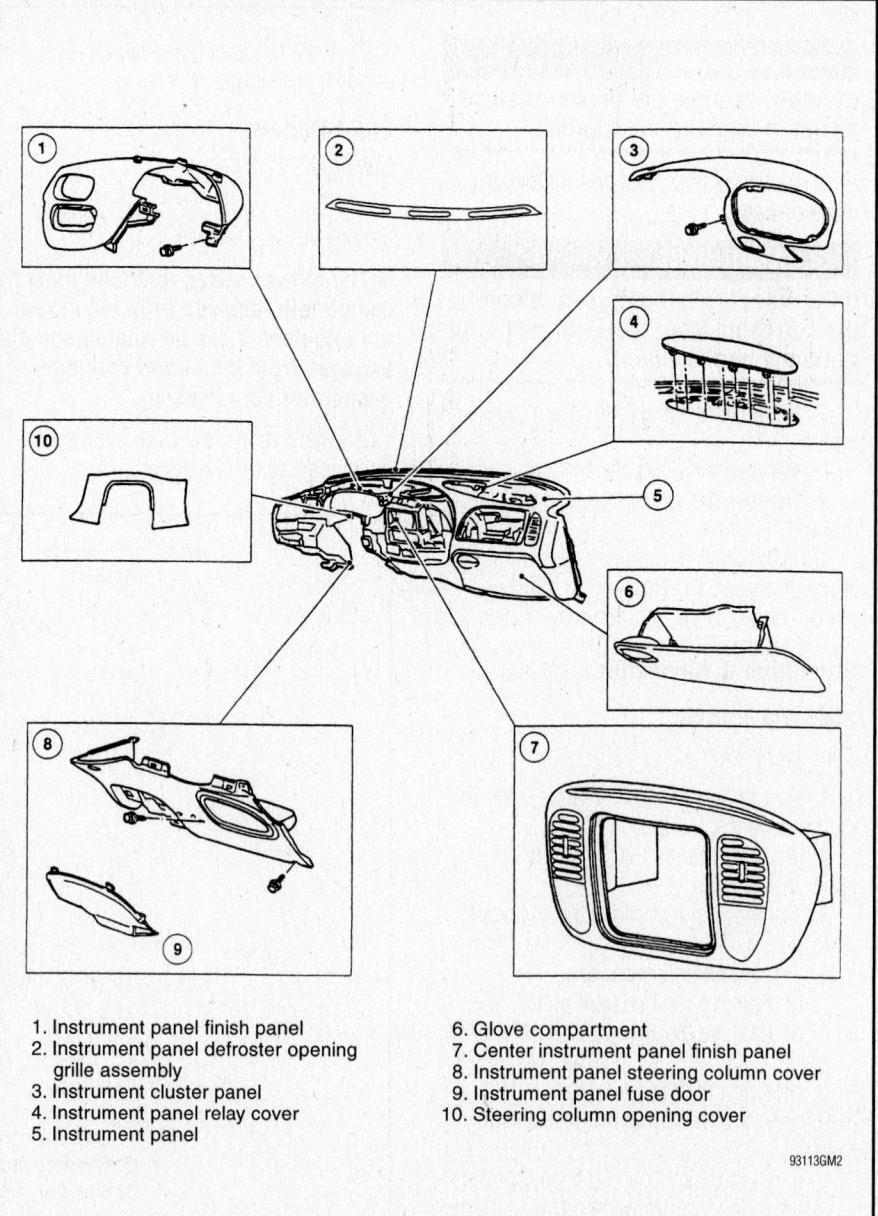

1. Instrument panel finish panel
2. Instrument panel defroster opening grille assembly
3. Instrument cluster panel
4. Instrument panel relay cover
5. Instrument panel
6. Glove compartment
7. Center instrument panel finish panel
8. Instrument panel steering column cover
9. Instrument panel fuse door
10. Steering column opening cover

93113GM2

Fig. 282 Exploded view of the instrument panel components—2005–06 Ford Expedition

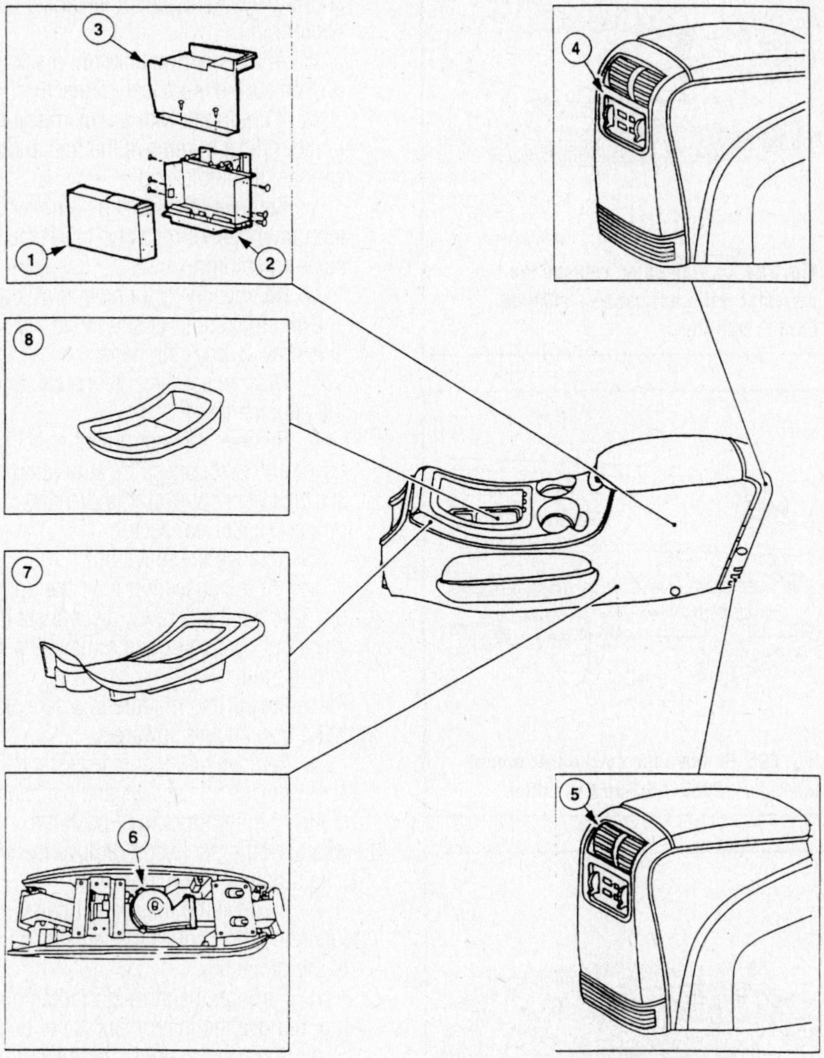

1. Digital audio compact disc player
2. Compact disc player mounting bracket
3. Compact disc player compartment trim panel
4. Radio and A/C integral control assembly
5. A/C register (upper)
6. Blower assembly
7. Center console finish panel
8. Console finish panel mat

93113GM3

Fig. 283 Exploded view of the floor console components—2005–06 Ford Expedition

91190G42

Fig. 286 Remove the instrument panel bolts through the steering column opening—2005–06 Ford Expedition

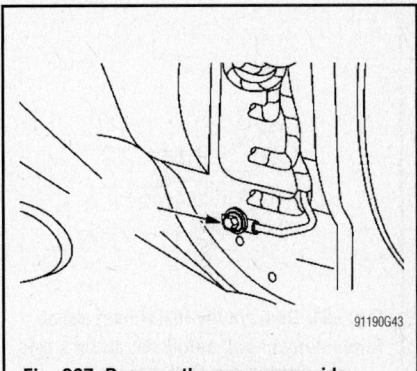

91190G43

Fig. 287 Remove the passenger side ground bolt—2005–06 Ford Expedition

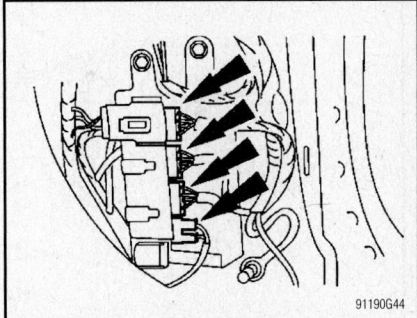

91190G44

Fig. 288 Detach the passenger side instrument panel main harness connectors—2005–06 Ford Expedition

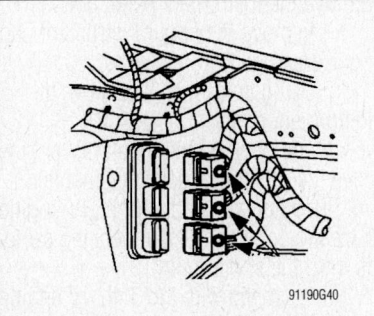

91190G40

Fig. 284 Remove the bulkhead electrical connectors from inside the engine compartment—2005–06 Ford Expedition

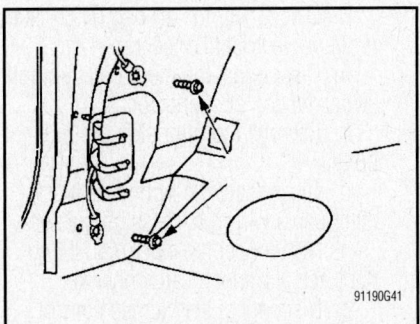

91190G41

Fig. 285 Remove the audio unit ground and the GEM/CTM ground bolts—2005–06 Ford Expedition

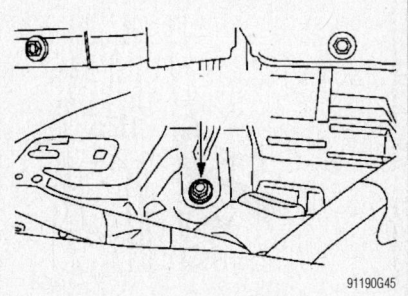

91190G45

Fig. 289 Remove the instrument panel bolt on the relay bracket—2005–06 Ford Expedition

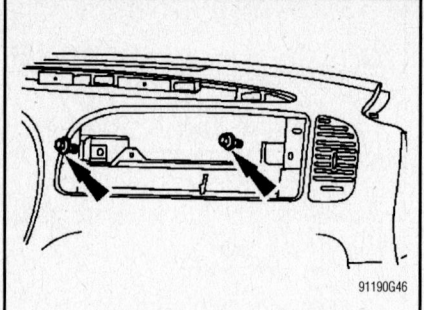

Fig. 290 Remove the instrument panel bolts through the passenger side air bag module opening—2005–06 Ford Expedition

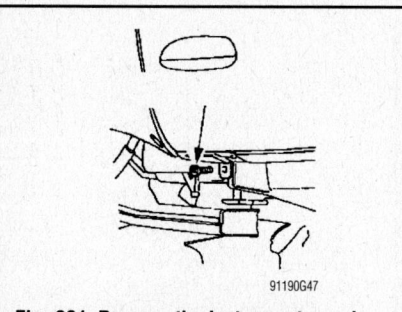

Fig. 291 Remove the instrument panel reinforcement bolt below the driver's side corner of the glove compartment—2005–06 Ford Expedition

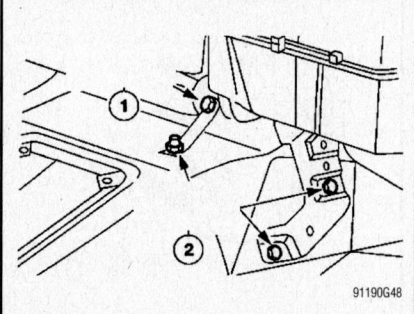

Fig. 292 Position the carpet aside and loosen the instrument panel floor brace—2005–06 Ford Expedition

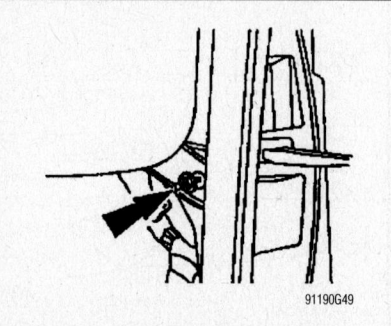

Fig. 293 Remove the passenger side instrument panel cowl side nut—2005–06 Ford Expedition

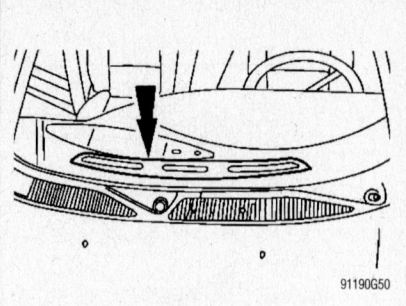

Fig. 294 On Navigator, remove the defroster grille assembly—2005–06 Ford Expedition

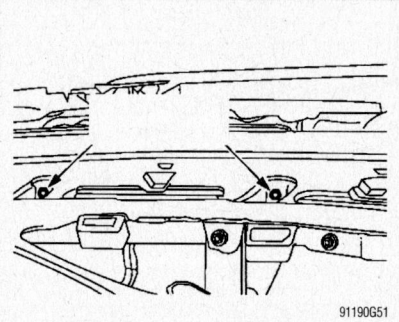

Fig. 295 Remove the cowl panel mounting bolts—2005–06 Ford Expedition

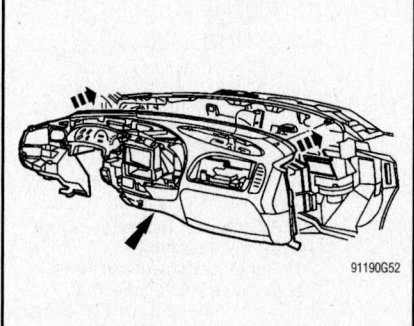

Fig. 296 Remove the instrument panel—2005–06 Ford Expedition

l. Disconnect the air bag diagnostic monitor electrical connector.

m. Disconnect the inertia fuel shutoff switch electrical connector.

n. Remove the right side ground bolts.

o. Disconnect the right side instrument panel wiring harness connectors.

p. Disconnect the electronic blend door actuator electrical connector.

q. Disconnect the climate control head vacuum harness connector.

r. Remove the steering column opening cover reinforcement nuts and the cover reinforcement.

s. At the base of the steering column, disconnect the air bag sliding contact and the anti-theft sensor electrical connectors.

t. At the steering column, disconnect the remaining electrical connectors.

u. If equipped with a transmission range indicator, remove the bolt and disconnect the cable.

v. Remove the steering column-to-instrument panel nuts and lower the steering column.

w. Remove the right side front fender splash shield screws and move the shield away from the panel.

x. Disconnect the antenna cable from the antenna base.

y. Remove the instrument panel relay cover and disconnect the auto lamp sensor electrical connector and/or the unload sensor connector.

z. Remove the glove box.

aa. At the passenger's air bag module, remove the screws, disconnect the electrical connector and remove the air bag module.

Place the air bag module in a safe place with the front facing upward.

a. Remove the right side assist handle screw covers, the screws and the handle.

b. At both doors, pull back the weather-strip seals and remove the windshield garnish moldings.

c. Remove the instrument panel reinforcement bolt below the left side corner of the glove box.

d. Through the air bag module opening, remove the instrument panel bolts.

e. Remove the upper instrument panel cowl covers and bolts.

f. At the relay bracket, remove the instrument panel bolt.

g. At the lower left side of the cigar lighter, remove the instrument panel bolt.

h. At the both sides, remove the instrument panel-to-cowl side nuts.

i. At the steering column opening, remove the instrument panel bolts.

j. Remove the upper instrument panel floor brace bolt.

k. Using an assistant, remove the instrument panel.

5. If equipped with the 5.4L 4V engine, remove the junction block splash shield.

6. If equipped with the 5.4L 4V engine, remove the bolts and disconnect the cable ends from the starter relay.

7. If equipped with the 5.4L 4V engine, remove the junction block bracket.

8. Compress the holding tabs and disconnect the heater hoses from the heater core.

9. Remove the air conditioning plenum screw and the air conditioning plenum demister adapter.

10. Disconnect the vacuum line.

11. Remove the heater core bracket screws and the bracket.

12. Remove the 13 heater housing plenum camber cover screws and the heater housing plenum chamber cover.

13. Remove the blend door assembly from the heater housing.

14. Remove the heater core.

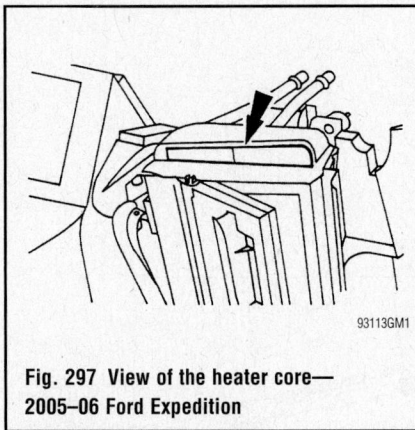

93113GM1

Fig. 297 View of the heater core—2005–06 Ford Expedition

To install:

15. Install the heater core.

16. Install the blend door assembly to the heater housing.

17. Install the 13 heater housing plenum camber cover and the heater housing plenum chamber cover screws.

18. Install the heater core bracket and the bracket screws.

19. Connect the vacuum line.

20. Install the air conditioning plenum demister adapter and the air conditioning plenum screw.

21. Connect the heater hoses to the heater core.

22. Install the instrument panel by performing the following procedure:

   a. Using an assistant, install the instrument panel.

   b. Install the upper instrument panel floor brace bolt.

   c. At the steering column opening, install the instrument panel bolts.

   d. At the both sides, install the instrument panel-to-cowl side nuts.

   e. At the lower left side of the cigar lighter, install the instrument panel bolt.

   f. At the relay bracket, install the instrument panel bolt.

   g. Install the upper instrument panel cowl bolts and covers.

   h. Through the air bag module opening, install the instrument panel bolts.

   i. Install the instrument panel reinforcement bolt below the left side corner of the glove box.

   j. At both doors, install the windshield garnish moldings and the weatherstrip seals.

   k. Install the right side assist handle, the screws and the handle screw covers.

   l. At the passenger's air bag module, install the air bag module, connect the electrical connector and install the air bag module screws.

   m. Install the glove box.

   n. Connect the auto lamp sensor electrical connector and/or the sunload sensor connector; then, install the instrument panel relay cover.

   o. Connect the antenna cable to the antenna base.

   p. Install the right side front fender splash shield and screws.

   q. Install the steering column and the steering column-to-instrument panel nuts.

   r. If equipped with a transmission range indicator, connect the cable and install the bolt.

   s. At the steering column, connect the remaining electrical connectors.

   t. At the base of the steering column, connect the air bag sliding contact and the anti-theft sensor electrical connectors.

   u. Install the steering column opening cover reinforcement and the cover reinforcement nuts.

   v. Connect the climate control head vacuum harness connector.

   w. Connect the electronic blend door actuator electrical connector.

   x. Connect the right side instrument panel wiring harness connectors.

   y. Install the right side ground bolts.

   z. Connect the inertia fuel shutoff switch electrical connector.

   aa. Connect the air bag diagnostic monitor electrical connector.

   bb. In the driver's compartment, install the bulkhead electrical connector to the instrument panel.

   cc. In the engine compartment, connect the bulkhead wiring harness connectors and the install wiring connector bolts.

   dd. Connect the left side instrument panel main wiring harness connector.

   ee. Install the radio ground and the GEM/CTM ground bolts.

   ff. Connect the electrical connector to the Brake Pedal Position (BPP) switch.

   gg. Install both side cowl trim panels.

   hh. Install both front door scuff plates.

   ii. Install the lower steering column cover and the cover bolts.

   jj. If equipped, install the floor console assembly.

23. Refill the cooling system.

24. Connect the negative battery cable.

25. Run the engine to normal operating temperatures; then, check the climate control operation and check for leaks.

2007 Models

See Figures 298 and 299.

1. Before servicing the vehicle, refer to the precautions in the beginning of this section.

2. Depower the supplemental restraint system (SRS).

3. Disconnect the negative battery cable.

4. Recover the refrigerant.

5. Drain the engine coolant.

6. If equipped with adjustable pedals, move the pedals to the full forward position.

7. Place the gear shift lever in NEUTRAL and apply the parking brake.

8. Position the front seat forward.

9. Remove the 2 front floor console rear bolts.

10. Position the front seats rearward.

11. Remove the 2 front floor console front bolts.

12. Remove the 2 bolt covers.

13. Remove the shifter trim ring.

14. Position the gear shift lever indicator bezel aside.

15. Release the 4 retainers and position aside.

16. Remove the front floor console tray mat.

17. Remove the front floor console screw.

18. Disconnect the shifter cable.

19. Remove the floor console front screws.

20. Loosen the bulkhead electrical connector bolt.

21. Disconnect the bulkhead electrical connector.

22. Disconnect the electrical connector.

23. Remove the front floor console.

24. Remove the instrument panel steering column cover.

25. Remove the screws.

26. Release the cover from the instrument panel.

27. Remove the hood release handle bolt and position aside.

28. Remove the instrument panel lower cover.

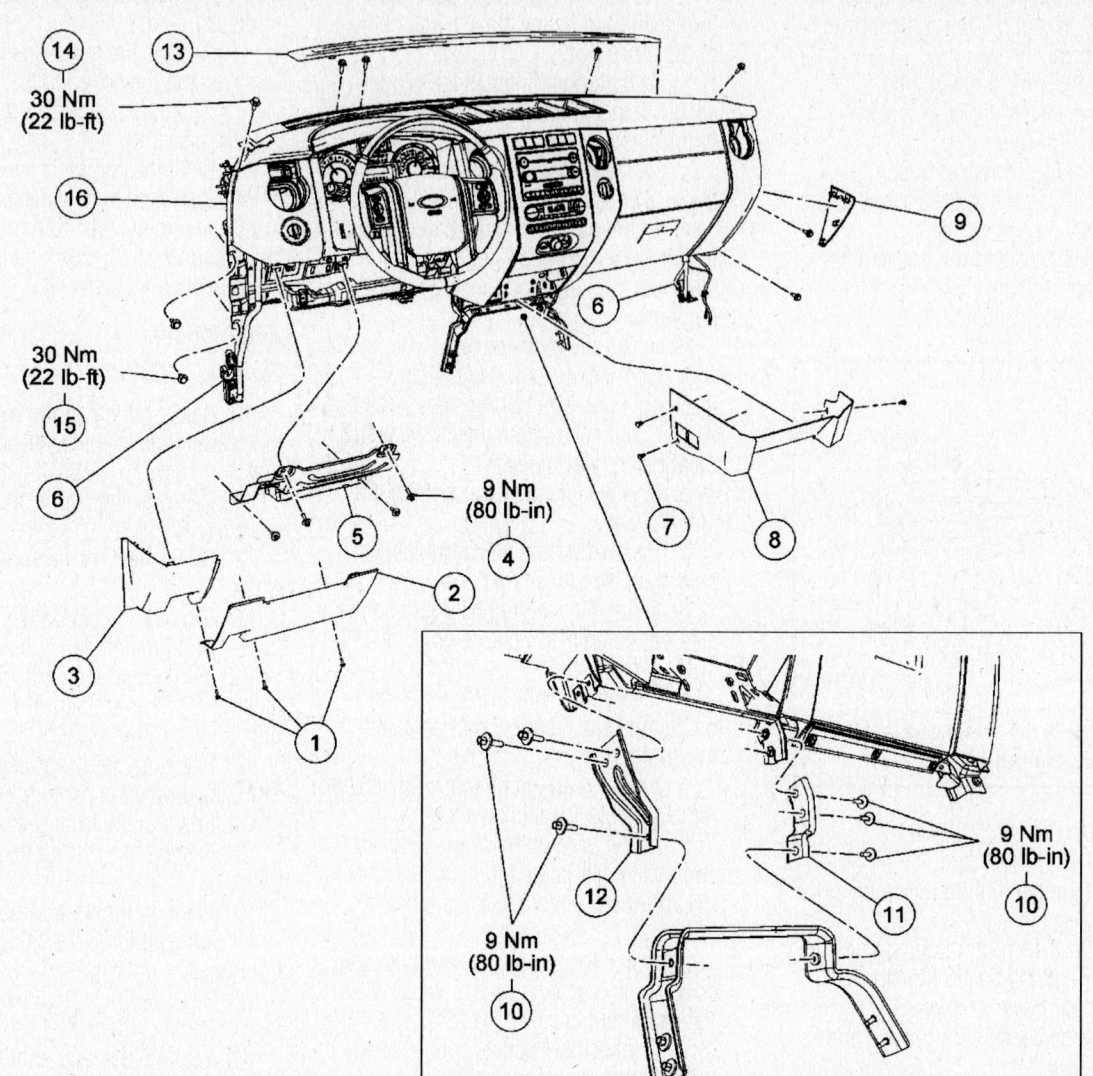

1. Instrument panel steering
   column cover screws (3 required)
2. Instrument panel steering column cover
3. Instrument panel lower cover
4. Steering column reinforcement
   panel bolt (4 required)
5. Steering column reinforcement panel
6. Instrument panel electrical
   wiring harness connectors
7. Pin-type retainer (3 required)
8. Valance panel
9. Instrument panel side finish panel
10. Instrument panel floor brace bolts (6 required)
11. Instrument panel floor brace RH
12. Instrument panel floor brace LH
13. Instrument panel defroster grille
14. Instrument panel cowl bolt (5 required)
15. Instrument panel bolt (4 required)
16. Instrument panel

22086_EXPD_G0124

Fig. 298 Expedition Instrument panel Exploded view

29. Remove the bolt from the parking brake handle and position aside.

30. Remove the bolts and the steering column reinforcement panel.

31. Loosen the bolt and disconnect the LH instrument panel bulkhead connector.

32. Disconnect the LH electrical connectors.

33. Disconnect the park brake indicator connector.

34. Disconnect the cruise control deactivator and the brake on/off switch electrical connector.

35. Disconnect the electrical connector located above the data link.

36. Disconnect the steering wheel position sensor electrical connector.

37. Disconnect the steering column shift cable from the shift lever.

38. Remove the steering column shift cable and position aside.

39. Remove the shift cable from the bracket.

40. Remove the shift cable and retainer from the steering column.

Secure the steering wheel to prevent any rotation or damage to the clockspring.

41. Remove the pinch bolt and separate the intermediate shaft from the steering column.

42. If equipped, remove the 3 pin-type retainers and the valance panel.

43. If equipped, disconnect the electronic automatic temperature control (EATC) hose from the evaporator case.

44. Disconnect the stability control sensor cluster electrical connector.

45. Disconnect the wiring harness from the console bracket.

46. Remove the satellite radio antenna from the wiring harness, if equipped.

47. Remove the RH instrument panel side finish panel.

48. Disconnect the RH instrument panel electrical connectors.

49. Remove the RH ground bolt.

50. Disconnect the in-line antenna connector.

51. Lower the glove compartment.

52. Disconnect the electrical connectors.

➡**There are 6 electrical connectors.**

53. Position the carpet aside, remove the bolts and the instrument panel floor brace.

54. Remove the instrument panel defroster grille.

55. Remove the instrument panel cowl bolts.

56. Remove the LH instrument panel bolts.

57. Remove the RH instrument panel bolts.

➡**This step requires an assistant.**

58. Remove the instrument panel.

➡**Two bullet connectors align the instrument panel to the bulkhead.**

59. Disconnect the 2 heater hose quick disconnect fittings at the heater core.

60. Remove the auxiliary evaporator outlet and inlet line fitting nuts and disconnect the fittings.

61. Disconnect the evaporator outlet and inlet fittings.

62. Detach the thermostatic expansion valve (TXV) manifold and tube assembly from the line 2 brackets.

63. Detach the TXV manifold and tube assembly bracket from the heater core and evaporator core housing stud at the dash panel.

64. Remove the 3 heater core and evaporator core housing nuts.

65. Detach the 4 satellite radio antenna cable pin-type retainers from the heater core and evaporator core housing (if equipped).

66. Detach the 3 body harness electrical connectors from the bracket below the air inlet duct.

67. Remove the air inlet duct bracket nut.

68. Remove the 4 tunnel instrument panel bracket bolts and the tunnel instrument panel bracket.

69. Detach the rear foot well duct from the heater core and evaporator core housing.

70. Remove the plenum chamber nut.

71. Remove the heater core and evaporator core housing.

72. Remove the 8 plenum chamber screws.

73. Release the plenum chamber clip and position the plenum chamber aside.

74. Remove 2 heater core fitting clips and the dash panel seal.

75. Remove the heater core tube bracket screw and the heater core tube bracket.

76. Remove the heater core bracket screw and the heater core bracket.

77. Remove the heater core.

To install:

78. Install the heater core.

79. Install the heater core bracket screws and bracket.

80. Install the heater core tube bracket and screws.

81. Install the heater core fitting clips and dash panel seal.

82. Install the plenum chamber clip and reposition the plenum chamber.

83. Install the plenum chamber screws.

84. Install the heater core and evaporator core housing.

85. Install the plenum chamber nut.

86. Install the rear foot well duct from the heater core and evaporator core housing.

87. Install the four tunnel instrument panel bracket bolts and the tunnel instrument panel bracket.

88. Install the air inlet duct bracket nut.

89. Reattach the three body harness electrical connectors to the bracket below the air inlet duct.

90. Install the four satellite radio antenna cable pin-type retainers to the

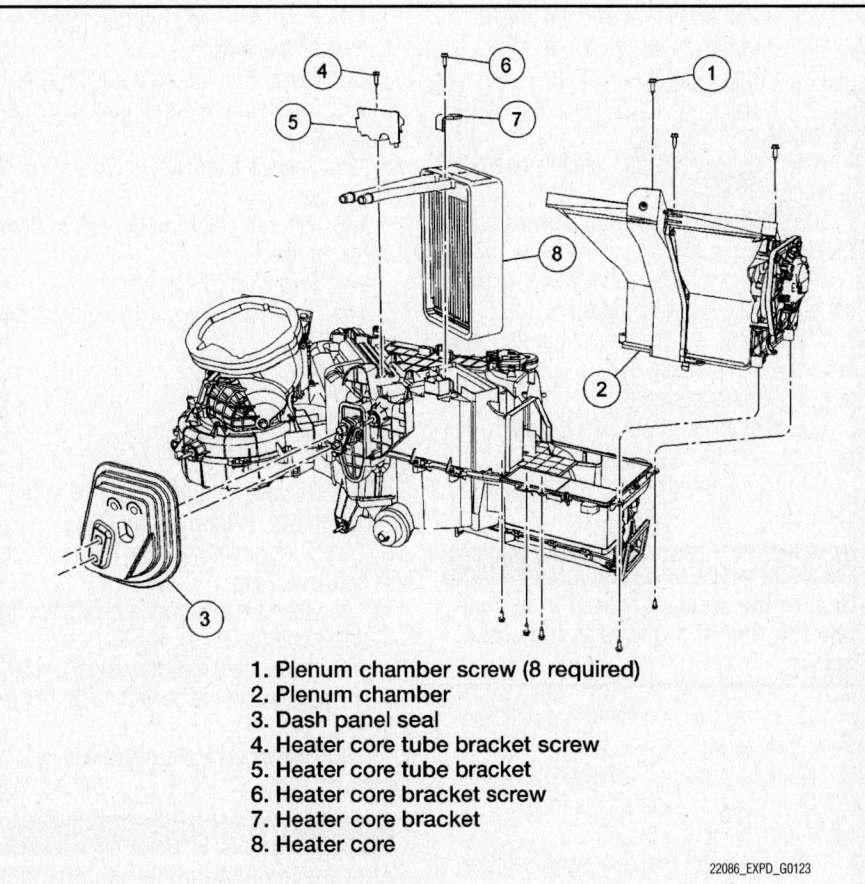

1. Plenum chamber screw (8 required)
2. Plenum chamber
3. Dash panel seal
4. Heater core tube bracket screw
5. Heater core tube bracket
6. Heater core bracket screw
7. Heater core bracket
8. Heater core

22086_EXPD_G0123

Fig. 299 Heater core and Evaporator core housing heater core removal shown

heater core and evaporator core housing (if equipped).

91. Install the three heater core and evaporator core housing nuts.

92. Install the TXV manifold and tube assembly bracket to the heater core and evaporator core housing stud at the dash panel.

93. Install the thermostatic expansion valve (TXV) manifold and tube assembly to the line brackets.

94. Reconnect the evaporator outlet and inlet fittings.

95. Install the auxiliary evaporator outlet and inlet line fitting nuts and connect the fittings.

96. Reconnect the two heater hose quick disconnect fittings at the heater core.

➡**Two bullet connectors align the instrument panel to the bulkhead.**

97. With the help of an assistant install the instrument panel.

98. Install the right and left panel bolts.

99. Install cowl bolts.

100. Install instrument panel defroster grill.

101. Reposition carpet install floor brace and bolts.

102. Reconnect the six electrical connectors.

103. Install lower glove compartment.

104. Reconnect antenna connector.

105. Install right ground bolt.

106. Install right finish panel and electrical connector.

107. If removed. Install satellite radio antenna.

108. Reconnect the wiring harness from the console bracket.

109. Reconnect the stability control sensor cluster electrical connector.

110. If removed, Reconnect the electronic automatic temperature control (EATC) hose from the evaporator case.

111. If removed, install the three pin-type retainers and the valance panel.

112. Install the steering intermediate shaft pinch bolt.

✳✳ WARNING

Secure the steering wheel to prevent any rotation or damage to the clockspring.

113. Install the shift cable and retainer from the steering column.

114. Install the shift cable in the bracket.

115. Install the steering column shift cable into the shift lever.

116. Reconnect the steering wheel position sensor electrical connector.

117. Reconnect the electrical connector located above the data link.

118. Reconnect the cruise control deactivator and the brake on/off switch electrical connector.

119. Reconnect the park brake indicator connector.

120. Reconnect the left side electrical connectors.

121. Reconnect the left side instrument panel bulkhead connector and tighten bolt.

122. Install the bolts and the steering column reinforcement panel.

123. Install hood release and parking brake handles. Tighten mounting screws, if equipped install electrical connector.

124. Install the instrument panel lower cover.

125. Install the instrument panel steering column cover.

126. Install the front floor console.

127. Reconnect the bulk head electrical connector and bolt.

128. Tighten the floor console front screws.

129. Reconnect the shifter cable.

130. Install the front floor console screw.

131. Install the front floor console tray mat.

132. Reconnect the four retainers.

133. Install the shifter trim ring.

134. Install the two front floor console front bolts and covers.

135. Reposition the front seats forward.

136. Install the two front floor console rear bolts.

137. Replace antifreeze and bleed cooling system.

138. Vacuum and recharge A/C system, check for leaks.

139. Power up (SRS) System.

140. Connect the negative battery cable.

Navigator

2005–06 Models

See Figures 300 through 315.

1. Remove the instrument panel by performing the following procedure:

   a. If equipped, remove the floor console assembly.

   b. Remove the lower steering column cover bolts and the cover.

2. Before servicing the vehicle, refer to the precautions in the beginning of this section.

3. Disconnect the negative battery cable.

✳✳ CAUTION

After disconnecting the negative battery cable, wait 1 minute for the SRS module to deplete its energy.

4. Drain the cooling system into a clean container for reuse.

5. Remove the instrument panel by performing the following procedure:

   a. If equipped, remove the floor console assembly.

   b. Remove the lower steering column cover bolts and the cover.

   c. Remove both front door scuff plates.

   d. Remove both side cowl trim panels.

   e. Disconnect the electrical connector from the Brake Pedal Position (BPP) switch.

   f. Remove the radio ground and the GEM/CTM ground bolts.

   g. Disconnect the left side instrument panel main wiring harness connector.

   h. In the engine compartment, remove the bulkhead wiring harness connector bolts and disconnect the wiring connectors.

   i. In the driver's compartment, release the 6 locking tabs and remove the bulkhead electrical connector from the instrument panel.

   j. Disconnect the air bag diagnostic monitor electrical connector.

   k. Disconnect the inertia fuel shutoff switch electrical connector.

   l. Remove the right side ground bolts.

   m. Disconnect the right side instrument panel wiring harness connectors.

   n. Disconnect the electronic blend door actuator electrical connector.

   o. Disconnect the climate control head vacuum harness connector.

   p. Remove the steering column opening cover reinforcement nuts and the cover reinforcement.

   q. At the base of the steering column, disconnect the air bag sliding contact and the anti-theft sensor electrical connectors.

   r. At the steering column, disconnect the remaining electrical connectors.

   s. If equipped with a transmission range indicator, remove the bolt and disconnect the cable.

   t. Remove the steering column-to-instrument panel nuts and lower the steering column.

   u. Remove the right side front fender splash shield screws and move the shield away from the panel.

   v. Disconnect the antenna cable from the antenna base.

   w. Remove the instrument panel relay cover and disconnect the auto lamp

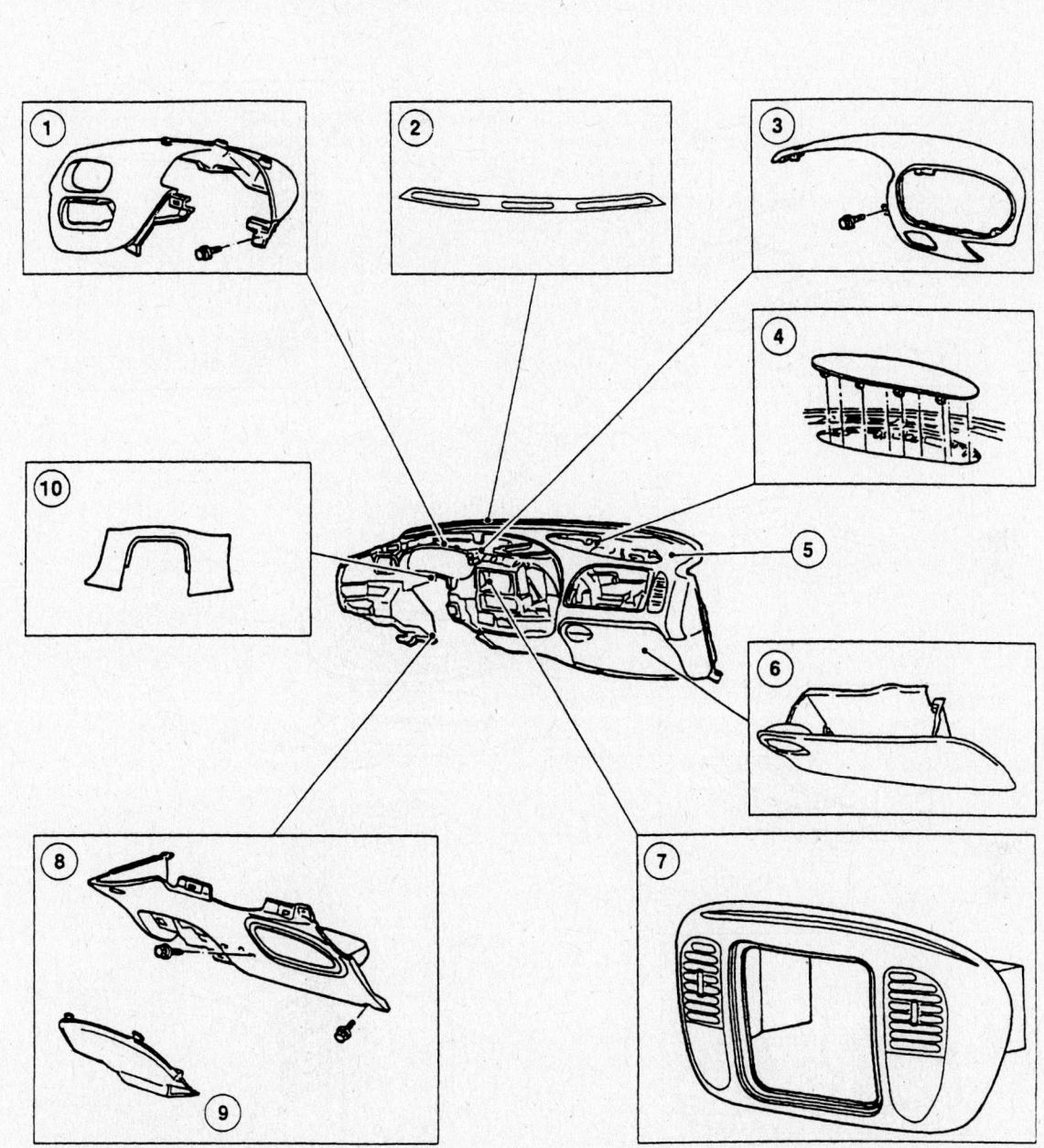

1. Instrument panel finish panel
2. Instrument panel defroster opening grille assembly
3. Instrument cluster panel
4. Instrument panel relay cover
5. Instrument panel
6. Glove compartment
7. Center instrument panel finish panel
8. Instrument panel steering column cover
9. Instrument panel fuse door
10. Steering column opening cover

93113GM2

Fig. 300 Exploded view of the instrument panel components—2005–06 Lincoln Navigator

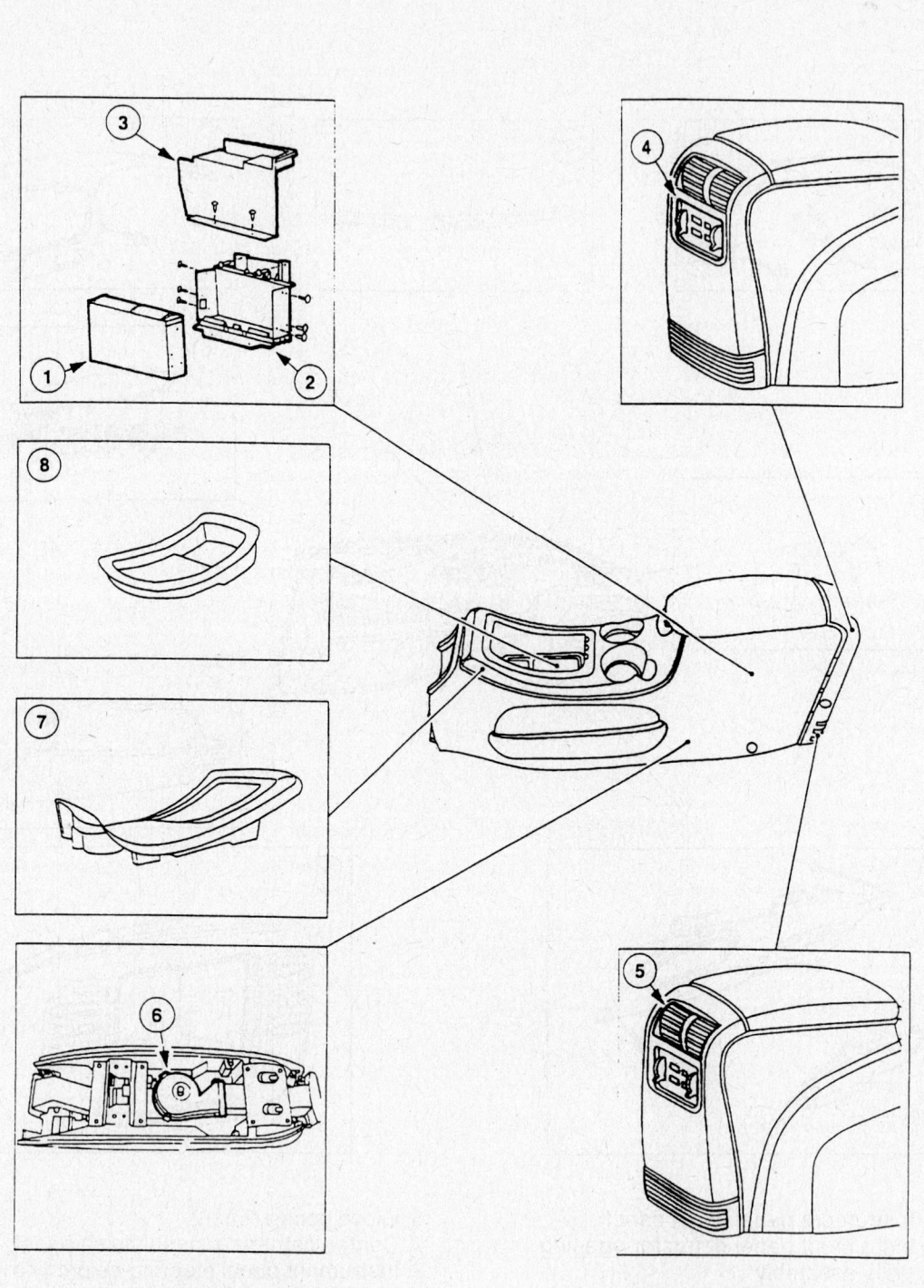

1. Digital audio compact disc player
2. Compact disc player mounting bracket
3. Compact disc player compartment trim panel
4. Radio and A/C integral control assembly
5. A/C register (upper)
6. Blower assembly
7. Center console finish panel
8. Console finish panel mat

93113GM3

Fig. 301 Exploded view of the floor console components—2005–06 Lincoln Navigator

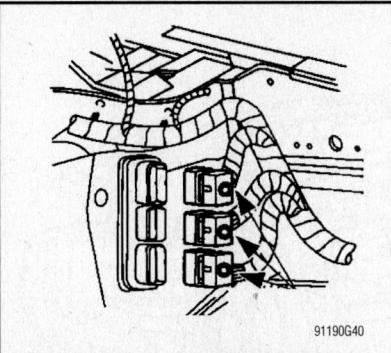

Fig. 302 Remove the bulkhead electrical connectors from inside the engine compartment—2005–06 Lincoln Navigator

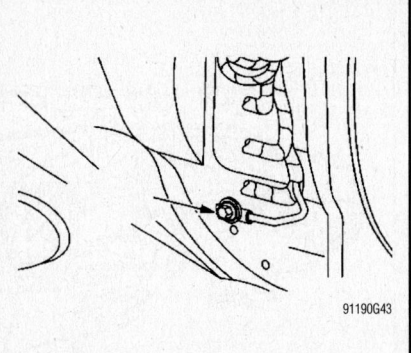

Fig. 305 Remove the passenger side ground bolt—2005–06 Lincoln Navigator

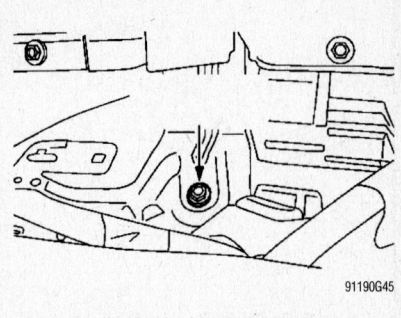

Fig. 307 Remove the instrument panel bolt on the relay bracket—2005–06 Lincoln Navigator

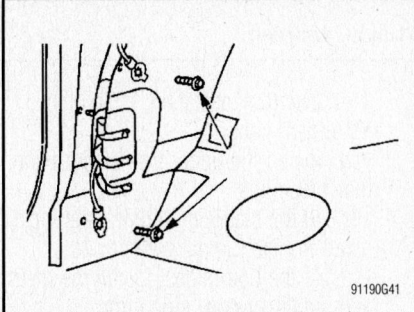

Fig. 303 Remove the audio unit ground and the GEM/CTM ground bolts—2005–06 Lincoln Navigator

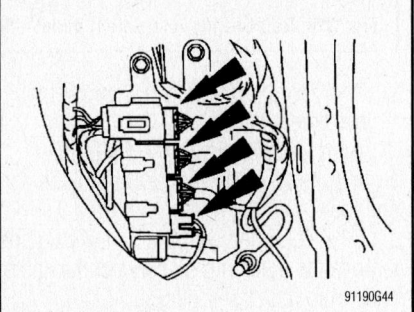

Fig. 306 Detach the passenger side instrument panel main harness connectors—2005–06 Lincoln Navigator

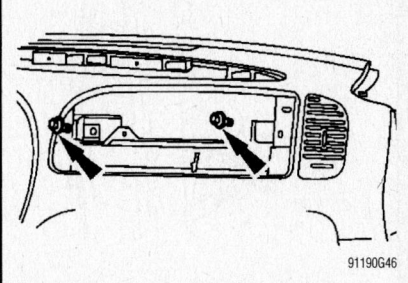

Fig. 308 Remove the instrument panel bolts through the passenger side air bag module opening—2005–06 Lincoln Navigator

sensor electrical connector and/or the sunload sensor connector.

x. Remove the glove box.

y. At the passenger's air bag module, remove the screws, disconnect the electrical connector and remove the air bag module.

Place the air bag module in a safe place with the front facing upward.

a. Remove the right side assist handle screw covers, the screws and the handle.

b. At both doors, pull back the weather-strip seals and remove the windshield garnish moldings.

c. Remove the instrument panel reinforcement bolt below the left side corner of the glove box.

d. Through the air bag module opening, remove the instrument panel bolts.

e. Remove the instrument panel defroster grille assembly and the instrument panel cowl top bolts.

f. At the relay bracket, remove the instrument panel bolt.

g. At the lower left side of the cigar lighter, remove the instrument panel bolt.

h. At the both sides, remove the instrument panel-to-cowl side nuts.

i. At the steering column opening, remove the instrument panel bolts.

j. Remove the upper instrument panel floor brace bolt.

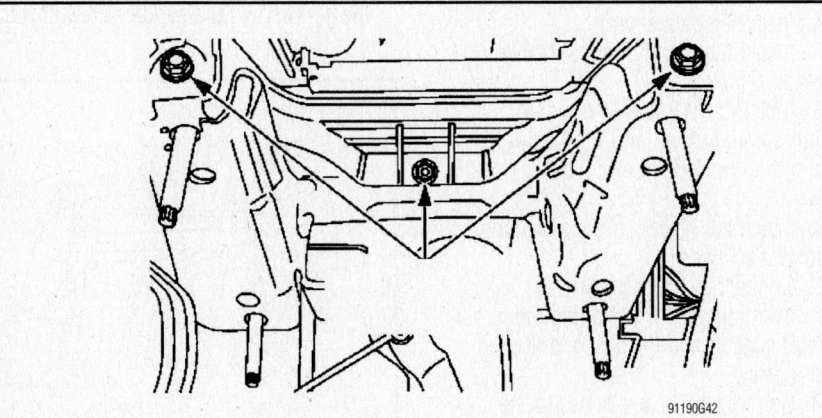

Fig. 304 Remove the instrument panel bolts through the steering column opening—2005–06 Lincoln Navigator

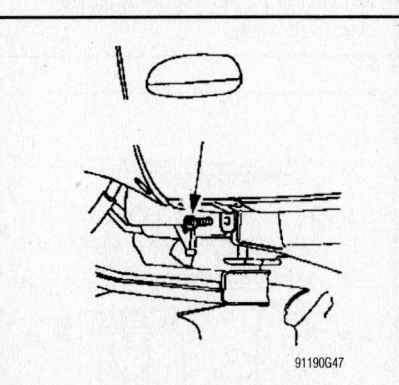

Fig. 309 Remove the instrument panel reinforcement bolt below the driver's side corner of the glove compartment—2005–06 Lincoln Navigator

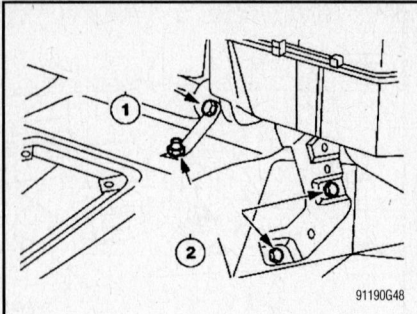

Fig. 310 Position the carpet aside and loosen the instrument panel floor brace—2005–06 Lincoln Navigator

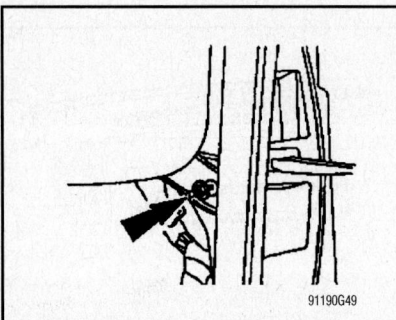

Fig. 311 Remove the passenger side instrument panel cowl side nut—2005–06 Lincoln Navigator

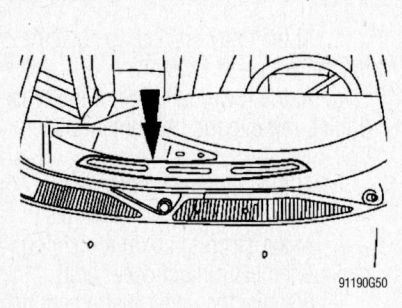

Fig. 312 On Navigator, remove the defroster grille assembly—2005–06 Lincoln Navigator

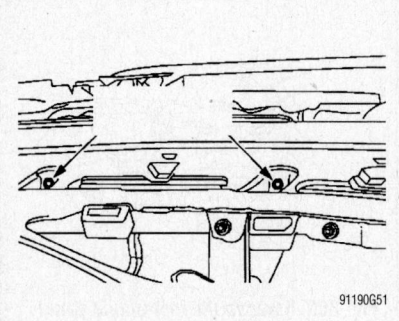

Fig. 313 Remove the cowl panel mounting bolts—2005–06 Lincoln Navigator

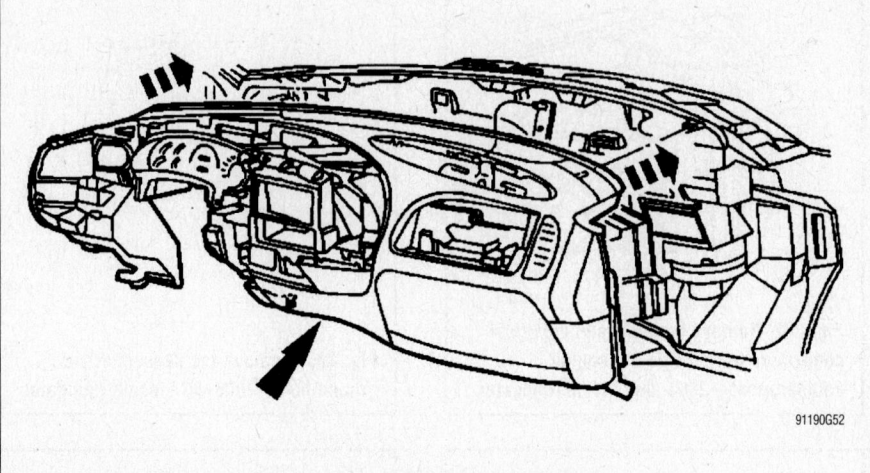

Fig. 314 Remove the instrument panel—2005–06 Lincoln Navigator

  k. Using an assistant, remove the instrument panel.

6. If equipped with the 5.4L 4V engine, remove the junction block splash shield.

7. If equipped with the 5.4L 4V engine, remove the bolts and disconnect the cable ends from the starter relay.

8. If equipped with the 5.4L 4V engine, remove the junction block bracket.

9. Compress the holding tabs and disconnect the heater hoses from the heater core.

10. Remove the air conditioning plenum screw and the air conditioning plenum demister adapter.

11. Disconnect the vacuum line.

12. Remove the heater core bracket screws and the bracket.

13. Remove the 13 heater housing plenum camber cover screws and the heater housing plenum chamber cover.

14. Remove the blend door assembly from the heater housing.

15. Remove the heater core.

To install:

16. Install the heater core.

17. Install the blend door assembly to the heater housing.

18. Install the 13 heater housing plenum camber cover and the heater housing plenum chamber cover screws.

19. Install the heater core bracket and the bracket screws.

20. Connect the vacuum line.

21. Install the air conditioning plenum demister adapter and the air conditioning plenum screw.

22. Connect the heater hoses to the heater core.

23. Install the instrument panel by performing the following procedure:

  a. Using an assistant, install the instrument panel.

  b. Install the upper instrument panel floor brace bolt.

  c. At the steering column opening, install the instrument panel bolts.

  d. At the both sides, install the instrument panel-to-cowl side nuts.

  e. At the lower left side of the cigar lighter, install the instrument panel bolt.

  f. At the relay bracket, install the instrument panel bolt.

  g. Install the instrument panel cowl top bolts and the instrument panel defroster grille assembly.

  h. Through the air bag module opening, install the instrument panel bolts.

  i. Install the instrument panel reinforcement bolt below the left side corner of the glove box.

  j. At both doors, install the windshield garnish moldings and the weatherstrip seals.

  k. Install the right side assist handle, the screws and the handle screw covers.

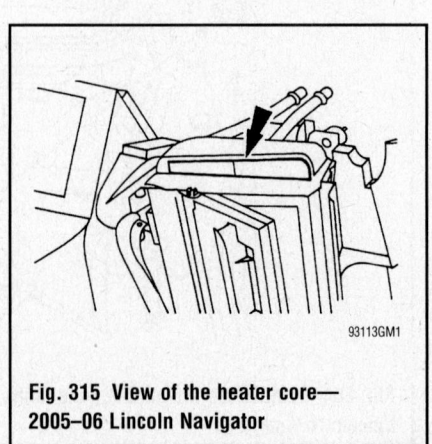

Fig. 315 View of the heater core—2005–06 Lincoln Navigator

l.   At the passenger's air bag module, install the air bag module, connect the electrical connector and install the air bag module screws.

m. Install the glove box.

n. Connect the auto lamp sensor electrical connector and/or the sunload sensor connector; then, install the instrument panel relay cover.

o. Connect the antenna cable to the antenna base.

p. Install the right side front fender splash shield and screws.

q. Install the steering column and the steering column-to-instrument panel nuts.

r.   If equipped with a transmission range indicator, connect the cable and install the bolt.

s. At the steering column, connect the remaining electrical connectors.

t.   At the base of the steering column, connect the air bag sliding contact and the anti-theft sensor electrical connectors.

u. Install the steering column opening cover reinforcement and the cover reinforcement nuts.

v. Connect the climate control head vacuum harness connector.

w. Connect the electronic blend door actuator electrical connector.

x. Connect the right side instrument panel wiring harness connectors.

y. Install the right side ground bolts.

z. Connect the inertia fuel shutoff switch electrical connector.

aa. Connect the air bag diagnostic monitor electrical connector.

bb. In the driver's compartment, install the bulkhead electrical connector to the instrument panel.

cc. In the engine compartment, connect the bulkhead wiring harness connectors and the install wiring connector bolts.

dd. Connect the left side instrument panel main wiring harness connector.

ee. Install the radio ground and the GEM/CTM ground bolts.

ff. Connect the electrical connector to the Brake Pedal Position (BPP) switch.

gg. Install both side cowl trim panels.

hh. Install both front door scuff plates.

ii. Install the lower steering column cover and the cover bolts.

jj. If equipped, install the floor console assembly.

24. Refill the cooling system.

25. Connect the negative battery cable.

26. Run the engine to normal operating temperatures; then, check the climate control operation and check for leaks.

2007 Models

See Figures 316 and 317.

1. Before servicing the vehicle, refer to the precautions in the beginning of this section.

2. Depower the supplemental restraint system (SRS).

3. Disconnect the negative battery cable.

4. Recover the refrigerant.

5. Drain the engine coolant.

6. If equipped with adjustable pedals, move the pedals to the full forward position.

7. Place the shift lever in NEUTRAL and apply the parking brake.

8. Position the front seat forward.

9. Remove the two front floor console rear bolts.

10. Position the front seats rearward.

11. Remove the shifter trim ring.

12. Remove the front floor console finish panel.

13. Pull upward on the rear of the finish panel to release the retainers.

14. Position the shifter lever indicator bezel aside.

15. Disconnect the shift cable.

16. Remove the front floor console front screws.

17. Loosen the bulkhead electrical connector bolt.

18. Disconnect the bulkhead electrical connector.

19. Disconnect the electrical connector.

20. Remove the left and right front floor console side finish panels.

21. If equipped, disconnect the electrical connector.

22. Remove the left and right front floor console front bolts and the floor console.

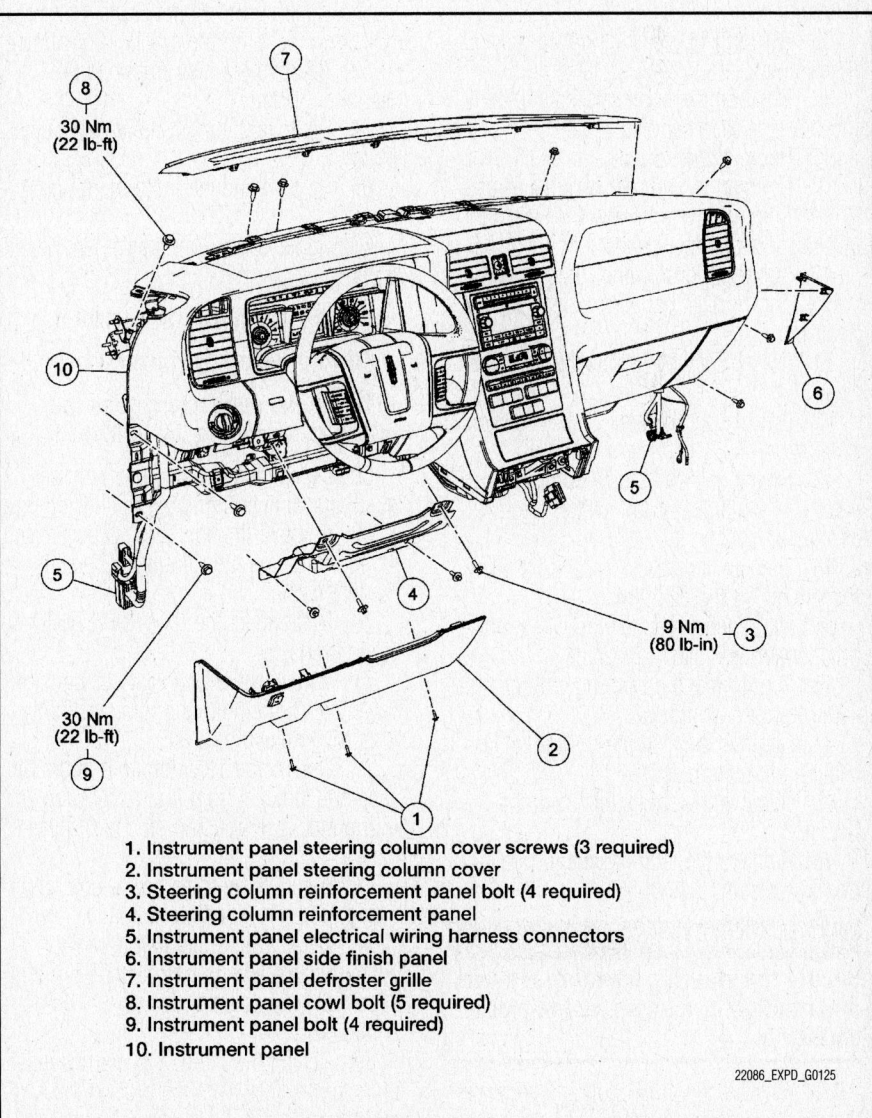

1. Instrument panel steering column cover screws (3 required)
2. Instrument panel steering column cover
3. Steering column reinforcement panel bolt (4 required)
4. Steering column reinforcement panel
5. Instrument panel electrical wiring harness connectors
6. Instrument panel side finish panel
7. Instrument panel defroster grille
8. Instrument panel cowl bolt (5 required)
9. Instrument panel bolt (4 required)
10. Instrument panel

22086_EXPD_G0125

Fig. 316 Navigator Instrument panel Exploded view

23. If equipped, remove the right instrument panel insulator.

24. Disconnect the instrument panel insulator lamp.

25. Remove the left and right cowl trim panels.

26. Remove the scuff plate.

27. Remove the cowl trim panel.

28. Position the left and right door weather-strip seals aside.

29. Remove the left and right assist handles.

30. Remove the covers.

31. Remove the bolts.

➡**Release the top attachments by pulling inboard first and then upward to release the lower hook.**

32. Remove the instrument panel steering column cover.

33. Remove the screws.

34. Release the cover from the instrument panel.

35. Disconnect the electrical connector, if equipped

36. Position the hood release and parking brake release handles aside.

37. Remove the screws.

38. Position the release handles aside.

39. Remove the bolts and the steering column reinforcement panel.

40. Loosen the bolt and disconnect the left instrument panel bulkhead connector.

41. Disconnect the left electrical connectors.

42. Disconnect the park brake indicator connector.

43. Disconnect the cruise control deactivator and the brake on/off switch electrical connector.

44. Disconnect the electrical connector located above the data link.

45. Disconnect the steering wheel position sensor electrical connector.

46. Disconnect the steering column shift cable from the shift lever.

47. Remove the steering column shift cable and position aside.

48. Remove the shift cable from the bracket.

49. Remove the shift cable and retainer from the steering column.

✳✳ WARNING

Secure the steering wheel to prevent any rotation or damage to the clockspring.

50. Remove the pinch bolt and separate the intermediate shaft from the steering column.

51. If equipped, remove the three pin-type retainers and the valance panel.

52. If equipped, disconnect the electronic automatic temperature control (EATC) hose from the evaporator case.

53. Disconnect the stability control sensor cluster electrical connector.

54. Disconnect the wiring harness from the console bracket.

55. Remove the satellite radio antenna from the wiring harness, if equipped.

56. Remove the right instrument panel side finish panel.

57. Disconnect the right instrument panel electrical connectors.

58. Remove the right ground bolt.

59. Disconnect the in-line antenna connector.

60. Lower the glove compartment.

61. Disconnect the electrical connectors.

➡**There are six electrical connectors.**

62. Position the carpet aside, remove the bolts and the instrument panel floor brace.

63. Remove the instrument panel defroster grille.

64. Remove the instrument panel cowl bolts.

65. Remove the left instrument panel bolts.

66. Remove the right instrument panel bolts.

➡**This step requires an assistant.**

67. Remove the instrument panel.

➡**Two bullet connectors align the instrument panel to the bulkhead.**

68. Disconnect the two heater hose quick disconnect fittings at the heater core.

69. Remove the auxiliary evaporator outlet and inlet line fitting nuts and disconnect the fittings.

70. Disconnect the evaporator outlet and inlet fittings.

71. Detach the thermostatic expansion valve (TXV) manifold and tube assembly from the line two brackets.

72. Detach the TXV manifold and tube assembly bracket from the heater core and evaporator core housing stud at the dash panel.

73. Remove the three heater core and evaporator core housing nuts.

74. Detach the four satellite radio antenna cable pin-type retainers from the heater core and evaporator core housing (if equipped).

75. Detach the three body harness electrical connectors from the bracket below the air inlet duct.

76. Remove the air inlet duct bracket nut.

77. Remove the plenum chamber nut.

78. Remove the four tunnel instrument panel bracket bolts and the tunnel instrument panel bracket.

79. Detach the rear foot well duct from the heater core and evaporator core housing.

80. Remove the plenum chamber nut.

81. Remove the heater core and evaporator core housing.

82. Remove the plenum chamber screws.

83. Release the plenum chamber clip and position the plenum chamber aside.

84. Remove the heater core fitting clips and the dash panel seal.

85. Remove the heater core tube bracket screw and the heater core tube bracket.

86. Remove the heater core bracket screw and the heater core bracket.

87. Remove the heater core.

To install:

88. Install the heater core.

89. Install the heater core bracket screws and bracket.

90. Install the heater core tube bracket and screws.

91. Install the heater core fitting clips and dash panel seal.

92. Install the plenum chamber clip and reposition the plenum chamber.

93. Install the plenum chamber screws.

94. Install the heater core and evaporator core housing.

95. Install the plenum chamber nut.

96. Install the rear foot well duct from the heater core and evaporator core housing.

97. Install the four tunnel instrument panel bracket bolts and the tunnel instrument panel bracket.

98. Install the air inlet duct bracket nut.

99. Reattach the three body harness electrical connectors to the bracket below the air inlet duct.

100. Install the four satellite radio antenna cable pin-type retainers to the heater core and evaporator core housing (if equipped).

101. Install the three heater core and evaporator core housing nuts.

102. Install the TXV manifold and tube assembly bracket to the heater core and evaporator core housing stud at the dash panel.

103. Install the thermostatic expansion valve (TXV) manifold and tube assembly to the line brackets.

104. Reconnect the evaporator outlet and inlet fittings.

105. Install the auxiliary evaporator outlet and inlet line fitting nuts and connect the fittings.

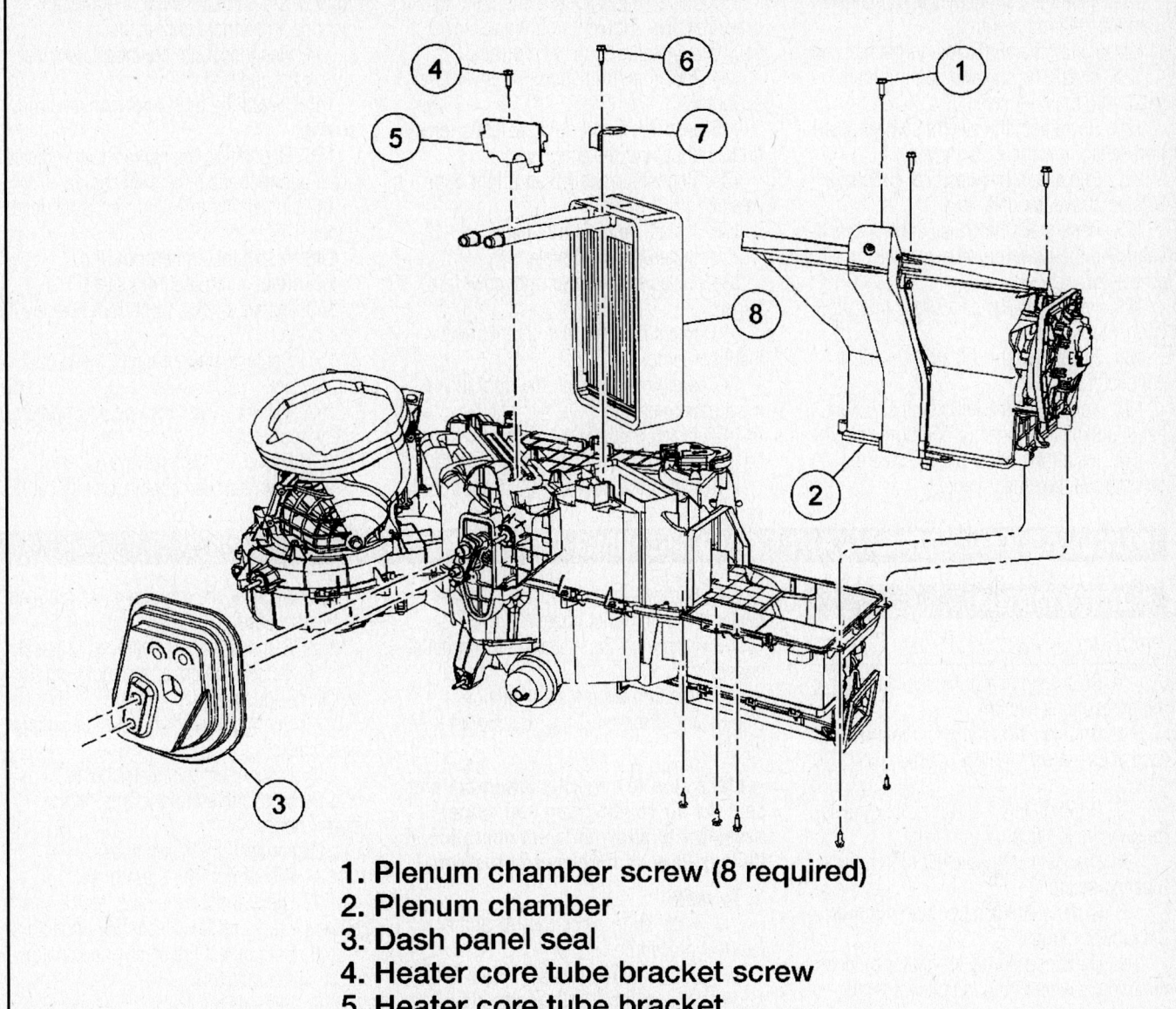

1. Plenum chamber screw (8 required)
2. Plenum chamber
3. Dash panel seal
4. Heater core tube bracket screw
5. Heater core tube bracket
6. Heater core bracket screw
7. Heater core bracket
8. Heater core

22086_EXPD_G0123

Fig. 317 Heater core and Evaporator core housing heater core removal shown

106. Reconnect the two heater hose quick disconnect fittings at the heater core.

➡**Two bullet connectors align the instrument panel to the bulkhead.**

107. With the help of an assistant install the instrument panel.
108. Install the right and left panel bolts.
109. Install cowl bolts.
110. Install instrument panel defroster grill.
111. Reposition carpet install floor brace and bolts.

112. Reconnect the six electrical connectors.
113. Install lower glove compartment.
114. Reconnect antenna connector.
115. Install right ground bolt.
116. Install right finish panel and electrical connector.
117. If removed. Install satellite radio antenna.
118. Reconnect the wiring harness from the console bracket.
119. Reconnect the stability control sensor cluster electrical connector.

120. If removed, Reconnect the electronic automatic temperature control (EATC) hose from the evaporator case.
121. If removed, install the three pin-type retainers and the valance panel.
122. Install the steering intermediate shaft pinch bolt.

❄❄ **WARNING**

Secure the steering wheel to prevent any rotation or damage to the clockspring.

123. Install the shift cable and retainer from the steering column.

124. Install the shift cable in the bracket.

125. Install the steering column shift cable into the shift lever.

126. Reconnect the steering wheel position sensor electrical connector.

127. Reconnect the electrical connector located above the data link.

128. Reconnect the cruise control deactivator and the brake on/off switch electrical connector.

129. Reconnect the park brake indicator connector.

130. Reconnect the left side electrical connectors.

131. Reconnect the left side instrument panel bulkhead connector and tighten bolt.

132. Install the bolts and the steering column reinforcement panel.

133. Install hood release and parking brake handles. Tighten mounting screws, if equipped install electrical connector.

134. Install instrument panel cover and screws.

135. Install left and right assist handles, tighten bolts and replace covers.

136. Reposition the left and right door weather-strip seals.

137. Install the cowl trim panel.

138. Install the scuff plate.

139. Install the left and right cowl trim panels.

140. Reconnect the instrument panel insulator lamp.

141. If removed, install the right instrument panel insulator.

142. Install the left and right front floor console front bolts and the floor console.

143. Install the left and right front floor console side finish panels, if equipped reconnect electrical connector.

144. Reconnect the bulkhead electrical connector and bolt.

145. Install the front floor console front screws.

146. Reposition the shifter lever indicator bezel and reconnect the shift cable.

147. Install the front floor console finish panel.

148. Install the shifter trim ring.

149. Reposition the front seats.

150. Install the two front floor console rear bolts.

151. Replace antifreeze and bleed cooling system.

152. Vacuum and recharge A/C system, check for leaks.

153. Power up (SRS) System.

154. Connect the negative battery cable.

AUXILIARY HEATING & AIR CONDITIONING COMPONENTS

BLOWER MOTOR

REMOVAL & INSTALLATION

1. Before servicing the vehicle, refer to the precautions section.

2. On Excursion models, remove the access panel from the RH quarter trim panel.

3. On Expedition & Navigator models, remove the RH quarter trim panel.

4. Disconnect the blower motor electrical connector.

5. Remove the screws, then remove the blower motor.

6. On Expedition & Navigator models remove the wheel from the blower motor, as follows:

   a. Remove the push clip.

   b. Remove the wheel.

7. Installation is the reverse of the removal procedure. Use a new push clip to install the wheel onto the blower motor.

HEATER CORE

REMOVAL & INSTALLATION

Excursion

1. Before servicing the vehicle, refer to the precautions section.

2. Remove the third row seat.

3. Position aside the RH rear quarter trim panel.

4. Remove the heater core cover:

   a. Remove the 8 screws.

   b. Remove the heater core cover.

5. Remove the heater core from the housing.

6. Remove the heater core from the heater inlet and outlet hoses.

7. Clamp off the heater inlet and outlet hoses.

8. Position the constant tension clamps and disconnect the hoses from the heater core.

➡**Make sure to correctly assemble and seal the air conditioning and heater assembly to allow efficient operation of the auxiliary climate control system.**

To install:

9. Installation is the reverse of the removal procedure.

10. Lubricate the coolant hoses with MERPOL® meeting Ford specification ESE-M99B144-B or plain water only, if needed.

11. Top-off the engine cooling system.

Expedition & Navigator

2005–06 Models

See Figures 318 through 320.

✳✳ WARNING

Before beginning this procedure, please refer to the Precautions at the beginning of this section.

✳✳ CAUTION

Do not open the cooling system while it is hot or while the engine is running. Failure to follow these instructions can result in personal injury.

1. Recover the refrigerant, as outlined in this section.

2. Remove the RH quarter trim panel.

3. Detach the upper air duct from the auxiliary housing.

4. Remove the bolts and the auxiliary line bracket.

5. Disconnect the heater hoses:

   a. Using suitable tools, clamp off heater hoses.

   b. Disconnect the heater hoses.

6. Disconnect the drain hose.

7. Disconnect the blower motor and blower motor resistor electrical connectors.

8. Disconnect the electrical actuator electrical connectors.

9. Remove the bolt.

10. Remove the bolt and the auxiliary climate control housing.

11. Remove the screws and the evaporator/heater core access cover.

12. Remove the heater core.

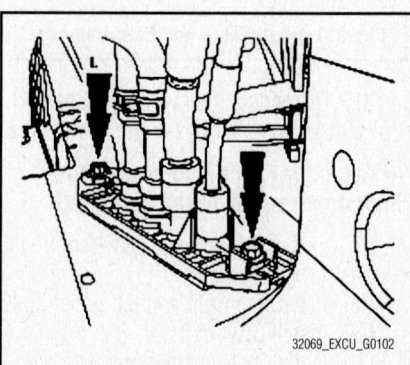

32069_EXCU_G0102

Fig. 318 Remove the bolts and the auxiliary line bracket

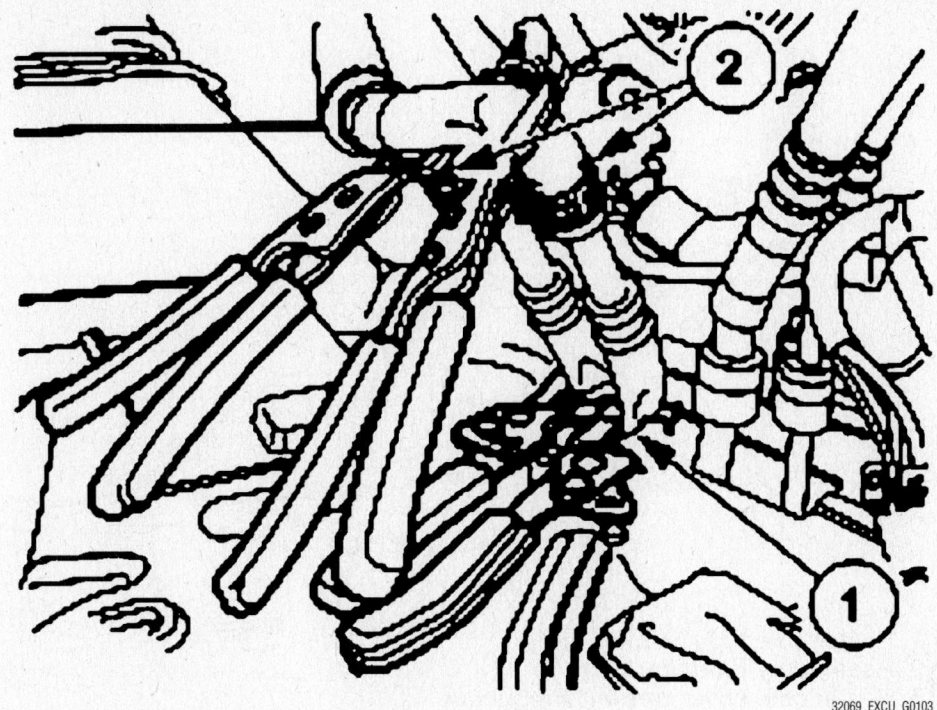

Fig. 319 Using suitable tools, clamp off the heater hoses, then disconnect the heater hoses

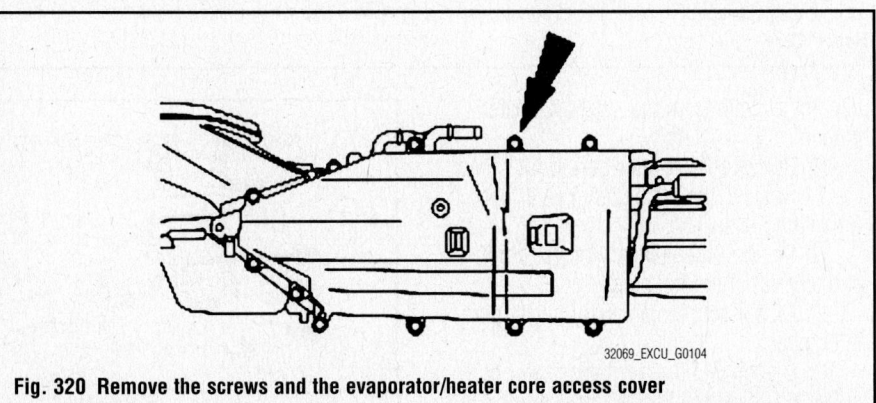

Fig. 320 Remove the screws and the evaporator/heater core access cover

To install:

13. Installation is the reverse of the removal procedure.

14. Install new O-ring seals.

15. Clean and lubricate the coolant hoses with plain water only if needed.

16. Lubricate the refrigerant system with the correct amount of clean PAG oil.

17. Fill the engine coolant level.

18. Evacuate, leak test and charge the refrigerant system, as outlined in this section

2007 Models—Except Expedition EL & Navigator L

See Figure 321.

1. Before servicing the vehicle, refer to the precautions section.

2. With the vehicle in NEUTRAL, position it on a hoist.

3. Recover the refrigerant.

4. Drain the engine coolant.

➡**Allow any residual coolant to drain from the auxiliary heater core after disconnecting the auxiliary heater hose fittings.**

5. Position a suitable drain pan and disconnect the 2 auxiliary heater hose fittings at the floor pan connection.

6. Disconnect the 2 auxiliary evaporator line fittings at the floor pan connection. Discard the O-ring seals.

7. Remove the 2 floor pan bracket bolts.

8. Remove the auxiliary headliner duct pin-type retainer and disconnect the duct.

9. Disconnect the auxiliary mode door actuator electrical connector.

10. Disconnect the auxiliary temperature blend door actuator electrical connector.

11. Disconnect the auxiliary blower motor resistor electrical connector.

12. Disconnect the auxiliary blower motor electrical connector and detach the wire harness from the housing.

13. Remove the 2 auxiliary heater core and evaporator core housing bolts.

14. Remove the auxiliary heater core and evaporator core housing.

15. Release the clip and open the floor pan bracket.

16. Remove the heater core tube bracket screw and the heater core tube bracket.

17. Remove the 12 evaporator/heater core access cover screws.

18. Remove the evaporator/heater core access cover.

19. Remove the heater core.

20. To install, reverse the removal procedure and note the following:

    a. Vacuum and recharge A/C system.

    b. Refill and bleed the cooling system.

    c. Install new O-ring seals.

    d. Lubricate the refrigerant system with the correct amount of clean PAG oil.

    e. Tighten the 2 auxiliary heater core and evaporator core housing bolts to 71 inch. lbs. (8 Nm).

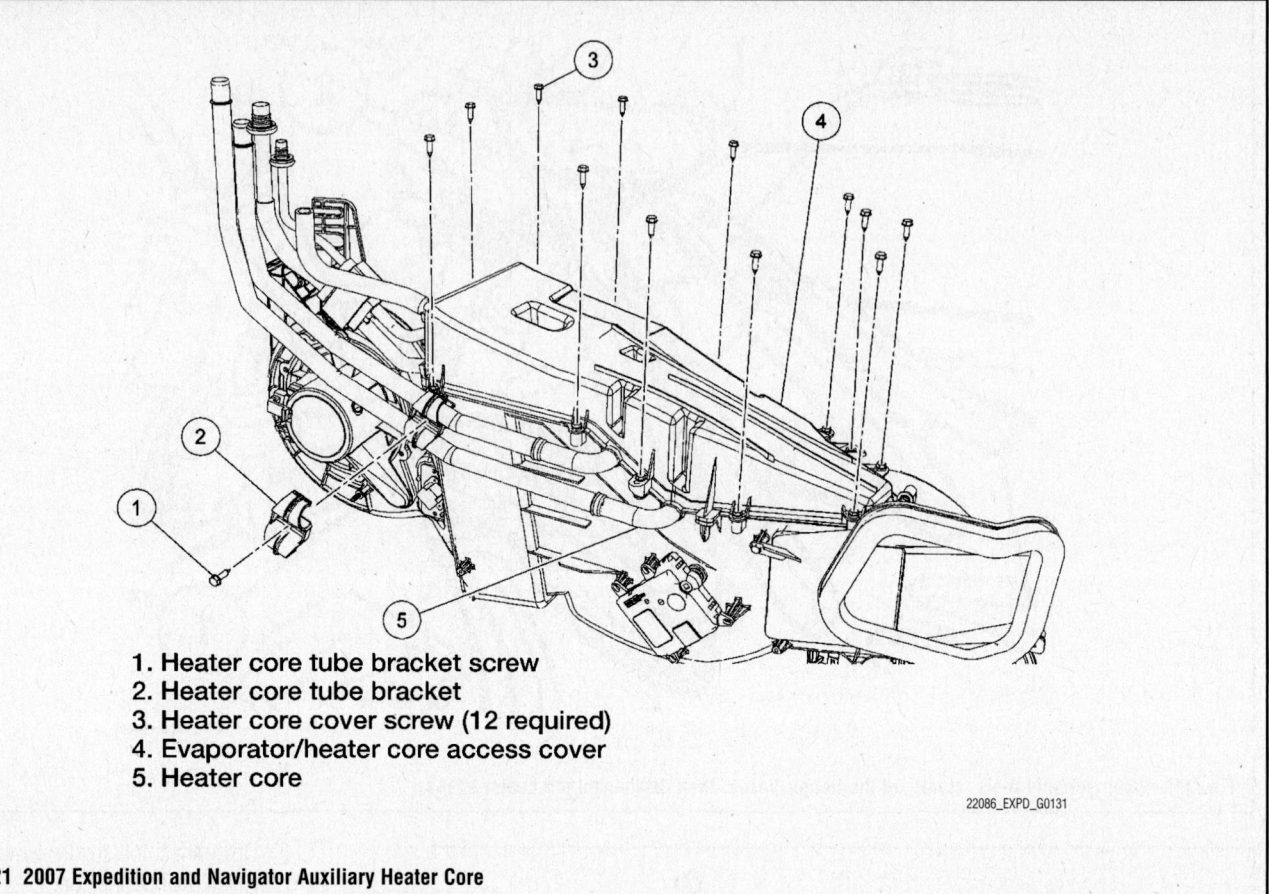

1. Heater core tube bracket screw
2. Heater core tube bracket
3. Heater core cover screw (12 required)
4. Evaporator/heater core access cover
5. Heater core

22086_EXPD_G0131

Fig. 321 2007 Expedition and Navigator Auxiliary Heater Core

2007 Expedition EL & Navigator L

See Figure 322.

1. Before servicing the vehicle, refer to the precautions section.

➡It is not necessary to install the new heater core tubes contained in the heater core service kit unless there is evidence of damage to the heater core tubes. New O-ring seals must be installed any time the heater core tubes are detached from the heater core.

2. With the vehicle in NEUTRAL, position it on a hoist.

3. Drain the engine coolant.

4. Remove the RH quarter trim panel.

5. Position a suitable drain pan and disconnect the 2 auxiliary heater outlet and inlet line quick disconnect fittings at the floor pan connections to allow any residual coolant to drain from the auxiliary heater core.

6. Remove the heater core door screw.

7. Remove the 2 auxiliary heater core tube fitting clips.

8. Position the auxiliary heater core partially out of the housing.

9. Disconnect the auxiliary heater core inlet tube.

10. Disconnect the auxiliary heater core outlet tube. Discard the O-ring seals.

11. Remove the auxiliary heater core.

➡Use only the O-ring seals contained in the auxiliary heater core service kit.

12. Verify that the heater core tube fittings are completely seated in the heater core before installing the heater core tube fitting clips.

13. To install, reverse the removal procedure and note the following:

   a. Refill and bleed the cooling system.

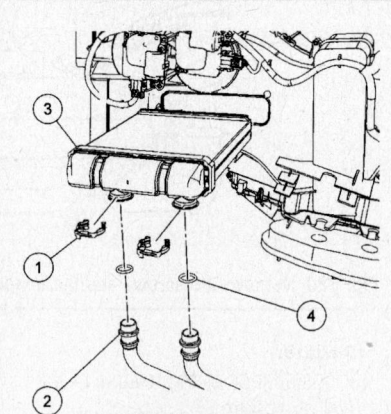

1 Auxiliary heater core tube fitting clip (2 required)
2 Auxiliary heater core tube (2 required)
3 Auxiliary heater core
4 O-ring seal (2 required)

22086_EXPD_G0132

Fig. 322 2007 Expedition EL & Navigator L Auxiliary Heater Core.

STEERING

POWER STEERING GEAR

REMOVAL & INSTALLATION

Excursion

1. Before servicing the vehicle, refer to the precautions in the beginning of this section.

➡**New O-ring seals must be installed any time the lines are disconnected from the steering gear.**

2. Remove the air cleaner assembly.
3. Disengage the steering coupling shield from the line fitting and slide upward on the steering shaft.
4. Remove the pinch bolt. Turn the steering wheel as necessary to access the bolt.
5. Make sure the steering column is locked.
6. Disconnect the lines.
7. Discard the O-ring seals.
8. Remove the tie rod cotter pin and nut. Discard the cotter pin.
9. Using tool 211-003, disconnect the drag link.
10. Remove the bolts, washers and the steering gear.
11. Remove the pitman arm nut.
12. Using tool 211-003, remove the steering gear sector shaft arm.

To install:
13. Install the steering gear sector shaft arm.
14. Install the pitman arm nut. Tighten the nut to 199 ft. lbs. (270 Nm).
15. Install steering gear, bolts and washers. Tighten to 59 ft. lbs. (80 Nm).
16. Connect the drag link.
17. Install the tie rod nut and new cotter pin. Tighten to 66 ft. lbs. (90 Nm).
18. Install a new high pressure hose O-ring seal and a new return hose O-ring seal.
19. Connect the lines. Tighten to 26 ft. lbs. (35 Nm).
20. Make sure the steering column is locked.
21. Connect the pinch bolt. Tighten to 36 ft. lbs. (48 Nm).
22. Engage the steering coupling shield to the line fitting.
23. Install the air cleaner assembly.
24. Fill and leak check the system.

2005–06 Expedition & Navigator

2WD Models

1. Before servicing the vehicle, refer to the precautions in the beginning of this section.

❊❊ **CAUTION**

While repairing the power steering system, care should be taken to prevent the entry of contaminants or premature failure of the power steering components can result.

➡**New O-ring seals must be installed any time the lines are disconnected from the steering gear.**

2. Place the front wheels in the straight-ahead position and the ignition switch in the OFF position.

❊❊ **WARNING**

The electrical power to the air suspension system must be shut off prior to hoisting, jacking or towing an air suspension vehicle. This can be accomplished by turning off the air suspension switch located near the jack storage area in the rear of the passenger compartment. Failure to do so can result in unexpected inflation or deflation of the air springs, which can result in shifting of the vehicle during these operations. Failure to follow these instructions may result in personal injury.

3. Turn the air suspension switch to the OFF position, if equipped.
4. With the vehicle in NEUTRAL, position the vehicle on a hoist.

➡**The hex holding feature can be used to prevent turning of the stud while removing the nut.**

5. Remove the 2 nuts and disconnect the tie-rod ends from the wheel knuckles.
6. Remove the 2 bolts and the oil drip shield.
7. Disconnect the lines from the frame rail retainers.

❊❊ **CAUTION**

Do not allow the intermediate shaft to rotate while it is disconnected from the gear or damage to the clockspring can occur.

8. Remove the intermediate shaft-to-gear pinch bolt and disconnect the intermediate shaft from the steering gear.

9. Remove the steering line clamp plate bolt and disconnect the power steering lines. Discard the O-ring seals.
10. On Navigator models, disconnect the electrical connector by rotating the actuator until the connector housing is facing the steering gear input shaft.
11. Remove the 2 steering gear bracket-to-crossmember nuts and bolts and discard the nuts.

❊❊ **CAUTION**

Make sure the steering lines are clear from the removal path of the gear or damage to the lines can result.

12. Remove the 2 steering gear bracket-to-gear nuts, bolts, and brackets and discard the nuts.
13. Remove the steering gear.

To install:
14. Installation is the reverse of removal, please note the following points and torque specifications:

❊❊ **CAUTION**

Make sure to tighten the bracket-to-steering gear bolts (M14) before tightening the bracket-to-crossmember bolts (M12) or damage to the steering gear can result.

  b. Install a new high pressure line O-ring seal and a new return line O-ring seal.
  c. Tighten the 2 new steering gear bracket-to-gear nuts and bolts to 111 ft. lbs. (150 Nm).
  d. Tighten the 2 new steering gear bracket-to-crossmember nuts and bolts to 76 ft. lbs. (103 Nm).
  e. Tighten the steering line clamp bolt to 17 ft. lbs. (23 Nm).
  f. Tighten the intermediate shat-to-gear pinch bolt to 22 ft. lbs. (30 Nm).
  g. Tighten the new tie rod nuts to 111 ft. lbs. (150 Nm).
  h. Fill the power steering system.

4WD Models

1. Before servicing the vehicle, refer to the precautions in the beginning of this section.

❊❊ **CAUTION**

While repairing the power steering system, care should be taken to prevent the entry of contaminants or premature failure of the power steering components can result.

➡New O-ring seals must be installed any time the lines are disconnected from the steering gear.

2. Place the front wheels in the straight-ahead position and the ignition switch in the OFF position.

❋❋ WARNING

The electrical power to the air suspension system must be shut off prior to hoisting, jacking or towing an air suspension vehicle. This can be accomplished by turning off the air suspension switch located near the jack storage area in the rear of the passenger compartment. Failure to do so can result in unexpected inflation or deflation of the air springs, which can result in shifting of the vehicle during these operations. Failure to follow these instructions may result in personal injury.

3. Turn the air suspension switch to the OFF position, if equipped.
4. Remove the engine cooling fan.

➡The hex holding feature can be used to prevent turning of the stud while removing the nut.

5. Remove the 2 nuts and disconnect the tie-rod ends from the wheel knuckles.
6. Remove the 2 bolts and the oil drip shield.
7. Disconnect the lines from the frame rail retainers.

❋❋ CAUTION

Do not allow the intermediate shaft to rotate while it is disconnected from the gear or damage to the clockspring can occur. If there is evidence that the intermediate shaft has rotated, the clockspring must be removed and recentered.

8. Remove the intermediate shaft-to-gear pinch bolt and disconnect the intermediate shaft from the gear.
9. Remove the steering line clamp plate bolt and disconnect the power steering lines. Position the lines aside and discard the O-ring seals.
10. On Navigator models:
    a. Disconnect the electrical connector. Rotate the actuator until the connector housing is facing the steering gear input shaft.
    b. Remove the left hand lower arm-to-frame nut and bolt. Discard the nut.
    c. Insert a block of wood between the left hand lower arm and the frame.

11. Remove the 2 steering gear bracket-to-crossmember nuts and bolts. Discard the nuts.

❋❋ CAUTION

Make sure the steering lines are clear from the removal path of the gear or damage to the lines can result.

12. Remove the 2 steering gear bracket-to-gear nuts, bolts, and brackets. Discard the nuts.
13. Remove the steering gear from the left hand side of the vehicle.

❋❋ CAUTION

Make sure that the wheel end vacuum line is clear of the steering gear mounting fasteners before tightening the bolts or damage to the line can result.

To install:

❋❋ CAUTION

Make sure to tighten the bracket-to-steering gear bolts (M14) before tightening the bracket-to-crossmember bolts (M12) or damage to the steering gear can result.

14. Installation is the reverse of removal, note the following torque specifications:
    a. Tighten the 2 new steering gear bracket-to-gear nuts, bolts to 150 Nm (111 lb-ft).
    b. Tighten the 2 new steering gear bracket-to-crossmember nuts and bolts to 103 Nm (76 lb-ft).
    c. Tighten the new left hand lower arm-to-frame nut and bolt to 200 Nm (148 lb-ft).
    d. Install new O-rings and tighten the steering line clamp plate bolt to 17 ft. lbs. (23 Nm).
    e. Tighten the intermediate shaft-to-gear pinch bolt to 22 ft. lbs. (30 Nm).
    f. Tighten the 2 tie-rod ends to wheel knuckle nuts to 150 Nm (111 lb-ft).
15. Fill and leak check the system.

2007 Expedition & Navigator

1. Before servicing the vehicle, refer to the precautions in the beginning of this section.
2. With the vehicle in NEUTRAL, position it on a hoist.
3. Hold the steering wheel in the straight ahead position using a suitable holding device.

❋❋ WARNING

Do not allow the steering column shaft to rotate while disconnected from the gear or damage to the clockspring can occur. if there is evidence that the steering column shaft has rotated, the clockspring must be recentered.

4. Remove and discard the tie-rod end nuts.
5. Using the special tool 204-592, disconnect the tie-rod ends from the wheel knuckles.
6. Release the lower cooling fan shroud tab and rotate the shroud upward.
7. Remove the 2 bolts and the oil drip shield.
8. Remove the steering column shaft-to-steering gear bolt and disconnect the steering column shaft from the steering gear.
9. Remove the steering line clamp plate bolt, rotate the clamp plate and disconnect the power steering lines.
10. Remove the 2 steering gear bolts and remove the steering gear.

To install:

❋❋ WARNING

New O-ring seals must be installed any time the lines are disconnected from the steering gear.

11. Position the steering gear and install the 2 steering gear bolts. Tighten bolts to 325 ft. lbs. (440 Nm).
12. Connect the steering column shaft and install the bolt.
13. Connect the steering lines, rotate the clamp plate and install the clamp plate bolt. Tighten the bolt to 17 ft. lbs. (23 Nm).
14. Install the oil drip shield and tighten the 2 bolts to 8 ft. lbs. (11 Nm).
15. Release the lower cooling fan shroud tab and rotate the shroud downward.
16. Connect the tie-rod ends to the wheel knuckles, install and tighten the nuts to 85 ft. lbs. (115 Nm).
17. Fill the power steering system.
18. Check and, if necessary, align the front end.

POWER STEERING PUMP

REMOVAL & INSTALLATION

Excursion

See Figure 323.

1. Before servicing the vehicle, refer to the precautions in the beginning of this section.

2. Remove the power steering pump pulley, as follows:

a. If equipped with A/C, rotate the tensioner clockwise and remove the belt from the power steering pump pulley. If not equipped with A/C, rotate the tensioner counterclockwise and remove the belt from the power steering pump pulley.

b. Using Power Steering Pump Pulley Removal tool no. 211-016 (T69L-10300-B), or equivalent, remove the power steering pump pulley.

➡**Replacement of the power steering pump pulley is necessary after being removed and installed two times.**

3. Loosen the clamps and remove the air cleaner outlet tube.

4. Remove the inlet air tube:

a. Loosen the clamp.

b. Detach the ducts from the charge air cooler and remove the inlet air tube.

5. Remove the return hose.

6. Place a pan under the power steering pump and drain the pump.

7. Disconnect the power steering high-pressure line.

8. Remove the bolts and detach the pump from the bracket.

9. Disconnect the power steering oil cooler return hose and remove the pump.

To install:

10. To install, reverse the removal procedure.

11. Tighten the power steering pump mounting bolts to 60 ft. lbs. (80 Nm).

a. When connecting a fitting with a Teflon® seal, a new ring must be installed. Using Teflon® Seal Installer Stet 211-D027, or equivalent special tool, install a Teflon® seal over a fitting.

12. Fill and leak check the power steering system.

Expedition & Navigator

2005–06 Models

See Figures 323 through 325.

1. Before servicing the vehicle, refer to the precautions in the beginning of this section.

❄❄ **WARNING**

While repairing the power steering system, care should be taken to prevent the entry of contaminants or premature failure of the power steering components can result.

2. Remove the engine cooling fan, as outlined in the Engine Mechanical Section.

3. Remove the power steering pump pulley, as follows:

a. Rotate the tensioner clockwise and remove the engine accessory drive belt from the power steering pump pulley.

b. Remove the air cleaner intake pipe.

c. Using the special tool, remove the power steering pump pulley.

4. Disconnect the clamp and remove the supply hose. Allow the fluid to drain into a suitable container.

5. Remove the pressure line bracket-to-engine nut.

6. Disconnect the pressure line-to-pump fitting. Discard the Teflon® seal.

7. Remove the 3 pump bolts.

8. Disconnect the harness retainer and remove the power steering pump.

To install:

9. Installation of the power steering pump is the reverse of the removal procedure. Please note the following:

a. Tighten the power steering pump mounting bolts to 18 ft. lbs. (25 Nm).

b. Use Teflon® Seal Installer Set 211-D207 (D90P-3517-A) or equivalent to install a new Teflon® seal on the pressure line-to-pump fitting.

c. Tighten the pressure line-to-pump fitting to 48 ft. lbs. (65 Nm).

d. Tighten the pressure line bracket-to-engine nut to 30 ft. lbs. (40 Nm).

10. Install the power steering pump pulley, as follows:

❄❄ **WARNING**

If the pulley has been removed and installed twice, install a new power steering pump pulley.

e. Using the special tool, install the power steering pump pulley. Inspect the pulley for paint marks in the web area near the hub. If there are 2 paint marks, install a new pulley. If there is 1 paint mark or none at all, use a paint pencil to mark the web area of the pulley near the hub.

f. Install the air cleaner element.

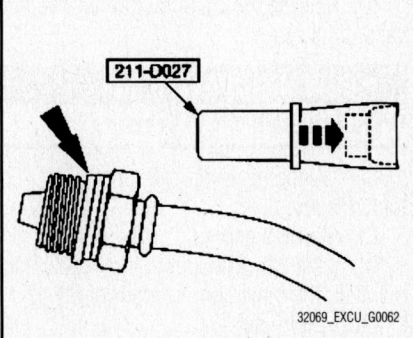

32069_EXCU_G0062

Fig. 323 Using the special tool, install a new Teflon® seal on the pressure line-to-pump fitting

32069_EXCU_G0061

Fig. 324 Use the special tool remove the power steering pump pulley

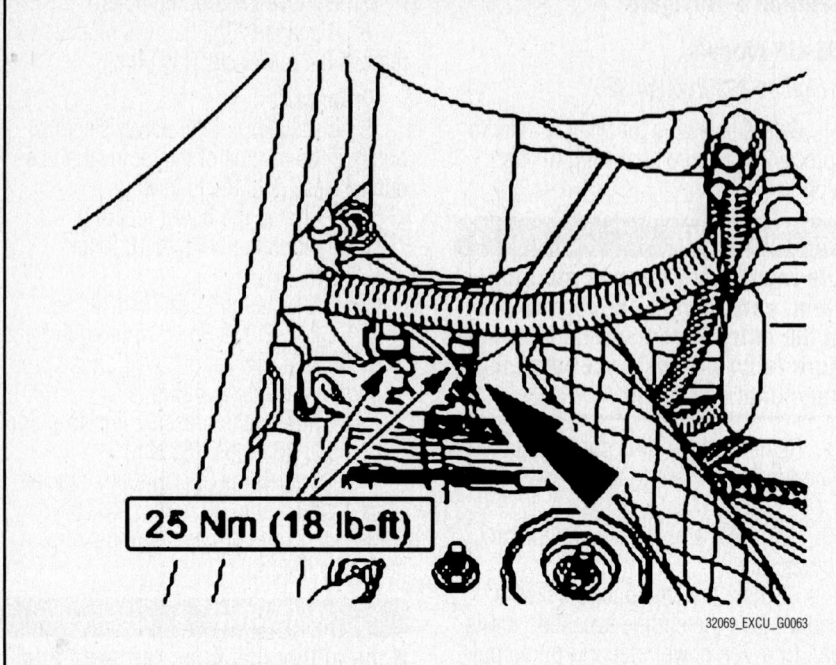

25 Nm (18 lb-ft)

32069_EXCU_G0063

Fig. 325 Remove the bolts, detach the harness retainer and remove the power steering pump

g. Rotate the tensioner clockwise and install the engine accessory drive belt on the power steering pump pulley.

11. Fill the power steering system.

2007 Models

1. Before servicing the vehicle, refer to the precautions in the beginning of this section.

2. With the vehicle in NEUTRAL , position it on a hoist.

3. Remove the 10 upper air deflector pushpin-type retainers.

4. Remove the upper air deflector.

5. Remove the air cleaner outlet pipe.

6. Remove the 2 upper cooling fan shroud bolts.

7. Release the lower cooling fan shroud tab and rotate the shroud upwards.

8. Rotate the accessory drive belt tensioner clockwise and remove the accessory drive belt from the power steering pump pulley.

9. Position the cooling fan shroud assembly upward to gain clearance to install the special tool.

10. Using the special tool 211-016, remove the power steering pump pulley.

11. Release the clamp and disconnect the supply hose from power steering pump.

12. Remove the power steering pressure line bracket-to-engine nut.

➡A new Teflon® O-ring seal must be installed any time the line is disconnected from the power steering pump.

13. Disconnect the power steering pressure line-to-power steering pump fitting. Discard the Teflon® O-ring seal.

14. Remove the 3 bolts and the power steering pump.

To install:

15. Install the power steering pump and mounting bolts, tighten the bolts to 18 ft. lbs. (25 Nm).

16. Using the special tool 211-D027, install a new Teflon® O-ring on the pressure line-to-pump fitting.

17. Install the power steering pressure line-to-power steering pump fitting and tighten to 48 ft. lbs. (65 Nm).

18. Install the power steering pressure line bracket-to-engine nut and tighten to 30 ft. lbs. (40 Nm).

19. Connect and clamp the supply hose to the power steering pump.

20. Using the special tool 211-185, install the power steering pump pulley.

21. Rotate the accessory drive belt tensioner clockwise and install the accessory drive belt to the power steering pump pulley.

22. Lower the cooling fan shroud assembly.

23. Release the lower cooling fan shroud tab, rotate shroud downward

24. Install the 2 upper cooling fan shroud bolts and tighten to 27 inch. lbs. (3 Nm).

25. Install the air cleaner outlet pipe.

26. Install the upper air deflector and the 10 pushpin-type retainers.

BLEEDING

See Figure 326.

> ❊❊ **WARNING**
>
> **If the air is not purged from the power steering system correctly, premature power steering pump failure can result. The condition can occur on pre-delivery vehicles with evidence of aerated fluid or on vehicles that have had steering component repairs.**

➡A whine heard from the power steering pump can be caused by air in the system. The power steering purge procedure must be carried out prior to any component repair for which power steering noise complaints are accompanied by evidence of aerated fluid.

1. Before servicing the vehicle, refer to the precautions in the beginning of this section.

2. Remove the power steering pump reservoir cap. Check the fluid.

3. Raise the front wheels off the floor.

4. Tightly insert the stopper of the vacuum pump into the reservoir.

5. Start the engine.

6. Install the vacuum pump, apply vacuum and maintain the maximum vacuum of 68-85 kPa (20-25 in-Hg).

7. If equipped with Hydro-Boost®, apply the brake pedal twice.

> ❊❊ **WARNING**
>
> **Do not hold the steering wheel against the stops for more than 3 to 5 seconds at a time. Damage to the power steering pump can occur.**

8. Cycle the steering wheel fully from stop-to-stop 10 times.

9. Stop the engine.

10. Release the vacuum and remove the vacuum pump.

> ❊❊ **WARNING**
>
> **Do not overfill the reservoir.**

11. Fill the reservoir with approved transmission fluid.

12. Start the engine.

13. Install the vacuum pump. Apply and maintain the maximum vacuum of 68-85 kPa (20-25 in-Hg).

14. Cycle the steering wheel fully from stop-to-stop 10 times.

15. Fill the reservoir as needed and install the reservoir cap.

Required tools for power steering system bleeding

	Vacuum Pump Kit 416-D002 (D95L-7559-A) or equivalent
	Evacuation Cap, Power Steering 211-265 or equivalent

22086_EXPD_G0117

Fig. 326 Power steering system bleeding tools

16. Visually inspect the power steering system for leaks.

17. Fill the reservoir as needed and visually inspect the power steering system for leaks.

18. Install the power steering reservoir cap.

FLUSHING

1. Before servicing the vehicle, refer to the precautions in the beginning of this section.

2. Remove the power steering fluid reservoir cap.

3. Using a suitable suction device, remove the power steering fluid from the reservoir.

4. Disconnect the power steering fluid return hose from the reservoir.

5. Plug the power steering fluid reservoir inlet port.

6. Attach an extension hose to the power steering return hose.

➡**Do not reuse the power steering fluid that has been flushed from the power steering system.**

7. Fill the power steering fluid reservoir with new fluid.

8. Do not allow the power steering pump to run completely dry of power steering fluid.

9. Start the engine while simultaneously turning the steering wheel to lock and then immediately turn the ignition switch to the OFF position.

✳✳ WARNING

Avoid turning the steering wheel without the engine running as this may cause air to be pulled into the steering gear.

10. Fill the power steering fluid reservoir with the approved power steering fluid. Do not overfill.

11. Repeat Steps 8 and 9, turning the steering wheel in the opposite direction each time, until the fluid exiting the power steering fluid return hose is clean and clear of foreign material.

12. Remove the extension hose from the power steering return hose.

13. Remove the plug from the power steering fluid reservoir inlet port.

14. Install the power steering return hose to the reservoir and the retaining clamp.

➡**It is necessary to correctly fill the power steering system to remove any trapped air and completely fill the power steering system components.**

15. If, after correctly filling the power steering system, there is power steering noise accompanied by evidence of aerated fluid and there are no fluid leaks, it may be necessary to purge the power steering system.

16. Fill the power steering system.

FILLING

See Figure 327.

1. Before servicing the vehicle, refer to the precautions in the beginning of this section.

✳✳ WARNING

If the air is not purged from the power steering system correctly, premature power steering pump failure can result. The condition can occur on pre-delivery vehicles with evidence of aerated fluid or on vehicles that have had steering component repairs.

2. Remove the power steering pump reservoir cap.

3. Tightly install the evacuation cap to the power steering pump reservoir.

4. Install the hose from the fill adapter manifold tee to the evacuation cap on the power steering pump reservoir.

5. Install the vacuum pump to the fill adapter manifold control valve.

6. Install the hose to the opposite fill adapter manifold control valve and submerge the open end of the hose into a container of new power steering fluid.

➡**The fill adapter manifold control valves are in the open position when the point of the handles face the center of the fill adapter manifold.**

7. Close the fill adapter manifold control valve connected to the power steering fluid container.

8. Open the fill adapter manifold control valve connected to the vacuum pump.

9. Using the vacuum pump, apply 68-85 kPa (20-25 in-Hg) of vacuum to the power steering system. Observe the vacuum gauge for 30 seconds.

10. If the vacuum gauge reading drops more than 3 kPa (0.88 in-Hg), correct any leaks in the power steering system or the filling tools before proceeding.

➡**The vacuum pump gauge reading will drop slightly during this step.**

11. Slowly open the fill adapter manifold control valve connected to the power steering fluid container until power steering fluid completely fills the hose.

12. Close the fill adapter manifold control valve connected to the power steering fluid container.

13. Using the vacuum pump, apply 68-85 kPa (20-25 in-Hg) of vacuum to the power steering system.

Tools required for power steering filling

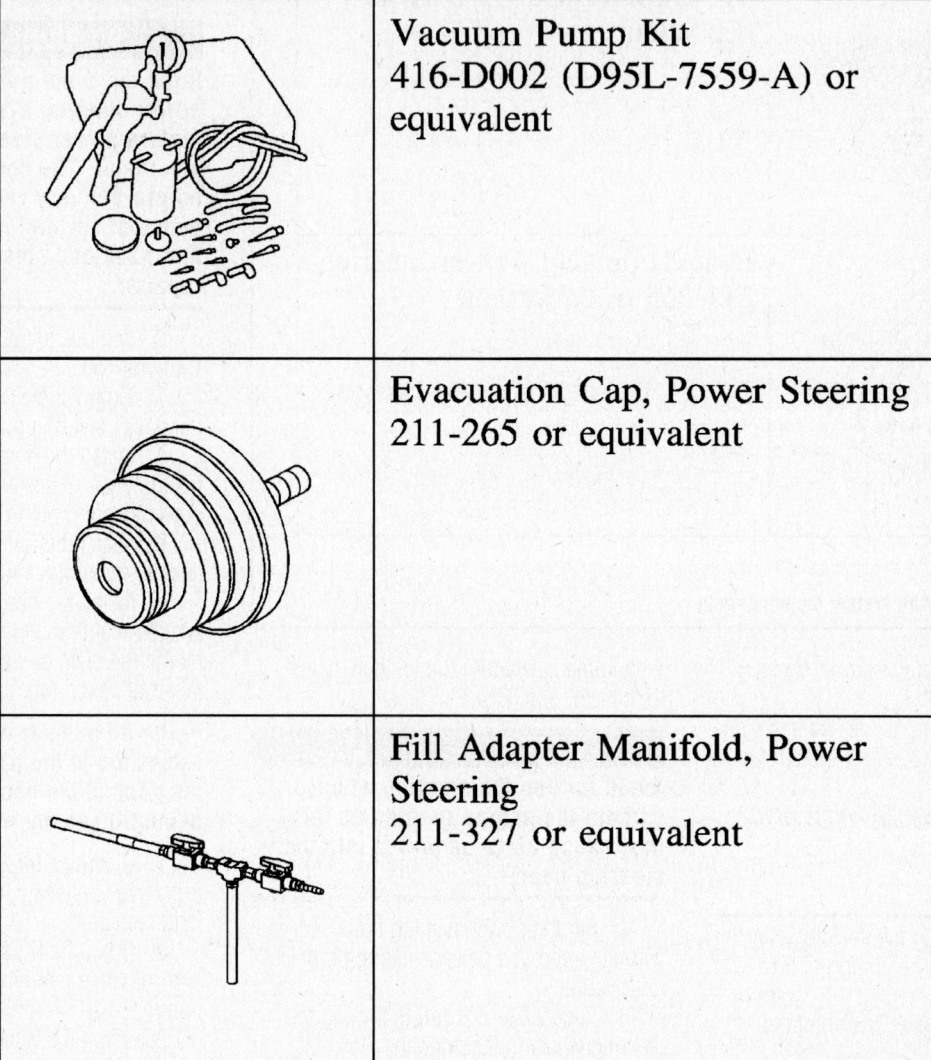

	Vacuum Pump Kit 416-D002 (D95L-7559-A) or equivalent
	Evacuation Cap, Power Steering 211-265 or equivalent
	Fill Adapter Manifold, Power Steering 211-327 or equivalent

22086_EXPD_G0118

Fig. 327 Power steering fluid filling tools

14. Close the fill adapter manifold control valve connected to the vacuum pump.

15. Slowly open the fill adapter manifold control valve connected to the power steering fluid container.

16. When the power steering fluid has drained from the hose connected to the power steering fluid container, close the fill adapter manifold control valve connected to the power steering fluid container.

17. Remove the tools from the vehicle.

18. Install the power steering reservoir cap.

✳✳ WARNING

Do not hold the steering wheel against the stops for more than 3 to 5 seconds at a time. Damage to the power steering pump can occur.

➡**There will be a slight drop in the power steering fluid level in the power steering fluid reservoir when the engine is started.**

19. Start the engine and turn the steering wheel from stop-to-stop.

20. If equipped with Hydro-Boost®, apply the brake pedal twice.

21. Turn the ignition switch to the OFF position.

✳✳ WARNING

Do not overfill the reservoir.

22. Remove the power steering reservoir cap and fill the reservoir.

23. Install the power steering reservoir cap.

SUSPENSION

FRONT SUSPENSION

COIL SPRING

REMOVAL & INSTALLATION

Excursion

1. Before servicing the vehicle, refer to the precautions section.

> ✴✴ **WARNING**
>
> **Suspension fasteners are critical parts because they affect performance of vital components and systems and their failure can result in major service expense. Install new parts with the same part number or an equivalent part if installation is necessary. Do not install a part of lesser quality or substitute design.**

2. Remove the wheel and tire assembly.
3. Use a suitable jack to support the front axle assembly.
4. Remove the nut and detach the shock from the mounting stud.
5. Remove the upper spring retainer.
6. Lower the front axle until the spring is free of the upper spring seat.
7. Using an extension through the top of the spring, remove the lower spring retainer.
8. Remove the front spring.
9. Installation is the reverse of removal procedure and note the following:
    a. Tighten the lower spring retainer to 99 ft. lbs. (133 Nm).
    b. Tighten the upper retainer to 26 ft. lbs. (35 Nm) and the lower shock bolt to 60 ft. lbs. (80 Nm).

Expedition & Navigator

2005–06 Models

See Figures 328 and 329.

1. Before servicing the vehicle, refer to the precautions section.
2. Remove the wheel and tire assembly.
3. Remove and discard the upper shock absorber nuts.
4. Remove the nut and detach the tie-rod from the wheel knuckle. Discard the nut.
5. Remove the nut, bolt and shock absorber/spring assembly. Discard the nut.
6. For reference during assembly, index the upper mount, spring and shock absorber.
7. Using a suitable spring compressor, compress the spring until the tension is released from the shock absorber.
8. While holding the shock rod, remove the nut and washer.

9. Remove the shock absorber. Discard the nut.
10. Remove the upper mount, dust shield and insulator.
11. Remove coil spring.
12. Installation is the reverse of removal procedure and note the following:
    a. Tighten the shock rod nut to 22 ft. lbs. (30 Nm).
    b. Tighten the shock absorber nut and bolt to 295 ft. lbs. (400 Nm).
    c. Tighten the tie rod nut to 111 ft. lbs. (150 Nm) and the new upper shock absorber nuts to 26 ft. lbs. (35 Nm).

2007 Models

> ✴✴ **WARNING**
>
> **Suspension fasteners are critical parts because they affect performance of vital parts and systems and their failure can result in major service expense. A new part with the same part number must be installed if installation becomes necessary. Do not use a replacement part of lesser quality or substitute design. Torque values must be used as specified during reassembly to make sure of correct retention of these parts.**

> ✴✴ **WARNING**
>
> **Do not tighten the lower shock nut until the installation procedure is complete and the weight of the vehicle is resting on the wheel and tire assemblies.**

1. Before servicing the vehicle, refer to the precautions section.
2. With the vehicle in NEUTRAL, position it on a hoist.
3. Remove and discard the shock absorber and spring assembly upper nuts.
4. Remove and discard the tie-rod end nut.
5. Using the special tool 204-592, separate the upper ball joint from the wheel knuckle.
6. Remove and discard the upper ball joint nut.
7. Remove and discard the shock absorber and spring assembly lower nut and bolt.
8. Using the special tool, disconnect the upper arm from the wheel knuckle and remove the shock absorber and spring assembly.

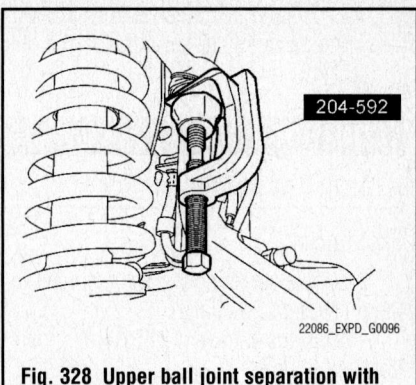

Fig. 328 Upper ball joint separation with special tool

➡ For reference during assembly, index the upper mount, spring and shock absorber.

9. Using a suitable spring compressor, compress the spring until the tension is released from the shock absorber.

➡ Use the hex holding feature to prevent the shock rod from turning while removing the nut.

10. While holding the shock rod, remove the nut and the shock absorber. Discard the nut.
11. Remove the upper mount, dust boot and insulator.
12. Remove coil spring.
13. To install, reverse the removal procedure and note the following:
    a. Tighten shock absorber nut to 41 ft. lbs. (56 Nm).
    b. Tighten lower shock absorber nut and bolt to 295 ft. lbs. (475 Nm).
    c. Tighten upper ball joint nut to 85 ft. lbs. (115 Nm).

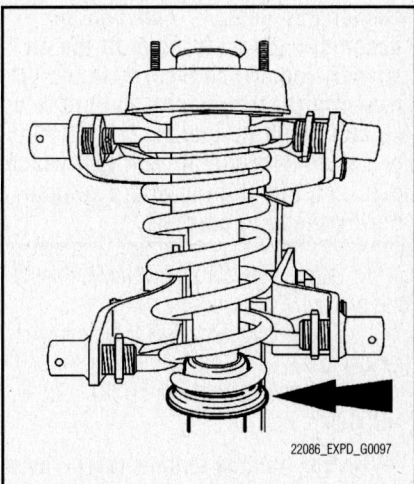

Fig. 329 Spring compression with spring compressor tool

d. Tighten tie-rod end nut to 111 ft lbs. (150 Nm).

e. Tighten the shock absorber and spring assembly upper nuts to 30 ft. lbs. (40 Nm).

CONTROL LINKS

REMOVAL & INSTALLATION

Excursion

1. Before servicing the vehicle, refer to the precautions section.

2. With the vehicle in NEUTRAL, position it on a hoist.

3. Remove the nut, washer and bolt, and disconnect the stabilizer bar link from the stabilizer bar.

4. Remove the nut.

➡ **For 2WD models the right-hand stabilizer bar link is equipped with a dished washer (heat shield). The washer must be installed during installation of the stabilizer bar link.**

5. Remove the bolt and the stabilizer bar link.

6. To install, reverse the removal procedure and note the following:

a. For 2WD models tighten the mounting nuts and bolts to 80 ft. lbs. (109 Nm).

b. For 4WD models tighten the mounting nuts and bolts to 85 ft. lbs. (115 Nm).

Expedition & Navigator

2005–06 Models

✳✳ WARNING

The electrical power to the air suspension system must be shut off prior to hoisting, jacking or towing an air suspension vehicle. This can be accomplished by turning off the air suspension switch located in the LH rear quarter trim panel. Failure to do so can result in unexpected inflation or deflation of the air springs, which can result in shifting of the vehicle during these operations.

1. Before servicing the vehicle, refer to the precautions section.

2. If equipped, turn the air suspension switch to the OFF position.

3. With the vehicle in NEUTRAL, position it on a hoist.

➡ **The hex holding feature can be used to prevent turning of the stud while removing the nut.**

4. Remove and discard the 2 stabilizer bar link upper nuts.

5. Remove and discard the 2 stabilizer bar link lower nuts and remove the 2 stabilizer bar links.

6. To install, reverse the removal procedure and note the following:

a. Tighten the 2 stabilizer bar link upper nuts to 148 ft. lbs. (200 Nm).

b. Tighten the 2 stabilizer bar link lower nuts to 66 ft. lbs. (90 Nm).

2007 Models

1. Before servicing the vehicle, refer to the precautions section.

2. With the vehicle in NEUTRAL, position it on a hoist.

➡ **The hex holding feature can be used to prevent turning of the stud while removing the nut.**

3. Remove and discard the 2 stabilizer bar link upper nuts.

4. Remove and discard the 2 stabilizer bar link lower nuts and remove the 2 stabilizer bar links.

5. To install, reverse the removal procedure and note the following:

a. Tighten upper and lower link nuts to 59 ft. lbs. (80 Nm).

LEAF SPRING

REMOVAL & INSTALLATION

Excursion

See Figures 330 through 332.

1. Before servicing the vehicle, refer to the precautions section.

2. With the vehicle in NEUTRAL, position it on a hoist.

3. Position jack stands under the axle housing.

➡ **The following step is for the left-hand shock only.**

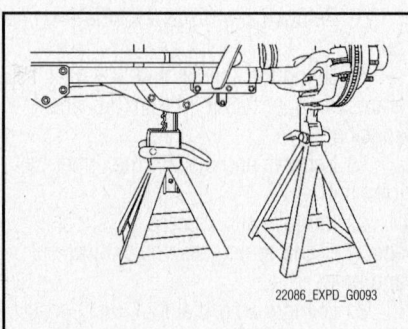

Fig. 330 Jack stand positioning under front axle

4. Remove the shock:
- Remove the nut and bolt.
- Remove the shock from the front spring cap.

✳✳ WARNING

Never reuse U-bolts. The U-bolts are a torque-to-yield design and cannot be retightened. Failure to use a new U-bolt can result in loose or broken springs and suspension components.

5. Remove the U-bolts:
- Remove the four nuts.
- Remove the two U-bolts and the front spring spacer. Discard the U-bolts.

6. Disconnect the front driveshaft:
- Remove the four bolts and the two straps.
- Remove the driveshaft from the pinion flange.

7. Disconnect the spring shackle:
- Remove the nut and bolt.
- Position the spring shackle away from the spring.

8. Detach the pushpin and remove the bolt and condenser bracket.

9. Disconnect the spring hanger:
- Remove the nut and bolt.
- Using a hammer, tap the spring until the spring is free from the hanger bracket.

10. Remove the spring from the vehicle.

To install:

11. Position the spring in the vehicle.

12. Install the spring into the spring hanger:
- Position the spring into the hanger.
- Install the bolt and nut. Do not tighten the nut and bolt at this time.

13. Install the bracket and bolt and the push pin.

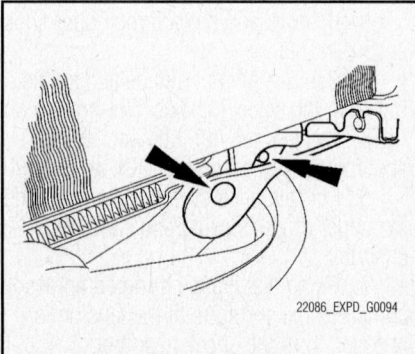

Fig. 331 Push pin location view

14. Install the spring into the spring shackle:
- Position the shackle.
- Install the bolt and nut. Do not tighten the nut and bolt at this time.

➡**The U-bolts insert through the front spring cap on the left-hand side and through the axle assembly bracket on the right-hand side.**

15. Install the upper front spring spacer and U-bolts:
- Position the front spring spacer and the new U-bolts.
- Install the four nuts. Do not tighten the nuts at this time.

➡**The following step is for the left-hand shock only. The right-hand shock is similar.**

16. Install the shock, bolt and nut onto the spring cap.

➡**The suspension must be loaded with the weight of the vehicle before the U-bolts and the leaf spring mounting bolts can be tightened. Make sure that the locating pin is correctly aligned with the axle.**

17. Lower the vehicle onto the jack stands until the front suspension is supporting the weight of the vehicle.

➡**The U-bolts must be tightened in a crisscross sequence. This will tighten the U-bolts evenly.**

18. Tighten the U-bolts in sequence to 99 ft. lbs. (133 Nm).
19. Tighten the leaf spring rear retaining bolt and nut to 185 ft. lbs. (250 Nm).
20. Tighten the leaf spring front retaining bolt and nut to 203 ft. lbs. (275 Nm).
21. Install the front driveshaft:
- Position the driveshaft onto the pinion flange.

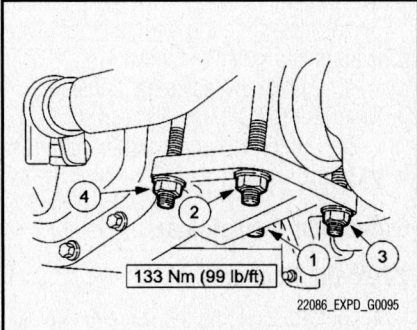

Fig. 332 U-bolt tightening sequence

- Install the two straps and the four bolts.
- Tighten the bolts to 76 ft. lbs. (102 Nm).

LOWER BALL JOINT

REMOVAL & INSTALLATION

2005–06 Expedition & Navigator

The lower ball joints on these models are an integral part of the control am. If found to be defective the control arm must be replaced. Refer to control arm removal and installation.

2007 Expedition & Navigator

See Figures 333 and 334.

1. Remove the wheel knuckle.
2. Remove and discard the lower ball joint snap ring.
3. Using the special tools 205-086 and 204-358, remove the lower ball joint.
4. Clean and inspect the lower arm lower ball joint bore for damage before installing a new ball joint.
5. To install, reverse the removal procedure.

➡**Make sure the lower ball joint is fully seated in the lower control arm, and**

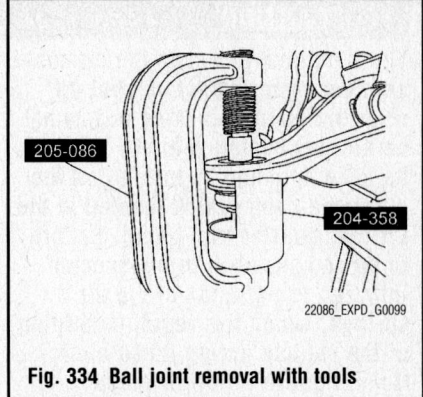

Fig. 334 Ball joint removal with tools

new lower ball joint snap ring is fully seated.

✳✳ WARNING

Always install new nuts and cotter pins.

LOWER CONTROL ARM

REMOVAL & INSTALLATION

Expedition & Navigator

See Figure 335.

1. Before servicing the vehicle, refer to the precautions section.

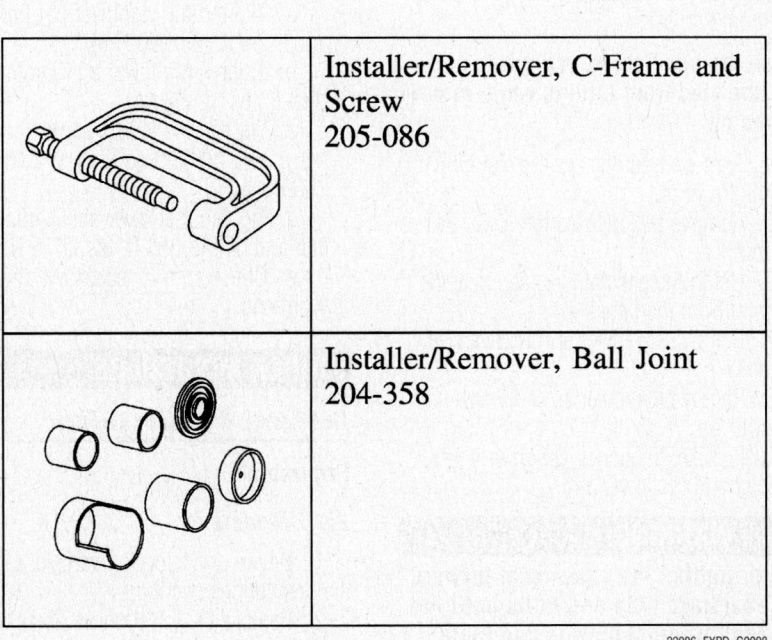

| Installer/Remover, C-Frame and Screw 205-086 |
| Installer/Remover, Ball Joint 204-358 |

Fig. 333 Ball joint removal tools

❋ CAUTION

The electrical power to the air suspension system must be shut off prior to hoisting, jacking or towing an air suspension vehicle. This can be accomplished by turning off the air suspension switch located in the LH rear quarter trim panel. Failure to do so can result in unexpected inflation or deflation of the air springs, which can result in shifting of the vehicle during these operations. Failure to follow these instructions may result in personal injury.

❋ WARNING

Suspension fasteners are critical parts because they affect performance of vital parts and systems and their failure can result in major service expense. A new part with the same part number must be installed if installation becomes necessary. Do not use a replacement part of lesser quality or substitute design. Torque values must be used as specified during reassembly to make sure of correct retention of these parts.

2. If equipped, turn the air suspension switch to the OFF position.

3. With the vehicle in NEUTRAL, position it on a hoist.

➡**Use the hex holding feature to prevent the stud from turning while removing the nut.**

4. Remove and discard the stabilizer bar link lower nut.

5. Remove and discard the lower ball joint nut.

6. Using the special tool, separate the ball joint from the knuckle.

7. Remove the lower arm rearward nut and bolt.

8. Remove the lower arm forward nut and bolt.

9. Remove the shock absorber lower nut, bolt and the lower arm.

❋❋ WARNING

Do not tighten the lower arm forward and rearward nuts and bolts until the installation procedure is complete and the weight of the vehicle is resting on the wheel and tire assemblies.

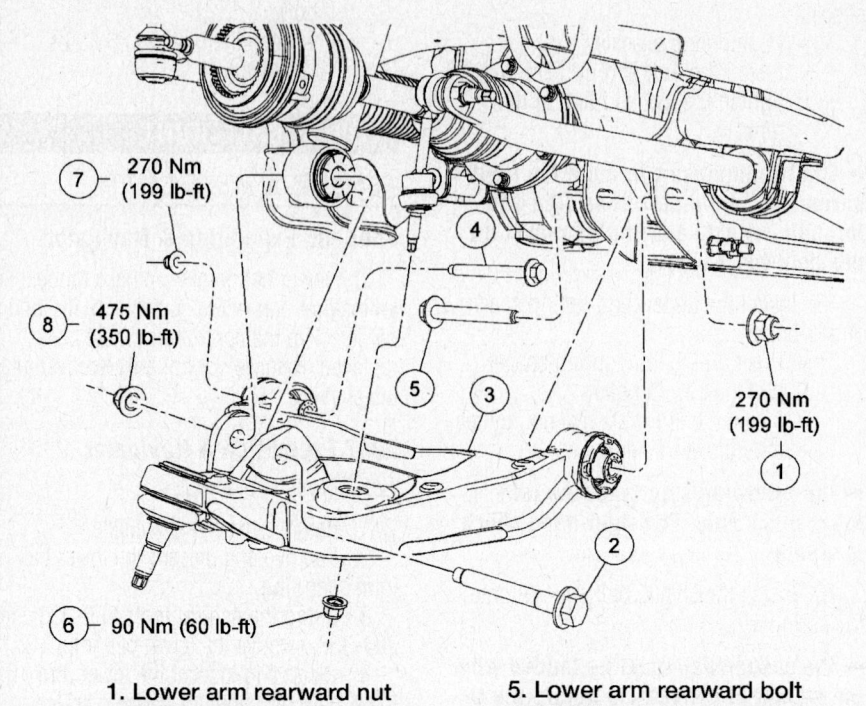

1. Lower arm rearward nut
2. Shock absorber lower bolt
3. Lower arm
4. Lower arm forward bolt
5. Lower arm rearward bolt
6. Stabilizer bar link lower nut
7. Lower arm forward nut
8. Shock absorber lower nut

22086_EXPD_G0101

Fig. 335 Lower control arm and related parts

To install:

10. To install, reverse the removal procedure and note the following:

a. Tighten the stabilizer bar link lower nut to 59 ft. lbs. (80 Nm).

b. Tighten the lower ball joint nut to 148 ft. lbs. (200 Nm).

c. Tighten the lower rearward and forward arm, nut and bolt to 285 ft. lbs. (350Nm).

d. Tighten the lower shock absorber nut and bolt to 350 ft. lbs. (475 Nm).

e. Check and, if necessary, align the front end.

SHOCK ABSORBERS

REMOVAL & INSTALLATION

Excursion

2WD Models

1. Before servicing the vehicle, refer to the precautions section.

2. Remove the lower shock absorber retaining nut and remove the shock absorber.

3. Remove the upper shock absorber retaining nut and upper shock absorber insulator.

To install:

4. Installation is the reverse of removal. Using new fasteners, tighten the lower and upper nuts to 76 ft. lbs. (103 Nm).

4WD Models

1. Before servicing the vehicle, refer to the precautions section.

2. Remove the upper shock absorber retaining nut and upper shock absorber insulator.

3. Raise and support the vehicle.

4. Remove the lower shock absorber retaining nut and remove the shock absorber.

To install:

5. Installation is the reverse of removal procedure and note the following:

a. Using new fasteners, tighten the lower nut to 60 ft. lbs. (80 Nm).

b. Tighten the upper nut to 30 ft. lbs. (40 Nm).

Expedition & Navigator

2005–06 Models

1. Before servicing the vehicle, refer to the precautions section.

2. Remove the wheel assembly.

3. Remove and discard the upper shock nuts. Tighten to 26 ft. lbs. (35 Nm).

➡**Use the hex holding feature to prevent the stud from turning while removing the nut.**

4. Remove the nut and detach the tie-rod end from the wheel knuckle. Discard the nut.
5. Remove the lower nut, bolt and the shock absorber and spring assembly. Discard the nut.

To install:

6. Installation is the reverse of removal, please note the following torque specifications:
   a. New lower nut, bolt and tighten to 400 Nm (295 ft. lbs.).
   b. New tie-rod end nut and tighten to 111 ft. lbs. (150 Nm).
   c. New upper shock nuts and tighten to 26 ft. lbs. (35 Nm).

2007 Models

1. Before servicing the vehicle, refer to the precautions section.

⁂ WARNING

Suspension fasteners are critical parts because they affect performance of vital parts and systems and their failure can result in major service expense. A new part with the same part number must be installed if installation becomes necessary. Do not use a replacement part of lesser quality or substitute design. Torque values must be used as specified during reassembly to make sure of correct retention of these parts.

⁂ WARNING

Do not tighten the lower shock nut until the installation procedure is complete and the weight of the vehicle is resting on the wheel and tire assemblies.

2. Before servicing the vehicle, refer to the precautions section.
3. With the vehicle in NEUTRAL, position it on a hoist.
4. Remove and discard the shock absorber and spring assembly upper nuts.
5. Remove and discard the tie-rod end nut.
6. Using the special tool 204-592, separate the upper ball joint from the wheel knuckle.
7. Remove and discard the upper ball joint nut.
8. Remove and discard the shock absorber and spring assembly lower nut and bolt.
9. Using the special tool, disconnect the upper arm from the wheel knuckle and remove the shock absorber and spring assembly.
10. To install, reverse the removal procedure and note the following:
   a. Tighten lower shock absorber nut and bolt to 295 ft. lbs. (475 Nm).
   b. Tighten upper ball joint nut to 85 ft. lbs. (115 Nm).
   c. Tighten tie-rod end nut to 111 ft lbs. (150 Nm).
   d. Tighten the shock absorber and spring assembly upper nuts to 30 ft. lbs. (40 Nm).

TESTING

1. Road test the vehicle.
2. On a smooth road see if any vibrations are present.
3. Use your hands in order to lift up and push down each corner of the vehicle 3 times.
4. Remove your hands from the vehicle.
5. Replace any shock that exceeds more than two bounces.
6. Raise vehicle for inspection.
7. Inspect each shock absorber for external fluid leakage.
8. Inspect for deformation or damage.
9. Inspect bushings for wear or damage.
10. Replace as necessary.

STABILIZER BAR

REMOVAL & INSTALLATION

Excursion

2WD Models

⁂ WARNING

Suspension fasteners are critical parts because they affect performance of vital components and systems and their failure can result in major service expense. They must be replaced with the same part number or an equivalent part if replacement is necessary. Do not use a replacement part of lesser quality or substitute design. Torque values must be used as specified during reassembly to ensure proper retention of these parts.

1. Raise and support the vehicle.
2. Remove the bolts and the retainer brackets.
3. Remove the nuts, bolts, washers and the stabilizer bar and links.
4. To install, reverse the removal procedure:
   a. Tighten the stabilizer bar nuts to 80 ft. lbs. (109 Nm) and the retainer bracket bolts to 32 ft. lbs. (43 Nm).

4WD Models

1. Raise and safely support the vehicle .
2. Remove the nuts, washers and bolts, and then disconnect the stabilizer bar links.
3. Remove the bolts and the stabilizer bar.
4. To install, reverse the removal procedure and note the following:
   a. Tighten the stabilizer bar bolts to 41 ft. lbs. (50 N) and the stabilizer link nuts to 85 ft. lbs. (115 Nm).

Expedition & Navigator

2005–06 Models

See Figure 336.

⁂ CAUTION

The electrical power to the air suspension system must be shut off prior to hoisting, jacking or towing an air suspension vehicle. This can be accomplished by turning off the air suspension switch located in the LH rear quarter trim panel. Failure to do so can result in unexpected inflation or deflation of the air springs, which can result in shifting of the vehicle during these operations.

1. If equipped, turn the air suspension switch to the OFF position.
2. Raise and support the vehicle.

➡**The hex holding feature can be used to prevent turning of the stud while removing the nut.**

3. Remove and discard the two stabilizer bar link-to-bar nuts.

➡**Use the hex holding feature to prevent the stud from turning while removing the nut.**

4. Remove the stabilizer link-to-control arm nuts and the stabilizer bar links. Discard the nuts.
5. Remove the four nuts, brackets, bushings and the stabilizer bar. Discard the nuts.
6. Inspect and, if necessary, install new stabilizer bar bushings.

To install:

7. Installation is the reverse of the removal procedure. Please note the following tightening specifications and make sure to use new retainers:

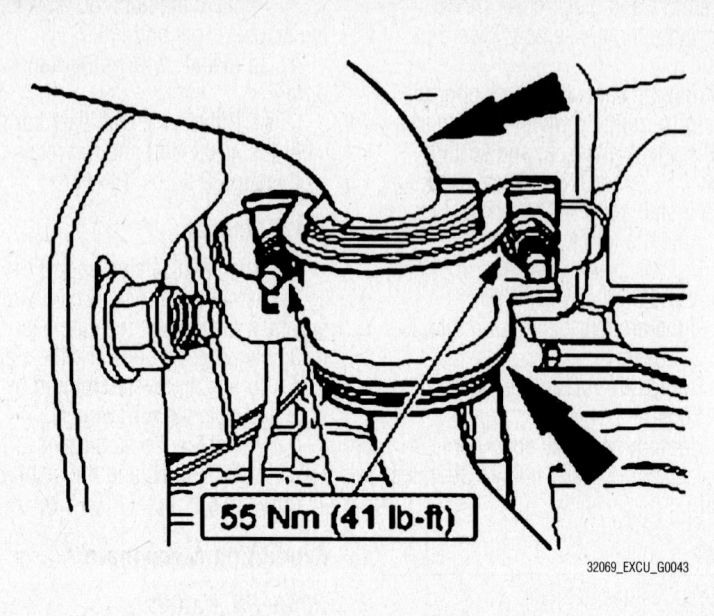

55 Nm (41 lb-ft)

32069_EXCU_G0043

Fig. 336 Remove the four nuts, brackets, bushings and the stabilizer bar

a. Stabilizer bar nuts: 41 ft. lbs. (55 Nm)

b. Stabilizer bar link-to-control arm nuts: 66 ft. lbs. (90 Nm)

c. Stabilizer bar link-to-bar nuts: 148 ft. lbs. (200 Nm)

2007 Expedition & Navigator

1. Before servicing the vehicle, refer to the precautions section.

2. With the vehicle in NEUTRAL, position it on a hoist.

➡**The hex holding feature can be used to prevent turning of the stud while removing the nut.**

3. Remove and discard the 2 stabilizer bar link upper nuts.

4. Remove and discard the 2 stabilizer bar link lower nuts and remove the 2 stabilizer bar links.

5. Remove the 4 stabilizer bar bracket nuts, brackets and the stabilizer bar. Discard the nuts.

6. Remove and discard the stabilizer bracket bolt plates.

➡**Make sure the stabilizer bar bushing upset is installed into the bracket groove.**

7. Inspect and, if necessary, install new stabilizer bar bushings.

8. To install, reverse the removal procedure and note the following:

a. Tighten upper and lower link nuts to 59 ft. lbs. (80 Nm).

b. Tighten the stabilizer bar bracket nuts to 41 ft. lbs. (55 Nm).

STEERING KNUCKLE

REMOVAL & INSTALLATION

Excursion

2WD Models

See Figures 337 and 338.

❊❊ **WARNING**

Suspension fasteners are critical parts because they affect performance of vital components and systems and their failure can result in major service expense. They must be replaced with the same part number or an equivalent part if replacement is necessary. Do not use a replacement part of lesser quality or substitute design. Torque values must be used as specified during reassembly to ensure proper retention of these parts.

1. Before servicing the vehicle, refer to the precautions section.

2. Raise and support the vehicle.

3. Remove the wheel and tire assembly.

4. Remove the disc brake caliper and the front disc brake hub and rotor.

5. Remove the front disc brake rotor shield.

6. If equipped, remove the ABS sensor retaining bolt, ABS sensor harness retaining bolt and the ABS sensor. Position out of the way.

7. Disconnect the tie rod end, as follows:

a. Remove and discard the cotter pin.

b. Remove the castellated nut.

c. Using the Pitman Arm Puller, remove the tie rod end.

8. Remove the pinch bolt.

9. Remove the camber adjuster.

❊❊ **WARNING**

To prevent damage to the ball joint seal and the ball joint socket, do not use a pickle fork-type remover to loosen the ball joints.

10. Remove the front wheel spindle, as follows:

a. Loosen, but do not remove, the castellated nut.

b. Remove and discard the cotter pin.

c. Strike the lower end of the front axle to loosen the ball joint.

d. Remove the castellated nut and the front wheel spindle.

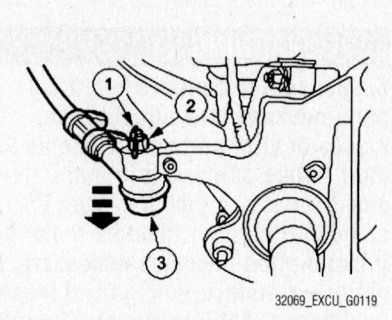

32069_EXCU_G0119

Fig. 337 Remove and discard the cotter pin (1), remove the castellated nut (2), then use the Pitman Arm Puller, to remove the tie rod end (3)

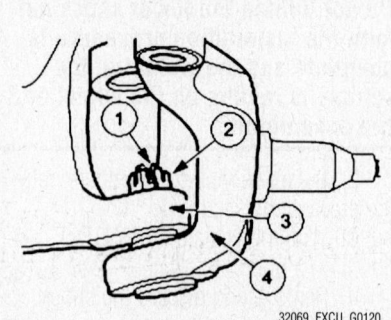

32069_EXCU_G0120

Fig. 338 Loosen, but do not remove, the castellated nut (2), remove and discard the cotter pin (1), strike the lower end of the front axle to loosen the ball joint (2), then remove the castellated nut and the front wheel spindle (4)

To install:

➡ **Tighten the ball joint nut further, if necessary, in order to insert a new cotter pin.**

11. Using new fasteners, follow the removal procedure in reverse order. Tighten as follows:

a. Front wheel spindle castellated nut: 99 ft. lbs. (133 Nm).

b. Pinch bolt: 60 ft. lbs. (80 Nm).

c. Tie rod end nut: 67 ft. lbs. (90 Nm).

d. ABS sensor bolt: 71 inch lbs. (8 Nm).

e. Rotor shield bolts: 71 inch lbs. (8 Nm).

12. Check the front end alignment.

4WD Models

See Figures 339 and 340.

1. Before servicing the vehicle, refer to the precautions section.

2. Raise and safely support the vehicle.

3. Remove the front brake disc.

4. Remove the wheel hub and bearing.

5. Using a drift, drive the axle shaft main seal out of the wheel knuckle.

6. Remove the axle shaft and main seal.

7. Remove the tie-rod end castellated nut:

a. Remove the cotter pin.

b. Remove the castellated nut.

8. Using a suitable puller, disconnect the tie-rod end from the wheel knuckle.

9. Remove the upper ball joint castellated nut and the insert:

a. Remove the cotter pin.

b. Remove the nut.

c. Remove the insert.

d. Remove the wheel knuckle, as follows:

e. Remove the lower ball joint nut.

f. Remove the knuckle.

10. Clean and inspect the wheel knuckle ball joint bores.

To install:

11. Position the wheel knuckle onto the axle housing.

12. Install the nut onto the lower ball joint. Do not tighten the nut at this time.

13. Install the insert and the castellated nut onto the upper ball joint. Do not tighten the nut at this time.

14. Tighten the lower ball joint retaining nut. Pre-tighten the nut to 47 ft. lbs. (64 Nm).

➡ **Never loosen the castellated nut to install the cotter pin.**

15. Install the cotter pin into the upper ball joint.

16. Tighten the upper ball joint castellated nut to 69 ft. lbs. (94 Nm).

17. Install the cotter pin. If necessary, tighten the castellated nut until the cotter pin can be installed.

18. Tighten the lower ball joint nut to 204 Nm (150 lb-ft).

19. Install the tie-rod end onto the wheel knuckle:

a. Position the tie-rod end into the wheel knuckle.

b. Install and tighten the castellated nut to 52 ft. lbs. (70 Nm).

c. Install the cotter pin.

20. Install the new main seal onto the axle shaft:

a. Position the main seal onto the axle shaft.

b. Using the special tools and a hammer, seat the main seal onto the axle shaft.

21. Position the axle shaft into the axle housing.

22. Using the special tools and a hammer, install the main seal into the wheel knuckle.

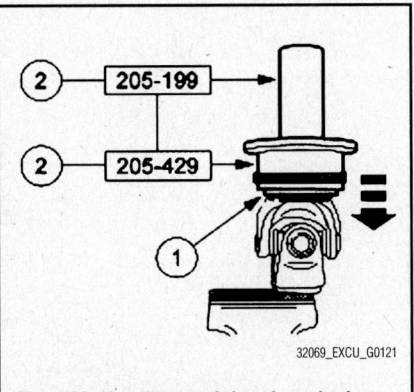

Fig. 339 Use the special tools and a hammer, seat the main seal onto the axle shaft.

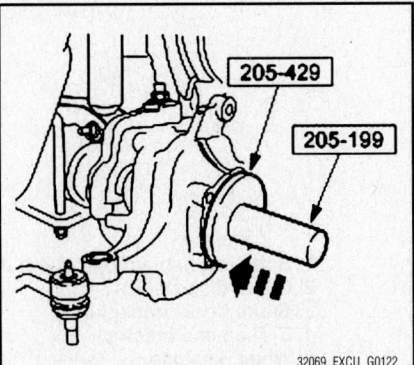

Fig. 340 Using the special tools and a hammer, install the main seal into the wheel knuckle

23. Install the wheel hub and bearing.

24. Install the front brake disc.

Expedition & Navigator

2WD Models

> ⁂ **CAUTION**
>
> **The electrical power to the air suspension system must be shut off prior to hoisting, jacking or towing an air suspension vehicle. This can be accomplished by turning off the air suspension switch located in the LH rear quarter trim panel. Failure to do so can result in unexpected inflation or deflation of the air springs, which can result in shifting of the vehicle during these operations.**

1. Before servicing the vehicle, refer to the precautions section.

2. If equipped, turn the air suspension to the OFF position.

3. Remove the wheel speed sensor harness bolt and detach the harness from the retainers.

4. Remove the wheel hub and bearing, as outlined in this section.

➡ **Use the hex holding feature to prevent the stud from turning while removing the nut.**

5. Remove the nut and detach the tie-rod from the wheel knuckle. Discard the nut.

6. Remove the bolt and position the brake hose aside.

➡ **Use the hex holding feature to prevent the stud from turning while removing the nut.**

7. Remove and discard the stabilizer bar link lower nut. Discard the nut.

8. Remove the shock absorber-to-lower arm nut and bolt. Discard the nut.

➡ **Use the hex holding feature to prevent the stud from turning while removing the nut.**

➡ **To separate the ball joints from the wheel knuckle, use tool 204-592.**

9. Remove the nut and separate the ball joint from the knuckle. Discard the nut.

➡ **Use the hex holding feature to prevent the stud from turning while removing the nut.**

10. Remove the nut and the wheel knuckle. Discard the nut.

11. If necessary, remove the 3 brake disc shield bolts and remove the brake disc shield.

To install:

➡ Do not tighten the lower shock nut until the installation procedure is complete and the weight of the vehicle is resting on the wheel and tire assemblies.

12. To install, reverse the removal procedure and note the following:

    a. Upper ball joint nut: 85 ft. lbs. (115 Nm).

    b. Lower ball joint nut: 148 ft. lbs. (200 Nm).

    c. Lower ball joint nut 2007 models: 111 ft. lbs. (150 Nm).

    d. Wheel bearing-to-knuckle bolts: 148 ft. lbs. (200 Nm).

    e. Shock absorber-to-lower control arm bolt and nut: 350 ft. lbs. (475 Nm).

    f. Stabilizer bar link-to-control arm nuts: 66 ft. lbs. (90 Nm).

    g. Brake hose bracket bolt: 9 ft. lbs. (12 Nm).

    h. Tie rod end nuts: 85 ft. lbs. (115 Nm).

    i. The brake disc shield bolts: 9 ft. lbs. (12 Nm).

13. Check and, if necessary, align the front end.

4WD Models

See Figure 341.

> **✳✳ CAUTION**
>
> The electrical power to the air suspension system must be shut off prior to hoisting, jacking or towing an air suspension vehicle. This can be accomplished by turning off the air suspension switch located in the LH rear quarter trim panel. Failure to do so can result in unexpected inflation or deflation of the air springs, which can result in shifting of the vehicle during these operations.

1. Before servicing the vehicle, refer to the precautions section.

2. If equipped, turn the air suspension to the OFF position.

3. Remove the wheel hub and bearing, as outlined in this section.

➡ Use the hex holding feature to prevent the stud from turning while removing the nut.

4. Remove and discard the tie rod end nut.

5. Remove the bolt and position the brake hose aside.

➡ Use the hex holding feature to prevent the stud from turning while removing the nut.

6. Remove and discard the stabilizer bar link-to-lower arm nut.

7. Remove the shock absorber-to-lower arm nut and bolt. Discard the nut.

8. Remove the three wheel end actuator-to-wheel knuckle bolts.

➡ Use the hex holding feature to prevent the stud from turning while removing the nut.

9. Remove and discard the lower ball joint nut.

➡ Use the hex holding feature to prevent the stud from turning while removing the nut.

➡ To separate the ball joints from the wheel knuckle, use tool 204-592.

10. Remove the upper ball joint nut and the wheel knuckle. Discard the nut.

To install:

➡ Do not tighten the lower shock nut until the installation procedure is complete and the weight of the vehicle is resting on the wheel and tire assemblies.

11. To install, reverse the removal procedure and note the following:

    a. Upper ball joint nut: 111 ft. lbs. (150 Nm).

    b. Lower ball joint nut: 148 ft. lbs. (200 Nm).

    c. Lower ball joint nut 2007 models: 111 ft. lbs. (150 Nm).

    d. Wheel end actuator-to-wheel knuckle bolts and shield: 9 ft. lbs. (12 Nm).

    e. Shock absorber-to-lower arm nut and bolt: 350 ft. lbs. (475 Nm).

    f. Stabilizer bar link-to-lower arm nut: 66 ft. lbs. (90 Nm).

    g. Brake hose bracket bolt: 9 ft. lbs. (12 Nm).

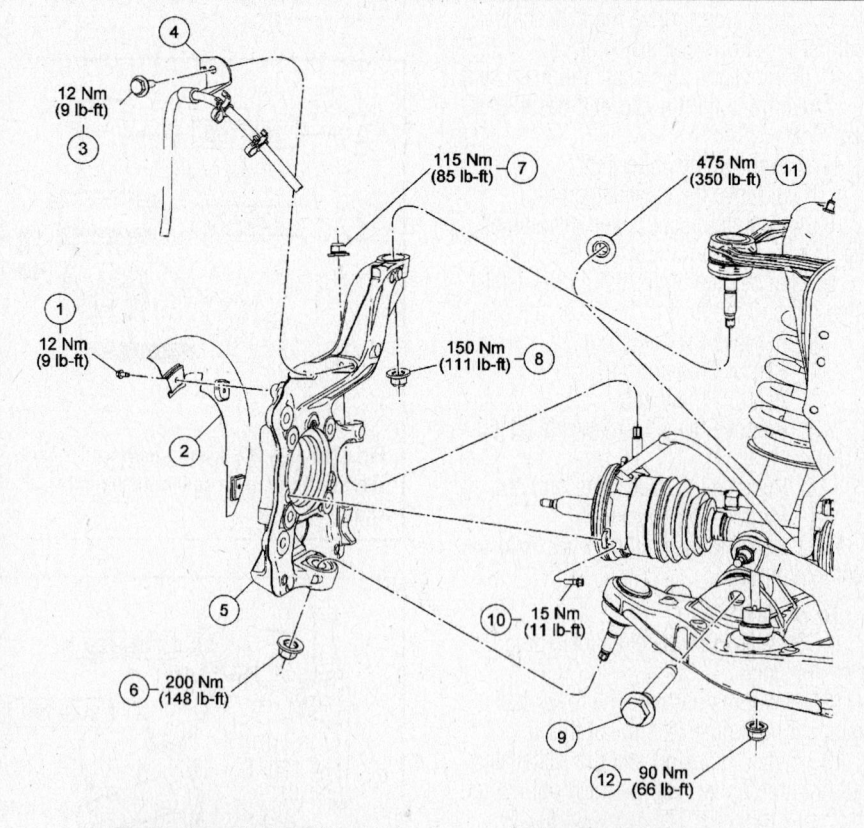

1. Brake disc shield bolt (3 required)
2. Brake disc shield
3. Brake hose bracket bolt
4. Brake hose bracket
5. Wheel knuckle
6. Lower ball joint nut
7. Tie-rod end nut
8. Upper ball joint nut
9. Shock absorber lower bolt
10. Integrated wheel end disconnect bolt (3 required)
11. Shock absorber lower nut
12. Stabilizer bar link lower nut

22086_EXPD_G0103

Fig. 341 2005–06 Wheel Knuckle and related parts

h. Tie rod end nut: 85 ft. lbs.
(115 Nm).
12. Check and, if necessary, align the
front end.

TRACK BAR

REMOVAL & INSTALLATION

Excursion

1. Before servicing the vehicle, refer to
the precautions section.

❋❋ CAUTION

**The electrical power to the air sus-
pension system must be shut off prior
to hoisting, jacking or towing an air
suspension vehicle. This can be
accomplished by turning off the air
suspension switch located in the
PASSENGER SIDE kick panel area.
Failure to do so can result in unexpected inflation or deflation of the air
springs, which can result in shifting
of the vehicle during these operations.**

2. Raise and support the vehicle.

❋ WARNING

**The air suspension height sensor has
a plastic harness retainer to suspension that must be unclipped prior to
removal.**

3. Remove or disconnect the following:
- Air suspension height sensor elec-
trical connector
- Metal retaining tabs and remove
the air suspension height sensor
from the ball studs
- Passenger side track bar bolt
- Driver's side track bar nut and bolt
- Track bar from the vehicle

To install:
4. To install, reverse the removal procedure and note the following:
a. Tighten the upper and lower track
bar bolts to 406 ft. lbs. (550 Nm).

UPPER BALL JOINT

REMOVAL & INSTALLATION

Expedition & Navigator

2005–06 Models

The upper ball joints on these models are
an integral part of the control arm. If found to
be defective the control arm must be
replaced. Refer to control arm removal and
installation.

2007 Models

The upper ball joints on these models are
an integral part of the control am. If found to
be defective the control arm must be replaced.
Refer to control arm removal and installation.

UPPER & LOWER BALL JOINTS

REMOVAL & INSTALLATION

Excursion

2WD Models

See Figures 342 and 343.

1. Before servicing the vehicle, refer to
the precautions in the beginning of this section.
2. Remove the wheel and tire assembly.
3. Remove the disc brake caliper and
the front disc brake hub and rotor.
4. Remove the wheel hub and bearing.
5. Using a drift, drive the axle shaft
main seal out of the wheel knuckle.
6. Remove the axle shaft and main seal.
7. Remove the tie-rod end castellated
nut. Discard the cotter pin.
8. Using the tool 211-003, disconnect
the tie-rod end from the wheel knuckle.
9. Remove the upper ball joint castellated nut and the insert.
10. Remove the wheel knuckle.
11. Position the front wheel spindle in a
vise, and remove the snapring from the
lower ball joint.

❋❋ WARNING

**To avoid damage to the components,
do not use heat to aid ball joint
removal.**

12. Using the removal/installation tool
205-086 and suitable receiver cup, remove
the lower ball joint from the front wheel
spindle.
13. Using the removal/installation tool
205-086 and suitable receiver cup, remove
the upper ball joint.

To install:

❋❋ WARNING

**To avoid damage to components, do
not use heat to aid installation.**

14. Clean the wheel knuckle ball joint
bores.

➡**The lower ball joint must be installed
first.**

15. Using the removal/installation tool
205-086 with suitable receiver cups, install
the lower ball joint.

16. Using the removal/installation tool
205-086 with suitable receiver cups, install
the upper ball joint.
17. Install the snapring in the groove at
the bottom of the ball joint.
18. Position the wheel knuckle onto the
axle housing.
19. Install the nut onto the lower ball
joint. Do not tighten the nut at this time.
20. Install the insert and the castellated
nut onto the upper ball joint. Do not tighten
the nut at this time.
21. Tighten the lower ball joint retaining
nut. Pre-tighten the nut to 35 ft. lbs (47 Nm)
on 2001–04 models or 47 ft. lbs (64 Nm)
on 2005 models.

➡**Do not loosen the castellated nut to
install the cotter pin.**

22. Install the cotter pin into the upper
ball joint.
23. Tighten the upper ball joint castellated nut to 69 ft. lbs. (94 Nm). Install the
cotter pin. If necessary, tighten the castellated nut until the cotter pin can be
installed.
24. Tighten the lower ball joint nut to
150 ft. lbs. (204 Nm).
25. Install the tie-rod end onto the wheel
knuckle.
26. Position the tie-rod end into the
wheel knuckle. Tighten the castellated nut to
52 ft. lbs. (70 Nm). Install a new cotter pin.
27. Position a new main seal onto the
axle shaft. Using the tools illustrated and a
hammer, seat the main seal onto the axle
shaft.
28. Position the axle shaft into the axle
housing. Using the tools illustrated and a
hammer, install the main seal into the wheel
knuckle.
29. Install the wheel hub and bearing.
30. Install the front brake disc.
31. Install the wheel and tire assembly.

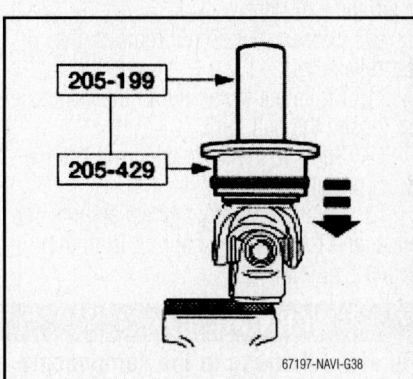

**Fig. 342 Using the tools shown and a
hammer, seat the main seal onto the axle
shaft—4WD Excursion**

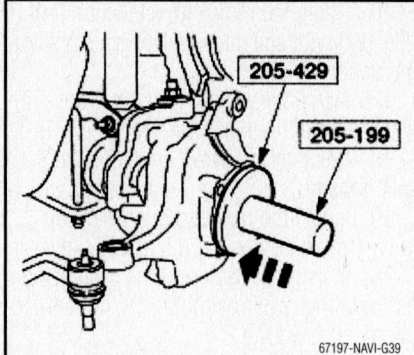

Fig. 343 Using the tools shown and a hammer, install the main seal into the wheel knuckle—4WD Excursion

67197-NAVI-G39

4WD Models

1. Before servicing the vehicle, refer to the precautions in the beginning of this section.

2. Remove the wheel and tire assembly.

3. Remove the disc brake caliper and the front disc brake hub and rotor.

4. Remove the front disc brake rotor shield.

5. Remove the ABS sensor retaining bolt, sensor harness retaining bolt and the sensor, if equipped and position out of the way.

6. Disconnect the tie rod end. Remove and discard the cotter pin.

7. Using a Pitman Arm Puller, remove the tie rod end.

8. Remove the pinch bolt and the camber adjuster.

✷ WARNING

To prevent damage to the ball joint seal and the ball joint socket, do not use a pickle fork-type remover to loosen the ball joints.

9. Remove and discard the cotter pin from the ball joint.

10. Loosen, but do not remove, the castellated nut.

11. Strike the lower end of the front axle to loosen the ball joint.

12. Remove the castellated nut and the front wheel spindle.

13. Position the front wheel spindle in a vise, and remove the snapring from the lower ball joint.

✷ WARNING

To avoid damage to the components, do not use heat to aid ball joint removal.

14. Using the removal/installation tool 205-086 and suitable receiver cup, remove the lower ball joint from the front wheel spindle.

15. Using the removal/installation tool 205-086 and suitable receiver cup, remove the upper ball joint.

To install:

✷ WARNING

To avoid damage to components, do not use heat to aid installation.

16. Clean the wheel knuckle ball joint bores.

➡ **The lower ball joint must be installed first.**

17. Using the removal/installation tool 205-086 with suitable receiver cups, install the lower ball joint.

18. Using the removal/installation tool 205-086 with suitable receiver cups, install the upper ball joint.

19. Install the snapring in the groove at the bottom of the ball joint.

20. Install the front wheel spindle. Tighten the nut to 99 ft. lbs. (133 Nm). Install a new cotter pin.

21. Install the camber adjuster and pinch bolt. Tighten to 60 ft. lbs. (80 Nm).

22. Connect the tie rod end. Tighten the nut to 67 ft. lbs (90 Nm). Install a new cotter pin.

23. Install the ABS sensor, if equipped.

24. Install the front disc brake rotor shield.

UPPER CONTROL ARM

REMOVAL & INSTALLATION

Expedition & Navigator

See Figures 344 and 345.

➡ **Before tightening any suspension bushing fasteners, use a suitable jack to raise the suspension until the distance between the center of the hub and the lip of the fender is equal to the measurement taken in Step 1 (curb height).**

1. Measure the distance from the center of the hub to the lip of the fender with the vehicle in a level, static ground position (curb height).

2. Before servicing the vehicle, refer to the precautions section.

✷ CAUTION

The electrical power to the air suspension system must be shut off prior to hoisting, jacking or towing an air suspension vehicle. This can be

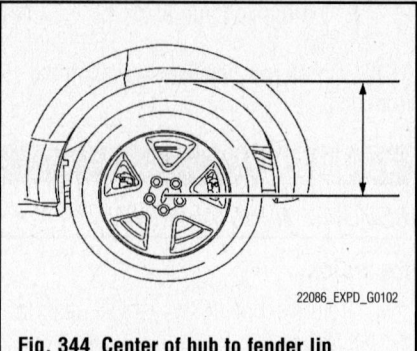

Fig. 344 Center of hub to fender lip measurement shown

22086_EXPD_G0102

accomplished by turning off the air suspension switch located in the LH rear quarter trim panel. Failure to do so can result in unexpected inflation or deflation of the air springs, which can result in shifting of the vehicle during these operations. Failure to follow these instructions may result in personal injury.

✷ WARNING

Suspension fasteners are critical parts because they affect performance of vital parts and systems and their failure can result in major service expense. A new part with the same part number must be installed if installation becomes necessary. Do not use a replacement part of lesser quality or substitute design. Torque values must be used as specified during reassembly to make sure of correct retention of these parts.

3. Raise and safely support the vehicle.

4. Remove the wheel and tire assembly.

5. Remove the shock absorber and spring assembly.

6. On models with an air suspension, detach the height sensor from the upper arm.

➡ **Use the hex holding feature to prevent the stud from turning while removing the nut.**

7. Remove and discard the upper ball joint nut.

8. Using the special tool 204-592, separate the upper ball joint from the wheel knuckle.

9. Remove the rearward upper arm-to-frame nut and bolt. Discard the nut.

10. Remove the forward upper arm-to-frame nut, bolt and the upper arm. Discard the nut.

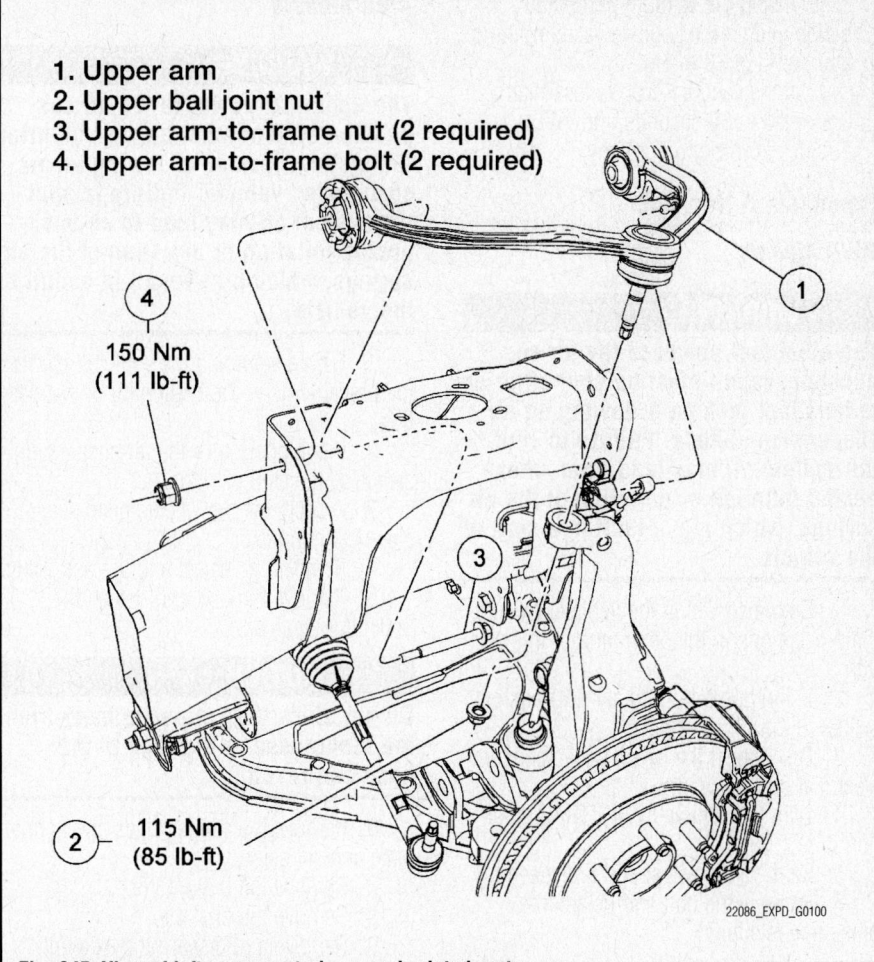

1. Upper arm
2. Upper ball joint nut
3. Upper arm-to-frame nut (2 required)
4. Upper arm-to-frame bolt (2 required)

④ 150 Nm (111 lb-ft)

② 115 Nm (85 lb-ft)

22086_EXPD_G0100

Fig. 345 View of left upper control arm and related parts

To install:

11. To install, reverse the removal procedure and note the following:

a. Tighten the control arm nuts/bolts to 111 ft. lbs. (150 Nm).

b. Tighten the upper control arm nut to 85 ft. lbs. (115 Nm).

c. Check and, if necessary, align the front end.

WHEEL BEARINGS

REMOVAL & INSTALLATION

Excursion

2WD Models

1. Before servicing the vehicle, refer to the precautions in the beginning of this section.

2. Remove the front wheel and tire assemblies.

3. Remove the front disc brake caliper and rotor, and position the caliper out of the way.

4. Remove the hub cap from the hub assembly.

5. Remove the cotter pin, adjusting nut and flat washer.

→**Inspect the condition of the spindle and nut threads to ensure a free turning nut when reassembling.**

6. Remove the outer bearing cone and roller assembly, and pull the hub assembly from the spindle.

7. Using care not to damage the bearing cage, use a suitable slide hammer and bearing seal remover to remove the inner bearing cone and bearing seal.

To install:

⁜⁜ CAUTION

Do not spin the bearing dry with compressed air.

→ **Remove all traces of lubricant from the bearings, hub and axle spindle. Inspect bearings and bearing cups for pitting or unusual wear. If either bearings or bearing cups are worn or damaged, replace both bearings and bearing cups.**

→**It is recommended that bearings and bearing cups be replaced in sets. If cups are worn or damaged, install the inner and outer bearing cups in the hub with an appropriate bearing cup driver tool. Check for proper seating of new bearing cups by trying to insert a 0.0015 inch (0.38-mm) feeler gauge between the bottom face of the cup and wheel hub seat. You should not be able to insert the feeler gauge.**

8. Remove all burrs, nicks or scratches from the shoulder of the spindle and seal bore in the hub with emery cloth.

9. Pack the inside of the hub with lithium-base wheel bearing grease. Fill the hub until the grease is flush with the inside diameters of both bearing cups.

10. Pack the bearing cone and roller assemblies with wheel bearing grease. Use a bearing packer for this operation. If a packer is not available, work as much lubricant as possible between the rollers and cages.

⁜⁜ CAUTION

Keep the hub centered on the spindle to prevent damage to the grease seal or spindle threads.

11. Place the inner bearing cone and roller assembly in the inner cup and install the wheel bearing hub seal, using a suitable seal replacer. Make sure seal is fully seated and lubricated.

12. Install the hub assembly.

13. Install the outer bearing cone and roller assembly and the flat washer on the spindle and install the adjusting nut. Install a new cotter pin.

14. Install the hub cap.

15. Install the front disc brake caliper and rotor.

16. Install the front wheel and tire assemblies.

4WD Models

1. Before servicing the vehicle, refer to the precautions section.

2. Remove or disconnect the following:
- Front brake rotor
- Hub lock by pulling out the retainer ring. And then the hub lock
- Snapring and the axle shaft thrust washers
- ABS wheel sensor harness and routing clips, if equipped

→**The wheel hub and bearing is a slip fit design and should not require a puller to remove it.**

- Four lock nuts
- Wheel hub and bearing
- Brake rotor shield
- Bolt and the Anti-lock Brake System (ABS) sensor, if equipped

3. Place the hub in a soft-jawed vise.

4. Install two nuts on the studs and use the inner nut to remove the studs.

5. Remove and discard the O-ring.

To install:

→**Any time the wheel hub is removed for any reason, a new O-ring seal must be installed. Failure to do so can cause a vacuum leak and loss of four wheel drive operations.**

6. Install a new O-ring.

7. Place the hub in a soft-jawed vise.

8. Install two nuts on the studs and use the outer nut to install the studs.

9. Install or connect the following:
- ABS sensor and the bolt. Tighten the bolt to 13 ft. lbs. (18 Nm).
- Brake rotor shield.

10. Apply a coat of High Temperature 4WD Front Axle and Wheel Bearing Grease E8TZ-19590-A to the O-ring area of the wheel hub and bearing before installing the hub and bearing.
- Wheel hub and bearing
- Four lock nuts and tighten to 133 ft. lbs. (180 Nm)
- ABS sensor harness and routing clips, if equipped

✳✳ WARNING

The non-metallic thrust washer must be installed between the two metal thrust washers. Failure to do so will cause severe wear to the non-metallic thrust washer, allowing the axle shaft to travel further in and out during torque thrust causing damage to the wheel hub and bearing, the axle shaft end seal and the axle shaft.

- Three thrust washers onto the axle shaft
- Snapring

→**Any time the hub lock is removed, a new O-ring seal must be installed. Failure to do so can cause a vacuum leak and loss of four wheel drive functions.**

- New O-ring seal
- Hub lock and the retainer ring
- Brake rotor

11. Perform a wheel-end vacuum leak test as follows:

a. Install the vacuum pump and gauge line on the knuckle vacuum fitting and pump to 20 in-Hg.

b. If the vacuum drop is less than 0.5 in-Hg in 30 seconds, the 4WD hublock is working correctly.

Expedition & Navigator

2WD Models

✳✳ WARNING

The electrical power to the air suspension system must be shut off prior to hoisting, jacking or towing an air suspension vehicle. Failure to shut the system off may lead to an unexpected inflation or deflation of the air springs, which may result in a shift of the vehicle.

1. Before servicing the vehicle, refer to the precautions in the beginning of this section.

2. If equipped, turn the air suspension switch to the OFF position.

3. Disconnect the wheel speed sensor electrical connector.

4. With the vehicle in NEUTRAL, position it on a hoist.

5. Remove the wheel and tire assembly.

6. Remove the bolt and detach the brake line retainers.

✳✳ CAUTION

Do not allow the caliper to hang from the brake hose or damage to the hose can result.

7. Remove the caliper, pads and anchor plate and set aside.

8. Remove the brake rotor.

9. Remove the bolts and the wheel bearing and hub assembly.

10. If installing a new wheel bearing and wheel hub, remove the wheel speed sensor bolt and the wheel speed sensor.

To install:

→**If the original wheel bearing and hub is being reinstalled, make sure to install a new O-ring.**

11. To install, reverse the removal procedure and note the following:

a. Wheel bearing/hub assembly bolts: 111 ft. lbs. (150 Nm).

b. Brake anchor plate: 148 ft. lbs. (200 Nm).

c. Speed sensor bolt: 13 ft. lbs. (18 Nm).

d. Retainer bracket bolts: 9 ft. lbs. (12 Nm).

4WD Models

✳✳ WARNING

The electrical power to the air suspension system must be shut off prior to hoisting, jacking or towing an air suspension vehicle. Failure to shut the system off may lead to an unexpected inflation or deflation of the air springs, which may result in a shift of the vehicle.

1. Before servicing the vehicle, refer to the precautions in the beginning of this section.

2. If equipped, turn the air suspension switch to the OFF position.

3. Disconnect the wheel speed sensor electrical connector.

4. Remove the wheel and tire assembly.

5. Remove the bolt and detach the brake line retainers.

✳✳ CAUTION

Do not allow the caliper to hang from the brake hose or damage to the hose can result.

6. Remove the caliper, pads and anchor plate and set aside.

7. Remove the brake rotor.

8. Remove the dust cap.

9. Remove and discard the axle nut.

10. Remove the bolts and the wheel bearing and hub assembly.

To install:

✳✳ CAUTION

If the original wheel bearing and hub is being reinstalled, make sure to install a new O-ring.

11. To install, reverse the removal procedure and note the following:

a. Wheel bearing/hub assembly bolts: 148 ft. lbs. (200 Nm).

b. Axle nut: 20 ft. lbs. (27 Nm).

c. Brake anchor plate: 148 ft. lbs. (200 Nm).

ADJUSTMENT

2005 Excursion—2WD Models Only

✳✳ WARNING

If bearings are adjusted too tightly, they will overheat and wear rapidly. An adjustment that is excessively loose can cause pounding and contribute to uneven tire wear, steering difficulties and inefficient brakes. Check bearing adjustment at regular

inspection intervals. New wheel seals must be installed when the hub is removed. A damaged or worn seal can permit bearing lubricant to reach the brake linings, resulting in ineffective brake operation and necessitating premature replacement of linings. To check the wheel bearing adjustment, raise the front of the vehicle. Grasp the tire at the sides, and alternately push inward and pull outward on the tire. If any looseness is felt, adjust the front wheel bearings as follows.

1. Remove the hub cap from the hub.
2. Remove the cotter pin and the castellated nut.
3. While rotating the wheel, tighten the adjusting nut to specification as illustrated to seat the bearings.
4. Back off the adjusting nut until loose.
5. While rotating the wheel, tighten the adjusting nut to 18 inch. lbs. (2 Nm).
6. Install the castellated nut and insert a new cotter pin.
7. Install the hub cap.

REPACKING

2005 Excursion—4WD Models Only

Pack the inside of the hub with lithium-base wheel bearing grease such as Motorcraft Premium Long-Life Grease XG-1-C or -K or equivalent meeting Ford specifications. Fill the hub until the grease is flush with the inside diameters of both bearing cups.

Pack the bearing cone and roller assemblies with wheel bearing grease. Use a bearing packer for this operation. If a packer is not available, work as much lubricant as possible between the rollers and cages.

SUSPENSION

COIL SPRING

REMOVAL & INSTALLATION

Expedition & Navigator

2005–06 Models

See Figure 346.

1. Before servicing the vehicle, refer to the precautions section.

> ❋❋ **WARNING**
>
> The electrical power to the air suspension system must be shut off prior to hoisting, jacking or towing an air suspension vehicle. This can be accomplished by turning off the air suspension switch located in the left rear quarter trim panel. Failure to do so can result in unexpected inflation

or deflation of the air springs, which can result in shifting of the vehicle during these operations.

2. If equipped, turn the air suspension switch to the OFF position.
3. Remove the wheel and tire assembly.
4. Remove and discard the upper shock absorber nuts.
5. Remove the nut, bolt and shock absorber/spring assembly. Discard the nut.
6. For reference during assembly, index the upper mount, spring and shock absorber.
7. Using a suitable spring compressor, compress the spring until the tension is released from the shock absorber.
8. While holding the shock rod, remove the nut and washer.

REAR SUSPENSION

9. Remove the shock absorber. Discard the nut.
10. Remove the upper mount, dust shield and insulator.
11. To install, reverse the removal procedure and note the following:
   a. Tighten the shock rod nut to 22 ft. lbs. (30 Nm).
   b. Tighten the shock absorber nut and bolt to 350 ft. lbs. (475 Nm).
   c. Tighten the new upper shock absorber nuts to 30 ft. lbs. (40 Nm).

2007 Models

See Figure 347.

> ❋❋ **WARNING**
>
> Do not tighten the lower arm-to-frame bolt or shock absorber lower nut until the installation procedure is complete and the weight of the vehicle is resting on the wheel and tire assemblies.

> ❋❋ **WARNING**
>
> Suspension fasteners are critical parts because they affect performance of vital parts and systems and their failure can result in major service expense. A new part with the same part number must be installed if installation becomes necessary. Do not use a replacement part of lesser quality or substitute design. Torque values must be used as specified during reassembly to make sure of correct retention of these parts.

1. Before servicing the vehicle, refer to the precautions section.
2. With the vehicle in NEUTRAL, position it on a hoist.

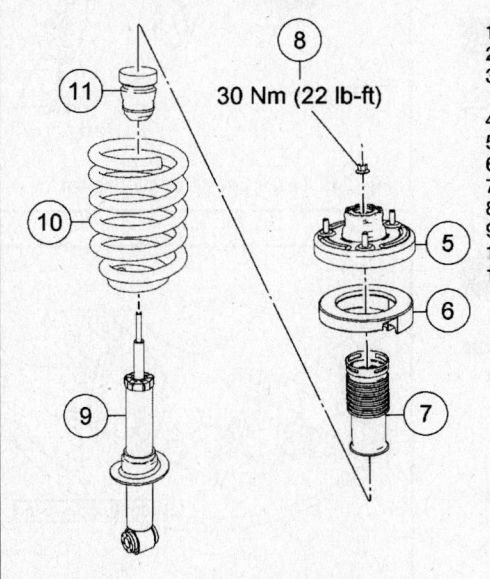

30 Nm (22 lb-ft)

1. Shock absorber and spring assembly
2. Shock absorber lower nut
3. Shock and spring assembly upper nut (3 required)
4. Shock absorber lower bolt
5. Upper mount
6. Insulator
7. Dust boot
8. Shock rod nut
9. Shock absorber
10. Spring
11. Jounce bumper

22086_EXPD_G0104

Fig. 346 Rear coil spring and related shock parts

3. If equipped, disconnect the air suspension height sensor connecting link from the lower arm.

4. Remove and discard the shock absorber lower bolt and flagnut.

5. Remove and discard the lower arm-to-frame bolt and flagnut.

6. Remove and discard the lower ball joint nut.

✳✳ WARNING

Do not damage the ball joint boot while installing the special tool.

7. Using the special tool 204-592, separate the lower ball joint from the wheel knuckle.

8. Swing the lower arm to the rear of the vehicle and remove the lower arm.

9. Remove and discard the upper mount nuts.

10. Remove the shock absorber and spring assembly.

➡**For reference during assembly, index the upper mount, spring and shock absorber.**

11. Using a suitable spring compressor, compress the spring until the tension is released from the shock absorber.

12. While holding the shock rod, remove the nut and washer.

13. Remove the shock absorber and discard the nut.

14. Remove the upper mount, dust boot and insulator.

15. To install, reverse the removal procedure and note the following:

   a. Tighten the new upper mount nuts to 30 ft. lbs. (40 Nm).

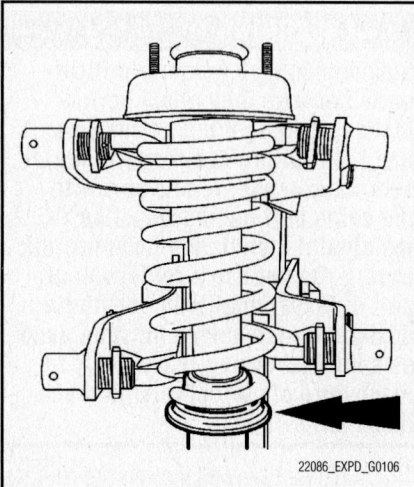

Fig. 347 Shock assembly view showing spring compression

   b. Tighten the new shock absorber lower bolt and nut to 350 ft. lbs. (475 Nm).

   c. Tighten the new lower ball joint nut to 111 ft. lbs. (150 Nm).

   d. Tighten the new lower arm-to-frame bolt to 221 ft. lbs. (300 Nm).

   e. Tighten the new shock rod nut to 41 ft. lbs. (56 Nm).

LEAF SPRING

REMOVAL & INSTALLATION

Excursion

1. Before servicing the vehicle, refer to the precautions section.

2. With the vehicle in NEUTRAL, position it on a hoist.

3. Remove the wheel and tire assembly.

4. Support the rear axle with a suitable jack.

5. Remove the U-bolt retaining nuts and remove the U-bolts.

6. Remove the rear spring upper plate.

7. Remove the nut and bolt from the rear spring front hanger bracket.

8. Remove the lower nut and bolt from the rear spring shackle bracket. Remove the rear spring assembly.

9. Remove the nut and bolt from the rear spring shackle assembly and remove the rear spring shackle.

10. To install, reverse the removal procedure and note the following:

   a. Tighten the new rear spring shackle bolts and nuts to 185 ft. lbs. (250 Nm).

   b. Tighten the new U-bolts and retaining nuts to 148 ft. lbs. (200 Nm).

LOWER CONTROL ARM

REMOVAL & INSTALLATION

Expedition & Navigator

2005–06 Models

See Figures 348 through 350.

✳✳ CAUTION

The electrical power to the air suspension system must be shut off prior to hoisting, jacking or towing an air suspension vehicle. This can be accomplished by turning off the air suspension switch located in the LH rear quarter trim panel. Failure to do so can result in unexpected inflation or deflation of the air springs, which can result in shifting of the vehicle during these operations.

1. If equipped, turn the air suspension switch to the OFF position.

2. Remove the wheel and tire assembly.

➡**Use the hex holding feature to prevent the stud from turning while removing the nut.**

3. Remove and discard the stabilizer bar link nut.

4. Remove the shock absorber-to-lower arm bolt and flag nut. Discard the flag nut.

5. Remove the lower arm-to-frame flag nuts and bolts. Discard the nut.

6. Remove the lower arm-to-knuckle bolt, flag nut and the lower arm. Discard the flag nut.

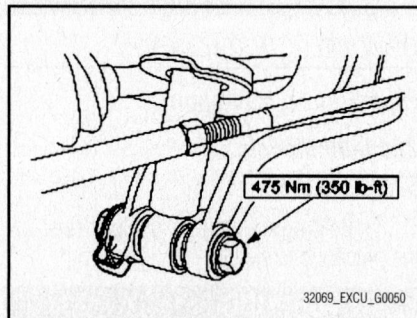

Fig. 348 View of the shock absorber-to-lower arm bolt and flag nut

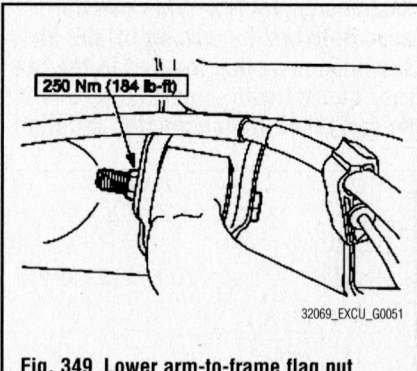

Fig. 349 Lower arm-to-frame flag nut

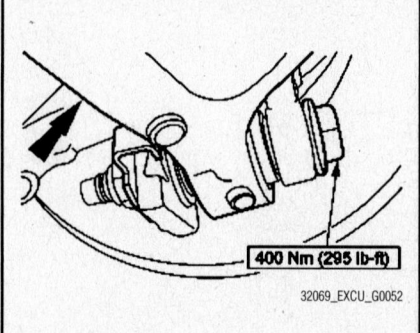

Fig. 350 Lower arm-to-knuckle bolt

7. If necessary, using a suitable press and adapters, remove the lower ball joint.

To install:

➥**Snug the lower arm-to-frame pivot nuts and bolts. Do not tighten to specification until installation procedure is complete and the vehicle is at curb ride height.**

8. Installation is the reverse of the removal procedure. Please note the following torque specifications:

    a. Lower arm-to-knuckle bolt and flag nut: 295 ft. lbs. (400 Nm)

    b. Lower arm-to-frame flag nuts and bolts: 184 ft. lbs. (250 Nm)

    c. Shock absorber-to-lower arm bolt and flag nut: 350 ft. lbs. (475 Nm)

    d. Stabilizer bar link nut: 66 ft. lbs. (90 Nm)

9. Check and, if necessary, adjust the rear alignment.

2007 Models

See Figures 351 and 352.

❋❋ WARNING

Suspension fasteners are critical parts because they affect performance of vital parts and systems and their failure can result in major service expense. A new part with the same part number must be installed if installation becomes necessary. Do not use a replacement part of lesser quality or substitute design. Torque values must be used as specified during reassembly to make sure of correct retention of these parts. Orientation of the suspension fasteners is important. Make sure the fasteners are installed in the same direction as they were in when removed.

1. Before servicing the vehicle, refer to the precautions section.

2. With the vehicle in NEUTRAL, position it on a hoist.

3. If equipped, disconnect the air suspension height sensor connecting link from the lower arm.

4. Remove and discard the shock absorber lower bolt and flagnut.

5. Remove and discard the lower arm-to-frame bolt and flagnut.

6. Remove and discard the lower ball joint nut.

❋❋ WARNING

Do not damage the ball joint boot while installing the special tool.

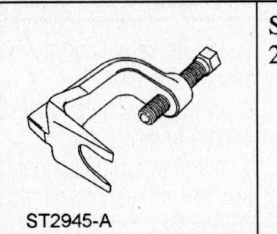

Special Tool(s)

ST2945-A	Separator, Ball Joint 204-592

22086_EXPD_G0108

Fig. 351 Ball joint separator tool

7. Using the special tool, separate the lower ball joint from the wheel knuckle.

8. Swing the lower arm to the rear of the vehicle and remove the lower arm.

To install:

9. Position the lower arm ball joint onto the wheel knuckle and install the lower ball joint nut, tighten the new nut to 111 ft. lbs. (150 Nm).

➥**Do not tighten the lower arm-to-frame bolt at this time.**

10. Install the lower arm-to-frame bolt and flagnut, tighten to 37 ft. lbs. (50 Nm).

➥**Do not tighten the shock absorber lower nut at this time.**

11. Position the lower arm and install a new shock absorber lower bolt and nut.

12. Lower the vehicle so that the weight of the vehicle is on the wheel and tire assemblies.

13. Tighten the lower arm-to-frame bolt to 221 ft. lbs. (300 Nm).

14. Tighten the shock absorber lower bolt to 350 ft. lbs. (475 Nm).

15. If equipped, connect the air suspension height sensor connecting link to the lower arm.

16. Check and, if necessary, align the rear end.

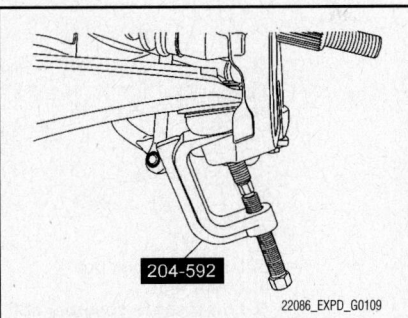

204-592

22086_EXPD_G0109

Fig. 352 Ball joint removal with separator tool

SHOCK ABSORBER

REMOVAL & INSTALLATION

Excursion

1. Before servicing the vehicle, refer to the precautions section.

❋❋ CAUTION

Suspension fasteners are critical parts because they affect performance of vital components and systems and their failure can result in major service expense. Install new parts with the same part number or an equivalent part if installation is necessary. Do not use an installation part of lesser quality or substitute design. Torque values must be used as specified during reassembly to make sure of correct retention of these parts.

❋❋ CAUTION

The low pressure gas shock absorbers are charged with nitrogen gas. Do not attempt to open, puncture or apply heat to shock absorbers.

2. Using a suitable jack, support the rear axle.

3. Remove the shock absorber lower retaining nut and bolt. Tighten to 66 ft. lbs. (90 Nm).

4. Remove the two shock absorber-to-frame mounting bolts. Tighten to 17 ft. lbs. (23 Nm).

To install:

5. Installation is the reverse of removal, please note the following torque specifications:

    a. Tighten the two shock absorber-to-frame mounting bolts to 17 ft. lbs. (23 Nm).

b. Tighten the shock absorber lower retaining nut and bolt to 66 ft. lbs. (90 Nm).

Expedition & Navigator

2005–06 Models

1. Before servicing the vehicle, refer to the precautions section.

> ❋❋ **WARNING**
>
> **The electrical power to the air suspension system must be shut off prior to hoisting, jacking or towing an air suspension vehicle. This can be accomplished by turning off the air suspension switch located in the left rear quarter trim panel. Failure to do so can result in unexpected inflation or deflation of the air springs, which can result in shifting of the vehicle during these operations.**

2. If equipped, turn the air suspension switch to the OFF position.
3. Remove the wheel assembly.
4. Remove and discard the upper nuts.
5. Remove the lower bolt and flag nut. Discard the flag nut.
6. Remove the shock absorber and spring assembly.

To install:

7. Installation is the reverse of removal, please note the following torque specifications:

   a. New lower bolt and flag nut and tighten to 475 Nm (350 ft. lbs.).
   b. New upper shock nuts and tighten to 30 ft. lbs. (40 Nm).

2007 Models

See Figure 353.

> ❋❋ **WARNING**
>
> **Do not tighten the lower arm-to-frame bolt or shock absorber lower nut until the installation procedure is complete and the weight of the vehicle is resting on the wheel and tire assemblies.**

> ❋❋ **WARNING**
>
> **Suspension fasteners are critical parts because they affect performance of vital parts and systems and their failure can result in major service expense. A new part with the same part number must be installed if installation becomes necessary. Do not use a replacement part of lesser quality or substitute design. Torque**

values must be used as specified during reassembly to make sure of correct retention of these parts.

1. Before servicing the vehicle, refer to the precautions section.
2. With the vehicle in NEUTRAL, position it on a hoist.
3. If equipped, disconnect the air suspension height sensor connecting link from the lower arm.
4. Remove and discard the shock absorber lower bolt and flagnut.
5. Remove and discard the lower arm-to-frame bolt and flagnut.
6. Remove and discard the lower ball joint nut.

> ❋❋ **WARNING**
>
> **Do not damage the ball joint boot while installing the special tool.**

7. Using the special tool 204-592, separate the lower ball joint from the wheel knuckle.
8. Swing the lower arm to the rear of the vehicle and remove the lower arm.
9. Remove and discard the upper mount nuts.
10. Remove the shock absorber and spring assembly.
11. To install, reverse the removal procedure and note the following:

    a. Tighten the new upper mount nuts to 30 ft. lbs. (40 Nm).
    b. Tighten the shock absorber lower bolt to 350 ft. lbs. (475 Nm).

c. Tighten the lower ball joint nut to 111 ft. lbs. (150 Nm).
d. Tighten the lower arm-to-frame bolt to 221 ft. lbs. (300 Nm).

TESTING

1. Road test the vehicle.
2. On a smooth road see if any vibrations are present.
3. Use your hands in order to lift up and push down each corner of the vehicle 3 times.
4. Remove your hands from the vehicle.
5. Replace any shock that exceeds more than two bounces.
6. Raise vehicle for inspection.
7. Inspect each shock absorber for external fluid leakage.
8. Inspect for deformation or damage.
9. Inspect bushings for wear or damage.
10. Replace as necessary.

TOE LINK

REMOVAL & INSTALLATION

Expedition & Navigator

2005–06 Models

See Figures 354 and 355.

> ❋❋ **CAUTION**
>
> **The electrical power to the air suspension system must be shut off prior to hoisting, jacking or towing an air**

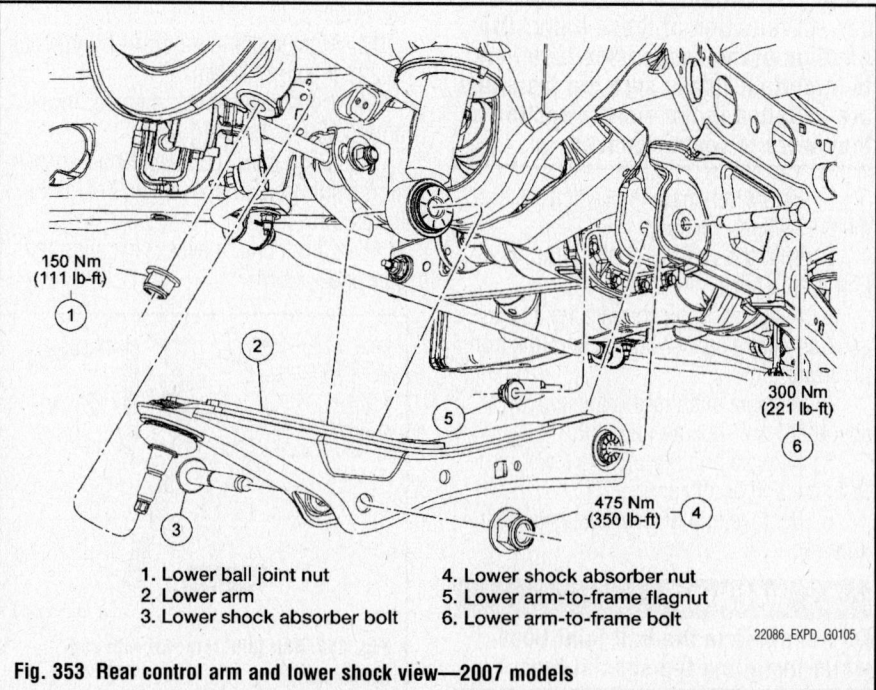

1. Lower ball joint nut
2. Lower arm
3. Lower shock absorber bolt
4. Lower shock absorber nut
5. Lower arm-to-frame flagnut
6. Lower arm-to-frame bolt

22086_EXPD_G0105

Fig. 353 Rear control arm and lower shock view—2007 models

suspension vehicle. This can be accomplished by turning off the air suspension switch located in the LH rear quarter trim panel. Failure to do so can result in unexpected inflation or deflation of the air springs, which can result in shifting of the vehicle during these operations.

1. If equipped, turn the air suspension switch to the OFF position.
2. Remove the wheel and tire assembly.

➡**Use the hex holding feature to prevent the stud from turning while removing the nut.**

3. Remove the nut and separate the toe link from the wheel knuckle.
4. Remove the nut and the toe link.

To install:

5. Install the toe link and tighten the nut to 66 ft. lbs. (90 Nm).
6. Install the toe link to the steering knuckle and tighten the nut to 41 ft. lbs. (55 Nm).
7. Install the wheel and tire assembly.
8. If equipped, turn the air suspension to the ON position.
9. Check and, if necessary, adjust the rear toe.

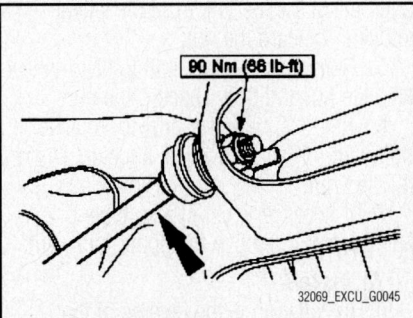

Fig. 354 Remove the nut and separate the toe link from the knuckle

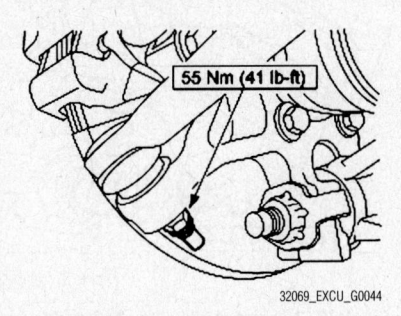

Fig. 355 View of the toe link nut and tightening specification

2007 Models

⁜ **WARNING**

Do not tighten the toe link-to-frame cam bolt or toe link-to-wheel knuckle bolt until the installation procedure is complete and the weight of the vehicle is resting on the wheel and tire assemblies.

1. Before servicing the vehicle, refer to the precautions section.
2. With the vehicle in NEUTRAL, position it on a hoist.
3. Index-mark the cam bolt and cam washer positions.
4. Remove and discard the bolt and washer.
5. Remove the toe link-to-frame cam bolt, cam washer and nut.
6. Remove the toe link.

➡**Using the index marks, transfer the marks onto the new cam bolt and cam washer. Use these index marks when installing the toe link.**

7. To install, reverse the removal procedure and note the following:
    a. Tighten the cam bolt to 166 ft. lbs. (225 Nm).
    b. Tighten the toe link-to-frame cam bolt to 203 ft. lbs. (275 Nm).
    c. Check and, if necessary, adjust the rear toe.

UPPER CONTROL ARM

REMOVAL & INSTALLATION

Expedition & Navigator

2005–06 Models
See Figures 356 through 358.

⁜ **WARNING**

The electrical power to the air suspension system must be shut off prior to hoisting, jacking or towing an air suspension vehicle. This can be accomplished by turning off the air suspension switch located in the LH rear quarter trim panel. Failure to do so can result in unexpected inflation or deflation of the air springs, which can result in shifting of the vehicle during these operations.

1. Before servicing the vehicle, refer to the precautions section.
2. If equipped, turn the air suspension switch to the OFF position.

3. Remove the wheel and tire assembly.
4. Remove the upper ball joint-to-knuckle nut and bolt. Discard the nut.
5. Remove the forward upper arm-to-frame nut and bolt and discard the nut.
6. Remove the upper arm-to-frame nut, bolt and the upper arm. Discard the nut.

To install:

7. Installation is the reverse of the removal procedure. Please note the following tightening specifications:
    a. Upper arm-to-frame bolt and nut: 184 ft. lbs. (250 Nm)
    b. Forward upper arm-to-frame bolt and nut: 111 ft. lbs. (150 Nm)

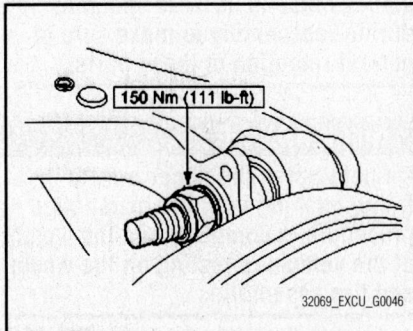

Fig. 356 Remove the upper ball joint-to-knuckle nut and bolt, then discard the nut

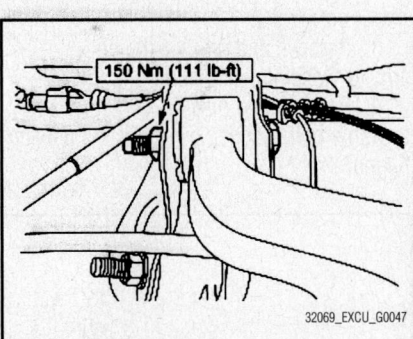

Fig. 357 Remove the forward upper arm-to-frame nut and bolt and discard the nut

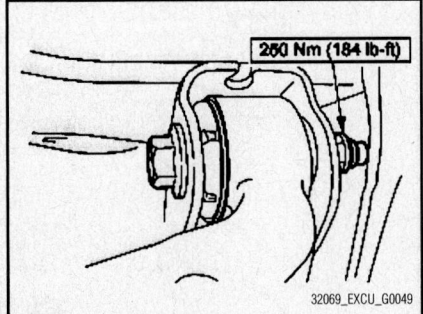

Fig. 358 Remove the nut, bolt and the upper arm. Discard the nut

c. Upper ball joint-to-knuckle bolt and nut: 111 ft. lbs. (150 Nm)

8. Check and, if necessary, adjust the rear alignment.

2007 Models

See Figure 359.

> **⁂ WARNING**
>
> Suspension fasteners are critical parts because they affect performance of vital parts and systems and their failure can result in major service expense. A new part with the same part number must be installed if installation becomes necessary. Do not use a replacement part of lesser quality or substitute design. Torque values must be used as specified during reassembly to make sure of correct retention of these parts.

> **⁂ WARNING**
>
> Do not tighten the upper arm-to-frame bushing until the installation procedure is complete and the weight of the vehicle is resting on the wheel and tire assemblies.

1. Before servicing the vehicle, refer to the precautions section.

2. With the vehicle in NEUTRAL, position it on a hoist.

3. Remove and discard the upper arm-to-wheel knuckle nut.

4. Remove and discard the upper arm-to-frame bolt, washer, camber set shim and flagnut.

5. Remove the upper arm.

6. To install, reverse the removal procedure and note the following:

a. Tighten the upper arm-to-frame bolt to 221 ft. lbs. (300 Nm).

b. Tighten the upper arm-to-wheel knuckle nut to 76 ft. lbs. (103 Nm).

WHEEL KNUCKLE

REMOVAL & INSTALLATION

Expedition & Navigator

2005–06 Models

See Figures 360 through 363.

> **⁂ CAUTION**
>
> The electrical power to the air suspension system must be shut off prior to hoisting, jacking or towing an air suspension vehicle. This can be accomplished by turning off the air suspension switch located in the LH rear quarter trim panel. Failure to do so can result in unexpected inflation or deflation of the air springs, which can result in shifting of the vehicle during these operations.

1. Remove the wheel bearing, as outlined in this section.

2. Remove the springs, adjuster and the parking brake shoes.

3. Depress the tabs and detach the parking brake cable from the wheel knuckle.

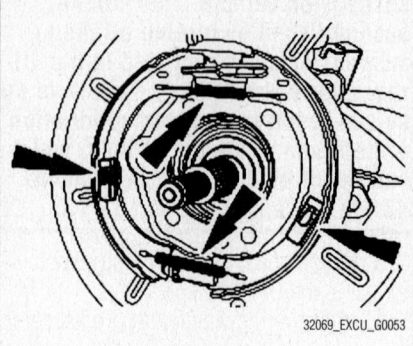

Fig. 360 Remove the springs, adjuster and the parking brake shoes

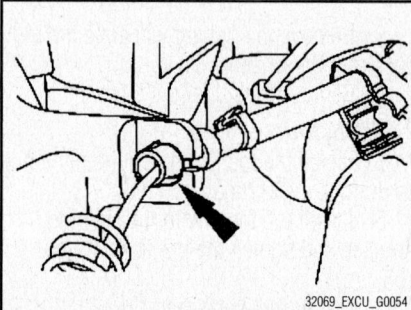

Fig. 361 Depress the tabs and detach the parking brake cable from the wheel knuckle

4. Remove the toe link-to-knuckle nut and detach the toe link from the wheel knuckle. Discard the nut.

5. Remove the upper ball joint-to-wheel knuckle nut and bolt. Discard the nut.

6. Remove the lower arm-to-knuckle bolt, flag nut and the wheel knuckle. Discard the flag nut.

7. If necessary, using a suitable press and adapters, remove the upper ball joint.

To install:

8. Installation is the reverse of the removal procedure. Please note the following tightening specifications:

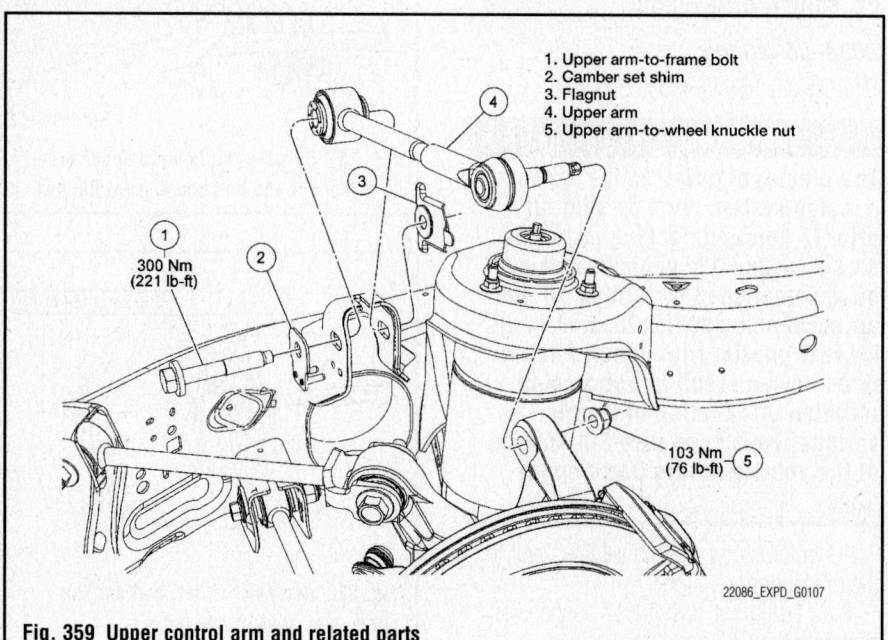

1. Upper arm-to-frame bolt
2. Camber set shim
3. Flagnut
4. Upper arm
5. Upper arm-to-wheel knuckle nut

300 Nm (221 lb-ft)

103 Nm (76 lb-ft)

22086_EXPD_G0107

Fig. 359 Upper control arm and related parts

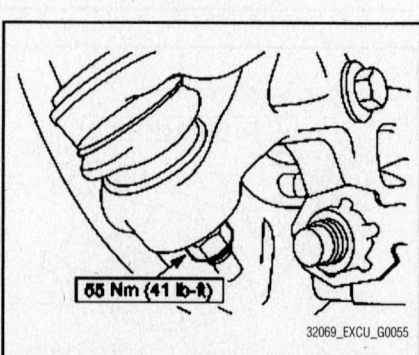

55 Nm (41 lb-ft)

32069_EXCU_G0055

Fig. 362 Remove the toe link-to-knuckle nut and detach the toe link from the wheel knuckle

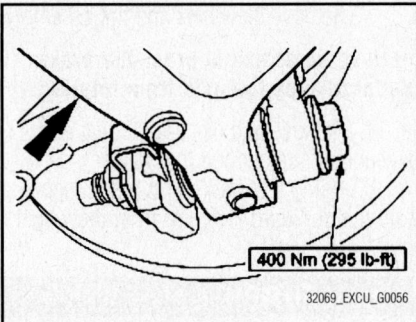

Fig. 363 Remove the lower arm-to-knuckle bolt, flag nut and the wheel knuckle

a. Lower arm-to-knuckle bolt and flag nut: 295 ft. lbs. (400 Nm)

b. Upper ball joint-to-wheel knuckle nut and bolt: 111 ft. lbs. (150 Nm)

c. Toe link-to-knuckle nut: 41 ft. lbs. (55 Nm)

9. Check and, if necessary, adjust the rear alignment.

2007 Models

✳✳ WARNING

Suspension fasteners are critical parts because they affect performance of vital parts and systems and their failure can result in major service expense. A new part with the same part number must be installed if installation becomes necessary. Do not use a replacement part of lesser quality or substitute design. Torque values must be used as specified during reassembly to make sure of correct retention of these parts.

1. Before servicing the vehicle, refer to the precautions section.

2. Remove the wheel bearing and wheel hub assembly.

3. Remove the parking brake shoes.

4. Remove the brake disc shield.

5. Compress the spring and depress the retaining tabs and detach the parking brake cable from the wheel knuckle.

6. Remove and discard the upper arm-to-wheel knuckle nut.

7. Using the special tool, separate the upper arm from the wheel knuckle.

8. Remove and discard the lower ball joint nut.

9. Using the special tool 204-592, separate the lower ball joint from the wheel knuckle.

10. Remove and discard the 2 bolts and disconnect the lower trailing arm from the wheel knuckle.

11. Remove and discard the bolt and disconnect the toe link from the wheel knuckle.

➡**Use the hex holding feature to prevent the stud from turning while removing the nut.**

12. Remove the upper trailing arm-to-wheel knuckle bolt and the wheel knuckle. Discard the bolt.

✳✳ WARNING

Do not tighten the upper arm-to-wheel knuckle bolt or the toe link-to-wheel knuckle bolt until the installation procedure is complete and the weight of the vehicle is resting on the wheel and tire assemblies.

To install:

13. To install, reverse the removal procedure and note the following:

a. Tighten upper arm-to-wheel knuckle nut to 76 ft. lbs. (103 Nm).

b. Tighten the lower ball joint nut to 111 ft. lbs. (150 Nm).

c. Tighten the lower trailing arm from the wheel knuckle bolts to 76 ft. lbs. (103 Nm).

d. Tighten the toe link-to-wheel knuckle bolt to 166 ft. lbs. (225 Nm).

e. Tighten the stabilizer bar link nut to 46 ft. lbs. (63 Nm).

f. Tighten the upper trailing arm-to-wheel knuckle bolt to 184 ft. lbs. (250 Nm).

14. Check and, if necessary, adjust the rear alignment.

WHEEL KNUCKLE BUSHING

REMOVAL & INSTALLATION

Expedition & Navigator

2007 Models

See Figures 364 through 367.

✳✳ WARNING

Do not tighten the upper trailing arm-to-knuckle bolt until the installation procedure is complete and the weight of the vehicle is resting on the wheel and tire assemblies.

1. Before servicing the vehicle, refer to the precautions section.

2. With the vehicle in NEUTRAL, position it on a hoist.

3. Remove and discard the upper trailing arm-to-wheel knuckle bolt.

4. Using the special tools 205-813,

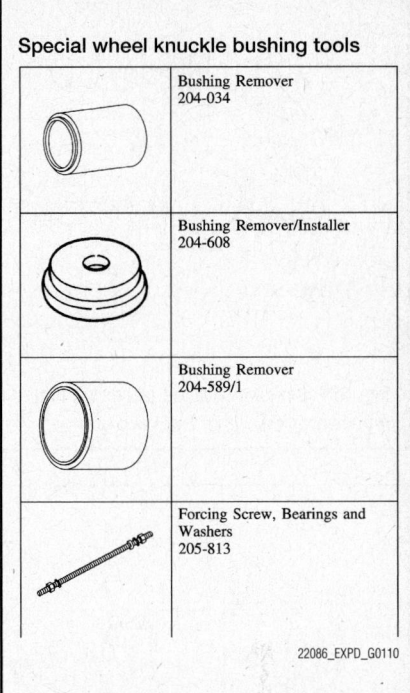

Special wheel knuckle bushing tools

	Bushing Remover 204-034
	Bushing Remover/Installer 204-608
	Bushing Remover 204-589/1
	Forcing Screw, Bearings and Washers 205-813

22086_EXPD_G0110

Fig. 364 Wheel knuckle bushing tools

204-608 and 204-034, remove the wheel knuckle bushing.

To install:

5. Clean and inspect the wheel knuckle bushing bore for damage or excessive wear.

6. Position the new wheel knuckle bushing with the larger void facing towards the upper trailing arm.

7. Install the special tools.

✳✳ WARNING

Do not use the forward forcing screw nut to install the bushing. The forward forcing screw nut is only used to properly position and align the bushing for installation.

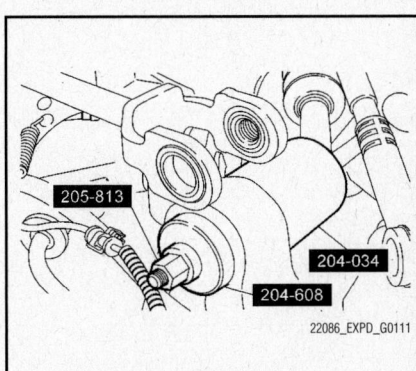

205-813
204-034
204-608

22086_EXPD_G0111

Fig. 365 Wheel knuckle removal with special tools

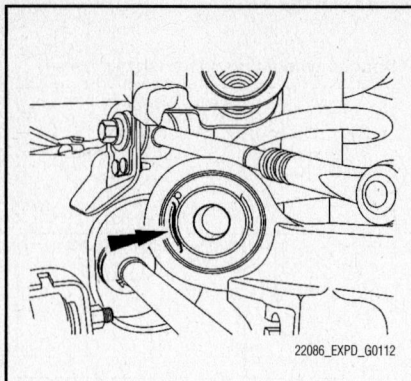

Fig. 366 Bushing with the larger void facing towards the upper trailing arm

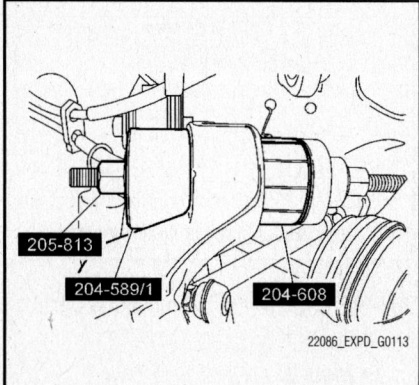

Fig. 367 Wheel knuckle installation with special tools

8. Hand tighten the forward forcing screw nut to align the bushing with the rearward side of the wheel knuckle bore.

✳✳ WARNING

Use the rearward forcing screw nut to install the bushing or damage to the bushing and/or the wheel knuckle bushing bore can result.

9. Tighten the rearward forcing screw nut and install the bushing until it is centered in the wheel knuckle.

➡**After installing the wheel knuckle bushing, make sure to measure the bushings position in the wheel knuckle bore. The measurement from the bushings outer metal surface to the machined face surface of knuckle bore should be 0.16 inch. (2.54 mm) +/- 0.01 inch. (0.25 mm).**

10. If necessary, use the special tool to adjust the bushing position in the wheel knuckle bushing bore.

11. Connect the upper trailing arm to the wheel knuckle.

12. Remove the jack stand from under the lower arm.

WHEEL HUB AND BEARING

REMOVAL & INSTALLATION

Expedition & Navigator

✳✳ WARNING

The electrical power to the air suspension system must be shut off prior to hoisting, jacking or towing an air suspension vehicle. This can be accomplished by turning off the air suspension switch located in the left hand rear quarter trim panel. Failure to do so can result in unexpected inflation or deflation of the air springs, which can result in shifting of the vehicle during these operations.

1. Before servicing the vehicle, refer to the precautions section.

2. If equipped, turn the air suspension switch to the OFF position.

3. Remove the wheel and tire assembly.

➡**Have an assistant press the brake pedal to keep the axle from rotating.**

4. Remove and discard the rear axle wheel hub retainer and the washer.

5. Using a suitable hub puller, separate the outboard CV joint from the wheel hub.

✳✳ CAUTION

Do not allow the caliper to hang from the brake hose or damage to the hose can result.

6. Remove the caliper anchor plate bolts, and position the caliper, pads and anchor plate aside.

7. Remove the rotor.

8. Disconnect the wheel speed sensor electrical connector and detach the retainer.

9. Remove the bolt and detach brake line the retainers.

10. Remove the bolts, the wheel bearing and the wheel speed sensor as an assembly.

11. Route the sensor wiring through the access hole in the brake shield and discard the bolts.

To install:

12. Installation is the reverse of removal, please note the following torque specifications:

   a. Wheel bearing bolts: tighten to 185 Nm (136 ft. lbs.).

   b. Caliper anchor plate bolts: Tighten to 190 Nm (140 ft. lbs.).

   c. New rear axle wheel hub retainer and the washer: Tighten to 300 Nm (221 ft. lbs.).

ADJUSTMENT

This is a sealed unit and no adjustment is required or possible.

SPECIFICATIONS AND MAINTENANCE CHARTS

VEHICLE AND ENGINE IDENTIFICATION CHART

		Engine							Model Year	
Code	Liters	Cu. In.	Cyl.	Fuel Sys.	Engine Type	Eng. Mfg.		Code		Year
1	3.0	183	6	SEFI	DOHC	Ford		5		2005
								6		2006
								7		2007

SEFI: Sequential Multi-port Fuel Injection

DOHC: Dual overhead cam

22086_FIVE_C0001

GENERAL ENGINE SPECIFICATIONS

Year	Engine Displacement Liters	Engine VIN	Net Horsepower @ rpm	Net Torque @ rpm (ft. lbs.)	Bore x Stroke (in.)	Compression Ratio	Oil Pressure @ rpm
2005	3.0	1	203@5750	207@4500	3.50x3.13	10.0:1	11@1500
2006	3.0	1	203@5750	207@4500	3.50x3.13	10.0:1	11@1500
2007	3.0	1	203@5750	207@4500	3.50x3.13	10.0:1	11@1500

22086_FIVE_C0002

GASOLINE ENGINE TUNE-UP SPECIFICATIONS

Year	Engine Displacement Liters	Engine VIN	Spark Plugs Gap (in.)	Ignition Timing (deg.) MT	Ignition Timing (deg.) AT	Fuel Pump (psi)	Idle Speed (rpm) MT	Idle Speed (rpm) AT	Valve Clearance In.	Valve Clearance Ex.
2005	3.0	1	0.052-0.056	—	①	②	—	①	HYD	HYD
2006	3.0	1	0.052-0.056	—	①	②	—	①	HYD	HYD
2007	3.0	1	0.052-0.056	—	①	②	—	①	HYD	HYD

NOTE: The Vehicle Emission Control Information label often reflects specification changes changes made during production.

The label figures must be used if they differ from those in this chart.

B: Before top dead center

HYD: Hydraulic

① Controlled by the Powertrain Control Module (PCM) and cannot be manually adjusted.

② Engine running: 40 psi

Key On, Engine Off (KOEO): 40 psi

22086_FIVE_C0004

CAPACITIES

Year	Model	Engine Displacement Liters	Engine ID/VIN	Engine Oil with Filter (qts.)	Transmission (pts.) 4-Spd	5-Spd	Auto.	Drive Axle Front (pts.)	Rear (pts.)	Fuel Tank (gal.)	Cooling System (qts.)
2005	Five Hundred	3.0	1	6.0	—	—	①	1.5	1.5	20	10.6
	Montego	3.0	1	6.0	—	—	①	1.5	1.5	20	10.6
2006	Five Hundred	3.0	1	6.0	—	—	①	1.5	1.5	20	10.6
	Montego	3.0	1	6.0	—	—	①	1.5	1.5	20	10.6
2007	Five Hundred	3.0	1	6.0	—	—	①	1.5	1.5	20	10.6
	Montego	3.0	1	6.0	—	—	①	1.5	1.5	20	10.6

NOTE: All capacities are approximate. Add fluid gradually and check to be sure a proper fluid level is obtained.

① CVT transmission: 20
  6-spd. Transmission: 15.8

22086_FIVE_C0003

FLUID SPECIFICATIONS

Year	Model	Engine Displacement Liters (VIN)	Engine Oil	Auto. Trans.	Drive Axle	Power Steering Fluid	Brake Master Cylinder
2005	Five Hundred	3.0 (1)	①	②	80W-90	Mercon® ATF Fluid	DOT 3
	Montego	3.0 (1)	①	②	80W-90	Mercon® ATF Fluid	DOT 3
2006	Five Hundred	3.0 (1)	①	②	80W-90	Mercon® ATF Fluid	DOT 3
	Montego	3.0 (1)	①	②	80W-90	Mercon® ATF Fluid	DOT 3
2007	Five Hundred	3.0 (1)	①	②	80W-90	Mercon® ATF Fluid	DOT 3
	Montego	3.0 (1)	①	②	80W-90	Mercon® ATF Fluid	DOT 3

DOT: Department Of Transpotation

① 5W-20 Premium Synthetic Blend Motor Oil (US) or 5W-20 Super Premium Motor Oil (Canada)

② Motorcraft Continuously Variable Chain Type Transmission Fluid XT-7-QCFT (US); CXT-7-LCF12 (Canada) on models with a CVT transmission

Motorcraft Premium Automatic Transmission Fluid XT-8-QAW (US); CXT-8-LAW12 (Canada) on 6 speed models

③ Motorcraft Continuously Variable Chain Type Transmission Fluid XT-7-QCFT (US); CXT-7-LCF12 (Canada) on models with a CVT transmission

22086_FIVE_C0014

VALVE SPECIFICATIONS

Year	Engine VIN	Engine Displacement Liters	Seat Angle (deg.)	Face Angle (deg.)	Spring Test Pressure (lbs. @ in.)	Spring Installed Height (in.)	Stem-to-Guide Clearance (in.) Intake	Exhaust	Stem Diameter (in.) Intake	Exhaust
2005	1	3.0	44.50-45.0	45.25-45.75	156@1.18	1.562-1.577	0.0007-0.0027	0.0018-0.0037	0.2350-0.2358	0.2343-0.2350
2006	1	3.0	44.50-45.0	45.25-45.75	156@1.18	1.562-1.577	0.0007-0.0027	0.0018-0.0037	0.2350-0.2358	0.2343-0.2350
2007	1	3.0	44.50-45.0	45.25-45.75	156@1.18	1.562-1.577	0.0007-0.0027	0.0018-0.0037	0.2350-0.2358	0.2343-0.2350

22086_FIVE_C0005

CRANKSHAFT AND CONNECTING ROD SPECIFICATIONS

All measurements are given in inches.

Year	Engine Displ. Liters	Engine VIN	Crankshaft				Connecting Rod		
			Main Brg. Journal Dia.	Main Brg. Oil Clearance	Shaft End-play	Thrust on No.	Journal Diameter	Oil Clearance	Side Clearance
2005	3.0	1	2.4790- 2.4800	0.0010- 0.0016	0.0050- 0.0010	3	1.9670- 2.9680	0.0010- 0.0025	0.0039- 0.0118
2006	3.0	1	2.4790- 2.4800	0.0010- 0.0016	0.0050- 0.0010	3	1.9670- 2.9680	0.0010- 0.0025	0.0039- 0.0118
2007	3.0	1	2.4790- 2.4800	0.0010- 0.0016	0.0050- 0.0010	3	1.9670- 2.9680	0.0010- 0.0025	0.0039- 0.0118

22086_FIVE_C0006

PISTON AND RING SPECIFICATIONS

All measurements are given in inches.

Year	Engine Displ. Liters	Engine VIN	Piston Clearance	Ring Gap			Ring Side Clearance		
				Top Comp.	Bottom Comp.	Oil Control	Top Comp.	Bottom Comp.	Oil Control
2005	3.0	1	0.0007- 0.0016	0.0039- 0.0098	0.0106- 0.0165	0.0059- 0.0255	NA	NA	NA
2006	3.0	1	0.0007- 0.0016	0.0039- 0.0098	0.0106- 0.0165	0.0059- 0.0255	NA	NA	NA
2007	3.0	1	0.0007- 0.0016	0.0039- 0.0098	0.0106- 0.0165	0.0059- 0.0255	NA	NA	NA

NA: Not Available

22086_FIVE_C0007

TORQUE SPECIFICATIONS

All readings in ft. lbs.

Year	Engine VIN	Engine Displacement Liters	Cylinder Head Bolts	Main Bearing Bolts	Rod Bearing Bolts	Crankshaft Damper Bolts	Flywheel Bolts	Manifold		Spark Plugs	Oil Pan Drain Plug
								Intake	Exhaust		
2005	1	3.0	①	N/A	N/A	②	59	③	15	11	19
2006	1	3.0	①	N/A	N/A	②	59	③	15	11	19
2007	1	3.0	①	N/A	N/A	②	59	③	15	11	19

① Step 1: 30 ft. lbs.
   Step 2: plus 90 degrees
   Step 3: loosen all bolts 1 turn
   Step 4: 30 ft. lbs.
   Step 5: plus 90 degrees.
   Step 6: plus 90 degrees.

② Step 1: 86 ft. lbs.
   Step 2: loosen 1 turn
   Step 3: 37 ft. lbs.
   Step 4: plus 90 degrees

③ Upper and lower manifold: 89 INCH lbs.

22086_FIVE_C0008

WHEEL ALIGNMENT

Year	Model			Caster Range (+/-Deg.)	Caster Preferred Setting (Deg.)	Camber Range (+/-Deg.)	Camber Preferred Setting (Deg.)	Toe-in (Deg.)
2005	Five Hundred	Front	AWD	0.75	+3.5	0.75	-0.40	+0.20+/-0.20
			FWD	0.75	+3.3	0.75	-0.60	+0.20+/-0.20
		Rear	AWD	—	—	0.75	-0.70	0.10+/-0.20
			FWD	—	—	0.75	-0.35	0.10+/-0.20
	Montego	Front	AWD	0.75	+3.5	0.75	-0.40	+0.20+/-0.20
			FWD	0.75	+3.3	0.75	-0.60	+0.20+/-0.20
		Rear	AWD	—	—	0.75	-0.70	0.10+/-0.20
			FWD	—	—	0.75	-0.35	0.10+/-0.20
2006	Five Hundred	Front	AWD	0.75	+3.5	0.75	-0.40	+0.20+/-0.20
			FWD	0.75	+3.3	0.75	-0.60	+0.20+/-0.20
		Rear	AWD	—	—	0.75	-0.70	0.10+/-0.20
			FWD	—	—	0.75	-0.35	0.10+/-0.20
	Montego	Front	AWD	0.75	+3.5	0.75	-0.40	+0.20+/-0.20
			FWD	0.75	+3.3	0.75	-0.60	+0.20+/-0.20
		Rear	AWD	—	—	0.75	-0.70	0.10+/-0.20
			FWD	—	—	0.75	-0.35	0.10+/-0.20
2007	Five Hundred	Front	AWD	0.75	+3.5	0.75	-0.40	+0.20+/-0.20
			FWD	0.75	+3.3	0.75	-0.60	+0.20+/-0.20
		Rear	AWD	—	—	0.75	-0.70	0.10+/-0.20
			FWD	—	—	0.75	-0.35	0.10+/-0.20
	Montego	Front	AWD	0.75	+3.5	0.75	-0.40	+0.20+/-0.20
			FWD	0.75	+3.3	0.75	-0.60	+0.20+/-0.20
		Rear	AWD	—	—	0.75	-0.70	0.10+/-0.20
			FWD	—	—	0.75	-0.35	0.10+/-0.20

22086_FIVE_C0011

TIRE AND WHEEL SPECIFICATIONS

Year	Model	OEM Tires Standard	OEM Tires Optional	Tire Pressures (psi) Front	Tire Pressures (psi) Rear	Wheel Size	Wheel Lug Nut Torque (ft. lbs.)
2005	Five Hundred	P225/55R18	①	35	35	①	95
	Montego	P225/55R18	①	35	35	①	95
2006	Five Hundred	P225/55R18	①	35	35	①	95
	Montego	P225/55R18	①	35	35	①	95
2007	Five Hundred	P225/55R18	①	35	35	①	95
	Montego	P225/55R18	①	35	35	①	95

OEM: Original Equipment Manufacturer

PSI: Pounds Per Square Inch

STD: Standard

OPT: Optional

① Not available

22086_FIVE_C0012

BRAKE SPECIFICATIONS

All measurements in inches unless noted

Year	Model		Brake Disc Original Thickness	Brake Disc Minimum Thickness	Brake Disc Maximum Runout	Minimum Lining Thickness Front	Minimum Lining Thickness Rear	Brake Caliper Bracket Bolts (ft. lbs.)	Brake Caliper Mounting Bolts (ft. lbs.)
2005	Five Hundred	F	①	1.040	0.002	0.118	—	74	44
		R	①	0.394	0.002	—	0.118	81	23
	Montego	F	①	1.040	0.002	0.118	—	74	44
		R	①	0.394	0.002	—	0.118	81	23
2006	Five Hundred	F	①	1.040	0.002	0.118	—	74	44
		R	①	0.394	0.002	—	0.118	81	23
	Montego	F	①	1.040	0.002	0.118	—	74	44
		R	①	0.394	0.002	—	0.118	81	23
2007	Five Hundred	F	①	1.040	0.002	0.118	—	74	44
		R	①	0.394	0.002	—	0.118	81	23
	Montego	F	①	1.040	0.002	0.118	—	74	44
		R	①	0.394	0.002	—	0.118	81	23

① Not available

22086_FIVE_C0013

SCHEDULED MAINTENANCE INTERVALS
FORD FIVE HUNDRED & MERCURY MONTEGO

TO BE SERVICED	TYPE OF SERVICE	VEHICLE MILEAGE INTERVAL (x1000)																	
		5	10	15	20	25	30	35	40	45	50	55	60	65	70	75	80	85	90
Engine oil & filter ①	R																		
Rotate tires	S/I	✓	✓	✓	✓	✓	✓	✓	✓	✓	✓	✓	✓	✓	✓	✓	✓	✓	✓
Engine coolant strength hoses & clamps	S/I			✓			✓			✓			✓				✓		✓
Air cleaner filter	R						✓						✓						✓
Automatic transmission fluid & filter	R						✓						✓						✓
Engine coolant ②	R																		
PCV valve	R												✓						✓
Spark plugs ③	R																		
Drive belts	S/I						✓						✓						✓
Exhaust system & heat shields	S/I						✓						✓						✓
Front & rear brakes	S/I	✓	✓	✓	✓	✓	✓	✓	✓	✓	✓	✓	✓	✓	✓	✓	✓	✓	✓
Fuel filter	R			✓			✓			✓			✓			✓			✓

R: Replace   S/I: Service or Inspect

① Engine oil and filter: replace every 3000 miles.

② Engine coolant: change initially at 100,000 miles or 5 years.

③ Spark plugs: replace every 100,000 miles.

Special Operating Condition Requirements

During extensive idling and/or low speed driving for long distances, as in heavy commercial use such as delivery, taxi, patrol car or livery:

Lube front lower control arm and steering linkage ball joints with

Zerk fittings (if equipped) every 4,800 km (3,000 miles) or 3 months.

Inspect brake system and check battery electrolyte level (Patrol cars) every 8,000 km (5,000 miles).

Install a new cabin air filter as required.

When operating in dusty conditions such as unpaved or dusty roads:

Install a new engine air filter as required.

Install a new cabin air filter as required.

When operating in off-road conditions:

Change automatic transmission fluid every 48,000 km (30,000 miles).

Install a new cabin air filter as required.

Inspect and lubricate U-joints.

Inspect and lubricate steering linkage ball joints with zerk fittings.

22086_FIVE_C0010

PRECAUTIONS

Before servicing any vehicle, please be sure to read all of the following precautions, which deal with personal safety, prevention of component damage, and important points to take into consideration when servicing a motor vehicle:

• Never open, service or drain the radiator or cooling system when the engine is hot; serious burns can occur from the steam and hot coolant.

• Observe all applicable safety precautions when working around fuel. Whenever servicing the fuel system, always work in a well-ventilated area. Do not allow fuel spray or vapors to come in contact with a spark, open flame, or excessive heat (a hot drop light, for example). Keep a dry chemical fire extinguisher near the work area. Always keep fuel in a container specifically designed for fuel storage; also, always properly seal fuel containers to avoid the possibility of fire or explosion. Refer to the additional fuel system precautions later in this section.

• Fuel injection systems often remain pressurized, even after the engine has been turned **OFF**. The fuel system pressure must be relieved before disconnecting any fuel lines. Failure to do so may result in fire and/or personal injury.

• Brake fluid often contains polyglycol ethers and polyglycols. Avoid contact with the eyes and wash your hands thoroughly after handling brake fluid. If you do get brake fluid in your eyes, flush your eyes with clean, running water for 15 minutes. If eye irritation persists, or if you have taken brake fluid internally, IMMEDIATELY seek medical assistance.

• The EPA warns that prolonged contact with used engine oil may cause a number of skin disorders, including cancer. You should make every effort to minimize your exposure to used engine oil. Protective gloves should be worn when changing oil. Wash your hands and any other exposed skin areas as soon as possible after exposure to used engine oil. Soap and water, or waterless hand cleaner should be used.

• All new vehicles are now equipped with an air bag system, often referred to as a Supplemental Restraint System (SRS) or Supplemental Inflatable Restraint (SIR) system. The system must be disabled before performing service on or around system components, steering column, instrument panel components, wiring and sensors. Failure to follow safety and disabling procedures could result in accidental air bag deployment, possible personal injury and unnecessary system repairs.

• Always wear safety goggles when working with, or around, the air bag system. When carrying a non-deployed air bag, be sure the bag and trim cover are pointed away from your body. When placing a non-deployed air bag on a work surface, always face the bag and trim cover upward, away from the surface. This will reduce the motion of the module if it is accidentally deployed. Refer to the additional air bag system precautions later in this section.

• Clean, high quality brake fluid from a sealed container is essential to the safe and proper operation of the brake system. You should always buy the correct type of brake fluid for your vehicle. If the brake fluid becomes contaminated, completely flush the system with new fluid. Never reuse any brake fluid. Any brake fluid that is removed from the system should be discarded. Also, do not allow any brake fluid to come in contact with a painted surface; it will damage the paint.

• Never operate the engine without the proper amount and type of engine oil; doing so WILL result in severe engine damage.

• Timing belt maintenance is extremely important. Many models utilize an interference-type, non-freewheeling engine. If the timing belt breaks, the valves in the cylinder head may strike the pistons, causing potentially serious (also time-consuming and expensive) engine damage. Refer to the maintenance interval charts for the recommended replacement interval for the timing belt, and to the timing belt section for belt replacement and inspection.

• Disconnecting the negative battery cable on some vehicles may interfere with the functions of the on-board computer system(s) and may require the computer to undergo a relearning process once the negative battery cable is reconnected.

• When servicing drum brakes, only disassemble and assemble one side at a time, leaving the remaining side intact for reference.

• Only an MVAC-trained, EPA-certified automotive technician should service the air conditioning system or its components.

BRAKES

GENERAL INFORMATION

PRECAUTIONS

• Certain components within the ABS system are not intended to be serviced or repaired individually.

• Do not use rubber hoses or other parts not specifically specified for and ABS system. When using repair kits, replace all parts included in the kit. Partial or incorrect repair may lead to functional problems and require the replacement of components.

• Lubricate rubber parts with clean, fresh brake fluid to ease assembly. Do not use shop air to clean parts; damage to rubber components may result.

• Use only DOT 3 brake fluid from an unopened container.

• If any hydraulic component or line is removed or replaced, it may be necessary to bleed the entire system.

• A clean repair area is essential. Always clean the reservoir and cap thoroughly before removing the cap. The slightest amount of dirt in the fluid may plug an orifice and impair the system function. Perform repairs after components have been thoroughly cleaned; use only denatured alcohol to clean components. Do not allow ABS components to come into contact with any substance containing mineral oil; this includes used shop rags.

• The Anti-Lock control unit is a microprocessor similar to other computer units in the vehicle. Ensure that the ignition switch is **OFF** before removing or installing controller harnesses. Avoid static electricity discharge at or near the controller.

ANTI-LOCK BRAKE SYSTEM (ABS)

• If any arc welding is to be done on the vehicle, the control unit should be unplugged before welding operations begin.

SPEED SENSORS

REMOVAL & INSTALLATION

Front

1. With the vehicle in NEUTRAL, position it on a hoist.
2. Disconnect the wheel speed sensor electrical connector.
3. Remove the 2 rivets and position aside the fender splash shield.
4. Remove the wheel speed sensor harness pin-type retainer.
5. Remove the 2 wheel speed sensor harness retainers.

6. Remove the bolt and the wheel speed sensor.

7. To install, reverse the removal procedure and tighten the speed sensor bolt to 71 ft, lbs. (8 Nm).

Rear

Front Wheel Drive

1. With the vehicle in NEUTRAL, position it on a hoist.

2. Disconnect the wheel speed sensor electrical connector.

3. Remove the 2 rivets and position aside the fender splash shield.

4. Remove the wheel speed sensor harness pin-type retainer.

5. Remove the 2 wheel speed sensor harness retainers.

6. Remove the bolt and the wheel speed sensor.

7. To install, reverse the removal procedure and tighten the speed sensor bolt to 71 ft, lbs. (8 Nm).

All Wheel Drive

1. With the vehicle in NEUTRAL, position it on a hoist.

2. Disconnect the wheel speed sensor electrical connector.

3. Remove the wheel speed sensor bolt.

4. On the left side, release the wheel speed sensor harness spring clip and the 2 pin-type retainers from the rear control arm.

5. Release the wheel speed sensor harness spring clip and the 2 pin-type retainers from the rear control arm.

6. On the right side, release the 3 pin-type retainers and remove the wheel speed sensor.

7. To install, reverse the removal procedure and tighten the speed sensor bolt to 71 ft, lbs. (8 Nm).

BRAKES

BLEEDING THE BRAKE SYSTEM

BLEEDING PROCEDURE

BLEEDING PROCEDURE

1. Clean all the dirt from the area, remove the brake master cylinder reservoir cap and fill the brake master cylinder reservoir with the specified brake fluid.

2. Remove the rear bleeder cap and place a box end wrench on the RH rear bleeder screw. Attach a rubber drain tube to the RH rear bleeder screw and submerge the free end of the tube in a container partially filled with clean brake fluid.

3. Have an assistant hold firm pressure on the brake pedal.

4. Loosen the RH rear bleeder screw until a stream of brake fluid comes out. While the assistant maintains pressure on the brake pedal, tighten the RH rear bleeder screw.

5. Press and release the parking brake 5 times.

6. Repeat until clear, bubble-free fluid comes out.

7. Refill the brake master cylinder reservoir as necessary.

8. Tighten the RH rear bleeder screw and install the bleeder cap.

9. Repeat Steps 3, 4, 5 and 6 for the LH rear bleeder screw.

10. Remove the rear bleeder cap and place a box end wrench on the RH front brake caliper bleeder screw. Attach a rubber drain tube to the RH front brake caliper bleeder screw, and submerge the free end of the tube in a container partially filled with clean brake fluid.

11. Have an assistant hold firm pressure on the brake pedal.

12. Loosen the RH front brake caliper bleeder screw until a stream of brake fluid comes out. While the assistant maintains pressure on the brake pedal, tighten the RH front brake caliper bleeder screw.

13. Repeat until clear, bubble-free fluid comes out.

14. Refill the brake master cylinder reservoir as necessary.

15. Tighten the RH front brake caliper bleeder screw and install the bleeder cap.

16. Repeat Steps 8, 9, 10 and 11 for the LH front brake caliper bleeder screw.

BLEEDING THE ABS SYSTEM

1. Clean all the dirt from the area and remove the brake master cylinder filler cap. Fill the brake master cylinder reservoir with the specified brake fluid.

➡**Master cylinder pressure bleeder adapter tools are available from various manufacturers of pressure bleeding equipment. Follow the instructions of the manufacturer when installing the adapter.**

2. Install the bleeder adapter to the brake master cylinder reservoir, and attach the bleeder tank hose to the fitting on the adapter.

3. Bleed the longest line first. Make sure the bleeder tank contains enough specified brake fluid to complete the bleeding operation.

4. Place a box end wrench on the RH rear bleeder screw. Attach a rubber drain tube to the RH rear bleeder screw, and submerge the free end of the tube in a container partially filled with clean brake fluid.

5. Open the valve on the bleeder tank.

6. Loosen the RH rear bleeder screw. Leave open until clear, bubble-free brake fluid flows, then tighten the RH rear bleeder screw and remove the rubber hose.

7. Press and release the parking brake 5 times.

8. Repeat until clear, bubble-free fluid comes out.

9. Tighten the RH rear bleeder screw and install the bleeder cap.

10. Repeat Steps 5 and 6 for the LH rear bleeder screw.

11. Continue bleeding the front of the system, going in order from the RH front disc brake caliper bleeder screw, ending with the LH front brake caliper bleeder screw.

12. Close the bleeder tank valve. Remove the tank hose from the adapter, and remove the adapter.

BRAKES   **FRONT DISC BRAKES**

BRAKE CALIPER

REMOVAL & INSTALLATION

See Figure 1.

➡The brake pads are a onetime use only type. If the pads are separated from the caliper the pads must be replaced.

  1. Remove and discard ½ of the brake fluid from the brake master cylinder reservoir.
  2. Raise and safely support the vehicle.
  3. Remove the wheel and tire assembly.
  4. Mark the disc brake caliper to avoid mixing the left-hand and right-hand components.
  5. Loosen the brake caliper bolts.
  6. Disconnect the brake hose from the brake line fitting.
  7. Remove and discard the caliper anchor bolts and position the caliper, anchor plate and pads aside. Support the steering stop when the anchor plate bolts are removed.
  8. Separate the brake pads from the caliper.
  9. Remove the caliper bolts from the caliper and anchor plate.
  10. Remove the brake pads and spring clips.

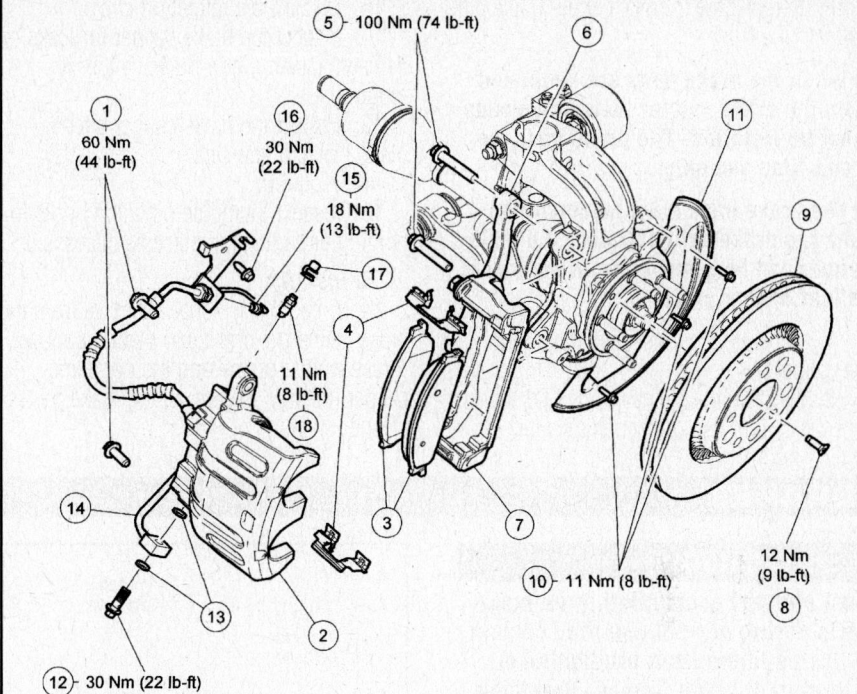

1	Brake caliper bolts (2 required)
2	Brake caliper RH/LH
3	Brake pads
4	Spring clips (2 required)
5	Brake caliper anchor plate bolts (2 required)
6	Steering stop
7	Brake caliper anchor plate
8	Brake disc screw
9	Brake disc
10	Brake disc shield bolts (3 required)
11	Brake disc shield (RH/LH)
12	Brake caliper flow bolt
13	Copper washers (2 required)
14	Brake flexible hose RH/LH
15	Brake line fitting
16	Brake flexible hose bracket bolt
17	Bleeder screw cap
18	Bleeder screw

06017-FREE-G51

Fig. 1 Exploded view of front disc brake assembly

To install:

  11. Compress the caliper pistons into the caliper bore.
  12. Install the spring clips and brake pads in the caliper and anchor plate assembly.
  13. Install the brake caliper anchor. Tighten the anchor bolts to 74 ft. lbs. (100 Nm).
  14. Install the caliper and new guide pins and tighten the bolts to 44 ft. lbs. (60 Nm).
  15. Install new copper washers in the brake flexible hoses and connect the hoses and install the flow bolt to 22 ft. lbs. (30 Nm).
  16. Bleed the brake system.
  17. Lower the vehicle.
  18. Pump the brake pedal several times to position the brake pads before attempting to move the vehicle.

  19. Check and fill the brake master cylinder as required.
  20. Road-test the vehicle and check for proper brake operation.

DISC BRAKE PADS

REMOVAL & INSTALLATION

See Figure 1.

  1. Check the brake fluid level in the brake master cylinder reservoir.
  2. If required, remove the fluid until the brake master cylinder reservoir is half full.
  3. With the vehicle in NEUTRAL, position it on a hoist.
  4. Using the large C-clamp, compress the pistons into the caliper housing.
  5. Position one end of the C-clamp on the outer pad between the caliper fingers,

the other end on the caliper housing. During this process, the outer brake pad will separate from the caliper housing.

6. Remove the 2 brake caliper guide pin bolts.

➡ When the brake pads are separated from the brake caliper, new brake pads must be installed. The brake pads are a one-time use only.

➡ The brake pads must be separated from the brake caliper before the brake caliper can be removed from the brake caliper anchor plate.

7. Separate the inner brake pad from the caliper.

8. Position the caliper aside and support the caliper using mechanic's wire.

9. Remove the 2 brake pads and spring clips from the brake caliper anchor plate.

10. Discard the retraction clips.

11. Inspect the brake caliper for leaks or damage. Install a new brake caliper if required.

12. Inspect the brake caliper anchor plate. Install a new brake caliper anchor plate if required.

13. Inspect the guide pins and boots for binding or damage, replace as necessary.

To install:

14. Clean the residual adhesive from the brake caliper-to-brake pad mating surfaces (brake caliper piston and the opposing caliper housing fingers) using brake parts cleaner.

15. If installing new brake pads, install all new hardware as supplied with the brake pad kit.

16. Install the new spring clips and brake pads to the brake caliper anchor plate.

17. Position the brake caliper onto the brake caliper anchor plate and install the 2 caliper guide pin bolts and tighten to 44 ft. lbs. (60 Nm).

18. If necessary, fill the brake master cylinder reservoir with clean brake fluid.

19. With the vehicles engine running, apply 89-133 N (20-30 lb) of pressure on the brake pedal for one minute to make sure the brake pads adhere to the brake caliper before any contamination can be introduced.

20. Test the brakes for normal operation.

BRAKES   REAR DISC BRAKES

✳✳ CAUTION

Dust and dirt accumulating on brake parts during normal use may contain asbestos fibers from production or aftermarket brake linings. Breathing excessive concentrations of asbestos fibers can cause serious bodily harm. Exercise care when servicing brake parts. Do not sand or grind brake lining unless equipment used is designed to contain the dust residue. Do not clean brake parts with compressed air or by dry brushing. Cleaning should be done by dampening the brake components with a fine mist of water, then wiping the brake components clean with a dampened cloth. Dispose of cloth and all residue containing asbestos fibers in an impermeable container with the appropriate label. Follow practices prescribed by the Occupational Safety and Health Administration (OSHA) and the Environmental Protection Agency (EPA) for the handling, processing, and disposing of dust or debris that may contain asbestos fibers.

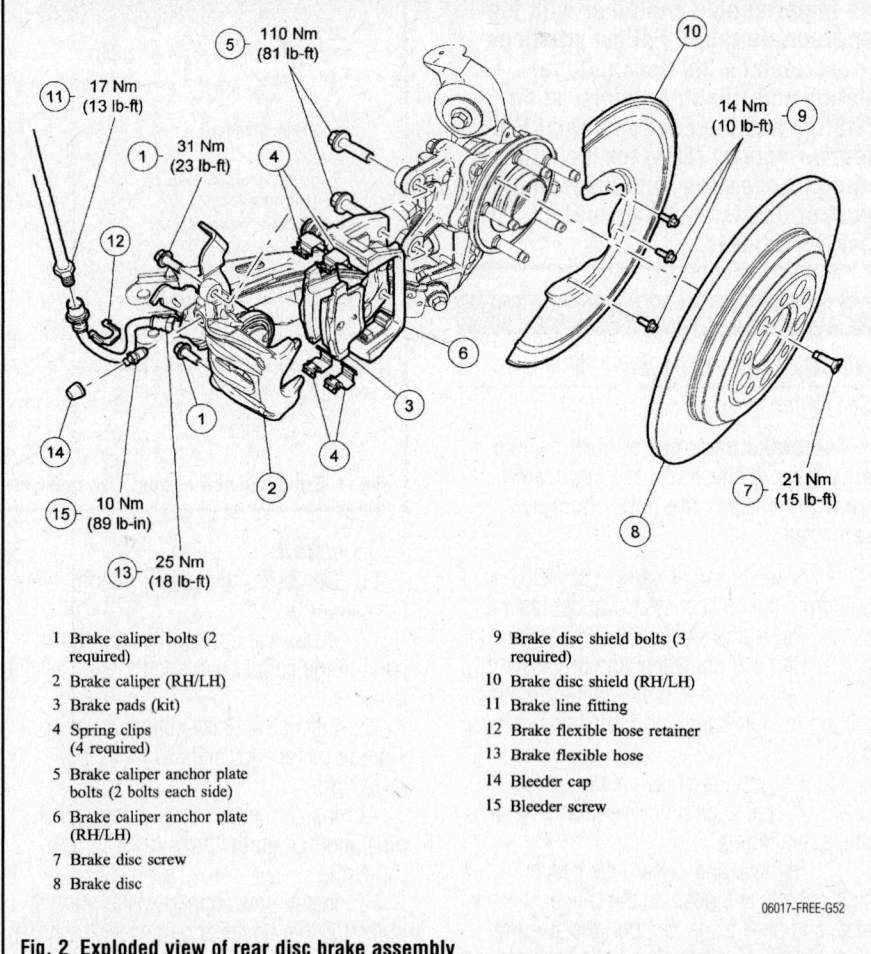

1 Brake caliper bolts (2 required)
2 Brake caliper (RH/LH)
3 Brake pads (kit)
4 Spring clips (4 required)
5 Brake caliper anchor plate bolts (2 bolts each side)
6 Brake caliper anchor plate (RH/LH)
7 Brake disc screw
8 Brake disc
9 Brake disc shield bolts (3 required)
10 Brake disc shield (RH/LH)
11 Brake line fitting
12 Brake flexible hose retainer
13 Brake flexible hose
14 Bleeder cap
15 Bleeder screw

06017-FREE-G52

Fig. 2 Exploded view of rear disc brake assembly

BRAKE CALIPER

REMOVAL & INSTALLATION

See Figures 2 and 3.

1. Remove and discard ½ of the brake fluid from the brake master cylinder reservoir.

2. Raise and safely support the vehicle.

3. Remove the wheel and tire assembly.

4. Release the tension on the parking brake cable.

5. Disconnect the parking brake cable end from the caliper lever and release the cable retainer from the caliper bracket.

6. Loosen the brake caliper bolts.

7. Remove and discard the caliper anchor bolts.

8. Remove the brake pads from the caliper.

9. Remove the caliper bolts and separate the caliper from the anchor plate.

To install:

10. Compress the caliper pistons into the caliper bore.

11. Install the anchor plate and tighten the bolts to 81 ft. lbs. (110 Nm).

12. Retract the disc brake caliper piston fully into the caliper bore using tool no. 206-026.

13. Install the spring clips and brake pads in the caliper.

14. Install the caliper and tighten the guide pins to 23 ft. lbs. (31 Nm).

15. Install the parking brake cable to the caliper.

16. Reload the tension on the parking brake cable.

17. Bleed the brake system and install the rubber bleeder screw caps when complete.

18. Install the wheel and tire assembly.

19. Lower the vehicle.

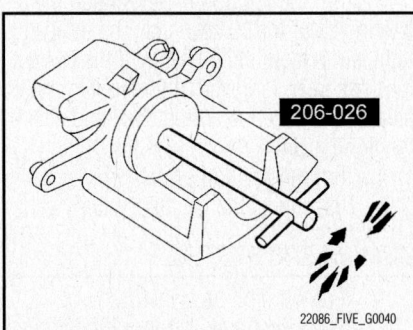

22086_FIVE_G0040

Fig. 3 Retract the disc brake caliper piston fully into the caliper bore using tool no. 206-026

20. Pump the brake pedal several times to position the brake pads before attempting to move the vehicle.

21. Check and fill the brake master cylinder as required.

22. Road-test the vehicle and check for proper brake operation.

DISC BRAKE PADS

REMOVAL & INSTALLATION
See Figure 2.

1. Check the brake fluid level in the brake fluid reservoir.

2. If required, remove fluid until the brake master cylinder reservoir is half full.

3. Remove the brake caliper bolts.

✳✳ CAUTION

Care must be taken when servicing rear brake components without disconnecting the parking brake cable from the brake caliper lever. Carefully position the caliper aside using a suitable support or damage to the parking brake cable end fittings can occur.

4. Using hand force and a rocking motion, separate the brake caliper from the anchor plate. Position the brake caliper aside.

5. Support the caliper with mechanic's wire.

✳✳ CAUTION

When the brake pads are separated from the brake caliper, new brake pads must be installed. The brake pads are one-time use only.

6. Remove and discard the brake pads and spring clips from the brake caliper anchor plate.

7. Do not remove the anchor plate guide pins. The guide pins are press fit to the brake caliper anchor plate. If the guide pins are damaged a new anchor plate must be installed.

8. Inspect the brake caliper anchor plate assembly.

9. Check the guide pins and boots for binding or damage.

10. Install a new brake caliper anchor plate if it is worn or damaged.

To install:

➡️**The LH caliper piston turns clockwise and the RH caliper piston turns counterclockwise.**

11. Compress the brake caliper piston into its cylinder.

12. Clean the residual adhesive from the brake caliper fingers and pistons using the specified brake parts cleaner.

13. Install the new spring clips and brake pads.

14. Position the brake caliper and install the 2 bolts and tighten to 23 ft. lbs. (31 Nm).

15. If necessary, fill the brake fluid reservoir with clean specified brake fluid.

16. With the vehicle engine running, apply 89-133 N (20-30 lb) of pressure on the brakes for approximately 1 minute, to make sure the brake pads adhere to the caliper before any contamination can be introduced.

17. Test the brakes for normal operation.

BRAKES

PARKING BRAKE

PARKING BRAKE CABLES

The parking brake system is a mechanical system that activates a self-adjusting brake ratchet system within the rear brake caliper.

The parking brake is a cable actuated system and is controlled by a foot-operated parking brake lever. The parking brake system is actuated when the parking brake control is pressed and released by pressing the parking brake lever again.

The parking brake control applies tension to rear parking brake shoes through the front parking brake cable and conduit and the left hand and right hand rear parking brake cables. The rear parking brake assemblies are then applied.

The parking brake cable tension is self-adjusting inside the parking brake control.

PARKING BRAKE SHOES

The parking brake control applies tension to rear parking brake shoes through the front parking brake cable and conduit and the left hand and right hand rear parking brake cables. The rear parking brake assemblies are then applied.

CHASSIS ELECTRICAL　AIR BAG (SUPPLEMENTAL RESTRAINT SYSTEM)

GENERAL INFORMATION

✳✳ CAUTION

These vehicles are equipped with an air bag system. The system must be disarmed before performing service on, or around, system components, the steering column, instrument panel components, wiring and sensors. Failure to follow the safety precautions and the disarming procedure could result in accidental air bag deployment, possible injury and unnecessary system repairs.

SERVICE PRECAUTIONS

Disconnect and isolate the battery negative cable before beginning any airbag system component diagnosis, testing, removal, or installation procedures. Allow system capacitor to discharge for two minutes before beginning any component service. This will disable the airbag system. Failure to disable the airbag system may result in accidental airbag deployment, personal injury, or death.

Do not place an intact undeployed airbag face down on a solid surface. The airbag will propel into the air if accidentally deployed and may result in personal injury or death.

When carrying or handling an undeployed airbag, the trim side (face) of the airbag should be pointing towards the body to minimize possibility of injury if accidental deployment occurs. Failure to do this may result in personal injury or death.

Replace airbag system components with OEM replacement parts. Substitute parts may appear interchangeable, but internal differences may result in inferior occupant protection. Failure to do so may result in occupant personal injury or death.

Wear safety glasses, rubber gloves, and long sleeved clothing when cleaning powder residue from vehicle after an airbag deployment. Powder residue emitted from a deployed airbag can cause skin irritation. Flush affected area with cool water if irritation is experienced. If nasal or throat irritation is experienced, exit the vehicle for fresh air until the irritation ceases. If irritation continues, see a physician.

Do not use a replacement airbag that is not in the original packaging. This may result in improper deployment, personal injury, or death.

The factory installed fasteners, screws and bolts used to fasten airbag components have a special coating and are specifically designed for the airbag system. Do not use substitute fasteners. Use only original equipment fasteners listed in the parts catalog when fastener replacement is required.

During, and following, any child restraint anchor service, due to impact event or vehicle repair, carefully inspect all mounting hardware, tether straps, and anchors for proper installation, operation, or damage. If a child restraint anchor is found damaged in any way, the anchor must be replaced. Failure to do this may result in personal injury or death.

Deployed and non-deployed airbags may or may not have live pyrotechnic material within the airbag inflator.

Do not dispose of driver/passenger/curtain airbags or seat belt tensioners unless you are sure of complete deployment. Refer to the Hazardous Substance Control System for proper disposal.

Dispose of deployed airbags and tensioners consistent with state, provincial, local, and federal regulations.

After any airbag component testing or service, do not connect the battery negative cable. Personal injury or death may result if the system test is not performed first.

If the vehicle is equipped with the Occupant Classification System (OCS), do not connect the battery negative cable before performing the OCS Verification Test using the scan tool and the appropriate diagnostic information. Personal injury or death may result if the system test is not performed properly.

Never replace both the Occupant Restraint Controller (ORC) and the Occupant Classification Module (OCM) at the same time. If both require replacement, replace one, then perform the Airbag System test before replacing the other.

Both the ORC and the OCM store Occupant Classification System (OCS) calibration data, which they transfer to one another when one of them is replaced. If both are replaced at the same time, an irreversible fault will be set in both modules and the OCS may malfunction and cause personal injury or death.

If equipped with OCS, the Seat Weight Sensor is a sensitive, calibrated unit and must be handled carefully. Do not drop or handle roughly. If dropped or damaged, replace with another sensor. Failure to do so may result in occupant injury or death.

If equipped with OCS, the front passenger seat must be handled carefully as well. When removing the seat, be careful when setting on floor not to drop. If dropped, the sensor may be inoperative, could result in occupant injury, or possibly death.

If equipped with OCS, when the passenger front seat is on the floor, no one should sit in the front passenger seat. This uneven force may damage the sensing ability of the seat weight sensors. If sat on and damaged, the sensor may be inoperative, could result in occupant injury, or possibly death.

DISARMING THE SYSTEM

1. Ensure the ignition is off.
2. Remove the Smart Junction Box (SJB) cover located below the left side of the instrument panel. Remove the Restraints Control Module (RCM) fuse no. F2.21.
3. Turn the ignition on and watch the air bag indicator for 30 seconds. The indicator light will remain lit constantly if the correct fuse has been removed. If the light is not on steadily, remove the correct fuse and check the light again.
4. Turn the ignition switch off.
5. Disconnect the negative battery cable.

ARMING THE SYSTEM

1. Turn the ignition switch on.
2. Install Restraints Control Module (RCM) fuse no. F2.21 and the fuse cover.
3. Turn the ignition off.
4. Connect the negative battery cable.
5. Turn the ignition on and then off. Wait 10 seconds and turn the key back on. Watch the air bag indicator. The indicator light will remain lit constantly for 6 seconds and then go off. If the indicator does not turn on and then off, diagnose the air bag system
6. Clear all Diagnostic Trouble Codes (DTC) using a diagnostic tool.

CLOCKSPRING CENTERING

See Figures 4 through 8.

1. Place the steering wheel in the straight-ahead position and remove the ignition key.
2. Disarm the air bag system.
3. Remove the steering wheel access cover.
4. Release one side of the driver air bag module wire clip. While actuating the horn at the lower part of the air bag cover, use a suitable tool (needle nose pliers, etc.) to

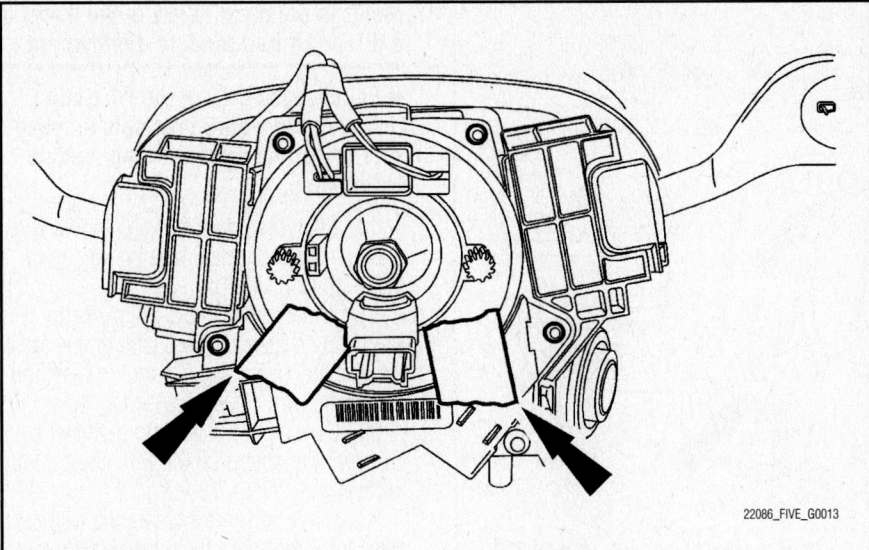

22086_FIVE_G0013

Fig. 4 If reusing the clockspring, tape the clockspring center rotor to the outer housing to keep it from rotating

release the wire clip until it touches the center post.

5. Release the horn and using a suitable tool, lift the end of the wire clip over the post.

6. Release the other side of the driver air bag module wire clip. While actuating the horn at the lower part of the air bag cover, use a suitable tool to release the other side of the wire clip until it touches the center post.

7. Release the horn and with a suitable tool, lift the end of the wire clip over the post causing both ends of the wire clip to overlap.

8. When the driver air bag module wire clip is released correctly, the wire clip will easily slide into place and the 2 wire clip hook ends will come to rest between the 2 inner posts.

9. With the wire clip ends in the overlapped position, actuate the horn at the upper part of the air bag cover, then push on both ends of the wire clip inward (toward the center of the steering wheel) to release the driver air bag module from the steering wheel.

10. Label the driver air bag module squib number on the driver air bag module electrical connectors before disconnecting.

11. Release the two retaining tabs on each driver air bag module electrical connector and disconnect both connectors.

12. Disconnect the horn and accessories electrical connectors and remove the driver air bag module.

13. Remove and discard the steering wheel bolt.

14. Remove the steering wheel. Route the 2 driver air bag module electrical connectors through the steering wheel.

15. Remove the cluster finish panel.

16. Remove the 3 screws and the lower steering column shroud.

17. If the clockspring is to be reinstalled, do not allow the clockspring to turn from its removal position.

18. If reusing the clockspring, tape the clockspring center rotor to the outer housing to keep it from rotating.

19. Disconnect the 2 clockspring electrical connectors.

20. Remove the 4 clockspring screws and remove the clockspring.

To install:

❋❋ WARNING

Incorrect centralization may result in premature component failure. If in doubt when centralizing the clockspring, repeat the centralizing procedure. Failure to follow this

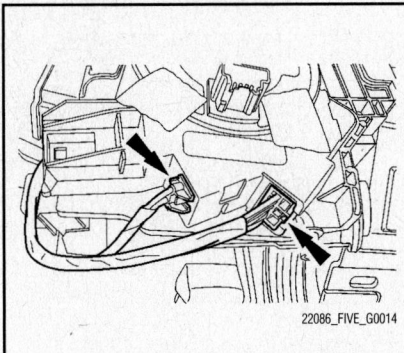

22086_FIVE_G0014

Fig. 5 Unplug the clockspring connectors

instruction may result in personal injury.

❋❋ CAUTION

Make sure the road wheels are in the straight-ahead position.

21. If the vehicle's clockspring has rotated out of center, perform the following to center the clockspring:

　a. Hold the clockspring outer housing stationary. Step 1 in the illustration.

❋❋ CAUTION

Overturning will destroy the clockspring. The internal ribbon wire acts as the stop and can be broken from its internal connection.

　b. While turning the rotor counter clockwise, carefully feel for the ribbon wire to run out of length and for a slight resistance. Stop turning at this point. Step 2 in the illustration.

　c. Turn the clockspring approximately 3 turns clockwise until the ribbon wire shows anywhere across the window (the window will be near the 2 o'clock position) and the arrow on the rotor lines up with the arrow on the bottom left of the housing. The clockspring is now centered. Step 3 in the illustration.

　d. Do not allow the rotor to turn from this position.

22. Install the clockspring and the 4 screws.

23. Connect the 2 clockspring electrical connectors.

24. On a repair reusing the same clockspring, remove the tape applied during clockspring removal.

➡ **When the tape is removed, do not allow the clockspring to turn.**

25. On a repair installing a new clockspring:

❋❋ CAUTION

Do not rotate the new clockspring between removing the sealing key and installing the steering wheel. If the vehicle is left unattended by the technician between removing the sealing key and installing the steering wheel, carry out the centralizing procedure.

　e. Remove the sealing key.

26. Install the lower steering column shroud and the 3 screws.

27. Install the cluster finish panel.

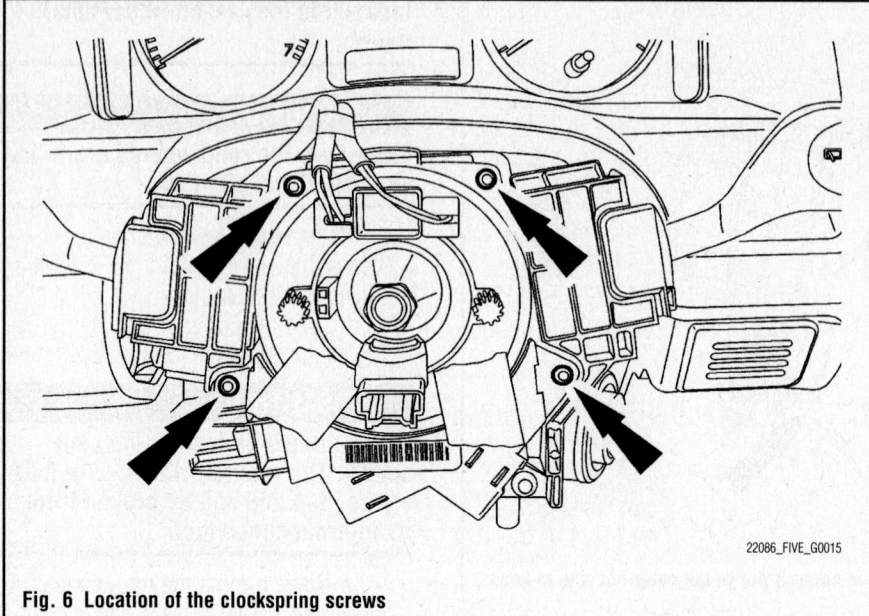

Fig. 6 Location of the clockspring screws

22086_FIVE_G0015

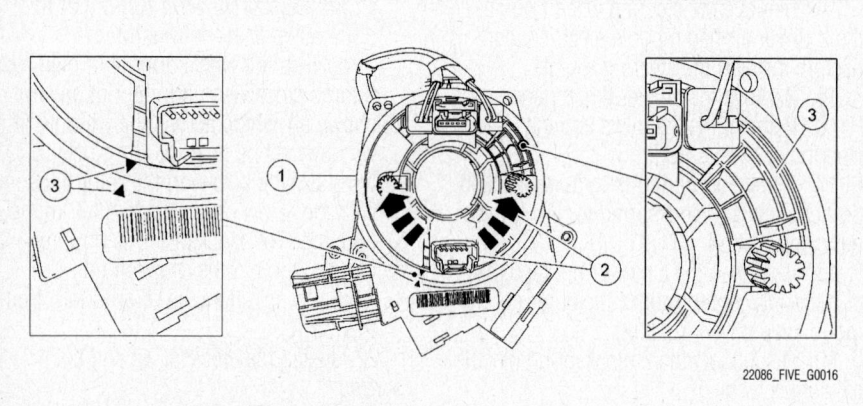

Fig. 7 The 3 steps of clockspring centering. Refer to the text for step by step instructions.

22086_FIVE_G0016

result in personal injury in the event of a driver air bag module deployment.

➡Follow each step of the wire clip resetting procedure precisely to make sure of correct driver air bag module installation.

30. Push the driver air bag module wire clip fully back on the 6 tabs on the top of the module.

31. While making sure the wire clip stays fully seated on the 6 tabs on the top of the module, use a suitable tool to reset the end of the wire clip that is on the top.

32. Carefully lift the 1 end of the wire clip over the post. Pull the wire clip outward to reset.

33. While still making sure the wire clip stays fully seated on the 6 tabs on the top of the module, use a suitable tool to reset the other end of the wire clip.

34. Carefully lift the other end of the wire clip over the post.

35. Pull the wire clip outward to reset.

36. Make sure the wire clip hook ends are evenly spaced from the center post.

37. Make sure the driver air bag module wire clip is fully seated on all of the tabs and guides.

38. Connect the horn and accessories electrical connectors.

✳✳ CAUTION

The clockspring electrical connectors are unique and cannot be reversed when connected to the driver air bag module. Match the electrical connector key to the keyway in the driver air

✳✳ CAUTION

If the vehicle is left unattended by the technician between centralizing the clockspring and installing the steering wheel, the centralizing procedure must be repeated.

28. Route the 2 driver air bag module electrical connectors through the steering wheel and install the steering wheel.

29. Tighten the steering wheel bolt to 30 ft. lbs. (40 Nm).

✳✳ CAUTION

Prior to reinstalling a previously removed driver air bag module, make sure to correctly position the wire clip that retains the driver air bag module to the steering wheel. Failure to follow this instruction
will result in incorrect installation of the driver air bag module and may

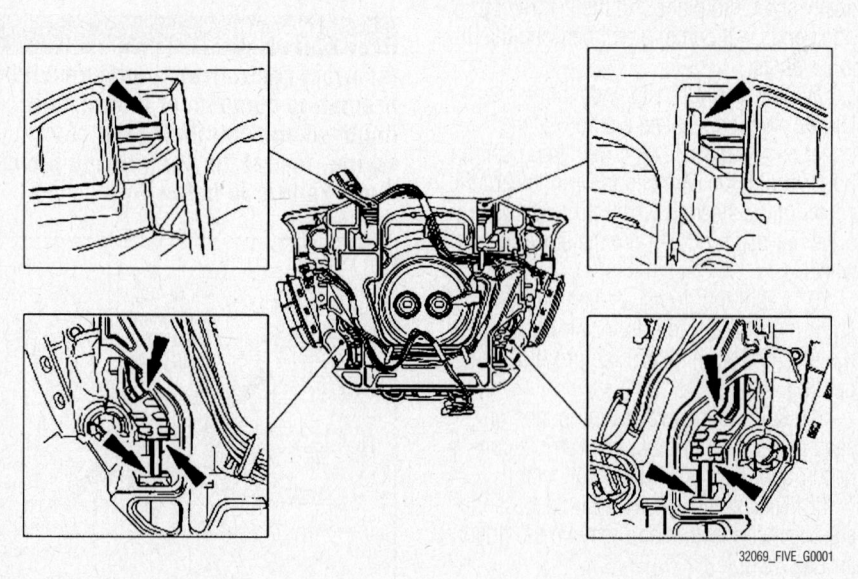

32069_FIVE_G0001

Fig. 8 Ensuring the driver air bag module wire clip is fully seated on all of the tabs and guides

bag module. Do not force the electrical connectors into the driver air bag module.

✳✳ CAUTION

Make sure the driver air bag module wiring is routed clear of the driver air bag mounting hooks on the steering wheel so that the wiring is not pinched during driver air bag module installation.

39. Connect the driver air bag module electrical connectors as noted in removal.

40. Make sure that all 4 retaining points of the driver air bag module wire clip are fully engaged and seated correctly to the steering wheel.

➡**Audible clicks will be heard when the locking tabs are fully engaged.**

41. Attach the driver air bag module to the steering wheel.

42. Align the driver air bag module to the 4 hooks on the steering wheel and press in until the driver air bag module wire clip is fully engaged to the steering wheel.

43. Check the driver air bag module and horn switch cover for clearance and correct movement.

44. Install the steering wheel access cover.

45. Rearm the air bag system.

DRIVETRAIN

AUTOMATIC TRANSAXLE ASSEMBLY

REMOVAL & INSTALLATION

CVT Transaxle

See Figure 9.

1. Place the vehicle on a hoist.
2. Drain the transaxle fluid.
3. Remove or disconnect the following:
   - Battery and battery tray
   - Air cleaner assembly and outlet pipe
   - Cowl grille panel
   - Upper roll restrictor bolt
   - Roll restrictor brace bolts and brace
   - Shift cable end
   - Electrical connector from shift cable bracket
   - Shift able bracket and position the cable and bracket aside
   - Transaxle wiring harnesses
   - Auxiliary coolant flow pump assembly, if equipped
   - Roll restrictor bracket and roll restrictor
   - PCV hose
   - Throttle body vacuum hoses
   - Power steering line bracket
   - Starter wiring and starter
   - Transaxle fluid cooler tube bracket
   - Ground cable
   - Transaxle bulkhead electrical connector
   - 4 upper transaxle mounting bolts
   - Left and right side halfshafts
   - Front and rear exhaust pipe nuts and discard
   - Catalytic converter pipe
4. On AWD models, remove the 2 outer bolts for the driveshaft brace.
5. Index mark the rear driveshaft flange to the Power Transfer Unit (PTU).
6. Remove and the discard 6 bolts from the front driveshaft flange.

7. Remove the PTU.
8. Wire the rear driveshaft to the chassis.
9. On all models, remove or disconnect the following:
   - Engine block heater connector
   - Knock sensor heat shield and knock sensor
   - Knock sensor wiring harness from transaxle
   - Transaxle-to-engine bolt
   - Power steering hose bolt
10. Install engine lifting eyes no. 134-00243 to the left and right cylinder heads.
11. Install lifting brackets no. 303-1140 to front of the engine.

12. Install engine support tools to the engine as shown.
13. Remove or disconnect the following:
   - Disconnect the lower radiator hose from its retainers and position aside
   - Power steering line from subframe
   - Wiring harness from left front subframe
   - Power steering rack retainers and wire the rack to the chassis
   - Oxygen sensor connector
   - Splash shield
   - Front motor mount nut
   - Lower stabilizer mount bolts
   - Rear motor mount nut

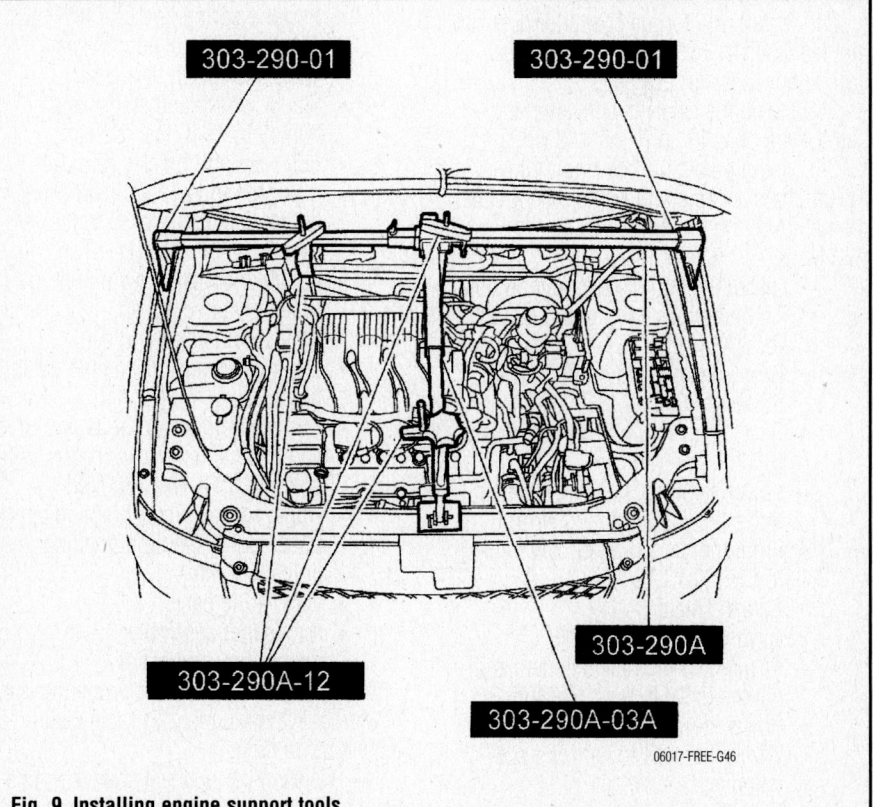

303-290-01   303-290-01

303-290A

303-290A-12

303-290A-03A

06017-FREE-G46

Fig. 9 Installing engine support tools

- Rear transaxle mount bolts
- Rear subframe mounting bolts on both sides
- Stabilizer bar links nuts from both sides and discard the nuts.
- Stabilizer bar from struts

14. Using a suitable powertrain lift, remove 4 subframe mounting bolts and remove the subframe.

15. Remove the catalytic converter.

16. Remove the torque converter access plug and remove and discard the 4 torque converter nuts.

17. Disconnect the transaxle fluid cooler tubes from the transaxle.

18. Securely fasten the transaxle to a suitable high lift transmission jack.

19. Remove the 3 engine-to-transaxle bolts, and remove the transaxle.

To install:

➡**If a different transaxle is being installed, transfer the appropriate external components to the new transaxle.**

20. Apply multi-purpose grease to the torque converter pilot hub.

21. Place the transaxle on a suitable jack and carefully raise it into position.

22. Install 3 engine-to-transaxle mounting bolts and tighten to 30 ft. lbs. (40 Nm).

23. Install new transaxle fluid cooler tube seals and connect the tubes.

24. Install new torque converter nuts and tighten to 27 ft. lbs. (36 Nm). Install the torque converter access plug.

25. Install the catalytic converter and tighten the bolts to 30 ft. lbs. (40 Nm).

26. Using a suitable powertrain lift, install the subframe and tighten the 4 subframe mounting bolts to 66 ft. lbs. (90 Nm).

- Install the subframe mounting bolts on both sides and tighten to 35 ft. lbs. (48 Nm).
- Rear transaxle mount bolts and tighten to 66 ft. lbs. (90 Nm).
- Rear motor mount nut and tighten to 52 ft. lbs. (70 Nm).
- Lower stabilizer mount bolts and tighten to 52 ft. lbs. (70 Nm).
- Front motor mount nut and tighten to 52 ft. lbs. (70 Nm).
- Splash shield
- Oxygen sensor connector
- Power steering rack retainers and tighten to 98 ft. lbs. (133 Nm)
- Power steering line to subframe
- Wiring harness to left front subframe
- Lower radiator hose

- Stabilizer bar to struts
- Stabilizer bar link nuts and tighten to 41 ft. lbs. (55 Nm)

27. Remove the all the special lifting tools from the engine and cylinder heads.

28. Install or connect the following:
- Transaxle-to-engine bolt and tighten to 30 ft. lbs. (40 Nm)
- Power steering hose bolt
- Knock sensor wiring harness to transaxle
- Knock sensor and heat shield
- Engine block heater connector

29. On AWD models, install the PTU and rear driveshaft. Tighten the bolts to 66 ft. lbs. (90 Nm).

30. Install the 2 outer bolts for the driveshaft brace and tighten to 18 ft. lbs. (25 Nm).

31. Install new bolts to the front driveshaft flange and tighten in a criss-cross pattern to 18 ft. lbs. (25 Nm).

32. On all models, install or connect the following:
- Front and rear exhaust pipe nuts and tighten to 30 ft. lbs. (40 Nm)
- Left and right side halfshafts
- 4 upper transaxle mounting bolts and tighten to 30 ft. lbs. (40 Nm)
- Transaxle bulkhead electrical connector
- Ground cable
- Transaxle fluid cooler tube bracket
- PCV hose
- Power steering line bracket
- Throttle body vacuum hoses
- Transaxle wiring harnesses
- Starter wiring and starter and tighten to 19 ft. lbs. (26 Nm)
- Roll restrictor bracket and roll restrictor and apply threadlocker before tightening to 30 ft. lbs. (40 Nm)
- Auxiliary coolant flow pump assembly, if equipped
- Shift able bracket and cable
- Electrical connector to shift cable bracket
- Roll restrictor brace bolts and brace and apply threadlocker before tightening to 30 ft. lbs. (40 Nm)
- Upper roll restrictor bolt and apply threadlocker before tightening to 30 ft. lbs. (40 Nm)
- Cowl grille panel
- Air cleaner assembly
- Battery tray and battery

33. Fill the transaxle with proper amount of Mercon®Continuously Variable chain type transmission fluid.

34. Connect the positive, then the negative battery cable. Start the engine and check for leaks.

6-Speed Transaxle

See Figure 9.

1. Place the vehicle on a hoist.

2. Drain the transaxle fluid.

3. Remove or disconnect the following:
- Battery and battery tray
- Air cleaner assembly and outlet pipe
- Cowl grille panel
- Upper roll restrictor bolt
- Roll restrictor brace bolts and brace
- Shift cable end
- Electrical connector from shift cable bracket
- Shift able bracket and position the cable and bracket aside
- Transaxle Control Module (TCM) wiring harness
- Transaxle wiring harnesses
- Roll restrictor bracket and roll restrictor
- PCV hose
- Throttle body vacuum hoses
- Power steering line bracket
- Starter wiring and starter
- Ground cable
- 4 upper transaxle mounting bolts
- Left and right side halfshafts
- Front and rear exhaust pipe nuts and discard
- Catalytic converter pipe
- Engine block heater connector
- Knock sensor heat shield and knock sensor
- Knock sensor wiring harness from transaxle
- Transaxle-to-engine bolt
- Power steering hose bolt

4. Install engine lifting eyes no. 134-00243 to the left and right cylinder heads.

5. Install lifting brackets no. 303-1140 to front of the engine.

6. Install engine support tools to the engine as shown.

7. Remove or disconnect the following:
- Disconnect the lower radiator hose from its retainers and position aside
- Power steering line from subframe
- Wiring harness from left front subframe
- Power steering rack retainers and wire the rack to the chassis
- Oxygen sensor connector
- Splash shield
- Front motor mount nut
- Lower stabilizer mount bolts
- Rear motor mount nut
- Rear transaxle mount bolts
- Rear subframe mounting bolts on both sides

- Stabilizer bar links nuts from both sides and discard the nuts.
- Stabilizer bar from struts

8. Using a suitable powertrain lift, remove 4 subframe mounting bolts and remove the subframe.

9. Remove the catalytic converter.

10. Remove the torque converter access plug and remove and discard the 4 torque converter nuts.

11. Disconnect the transaxle fluid cooler tubes from the transaxle.

12. Securely fasten the transaxle to a suitable high lift transmission jack.

13. Remove the 3 engine-to-transaxle bolts, and remove the transaxle.

To install:

→**If a different transaxle is being installed, transfer the appropriate external components to the new transaxle.**

14. Apply multi-purpose grease to the torque converter pilot hub.

15. Place the transaxle on a suitable jack and carefully raise it into position.

16. Install 3 engine-to-transaxle mounting bolts and tighten to 30 ft. lbs. (40 Nm).

17. Install new transaxle fluid cooler tube seals and connect the tubes.

18. Install new torque converter nuts and tighten to 27 ft. lbs. (36 Nm). Install the torque converter access plug.

19. Install the catalytic converter and tighten the bolts to 30 ft. lbs. (40 Nm).

20. Using a suitable powertrain lift, install the subframe and tighten the 4 subframe mounting bolts to 66 ft. lbs. (90 Nm).

- Install the subframe mounting bolts on both sides and tighten to 35 ft. lbs. (48 Nm).
- Rear transaxle mount bolts and tighten to 66 ft. lbs. (90 Nm).
- Rear motor mount nut and tighten to 52 ft. lbs. (70 Nm).
- Lower stabilizer mount bolts and tighten to 52 ft. lbs. (70 Nm).
- Front motor mount nut and tighten to 52 ft. lbs. (70 Nm).
- Splash shield
- Oxygen sensor connector
- Power steering rack retainers and tighten to 98 ft. lbs. (133 Nm)
- Power steering line to subframe
- Wiring harness to left front subframe
- Lower radiator hose
- Stabilizer bar to struts
- Stabilizer bar link nuts and tighten to 41 ft. lbs. (55 Nm)

21. Remove the all the special lifting tools from the engine and cylinder heads.

22. Install or connect the following:

- Transaxle-to-engine bolt and tighten to 30 ft. lbs. (40 Nm)
- Power steering hose bolt
- Knock sensor wiring harness to transaxle
- Knock sensor and heat shield
- Engine block heater connector
- Front and rear exhaust pipe nuts and tighten to 30 ft. lbs. (40 Nm)
- Left and right side halfshafts
- 4 upper transaxle mounting bolts and tighten to 30 ft. lbs. (40 Nm)
- Transaxle bulkhead electrical connector
- Ground cable
- Transaxle fluid cooler tube bracket
- PCV hose
- Power steering line bracket
- Throttle body vacuum hoses
- Transaxle wiring harnesses
- Starter wiring and starter and tighten to 19 ft. lbs. (26 Nm)
- Roll restrictor bracket and roll restrictor and apply threadlocker before tightening to 30 ft. lbs. (40 Nm)
- Auxiliary coolant flow pump assembly, if equipped
- Shift able bracket and cable
- Electrical connector to shift cable bracket
- Roll restrictor brace bolts and brace and apply threadlocker before tightening to 30 ft. lbs. (40 Nm)
- Upper roll restrictor bolt and apply threadlocker before tightening to 30 ft. lbs. (40 Nm)
- Cowl grille panel
- Air cleaner assembly
- Battery tray and battery

23. Fill the transaxle with proper amount of Motorcraft®Premium automatic transmission no. XT-8-QAW.

24. Connect the positive, then the negative battery cable.

Start the engine and check for leaks.

POWER TRANSFER UNIT

REMOVAL & INSTALLATION

1. Raise the vehicle on a hoist.
2. Remove the left and right halfshafts
3. Remove the front and rear exhaust pipe nuts.
4. Remove the catalytic converter pipe.
5. Index mark the driveshaft flange to the output flange.
6. Remove the 2 outer driveshaft brace bolts.

7. Remove the 6 bolts from the driveshaft flange.

8. Remove the upper PTU bracket bolts and the bracket.

9. Remove 4 PTU mounting bolts and the PTU.

10. Remove the input shaft oil slinger and seal.

To install:

11. Using a seal installer, install the input shaft seal and oil slinger.

12. Position the PTU in place and tighten the bolts to 66 ft. lbs. (90 Nm).

13. Install the upper PTU bracket bolts and the bracket and tighten to 41 ft. lbs. (55 Nm).

14. Install the left and right halfshafts

15. Install the 2 outer driveshaft brace bolts and tighten to 18 ft. lbs. (25 Nm).

16. Install the 6 bolts to the driveshaft flange and tighten in a criss-cross pattern to 18 ft. lbs. (25 Nm).

17. Install the catalytic converter pipe, front and rear exhaust pipe nuts and tighten all fasteners to 30 ft. lbs. (40 Nm).

HALFSHAFTS

REMOVAL & INSTALLATION

Front

See Figures 10 through 13.

→**Do not begin this removal procedure unless a new wheel hub retainer nut, a new retainer circlip and a new lower ball joint-to-front wheel knuckle retaining bolt and nut are available. Once removed, these parts must not be reused during assembly. Their torque holding ability, or retention capability, is diminished during removal.**

1. Remove or disconnect the following:
   - Front wheels
   - ABS sensor
   - Brake caliper and wire aside
   - Axle hub nut and washer. Discard the nut.

2. Separate the halfshaft from the hub using tool no. 205-D070.

3. Remove and discard the lower ball joint nut.

4. Disconnect the lower control arm.

5. On the left side, on 6-speed models, use a slide hammer and remove the halfshaft from the transaxle.

6. On the left side on CVT models, use a slide hammer and halfshaft fork no. 205-241 and remove the shaft from the transaxle.

7. On the right side, remove the halfshaft bearing nuts and remove the halfshaft.

8. On both sides, inspect the halfshaft seal and replace if necessary.

To install:

✳✳ WARNING

Do not reuse the retainer circlip. A new circlip must be installed each time the inboard CV-joint stub shaft is installed into the transaxle differential.

9. Install a new retainer circlip on the inboard CV-joint stub shaft by starting one

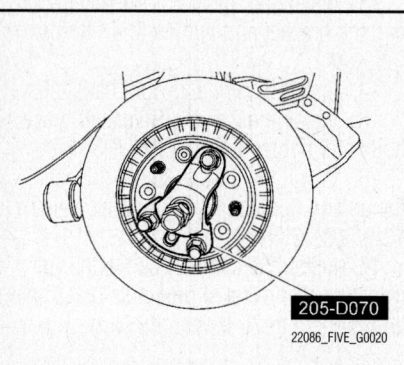

205-D070

22086_FIVE_G0020

Fig. 10 Separate the front halfshaft from the hub using tool no. 205-D070

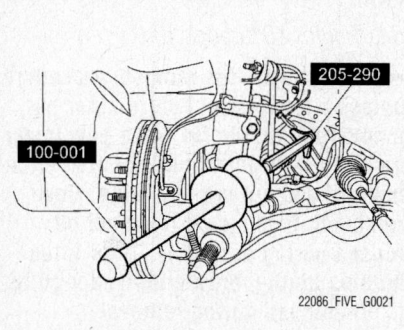

205-290

100-001

22086_FIVE_G0021

Fig. 11 On the left front side of 6-speed models, use a slide hammer to remove the halfshaft from the transaxle

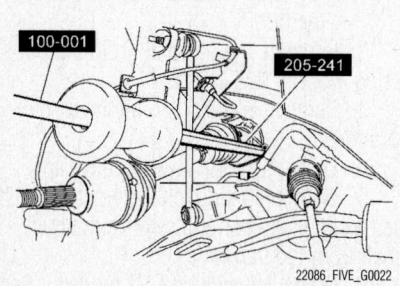

100-001

205-241

22086_FIVE_G0022

Fig. 12 On the left front side of CVT models, use a slide hammer and halfshaft fork no. 205-241 to remove the halfshaft from the transaxle

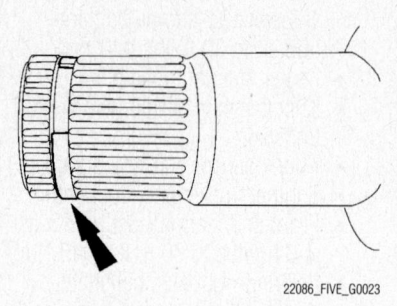

22086_FIVE_G0023

Fig. 13 Install a new retainer circlip on the front halfshaft inboard CV-joint stub shaft

end in the groove and working the retainer circlip over the inboard shaft housing end and into the groove. This will avoid over-expanding the circlip.

➡**A non-metallic mallet may be used to aid in seating the retainer circlip into the differential side gear groove. If a mallet is necessary, tap only on the outboard CV-joint shaft.**

10. Install the halfshaft.

11. On the right side install the halfshaft bearing nuts and tighten to 20 ft. lbs. (27 Nm).

12. On both sides install the halfshaft into the hub.

13. Connect the lower control arm to the knuckle and install a new ball joint nut. Tighten the nut to 59 ft. lbs. (80 Nm).

14. Using the old axle nut and washer tighten the nut to seat the halfshaft in the hub.

15. Remove the old nut and washer.

16. Install a new axle nut and washer and in a continuous motion, tighten the nut to 259 ft. lbs. (350 Nm).

17. Install the brake caliper and tighten to 74 ft. lbs. (100 Nm).

18. Install the front wheels and lower the vehicle.

Rear

➡**Do not begin this removal procedure unless a new wheel hub retainer nut is available. Once removed, the nut must not be reused during assembly. The torque holding ability, or retention capability, is diminished during removal.**

1. Remove or disconnect the following:
   • Rear wheel
   • Brake caliper and wire aside
   • Axle hub nut and washer. Discard the nut.
   • ABS sensor

2. Using a hub remover, press the half-shaft out until it is loose in the hub.

3. Remove the brake disc.

4. Remove the 4 hub bolts and remove the hub.

5. Using a prybar, separate the halfshaft from the axle, and remove the halfshaft.

To install:

✳✳ WARNING

Do not reuse the retainer circlip. A new circlip must be installed each time.

6. Install a new retainer circlip on the CV-joint stub shaft by starting one end in the groove and working the retainer circlip over the inboard shaft housing end and into the groove. This will avoid over-expanding the circlip.

7. Install the halfshaft.

8. Install the hub and the hub bolts and tighten to 89 ft. lbs. (120 Nm).

9. Install the brake disc and tighten to 16 ft. lbs. (21 Nm).

10. Using the old axle nut and washer tighten the nut to seat the halfshaft in the hub.

11. Remove the old nut and washer.

12. Install a new axle nut and washer and in a continuous motion, tighten the nut to 148 ft. lbs. (200 Nm).

13. Install the ABS sensor.

14. Install the caliper and tighten to 81 ft. lbs. (110 Nm).

15. Install the rear wheel.

CV-JOINT

OVERHAUL

➡**Overhaul procedures are not available from the manufacturer.**

DRIVESHAFT, PINION FLANGE AND SEAL

REMOVAL & INSTALLATION

See Figures 14, 15 and 16.

1. Place the vehicle on a hoist.

2. Remove the exhaust system at the flex pipe.

3. Remove the exhaust support brace.

4. Index mark the driveshaft to the rear axle pinion flange, PTU flange and center bearing bracket.

5. Disconnect the driveshaft from the rear pinion flange and discard the bolts.

6. Remove the driveshaft flange bolts from the PTU flange and discard the bolts.

7. Disconnect the driveshaft from the PTU flange.

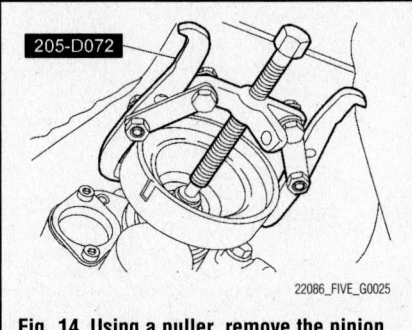

Fig. 14 Using a puller, remove the pinion flange

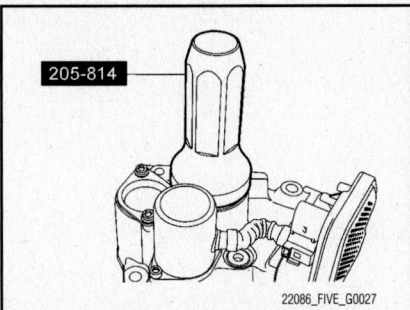

Fig. 16 Using a seal installer, install the pinion seal

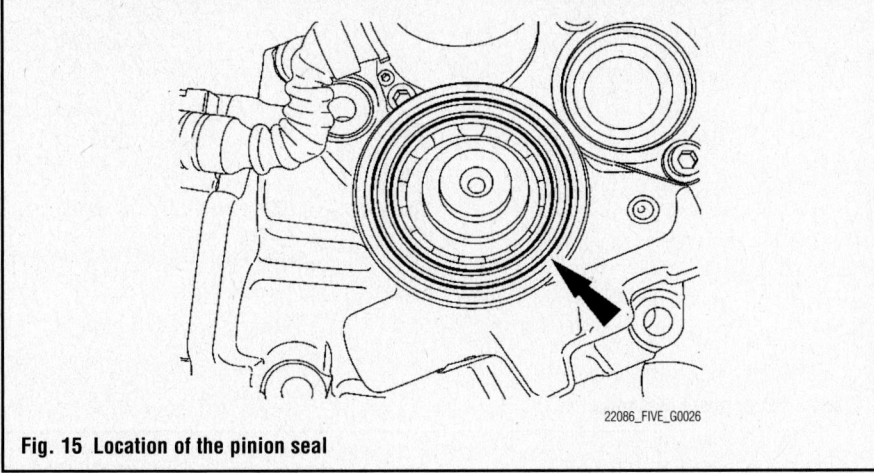

Fig. 15 Location of the pinion seal

8. Remove the center bearing bracket bolts and remove the driveshaft.

9. Remove and discard the pinion flange nut.

10. Using a puller, remove the pinion flange.

11. Remove the pinion seal.

To install:

12. Using a seal installer, install the pinion seal.

13. Install the drive pinion flange using a new nut. Tighten the nut to 74 ft. lbs. (100 Nm).

14. Install the driveshaft.

15. Install the center bearing bracket and loosely tighten the bolts. bolts and remove the driveshaft.

16. Using the index marks made on removal, connect the driveshaft to the PTU flange and rear pinion flange and hand tighten the bolts..

17. Tighten the center bearing bracket bolts to 15 ft. lbs. (20 Nm).

18. Tighten the driveshaft to rear pinion flange and PTU flange bolts to 18 ft. lbs. (25 Nm).

19. Install the exhaust support brace and tighten the bolts to 22 ft. lbs. (30 Nm).

20. Install the exhaust system.

21. Lower the vehicle.

OUTPUT SHAFT SEAL AND FLANGE

REMOVAL & INSTALLATION

1. Remove the driveshaft.

2. Remove the output flange nut and flange.

3. Remove the output shaft seal.

To install:

4. Clean the output shaft seal bore and shaft.

5. Use a seal installer and install the output shaft seal.

6. Install the output flange and tighten the nut to 74 ft. lbs. (100 Nm).

7. Install the driveshaft.

ENGINE COOLING

ENGINE FAN

REMOVAL & INSTALLATION

1. Disconnect the battery ground cable.

2. Disconnect the 2 coolant hose retainers from the fan shroud and position aside.

3. Disconnect the cooling fan motor electrical connector.

4. Remove the 2 cooling fan motor and shroud bolts and release the cooling fan motor and shroud from the lower brackets.

5. To install, reverse the removal procedure.

RADIATOR

REMOVAL & INSTALLATION

1. Drain the cooling system.

2. Remove the air cleaner assembly.

3. Remove the cooling fan motor and shroud.

4. Remove the front grille.

5. Disconnect the upper radiator hose and position aside.

6. Disconnect the lower radiator hose and position aside.

7. Disconnect the horn assembly electrical connector.

8. Remove the horn assembly bolt and the horn assembly.

9. Remove the 2 A/C condenser retaining bolts and position aside the A/C condenser.

10. Remove the 2 radiator support bracket bolts.

11. Remove the 2 radiator support brackets and position the radiator forward.

12. Remove the transmission cooler bracket bolt.

13. Lift the transmission cooler.

14. Remove the radiator.

To install:

15. To install, reverse the removal procedure.

16. Tighten the condenser, radiator bracket and transmission cooler bracket to 53 inch lbs. (6 Nm).

17. Fill and bleed the cooling system.

THERMOSTAT

REMOVAL & INSTALLATION

1. Drain the cooling system.

2. Remove the air cleaner assembly.

3. Disconnect the degas bottle-to-thermostat housing hose and position aside.

4. Disconnect the throttle body-to-thermostat housing hose and position aside.

5. Disconnect the upper radiator-to-thermostat housing hose and position aside.

6. Disconnect the bypass tube-to-thermostat housing hose and position aside.

7. Disconnect the heater hose from the thermostat housing and position aside.

8. Disconnect the lower radiator-to-thermostat housing hose and position aside.

9. Remove the 2 bolts and the thermostat housing.

10. Discard the O-ring seal.

11. Remove the 3 thermostat housing bolts and separate the upper and lower thermostat housing.

12. Remove the thermostat.

13. Remove the O-ring seal and discard.

To install:

14. Align the thermostat bridge with the alignment marks and install it in the upper housing.

15. Lubricate a new O-ring seal with clean engine coolant and install it in the upper housing.

16. Install the lower thermostat housing and the 3 bolts and tighten to 89 inch lbs. (10 Nm).

17. Reverse the removal procedure to complete installation.

18. Fill the engine with coolant.

WATER PUMP

REMOVAL & INSTALLATION

See Figure 17.

1. Remove or disconnect the following:

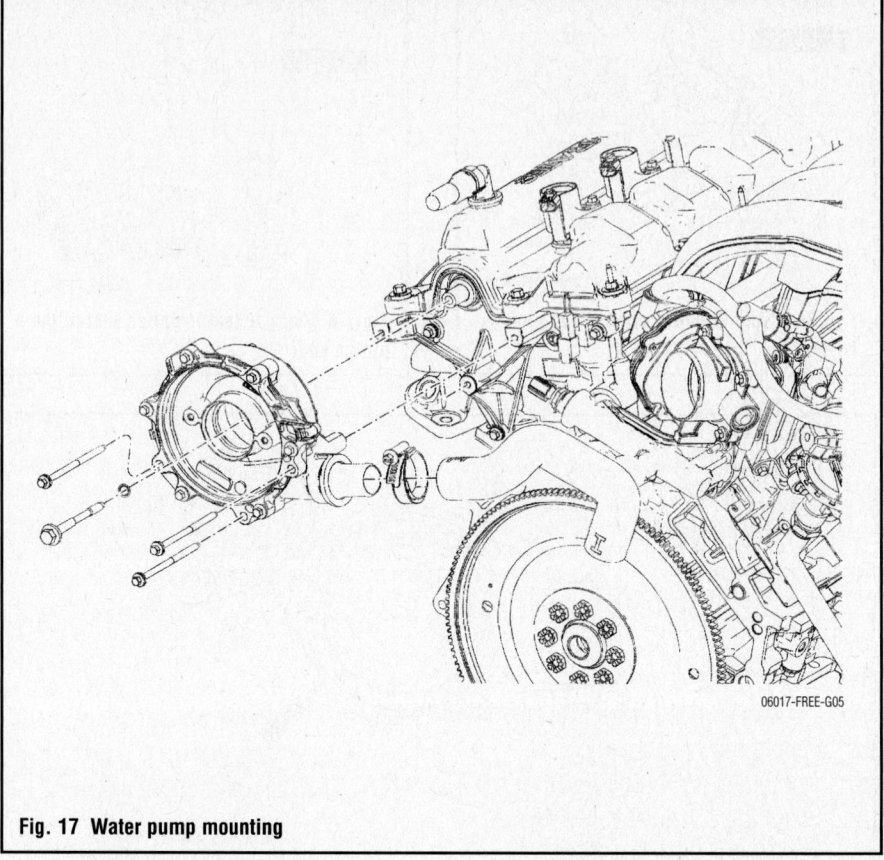

Fig. 17 Water pump mounting

06017-FREE-G05

- Negative battery cable
- Coolant
- Accessory drive belt
- Air cleaner assembly
- Lower radiator hose
- Thermostat hoses
- Thermostat housing
- Water pump

To install:

2. Position a new water pump housing gasket on the water pump sealing surface using gasket sealant to hold the gasket in place.

3. Install the water pump and tighten the bolts in the following sequence: tighten the center bolt to 35 inch lbs. (4 nm), loosely install the outer bolts, retighten the center bolt to 18 ft. lbs. (25 Nm), tighten the outer bolts to 89 inch lbs. (10 Nm).

4. The remainder of the installation is the reverse of removal.

5. Fill and bleed the cooling system.

6. Connect the negative battery cable.

7. Start the engine and check for leaks.

ENGINE ELECTRICAL | **CHARGING SYSTEM**

ALTERNATOR

REMOVAL & INSTALLATION

See Figure 18.

1. Disconnect the negative battery cable.
2. Raise and support the vehicle.
3. Rotate the drive belt tensioner counterclockwise and remove the accessory drive belt.
4. Remove the right lower splash shield.
5. Disconnect the crankshaft position sensor.
6. Disconnect the wiring harness locators from the alternator splash shield.
7. Detach the alternator wiring connector.
8. Remove the positive cable nut.
9. Remove the alternator splash shield and the alternator.

To install:

10. Position the alternator on the engine.
11. Install the alternator mounting bolts.

Tighten the stud bolts to 71 INCH lbs. (8 Nm) and the bolts to 35 ft. lbs. (47 Nm).

12. Tighten the positive cable nut to 71 INCH lbs. (8 Nm).
13. Connect the wiring connector.
14. Install the wiring harness locators.
15. Connect the crankshaft position sensor.
16. Install the lower right splash shield.
17. Install and tension the accessory drive belt.
18. Connect the negative battery cable.

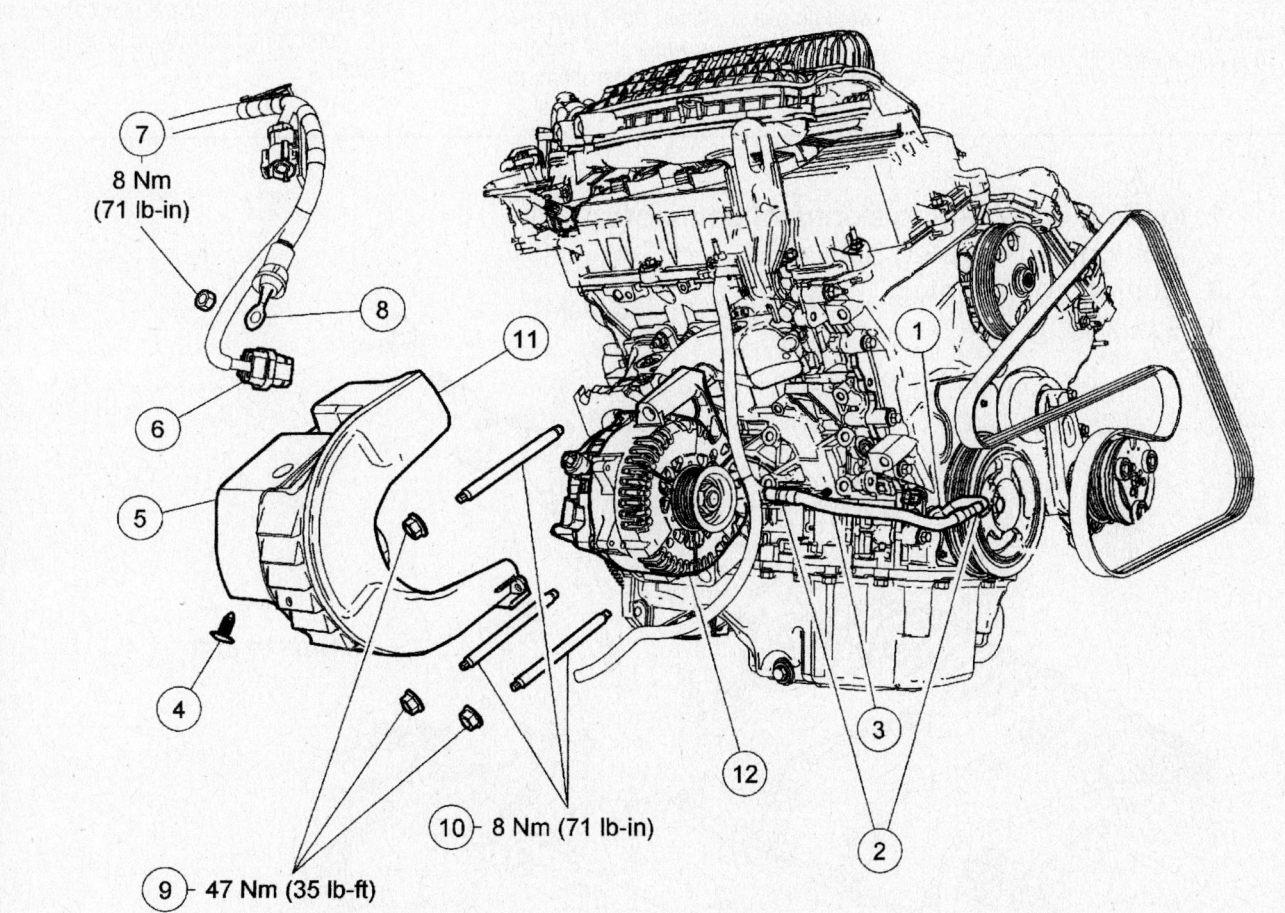

8 Nm (71 lb-in)

10 – 8 Nm (71 lb-in)

9 – 47 Nm (35 lb-ft)

1 Crankshaft position sensor connector	7 Generator B+ nut
2 Harness locators (2 required)	8 Generator B+ terminal
3 Engine control harness	9 Generator stud nuts (3 required)
4 Lower generator boot pin-type retainer	10 Generator studs (3 required)
5 Generator boot	11 Generator shield
6 Generator electrical connector	12 Generator

06017-FREE-G02

Fig. 18 Alternator mounting

ENGINE ELECTRICAL   **IGNITION SYSTEM**

IGNITION COIL

REMOVAL & INSTALLATION

See Figure 19.

1. Disconnect the negative battery cable.
2. Remove the upper intake manifold.
3. Disconnect the ignition coil electrical connectors.
4. Remove the ignition coil bolts.
5. When removing the ignition coils, a slight twisting motion will break the seal and ease removal.
6. Remove the ignition coils.

To install:

7. To install, reverse the removal procedure. Tighten the spark plugs to 11 ft. lbs. (15 Nm).

IGNITION TIMING

ADJUSTMENT

The ignition timing is controlled by the Powertrain Control Module (PCM). No adjustment is necessary or possible.

SPARK PLUGS

REMOVAL & INSTALLATION

When you're removing spark plugs, work on one at a time. Don't start by removing the plug wires all at once, because, unless you number them, they may become mixed up. Take a minute before you begin and number the wires with tape.

1. Disconnect the negative battery cable.
2. Remove the upper intake manifold.
3. Disconnect the ignition coil electrical connectors.
4. Remove the ignition coil bolts.
5. When removing the ignition coils, a slight twisting motion will break the seal and ease removal.
6. Remove the ignition coils.
7. Remove the spark plugs.

To install:

8. To install, reverse the removal procedure. Tighten the spark plugs to 11 ft. lbs. (15 Nm).

1. Ignition coil-on-plug electrical connector
2. Ignition coil-on-plug bolt
3. Ignition coil-on-plug
4. Spark plug

2 – 6 Nm (53 lb-in)

15 Nm (11 lb-ft) – 4

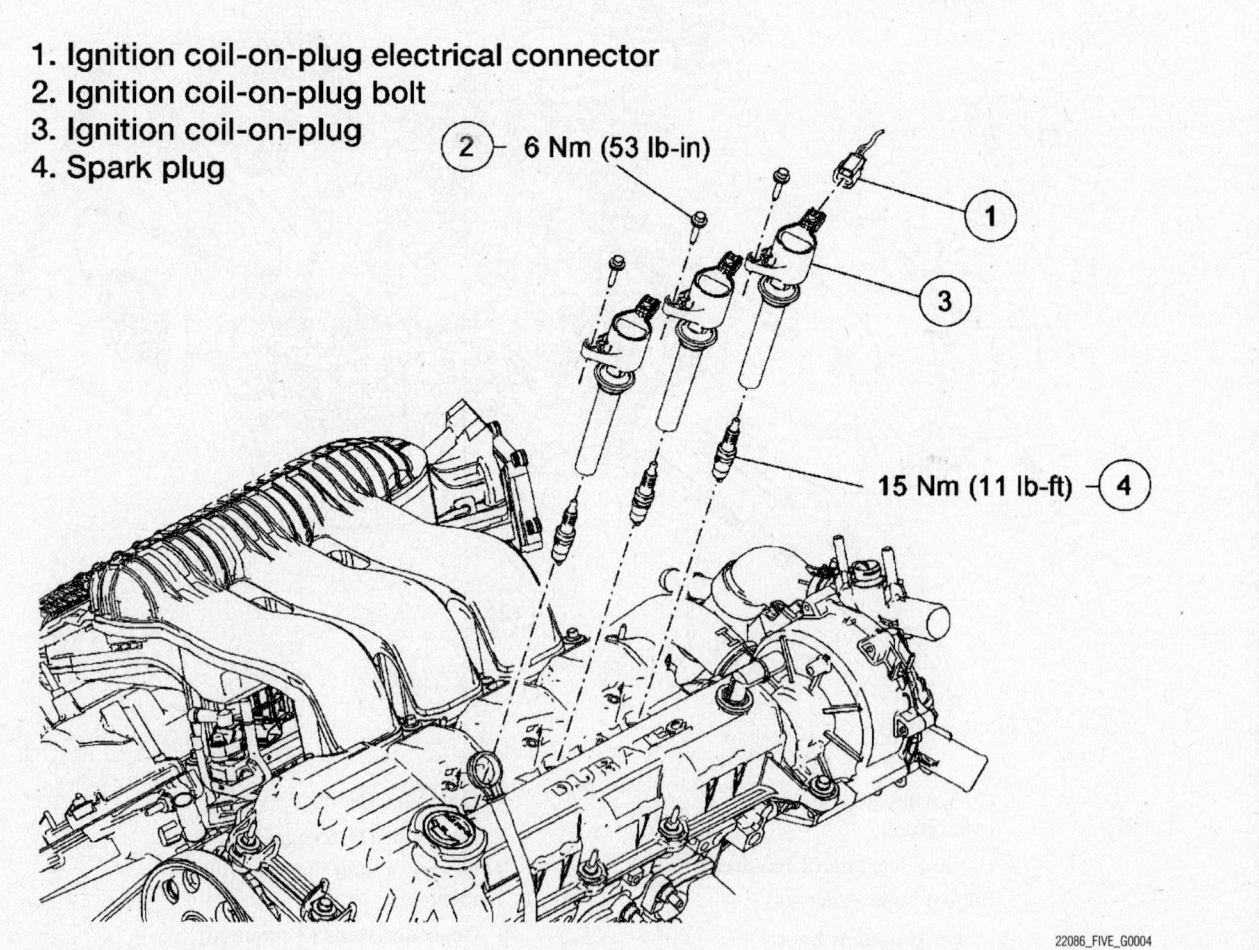

22086_FIVE_G0004

Fig. 19 Ignition coil on plug mounting

ENGINE ELECTRICAL | **STARTING SYSTEM**

STARTER

REMOVAL & INSTALLATION

CVT Transmission Models

See Figure 20.

1. Disconnect the negative battery cable.
2. Remove the air cleaner assembly.
3. Remove the starter cover.
4. Disconnect the starter electrical connectors.
5. Remove the starter bolts.
6. Remove the starter from the vehicle.

To install:

7. Position the starter in the vehicle.

8. Install the bolts. Tighten to 18 ft. lbs. (25 Nm).
9. Connect the starter electrical connectors.
10. Install the starter cover.
11. Install the air cleaner assembly.
12. Connect the negative battery cable.

6-Speed Transmission Models

See Figure 21.

1. Disconnect the negative battery cable.
2. Remove the air cleaner outlet pipe.
3. Remove the transaxle roll restrictor bolts and the cross brace assembly.
4. Remove the starter cover.

5. Disconnect the starter electrical connectors.
6. Remove the starter bolts.
7. Remove the starter from the vehicle.

To install:

8. Position the starter in the vehicle.
9. Install the bolts. Tighten to 18 ft. lbs. (25 Nm).
10. Connect the starter electrical connectors.
11. Install the starter cover.
12. Install the cross brace assembly and transaxle roll restrictor bolts.
13. Install the air cleaner outlet pipe.
14. Connect the negative battery cable.

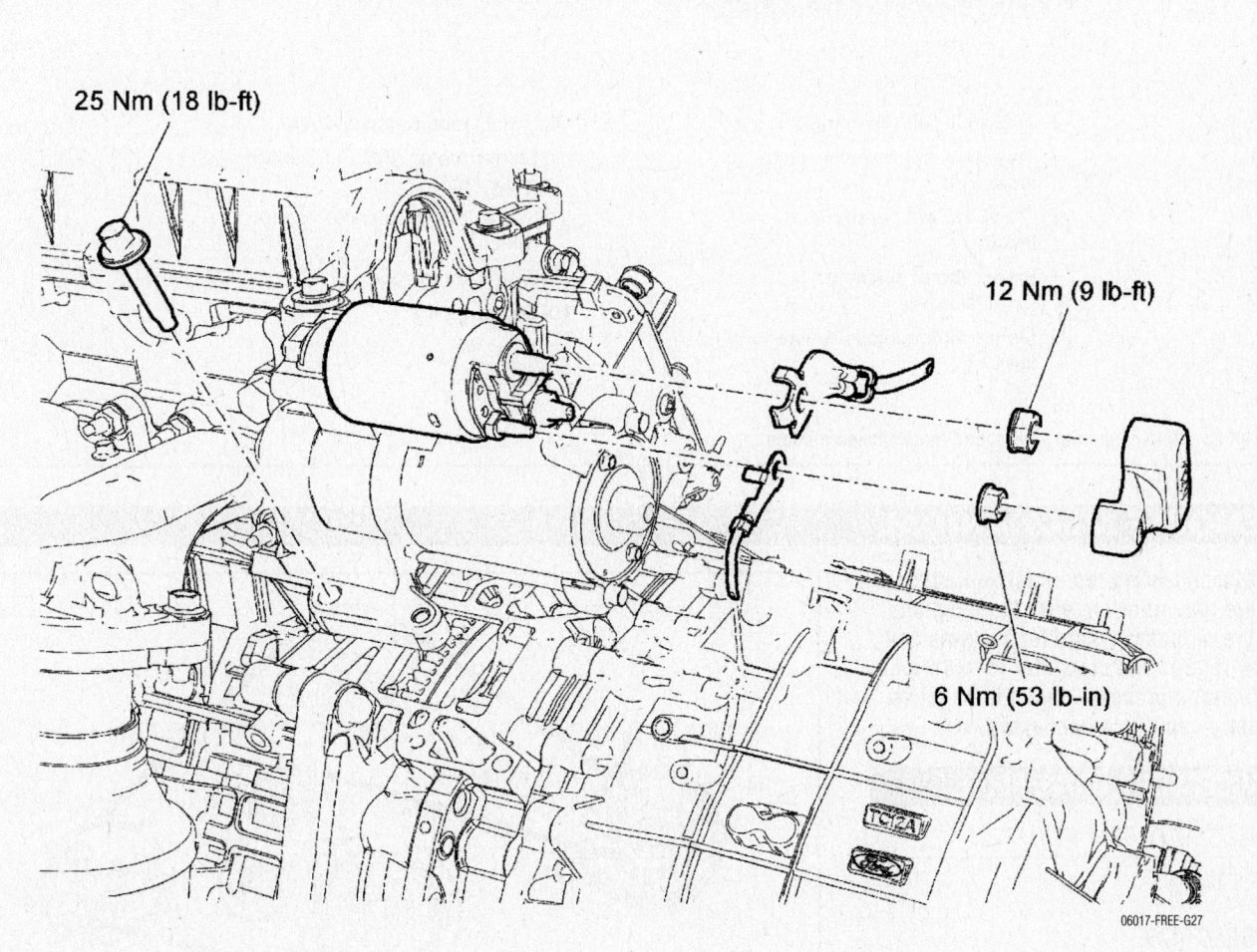

25 Nm (18 lb-ft)

12 Nm (9 lb-ft)

6 Nm (53 lb-in)

06017-FREE-G27

Fig. 20 Starter mounting—CVT transmission models

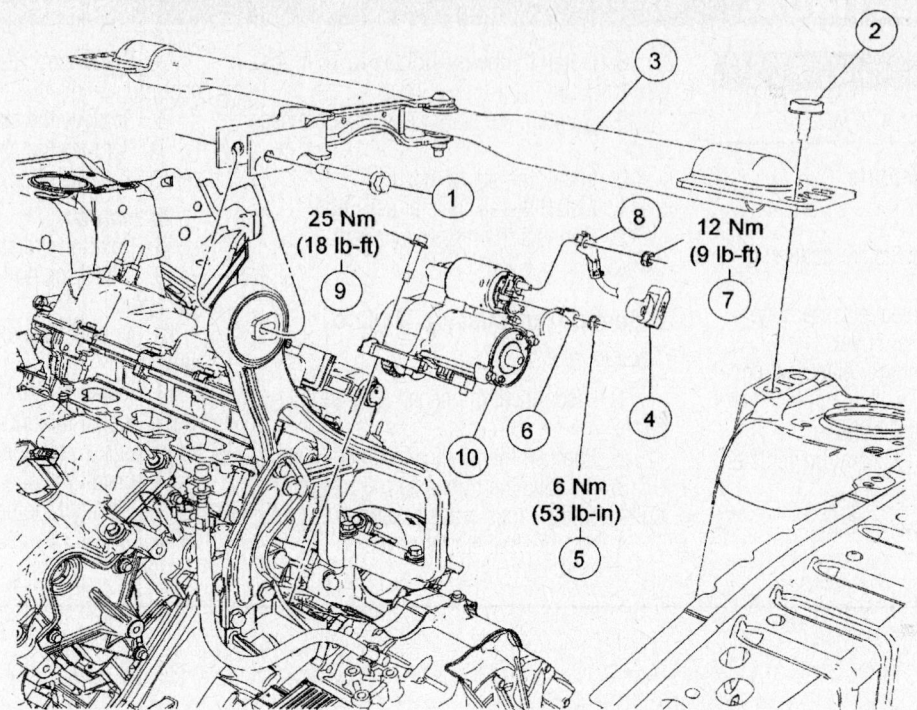

25 Nm
(18 lb-ft)

12 Nm
(9 lb-ft)

6 Nm
(53 lb-in)

1 Transaxle roll restrictor bolt

2 Transaxle roll restrictor cross
   brace bolt

3 Transaxle roll restrictor cross
   brace

4 Starter motor solenoid
   terminal cover

5 Starter motor solenoid wire
   nut

6 Starter motor solenoid wire

7 Starter motor solenoid battery
   cable nut

8 Starter motor solenoid battery
   cable

9 Starter motor bolt

10 Starter motor

06017-FREE-G28

Fig. 21 Starter mounting—6-speed transmission models

ENGINE MECHANICAL

→**Disconnecting the negative battery
cable may interfere with the functions
of the on board computer systems and
may require the computer to undergo a
relearning process, once the negative
battery cable is reconnected.**

ACCESSORY DRIVE BELTS

ACCESSORY BELT ROUTING

See Figure 22.

INSPECTION

Inspect the drive belt for signs of glazing
or cracking. A glazed belt will be perfectly
smooth from slippage, while a good belt will
have a slight texture of fabric visible. Cracks

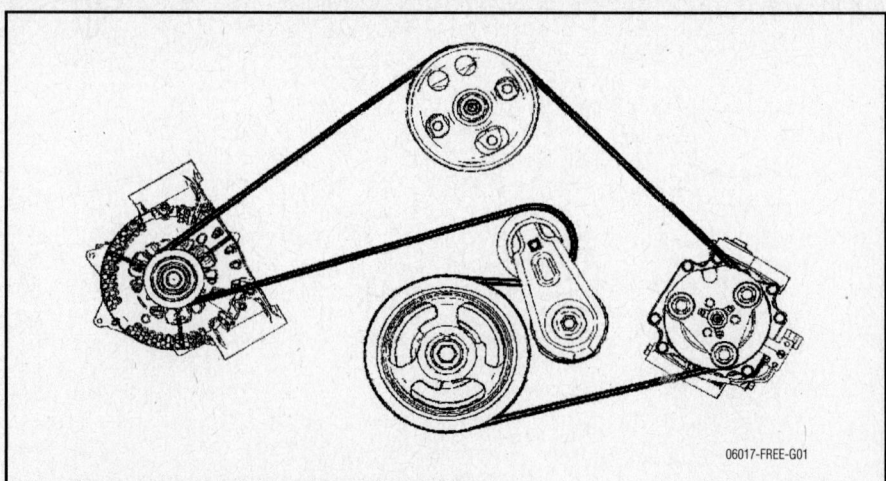

06017-FREE-G01

Fig. 22 Accessory drive belt routing—3.0L engine

will usually start at the inner edge of the belt and run outward. All worn or damaged drive belts should be replaced immediately.

REMOVAL & INSTALLATION

1. With the vehicle in NEUTRAL, position it on a hoist.
2. Remove the 7 pin-type retainers and the RH splash shield.
3. If equipped, remove the 3 A/C compressor pulley shield retainers and the shield.
4. Using a suitable belt tensioner release tool, rotate the accessory drive belt tensioner counterclockwise and remove the accessory drive belt.

To install:
5. To install, reverse the removal procedure.

CAMSHAFT AND VALVE LIFTERS

REMOVAL & INSTALLATION

Right Side

See Figures 23 through 25.

1. Disconnect the negative battery cable.
2. Remove the engine front cover.
3. Remove the timing chains.
4. Loosen the camshaft bearing cap bolts evenly in the sequence shown and remove the bearing caps.

➡**The bearing caps are numbered for correct positioning.**

5. Remove the camshafts.

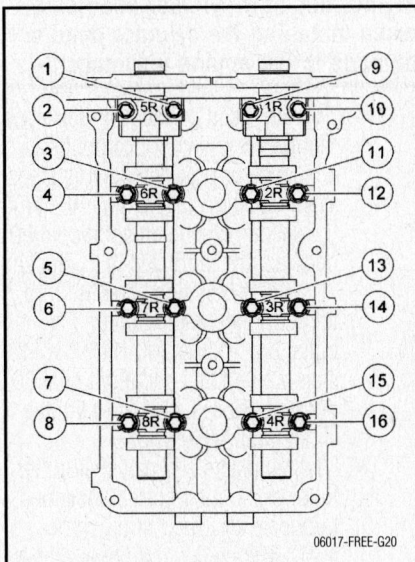

Fig. 23 Right side camshaft bearing cap removal sequence

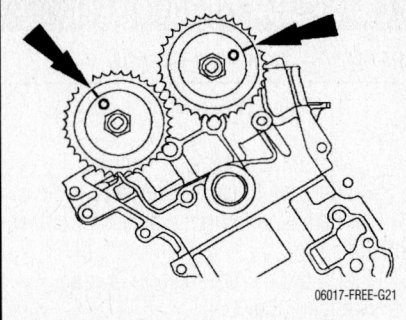

Fig. 24 Right side camshaft sprocket mark positioning

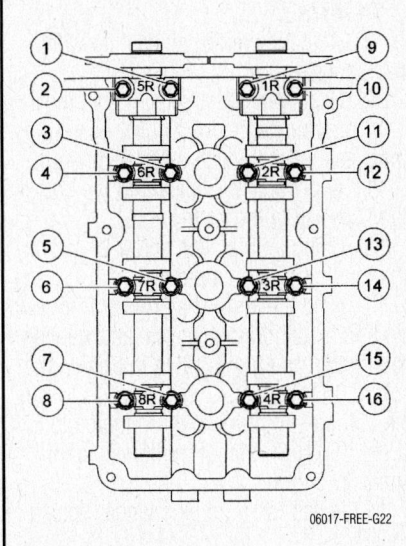

Fig. 25 Right side camshaft bearing cap tightening sequence

To install:
6. Clean and inspect all parts before installation.
7. Lubricate the camshaft lobes and journals with clean engine oil.
8. Carefully install the camshafts.
9. Align the camshaft sprocket marks as shown.
10. Lubricate the bearing surfaces of the bearing caps with clean engine oil.
11. Position the bearing caps in their proper locations and loosely install the bearing cap bolts.
12. Tighten the bearing caps bolts in sequence to 89 inch lbs. (10 Nm).
13. Install the timing chains.
14. Install the engine front cover.
15. Connect the negative battery cable.

Left Side

See Figures 26 through 29.

1. Disconnect the negative battery cable.
2. Remove the water pump.

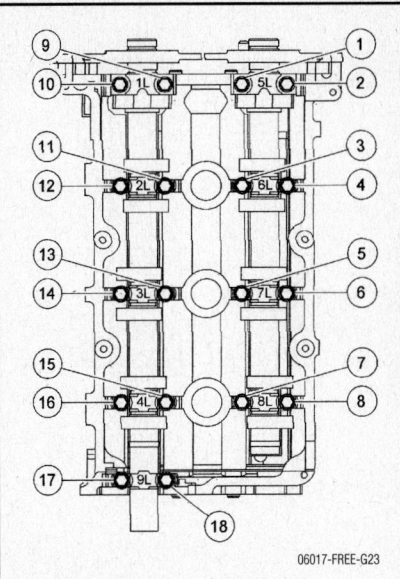

Fig. 26 Left side camshaft bearing cap removal sequence

3. Remove the engine front cover.
4. Remove the timing chains.
5. Remove the 3 bolts and the camshaft oil seal retainer.
6. Using a press, remove the oil seal from the retainer and discard.
7. Loosen the camshaft bearing cap bolts evenly in the sequence shown and remove the bearing caps.

➡**The bearing caps are numbered for correct positioning.**

8. Remove the camshafts.

To install:
9. Clean and inspect all parts before installation.
10. Lubricate the camshaft lobes and journals with clean engine oil.
11. Carefully install the camshafts.
12. Align the camshaft sprocket marks as shown.
13. Lubricate the bearing surfaces of the bearing caps with clean engine oil.

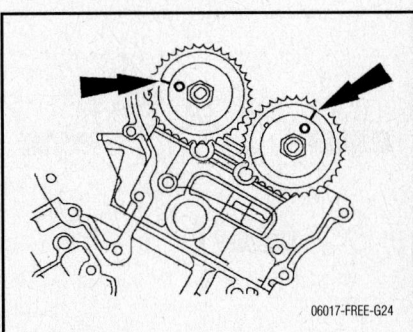

Fig. 27 Left side camshaft sprocket mark positioning

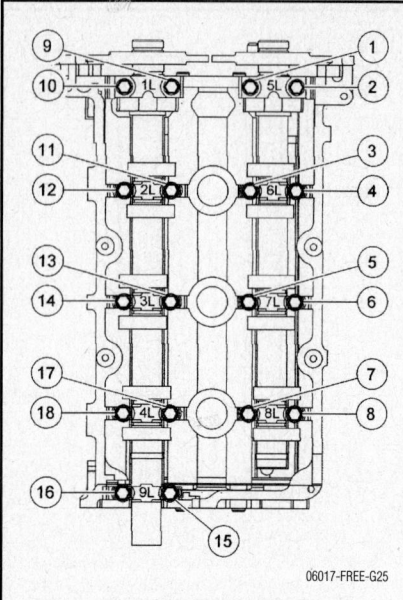

Fig. 28 Left side camshaft bearing cap tightening sequence

14. Position the bearing caps in their proper locations and loosely install the bearing cap bolts.

15. Tighten the bearing caps bolts in sequence to 89 inch lbs. (10 Nm).

16. Install the camshaft oil seal retainer and tighten the bolts 89 inch lbs. (10 Nm).

17. Lubricate the oil seal with clean engine oil and position the seal on installer tool no. 303-463.

18. Position the installer tool and oil seal on the camshaft.

19. Using installer tools no. 303-1139, 211-185 and 303-458, install the camshaft oil seal.

20. Remove the special tools.
21. Install the timing chains.
22. Install the engine front cover.
23. Install the water pump.
24. Connect the negative battery cable.

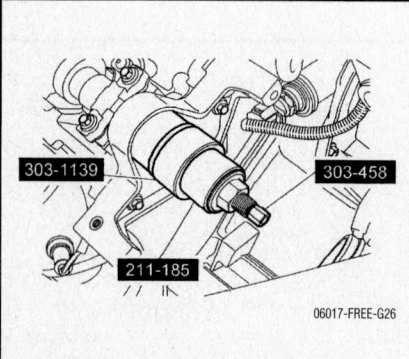

Fig. 29 Left side camshaft oil seal installation

CRANKSHAFT FRONT SEAL

REMOVAL & INSTALLATION

1. Disconnect the negative battery cable.

2. Raise the vehicle on a hoist.

3. Remove the accessory drive belt.

4. Remove the right side fender splash shield.

5. Hold the crankshaft pulley and remove the pulley bolt.

6. Using a puller, remove the crankshaft pulley.

7. Use a seal replacer and pull out the oil seal.

To install:

8. Coat the crankshaft seal lip with clean engine oil.

9. Using a seal installer, install the seal.

10. Lubricate the front cover and crankshaft seal inner lip with clean engine oil.

11. Apply silicone sealant to the crankshaft keyway in the pulley.

12. Using an installer, screw the crankshaft pulley on the crankshaft.

13. Hold the crankshaft pulley from turning and install the pulley bolt and washer and tighten as follows: Step 1; tighten the bolt to 86 ft. lbs. (120 Nm). Step 2; loosen the bolt one full turn. Step 3; tighten to 37 ft. lbs. (50 Nm). Step 4; tighten an additional 90 degrees.

14. Install the right side fender splash shield.

15. Install the accessory drive belt.

16. Lower the vehicle.

CYLINDER HEAD

REMOVAL & INSTALLATION

Left Side

See Figures 30 through 32.

1. Relieve the fuel system pressure.

2. Disconnect the negative battery cable.

3. Drain the engine coolant.

4. Remove or disconnect the following:
   - Accessory drive belt
   - Upper and lower intake manifolds
   - Coolant bypass tube
   - Ignition coil on plugs
   - Valve cover wiring harness
   - 6 bolts and 8 stud bolts, and remove the valve cover
   - Camshafts
   - Exhaust manifold
   - Oil dipstick and tube
   - Mark the location of the camshaft roller followers and remove them

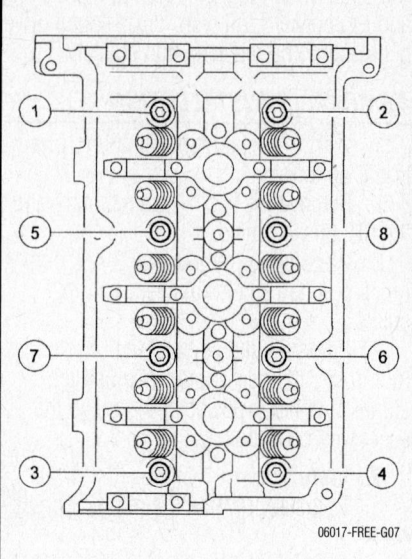

Fig. 30 Left side cylinder head bolt removal sequence

   - Hydraulic lash adjusters
   - Cylinder head bolts in the sequence shown
   - Cylinder head from the engine block and discard the gaskets and bolts

To install:

5. The cylinder head should be cleaned and inspected prior to installation.

6. Clean all gasket mating surfaces thoroughly.

7. Install or connect the following:
   - New head gaskets on the cylinder block

❊❊ WARNING

Always use new cylinder head bolts when installing the cylinder head or damage to the engine may occur.

   - Cylinder head on the cylinder block
   - Tighten the cylinder head bolts in sequence using the following steps. The first step is 30 ft. lbs. (40 Nm), the second step is an additional 90 degrees, the third step is to loosen all bolts in sequence one full turn, the fourth step is to tighten the bolts to 30 ft. lbs. (40 Nm), the fifth step is to tighten and additional 90 degrees, the last step is to tighten an addition 90 degrees.
   - Lash adjusters and camshaft roller followers in their correct locations. Lubricate all rocker arm components with engine assembly lubricant.
   - Oil dipstick and tube

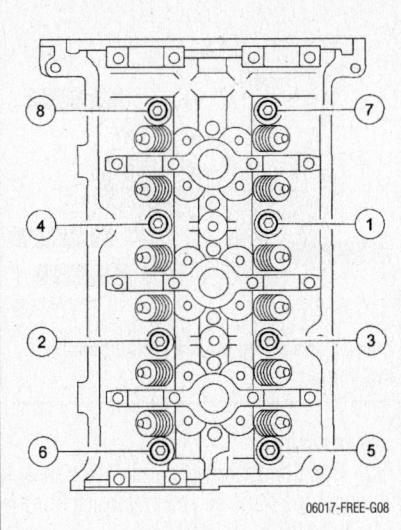

Fig. 31 Left side cylinder head bolt installation sequence

- Exhaust manifold
- Camshafts
- Place a bead of silicone gasket sealant to the front cover-to-cylinder head surface
- Valve cover. Install the 6 bolts and 8 stud bolts, and tighten in sequence to 89 inch lbs. (10 Nm).
- Valve cover wiring harness
- Ignition coil on plugs
- Coolant bypass tube
- Upper and lower intake manifolds
- Accessory drive belt

8. Fill and bleed the cooling system.

➡**Engine coolant is corrosive to engine bearing material. Replace the engine oil after removal of any coolant-carrying component to help prevent potential bearing damage.**

9. Change the engine oil and filter
10. Connect the negative battery cable.
11. Start the engine and check for leaks.

Right Side

See Figures 33 through 35.

1. Relieve the fuel system pressure.
2. Disconnect the negative battery cable.
3. Drain the engine coolant.
4. Remove or disconnect the following:

- Accessory drive belt
- Upper and lower intake manifolds
- Coolant bypass tube
- Ignition coil on plugs
- PCV connector and tube
- Power steering reservoir bracket and stud bolts
- Power steering pressure tube bracket
- Wiring harness and retainers from valve cover
- Valve cover bolts and stud bolts
- Valve cover
- Camshafts
- Exhaust manifold
- Mark the location of the camshaft roller followers and remove them
- Hydraulic lash adjusters
- Cylinder head bolts in the sequence shown
- Cylinder head from the engine block and discard the gaskets and bolts

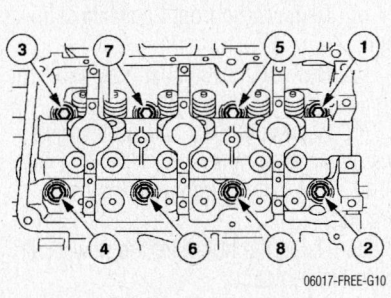

Fig. 33 Right side cylinder head bolt removal sequence

To install:

5. The cylinder head should be cleaned and inspected prior to installation.
6. Clean all gasket mating surfaces thoroughly.
7. Install or connect the following:
- New head gaskets on the cylinder block

※※ WARNING

Always use new cylinder head bolts when installing the cylinder head or damage to the engine may occur.

- Cylinder head on the cylinder block
- Tighten the cylinder head bolts in sequence using the following steps. The first step is 30 ft. lbs. (40 Nm), the second step is an additional 90 degrees, the third step is to loosen all bolts in sequence one full turn, the fourth step is to tighten the bolts to 30 ft. lbs. (40 Nm), the fifth step is to tighten and additional 90 degrees, the last step is to tighten an addition 90 degrees.
- Lash adjusters and camshaft roller followers in their correct locations. Lubricate all rocker arm components with engine assembly lubricant.
- Exhaust manifold
- Camshafts
- Place a bead of silicone gasket sealant to the front cover-to-cylinder head surface
- Valve cover. Install the 9 bolts and 5 stud bolts, and tighten in sequence to 89 inch lbs. (10 Nm).
- Power steering pressure tube bracket
- Power steering reservoir bracket and stud bolts
- PCV connector and tube
- Ignition coil on plugs

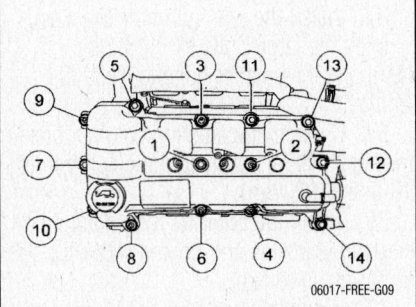

Fig. 32 Left side valve cover bolt installation sequence

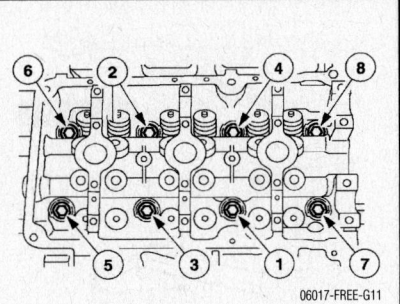

Fig. 34 Right side cylinder head bolt installation sequence

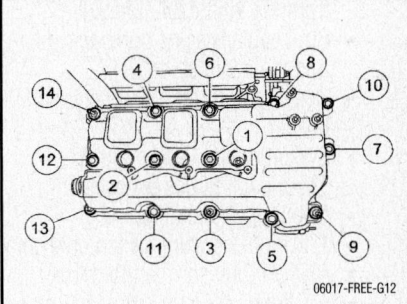

Fig. 35 Right side valve cover bolt installation sequence

- Coolant bypass tube
- Upper and lower intake manifolds
- Accessory drive belt

8. Fill and bleed the cooling system.

➡**Engine coolant is corrosive to engine bearing material. Replace the engine oil after removal of any coolant-carrying component to help prevent potential bearing damage.**

9. Change the engine oil and filter
10. Connect the negative battery cable.
11. Start the engine and check for leaks.

ENGINE ASSEMBLY

REMOVAL & INSTALLATION

See Figures 36 and 37.

1. Relieve the fuel system pressure.
2. Drain the engine coolant.
3. Drain the engine oil.
4. Recover the air conditioning refrigerant, into a refrigerant recovery station.
5. Place the transmission in neutral and raise the vehicle on a hoist.
6. Remove or disconnect the following:
   - Both battery cables
   - B+ terminal from the battery cable
   - Air cleaner outlet pipe and air cleaner
   - Cowl vent screen
   - Left and right halfshafts
   - Exhaust flex pipe
   - Left side catalytic converter
   - Roll restrictor cross brace-to-roll restrictor bolt and discard
   - Roll restrictor cross brace
   - Right and left fender ground straps
   - Fuel tube from the fuel rail
   - Vapor tube from the purge valve
   - Powertrain Control Module (PCM) connectors and wiring conduit
   - Power steering reservoir hose and retainers
   - Disconnect the transmission shift cable
   - Electrical connector and retainers from the shift cable bracket
   - Shift cable bracket bolts and position the cable aside
   - Heater and throttle body coolant hoses
   - Brake booster vacuum hose
   - Thermostat housing hoses
   - Cooling tube retainers
   - A/C high pressure switch connector
   - A/C compressor manifold tube
   - A/C tube retaining nuts and position the tubes aside
   - Transmission cooler lines
   - Power steering cooler hose

- Engine block heater connector and harness
- Torque converter lower access plug
- Torque converter attaching nuts
- 3 engine-to-transaxle mounting bolts
- Left catalytic converter bracket
- Driveshaft support bracket bolts and the driveshaft, if equipped
- Stabilizer bar links from the struts
- Outer tie rod ends from the steering knuckles
- Steering column intermediate shaft bolt and separate the shaft from the steering gear

7. Position subframe support tool 014-00765 under subframe and powertrain assembly.
8. Remove the subframe bolts and rear subframe brackets.
9. Lower the powertrain and subframe assembly from the vehicle.
10. To separate the engine from the transaxle and subframe assembly, disconnect all necessary electrical connectors, fluid lines and starter wiring. Remove the starter and engine roll restrictor brackets
11. Install engine lifting eyes no. 134-00243 to the left and right cylinder heads.
12. Install lifting brackets no. 303-1140 to front of the engine.
13. Install an engine hoist and lifting bar no. 303-D089 to the engine.
14. Remove the front transaxle stabilizer bolt.
15. Remove the exhaust manifold heat shield.
16. Remove the left and right engine insulator upper nuts.
17. Remove the transaxle insulator bracket.
18. Using the hoist, lift the powertrain from the subframe.
19. Remove the transaxle-to-engine mounting bolts and separate the engine and transaxle.

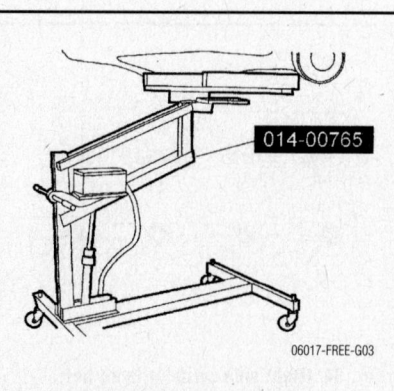

Fig. 36 Installing subframe support tool

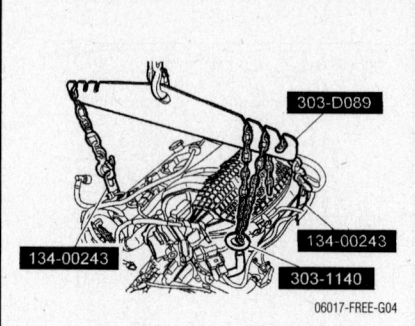

Fig. 37 Installing engine lifting tools to the engine

To install:

20. Position the engine onto the transaxle and install the transaxle mount bolts. Torque the bolts to 30 ft. lbs. (40 Nm).
21. Install the exhaust manifold heat shield.
22. Using the hoist, position the powertrain to the subframe.
23. Install the left and right engine insulator upper nuts and tighten to 62 ft. lbs. (70 Nm).
24. Install the front transaxle stabilizer bolt and tighten to 30 ft. lbs. (40 Nm).
25. Install the transaxle insulator bracket and tighten the bolts to 41 ft. lbs. (55 Nm).
26. Install the starter and tighten the bolts to 18 ft. lbs. (25 Nm).
27. Connect the starter wiring and terminal cover.
28. Apply thread lock to the roll restrictor bolts and install the restrictor bracket and tighten the bolts to 41 ft. lbs. (55 Nm).
29. Reconnect all necessary electrical connectors, fluid lines and retainers.
30. Remove the engine hoist and lifting tools.
31. Using subframe support tool 014-00765, raise the subframe and powertrain assembly into the vehicle
32. Install the front subframe bolts and tighten the bolts to 148 ft. lbs. (200 Nm).
33. Install the rear subframe brackets. Tighten the large bolts to 111 ft. lbs. (150 Nm), and the smaller bolts to 41 ft. lbs. (55 Nm).
34. Connect the steering column intermediate shaft and tighten the pinch bolt to 18 ft. lbs. (25 Nm).
35. Install the outer tie rod ends to the steering knuckles and tighten NEW nuts to 85 ft. lbs. (115 Nm).
36. Install the stabilizer bar links to the struts using NEW nuts and tighten to 41 ft. lbs. (55 Nm).

37. Install the driveshaft and tighten the bolts to 18 ft. lbs. (25 Nm).

38. Install the driveshaft support bracket bolts and tighten the bolts to 18 ft. lbs. (25 Nm).

39. Install or connect the following:
- NEW torque converter attaching nuts and tighten to 27 ft. lbs. (36 Nm)
- Torque converter lower access plug
- Engine block heater connector and harness
- Power steering cooler hose
- Transmission cooler lines
- A/C tube and retaining nuts
- A/C compressor manifold tube
- A/C high pressure switch connector
- Cooling tube retainers
- Thermostat housing hoses
- Brake booster vacuum hose
- Heater and throttle body coolant hoses
- Shift cable and bracket bolts and tighten the bolts to 18 ft. lbs. (25 Nm)
- Electrical connector and retainers to the shift cable bracket
- Connect the transmission shift cable
- Power steering reservoir hose and retainers
- Powertrain Control Module (PCM) connectors and wiring conduit
- Vapor tube from the purge valve
- Fuel tube from the fuel rail
- Right and left fender ground straps
- Roll restrictor cross brace
- NEW roll restrictor cross brace-to-roll restrictor bolts and tighten to 41 ft. lbs. (55 Nm)
- Left catalytic converter bracket
- Left side catalytic converter
- Exhaust flex pipe
- Left and right halfshafts
- Cowl vent screen
- Air cleaner outlet pipe and air cleaner
- B+ terminal to the battery cable
- Both battery cables

40. Refill the engine, transaxle and cooling system with the correct amount of the appropriate fluids before starting the engine. Recharge the A/C system using approved recycling equipment.

EXHAUST MANIFOLD

REMOVAL & INSTALLATION

➡ **Spray the exhaust system fasteners with penetrating lubricant before removing them to help prevent broken studs and bolts. The use of a 6-point socket is highly recommended when removing exhaust system fasteners.**

❊❊ CAUTION

To prevent serious burns, allow the exhaust manifold to cool down before attempting to remove it.

Left Manifold

See Figure 38.

1. Disconnect the negative battery cable.
2. Remove the coolant hose retainers from the fan shroud and position aside.
3. Disconnect the cooling fan electrical connectors.
4. Remove the cooling fans.
5. Disconnect the oxygen sensor connector.
6. Remove the 2 exhaust manifold-to-catalytic converter bolts.
7. Remove 6 exhaust manifold nuts and remove the exhaust manifold.

To install:

8. Clean all gasket mating surfaces thoroughly.
9. Install a new exhaust manifold gasket and the exhaust manifold on the cylinder head. Start 2 nuts to hold the manifold in position.
10. Install the remaining nuts. Tighten the nuts in the sequence shown to 15 ft. lbs. (20 Nm).
11. Install the 2 exhaust manifold-to-catalytic converter bolts and tighten to 30 ft. lbs. (40 Nm).

12. Connect the oxygen sensor connector.
13. Install the cooling fans.
14. Connect the cooling fan electrical connectors.
15. Install the coolant hose retainers to the fan shroud.
16. Connect the negative battery cable.
17. Start the engine and check for exhaust leaks.

Right Manifold

See Figure 39.

1. Disconnect the negative battery cable.
2. Raise the vehicle on a hoist.
3. Remove the right side catalytic converter.
4. Disconnect the oxygen sensor connector.
5. Remove the exhaust manifold heat shield.
6. Disconnect the EGR tube from the manifold.
7. Remove the exhaust manifold.

To install:

8. Clean all gasket mating surfaces thoroughly.
9. Install a new gasket and the exhaust manifold on the cylinder head. Start 2 nuts to hold the manifold in position.
10. Install the remaining nuts. Tighten the nuts in the sequence shown to 15 ft. lbs. (20 Nm).
11. Connect the EGR tube from the manifold.

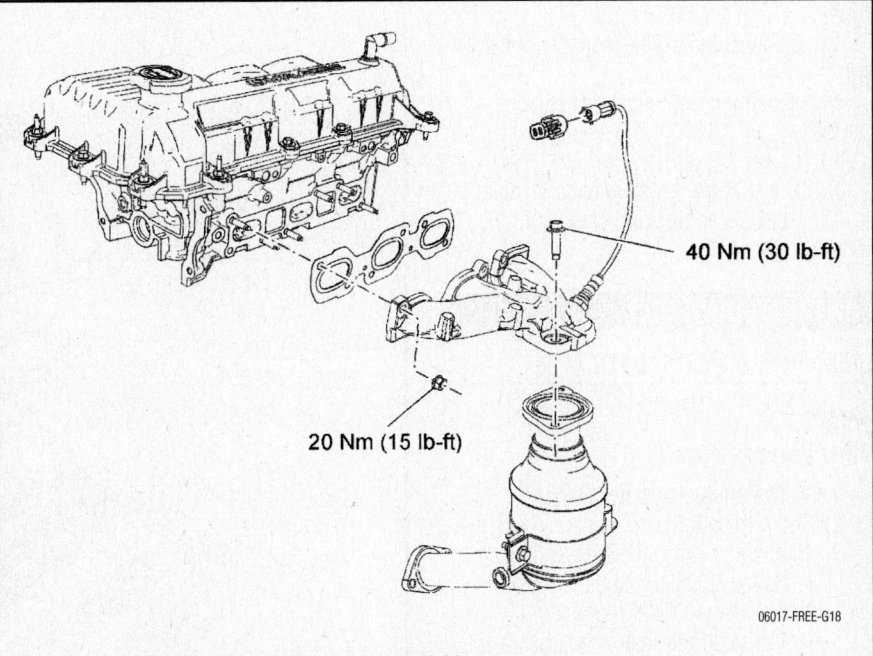

40 Nm (30 lb-ft)

20 Nm (15 lb-ft)

06017-FREE-G18

Fig. 38 Exploded view of the left exhaust manifold

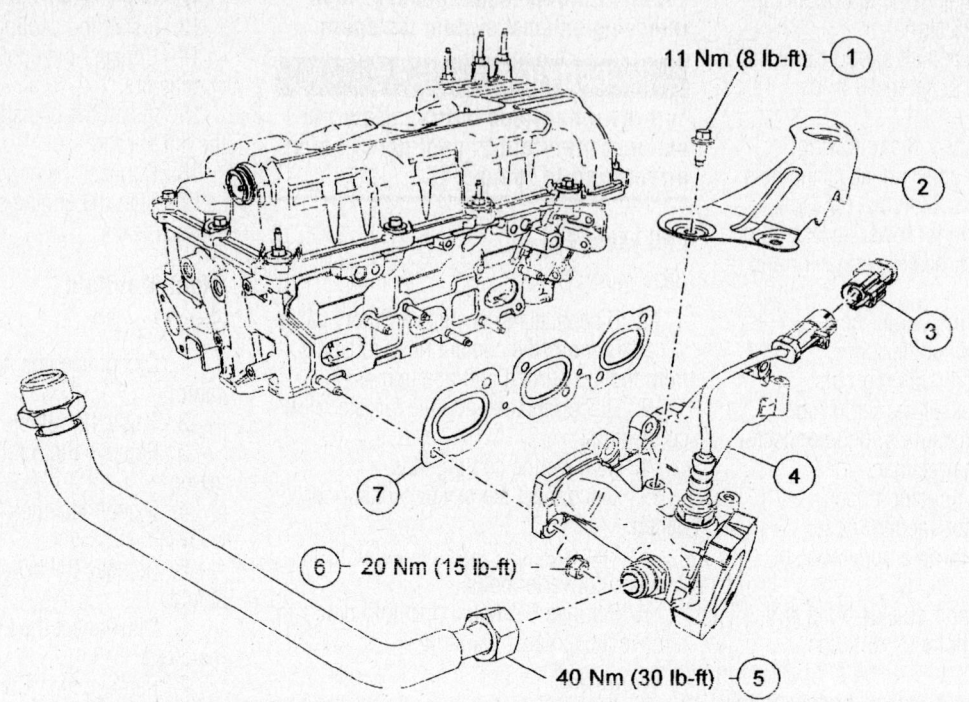

1. RH exhaust manifold heat shield (2 required)
2. RH exhaust manifold heat shield
3. Heated oxygen sensor (HO2S) electrical connector
4. RH exhaust manifold
5. Exhaust gas recirculation (EGR) system module tube fitting
6. RH exhaust manifold nut (6 required)
7. RH exhaust manifold gasket

06017-FREE-G19

Fig. 39 Exploded view of the right exhaust manifold

12. Install the exhaust manifold heat shield.
13. Connect the oxygen sensor connector.
14. Install the right side catalytic converter.
15. Lower the vehicle.
16. Connect the negative battery cable.
17. Start the engine and check for exhaust leaks.

INTAKE MANIFOLD

REMOVAL & INSTALLATION

Upper

See Figures 40 through 42.

1. Relive the fuel system pressure.
2. Drain the engine coolant.
3. Remove or disconnect the following:
   - Negative battery cable
   - Air cleaner outlet pipe
   - Transaxle roll restrictor cross brace bolts and cross brace
   - EVAP purge valve tube

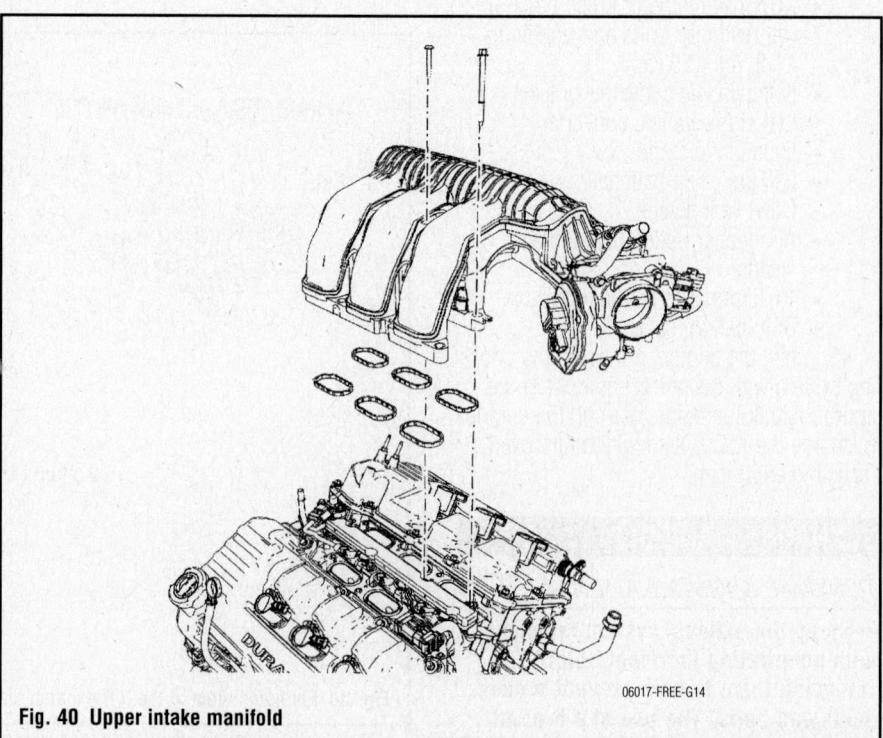

06017-FREE-G14

Fig. 40 Upper intake manifold

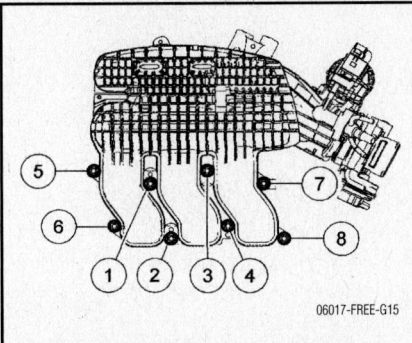

Fig. 41 Upper intake manifold tightening sequence

- PCV, brake booster and vacuum harness tubes from the manifold
- Fuel tube retainer
- EGR connector and vacuum tube
- Throttle body and PCV coolant hoses
- Throttle body electrical connector
- Upper-to-lower intake manifold attaching screws
- Intake manifold

To install:

4. Installation is the reverse of the removal procedure, using the following torque specifications.
- Intake manifold bolts and tighten all bolts in steps in sequence to 89 inch lbs. (10 Nm)
- Transaxle roll restrictor roll brace and tighten the bolts as shown

5. Fill and bleed the engine cooling system.

6. Connect the negative battery cable.

7. Start the engine and check for leaks.

Lower

See Figure 43.

1. Remove or disconnect the following:
- Coolant
- Fuel system pressure

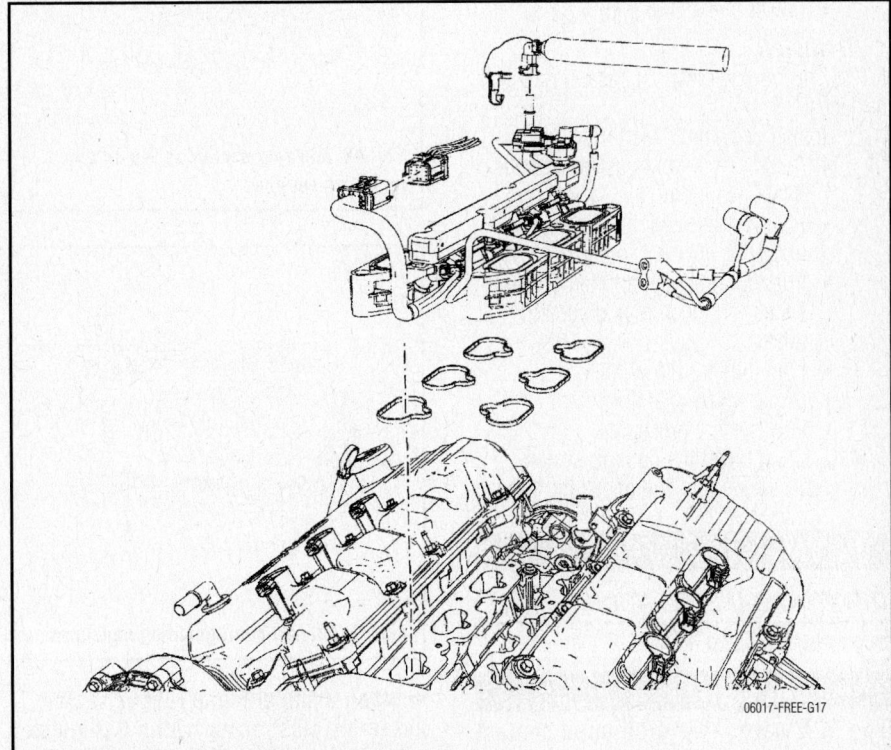

Fig. 43 Lower intake manifold and related components

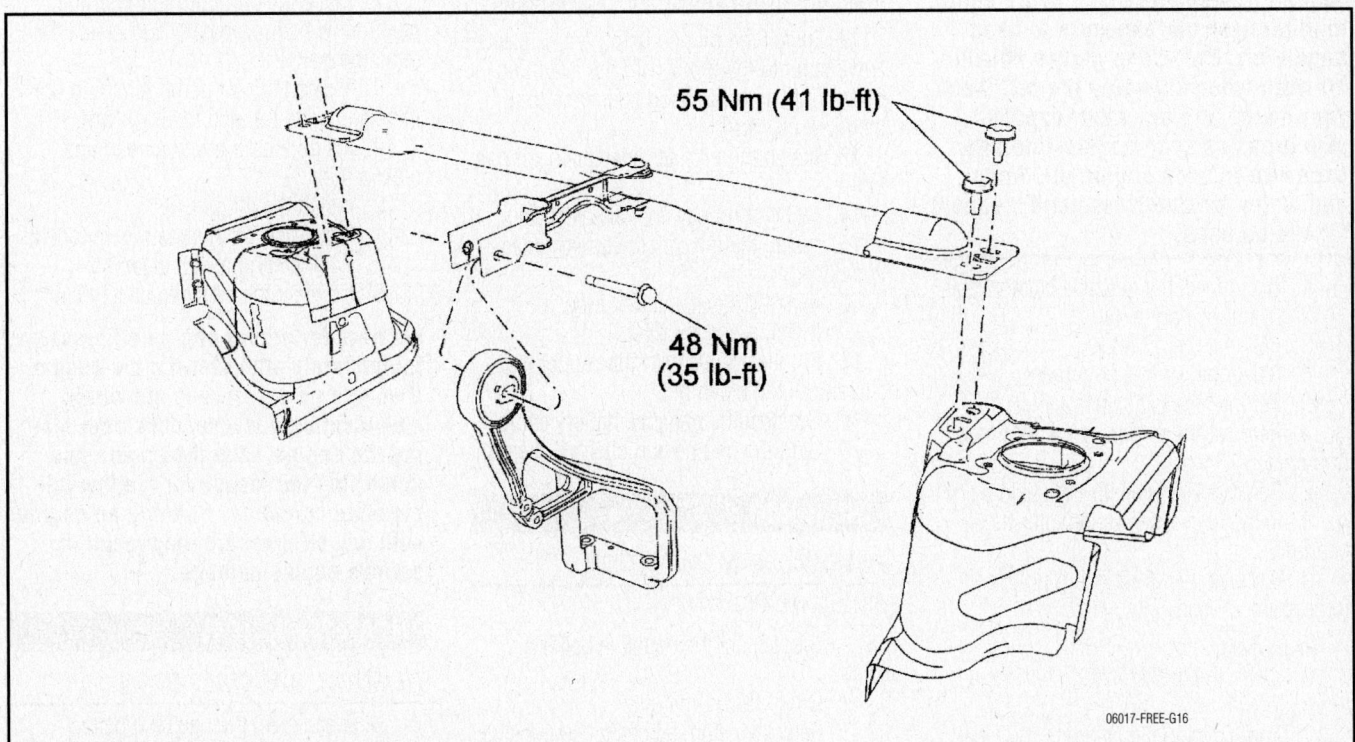

Fig. 42 Transaxle roll restrictor brace bolt tightening

55 Nm (41 lb-ft)

48 Nm (35 lb-ft)

- Upper intake manifold
- Fuel tube from fuel rail
- Fuel rail pressure and temperature sensor connectors and vacuum tube
- Fuel charging wiring harness connector
- Lower intake manifold

To install:

2. Thoroughly clean all gasket mating surfaces.

3. Install or connect the following:

- 6 intake manifold gaskets and the intake manifold
- Fuel charging wiring harness connector
- Fuel rail pressure and temperature sensor connectors and vacuum tube
- Fuel tube from fuel rail
- Upper intake manifold
- Fuel system pressure

4. Fill and bleed the cooling system.

5. Start the engine and check for leaks.

OIL PAN

REMOVAL & INSTALLATION

See Figures 44 and 45.

✳✳ CAUTION

The EPA warns that prolonged contact with used engine oil may cause a number of skin disorders, including cancer! You should make every effort to minimize your exposure to used engine oil. Protective gloves should be worn when changing the oil. Wash your hands and any other exposed skin areas as soon as possible after exposure to used engine oil. Soap and water, or waterless hand cleaner, should be used.

1. Disconnect the negative battery cable.
2. Drain the engine oil.
3. Remove the oil filter.
4. Raise the vehicle on a hoist.
5. Remove the exhaust flex pipe.
6. Remove the torque converter inspection cover.
7. Remove 2 oil pan-to-transaxle bolts.
8. Remove the oil filter adapter-to-oil pan bolt.
9. Remove the 15 retaining bolts and remove the oil pan.

To install:

10. Clean the gasket mating surfaces thoroughly.
11. Apply a drop of sealant to the locations shown.

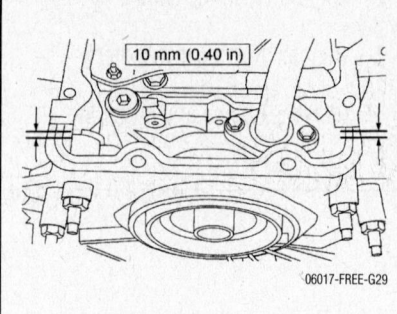

Fig. 44 Applying sealant to the oil pan mounting surface

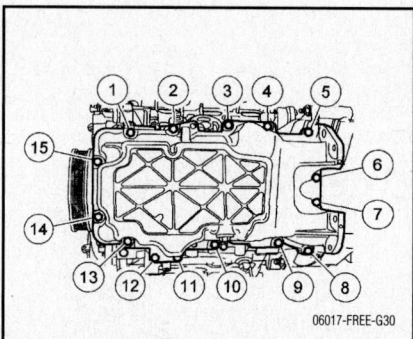

Fig. 45 Oil pan bolt tightening sequence

➡ **When using silicone rubber sealer, assembly must occur within 5 minutes after sealer application. After this time, the sealer may start to harden and its sealing effectiveness may be reduced.**

12. Install the oil pan using a new gasket and secure to the block with the attaching bolts. Tighten the bolts in sequence to 89 inch lbs. (10 Nm).
13. Install the oil filter adapter-to-oil pan bolt.
14. Install 2 oil pan-to-transaxle bolts.
15. Install the torque converter inspection cover.
16. Install the exhaust flex pipe.
17. Install a new oil filter.
18. Fill the engine with the proper type and amount of clean oil.
19. Connect the negative battery cable.
20. Start the engine and check for leaks.

OIL PUMP

REMOVAL & INSTALLATION

See Figures 46 and 47.

1. Disconnect the negative battery cable.
2. Drain the engine oil.
3. Remove the timing chain components.
4. Remove the oil pan.

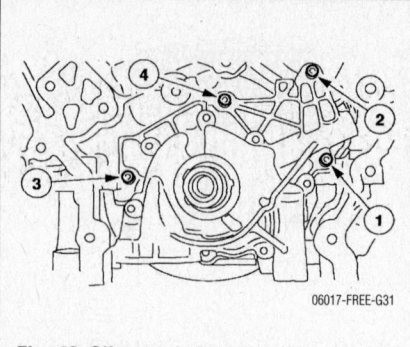

Fig. 46 Oil pump bolt removal sequence

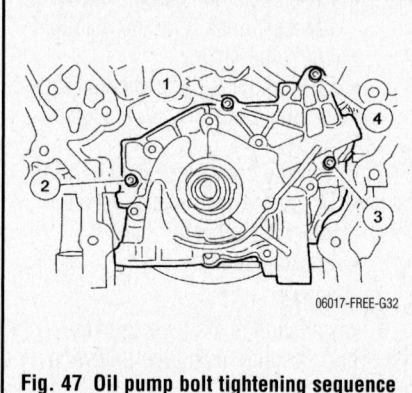

Fig. 47 Oil pump bolt tightening sequence

5. Remove the oil pump screen and pickup tube.
6. Remove the oil pump attaching bolts in the sequence shown.
7. Place the oil pump in the proper position with a new gasket and install the retaining bolts.
8. Tighten the oil pump retaining bolts in sequence to 89 inch lbs. (10 Nm).
9. Install the oil pump screen and pickup tube.
10. Install the oil pan.
11. Install the timing chain components.
12. Fill the engine with clean oil.
13. Connect the negative battery cable.

➡ **Check for proper engine oil pressure immediately after starting the engine. If engine oil pressure is not within specification a few seconds after starting the engine, stop the engine and determine the reason for the low oil pressure condition. Running an engine with low oil pressure may result in serious engine damage.**

REAR MAIN SEAL

REMOVAL & INSTALLATION

1. Disconnect the negative battery cable.

2. Raise the vehicle on a hoist.
3. Remove the transaxle.
4. Remove the flexplate.

WARNING

Use caution when working near the crankshaft sealing surface. If the surface becomes damaged, an oil leak may occur.

5. Screw in the threaded end of a crankshaft rear seal replacer tool, then use the tool to remove the seal.

To install:

6. Inspect the crankshaft seal area for any damage that may cause the seal to leak. If damage is evident, service or replace the crankshaft as necessary.
7. Coat the crankshaft seal area and the seal lip with engine oil.
8. Using a crankshaft seal replacer tool, install the seal. Tighten the bolts of the seal installer tool evenly so the seal is straight and seats without misalignment.
9. Install the flexplate and tighten the bolts to 59 ft. lbs. (80 Nm).
10. Install the transaxle, lower the vehicle and connect the battery.

TIMING CHAINS AND FRONT COVER

REMOVAL & INSTALLATION

See Figures 48 through 56.

1. Raise the vehicle on a hoist.
2. Disconnect the negative battery cable.
3. Remove the accessory drive belt.
4. Remove the oil pan.
5. Remove the crankshaft front oil seal.
6. Remove both valve covers. See the procedure in cylinder head.
7. Remove the accessory drive belt tensioner.
8. Disconnect the power steering pump and reservoir without disconnecting the lines, and position aside.
9. Disconnect the crankshaft and camshaft position sensor electrical connectors.
10. Remove the alternator-to-front cover stud nut and stud.
11. Remove the radiator splash shield.
12. Remove the A/C compressor bolts and without disconnecting the lines, position the compressor aside.
13. Remove the compressor bracket.
14. Remove the ground wire from the front cover.
15. Remove the 14 bolts, stud bolt and remove the engine front cover.

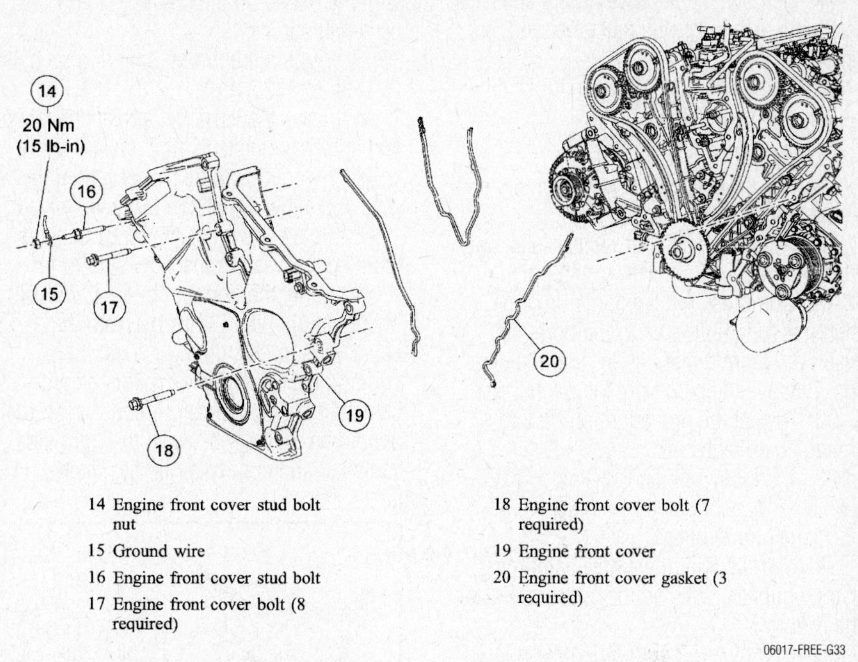
14
20 Nm
(15 lb-in)
16
15
17
18
19
20
14 Engine front cover stud bolt nut
15 Ground wire
16 Engine front cover stud bolt
17 Engine front cover bolt (8 required)
18 Engine front cover bolt (7 required)
19 Engine front cover
20 Engine front cover gasket (3 required)
06017-FREE-G33

Fig. 48 Exploded view of engine front cover

16. Remove the ignition pulse wheel.
17. Install the crankshaft damper bolt.
18. Remove the spark plugs.
19. Rotate the crankshaft clockwise to position the crankshaft keyway in the 11 o'clock position.

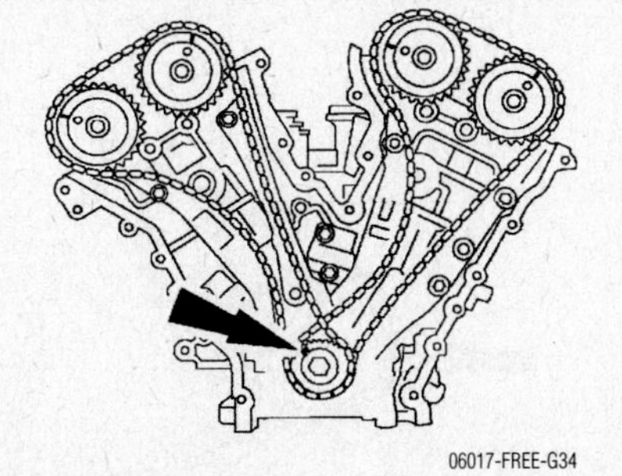
06017-FREE-G34

Fig. 49 Crankshaft and camshaft sprocket timing marks

20. Position the camshaft sprockets timing marks in the correct position so the no. 1 cylinder is a TDC of the compression stroke.
21. Ensure all timing marks are correctly located. If not, rotate the crankshaft one additional turn and recheck the marks.
22. Rotate the crankshaft clockwise 120 degrees to the 3 o'clock position to place the right side camshafts in the neutral position.
23. Ensure the camshafts are correctly located.
24. Remove the right side timing chain tensioner arm bolts, the tensioner and the tensioner arm.
25. Remove the right side timing chain guide and timing chain.
26. Rotate the crankshaft clockwise 600 degrees to position the left side camshafts in the neutral position.

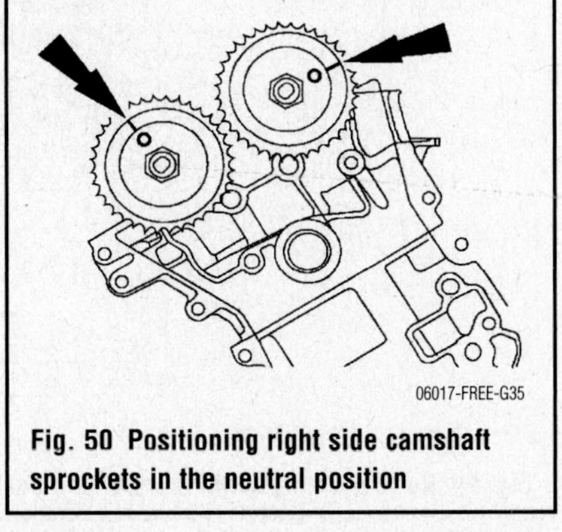
06017-FREE-G35

Fig. 50 Positioning right side camshaft sprockets in the neutral position

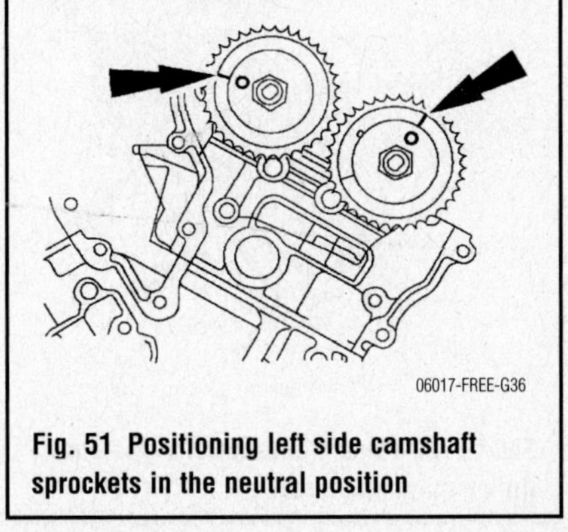
06017-FREE-G36

Fig. 51 Positioning left side camshaft sprockets in the neutral position

27. Remove the left side timing chain tensioner arm bolts, the tensioner and the tensioner arm.

28. Remove the left side timing chain guide and timing chain.

To install:

29. Place the timing chain tensioner in a soft-jawed vise.

30. Hold the tensioner ratchet lock away from the ratchet stem with a small pick.

31. Compress the tensioner until the piston is fully bottomed in the bore and insert a 1.5mm paper clip to hold the piston. Remove the pick from the ratchet stem.

32. Repeat the procedure on the other timing chain tensioner.

33. Mark any link on the timing chain with a permanent marker to indicate the crankshaft timing mark.

34. Starting with the crankshaft timing mark, count 29 links on the chain and mark the link.

35. Continue to count to the 42nd link and mark the link. Repeat this procedure on the other timing chain.

36. Ensure the left side camshaft sprocket timing marks are still aligned.

37. Install the left side timing chain and guide and install the bolts.

38. Align the marks on the timing chain with the marks on the crankshaft and camshaft sprockets.

39. Tighten the timing chain guide bolts to 18 ft. lbs. (25 Nm).

40. Install the tensioner arm and tensioner and tighten the bolts to 18 ft. lbs. (25 Nm).

41. Rotate the crankshaft 120 degrees clockwise until the crankshaft keyway is in the 3 o'clock position.

42. Ensure the right side camshaft sprocket timing marks are still aligned.

43. Install the right side timing chain and guide and install the bolts.

44. Align the marks on the timing chain

with the marks on the crankshaft and camshaft sprockets.

45. Tighten the timing chain guide bolts to 18 ft. lbs. (25 Nm).

46. Install the tensioner arm and tensioner and tighten the bolts to 18 ft. lbs. (25 Nm).

47. Remove both tensioner retaining pins and allow the piston to move.

48. Rotate the crankshaft 120 degrees counterclockwise to the TDC position.

49. Verify the correct timing as follows: There should be 12 links between the camshaft sprocket timing marks; there should be 27 links between the left side camshaft and crankshaft timing marks; there should be 30 links between the right side camshaft and crankshaft timing marks.

50. Remove the crankshaft damper bolt and install the ignition pulse wheel. Install the pulse wheel with the keyway in the slot stamped "30" or "30FF."

51. Install the spark plugs and tighten to 11 ft. lbs. (15 Nm).

52. Clean the front cover gasket mating surfaces.

53. Place silicone gasket sealant on the cylinder head and cylinder block mating surfaces as shown.

54. Install the front cover and tighten the bolts and stud bolt in the sequence shown to 18 ft. lbs. (25 Nm).

55. Install the ground wire to the front cover.

56. Install the A/C compressor bracket.

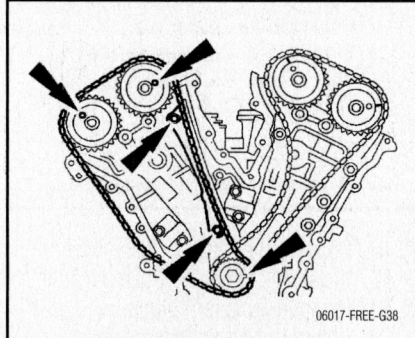

Fig. 53 Right side crankshaft and camshaft timing mark alignment

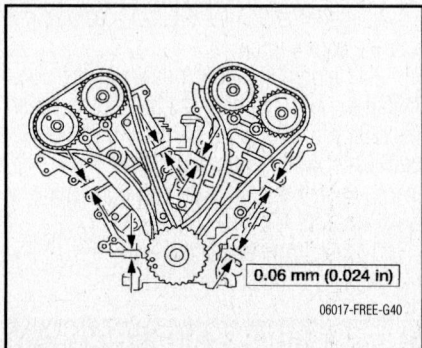

Fig. 55 Applying sealant to block and head front cover mating surfaces

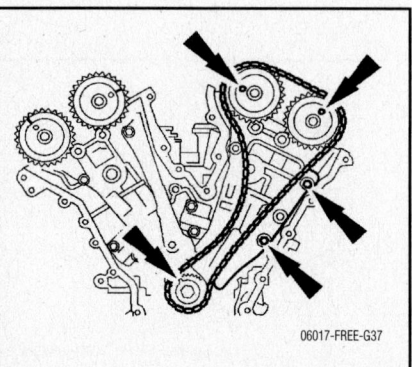

Fig. 52 Left side crankshaft and camshaft timing mark alignment

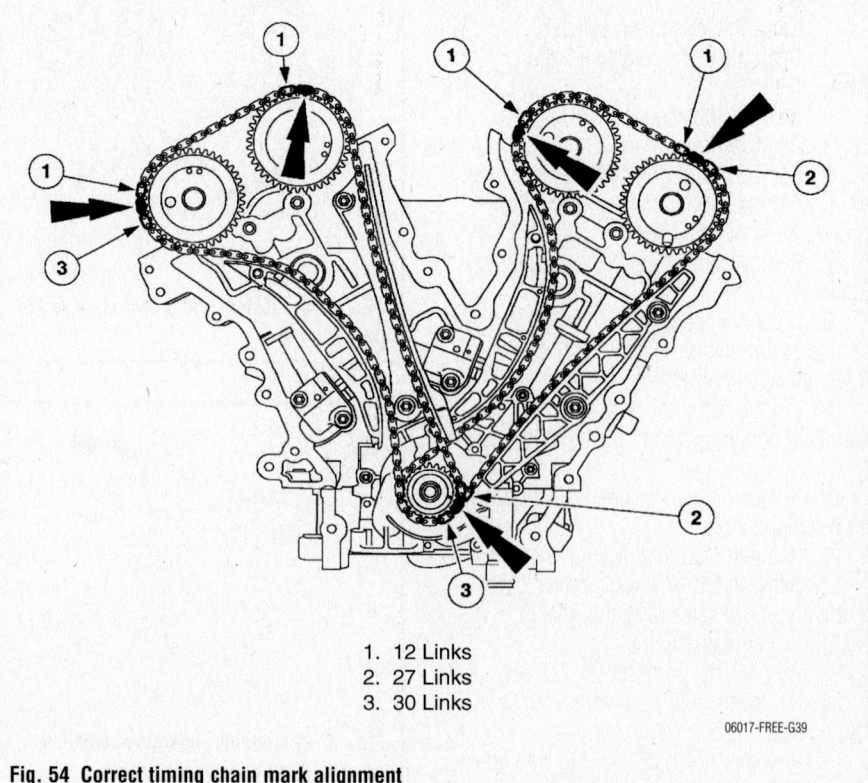

1. 12 Links
2. 27 Links
3. 30 Links

Fig. 54 Correct timing chain mark alignment

14
15
13
16
10
12
9
11
4
7
8
3
1
2
6
5
06017-FREE-G41

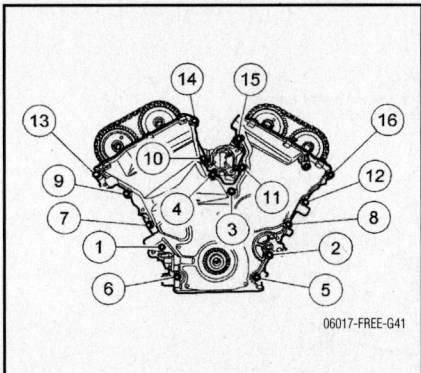

Fig. 56 Front cover bolt torque sequence

57. Install the A/C compressor.
58. Install the radiator splash shield.
59. Install the alternator-to-front cover stud nut and stud.
60. Connect the crankshaft and camshaft position sensor electrical connectors.
61. Connect the power steering pump and reservoir
62. Install the accessory drive belt tensioner.
63. Install both valve covers.
64. Install the crankshaft front oil seal.
65. Install the oil pan.
66. Install the accessory drive belt.
67. Fill the crankcase with the proper type and quantity of engine oil. Fill and bleed the cooling system. Connect the negative battery cable.
68. Start the engine and check for leaks. Check the ignition timing and curb idle speed and adjust, as necessary.

VALVE LASH

ADJUSTMENT

The lash adjusters are hydraulic and are not adjustable.

ENGINE PERFORMANCE & EMISSION CONTROL

COMPONENT LOCATIONS

See Figures 57 through 59.

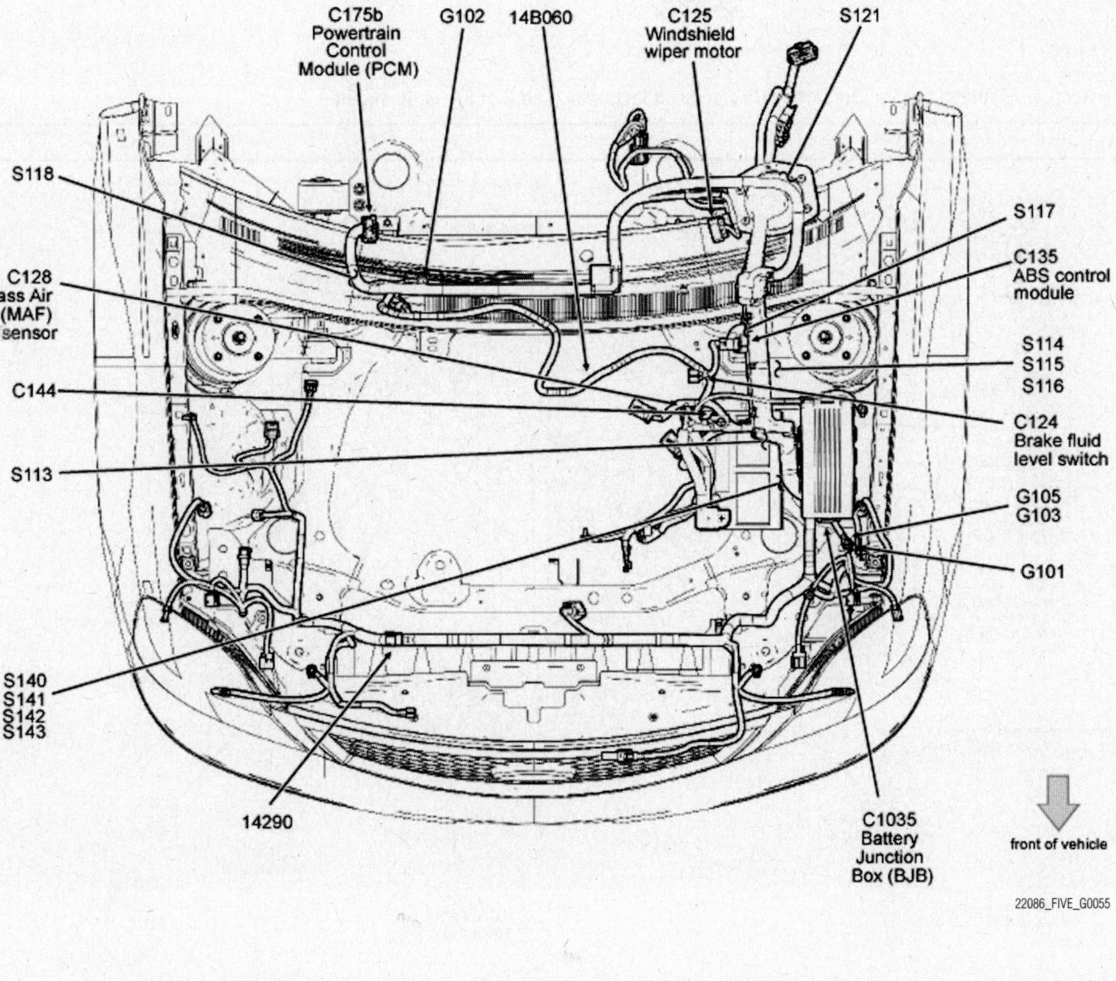

C175b
Powertrain
Control
Module (PCM)
G102
14B060
C125
Windshield
wiper motor
S121
S118
S117
C135
ABS control
module
C128
Mass Air
Flow (MAF)
sensor
S114
S115
S116
C144
C124
Brake fluid
level switch
S113
G105
G103
G101
S112 S140
S119 S141
S122 S142
S124 S143
14290
C1035
Battery
Junction
Box (BJB)
front of vehicle
22086_FIVE_G0055

Fig. 57 Five Hundred/Montego engine compartment component locations (part 1 of 3)—3.0L engine

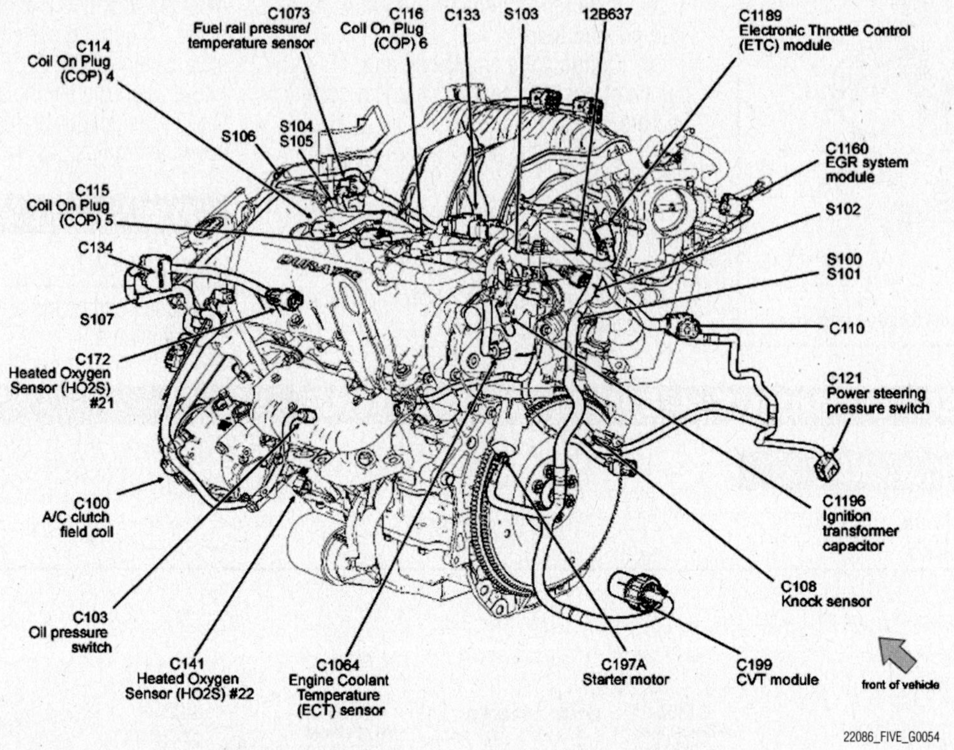

C114
Coil On Plug
(COP) 4

C1073
Fuel rail pressure/
temperature sensor

C116
Coil On Plug
(COP) 6

C133 S103 12B637

C1189
Electronic Throttle Control
(ETC) module

S106 S104
S105

C115
Coil On Plug
(COP) 5

C1160
EGR system
module

C134

S102

S100
S101

S107

C110

C172
Heated Oxygen
Sensor (HO2S)
#21

C121
Power steering
pressure switch

C100
A/C clutch
field coil

C1196
Ignition
transformer
capacitor

C103
Oil pressure
switch

C108
Knock sensor

C141
Heated Oxygen
Sensor (HO2S) #22

C1064
Engine Coolant
Temperature
(ECT) sensor

C197A
Starter motor

C199
CVT module

front of vehicle

22086_FIVE_G0054

Fig. 58 Five Hundred/Montego engine compartment component locations (part 2 of 3)—3.0L engine

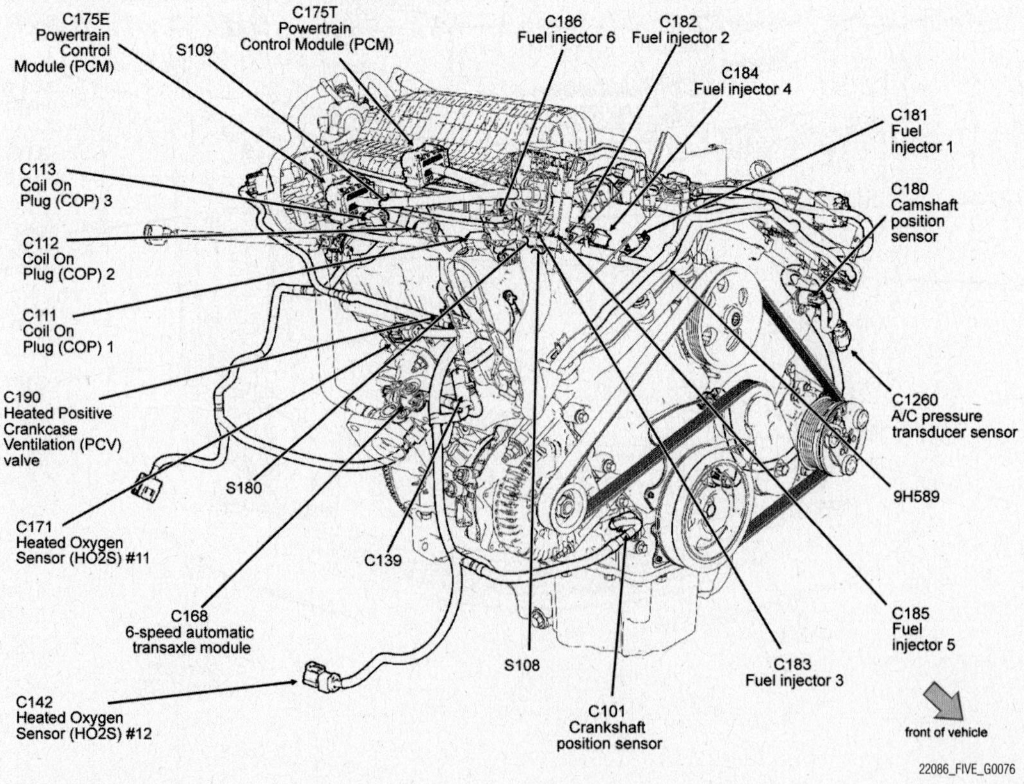

C175E
Powertrain
Control
Module (PCM)

S109

C175T
Powertrain
Control Module (PCM)

C186
Fuel injector 6

C182
Fuel injector 2

C184
Fuel injector 4

C181
Fuel
injector 1

C113
Coil On
Plug (COP) 3

C180
Camshaft
position
sensor

C112
Coil On
Plug (COP) 2

C111
Coil On
Plug (COP) 1

C190
Heated Positive
Crankcase
Ventilation (PCV)
valve

C1260
A/C pressure
transducer sensor

S180

9H589

C171
Heated Oxygen
Sensor (HO2S) #11

C139

C168
6-speed automatic
transaxle module

C185
Fuel
injector 5

C142
Heated Oxygen
Sensor (HO2S) #12

S108

C101
Crankshaft
position sensor

C183
Fuel injector 3

front of vehicle

22086_FIVE_G0076

Fig. 59 Five Hundred/Montego engine compartment component locations (part 3 of 3)—3.0L engine

CAMSHAFT POSITION (CMP) SENSOR

LOCATION

The Camshaft Position (CMP) sensor is located on the front right of the engine. Refer to the illustration for detailed information.

OPERATION

The CMP sensor detects the position of the camshaft. The CMP sensor identifies when piston number 1 is on its compression stroke. A signal is then sent to the PCM and used for synchronizing the sequential firing of the fuel injectors. Coil-on-plug (COP) ignition applications use the CMP signal to select the correct ignition coil to fire.

REMOVAL & INSTALLATION

1. Disconnect the negative battery cable.
2. Disconnect the CMP sensor electrical connector.
3. Remove the bolt and the CMP sensor.

To install:
4. Installation is the reverse of removal.

TESTING

See Figures 60 and 61.

1. Check the condition of the connector. Make sure the connector is firmly attached. Check for broken or bent connector pins. Repair any connector damage before continuing with troubleshooting the issue.
2. Check the condition of the wiring to the connector. If the wiring is damaged, repair the wiring before continuing with any further tests.
3. Monitor the generator for an audible electric noise.
4. Key in OFF position.
5. CMP Sensor connector disconnected.
6. Measure the resistance between the CMP sensor signal return and VR signal return. The resistance should be between 250–1000 Ohms. If the resistance is not within specification, replace the sensor.
7. Key in OFF position.
8. Generator/regulator B+ connector connected.
9. CMP Sensor connector disconnected.
10. Key ON, engine running.
11. Connect a Digital multimeter (DMM) set on low voltage AC scale.
12. Measure the voltage between the CMP sensor positive terminal and the signal return or negative terminal on the component and measure the voltage between the CMP sensor positive terminal and the VR

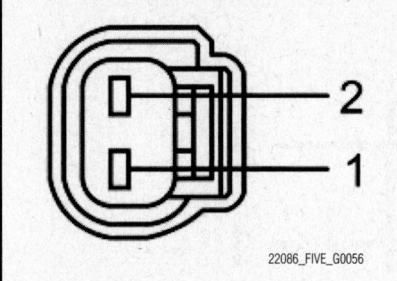

Fig. 60 Camshaft Position (CMP) sensor terminal locations. Terminal 1 is SIGRTN and terminal 2 is CMP

Fig. 61 Camshaft Position (CMP) sensor harness terminal locations. Pin 1 is signal return and Pin 2 is the CMP sensor signal

signal return or negative terminal. or negative terminal on the component while running the engine at approximately 2,500 RPM.
13. If the voltage is not greater than 0.25 volts, replace the CMP.
14. PCM connector disconnected.
15. Key ON, engine OFF.
16. Measure the voltage between CMP positive terminal and battery ground. If the voltage is not at least 1 volt, there is a short in the harness side wiring.
17. Key in OFF position.
18. Measure the resistance between the PCM positive terminal on the harness side and the CMP sensor connector negative terminal on the harness side. Measure the resistance between the PCM signal return on the harness side and CMP sensor signal return on the harness side. Measure the resistance between the PCM VR signal return on the harness side and CMP VR sensor signal return on the harness side. If the resistance is not less than 5 Ohms, there is an open circuit in the harness side.

CRANKSHAFT POSITION (CKP) SENSOR

LOCATION

The Crankshaft Position (CKP) sensor is located just to the right of the alternator

(looking from at the front of the engine) on the timing cover. Refer to the illustration for detailed information.

OPERATION

The CKP sensor is a magnetic transducer mounted on the engine block adjacent to a pulse wheel located on the crankshaft. By monitoring the crankshaft mounted pulse wheel, the CKP is the primary sensor for ignition information to the PCM. The pulse wheel has a total of 35 teeth spaced 10 degrees apart with one empty space for a missing tooth. By monitoring the pulse wheel, the CKP sensor signal indicates crankshaft position and speed information to the PCM. By monitoring the missing tooth, the CKP sensor is also able to identify piston travel in order to synchronize the ignition system and provide a way of tracking the angular position of the crankshaft relative to a fixed reference for the CKP sensor configuration. The PCM also uses the CKP signal to determine if a misfire has occurred by measuring rapid decelerations between teeth.

REMOVAL & INSTALLATION

1. With vehicle in NEUTRAL, position it on a hoist.
2. Disconnect the negative battery cable.
3. Remove the 7 pin-type retainers and the right side splash shield.
4. Disconnect the crankshaft position (CKP) sensor electrical connector.
5. Remove the bolt and the CKP sensor.

To install:
6. Installation is the reverse of removal.

TESTING

See Figures 62 and 63.

1. Check the condition of the connector. Make sure the connector is firmly attached. Check for broken or bent connector pins. Repair any connector damage before continuing with troubleshooting the issue.
2. Check the condition of the wiring to the connector. If the wiring is damaged, repair the wiring before continuing with any further tests.
3. The battery should be fully charged and the starting system should be functioning properly.
4. Visually check the timing cover, CKP sensor and external trigger wheel (outside the timing cover) for obvious physical damage. Repair as needed.
5. Key in OFF position.

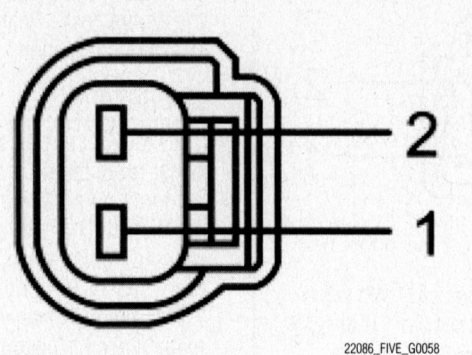

22086_FIVE_G0058

Fig. 62 Crankshaft Position (CKP) sensor terminal locations. Terminal 1 is the negative terminal and terminal 2 is the positive terminal

22086_FIVE_G0059

Fig. 63 Crankshaft Position (CKP) sensor harness terminal locations. Pin 1 is CKP negative terminal and Pin 2 is the CKP positive terminal

6. Measure the resistance between the positive terminal on the CKP sensor connector, component side and the negative terminal CKP sensor, component side. The resistance should be between 250–1000 Ohms. If the resistance is not within specification, replace the sensor.

7. Measure the resistance between the positive terminal on the CKP_SHLD assembly connector on the harness side and ground. If the resistance is not less than 5 Ohms, repair the open circuit in the CKP_SHLD assembly.

8. PCM connector disconnected.

9. Measure the resistance between the positive terminal of the CKP sensor connector on the harness side and the negative terminal of the CKP connector on the harness side. If the resistance is not greater than 10 KOhms, repair the short circuit in the harness.

10. Measure the resistance between: the positive terminal of the CKP sensor on the harness side and the negative terminal of the PCM connector on the harness side. If the resistance is not less than 5 Ohms, repair the open circuit in the harness.

11. Measure the resistance between the positive terminal of the CKP sensor connector on the harness side and the negative battery terminal and the resistance between the CKP sensor negative terminal and the negative battery terminal. If the resistance is not greater than 10 KOhms, repair the short circuit in the harness.

12. Key ON, engine OFF.

13. Measure the voltage between: the positive terminal of the PCM positive connector on the harness side and battery ground terminal. Measure the voltage between: the negative terminal of the PCM positive connector on the harness side and battery ground terminal. If the is voltage present, repair the short circuit in the wiring.

ENGINE COOLANT TEMPERATURE (ECT) SENSOR

LOCATION

The Engine Coolant Temperature (ECT) sensor is located on the rear left of the engine. Refer to the illustration for detailed information.

OPERATION

The ECT sensor is a thermistor device in which resistance changes with temperature. The electrical resistance of a thermistor decreases as the temperature increases, and the resistance increases as the temperature decreases. The varying resistance changes the voltage drop across the sensor terminals and provides electrical signals to the PCM corresponding to temperature. The ECT measures the temperature of the engine coolant. The PCM uses the ECT input for fuel control and for cooling fan control

REMOVAL & INSTALLATION

1. Drain and recycle the engine coolant.

⁂ CAUTION

The brake aspirator tube must be fully seated in the air cleaner outlet pipe or a vacuum leak will occur.

2. Disconnect the positive crankcase ventilation (PCV) and brake aspirator tubes from the air cleaner outlet pipe.

3. Disconnect the mass air flow (MAF) sensor electrical connector.

4. Loosen the air cleaner outlet tube clamp at the electronic throttle body.

5. Remove the air cleaner housing cover and outlet tube assembly.

6. Disconnect the engine coolant temperature (ECT) sensor electrical connector.

7. Remove the hairpin clip and the ECT sensor.

To install:

8. Installation is the reverse of removal.

9. Use the alignment notches to correctly align the air cleaner housing cover to the air cleaner tray.

10. Lubricate the O-ring seal with clean engine coolant.

TESTING

See Figures 64 and 65.

1. Before servicing the vehicle, refer to the precautions section.

2. Drain and recycle the engine coolant.

3. Remove the coolant temperature sensor.

4. Place the sensor in a container of water with a temperature approximately 20 degrees C (68 F).

5. Using an ohmmeter, check resistance between the terminals. The resistance should be 37.30 Kohms.

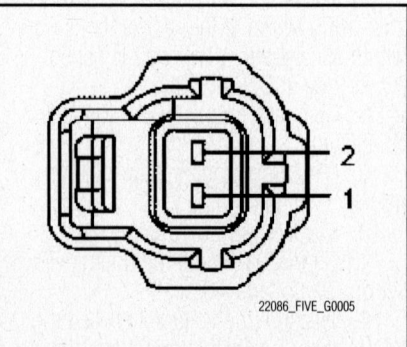

22086_FIVE_G0005

Fig. 64 Coolant temperature sensor pin locations

TEMPERATURE SENSOR VOLTAGE AND RESISTANCE SPECIFICATIONS

Temperature		Temperature Sensor Values	
°C	°F	Voltage	Resistance (K ohms)
120	248	0.28	1.18
110	230	0.36	1.55
100	212	0.47	2.07
90	194	0.61	2.80
80	176	0.80	3.84
70	158	1.05	5.37
60	140	1.37	7.70
50	122	1.77	10.97
40	104	2.23	16.15
30	86	2.74	24.27
20	68	3.26	37.30
10	50	3.73	58.75
0	32	4.14	95.85
-10	14	4.45	160.31

22086_FIVE_G0006

Fig. 65 Ford temperature sensor voltage and resistance specification chart

6. Raise the temperature of the container of water to approximately 80 degrees C (176F).

7. Using an ohmmeter, check resistance between the terminals. The resistance should be 3.84 Kohms.

8. If the resistance is not as specified, replace the sensor.

EGR SYSTEM MODULE

LOCATION

The EGR system module sensor is located on the rear right of the engine. Refer to the illustration for detailed information.

OPERATION

The ESM is an integrated differential pressure feedback EGR system that functions in the same manner as a conventional differential pressure feedback EGR system. The various system components have been integrated into a single component called the ESM. The flange of the valve portion of the ESM bolts directly to the intake manifold with a metal gasket that forms the metering orifice. This arrangement increases system reliability, response time, and system precision. By relocating the EGR orifice from the exhaust to the intake side of the EGR valve, the downstream pressure signal measures manifold absolute pressure (MAP). This MAP signal is used for EGR correction and inferred barometric pressure (BARO) at key on. The system provides the powertrain control module (PCM) with a differential pressure feedback EGR signal, identical to a traditional differential pressure feedback EGR system

TESTING

See Figures 66 through 68.

1. Check the condition of the connector. Make sure the connector is firmly attached. Check for broken or bent connector pins. Repair any connector damage before continuing with troubleshooting the issue.

2. Check the condition of the wiring to the connector. If the wiring is damaged, repair the wiring before continuing with any further tests.

3. The battery should be fully charged and the starting system should be functioning properly.

4. Check the DPFE circuit for a short to SIGNRTN or GND in the harness as follows:
   a. Key in OFF position.
   b. PCM connector disconnected.
   c. Measure the resistance between the positive DPFE terminal on the PCM connector on the harness side and the negative SIGRTN terminal on the PCM connector on the harness side. If the resistance is not greater than 10 KOhms, there is a short circuit.

   d. Measure the resistance between the positive DPFE terminal on the PCM connector on the harness side and the negative battery terminal. If the resistance is not KOhms, there is a short circuit.

5. Check the VREF voltage to the ESM as follows:
   a. Key in OFF position.
   b. ESM connector disconnected.
   c. Key ON, engine OFF.
   d. Measure the voltage between the positive VREF Pin 2 terminal on the ESM connector on the harness side and the negative battery terminal. If the voltage is not 4–5.5 volts, there is a open circuit.

6. Check the DPFE circuit for a short to voltage as follows:
   a. Key in OFF position.
   b. PCM connector disconnected.
   c. Key ON, engine OFF.
   d. Measure the voltage between the positive DPFE Pin 5 terminal on the ESM connector on the harness side and the negative battery terminal. If the voltage is not less than 1 volt, there is a short circuit.

7. Simulate the differential pressure feedback EGR sensor signal with a vacuum pump as follows:
   a. Disconnect the downstream differential pressure feedback EGR sensor port hose at the ESM.
   b. Verify the hose and port are clear and free of obstructions.
   c. Connect a vacuum pump to the downstream differential pressure feedback EGR sensor port.
   d. Key ON, engine OFF.
   e. Access the PCM and monitor the DPFEGR PID.
   f. Apply 27 - 30 kPa (8 - 9 in-Hg) vacuum to the differential pressure feedback EGR sensor and hold for 10 seconds.
   g. Quickly release the vacuum.
   h. The DPFEGR PID voltage must be between 0.25 and 1.3 volts with the key ON and no vacuum applied.
   i. The DPFEGR PID voltage must increase to greater than 4 volts with the vacuum applied.
   j. The DPFEGR PID must drop to less than 1.5 volts in less than 3 seconds when the vacuum is released.
   k. If the DPFEGR PID voltage does not read as specified, replace the DPFE sensor.

8. Inspect the EGR vacuum regulator solenoid vent for blockage as follows:

➡ **When the EGR valve is closed, the EGR vacuum regulator solenoid vacuum is vented through the solenoid vent to the atmosphere. A plugged EGR vacuum regulator solenoid vent does**

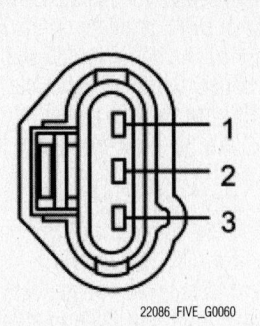

22086_FIVE_G0060

Fig. 66 DPFE sensor connector terminal locations. Pin 1 is VREF Pin 2 is the SGN-RTN and Pin 3 is DPFE

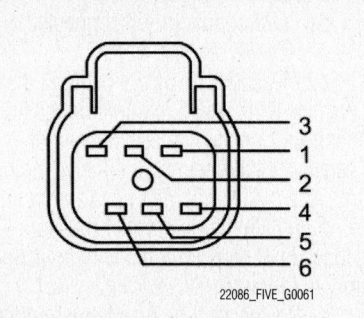

22086_FIVE_G0061

Fig. 67 EGR module connector terminal locations. Pin 1 is EVR Pin 2 is the VPWR and Pin 6 is SGNRTN, Pin 5 is DPFE and Pin 2 is VREF

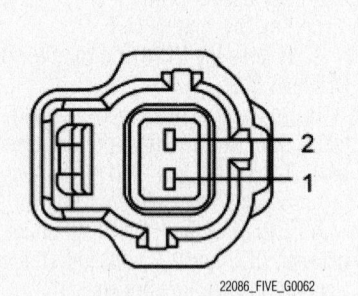

22086_FIVE_G0062

Fig. 68 EGR vacuum regulator solenoid connector terminal locations. Pin 1 is VPWR Pin 2 is the EVR and Pin 6 is SGN-RTN, Pin 5 is DPFE and Pin 2 is VREF

not allow EGR vacuum to vent to the atmosphere.

a. EGR vacuum regulator vacuum hoses disconnected.

b. Connect a hand vacuum pump to the EGR vacuum regulator source port.

c. Apply 34 to 51 kPa (10 to 15 in-Hg) vacuum.

d. If the EGR vacuum regulator solenoid vacuum not bleed off?, install a new EGR vacuum regulator solenoid.

ELECTRONIC THROTTLE BODY (ETB) POSITION SENSOR

LOCATION

The ETB position sensor is attached to the throttle body by screws.

OPERATION

The ETB position sensor has 2 signal circuits in the sensor for redundancy. The redundant ETB position signals are required for increased monitoring. The first ETB position sensor signal (TP1) has a negative slope (increasing angle, decreasing voltage) and the second signal (TP2) has a positive slope (increasing angle, increasing voltage). During normal operation the negative slope ETB position sensor signal (TP1) is used by the control strategy as the indication of throttle position. The 2 ETB position sensor signals make sure the PCM receives a correct input even if 1 signal has a concern. There is 1 reference voltage circuit and 1 signal return circuit for the sensor.

REMOVAL & INSTALLATION

1. Disconnect the negative battery cable.
2. Disconnect sensor electrical connector.
3. Remove the 2 screws and the sensor.

To install:
4. Installation is the reverse of removal.

TESTING

See Figures 69 through 72.

1. Check the condition of the connector. Make sure the connector is firmly attached. Check for broken or bent connector pins. Repair any connector damage before continuing with troubleshooting the issue.

2. Check the condition of the wiring to the connector. If the wiring is damaged, repair the wiring before continuing with any further tests.

3. The battery should be fully charged and the starting system should be functioning properly.

4. Key in OFF position.

5. Remove the inlet tube from the throttle body.

6. Visually inspect for throttle plate obstructions or sludge.

7. Slowly, push the throttle plate to wide open and release.

8. The throttle plate should move freely to wide open and back. Repair as needed.

9. ETBTPS connector disconnected.

10. Key ON, engine OFF.

11. Measure the voltage between the positive ETCREF terminal on the ETBTPS connector on the harness side and the negative ETCRTN terminal on the ETBTPS connector on the harness side. There should be 4–6 volts.

12. There are 2 types of ETBTPS available. Look at the sensor housing of the ETBTPS on the vehicle and compare to the accompanying illustrations.

13. Check the resistance of the type 1 ETBTPS as follows:

a. Key in OFF position.

➡ **Do not move the throttle plate during the resistance measurement. Measure the sensor resistance with the throttle plate at the default position.**

b. ETBTPS connector disconnected.

c. Measure the resistance between the positive TP 1 terminal on the ETBTPS connector component side and the negative ETCREF terminal on the ETBTPS connector component side. The resistance should be 1,100–3,500 Ohms.

d. Measure the resistance between the positive TP 1 terminal on the ETBTPS connector component side and the negative ETCRTN terminal on the ETBTPS connector component side. The resistance should be 2,500–5,900 Ohms.

e. Measure the resistance between the positive TP 2 terminal on the ETBTPS connector component side and the negative ETCREF terminal on the ETBTPS connector component side. The resistance should be 1,800–4,900 Ohms.

f. Measure the resistance between the positive TP 2 terminal on the ETBTPS connector component side and the negative ETCRTN terminal on the ETBTPS connector component side. The resistance should be 800–2,800 Ohms.

g. Measure the resistance between the positive ETCREF terminal on the ETBTPS connector component side and the negative ETCRTN terminal on the ETBTPS connector component side. The resistance should be 1,800–4,900 Ohms.

h. If not within specification, replace the sensor.

14. Check the resistance of the type 2 ETBTPS as follows:

a. Key in OFF position.

➡ **Do not move the throttle plate during the resistance measurement. Measure the sensor resistance with the throttle plate at the default position.**

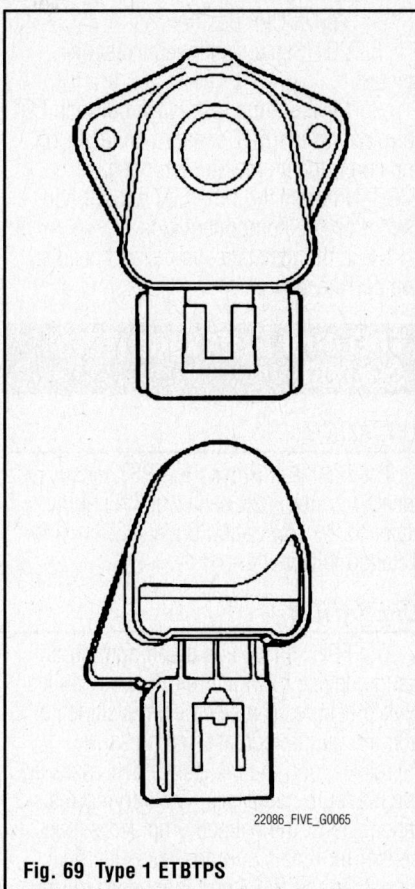

Fig. 69 Type 1 ETBTPS

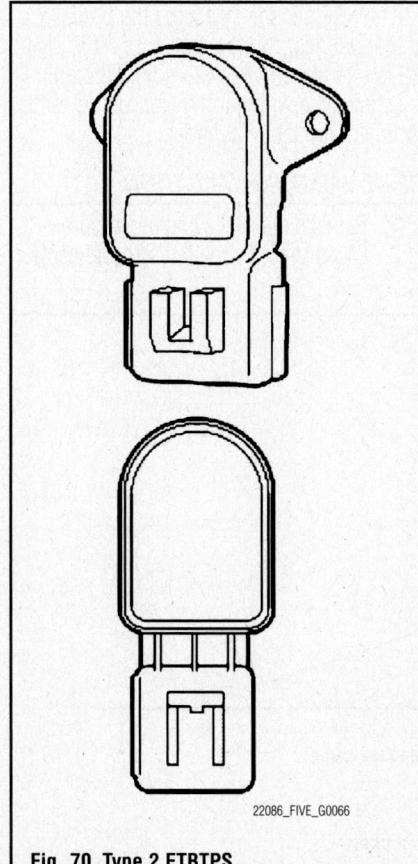

Fig. 70 Type 2 ETBTPS

b. ETBTPS connector disconnected.

c. Measure the resistance between the positive TP 1 terminal on the ETBTPS connector component side and the negative ETCREF terminal on the ETBTPS connector component side. The resistance should be 700–1,800 Ohms.

d. Measure the resistance between the positive TP 1 terminal on the ETBTPS connector component side and the negative ETCRTN terminal on the ETBTPS connector component side. The resistance should be 1,300–2,800 Ohms.

e. Measure the resistance between the positive TP 2 terminal on the ETBTPS connector component side and the negative ETCREF terminal on the ETBTPS connector component side. The resistance should be 1,000–2,400 Ohms.

f. Measure the resistance between the positive TP 2 terminal on the ETBTPS connector component side and the negative ETCRTN terminal on the ETBTPS connector component side. The resistance should be 500–1,500 Ohms.

g. Measure the resistance between the positive ETCREF terminal on the ETBTPS connector component side and the negative ETCRTN terminal on the ETBTPS connector component side. The resistance should be 700–2,100 Ohms.

h. If not within specification, replace the sensor.

15. Check the TP1 and TP2 circuits for a short to voltage in the harness as follows:

a. PCM connector disconnected.

b. Key ON, engine OFF.

c. Measure the voltage between the positive TP1 or TP2 terminal on the ETBTPS connector on the harness side and ground. If voltage is present the there is a short to voltage.

16. Check the TP1 and TP2 circuits for an open in the harness as follows:

a. Key in OFF position.

b. Measure the resistance between the positive TP1 or TP2 terminal on the ETBTPS connector on the harness side and the negative TP 1 or TP2 terminal on the PCM connector on the harness side. If the resistance is not 5 Ohms, there is an open circuit.

17. Check the tp1 and tp2 circuits for a short to ground in the harness as follows:

a. Measure the resistance between the positive TP1 or TP2 terminal on the ETBTPS connector on the harness side and the negative battery terminal. If the resistance is not greater that 10 KOhms, there is a short circuit.

18. Check the TP circuits for a short together as follows:

a. Measure the resistance between the following terminals:

- Positive TP1 terminal on the ETBTPS connector on the harness side and the negative TP2 terminal on the PCM connector on the harness side.
- Positive TP1 terminal on the ETBTPS connector on the harness side and the negative ETCREF terminal on the PCM connector on the harness side.
- Positive TP1 terminal on the ETBTPS connector on the harness side and the negative ETCRTN terminal on the PCM connector on the harness side.
- Positive TP2 terminal on the ETBTPS connector on the harness side and the negative ETCREF terminal on the PCM connector on the harness side.
- Positive TP2 terminal on the ETBTPS connector on the harness side and the negative ETCRTN terminal on the PCM connector on the harness side.

b. If the resistance is not greater that 10 KOhms, there is a short circuit.

19. Check the air inlet system for leaks. Repair as needed.

20. Listen for air noise around the Mass Air Flow (MAF) sensor and throttle body while the engine is running. Repair as needed.

21. Check the Throttle Actuator Control Motor (TACM) visually.

➡**Make sure the TACM harness connector is properly connected.**

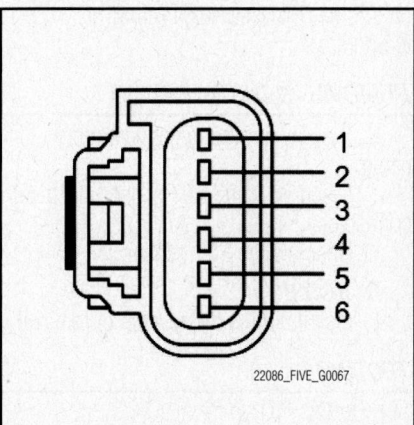

Fig. 71 EETBTPS connector terminal locations. Pin 3 is TP1 Pin 4 is the ECTRTN, Pin 5 is ECTREF and Pin 6 TP2

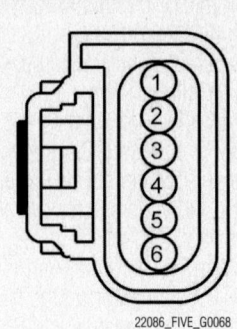

22086_FIVE_G0068

Fig. 72 EETBTPS harness connector terminal locations. Pin 2 is Tach + Pin 2 is Tach −, Pin 3 is Throttle position signal 1, Pin 4 is ETC reference voltage, Pin 5 is ETC reference voltage and PIN 6 is Throttle position signal 2

22. Key in OFF position.
23. Inspect the TACM for damaged housing, harness connector, and harness. Repair as needed.

ENGINE OIL TEMPERATURE (EOT) SENSOR

LOCATION

The Engine Oil Temperature (EOT) sensor is located on the front right of the engine. Refer to the illustration for detailed information.

OPERATION

The EOT sensor is a thermistor device in which resistance changes with temperature. The electrical resistance of a thermistor decreases as the temperature increases and the resistance increases as the temperature decreases. The varying resistance changes the voltage drop across the sensor terminals and provides electrical signals to the PCM corresponding to temperature.

REMOVAL & INSTALLATION

1. Disconnect the negative battery cable.
2. Disconnect the EOT sensor electrical connector.
3. Unscrew the EOT sensor.

To install:
4. Installation is the reverse of removal.

TESTING

See Figures 73 and 74.

1. Check the condition of the connector. Make sure the connector is firmly attached. Check for broken or bent connector pins. Repair any connector damage before continuing with troubleshooting the issue.
2. Check the condition of the wiring to the connector. If the wiring is damaged, repair the wiring before continuing with any further tests.
3. The battery should be fully charged and the starting system should be functioning properly.
4. Run the engine until the engine temperature stabilizes.
5. Verify the radiator hoses are hot and the cooling system is pressurized.
6. Check the sensor signal for a short to ground as follows:
   a. PCM connector disconnected.
   b. Measure the resistance between the positive EOT terminal on the EOT sensor connector on the harness side and the negative SIGRTN terminal on the EOT sensor connector on the harness side. The resistance should not be greater than 10 KOhms or there is a short circuit in the harness.

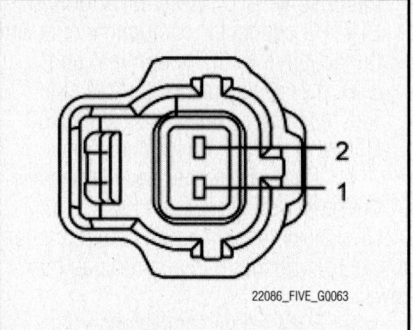

22086_FIVE_G0063

Fig. 73 EOT connector terminal locations. Pin 1 is EOT and Pin 2 is SGNRTN

7. Key in OFF position.
8. EOT Sensor connector disconnected.
9. Measure the resistance between EOT terminal on the EOT sensor connector on the component side and the negative SIGRTN terminal on the EOT sensor connector on the component side.
10. If the resistance is not as specified, replace the sensor.

FUEL RAIL PRESSURE (FRP) SENSOR

LOCATION

The Fuel Rail Pressure (FPS) sensor is located on the front center of the engine. Refer to the illustration under TESTING for detailed information.

OPERATION

The FRP sensor is a diaphragm strain gauge device in which resistance changes with pressure. The electrical resistance of a strain gauge increases as pressure increases, and the resistance decreases as the pressure decreases. The varying resistance affects the voltage drop across the sensor terminals and provides electrical signals to the PCM corresponding to pressure.

The FRP sensor measures the pressure of the fuel near the fuel injectors. This signal is used by the PCM to adjust the fuel injector pulse width and meter fuel to each engine combustion cylinder.

REMOVAL & INSTALLATION

1. Release the fuel system pressure.
2. Disconnect the battery ground cable.

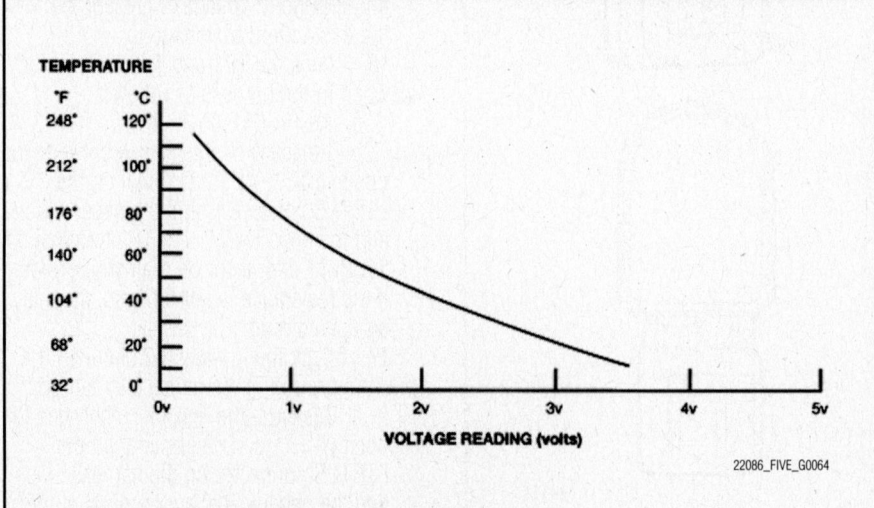

22086_FIVE_G0064

Fig. 74 Ford temperature sensor voltage specification chart

3. Disconnect the fuel rail pressure and temperature sensor electrical and vacuum connectors.

4. Remove the 2 bolts and the fuel rail pressure and temperature sensor.

5. To install, reverse the removal procedure. Lubricate the O-ring seal with clean engine oil.

TESTING

See Figures 75 and 76.

1. Before servicing the vehicle, refer to the precautions section.

2. Check all electrical connections are clean and tight. Repair and broken, cracked or loose connections or damaged wiring.

3. Turn the key on and let the engine idle for two minutes.

4. Inspect the fuel rail pressure sensor vacuum hose between the intake manifold and the fuel rail pressure sensor for air leaks and correct connection.

5. Turn the key off.

6. Remove the vacuum hose from the fuel rail pressure sensor. Inspect the fuel rail pressure sensor and vacuum hose for traces of fuel.

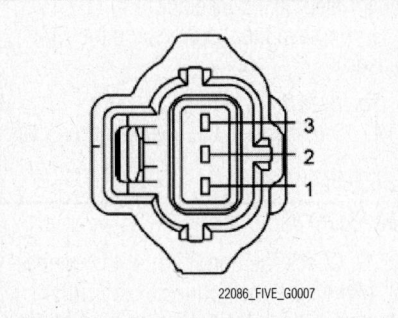

Fig. 75 Exploded view of the fuel pressure sensor electrical connector pin locations. Pin 1 is reference voltage and Pin 2 is the signal return

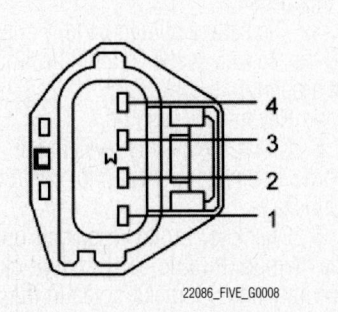

Fig. 76 Exploded view of the fuel pressure sensor pin locations. Pin 2 is reference voltage and Pin 4 is the signal return

7. If fuel is found replace the fuel rail pressure sensor.

8. Turn the key off.

9. Connect a 5 amp fused jumper wire between the Pin 1 on the sensor harness side and Pin 3 on the harness side of the fuel rail pressure sensor.

10. If the voltage greater than 4.5 V? replace the fuel rail pressure sensor.

HEATED OXYGEN (HO2S) SENSOR

LOCATION

The Heated Oxygen (HO2S) sensor is located on the front right of the engine. Refer to the illustration for detailed information.

OPERATION

The HO2S detects the presence of oxygen in the exhaust and produces a variable voltage according to the amount of oxygen detected. A high concentration of oxygen (lean air/fuel ratio) in the exhaust produces a voltage signal less than 0.4 volt. A low concentration of oxygen (rich air/fuel ratio) produces a voltage signal greater than 0.6 volt. The HO2S provides feedback to the PCM indicating air/fuel ratio in order to achieve a near stoichiometric air/fuel ratio of 14.7:1 during closed loop engine operation. The HO2S generates a voltage between 0.0 and 1.1 volts.

REMOVAL & INSTALLATION

1. With vehicle in NEUTRAL, position it on a hoist.

2. Disconnect the negative battery cable.

3. Disconnect the heated oxygen sensor (HO2S) electrical connector.

➡**If necessary, lubricate the HO2S with lock lubricant to aid in removal.**

4. Remove the HO2S from the exhaust manifold using an oxygen sensor wrench.

➡**Never reuse an oxygen sensor when removed, always install a new sensor.**

To install:

5. Installation is the reverse of removal, tighten the sensor to 35 ft. lbs. (48 Nm).

TESTING

See Figures 77 and 78.

1. Check the condition of the connector. Make sure the connector is firmly attached. Check for broken or bent connector pins. Repair any connector damage before continuing with troubleshooting the issue.

2. Check the condition of the wiring to

the connector. If the wiring is damaged, repair the wiring before continuing with any further tests.

3. The battery should be fully charged and the starting system should be functioning properly.

4. Check for leaks at the following:
- Hoses connecting to the mass air flow (MAF) sensor assembly
- Hoses connecting to the throttle body
- Intake manifold gasket leaks
- PCV system
- Disconnected vacuum lines
- Improperly seated engine oil dipstick, tube or oil fill cap
- Exhaust leaks at flanges and gaskets

5. Measure the resistance between: the HO2S positive terminal connector on the component side and the HO2S negative terminal connector on the component side. If the resistance is not between 3–30 Ohms, replace the sensor.

6. Measure the resistance between the positive terminal of the PCM connector on the harness side and the negative terminal

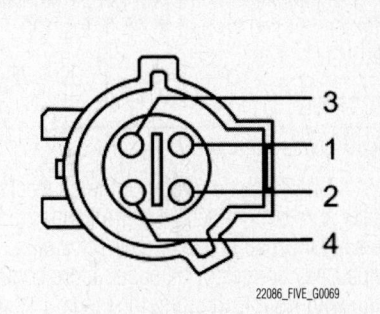

Fig. 77 Heated Oxygen (HO2S) sensor terminal locations. Pin 1 is HO2S heater, Pin 2 is VPWR, Pin 3 is HO2S signal and Pin 4 is SIGNRTN

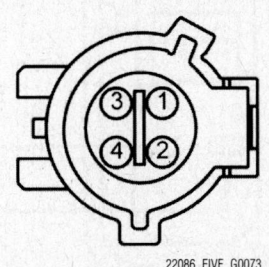

Fig. 78 Heated Oxygen (HO2S) sensor harness terminal locations. Pin 1 is HO2s heater control, Pin 2 is voltage supplied at start and run overload protect, Pin 3 is HO2S signal and Pin 4 is signal return

of the HO2S connector on the harness side. If the resistance is not less than 5Ohms, repair the open circuit in the wiring harness.

KNOCK SENSOR (KS)

LOCATION

The Knock (KS) sensor is located on the rear of the engine. Refer to the illustration for detailed information.

OPERATION

The KS is a tuned accelerometer on the engine which converts engine vibration to an electrical signal. The PCM uses this signal to determine the presence of engine knock and to retard spark timing.

REMOVAL & INSTALLATION

1. With the vehicle in NEUTRAL, position it on a hoist.
2. Disconnect the negative battery cable.
3. Position the knock sensor (KS) heat shield aside.
4. Disconnect the KS electrical connector.
5. Remove the bolt and the KS.

To install:
6. Installation is the reverse of removal. Tighten the sensor bolt to 15 ft. lbs. (20 Nm).

TESTING

See Figures 79 and 80.

1. Check the condition of the connector. Make sure the connector is firmly attached. Check for broken or bent connector pins. Repair any connector damage before continuing with troubleshooting the issue.
2. Check the condition of the wiring to the connector. If the wiring is damaged,

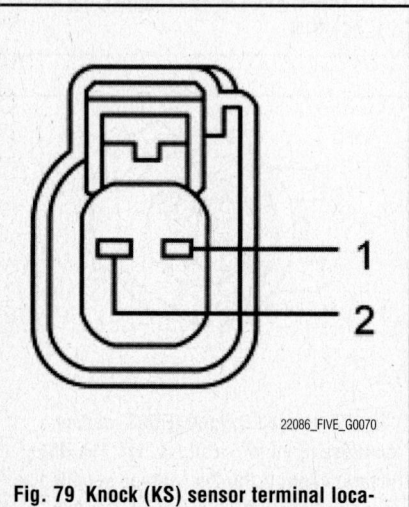

Fig. 79 Knock (KS) sensor terminal locations. Pin 1 is KS + and Pin 2 is KS −

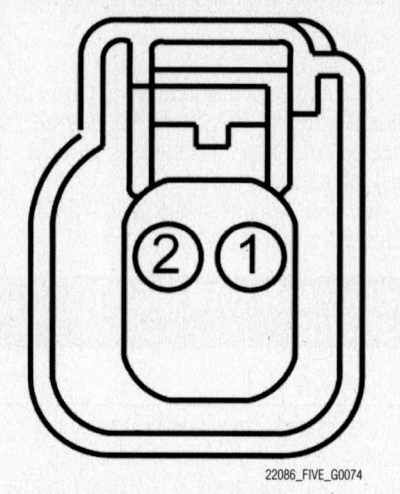

22086_FIVE_G0074

Fig. 80 Knock (KS) sensor harness terminal locations. Pin 1 is KS + and Pin 2 is KS −

repair the wiring before continuing with any further tests.
3. The battery should be fully charged and the starting system should be functioning properly.
4. KS connector disconnected.
5. Measure the resistance between: the positive terminal of the KS connector on the component side and the negative terminal of the KS connector on the components side. If the resistance is not between 4.39–5.35 MOhms, replace the sensor.
6. Key in OFF position.
7. PCM connector disconnected.
Measure the resistance between positive terminal of the KS connector on the harness side and the negative terminal of the KS connector on the harness side. If the resistance is not less than 5 Ohms, repair the open circuit in the harness.
8. Measure the resistance between positive terminal of the KS connector on the harness side and the negative terminal of the PCM connector on the harness side. If the resistance is not less than 5 Ohms, repair the open circuit in the harness.
9. Measure the resistance between positive terminal of the KS connector on the harness side and the negative terminal of the battery. If the resistance is not greater than 10 KOhms, repair the short circuit in the harness.

MASS AIR FLOW (MAF) SENSOR

LOCATION

The Mass Air Flow (MAF) sensor is located between the air cleaner and the throttle body or inside the air cleaner assembly. Refer to the illustration for detailed information.

OPERATION

The MAF sensor uses a hot wire sensing element to measure the amount of air entering the engine. Air passing over the hot wire causes it to cool. This hot wire is maintained at 200°C (392°F) above the ambient temperature as measured by a constant cold wire. The current required to maintain the temperature of the hot wire is proportional to the mass air flow. The MAF sensor then outputs an analog voltage signal to the PCM proportional to the intake air mass. The PCM calculates the required fuel injector pulse width in order to provide the desired air/fuel ratio. This input is also used in determining transmission electronic pressure control (EPC), shift and torque converter clutch scheduling.

REMOVAL & INSTALLATION

1. Disconnect the negative battery cable.
2. Disconnect the mass air flow (MAF) sensor electrical connector.
3. Remove the 2 screws and the MAF sensor.

To install:
4. Installation is the reverse of removal.

TESTING

See Figure 82.

1. Check the condition of the connector. Make sure the connector is firmly attached. Check for broken or bent connector pins. Repair any connector damage before continuing with troubleshooting the issue.
2. Check the condition of the wiring to the connector. If the wiring is damaged, repair the wiring before continuing with any further tests.
3. The battery should be fully charged and the starting system should be functioning properly.
4. Key in OFF position.
5. Check the air inlet system (air cleaner, housing, ductwork) for obstructions or blockage.
6. Check for broken/loose air outlet tube clamps (throttle body and air cleaner assembly ends), cracks/holes in the air outlet tube, and worn gaskets between the MAF sensor and the air cleaner assembly.
7. Check the throttle body bore for

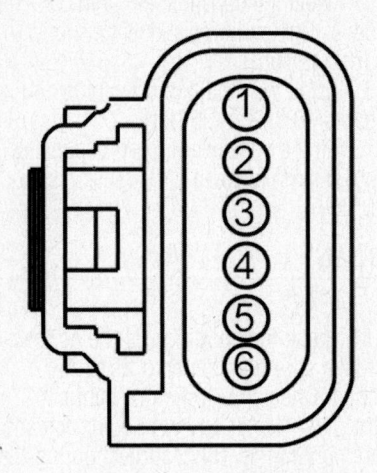

Fig. 82 Mass Air Flow (MAF) sensor harness terminal locations. Pin 1 is IAT reference voltage, Pin 2 is SIGRTN, Pin 3 is MAF reference voltage, Pin 4 is MAF signal return, Pin 5 is ground and Pin 6 is VPWR

sludge. Verify the MAF sensor is connected. Repair as necessary.

8. Key in OFF position.

9. MAF/IAT Sensor connector disconnected.

10. Key ON, engine OFF.

11. Measure the voltage between the positive terminal of the MAF sensor connector on the harness side and battery ground terminal. If the voltage is not greater than 1 volt, repair the open circuit in the harness.

12. Measure the voltage between the positive terminal of the battery and the negative terminal of the MAF sensor connector on the harness side. If the voltage is not greater than 10 volts, repair the open circuit in the harness.

13. Measure the resistance between the positive terminal of the PCM connector on the harness side and the negative terminal of the MAF sensor connector on the harness side. If the resistance is not less than 5 Ohms, repair the open circuit.

14. If the harness and connector are not damaged, replace the sensor.

POWERTRAIN CONTROL MODULE (PCM)

LOCATION

The PCM is located in the engine compartment, passenger side, mounted to the cowl.

OPERATION

The center of the electronic engine control system is a microprocessor called the PCM. The PCM receives input from sensors and other electronic components (switches, relays). Based on the information received and programmed into its memory, the PCM generates output signals to control various relays, solenoids and actuators.

REMOVAL & INSTALLATION

1. Retrieve the module configuration.
2. Remove the cowl panel grille.
3. Disconnect the 3 PCM electrical connectors.
4. Remove the bolt and the PCM.

To install:

5. Installation is the reverse of removal.

TESTING

1. Check the condition of the connector. Make sure the connector is firmly attached. Check for broken or bent connector pins. Repair any connector damage before continuing with troubleshooting the issue.

2. Check the condition of the wiring to the connector. If the wiring is damaged, repair the wiring before continuing with any further tests.

3. The battery should be fully charged and the starting system should be functioning properly.

4. Key in OFF position.

5. PCM Power Relay connector disconnected.

6. Key ON, engine OFF.

7. Measure the voltage between: the positive terminal of the PCM power relay connector on the harness side. The voltages should be greater than 10 V. If not there is a open circuit.

8. Check the PCMRC circuit for an open in the harness as follows:

   a. Key in OFF position.

   b. PCM connector disconnected.

   c. Measure the resistance between the positive PCMRC terminal on the Power Relay Connector on the harness side and the negative PCMRC terminal on the Power Relay Connector on the harness side. If the resistance is not less than 5Ohms, there is a open in the circuit.

9. Check the PCMRC circuit for a short to voltage in the harness as follows:

   a. Key ON, engine OFF.

   b. Measure the voltage between the positive PCMRC terminal on the Power

Relay Connector on the harness side and the negative battery terminal. If there is voltage present, there is a short in the circuit.

10. Check the ISP-R voltage at the PCM harness connector as follows:

   a. Key ON, engine OFF.

   b. PCM Power Relay connector connected.

   c. Key OFF.

   d. Measure the voltage between the positive ISP-R terminal on the Power Relay Connector on the harness side and the negative battery terminal. If the voltage is greater than 10 volts, there is a open in the circuit.

11. Check the PCM power relay ground circuit for an open as follows:

   a. Measure the voltage between the positive terminal on the Power Relay Connector on the harness side and the negative terminal of the PCM power relay connector on the harness side. If the voltage is greater than 10 volts, there is a open in the circuit.

12. Check for an open VPWR circuit between the PCM and power relay as follows:

   a. Key OFF.

   b. PCM connector disconnected.

   c. Measure the resistance between the positive VPWR terminal on the Power Relay Connector on the harness side and the negative VPWR PCM terminal on the harness side. If the resistance is not less than 5 Ohms, there is an open circuit.

13. Check the PCMRC circuit for a short to ground in the harness as follows:

   a. Key in OFF position.

   b. PCM Power Relay connector disconnected.

   c. PCM connector disconnected.

   d. Measure the resistance between the positive PCMRC terminal of the PCM connector and battery ground. If the resistance is not greater than 10 KOhms, there is a short circuit.

14. Check the ISP-R circuit for a short to voltage in the harness as follows:

   a. Key in OFF position.

   b. Measure the voltage between the positive ISP-R terminal of the PCM connector and battery ground. If there is voltage present, there is a short circuit.

15. Check the injpwrm circuit for an open in the harness as follows:

   a. INJ connector disconnected.

   b. Measure the resistance between the INJPWRM positive terminal on the Power Relay Connector on the harness side and the negative INJ VPWR connector terminal on the harness side. If the resistance is not less than 5 Ohms, there is an open circuit.

16. Check for correct PCM operation as follows:

    a. Key in OFF position.

    b. Disconnect all the PCM connectors.

    c. Connect all the PCM connectors and make sure they seat correctly.

    d. Carry out the PCM self-test and verify the concern is still present.

    e. If the concern still present, replace the PCM.

OUTPUT SHAFT SPEED SENSOR (OSS)

LOCATION

The Output Shaft Speed (OSS) sensor is located under the transmission filter. To access and remove the sensor the transmission fluid pan and filter must be removed.

OPERATION

The OSS sensor provides the PCM with information about the rotational speed of an output shaft. The PCM uses the information to control and diagnose powertrain behavior. In some applications, the sensor is also used as the source of vehicle speed.

REMOVAL & INSTALLATION

1. With the vehicle in NEUTRAL, position it on a hoist.

2. Disconnect the negative battery cable.

3. Remove the transmission fluid pan drain plug and allow the continuously variable transaxle (CVT) transmission fluid to drain.

4. Remove the transmission fluid pan bolts and the transmission fluid pan.

5. Remove and discard the transmission fluid pan gasket.

➡**Check the transaxle case to see if the filter pickup tube seal is stuck in the case. If the pickup tube seal is in the case it will need to be removed.**

6. Remove and discard the transmission fluid filter.

7. Use a suitable seal pick to remove the seal if it is stuck in the case.

⁕⁕ **CAUTION**

Do not pull up on the wire harness. Damage to the wiring harness could result.

8. Depress the tab on the electrical connector and pull up on the output shaft speed (OSS) connector to disconnect.

⁕⁕ **CAUTION**

The OSS sensor has a spacer under the sensor for the bolt. This is used for keeping the sensor a specific distance from the differential gears.

9. Remove the OSS sensor bolt, sensor and spacer.

To install:

⁕⁕ **CAUTION**

The OSS sensor has a spacer under the sensor for the bolt. This is used for keeping the sensor a specific distance from the differential gears.

10. Install the OSS sensor spacer, sensor and bolt. Tighten to 71 inch lbs. (8 Nm). Tighten to 8 Nm (71 lb-in).

11. Connect the electrical connectors.

⁕⁕ **CAUTION**

Make sure that the transmission fluid filter pickup tube seal was removed from the bore when the transmission fluid filter was removed. Failure to remove the seal prior to installing the new transmission fluid filter will result in transaxle failure.

⁕⁕ **CAUTION**

Make sure that the transmission fluid filter is fully seated into the bore. If the transmission fluid filter is not correctly installed, internal transaxle damage will occur.

12. Install a new transmission fluid filter and seal assembly.

13. Make sure that the transmission fluid filter is seated over one of the mechatronic bolts.

⁕⁕ **CAUTION**

Use care when cleaning the gasket surface not to scratch or gouge it, a transmission leak could result.

➡**Using a plastic scraper, make sure that all gasket material is removed from the case.**

14. Install a new transmission fluid pan gasket.

15. Install the transmission fluid pan and the bolts. Tighten in the sequence shown to 9 ft. lbs. (12 Nm).

16. Install the fluid pan drain plug and tighten to 18 ft. lbs. (25 Nm).

17. Fill the transaxle with approximately 4.7L (5 quarts) of clean CVT transmission fluid.

TESTING

See Figure 83.

1. Check the condition of the connector. Make sure the connector is firmly attached. Check for broken or bent connector pins. Repair any connector damage before continuing with troubleshooting the issue.

2. Check the condition of the wiring to the connector. If the wiring is damaged, repair the wiring before continuing with any further tests.

3. The battery should be fully charged and the starting system should be functioning properly.

4. Check the VSS harness routing:

5. Verify the harness is not routed adjacent to any high current wires such as ignition wires or generator wiring.

6. Verify the VSS harness is shielded and grounded, if applicable.

➡**The Variable Reluctance (VR) sensors have 2-wire connectors, Hall-effect sensors have 3-wire connectors.**

7. Check the sensor voltage as follows:

    a. Key in OFF position.

    b. OSS/VSS connector disconnected.

    c. Key ON, engine OFF.

    d. Measure the voltage between the positive VPWR terminal on the OSS/VSS connector on the harness side and the negative battery terminal.

    e. If the voltage is not greater than 10 volts there is an open circuit.

8. Check the VPWR ground to the sensor as follows:

    a. Key in OFF position.

    b. Measure the resistance between the positive PWRGND terminal on the sensor connector on the harness side and the negative battery terminal.

    c. If the resistance is not less than 5 Ohms, there is an open circuit.

9. Check the sensor circuit for a short to Vref and voltage in the harness as follows:

    a. Key ON, engine OFF.

    b. Sensor connector disconnected.

    c. Measure the voltage between the positive OSS/VSS terminal on the sensor connector on the harness side and the negative battery terminal.

  d. If the voltage is not less than 1 volt there is an short circuit.

10. Check the Sensor circuit(s) for an open in the harness as follows:

➡️**Hall-effect sensors are not equipped with a SIGRTN circuit. Disregard the SIGRTN measurement.**

  a. Key in OFF position.
  b. PCM connector disconnected.
  c. Sensor connector disconnected.
  d. Measure the resistance between the following:

  • Positive OSS/VSS terminal on the PCM connector on the harness side and negative OSS/VSS terminal on the OSS/VSS connector on the harness side.
  • Positive SIGRTN terminal on the PCM connector on the harness side and negative SIGRTN terminal on the OSS/VSS connector on the harness side.
  • Positive PWRGND terminal on the PCM connector on the harness side and negative PWRGND terminal on the OSS/VSS connector on the harness side.

  e. If the resistance is not less than 5 Ohms, there is an open circuit.

11. Check the sensor signal output to the PCM, hall-effect type sensor as follows:

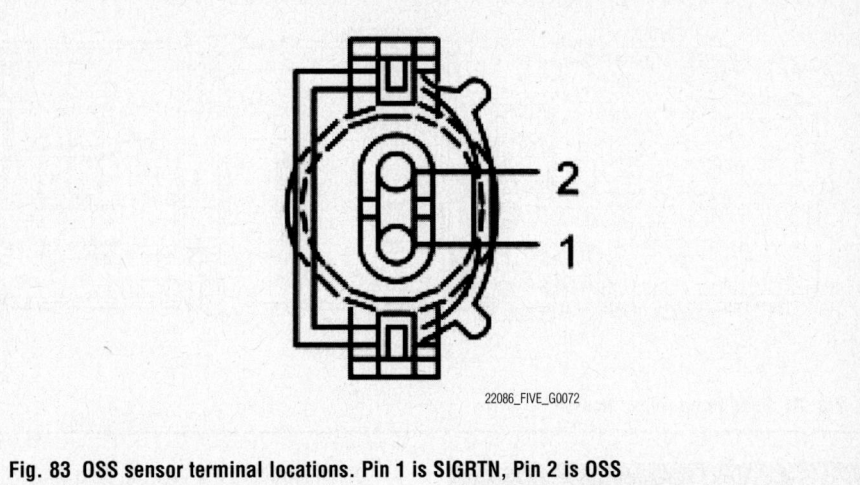

22086_FIVE_G0072

Fig. 83 OSS sensor terminal locations. Pin 1 is SIGRTN, Pin 2 is OSS

➡️**The opposite wheel must be held stationary.**

  a. PCM connector disconnected.
  b. Raise the vehicle to allow for the rotation of the front drive wheels.
  c. Key ON, engine OFF.
  d. Transmission gear selector in NEUTRAL.
  e. Measure the voltage between the positive OSS/VSS terminal on the PCM connector on the harness side and the negative PWRGND terminal on the PCM connector on the harness side.
  f. The voltage should rise above 5 volts and fall below 1 volt in a regular cycle. If the voltage is not as specified, inspect the target wheel. If the target wheel is good, replace the sensor.

12. Check the resistance of the sensor as follows:

  a. Measure the resistance between the OSS/VSS positive terminal on the OSS/VSS connector on the component side and the negative SIGRTN terminal on the OSS/VSS connector on the component side. The resistance should be 170–270 Ohms on a VSS or 400–1.25 KOhms on a OSS. If the resistance is not as specified, inspect the target wheel. If the target wheel is good, replace the sensor.

FUEL   GASOLINE FUEL INJECTION SYSTEM

FUEL SYSTEM SERVICE PRECAUTIONS

Safety is the most important factor when performing not only fuel system maintenance but any type of maintenance. Failure to conduct maintenance and repairs in a safe manner may result in serious personal injury or death. Maintenance and testing of the vehicle's fuel system components can be accomplished safely and effectively by adhering to the following rules and guidelines.

  • To avoid the possibility of fire and personal injury, always disconnect the negative battery cable unless the repair or test procedure requires that battery voltage be applied.

  • Always relieve the fuel system pressure prior to disconnecting any fuel system component (injector, fuel rail, pressure regulator, etc.), fitting or fuel line connection. Exercise extreme caution whenever relieving fuel system pressure to avoid exposing skin, face and eyes to fuel spray. Please be advised that fuel under pressure may penetrate the skin or any part of the body that it contacts.

  • Always place a shop towel or cloth around the fitting or connection prior to loosening to absorb any excess fuel due to spillage. Ensure that all fuel spillage (should it occur) is quickly removed from engine surfaces. Ensure that all fuel soaked cloths or towels are deposited into a suitable waste container.

  • Always keep a dry chemical (Class B) fire extinguisher near the work area.

  • Do not allow fuel spray or fuel vapors to come into contact with a spark or open flame.

  • Always use a back-up wrench when loosening and tightening fuel line connection fittings. This will prevent unnecessary stress and torsion to fuel line piping.

  • Always replace worn fuel fitting O-rings with new Do not substitute fuel hose or equivalent where fuel pipe is installed.

  Before servicing the vehicle, make sure to also refer to the precautions in the beginning of this section as well.

RELIEVING FUEL SYSTEM PRESSURE

See Figure 84.

  Locate the fuel pump relay in the engine compartment power distribution box relay no. 53. Remove the fuel pump relay. Start the engine and allow it to idle until it stalls. Crank the engine for 5 seconds to ensure fuel supply manifold pressure is released. When vehicle service is complete, reinstall the fuel pump relay and turn the ignition on to pressurize the fuel system. Start the vehicle and check the system for leaks.

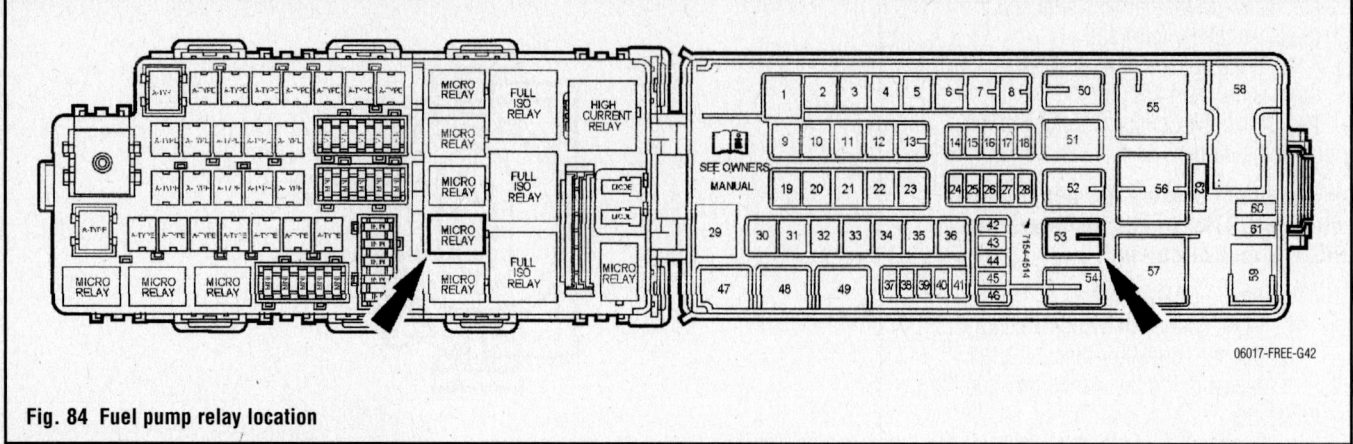

Fig. 84 Fuel pump relay location

FUEL FILTER

REMOVAL & INSTALLATION

1. Place the vehicle in neutral and position it on a hoist
2. Relieve the fuel system pressure.
3. Disconnect the negative battery cable.

➡**The fuel lines and filter may contain some fuel after the fuel system pressure is released. After disconnecting the lines or removing the filter, carefully drain the residual fuel into a suitable container.**

4. Disconnect the fuel supply line-to-fuel filter inlet quick connect coupling.
5. Disconnect the fuel supply line-to-fuel filter outlet quick connect coupling.
6. Loosen the fuel filter retaining clamp.
7. Remove the fuel filter.

To install:

8. Installation is the reverse of removal. Tighten the filter retaining clamp to 27 inch lbs. (3 Nm).
9. Start the vehicle and check for leaks.

FUEL INJECTORS

REMOVAL & INSTALLATION

See Figure 85.

1. Relieve the fuel system pressure.
2. Disconnect the negative battery cable.
3. Remove the upper and lower intake manifolds.
4. Disconnect the fuel rail temperature and pressure sensor connectors.
5. Remove the vacuum harness.
6. Remove the fuel rail attaching bolts.
7. Separate the fuel rail and injectors from the lower intake manifold.
8. Disconnect the fuel injector connectors.

9. Disconnect the fuel rail charging wiring harness.
10. Remove the retaining clips and separate the injectors from the supply manifold. Discard the O-rings.

To install:

11. Lubricate NEW O-rings with clean engine oil and position fuel injectors on the supply manifold. Install the retaining clips.

12. Connect the fuel rail charging wiring harness.
13. Connect the fuel injector connectors.
14. Connect the fuel rail and injectors to the lower intake manifold.
15. Install the fuel rail attaching bolts and tighten to 89 inch lbs. (19 Nm).
16. Install the vacuum harness.

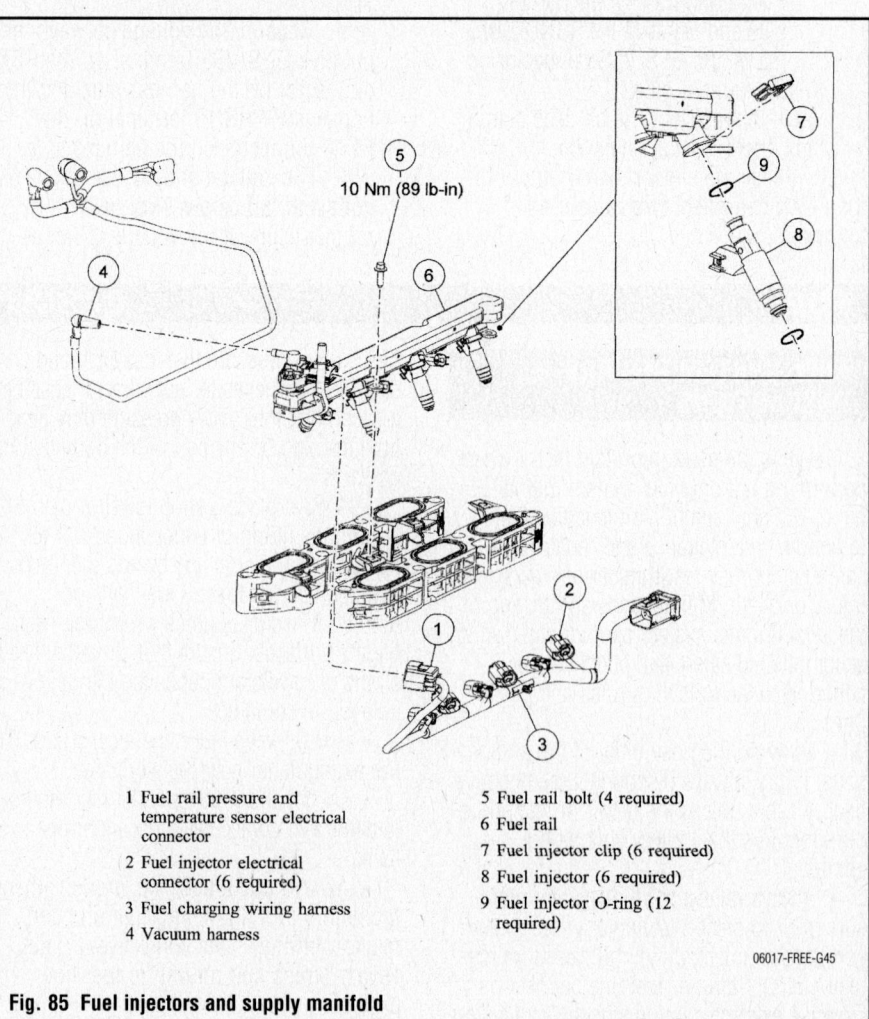

1 Fuel rail pressure and temperature sensor electrical connector
2 Fuel injector electrical connector (6 required)
3 Fuel charging wiring harness
4 Vacuum harness
5 Fuel rail bolt (4 required)
6 Fuel rail
7 Fuel injector clip (6 required)
8 Fuel injector (6 required)
9 Fuel injector O-ring (12 required)

Fig. 85 Fuel injectors and supply manifold

17. Connect the fuel rail temperature and pressure sensor connectors.

18. Install the upper and lower intake manifolds.

19. Connect the negative battery cable.

20. Start the engine and check for fuel leaks.

FUEL PUMP

REMOVAL & INSTALLATION

See Figure 86.

1. Disconnect the negative battery cable.

2. Drain the fuel tank.

3. Remove the rear lower seat cushion.

4. Remove the fuel pump module cover.

5. Remove any dirt that has accumulated around the fuel pump module attaching flange to prevent it from entering the tank during service.

6. Disconnect the fuel pump electrical connectors.

7. Disconnect the fuel pump quick connect coupling from the fuel pump module.

8. Disconnect the fuel vapor tube quick connect coupling from the fuel pump module.

9. Turn the fuel pump module locking ring using a locking ring removal tool, and remove the locking ring.

10. Remove the fuel pump module and disconnect the quick connect fittings from the bottom of the fuel pump.

To install:

11. Connect the quick connect fittings to the bottom of the fuel pump. Insert the fuel pump module into the fuel tank and align the arrows on the fuel pump with the arrows on the fuel tank. Secure it in place with the locking ring.

12. Connect the fuel vapor tube quick connect coupling to the fuel pump module.

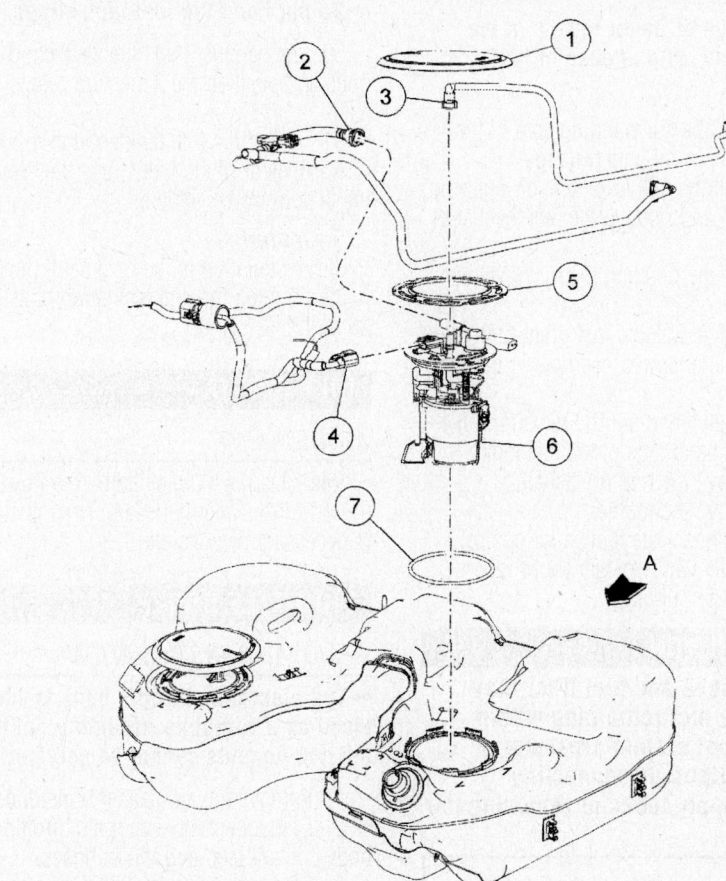

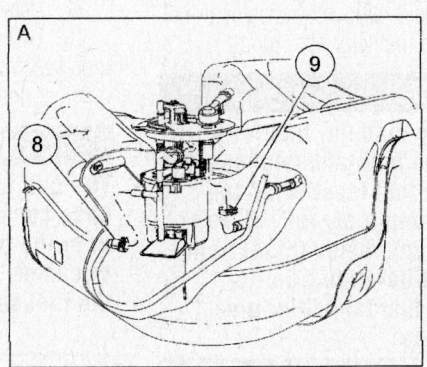

1 Fuel pump module access cover

2 Fuel vapor control tube assembly valve quick connect coupling

3 Fuel supply tube quick release coupling

4 Fuel pump module electrical connector

5 Fuel pump module lock ring

6 Fuel pump module

7 Fuel pump module O-ring seal

8 Fuel transfer supply tube quick connect coupling

9 Fuel vapor tube quick connect coupling

06017-FREE-G44

Fig. 86 In-tank electric fuel pump and related components

13. Connect the fuel pump quick connect coupling to the fuel pump module.

14. Connect the fuel pump electrical connectors.

15. Install the fuel pump module cover.

16. Install the rear seat latching bracket bolts and brackets and tighten to 13 ft. lbs. (17 Nm).

17. Install a minimum of 10 gallons (38L) of fuel and check for leaks.

18. Check for fuel leaks at the fittings.

19. Start the engine and check for fuel leaks.

FUEL TANK

REMOVAL & INSTALLATION

See Figure 87.

1. With the vehicle in NEUTRAL, position it on a hoist.

2. Properly relieve the fuel system pressure.

3. Disconnect the negative battery cable.

4. Release the fuel tank filler cap and position aside.

5. Insert a suitable fuel drain tube into the fuel tank filler pipe until it reaches the fuel tank inlet spout.

➡ **When the fuel tank is completely full, this step will remove approximately 1/8 of the fuel from the fuel tank.**

6. Attach the fuel storage tanker to the fuel drain tube and remove any residual fuel remaining in the fuel tank filler pipe.

❊ CAUTION

The fuel pump module, fuel level sensor and the fuel tank inlet spout are below the fuel level when the fuel tank is completely full. Make sure to drain any residual fuel from the fuel tank filler pipe prior to removing the fuel tank filler pipe clamp and hose.

7. Release the fuel tank filler pipe hose-to-fuel tank inlet spout clamp.

➡ **The fuel tank filler pipe may have some residual fuel remaining in it after draining. Upon disconnecting the fuel tank filler pipe hose, carefully drain the residual fuel into a suitable container.**

8. Remove the fuel tank filler pipe hose from the fuel tank inlet spout.

9. Insert a suitable fuel drain tube into the fuel tank inlet spout.

➡ **When draining a completely full fuel tank, this step will drain most of the**

fuel from the right hand side of the fuel tank, and partially drain the left hand side of the fuel tank, due to the siphoning effect from the fuel crossover tube.

10. Attach the fuel storage tanker to the fuel drain tube and drain the fuel from the RH side of the fuel tank.

11. Remove the rear lower seat cushion.

12. Release the latches and pull upward on the rear lower seat cushion and remove.

13. Position the rear floor carpet and any padding or insulation covering the fuel level sensor access cover aside.

14. Remove the fuel level sensor access cover.

15. Disconnect the fuel level sensor electrical connector.

➡ **Place rags or paper towels in the general work area in case of fuel spillage.**

16. Clean the surrounding area of the fuel level sensor mounting flange.

17. Install the fuel level sensor lock ring removal tool and remove the fuel level sensor lock ring.

18. Carefully position the fuel level sensor aside.

19. Install a suitable fuel drain tube into the fuel level sensor access hole in the fuel tank.

20. Completely drain the remaining fuel from the left hand side of the fuel tank.

21. Remove the rear driveshaft.

22. Remove the muffler.

23. Disconnect the fuel vapor control tube assembly valve-to-fuel vapor tube quick connect coupling.

❊ CAUTION

The fuel tubes and fuel filter may have some fuel remaining within after the fuel system pressure is released. Upon disconnecting the fuel supply tubes or removing the

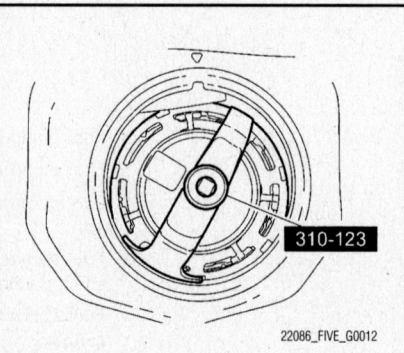

Fig. 87 Removing the fuel level sensor lock ring

22086_FIVE_G0012

fuel filter, carefully drain the residual fuel into a suitable container.

24. Disconnect the fuel supply tube-to-fuel filter quick connect coupling.

25. Disconnect the fuel vapor tube-to-fuel vapor control tube assembly valve quick connect coupling.

26. Disconnect the fuel tank wiring harness electrical connector at the rear of the fuel tank.

27. Remove the fuel tank filler pipe hose from the fuel tank.

28. Place a suitable lifting device under the fuel tank.

29. Remove the 2 front fuel tank strap bolts.

➡ **Do not bend the fuel tank straps.**

30. Loosen the 2 rear fuel tank strap bolts and position the 2 fuel tank straps aside.

31. Lower the fuel tank enough to move forward, clear of the fuel straps then remove the tank from the vehicle.

To install:

32. Installation is the reverse of removal.

33. Tighten the fuel tank strap bolts to 26 ft. lbs. (35 Nm).

IDLE SPEED

ADJUSTMENT

Idle speed is maintained by the Powertrain Control Module (PCM). No adjustment is necessary or possible.

THROTTLE BODY

REMOVAL & INSTALLATION

➡ **The electronic throttle body is serviced as a complete assembly. Individual components cannot be serviced.**

1. Remove the air cleaner outlet pipe.

2. Disconnect the electronic throttle body coolant feed and return hoses.

3. Disconnect the coolant hoses and plug the coolant hoses.

4. Disconnect the electronic throttle body electrical connector.

5. Remove the bolts and the throttle body.

6. Remove and discard the throttle body gasket.

7. Clean and inspect the sealing surfaces.

8. To install, reverse the removal procedure. Install a new throttle body gasket. Tighten the bolts to 89 inch lbs. (10 Nm).

HEATING & AIR CONDITIONING SYSTEM

BLOWER MOTOR

REMOVAL & INSTALLATION

1. Remove the RH cowl side trim panel.
2. Remove the RH lower instrument panel insulator.
3. Disconnect the blower motor electrical connector.
4. Remove the 3 blower motor screws.
5. Remove the blower motor.
6. Remove the blower motor wheel clip.
7. Remove the blower motor wheel.
8. To install, reverse the removal procedure.

HEATER CORE

REMOVAL & INSTALLATION

See Figure 88.

1. Ensure the ignition is off.
2. Remove the Smart Junction Box (SJB) cover located below the left side of the instrument panel. Remove the Restraints Control Module (RCM) fuse no. F2.21.
3. Turn the ignition on and watch the air bag indicator for 30 seconds. The indicator light will remain lit constantly if the correct fuse has been removed. If the light is not on steadily, remove the correct fuse and check the light again.
4. Turn the ignition switch off.
5. Disconnect the negative battery cable.
6. Drain the cooling system into a clean container for reuse.
7. Recover the air conditioning refrigerant, into a refrigerant recovery station.
8. Disconnect the heater hoses from the heater core inlet and outlet tubes in the engine compartment.
9. Remove the steering wheel access cover.
10. Release one side of the driver air bag module clip using needle nose pliers.
11. Lift the end of the clip over the center post.
12. Repeat the procedure on the opposite wide wire clip.

➡ **When the clips are released correctly, the clip ends will come to rest between the center two inner posts.**

13. Push on the horn at the upper part of the air bag cover and push both ends of the wire clips inward to release the driver air bag module from the steering wheel.
14. Disconnect the air bag electrical connectors, horn and accessories

connectors, and remove the driver air bag module.
15. Remove and discard the steering wheel bolt.
16. Remove the steering wheel.
17. Remove the upper and lower steering column covers.
18. Disconnect the multi-function switch connectors and remove the multi-function switch.
19. Remove or disconnect the following:
- Cowl trim panels and disconnect the electrical connectors
- Lower instrument panel insulator
- Front floor console
- Floor shifter
- Instrument panel center finish panel
- Audio unit and disconnect the electrical and antenna connectors
- Instrument panel side panels
- A pillar trim panels
- Steering column cover
- Hood release handle
- Headlight switch
- Instrument cluster finish panel
- Glove box door
- Passenger air bag module connectors
- Two air bag module bolts
- Passenger air bag module
- Passenger assist handle
- Left side main wiring harness connectors
- 12 screws attaching the upper instrument panel section and remove the upper section
- Thermostatic expansion valve bolt
- Powertrain Control Module (PCM)
- Transaxle roll restrictor bolt
- Transaxle roll restrictor bar bolts
- Instrument panel cowl top bolts from both sides
- Steering column pinch bolt
- A/C floor duct
- Four floor tunnel brace bolts
- Restraints Control Module (RCM) small and large electrical connectors
20. Mark the location of the instrument panel cross beam bolts.
21. With the help of an assistant, remove the bolts from one side of the cross beam and while supporting the beam, remove the other side bolts and remove the cross beam.
22. Remove the dash panel seal from the heater core tubes.
23. Remove the heater core tube bracket.
24. Disconnect the evaporator discharge air temperature sensor connector.

25. Remove the left side blend door actuator.
26. Remove the heater core cover screws.
27. Remove the heater core cover and the heater core.

To install:

28. Install the heater core cover and the heater core.
29. Install the heater core cover screws.
30. Install the left side blend door actuator.
31. Connect the evaporator discharge air temperature sensor connector.
32. Install the heater core tube bracket.
33. Install the dash panel seal to the heater core tubes.
34. With the help of an assistant, install the bolts from one side of the cross beam and while supporting the beam, install the other side bolts using the locations marked previously. Tighten the bolts to 18 ft. lbs. (25 Nm).
35. Connect the RCM small and large electrical connectors.
36. Install or connect the following:
- Four floor tunnel brace bolts
- A/C floor duct
- Steering column pinch bolt and tighten to 18 ft. lbs. (25 Nm)
- Instrument panel cowl top bolts to both sides and tighten to 18 ft. lbs. (25 Nm)
- Transaxle roll restrictor bar bolts and tighten to 40 ft. lbs. (55 Nm)
- Transaxle roll restrictor bolt and tighten to 35 ft. lbs. (48 Nm)
- Powertrain Control Module (PCM)
- Thermostatic expansion valve bolt
- Instrument panel upper section and 12 screws
- Left side main wiring harness connectors
- Passenger assist handle
- Passenger air bag module
- Two air bag module bolts and tighten to 80 inch lbs. (9 Nm)
- Passenger air bag module connectors
- Glove box door
- Instrument cluster finish panel
- Headlight switch
- Hood release handle
- Steering column cover
- A pillar trim panels
- Instrument panel side panels
- Audio unit and connect the electrical and antenna connectors
- Instrument panel center finish panel

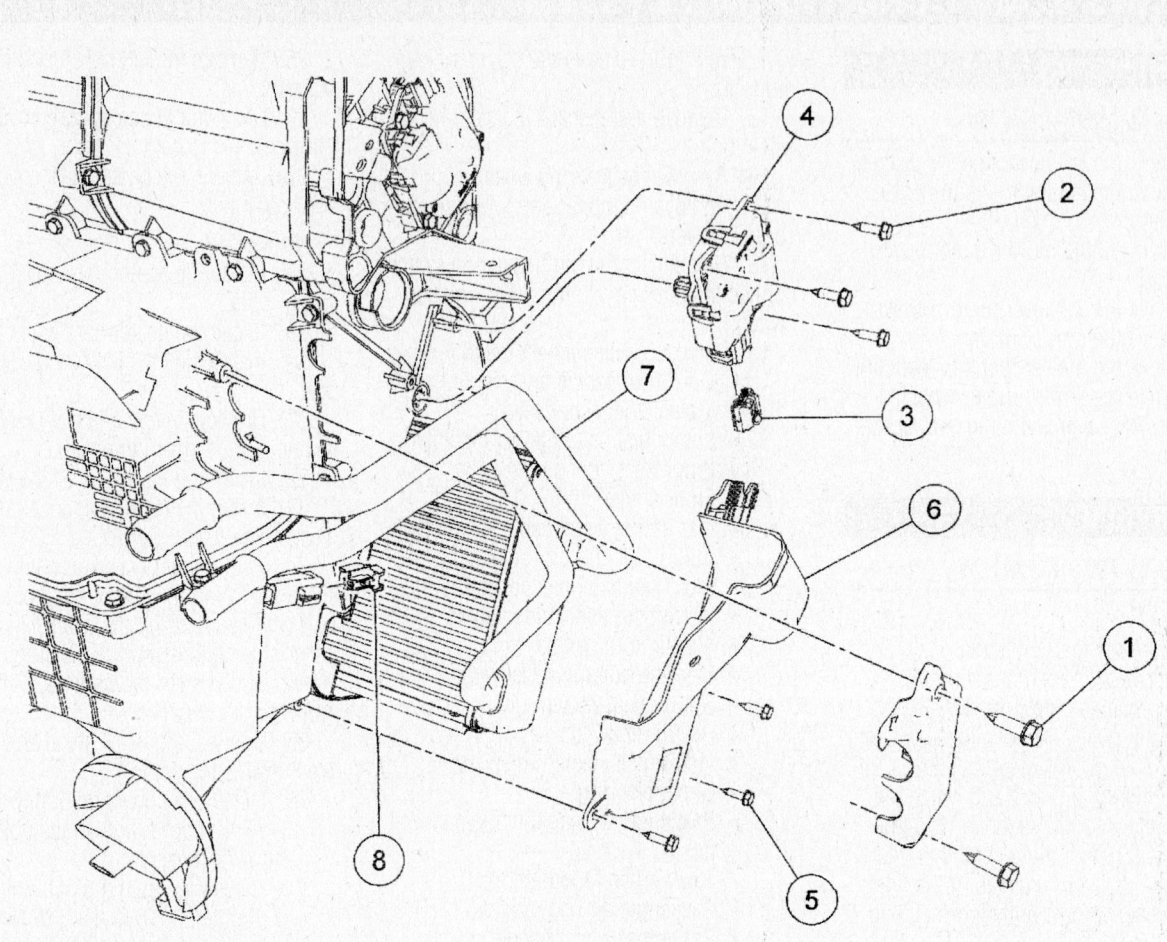

1 Heater tube bracket screw

2 LH temperature blend door actuator screw

3 LH temperature blend door actuator electrical connector

4 LH temperature blend door actuator

5 Heater core cover screw

6 Heater core cover

7 Heater core

8 Evaporator discharge air temperature sensor electrical connector

06017-FREE-G06

Fig. 88 Exploded view of heater core mounting

- Floor shifter
- Front floor console
- Lower instrument panel insulator
- Cowl trim panels and connect the electrical connectors
- Multi-function switch and connectors
- Upper and lower steering column covers
- Steering wheel and tighten the NEW bolt to 30 ft. lbs. (40 Nm)
- Connect the air bag electrical connectors, horn and accessories connectors, and install the driver air bag module. Make the clips are released from the center post and back in position on both sides of the air bag.
- Steering wheel access cover
- Heater hoses to the heater core inlet and outlet tubes

37. Recharge the air conditioning refrigerant.

38. Refill the coolant system.

39. Disconnect the negative battery cable.

40. Turn the ignition switch on.

41. Install Restraints Control Module (RCM) fuse no. F2.21 and the fuse cover.

42. Turn the ignition off.

43. Connect the negative battery cable.

44. Turn the ignition on and then off. Wait 10 seconds and turn the key back on. Watch the air bag indicator. The indicator light will remain lit constantly for 6 seconds and then go off. If the indicator does not turn on and then off, diagnose the air bag system

45. Clear all Diagnostic Trouble Codes (DTC) using a diagnostic tool.

STEERING

POWER STEERING GEAR

REMOVAL & INSTALLATION

See Figure 89.

✳✳ WARNING

Do not allow the steering wheel to rotate when the intermediate shaft is being disconnected, or damage to the clockspring can result. If it is suspected that the shaft has rotated, the clockspring must be removed and re-centered.

1. Place the steering wheel in the straight ahead position and remove the ignition key.

2. Raise the vehicle on a hoist.
3. Remove or disconnect the following:
   • Front wheels
   • Tie rod end cotter pins and castle nuts
   • Tie rod ends from the knuckles
   • Power steering line clamp plate bolt
4. Place a drain pan under the vehicle and disconnect the power steering lines.
5. Release the steering shaft intermediate boot bearing clamp and release the boot from the shaft.
6. Retain the bearing boot clamp in the open position.
7. Remove the pinch bolt retaining the steering column intermediate shaft coupling.

8. Remove the steering gear mounting nuts and bolts.
9. Remove the steering gear through the left side of the vehicle.
driver's side of the vehicle.

To install:

10. Install new O-rings on the power steering line fittings.
11. Place the steering gear in the vehicle through the left side.
12. Tighten the steering gear mounting bolts and nuts to 86 ft. lbs. (117 Nm).
13. Install the pinch bolt retaining the steering column intermediate shaft coupling and tighten to 18 ft. lbs. (25 Nm).

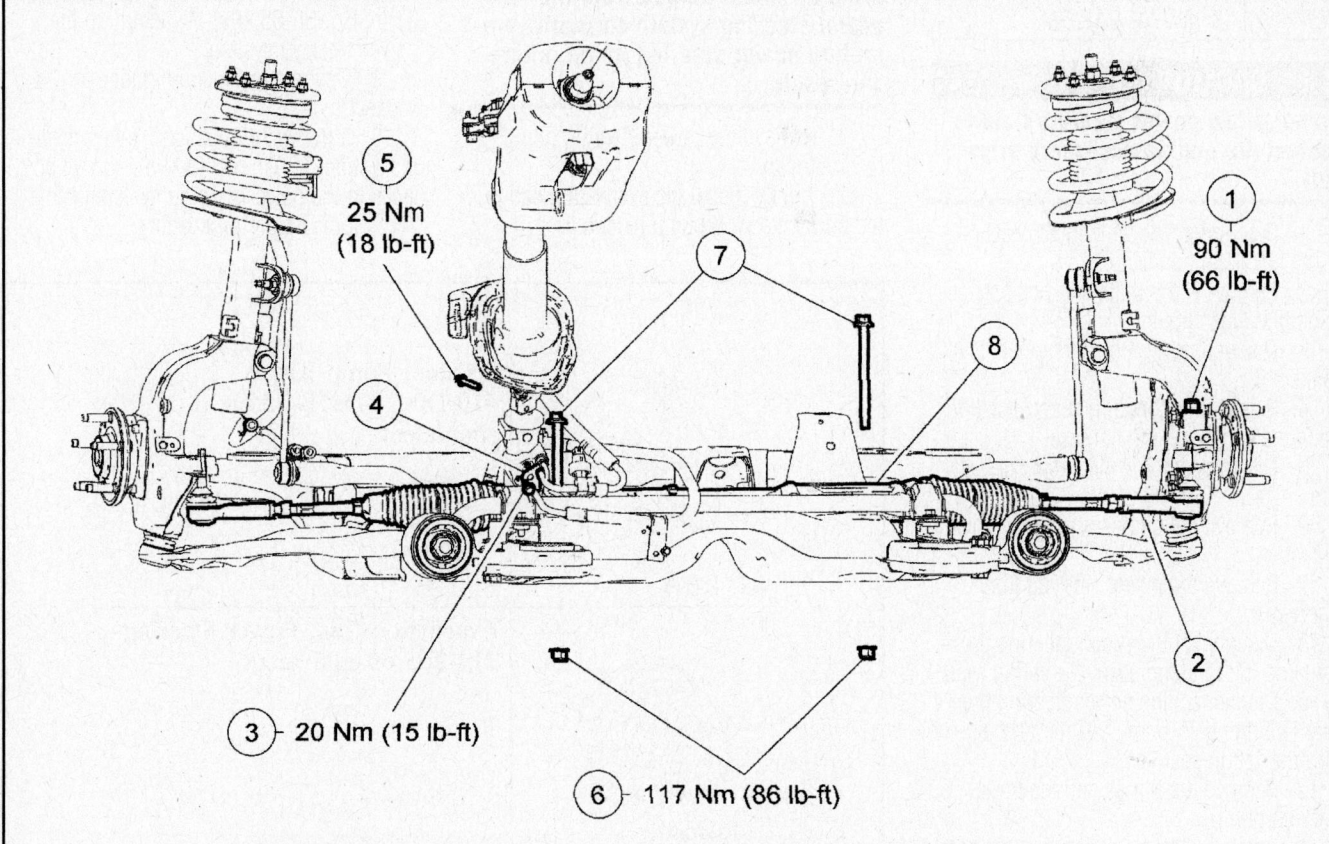

1 Tie-rod end nuts (2 required)

2 Tie-rod ends (2 required)

3 Power steering line clamp plate bolt

4 O-ring seals (2 required)

5 Intermediate shaft-to-steering gear bolt

6 Steering gear nuts (2 required)

7 Steering gear bolts (2 required)

8 Steering gear

06017-FREE-G47

Fig. 89 Exploded view of the rack and pinion steering gear mounting on the front subframe of the vehicle

14. Position the bearing boot in the retention groove so the outer bearing race is not exposed from the groove.

15. Install boot bearing clamp and ensure the end tabs do not contact the boot.

16. Using new o-rings, install the power steering lines.

17. Install the power steering line clamp plate bolt and tighten to 15 ft. lbs. (20 Nm).

18. Connect the tie rods.

19. Install the tie rod end nuts and tighten to 66 ft. lbs. (90 Nm).

20. Install the front wheels.

21. Lower the vehicle.

22. Fill the power steering oil reservoir.

23. Start the vehicle and check for leaks.

24. Check for proper wheel alignment and steering wheel position.

POWER STEERING PUMP

REMOVAL & INSTALLATION

✳✳ CAUTION

Do not allow power steering fluid to contact the engine accessory drive belt.

1. Disconnect the windshield washer motor electrical connector.

2. Remove the 2 bolts and position aside the degas bottle.

3. Disconnect the fill sensor electrical connector.

4. Release the 2 retainers and position aside the engine wiring harness.

5. Disconnect the 4 electrical connectors.

6. Remove the engine accessory drive belt.

7. Remove the power steering fluid reservoir.

8. Disconnect the power steering pressure line fitting and discard the Teflon seal.

9. Disconnect the power steering pressure line fitting-to-pump adapter and discard the Teflon seal.

10. Remove the 3 nuts and the power steering pump.

11. Rotate the power steering pump pulley to access the nuts through the holes.

To install:

12. Install a new Teflon® seal on the power steering pressure line fitting and the power steering pressure line fitting-to-pump adapter.

13. Install the power steering pump and the 3 nuts.

14. Rotate the power steering pump pulley to access the nuts through the holes and tighten to 18 ft. lbs. (25 Nm).

15. Install the power steering pressure line fitting-to-pump adapter and tighten to 48 ft. lbs. (65 Nm).

16. Connect the power steering pressure line fitting and tighten to 48 ft. lbs. (65 Nm).

17. Install the power steering fluid reservoir.

18. Install the engine accessory drive belt.

19. Position the degas bottle and install the 2 bolts.

20. Connect the fill sensor electrical connector.

21. Connect the windshield washer motor electrical connector.

22. Fill the power steering system.

BLEEDING

See Figure 90.

✳✳ CAUTION

If the air is not purged from the power steering system correctly, premature power steering pump failure can result.

1. Remove the power steering pump reservoir cap.

2. Tightly install the evacuation cap to the power steering pump reservoir.

3. Install the hose from the fill adapter manifold tee to the evacuation cap on the power steering pump reservoir.

4. Install the vacuum pump to the fill adapter manifold control valve.

5. Install the hose to the opposite fill adapter manifold control valve and submerge the open end of the hose into a container of new power steering fluid.

➡**The fill adapter manifold control valves are in the open position when the point of the handles face the center of the fill adapter manifold.**

6. Close the fill adapter manifold control valve connected to the power steering fluid container.

7. Open the fill adapter manifold control valve connected to the vacuum pump.

8. Using the vacuum pump, apply 20-25 in. Hg (68-85 kPa) of vacuum to the power steering system.

9. Observe the vacuum gauge for 30 seconds.

10. If the vacuum gauge reading drops more than 0.88 in. Hg (3 kPa), correct any leaks in the power steering system or the filling tools before proceeding.

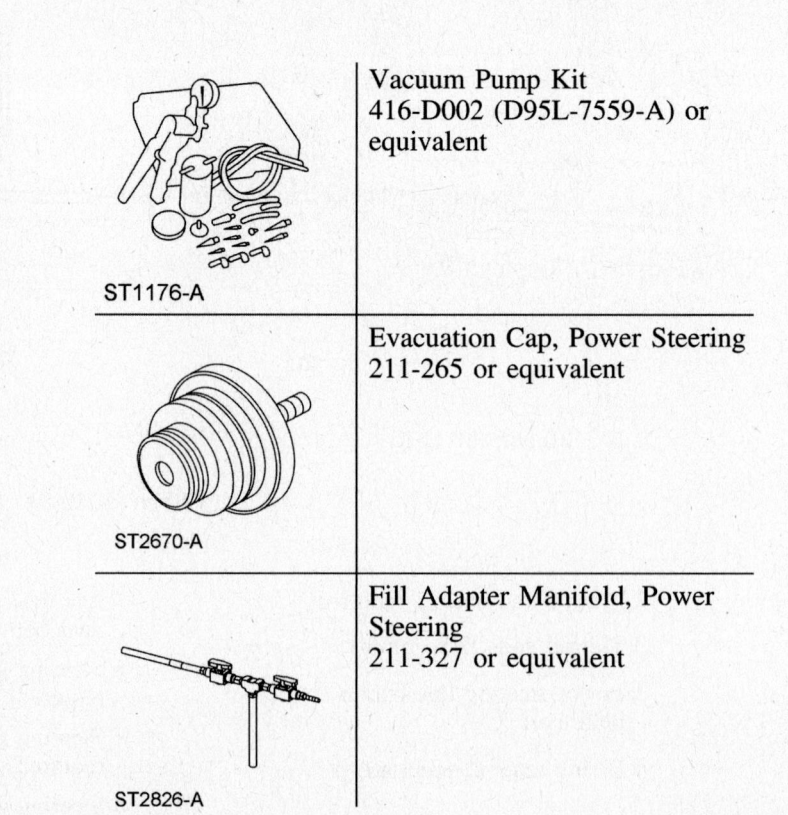

ST1176-A	Vacuum Pump Kit 416-D002 (D95L-7559-A) or equivalent
ST2670-A	Evacuation Cap, Power Steering 211-265 or equivalent
ST2826-A	Fill Adapter Manifold, Power Steering 211-327 or equivalent

22086_FIVE_G0039

Fig. 90 Tools needed to bleed the power steering system

➡**The vacuum pump gauge reading will drop slightly during this step.**

11. Slowly open the fill adapter manifold control valve connected to the power steering fluid container until power steering fluid completely fills the hose.
12. Close the fill adapter manifold control valve connected to the power steering fluid container.
13. Using the vacuum pump, apply 20-25 in. Hg (68-85 kPa) of vacuum to the power steering system.
14. Close the fill adapter manifold control valve connected to the vacuum pump.
15. Slowly open the fill adapter manifold control valve connected to the power steering fluid container.
16. When the power steering fluid has drained from the hose connected to the power steering fluid container, close the fill adapter manifold control valve connected to the power steering fluid container.
17. Remove the tools from the vehicle.
18. Install the power steering reservoir cap.

⁂ CAUTION

Do not hold the steering wheel against the stops for more than 3 - 5 seconds at a time. Damage to the power steering pump can occur.

➡**There will be a slight drop in the power steering fluid level in the power steering fluid reservoir when the engine is started.**

19. Start the engine and turn the steering wheel from stop-to-stop.
20. If equipped with Hydro-Boost®, apply the brake pedal twice.
21. Turn the ignition switch to the OFF position.

⁂ CAUTION

Do not overfill the reservoir.

22. Remove the power steering reservoir cap and fill the reservoir.
23. Install the power steering reservoir cap.

SUSPENSION

FRONT SUSPENSION

See Figure 91.

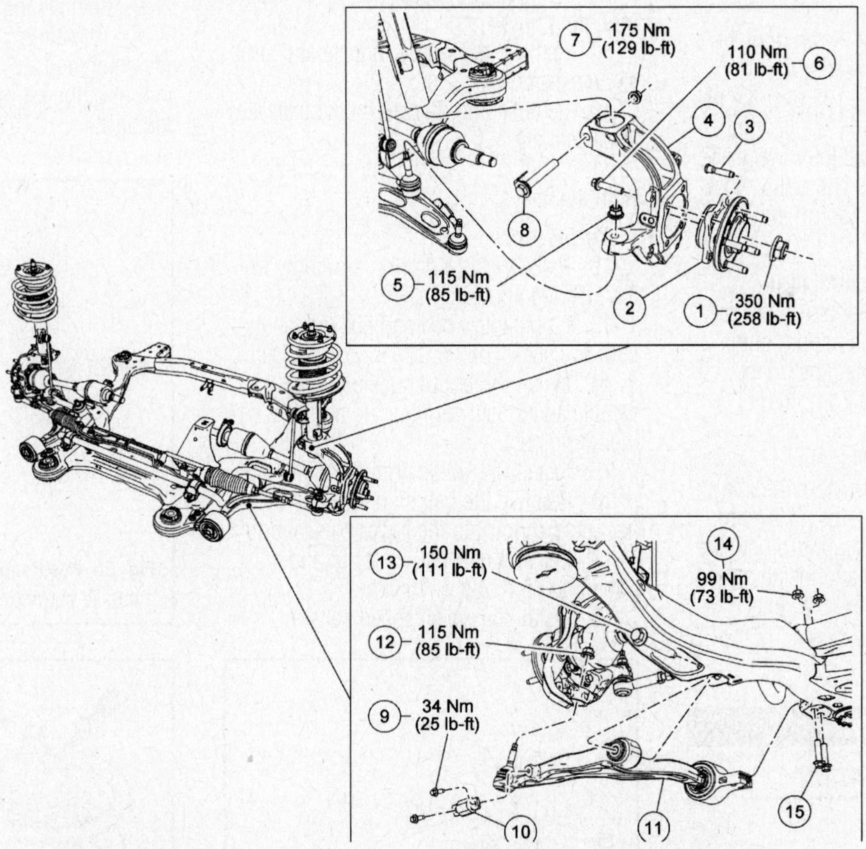
175 Nm (129 lb-ft)
110 Nm (81 lb-ft)
115 Nm (85 lb-ft)
350 Nm (258 lb-ft)
150 Nm (111 lb-ft)
99 Nm (73 lb-ft)
115 Nm (85 lb-ft)
34 Nm (25 lb-ft)
1. Wheel hub nut
2. Wheel hub and wheel bearing
3. Wheel stud (5 required)
4. Wheel knuckle
5. Tie-rod end nut
6. Wheel bearing and hub bolt (4 required)
7. Strut-to-wheel knuckle nut
8. Strut-to-wheel knuckle flag bolt
9. Steering limiter bolt (2 required)
10. Steering limiter nut (2 required)
11. Lower control arm
12. Lower ball joint nut
13. Lower arm rearward bolt
14. Lower arm bushing forward nut (2 required)
15. Lower arm bushing forward bolt (2 required)
22086_FIVE_G0029

Fig. 91 Exploded view of the front suspension components

LOWER BALL JOINT

REMOVAL & INSTALLATION

The lower ball joint is an integral part of the lower control and cannot be replaced separately. If the lower ball joint is defective, the entire lower control arm must be replaced. Refer to the lower control arm procedure.

LOWER CONTROL ARM

REMOVAL & INSTALLATION

See Figure 91.

✳✳ WARNING

Always use new bolts and nuts on the suspension components.

1. Raise the vehicle on a hoist.
2. Remove the wheel assembly.
3. Remove the lower ball joint nut using a crow's foot wrench, and discard the nut
4. Push the lower arm down until the ball joint is clear of the lower arm.
5. Install tool no. 307-102 over the ball stud.
6. Remove and discard the lower arm bushing-to-subframe nuts and bolts.
7. Remove the lower control arm.

To install:

8. Install the lower control arm.
9. Install the new lower arm bushing-to-subframe bolts from the bottom of the lower arm bushing with the nuts on top.
10. Tighten the nuts to 73 ft. lbs. (99 Nm).
11. Remove the special tool.
12. Install the lower arm-to-subframe bolts and tighten to 111 ft. lbs. (150 Nm).
13. Push the lower arm upward until the ball joint is up in the arm and install a new ball joint nut and tighten to 85 ft. lbs. (115 Nm).
14. Lower the vehicle.

MACPHERSON STRUT

REMOVAL & INSTALLATION

See Figures 91 and 92.

➡ **Do not allow the axle shaft to move outward as damage to the CV joint may result.**

✳✳ WARNING

Always use new bolts and nuts on the suspension components.

1. Turn the ignition switch **OFF** and

place the steering column in the unlocked position.
2. Loosen the strut/spring upper mounting nuts.
3. Raise the vehicle on a hoist.
4. Remove or disconnect the following:
   - Front wheel
   - Front wheel axle hub nut and discard
   - Tie rod-to-wheel knuckle nut
   - Separate the tie rod from the knuckle
   - Brake disc
   - Wheel speed sensor and wire aside
   - Lower ball joint nut using a crow's foot wrench, and discard the nut
5. Push the lower arm down until the ball joint is clear of the lower arm.
6. Install tool no. 307-102 over the ball stud.
7. Use a puller and press the halfshaft from the wheel hub and support the halfshaft level.
8. Remove and discard the strut upper mounting nuts.
9. Remove the wheel knuckle and strut as an assembly.
10. Remove and discard the knuckle-to-strut bolt and nut.
11. Separate the spring/strut assembly from the knuckle.

To install:

12. Place the strut/spring assembly in the steering knuckle.
13. Using a new bolt and nut, tighten the strut-to-knuckle bolt to 129 ft. lbs. (175 Nm).
14. Install the strut/knuckle in the vehicle and loosely tighten the new top mounting nuts.
15. Install the halfshaft in the wheel hub.
16. Remove the ball stud tool and connect the ball joint to the lower control arm.
17. Install a new ball joint nut and tighten to 85 ft. lbs. (115 Nm).
18. Install the wheel speed sensor.

19. Install the brake disc.
20. Install the tie rod to the wheel knuckle and tighten the new nut to 85 ft. lbs. (115 Nm).
21. Install a new axle hub nut and tighten to 258 ft. lbs. (350 Nm).
22. Install the front wheel.
23. Lower the vehicle.
24. Tighten the upper strut nuts to 22 ft. lbs. (30 Nm).
25. Check the wheel alignment.

OVERHAUL

See Figures 93 and 94.

1. Using a spring compressor, compress the spring and loosen the strut rod nut.
2. Compress the spring until all tension is relieved.
3. Remove the strut rod appearance cap.
4. Remove and discard the upper strut rod nut.
5. Separate the strut, spring mount and washer.
6. Remove the spring.
7. To maintain wheel camber, position the notch and arrow on the upper strut mount outboard opposite the locator tab on the strut.

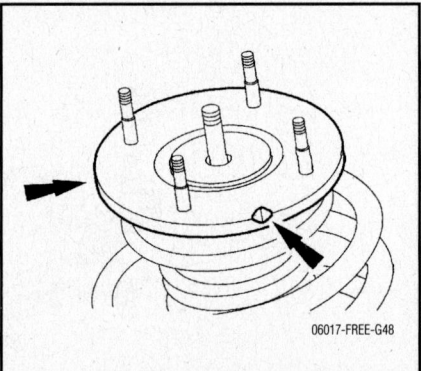

Fig. 93 Positioning upper strut mount outboard to maintain wheel camber

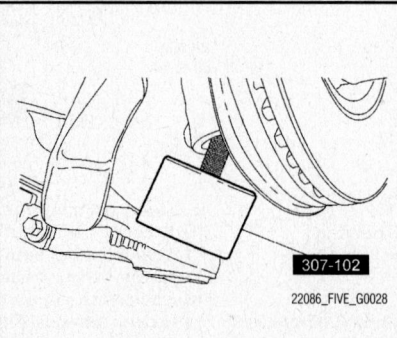

Fig. 92 Install tool no. 307-102 over the front ball stud

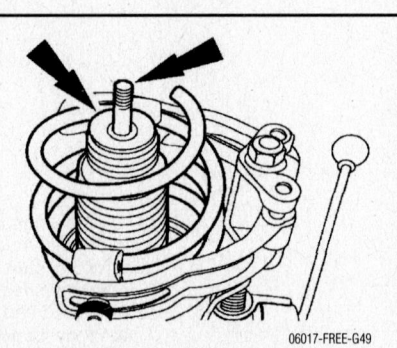

Fig. 94 Positioning upper strut mount inboard to adjust wheel camber +0.5 degrees

8. To adjust camber +0.5 degrees, position the notch and arrow on the upper strut mount inboard aligned with the locator tab on the strut.

9. To reassemble, reverse the disassembly procedure. Make sure the spring is correctly seated in both spring seats. Tighten the new strut top retaining nut to 59 ft. lbs. (80 Nm).

STABILIZER BAR

REMOVAL & INSTALLATION

See Figures 95 and 96.

❊❊ WARNING

Always use new bolts and nuts on the suspension components.

1. Place the steering wheel in the UNLOCKED position.
2. Raise and safely support the vehicle.
3. Remove the wheels.
4. Unplug the heated oxygen sensor connector and unclip the connector from the subframe.
5. Remove the stabilizer bar link nuts.
6. Remove and discard the tie rod nut and separate the tie rod from the knuckle.
7. Remove and discard the lower arm bushing-to-subframe nuts and bolts.
8. Remove and discard the lower arm-to-subframe bolt.

9. Remove and discard the rear subframe to body bolts.
10. Lower the subframe about 2 inches.
11. Remove and discard the stabilizer bar bracket bolts.
12. Remove the stabilizer bar from the right side of the vehicle.

To install:

13. Install the stabilizer bar from the right side of the vehicle.
14. Install the stabilizer bar bracket bolts and tighten to 37 ft. lbs. (50 Nm).
15. Raise the subframe about 2 inches.
16. Install the rear subframe-to-body bolts.
17. Install the lower arm-to-subframe bolt and tighten to 111 ft. lbs. (150 Nm).

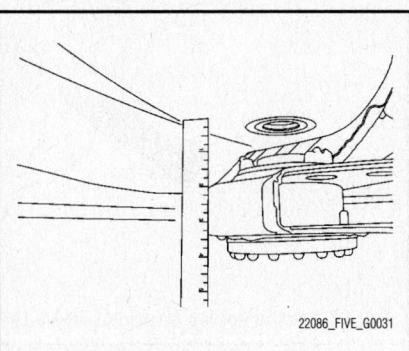

Fig. 96 Lower the subframe about 2 inches

18. Install the lower arm bushing-to-subframe nuts and bolts and tighten to 73 ft. lbs. (99 Nm).
19. Connect the tie rod to the knuckle and tighten the tie rod nut to 85 ft. lbs. (115 Nm).
20. Install the stabilizer bar link nuts and tighten to 41 ft. lbs. (55 Nm).
21. Install the wheels.
22. Lower the vehicle.

STEERING KNUCKLE

REMOVAL & INSTALLATION

❊❊ WARNING

Always use new bolts and nuts on the suspension components.

1. Raise and support the vehicle.
2. Remove the front wheel.
3. Remove and discard the axle hub nut.
4. Remove the tie rod-to-wheel nut and separate the tie rod from the knuckle.
5. Remove the brake disc.
6. Remove the wheel speed sensor and wire aside.
7. Remove the lower ball joint nut using a crow's foot wrench, and discard the nut
8. Push the lower arm down until the ball joint is clear of the lower arm.
9. Install tool no. 307-102 over the ball stud.
10. Use a puller and press the halfshaft from the wheel hub and support the halfshaft level.
11. Remove and discard the wheel knuckle-to-strut nut and bolt.
12. Remove the wheel knuckle.

To install:

13. Install the wheel knuckle.
14. Install and the wheel knuckle-to-strut nut and bolt and tighten to 129 ft. lbs. (175 Nm).
15. Install the halfshaft in the wheel hub.
16. Remove the ball stud tool and connect the ball joint to the lower control arm
17. Install a new ball joint nut and tighten to 85 ft. lbs. (115 Nm).
18. Install the wheel speed sensor.
19. Install the brake disc.
20. Install the tie rod to the wheel knuckle and tighten the new nut to 85 ft. lbs. (115 Nm).
21. Install a new axle hub nut and tighten to 258 ft. lbs. (350 Nm).
22. Install the front wheel.
23. Lower the vehicle.

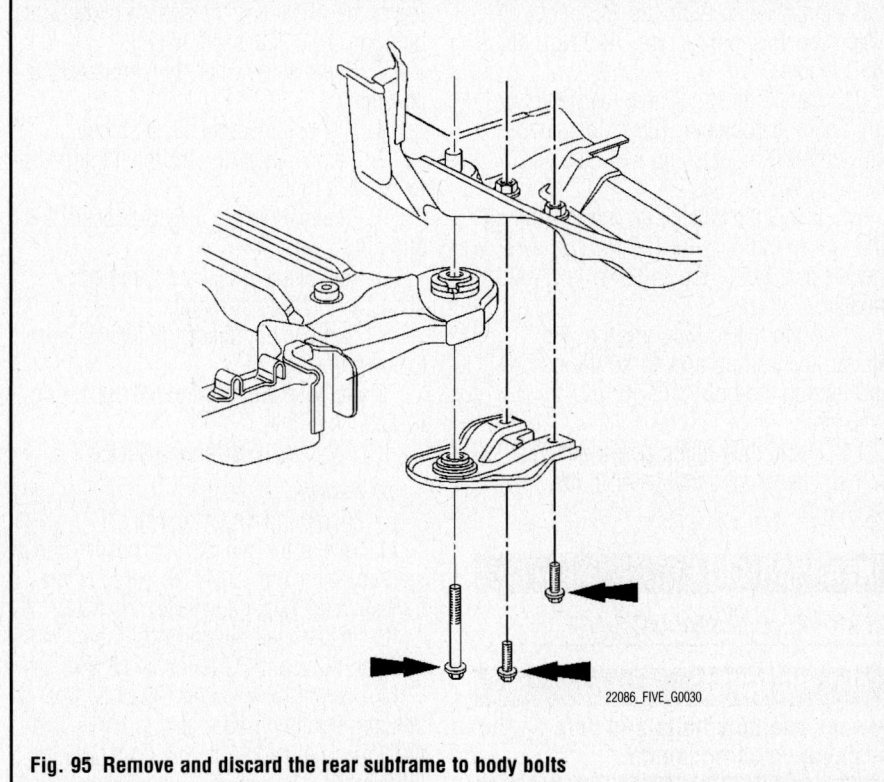

Fig. 95 Remove and discard the rear subframe to body bolts

WHEEL HUB AND BEARING

REMOVAL & INSTALLATION

See Figure 97.

The wheel bearing is integral with the wheel hub and cannot be replaced separately. If the wheel bearing is found to be defective, the wheel hub must be replaced as an assembly.

✴ WARNING

Always use new bolts and nuts on the suspension components.

1. Raise and safely support the vehicle.
2. Remove the wheel and tire assembly.
3. Remove the steering knuckle.
4. Remove and discard the wheel hub-to-knuckle bolts and separate the knuckle from the hub.

To install:

5. Clean the steering knuckle bore.
6. Install the wheel hub-to-the steering knuckle.
7. Install the wheel hub-to-knuckle bolts and tighten to 81 ft. lbs. (110 Nm).
8. Install the steering knuckle.
9. Install the wheel and tire.

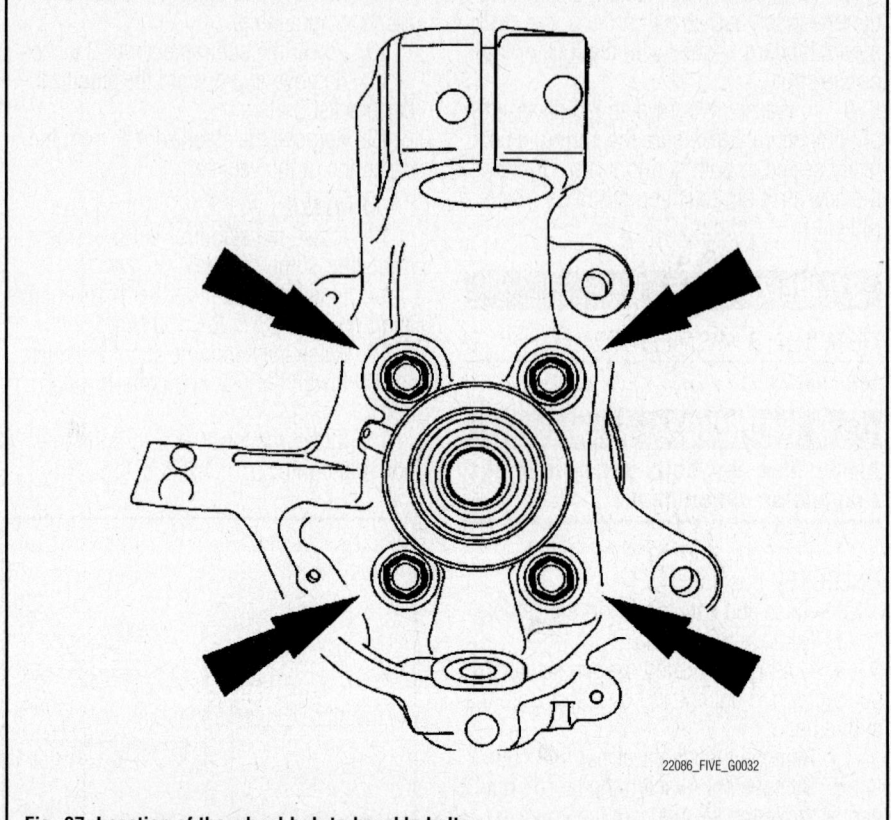

22086_FIVE_G0032

Fig. 97 Location of the wheel hub-to-knuckle bolts

SUSPENSION

REAR SUSPENSION

LOWER CONTROL ARM

REMOVAL & INSTALLATION

✴ WARNING

Always use new bolts and nuts on the suspension components.

1. Measure the distance between the top of the wheel and the bottom of the wheel opening. This is the trim height.
2. Remove and discard the trailing arm-to-knuckle bolt.
3. Loosen the trailing arm-to-subframe bolt and allow it to swing down.
4. Remove and discard the knuckle-to-lower arm bolt.
5. Remove and discard the shock absorber-to-lower arm bolt.
6. Remove and discard the lower arm-to-subframe bolt.
7. Remove the lower arm.

To install:

8. Install the lower control arm.
9. Use a jack and raise the suspension to the trim height previously measured before tightening the lower arm bolts.

10. Install the lower arm-to-subframe bolt and tighten to 98 ft. lbs. (133 Nm) on AWD models and 92 ft. lbs. (125 Nm) on 2WD models.
11. Install the shock absorber-to-lower arm bolt and tighten to 105 ft. lbs. (142 Nm) on AWD models and 81 ft. lbs. (110 Nm) on 2WD models.
12. Install the knuckle-to-lower arm bolt and tighten to 66 ft. lbs. (90 Nm) on AWD models and 118 ft. lbs. (160 Nm) on 2WD models.
13. Bring the trailing arm up and tighten the trailing arm-to-subframe bolt and tighten the bolt to 81 ft. lbs. (110 Nm).
14. Install the trailing arm-to-knuckle bolt and tighten the bolt to 77 ft. lbs. (105 Nm).

REAR KNUCKLE

REMOVAL & INSTALLATION

✴ WARNING

Always use new bolts and nuts on the suspension components.

1. Measure the distance between the top of the wheel and the bottom of the wheel opening. This is the trim height.
2. Remove the wheel hub and bearing assembly.
3. Remove the brake dust shield.
4. Remove and discard the trailing arm-to-knuckle bolt.
5. Remove the toe link-to-knuckle bolt and nut.
6. Remove and discard the shock absorber-to-lower arm bolt.
7. Remove and discard the lower arm-to-subframe bolt.
8. Remove and discard the upper arm-to-subframe bolt.
9. Remove the steering knuckle.

To install:

10. Install the wheel knuckle.
11. Use a jack and raise the suspension to the trim height previously measured before tightening the upper and lower arm bolts.
12. Install the upper arm-to-subframe bolt and tighten to 81 ft. lbs. (110 Nm).
13. Install the lower arm-to-subframe bolt and tighten to 98 ft. lbs. (133 Nm) on AWD models, and 92 ft. lbs. (125 Nm) on 2WD models.

14. Install the shock absorber-to-lower arm bolt and tighten to 105 ft. lbs. (142 Nm) on AWD models, and 81 ft. lbs. (110 Nm) on 2WD models.

15. Install the toe link-to-knuckle bolt and nut and tighten to 74 ft. lbs. (100 Nm).

16. Install the trailing arm-to-knuckle bolt and tighten to 77 ft. lbs. (105 Nm).

17. Install the brake dust shield.

18. Install the wheel hub and bearing assembly.

SHOCK ABSORBER & COIL SPRING ASSEMBLY

REMOVAL & INSTALLATION

See Figure 98.

✳✳ WARNING

Always use new bolts and nuts on the suspension components.

1. Measure the distance between the top of the wheel and the bottom of the wheel opening. This is the trim height.

2. Loosen the lug nuts on the rear wheels.

3. Remove the interior trim panel to access the upper shock nut, then remove and discard the nut.

4. Raise the vehicle on a hoist.

5. Remove the rear wheels.

6. Remove the brake caliper and wire aside.

7. Position a jack under the wheel knuckle at the trailing arm and knuckle attachment point.

8. Raise the wheel knuckle until the toe link is parallel to the ground.

9. Remove and discard the trailing arm-to-knuckle bolt.

10. Lower the suspension jack.

11. Remove and discard the trailing arm-to-subframe bolt.

12. Position a jack under the lower shock mount and raise it enough to compress the spring.

13. Remove and discard the lower arm-to-knuckle bolt.

14. Remove and discard the lower arm-to-subframe bolt.

15. Remove and discard the lower shock mounting bolt.

16. Hold the shock absorber and swing the lower arm down to access and remove the shock/spring assembly.

To install:

17. Tape the spring to the upper spring seat.

18. Position the spring and upper rubber seat on the shock.

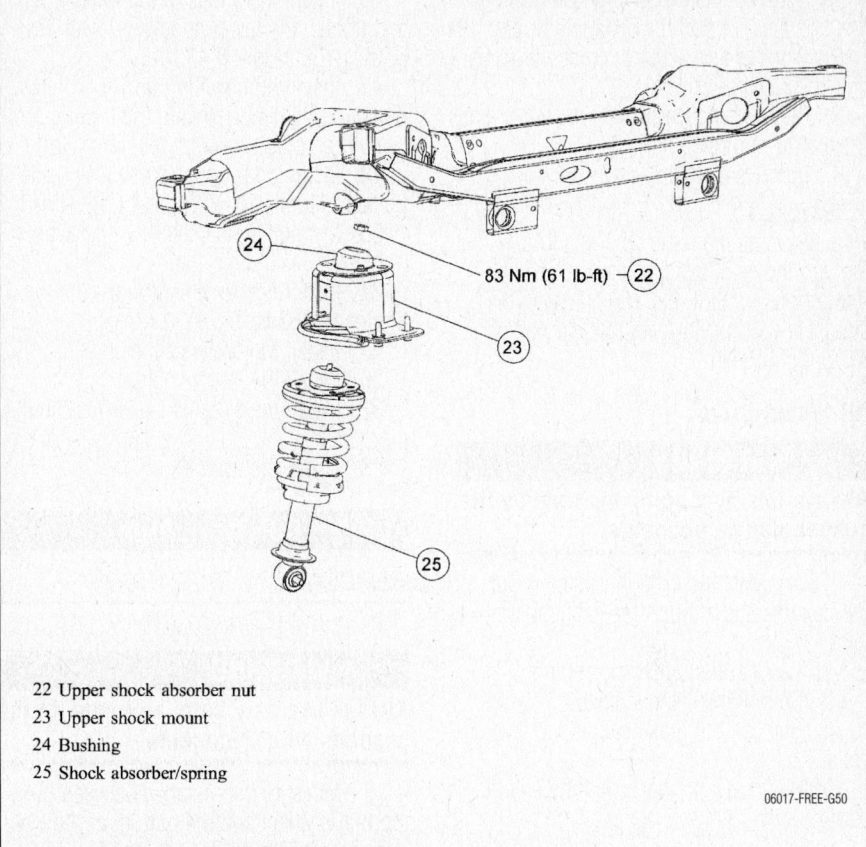

22 Upper shock absorber nut
23 Upper shock mount
24 Bushing
25 Shock absorber/spring

83 Nm (61 lb-ft) — 22

06017-FREE-G50

Fig. 98 Rear shock absorber/spring mounting

19. Install a new lower arm-to-knuckle bolt in the lower arm.

20. Position a jack under the lower arm.

21. Install the shock/spring assembly into alignment with the upper mount.

22. Swing the lower arm into position under the shock/spring assembly.

23. Remove the jack.

24. Partially lower the hoist.

25. Place a floor jack under the lower arm at the lowest point.

26. Raise the jack until the top of the shock makes contact with the inside surface of the upper mount.

27. With the help of an assistant guiding the shock assembly, raise the jack until the shock seats in the upper mount.

28. Install a new top nut and tighten to 61 ft. lbs. (83 Nm).

29. Remove the floor jack.

30. Raise the vehicle.

31. Position a jack under the wheel knuckle at the trailing arm and knuckle attachment point.

32. Remove the lower arm bolt, install the shock/spring in the lower arm and install the bolt.

33. Loosen the lower arm-to-subframe bolt.

Raise the jack under the center of the wheel hub is at the proper trim height.

34. Tighten the lower arm-to-subframe bolt to 92 ft. lbs. (125 Nm).

35. Tighten the lower arm-to-knuckle bolt to 81 ft. lbs. (110 Nm).

36. Position the trailing arm to the knuckle and loosely install the bolt.

37. Place a jack under the lower arm and raise it until the trailing arm and subframe bushing are aligned.

38. Install a new trailing arm-to-subframe bolt and tighten to 81 ft. lbs. (100 Nm).

39. Install the trailing arm-to-knuckle bolt and tighten to 77 ft. lbs. (105 Nm).

40. Install the brake caliper.

41. Install the wheel.

42. Lower the vehicle.

STABILIZER BAR

REMOVAL & INSTALLATION

Front Wheel Drive

✳✳ WARNING

Always use new bolts and nuts on the suspension components.

1. Separate the exhaust system from the flexpipe and support the exhaust system.

2. Remove and discard the stabilizer bar link-to-stabilizer bar nuts.

3. Remove and discard the stabilizer bar bracket-to-subframe bolts.

4. Remove the stabilizer bar.

To install:

5. Reverse the removal procedure. Tighten the stabilizer bar bracket-to-subframe bolts to 43 ft. lbs. (58 Nm) and the stabilizer bar link-to-stabilizer bar nuts to 41 ft. lbs. (55 Nm).

All Wheel Drive

> ❊❊ **WARNING**
>
> **Always use new bolts and nuts on the suspension components.**

1. Separate the exhaust system from the flexpipe and support the exhaust system.

2. Raise and support the vehicle.

3. Remove the rear wheels.

4. Remove the brake calipers and wire aside.

5. Remove both rear axle nuts and discard.

6. Using a hub remover, press the axle shaft from the wheel hub.

7. Remove and discard both upper arm-to-knuckle bolts.

8. Remove and discard both trailing arm-to-knuckle bolts and loosen the trailing arm-to-subframe bolt.

9. Remove and discard the lower shock-to-lower arm nuts and remove it from the lower arm.

10. Loosen both toe link-to-subframe bolts and allow the wheel knuckles to hang in a downward position.

11. Remove the rear subframe cross brace bolts and cross brace.

12. Remove and discard the stabilizer bar link-to-stabilizer bar nuts.

13. Remove and discard the stabilizer bar bracket-to-subframe bolts.

14. Remove the stabilizer bar.

To install:

15. Install the stabilizer bar.

16. Install the stabilizer bar bracket-to-subframe bolts and tighten to 43 ft. lbs. (58 Nm).

17. Install the stabilizer bar link-to-stabilizer bar nuts.

18. Install the rear subframe cross brace and bolts and tighten to 46 ft. lbs. (63 Nm).

19. Bring the wheel knuckles up and tighten both toe link-to-subframe bolts to 74 ft. lbs. (100 Nm).

20. Install the shock to the lower arm and tighten the lower shock-to-lower arm nuts to 105 ft. lbs. (142 Nm).

21. Install both trailing arm-to-knuckle bolts and tighten them and the trailing arm-to-subframe bolt to 77 ft. lbs. (110 Nm).

22. Install both upper arm-to-knuckle bolts and tighten to 77 ft. lbs. (105 Nm).

23. Install the axle shaft into the wheel hub.

24. Install new axle shaft nuts and tighten to 258 ft. lbs. (350 Nm).

25. Install the brake calipers.

26. Install the rear wheels.

27. Install the exhaust system to the flex pipe.

28. Lower the vehicle.

UPPER CONTROL ARM

REMOVAL & INSTALLATION

See Figures 99 through 104.

> ❊❊ **WARNING**
>
> **Always use new bolts and nuts on the suspension components.**

1. Measure the distance between the top of the wheel and the bottom of the wheel opening. This is the trim height.

2. Remove the rear wheels.

3. With a wax pencil, mark the relational alignment of the rear subframe to the underbody at the mounting locations.

4. Remove the 2 catalytic converter nuts.

5. Disconnect the muffler and tailpipe assembly from the isolators.

6. Remove the catalytic converter, muffler and tailpipe assembly.

➡**Index the driveshaft before disconnecting from the rear drive axle. It is necessary to install new driveshaft bolts during installation. Reuse of the driveshaft bolts is not recommended.**

7. Remove the 6 driveshaft bolts.

8. Loosen the trailing link-to-subframe bolts.

9. Support and raise the knuckle with a suitable jack.

10. Raise the knuckle until the tilt angle of the trailing link is horizontal to the body.

11. Remove the trailing link-to-knuckle bolts.

12. Position the trailing link aside.

13. Remove the rear shock-to-lower control arm bolts.

14. Disconnect the rear wheel speed sensor electrical connectors.

15. On AWD vehicles, remove the rear axle assembly.

16. Release the park brake cable tension.

17. Disconnect the intermediate park brake cable from the front park brake cable.

18. Disconnect the intermediate cable from the body bracket.

19. Remove the park brake cable-to-body bracket.

20. Disconnect the rear park brake cables at the equalizer.

21. Disconnect the rear park brake cables from the park brake levers at the rear calipers.

22. Disconnect the rear park brake cables from the park brake brackets.

23. Remove the rear brake caliper pins.

24. Remove the rear calipers and the rear caliper brackets and attach aside to the body with mechanic's wire. It is not necessary to disconnect the hydraulic brake lines.

25. On AWD vehicles remove the 4 rear subframe bracket bolts.

> ❊❊ **CAUTION**
>
> **When positioning the lifting table, be sure to support the rear subframe on the subframe rails. Do not lift on the rear differential or rear control arms, damage may occur.**

26. Position a lifting table.

27. Remove the 4 rear subframe bolts.

28. On AWD vehicles remove the 2 rear subframe brackets.

29. Remove the rear subframe assembly.

30. Place a suitable support under the wheel knuckle.

31. Remove and discard the stabilizer bar link upper nut and separate the link from the upper arm.

32. Remove and discard the upper arm-to-subframe bolts.

33. On FWD vehicles, remove and discard the upper arm-to-knuckle bolt and separate the upper arm from the wheel knuckle.

34. On AWD vehicles, remove and discard the wheel knuckle ball joint nut.

➡**It may be necessary to tap the knuckle to disconnect the upper arm.**

35. Using the tools shown, separate the wheel knuckle from the upper arm.

36. Using the tool shown, separate the upper arm and front bushing from the rear bushing. Once the upper arm and front bushing are separated from the rear bushing, use the special tool to pull the arm and bushing out of the bushing bore.

37. Using the tool shown, separate the upper arm front bushing from the upper arm.

38. Remove the upper arm from the subframe.

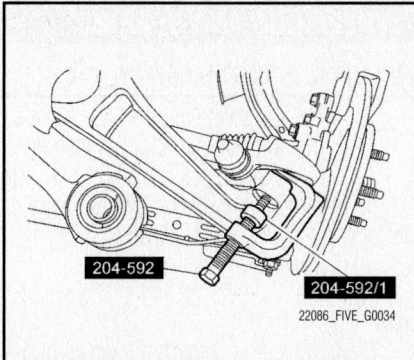

Fig. 99 Using the tools shown, separate the wheel knuckle from the upper arm

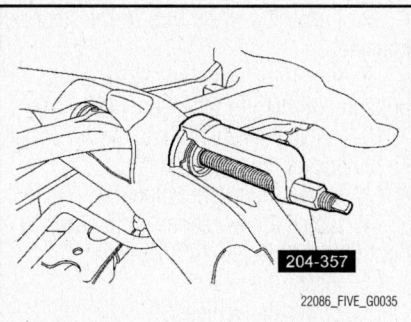

Fig. 100 Using the tools shown, separate the upper arm and front bushing from the rear bushing

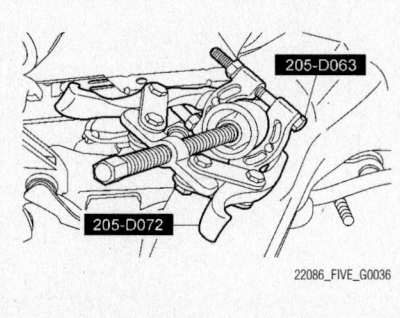

Fig. 101 Using the tools shown, separate the upper arm front bushing from the upper arm

39. Using the tools shown, remove the upper arm rear bushing from the sub-frame.

To install:

40. Use only liquid soap, if necessary, to lubricate the bushing. Do not use any other types of lubricants or damage to the bore or bushing may occur.

➡Make sure the bushing bore on the subframe is clean and free of foreign materials. To aid in installation, a small amount of liquid soap may be applied to the outer diameter of the bushing.

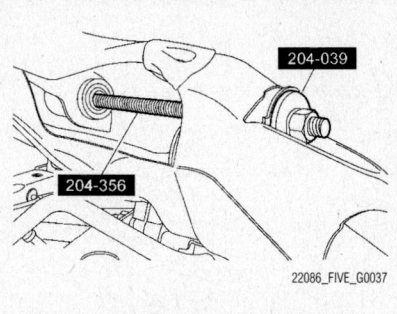

Fig. 102 Using the tools shown, remove the upper arm rear bushing from the sub-frame

41. Position the upper arm rear bushing into the bushing bore from the rear of the subframe and, using the special tools, install the bushing into the subframe.

42. Use the opposite side bushing as a guide to install the bushing to the correct depth in the subframe.

✳✳ CAUTION

Do not fully tighten the nut at this time or incorrect clamp load or bushing damage may occur.

43. On AWD vehicles, position the upper arm into the forward bushing bore and into the rear bushing, then position the upper arm onto the wheel knuckle ball joint stud and install the ball joint nut. Tighten the nut until snug.

44. On FWD vehicles, position the upper arm into the forward bushing bore and into the rear bushing, then position the upper arm onto the wheel knuckle and install the upper arm-to-knuckle bolt. Tighten the bolt until snug.

45. Loosely install the upper arm-to-subframe rear bolt.

➡The upper arm height setting is measured from the top of the subframe to the bottom of the upper arm.

While an assistant holds the upper arm, adjust it to the correct height. On FWD models the measurement is 5.7 inches (147 mm). On AWD models the measurement is 5.4 inches (138 mm).

46. Tighten the upper arm-to-subframe rear bolt to 81 ft. lbs. (110 Nm).

47. While an assistant holds the upper arm in the center of the bushing bore, use the tools to install the upper arm front bushing into the subframe.

48. Install the forward upper arm bushing to the correct depth in the subframe.

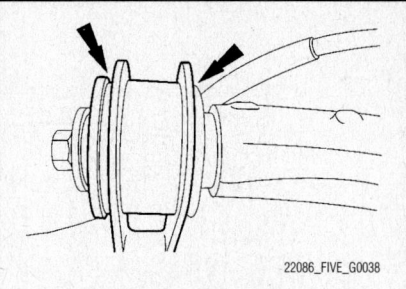

Fig. 103 Install the forward upper arm bushing to the correct depth in the subframe. Use the opposite side bushing as a guide

Use the opposite side bushing as a guide.

49. Install the upper arm-to-subframe front bolt and tighten to 81 ft. lbs. (110 Nm).

50. On AWD vehicles, tighten the wheel knuckle ball joint nut to 81 ft. lbs. (110 Nm).

51. On FWD vehicles, tighten upper arm-to-wheel knuckle bolt to 81 ft. lbs. (110 Nm).

52. Position the stabilizer bar link and install the stabilizer bar link upper nut. Tighten to 28 ft. lbs. (38 Nm).

➡Install new suspension fasteners during assembly.

➡Before tightening the upper control, toe link, trailing arm and lower control arm bolts, use a jackstand to raise the rear suspension to ride height.

53. Install the subframe in the reverse order of removal keeping in mind the following:

    a. Align the subframe to the body following the alignment specification.

    b. Install the 4 rear subframe bolts and tighten to 85 ft. lbs. (115 Nm).

    c. On AWD vehicles install the 4 rear subframe bracket bolts and tighten to 41 ft. lbs. (55 Nm).

    d. Install the rear shock-to-lower control arm bolts. On AWD models tighten to 105 ft. lbs. (142 Nm) or 81 ft. lbs. 110 Nm) on FWD models.

    e. Install the trailing link-to-knuckle bolts and tighten to 77 ft. lbs. (105 Nm).

    f. Install the trailing link-to-subframe bolts and tighten to 77 ft. lbs. (105 Nm).

    g. Install the 6 driveshaft bolts and tighten to 18 ft. lbs. (25 Nm)

    h. Install the 2 catalytic converter nuts and tighten to 30 ft. lbs. (40 Nm).

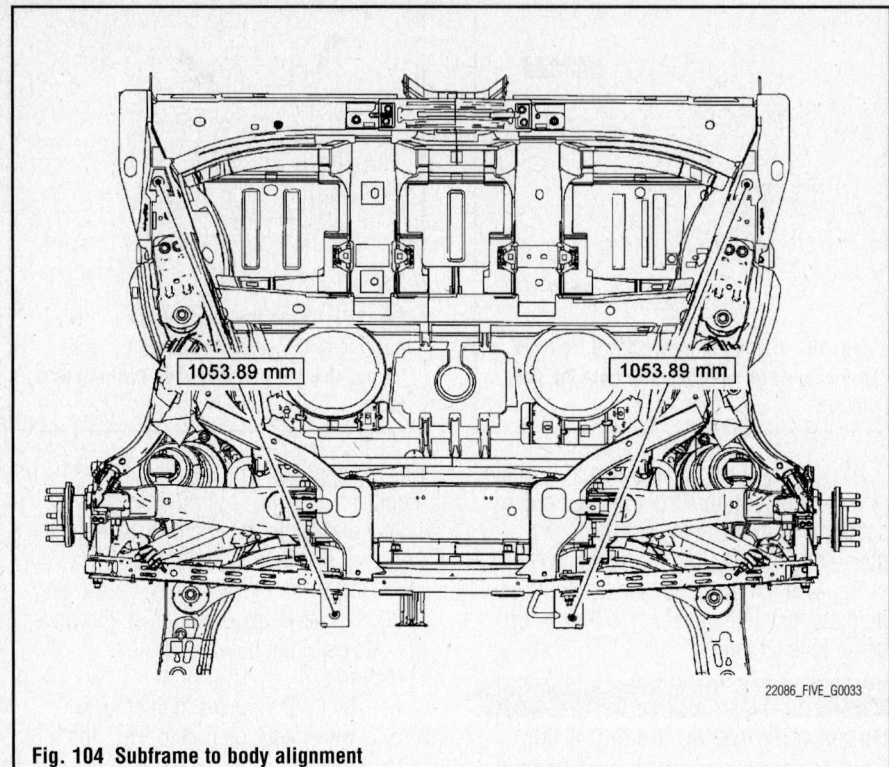

1053.89 mm   1053.89 mm

22086_FIVE_G0033

Fig. 104 Subframe to body alignment

WHEEL HUB AND BEARING

REMOVAL & INSTALLATION

1. Raise and safely support the vehicle.
2. Remove the wheel and tire assembly.
3. Remove and discard the rear axle nut.
4. Remove the brake caliper and wire it out of the way.
5. Remove the brake rotor.
6. Press the halfshaft out of the wheel hub.
7. Remove and discard the wheel hub-to-knuckle bolts and separate the hub from the knuckle.

To install:

8. Install the wheel hub-to-the steering knuckle.
9. Install the wheel hub-to-knuckle bolts and tighten to 89 ft. lbs. (120 Nm).
10. Install the halfshaft into the wheel hub.
11. Install the brake disc.
12. Install the brake caliper.
13. Install a new rear axle nut and tighten to 148 ft. lbs. (200 Nm).
14. Install the wheel.
15. Lower the vehicle.

FORD

Focus

10

SPECIFICATIONS AND MAINTENANCE CHARTS

ENGINE AND VEHICLE IDENTIFICATION

Engine							Model Year	
Code ①	Liters	Cu. In.	Cyl.	Fuel Sys.	Type	Eng. Mfg.	Code ②	Year
N	2.0	122	4	SEFI	DOHC	Ford	5	2005
Z	2.3	140	4	SEFI	DOHC	Ford	6	2006
							7	2007
							8	2008

SEFI: Sequential Electronic Fuel Injection

DOHC: Dual Overhead Camshaft

① 8th digit of the Vehicle Identification Number (VIN)

② 10th digit of the Vehicle Identification Number (VIN)

22086_FOCU_C0001

GENERAL ENGINE SPECIFICATIONS

Year	Model	Engine Displacement Liters	Engine ID/VIN	Net Horsepower @ rpm	Net Torque @ rpm (ft. lbs.)	Bore x Stroke (in.)	Compression Ratio	Oil Pressure @ rpm
2005	Focus ZX3	2.0	N	130@6000	133@4500	3.44X3.27	10.0:1	29-39@2000
	Focus ZX5	2.0	N	130@6000	133@4500	3.44x3.27	10.0:1	29-39@2000
	Focus ZX4	2.3	Z	151@5750	154@4250	3.44x3.70	9.7:1	29-39@2000
2006	Focus ZX3	2.0	N	130@6000	133@4500	3.44X3.27	10.0:1	29-39@2000
	Focus ZX5	2.0	N	130@6000	133@4500	3.44x3.27	10.0:1	29-39@2000
	Focus ZX4	2.3	Z	151@5750	154@4250	3.44x3.70	9.7:1	29-39@2000
2007	Focus ZX3	2.0	N	130@6000	133@4500	3.44X3.27	10.0:1	29-39@2000
	Focus ZX5	2.0	N	130@6000	133@4500	3.44x3.27	10.0:1	29-39@2000
	Focus ZX4	2.3	Z	151@5750	154@4250	3.44x3.70	9.7:1	29-39@2000

22086_FOCU_C0002

ENGINE TUNE-UP SPECIFICATIONS

Year	Engine Displacement Liters	Engine ID/VIN	Spark Plug Gap (in.)	Ignition Timing (deg.) MT	Ignition Timing (deg.) AT	Fuel Pump (psi)	Idle Speed (rpm) MT	Idle Speed (rpm) AT	Valve Clearance (in.) In.	Valve Clearance (in.) Ex.
2005	2.0	N	0.049-0.053	10B	10B	25-40 ①	②	②	0.008-0.011	0.010-0.013
	2.3	Z	0.049-0.053	10B	10B	25-40 ①	②	②	0.008-0.011	0.010-0.013
2006	2.0	N	0.049-0.053	10B	10B	25-40 ①	②	②	0.008-0.011	0.010-0.013
	2.3	Z	0.049-0.053	10B	10B	25-40 ①	②	②	0.008-0.011	0.010-0.013
2007	2.0	N	0.049-0.053	10B	10B	25-40 ①	②	②	0.008-0.011	0.010-0.013
	2.3	Z	0.049-0.053	10B	10B	25-40 ①	②	②	0.008-0.011	0.010-0.013

NOTE: The Vehicle Emission Control Information label often reflects specification changes made during production. The label figures must be used if they differ from those in this chart.

B: Before Top Dead Center

① Fuel pressure with engine running

② Idle speed is electronically controlled and is not adjustable

22086_FOCU_C0003

CAPACITIES

Year	Model	Engine Displacement Liters	Engine ID/VIN	Engine Oil with Filter (qts.)	Transmission (pts.)		Front Drive Axle (pts.)	Fuel Tank (gal.)	Cooling System (qts.)
					Manual	Auto.			
2005	Focus ZX3	2.0	N	4.5	4.0	14.0	—	14.0	7.2
	Focus ZX4	2.0	N	4.5	4.0	14.0	—	14.0	7.2
	Focus ZX5	2.0	N	4.5	4.0	14.0	—	14.0	7.2
	Focus ZX4 ST	2.3	Z	4.5	4.0	14.0	—	14.0	7.6
2006	Focus ZX3	2.0	N	4.5	4.0	14.0	—	14.0	7.2
	Focus ZX4	2.0	N	4.5	4.0	14.0	—	14.0	7.2
	Focus ZX5	2.0	N	4.5	4.0	14.0	—	14.0	7.2
	Focus ZX4 ST	2.3	Z	4.5	4.0	14.0	—	14.0	7.6
2007	Focus ZX3	2.0	N	4.5	4.0	14.0	—	14.0	7.2
	Focus ZX4	2.0	N	4.5	4.0	14.0	—	14.0	7.2
	Focus ZX5	2.0	N	4.5	4.0	14.0	—	14.0	7.2
	Focus ZX4 ST	2.3	Z	4.5	4.0	14.0	—	14.0	7.6

Note: All capacities are approximates. Add fluid gradually and ensure a proper fluid level is obtained.

22086_FOCU_C0004

FLUID SPECIFICATIONS

Year	Model	Engine Displacement Liters	Engine ID/VIN	Engine Oil	Auto. Trans.	Drive Axle	Power Steering Fluid	Brake Master Cylinder
2005	Focus ZX3	2.0L	N	5W-20	Mercon®V	Mercon®V	Mercon® ATF	DOT 3
	Focus ZX4	2.0L	N	5W-20	Mercon®V	Mercon®V	Mercon® ATF	DOT 3
	Focus ZX5	2.0L	N	5W-20	Mercon®V	Mercon®V	Mercon® ATF	DOT 3
	Focus ZX4 ST	2.3L	Z	5W-20	Mercon®V	Mercon®V	Mercon® ATF	DOT 3
2006	Focus ZX3	2.0L	N	5W-20	Mercon®V	Mercon®V	Mercon® ATF	DOT 3
	Focus ZX4	2.0L	N	5W-20	Mercon®V	Mercon®V	Mercon® ATF	DOT 3
	Focus ZX5	2.0L	N	5W-20	Mercon®V	Mercon®V	Mercon® ATF	DOT 3
	Focus ZX4 ST	2.3L	Z	5W-20	Mercon®V	Mercon®V	Mercon® ATF	DOT 3
2007	Focus ZX3	2.0L	N	5W-20	Mercon®V	Mercon®V	Mercon® ATF	DOT 3
	Focus ZX4	2.0L	N	5W-20	Mercon®V	Mercon®V	Mercon® ATF	DOT 3
	Focus ZX5	2.0L	N	5W-20	Mercon®V	Mercon®V	Mercon® ATF	DOT 3
	Focus ZX4 ST	2.3L	Z	5W-20	Mercon®V	Mercon®V	Mercon® ATF	DOT 3

DOT: Department Of Transpotation

22086_FOCU_C0005

VALVE SPECIFICATIONS

Year	Engine Displacement Liters	Engine ID/VIN	Seat Angle (deg.)	Face Angle (deg.)	Spring Test Pressure (lbs. @ in.)	Spring Installed Height (in.)	Stem-to-Guide Clearance (in.)		Stem Diameter (in.)	
							Intake	Exhaust	Intake	Exhaust
2005	2.0	N	45	45	①	1.492	0.0001	0.00011	0.2153-0.2159	0.2151-0.2157
	2.3	Z	45	45	①	1.492	0.00011	0.0011	0.2153-0.2159	0.2151-0.2157
2006	2.0	N	45	45	①	1.492	0.0001	0.00011	0.2153-0.2159	0.2151-0.2157
	2.3	Z	45	45	①	1.492	0.00011	0.0011	0.2153-0.2159	0.2151-0.2157
2007	2.0	N	45	45	①	1.492	0.0001	0.00011	0.2153-0.2159	0.2151-0.2157
	2.3	Z	45	45	①	1.492	0.00011	0.0011	0.2153-0.2159	0.2151-0.2157

① Intake: 0.35 in. @ 97.03 lbs.; exhaust: 0.29 in. @ 93.34 lbs.

22086_FOCU_C0007

CAMSHAFT AND BEARING SPECIFICATIONS CHART

All measurements are given in inches.

Year	Engine Displ. Liters	Engine VIN	Journal Dia.	Brg. Oil Clearance	Shaft End-play	Runout	Journal Bore	Lobe Height	
								Intake	Exhaust
2005	2.0	N	0.982-0.983	0.001-0.003	0.003-0.009	0.001	0.984-0.985	0.324	0.307
	2.3	Z	0.982-0.983	0.001-0.003	0.003-0.009	0.001	0.984-0.985	0.324	0.307
2006	2.0	N	0.982-0.983	0.001-0.003	0.003-0.009	0.001	0.984-0.985	0.324	0.307
	2.3	Z	0.982-0.983	0.001-0.003	0.003-0.009	0.001	0.984-0.985	0.324	0.307
2007	2.0	N	0.982-0.983	0.001-0.003	0.003-0.009	0.001	0.984-0.985	0.324	0.307
	2.3	Z	0.982-0.983	0.001-0.003	0.003-0.009	0.001	0.984-0.985	0.324	0.307

22086_FOCU_C0008

CRANKSHAFT AND CONNECTING ROD SPECIFICATIONS

All measurements are given in inches.

Year	Engine Displacement Liters	Engine ID/VIN	Crankshaft				Connecting Rod		
			Main Brg. Journal Dia.	Main Brg. Oil Clearance	Shaft End-play	Thrust on No.	Journal Diameter	Oil Clearance	Side Clearance
2005	2.0	N	2.0460-2.0470	0.0007-0.0013	0.0080-0.0160	3	1.967-1.9680	0.001-0.002	0.076-0.120
	2.3	Z	2.0460-2.0470	0.0007-0.0013	0.0080-0.0160	3	1.967-1.9680	0.001-0.002	0.076-0.120
2006	2.0	N	2.0460-2.0470	0.0007-0.0013	0.0080-0.0160	3	1.967-1.9680	0.001-0.002	0.076-0.120
	2.3	Z	2.0460-2.0470	0.0007-0.0013	0.0080-0.0160	3	1.967-1.9680	0.001-0.002	0.076-0.120
2007	2.0	N	2.0460-2.0470	0.0007-0.0013	0.0080-0.0160	3	1.967-1.9680	0.001-0.002	0.076-0.120
	2.3	Z	2.0460-2.0470	0.0007-0.0013	0.0080-0.0160	3	1.967-1.9680	0.001-0.002	0.076-0.120

22086_FOCU_C0006

PISTON AND RING SPECIFICATIONS

All measurements are given in inches.

Year	Engine Displacement Liters	Engine ID/VIN	Piston Clearance	Ring Gap			Ring Side Clearance		
				Top Compression	Bottom Compression	Oil Control	Top Compression	Bottom Compression	Oil Control
2005	2.0	N	0.0009-0.0017	NA	NA	NA	NA	NA	NA
	2.3	Z	0.0009-0.0017	NA	NA	NA	NA	NA	NA
2006	2.0	N	0.0009-0.0017	NA	NA	NA	NA	NA	NA
	2.3	Z	0.0009-0.0017	NA	NA	NA	NA	NA	NA
2007	2.0	N	0.0009-0.0017	NA	NA	NA	NA	NA	NA
	2.3	Z	0.0009-0.0017	NA	NA	NA	NA	NA	NA

22086_FOCU_C0009

TORQUE SPECIFICATIONS
All readings in ft. lbs.

Year	Engine Displacement Liters	Engine ID/VIN	Cylinder Head Bolts	Main Bearing Bolts	Rod Bearing Bolts	Crankshaft Damper Bolts	Flywheel Bolts	Manifold Intake	Manifold Exhaust	Spark Plugs	Oil Pan Drain Plug
2005	2.0	N	①	NA	NA	②	③	13	41	9	④
	2.3	Z	①	NA	NA	②	③	13	41	9	④
2006	2.0	N	①	NA	NA	②	③	13	41	9	④
	2.3	Z	①	NA	NA	②	③	13	41	9	④
2007	2.0	N	①	NA	NA	②	③	13	41	9	④
	2.3	Z	①	NA	NA	②	③	13	41	9	④

NA: Not Available

① Step 1: 44 inch lbs.
Step 2: 11 ft. lbs.
Step 3: 33 ft. lbs.
Step 4: Plus 90 degrees
Step 5: Plus 90 degrees

② Step 1: 74 ft. lbs.
Step 2: Plus 90 degrees

③ Step 1: 37 ft. lbs.
Step 2: 50 ft. lbs.
Step 3: 83 ft. lbs.

④ 4 front bolts to engine cover: 89 inch lbs.
All pan bolts: 18 ft. lbs.

22086_FOCU_C0010

WHEEL ALIGNMENT

Year	Model		Caster Range (+/-Deg.)	Caster Preferred Setting (Deg.)	Camber Range (+/-Deg.)	Camber Preferred Setting (Deg.)	Toe-in (Deg.)
2005	Sedan	F	1.00	+2.75	1.25	-0.50	0 +/- 0.20
		R	—	—	0.30	-1.02	0.36 +/- 0.18
	Wagon	F	1.30	+2.75	1.25	-0.50	0 +/- 0.20
		R	—	—	0.75	-0.94	0.36 +/- 0.18
2006	Sedan	F	0.75	+2.75	0.75	-0.50	0 +/- 0.20
		R	—	—	0.75	-1.0	0.36 +/- 0.18
	Wagon	F	1.30	+2.75	1.25	-0.50	0 +/- 0.20
		R	—	—	0.75	-0.94	0.36 +/- 0.18
2007	Sedan	F	1.00	+2.75	1.25	-0.50	0 +/- 0.20
		R	—	—	0.30	-1.02	0.36 +/- 0.18
	Wagon	F	1.30	+2.75	1.25	-0.50	0 +/- 0.20
		R	—	—	0.75	-0.94	0.36 +/- 0.18

22086_FOCU_C0011

TIRE, WHEEL AND BALL JOINT SPECIFICATIONS

| Year | Model | OEM Tires | | Tire Pressures (psi) | | Wheel Size | Ball Joint Inspection | Lug Nut Torque (ft. lbs.) |
		Standard	Optional	Front	Rear			
2005	Focus ZX	P195/60/R15	P205/50R16	①	①	NA	②	94
	Focus ZX4 ST	P205/50R16	—	①	①	NA	②	94
2006	Focus ZX	P195/60/R15	P205/50R16	①	①	NA	②	94
	Focus ZX4 ST	P205/50R16	—	①	①	NA	②	94
2007	Focus ZX	P195/60/R15	P205/50R16	①	①	NA	②	94
	Focus ZX4 ST	P205/50R16	—	①	①	NA	②	94

OEM: Original Equipment Manufacturer

NA: Not available

PSI: Pounds Per Square Inch

① Always refer to the owner's manual and/or vehicle label

② Replace if any measurable movement is found

22086_FOCU_C0012

BRAKE SPECIFICATIONS
All measurements in inches unless noted

| Year | Model | | Brake Disc | | | Brake Drum Diameter | | | Minimum Lining Thickness | | Brake Caliper Mounting Bolts (ft. lbs.) |
			Original Thickness	Minimum Thickness	Maximum Runout	Original Inside Diameter	Max. Wear Limit	Maximum Machine Diameter	Front	Rear	
2005	Focus	F	NA	0.910	0.002	—	—	—	①	—	21
		R	NA	0.350	0.002	NA	8.03	—	—	②	26
2006	Focus	F	NA	0.910	0.002	—	—	—	①	—	21
		R	NA	0.350	0.002	NA	8.03	—	—	②	26
2007	Focus	F	NA	0.910	0.002	—	—	—	①	—	21
		R	NA	0.350	0.002	NA	8.03	—	—	②	26

① Disc pads: 0.118 in.

② Disc pads: 0.118 in.

Drum brake linings: 0.140 in.

22086_FOCU_C0013

SCHEDULED MAINTENANCE INTERVALS
Ford—Focus

TO BE SERVICED	TYPE OF SERVICE	VEHICLE MILEAGE INTERVAL (x1000)												
		5	10	15	20	25	30	35	40	45	50	55	60	65
Air cleaner filter	R						✔						✔	
Accessory drive belt	S/I												✔	
Brake system ①	S/I			✔			✔			✔			✔	
Clutch pedal operation	S/I						✔						✔	
Cooling fan operation	S/I		✔		✔		✔		✔		✔		✔	
Cooling system hoses & clamps	S/I			✔			✔			✔			✔	
CV-joint boots & axle seals	S/I						✔						✔	
Engine coolant	R	Ten years or 150,000 miles												
Engine oil & filter	R	✔	✔	✔	✔	✔	✔	✔	✔	✔	✔	✔	✔	✔
Exterior Lights	S/I	Check monthly												
PCV valve	S/I												✔	
Exhaust system & heat shields	S/I						✔						✔	
Parking brake system	S/I	Every 6 months												
Power steering fluid	S/I	Every 6 months												
Rotate tires	S/I	✔		✔		✔		✔		✔		✔		✔
Steering linkage	S/I						✔						✔	
Spark plugs	R	Change at 100,000 miles												
Suspension components	S/I						✔						✔	

R: Replace   S/I: Inspect and service, if necessary   L: Lubricate   A: Adjust   C: Clean

① Inspect the reservoir fluid level, rotor and or drum, brake lines, hoses, calipers and or wheel cylinders

FREQUENT OPERATION MAINTENANCE (SEVERE SERVICE)
  If a vehicle is operated under any of the following conditions it is considered severe service:
- **Extremely dusty areas.**
- **50% or more of the vehicle operation is in 32°C (90°F) or higher temperatures, or constant operation in temperatures below 0°C (32°F)**
- **Prolonged idling (vehicle operation in stop and go traffic).**
- **Frequent short running periods (engine does not warm to normal operating temperatures).**
- **Police, taxi, delivery usage or trailer towing usage.**
Oil & oil filter change: change every 3000 miles.
Air filter element: change every 15,000 miles.

22086_FOCU_C0014

PRECAUTIONS

Before servicing any vehicle, please be sure to read all of the following precautions, which deal with personal safety, prevention of component damage, and important points to take into consideration when servicing a motor vehicle:

• Never open, service or drain the radiator or cooling system when the engine is hot; serious burns can occur from the steam and hot coolant.

• Observe all applicable safety precautions when working around fuel. Whenever servicing the fuel system, always work in a well-ventilated area. Do not allow fuel spray or vapors to come in contact with a spark, open flame, or excessive heat (a hot drop light, for example). Keep a dry chemical fire extinguisher near the work area. Always keep fuel in a container specifically designed for fuel storage; also, always properly seal fuel containers to avoid the possibility of fire or explosion. Refer to the additional fuel system precautions later in this section.

• Fuel injection systems often remain pressurized, even after the engine has been turned **OFF**. The fuel system pressure must be relieved before disconnecting any fuel lines. Failure to do so may result in fire and/or personal injury.

• Brake fluid often contains polyglycol ethers and polyglycols. Avoid contact with the eyes and wash your hands thoroughly after handling brake fluid. If you do get brake fluid in your eyes, flush your eyes with clean, running water for 15 minutes. If eye irritation persists, or if you have taken

brake fluid internally, IMMEDIATELY seek medical assistance.

• The EPA warns that prolonged contact with used engine oil may cause a number of skin disorders, including cancer. You should make every effort to minimize your exposure to used engine oil. Protective gloves should be worn when changing oil. Wash your hands and any other exposed skin areas as soon as possible after exposure to used engine oil. Soap and water, or waterless hand cleaner should be used.

• All new vehicles are now equipped with an air bag system, often referred to as a Supplemental Restraint System (SRS) or Supplemental Inflatable Restraint (SIR) system. The system must be disabled before performing service on or around system components, steering column, instrument panel components, wiring and sensors. Failure to follow safety and disabling procedures could result in accidental air bag deployment, possible personal injury and unnecessary system repairs.

• Always wear safety goggles when working with, or around, the air bag system. When carrying a non-deployed air bag, be sure the bag and trim cover are pointed away from your body. When placing a non-deployed air bag on a work surface, always face the bag and trim cover upward, away from the surface. This will reduce the motion of the module if it is accidentally deployed. Refer to the additional air bag system precautions later in this section.

• Clean, high quality brake fluid from a sealed container is essential to the safe and

proper operation of the brake system. You should always buy the correct type of brake fluid for your vehicle. If the brake fluid becomes contaminated, completely flush the system with new fluid. Never reuse any brake fluid. Any brake fluid that is removed from the system should be discarded. Also, do not allow any brake fluid to come in contact with a painted surface; it will damage the paint.

• Never operate the engine without the proper amount and type of engine oil; doing so WILL result in severe engine damage.

• Timing belt maintenance is extremely important. Many models utilize an interference-type, non-freewheeling engine. If the timing belt breaks, the valves in the cylinder head may strike the pistons, causing potentially serious (also time-consuming and expensive) engine damage. Refer to the maintenance interval charts for the recommended replacement interval for the timing belt, and to the timing belt section for belt replacement and inspection.

• Disconnecting the negative battery cable on some vehicles may interfere with the functions of the on-board computer system(s) and may require the computer to undergo a relearning process once the negative battery cable is reconnected.

• When servicing drum brakes, only disassemble and assemble one side at a time, leaving the remaining side intact for reference.

• Only an MVAC-trained, EPA-certified automotive technician should service the air conditioning system or its components.

BRAKES   ANTI-LOCK BRAKE SYSTEM (ABS)

GENERAL INFORMATION

ABS SYSTEM OVERVIEW

The ABS module executes control of the anti-lock brakes and full speed traction control functions to enhance driver control of the vehicle. The ABS module manages the interactions between the anti-lock, traction control, and engine control systems to optimize the vehicle traction during deceleration and acceleration.

The ABS module continuously monitors and compares the rotational speed of each wheel. The rotational wheel speed is measured by the wheel speed sensor which electrically senses the pole pairs of the magnetic encoder ring passing the sensor head.

The ABS module is self-monitoring.

When the ignition switch is turned to the RUN position, the ABS module carries out a preliminary electrical check. At approximately 20 km/h (12 mph) the pump motor is turned on for approximately 0.5 second. Any concern with the ABS causes the ABS module to shut off, the ABS warning indicator to illuminate, and the power assist braking system to function normally.

TRACTION CONTROL

The traction control system helps maintain vehicle traction at the limits of tire adhesion. System effectiveness varies with vehicle speed, road conditions, and steering inputs.

The ABS module defaults to ON when the engine is started. The traction control switch (TCS) allows the driver to control the ON/OFF operation of the traction control

system by pressing the switch for a minimum of 1 second, independent of the ABS function. The ABS control system cannot be switched off by the driver.

The traction control system status is indicated by a traction control system warning light. An illuminated traction control warning light in the instrument cluster indicates that the system has been switched off by the traction control switch, or a system error has been detected and the system function is disabled. A flashing warning light indicates that wheel slip has occurred. The warning light remains flashing until traction control intervention is no longer required.

The ABS module communicates with the powertrain control module (PCM) requesting assistance with traction control. At speeds under 40 km/h (25 mph) the ABS module requests the PCM to reduce engine torque, while simultaneously applying and releasing the appropriate brake to restore traction when one or both drive wheels lose traction and begin to spin. The PCM accomplishes this by minor incremental ignition timing changes and fewer fuel injector pulses until the driven wheel speed returns to normal and the traction control module ends the request. After the vehicle speed exceeds 40 km/h (25 mph), the traction control is accomplished only by the PCM controlling the torque.

During a traction control event you may experience any of the following normal behaviors:

• a rumble or grinding sound much like ABS
• a small deceleration of the vehicle
• the traction control indicator will flash

The ABS module continually monitors all sensors and actuators used to improve the traction control of the vehicle. Some drivers may notice a slight movement of the brake pedal when the system checks itself. If the brake system has not been bled correctly, the brake pedal movement may become more significant.

The ABS function continues to work as designed unless the yellow ABS warning indicator is also illuminated. The normal brake function should always occur, unless the red brake warning indicator is illuminated.

ELECTRONIC BRAKE DISTRIBUTION (EBD)

The EBD controls rear brake pressure and acts as an electronic proportioning valve. It is controlled by the ABS module.

When EBD is disabled, the amber ABS warning indicator and the red brake warning indicator will illuminate.

SPEED SENSORS

REMOVAL & INSTALLATION

Front

See Figure 1.

1. Before servicing the vehicle, refer to the precautions in the beginning of this section.
2. Disconnect battery negative cable from battery and properly isolate to prevent accidental reconnection.
3. Raise and support the vehicle.
4. Disconnect the wheel speed sensor electrical connector
5. Remove the wheel speed sensor.

To install:

6. Install the wheel speed sensor and tighten the bolt to 80 inch lbs. (9 Nm)

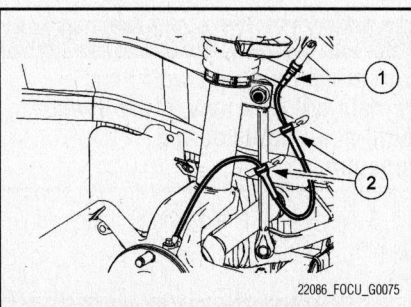

22086_FOCU_G0075

Fig. 1 Showing the front speed sensor wiring harness with the connector (1) and retaining clips (2)

7. Connect the electrical connector.
8. Lower the vehicle and reattach the negative battery cable.

Rear

See Figure 2.

1. Before servicing the vehicle, refer to the precautions in the beginning of this section.
2. Disconnect battery negative cable from battery and properly isolate to prevent accidental reconnection.
3. Raise and support the vehicle.
4. Remove the wheel speed sensor.

To install:

5. Install the wheel speed sensor and tighten the bolt to 80 inch lbs. (9 Nm)
6. Connect the electrical connector.
7. Lower the vehicle and reattach the negative battery cable.

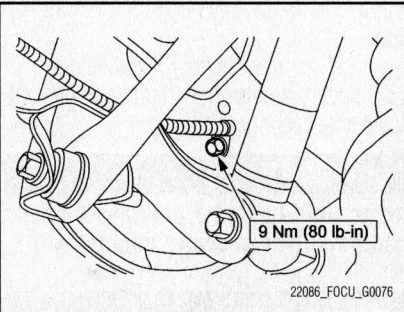

9 Nm (80 lb-in)

22086_FOCU_G0076

Fig. 2 Showing the rear speed sensor bolt location

BRAKES

BLEEDING THE BRAKE SYSTEM

BLEEDING PROCEDURE

BRAKE LINE BLEEDING

1. Before servicing the vehicle, refer to the precautions in the beginning of this section.
2. Disconnect battery negative cable from battery and properly isolate to prevent accidental reconnection.

❋❋ CAUTION

Brake fluid contains polyglycol ethers and polyglycols. Avoid contact with the eyes. Wash hands thoroughly after handling. If brake fluid contacts the eyes, flush the eyes for 15 minutes with cold running water. Get medical attention if irritation persists. If taken internally,

drink water and induce vomiting. Get medical attention immediately. Failure to follow these instructions may result in personal injury.

❋❋ WARNING

If brake fluid is spilled on the paintwork, the affected area must be immediately washed down with cold water.

➡Make sure that the vehicle is standing on a level surface.

➡The system consists of separate circuits for each front and diagonally opposite rear wheel. Each circuit can be bled independently.

❋❋ WARNING

The brake fluid reservoir must remain full with new, clean brake fluid at all times during bleeding.

3. Install the bleed tube to the bleed nipple.
4. Immerse the end of the bleed tube in a bleed jar containing a small quantity of approved brake fluid.
5. Position the bleed jar base at least 12 inches (300 mm) above the bleed nipple to maintain fluid pressure and prevent air leaking past the threads of the bleed nipple.
6. Loosen the bleed nipple by one-half turn.
7. Operate the brake pedal fully (pumping brake fluid and air into the bleed jar)

and allow the brake pedal to return to the rest position.

8. Fill the brake fluid reservoir to the MAX mark.

9. Continue operating the brake pedal until air-free fluid is being pumped into the bleed jar.

10. With the brake pedal fully depressed tighten the bleed nipple.

✳ WARNING

Make sure the bleed nipple cap is installed after bleeding the brake line(s). This will prevent corrosion to the bleed nipple. Failure to follow this instruction may result in the bleed nipple becoming seized.

11. Repeat the procedure for the remaining brake lines.

12. Connect the battery ground cable.

BLEEDING THE ABS SYSTEM

1. Before servicing the vehicle, refer to the precautions in the beginning of this section.

2. Disconnect battery negative cable from battery and properly isolate to prevent accidental reconnection.

✳ CAUTION

Brake fluid contains polyglycol ethers and polyglycols. Avoid contact with

the eyes. Wash hands thoroughly after handling. If brake fluid contacts the eyes, flush the eyes for 15 minutes with cold running water. Get medical attention if irritation persists. If taken internally, drink water and induce vomiting. Get medical attention immediately. Failure to follow these instructions may result in personal injury.

✳✳ WARNING

If brake fluid is spilled on the paintwork, the affected area must be immediately washed down with cold water.

➡ Make sure that the vehicle is standing on a level surface.

➡ The system consists of separate circuits for each front and diagonally opposite rear wheel. Each circuit can be bled independently.

✳✳ WARNING

The brake fluid reservoir must remain full with new, clean brake fluid at all times during bleeding.

3. Install the bleed tube to the bleed nipple.

4. Immerse the end of the bleed tube in a bleed jar containing a small quantity of approved brake fluid.

5. Position the bleed jar base at least 12 inches (300 mm) above the bleed nipple to maintain fluid pressure and prevent air leaking past the threads of the bleed nipple.

6. Loosen the bleed nipple by one-half turn.

7. Operate the brake pedal fully (pumping brake fluid and air into the bleed jar) and allow the brake pedal to return to the rest position.

8. Fill the brake fluid reservoir to the MAX mark.

9. Continue operating the brake pedal until air-free fluid is being pumped into the bleed jar.

10. With the brake pedal fully depressed tighten the bleed nipple.

✳✳ WARNING

Make sure the bleed nipple cap is installed after bleeding the brake line(s). This will prevent corrosion to the bleed nipple. Failure to follow this instruction may result in the bleed nipple becoming seized.

11. Repeat the procedure for the remaining brake lines.

12. Connect the battery ground cable.

BRAKES

✳✳ CAUTION

Dust and dirt accumulating on brake parts during normal use may contain asbestos fibers from production or aftermarket brake linings. Breathing excessive concentrations of asbestos fibers can cause serious bodily harm. Exercise care when servicing brake parts. Do not sand or grind brake lining unless equipment used is designed to contain the dust residue. Do not clean brake parts with compressed air or by dry brushing. Cleaning should be done by dampening the brake components with a fine mist of water, then wiping the brake components clean with a dampened cloth. Dispose of cloth and all residue containing asbestos fibers in an impermeable container with the appropriate label. Follow practices prescribed by the Occupational Safety and Health Administration (OSHA) and the Environmental Protection Agency

(EPA) for the handling, processing, and disposing of dust or debris that may contain asbestos fibers.

BRAKE CALIPER

REMOVAL & INSTALLATION

1. Before servicing the vehicle, refer to the Precautions Section.

2. Remove the wheel and tire assembly.

3. Loosen the brake flexible hose

4. Remove the front brake pads.

✳✳ CAUTION

Cap the brake hose to prevent fluid loss and dirt contamination.

5. Disconnect the caliper from the brake flexible hose.

6. Remove the caliper.

To install:

7. Position the caliper in place.

FRONT DISC BRAKES

8. Install or connect the following:
- Brake hose to the caliper. Tighten the fitting to 11 ft. lbs. (15 Nm).
- Brake pads
- Brake caliper to the steering knuckle. Tighten the bolts to 21 ft. lbs. (28 Nm).
- Brake hose to the support bracket
- Front wheel

9. Bleed the brakes and check for proper operation.

DISC BRAKE PADS

REMOVAL & INSTALLATION

1. Before servicing the vehicle, refer to the Precautions Section.

2. Siphon fluid from the master cylinder until it is about one-half full.

3. Remove or disconnect the following:
- Front wheel
- Brake hose from the support bracket

- Outer brake pad retaining clip
- Brake caliper
- Inner and outer brake pads

To install:

4. Compress the caliper piston into the caliper bore.
5. Install or connect the following:
   - Inner and outer brake pads

- Brake caliper. Tighten the bolts to 21 ft. lbs. (28 Nm).
- Brake hose to the support bracket
- Front wheel

6. Refill the master cylinder and bleed the system.

BRAKES

☀☀ CAUTION

Dust and dirt accumulating on brake parts during normal use may contain asbestos fibers from production or aftermarket brake linings. Breathing excessive concentrations of asbestos fibers can cause serious bodily harm. Exercise care when servicing brake parts. Do not sand or grind brake lining unless equipment used is designed to contain the dust residue. Do not clean brake parts with compressed air or by dry brushing. Cleaning should be done by dampening the brake components with a fine mist of water, then wiping the brake components clean with a dampened cloth. Dispose of cloth and all residue containing asbestos fibers in an impermeable container with the appropriate label. Follow practices prescribed by the Occupational Safety and Health Administration (OSHA) and the Environmental Protection Agency (EPA) for the handling, processing, and disposing of dust or debris that may contain asbestos fibers.

BRAKE CALIPER

REMOVAL & INSTALLATION

1. Remove the wheel and tire.
2. Loosen the flexible brake hose fitting.
3. Remove the rear brake pads.

☀☀ CAUTION

Cap the brake hose to prevent fluid loss and dirt contamination.

4. Disconnect the caliper from the flexible brake hose.
5. Remove the brake caliper.

To install:

6. Loosely connect the brake hose to the brake caliper.
7. Install the caliper and tighten the bolts to 26 ft. lbs. (35 Nm).

8. Tighten the brake hose union to 11 ft. lbs. (15 Nm).
9. Remove the brake hose clamp.
10. Install the wheel and tire.
11. Bleed the brake system.

DISC BRAKE PADS

REMOVAL & INSTALLATION
See Figure 3.

1. Before servicing the vehicle, refer to the Precautions Section.
2. Remove the rear wheel and tire.
3. Detach the parking brake cable from the brake caliper.
4. Loosen the brake hose union.
5. Detach the brake caliper from the brake anchor plate.

REAR DISC BRAKES

6. Remove the brake caliper.
7. Remove the brake pads.

To install:

➡ **When the brake caliper piston is retracted into the piston housing, brake fluid will be displaced into the brake fluid reservoir.**

8. Using the Rear Caliper Piston Adjuster 206-010 and Adapter 206-026, retract the brake caliper piston.
9. Install the brake pads.
10. Install the caliper and tighten the bolts to 26 ft. lbs. (35 Nm).
11. Attach the parking brake cable to the brake caliper.
12. Install the wheel and tire.
13. Bleed the brake system.

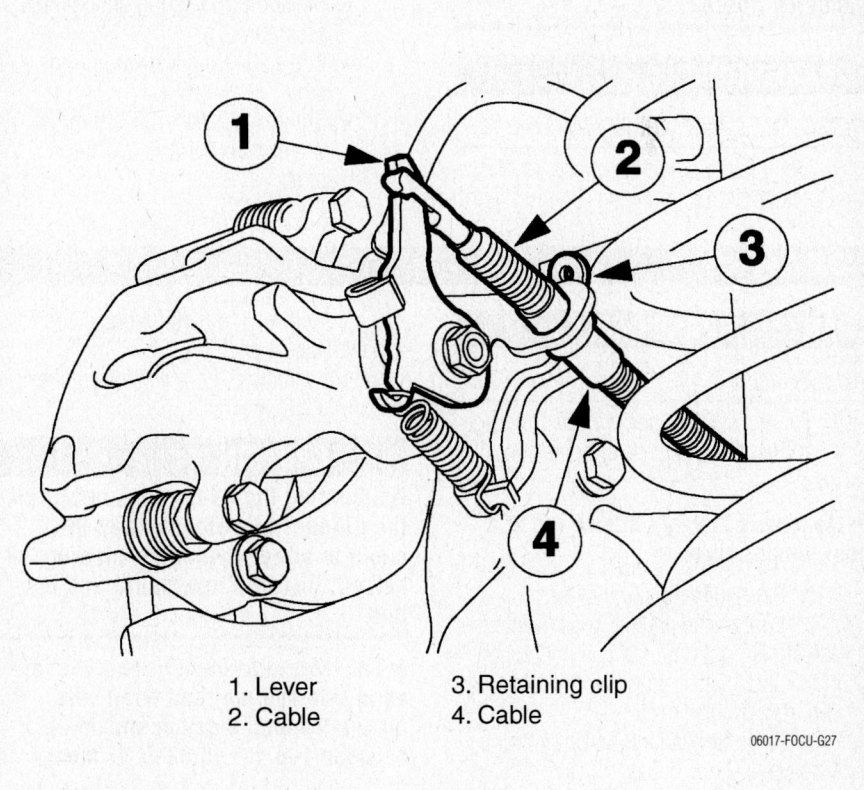

1. Lever
2. Cable
3. Retaining clip
4. Cable

06017-FOCU-G27

Fig. 3 Detaching the parking brake cable from the caliper

BRAKES

✳✳ CAUTION

Dust and dirt accumulating on brake parts during normal use may contain asbestos fibers from production or aftermarket brake linings. Breathing excessive concentrations of asbestos fibers can cause serious bodily harm. Exercise care when servicing brake parts. Do not sand or grind brake lining unless equipment used is designed to contain the dust residue. Do not clean brake parts with compressed air or by dry brushing. Cleaning should be done by dampening the brake components with a fine mist of water, then wiping the brake components clean with a dampened cloth. Dispose of cloth and all residue containing asbestos fibers in an impermeable container with the appropriate label. Follow practices prescribed by the Occupational Safety and Health Administration (OSHA) and the Environmental Protection Agency (EPA) for the handling, processing, and disposing of dust or debris that may contain asbestos fibers.

BRAKE DRUM

REMOVAL & INSTALLATION

1. Before servicing the vehicle, refer to the Precautions Section.

2. Remove or disconnect the following:
   - Rear wheel
   - Wheel speed sensor, if equipped
   - Brake drum, bearing and spindle assembly.

To install:

3. Install or connect the following:
   - Brake drum, bearing and spindle assembly. Tighten the bolts to 49 ft. lbs. (66 Nm).
   - Wheel speed sensor, if equipped
   - Rear wheel

BRAKE SHOES

REMOVAL & INSTALLATION

1. Before servicing the vehicle, refer to the Precautions Section.
2. Remove or disconnect the following:
   - Rear wheel
   - Wheel speed sensor, if equipped
   - Brake drum, bearing and spindle assembly
   - Brake shoe hold-down springs and pins
   - Brake shoe assembly from the wheel cylinder and anchor block

   - Parking brake cable
   - Lower return spring
   - Upper return spring
   - Primary shoe from the strut and brake shoe adjuster
   - Parking brake return spring
   - Secondary shoe from the strut support

To install:

3. Install or connect the following:
   - Secondary shoe to the strut support
   - Parking brake return spring
   - Primary shoe to the strut and brake shoe adjuster. Rotate the adjuster fully clockwise.
   - Upper return spring
   - Lower return spring
   - Parking brake cable
   - Brake shoe assembly to the wheel cylinder and anchor block
   - Brake shoe hold-down springs and pins
   - Brake drum, bearing and spindle assembly. Tighten the bolts to 49 ft. lbs. (66 Nm).
   - Wheel speed sensor, if equipped
   - Rear wheel

4. Operate the brake pedal to adjust the rear brakes.

BRAKES

PARKING BRAKE CABLES

ADJUSTMENT

1. On all vehicles, perform the following:
   a. Remove the parking brake control boot.

➡**Make sure the rear brakes are at a cool temperature.**

   b. Release the parking brake.
   c. Loosen the parking brake cable adjustment nut until there is no tension in the cable, after removing the retaining clip. Remove the nut.
   d. Raise the parking brake control up 4 notches.
   e. Tighten the parking brake cable adjustment nut to the specified torque.
   f. Apply and release the hand brake lever several times with sufficient force to settle the parking brake system.

   g. Release the parking brake control to its lowest position.
2. On vehicles with rear drum brakes, perform the following:

✳✳ CAUTION

If adjusting the cable does not affect the plunger movement, then the cable is either damaged, binding, or seized. Install a new cable and conduit.

➡**The total movement of both the left-hand side and the right-hand side plungers added together should be between 1–8 mm (0.03–0.31 inch).**

   h. Check the movement of the plunger in the left-hand side and the right-hand side backing plates. If further adjustment is required, adjust the cable using the parking brake cable adjustment nut.

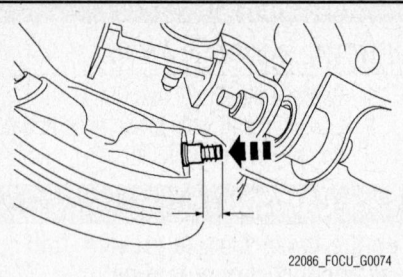

22086_FOCU_G0074

Fig. 4 Check the movement of the plunger in the left-hand side and the right-hand side backing plates

3. On vehicles with rear disc brakes, perform the following:

✳✳ CAUTION

If adjusting the cable does not affect the caliper parking brake lever movement, then the cable is either dam-

aged, binding, or seized. Install a new cable and conduit.

➡️**The total movement between both the left-hand side and the right-hand side caliper parking brake lever and the stop added together should be between 0.5–2 mm (0.01–0.07 inch).**

i. Check the movement of the caliper parking brake lever on the left-hand side

and right-hand side. If further adjustment is required, adjust the cable using the parking brake cable adjustment nut.

4. On all vehicles, perform the following:

5. Rotate the rear wheels to make sure that no brake drag is apparent.

6. Make sure the parking brake adjustment nut is in the correct position after adjustment. Install the parking brake adjustment nut retaining clip.

7. Install the parking brake control boot.

PARKING BRAKE SHOES

REMOVAL & INSTALLATION

The rear drum brake shoes serve as the parking brakes. Refer to the procedure under "Rear Drum Brakes".

CHASSIS ELECTRICAL

GENERAL INFORMATION

✳✳ CAUTION

These vehicles are equipped with an air bag system. The system must be disarmed before performing service on, or around, system components, the steering column, instrument panel components, wiring and sensors. Failure to follow the safety precautions and the disarming procedure could result in accidental air bag deployment, possible injury and unnecessary system repairs.

SERVICE PRECAUTIONS

Disconnect and isolate the battery negative cable before beginning any airbag system component diagnosis, testing, removal, or installation procedures. Allow system capacitor to discharge for two minutes before beginning any component service. This will disable the airbag system. Failure to disable the airbag system may result in accidental airbag deployment, personal injury, or death.

Do not place an intact undeployed airbag face down on a solid surface. The airbag will propel into the air if accidentally deployed and may result in personal injury or death.

When carrying or handling an undeployed airbag, the trim side (face) of the airbag should be pointing towards the body to minimize possibility of injury if accidental deployment occurs. Failure to do this may result in personal injury or death.

Replace airbag system components with OEM replacement parts. Substitute parts may appear interchangeable, but internal differences may result in inferior occupant protection. Failure to do so may result in occupant personal injury or death.

Wear safety glasses, rubber gloves, and long sleeved clothing when cleaning powder residue from vehicle after an airbag

AIR BAG (SUPPLEMENTAL RESTRAINT SYSTEM)

deployment. Powder residue emitted from a deployed airbag can cause skin irritation. Flush affected area with cool water if irritation is experienced. If nasal or throat irritation is experienced, exit the vehicle for fresh air until the irritation ceases. If irritation continues, see a physician.

Do not use a replacement airbag that is not in the original packaging. This may result in improper deployment, personal injury, or death.

The factory installed fasteners, screws and bolts used to fasten airbag components have a special coating and are specifically designed for the airbag system. Do not use substitute fasteners. Use only original equipment fasteners listed in the parts catalog when fastener replacement is required.

During, and following, any child restraint anchor service, due to impact event or vehicle repair, carefully inspect all mounting hardware, tether straps, and anchors for proper installation, operation, or damage. If a child restraint anchor is found damaged in any way, the anchor must be replaced. Failure to do this may result in personal injury or death.

Deployed and non-deployed airbags may or may not have live pyrotechnic material within the airbag inflator.

Do not dispose of driver/passenger/curtain airbags or seat belt tensioners unless you are sure of complete deployment. Refer to the Hazardous Substance Control System for proper disposal.

Dispose of deployed airbags and tensioners consistent with state, provincial, local, and federal regulations.

After any airbag component testing or service, do not connect the battery negative cable. Personal injury or death may result if the system test is not performed first.

If the vehicle is equipped with the Occupant Classification System (OCS), do not connect the battery negative cable before performing the OCS Verification Test using the scan tool and the appropriate diagnostic information. Personal injury or death may

result if the system test is not performed properly.

Never replace both the Occupant Restraint Controller (ORC) and the Occupant Classification Module (OCM) at the same time. If both require replacement, replace one, then perform the Airbag System test before replacing the other.

Both the ORC and the OCM store Occupant Classification System (OCS) calibration data, which they transfer to one another when one of them is replaced. If both are replaced at the same time, an irreversible fault will be set in both modules and the OCS may malfunction and cause personal injury or death.

If equipped with OCS, the Seat Weight Sensor is a sensitive, calibrated unit and must be handled carefully. Do not drop or handle roughly. If dropped or damaged, replace with another sensor. Failure to do so may result in occupant injury or death.

If equipped with OCS, the front passenger seat must be handled carefully as well. When removing the seat, be careful when setting on floor not to drop. If dropped, the sensor may be inoperative, could result in occupant injury, or possibly death.

If equipped with OCS, when the passenger front seat is on the floor, no one should sit in the front passenger seat. This uneven force may damage the sensing ability of the seat weight sensors. If sat on and damaged, the sensor may be inoperative, could result in occupant injury, or possibly death.

DISARMING (DEPOWERING) THE SYSTEM

1. Before servicing the vehicle, refer to the Precautions Section.

✳✳ CAUTION

If a seat equipped with a Supplemental Restraint System (SRS) component is being serviced, the SRS must be depowered.

→The air bag warning lamp illuminates when the RCM fuse is removed and the ignition switch is ON. This is normal operation and does not indicate a Supplemental Restraint System (SRS) fault.

→The SRS must be fully operational and free of faults before releasing the vehicle to the customer.

2. Turn all vehicle accessories OFF.

3. Turn the ignition switch to OFF.

4. At the central junction box (CJB), located below the LH side of the instrument panel, remove the cover and the restraints control module (RCM) fuse F2.60 (7.5A) from the CJB.

5. Turn the ignition ON and visually monitor the air bag indicator for at least 30 seconds. The air bag indicator will remain lit continuously (no flashing) if the correct RCM fuse has been removed. If the air bag indicator does not remain lit continuously, remove the correct RCM fuse before proceeding.

6. Turn the ignition OFF.

❊❊ WARNING

To avoid accidental deployment and possible personal injury, the backup power supply must be depleted before repairing or replacing any front or side air bag Supplemental Restraint System (SRS) components and before servicing, replacing, adjusting or striking components near the front or side air bag sensors, such as doors, instrument panel, console, door latches, strikers, seats and hood latches.

→The side impact sensors (if equipped) are located at or near the base of the B-pillars.

7. Disconnect the battery ground cable (14301) and wait at least one minute.

8. Be sure to disconnect auxiliary batteries and power supplies (if equipped).

ARMING (REPOWERING) THE SYSTEM

❊❊ WARNING

The restraint system diagnostic tool is for restraint system service only. Remove from vehicle prior to road use. Failure to remove could result in injury and possible violation of vehicle safety standards.

❊❊ CAUTION

Make sure all restraint system diagnostic tool(s) that may have been installed during the repair have been removed from the vehicle and all SRS components are connected.

1. Turn the ignition switch from OFF to ON.
Install the RCM fuse F2.60 (7.5A) to the CJB and install the cover.

❊❊ WARNING

Be sure that nobody is in the vehicle and that there is nothing blocking or set in front of any air bag module when the battery ground cable is connected.

2. Connect the battery ground cable.

3. Prove out the Supplemental Restraint System (SRS) as follows:

a. Turn the ignition key from ON to OFF. Wait 10 seconds, then turn the key back to ON and visually monitor the air bag indicator with the air bag modules installed. The air bag indicator will light continuously for approximately six seconds and then turn off. If an air bag Supplemental Restraint System (SRS) fault is present, the air bag indicator will either:

- Fail to light
- Remain lit continuously
- Flash at a 5 Hz rate (RCM not configured)

→The air bag indicator may not illuminate until approximately 30 seconds after the ignition switch has been turned from the OFF to the ON position. This is the time required for the

restraints control module (RCM) to complete the testing of the SRS. If the air bag indicator is inoperative and a SRS fault exists, a chime will sound in a pattern of five sets of five beeps. If this occurs, the air bag indicator and any SRS fault discovered must be diagnosed and repaired.

4. Clear all continuous DTCs from the restraints control module using a scan tool.

CLOCKSPRING CENTERING

See Figure 5.

1. Before servicing the vehicle, refer to the Precautions Section.

❊❊ WARNING

Incorrect centralization may result in premature component failure. If in doubt when centralizing the clockspring, repeat the centralizing procedure. Failure to follow this instruction may result in personal injury.

❊❊ CAUTION

Make sure the road wheels are in the straight ahead position.

2. If a clockspring has rotated out of center, centralize the clockspring as follows:

a. Turn the clockspring in a counterclockwise direction until resistance is felt.

b. Turn the clockspring in a clockwise direction, until the arrow marked on the rotor of the clockspring aligns with the raised "V" section at the 12 o'clock position on the outer cover of the clockspring (approximately two and one half turns).

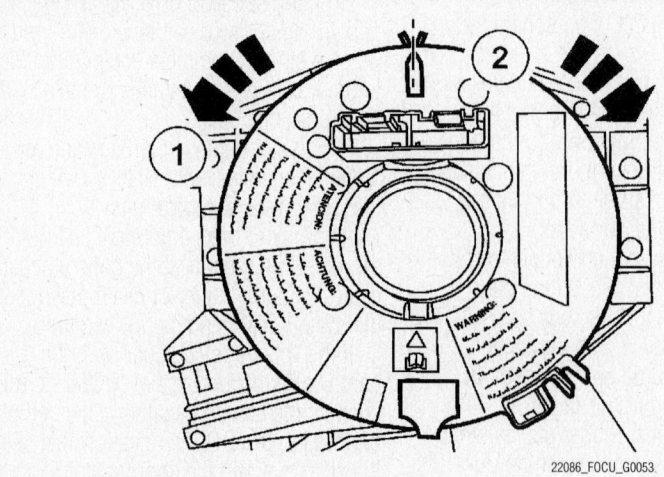

22086_FOCU_G0053

Fig. 5 Centering the clockspring

AUTOMATIC TRANSAXLE ASSEMBLY

REMOVAL & INSTALLATION

See Figures 6 through 12.

1. Before servicing the vehicle, refer to the Precautions Section.
2. Remove or disconnect the following:
   - Negative battery cable
   - Battery tray
   - Air cleaner resonator
   - LH strut and spring assembly top mount nuts by four turns
   - Transmission Range (TR) sensor
   - Transaxle solenoid connector
   - Turbine Shaft Speed (TSS) sensor
   - Electrical connector bracket nuts and move aside
   - Upper center converter housing bolts
3. Using special tool 303-290, or a suitable harness and crane, support the engine from above.
4. Remove or disconnect the following:
   - Transmission fluid fill tube
   - Shift cable bracket bolts
   - Starter motor and isolator
   - Right hand engine support insulator

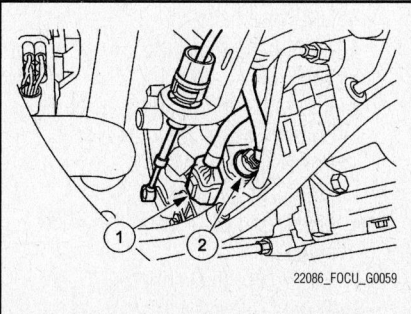

Fig. 6 Showing the location of the TR sensor (1) and the solenoid connector (2)

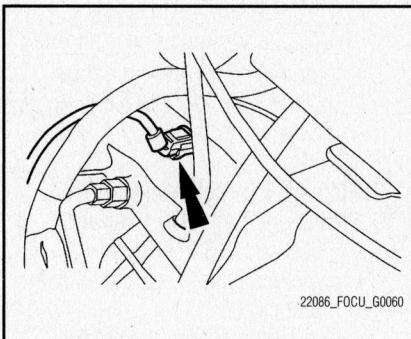

Fig. 7 Disconnect the TSS sensor

Fig. 8 Remove the upper center convert housing bolts

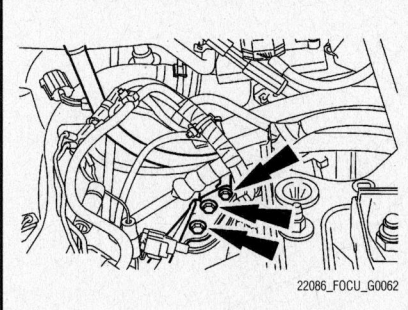

Fig. 9 Remove the shift cable bracket bolts

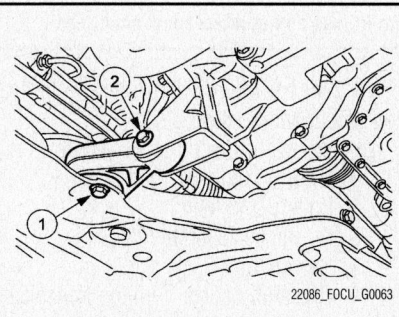

Fig. 10 Remove the RH engine support insulator bolts and nut (1, 2)

   - Left hand stabilizer bar at the strut
   - Tie rod ends from the knuckles, using Special Tool 211-001
   - Lower control arms from the knuckles
   - Right hand halfshaft from the transmission and hang securely aside
   - Left hand halfshaft from the transmission and hang securely aside

➡**Plug the transaxle openings to prevent contamination.**

   - Output Speed Sensor (OSS) connector
   - Transmission cooler lines
   - Shift cable from manual control lever
5. Remove the plastic cover and rotate the crankshaft to gain access to the converter nuts. Remove the four nuts.

➡**Before removal, mark one stud location to the flexplate for reinstallation reference.**

6. Remove the rear engine mount and lower the engine/transaxle assembly slightly.
7. Remove the rear engine mount bracket.
8. Secure the transaxle to a jack or suitable lifting device using a safety strap.
9. Remove the converter housing bolts and separate the transaxle from the engine.

➡**Note the locations of the different bolt lengths.**

10. Install the holding tool, 307-346, to prevent damage to the torque converter.

To install:

11. Position the transaxle into position onto the engine assembly.
12. Install the converter housing bolts and tighten to 35 ft. lbs. (47 Nm).
13. Using new self-locking nuts, install the torque converter to the flexplate. Tighten the nuts to 27 ft. lbs. (37 Nm).
14. Raise the engine/transaxle assembly into place and install the rear engine mount. Tighten the bracket bolts to 59 ft. lbs. (80 Nm). Tighten the outer engine mount bolts to 35 ft. lbs. (48 Nm). Tighten the center nut to 98 ft. lbs. (133 Nm).
15. Install or connect the following:
   - Transmission cooler lines
   - OSS connecter
   - Left hand halfshaft
   - Right hand halfshaft
   - Lower control arms to the knuckles
   - Tie rod ends to the knuckles
   - Stabilizer bar to the strut
   - Right hand engine support isolator and tighten to 35 ft. lbs. (48 Nm)
   - Starter motor
   - Transmission fluid fill tube
   - Shift cable bracket bolts
   - Upper center converter housing bolts and tighten to 35 ft. lbs. (47 Nm)
   - Electrical connector bracket
   - TSS sensor
   - TR sensor
   - Transaxle solenoid connector
   - LH strut upper mounting nuts; tighten to 22 ft. lbs. (30 Nm)
   - Air cleaner resonator

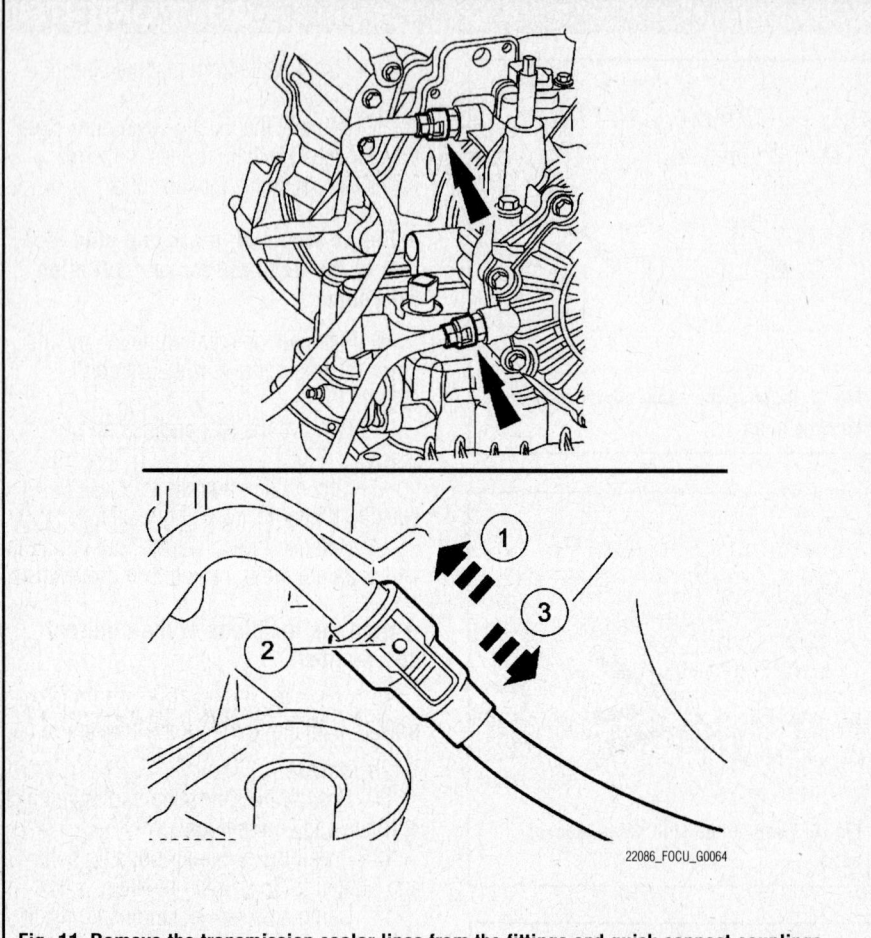

Fig. 11 Remove the transmission cooler lines from the fittings and quick-connect couplings

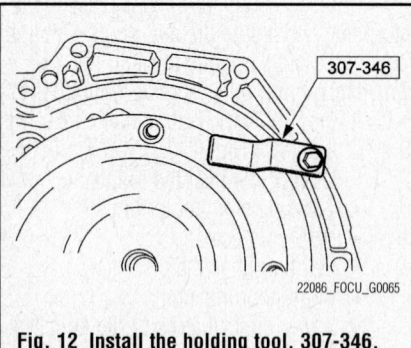

Fig. 12 Install the holding tool, 307-346, to prevent damage to the torque converter

- Battery tray
- Negative battery cable

16. Fill the transmission to the correct level.

17. Start the engine and check for leaks.

MANUAL TRANSAXLE ASSEMBLY

REMOVAL & INSTALLATION

See Figure 13.

1. Before servicing the vehicle, refer to the Precautions Section.
2. Remove or disconnect the following:
   - Steering column shaft bolt
   - Battery and tray
   - Air intake assembly
   - Resonator
   - Gearshift cables from the transaxle
   - Gearshift cables from the bracket
   - Hydraulic clutch line from retaining bracket
   - Heated Oxygen Sensors (HO2S) and Catalyst Monitor Sensor (CMS) connections
3. Support the engine using Special Tools 303-290.
4. Remove or disconnect the following:
   - Rear engine mount and mount bracket
   - Reverse lamp switch
   - Upper transmission to engine bolts
   - Tire and wheels
   - Engine roll restrictor
   - Tie rods from the knuckles
   - Lower control arms from the wheel knuckles
   - Stabilizer bar from the strut
   - Power steering lines from the steering gear

➡**Matchmark the subframe to the chassis.**

5. Support the subframe with a suitable lifting device.
6. Remove the six subframe bolts and lower the subframe from the vehicle.
7. Remove or disconnect the following:
   - Vehicle Speed Sensor (VSS)
   - Right hand halfshaft from the transmission and hang securely aside
   - Left hand halfshaft from the transmission and hang securely aside
8. Loosen, but do not remove, the starter mounting bolts.
9. Disconnect the clutch hydraulic line.
10. Secure the transmission to a jack or suitable lifting device.
11. Remove the 10 transmission-to-engine bolts.
12. Pull the transmission rearward until the input shaft is clear of the pressure plate, then lower the transmission from the vehicle.

To install:

13. Lift the transmission into the vehicle.
14. Tighten the transmission-to-engine bolts to 35 ft. lbs. (48 Nm).
15. Connect the clutch hydraulic line.
16. Tighten the starter motor mounting bolts to 18 ft. lbs. (25 Nm).
17. Install or connect the following:
   - Left hand halfshaft
   - Right hand halfshaft
   - VSS
   - Subframe and tighten mounting bolts to 148 ft. lbs. (200 Nm)
   - Power steering lines
   - Stabilizer bar to the strut
   - Lower control arms to the wheel knuckles
   - Tie rods to the knuckles
   - Engine roll restrictor
   - Upper transmission-to-engine bolts and tighten to 35 ft. lbs. (48 Nm)
   - Reverse lamp switch
   - Rear engine mount bracket and tighten bolts to 59 ft. lbs. (80 Nm)
   - Rear engine mount and tighten bolts to 35 ft. lbs. (48 Nm). Tighten the center nut to 98 ft. lbs. (133 Nm).
18. Remove the engine support tools.
19. Install or connect the following:
   - HO2S and CMS sensors
   - Hydraulic clutch line to the retaining bracket
   - Gearshift cables to the bracket
   - Gearshift cables to the transaxle

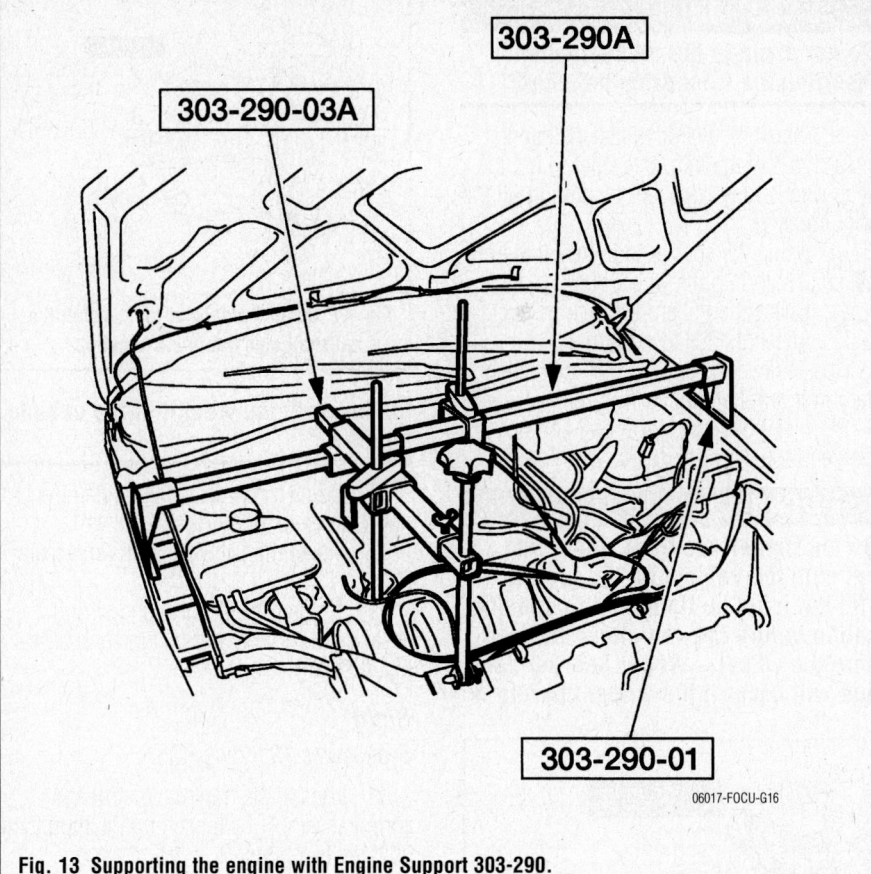

Fig. 13 Supporting the engine with Engine Support 303-290.

- Resonator and tighten bolts to 8 ft. lbs. (11 Nm)
- Air intake assembly
- Battery tray
- Steering column shaft bolt
- Negative battery cable

20. Fill the transmission to the correct level.
21. Adjust the shift linkage if necessary.
22. Start the engine and check for leaks.

CLUTCH

REMOVAL & INSTALLATION

1. Before servicing the vehicle, refer to the Precautions Section.
2. Remove or disconnect the following:
   - Negative battery cable
   - Transaxle; see "Manual Transaxle Assembly" section
   - Loosen the pressure plate to flexplate bolts evenly in ½ turn steps.
   - Pressure plate and clutch disc

To install:

3. Install the clutch disc and pressure plate, using a proper clutch alignment tool.
4. Tighten the pressure plate bolts evenly in ½ turns to 21 ft. lbs. (29 Nm).

5. Install the transaxle. See "Manual Transaxle Assembly" section.
6. Connect the negative battery cable.

ADJUSTMENTS

The clutch system is hydraulically actuated and no adjustments are necessary or possible.

HYDRAULIC CLUTCH SYSTEM

BLEEDING

1. Before servicing the vehicle, refer to the Precautions Section.
2. Remove or disconnect the following:
   - Air cleaner assembly
   - Mass Air Flow (MAF) sensor connector
   - Air intake pipe
3. Remove fluid from the brake fluid reservoir until the level reaches the **MIN** mark.
4. Fill the reservoir of Special Tool 416-D002 with DOT 4 brake fluid.
5. Attach the tool to the slave cylinder bleed nipple.
6. Open the bleed nipple and pump 80 ml brake fluid into the clutch control system.

7. Tighten the bleed nipple to 88 inch lbs. (10 Nm) and remove the tool.
8. Have an assistant depress the clutch pedal 4–5 times and hold the pedal at full travel.
9. Close the bleeder before releasing the clutch pedal.
10. Repeat the procedure until no more air bubbles are seen.
11. Check the clutch for proper operation.
12. Check the brake fluid reservoir level and fill with DOT 4 brake fluid, as necessary.
13. Install or connect the following:
   - Air intake pipe
   - MAF sensor connector
   - Air cleaner assembly

HALFSHAFT

REMOVAL & INSTALLATION

With Automatic Transaxle

Left Side

See Figures 14 through 17.

➡**The hub nut may be reused 4 times. Mark the nut at removal and only use hub nuts with 3 or fewer marks for assembly.**

1. Before servicing the vehicle, refer to the Precautions Section.
2. Loosen the LH strut and spring assembly mounting nuts by 4 turns.
3. Remove or disconnect the following:
   - Front wheel
   - Hub retainer nut. Mark the nut.
   - Lower ball joint from the knuckle
4. After separating the lower control arm from the wheel knuckle, immediately install the special tool over the ball stud before releasing the lower control arm and knuckle into rest positions. Leave the special tool in place during service and only remove prior to reassembly.

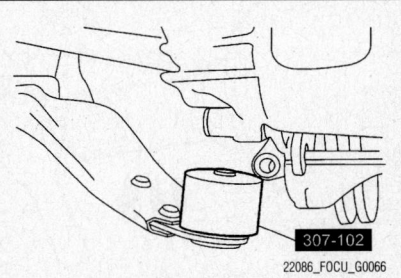

Fig. 14 Install the special tool over the ball stud prior to releasing the lower control arm and knuckle

5. Remove the hub nut, and then press the stub shaft out of the wheel hub.

※※ CAUTION

Support the halfshaft. The inner joint must not be bent at more than 18 degrees.

6. Separate the inner CV-joint from the transaxle as follows:

7. Remove the LH drive halfshaft from the transaxle, using a slide hammer as shown.

8. Close off the transaxle opening with an auxiliary plug.

To install:

→Replace the self-locking nuts and circlip for assembly.

※※ CAUTION

Support the halfshaft. The inner halfshaft joint must not be bent by more than 18 degrees.

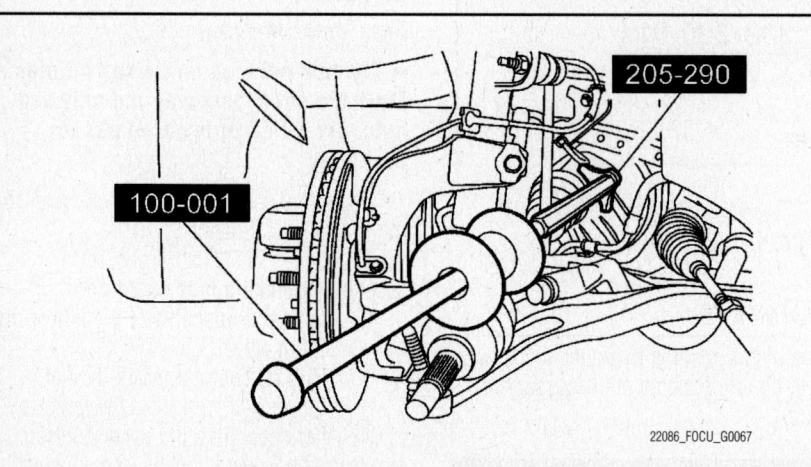

Fig. 15 Remove the LH drive halfshaft from the transaxle, using a slide hammer as shown

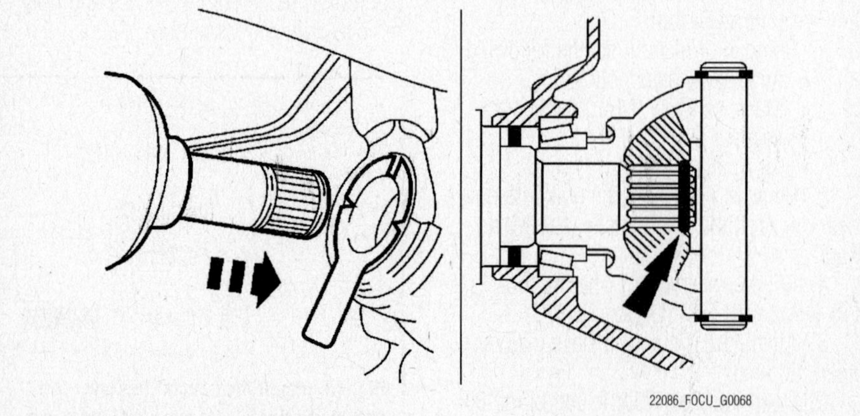

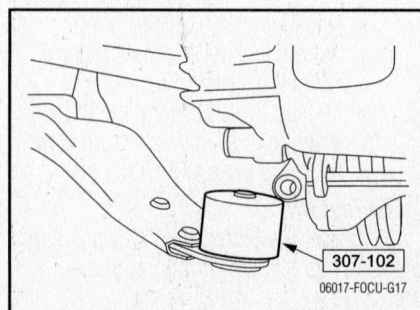

Fig. 16 Install the LH drive halfshaft and snap ring into the transaxle; make sure the snap ring is fully engaged, by pulling on the joint housing

※※ CAUTION

Do not damage the oil seal when inserting the front drive halfshaft.

9. Install the LH drive halfshaft and snap ring into the transaxle. Make sure the snap ring is fully engaged, by pulling on the joint housing.

10. Using the special tool, install the LH halfshaft stub into the wheel hub.

11. Check the transmission fluid level.

12. Attach the LH lower arm.

13. Remove the special tool and attach the lower arm ball joint.

14. Install the lower arm bolt and nut. Tighten to 48 Nm (35 lb-ft).

※※ CAUTION

Do not tighten the front wheel hub nut with the vehicle on the ground. The nut must be tightened to specification before the vehicle is lowered onto the wheels. Wheel bearing damage will occur if the wheel bearing is

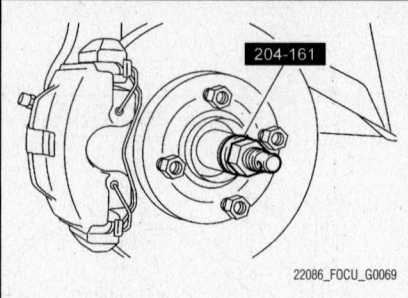

Fig. 17 Using the special tool, install the LH halfshaft stub into the wheel hub

loaded with the weight of the vehicle applied.

15. Install a new wheel hub retaining nut. Tighten to 199 ft. lbs. (270 Nm).

16. Install the LH wheel and tire assembly.

17. Tighten the LH strut and spring assembly-to-mount nuts. Tighten to 22 ft. lbs. (30 Nm).

Right

See Figures 18 through 20.

1. Loosen the right hand strut and spring assembly by loosening the mounting bolts by five turns.

2. Loosen the hub nut.

3. Remove the right hand tire.

4. Remove the lower ball joint nut and detach the lower control arm.

※※ CAUTION

Do not use a prying device or separator fork between the lower ball joint and knuckle. Use a pry bar by inserting it into the lower control arm opening.

5. Install Special Tool 307-102 over the ball stud before releasing the lower control arm and knuckle into rest positions.

6. Unscrew the hub nut and detach the right hand halfshaft from the wheel hub using a suitable puller.

Fig. 18 Installing Special Tool 307-102 on the lower ball stud.

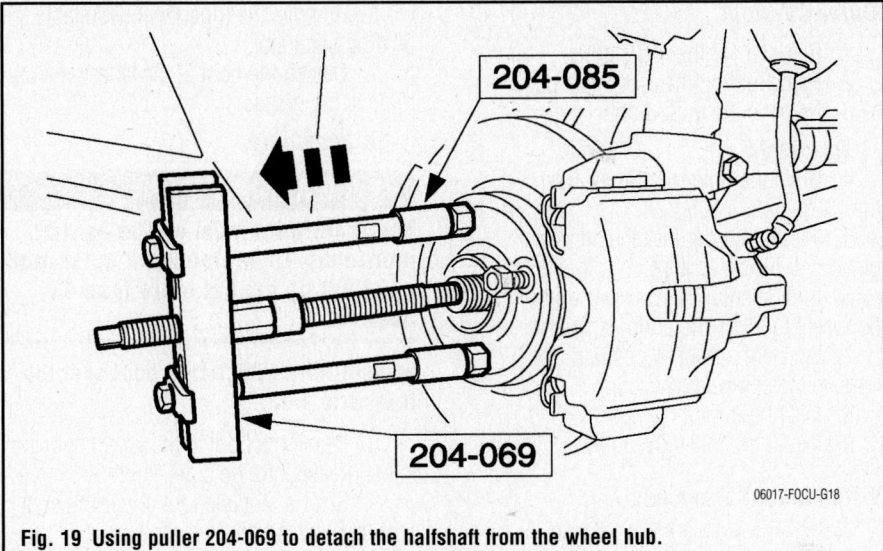

Fig. 19 Using puller 204-069 to detach the halfshaft from the wheel hub.

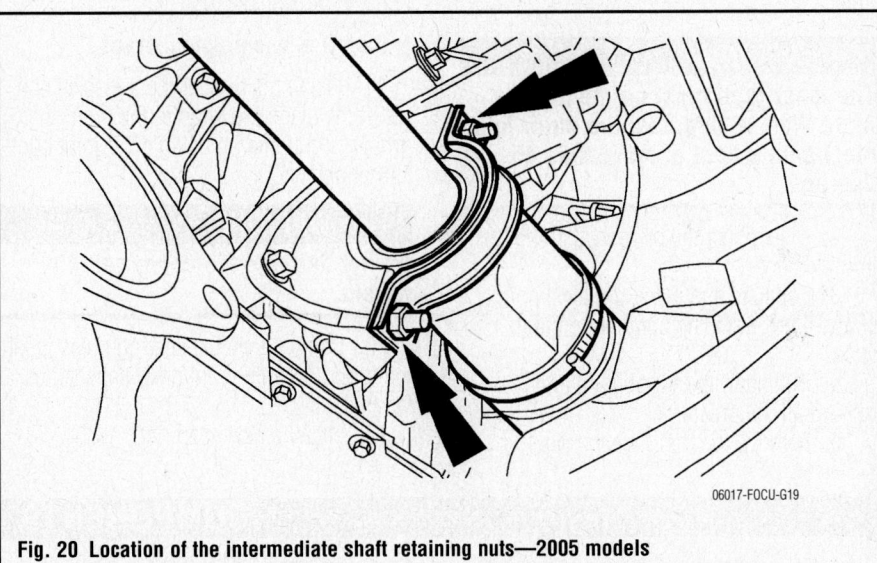

Fig. 20 Location of the intermediate shaft retaining nuts—2005 models

7. Remove the retaining clip nuts.
8. Pull out the right hand halfshaft and intermediate shaft as an assembly.

✳✳ CAUTION

Support the halfshaft. The inner half-shaft joint must not be bent by more than 18 degrees.

To install:
9. Install the halfshaft/intermediate shaft assembly.
10. Using new nuts, install the retaining clip and tighten to 18 ft. lbs. (25 Nm).
11. Install or connect the following:
   • Wheel hub retaining nut
   • Lower control arm
   • Lower ball joint
12. Tighten the right hand strut and spring assembly mounting bolts.

With Manual Transaxle

1. Before servicing the vehicle, refer to the precautions in the beginning of this section.
2. Disconnect battery negative cable from battery and properly isolate to prevent accidental reconnection.
3. Loosen the strut and spring assembly top mount nuts by four turns.
4. Loosen the wheel nuts.
5. Loosen the wheel hub retaining nut.
6. Raise and support the vehicle.
7. Remove the wheel.

✳✳ WARNING

Protect the ball joint seat using a soft cloth to prevent damage.

8. Detach the lower arm ball joint.

➡ The wheel hub retaining nut can be reused four times; mark the retaining nut.

9. Press the halfshaft out of the wheel hub.

✳✳ WARNING

Support the halfshaft. The inner half-shaft joint must not be bent by more than 18 degrees.

10. Allow the oil to drain into a suitable container.
11. Remove the front drive halfshaft from the transaxle.

➡ On vehicles equipped with an intermediate shaft, the intermediate shaft and halfshaft are removed as an assembly.

12. Close off the transaxle with auxiliary plugs.

To install:
13. Install new self locking nuts and snap ring.

✳✳ WARNING

Do not damage the oil seal when inserting the front drive half-shaft.

14. Make sure the snap ring is fully engaged, by pulling on the joint housing.
15. Remove the auxiliary plug from the transaxle opening.
16. Install the halfshaft and snap ring into the transaxle.

➡ The wheel hub retaining nut can be reused four times, inspect the markings on the retaining nut and install a new nut if necessary.

17. Do not fully tighten the wheel hub retaining nut.
18. Install the halfshaft stub into the wheel hub.
19. Loosely install the wheel hub retaining nut. Do not fully tighten.
20. Check the transmission fluid level.
21. Attach the lower arm ball joint and tighten the bolt to 37 ft. lbs. (50 Nm)
22. Install the wheel and loosely install the nuts. Do not fully tighten.
23. Tighten the wheel hub retaining nut to 233 ft. lbs. (316 Nm)
24. Tighten the wheel nuts to 94 ft. lbs. (128 Nm)
25. Lower the vehicle.

26. Tighten the strut and spring assembly to mount nuts to 18 ft. lbs. (25 Nm)

27. Reconnect negative battery cable.

CV-JOINTS

OVERHAUL

With Automatic Transaxle

Inner Tripod Joint

1. Before servicing the vehicle, refer to the Precautions Section.

2. Remove the axle halfshaft from the vehicle and place it in a vise.

3. Remove or disconnect the following:
- Tripod joint boot clamps
- Tripod joint boot
- Tripod joint housing
- Snap ring
- Tripod joint

To install:

➡Use new snap rings and boot clamps for assembly.

4. Install or connect the following:
- Tripod joint
- Snap ring
- Tripod joint housing. Fill the joint housing with grease.
- Tripod joint boot
- Tripod joint boot clamps

5. Install the halfshaft.

Outer CV-Joint

1. Remove the Inner CV-Joint.
2. Remove the outer boot clamps.
3. Remove the outer boot.

To install:

4. Slide the outer boot outwards over the CV-joint.

5. Press the boot into the annular groove on the drive joint.

6. Slide a small screwdriver under the boot seat to allow the air to escape.

7. Locate the boot in position and remove the screwdriver.

8. Install the boot clamps.

9. Install the inner CV-Joint.

With Manual Transaxle

1. Before servicing the vehicle, refer to the precautions in the beginning of this section.

✳✳ WARNING

The inner joint must not be bent at more than 18 degrees; the outer joint must not be bent at more than 45 degrees.

2. Disconnect the driveshaft at the transaxle end.

3. Separate and discard the clamping straps. Push back the boot along the shaft.

4. Pull apart the tripod joint and remove all the grease.

5. Remove the tripod snap ring.

6. Remove the tripod with a suitable bearing separator.

7. Detach the boot at the wheel end and remove the grease.

To assemble:

✳✳ WARNING

The inner joint must not be bent at more than 18 degrees; the outer joint must not be bent at more than 45 degrees.

➡Install the wheel-side boot over the transaxle side.

8. Install the boot at the wheel end and inject grease into the outer joint.

9. Slide a suitable tool under the boot seat to allow the air to escape.

10. Locate the boot in position and remove the suitable tool.

➡Install new clamping straps.

11. Install the boot at the transaxle end, insert the clamping strap in the boot ring groove and tighten it using a CV joint boot strap tightener.

✳✳ WARNING

Do not damage the universal joint rollers.

12. Using a suitable bearing press, push the tripod onto the front drive halfshaft as far as it will go.

13. Install a new snap ring.

ENGINE COOLING

ENGINE FAN

REMOVAL & INSTALLATION

1. Before servicing the vehicle, refer to the precautions in the beginning of this section.

2. Disconnect battery negative cable from battery and properly isolate to prevent accidental reconnection.

➡The fan shroud and electric cooling fans are serviced as an assembly.

3. Raise the vehicle.

4. Disconnect the dual electric cooling fan electrical connectors.

5. Lift and remove the cooling fan motors and shroud from the retainer brackets and lower from the vehicle.

To install:

6. Place the motor and shroud assembly into the retainer brackets.

7. Connect dual electric cooling fan electrical connectors.

8. Lower the vehicle.

9. Reconnect negative battery cable.

RADIATOR

REMOVAL & INSTALLATION

See Figure 21.

1. Before servicing the vehicle, refer to the precautions in the beginning of this section.

2. Disconnect battery negative cable from battery and properly isolate to prevent accidental reconnection.

3. Raise the vehicle.

4. Drain the cooling system.

5. Lift and remove the cooling fan motors and shroud from the retainer brackets and lower from the vehicle.

6. Remove or disconnect the following:
- Electrical connector from the horn
- Upper hose from the radiator
- Lower hose from the radiator

COMPONENTS

- Push-type pins and the lower radiator splash shield

7. Detach and support the air conditioning condenser, if equipped.

8. Detach the wiring harness retaining clip from the radiator support bracket.

9. If equipped with automatic transaxle, detach the transmission fluid cooler from the two RH and the one LH brackets and support the fluid cooler.

10. Remove the four bolts and the lower core support.

11. Remove the radiator.

To install:

12. Install or connect the following:
- Radiator
- Four bolts and lower core support
- Transmission fluid cooler, if equipped
- Air conditioning condenser, if equipped
- Lower radiator splash shield

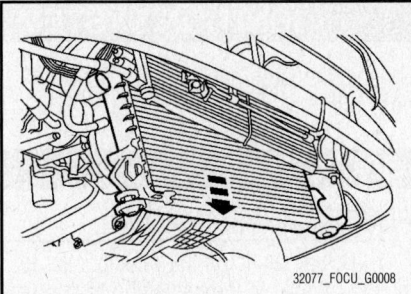

Fig. 21 The radiator is removed from beneath the vehicle.

- Upper and lower radiator hoses
- Horn electrical connector
- Cooling fan motors and shroud
13. Fill and bleed the cooling system.
14. Lower the vehicle.
15. Reconnect the negative battery cable.

THERMOSTAT

REMOVAL & INSTALLATION

1. Before servicing the vehicle, refer to the precautions in the beginning of this section.
2. Disconnect battery negative cable from battery and properly isolate to prevent accidental reconnection.

ENGINE ELECTRICAL

ALTERNATOR

REMOVAL & INSTALLATION

1. Before servicing the vehicle, refer to the Precautions Section.
2. Remove or disconnect the following:
   - Negative battery cable
   - Upper alternator mounting nut
3. Raise and support the vehicle.
4. Remove the accessory drive shield.
5. Release the tension and remove the accessory drive belt from the alternator pulley.
6. Release the two air intake tube retainers and remove the air intake tube assembly.

➡ **The thermostat and thermostat housing are serviced as an assembly.**

3. Drain the cooling system.
4. Raise vehicle.
5. Remove or disconnect the following:
   - Accessory drive belt shield
   - Accessory drive belt
   - Two power steering hose bracket retaining nuts and position the hose and brackets aside.
   - Cooling fan motor and shroud
   - 3 A/C compressor bolts and position the compressor aside
   - Hoses from the thermostat housing
6. Remove the bolts, the thermostat housing and the thermostat as an assembly.

To install:

➡ **Lubricate the thermostat housing O-ring with clean engine coolant.**

7. Install or connect the following:
   - New thermostat/housing assembly and tighten the bolts to 89 inch lbs. (10 Nm)
   - Hoses to the thermostat housing
   - A/C compressor bracket and compressor and tighten the bolts to 18 ft. lbs. (25 Nm)
   - Cooling fan motor and shroud
   - Power steering hose, bracket and

7. Remove and discard the generator B+ cable nut and disconnect the B+ cable.
8. Remove or disconnect the following:
   - Alternator electrical connector
   - 2 alternator nuts and bolts
   - Engine roll restrictor mount bolt
9. With an assistant, position the engine forward and remove the alternator from its mounting.
10. Remove the lower air duct and remove the alternator.
11. Remove the radial adapter (B+ connection extension).

To install:

Install or connect the following:
   - Radial adapter to the alternator

tighten the nuts to 89 inch lbs. (10 Nm)
8. Fill and bleed the cooling system.
9. Reconnect the negative battery cable.

WATER PUMP

REMOVAL & INSTALLATION

1. Before servicing the vehicle, refer to the Precautions Section.
2. Drain the cooling system.
3. Remove or disconnect the following:
   - Negative battery cable
   - Accessory drive belt
   - Water pump pulley
   - Water pump mounting bolts
   - Water pump

To install:

4. Install or connect the following:
   - Water pump with new O-ring. Tighten the bolts to 89 inch lbs. (10 Nm).
   - Water pump pulley. Tighten the bolts to 18 ft. lbs. (25 Nm).
   - Accessory drive belt
   - Negative battery cable
5. Fill the cooling system to the correct level.
6. Start the engine and check for leaks.

CHARGING SYSTEM

   - Lower air duct
   - Alternator; tighten the 2 bolts and nuts to 35 ft. lbs. (48 Nm)
   - Alternator electrical connector
   - Alternator B+ cable and new nut
12. Reposition the engine. Tighten the engine roll restrictor mount bolt to 35 ft. lbs. (48 Nm).
13. Install or connect the following:
   - Air intake tube and retainers
   - Accessory drive belt
   - Accessory drive belt
14. Lower the vehicle.
15. Install the alternator upper mounting nut. Tighten to 35 ft. lbs. (48 Nm).
16. Reconnect the negative battery cable.

FIRING ORDER

See Figure 22.

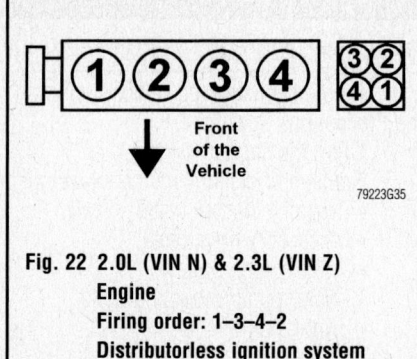

**Fig. 22 2.0L (VIN N) & 2.3L (VIN Z)
Engine
Firing order: 1–3–4–2
Distributorless ignition system**

IGNITION COIL

REMOVAL & INSTALLATION

2.0L (VIN N) Engine

1. Before servicing the vehicle, refer to the precautions in the beginning of this section.
2. Disconnect battery negative cable

from battery and properly isolate to prevent accidental reconnection.
3. Remove the ignition coil-on plug electrical connector.
4. Remove the retaining bolt.
5. Remove the ignition coil-on plug.
6. Installation is the reverse of the removal procedure.

2.3L (VIN Z) Engine

1. Before servicing the vehicle, refer to the precautions in the beginning of this section.
2. Disconnect battery negative cable from battery and properly isolate to prevent accidental reconnection.
3. Remove the ignition coil-on plug electrical connector.
4. Remove the retaining bolt.
5. Remove the ignition coil-on plug.
6. Installation is the reverse of the removal procedure.

IGNITION TIMING

ADJUSTMENT

The ignition timing is controlled by the Powertrain Control Module (PCM).

No adjustment is necessary or possible.

SPARK PLUGS

REMOVAL & INSTALLATION

1. Before servicing the vehicle, refer to the precautions in the beginning of this section.
2. Disconnect battery negative cable from battery and properly isolate to prevent accidental reconnection.
3. Remove the ignition coil.
4. Remove foreign material from the spark plug well with compressed air.
5. Remove the spark plug.

To install:

6. Check and adjust the spark plug gap as necessary.

➡ **Spark plug gap should be 0.041–0.045 inch (1.05–1.15mm)**

7. Install spark plugs and tighten to 9 ft. lbs. (12 Nm)
8. Reinstall ignition coil.

STARTER

REMOVAL & INSTALLATION

See Figure 23.

1. Before servicing the vehicle, refer to the Precautions Section.
2. Disconnect the battery ground cable.
3. Remove the terminal nuts and disconnect the wiring.
4. Remove the nuts and disconnect the power steering pressure line brackets from the stud bolts.
5. Remove the bolts and the starter motor.
6. To install, reverse the removal procedure. Tighten the starter bolts to 18 ft. lbs. (25 Nm).

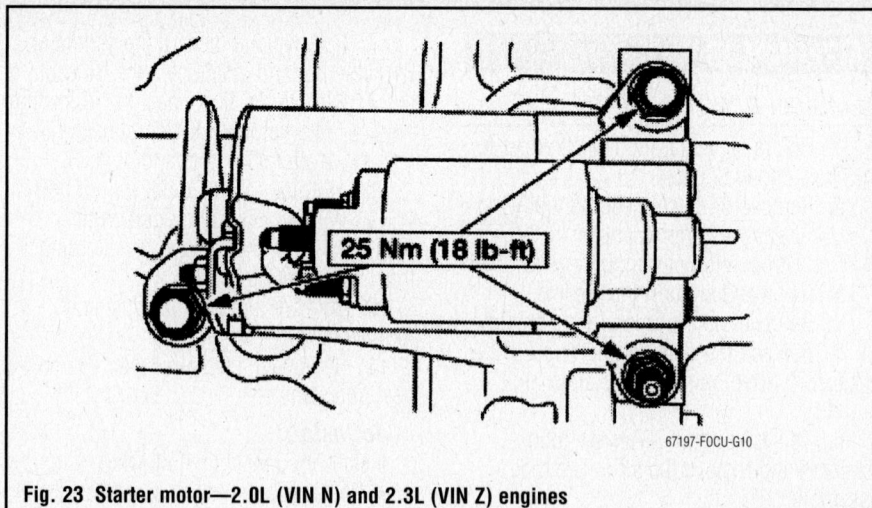

Fig. 23 Starter motor—2.0L (VIN N) and 2.3L (VIN Z) engines

ENGINE MECHANICAL **COMPONENTS**

➡**Disconnecting the negative battery cable may interfere with the functions of the on board computer systems and may require the computer to undergo a relearning process, once the negative battery cable is reconnected.**

ACCESSORY DRIVE BELTS

ACCESSORY BELT ROUTING

See Figure 24.

INSPECTION

Inspect the drive belt for signs of glazing or cracking. A glazed belt will be perfectly smooth from slippage, while a good belt will have a slight texture of fabric visible. Cracks will usually start at the inner edge of the belt and run outward. All worn or damaged drive belts should be replaced immediately.

ADJUSTMENT

Belt tension is automatically maintained by a spring-loaded tensioner. No adjustment is necessary.

REMOVAL & INSTALLATION

See Figure 25.

1. Before servicing the vehicle, refer to the precautions in the beginning of this section.

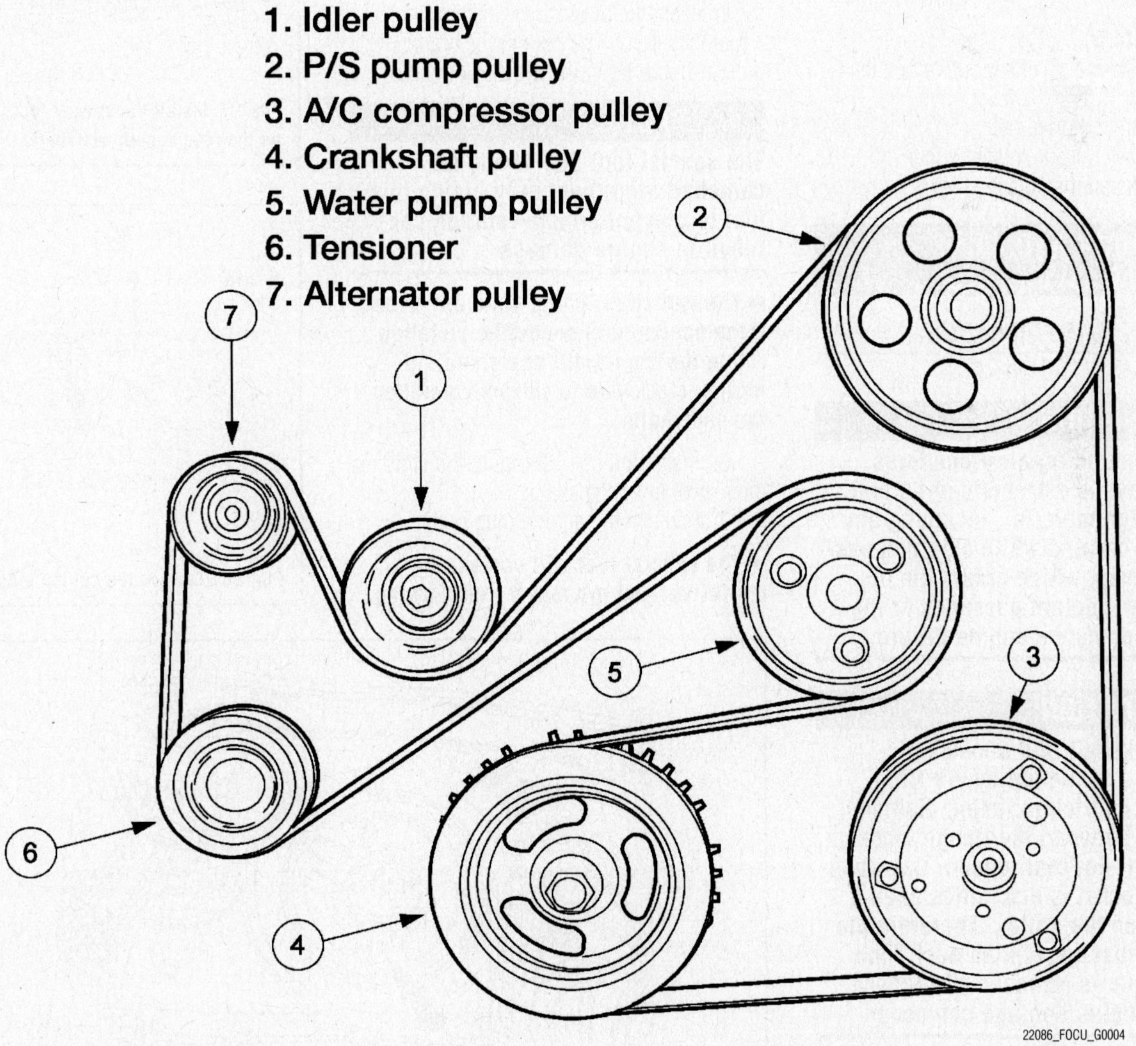

1. Idler pulley
2. P/S pump pulley
3. A/C compressor pulley
4. Crankshaft pulley
5. Water pump pulley
6. Tensioner
7. Alternator pulley

22086_FOCU_G0004

Fig. 24 Accessory drive belt routing—2.0L (VIN N) and 2.3L (VIN Z) engines

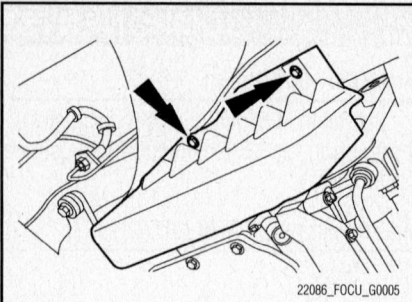

Fig. 25 Location of splash shield and removal

2. With the vehicle in NEUTRAL, position it on a hoist.
3. Remove the splash shield
4. Rotate the accessory drive belt tensioner.
5. Remove the accessory drive belt.

To install:

6. Rotate the accessory drive belt tensioner.
7. Route the drive belt.
8. Slowly release the tensioner
9. Reinstall the splash shield.

CAMSHAFT AND VALVE LIFTERS

REMOVAL & INSTALLATION

See Figures 26 through 33.

✳✳ CAUTION

During engine repair procedures, cleanliness is extremely important. Any foreign material, including any material created while cleaning gasket surfaces, which enters the oil passages, coolant passages or the oil pan can cause engine failure.

✳✳ CAUTION

The crankshaft, the crankshaft sprocket and the pulley are fitted together by friction, using diamond washers between the flange faces on each part. For that reason, the crankshaft sprocket is also unfastened if you loosen the pulley. Therefore the engine must be retimed each time the damper is removed. Otherwise severe engine damage can occur.

✳✳ CAUTION

Do not rotate the camshafts unless instructed to in this procedure. Rotating the camshafts or crankshaft with timing components loosened or

removed can cause serious damage to the valves and pistons.

1. Before servicing the vehicle, refer to the Precautions Section.
2. With the vehicle in NEUTRAL, position it on a hoist.
3. Disconnect the battery negative cable.
4. Remove the degas bottle.
5. Check the valve clearance.
6. Remove the accessory drive belt.

✳✳ CAUTION

Failure to position the No. 1 piston at Top Dead Center (TDC) can result in damage to the engine. Turn the engine in the normal direction of rotation only.

7. Using the crankshaft pulley bolt, turn the crankshaft clockwise to position the No. 1 piston at TDC. The hole in the crankshaft pulley should be in the 6 o'clock position.

✳✳ CAUTION

The special tool 303-465 is for camshaft alignment only. Using this tool to prevent engine rotation can result in engine damage.

➡The camshaft timing slots are offset. If the special tool cannot be installed, rotate the crankshaft one complete revolution clockwise to correctly position the camshafts.

8. Install the special tool in the slots on the rear of both camshafts.
9. Remove the engine plug bolt.

➡The special tool will contact the crankshaft and prevent it from turning

past TDC. However, the crankshaft can still be rotated in the counterclockwise direction. The crankshaft must remain at the TDC position during the camshaft removal and installation.

10. Install the special tool.
11. Install a standard 6 mm (0.23 in) x 18 mm (0.7 in) bolt through the crankshaft pulley and thread it into the front cover.

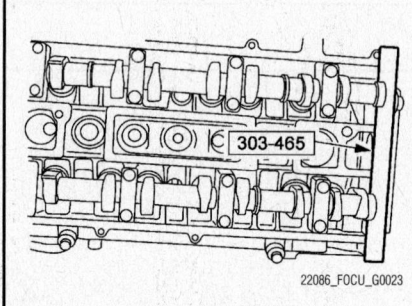

Fig. 27 Install the special tool in the slots on the rear of both camshafts

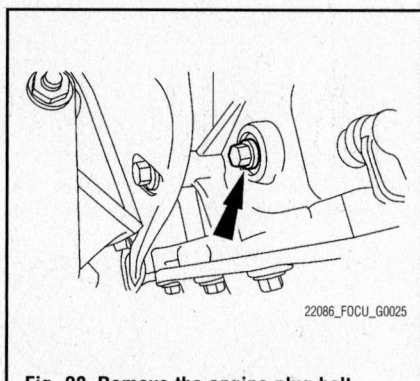

Fig. 28 Remove the engine plug bolt

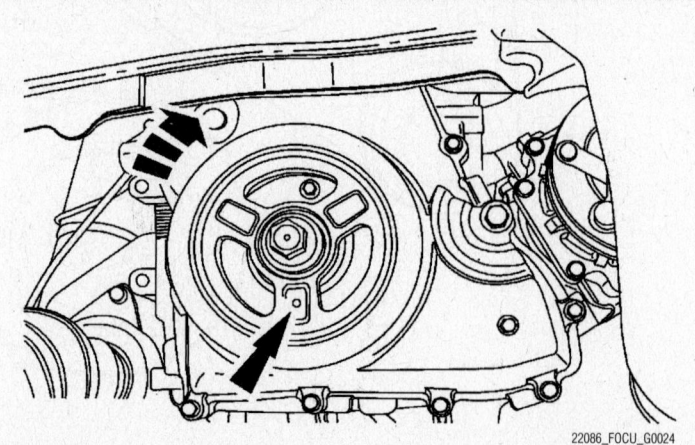

Fig. 26 Using the crankshaft pulley bolt, turn the crankshaft clockwise to position the No. 1 piston at TDC, with the hole in the crankshaft pulley at the 6 o'clock position —2.0L (VIN N) and 2.3L (VIN Z) engine

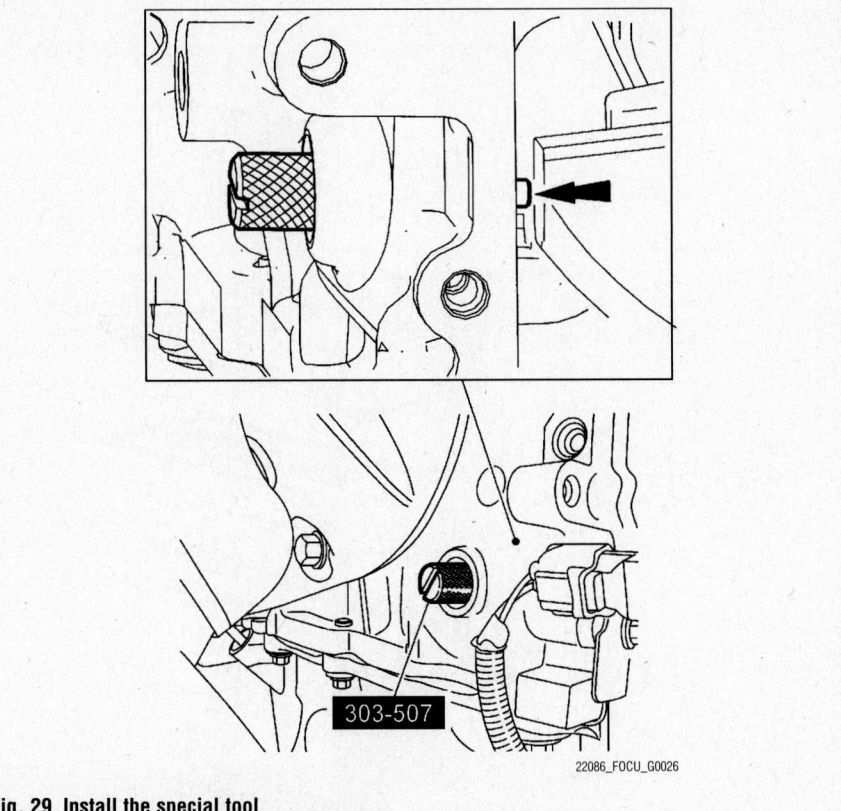

Fig. 29 Install the special tool

⁕⁕ CAUTION

Only hand-tighten the bolt or damage to the front cover can occur.

12. Remove the lower and upper front cover timing hole plugs from the engine front covers.

13. Reposition the special camshaft holding tool to the slot on the rear of the intake camshaft only.

➡**Releasing the ratcheting mechanism in the timing chain tensioner allows the plunger to collapse and create slack in the timing chain. Installing an M6 × 30 mm (1.18 in) bolt into the upper front cover timing hole will hold the tensioner arm in a retracted position and allow enough slack in the timing chain for removal of the exhaust camshaft gear.**

14. Using a small pick tool, unlock the chain tensioner ratchet through the lower front cover timing hole.

15. Using the flats of the camshaft, have an assistant rotate the exhaust camshaft clockwise to collapse the timing chain tensioner plunger.

16. Insert an M6 × 30 mm (1.18 in) bolt into the upper front cover timing hole to hold the tensioner arm in place.

17. Remove the camshaft holding tool.

18. Using the flats on the camshaft to prevent camshaft rotation, remove the bolt and exhaust camshaft drive gear.

19. Remove the timing chain from the intake camshaft drive gear.

20. Using the flats on the camshaft to prevent camshaft rotation, remove the bolt and intake camshaft drive gear.

21. Mark the position of the camshaft lobes on the No. 1 cylinder for installation reference.

⁕⁕ WARNING

Failure to follow the camshaft loosening procedure can result in damage to the camshafts.

22. Remove the camshafts from the engine, using only the following procedure:

    a. Loosen the camshaft bearing cap bolts, in sequence, one turn at a time.

    b. Repeat the first step until all tension is released from the camshaft bearing caps.

    c. Remove the camshaft bearing caps.

    d. Remove the camshafts.

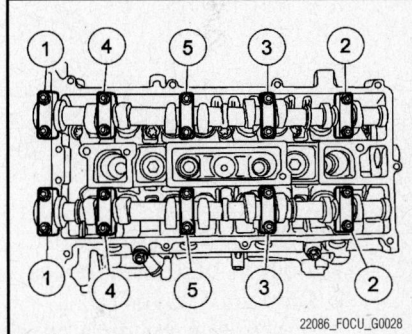

Fig. 31 Showing the camshaft bolt loosening sequence

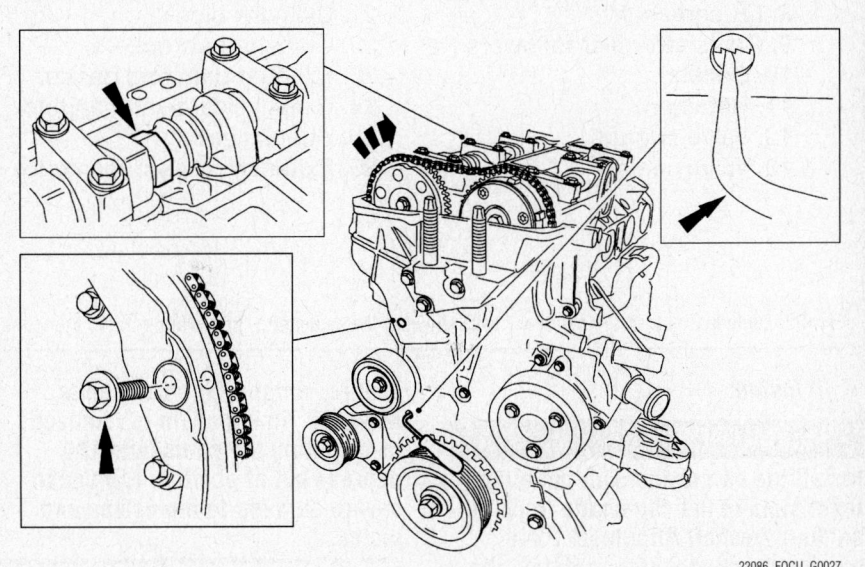

Fig. 30 Insert an M6 × 30 mm (1.18 in) bolt into the upper front cover timing hole to hold the tensioner arm in place

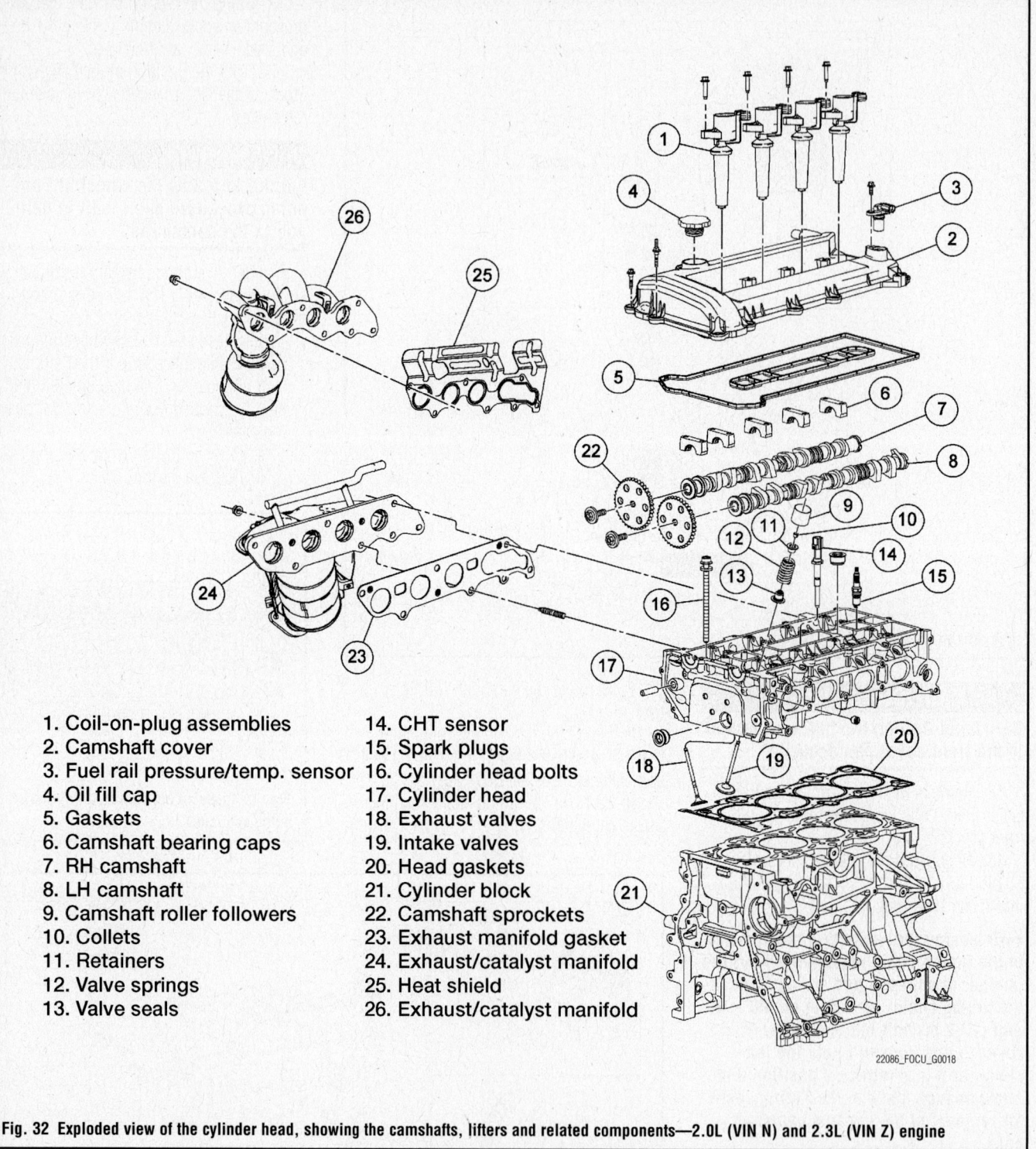

1. Coil-on-plug assemblies
2. Camshaft cover
3. Fuel rail pressure/temp. sensor
4. Oil fill cap
5. Gaskets
6. Camshaft bearing caps
7. RH camshaft
8. LH camshaft
9. Camshaft roller followers
10. Collets
11. Retainers
12. Valve springs
13. Valve seals
14. CHT sensor
15. Spark plugs
16. Cylinder head bolts
17. Cylinder head
18. Exhaust valves
19. Intake valves
20. Head gaskets
21. Cylinder block
22. Camshaft sprockets
23. Exhaust manifold gasket
24. Exhaust/catalyst manifold
25. Heat shield
26. Exhaust/catalyst manifold

22086_FOCU_G0018

Fig. 32 Exploded view of the cylinder head, showing the camshafts, lifters and related components—2.0L (VIN N) and 2.3L (VIN Z) engine

To install:

> ⁂ **CAUTION**
>
> Install the camshafts with the alignment slots in the camshafts lined up so the Camshaft Alignment Plate can be installed without rotating the camshafts. Make sure the lobes on the No. 1 cylinder are in the same position as noted in the removal pro-

cedure. Rotating the camshafts when the timing chain is removed, or installing the camshafts 180 degrees out of position can cause severe damage to the valves and pistons.

➥Lubricate the camshaft journals and bearing caps with clean engine oil.

23. Install the camshafts and bearing caps. Tighten the bearing caps in the sequence shown in 3 stages:

a. Stage 1: Tighten the camshaft bearing cap bolts one turn at a time until finger tight.

b. Stage 2: Tighten to 62 inch lbs. (7 Nm).

c. Stage 3: Tighten to 12 ft. lbs. (16 Nm).

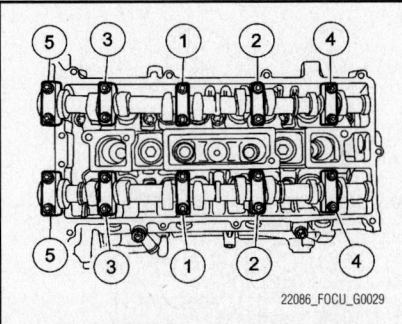

Fig. 33 Showing the camshaft bolt tightening sequence

24. Install the special camshaft holding tool to the rear of the camshafts.

25. Install the intake camshaft drive gear and hand-tighten the bolt.

26. Install the timing chain on the intake camshaft drive gear.

➡ **The timing chain must be correctly engaged on the teeth of the crankshaft timing sprocket and the intake camshaft drive gear in order to install the exhaust camshaft drive gear onto the exhaust camshaft.**

27. Position the exhaust camshaft drive gear in the timing chain and install the gear and bolt on the exhaust camshaft. Hand-tighten the bolt.

28. Releasing the tensioner arm will remove the slack from the timing chain release.

29. Remove the M6 × 30 mm bolt from the upper front cover timing hole to unlock the tensioner arm.

✳✳ CAUTION

The special tool 303-465 is for camshaft alignment only. Using this tool to prevent engine rotation can result in engine damage.

30. Using the flats on the camshafts to prevent camshaft rotation, tighten the bolts. Tighten to 53 ft. lbs. (72 Nm).

31. Remove the special camshaft holding tool.

32. Remove the 6 mm (0.23 in) × 18 mm (0.7 in) bolt from the crankshaft damper.

33. Remove the special tool from the engine plug bore.

34. Install the upper front cover timing hole plug. Tighten to 89 inch lbs. (10 Nm).

35. Apply silicone gasket and sealant to the threads of the lower front cover timing hole plug.

36. Install the plug and tighten to 9 ft. lbs. (12 Nm).

37. Install the engine plug bolt. Tighten to 15 ft. lbs. (20 Nm).

38. Install the accessory drive belt.

39. Install the valve cover.

40. Install the degas bottle.

41. Connect the battery negative cable.

CRANKSHAFT FRONT SEAL

REMOVAL & INSTALLATION

See Figures 34 and 35.

1. Before servicing the vehicle, refer to the Precautions Section.

➡ **The crankshaft, crankshaft sprocket and the pulley are fitted together by friction, using diamond washers** between the flange faces on each part. For that reason, the crankshaft sprocket is also unfastened if you loosen the pulley. Therefore, the engine must be retimed each time the damper is removed.

2. Remove the crankshaft pulley. See "Crankshaft Damper" in this section.

3. Remove the crankshaft seal using Special Tool 303-409.

To install:

4. Install the front crankshaft seal using Special Tool 303-096.

5. Install the crankshaft pulley.

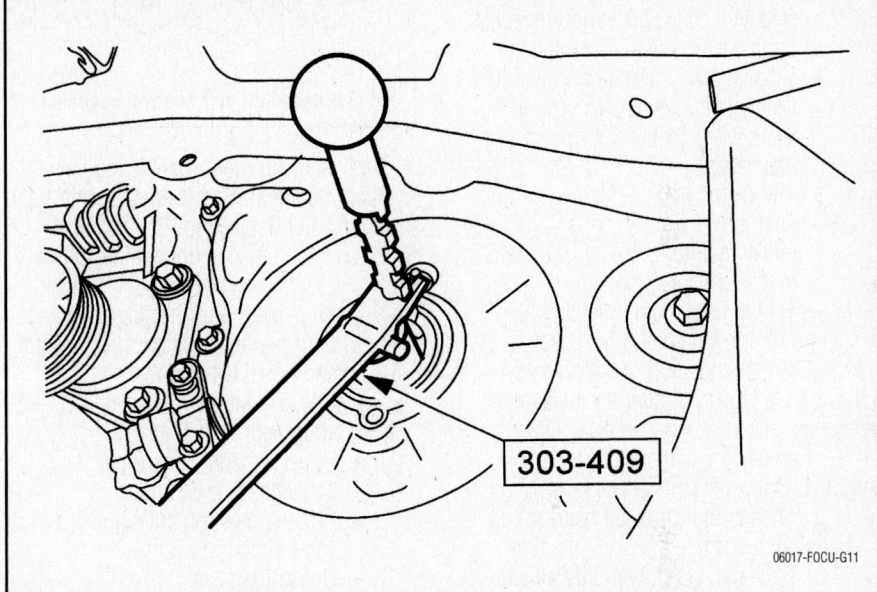

Fig. 34 Remove the crankshaft seal using Seal Remover 303-409—2005 models

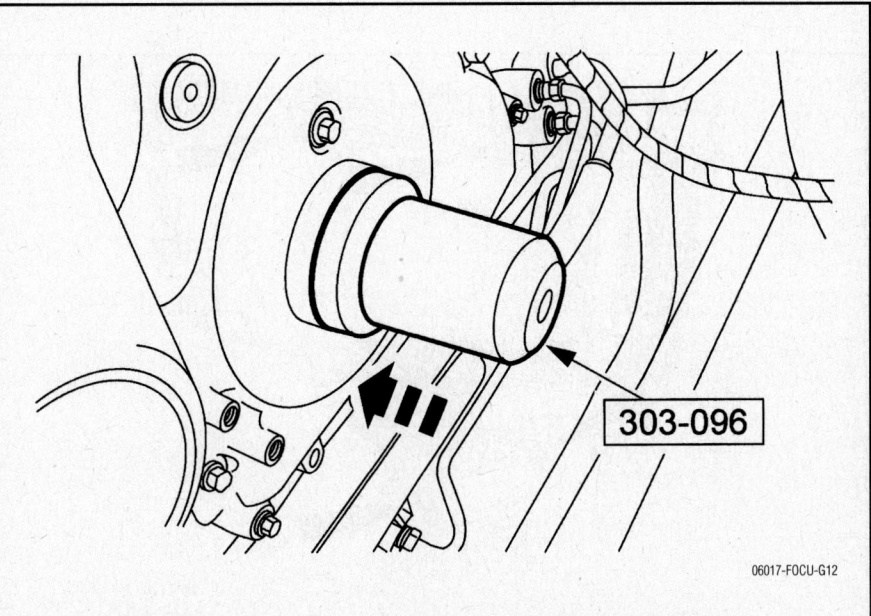

Fig. 35 Installing the crankshaft seal using Special Tool 303-096—2005 models

CYLINDER HEAD

REMOVAL & INSTALLATION

2.0L (VIN N) Engine

See Figures 36 through 38.

1. Before servicing the vehicle, refer to the Precautions Section.
2. Drain the cooling system.
3. Relieve the fuel system pressure.
4. Remove or disconnect the following:
   - Negative battery cable
   - Battery tray
   - Cooling fans
   - Catalytic converter from the muffler assembly
   - Catalytic converter support bracket
   - Engine heat shield, if equipped
   - Exhaust sensor electrical connectors
   - Catalytic converter and secure it aside with mechanic's wire or equivalent
   - Alternator
   - Fuel rail
   - Intake manifold; see "Intake Manifold" in this section
   - Timing drive components; see "Timing Chain and Sprockets"
5. Mark the position of the camshaft lobes on the No. 1 cylinder for installation reference.
6. Remove the camshafts from the engine by following this procedure:
   a. Loosen the camshaft bearing cap bolts, in sequence, one turn at a time.
   b. Repeat the first step until all tension is released from the camshaft bearing caps.
   c. Remove the camshaft bearing caps.

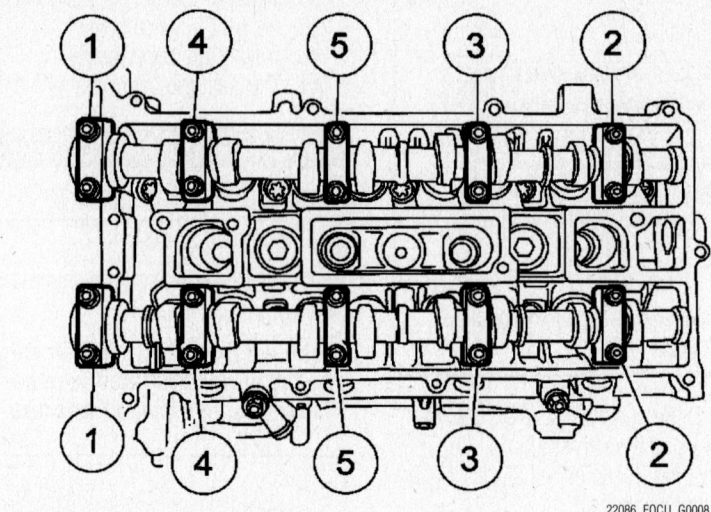

Fig. 37 Camshaft bolt removal sequence—2.0L (VIN N) engine

22086_FOCU_G0008

   d. Remove the camshaft and valve lifters (tappets). See "Camshaft and Valve Lifters" in this section.
7. Remove or disconnect the following:

   - Secondary air injection (AIR) vacuum regulator electrical connector and hose, if equipped
   - Hoses from the AIR valve, if equipped
   - Upper exhaust sensor electrical connectors, if equipped
   - Exhaust gas recirculation (EGR) valve electrical connector
   - Coolant bypass
   - EGR coolant hose
   - Cylinder head bolts
   - Cylinder head

To install:

8. Inspect the cylinder head mating surfaces.
9. Apply silicone gasket sealant to the locations shown.
10. Install a new cylinder head gasket and cylinder head.
11. Using new bolts, tighten the cylinder bolts as follows:
    a. Step 1: 44 inch lbs. (5 Nm)
    b. Step 2: 11 ft. lbs. (15 Nm)
    c. Step 3: 33 ft. lbs. (45 Nm)
    d. Step 4: Plus 90 degrees
    e. Step 5: Plus 90 degrees again
12. Install or connect the following:
    - EGR coolant hose
    - Coolant bypass, using new gasket. Tighten to 89 inch lbs. (10 Nm).
    - EGR valve electrical connector
    - Catalytic converter, using new gasket and nuts. Tighten nuts to 41 ft. lbs. (55 Nm).
    - Exhaust sensor electrical connectors
    - Upper exhaust sensor electrical connectors, if equipped
    - Hoses to the AIR valve, if equipped

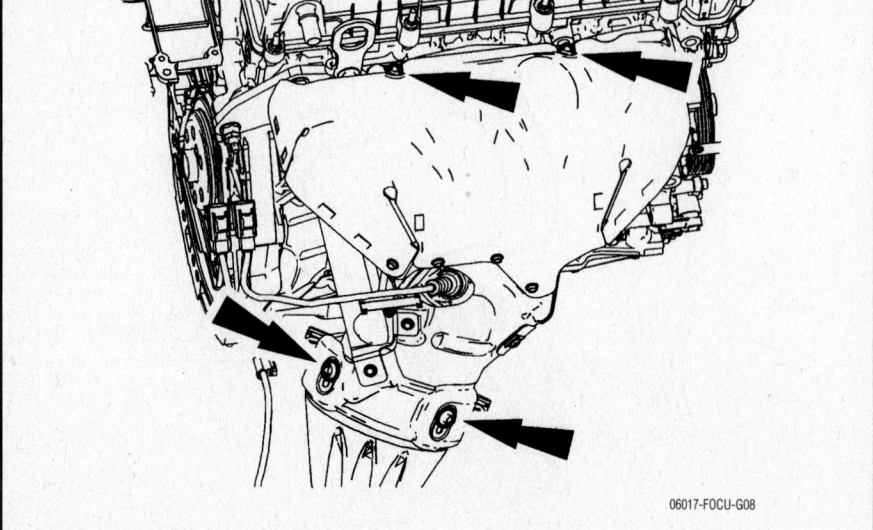

06017-FOCU-G08

Fig. 36 Removing the engine heat shield from 2.0L (VIN N) engines

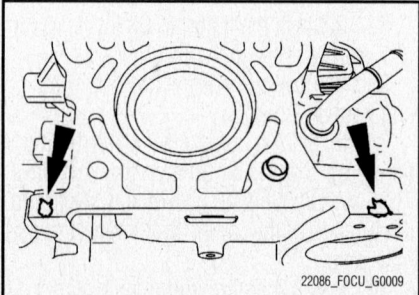

22086_FOCU_G0009

Fig. 38 Applying silicone gasket sealant for cylinder head installation

- Secondary air injection (AIR) vacuum regulator electrical connector and hose, if equipped
- Engine heat shield, if equipped
- Catalytic converter support bracket and tighten bolts to 35 ft. lbs. (47 Nm)
- Catalytic converter to muffler assembly, using new gasket and nuts
- Valve lifters and camshafts
- Intake manifold
- Fuel rail
- Alternator
- Cooling fan
- Battery tray
- Negative battery cable

13. Drain the engine oil.

14. Change the oil filter and fill the engine with oil.

15. Fill and bleed the cooling system to the correct level.

16. Start the engine and check for leaks.

2.3L (VIN Z) Engine

1. Before servicing the vehicle, refer to the Precautions Section.

2. Drain the cooling system.

3. Relieve the fuel system pressure.

4. Remove or disconnect the following:
- Negative battery cable
- Battery tray
- Cooling fan
- Catalytic converter from the muffler assembly
- Catalytic converter support bracket
- Engine heat shield
- Exhaust sensor electrical connectors
- Catalytic converter and secure it aside with mechanic's wire or equivalent
- Alternator
- Fuel rail
- Intake manifold
- Valve lifters
- Exhaust gas recirculation (EGR) valve electrical connector
- Coolant bypass
- EGR coolant hose
- Cylinder head bolts
- Cylinder head

To install:

5. Inspect the cylinder head mating surfaces.

6. Apply silicone gasket sealant to the locations shown.

7. Install a new cylinder head gasket and cylinder head.

8. Using new bolts, tighten the cylinder bolts as follows:

a. Step 1: 44 inch lbs. (5 Nm)
b. Step 2: 11 ft. lbs. (15 Nm)
c. Step 3: 33 ft. lbs. (45 Nm)
d. Step 4: Plus 90 degrees
e. Step 5: Plus 90 degrees again

9. Install or connect the following:
- EGR coolant hose
- Coolant bypass, using new gasket. Tighten to 89 inch lbs. (10 Nm).
- EGR valve electrical connector
- Catalytic converter, using new gasket and nuts. Tighten nuts to 41 ft. lbs. (55 Nm).
- Exhaust sensor electrical connectors
- Engine heat shield
- Catalytic converter support bracket and tighten bolts to 35 ft. lbs. (47 Nm)
- Catalytic converter to muffler assembly, using new gasket and nuts
- Valve lifters
- Intake manifold
- Fuel rail
- Alternator
- Cooling fan
- Battery tray
- Negative battery cable

10. Drain the engine oil.

11. Change the oil filter and fill the engine with oil.

12. Fill the cooling system to the correct level.

13. Start the engine and check for leaks.

ENGINE ASSEMBLY

REMOVAL & INSTALLATION

See Figures 39 through 45.

1. Before servicing the vehicle, refer to the Precautions Section.

2. Drain the engine oil. Reinstall the drain plug.

3. Drain the cooling system.

4. Relieve the fuel system pressure.

5. Recover the A/C refrigerant, if equipped.

6. Remove or disconnect the following:
- Battery and battery tray
- Accessory drive belt splash guard
- Accessory drive belt
- Catalytic converter from the muffler assembly
- Catalytic converter support bracket
- Catalytic convert heat shield, if equipped
- Exhaust sensor electrical connectors
- Upper exhaust sensor electrical connector and retainer, if equipped

- Secondary air injection (AIR) hose, if equipped
- Catalytic converter-to-engine nuts
- Vent tube from the air cleaner outlet pipe
- Air intake resonator
- Accelerator control snow shield
- Throttle cable
- Cruise control cable, if equipped
- Fuel supply hose quick release coupling from the fuel rail. Position the fuel hose aside.
- Evaporative emissions hose
- AIR hose, if equipped
- AIR vacuum regulator electrical connector, if equipped
- Power brake booster vacuum hose
- Exhaust Gas Recirculation (EGR) valve electrical connector
- Upper radiator hose
- Ground strap (near shock tower)
- Heater hoses
- Fuel charging wiring harness
- Power distribution wiring harness electrical connector
- Wiring harness retainers
- Power distribution wiring harness eyelet
- Three main engine wiring harness electrical connectors
- Gearshift cables from transmission and retaining bracket (M/T)
- Clutch slave cylinder supply hose (M/T)
- Reverse lamp switch electrical connector
- Transmission shifter cable and position it out of the way (A/T)
- Transmission cooler hoses (A/T)
- Heater hose from the "T" fitting and position it out of the way
- Coolant expansion tank
- Power steering pump pulley, using Special Tool 211-016
- Power steering pump (position out of the way)
- Cooling fan
- Lower radiator hose
- Ground strap connection at engine
- Alternator cooling pipe
- Starter motor electrical connectors
- Power steering pressure hose
- A/C compressor, if equipped
- Left hand brake hose support bracket
- Left hand brake caliper and support aside

7. Loosen the left hand strut and spring assembly top mounting bolts by four turns.

8. Disconnect the left hand stabilizer bar at the strut.

9. Remove the left and right tie rod end nuts.

10. Disconnect the both tie rods from the knuckles using special tool 211-001

11. Disconnect the lower control arms from the knuckles.

12. Remove the intermediate shaft and right hand half shaft assembly from the transmission.

13. Remove the left hand halfshaft from the transmission using Special Tools 100-001 and 205-241.

➡ **Support both halfshafts to one side with mechanic's wire or suitable equivalent.**

➡ **Install a plug into the transmission openings.**

14. Remove or disconnect the following:
   - Transmission roll restrictor
   - Starter and starter isolator
   - Two lower bell housing bolts
   - Two oil pan-to-bell housing bolts

15. Using Special Tool 014-0000, fasten the engine to the lift table

16. Remove or disconnect the following:
   - Motor mount nuts
   - Transmission mount center nut

17. Lower the engine and transmission assembly from the vehicle.

18. Disconnect the vehicle speed sensor (VSS) connector.

19. Heater hose from the "T" fitting and position it out of the way; mark one of the bolt to flexplate location for replacement reference (A/T).

20. Disconnect the output shaft speed (OSS) sensor, turbine shaft speed (TSS) sensor, the solenoid body and the transmission range (TR) sensor electrical connectors (A/T).

21. Lower the engine on the lifting table to within a few inches of the floor. Using the engine crane, remove the engine from the lift table.

22. Remove the remaining bell housing bolts and separate the engine and transmission (M/T).

23. Install the flywheel holding tool (307-346) to retain flywheel position (A/T).

To install:

24. On 2.0L with automatic transaxle, perform the following:
   a. Lubricate the torque converter pilot hub with multi-purpose grease.
   b. Check the depth of the torque converter position by laying a straightedge on the automatic transaxle flange.
   c. Check the installation depth between the transaxle flange and the

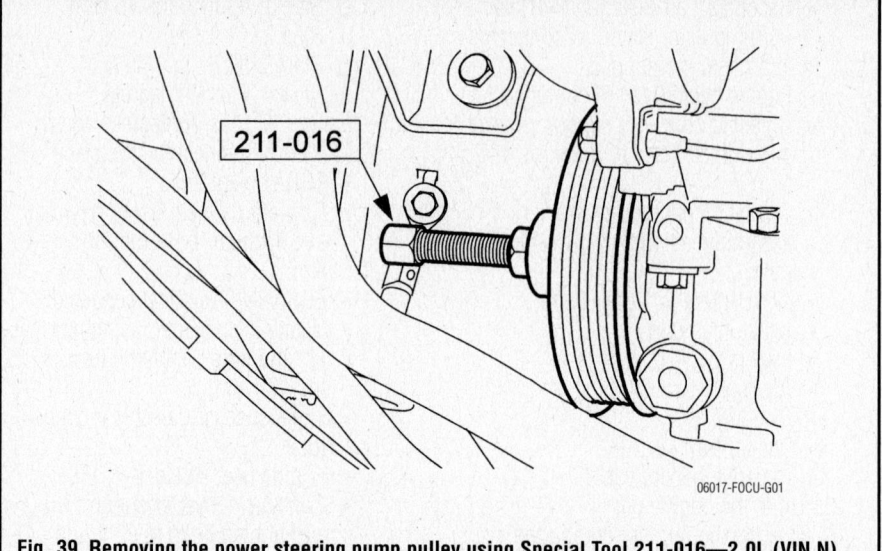

Fig. 39 Removing the power steering pump pulley using Special Tool 211-016—2.0L (VIN N).

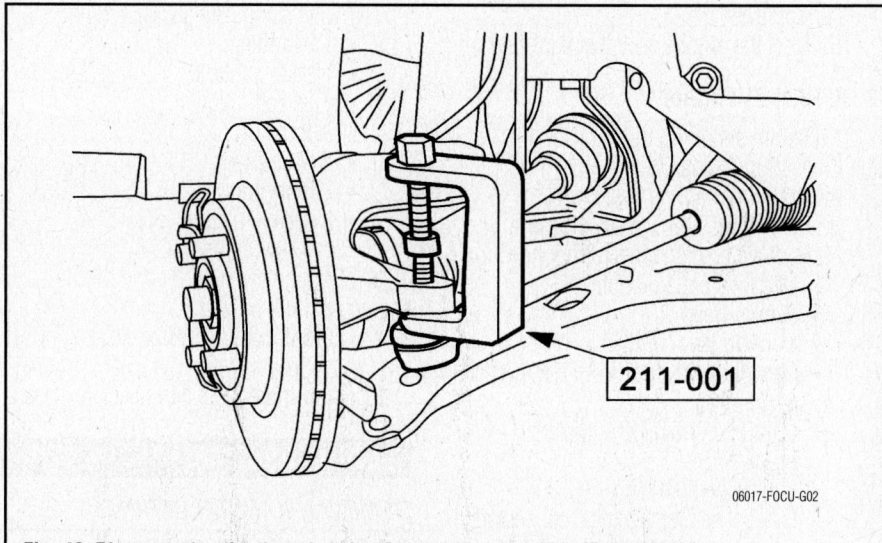

Fig. 40 Disconnecting the tie rods using Special Tool 211-001—2.0L (VIN N)

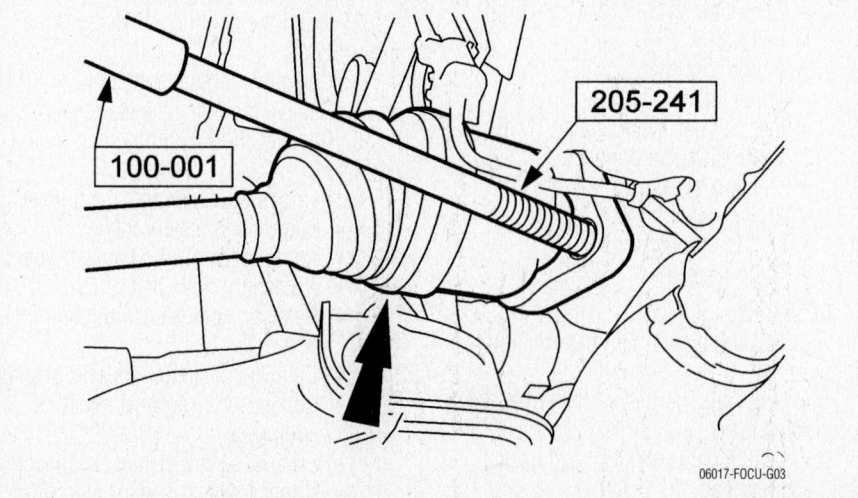

Fig. 41 Removing the left hand halfshaft from the transaxle using Removal Tools 100-001 and 205-241.

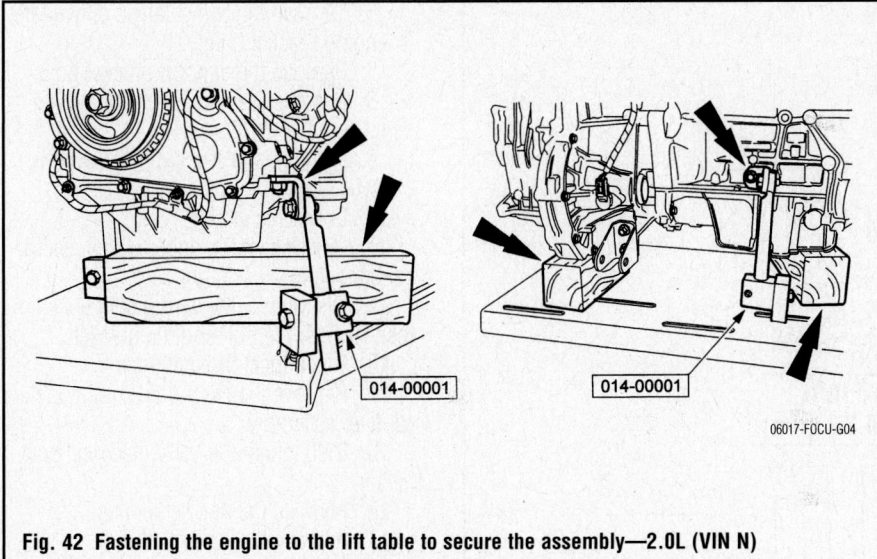

Fig. 42 Fastening the engine to the lift table to secure the assembly—2.0L (VIN N)

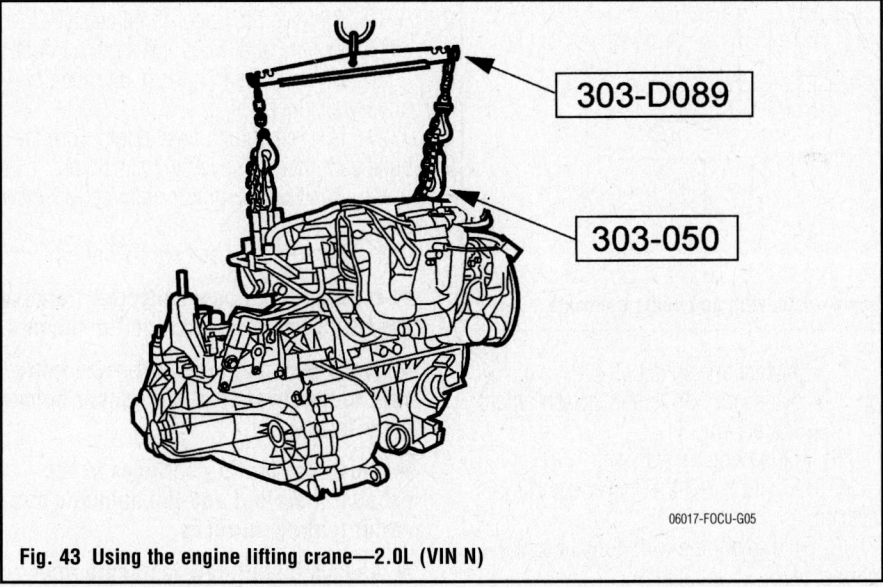

303-D089

303-050

Fig. 43 Using the engine lifting crane—2.0L (VIN N)

torque converter centering spigot for the correct clearance.

25. For all models, install new dowel pins in the engine block on either side of the flywheel.

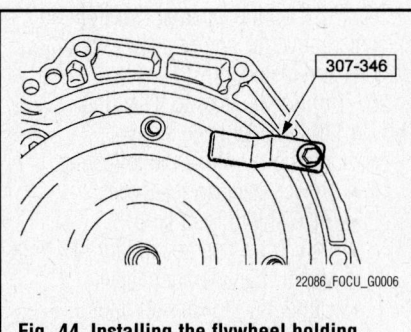

307-346

22086_FOCU_G0006

Fig. 44 Installing the flywheel holding tool—2.0L (VIN N) with automatic transaxle

26. Install the transmission onto the engine and tighten the bell housing bolts to 35 ft. lbs. (48 Nm).

27. Using engine crane, raise the engine and transmission assembly onto the lifting table.

28. Secure the engine assembly to the lift table using Special Tool 014-00001.

29. On 2.0L models with automatic transaxle, perform the following:

    a. Connect the solenoid body and transmission range (TR) sensor connectors.

    b. Connect Turbine shaft speed (TSS) connector.

    c. Connect the output shaft speed (OSS) connector.

    d. Install the four torque converter nuts and tighten to 26 ft. lbs. (35 Nm).

30. Using the lift table, position the engine and transmission assembly into the vehicle.

31. Connect the VSS connector (M/T).

32. Using the lift table, position the engine and transmission assembly into the vehicle.

33. Install or connect the following:

- Transmission center mount and nut and tighten to 98 ft. lbs. (133 Nm)
- Motor mount nuts and tighten to 59 ft. lbs. (80 Nm)
- Remaining bell housing bolts and tighten to 35 ft. lbs. (48 Nm)
- Starter motor isolator and starter motor. Tighten the bolts to 18 ft. lbs. (25 Nm).
- Transmission roll restrictor and tighten the bolts to 35 ft. lbs. (48 Nm)
- Left hand halfshaft
- Right hand halfshaft and intermediate shaft. Tighten the mounting bracket to 18 ft. lbs. (25 Nm).
- Lower control arms
- Tie rod ends
- Stabilizer bar at the struts

34. Tighten the left hand strut and spring assembly top mounting nuts to 18 ft. lbs. (25 Nm).

35. Install or connect the following:

- Brake caliper
- Brake hose support bracket
- A/C compressor, if equipped. Tighten the bolts to 18 ft. lbs. (25 Nm).
- PSP tube and tighten the nuts to 10 ft. lbs. (13 Nm)
- Starter motor electrical connections
- Alternator coolant pipe
- Engine ground cable and tighten to 35 ft. lbs. (48 Nm)
- Lower radiator hose
- Cooling fan
- Power steering pump and tighten to 13 ft. lbs. (18 Nm)

➡ Use new O-rings when connecting the PSP hose.

- Power steering pump pulley using Special Tool 211-185
- Coolant expansion tank
- Reversing lamp electrical connector
- Clutch slave cylinder supply hose
- Transmission cables
- Transmission cooler hoses (A/T)
- Automatic transaxle shifter cable (A/T)
- Three main wiring harness connectors
- Power distribution wiring harness eyelet
- Wiring harness retainers
- Power distribution wiring harness electrical connector

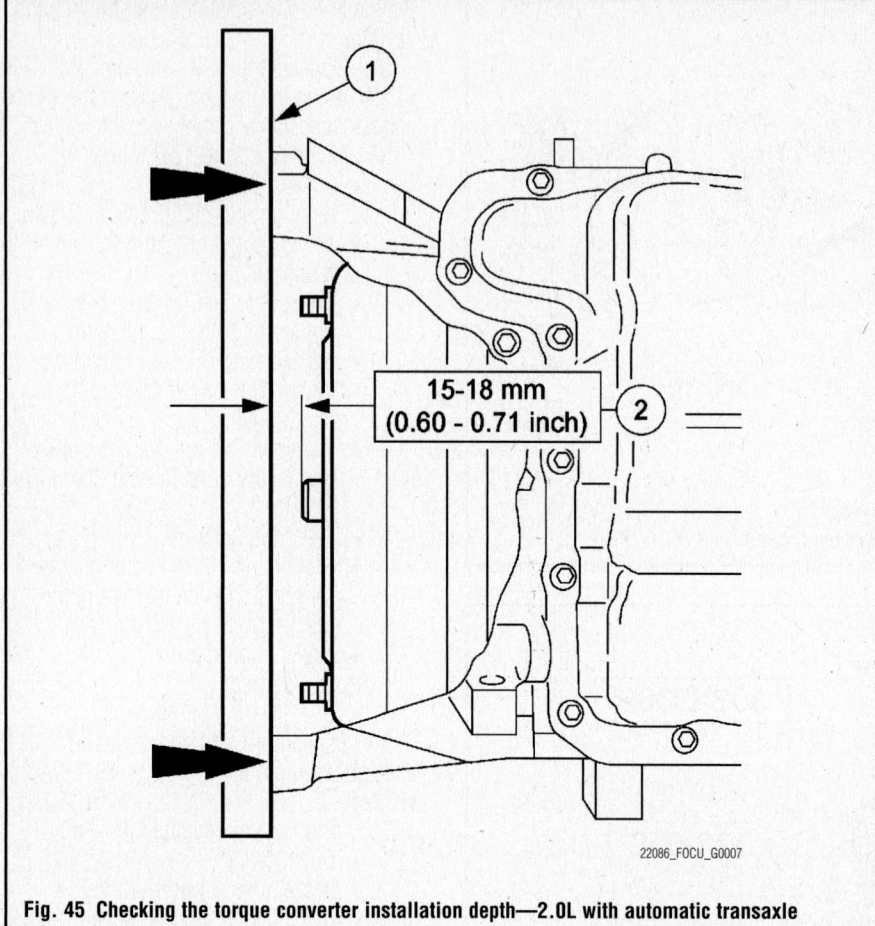

Fig. 45 Checking the torque converter installation depth—2.0L with automatic transaxle

- Fuel charging wiring harness
- Upper radiator hose
- Heater hoses
- Coolant vent hose
- EGR electrical connector
- Power brake booster vacuum hose
- Secondary AIR electrical connector, if equipped
- AIR hose, if equipped
- Evaporative emission hose
- Fuel supply hose
- Throttle cable
- Cruise control cable, if equipped
- Accelerator control snow shield and tighten to 89 inch lbs. (10 Nm)
- Air intake resonator
- Air cleaner outlet pipe
- Catalytic converter, using new gasket and nuts. Tighten to 41 ft. lbs. (55 Nm).
- Upper exhaust sensor electrical connector, if equipped
- Exhaust sensor electrical connectors
- Catalytic converter heat shield, if equipped
- Catalytic converter support bracket
- Catalytic converter to muffler assembly using a new gasket and nuts

- Accessory drive belt
- Accessory drive belt splash shield
- Battery tray

36. Fill the engine with oil.
37. Fill and bleed the power steering system.
38. Fill the engine with coolant to the correct level.
39. Charge the A/C system.
40. Start the engine and check for leaks.

EXHAUST MANIFOLD

REMOVAL & INSTALLATION

See Figure 46.

➡ **The exhaust manifold is integral to the catalytic converter.**

1. Before servicing the vehicle, refer to the Precautions Section.
2. Position the vehicle on a hoist.
3. Relieve the fuel system pressure.
4. Remove the two catalytic converter-to-muffler assembly flange nuts. Discard the nuts.
5. Disconnect the catalyst monitor and the Heated Oxygen Sensor (HO2S) electrical connectors.

6. Remove the two catalytic converter-to-engine bracket bolts.
7. Remove the support bracket bolts.
8. Remove the two lower heat shield screws.
9. Remove and discard the lower two catalytic converter nuts.
10. Lower the vehicle.
11. Disconnect the upper HO2S electrical connector.
12. Disconnect the wiring connector, then remove the bolt and the bracket.
13. Disconnect the fuel lines.
14. Remove the two bolts and the fuel canister assembly.
15. Disconnect the VMV electrical connector.
16. Remove the upper fuel line.
17. Remove the lower fuel line.
18. Remove the two VMV bolts and the VMV.
19. Remove the upper three catalytic converter nuts and studs. Discard the nuts.
20. Remove the PCV hose and the secondary air hose.
21. Disconnect the heat shield from the bulkhead, then remove the heat shield.
22. Position the power steering reservoir aside.
23. Remove the catalytic converter.

➡ **If installing a new converter, remove the HO2S and catalyst monitor sensors.**

➡ **Make sure to apply anti-seize lubricant to the threads of the sensor before installation.**

➡ **Clean the mating surfaces of the exhaust manifold and the catalytic converter mating surfaces.**

➡ **Always install new fasteners and gaskets.**

➡ **Do not tighten the fasteners until all components are assembled. Make sure to tighten all fasteners beginning at the front of the vehicle.**

To install:
24. Position the exhaust manifold and catalytic converter into position, with new gaskets and fasteners.
25. Tighten the nuts to 41 ft. lbs. (55 Nm) in the sequence shown.
26. Install or connect the following:
- Power steering reservoir
- Heat shield to bulkhead
- PCV hose and secondary AIR hose
- Vapor management valve
- Upper and lower fuel lines
- VMV electrical connector
- Fuel canister
- Fuel lines

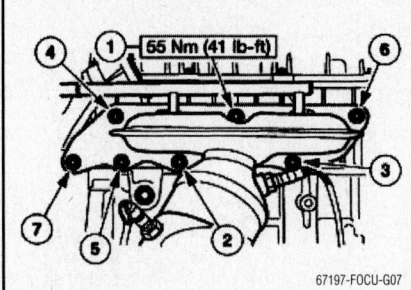

Fig. 46 Exhaust manifold/catalytic converter torque sequence—2.0L (VIN N) and 2.3L (VIN Z) engines

- Wiring harness connector
- HO2S connector

27. Raise and support the vehicle.
28. Install or connect the following:
- 2 lower catalytic converter nuts
- 2 lower heat shield screws
- Catalytic converter brackets

29. Lower the vehicle.

INTAKE MANIFOLD

REMOVAL & INSTALLATION

2.0L (VIN N) Engine

See Figures 47 and 48.

1. Before servicing the vehicle, refer to the Precautions Section.
2. Remove or disconnect the following:
- Cooling fan motor and shroud
- Lower intake manifold bolt
- Air cleaner outlet tube
- Accelerator control snow shield
- Emissions breather tube
- Throttle cable and cruise control cable, if equipped, from the throttle linkage
- Throttle position (TP) sensor electrical connector and position the wiring harness aside
- Idle air control (IAC) valve electrical connector and position the wiring harness aside
- Evaporative emissions hose
- Power brake booster vacuum hose
- Vacuum hose from the fuel pressure regulator
- Intake manifold runner control (IMRC) actuator electrical connector
- Manifold absolute pressure (MAP) sensor electrical connector
- Secondary air injection (AIR) vacuum supply hose, if equipped
- Swirl control valve electrical connector
- Oil level indicator tube

➡ **There are 3 different size bolts used. Mark the location of the bolts to ensure installation in the correct location.**

- Seven intake manifold bolts

3. Raise the intake manifold enough to gain clearance to disconnect the Knock Sensor (KS) wiring harness.
4. Disconnect the positive crankcase ventilation (PCV) hose.
5. Remove the exhaust gas recirculation (EGR) tube.
6. Remove the intake manifold.

To install:

7. Inspect and install new intake manifold gaskets, if necessary.
8. Position the intake manifold and install the PCV hose and then install the exhaust gas recirculation (EGR) tube. Tighten the EGR tube to 41 ft. lbs. (55 Nm).
9. Connect the KS wiring harness.

➡ **Be sure to install the bolts in the previously marked locations.**

10. Install the seven mounting bolts. Tighten the bolts to 13 ft. lbs. (18 Nm).
11. Install or connect the following:
- Oil level indicator tube
- Swirl control valve electrical connectors

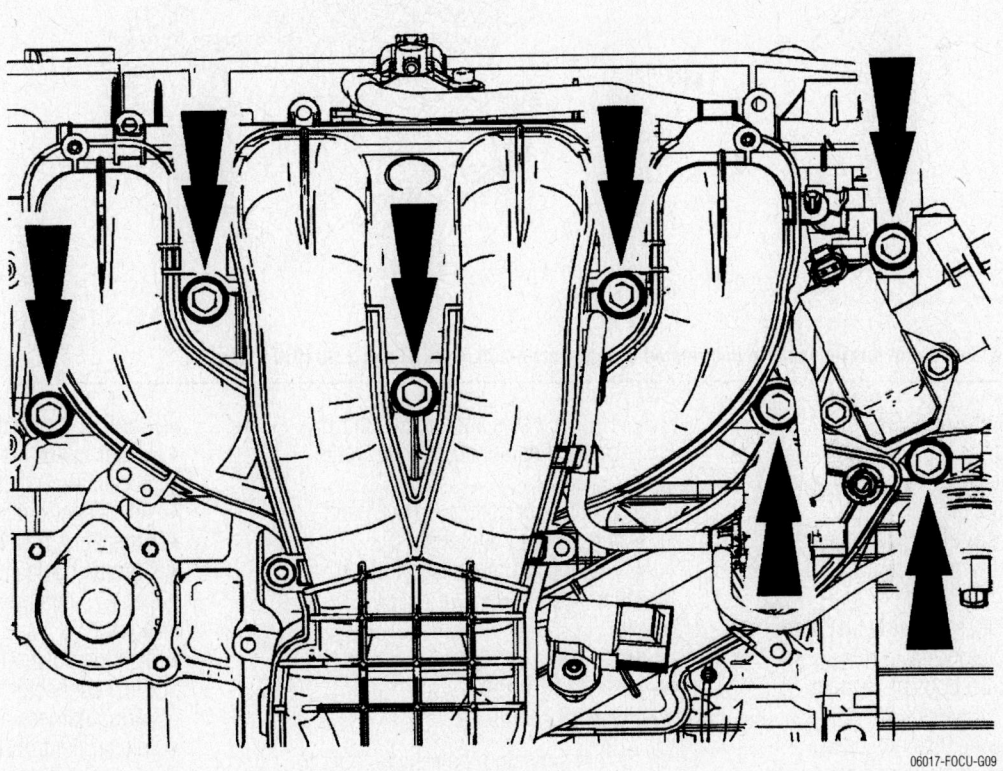

Fig. 47 Location of the intake manifold mounting bolts—2.0L (VIN N) engine.

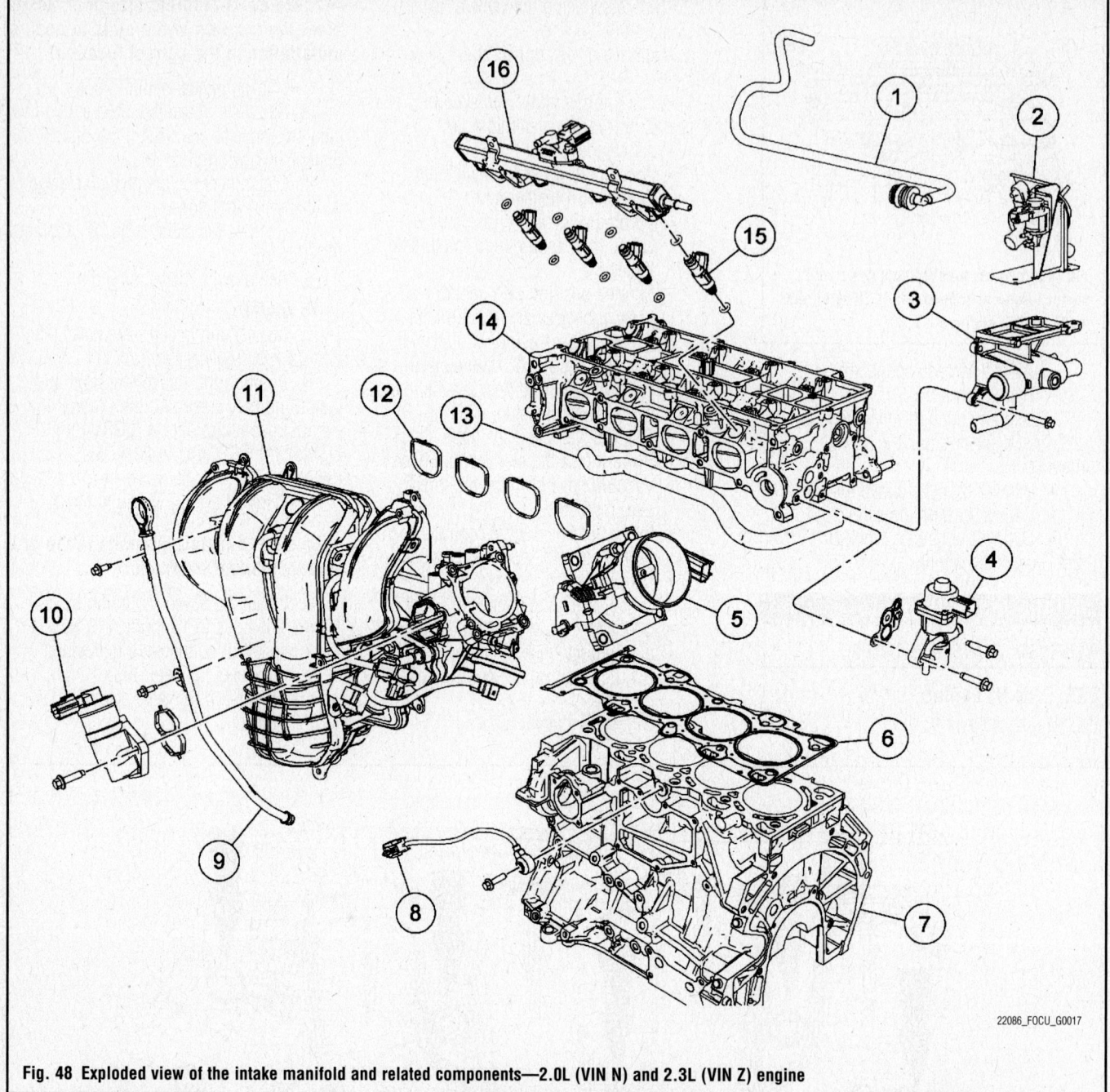

Fig. 48 Exploded view of the intake manifold and related components—2.0L (VIN N) and 2.3L (VIN Z) engine

- AIR vacuum supply hose, if equipped
- Lower intake bolt and tighten to 13 ft. lbs. (18 Nm)
- MAP sensor electrical connector
- IMRC actuator electrical connector
- Vacuum hose from the fuel pressure regulator
- Power brake booster vacuum hose
- Evaporative emissions hose
- IAC wiring harness and connector
- TP sensor electrical wiring harness and connector

- Throttle cable and cruise control cable, if equipped, to the throttle linkage
- Accelerator control snow shield
- Air cleaner outlet tube
- Cooling fan motor and shroud

12. Start the engine and check for leaks.

2.3L (VIN Z) Engine

See Figures 48 and 49.

1. Before servicing the vehicle, refer to the Precautions Section.
2. Remove or disconnect the following:

- Cooling fan motor and shroud
- Lower intake manifold bolt
- Accelerator control snow shield
- Air cleaner outlet tube
- Emissions breather tube
- Throttle cable and cruise control cable, if equipped, from the throttle linkage
- Throttle position (TP) sensor electrical connector and position the wiring harness aside
- Idle air control (IAC) valve electrical connector and position the wiring harness aside
- Evaporative emissions hose

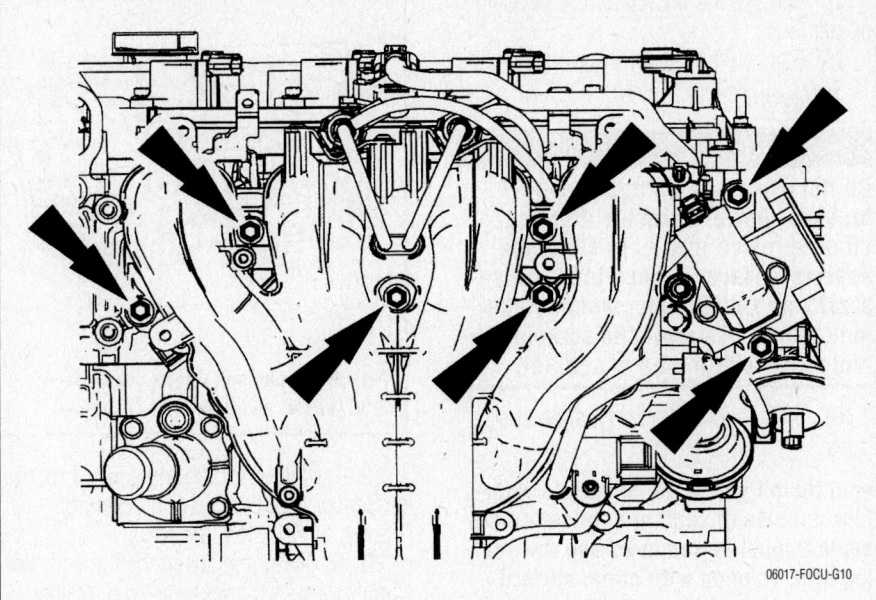

Fig. 49 Intake manifold mounting bolt locations—2.3L engine

- Power brake booster vacuum hose
- Vacuum hose from the fuel pressure regulator
- Intake manifold runner control (IMRC) actuator electrical connector
- Manifold absolute pressure (MAP) sensor electrical connector
- Swirl control valve electrical connectors and pin-type retainers
- Oil level indicator tube

➡There are 3 different size bolts used. Mark the location of the bolts to ensure installation in the correct location.

- Seven intake manifold bolts

3. Raise the intake manifold enough to gain clearance to disconnect the Knock Sensor (KS) wiring harness.

4. Disconnect the positive crankcase ventilation (PCV) hose.

5. Remove the exhaust gas recirculation (EGR) tube.

6. Remove the intake manifold.

To install:

7. Inspect and install new intake manifold gaskets, if necessary.

8. Position the intake manifold and install the PCV hose and then install the exhaust gas recirculation (EGR) tube. Tighten the EGR tube to 41 ft. lbs. (55 Nm).

9. Connect the KS wiring harness.

➡Be sure to install the bolts in the previously marked locations.

➡To ease the installation of the lower center mounting bolt, use a 6-inch long, 5⁄16-inch diameter hose.

10. Install the seven mounting bolts. Tighten the bolts to 13 ft. lbs. (18 Nm).

11. Install or connect the following:
- Oil level indicator tube
- Swirl control valve electrical connectors and pin-type retainers
- Lower intake bolt and tighten to 13 ft. lbs. (18 Nm)
- MAP sensor electrical connector
- IMRC actuator electrical connector
- Vacuum hose from the fuel pressure regulator
- Power brake booster vacuum hose
- Evaporative emissions hose
- IAC wiring harness and connector
- TP sensor electrical wiring harness and connector
- Throttle cable and cruise control cable, if equipped, to the throttle linkage
- Accelerator control snow shield
- Air cleaner outlet tube
- Cooling fan motor and shroud

12. Start the engine and check for leaks.

OIL PAN

REMOVAL & INSTALLATION

See Figures 50 through 56.

1. Before servicing the vehicle, refer to the Precautions Section.

2. With the vehicle in NEUTRAL, position it on a hoist.

3. Remove the battery tray.

4. Detach the 2 positive battery cable pin-type retainers and position aside.

5. Detach the transmission connector wire harness pin-type retainer and position aside.

6. Remove the nut from the Heated Oxygen Sensor (HO2S) and catalyst monitor sensor wire connector bracket.

7. Remove the nut and position the HO2S and catalyst monitor sensor wire connector bracket aside.

8. Loosen the upper bellhousing-to-engine bolt and stud bolt 0.19 in. (5mm) maximum.

9. Remove the oil level indicator and tube.

10. Loosen the 2 (automatic transaxle) or 3 (manual transaxle) front lower bellhousing-to-engine bolts 0.19 in. (5mm).

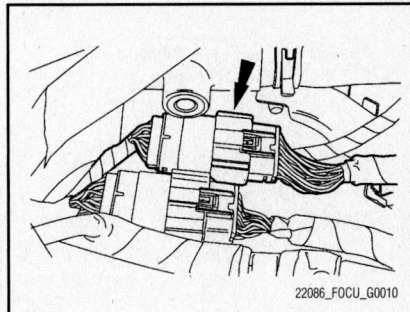

Fig. 50 Detach the transmission connector wire harness pin-type retainer and position aside

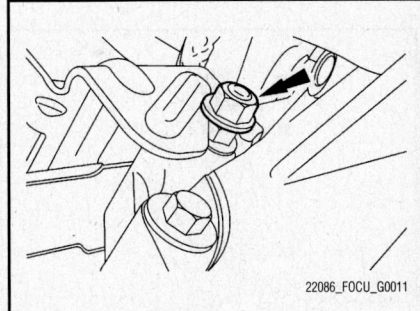

Fig. 51 Remove the nut from the Heated Oxygen Sensor (HO2S) and catalyst monitor sensor wire connector bracket

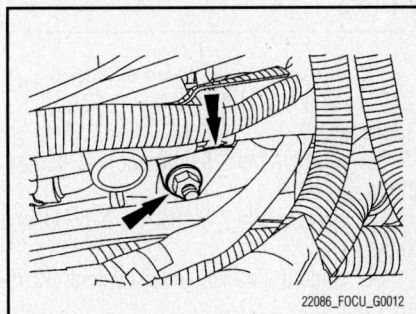

Fig. 52 Remove the nut and position the HO2S and catalyst monitor sensor wire connector bracket aside

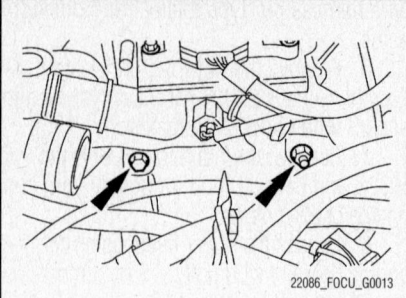

Fig. 53 Loosen the upper bellhousing-to-engine bolt and stud bolt 0.19 in. (5mm) maximum

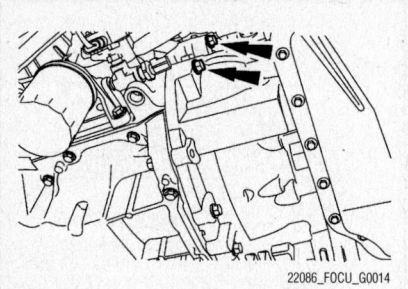

Fig. 54 Loosen the 2 (automatic transaxle) or 3 (manual transaxle) front lower bellhousing-to-engine bolts 0.19 in. (5mm)

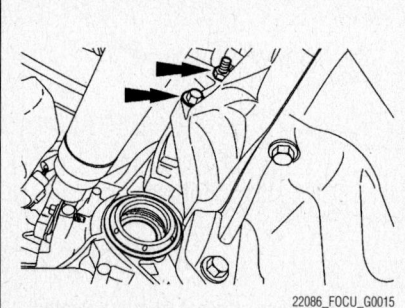

Fig. 55 Loosen the rear lower engine-to-bellhousing bolt and stud bolt 0.19 in. (5mm)

11. Loosen the rear lower engine-to-bellhousing bolt and stud bolt 0.19 in. (5mm).

12. Remove the 2 bellhousing-to-oil pan bolts and the 2 oil pan bolts.

13. Remove the 2 oil pan-to-bellhousing bolts.

14. Slide the transmission rearward 0.19 in. (5mm).

15. Remove the 2 bolts and the accessory drive belt splash shield.

16. Drain the engine oil. Install the drain plug; tighten to 21 ft. lbs. (28 Nm).

17. Remove the 4 engine front cover-to-oil pan bolts.

18. Remove the 11 bolts and the oil pan.

To install:

※ CAUTION

Do not use metal scrapers, wire brushes, power abrasive discs or other abrasive means to clean the sealing surfaces. These tools cause scratches and gouges, which make leak paths. Use a plastic scraping tool to remove traces of sealant.

19. Clean and inspect all mating surfaces.

➡ **If the oil pan is not secured within four minutes of sealant application the sealant must be removed and the sealing area cleaned with metal surface cleaner. Allow to dry until there is no sign of wetness, or four minutes, whichever is longer. Failure to follow this procedure can cause future oil leakage.**

20. Apply a 2.5mm bead of silicone gasket and sealant to the entire oil pan mating surface, avoiding the bolt holes.

21. Position the oil pan onto the engine and install the oil pan bolts finger-tight.

22. Install the 4 engine front cover-to-oil pan bolts. Tighten to 89 inch lbs. (10 Nm).

23. Tighten the oil pan bolts in sequence to 18 ft. lbs. (25 Nm).

24. Install the accessory drive belt splash shield and the 2 bolts.

25. Alternately tighten the 1 front bellhousing-to-engine and 1 rear engine-to-bellhousing lower bolts to slide the transmission and engine together. Tighten to 35 ft. lbs. (48 Nm).

26. Tighten the remaining 1 (automatic transaxle) or 2 (manual transaxle) lower front bellhousing-to-engine bolts. Tighten to 35 ft. lbs. (48 Nm).

27. Tighten the remaining rear engine-to-bellhousing stud bolt. Tighten to 35 ft. lbs. (48 Nm).

28. Install the 2 bellhousing-to-oil pan bolts and the 2 oil pan-to-bellhousing bolts. Tighten to 35 ft. lbs. (48 Nm).

29. Install the oil level indicator and tube.

30. Tighten the top bellhousing-to-engine bolt and stud bolt to 35 ft. lbs. (48 Nm).

31. Position the HO2S and catalyst monitor sensor wire connector bracket and install the nut. Tighten to 18 ft. lbs. (25 Nm).

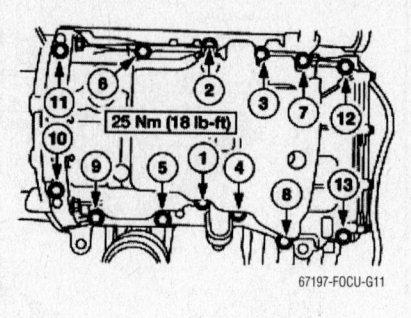

Fig. 56 Oil pan bolt torque sequence—2.0L (VIN N) and 2.3L (VIN Z) engines

32. Install the HO2S and catalyst monitor sensor wire connector bracket nut. Tighten to 18 ft. lbs. (25 Nm).

33. Position and attach the transmission connector wire harness pin-type retainer.

34. Position and attach the 2 positive battery cable pin-type retainers.

35. Install the battery tray.

36. Fill the engine with new oil.

OIL PUMP

REMOVAL & INSTALLATION

See Figure 57.

1. Before servicing the vehicle, refer to the Precautions Section.

2. Remove the engine from the vehicle and mount it on an engine stand.

3. Remove or disconnect the following:
- Oil pan
- Oil pump pickup tube and screen
- Front cover and the timing chain

4. Release the tension on the tensioner spring.

5. Remove the tensioner and the shoulder bolt.

6. Remove the guide.

➡**The oil pump chain sprocket must be held in place.**

7. Remove the following:
- Oil pump chain and sprockets
- Oil pump assembly and gasket

To install:

8. Install the oil pump with a new gasket. Tighten the bolts in sequence as follows:
- a. Step 1: 89 inch lbs. (10 Nm).
- b. Step 2: 17 ft. lbs. (23 Nm).

9. Install the pump chain and sprockets. Tighten the pump sprocket bolt to 18 ft. lbs. (25 Nm).

10. Install the chain guide, tensioner, and shoulder bolt. Tighten the bolts to 89 inch lbs. (10 Nm).

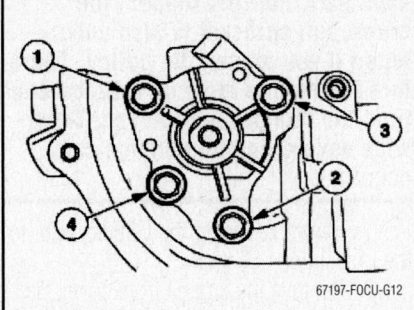

Fig. 57 Oil pump torque sequence—2.0L (VIN N) and 2.3L (VIN Z) engines

11. Hook the tensioner spring around the shoulder bolt.

12. Install the oil pump pickup tube and screen with a new gasket. Tighten the bolts to 89 ft. lbs. (10 Nm).

13. Install the oil pan.

14. Install the timing chain and front cover.

15. Install the engine into the vehicle.

PISTON AND RING

POSITIONING

See Figure 58.

REAR MAIN SEAL

REMOVAL & INSTALLATION

See Figures 59 and 60.

1. Before servicing the vehicle, refer to the Precautions Section.

2. Remove the transaxle.

3. Remove the flywheel or flexplate.

4. Remove the oil level indicator and tube.

✳✳ CAUTION

If the oil pan is not removed, damage to the rear seal retainer joint can occur.

5. Remove the oil pan.

6. Remove the bolts and the crankshaft rear oil seal.

To install:

7. Install the crankshaft rear oil seal on the Crankshaft Rear Main Oil Seal Installer 303-328.

8. Install the Crankshaft Rear Main Oil Seal Installer and the crankshaft rear oil seal on the crankshaft. Tighten the bolts, in the sequence shown, to 10 Nm (89 inch lbs.).

9. Remove the Crankshaft Rear Main Oil Seal Installer.

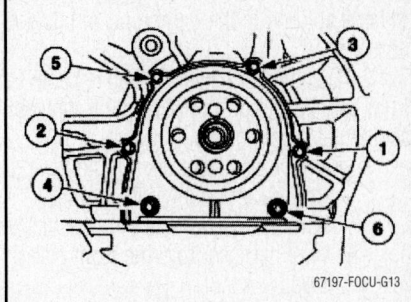

Fig. 59 Seal retainer torque sequence—2.0L (VIN N) and 2.3L (VIN Z) engine

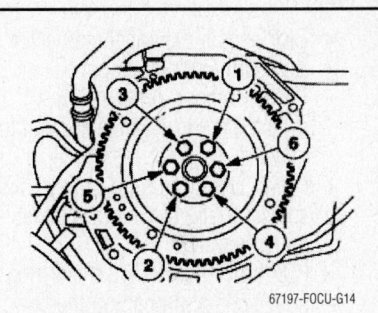

Fig. 60 Flywheel/Flexplate torque sequence—2.0L (VIN N) and 2.3L (VIN Z) engine

10. Install the oil pan.

11. Install the flywheel or flexplate. Tighten the bolts in the sequence shown as follows:.

   a. Step 1: Tighten to 37 ft. lbs. (50 Nm).

   b. Step 2: Tighten to 50 ft. lbs. (80 Nm).

   c. Step 3: Tighten to 83 ft. lbs. (112 Nm).

12. Install the transaxle.

13. Fill the engine with clean oil.

TIMING CHAIN COVER AND SEAL

REMOVAL & INSTALLATION

2.0L (VIN N) and 2.3L (VIN Z) Engine

See Figure 61.

✳✳ WARNING

The crankshaft, the crankshaft sprocket and the pulley are fitted together by friction, using diamond washers between the flange faces on each part. For that reason, the crankshaft sprocket is also unfastened if you loosen the pulley. Therefore the engine must be retimed each time the damper is removed. Otherwise severe engine damage can occur.

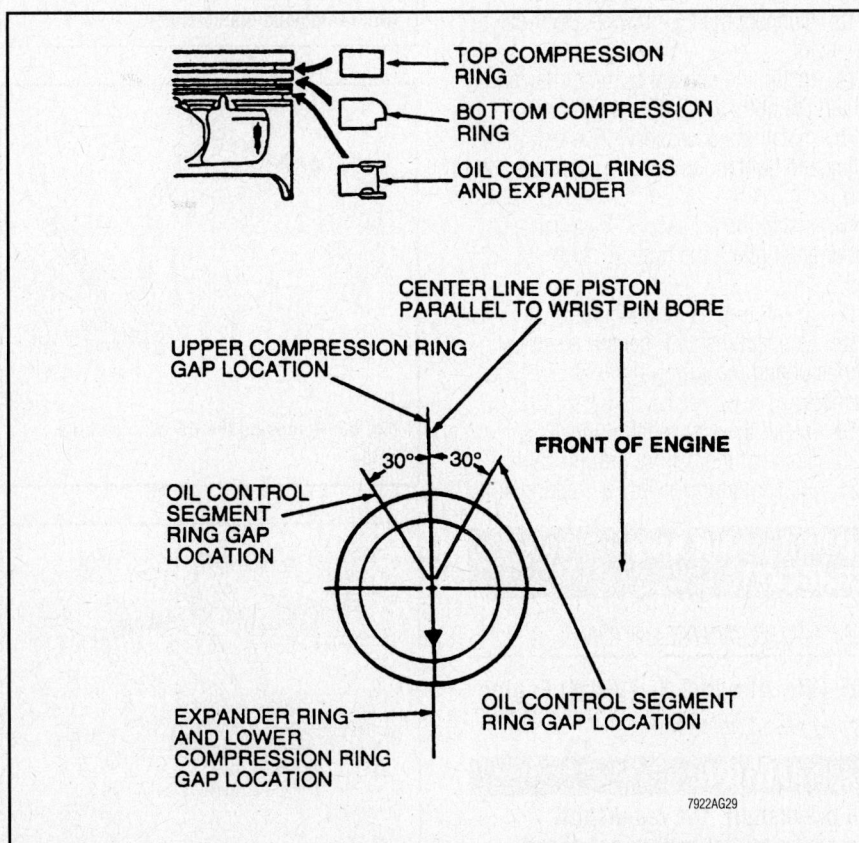

Fig. 58 Ford 2.0L (VIN N) and 2.3L (VIN Z) engines—piston ring positioning, end-gap spacing and piston positioning. The small directional arrow must face the front of the engine.

1. Before servicing the vehicle, refer to the precautions in the beginning of this section.

2. Disconnect battery negative cable from battery and properly isolate to prevent accidental reconnection.

3. Remove or disconnect the following:
- Crankshaft pulley/damper; see "Crankshaft Damper" in this section
- Wire harness from the front cover studs

➡️If the crankshaft position (CKP) sensor is damaged during engine front cover removal a new CKP sensor must be installed.

- CKP sensor electrical connector
- Accessory belt tensioner
- Power steering pressure (PSP) switch electrical connector and tube bracket
- Power steering pump pulley using special tool 211-016 or a suitable pulley remover
- PSP tube and discard the O-ring
- Four bolts and position the power steering pump aside
- Coolant pump pulley
- RH motor mount
- Accessory drive belt idler pulley
- Retainers and the engine front cover

To install:

❋❋ WARNING

Do not use metal scrapers, wire brushes, power abrasive disks or other abrasive means to clean sealing surfaces. These tools cause scratches and gouges which make leak paths.

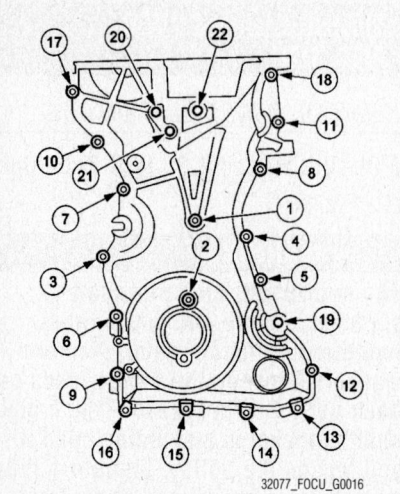

Fig. 61 Tightening sequence of front cover bolts

4. Clean and inspect the mounting surfaces of the engine and the front cover.

➡️**The engine front cover must be installed and the bolts tightened within four minutes of applying the silicone gasket and sealant.**

5. Apply a 2.5-mm bead of silicone gasket and sealant to the cylinder head and oil pan joint areas.

6. Apply a 2.5-mm bead of silicone gasket and sealant to the front cover.

7. Install the front cover. Tighten the bolts in the sequence shown to the following specifications:
- Tighten the 8 mm bolts to 89 inch lbs. (10 Nm)
- Tighten the 13 mm bolts to 35 ft. lbs. (48 Nm)

8. Position the power steering pump and tighten the bolts to 18 ft. lbs. (25 Nm)

9. Install a new O-ring on the PSP tube fitting.

10. Connect the power steering PSP tube fitting and tighten the nut to 15 ft. lbs. (20 Nm)

11. Install the power steering pump pulley using special tool 211-185 or a suitable pulley installer.

12. Attach the PSP tube bracket and tighten the nut to 10 inch lbs. (13 Nm)

13. Connect the PSP switch electrical connector.

14. Install the coolant pump pulley and tighten the bolts to 18 ft. lbs. (25 Nm)

15. Install the accessory drive belt idler pulley and tighten the bolts to 18 ft. lbs. (25 Nm)

16. Install the accessory drive belt tensioner and tighten the bolts to 18 ft. lbs. (25 Nm)

17. Install the RH motor mount

18. Connect the CKP sensor electrical connector and the wiring harness pin-type retainers.

19. Install the crankshaft pulley.

20. Connect the battery ground cable.

21. Fill and purge the power steering fluid.

TIMING CHAIN AND SPROCKETS

REMOVAL & INSTALLATION

2.0L (VIN N) and 2.3L (VIN Z) Engine

See Figures 62 through 67.

❋❋ CAUTION

The crankshaft, the crankshaft sprocket and the pulley are fitted together by friction, using diamond washers between the flange faces on

each part. For that reason, the crankshaft sprocket is also unfastened if you loosen the pulley. Therefore the engine must be retimed each time the damper is removed. Otherwise severe engine damage can occur.

1. Before servicing the vehicle, refer to the Precautions Section.

2. Remove the engine front cover. See "Timing Chain Cover and Seal" in this section.

3. Remove the timing chain tensioner:
   a. Compress the timing chain tensioner and insert a paper clip into the hole.

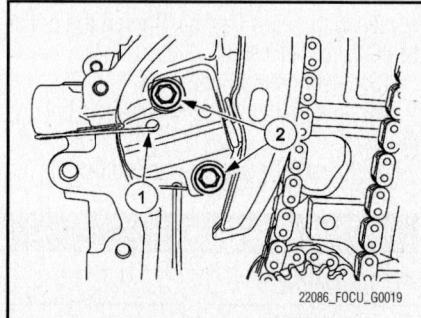

Fig. 62 Removing the timing chain tension, using a paper clip (1) as a holder while removing the bolts (2)

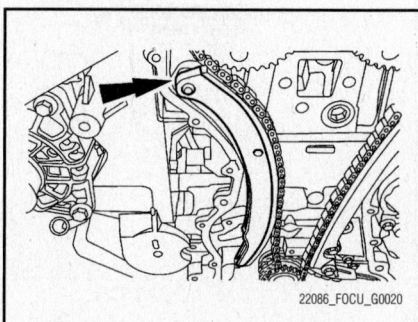

Fig. 63 Removing the RH timing chain guide

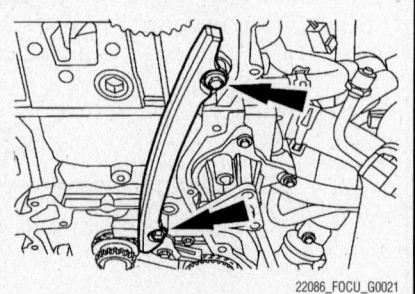

Fig. 64 Removing the LH timing chain guide

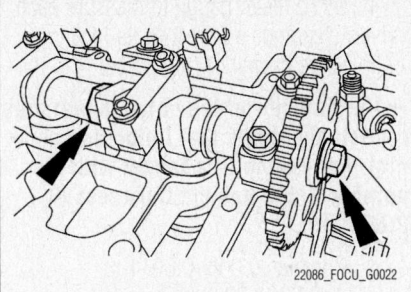

Fig. 65 If necessary, remove the bolts and the camshaft sprockets. Use the flats on the camshaft to prevent camshaft rotation

22086_FOCU_G0022

b. Remove the bolts and timing chain tensioner.

4. Remove the RH timing chain guide.

5. Remove the timing chain.

6. Remove the bolts and the LH timing chain guide.

7. If necessary, remove the bolts and the camshaft sprockets. Use the flats on the camshaft to prevent camshaft rotation.

To install:

8. If installed on the camshaft, remove the special holding tool.

✳✳ CAUTION

Do not rotate the camshafts. Damage to the valves and pistons can occur.

9. If the camshaft sprockets were not removed, use the flats on the camshafts to prevent camshaft rotation and loosen the sprocket bolts.

10. If removed, install the camshaft sprockets and the bolts. Do not tighten the bolts at this time.

11. Install the LH timing chain guide and bolts. Tighten to 89 inch lbs. (10 Nm).

12. Install the timing chain.

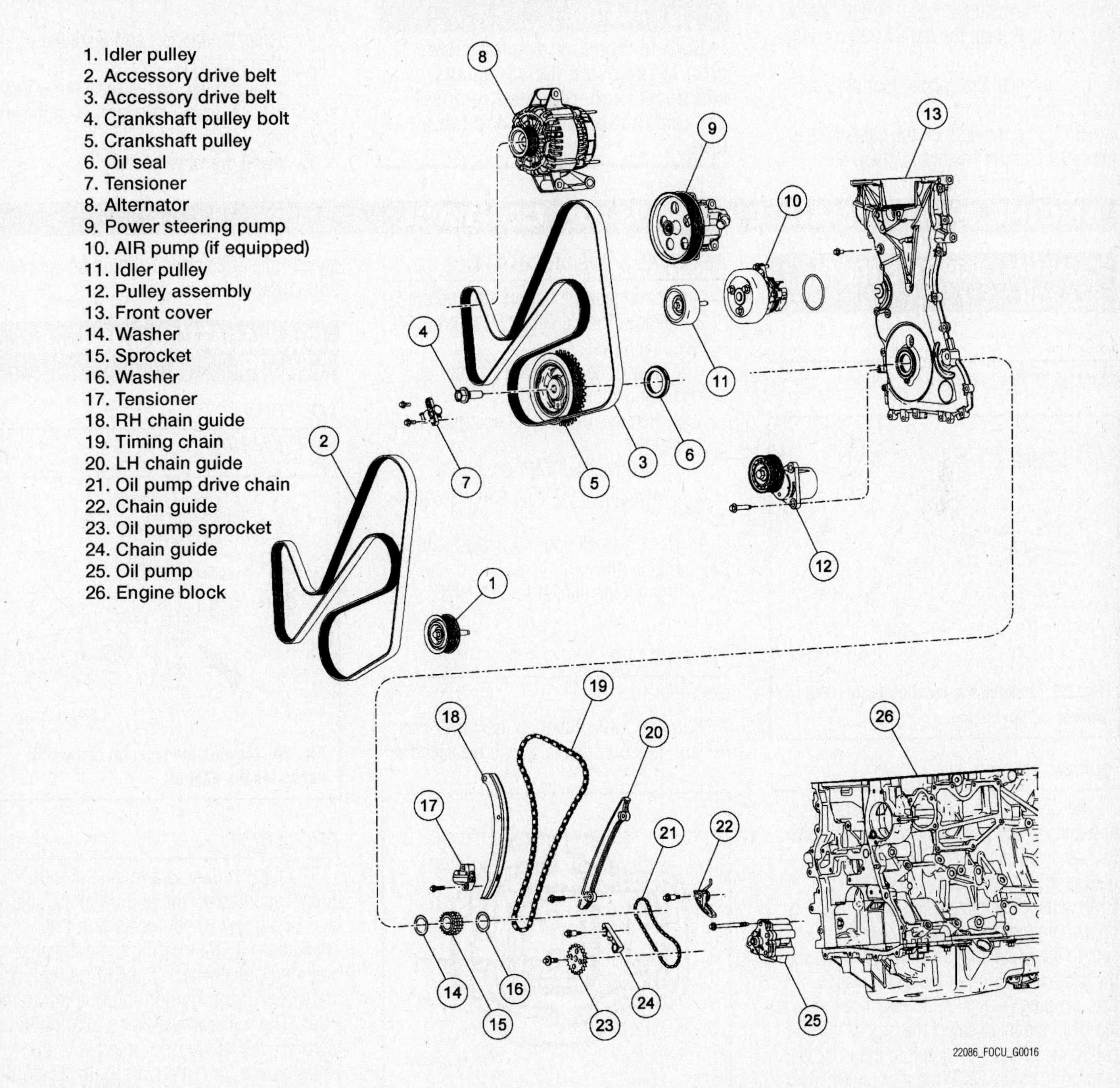

1. Idler pulley
2. Accessory drive belt
3. Accessory drive belt
4. Crankshaft pulley bolt
5. Crankshaft pulley
6. Oil seal
7. Tensioner
8. Alternator
9. Power steering pump
10. AIR pump (if equipped)
11. Idler pulley
12. Pulley assembly
13. Front cover
14. Washer
15. Sprocket
16. Washer
17. Tensioner
18. RH chain guide
19. Timing chain
20. LH chain guide
21. Oil pump drive chain
22. Chain guide
23. Oil pump sprocket
24. Chain guide
25. Oil pump
26. Engine block

Fig. 66 Exploded view of the front cover, timing chain, oil pump and related components—2.0L (VIN N) and 2.3L (VIN Z) engine

22086_FOCU_G0016

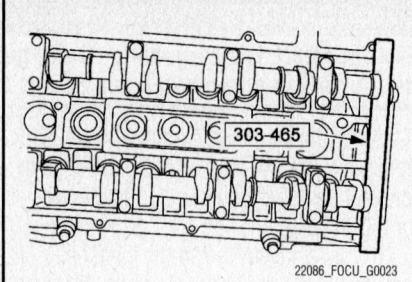

Fig. 67 Reinstall the special tool onto the camshafts

13. Install the RH timing chain guide.

14. Install the timing chain tensioner and the bolts. Remove the paper clip to release the piston. Tighten the bolts to 89 inch lbs. (10 Nm).

15. Reinstall the special tool onto the camshafts.

16. Using the flats on the camshafts to prevent camshaft rotation, tighten the camshaft sprocket bolts to 53 ft. lbs. (72 Nm).

17. Install the front cover. See "Timing Chain Cover and Seal".

VALVE LASH

INSPECTION/ADJUSTMENT

1. Before servicing the vehicle, refer to the Precautions Section.

2. Remove the valve cover.

3. Measure each valve's clearance at base circle, with the lobe pointed away from the tappet, before removing the camshafts.

☀☀ CAUTION

Failure to measure all clearances prior to removing the camshafts will necessitate repeated removal and installation and wasted labor time.

4. Use a feeler gauge to measure each valve's clearance and record its location.

5. Valve clearance should be:

➡**The number on the valve tappet only reflects the digits that follow the decimal. For example, a tappet with the number 0.650 has the thickness of 3.650 mm.**

- Intake: 0.008–0.0011 in. (0.22–0.28 mm)
- Exhaust: 0.010–0.013 in. (0.27–0.33 mm)

6. Select tappets using this formula: tappet thickness = measured clearance + the base tappet thickness - most desirable thickness.

7. Select the tappets and mark the installation location.

8. If any tappets do not measure within specifications, install new tappets in these locations.

9. Install the valve cover.

ENGINE PERFORMANCE & EMISSION CONTROL

CAMSHAFT POSITION (CMP) SENSOR

LOCATION

See Figure 68.

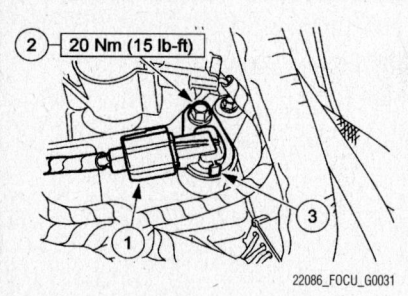

Fig. 68 Showing the location of the CMP sensor on the engine

OPERATION

The CMP sensor provides camshaft position information which is used by the PCM for fuel synchronization. The CMP sensor detects the position of the camshaft. The CMP sensor identifies when piston No. 1 is on its compression stroke. A signal is then sent to the PCM and used for synchronizing the sequential firing of the fuel injectors. Coil-on-plug (COP) ignition applications use the CMP signal to select the proper ignition coil to fire. The input circuit to the PCM is referred to as the CMP input or circuit. DTC P0340 is associated with this sensor.

REMOVAL & INSTALLATION

1. Disconnect the battery ground cable.

2. Remove the Camshaft Position (CMP) sensor as follows:

   a. Disconnect the CMP sensor electrical connector (1).

   b. Remove the bolt retaining the CMP sensor (2).

   c. Remove the CMP sensor (3).

3. To install, reverse the removal procedure.

4. Use a new O-ring, lubricated with clean engine oil.

5. Tighten the sensor to 15 ft. lbs. (20 Nm).

TESTING

See Figure 69.

With the CMP sensor connector disconnected, measure the resistance between the

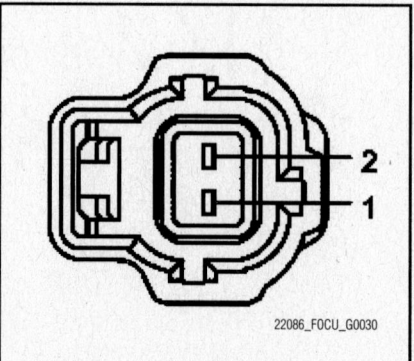

Fig. 69 Showing the CMP sensor pins

sensor pins. Resistance should be between 250–1000 ohms.

CRANKSHAFT POSITION (CKP) SENSOR

LOCATION

See Figure 70.

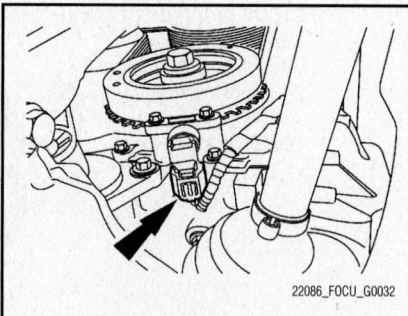

Fig. 70 Showing the location of the CKP sensor on the engine

OPERATION

The CKP sensor is a magnetic transducer mounted on the engine block adjacent to a pulse wheel located on the crankshaft. By monitoring the crankshaft mounted pulse wheel, the CKP is the primary sensor for ignition information to the PCM. The pulse wheel has a total of 35 teeth spaced 10 degrees apart with one empty space for a missing tooth. The 6.8L 10-cylinder pulse wheel has 39 teeth spaced 9 degrees apart and one 9 degree empty space for a missing tooth. By monitoring the pulse wheel, the CKP sensor signal indicates crankshaft position and speed information to the PCM. By monitoring the missing tooth, the CKP sensor is also able to identify piston travel in order to synchronize the ignition system and provide a way of tracking the angular position of the crankshaft relative to a fixed reference for the CKP sensor configuration. The PCM also uses the CKP signal to determine if a misfire has occurred by measuring rapid decelerations between teeth.

REMOVAL & INSTALLATION

See Figures 71 through 73.

1. With the vehicle in NEUTRAL, position it on a hoist.
2. Disconnect the battery ground cable.
3. Remove the two retaining screws and the crankshaft pulley shield.
4. Disconnect the crankshaft position (CKP) sensor electrical connector.
5. Remove the engine plug bolt.
6. Turn the crankshaft pulley bolt to position the number one cylinder at top dead center, and install the special tool into the engine plug bolt bore.
7. Remove the CKP sensor retaining bolts and the sensor.

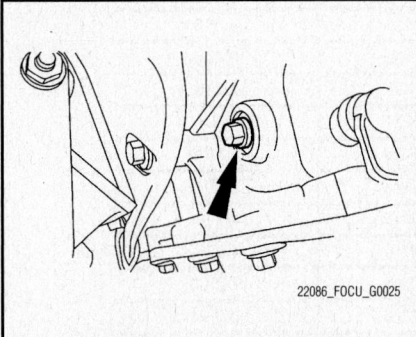

Fig. 71 Remove the engine plug bolt

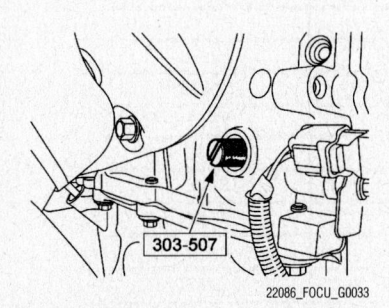

Fig. 72 Install the special tool into the engine plug bolt bore

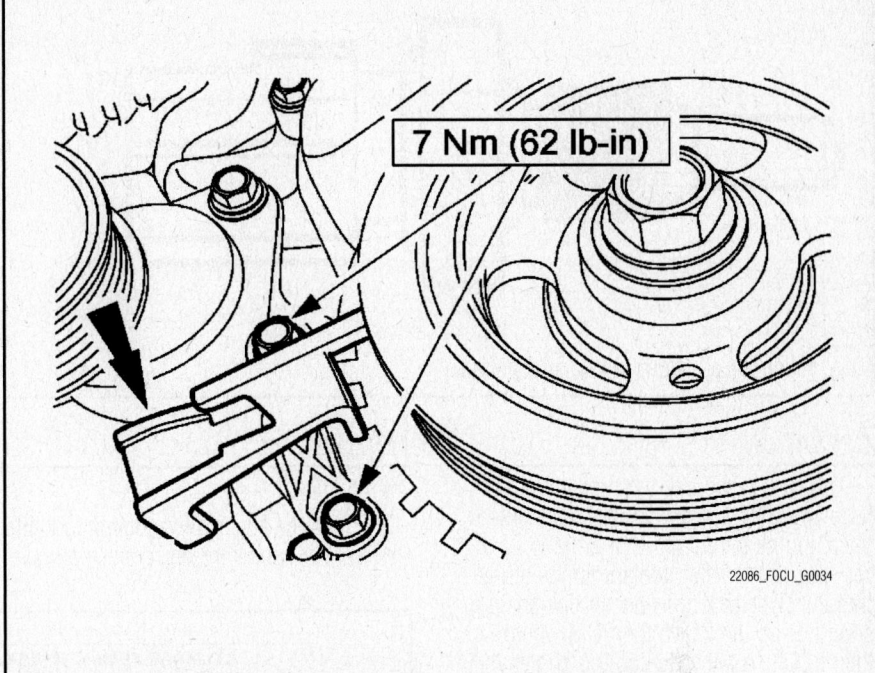

Fig. 73 Adjust the CKP sensor with the alignment tool and tighten the bolts

8. Install and hand-tighten a 6 mm x 18 mm standard bolt into the crankshaft damper to hold its position.

To install:

➡**Whenever the crankshaft position (CKP) sensor is removed, a new one must be installed using the alignment tool supplied with the new part.**

9. Install a new CKP sensor, but do not tighten the bolts at this time.

➡**The crankshaft position (CKP) sensor alignment tool is supplied with the new sensor and is not available separately.**

10. Adjust the CKP sensor with the alignment tool and tighten the bolts.
11. Connect the CKP sensor electrical connector.
12. Remove the holding bolt from the crankshaft damper.
13. Remove the special tool from the engine plug bolt bore.
14. Install the engine plug bolt and tighten to 15 ft. lbs. (20 Nm).
15. Install the crankshaft pulley shield.

TESTING

See Figure 74.

1. With the CKP sensor connector disconnected, the Key ON and the engine

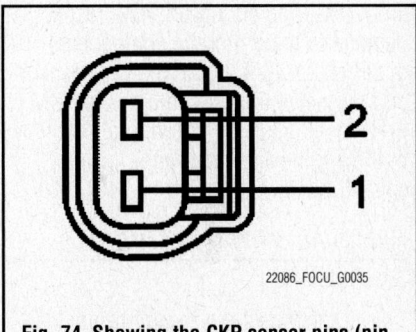

Fig. 74 Showing the CKP sensor pins (pin 1 is negative; pin 2 is positive)

OFF, measure the voltage between the sensor pins on the harness side of the connector. Voltage should be between 1–3 volts.

2. With Key in OFF position, disconnect the CKP sensor connector and measure the resistance between the sensor pins. The CKP sensor resistance values change significantly with temperature rise. The resistance should be between 250–1000 ohms.

CYLINDER HEAD TEMPERATURE (CHT) SENSOR

LOCATION

See Figure 75.

The CHT sensor is installed in the aluminum cylinder head.

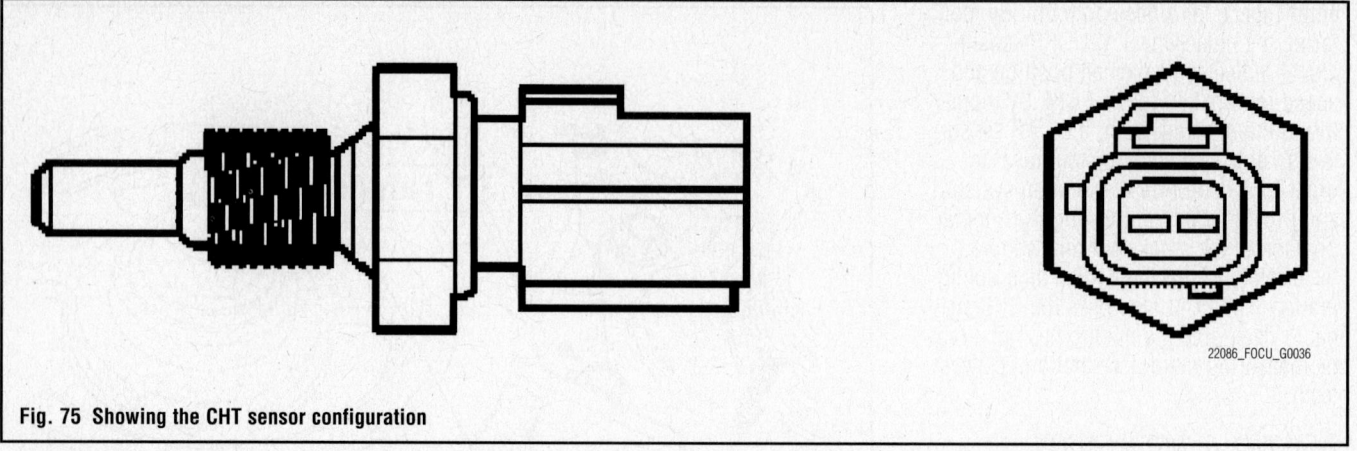

Fig. 75 Showing the CHT sensor configuration

OPERATION

The CHT measures the metal temperature. The CHT sensor can provide complete engine temperature information and can be used to infer coolant temperature. If the CHT sensor conveys an overheating condition to the PCM, the PCM would then initiate a fail-safe cooling strategy based on information from the CHT sensor. A cooling system failure such as low coolant or coolant loss could cause an overheating condition. As a result, damage to major engine components could occur. Using both the CHT sensor and fail-safe cooling strategy, the PCM prevents damage by allowing air cooling of the engine and limp home capability.

REMOVAL & INSTALLATION

See Figure 76.

1. Disconnect the battery ground cable.
2. Pull back the cylinder head temperature (CHT) sensor cover and disconnect the electrical connector.
3. Remove and discard the CHT sensor.
4. To install, reverse the removal procedure.

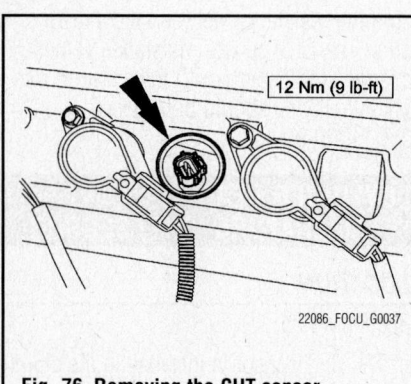

Fig. 76 Removing the CHT sensor

TESTING

See Figure 77.

1. With the key in OFF position and the CHT sensor connector disconnected, measure the resistance between the sensor pins.
2. Normal resistance is related to engine temperature. See the chart for normal resistance readings.

CYLINDER HEAD TEMPERATURE SENSOR EXPECTED VALUES				
Temperature		CHT Sensor Values		
°C	°F	Cold End (volts)	Hot End (volts)	Resistance (K ohms)
0	32	4.14	-	96.255
10	50	3.73	-	59.175
20	68	3.26	-	37.387
30	86	2.74	-	24.215
40	104	2.23	-	16.043
50	122	1.76	-	10.85
60	140	1.36	-	7.487
70	158	1.04	-	5.268
80	176	0.79	3.99	3.775
85	185	0.69	3.86	3.215
90	194	0.60	3.71	2.75
95	203	0.53	3.56	2.361
100	212	0.46	3.41	2.034
110	230	-	3.07	1.523
120	248	-	2.74	1.155
130	266	-	2.41	0.8866
140	284	-	2.10	0.6891
150	302	-	1.81	0.5417
160	320	-	1.55	0.4301
170	338	-	1.33	0.3449
180	356	-	1.13	0.2791
190	374	-	0.96	0.2278
200	392	-	0.82	0.1875
210	410	-	0.70	0.155
220	428	-	0.60	0.130
230	446	-	0.51	0.109
240	464	-	0.44	0.092
250	482		0.35	0.078
260	500		0.33	0.067

Fig. 77 Cylinder Head Temperature (CHT) Sensor expected values

FUEL RAIL PRESSURE AND TEMPERATURE (FRPT) SENSOR

LOCATION

See Figure 78.

The fuel rail pressure and temperature sensor is mounted on the fuel rail.

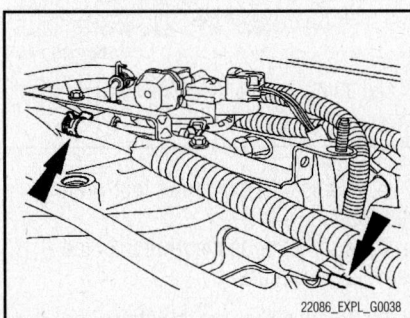

Fig. 78 Fuel rail temperature and pressure sensor location

OPERATION

The FRPT sensor measures the pressure and temperature of the fuel in the fuel rail and sends these signals to the PCM. The sensor uses the intake manifold vacuum as a reference to determine the pressure difference between the fuel rail and the intake manifold. The fuel return line to the fuel tank has been deleted in this type of fuel system. The relationship between fuel pressure and fuel temperature is used to determine the possible presence of fuel vapor in the fuel rail. Both pressure and temperature signals are used to control the speed of the fuel pump. The speed of the fuel pump sustains fuel rail pressure which preserves fuel in its liquid state. The dynamic range of the fuel injectors increase because of the higher rail pressure, which allows the injector pulse width to decrease.

REMOVAL & INSTALLATION

1. Release the fuel system pressure.
2. Disconnect the battery ground cable.
3. Disconnect the fuel rail pressure and temperature sensor electrical connector and vacuum tube.
4. Remove the bolts and the fuel rail pressure and temperature sensor.
5. Inspect, and if necessary, install a new O-ring seal.
6. Installation is the reverse of the removal procedure.

TESTING

See Figures 79 and 80.

1. Connect the vacuum hose to the FRP.

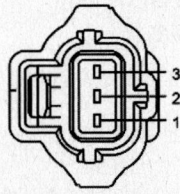

Pin	Circuit
3	FRP (Fuel Rail Pressure)
2	SIGRTN (Signal Return)
1	VREF (Reference Voltage)

Fuel Rail Pressure (FRP) Sensor Connector

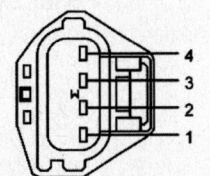

Pin	Circuit
3	FRT (Fuel Rail Temperature)
1	FRP (Fuel Rail Pressure)
4	SIGRTN (Signal Return)
2	VREF (Reference Voltage)

Fuel Rail Pressure/Temperature (FRPT) Sensor Connector

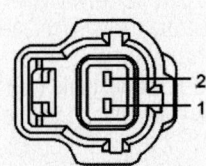

Pin	Circuit
2	SIGRTN (Signal Return)
1	FRT (Fuel Rail Temperature)

Fuel Rail Temperature (FRT) Sensor Connector

22086_EXPL_G0273

Fig. 79 Fuel rail pressure and temperature sensor pin identification

FPRT SENSOR TEMPERATURE, VOLTAGE & RESISTANCE SPECIFICATIONS

Temperature		Sensor	
°C	°F	Volts	K Ohms
100	212	0.47	2.073
95	203	0.54	2.405
90	194	0.61	2.800
85	185	0.70	3.273
80	176	0.80	3.840
75	167	0.92	4.524
70	158	1.06	5.351
65	149	1.21	6.356
60	140	1.38	7.584
55	131	1.56	9.091
50	122	1.77	10.949
45	113	1.99	13.252
40	104	2.23	16.123
35	95	2.48	19.720
30	86	2.74	24.253
25	77	3.00	30.000
20	68	3.26	37.332
15	59	3.50	46.745
10	50	3.73	58.911
5	41	3.95	74.745
0	32	4.13	95.501

22086_FOCU_G0101

Fig. 80 FRPT sensor temperature, voltage and resistance specifications

2. Disconnect the FRP sensor connector.

3. Turn the key ON, engine OFF.

4. Measure the voltage between the harness connector pins.

5. The voltage should be as shown in the chart, according to temperature.

HEATED OXYGEN SENSOR (HO2S)

LOCATION

See Figure 81.

The oxygen sensors are located in the exhaust pipe, before and after the catalytic converter.

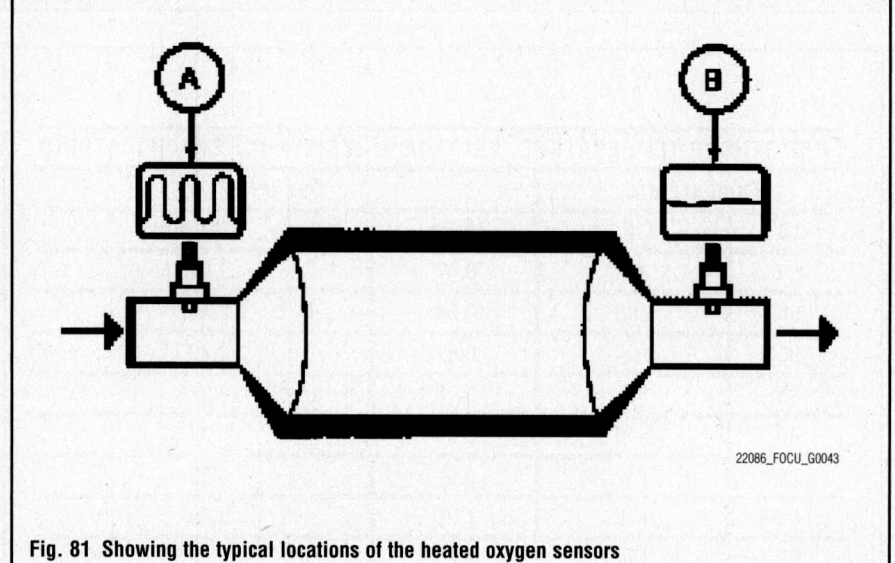

Fig. 81 Showing the typical locations of the heated oxygen sensors

OPERATION

The catalyst efficiency monitor uses pre and post-catalyst heated oxygen sensors (HO2S) to infer the hydrocarbon (HC) efficiency based on the oxygen storage capacity of the catalyst. Under normal, closed-loop fuel conditions, high efficiency catalysts have significant oxygen storage. This makes the switching frequency of the post-catalyst HO2S (B) very slow and reduces the amplitude of those switches as compared to the switching frequency and amplitude of the pre-catalyst HO2S (A). As catalyst efficiency deteriorates due to thermal and chemical deterioration, its ability to store oxygen declines. The post-catalyst HO2S (B) signal begins to switch more rapidly with increasing amplitude, approaching the switching frequency and amplitude of the pre-catalyst HO2S (A).

REMOVAL & INSTALLATION

With Secondary AIR System

See Figures 82 and 83.

1. Disconnect the battery ground cable.

2. Disconnect the electrical connector and detach the wiring retainer.

3. Remove the evaporative emissions (EVAP) canister purge valve heat shield.

4. Remove the four bolts and position the exhaust manifold heat shield aside.

➡**If necessary, lubricate the Heated Oxygen Sensor (HO2S) with penetrating and lock lubricant to assist in removal.**

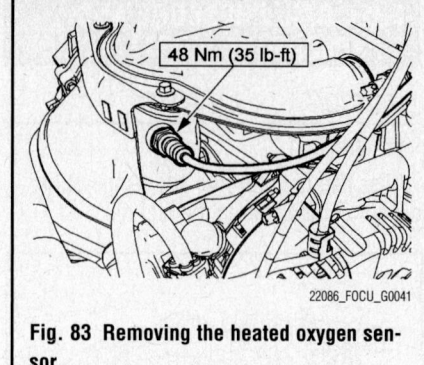

Fig. 83 Removing the heated oxygen sensor

5. Using a 22mm crows foot wrench, remove the HO2S.

6. Installation is the reverse of the removal procedure.

➡**Make sure that the electrical connector locking tab is engaged.**

✳✳ CAUTION

Make sure that the sensor wiring is secured with all retainers and routed away from hot surfaces and sharp edges.

➡**Make sure to apply anti-seize lubricant to the threads of the sensors before installation.**

Without Secondary AIR System

See Figures 84 and 85.

1. Disconnect the battery ground cable.

2. Raise and support the vehicle on a hoist.

3. Unsnap the electrical connector heat shield.

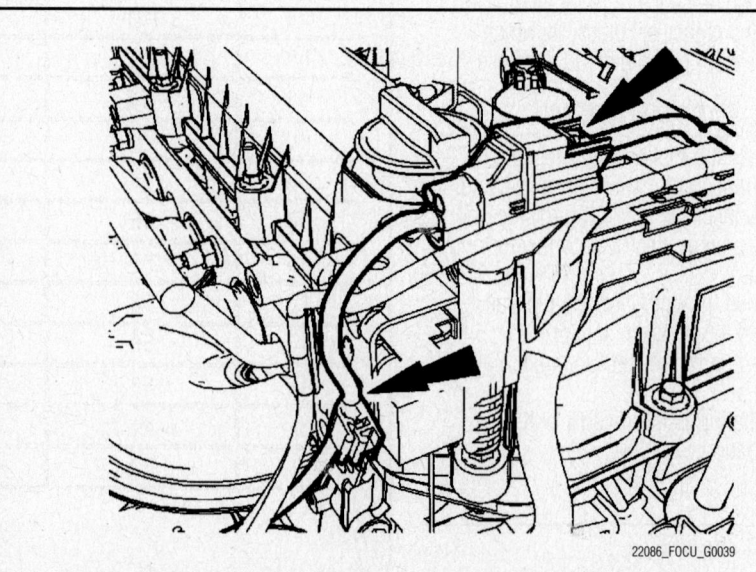

Fig. 82 Disconnect the electrical connector and detach the wiring retainer

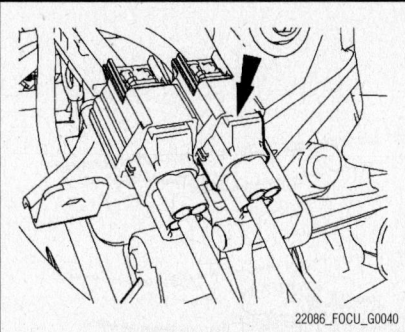

Fig. 84 Disconnect the electrical connector and detach the wiring retainer

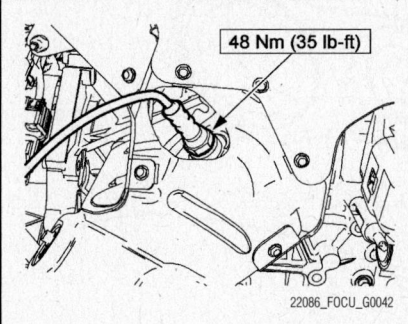

Fig. 85 Removing the heated oxygen sensor

4. Disconnect the electrical connector and detach the wiring retainer.

➡If necessary, lubricate the Heated Oxygen Sensor (HO2S) with penetrating and lock lubricant to assist in removal.

5. Using a 22mm crows foot wrench, remove the HO2S.
6. Installation is the reverse of the removal procedure.

➡Make sure that the electrical connector locking tab is engaged.

❋❋ CAUTION

Make sure that the sensor wiring is secured with all retainers and routed away from hot surfaces and sharp edges.

➡Make sure to apply anti-seize lubricant to the threads of the sensors before installation.

IDLE AIR CONTROL (IAC) VALVE

LOCATION

The Idle Air Control (IAC) valve is located on the throttle body assembly, under the snow shield.

REMOVAL & INSTALLATION
See Figure 86.

1. Disconnect the battery ground cable.
2. Remove throttle body snow shield as follows:
   a. Remove the retaining screw.
   b. Detach the emission tube retainer from the snow shield.
   c. Remove the snow shield.
3. Remove the Idle Air Control (IAC) valve as follows:
   a. Disconnect the IAC electrical connector (1).
   b. Remove the two IAC retaining screws (2).
   c. Remove the IAC valve (3).
4. Installation is the reverse of the removal procedure. Use a new gasket.

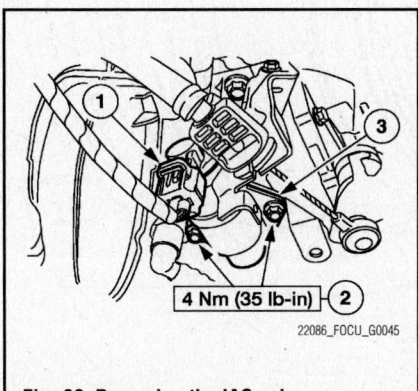

Fig. 86 Removing the IAC valve

TESTING
See Figure 87.

1. Disconnect the IAC valve connector
2. Using a DVOM, measure the resistance between the valve pins.
3. The resistance should be between 6–15 ohms.
4. If the resistance is not as specified, the IAC valve should be replaced.

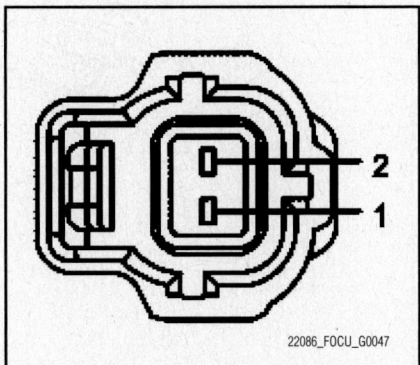

Fig. 87 Identifying the IAC valve pins

KNOCK SENSOR (KS)

LOCATION

The Knock Sensor (KS) is located on the side of the cylinder head.

OPERATION

The KS is a tuned accelerometer on the engine which converts engine vibration to an electrical signal. The PCM uses this signal to determine the presence of engine knock and to retard spark timing.

REMOVAL & INSTALLATION
See Figure 88.

1. Disconnect the battery ground cable.
2. Remove the intake manifold.
3. Remove the Knock Sensor (KS).
4. Remove the retaining bolt, then remove the KS.
5. Installation is the reverse of the removal procedure. Tighten the sensor to 15 ft. lbs. (20 Nm).

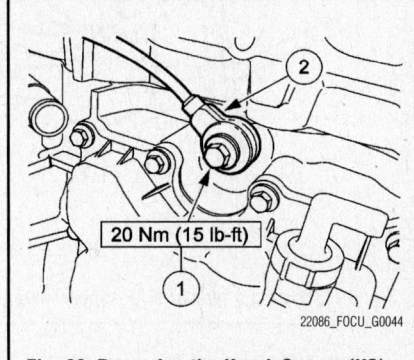

Fig. 88 Removing the Knock Sensor (KS)

TESTING

1. Verify that the Knock Sensor (KS) is properly installed.
2. Disconnect the sensor connector.
3. Using a DVOM, measure the resistance between the sensor pins. It should be between 4.39–5.35 m/ohms.
4. If the sensor does not test within this range, it should be replaced.

MASS AIR FLOW (MAF) SENSOR

LOCATION

The MAF sensor is located on the inlet tube of the intake air system.

OPERATION
See Figure 89.

The MAF sensor uses a hot wire sensing element to measure the amount of

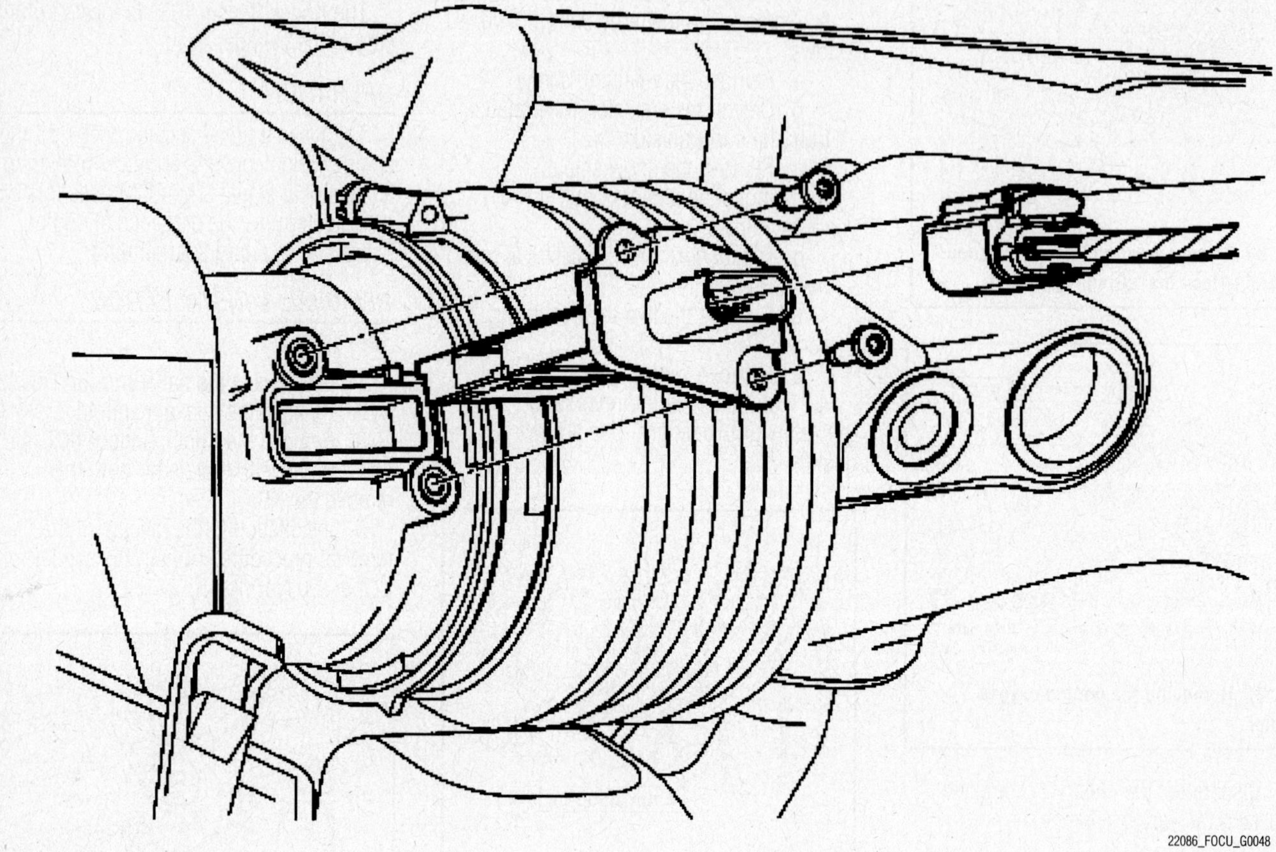

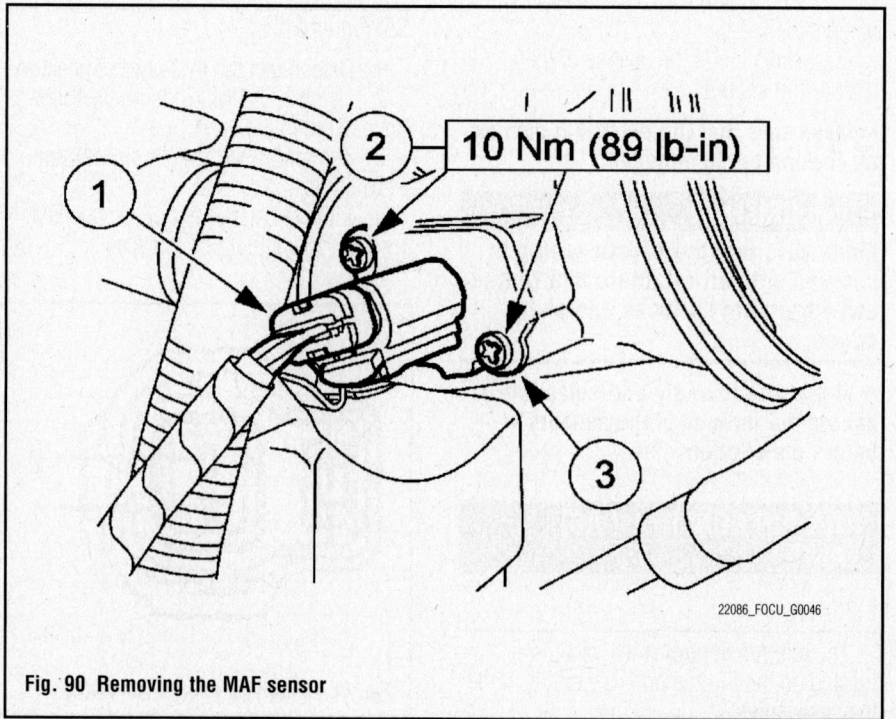

Fig. 89 Showing a typical MAF sensor installation

22086_FOCU_G0048

air entering the engine. Air passing over the hot wire causes it to cool. This hot wire is maintained at 200°C (392°F) above the ambient temperature as measured by a constant cold wire. If the hot wire electronic sensing element must be replaced, then the entire assembly must be replaced. Replacing only the element may change the air flow calibration.

REMOVAL & INSTALLATION

See Figure 90.

1. Disconnect the battery ground cable.

2. With the vehicle in NEUTRAL, position it on a hoist.

3. Disconnect the MAF sensor electrical connector.

4. Remove the two MAF sensor retaining screws.

5. Remove the MAF sensor.

6. Installation is the reverse of the removal procedure.

10 Nm (89 lb-in)

22086_FOCU_G0046

Fig. 90 Removing the MAF sensor

TESTING

See Figure 91.

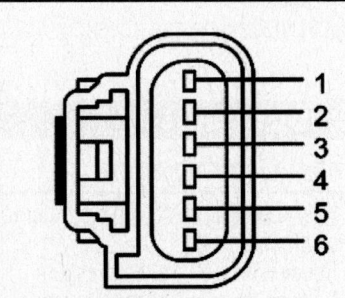

MAF Sensor Pin Connections

Pin	Circuit
1	IAT
2	SIGRTN
3	MAF
4	MAF RTN
5	PWRGND
6	VPWR

MAF Sensor Pin Connections

22086_EXPL_G0284

Fig. 91 Showing the MAF sensor pin and circuit identification

POWERTRAIN CONTROL MODULE

LOCATION

The PCM is located behind the cowl trim (kick panel) on the passenger side of the vehicle.

OPERATION

The center of the Electronic Engine Control (EEC) system is a microprocessor called the PCM. The PCM uses a 150-pin connector and receives input from sensors and other electronic components (switches, relays). Based on the information received and programmed into its memory, the PCM generates output signals to control various relays, solenoids and actuators.

REMOVAL & INSTALLATION

See Figure 92.

1. Disconnect the battery ground cable.
2. Remove the instrument panel side trim strip.
3. Remove the cowl side trim panel (kick panel).
4. Remove the glove box.
5. Remove the passenger side lower foot well trim panel.
6. Remove the two retaining nuts.

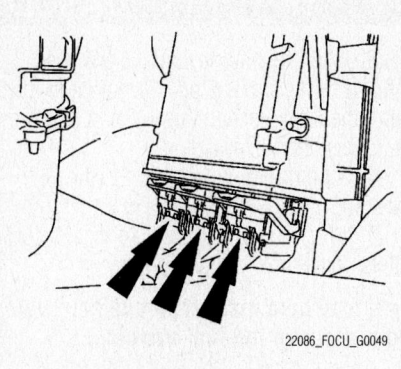

22086_FOCU_G0049

Fig. 92 Showing the MAF sensor pin and circuit identification

7. Remove the generic electronic module (GEM0 and the bracket and position aside.
8. Disconnect the 3 powertrain control (PCM) module electrical connectors and remove the PCM.
9. Installation is the reverse of the removal procedure.

> ✲✲✲ **CAUTION**
>
> **Make sure that the PCM electrical connectors do not unlock when installing the GEM module.**

TESTING

See Figure 93.

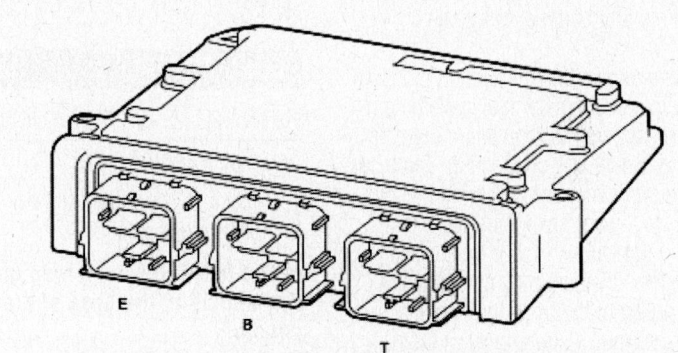

150 PIN PCM HARNESS CONNECTORS

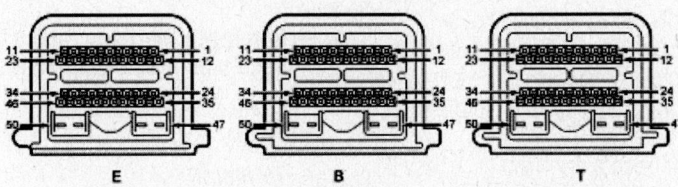

| ENGINE | BODY / COWL | TRANSMISSION |

150-PIN PCM POWER AND GROUNDS		
Function	**Description**	**Connector/Pin**
VPWR	Voltage input to module	B35
VPWR	Voltage input to module	B36
PWRGND	Power ground	B47
PWRGND	Power ground	B48
PWRGND	Power ground	B49
CSEGND	Case ground	B10
SIGRTN	Connector B signal return	B41
SIGRTN	Connector T signal return	T41
SIGRTN	Connector E signal return	E41
VREF	Connector buffered 5.0-volt reference	B40
VREF	Connector E buffered 5.0-volt reference	E40
KAPWR	Keep alive power	B45

PCM Pin Identification

22086_EXPL_G0288

Fig. 93 PCM connector pin identification

FUEL SYSTEM SERVICE PRECAUTIONS

Safety is the most important factor when performing not only fuel system maintenance but any type of maintenance. Failure to conduct maintenance and repairs in a safe manner may result in serious personal injury or death. Maintenance and testing of the vehicle's fuel system components can be accomplished safely and effectively by adhering to the following rules and guidelines.

• To avoid the possibility of fire and personal injury, always disconnect the negative battery cable unless the repair or test procedure requires that battery voltage be applied.

• Always relieve the fuel system pressure prior to disconnecting any fuel system component (injector, fuel rail, pressure regulator, etc.), fitting or fuel line connection. Exercise extreme caution whenever relieving fuel system pressure to avoid exposing skin, face and eyes to fuel spray. Please be advised that fuel under pressure may penetrate the skin or any part of the body that it contacts.

• Always place a shop towel or cloth around the fitting or connection prior to loosening to absorb any excess fuel due to spillage. Ensure that all fuel spillage (should it occur) is quickly removed from engine surfaces. Ensure that all fuel soaked cloths or towels are deposited into a suitable waste container.

• Always keep a dry chemical (Class B) fire extinguisher near the work area.

• Do not allow fuel spray or fuel vapors to come into contact with a spark or open flame.

• Always use a back-up wrench when loosening and tightening fuel line connection fittings. This will prevent unnecessary stress and torsion to fuel line piping.

• Always replace worn fuel fitting O-rings with new Do not substitute fuel hose or equivalent where fuel pipe is installed.

Before servicing the vehicle, make sure to also refer to the precautions in the beginning of this section as well.

RELIEVING FUEL SYSTEM PRESSURE

➡The fuel pump relay is located in the engine compartment, in the battery junction box, relay C1051.

1. Remove the fuel pump relay.
2. Start the engine and allow to idle until the engine stalls.

3. After the engine stalls, crank the engine for approximately 5 seconds to make sure the fuel injection supply manifold pressure has been released.
4. Turn the ignition switch to the OFF position.
5. When the fuel system service is complete, install the fuel pump relay.

➡It may take more than one key cycle to pressurize the fuel system.

6. Cycle the ignition key and wait 3 seconds to pressurize the fuel system. Check for leaks before starting the engine.
7. Start the engine and check the fuel system for leaks.

FUEL FILTER

REMOVAL & INSTALLATION

See Figure 94.

1. Before servicing the vehicle, refer to the Precautions Section.

➡The fuel filter is located underneath the vehicle in the area of the rear suspension.

2. Relieve the fuel system pressure.
3. Raise the vehicle.

➡To remove the lines, press the quick-release tabs on the connectors.

4. Remove the fuel filter bolt and remove it from the bracket.

To install:

5. Position the fuel filter into the bracket. Ensure the fuel flow direction is properly aligned.
6. Install and tighten the fuel pump bracket bolt.
7. Lubricate the fuel tube fittings with clean engine oil. Align the fuel tube fittings and press together until a click is heard and

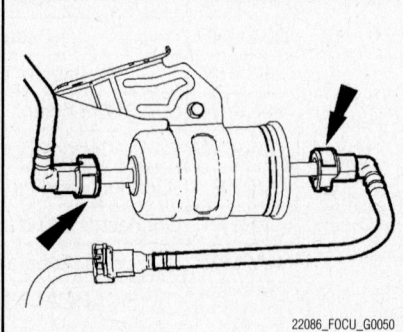

22086_FOCU_G0050

Fig. 94 Location of fuel filter and lines.

then pull on the fittings to make sure they are fully engaged.
8. Start the engine and check for leaks.

FUEL INJECTORS

REMOVAL & INSTALLATION

1. Before servicing the vehicle, refer to the Precautions Section.
2. Relieve the fuel system pressure
3. Release the fuel system pressure.
4. Disconnect the battery ground cable.
5. Disconnect the fuel tube quick release coupling from the fuel rail and position the tube aside.
6. Disconnect the fuel injector electrical connectors.
7. Disconnect the fuel rail pressure and temperature sensor electrical connector and vacuum tube.
8. Remove the bolts and the fuel rail and injectors.
9. Remove the spacers.
10. If necessary, remove the fuel injector retaining clips and the fuel injectors. Remove and discard the O-ring seals.
11. To install, reverse the removal procedure. Tighten the fuel rail bolts to 18 ft. lbs. (25 Nm).

FUEL PUMP

REMOVAL & INSTALLATION

1. Before servicing the vehicle, refer to the Precautions Section.
2. Relieve the fuel system pressure.
3. With the vehicle in NEUTRAL, position it on a hoist.
4. Remove the fuel tank. See "Fuel Tank" in this section.
5. Press the quick connect coupling release tab and disconnect the fuel tube.

✳✳ CAUTION

Make sure that the float, arm or flange are not damaged while removing the fuel pump module.

6. Using a suitable fuel pump lock ring remover, rotate the lock ring counterclockwise and remove the fuel pump module.
7. Discard the locking ring and seal.

To install:

8. Installation is the reverse of the removal procedure.

9. Inspect the surfaces of the fuel pump module flange and fuel tank O-ring contact surfaces. Do not polish or adjust the O-ring contact area of the fuel pump flange or the fuel tank. Install a new fuel pump module or the fuel tank if the O-ring contact area is bent, scratched or corroded.

10. Installation is the reverse of the removal procedure.

11. Lubricate the fuel tube quick connect coupling with clean engine oil. Align the fuel tube and the quick connect coupling and press together until an audible click is heard and then pull on the fittings to make sure they are fully engaged.

12. Start the engine and check for leaks.

FUEL TANK

REMOVAL & INSTALLATION

See Figures 95 and 96.

1. With the vehicle in NEUTRAL, position it on a hoist.
2. Release the fuel system pressure.
3. Drain the fuel tank.
4. Disconnect the fuel pump module electrical connector.
5. Remove the heat shield retainer nut.
6. Loosen the clamp and disconnect the filler pipe.
7. Press the quick connect coupling release tab and disconnect the vent tube.
8. Press the quick connect coupling release tab and disconnect the fuel feed tube.
9. Support the fuel tank using a suitable high-lift jack.

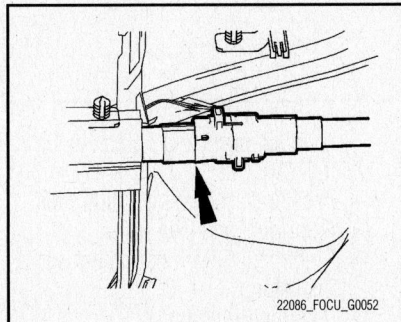

Fig. 95 Disconnect the fuel pump module electrical connector

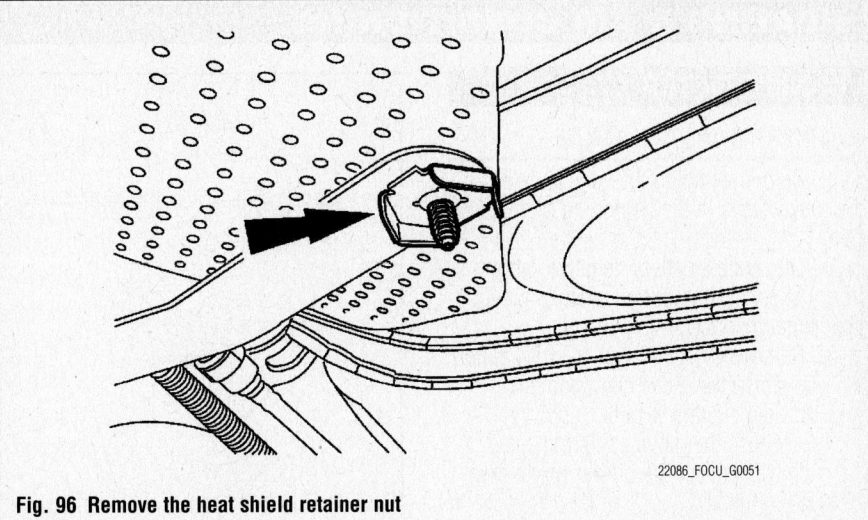

22086_FOCU_G0051

Fig. 96 Remove the heat shield retainer nut

➡**Make sure not to bend or deform the fuel tank straps during the removal of the tank.**

10. Remove the bolt and position aside the fuel tank straps.
11. Remove the fuel tank.

To install:

12. Position the fuel tank and use the jack to hold it in place.
13. Install the fuel tank strap bolts. Tighten the bolts to 18 ft. lbs. (25 Nm).
14. Remove the hi-lift jack.
15. Reconnect the quick-connect couplings to the feed and vent tubes.

✳✳ CAUTION

The orientation marks on the fuel fill and vent hoses must be aligned with the orientation marks on the fuel tank during installation. If the installation of a new hose clamp is necessary, a new stainless steel clamp is required.

16. Install the heat shield retainer nut.
17. Reconnect the fuel pump module electrical connector.
18. Fill the fuel tank.
19. Repressurize the fuel system as follows:
   a. Cycle the ignition key and wait 3 seconds to pressurize the fuel system. Check for leaks before starting the engine.
20. Start the engine and check the fuel system for leaks.

21. Carry out an evaporative emission system leak test.

IDLE SPEED

ADJUSTMENT

Idle speed is maintained by the Powertrain Control Module (PCM). No adjustment is necessary or possible.

THROTTLE BODY

REMOVAL & INSTALLATION

1. Before servicing the vehicle, refer to the precautions in the beginning of this section.
2. Disconnect battery negative cable from battery and properly isolate to prevent accidental reconnection.
3. Remove or disconnect the following:

   • Air cleaner outlet tube
   • Accelerator cable and speed control cable (if equipped)
   • Throttle position (TP) sensor electrical connector
   • Throttle body

4. Remove and discard the throttle body gasket.

To install:

5. Installation is the reverse of the removal procedure, noting the following:
   a. Install a new throttle body gasket.
   b. Tighten the throttle body retaining bolts to 89 inch lbs. (10 Nm).

BLOWER MOTOR

REMOVAL & INSTALLATION

1. Before servicing the vehicle, refer to the precautions in the beginning of this section.

2. Disconnect battery negative cable from battery and properly isolate to prevent accidental reconnection.

3. Remove the RH lower I/P trim panel.
   a. Open the glove compartment.
   b. Remove the RH floor duct.
   c. Close the glove compartment.
   d. Disconnect the blower motor electrical connector.

4. Remove the blower motor.

To install:

5. Install the blower motor and securely tighten the screws.

6. Connect the blower motor electrical connector.

7. Open the glove compartment and attach the floor air duct.

8. Close the glove compartment.

9. Install the RH lower trim panel.

HEATER CORE

REMOVAL & INSTALLATION

See Figures 97 through 99.

1. Before servicing the vehicle, refer to the Precautions Section.

2. Remove or disconnect the following:
   - Clamp off or remove the coolant hoses from heater core
   - Floor console; see "Console" under the "Body" section
   - Rear armrest bracket nuts, if equipped
   - Rear footwell duct between the front seats
   - Right hand lower instrument panel insulator
   - Floor duct and trim panel

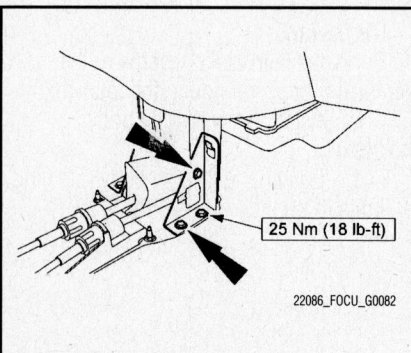

Fig. 97 Remove the LH and RH brackets

25 Nm (18 lb-ft)

22086_FOCU_G0082

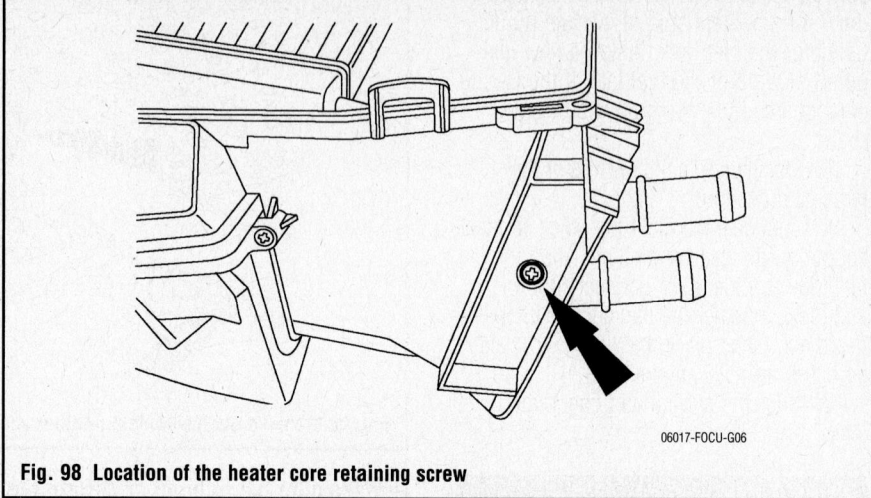

Fig. 98 Location of the heater core retaining screw

06017-FOCU-G06

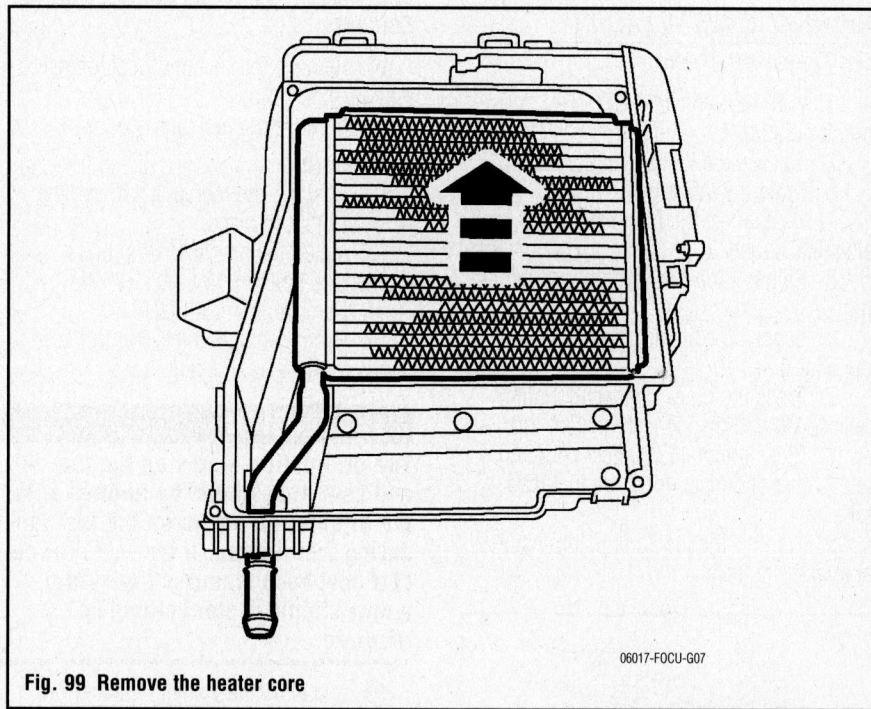

Fig. 99 Remove the heater core

06017-FOCU-G07

- Accelerator pedal mounting nuts and position the pedal aside
- Left and right hand instrument panel brackets
- Left hand floor duct
- Right hand floor duct
- Heater core cover
- Heater core retaining screw
- Heater core

To install:

3. Install or connect the following:
   - Heater core and retaining screw
   - Heater core cover
   - Right hand floor duct
   - Left hand floor duct
   - Left and right hand instrument panel brackets and tighten to 12 ft. lbs. (16 Nm)
   - Accelerator pedal mounting nuts
   - Floor duct and trim panel
   - Right hand lower instrument panel insulator
   - Rear footwell duct
   - Rear armrest bracket nuts, if equipped
   - Floor console
   - Coolant hoses to the heater core
   - Negative battery cable

4. Fill the cooling system to the correct level.

5. Start the engine and check for leaks.

POWER STEERING GEAR

REMOVAL & INSTALLATION

See Figure 100.

1. Before servicing the vehicle, refer to the precautions in the beginning of this section.

2. Disconnect battery negative cable from battery and properly isolate to prevent accidental reconnection.

3. Center the steering wheel.

4. Disconnect the steering column shaft from the steering gear pinion extension.

5. Loosen the front wheel nuts.

6. Raise and support the vehicle.

7. Remove the wheels.

8. Remove the tie rod end retaining nuts.

✳ WARNING

When the tie rod ends are detached from the wheel knuckles, the ball joint seals must be wrapped in cloth to protect them.

9. Detach the tie rod ends from the wheel knuckles using a suitable ball joint press.

10. Detach the stabilizer bar links from the strut and spring assemblies.

11. Disconnect the fluid cooler hose using a suitable hose fitting tool and allow the fluid to drain into a suitable container.

12. Remove the support insulator to transaxle center bolt.

13. Remove the steering gear heat shield.

14. Detach the hose support clamp.

15. Detach the power steering hoses from the steering gear.

16. Using a suitable jack, support the crossmember.

17. Remove the six crossmember bolts.

18. Lower the crossmember.

19. Remove the steering column coupling shaft and floor seal.

20. Remove the steering gear.

To install:

➡**New O-ring seals must be installed any time the lines are disconnected from the steering gear.**

21. Install a new high pressure hose O-ring seal (3F886-AA) and a new return hose O-ring seal (3F886-BA).

22. Install the steering gear and torque the bolts to 59 ft. lbs. (80 Nm)

➡**Visually inspect the floor seal before installation. Make sure the sealing sur-**

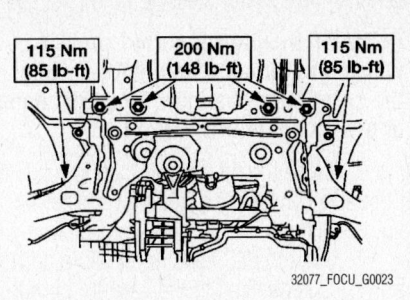

Fig. 100 Tighten crossmember bolts as shown

face of the floor seal is clean and not permanently deformed. The foam portion of the floor seal should be between 20-25mm.

23. Install a new floor seal if below the specified value.

24. Install the steering column coupling shaft and floor seal.

25. Align the crossmember using suitable alignment pins.

26. Raise the crossmember, engaging the guide pins into the chassis aligning holes.

27. Install the crossmember bolts and tighten to 85 ft. lbs. (115 Nm) and 148 ft. lbs. (200 Nm) as shown in the diagram.

28. Remove the transmission jack.

29. Remove the subframe alignment pins.

30. Install the power steering hoses.

31. Install the hose support clamp and securely tighten.

32. Install the steering gear heat shield.

33. Install the support insulator to transaxle center bolt and tighten to 37 ft. lbs. (50 Nm)

34. Connect the fluid cooler hose.

35. Install the stabilizer bar links to the strut and spring assemblies and tighten to 37 ft. lbs. (50 Nm)

✳✳ CAUTION

Install new tie rod end retaining nuts. Failure to follow this instruction may result in personal injury.

36. Install the tie rod ends and tighten the nuts to 35 ft. lbs. (47 Nm)

37. Install the wheels and tighten the nuts to 94 ft. lbs. (128 Nm)

➡**Make sure the steering is in the straight-ahead position before lowering the vehicle.**

38. Lower the vehicle.

39. Using a new clamp bolt, connect the steering column coupling shaft to the steering gear pinion extension and tighten to 21 ft. lbs. (28 Nm)

40. Install the instrument panel lower panel.

41. Fill the system.

42. If a new steering gear has been installed, check the toe adjustment.

POWER STEERING PUMP

REMOVAL & INSTALLATION

✳✳ CAUTION

While repairing the power steering system, care should be taken to prevent the entry of contaminants, or premature failure of the power steering components can result.

✳✳ CAUTION

Whenever the hoses are disconnected from the power steering pump. Make sure the accessory drive belt is not contaminated with power steering fluid.

1. With the vehicle in NEUTRAL, position it on a hoist.

2. Siphon the power steering fluid from the power steering reservoir.

3. Remove the power steering pump pulley.

4. Disconnect the power steering pressure switch electrical connector.

5. Remove the power steering line bracket nuts.

➡**A new Teflon® O-ring seal must be installed any time the power steering pressure line is disconnected from the power steering pump.**

6. Disconnect the power steering pressure line from the power steering pump.

7. Remove and discard the Teflon O-ring seal

8. Release the clamp and disconnect the power steering fluid supply hose.

9. Remove the 2 lower power steering pump mounting bolts.

10. Remove the 2 upper power steering pump mounting bolts and the power steering pump.

To install:

11. Position the power steering pump into position.

12. Install the 2 upper mounting bolts. Tighten the bolts to 18 ft. lbs. (25 Nm).

13. Install the 2 lower mounting bolts. Tighten the bolts to 18 ft. lbs. (25 Nm).

14. With a new O-ring, connect the power steering pressure line to the pump. Tighten the fitting to 48 ft. lbs. (65 Nm).

15. Install or connect the following: RL-BS0

- P/S line bracket and nuts
- PSP switch connector
- P/S pump pulley and accessory belt

16. Fill and bleed the power steering system.

BLEEDING

> ❋ **CAUTION**
>
> **If the air is not purged from the power steering system correctly, premature power steering pump failure can result. The condition can occur on pre-delivery vehicles with evidence of aerated fluid or on vehicles that have had steering component repairs.**

1. Remove the power steering pump reservoir cap.

2. Tightly install the evacuation cap to the power steering pump reservoir.

3. Install the hose from the fill adapter manifold tee to the evacuation cap on the power steering pump reservoir.

4. Install the vacuum pump to the fill adapter manifold control valve.

5. Install the hose to the opposite fill adapter manifold control valve and submerge the open end of the hose into a container of new power steering fluid.

➡ **The fill adapter manifold control valves are in the open position when the point of the handles face the center of the fill adapter manifold.**

6. Close the fill adapter manifold control valve connected to the power steering fluid container.

7. Open the fill adapter manifold control valve connected to the vacuum pump.

8. Using the vacuum pump, apply 68-85 kPa (20-25 in-Hg) of vacuum to the power steering system.

9. Observe the vacuum gauge for 30 seconds.

10. If the vacuum gauge reading drops more than 3 kPa (0.88 in-Hg), correct any leaks in the power steering system or the filling tools before proceeding.

➡ **The vacuum pump gauge reading will drop slightly during this step.**

11. Slowly open the fill adapter manifold control valve connected to the power steering fluid container until power steering fluid completely fills the hose.

12. Close the fill adapter manifold control valve connected to the power steering fluid container.

13. Using the vacuum pump, apply 68-85 kPa (20-25 in-Hg) of vacuum to the power steering system.

14. Close the fill adapter manifold control valve connected to the vacuum pump.

15. Slowly open the fill adapter manifold control valve connected to the power steering fluid container.

16. When the power steering fluid has drained from the hose connected to the power steering fluid container, close the fill adapter manifold control valve connected to the power steering fluid container.

17. Remove the tools from the vehicle.

18. Install the power steering reservoir cap.

> ❋❋ **CAUTION**
>
> **Do not hold the steering wheel against the stops for more than 3 to 5 seconds at a time. Damage to the power steering pump can occur.**

➡ **There will be a slight drop in the power steering fluid level in the power steering fluid reservoir when the engine is started.**

19. Start the engine and turn the steering wheel from stop-to-stop.

20. If equipped with Hydro-Boost, apply the brake pedal twice.

21. Turn the ignition switch to the OFF position.

> ❋❋ **CAUTION**
>
> **Do not overfill the reservoir.**

22. Remove the power steering reservoir cap and fill the reservoir.

23. Install the power steering reservoir cap.

SUSPENSION

COIL SPRING

REMOVAL & INSTALLATION

See Figure 101.

1. Before servicing the vehicle, refer to the precautions in the beginning of this section.

2. Disconnect battery negative cable from battery and properly isolate to prevent accidental reconnection.

3. Remove the strut assembly from the vehicle.

> ❋❋ **CAUTION**
>
> **As the spring is under extreme tension care must be taken at all times. Failure to follow this instruction may result in personal injury.**

4. Using a suitable coil spring compressor, compress the spring.

5. Loosen the thrust bearing nut using an Allen key to prevent shaft rotation.

6. Disassemble the strut and spring assembly as follows:

- Remove the thrust bearing nut.
- Remove the top mount.
- Remove the thrust bearing.
- Remove the strut.
- Remove the bump stop.
- Remove the boot.

To assemble:

7. The strut unit is assembled in the reverse order of disassembly.

   a. Make sure the top mount is correctly seated onto the thrust bearing before assembly.

   b. Make sure the spring ends butt correctly against the spring seats, color code at the bottom.

   c. Make sure the bump stop is installed with the flat surface uppermost.

FRONT SUSPENSION

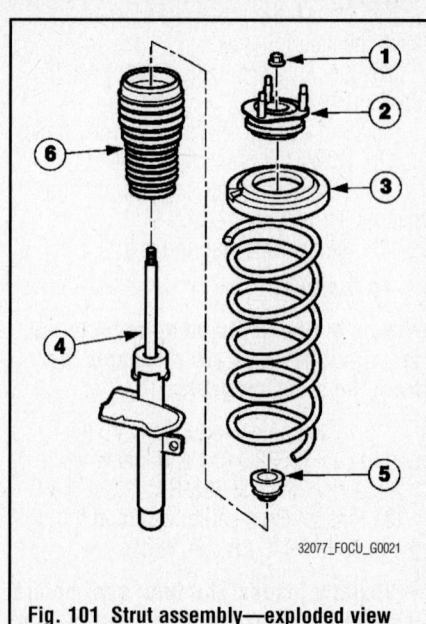

32077_FOCU_G0021

Fig. 101 Strut assembly—exploded view

8. Install a new thrust bearing nut and tighten to 35 ft. lbs. (38 Nm).

9. Install the strut assembly.

LOWER BALL JOINT

REMOVAL & INSTALLATION

The lower ball joint is replaced with the lower control arm as an assembly.

LOWER CONTROL ARM

REMOVAL & INSTALLATION

1. Before servicing the vehicle, refer to the Precautions Section.

2. Remove the wheel.

3. Remove the pinch bolt and separate the lower ball joint from the wheel knuckle.

❊❊ CAUTION

Do not use a prying device or separator fork between the lower ball joint and knuckle. Use a pry bar by inserting it into the lower control arm opening.

4. Install Special Tool 307-102 over the ball stud before releasing the lower control arm and knuckle into rest positions.

5. Remove the lower control arm bolts.

6. Remove the control arm.

To install:

➡️**Use new nuts, bolts and ball bearing washers for assembly.**

7. Install the control arm and tighten the bolts as follows:

   a. Tighten the front pivot bolt to 103 ft. lbs. (140 Nm).

   b. Tighten the rear inboard nut to 133 ft. lbs. (180 Nm).

   c. Tighten the rear outboard nut to 92 ft. lbs. (125 Nm).

8. Install the lower ball joint and tighten the pinch bolt to 35 ft. lbs. (48 Nm).

9. Install the wheel.

CONTROL ARM BUSHING REPLACEMENT

The lower control arm bushings are replaced with the lower control arm as an assembly.

MACPHERSON STRUT

REMOVAL & INSTALLATION

1. Before servicing the vehicle, refer to the Precautions Section.

2. Remove or disconnect the following:

- Front wheel
- Brake hose from the support bracket
- Stabilizer bar connecting link
- Wheel knuckle bolt
- Wheel knuckle
- Strut tower nuts
- Strut and spring assembly

To install:

3. Install or connect the following:

- Strut and spring assembly
- Strut tower nuts and tighten to 22 ft. lbs. (30 Nm)
- Wheel knuckle
- Wheel knuckle bolt and tighten to 85 ft. lbs. (115 Nm)
- Stabilizer bar connecting link and tighten to 41 ft. lbs. (55 Nm)
- Brake hose to the support bracket
- Front wheel

4. Check the wheel alignment and adjust as necessary.

SHOCK ABSORBERS

REMOVAL & INSTALLATION

See Figure 102.

1. Before servicing the vehicle, refer to the precautions in the beginning of this section.

2. Disconnect battery negative cable from battery and properly isolate to prevent accidental reconnection.

3. Remove the strut assembly from the vehicle.

❊❊ CAUTION

As the spring is under extreme tension care must be taken at all times. Failure to follow this instruction may result in personal injury.

4. Using a suitable coil spring compressor, compress the spring.

5. Loosen the thrust bearing nut using an Allen key to prevent shaft rotation.

6. Disassemble the strut and spring assembly as follows:

- Remove the thrust bearing nut.
- Remove the top mount.
- Remove the thrust bearing.
- Remove the strut.
- Remove the bump stop.
- Remove the boot.

To assemble:

7. The strut unit is assembled in the reverse order of disassembly.

   a. Make sure the top mount is correctly seated onto the thrust bearing before assembly.

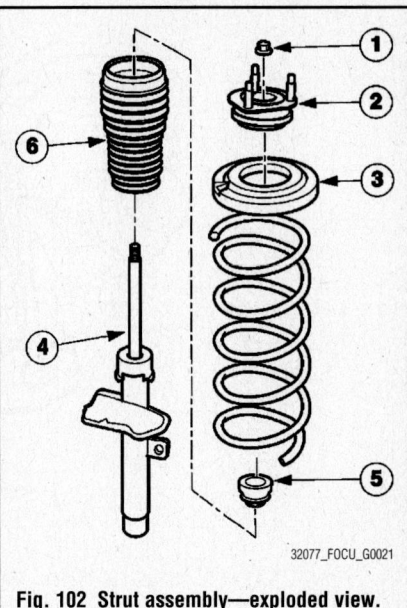

Fig. 102 Strut assembly—exploded view.

   b. Make sure the spring ends butt correctly against the spring seats, color code at the bottom.

   c. Make sure the bump stop is installed with the flat surface uppermost.

8. Install a new thrust bearing nut and tighten to 49 ft. lbs. (66 Nm)

9. Install the strut assembly.

STABILIZER BAR

REMOVAL & INSTALLATION

See Figures 103 through 105.

1. Before servicing the vehicle, refer to the precautions in the beginning of this section.

2. Disconnect battery negative cable from battery and properly isolate to prevent accidental reconnection.

3. Make sure the road wheels are in the straight ahead position.

4. Disconnect the steering column shaft from the steering gear pinion extension.

   a. Remove the bolt.

   b. Release the pinion shaft extension from the steering column.

   c. Discard the bolt.

5. Remove the front wheels and tires.

6. Loosen the tie rod end retaining nuts.

7. Detach the tie rod ends from the wheel knuckles and discard the retaining nuts.

8. Detach the stabilizer bar connecting links from the stabilizer bar.

9. Detach the lower arm ball joints from the wheel knuckles and remove the brake heat shield.

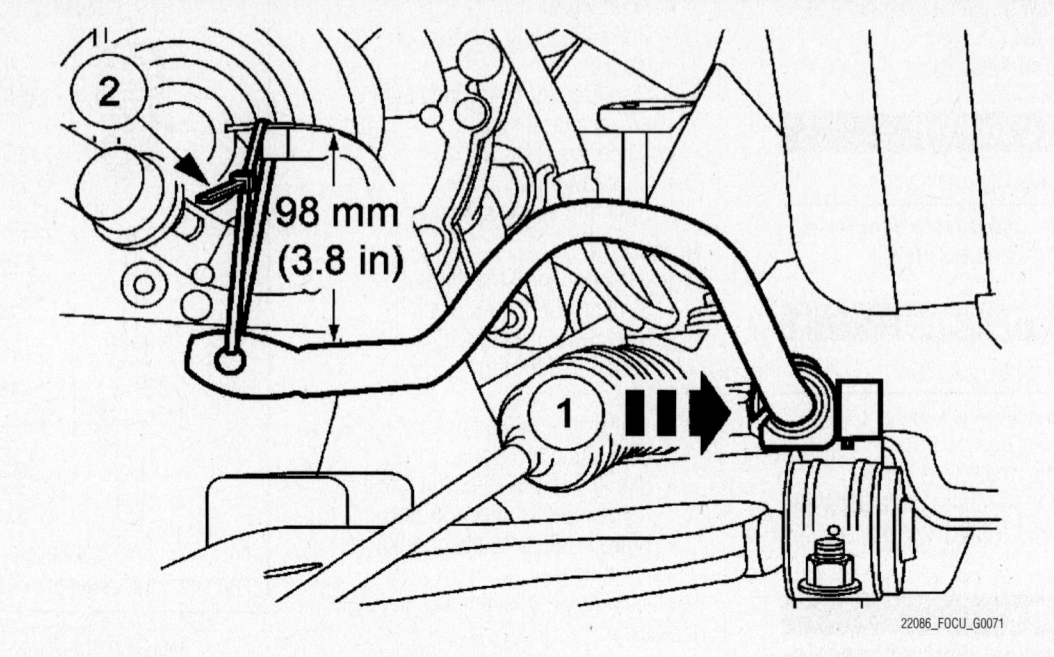

Fig. 103 Position the bushings and use cable ties to support the stabilizer bar

10. Remove the support insulator to transaxle center bolt.

11. Using a suitable transmission jack, support the crossmember.

12. Remove the six crossmember bolts.

❋❋ WARNING

The power steering lines are attached to the steering gear.

13. Lower the crossmember to gain access to the stabilizer bar.

14. Remove the stabilizer bar.

15. Remove the stabilizer bar bushings.

To install:

➡**The stabilizer bar bushings must be located correctly on the flats of the stabilizer bar with no lubricant.**

16. Install the stabilizer bar bushings (both sides).

17. Install the stabilizer bar as follows:
- Locate the bushing against the spacer (both sides).
- Using suitable cable ties, support the stabilizer bar to specification (both sides).

18. Install the stabilizer bar clamps.

19. Install the stabilizer bar clamp rear retaining bolts and tighten to 41 ft. lbs. (55 Nm)

➡**Do not fully tighten stabilizer bar clamp front retaining bolts at this stage.**

20. Install the stabilizer bar clamp front retaining bolts.

21. Tighten the bolts in two stages:
- Stage 1: Tighten bolts to 22 ft. lbs. (30 Nm)
- Stage 2: Tighten bolts to 41 ft. lbs. (55 Nm)

22. Remove the cable ties supporting the stabilizer bar.

23. Using the special tools, align the subframe as follows:

a. Insert the guide pins through the subframe alignment holes.

b. Slide the locking plates into the grooves and tighten the guide pin sleeve.

c. Raise the subframe, engaging the guide pins into the chassis alignment holes.

➡**Do not fully tighten the subframe retaining bolts at this stage.**

24. Install the subframe retaining bolts.

25. Remove the subframe RH alignment pin.

26. Tighten the subframe retaining bolts.

27. Lower and remove the transmission jack.

28. Remove the subframe LH alignment pin.

29. Install the support insulator to transaxle center bolt and tighten to 37 ft. lbs. (50 Nm)

30. Install the lower arm ball joint.

31. Attach the stabilizer bar connecting links to the stabilizer bar. Tighten the bolt to 41 ft. lbs. (55 Nm).

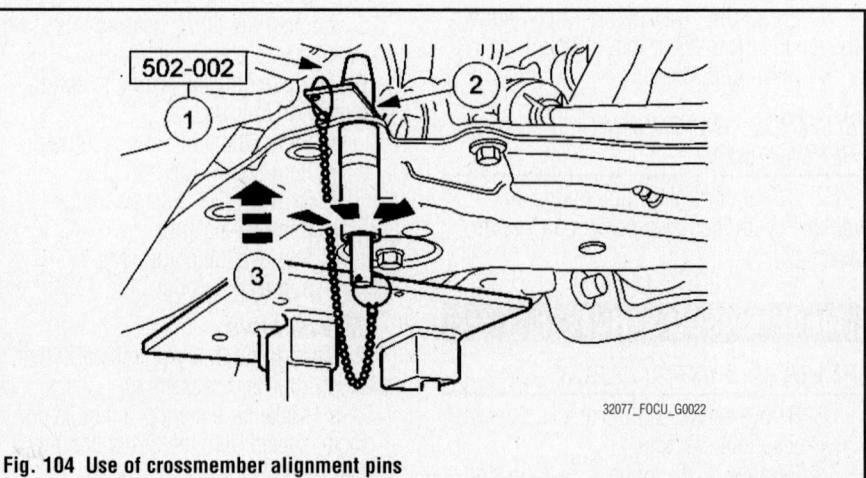

Fig. 104 Use of crossmember alignment pins

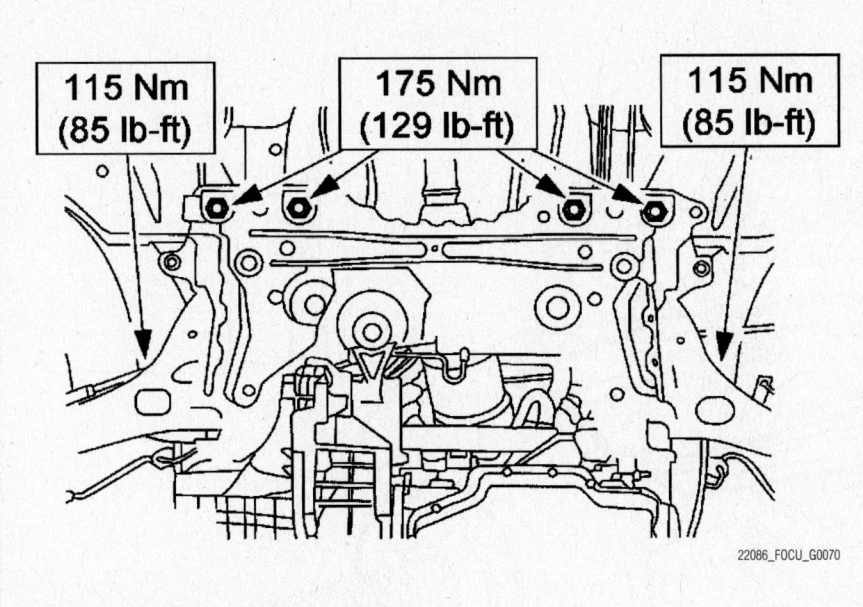

115 Nm (85 lb-ft) 175 Nm (129 lb-ft) 115 Nm (85 lb-ft)

22086_FOCU_G0070

Fig. 105 Tighten subframe bolts as shown

✳✳ CAUTION

Install new tie rod end retaining nuts. Failure to follow this instruction may result in personal injury.

32. Attach the tie rod ends to the wheel knuckles and tighten to 35 ft. lbs. (47 Nm)
33. Install the front wheels and tires.
34. Make sure the vehicle is in the straight-ahead position, before lowering the vehicle.
35. Lower the vehicle.

✳✳ CAUTION

Install a new steering column pinch bolt. Failure to follow this instruction may result in personal injury.

36. Connect the steering column shaft to the steering gear pinion extension.
37. Connect the pinion shaft extension to the steering column.
38. Install the bolt and tighten to 21 ft. lbs. (28 Nm)
39. Connect the battery ground cable.

STEERING KNUCKLE

REMOVAL & INSTALLATION

1. Before servicing the vehicle, refer to the precautions in the beginning of this section.
2. Disconnect battery negative cable from battery and properly isolate to prevent accidental reconnection.
3. Loosen the strut tower nuts by at least five turns.

4. Loosen the wheel hub retaining nut.
5. Remove the brake disc.
6. Detach the wheel speed sensor, if equipped.
7. Remove the tie rod end retaining nut.
8. Detach the tie rod ball joint end using a suitable ball joint press.

➡The wheel hub retaining nut can be reused four times, mark the retaining nut.

9. Remove the wheel hub retaining nut.

➡Make sure that the halfshaft does not disengage from the inner constant velocity joint.

10. Using a suitable puller, separate the wheel hub from the halfshaft.
11. Remove the wheel knuckle bolt.
12. Remove the wheel knuckle.
13. Support the halfshaft out of the way.

To install:
14. Install the wheel knuckle to strut pinch bolt and tighten to 85 ft. lbs. (115 Nm).
15. Install the halfshaft.

✳✳ WARNING

The wheel hub retaining nut can be re-used four times, inspect the markings on the retaining nut and install a new retaining nut if necessary.

16. Install the wheel hub retaining nut but do not fully tighten.

17. Install the lower arm to wheel knuckle nut and bolt and tighten to 35 ft. lbs. (48 Nm)

✳✳ CAUTION

Install a new tie rod end retaining nut. Failure to follow this instruction may result in personal injury.

18. Install the tie rod end and tighten nut to 35 ft. lbs. (48 Nm)
19. Attach the wheel speed sensor, if equipped.
20. Install the brake disc.
21. Tighten the wheel hub retaining nut to 199 ft. lbs. (270 Nm)
22. Tighten the strut tower nuts to 22 ft. lbs. (30 Nm)

WHEEL BEARINGS

REMOVAL & INSTALLATION

See Figures 106 through 110.

➡The hub nut may be reused 4 times. Mark the nut at removal and only use hub nuts with 3 or fewer marks for assembly.

1. Before servicing the vehicle, refer to the Precautions Section.
2. Loosen the strut center nut 5 turns.
3. Loose the wheel hub retaining nut.
4. Remove or disconnect the following:

- Front wheel
- Wheel speed sensor, if equipped
- Hub retainer nut. Mark the nut.
- Brake caliper and rotor
- Outer tie rod end
- Lower ball joint

5. Separate the wheel hub from the halfshaft using a suitable puller.
6. Remove the steering knuckle pinch bolt
7. Release the knuckle using a suitable lever and remove from the vehicle.
8. Remove the wheel hub and outer bearing race using Special Tool 205-D064
9. Remove the bearing inner ring using Special Tools 204-180 and 205-D064
10. Remove the snap ring from the knuckle.
11. Reassemble the bearing cage to the bearing inner and install to the wheel knuckle.
12. Using Special Tools 205-153, 204-023 and 206-054, remove the bearing outer ring from the wheel knuckle.

To install:
13. Press the bearing into the hub using Special Tools 205-153 and 205-140.
14. Install the snap ring.

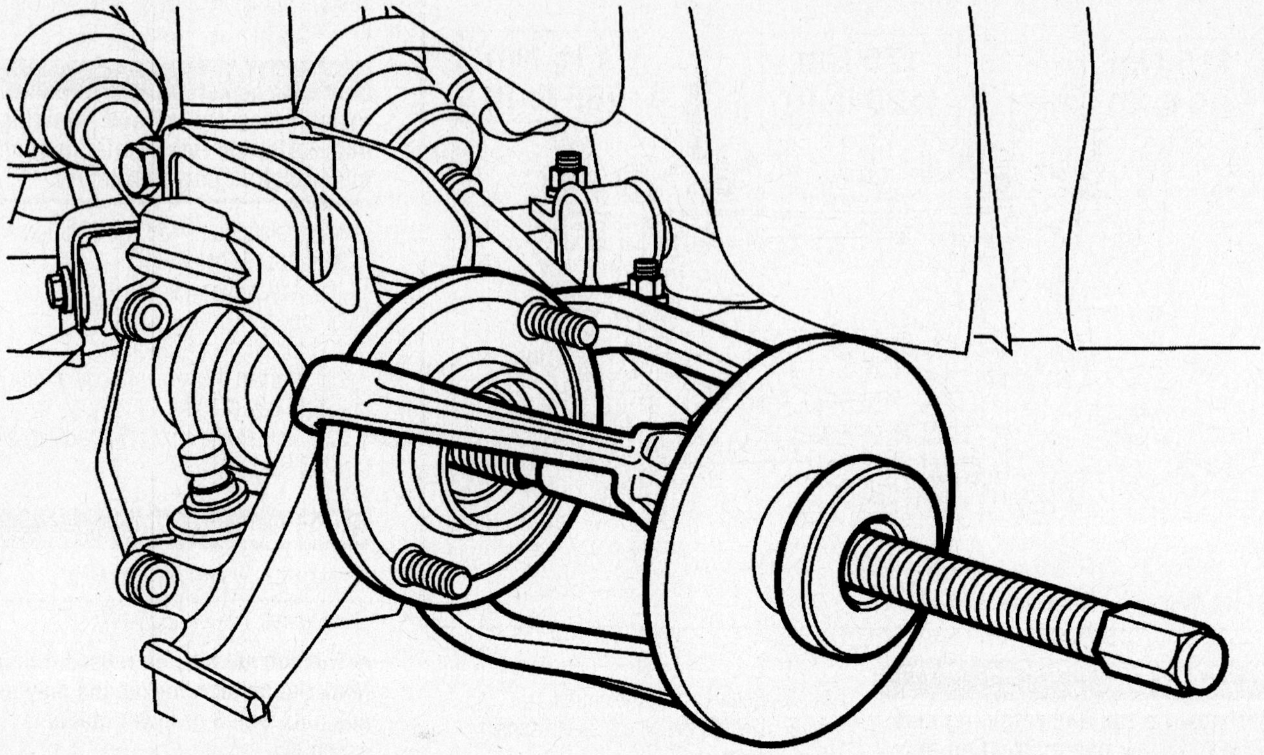

06017-FOCU-G20

Fig. 106 Removing hub using a suitable puller

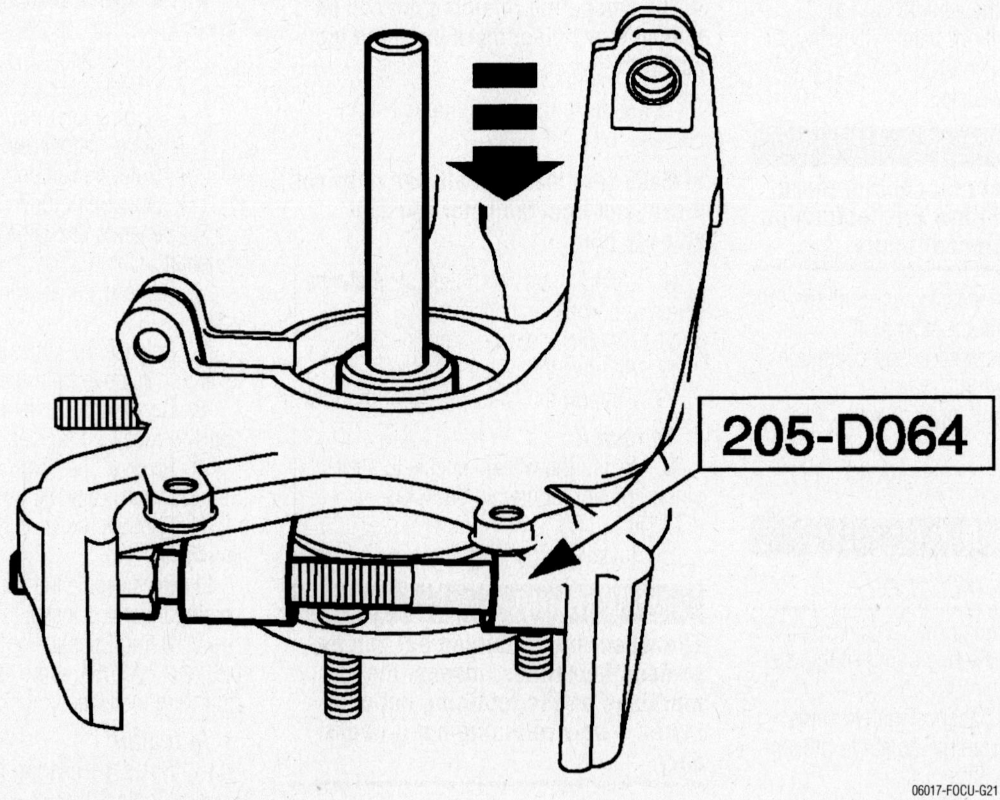

205-D064

06017-FOCU-G21

Fig. 107 Removing outer bearing race using puller 205-D064

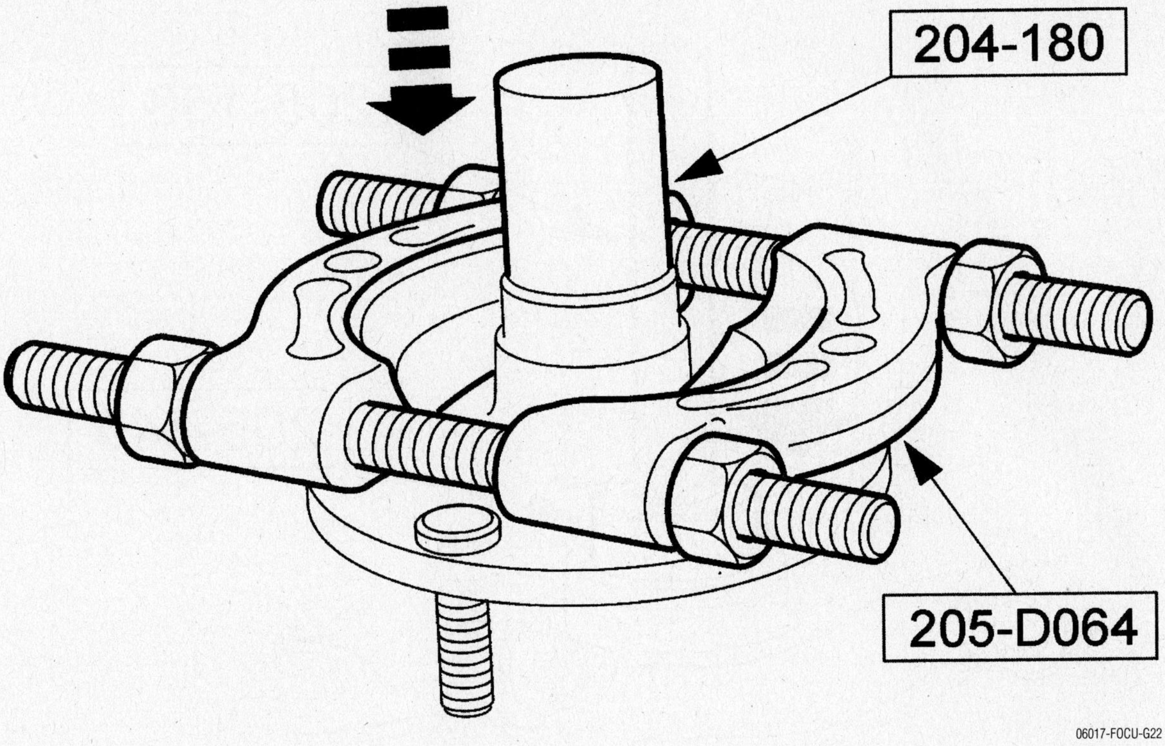

204-180

205-D064

06017-FOCU-G22

Fig. 108 Removing the bearing inner ring using Special Tool 204-180

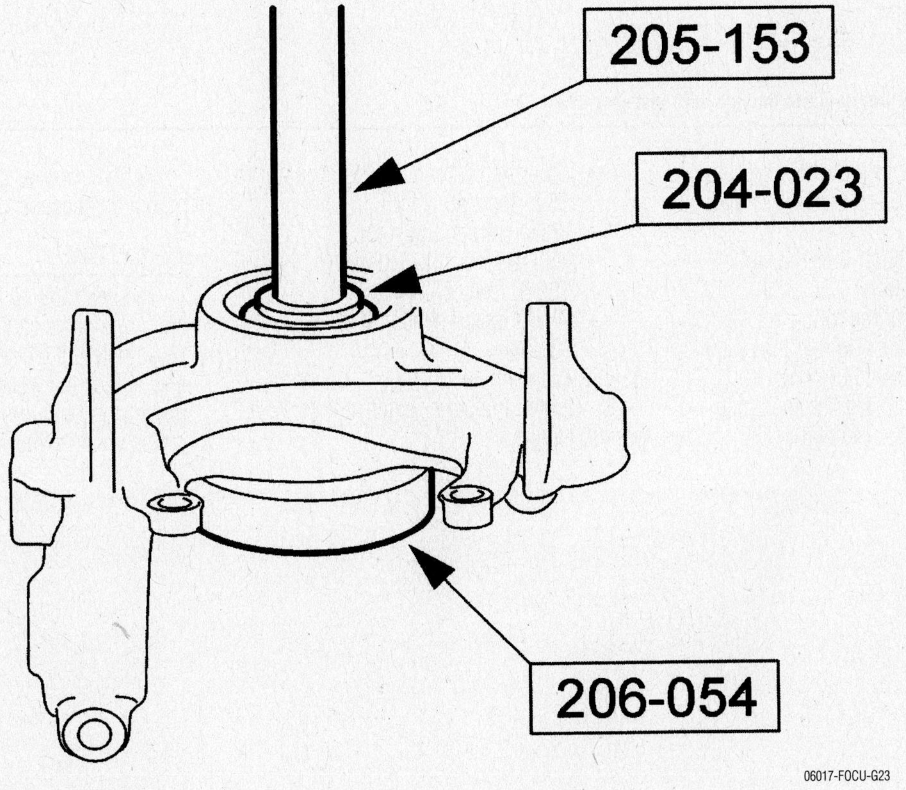

205-153

204-023

206-054

06017-FOCU-G23

Fig. 109 Removing the bearing outer ring from the wheel knuckle

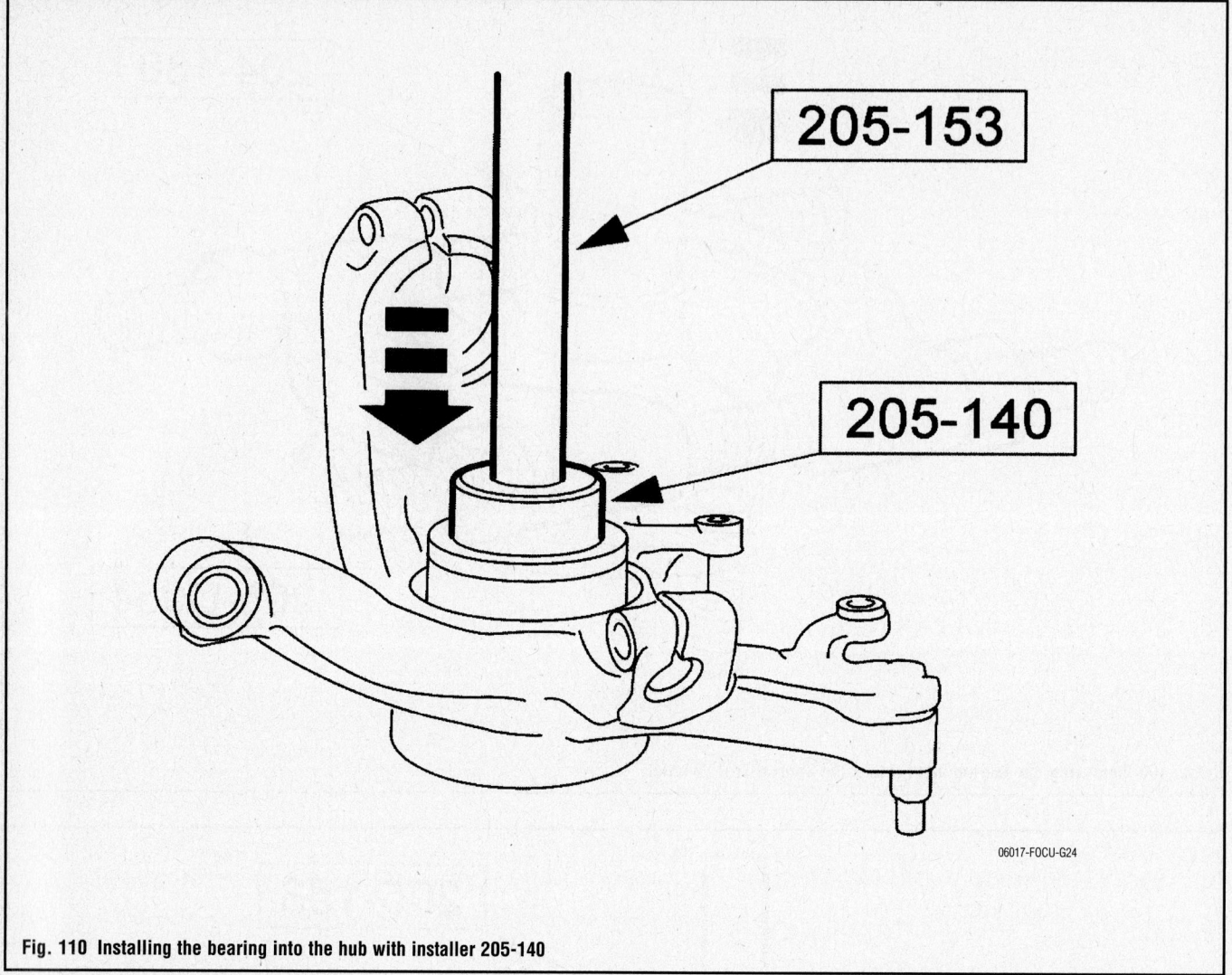

205-153

205-140

06017-FOCU-G24

Fig. 110 Installing the bearing into the hub with installer 205-140

15. Press the hub into the wheel bearing using Special Tools 205-153, 204-023 and 206-054.

16. Draw the stub shaft into the wheel hub with Halfshaft installer 205-379.

17. Install or connect the following:
- Steering knuckle. Tighten the pinch bolt to 85 ft. lbs. (115 Nm).
- Lower ball joint. Tighten the pinch bolt to 35 ft. lbs. (48 Nm).
- Outer tie rod end. Tighten the nut to 35 ft. lbs. (48 Nm).
- Brake caliper and rotor
- Hub retainer nut. Tighten the nut to 199 ft. lbs. (270 Nm).
- Wheel speed sensor, if equipped
- Front wheel

18. Tighten the strut center nuts to 22 ft. lbs. (30 Nm).

19. Check the wheel alignment and adjust as necessary.

ADJUSTMENT

The bearings on the front and rear wheels are a one piece cartridge design and cannot be adjusted. If wheel bearing play is excessive, check the wheel hub retainer nut for proper torque. If the torque is correct, replacement of the wheel bearing is required.

SUSPENSION

COIL SPRING

REMOVAL & INSTALLATION

Except Wagon

See Figure 111.

1. Before servicing the vehicle, refer to the Precautions Section.

2. Raise and support the vehicle.

3. Install spring compressor 204-167 with Adapters 204-215.

4. If necessary, remove the lower shock mounting bolt and nut.

5. Compress the coil spring and remove it.

6. Installation is the reverse of the removal procedure.

Wagon

1. Before servicing the vehicle, refer to the Precautions Section.

2. Remove the rear wheel.

3. Detach the stabilizer bar from the rear lower arms.

4. Using a transmission jack or suitable lifting device, raise the rear lower arm 1.25 inches (32 mm).

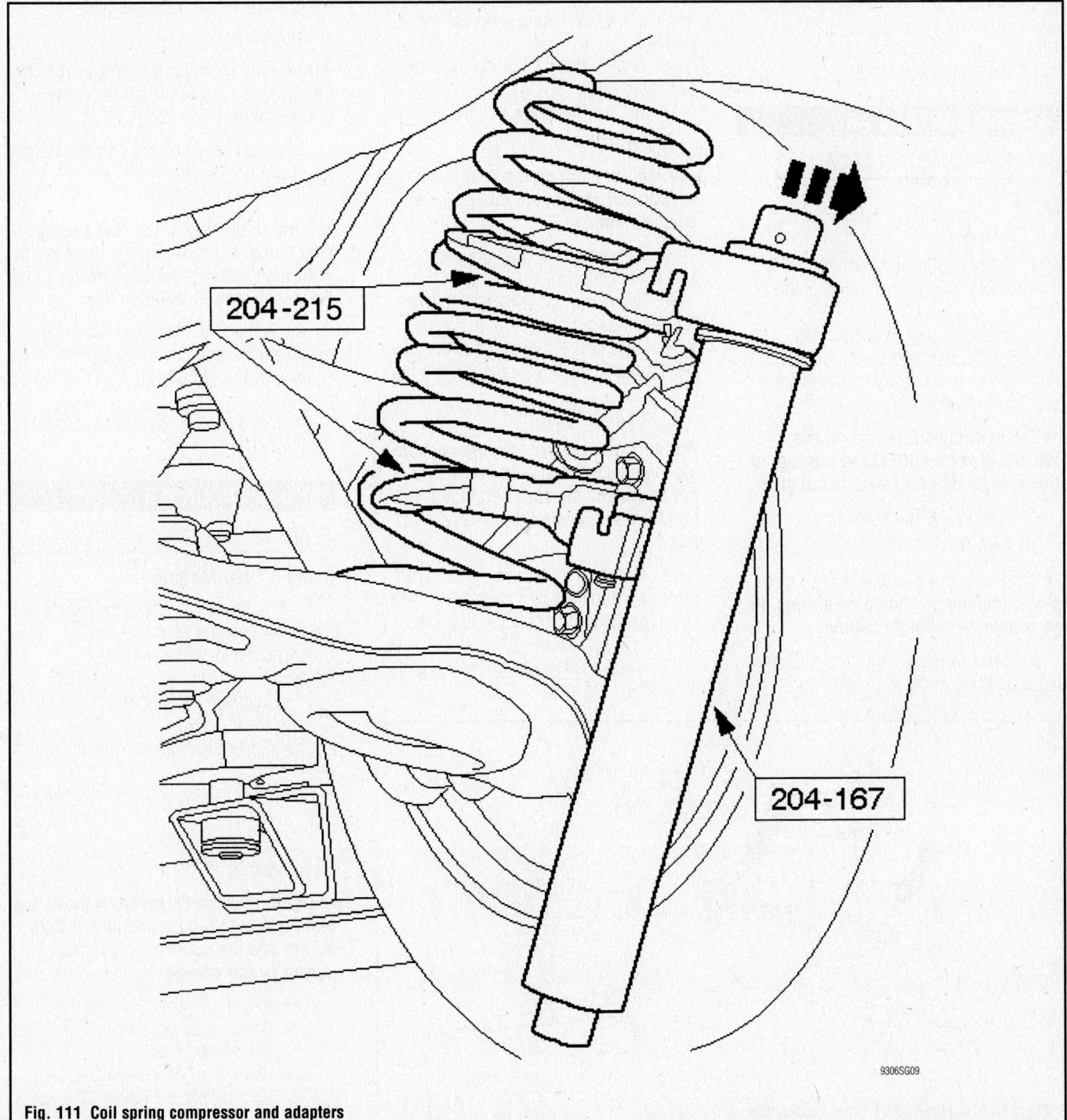

Fig. 111 Coil spring compressor and adapters

9306SG09

5. Detach the rear lower arm from the wheel knuckle.

6. Lower the rear lower arm.

7. Remove the spring.

To install:

8. Install the spring.

9. Raise the rear lower arm using a transmission jack or suitable lifting device.

10. Attach the rear lower arm to the wheel knuckle and tighten bolt to 85 ft. lbs. (115 Nm).

11. Attach the stabilizer bar to the rear lower arms and tighten to 11 ft. lbs. (15 Nm).

12. Install the rear wheel.

LOWER CONTROL ARM

REMOVAL & INSTALLATION

Front

See Figure 112.

1. Before servicing the vehicle, refer to the precautions in the beginning of this section.

2. Raise and support the vehicle.

3. Disconnect battery negative cable from battery and properly isolate to prevent accidental reconnection.

➡**The front lower arm is marked FRONT. Make a note of the position of the front lower arm to aid installation.**

4. Remove the front lower arm.

To install:

➡**Final tightening of the rear suspension components should be carried out at or near curb height setting.**

5. Install the front lower arm and tighten the bolts to 85 ft. lbs. (115 Nm)

Rear

Except Wagon

1. Before servicing the vehicle, refer to the precautions in the beginning of this section.

2. Raise and support the vehicle.

3. Disconnect battery negative cable from battery and properly isolate to prevent accidental reconnection.

4. Remove the spring.

5. Mark the position of the rear lower arm adjustment cam to the cross-member.

6. Detach the stabilizer bar from the rear lower arm.

7. Remove the rear lower arm.

To install:

➡**Align the mark on the rear lower arm adjustment cam to the mark on the crossmember.**

8. Install the rear lower arm but do not fully tighten the bolts

9. Install the rear lower arm-to-wheel knuckle retaining bolt.

10. Attach the stabilizer bar to the rear lower arm and tighten the nut to 11 ft. lbs. (15 Nm)

11. Install the spring.

➡**Final tightening of the rear suspension components should be carried out at or near the curb height setting. Load the suspension to achieve this.**

12. Tighten the rear lower arm adjustment cam nut and rear lower arm-to-wheel knuckle retaining bolts 85 ft. lbs. (115 Nm)

13. Check the toe setting and adjust as necessary.

Wagon

1. Before servicing the vehicle, refer to the precautions in the beginning of this section.

2. Raise and support the vehicle.

3. Disconnect battery negative cable from battery and properly isolate to prevent accidental reconnection.

4. Remove the spring.

5. Mark the position of the rear lower arm adjustment cam to the cross-member.

6. Remove the rear lower arm.

To install:

➡**Align the mark on the rear lower arm adjustment cam to the mark on the crossmember.**

7. Install the rear lower arm but do not fully tighten the bolts

8. Install the spring.

➡**Final tightening of the rear suspension components should be carried out at or near the curb height setting. Load the suspension to achieve this.**

9. Tighten the rear lower arm adjustment cam nut and rear lower arm-to-wheel knuckle retaining bolts 85 ft. lbs. (115 Nm)

10. Check the toe setting and adjust as necessary.

SHOCK ABSORBER

REMOVAL & INSTALLATION

3 and 4-Door Models

1. Before servicing the vehicle, refer to the Precautions Section.

2. Remove or disconnect the following:
   - Luggage compartment interior trim panel
   - Upper shock absorber mounting nut
   - Lower shock absorber mounting bolt
   - Shock absorber

To install:

➡**Tighten the shock absorber mounting fasteners with the suspension at curb height and the vehicle weight supported by the wheels.**

3. Install or connect the following:
   - Shock absorber. Guide the rod into the locating hole.
   - Lower shock absorber mounting bolt. Tighten the bolt to 85 ft. lbs. (115 Nm).

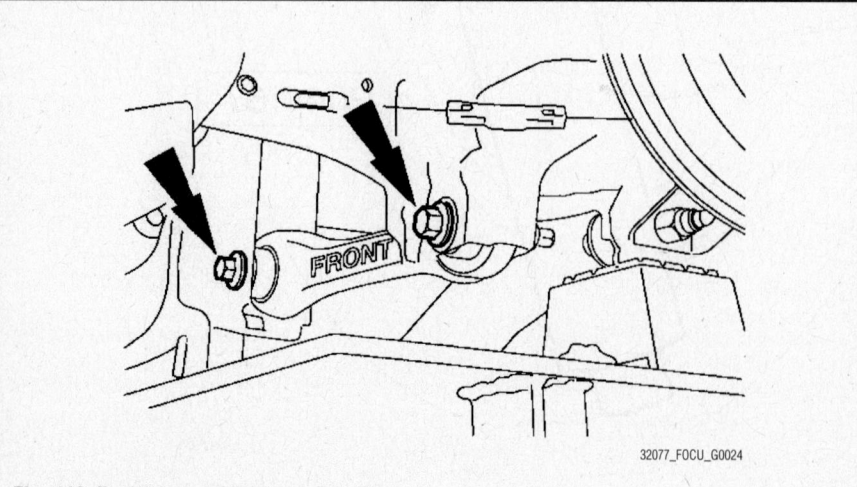

Fig. 112 Front lower arm—rear suspension

32077_FOCU_G0024

- Upper shock absorber mounting nut. Tighten the nut to 13 ft. lbs. (18 Nm).
- Luggage compartment interior trim panel

Wagon

1. Before servicing the vehicle, refer to the Precautions Section.
2. Remove the rear tire.
3. Detach the exhaust system from the rear hanger, left side only.
4. Remove the exhaust heat shield, left side only.
5. Using a transmission jack or suitable lifting device, support the lower control arm.
6. Remove the upper and lower mounting bolts.
7. Remove the shock absorber.

To install:

8. Install the shock absorber and tighten the upper mounting bolt to 85 ft. lbs. (115 Nm).
9. Lower the control arm and remove the jack.
10. Install the exhaust heat shield, if removed.
11. Attach the exhaust system to the rear hanger, if removed.
12. Install the rear tire.
13. Tighten the lower mounting bolt to 85 ft. lbs. (115 Nm).

UPPER CONTROL ARM

REMOVAL & INSTALLATION

Except Wagon

1. Before servicing the vehicle, refer to the precautions in the beginning of this section.
2. Raise and support the vehicle.
3. Disconnect battery negative cable from battery and properly isolate to prevent accidental reconnection.
4. Remove the rear wheel and tire.
5. Detach the upper arm from the wheel knuckle.

➡**Make a note of the position of the upper arm to aid installation.**

6. Remove the upper arm.

To install:

➡**Final tightening of the rear suspension components should be carried out at the design height setting. Load the suspension to achieve this.**

➡**Do not fully tighten the upper arm-to-wheel knuckle retaining bolt at this stage.**

7. Attach the upper arm to the wheel knuckle but to not fully tighten the bolts.
8. Install the wheel and tire.
9. Lower the vehicle and tighten the upper arm retaining bolt to 85 ft. lbs. (115 Nm)
10. Tighten the upper arm-to-wheel knuckle retaining bolt to 85 ft. lbs. (115 Nm)

Wagon

1. Before servicing the vehicle, refer to the precautions in the beginning of this section.
2. Raise and support the vehicle.
3. Disconnect battery negative cable from battery and properly isolate to prevent accidental reconnection.
4. Remove the rear wheel and tire.
5. Detach the upper arm from the wheel knuckle.
6. Detach the shock absorber from the wheel knuckle and position it aside.

➡**Make a note of the position of the upper arm to aid installation.**

7. Remove the upper arm.

To install:

➡**Final tightening of the rear suspension components should be carried out at the design height setting. Load the suspension to achieve this.**

➡**Do not fully tighten the upper arm-to-wheel knuckle retaining bolt at this stage.**

8. Attach the upper arm to the wheel knuckle but to not fully tighten the bolts.
9. Attach the shock absorber to the wheel knuckle but do not fully tighten the bolt.
10. Install the wheel and tire.
11. Lower the vehicle and tighten the upper arm retaining bolt to 85 ft. lbs. (115 Nm)
12. Tighten the upper arm-to-wheel knuckle retaining bolt to 85 ft. lbs. (115 Nm)
13. Tighten the shock absorber bolt to 85 ft. lbs. (115 Nm)

WHEEL HUB

REMOVAL & INSTALLATION

1. Before servicing the vehicle, refer to the precautions in the beginning of this section.
2. Remove the dust cap.
3. On rear disc brake models, perform the following:

4. Remove the wheel and tire.
5. Remove the brake caliper and disc.
6. Remove the wheel hub.
7. On rear drum brake models, perform the following:
   a. Remove the wheel and tire.
   b. Remove the parking brake.
   c. Remove the wheel hub.

To install:

※※ CAUTION

If equipped, avoid any impact on the wheel speed sensor ring. Ensure the ring is clean before hub installation.

➡**The wheel hub retaining nut can be re-used four times, mark the wheel hub retaining nut. The nut should be scribed with a mark each time it is reinstalled. Do not exceed four uses.**

8. On models with rear drum brakes, perform the following:
   a. Install the wheel hub. Do not fully tighten the wheel hub retaining nut at this stage.
   b. Tighten the wheel hub retaining nut while rotating the brake drum 10 times in the opposite direction when tightening the wheel hub retaining nut to prevent damage to the bearing. Tighten the nut to 173 ft. lbs. (235 Nm).
   c. Apply the parking brake.
   d. Install the wheel and tire.
9. On models with rear disc brakes, perform the following:
   a. Install the wheel hub. Do not fully tighten the wheel hub retaining nut at this stage.
   b. Now, tighten the wheel hub retaining nut while rotating the brake drum 10 times in the opposite direction when tightening the wheel hub retaining nut to prevent damage to the bearing. Tighten the nut to 173 ft. lbs. (235 Nm).
   c. Install the rear disc and caliper.
   d. Install the wheel and tire.

WHEEL HUB AND BEARING

REMOVAL & INSTALLATION

See Figure 113.

1. Before servicing the vehicle, refer to the Precautions Section.
2. Remove or disconnect the following:
   - Rear wheel
   - Dust cap

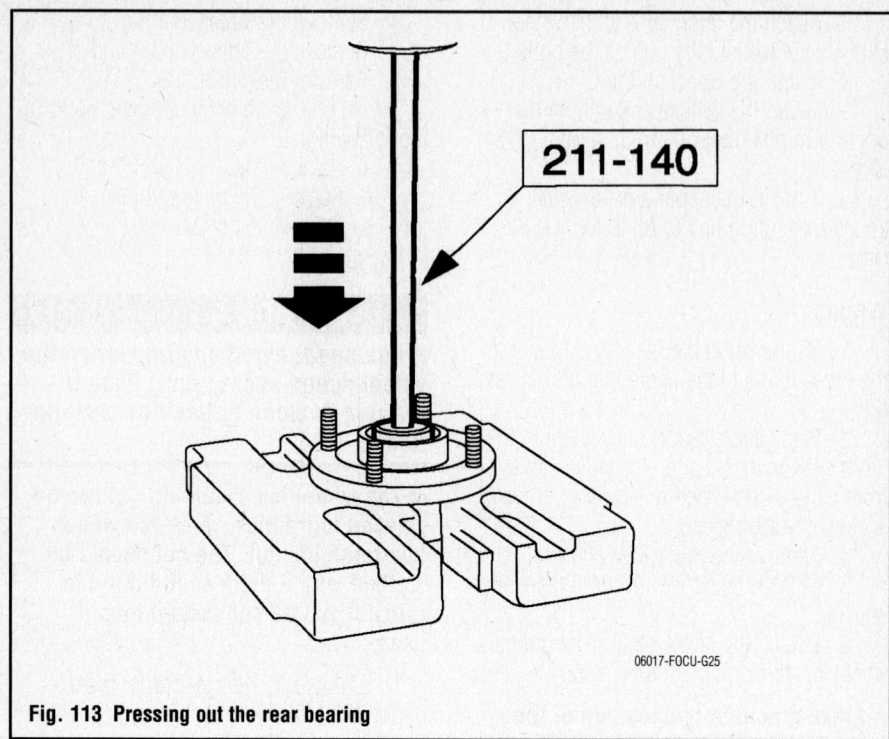

211-140

06017-FOCU-G25

Fig. 113 Pressing out the rear bearing

- Brake caliper and rotor, if equipped
- Brake drum, if equipped
- Hub nut and hub
- Wheel speed sensor tone ring, if equipped with ABS
- Snap ring

3. Remove the wheel bearing with a press.

To install:

➡ **Use a new wheel speed sensor tone ring for assembly.**

4. Press the wheel bearing into the brake drum hub.

5. Install or connect the following:
- Snap ring
- Wheel speed sensor tone ring, if equipped with ABS
- Brake drum, if equipped
- Hub nut. Tighten the hub nut to 173 ft. lbs. (235 Nm).
- Brake caliper, if equipped
- Dust cap
- Rear wheel

SPECIFICATIONS AND MAINTENANCE CHARTS

VEHICLE AND ENGINE IDENTIFICATION CHART

			Engine					Model Year	
Code	Liters	Cu. In.	Cyl.	Fuel Sys.	Engine Type	Eng. Mfg.		Code	Year
6	3.9	238	6	SEFI	OHV	Ford		5	2005
2	4.2	256	6	SEFI	OHV	Ford		6	2006
								7	2007

SEFI: Sequential Multi-port Fuel Injection

22086_FREE_C0001

GENERAL ENGINE SPECIFICATIONS

Year	Engine Displacement Liters	Engine VIN	Net Horsepower @ rpm	Net Torque @ rpm (ft. lbs.)	Bore x Stroke (in.)	Com-pression Ratio	Oil Pressure @ rpm
2005	3.9	6	193@4500	240@3500	3.81x3.46	9.3:1	40-125@2500
	4.2	2	201@4250	263@3650	3.81x3.80	9.3:1	40-125@2500
2006	3.9	6	193@4500	240@3500	3.81x3.46	9.3:1	40-125@2500
	4.2	2	201@4250	263@3650	3.81x3.80	9.3:1	40-125@2500
2007	3.9	6	193@4500	240@3500	3.81x3.46	9.3:1	40-125@2500
	4.2	2	201@4250	263@3650	3.81x3.80	9.3:1	40-125@2500

22086_FREE_C0002

GASOLINE ENGINE TUNE-UP SPECIFICATIONS

Year	Engine Displacement Liters	Engine VIN	Spark Plugs Gap (in.)	Ignition Timing (deg.) MT	Ignition Timing (deg.) AT	Fuel Pump (psi)	Idle Speed (rpm) MT	Idle Speed (rpm) AT	Valve Clearance In.	Valve Clearance Ex.
2005	3.9	6	0.052-0.056	—	①	②	—	①	HYD	HYD
	4.2	2	0.052-0.056	—	①	②	—	①	HYD	HYD
2006	3.9	6	0.052-0.056	—	①	②	—	①	HYD	HYD
	4.2	2	0.052-0.056	—	①	②	—	①	HYD	HYD
2007	3.9	6	0.052-0.056	—	①	②	—	①	HYD	HYD
	4.2	2	0.052-0.056	—	①	②	—	①	HYD	HYD

NOTE: The Vehicle Emission Control Information label often reflects specification changes changes made during production.

The label figures must be used if they differ from those in this chart.

HYD: Hydraulic

① Controlled by the Powertrain Control Module (PCM) and cannot be manually adjusted.

② Engine running: 58 psi
   Key On, Engine Off (KOEO): 67 psi

22086_FREE_C0003

CAPACITIES

Year	Model	Engine Displacement Liters	Engine ID/VIN	Engine Oil with Filter (qts.)	Transmission (pts.) 4-Spd	5-Spd	Auto.	Drive Axle Front (pts.)	Rear (pts.)	Fuel Tank (gal.)	Cooling System (qts.)
2005	Freestar	3.9	6	5.0	—	—	12.25	①	—	26	②
		4.2	2	5.0	—	—	12.25	①	—	26	②
	Monterey	3.9	6	5.0	—	—	12.25	①	—	26	②
		4.2	2	5.0	—	—	12.25	①	—	26	②
2006	Freestar	3.9	6	5.0	—	—	12.25	①	—	26	②
		4.2	2	5.0	—	—	12.25	①	—	26	②
	Monterey	3.9	6	5.0	—	—	12.25	①	—	26	②
		4.2	2	5.0	—	—	12.25	①	—	26	②
2007	Freestar	3.9	6	5.0	—	—	12.25	①	—	26	②
		4.2	2	5.0	—	—	12.25	①	—	26	②
	Monterey	3.9	6	5.0	—	—	12.25	①	—	26	②
		4.2	2	5.0	—	—	12.25	①	—	26	②

NOTE: All capacities are approximate. Add fluid gradually and check to be sure a proper fluid level is obtained.

① Included in transaxle capacity

② w/auxiliary heater: 16.0
   wo/auxiliary heater: 15.0

22086_FREE_C0004

FLUID SPECIFICATIONS

Year	Model	Engine Displacement Liters	Engine ID/VIN	Engine Oil	Auto. Trans. ①	Drive Axle	Power Steering Fluid	Brake Master Cylinder
2005	Freestar	3.9	6	5W-20	MERCON V	MERCON V	MERCON	DOT 3
		4.2	2	5W-20	MERCON V	MERCON V	MERCON	DOT 3
	Monterey	3.9	6	5W-20	MERCON V	MERCON V	MERCON	DOT 3
		4.2	2	5W-20	MERCON V	MERCON V	MERCON	DOT 3
2006	Freestar	3.9	6	5W-20	MERCON V	MERCON V	MERCON	DOT 3
		4.2	2	5W-20	MERCON V	MERCON V	MERCON	DOT 3
	Monterey	3.9	6	5W-20	MERCON V	MERCON V	MERCON	DOT 3
		4.2	2	5W-20	MERCON V	MERCON V	MERCON	DOT 3
2007	Freestar	3.9	6	5W-20	MERCON V	MERCON V	MERCON	DOT 3
		4.2	2	5W-20	MERCON V	MERCON V	MERCON	DOT 3
	Monterey	3.9	6	5W-20	MERCON V	MERCON V	MERCON	DOT 3
		4.2	2	5W-20	MERCON V	MERCON V	MERCON	DOT 3

22086_FREE_C0013

VALVE SPECIFICATIONS

Year	Engine VIN	Engine Displ. Liters	Seat Angle (deg.)	Face Angle (deg.)	Spring Test Pressure (lbs. @ in.)	Spring Installed Height (in.)	Stem-to-Guide Clearance (in.)		Stem Diameter (in.)	
							Intake	Exhaust	Intake	Exhaust
2005	6	3.9	44.75	45.6	224@1.16	1.620	0.0008-0.0027	0.0018-0.0037	0.2746-0.2754	0.2735-0.2744
	2	4.2	44.75	45.6	224@1.16	1.620	0.0008-0.0027	0.0018-0.0037	0.2746-0.2754	0.2735-0.2744
2006	6	3.9	44.75	45.6	224@1.16	1.620	0.0008-0.0027	0.0080-0.0037	0.2746-0.2754	0.2735-0.2744
	2	4.2	44.75	45.6	224@1.16	1.620	0.0008-0.0027	0.0080-0.0037	0.2746-0.2754	0.2735-0.2744
2007	6	3.9	44.75	45.6	224@1.16	1.620	0.0008-0.0027	0.0080-0.0037	0.2746-0.2754	0.2735-0.2744
	2	4.2	44.75	45.6	224@1.16	1.620	0.0008-0.0027	0.0080-0.0037	0.2746-0.2754	0.2735-0.2744

22086_FREE_C0007

CAMSHAFT AND BEARING SPECIFICATIONS CHART

All measurements are given in inches.

Year	Engine Displ. Liters	Engine ID/VIN	Journal Dia.	Brg. Oil Clearance	Shaft End-play	Runout	Journal Bore	Lobe Height	
								Intake	Exhaust
2005	3.9	6	2.0505 - 2.0515	NA	0.001 - 0.006	0.0005	①	NA	NA
	4.2	2	2.0505 - 2.0515	NA	0.001 - 0.006	0.0005	①	NA	NA
2006	3.9	6	2.0505 - 2.0515	NA	0.001 - 0.006	0.0005	①	NA	NA
	4.2	2	2.0505 - 2.0515	NA	0.001 - 0.006	0.0005	①	NA	NA
2007	3.9	6	2.0505 - 2.0515	NA	0.001 - 0.006	0.0005	①	NA	NA
	4.2	2	2.0505 - 2.0515	NA	0.001 - 0.006	0.0005	①	NA	NA

NA: Not Available

① Intake Journals: 1.85 - 1.8542
   Exhaust Journals: 1.56 - 1.5645

22086_FREE_C0014

CRANKSHAFT AND CONNECTING ROD SPECIFICATIONS

All measurements are given in inches.

Year	Engine Displ. Liters	Engine VIN	Crankshaft				Connecting Rod		
			Main Brg. Journal Dia.	Main Brg. Oil Clearance	Shaft End-play	Thrust on No.	Journal Diameter	Oil Clearance	Side Clearance
2005	3.9	6	2.5188-2.5196	0.0010-0.0014	0.0040-0.0080	3	2.3103-2.3111	0.0010-0.0014	0.0047-0.0193
	4.2	2	2.5188-2.5196	0.0010-0.0014	0.0040-0.0080	3	2.3103-2.3111	0.0010-0.0030	0.0047-0.0193
2006	3.9	6	2.5188-2.5196	0.0010-0.0014	0.0040-0.0080	3	2.3103-2.3111	0.0010-0.0014	0.0047-0.0193
	4.2	2	2.5188-2.5196	0.0010-0.0014	0.0040-0.0080	3	2.3103-2.3111	0.0010-0.0030	0.0047-0.0193
2007	3.9	6	2.5188-2.5196	0.0010-0.0014	0.0040-0.0080	3	2.3103-2.3111	0.0010-0.0014	0.0047-0.0193
	4.2	2	2.5188-2.5196	0.0010-0.0014	0.0040-0.0080	3	2.3103-2.3111	0.0010-0.0030	0.0047-0.0193

22086_FREE_C0006

PISTON AND RING SPECIFICATIONS

All measurements are given in inches.

Year	Engine Displ. Liters	Engine VIN	Piston Clearance	Ring Gap			Ring Side Clearance		
				Top Comp.	Bottom Comp.	Oil Control	Top Comp.	Bottom Comp.	Oil Control
2005	3.9	6	0.0007-0.0017	0.0067-0.0130	0.0118-0.0217	0.0059-0.0256	0.0012-0.0026	0.0012-0.0028	Snug
	4.2	2	0.0007-0.0017	0.0066-0.0129	0.0118-0.0217	0.0059-0.0255	0.0012-0.0031	0.0012-0.0028	Snug
2006	3.9	6	0.0007-0.0017	0.0067-0.0130	0.0118-0.0217	0.0059-0.0256	0.0012-0.0026	0.0012-0.0028	Snug
	4.2	2	0.0007-0.0017	0.0066-0.0129	0.0118-0.0217	0.0059-0.0255	0.0012-0.0031	0.0012-0.0028	Snug
2007	3.9	6	0.0007-0.0017	0.0067-0.0130	0.0118-0.0217	0.0059-0.0256	0.0012-0.0026	0.0012-0.0028	Snug
	4.2	2	0.0007-0.0017	0.0066-0.0129	0.0118-0.0217	0.0059-0.0255	0.0012-0.0031	0.0012-0.0028	Snug

22086_FREE_C0005

TORQUE SPECIFICATIONS
All readings in ft. lbs.

Year	Engine VIN	Engine Disp. Liters	Cylinder Head Bolts	Main Bearing Bolts	Rod Bearing Bolts	Crankshaft Damper Bolts	Flywheel Bolts	Manifold Intake	Exhaust	Spark Plugs	Oil Pan Drain Plug
2005	6	3.9	①	②	③	118	59	④	18	12	19
	2	4.2	①	②	③	118	59	④	18	12	19
2006	6	3.9	①	②	③	118	59	④	18	12	19
	2	4.2	①	②	③	118	59	④	18	12	19
2007	6	3.9	①	②	③	118	59	④	18	12	19
	2	4.2	①	②	③	118	59	④	18	12	19

① Step 1: 14 ft. lbs.
Step 2: 29 ft. lbs.
Step 3: 36 ft. lbs.
Step 4: Loosen bolt no. 1 bolt 3 turns
Step 5: Tighten no. 1 bolt as listed in step 7
Step 6: Repeat steps 4 and 5 for each bolt in sequence
Step 7: Long bolts to 30 ft. lbs. plus 1/2 turn; short bolts to 18 ft. lbs. plus 1/2 turn

② Step 1: 37 ft. lbs.
Step 2: plus 120 degrees
③ Step 1: 18 ft. lbs.
Step 2: 33 ft. lbs.
Step 3: plus 105 degrees

④ Upper manifold :Step 1: 53 INCH lbs.
Step 2: 89 INCH lbs.
Lower manifold: Step 1: 44 INCH lbs
Step 2: 89 INCH lbs.

22086_FREE_C0008

WHEEL ALIGNMENT

Year	Model			Caster Range (+/-Deg.)	Caster Preferred Setting (Deg.)	Camber Range (+/-Deg.)	Camber Preferred Setting (Deg.)	Toe-in (Deg.)
2005	Freestar	Front	L	0.75	+3.2	0.75	-0.40	-0.15+/-0.25
			R	0.75	+3.2	0.75	-0.40	-0.15+/-0.25
		Rear		—	—	0.75	-0.30	-0.14+/-0.20
	Monterey	Front	L	0.75	+3.2	0.75	-0.40	-0.15+/-0.25
			R	0.75	+3.2	0.75	-0.40	-0.15+/-0.25
		Rear		—	—	0.75	-0.30	-0.14+/-0.20
2006	Freestar	Front	L	0.75	+3.6	0.75	-0.40	-0.15+/-0.25
			R	0.75	+3.6	0.75	-0.40	-0.15+/-0.25
		Rear		—	—	0.75	-0.30	-0.14+/-0.20
	Monterey	Front	L	0.75	+3.6	0.75	-0.40	-0.15+/-0.25
			R	0.75	+3.6	0.75	-0.40	-0.15+/-0.25
		Rear		—	—	0.75	-0.30	-0.14+/-0.20
2007	Freestar	Front	L	0.75	+3.5	0.75	-0.40	-0.15+/-0.20
			R	0.75	+3.5	0.75	-0.40	-0.15+/-0.20
		Rear		—	—	0.75	-0.30	-0.14+/-0.25
	Monterey	Front	L	0.75	+3.5	0.75	-0.40	-0.15+/-0.20
			R	0.75	+3.5	0.75	-0.40	-0.15+/-0.20
		Rear		—	—	0.75	-0.30	-0.14+/-0.25

L: Left
R: Right

22086_FREE_C0009

TIRE AND WHEEL SPECIFICATIONS

| Year | Model | OEM Tires | | Tire Pressures (psi) | | Wheel Size | Lug Nut (Ft. Lbs.) |
		Standard	Optional	Front	Rear		
2005	Freestar	P225/60R16	P235/60R16	35	35	①	100
	Monterey	P225/60R16	P235/60R16	35	35	①	100
2006	Freestar	P225/60R16	P235/60R16	35	35	①	100
	Monterey	P225/60R16	P235/60R16	35	35	①	100
2007	Freestar	P225/60R16	P235/60R16	35	35	①	100
	Monterey	P225/60R16	P235/60R16	35	35	①	100

OEM: Original Equipment Manufacturer

PSI: Pounds Per Square Inch

STD: Standard

OPT: Optional

① Not available

22086_FREE_C0011

BRAKE SPECIFICATIONS
All measurements in inches unless noted

| Year | Model | | Brake Disc | | | Minimum Lining Thickness | | Brake Caliper | |
			Original Thickness	Minimum Thickness	Maximum Runout	Front	Rear	Bracket Bolts (ft. lbs.)	Mounting Bolts (ft. lbs.)
2005	Freestar	F	①	1.110	0.002	0.118	—	136	26
		R	①	0.720	0.002	—	0.118	75	24
	Monterey	F	①	1.110	0.002	0.118	—	136	26
		R	①	0.720	0.002	—	0.118	75	24
2006	Freestar	F	①	1.110	0.002	0.118	—	136	26
		R	①	0.720	0.002	—	0.118	75	24
	Monterey	F	①	1.110	0.002	0.118	—	136	26
		R	①	0.720	0.002	—	0.118	75	24
2007	Freestar	F	①	1.110	0.002	0.118	—	136	26
		R	①	0.720	0.002	—	0.118	75	24
	Monterey	F	①	1.110	0.002	0.118	—	136	26
		R	①	0.720	0.002	—	0.118	75	24

① Not available

22086_FREE_C0010

SCHEDULED MAINTENANCE INTERVALS
FORD FREESTAR, MERCURY MONTEREY

TO BE SERVICED	TYPE OF SERVICE	VEHICLE MILEAGE INTERVAL (x1000)																	
		5	10	15	20	25	30	35	40	45	50	55	60	65	70	75	80	85	90
Engine oil & filter ①	R																		
Rotate tires	S/I	✓	✓	✓	✓	✓	✓	✓	✓	✓	✓	✓	✓	✓	✓	✓	✓	✓	✓
Engine coolant strength hoses & clamps	S/I			✓			✓			✓			✓			✓			✓
Air cleaner filter	R						✓						✓						✓
Automatic transmission fluid & filter	R						✓						✓						✓
Engine coolant ②	R																		
PCV valve	R												✓						✓
Spark plugs ③	R																		
Drive belts	S/I						✓						✓						✓
Exhaust system & heat shields	S/I						✓						✓						✓
Front & rear brakes	S/I	✓	✓	✓	✓	✓	✓	✓	✓	✓	✓	✓	✓	✓	✓	✓	✓	✓	✓
Fuel filter	R			✓			✓			✓			✓			✓			✓

R: Replace   S/I: Service or Inspect

① Engine oil and filter: replace every 3000 miles.

② Engine coolant: change initially at 100,000 miles or 5 years.

③ Spark plugs: replace every 100,000 miles.

Special Operating Condition Requirements

During extensive idling and/or low speed driving for long distances, as in heavy commercial use such as delivery, taxi, patrol car or livery:

Lube front lower control arm and steering linkage ball joints with

Zerk fittings (if equipped) every 4,800 km (3,000 miles) or 3 months.

Inspect brake system and check battery electrolyte level (Patrol cars) every 8,000 km (5,000 miles).

Install a new cabin air filter as required.

When operating in dusty conditions such as unpaved or dusty roads:

Install a new engine air filter as required.

Install a new cabin air filter as required.

When operating in off-road conditions:

Change automatic transmission fluid every 48,000 km (30,000 miles).

Install a new cabin air filter as required.

Inspect and lubricate U-joints.

Inspect and lubricate steering linkage ball joints with zerk fittings.

22086_FREE_C0012

PRECAUTIONS

Before servicing any vehicle, please be sure to read all of the following precautions, which deal with personal safety, prevention of component damage, and important points to take into consideration when servicing a motor vehicle:

• Never open, service or drain the radiator or cooling system when the engine is hot; serious burns can occur from the steam and hot coolant.

• Observe all applicable safety precautions when working around fuel. Whenever servicing the fuel system, always work in a well-ventilated area. Do not allow fuel spray or vapors to come in contact with a spark, open flame, or excessive heat (a hot drop light, for example). Keep a dry chemical fire extinguisher near the work area. Always keep fuel in a container specifically designed for fuel storage; also, always properly seal fuel containers to avoid the possibility of fire or explosion. Refer to the additional fuel system precautions later in this section.

• Fuel injection systems often remain pressurized, even after the engine has been turned **OFF**. The fuel system pressure must be relieved before disconnecting any fuel lines. Failure to do so may result in fire and/or personal injury.

• Brake fluid often contains polyglycol ethers and polyglycols. Avoid contact with the eyes and wash your hands thoroughly after handling brake fluid. If you do get brake fluid in your eyes, flush your eyes with clean, running water for 15 minutes. If eye irritation persists, or if you have taken brake fluid internally, IMMEDIATELY seek medical assistance.

• The EPA warns that prolonged contact with used engine oil may cause a number of skin disorders, including cancer. You should make every effort to minimize your exposure to used engine oil. Protective gloves should be worn when changing oil. Wash your hands and any other exposed skin areas as soon as possible after exposure to used engine oil. Soap and water, or waterless hand cleaner should be used.

• All new vehicles are now equipped with an air bag system, often referred to as a Supplemental Restraint System (SRS) or Supplemental Inflatable Restraint (SIR) system. The system must be disabled before performing service on or around system components, steering column, instrument panel components, wiring and sensors. Failure to follow safety and disabling procedures could result in accidental air bag deployment, possible personal injury and unnecessary system repairs.

• Always wear safety goggles when working with, or around, the air bag system. When carrying a non-deployed air bag, be sure the bag and trim cover are pointed away from your body. When placing a non-deployed air bag on a work surface, always face the bag and trim cover upward, away from the surface. This will reduce the motion of the module if it is accidentally deployed. Refer to the additional air bag system precautions later in this section.

• Clean, high quality brake fluid from a sealed container is essential to the safe and proper operation of the brake system. You should always buy the correct type of brake fluid for your vehicle. If the brake fluid becomes contaminated, completely flush the system with new fluid. Never reuse any brake fluid. Any brake fluid that is removed from the system should be discarded. Also, do not allow any brake fluid to come in contact with a painted surface; it will damage the paint.

• Never operate the engine without the proper amount and type of engine oil; doing so WILL result in severe engine damage.

• Timing belt maintenance is extremely important. Many models utilize an interference-type, non-freewheeling engine. If the timing belt breaks, the valves in the cylinder head may strike the pistons, causing potentially serious (also time-consuming and expensive) engine damage. Refer to the maintenance interval charts for the recommended replacement interval for the timing belt, and to the timing belt section for belt replacement and inspection.

• Disconnecting the negative battery cable on some vehicles may interfere with the functions of the on-board computer system(s) and may require the computer to undergo a relearning process once the negative battery cable is reconnected.

• When servicing drum brakes, only disassemble and assemble one side at a time, leaving the remaining side intact for reference.

• Only an MVAC-trained, EPA-certified automotive technician should service the air conditioning system or its components.

BRAKES

GENERAL INFORMATION

The Anti-lock Brake System (ABS) module, with or without stability assist, simultaneously manages the anti-lock braking, traction control and engine control systems to maintain vehicle control during deceleration and acceleration.

When the ignition switch is in the **RUN** position, the module carries out a preliminary electrical check and, at approximately 12 mph (20 km/h), the hydraulic pump motor is turned on for approximately one half-second. Any malfunction of the anti-lock brake system disables the traction control and stability assist (if equipped) and the anti-lock brake warning indicator illuminates. However, the power-assist braking system functions normally.

The Anti-lock Brake System (ABS) consists of the following components:
• Hydraulic Control Unit (HCU)
• ABS module
• Front wheel speed sensors and sensor rings (part of the front hub and bearing assembly)
• Rear wheel speed sensors
• Rear wheel speed sensor rings (part of the rear hub and bearing assembly)
• Yellow ABS warning indicator

ANTI-LOCK BRAKE SYSTEM (ABS)

The front wheel speed sensors and front wheel speed sensor rings are integral to the front hub and bearing assemblies.

The rear wheel speed sensor rings are integral to the rear hub and bearing assembly.

The ABS with traction control and stability assist consists of these additional components:
• Accelerometer
• Yaw rate sensor (contained in the accelerometer)
• Steering wheel rotation sensor
• Traction control switch
• Trac off indicator

SPEED SENSORS

REMOVAL & INSTALLATION

Rear

See Figure 1.

1. Raise and safely support the vehicle.
2. Disconnect the wheel speed sensor electrical connector.
3. Remove the 3 wheel speed sensor harness pin-type retainers.
4. Remove the 2 wheel speed sensor harness retainers.
5. Disconnect the wheel speed sensor at the wheel.
6. Remove the wheel speed sensor and harness assembly.
7. Installation is the reverse of the removal procedure.

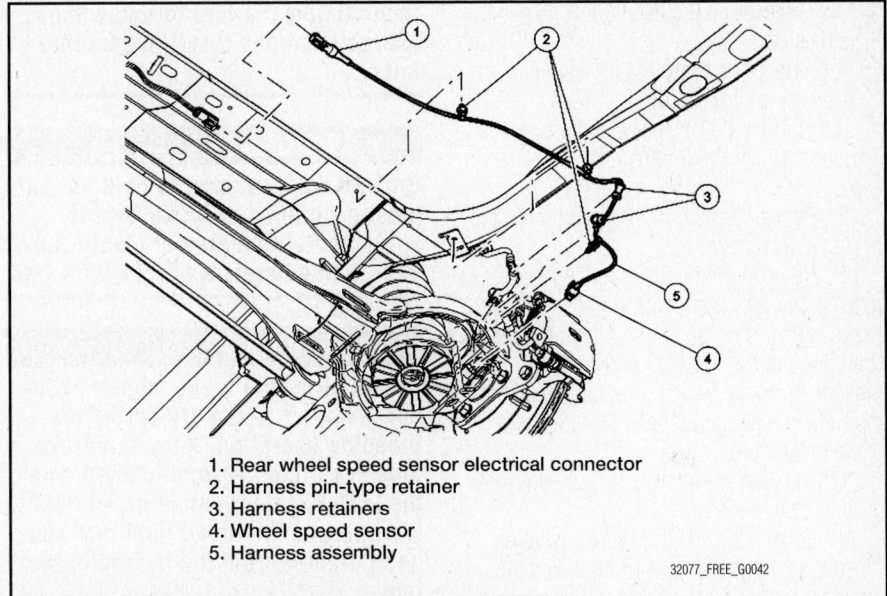

1. Rear wheel speed sensor electrical connector
2. Harness pin-type retainer
3. Harness retainers
4. Wheel speed sensor
5. Harness assembly

32077_FREE_G0042

Fig. 1 Rear wheel speed sensor and related components

BRAKES

BLEEDING THE BRAKE SYSTEM

BLEEDING PROCEDURE

BLEEDING PROCEDURE

Manual Bleeding

1. This procedure requires the use of the following special tools or their equivalents: Worldwide Diagnostic System (WDS) and Vehicle Communication Module (VCM) with proper adapters or equivalent diagnostic scan tool.

> ✳ **CAUTION**
>
> Use of any other than approved DOT 3 motor vehicle brake fluid will cause permanent damage to brake components and will render the brakes inoperative. Failure to follow these instructions may result in personal injury.

> ✳ **CAUTION**
>
> Brake fluid contains polyglycol ethers and polyglycols. Avoid contact with eyes. Wash hands thoroughly after handling. If brake fluid contacts eyes, flush eyes with running water for 15 minutes. Get medical attention if irritation persists. If taken internally, drink water and induce vomiting. Get medical attention immediately. Failure to follow these instructions may result in personal injury.

> ✳ **WARNING**
>
> Brake fluid is harmful to painted and plastic surfaces. If brake fluid is spilled onto a painted or plastic surface, immediately wash it with water.

> ✳ **WARNING**
>
> Do not allow the brake master cylinder reservoir to run dry during the bleeding operation. Keep the brake master cylinder reservoir filled with the DOT 3 motor vehicle brake fluid. Never reuse the brake fluid that has been drained from the hydraulic system.

> ✳ **WARNING**
>
> After a hydraulic control unit replacement (ABS or IVD unit), conduct the Brake System Pressure Bleeding procedure before the diagnostic tool based bleed procedure. A diagnostic tool based bleed procedure is then required to completely bleed the system. Follow the instructions from the diagnostic tool to ensure a correct bleed.

➡ If the Hydraulic Control Unit (HCU), or any component upstream of the HCU are installed new, carry out the Brake System Pressure Bleeding procedure first without the scan tool, followed by the Brake System Bleed procedure using the scan tool. The Component Bleeding - Rear Brake Caliper procedure is not required as the rear calipers were not replaced.

➡ When any part of the hydraulic system has been disconnected for repair or installation of new components, air can get into the system and cause spongy brake pedal action. This requires bleeding of the hydraulic system after it has been correctly connected. The hydraulic system can be bled manually or with pressure bleeding equipment. Bleeding the system with pressure bleeding equipment is the preferred method.

2. Connect the diagnostic tool cable adapter into the vehicle Data Link Connector (DLC) under the dash and follow the diagnostic tool instructions.
3. Clean all the dirt from the area, remove the brake master cylinder reservoir cap and fill the brake master cylinder reservoir with the specified brake fluid.
4. Remove the rear bleeder cap and place a box end wrench on the RH rear bleeder screw. Attach a rubber drain tube to the RH rear bleeder screw and submerge the free end of the tube in a container partially filled with clean brake fluid.
5. Have an assistant hold firm pressure on the brake pedal.
6. Loosen the RH rear bleeder screw until a stream of brake fluid comes out. While the assistant maintains pressure on the brake pedal, tighten the RH rear bleeder screw.

a. Repeat until clear, bubble-free fluid comes out.

b. Refill the brake master cylinder reservoir as necessary.

7. Tighten the RH rear bleeder screw to 7 ft. lbs. (10 Nm) and reinstall the bleeder cap.

8. Repeat Steps 3, 4, 5 and 6 for the LH rear bleeder screw.

9. Remove the rear bleeder cap and place a box end wrench on the RH front brake caliper bleeder screw. Attach a rubber drain tube to the RH front brake caliper bleeder screw, and submerge the free end of the tube in a container partially filled with clean brake fluid.

10. Have an assistant hold firm pressure on the brake pedal.

11. Loosen the RH front brake caliper bleeder screw until a stream of brake fluid comes out. While the assistant maintains pressure on the brake pedal, tighten the RH front brake caliper bleeder screw.

a. Repeat until clear, bubble-free fluid comes out.

b. Refill the brake master cylinder reservoir as necessary.

12. Tighten the RH front brake caliper bleeder screw to 7 ft. lbs. (10 Nm) and reinstall the bleeder cap.

13. Repeat Steps 8, 9, 10 and 11 for the LH front brake caliper bleeder screw.

Pressure Bleeding

1. This procedure requires the use of the following special tools or their equivalents: Worldwide Diagnostic System (WDS) and Vehicle Communication Module (VCM) with proper adapters or equivalent diagnostic scan tool.

**** CAUTION**

Use of any other than approved DOT 3 motor vehicle brake fluid will cause permanent damage to brake components and will render the brakes inoperative. Failure to follow these instructions may result in personal injury.

**** CAUTION**

Brake fluid contains polyglycol ethers and polyglycols. Avoid contact with eyes. Wash hands thoroughly after handling. If brake fluid contacts eyes, flush eyes with running water for 15 minutes. Get medical attention if irritation persists. If taken internally, drink water and induce vomiting. Get medical attention immediately. Failure to follow these instructions may result in personal injury.

**** WARNING**

Brake fluid is harmful to painted and plastic surfaces. If brake fluid is spilled onto a painted or plastic surface, immediately wash it with water.

**** WARNING**

Do not allow the brake master cylinder reservoir to run dry during the bleeding operation. Keep the brake master cylinder reservoir filled with the DOT 3 motor vehicle brake fluid. Never reuse the brake fluid that has been drained from the hydraulic system.

2. Clean all the dirt from the area and remove the brake master cylinder filler cap. Fill the brake master cylinder reservoir with the specified brake fluid.

➡Master cylinder pressure bleeder adapter tools are available from various manufacturers of pressure bleeding equipment. Follow the instructions of the manufacturer when installing the adapter.

3. Install the bleeder adapter to the brake master cylinder reservoir, and attach the bleeder tank hose to the fitting on the adapter.

➡Bleed the longest line first. Make sure the bleeder tank contains enough specified brake fluid to complete the bleeding operation.

4. Place a box end wrench on the RH rear bleeder screw. Attach a rubber drain tube to the RH rear bleeder screw, and submerge the free end of the tube in a container partially filled with clean brake fluid.

5. Open the valve on the bleeder tank.

6. Loosen the RH rear bleeder screw. Leave open until clear, bubble-free brake fluid flows, then tighten the RH rear bleeder screw to 7 ft. lbs. (10 Nm) and remove the rubber hose.

7. Continue bleeding the rear of the system, going in order from the LH rear bleeder screw to the RH front disc brake caliper bleeder screw ending with the LH front brake caliper bleeder screw.

8. Close the bleeder tank valve. Remove the tank hose from the adapter, and remove the adapter.

Master Cylinder

1. This procedure requires the use of the following special tools or their equivalents: Worldwide Diagnostic System (WDS) and Vehicle Communication Module (VCM) with proper adapters or equivalent diagnostic scan tool.

**** CAUTION**

Use of any other than approved DOT 3 motor vehicle brake fluid will cause permanent damage to brake components and will render the brakes inoperative. Failure to follow these instructions may result in personal injury.

**** CAUTION**

Brake fluid contains polyglycol ethers and polyglycols. Avoid contact with eyes. Wash hands thoroughly after handling. If brake fluid contacts eyes, flush eyes with running water for 15 minutes. Get medical attention if irritation persists. If taken internally, drink water and induce vomiting. Get medical attention immediately. Failure to follow these instructions may result in personal injury.

**** WARNING**

Brake fluid is harmful to painted and plastic surfaces. If brake fluid is spilled onto a painted or plastic surface, immediately wash it with water.

➡When any part of the hydraulic system has been disconnected for repair or installation of new components, air can enter the system and cause spongy brake pedal action. This requires bleeding of the hydraulic system after it has been correctly connected. The hydraulic system can be bled manually or with pressure bleeding equipment.

➡When a new brake master cylinder has been installed or the system has been emptied, or partially emptied, it should be primed to prevent air from entering the system.

2. For in-vehicle priming, disconnect the brake lines.

3. For bench priming, mount the brake master cylinder in a vise.

4. Install short brake tubes onto the primary and secondary ports with the ends submerged in the brake master cylinder reservoir.

5. Fill the brake master cylinder reservoir with DOT 3 motor vehicle brake fluid.

6. Have an assistant pump the brake pedal, or slowly press the primary piston until clear fluid flows from the brake tubes, without air bubbles.

7. If the brake master cylinder has been primed at the bench, install it in the vehicle.

8. Remove the short brake tubes, and install the master cylinder brake tubes. Tighten to 13 ft. lbs. (17 Nm).

9. Bleed each brake tube at the brake master cylinder as follows:

a. Have an assistant pump the brake pedal, and then hold firm pressure on the brake pedal.

b. Loosen the rear-most brake tube fittings until a stream of brake fluid comes out. While the assistant maintains pressure on the brake pedal, tighten the brake tube fitting.

c. Repeat this operation until clear, bubble-free fluid comes out.

d. Refill the brake master cylinder reservoir as necessary. Repeat the bleeding operation at the front brake tube.

Rear Brake Caliper

See Figure 2.

➡ This procedure requires the use of a Rear Brake Caliper Piston Adapter for Adjuster 206-026 (T87P-2588-A), or equivalent.

✳✳ CAUTION

Use of any other than approved DOT 3 motor vehicle brake fluid will cause permanent damage to brake components and will render the brakes inoperative. Failure to follow these instructions may result in personal injury.

✳✳ CAUTION

Brake fluid contains polyglycol ethers and polyglycols. Avoid contact with eyes. Wash hands thoroughly after handling. If brake fluid contacts eyes, flush eyes with running water for 15 minutes. Get medical attention if irritation persists. If taken internally, drink water and induce vomiting. Get medical attention immediately. Failure to follow these instructions may result in personal injury.

✳✳ WARNING

Brake fluid is harmful to painted and plastic surfaces. If brake fluid is spilled onto a painted or plastic surface, immediately wash it with water.

✳✳ WARNING

Do not allow the brake master cylinder reservoir to run dry during the bleeding operation. Keep the brake master cylinder reservoir filled with the DOT 3 motor vehicle brake fluid. Never reuse the brake fluid that has been drained from the hydraulic system.

➡ When any part of the hydraulic system has been disconnected for repair or installation of new components, air can get into the system and cause spongy brake pedal action. This requires bleeding of the hydraulic system after it has been correctly connected. The hydraulic system can be bled manually or with pressure bleeding equipment.

➡ Due to the complexity of the fluid path within the rear integral parking brake calipers, it may be necessary to follow this procedure when new calipers are installed.

➡ This procedure is necessary only when installing a new rear brake caliper. To bleed the brake system, refer to Manual or Pressure Bleeding in this section.

1. Raise and safely support the vehicle.

2. Remove the 2 brake caliper bolts and position the brake caliper aside.

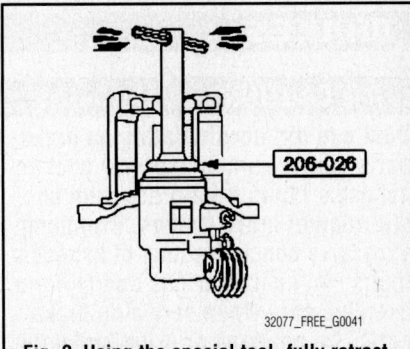

Fig. 2 Using the special tool, fully retract the brake caliper piston and tighten the bleeder screw

3. Remove the outer brake pad.

➡ Place a shop towel between the caliper and the brake disc.

4. Install the brake caliper using the 2 brake caliper bolts and torque to 24 ft. lbs. (33 Nm).

5. Slowly apply the brake pedal to extend the brake caliper piston out.

6. Remove the 2 brake caliper bolts and position the brake caliper aside.

7. Bleed the brake caliper:

a. Remove the bleeder screw cap and place a box end wrench on the brake caliper bleeder screw. Attach a rubber drain tube to the brake caliper bleeder screw and submerge the free end of the tube in a container partially filled with clean brake fluid.

8. Loosen the brake caliper bleeder screw:

a. Using the special tool, fully retract the brake caliper piston and tighten the bleeder screw to 7 ft. lbs. (10 Nm).

9. Refill the brake master cylinder reservoir as necessary.

10. Repeat steps 5 through 9 until clear, bubble free fluid comes out. Install the bleeder screw cap.

11. Install the outer brake pad.

12. Position the brake caliper and install the 2 brake caliper bolts. Torque to 24 ft. lbs. (33 Nm).

BRAKES

✳✳ CAUTION

Dust and dirt accumulating on brake parts during normal use may contain asbestos fibers from production or aftermarket brake linings. Breathing excessive concentrations of asbestos fibers can cause serious bodily harm. Exercise care when servicing brake parts. Do not sand or grind brake lin- ing unless equipment used is designed to contain the dust residue. Do not clean brake parts with com- pressed air or by dry brushing. Clean- ing should be done by dampening the brake components with a fine mist of water, then wiping the brake compo- nents clean with a dampened cloth. Dispose of cloth and all residue con- taining asbestos fibers in an imper- meable container with the appropriate label. Follow practices prescribed by the Occupational Safety and Health Administration (OSHA) and the Envi- ronmental Protection Agency (EPA) for the handling, processing, and dis- posing of dust or debris that may con- tain asbestos fibers.

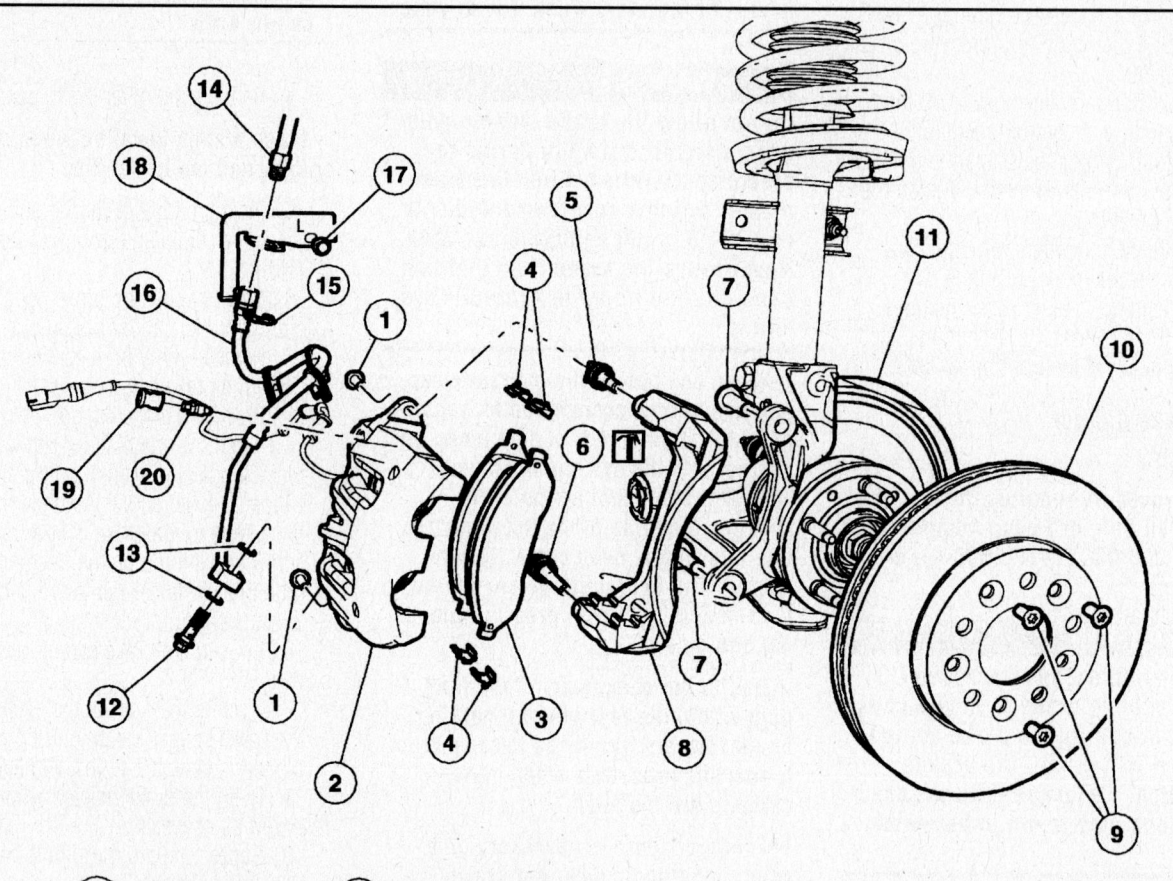

①	35 Nm (26 lb-ft)	⑭	17 Nm (13 lb-ft)
⑦	185 Nm (136 lb-ft)	⑰	17 Nm (13 lb-ft)
⑫	55 Nm (41 lb-ft)	⑳	10 Nm (7 lb-ft)

Item	Description	Item	Description	Item	Description
1	Brake caliper bolt (two required for each side)	7	Brake caliper anchor bracket bolts (2 required each side)	13	Copper washers
2	Brake caliper RH/LH	8	Brake caliper anchor bracket RH/LH	14	Brake line fitting
3	Brake pads	9	Brake disc screws (if equipped)	15	Retainer clip
4	Slippers (4 required each side)	10	Brake disc	16	Front brake hose RH/LH
5	Guide pin	11	Dust shield (RH/LH)	17	Brake hose bracket bolt
6	Locator pin	12	Flow bolt	18	Brake hose bracket
				19	Bleeder screw dust cover
				20	Bleeder screw

Fig. 3 Exploded view of the front disc brake caliper assembly—Freestar and Monterey

67197-FREE-G37

BRAKE CALIPER

REMOVAL & INSTALLATION

See Figure 3.

1. Raise and safely support the vehicle.
2. Remove the wheel and tire assembly.
3. Mark the disc brake caliper to avoid mixing the left-hand and right-hand components.
4. Disconnect the brake hose from the disc brake caliper by loosening and removing the hollow retaining bolt. Discard the 2 copper sealing washers and plug the brake hose.
5. Remove the 2 brake pin retainer bolts.
6. Lift the disc brake caliper off of the disc brake rotor using a rotating motion. Do not pry against the caliper piston. Prying may damage the piston or seals.
7. Remove the disc brake caliper from the vehicle.
8. Remove the caliper anchor bracket, if necessary.

To install:

9. Install the brake caliper anchor, if removed. Tighten the anchor bolts to 136 ft. lbs. (185 Nm).
10. Retract the caliper piston fully into the caliper bore using a C-clamp and block of wood or equivalent.
11. Ensure that the disc brake pads are properly positioned and that the lining material is facing the rotor.
12. Place the disc brake caliper over the rotor and hand-start 2 brake pin retainer bolts. Starting with the bottom bolt first, tighten the brake pin retainer bolts-to-guide pin bolts to 26 ft. lbs. (35 Nm).

➡**If both disc brake calipers were removed, make sure that they are mounted to the proper side. The brake bleeder on the caliper when properly installed should be on top of the caliper for proper bleeding of air.**

13. Unplug and install the brake hose and hollow retaining bolt to the disc brake caliper using a new copper sealing washer on each side of the hose fitting.
14. Bleed the brake system and install the rubber bleeder screw caps when complete.
15. Install the wheel and tire assembly. Torque the lug nuts to 100 ft. lbs. (136 Nm).
16. Lower the vehicle.
17. Pump the brake pedal several times to position the brake pads before attempting to move the vehicle.
18. Check and fill the brake master cylinder as required.
19. Road-test the vehicle and check for proper brake operation.

DISC BRAKE PADS

REMOVAL AND INSTALLATION

See Figure 3.

1. Remove ½ of the brake fluid from the brake master cylinder reservoir. Properly dispose of the brake fluid.
2. Raise and safely support the vehicle.
3. Remove the wheel and tire assembly.
4. Remove 2 disc brake caliper brake pin retainers. Do not remove the brake hose from the caliper.

5. Lift the disc brake caliper off of the disc brake rotor using a rotating motion. Do not pry against the caliper piston. Prying may damage the piston or seals.
6. Hang the disc brake caliper with a length of wire or equivalent to prevent damage to the brake hose.
7. Remove the inner and outer disc brake pads and the anti-rattle clip.
8. Inspect the disc brake rotor surfaces for grooves, cracks or glazing. Resurface or replace as required. If resurfacing, observe the minimum thickness specification.

To install:

9. Retract the caliper piston fully into the caliper bore using a C-clamp and wood block or equivalent. This will allow room for the new disc brake pads.
10. Install new inner and outer disc brake pads and the anti-rattle clip. Ensure that the disc brake pads are properly positioned and that the lining material is facing the rotor.
11. Place the disc brake caliper over the rotor and install 2 disc brake caliper brake pin retainers. Tighten the brake pin retainers to 26 ft. lbs. (35 Nm).
12. Install the wheel and tire assembly. Torque the lug nuts to 100 ft. lbs. (136 Nm).
13. Lower the vehicle.
14. Pump the brake pedal to position the brake pads before attempting to move the vehicle.
15. Check and fill the brake master cylinder reservoir, as required.
16. Road-test the vehicle and check for proper brake system operation.

BRAKES

✳✳ CAUTION

Dust and dirt accumulating on brake parts during normal use may contain asbestos fibers from production or aftermarket brake linings. Breathing excessive concentrations of asbestos fibers can cause serious bodily harm. Exercise care when servicing brake parts. Do not sand or grind brake lining unless equipment used is designed to contain the dust residue. Do not clean brake parts with compressed air or by dry brushing. Cleaning should be done by dampening the brake components with a fine mist of water, then wiping the brake components clean with a dampened cloth. Dispose of cloth and all residue containing asbestos fibers in an impermeable container with the appropriate label. Follow practices prescribed by the Occupational Safety and Health Administration (OSHA) and the Environmental Protection Agency (EPA) for the handling, processing, and disposing of dust or debris that may contain asbestos fibers.

BRAKE CALIPER

REMOVAL & INSTALLATION

See Figure 4.

1. Remove and discard ½ of the brake fluid from the brake master cylinder reservoir.

REAR DISC BRAKES

2. Raise and safely support the vehicle.
3. Remove the wheel and tire assembly.
4. Disconnect the brake hose from the disc brake caliper by loosening and removing the hollow retaining bolt. Discard 2 copper sealing washers and plug the brake hose.
5. Using a C-clamp or equivalent, position the clamp frame on the inboard side of the disc brake caliper housing. Place the clamp screw on the outboard disc brake pad and tighten the clamp enough to press the caliper piston into the caliper housing releasing pressure on the disc brake pads.
6. Disconnect the parking brake cable from the caliper.
7. Remove 2 disc brake caliper retaining bolts.

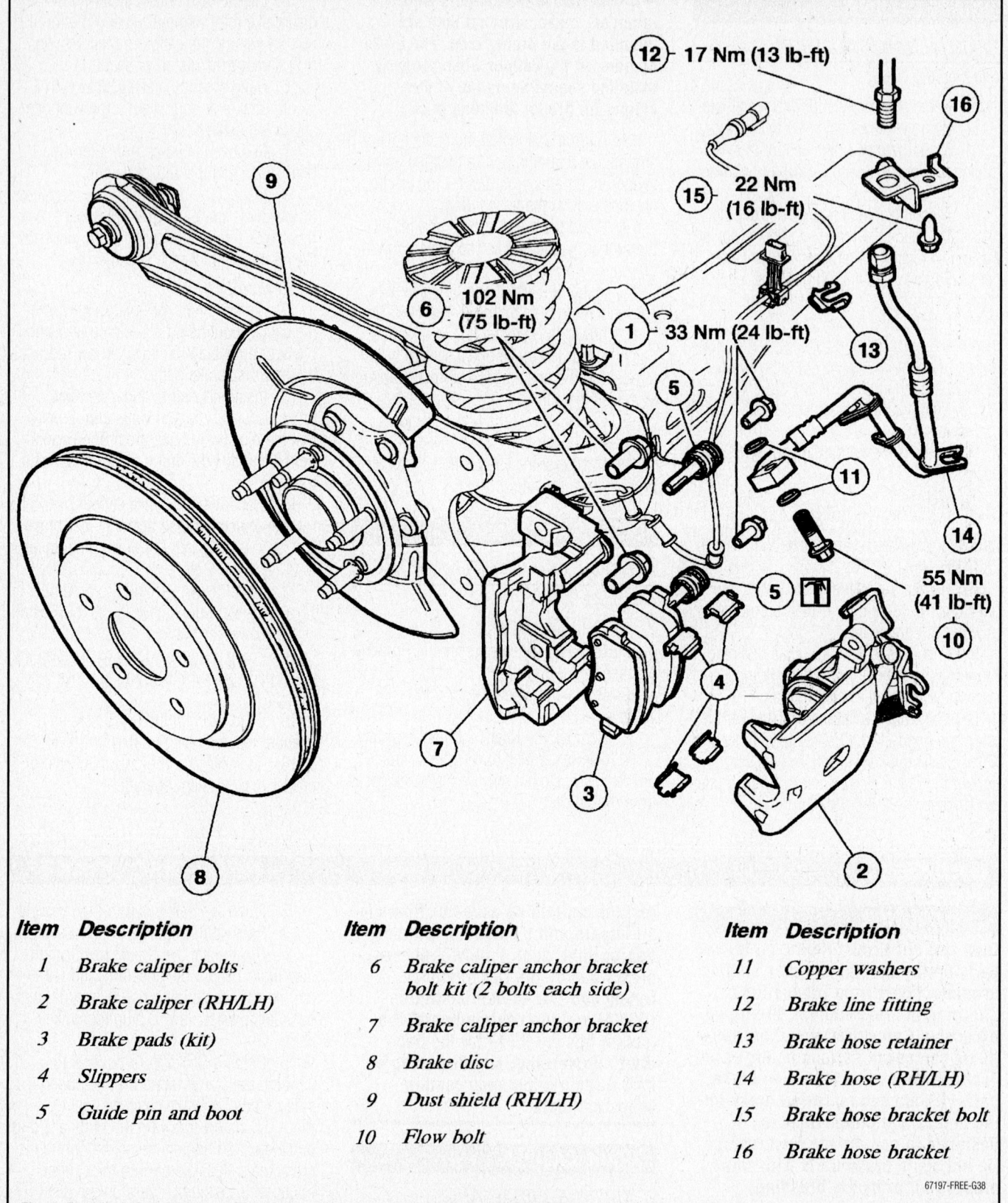

Fig. 4 Exploded view of the rear disc brake caliper assembly—Freestar and Monterey

67197-FREE-G38

Item	Description
1	Brake caliper bolts
2	Brake caliper (RH/LH)
3	Brake pads (kit)
4	Slippers
5	Guide pin and boot

Item	Description
6	Brake caliper anchor bracket bolt kit (2 bolts each side)
7	Brake caliper anchor bracket
8	Brake disc
9	Dust shield (RH/LH)
10	Flow bolt

Item	Description
11	Copper washers
12	Brake line fitting
13	Brake hose retainer
14	Brake hose (RH/LH)
15	Brake hose bracket bolt
16	Brake hose bracket

8. Remove the caliper by swinging out the bottom of the caliper first.

9. Remove the disc brake pads, if necessary.

10. Remove the caliper anchor bracket, if necessary.

To install:

11. If removed, install the caliper anchor bracket. Tighten the bolts to 75 ft. lbs. (102 Nm).

12. Retract the disc brake caliper piston fully into the caliper bore using a C-clamp and block of wood or equivalent.

13. Ensure that the disc brake pads are properly positioned and that the lining material is facing the rotor.

14. Install the caliper over the disc brake rotor and position on the brake adapter. Install 2 disc brake caliper retaining bolts and starting with the bottom bolt first, tighten to 24 ft. lbs. (33 Nm).

15. Install the parking brake cable to the caliper.

16. Unplug and install the brake hose and hollow retaining bolt to the disc brake caliper using a new copper sealing washer on each side of the hose fitting. Tighten the retaining bolt to 41 ft. lbs. (55 Nm).

17. Bleed the brake system and install the rubber bleeder screw caps when complete.

18. Install the wheel and tire assembly. Torque the lug nuts to 100 ft. lbs. (136 Nm).

19. Lower the vehicle.

20. Pump the brake pedal several times to position the brake pads before attempting to move the vehicle.

21. Check and fill the brake master cylinder as required.

22. Road-test the vehicle and check for proper brake operation.

DISC BRAKE PADS

REMOVAL AND INSTALLATION

See Figure 4.

1. Remove ½ of the brake fluid from the brake master cylinder reservoir. Properly dispose of the brake fluid.

2. Raise and safely support the vehicle.

3. Remove the wheel and tire assembly.

4. Using a C-clamp or equivalent, position the clamp frame on the inboard side of the disc brake caliper housing. Place the clamp screw on the outboard disc brake pad and tighten the clamp enough to press the caliper piston into the caliper housing releasing pressure on the disc brake pads.

5. Remove 2 disc brake caliper retaining bolts. Do not remove the disc brake caliper brake hose from the caliper.

6. Work the disc brake caliper off the brake rotor and disc brake adapter. Move the disc brake caliper aside and secure with wire or equivalent to prevent damage to the brake hose.

7. Remove the slippers from the anchor plate abutments by gently prying them off the rails and discard the slippers.

8. Remove the inner and outer disc brake pads.

9. Inspect the disc brake rotor surfaces for grooves, cracks or glazing. Resurface or replace as required. If resurfacing, observe the minimum thickness specification.

To install:

10. Retract the disc brake caliper piston fully into the caliper bore using a C-clamp and block of wood or equivalent. This will make room for the new disc brake pads.

11. Install new anti-wear slippers on the rail abutments by snapping them in place.

12. Install new inner and outer disc brake pads. Ensure that the disc brake pads are properly positioned and that the lining material is facing the rotor.

13. Install the disc brake caliper over the brake rotor and place on the brake adapter. Ensure that the notches on the upper ends of the brake pads are seated over the upper ledge of the disc brake adapter and the lower tabs are placed on the lower ledge of the disc brake adapter.

14. Lubricate 2 disc brake caliper retaining bolts with a suitable grease and install. Tighten the retaining bolts to 41 ft. lbs. (55 Nm).

15. Install the wheel and tire assembly. Torque the lug nuts to 100 ft. lbs. (136 Nm).

16. Lower the vehicle.

17. Pump the brake pedal several times to position the brake pads before attempting to move the vehicle.

18. Check and fill the brake master cylinder reservoir, as required.

19. Road-test the vehicle and check for proper brake operation.

BRAKES   PARKING BRAKE

PARKING BRAKE CABLES

ADJUSTMENT

The rear disc brake pads serve as the parking brakes. Refer to the procedures under Rear Disc Brakes.

PARKING BRAKE SHOES

REMOVAL & INSTALLATION

The rear disc brake pads serve as the parking brakes. Refer to the procedures under Rear Disc Brakes.

CHASSIS ELECTRICAL   AIR BAG (SUPPLEMENTAL RESTRAINT SYSTEM)

GENERAL INFORMATION

❈❈ CAUTION

These vehicles are equipped with an air bag system. The system must be disarmed before performing service on, or around, system compo- nents, the steering column, instrument panel components, wiring and sensors. Failure to follow the safety precautions and the disarming procedure could result in accidental air bag deployment, possible injury and unnecessary system repairs.

SERVICE PRECAUTIONS

Disconnect and isolate the battery negative cable before beginning any airbag system component diagnosis, testing, removal, or installation procedures. Allow system capacitor to discharge for two minutes before beginning any component service.

This will disable the airbag system. Failure to disable the airbag system may result in accidental airbag deployment, personal injury, or death.

Do not place an intact undeployed airbag face down on a solid surface. The airbag will propel into the air if accidentally deployed and may result in personal injury or death.

When carrying or handling an undeployed airbag, the trim side (face) of the airbag should be pointing towards the body to minimize possibility of injury if accidental deployment occurs. Failure to do this may result in personal injury or death.

Replace airbag system components with OEM replacement parts. Substitute parts may appear interchangeable, but internal differences may result in inferior occupant protection. Failure to do so may result in occupant personal injury or death.

Wear safety glasses, rubber gloves, and long sleeved clothing when cleaning powder residue from vehicle after an airbag deployment. Powder residue emitted from a deployed airbag can cause skin irritation. Flush affected area with cool water if irritation is experienced. If nasal or throat irritation is experienced, exit the vehicle for fresh air until the irritation ceases. If irritation continues, see a physician.

Do not use a replacement airbag that is not in the original packaging. This may result in improper deployment, personal injury, or death.

The factory installed fasteners, screws and bolts used to fasten airbag components have a special coating and are specifically designed for the airbag system. Do not use substitute fasteners. Use only original equipment fasteners listed in the parts catalog when fastener replacement is required.

During, and following, any child restraint anchor service, due to impact event or vehicle repair, carefully inspect all mounting hardware, tether straps, and anchors for proper installation, operation, or damage. If a child restraint anchor is found damaged in any way, the anchor must be replaced. Failure to do this may result in personal injury or death.

Deployed and non-deployed airbags may or may not have live pyrotechnic material within the airbag inflator.

Do not dispose of driver/passenger/curtain airbags or seat belt tensioners unless you are sure of complete deployment. Refer to the Hazardous Substance Control System for proper disposal.

Dispose of deployed airbags and tensioners consistent with state, provincial, local, and federal regulations.

After any airbag component testing or service, do not connect the battery negative cable. Personal injury or death may result if the system test is not performed first.

If the vehicle is equipped with the Occupant Classification System (OCS), do not connect the battery negative cable before performing the OCS Verification Test using the scan tool and the appropriate diagnostic information. Personal injury or death may result if the system test is not performed properly.

Never replace both the Occupant Restraint Controller (ORC) and the Occupant Classification Module (OCM) at the same time. If both require replacement, replace one, then perform the Airbag System test before replacing the other.

Both the ORC and the OCM store Occupant Classification System (OCS) calibration data, which they transfer to one another when one of them is replaced. If both are replaced at the same time, an irreversible fault will be set in both modules and the OCS may malfunction and cause personal injury or death.

If equipped with OCS, the Seat Weight Sensor is a sensitive, calibrated unit and must be handled carefully. Do not drop or handle roughly. If dropped or damaged, replace with another sensor. Failure to do so may result in occupant injury or death.

If equipped with OCS, the front passenger seat must be handled carefully as well. When removing the seat, be careful when setting on floor not to drop. If dropped, the sensor may be inoperative, could result in occupant injury, or possibly death.

If equipped with OCS, when the passenger front seat is on the floor, no one should sit in the front passenger seat. This uneven force may damage the sensing ability of the seat weight sensors. If sat on and damaged, the sensor may be inoperative, could result in occupant injury, or possibly death.

DISARMING THE SYSTEM

1. Disconnect the negative battery cable from the battery.
2. Disconnect the positive battery cable from the battery.
3. Wait 1 minute. This time is required for the back-up power supply in the air bag diagnostic monitor to completely drain. The system is now disarmed.

ARMING THE SYSTEM

1. Connect the positive battery cable.
2. Connect the negative battery cable.
3. Stand outside the vehicle and carefully turn the ignition to the **RUN** position. Be sure that no part of your body is in front of the air bag module on the steering wheel, to prevent injury in case of an accidental air bag deployment.
4. Ensure the air bag indicator light turns off after approximately 6 seconds. If the light does not illuminate at all, does not turn off, or starts to flash, diagnose the problem. If the light does turn off after 6 seconds and does not flash, the SRS is working properly.

DRIVE TRAIN

AUTOMATIC TRANSAXLE ASSEMBLY

REMOVAL & INSTALLATION

See Figure 5.

1. Remove or disconnect the following:

- Battery and battery tray
- Air cleaner assembly
- All transaxle electrical harnesses
- Transaxle shift cable from the lever by unsnapping the shift cable end from the lever ball stud
- Manual control lever
- Hood
- Wiper arm and pivot assembly
- Passenger side air intake box
- Air intake tube
- Upper radiator shield
- Hood latch and oil filler cap

➡**Install engine lifting eyes to support the engine during transaxle removal.**

2. Install an engine support kit and suitably support the engine.

3. Remove or disconnect the following:
- Transaxle filer tube
- Transaxle cooler lines
- The 2 upper transaxle-to-engine bolts
- Raise and support the vehicle

- Anti-roll bracket under the vehicle
- Rear transaxle support nut
- Transaxle fluid
- Catalytic converter assembly
- Front wheels

4. Disconnect the left and right tie rod ends from the knuckles.

5. Disconnect the sway bar ends from the knuckles.

6. Remove the left and right knuckle pinch bolts.

7. Remove or disconnect the following:

- Steering rack bolts
- Power steering hose retainers
- Front and rear engine mount nuts
- Place a jack under the subframe to support it
- 4 subframe mounting bolts

8. Partially lower the subframe and remove the sway bar mounting bolts. Remove the sway bar.

9. Lower the subframe from the vehicle.

10. Remove or disconnect the following:
- Wire the steering rack in place
- Starter
- Halfshafts from the transaxle and support them out of the way
- Torque converter nuts and discard them
- Transaxle electrical connectors

11. Position a transaxle jack to support

the transaxle and remove the transaxle mounting nuts.

12. Remove the oil pan-to-transaxle bolt.

13. Separate the transaxle from the engine block by carefully moving the transaxle rearward until enough clearance exists to remove the transaxle from the engine compartment.

To install:

➡**If a different transaxle is being installed, transfer the heat shield to the new transaxle.**

14. Place the transaxle on a suitable jack and carefully raise it into position.

15. Install or connect the following:
- Oil pan-to-transaxle bolt, and tighten the bolt to 46 ft. lbs. (62 Nm).
- Engine bracket-to-transaxle bolts, and tighten the bolts to 46 ft. lbs. (62 Nm)
- Transaxle-to-engine bolts, and tighten the bolts to 35 ft. lbs. (47 Nm)
- Transaxle mounting bolts, and tighten the bolts to 46 ft. lbs. (62 Nm).
- Transaxle electrical connectors
- NEW torque converter nuts, and tighten them to 26 ft. lbs. (35 Nm)
- Transaxle housing cover, and

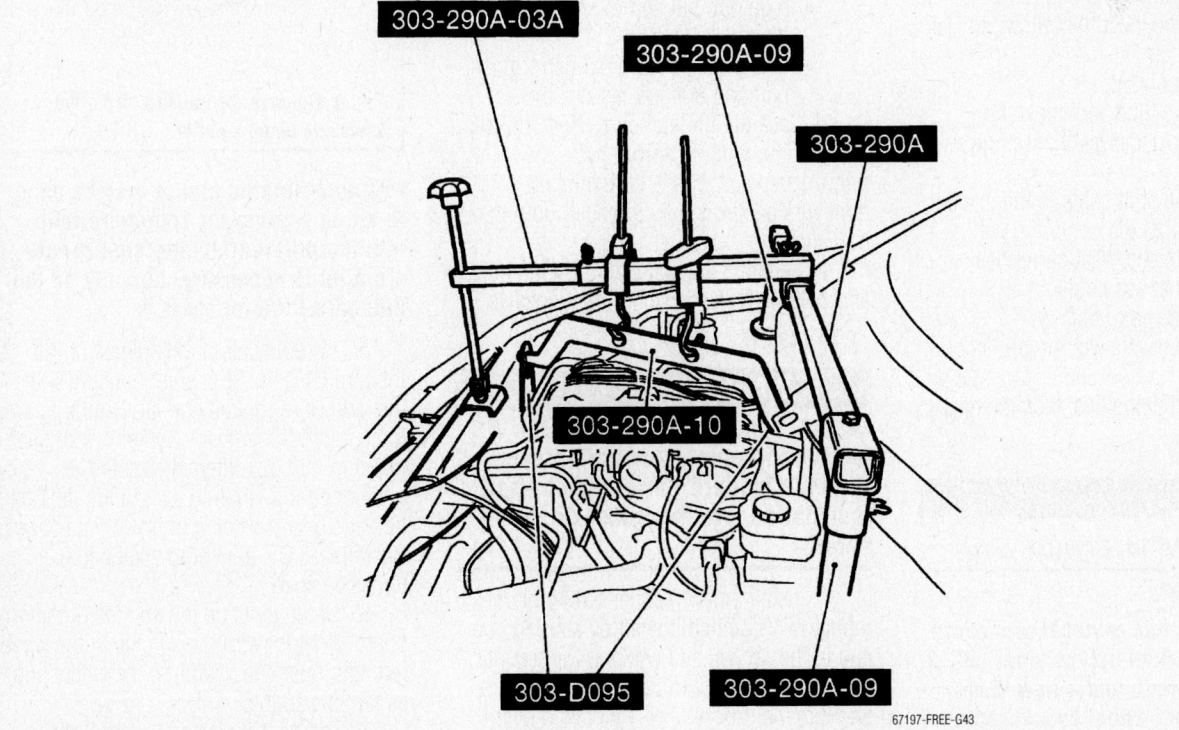

303-290A-03A
303-290A-09
303-290A
303-290A-10
303-D095
303-290A-09

67197-FREE-G43

Fig. 5 Installing engine support kit—3.9L and 4.2L engines

tighten the bolts to 89 inch lbs. (10 Nm)

- Both halfshafts
- Starter motor, and connect the electrical harness
- Speedometer cable
- Front subframe
- Sway bar mounting bolts, and tighten the bolts to 46 ft. lbs. (62 Nm)
- The 4 subframe bolts, and tighten them to 66 ft. lbs. (90 Nm)
- Front and rear engine mount bolts, and tighten them to 66 ft. lbs. (90 Nm)
- Power steering hose retainers
- Steering rack bolts, and tighten them to 98 ft. lbs. 133 Nm).
- Left and right knuckle pinch bolts, and tighten the bolts to 46 ft. lbs. (62 Nm).
- Sway bar end mounting nuts, and tighten the bolts to 41 ft. lbs. (55 Nm).
- Tie rod end nuts, and tighten the nuts to 41 ft. lbs. (55 Nm).
- Catalytic converter
- Rear transaxle mounting nut, and tighten to 66 ft. lbs. (90 Nm)
- Anti-roll bracket
- Upper transaxle-to-engine bolts, and tighten the bolts to 46 ft. lbs. (62 Nm)
- Fluid cooler-to-transaxle lines
- Front wheels and lower the vehicle

16. Remove the engine support kit.
17. Install or connect the following:
- Hood latch
- Radiator shield
- Air intake tube and intake box
- Wiper arm and pivot assembly
- Hood
- Transaxle shift cable to the manual lever ball stud
- Transaxle electrical harnesses
- Air cleaner assembly
- Battery tray and battery

18. Fill the transaxle with proper amount of Mercon®V fluid.
19. Connect the positive, then the negative battery cable.

HALFSHAFT

REMOVAL & INSTALLATION

See Figures 6 and 7.

➡**Do not begin this removal procedure unless a new wheel hub retainer nut, a new retainer circlip and a new lower ball joint-to-front wheel knuckle retaining bolt and nut are available. Once**

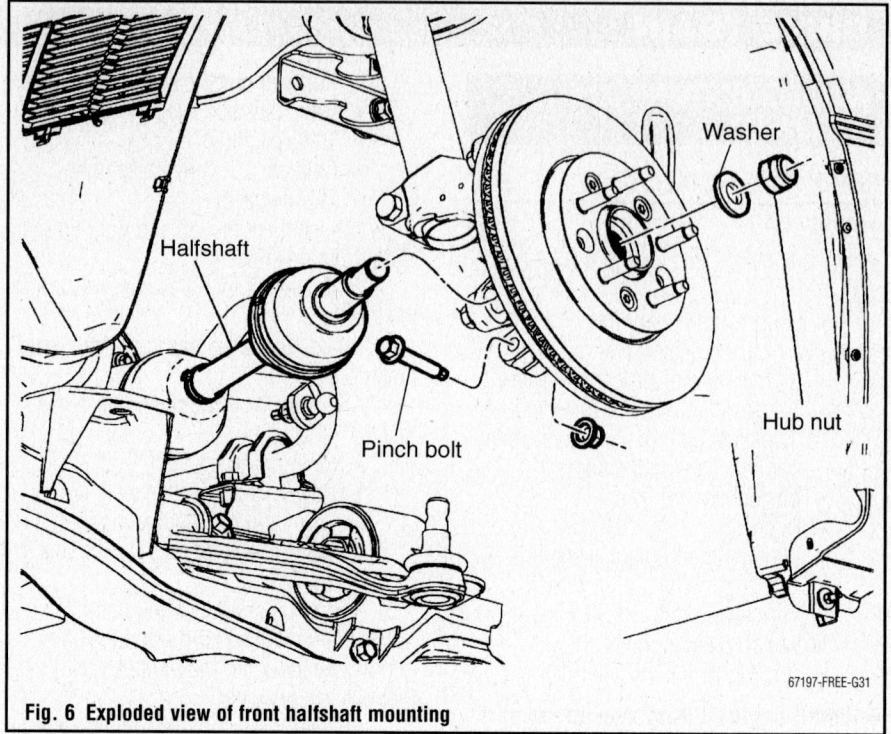

Fig. 6 Exploded view of front halfshaft mounting

removed, these parts must not be reused during assembly. Their torque holding ability, or retention capability, is diminished during removal.

1. Remove or disconnect the following:
- Front wheels
- ABS sensor
- Brake caliper and wire aside
- Axle hub nut and washer. Discard the nut.
- Lower control arm ball joint pinch bolt and nut and discard them

2. Separate the outboard CV-joint from the wheel hub using a front hub remover/replacer. Make sure the hub remover adapter is fully threaded onto the hub stud.

3. Separate the halfshaft from the hub, and pull the halfshaft out of the transaxle.

To install:

✳✳ WARNING

Do not reuse the retainer circlip. A new circlip must be installed each time the inboard CV-joint stub shaft is installed into the transaxle differential.

4. Install a new retainer circlip on the inboard CV-joint stub shaft by starting one end in the groove and working the retainer circlip over the inboard shaft housing end and into the groove. This will avoid over-expanding the circlip.

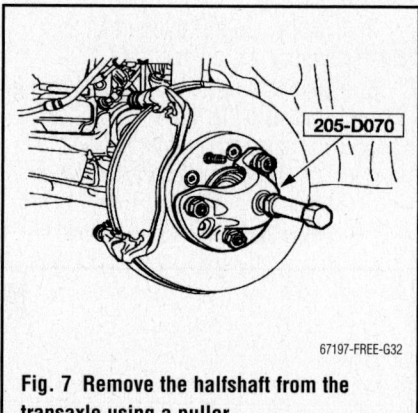

Fig. 7 Remove the halfshaft from the transaxle using a puller

➡**A non-metallic mallet may be used to aid in seating the retainer circlip into the differential side gear groove. If a mallet is necessary, tap only on the outboard CV-joint shaft.**

5. Carefully align the splines of the inboard CV-joint stub shaft housing with the splines in the differential. Exerting some force, push the inboard CV-joint stub shaft housing into the differential until the retainer circlip is felt to seat in the differential side gear. Use care to prevent damage to the inboard CV-joint stub shaft and transaxle seal.

6. Carefully align the splines of the outboard CV-joint with the splines in the wheel hub and push the shaft into the wheel hub as far as possible.

7. Temporarily fasten the front disc brake rotor to the wheel hub with washers

and 2 lug nuts. Insert a steel rod into the front disc brake rotor and rotate clockwise to contact the front wheel knuckle to prevent the front disc brake rotor from turning when the nut is tightened.

➡**A new front axle wheel hub retaining nut must be installed.**

8. Manually thread the front axle wheel hub retaining nut onto the outboard CV-joint stub shaft housing as far as possible.

➡**A new bolt and nut must be used to connect the front suspension arm to the knuckle.**

9. Connect the front suspension lower arm to the front wheel knuckle. Tighten the nut and bolt to 46 ft. lbs. (63 Nm).

10. Install the front brake anti-lock sensor.

➡**Do not use power or impact tools to tighten the hub nut.**

11. Tighten front axle wheel hub retaining nut to 111 ft. lbs. (150 Nm).

12. Install the front wheels and lower the vehicle.

13. Fill the transaxle to the proper level with Mercon®V automatic transmission fluid.

CV-JOINTS

OVERHAUL

➡**Overhaul procedures are not available from manufacturer. The assembled length of the left side halfshaft should**
be 24.07 inches (611.37 mm), and the assembled length of the right halfshaft should be 28 inches (711.2 mm).

CV-BOOTS INSPECTION

The CV (Constant Velocity) boots should be checked for damage each time the oil is changed and any other time the vehicle is raised for service. These boots keep water, grime, dirt and other damaging matter from entering the CV-joints. Any of these could cause early CV-joint failure which can be expensive to repair. Heavy grease thrown around the inside of the front wheel(s) and on the brake caliper/drum can be an indication of a torn boot. Thoroughly check the boots for missing clamps and tears. If the boot is damaged, it should be replaced immediately.

REAR AXLE HOUSING

REMOVAL & INSTALLATION

1. With the vehicle in NEUTRAL, position it on a hoist.
2. Remove the rear brake discs.
3. Disconnect the brake lines and rear wheel speed sensor wire harness from the rear axle assembly.

❄ CAUTION

The rear axle assembly must be supported before removal of the trackbar arm or the retaining bolts to prevent damage to the vehicle components.

4. Secure the axle to a suitable highlift jack.

5. Remove the trackbar arm bolt. Remove the trackbar arm from the axle mounting bracket.

6. Remove the shock absorber lower bolts and nuts.

7. Remove the nuts and the parking brake cable brackets.

8. Remove the rear springs. The spring insulators may come out with the spring when the spring is removed.

9. Slowly lower the axle assembly.

10. Remove the trailing arm nuts and bolts.

11. Remove the axle assembly.

To install:

12. Install the axle assembly, making sure it is supported.

13. Install the trailing arm nuts and bolts and tighten to 98 ft. lbs. (133 Nm).

14. Slowly raise the axle assembly.

15. Install the rear springs. The spring insulators must be inserted when the spring is installed.

16. Install the nuts and the parking brake cable brackets and tighten to 18 ft. lbs. (25 Nm).

17. Install the shock absorber lower bolts and nuts and tighten to 59 ft. lbs. (80 Nm).

18. Install the trackbar arm to the axle mounting bracket. Install the trackbar arm bolt and tighten to 76 ft. lbs. (103 Nm).

19. Connect the brake lines and rear wheel speed sensor wire harness to the rear axle assembly.

20. Install the rear brake discs.

ENGINE COOLING

ENGINE FAN

REMOVAL & INSTALLATION

1. Raise and safely support the vehicle.
2. Remove the radiator, as outlined in this section.
3. Remove the 2 cooling fan shroud-to-radiator bolts.
4. Remove the cooling fan and shroud assembly.

To install:

5. Install the cooling fan and shroud assembly.

6. Tighten the 2 cooling fan shroud-to-radiator bolts to 8 ft. lbs. (11 Nm).

7. Install the radiator.

RADIATOR

REMOVAL & INSTALLATION

See Figures 8 through 11.

1. Raise and safely support the vehicle.
2. Drain the cooling system.
3. Remove the 8 pin-type retainers and the upper radiator sight shield.
4. Disconnect the cooling fan electrical connectors.
5. Disconnect the harness retainers from the fan shroud.
   To install, tighten to 10 Nm (89 lb-in).
6. Disconnect the upper radiator hose.
7. Remove the radiator alignment pins, as follows:

a. Using mechanic's wire, tie the radiator and the condenser to the upper radiator support separately.

b. Allow 2 inches of slack in the condenser wire to allow for movement.

c. Remove the radiator alignment pins.

8. Disconnect the radiator vent hose from the radiator.

9. Disconnect the degas bottle return hose.

10. Disconnect the lower radiator hose.

11. Detach the transmission cooler tube clips.

12. Disconnect the transmission cooler tubes, as follows:

a. Disconnect the fluid cooler tubes from the connector assembly.

b. Push the fluid cooler tube inward slightly, squeeze the retaining clip, and with a slight twisting motion, pull the fluid cooler tube out of the connector.

13. Detach the transmission cooler tube pin-type retainers.

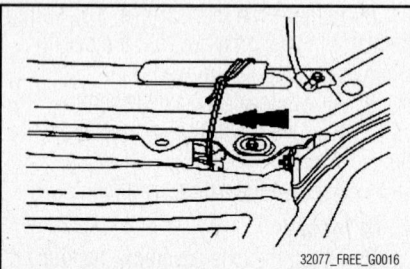

Fig. 8 Remove the radiator alignment pins

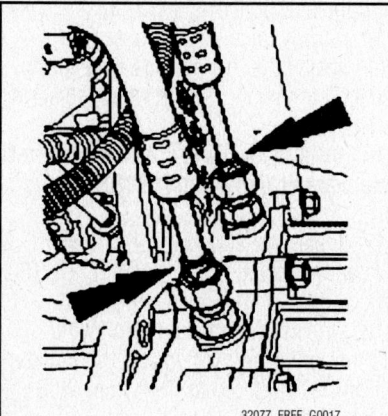

Fig. 9 Disconnect the transmission cooler tubes

Fig. 10 Detach the power steering tubes from both sides of the radiator lower support

Fig. 11 Remove the screws

14. Detach the power steering tubes from both sides of the radiator lower support.

15. Remove the bolt and reposition the A/C muffler bracket aside.

16. Remove the screws.

➡**Power steering cooler shown, auxiliary transmission fluid cooler is similar.**

17. Remove the bolts and position the cooler aside.

18. Remove the 4 bolts and the lower radiator support and insulators.

19. Remove the 2 radiator-to-condenser bolts.

20. Remove the radiator.

21. Lower the vehicle, cut the mechanics wire on the radiator and remove the radiator, cooling fans and shroud as an assembly.

22. Installation is the reverse of the removal procedure. Observe the following steps and tightening specifications.

a. Radiator-to-condenser bolts: 89 inch lbs. (10 Nm)

b. Radiator lower support and insulator bolts: 18 ft. lbs. (25 Nm)

c. Power steering and/or auxiliary transmission fluid cooler bolts: 71 inch lbs. (8 Nm)

d. A/C muffler bracket bolt: 71 inch lbs. (8 Nm)

e. Fan shroud retainers: 89 inch lbs. (10 Nm)

23. Fill the transaxle using clean automatic transmission fluid.

24. Fill and bleed the cooling system.

THERMOSTAT

REMOVAL & INSTALLATION

See Figure 12.

1. Partially drain the cooling system to a level below the thermostat.

2. Remove the air cleaner outlet tube.

3. Disconnect the upper radiator hose from the thermostat housing.

4. Remove the thermostat housing-to-engine bolts and the thermostat housing.

➡**Mark the location of the vent pin before removing the thermostat.**

5. Remove the thermostat.

6. Discard the gasket.

To install:

7. Position a new gasket.

8. Install the thermostat. Tighten the thermostat housing-to-engine bolts in two stages:

a. Stage 1: Tighten the thermostat housing-to-engine bolts to 71 inch lbs. (8 Nm).

b. Stage 2: Tighten an additional 60 degrees.

9. Connect the upper radiator hose to the thermostat housing.

10. Install the air cleaner outlet tube.

11. Fill and bleed the cooling system.

WATER PUMP

REMOVAL & INSTALLATION

See Figure 13.

1. Remove or disconnect the following:

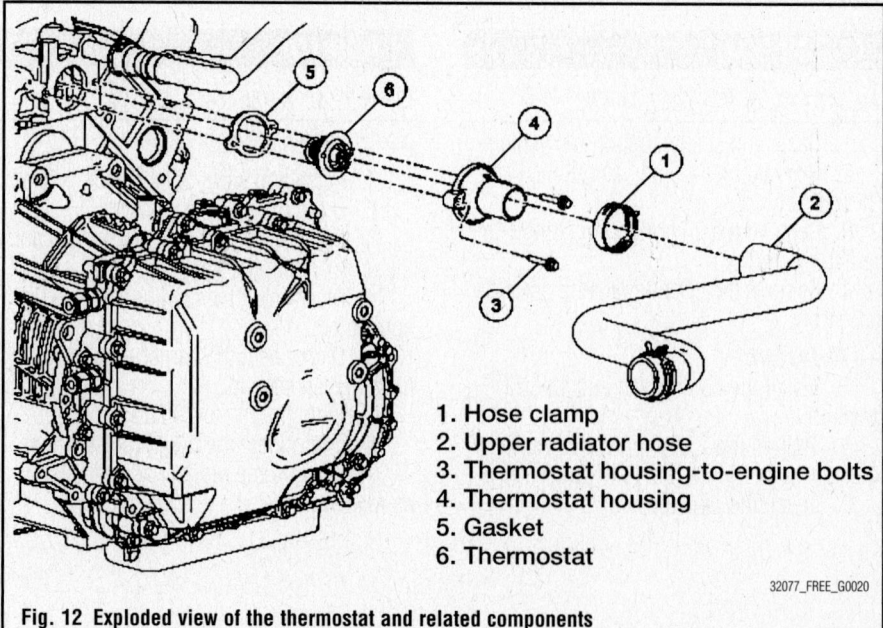

1. Hose clamp
2. Upper radiator hose
3. Thermostat housing-to-engine bolts
4. Thermostat housing
5. Gasket
6. Thermostat

Fig. 12 Exploded view of the thermostat and related components

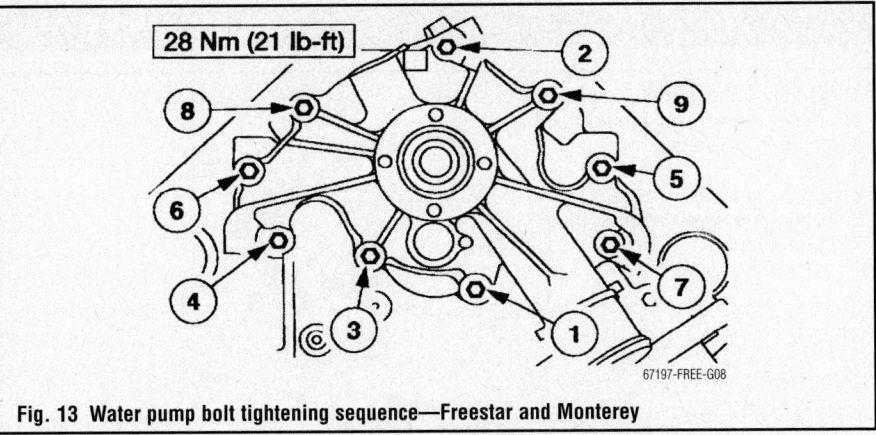

Fig. 13 Water pump bolt tightening sequence—Freestar and Monterey

- Negative battery cable
- Coolant
- Accessory drive belt
- Lower radiator hose
- Idler pulley
- Generator bracket
- Lower engine mount nuts

➡Install a suitable engine lifting device and raise the engine approximately 5 inches to gain access to the water pump pulley bolts.

- Water pump pulley
- Bypass hoses
- Water pump

To install:

✳✳ WARNING

Be careful not to gouge the aluminum surfaces when scraping the old gasket material from the mating surfaces of the water pump and front cover.

2. Clean the gasket surfaces on the water pump and front cover.
3. Position a new water pump housing gasket on the water pump sealing surface using gasket sealant to hold the gasket in place.
4. Install the water pump and tighten the bolts in sequence shown to 21 ft. lbs. (28 Nm).
5. The remainder of the installation is the reverse of removal.
6. Fill and bleed the cooling system.
7. Connect the negative battery cable.
8. Start the engine and check for leaks.

ENGINE ELECTRICAL

CHARGING SYSTEM

ALTERNATOR

REMOVAL & INSTALLATION

See Figure 14.

1. Disconnect the negative battery cable.
2. Disconnect the accessory drive belt.
3. Detach the alternator wiring connector.
4. Remove the positive cable nut.
5. Remove the alternator.

To install:

6. Position the alternator on the engine.
7. Install the alternator mounting bolts. Tighten the bolts to 18 ft. lbs. (25 Nm) on 2005 models, or 35 ft. lbs. (47 Nm) on 2006–07 models.
8. Tighten the positive cable nut to 71 inch lbs. (8 Nm).
9. Connect the wiring connector.
10. Install and tension the accessory drive belt.
11. Connect the negative battery cable.

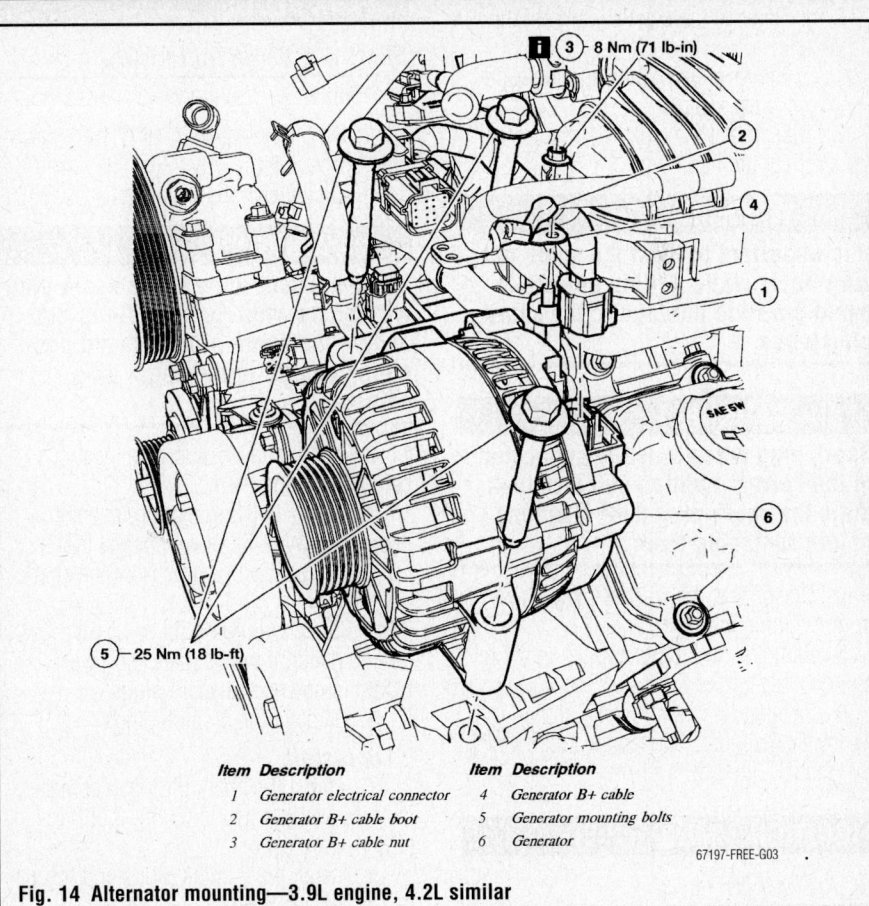

Item	Description	Item	Description
1	Generator electrical connector	4	Generator B+ cable
2	Generator B+ cable boot	5	Generator mounting bolts
3	Generator B+ cable nut	6	Generator

Fig. 14 Alternator mounting—3.9L engine, 4.2L similar

ENGINE ELECTRICAL   IGNITION SYSTEM

IGNITION COIL

REMOVAL & INSTALLATION

See Figure 15.

1. Disconnect the negative battery cable.
2. Remove the wiper motor and pivot assembly, as follows:

   a. Remove the windshield wiper arms.

➥**Disconnect the washer hose before removing the cowl panel grille.**

   b. Remove the pushpin-type retainers and the cowl panel grille.

   c. Remove the washer hose grommet from the cowl panel and position aside the washer hose.

   d. If equipped, remove the A/C air inlet filter.

   e. Remove the 9 cowl panel bolts and position aside the cowl panel.

   f. Disconnect the windshield wiper motor electrical connector.

   g. Remove the cowl panel from the vehicle.

   h. Remove the 4 bolts and the windshield wiper motor.

3. Disconnect the electrical connector from the ignition coil.

> ✳✳ **WARNING**
>
> **It is important to twist the spark plug wire boots while pulling upward to avoid possible damage to the spark plug wires.**

> ✳✳ **WARNING**
>
> **Spark plug wires must be connected to the correct ignition coil terminal. Mark the spark plug wire locations before removing them.**

4. Disconnect the 6 spark plug wires from the ignition coil.
5. Remove the 3 bolts and the ignition coil.
6. Installation is the reverse of the removal procedure. Tighten the coil bolts to 62 inch lbs. (7 Nm).

IGNITION TIMING

ADJUSTMENT

The ignition timing is controlled by the Powertrain Control Module (PCM). No adjustment is necessary or possible.

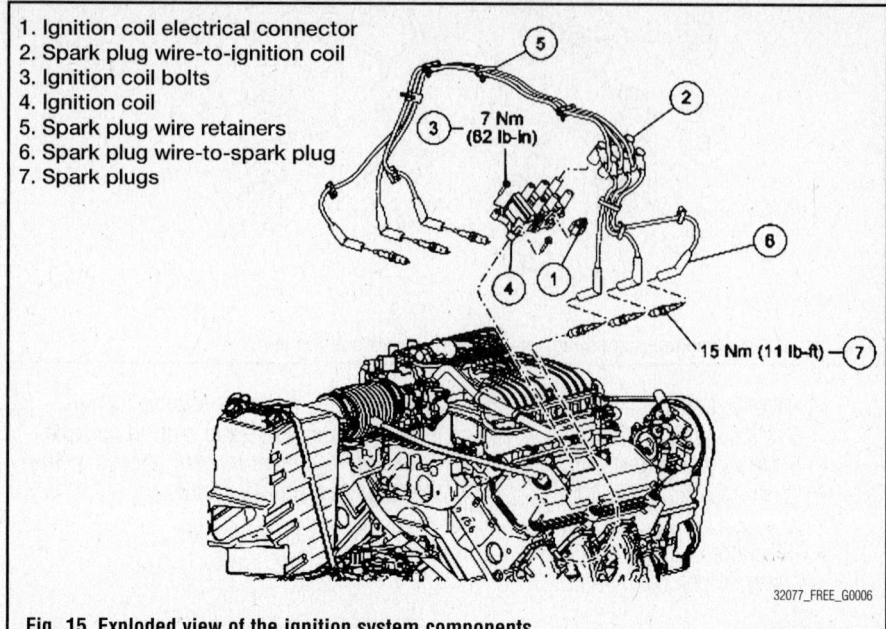

1. Ignition coil electrical connector
2. Spark plug wire-to-ignition coil
3. Ignition coil bolts
4. Ignition coil
5. Spark plug wire retainers
6. Spark plug wire-to-spark plug
7. Spark plugs

7 Nm (62 lb-in)

15 Nm (11 lb-ft) — 7

32077_FREE_G0006

Fig. 15 Exploded view of the ignition system components

SPARK PLUGS

REMOVAL & INSTALLATION

See Figures 15, 16 and 17.

1. With the vehicle in NEUTRAL, position it on a hoist.
2. Disconnect the negative battery cable.

> ✳✳ **WARNING**
>
> **It is important to twist the spark plug wire boots while pulling along the axis of the spark plug to avoid possible damage to the spark plug wires.**

3. Tag the spark plug wire locations before removing them.
4. With a twisting motion, use the Spark Plug Wire Remover special tool to pull the 6 spark plug wires from the spark plugs.
5. Use compressed air to remove any foreign material in the spark plug well before removing the spark plugs.
6. Remove the 6 spark plugs.

To install:

7. Adjust the spark plug gap as necessary. The proper gap is 0.052–0.056 in. (1.3–1.4mm).
8. Install the 6 spark plugs and torque to 11 ft. lbs. (15 Nm).
9. Apply dielectric grease to the inside of the spark plug wire boots before attaching to the spark plugs.

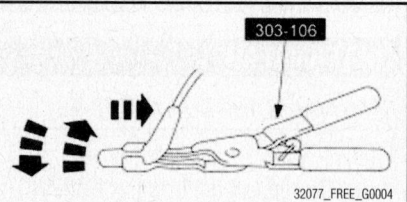

303-106

32077_FREE_G0004

Fig. 16 Use the Spark Plug Wire Removal tool to properly remove the wires from the plugs

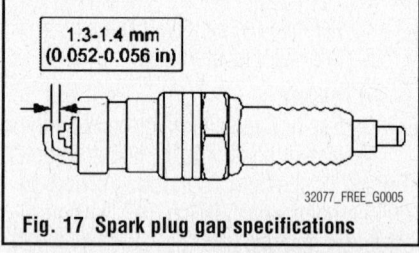

1.3-1.4 mm
(0.052-0.056 in)

32077_FREE_G0005

Fig. 17 Spark plug gap specifications

> ✳✳ **WARNING**
>
> **Spark plug wires must be connected to the correct spark plug. Mark spark plug wire locations before removing them.**

> ✳✳ **WARNING**
>
> **Make sure the spark plug boots are positioned so the spark plug wires do not contact the exhaust manifold.**

10. Connect the 6 spark plug wires to the spark plugs.
11. Connect the negative battery cable.

ENGINE ELECTRICAL

STARTER

REMOVAL & INSTALLATION

See Figure 18.

1. Disconnect the negative battery cable.
2. Raise and support the vehicle safely.
3. Disconnect the starter electrical harness.
4. Remove the upper starter bolt.
5. Support the starter and remove the lower bolt.
6. Remove the starter from the vehicle.

To install:

7. Position the starter in the vehicle.
8. Install the upper and lower bolts. Tighten to 21 ft. lbs. (28 Nm).
9. Connect the starter electrical harness.
10. Lower the vehicle.
11. Connect the negative battery cable.

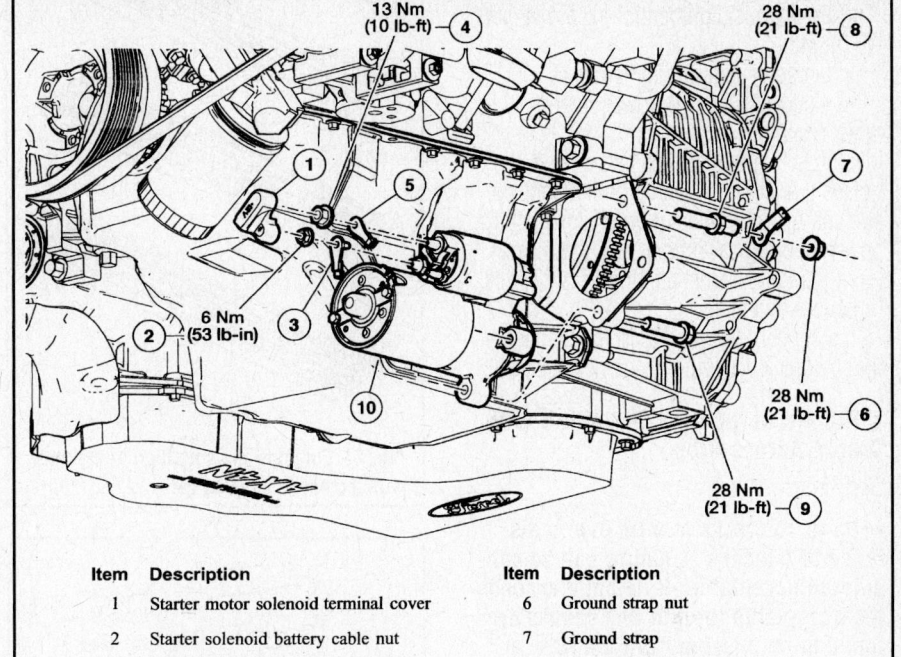

Item	Description	Item	Description
1	Starter motor solenoid terminal cover	6	Ground strap nut
2	Starter solenoid battery cable nut	7	Ground strap
3	Starter solenoid battery cable	8	Starter motor stud bolt
4	Starter solenoid wire nut	9	Starter motor bolt
5	Starter solenoid wire	10	Starter motor

Fig. 18 Starter motor mounting—3.9L and 4.2L engines

67197-FREE-G40

ENGINE MECHANICAL

➡**Disconnecting the negative battery cable may interfere with the functions of the on board computer systems and may require the computer to undergo a relearning process, once the negative battery cable is reconnected.**

ACCESSORY DRIVE BELTS

ACCESSORY BELT ROUTING

See Figure 19.

INSPECTION

❋❋ WARNING

Under no circumstances should the accessory drive belt, tensioner or pulleys be lubricated as potential damage to the belt material and tensioner damping mechanism will occur. Do not apply any fluids or belt dressing to the accessory drive belt or pulleys.

Visual Inspection

Visually inspect the belt for obvious signs of mechanical damage:

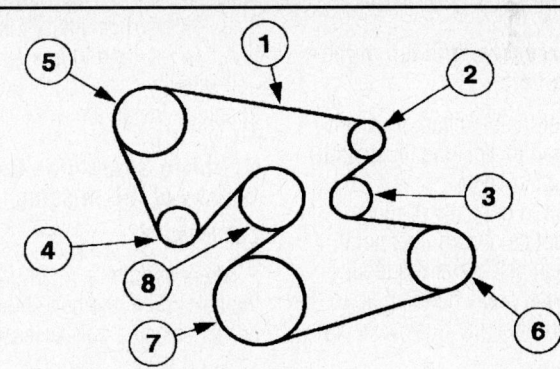

Item	Description
1	Drive belt
2	Generator pulley
3	Idler pulley
4	Drive belt tensioner
5	Power steering pump pulley
6	A/C clutch pulley
7	Crankshaft vibration damper pulley
8	Coolant pump pulley

67197-FREE-G01

Fig. 19 3.9L and 4.2L engine accessory drive belt routing

- Drive belt cracking/chunking/wear
- Belt/pulley contamination
- Incorrectly routed belt
- Pulley misalignment or excessive pulley runout
- Loose or mislocated hardware
- Incorrectly routed power steering tubes (rubbing)

Eliminate all other non-belt related noises that could cause belt misdiagnosis, such as A/C compressor engagement chirp, power steering cavitations at low temperatures, Variable Camshaft Timing (VCT) tick or generator whine.

If a concern is found, correct the condition before proceeding to the next section.

V-Ribbed Serpentine Drive Belt With Cracks Across Ribs

See Figure 20.

➡**Up to 15 cracks in a rib over a distance of 4 inches (100mm) can be considered acceptable. If damage exceeds the acceptable limit or any chunks are found to be missing from the ribs, a new belt must be installed.**

1. Check the belt for cracks. Up to 15 cracks in a rib over a distance of 4 inches (100mm) can be considered acceptable. If cracks exceed this standard, install a new belt.

V- Ribbed Serpentine Belt With Piling

See Figure 21.

➡**Piling is an excessive buildup in the V-grooves of the belt.**

The condition of the V-ribbed drive belt should be compared against the illustration and appropriate action taken.

1. Small scattered deposits of rubber material. This is not a concern, therefore, installation of a new belt is not required.

2. Longer deposit areas building up to 50 percent of the rib height. This is not con-

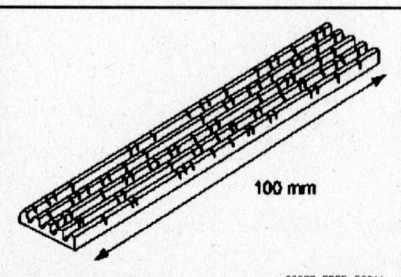

Fig. 20 Up to 15 cracks in a rib over a distance of 4 inches (100mm) can be considered acceptable. If cracks exceed this standard, install a new belt

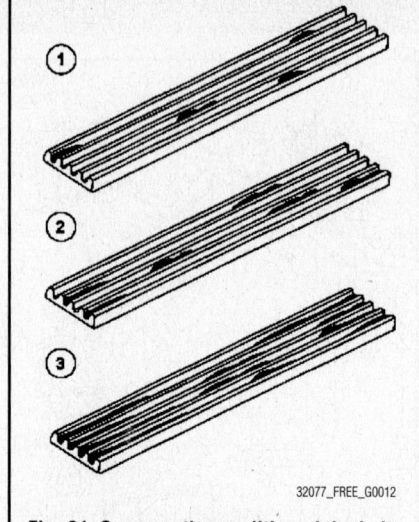

Fig. 21 Compare the condition of the belt with the accompanying text

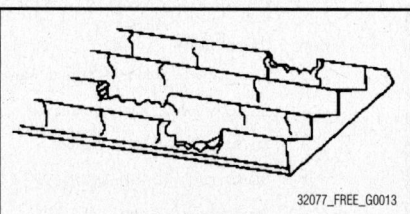

Fig. 22 Replace the belt if missing chunks are found during inspection

sidered a concern but it can result in excessive noise. If noise is apparent, install a new belt.

3. Heavy deposits building up along the grooves resulting in a possible noise and belt stability concern. If heavy deposits are apparent, install a new belt.

V-Ribbed Serpentine Belt With Chunks of Rib Missing

See Figure 22.

There should be no chunks missing from the belt ribs. If the belt shows any evidence of this, install a new accessory drive belt.

ADJUSTMENT

The belts used on these vehicle are equipped with automatic (spring load) tensioners which maintain tension. No adjustment is necessary or possible.

REMOVAL & INSTALLATION

See Figures 19 and 23.

1. Rotate the accessory drive belt tensioner counterclockwise.

2. Push the spring clip toward the belt tensioner to lock the accessory drive belt tensioner in place.

3. Remove the drive belt.

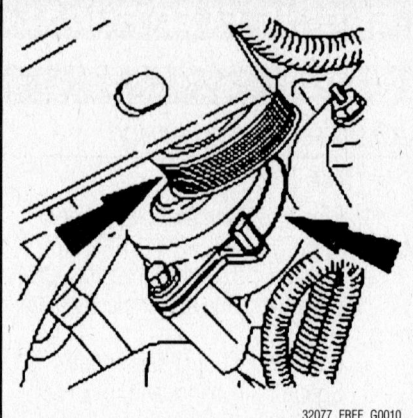

Fig. 23 To remove the belt, rotate the accessory drive belt tensioner counterclockwise, then push the spring clip toward the belt tensioner to lock the accessory drive belt tensioner in place

4. Installation is the reverse of the removal procedure. Make sure the belt is routed properly.

CAMSHAFT AND VALVE LIFTERS

REMOVAL & INSTALLATION

See Figure 24.

1. Rotate the crankshaft until the No. 1 piston is at the TDC on its compression stroke and the timing marks are aligned.

2. Remove or disconnect the following:
- Engine from the vehicle
- Valve covers
- Intake manifolds
- Pushrods
- Tappet guide plate and retainer
- Tappets
- Crankshaft pulley and damper
- Engine front cover assembly

3. Check the camshaft end-play as follows:

a. Push the camshaft toward the rear of the engine and install a dial indicator, so the indicator point is on the camshaft sprocket attaching screw.

b. Zero the dial indicator. Position a small prybar between the camshaft sprocket or gear and block.

c. Pull the camshaft forward and release it. Camshaft end-play should be 0.001–0.006 in. (0.025–0.15mm).

d. If the camshaft end-play is not within specification, replace the thrust plate upon reassembly.

4. Remove or disconnect the following:
- Timing chain and sprockets
- Balance shaft drive gear
- Camshaft keyway

Fig. 24 Aligning balance shaft drive gear and driven gear—3.9L and 4.2L engines

- Balance shaft driven gear, thrust plate and balance shaft as an assembly
- Camshaft thrust plate and spacer

5. Carefully remove the camshaft by pulling it toward the front of the engine. Remove it slowly to avoid damaging the bearings, journals and lobes.

To install:

6. Clean and inspect all parts before installation.

7. Lubricate the camshaft lobes and journals with Molylube® or heavy engine oil.

8. Carefully install the camshaft, spacer and camshaft key.

➡**If a new camshaft is being installed, recheck camshaft end-play.**

9. Lubricate the engine thrust plate with engine assembly lubricant, then install the thrust plate. Tighten the retaining bolts to 71 inch lbs. (8 Nm).

10. Install the timing chain and sprockets.

11. Install the balance shaft assembly. Tighten the bolts to 71 inch lbs. (8 Nm).

12. Install the balance shaft drive gear, ensuring that the timing marks are correctly located as shown.

➡**Check the camshaft sprocket bolt for blockage of the drilled oil passages prior to installation, and clean if necessary.**

13. Install or connect the following:
- Engine front cover
- Crankshaft damper and pulley
- Hydraulic tappets into their original bores
- Align the valve tappet flats and install the tappet guide plate with the word **UP** facing you
- Install the intake manifold assembly

- Lubricate and install the pushrods and rocker arms
- Install the valve covers
- Install the engine assembly into the vehicle

CYLINDER HEAD

REMOVAL & INSTALLATION

Left Side

See Figure 25.

1. Relieve the fuel system pressure.
2. Remove or disconnect the following:
- Negative battery cable
- Coolant
- Dual converter Y-pipe.
- Exhaust manifold
- Upper and lower intake manifolds
- Alternator and mounting bracket
- A/C compressor and mounting bracket
- Valve covers

➡**Pushrods must be installed in their original positions. Note pushrod location during removal.**

- Pushrods
- Rotate tensioner clockwise and remove accessory drive belt
- Automatic belt tensioner assembly
- Lower exhaust manifold mounting studs
- Spark plugs
- Cylinder head bolts
- Cylinder head from the engine block and discard the gaskets

To install:

3. The cylinder head should be cleaned and inspected prior to installation.

4. Lightly oil all bolt and stud bolt threads before installation.

5. Clean all gasket mating surfaces thoroughly.

6. Install or connect the following:
- New head gaskets on the cylinder block.

✲✲ WARNING

Always use new cylinder head bolts when installing the cylinder head or damage to the engine may occur.

- Cylinder head on the cylinder block.

➡**Long bolts go in the inside of the cylinder head and short bolts go on the outside.**

- Tighten the cylinder head bolts in steps following the proper torque

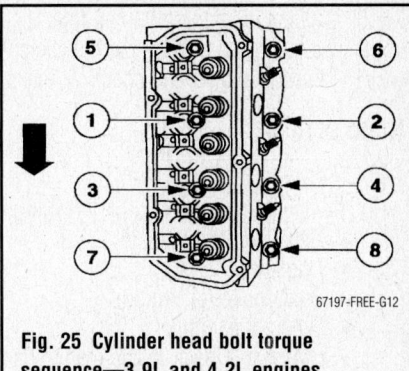

Fig. 25 Cylinder head bolt torque sequence—3.9L and 4.2L engines

sequence. The first step is 14 ft. lbs. (20 Nm), the second step is 29 ft. lbs. (40 Nm), the third step is 36 ft. lbs. (50 Nm).

- Using the torque sequence, loosen the first long bolt 3 turns, then tighten the bolt to 30 ft. lbs. (40 Nm). Tighten the bolt an additional 180 degrees. Using the torque sequence, loosen the first short bolt 3 turns, then tighten the bolt to 18 ft. lbs. (25 Nm). Tighten the bolt an additional 180 degrees. Repeat these steps for each bolt in sequence using the proper torque for long and short bolts.
- Lower exhaust manifold mounting studs
- Pushrods. Dip each end in engine assembly lubricant.
- Rocker arms, seats and retaining bolts. Lubricate all rocker arm components with engine assembly lubricant. Tighten the bolts to 44 inch lbs. (5 Nm).

➡**The rocker arm seats must be fully seated in the cylinder head and the pushrods must be seated in the rocker arm sockets prior to the final tightening.**

- Final tighten all rocker arm retaining bolts to 24 ft. lbs. (32 Nm)
- Automatic belt tensioner assembly
- Accessory drive belt
- Valve covers
- A/C compressor and mounting bracket
- Alternator and mounting bracket
- Upper and lower intake manifolds
- Exhaust manifold
- Dual converter Y-pipe.

7. Fill and bleed the cooling system.

➡**Engine coolant is corrosive to engine bearing material. Replace the engine oil after removal of any coolant-carrying component to help prevent potential bearing damage.**

8. Change the engine oil and filter
9. Connect the negative battery cable.
10. Start the engine and check for leaks.

Right Side

See Figure 25.

1. Remove or disconnect the following:
   - Negative battery cable
   - Coolant
   - Dual converter Y-pipe.
   - Exhaust manifold
   - Upper and lower intake manifolds
   - Power steering pump and mounting bracket
   - Valve covers

➡**Pushrods must be installed in their original positions. Note pushrod location during removal.**

   - Pushrods
   - Rotate tensioner clockwise and remove accessory drive belt
   - Automatic belt tensioner assembly
   - Lower exhaust manifold mounting studs
   - Spark plugs
   - Cylinder head bolts
   - Cylinder head from the engine block and discard the gaskets

To install:

2. The cylinder head should be cleaned and inspected prior to installation.
3. Lightly oil all bolt and stud bolt threads before installation.
4. Clean all gasket mating surfaces thoroughly.
5. Install or connect the following:
   - New head gaskets on the cylinder block.

✳✳ WARNING

Always use new cylinder head bolts when installing the cylinder head or damage to the engine may occur.

   - Cylinder head on the cylinder block.

➡**Long bolts go in the inside of the cylinder head and short bolts go on the outside.**

   - Tighten the cylinder head bolts in steps following the proper torque sequence. The first step is 14 ft. lbs. (20 Nm), the second step is 29 ft. lbs. (40 Nm), the third step is 36 ft. lbs. (50 Nm).
   - Using the torque sequence, loosen the first long bolt 3 turns, then tighten the bolt to 30 ft. lbs. (40

Nm). Tighten the bolt an additional 180 degrees. Using the torque sequence, loosen the first short bolt 3 turns, then tighten the bolt to 18 ft. lbs. (25 Nm). Tighten the bolt an additional 180 degrees. Repeat these steps for each bolt in sequence using the proper torque for long and short bolts.
   - Lower exhaust manifold mounting studs
   - Pushrods. Dip each end in engine assembly lubricant.
   - Rocker arms, seats and retaining bolts. Lubricate all rocker arm components with engine assembly lubricant. Tighten the bolts to 44 inch lbs. (5 Nm).

➡**The rocker arm seats must be fully seated in the cylinder head and the pushrods must be seated in the rocker arm sockets prior to the final tightening.**

   - Final tighten all rocker arm retaining bolts to 24 ft. lbs. (32 Nm)
   - Automatic belt tensioner assembly
   - Accessory drive belt
   - Valve covers
   - Power steering pump and mounting bracket
   - Upper and lower intake manifolds
   - Exhaust manifold
   - Dual converter Y-pipe.
6. Fill and bleed the cooling system.

➡**Engine coolant is corrosive to engine bearing material. Replace the engine oil after removal of any coolant-carrying component to help prevent potential bearing damage.**

7. Change the engine oil and filter
8. Connect the negative battery cable.
9. Start the engine and check for leaks.

ENGINE ASSEMBLY

REMOVAL & INSTALLATION

See Figures 26 through 29.

1. Relieve the fuel system pressure.
2. Drain the engine coolant.
3. Recover the air conditioning refrigerant, into a refrigerant recovery station
4. Remove or disconnect the following:
   - Both battery cables
   - Wiper motor
   - Cowl top panel
   - Air cleaner assembly
   - Fuel supply manifold lines
   - Power steering pump
   - Starter

➡**Do not allow the flex connector of the duel converter Y-pipe to hang unsupported or damage to the flex joint will result.**

   - Dual converter Y-pipe and support it from the body
   - Accelerator and cruise control cables from throttle assembly
   - Accelerator cable bracket
   - Upper and lower radiator hoses from the engine
   - Heater water hoses and secure to body
   - Positive terminal from Power Distribution Box (PDB)
   - PDB 68-pin connector
   - Engine wiring retainers
   - Shift cable
   - Evaporative (EVAP) return tube
   - EVAP canister connector and vacuum line
   - Brake booster vacuum line
   - Powertrain Control Module (PCM)
   - Engine grounds (3)
   - Radiator shield
   - Passenger side engine roll restrictor
   - A/C compressor and wire aside
   - Power steering cooler line
   - Transaxle cooler lines
   - Steering column pinch bolt
   - Oil pan-to-transaxle bolts
   - Torque converter nuts (4)
   - Brake calipers and wire aside

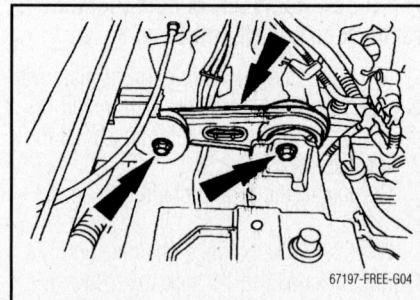

Fig. 26 Removing passenger side engine roll restrictor—Freestar and Monterey

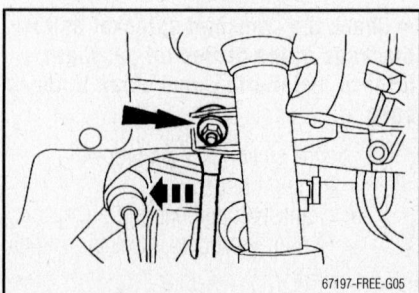

Fig. 27 Removing stabilizer bar links— Freestar and Monterey

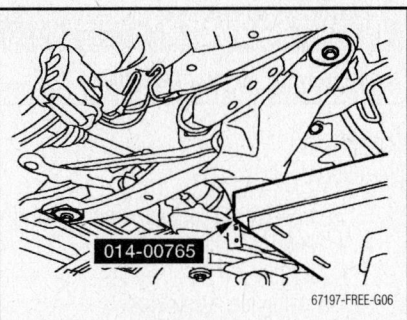

Fig. 28 Installing subframe support tool—Freestar and Monterey

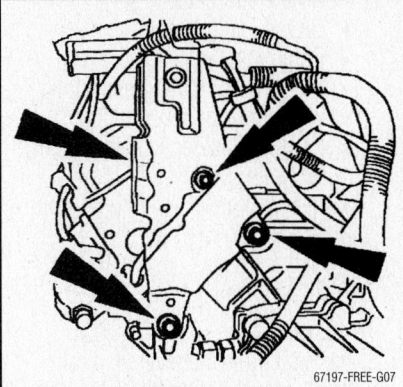

Fig. 29 Removing driver side engine roll restrictor—Freestar and Monterey

- ABS connectors
- Stabilizer bar links
- Lower strut bolts on both sides
- Position subframe support tool 014-00765 under subframe
- Subframe bolts and lower the engine, transaxle and subframe assembly
- Alternator brace
- A/C compressor and wire aside
- Driver side engine roll restrictor
- Label and remove remaining electrical connectors
- Transaxle fluid level tube
- Install suitable engine lifting device
- Bell housing bolts (4)
- Engine mount bolts
- Transaxle mount bolts
- Engine

To install:

5. Position the engine onto the transaxle and subframe assembly.

6. Install the transaxle mount bolts. Torque the bolts to 46 ft. lbs. (63 Nm).

7. Install the oil pan-to-transaxle bolt. Torque the bolt to 33 ft. lbs. (45 Nm).

8. Install the engine mount bolts. Torque the bolts to 66 ft. lbs. (90 Nm).

9. Install the bell housing bolts. Torque the bolts to 37 ft. lbs. (50 Nm).

10. Install or connect the following:
- Transaxle fluid level tube
- Under vehicle electrical connectors
- Driver side roll restrictor bracket. Torque the bolts to 37 ft. lbs. (50 Nm).
- A/C compressor. Torque the bolts to 18 ft. lbs. (25 Nm).
- Generator brace
- Raise the engine, transaxle and subframe assembly
- Subframe bolts. Torque the bolts to 66 ft. lbs. (90 Nm).
- Lower strut bolts. Torque the bolts to 91 ft. lbs. (124 Nm).
- Stabilizer bar link bolts. Torque the bolts to 70 ft. lbs. (95 Nm).
- ABS connectors
- Brake calipers. Torque the bolts to 26 ft. lbs. (35 Nm).
- Torque converter bolts. Torque the bolts to 27 ft. lbs. (36 Nm).
- Oil pan-to-transaxle bolts. Torque the bolts to 33 ft. lbs. (45 Nm).
- Steering column pinch bolt. Torque the bolts to 30 ft. lbs. (40 Nm).

11. The remainder of the installation is the reverse of removal.

12. Please note the following torque specifications:
- Passenger side roll restrictor. Torque the bolts to 46 ft. lbs. (63 Nm).

13. Refill the engine, transaxle and cooling system with the correct amount of the appropriate fluids before starting the engine. Recharge the A/C system using approved recycling equipment.

EXHAUST MANIFOLD

REMOVAL & INSTALLATION

Left Manifold

See Figure 30.

➡Spray the exhaust system fasteners with penetrating lubricant before removing them to help prevent broken studs and bolts. The use of a 6-point socket is highly recommended when removing exhaust system fasteners.

✳✳ CAUTION

To prevent serious burns, allow the exhaust manifold to cool down before attempting to remove it.

1. Disconnect the negative battery cable.
2. Remove the dipstick tube bolt.
3. Disconnect the EGR tube from the manifold.
4. Raise and support the vehicle safely on jackstands.
5. Disconnect the dual converter Y-pipe from the exhaust manifold.
6. Lower the vehicle.
7. Remove the exhaust manifold.

To install:

8. Clean all gasket mating surfaces thoroughly.

9. Install a new exhaust manifold gasket and the exhaust manifold on the cylinder head. Start 2 nuts to hold the manifold in position.

10. Install the remaining nuts. Tighten the nuts in the sequence shown to 18 ft. lbs. (25 Nm).

11. Raise and support the vehicle safely.
12. Connect the dual converter Y-pipe.
13. Lower the vehicle.
14. Install the EGR tube.
15. Install the dipstick bolt.
16. Connect the negative battery cable.
17. Start the engine and check for exhaust leaks.

Right Manifold

See Figure 31.

➡Spray the exhaust system fasteners with penetrating lubricant before removing them to help prevent broken studs and bolts. The use of a 6-point socket is highly recommended when removing exhaust system fasteners.

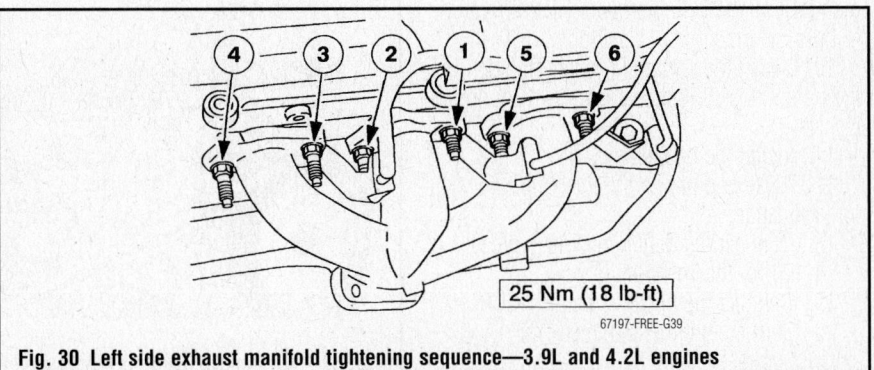

25 Nm (18 lb-ft)

Fig. 30 Left side exhaust manifold tightening sequence—3.9L and 4.2L engines

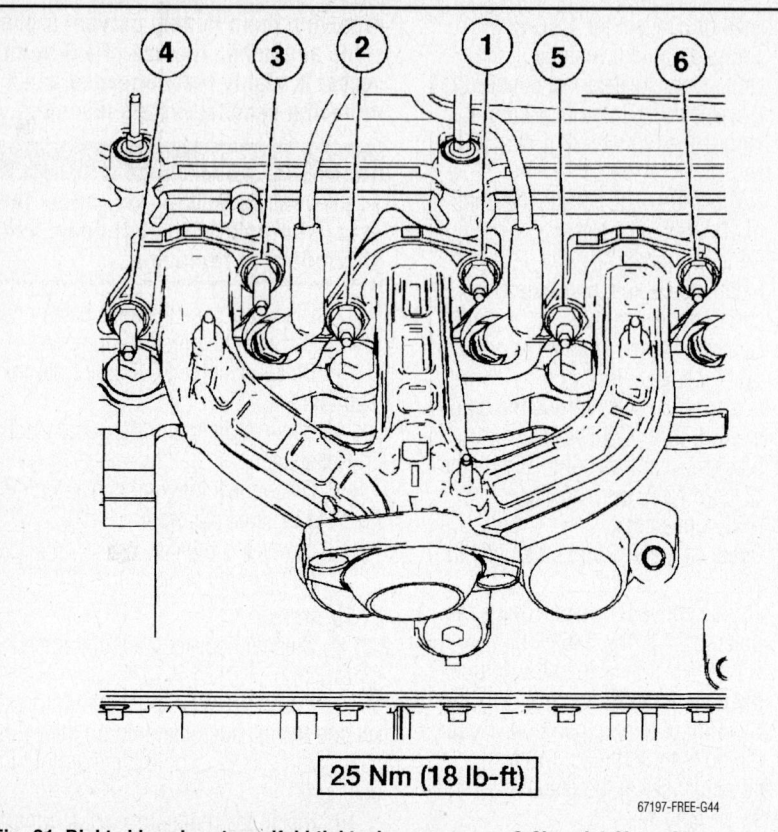

25 Nm (18 lb-ft)

67197-FREE-G44

Fig. 31 Right side exhaust manifold tightening sequence—3.9L and 4.2L engines

INTAKE MANIFOLD

REMOVAL & INSTALLATION

Upper

See Figures 32 and 33.

1. Remove or disconnect the following:
   - Negative battery cable
   - Coolant
   - Fuel system pressure
   - Wiper motor and pivot assembly
   - Cowl top panel
   - Air cleaner outlet tube
   - Accelerator cable
   - Cruise control cable
   - Cable bracket
   - Evaporative (EVAP) return tube
   - Brake booster vacuum hose
   - Exhaust Gas Recirculation (EGR) tubes and connector
   - Remaining electrical connectors
   - Spark plug wires
   - Coolant hoses
   - Intake manifold

To install:

2. Installation is the reverse of the removal procedure, using the following torque specifications.

☀☀ CAUTION

To prevent serious burns, allow the exhaust manifold to cool down before attempting to remove it.

1. Disconnect the negative battery cable.
2. Raise and support the vehicle safely on jackstands.
3. Remove the cowl top panel.
4. Disconnect the dual converter Y-pipe from the exhaust manifold.
5. Lower the vehicle.
6. Remove the heat shield.
7. Remove the exhaust manifold.

To install:

8. Clean all gasket mating surfaces thoroughly.
9. Install a new gasket and the exhaust manifold on the cylinder head. Start 2 nuts to hold the manifold in position.
10. Install the remaining nuts. Tighten the nuts in the sequence shown to 18 ft. lbs. (25 Nm).
11. Install the heat shield.
12. Raise and support the vehicle safely on jackstands.
13. Connect the dual converter Y-pipe.
14. Lower the vehicle.
15. Connect the negative battery cable.
16. Start the engine and check for exhaust leaks.

67197-FREE-G13

Fig. 32 Upper intake manifold—3.9L and 4.2L engines

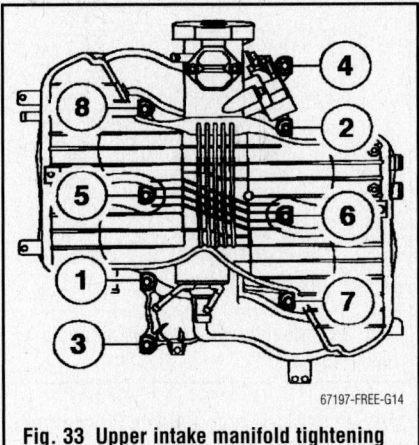

Fig. 33 Upper intake manifold tightening sequence—3.9L and 4.2L engines

- Intake manifold bolts and tighten all bolts in steps in sequence to 53 inch lbs. (6 Nm), then to 89 inch lbs. (10 Nm).
3. Fill and bleed the engine cooling system.
4. Connect the negative battery cable.
5. Start the engine and check for leaks.

Lower

See Figures 34 and 35.

1. Remove or disconnect the following:
   - Coolant
   - Fuel system pressure
   - Upper intake manifold
   - Fuel supply manifold
   - Water bypass tube from the heater water outlet tube
   - Heater hoses from manifold
   - Upper radiator hose
   - Electrical wiring harnesses
   - Lower intake manifold retaining bolts. Note the location of the 6 long bolts and 8 short bolts.

➡ **The lower intake manifold is sealed at each corner with sealer. To break the seal it may be necessary to pry on the front of the intake manifold with a pry-bar. If it is necessary, use care to prevent damage to the machined surfaces.**

   - Lower intake manifold

To install:

2. Thoroughly clean all gasket mating surfaces.

➡ **When using silicone rubber sealer, assembly must occur within 5 minutes after sealer application. After this time, the sealer may start to set up and its sealing effectiveness may be reduced.**

3. Install or connect the following:
   - Apply a 3mm bead of RTV silicone sealer at each corner where the

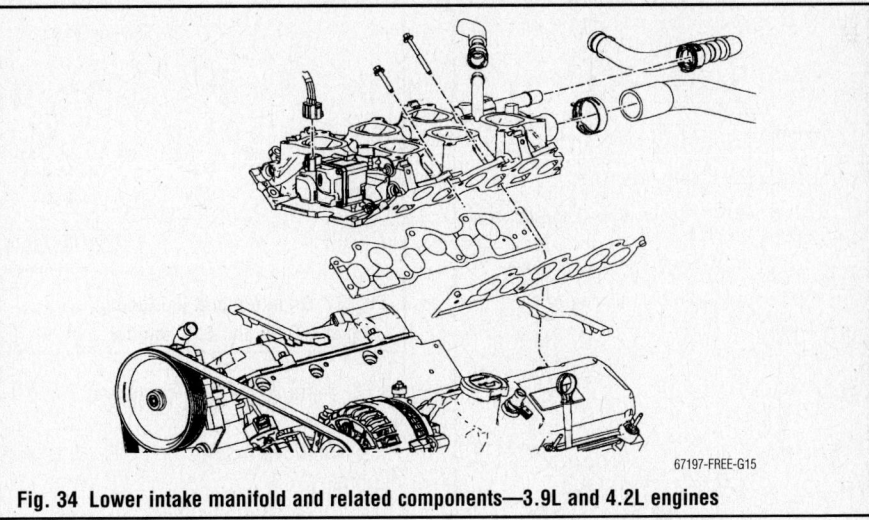

Fig. 34 Lower intake manifold and related components—3.9L and 4.2L engines

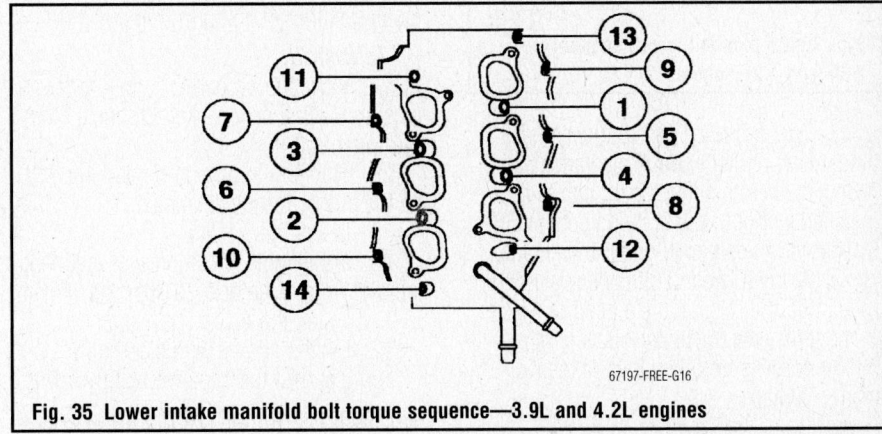

Fig. 35 Lower intake manifold bolt torque sequence—3.9L and 4.2L engines

cylinder head joins the engine block
   - Front and rear intake manifold seals
   - Lower intake manifold into position on the cylinder block, using new gaskets
   - Install intake bolts in their original locations. Tighten in 2 steps in sequence to 44 inch lbs. (5 Nm), then again to 89 inch lbs. (10 Nm).
   - Heater hoses
   - Water bypass hose
   - Fuel supply manifold
   - Upper intake manifold
   - Upper radiator hose
4. Fill and bleed the cooling system.
5. Start the engine and check for leaks.

OIL PAN

REMOVAL & INSTALLATION

See Figure 36.

✴✴ CAUTION

The EPA warns that prolonged contact with used engine oil may cause a number of skin disorders, including

cancer! You should make every effort to minimize your exposure to used engine oil. Protective gloves should be worn when changing the oil. Wash your hands and any other exposed skin areas as soon as possible after exposure to used engine oil. Soap and water, or waterless hand cleaner, should be used.

1. Disconnect the negative battery cable.
2. Raise and support the vehicle safely on jackstands.
3. Drain the engine oil.
4. Remove the oil filter.
5. Remove the dual converter Y-pipe assembly.
6. Remove the starter motor.
7. Remove the engine rear plate/converter housing cover.
8. Remove the 3 oil pan-to-transaxle bolts.
9. Remove the retaining bolts and remove the oil pan.

To install:

10. Clean the gasket mating surfaces thoroughly.

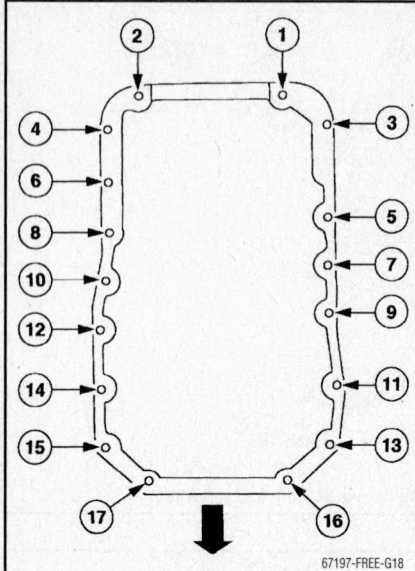

Fig. 36 Oil pan bolt torque sequence— 3.9L and 4.2L engines

11. Trial fit the oil pan to the cylinder block. Ensure that enough clearance has been provided to allow the oil pan to be installed without sealant being scraped off when pan is positioned under the engine.

12. Apply a bead of silicone sealer to the oil pan flange. Also apply a bead of sealer to the front cover/cylinder block joint and fill the grooves on both sides of the rear main seal cap.

➡**When using silicone rubber sealer, assembly must occur within 5 minutes after sealer application. After this time, the sealer may start to harden and its sealing effectiveness may be reduced.**

13. Install the oil pan and secure to the block with the attaching bolts. Tighten the bolts in sequence to 89 inch lbs. (10 Nm).

14. Install the oil pan-to-transaxle bolts and tighten to 33 ft. lbs. (45 Nm).

15. Install a new oil filter.

16. Install the engine rear plate/converter housing cover.

17. Install the starter motor.

18. Install the Y-pipe converter assembly.

19. Lower the vehicle.

20. Fill the engine with the proper type and amount of clean oil.

21. Connect the negative battery cable.

22. Start the engine and check for leaks.

OIL PUMP

REMOVAL & INSTALLATION

See Figure 37.

1. Disconnect the negative battery cable.
2. Drain the engine oil.

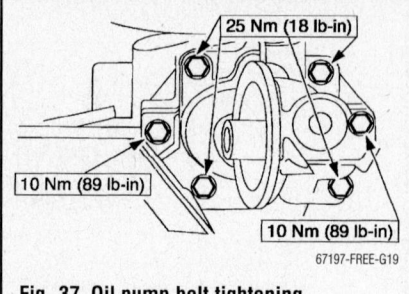

Fig. 37 Oil pump bolt tightening torques—3.9L and 4.2L engines

3. Remove the A/C compressor and wire aside.

4. Remove the A/C compressor mounting bracket

5. Remove the oil filter.

6. Remove the oil pump attaching bolts. Lift the oil pump from the engine.

To install:

7. Place the oil pump in the proper position with a new gasket and install the retaining bolt.

8. Tighten the oil pump retaining bolt to the proper torque as shown.

9. Install the oil filter.

10. Install the A/C compressor mounting bracket. Torque the bolts to 35 ft. lbs. 47 Nm).

11. Install the A/C compressor.

12. Fill the engine with clean oil.

13. Connect the negative battery cable.

➡**Check for proper engine oil pressure immediately after starting the engine. If engine oil pressure is not within specification a few seconds after starting the engine, stop the engine and determine the reason for the low oil pressure condition. Running an engine with low oil pressure may result in serious engine damage.**

14. Start the engine and check for leaks.

INSPECTION

See Figures 38 and 39.

Once the oil pump is removed, inspect the oil pump drive gear, driven gear and

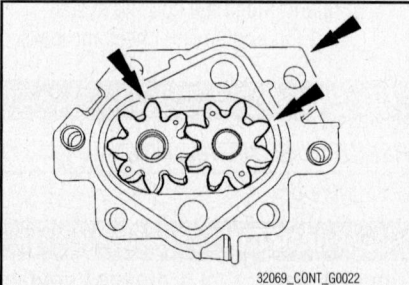

Fig. 38 Inspect the oil pump drive gear, driven gear and cover

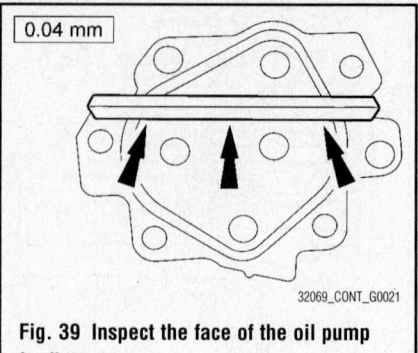

Fig. 39 Inspect the face of the oil pump for flatness

cover. Install new components if necessary. Also, inspect the face of the oil pump for flatness.

PISTON AND RING

POSITIONING

See Figure 40.

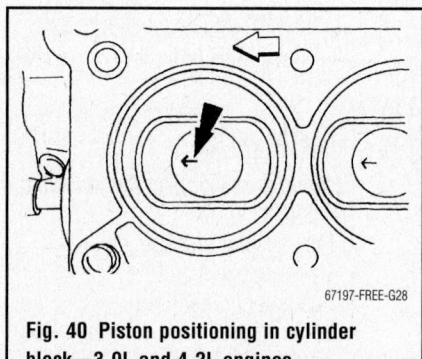

Fig. 40 Piston positioning in cylinder block—3.9L and 4.2L engines

REAR MAIN SEAL

REMOVAL & INSTALLATION

See Figure 41.

1. Disconnect the negative battery cable.
2. Raise and support the vehicle safely on jackstands.
3. Remove the transaxle.
4. Remove the flexplate and the rear cover plate, if necessary.

✳✳ WARNING

Use caution when working near the crankshaft sealing surface. If the surface becomes damaged, an oil leak may occur.

5. Screw in the threaded end of a crankshaft rear seal replacer tool, then use the tool to remove the seal.

To install:

6. Inspect the crankshaft seal area for any damage that may cause the seal to leak.

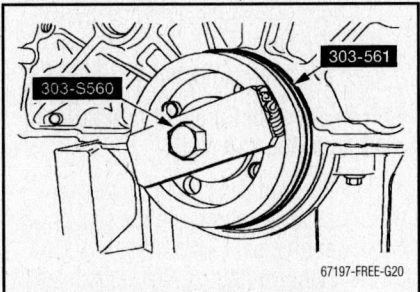

Fig. 41 The rear main seal must be installed with the proper tools to avoid damaging the seal or crankshaft

If damage is evident, service or replace the crankshaft as necessary.

7. Coat the crankshaft seal area and the seal lip with engine oil.

8. Using a crankshaft seal replacer tool, install the seal. Tighten the bolts of the seal installer tool evenly so the seal is straight and seats without misalignment.

9. Install the flexplate.

10. Install the rear cover plate, if necessary.

11. Install the transaxle, lower the vehicle and connect the battery.

TIMING CHAIN, SPROCKETS, FRONT COVER AND SEAL

REMOVAL & INSTALLATION

See Figures 42 through 48.

1. Rotate the crankshaft until No. 1 cylinder is at TDC on compression stroke.

2. Remove or disconnect the following:
- Negative battery cable
- Coolant
- Air cleaner assembly and air intake duct
- Alternator
- Coolant hoses
- Water pump
- Camshaft position sensor
- Power steering pump and position aside
- Camshaft synchronizer
- Alternator mounting bracket
- Accessory drive belt and tensioner
- Oil filter
- Right side ABS connector
- Place safety stand under right side of subframe
- Remove 2 subframe bolts and lower right side of subframe about 2 inches
- Crankshaft pulley
- Raise subframe and reinstall bolts
- Crankshaft front seal
- Front oil pan bolts
- Front cover

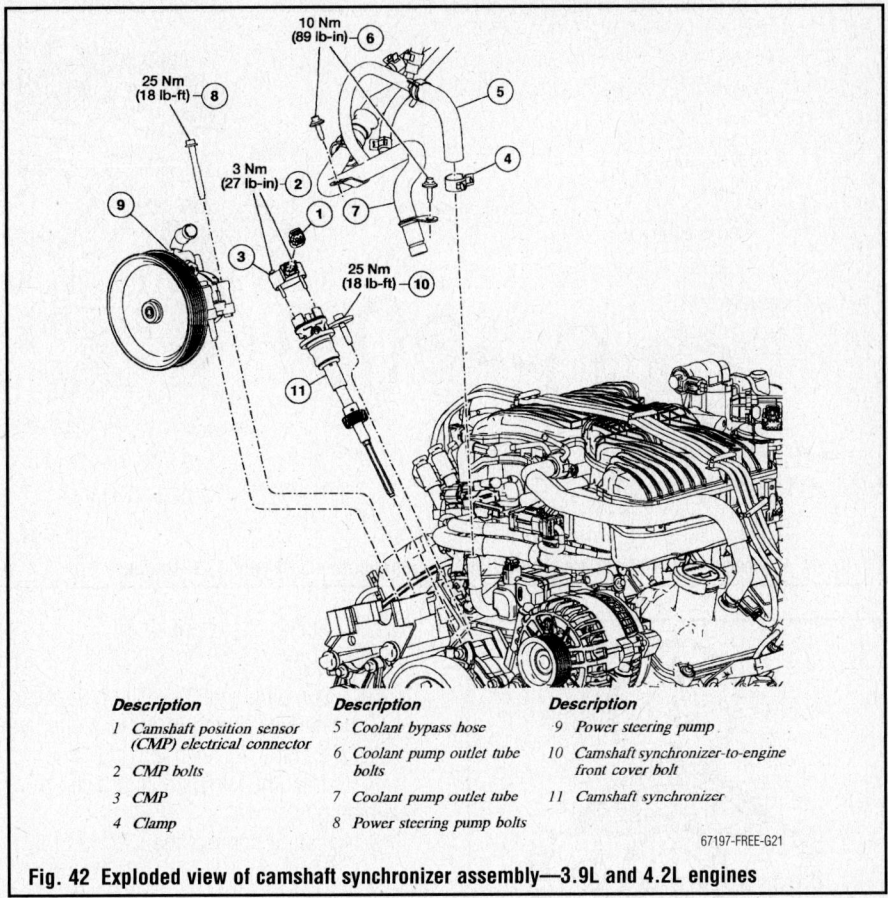

Description	Description	Description
1 Camshaft position sensor (CMP) electrical connector	5 Coolant bypass hose	9 Power steering pump
2 CMP bolts	6 Coolant pump outlet tube bolts	10 Camshaft synchronizer-to-engine front cover bolt
3 CMP	7 Coolant pump outlet tube	11 Camshaft synchronizer
4 Clamp	8 Power steering pump bolts	

Fig. 42 Exploded view of camshaft synchronizer assembly—3.9L and 4.2L engines

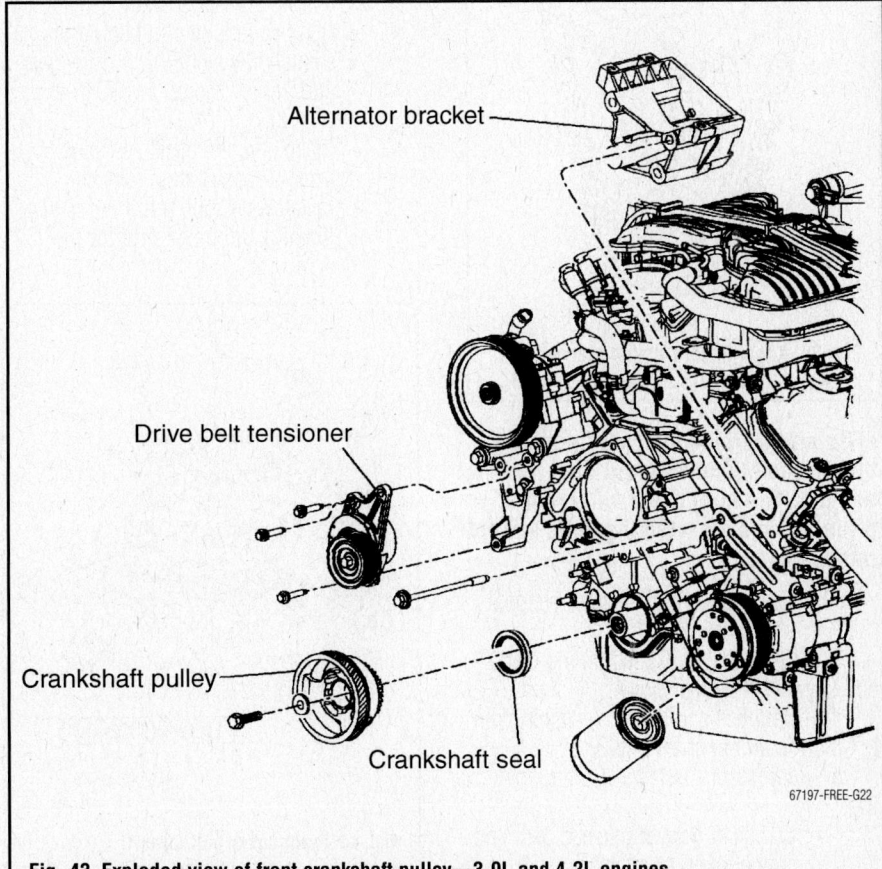

Fig. 43 Exploded view of front crankshaft pulley—3.9L and 4.2L engines

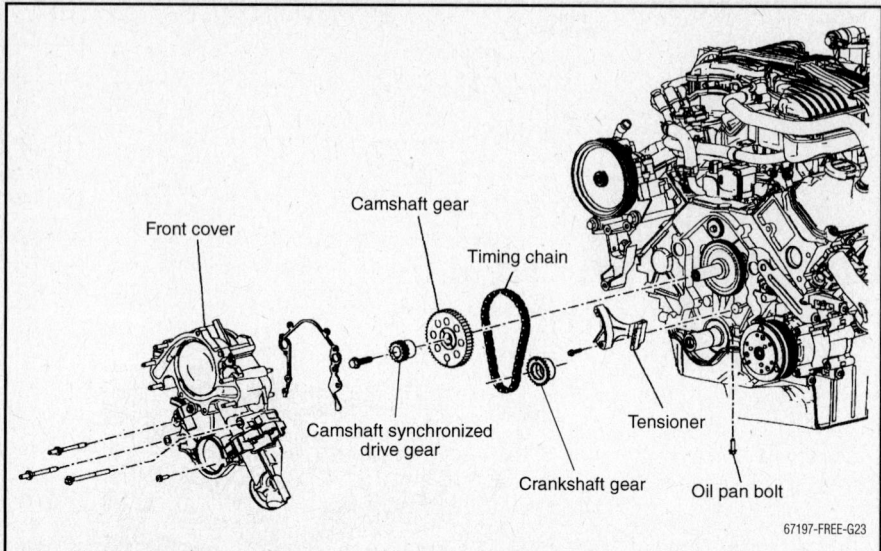

Fig. 44 Exploded view of front cover and timing components—3.9L and 4.2L engines

67197-FREE-G23

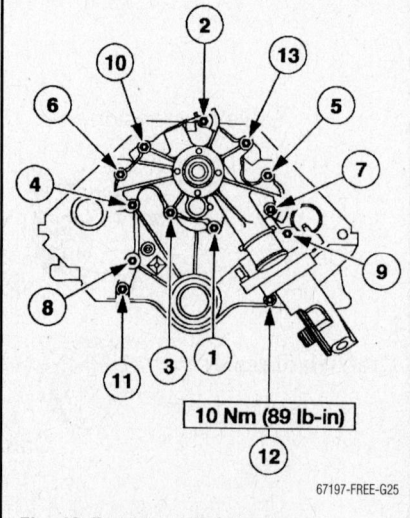

Fig. 45 Aligning gear timing marks and keyway—3.9L and 4.2L engines

67197-FREE-G24

➡**Do not overlook the cover retaining bolt located behind the oil filter adapter. The front cover will break if pried on, and all retaining bolts are not removed.**

- Camshaft synchronizer drive gear
- Camshaft gear

3. Ensure the crankshaft timing marks and keyways align as shown.

4. Compress and install a retaining pin to hold the timing chain tensioner.

5. Remove or disconnect the following:

- Camshaft gear, crankshaft gear and timing chain as an assembly

- Timing chain tensioner

To install:

6. Clean all the gasket mating surfaces.

7. Install the timing chain tensioner and tighten the bolt to 71 inch lbs. (11 Nm).

8. Retract the tensioner and insert a retaining pin.

9. Install or connect the following:

- Camshaft sprocket, crankshaft sprocket and timing chain. Be sure the timing marks align.
- Remove tensioner retaining pin
- Camshaft synchronizer drive gear and tighten the bolt to 33 ft. lbs. (45 Nm)
- Place silicone gasket sealant on front oil pan mating surface
- Install water pump to front cover
- Install front cover and torque

bolts in sequence to 21 ft. lbs. (28 Nm)
- Front oil pan bolts

➡**Front cover bolt no. 12 is tightened to 89 inch lbs. (10 Nm)**

- New crankshaft seal in the front cover and lubricate the seal lip with engine oil
- Remove right subframe bolts and lower subframe again about 2 inches
- Crankshaft pulley and tighten the bolt to 118 ft. lbs. (160 Nm)
- Raise subframe, install bolts and tighten to 66 ft. lbs. (90 Nm)
- Right side ABS connector
- Oil filter

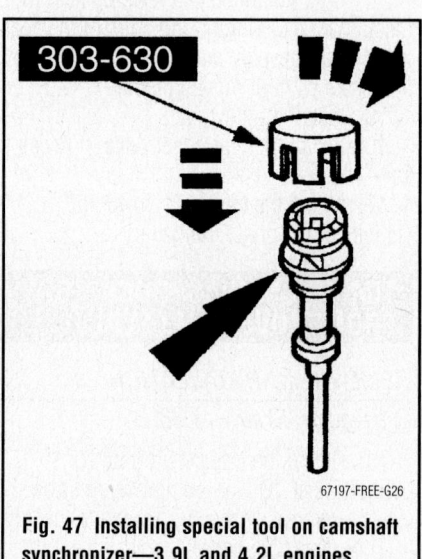

Fig. 47 Installing special tool on camshaft synchronizer—3.9L and 4.2L engines

67197-FREE-G26

- Accessory drive belt and tensioner
- Alternator mounting bracket
- Camshaft synchronizer

10. Coat the camshaft synchronizer gear with clean engine oil.

11. Install the special tool 303-630 onto the top of the camshaft synchronizer.

➡**During installation the arrow on the special tool will rotate clockwise until the oil pump intermediate shaft engages the camshaft gear.**

12. Install the camshaft synchronizer until the arrow on the special tool is at 54 degrees from the centerline of the engine as shown.

13. Install or connect the following:

- Power steering pump
- Camshaft position sensor
- Coolant hoses
- Alternator
- Air cleaner assembly and air intake duct

10 Nm (89 lb-in)

Fig. 46 Front cover bolt torque sequence—3.9L and 4.2L engine

67197-FREE-G25

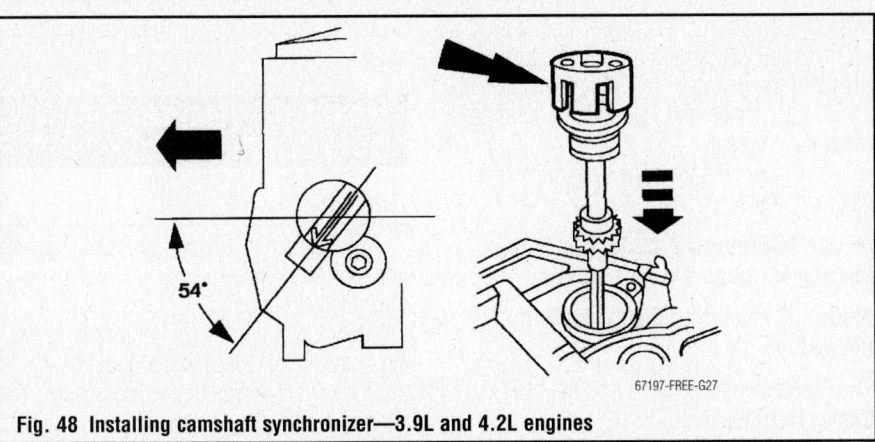

Fig. 48 Installing camshaft synchronizer—3.9L and 4.2L engines

14. Fill the crankcase with the proper type and quantity of engine oil. Fill and bleed the cooling system. Connect the negative battery cable.

15. Start the engine and check for leaks. Check the ignition timing and curb idle speed and adjust, as necessary.

VALVE LASH

ADJUSTMENT

The 3.9L and 4.2L engine uses hydraulic valve lash adjusters that do not require any adjustment.

ENGINE PERFORMANCE & EMISSION CONTROL

ACCELERATOR PEDAL POSITION (APP) SENSOR

OPERATION

The Accelerator Pedal Position (APP) sensor is an input to the Powertrain Control Module (PCM) and is used to determine the torque demand. There are 3 pedal position signals in the sensor. Signal 1, APPS1, has a negative slope (increasing angle, decreasing voltage) and signals 2 and 3, APPS2 and APPS3, both have a positive slope (increasing angle, increasing voltage). During normal operation APPS1 is used as the indication of pedal position by the strategy. The 3 pedal position signals make sure the PCM receives a correct input even if 1 signal has a concern. There are 2 reference voltage circuits and 2 signal return circuits for the sensor.

CAMSHAFT POSITION (CMP) SENSOR

LOCATION

The Camshaft Position (CMP) Sensor is located at the front of the engine block.

OPERATION

The CMP sensor detects the position of the camshaft. The CMP sensor identifies when piston number 1 is on its compression stroke. A signal is then sent to the PCM and used for synchronizing the sequential firing of the fuel injectors. Coil-on-plug (COP) ignition applications use the CMP signal to select the correct ignition coil to fire.

Vehicles with 2 CMP sensors are equipped with variable camshaft timing (VCT). They use the second sensor to iden-

tify the position of the camshaft on bank 2 as an input to the PCM.

There are 2 types of CMP sensors: the 3-pin connector Hall-effect type sensor and the 2-pin connector variable reluctance type sensor.

REMOVAL & INSTALLATION

1. Disconnect the negative battery cable.
2. Disconnect the camshaft position sensor (CMP) electrical connector.
3. Remove the 2 CMP sensor bolts and the CMP sensor.
4. To install, reverse the removal procedure. Tighten the sensor bolts to 27 inch lbs. (3 Nm).

CRANKSHAFT POSITION (CKP) SENSOR

LOCATION

See Figure 49.

Refer to the accompanying illustration for Crankshaft Position Sensor (CKP) location.

OPERATION

The CKP sensor is a magnetic transducer mounted on the engine block adjacent to a pulse wheel located on the crankshaft. By monitoring the crankshaft mounted pulse wheel, the CKP is the primary sensor for ignition information to the PCM. The pulse

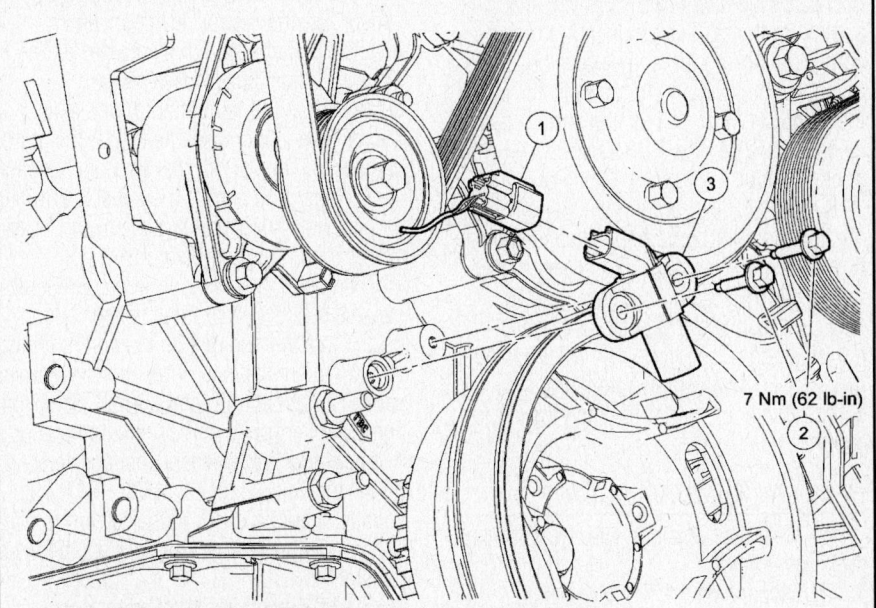

1. Crankshaft Position (CKP) Sensor electrical connector
2. CKP sensor bolts (2 required)
3. CKP sensor*

Fig. 49 Crankshaft Position (CKP) Sensor location

wheel has a total of 35 teeth spaced 10 degrees apart with one empty space for a missing tooth. By monitoring the pulse wheel, the CKP sensor signal indicates crankshaft position and speed information to the PCM. By monitoring the missing tooth, the CKP sensor is also able to identify piston travel in order to synchronize the ignition system and provide a way of tracking the angular position of the crankshaft relative to a fixed reference for the CKP sensor configuration. The PCM also uses the CKP signal to determine if a misfire has occurred by measuring rapid decelerations between teeth.

REMOVAL & INSTALLATION

1. With the vehicle in NEUTRAL, position it on a hoist.
2. Disconnect the negative battery cable.
3. Disconnect the CKP sensor electrical connector.
4. Remove the 2 CKP sensor bolts.
5. Remove the CKP sensor.
6. To install, reverse the removal procedure. Tighten the sensor bolts to 62 inch lbs. (7 Nm).

EGR VALVE POSITION (EVP) SENSOR

OPERATION

The EGR valve in the differential pressure feedback EGR system is a conventional, vacuum-actuated. The valve increases or decreases the flow of EGR. As vacuum applied to the EGR valve diaphragm overcomes the spring force, the valve begins to open. As the vacuum signal weakens, at 1.6 inch Hg (5.4 kPa) or less, the spring force closes the valve. The EGR valve is fully open at about 4.5 inch Hg (15 kPa).

Since EGR flow requirement varies greatly, providing repair specifications on flow rate is impractical. The on board diagnostic (OBD) system monitors the EGR valve function and triggers a diagnostic trouble code (DTC) if the test criteria is not met. The EGR valve flow rate is not measured directly as part of the diagnostic procedures.

REMOVAL & INSTALLATION

1. With the vehicle in NEUTRAL, position it on a hoist.
2. Disconnect the negative battery cable.
3. Disconnect the Exhaust Gas Recirculation (EGR) system module-to-exhaust manifold tube upper nut.
4. Disconnect the EGR system module-

to-exhaust manifold tube lower nut and remove the EGR system module-to-exhaust manifold tube.

5. Disconnect the EGR system module electrical connector.
6. Disconnect the EGR system module vacuum connector.

➡ **The EGR system module gasket sealing surfaces are soft metals.**

➡ **Do not reuse the EGR system module gasket.**

7. Remove the 2 bolts and the EGR system module.
8. Remove and discard the EGR system module gasket.
9. Carefully clean the EGR system module gasket sealing surfaces.

To install:

10. To install, reverse the removal procedure, noting the following:
   a. Install a new EGR system module gasket with the side with the raised circle facing the intake manifold.
   b. Tighten the EGR system module bolts to 18 ft. lbs. (25 Nm).
   c. Tighten the EGR system module-to-exhaust manifold upper and lower tube nuts to 30 ft. lbs. (40 Nm).

ENGINE COOLANT TEMPERATURE (ECT) SENSOR

OPERATION

The Engine Coolant Temperature (ECT) sensor is a thermistor device in which resistance changes with temperature. The electrical resistance of a thermistor decreases as the temperature increases, and the resistance increases as the temperature decreases. The varying resistance changes the voltage drop across the sensor terminals and provides electrical signals to the PCM corresponding to temperature.

Thermistor-type sensors are considered passive sensors. A passive sensor is connected to a voltage divider network so that varying the resistance of the passive sensor causes a variation in total current flow. Voltage that is dropped across a fixed resistor in a series with the sensor resistor determines the voltage signal at the PCM. This voltage signal is equal to the reference voltage minus the voltage drop across the fixed resistor.

The ECT measures the temperature of the engine coolant. The PCM uses the ECT input for fuel control and for cooling fan control. There are 3 types of ECT sensors, threaded, push-in, and twist-lock. The ECT

sensor is located in an engine coolant passage

ENGINE OIL TEMPERATURE (EOT) SENSOR

OPERATION

The Engine Oil Temperature (EOT) sensor is a thermistor device in which resistance changes with temperature. The electrical resistance of a thermistor decreases as the temperature increases and the resistance increases as the temperature decreases. The varying resistance changes the voltage drop across the sensor terminals and provides electrical signals to the PCM corresponding to temperature.

Thermistor-type sensors are considered passive sensors. A passive sensor is connected to a voltage divider network so that varying the resistance of the passive sensor causes a variation in total current flow. Voltage that is dropped across a fixed resistor in a series with the sensor resistor determines the voltage signal at the PCM. This voltage signal is equal to the reference voltage minus the voltage drop across the fixed resistor.

The EOT sensor measures the temperature of the engine oil. The sensor is typically threaded into the engine oil lubrication system. The PCM can use the EOT sensor input to determine the following:

• The PCM can use EOT sensor input in conjunction with other PCM inputs to determine oil degradation.
• The PCM can use EOT sensor input to initiate a soft engine shutdown. To prevent engine damage from occurring as a result of high oil temperatures, the PCM has the ability to initiate a soft engine shutdown. Whenever engine RPM exceeds a calibrated level for a certain period of time, the PCM begins reducing power by disabling engine cylinders.

HEATED OXYGEN (HO2S) SENSOR

LOCATION

Three Heated Oxygen Sensors (HO2S) are used. They are located in the exhaust system.

OPERATION

The HO2S detects the presence of oxygen in the exhaust and produces a variable voltage according to the amount of oxygen detected. A high concentration of oxygen (lean air/fuel ratio) in the exhaust produces a voltage signal less than 0.4 volt. A low

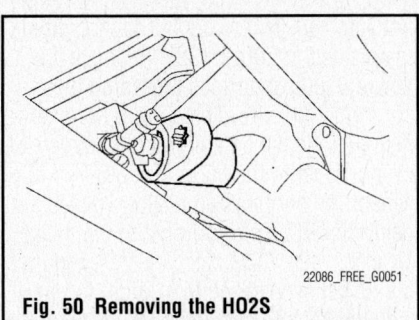

Fig. 50 Removing the HO2S

concentration of oxygen (rich air/fuel ratio) produces a voltage signal greater than 0.6 volt. The HO2S provides feedback to the PCM indicating air/fuel ratio in order to achieve a near stoichiometric air/fuel ratio of 14.7:1 during closed loop engine operation. The HO2S generates a voltage between 0.0 and 1.1 volts.

Embedded with the sensing element is the HO2S heater. The heating element heats the sensor to a temperature of 1,472°F (800°C). At approximately 572°F (300°C) the engine can enter closed loop operation. The VPWR circuit supplies voltage to the heater. The PCM turns the heater on by providing the ground when the correct conditions occur. The heater allows the engine to enter closed loop operation sooner. The use of this heater requires the HO2S heater control to be duty cycled, to prevent damage to the heater.

REMOVAL & INSTALLATION
See Figure 50.

1. With the vehicle in NEUTRAL, position it on a hoist.
2. Disconnect the negative battery cable.
3. Disconnect the heated oxygen sensor (HO2S) electrical connector.
4. Using the special tool, remove the HO2S sensor.

➡**Apply a light coat of anti-seize lubricant to the threads of the HO2S sensor prior to installation.**

5. To install, reverse the removal procedure. Tighten the sensor to 34 ft. lbs. (46 Nm).

IDLE AIR CONTROL (IAC) VALVE

LOCATION

The Idle Air Control (IAC) valve is located at the top rear of the intake manifold assembly.

OPERATION

➡**The IAC valve assembly is not adjustable and cannot be cleaned, also some IAC valves are normally open and**

others are normally closed. Some IAC valves require engine vacuum to operate.

The IAC valve assembly controls the engine idle speed and provides a dashpot function. The IAC valve assembly meters intake air around the throttle plate through a bypass within the IAC valve assembly and throttle body. The PCM determines the desired idle speed or bypass air and signals the IAC valve assembly through a specified duty cycle. The IAC valve responds by positioning the IAC valve to control the amount of bypassed air. The PCM monitors engine RPM and increases or decreases the IAC duty cycle in order to achieve the desired RPM

The PCM uses the IAC valve assembly to control:

- no touch start
- cold engine fast idle for rapid warm-up
- idle (corrects for engine load)
- stumble or stalling on deceleration (provides a dashpot function)
- over-temperature idle boost

REMOVAL & INSTALLATION

1. Disconnect the battery ground cable.
2. Disconnect the IAC valve electrical connector.

3. Remove the 2 IAC valve bolts and the IAC valve.
4. Remove and discard the IAC valve gasket.
5. To install, reverse the removal procedure. Tighten the IAC valve bolts to 8 ft. lbs. (11 Nm).

KNOCK SENSOR (KS)

LOCATION

The Knock Sensor (KS) is located at the throttle body.

OPERATION

The KS is a tuned accelerometer on the engine which converts engine vibration to an electrical signal. The PCM uses this signal to determine the presence of engine knock and to retard spark timing.

REMOVAL & INSTALLATION
See Figures 51 and 52.

1. Disconnect the battery ground cable.
2. Remove the air cleaner outlet pipe.
3. Remove the front and rear roll restrictor bolts and the roll restrictor.
4. Remove the upper and lower roll

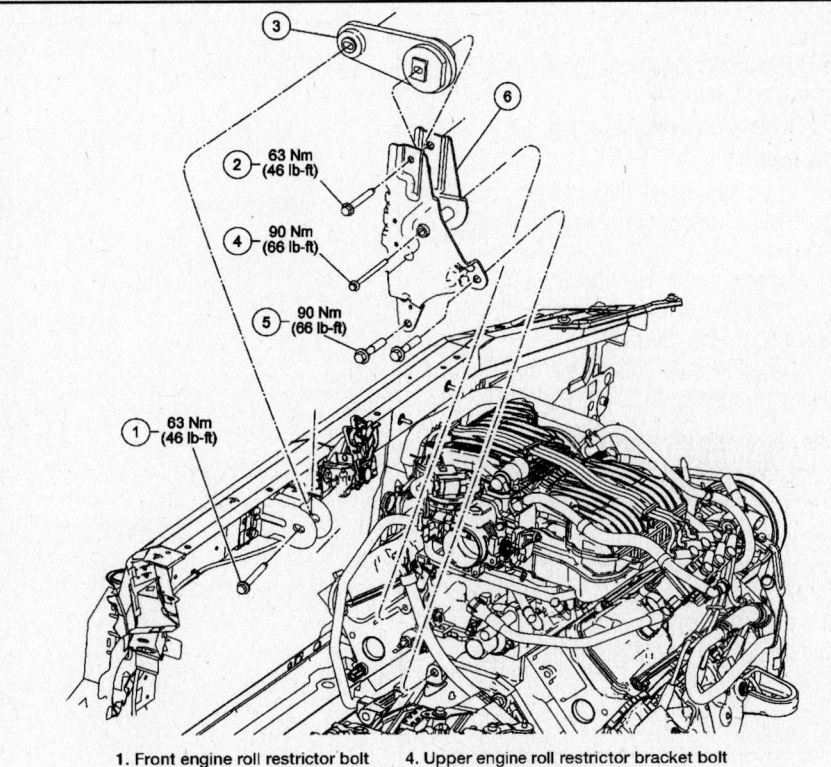

1. Front engine roll restrictor bolt
2. Rear engine roll restrictor bolt
3. Engine roll restrictor
4. Upper engine roll restrictor bracket bolt
5. Lower engine roll restrictor bracket bolt (2 required)
6. Engine roll restrictor

Fig. 51 Removing the Knock Sensor (KS)—1 of 2

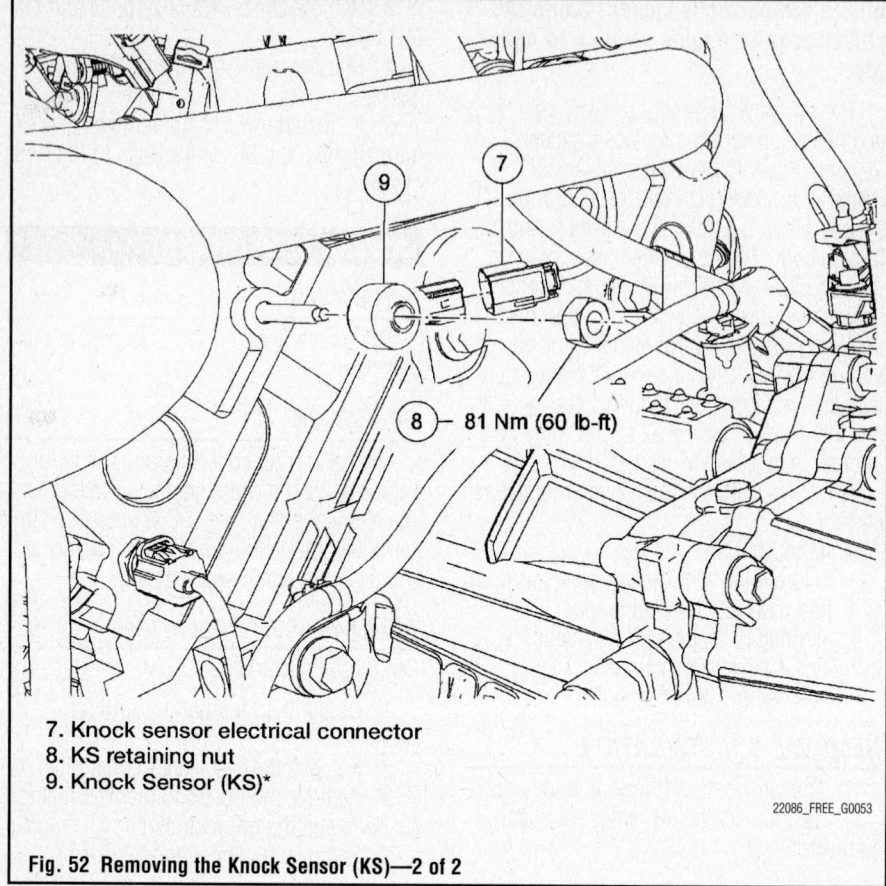

7. Knock sensor electrical connector
8. KS retaining nut
9. Knock Sensor (KS)*

22086_FREE_G0053

Fig. 52 Removing the Knock Sensor (KS)—2 of 2

restrictor bolts and the roll restrictor bracket.

5. Disconnect the Knock Sensor (KS) electrical connector

6. Remove the nut and the KS.

To install:

7. To install, reverse the removal procedure. Note the following tightening specifications:

　　a. Sensor nut: 15 ft. lbs. (20 Nm)

　　b. Upper and lower roll restrictor bolts: 66 ft. lbs. (90 Nm)

　　c. Tighten the front and rear roll restrictor bolts to 46 ft. lbs. (63 Nm).

MASS AIR FLOW (MAF) SENSOR

LOCATION

See Figure 53.

Refer to the accompanying illustration for the Mass Air Flow (MAF) sensor location.

OPERATION

See Figures 54 through 56.

The MAF sensor uses a hot wire sensing element to measure the amount of air entering the engine. Air passing over the

hot wire causes it to cool. This hot wire is maintained at 200°C (392°F) above the ambient temperature as measured by a constant cold wire. The current required to maintain the temperature of the hot wire is proportional to the mass air flow. The MAF sensor then outputs an analog voltage signal to the PCM proportional to the intake air mass. The PCM calculates the required fuel injector pulse width in order to provide the desired air/fuel ratio. This input is also used in determining transmission electronic pressure control (EPC), shift and torque converter clutch scheduling.

The MAF sensor is located between the air cleaner and the throttle body or inside the air cleaner assembly. Most MAF sensors have integrated bypass technology with an integrated Intake Air Temperature (IAT) sensor. The hot wire electronic sensing element must be replaced as an assembly. Replacing only the element may change the air flow calibration.

REMOVAL & INSTALLATION

1. Disconnect the battery ground cable.

2. Disconnect the Mass Air Flow (MAF) sensor electrical connector.

3. Remove the 2 MAF sensor screws and the MAF sensor.

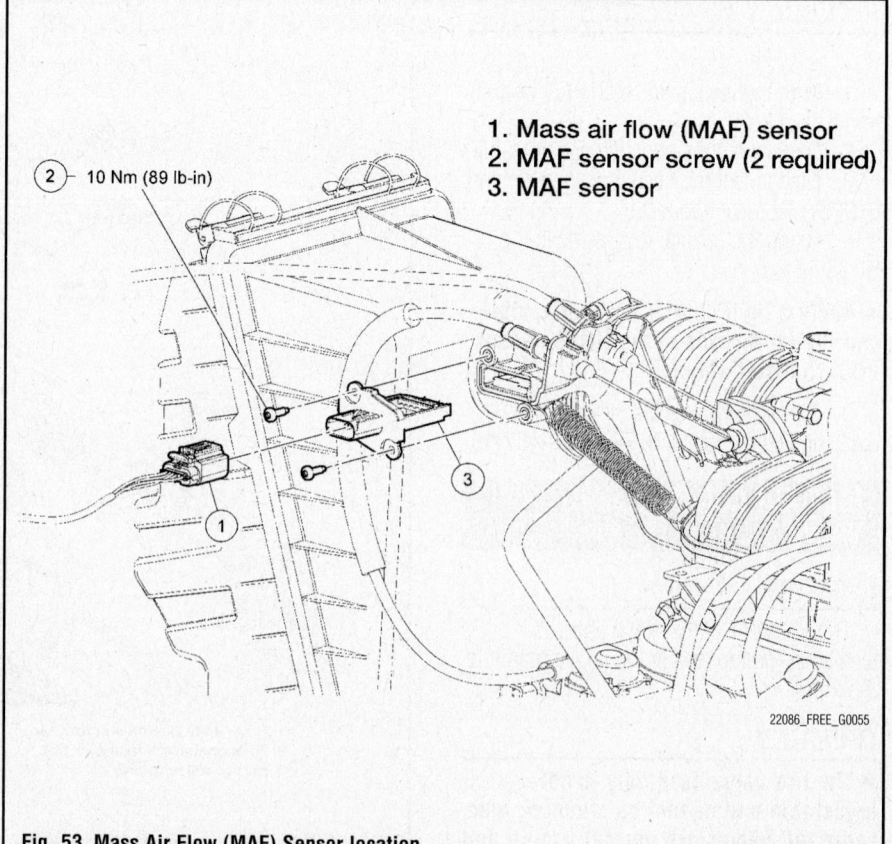

1. Mass air flow (MAF) sensor
2. MAF sensor screw (2 required)
3. MAF sensor

22086_FREE_G0055

Fig. 53 Mass Air Flow (MAF) Sensor location

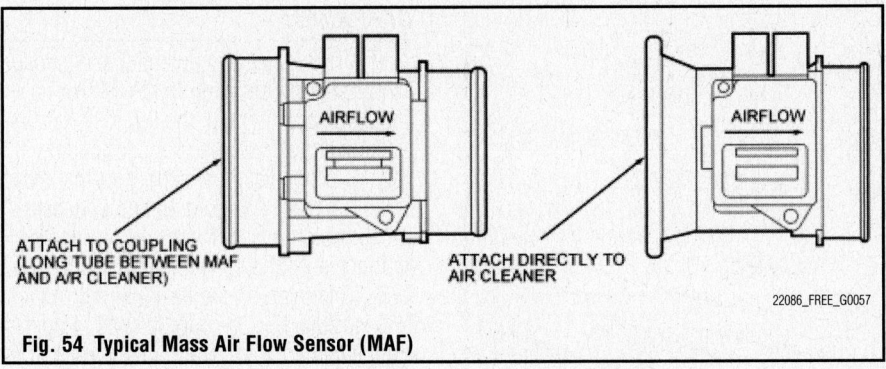

Fig. 54 Typical Mass Air Flow Sensor (MAF)

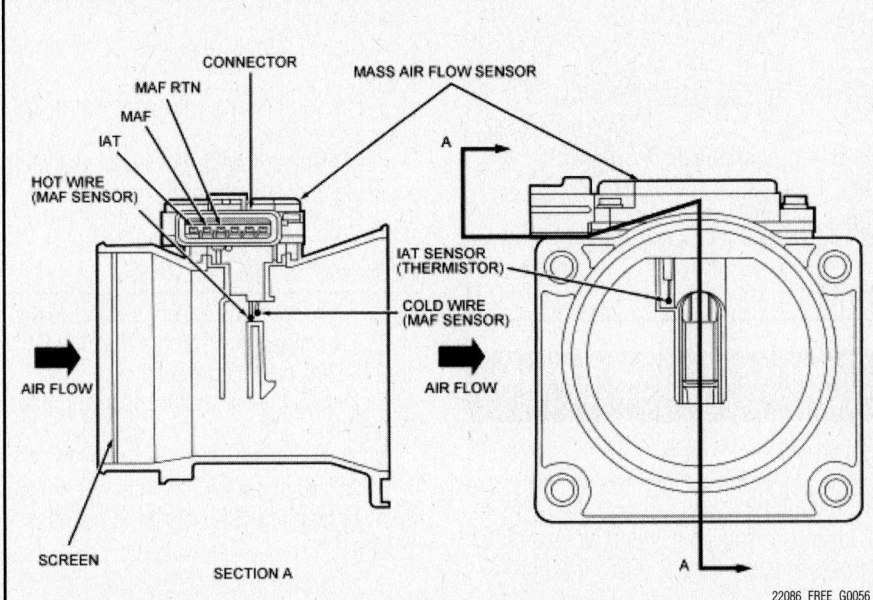

Fig. 55 Identifying air flow through throttle body contacting MAF sensor hot and cold wire terminals

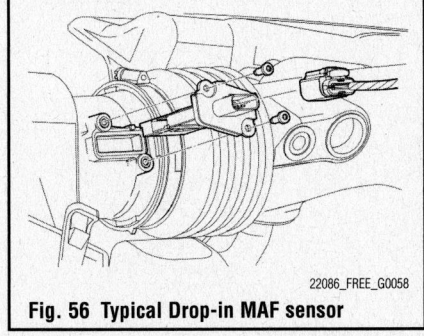

Fig. 56 Typical Drop-in MAF sensor

4. To install, reverse the removal procedure. Tighten the MAF sensor screws to 89 inch lbs. (10 Nm).

POWERTRAIN CONTROL MODULE (PCM)

LOCATION

The Powertrain Control Module (PCM) is located at the rear of the engine compartment on the passenger side.

OPERATION

The center of the Electronic Engine Control (EEC) system is a microprocessor called the PCM. The PCM receives input from sensors and other electronic components (switches, relays). Based on the information received and programmed into its memory, the PCM generates output signals to control various relays, solenoids and actuators. There are several different types of PCMs in use for this model year.

REMOVAL & INSTALLATION

See Figures 57 and 58.

➡️**Any PCM replacement will require that ALL customer keys are available to be programmed at the time of installation. PCM replacement DOES NOT require new keys.**

1. Retrieve the module configuration. Carry out the module configuration retrieval steps of the Programmable Module Installation procedure.
2. Remove the 3 bolts and position aside the suction accumulator.
3. Remove the bolt and position aside the power steering reservoir.
4. Loosen the bolt and disconnect the PCM electrical connector.
5. Remove the 2 PCM retaining nuts and the PCM.

To install:

6. Install the PCM and the 2 retaining nuts. Tighten to 44 inch lbs. (5 Nm).
7. Connect the PCM electrical connec-

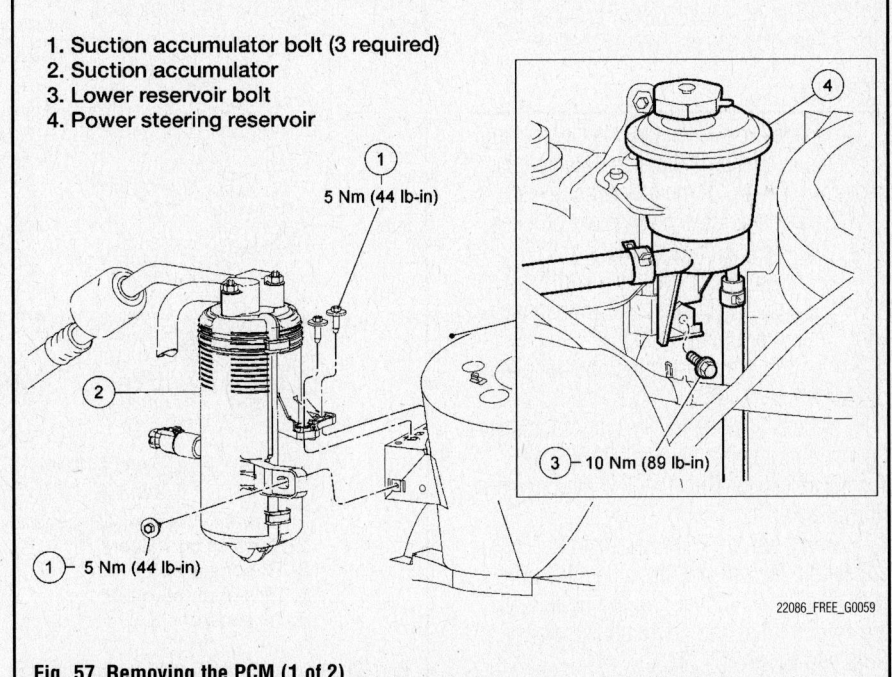

1. Suction accumulator bolt (3 required)
2. Suction accumulator
3. Lower reservoir bolt
4. Power steering reservoir

Fig. 57 Removing the PCM (1 of 2)

5. Powertrain control module (PCM) electrical connector
6. PCM retaining nut (2 required)
7. PCM*

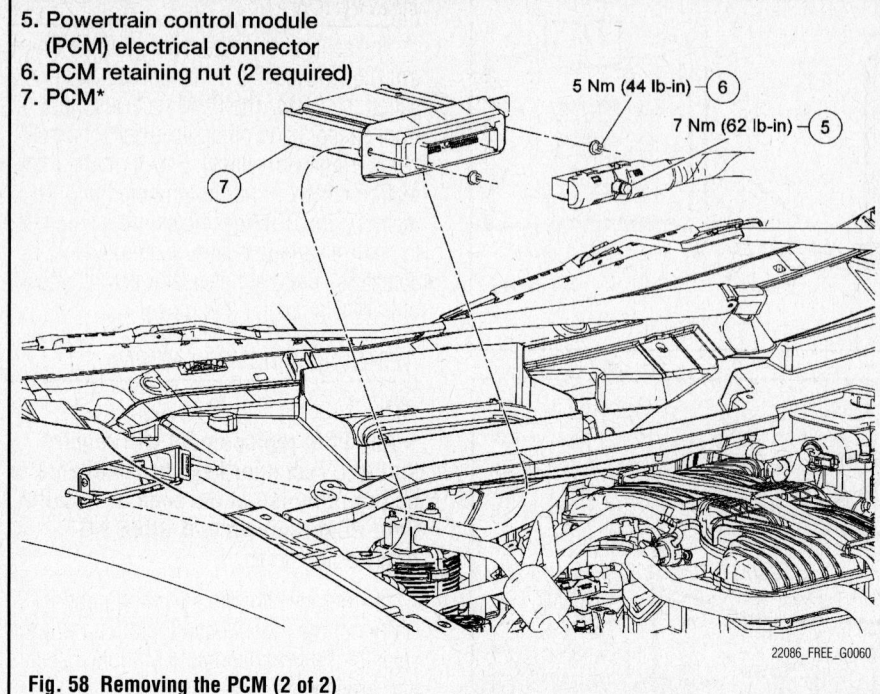

5 Nm (44 lb-in) — 6
7 Nm (62 lb-in) — 5

Fig. 58 Removing the PCM (2 of 2)

tor and tighten the bolt. Tighten to 62 inch lbs. (7 Nm).

8. Position the power steering reservoir and install the bolt. Tighten to 89 inch lbs. (10 Nm).

9. Position the suction accumulator and install the 3 bolts. Tighten to 44 inch lbs. (5 Nm).

10. Restore the module configuration. Carry out the module configuration restore steps of the Programmable Module Installation procedure.

11. Reprogram the Passive Anti-Theft System (PATS). Carry out the Key Programming Using Two Programmed Keys procedure.

TESTING

Complete the preliminary checks looking for obvious concerns that may relate to the symptom. Check for the following items:
- Related electrical connectors or fuses
- Vacuum lines (leaks, routing)
- Air intake system (leaks, restrictions)
- Fuel quality (octane, contamination, winter/summer blend)
- Cooling system (engine operating at proper temperature)
- Access any related On-line Automotive Service Information System (OASIS) or Technical Service Bulletin (TSB) information (if available).
- Carry out the PCM self-test to access any DTCs. Record any key on engine off (KOEO), key on engine running (KOER) (if the engine runs) and continuous memory (MIL and non-MIL) DTCs.

THROTTLE POSITION SENSOR (TPS)

LOCATION

See Figure 59.

Refer to the accompanying illustration for Throttle Position Sensor (TPS) location.

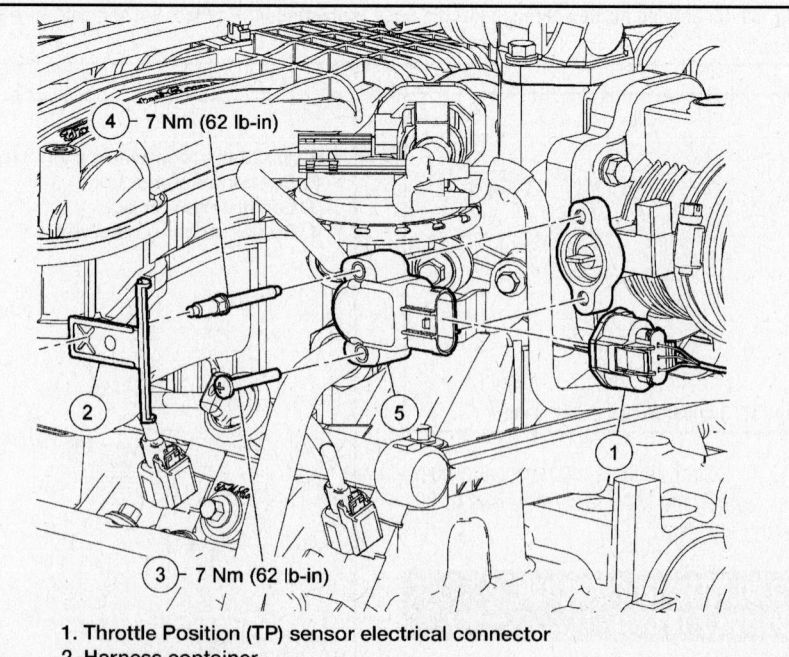

4 — 7 Nm (62 lb-in)
3 — 7 Nm (62 lb-in)

1. Throttle Position (TP) sensor electrical connector
2. Harness container
3. TP sensor bolt
4. TP sensor stud bolt
5. TP sensor*

Fig. 59 Throttle Position (TP) sensor location

OPERATION

The TPS is a rotary potentiometer sensor that provides a signal to the PCM that is linearly proportional to the throttle plate/shaft position. The sensor housing has a 3-blade electrical connector that may be gold plated. The gold plating increases the corrosion resistance on the terminals and increases the connector durability. The TPS is mounted on the throttle body. As the TPS is rotated by the throttle shaft, 4 operating conditions are determined by the PCM from the throttle position. The operating conditions are:
- Closed throttle (includes idle or deceleration)
- Part throttle (includes cruise or moderate acceleration)
- Wide open throttle (includes maximum acceleration or de-choke on crank)
- Throttle angle rate

REMOVAL & INSTALLATION

1. Disconnect the battery ground cable.
2. Disconnect the Throttle Position Sensor (TPS) electrical connector.
3. Detach the harness retainer from the stud bolt.
4. Remove the 2 TPS bolts and the TPS.
5. To install, reverse the removal procedure. Tighten the TPS bolts to 62 inch lbs. (7 Nm).

VEHICLE SPEED SENSOR (VSS)

LOCATION

The Vehicle Speed Sensor (VSS) is located at the front bottom of the transmission on the driver side. This sensor may also be referred to as the Output Shaft Speed Sensor (OSS).

REMOVAL & INSTALLATION

1. Remove the catalytic converter.
2. Remove the heat shield.
3. Disconnect the Vehicle Speed Sensor (VSS)/Output Shaft Speed (OSS) sensor connector.
4. Remove the VSS/OSS cover.
5. Remove the connector, the bolt and the cover.
6. Remove the VSS/OSS sensor.
7. To install, reverse the removal procedure.

FUEL SYSTEMS

GASOLINE FUEL INJECTION SYSTEM

FUEL SYSTEM SERVICE PRECAUTIONS

Safety is the most important factor when performing not only fuel system maintenance but any type of maintenance. Failure to conduct maintenance and repairs in a safe manner may result in serious personal injury or death. Maintenance and testing of the vehicle's fuel system components can be accomplished safely and effectively by adhering to the following rules and guidelines.

• To avoid the possibility of fire and personal injury, always disconnect the negative battery cable unless the repair or test procedure requires that battery voltage be applied.

• Always relieve the fuel system pressure prior to disconnecting any fuel system component (injector, fuel rail, pressure regulator, etc.), fitting or fuel line connection. Exercise extreme caution whenever relieving fuel system pressure to avoid exposing skin, face and eyes to fuel spray. Please be advised that fuel under pressure may penetrate the skin or any part of the body that it contacts.

• Always place a shop towel or cloth around the fitting or connection prior to loosening to absorb any excess fuel due to spillage. Ensure that all fuel spillage (should it occur) is quickly removed from engine surfaces. Ensure that all fuel soaked cloths or towels are deposited into a suitable waste container.

• Always keep a dry chemical (Class B) fire extinguisher near the work area.

• Do not allow fuel spray or fuel vapors to come into contact with a spark or open flame.

• Always use a back-up wrench when loosening and tightening fuel line connection fittings. This will prevent unnecessary stress and torsion to fuel line piping.

• Always replace worn fuel fitting O-rings with new Do not substitute fuel hose or equivalent where fuel pipe is installed.

Before servicing the vehicle, make sure to also refer to the precautions in the beginning of this section as well.

RELIEVING FUEL SYSTEM PRESSURE

2005 Models

Locate the fuel pump relay in the engine compartment fuse block at location K4/C-1051. Remove the fuel pump relay. Start the engine and allow it to idle until it stalls. Crank the engine for 5 seconds to ensure fuel supply manifold pressure is released. When vehicle service is complete, reinstall the fuel pump relay and turn the ignition on to pressurize the fuel system. Start the vehicle and check the system for leaks.

2006–07 Models

Remove the Schrader valve cap from the fuel rail. Install fuel pressure gauge no. 310-012. Slowly open the manual valve to release the pressure, using a container to catch any residual fuel. When servicing is complete, remove the gauge, install the cap and start the engine. Check for leaks.

FUEL FILTER

REMOVAL & INSTALLATION

See Figures 60 and 61.

1. Relieve the fuel system pressure.
2. Raise and support the vehicle safely on jackstands.
3. Place a rag under the fuel filter to catch any residual fuel that may leak out when the filter is removed.
4. Remove the quick-connect fittings at both ends of the fuel filter.
5. Install retainer clips in each fitting.

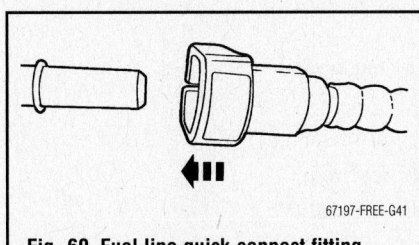

Fig. 60 Fuel line quick-connect fitting removal—3.9L and 4.2L engines

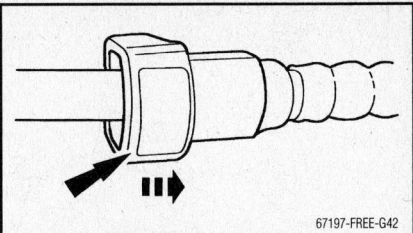

Fig. 61 Fuel line quick-connect fitting installation—3.9L and 4.2L engines

6. Note the flow arrow direction for installation reference.
7. Remove the fuel filter by pulling it from the bracket.

To install:

8. Install the fuel filter in its bracket, ensuring proper direction of flow as noted earlier.
9. Apply clean engine oil to end of fuel line and install the quick-connect fittings at both ends of the fuel filter. Ensure the fuel line clicks into place and is fully seated.
10. Start the engine and check the filter connections for leaks by running the tip of your finger around each connection.
11. Turn the engine off and lower the vehicle.

FUEL INJECTORS

REMOVAL & INSTALLATION

See Figures 62 and 63.

1. Disconnect the negative battery cable.
2. Relieve the fuel system pressure.
3. Disconnect the fuel charging wiring harness.
4. Remove the fuel pressure vacuum connector and fuel supply line.
5. Remove the fuel injection supply manifold, with injectors attached.
6. Remove the retaining clips and separate the injectors from the supply manifold.

To install:

7. Inspect fuel injector O-rings for signs of deterioration and replace as required.

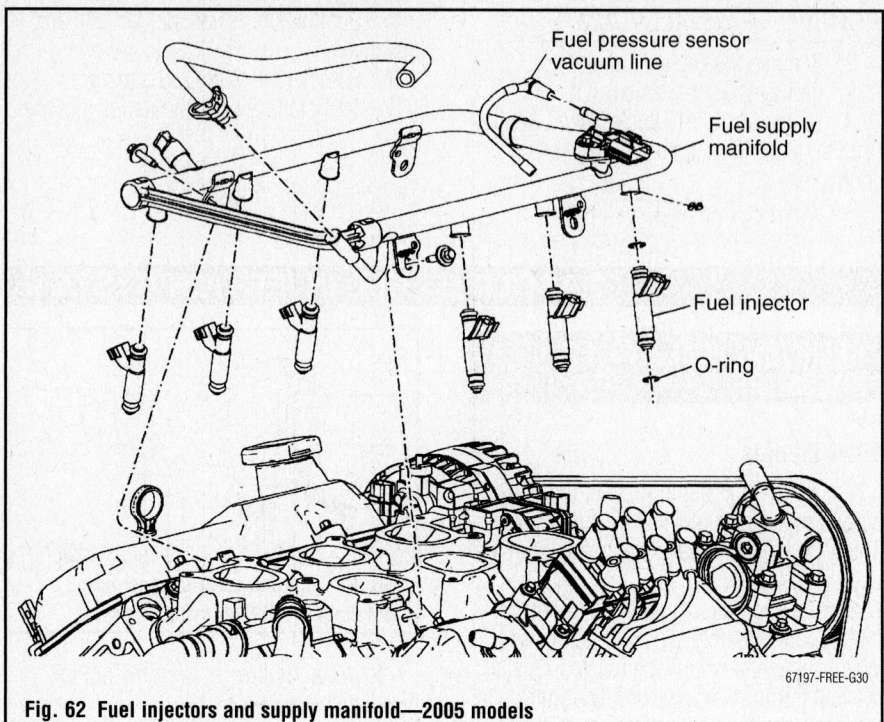

Fig. 62 Fuel injectors and supply manifold—2005 models

67197-FREE-G30

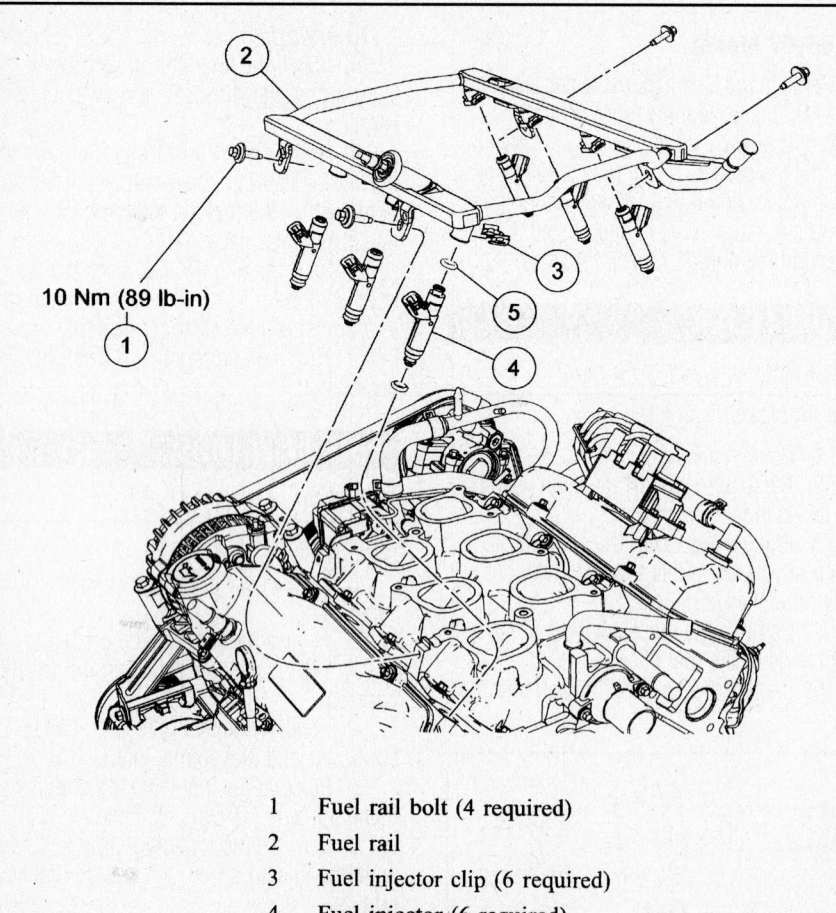

10 Nm (89 lb-in)

1	Fuel rail bolt (4 required)
2	Fuel rail
3	Fuel injector clip (6 required)
4	Fuel injector (6 required)
5	Fuel injector O-ring seal (12 required)

06017FRSTG02

Fig. 63 Fuel injectors and supply manifold—2006–07 models

➡**Never use silicone grease on fuel injectors.**

8. Lubricate O-rings with clean engine oil and position fuel injectors on the supply manifold. Install the retaining clips.

9. Install the fuel injection supply manifold, making sure the injectors are seated properly. A slight rocking motion helps seat the injectors.

10. Install the fuel pressure vacuum connector and fuel supply line.

11. Install the fuel charging wiring connectors.

12. Start the engine and check for fuel leaks.

FUEL PUMP

REMOVAL & INSTALLATION

See Figures 64 and 65.

➡**To gain access to the fuel pump, it is necessary to remove the fuel tank. The fuel tank is equipped with a composite protective shield mounted with the support straps and retainers on the right side of the tank. Make sure the shield is correctly installed when installing the tank.**

1. Disconnect the negative battery cable.

2. Depressurize the fuel system and drain the fuel into a suitable container.

3. Remove the fuel filler pipe.

✴✴ CAUTION

Some fuel may remain in the filler pipe.

4. Support the fuel tank.

5. Disconnect the electrical connectors and fuel line fittings.

6. Disconnect the retaining straps and lower the tank.

7. Remove any dirt that has accumulated around the fuel pump module attaching flange to prevent it from entering the tank during service.

8. Turn the fuel pump module locking ring counterclockwise using a locking ring removal tool, and remove the locking ring.

9. Remove the fuel pump module.

10. Remove the seal gasket and discard it.

To install:

11. Put a light coating of grease on a new seal ring to hold it in place during assembly. Install it in the fuel tank ring groove.

12. Insert the fuel pump module into the fuel tank, then secure it in place with the locking ring. Tighten the ring to 60 ft. lbs. (81 Nm).

13. Install the tank in the vehicle.

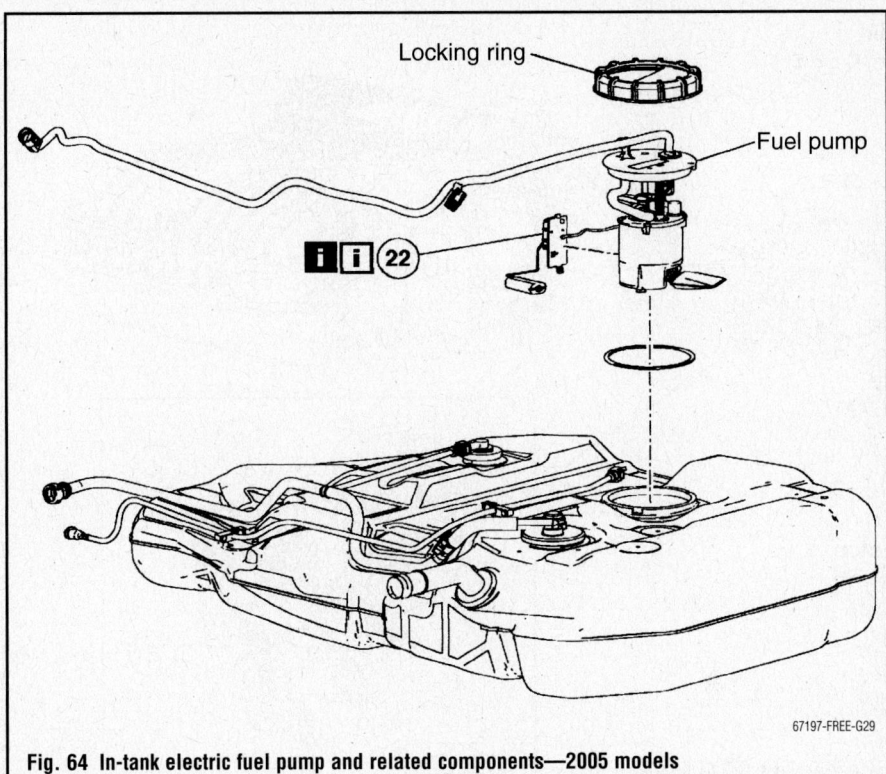

Fig. 64 In-tank electric fuel pump and related components—2005 models

67197-FREE-G29

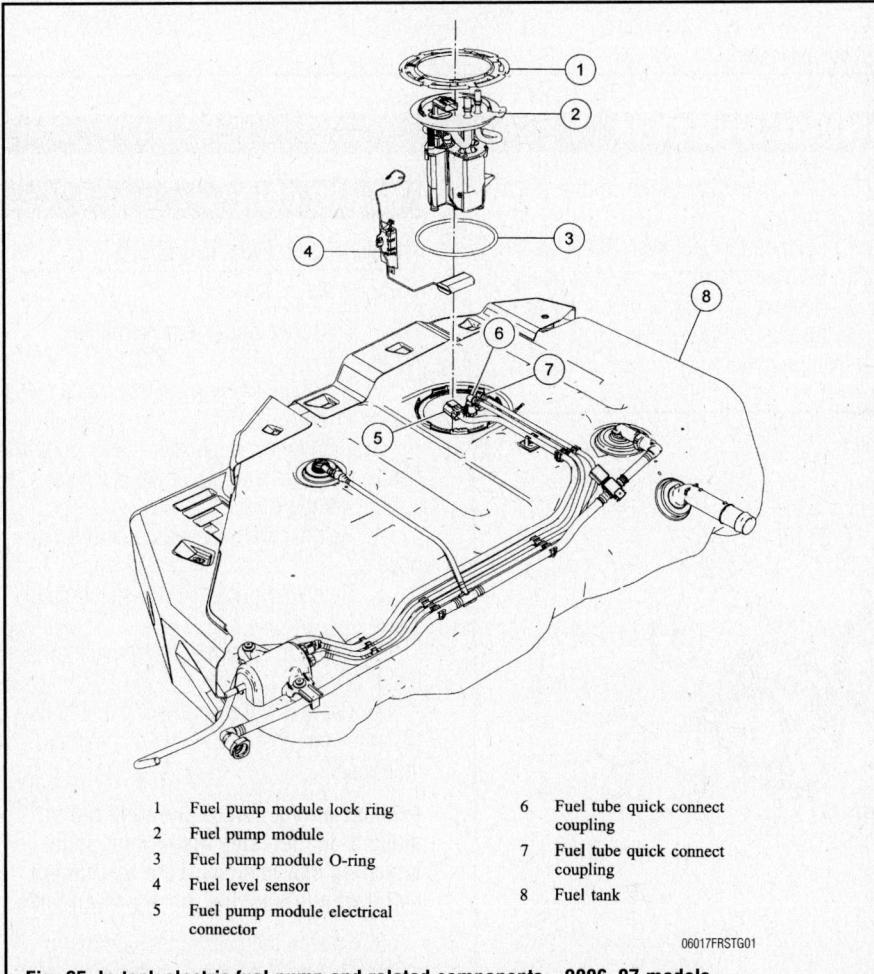

1	Fuel pump module lock ring	6	Fuel tube quick connect coupling
2	Fuel pump module	7	Fuel tube quick connect coupling
3	Fuel pump module O-ring	8	Fuel tank
4	Fuel level sensor		
5	Fuel pump module electrical connector		

06017FRSTG01

Fig. 65 In-tank electric fuel pump and related components—2006–07 models

14. Install a minimum of 10 gallons (38L) of fuel and check for leaks.

15. Check for fuel leaks at the fittings.

16. Start the engine and check for fuel leaks.

IDLE SPEED

ADJUSTMENT

Idle speed is maintained by the Powertrain Control Module (PCM). No adjustment is necessary or possible.

THROTTLE BODY

REMOVAL & INSTALLATION

See Figure 66.

✳ WARNING

Throttle body bore and plate area have a special coating and cannot be cleaned, or possible damage to the throttle body can occur.

1. Disconnect the negative battery cable.

2. Remove the air cleaner outlet pipe.

3. Detach the harness retainer from the cable bracket stud bolt.

4. Disconnect the Throttle Position (TP) sensor electrical connector.

5. Disconnect the throttle return spring from the throttle body.

6. Disconnect the speed control cable from the throttle body.

7. Disconnect the accelerator cable from the throttle body.

8. Remove the 2 cable bracket bolts and position the bracket and cables aside.

9. Remove the 4 throttle body-to-upper intake manifold bolts and the throttle body.

10. Remove the throttle body gasket.

11. Inspect the gasket and install new if necessary.

To install:

12. Install the throttle body gasket and throttle body. Tighten the mounting bolts to 89 inch lbs. (10 Nm).

13. Install the cable bracket and tighten the bolts to 11 ft. lbs. (15 Nm).

14. Attach the accelerator cable to the throttle body.

15. Connect the speed control cable to the throttle body.

16. Connect the throttle return spring to the throttle body.

17. Attach the TP sensor electrical connector.

18. Attach the harness retainer to the cable bracket stud bolt.

19. Install the air cleaner outlet pipe.

20. Connect the negative battery cable.

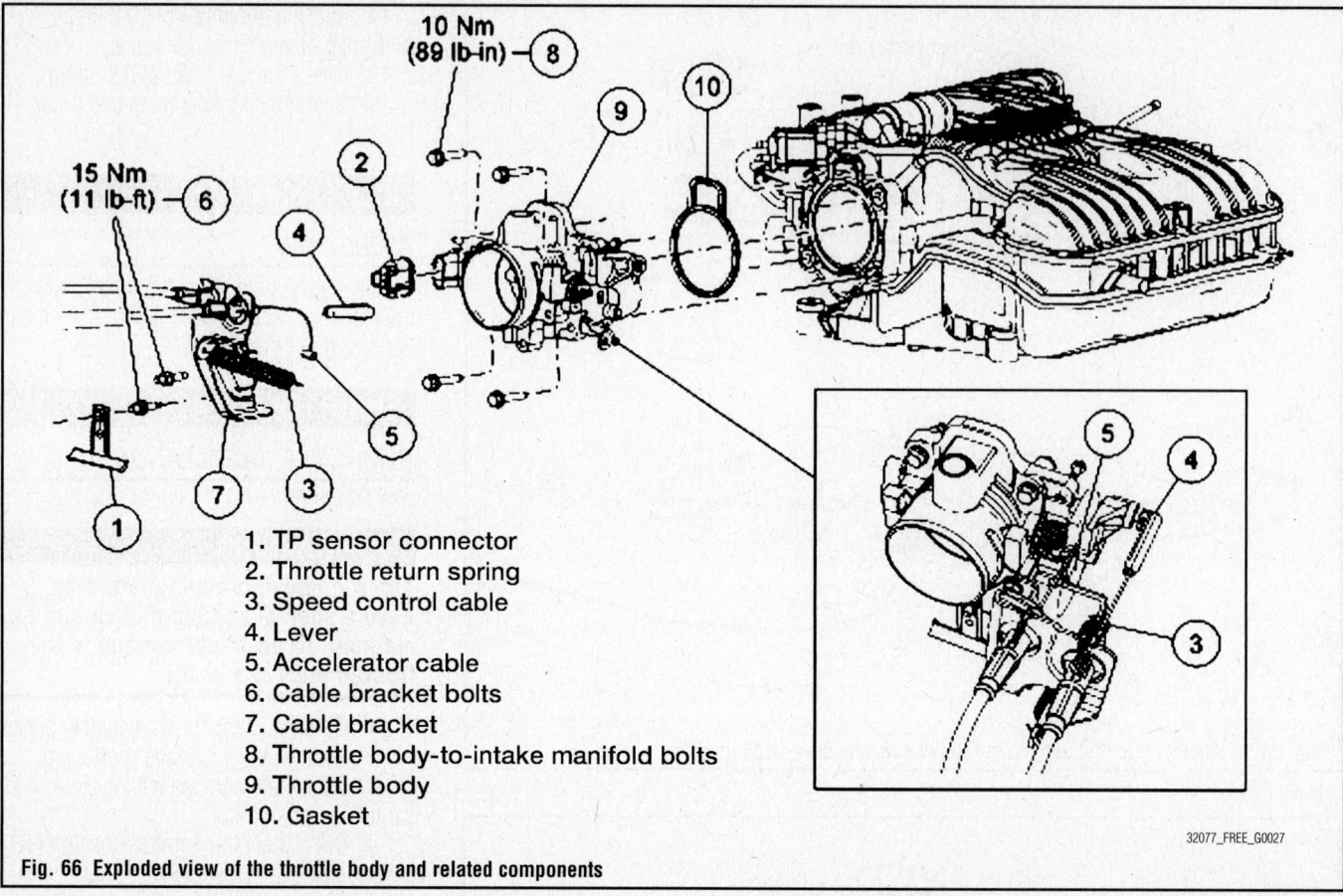

1. TP sensor connector
2. Throttle return spring
3. Speed control cable
4. Lever
5. Accelerator cable
6. Cable bracket bolts
7. Cable bracket
8. Throttle body-to-intake manifold bolts
9. Throttle body
10. Gasket

32077_FREE_G0027

Fig. 66 Exploded view of the throttle body and related components

HEATING & AIR CONDITIONING SYSTEM

BLOWER MOTOR

REMOVAL & INSTALLATION

See Figure 67.

1. Lower the glove compartment.
2. Detach the electrical connector.
3. Disconnect the blower motor electrical connector.
4. Remove the 3 blower motor screws.
5. Remove the blower motor wheel clip.
6. Remove the blower motor wheel.
7. Installation is the reverse of the removal procedure.

1. Blower motor electrical connector
2. Blower motor screws
3. Blower motor
4. Blower motor wheel clip
5. Blower motor wheel

32077_FREE_G0051

Fig. 67 Exploded view of the blower motor

HEATER CORE

REMOVAL & INSTALLATION

See Figures 68 and 69.

1. Disconnect the negative battery cable.
2. Drain the cooling system into a clean container for reuse.
3. Disconnect the heater hoses from the heater core inlet and outlet tubes in the engine compartment.
4. Remove the steering column lower covers.
5. Remove the center storage compartment
6. Remove the upper instrument panel finish cover.
7. Remove the instrument panel bolts (9) at the top and driver side of the instrument panel.

→Insert a long bolt or threaded rod in place of the left side instrument panel attaching bolt to support the instrument panel when removing the attaching bolts.

8. Loosen the passenger side instrument panel bolts approximately halfway.

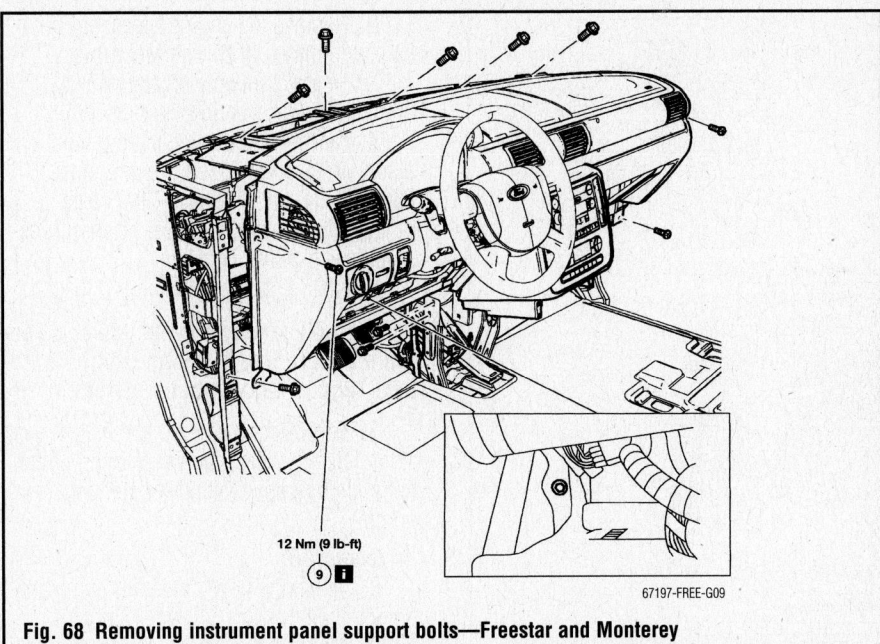

12 Nm (9 lb-ft)
⑨ ⓘ
67197-FREE-G09

Fig. 68 Removing instrument panel support bolts—Freestar and Monterey

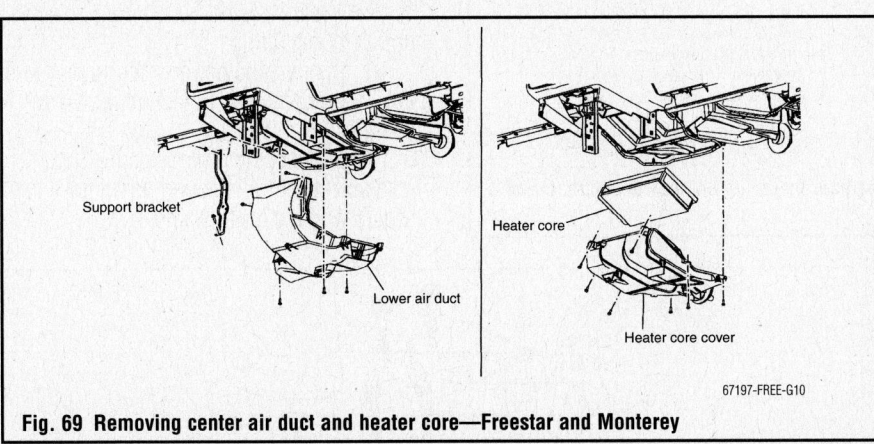

Support bracket

Lower air duct

Heater core

Heater core cover

67197-FREE-G10

Fig. 69 Removing center air duct and heater core—Freestar and Monterey

9. Remove the center instrument panel support brace.

10. From inside the glove box, remove the attaching bolt.

11. Pull the instrument panel outward approximately 3 inches.

12. Remove the lower center air duct.

13. Disconnect the heater core wiring connector.

14. Remove the heater core cover and heater core.

To install:

15. Installation is the reverse of removal.

16. Please note the following torque specifications:

- Upper instrument panel bolts. Torque the bolts to 44 inch lbs. (5 Nm).
- Side and lower instrument panel bolts. Torque the bolts to 9 ft. lbs. (12 Nm).

17. Refill the cooling system.

18. Connect the negative battery cable.

19. Run the engine to normal operating temperatures; then, check the climate control operation and check for leaks.

STEERING

POWER STEERING GEAR

REMOVAL & INSTALLATION

See Figure 70.

✳✳ WARNING

Do not allow the steering wheel to rotate when the intermediate shaft is disconnect, or damage to the clockspring can result. If it is suspected that the shaft has rotated, the clockspring must be removed and re-centered.

1. Remove or disconnect the following:
   - Front wheels
   - Tie rod end cotter pins and castle nuts
   - Tie rod ends from the knuckles

2. Position the dash opening weather seal for the steering column out of the way.

3. Remove or disconnect the following:
   - Pinch bolt retaining the steering column intermediate shaft coupling
   - Steering gear retaining nuts/bolts

4. Rotate the rack and pinion assembly to clear the bolts from the front crossmember, and pull toward the driver's side of the vehicle.

5. Place a drain pan under the vehicle and disconnect the power steering lines.

6. Remove the rack and pinion assembly through the driver's side of the vehicle.

To install:

7. Install new Teflon® O-rings on the power steering line fittings.

8. Place the rack and pinion retaining bolts in the gear housing.

9. Install or connect the following:
   - Rack and pinion assembly through the driver's side of the vehicle

   - Power steering lines on the rack and pinion assembly
   - Rack and pinion assembly on the crossmember
   - Tie rod ends to the knuckles. Tighten the castle nuts to 59 ft. lbs. (80 Nm) and install the cotter pins.
   - Rack and pinion assembly retaining bolts, and tighten them to 129 ft. lbs. (175 Nm).
   - Front wheels

10. Using a new pinch bolt, install the steering column intermediate shaft coupling on the rack input shaft. Tighten the pinch bolt to 22 ft. lbs. (30 Nm).

11. Position the steering column opening weather seal over the steering gear housing.

12. Lower the vehicle.

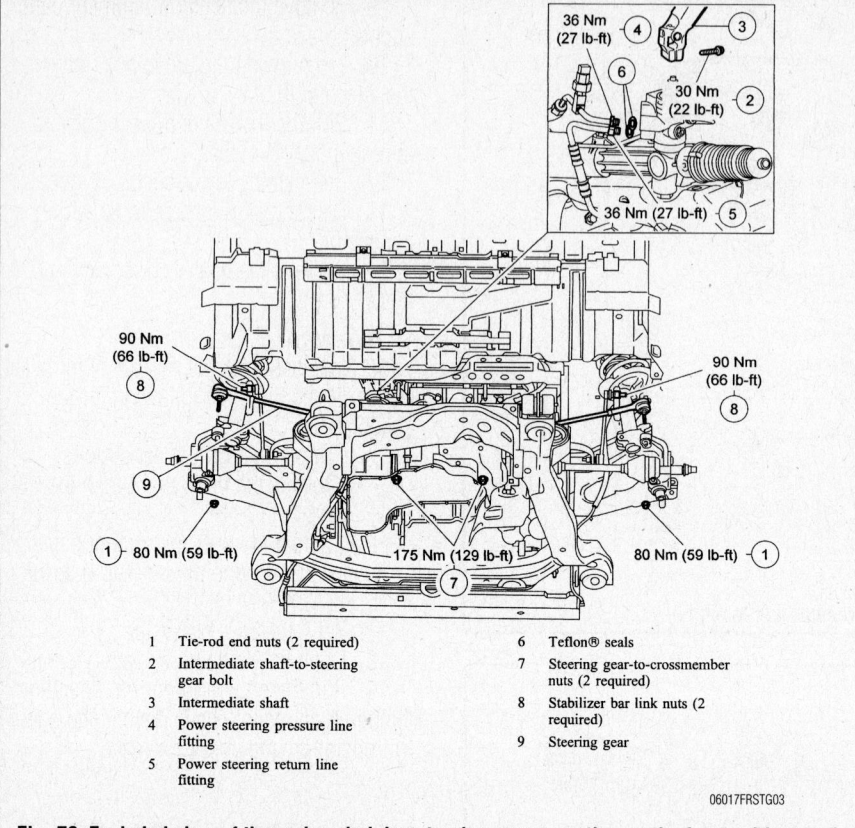

Fig. 70 Exploded view of the rack and pinion steering gear mounting on the front subframe of the vehicle—Freestar and Monterey

1 Tie-rod end nuts (2 required)
2 Intermediate shaft-to-steering gear bolt
3 Intermediate shaft
4 Power steering pressure line fitting
5 Power steering return line fitting
6 Teflon® seals
7 Steering gear-to-crossmember nuts (2 required)
8 Stabilizer bar link nuts (2 required)
9 Steering gear

06017FRSTG03

2. Remove the engine accessory drive belt, as outlined in Engine Mechanical.

3. Using a suitable suction device, drain the power steering fluid reservoir.

4. Release the power steering fluid reservoir-to-power steering pump hose lower clamp and disconnect the hose.

5. Disconnect the power steering pressure line-to-pump fitting.

To install, tighten to 65 Nm (48 lb-ft).

➡ **When disconnecting the power steering pressure line-to-pump fitting, a new Teflon® seal must be installed.**

6. Remove and discard the Teflon® seal.

7. Remove the 4 power steering pump bolts, then remove the power steering pump.

To install:

8. Install the power steering pump and tighten the bolts to 18 ft. lbs. (25 Nm).

9. Using the special tool, install a new Teflon® seal on the power steering pressure line-to-pump fitting.

10. Connect the power steering pressure line-to-pump fitting. Tighten to 48 ft. lbs. (65 Nm).

11. Connect the power steering fluid reservoir-to-power steering pump hose and secure with the lower clamp.

13. Fill the power steering oil reservoir.

14. Start the vehicle and check for leaks.

15. Check for proper wheel alignment and steering wheel position.

POWER STEERING PUMP

REMOVAL & INSTALLATION

See Figures 71 and 72.

➡ **This procedure requires Teflon® Seal Installer Set 211-D027 (D90P-3517) or equivalent.**

✳✳ WARNING

When repairing the power steering system, be careful to avoid the entry of contaminants or premature failure of the power steering components can result.

1. Remove the cowl panel grille, as follows:

a. Remove the 2 windshield wiper arm nuts.

b. Remove the LH and RH windshield wiper arms.

c. Remove the 4 cowl panel grille push pins.

d. Remove the cowl panel grille. Disconnect the washer hose.

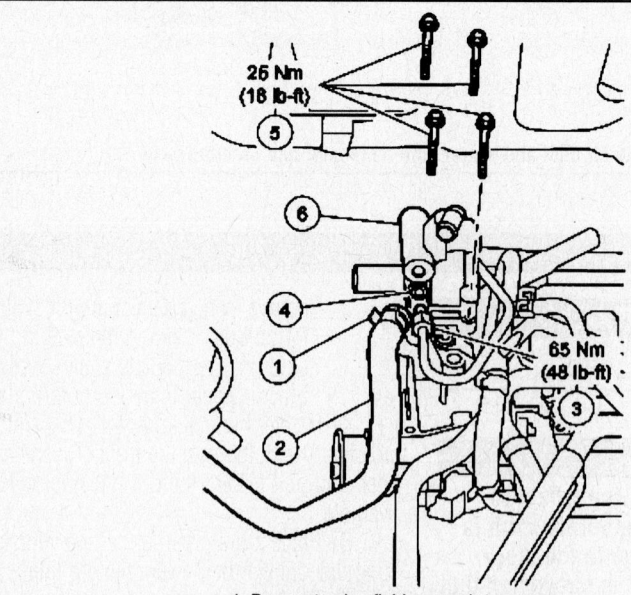

1. Power steering fluid reservoir-to-power steering pump hose lower clamp
2. Power steering fluid reservoir-to-power steering pump hose
3. Power steering pressure line-to-pump fitting
4. Teflon® seal
5. Power steering pump bolts
6. Power steering pump

Note: The power steering pump pulley has been removed for clarity

32077_FREE_G0039

Fig. 71 View of the power steering pump and related components—Note: The power steering pump pulley has been removed for clarity.

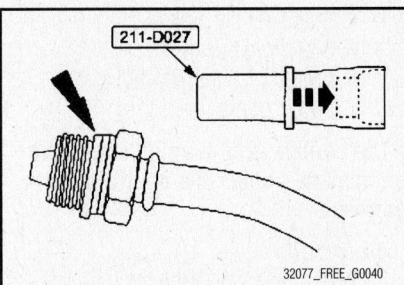

Fig. 72 Using a suitable Teflon® seal installer tool, install a new Teflon® seal on the power steering pressure line-to-pump fitting

12. Install the engine accessory drive belt, as outlined in Engine Mechanical.

13. Install the cowl panel grille, as follows:

   a. Install the cowl panel grille.

   b. Connect the washer hose.

   c. Install the 4 cowl panel grille push pins.

   d. Install the LH and RH windshield wiper arms.

   e. Cycle and park the windshield wipers.

   f. Install the 2 windshield wiper arm nuts and tighten to 18 ft. lbs. (25 Nm).

14. Fill the power steering system, as outlined under Bleeding.

BLEEDING

Filling the System

➡This procedure requires the use of the following special tools or their equivalents. Vacuum Pump Kit 416-D002 (D95L-7559-A), Power Steering Evacuation Cap 211-265, and Power Steering Fill Adapter Manifold 211-327.

✳✳ WARNING

If the air is not purged from the power steering system correctly, premature

power steering pump failure can result. The condition can occur on pre-delivery vehicles with evidence of aerated fluid or on vehicles that have had steering component repairs.

1. Remove the power steering pump reservoir cap.

2. Tightly install the evacuation cap to the power steering pump reservoir.

3. Install the hose from the fill adapter manifold tee to the evacuation cap on the power steering pump reservoir.

4. Install the vacuum pump to the fill adapter manifold control valve.

5. Install the hose to the opposite fill adapter manifold control valve and submerge the open end of the hose into a container of new power steering fluid.

➡The fill adapter manifold control valves are in the open position when the point of the handles face the center of the fill adapter manifold.

6. Close the fill adapter manifold control valve connected to the power steering fluid container.

7. Open the fill adapter manifold control valve connected to the vacuum pump.

8. Using the vacuum pump, apply 20–25 in. Hg (68–85 kPa) of vacuum to the power steering system. Observe the vacuum gauge for 30 seconds.

9. If the vacuum gauge reading drops more than 0.88 in. Hg (3 kPa), correct any leaks in the power steering system or the filling tools before proceeding.

➡The vacuum pump gauge reading will drop slightly during this step.

10. Slowly open the fill adapter manifold control valve connected to the power steering fluid container until power steering fluid completely fills the hose.

11. Close the fill adapter manifold control valve connected to the power steering fluid container.

12. Using the vacuum pump, 20–25 in. Hg (68–85 kPa) of vacuum to the power steering system.

13. Close the fill adapter manifold control valve connected to the vacuum pump.

14. Slowly open the fill adapter manifold control valve connected to the power steering fluid container.

15. When the power steering fluid has drained from the hose connected to the power steering fluid container, close the fill adapter manifold control valve connected to the power steering fluid container.

16. Remove the tools from the vehicle.

17. Install the power steering reservoir cap.

✳✳ WARNING

Do not hold the steering wheel against the stops for more than 3 to 5 seconds at a time. Damage to the power steering pump can occur.

➡There will be a slight drop in the power steering fluid level in the power steering fluid reservoir when the engine is started.

18. Start the engine and turn the steering wheel from stop-to-stop.

19. If equipped with Hydro-Boost®, apply the brake pedal twice.

20. Turn the ignition switch to the **OFF** position.

✳✳ WARNING

Do not overfill the reservoir.

21. Remove the power steering reservoir cap and fill the reservoir.

22. Install the power steering reservoir cap.

SUSPENSION

FRONT SUSPENSION

COIL SPRING & SHOCK ABSORBER

REMOVAL & INSTALLATION

See Figure 73.

➡Do not allow the axle shaft to move outward as damage to the CV-joint may result.

1. Turn the ignition switch **OFF** and place the steering column in the unlocked position.

2. Remove or disconnect the following:

   • Front wheel

   • Stabilizer bar link nut

   • Support the steering knuckle and remove the pinch bolt

   • Upper strut mounting nuts

3. Push down on the steering knuckle until the strut is free of the steering knuckle and remove the strut.

To install:

4. Push down on the steering knuckle and insert the bottom of the strut into the steering knuckle.

5. Install the upper strut mounting nuts and tighten them to 26 ft. lbs. (35 Nm).

6. Install strut-to-wheel knuckle pinch bolt and tighten to 85 ft. lbs. (115 Nm).

7. Install or connect the following:

   • Stabilizer bar link nut and tighten to 66 ft. lbs. (90 Nm).

   • Rotor

   • Caliper

   • Wheels

8. Check the wheel alignment.

OVERHAUL

1. Position a suitable pass through socket wrench onto the strut shaft nut.

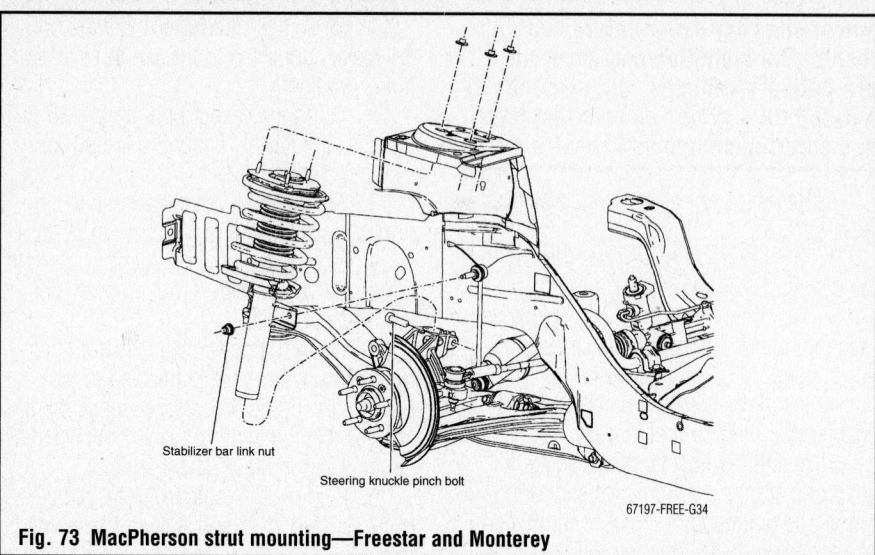

Fig. 73 MacPherson strut mounting—Freestar and Monterey

67197-FREE-G34

- Stabilizer bar link nut
- Steering knuckle
- Lower arm bushing bolts
- Lower control arm

➡ **The control arm bushing should be replaced whenever the control arm is removed.**

To install:

2. Install or connect the following:
   - Lower control arm
   - Lower arm bushing bolts. Tighten NEW bolts to 66 ft. lbs. (90 Nm).
   - Steering knuckle. Tighten NEW ball joint stud-to-knuckle bolt to 66 ft. lbs. (90 Nm).
   - Stabilizer bar link nut. Tighten NEW bolt to 66 ft. lbs. (90 Nm).

2. Place a 10 mm six point deep socket on the strut top retaining nut.

3. Remove the strut shaft while holding the retaining nut in place.

4. Remove the shock absorber.

5. Remove the upper shock mount and bearing assembly.

6. Remove the coil spring.

7. To reassemble, reverse the disassembly procedure. Tighten the strut top retaining nut to 37 ft. lbs. (50 Nm).

LOWER BALL JOINT

REMOVAL & INSTALLATION

The lower ball joint and seal are an integral part of the lower control arm assembly, and cannot be replaced separately. If the lower ball joint or seal is found to be defective, the lower control arm must be replaced as an assembly.

LOWER CONTROL ARM, CONTROL ARM BUSHING & STEERING KNUCKLE

REMOVAL AND & INSTALLATION

See Figure 74.

➡ **Do not begin the removal procedure unless a new strut-to-lower arm nut, a new ball joint pinch bolt/nut and a new lower arm-to-front subframe bolt/nut are available.**

1. Remove or disconnect the following:
   - Wheel
   - Brake caliper
   - Rotor
   - Axle shaft nut
   - Wheel hub and bearing
   - Tie rod nut
   - Steering knuckle pinch bolt

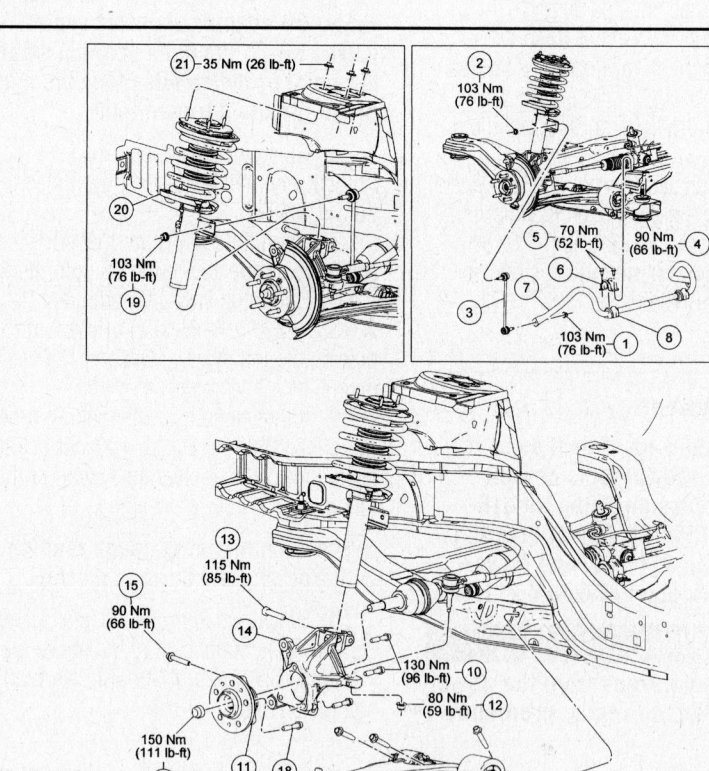

1	Stabilizer bar link lower nut	12	Tie-rod end nut
2	Stabilizer bar link upper nut	13	Wheel knuckle pinch bolt
3	Stabilizer bar link (2 required)	14	Wheel knuckle (LH/RH)
4	Subframe bolt	15	Lower ball joint pinch bolt
5	Stabilizer bar bracket bolts	16	Lower arm bushing bolt (4 required)
6	Stabilizer bar bracket	17	Lower arm (LH/RH)
7	Stabilizer bar	18	Wheel stud
8	Stabilizer bar bushing	19	Stabilizer bar link upper nut
9	Axle shaft nut	20	Shock absorber and spring assembly
10	Wheel bearing and hub-to-wheel knuckle bolts (3 required)	21	Shock absorber upper nut
11	Wheel bearing and hub assembly		

06017FRSTG04

Fig. 74 Exploded view of the front suspension—Freestar and Monterey

- Steering knuckle pinch bolt. Tighten NEW bolt to 85 ft. lbs. (115 Nm).
- Tie rod nut. Tighten NEW nut to 59 ft. lbs. (80 Nm).
- Wheel hub and bearing. Tighten the bolts to 85 ft. lbs. (115 Nm).
- Axle shaft nut. Tighten NEW bolt to 185 ft. lbs. (250 Nm).
- Rotor
- Brake caliper

3. Install the wheels.
4. Lower the vehicle.

STABILIZER BAR

REMOVAL & INSTALLATION

1. Raise and safely support the vehicle.
2. Remove the wheels.
3. Remove the stabilizer bar link nuts.
4. Remove the stabilizer bar links.

➡**The subframe will need to be supported when the mounting bolts are removed.**

5. Remove the rear subframe mounting bolts and lower the rear of the subframe about 2-3 inches.
6. Remove the stabilizer bar brackets.
7. Remove the stabilizer bar.

To install:

8. Install or connect the following:
- Stabilizer bar and brackets. Tighten the bracket bolts to 46 ft. lbs. (63 Nm).
- NEW subframe bolts. Tighten the bracket bolts to 66 ft. lbs. (89 Nm).
- Stabilizer bar links. Tighten the bracket bolts to 66 ft. lbs. (89 Nm).
- ABS speed sensor
- Brake rotor and caliper
- Wheels
- Lower the vehicle

WHEEL HUB AND BEARING

REMOVAL & INSTALLATION

The wheel bearing is integral with the wheel hub and cannot be replaced separately. If the wheel bearing is found to be defective, the wheel hub must be replaced as an assembly.

1. With the vehicle on the ground, remove and discard the axle shaft nut.
2. Raise and safely support the vehicle.
3. Remove the wheel and tire assembly.
4. Remove the brake caliper and wire it out of the way.
5. Remove the brake rotor.
6. Using a puller, remove the driveshaft from the hub and bearing housing.
7. Remove 3 hub attaching bolts, and remove the hub and bearing assembly.

To install:

8. Position the dust shield over the hub and fit the hub and bearing into the knuckle and seat it fully before installing the attaching bolts. Tighten the bolts to 85 ft. lbs. (115 Nm).
9. Install or connect the following:
- Driveshaft
- Brake rotor
- Brake caliper
- Wheel and tire. Tighten the lug nuts to 100 ft. lbs. (135 Nm).
- Install the axle nut and tighten the nut to 96 ft. lbs. (130 Nm).

SUSPENSION

REAR SUSPENSION

COIL SPRING

REMOVAL & INSTALLATION

See Figure 75.

1. Raise and safely support the vehicle.
2. Remove the rear wheels.
3. Remove the brake caliper and wire aside.
4. Remove the brake rotor.
5. Disconnect the ABS speed sensor.

➡**The rear axle will need to be supported when the shock absorbers are removed.**

6. Remove the wheel hub and bearing assembly.
7. Remove the shock absorber.
8. Slowly lower the rear axle assembly until the rear spring can be removed.
9. Remove the rear spring.

To install:

10. Position the rear spring insulator on the rear axle assembly and press the insulator downward into place. Verify rear spring insulator is properly seated into correct position.
11. Slowly raise the rear axle assembly with a jack, and guide the upper rear spring insulator onto the upper spring seat on the underbody.

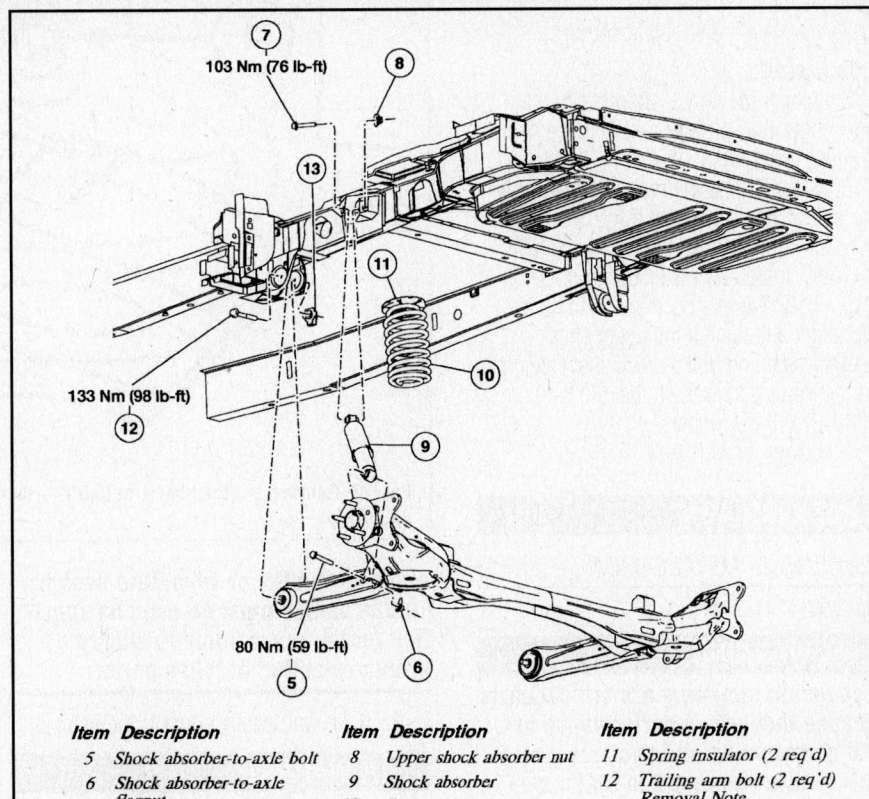

Item	Description	Item	Description	Item	Description
5	Shock absorber-to-axle bolt	8	Upper shock absorber nut	11	Spring insulator (2 req'd)
6	Shock absorber-to-axle flagnut	9	Shock absorber	12	Trailing arm bolt (2 req'd) Removal Note
7	Upper shock absorber bolt	10	Spring	13	Trailing arm nut (2 req'd)

67197-FREE-G35

Fig. 75 Exploded view of the rear coil spring ford shock absorber mounting—Freestar and Monterey

12. Position the shock absorber on the lower rear axle assembly and tighten the upper shock absorber retaining bolt to 76 ft. lbs. (103 Nm), and the lower bolt to 59 ft. lbs. (80 Nm).

13. Install the wheel hub and bearing assembly and tighten the bolts to 85 ft. lbs. (115 Nm).

14. Connect the ABS speed sensor.

15. Install the brake rotor and caliper.

16. Install the wheels.

17. Lower the vehicle.

SHOCK ABSORBER

REMOVAL & INSTALLATION

See Figure 75.

1. Loosen the lug nuts on the rear wheels.

2. Raise and safely support the vehicle.

3. Remove the rear wheels.

4. Position a jack under the rear axle assembly and raise it slightly to put the suspension at normal ride height.

5. Remove the lower shock absorber bolt/nut and disconnect the shock from the rear axle.

6. Lower the rear axle slightly to help aid removal of the upper shock absorber bolt/nut.

7. Remove the shock absorber.

To install:

8. Attach the shock absorber to the upper mounting bracket and install a new retaining bolt/nut.

9. Slowly raise the rear axle assembly with a jack, and guide the lower shock absorber into the bracket on the rear axle assembly. Install a new retaining bolt/nut.

10. Raise the rear suspension to normal ride height and tighten the upper shock absorber retaining bolt to 76 ft. lbs. (103 Nm), and the lower bolt to 59 ft. lbs. (80 Nm).

11. Install the wheels.

12. Lower the vehicle.

TRACKBAR ARM

REMOVAL & INSTALLATION

See Figures 76 and 77.

✷✷ WARNING

Suspension fasteners are critical parts because they affect performance of vital components and systems and their failure can result in major service expense. They must be replaced with the same part number, or an equivalent part, if replacement is necessary. Do not use a replacement part

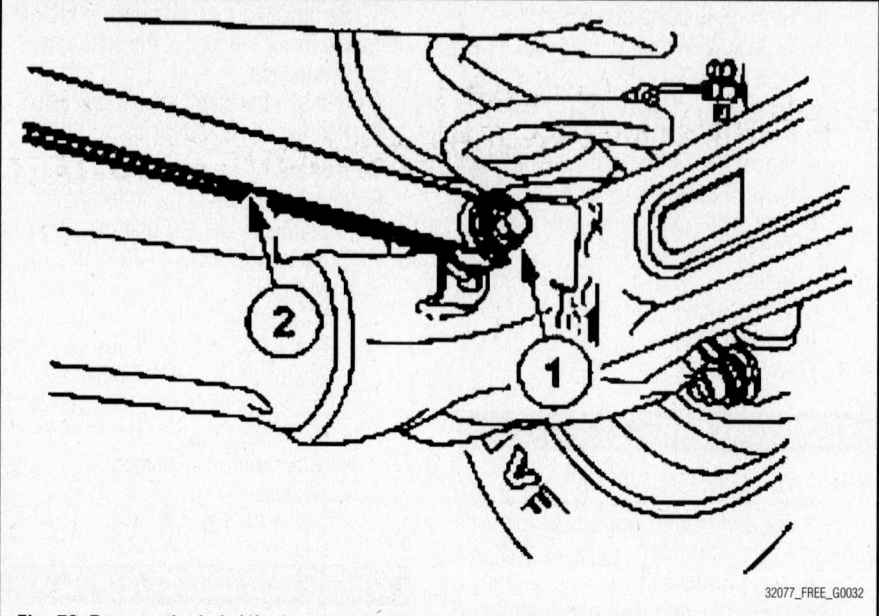

Fig. 76 Remove the bolt (1), then remove the trackbar (2) arm from the axle mounting bracket

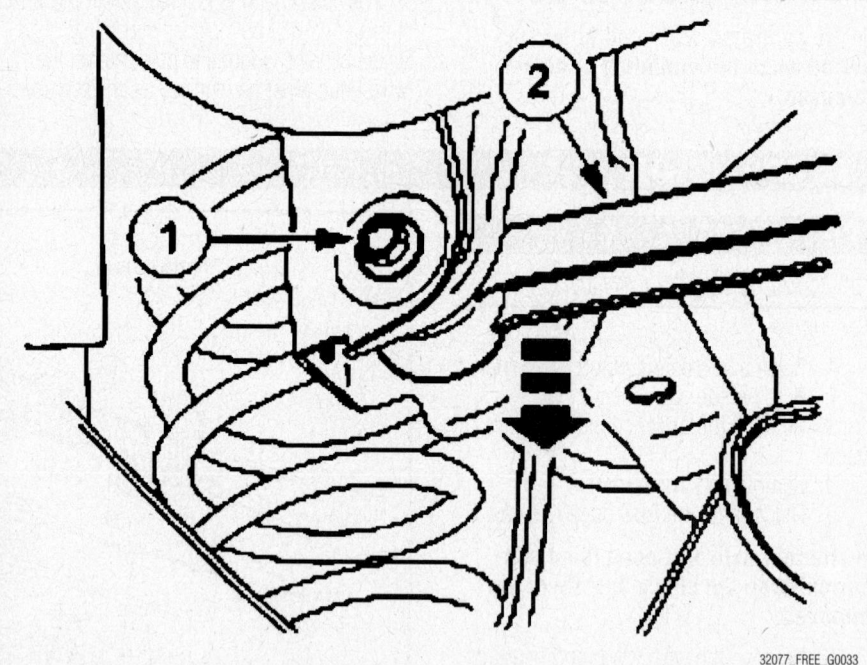

Fig. 77 Remove the trackbar arm bolt (1), then remove the trackbar arm from the mounting bracket (2)

of lesser quality or substitute design. Torque values must be used as specified during reassembly to ensure proper retention of these parts.

1. Raise and safely support the vehicle.

✷✷ WARNING

The rear axle assembly must be supported before removal of the trackbar arm or the retaining bolts to prevent damage to the vehicle components.

The rear axle U-channel must fit completely into the saddle of the jack stand to prevent damage to the rear axle.

2. Support the rear axle with a jack stand.

3. Disconnect the trackbar arm from the rear axle, as follows:

   a. Remove the trackbar bolt.

   b. Remove the trackbar arm from the axle mounting bracket.

4. Remove the trackbar from the mounting bracket:

    a. Remove the trackbar arm bolt.

    b. Remove the trackbar arm.

To install:

5. Installation is the reverse of the removal procedure. Please observe the following tightening specifications:

    a. Track arm bolt: 66 ft. lbs. (90 Nm)

    b. Trackbar arm-to-axle mounting bracket bolt: 76 ft. lbs. (103 Nm)

TRAILING ARM BUSHING

REMOVAL & INSTALLATION

See Figures 78 through 80.

➡This procedure requires the following special tools, or their equivalents. Bushing Replacer 204-189 (T95T-5638-DH), Bushing Remover/Replacer 204-191 (T95T-5638-FH), Forcing Screws 204-044 (T79P-5638-AR), Rotunda High Lift Jack 014-00942.

✴✴ WARNING

Suspension fasteners are critical parts because they affect performance of vital components and systems and their failure can result in major service expense. They must be replaced with the same part number, or an equivalent part, if replacement is necessary. Do not use a replacement part of lesser quality or substitute design. Torque values must be used as specified during reassembly to ensure proper retention of these parts.

✴✴ WARNING

The rear axle assembly must be supported to prevent damage to the vehicle. The rear axle U-channel must fit completely into the saddle of the jack stand to prevent damage to the rear axle.

1. Raise and safely support the vehicle.

2. Remove the rear brake disc (rotor), as outlined in brakes.

3. Using the special tool or equivalent jack stand, support the rear axle.

4. Remove the shock absorber lower bolt and nut.

5. Remove the trailing arm bushing bolt and nut.

6. If necessary, use a pry bar to remove the trailing arm and bushing from the body bracket.

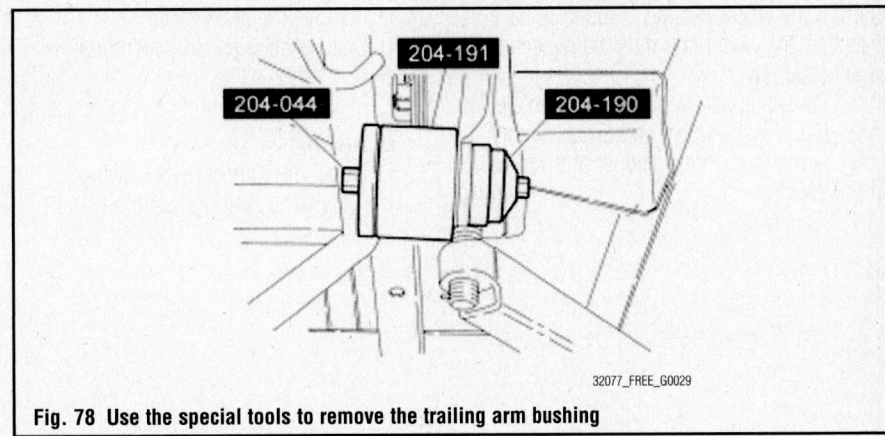

Fig. 78 Use the special tools to remove the trailing arm bushing

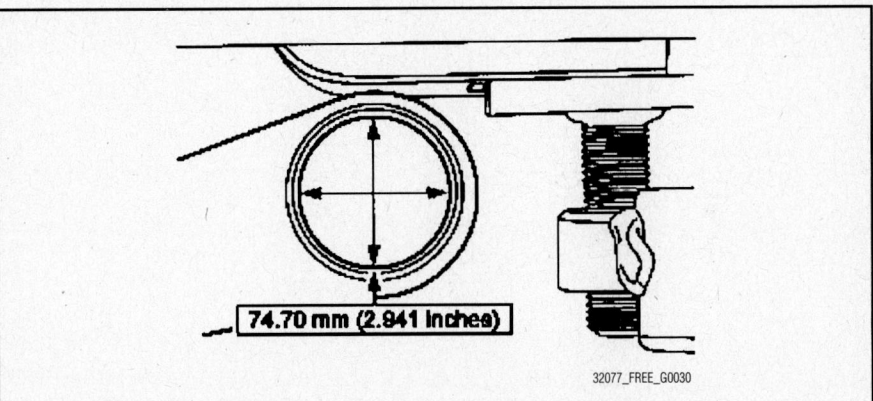

Fig. 79 Using a suitable calibrated telescoping micrometer, measure the trailing arm bushing bore. If the measurement exceeds the specification, install a new rear axle assembly

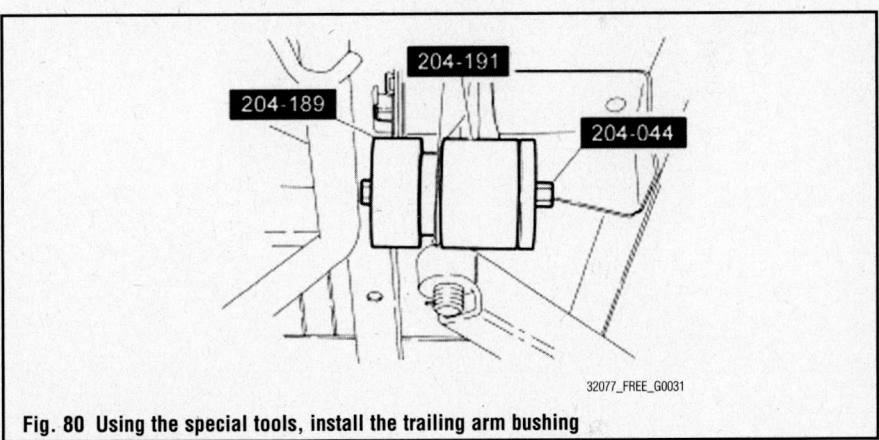

Fig. 80 Using the special tools, install the trailing arm bushing

7. Using the special tools, remove the trailing arm bushing.

8. Using a suitable calibrated telescoping micrometer, measure the trailing arm bushing bore. If the measurement exceeds the specification, install a new rear axle assembly.

To install:

9. Using the special tools, install the trailing arm bushing.

➡Make sure the coil spring is correctly seated before raising the axle assembly.

10. Raise the rear axle assembly into position and install the trailing arm bolt and nut. Tighten to 98 ft. lbs. (133 Nm).

11. Install the shock absorber lower bolt. Tighten to 59 ft. lbs. (80 Nm).

12. Install the rear brake disc (rotor)

13. Carefully lower the vehicle.

WHEEL HUB AND BEARING

REMOVAL & INSTALLATION

The wheel bearing is integral with the wheel hub and cannot be replaced separately. If the wheel bearing is found to be defective, the wheel hub must be replaced as an assembly.

1. Raise and safely support the vehicle.
2. Remove the wheel and tire assembly.
3. Remove the brake caliper and wire it out of the way.

4. Remove the brake rotor.
5. Disconnect the ABS sensor connector.
6. Remove the hub and bearing assembly.

To install:
7. Install or connect the following:
   • Hub and bearing assembly and

tighten the bolts to 85 ft. lbs. (115 Nm).
- ABS sensor connector
- Brake rotor
- Brake caliper
- Wheel and tire. Tighten the lug nuts to 100 ft. lbs. (135 Nm).

FORD

Freestyle

12

SPECIFICATIONS AND MAINTENANCE CHARTS

VEHICLE AND ENGINE IDENTIFICATION CHART

		Engine							Model Year	
Code	Liters	Cu. In.	Cyl.	Fuel Sys.	Engine Type	Eng. Mfg.		Code		Year
1	3.0	183	6	SEFI	DOHC	Ford		5		2005
								6		2006
								7		2007

SEFI: Sequential Multi-port Fuel Injection

DOHC: Dual overhead cam

22086_FRST_C0001

GENERAL ENGINE SPECIFICATIONS

Year	Engine Displacement Liters	Engine VIN	Net Horsepower @ rpm	Net Torque @ rpm (ft. lbs.)	Bore x Stroke (in.)	Compression Ratio	Oil Pressure @ rpm
2005	3.0	1	203@5750	207@4500	3.50x3.13	10.0:1	11@1500
2006	3.0	1	203@5750	207@4500	3.50x3.13	10.0:1	11@1500
2007	3.0	1	203@5750	207@4500	3.50x3.13	10.0:1	11@1500

22086_FRST_C0002

GASOLINE ENGINE TUNE-UP SPECIFICATIONS

Year	Engine Displacement Liters	Engine VIN	Spark Plugs Gap (in.)	Ignition Timing (deg.) MT	AT	Fuel Pump (psi)	Idle Speed (rpm) MT	AT	Valve Clearance In.	Ex.
2005	3.0	1	0.052-0.056	—	①	②	—	①	HYD	HYD
2006	3.0	1	0.052-0.056	—	①	②	—	①	HYD	HYD
2007	3.0	1	0.052-0.056	—	①	②	—	①	HYD	HYD

The label figures must be used if they differ from those in this chart.

B: Before top dead center

HYD: Hydraulic

① Controlled by the Powertrain Control Module (PCM) and cannot be manually adjusted.

② Engine running: 40 psi

Key On, Engine Off (KOEO): 40 psi

22086_FRST_C0004

CAPACITIES

Year	Model	Engine Displacement Liters	Engine ID/VIN	Engine Oil with Filter (qts.)	Transmission (pts.)			Drive Axle		Fuel Tank (gal.)	Cooling System (qts.)
					4-Spd	5-Spd	Auto.	Front (pts.)	Rear (pts.)		
2005	Freesyle	3.0	1	6.0	—	—	①	1.5	1.5	19	③
2006	Freesyle	3.0	1	6.0	—	—	①	1.5	1.5	19	③
2007	Freesyle	3.0	1	6.0	—	—	①	1.5	1.5	19	③

NOTE: All capacities are approximate. Add fluid gradually and check to be sure a proper fluid level is obtained.

① CVT transmission: 20   ② w/auxiliary heater: 12.7
   6-spd. Transmission: 15.8   wo/auxiliary heater: 10.6

22086_FRST_C0003

FLUID SPECIFICATIONS

Year	Model	Engine Displacement Liters (VIN)	Engine Oil	Auto. Trans.	Drive Axle	Power Steering Fluid	Brake Master Cylinder
2005	Freestyle	3.0 (1)	①	②	80W-90	Mercon® ATF Fluid	DOT 3
2006	Freestyle	3.0 (1)	①	②	80W-90	Mercon® ATF Fluid	DOT 3
2007	Freestyle	3.0 (1)	①	②	80W-90	Mercon® ATF Fluid	DOT 3

DOT: Department Of Transpotation

① 5W-20 Premium Synthetic Blend Motor Oil (US) or 5W-20 Super Premium Motor Oil (Canada)

② Motorcraft Continuously Variable Chain Type Transmission Fluid XT-7-QCFT (US); CXT-7-LCF12 (Canada) on models with a CVT transmission

Motorcraft Premium Automatic Transmission Fluid XT-8-QAW (US); CXT-8-LAW12 (Canada) on 6 speed models

③ Motorcraft Continuously Variable Chain Type Transmission Fluid XT-7-QCFT (US); CXT-7-LCF12 (Canada) on models with a CVT transmission

22086_FRST_C0014

VALVE SPECIFICATIONS

Year	Engine VIN	Engine Displacement Liters	Seat Angle (deg.)	Face Angle (deg.)	Spring Test Pressure (lbs. @ in.)	Spring Installed Height (in.)	Stem-to-Guide Clearance (in.)		Stem Diameter (in.)	
							Intake	Exhaust	Intake	Exhaust
2005	1	3.0	44.50-45.0	45.25-45.75	156@ 1.18	1.562-1.577	0.0007-0.0027	0.0018-0.0037	0.2350-0.2358	0.2343-0.2350
2006	1	3.0	44.50-45.0	45.25-45.75	156@ 1.18	1.562-1.577	0.0007-0.0027	0.0018-0.0037	0.2350-0.2358	0.2343-0.2350
2007	1	3.0	44.50-45.0	45.25-45.75	156@ 1.18	1.562-1.577	0.0007-0.0027	0.0018-0.0037	0.2350-0.2358	0.2343-0.2350

22086_FRST_C0005

CRANKSHAFT AND CONNECTING ROD SPECIFICATIONS
All measurements are given in inches.

| Year | Engine Displ. Liters | Engine VIN | Crankshaft | | | | Connecting Rod | | |
			Main Brg. Journal Dia.	Main Brg. Oil Clearance	Shaft End-play	Thrust on No.	Journal Diameter	Oil Clearance	Side Clearance
2005	3.0	1	2.4790-2.4800	0.0010-0.0016	0.0050-0.0010	3	1.9670-2.9680	0.0010-0.0025	0.0039-0.0118
2006	3.0	1	2.4790-2.4800	0.0010-0.0016	0.0050-0.0010	3	1.9670-2.9680	0.0010-0.0025	0.0039-0.0118
2007	3.0	1	2.4790-2.4800	0.0010-0.0016	0.0050-0.0010	3	1.9670-2.9680	0.0010-0.0025	0.0039-0.0118

22086_FRST_C0006

PISTON AND RING SPECIFICATIONS
All measurements are given in inches.

| Year | Engine Displ. Liters | Engine VIN | Piston Clearance | Ring Gap | | | Ring Side Clearance | | |
				Top Comp.	Bottom Comp.	Oil Control	Top Comp.	Bottom Comp.	Oil Control
2005	3.0	1	0.0007-0.0016	0.0039-0.0098	0.0106-0.0165	0.0059-0.0255	NA	NA	NA
2006	3.0	1	0.0007-0.0016	0.0039-0.0098	0.0106-0.0165	0.0059-0.0255	NA	NA	NA
2007	3.0	1	0.0007-0.0016	0.0039-0.0098	0.0106-0.0165	0.0059-0.0255	NA	NA	NA

NA: Not Available

22086_FRST_C0007

TORQUE SPECIFICATIONS
All readings in ft. lbs.

| Year | Engine VIN | Engine Displacement Liters | Cylinder Head Bolts | Main Bearing Bolts | Rod Bearing Bolts | Crankshaft Damper Bolts | Flywheel Bolts | Manifold | | Spark Plugs | Oil Pan Drain Drain |
								Intake	Exhaust		
2005	1	3.0	①	NA	NA	②	59	③	15	11	19
2006	1	3.0	①	NA	NA	②	59	③	15	11	19
2007	1	3.0	①	NA	NA	②	59	③	15	11	19

NA: Not Available

① Step 1: 30 ft. lbs.
   Step 2: plus 90 degrees
   Step 3: loosen all bolts 1 turn
   Step 4: 30 ft. lbs.
   Step 5: plus 90 degrees.
   Step 6: plus 90 degrees.

② Step 1: 86 ft. lbs.
   Step 2: loosen 1 turn
   Step 3: 37 ft. lbs.
   Step 4: plus 90 degrees

③ Upper and lower manifold: 89 INCH lbs.

22086_FRST_C0008

WHEEL ALIGNMENT

Year	Model			Caster Range (+/-Deg.)	Caster Preferred Setting (Deg.)	Camber Range (+/-Deg.)	Camber Preferred Setting (Deg.)	Toe-in (Deg.)
2005	Freestyle	Front	AWD	0.75	+3.0	0.75	-0.32	+0.20+/-0.20
			FWD	0.75	+3.1	0.75	-0.28	+0.20+/-0.20
		Rear	AWD	—	—	0.75	0.00	0.10+/-0.20
			FWD	—	—	0.75	-0.57	0.10+/-0.20
2006	Freestyle	Front	AWD	0.75	+3.0	0.75	-0.32	+0.20+/-0.20
			FWD	0.75	+3.1	0.75	-0.28	+0.20+/-0.20
		Rear	AWD	—	—	0.75	0.00	0.10+/-0.20
			FWD	—	—	0.75	-0.57	0.10+/-0.20
2007	Freestyle	Front	AWD	0.75	+3.0	0.75	-0.32	+0.20+/-0.20
			FWD	0.75	+3.1	0.75	-0.28	+0.20+/-0.20
		Rear	AWD	—	—	0.75	0.00	0.10+/-0.20
			FWD	—	—	0.75	-0.57	0.10+/-0.20

22086_FRST_C0009

TIRE AND WHEEL SPECIFICATIONS

Year	Model	OEM Tires Standard	OEM Tires Optional	Tire Pressures (psi) Front	Tire Pressures (psi) Rear	Wheel Size	Wheel Lug Nut Torque (ft. lbs.)
2005	Freestyle	P215/65R17	P225/60R18	35	35	①	95
2006	Freestyle	P215/65R17	P225/60R18	35	35	①	95
2007	Freestyle	P215/65R17	P225/60R18	35	35	①	95

OEM: Original Equipment Manufacturer

PSI: Pounds Per Square Inch

STD: Standard

OPT: Optional

① Not available

22086_FRST_C0013

BRAKE SPECIFICATIONS

All measurements in inches unless noted

Year	Model		Brake Disc Original Thickness	Brake Disc Minimum Thickness	Brake Disc Maximum Runout	Minimum Lining Thickness Front	Minimum Lining Thickness Rear	Brake Caliper Bracket Bolts (ft. lbs.)	Brake Caliper Mounting Bolts (ft. lbs.)
2005	Freestyle	F	①	1.040	0.002	0.118	—	74	44
		R	①	0.394	0.002	—	0.118	81	23
2006	Freestyle	F	①	1.040	0.002	0.118	—	74	44
		R	①	0.394	0.002	—	0.118	81	23
2007	Freestyle	F	①	1.040	0.002	0.118	—	74	44
		R	①	0.394	0.002	—	0.118	81	23

① Not available

22086_FRST_C0011

SCHEDULED MAINTENANCE INTERVALS
FORD FREESTYLE

TO BE SERVICED	TYPE OF SERVICE	VEHICLE MILEAGE INTERVAL (x1000)																	
		5	10	15	20	25	30	35	40	45	50	55	60	65	70	75	80	85	90
Engine oil & filter ①	R																		
Rotate tires	S/I	✓	✓	✓	✓	✓	✓	✓	✓	✓	✓	✓	✓	✓	✓	✓	✓	✓	✓
Engine coolant strength hoses & clamps	S/I			✓			✓			✓			✓				✓		✓
Air cleaner filter	R						✓						✓						✓
Automatic transmission fluid & filter	R						✓						✓						✓
Engine coolant ②	R																		
PCV valve	R												✓						✓
Spark plugs ③	R																		
Drive belts	S/I						✓						✓						✓
Exhaust system & heat shields	S/I						✓						✓						✓
Front & rear brakes	S/I	✓	✓	✓	✓	✓	✓	✓	✓	✓	✓	✓	✓	✓	✓	✓	✓	✓	✓
Fuel filter	R			✓			✓			✓			✓			✓			✓

R: Replace   S/I: Service or Inspect

① Engine oil and filter: replace every 3000 miles.

② Engine coolant: change initially at 100,000 miles or 5 years.

③ Spark plugs: replace every 100,000 miles.

Special Operating Condition Requirements

During extensive idling and/or low speed driving for long distances, as in heavy commercial use such as delivery, taxi, patrol car or livery:

Lube front lower control arm and steering linkage ball joints with

Zerk fittings (if equipped) every 4,800 km (3,000 miles) or 3 months.

Inspect brake system and check battery electrolyte level (Patrol cars) every 8,000 km (5,000 miles).

Install a new cabin air filter as required.

When operating in dusty conditions such as unpaved or dusty roads:

Install a new engine air filter as required.

Install a new cabin air filter as required.

When operating in off-road conditions:

Change automatic transmission fluid every 48,000 km (30,000 miles).

Install a new cabin air filter as required.

Inspect and lubricate U-joints.

Inspect and lubricate steering linkage ball joints with zerk fittings.

22086_FRST_C0010

PRECAUTIONS

Before servicing any vehicle, please be sure to read all of the following precautions, which deal with personal safety, prevention of component damage, and important points to take into consideration when servicing a motor vehicle:

• Never open, service or drain the radiator or cooling system when the engine is hot; serious burns can occur from the steam and hot coolant.

• Observe all applicable safety precautions when working around fuel. Whenever servicing the fuel system, always work in a well-ventilated area. Do not allow fuel spray or vapors to come in contact with a spark, open flame, or excessive heat (a hot drop light, for example). Keep a dry chemical fire extinguisher near the work area. Always keep fuel in a container specifically designed for fuel storage; also, always properly seal fuel containers to avoid the possibility of fire or explosion. Refer to the additional fuel system precautions later in this section.

• Fuel injection systems often remain pressurized, even after the engine has been turned **OFF**. The fuel system pressure must be relieved before disconnecting any fuel lines. Failure to do so may result in fire and/or personal injury.

• Brake fluid often contains polyglycol ethers and polyglycols. Avoid contact with the eyes and wash your hands thoroughly after handling brake fluid. If you do get brake fluid in your eyes, flush your eyes with clean, running water for 15 minutes. If eye irritation persists, or if you have taken brake fluid internally, IMMEDIATELY seek medical assistance.

• The EPA warns that prolonged contact with used engine oil may cause a number of skin disorders, including cancer. You should make every effort to minimize your exposure to used engine oil. Protective gloves should be worn when changing oil. Wash your hands and any other exposed skin areas as soon as possible after exposure to used engine oil. Soap and water, or waterless hand cleaner should be used.

• All new vehicles are now equipped with an air bag system, often referred to as a Supplemental Restraint System (SRS) or Supplemental Inflatable Restraint (SIR) system. The system must be disabled before performing service on or around system components, steering column, instrument panel components, wiring and sensors. Failure to follow safety and disabling procedures could result in accidental air bag deployment, possible personal injury and unnecessary system repairs.

• Always wear safety goggles when working with, or around, the air bag system. When carrying a non-deployed air bag, be sure the bag and trim cover are pointed away from your body. When placing a non-deployed air bag on a work surface, always face the bag and trim cover upward, away from the surface. This will reduce the motion of the module if it is accidentally deployed. Refer to the additional air bag system precautions later in this section.

• Clean, high quality brake fluid from a sealed container is essential to the safe and proper operation of the brake system. You should always buy the correct type of brake fluid for your vehicle. If the brake fluid becomes contaminated, completely flush the system with new fluid. Never reuse any brake fluid. Any brake fluid that is removed from the system should be discarded. Also, do not allow any brake fluid to come in contact with a painted surface; it will damage the paint.

• Never operate the engine without the proper amount and type of engine oil; doing so WILL result in severe engine damage.

• Timing belt maintenance is extremely important. Many models utilize an interference-type, non-freewheeling engine. If the timing belt breaks, the valves in the cylinder head may strike the pistons, causing potentially serious (also time-consuming and expensive) engine damage. Refer to the maintenance interval charts for the recommended replacement interval for the timing belt, and to the timing belt section for belt replacement and inspection.

• Disconnecting the negative battery cable on some vehicles may interfere with the functions of the on-board computer system(s) and may require the computer to undergo a relearning process once the negative battery cable is reconnected.

• When servicing drum brakes, only disassemble and assemble one side at a time, leaving the remaining side intact for reference.

• Only an MVAC-trained, EPA-certified automotive technician should service the air conditioning system or its components.

BRAKES

GENERAL INFORMATION

PRECAUTIONS

• Certain components within the ABS system are not intended to be serviced or repaired individually.

• Do not use rubber hoses or other parts not specifically specified for and ABS system. When using repair kits, replace all parts included in the kit. Partial or incorrect repair may lead to functional problems and require the replacement of components.

• Lubricate rubber parts with clean, fresh brake fluid to ease assembly. Do not use shop air to clean parts; damage to rubber components may result.

• Use only DOT 3 brake fluid from an unopened container.

• If any hydraulic component or line is removed or replaced, it may be necessary to bleed the entire system.

• A clean repair area is essential. Always clean the reservoir and cap thoroughly before removing the cap. The slightest amount of dirt in the fluid may plug an orifice and impair the system function. Perform repairs after components have been thoroughly cleaned; use only denatured alcohol to clean components. Do not allow ABS components to come into contact with any substance containing mineral oil; this includes used shop rags.

• The Anti-Lock control unit is a microprocessor similar to other computer units in the vehicle. Ensure that the ignition switch is **OFF** before removing or installing controller harnesses. Avoid static electricity discharge at or near the controller.

• If any arc welding is to be done on the vehicle, the control unit should be unplugged before welding operations begin.

ANTI-LOCK BRAKE SYSTEM (ABS)

SPEED SENSORS

REMOVAL & INSTALLATION

Front

1. With the vehicle in NEUTRAL, position it on a hoist.

2. Disconnect the wheel speed sensor electrical connector.

3. Remove the 2 rivets and position aside the fender splash shield.

4. Remove the wheel speed sensor harness pin-type retainer.

5. Remove the 2 wheel speed sensor harness retainers.

6. Remove the bolt and the wheel speed sensor.

7. To install, reverse the removal procedure and tighten the speed sensor bolt to 71 ft, lbs. (8 Nm).

Rear

Front Wheel Drive

1. With the vehicle in NEUTRAL, position it on a hoist.

2. Disconnect the wheel speed sensor electrical connector.

3. Remove the 2 rivets and position aside the fender splash shield.

4. Remove the wheel speed sensor harness pin-type retainer.

5. Remove the 2 wheel speed sensor harness retainers.

6. Remove the bolt and the wheel speed sensor.

7. To install, reverse the removal procedure and tighten the speed sensor bolt to 71 ft, lbs. (8 Nm).

All Wheel Drive

1. With the vehicle in NEUTRAL, position it on a hoist.

2. Disconnect the wheel speed sensor electrical connector.

3. Remove the wheel speed sensor bolt.

4. On the left side, release the wheel speed sensor harness spring clip and the 2 pin-type retainers from the rear control arm.

5. Release the wheel speed sensor harness spring clip and the 2 pin-type retainers from the rear control arm.

6. On the right side, release the 3 pin-type retainers and remove the wheel speed sensor.

7. To install, reverse the removal procedure and tighten the speed sensor bolt to 71 ft, lbs. (8 Nm).

BRAKES   BLEEDING THE BRAKE SYSTEM

BLEEDING PROCEDURE

BLEEDING PROCEDURE

1. Clean all the dirt from the area, remove the brake master cylinder reservoir cap and fill the brake master cylinder reservoir with the specified brake fluid.

2. Remove the rear bleeder cap and place a box end wrench on the RH rear bleeder screw. Attach a rubber drain tube to the RH rear bleeder screw and submerge the free end of the tube in a container partially filled with clean brake fluid.

3. Have an assistant hold firm pressure on the brake pedal.

4. Loosen the RH rear bleeder screw until a stream of brake fluid comes out. While the assistant maintains pressure on the brake pedal, tighten the RH rear bleeder screw.

5. Press and release the parking brake 5 times.

6. Repeat until clear, bubble-free fluid comes out.

7. Refill the brake master cylinder reservoir as necessary.

8. Tighten the RH rear bleeder screw and install the bleeder cap.

9. Repeat Steps 3, 4, 5 and 6 for the LH rear bleeder screw.

10. Remove the rear bleeder cap and place a box end wrench on the RH front brake caliper bleeder screw. Attach a rubber drain tube to the RH front brake caliper bleeder screw, and submerge the free end of the tube in a container partially filled with clean brake fluid.

11. Have an assistant hold firm pressure on the brake pedal.

12. Loosen the RH front brake caliper bleeder screw until a stream of brake fluid comes out. While the assistant maintains pressure on the brake pedal, tighten the RH front brake caliper bleeder screw.

13. Repeat until clear, bubble-free fluid comes out.

14. Refill the brake master cylinder reservoir as necessary.

15. Tighten the RH front brake caliper bleeder screw and install the bleeder cap.

16. Repeat Steps 8, 9, 10 and 11 for the LH front brake caliper bleeder screw.

BLEEDING THE ABS SYSTEM

1. Clean all the dirt from the area and remove the brake master cylinder filler cap. Fill the brake master cylinder reservoir with the specified brake fluid.

➡**Master cylinder pressure bleeder adapter tools are available from various manufacturers of pressure bleeding equipment. Follow the instructions of the manufacturer when installing the adapter.**

2. Install the bleeder adapter to the brake master cylinder reservoir, and attach the bleeder tank hose to the fitting on the adapter.

3. Bleed the longest line first. Make sure the bleeder tank contains enough specified brake fluid to complete the bleeding operation.

4. Place a box end wrench on the RH rear bleeder screw. Attach a rubber drain tube to the RH rear bleeder screw, and submerge the free end of the tube in a container partially filled with clean brake fluid.

5. Open the valve on the bleeder tank.

6. Loosen the RH rear bleeder screw. Leave open until clear, bubble-free brake fluid flows, then tighten the RH rear bleeder screw and remove the rubber hose.

7. Press and release the parking brake 5 times.

8. Repeat until clear, bubble-free fluid comes out.

9. Tighten the RH rear bleeder screw and install the bleeder cap.

10. Repeat Steps 5 and 6 for the LH rear bleeder screw.

11. Continue bleeding the front of the system, going in order from the RH front disc brake caliper bleeder screw, ending with the LH front brake caliper bleeder screw.

12. Close the bleeder tank valve. Remove the tank hose from the adapter, and remove the adapter.

※※ CAUTION

Dust and dirt accumulating on brake parts during normal use may contain asbestos fibers from production or aftermarket brake linings. Breathing excessive concentrations of asbestos fibers can cause serious bodily harm. Exercise care when servicing brake parts. Do not sand or grind brake lining unless equipment used is designed to contain the dust residue. Do not clean brake parts with compressed air or by dry brushing. Cleaning should be done by dampening the brake components with a fine mist of water, then wiping the brake components clean with a dampened cloth. Dispose of cloth and all residue containing asbestos fibers in an impermeable container with the appropriate label. Follow practices prescribed by the Occupational Safety and Health Administration (OSHA) and the Environmental Protection Agency (EPA) for the handling, processing, and disposing of dust or debris that may contain asbestos fibers.

BRAKE CALIPER

REMOVAL & INSTALLATION

See Figure 1.

➡The brake pads are a onetime use only type. If the pads are separated from the caliper the pads must be replaced.

1. Remove and discard ½ of the brake fluid from the brake master cylinder reservoir.
2. Raise and safely support the vehicle.
3. Remove the wheel and tire assembly.
4. Mark the disc brake caliper to avoid mixing the left-hand and right-hand components.
5. Loosen the brake caliper bolts.
6. Disconnect the brake hose from the brake line fitting.
7. Remove and discard the caliper anchor bolts and position the caliper, anchor plate and pads aside. Support the steering stop when the anchor plate bolts are removed.
8. Separate the brake pads from the caliper.
9. Remove the caliper bolts from the caliper and anchor plate.
10. Remove the brake pads and spring clips.

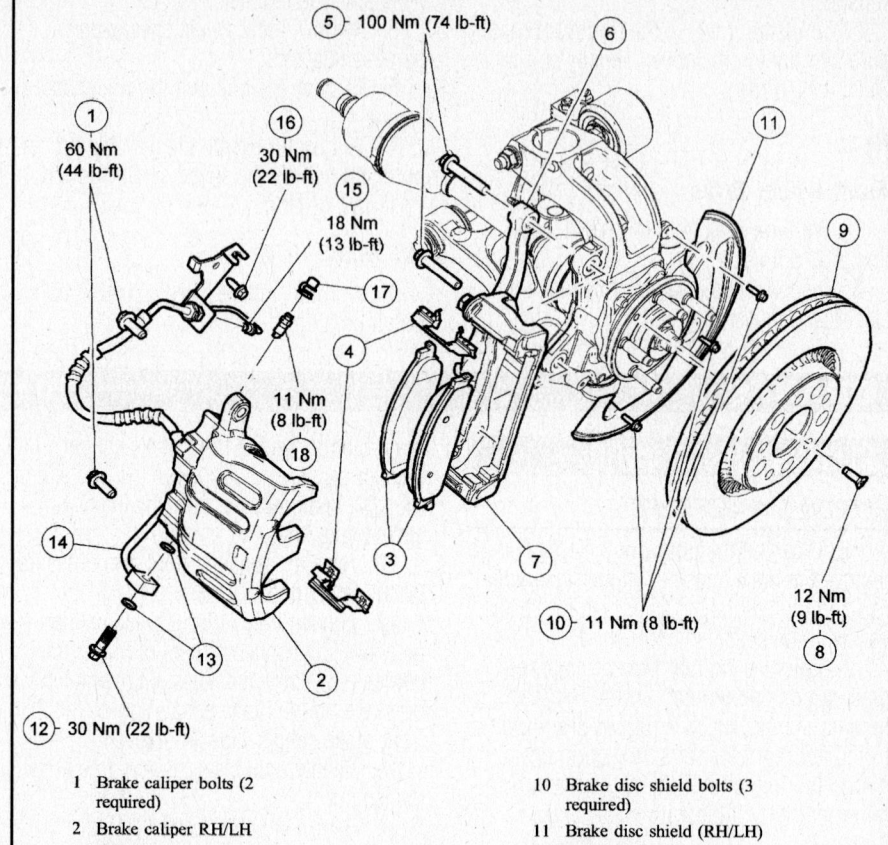

Fig. 1 Exploded view of front disc brake assembly

1	Brake caliper bolts (2 required)	10	Brake disc shield bolts (3 required)
2	Brake caliper RH/LH	11	Brake disc shield (RH/LH)
3	Brake pads	12	Brake caliper flow bolt
4	Spring clips (2 required)	13	Copper washers (2 required)
5	Brake caliper anchor plate bolts (2 required)	14	Brake flexible hose RH/LH
6	Steering stop	15	Brake line fitting
7	Brake caliper anchor plate	16	Brake flexible hose bracket bolt
8	Brake disc screw	17	Bleeder screw cap
9	Brake disc	18	Bleeder screw

06017-FREE-G51

To install:

11. Compress the caliper pistons into the caliper bore.
12. Install the spring clips and brake pads in the caliper and anchor plate assembly.
13. Install the brake caliper anchor. Tighten the anchor bolts to 74 ft. lbs. (100 Nm).
14. Install the caliper and new guide pins and tighten the bolts to 44 ft. lbs. (60 Nm).
15. Install new copper washers in the brake flexible hoses and connect the hoses and install the flow bolt to 22 ft. lbs. (30 Nm).
16. Bleed the brake system.
17. Lower the vehicle.
18. Pump the brake pedal several times to position the brake pads before attempting to move the vehicle.

19. Check and fill the brake master cylinder as required.
20. Road-test the vehicle and check for proper brake operation.

DISC BRAKE PADS

REMOVAL & INSTALLATION

See Figure 1.

1. Check the brake fluid level in the brake master cylinder reservoir.
2. If required, remove the fluid until the brake master cylinder reservoir is half full.
3. With the vehicle in NEUTRAL, position it on a hoist.
4. Using the large C-clamp, compress the pistons into the caliper housing.

5. Position one end of the C-clamp on the outer pad between the caliper fingers, the other end on the caliper housing. During this process, the outer brake pad will separate from the caliper housing.

6. Remove the 2 brake caliper guide pin bolts.

➡**When the brake pads are separated from the brake caliper, new brake pads must be installed. The brake pads are a one-time use only.**

➡**The brake pads must be separated from the brake caliper before the brake caliper can be removed from the brake caliper anchor plate.**

7. Separate the inner brake pad from the caliper.

8. Position the caliper aside and support the caliper using mechanic's wire.

9. Remove the 2 brake pads and spring clips from the brake caliper anchor plate.

10. Discard the retraction clips.

11. Inspect the brake caliper for leaks or damage. Install a new brake caliper if required.

12. Inspect the brake caliper anchor plate. Install a new brake caliper anchor plate if required.

13. Inspect the guide pins and boots for binding or damage, replace as necessary.

To install:

14. Clean the residual adhesive from the brake caliper-to-brake pad mating surfaces (brake caliper piston and the opposing caliper housing fingers) using brake parts cleaner.

15. If installing new brake pads, install all new hardware as supplied with the brake pad kit.

16. Install the new spring clips and brake pads to the brake caliper anchor plate.

17. Position the brake caliper onto the brake caliper anchor plate and install the 2 caliper guide pin bolts and tighten to 44 ft. lbs. (60 Nm).

18. If necessary, fill the brake master cylinder reservoir with clean brake fluid.

19. With the vehicles engine running, apply 89-133 N (20-30 lb) of pressure on the brake pedal for one minute to make sure the brake pads adhere to the brake caliper before any contamination can be introduced.

20. Test the brakes for normal operation.

BRAKES

❄❄ CAUTION

Dust and dirt accumulating on brake parts during normal use may contain asbestos fibers from production or aftermarket brake linings. Breathing excessive concentrations of asbestos fibers can cause serious bodily harm. Exercise care when servicing brake parts. Do not sand or grind brake lining unless equipment used is designed to contain the dust residue. Do not clean brake parts with compressed air or by dry brushing. Cleaning should be done by dampening the brake components with a fine mist of water, then wiping the brake components clean with a dampened cloth. Dispose of cloth and all residue containing asbestos fibers in an impermeable container with the appropriate label. Follow practices prescribed by the Occupational Safety and Health Administration (OSHA) and the Environmental Protection Agency (EPA) for the handling, processing, and disposing of dust or debris that may contain asbestos fibers.

BRAKE CALIPER

REMOVAL & INSTALLATION

See Figure 2.

1. Remove and discard ½ of the brake fluid from the brake master cylinder reservoir.

2. Raise and safely support the vehicle.

3. Remove the wheel and tire assembly.

4. Release the tension on the parking brake cable.

5. Disconnect the parking brake cable end from the caliper lever and release the cable retainer from the caliper bracket.

6. Loosen the brake caliper bolts.

REAR DISC BRAKES

7. Remove and discard the caliper anchor bolts.

8. Remove the brake pads from the caliper.

9. Remove the caliper bolts and separate the caliper from the anchor plate.

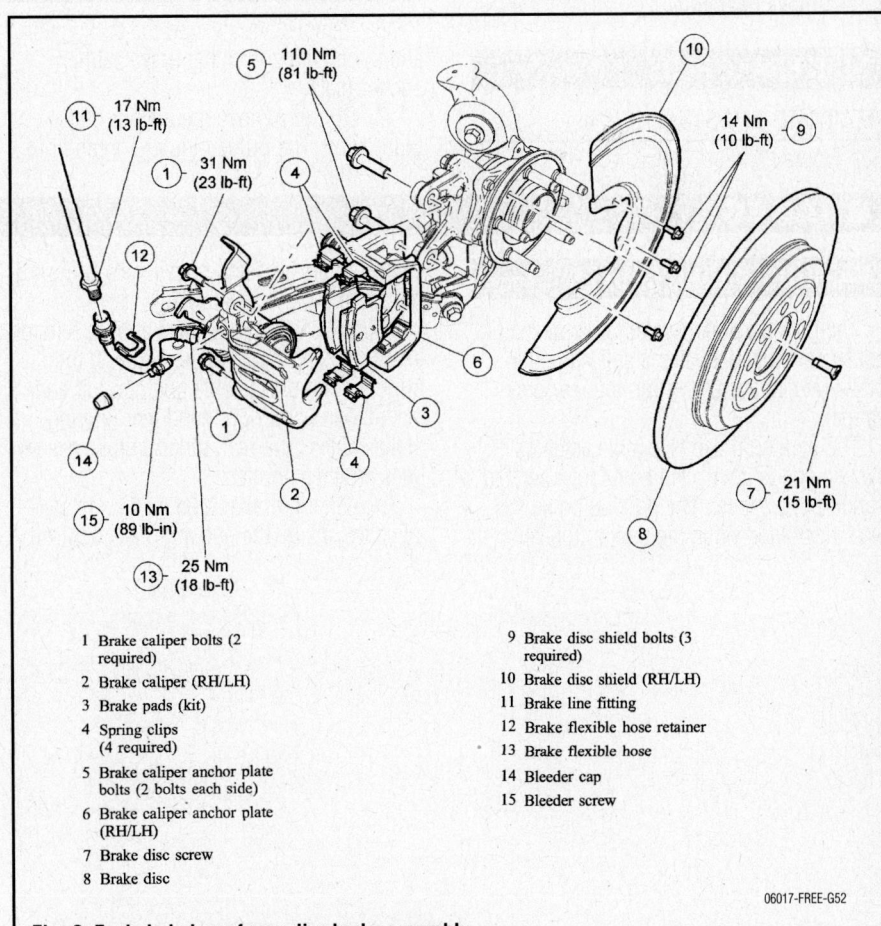

1 Brake caliper bolts (2 required)
2 Brake caliper (RH/LH)
3 Brake pads (kit)
4 Spring clips (4 required)
5 Brake caliper anchor plate bolts (2 bolts each side)
6 Brake caliper anchor plate (RH/LH)
7 Brake disc screw
8 Brake disc
9 Brake disc shield bolts (3 required)
10 Brake disc shield (RH/LH)
11 Brake line fitting
12 Brake flexible hose retainer
13 Brake flexible hose
14 Bleeder cap
15 Bleeder screw

06017-FREE-G52

Fig. 2 Exploded view of rear disc brake assembly

To install:

10. Compress the caliper pistons into the caliper bore.

11. Install the anchor plate and tighten the bolts to 81 ft. lbs. (110 Nm).

12. Retract the disc brake caliper piston fully into the caliper bore using tool no. 206-026.

13. Install the spring clips and brake pads in the caliper.

14. Install the caliper and tighten the guide pins to 23 ft. lbs. (31 Nm).

15. Install the parking brake cable to the caliper.

16. Reload the tension on the parking brake cable.

17. Bleed the brake system and install the rubber bleeder screw caps when complete.

18. Install the wheel and tire assembly.

19. Lower the vehicle.

20. Pump the brake pedal several times to position the brake pads before attempting to move the vehicle.

21. Check and fill the brake master cylinder as required.

22. Road-test the vehicle and check for proper brake operation.

DISC BRAKE PADS

REMOVAL & INSTALLATION
See Figure 2.

1. Check the brake fluid level in the brake fluid reservoir.

2. If required, remove fluid until the brake master cylinder reservoir is half full.

3. Remove the brake caliper bolts.

✳✳ CAUTION
Care must be taken when servicing rear brake components without disconnecting the parking brake cable from the brake caliper lever. Carefully position the caliper aside using a suitable support or damage to the parking brake cable end fittings can occur.

4. Using hand force and a rocking motion, separate the brake caliper from the anchor plate. Position the brake caliper aside.

5. Support the caliper with mechanic's wire.

✳✳ CAUTION
When the brake pads are separated from the brake caliper, new brake pads must be installed. The brake pads are one-time use only.

6. Remove and discard the brake pads and spring clips from the brake caliper anchor plate.

7. Do not remove the anchor plate guide pins. The guide pins are press fit to the brake caliper anchor plate. If the guide pins are damaged a new anchor plate must be installed.

8. Inspect the brake caliper anchor plate assembly.

9. Check the guide pins and boots for binding or damage.

10. Install a new brake caliper anchor plate if it is worn or damaged.

To install:

➡ The LH caliper piston turns clockwise and the RH caliper piston turns counterclockwise.

11. Compress the brake caliper piston into its cylinder.

12. Clean the residual adhesive from the brake caliper fingers and pistons using the specified brake parts cleaner.

13. Install the new spring clips and brake pads.

14. Position the brake caliper and install the 2 bolts and tighten to 23 ft. lbs. (31 Nm).

15. If necessary, fill the brake fluid reservoir with clean specified brake fluid.

16. With the vehicle engine running, apply 89-133 N (20-30 lb) of pressure on the brakes for approximately 1 minute, to make sure the brake pads adhere to the caliper before any contamination can be introduced.

17. Test the brakes for normal operation.

BRAKES

PARKING BRAKE CABLES

The parking brake system is a mechanical system that activates a self-adjusting brake ratchet system within the rear brake caliper.

The parking brake is a cable actuated system and is controlled by a foot-operated parking brake lever. The parking brake system is actuated when the parking brake control is pressed and released by pressing the parking brake lever again.

The parking brake control applies tension to rear parking brake shoes through the front parking brake cable and conduit and the left hand and right hand rear parking brake cables. The rear parking brake assemblies are then applied.

The parking brake cable tension is self-adjusting inside the parking brake control.

PARKING BRAKE

PARKING BRAKE SHOES

The parking brake control applies tension to rear parking brake shoes through the front parking brake cable and conduit and the left hand and right hand rear parking brake cables. The rear parking brake assemblies are then applied.

CHASSIS ELECTRICAL   AIR BAG (SUPPLEMENTAL RESTRAINT SYSTEM)

GENERAL INFORMATION

✷✷ CAUTION

These vehicles are equipped with an air bag system. The system must be disarmed before performing service on, or around, system components, the steering column, instrument panel components, wiring and sensors. Failure to follow the safety precautions and the disarming procedure could result in accidental air bag deployment, possible injury and unnecessary system repairs.

SERVICE PRECAUTIONS

Disconnect and isolate the battery negative cable before beginning any airbag system component diagnosis, testing, removal, or installation procedures. Allow system capacitor to discharge for two minutes before beginning any component service. This will disable the airbag system. Failure to disable the airbag system may result in accidental airbag deployment, personal injury, or death.

Do not place an intact undeployed airbag face down on a solid surface. The airbag will propel into the air if accidentally deployed and may result in personal injury or death.

When carrying or handling an undeployed airbag, the trim side (face) of the airbag should be pointing towards the body to minimize possibility of injury if accidental deployment occurs. Failure to do this may result in personal injury or death.

Replace airbag system components with OEM replacement parts. Substitute parts may appear interchangeable, but internal differences may result in inferior occupant protection. Failure to do so may result in occupant personal injury or death.

Wear safety glasses, rubber gloves, and long sleeved clothing when cleaning powder residue from vehicle after an airbag deployment. Powder residue emitted from a deployed airbag can cause skin irritation. Flush affected area with cool water if irritation is experienced. If nasal or throat irritation is experienced, exit the vehicle for fresh air until the irritation ceases. If irritation continues, see a physician.

Do not use a replacement airbag that is not in the original packaging. This may result in improper deployment, personal injury, or death.

The factory installed fasteners, screws and bolts used to fasten airbag components have a special coating and are specifically designed for the airbag system. Do not use substitute fasteners. Use only original equipment fasteners listed in the parts catalog when fastener replacement is required.

During, and following, any child restraint anchor service, due to impact event or vehicle repair, carefully inspect all mounting hardware, tether straps, and anchors for proper installation, operation, or damage. If a child restraint anchor is found damaged in any way, the anchor must be replaced. Failure to do this may result in personal injury or death.

Deployed and non-deployed airbags may or may not have live pyrotechnic material within the airbag inflator.

Do not dispose of driver/passenger/curtain airbags or seat belt tensioners unless you are sure of complete deployment. Refer to the Hazardous Substance Control System for proper disposal.

Dispose of deployed airbags and tensioners consistent with state, provincial, local, and federal regulations.

After any airbag component testing or service, do not connect the battery negative cable. Personal injury or death may result if the system test is not performed first.

If the vehicle is equipped with the Occupant Classification System (OCS), do not connect the battery negative cable before performing the OCS Verification Test using the scan tool and the appropriate diagnostic information. Personal injury or death may result if the system test is not performed properly.

Never replace both the Occupant Restraint Controller (ORC) and the Occupant Classification Module (OCM) at the same time. If both require replacement, replace one, then perform the Airbag System test before replacing the other.

Both the ORC and the OCM store Occupant Classification System (OCS) calibration data, which they transfer to one another when one of them is replaced. If both are replaced at the same time, an irreversible fault will be set in both modules and the OCS may malfunction and cause personal injury or death.

If equipped with OCS, the Seat Weight Sensor is a sensitive, calibrated unit and must be handled carefully. Do not drop or handle roughly. If dropped or damaged, replace with another sensor. Failure to do so may result in occupant injury or death.

If equipped with OCS, the front passenger seat must be handled carefully as well.

When removing the seat, be careful when setting on floor not to drop. If dropped, the sensor may be inoperative, could result in occupant injury, or possibly death.

If equipped with OCS, when the passenger front seat is on the floor, no one should sit in the front passenger seat. This uneven force may damage the sensing ability of the seat weight sensors. If sat on and damaged, the sensor may be inoperative, could result in occupant injury, or possibly death.

DISARMING THE SYSTEM

1. Ensure the ignition is off.
2. Remove the Smart Junction Box (SJB) cover located below the left side of the instrument panel. Remove the Restraints Control Module (RCM) fuse no. F2.21.
3. Turn the ignition on and watch the air bag indicator for 30 seconds. The indicator light will remain lit constantly if the correct fuse has been removed. If the light is not on steadily, remove the correct fuse and check the light again.
4. Turn the ignition switch off.
5. Disconnect the negative battery cable.

ARMING THE SYSTEM

1. Turn the ignition switch on.
2. Install Restraints Control Module (RCM) fuse no. F2.21 and the fuse cover.
3. Turn the ignition off.
4. Connect the negative battery cable.
5. Turn the ignition on and then off. Wait 10 seconds and turn the key back on. Watch the air bag indicator. The indicator light will remain lit constantly for 6 seconds and then go off. If the indicator does not turn on and then off, diagnose the air bag system
6. Clear all Diagnostic Trouble Codes (DTC) using a diagnostic tool.

CLOCKSPRING CENTERING

See Figures 3 through 7.

1. Place the steering wheel in the straight-ahead position and remove the ignition key.
2. Disarm the air bag system.
3. Remove the steering wheel access cover.
4. Release one side of the driver air bag module wire clip. While actuating the horn at the lower part of the air bag cover, use a suitable tool (needle nose pliers, etc.) to release the wire clip until it touches the center post.

5. Release the horn and using a suitable tool, lift the end of the wire clip over the post.

6. Release the other side of the driver air bag module wire clip. While actuating the horn at the lower part of the air bag cover, use a suitable tool to release the other side of the wire clip until it touches the center post.

7. Release the horn and with a suitable tool, lift the end of the wire clip over the post causing both ends of the wire clip to overlap.

8. When the driver air bag module wire clip is released correctly, the wire clip will easily slide into place and the 2 wire clip hook ends will come to rest between the 2 inner posts.

9. With the wire clip ends in the overlapped position, actuate the horn at the upper part of the air bag cover, then push on both ends of the wire clip inward (toward the center of the steering wheel) to release the driver air bag module from the steering wheel.

10. Label the driver air bag module squib number on the driver air bag module electrical connectors before disconnecting.

11. Release the two retaining tabs on each driver air bag module electrical connector and disconnect both connectors

12. Disconnect the horn and accessories electrical connectors and remove the driver air bag module.

13. Remove and discard the steering wheel bolt.

14. Remove the steering wheel. Route the 2 driver air bag module electrical connectors through the steering wheel.

15. Remove the cluster finish panel.

16. Remove the 3 screws and the lower steering column shroud.

17. If the clockspring is to be reinstalled, do not allow the clockspring to turn from its removal position.

18. If reusing the clockspring, tape the clockspring center rotor to the outer housing to keep it from rotating.

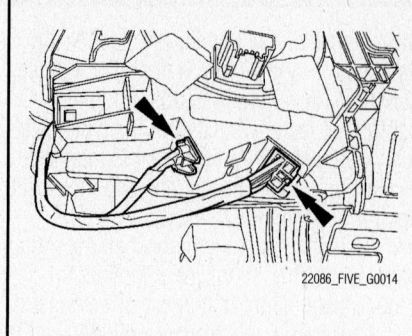

Fig. 4 Unplug the clockspring connectors

19. Disconnect the 2 clockspring electrical connectors.

20. Remove the 4 clockspring screws and remove the clockspring.

To install:

⁎⁎ **WARNING**

Incorrect centralization may result in premature component failure. If in doubt when centralizing the clockspring, repeat the centralizing procedure. Failure to follow this instruction may result in personal injury.

⁎⁎ **CAUTION**

Make sure the road wheels are in the straight-ahead position.

21. If the vehicle's clockspring has rotated out of center, perform the following to center the clockspring:

    a. Hold the clockspring outer housing stationary. Step 1 in the illustration.

⁎⁎ **CAUTION**

Overturning will destroy the clockspring. The internal ribbon wire acts

as the stop and can be broken from its internal connection.

    b. While turning the rotor counter clockwise, carefully feel for the ribbon wire to run out of length and for a slight resistance. Stop turning at this point. Step 2 in the illustration.

    c. Turn the clockspring approximately 3 turns clockwise until the ribbon wire shows anywhere across the window (the window will be near the 2 o'clock position) and the arrow on the rotor lines up with the arrow on the bottom left of the housing. The clockspring is now centered. Step 3 in the illustration.

    d. Do not allow the rotor to turn from this position.

22. Install the clockspring and the 4 screws.

23. Connect the 2 clockspring electrical connectors.

24. On a repair reusing the same clockspring, remove the tape applied during clockspring removal.

➡ **When the tape is removed, do not allow the clockspring to turn.**

25. On a repair installing a new clockspring:

⁎⁎ **CAUTION**

Do not rotate the new clockspring between removing the sealing key and installing the steering wheel. If the vehicle is left unattended by the technician between removing the sealing key and installing the steering wheel, carry out the centralizing procedure.

    e. Remove the sealing key.

26. Install the lower steering column shroud and the 3 screws.

27. Install the cluster finish panel.

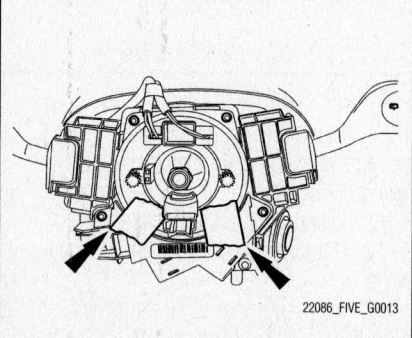

Fig. 3 If reusing the clockspring, tape the clockspring center rotor to the outer housing to keep it from rotating

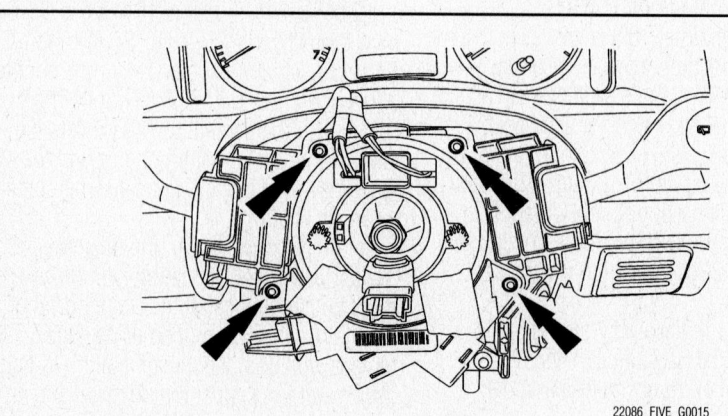

Fig. 5 Location of the clockspring screws

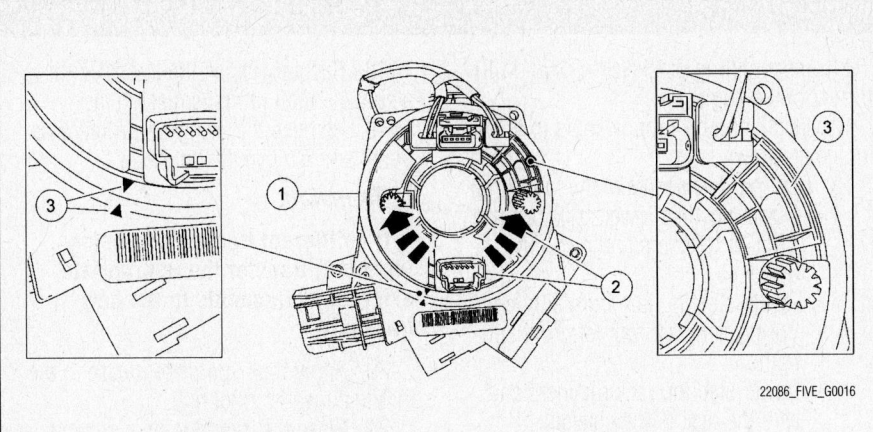

Fig. 6 The 3 steps of clockspring centering. Refer to the text for step by step instructions.

※ **CAUTION**

If the vehicle is left unattended by the technician between centralizing the clockspring and installing the steering wheel, the centralizing procedure must be repeated.

28. Route the 2 driver air bag module electrical connectors through the steering wheel and install the steering wheel.
29. Tighten the steering wheel bolt to 30 ft. lbs. (40 Nm).

※ **CAUTION**

Prior to reinstalling a previously removed driver air bag module, make sure to correctly position the wire clip that retains the driver air bag module to the steering wheel. Failure to follow this instruction will result in incorrect installation of the driver air bag module and may result in personal injury in the event of a driver air bag module deployment.

➡**Follow each step of the wire clip resetting procedure precisely to make sure of correct driver air bag module installation.**

30. Push the driver air bag module wire clip fully back on the 6 tabs on the top of the module.
31. While making sure the wire clip stays fully seated on the 6 tabs on the top of the module, use a suitable tool to reset the end of the wire clip that is on the top.
32. Carefully lift the 1 end of the wire clip over the post. Pull the wire clip outward to reset.
33. While still making sure the wire clip stays fully seated on the 6 tabs on the top of

the module, use a suitable tool to reset the other end of the wire clip.
34. Carefully lift the other end of the wire clip over the post.
35. Pull the wire clip outward to reset.
36. Make sure the wire clip hook ends are evenly spaced from the center post.
37. Make sure the driver air bag module wire clip is fully seated on all of the tabs and guides.
38. Connect the horn and accessories electrical connectors.

※ **CAUTION**

The clockspring electrical connectors are unique and cannot be reversed when connected to the driver air bag

module. Match the electrical connector key to the keyway in the driver air bag module. Do not force the electrical connectors into the driver air bag module.

※ **CAUTION**

Make sure the driver air bag module wiring is routed clear of the driver air bag mounting hooks on the steering wheel so that the wiring is not pinched during driver air bag module installation.

39. Connect the driver air bag module electrical connectors as noted in removal.
40. Make sure that all 4 retaining points of the driver air bag module wire clip are fully engaged and seated correctly to the steering wheel.

➡**Audible clicks will be heard when the locking tabs are fully engaged.**

41. Attach the driver air bag module to the steering wheel.
42. Align the driver air bag module to the 4 hooks on the steering wheel and press in until the driver air bag module wire clip is fully engaged to the steering wheel.
43. Check the driver air bag module and horn switch cover for clearance and correct movement.
44. Install the steering wheel access cover.
45. Rearm the air bag system.

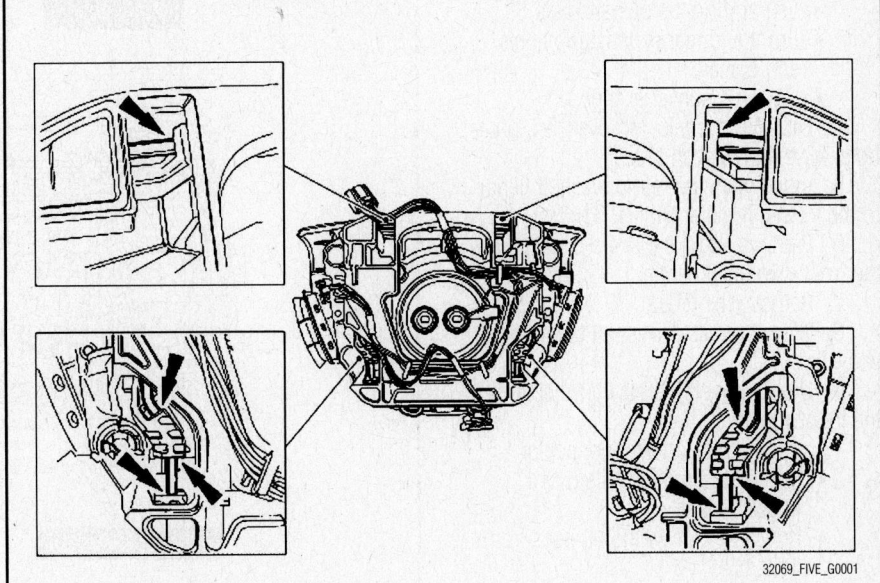

Fig. 7 Ensuring the driver air bag module wire clip is fully seated on all of the tabs and guides

DRIVETRAIN

AUTOMATIC TRANSAXLE ASSEMBLY

REMOVAL & INSTALLATION

CVT Transaxle

See Figure 8.

1. Place the vehicle on a hoist.
2. Drain the transaxle fluid.
3. Remove or disconnect the following:
   - Battery and battery tray
   - Air cleaner assembly and outlet pipe
   - Cowl grille panel
   - Upper roll restrictor bolt
   - Roll restrictor brace bolts and brace
   - Shift cable end
   - Electrical connector from shift cable bracket
   - Shift able bracket and position the cable and bracket aside
   - Transaxle wiring harnesses
   - Auxiliary coolant flow pump assembly, if equipped
   - Roll restrictor bracket and roll restrictor
   - PCV hose
   - Throttle body vacuum hoses
   - Power steering line bracket
   - Starter wiring and starter
   - Transaxle fluid cooler tube bracket
   - Ground cable
   - Transaxle bulkhead electrical connector
   - 4 upper transaxle mounting bolts
   - Left and right side halfshafts
   - Front and rear exhaust pipe nuts and discard
   - Catalytic converter pipe
4. On AWD models, remove the 2 outer bolts for the driveshaft brace.
5. Index mark the rear driveshaft flange to the Power Transfer Unit (PTU).
6. Remove and the discard 6 bolts from the front driveshaft flange.
7. Remove the PTU.
8. Wire the rear driveshaft to the chassis.
9. On all models, remove or disconnect the following:
   - Engine block heater connector
   - Knock sensor heat shield and knock sensor
   - Knock sensor wiring harness from transaxle
   - Transaxle-to-engine bolt
   - Power steering hose bolt
10. Install engine lifting eyes no. 134-00243 to the left and right cylinder heads.

11. Install lifting brackets no. 303-1140 to front of the engine.
12. Install engine support tools to the engine as shown.
13. Remove or disconnect the following:
    - Disconnect the lower radiator hose from its retainers and position aside
    - Power steering line from subframe
    - Wiring harness from left front subframe
    - Power steering rack retainers and wire the rack to the chassis
    - Oxygen sensor connector
    - Splash shield
    - Front motor mount nut
    - Lower stabilizer mount bolts
    - Rear motor mount nut
    - Rear transaxle mount bolts
    - Rear subframe mounting bolts on both sides
    - Stabilizer bar links nuts from both sides and discard the nuts.
    - Stabilizer bar from struts
14. Using a suitable powertrain lift, remove 4 subframe mounting bolts and remove the subframe.
15. Remove the catalytic converter.
16. Remove the torque converter access plug and remove and discard the 4 torque converter nuts.
17. Disconnect the transaxle fluid cooler tubes from the transaxle.

18. Securely fasten the transaxle to a suitable high lift transmission jack.
19. Remove the 3 engine-to-transaxle bolts, and remove the transaxle.

To install:

➡ **If a different transaxle is being installed, transfer the appropriate external components to the new transaxle.**

20. Apply multi-purpose grease to the torque converter pilot hub.
21. Place the transaxle on a suitable jack and carefully raise it into position.
22. Install 3 engine-to-transaxle mounting bolts and tighten to 30 ft. lbs. (40 Nm).
23. Install new transaxle fluid cooler tube seals and connect the tubes.
24. Install new torque converter nuts and tighten to 27 ft. lbs. (36 Nm). Install the torque converter access plug.
25. Install the catalytic converter and tighten the bolts to 30 ft. lbs. (40 Nm).
26. Using a suitable powertrain lift, install the subframe and tighten the 4 subframe mounting bolts to 66 ft. lbs. (90 Nm).
    - Install the subframe mounting bolts on both sides and tighten to 35 ft. lbs. (48 Nm).
    - Rear transaxle mount bolts and tighten to 66 ft. lbs. (90 Nm).

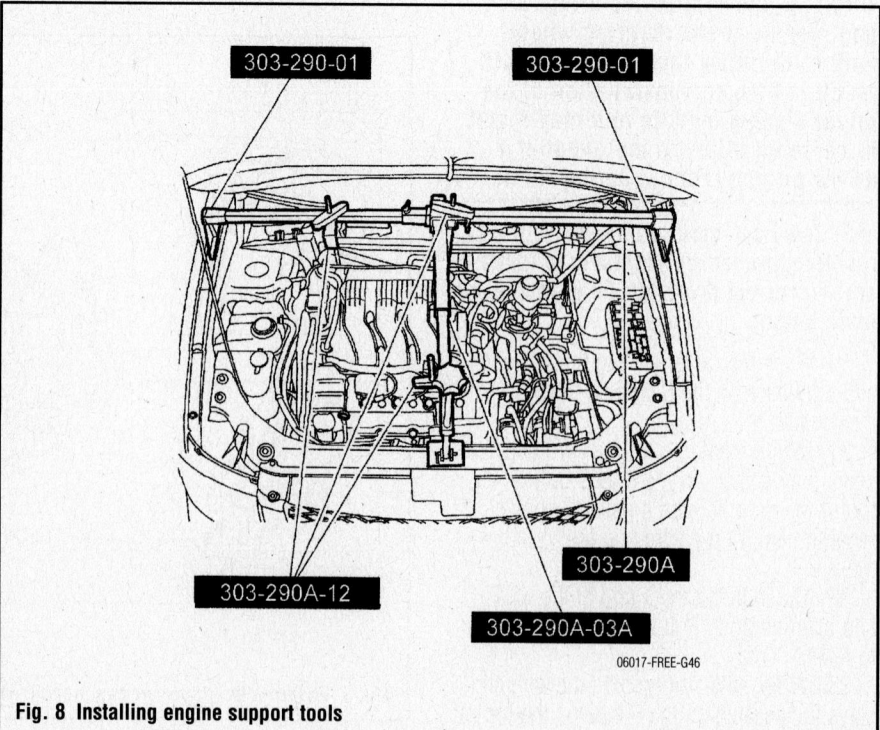

303-290-01 303-290-01 303-290A 303-290A-12 303-290A-03A

06017-FREE-G46

Fig. 8 Installing engine support tools

- Rear motor mount nut and tighten to 52 ft. lbs. (70 Nm).
- Lower stabilizer mount bolts and tighten to 52 ft. lbs. (70 Nm).
- Front motor mount nut and tighten to 52 ft. lbs. (70 Nm).
- Splash shield
- Oxygen sensor connector
- Power steering rack retainers and tighten to 98 ft. lbs. (133 Nm)
- Power steering line to subframe
- Wiring harness to left front subframe
- Lower radiator hose
- Stabilizer bar to struts
- Stabilizer bar link nuts and tighten to 41 ft. lbs. (55 Nm)

27. Remove the all the special lifting tools from the engine and cylinder heads.

28. Install or connect the following:
- Transaxle-to-engine bolt and tighten to 30 ft. lbs. (40 Nm)
- Power steering hose bolt
- Knock sensor wiring harness to transaxle
- Knock sensor and heat shield
- Engine block heater connector

29. On AWD models, install the PTU and rear driveshaft. Tighten the bolts to 66 ft. lbs. (90 Nm).

30. Install the 2 outer bolts for the driveshaft brace and tighten to 18 ft. lbs. (25 Nm).

31. Install new bolts to the front driveshaft flange and tighten in a criss-cross pattern to 18 ft. lbs. (25 Nm).

32. On all models, install or connect the following:
- Front and rear exhaust pipe nuts and tighten to 30 ft. lbs. (40 Nm)
- Left and right side halfshafts
- 4 upper transaxle mounting bolts and tighten to 30 ft. lbs. (40 Nm)
- Transaxle bulkhead electrical connector
- Ground cable
- Transaxle fluid cooler tube bracket
- PCV hose
- Power steering line bracket
- Throttle body vacuum hoses
- Transaxle wiring harnesses
- Starter wiring and starter and tighten to 19 ft. lbs. (26 Nm)
- Roll restrictor bracket and roll restrictor and apply threadlocker before tightening to 30 ft. lbs. (40 Nm)
- Auxiliary coolant flow pump assembly, if equipped
- Shift able bracket and cable
- Electrical connector to shift cable bracket

- Roll restrictor brace bolts and brace and apply threadlocker before tightening to 30 ft. lbs. (40 Nm)
- Upper roll restrictor bolt and apply threadlocker before tightening to 30 ft. lbs. (40 Nm)
- Cowl grille panel
- Air cleaner assembly
- Battery tray and battery

33. Fill the transaxle with proper amount of Mercon®Continuously Variable chain type transmission fluid.

34. Connect the positive, then the negative battery cable.

Start the engine and check for leaks.

6-Speed Transaxle

See Figure 8.

1. Place the vehicle on a hoist.
2. Drain the transaxle fluid.
3. Remove or disconnect the following:
- Battery and battery tray
- Air cleaner assembly and outlet pipe
- Cowl grille panel
- Upper roll restrictor bolt
- Roll restrictor brace bolts and brace
- Shift cable end
- Electrical connector from shift cable bracket
- Shift able bracket and position the cable and bracket aside
- Transaxle Control Module (TCM) wiring harness
- Transaxle wiring harnesses
- Roll restrictor bracket and roll restrictor
- PCV hose
- Throttle body vacuum hoses
- Power steering line bracket
- Starter wiring and starter
- Ground cable
- 4 upper transaxle mounting bolts
- Left and right side halfshafts
- Front and rear exhaust pipe nuts and discard
- Catalytic converter pipe
- Engine block heater connector
- Knock sensor heat shield and knock sensor
- Knock sensor wiring harness from transaxle
- Transaxle-to-engine bolt
- Power steering hose bolt

4. Install engine lifting eyes no. 134-00243 to the left and right cylinder heads.

5. Install lifting brackets no. 303-1140 to front of the engine.

6. Install engine support tools to the engine as shown.

7. Remove or disconnect the following:
- Disconnect the lower radiator hose from its retainers and position aside

- Power steering line from subframe
- Wiring harness from left front subframe
- Power steering rack retainers and wire the rack to the chassis
- Oxygen sensor connector
- Splash shield
- Front motor mount nut
- Lower stabilizer mount bolts
- Rear motor mount nut
- Rear transaxle mount bolts
- Rear subframe mounting bolts on both sides
- Stabilizer bar links nuts from both sides and discard the nuts.
- Stabilizer bar from struts

8. Using a suitable powertrain lift, remove 4 subframe mounting bolts and remove the subframe.

9. Remove the catalytic converter.

10. Remove the torque converter access plug and remove and discard the 4 torque converter nuts.

11. Disconnect the transaxle fluid cooler tubes from the transaxle.

12. Securely fasten the transaxle to a suitable high lift transmission jack.

13. Remove the 3 engine-to-transaxle bolts, and remove the transaxle.

To install:

➡ **If a different transaxle is being installed, transfer the appropriate external components to the new transaxle.**

14. Apply multi-purpose grease to the torque converter pilot hub.

15. Place the transaxle on a suitable jack and carefully raise it into position.

16. Install 3 engine-to-transaxle mounting bolts and tighten to 30 ft. lbs. (40 Nm).

17. Install new transaxle fluid cooler tube seals and connect the tubes.

18. Install new torque converter nuts and tighten to 27 ft. lbs. (36 Nm). Install the torque converter access plug.

19. Install the catalytic converter and tighten the bolts to 30 ft. lbs. (40 Nm).

20. Using a suitable powertrain lift, install the subframe and tighten the 4 subframe mounting bolts to 66 ft. lbs. (90 Nm).
- Install the subframe mounting bolts on both sides and tighten to 35 ft. lbs. (48 Nm).
- Rear transaxle mount bolts and tighten to 66 ft. lbs. (90 Nm).
- Rear motor mount nut and tighten to 52 ft. lbs. (70 Nm).
- Lower stabilizer mount bolts and tighten to 52 ft. lbs. (70 Nm).

- Front motor mount nut and tighten to 52 ft. lbs. (70 Nm).
- Splash shield
- Oxygen sensor connector
- Power steering rack retainers and tighten to 98 ft. lbs. (133 Nm)
- Power steering line to subframe
- Wiring harness to left front subframe
- Lower radiator hose
- Stabilizer bar to struts
- Stabilizer bar link nuts and tighten to 41 ft. lbs. (55 Nm)

21. Remove the all the special lifting tools from the engine and cylinder heads.

22. Install or connect the following:
- Transaxle-to-engine bolt and tighten to 30 ft. lbs. (40 Nm)
- Power steering hose bolt
- Knock sensor wiring harness to transaxle
- Knock sensor and heat shield
- Engine block heater connector
- Front and rear exhaust pipe nuts and tighten to 30 ft. lbs. (40 Nm)
- Left and right side halfshafts
- 4 upper transaxle mounting bolts and tighten to 30 ft. lbs. (40 Nm)
- Transaxle bulkhead electrical connector
- Ground cable
- Transaxle fluid cooler tube bracket
- PCV hose
- Power steering line bracket
- Throttle body vacuum hoses
- Transaxle wiring harnesses
- Starter wiring and starter and tighten to 19 ft. lbs. (26 Nm)
- Roll restrictor bracket and roll restrictor and apply threadlocker before tightening to 30 ft. lbs. (40 Nm)
- Auxiliary coolant flow pump assembly, if equipped
- Shift able bracket and cable
- Electrical connector to shift cable bracket
- Roll restrictor brace bolts and brace and apply threadlocker before tightening to 30 ft. lbs. (40 Nm)
- Upper roll restrictor bolt and apply threadlocker before tightening to 30 ft. lbs. (40 Nm)
- Cowl grille panel
- Air cleaner assembly
- Battery tray and battery

23. Fill the transaxle with proper amount of Motorcraft®Premium automatic transmission no. XT-8-QAW.

24. Connect the positive, then the negative battery cable.

25. Start the engine and check for leaks.

POWER TRANSFER UNIT

REMOVAL & INSTALLATION

1. Raise the vehicle on a hoist.
2. Remove the left and right halfshafts
3. Remove the front and rear exhaust pipe nuts.
4. Remove the catalytic converter pipe.
5. Index mark the driveshaft flange to the output flange.
6. Remove the 2 outer driveshaft brace bolts.
7. Remove the 6 bolts from the driveshaft flange.
8. Remove the upper PTU bracket bolts and the bracket.
9. Remove 4 PTU mounting bolts and the PTU.
10. Remove the input shaft oil slinger and seal.

To install:

11. Using a seal installer, install the input shaft seal and oil slinger.
12. Position the PTU in place and tighten the bolts to 66 ft. lbs. (90 Nm).
13. Install the upper PTU bracket bolts and the bracket and tighten to 41 ft. lbs. (55 Nm).
14. Install the left and right halfshafts
15. Install the 2 outer driveshaft brace bolts and tighten to 18 ft. lbs. (25 Nm).
16. Install the 6 bolts to the driveshaft flange and tighten in a criss-cross pattern to 18 ft. lbs. (25 Nm).
17. Install the catalytic converter pipe, front and rear exhaust pipe nuts and tighten all fasteners to 30 ft. lbs. (40 Nm).

HALFSHAFTS

REMOVAL & INSTALLATION

Front

➡Do not begin this removal procedure unless a new wheel hub retainer nut, a new retainer circlip and a new lower ball joint-to-front wheel knuckle retaining bolt and nut are available. Once removed, these parts must not be reused during assembly. Their torque holding ability, or retention capability, is diminished during removal.

1. Remove or disconnect the following:
- Front wheels
- ABS sensor
- Brake caliper and wire aside
- Axle hub nut and washer. Discard the nut.

2. Separate the halfshaft from the hub using tool no. 205-D070.

3. Remove and discard the lower ball joint nut.
4. Disconnect the lower control arm.
5. On the left side, on 6-speed models, use a slide hammer and remove the halfshaft from the transaxle.
6. On the left side on CVT models, use a slide hammer and halfshaft fork no. 205-241 and remove the shaft from the transaxle.
7. On the right side, remove the halfshaft bearing nuts and remove the halfshaft.
8. On both sides, inspect the halfshaft seal and replace if necessary.

To install:

※※ WARNING

Do not reuse the retainer circlip. A new circlip must be installed each time the inboard CV-joint stub shaft is installed into the transaxle differential.

9. Install a new retainer circlip on the inboard CV-joint stub shaft by starting one end in the groove and working the retainer circlip over the inboard shaft housing end and into the groove. This will avoid over-expanding the circlip.

➡**A non-metallic mallet may be used to aid in seating the retainer circlip into the differential side gear groove. If a mallet is necessary, tap only on the outboard CV-joint shaft.**

10. Install the halfshaft.
11. On the right side install the halfshaft bearing nuts and tighten to 20 ft. lbs. (27 Nm).
12. On both sides install the halfshaft into the hub.
13. Connect the lower control arm to the knuckle and install a new ball joint nut. Tighten the nut to 59 ft. lbs. (80 Nm).
14. Using the old axle nut and washer tighten the nut to seat the halfshaft in the hub.
15. Remove the old nut and washer.
16. Install a new axle nut and washer and in a continuous motion, tighten the nut to 259 ft. lbs. (350 Nm).
17. Install the brake caliper and tighten to 74 ft. lbs. (100 Nm).
18. Install the front wheels and lower the vehicle.

Rear

➡Do not begin this removal procedure unless a new wheel hub retainer nut is available. Once removed, the nut must not be reused during assembly. The torque holding ability, or retention capability, is diminished during removal.

1. Remove or disconnect the following:

- Rear wheel
- Brake caliper and wire aside
- Axle hub nut and washer. Discard the nut.
- ABS sensor

2. Using a hub remover, press the halfshaft out until it is loose in the hub.

3. Remove the brake disc.

4. Remove the 4 hub bolts and remove the hub.

5. Using a prybar, separate the halfshaft from the axle, and remove the halfshaft.

To install:

⁘ WARNING

Do not reuse the retainer circlip. A new circlip must be installed each time.

6. Install a new retainer circlip on the CV-joint stub shaft by starting one end in the groove and working the retainer circlip over the inboard shaft housing end and into the groove. This will avoid over-expanding the circlip.

7. Install the halfshaft.

8. Install the hub and the hub bolts and tighten to 89 ft. lbs. (120 Nm).

9. Install the brake disc and tighten to 16 ft. lbs. (21 Nm).

10. Using the old axle nut and washer tighten the nut to seat the halfshaft in the hub.

11. Remove the old nut and washer.

12. Install a new axle nut and washer and in a continuous motion, tighten the nut to 148 ft. lbs. (200 Nm).

13. Install the ABS sensor.

14. Install the caliper and tighten to 81 ft. lbs. (110 Nm).

15. Install the rear wheel.

CV-JOINTS OVERHAUL

➡**Overhaul procedures are not available from the manufacturer.**

OUTPUT SHAFT SEAL AND FLANGE

REMOVAL & INSTALLATION

1. Remove the driveshaft.

2. Remove the output flange nut and flange.

3. Remove the output shaft seal.

To install:

4. Clean the output shaft seal bore and shaft.

5. Use a seal installer and install the output shaft seal.

6. Install the output flange and tighten the nut to 74 ft. lbs. (100 Nm).

7. Install the driveshaft.

DRIVESHAFT, PINION FLANGE AND SEAL

REMOVAL & INSTALLATION

1. Place the vehicle on a hoist.

2. Remove the exhaust system at the flex pipe.

3. Remove the exhaust support brace.

4. Index mark the driveshaft to the rear axle pinion flange, PTU flange and center bearing bracket.

5. Disconnect the driveshaft from the rear pinion flange and discard the bolts.

6. Remove the driveshaft flange bolts from the PTU flange and discard the bolts.

7. Disconnect the driveshaft from the PTU flange.

8. Remove the center bearing bracket bolts and remove the driveshaft.

9. Remove and discard the pinion flange nut.

10. Using a puller, remove the pinion flange.

11. Remove the pinion seal.

To install:

12. Using a seal installer, install the pinion seal.

13. Install the drive pinion flange using a new nut. Tighten the nut to 74 ft. lbs. (100 Nm).

14. Install the driveshaft.

15. Install the center bearing bracket and loosely tighten the bolts.

bolts and remove the driveshaft.

16. Using the index marks made on removal, connect the driveshaft to the PTU flange and rear pinion flange and hand tighten the bolts.

17. Tighten the center bearing bracket bolts to 15 ft. lbs. (20 Nm).

18. Tighten the driveshaft to rear pinion flange and PTU flange bolts to 18 ft. lbs. (25 Nm).

19. Install the exhaust support brace and tighten the bolts to 22 ft. lbs. (30 Nm).

20. Install the exhaust system.

21. Lower the vehicle.

ENGINE COOLING

ENGINE FAN

REMOVAL & INSTALLATION

1. Disconnect the battery ground cable.

2. Disconnect the 2 coolant hose retainers from the fan shroud and position aside.

3. Disconnect the cooling fan motor electrical connector.

4. Remove the 2 cooling fan motor and shroud bolts and release the cooling fan motor and shroud from the lower brackets.

5. To install, reverse the removal procedure.

RADIATOR

REMOVAL & INSTALLATION

1. Drain the cooling system.

2. Remove the air cleaner assembly.

3. Remove the cooling fan motor and shroud.

4. Remove the front grille.

5. Disconnect the upper radiator hose and position aside.

6. Disconnect the lower radiator hose and position aside.

7. Disconnect the horn assembly electrical connector.

8. Remove the horn assembly bolt and the horn assembly.

9. Remove the 2 A/C condenser retaining bolts and position aside the A/C condenser.

10. Remove the 2 radiator support bracket bolts.

11. Remove the 2 radiator support brackets and position the radiator forward.

12. Remove the transmission cooler bracket bolt.

13. Lift the transmission cooler.

14. Remove the radiator.

To install:

15. To install, reverse the removal procedure.

16. Tighten the condenser, radiator bracket and transmission cooler bracket to 53 inch lbs. (6 Nm).

17. Fill and bleed the cooling system.

THERMOSTAT

REMOVAL & INSTALLATION

1. Drain the cooling system.

2. Remove the air cleaner assembly.

3. Disconnect the degas bottle-to-thermostat housing hose and position aside.

4. Disconnect the throttle body-to-thermostat housing hose and position aside.

5. Disconnect the upper radiator-to-thermostat housing hose and position aside.

6. Disconnect the bypass tube-to-thermostat housing hose and position aside.

7. Disconnect the heater hose from the thermostat housing and position aside.

8. Disconnect the lower radiator-to-thermostat housing hose and position aside.

9. Remove the 2 bolts and the thermostat housing.

10. Discard the O-ring seal.

11. Remove the 3 thermostat housing bolts and separate the upper and lower thermostat housing.

12. Remove the thermostat.

13. Remove the O-ring seal and discard.

To install:

14. Align the thermostat bridge with the alignment marks and install it in the upper housing.

15. Lubricate a new O-ring seal with clean engine coolant and install it in the upper housing.

16. Install the lower thermostat housing and the 3 bolts and tighten to 89 inch lbs. (10 Nm).

17. Reverse the removal procedure to complete installation.

18. Fill the engine with coolant.

WATER PUMP

REMOVAL & INSTALLATION

See Figure 9.

1. Remove or disconnect the following:

- Negative battery cable
- Coolant
- Accessory drive belt
- Air cleaner assembly
- Lower radiator hose
- Thermostat hoses
- Thermostat housing
- Water pump

To install:

2. Position a new water pump housing gasket on the water pump sealing surface using gasket sealant to hold the gasket in place.

3. Install the water pump and tighten the bolts in the following sequence: tighten the center bolt to 35 inch lbs. (4 nm), loosely install the outer bolts, retighten the center bolt to 18 ft. lbs. (25 Nm), tighten the outer bolts to 89 inch lbs. (10 Nm).

4. The remainder of the installation is the reverse of removal.

5. Fill and bleed the cooling system.

6. Connect the negative battery cable.

7. Start the engine and check for leaks.

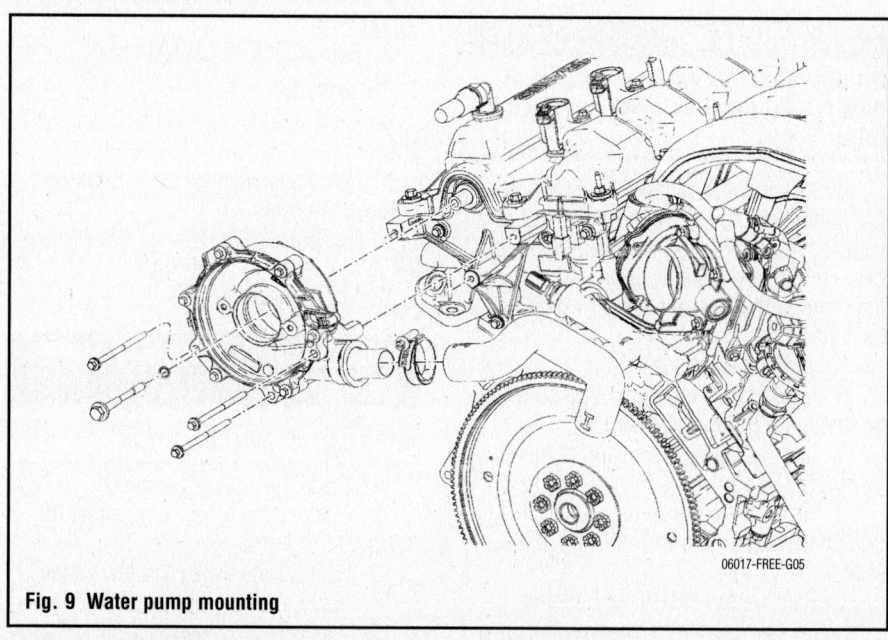

Fig. 9 Water pump mounting

06017-FREE-G05

ENGINE ELECTRICAL

CHARGING SYSTEM

ALTERNATOR

REMOVAL & INSTALLATION

See Figure 10.

1. Disconnect the negative battery cable.

2. Raise and support the vehicle.

3. Rotate the drive belt tensioner counterclockwise and remove the accessory drive belt.

4. Remove the right lower splash shield.

5. Disconnect the crankshaft position sensor.

6. Disconnect the wiring harness locators from the alternator splash shield.

7. Detach the alternator wiring connector.

8. Remove the positive cable nut.

9. Remove the alternator splash shield and the alternator.

To install:

10. Position the alternator on the engine.

11. Install the alternator mounting bolts. Tighten the stud bolts to 71 INCH lbs. (8 Nm) and the bolts to 35 ft. lbs. (47 Nm).

12. Tighten the positive cable nut to 71 INCH lbs. (8 Nm).

13. Connect the wiring connector.

14. Install the wiring harness locators.

15. Connect the crankshaft position sensor.

16. Install the lower right splash shield.

17. Install and tension the accessory drive belt.

18. Connect the negative battery cable.

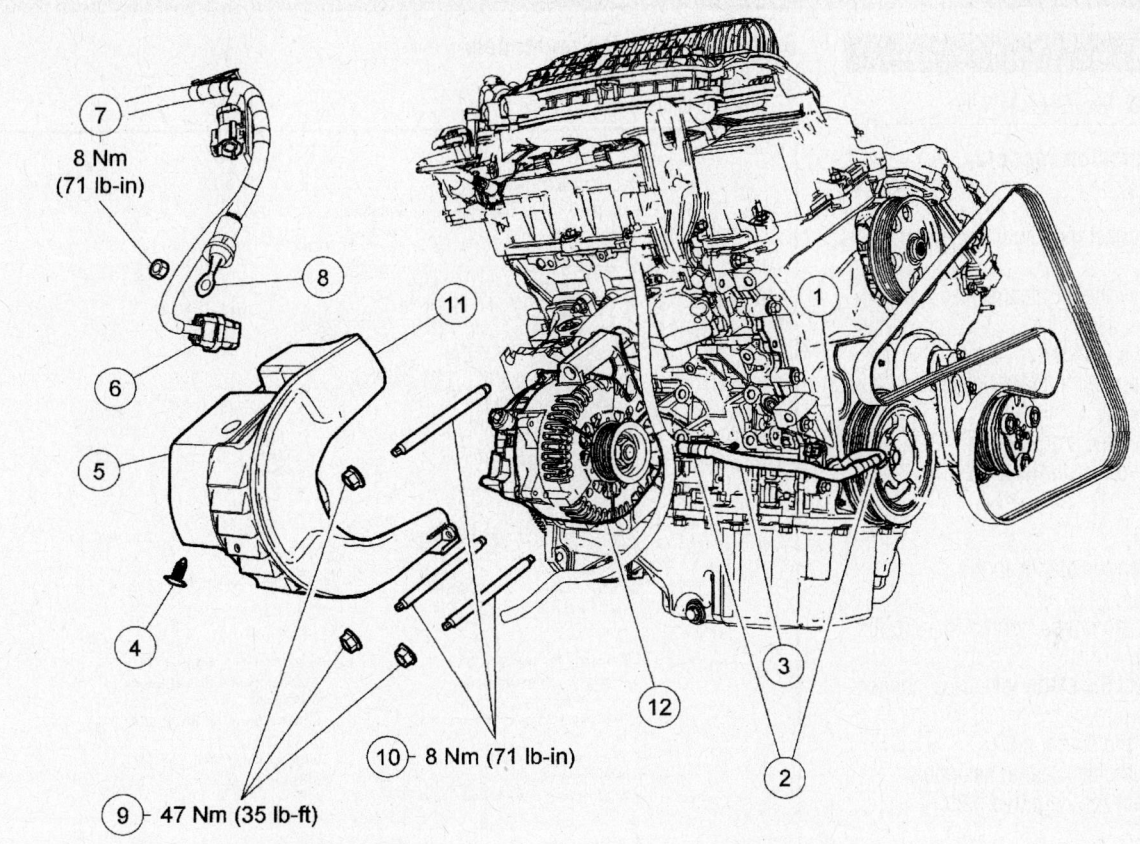

1 Crankshaft position sensor
  connector
2 Harness locators (2 required)
3 Engine control harness
4 Lower generator boot
  pin-type retainer
5 Generator boot
6 Generator electrical connector

7 Generator B+ nut
8 Generator B+ terminal
9 Generator stud nuts (3
  required)
10 Generator studs (3 required)
11 Generator shield
12 Generator

06017-FREE-G02

Fig. 10 Alternator mounting

ENGINE ELECTRICAL

IGNITION SYSTEM

IGNITION COIL

REMOVAL & INSTALLATION

1. Disconnect the negative battery cable.
2. Remove the upper intake manifold.
3. Disconnect the ignition coil electrical connectors.
4. Remove the ignition coil bolts.
5. When removing the ignition coils, a slight twisting motion will break the seal and ease removal.
6. Remove the ignition coils.

To install:

7. To install, reverse the removal procedure. Tighten the spark plugs to 11 ft. lbs. (15 Nm)

IGNITION TIMING

ADJUSTMENT

The ignition timing is controlled by the Powertrain Control Module (PCM). No adjustment is necessary or possible.

SPARK PLUGS

REMOVAL & INSTALLATION

When you're removing spark plugs, work on one at a time. Don't start by removing the plug wires all at once, because, unless you number them, they may become mixed up. Take a minute before you begin and number the wires with tape.

1. Disconnect the negative battery cable.
2. Remove the upper intake manifold.
3. Disconnect the ignition coil electrical connectors.
4. Remove the ignition coil bolts.
5. When removing the ignition coils, a slight twisting motion will break the seal and ease removal.
6. Remove the ignition coils.
7. Remove the spark plugs.

To install:

8. To install, reverse the removal procedure. Tighten the spark plugs to 11 ft. lbs. (15 Nm).

STARTER

REMOVAL & INSTALLATION

CVT Transmission Models

See Figure 11.

1. Disconnect the negative battery cable.
2. Remove the air cleaner assembly.
3. Remove the starter cover.
4. Disconnect the starter electrical connectors.
5. Remove the starter bolts.
6. Remove the starter from the vehicle.

To install:

7. Position the starter in the vehicle.
8. Install the bolts. Tighten to 18 ft. lbs. (25 Nm).
9. Connect the starter electrical connectors.
10. Install the starter cover.
11. Install the air cleaner assembly.
12. Connect the negative battery cable.

6-Speed Transmission Models

See Figure 12.

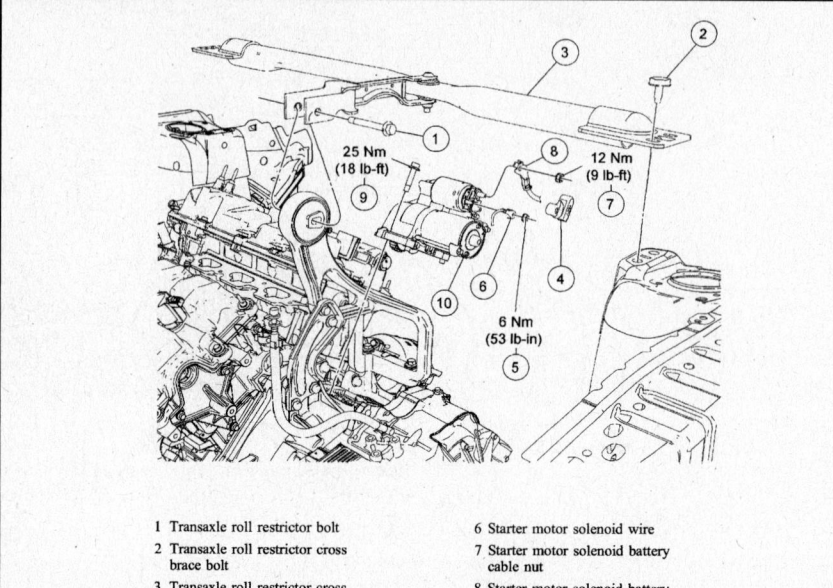

1 Transaxle roll restrictor bolt	6 Starter motor solenoid wire
2 Transaxle roll restrictor cross brace bolt	7 Starter motor solenoid battery cable nut
3 Transaxle roll restrictor cross brace	8 Starter motor solenoid battery cable
4 Starter motor solenoid terminal cover	9 Starter motor bolt
5 Starter motor solenoid wire nut	10 Starter motor

06017-FREE-G28

Fig. 12 Starter mounting—6-speed transmission models

25 Nm (18 lb-ft)

12 Nm (9 lb-ft)

6 Nm (53 lb-in)

06017-FREE-G27

Fig. 11 Starter mounting—CVT transmission models

1. Disconnect the negative battery cable.
2. Remove the air cleaner outlet pipe.
3. Remove the transaxle roll restrictor bolts and the cross brace assembly.
4. Remove the starter cover.
5. Disconnect the starter electrical connectors.
6. Remove the starter bolts.
7. Remove the starter from the vehicle.

To install:

8. Position the starter in the vehicle.
9. Install the bolts. Tighten to 18 ft. lbs. (25 Nm).
10. Connect the starter electrical connectors.
11. Install the starter cover.
12. Install the cross brace assembly and transaxle roll restrictor bolts.
13. Install the air cleaner outlet pipe.
14. Connect the negative battery cable.

ENGINE MECHANICAL

➡️**Disconnecting the negative battery cable may interfere with the functions of the on board computer systems and may require the computer to undergo a relearning process, once the negative battery cable is reconnected.**

ACCESSORY DRIVE BELTS

ACCESSORY BELT ROUTING

See Figure 13.

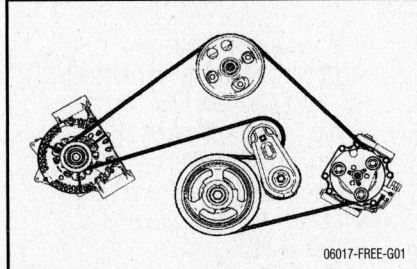

Fig. 13 Accessory drive belt routing— 3.0L engine

INSPECTION

Inspect the drive belt for signs of glazing or cracking. A glazed belt will be perfectly smooth from slippage, while a good belt will have a slight texture of fabric visible. Cracks will usually start at the inner edge of the belt and run outward. All worn or damaged drive belts should be replaced immediately.

REMOVAL & INSTALLATION

1. With the vehicle in NEUTRAL, position it on a hoist.
2. Remove the 7 pin-type retainers and the RH splash shield.
3. If equipped, remove the 3 A/C compressor pulley shield retainers and the shield.
4. Using a suitable belt tensioner release tool, rotate the accessory drive belt tensioner counterclockwise and remove the accessory drive belt.

To install:
5. To install, reverse the removal procedure.

CAMSHAFT AND VALVE LIFTERS

REMOVAL & INSTALLATION

Right Side

See Figures 14 through 16.

1. Disconnect the negative battery cable.
2. Remove the engine front cover.

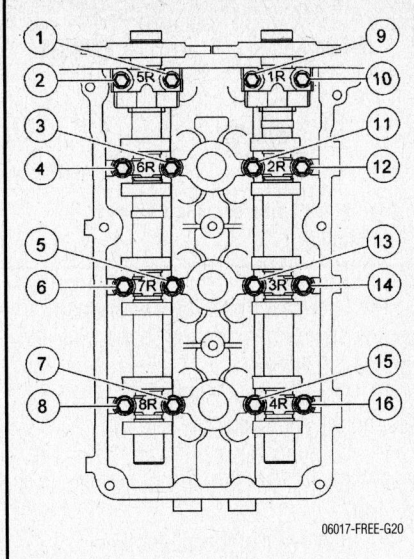

Fig. 14 Right side camshaft bearing cap removal sequence

3. Remove the timing chains.
4. Loosen the camshaft bearing cap bolts evenly in the sequence shown and remove the bearing caps.

➡️**The bearing caps are numbered for correct positioning.**

5. Remove the camshafts.

To install:
6. Clean and inspect all parts before installation.
7. Lubricate the camshaft lobes and journals with clean engine oil.
8. Carefully install the camshafts.
9. Align the camshaft sprocket marks as shown.
10. Lubricate the bearing surfaces of the bearing caps with clean engine oil.
11. Position the bearing caps in their proper locations and loosely install the bearing cap bolts.
12. Tighten the bearing caps bolts in sequence to 89 inch lbs. (10 Nm).

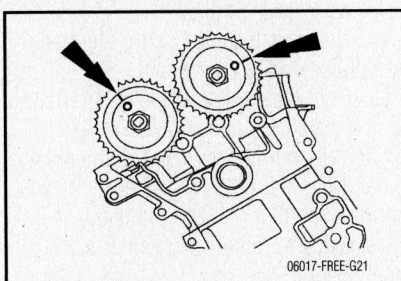

Fig. 15 Right side camshaft sprocket mark positioning

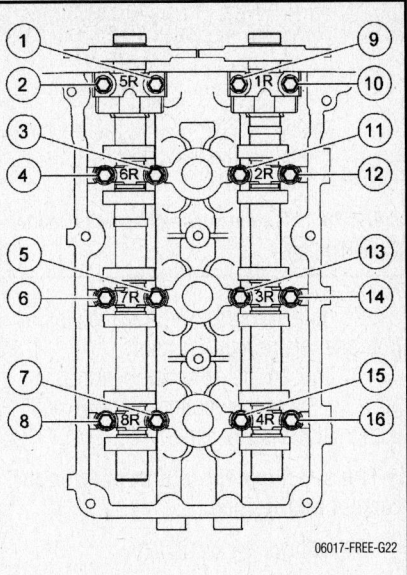

Fig. 16 Right side camshaft bearing cap tightening sequence

13. Install the timing chains.
14. Install the engine front cover.
15. Connect the negative battery cable.

Left Side

See Figures 17 through 20.

1. Disconnect the negative battery cable.
2. Remove the water pump.
3. Remove the engine front cover.
4. Remove the timing chains.
5. Remove the 3 bolts and the camshaft oil seal retainer.

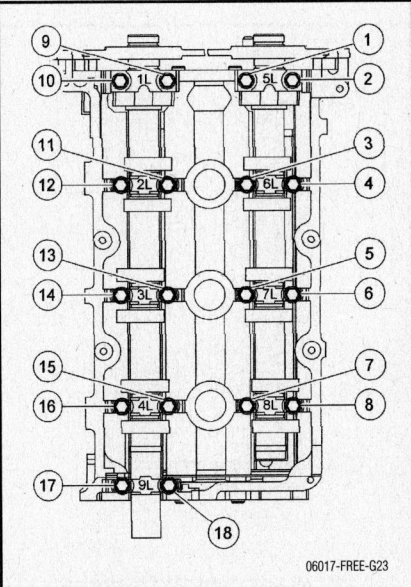

Fig. 17 Left side camshaft bearing cap removal sequence

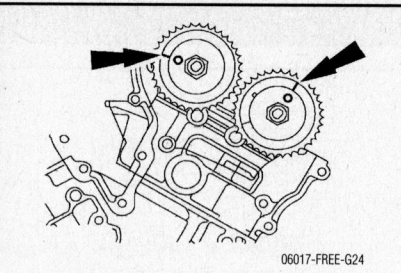

Fig. 18 Left side camshaft sprocket mark positioning

6. Using a press, remove the oil seal from the retainer and discard.

7. Loosen the camshaft bearing cap bolts evenly in the sequence shown and remove the bearing caps.

➡️**The bearing caps are numbered for correct positioning.**

8. Remove the camshafts.

To install:

9. Clean and inspect all parts before installation.

10. Lubricate the camshaft lobes and journals with clean engine oil.

11. Carefully install the camshafts.

12. Align the camshaft sprocket marks as shown.

13. Lubricate the bearing surfaces of the bearing caps with clean engine oil.

14. Position the bearing caps in their proper locations and loosely install the bearing cap bolts.

15. Tighten the bearing caps bolts in sequence to 89 inch lbs. (10 Nm).

16. Install the camshaft oil seal retainer and tighten the bolts 89 inch lbs. (10 Nm).

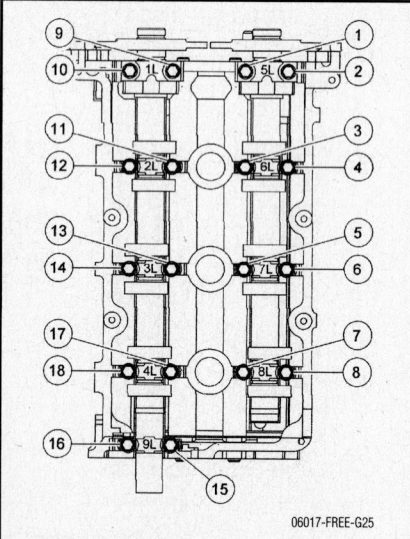

Fig. 19 Left side camshaft bearing cap tightening sequence

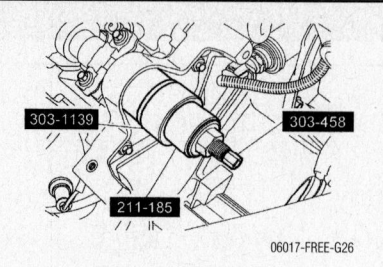

Fig. 20 Left side camshaft oil seal installation

17. Lubricate the oil seal with clean engine oil and position the seal on installer tool no. 303-463.

18. Position the installer tool and oil seal on the camshaft.

19. Using installer tools no. 303-1139, 211-185 and 303-458, install the camshaft oil seal.

20. Remove the special tools.

21. Install the timing chains.

22. Install the engine front cover.

23. Install the water pump.

24. Connect the negative battery cable.

CRANKSHAFT FRONT SEAL

REMOVAL & INSTALLATION

1. Disconnect the negative battery cable.

2. Raise the vehicle on a hoist.

3. Remove the accessory drive belt.

4. Remove the right side fender splash shield.

5. Hold the crankshaft pulley and remove the pulley bolt.

6. Using a puller, remove the crankshaft pulley.

7. Use a seal replacer and pull out the oil seal.

To install:

8. Coat the crankshaft seal lip with clean engine oil.

9. Using a seal installer, install the seal.

10. Lubricate the front cover and crankshaft seal inner lip with clean engine oil.

11. Apply silicone sealant to the crankshaft keyway in the pulley.

12. Using an installer, screw the crankshaft pulley on the crankshaft.

13. Hold the crankshaft pulley from turning and install the pulley bolt and washer and tighten as follows: Step 1; tighten the bolt to 86 ft. lbs. (120 Nm). Step 2; loosen the bolt one full turn. Step 3; tighten to 37 ft. lbs. (50 Nm). Step 4; tighten an additional 90 degrees.

14. Install the right side fender splash shield.

15. Install the accessory drive belt.

16. Lower the vehicle.

CYLINDER HEAD

REMOVAL & INSTALLATION

Left Side

See Figures 21 through 23.

1. Relieve the fuel system pressure.

2. Disconnect the negative battery cable.

3. Drain the engine coolant.

4. Remove or disconnect the following:

- Accessory drive belt
- Upper and lower intake manifolds
- Coolant bypass tube
- Ignition coil on plugs
- Valve cover wiring harness
- 6 bolts and 8 stud bolts, and remove the valve cover
- Camshafts
- Exhaust manifold
- Oil dipstick and tube
- Mark the location of the camshaft roller followers and remove them
- Hydraulic lash adjusters
- Cylinder head bolts in the sequence shown
- Cylinder head from the engine block and discard the gaskets and bolts

To install:

5. The cylinder head should be cleaned and inspected prior to installation.

6. Clean all gasket mating surfaces thoroughly.

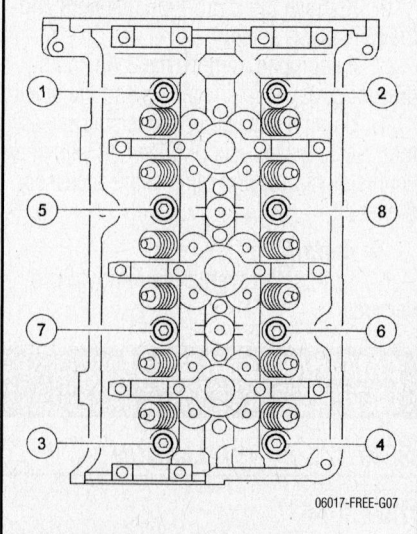

Fig. 21 Left side cylinder head bolt removal sequence

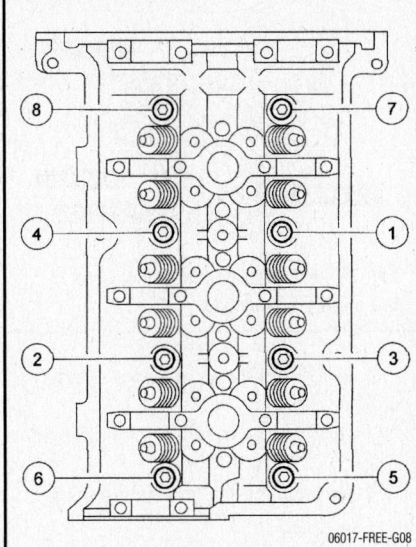

Fig. 22 Left side cylinder head bolt installation sequence

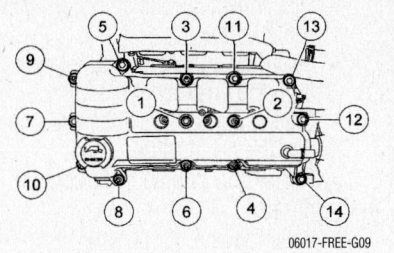

Fig. 23 Left side valve cover bolt installation sequence

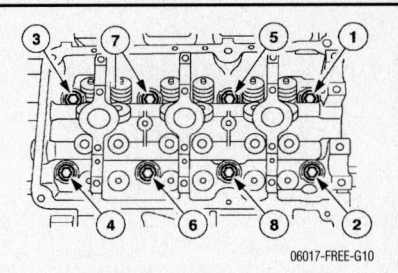

Fig. 24 Right side cylinder head bolt removal sequence

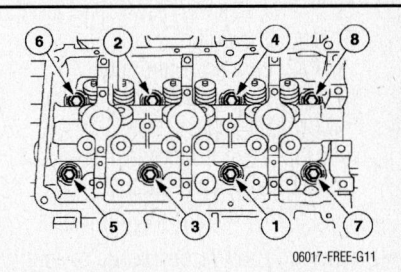

Fig. 25 Right side cylinder head bolt installation sequence

7. Install or connect the following:
   - New head gaskets on the cylinder block

✳✳ WARNING

Always use new cylinder head bolts when installing the cylinder head or damage to the engine may occur.

- Cylinder head on the cylinder block
- Tighten the cylinder head bolts in sequence using the following steps. The first step is 30 ft. lbs. (40 Nm), the second step is an additional 90 degrees, the third step is to loosen all bolts in sequence one full turn, the fourth step is to tighten the bolts to 30 ft. lbs. (40 Nm), the fifth step is to tighten and additional 90 degrees, the last step is to tighten an addition 90 degrees.
- Lash adjusters and camshaft roller followers in their correct locations. Lubricate all rocker arm components with engine assembly lubricant.
- Oil dipstick and tube
- Exhaust manifold
- Camshafts
- Place a bead of silicone gasket sealant to the front cover-to-cylinder head surface
- Valve cover. Install the 6 bolts and 8 stud bolts, and tighten in sequence to 89 inch lbs. (10 Nm).
- Valve cover wiring harness
- Ignition coil on plugs
- Coolant bypass tube

- Upper and lower intake manifolds
- Accessory drive belt
8. Fill and bleed the cooling system.

➡**Engine coolant is corrosive to engine bearing material. Replace the engine oil after removal of any coolant-carrying component to help prevent potential bearing damage.**

9. Change the engine oil and filter
10. Connect the negative battery cable.
11. Start the engine and check for leaks.

Right Side

See Figures 24 through 26.

1. Relieve the fuel system pressure.
2. Disconnect the negative battery cable.
3. Drain the engine coolant.
4. Remove or disconnect the following:
   - Accessory drive belt
   - Upper and lower intake manifolds
   - Coolant bypass tube
   - Ignition coil on plugs
   - PCV connector and tube
   - Power steering reservoir bracket and stud bolts
   - Power steering pressure tube bracket
   - Wiring harness and retainers from valve cover
   - Valve cover bolts and stud bolts
   - Valve cover
   - Camshafts
   - Exhaust manifold
   - Mark the location of the camshaft roller followers and remove them
   - Hydraulic lash adjusters
   - Cylinder head bolts in the sequence shown
   - Cylinder head from the engine block and discard the gaskets and bolts

To install:

5. The cylinder head should be cleaned and inspected prior to installation.
6. Clean all gasket mating surfaces thoroughly.

7. Install or connect the following:
   - New head gaskets on the cylinder block

✳✳ WARNING

Always use new cylinder head bolts when installing the cylinder head or damage to the engine may occur.

- Cylinder head on the cylinder block
- Tighten the cylinder head bolts in sequence using the following steps. The first step is 30 ft. lbs. (40 Nm), the second step is an additional 90 degrees, the third step is to loosen all bolts in sequence one full turn, the fourth step is to tighten the bolts to 30 ft. lbs. (40 Nm), the fifth step is to tighten and additional 90 degrees, the last step is to tighten an addition 90 degrees.
- Lash adjusters and camshaft roller followers in their correct locations. Lubricate all rocker arm components with engine assembly lubricant.
- Exhaust manifold
- Camshafts
- Place a bead of silicone gasket sealant to the front cover-to-cylinder head surface
- Valve cover. Install the 9 bolts and 5 stud bolts, and tighten in sequence to 89 inch lbs. (10 Nm).
- Power steering pressure tube bracket

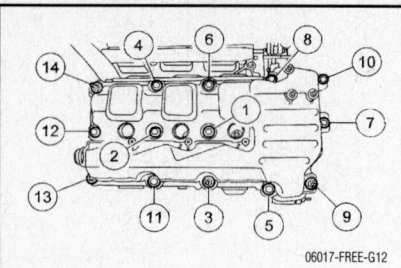

Fig. 26 Right side valve cover bolt installation sequence

- Power steering reservoir bracket and stud bolts
- PCV connector and tube
- Ignition coil on plugs
- Coolant bypass tube
- Upper and lower intake manifolds
- Accessory drive belt
8. Fill and bleed the cooling system.

➡**Engine coolant is corrosive to engine bearing material. Replace the engine oil after removal of any coolant-carrying component to help prevent potential bearing damage.**

9. Change the engine oil and filter
10. Connect the negative battery cable.
11. Start the engine and check for leaks.

ENGINE ASSEMBLY

REMOVAL & INSTALLATION

See Figures 27 and 28.

1. Relieve the fuel system pressure.
2. Drain the engine coolant.
3. Drain the engine oil.
4. Recover the air conditioning refrigerant, into a refrigerant recovery station.
5. Place the transmission in neutral and raise the vehicle on a hoist.
6. Remove or disconnect the following:
   - Both battery cables
   - B+ terminal from the battery cable
   - Air cleaner outlet pipe and air cleaner
   - Cowl vent screen
   - Left and right halfshafts
   - Exhaust flex pipe
   - Left side catalytic converter
   - Roll restrictor cross brace-to-roll restrictor bolt and discard
   - Roll restrictor cross brace
   - Right and left fender ground straps
   - Fuel tube from the fuel rail
   - Vapor tube from the purge valve
   - Powertrain Control Module (PCM) connectors and wiring conduit
   - Power steering reservoir hose and retainers

- Disconnect the transmission shift cable
- Electrical connector and retainers from the shift cable bracket
- Shift cable bracket bolts and position the cable aside
- Heater and throttle body coolant hoses
- Brake booster vacuum hose
- Thermostat housing hoses
- Cooling tube retainers
- A/C high pressure switch connector
- A/C compressor manifold tube
- A/C tube retaining nuts and position the tubes aside
- Transmission cooler lines
- Power steering cooler hose
- Engine block heater connector and harness
- Torque converter lower access plug
- Torque converter attaching nuts
- 3 engine-to-transaxle mounting bolts
- Left catalytic converter bracket
- Driveshaft support bracket bolts and the driveshaft, if equipped
- Stabilizer bar links from the struts
- Outer tie rod ends from the steering knuckles
- Steering column intermediate shaft bolt and separate the shaft from the steering gear

7. Position subframe support tool 014-00765 under subframe and powertrain assembly.
8. Remove the subframe bolts and rear subframe brackets.
9. Lower the powertrain and subframe assembly from the vehicle.
10. To separate the engine from the transaxle and subframe assembly, disconnect all necessary electrical connectors, fluid lines and starter wiring. Remove the starter and engine roll restrictor brackets
11. Install engine lifting eyes no. 134-00243 to the left and right cylinder heads.
12. Install lifting brackets no. 303-1140 to front of the engine.
13. Install an engine hoist and lifting bar no. 303-D089 to the engine.

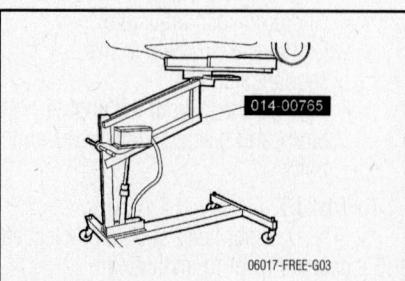

Fig. 27 Installing subframe support tool—Freestyle

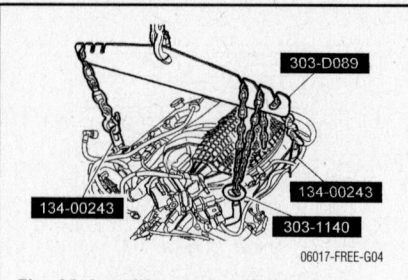

Fig. 28 Installing engine lifting tools to the engine—Freestyle

14. Remove the front transaxle stabilizer bolt.
15. Remove the exhaust manifold heat shield.
16. Remove the left and right engine insulator upper nuts.
17. Remove the transaxle insulator bracket.
18. Using the hoist, lift the powertrain from the subframe.
19. Remove the transaxle-to-engine mounting bolts and separate the engine and transaxle.

To install:

20. Position the engine onto the transaxle and install the transaxle mount bolts. Torque the bolts to 30 ft. lbs. (40 Nm).
21. Install the exhaust manifold heat shield.
22. Using the hoist, position the powertrain to the subframe.
23. Install the left and right engine insulator upper nuts and tighten to 62 ft. lbs. (70 Nm).
24. Install the front transaxle stabilizer bolt and tighten to 30 ft. lbs. (40 Nm).
25. Install the transaxle insulator bracket and tighten the bolts to 41 ft. lbs. (55 Nm).
26. Install the starter and tighten the bolts to 18 ft. lbs. (25 Nm).
27. Connect the starter wiring and terminal cover.
28. Apply thread lock to the roll restrictor bolts and install the restrictor bracket and tighten the bolts to 41 ft. lbs. (55 Nm).
29. Reconnect all necessary electrical connectors, fluid lines and retainers.
30. Remove the engine hoist and lifting tools.
31. Using subframe support tool 014-00765, raise the subframe and powertrain assembly into the vehicle
32. Install the front subframe bolts and tighten the bolts to 148 ft. lbs. (200 Nm).
33. Install the rear subframe brackets. Tighten the large bolts to 111 ft. lbs. (150 Nm), and the smaller bolts to 41 ft. lbs. (55 Nm).

34. Connect the steering column intermediate shaft and tighten the pinch bolt to 18 ft. lbs. (25 Nm).

35. Install the outer tie rod ends to the steering knuckles and tighten NEW nuts to 85 ft. lbs. (115 Nm).

36. Install the stabilizer bar links to the struts using NEW nuts and tighten to 41 ft. lbs. (55 Nm).

37. Install the driveshaft and tighten the bolts to 18 ft. lbs. (25 Nm).

38. Install the driveshaft support bracket bolts and tighten the bolts to 18 ft. lbs. (25 Nm).

39. Install or connect the following:
- NEW torque converter attaching nuts and tighten to 27 ft. lbs. (36 Nm)
- Torque converter lower access plug
- Engine block heater connector and harness
- Power steering cooler hose
- Transmission cooler lines
- A/C tube and retaining nuts
- A/C compressor manifold tube
- A/C high pressure switch connector
- Cooling tube retainers
- Thermostat housing hoses
- Brake booster vacuum hose
- Heater and throttle body coolant hoses
- Shift cable and bracket bolts and tighten the bolts to 18 ft. lbs. (25 Nm)
- Electrical connector and retainers to the shift cable bracket
- Connect the transmission shift cable
- Power steering reservoir hose and retainers
- Powertrain Control Module (PCM) connectors and wiring conduit
- Vapor tube from the purge valve
- Fuel tube from the fuel rail
- Right and left fender ground straps
- Roll restrictor cross brace
- NEW roll restrictor cross brace-to-roll restrictor bolts and tighten to 41 ft. lbs. (55 Nm)
- Left catalytic converter bracket
- Left side catalytic converter
- Exhaust flex pipe
- Left and right halfshafts
- Cowl vent screen
- Air cleaner outlet pipe and air cleaner
- B+ terminal to the battery cable
- Both battery cables

40. Refill the engine, transaxle and cooling system with the correct amount of the appropriate fluids before starting the engine. Recharge the A/C system using approved recycling equipment.

EXHAUST MANIFOLD

REMOVAL & INSTALLATION

➡Spray the exhaust system fasteners with penetrating lubricant before removing them to help prevent broken studs and bolts. The use of a 6-point socket is highly recommended when removing exhaust system fasteners.

❊❊ CAUTION

To prevent serious burns, allow the exhaust manifold to cool down before attempting to remove it.

Left Manifold

See Figure 29.

1. Disconnect the negative battery cable.
2. Remove the coolant hose retainers from the fan shroud and position aside.
3. Disconnect the cooling fan electrical connectors.
4. Remove the cooling fans.
5. Disconnect the oxygen sensor connector.
6. Remove the 2 exhaust manifold-to-catalytic converter bolts.
7. Remove 6 exhaust manifold nuts and remove the exhaust manifold.

To install:
8. Clean all gasket mating surfaces thoroughly.
9. Install a new exhaust manifold gasket and the exhaust manifold on the cylinder head. Start 2 nuts to hold the manifold in position.
10. Install the remaining nuts. Tighten the nuts in the sequence shown to 15 ft. lbs. (20 Nm).
11. Install the 2 exhaust manifold-to-catalytic converter bolts and tighten to 30 ft. lbs. (40 Nm).
12. Connect the oxygen sensor connector.
13. Install the cooling fans.
14. Connect the cooling fan electrical connectors.
15. Install the coolant hose retainers to the fan shroud.
16. Connect the negative battery cable.
17. Start the engine and check for exhaust leaks.

Right Manifold

See Figure 30.

1. Disconnect the negative battery cable.
2. Raise the vehicle on a hoist.
3. Remove the right side catalytic converter.
4. Disconnect the oxygen sensor connector.
5. Remove the exhaust manifold heat shield.
6. Disconnect the EGR tube from the manifold.
7. Remove the exhaust manifold.

To install:
8. Clean all gasket mating surfaces thoroughly.

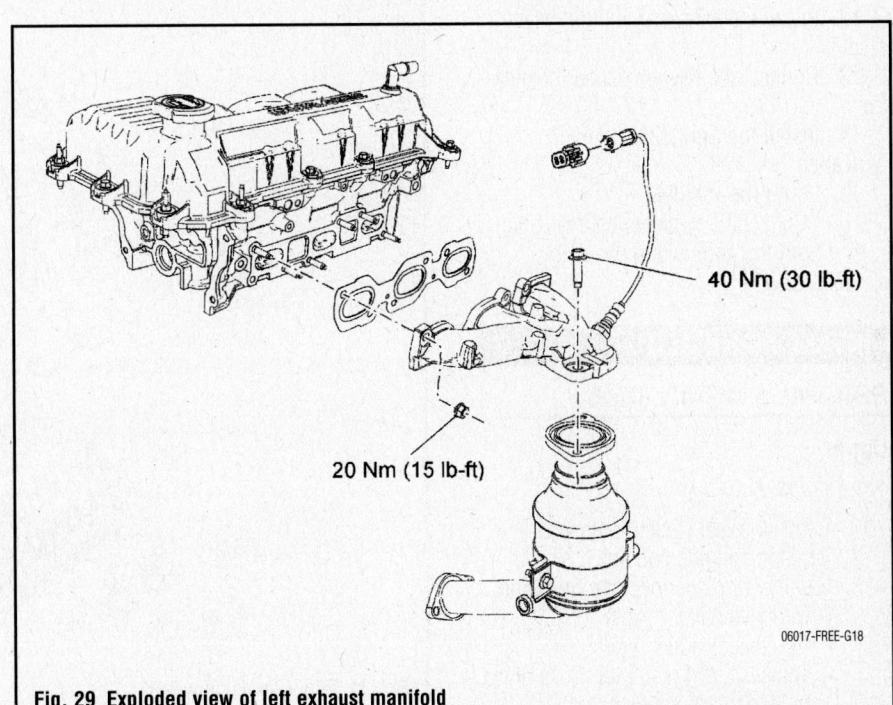

40 Nm (30 lb-ft)

20 Nm (15 lb-ft)

06017-FREE-G18

Fig. 29 Exploded view of left exhaust manifold

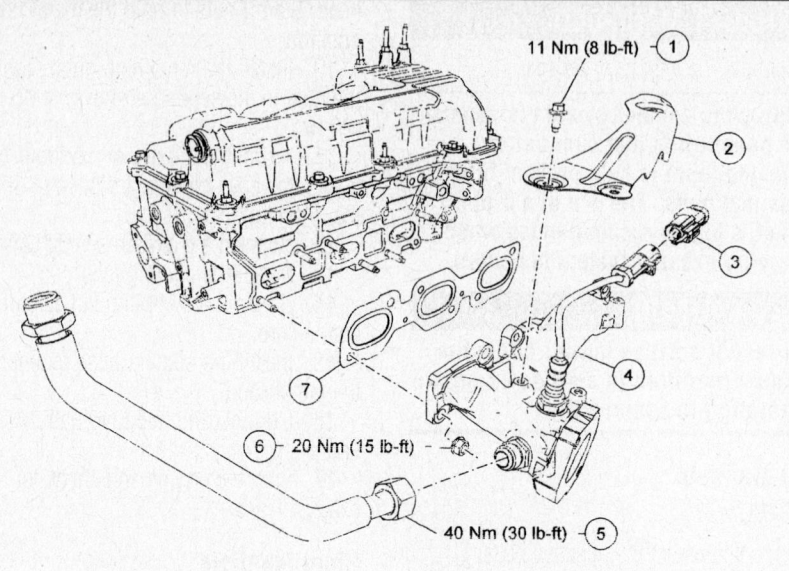

11 Nm (8 lb-ft) — ①

6 — 20 Nm (15 lb-ft)

40 Nm (30 lb-ft) — ⑤

1 RH exhaust manifold heat shield (2 required)

2 RH exhaust manifold heat shield

3 Heated oxygen sensor (HO2S) electrical connector

4 RH exhaust manifold

5 Exhaust gas recirculation (EGR) system module tube fitting

6 RH exhaust manifold nut (6 required)

7 RH exhaust manifold gasket

06017-FREE-G19

Fig. 30 Exploded view of right exhaust manifold

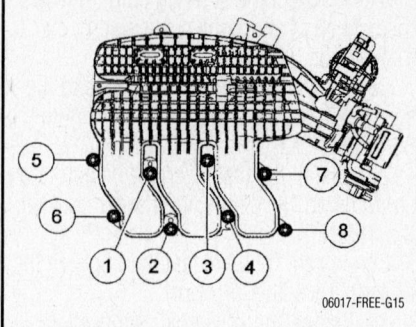

06017-FREE-G15

Fig. 32 Upper intake manifold tightening sequence

- Throttle body and PCV coolant hoses
- Throttle body electrical connector
- Upper-to-lower intake manifold attaching screws
- Intake manifold

To install:

4. Installation is the reverse of the removal procedure, using the following torque specifications.

- Intake manifold bolts and tighten all bolts in steps in sequence to 89 inch lbs. (10 Nm)
- Transaxle roll restrictor roll brace and tighten the bolts as shown

5. Fill and bleed the engine cooling system.

6. Connect the negative battery cable.

9. Install a new gasket and the exhaust manifold on the cylinder head. Start 2 nuts to hold the manifold in position.

10. Install the remaining nuts. Tighten the nuts in the sequence shown to 15 ft. lbs. (20 Nm).

11. Connect the EGR tube from the manifold.

12. Install the exhaust manifold heat shield.

13. Connect the oxygen sensor connector.

14. Install the right side catalytic converter.

15. Lower the vehicle.

16. Connect the negative battery cable.

17. Start the engine and check for exhaust leaks.

INTAKE MANIFOLD

REMOVAL & INSTALLATION

Upper

See Figures 31 through 33.

1. Relive the fuel system pressure.
2. Drain the engine coolant.
3. Remove or disconnect the following:
   - Negative battery cable
   - Air cleaner outlet pipe
   - Transaxle roll restrictor cross brace bolts and cross brace

- EVAP purge valve tube
- PCV, brake booster and vacuum harness tubes from the manifold
- Fuel tube retainer
- EGR connector and vacuum tube

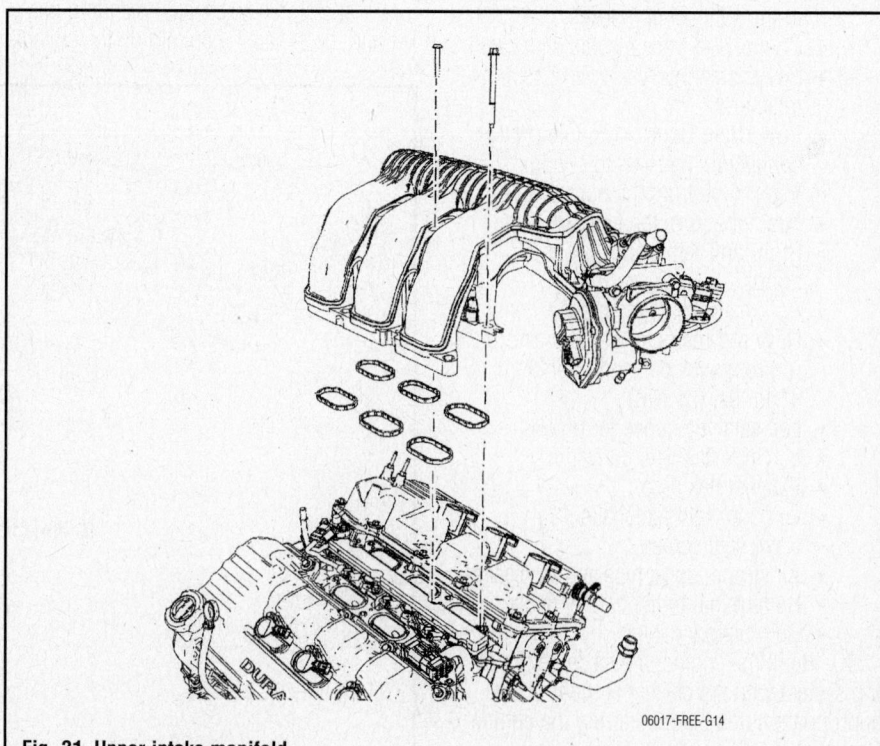

06017-FREE-G14

Fig. 31 Upper intake manifold

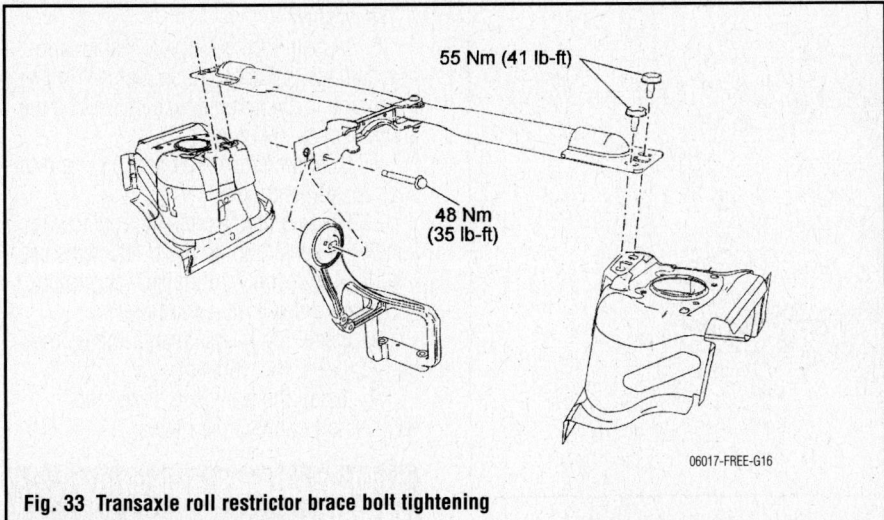

Fig. 33 Transaxle roll restrictor brace bolt tightening

55 Nm (41 lb-ft)

48 Nm (35 lb-ft)

06017-FREE-G16

7. Start the engine and check for leaks.

Lower

See Figure 34.

1. Remove or disconnect the following:
   - Coolant
   - Fuel system pressure
   - Upper intake manifold
   - Fuel tube from fuel rail
   - Fuel rail pressure and temperature sensor connectors and vacuum tube
   - Fuel charging wiring harness connector
   - Lower intake manifold

To install:

2. Thoroughly clean all gasket mating surfaces.
3. Install or connect the following:

- 6 intake manifold gaskets and the intake manifold
- Fuel charging wiring harness connector
- Fuel rail pressure and temperature sensor connectors and vacuum tube
- Fuel tube from fuel rail
- Upper intake manifold
- Fuel system pressure

4. Fill and bleed the cooling system.
5. Start the engine and check for leaks.

OIL PAN

REMOVAL & INSTALLATION

See Figures 35 and 36.

✳✳ CAUTION

The EPA warns that prolonged contact with used engine oil may cause

a number of skin disorders, including cancer! You should make every effort to minimize your exposure to used engine oil. Protective gloves should be worn when changing the oil. Wash your hands and any other exposed skin areas as soon as possible after exposure to used engine oil. Soap and water, or waterless hand cleaner, should be used.

1. Disconnect the negative battery cable.
2. Drain the engine oil.
3. Remove the oil filter.
4. Raise the vehicle on a hoist.
5. Remove the exhaust flex pipe.
6. Remove the torque converter inspection cover.
7. Remove 2 oil pan-to-transaxle bolts.
8. Remove the oil filter adapter-to-oil pan bolt.
9. Remove the 15 retaining bolts and remove the oil pan.

To install:

10. Clean the gasket mating surfaces thoroughly.
11. Apply a drop of sealant to the locations shown.

➡**When using silicone rubber sealer, assembly must occur within 5 minutes after sealer application. After this time, the sealer may start to harden and its sealing effectiveness may be reduced.**

12. Install the oil pan using a new gasket and secure to the block with the attaching bolts. Tighten the bolts in sequence to 89 inch lbs. (10 Nm).
13. Install the oil filter adapter-to-oil pan bolt.
14. Install 2 oil pan-to-transaxle bolts.
15. Install the torque converter inspection cover.
16. Install the exhaust flex pipe.
17. Install a new oil filter.

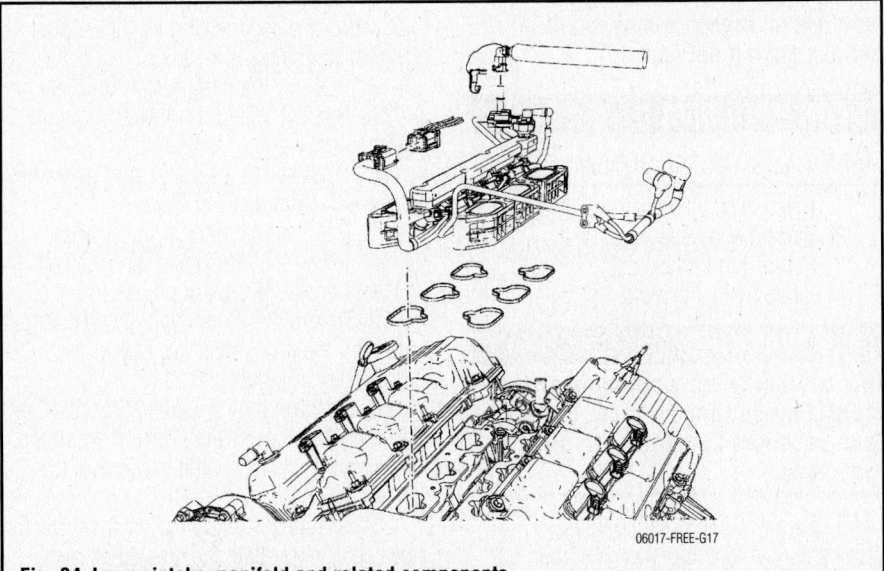

Fig. 34 Lower intake manifold and related components

06017-FREE-G17

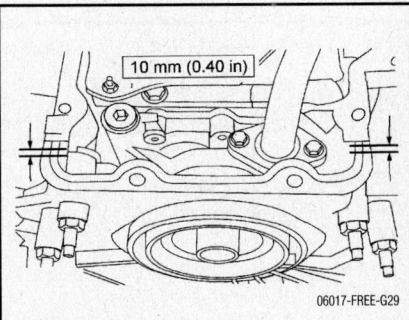

10 mm (0.40 in)

06017-FREE-G29

Fig. 35 Applying sealant to the oil pan mounting surface

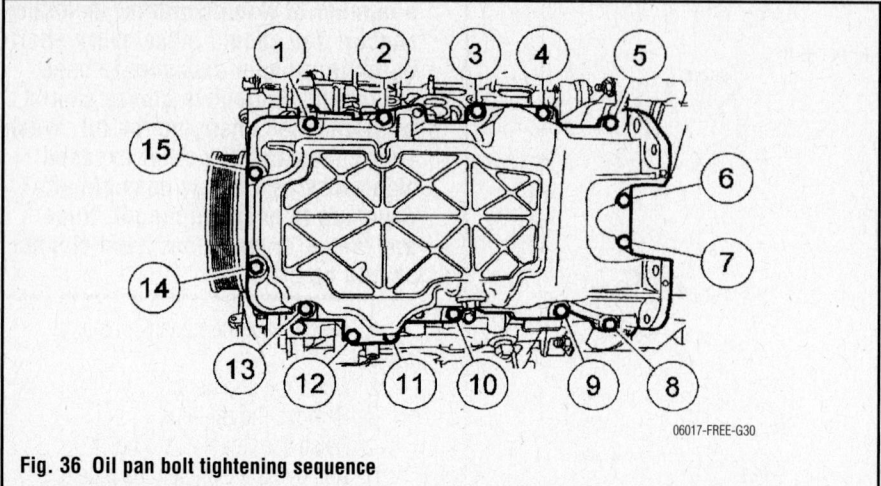

Fig. 36 Oil pan bolt tightening sequence

18. Fill the engine with the proper type and amount of clean oil.
19. Connect the negative battery cable.
20. Start the engine and check for leaks.

OIL PUMP

REMOVAL & INSTALLATION

See Figures 37 and 38.

1. Disconnect the negative battery cable.
2. Drain the engine oil.
3. Remove the timing chain components.
4. Remove the oil pan.
5. Remove the oil pump screen and pickup tube.
6. Remove the oil pump attaching bolts in the sequence shown.
7. Place the oil pump in the proper position with a new gasket and install the retaining bolts.
8. Tighten the oil pump retaining bolts in sequence to 89 inch lbs. (10 Nm).
9. Install the oil pump screen and pickup tube.
10. Install the oil pan.
11. Install the timing chain components.

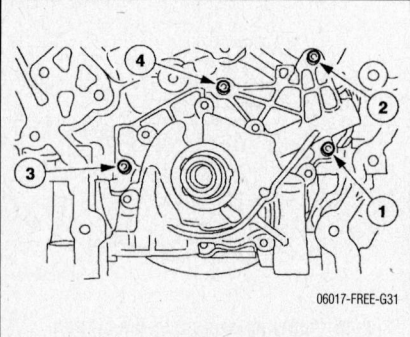

Fig. 37 Oil pump bolt removal sequence

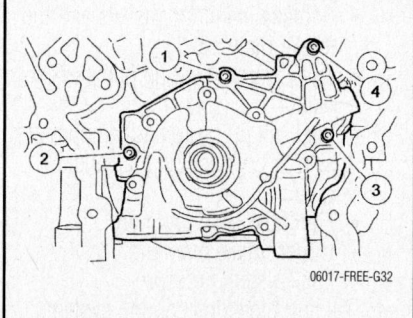

Fig. 38 Oil pump bolt tightening sequence

12. Fill the engine with clean oil.
13. Connect the negative battery cable.

➡ **Check for proper engine oil pressure immediately after starting the engine. If engine oil pressure is not within specification a few seconds after starting the engine, stop the engine and determine the reason for the low oil pressure condition. Running an engine with low oil pressure may result in serious engine damage.**

REAR MAIN SEAL

REMOVAL & INSTALLATION

1. Disconnect the negative battery cable.
2. Raise the vehicle on a hoist.
3. Remove the transaxle.
4. Remove the flexplate.

✳✳ WARNING

Use caution when working near the crankshaft sealing surface. If the surface becomes damaged, an oil leak may occur.

5. Screw in the threaded end of a crankshaft rear seal replacer tool, then use the tool to remove the seal.

To install:

6. Inspect the crankshaft seal area for any damage that may cause the seal to leak. If damage is evident, service or replace the crankshaft as necessary.
7. Coat the crankshaft seal area and the seal lip with engine oil.
8. Using a crankshaft seal replacer tool, install the seal. Tighten the bolts of the seal installer tool evenly so the seal is straight and seats without misalignment.
9. Install the flexplate and tighten the bolts to 59 ft. lbs. (80 Nm).
10. Install the transaxle, lower the vehicle and connect the battery.

TIMING CHAINS AND FRONT COVER

REMOVAL & INSTALLATION

See Figures 39 through 47.

1. Raise the vehicle on a hoist.
2. Disconnect the negative battery cable.
3. Remove the accessory drive belt.
4. Remove the oil pan.
5. Remove the crankshaft front oil seal.
6. Remove both valve covers. See the procedure in cylinder head.
7. Remove the accessory drive belt tensioner.
8. Disconnect the power steering pump and reservoir without disconnecting the lines, and position aside.
9. Disconnect the crankshaft and camshaft position sensor electrical connectors.
10. Remove the alternator-to-front cover stud nut and stud.
11. Remove the radiator splash shield.
12. Remove the A/C compressor bolts and without disconnecting the lines, position the compressor aside.
13. Remove the compressor bracket.
14. Remove the ground wire from the front cover.
15. Remove the 14 bolts, stud bolt and remove the engine front cover.
16. Remove the ignition pulse wheel.
17. Install the crankshaft damper bolt.
18. Remove the spark plugs.
19. Rotate the crankshaft clockwise to position the crankshaft keyway in the 11 o'clock position.
20. Position the camshaft sprockets timing marks in the correct position so the no. 1 cylinder is a TDC of the compression stroke.
21. Ensure all timing marks are correctly located. If not, rotate the crankshaft one additional turn and recheck the marks.

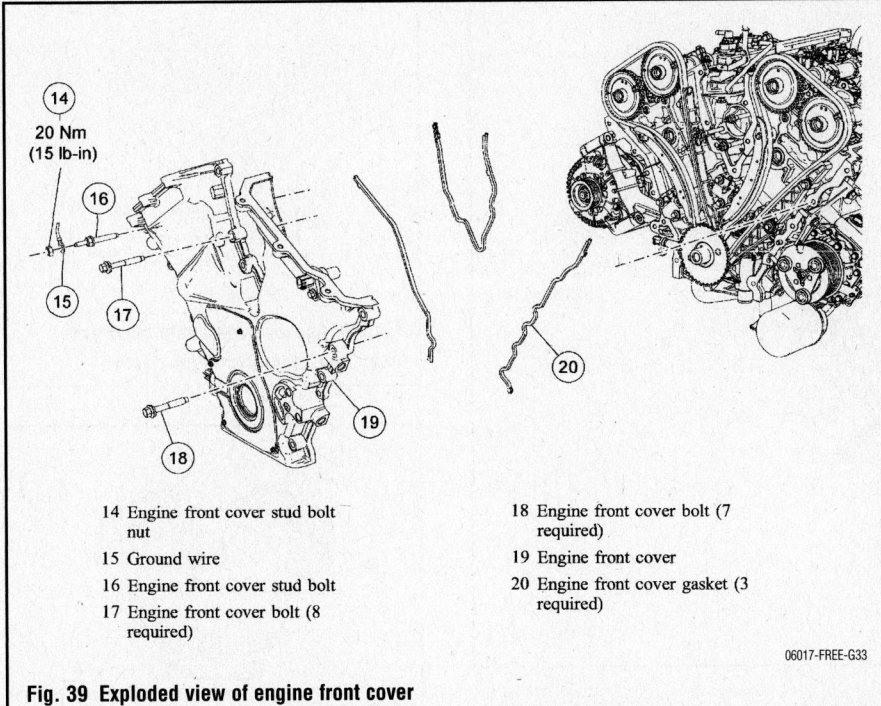

14 Engine front cover stud bolt nut
15 Ground wire
16 Engine front cover stud bolt
17 Engine front cover bolt (8 required)

18 Engine front cover bolt (7 required)
19 Engine front cover
20 Engine front cover gasket (3 required)

06017-FREE-G33

Fig. 39 Exploded view of engine front cover

33. Mark any link on the timing chain with a permanent marker to indicate the crankshaft timing mark.

34. Starting with the crankshaft timing mark, count 29 links on the chain and mark the link.

35. Continue to count to the 42nd link and mark the link. Repeat this procedure on the other timing chain.

36. Ensure the left side camshaft sprocket timing marks are still aligned.

37. Install the left side timing chain and guide and install the bolts.

38. Align the marks on the timing chain with the marks on the crankshaft and camshaft sprockets.

39. Tighten the timing chain guide bolts to 18 ft. lbs. (25 Nm).

40. Install the tensioner arm and tensioner and tighten the bolts to 18 ft. lbs. (25 Nm).

41. Rotate the crankshaft 120 degrees clockwise until the crankshaft keyway is in the 3 o'clock position.

42. Ensure the right side camshaft sprocket timing marks are still aligned.

43. Install the right side timing chain and guide and install the bolts.

44. Align the marks on the timing chain with the marks on the crankshaft and camshaft sprockets.

45. Tighten the timing chain guide bolts to 18 ft. lbs. (25 Nm).

46. Install the tensioner arm and tensioner and tighten the bolts to 18 ft. lbs. (25 Nm).

22. Rotate the crankshaft clockwise 120 degrees to the 3 o'clock position to place the right side camshafts in the neutral position.

23. Ensure the camshafts are correctly located.

24. Remove the right side timing chain tensioner arm bolts, the tensioner and the tensioner arm.

25. Remove the right side timing chain guide and timing chain.

26. Rotate the crankshaft clockwise 600 degrees to position the left side camshafts in the neutral position.

27. Remove the left side timing chain tensioner arm bolts, the tensioner and the tensioner arm.

28. Remove the left side timing chain guide and timing chain.

To install:

29. Place the timing chain tensioner in a soft-jawed vise.

30. Hold the tensioner ratchet lock away from the ratchet stem with a small pick.

31. Compress the tensioner until the piston is fully bottomed in the bore and insert a 1.5mm paper clip to hold the piston. Remove the pick from the ratchet stem.

32. Repeat the procedure on the other timing chain tensioner.

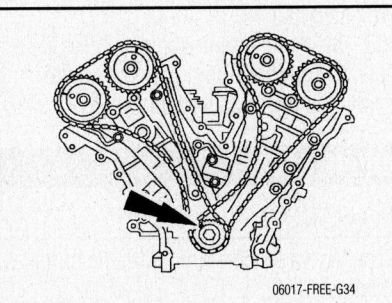

06017-FREE-G34

Fig. 40 Crankshaft and camshaft sprocket timing marks

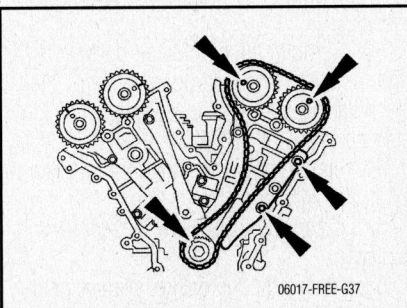

06017-FREE-G37

Fig. 43 Left side crankshaft and camshaft timing mark alignment

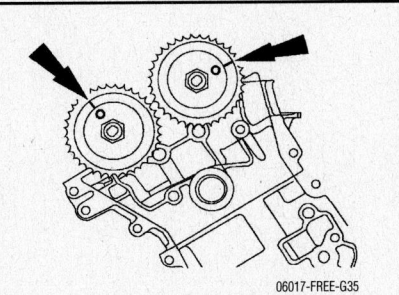

06017-FREE-G35

Fig. 41 Positioning right side camshaft sprockets in the neutral position

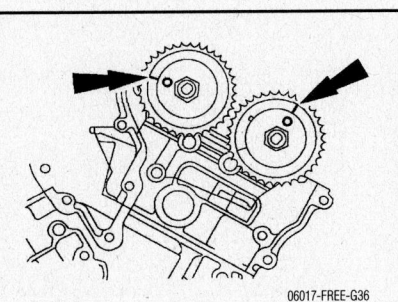

06017-FREE-G36

Fig. 42 Positioning left side camshaft sprockets in the neutral position

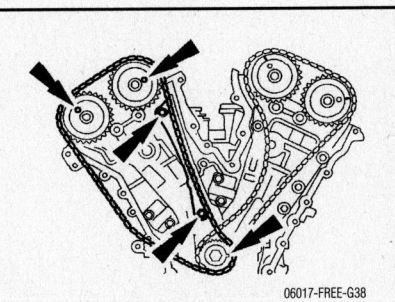

06017-FREE-G38

Fig. 44 Right side crankshaft and camshaft timing mark alignment

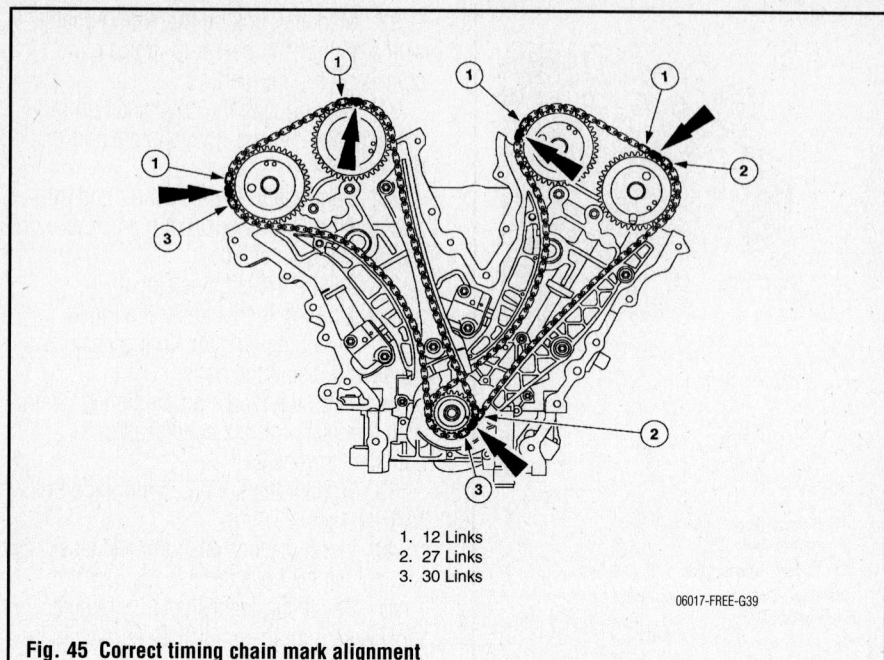

1. 12 Links
2. 27 Links
3. 30 Links

06017-FREE-G39

Fig. 45 Correct timing chain mark alignment

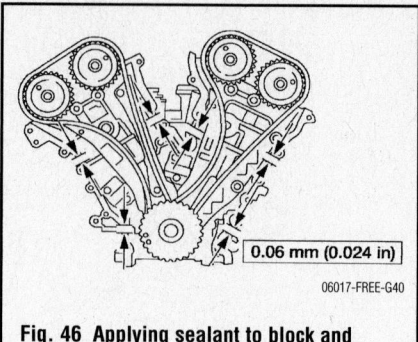

0.06 mm (0.024 in)

06017-FREE-G40

Fig. 46 Applying sealant to block and head front cover mating surfaces

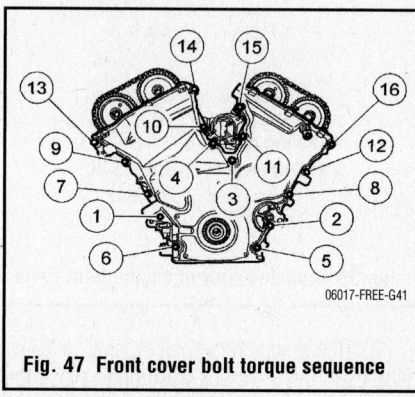

06017-FREE-G41

Fig. 47 Front cover bolt torque sequence

47. Remove both tensioner retaining pins and allow the piston to move.

48. Rotate the crankshaft 120 degrees counterclockwise to the TDC position.

49. Verify the correct timing as follows: There should be 12 links between the camshaft sprocket timing marks; there should be 27 links between the left side camshaft and crankshaft timing marks; there should be 30 links between the right side camshaft and crankshaft timing marks.

50. Remove the crankshaft damper bolt and install the ignition pulse wheel. Install the pulse wheel with the keyway in the slot stamped "30" or "30FF."

51. Install the spark plugs and tighten to 11 ft. lbs. (15 Nm).

52. Clean the front cover gasket mating surfaces.

53. Place silicone gasket sealant on the cylinder head and cylinder block mating surfaces as shown.

54. Install the front cover and tighten the bolts and stud bolt in the sequence shown to 18 ft. lbs. (25 Nm).

55. Install the ground wire to the front cover.

56. Install the A/C compressor bracket.

57. Install the A/C compressor.

58. Install the radiator splash shield.

59. Install the alternator-to-front cover stud nut and stud.

60. Connect the crankshaft and camshaft position sensor electrical connectors.

61. Connect the power steering pump and reservoir

62. Install the accessory drive belt tensioner.

63. Install both valve covers.

64. Install the crankshaft front oil seal.

65. Install the oil pan.

66. Install the accessory drive belt.

67. Fill the crankcase with the proper type and quantity of engine oil. Fill and bleed the cooling system. Connect the negative battery cable.

68. Start the engine and check for leaks. Check the ignition timing and curb idle speed and adjust, as necessary.

VALVE LASH

ADJUSTMENT

The lash adjusters are hydraulic and are not adjustable.

ENGINE PERFORMANCE & EMISSION CONTROL

COMPONENT LOCATIONS

See Figures 48 through 50.

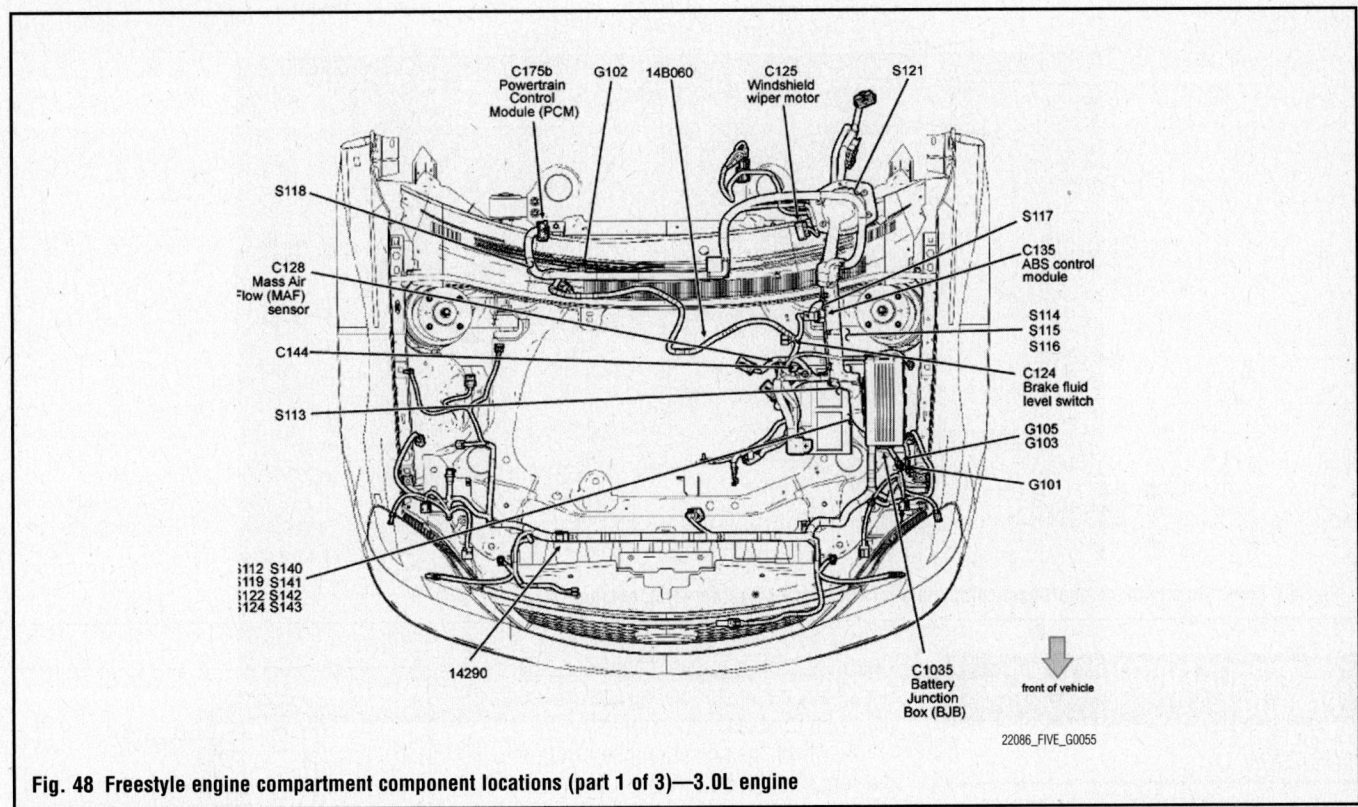

Fig. 48 Freestyle engine compartment component locations (part 1 of 3)—3.0L engine

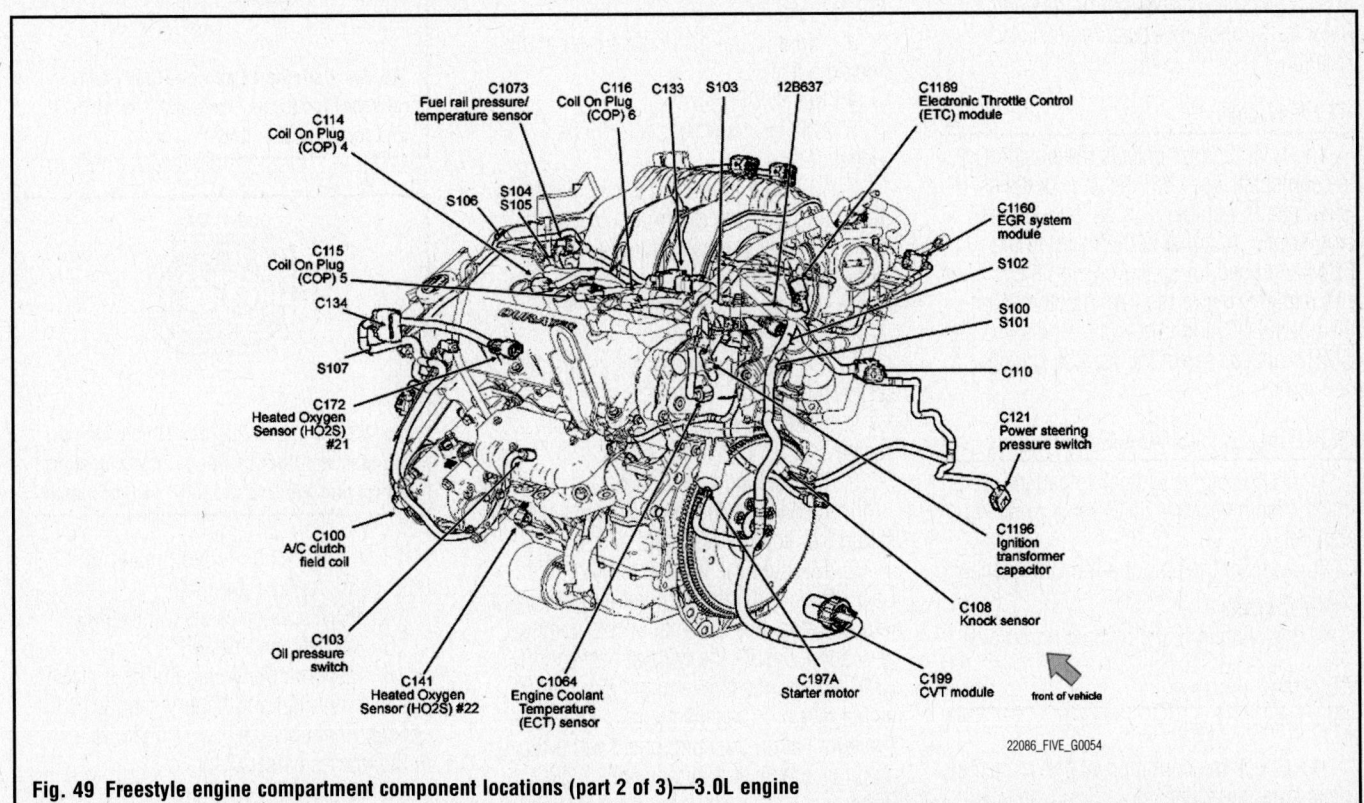

Fig. 49 Freestyle engine compartment component locations (part 2 of 3)—3.0L engine

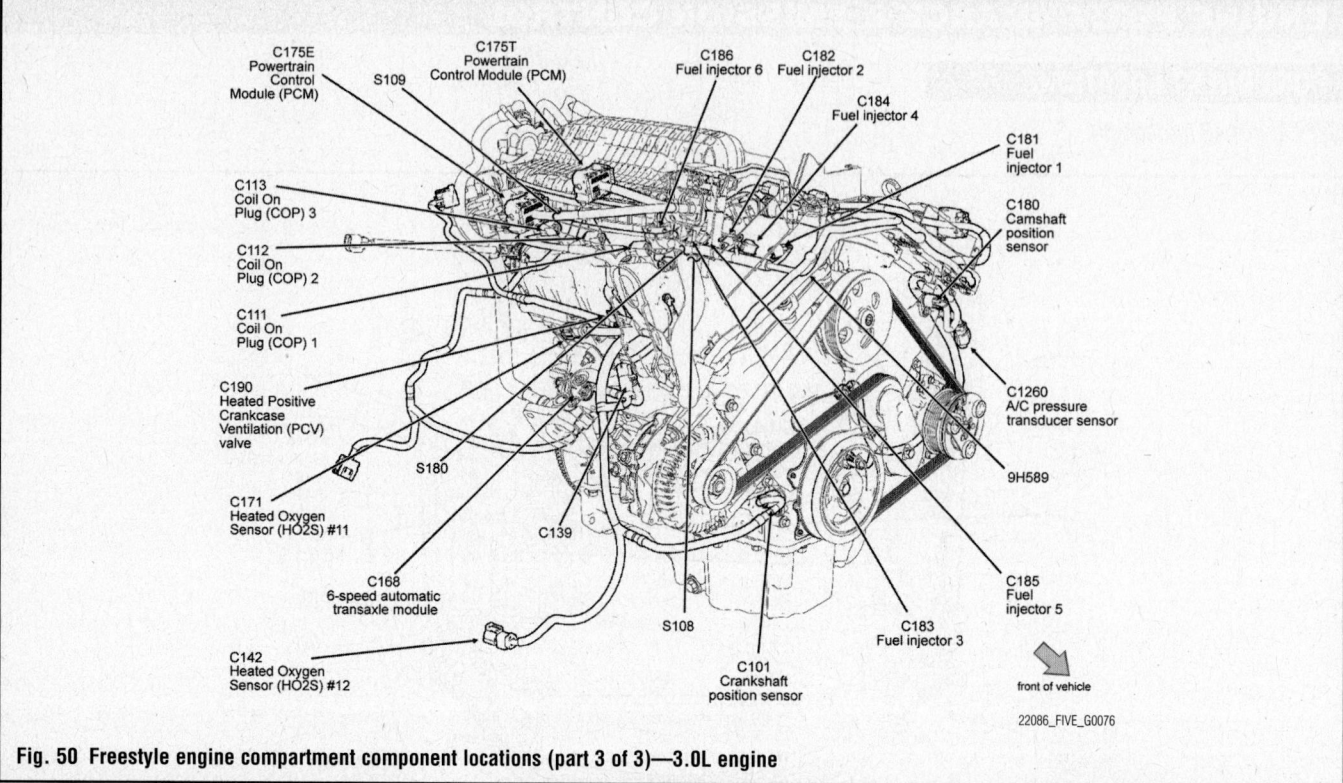

Fig. 50 Freestyle engine compartment component locations (part 3 of 3)—3.0L engine

CAMSHAFT POSITION (CMP) SENSOR

LOCATION

The Camshaft Position (CMP) sensor is located on the front right of the engine. Refer to Component Locations for exact location.

OPERATION

The CMP sensor detects the position of the camshaft. The CMP sensor identifies when piston number 1 is on its compression stroke. A signal is then sent to the PCM and used for synchronizing the sequential firing of the fuel injectors. Coil-on-plug (COP) ignition applications use the CMP signal to select the correct ignition coil to fire.

REMOVAL & INSTALLATION

1. Disconnect the negative battery cable.
2. Disconnect the CMP sensor electrical connector.
3. Remove the bolt and the CMP sensor.

To install:
4. Installation is the reverse of removal.

TESTING

See Figures 51 and 52.

1. Check the condition of the connector. Make sure the connector is firmly attached.

Check for broken or bent connector pins. Repair any connector damage before continuing with troubleshooting the issue.

2. Check the condition of the wiring to the connector. If the wiring is damaged, repair the wiring before continuing with any further tests.
3. Monitor the generator for an audible electric noise.
4. Key in OFF position.
5. CMP Sensor connector disconnected.
6. Measure the resistance between the CMP sensor signal return and VR signal return. The resistance should be between 250–1000 ohms. If the resistance is not within specification, replace the sensor.
7. Key in OFF position.
8. Generator/regulator B+ connector connected.
9. CMP Sensor connector disconnected.
10. Key ON, engine running.
11. Connect a Digital multimeter (DMM) set on low voltage AC scale.
12. Measure the voltage between the CMP sensor positive terminal and the signal return or negative terminal on the component and measure the voltage between the CMP sensor positive terminal and the VR signal return or negative terminal. or negative terminal on the component while running the engine at approximately 2,500 RPM.

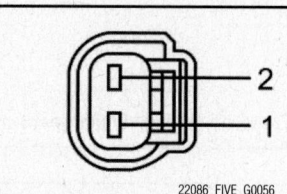

Fig. 51 Camshaft Position (CMP) sensor terminal locations. Terminal 1 is SIGRTN and terminal 2 is CMP

Fig. 52 Camshaft Position (CMP) sensor harness terminal locations. Pin 1 is signal return and Pin 2 is the CMP sensor signal

13. If the voltage is not greater than 0.25 volts, replace the CMP.
14. PCM connector disconnected.
15. Key ON, engine OFF.
16. Measure the voltage between CMP positive terminal and battery ground. If the voltage is not at least 1 volt, there is a short in the harness side wiring.
17. Key in OFF position.

18. Measure the resistance between the PCM positive terminal on the harness side and the CMP sensor connector negative terminal on the harness side. Measure the resistance between the PCM signal return on the harness side and CMP sensor signal return on the harness side. Measure the resistance between the PCM VR signal return on the harness side and CMP VR sensor signal return on the harness side. If the resistance is not less than 5 ohms, there is an open circuit in the harness side.

CRANKSHAFT POSITION (CKP) SENSOR

LOCATION

The Crankshaft Position (CKP) sensor is located just to the right of the alternator (looking from at the front of the engine) on the timing cover. Refer to Component Locations for exact location.

OPERATION

The CKP sensor is a magnetic transducer mounted on the engine block adjacent to a pulse wheel located on the crankshaft. By monitoring the crankshaft mounted pulse wheel, the CKP is the primary sensor for ignition information to the PCM. The pulse wheel has a total of 35 teeth spaced 10 degrees apart with one empty space for a missing tooth. By monitoring the pulse wheel, the CKP sensor signal indicates crankshaft position and speed information to the PCM. By monitoring the missing tooth, the CKP sensor is also able to identify piston travel in order to synchronize the ignition system and provide a way of tracking the angular position of the crankshaft relative to a fixed reference for the CKP sensor configuration. The PCM also uses the CKP signal to determine if a misfire has occurred by measuring rapid decelerations between teeth.

REMOVAL & INSTALLATION

1. With vehicle in NEUTRAL, position it on a hoist.
2. Disconnect the negative battery cable.
3. Remove the 7 pin-type retainers and the right side splash shield.
4. Disconnect the crankshaft position (CKP) sensor electrical connector.
5. Remove the bolt and the CKP sensor.

To install:
6. Installation is the reverse of removal.

TESTING

See Figures 53 and 54.

1. Check the condition of the connector.

Make sure the connector is firmly attached. Check for broken or bent connector pins. Repair any connector damage before continuing with troubleshooting the issue.

2. Check the condition of the wiring to the connector. If the wiring is damaged, repair the wiring before continuing with any further tests.

3. The battery should be fully charged and the starting system should be functioning properly.

4. Visually check the timing cover, CKP sensor and external trigger wheel (outside the timing cover) for obvious physical damage. Repair as needed.

5. Key in OFF position.

6. Measure the resistance between the positive terminal on the CKP sensor connector, component side and the negative terminal CKP sensor, component side. The resistance should be between 250–1000 ohms. If the resistance is not within specification, replace the sensor.

7. Measure the resistance between the positive terminal on the CKP_SHLD assembly connector on the harness side and ground. If the resistance is not less than 5 ohms, repair the open circuit in the CKP_SHLD assembly.

8. PCM connector disconnected.

9. Measure the resistance between the positive terminal of the CKP sensor connector on the harness side and the negative terminal of the CKP connector on the harness side. If the resistance is not greater than 10 Kohms, repair the short circuit in the harness.

10. Measure the resistance between: the positive terminal of the CKP sensor on the harness side and the negative terminal of the PCM connector on the harness side. If the resistance is not less than 5 ohms, repair the open circuit in the harness.

11. Measure the resistance between the positive terminal of the CKP sensor connector on the harness side and the negative

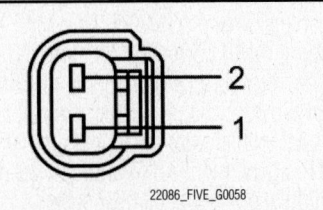

Fig. 53 Crankshaft Position (CKP) sensor terminal locations. Terminal 1 is the negative terminal and terminal 2 is the positive terminal

22086_FIVE_G0059

Fig. 54 Crankshaft Position (CKP) sensor harness terminal locations. Pin 1 is CKP negative terminal and Pin 2 is the CKP positive terminal

battery terminal and the resistance between the CKP sensor negative terminal and the negative battery terminal. If the resistance is not greater than 10 Kohms, repair the short circuit in the harness.

12. Key ON, engine OFF.

13. Measure the voltage between: the positive terminal of the PCM positive connector on the harness side and battery ground terminal. Measure the voltage between: the negative terminal of the PCM positive connector on the harness side and battery ground terminal. If the is voltage present, repair the short circuit in the wiring.

ENGINE COOLANT TEMPERATURE (ECT) SENSOR

LOCATION

The Engine Coolant Temperature (ECT) sensor is located on the rear left of the engine. Refer to Component Locations for exact location.

OPERATION

The ECT sensor is a thermistor device in which resistance changes with temperature. The electrical resistance of a thermistor decreases as the temperature increases, and the resistance increases as the temperature decreases. The varying resistance changes the voltage drop across the sensor terminals and provides electrical signals to the PCM corresponding to temperature. The ECT measures the temperature of the engine coolant. The PCM uses the ECT input for fuel control and for cooling fan control

REMOVAL & INSTALLATION

1. Drain and recycle the engine coolant.

⁂ **CAUTION**

The brake aspirator tube must be fully seated in the air cleaner outlet pipe or a vacuum leak will occur.

2. Disconnect the positive crankcase ventilation (PCV) and brake aspirator tubes from the air cleaner outlet pipe.

3. Disconnect the mass air flow (MAF) sensor electrical connector.

4. Loosen the air cleaner outlet tube clamp at the electronic throttle body.

5. Remove the air cleaner housing cover and outlet tube assembly.

6. Disconnect the engine coolant temperature (ECT) sensor electrical connector.

7. Remove the hairpin clip and the ECT sensor.

To install:

8. Installation is the reverse of removal.

9. Use the alignment notches to correctly align the air cleaner housing cover to the air cleaner tray.

10. Lubricate the O-ring seal with clean engine coolant.

TESTING

See Figures 55 and 56.

1. Before servicing the vehicle, refer to the precautions section.

2. Drain and recycle the engine coolant.

3. Remove the coolant temperature sensor.

4. Place the sensor in a container of water with a temperature approximately 20 degrees C (68 F).

5. Using an ohmmeter, check resistance between the terminals. The resistance should be 37.30 Kohms.

6. Raise the temperature of the container of water to approximately 80 degrees C (176F).

7. Using an ohmmeter, check resistance between the terminals. The resistance should be 3.84 Kohms.

8. If the resistance is not as specified, replace the sensor.

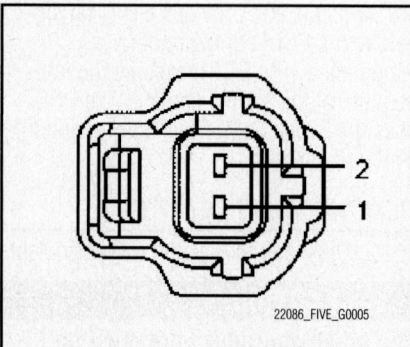

Fig. 55 Coolant temperature sensor pin locations

TEMPERATURE SENSOR VOLTAGE AND RESISTANCE SPECIFICATIONS			
Temperature		Temperature Sensor Values	
°C	°F	Voltage	Resistance (K ohms)
120	248	0.28	1.18
110	230	0.36	1.55
100	212	0.47	2.07
90	194	0.61	2.80
80	176	0.80	3.84
70	158	1.05	5.37
60	140	1.37	7.70
50	122	1.77	10.97
40	104	2.23	16.15
30	86	2.74	24.27
20	68	3.26	37.30
10	50	3.73	58.75
0	32	4.14	95.85
-10	14	4.45	160.31

22086_FIVE_G0006

Fig. 56 Ford temperature sensor voltage and resistance specification chart

EGR SYSTEM MODULE

LOCATION

The EGR system module sensor is located on the rear right of the engine. Refer to Component Locations for exact location.

OPERATION

The ESM is an integrated differential pressure feedback EGR system that functions in the same manner as a conventional differential pressure feedback EGR system. The various system components have been integrated into a single component called the ESM. The flange of the valve portion of the ESM bolts directly to the intake manifold with a metal gasket that forms the metering orifice. This arrangement increases system reliability, response time, and system precision. By relocating the EGR orifice from the exhaust to the intake side of the EGR valve, the downstream pressure signal measures manifold absolute pressure (MAP). This MAP signal is used for EGR correction and inferred barometric pressure (BARO) at key on. The system provides the powertrain control module (PCM) with a differential pressure feedback EGR signal, identical to a traditional differential pressure feedback EGR system

TESTING

See Figures 57 through 59.

1. Check the condition of the connector. Make sure the connector is firmly attached.

Check for broken or bent connector pins. Repair any connector damage before continuing with troubleshooting the issue.

2. Check the condition of the wiring to the connector. If the wiring is damaged, repair the wiring before continuing with any further tests.

3. The battery should be fully charged and the starting system should be functioning properly.

4. Check the DPFE circuit for a short to SIGNRTN or GND in the harness as follows:

    a. Key in OFF position.

    b. PCM connector disconnected.

    c. Measure the resistance between the positive DPFE terminal on the PCM connector on the harness side and the negative SIGRTN terminal on the PCM connector on the harness side. If the resistance is not greater than 10 Kohms, there is a short circuit.

    d. Measure the resistance between the positive DPFE terminal on the PCM connector on the harness side and the negative battery terminal. If the resistance is not Kohms, there is a short circuit.

5. Check the VREF voltage to the ESM as follows:

    a. Key in OFF position.

    b. ESM connector disconnected.

    c. Key ON, engine OFF.

    d. Measure the voltage between the positive VREF Pin 2 terminal on the ESM connector on the harness side and the negative battery terminal. If the voltage is not 4–5.5 volts, there is a open circuit.

6. Check the DPFE circuit for a short to voltage as follows:

    a. Key in OFF position.

    b. PCM connector disconnected.

    c. Key ON, engine OFF.

    d. Measure the voltage between the positive DPFE Pin 5 terminal on the ESM connector on the harness side and the negative battery terminal. If the voltage is not less than 1 volt, there is a short circuit.

7. Simulate the differential pressure feedback EGR sensor signal with a vacuum pump as follows:

    a. Disconnect the downstream differential pressure feedback EGR sensor port hose at the ESM.

    b. Verify the hose and port are clear and free of obstructions.

    c. Connect a vacuum pump to the downstream differential pressure feedback EGR sensor port.

    d. Key ON, engine OFF.

    e. Access the PCM and monitor the DPFEGR PID.

    f. Apply 27 - 30 kPa (8 - 9 in-Hg) vacuum to the differential pressure feedback EGR sensor and hold for 10 seconds.

    g. Quickly release the vacuum.

    h. The DPFEGR PID voltage must be between 0.25 and 1.3 volts with the key ON and no vacuum applied.

    i. The DPFEGR PID voltage must increase to greater than 4 volts with the vacuum applied.

    j. The DPFEGR PID must drop to less than 1.5 volts in less than 3 seconds when the vacuum is released.

    k. If the DPFEGR PID voltage does not read as specified, replace the DPFE sensor.

8. Inspect the EGR vacuum regulator solenoid vent for blockage as follows:

➡**When the EGR valve is closed, the EGR vacuum regulator solenoid vacuum is vented through the solenoid vent to the atmosphere. A plugged EGR vacuum regulator solenoid vent does not allow EGR vacuum to vent to the atmosphere.**

    a. EGR vacuum regulator vacuum hoses disconnected.

    b. Connect a hand vacuum pump to the EGR vacuum regulator source port.

    c. Apply 34 to 51 kPa (10 to 15 in-Hg) vacuum.

    d. If the EGR vacuum regulator solenoid vacuum not bleed off?, install a new EGR vacuum regulator solenoid.

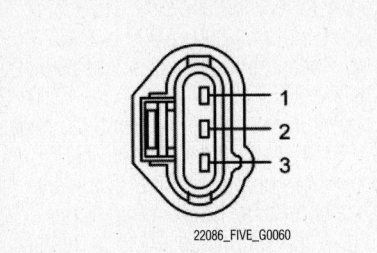

Fig. 57 DPFE sensor connector terminal locations. Pin 1 is VREF Pin 2 is the SGNRTN and Pin 3 is DPFE

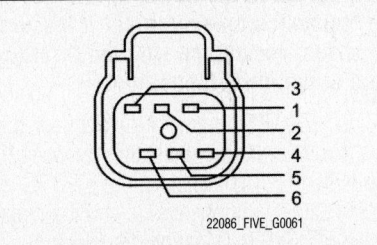

Fig. 58 EGR module connector terminal locations. Pin 1 is EVR Pin 2 is the VPWR and Pin 6 is SGNRTN, Pin 5 is DPFE and Pin 2 is VREF

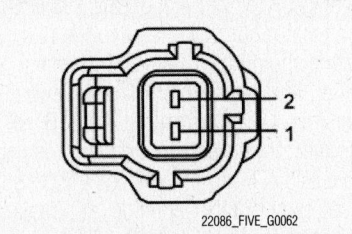

Fig. 59 EGR vacuum regulator solenoid connector terminal locations. Pin 1 is VPWR Pin 2 is the EVR and Pin 6 is SGNRTN, Pin 5 is DPFE and Pin 2 is VREF

ELECTRONIC THROTTLE BODY (ETB) POSITION SENSOR

LOCATION

The ETB position sensor is attached to the throttle body by screws.

OPERATION

The ETB position sensor has 2 signal circuits in the sensor for redundancy. The redundant ETB position signals are required for increased monitoring. The first ETB position sensor signal (TP1) has a negative slope (increasing angle, decreasing voltage) and the second signal (TP2) has a positive slope (increasing angle, increasing voltage). During normal operation the negative slope ETB position sensor signal (TP1) is used by the control strategy as the indication of

throttle position. The 2 ETB position sensor signals make sure the PCM receives a correct input even if 1 signal has a concern. There is 1 reference voltage circuit and 1 signal return circuit for the sensor.

REMOVAL & INSTALLATION

1. Disconnect the negative battery cable.
2. Disconnect sensor electrical connector.
3. Remove the 2 screws and the sensor.

To install:

4. Installation is the reverse of removal.

TESTING

See Figures 60 through 63.

1. Check the condition of the connector. Make sure the connector is firmly attached. Check for broken or bent connector pins. Repair any connector damage before continuing with troubleshooting the issue.

2. Check the condition of the wiring to the connector. If the wiring is damaged, repair the wiring before continuing with any further tests.

3. The battery should be fully charged and the starting system should be functioning properly.

4. Key in OFF position.

5. Remove the inlet tube from the throttle body.

6. Visually inspect for throttle plate obstructions or sludge.

7. Slowly, push the throttle plate to wide open and release.

8. The throttle plate should move freely to wide open and back. Repair as needed.

9. ETBTPS connector disconnected.

10. Key ON, engine OFF.

11. Measure the voltage between the positive ETCREF terminal on the ETBTPS connector on the harness side and the negative ETCRTN terminal on the ETBTPS connector on the harness side. There should be 4–6 volts.

12. There are 2 types of ETBTPS available. Look at the sensor housing of the ETBTPS on the vehicle and compare to the accompanying illustrations.

13. Check the resistance of the type 1 ETBTPS as follows:

    a. Key in OFF position.

➡**Do not move the throttle plate during the resistance measurement. Measure the sensor resistance with the throttle plate at the default position.**

    b. ETBTPS connector disconnected.

    c. Measure the resistance between the positive TP 1 terminal on the ETBTPS connector component side and the negative ETCREF terminal on the ETBTPS

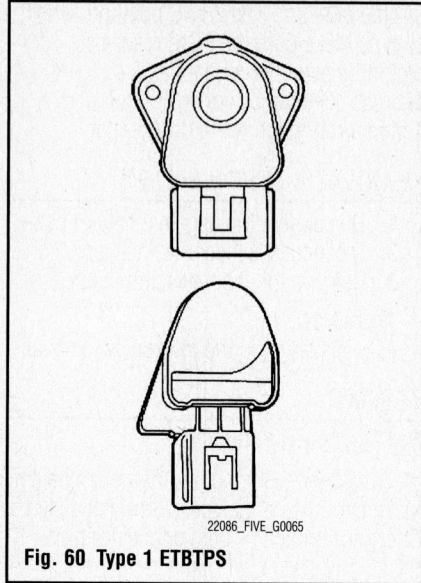

Fig. 60 Type 1 ETBTPS

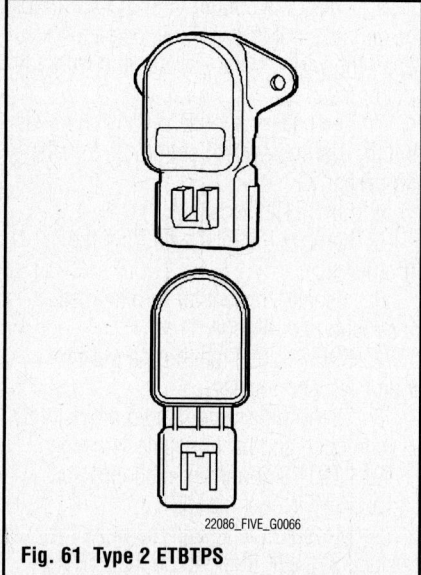

Fig. 61 Type 2 ETBTPS

connector component side. The resistance should be 1,100–3,500 ohms.

d. Measure the resistance between the positive TP 1 terminal on the ETBTPS connector component side and the negative ETCRTN terminal on the ETBTPS connector component side. The resistance should be 2,500–5,900 ohms.

e. Measure the resistance between the positive TP 2 terminal on the ETBTPS connector component side and the negative ETCREF terminal on the ETBTPS connector component side. The resistance should be 1,800–4,900 ohms.

f. Measure the resistance between the positive TP 2 terminal on the ETBTPS connector component side and the negative ETCRTN terminal on the ETBTPS

connector component side. The resistance should be 800–2,800 ohms.

g. Measure the resistance between the positive ETCREF terminal on the ETBTPS connector component side and the negative ETCRTN terminal on the ETBTPS connector component side. The resistance should be 1,800–4,900 ohms.

h. If not within specification, replace the sensor.

14. Check the resistance of the type 2 ETBTPS as follows:

a. Key in OFF position.

➡**Do not move the throttle plate during the resistance measurement. Measure the sensor resistance with the throttle plate at the default position.**

b. ETBTPS connector disconnected.

c. Measure the resistance between the positive TP 1 terminal on the ETBTPS connector component side and the negative ETCREF terminal on the ETBTPS connector component side. The resistance should be 700–1,800 ohms.

d. Measure the resistance between the positive TP 1 terminal on the ETBTPS connector component side and the negative ETCRTN terminal on the ETBTPS connector component side. The resistance should be 1,300–2,800 ohms.

e. Measure the resistance between the positive TP 2 terminal on the ETBTPS connector component side and the negative ETCREF terminal on the ETBTPS connector component side. The resistance should be 1,000–2,400 ohms.

f. Measure the resistance between the positive TP 2 terminal on the ETBTPS connector component side and the negative ETCRTN terminal on the ETBTPS connector component side. The resistance should be 500–1,500 ohms.

g. Measure the resistance between the positive ETCREF terminal on the ETBTPS connector component side and the negative ETCRTN terminal on the ETBTPS connector component side. The resistance should be 700–2,100 ohms.

h. If not within specification, replace the sensor.

15. Check the TP1 and TP2 circuits for a short to voltage in the harness as follows:

a. PCM connector disconnected.

b. Key ON, engine OFF.

c. Measure the voltage between the positive TP1 or TP2 terminal on the ETBTPS connector on the harness side and ground. If voltage is present the there is a short to voltage.

16. Check the TP1 and TP2 circuits for an open in the harness as follows:

a. Key in OFF position.

b. Measure the resistance between the positive TP1 or TP2 terminal on the ETBTPS connector on the harness side and the negative TP 1 or TP2 terminal on the PCM connector on the harness side. If the resistance is not 5 ohms, there is an open circuit.

17. Check the tp1 and tp2 circuits for a short to ground in the harness as follows:

a. Measure the resistance between the positive TP1 or TP2 terminal on the ETBTPS connector on the harness side and the negative battery terminal. If the resistance is not greater that 10 Kohms, there is a short circuit.

18. Check the TP circuits for a short together as follows:

a. Measure the resistance between the following terminals:

- Positive TP1 terminal on the ETBTPS connector on the harness side and the negative TP2 terminal on the PCM connector on the harness side.
- Positive TP1 terminal on the ETBTPS connector on the harness side and the negative ETCREF terminal on the PCM connector on the harness side.
- Positive TP1 terminal on the ETBTPS connector on the harness side and the negative ETCRTN terminal on the PCM connector on the harness side.
- Positive TP2 terminal on the ETBTPS connector on the harness side and the negative ETCREF terminal on the PCM connector on the harness side.
- Positive TP2 terminal on the ETBTPS connector on the harness side and the negative ETCRTN terminal on the PCM connector on the harness side.

b. If the resistance is not greater that 10 Kohms, there is a short circuit.

19. Check the air inlet system for leaks. Repair as needed.

20. Listen for air noise around the Mass Air Flow (MAF) sensor and throttle body while the engine is running. Repair as needed.

21. Check the Throttle Actuator Control Motor (TACM) visually

➡**Make sure the TACM harness connector is properly connected.**

22. Key in OFF position.

23. Inspect the TACM for damaged housing, harness connector, and harness. Repair as needed.

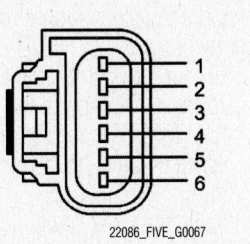

Fig. 62 EETBTPS connector terminal locations. Pin 3 is TP1 Pin 4 is the ECTRTN, Pin 5 is ECTREF and Pin 6 TP2

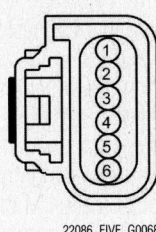

Fig. 63 EETBTPS harness connector terminal locations. Pin 2 is Tach + Pin 2 is Tach -, Pin 3 is Throttle position signal 1, Pin 4 is ETC reference voltage, Pin 5 is ETC reference voltage and PIN 6 is Throttle position signal 2

ENGINE OIL TEMPERATURE (EOT) SENSOR

LOCATION

The Engine Oil Temperature (EOT) sensor is located on the front right of the engine. Refer to Component Locations for exact location.

OPERATION

The EOT sensor is a thermistor device in which resistance changes with temperature. The electrical resistance of a thermistor decreases as the temperature increases and the resistance increases as the temperature decreases. The varying resistance changes the voltage drop across the sensor terminals and provides electrical signals to the PCM corresponding to temperature.

REMOVAL & INSTALLATION

1. Disconnect the negative battery cable.
2. Disconnect the EOT sensor electrical connector.
3. Unscrew the EOT sensor.

To install:
4. Installation is the reverse of removal.

TESTING

See Figures 64 and 65.

1. Check the condition of the connector. Make sure the connector is firmly attached. Check for broken or bent connector pins. Repair any connector damage before continuing with troubleshooting the issue.
2. Check the condition of the wiring to the connector. If the wiring is damaged, repair the wiring before continuing with any further tests.
3. The battery should be fully charged and the starting system should be functioning properly.
4. Run the engine until the engine temperature stabilizes.
5. Verify the radiator hoses are hot and the cooling system is pressurized.
6. Check the sensor signal for a short to ground as follows:
   a. PCM connector disconnected.
   b. Measure the resistance between the positive EOT terminal on the EOT sensor connector on the harness side and the negative SIGRTN terminal on the EOT sensor connector on the harness side. The resistance should not be greater than

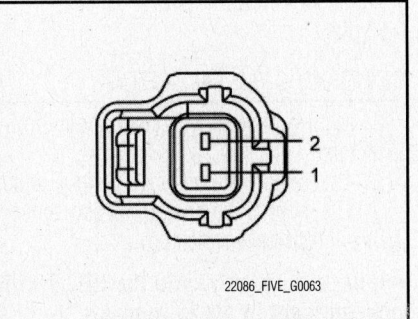

Fig. 64 EOT connector terminal locations. Pin 1 is EOT and Pin 2 is SGNRTN

10 Kohms or there is a short circuit in the harness.
7. Key in OFF position.
8. EOT Sensor connector disconnected.
9. Measure the resistance between EOT terminal on the EOT sensor connector on the component side and the negative SIGRTN terminal on the EOT sensor connector on the component side.
10. If the resistance is not as specified, replace the sensor.

FUEL RAIL PRESSURE (FRP) SENSOR

LOCATION

The Fuel Rail Pressure (FPS) sensor is located on the front center of the engine. Refer to Component Locations for exact location.

OPERATION

The FRP sensor is a diaphragm strain gauge device in which resistance changes with pressure. The electrical resistance of a strain gauge increases as pressure increases, and the resistance decreases as the pressure decreases. The varying resistance affects the voltage drop across the sensor terminals and provides electrical signals to the PCM corresponding to pressure.

The FRP sensor measures the pressure of the fuel near the fuel injectors. This signal is used by the PCM to adjust the fuel injector pulse width and meter fuel to each engine combustion cylinder.

REMOVAL & INSTALLATION

1. Release the fuel system pressure.
2. Disconnect the battery ground cable.

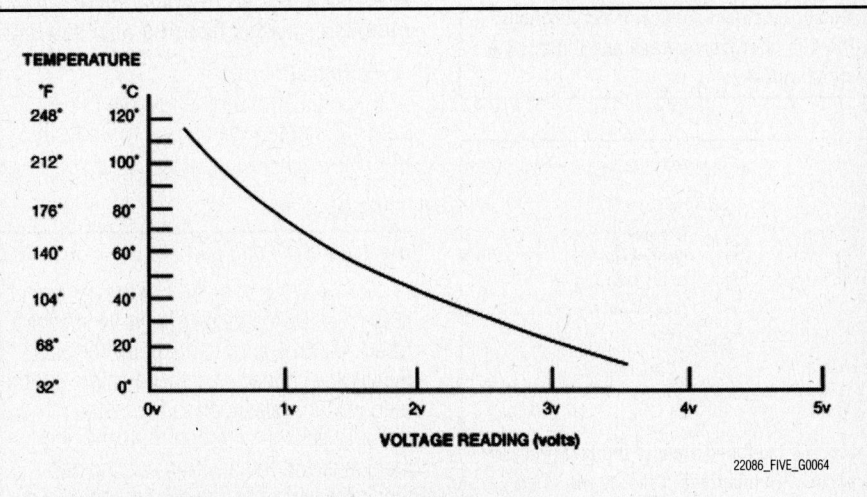

Fig. 65 Ford temperature sensor voltage specification chart

3. Disconnect the fuel rail pressure and temperature sensor electrical and vacuum connectors.

4. Remove the 2 bolts and the fuel rail pressure and temperature sensor.

5. To install, reverse the removal procedure. Lubricate the O-ring seal with clean engine oil.

TESTING

See Figures 66 and 67.

1. Before servicing the vehicle, refer to the precautions section.

2. Check all electrical connections are clean and tight. Repair and broken, cracked or loose connections or damaged wiring.

3. Turn the key on and let the engine idle for two minutes.

4. Inspect the fuel rail pressure sensor vacuum hose between the intake manifold and the fuel rail pressure sensor for air leaks and correct connection.

5. Turn the key off.

6. Remove the vacuum hose from the fuel rail pressure sensor. Inspect the fuel rail pressure sensor and vacuum hose for traces of fuel.

7. If fuel is found replace the fuel rail pressure sensor.

8. Turn the key off.

9. Connect a 5 amp fused jumper wire between the Pin 1 on the sensor harness

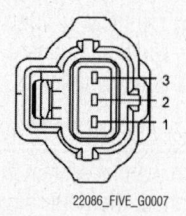

22086_FIVE_G0007

Fig. 66 Exploded view of the fuel pressure sensor electrical connector pin locations. Pin 1 is reference voltage and Pin 2 is the signal return

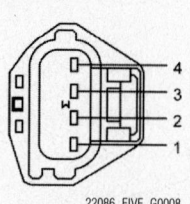

22086_FIVE_G0008

Fig. 67 Exploded view of the fuel pressure sensor pin locations. Pin 2 is reference voltage and Pin 4 is the signal return

side and Pin 3 on the harness side of the fuel rail pressure sensor.

10. If the voltage greater than 4.5 V? replace the fuel rail pressure sensor.

HEATED OXYGEN (HO2S) SENSOR

LOCATION

The Heated Oxygen Sensor (HO2S) is located on the front right of the engine. Refer to Component Locations for exact location.

OPERATION

The HO2S detects the presence of oxygen in the exhaust and produces a variable voltage according to the amount of oxygen detected. A high concentration of oxygen (lean air/fuel ratio) in the exhaust produces a voltage signal less than 0.4 volt. A low concentration of oxygen (rich air/fuel ratio) produces a voltage signal greater than 0.6 volt. The HO2S provides feedback to the PCM indicating air/fuel ratio in order to achieve a near stoichiometric air/fuel ratio of 14.7:1 during closed loop engine operation. The HO2S generates a voltage between 0.0 and 1.1 volts.

REMOVAL & INSTALLATION

1. With vehicle in NEUTRAL, position it on a hoist.

2. Disconnect the negative battery cable.

3. Disconnect the heated oxygen sensor (HO2S) electrical connector.

➡**If necessary, lubricate the HO2S with lock lubricant to aid in removal.**

4. Remove the HO2S from the exhaust manifold using an oxygen sensor wrench.

➡**Never reuse an oxygen sensor when removed, always install a new sensor.**

To install:

5. Installation is the reverse of removal, tighten the sensor to 35 ft. lbs. (48 Nm).

TESTING

See Figures 68 and 69.

1. Check the condition of the connector. Make sure the connector is firmly attached. Check for broken or bent connector pins. Repair any connector damage before continuing with troubleshooting the issue.

2. Check the condition of the wiring to the connector. If the wiring is damaged, repair the wiring before continuing with any further tests.

3. The battery should be fully charged and the starting system should be functioning properly.

4. Check for leaks at the following:
- Hoses connecting to the mass air flow (MAF) sensor assembly
- Hoses connecting to the throttle body
- Intake manifold gasket leaks
- PCV system
- Disconnected vacuum lines
- Improperly seated engine oil dipstick, tube or oil fill cap
- Exhaust leaks at flanges and gaskets

5. Measure the resistance between: the HO2S positive terminal connector on the component side and the HO2S negative terminal connector on the component side. If the resistance is not between 3–30 ohms, replace the sensor.

6. Measure the resistance between the positive terminal of the PCM connector on the harness side and the negative terminal of the HO2S connector on the harness side. If the resistance is not less than 5 ohms, repair the open circuit in the wiring harness.

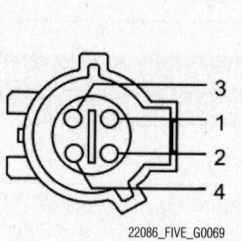

22086_FIVE_G0069

Fig. 68 Heated Oxygen Sensor (HO2S) terminal locations. Pin 1 is HO2S heater, Pin 2 is VPWR, Pin 3 is HO2S signal and Pin 4 is SIGNRTN

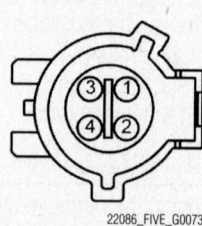

22086_FIVE_G0073

Fig. 69 Heated Oxygen Sensor (HO2S) harness terminal locations. Pin 1 is HO2s heater control, Pin 2 is voltage supplied at start and run overload protect , Pin 3 is HO2S signal and Pin 4 is signal return

KNOCK SENSOR (KS)

LOCATION

The Knock (KS) sensor is located on the rear of the engine. Refer to Component Locations for exact location.

OPERATION

The KS is a tuned accelerometer on the engine which converts engine vibration to an electrical signal. The PCM uses this signal to determine the presence of engine knock and to retard spark timing.

REMOVAL & INSTALLATION

1. With the vehicle in NEUTRAL, position it on a hoist.
2. Disconnect the negative battery cable.
3. Position the knock sensor (KS) heat shield aside.
4. Disconnect the KS electrical connector.
5. Remove the bolt and the KS.

To install:
6. Installation is the reverse of removal. Tighten the sensor bolt to 15 ft. lbs. (20 Nm).

TESTING

See Figures 70 and 71.

1. Check the condition of the connector. Make sure the connector is firmly attached. Check for broken or bent connector pins. Repair any connector damage before continuing with troubleshooting the issue.
2. Check the condition of the wiring to the connector. If the wiring is damaged, repair the wiring before continuing with any further tests.
3. The battery should be fully charged and the starting system should be functioning properly.
4. KS connector disconnected.
5. Measure the resistance between: the positive terminal of the KS connector on the component side and the negative terminal of the KS connector on the components side.

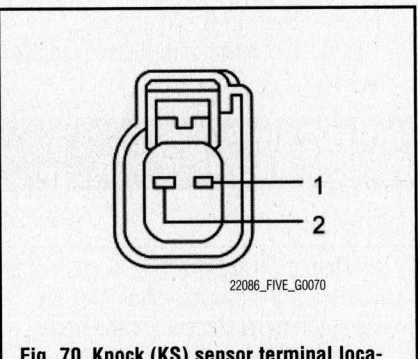

Fig. 70 Knock (KS) sensor terminal locations. Pin 1 is KS + and Pin 2 is KS −

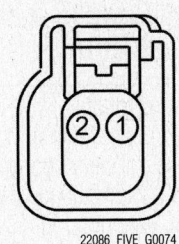

22086_FIVE_G0074

Fig. 71 Knock (KS) sensor harness terminal locations. Pin 1 is KS + and Pin 2 is KS −

If the resistance is not between 4.39–5.35 Mohms, replace the sensor.

6. Key in OFF position.
7. PCM connector disconnected.
Measure the resistance between positive terminal of the KS connector on the harness side and the negative terminal of the KS connector on the harness side. If the resistance is not less than 5 ohms, repair the open circuit in the harness.
8. Measure the resistance between positive terminal of the KS connector on the harness side and the negative terminal of the PCM connector on the harness side. If the resistance is not less than 5 ohms, repair the open circuit in the harness.
9. Measure the resistance between positive terminal of the KS connector on the harness side and the negative terminal of the battery. If the resistance is not greater than 10 Kohms, repair the short circuit in the harness.

MASS AIR FLOW (MAF) SENSOR

LOCATION

The Mass Air Flow (MAF) sensor is located between the air cleaner and the throttle body or inside the air cleaner assembly. Refer to Component Locations for exact location.

OPERATION

The MAF sensor uses a hot wire sensing element to measure the amount of air entering the engine. Air passing over the hot wire causes it to cool. This hot wire is maintained at 200°C (392°F) above the ambient temperature as measured by a constant cold wire. The current required to maintain the temperature of the hot wire is proportional to the mass air flow. The MAF sensor then outputs an analog voltage signal to the PCM proportional to the intake air mass. The PCM calculates the required fuel injector pulse width in order to provide the

desired air/fuel ratio. This input is also used in determining transmission electronic pressure control (EPC), shift and torque converter clutch scheduling.

REMOVAL & INSTALLATION

1. Disconnect the negative battery cable.
2. Disconnect the mass air flow (MAF) sensor electrical connector.
3. Remove the 2 screws and the MAF sensor.

To install:
4. Installation is the reverse of removal.

TESTING

See Figures 72 and 73.

1. Check the condition of the connector. Make sure the connector is firmly attached. Check for broken or bent connector pins. Repair any connector damage before continuing with troubleshooting the issue.
2. Check the condition of the wiring to the connector. If the wiring is damaged, repair the wiring before continuing with any further tests.
3. The battery should be fully charged and the starting system should be functioning properly.
4. Key in OFF position.
5. Check the air inlet system (air cleaner, housing, ductwork) for obstructions or blockage.
6. Check for broken/loose air outlet tube clamps (throttle body and air cleaner assembly ends), cracks/holes in the air outlet tube, and worn gaskets between the MAF sensor and the air cleaner assembly.
7. Check the throttle body bore for sludge. Verify the MAF sensor is connected. Repair as necessary.
8. Key in OFF position.
9. MAF/IAT Sensor connector disconnected.
10. Key ON, engine OFF.
11. Measure the voltage between the positive terminal of the MAF sensor connector on the harness side and battery ground terminal. If the voltage is not greater than 1 volt, repair the open circuit in the harness.
12. Measure the voltage between the positive terminal of the battery and the negative terminal of the MAF sensor connector on the harness side. If the voltage is not greater than 10 volts, repair the open circuit in the harness.
13. Measure the resistance between the positive terminal of the PCM connector on the harness side and the negative terminal of the MAF sensor connector on the harness side. If the resistance is not less than 5 ohms, repair the open circuit.

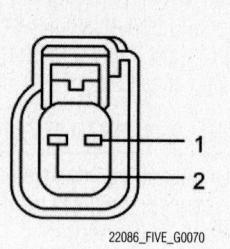

Fig. 72 Mass Air Flow (MAF) sensor terminal locations. Pin 1 is IAT, Pin 2 is SIGRTN, Pin 3 is MAF, Pin 4 is MAF RTN, Pin 5 is PWRGDN and Pin 6 is VPWR

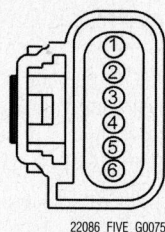

Fig. 73 Mass Air Flow (MAF) sensor harness terminal locations. Pin 1 is IAT reference voltage, Pin 2 is SIGRTN, Pin 3 is MAF reference voltage, Pin 4 is MAF signal return, Pin 5 is ground and Pin 6 is VPWR

14. If the harness and connector are not damaged, replace the sensor.

POWERTRAIN CONTROL MODULE (PCM)

LOCATION

The PCM is located in the engine compartment, passenger side, mounted to the cowl.

OPERATION

The center of the electronic engine control system is a microprocessor called the PCM. The PCM receives input from sensors and other electronic components (switches, relays). Based on the information received and programmed into its memory, the PCM generates output signals to control various relays, solenoids and actuators.

REMOVAL & INSTALLATION

1. Retrieve the module configuration.
2. Remove the cowl panel grille.
3. Disconnect the 3 PCM electrical connectors.
4. Remove the bolt and the PCM.

To install:

5. Installation is the reverse of removal.

TESTING

1. Check the condition of the connector. Make sure the connector is firmly attached. Check for broken or bent connector pins. Repair any connector damage before continuing with troubleshooting the issue.
2. Check the condition of the wiring to the connector. If the wiring is damaged, repair the wiring before continuing with any further tests.
3. The battery should be fully charged and the starting system should be functioning properly.
4. Key in OFF position.
5. PCM Power Relay connector disconnected.
6. Key ON, engine OFF.
7. Measure the voltage between: the positive terminal of the PCM power relay connector on the harness side. The voltages should be greater than 10 V. If not there is a open circuit.
8. Check the PCMRC circuit for an open in the harness as follows:
   a. Key in OFF position.
   b. PCM connector disconnected.
   c. Measure the resistance between the positive PCMRC terminal on the Power Relay Connector on the harness side and the negative PCMRC terminal on the Power Relay Connector on the harness side. If the resistance is not less than 5ohms, there is a open in the circuit.
9. Check the PCMRC circuit for a short to voltage in the harness as follows:
   a. Key ON, engine OFF.
   b. Measure the voltage between the positive PCMRC terminal on the Power Relay Connector on the harness side and the negative battery terminal. If there is voltage present, there is a short in the circuit.
10. Check the ISP-R voltage at the PCM harness connector as follows:
   a. Key ON, engine OFF.
   b. PCM Power Relay connector connected.
   c. Key OFF.
   d. Measure the voltage between the positive ISP-R terminal on the Power Relay Connector on the harness side and the negative battery terminal. If the voltage is greater than 10 volts, there is a open in the circuit.
11. Check the PCM power relay ground circuit for an open as follows:
   a. Measure the voltage between the positive terminal on the Power Relay Connector on the harness side and the

negative terminal of the PCM power relay connector on the harness side. If the voltage is greater than 10 volts, there is a open in the circuit.
12. Check for an open VPWR circuit between the PCM and power relay as follows:
   a. Key OFF.
   b. PCM connector disconnected.
   c. Measure the resistance between the positive VPWR terminal on the Power Relay Connector on the harness side and the negative VPWR PCM terminal on the harness side. If the resistance is not less than 5 ohms, there is an open circuit.
13. Check the PCMRC circuit for a short to ground in the harness as follows:
   a. Key in OFF position.
   b. PCM Power Relay connector disconnected.
   c. PCM connector disconnected.
   d. Measure the resistance between the positive PCMRC terminal of the PCM connector and battery ground. If the resistance is not greater than 10 Kohms, there is a short circuit.
14. Check the ISP-R circuit for a short to voltage in the harness as follows:
   a. Key in OFF position.
   b. Measure the voltage between the positive ISP-R terminal of the PCM connector and battery ground. If there is voltage present, there is a short circuit.
15. Check the injpwrm circuit for an open in the harness as follows:
   a. INJ connector disconnected.
   b. Measure the resistance between the INJPWRM positive terminal on the Power Relay Connector on the harness side and the negative INJ VPWR connector terminal on the harness side. If the resistance is not less than 5 ohms, there is an open circuit.
16. Check for correct PCM operation as follows:
   a. Key in OFF position.
   b. Disconnect all the PCM connectors.
   c. Connect all the PCM connectors and make sure they seat correctly.
   d. Carry out the PCM self-test and verify the concern is still present.
   e. If the concern still present, replace the PCM.

OUTPUT SHAFT SPEED SENSOR (OSS)

LOCATION

The Output Shaft Speed (OSS) sensor is located under the transmission filter. To access and remove the sensor the transmissions fluid pan and filter must be removed.

OPERATION

The OSS sensor provides the PCM with information about the rotational speed of an output shaft. The PCM uses the information to control and diagnose powertrain behavior. In some applications, the sensor is also used as the source of vehicle speed.

REMOVAL & INSTALLATION

1. With the vehicle in NEUTRAL, position it on a hoist.
2. Disconnect the negative battery cable.
3. Remove the transmission fluid pan drain plug and allow the continuously variable transaxle (CVT) transmission fluid to drain.
4. Remove the transmission fluid pan bolts and the transmission fluid pan.
5. Remove and discard the transmission fluid pan gasket.

➡ **Check the transaxle case to see if the filter pickup tube seal is stuck in the case. If the pickup tube seal is in the case it will need to be removed.**

6. Remove and discard the transmission fluid filter.
7. Use a suitable seal pick to remove the seal if it is stuck in the case.

❈ CAUTION

Do not pull up on the wire harness. Damage to the wiring harness could result.

8. Depress the tab on the electrical connector and pull up on the output shaft speed (OSS) connector to disconnect.

❈❈ CAUTION

The OSS sensor has a spacer under the sensor for the bolt. This is used for keeping the sensor a specific distance from the differential gears.

9. Remove the OSS sensor bolt, sensor and spacer.

To install:

❈ CAUTION

The OSS sensor has a spacer under the sensor for the bolt. This is used for keeping the sensor a specific distance from the differential gears.

10. Install the OSS sensor spacer, sensor and bolt. Tighten to 71 inch lbs. (8 Nm).Tighten to 8 Nm (71 lb-in).
11. Connect the electrical connectors.

❈❈ CAUTION

Make sure that the transmission fluid filter pickup tube seal was removed from the bore when the transmission fluid filter was removed. Failure to remove the seal prior to installing the new transmission fluid filter will result in transaxle failure.

❈❈ CAUTION

Make sure that the transmission fluid filter is fully seated into the bore. If the transmission fluid filter is not correctly installed, internal transaxle damage will occur.

12. Install a new transmission fluid filter and seal assembly.
13. Make sure that the transmission fluid filter is seated over one of the mechatronic bolts.

❈❈ CAUTION

Use care when cleaning the gasket surface not to scratch or gouge it, a transmission leak could result.

NOTE: Using a plastic scraper, make sure that all gasket material is removed from the case.

14. Install a new transmission fluid pan gasket.
15. Install the transmission fluid pan and the bolts. Tighten in the sequence shown to 9 ft. lbs. (12 Nm). Tighten to 12 Nm (9 lb-ft).
16. Install the fluid pan drain plug and tighten to 18 ft. lbs. (25 Nm).
17. Fill the transaxle with approximately 4.7L (5 quarts) of clean CVT transmission fluid.

TESTING

See Figure 74.

1. Check the condition of the connector. Make sure the connector is firmly attached. Check for broken or bent connector pins. Repair any connector damage before continuing with troubleshooting the issue.
2. Check the condition of the wiring to the connector. If the wiring is damaged, repair the wiring before continuing with any further tests.
3. The battery should be fully charged and the starting system should be functioning properly.
4. Check the VSS harness routing:
5. Verify the harness is not routed adjacent to any high current wires such as ignition wires or generator wiring.

6. Verify the VSS harness is shielded and grounded, if applicable.

➡ **The Variable Reluctance (VR) sensors have 2-wire connectors, Hall-effect sensors have 3-wire connectors.**

7. Check the sensor voltage as follows:
   a. Key in OFF position.
   b. OSS/VSS connector disconnected.
   c. Key ON, engine OFF.
   d. Measure the voltage between the positive VPWR terminal on the OSS/VSS connector on the harness side and the negative battery terminal.
   e. If the voltage is not greater than 10 volts there is an open circuit.
8. Check the VPWR ground to the sensor as follows:
   a. Key in OFF position.
   b. Measure the resistance between the positive PWRGND terminal on the sensor connector on the harness side and the negative battery terminal.
   c. If the resistance is not less than 5 ohms, there is an open circuit.
9. Check the sensor circuit for a short to Vref and voltage in the harness as follows:
   a. Key ON, engine OFF.
   b. Sensor connector disconnected.
   c. Measure the voltage between the positive OSS/VSS terminal on the sensor connector on the harness side and the negative battery terminal.
   d. If the voltage is not less than 1 volt there is an short circuit.
10. Check the Sensor circuit(s) for an open in the harness as follows:

➡ **Hall-effect sensors are not equipped with a SIGRTN circuit. Disregard the SIGRTN measurement.**

   a. Key in OFF position.
   b. PCM connector disconnected.
   c. Sensor connector disconnected.
   d. Measure the resistance between the following:
   - Positive OSS/VSS terminal on the PCM connector on the harness side and negative OSS/VSS terminal on the OSS/VSS connector on the harness side.
   - Positive SIGRTN terminal on the PCM connector on the harness side and negative SIGRTN terminal on the OSS/VSS connector on the harness side.
   - Positive PWRGND terminal on the PCM connector on the harness side and negative PWRGND

terminal on the OSS/VSS connector on the harness side.

e. If the resistance is not less than 5 ohms, there is an open circuit.

11. Check the sensor signal output to the PCM, hall-effect type sensor as follows:

➡**The opposite wheel must be held stationary.**

a. PCM connector disconnected.

b. Raise the vehicle to allow for the rotation of the front drive wheels.

c. Key ON, engine OFF.

d. Transmission gear selector in NEUTRAL.

e. Measure the voltage between the positive OSS/VSS terminal on the PCM connector on the harness side and the negative PWRGND terminal on the PCM connector on the harness side.

f. The voltage should rise above 5 volts and fall below 1 volt in a regular cycle. If the voltage is not as specified, inspect the target wheel. If the target wheel is good, replace the sensor.

12. Check the resistance of the sensor as follows:

a. Measure the resistance between the OSS/VSS positive terminal on the OSS/VSS connector on the component side and the negative SIGRTN terminal on the OSS/VSS connector on the component side. The resistance should be 170–270 ohms on a VSS or 400–1.25 Kohms on a OSS. If the resistance is not as specified, inspect the target wheel. If the target wheel is good, replace the sensor.

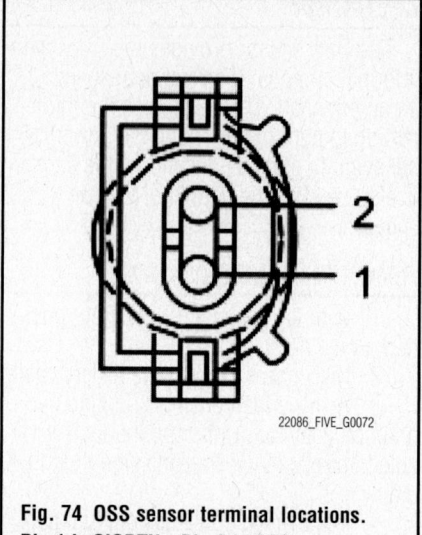

22086_FIVE_G0072

Fig. 74 OSS sensor terminal locations. Pin 1 is SIGRTN,, Pin 2 is OSS

FUEL GASOLINE FUEL INJECTION SYSTEM

FUEL SYSTEM SERVICE PRECAUTIONS

Safety is the most important factor when performing not only fuel system maintenance but any type of maintenance. Failure to conduct maintenance and repairs in a safe manner may result in serious personal injury or death. Maintenance and testing of the vehicle's fuel system components can be accomplished safely and effectively by adhering to the following rules and guidelines.

• To avoid the possibility of fire and personal injury, always disconnect the negative battery cable unless the repair or test procedure requires that battery voltage be applied.

• Always relieve the fuel system pressure prior to disconnecting any fuel system component (injector, fuel rail, pressure regulator, etc.), fitting or fuel line connection. Exercise extreme caution whenever relieving fuel

system pressure to avoid exposing skin, face and eyes to fuel spray. Please be advised that fuel under pressure may penetrate the skin or any part of the body that it contacts.

• Always place a shop towel or cloth around the fitting or connection prior to loosening to absorb any excess fuel due to spillage. Ensure that all fuel spillage (should it occur) is quickly removed from engine surfaces. Ensure that all fuel soaked cloths or towels are deposited into a suitable waste container.

• Always keep a dry chemical (Class B) fire extinguisher near the work area.

• Do not allow fuel spray or fuel vapors to come into contact with a spark or open flame.

• Always use a back-up wrench when loosening and tightening fuel line connection fittings. This will prevent unnecessary stress and torsion to fuel line piping.

• Always replace worn fuel fitting O-rings with new Do not substitute fuel hose or equivalent where fuel pipe is installed.

Before servicing the vehicle, make sure to also refer to the precautions in the beginning of this section as well.

RELIEVING FUEL SYSTEM PRESSURE

See Figure 75.

Locate the fuel pump relay in the engine compartment power distribution box relay no. 53. Remove the fuel pump relay. Start the engine and allow it to idle until it stalls. Crank the engine for 5 seconds to ensure fuel supply manifold pressure is released. When vehicle service is complete, reinstall the fuel pump relay and turn the ignition on to pressurize the fuel system. Start the vehicle and check the system for leaks.

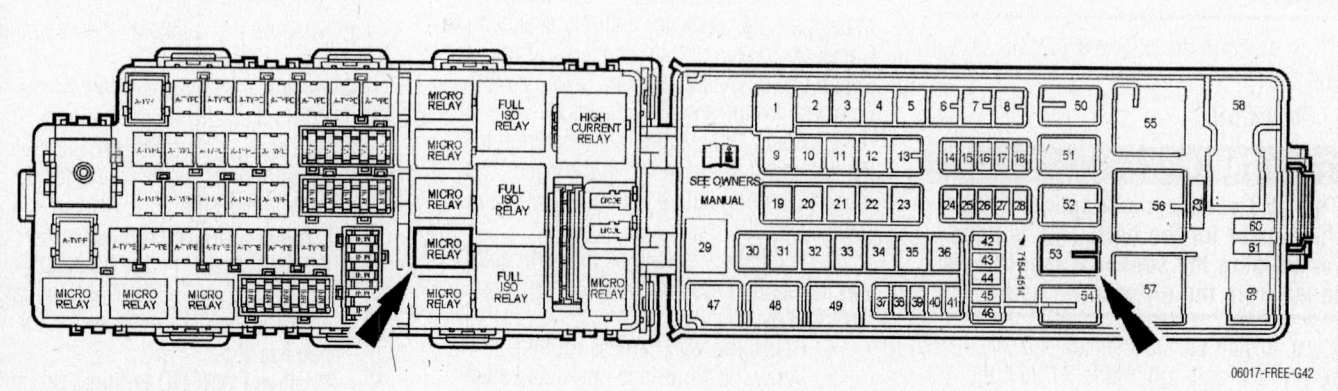

06017-FREE-G42

Fig. 75 Fuel pump relay location

FUEL FILTER

REMOVAL & INSTALLATION

See Figure 76.

1. Relieve the fuel system pressure.
2. Disconnect the negative battery cable.
3. Raise and support the vehicle safely on jackstands.
4. Place a rag under the fuel filter to catch any residual fuel that may leak out when the filter is removed.
5. Remove the quick-connect fittings at both ends of the fuel filter.
6. Note the flow arrow direction for installation reference.
7. Remove the fuel filter by loosening the retaining clamp and pulling it from the bracket.

To install:

8. Install the fuel filter in its bracket, ensuring proper direction of flow as noted earlier.
9. Install the quick-connect fittings at both ends of the fuel filter. Ensure the fuel line clicks into place and is fully seated.
10. Start the engine and check the filter connections for leaks by running the tip of your finger around each connection.
11. Turn the engine off and lower the vehicle.

FUEL INJECTORS

REMOVAL & INSTALLATION

See Figure 77.

1. Relieve the fuel system pressure.
2. Disconnect the negative battery cable.
3. Remove the upper and lower intake manifolds.
4. Disconnect the fuel rail temperature and pressure sensor connectors.
5. Remove the vacuum harness.
6. Remove the fuel rail attaching bolts.
7. Separate the fuel rail and injectors from the lower intake manifold.
8. Disconnect the fuel injector connectors.
9. Disconnect the fuel rail charging wiring harness.
10. Remove the retaining clips and separate the injectors from the supply manifold. Discard the O-rings.

To install:

11. Lubricate NEW O-rings with clean engine oil and position fuel injectors on the supply manifold. Install the retaining clips.

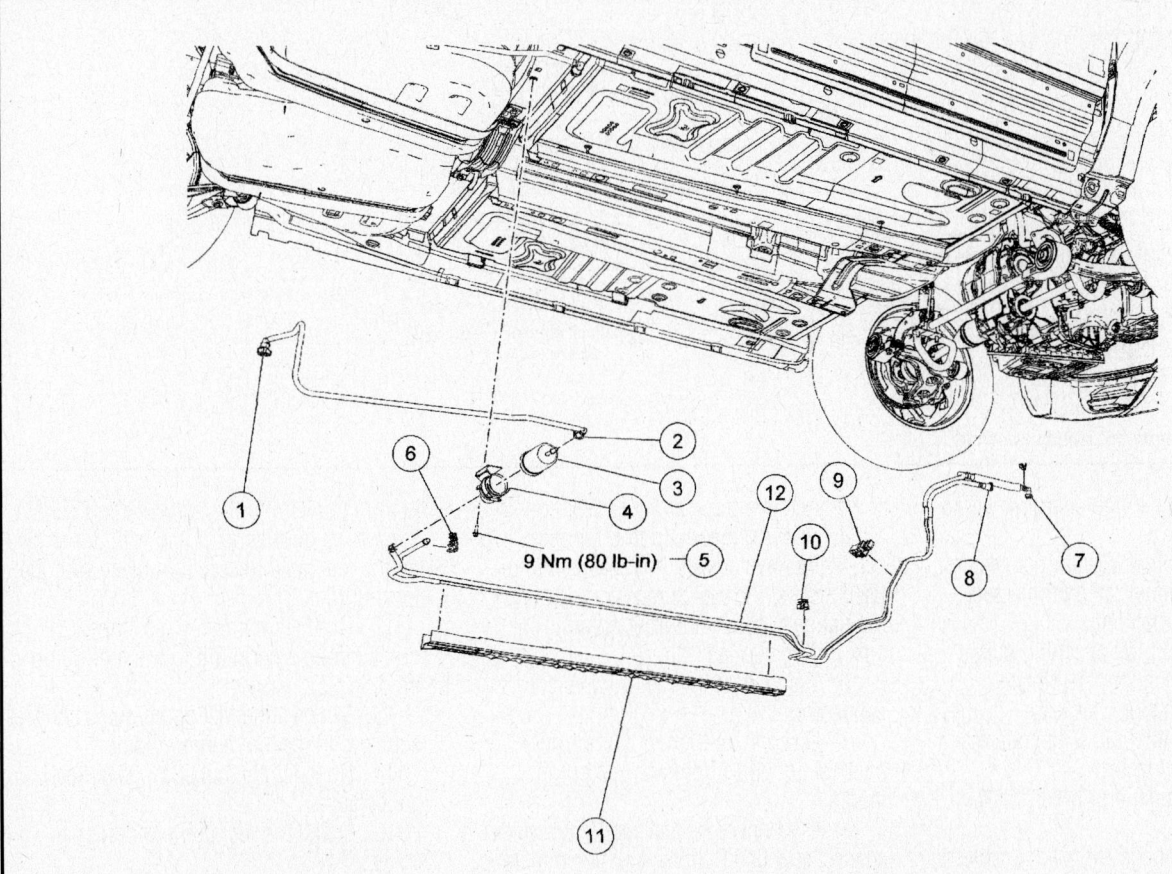

9 Nm (80 lb-in)

1 Fuel supply tube quick connect coupling
2 Fuel supply tube quick connect coupling
3 Fuel filter
4 Fuel filter bracket
5 Fuel filter bracket bolt
6 Fuel tube retainer clip
7 Fuel supply tube quick connect coupling with redundant clip

06017-FREE-G43

Fig. 76 Exploded view of fuel filter mounting

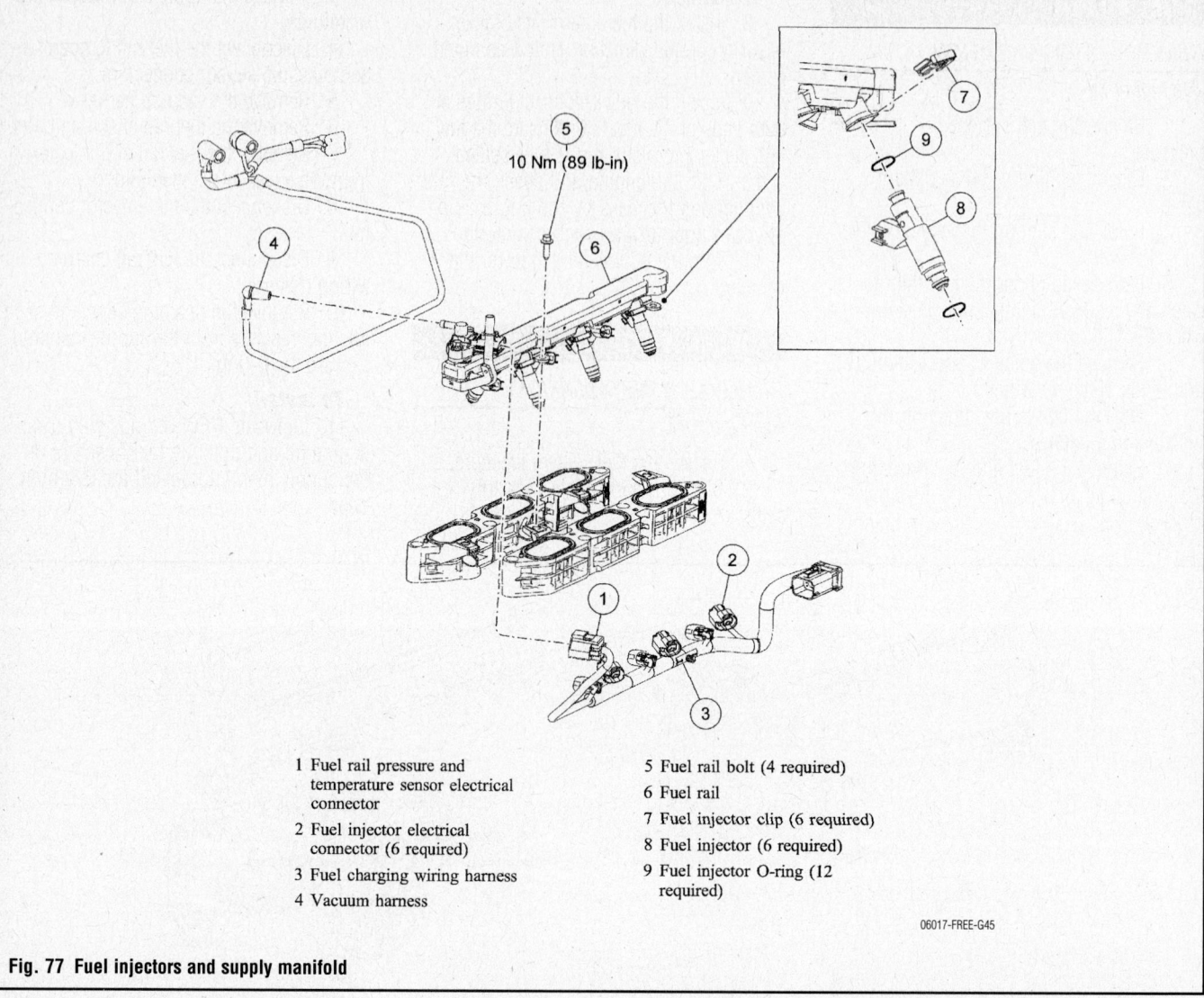

10 Nm (89 lb-in)

1 Fuel rail pressure and
temperature sensor electrical
connector
2 Fuel injector electrical
connector (6 required)
3 Fuel charging wiring harness
4 Vacuum harness

5 Fuel rail bolt (4 required)
6 Fuel rail
7 Fuel injector clip (6 required)
8 Fuel injector (6 required)
9 Fuel injector O-ring (12
required)

06017-FREE-G45

Fig. 77 Fuel injectors and supply manifold

12. Connect the fuel rail charging wiring harness.

13. Connect the fuel injector connectors.

14. Connect the fuel rail and injectors to the lower intake manifold.

15. Install the fuel rail attaching bolts and tighten to 89 inch lbs. (19 Nm).

16. Install the vacuum harness.

17. Connect the fuel rail temperature and pressure sensor connectors.

18. Install the upper and lower intake manifolds.

19. Connect the negative battery cable.

20. Start the engine and check for fuel leaks.

FUEL PUMP

REMOVAL & INSTALLATION

See Figure 78.

1. Disconnect the negative battery cable.
2. Drain the fuel tank.

3. Remove the rear lower seat cushion.

4. Remove the fuel pump module cover.

5. Remove any dirt that has accumulated around the fuel pump module attaching flange to prevent it from entering the tank during service.

6. Disconnect the fuel pump electrical connectors.

7. Disconnect the fuel pump quick connect coupling from the fuel pump module.

8. Disconnect the fuel vapor tube quick connect coupling from the fuel pump module.

9. Turn the fuel pump module locking ring using a locking ring removal tool, and remove the locking ring.

10. Remove the fuel pump module and disconnect the quick connect fittings from the bottom of the fuel pump.

To install:

11. Connect the quick connect fittings to the bottom of the fuel pump. Insert the fuel

pump module into the fuel tank and align the arrows on the fuel pump with the arrows on the fuel tank. Secure it in place with the locking ring.

12. Connect the fuel vapor tube quick connect coupling to the fuel pump module.

13. Connect the fuel pump quick connect coupling to the fuel pump module.

14. Connect the fuel pump electrical connectors.

15. Install the fuel pump module cover.

16. Install the rear seat latching bracket bolts and brackets and tighten to 13 ft. lbs. (17 Nm).

17. Install a minimum of 10 gallons (38L) of fuel and check for leaks.

18. Check for fuel leaks at the fittings.

19. Start the engine and check for fuel leaks.

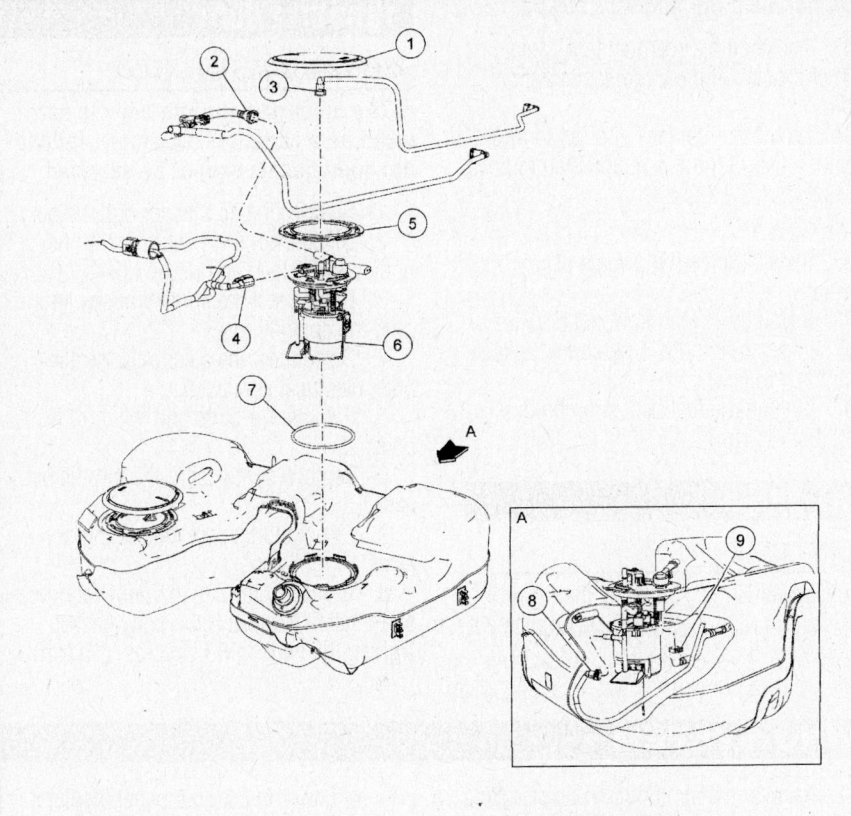

1 Fuel pump module access
   cover
2 Fuel vapor control tube
   assembly valve quick connect
   coupling
3 Fuel supply tube quick
   release coupling
4 Fuel pump module electrical
   connector

5 Fuel pump module lock ring
6 Fuel pump module
7 Fuel pump module O-ring
   seal
8 Fuel transfer supply tube
   quick connect coupling
9 Fuel vapor tube quick connect
   coupling

06017-FREE-G44

Fig. 78 In-tank electric fuel pump and related components

FUEL TANK

REMOVAL & INSTALLATION

See Figure 79.

1. With the vehicle in NEUTRAL, position it on a hoist.

2. Properly relieve the fuel system pressure.

3. Disconnect the negative battery cable.

4. Release the fuel tank filler cap and position aside.

5. Insert a suitable fuel drain tube into the fuel tank filler pipe until it reaches the fuel tank inlet spout.

➡**When the fuel tank is completely full, this step will remove approximately 1/8 of the fuel from the fuel tank.**

6. Attach the fuel storage tanker to the fuel drain tube and remove any residual fuel remaining in the fuel tank filler pipe.

✳✳ CAUTION

The fuel pump module, fuel level sensor and the fuel tank inlet spout are below the fuel level when the fuel tank is completely full. Make sure to drain any residual fuel from the fuel tank filler pipe prior to removing the fuel tank filler pipe clamp and hose.

7. Release the fuel tank filler pipe hose-to-fuel tank inlet spout clamp.

➡**The fuel tank filler pipe may have some residual fuel remaining in it after draining. Upon disconnecting the fuel tank filler pipe hose, carefully drain the residual fuel into a suitable container.**

8. Remove the fuel tank filler pipe hose from the fuel tank inlet spout.

9. Insert a suitable fuel drain tube into the fuel tank inlet spout.

➡When draining a completely full fuel tank, this step will drain most of the fuel from the right hand side of the fuel tank, and partially drain the left hand side of the fuel tank, due to the siphoning effect from the fuel crossover tube.

10. Attach the fuel storage tanker to the fuel drain tube and drain the fuel from the RH side of the fuel tank.

11. Position the second row seats to the forward folded position.

12. Release the 2 load floor support brackets and position the load floor upward.

13. Position the third row seats into the load floor.

14. Remove the 4 load floor support-to-floor pan retaining nuts.

15. Remove the 2 load floor support brackets

16. Position the rear floor carpet and any padding or insulation covering the fuel level sensor access cover aside.

17. Remove the fuel level sensor access cover.

18. Disconnect the fuel level sensor electrical connector.

➡**Place rags or paper towels in the general work area in case of fuel spillage.**

19. Clean the surrounding area of the fuel level sensor mounting flange.

20. Install the fuel level sensor lock ring removal tool and remove the fuel level sensor lock ring.

21. Carefully position the fuel level sensor aside.

22. Install a suitable fuel drain tube into the fuel level sensor access hole in the fuel tank.

23. Completely drain the remaining fuel from the left hand side of the fuel tank.

24. Remove the rear driveshaft.

25. Remove the muffler.

26. Disconnect the fuel vapor control tube assembly valve-to-fuel vapor tube quick connect coupling.

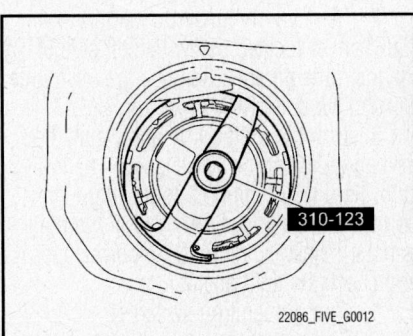

310-123

22086_FIVE_G0012

Fig. 79 Removing the fuel level sensor lock ring

❉❉ CAUTION

The fuel tubes and fuel filter may have some fuel remaining within after the fuel system pressure is released. Upon disconnecting the fuel supply tubes or removing the fuel filter, carefully drain the residual fuel into a suitable container.

27. Disconnect the fuel supply tube-to-fuel filter quick connect coupling.
28. Disconnect the fuel vapor tube-to-fuel vapor control tube assembly valve quick connect coupling.
29. Disconnect the fuel tank wiring harness electrical connector at the rear of the fuel tank.
30. Remove the fuel tank filler pipe hose from the fuel tank.
31. Place a suitable lifting device under the fuel tank.
32. Remove the 2 front fuel tank strap bolts.

➡ **Do not bend the fuel tank straps.**

33. Loosen the 2 rear fuel tank strap bolts and position the 2 fuel tank straps aside.
34. Lower the fuel tank enough to move forward, clear of the fuel straps then remove the tank from the vehicle.

To install:
35. Installation is the reverse of removal.
36. Install the 4 load floor support-to-floor pan retaining nuts. Tighten the bolts to 13 ft. lbs. (18 Nm).
37. Tighten the fuel tank strap bolts to 26 ft. lbs. (35 Nm).

IDLE SPEED

ADJUSTMENT

Idle speed is maintained by the Powertrain Control Module (PCM). No adjustment is necessary or possible.

THROTTLE BODY

REMOVAL & INSTALLATION

➡ **The electronic throttle body is serviced as a complete assembly. Individual components cannot be serviced.**

1. Remove the air cleaner outlet pipe.
2. Disconnect the electronic throttle body coolant feed and return hoses.
3. Disconnect the coolant hoses and plug the coolant hoses.
4. Disconnect the electronic throttle body electrical connector.
5. Remove the bolts and the throttle body.
6. Remove and discard the throttle body gasket.
7. Clean and inspect the sealing surfaces.
8. To install, reverse the removal procedure. Install a new throttle body gasket. Tighten the bolts to 89 inch lbs. (10 Nm).

HEATING & AIR CONDITIONING SYSTEM

BLOWER MOTOR

REMOVAL & INSTALLATION

1. Remove the RH cowl side trim panel.
2. Remove the RH lower instrument panel insulator.
3. Disconnect the blower motor electrical connector.
4. Remove the 3 blower motor screws.
5. Remove the blower motor.
6. Remove the blower motor wheel clip.
7. Remove the blower motor wheel.
8. To install, reverse the removal procedure.

HEATER CORE

REMOVAL & INSTALLATION

See Figure 80.

1. Ensure the ignition is off.
2. Remove the Smart Junction Box (SJB) cover located below the left side of the instrument panel. Remove the Restraints Control Module (RCM) fuse no. F2.21.
3. Turn the ignition on and watch the air bag indicator for 30 seconds. The indicator light will remain lit constantly if the correct fuse has been removed. If the light is not on steadily, remove the correct fuse and check the light again.
4. Turn the ignition switch off.
5. Disconnect the negative battery cable.
6. Drain the cooling system into a clean container for reuse.

7. Recover the air conditioning refrigerant, into a refrigerant recovery station.
8. Disconnect the heater hoses from the heater core inlet and outlet tubes in the engine compartment.
9. Remove the steering wheel access cover.
10. Release one side of the driver air bag module clip using needle nose pliers.
11. Lift the end of the clip over the center post.
12. Repeat the procedure on the opposite wide wire clip.

➡ **When the clips are released correctly, the clip ends will come to rest between the center two inner posts.**

13. Push on the horn at the upper part of the air bag cover and push both ends of the wire clips inward to release the driver air bag module from the steering wheel.
14. Disconnect the air bag electrical connectors, horn and accessories connectors, and remove the driver air bag module.
15. Remove and discard the steering wheel bolt.
16. Remove the steering wheel.
17. Remove the upper and lower steering column covers.
18. Disconnect the multi-function switch connectors and remove the multi-function switch.
19. Remove or disconnect the following:
- Cowl trim panels and disconnect the electrical connectors

- Lower instrument panel insulator
- Front floor console
- Floor shifter
- Instrument panel center finish panel
- Audio unit and disconnect the electrical and antenna connectors
- Instrument panel side panels
- A pillar trim panels
- Steering column cover
- Hood release handle
- Headlight switch
- Instrument cluster finish panel
- Glove box door
- Passenger air bag module connectors
- Two air bag module bolts
- Passenger air bag module
- Passenger assist handle
- Left side main wiring harness connectors
- 12 screws attaching the upper instrument panel section and remove the upper section
- Thermostatic expansion valve bolt
- Powertrain Control Module (PCM)
- Transaxle roll restrictor bolt
- Transaxle roll restrictor bar bolts
- Instrument panel cowl top bolts from both sides
- Steering column pinch bolt
- A/C floor duct
- Four floor tunnel brace bolts
- Restraints Control Module (RCM) small and large electrical connectors

20. Mark the location of the instrument panel cross beam bolts.

21. With the help of an assistant, remove the bolts from one side of the cross beam and while supporting the beam, remove the other side bolts and remove the cross beam.

22. Remove the dash panel seal from the heater core tubes.

23. Remove the heater core tube bracket.

24. Disconnect the evaporator discharge air temperature sensor connector.

25. Remove the left side blend door actuator.

26. Remove the heater core cover screws.

27. Remove the heater core cover and the heater core.

To install:

28. Install the heater core cover and the heater core.

29. Install the heater core cover screws.

30. Install the left side blend door actuator.

31. Connect the evaporator discharge air temperature sensor connector.

32. Install the heater core tube bracket.

33. Install the dash panel seal to the heater core tubes.

34. With the help of an assistant, install the bolts from one side of the cross beam and while supporting the beam, install the other side bolts using the locations marked previously. Tighten the bolts to 18 ft. lbs. (25 Nm).

35. Connect the RCM small and large electrical connectors.

36. Install or connect the following:
   - Four floor tunnel brace bolts
   - A/C floor duct
   - Steering column pinch bolt and tighten to 18 ft. lbs. (25 Nm)
   - Instrument panel cowl top bolts to both sides and tighten to 18 ft. lbs. (25 Nm)
   - Transaxle roll restrictor bar bolts and tighten to 40 ft. lbs. (55 Nm)
   - Transaxle roll restrictor bolt and tighten to 35 ft. lbs. (48 Nm)
   - Powertrain Control Module (PCM)
   - Thermostatic expansion valve bolt
   - Instrument panel upper section and 12 screws
   - Left side main wiring harness connectors
   - Passenger assist handle
   - Passenger air bag module
   - Two air bag module bolts and tighten to 80 inch lbs. (9 Nm)
   - Passenger air bag module connectors
   - Glove box door
   - Instrument cluster finish panel
   - Headlight switch
   - Hood release handle
   - Steering column cover
   - A pillar trim panels
   - Instrument panel side panels
   - Audio unit and connect the electrical and antenna connectors
   - Instrument panel center finish panel
   - Floor shifter
   - Front floor console
   - Lower instrument panel insulator
   - Cowl trim panels and connect the electrical connectors
   - Multi-function switch and connectors
   - Upper and lower steering column covers
   - Steering wheel and tighten the NEW bolt to 30 ft. lbs. (40 Nm)
   - Connect the air bag electrical connectors, horn and accessories connectors, and install the driver air bag module. Make the clips are released from the center post and back in position on both sides of the air bag.
   - Steering wheel access cover
   - Heater hoses to the heater core inlet and outlet tubes

37. Recharge the air conditioning refrigerant.

38. Refill the coolant system.

39. Disconnect the negative battery cable.

40. Turn the ignition switch on.

41. Install Restraints Control Module (RCM) fuse no. F2.21 and the fuse cover.

42. Turn the ignition off.

43. Connect the negative battery cable.

44. Turn the ignition on and then off. Wait 10 seconds and turn the key back on. Watch the air bag indicator. The indicator light will remain lit constantly for 6 seconds and then go off. If the indicator does not turn on and then off, diagnose the air bag system

45. Clear all Diagnostic Trouble Codes (DTC) using a diagnostic tool.

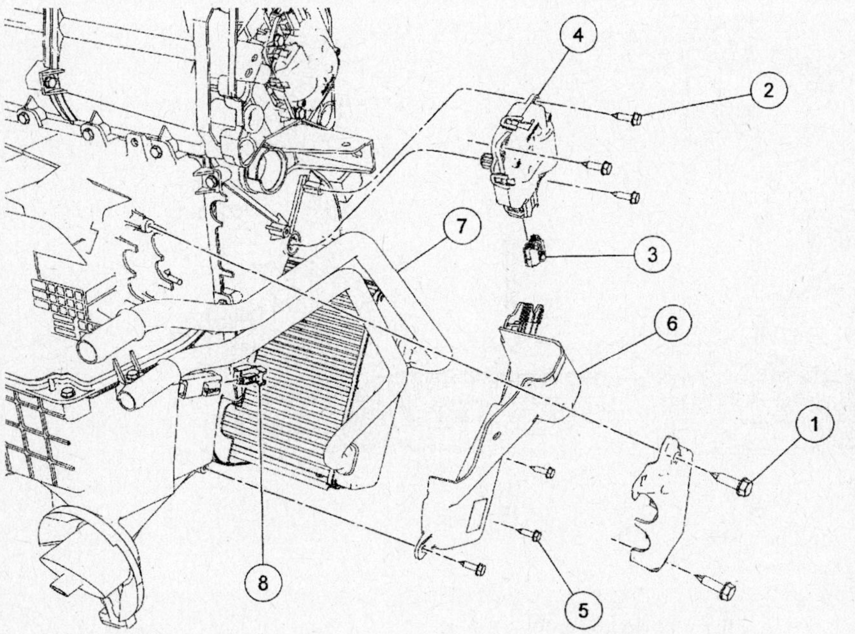

1 Heater tube bracket screw	5 Heater core cover screw
2 LH temperature blend door actuator screw	6 Heater core cover
3 LH temperature blend door actuator electrical connector	7 Heater core
4 LH temperature blend door actuator	8 Evaporator discharge air temperature sensor electrical connector

06017-FREE-G06

Fig. 80 Exploded view of heater core mounting—Freestyle

STEERING

POWER STEERING GEAR

REMOVAL & INSTALLATION

See Figure 81.

✳ WARNING

Do not allow the steering wheel to rotate when the intermediate shaft is disconnected, or damage to the clockspring can result. If it is suspected that the shaft has rotated, the clockspring must be removed and re-centered.

1. Place the steering wheel in the straight ahead position and remove the ignition key.
2. Raise the vehicle on a hoist.
3. Remove or disconnect the following:
   - Front wheels
   - Tie rod end cotter pins and castle nuts
   - Tie rod ends from the knuckles
   - Power steering line clamp plate bolt
4. Place a drain pan under the vehicle and disconnect the power steering lines.

5. Release the steering shaft intermediate boot bearing clamp and release the boot from the shaft.
6. Retain the bearing boot clamp in the open position.
7. Remove the pinch bolt retaining the steering column intermediate shaft coupling.
8. Remove the steering gear mounting nuts and bolts.
9. Remove the steering gear through the left side of the vehicle.
   driver's side of the vehicle.

To install:

10. Install new O-rings on the power steering line fittings.
11. Place the steering gear in the vehicle through the left side.
12. Tighten the steering gear mounting bolts and nuts to 86 ft. lbs. (117 Nm).
13. Install the pinch bolt retaining the steering column intermediate shaft coupling and tighten to 18 ft. lbs. (25 Nm).
14. Position the bearing boot in the retention groove so the outer bearing race is not exposed from the groove.

15. Install boot bearing clamp and ensure the end tabs do not contact the boot.
16. Using new o-rings, install the power steering lines.
17. Install the power steering line clamp plate bolt and tighten to 15 ft. lbs. (20 Nm).
18. Connect the tie rods.
19. Install the tie rod end nuts and tighten to 66 ft. lbs. (90 Nm).
20. Install the front wheels.
21. Lower the vehicle.
22. Fill the power steering oil reservoir.
23. Start the vehicle and check for leaks.
24. Check for proper wheel alignment and steering wheel position.

POWER STEERING PUMP

REMOVAL & INSTALLATION

✳ CAUTION

Do not allow power steering fluid to contact the engine accessory drive belt.

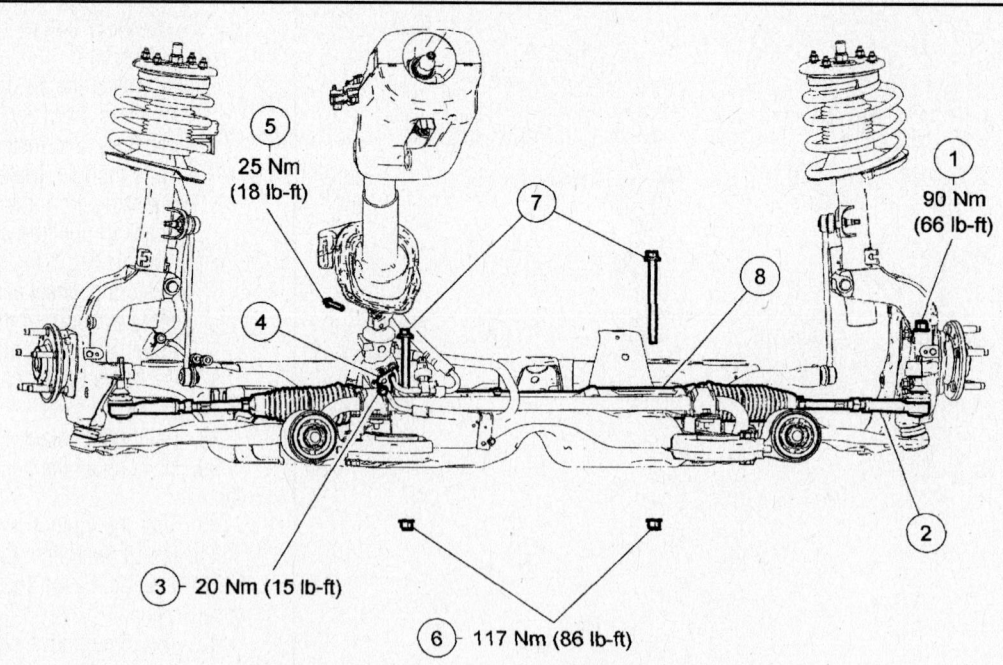

1 Tie-rod end nuts (2 required)

2 Tie-rod ends (2 required)

3 Power steering line clamp plate bolt

4 O-ring seals (2 required)

5 Intermediate shaft-to-steering gear bolt

6 Steering gear nuts (2 required)

7 Steering gear bolts (2 required)

8 Steering gear

06017-FREE-G47

Fig. 81 Exploded view of the rack and pinion steering gear mounting on the front subframe of the vehicle

1. Disconnect the windshield washer motor electrical connector.
2. Remove the 2 bolts and position aside the degas bottle.
3. Disconnect the fill sensor electrical connector.
4. Release the 2 retainers and position aside the engine wiring harness.
5. Disconnect the 4 electrical connectors.
6. Remove the engine accessory drive belt.
7. Remove the power steering fluid reservoir.
8. Disconnect the power steering pressure line fitting and discard the Teflon seal.
9. Disconnect the power steering pressure line fitting-to-pump adapter and discard the Teflon seal.
10. Remove the 3 nuts and the power steering pump.

11. Rotate the power steering pump pulley to access the nuts through the holes.

To install:

12. Install a new Teflon® seal on the power steering pressure line fitting and the power steering pressure line fitting-to-pump adapter.
13. Install the power steering pump and the 3 nuts.
14. Rotate the power steering pump pulley to access the nuts through the holes and tighten to 18 ft. lbs. (25 Nm).
15. Install the power steering pressure line fitting-to-pump adapter and tighten to 48 ft. lbs. (65 Nm).
16. Connect the power steering pressure line fitting and tighten to 48 ft. lbs. (65 Nm).
17. Install the power steering fluid reservoir.
18. Install the engine accessory drive belt.

19. Position the degas bottle and install the 2 bolts.
20. Connect the fill sensor electrical connector.
21. Connect the windshield washer motor electrical connector.
22. Fill the power steering system.

BLEEDING

See Figure 82.

> ❊❊ **CAUTION**
>
> **If the air is not purged from the power steering system correctly, premature power steering pump failure can result.**

1. Remove the power steering pump reservoir cap.
2. Tightly install the evacuation cap to the power steering pump reservoir.
3. Install the hose from the fill adapter manifold tee to the evacuation cap on the power steering pump reservoir.
4. Install the vacuum pump to the fill adapter manifold control valve.
5. Install the hose to the opposite fill adapter manifold control valve and submerge the open end of the hose into a container of new power steering fluid.

➡ **The fill adapter manifold control valves are in the open position when the point of the handles face the center of the fill adapter manifold.**

6. Close the fill adapter manifold control valve connected to the power steering fluid container.
7. Open the fill adapter manifold control valve connected to the vacuum pump.
8. Using the vacuum pump, apply 20-25 in. Hg (68-85 kPa) of vacuum to the power steering system.
9. Observe the vacuum gauge for 30 seconds.
10. If the vacuum gauge reading drops more than 0.88 in. Hg (3 kPa), correct any leaks in the power steering system or the filling tools before proceeding.

➡ **The vacuum pump gauge reading will drop slightly during this step.**

11. Slowly open the fill adapter manifold control valve connected to the power steering fluid container until power steering fluid completely fills the hose.
12. Close the fill adapter manifold control valve connected to the power steering fluid container.
13. Using the vacuum pump, apply 20-25 in. Hg (68-85 kPa) of vacuum to the power steering system.

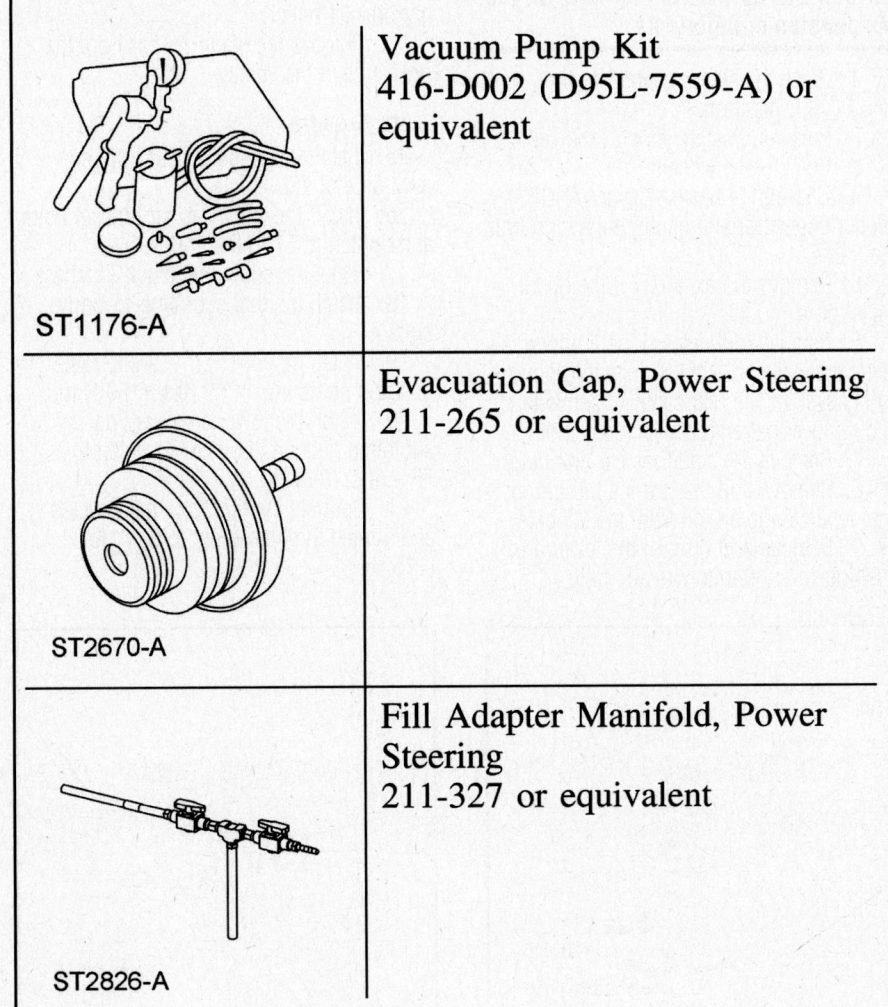

ST1176-A	Vacuum Pump Kit 416-D002 (D95L-7559-A) or equivalent
ST2670-A	Evacuation Cap, Power Steering 211-265 or equivalent
ST2826-A	Fill Adapter Manifold, Power Steering 211-327 or equivalent

22086_FIVE_G0039

Fig. 82 Tools needed to bleed the power steering system

14. Close the fill adapter manifold control valve connected to the vacuum pump.

15. Slowly open the fill adapter manifold control valve connected to the power steering fluid container.

16. When the power steering fluid has drained from the hose connected to the power steering fluid container, close the fill adapter manifold control valve connected to the power steering fluid container.

17. Remove the tools from the vehicle.

18. Install the power steering reservoir cap.

✳✳ CAUTION

Do not hold the steering wheel against the stops for more than 3 - 5 seconds at a time. Damage to the power steering pump can occur.

➡There will be a slight drop in the power steering fluid level in the power steering fluid reservoir when the engine is started.

19. Start the engine and turn the steering wheel from stop-to-stop.

20. If equipped with Hydro-Boost®, apply the brake pedal twice.

21. Turn the ignition switch to the OFF position.

✳✳ CAUTION

Do not overfill the reservoir.

22. Remove the power steering reservoir cap and fill the reservoir.

23. Install the power steering reservoir cap.

SUSPENSION   FRONT SUSPENSION

LOWER BALL JOINT

REMOVAL & INSTALLATION

The lower ball joint is an integral part of the lower control and cannot be replaced separately. If the lower ball joint is defective, the entire lower control arm must be replaced. Refer to the lower control arm procedure.

LOWER CONTROL ARM

REMOVAL AND & INSTALLATION

✳✳ WARNING

Always use new bolts and nuts on the suspension components.

1. Raise the vehicle on a hoist.

2. Remove the lower ball joint nut using a crow's foot wrench, and discard the nut

3. Push the lower arm down until the ball joint is clear of the lower arm.

4. Install tool no. 307-102 over the ball stud.

5. Remove and discard the lower arm bushing-to-subframe nuts and bolts.

6. Remove the lower control arm.

To install:

7. Install the lower control arm.

8. Install the new lower arm bushing-to-subframe bolts from the bottom of the lower arm bushing with the nuts on top.

9. Tighten the nuts to 73 ft. lbs. (99 Nm).

10. Remove the special tool.

11. Install the lower arm-to-subframe bolts and tighten to 111 ft. lbs. (150 Nm).

12. Push the lower arm upward until the ball joint is up in the arm and install a new ball joint nut and tighten to 85 ft. lbs. (115 Nm).

13. Lower the vehicle.

STABILIZER BAR

REMOVAL & INSTALLATION
See Figure 84.

✳✳ WARNING

Always use new bolts and nuts on the suspension components.

1. Place the steering wheel in the UNLOCKED position.

2. Raise and safely support the vehicle.

3. Remove the wheels.

4. Unplug the heated Oxygen (HO2S) sensor connector and unclip the wiring from the frame.

5. Remove the exhaust Y-pipe on all wheel drive models.

6. Remove and discard the 2 upper catalytic converter-to-exhaust manifold bolts and gasket for the rear catalytic converter and remove the rear catalytic converter.

7. Remove the stabilizer bar link nuts.

8. Remove and discard the tie rod nut and separate the tie rod from the knuckle.

9. Remove and discard the lower arm bushing-to-subframe nuts and bolts.

10. Remove and discard the lower arm-to-subframe bolt.

11. Remove and discard the rear subframe to body bolts.

12. Lower the subframe about 2 inches.

13. Remove and discard the stabilizer bar bracket bolts.

14. Remove the stabilizer bar from the right side of the vehicle.

To install:

15. Install the stabilizer bar from the right side of the vehicle.

16. Install the stabilizer bar bracket bolts and tighten to 37 ft. lbs. (50 Nm).

17. Raise the subframe about 2 inches.

18. Install the rear subframe-to-body bolts.

19. Install the lower arm-to-subframe bolt and tighten to 111 ft. lbs. (150 Nm).

20. Install the lower arm bushing-to-subframe nuts and bolts and tighten to 73 ft. lbs. (99 Nm).

21. Connect the tie rod to the knuckle and tighten the tie rod nut to 85 ft. lbs. (115 Nm).

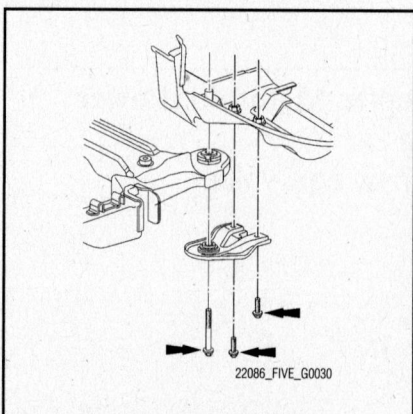

22086_FIVE_G0030

Fig. 83 Remove and discard the rear subframe to body bolts

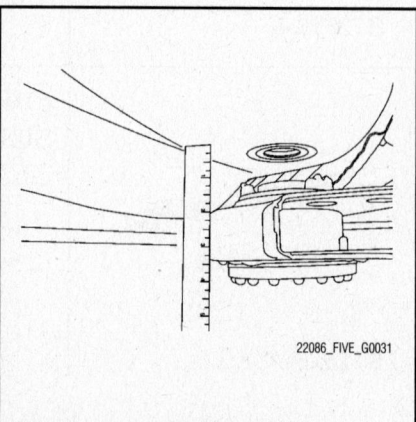

22086_FIVE_G0031

Fig. 84 Lower the subframe about 2 inches

22. Install the stabilizer bar link nuts and tighten to 41 ft. lbs. (55 Nm).
23. Install the wheels.
24. Lower the vehicle.

STEERING KNUCKLE

REMOVAL & INSTALLATION

❊❊ WARNING

Always use new bolts and nuts on the suspension components.

1. Raise and support the vehicle.
2. Remove the front wheel.
3. Remove and discard the axle hub nut.
4. Remove the tie rod-to-wheel nut and separate the tie rod from the knuckle.
5. Remove the brake disc.
6. Remove the wheel speed sensor and wire aside.
7. Remove the lower ball joint nut using a crow's foot wrench, and discard the nut
8. Push the lower arm down until the ball joint is clear of the lower arm.
9. Install tool no. 307-102 over the ball stud.
10. Use a puller and press the halfshaft from the wheel hub and support the half-shaft level.
11. Remove and discard the wheel knuckle-to-strut nut and bolt.
12. Remove the wheel knuckle.

To install:

13. Install the wheel knuckle.
14. Install and the wheel knuckle-to-strut nut and bolt and tighten to 129 ft. lbs. (175 Nm).
15. Install the halfshaft in the wheel hub.
16. Remove the ball stud tool and connect the ball joint to the lower control arm
17. Install a new ball joint nut and tighten to 85 ft. lbs. (115 Nm).
18. Install the wheel speed sensor.
19. Install the brake disc.
20. Install the tie rod to the wheel knuckle and tighten the new nut to 85 ft. lbs. (115 Nm).
21. Install a new axle hub nut and tighten to 259 ft. lbs. (350 Nm).
22. Install the front wheel.
23. Lower the vehicle.

STRUT & SPRING ASSEMBLY

REMOVAL & INSTALLATION

➡**Do not allow the axle shaft to move outward as damage to the CV joint may result.**

❊❊ WARNING

Always use new bolts and nuts on the suspension components.

1. Turn the ignition switch **OFF** and place the steering column in the unlocked position.
2. Loosen the strut/spring upper mounting nuts.
3. Raise the vehicle on a hoist.
4. Remove or disconnect the following:
   • Front wheel
   • Front wheel axle hub nut and discard
   • Tie rod-to-wheel knuckle nut
   • Separate the tie rod from the knuckle
   • Brake disc
   • Wheel speed sensor and wire aside
   • Lower ball joint nut using a crow's foot wrench, and discard the nut
5. Push the lower arm down until the ball joint is clear of the lower arm.
6. Install tool no. 307-102 over the ball stud.
7. Use a puller and press the halfshaft from the wheel hub and support the half-shaft level.
8. Remove and discard the strut upper mounting nuts.
9. Remove the wheel knuckle and strut as an assembly.
10. Remove and discard the knuckle-to-strut bolt and nut.
11. Separate the spring/strut assembly from the knuckle.

To install:

12. Place the strut/spring assembly in the steering knuckle.
13. Using a new bolt and nut, tighten the strut-to-knuckle bolt to 129 ft. lbs. (175 Nm).
14. Install the strut/knuckle in the vehicle and loosely tighten the new top mounting nuts.
15. Install the halfshaft in the wheel hub.
16. Remove the ball stud tool and connect the ball joint to the lower control arm
17. Install a new ball joint nut and tighten to 85 ft. lbs. (115 Nm).
18. Install the wheel speed sensor.
19. Install the brake disc.
20. Install the tie rod to the wheel knuckle and tighten the new nut to 85 ft. lbs. (115 Nm).
21. Install a new axle hub nut and tighten to 148 ft. lbs. (200 Nm).
22. Install the front wheel.
23. Lower the vehicle.
24. Tighten the upper strut nuts to 18 ft. lbs. (25 Nm).
25. Check the wheel alignment.

OVERHAUL

See Figures 85 and 86.

1. Using a spring compressor, compress the spring and loosen the strut rod nut.
2. Compress the spring until all tension is relieved.
3. Remove the strut rod appearance cap.
4. Remove and discard the upper strut rod nut.
5. Separate the strut, spring mount and washer.
6. Remove the spring.
7. To maintain wheel camber, position the notch and arrow on the upper strut mount outboard opposite the locator tab on the strut.
8. To adjust camber +0.5 degrees, position the notch and arrow on the upper strut mount inboard aligned with the locator tab on the strut.
9. To reassemble, reverse the disassembly procedure. Make sure the spring is correctly seated in both spring seats. Tighten the new strut top retaining nut to 59 ft. lbs. (80 Nm).

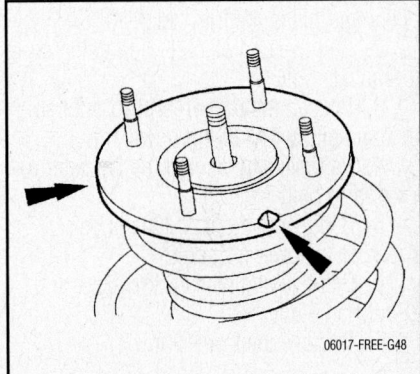

06017-FREE-G48

Fig. 85 Positioning upper strut mount outboard to maintain wheel camber

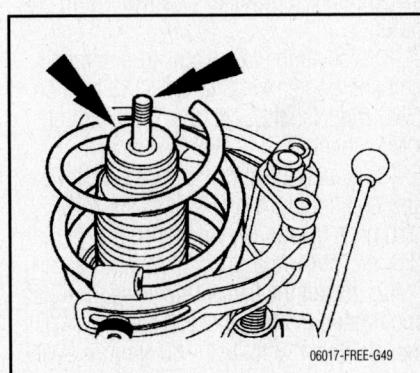

06017-FREE-G49

Fig. 86 Positioning upper strut mount inboard to adjust wheel camber +0.5 degrees

WHEEL HUB AND BEARING

REMOVAL & INSTALLATION

See Figure 87.

The wheel bearing is integral with the wheel hub and cannot be replaced separately. If the wheel bearing is found to be defective, the wheel hub must be replaced as an assembly.

✳ WARNING

Always use new bolts and nuts on the suspension components.

1. Raise and safely support the vehicle.
2. Remove the wheel and tire assembly.
3. Remove the steering knuckle.
4. Remove and discard the wheel hub-to-knuckle bolts and separate the knuckle from the hub.

To install:

5. Clean the steering knuckle bore.
6. Install the wheel hub-to-the steering knuckle.
7. Install the wheel hub-to-knuckle bolts and tighten to 81 ft. lbs. (110 Nm).
8. Install the steering knuckle.
9. Install the wheel and tire.

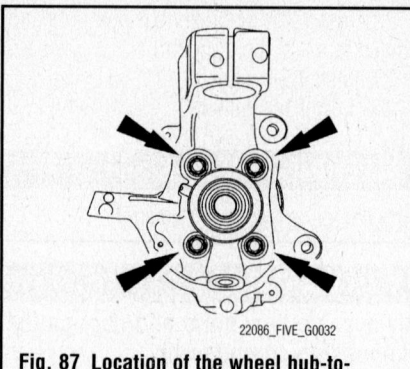

22086_FIVE_G0032

Fig. 87 Location of the wheel hub-to-knuckle bolts

SUSPENSION

LOWER CONTROL ARM

REMOVAL & INSTALLATION

✳ WARNING

Always use new bolts and nuts on the suspension components.

1. Measure the distance between the top of the wheel and the bottom of the wheel opening. This is the trim height.
2. Remove and discard the trailing arm-to-knuckle bolt.
3. Loosen the trailing arm-to-subframe bolt and allow it to swing down.
4. Remove and discard the knuckle-to-lower arm bolt.
5. Remove and discard the shock absorber-to-lower arm bolt.
6. Remove and discard the lower arm-to-subframe bolt.
7. Remove the lower arm.

To install:

8. Install the lower control arm.
9. Use a jack and raise the suspension to the trim height previously measured before tightening the lower arm bolts.
10. Install the lower arm-to-subframe bolt and tighten to 98 ft. lbs. (133 Nm) on AWD models and 92 ft. lbs. (125 Nm) on 2WD models.
11. Install the shock absorber-to-lower arm bolt and tighten to 105 ft. lbs. (142 Nm) on AWD models and 81 ft. lbs. (110 Nm) on 2WD models.
12. Install the knuckle-to-lower arm bolt and tighten to 66 ft. lbs. (90 Nm) on AWD models and 118 ft. lbs. (160 Nm) on 2WD models.
13. Bring the trailing arm up and tighten the trailing arm-to-subframe bolt and tighten the bolt to 81 ft. lbs. (110 Nm).

14. Install the trailing arm-to-knuckle bolt and tighten the bolt to 77 ft. lbs. (105 Nm).

REAR KNUCKLE

REMOVAL & INSTALLATION

✳ WARNING

Always use new bolts and nuts on the suspension components.

1. Measure the distance between the top of the wheel and the bottom of the wheel opening. This is the trim height.
2. Remove the wheel hub and bearing assembly.
3. Remove the brake dust shield.
4. Remove and discard the trailing arm-to-knuckle bolt.
5. Remove the toe link-to-knuckle bolt and nut.
6. Remove and discard the shock absorber-to-lower arm bolt.
7. Remove and discard the lower arm-to-subframe bolt.
8. Remove and discard the upper arm-to-subframe bolt.
9. Remove the steering knuckle.

To install:

10. Install the wheel knuckle.
11. Use a jack and raise the suspension to the trim height previously measured before tightening the upper and lower arm bolts.
12. Install the upper arm-to-subframe bolt and tighten to 81 ft. lbs. (110 Nm).
13. Install the lower arm-to-subframe bolt and tighten to 98 ft. lbs. (133 Nm) on AWD models, and 92 ft. lbs. (125 Nm) on 2WD models.
14. Install the shock absorber-to-lower arm bolt and tighten to 105 ft. lbs. (142

REAR SUSPENSION

Nm) on AWD models, and 81 ft. lbs. (110 Nm) on 2WD models.

15. Install the toe link-to-knuckle bolt and nut and tighten to 74 ft. lbs. (100 Nm).
16. Install the trailing arm-to-knuckle bolt and tighten to 77 ft. lbs. (105 Nm).
17. Install the brake dust shield.
18. Install the wheel hub and bearing assembly.

SHOCK & SPRING ASSEMBLY

REMOVAL & INSTALLATION

See Figure 88.

✳ WARNING

Always use new bolts and nuts on the suspension components.

1. Measure the distance between the top of the wheel and the bottom of the wheel opening. This is the trim height.
2. Loosen the lug nuts on the rear wheels.
3. Remove the interior trim panel to access the upper shock nut, then remove and discard the nut.
4. Raise the vehicle on a hoist.
5. Remove the rear wheels.
6. Remove the brake caliper and wire aside.
7. Position a jack under the wheel knuckle at the trailing arm and knuckle attachment point.
8. Raise the wheel knuckle until the toe link is parallel to the ground.
9. Remove and discard the trailing arm-to-knuckle bolt.
10. Lower the suspension jack.
11. Remove and discard the trailing arm-to-subframe bolt.

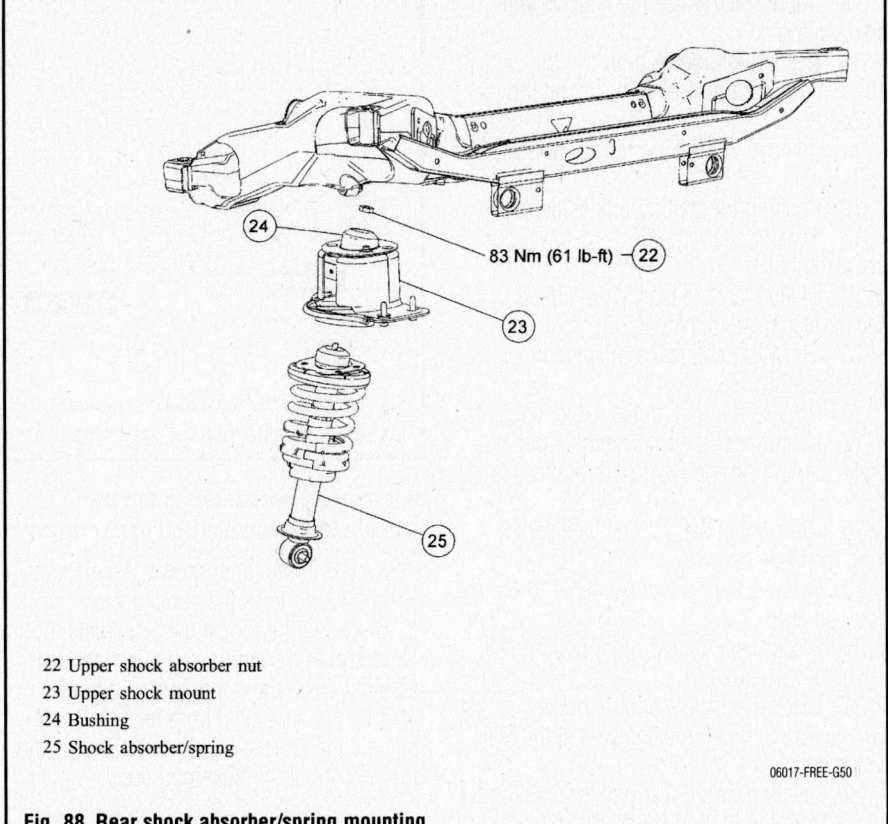

22 Upper shock absorber nut
23 Upper shock mount
24 Bushing
25 Shock absorber/spring

83 Nm (61 lb-ft) — 22

06017-FREE-G50

Fig. 88 Rear shock absorber/spring mounting

12. Position a jack under the lower shock mount and raise it enough to compress the spring.

13. Remove and discard the lower arm-to-knuckle bolt.

14. Remove and discard the lower arm-to-subframe bolt.

15. Remove and discard the lower shock mounting bolt.

16. Hold the shock absorber and swing the lower arm down to access and remove the shock/spring assembly.

To install:

17. Tape the spring to the upper spring seat.

18. Position the spring and upper rubber seat on the shock.

19. Install a new lower arm-to-knuckle bolt in the lower arm.

20. Position a jack under the lower arm.

21. Install the shock/spring assembly into alignment with the upper mount.

22. Swing the lower arm into position under the shock/spring assembly.

23. Remove the jack.

24. Partially lower the hoist.

25. Place a floor jack under the lower arm at the lowest point.

26. Raise the jack until the top of the shock makes contact with the inside surface of the upper mount.

27. With the help of an assistant guiding the shock assembly, raise the jack until the shock seats in the upper mount.

28. Install a new top nut and tighten to 61 ft. lbs. (83 Nm).

29. Remove the floor jack.

30. Raise the vehicle.

31. Position a jack under the wheel knuckle at the trailing arm and knuckle attachment point.

32. Remove the lower arm bolt, install the shock/spring in the lower arm and install the bolt.

33. Loosen the lower arm-to-subframe bolt. Raise the jack under the center of the wheel hub is at the proper trim height.

34. Tighten the lower arm-to-subframe bolt to 92 ft. lbs. (125 Nm).

35. Tighten the lower arm-to-knuckle bolt to 81 ft. lbs. (110 Nm).

36. Position the trailing arm to the knuckle and loosely install the bolt.

37. Place a jack under the lower arm and raise it until the trailing arm and subframe bushing are aligned.

38. Install a new trailing arm-to-subframe bolt and tighten to 81 ft. lbs. (100 Nm).

39. Install the trailing arm-to-knuckle bolt and tighten to 77 ft. lbs. (105 Nm).

40. Install the brake caliper.

41. Install the wheel.

42. Lower the vehicle.

STABILIZER BAR

REMOVAL & INSTALLATION

Front Wheel Drive

❊❊ WARNING

Always use new bolts and nuts on the suspension components.

1. Separate the exhaust system from the flexpipe and support the exhaust system.

2. Remove and discard the stabilizer bar link-to-stabilizer bar nuts.

3. Remove and discard the stabilizer bar bracket-to-subframe bolts.

4. Remove the stabilizer bar.

To install:

5. Reverse the removal procedure. Tighten the stabilizer bar bracket-to-subframe bolts to 43 ft. lbs. (58 Nm).

All Wheel Drive

❊❊ WARNING

Always use new bolts and nuts on the suspension components.

1. Separate the exhaust system from the flexpipe and support the exhaust system.

2. Raise and support the vehicle.

3. Remove the rear wheels.

4. Remove the brake calipers and wire aside.

5. Remove both rear axles nuts and discard.

6. Using a hub remover, press the axle shaft from the wheel hub.

7. Remove and discard both upper arm-to- knuckle bolts.

8. Remove and discard both trailing arm-to-knuckle bolts and loosen the trailing arm-to-subframe bolt.

9. Remove and discard the lower shock-to-lower arm nuts and remove it from the lower arm.

10. Loosen both toe link-to-subframe bolts and allow the wheel knuckles to hang in a downward position.

11. Remove the rear subframe cross brace bolts and cross brace.

12. Remove and discard the stabilizer bar link-to-stabilizer bar nuts.

13. Remove and discard the stabilizer bar bracket-to-subframe bolts.

14. Remove the stabilizer bar.

To install:

15. Install the stabilizer bar.

16. Install the stabilizer bar bracket-to-subframe bolts and tighten to 43 ft. lbs. (58 Nm).

17. Install the stabilizer bar link-to-stabilizer bar nuts.

18. Install the rear subframe cross brace and bolts and tighten to 46 ft. lbs. (63 Nm).

19. Bring the wheel knuckles up and tighten both toe link-to-subframe bolts to 74 ft. lbs. (100 Nm).

20. Install the shock to the lower arm and tighten the lower shock-to-lower arm nuts to 105 ft. lbs. (142 Nm).

21. Install both trailing arm-to-knuckle bolts and tighten them and the trailing arm-to-subframe bolt to 77 ft. lbs. (110 Nm).

22. Install both upper arm-to- knuckle bolts and tighten to 77 ft. lbs. (105 Nm).

23. Install the axle shaft into the wheel hub.

24. Install new axle shaft nuts and tighten to 148 ft. lbs. (200 Nm).

25. Install the brake calipers.

26. Install the rear wheels.

27. Install the exhaust system to the flex pipe.

28. Lower the vehicle.

UPPER CONTROL ARM

REMOVAL & INSTALLATION

See Figures 89 through 94.

✳✳ WARNING

Always use new bolts and nuts on the suspension components.

1. Measure the distance between the top of the wheel and the bottom of the wheel opening. This is the trim height.

2. Remove the rear wheels.

3. With a wax pencil, mark the relational alignment of the rear subframe to the underbody at the mounting locations.

4. Remove the 2 catalytic converter nuts.

5. Disconnect the muffler and tailpipe assembly from the isolators.

6. Remove the catalytic converter, muffler and tailpipe assembly.

➡**Index the driveshaft before disconnecting from the rear drive axle. It is necessary to install new driveshaft bolts during installation. Reuse of the driveshaft bolts is not recommended.**

7. Remove the 6 driveshaft bolts.

8. Loosen the trailing link-to-subframe bolts.

9. Support and raise the knuckle with a suitable jack.

10. Raise the knuckle until the tilt angle of the trailing link is horizontal to the body.

11. Remove the trailing link-to-knuckle bolts.

12. Position the trailing link aside.

13. Remove the rear shock-to-lower control arm bolts.

14. Disconnect the rear wheel speed sensor electrical connectors.

15. On AWD vehicles, remove the rear axle assembly.

16. Release the park brake cable tension.

17. Disconnect the intermediate park brake cable from the front park brake cable.

18. Disconnect the intermediate cable from the body bracket.

19. Remove the park brake cable-to-body bracket.

20. Disconnect the rear park brake cables at the equalizer.

21. Disconnect the rear park brake cables from the park brake levers at the rear calipers.

22. Disconnect the rear park brake cables from the park brake brackets.

23. Remove the rear brake caliper pins.

24. Remove the rear calipers and the rear caliper brackets and attach aside to the body with mechanic's wire. It is not necessary to disconnect the hydraulic brake lines.

25. On AWD vehicles remove the 4 rear subframe bracket bolts.

✳✳ CAUTION

When positioning the lifting table, be sure to support the rear subframe on the subframe rails. Do not lift on the rear differential or rear control arms, damage may occur.

26. Position a lifting table.

27. Remove the 4 rear subframe bolts.

28. On AWD vehicles remove the 2 rear subframe brackets.

29. Remove the rear subframe assembly.

30. Place a suitable support under the wheel knuckle.

31. Remove and discard the stabilizer bar link upper nut and separate the link from the upper arm.

32. Remove and discard the upper arm-to-subframe bolts.

33. On FWD vehicles, remove and discard the upper arm-to-knuckle bolt and separate the upper arm from the wheel knuckle.

34. On AWD vehicles , remove and discard the wheel knuckle ball joint nut.

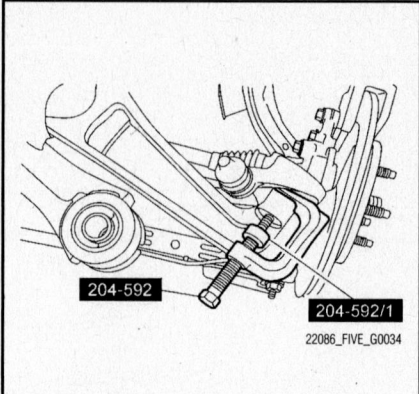

Fig. 89 Using the tools shown, separate the wheel knuckle from the upper arm

➡**It may be necessary to tap the knuckle to disconnect the upper arm.**

35. Using the tools shown, separate the wheel knuckle from the upper arm.

36. Using the tool shown, separate the upper arm and front bushing from the rear bushing. Once the upper arm and front bushing are separated from the rear bushing, use the special tool to pull the arm and bushing out of the bushing bore.

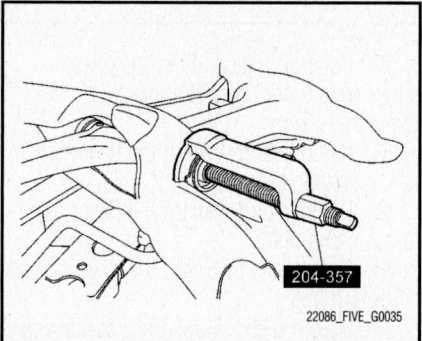

Fig. 90 Using the tools shown, separate the upper arm and front bushing from the rear bushing

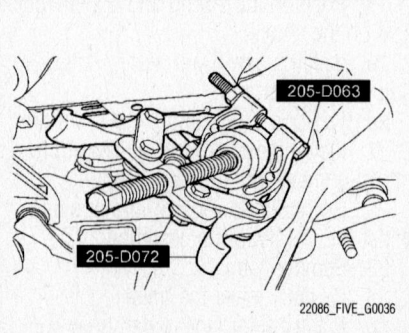

Fig. 91 Using the tools shown, separate the upper arm front bushing from the upper arm

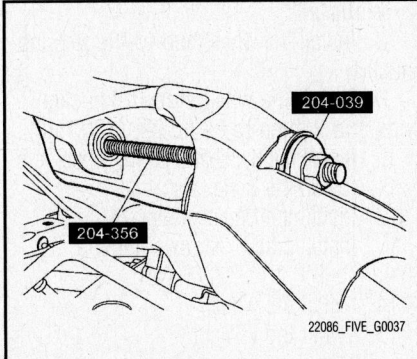

Fig. 92 Using the tools shown, remove the upper arm rear bushing from the subframe

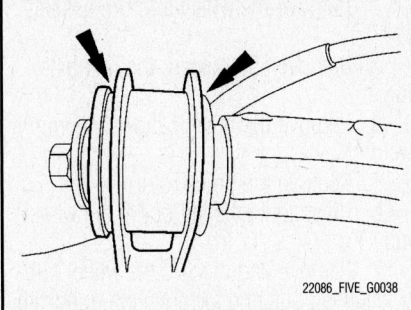

Fig. 93 Install the forward upper arm bushing to the correct depth in the subframe. Use the opposite side bushing as a guide

37. Using the tool shown, separate the upper arm front bushing from the upper arm.

38. Remove the upper arm from the subframe.

39. Using the tools shown, remove the upper arm rear bushing from the subframe.

To install:

40. Use only liquid soap, if necessary, to lubricate the bushing. Do not use any other types of lubricants or damage to the bore or bushing may occur.

➡ Make sure the bushing bore on the subframe is clean and free of foreign materials. To aid in installation, a small amount of liquid soap may be applied to the outer diameter of the bushing.

41. Position the upper arm rear bushing into the bushing bore from the rear of the subframe and, using the special tools, install the bushing into the subframe.

42. Use the opposite side bushing as a guide to install the bushing to the correct depth in the subframe.

❋❋ CAUTION

Do not fully tighten the nut at this time or incorrect clamp load or bushing damage may occur.

43. On AWD vehicles, position the upper arm into the forward bushing bore and into the rear bushing, then position the upper arm onto the wheel knuckle ball joint stud and install the ball joint nut. Tighten the nut until snug.

44. On FWD vehicles, position the upper arm into the forward bushing bore and into the rear bushing, then position the upper arm onto the wheel knuckle and install the upper arm-to-knuckle bolt. Tighten the bolt until snug.

45. Loosely install the upper arm-to-subframe rear bolt.

➡ The upper arm height setting is measured from the top of the subframe to the bottom of the upper arm. While an assistant holds the upper arm, adjust it to the correct height. On FWD models the measurement is 6.4 inches (163 mm). On AWD models the measurement is 6.2 inches (158 mm).

46. Tighten the upper arm-to-subframe rear bolt to 81 ft. lbs. (110 Nm).

47. While an assistant holds the upper arm in the center of the bushing bore, use the tools to install the upper arm front bushing into the subframe.

48. Install the forward upper arm bushing to the correct depth in the subframe. Use the opposite side bushing as a guide.

49. Install the upper arm-to-subframe front bolt and tighten to 81 ft. lbs. (110 Nm).

50. On AWD vehicles, tighten the wheel knuckle ball joint nut to 81 ft. lbs. (110 Nm).

51. On FWD vehicles, tighten upper arm-to-wheel knuckle bolt to 81 ft. lbs. (110 Nm).

52. Position the stabilizer bar link and install the stabilizer bar link upper nut. Tighten to 28 ft. lbs. (38 Nm).

➡ Install new suspension fasteners during assembly.

➡ Before tightening the upper control, toe link, trailing arm and lower control arm bolts, use a jackstand to raise the rear suspension to ride height.

53. Install the subframe in the reverse order of removal keeping in mind the following:

a. Align the subframe to the body following the alignment specification.

b. Install the 4 rear subframe bolts and tighten to 85 ft. lbs. (115 Nm).

c. On AWD vehicles install the 4 rear subframe bracket bolts and tighten to 41 ft. lbs. (55 Nm).

d. Install the rear shock-to-lower control arm bolts. On AWD models tighten to 105 ft. lbs. (142 Nm) or 81 ft. lbs. 110 Nm) on FWD models.

e. Install the trailing link-to-knuckle bolts and tighten to 77 ft. lbs. (105 Nm).

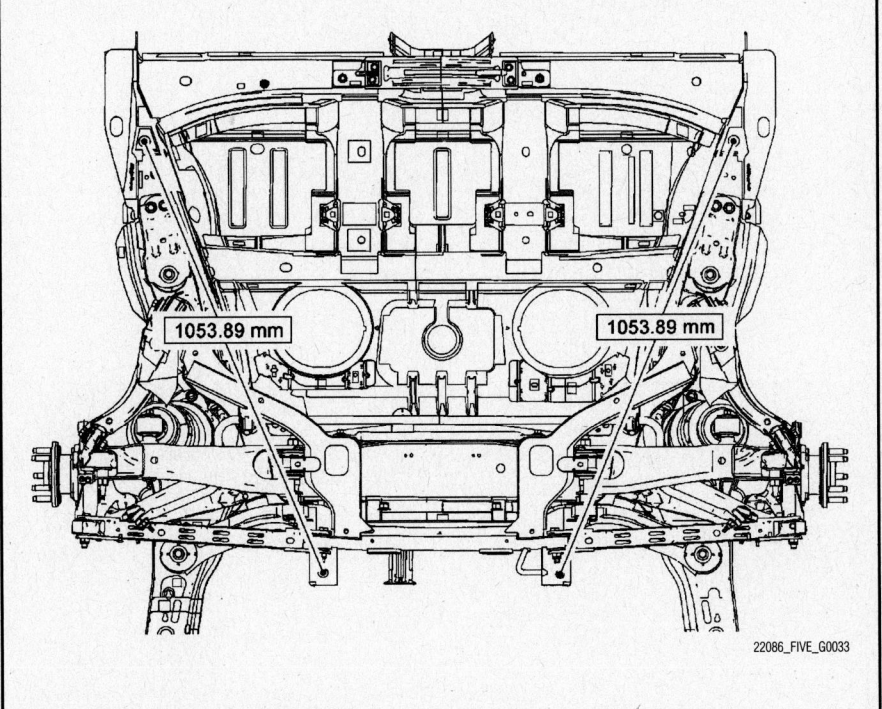

Fig. 94 Subframe to body alignment

f. Install the trailing link-to-subframe bolts and tighten to 77 ft. lbs. (105 Nm).

g. Install the 6 driveshaft bolts and tighten to 18 ft. lbs. (25 Nm)

h. Install the 2 catalytic converter nuts and tighten to 30 ft. lbs. (40 Nm).

WHEEL HUB AND BEARING

REMOVAL & INSTALLATION

1. Raise and safely support the vehicle.

2. Remove the wheel and tire assembly.

3. Remove and discard the rear axle nut.

4. Remove the brake caliper and wire it out of the way.

5. Remove the brake rotor.

6. Press the halfshaft out of the wheel hub.

7. Remove and discard the wheel hub-to-knuckle bolts and separate the hub from the knuckle.

To install:

8. Install the wheel hub-to-the steering knuckle.

9. Install the wheel hub-to-knuckle bolts and tighten to 89 ft. lbs. (120 Nm).

10. Install the halfshaft into the wheel hub.

11. Install the brake disc.

12. Install the brake caliper.

13. Install a new rear axle nut and tighten to 148 ft. lbs. (200 Nm).

14. Install the wheel.

15. Lower the vehicle.

SPECIFICATIONS AND MAINTENANCE CHARTS

ENGINE AND VEHICLE IDENTIFICATION CHART

		Engine Code					Model Year	
Code	Liters (cc)	Cu. In.	Cyl.	Fuel Sys.	Engine Type	Eng. Mfg.	Code ①	Year
Z	2.3 (2300)	139	4	SMFI	DOHC	Ford Motor Co.	6	2006
1	3.0 (3000)	182	6	SMFI	DOHC	Ford Motor Co.	7	2007
T	3.5 (3500)	214	6	SMFI	DOHC	Ford Motor Co.		

DOHC: Double Overhead Cam

SMFI: Sequential Multi-port Fuel Injection

① 10th position of VIN

22086_FUSI_C0001

GENERAL ENGINE SPECIFICATIONS

Year	Model	Engine Displacement Liters (VIN)	Net Horsepower @ rpm	Net Torque @ rpm (ft. lbs.)	Bore x Stroke (in.)	Compression Ratio	Oil Pressure @ rpm
2006	Fusion	2.3 (Z)	160@6250	156@4250	3.44x3.70	9.7:1	①
		3.0 (1)	221@3250	205@4800	3.50x3.13	9.86:1	②
	Milan	2.3 (Z)	160@6250	156@4250	3.44x3.70	9.7:1	①
		3.0 (1)	221@3250	205@4800	3.50x3.13	9.86:1	②
	Zephyr	3.0 (1)	221@3250	205@4800	3.50x3.13	9.86:1	②
2007	Fusion	2.3 (Z)	160@6250	156@4250	3.44x3.70	9.7:1	①
		3.0 (1)	221@3250	205@4800	3.50x3.13	9.86:1	②
	Milan	2.3 (Z)	160@6250	156@4250	3.44x3.70	9.7:1	①
		3.0 (1)	221@3250	205@4800	3.50x3.13	9.86:1	②
	MKZ	3.5 (T)	263@6250	249@4500	3.64x3.41	10.3:1	NA

NA - Not Available

① 29-39 psi @ 2000 rpm

② 11 psi, minimum @ 1,500 rpm with engine warmed up after 10 minutes of idling

22086_FUSI_C0002

ENGINE TUNE-UP SPECIFICATIONS

Year	Engine Displacement Liters (VIN)	Spark Plug Gap (in.)	Ignition Timing (deg.) MT	AT	Fuel Pump (psi)	Idle Speed (rpm) MT	AT	Valve Clearance (in.) Intake	Exhaust
2006	2.3 (Z)	0.049-0.053	NA	NA	57	NA	NA	0.008-0.011	0.010-0.013
	3.0 (1)	0.052-0.056	NA	NA	65	NA	NA	NA	NA
2007	2.3 (Z)	0.049-0.053	NA	NA	57	NA	NA	0.008-0.011	0.010-0.013
	3.0 (1)	0.052-0.056	NA	NA	65	NA	NA	NA	NA
	3.5 (T)	0.051-0.057	—	NA	65	—	NA	0.006-0.010	0.0118-0.0157

NOTE: The Vehicle Emission Control Information label often reflects changes made during production and must be used if they differ from this chart.

NOTE: The fuel pressure readings are with the engine running

NA - Not Available

22086_FUSI_C0003

CAPACITIES

Year	Model	Engine Displacement Liters (VIN)	Engine Oil with Filter (qts.)	Transmission (pts.) 5-Spd	Transmission (pts.) Auto.	Transfer Case (pts.)	Drive Axle Front (pts.)	Drive Axle Rear (pts.)	Fuel Tank (gal.)	Cooling System (qts.)
2006	Fusion	2.3 (Z)	4.5	NA	14.0	—	—	—	16.5	8.6
		3.0 (1)	6.0	—	14.8	—	—	—	16.5	9.7
	Milan	2.3 (Z)	4.6	NA	14.0	—	—	—	16.5	8.6
		3.0 (1)	6.0	—	14.8	—	—	—	16.5	9.7
	Zephyr	3.0 (1)	6.0	—	14.8	—	—	—	16.5	9.7
2007	Fusion	2.3 (Z)	4.5	NA	14.0	—	—	—	16.5	8.6
		3.0 (1)	6.0	—	14.8	①	—	2.43	②	9.7
	Milan	2.3 (Z)	4.6	NA	14.0	—	—	—	16.5	8.6
		3.0 (1)	6.0	—	14.8	①	—	2.43	②	9.7
	MKZ	3.5 (T)	5.5	—	14.8	①	—	2.43	②	10.0

NOTE: All capacities are approximate. Add fluid gradually and check to be sure a proper fluid level is obtained.

NA: Not Available

① Power Transfer Unit (PTU): 18 ounces

② Front Wheel Drive (FWD): 16.5 gallons

 All Wheel Drive (AWD): 17.5 gallons

22086_FUSI_C0004

FLUID SPECIFICATIONS

Year	Model	Engine Displacement Liters (VIN)	Engine Oil	Auto. Trans.	Drive Axle	Power Steering Fluid	Brake Master Cylinder
2006	Fusion	2.3L (Z)	①	Mercon® ATF Fluid	80W-90	Mercon® ATF Fluid	DOT 3
		3.0L (1)	①	Mercon® ATF Fluid	80W-90	Mercon® ATF Fluid	DOT 3
	Milan	2.3L (Z)	①	Mercon® ATF Fluid	80W-90	Mercon® ATF Fluid	DOT 3
		3.0L (1)	①	Mercon® ATF Fluid	80W-90	Mercon® ATF Fluid	DOT 3
	Zephyr	3.0L (1)	①	Mercon® ATF Fluid	80W-90	Mercon® ATF Fluid	DOT 3
2007	Fusion	2.3L (Z)	①	Mercon® ATF Fluid	80W-90	Mercon® ATF Fluid	DOT 3
		3.0L (1)	①	Mercon® ATF Fluid	80W-90	Mercon® ATF Fluid	DOT 3
	Milan	2.3L (Z)	①	Mercon® ATF Fluid	80W-90	Mercon® ATF Fluid	DOT 3
		3.0L (1)	①	Mercon® ATF Fluid	80W-90	Mercon® ATF Fluid	DOT 3
	MKZ	3.5L (T)	①	Mercon® ATF Fluid	80W-90	Mercon® ATF Fluid	DOT 3

DOT: Department Of Transpotation

① 5W-20 Premium Synthetic Blend Motor Oil (US) or 5W-20 Super Premium Motor Oil (Canada)

22086_FUSI_C0005

VALVE SPECIFICATIONS

Year	Engine Displacement Liters (VIN)	Seat Angle (deg.)	Face Angle (deg.)	Spring Test Pressure (lbs. @ in.)	Spring Installed Height (in.)	Stem-to-Guide Clearance (in.)		Stem Diameter (in.)	
						Intake	Exhaust	Intake	Exhaust
2006	2.3 (Z)	45	45	NA	1.492	0.0009	0.0011	0.2153-0.2159	0.2151-0.2157
	3.0 (1)	44.75	45.5	156 @ 1.18	1.570	0.0007-0.0027	0.0017-0.0370	0.2350-0.2358	0.2343-0.235
2007	2.3 (Z)	45	45	NA	1.492	0.0009	0.0011	0.2153-0.2159	0.2151-0.2157
	3.0 (1)	44.75	45.5	156 @ 1.18	1.570	0.0007-0.0027	0.0017-0.0370	0.2350-0.2358	0.2343-0.235
	3.5 (T)	89.0-91.0	90.50-91.50	115 @ 1.08	1.450	0.0008-0.0027	0.0013-0.0320	0.2157-0.2164	0.2151-0.2159

NA: Not Available

22086_FUSI_C0006

CAMSHAFT SPECIFICATIONS

All measurements are given in inches

Year	Engine Displacement Liters (VIN)	Journal Diameter	Bearing Oil Clearance	Shaft End-play	Runout	Lobe Height	
						Intake	Exhaust
2006	2.3 (Z)	0.982-0.983	0.001-0.0020	0.003-0.009	0.001	0.324	0.307
	3.0 (1)	1.061-1.060	0.001-0.0029	0.00748	NA	0.189	0.189
2007	2.3 (Z)	0.982-0.983	0.001-0.0020	0.003-0.009	0.001	0.324	0.307
	3.0 (1)	1.061-1.060	0.001-0.0029	0.00748	NA	0.189	0.189
	3.5 (T)	①	②	0.0012-0.0066	0.0015	0.380	0.380

NA: Not Available

① 1st journal: 1.2202-1.2209 in.
Intermediate journals: 1.021-1.022 in.

② 1st journal: 0.0027 MAX
Intermediate journals: 0.0029 MAX

22086_FUSI_C0007

CRANKSHAFT AND CONNECTING ROD SPECIFICATIONS

All measurements are given in inches

Year	Engine Displacement Liters (VIN)	Crankshaft				Connecting Rod		
		Main Brg. Journal Dia.	Main Brg. Oil Clearance	Shaft End-play	Thrust on No.	Journal Diameter	Oil Clearance	Side Clearance
2006	2.3 (Z)	2.046-2.047	0.0007-0.0013	0.008-0.016	NA	1.967-1.968	0.001-0.002	0.076-0.120
	3.0 (1)	2.467-2.479	0.0009-0.0030	0.005-0.010	NA	1.967-1.968	0.001-0.0025	0.0039-0.0118
2007	2.3 (Z)	2.046-2.047	0.0007-0.0013	0.008-0.016	NA	1.967-1.968	0.001-0.002	0.076-0.120
	3.0 (1)	2.467-2.479	0.0009-0.0030	0.005-0.010	NA	1.967-1.968	0.001-0.0025	0.0039-0.0118
	3.5 (T)	2.657	NA	0.0039-0.0114	NA	2.204-2.205	NA	0.0068-0.0167

NA - Not Available

22086_FUSI_C0008

PISTON AND RING SPECIFICATIONS

All measurements are given in inches

Year	Engine Displacement Liters (VIN)	Piston Clearance	Ring Gap			Ring Side Clearance		
			Top Compression	Bottom Compression	Oil Control	Top Compression	Bottom Compression	Oil Control
2006	2.3 (Z)	0.0009-0.0017	0.006-0.012	0.012-0.018	0.007-0.027	NA	NA	NA
	3.0 (1)	0.0005-0.0009	0.0039-0.0098	0.0106-0.0165	0.0059-0.0255	NA	NA	NA
2007	2.3 (Z)	0.0009-0.0017	0.006-0.012	0.012-0.018	0.007-0.027	NA	NA	NA
	3.0 (1)	0.0005-0.0009	0.0039-0.0098	0.0106-0.0165	0.0059-0.0255	NA	NA	NA
	3.5 (T)	0.0003-0.0017	0.0059-0.0098	0.0118-0.0216	0.0059-0.0177	NA	NA	NA

NA: Not Available

22086_FUSI_C0009

TORQUE SPECIFICATIONS
All readings in ft. lbs.

Year	Engine Displacement Liters (VIN)	Cylinder Head Bolts	Main Bearing Bolts	Rod Bearing Bolts	Crankshaft Damper Bolts	Flywheel Bolts	Manifold Intake	Manifold Exhaust	Spark Plugs	Oil Pan Drain Plug
2006	2.3 (Z)	①	NA	NA	②	③	13	41	9	27
	3.0 (1)	④	NA	NA	⑤	59	⑥	15	11	19
2007	2.3 (Z)	①	NA	NA	②	③	13	41	9	27
	3.0 (1)	④	NA	NA	⑤	59	⑥	15	11	19
	3.5 (T)	⑦	NA	NA	⑤	59	⑥	⑧	11	20

① Step 1: 62 INCH lbs.
   Step 2: 11 ft. lbs.
   Step 3: 33 ft. lbs.
   Step 4: +90 degrees
   Step 4: +90 degrees

② Step 1: 74 ft. lbs.
   Step 2: +90 degrees

③ Step 1: 37 ft. lbs.
   Step 2: 59 ft. lbs.
   Step 3: 83 ft. lbs.

④ Step 1: 30 ft. lbs.
   Step 2: +90 degrees
   Step 3: Loosen 1 full turn
   Step 4: 30 ft. lbs.
   Step 5: +90 degrees
   Step 6: +90 degrees

⑤ Step 1: 89 ft. lbs.
   Step 2: Loosen 1 full turn
   Step 3: 37 ft. lbs
   Step 4: +90 degrees

⑥ Upper intake manifold: 89 inch lbs.
   Lower intake manifold: 89 inch lbs.

⑦ Step 1: 15 ft. lbs.
   Step 2: 26 ft. lbs.
   Step 3: +90 degrees
   Step 4: +90 degrees
   Step 5: +90 degrees

⑧ Studs: 9 ft. lbs.
   Nuts: 15 ft. lbs.

22086_FUSI_C0010

TIRE, WHEEL AND BALL JOINT SPECIFICATIONS

Year	Model	OEM Tires Standard	OEM Tires Optional	Tire Pressures (psi) Front	Tire Pressures (psi) Rear	Wheel Size	Ball Joint Inspection	Lug Nut (ft. lbs.)
2006	Fusion	P205/60R16	P225/50R17	①	①	NS	NS	98
	Milan	P205/60R16	P225/50R17	①	①	NS	NS	98
	Zephyr	P225/50VR17	NA	①	①	NS	NS	98
2007	Fusion	P205/60R16	P225/50R17	①	①	NS	NS	98
	Milan	P205/60R16	P225/50R17	①	①	NS	NS	98
	MKZ	P225/50VR17	NA	①	①	NS	NS	98

OEM: Original Equipment Manufacturer

PSI: Pounds Per Square Inch

NS: Not specified by manufacturer

① See the safety certification label on the driver side door jamb for tire pressures.

22086_FUSI_C0011

BRAKE SPECIFICATIONS

All measurements in inches unless noted

Year	Model		Brake Disc Original Thickness	Brake Disc Minimum Thickness	Brake Disc Maximum Runout	Brake Drum Diameter Original Inside Diameter	Brake Drum Diameter Max. Wear Limit	Brake Drum Diameter Maximum Machine Diameter	Minimum Lining Thickness Front	Minimum Lining Thickness Rear	Brake Caliper Bracket Bolts (ft. lbs.)	Brake Caliper Mounting Bolts (ft. lbs.)
2006	Fusion	F	0.984	0.905	NA	—	—	—	0.118	—	①	②
		R	0.393	0.314	NA	—	—	—	—	0.118	③	④
	Milan	F	0.984	0.905	NA	—	—	—	0.118	—	①	②
		R	0.393	0.314	NA	—	—	—	—	0.118	③	④
	Zephyr	F	0.984	0.905	NA	—	—	—	0.118	—	①	②
		R	0.393	0.314	NA	—	—	—	—	0.118	③	④
2007	Fusion	F	0.984	0.905	NA	—	—	—	0.118	—	①	②
		R	0.393	0.314	NA	—	—	—	—	0.118	③	④
	Milan	F	0.984	0.905	NA	—	—	—	0.118	—	①	②
		R	0.393	0.314	NA	—	—	—	—	0.118	③	④
	MKZ	F	0.984	0.905	NA	—	—	—	0.118	—	①	②
		R	0.393	0.314	NA	—	—	—	—	0.118	③	④

F: Front

R: Rear

① Front brake caliper guide pin bolts: 20 ft. lbs.

② Rear brake caliper guide pin bolts: 19 ft. lbs.

③ Front brake anchor plate bolts: 66 ft. lbs.

④ Rear brake anchor plate bolts: 52 ft. lbs.

22086_FUSI_C0012

SCHEDULED MAINTENANCE INTERVALS

FORD FUSION, LINCOLN ZEPHYR AND MKZ, MERCURY MILAN

TO BE SERVICED	TYPE OF SERVICE	VEHICLE MILEAGE INTERVAL (x1000)											
		10	20	30	40	50	60	70	80	90	100	110	120
Accessory drive belts	I & A			✓			✓			✓			✓
Air cleaner element	R			✓			✓			✓			✓
Air conditioning filter	R			✓			✓			✓			✓
Brake fluid	R											✓	
Brake hoses & lines (including ABS)	I		✓		✓		✓		✓		✓		
Cooling system hoses & connections	I		✓		✓		✓		✓		✓		
Engine coolant	R												✓
Engine oil	R	✓	✓	✓	✓	✓	✓	✓	✓	✓	✓	✓	✓
Engine oil and coolant levels	I	Inspect at each fuel stop											
Engine oil filter	R		✓		✓		✓		✓		✓		
Exhaust system	I		✓		✓		✓		✓		✓		
Fluid levels and condition	I		✓		✓		✓		✓		✓		
Front and rear brakes	I		✓		✓		✓		✓		✓		
Fuel lines & connection	I		✓		✓		✓		✓		✓		
Halfshaft boots	I		✓		✓		✓		✓		✓		
Idle speed	I & A											✓	
Parking brake system	I & A		✓		✓		✓		✓		✓		
Rear differential fluid	R										✓		
Rotate and inspect tires	I	✓	✓	✓	✓	✓	✓	✓	✓	✓	✓	✓	✓
Spark plugs	R											✓	
Suspension components	I		✓		✓		✓		✓		✓		
Tie rod ends, steering gear box & boots	I		✓		✓		✓		✓		✓		
Transmission fluid	R												✓
Valve clearance	I											✓	

R: Replace   I: Inspect   A: Adjust

FREQUENT OPERATION MAINTENANCE (SEVERE SERVICE)

If a vehicle is operated under any of the following conditions it is considered severe service:

- Towing a trailer or using a camper or car-top carrier.
- Repeated short trips of less than 5 miles in temperatures below freezing, or trips of less than 10 miles in any temperature.
- Extensive idling or low-speed driving for long distances as in heavy commercial use, such as delivery, taxi or police cars.
- Operating on rough, muddy or salt-covered roads.
- Operating on unpaved or dusty roads.
- Driving in extremely hot (over 90°) conditions.

Air cleaner element: replace every 15,000 miles

Engine oil and filter: replace every 3750 miles or 6 months, whichever occurs first.

Timing belt: replace every 60,000 miles if the vehicle is regularly driven in temperatures above 110°F or below -20°F.

Transmission fluid: replace every 30,000 miles.

Rear differential fluid: replace every 60,000 miles.

Front and rear brakes: inspect every 7500 miles or 6 months, whichever occurs first.

Locks and hinges: lubricate every 15,000 miles.

Tie rods, steering gear box, boots: inspect every 7500 miles or 6 months, whichever occurs first.

Suspension components: inspect every 7500 miles or 6 months, whichever occurs first.

Halfshaft boots: inspect every 7500 miles or 6 months, whichever occurs first.

PRECAUTIONS

Before servicing any vehicle, please be sure to read all of the following precautions, which deal with personal safety, prevention of component damage, and important points to take into consideration when servicing a motor vehicle:

• Never open, service or drain the radiator or cooling system when the engine is hot; serious burns can occur from the steam and hot coolant.

• Observe all applicable safety precautions when working around fuel. Whenever servicing the fuel system, always work in a well-ventilated area. Do not allow fuel spray or vapors to come in contact with a spark, open flame, or excessive heat (a hot drop light, for example). Keep a dry chemical fire extinguisher near the work area. Always keep fuel in a container specifically designed for fuel storage; also, always properly seal fuel containers to avoid the possibility of fire or explosion. Refer to the additional fuel system precautions later in this section.

• Fuel injection systems often remain pressurized, even after the engine has been turned **OFF**. The fuel system pressure must be relieved before disconnecting any fuel lines. Failure to do so may result in fire and/or personal injury.

• Brake fluid often contains polyglycol ethers and polyglycols. Avoid contact with the eyes and wash your hands thoroughly after handling brake fluid. If you do get brake fluid in your eyes, flush your eyes with clean, running water for 15 minutes. If eye irritation persists, or if you have taken brake fluid internally, IMMEDIATELY seek medical assistance.

• The EPA warns that prolonged contact with used engine oil may cause a number of skin disorders, including cancer. You should make every effort to minimize your exposure to used engine oil. Protective gloves should be worn when changing oil. Wash your hands and any other exposed skin areas as soon as possible after exposure to used engine oil. Soap and water, or waterless hand cleaner should be used.

• All new vehicles are now equipped with an air bag system, often referred to as a Supplemental Restraint System (SRS) or Supplemental Inflatable Restraint (SIR) system. The system must be disabled before performing service on or around system components, steering column, instrument panel components, wiring and sensors. Failure to follow safety and disabling procedures could result in accidental air bag deployment, possible personal injury and unnecessary system repairs.

• Always wear safety goggles when working with, or around, the air bag system. When carrying a non-deployed air bag, be sure the bag and trim cover are pointed away from your body. When placing a non-deployed air bag on a work surface, always face the bag and trim cover upward, away from the surface. This will reduce the motion of the module if it is accidentally deployed. Refer to the additional air bag system precautions later in this section.

• Clean, high quality brake fluid from a sealed container is essential to the safe and proper operation of the brake system. You should always buy the correct type of brake fluid for your vehicle. If the brake fluid becomes contaminated, completely flush the system with new fluid. Never reuse any brake fluid. Any brake fluid that is removed from the system should be discarded. Also, do not allow any brake fluid to come in contact with a painted surface; it will damage the paint.

• Never operate the engine without the proper amount and type of engine oil; doing so WILL result in severe engine damage.

• Timing belt maintenance is extremely important. Many models utilize an interference-type, non-freewheeling engine. If the timing belt breaks, the valves in the cylinder head may strike the pistons, causing potentially serious (also time-consuming and expensive) engine damage. Refer to the maintenance interval charts for the recommended replacement interval for the timing belt, and to the timing belt section for belt replacement and inspection.

• Disconnecting the negative battery cable on some vehicles may interfere with the functions of the on-board computer system(s) and may require the computer to undergo a relearning process once the negative battery cable is reconnected.

• When servicing drum brakes, only disassemble and assemble one side at a time, leaving the remaining side intact for reference.

• Only an MVAC-trained, EPA-certified automotive technician should service the air conditioning system or its components.

BRAKES

GENERAL INFORMATION

PRECAUTIONS

The Anti-lock Brake System (ABS) with Roll Stability Control (RSC) and traction assist consists of the following components:

• Hydraulic Control Unit (HCU)
• ABS module (also controls the RSC system and traction assist system)
• Stability/traction control switch
• Steering wheel rotation sensor
• Stability control sensor cluster (contains the accelerometer[s], roll rate sensor and yaw rate sensor)
• Front wheel speed sensors
• Front wheel speed sensor tone rings (integral to the halfshafts)
• Rear wheel speed sensors
• Rear wheel speed sensor tone rings (integral to the halfshafts)
• Brake pressure transducer (integral to the HCU)
• Brake fluid level switch
• Red brake warning indicator
• Yellow ABS warning indicator
• Traction assist/roll stability control indicator ("sliding car" indicator)

SPEED SENSORS

REMOVAL & INSTALLATION

Front

See Figure 1.

1. Disconnect the negative battery cable.
2. Raise and safely support the vehicle.
3. Remove the wheel and tire assembly.

ANTI-LOCK BRAKE SYSTEM (ABS)

4. Remove the retainers and position the fender splash shield aside.
5. Disconnect the wheel speed sensor electrical connector.
6. Remove the 2 wheel speed sensor harness bracket bolts.

To install:

7. Remove the front wheel speed sensor bolt from the knuckle and remove the wheel speed sensor.
8. Installation is the reverse of the removal procedure. Tighten the retainers as follows:

   a. Speed sensor-to-knuckle bolt to 23 Nm (17 ft. lbs.)

   b. Speed sensor bracket-to-body bolt: 7 Nm (62 inch lbs.)

   c. Speed sensor bracket-to-knuckle bolt: 23 Nm (17 ft. lbs.)

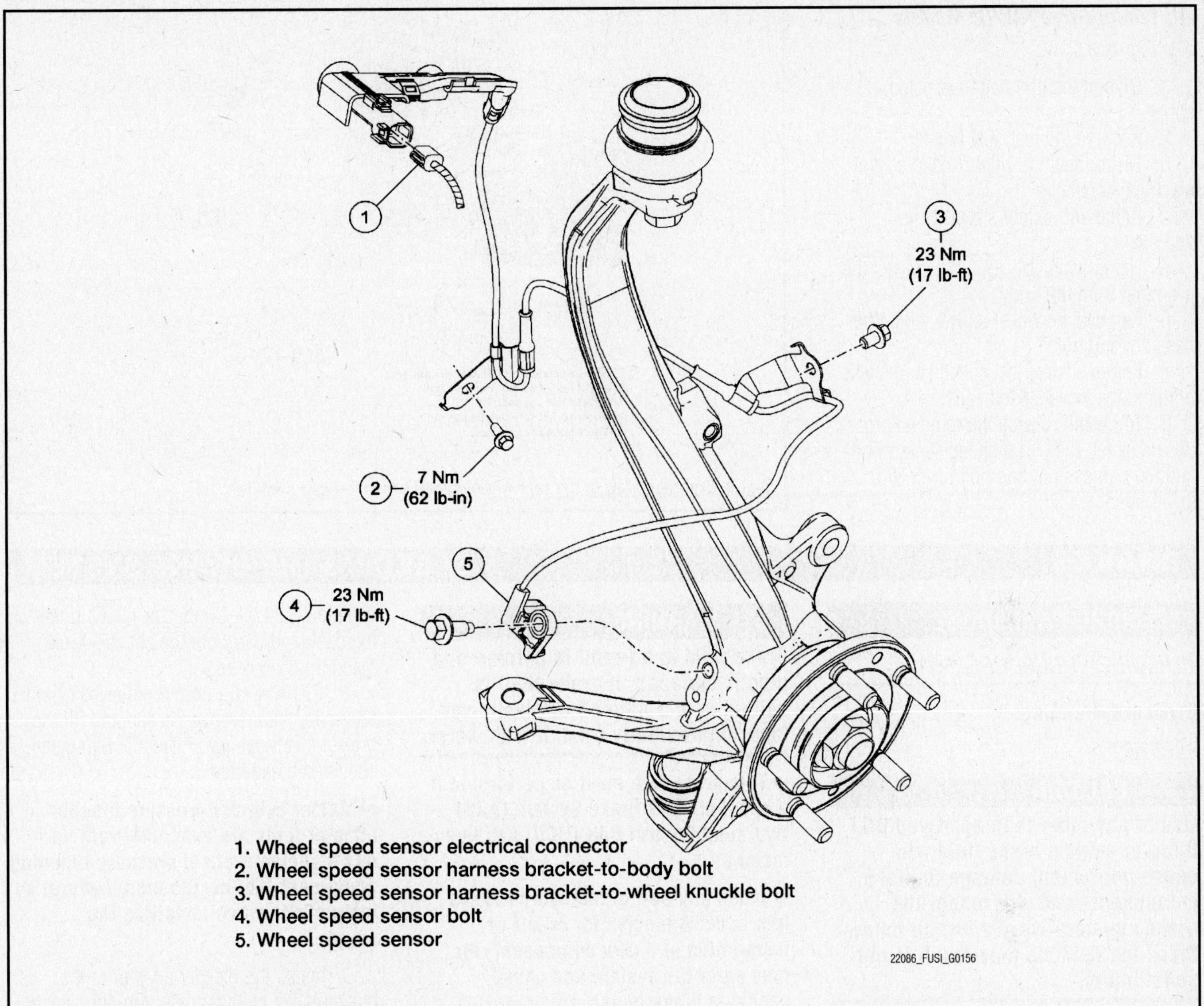

1. Wheel speed sensor electrical connector
2. Wheel speed sensor harness bracket-to-body bolt
3. Wheel speed sensor harness bracket-to-wheel knuckle bolt
4. Wheel speed sensor bolt
5. Wheel speed sensor

22086_FUSI_G0156

Fig. 1 Exploded view of the front wheel speed sensor

Rear

Front Wheel Drive (FWD) Models

See Figure 2.

1. Disconnect the negative battery cable.
2. Remove the rear seat bolster.
3. Disconnect the wheel speed sensor electrical connector.
4. Raise and safely support the vehicle.
5. Using a suitable tool, disconnect the grommet from the body.

➡ **It is not necessary to remove the harness routing brackets.**

6. Disconnect the wheel speed sensor harness from the brackets.
7. Remove the wheel speed sensor wire bolt and the wheel speed sensor.
8. To install, reverse the removal procedure. Tighten the wheel speed sensor bolt to 23 Nm (17 ft. lbs.).

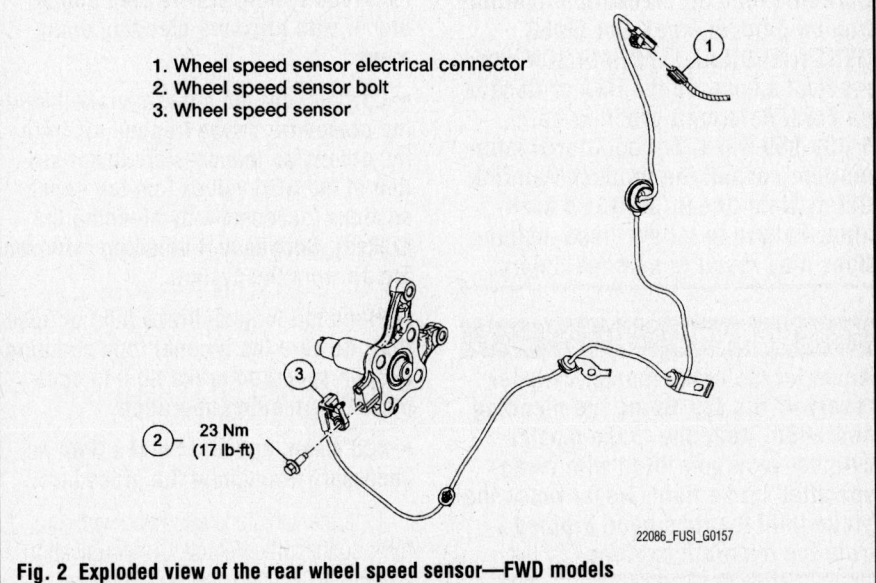

1. Wheel speed sensor electrical connector
2. Wheel speed sensor bolt
3. Wheel speed sensor

23 Nm
(17 lb-ft)

22086_FUSI_G0157

Fig. 2 Exploded view of the rear wheel speed sensor—FWD models

All Wheel Drive (AWD) Models

See Figure 3.

1. Disconnect the negative battery cable.
2. Remove the rear seat bolster.
3. Disconnect the wheel speed sensor electrical connector.
4. Raise and safely support the vehicle.
5. Using a suitable tool, disconnect the grommet from the body.
6. Remove the wheel speed sensor harness nut and bolt.
7. Remove the wheel speed sensor wire bolt and the wheel speed sensor.
8. To install, reverse the removal procedure. Tighten the wheel speed sensor bolt and the harness nut and bolt to 23 Nm (17 ft. lbs.).

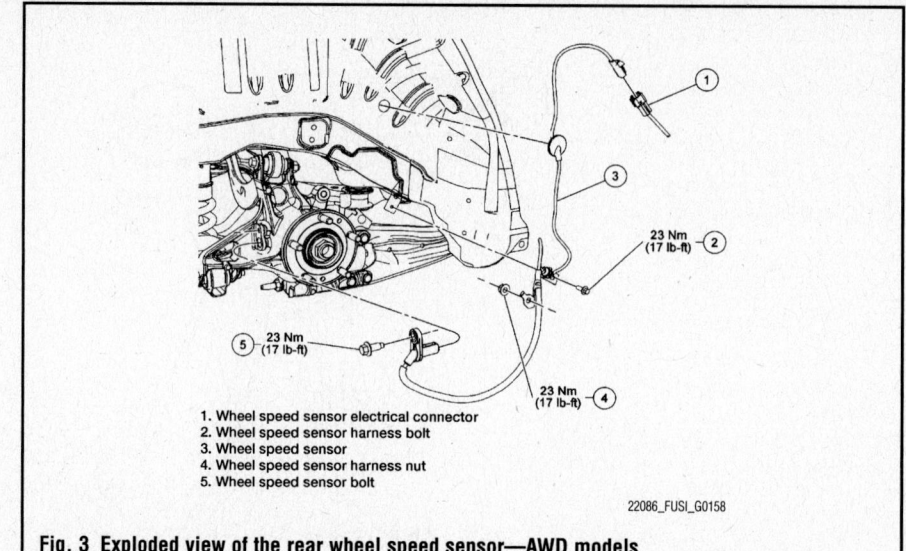

1. Wheel speed sensor electrical connector
2. Wheel speed sensor harness bolt
3. Wheel speed sensor
4. Wheel speed sensor harness nut
5. Wheel speed sensor bolt

22086_FUSI_G0158

Fig. 3 Exploded view of the rear wheel speed sensor—AWD models

---

BRAKES

BLEEDING THE BRAKE SYSTEM

BLEEDING PROCEDURE

BLEEDING PROCEDURE

Pressure Bleeding

See Figure 4.

> ※※ **CAUTION**
>
> Use of any other than approved DOT 3 motor vehicle brake fluid will cause permanent damage to brake components and will render the brakes inoperative. Failure to follow these instructions may result in personal injury.

> ※ **CAUTION**
>
> Carefully read all precaution information on product label. For EMERGENCY MEDICAL INFORMATION seek medical advice. In the USA or Canada on Ford/Motorcraft products call: 1-800-959-3673. For additional information, consult the product Material Safety Data Sheet (MSDS) if available. Failure to follow these instructions may result in personal injury.

> ※※ **WARNING**
>
> Never let the brake master cylinder reservoir run dry during the bleeding operation. Keep the brake master cylinder reservoir filled with clean, specified brake fluid. Never reuse the brake fluid that has been drained from the hydraulic system.

> ※※ **WARNING**
>
> Brake fluid is harmful to painted and plastic surfaces. If brake fluid is spilled onto a painted or plastic surface, immediately wash it with water.

➡ This procedure must be performed if a new Anti-lock Brake System (ABS) Hydraulic Control Unit (HCU) has been installed.

➡ When any part of the hydraulic system is disconnected for repair or installation of a new component, air may enter the system and cause spongy a brake pedal. This requires bleeding of the hydraulic system after it has been correctly connected. The hydraulic system can be bled manually or with pressure bleeding equipment.

➡ Carrying out the chassis brake bleeding procedure drives trapped air from the otherwise inaccessible lower section of the HCU valves into the upper sections (accessible by bleeding the brakes). Subsequent bleeding removes the air from the system.

➡ Bleed the longest brake tube or hose first. Be sure the bleeder tank contains enough specified brake fluid to complete the bleeding operation.

➡ Add clean, specified brake fluid as necessary throughout the procedure.

1. If the vehicle is equipped with an ABS, connect the Vehicle Communication Module (VCM) and scan tool into the vehicle Data Link Connector (DLC) under the dash and carry out the chassis brake bleeding procedure.
2. Clean all dirt from the master cylinder filler cap, then remove the cap and fill the brake master cylinder reservoir with clean, specified brake fluid.

➡ Master cylinder pressure bleeder adapter tools are available from various manufacturers of pressure bleeding equipment. Follow the manufacturer's instructions when installing the adapter.

3. Install the bleeder adapter to the brake master cylinder reservoir and attach the bleeder tank hose to the fitting on the adapter.
4. Place a box-end wrench on the RH rear disc brake caliper bleeder screw. Attach a rubber hose to the RH rear disc brake caliper bleeder screw and submerge the free end of the hose in a container partially filled with clean, specified brake fluid.
5. Open the valve on the bleeder tank.
6. Loosen the rear disc brake caliper bleeder screw. Leave the bleeder screw open until clear, bubble-free brake fluid flows into the container, then tighten the rear disc brake caliper bleeder screw and remove the rubber hose. Tighten to 8 Nm (71 inch lbs.).
7. Continue bleeding the rest of the system, going in order from the LH rear disc brake caliper to the RH front disc brake caliper, ending with the LH front disc brake caliper.

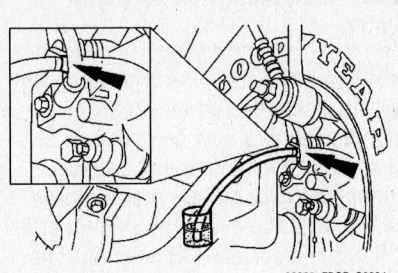

Fig. 4 Place a box-end wrench on the RH rear disc brake caliper bleeder screw. Attach a rubber hose to the RH rear disc brake caliper bleeder screw and submerge the free end of the hose in a container partially filled with clean, specified brake fluid

8. Close the bleeder tank valve and remove the tank hose from the adapter and remove the adapter.

9. Fill the brake master cylinder reservoir with clean, specified brake fluid and install the cap.

Manual Bleeding
See Figure 4.

✳ CAUTION

Use of any other than approved DOT 3 motor vehicle brake fluid will cause permanent damage to brake components and will render the brakes inoperative. Failure to follow these instructions may result in personal injury.

✳ CAUTION

Carefully read all precaution information on product label. For EMERGENCY MEDICAL INFORMATION seek medical advice. In the USA or Canada on Ford/Motorcraft products call: 1-800-959-3673. For additional information, consult the product Material Safety Data Sheet (MSDS) if available. Failure to follow these instructions may result in personal injury.

✳ WARNING

Never let the brake master cylinder reservoir run dry during the bleeding operation. Keep the brake master cylinder reservoir filled with clean, specified brake fluid. Never reuse the brake fluid that has been drained from the hydraulic system.

✳ WARNING

Brake fluid is harmful to painted and plastic surfaces. If brake fluid is spilled onto a painted or plastic surface, immediately wash it with water.

➡ This procedure must be performed if a new Anti-lock Brake System (ABS) Hydraulic Control Unit (HCU) has been installed.

➡ When any part of the hydraulic system is disconnected for repair or installation of a new component, air may enter the system and cause spongy a brake pedal. This requires bleeding of the hydraulic system after it has been correctly connected. The hydraulic system can be bled manually or with pressure bleeding equipment.

➡ Carrying out the chassis brake bleeding procedure drives trapped air from the otherwise inaccessible lower section of the HCU valves into the upper sections (accessible by bleeding the brakes). Subsequent bleeding removes the air from the system.

➡ Bleed the longest brake tube or hose first. Be sure the bleeder tank contains enough specified brake fluid to complete the bleeding operation.

➡ Add clean, specified brake fluid as necessary throughout the procedure.

1. Clean all dirt from the master cylinder filler cap, then remove the cap and fill the brake master cylinder reservoir with clean, specified brake fluid. Install the master cylinder filler cap.

2. If the vehicle is equipped with an ABS, connect the Vehicle Communication Module (VCM) and scan tool into the vehicle Data Link Connector (DLC) under the dash and carry out the chassis brake bleeding procedure.

3. Place a box-end wrench on the RH rear disc brake caliper bleeder screw. Attach a rubber hose to the RH rear disc brake caliper bleeder screw and submerge the free end of the hose in a container partially filled with clean, specified brake fluid.

4. Have an assistant pump the brake pedal and then hold firm pressure on the brake pedal.

5. Loosen the RH rear disc brake caliper bleeder screw until a stream of brake fluid comes out. Have an assistant maintain pressure on the brake pedal while tightening

the RH rear disc brake caliper bleeder screw:
    a. Repeat until clear, bubble-free fluid comes out.
    b. Refill the brake master cylinder reservoir as necessary.

6. Tighten the RH rear disc brake caliper bleeder screw. Tighten to 8 Nm (71 inch lbs.).

7. Repeat Steps 2 through 5 for the LH rear disc brake caliper.

8. Place a box-end wrench on the RH front disc brake caliper bleeder screw. Attach a rubber hose to the RH front disc brake caliper bleeder screw and submerge the free end of the hose in a container partially filled with clean, specified brake fluid.

9. Have an assistant pump the brake pedal and then hold firm pressure on the brake pedal.

10. Loosen the RH front disc brake caliper bleeder screw until a stream of brake fluid comes out. Have an assistant maintain pressure on the brake pedal while tightening the RH front disc brake caliper bleeder screw.
    a. Repeat until clear, bubble-free fluid comes out.
    b. Refill the brake master cylinder reservoir as necessary.

11. Tighten the RH front disc brake caliper bleeder screw to 8 Nm (71 inch lbs.).

12. Repeat Steps 7 through 10 for the LH front disc brake caliper.

Gravity Bleeding
See Figure 4.

✳ CAUTION

Use of any other than approved DOT 3 motor vehicle brake fluid will cause permanent damage to brake components and will render the brakes inoperative. Failure to follow these instructions may result in personal injury.

✳ CAUTION

Carefully read all precaution information on product label. For EMERGENCY MEDICAL INFORMATION seek medical advice. In the USA or Canada on Ford/Motorcraft products call: 1-800-959-3673. For additional information, consult the product Material Safety Data Sheet (MSDS) if available. Failure to follow these instructions may result in personal injury.

✳✳ WARNING

Never let the brake master cylinder reservoir run dry during the bleeding operation. Keep the brake master cylinder reservoir filled with clean, specified brake fluid. Never reuse the brake fluid that has been drained from the hydraulic system.

✳✳ WARNING

Brake fluid is harmful to painted and plastic surfaces. If brake fluid is spilled onto a painted or plastic surface, immediately wash it with water.

➡ When any part of the hydraulic system is disconnected for repair or installation of a new component, air may enter the system and cause spongy a brake pedal. This requires bleeding of the hydraulic system after it has been correctly connected. The hydraulic system can be bled manually or with pressure bleeding equipment.

➡ Performing the chassis brake bleeding procedure drives trapped air from the otherwise inaccessible lower section of the HCU valves into the upper sections (accessible by bleeding the brakes). Subsequent bleeding removes the air from the system.

➡ Add clean, specified brake fluid as necessary throughout the procedure.

1. Clean all dirt from the master cylinder filler cap, then remove the cap and fill the brake master cylinder reservoir with clean, specified brake fluid.

2. If the vehicle is equipped with an ABS, connect the Vehicle Communication Module (VCM) and scan tool into the vehicle Data Link Connector (DLC) under the dash and carry out the chassis brake bleeding procedure.

3. Bleed the rear disc brake calipers:
 a. Place a box-end wrench on the RH rear disc brake caliper bleeder screw.
 Attach a rubber hose to the RH rear disc brake caliper bleeder screw and submerge the free end of the hose in a container partially filled with clean, specified brake fluid.
 b. Open the bleeder screw and leave open until clear bubble-free brake fluid flows into the container.
 c. Repeat for the LH rear disc brake caliper.

4. Tighten the rear disc brake caliper bleeder screws to 8 Nm (71 inch lbs.).

5. Bleed the front disc brake calipers:
 a. Place a box-end wrench on the RH front disc brake caliper bleeder screw.
 b. Attach a rubber hose to the RH front disc brake caliper bleeder screw and submerge the free end of the hose in a container partially filled with clean, specified brake fluid.
 c. Open the bleeder screw and leave open until clear bubble-free brake fluid flows.
 d. Repeat for the LH front disc brake caliper.

6. Tighten the front disc brake caliper bleeder screws to 8 Nm (71 inch lbs.).

Bleeding the Master Cylinder

See Figure 5.

✳✳ CAUTION

Use of any other than approved DOT 3 motor vehicle brake fluid will cause permanent damage to brake components and will render the brakes inoperative. Failure to follow these instructions may result in personal injury.

✳✳ CAUTION

Carefully read all precaution information on product label. For EMERGENCY MEDICAL INFORMATION seek medical advice. In the USA or Canada on Ford/Motorcraft products call: 1-800-959-3673. For additional information, consult the product Material Safety Data Sheet (MSDS) if available. Failure to follow these instructions may result in personal injury.

✳✳ WARNING

Never let the brake master cylinder reservoir run dry during the bleeding operation. Keep the brake master cylinder reservoir filled with clean, specified brake fluid. Never reuse the brake fluid that has been drained from the hydraulic system.

✳✳ WARNING

Brake fluid is harmful to painted and plastic surfaces. If brake fluid is spilled onto a painted or plastic surface, immediately wash it with water.

➡ When any part of the hydraulic system is disconnected for repair or installation of a new component, air may enter the system and cause spongy a brake pedal. This requires bleeding of the hydraulic system after it has been correctly connected. The hydraulic system can be bled manually or with pressure bleeding equipment.

➡ Performing the chassis brake bleeding procedure drives trapped air from the otherwise inaccessible lower section of the HCU valves into the upper sections (accessible by bleeding the brakes). Subsequent bleeding removes the air from the system.

➡ Add clean, specified brake fluid as necessary throughout the procedure.

➡ When a new brake master cylinder has been installed or the system has been emptied, or partially emptied, it should be primed to prevent air from getting into the system.

1. Disconnect the brake master cylinder outlet tubes.

2. Install short brake tubes with ends submerged in the brake master cylinder reservoir and fill the brake master cylinder reservoir with clean, specified brake fluid.

3. Have an assistant pump the brake pedal until clear fluid flows from both brake tubes without air bubbles.

4. Remove the short brake tubes and install the brake outlet tubes.

5. Bleed each brake tube at the brake master cylinder as follows:
 a. Have an assistant pump the brake pedal and then hold firm pressure on the brake pedal.
 b. Loosen the rearmost brake tube

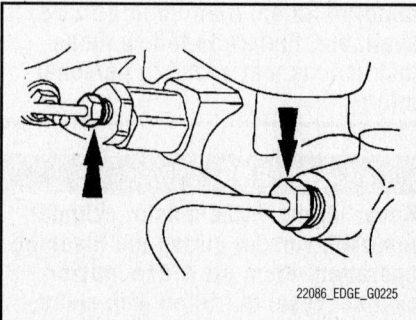

22086_EDGE_G0225

Fig. 5 Disconnect the brake master cylinder outlet tubes

fittings until a stream of brake fluid comes out. Have an assistant maintain pressure on the brake pedal while tightening the brake tube fitting.

c. Repeat this operation until clear, bubble-free fluid comes out.

d. Refill the brake master cylinder reservoir as necessary. Repeat the bleeding operation at the front brake tube.

e. While the assistant maintains pressure on the brake pedal, tighten

the brake tubes to 28 Nm (21 ft. lbs.).

BLEEDING THE ABS SYSTEM

Refer to the Bleeding Procedures located at the beginning of the Brakes Section.

BRAKES

❊❊ CAUTION

Dust and dirt accumulating on brake parts during normal use may contain asbestos fibers from production or aftermarket brake linings. Breathing excessive concentrations of asbestos fibers can cause serious bodily harm. Exercise care when servicing brake parts. Do not sand or grind brake lining unless equipment used is designed to contain the dust residue. Do not clean brake parts with compressed air or by dry brushing. Cleaning should be done by dampening the brake components with a fine mist of water, then wiping the brake components clean with a dampened cloth. Dispose of cloth and all residue containing asbestos fibers in an impermeable container with the appropriate label. Follow practices prescribed by the Occupational Safety and Health Administration (OSHA) and the Environmental Protection Agency (EPA) for the handling, processing, and disposing of dust or debris that may contain asbestos fibers.

BRAKE CALIPER

REMOVAL & INSTALLATION

See Figure 6.

❊❊ CAUTION

Use of any other than approved DOT 3 motor vehicle brake fluid will cause permanent damage to brake components and will render the brakes inoperative. Failure to follow these instructions may result in personal injury.

❊❊ CAUTION

Carefully read all precaution information on product label. For EMERGENCY MEDICAL INFORMATION seek medical advice. In the USA or Canada on Ford/Motorcraft products call: 1-800-959-3673. For additional

information, consult the product Material Safety Data Sheet (MSDS) if available. Failure to follow these instructions may result in personal injury.

❊❊ WARNING

Brake fluid is harmful to painted and plastic surfaces. If brake fluid is spilled onto a painted or plastic surface, immediately wash it with water.

1. Raise and safely support the vehicle.
2. Remove the wheel and tire assembly.
3. Remove the brake caliper flow bolt and position the hose aside.
4. Discard the 2 copper washers.
5. Remove the 2 brake caliper guide pin bolts.
6. Remove the brake caliper.
7. If a leaking or damaged caliper piston boot is found, install a new brake caliper.

❊❊ WARNING

The caliper guide pin boots must be seated correctly on the anchor plate or the guide pins may become contaminated.

8. Inspect the guide pin boots and make sure they are seated on the anchor

FRONT DISC BRAKES

plate correctly. The boot has a lip that fits under the edge of the anchor plate extension.

To install:

9. Installation is the reverse of the removal procedure, noting the following:

a. During installation, make sure that the brake caliper hose is not twisted.

b. Tighten the caliper guide pin bolts to 27 Nm (20 ft. lbs.). Make sure to install the longer/bigger bolt in the upper position.

c. Use new copper washers, then tighten the brake caliper flow bolts to 25 Nm (18 ft. lbs.).

d. Bleed the brake system, as outlined in the beginning of the Brake Section.

DISC BRAKE PADS

REMOVAL & INSTALLATION

See Figures 7 and 8.

1. Check the brake fluid level in the brake master cylinder reservoir.
2. If necessary, remove the fluid until the brake master cylinder reservoir is ½ full.
3. Raise and safely support the vehicle.
4. Remove the wheel and tire assembly.

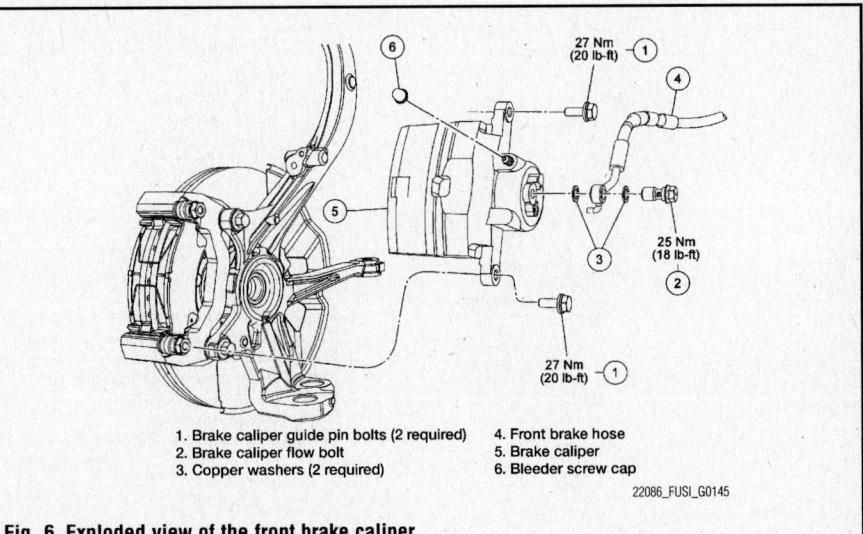

1. Brake caliper guide pin bolts (2 required)
2. Brake caliper flow bolt
3. Copper washers (2 required)
4. Front brake hose
5. Brake caliper
6. Bleeder screw cap

22086_FUSI_G0145

Fig. 6 Exploded view of the front brake caliper

> ❊❊ **WARNING**
>
> Do not pry in the caliper sight hole to retract the pistons as this can damage the pistons and boots.

> ❊ **WARNING**
>
> NEVER let the brake caliper hang from the brake hose or damage to the hose can occur.

5. Remove the 2 brake caliper guide pin bolts and position the caliper aside.
6. Support the caliper using a suitable piece of wire.
7. Remove the 2 brake pad retraction springs.
8. Remove the brake pads, brake pad shims and stainless steel shims.
9. Inspect the brake pads and shims for wear or contamination.
10. Remove the brake pad slides.
11. Remove the 4 brake pad slide clips.

To install:
12. Install the 4 brake pad slide clips.

> ❊ **WARNING**
>
> Protect the caliper piston and boots when pushing the caliper piston into the bores.

> ❊❊ **WARNING**
>
> Make sure that the caliper guide pin boots are fully seated or damage to

the caliper guide pin boots can occur.

13. If installing new brake pads, using a suitable tool and a worn brake, compress the disc brake caliper pistons into the caliper.
14. Install the brake pad slides.
15. Apply grease that is supplied to the pad backing plate and shims in the areas indicated.

   a. 1. Apply grease to the back of the brake pad.

   b. 2. Apply grease to the inner piston side stainless steel shim.

   c. 3. Apply grease to the outer stainless steel shim.

➡ **The cut shim is directional and used on the inboard pad only. The cut is positioned toward the leading side.**

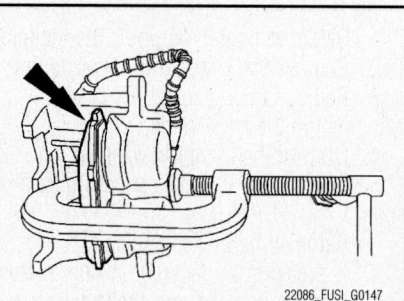

Fig. 8 If installing new brake pads, using a suitable tool and a worn brake, compress the disc brake caliper pistons into the caliper

Correct installation can be verified if the shim hole is positioned on the bottom side.

16. Install the brake pad shims and the stainless steel shims to the brake pads.
17. Install the 2 brake pad retraction springs.

> ❊❊ **WARNING**
>
> The caliper guide pin boots must be seated correctly on the anchor plate or the guide pins may become contaminated.

18. Inspect the guide pin boots and make sure they are seated on the anchor plate correctly. The boot has a lip that fits under the edge of the anchor plate extension.

➡ **Make sure that the brake caliper hose does not become twisted.**

19. Position the brake caliper and install the 2 guide pin bolts. Tighten to 27 Nm (20 ft. lbs.).
20. Install the wheel and tire assembly.
21. Fill the brake master cylinder reservoir with clean, specified brake fluid.
22. Test the brakes for normal operation

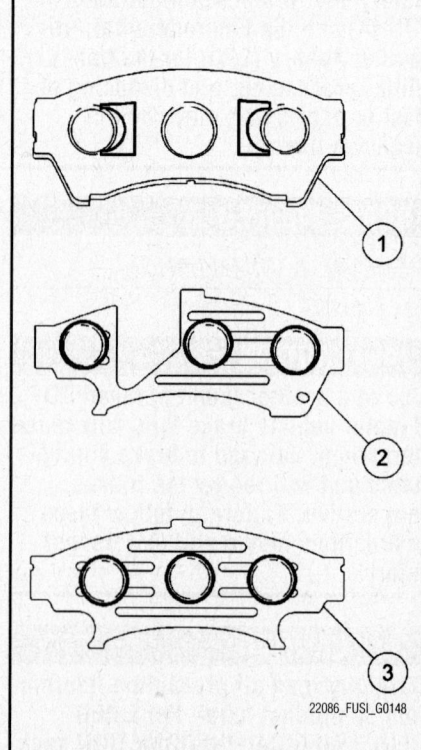

Fig. 9 Apply grease that is supplied to the pad backing plate and shims in the areas indicated. Refer to the procedure.

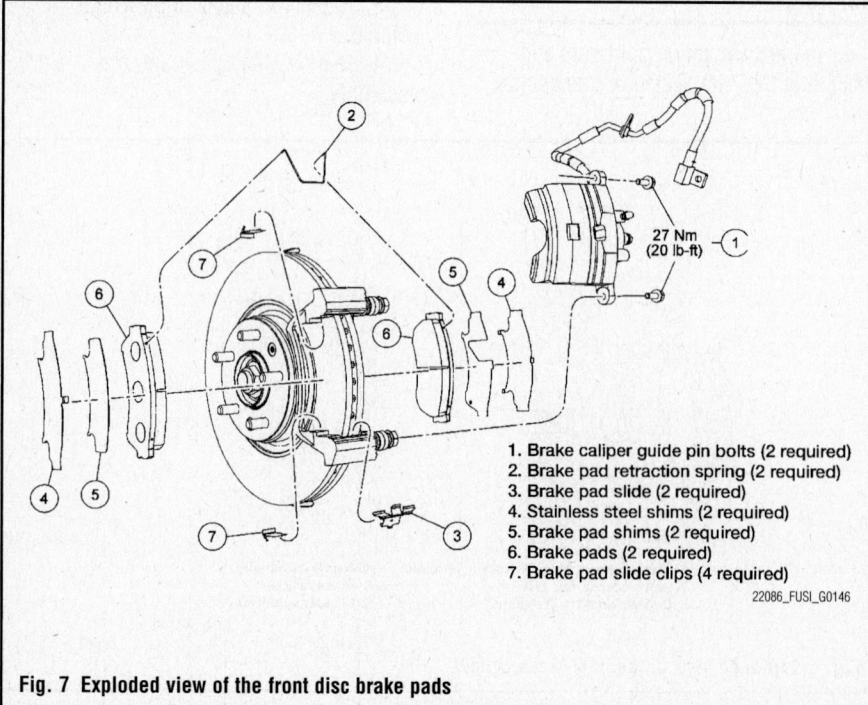

1. Brake caliper guide pin bolts (2 required)
2. Brake pad retraction spring (2 required)
3. Brake pad slide (2 required)
4. Stainless steel shims (2 required)
5. Brake pad shims (2 required)
6. Brake pads (2 required)
7. Brake pad slide clips (4 required)

22086_FUSI_G0146

27 Nm (20 lb-ft)

Fig. 7 Exploded view of the front disc brake pads

BRAKES   **REAR DISC BRAKES**

❉❉ CAUTION

Dust and dirt accumulating on brake parts during normal use may contain asbestos fibers from production or aftermarket brake linings. Breathing excessive concentrations of asbestos fibers can cause serious bodily harm. Exercise care when servicing brake parts. Do not sand or grind brake lining unless equipment used is designed to contain the dust residue. Do not clean brake parts with compressed air or by dry brushing. Cleaning should be done by dampening the brake components with a fine mist of water, then wiping the brake components clean with a dampened cloth. Dispose of cloth and all residue containing asbestos fibers in an impermeable container with the appropriate label. Follow practices prescribed by the Occupational Safety and Health Administration (OSHA) and the Environmental Protection Agency (EPA) for the handling, processing, and disposing of dust or debris that may contain asbestos fibers.

BRAKE CALIPER

REMOVAL & INSTALLATION
See Figures 10 and 11.

❉❉ CAUTION

Use of any other than approved DOT 3 motor vehicle brake fluid will cause permanent damage to brake components and will render the brakes inoperative. Failure to follow these instructions may result in personal injury.

❉❉ CAUTION

Carefully read all precaution information on product label. For EMERGENCY MEDICAL INFORMATION seek medical advice. In the USA or Canada on Ford/Motorcraft products call: 1-800-959-3673. For additional information, consult the product Material Safety Data Sheet (MSDS) if available. Failure to follow these instructions may result in personal injury.

❉❉ WARNING

Brake fluid is harmful to painted and plastic surfaces. If brake fluid is spilled onto a painted or plastic surface, immediately wash it with water.

1. Raise and safely support the vehicle.
2. Remove the wheel and tire assembly.
3. Disconnect the parking brake cable from the brake caliper:
    a. Pull back the parking brake lever.
    b. Disconnect the cable from the parking brake lever.
    c. Remove the cable conduit retaining clip.
    d. Disconnect the cable from the brake caliper.
4. Remove the brake caliper flow bolt and position the brake hose aside. Discard the 2 copper washers.
5. Remove the 2 brake caliper guide pin bolts and the brake caliper.
6. If a leaking or damaged caliper piston boot is found, install a new disc brake caliper.

To install:
7. Position the notch in the caliper piston so that it will correctly align with the pin on the backside of the inboard brake pad.

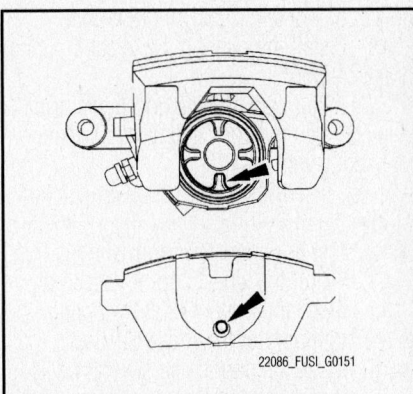

22086_FUSI_G0151

Fig. 11 Position the notch in the caliper piston so that it will correctly align with the pin on the backside of the inboard brake pad

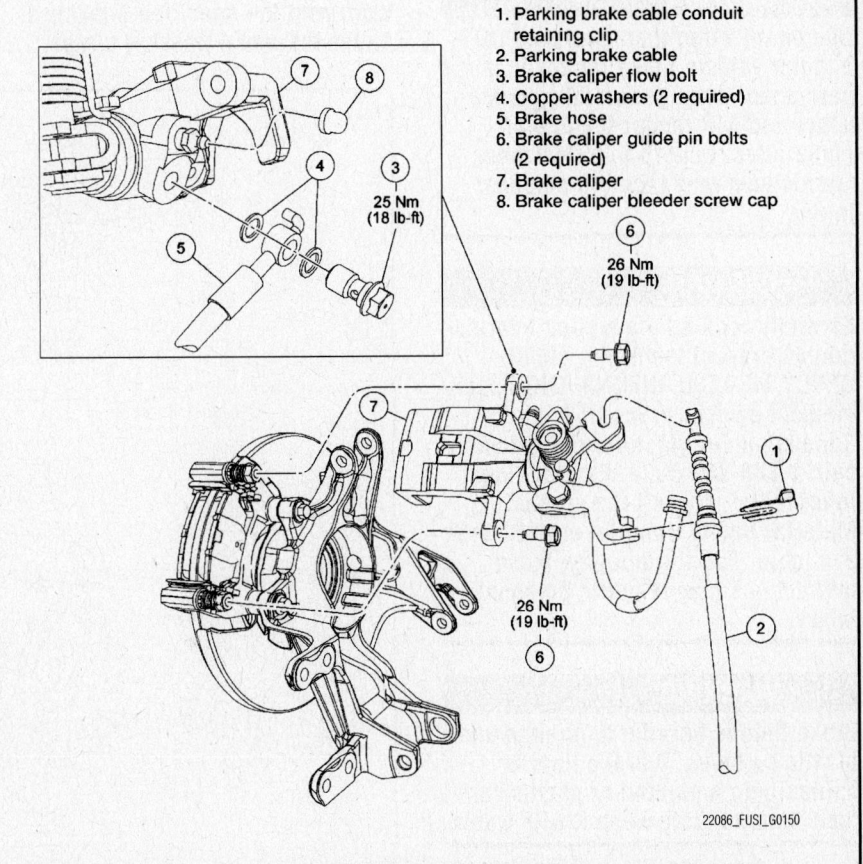

1. Parking brake cable conduit retaining clip
2. Parking brake cable
3. Brake caliper flow bolt
4. Copper washers (2 required)
5. Brake hose
6. Brake caliper guide pin bolts (2 required)
7. Brake caliper
8. Brake caliper bleeder screw cap

25 Nm (18 lb-ft)

26 Nm (19 lb-ft)

26 Nm (19 lb-ft)

22086_FUSI_G0150

Fig. 10 Exploded view of the rear disc brake caliper—FWD vehicle shown, AWD similar

➡Make sure that the brake caliper hose is not twisted.

8. Position the brake caliper onto the anchor plate.

9. Install the 2 brake caliper guide pin bolts and tighten to 26 Nm (19 ft. lbs.).

10. Using 2 new copper washers, position the brake hose and install the brake caliper flow bolt. Tighten to 25 Nm (18 ft. lbs.).

11. Install the parking brake cable to the brake caliper:

a. Pull back the parking brake lever.

b. Connect the cable to the parking brake lever.

c. Install the cable conduit retaining clip.

12. Test the brakes for normal operation

13. Install the wheel and tire assembly.

14. Bleed the brake system, as outlined at the beginning of the Brake Section.

15. Cycle the park brake several times to verify normal operation.

16. Test the brakes for normal operation

DISC BRAKE PADS

REMOVAL & INSTALLATION
See Figures 11 through 13.

✳ CAUTION

Use of any other than approved DOT 3 motor vehicle brake fluid will cause permanent damage to brake components and will render the brakes inoperative. Failure to follow these instructions may result in personal injury.

✳ CAUTION

Carefully read all precaution information on product label. For EMERGENCY MEDICAL INFORMATION seek medical advice. In the USA or Canada on Ford/Motorcraft products call: 1-800-959-3673. For additional information, consult the product Material Safety Data Sheet (MSDS) if available. Failure to follow these instructions may result in personal injury.

✳ WARNING

Brake fluid is harmful to painted and plastic surfaces. If brake fluid is spilled onto a painted or plastic surface, immediately wash it with water.

1. Check the brake fluid level in the brake master cylinder reservoir.

2. If necessary, remove the fluid until the brake master cylinder reservoir is ½ full.

3. Remove the wheel and tire assembly.

4. Disconnect the parking brake cable from the brake caliper:

a. Pull back the parking brake lever.

b. Disconnect the cable from the parking brake lever.

c. Remove the cable conduit retaining clip.

d. Disconnect the cable from the brake caliper.

✳ WARNING

Do not pry in the caliper sight hole to retract the pistons, as this can damage the pistons and boots.

✳ WARNING

Do not allow the brake caliper to hang from the brake hose or damage to the hose can occur.

5. Remove the 2 brake caliper guide pin bolts and position the caliper aside. Support the caliper using mechanic's wire.

✳ WARNING

Install new brake pads if they are worn past the specified thickness above the metal backing plates.

Install new brake pads in complete axle sets.

6. Remove the 2 brake pads, shims and retraction clips. Inspect the brake pads and shims for wear, damage or contamination.

7. Discard the slide clips.

8. Inspect the brake pads for wear and contamination.

To install:

➡Make sure the caliper piston boot is clean and free of foreign material.

9. Using the special tool, compress the brake caliper piston into the brake caliper bore.

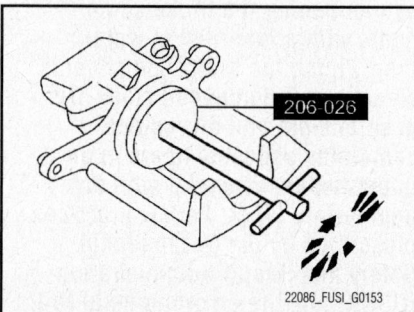

Fig. 13 Using the special tool, compress the brake caliper piston into the brake caliper bore.

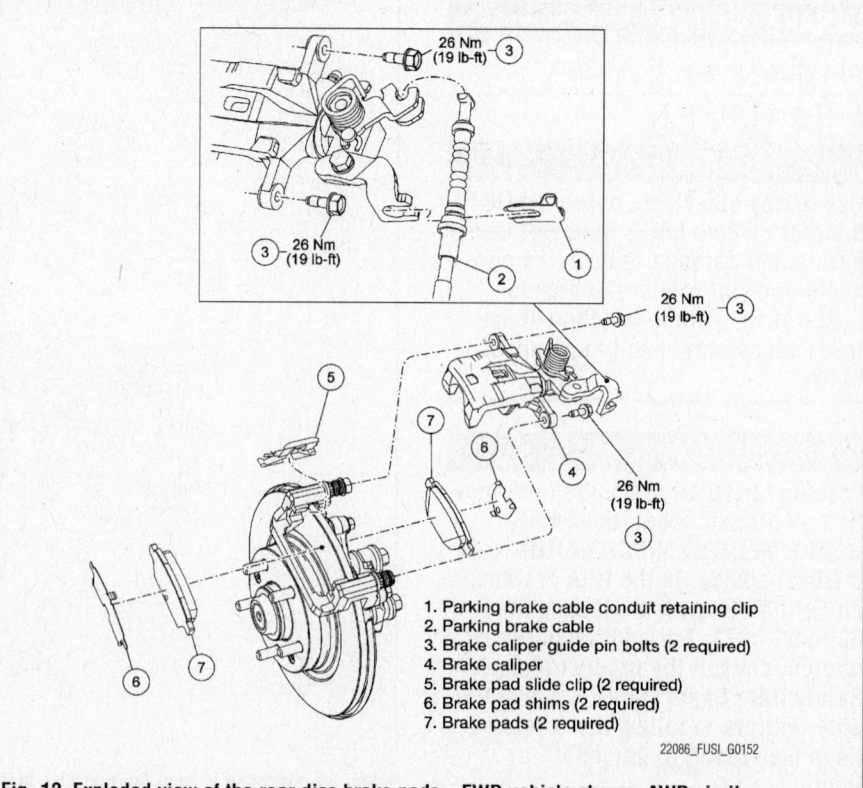

1. Parking brake cable conduit retaining clip
2. Parking brake cable
3. Brake caliper guide pin bolts (2 required)
4. Brake caliper
5. Brake pad slide clip (2 required)
6. Brake pad shims (2 required)
7. Brake pads (2 required)

22086_FUSI_G0152

Fig. 12 Exploded view of the rear disc brake pads—FWD vehicle shown, AWD similar

10. Position the notch in the caliper piston so that it will correctly align with the pin on the backside of the inboard brake pad.

11. Install the 2 brake pads, shims and slide clips to the brake caliper anchor plate.

➡**Make sure that the brake caliper hose is not twisted.**

12. Position the brake caliper on the anchor plate and install the 2 bolts. Tighten to 26 Nm (19 ft. lbs.).

13. Install the parking brake cable to the brake caliper:

   a. Pull back the parking brake lever.

   b. Connect the cable to the parking brake lever.

   c. Install the cable conduit retaining clip.

14. Fill the brake master cylinder reservoir with clean, specified brake fluid.

15. Install the wheel and tire assembly.

16. Fill the brake master cylinder reservoir with clean, specified brake fluid.

17. Cycle the park brake several times to verify normal operation.

18. Test the brakes for normal operation

BRAKES   PARKING BRAKE

PARKING BRAKE CABLES

ADJUSTMENT

See Figures 14 and 15.

➡**Do not pry at the floor console rear access panel with a screwdriver or damage to the panel may occur.**

1. Remove the floor console rear access panel.

2. Raise and safely support the vehicle.

➡**The dimension will vary depending on the amount of cable stretch. New cables require cycling the parking brake control 5-10 times to remove the cable slack.**

3. Adjust the parking brake adjustment nut as shown in the accompanying illustration.

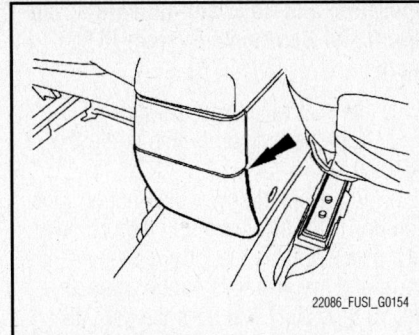

Fig. 14 Remove the floor console rear access panel

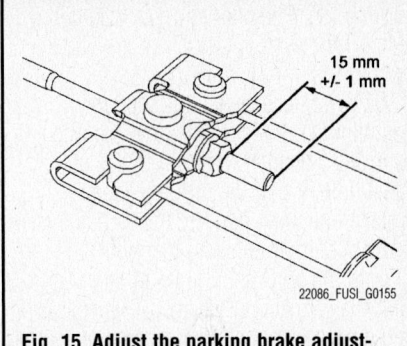

Fig. 15 Adjust the parking brake adjustment nut as shown

4. Verify correct operation of the parking brake system:

   a. At 2 clicks of the parking brake control, slight drag at the rear wheels should be present.

   b. At 5 clicks of the parking brake control, no movement at the rear wheels should be present.

5. Install the floor console rear access panel

CHASSIS ELECTRICAL   AIR BAG (SUPPLEMENTAL RESTRAINT SYSTEM)

GENERAL INFORMATION

✳ CAUTION

These vehicles are equipped with an air bag system. The system must be disarmed before performing service on, or around, system components, the steering column, instrument panel components, wiring and sensors. Failure to follow the safety precautions and the disarming procedure could result in accidental air bag deployment, possible injury and unnecessary system repairs.

SERVICE PRECAUTIONS

Disconnect and isolate the battery negative cable before beginning any airbag system component diagnosis, testing, removal, or installation procedures. Allow system capacitor to discharge for two minutes before beginning any component service. This will disable the airbag system. Failure to disable the airbag system may result in accidental airbag deployment, personal injury, or death.

Do not place an intact undeployed airbag face down on a solid surface. The airbag will propel into the air if accidentally deployed and may result in personal injury or death.

When carrying or handling an undeployed airbag, the trim side (face) of the airbag should be pointing towards the body to minimize possibility of injury if accidental deployment occurs. Failure to do this may result in personal injury or death.

Replace airbag system components with OEM replacement parts. Substitute parts may appear interchangeable, but internal differences may result in inferior occupant protection. Failure to do so may result in occupant personal injury or death.

Wear safety glasses, rubber gloves, and long sleeved clothing when cleaning powder residue from vehicle after an airbag deployment. Powder residue emitted from a deployed airbag can cause skin irritation. Flush affected area with cool water if irritation is experienced. If nasal or throat irritation is experienced, exit the vehicle for fresh air until the irritation ceases. If irritation continues, see a physician.

Do not use a replacement airbag that is not in the original packaging. This may result in improper deployment, personal injury, or death.

The factory installed fasteners, screws and bolts used to fasten airbag components have a special coating and are specifically designed for the airbag system. Do not use substitute fasteners. Use only original equipment fasteners listed in the parts catalog when fastener replacement is required.

During, and following, any child restraint anchor service, due to impact event or vehicle repair, carefully inspect all mounting hardware, tether straps, and anchors for proper installation, operation, or damage. If a child restraint anchor is found damaged in any way, the anchor must be replaced. Failure to do this may result in personal injury or death.

Deployed and non-deployed airbags may or may not have live pyrotechnic material within the airbag inflator.

Do not dispose of driver/passenger/ curtain airbags or seat belt tensioners unless you are sure of complete deployment. Refer to the Hazardous Substance Control System for proper disposal.

Dispose of deployed airbags and tensioners consistent with state, provincial, local, and federal regulations.

After any airbag component testing or service, do not connect the battery negative cable. Personal injury or death may result if the system test is not performed first.

If the vehicle is equipped with the Occupant Classification System (OCS), do not connect the battery negative cable before performing the OCS Verification Test using the scan tool and the appropriate diagnostic information. Personal injury or death may result if the system test is not performed properly.

Never replace both the Occupant Restraint Controller (ORC) and the Occupant Classification Module (OCM) at the same time. If both require replacement, replace one, then perform the Airbag System test before replacing the other.

Both the ORC and the OCM store Occupant Classification System (OCS) calibration data, which they transfer to one another when one of them is replaced. If both are replaced at the same time, an irreversible fault will be set in both modules and the OCS may malfunction and cause personal injury or death.

If equipped with OCS, the Seat Weight Sensor is a sensitive, calibrated unit and must be handled carefully. Do not drop or handle roughly. If dropped or damaged, replace with another sensor. Failure to do so may result in occupant injury or death.

If equipped with OCS, the front passenger seat must be handled carefully as well. When removing the seat, be careful when setting on floor not to drop. If dropped, the sensor may be inoperative, could result in occupant injury, or possibly death.

If equipped with OCS, when the passenger front seat is on the floor, no one should sit in the front passenger seat. This uneven force may damage the sensing ability of the seat weight sensors. If sat on and damaged, the sensor may be inoperative, could result in occupant injury, or possibly death.

DISARMING THE SYSTEM

✳✳ CAUTION

Never probe the electrical connectors on air bag, safety canopy or side air curtain modules. Failure to follow this instruction may result in the accidental deployment of these modules, which increases the risk of serious personal injury or death.

✳✳ CAUTION

To reduce the risk of accidental deployment, do not use any memory saver devices. Failure to follow this instruction may result in serious personal injury or death.

➡The air bag warning indicator illuminates when the Restraints Control Module (RCM) fuse is removed and the ignition switch is ON. This is normal operation and does not indicate a Supplemental Restraints System (SRS) fault.

1. Turn all vehicle accessories OFF.
2. Turn the ignition switch to the **OFF** position.
3. At the smart power distribution junction box (SPDJB), located in the LH lower kick panel, remove the lower kick panel fuse cover and the restraints control module (RCM) fuse 46 (7.5A) from the (SPDJB).
4. Turn the ignition **ON** and make sure that the air bag warning indicator lights up for at least 30 seconds. The air bag warning indicator will remain lit continuously (no flashing) if the correct RCM fuse has been removed. If the air bag warning indicator does not remain lit continuously, remove the correct RCM fuse before proceeding.
5. Turn the ignition switch to the **OFF** position.

✳✳ WARNING

To avoid accidental deployment and possible personal injury, the backup power supply MUST be depleted before repairing or installing any new front or side air bag SRS components and before servicing, installing, adjusting or striking components near the front or side air bag sensors, such as doors, instrument panel, console, door latches, strikers, seats and hood latches. Failure to follow this instruction may result in serious personal injury. The front impact severity sensors are located on the radiator support under the front bumper cover. The first row side impact sensors are located at or near the base of the B-pillars. The second row side impact sensors are located on the C-pillars.

6. To deplete the backup power supply energy, disconnect the negative battery cable and wait at least one minute. Be sure to disconnect auxiliary batteries and power supplies (if equipped).

7. Disconnect the negative battery cable and wait at least one minute.

ARMING THE SYSTEM

1. Turn the ignition switch from the **OFF** position to the **ON** position.
2. Install RCM fuse 46 (7.5A) to the SPDJB and install the lower kick panel fuse cover.

✳✳ CAUTION

Make sure that nobody is in the vehicle and that there is nothing blocking or set in front of any air bag module when the negative battery cable is connected. Failure to follow this instruction may result in serious personal injury.

3. Connect the negative battery cable.
4. Prove out the SRS as follows:
   a. Turn the ignition switch from ON to OFF. Wait 10 seconds, then turn the ignition switch back to ON and visually monitor the air bag warning indicator with the air bag modules installed. The air bag warning indicator will light continuously for approximately 6 seconds and then turn OFF. If an air bag SRS fault is present, the air bag warning indicator will:
   • Fail to light.
   • Remain lit continuously.
   • Flash at a 5 Hz rate (RCM not configured).

5. The air bag warning indicator might not light until approximately 30 seconds after the ignition switch has been turned from the OFF to the ON position. This is the time required for the RCM to complete the testing of the SRS. If the air bag warning indicator is inoperative and a SRS fault exists, a chime will sound in a pattern of 5 sets of 5 beeps. If this occurs, the air bag warning indicator and any SRS fault discovered must be diagnosed and repaired.

6. Clear all continuous Diagnostic Trouble Codes (DTCs) from the RCM and Occupant Classification Sensor (OCS) module using a scan tool.

CLOCKSPRING CENTERING

See Figures 16 through 18.

➡This procedure covers removal and installation, and centering of the clockspring.

✳✳ CAUTION

To reduce the risk of accidental deployment, do not use any memory

saver devices. Failure to follow this instruction may result in serious personal injury or death.

→The air bag warning indicator illuminates when the Restraints Control Module (RCM) fuse is removed and the ignition switch is ON. This is normal operation and does not indicate a Supplemental Restraint System (SRS) fault.

→Repair is made by installing a new part only. If the new part does not correct the condition, install the original part and carry out the diagnostic procedure again.

1. Disarm the SRS, as outlined in this section.

2. Tilt the steering wheel in the downward position and lock the tilt handle.

3. Remove the driver air bag module, as follows:

a. Using a 3-mm Allen wrench or a suitable tool through the access hole on the backside of the steering wheel, position the tool against the spring clip and push in, disengaging the clip from the locking pin. With the spring clip disengaged from the locking pin, gently pull back on that side of the driver air bag module to release it from the steering wheel. Repeat for the other locking pin.

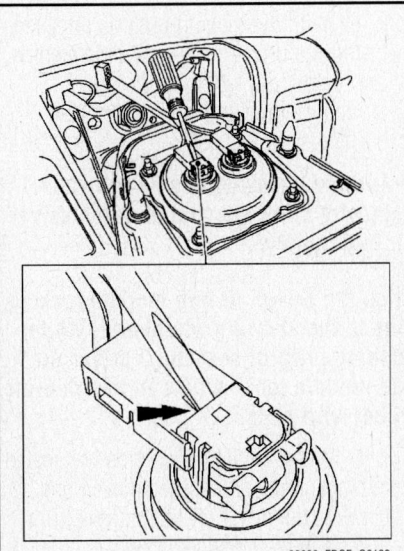

Fig. 16 Using a small screwdriver as shown, lift up and release the locking buttons on the driver air bag module electrical connectors. With the locking buttons released, remove the electrical connectors and the driver air bag module

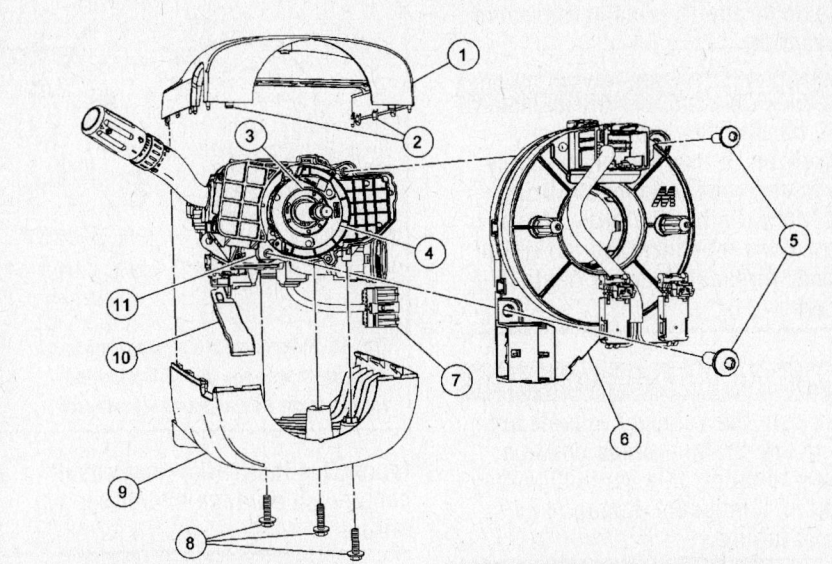

1. Upper steering column shroud
2. Upper steering column shroud tabs (2)
3. Absolute steering angle sensor
4. Absolute steering angle sensor ring
5. Clockspring screws (2)
6. Clockspring
7. Clockspring electrical connector
8. Lower steering column shroud screws (3)
9. Lower steering column shroud
10. Steering column tilt lock/unlock handle
11. Multi-function switch housing

22086_EDGE_G0128

Fig. 17 Exploded view of the SRS clockspring and related components

❉❉ WARNING

NEVER pull the driver air bag module electrical connectors out by the locking buttons. Damage to the locking buttons can occur.

b. Using a small screwdriver as shown, lift up and release the locking buttons on the driver air bag module electrical connectors. With the locking buttons released, remove the electrical connectors and the driver air bag module.

❉❉ WARNING

Vehicles with absolute steering angle sensor and/or adaptive headlamps, do not allow the clockspring rotor to turn from the straight-ahead position after the steering wheel is removed. Failure to follow this instruction may result in component damage and/or system failure.

→Make sure the vehicle's wheels are in the straight-ahead position.

4. Remove the steering wheel, as outlined in the Steering Section.

5. Tape the clockspring rotor to the steering column shaft to prevent the clockspring rotor from moving out of center.

6. Release the 2 tabs and position the upper steering column shroud upward.

7. Remove the 3 screws and the lower steering column shroud.

8. Disconnect the clockspring electrical connector.

9. Remove the tape from the clockspring rotor to the steering column shaft. Do not allow the clockspring rotor to move from center after tape is removed.

❉❉ WARNING

Vehicles with absolute steering angle sensor and/or adaptive headlamps, do not allow the clockspring rotor to turn from the straight-ahead position after the steering wheel is removed. Failure to follow this instruction may result in component damage and/or system failure.

→Vehicles with absolute steering angle sensor and/or adaptive headlamps, after the clockspring has been removed make sure the arrow on the absolute steering angle sensor ring is lined up with the arrow on the absolute steering angle sensor housing as shown.

10. Remove the 2 clockspring screws and remove the clockspring.

To install:
Vehicle repairs re-using the same clockspring:

✳✳ CAUTION

If the clockspring is not correctly centralized, it may fail prematurely. If in doubt, repeat the centralizing procedure. Failure to follow these instructions may increase the risk of serious personal injury or death in a crash.

✳✳ WARNING

Make sure the vehicle's wheels are still in the straight-ahead position. Failure to follow this instruction may result in component damage and/or system failure.

11. If the vehicle's clockspring has rotated out of center, follow these steps to center the clockspring.

    a. Hold the clockspring outer housing stationary.

✳✳ WARNING

Overturning will destroy the clockspring. The internal ribbon wire acts as the stop and can be broken from its internal connection.

    b. While turning the rotor counter-clockwise, carefully feel for the ribbon wire to run out of length and for a slight resistance. Stop turning at this point.

    c. Turn the clockspring clockwise (approximately 2.25 turns) until the clockspring rotor wiring and connector are in the 12 o'clock position. Clockspring is now centered.

    d. Do not allow the rotor to turn from this position.

➡Slight rotation of the absolute steering angle sensor ring is allowed to align the 2 arrows.

12. Make sure the sensor ring arrow is lined up with the absolute steering angle sensor housing arrow as shown.

✳✳ WARNING

If the clockspring is left unattended between centralizing the clockspring and installing it to the multi-function switch housing, the centralizing procedure must be repeated. Failure to

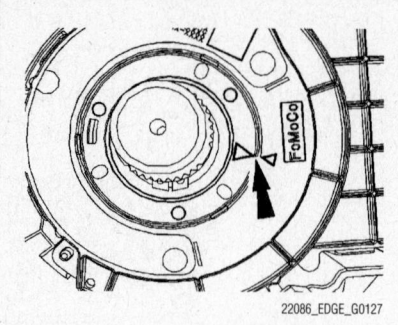

Fig. 18 Make sure the sensor ring arrow is lined up with the absolute steering angle sensor housing arrow as shown

follow this instruction may result in component damage and/or system failure.

➡On vehicles with absolute steering angle sensor and/or adaptive headlamps, slight rotation of the clockspring rotor might be needed to seat the clockspring 3 locator pins into the absolute steering angle sensor and or adaptive headlamps sensor ring. Very slight rotation is possible on a new clockspring with the sealing key installed.

➡Make sure the clockspring is fully seated into the multi-function switch housing before installing the clockspring screws.

13. Install the clockspring and the 2 screws.

14. Connect the clockspring electrical connector.

15. Install the lower steering column shroud and the 3 screws.

16. Attach the upper steering column shroud to the lower steering column shroud.

✳✳ WARNING

If not installing a new clockspring, and the vehicle is left unattended between the installation of the clockspring to the multi-function switch housing and installing the steering wheel, the centralizing procedure can be repeated at this time with the clockspring being installed in the multi-function switch housing. Failure to follow this instruction may result in component damage and/or system failure.

17. Install the steering wheel, as outlined in the Steering Section.

18. If a new clockspring is being installed, and after the steering wheel installation, remove the clockspring sealing key.

19. Install the driver air bag module, as follows:

✳✳ WARNING

Do not install the driver air bag module electrical connectors by the locking buttons. Damage to the locking buttons can occur.

✳✳ WARNING

The driver air bag module electrical connector locking buttons must be in the released position when the connector is being installed or connector damage may occur.

✳✳ WARNING

The driver air bag module electrical connectors are unique and cannot be reversed when connected to the driver air bag module. Match the electrical connector key to the keyway in the driver air bag module. Do not force the electrical connectors into the driver air bag module. Damage to the connector or component may occur.

    e. With the locking buttons released, install the driver air bag module electrical connectors fully into the driver air bag module and seat the locking buttons.

➡Audible clicks will be heard when both wire clips are seated in the driver air bag module.

Align the driver air bag module locking pins to the steering wheel and, while pushing inward, seat the 2 driver air bag module locking pins to the steering wheel wire clips.

    f. When the 2 locking pins are seated in place, there should be an even gap between the driver air bag module trim cover and the steering wheel

20. Rearm the SRS, as outlined in this section.

DRIVETRAIN

AUTOMATIC TRANSAXLE ASSEMBLY

REMOVAL & INSTALLATION

FNR5 Transaxle

See Figures 19 through 23.

1. Raise and safely support the vehicle.
2. Remove the air cleaner assembly:
   a. Disconnect the mass air flow (MAF) sensor electrical connector.
   b. Disconnect the engine breather.
   c. Disconnect the brake booster vacuum hose.
   d. Loosen the clamp and remove the air cleaner assembly.
3. Remove the battery.
4. Remove the battery tray:
   a. Disconnect the positive battery cable fastener from the battery tray.
   b. Disconnect the 3 wiring harness retainers.
   c. Remove the nut.
   d. Remove the bolt and remove the battery tray.
5. Disconnect the selector lever cable end from the manual lever.
6. Remove the 2 bolts, disconnect the harness and position the selector lever cable and bracket aside.
7. Disconnect the transmission range (TR) sensor electrical connector, transmission main valve body electrical connector, and disconnect the harness retainer from the transaxle and position the harness aside.
8. Disconnect the turbine shaft speed (TSS) sensor, intermediate shaft speed sensor and 5th gear valve body electrical connector and position the harness aside.
9. Remove the ground strap.
10. Remove the 3 top bellhousing bolts.
11. Remove the 2 roll restrictor bracket bolts.
12. Install the special tool.
13. Remove the 2 transaxle insulator bolts and lower the transaxle.
14. Remove the 3 nuts and remove the transaxle insulator bracket.
15. Disconnect the pressure switch electrical connector.
16. Disconnect the output shaft speed (OSS) sensor electrical connector.
17. Remove the 4 screws and position the RH fender splash shield aside.
18. Remove the 6 pin-type retainers and the RH front structure-to-subframe splash shield.
19. Remove the 4 screws and position the LH fender splash shield aside.

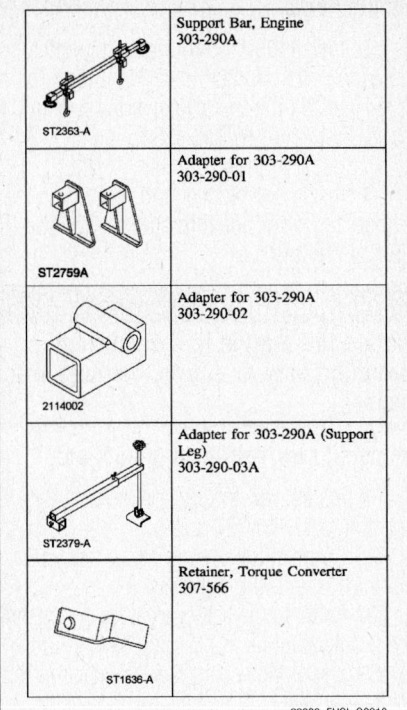

Support Bar, Engine 303-290A	ST2363-A
Adapter for 303-290A 303-290-01	ST2759A
Adapter for 303-290A 303-290-02	2114002
Adapter for 303-290A (Support Leg) 303-290-03A	ST2379-A
Retainer, Torque Converter 307-566	ST1636-A

22086_FUSI_G0218

Fig. 19 Special tools necessary for transaxle removal and installation

20. Remove the 6 pin-type retainers and the LH front structure-to-subframe splash shield.
21. Remove the LH front power steering bracket bolt.
22. Remove the 2 LH power steering tube bracket bolts.
23. Remove the RH power steering tube bracket bolt.

➡ **If installation of a new transmission is necessary, the transmission fluid will need to be drained.**

24. Remove the transmission fluid pan drain plug and allow the fluid to drain.
25. Install the fluid drain plug and tighten to 29 Nm (21 ft. lbs.).

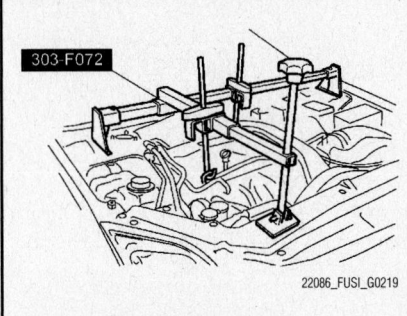

303-F072

22086_FUSI_G0219

Fig. 20 Install the special tool

26. Remove the 2 LH bolts and the RH bolt and position the steering gear aside using mechanic's wire.
27. Remove the nuts and disconnect the sway bar links from the front struts.
28. Remove the RH halfshaft, as outlined in this section.

☀ WARNING

Failure to hold the differential side gears can allow the side gears to rotate and fall out of the differential carrier.

29. Insert a suitable tool into the RH side of the differential to hold the differential side gears in place.
30. Remove the LH halfshaft, as outlined in this section.
31. Support the subframe with a suitable powertrain lift.
32. Remove the 2 rear subframe nuts.
33. Remove the 4 bolts and the subframe support brackets.
34. Remove front subframe nuts.
35. Lower the subframe and remove it from the vehicle.
36. Position the boot aside and remove the starter terminals.
37. Remove the wiring harness retainer from the starter stud.
38. Remove the 2 stud bolts and the starter.
39. Disconnect the transmission fluid cooler hoses from the transmission.

☀ WARNING

Only rotate the engine in a clockwise direction or engine damage will occur.

➡ **Mark one stud and the flexplate for assembly reference.**

40. Remove and discard the 4 torque converter nuts.
41. Remove the nut and the bracket from the torque converter housing stud bolt.
42. Support the transaxle with a suitable transmission jack.
43. Remove the 3 back torque converter housing bolts.
44. Remove the 3 front torque converter housing bolts.
45. Separate the transaxle from the engine and install the special tool.
46. Remove the transaxle from the vehicle.
47. If installing a new transaxle, the fluid cooler will need to be backflushed and cleaned

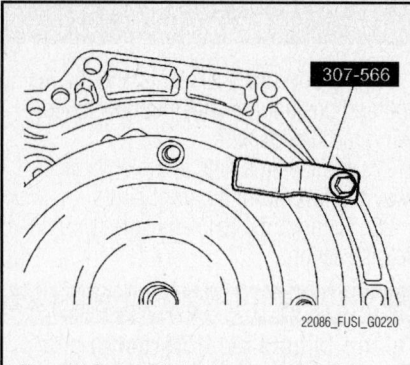

Fig. 21 Separate the transaxle from the engine and install the special tool.

To install:

48. Make sure that the torque converter is installed correctly.

➡**Lubricate the torque converter pilot hub with multi-purpose grease.**

49. Check the installation depth of the torque converter, as follows:

   a. 1. Lay a steel straightedge on the automatic transaxle flange.

   b. 2. Check the installation depth between the transaxle flange and the torque converter centering spigot for the correct clearance.

50. Using a high-lift jack, secure the transaxle using a safety strap.

51. Remove the special tool.

➡**Make sure that the dowel pins are installed in the engine block prior to installing the transaxle.**

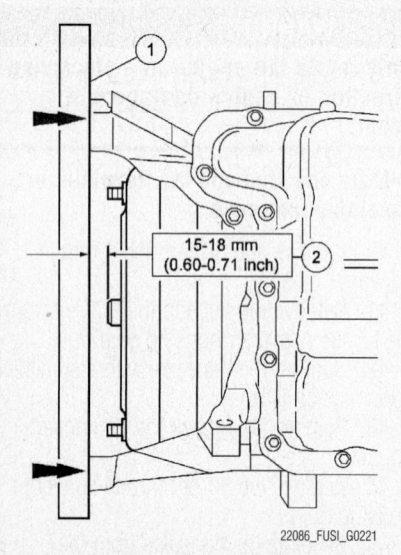

Fig. 22 1. Lay a steel straightedge on the automatic transaxle flange. 2. Check the installation depth between the transaxle flange and the torque converter centering spigot for the correct clearance.

52. Move the transaxle into position.

➡**Note the location of the different length bolts.**

53. Install the 3 front torque converter housing bolts. Tighten to 47 Nm (35 ft. lbs.).

54. Install the 3 rear converter housing bolts. Tighten to 47 Nm (35 ft. lbs.).

55. Remove the transmission jack.

56. Install the bracket and the nut on the torque converter housing stud. Tighten to 25 Nm (18 ft. lbs.).

✳✳ WARNING

Rotate the engine in a clockwise direction only or engine damage will occur.

➡**Install new self-locking nuts only.**

57. Install new torque converter nuts. Tighten to 37 Nm (27 ft. lbs.).

58. Connect the transmission fluid cooler hoses to the transmission.

59. Position the starter in place and install the 2 bolts. Tighten to 35 Nm (26 ft. lbs.).

60. Install the wiring harness fastener on the starter stud.

61. Install the starter terminals and install the boot back into position:

   a. Tighten nut (1) in the accompanying illustration to 12 Nm (9 ft. lbs.).

   b. Tighten nut (2) in the accompanying illustration to 5 Nm (44 lb-in).

62. Position the subframe in place using a suitable powertrain lift.

63. Install the front subframe nuts and tighten to 150 Nm (111 ft. lbs.).

64. Position the subframe support brackets in place and loosely install the bolts.

65. Install the rear subframe nuts. Tighten to 150 Nm (111 ft. lbs.).

66. Tighten the subframe support bracket bolts. Tighten to 103 Nm (76 ft. lbs.).

67. Install the LH halfshaft.

68. Remove the tool installed during removal of the transaxle to hold the differential side gears.

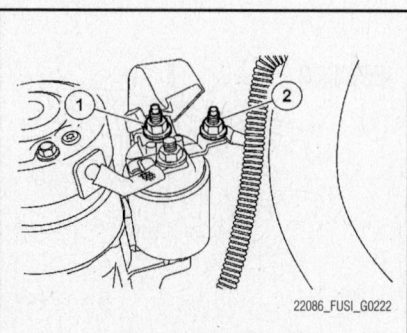

Fig. 23 Starter terminal nuts (1) and (2)

69. Install the RH halfshaft.

70. Install the sway bar links and nuts to the struts. Tighten to 40 Nm (30 ft. lbs.).

71. Position the steering gear in place and install the bolts. Tighten to 107 Nm (79 ft. lbs.).

72. Install the RH power steering tube bracket bolt. Tighten to 9 Nm (80 lb-in).

73. Install the 2 LH power steering tube bracket bolts. Tighten to 9 Nm (80 lb-in).

74. Install the LH power steering tube bracket bolt. Tighten to 9 Nm (80 lb-in).

75. Position the LH front structure-to-subframe splash shield in place and install the 6 pin-type retainers.

76. Position the LH splash shield in place and install the 4 screws.

77. Position the RH front structure-to-subframe splash shield in place and install the 6 pin-type retainers.

78. Position the RH splash shield in place and install the 4 screws.

79. Connect the OSS sensor electrical connector.

80. Connect the pressure switch electrical connector.

81. Position the transaxle support insulator bracket in place and install the 3 nuts. Tighten to 80 Nm (59 ft. lbs.).

82. Raise the transaxle and install the 2 transaxle insulator bolts. Tighten to 63 Nm (46 ft lbs.).

83. Install the 2 roll restrictor bracket bolts. Tighten to 90 Nm (66 ft. lbs.).

84. Install the 3 top torque converter housing bolts. Tighten to 47 Nm (35 ft. lbs.).

85. Install the ground strap. Tighten to 25 Nm (18 ft. lbs.).

86. Connect the TSS sensor, intermediate shaft speed sensor and the 5th gear valve body electrical connectors.

87. Connect the main valve body and the TR sensor electrical connectors and connect the wiring harness to the transmission.

88. Position the selector lever cable and bracket in place, and connect the electrical harness fastener and install the 2 bolts. Tighten to 20 Nm (15 ft. lbs.).

89. Connect the selector lever cable end to the manual lever.

90. Install the battery tray:

   a. Position the battery tray in place and install the bolt. Tighten to 9 Nm (80 lb-in).

   b. Install the nut. Tighten to 9 Nm (80 lb-in).

   c. Connect the 3 wiring harness retainers.

   d. Connect the positive battery cable fastener to the battery tray.

➡**When the battery has been disconnected and reconnected, some abnormal drive symptoms may occur while the vehicle relearns its adaptive strategy. The vehicle may need to be driven to relearn the strategy.**

91. Install the battery.

92. Fill the transaxle with clean automatic transmission fluid

6-Speed Transaxle

3.0L Engine

See Figures 24 through 31.

1. Raise and safely support the vehicle.

2. Remove the battery and battery tray.

3. Remove the air cleaner and the outlet pipe.

4. Disconnect the shift cable end.

5. Remove the 3 bolts for the shift cable bracket and position the cable and bracket aside.

6. Disconnect the wire harness from the transmission control module (TCM).

7. Remove the 2 ground strap bolts and position aside the ground straps.

8. Remove the electrical terminal cover for the starter motor electrical connectors.

9. Remove the starter terminals.

10. Remove the 2 bolts and the starter.

11. Remove the 3 upper torque converter housing bolts.

12. Disconnect the exhaust gas recirculation (EGR) valve electrical connector.

13. Disconnect the EGR tube nut from the valve.

14. Remove the 2 bolts and the EGR valve. Discard the gasket.

15. Remove the bolt from the power steering line bracket and position it aside.

16. Remove the 4 screws and position the RH fender splash shield aside.

17. Remove the 6 pin-type retainers and remove the RH front structure to subframe splash shield.

18. Remove the 4 screws and position the LH fender splash shield aside.

19. Remove the pin-type retainers and remove the LH front structure to subframe splash shield.

20. Remove the 2 nuts and separate the sway bar links from the struts.

➡**If a transaxle exchange or overhaul is required, the transmission fluid must be drained.**

21. Remove the drain plug and allow the fluid to drain. If removed, install the transmission fluid drain plug and tighten to 47 Nm (35 ft. lbs.).

22. Remove the LH halfshaft, as outlined in this section.

23. For All Wheel Drive (AWD) vehicles, perform the following:

a. Remove and discard the front wheel hub nut.

24. Remove the RH lower control arm nuts.

✳✳ WARNING

When the lower ball joint is separated from the wheel knuckle, the lower arm may strike the outer constant velocity (CV) joint boot with enough force to damage the boot clamp. This will result in a loss of grease from the outer CV joint. Place a block of wood, or similar item, between the lower arm and the outer CV joint to prevent the lower arm from striking the outer CV joint.

➡**Once pressure is applied to the ball joint with the special tool, it may be necessary to tap the wheel knuckle at the ball joint area to separate the ball joint from the wheel knuckle.**

25. Using the special tools, separate the 2 lower ball joints from the wheel knuckle and remove the wheel knuckle.

26. Remove the bolt connecting the RH damper fork to the lower control arm.

27. Remove the 2 Y-pipe bolts and nuts.

28. Remove the flexpipe nuts and the Y-pipe assembly.

29. If equipped, remove the 2 bolts and the roll restrictor heat shield.

30. Remove the 2 bolts from the engine roll restrictor bracket.

31. Remove the bolts and position the power steering cooler tube aside.

32. Remove the 3 steering gear bolts and position the steering gear aside with mechanic's wire.

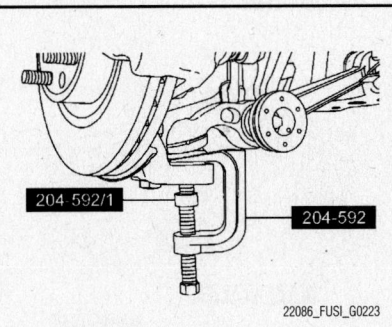

Fig. 24 Using the special tools, separate the 2 lower ball joints from the wheel knuckle and remove the wheel knuckle.

33. Position a suitable drivetrain lift table under the subframe.

34. Remove the 2 rear subframe nuts.

35. Remove the 4 bolts and the 2 subframe support brackets.

36. Remove the 2 front subframe nuts and remove the subframe.

37. Loosen the EGR tube nut at the RH exhaust manifold and remove the EGR tube.

38. For Front wheel drive (FWD) vehicles:

a. Remove the 2 bolts and the RH exhaust manifold heat shield.

b. Remove the 2 bolts and the catalytic converter band clamp.

c. Remove the 2 bolts and the catalytic converter-to-engine block bracket.

d. Disconnect the heated oxygen sensor (HO2S) electrical connector from the RH halfshaft bearing support bracket.

e. Remove the bolt retaining the brake caliper hose.

f. Remove the 2 bolts and remove the RH halfshaft from the transaxle and position it aside with mechanic's wire.

39. For AWD vehicles:

a. Using special tool 205-D070, separate the halfshaft from the wheel hub.

b. Remove the 2 bolts and the RH halfshaft.

c. Index the driveshaft, remove the 4 bolts from the driveshaft and position the driveshaft aside.

d. Disconnect the RH catalyst monitor sensor (CMS) electrical connector and detach the wiring retainer.

e. Using the special tool, remove the RH CMS.

f. Disconnect the RH heated oxygen sensor (HO2S) electrical connector.

g. Using the special tool, remove the RH HO2S.

h. Remove the 6 bolts and the RH exhaust heat shield

i. Remove the 3 nuts and the catalytic converter band clamp RH half.

j. Remove the 2 bolts and the catalytic converter band clamp LH half.

k. Remove the nuts and the RH catalytic converter.

l. Remove the 5 bolts and the power transfer unit (PTU) support bracket.

➡**A new halfshaft seal must be installed anytime the RH halfshaft is removed.**

➡**The seal deflector will be damaged during removal. Be careful not to damage the cover seal directly behind the seal deflector.**

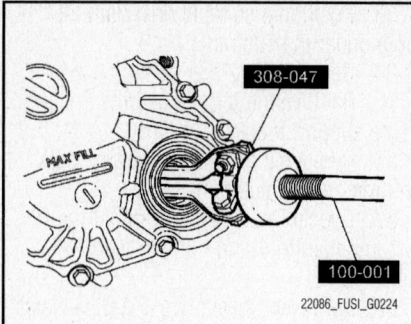

Fig. 25 Using the special tools, remove the halfshaft seal from the PTU

m. Remove the seal deflector.

n. Using the special tools, remove the halfshaft seal from the PTU.

o. Remove the 5 bolts and the PTU.

➡**When installing the lifting bracket, it will be easier to loosely install the upper bolt first, then install the lower bolt.**

40. Install the lower half of the lifting hook.

41. Install the upper half of the lifting hook.

42. Install the universal lifting brackets on the LH side of the engine.

43. Using the special tools, support the engine.

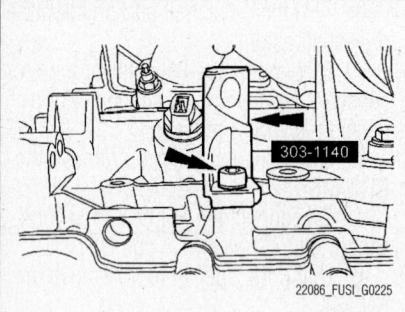

Fig. 26 Install the lower half of the lifting hook.

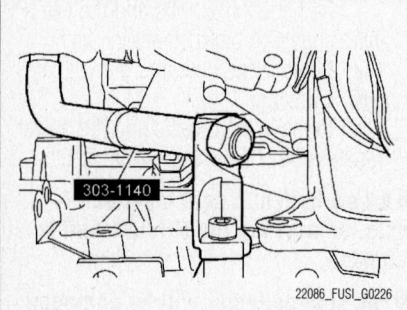

Fig. 27 Install the upper half of the lifting hook.

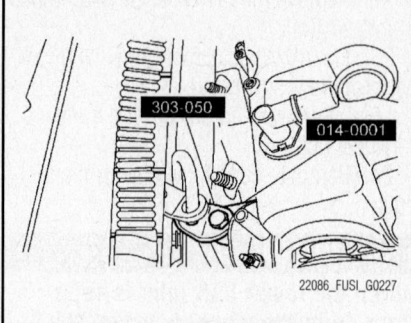

Fig. 28 Install the universal lifting brackets on the LH side of the engine.

44. Remove the 2 bolts from the transmission insulator.

45. Lower the transaxle and remove the 2 nuts and the bolt and remove the transaxle support insulator bracket.

46. Remove the HO2S bracket bolt and disconnect the wiring harness fastener.

47. Remove the inspection cover.

48. Remove and discard the 3 torque converter nuts.

49. Disconnect the transmission fluid cooler hoses.

50. Position a suitable high-lift transmission jack under the transaxle.

51. Remove the 5 torque converter housing bolts and remove the transmission.

52. If installing a new transaxle, the fluid cooler will need to be backflushed and cleaned. Carry out transmission fluid cooler tube backflushing and cleaning.

To install:

❊❊ WARNING

MERCON®, MERCON®V, MERCON®SP, Motorcraft Premium Automatic Transmission Fluid and Motorcraft

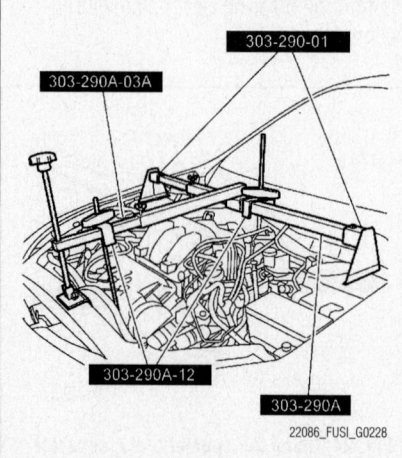

Fig. 29 Using the special tools, support the engine

Continuously Variable Chain Type Transmission Fluid are not interchangeable transmission fluids. The use of any fluid other than what is recommended for this transmission will cause transmission damage.

➡**If the transaxle was overhauled, or if installing a new transaxle and the transmission fluid cooler has not been flushed, flush the fluid cooler at this time.**

53. Prior to installing the transaxle, apply multi-purpose grease to the torque converter pilot hub.

54. Position the transaxle to the back of the engine.

55. Install the 5 transaxle-to-engine bolts. Tighten to 40 Nm (30 ft. lbs.).

56. Connect the transmission fluid cooler hoses to the transaxle.

57. Install 3 new torque converter nuts. Tighten to 36 Nm (27 ft. lbs.).

58. Install the inspection cover.

59. Connect the wiring harness fastener to the stud bolt and position the heated oxygen sensor (HO2S) bracket in place and install the bolt. Tighten to 12 Nm (9 ft. lbs.).

60. Position the transaxle insulator bracket in place. Apply threadlock to the threads and install the 2 nuts and the bolt. Tighten to 80 Nm (59 ft. lbs.).

61. Raise the transaxle. Apply threadlock to the threads and install the 2 bolts. Tighten to 62 Nm (46 ft. lbs.).

62. Remove the special tools.

63. Remove the special tools from the LH side of the engine.

64. Remove the upper half of the lifting hook.

65. Remove the lower half of the lifting hook.

66. For AWD vehicles:

a. Position the power transfer unit (PTU) in place and install the 5 bolts.

b. Tighten to 90 Nm (66 ft. lbs.).

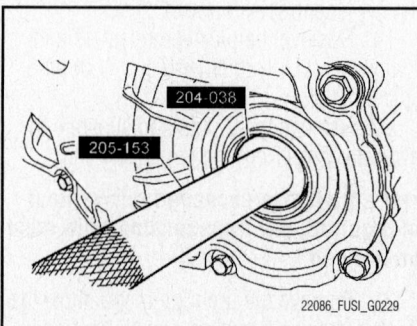

Fig. 30 Using the special tools, install a new intermediate shaft seal.

67. Using the special tools, install a new intermediate shaft seal.

➡**Do not overheat (melt) the seal deflector. If the deflector is damaged, a new one must be used.**

68. Using a suitable heat gun, heat the new seal deflector. Concentrate the heat across the back of the deflector near the white colored tabs. Install the seal deflector immediately after heating.

69. If necessary, use special tools 308-430 and 308-431 to seat the seal deflector. Make sure the deflector is fully seated and there are no cracks on the face or inner diameter white colored tab.

70. For an alternate method to heat the seal deflector, place the deflector in boiling water for 3 to 5 minutes. Dry off deflector and install.

71. Make sure the deflector is completely seated all the way around.

72. Position the PTU support bracket in place and install the 5 bolts. Tighten to 70 Nm (52 ft. lbs.).

73. Position the RH catalytic converter in place and install the nuts. Tighten to 40 Nm (30 ft. lbs.).

74. Install the catalytic converter band clamp LH half and the 2 bolts. Tighten to 40 Nm (30 ft. lbs.).

75. Install the catalytic converter band clamp RH half and install the 3 nuts. Tighten to 20 Nm (15 ft. lbs.).

76. Install the RH exhaust heat shield and the 6 bolts. Tighten to 11 Nm (8 ft. lbs.).

77. Using the special tool, install the RH HO2S. Tighten to 48 Nm (35 ft. lbs.).

78. Connect the RH HO2S electrical connector.

79. Using the special tool, install the RH catalyst monitor sensor (CMS). Tighten to 48 Nm (35 ft. lbs.).

80. Connect the RH CMS electrical connector and attach the wiring harness retainer.

81. Position the driveshaft in place, align the index marks made during removal and install the 4 bolts. Tighten to 70 Nm (52 ft. lbs.).

82. Position the RH driveshaft in place and install the 2 bolts. Tighten to 23 Nm (17 ft. lbs.).

83. For FWD vehicles :

   a. Position the RH halfshaft in the transaxle and install the 2 bolts. Tighten to 55 Nm (41 ft. lbs.).

   b. Install the bolt retaining the brake caliper hose. Tighten to 22 Nm (16 ft. lbs.).

   c. Connect the HO2S to the RH halfshaft bearing support bracket.

   d. Install the catalytic converter-to-engine block bracket and install the 2 bolts. Tighten to 35 Nm (26 ft. lbs.).

   e. Install the catalytic converter band clamp and the 2 bolts. Tighten to 20 Nm (15 ft. lbs.).

   f. Install the RH exhaust manifold heat shield and the 2 bolts. Tighten to 11 Nm (8 ft. lbs.).

84. Loosely install the exhaust gas recirculation (EGR) tube nut on the RH exhaust manifold.

85. Position the subframe in place using a suitable powertrain lift.

86. Install the front subframe nuts. Tighten to 150 Nm (111 ft. lbs.).

87. Position the subframe support brackets in place and loosely install the bolts.

88. Install the rear subframe nuts. Tighten to 150 Nm (111 ft. lbs.).

89. Tighten the subframe support bracket bolts. Tighten to 103 Nm (76 ft. lbs.).

90. Position the steering gear in place and install the 3 bolts. Tighten to 107 Nm (79 ft. lbs.).

91. Position the power steering cooler tube in place and install the bolts. Tighten to 9 Nm (80 lb-in).

92. Install the 2 roll restrictor bolts. Tighten to 90 Nm (66 ft. lbs.).

93. If equipped, install the roll restrictor heat shield and the bolts.

94. Position the Y-pipe assembly in place and install the 2 flexpipe nuts. Tighten to 40 Nm (30 ft. lbs.).

95. Install the 2 Y-pipe bolts and the 2 Y-pipe nuts. Tighten to 40 Nm (30 ft. lbs.).

96. Install the bolt connecting the RH damper fork to the lower control arm. Tighten to 103 Nm (76 ft. lbs.).

97. Position the lower control arms in the knuckle and install the nuts. Tighten to 200 Nm (148 ft. lbs.).

98. For AWD vehicles:

   a. Using the special tool, install the halfshaft in the wheel hub.

   b. Install the front RH wheel hub nut. Tighten 225 Nm (185 ft. lbs.).

99. Install the LH halfshaft.

100. Position the sway bar links in the struts and install the nuts. Tighten to 40 Nm (30 ft. lbs.).

101. Install the LH front structure to subframe splash shield and install the pin-type retainers.

102. Position the LH fender splash shield in place and install the 4 screws.

103. Position the RH front structure-to-subframe splash shield in place and install the 6 pin-type retainers.

104. Position the RH fender splash shield in place and install the 4 screws.

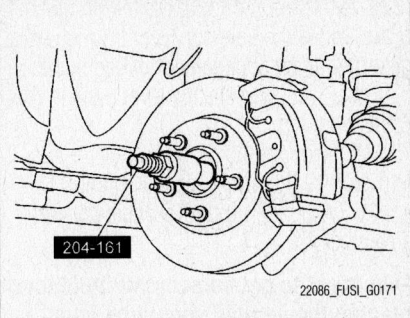

204-161

22086_FUSI_G0171

Fig. 31 Using the special tool, install the halfshaft in the wheel hub.

105. Position the power steering line bracket on the right cylinder head and install the bolt. Tighten to 7 Nm (62 lb-in).

106. Install a new gasket and the EGR valve and install the 2 bolts. Tighten to 25 Nm (18 ft. lbs.).

107. Install the EGR tube on the valve. Tighten to 40 Nm (30 ft. lbs.).

108. Connect the EGR valve electrical connector.

109. Tighten the EGR tube at the RH exhaust manifold. Tighten to 40 Nm (30 ft. lbs.).

110. Install the 3 upper transaxle-to-engine retaining bolts. Tighten to 40 Nm (30 ft. lbs.).

111. Install the starter and the 2 bolts. Tighten to 26 Nm (19 ft. lbs.).

112. Connect the 2 starter motor electrical connectors:

   a. Tighten the larger nut to 12 Nm (9 ft. lbs.).

   b. Tighten the smaller nut to 5 Nm (44 lb-in).

113. Install the electrical cover for the starter motor electrical connectors.

114. Install the 2 ground straps and ground strap bolts. Tighten to 12 Nm (9 ft. lbs.).

115. Connect the TCM electrical connector.

116. Position the shift cable and bracket in place and install the nut and 2 bolts. Tighten to 12 Nm (9 ft. lbs.).

117. Connect the shift cable end.

118. Remove the transmission fluid fill plug.

119. Fill the transaxle with clean automatic transmission fluid. Install the fluid fill plug and tighten to 39 Nm (29 ft. lbs.).

120. Install the air cleaner and outlet tube.

121. Install the battery tray and the battery.

122. Remove the fluid level indicator and make sure that the transaxle has fluid in it.

123. With the transaxle in PARK, the vehicle on a level surface, the engine at idle

(680-780 rpm) and foot pressed on the brake, move the selector lever through each gear and allow engagement of each gear.

124. Place the selector lever back in the PARK position.

125. Wipe the fluid level indicator cap and remove the fluid level indicator.

126. Wipe the fluid level indicator with a clean cloth.

➡In order to get an accurate fluid level reading the vehicle should be on a level surface. Idle the engine to reach the normal operating temperature. Using the scan tool, verify that the transaxle is at normal operating temperature 60°C-70°C (140°F-158°F), prior to adjusting the transmission fluid level.

127. If fluid needs to be added, add fluid in 0.25L (1/2 pint) increments through the fluid fill plug located on the top of the transaxle near the fluid level indicator. Do not overfill the fluid. Install the fluid level indicator back in the fluid filler tube until it is fully seated, then remove the indicator. The fluid level should be at the upper most mark on the fluid level indicator. Only fill to the upper most mark on the fluid indicator. Do not overfill. Damage to the transaxle will occur.

➡The correct transmission fluid level at normal operating temperature of 60°C-70°C (140°F-158°F) is between the top 2 marks on the fluid level indicator.

128. Fill the transaxle to the correct fluid level.

➡The correct transmission fluid level at cold operating temperature of 15°C-25°C (59°F-77°F) is at the bottom mark on the fluid level indicator.

129. If the transmission fluid temperature is low, fill the fluid to the cold range on the fluid level indicator. Recheck the fluid level when the transaxle has reached the normal operating temperature

3.5L Engine

See Figures 30 through 36.

1. Raise and safely support the vehicle..

2. Remove the battery and battery tray.

3. Remove the air cleaner and the outlet pipe.

4. Remove the upper intake manifold, as outlined in this section.

5. Disconnect the shift cable end.

6. Remove the 2 bolts and the nut for the shift cable bracket and position the cable and bracket aside.

7. Disconnect the wire harness from the Transmission Control Module (TCM).

8. Disconnect the wiring harness fasteners from the torque converter housing stud bolt and the starter motor.

9. Remove the 2 ground strap bolts and position aside the ground straps.

10. Position the boot back and remove the starter terminals from the starter.

11. Remove the 2 bolts and the starter.

12. Remove the 4 upper torque converter housing bolts.

13. Install the special tool on the LH cylinder head.

14. Install the special tools and support the engine.

15. Remove the transaxle support insulator through bolt.

16. Using the special tools, lower the transaxle and remove the 2 transaxle support insulator bracket nuts, the bolt and the bracket.

17. Remove the 4 screws and position the RH fender splash shield aside.

18. Remove the 6 pin-type retainers and remove the RH front structure to subframe splash shield.

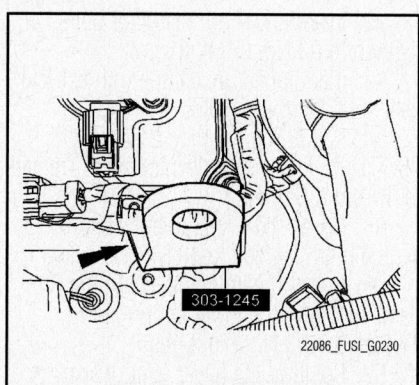

Fig. 32 Install the special tool on the LH cylinder head

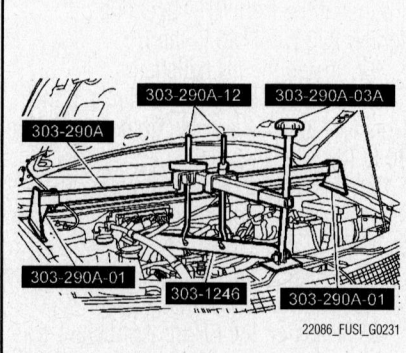

Fig. 33 Install the special tools and support the engine.

19. Remove the 4 screws and position the LH fender splash shield aside.

20. Remove the pin-type retainers and remove the LH front structure-to-subframe splash shield.

21. Remove the 6 Y-pipe nuts and the Y-pipe assembly.

22. Remove the nuts and separate the sway bar links from the struts.

23. If a transaxle exchange or overhaul is required, the transmission fluid must be drained. Remove the drain plug and allow the fluid to drain.

24. If removed, install the transmission fluid drain plug. Tighten to 47 Nm (35 ft. lbs.).

25. Remove the LH halfshaft.

26. For All Wheel Drive (AWD) vehicles, remove and discard the front wheel hub nut.

27. Remove the RH lower control arm nuts.

❋❋ WARNING

When the lower ball joint is separated from the wheel knuckle, the lower arm may strike the outer constant velocity (CV) joint boot with enough force to damage the boot clamp. This will result in a loss of grease from the outer CV joint. Place a block of wood, or similar item, between the lower arm and the outer CV joint to prevent the lower arm from striking the outer CV joint.

➡Once pressure is applied to the ball joint with the special tool, it may be necessary to tap the wheel knuckle at the ball joint area to separate the ball joint from the wheel knuckle.

28. Using the special tools, separate the 2 lower ball joints from the wheel knuckle and remove the wheel knuckle.

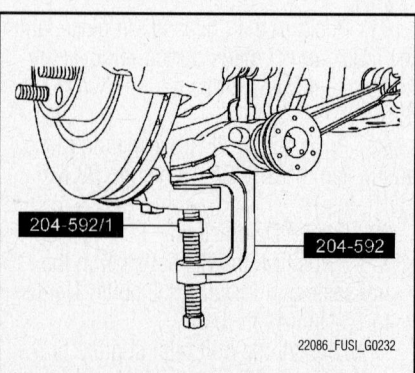

Fig. 34 Using the special tools, separate the 2 lower ball joints from the wheel knuckle and remove the wheel knuckle

29. Remove the bolt connecting the RH damper fork to the lower control arm.

30. Remove the 2 engine roll restrictor bracket bolts.

31. Remove the bolts and position the power steering cooler tube aside.

32. Remove the 3 steering gear bolts and position the steering gear aside with mechanic's wire.

33. Position a suitable drivetrain lift table under the subframe.

34. Remove the 2 rear subframe nuts.

35. Remove the 4 bolts and the 2 subframe support brackets.

36. Remove the 2 front subframe nuts and remove the subframe.

37. For Front Wheel Drive (FWD) vehicles:

   a. Remove the 2 catalytic converter bracket bolts.

   b. Remove the 2 nuts and remove the catalytic converter support bracket.

   c. Remove the 3 bolts and position the RH halfshaft aside.

38. For AWD vehicles:

   a. Using the special tool, press the halfshaft out of the wheel hub.

   b. Remove the 2 bolts and the RH halfshaft.

   c. Matchmark the installed position of the driveshaft, remove the 4 bolts and position the driveshaft aside.

   d. Disconnect the RH catalyst monitor electrical connector.

   e. Remove the 2 catalytic converter bracket bolts.

   f. Remove the 4 nuts and the RH catalytic converter.

   g. Remove the 5 bolts and the Power Transfer Unit (PTU) support bracket.

➥A new halfshaft seal must be installed anytime the RH halfshaft is removed. The seal deflector will be damaged during removal. Be careful not to damage the cover seal directly behind the seal deflector.

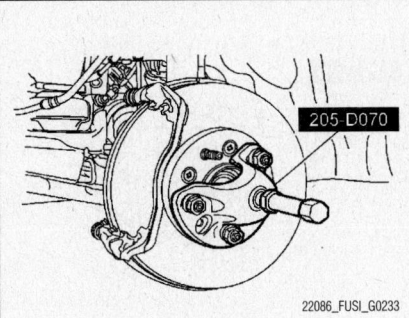

Fig. 35 Using the special tool, press the halfshaft out of the wheel hub

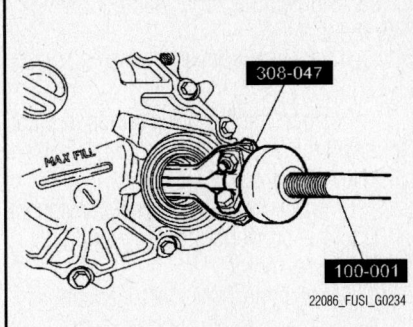

Fig. 36 Using the special tools, remove the halfshaft seal from the PTU

   h. Remove the seal deflector.

   i. Using the special tools, remove the halfshaft seal from the PTU.

   j. Remove the 5 bolts and the PTU.

39. Remove the 2 fasteners and the inspection cover.

40. Remove the 4 torque converter nuts.

41. Disconnect the transmission fluid cooler hoses.

42. Position a suitable high-lift transmission jack under the transaxle.

43. Remove the 7 torque converter housing bolts and remove the transaxle.

44. If installing a new transaxle, the fluid cooler will need to be backflushed and cleaned. Carry out transmission fluid cooler tube backflushing and cleaning.

To install:

❋❋ WARNING

MERCON®, MERCON®V, MERCON®SP, Motorcraft Premium Automatic Transmission Fluid and Motorcraft Continuously Variable Chain Type Transmission Fluid are not interchangeable transmission fluids. The use of any fluid other than what is recommended for this transmission will cause transmission damage.

➥If the transaxle was overhauled, or if installing a new transaxle and the transmission fluid cooler has not been flushed, flush the fluid cooler at this time.

45. Prior to installing the transaxle, apply multi-purpose grease to the torque converter pilot hub.

46. Position the transaxle to the back of the engine.

47. Install the 7 torque converter housing bolts. Tighten to 48 Nm (35 ft. lbs.).

48. Connect the transmission fluid cooler hoses to the transaxle.

49. Install 4 new torque converter nuts. Tighten to 36 Nm (27 ft. lbs.).

50. Position the inspection cover in place and install the 2 fasteners.

51. For AWD vehicles:

   a. Position the power transfer unit (PTU) in place and install the 5 bolts. Tighten to 90 Nm (66 ft. lbs.).

   b. Using the special tools, install a new intermediate shaft seal.

➥Do not overheat (melt) the seal deflector. If the deflector is damaged, a new one must be used.

   c. Using a suitable heat gun, heat the new seal deflector. Concentrate the heat across the back of the deflector near the white colored tabs. Install the seal deflector immediately after heating.

   • If necessary, use special tools 308-430 and 308-431 to seat the seal deflector. Make sure the deflector is fully seated and there are no cracks on the face or inner diameter white colored tab.

   • For an alternate method to heat the seal deflector, place the deflector in boiling water for 3 to 5 minutes. Dry off deflector and install.

   • Make sure the deflector is completely seated all the way around.

   d. Position the PTU support bracket in place and install the 5 bolts. Tighten to 70 Nm (52 ft. lbs.).

   e. Position the RH catalytic converter in place and install the 4 nuts. Tighten to 40 Nm (30 ft. lbs.).

   f. Install the 2 catalytic converter bracket bolts. Tighten to 20 Nm (15 ft. lbs.).

   g. Connect the RH catalyst monitor electrical connector.

   h. Position the driveshaft in place, align the index marks made during removal and install the bolts. Tighten to 70 Nm (52 ft. lbs.).

   i. Position the RH halfshaft in the transaxle and in the wheel hub and install the 2 bolts. Tighten to 23 Nm (17 ft. lbs.).

52. For FWD vehicles:

   a. Install the RH halfshaft in the transaxle and install the 3 bolts. Tighten to 55 Nm (41 ft. lbs.).

   b. Install the catalytic converter support bracket and install the 2 nuts. Tighten to 23 Nm (17 ft. lbs.).

   c. Install the 2 catalytic converter bracket bolts. Tighten to 20 Nm (15 ft. lbs.).

53. Position the subframe in place and install the 2 front subframe nuts. Tighten to 150 Nm (111 ft. lbs.).

54. Position the subframe support brackets in place and loosely install the bolts.

55. Install the rear subframe nuts. Tighten to 150 Nm (111 ft. lbs.).

56. Tighten the subframe support bracket bolts. Tighten to 103 Nm (76 ft. lbs.).

57. Position the steering gear in place and install the 3 bolts. Tighten to 107 Nm (79 ft. lbs.).

58. Position the power steering cooler tube in place and install the bolts. Tighten to 9 Nm (80 lb-in).

59. Install the 2 roll restrictor bracket bolts. Tighten to 90 Nm (66 ft. lbs.).

60. Install the bolt connecting the RH damper fork to the lower control arm. Tighten to 103 Nm (76 ft. lbs.).

61. Position the lower control arms in the knuckle and install the nuts. Tighten to 200 Nm (148 ft. lbs.).

62. For AWD vehicles:
   a. Using the special tool, install the halfshaft in the wheel hub.
   b. Install a new front wheel hub nut. Tighten to 255 Nm (185 ft. lbs.).

63. Install the LH halfshaft.

64. Position the sway bar links in the struts and install the nuts. Tighten to 40 Nm (30 ft. lbs.).

65. Position the Y-pipe in place and install the 6 Y-pipe nuts. Tighten to 40 Nm (30 ft. lbs.).

66. Install the LH front structure to subframe splash shield and install the pin-type retainers.

67. Position the LH fender splash shield in place and install the 4 screws.

68. Position the RH front structure-to-subframe splash shield in place and install the 6 pin-type retainers.

69. Position the RH fender splash shield in place and install the 4 screws.

70. Apply threadlock to the threads and install the transaxle support insulator bracket, the 2 nuts and the bolt. Tighten to 80 Nm (59 ft. lbs.).

71. Using the special tool, raise the transaxle. Apply threadlock to the threads and install the transaxle support insulator through bolt. Tighten to 130 Nm (96 ft. lbs.).

72. Remove the special tools.

73. Remove the special tool from the LH cylinder head.

74. Install the 4 upper torque converter housing bolts. Tighten to 48 Nm (35 ft. lbs.).

75. Install the starter and the 2 bolts. Tighten to 26 Nm (19 ft. lbs.).

76. Connect the 2 starter motor electrical connectors and position back the electrical terminal cover:

   a. Tighten the larger nut to 12 Nm (9 ft. lbs.).
   b. Tighten the smaller nut to 5 Nm (44 lb-in).

77. Position the 2 ground straps in place and install the 2 ground strap bolts. Tighten to 12 Nm (9 ft. lbs.).

78. Connect the wiring harness fasteners on the torque converter housing stud bolt and the starter motor.

79. Connect the TCM electrical connector.

80. Position the selector lever cable in place and install the 2 bolts and the nut. Tighten to 12 Nm (9 ft. lbs.).

81. Connect the shift cable end.

82. Remove the transmission fluid fill plug.

83. Fill the transaxle with clean automatic transmission fluid. Install the fluid fill plug and tighten to 39 Nm (29 ft. lbs.).

84. Install the upper intake manifold.

85. Install the air cleaner and outlet tube.

86. Install the battery tray and the battery.

87. Remove the fluid level indicator and make sure that the transaxle has fluid in it.

88. With the transaxle in PARK, the vehicle on a level surface, the engine at idle (680-780 rpm) and foot pressed on the brake, move the selector lever through each gear and allow engagement of each gear. Place the selector lever back in the PARK position.

89. Wipe the fluid level indicator cap and remove the fluid level indicator.

90. Wipe the fluid level indicator with a clean cloth.

➡ In order to get an accurate fluid level reading the vehicle should be on a level surface. Idle the engine to reach the normal operating temperature. Using the scan tool, verify that the transaxle is at normal operating temperature 60°C-70°C (140°F-158°F), prior to adjusting the transmission fluid level.

91. If fluid needs to be added, add fluid in 0.25L (1/2 pint) increments through the fluid fill plug located on the top of the transaxle near the fluid level indicator. Do not overfill the fluid. Install the fluid level indicator back in the fluid filler tube until it is fully seated, then remove the indicator. The fluid level should be at the upper most mark on the fluid level indicator. Only fill to the upper most mark on the fluid indicator. Do not overfill. Damage to the transaxle will occur.

➡ The correct transmission fluid level at normal operating temperature of

60°C-70°C (140°F-158°F) is between the top 2 marks on the fluid level indicator.

92. Fill the transaxle to the correct fluid level.

➡ The correct transmission fluid level at cold operating temperature of 15°C-25°C (59°F-77°F) is at the bottom mark on the fluid level indicator.

93. If the transmission fluid temperature is low, fill the fluid to the cold range on the fluid level indicator.

94. Recheck the fluid level when the transaxle has reached the normal operating temperature.

MANUAL TRANSAXLE ASSEMBLY

REMOVAL & INSTALLATION
See Figures 37 and 38.

1. Raise and safely support the vehicle.
2. Remove battery and the battery tray.
3. Remove the air cleaner assembly.

✳✳ WARNING
Carefully disconnect the spring clip.

4. Disconnect the gearshift cables from the shift mechanism:
   a. Pull the spring clip out of the groove. Lift upward to rotate the clip 90 degrees.

✳✳ WARNING
Carefully pry the retainer on the shift cable. Do not damage the shift cable retainers.

5. Disconnect the shift cables from the transaxle bracket.

6. Install special tool 303-F072, or equivalent support tool.

7. Remove the ground wire bolt.

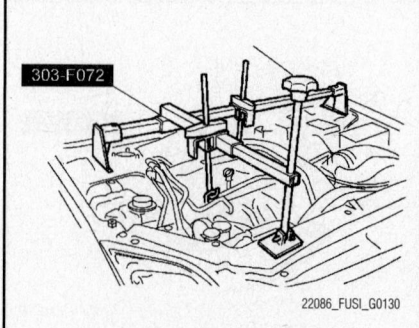

22086_FUSI_G0130

Fig. 37 Install special tool 303-F072, or equivalent support tool

8. Remove the radio frequency interference capacitor and ground cable bolt.

9. Detach the wire harness from the transaxle.

10. Remove the 3 upper transaxle-to-engine bolts.

11. Remove the transaxle mount:

a. If the mount studs are removed or come out, do not reinstall the old stud. Install a new stud. Make sure the stud is properly seated in the case.

12. Raise the vehicle.

13. Remove the 7 bolts and the splash shield, if equipped.

14. If transmission disassembly is necessary, drain the transmission fluid.

15. Remove the clutch tube bracket bolts.

16. Remove the bolts and position the clutch slave cylinder aside.

17. Disconnect the reverse lamp switch electrical connector.

18. Loosen the starter motor bolts.

19. Remove the engine roll restrictor.

20. Remove the roll restrictor mount bracket.

21. Disconnect the Vehicle Speed Sensor (VSS) electrical connector.

22. Remove the front subframe.

23. Remove the LH halfshaft from the transaxle.

24. Remove the 2 intermediate shaft support bracket bolts, then remove the RH intermediate shaft from the transaxle.

✳✳ WARNING

Secure the transaxle to the transmission jack with a safety strap.

25. Install a transmission jack.

26. Remove the bellhousing-to-oil pan bolt.

27. Remove the 2 oil pan-to-bellhousing bolts.

28. Remove the remaining 7 transaxle-to-engine bolts.

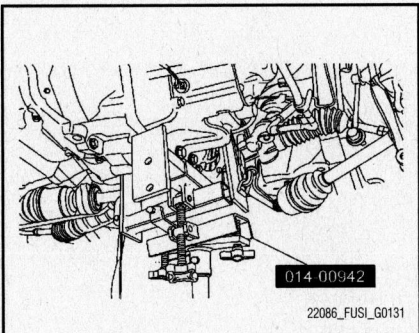

014 00942

22086_FUSI_G0131

Fig. 38 Install a suitable transmission jack

29. Move the transaxle away from the engine and lower it from the vehicle.

To install:

30. Apply a very small amount of grease on the input shaft splines. Wipe off excess grease. The splines should have a thin film of grease only. Excess grease can contaminate the clutch facing and affect clutch function.

✳✳ WARNING

Secure the transaxle to the transmission jack with a safety strap.

31. Raise and position the transaxle to the engine.

32. Install the bellhousing-to-oil pan bolt. Tighten to 48 Nm (35 ft. lbs.).

33. Install the 2 oil pan-to-bellhousing bolts. Tighten to 48 Nm (35 ft. lbs.).

34. Install the 7 remaining transaxle-to-engine bolts. Tighten to 48 Nm (35 ft. lbs.).

35. Install the transmission lower mount to the transaxle. Do not tighten the bolts at this time.

36. Position the slave cylinder to the clutch release arm and install the bolts. Tighten to 20 Nm (15 ft. lbs.).

37. Install the clutch tube bracket bolts. Tighten to 22 Nm (16 ft. lbs.).

38. Tighten the starter motor bolts to 25 Nm (18 ft. lbs.).

39. Remove the transmission jack.

➡ Install a new stub shaft circlip.

40. Install the LH halfshaft into the transaxle.

➡ Install a new stub shaft circlip.

41. Install the RH intermediate shaft into the transaxle. Install the 2 intermediate shaft support bracket bolts.

42. Install the roll restrictor mount bracket.

43. Install the front subframe.

44. Remove the lift table.

45. Install the engine roll-restrictor. Tighten to 90 Nm (66 ft. lbs.).

46. Connect the reverse lamp switch electrical connector.

47. Connect the VSS electrical connector.

48. Working in the engine compartment, position the transaxle lower mount to the upper mount and install the 2 bolts. Tighten all 5 bolts to 80 Nm (59 ft. lbs.).

49. Install the ground wire and ground wire bolt. Tighten to 10 Nm (89 lb-in).

50. Install the radio frequency interference capacitor, the ground cable and the bolt. Tighten to 10 Nm (89 lb-in).

51. Install the 3 upper transaxle-to-engine bolts. Tighten to 48 Nm (35 ft. lbs.).

52. Attach the wire harness to the transaxle.

53. Remove the special support tool.

54. Install the shift and selector cables. Make sure the cables are engaged in the shift bracket and the spring clips are seated in the groove.

55. Install battery tray and the battery.

56. Install the air cleaner assembly.

57. Fill the transaxle proper amount of SAE 75W-90 Premium Gear Oil.

58. Install the splash shield and the 7 bolts, if equipped.

59. Check the vehicle for normal operation

CLUTCH

REMOVAL & INSTALLATION

See Figures 39 through 43.

1. Remove the transaxle, as outlined in this section.

2. Inspect the clutch pressure plate:

a. Check the diaphragm spring fingers for discoloration, scoring, bent or broken segments.

b. Using the special tool, rotate the flywheel and check for spring ends that are higher or lower than the rest.

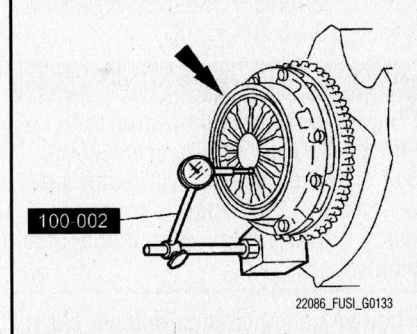

100-002

22086_FUSI_G0133

Fig. 39 Using the special tool, rotate the flywheel and check for spring ends that are higher or lower than the rest

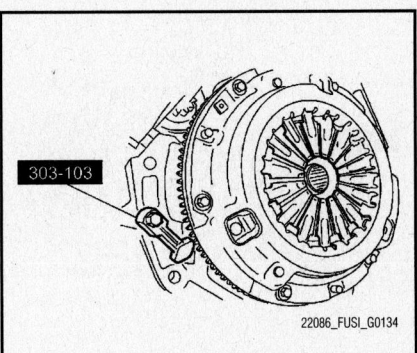

303-103

22086_FUSI_G0134

Fig. 40 Using the special tool, lock the flywheel to the engine

c. The specification is 0.6 mm (0.02 in) maximum.

3. Using the special tool, lock the flywheel to the engine.

⁂ CAUTION

The clutch disc and clutch pressure plate are heavy and may fall if not held when the bolts are removed. Failure to follow these instructions may result in personal injury.

⚡ WARNING

Loosen each bolt, one turn at a time in a star pattern, until spring tension is released.

4. Using a suitable clutch disc aligner, remove the bolts, the clutch pressure plate and the clutch disc.

⁂ WARNING

Do not use cleaners with a petroleum base and do not immerse the clutch pressure plate in solvent.

5. Using a suitable commercial alcohol-based solvent, clean the clutch pressure plate.

6. Inspect the clutch pressure plate surface for burn marks, scores, flatness, ridges or cracks. Maximum clearance for flatness check is 0.3 mm (0.012 in).

⚡ WARNING

If the clutch disc is saturated with oil, inspect the rear engine crankshaft seal or transmission input shaft seal for leakage. If leakage is found, install a new seal prior to clutch disc installation.

➡Use an emery cloth to remove minor imperfections in the clutch disc lining surface.

➡Install a new clutch disc if any of the following conditions are present.

7. Inspect the clutch disc for the following:

   a. Oil or grease saturation.
   b. Worn or loose facings.
   c. Warpage or loose rivets at the hub.
   d. Wear or rust on the splines.

8. Check the clutch disc runout.

9. If necessary, conduct a flywheel runout check.

10. Remove the clutch release bearing.

11. Inspect the clutch release bearing for wear or damage. Rotate the bearing while applying pressure in the axial direction. If the bearing feels rough, sticks or has excessive resistance, install a new bearing.

12. Inspect the release bearing guide tube for wear or damage. Slide the release bearing on the guide tube. Check for roughness or sticking.

13. Remove the clutch release fork. Inspect the fork for wear or damage.

To install:

14. Apply a very small amount of grease in the clutch disc hub. Wipe off excess grease to avoid contaminating the clutch disc and affecting clutch function.

15. Using a suitable clutch disc aligner, position the clutch disc on the flywheel.

16. Position the clutch pressure plate on the flywheel and to the dowels. Install the clutch pressure plate bolts. Tighten the bolts one turn at a time in a star pattern. Tighten to 29 Nm (21 ft. lbs.).

17. Apply a small amount of grease to:

   a. the clutch release fork fingers.
   b. the clutch release fork spring.
   c. the guide tube.
   d. the clutch slave cylinder end that contacts the release fork.

18. Install the clutch release bearing and the clutch release fork.

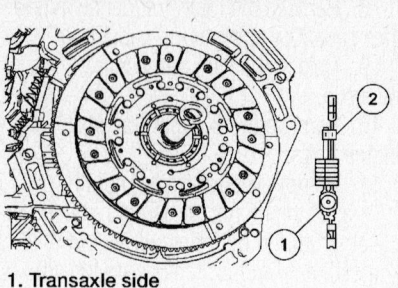

1. Transaxle side
2. Engine side

22086_FUSI_G0136

Fig. 43 Using a suitable clutch disc aligner, position the clutch disc on the flywheel

19. Install the transaxle. Apply a very small amount of grease to the transmission input shaft end and on the splines

BLEEDING

See Figure 44.

⁂ CAUTION

Use of any other than approved DOT 3 motor vehicle brake fluid will cause permanent damage to brake components and will render the brakes inoperative. Failure to follow these instructions may result in personal injury.

⁂ CAUTION

Carefully read cautionary information on product label. For EMERGENCY MEDICAL INFORMATION seek medical advice. In the USA or Canada on Ford/Motorcraft products call: 1-800-959-3673. For additional information, consult the product Material Safety Data Sheet (MSDS) if available. Failure to follow these instructions may result in personal injury.

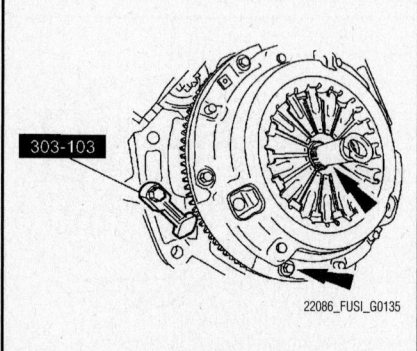

303-103

22086_FUSI_G0135

Fig. 41 Using a suitable clutch disc aligner, remove the bolts, the clutch pressure plate and the clutch disc

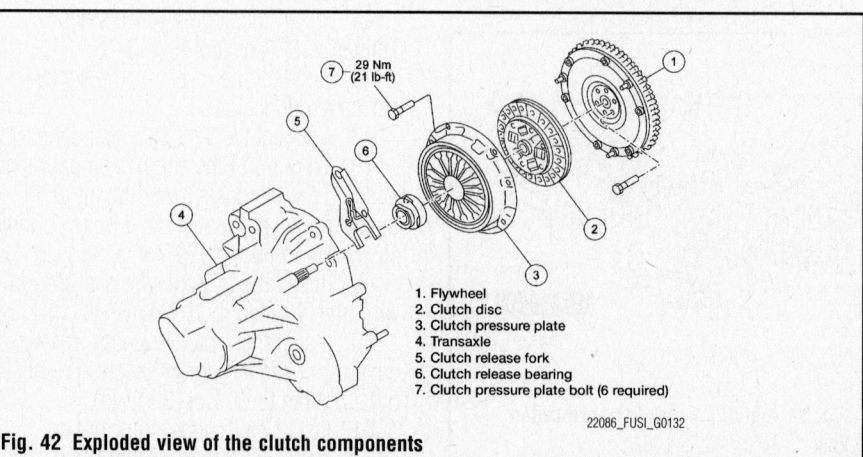

7 — 29 Nm (21 lb-ft)

1. Flywheel
2. Clutch disc
3. Clutch pressure plate
4. Transaxle
5. Clutch release fork
6. Clutch release bearing
7. Clutch pressure plate bolt (6 required)

22086_FUSI_G0132

Fig. 42 Exploded view of the clutch components

❋❋ WARNING

Do not let the brake master cylinder reservoir to run dry during the bleeding operation. Keep the brake master cylinder reservoir filled with clean, specified brake fluid. Never reuse the brake fluid that has been drained from the hydraulic system.

❋❋ WARNING

Brake fluid is harmful to painted and plastic surfaces. If brake fluid is spilled onto a painted or plastic surface, immediately wash it with water.

➡ When any part of the hydraulic system has been disconnected for repair or new installation, air may get into the system and cause spongy brake pedal action. This requires bleeding of the hydraulic system after it has been correctly connected. The hydraulic system can be bled manually or with pressure bleeding equipment.

1. Attach a rubber drain hose to the bleeder screw and submerge the free end of the hose in a container partially filled with clean brake fluid.
2. Slowly pump the clutch pedal to the floor several times and hold it.
3. With the clutch pedal held to the floor, loosen the bleeder screw until fluid and air are expelled from the system.
4. With the clutch pedal held to the floor, tighten the bleeder screw.
5. Repeat Steps 2 through 4 until no air bubbles appear in the fluid.
6. Tighten the bleeder screw to 7 Nm (62 lb-in).
7. Add brake fluid to the reservoir. Fill to the level in between the MIN and MAX lines.
8. Check system for normal operation.

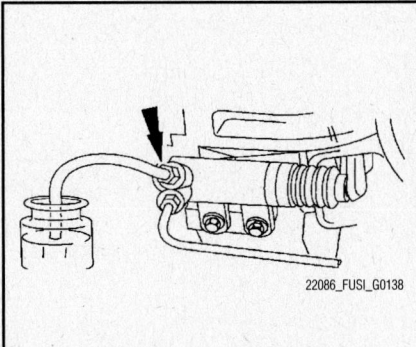

Fig. 44 Bleeding the clutch system

CLUTCH MASTER CYLINDER

REMOVAL & INSTALLATION
See Figure 45.

❋❋ CAUTION

Use of any other than approved DOT 3 motor vehicle brake fluid will cause permanent damage to brake components and will render the brakes inoperative. Failure to follow these instructions may result in personal injury.

❋❋ WARNING

Brake fluid is harmful to painted and plastic surfaces. If brake fluid is spilled onto a painted or plastic surface, wash it immediately with water.

❋❋ CAUTION

Do not allow the brake master cylinder reservoir to run dry during the bleeding operation. Keep the brake master cylinder reservoir filled with clean specified brake fluid. Never reuse the brake fluid that has been drained from the hydraulic system.

➡ When any part of the hydraulic system has been disconnected for repair or new installation, air may get into the system and cause spongy brake pedal action. This requires bleeding of the hydraulic system after it has been correctly connected. The hydraulic system can be bled manually or with pressure bleeding equipment.

1. Working under the instrument panel, remove the clutch master cylinder nut.
   a. To install, tighten to 21 Nm (15 ft. lbs.).
2. Using a suitable suction tool, remove the brake fluid to just below the clutch reservoir hose.
3. Remove the battery and the battery tray.
4. Remove the Powertrain Control Module (PCM).
   a. Disconnect the electrical connectors.
   b. Remove the PCM bolts.
5. Remove the PCM bracket.
6. Disconnect the clutch master cylinder-to-clutch slave cylinder hydraulic line.
   a. To install, tighten to 17 Nm (13 ft. lbs.).
7. Disconnect the clutch master cylinder-to-clutch reservoir hose.

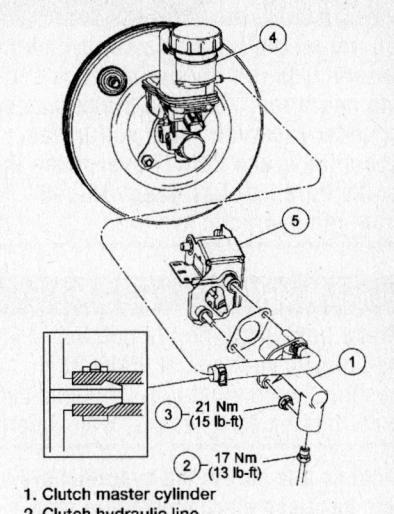

1. Clutch master cylinder
2. Clutch hydraulic line
3. Clutch master cylinder nut (2 required)
4. Clutch system reservoir
5. Clutch pedal and bracket

22086_FUSI_G0137

Fig. 45 Exploded view of the clutch master cylinder

8. Remove the clutch master cylinder nut.
   a. To install, tighten to 21 Nm (15 ft. lbs.).
9. Remove the clutch master cylinder assembly.
10. To install, reverse the removal procedure. Bleed the clutch hydraulic system, as outlined in this section.

CLUTCH SLAVE CYLINDER

REMOVAL & INSTALLATION
See Figure 46.

❋❋ CAUTION

Use of any other than approved DOT 3 motor vehicle brake fluid will cause permanent damage to brake components and will render the brakes inoperative. Failure to follow these instructions may result in personal injury.

❋❋ CAUTION

Carefully read cautionary information on product label. For EMERGENCY MEDICAL INFORMATION seek medical advice. In the USA or Canada on Ford/Motorcraft products call: 1-800-959-3673. For additional information, consult the product Material Safety Data Sheet (MSDS) if available. Failure to follow these instructions may result in personal injury.

❋❋ WARNING

Do not let the brake master cylinder reservoir to run dry during the bleeding operation. Keep the brake master cylinder reservoir filled with clean, specified brake fluid. Never reuse the brake fluid that has been drained from the hydraulic system.

❋❋ WARNING

Brake fluid is harmful to painted and plastic surfaces. If brake fluid is spilled onto a painted or plastic surface, immediately wash it with water.

➡When any part of the hydraulic system has been disconnected for repair or new installation, air may get into the system and cause spongy brake pedal action. This requires bleeding of the hydraulic system after it has been correctly connected. The hydraulic system can be bled manually or with pressure bleeding equipment.

1. Using a suitable suction tool, remove the brake fluid to just below the clutch reservoir hose.

2. Disconnect the clutch slave cylinder-to-clutch master cylinder line.

3. Remove the 2 clutch slave cylinder bolts and the clutch slave cylinder.

    a. To install, tighten to 19 Nm (14 ft. lbs.).

4. To install, reverse the removal procedure, noting the following:

    a. Apply a small amount of grease on the end of the slave cylinder push rod.

    b. Bleed the air from the system, as outlined in this section.

POWER TRANSFER UNIT

REMOVAL & INSTALLATION

See Figure 47.

➡This procedure covers Removal and Installation of the Power Transfer Unit (PTU).

1. Raise and safely support the vehicle.

❋❋ WARNING

A new Power Transfer Unit (PTU) intermediate shaft seal must be installed whenever the intermediate shaft or PTU is removed from the vehicle. Refer to the procedure in this section.

17 Nm (13 lb-ft) ─①

19 Nm (14 lb-ft) ─③

1. Clutch hydraulic line
2. Clutch slave cylinder
3. Clutch slave cylinder bolts (2 required)

22086_FUSI_G0139

Fig. 46 Exploded view of the slave cylinder

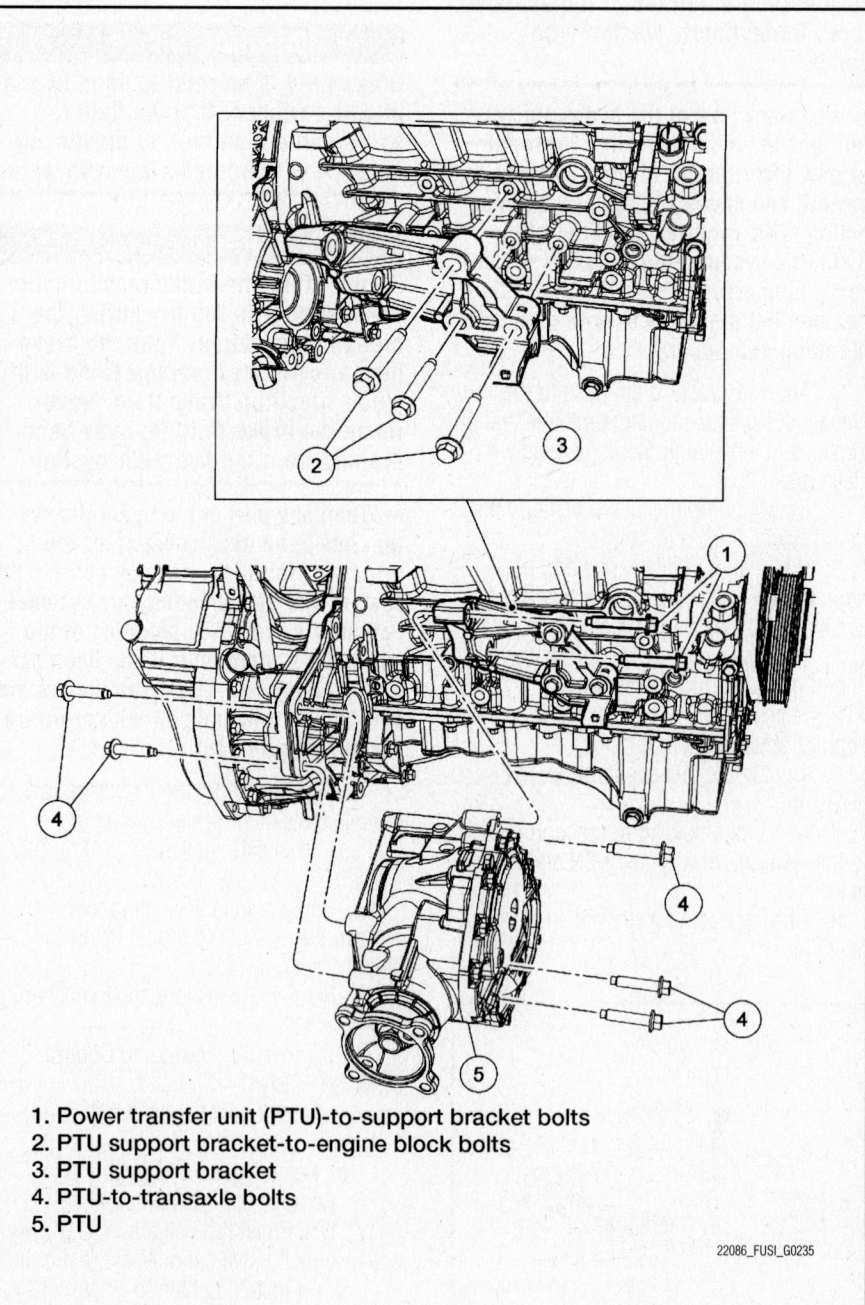

1. Power transfer unit (PTU)-to-support bracket bolts
2. PTU support bracket-to-engine block bolts
3. PTU support bracket
4. PTU-to-transaxle bolts
5. PTU

22086_FUSI_G0235

Fig. 47 Exploded view of the Power Transfer Unit (PTU)

2. Remove the driveshaft.
3. Remove the RH catalytic converter.
4. Remove the 2 PTU-to-support bracket bolts.
5. Remove the 3 PTU support bracket bolts and the PTU support bracket.
6. Remove the 5 PTU-to-transaxle bolts.
7. Separate the PTU from the transaxle. Remove the PTU.

To install:

❊ WARNING

A new Power Transfer Unit (PTU) intermediate shaft seal and deflector must be installed whenever the intermediate shaft or PTU is removed from the vehicle.

8. Position the power transfer unit (PTU) to the transaxle. Install the 5 PTU-to-transaxle bolts. Tighten to 90 Nm (66 ft. lbs.).
9. Position the PTU support bracket into place and install the 5 PTU support bracket bolts. Tighten to 5 Nm (44 lb-in).
10. Tighten the bolts to the transaxle to 70 Nm (52 ft. lbs.).
11. Tighten the bolts to the engine to 70 Nm (52 ft. lbs.).
12. Install the driveshaft.
13. Install the RH catalytic converter.
14. Fill the PTU, if necessary

POWER TRANSFER UNIT SEAL

REMOVAL & INSTALLATION

See Figures 48 through 50.
See Figures 51 and 52.

➡**This procedure will not affect the fluid level of the power transfer unit (PTU). Automatic transmission fluid (ATF) will leak when the intermediate shaft seal is removed. Add ATF to the transmission if necessary.**

1. Raise and safely support the vehicle.
2. Remove the intermediate shaft.

➡**The seal deflector will be damaged during removal. Be careful not to damage the cover seal directly behind the seal deflector.**

3. Using the heat gun, warm the seal deflector. Using a crow's foot bar, remove the seal deflector.

➡**The removal of the intermediate shaft can unseat the seal. Check the seal before installing the special tools.**

4. Using the special tools, remove the intermediate shaft seal. Clean the area around the seal deflector and seal.

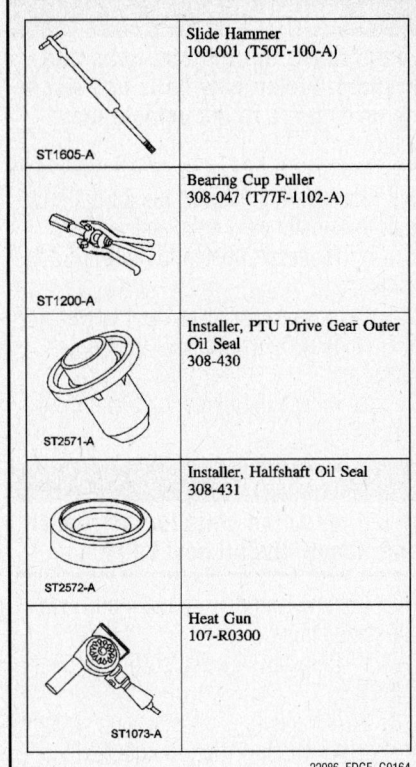

Fig. 48 Special tools are required to remove the PTU seal

➡**There is a bearing inside the PTU, directly behind the cover seal. The bearing is not serviced.**

5. If necessary, carefully remove the cover seal.

To install:
6. If necessary, install a new cover seal. Using the special tools, seat the cover seal.
7. Use a suitable socket to install the intermediate shaft seal. The socket should be 39.5 mm (1.5 in) to 40.5 mm (1.6 in) in diameter. Index-mark the socket at 18 mm (0.71 in).

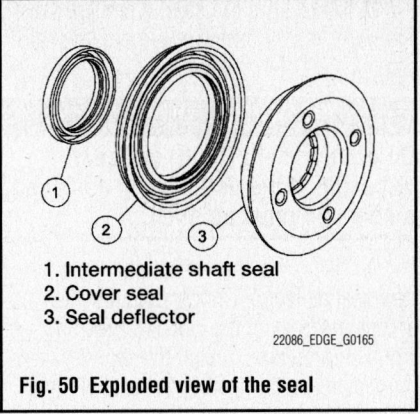

1. Intermediate shaft seal
2. Cover seal
3. Seal deflector

Fig. 50 Exploded view of the seal

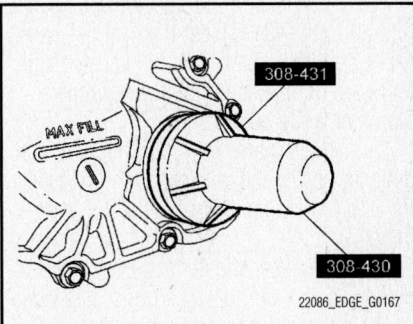

Fig. 51 Using the special tools, seat the cover seal

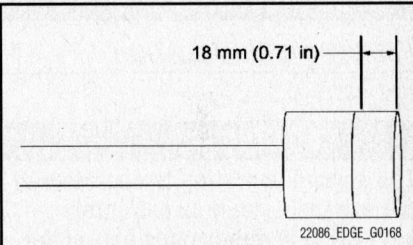

Fig. 52 Use a suitable socket to install the intermediate shaft seal. The socket should be 39.5 mm (1.5 in) to 40.5 mm (1.6 in) in diameter. Index-mark the socket at 18 mm (0.71 in)

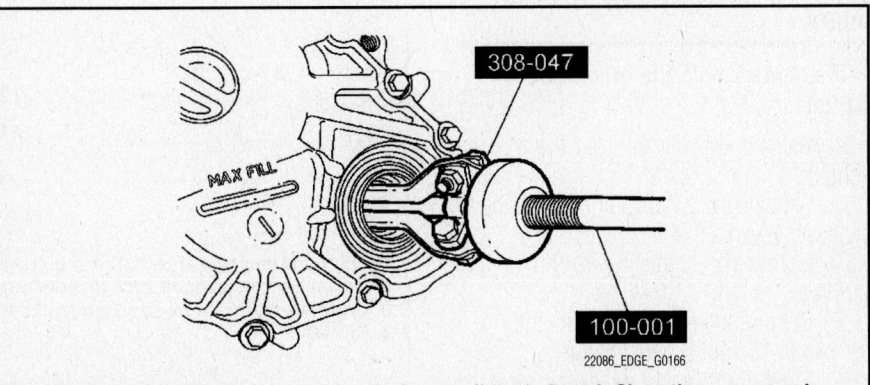

Fig. 49 Using the special tools, remove the intermediate shaft seal. Clean the area around the seal deflector and seal

8. Make sure the seal is centered in the bore. Install a new intermediate shaft seal.

✳✳ WARNING

Do not overheat (melt) the seal deflector. If the deflector is damaged, a new one must be used.

9. Using a suitable heat gun, heat the new seal deflector. Concentrate the heat across the back of the deflector near the white colored tabs. Install the seal deflector immediately after heating. An audible snap should be heard.

10. If necessary, use special tools 308-430 and 308-431 to seat the seal deflector. Make sure the deflector is fully seated and there are no cracks on the face or inner diameter white colored tab.

11. An alternate method to heat the seal deflector, place the deflector in boiling water for 3 to 5 minutes. Dry off deflector and install.

12. Make sure the deflector is completely seated all the way around. It is correctly installed when the face of the deflector is recessed into the pocket.

13. Install the intermediate shaft.

FRONT DRIVESHAFT

REMOVAL & INSTALLATION
See Figure 53.

✳✳ CAUTION

The normal operating temperature of the exhaust system is extremely high. NEVER remove any part of the system until it has cooled. Be especially cautious when working around the catalytic converters. The temperature of the converter is very high after only a few minutes of engine operation. Failure to follow these precautions may result in personal injury.

➡**Matchmark both the driveshaft flanges.**

1. Raise and safely support the vehicle.

2. Remove the 2 nuts and separate the exhaust system at the flex pipe.
    a. To install, tighten to 40 Nm (30 ft. lbs.).

3. Support the exhaust system and remove the 2 front exhaust hangers.

4. Carefully lower the exhaust system to allow clearance for removal of the drive-shaft.

✳✳ WARNING

Do not reuse the CV joint bolts and washers. Install new bolts and washers or damage to the vehicle may occur.

5. Remove and discard the 4 front drive-shaft-to-transfer case bolts and washers.
    a. To install, tighten to 70 Nm (52 ft. lbs.).

6. Remove and discard the 4 universal joint flange bolts and remove the front driveshaft.
    a. To install, tighten to 70 Nm (52 ft. lbs.).

✳✳ WARNING

Do not reuse the bolts for the rear U-joint flange. Install new bolts.

7. Remove and discard the 4 universal joint flange bolts.
    a. To install, tighten to 70 Nm (52 ft. lbs.).

8. With the help of an assistant, remove the 4 center bearing support nuts and the driveshaft.
    a. To install, tighten to 55 Nm (41 ft. lbs.).

➡**If a driveshaft is installed and drive-shaft vibration is encountered after installation, index the driveshaft.**

9. Installation is the reverse of the removal procedure.

FRONT HALFSHAFT

REMOVAL & INSTALLATION

Left Side
See Figures 54 through 59.

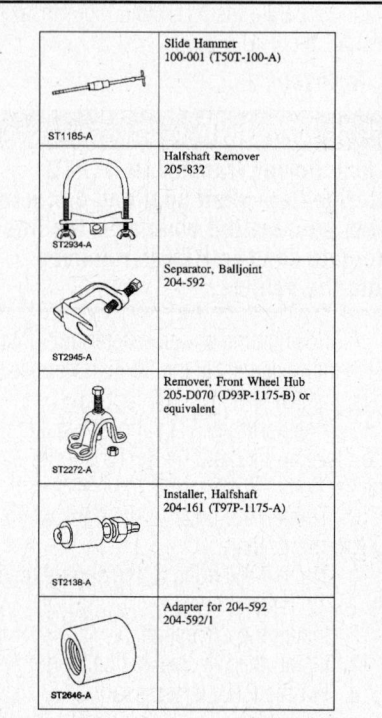

Slide Hammer 100-001 (T50T-100-A)	
ST1185-A	
Halfshaft Remover 205-832	
ST2934-A	
Separator, Balljoint 204-592	
ST2945-A	
Remover, Front Wheel Hub 205-D070 (D93P-1175-B) or equivalent	
ST2272-A	
Installer, Halfshaft 204-161 (T97P-1175-A)	
ST2138-A	
Adapter for 204-592 204-592/1	
ST2646-A	

22086_FUSI_G0166

Fig. 54 Special tools required for this procedure

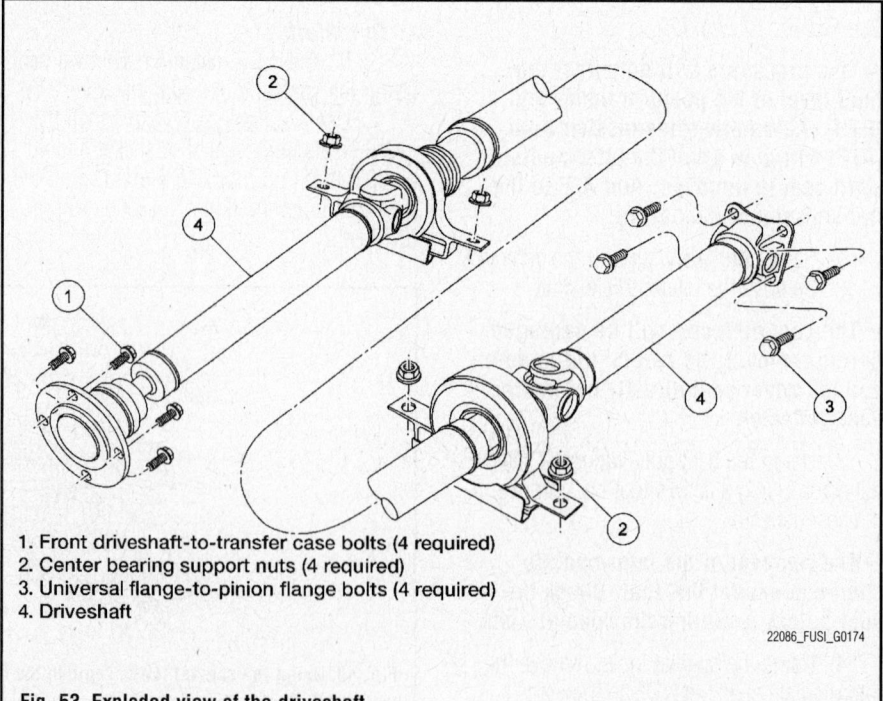

1. Front driveshaft-to-transfer case bolts (4 required)
2. Center bearing support nuts (4 required)
3. Universal flange-to-pinion flange bolts (4 required)
4. Driveshaft

22086_FUSI_G0174

Fig. 53 Exploded view of the driveshaft

➡This procedure requires are variety of special tools.

1. Remove the front tire and wheel.

➡Apply the brake to keep the halfshaft from rotating.

2. Remove and discard the front wheel hub nut.

3. Remove the front and rear lower control arm nuts.

➡Once pressure is applied to the ball joint with the special tool, it may be necessary to tap the wheel knuckle at the ball joint area to separate the ball joint from the wheel knuckle.

4. Using special tools 204-592/1 and 204-592, or equivalent, disconnect the 2 ball joints.

5. Using special tool 205-D070, or equivalent, separate the halfshaft from the wheel hub.

✳✳ WARNING

When the lower ball joint is separated from the wheel knuckle, the lower arm may strike the outer constant velocity (CV) joint boot with enough force to damage the boot clamp. This will result in a loss of grease from the outer CV joint. Place a block of wood, or similar item,

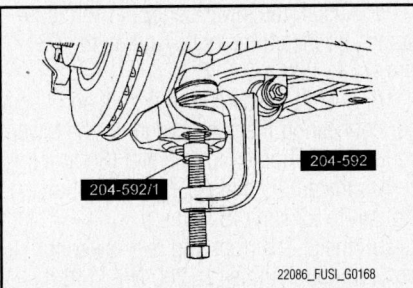

Fig. 55 Using special tools 204-592/1 and 204-592, or equivalent, disconnect the 2 ball joints

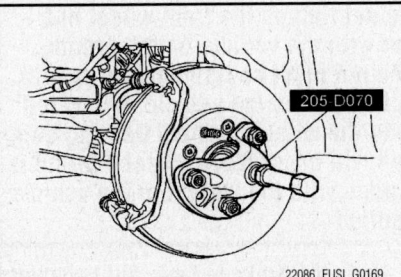

Fig. 56 Using special tool 205-D070, or equivalent, separate the halfshaft from the wheel hub

between the lower arm and the outer CV joint to prevent the lower arm from striking the outer CV joint.

6. Remove the damper fork bolt and flagnut connecting the damper fork to the lower control arm.

7. Remove the brake caliper hose bolt.

➡Support the knuckle with a suitable jackstand.

8. Pull the knuckle outboard and rotate it toward the rear of the vehicle.

9. Remove the lower control arm-to-subframe bolt. Remove the lower control arm.

10. Remove the 4 pushpins and position the splash shield aside.

✳✳ WARNING

The sharp edges on the stub shaft splines can slice or puncture the oil seal. Use care when inserting the stub shaft into the transmission.

Fig. 57 Using special tools 100-001 and 205-832, or equivalent, remove the half-shaft from the transmission

11. Using special tools 100-001 and 205-832, or equivalent, remove the halfshaft from the transmission.

12. Remove and discard the circlip from the stub shaft.

To install:

✳✳ WARNING

Make sure to install the correct circlip for each application. Failure to use the correct diameter circlip may result in shaft removal concerns or shaft separation during vehicle operation.

13. Install a new stub shaft circlip.

14. Insert the halfshaft into the wheel hub.

➡After insertion, pull the halfshaft inner end to make sure the circlip is locked.

15. Push the stub shaft into the transmission so the circlip locks into the differential side gear.

16. Install the splash shield and pushpins.

17. Rotate the knuckle into position.

18. Install the lower control arm bolt and nut to the subframe. Tighten to 103 Nm (76 ft. lbs.).

19. Install the damper fork bolt connecting the damper fork to the lower control arm. Tighten to 109 Nm (80 ft. lbs.).

20. Install the brake caliper hose bolt. Tighten to 22 Nm (16 ft. lbs.).

21. Using the special tool, install the halfshaft in the wheel hub.

22. Install the front and rear lower control arm nuts. Tighten to 200 Nm (148 ft. lbs.).

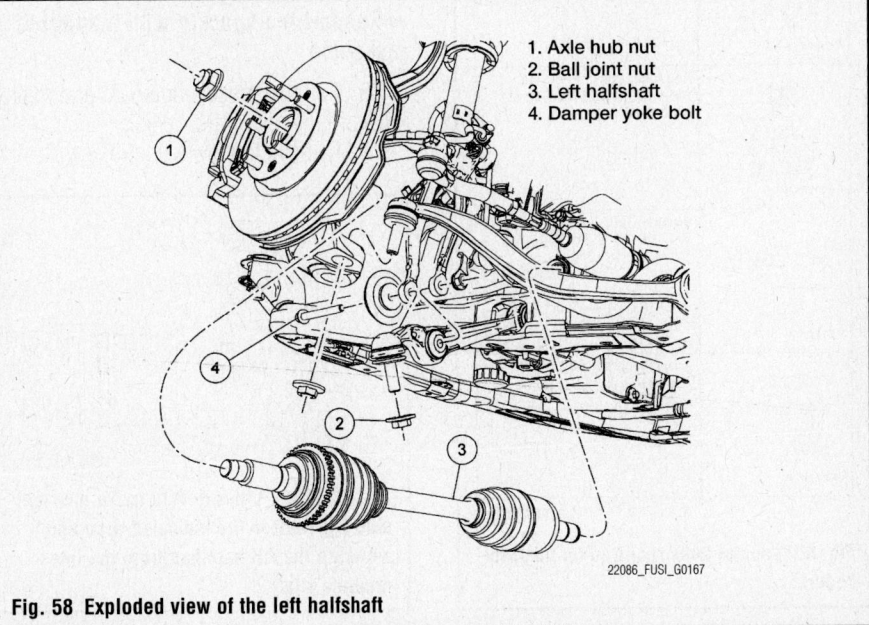

1. Axle hub nut
2. Ball joint nut
3. Left halfshaft
4. Damper yoke bolt

Fig. 58 Exploded view of the left halfshaft

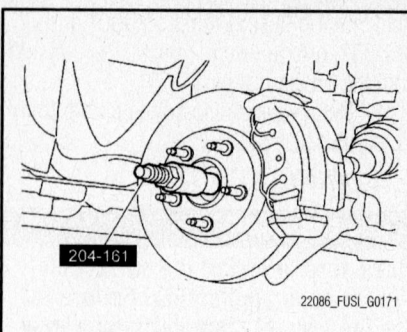

Fig. 59 Using the special tool, install the halfshaft in the wheel hub.

✳✳ WARNING

Do not tighten the front wheel hub nut with the vehicle on the ground. The nut must be tightened to specification before the vehicle is lowered onto the wheels. Wheel bearing damage will occur if the wheel bearing is loaded with the weight of the vehicle applied.

➡**Apply the brake to keep the halfshaft from rotating.**

23. Install the new front wheel hub nut. Tighten to 255 Nm (185 ft. lbs.).

24. Stake the new nut in line with the keyway.

25. Install the front tire and wheel

Right Side

See Figures 55, 56 and 59 through 61.

ST2945-A	Separator, Ball Joint 204-592
ST2272-A	Remover, Front Wheel Hub 205-D070 (D93P-1175-B) or equivalent
ST2138-A	Installer, Halfshaft 204-161 (T97P-1175-A)
ST2646-A	Adapter for 204-592 204-592/1

22086_FUSI_G0172

Fig. 60 Special tools required for this procedure

➡**This procedure requires are variety of special tools.**

1. Remove the front tire and wheel.

➡**Apply the brake to keep the halfshaft from rotating.**

2. Remove and discard the front wheel hub nut.

3. Remove the front and rear lower control arm nuts.

➡**Once pressure is applied to the ball joint with the special tool, it may be necessary to tap the wheel knuckle at the ball joint area to separate the ball joint from the wheel knuckle.**

4. Using special tools 204-592/1 and 204-592, or equivalent, disconnect the 2 ball joints.

5. Using special tool 205-D070, or equivalent, separate the halfshaft from the wheel hub.

✳✳ WARNING

When the lower ball joint is separated from the wheel knuckle, the lower arm may strike the outer constant velocity (CV) joint boot with enough force to damage the boot clamp. This will result in a loss of grease from the outer CV joint. Place a block of wood, or similar item, between the lower arm and the outer CV joint to prevent the lower arm from striking the outer CV joint.

---

6. Remove the damper fork bolt and flagnut connecting the damper fork to the lower control arm.

7. Remove the brake caliper hose bolt.

➡**Support the knuckle with a suitable jackstand.**

8. Pull the knuckle outboard and rotate it toward the rear of the vehicle.

9. Remove the lower control arm-to-

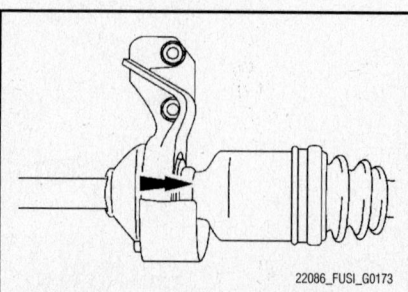

22086_FUSI_G0173

Fig. 61 Use a brass drift to strike the right side halfshaft in the indicated area and separate the RH halfshaft from the intermediate shaft

---

subframe bolt. Remove the lower control arm.

10. Use a brass drift to strike the right side halfshaft in the indicated area and separate the RH halfshaft from the intermediate shaft.

11. Pull the strut forward, remove the halfshaft from the damper fork. Position the halfshaft in front of the damper fork towards the front of the vehicle.

12. Remove and discard the circlip from the intermediate shaft.

To install:

✳✳ WARNING

Make sure to install the correct circlip for each application. Failure to use the correct diameter circlip may result in shaft removal concerns or shaft separation during vehicle operation.

---

13. Install a new intermediate shaft circlip.

➡**Pull the right side shaft outward to make sure the circlip is locked.**

14. Align the splines on the right side shaft with the intermediate shaft and push the stub shaft in until the circlip locks the shafts together.

15. Insert the halfshaft into the wheel hub.

16. Rotate the knuckle into position.

17. Install the lower control arm to subframe and install the bolt. Tighten to 103 Nm (76 ft. lbs.).

18. Install the damper fork bolt and flag nut connecting the damper fork to the lower control arm. Tighten to 109 Nm (80 ft. lbs.).

19. Install the brake caliper hose bolt. Tighten to 22 Nm (16 ft. lbs.).

20. Install the front and rear lower control arm nuts. Tighten to 200 Nm (148 ft. lbs.).

21. Using the special tool, install the halfshaft in the wheel hub.

✳✳ WARNING

Do not tighten the front wheel hub nut with the vehicle on the ground. The nut must be tightened to specification before the vehicle is lowered onto the wheels. Wheel bearing damage will occur if the wheel bearing is loaded with the weight of the vehicle applied.

➡**Apply the brake to keep the halfshaft from rotating.**

22. Install a new front wheel hub nut Tighten to 255 Nm (185 ft. lbs.).

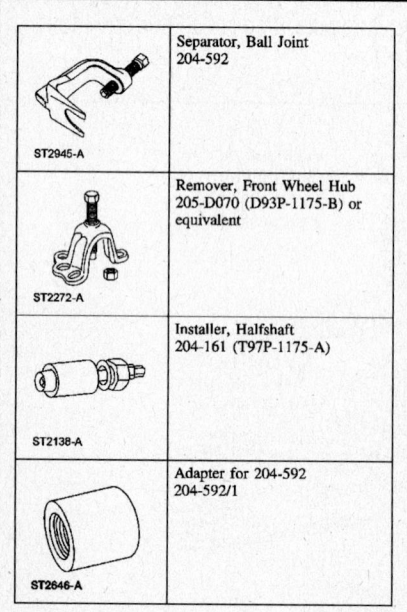

23. Stake the new nut in line with the keyway.

24. Install the front tires and wheels

INTERMEDIATE SHAFT

REMOVAL & INSTALLATION

Front Wheel Drive (FWD) Models

1. Remove the right halfshaft, as outlined in this section.

2. For vehicles with the 3.0L engine, remove the 2 bolts from the intermediate shaft support bearing bracket.

3. For vehicles with the 3.5L engine:

a. Remove the 2 catalytic converter bracket bolts.

b. Remove the 2 nuts and remove the catalytic converter support bracket.

c. Remove the 3 bolts from the intermediate shaft bearing support bracket.

➡ **Do not damage the transaxle seals when removing the intermediate shaft.**

4. Carefully remove the intermediate shaft while supporting both ends of the intermediate shaft.

5. Remove and discard the circlip from the outboard end of the intermediate shaft.

To install:

❊❊ WARNING

Make sure to install the correct circlip for each application. Failure to use the correct diameter circlip may result in shaft removal concerns or shaft separation during vehicle operation.

6. Install as new circlip on the outboard end of the intermediate shaft.

7. Position the intermediate shaft in the transaxle and engage the intermediate shaft splines with the transaxle side gears. Make sure the circlip is locked in the gear.

8. For 3.0L engines, install the 2 intermediate shaft support bracket bolts. Tighten to 40 Nm (30 ft. lbs.).

9. For 3.5L engines:

a. Install the 3 intermediate shaft bearing support bracket bolts. Tighten to 40 Nm (30 ft. lbs.).

b. Install the catalytic converter support bracket and install the 2 nuts. Tighten to 23 Nm (17 ft. lbs.).

c. Install the 2 catalytic converter bracket bolts. Tighten to 20 Nm (15 ft. lbs.).

10. Install the right halfshaft.

All Wheel Drive (AWD) Models

❊❊ WARNING

The intermediate shaft seal in the Power Transfer Unit (PTU) must be replaced whenever the intermediate shaft is removed. Refer to the Power Transfer Unit Seal Replacement procedure under the Transfer Case Section.

1. Remove the right halfshaft assembly.

2. Remove the right halfshaft.

3. Remove the 2 bolts from the intermediate shaft support bearing bracket.

➡ **Do not damage the transaxle seals when removing the intermediate shaft.**

4. Carefully remove the intermediate shaft while supporting both ends of the intermediate shaft.

5. Remove and discard the circlip from the outboard end of the intermediate shaft.

To install:

❊❊ WARNING

Make sure to install the correct circlip for each application. Failure to use the correct diameter circlip may result in shaft removal concerns or shaft separation during vehicle operation.

6. Install a new circlip on the outboard end of the intermediate shaft.

7. Install a new intermediate shaft seal.

8. Position the intermediate shaft in the transaxle and engage the intermediate shaft splines with the transaxle side gears. Make sure the circlip is locked in the gear.

9. Install the 2 intermediate shaft support bracket bolts. Tighten to 40 Nm (30 ft. lbs.).

10. Install the right halfshaft.

REAR HALFSHAFT

REMOVAL & INSTALLATION
See Figures 62 and 63.

❊❊ WARNING

When performing this procedure, please note the following to avoid damaging the halfshaft and/or CV-Joints:

• Never pick up or hold the halfshaft by only the inner or outer Constant Velocity (CV) joint.

• Handle the halfshaft by only the interconnecting shaft to avoid pulling

apart and potential damage to the CV joints.

• Do not over-angle the CV joints.

• Damage will occur to an assembled inner CV joint if it is over-plunged outward from the joint housing.

• Never use a hammer to remove or install the halfshafts.

• Never use the halfshaft assembly as a lever to position other components. Always support the free-ends of the halfshaft.

• Do not allow the boots to contact sharp edges or hot exhaust components.

• Do not drop assembled halfshafts. The impact may cut the boots from the inside without evidence of external damage.

1. Raise and safely support the vehicle.

2. Remove the tire and wheel.

3. Remove and discard the rear wheel hub nut.

4. Remove the bolt and position aside the shaft speed sensor.

5. Remove the nut and lower shock absorber bolt.

6. Support the lower arm and remove the nut and bolt from the knuckle.

7. Remove the 4 toe link bracket nuts.

8. Using a suitable front hub removal tool, separate the halfshaft from the rear axle hub assembly.

❊❊ WARNING

Do not damage the oil seal protector when removing the axle halfshaft from the differential.

9. Using a suitable pry bar, remove the halfshaft.

10. Remove and discard the circlip from the stub shaft.

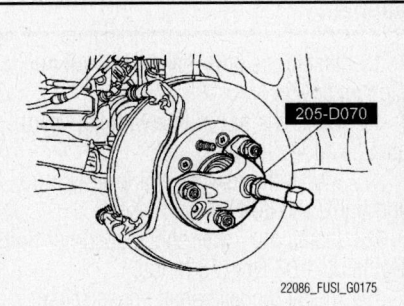

205-D070

22086_FUSI_G0175

Fig. 62 Using a suitable front hub removal tool, separate the halfshaft from the rear axle hub assembly

To install:

❊❊ WARNING

Make sure to install the correct circlip for each application. Failure to use the correct diameter circlip may result in shaft removal concerns or shaft separation during vehicle operation.

11. Install a new circlip on the stub shaft.

12. Install the stub shaft in the rear drive unit. Make sure the circlip locks in the side gear.

13. Using the special tool, install the outer halfshaft end into the hub assembly.

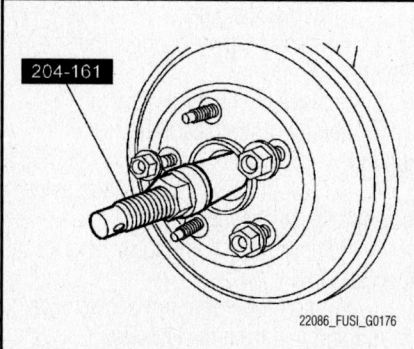

Fig. 63 Using the special tool, install the outer halfshaft end into the hub assembly

14. Position the lower arm and install the lower arm bolt and nut. Tighten to 103 Nm (76 ft. lbs.).

❊❊ WARNING

Do not tighten the rear wheel hub nut with the vehicle on the ground. The nut must be tightened to specification before the vehicle is lowered to the ground. Wheel bearing damage will occur if the wheel bearing is loaded with the weight of the vehicle applied.

15. Install the new rear wheel hub nut. Tighten to 255 Nm (188 ft. lbs.).

16. Stake the nut in line with keyway to engage added locking.

17. Install the rear toe link bracket nuts and tighten to 80 Nm (59 ft. lbs.).

18. Install the lower shock absorber bolt. Tighten to 103 Nm (76 ft. lbs.).

19. Install the axle shaft speed sensor. Tighten to 23 Nm (17 ft. lbs.).

20. Fill the axle with the specified quantity of the specified lubricant.

21. Install the tire and wheel.

REAR PINION SEAL

REMOVAL & INSTALLATION

See Figures 64 and 65.

1. Raise and safely support the vehicle.

2. Remove and discard the 4 rear driveshaft universal joint flange bolts. Support the driveshaft.

➡**Discard the nut after removing it. Install a new nut during installation.**

3. Using the special tool, hold the pinion flange while removing the nut. Remove the nut, then discard it.

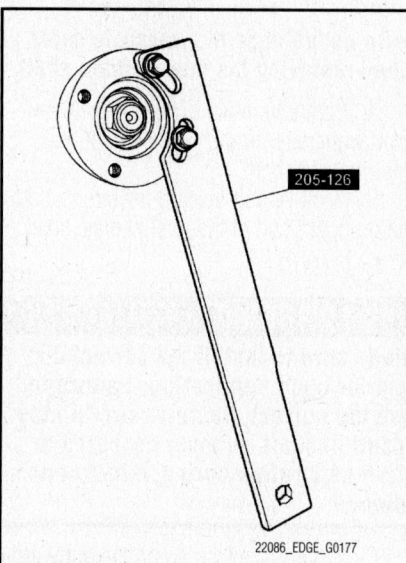

Fig. 64 Using the special tool, hold the pinion flange while removing the nut. Remove the nut, then discard it

4. Matchmark the location of the pinion to the yoke.

5. Using a suitable 2-jawed puller, remove the pinion flange.

6. Using the special tools, remove the seal.

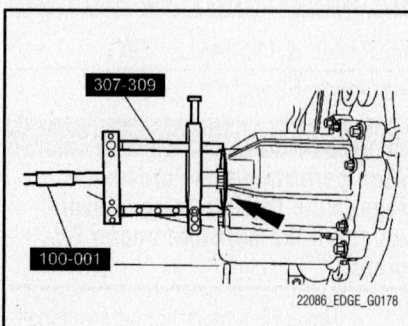

Fig. 65 Using the special tools, remove the seal

To install:

➡**Make sure that the mating surface is clean before installing the new seal.**

7. Using the special Pinion Seal Installation tool, install the seal.

➡**Lubricate the pinion flange with premium long-life grease.**

8. Align the matchmarks and position the pinion flange.

9. Using the special tool, install the pinion nut and tighten to 244 Nm (180 ft. lbs.).

10. Align the matchmarks and install the rear driveshaft universal joint flange. Tighten the bolts to 70 Nm (52 ft. lbs.).

REAR STUB SHAFT, PILOT BEARING & SEAL

REMOVAL & INSTALLATION

See Figures 66 through 68.

➡**This procedure covers replacement of the Stub Shaft, Bearing and Seal.**

1. Remove the halfshaft assembly.

2. To remove the seal, use the special tool to remove the stub shaft seal. The stub shaft pilot bearing is not serviced.

To install:

➡**Lubricate the new stub shaft pilot bearing housing seal with grease.**

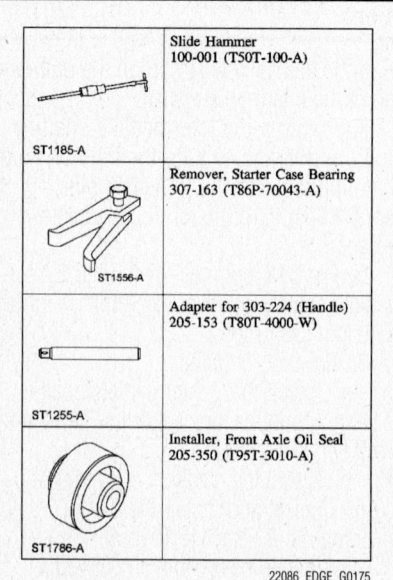

Fig. 66 Special tools needed for seal replacement

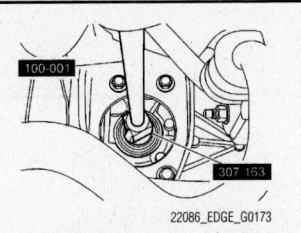

Fig. 67 To remove the seal, use the special tool to remove the stub shaft seal. The stub shaft pilot bearing is not serviced

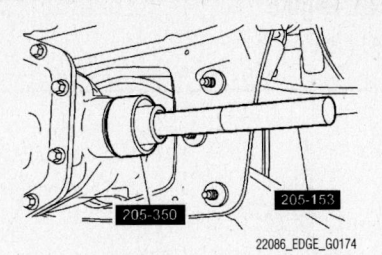

Fig. 68 Using the special tools, install the stub shaft pilot bearing housing seal

3. Using the special tools, install the stub shaft pilot bearing housing seal.

✷✷ WARNING

Inspect the inboard CV joint seal journal for rust or nicks/scratches prior to installing the halfshaft. If necessary, polish the seal journal with fine crocus cloth.

4. Install the halfshaft assembly.

ENGINE COOLING

ENGINE FAN

REMOVAL & INSTALLATION

See Figure 69.

1. Disconnect the negative battery cable.
2. Remove the air cleaner assembly.
3. If equipped, detach the 2 block heater wiring clips from the radiator support.
4. Detach the 5 wiring harness retainers and position the harness aside.
5. Position aside the upper radiator hose from the cooling fan motor and shroud.
6. Disconnect the cooling fan motor and shroud electrical connector.
7. If equipped, remove the bolt and position aside the oil cooler bracket.
8. Remove the 2 bolts and the cooling fan motor and shroud.

To install:

9. Installation is the reverse of the removal procedure, noting the following tightening specifications:
   a. Cooling fan motor and shroud bolts: 6 Nm (53 inch lbs.)
   b. Oil cooler bracket bolt: 6 Nm (53 inch lbs.)

RADIATOR

REMOVAL & INSTALLATION

1. Drain the cooling system.
2. Remove the cooling fan motor and shroud, as outlined in this section.
3. Remove the front bumper cover, as follows:
   a. Raise and safely support the vehicle..
   b. Remove the 2 bolts from the top of the radiator grille.
   c. Remove the 4 scrivets from the top of the radiator grille.
   d. Remove the 3 lower pin-type retainers.
   e. Remove the 6 fender splash shield screws (3 each side).
   f. Remove the 4 lower screws (2 each side).
   g. Disconnect the side marker lamp electrical connectors, if equipped.
   h. Disconnect the fog lamp electrical connectors, if equipped.
   i. Remove the front bumper cover.
   j. Pull the corner of the bumper cover from the bracket.
4. Disconnect the upper radiator hose and lower degas bottle hose from the radiator.
5. Disconnect the lower radiator hose from the radiator.
6. Lift and remove the tabs from the radiator support and position the radiator towards the engine.
7. Remove the 2 A/C condenser bolts from the radiator and separate the condenser from the radiator.

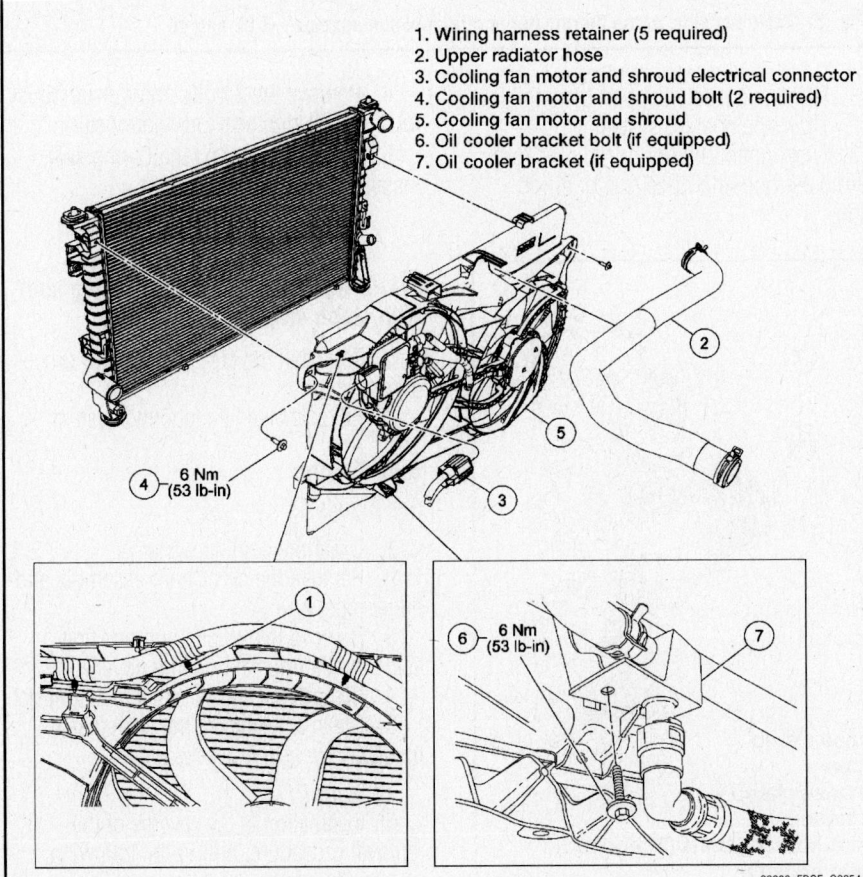

1. Wiring harness retainer (5 required)
2. Upper radiator hose
3. Cooling fan motor and shroud electrical connector
4. Cooling fan motor and shroud bolt (2 required)
5. Cooling fan motor and shroud
6. Oil cooler bracket bolt (if equipped)
7. Oil cooler bracket (if equipped)

6 Nm (53 lb-in)

Fig. 69 Exploded view of the engine cooling fan and shroud and related components

To install, tighten to 10 Nm (89 inch lbs.).

8. Remove the radiator.

To install:

9. Installation is the reverse of the removal procedure, noting the following:

a. Tighten the A/C condenser-to-radiator bolts to 10 Nm (89 inch lbs.)

b. Fill and bleed the cooling system.

THERMOSTAT

REMOVAL & INSTALLATION

2.3L Engine

See Figure 70.

1. Raise and safely support the vehicle.
2. Drain the cooling system.
3. Remove the 3 bolts and reposition the thermostat housing to gain access to the hose clamps.
4. Remove and discard the gasket.

a. To install, tighten the bolts to 10 Nm (89 lb-in).

5. Disconnect the heater hose from the thermostat housing.
6. Disconnect the lower radiator hose from the thermostat housing and remove the thermostat housing.

To install:

7. To install, reverse the removal procedure.
8. Install a new thermostat housing gasket.
9. Fill and bleed the cooling system

3.0L Engine

See Figure 71.

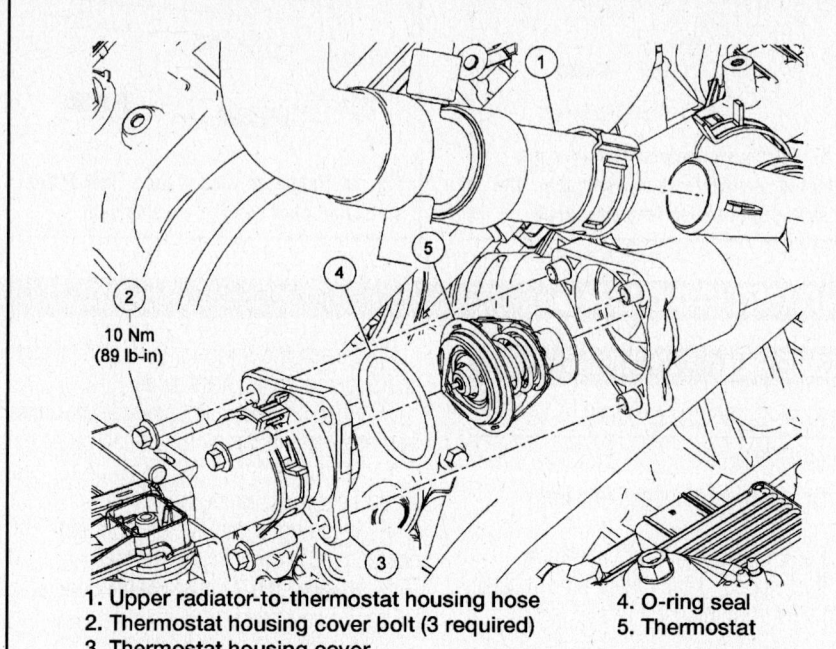

1. Upper radiator-to-thermostat housing hose
2. Thermostat housing cover bolt (3 required)
3. Thermostat housing cover
4. O-ring seal
5. Thermostat

22086_FUSI_G0053

Fig. 71 Exploded view of the thermostat and related components—3.0L engine

1. Raise and safely support the vehicle.
2. Drain the cooling system.
3. Disconnect the upper radiator-to-thermostat housing hose and position aside.

4. Remove the 3 bolts, thermostat housing cover, O-ring seal and thermostat.
5. Clean and inspect the O-ring seal. Install a new seal if necessary.

a. To install, tighten to 10 Nm (89 lb-in).

➡ **Lubricate the thermostat O-ring seal with clean engine coolant.**

6. To install, reverse the removal procedure.
7. Fill and bleed the cooling system

3.5L Engine

See Figure 72.

1. Drain the cooling system.
2. Remove the air cleaner assembly and outlet pipe.
3. Remove the 2 bolts and position aside the thermostat housing cover.
4. Remove the O-ring seal and thermostat.
5. Clean and inspect the O-ring seal. Install a new seal if necessary.

To install:

6. Installation is the reverse of the removal procedure, noting the following:

a. Lubricate the thermostat O-ring seal with clean engine coolant.

b. Tighten the thermostat housing cover to 10 Nm (89 inch lbs.).

c. Fill and bleed the cooling system.

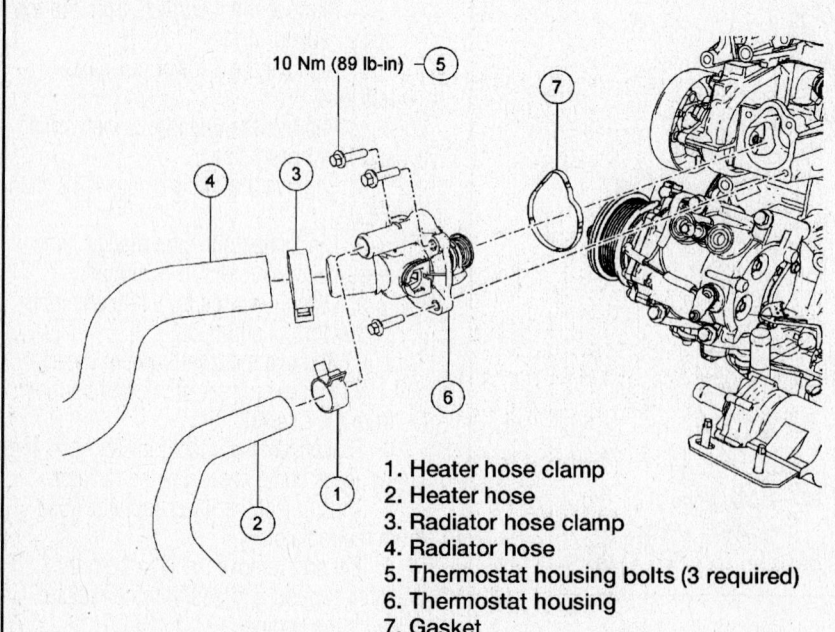

1. Heater hose clamp
2. Heater hose
3. Radiator hose clamp
4. Radiator hose
5. Thermostat housing bolts (3 required)
6. Thermostat housing
7. Gasket

22086_FUSI_G0052

Fig. 70 Thermostat housing and related components—2.3L engine

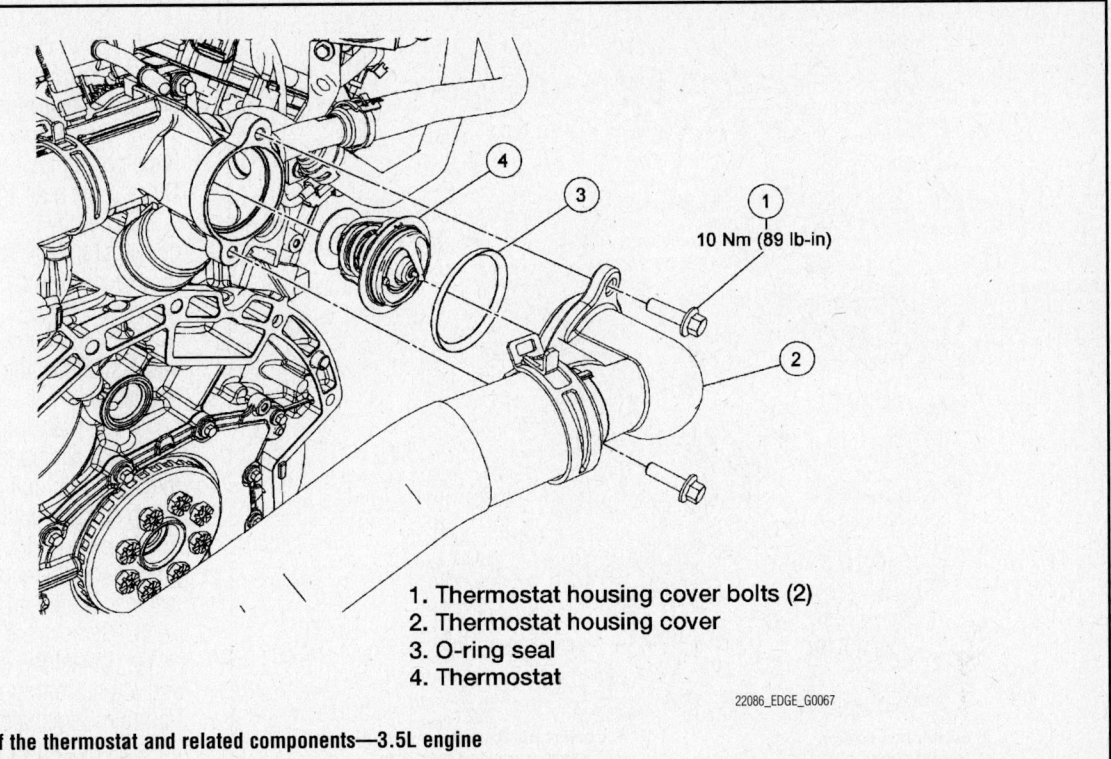

1. Thermostat housing cover bolts (2)
2. Thermostat housing cover
3. O-ring seal
4. Thermostat

22086_EDGE_G0067

Fig. 72 Exploded view of the thermostat and related components—3.5L engine

WATER PUMP

REMOVAL & INSTALLATION

2.3L Engine

See Figure 73.

1. Raise and safely support the vehicle.
2. Drain the cooling system.
3. Loosen the 3 coolant pump pulley bolts.

4. Remove the accessory drive belt.
5. Remove the 3 bolts and the coolant pump pulley.
   a. To install, tighten to 20 Nm (15 ft. lbs.).
6. Remove the 3 bolts and the coolant pump.
7. Remove and discard the O-ring seal.
   a. To install, tighten to 10 Nm (89 lb-in).

To install:

8. To install, reverse the removal procedure.
9. Lubricate the O-ring seal with clean engine coolant.
10. Fill and bleed the cooling system

3.0L Engine

See Figures 74, 75 and 76.

1. Raise and safely support the vehicle.
2. Drain the cooling system.
3. Remove the coolant pump belt.
4. Using Special tool 303-S455, or equivalent, remove the coolant pump drive pulley.

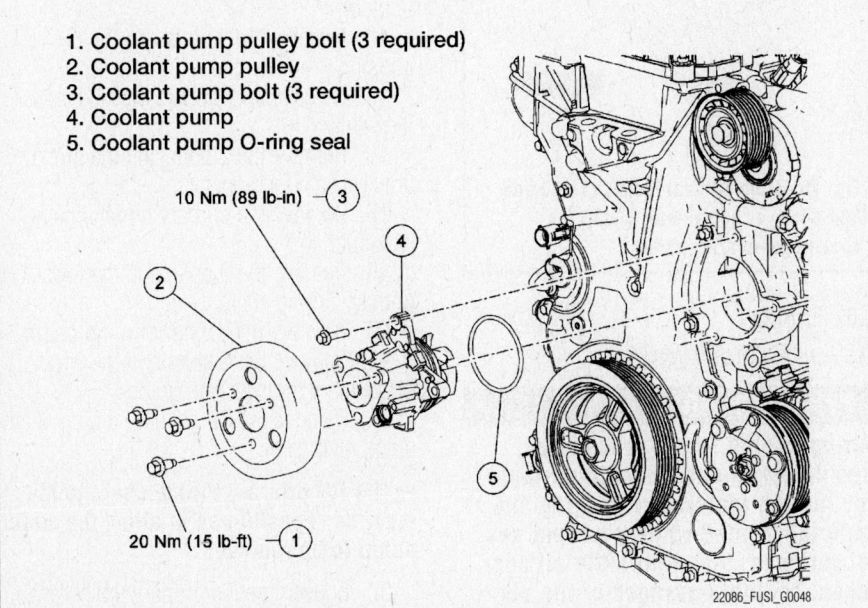

1. Coolant pump pulley bolt (3 required)
2. Coolant pump pulley
3. Coolant pump bolt (3 required)
4. Coolant pump
5. Coolant pump O-ring seal

10 Nm (89 lb-in) — 3

20 Nm (15 lb-ft) — 1

22086_FUSI_G0048

Fig. 73 Exploded view of the water pump—2.3L engine

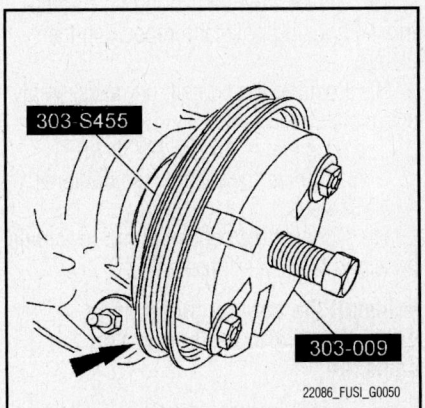

303-S455

303-009

22086_FUSI_G0050

Fig. 74 Using Special tool 303-S455, or equivalent, remove the coolant pump drive pulley

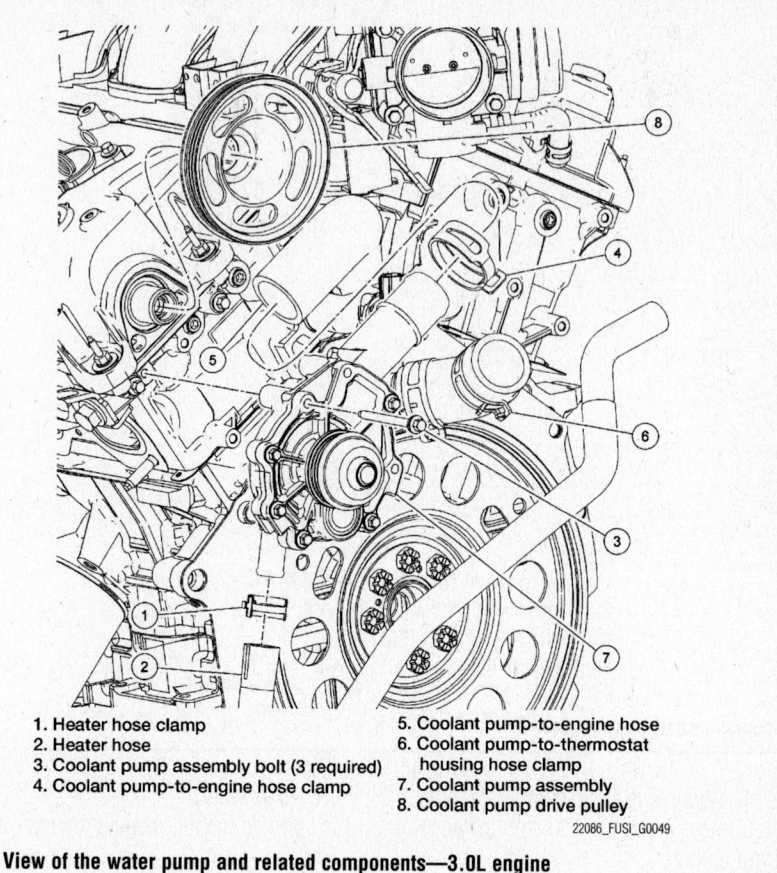

1. Heater hose clamp
2. Heater hose
3. Coolant pump assembly bolt (3 required)
4. Coolant pump-to-engine hose clamp
5. Coolant pump-to-engine hose
6. Coolant pump-to-thermostat housing hose clamp
7. Coolant pump assembly
8. Coolant pump drive pulley

22086_FUSI_G0049

Fig. 75 View of the water pump and related components—3.0L engine

5. Disconnect the heater hose from the coolant pump.

6. Disconnect the coolant pump-to-engine hose and position aside.

7. Remove the 3 bolts from the coolant pump assembly.

8. Reposition the coolant pump-to-thermostat housing hose clamp and remove the coolant pump and hose as an assembly.

To install:

9. Connect the coolant pump-to-thermostat housing hose and reposition the clamp.

10. Position the coolant pump assembly and install the 3 bolts:

   a. Tighten to 10 Nm (89 lb-in).

   b. Tighten the 3 bolts an additional 90 degrees.

11. Connect the coolant pump-to-engine hose and the heater hose.

➡**Install the coolant pump drive pulley flush with the end of the camshaft.**

12. Using Special tools 211-185 and 303-S455, or equivalent, install the coolant pump drive pulley.

13. Install the coolant pump belt.

14. Fill and bleed the cooling system.

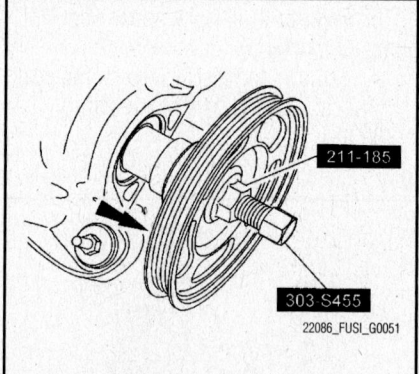

211-185

303-S455

22086_FUSI_G0051

Fig. 76 Using Special tools 211-185 and 303-S455, or equivalent, install the coolant pump drive pulley

3.5L Engine

See Figures 77 through 88.

※※ WARNING

During engine repair procedures, cleanliness is extremely important. Any foreign material, including any material created while cleaning gasket surfaces, that enters the oil passages, coolant passages or the oil pan can cause engine failure.

1. Raise and safely support the vehicle.

2. Drain the cooling system.

3. Loosen the exhaust flexible pipe clamp and disconnect the 2 exhaust hangers.

4. Remove the 4 nuts, the exhaust flexible pipe and the Y-pipe as an assembly. Discard the nuts and the gasket.

5. Remove the LH and RH catalytic converters. Refer to the Exhaust Manifold procedure for more information on catalytic converter removal.

6. If equipped, remove the heat shield and disconnect the block heater electrical connector.

7. Remove the RH cylinder block drain plug or, if equipped, the block heater. Allow the coolant to drain from the cylinder block into a suitable container.

8. Remove the LH cylinder block drain plug. Allow the coolant to drain from the cylinder block into a suitable container.

9. Remove the engine front cover.

10. Rotate the crankshaft clockwise and align the timing marks on the Variable Camshaft Timing (VCT) assemblies as shown in the accompanying illustration.

➡**The special tool will hold the camshafts in the Top Dead Center (TDC) position.**

11. Install the special tool onto the flats of the LH camshafts.

➡**The special tool will hold the camshafts in the TDC position.**

12. Install the special tool onto the flats of the RH camshafts.

13. Remove the 3 bolts and the RH VCT housing.

14. Remove the 3 bolts and the LH VCT housing.

15. Remove and discard the VCT housing seals.

16. Remove the 2 bolts and the primary timing chain tensioner.

17. Remove the primary timing chain tensioner arm.

18. Remove the 2 bolts and the lower LH primary timing chain guide.

19. Remove the primary timing chain.

20. Remove the 2 bolts and the upper LH primary timing chain guide.

21. Remove the RH primary timing chain guide lower bolt.

➡**The RH primary timing chain guide must be repositioned to allow the water pump to be removed.**

22. Loosen the RH primary timing chain guide upper bolt. Rotate the guide and tighten the bolt.

Fig. 77 Rotate the crankshaft clockwise and align the timing marks on the Variable Camshaft Timing (VCT) assemblies as shown

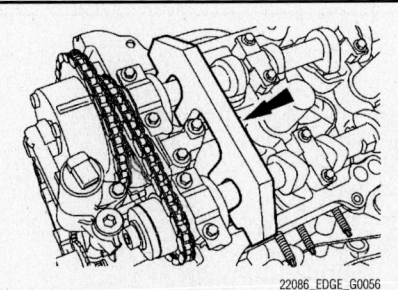

Fig. 78 Install the special tool onto the flats of the camshafts—left side shown, right side similar

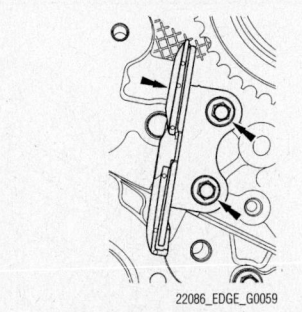

Fig. 81 Remove the 2 bolts and the upper LH primary timing chain guide

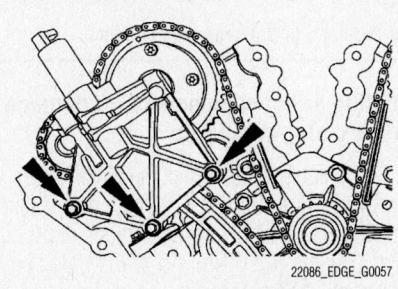

Fig. 79 Remove the 3 bolts and the VCT housing—right side shown, left side similar

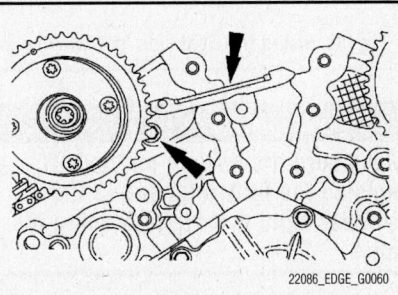

Fig. 82 Loosen the RH primary timing chain guide upper bolt. Rotate the guide and tighten the bolt

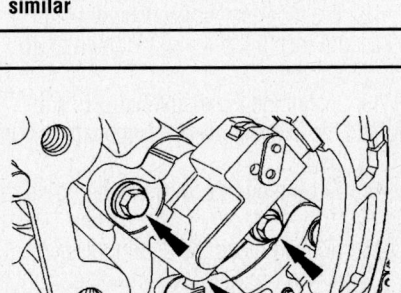

Fig. 80 Remove the 2 bolts and the primary timing chain tensioner

23. Remove the 8 bolts and the water pump.

24. Thoroughly clean and inspect all mating surfaces.

To install:

25. Install the water pump and the 8 bolts. Tighten in the sequence shown to 10 Nm (89 inch lbs.).

26. Loosen the RH primary timing chain guide upper bolt.

27. Position the RH primary timing chain guide and install the lower bolt. Tighten the 2 bolts to 10 Nm (89 inch lbs.).

28. Install the primary timing chain with the colored links aligned with the timing marks on the VCT assemblies and the crankshaft sprocket.

29. Install the upper LH primary timing chain guide and the 2 bolts. Tighten to 10 Nm (89 inch lbs.).

30. Install the lower LH primary timing chain guide and the 2 bolts. Tighten to 10 Nm (89 inch lbs.).

31. Install the primary timing chain tensioner arm.

32. Reset the primary timing chain tensioner, as follows:

   a. Rotate the lever counterclockwise.

   b. Using a soft-jawed vise, compress the plunger.

   c. Align the hole in the lever with the hole in the tensioner housing.

   d. Install a suitable lock pin.

➡ **It may be necessary to rotate the crankshaft slightly to remove slack from the timing chain and install the tensioner.**

   e. Install the primary tensioner and the 2 bolts. Tighten to 10 Nm (89 inch lbs.).

   f. Remove the lock pin.

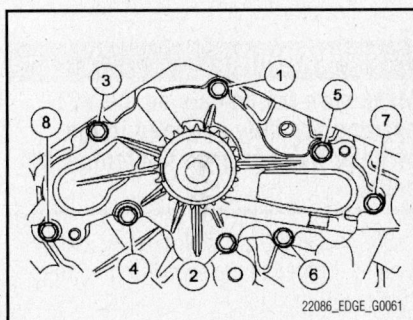

Fig. 83 Water pump bolt tightening sequence

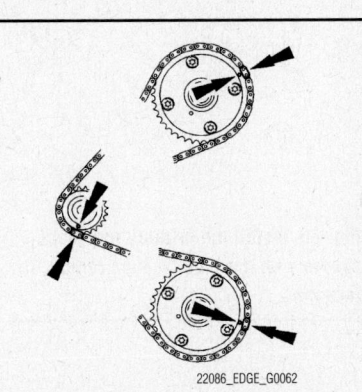

Fig. 84 Install the primary timing chain with the colored links aligned with the timing marks on the VCT assemblies and the crankshaft sprocket

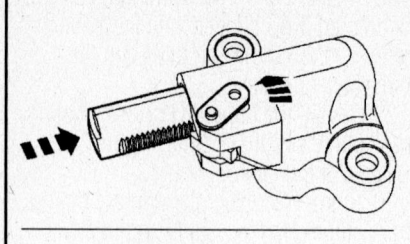

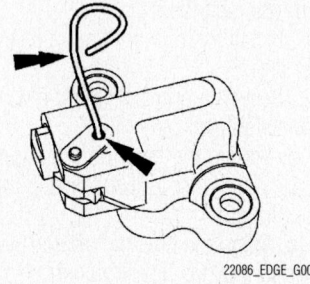

Fig. 85 Rotate the lever counterclockwise. Using a soft-jawed vise, compress the plunger. Align the hole in the lever with the hole in the tensioner housing, then insert a lock pin

33. As a post check, verify correct alignment of all timing marks.

34. Install new VCT housing seals.

※ WARNING

Make sure the dowels on the VCT housing are fully engaged in the cylinder head prior to tightening the bolts.

35. Install the LH VCT housing and the 3 bolts. Tighten in the sequence shown to 10 Nm (89 inch lbs.).

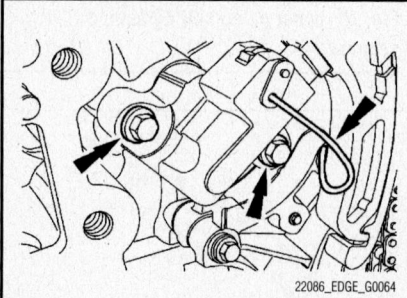

Fig. 86 Install the primary tensioner, secure with the 2 bolts, then remove the lock pin

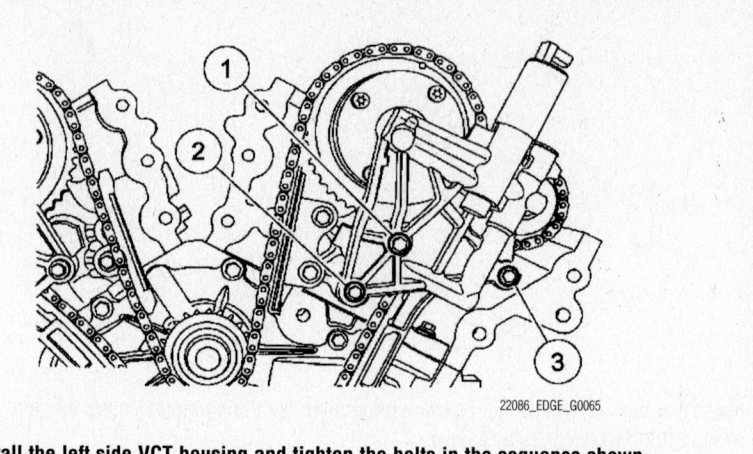

Fig. 87 Install the left side VCT housing and tighten the bolts in the sequence shown

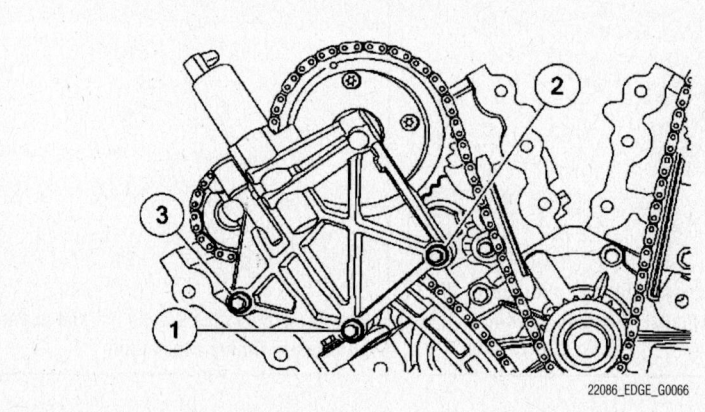

Fig. 88 Install the right side VCT housing and tighten the bolts in the sequence shown

※ WARNING

Make sure the dowels on the VCT housing are fully engaged in the cylinder head prior to tightening the bolts.

36. Install the RH VCT housing and the 3 bolts. Tighten in the sequence shown to 10 Nm (89 inch lbs.).

37. Install the engine front cover.

38. Install the RH cylinder block drain plug or, if equipped, the block heater. Tighten the cylinder block drain plug to 20 Nm (15 ft. lbs.). Tighten the block heater to 41 Nm (30 ft. lbs.).

➡Make sure that the block heater wiring is routed and secured away from rotating or hot components, or damage to the wiring can occur.

39. If equipped, connect the block heater electrical connector and install the heat shield.

40. Install the LH cylinder block drain plug. Tighten to 20 Nm (15 ft. lbs.) plus an additional 180 degrees.

41. Install the LH and RH catalytic converters.

42. Position the Y-pipe assembly in place and install the 4 nuts. Tighten to 40 Nm (30 ft. lbs.).

43. Install the 2 exhaust hangers and tighten the exhaust clamp. Tighten to 40 Nm (30 ft. lbs.).

44. Fill the engine with clean engine oil.

45. Fill and bleed the cooling system

ENGINE ELECTRICAL   **CHARGING SYSTEM**

ALTERNATOR

REMOVAL & INSTALLATION

2.3L Engine

See Figure 89.

1. Disconnect the battery.
2. Remove the bolt, the 2 nuts and the generator upper air duct.
3. Rotate the front end accessory drive belt tensioner clockwise and position the accessory drive belt aside.
4. Remove the 2 nuts and the generator shield.

5. Press the locking tabs and remove the generator intermediate air duct.
6. Position the generator protective cover aside, remove the nut and position the generator B+ terminal aside.
7. Release the generator harness locator from the generator.
8. Disconnect the generator electrical connector.
9. Release the generator harness locator from the engine block.
10. Disconnect the Crankshaft Position (CKP) sensor connector and position the generator harness aside.

11. Remove the bolt, 2 nuts, and the generator.
12. If necessary, remove the 3 bolts and the generator lower air duct.
13. If necessary, remove the 2 generator stud bolts.

To install:

14. Installation is the reverse of the removal procedure, noting the following tightening specifications:
   a. Generator stud bolts: 24 Nm (18 ft. lbs.)
   b. Generator lower air duct: 4 Nm (35 lb-in)

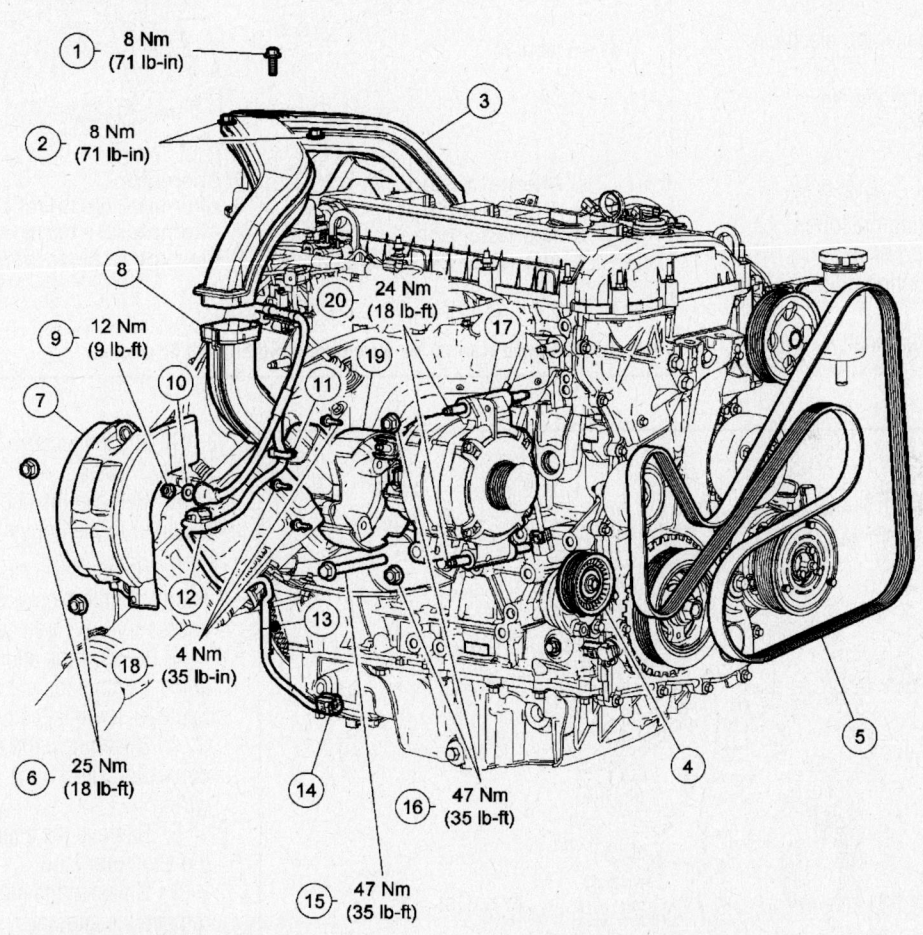

1. Generator upper air duct bolt
2. Generator upper air duct nuts (2 required)
3. Generator upper air duct
4. Front end accessory drive belt tensioner
5. Front end accessory drive belt
6. Generator shield nuts (2 required)
7. Generator shield
8. Generator intermediate air duct
9. Generator B+ terminal nut
10. Generator B+ terminal
11. Generator harness locator
12. Generator electrical connector
13. Generator harness locator
14. Crankshaft position (CKP) electrical connector
15. Generator bolt
16. Generator nuts (2 required)
17. Generator
18. Generator lower air duct bolts (3 required)
19. Generator lower air duct
20. Generator stud bolts (2 required)

22086_FUSI_G0005

Fig. 89 Exploded view of the alternator mounting—2.3L engine

c. Generator mounting bolt and nuts: 47 Nm (35 ft. lbs.)

d. Generator B+ terminal: tighten to 12 Nm (9 ft. lbs.)

e. Generator shield: tighten to 25 Nm (18 ft. lbs.)

f. Generator upper air duct: 8 Nm (71 lb-in)

3.0L Engine

See Figure 90.

1. Remove the A/C compressor, as outlined in the Heating & Air Conditioning Section.

2. Disconnect the battery.

3. Position the generator protective cover aside, remove the nut and position the generator B+ terminal aside.

4. Disconnect the generator electrical connector.

5. Remove the 3 bolts and the generator.

To install:

6. Installation is the reverse of the removal procedure, noting the following tightening specifications:

a. Generator mounting bolts: 47 Nm (35 ft. lbs.)

b. Generator B+ terminal: 12 Nm (9 ft. lbs.)

3.5L Engine

See Figure 91.

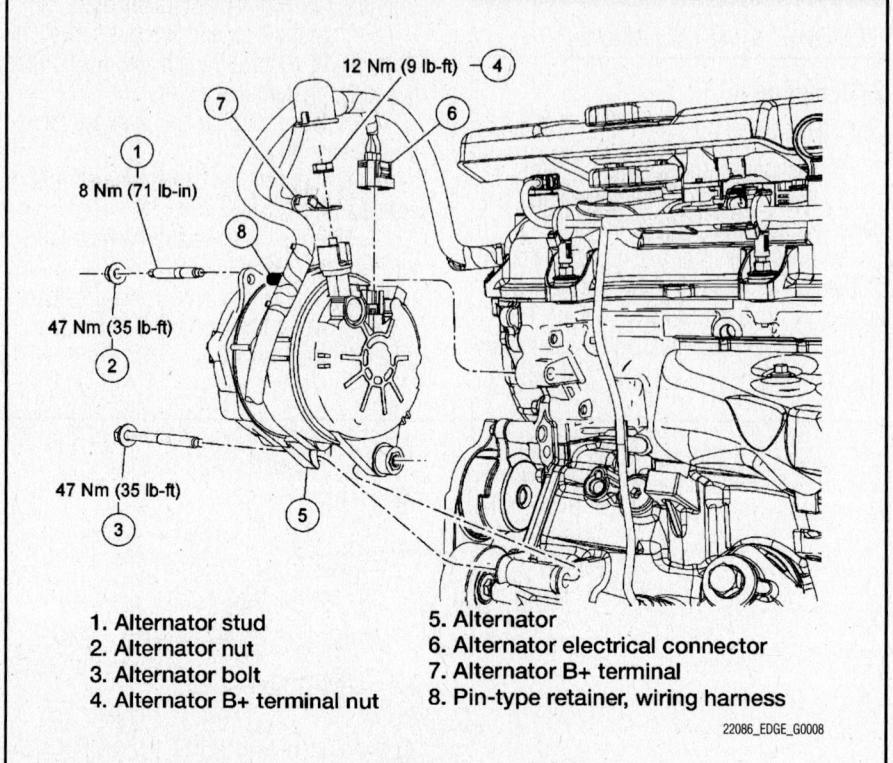

1. Alternator stud
2. Alternator nut
3. Alternator bolt
4. Alternator B+ terminal nut
5. Alternator
6. Alternator electrical connector
7. Alternator B+ terminal
8. Pin-type retainer, wiring harness

22086_EDGE_G0008

Fig. 91 Exploded view of the alternator mounting—3.5L engine

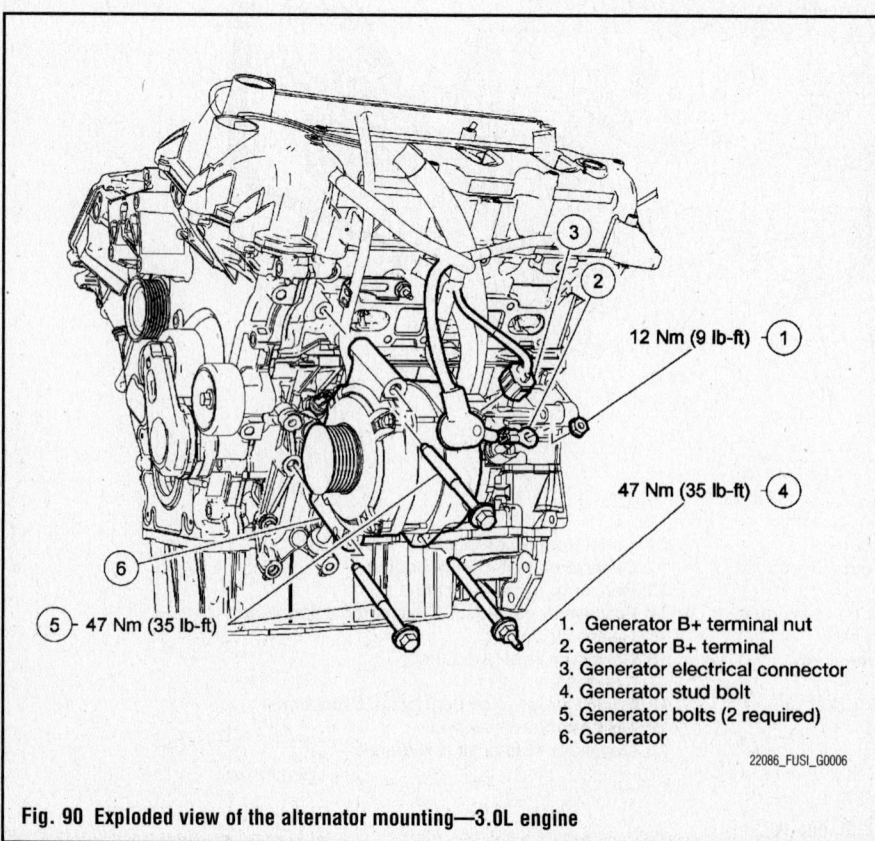

1. Generator B+ terminal nut
2. Generator B+ terminal
3. Generator electrical connector
4. Generator stud bolt
5. Generator bolts (2 required)
6. Generator

22086_FUSI_G0006

Fig. 90 Exploded view of the alternator mounting—3.0L engine

1. Disconnect the positive and negative battery cables.

2. Remove the engine cooling fan, as outlined in the Engine Mechanical Section..

3. Rotate the accessory drive belt tensioner counterclockwise and position the accessory drive belt aside.

4. Position the alternator protective cover aside, remove the nut and position the alternator B+ terminal aside.

5. Disconnect the alternator electrical connector. Detach the pin-type retainer and wiring

6. Remove the alternator stud nut and the alternator stud.

7. Unfasten the mounting bolts and remove the alternator.

To install:

7. Installation is the reverse of the removal procedure, noting the following tightening specifications:

a. Alternator mounting bolt: 35 ft. lbs. (47 Nm)

b. Alternator stud: 71 inch lbs. (8 Nm)

c. Alternator stud nut: 35 ft. lbs. (47 Nm)

d. Alternator B+ terminal nut: 9 ft. lbs. (12 Nm)

ENGINE ELECTRICAL | **IGNITION SYSTEM**

IGNITION COIL

REMOVAL & INSTALLATION

2.3L Engine

See Figure 92.

1. Disconnect the negative battery cable.
2. Remove the 2 nuts, the bolt and the generator air inlet duct.
3. Disconnect the 4 ignition coil-on-plug electrical connectors.

➡**When removing the ignition coil-on-plugs, a slight twisting motion will break the seal and ease removal.**

4. Remove the 4 bolts and the ignition coil-on-plugs.

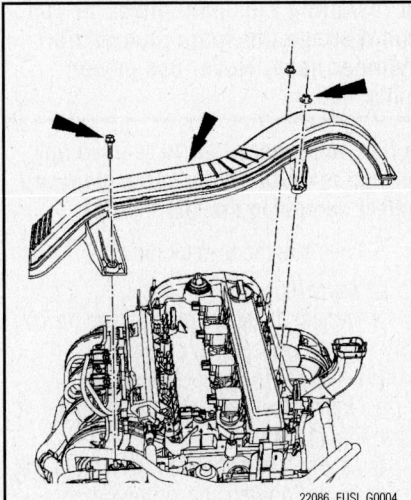

Fig. 92 Remove the 2 nuts, the bolt and the alternator air inlet duct—2.3L engine

To install:

5. Installation is the reverse of the removal procedure, noting the following:

 a. Apply a small amount of dielectric grease to the inside of the ignition coil-on-plug boots before attaching to the spark plugs.

 b. Tighten the ignition coil-on-plugs to 10 Nm (89 lb-in).

 c. Tighten the alternator air inlet duct retainers to 6 Nm (53 lb-in).

3.0L Engine

➡**The upper intake manifold must be removed to access the RH ignition coil-on-plugs only.**

1. Disconnect the negative battery cable.
2. Remove the upper intake manifold, if removing the RH coil-on-plugs.

3. Disconnect the 6 ignition coil-on-plug electrical connectors.

➡**When removing the ignition coil-on-plugs, a slight twisting motion will break the seal and ease removal.**

4. Remove the 6 bolts and the 6 ignition coil-on-plugs.
5. Installation is the reverse of the removal procedure, noting the following:

 a. Tighten the coil-on-plug bolts to 7 Nm (62 lb-in).

 b. Apply a small amount of dielectric grease to the inside of the ignition coil-on-plug boots before attaching to the spark plugs.

3.5L Engine

See Figure 93.

1. Disconnect the negative battery cable.
2. If removing the left side ignition coils, disconnect the crankcase vent tube quick connect coupling from the valve cover fitting and position it aside.
3. If removing the right side ignition coils, remove the upper intake manifold, as outlined in the Engine Mechanical Section.

➡**The upper intake manifold must be removed to access the right side ignition coils only.**

4. Detach the 6 ignition coil-on-plug electrical connectors and unfasten the mounting bolts, then remove the ignition coils from the vehicle.

➡**When removing the ignition coil-on-plugs, use a slight twisting motion to help break the seal and make removal easier.**

To install:

5. Install the 6 ignition coil-on-plugs and the 6 bolts, then tighten to 62 inch lbs. (7 Nm).
6. Attach the 6 ignition coil-on-plug electrical connectors.
7. If removed, install the upper intake manifold, as outlined in the Engine Mechanical Section.
8. If disconnected, position and connect the crankcase vent tube quick connect coupling to the valve cover
9. Connect the negative battery cable.

IGNITION TIMING

ADJUSTMENT

The ignition timing is controlled by the Powertrain Control Module (PCM). No adjustment is necessary or possible.

SPARK PLUGS

REMOVAL & INSTALLATION

2.3L Engine

See Figure 92.

1. Disconnect the negative battery cable.
2. Remove the 2 nuts, the bolt and the alternator air inlet duct.
3. Disconnect the 4 ignition coil-on-plug electrical connectors.

➡**When removing the ignition coil-on-plugs, a slight twisting motion will break the seal and ease removal.**

Remove the 4 bolts and the ignition coil-on-plugs.

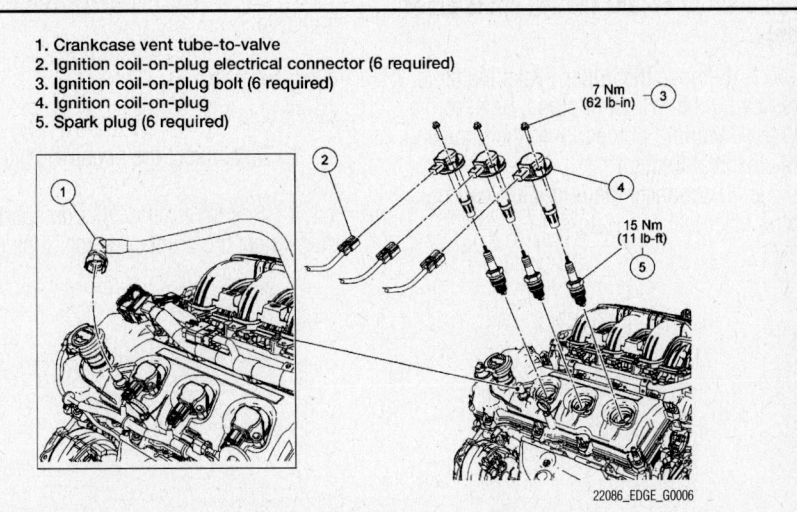

1. Crankcase vent tube-to-valve
2. Ignition coil-on-plug electrical connector (6 required)
3. Ignition coil-on-plug bolt (6 required)
4. Ignition coil-on-plug
5. Spark plug (6 required)

7 Nm (62 lb-in) — 3

15 Nm (11 lb-ft) — 5

Fig. 93 Exploded view of the ignition system components—left side shown, right side similar

✳✳ WARNING

Only use hand tools when removing or installing the spark plugs, or damage can occur to the cylinder head or spark plug.

➡ **Use compressed air to remove any foreign material in the spark plug well before removing the spark plugs.**

4. Remove the 4 spark plugs.

To install:

5. Inspect the spark plugs, as outlined in this section.

6. Adjust the spark plug gap, as necessary, to 1.25–1.35mm (0.049–0.053 in.).

✳✳ WARNING

Only use hand tools when removing or installing the spark plugs, or damage can occur to the cylinder head or spark plug.

7. Install the spark plugs and tighten to 12 Nm (9 ft. lbs.).

➡ **Apply a small amount of dielectric grease to the inside of the ignition coil-on-plug boots before attaching to the spark plugs.**

8. Install the 4 ignition coils and bolts and tighten to 10 Nm (89 lb-in).

9. Connect the 4 ignition coil electrical connectors.

10. Install the alternator air inlet duct and the 2 nuts and the bolt. Tighten to 6 Nm (53 lb-in).

11. Connect the negative battery cable.

3.0L Engine

➡ **The upper intake manifold must be removed to access the RH spark plugs only.**

1. Remove the upper intake manifold, if removing the RH spark plugs. Refer to the Intake Manifold procedure in the Engine Mechanical Section

2. Disconnect the 6 ignition coil-on-plug electrical connectors.

➡ **When removing the ignition coil-on-plugs, a slight twisting motion will break the seal and ease removal.**

3. Remove the 6 bolts and the 6 ignition coil-on-plugs.

✳✳ WARNING

Only use hand tools when removing or installing the spark plugs, or damage can occur to the cylinder head or spark plug.

➡ **Use compressed air to remove any foreign material in the spark plug well before removing the spark plugs.**

4. Remove the 6 spark plugs.

To install:

5. Inspect the spark plugs, as outlined in this section.

6. Inspect the 6 spark plugs.

7. Adjust the spark plug gap, as necessary, to 1.32–1.42mm (0.052–0.056 in.).

✳✳ WARNING

Only use hand tools when removing or installing the spark plugs, or damage can occur to the cylinder head or spark plug.

8. Install the 6 spark plugs. Tighten to 15 Nm (11 ft. lbs.).

➡ **Apply a small amount of dielectric grease to the inside of the ignition coil-on-plug boots before attaching to the spark plugs.**

9. Install the 6 ignition coil-on-plugs and the 6 bolts. Tighten to 7 Nm (62 lb-in).

10. Connect the 6 ignition coil-on-plug electrical connectors.

11. If removed, install the upper intake manifold

3.5L Engine
See Figure 93.

1. Disconnect the negative battery cable.

2. If removing the left side spark plugs, disconnect the crankcase vent tube quick connect coupling from the valve cover fitting and position it aside.

3. If removing the right side spark plugs, remove the upper intake manifold, as outlined in the Engine Mechanical Section.

➡ **The upper intake manifold must be removed to access the right side spark plugs only.**

4. Detach the 6 ignition coil-on-plug electrical connectors and unfasten the mounting bolts, then remove the ignition coils from the vehicle.

➡ **When removing the ignition coil-on-plugs, a slight twisting motion will help break the seal and make removal easier.**

✳✳ CAUTION

Only use hand tools when removing or installing the spark plugs, or you can damage the spark plug and/or cylinder head. Never use power tools.

➡ **Use compressed air to remove any foreign material in the spark plug well before removing the spark plugs.**

5. Remove the 6 spark plugs.

To install:

6. Adjust the spark plug gap as necessary. The proper spark plug gap is 0.0051–0.0057 in. (1.29–1.45mm).

7. Install the spark plugs and tighten to 11 ft. lbs. (15 Nm).

8. Apply a little dielectric grease to the inside of the ignition coil-on-plug boots before attaching to the spark plugs.

9. Install the 6 ignition coil-on-plugs and the 6 bolts, then tighten to 62 inch lbs. (7 Nm).

10. Attach the 6 ignition coil-on-plug electrical connectors.

11. If removed, install the upper intake manifold, as outlined in the Engine Mechanical Section.

12. If disconnected, position and connect the crankcase vent tube quick connect coupling to the valve cover

13. Connect the negative battery cable.

ENGINE ELECTRICAL   **STARTING SYSTEM**

STARTER

REMOVAL & INSTALLATION

2.3L Engine

See Figure 94.

1. Raise and safely support the vehicle.
2. Disconnect the negative battery cable.
3. If equipped, remove the 7 screws and the underbody cover.
4. Remove the starter motor solenoid wire nut and position the wire aside.
5. Position the starter motor solenoid battery cable terminal cover aside.
6. Remove the starter motor solenoid battery cable nut and position the cable aside.
7. Disconnect the wiring harness retainer from the top and bottom starter motor stud bolt and position the wiring harness aside.
8. Remove the starter motor stud bolt, bolt and the starter motor.

To install:

9. Installation is the reverse of the removal procedure, noting the following tightening specifications:
   a. Starter motor bolt and stud bolts: 25 Nm (18 ft. lbs.)
   b. Starter motor solenoid battery cable nut: 12 Nm (9 ft. lbs.)
   c. Starter motor solenoid wire nut: 5 Nm (44 lb-in)

3.0L Engine

See Figure 95.

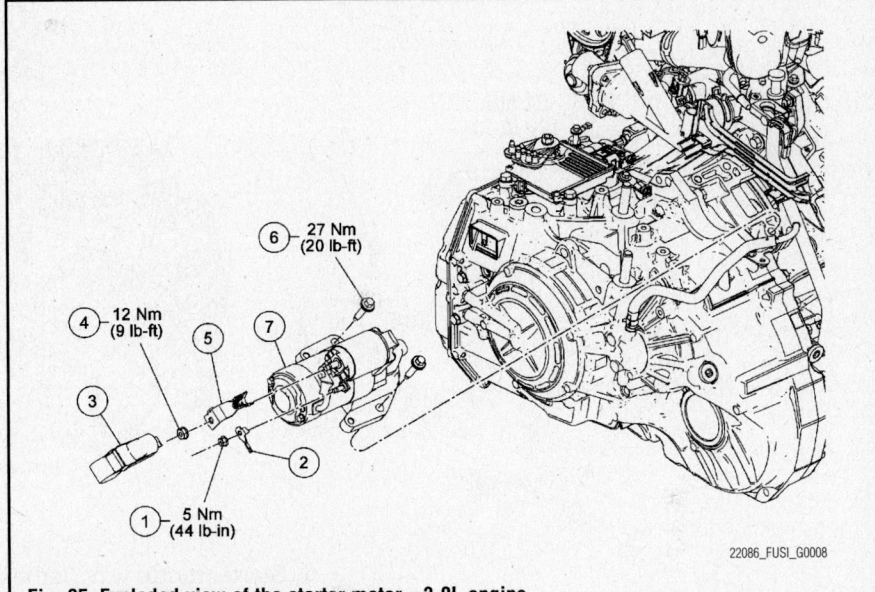

Fig. 95 Exploded view of the starter motor—3.0L engine

22086_FUSI_G0008

❈❈ CAUTION

When performing work on the starting system, be aware that the heavy gauge leads are connected directly to the battery. Make sure the protective caps are in place when maintenance is completed.

---

1. Disconnect the negative, then the positive battery cables.
2. Remove the battery tray.
3. On the 3.5L engine, detach the starter motor wire harness pin-type retainer.
4. Remove the starter motor solenoid wire nut and position the wire aside.
5. Position the starter motor solenoid terminal battery cable cover aside.
6. Remove the starter motor solenoid battery cable nut and position aside the cable.
7. Remove the 2 starter motor bolts and the starter motor.

To install:

8. Installation is the reverse of the removal procedure, noting the following tightening specifications:
   a. Starter motor bolts: 27 Nm (20 ft. lbs.)
   b. Starter motor solenoid battery cable nut: 12 Nm (9 ft. lbs.)
   c. Starter motor solenoid wire nut: 5 Nm (44 lb-in)

3.5L Engine

See Figure 96.

1. Disconnect the negative, then the positive battery cables.
2. Remove the battery tray.
3. Detach the starter motor wire harness pin-type retainer.

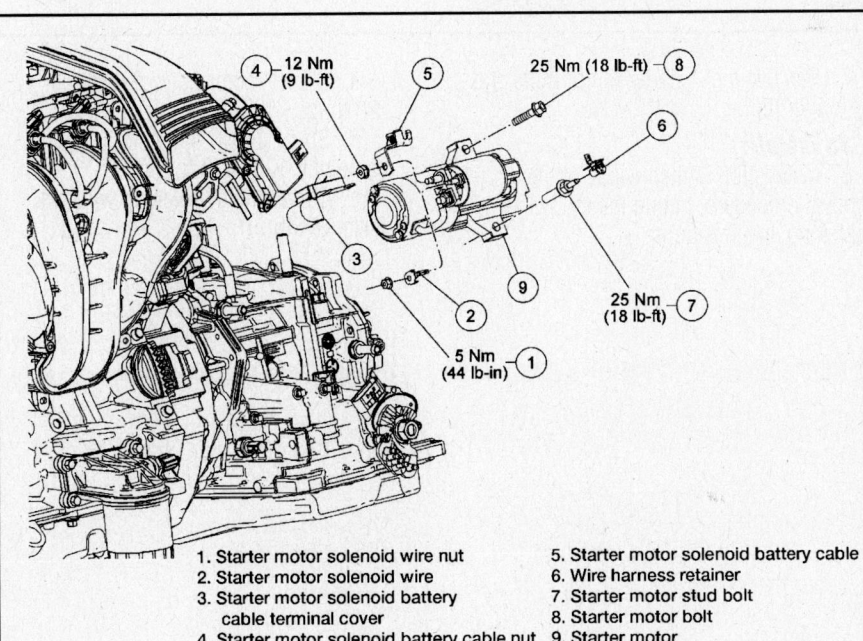

1. Starter motor solenoid wire nut
2. Starter motor solenoid wire
3. Starter motor solenoid battery cable terminal cover
4. Starter motor solenoid battery cable nut
5. Starter motor solenoid battery cable
6. Wire harness retainer
7. Starter motor stud bolt
8. Starter motor bolt
9. Starter motor

22086_FUSI_G0007

Fig. 94 Exploded view of the starter motor—2.3L engine

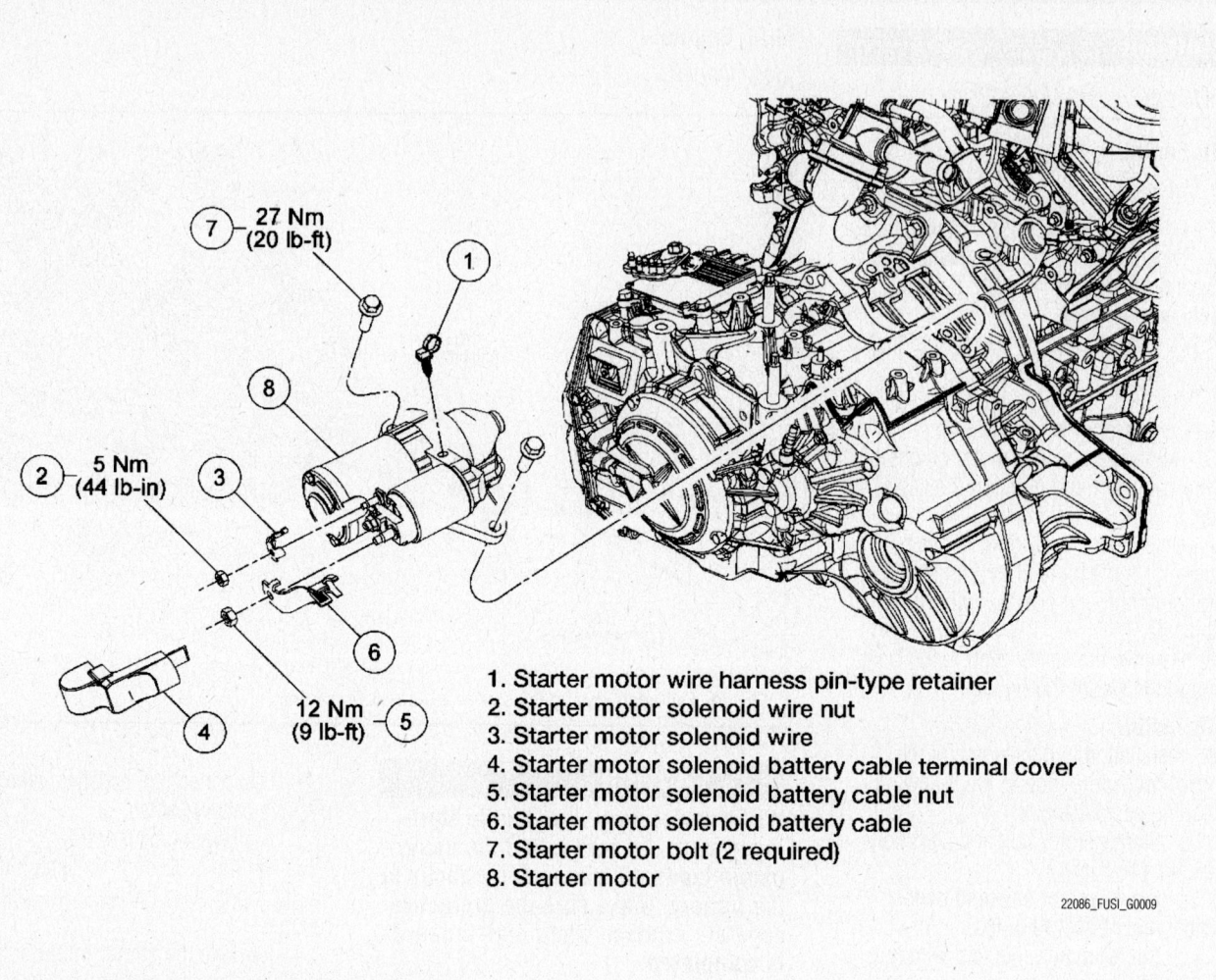

1. Starter motor wire harness pin-type retainer
2. Starter motor solenoid wire nut
3. Starter motor solenoid wire
4. Starter motor solenoid battery cable terminal cover
5. Starter motor solenoid battery cable nut
6. Starter motor solenoid battery cable
7. Starter motor bolt (2 required)
8. Starter motor

22086_FUSI_G0009

Fig. 96 Exploded view of the starter motor—3.5L engine

4. Remove the starter motor solenoid wire nut and position the wire aside.

5. Position the starter motor solenoid terminal battery cable cover aside.

6. Remove the starter motor solenoid battery cable nut and position aside the cable.

7. Remove the 2 starter motor bolts and the starter motor.

To install:

8. Installation is the reverse of the removal procedure, noting the following tightening specifications:

a. Starter motor bolts: 27 Nm (20 ft. lbs.)

b. Starter motor solenoid battery cable nut: 12 Nm (9 ft. lbs.)

c. Starter motor solenoid wire nut: 5 Nm (44 lb-in)

ENGINE MECHANICAL

➡**Disconnecting the negative battery cable may interfere with the functions of the on board computer systems and may require the computer to undergo a relearning process, once the negative battery cable is reconnected.**

ACCESSORY DRIVE BELTS

ACCESSORY BELT ROUTING

See Figures 97 through 100.

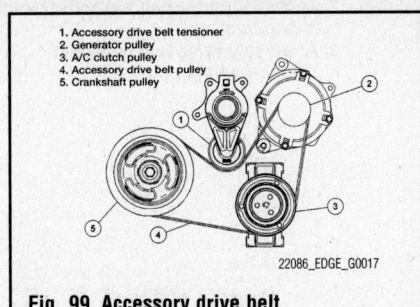

1. Accessory drive belt tensioner
2. Generator pulley
3. A/C clutch pulley
4. Accessory drive belt pulley
5. Crankshaft pulley

22086_EDGE_G0017

Fig. 99 Accessory drive belt routing—3.5L engine

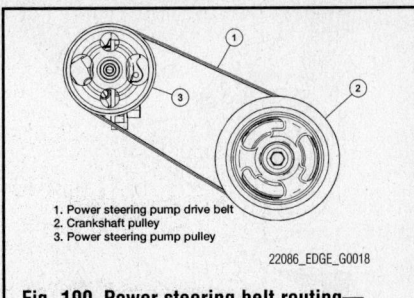

1. Power steering pump drive belt
2. Crankshaft pulley
3. Power steering pump pulley

22086_EDGE_G0018

Fig. 100 Power steering belt routing—3.5L engine

INSPECTION

Inspect the drive belt for signs of glazing or cracking. A glazed belt will be perfectly smooth from slippage, while a good belt will have a slight texture of fabric visible. Cracks will usually start at the inner edge of the belt and run outward. All worn or damaged drive belts should be replaced immediately.

ADJUSTMENT

Belt tension is maintained by an automatic belt tensioner. No adjustments are necessary.

REMOVAL & INSTALLATION

Accessory Drive Belt

2.3L Engine

See Figure 101.

⁎⁎ WARNING

NEVER lubricate the accessory drive belt, tensioner or pulleys as this will cause potential damage to the belt material and tensioner damping mechanism. Do not apply any fluids or any type of belt dressing to the accessory drive belt or pulleys.

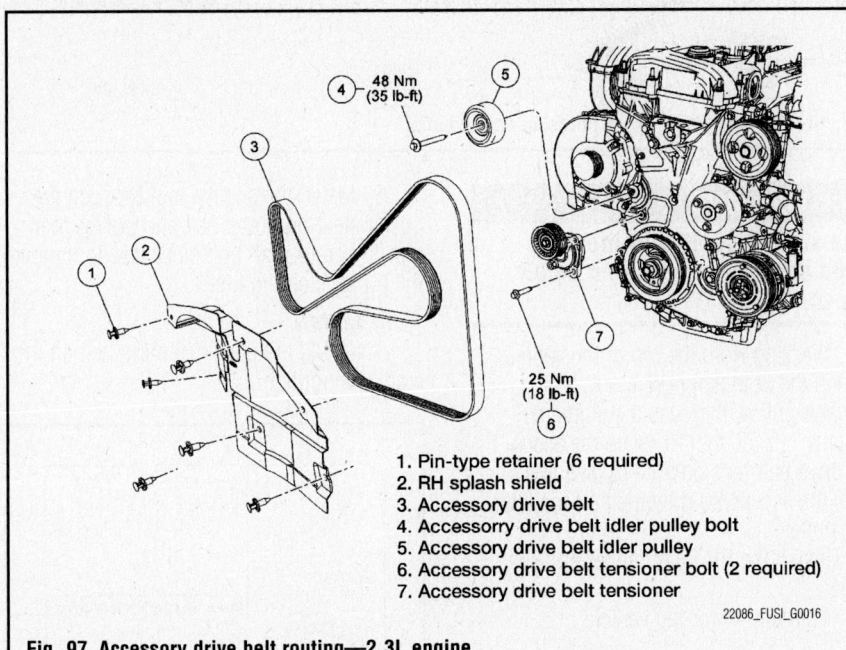

48 Nm (35 lb-ft)

25 Nm (18 lb-ft)

1. Pin-type retainer (6 required)
2. RH splash shield
3. Accessory drive belt
4. Accessorry drive belt idler pulley bolt
5. Accessory drive belt idler pulley
6. Accessory drive belt tensioner bolt (2 required)
7. Accessory drive belt tensioner

22086_FUSI_G0016

Fig. 97 Accessory drive belt routing—2.3L engine

1. Raise and safely support the vehicle.
2. Remove the 4 screws and position the RH fender splash shield aside.
3. Remove the 6 pin-type retainers and the RH splash shield.
4. Using the hex feature, rotate the accessory drive belt tensioner clockwise and remove the accessory drive belt from the coolant pump pulley.
5. Remove the accessory drive belt from the engine.
6. Installation is the reverse of the removal procedure. Make sure the belt is properly routed.

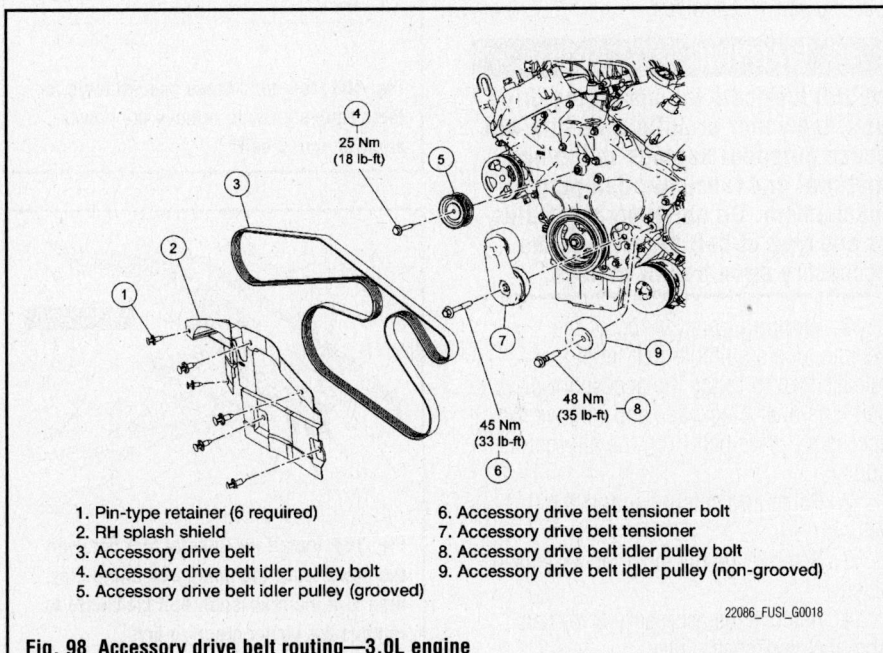

25 Nm (18 lb-ft)

45 Nm (33 lb-ft)

48 Nm (35 lb-ft)

1. Pin-type retainer (6 required)
2. RH splash shield
3. Accessory drive belt
4. Accessory drive belt idler pulley bolt
5. Accessory drive belt idler pulley (grooved)
6. Accessory drive belt tensioner bolt
7. Accessory drive belt tensioner
8. Accessory drive belt idler pulley bolt
9. Accessory drive belt idler pulley (non-grooved)

22086_FUSI_G0018

Fig. 98 Accessory drive belt routing—3.0L engine

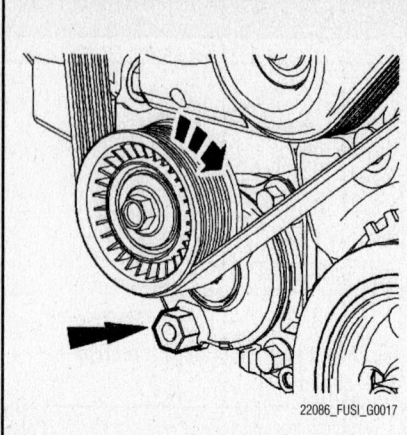

Fig. 101 Using the hex feature, rotate the accessory drive belt tensioner clockwise and remove the accessory drive belt from the coolant pump pulley

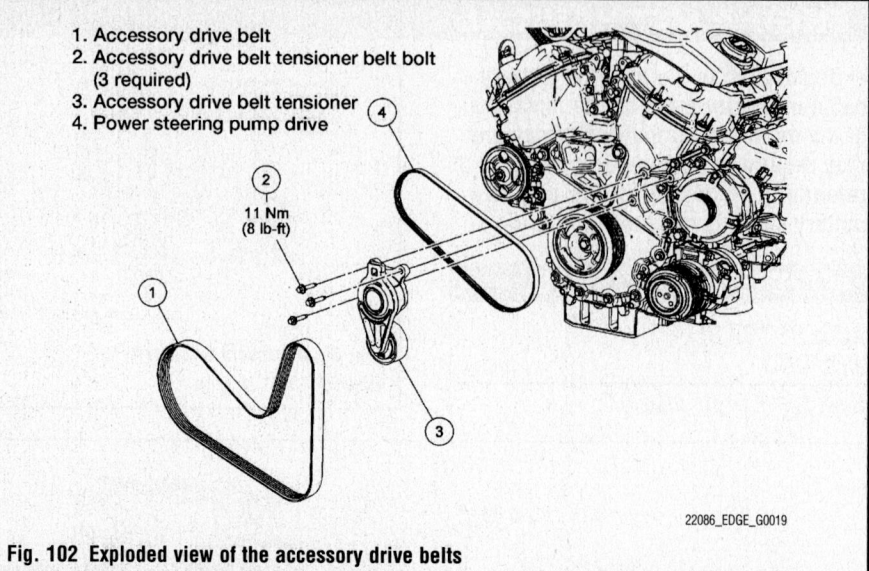

1. Accessory drive belt
2. Accessory drive belt tensioner belt bolt (3 required)
3. Accessory drive belt tensioner
4. Power steering pump drive

11 Nm (8 lb-ft)

Fig. 102 Exploded view of the accessory drive belts

3.0L Engine

1. Raise and safely support the vehicle.

2. Remove the 4 screws and position the RH fender splash shield aside.

3. Remove the 6 pin-type retainers and the RH splash shield.

4. Using a suitable belt tensioner release tool, rotate the accessory drive belt tensioner counterclockwise and remove the accessory drive belt.

5. To install, reverse the removal procedure. Make sure the belt is properly routed.

3.5L Engine

See Figure 102.

> **✳✳ WARNING**
>
> **NEVER lubricate the accessory drive belt, tensioner or pulleys as this will cause potential damage to the belt material and tensioner damping mechanism. Do not apply any fluids or any type of belt dressing to the accessory drive belt or pulleys.**

1. Raise and safely support the vehicle.

2. Working from the top of the vehicle, use a suitable belt tensioner release tool to rotate the accessory drive belt tensioner clockwise and remove the accessory drive belt from the alternator pulley.

3. Remove the RH inner fender splash shield..

4. Working from underneath the vehicle, remove the accessory drive belt.

To install:

5. Working from underneath the vehicle, install the accessory drive belt on all pulleys, except the alternator pulley.

> **✳✳ WARNING**
>
> **Make sure the belt is properly routed and correctly seated on all pulleys.**

6. Working from the top of the vehicle, position the accessory drive belt on the alternator pulley, then use a suitable belt tensioner release tool to rotate the accessory drive belt tensioner clockwise and install the accessory drive belt on the alternator pulley.

7. Install the RH inner fender splash shield.

8. Carefully lower the vehicle.

Power Steering Pump Belt

See Figures 103 and 104.

> **✳✳ WARNING**
>
> **NEVER lubricate the accessory drive belt, tensioner or pulleys as this will cause potential damage to the belt material and tensioner damping mechanism. Do not apply any fluids or any type of belt dressing to the accessory drive belt or pulleys.**

1. Working from the top of the vehicle, use a suitable belt tensioner release tool to rotate the accessory drive belt tensioner clockwise and remove the accessory drive belt from the alternator pulley.

2. Raise and safely support the vehicle.

3. Remove the RH inner fender splash shield..

4. Remove the accessory drive belt from the crankshaft pulley.

5. Install the special tool between the power steering pump belt and pulley, then turn the crankshaft bolt clockwise to remove the power steering belt.

To install:

6. Install the power steering belt on the crankshaft pulley.

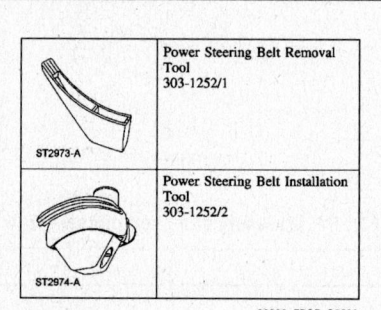

ST2973-A	Power Steering Belt Removal Tool 303-1252/1
ST2974-A	Power Steering Belt Installation Tool 303-1252/2

Fig. 103 You need these special tools, or their equivalents, to remove the power steering pump belt

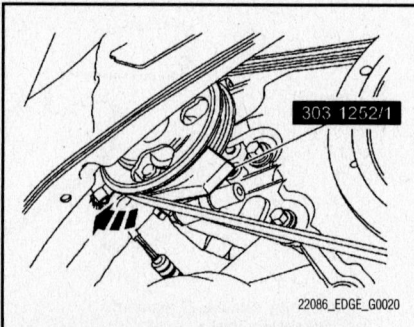

303-1252/1

Fig. 104 Install the special tool between the power steering pump belt and pulley, then turn the crankshaft bolt clockwise to remove the power steering belt

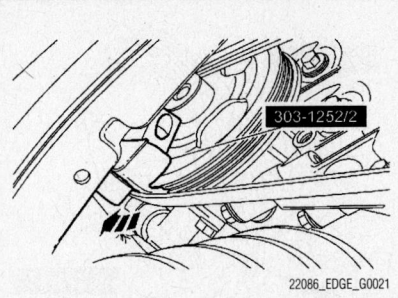

303-1252/2

22086_EDGE_G0021

Fig. 105 Position the power steering belt around the special tool and the power steering pulley. Make sure that the belt is engaged with the power steering pulley and rotate the crankshaft clockwise to install the power steering belt

✳✳ **WARNING**

Make sure the belt is correctly seated on the crankshaft and power steering pulleys.

7. Position the power steering belt around the special tool and the power steering pulley. Make sure that the belt is engaged with the power steering pulley and rotate the crankshaft clockwise to install the power steering belt.

8. Install the accessory drive belt on the crankshaft pulley.

✳✳ **WARNING**

Make sure the belt is properly routed and correctly seated on all pulleys.

9. Working from the top of the vehicle, place the accessory drive belt on the alternator pulley. Using a suitable belt tensioner release tool, rotate the accessory drive belt tensioner clockwise and install the accessory drive belt on the alternator pulley.

10. Install the RH inner fender splash shield.

Coolant Pump Belt

3.0L Engine

1. Raise and safely support the vehicle.
2. If equipped, remove the 2 nuts and the coolant belt pump shield.
3. Cut and remove the coolant pump belt.
4. Discard the belt.

To install:

➡To install the coolant pump belt, remove the 2 splash shields for access to the crankshaft bolt.

5. Remove the 4 screws and position the RH fender splash shield aside.

6. Remove the 6 pin-type retainers (4 shown) and the RH splash shield.

7. Install the coolant pump belt on the coolant pump pulley and position it on the camshaft pulley.

✳✳ **WARNING**

Do not use any screwdrivers, pliers or other metal objects that could cause damage to the belt or camshaft pulley while installing the belt.

8. Rotate the crankshaft clockwise to seat the coolant pump belt on the camshaft pulley.

9. If equipped, install the coolant pump belt shield and the nuts. Tighten to 6 Nm (53 lb-in).

10. Install the RH splash shield and the 6 pin-type retainers.

11. Position the RH fender splash shield and install the 4 screws.

CAMSHAFT AND VALVE LIFTERS

REMOVAL & INSTALLATION

2.3L Engine

See Figures 106 and 107.

✳✳ **WARNING**

Do not loosen or remove the crankshaft pulley bolt without first installing the special tools as instructed in this procedure. The crankshaft pulley and the crankshaft timing sprocket are not keyed to the crankshaft. The crankshaft, the crankshaft sprocket and the pulley are fitted together by friction, using diamond washers between the flange faces on each part. For that reason, the crankshaft sprocket is also unfastened if you loosen the pulley bolt. Before any repair requiring loosening or removal of the crankshaft pulley bolt, the crankshaft and camshafts must be locked in place by the special service tools, otherwise severe engine damage can occur.

✳✳ **WARNING**

During engine repair procedures, cleanliness is extremely important. Any foreign material, including any material created while cleaning gasket surfaces, that enters the oil passages, coolant passages or the oil pan can cause engine failure.

1. Raise and safely support the vehicle.
2. Release the fuel system pressure, as outlined in the Fuel Section.
3. Check the valve clearance.
4. Remove the degas bottle.
5. Remove the catalytic converter.
6. Remove the generator.
7. Remove the fuel supply rail.
8. Remove the intake manifold.
9. On Vehicles with secondary air injection (AIR):
   a. Disconnect the secondary air injection (AIR) pump electrical connector.
   b. Remove the 3 bolts and position the AIR pump aside.
10. Remove the bolt and the radio frequency interference capacitor from the engine mount bracket.
11. Remove the engine mount bracket bolt.
12. Install the special tool (303-050) and a suitable length of chain to the threaded hole in the LH side of the engine block.
13. Install the special tools 313-F072 and 303-050, or equivalent, then using the special tool, lift the engine 25 mm (0.98 in).
14. Remove the nut, 2 bolts and the engine mount.
15. Lower the engine 25 mm (0.98 in).
16. Remove the 2 nuts and the engine mount bracket.
17. Remove the timing drive components.
18. Remove the special tool.
19. Mark the position of the camshaft lobes on the No. 1 cylinder for installation reference.
20. Remove the bolt and the variable camshaft timing (VCT) solenoid.

✳✳ **WARNING**

Failure to follow the camshaft loosening procedure can result in damage to the camshafts.

21. Remove the camshafts from the engine.
22. Loosen the camshaft bearing cap bolts, in the sequence shown, one turn at a time until all tension is released from the camshaft bearing caps.
23. Remove the bolts and the camshaft bearing caps.
24. Remove the camshafts.

✳✳ **WARNING**

If the camshafts and valve tappets are to be reused, mark the location of the valve tappets to make sure they are assembled in their original positions.

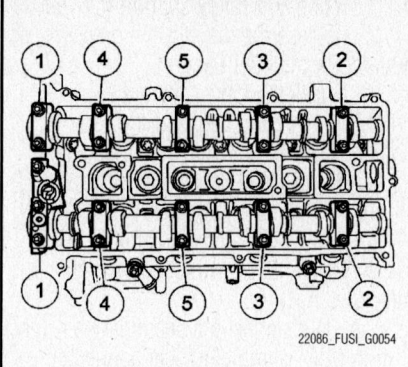

Fig. 106 Camshaft bearing bolt loosening sequence—2.3L engine

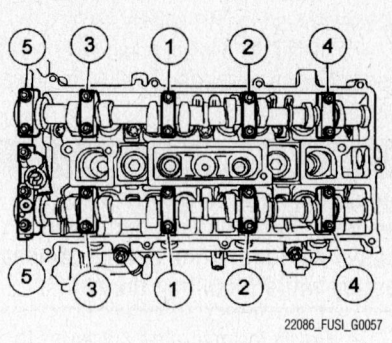

Fig. 107 Camshaft bearing cap bolt tightening sequence—2.3L engine

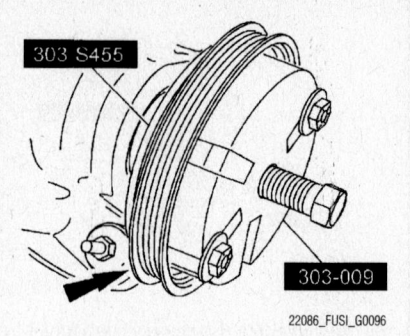

Fig. 108 Using the special tools, remove the coolant pump drive pulley from the camshaft

→The number on the valve tappets only reflects the digits that follow the decimal. For example, a tappet with the number 0.650 has the thickness of 3.650 mm.

25. Remove and inspect the valve tappets.

To install:

→Coat the valve tappets with clean engine oil prior to installation.

26. Install the valve tappets.

⁑ WARNING

Install the camshafts with the alignment slots in the camshafts lined up so the Camshaft Alignment Plate can be installed without rotating the camshafts. Make sure the lobes on the No. 1 cylinder are in the same position as noted in the removal procedure. Rotating the camshafts when the timing chain is removed, or installing the camshafts 180 degrees out of position can cause severe damage to the valves and pistons.

→Lubricate the camshaft journals and bearing caps with clean engine oil.

27. Install the camshafts and bearing caps. Tighten the camshaft bearing caps in the sequence shown in 3 stages:
  a. Stages 1: Tighten the camshaft bearing cap bolts until finger tight.
  b. Stages 2: Tighten to 7 Nm (62 lb-in).
  c. Stages 3: Tighten to 16 Nm (12 ft. lbs.).
28. Install the special tool 303-465, or equivalent..
29. Install the VCT solenoid and bolt. Tighten to 10 Nm (89 lb-in).
30. Install the timing drive components.

31. Install the engine mount bracket and the 2 nuts. Tighten to 103 Nm (76 ft. lbs.).
32. Using the special too, lift the engine 25 mm (0.98 in).
33. Install the engine mount, nut and 2 bolts. Tighten to 55 Nm (41 ft. lbs.).
34. Lower the engine 25 mm (0.98 in).
35. Install the engine mount bracket bolt. Tighten to 115 Nm (85 ft. lbs.).
36. Install the radio frequency interference capacitor and bolt to the engine mount bracket. Tighten to 10 Nm (89 lb-in).
37. On Vehicles with secondary air injection (AIR):
  a. Install the AIR pump and the 3 bolts.
  b. Tighten to 30 Nm (22 ft. lbs.).
  c. Connect the AIR pump electrical connector.
38. Install the intake manifold.
39. Install the fuel supply rail.
40. Install the generator.
41. Install the catalytic converter.
42. Install the degas bottle.
43. Fill and bleed the engine cooling system

3.0L Engine

Left Side

See Figures 108 through 114.

1. Remove the timing drive components (timing chain and sprockets), as outlined in this section.
2. Cut and discard the coolant pump belt.
3. Using the special tools, remove the coolant pump drive pulley from the camshaft.

→To make sure of correct sealing, do not scratch the camshaft.

4. Using the special tools, remove and discard the camshaft oil seal.
5. Remove the 2 bolts and the camshaft oil seal retainer.

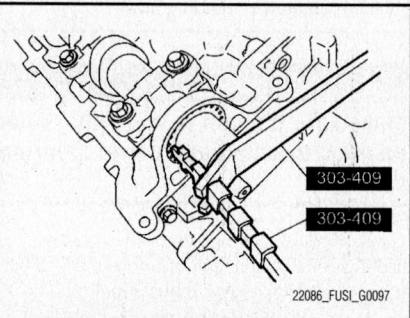

Fig. 109 Using the special tools, remove and discard the camshaft oil seal

6. Discard the press-in-place gasket.

⁑ WARNING

The camshafts must be in the neutral position before removing the bearing caps.

7. Verify the camshafts are in the neutral position.

⁑ WARNING

Do not allow the camshaft to rotate from the neutral position while removing the variable camshaft timing (VCT) actuator.

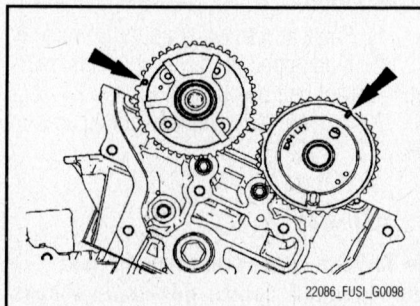

Fig. 110 Verify the camshafts are in the neutral position

➡Install a 3/8-in ratchet and extension into the D-slot on the rear of the intake camshaft to hold the camshaft in place for removal of the VCT actuator bolt.

8. Remove the bolt and the variable camshaft timing (VCT) actuator.

✲✲ WARNING

Cylinder head camshaft bearing caps are numbered to verify that they are assembled in their original positions. If the numbers cannot be seen, mark the camshaft bearing caps prior to removing them.

✲✲ WARNING

After loosening all of the camshaft bearing cap bolts, remove the camshaft bearing thrust caps (1L and 6L) first, or damage to the thrust caps may occur.

9. Loosen the bolts evenly in the sequence shown:
   a. Remove the camshaft bearing thrust caps (1L and 6L).
   b. Remove the remaining camshaft bearing caps.
   c. Remove the camshafts from the cylinder head.

To install:

10. Position the VCT actuator onto the intake camshaft. Install the bolt finger-tight.

✲✲ WARNING

The camshafts must be installed in the neutral position.

11. Lubricate the camshafts with clean engine oil and carefully position the camshafts into the cylinder head.
12. Align the camshafts in the neutral position.

✲✲ WARNING

The camshaft caps must be installed in their original positions or damage to the engine may occur.

✲✲ WARNING

Do not install the camshaft bearing thrust caps until all of the camshaft bearing caps have been installed, or damage to the thrust caps may occur.

➡Lubricate the bearing surfaces of the camshaft bearing caps with clean engine oil.

13. Install the camshaft bearing caps and loosely install the bolts.

➡Lubricate the bearing surfaces of the camshaft bearing thrust caps with clean engine oil.

14. Install the camshaft bearing thrust caps. Loosely install the bolts.
15. Tighten the camshaft bearing cap bolts in the sequence shown to 10 Nm (89 lb-in).

✲✲ WARNING

Do not allow the camshaft to rotate from the neutral position while tightening the VCT actuator bolt.

➡Install a 3/8-in ratchet and extension into the D-slot on the rear of the intake camshaft to hold the camshaft in place for tightening of the VCT actuator bolt.

16. Tighten the VCT actuator bolt to 40 Nm (30 ft. lbs.) plus an additional 90 degrees.

➡Clean the sealing surface with metal surface cleaner before installing a new press-in-place gasket.

17. Install the camshaft oil seal retainer and the 2 bolts. Tighten to 10 Nm (89 lb-in).
18. Apply clean engine oil to the seal lip and seal bore before installing the seal.
19. Using the special tools, install a new camshaft oil seal.

303-464
303-463
211-185
22086_FUSI_G0101

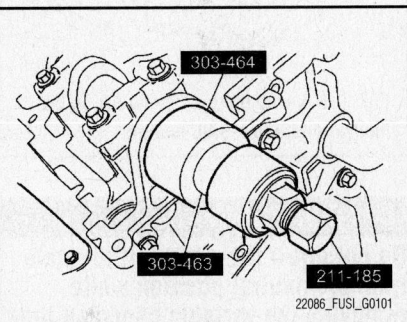

Fig. 113 Using the special tools, install a new camshaft oil seal

✲✲ WARNING

The pulley is pressed on flush to the end of the camshaft.

20. Using the special tool, install the coolant pump drive pulley.
21. Install the timing drive components (timing chain), as outlined in this section.
22. Install the coolant pump belt

1L
6L
2L
7L
3L
8L
4L
9L
5L
22086_FUSI_G0099

Fig. 111 Left side camshaft bearing cap loosening sequence—3.0L engine

1L
6L
2L
7L
3L
8L
4L
9L
5L
22086_FUSI_G0100

Fig. 112 Tighten the left side camshaft bearing cap bolts in the sequence shown to 10 Nm (89 lb-in)—3.0L engine

211-185
303-S455
22086_FUSI_G0102

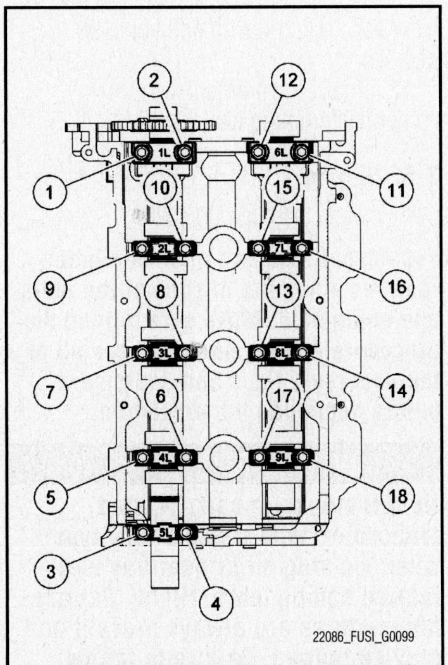

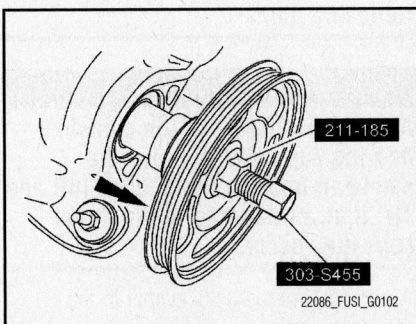

Fig. 114 Using the special tool, install the coolant pump drive pulley.

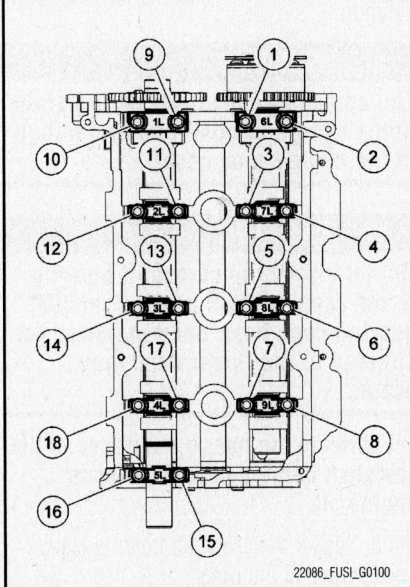

Right Side

See Figures 115 through 117.

1. Remove the timing drive components/timing chain, as outlined in this section.

> **✳✳ WARNING**
>
> The camshafts must be in the neutral position before removing the bearing caps.

2. Verify the camshafts are in the neutral position.

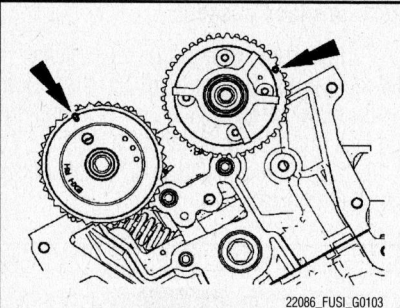

Fig. 115 Verify the camshafts are in the neutral position—3.0L engine

> **✳✳ WARNING**
>
> Do not allow the camshaft to rotate from the neutral position while removing the variable camshaft timing (VCT) actuator.

➡ Install a 3/8-in ratchet and extension into the D-slot on the rear of the intake camshaft to hold the camshaft in place for removal of the VCT actuator bolt.

3. Remove the bolt and the VCT actuator.

> **✳✳ WARNING**
>
> Cylinder head camshaft bearing caps are numbered to verify that they are assembled in their original positions. If the numbers cannot be seen, mark the camshaft bearing caps prior to removing them.

> **✳✳ WARNING**
>
> After loosening all of the camshaft bearing cap bolts, remove the camshaft bearing thrust caps (5R and 1R) first, or damage to the thrust caps may occur.

4. Loosen the bolts evenly in the sequence shown:

   a. Remove the camshaft bearing thrust caps (5R and 1R).

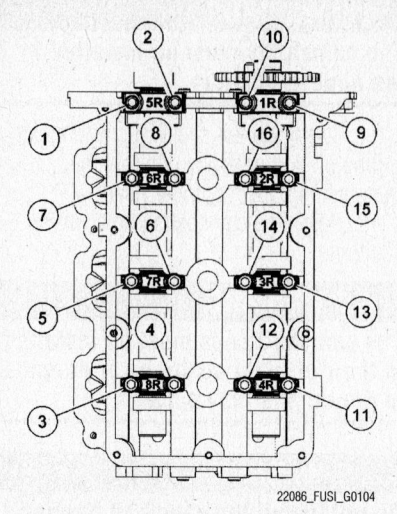

Fig. 116 Right side camshaft bearing cap loosening sequence—3.0L engine

   b. Remove the remaining camshaft bearing caps.

   c. Remove the camshafts from the cylinder head.

To install:

5. Position the VCT actuator onto the intake camshaft. Install the bolt finger-tight.

> **✳✳ WARNING**
>
> The camshafts must be installed in the neutral position.

6. Lubricate the camshafts with clean engine oil and carefully position the camshafts onto the cylinder head.

7. Align the camshafts in the neutral position.

> **✳✳ WARNING**
>
> The camshaft caps must be installed in their original positions or damage to the engine may occur.

> **✳✳ WARNING**
>
> Do not install the camshaft bearing thrust caps until all of the camshaft bearing caps have been installed, or damage to the thrust caps may occur.

➡ Lubricate the bearing surfaces of the camshaft bearing caps with clean engine oil.

8. Install the camshaft bearing caps. Loosely install the bolts.

➡ Lubricate the bearing surfaces of the camshaft bearing thrust caps with clean engine oil.

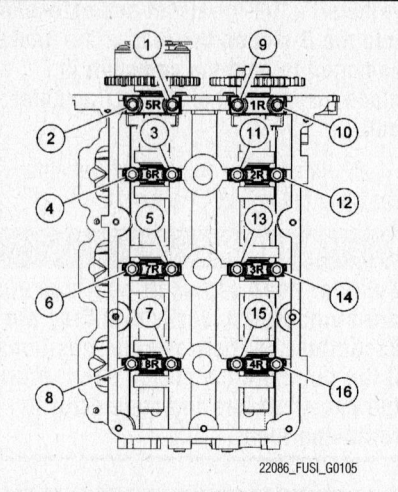

Fig. 117 Tighten the right side camshaft bearing cap bolts in the sequence shown to 10 Nm (89 lb-in)—3.0L engine

9. Install the camshaft bearing thrust caps. Loosely install the bolts.

10. Tighten the camshaft bearing cap bolts in the sequence shown to 10 Nm (89 lb-in).

> **✳✳ WARNING**
>
> Do not allow the camshaft to rotate from the neutral position while tightening the VCT actuator bolt.

➡ Install a 3/8-in ratchet and extension into the D-slot on the rear of the intake camshaft to hold the camshaft in place for tightening of the VCT actuator bolt.

11. Tighten the VCT actuator bolt to 40 Nm (30 ft. lbs.) plus an additional 90 degrees.

12. Install the timing drive components/timing chain.

3.5L Engine

See Figures 118 through 138.

➡ Camshaft removal and installation requires a number of specialized tools and equipment. Make sure to read the procedure and be sure you have all of the necessary tools and equipment before beginning the procedure.

> **✳✳ WARNING**
>
> NEVER smoke or carry lighted tobacco or open flame of any type when working on or near any fuel-related components. Highly flammable mixtures are always present and may be ignited. Failure to follow these precautions may result in personal injury or death.

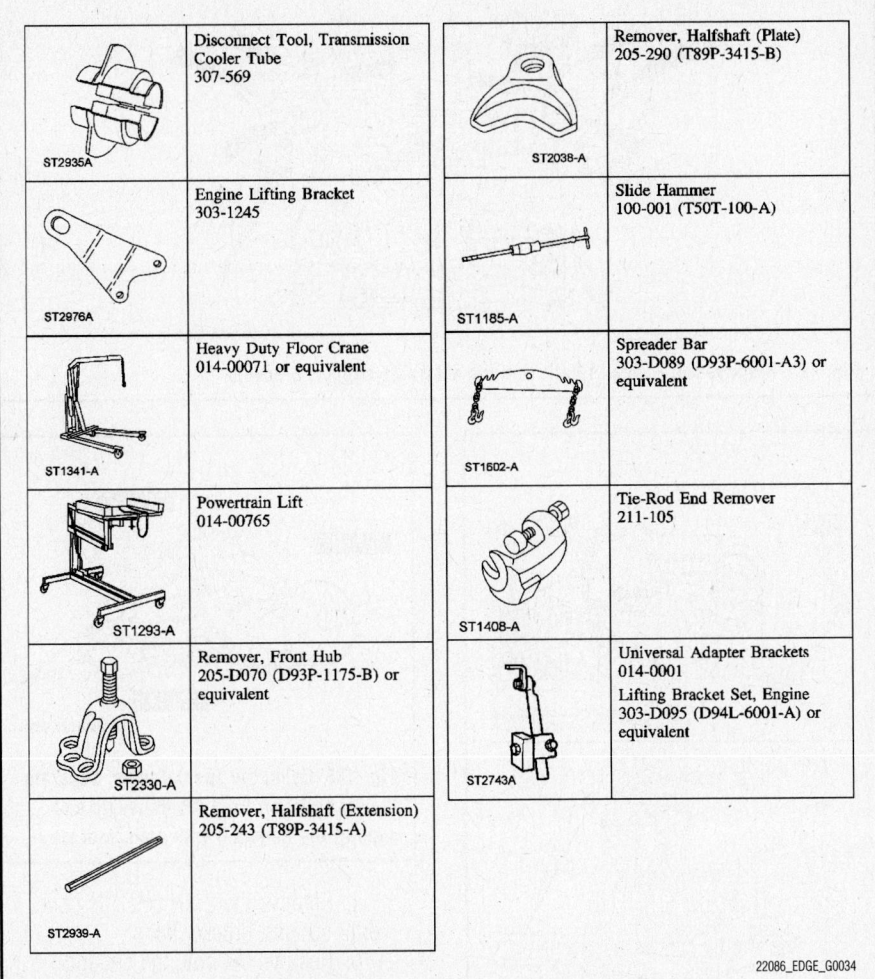

Disconnect Tool, Transmission Cooler Tube 307-569	Remover, Halfshaft (Plate) 205-290 (T89P-3415-B)
ST2935A	ST2038-A
Engine Lifting Bracket 303-1245	Slide Hammer 100-001 (T50T-100-A)
ST2976A	ST1185-A
Heavy Duty Floor Crane 014-00071 or equivalent	Spreader Bar 303-D089 (D93P-6001-A3) or equivalent
ST1341-A	ST1602-A
Powertrain Lift 014-00765	Tie-Rod End Remover 211-105
ST1293-A	ST1408-A
Remover, Front Hub 205-D070 (D93P-1175-B) or equivalent	Universal Adapter Brackets 014-0001 Lifting Bracket Set, Engine 303-D095 (D94L-6001-A) or equivalent
ST2330-A	ST2743A
Remover, Halfshaft (Extension) 205-243 (T89P-3415-A)	
ST2939-A	

22086_EDGE_G0034

Fig. 118 Special tools needed for camshaft removal and installation

⁂ WARNING

During engine repair procedures, cleanliness is extremely important. Any foreign material, including any material created while cleaning gasket surfaces that enters the oil passages, coolant passages or the oil pan, can cause engine failure.

1. Raise and safely support the vehicle.
2. Recover the air conditioning system using the proper equipment
3. Release the fuel system pressure, as outlined in the Fuel System Section.
4. Drain the engine cooling system.
5. Remove the accessory drive belt and the power steering belt, as outlined in this section.
6. Disconnect the power steering cooler hose and drain the power steering fluid into a suitable drain pan.
7. Remove the degas bottle.
8. Remove the engine air cleaner and air cleaner outlet pipe.

9. Remove the battery tray.
10. Disconnect the battery harness electrical connector.
11. Remove the nut and disconnect the power feed from the battery terminal.
12. Remove the bolt and the ground wire.
13. Detach the 2 wiring harness retainers from the cowl.
14. Disconnect the vacuum hose from the upper intake manifold.
15. Disconnect the upper Evaporative Emissions (EVAP) tube quick connect coupling from the purge valve.
16. Disconnect the upper radiator hose, lower radiator hose and 2 heater hoses from the thermostat housing.
17. Detach the wiring harness retainer from the transaxle control cable bracket.
18. Disconnect the transaxle control cable from the control lever. Detach the control cable from the bracket.
19. Disconnect the transaxle control electrical connector.

20. If equipped, detach the engine block heater harness retainers from the radiator support and the A/C suction tube.
21. Remove the nut and disconnect the A/C pressure tube fitting. Discard the O-ring seal.
22. Remove the safety clip from the A/C fitting. Disconnect the A/C suction tube fitting.
23. Disconnect the hose from the power steering reservoir.
24. Disconnect the fuel supply tube.
25. Disconnect the fuel hose routing clip from the transaxle stud and position the fuel hose aside.
26. Disconnect the 2 engine wiring harness electrical connectors.
27. Detach the electrical connector from the LH valve cover.
28. Remove the oil level indicator.
29. Detach the wiring harness retainer from the RH valve cover stud bolt.
30. Remove the bolt and the ground wire from the engine front cover.
31. Remove the nut, the ground wire and the radio interference capacitor wire from the engine front cover stud.
32. Loosen the exhaust flexible pipe clamp and disconnect the 2 exhaust hangers.
33. Remove the 4 nuts and the exhaust flexible pipe and Y-pipe as an assembly. Discard the nuts and the gasket.
34. Remove the 3 pin-type retainers, the 7 screws and the radiator splash shield.
35. Remove the LH inner splash shield.
36. Remove the 2 secondary latches from the transmission fluid cooler tubes.
37. Using the special tool shown in the accompanying illustration, disconnect the transaxle cooling tubes.
38. Remove the drain plug and drain the engine oil into a suitable container. Install the drain plug and tighten to 27 Nm (20 ft. lbs.).
39. Remove and discard the engine oil filter.

307-569

22086_EDGE_G0023

Fig. 119 Using the special tool shown, disconnect the transaxle cooling tubes

40. Remove the power steering cooler bracket bolt from the RH side of the sub-frame.

➡ **Matchmark the driveshaft for proper alignment during installation.**

41. For All Wheel Drive (AWD) vehicles, remove the 4 bolts and support the drive-shaft with a length of mechanic's wire.

42. Remove and discard the RH front halfshaft nut.

43. Remove the 2 nuts and the roll restrictor heat shield.

44. Remove the engine roll restrictor-to-subframe through bolt.

45. Remove and discard the Power Steering Pressure (PSP) tube-to-pump banjo bolt and the 2 seals.

❊❊ WARNING

Do not allow the intermediate shaft to rotate while it is disconnected from the gear or damage to the clock-spring can occur. If there is evidence that the intermediate shaft has rotated, the clockspring must be removed and recentered as outlined in the Chassis Electrical Section.

46. Remove and discard the steering intermediate shaft bolt.

47. Separate the steering intermediate shaft from the steering gear.

48. Remove and discard the cotter pins and tie-rod end nuts.

49. Using a suitable tie rod end removal tool, separate the tie-rod ends from the wheel knuckles.

50. Remove the 2 stabilizer link-to-lower control arm nuts and separate the stabilizer bar links from the lower control arms.

51. Remove the lower control arm-to-knuckle pinch bolts and separate the lower control arms from the knuckles.

52. Remove the 3 RH subframe-to-lower bumper nuts.

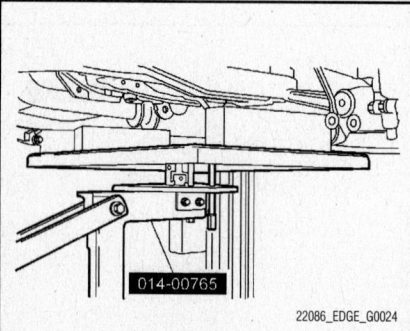

Fig. 120 Position the special tool under the subframe assembly

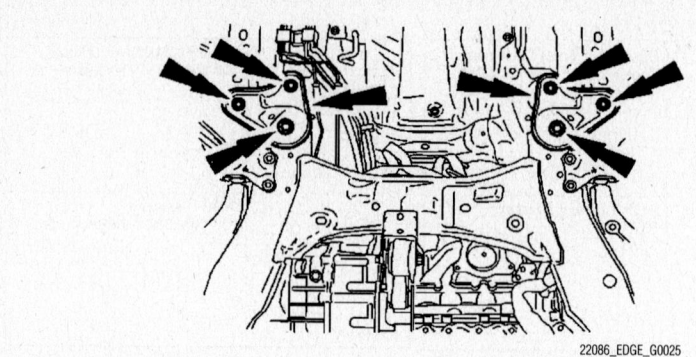

Fig. 121 Remove the 2 nuts, 4 bolts and the subframe support brackets

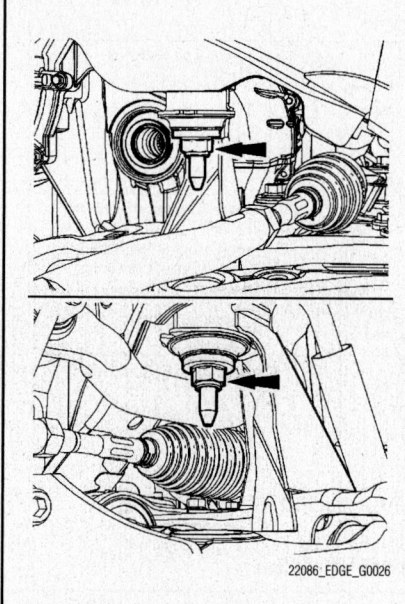

Fig. 122 Remove the 2 middle subframe nuts

53. Remove the 3 LH subframe-to-lower bumper nuts and separate the lower bumper from the subframe.

54. Position the special tool under the subframe assembly.

55. Remove the 2 nuts, 4 bolts and the subframe support brackets.

56. Remove the 2 front subframe nuts.

57. Remove the 2 middle subframe nuts.

58. Using the special tool, lower the subframe assembly from the vehicle.

59. If equipped, disconnect the oil cooler coolant hoses.

60. Using the special tools, or their equivalents, separate the LH halfshaft from the transaxle and support the halfshaft with a piece of wire.

61. Using the special tool, separate the RH halfshaft from the hub.

62. For Front Wheel Drive (FWD) vehicles, perform the following:

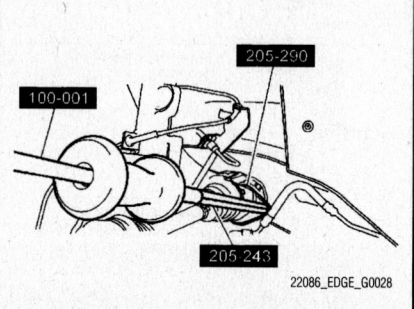

Fig. 123 Using the special tools, separate the LH halfshaft from the transaxle and support the halfshaft with a piece of wire

   a. Remove the 2 RH catalytic converter support bracket bolts.

   b. Remove the bolt, the nut and the RH catalytic converter support bracket.

   c. Remove the 2 stud bolts and the RH halfshaft/intermediate shaft assembly.

63. For AWD vehicles, remove the 2 RH halfshaft bearing support bracket bolts and the RH halfshaft/intermediate shaft assembly.

64. Position a block of wood under the transaxle. Install the special tools, or their equivalents, as shown in the accompanying illustration.

65. Remove the transaxle support insulator through bolt and nut.

66. Remove the 3 nuts, the bolt and the transaxle support insulator bracket.

67. Remove the nut, bolt and engine mount brace.

68. Remove the 4 engine mount nuts.

69. Remove the 3 bolts and the engine mount.

70. Lower the engine and transaxle assembly from the vehicle.

71. If equipped, detach the engine block heater wiring harness retainers and position the harness aside.

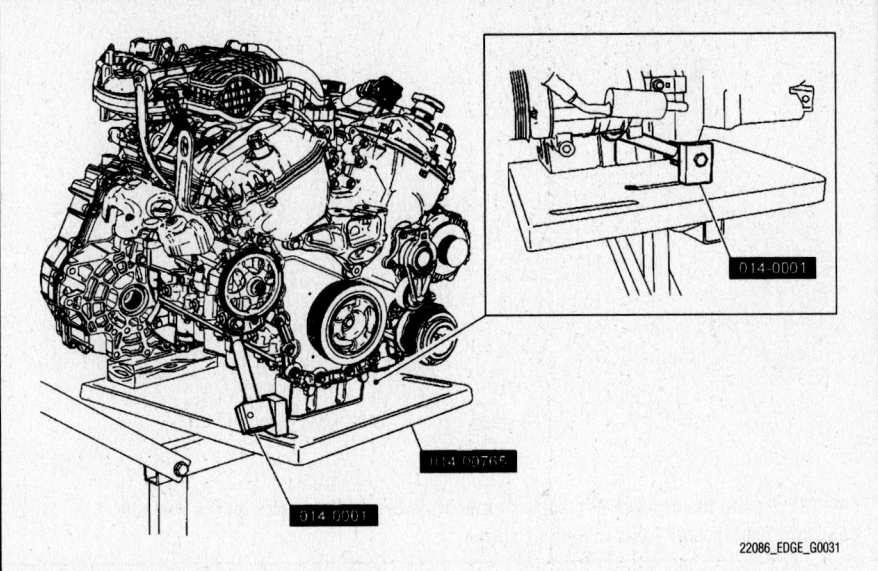

Fig. 124 Position a block of wood under the transaxle. Install the special tools, or their equivalents, as shown

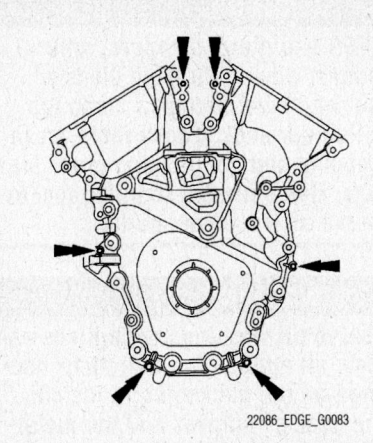

Fig. 126 Install 6 of the engine front cover bolts (finger tight) into the 6 threaded holes in the engine front cover. Tighten the bolts one turn at a time in a criss-cross pattern until the engine front cover-to-cylinder block seal is released

72. Disconnect the Positive Crankcase Ventilation (PCV) fitting electrical connector.

73. Disconnect the PCV hose from the PCV valve.

74. Disconnect the throttle body electrical connector.

75. Detach the wiring harness retainers from the upper intake manifold.

76. Remove the upper intake manifold support bracket bolt.

77. Remove the upper intake manifold support bracket bolt.

78. Remove the 6 bolts and the upper intake manifold. Discard the gaskets.

79. Disconnect the RH catalyst monitor electrical connector.

80. Disconnect the PSP switch electrical connector.

81. Disconnect the RH Variable Camshaft Timing (VCT) solenoid electrical connector.

82. Disconnect the 3 RH coil-on-plug electrical connectors.

83. Disconnect the heated PCV valve electrical connector.

84. Detach all of the wiring harness retainers from the RH valve cover and stud bolts.

85. Disconnect the LH VCT solenoid electrical connector.

86. Disconnect the 3 LH coil-on-plug electrical connectors.

87. Detach all of the wiring harness retainers from the LH valve cover and stud bolts.

88. Remove the 6 bolts and the 6 coil-on-plugs.

89. Remove the 11 stud bolts and the LH valve cover. Discard the gasket.

90. Remove the bolt, the 10 stud bolts and the RH valve cover. Discard the gasket.

91. Inspect the VCT solenoid seals and the spark plug tube seals. Install new seals if damaged.

Using the special tools, remove the seal(s).

92. Remove the 3 bolts and the power steering pump.

93. Remove the 3 bolts and the accessory drive belt tensioner.

94. Remove the crankshaft pulley, as outlined in this section.

95. Remove the crankshaft front seal, as outlined in this section.

96. Remove the 2 bolts and the engine mount bracket.

97. Remove the 2 engine mount studs.

98. Remove the 3 bolts and the engine mount bracket.

99. Remove the 22 engine front cover bolts.

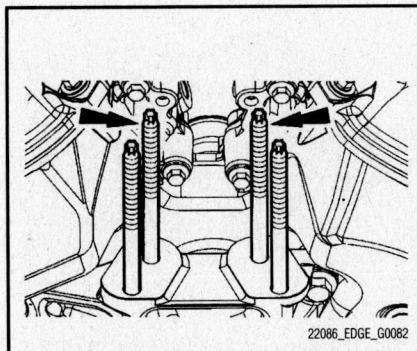

Fig. 125 Remove the 2 engine mount studs (arrows)

100. Install 6 of the engine front cover bolts (finger tight) into the 6 threaded holes in the engine front cover. Tighten the bolts one turn at a time in a criss-cross pattern until the engine front cover-to-cylinder block seal is released. Remove the engine front cover.

✲✲ WARNING

Only use a 3M Roloc® Bristle Disk, (2 inch, white, part number 07528) to clean the engine front cover. Do not use metal scrapers, wire brushes or any other power abrasive disk to clean the engine front cover. These tools cause scratches and gouges that make leak paths.

101. Clean the engine front cover using a 3M Roloc® Bristle Disk, (2 inch, white, part number 07528) in a suitable tool turning at the recommended speed of 15,000 rpm.

102. Thoroughly wash the engine front cover to remove any foreign material, including any abrasive particles created during the cleaning process.

✲✲ WARNING

Place clean, lint free shop towels over exposed engine cavities. Carefully remove the towels so foreign material is not dropped into the engine. Any foreign material (including any material created while cleaning gasket surfaces) that enters the oil passages or the oil pan, can cause engine failure.

> ✳✳ **WARNING**
>
> NEVER use metal scrapers, wire brushes, power abrasive discs or other abrasive means to clean the sealing surfaces. These tools cause scratches and gouges that make leak paths. Use a plastic scraping tool to remove all traces of sealant.

> ✳✳ **WARNING**
>
> Observe all warnings or cautions and follow all application directions contained on the packaging of the silicone gasket remover and the metal surface prep.

103. Clean the sealing surfaces of the cylinder block.

104. Remove any large deposits of silicone or gasket material with a plastic scraper.

105. Apply silicone gasket remover, following package directions, and allow to set for several minutes. Remove the silicone gasket remover with a plastic scraper. A second application of silicone gasket remover may be required if residual traces of silicone or gasket material remain.

106. Apply metal surface prep, following package directions, to remove any remaining traces of oil or coolant and to prepare the surfaces to bond. Do not attempt to make the metal shiny. Some staining of the metal surfaces is normal.

107. Make sure the 2 locating dowel pins are seated correctly in the cylinder block.

108. Rotate the crankshaft clockwise and align the timing marks on the variable camshaft timing (VCT) assemblies as shown.

➡ The special tool will hold the camshafts in the Top Dead Center (TDC) position.

109. Install the special tool onto the flats of the LH camshafts.

➡ The special tool will hold the camshafts in the TDC position.

110. Install the special tool onto the flats of the RH camshafts.

111. Remove the 3 bolts and the RH VCT housing.

112. Remove the 3 bolts and the LH VCT housing.

113. Remove and discard the VCT housing seals.

114. Remove the 2 bolts and the primary timing chain tensioner.

Fig. 127 Rotate the crankshaft clockwise and align the timing marks on the Variable Camshaft Timing (VCT) assemblies as shown

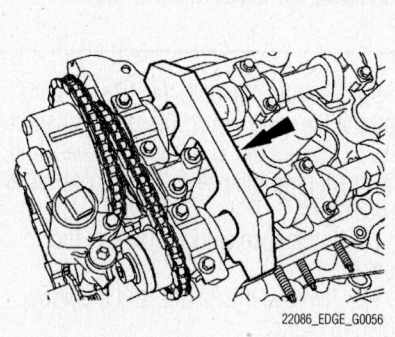

Fig. 128 Install the special tool onto the flats of the camshafts—left side shown, right side similar

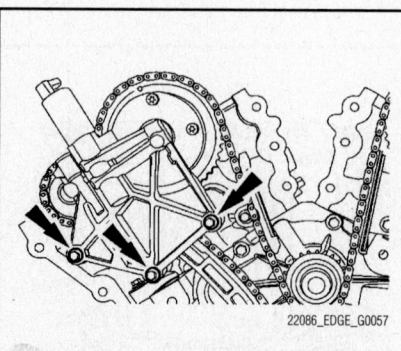

Fig. 129 Remove the 3 bolts and the VCT housing—right side shown, left side similar

115. Remove the primary timing chain tensioner arm.

116. Remove the 2 bolts and the lower LH primary timing chain guide.

117. Remove the primary timing chain. Refer to the Timing Chain procedure in this section for more details.

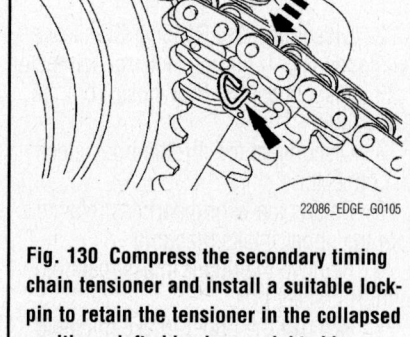

Fig. 130 Compress the secondary timing chain tensioner and install a suitable lock-pin to retain the tensioner in the collapsed position—left side shown, right side similar

118. To remove the LH camshafts, perform the following:

a. Compress the LH secondary timing chain tensioner and install a suitable lockpin to retain the tensioner in the collapsed position.

➡ The VCT bolt and the exhaust camshaft bolt must be discarded and new ones installed. However, the exhaust camshaft washer is reusable.

b. Remove and discard the LH VCT assembly bolt and the LH exhaust camshaft sprocket bolt.

c. Remove the LH VCT assembly, secondary timing chain and the LH exhaust camshaft sprocket as an assembly.

➡ When the special tool is removed, valve spring pressure will rotate the LH camshafts approximately 3 degrees to a neutral position.

d. Remove the special tool from the LH camshafts.

✳✳ WARNING

The camshafts must remain in the neutral position during removal.

e. Verify the LH camshafts are in the neutral position.

✳✳ WARNING

Cylinder head camshaft bearing caps are numbered to verify that they are assembled in their original positions.

f. Remove the bolts and the LH camshaft bearing caps.

g. Remove the LH camshafts.

119. To remove the RH camshafts, perform the following:

a. Compress the RH secondary timing chain tensioner and install a suitable lockpin to retain the tensioner in the collapsed position.

➡ **The VCT bolt and the exhaust camshaft bolt must be discarded and new ones installed. However, the exhaust camshaft washer is reusable.**

b. Remove and discard the RH VCT assembly bolt and the RH exhaust camshaft sprocket bolt.

c. Remove the RH VCT assembly, secondary timing chain and the RH exhaust camshaft sprocket as an assembly.

d. Remove the special tool from the RH camshafts.

➡ **The camshafts must remain in the neutral position during removal.**

e. Rotate the RH camshafts counterclockwise to the neutral position.

➡ **The cylinder head camshaft bearing caps are numbered to verify that they are assembled in their original positions.**

Fig. 131 Verify the camshafts are in the neutral position—left side shown, right side similar

f. Remove the bolts and the RH camshaft bearing caps.

g. Remove the RH camshafts.

To install:

✳✳ WARNING

The crankshaft MUST stay in the free-wheeling position (crankshaft dowel pin at 9 o'clock) until after the camshafts are installed and the valve clearance is checked/adjusted. Do NOT turn the crankshaft until instructed to do so. Failure to follow this process will result in severe engine damage.

120. Rotate the crankshaft counterclockwise until the crankshaft dowel pin is in the 9 o'clock position.

121. To install the LH camshafts, perform the following:

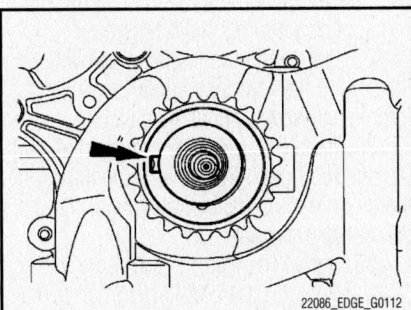

22086_EDGE_G0112

Fig. 132 Rotate the crankshaft counterclockwise until the crankshaft dowel pin is in the 9 o'clock position

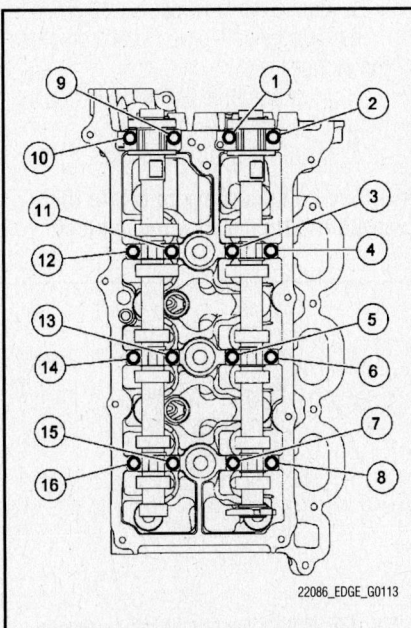

22086_EDGE_G0113

Fig. 133 Camshaft bearing cap tightening sequence—left side

✳✳ WARNING

The camshafts must remain in the neutral position during installation.

➡ **Coat the camshafts with clean engine oil prior to installation.**

h. Position the camshafts onto the LH cylinder head in the neutral position.

✳✳ WARNING

The cylinder head camshaft bearing caps are numbered to verify that they are assembled in their original positions.

i. Install the 8 camshaft caps and the 16 bolts. Tighten in the sequence shown to 10 Nm (89 inch lbs.).

122. To install the RH camshafts, perform the following:

✳✳ WARNING

The camshafts must remain in the neutral position during installation.

➡ **Coat the camshafts with clean engine oil prior to installation.**

j. Position the camshafts onto the RH cylinder head in the neutral position.

✳✳ WARNING

The cylinder head camshaft bearing caps are numbered to verify that they are assembled in their original positions.

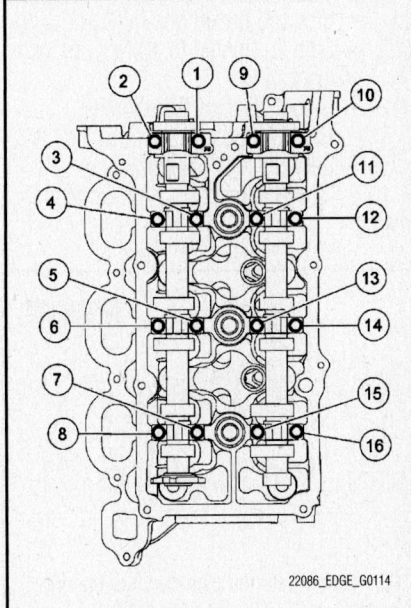

22086_EDGE_G0114

Fig. 134 Camshaft bearing cap tightening sequence—right side

123. Install the 8 camshaft caps and the 16 bolts. Tighten in the sequence shown to 10 Nm (89 inch lbs.).

✳✳ WARNING

If any components are installed new, the engine valve clearance must be checked/adjusted or engine damage can occur.

➡**Use a camshaft sprocket bolt to turn the camshafts.**

124. Using a feeler gauge, confirm that the valve tappet clearances are within specification. If valve tappet clearances are not within specification, the clearance must be adjusted by installing new valve tappet(s) of the correct size. Refer to the Valve Lash Adjustment procedure in this section.

125. For LH camshafts, perform the following:

➡**Use a camshaft sprocket bolt to turn the camshafts.**

k. Rotate the LH camshafts to the top dead center position and install the special tool on the flats of the camshafts.

l. Assemble the LH Variable camshaft timing (VCT) assembly, the LH exhaust camshaft sprocket and the LH secondary timing chain.

m. Align the colored links with the timing marks.

n. Position the LH secondary timing assembly onto the camshafts.

o. Install 2 new bolts and the original washer. Tighten in 4 steps, as follows:
- Step 1: Tighten to 40 Nm (30 ft. lbs.).
- Step 2: Loosen one full turn.
- Step 3: Tighten to 10 Nm (89 inch lbs.).
- Step 4: Tighten 90 degrees.

p. Remove the lockpin from the LH secondary timing chain tensioner.

126. For RH camshafts, perform the following:

➡**Use a camshaft sprocket bolt to turn the camshafts.**

q. Rotate the RH camshafts to the top dead center position and install the special tool on the flats of the camshafts.

r. Assemble the RH VCT assembly, the RH exhaust camshaft sprocket and the RH secondary timing chain.

s. Align the colored links with the timing marks.

t. Position the RH secondary timing assembly onto the camshafts.

u. Install 2 new bolts and the original washer. Tighten in 4 Steps.
- Step 1: Tighten to 40 Nm (30 ft. lbs.).
- Step 2: Loosen one full turn.
- Step 3: Tighten to 10 Nm (89 inch lbs.).
- Step 4: Tighten 90 degrees.

v. Remove the lockpin from the RH secondary timing chain tensioner.

127. Rotate the crankshaft clockwise 60 degrees to the top dead center position (crankshaft dowel pin at 11 o'clock).

128. Install the primary timing chain with the colored links aligned with the timing marks on the VCT assemblies and the crankshaft sprocket.

129. Install the lower LH primary timing chain guide and the 2 bolts. Tighten to 10 Nm (89 inch lbs.).

130. Install the primary timing chain tensioner arm.

131. Reset the primary timing chain tensioner, as follows:

a. Rotate the lever counterclockwise.

b. Using a soft-jawed vise, compress the plunger.

c. Align the hole in the lever with the hole in the tensioner housing.

d. Install a suitable lockpin.

➡**It may be necessary to rotate the crankshaft slightly to remove slack from the timing chain and install the tensioner.**

132. Install the primary tensioner and the 2 bolts. Tighten to 10 Nm (89 inch lbs.).

133. Remove the lockpin.

134. As a post-check, verify correct alignment of all timing marks.

135. Install new VCT housing seals.

✳✳ WARNING

Make sure the dowels on the VCT housing are fully engaged in the cylinder head prior to tightening the bolts.

136. Install the LH VCT housing and the 3 bolts. Tighten in the sequence shown to 10 Nm (89 inch lbs.).

✳✳ WARNING

Make sure the dowels on the VCT housing are fully engaged in the cylinder head prior to tightening the bolts.

137. Install the RH VCT housing and the 3 bolts. Tighten in the sequence shown to 10 Nm (89 inch lbs.).

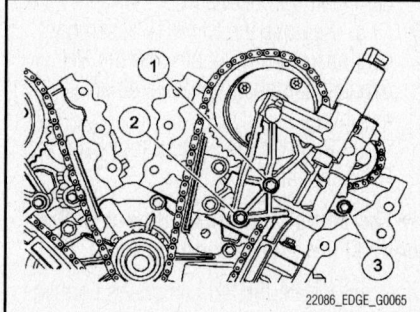

22086_EDGE_G0065

Fig. 137 Install the left side VCT housing and tighten the bolts in the sequence shown

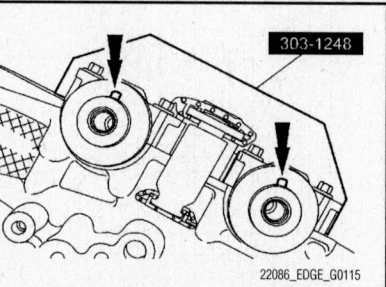

303-1248

22086_EDGE_G0115

Fig. 135 Rotate the camshafts to the top dead center position and install the special tool on the flats of the camshafts—left side shown, right side similar

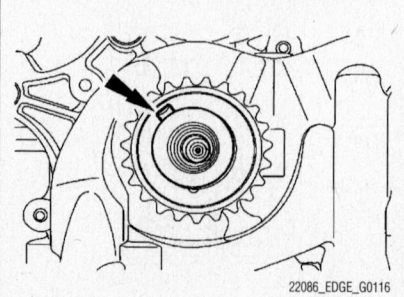

22086_EDGE_G0116

Fig. 136 Rotate the crankshaft clockwise 60 degrees to the top dead center position (crankshaft dowel pin at 11 o'clock)

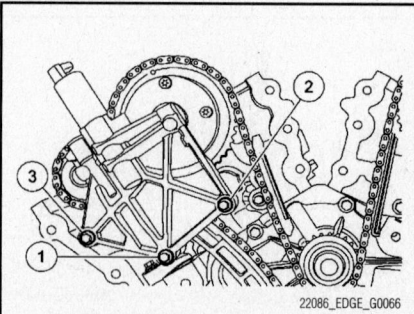

22086_EDGE_G0066

Fig. 138 Install the right side VCT housing and tighten the bolts in the sequence shown

138. Install the alignment dowels, or equivalent special tools.

❈❈ WARNING

Failure to use the correct RTV Silicone Sealant (TA-357) may cause the engine oil to foam excessively and result in serious engine damage.

139. Install the timing chain (engine front cover), as outlined in this section.

140. Install the engine mount bracket and the 2 bolts. Tighten to 24 Nm (18 ft. lbs.).

141. Install the 2 engine mount studs. Tighten to 18 Nm (13 ft. lbs.).

➡**Apply clean engine oil to the crankshaft front seal bore in the engine front cover.**

142. Install a new crankshaft front seal, as outlined in this section.

➡**Lubricate the outside diameter sealing surfaces with clean engine oil.**

143. Install the crankshaft pulley, as outlined in this section.

144. Install the accessory drive belt tensioner and the 3 bolts. Tighten to 11 Nm (8 ft. lbs.).

145. Install the power steering pump and the 3 bolts. Tighten to 24 Nm (18 ft. lbs.).

146. Install the right and left valve covers, as outlined in this section.

147. Install the 6 coil-on-plug assemblies and the 6 bolts. Tighten to 7 Nm (62 inch lbs.).

148. Attach all of the wiring harness retainers to the LH valve cover and stud bolts.

149. Connect the 3 LH coil-on-plug electrical connectors.

150. Connect the LH camshaft VCT solenoid electrical connector.

151. Attach all of the wiring harness retainers to the RH valve cover and stud bolts.

152. Connect the heated PCV valve electrical connector.

153. Connect the 3 RH coil-on-plug electrical connectors.

154. Connect the RH VCT solenoid electrical connector.

155. Connect the Power Steering Pressure (PSP) switch electrical connector.

156. Connect the RH catalyst monitor sensor electrical connector.

157. Using new gaskets, install the upper intake manifold and the 6 bolts. Tighten in the sequence given in the intake manifold procedure, to 10 Nm (89 inch lbs.).

158. Install the upper intake manifold support bracket bolt. Tighten to 10 Nm (89 inch lbs.).

159. Install the upper intake manifold support bracket bolt. Tighten to 10 Nm (89 inch lbs.).

160. Attach the wiring harness retainers to the upper intake manifold.

161. Connect the throttle body electrical connector.

162. Connect the PCV hose to the PCV valve.

163. Connect the PCV fitting electrical connector.

164. If equipped, attach the engine block heater wiring harness retainers.

165. Raise the engine and transaxle assembly into the vehicle.

166. Install the engine mount and the 3 bolts. Tighten to 90 Nm (66 ft. lbs.).

167. Install the 4 engine mount nuts. Tighten to 63 Nm (46 ft. lbs.).

168. Install the engine mount brace, the nut and the bolt. Tighten to 20 Nm (15 ft. lbs.).

169. Install the transaxle support insulator bracket, the 3 nuts and the bolt. Tighten to 63 Nm (46 ft. lbs.).

170. Install the transaxle support insulator through bolt and nut. Tighten to 175 Nm (129 ft. lbs.).

171. For AWD vehicles, perform the following:

❈❈ WARNING

A new Powertrain Transfer Unit (PTU) seal must be installed whenever the intermediate shaft is removed.

e. Install a new PTU seal.

➡**Before installing the halfshaft, inspect the halfshaft sealing surface for wear or damage and install new, if necessary.**

f. Position the RH halfshaft/intermediate shaft assembly in the PTU and in the steering knuckle and install the 2 bolts. Tighten to 40 Nm (30 ft. lbs.).

172. For FWD vehicles, perform the following:

➡**Before installing the halfshaft, inspect the halfshaft sealing surface for wear or damage and install new if necessary.**

g. Position the RH halfshaft/intermediate shaft assembly in the transaxle and in the steering knuckle and install the 2 stud bolts. Tighten to 55 Nm (41 ft. lbs.).

➡**Do not tighten the 2 catalytic converter support bracket bolts at this time.**

h. Install the converter support bracket and the 2 bolts.

i. Install the catalytic converter bracket bolt and the nut. Tighten the nut to 40 Nm (30 ft. lbs.). Tighten the bolt to 55 Nm (41 ft. lbs.).

j. Tighten the 2 RH catalytic converter support bracket bolts to 20 Nm (15 ft. lbs.).

➡**Before installing the halfshaft, inspect the halfshaft sealing surface for wear or damage and install new, if necessary.**

173. Install the LH halfshaft into the transaxle.

174. If equipped, connect the oil cooler coolant hoses.

175. Using the special tool, raise the subframe into the installed position. For more information, refer to the Engine Removal & Installation procedure in this section.

176. Install the 2 middle subframe nuts. Tighten to 133 Nm (98 ft. lbs.).

177. Install the 2 front subframe nuts. Tighten to 133 Nm (98 ft. lbs.).

178. Position the subframe support brackets in place and loosely install the 4 bolts.

179. Install the 2 rear subframe bracket nuts. Tighten to 133 Nm (98 ft. lbs.).

180. Tighten the 4 subframe support bracket bolts to 90 Nm (66 ft. lbs.).

181. Position the lower bumper on the subframe and install the 3 LH nuts. Tighten to 9 Nm (80 inch lbs.).

182. Install the 3 RH lower bumper-to-subframe nuts. Tighten to 9 Nm (80 inch lbs.).

183. Install the ball joints in the steering knuckles and install the pinch bolts. Tighten to 55 Nm (41 ft. lbs.).

184. Position the stabilizer bar links in the lower control arms and install the nuts. Tighten to 90 Nm (66 ft. lbs.).

185. Install the tie-rod ends and nuts. Tighten to 48 Nm (35 ft. lbs.). Install new cotter pins.

❈❈ WARNING

Do not let the intermediate shaft rotate while it is disconnected from the gear or damage to the clockspring can occur. If there is evidence that the intermediate shaft has rotated, the clockspring must be removed and recentered, as outlined in the Chassis Electrical Section.

186. Install the intermediate shaft onto the steering gear and install a new bolt. Tighten to 23 Nm (17 ft. lbs.).

187. Using a new banjo bolt and 2 new seals, install the PSP tube. Tighten to 48 Nm (35 ft. lbs.).

188. Install the engine roll restrictor-to-subframe through bolt. Tighten to 103 Nm (76 ft. lbs.).

189. Install the roll restrictor heat shield and the 2 nuts. Tighten to 11 Nm (8 ft. lbs.).

190. Apply the brake to keep the halfshaft from rotating. Install a new RH front halfshaft nut and tighten to 350 Nm (258 ft. lbs.).

191. For AWD vehicles, line up the index marks on the rear driveshaft to the index marks on the PTU flange made during removal and install the 4 bolts. Tighten to 70 Nm (52 ft. lbs.).

192. Install the power steering cooler bracket bolt to the RH side of the subframe. Tighten to 9 Nm (80 inch lbs.).

193. Connect the power steering cooler hose.

➡**Lubricate the engine oil filter gasket with clean engine oil prior to installing the oil filter.**

194. Install a new engine oil filter. Tighten to 5 Nm (44 inch lbs.) and then rotate an additional 180 degrees.

195. Connect the 2 transmission fluid cooler tubes.

196. Install the 2 secondary latches onto the transmission fluid cooler tubes.

197. Install the LH inner splash shield.

198. Install the radiator splash shield, the 3 pin-type retainers and the 7 screws.

199. Using a new gasket, install the Y-pipe and exhaust flexible pipe assembly and 4 new nuts. Tighten to 40 Nm (30 ft. lbs.).

200. Install the 2 exhaust hangers and tighten the exhaust clamp. Tighten to 40 Nm (30 ft. lbs.).

201. Install the ground wire, the radio interference capacitor wire and the nut to the engine front cover stud. Tighten to 10 Nm (89 inch lbs.).

202. Install the ground wire and bolt to the engine front cover. Tighten to 10 Nm (89 inch lbs.).

203. Attach the wiring harness retainer to the RH valve cover stud bolt.

204. Install the oil level indicator.

205. Connect the 2 engine wiring harness electrical connectors.

206. Attach the electrical connector to the LH valve cover.

207. Connect the fuel hose routing clip to the transaxle stud.

208. Connect the fuel supply tube.

209. Connect the hose to the power steering reservoir.

210. Connect the A/C suction tube fitting. Install the safety clip onto the A/C fitting.

211. Using a new O-ring seal, connect the A/C pressure tube fitting and install the nut. Tighten to 8 Nm (71 inch lbs.).

212. If equipped, attach the engine block heater harness retainers from to the radiator support and the A/C suction tube.

213. Connect the transaxle control electrical connector.

214. Attach the control cable to the bracket. Connect the transaxle control cable to the control lever.

215. Attach the wiring harness retainer to the transaxle control cable bracket.

216. Connect the upper radiator hose, lower radiator hose and 2 heater hoses to the thermostat housing.

217. Connect the upper EVAP tube quick connect coupling. to the purge valve.

218. Connect the vacuum hose to the upper intake manifold.

219. Install the ground wire and the bolt. Tighten to 10 Nm (89 inch lbs.).

220. Attach the 2 wiring harness retainers to the cowl.

221. Connect the power feed to the battery terminal and install the nut. Tighten to 8 Nm (71 inch lbs.).

222. Connect the battery harness electrical connector.

223. Install the battery tray.

224. Install the engine air cleaner and the air cleaner outlet pipe.

225. Install the degas bottle.

226. Install the accessory drive belt and the power steering belt, as outlined in this section.

❊❊ WARNING

Do not expose the RTV Silicone Sealant (TA-357) to engine oil for at least 90 minutes after installing the engine front cover. Failure to follow this instruction may cause oil leakage.

227. Fill the engine with clean engine oil.

228. Fill and bleed the cooling system.

229. Fill the power steering system, as outlined in the Steering Section.

230. Recharge the air conditioning system.

CRANKSHAFT FRONT SEAL

REMOVAL & INSTALLATION

2.3L Engine

See Figures 139 and 140.

❊❊ WARNING

Do not loosen or remove the crankshaft pulley bolt without first installing the special tools as instructed in this procedure. The

crankshaft pulley and the crankshaft timing sprocket are not keyed to the crankshaft. The crankshaft, the crankshaft sprocket and the pulley are fitted together by friction, using diamond washers between the flange faces on each part. For that reason, the crankshaft sprocket is also unfastened if you loosen the pulley bolt. Before any repair requiring loosening or removal of the crankshaft pulley bolt, the crankshaft and camshafts must be locked in place by the special service tools, otherwise severe engine damage can occur.

❊❊ WARNING

During engine repair procedures, cleanliness is extremely important. Any foreign material, including any material created while cleaning gasket surfaces, that enters the oil passages, coolant passages or the oil pan can cause engine failure.

1. Remove the crankshaft pulley, as outlined in this section.

❊❊ WARNING

Use care not to damage the engine front cover or the crankshaft when removing the seal.

2. Using special tool 303-409, or equivalent seal removal tool, remove the crankshaft front oil seal.

To install:

➡**Remove the through-bolt from the special tool.**

➡**Lubricate the oil seal with clean engine oil.**

3. Using special tool 303-096, or equivalent seal installation tool, install the crankshaft front oil seal.

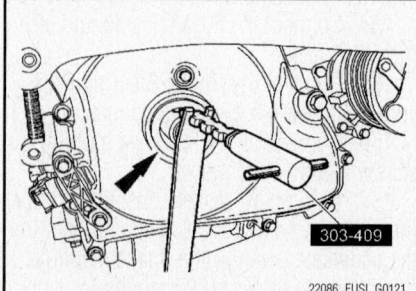

303-409

22086_FUSI_G0121

Fig. 139 Using special tool 303-409, or equivalent seal removal tool, remove the crankshaft front oil seal—3.0L engine

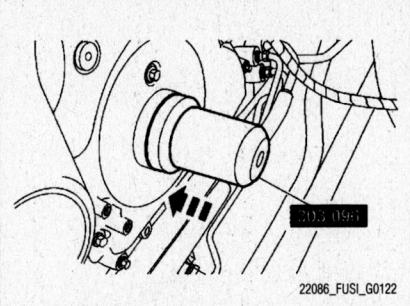

Fig. 140 Using special tool 303-096, or equivalent seal installation tool, install the crankshaft front oil seal—3.0L engine

4. Install the crankshaft pulley, as outlined in this section.

3.0L Engine

See Figures 141 and 142.

1. Raise and safely support the vehicle.
2. Remove the crankshaft pulley, as outlined in this section.

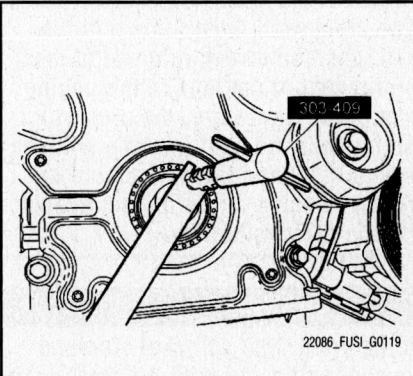

Fig. 141 Use the special tool to remove the crankshaft front seal—3.0L engine

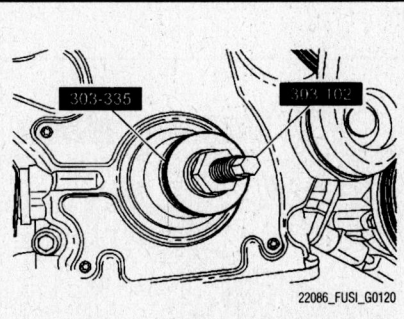

Fig. 142 Using special tools 303-335 and 303-102, or equivalent front cover seal installer and crankshaft damper replacer tools, install a new crankshaft front seal—3.0L engine

3. Using Special Tool 303-409, or equivalent oil seal remover, remove and discard the crankshaft front seal.

To install:

➡ **Clean all sealing surfaces with metal surface cleaner.**

4. Apply clean engine oil to the seal lip and seal bore before installing the seal.
5. Using special tools 303-335 and 303-102, or equivalent front cover seal installer and crankshaft damper replacer tools, install a new crankshaft front seal.
6. Install the crankshaft pulley, as outlined in this section.

3.5L Engine

See Figures 143 and 144.

➡ **This procedure requires the use of the following special tools or their equivalents:**

- Crankshaft Front Seal Installer 303-1251
- Oil Seal Remover 303-409 (T92C-6700CH)
- Crankshaft Damper Replacer 303-102 (T74P-6316-B)

1. Raise and safely support the vehicle.
2. Remove the crankshaft pulley, as outlined in this section.
3. Using the special tool shown, remove and discard the crankshaft front seal.
4. Thoroughly clean all sealing surfaces with a suitable metal surface cleaner.

To install:

➡ **Apply clean engine oil to the crankshaft front seal bore in the engine front cover.**

5. Using the special tools, install a new crankshaft front seal.

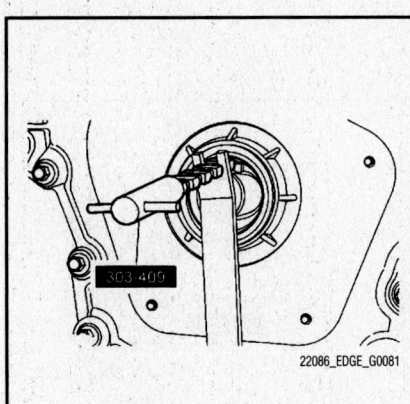

Fig. 143 Using the special tool, remove and discard the crankshaft front seal

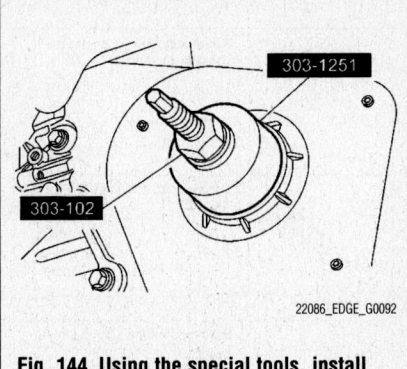

Fig. 144 Using the special tools, install a new crankshaft front seal

6. Install the crankshaft pulley, as outlined in this section.

CRANKSHAFT PULLEY

REMOVAL & INSTALLATION

2.3L Engine

See Figures 145 through 151.

➡ **A variety of special tools are required for this procedure. Make sure you have access to all necessary tools before beginning.**

❋❋ WARNING

Do not loosen or remove the crankshaft pulley bolt without first installing the special tools as instructed in this procedure. The crankshaft pulley and the crankshaft timing sprocket are not keyed to the crankshaft. The crankshaft, the crankshaft sprocket and the pulley are fitted together by friction, using diamond washers between the flange faces on each part. For that reason, the crankshaft sprocket is also unfastened if you loosen the pulley bolt. Before any repair requiring loosening or removal of the crankshaft pulley bolt, the crankshaft and camshafts must be locked in place by the special service tools, otherwise severe engine damage can occur.

❋❋ WARNING

During engine repair procedures, cleanliness is extremely important. Any foreign material, including any material created while cleaning gasket surfaces, that enters the oil passages, coolant passages or the oil pan can cause engine failure.

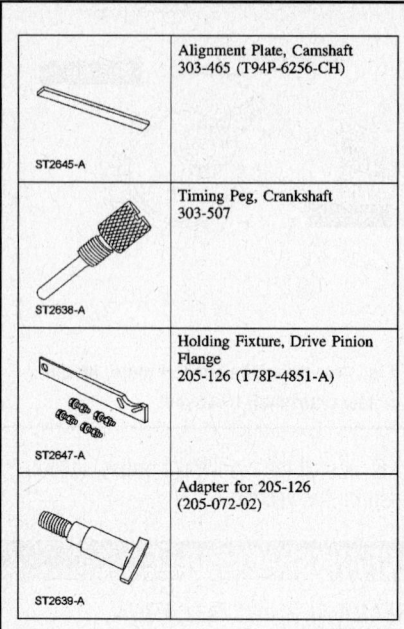

(ST2645-A)	Alignment Plate, Camshaft 303-465 (T94P-6256-CH)
(ST2638-A)	Timing Peg, Crankshaft 303-507
(ST2647-A)	Holding Fixture, Drive Pinion Flange 205-126 (T78P-4851-A)
(ST2639-A)	Adapter for 205-126 (205-072-02)

22086_FUSI_G0106

Fig. 145 Special tools (or their equivalents) necessary for crankshaft pulley removal and installation—2.3L engine

1. With the vehicle in NEUTRAL, position it on a hoist.

2. Remove the accessory drive belt.

3. If equipped, remove the 7 screws and the underbody cover.

4. Remove the valve cover.

✳ WARNING

Failure to position the No. 1 piston at top dead center (TDC) can result in damage to the engine. Turn the engine in the normal direction of rotation only.

5. Using the crankshaft pulley bolt, turn the crankshaft clockwise to position the No. 1 piston at TDC. The hole in the crankshaft pulley should be in the 6 o'clock position.

✳ WARNING

The special tool 303-465 is for camshaft alignment only. Using this tool to prevent engine rotation can result in engine damage.

➡ **The camshaft timing slots are offset. If the special tool cannot be installed, rotate the crankshaft one complete revolution clockwise to correctly position the camshafts.**

6. Install the special tool in the slots on the rear of both camshafts.

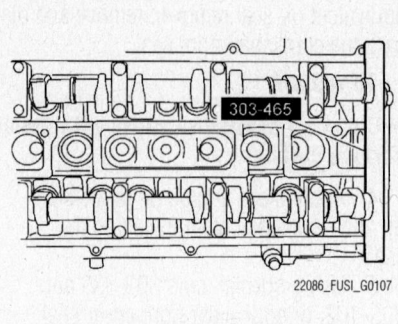

22086_FUSI_G0107

Fig. 146 Install the special tool in the slots on the rear of both camshafts—2.3L engine

7. On vehicles with A/T, remove the 2 halfshaft carrier bracket bolts and slide the RH halfshaft 12 mm (0.47 in) out of the transaxle.

8. Remove the engine plug bolt.

➡ **The special tool will contact the crankshaft and prevent it from turning past TDC. However, the crankshaft can still be rotated in the counterclockwise direction. The crankshaft must remain at the TDC position during the crankshaft pulley removal and installation.**

9. Install the special tool.

10. Assemble the special tools using 4 hardened washers in the locations shown.

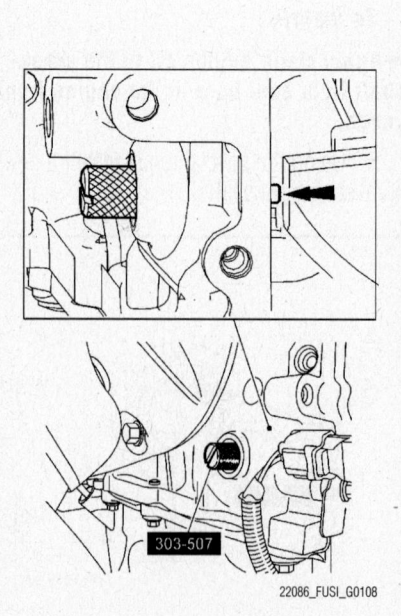

22086_FUSI_G0108

Fig. 147 Install the special tool 303-507, or equivalent—2.3L engine

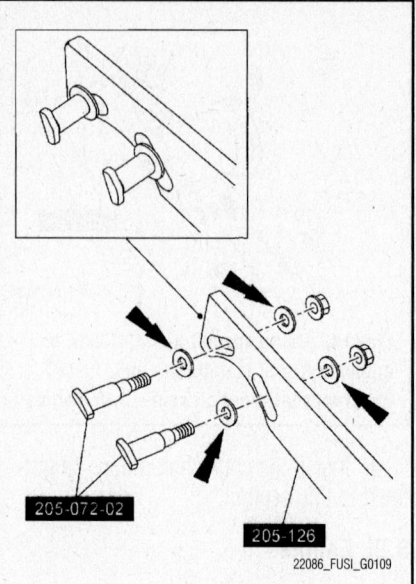

22086_FUSI_G0109

Fig. 148 Assemble the special tools using 4 hardened washers in the locations shown—2.3L engine

✳ WARNING

The crankshaft must remain in the TDC position during removal of the pulley bolt or damage to the engine can occur. Therefore, the crankshaft pulley must be held in place with the special tool and the bolt should be removed using an air impact wrench (1/2-in drive minimum).

✳ WARNING

If the crankshaft sprocket diamond washer comes off with the crankshaft pulley, it must be installed back onto the crankshaft.

11. Using the special tools and an air impact wrench, remove the crankshaft pulley.

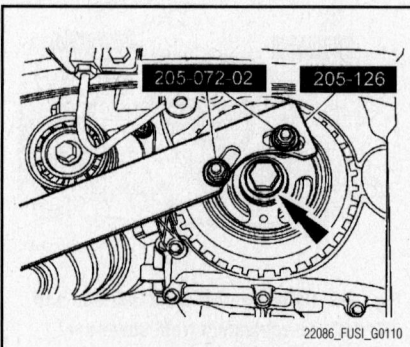

22086_FUSI_G0110

Fig. 149 Remove and discard the crankshaft pulley bolt and washer. Then, remove the crankshaft pulley.

a. Remove and discard the crankshaft pulley bolt and washer.
b. Remove the crankshaft pulley.

To install:

> ❊❊ **WARNING**
> **Do not install the crankshaft pulley bolt at this time.**

➡**Apply clean engine oil on the seal area before installing.**

12. Position the crankshaft pulley onto the crankshaft with the hole in the pulley at the 6 o'clock position.

> ❊❊ **WARNING**
> **Only hand-tighten the 6 mm (0.23 in) bolt or damage to the front cover can occur.**

➡**This step will correctly align the crankshaft pulley to the crankshaft.**

13. Install a standard 6 mm (0.23 in) x 18 mm (0.7 in) bolt through the crankshaft pulley and thread it into the front cover.

14. Assemble the special tools using 4 hardened washers in the locations shown.

> ❊❊ **WARNING**
> **The crankshaft must remain in the TDC position during installation of the pulley bolt or damage to the engine can occur. Therefore, the crankshaft pulley must be held in place with the special tool and the**

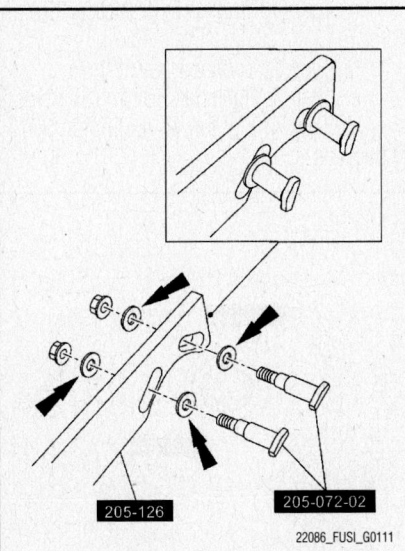

Fig. 150 Assemble the special tools using 4 hardened washers in the locations shown.

bolt should be installed using hand tools only.

> ❊❊ **WARNING**
> **Do not reuse the crankshaft pulley bolt.**

15. Install a new crankshaft pulley bolt. Using the special tools to hold the crankshaft pulley in place, tighten the crankshaft pulley bolt in 2 stages:
a. Stage 1: Tighten to 100 Nm (74 ft. lbs.).
b. Stage 2: Tighten an additional 90 degrees (1/4 turn).

16. Remove the 6 mm (0.23 in) x 18 mm (0.7 in) bolt.
17. Remove the special tools.

➡**Only turn the engine in the normal direction of rotation.**

18. Turn the crankshaft clockwise 1 and 3/4 turns.
19. Install the special tool 303-507.

➡**Only turn the engine in the normal direction of rotation.**

20. Turn the crankshaft clockwise until the crankshaft contacts the special tool.

> ❊❊ **WARNING**
> **Only hand-tighten the bolt or damage to the front cover can occur.**

21. Using the 6 mm (0.23 in) x 18 mm (0.7 in) bolt, check the position of the crankshaft pulley. If it is not possible to install the bolt, the engine valve timing must be corrected by repeating this procedure.

22. Using the special tool 303-465, or equivalent, check the position of the camshafts. If it is not possible to install

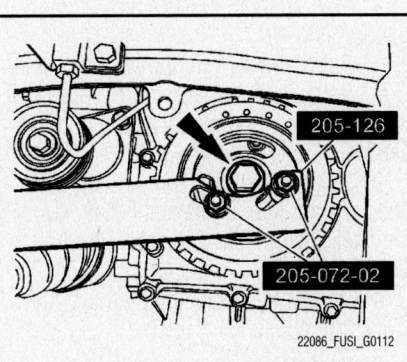

Fig. 151 Install a new crankshaft pulley bolt. Using the special tools to hold the crankshaft pulley in place, tighten the crankshaft pulley bolt in 2 stages

the special tool, the engine valve timing must be corrected by repeating this procedure.

23. Remove the special tool.
24. Remove the 6 mm (0.23 in) x 18 mm (0.7 in) bolt.
25. Remove the special tool 303-507.
26. Install the engine plug bolt and tighten to 20 Nm (15 ft. lbs.).
27. On A/T vehicles, install the RH half-shaft and the 2 halfshaft carrier bearing bracket bolts. Tighten to 40 Nm (30 ft. lbs.).
28. If equipped, install the underbody cover and the 7 screws.
29. Install the accessory drive belt.
30. Install the valve cover

3.0L Engine

See Figures 152 through 156.

➡**A variety of special tools are required for this procedure. Make sure you have access to all necessary tools before beginning.**

1. Raise and safely support the vehicle.
2. Remove the accessory drive belt.
3. Use the special tool to hold the crankshaft pulley and remove the crankshaft pulley bolt and washer.
4. Using the special tool, remove the crankshaft pulley.

To install:
5. Lubricate the crankshaft front seal inner lip with clean engine oil.

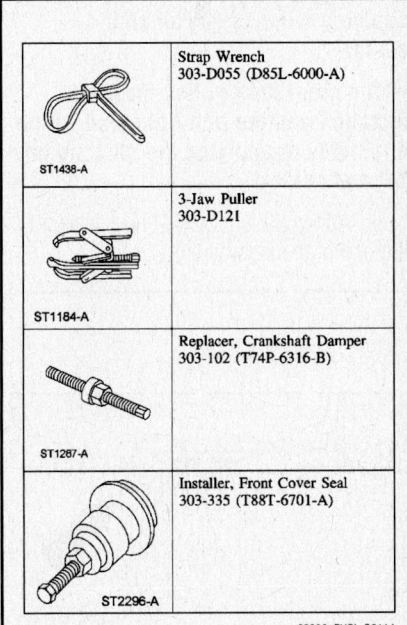

Fig. 152 Special tools (or their equivalents) necessary for crankshaft pulley removal and installation—3.0L engine

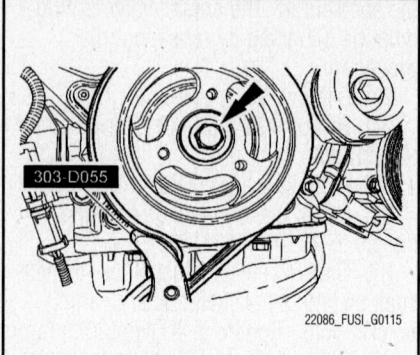

Fig. 153 Use the special tool to hold the crankshaft pulley and remove the crankshaft pulley bolt and washer—3.0L engine

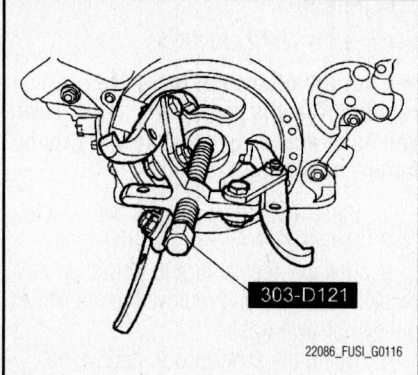

Fig. 154 Using the special tool, remove the crankshaft pulley—3.0L engine

➡ Clean the keyway and slot using metal surface cleaner before applying silicone gasket and sealer.

➡ The crankshaft pulley must be installed and the bolt tightened within 4 minutes of applying the silicone gasket and sealer.

6. Apply silicone gasket and sealant to the end of the keyway slot.

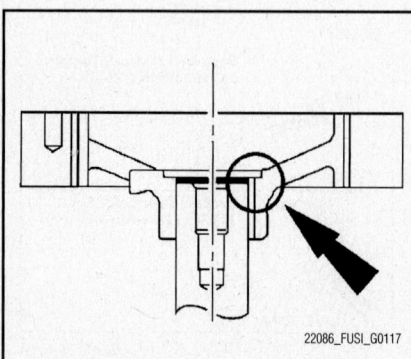

Fig. 155 Apply silicone gasket and sealant to the end of the keyway slot—3.0L engine

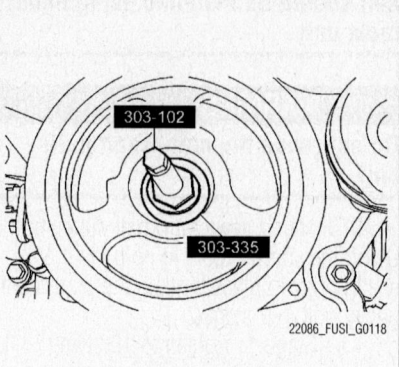

Fig. 156 Use the special tools to install the crankshaft pulley—3.0L engine

➡ Lubricate the outside diameter sealing surfaces with clean engine oil.

7. Using the special tools, install the crankshaft pulley.

8. Install the bolt and washer. Using the special tool 303-D055, or equivalent strap wrench, to hold the crankshaft pulley, tighten the bolt in 4 stages:

    a. Stage 1: Tighten to 120 Nm (89 ft. lbs.).

    b. Stage 2: Loosen one full turn.

    c. Stage 3: Tighten to 50 Nm (37 ft. lbs.).

    d. Stage 4: Tighten an additional 90 degrees.

9. Install the accessory drive belt

3.5L Engine

See Figures 157 through 160.

➡ This procedure requires the use of the following special tools or their equivalents:

- 3-Jaw Puller 303-D121
- Front Cover Oil Seal Installer 303-335
- Crankshaft Damper Replacer 303-102 (T74P-6316-B)
- Strap Wrench 303-D055 (D85L-6000-A)

1. Raise and safely support the vehicle.

2. Remove the accessory drive belt and the power steering belt, as outlined in this section.

3. Using the special tool, or equivalent strap wrench to hold the crankshaft, remove the crankshaft bolt and washer. Discard the bolt.

4. Using the special tool, remove the crankshaft pulley.

To install:

5. Lubricate the crankshaft front seal inner lip with clean engine oil. Lubricate the outside diameter sealing surfaces with clean engine oil.

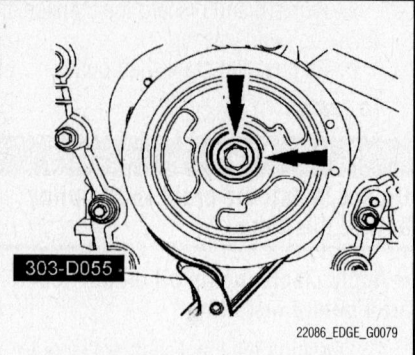

Fig. 157 Using the special tool, remove the crankshaft bolt and washer. Discard the bolt

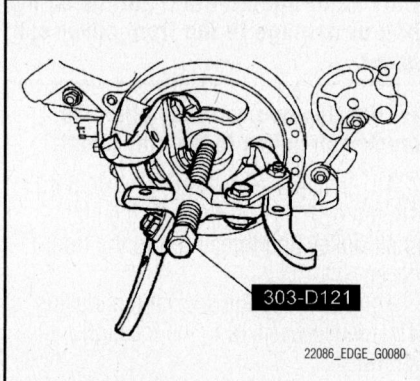

Fig. 158 Using the special tool, remove the crankshaft pulley

6. Using the special tools, install the crankshaft pulley.

7. Using the special tool, install the crankshaft pulley washer and new bolt and tighten in 4 steps.

    a. Step 1: Tighten to 120 Nm (89 (ft. lbs.).

    b. Step 2: Loosen one full turn.

    c. Step 3: Tighten to 50 Nm (37 ft. lbs.).

    d. Step 4: Tighten an additional 90 degrees.

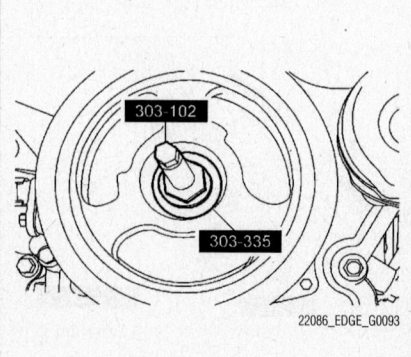

Fig. 159 Using the special tools, install the crankshaft pulley

Fig. 160 Using the special tool, install the crankshaft pulley washer and new bolt and tighten in 4 steps

8. Install the accessory drive belt and the power steering belt, as outlined in this section.

CYLINDER HEAD

REMOVAL & INSTALLATION

2.3L Engine

See Figures 161 through 164.

> ※※ **WARNING**
>
> **Do not loosen or remove the crankshaft pulley bolt without first installing the special tools as instructed in this procedure. The crankshaft pulley and the crankshaft timing sprocket are not keyed to the crankshaft. The crankshaft, the crankshaft sprocket and the pulley are fitted together by friction, using diamond washers between the flange faces on each part. For that reason, the crankshaft sprocket is also unfastened if you loosen the pulley bolt. Before any repair requiring loosening or removal of the crankshaft pulley bolt, the crankshaft and camshafts must be locked in place by the special service tools, otherwise severe engine damage can occur.**

> ※※ **WARNING**
>
> **During engine repair procedures, cleanliness is extremely important. Any foreign material, including any material created while cleaning gasket surfaces, that enters the oil passages, coolant passages or the oil pan can cause engine failure.**

1. Raise and safely support the vehicle.

2. Release the fuel system pressure, as outlined in the Fuel Section.
3. Check the valve clearance.
4. Remove the degas bottle.
5. Remove the catalytic converter.
6. Remove the generator.
7. Remove the fuel supply rail.
8. Remove the intake manifold.
9. On Vehicles with secondary air injection (AIR):
   a. Disconnect the secondary air injection (AIR) pump electrical connector.
   b. Remove the 3 bolts and position the AIR pump aside.
10. Remove the bolt and the radio frequency interference capacitor from the engine mount bracket.
11. Remove the engine mount bracket bolt.
12. Install the special tool (303-050) and a suitable length of chain to the threaded hole in the LH side of the engine block.
13. Install the special tools 313-F072 and 303-050, or equivalent, then using the special tool, lift the engine 25 mm (0.98 in).
14. Remove the nut, 2 bolts and the engine mount.
15. Lower the engine 25 mm (0.98 in).
16. Remove the 2 nuts and the engine mount bracket.
17. Remove the timing drive components.
18. Remove the special tool.
19. Mark the position of the camshaft lobes on the No. 1 cylinder for installation reference.
20. Remove the bolt and the variable camshaft timing (VCT) solenoid.

> ※※ **WARNING**
>
> **Failure to follow the camshaft loosening procedure can result in damage to the camshafts.**

21. Remove the camshafts from the engine.
22. Loosen the camshaft bearing cap bolts, in the sequence shown, one turn at a time until all tension is released from the camshaft bearing caps.
23. Remove the bolts and the camshaft bearing caps.
24. Remove the camshafts.

> ※※ **WARNING**
>
> **If the camshafts and valve tappets are to be reused, mark the location of the valve tappets to make sure they are assembled in their original positions.**

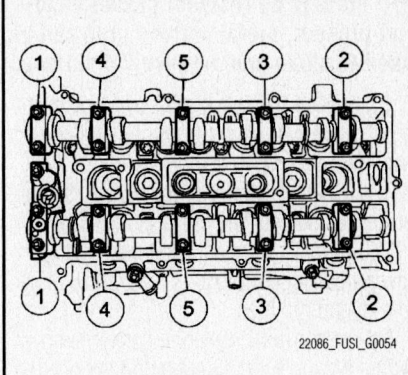

Fig. 161 Camshaft bearing bolt loosening sequence—2.3L engine

➡**The number on the valve tappets only reflects the digits that follow the decimal. For example, a tappet with the number 0.650 has the thickness of 3.650 mm.**

25. Remove and inspect the valve tappets.
26. Detach the retaining clip and position the Evaporative Emissions (EVAP) tube bundle aside.
27. Disconnect the upper radiator hose, coolant bypass hose, heater hose and coolant vent hose from the engine coolant outlet.
28. Disconnect the Engine Coolant Temperature sensor (ECT) electrical connector.
29. Disconnect the exhaust gas recirculation (EGR) valve electrical connector.
30. Disconnect the coolant hose from the EGR valve.
31. On Vehicles with secondary air injection (AIR):
   a. Remove the 2 bolts and position AIR valve bracket aside.
32. Remove the 10 bolts and the cylinder head. Discard the bolts.

To install:

> ※※ **WARNING**
>
> **Do not use metal scrapers, wire brushes, power abrasive discs or other abrasive means to clean the sealing surfaces. These tools cause scratches and gouges that make leak paths. Use a plastic scraping tool to remove all traces of the head gasket.**

> ※※ **WARNING**
>
> **Observe all warnings or cautions and follow all application directions contained on the packaging of the silicone gasket remover and the metal surface prep.**

➡️ If there is no residual gasket material present, metal surface prep can be used to clean and prepare the surfaces.

33. Clean the cylinder head-to-cylinder block mating surface of both the cylinder head and the cylinder block.

34. Remove any large deposits of silicone or gasket material with a plastic scraper.

35. Apply silicone gasket remover, following package directions, and allow to set for several minutes.

36. Remove the silicone gasket remover with a plastic scraper. A second application of silicone gasket remover may be required if residual traces of silicone or gasket material remain.

37. Apply metal surface prep, following package directions, to remove any traces of oil or coolant, and to prepare the surfaces to bond with the new gasket. Do not attempt to make the metal shiny. Some staining of the metal surfaces is normal.

38. Clean the cylinder head bolt holes in the cylinder block. Make sure all coolant, oil or other foreign material is removed.

39. Inspect the cylinder head for distortion.

40. Apply silicone gasket and sealant to the locations shown.

41. Install a new head gasket.

➡️ The cylinder head bolts are torque-to-yield and must not be reused. New cylinder head bolts must be installed.

➡️ Lubricate the bolts with clean engine oil prior to installation.

  b. Install 10 new cylinder head bolts. Tighten the bolts in the sequence shown in 5 stages:
  c. Stage 1: Tighten to 7 Nm (62 lb-in).
  d. Stage 2: Tighten to 15 Nm (11 ft. lbs.).
  e. Stage 3: Tighten to 45 Nm (33 ft. lbs.).

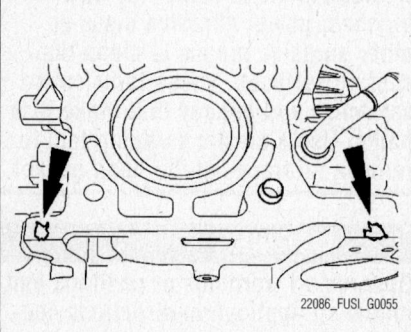

Fig. 162 Apply silicone gasket and sealant to the locations shown

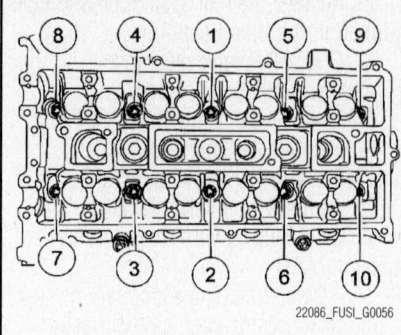

Fig. 163 Cylinder head bolt tightening sequence—2.3L engine

  f. Stage 4: Turn 90 degrees.
  g. Stage 5: Turn an additional 90 degrees.

42. On Vehicles with secondary air injection (AIR):
  a. Position AIR valve bracket and install the 2 bolts.
  b. Tighten to 10 Nm (89 lb-in).

43. Connect the coolant hose to the EGR valve.

44. Connect the EGR valve electrical connector.

45. Connect the ECT electrical connector.

46. Connect the upper radiator hose, coolant bypass hose, heater hose and coolant vent hose to the engine coolant outlet.

47. Attach the EVAP tube bundle retaining clip retaining clip.

➡️ Coat the valve tappets with clean engine oil prior to installation.

48. Install the valve tappets.

✳️✳️ WARNING

Install the camshafts with the alignment slots in the camshafts lined up so the Camshaft Alignment Plate can be installed without rotating the camshafts. Make sure the lobes on the No. 1 cylinder are in the same position as noted in the removal procedure. Rotating the camshafts when the timing chain is removed, or installing the camshafts 180 degrees out of position can cause severe damage to the valves and pistons.

➡️ Lubricate the camshaft journals and bearing caps with clean engine oil.

49. Install the camshafts and bearing caps. Tighten the camshaft bearing caps in the sequence shown in 3 stages:
  a. Stages 1: Tighten the camshaft bearing cap bolts until finger tight.

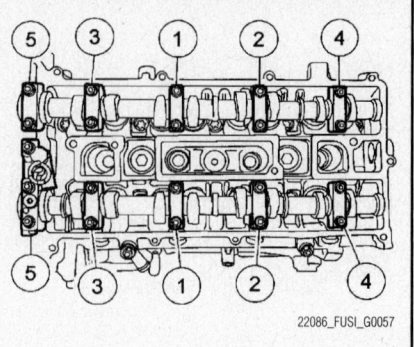

Fig. 164 Camshaft bearing cap bolt tightening sequence—2.3L engine

  b. Stages 2: Tighten to 7 Nm (62 lb-in).
  c. Stages 3: Tighten to 16 Nm (12 ft. lbs.).

50. Install the special tool 303-465, or equivalent..

51. Install the VCT solenoid and bolt. Tighten to 10 Nm (89 lb-in).

52. Install the timing drive components.

53. Install the engine mount bracket and the 2 nuts. Tighten to 103 Nm (76 ft. lbs.).

54. Using the special too, lift the engine 25 mm (0.98 in).

55. Install the engine mount, nut and 2 bolts. Tighten to 55 Nm (41 ft. lbs.).

56. Lower the engine 25 mm (0.98 in).

57. Install the engine mount bracket bolt. Tighten to 115 Nm (85 ft. lbs.).

58. Install the radio frequency interference capacitor and bolt to the engine mount bracket. Tighten to 10 Nm (89 lb-in).

59. On Vehicles with secondary air injection (AIR):
  a. Install the AIR pump and the 3 bolts.
  b. Tighten to 30 Nm (22 ft. lbs.).
  c. Connect the AIR pump electrical connector.

60. Install the intake manifold.

61. Install the fuel supply rail.

62. Install the generator.

63. Install the catalytic converter.

64. Install the degas bottle.

65. Fill and bleed the engine cooling system

3.0L Engine

Left Side

See Figures 165 through 167.

✳️✳️ WARNING

During engine repair procedures, cleanliness is extremely important. Any foreign material, including any material created while cleaning gas-

ket surfaces that enters the oil passages, coolant passages or the oil pan, can cause engine failure.

1. Raise and safely support the vehicle.
2. Remove the LH camshafts, as outlined in this section.
3. Remove the coolant bypass tube.
4. Remove the 3 bolts and position the coolant pump aside.
5. Remove the LH catalytic converter.

✵ WARNING
The camshaft roller followers must be installed in their original positions.

→ Mark the location of the roller followers, using a permanent-type marker.

6. Remove the camshaft roller followers.
7. Loosen the 8 bolts in the sequence shown and remove the cylinder head.
8. Discard the bolts and the gasket.

✵ WARNING
Do not use metal scrapers, wire brushes, power abrasive discs or other abrasive means to clean the sealing surfaces. These tools cause scratches and gouges that make leak paths. Use a plastic scraping tool to remove all traces of the head gasket.

✵ WARNING
Observe all warnings or cautions and follow all application directions contained on the packaging of the silicone gasket remover and the metal surface prep.

→ If there is no residual gasket material present, metal surface prep can be used to clean and prepare the surfaces.

9. Clean the cylinder head-to-cylinder block mating surface of both the cylinder head and the cylinder block.
10. Remove any large deposits of silicone or gasket material with a plastic scraper.
11. Apply silicone gasket remover, following package directions, and allow to set for several minutes.
12. Remove the silicone gasket remover with a plastic scraper. A second application of silicone gasket remover may be required if residual traces of silicone or gasket material remain.
13. Apply metal surface prep, following package directions, to remove any traces of oil or coolant, and to prepare the surfaces to bond with the new gasket. Do not attempt to make the metal shiny. Some staining of the metal surfaces is normal.
14. Support the cylinder head on a bench with the head gasket side up.

→ The straightedge used must be flat within 0.0051 mm (0.0002 in) per foot of tool length. Inspect all areas of the deck face with a straightedge and feeler gauge. The cylinder head must not have depressions deeper than 0.0254 mm (0.001 in) across a 38.1 mm (1.5 in) square area, or scratches more than 0.0254 mm (0.001 in).

To install:
15. Clean the cylinder head bolt holes in the cylinder block. Make sure all coolant, oil or other foreign material is removed.
16. Position a new gasket and the cylinder head on the engine.

→ **New cylinder head bolts must be installed. They are torque-to-yield designed and cannot be reused.**

17. Install the 8 bolts and tighten in 6 stages in the sequence shown.
  a. Stage 1: Tighten to 40 Nm (30 ft. lbs.).
  b. Stage 2: Tighten 90 degrees.
  c. Stage 3: Loosen one full turn.
  d. Stage 4: Tighten to 40 Nm (30 ft. lbs.).
  e. Stage 5: Tighten 90 degrees.
  f. Stage 6: Tighten 90 degrees.

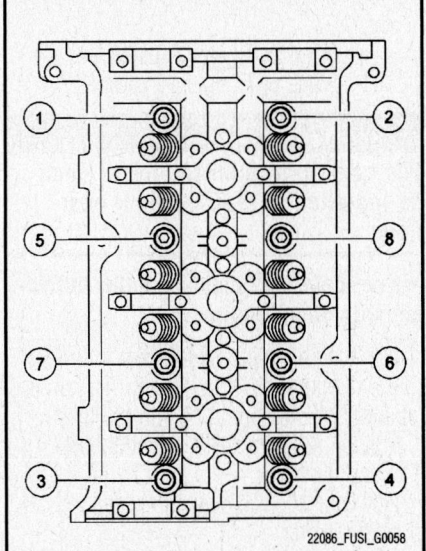

Fig. 165 Left side cylinder head bolt loosening sequence—3.0L engine

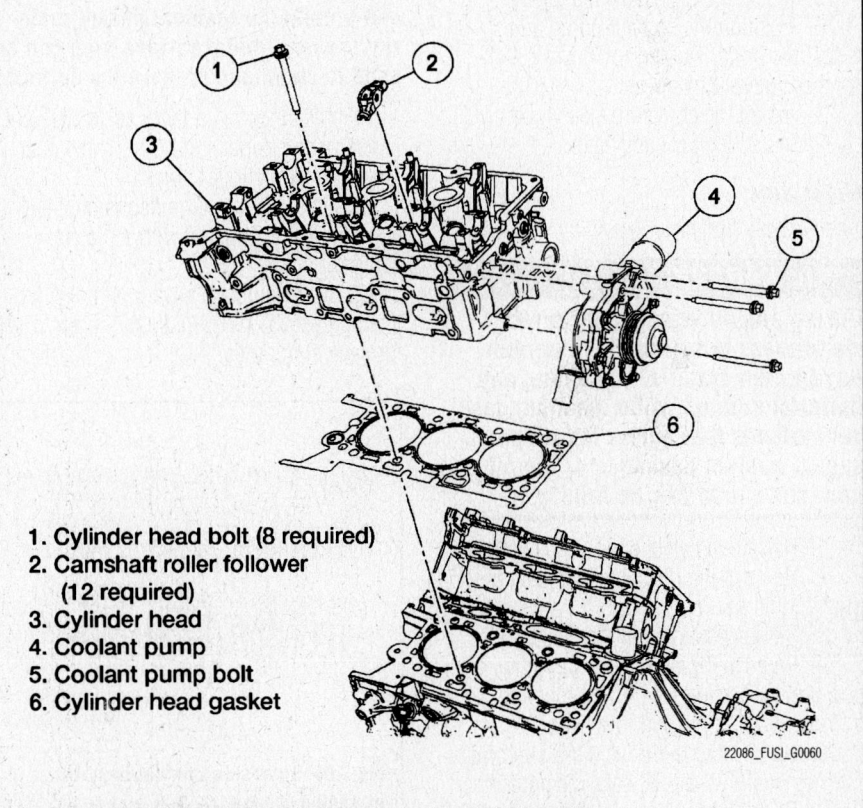

1. Cylinder head bolt (8 required)
2. Camshaft roller follower (12 required)
3. Cylinder head
4. Coolant pump
5. Coolant pump bolt
6. Cylinder head gasket

Fig. 166 Exploded view of the left side cylinder head—3.0L engine

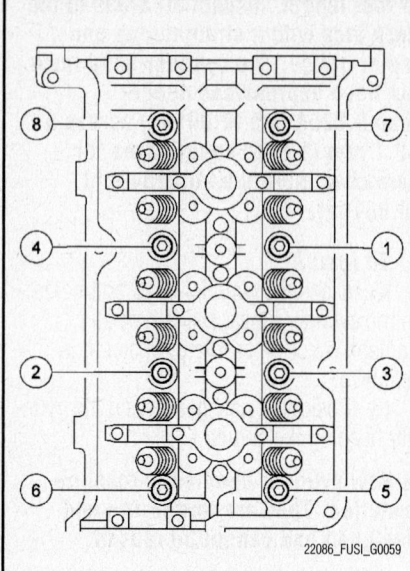

Fig. 167 Left side cylinder head bolt tightening sequence—3.0L engine

22086_FUSI_G0059

❋❋ WARNING

The camshaft roller followers must be installed in their original positions.

➡**Lubricate the camshaft roller followers with clean engine oil.**

18. Install the camshaft roller followers.
19. Install the LH catalytic converter.
20. Position the coolant pump and install the bolts. Tighten to 10 Nm (89 lb-in) then rotate 90 degrees.
21. Install the coolant bypass tube.
22. Install the LH camshafts.

Right Side

See Figures 168 through 170.

❋❋ WARNING

During engine repair procedures, cleanliness is extremely important. Any foreign material, including any material created while cleaning gasket surfaces that enters the oil passages, coolant passages or the oil pan, can cause engine failure.

1. Raise and safely support the vehicle.
2. Remove the RH camshafts, as outlined in this section.
3. Remove the coolant bypass tube.
4. Remove the bolt and detach the power steering pressure (PSP) tube bracket from the back of the cylinder head.
5. On Front wheel drive (FWD) vehicles:
   a. Remove the RH catalytic converter.
6. On All wheel drive (AWD) vehicles:

a. Remove the RH exhaust manifold.
7. If equipped, remove the wiring harness retainer bolt.

❋❋ WARNING

The camshaft roller followers must be installed in their original positions.

➡**Mark the location of the roller followers, using a permanent-type marker.**

8. Remove the camshaft roller followers.
9. Loosen the 8 bolts in the sequence shown and remove the cylinder head.
10. Discard the bolts and the gasket.

❋❋ WARNING

Do not use metal scrapers, wire brushes, power abrasive discs or other abrasive means to clean the sealing surfaces. These tools cause scratches and gouges that make leak paths. Use a plastic scraping tool to remove all traces of the head gasket.

❋❋ WARNING

Observe all warnings or cautions and follow all application directions contained on the packaging of the silicone gasket remover and the metal surface prep.

➡**If there is no residual gasket material present, metal surface prep can be used to clean and prepare the surfaces.**

11. Clean the cylinder head-to-cylinder block mating surface of both the cylinder head and the cylinder block.
12. Remove any large deposits of silicone or gasket material with a plastic scraper.
13. Apply silicone gasket remover, following package directions, and allow to set for several minutes.

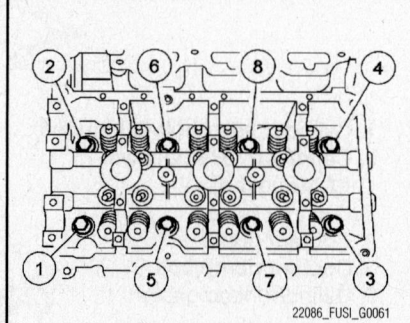

22086_FUSI_G0061

Fig. 168 Right side cylinder head bolt loosening sequence—3.0L engine

14. Remove the silicone gasket remover with a plastic scraper. A second application of silicone gasket remover may be required if residual traces of silicone or gasket material remain.
15. Apply metal surface prep, following package directions, to remove any traces of oil or coolant, and to prepare the surfaces to bond with the new gasket. Do not attempt to make the metal shiny. Some staining of the metal surfaces is normal.
16. Support the cylinder head on a bench with the head gasket side up.

➡**The straightedge used must be flat within 0.0051 mm (0.0002 in) per foot of tool length.**

17. Inspect all areas of the deck face with a straightedge and feeler gauge. The cylinder head must not have depressions deeper than 0.0254 mm (0.001 in) across a 38.1 mm (1.5 in) square area, or scratches more than 0.0254 mm (0.001 in).

To install:

18. Clean the cylinder head bolt holes in the cylinder block. Make sure all coolant, oil or other foreign material is removed.
19. Position a new gasket and the cylinder head on the engine.

➡**New cylinder head bolts must be installed. They are torque-to-yield designed and cannot be reused.**

20. Install the 8 bolts and tighten in 6 stages in the sequence shown:
   a. Stage 1: Tighten to 40 Nm (30 ft. lbs.).
   b. Stage 2: Tighten 90 degrees.
   c. Stage 3: Loosen one full turn.
   d. Stage 4: Tighten to 40 Nm (30 ft. lbs.).
   e. Stage 5: Tighten 90 degrees.
   f. Stage 6: Tighten 90 degrees.

❋❋ WARNING

The camshaft roller followers must be installed in their original positions.

➡**Lubricate the camshaft roller followers with clean engine oil.**

21. Install the camshaft roller followers.
22. If equipped, install the wiring harness retainer bolt. Tighten to 10 Nm (89 lb-in).
23. On AWD vehicles, install the RH exhaust manifold.
24. On FWD vehicles, install the RH catalytic converter.
25. Position the PSP tube bracket onto the rear of the cylinder head and install the bolt. Tighten to 9 Nm (80 lb-in).

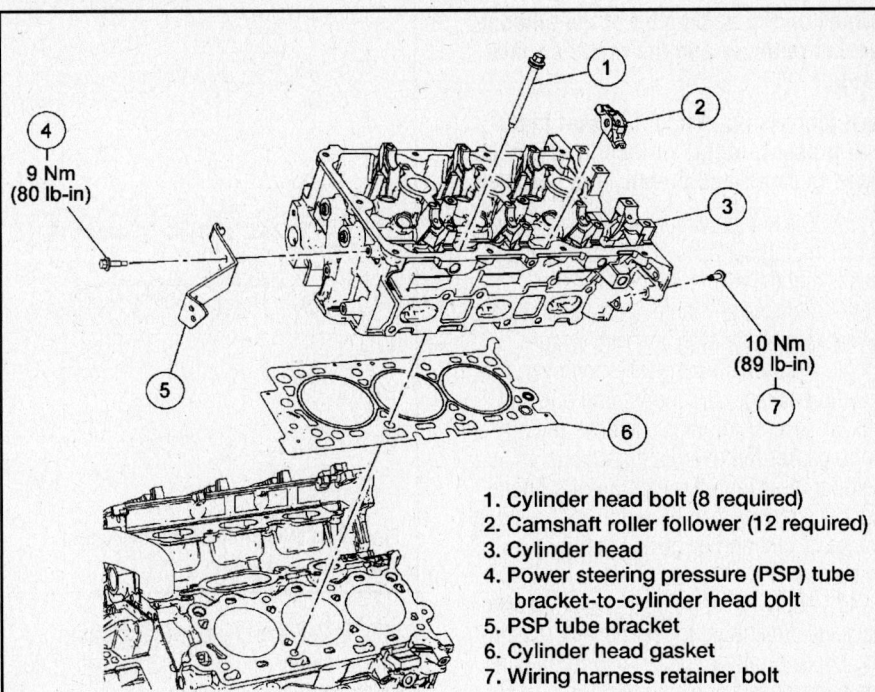

1. Cylinder head bolt (8 required)
2. Camshaft roller follower (12 required)
3. Cylinder head
4. Power steering pressure (PSP) tube bracket-to-cylinder head bolt
5. PSP tube bracket
6. Cylinder head gasket
7. Wiring harness retainer bolt

22086_FUSI_G0063

Fig. 169 Exploded view of the right side cylinder head—3.0L engine

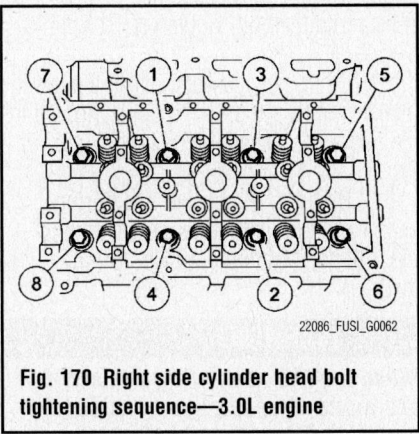

22086_FUSI_G0062

Fig. 170 Right side cylinder head bolt tightening sequence—3.0L engine

26. Install the coolant bypass tube.
27. Install the RH camshafts

3.5L Engine

Left Side

See Figures 171 through 175.

1. Remove the LH camshafts, as outlined in this section.

2. If equipped, remove the heat shield and disconnect the block heater electrical connector.

3. Remove the block heater wiring harness from the engine.

4. Tag and detach the 6 fuel injector electrical connectors.

5. Disconnect the Cylinder Head Temperature (CHT) sensor electrical connector.

6. Remove the bolt and position aside the LH radio interference capacitor.

7. Disconnect the LH CMP sensor electrical connector.

8. Disconnect the LH Heated Oxygen Sensor (HO2S) electrical connector.

9. Disconnect the LH catalyst monitor sensor electrical connector.

10. Remove the wiring harness retainer bolt from the rear of the LH cylinder head.

11. Disconnect the A/C compressor electrical connector.

12. Remove the nut and disconnect the alternator B+ cable.

13. Disconnect the alternator electrical connector.

14. Detach the wiring harness retainer from the alternator.

15. Disconnect the Engine Oil Pressure (EOP) switch electrical connector and the wiring harness pin-type retainer.

16. Remove the nut, 2 bolts and the A/C compressor. Position the compressor aside, but DO NOT disconnect the refrigerant lines.

17. Remove the nut, bolt and the alternator.

18. Remove the 2 LH catalytic converter bracket bolts.

19. Remove the 4 nuts (3 shown) and the LH catalytic converter. Discard the nuts and the gasket.

20. Remove the 3 bolts and the LH exhaust manifold heat shield.

21. Remove the 6 nuts and the LH exhaust manifold.

22. Discard the nuts and the exhaust manifold gasket.

23. Clean and inspect the LH exhaust manifold, as outlined under the Exhaust Manifold procedure in this section. Remove and discard the 6 LH exhaust manifold studs.

24. Remove the LH cylinder block drain plug. Allow the coolant to drain from the cylinder block into a suitable container.

25. Remove the 2 RH catalytic converter bracket bolts.

26. Remove the 4 nuts and the RH catalytic converter. Discard the nuts and the gasket.

27. Remove the RH cylinder block drain plug or, if equipped, the block heater. Allow the coolant to drain from the cylinder block into a suitable container.

28. Remove the 4 bolts and the fuel rail and injectors as an assembly.

29. Remove the 3 thermostat housing-to-lower intake manifold bolts.

30. Remove the thermostat housing and discard the gasket and O-ring seal.

31. Remove the 10 bolts and the lower intake manifold. Discard the gaskets.

32. Remove the bolt and the LH CMP sensor.

33. Remove the 2 bolts and the upper LH primary timing chain guide.

34. Remove the 2 bolts and the LH secondary timing chain tensioner.

35. Remove the valve tappets from the cylinder head.

36. Remove and discard the M6 bolt.

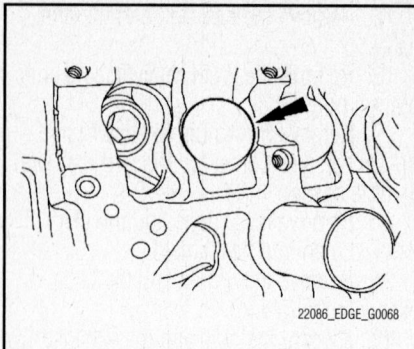

Fig. 171 Remove the valve tappets from the cylinder head

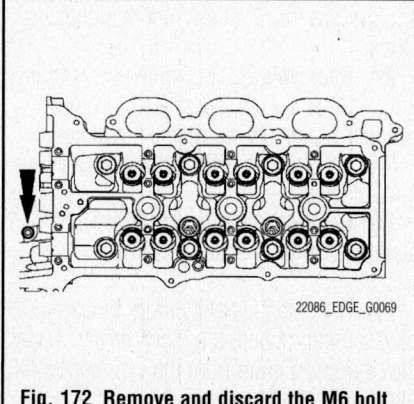

Fig. 172 Remove and discard the M6 bolt

❄ WARNING

The cylinder head bolts must be discarded and new bolts must be installed. They are tighten-to-yield designed and cannot be reused.

❄❄ WARNING

Aluminum surfaces are soft and can be easily scratched. Do NOT place the cylinder head gasket surface, unprotected, on a workbench surface.

37. Remove and discard the 8 bolts from the cylinder head.
38. Remove the cylinder head. Discard the cylinder head gasket.

❄ WARNING

NEVER use metal scrapers, wire brushes, power abrasive discs or other abrasive means to clean the sealing surfaces. These tools cause scratches and gouges that make leak paths. Use a plastic scraping tool to remove all traces of the head gasket.

➡ Observe all warnings or cautions and follow all application directions contained on the packaging of the silicone gasket remover and the metal surface prep.

➡ If there is no residual gasket material present, metal surface prep can be used to clean and prepare the surfaces.

39. Clean the cylinder head-to-cylinder block mating surfaces of both the cylinder heads and the cylinder block.
40. Remove any large deposits of silicone or gasket material with a plastic scraper.
41. Apply silicone gasket remover, following package directions, and allow to set for several minutes. Remove the silicone gasket remover with a plastic scraper. A second application of silicone gasket remover may be required if residual traces of silicone or gasket material remain.
42. Apply metal surface prep, following package directions, to remove any remaining traces of oil or coolant and to prepare the surfaces to bond with the new gasket. Do not attempt to make the metal shiny. Some staining of the metal surfaces is normal.
43. Support the cylinder head on a bench with the head gasket side up.

➡ The straightedge used must be flat within 0.0051 mm (0.0002 in) per foot of tool length. Inspect all areas of the deck face with a straightedge and feeler gauge. The cylinder head must not have depressions deeper than 0.0254 mm (0.001 in) across a 38.1 mm (1.5 in) square area, or scratches more than 0.0254 mm (0.001 in).

To install:

44. Install a new gasket, the LH cylinder head and 8 new bolts. Tighten in the sequence shown in 5 steps:
  a. Step 1: Tighten to 15 ft. lbs. (20 Nm).
  b. Step 2: Tighten to 26 ft. lbs. (35 Nm).
  c. Step 3: Tighten 90 degrees.
  d. Step 4: Tighten 90 degrees.
  e. Step 5: Tighten 90 degrees.
45. Install the M6 bolt and tighten to 10 Nm (89 inch lbs.).

❄❄ WARNING

The valve tappets must be installed in their original positions.

➡ Coat the valve tappets with clean engine oil prior to installation.

46. Install the valve tappets in their original positions.

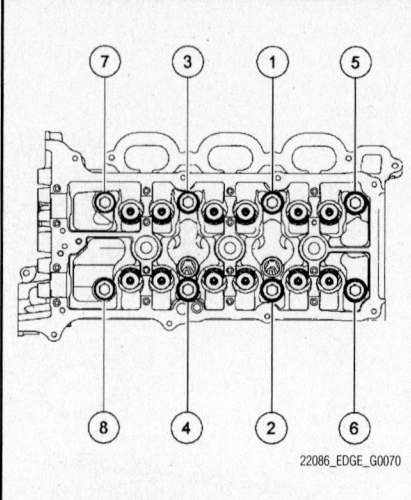

Fig. 173 Cylinder head bolt tightening sequence—left side

47. Install the LH secondary timing chain tensioner and the 2 bolts. Tighten to 10 Nm (89 inch lbs.).
48. Install the upper LH primary timing chain guide and the 2 bolts. Tighten to 10 Nm (89 inch lbs.).
49. Install LH camshaft position (CMP) sensor and the bolt. Tighten to 10 Nm (89 inch lbs.).
50. Using new gaskets, install the lower intake manifold and the 10 bolts. Tighten in the sequence shown to 10 Nm (89 inch lbs.).
51. Using a new gasket and O-ring seal, install the thermostat housing and the 3 bolts. Tighten to 10 Nm (89 inch lbs.).

❄❄ WARNING

Make sure to use O-ring seals that are made of special fuel-resistant material. Using regular O-rings can cause the fuel system to leak. Never reuse the O-ring seals.

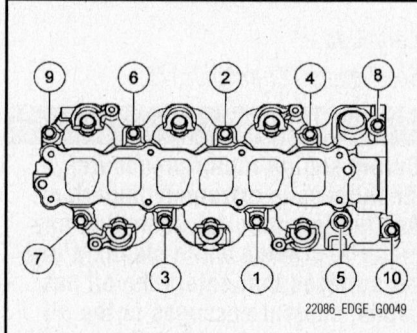

Fig. 174 Lower intake manifold bolt tightening sequence

The upper and lower O-ring seals are not interchangeable.

52. Install new fuel injector O-ring seals, as follows:

   a. Remove the retaining clips and separate the fuel injectors from the fuel rail.

   b. Remove and discard the O-ring seals.

   c. Install new O-ring seals and lubricate with clean engine oil.

   d. Install the fuel injectors and the retaining clips onto the fuel rail.

53. Install the fuel rail and injectors as an assembly and install the 4 bolts. Tighten to 10 Nm (89 inch lbs.).

54. Install the RH cylinder block drain plug or, if equipped, the block heater. Tighten to 40 Nm (30 ft. lbs.).

55. Install the 2 RH catalytic converter bracket bolts. Tighten the 4 catalytic converter nuts to 40 Nm (30 ft. lbs.). Tighten the 2 catalytic converter brackets to 20 Nm (15 ft. lbs.).

56. Using a new gasket, install the RH catalytic converter and 4 new nuts. Tighten to 40 Nm (30 ft. lbs.).

57. Install the LH cylinder block drain plug. Tighten to 20 Nm (15 ft. lbs.) plus an additional 180 degrees.

58. Install 6 new LH exhaust manifold studs. Tighten to 12 Nm (9 ft. lbs.).

59. Using a new gasket, install the LH exhaust manifold and 6 new nuts. Tighten in the sequence shown to 20 Nm (15 ft. lbs.).

60. Install the LH exhaust manifold heat shield and the 3 bolts. Tighten to 14 Nm (10 ft. lbs.).

61. Using a new gasket, install the LH catalytic converter and 4 new nuts. Tighten to 40 Nm (30 ft. lbs.).

62. Install the 2 LH catalytic converter bracket bolts. Tighten to 20 Nm (15 ft. lbs.).

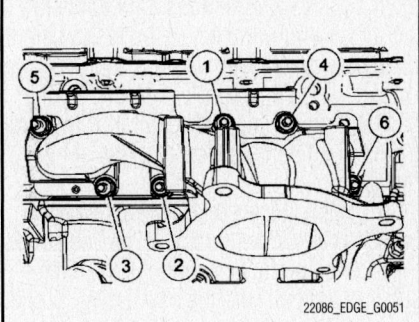

Fig. 175 Exhaust manifold tightening sequence—left side

63. Install the alternator, the bolt and the nut. Tighten to 47 Nm (35 ft. lbs.).

64. Install the A/C compressor, the nut and the 2 bolts. Tighten to 25 Nm (18 ft. lbs.).

65. Connect the EOP switch electrical connector and the wiring harness pin-type retainer.

66. Attach the wiring harness retainer to the alternator.

67. Connect the alternator electrical connector.

68. Connect the alternator B+ cable and install the nut. Tighten to 6 Nm (53 inch lbs.).

69. Connect the A/C compressor electrical connector.

70. Install the wiring harness retainer bolt on the rear of the LH cylinder head. Tighten to 10 Nm (89 inch lbs.).

71. Connect the LH catalyst monitor sensor electrical connector.

72. Connect the LH HO2S electrical connector.

73. Connect the LH CMP sensor electrical connector.

74. Install the LH radio interference capacitor and the bolt. Tighten to 10 Nm (89 inch lbs.).

75. Connect the CHT sensor electrical connector.

76. Connect the 6 fuel injector electrical connectors.

77. If equipped, install the block heater wiring harness onto the engine. Connect the block heater electrical connector and install the heat shield.

78. Install the LH camshafts, as outlined in this section.

Right Side

See Figures 174, 176 through 181 and 217.

During engine repair procedures, cleanliness is extremely important. Any foreign material, including any material created while cleaning gasket surfaces that enters the oil passages, coolant passages or the oil pan, can cause engine failure.

1. Remove the RH camshafts, as outlined in this section.

2. If equipped, remove the heat shield and disconnect the block heater electrical connector.

3. Remove the block heater wiring harness from the engine.

4. Disconnect the RH Heated Oxygen Sensor (HO2S) electrical connector.

5. Remove the bolt and position aside the RH radio interference capacitor.

6. Disconnect the RH Camshaft Position (CMP) sensor electrical connector.

7. Remove the bolt and the ground cable from the RH cylinder.

8. Tag and detach the 6 fuel injector electrical connectors.

9. Disconnect the Cylinder Head Temperature (CHT) sensor electrical connector.

10. Disconnect the LH catalyst monitor sensor electrical connector.

11. Remove the 2 LH catalytic converter bracket bolts.

12. Remove the 4 nuts (3 shown) and the LH catalytic converter. Discard the nuts and the gasket.

13. Remove the LH cylinder block drain plug. Allow the coolant to drain from the cylinder block into a suitable container.

14. Remove the 2 RH catalytic converter bracket bolts.

15. Remove the 4 nuts and the RH catalytic converter. Discard the nuts and the gasket.

16. Remove the RH cylinder block drain plug or, if equipped, the block heater. Allow the coolant to drain from the cylinder block into a suitable container.

17. Remove the 3 bolts and the RH exhaust manifold heat shield.

18. Remove the 6 nuts and the RH exhaust manifold. Discard the nuts and exhaust manifold gaskets.

19. Clean and inspect the RH exhaust manifold. Refer to the Exhaust Manifold procedure in this section.

20. Remove and discard the 6 RH exhaust manifold studs.

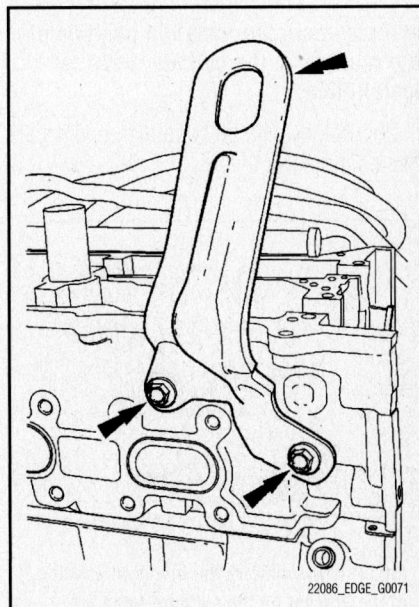

Fig. 176 Remove the 2 bolts and the engine lifting eye

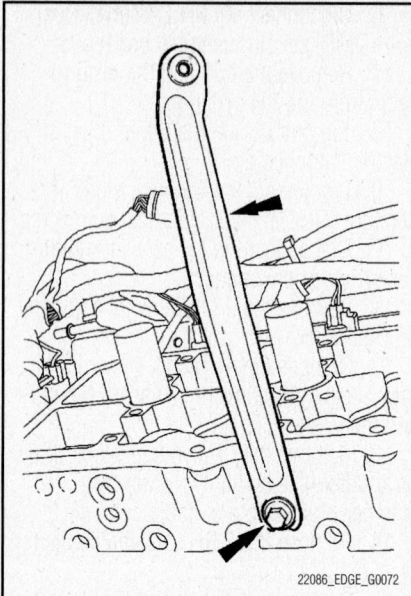

Fig. 177 Matchmark the installed position of the bracket on the cylinder head for installation, then remove the bolt and the upper intake manifold bracket

21. Remove the 2 bolts and the RH primary timing chain guide.
22. Remove the 2 bolts and the RH secondary timing chain tensioner.
23. Remove the 2 bolts and the engine lifting eye.

➡Matchmark the installed position of the bracket on the cylinder head for installation.

24. Remove the bolt and the upper intake manifold bracket.

➡Matchmark the installed position of the bracket on the cylinder head for installation.

25. Remove the bolt and the upper intake manifold bracket.

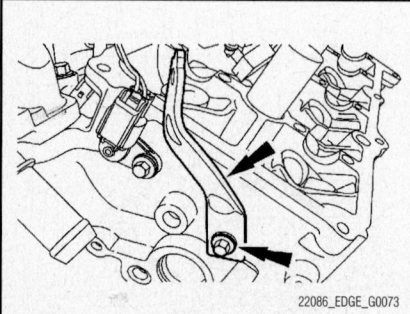

Fig. 178 Matchmark the installed position of the bracket on the cylinder head for installation, then remove the bolt and the upper intake manifold bracket

26. Remove the bolt and the RH CMP sensor.
27. Remove the 4 bolts and the fuel rail and injectors as an assembly.
28. Remove the 3 thermostat housing-to-lower intake manifold bolts. Remove the thermostat housing and discard the gasket and O-ring seal.
29. Remove the 10 bolts and the lower intake manifold. Discard the gaskets.
30. Disconnect and remove the CHT sensor jumper harness.

❊❊ WARNING

If the components are being reinstalled, they must be installed in the same positions. Mark the components for installation into their original positions.

31. Remove the valve tappets from the cylinder head.
32. Remove and discard the M6 bolt.

❊❊ WARNING

Place clean rags over any exposed engine cavities. Also, carefully remove the towels so foreign materials do not drop into the engine.

❊❊ WARNING

The cylinder head bolts must be discarded and new bolts must be installed. They are tighten-to-yield designed and cannot be reused.

❊❊ WARNING

Aluminum surfaces are soft and can be easily scratched. Do NOT place the cylinder head gasket surface, unprotected, on a workbench surface.

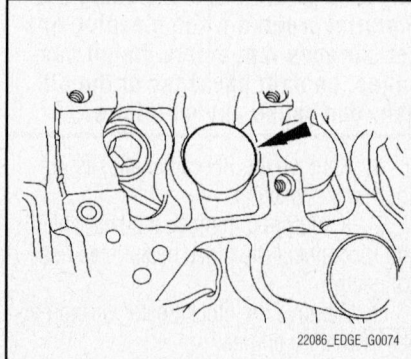

Fig. 179 Remove the valve tappets from the cylinder head

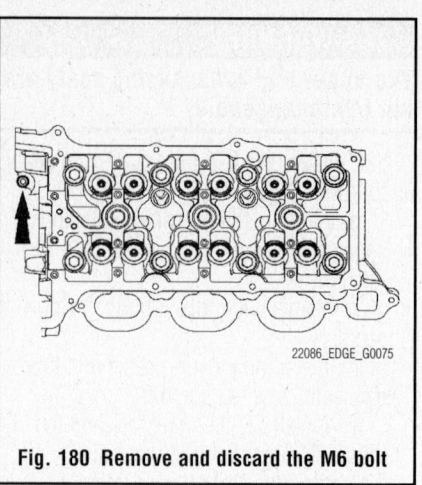

Fig. 180 Remove and discard the M6 bolt

33. Remove and discard the 8 bolts from the cylinder head. Remove the cylinder head. Discard the cylinder head gasket.

❊❊ WARNING

NEVER use metal scrapers, wire brushes, power abrasive discs or other abrasive means to clean the sealing surfaces. These tools cause scratches and gouges that make leak paths. Use a plastic scraping tool to remove all traces of the head gasket.

➡Observe all warnings or cautions and follow all application directions contained on the packaging of the silicone gasket remover and the metal surface prep.

➡If there is no residual gasket material present, metal surface prep can be used to clean and prepare the surfaces.

34. Clean the cylinder head-to-cylinder block mating surfaces of both the cylinder heads and the cylinder block.
35. Remove any large deposits of silicone or gasket material with a plastic scraper.
36. Apply silicone gasket remover, following package directions, and allow to set for several minutes. Remove the silicone gasket remover with a plastic scraper. A second application of silicone gasket remover may be required if residual traces of silicone or gasket material remain.
37. Apply metal surface prep, following package directions, to remove any remaining traces of oil or coolant and to prepare the surfaces to bond with the new gasket. Do not attempt to make the metal shiny. Some staining of the metal surfaces is normal.
38. Support the cylinder head on a bench with the head gasket side up.

➡The straightedge used must be flat within 0.0051 mm (0.0002 in) per foot of tool length. Inspect all areas of the deck face with a straightedge and feeler gauge. The cylinder head must not have depressions deeper than 0.0254 mm (0.001 in) across a 38.1 mm (1.5 in) square area, or scratches more than 0.0254 mm (0.001 in).

To install:

39. Install a new gasket, the RH cylinder head and 8 new bolts. Tighten in the sequence shown in 5 steps:
   a. Step 1: Tighten to 20 Nm (15 ft. lbs.).
   b. Step 2: Tighten to 35 Nm (26 ft. lbs.).
   c. Step 3: Tighten 90 degrees.
   d. Step 4: Tighten 90 degrees.
   e. Step 5: Tighten 90 degrees.

40. Install the M6 bolt and tighten to 10 Nm (89 inch lbs.).

✳ WARNING

The valve tappets must be installed in their original positions.

➡Coat the valve tappets with clean engine oil prior to installation.

41. Install the valve tappets in their original, installed positions.

42. Install and connect the CHT sensor jumper harness.

43. Using new gaskets, install the lower intake manifold and the 10 bolts. Tighten in the sequence shown to 10 Nm (89 inch lbs.).

44. Using a new gasket and O-ring seal, install the thermostat housing and

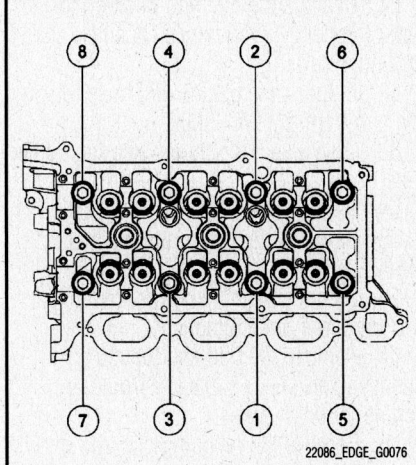

Fig. 181 Cylinder head bolt tightening sequence—right side

22086_EDGE_G0076

the 3 bolts. Tighten to 10 Nm (89 inch lbs.).

✳ WARNING

Only use O-ring seals that are made of special fuel-resistant material. Using regular O-rings can cause the fuel system to leak. Never reuse the O-ring seals.

✳ WARNING

The upper and lower O-ring seals are not interchangeable.

45. Install new fuel injector O-ring seals, as follows:
   a. Remove the retaining clips and separate the fuel injectors from the fuel rail.
   b. Remove and discard the O-ring seals.
   c. Install new O-ring seals and lubricate with clean engine oil.
   d. Install the fuel injectors and the retaining clips onto the fuel rail.

46. Install the fuel rail and injectors as an assembly and install the 4 bolts. Tighten to 10 Nm (89 inch lbs.).

47. Install the RH CMP sensor and the bolt. Tighten to 10 Nm (89 inch lbs.).

➡Align the bracket with the index mark made during removal.

48. Install the upper intake manifold bracket and the bolt. Tighten to 10 Nm (89 inch lbs.).

➡Align the bracket with the index mark made during removal.

49. Install the upper intake manifold bracket and the bolt. Tighten to 10 Nm (89 inch lbs.).

50. Install the engine lifting eye and the 2 bolts. Tighten to 24 Nm (18 ft. lbs.).

51. Install the RH secondary timing chain tensioner and the 2 bolts. Tighten to 10 Nm (89 inch lbs.).

52. Install the RH primary timing chain guide and the 2 bolts. Tighten to 10 Nm (89 inch lbs.).

53. Install 6 new RH exhaust manifold studs. Tighten to 12 Nm (9 ft. lbs.).

54. Using a new gasket, install the RH exhaust manifold and 6 new nuts. Tighten in the sequence shown to 20 Nm (15 ft. lbs.).

55. Install the RH exhaust manifold heat shield and the 3 bolts. Tighten to 14 Nm (10 ft. lbs.).

56. Install the RH cylinder block drain plug or, if equipped, the block heater. Tighten to 40 Nm (30 ft. lbs.).

➡Do not tighten the 4 catalytic converter nuts at this time.

57. Using a new gasket, install the RH catalytic converter and 4 new nuts.

58. Install the 2 RH catalytic converter bracket bolts. Tighten the 4 catalytic converter nuts to 40 Nm (30 ft. lbs.). Tighten the 2 catalytic converter brackets to 20 Nm (15 ft. lbs.).

59. Install the LH cylinder block drain plug. Tighten to 20 Nm (15 ft. lbs.) plus an additional 180 degrees.

60. Using a new gasket, install the LH catalytic converter and 4 new nuts (3 shown). Tighten to 40 Nm (30 ft. lbs.).

61. Install the 2 LH catalytic converter bracket bolts. Tighten to 20 Nm (15 ft. lbs.).

62. Connect the LH catalyst monitor sensor electrical connector.

63. Connect the CHT sensor electrical connector.

64. Connect the 6 fuel injector electrical connectors.

65. Install the ground cable and the bolt. Tighten to 10 Nm (89 inch lbs.).

66. Connect the RH CMP sensor electrical connector.

67. Install the RH radio interference capacitor and the bolt. Tighten to 10 Nm (89 inch lbs.).

68. Connect the RH HO2S electrical connector.

69. If equipped, install the block heater wiring harness onto the engine. Connect the block heater electrical connector and install the heat shield.

70. Install the RH camshafts, as outlined in this section.

ENGINE ASSEMBLY

REMOVAL & INSTALLATION

2.3L Engine

With Automatic Transaxle

See Figures 182 through 185.

1. Raise and safely support the vehicle.

2. Release the fuel system pressure, as outlined in the Fuel Section.

3. Disconnect the negative battery cable.

4. Recover the air conditioning system.

5. Place the steering wheel in the straight ahead position and the ignition key in the OFF position.

6. Remove the 2 nuts and the steering joint cover.

Do not allow the intermediate shaft to rotate while it is disconnected from the gear or damage to the clockspring can occur. If there is evidence that the intermediate shaft has rotated, the clockspring must be removed and recentered.

➡Matchmark the installed position of the steering column shaft position to the steering gear for reference during installation.

7. Remove the bolt and disconnect the steering column shaft from the steering gear.

8. Remove the bolt and disconnect the power steering pressure (PSP) tube from the power steering pump.

9. Route the PSP tube out the bottom of the engine compartment.

10. Drain the cooling system.

11. If equipped, remove the 7 screws and the underbody cover.

12. Remove the exhaust flexible pipe.

The steering gear-to-dash seal must be removed or it will be damaged when lowering the subframe.

13. Release the 4 clips and slide the steering gear-to-dash seal off of the steering gear and into the passenger compartment.

14. Remove the engine roll restrictor bolt.

15. Remove the 4 screws and position the RH fender splash shield aside.

16. Remove the 6 pin-type retainers (4 shown) and the RH splash shield.

17. Remove the 4 screws and position the LH fender splash shield aside.

18. Remove the 6 pin-type retainers (4 shown) and the LH splash shield.

19. Remove the cotter pins and nuts from the tie-rod ends.

20. Using a suitable tool, separate the tie-rod ends from the steering knuckles.

21. Disconnect the power steering cooler tube.

22. Remove the nuts and separate the sway bar links from the struts.

23. Remove the lower ball joint nuts.

When the lower ball joint is separated from the wheel knuckle, the lower arm may strike the outer constant velocity (CV) joint boot with enough force to damage the boot clamp. This will result in a loss of grease from the outer CV joint. Place a block of wood, or similar item, between the lower arm and the outer CV joint to prevent the lower arm from striking the outer CV joint.

➡Once pressure is applied to the ball joint with the special tool, it may be necessary to tap the wheel knuckle at the ball joint area to separate the ball joint from the wheel knuckle.

24. Using the special tools, separate the lower ball joints from the lower control arms.

25. Remove the through bolts from the lower control arms.

26. Position the special tool under the subframe assembly.

27. Remove the subframe bracket-to-body bolts.

28. Remove the subframe nuts and the subframe brackets.

29. Remove the front subframe nuts.

30. Lower the subframe assembly from the vehicle.

31. Remove the engine oil pan drain plug and drain the engine oil. Install the

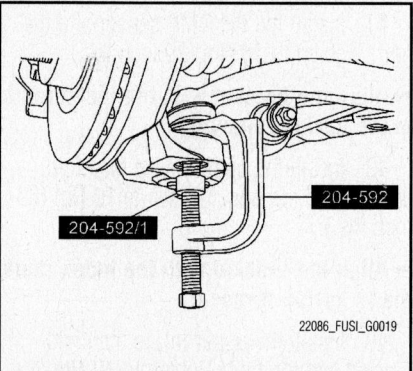

204-592/1   204-592

22086_FUSI_G0019

Fig. 182 Using the special tools, separate the lower ball joints from the lower control arms

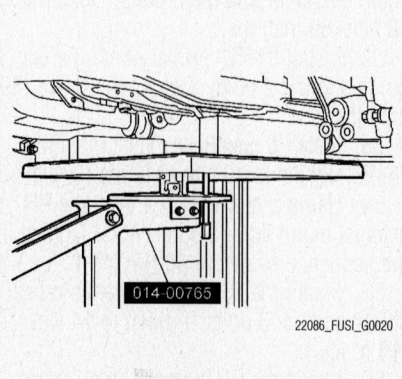

014-00765

22086_FUSI_G0020

Fig. 183 Position the special tool under the subframe assembly

drain plug and tighten to 28 Nm (21 ft. lbs.).

32. Remove the oil filter element.

33. Remove the bolt, 2 nuts and the generator air inlet duct.

34. Remove the engine air cleaner and air cleaner outlet pipe.

35. Remove the battery tray.

36. Remove the nut and disconnect the wire from the battery cable.

37. Disconnect the 2 engine wiring harness electrical connectors.

38. Remove the bolt and the ground wire.

39. Disconnect the Powertrain Control Module (PCM) electrical connector and the pin-type retainer.

40. Disconnect the fuel supply tube from the fuel rail.

41. Disconnect the crankcase vent tube from the valve cover.

42. Depress the locking ring and disconnect the brake booster vacuum supply tube from the intake manifold.

43. Disconnect the evaporative emissions (EVAP) tube from the intake manifold.

44. Detach the retaining clip and position the EVAP tube bundle aside.

45. Disconnect the upper radiator and heater hoses from the coolant bypass.

46. If equipped, disconnect the block heater electrical connector and detach the harness retaining clips from the heater hose.

47. Disconnect the heater hose inline connector.

48. Disconnect the transaxle control cable from the control lever.

49. Detach the control cable from the bracket.

50. Disconnect the transaxle cooler tubes.

51. Remove the bolt and position the radio frequency interference capacitor and ground wire aside.

52. Detach the coolant vent hose retaining clip from the A/C tube.

53. Disconnect the power steering cooler tube.

54. Remove the 2 A/C tube bracket bolts.

55. Remove the 2 nuts and disconnect the A/C tubes.

56. Remove the nut and disconnect the A/C tube from the condenser.

57. Remove the bolt and the radio frequency interference capacitor from the engine mount bracket.

58. Remove the retaining clip and disconnect the lower radiator hose.

59. Using a suitable tool, separate the LH halfshaft from the transaxle and support the halfshaft with a length of mechanic's wire.

60. Remove the 2 RH halfshaft carrier bearing bracket bolts.

61. Separate the RH halfshaft from the transaxle and support the halfshaft with a length of mechanic's wire.

62. Remove the bellhousing-to-oil pan bolt.

63. Remove the 2 oil pan-to-bellhousing bolts.

64. For vehicles with secondary Air Injection (AIR), disconnect the AIR pump electrical connector, then remove the 3 bolts and position the AIR pump aside.

➡**Position a suitable block of wood under the transaxle.**

65. Install the special tools onto the engine.

66. Raise the engine and transaxle 25.4 mm (1 in) to neutralize the engine and transaxle mounts.

67. Remove the 2 transaxle mount bolts.

68. Remove the bolt, 2 nuts and the engine mount bracket.

69. Lower the engine and transaxle from the vehicle.

70. Remove the 2 nuts and disconnect the starter wires.

71. Detach the 2 wiring harness retainers from the starter stud bolts.

72. Remove the 2 stud bolts and the starter.

73. Remove the 4 torque convertor nuts.

74. Remove the bolt and ground wire.

75. Remove the nut and position the engine wiring harness bracket aside.

76. Disconnect the transmission range (TR) sensor and primary control solenoid electrical connectors.

77. Disconnect the transaxle control electrical connectors.

78. Disconnect the Turbine Shaft Speed (TSS) sensor electrical connector.

79. Disconnect the Output Shaft Speed (OSS) sensor electrical connector.

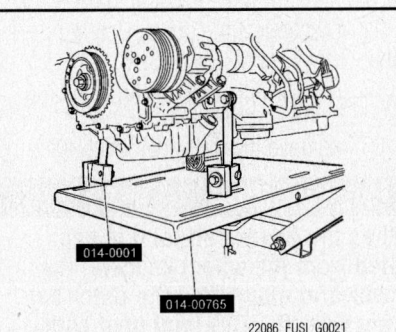

Fig. 184 Install the special tools onto the engine, then raise the engine and transaxle 25.4 mm (1 in) to neutralize the engine and transaxle mounts

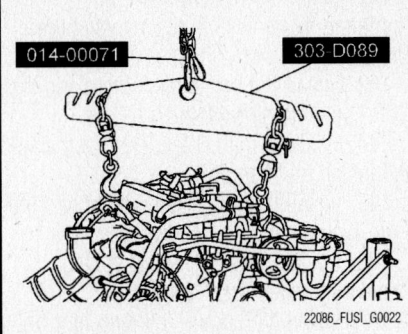

Fig. 185 Install the special tools and remove the engine and transaxle from the powertrain lift table

80. Disconnect the transaxle pressure switch electrical connector.

81. Install the special tools and remove the engine and transaxle from the power-train lift table.

82. Remove the bellhousing-to-engine retainers.

83. Separate the engine and transaxle.

To install:

> ❖❖❖ **CAUTION**

Do not smoke or carry lighted tobacco or open flame of any type when working on or near any fuel-related components. Highly flammable mixtures are always present and may be ignited. Failure to follow these instructions may result in personal injury.

84. Using the engine crane and spreader bar, position the engine and transaxle together. Install the engine-to-transaxle bolts. Tighten to 48 Nm (35 ft. lbs.).

85. Using the engine crane and spreader bar, position the engine and transaxle onto the lift table.

➡**Position a suitable block of wood under the transaxle.**

86. Install the special tools onto the engine.

87. Connect the transaxle pressure switch electrical connector.

88. Connect the OSS sensor electrical connector.

89. Connect the TSS sensor electrical connector.

90. Connect the transaxle control electrical connectors.

91. Connect the TR sensor and primary control solenoid electrical connectors.

92. Install the engine wiring harness bracket and nut. Tighten to 20 Nm (15 ft. lbs.).

93. Install the ground wire and bolt. Tighten to 10 Nm (89 lb-in).

94. Install new torque converter nuts. Tighten to 35 Nm (26 ft. lbs.).

95. Install the starter and the 2 stud bolts. Tighten to 25 Nm (18 ft. lbs.).

96. Connect the starter wires and install the 2 nuts:

   a. Tighten the large nut to 12 Nm (9 ft. lbs.).

   b. Tighten the small nut to 5 Nm (44 lb-in).

97. Attach the 2 wiring harness retainers to the starter stud bolts.

98. Raise the engine and transaxle into the vehicle.

99. Install the 2 transaxle mount bolts. Tighten to 90 Nm (66 ft. lbs.).

100. Install the engine mount bracket, 2 nuts and the bolt:

   a. Tighten the nuts to 103 Nm (76 ft. lbs.).

   b. Tighten the bolt to 115 Nm (85 ft. lbs.).

101. For vehicles with secondary AIR:

   a. Install the AIR pump and the 3 bolts and tighten to 30 Nm (22 ft. lbs.).

   b. Connect the AIR pump electrical connector.

102. Install the 2 oil pan-to-bellhousing bolts. Tighten to 48 Nm (35 ft. lbs.).

103. Install the bellhousing-to-oil pan bolt. Tighten to 48 Nm (35 ft. lbs.).

104. Install the RH halfshaft into the transaxle.

105. Install the 2 RH halfshaft carrier bearing bracket bolts. Tighten to 40 Nm (30 ft. lbs.).

➡**Start one end of the circlip in the groove and work the circlip over the halfshaft and into the groove to prevent the circlip from over expanding.**

106. Install a new circlip in the groove on the LH halfshaft.

107. Install LH halfshaft into the transaxle.

108. Connect the lower radiator hose and install the retaining clip.

109. Install the radio frequency interference capacitor and the bolt on the engine mount bracket. Tighten to 10 Nm (89 lb-in).

110. Connect the A/C tube to the condenser and install the nut. Tighten to 8 Nm (71 lb-in).

111. Connect the A/C tubes and install the 2 nuts. Tighten to 8 Nm (71 lb-in).

112. Install the 2 A/C tube bracket bolts. Tighten to 10 Nm (89 lb-in).

113. Attach the coolant vent hose retaining clip to the A/C tube.

114. Install the radio frequency interference capacitor, ground wire and the bolt. Tighten to 10 Nm (89 lb-in).

115. Connect the power steering cooler tube.

116. Connect the transaxle cooler tubes.

117. Connect the transaxle control cable to the bracket. Attach the control cable to the control lever.

118. Connect the heater hose inline connector.

119. If equipped, connect the block heater electrical connector and attach the harness retaining clips to the heater hose.

120. Connect the upper radiator and heater hoses to the coolant bypass.

121. Attach the EVAP tube bundle retaining clip to the bracket.

122. Connect the EVAP tube to the intake manifold.

123. Insert the brake booster vacuum supply tube into the locking ring on the intake manifold.

124. Connect the crankcase vent tube to the valve cover.

125. Connect the fuel supply tube to the fuel rail.

126. Connect the PCM electrical connector and the pin-type retainer.

127. Install the ground wire and the bolt. Tighten to 10 Nm (89 lb-in).

128. Connect the 2 engine wiring harness electrical connectors.

129. Connect the wire and install the nut on the battery cable. Tighten to 10 Nm (89 lb-in).

130. Install the battery tray.

131. Install the engine air cleaner and air cleaner outlet pipe.

132. Install the generator air inlet duct, bolt and the 2 nuts. Tighten to 6 Nm (53 lb-in).

133. Place the subframe assembly on the special tool and raise the subframe into the installed position.

134. Install the front subframe nuts. Tighten to 150 Nm (111 ft. lbs.).

135. Position the subframe brackets and install the bolts finger-tight.

136. Install the subframe nuts. Tighten to 150 Nm (111 ft. lbs.).

137. Tighten the subframe bracket-to-body bolts to 103 Nm (76 ft. lbs.).

138. Install the through bolts into the lower control arms. Tighten to 103 Nm (76 ft. lbs.).

139. Install the lower ball joint nuts. Tighten to 200 Nm (148 ft. lbs.).

140. Install the sway bar links and nuts to the struts. Tighten to 40 Nm (30 ft. lbs.).

141. Connect the power steering cooler tube.

142. Install tie-rod ends and nuts. Tighten to 48 Nm (35 ft. lbs.). Install the cotter pin.

143. Install the LH splash shield and the 6 pin-type retainers (4 shown).

144. Position the LH fender splash shield and install the 4 screws.

145. Install the RH splash shield and the 6 pin-type retainers (4 shown).

146. Position the RH fender splash shield and install the 4 screws.

147. Install the engine roll restrictor bolt. Tighten to 90 Nm (66 ft. lbs.).

148. Route the PSP tube up into the engine compartment.

149. Slide the steering gear-to-dash seal onto the steering gear and engage the 4 retaining clips into the body.

150. From under the vehicle, verify that the seal is properly installed on the steering gear and the retaining clips are fully engaged into the dash.

151. Install the oil filter element.

152. Install the exhaust flexible pipe.

153. If equipped, install the underbody cover and the 7 screws.

154. Connect the PSP tube to the power steering pump and install the bolt. Tighten to 35 Nm (26 ft. lbs.).

➡**Align the matchmarks made during removal.**

155. Install the steering intermediate shaft onto the steering gear and install the bolt. Tighten to 23 Nm (17 ft. lbs.).

156. Install the steering joint cover and the 2 nuts.

157. Fill the engine with clean engine oil.

158. Connect the battery ground cable.

159. Fill and bleed the cooling system.

160. Fill the power steering system.

161. Recharge the air conditioning system.

With Manual Transaxle
See Figures 182 through 186.

1. Raise and safely support the vehicle.

2. Release the fuel system pressure, as outlined in the Fuel Section.

3. Disconnect the negative battery cable.

4. Recover the air conditioning system.

5. Place the steering wheel in the straight ahead position and the ignition key in the OFF position.

6. Remove the 2 nuts and the steering joint cover.

✳✳ WARNING
Do not allow the intermediate shaft to rotate while it is disconnected from the gear or damage to the clock-

spring can occur. If there is evidence that the intermediate shaft has rotated, the clockspring must be removed and recentered. Refer to the Chassis Electrical Section for more information.

➡**Matchmark the installed position of the steering column shaft to the steering gear for reference during installation.**

7. Remove the bolt and disconnect the steering column shaft from the steering gear.

8. Remove the bolt and disconnect the Power Steering Pressure (PSP) tube from the power steering pump.

9. Route the PSP tube out the bottom of the engine compartment.

10. Drain the cooling system.

11. If equipped, remove the 7 screws and the underbody cover.

12. Remove the exhaust flexible pipe.

✳✳ WARNING
The steering gear-to-dash seal must be removed or it will be damaged when lowering the subframe.

13. Release the 4 clips and slide the steering gear-to-dash seal off of the steering gear and into the passenger compartment.

14. Remove the engine roll restrictor bolt.

15. Remove the 4 screws and position the RH fender splash shield aside.

16. Remove the 6 pin-type retainers and the RH splash shield.

17. Remove the 4 screws and position the LH fender splash shield aside.

18. Remove the 6 pin-type retainers and the LH splash shield.

19. Remove the cotter pins and nuts from the tie-rod ends.

20. Using the special tool, separate the tie-rod ends from the steering knuckles.

21. Disconnect the power steering cooler tube.

22. Remove the nuts and separate the sway bar links from the struts.

23. Remove the lower ball joint nuts.

✳✳ WARNING
When the lower ball joint is separated from the wheel knuckle, the lower arm may strike the outer constant velocity (CV) joint boot with enough force to damage the boot clamp. This will result in a loss of grease from the outer CV joint. Place a block of wood, or similar item,

between the lower arm and the outer CV joint to prevent the lower arm from striking the outer CV joint.

➡️**Once pressure is applied to the ball joint with the special tool, it may be necessary to tap the wheel knuckle at the ball joint area to separate the ball joint from the wheel knuckle.**

24. Using the special tools, separate the lower ball joints from the lower control arms.

25. Remove the through bolts from the lower control arms.

26. Position the special tool under the subframe assembly.

27. Remove the subframe bracket-to-body bolts.

28. Remove the rear subframe nuts and the subframe brackets.

29. Remove the front subframe nuts.

30. Lower the subframe assembly from the vehicle.

31. Remove the engine oil pan drain plug and drain the engine oil. Install the drain plug and tighten to 26 Nm (19 ft. lbs.).

32. Remove the oil filter element.

33. Remove the bolt, 2 nuts and the generator air inlet duct.

34. Remove the engine air cleaner and air cleaner outlet pipe.

35. Remove the battery tray.

36. Remove the nut and disconnect the wire from the battery cable.

37. Disconnect the 2 engine wiring harness electrical connectors.

38. Remove the bolt and the ground wire.

39. Disconnect the Powertrain Control Module (PCM) electrical connector and pin-type retainer.

40. Disconnect the fuel supply tube from the fuel rail.

41. Disconnect the crankcase vent tube from the valve cover.

42. Depress the locking ring and disconnect the brake booster vacuum supply tube from the intake manifold.

43. Disconnect the Evaporative emissions (EVAP) tube from the intake manifold.

44. Detach the retaining clip and position the EVAP tube bundle aside.

45. Disconnect the upper radiator and heater hoses from the coolant bypass.

46. If equipped, disconnect the block heater electrical connector and detach the harness retaining clips from the heater hose.

47. Disconnect the heater hose inline connector.

48. Remove the 2 clutch tube bracket bolts.

49. Remove the 2 bolts and position the clutch slave cylinder aside.

50. Disconnect the transaxle control cables from the control levers.

51. Detach the control cables from the bracket.

52. Disconnect the power steering cooler tube.

53. Remove the bolt and position the radio frequency interference capacitor and ground wire aside.

54. Detach the coolant vent hose retaining clip from the A/C tube.

55. Remove the 2 A/C tube bracket bolts.

56. Remove the 2 nuts and disconnect the A/C tubes.

57. Remove the nut and disconnect the A/C tube from the condenser.

58. Remove the bolt and the radio frequency interference capacitor from the engine mount bracket.

59. Remove the retaining clip and disconnect the lower radiator hose.

60. Using the special tools, separate the LH halfshaft from the transaxle and support the halfshaft with a length of mechanic's wire.

61. Remove the 2 RH halfshaft carrier bearing bracket bolts.

62. Separate the RH halfshaft from the transaxle and support the halfshaft with a length of mechanic's wire.

63. Remove the bellhousing-to-oil pan bolt.

64. Remove the 2 oil pan-to-bellhousing bolts.

➡️**Position a suitable block of wood under the transaxle.**

65. Install the special tools onto the engine.

66. Raise the engine and transaxle 25.4 mm (1 in) to neutralize the engine and transaxle mounts.

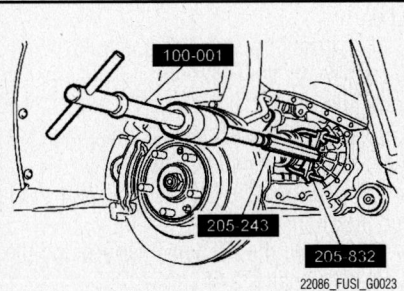

100-001
205-243
205-832
22086_FUSI_G0023

Fig. 186 Using the special tools, separate the LH halfshaft from the transaxle and support the halfshaft with a length of mechanic's wire

67. Remove the 2 transaxle mount bolts.

68. Remove the bolt, 2 nuts and the motor mount bracket.

69. Lower the engine and transaxle from the vehicle.

70. Remove the 2 nuts and disconnect the starter wires.

71. Detach the 2 wiring harness retainers from the starter stud bolts.

72. Remove the 2 bolts and the starter.

73. Remove the bolt and ground wire.

74. Remove the nut and position the engine wiring harness bracket aside.

75. Disconnect the backup lamp electrical connector.

76. Disconnect the Vehicle Speed Sensor (VSS) electrical connector.

77. Install the special tools and remove the engine and transaxle from the powertrain lift table.

78. Remove the bellhousing-to-engine retainers.

79. Separate the engine and transaxle

To install:

⚠️⚠️ **CAUTION**

Do not smoke or carry lighted tobacco or open flame of any type when working on or near any fuel-related components. Highly flammable mixtures are always present and may be ignited. Failure to follow these instructions may result in personal injury.

80. Using the engine crane and spreader bar, position the engine and transaxle together. Install the transaxle-to-engine bolts. Tighten to 48 Nm (35 ft. lbs.).

81. Using the engine crane and spreader bar, position the engine and transaxle onto the lift table.

➡️**Position a suitable block of wood under the transaxle.**

82. Install the special tools onto the engine.

83. Connect the VSS electrical connector.

84. Connect the backup lamp electrical connector.

85. Install the engine wiring harness bracket and nut. Tighten to 20 Nm (15 ft. lbs.).

86. Install the ground wire and bolt. Tighten to 10 Nm (89 lb-in).

87. Install the starter and the 2 stud bolts. Tighten to 25 Nm (18 ft. lbs.).

88. Connect the starter wires and install the 2 nuts:

　a. Tighten the large nut to 12 Nm (9 ft. lbs.).

b. Tighten the small nut to 5 Nm (44 lb-in).

89. Attach the 2 wiring harness retainers to the starter stud bolts.

90. Raise the engine and transaxle into the vehicle.

91. Install the 2 transaxle mount bolts. Tighten to 90 Nm (66 ft. lbs.). Install the engine mount bracket, 2 nuts and the bolt:

c. Tighten the nuts to 103 Nm (76 ft. lbs.).

d. Tighten the bolt to 115 Nm (85 ft. lbs.).

92. Install the 2 oil pan-to-bellhousing bolts. Tighten to 48 Nm (35 ft. lbs.).

93. Install the bellhousing-to-oil pan bolt. Tighten to 48 Nm (35 ft. lbs.).

94. Install the RH halfshaft into the transaxle.

95. Install the 2 RH halfshaft carrier bearing bracket bolts. Tighten to 40 Nm (30 ft. lbs.).

➡**Start one end of the circlip in the groove and work the circlip over the halfshaft and into the groove to prevent the circlip from over expanding.**

96. Install a new circlip in the groove on the LH halfshaft.

97. Install LH halfshaft into the transaxle.

98. Connect the lower radiator hose and install the retaining clip.

99. Install the radio frequency interference capacitor and the bolt on the engine mount bracket. Tighten to 10 Nm (89 lb-in).

100. Connect the A/C tube to the condenser and install the nut. Tighten to 8 Nm (71 lb-in).

101. Connect the A/C tubes and install the 2 nuts. Tighten to 8 Nm (71 lb-in).

102. Install the 2 A/C tube bracket bolts. Tighten to 10 Nm (89 lb-in).

103. Attach the coolant vent hose retaining clip to the A/C tube.

104. Install the radio frequency interference capacitor, ground wire and the bolt. Tighten to 10 Nm (89 lb-in).

105. Connect the power steering cooler tube.

106. Attach the transaxle control cables to the bracket. Connect the control cables to the control levers.

107. Install the clutch slave cylinder and the 2 bolts. Tighten to 22 Nm (16 ft. lbs.).

108. Install the 2 clutch tube bracket bolts. Tighten to 22 Nm (16 ft. lbs.).

109. Connect the heater hose inline connector.

110. If equipped, connect the block heater electrical connector and attach the harness retaining clips to the heater hose.

111. Connect the upper radiator and heater hoses to the coolant bypass.

112. Attach the EVAP tube bundle retaining clip to the bracket.

113. Connect the EVAP tube to the intake manifold.

114. Insert the brake booster vacuum supply tube into the locking ring on the intake manifold.

115. Connect the crankcase vent tube to the valve cover.

116. Connect the fuel supply tube to the fuel rail.

117. Connect the PCM electrical connector and the pin-type retainer.

118. Install the ground wire and the bolt. Tighten to 10 Nm (89 lb-in).

119. Connect the 2 engine wiring harness electrical connectors.

120. Connect the wire and install the nut on the battery cable. Tighten to 10 Nm (89 lb-in).

121. Install the battery tray.

122. Install the engine air cleaner and air cleaner outlet pipe.

123. Install the generator air inlet duct, bolt and the 2 nuts. Tighten to 6 Nm (53 lb-in).

124. Place the subframe assembly on the special tool and raise the subframe into the installed position.

125. Install the front subframe nuts. Tighten to 150 Nm (111 ft. lbs.).

126. Position the subframe brackets and install the bolts finger-tight.

127. Install the subframe nuts. Tighten to 150 Nm (111 ft. lbs.).

128. Tighten the subframe bracket-to-body bolts to 103 Nm (76 ft. lbs.).

129. Install the through bolts into the lower control arms. Tighten to 103 Nm (76 ft. lbs.).

130. Install the lower ball joint nuts. Tighten to 200 Nm (148 ft. lbs.).

131. Install the sway bar links and nuts to the struts. Tighten to 40 Nm (30 ft. lbs.).

132. Connect the power steering cooler tube.

133. Install tie-rod ends and nuts. Tighten to 48 Nm (35 ft. lbs.). Install the cotter pin.

134. Install the LH splash shield and the 6 pin-type retainers (4 shown).

135. Position the LH fender splash shield and install the 4 screws.

136. Install the RH splash shield and the 6 pin-type retainers (4 shown).

137. Position the RH fender splash shield and install the 4 screws.

138. Install the engine roll restrictor bolt. Tighten to 90 Nm (66 ft. lbs.).

139. Route the PSP tube up into the engine compartment.

140. Slide the steering gear-to-dash seal onto the steering gear and engage the 4 retaining clips into the body.

141. From under the vehicle, verify that the seal is properly installed on the steering gear and the retaining clips are fully engaged into the dash.

142. Install the oil filter element.

143. Install the exhaust flexible pipe.

144. If equipped, install the underbody cover and the 7 screws.

145. Connect the PSP tube to the power steering pump and install the bolt. Tighten to 35 Nm (26 ft. lbs.).

➡**Align the matchmarks made during removal.**

146. Install the steering intermediate shaft onto the steering gear and install the bolt. Tighten to 23 Nm (17 ft. lbs.).

147. Install the steering joint cover and the 2 nuts.

148. Fill the engine with clean engine oil.

149. Connect the battery ground cable.

150. Fill and bleed the cooling system.

151. Fill the power steering system.

152. Recharge the air conditioning system

3.0L Engine

See Figures 187 through 198.

✶✶ CAUTION

Do not smoke or carry lighted tobacco or open flame of any type when working on or near any fuel-related components. Highly flammable mixtures are always present and may be ignited. Failure to follow these instructions may result in personal injury.

1. With the vehicle in NEUTRAL, position it on a hoist.

2. Release the fuel system pressure.

3. Disconnect the battery ground cable.

4. Recover the air conditioning system.

5. Place the steering wheel in the straight ahead position and the ignition key in the OFF position.

6. Remove the 2 nuts and the steering joint cover.

✶✶ WARNING

Do not allow the intermediate shaft to rotate while it is disconnected from the gear or damage to the clockspring can occur. If there is evidence that the intermediate shaft has rotated, the clockspring must be removed and recentered.

➡ Matchmark the installed position of the steering column shaft position to the steering gear for reference during installation.

7. Remove the bolt and disconnect the steering column shaft from the steering gear.

8. Drain the cooling system.

9. Remove the 4 screws and position the RH fender splash shield aside.

10. Remove the 6 pin-type retainers (4 shown) and the RH splash shield.

11. Remove the 4 screws and position the LH fender splash shield aside.

12. Remove the 6 pin-type retainers (4 shown) and the LH splash shield.

13. Disconnect the power steering hose and drain the power steering fluid into a suitable drain pan.

14. Remove the exhaust flexible pipe.

15. For All wheel drive (AWD) vehicles:

➡ Matchmark the driveshaft for installation.

e. Remove the 4 bolts (3 shown) and support the driveshaft with a length of mechanic's wire.

✳✳ WARNING

The steering gear-to-dash seal must be removed or it will be damaged when lowering the subframe.

16. Release the 4 clips and slide the steering gear-to-dash seal off of the steering gear and into the passenger compartment.

17. Remove the Power Steering Pressure (PSP) hose bracket bolt.

18. Remove and discard the PSP hose banjo bolt and the 2 seals from the steering gear.

19. If equipped, remove the 2 bolts and the heat shield.

20. Remove the 2 bolts and the engine roll restrictor.

21. Remove the cotter pins and nuts from the tie-rod ends.

22. Using the a suitable tie-rod end removal tool, separate the tie-rod ends from the steering knuckles.

23. Remove the nuts and separate the stabilizer bar links from the struts.

24. Remove the lower ball joint nuts.

✳✳ WARNING

When the lower ball joint is separated from the wheel knuckle, the lower arm may strike the outer constant velocity (CV) joint boot with enough force to damage the boot clamp. This will result in a loss of grease from the outer CV joint. Place

a block of wood, or similar item, between the lower arm and the outer CV joint to prevent the lower arm from striking the outer CV joint.

➡ Once pressure is applied to the ball joint with the special tool, it may be necessary to tap the wheel knuckle at the ball joint area to separate the ball joint from the wheel knuckle.

25. Using the special tools, separate the lower ball joints from the lower control arms.

26. Remove the through bolts from the lower control arms.

27. Position the special tool under the subframe assembly.

28. Remove the subframe bracket-to-body bolts.

29. Remove the subframe nuts and the subframe brackets.

30. Remove the front subframe nuts.

31. Lower the subframe assembly from the vehicle.

32. Disconnect the transaxle cooler hoses.

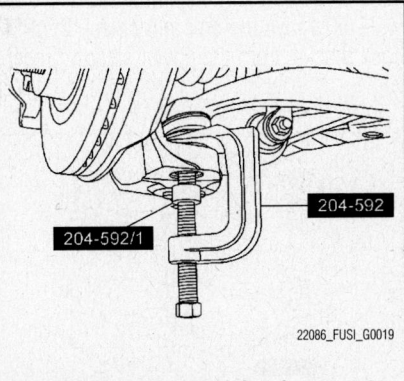

Fig. 187 Using the special tools, separate the lower ball joints from the lower control arms

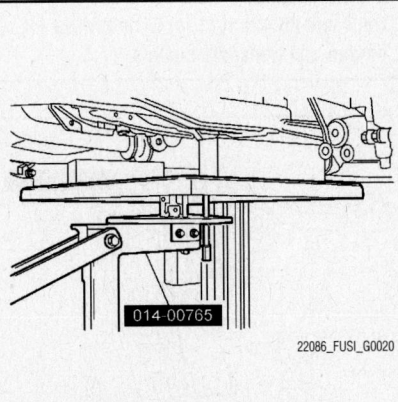

Fig. 188 Position the special tool under the subframe assembly

33. Remove the drain plug and drain the engine oil. Install the drain plug and tighten to 26 Nm (19 ft. lbs.).

34. Remove and discard the engine oil filter.

35. Remove the engine air cleaner and air cleaner outlet pipe.

36. Remove the battery tray.

37. Remove the nut and disconnect the power feed wire from the battery terminal.

38. Disconnect the 2 engine wiring harness electrical connectors.

39. Remove the bolt and position aside the ground wire.

40. Disconnect the Powertrain Control Module (PCM) electrical connector and the pin-type retainer.

41. Disconnect the fuel supply tube from the fuel rail.

42. Disconnect the heater hose from the thermostat housing.

43. Disconnect the heater hose inline connection.

44. Disconnect the throttle body coolant hose.

45. Disconnect the Evaporative emissions (EVAP) hose.

46. Disconnect the upper and lower radiator hoses from the thermostat housing.

47. Disconnect the transaxle control cable from the transaxle selector lever.

48. Remove the 3 transaxle control cable bracket bolts and position the cable aside.

49. Remove the bolt and position the ground wire aside.

50. Remove the vacuum tube bracket bolt.

51. Disconnect the vacuum hose from the intake manifold.

52. If equipped, detach the block heater cable retaining clips from the cooling fan shroud.

53. Disconnect the power steering hose from the power steering reservoir.

54. Detach the power steering hose retaining clip from the LH valve cover stud bolt and the engine wiring harness.

55. Disconnect the coolant hose from the degas bottle.

56. Detach the coolant hose retaining clip and position the coolant hose aside.

57. Remove the 2 A/C tube bracket bolts.

58. Remove the 2 nuts and disconnect the A/C tubes.

59. Remove the bolt and the ground wire from the engine mount bracket.

60. Remove the bolt and separate the A/C manifold from the A/C compressor.

61. Using the special tools, separate the LH halfshaft from the transaxle and support the halfshaft with a length of mechanic's wire.

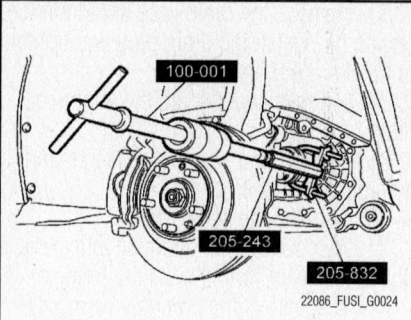

Fig. 189 Using the special tools, separate the LH halfshaft from the transaxle and support the halfshaft with a length of mechanic's wire

62. For early build Front Wheel Drive (FWD) vehicles:

a. Disconnect the Crankshaft Position (CKP) sensor electrical connector and pin-type retainer.

b. Disconnect the Power Steering Pressure (PSP) switch electrical connector.

c. Disconnect the catalyst monitor sensor electrical connector and pin-type retainer.

63. For FWD vehicles:

a. Remove the 2 RH halfshaft carrier bearing bracket bolts.

b. Separate the RH halfshaft from the transaxle and support the halfshaft with a length of mechanic's wire.

64. For AWD vehicles:

a. Disconnect the RH catalyst monitor sensor electrical connector and detach the wiring retainer.

b. Using the special sensor tool, remove the RH catalyst monitor sensor.

c. Disconnect the RH heated oxygen sensor (HO2S) electrical connector.

d. Using the special tool, remove the RH HO2S.

e. Remove the 6 bolts and the RH exhaust heat shield.

f. Remove the 3 nuts and the RH exhaust heat shield bracket (outboard half).

g. Remove the 2 bolts and the RH exhaust heat shield bracket (inboard half).

h. Remove the 3 nuts (2 shown) and the RH catalytic converter.

i. Discard the nuts and gasket.

j. Remove the 2 halfshaft carrier bearing bolts.

k. Separate the RH halfshaft from the power transfer unit (PTU) and support the halfshaft with a length of mechanic's wire.

l. Remove the 5 bolts and the PTU support bracket

m. Remove the 5 bolts and the PTU.

65. Remove the torque converter nut access plug.

66. Remove the 3 torque converter nuts.

67. Remove the 2 oil pan-to-transaxle bolts.

➡**Position a suitable block of wood under the transaxle.**

68. Install the special tools onto the engine.

69. Raise the engine and transaxle 25.4 mm (1 in) to neutralize the engine and transaxle mounts.

70. Remove the 2 transaxle mount bolts.

71. Remove the bolt and damper.

72. Remove the bolt, 3 nuts and the engine mount bracket.

73. Lower the engine and transaxle from the vehicle.

74. Install the special tools.

75. Detach the wiring harness retainer from the PSP hose bracket.

76. Remove the bolt and detach the PSP hose bracket from the cylinder head.

77. Remove the bolt and detach the PSP hose bracket from the cylinder head.

78. Remove the bolt and detach the PSP hose bracket from the power steering reservoir.

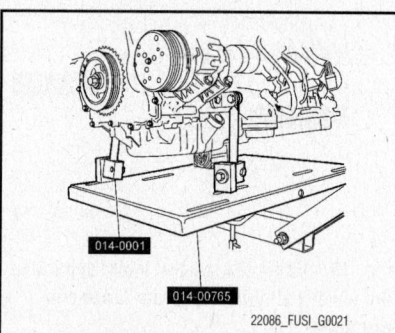

Fig. 190 Install the special tools onto the engine, then raise the engine and transaxle 25.4 mm (1 in) to neutralize the engine and transaxle mounts

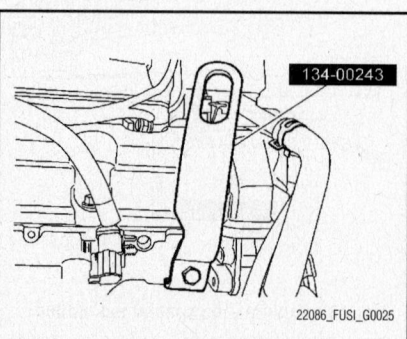

Fig. 191 Install the special tool

79. Remove the banjo bolt and the PSP hose. Discard the banjo bolt and 2 seals.

80. Install the special tool.

81. Disconnect the Exhaust Gas Recirculation (EGR) valve electrical connector.

82. Loosen the EGR tube-to-EGR valve nut.

83. Remove the 2 bolts and the EGR valve. Discard the gasket.

84. Loosen the EGR tube-to-catalytic converter nut and remove the EGR tube.

85. For FWD vehicles:

a. Remove the 2 bolts and the heat shield.

b. Remove the 2 bolts and the catalytic converter bracket.

c. Remove the 2 bolts and the catalytic converter bracket assembly.

➡**When installing the lower half of the lifting bracket it will be easier to loosely install the upper bolt first then install the lower bolt.**

86. Install the lower half of the special tool.

87. Install the upper half of the special tool.

88. Using the special tools and a suitable engine crane, remove the engine and transaxle from the lift table.

89. Remove the bolt and ground wire.

90. Remove the bolt and the catalyst monitor sensor electrical connector bracket.

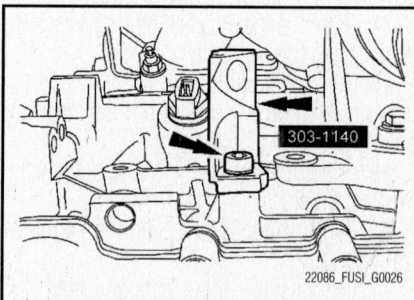

Fig. 192 Install the lower half of the special tool

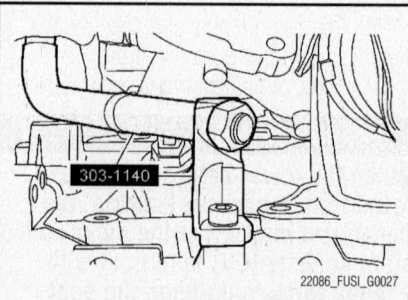

Fig. 193 Install the upper half of the special tool

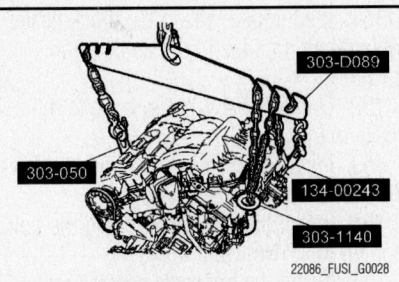

Fig. 194 Using the special tools and a suitable engine crane, remove the engine and transaxle from the lift table

91. Disconnect the Transmission Control Module (TCM) electrical connector.
92. Remove the 2 nuts and the starter motor wiring.
93. Remove the 2 bolts and the starter motor.
94. Remove the engine-to-transaxle bolt.
95. Remove the 3 transaxle-to-engine bolts.
96. Detach the wiring harness retainer from the stud bolt.
97. Remove the transaxle-to-engine stud bolt, bolt and nut.
98. Using the special tools and a suitable engine crane, separate the engine and transaxle.

To install:

✳ WARNING

If the oil pan was removed during engine disassembly, it must be installed after engine and transaxle are assembled and the transaxle-to-engine bolts are installed. Failure to follow this assembly sequence can result in engine oil leaks.

99. Using the special tools and a suitable engine crane, align the transaxle to the engine.
100. Install the transaxle-to-engine stud bolt, bolt and nut. Tighten to 48 Nm (35 ft. lbs.).
101. Attach the wiring harness retainer to the stud bolt.
102. Install the 3 transaxle-to-engine bolts. Tighten to 48 Nm (35 ft. lbs.).
103. Install the engine-to-transaxle bolt. Tighten to 48 Nm (35 ft. lbs.).

✳ WARNING

Do not use metal scrapers, wire brushes, power abrasive discs or other abrasive means to clean the sealing surfaces. These tools cause scratches and gouges which make leak paths.

104. Use a plastic scraping tool to remove all traces of the oil pan gasket.
105. Clean all sealing surfaces with metal surface cleaner and install a new oil pan gasket.

➡ **The oil pan must be installed and the bolts tightened within 4 minutes of sealant application.**

106. Apply a 10 mm (0.39 in) diameter dot of silicone sealant to the areas indicated.
107. Position the oil pan and install the 10 bolts and 5 stud bolts finger tight.
108. Install the 2 oil pan-to-transaxle bolts. Tighten to 48 Nm (35 ft. lbs.).
109. Tighten the 15 oil pan-to-engine bolts and stud bolts in the sequence shown to 25 Nm (18 ft. lbs.).
110. Install 6 new LH catalytic converter studs. Tighten to 12 Nm (9 ft. lbs.).
111. Install a new gasket, the LH catalytic converter and 6 new nuts. Tighten to 20 Nm (15 ft. lbs.) in the sequence shown.
112. Install the LH catalytic converter bracket and the 2 bolts. Tighten to 20 Nm (15 ft. lbs.).
113. Install the heat shield and the 4 bolts. Tighten to 11 Nm (8 ft. lbs.).
114. Connect the LH heated oxygen sensor (HO2S) electrical connector and pin-type retainer.
115. Connect the LH catalyst monitor sensor electrical connector.

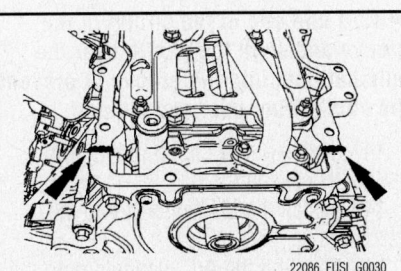

Fig. 195 Apply a 10 mm (0.39 in) diameter dot of silicone sealant to the areas indicated

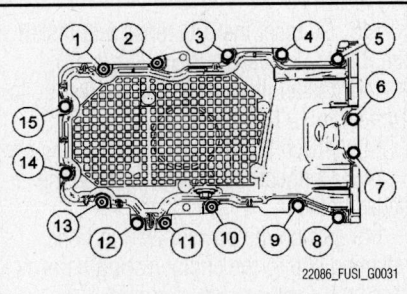

Fig. 196 Oil pan-to-engine retainer tightening sequence—3.0L engine

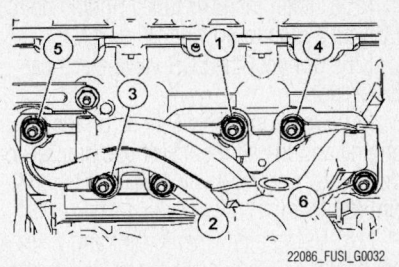

Fig. 197 Install a new gasket, the LH catalytic converter and 6 new nuts. Tighten to 20 Nm (15 ft. lbs.) in the proper sequence

116. Install the starter motor and the 2 bolts. Tighten to 27 Nm (20 ft. lbs.).
117. Connect the starter motor wiring and install the 2 nuts:
 a. Tighten the large nut to 12 Nm (9 ft. lbs.).
 b. Tighten the small nut to 5 Nm (44 lb-in).
118. Connect the Transmission Control Module (TCM) electrical connector.
119. Install the catalyst monitor sensor bracket and the bolt. Tighten to 12 Nm (9 ft. lbs.).
120. Install the ground wire and the bolt. Tighten to 12 Nm (9 ft. lbs.).
121. Using the special tools and a suitable engine crane, position the engine and transaxle onto the lift table.

➡ **Position a suitable block of wood under the transaxle.**

122. Install the special tools.
123. For FWD vehicles:
 a. Install the catalytic converter bracket assembly and the 2 bolts. Tighten to 35 Nm (26 ft. lbs.).
 b. Install the catalytic converter bracket and the 2 bolts. Tighten to 20 Nm (15 ft. lbs.).
 c. Install the heat shield and the 2 bolts. Tighten to 11 Nm (8 ft. lbs.).
124. Using a new gasket, install the EGR valve and the 2 bolts. Tighten to 25 Nm (18 ft. lbs.).

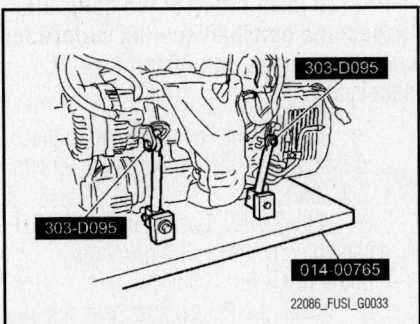

Fig. 198 Install the special tools

125. Install the EGR tube. Tighten both EGR tube nuts to 40 Nm (30 ft. lbs.).

126. Connect the EGR valve electrical connector.

127. Position the PSP hose on the engine and install the PSP hose bracket-to-power steering reservoir bolt. Tighten to 9 Nm (80 lb-in).

128. Using a new banjo bolt and 2 seals, connect the PSP hose to the power steering pump. Tighten to 37 Nm (27 ft. lbs.).

129. Attach the PSP hose bracket to the cylinder head and install the bolt. Tighten to 9 Nm (80 lb-in).

130. Attach the PSP hose bracket to the cylinder head and install the bolt. Tighten to 9 Nm (80 lb-in).

131. Attach the wiring harness retainer to the PSP hose bracket.

132. Raise the engine and transaxle up into the vehicle.

133. Install the engine mount bracket, 3 nuts and the bolt:

    a. Tighten the nuts to 63 Nm (46 ft. lbs.).

    b. Tighten the bolt to 115 Nm (85 ft. lbs.).

134. Install the damper and bolt. Tighten to 23 Nm (17 ft. lbs.).

135. Install the 2 transaxle mount bolts. Tighten to 90 Nm (66 ft. lbs.).

136. Install the 3 torque converter nuts. Tighten to 36 Nm (27 ft. lbs.).

137. Install the torque converter nut access plug.

138. For AWD vehicles:

    a. Install the power transfer unit (PTU) and the 5 bolts. Tighten to 90 Nm (66 ft. lbs.).

    b. Install the PTU support bracket and the 5 bolts. Tighten to 70 Nm (52 ft. lbs.).

✳✳ WARNING

A new power transfer unit (PTU) seal must be installed whenever the intermediate shaft is removed.

    c. Install a new PTU seal.

➡**Prior to installation of the halfshaft, inspect the halfshaft sealing surface for wear or damage and install new, if necessary.**

    d. Position the RH driveshaft in place and install the 2 bolts. Tighten to 23 Nm (17 ft. lbs.).

    e. Using a new gasket, install the RH catalytic converter and 3 new nuts. Tighten to 48 Nm (35 ft. lbs.).

    f. Install the RH exhaust heat shield bracket (inboard half) and the 2 bolts. Tighten to 40 Nm (30 ft. lbs.).

    g. Install the RH exhaust heat shield bracket (outboard half) and the 3 nuts. Tighten to 20 Nm (15 ft. lbs.).

    h. Install the RH exhaust heat shield and the 6 bolts. Tighten to 11 Nm (8 ft. lbs.).

    i. Using the special tool, install the RH HO2S. Tighten to 48 Nm (35 ft. lbs.).

    j. Connect the RH HO2S electrical connector.

    k. Using the special tool, install the RH catalytic monitor sensor. Tighten to 48 Nm (35 ft. lbs.).

    l. Connect the RH catalyst monitor sensor electrical connector and attach the wiring harness retainer.

139. For FWD vehicles:

    a. Install the RH halfshaft into the transaxle.

    b. Install the 2 RH halfshaft carrier bearing bracket bolts. Tighten to 55 Nm (41 ft. lbs.).

140. For Early build FWD vehicles:

    a. Connect the catalyst monitor sensor electrical connector and pin-type retainer.

    b. Connect the PSP switch electrical connector.

    c. Connect the CKP sensor electrical connector and pin-type retainer.

➡**Prior to installation of the halfshaft, inspect the halfshaft sealing surface for wear or damage and install new, if necessary.**

➡**Start one end of the circlip in the groove and work the circlip over the halfshaft and into the groove to prevent the circlip from over expanding.**

141. Install a new circlip in the groove on the LH halfshaft.

142. Install the LH halfshaft into transaxle.

143. Position the A/C manifold onto the A/C compressor and install the bolt. Tighten to 15 Nm (11 ft. lbs.).

144. Install the ground wire and bolt to the engine mount bracket. Tighten to 10 Nm (89 lb-in).

145. Connect the A/C tubes and install the 2 nuts. Tighten to 8 Nm (71 lb-in).

146. Install the 2 A/C tube bracket bolts. Tighten to 10 Nm (89 lb-in).

147. Attach the coolant hose retaining clip.

148. Connect the coolant hose to the degas bottle.

149. Attach the power steering hose retaining clip to the engine wiring harness and the LH valve cover stud bolt.

150. Connect the power steering hose to the power steering reservoir.

151. If equipped, attach the block heater cable retaining clips to the cooling fan shroud.

152. Connect the vacuum hose to the intake manifold.

153. Install the vacuum tube bracket bolt. Tighten to 10 Nm (89 lb-in).

154. Install the ground wire and the bolt. Tighten to 12 Nm (9 ft. lbs.).

155. Install the transaxle control cable bracket and the 3 bolts. Tighten to 8 Nm (71 lb-in).

156. Connect the transaxle control cable to the transaxle selector lever.

157. Connect the upper and lower radiator hoses to the thermostat housing.

158. Connect the EVAP hose.

159. Connect the throttle body coolant hose.

160. Connect the heater hose inline connection.

161. Connect the heater hose to the thermostat housing.

162. Connect the fuel supply tube to the fuel rail.

163. Connect the PCM electrical connector and the pin-type retainer.

164. Install the ground wire and bolt. Tighten to 10 Nm (89 lb-in).

165. Connect the 2 engine wiring harness electrical connectors.

166. Connect the power feed to the battery terminal and install the nut. Tighten to 6 Nm (53 lb-in).

167. Install the battery tray.

168. Install the engine air cleaner and air cleaner outlet pipe.

➡**Lubricate the engine oil filter gasket with clean engine oil prior to installing.**

169. Install a new engine oil filter. Tighten to 5 Nm (44 lb-in) and then rotate an additional 180 degrees.

170. Connect the transaxle cooler hoses.

171. Place the subframe assembly on the special tool and raise the subframe into the installed position.

172. Install the front subframe nuts. Tighten to 150 Nm (111 ft. lbs.).

173. Position the subframe brackets and install the bolts finger-tight.

174. Install the subframe nuts. Tighten to 150 Nm (111 ft. lbs.).

175. Tighten the subframe bracket-to-body bolts to 103 Nm (76 ft. lbs.).

176. Install the through bolts into the lower control arms. Tighten to 103 Nm (76 ft. lbs.).

177. Install the lower ball joint nuts. Tighten to 200 Nm (148 ft. lbs.).

178. Install the sway bar links and nuts to the struts. Tighten to 40 Nm (30 ft. lbs.).

179. Connect the power steering cooler hose.

180. Install the tie-rod ends and nuts. Tighten to 48 Nm (35 ft. lbs.). Install the cotter pin.

181. Install the LH splash shield and the 6 pin-type retainers (4 shown).

182. Position the LH fender splash shield and install the 4 screws.

183. Install the RH splash shield and the 6 pin-type retainers (4 shown).

184. Position the RH fender splash shield and install the 4 screws.

185. Install the engine roll restrictor and the 2 bolts. Tighten to 90 Nm (66 ft. lbs.).

186. If equipped, install the heat shield and the 2 bolts.

187. Using a new banjo bolt and 2 seals, connect the PSP hose to the power steering gear. Tighten to 37 Nm (27 ft. lbs.).

188. Position the PSP hose onto the steering gear and install the PSP hose bracket bolt. Tighten to 15 Nm (11 ft. lbs.).

189. Slide the steering gear-to-dash seal onto the steering gear and engage the 4 retaining clips into the body.

190. From under the vehicle, verify that the seal is properly installed on the steering gear and the retaining clips are fully engaged into the body.

191. For AWD vehicles:
   a. Line up the index marks on the rear driveshaft to the index marks on the PTU flange made during removal and install the 4 bolts (3 shown).
   b. Tighten to 70 Nm (52 ft. lbs.).

192. Install the exhaust flexible pipe.

➡**Align the index marks made during removal.**

193. Install the steering intermediate shaft onto the steering gear and install the bolt. Tighten to 23 Nm (17 ft. lbs.).

194. Install the steering joint cover and the 2 nuts.

195. Fill the engine with clean engine oil.

196. Connect the battery ground cable.

197. Fill and bleed the cooling system.

198. Fill the power steering system.

199. Check the transaxle fluid and add fluid if necessary.

200. Recharge the air conditioning system

3.5L Engine

See Figures 199 through 209.

➡**Engine removal and installation requires a number of specialized tools and equipment. Make sure to read the procedure and be sure you have all of the necessary tools and equipment before beginning the procedure.**

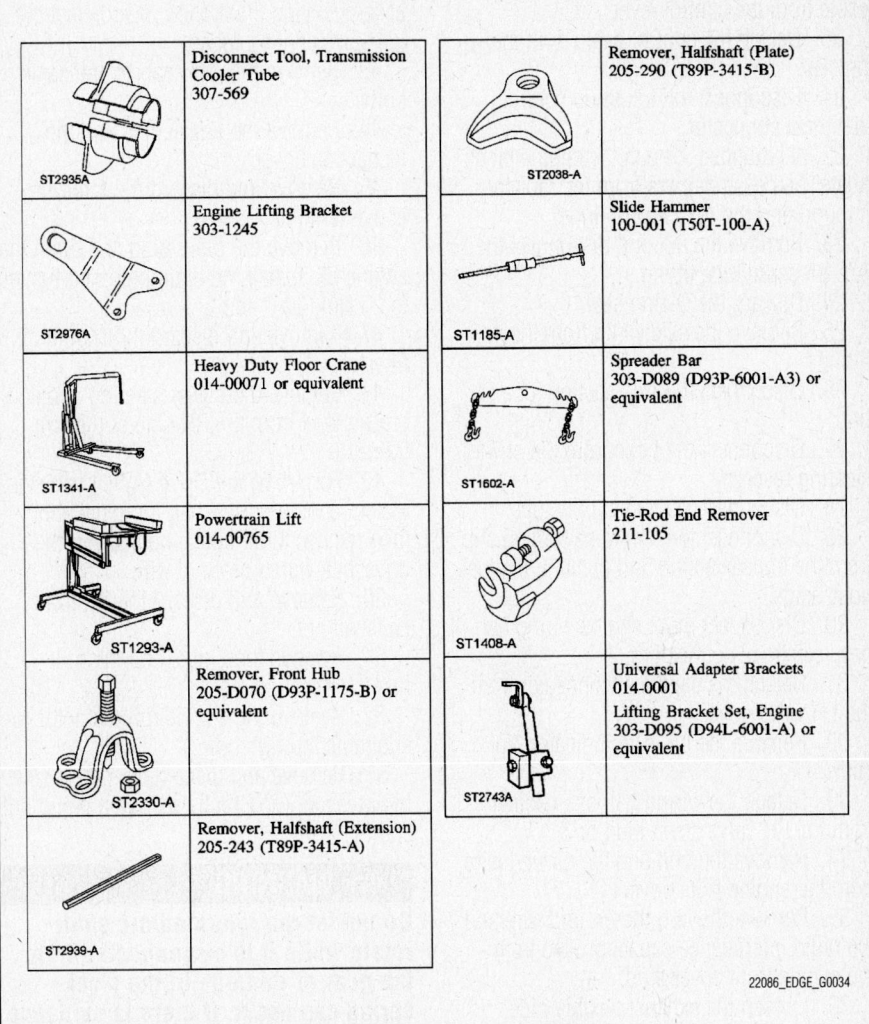

22086_EDGE_G0034

Fig. 199 Special tools needed for engine removal and installation

※※ CAUTION

NEVER smoke or carry lighted tobacco or open flame of any type when working on or near any fuel-related components. Highly flammable mixtures are always present and may be ignited. Failure to follow these instructions may result in personal injury or death.

1. Raise and safely support the vehicle..
2. Recover the air conditioning system.
3. Release the fuel system pressure, as outlined in the Fuel System Section..
4. Disconnect the negative, then the positive battery cables.
5. Drain the engine cooling system.
6. Remove the accessory drive belt and the power steering belt, as outlined in this section.
7. Disconnect the power steering cooler hose and drain the power steering fluid into a suitable drain pan.
8. Remove the degas bottle.
9. Remove the engine air cleaner and air cleaner outlet pipe.
10. Remove the battery and the battery tray.
11. Disconnect the battery harness electrical connector.
12. Remove the nut and disconnect the power feed from the battery terminal.
13. Remove the bolt and the ground wire.
14. Detach the 2 wiring harness retainers from the cowl.
15. Disconnect the vacuum hose from the upper intake manifold.
16. Disconnect the upper Evaporative Emissions (EVAP) tube quick connect coupling from the purge valve.
17. Disconnect the upper radiator hose, lower radiator hose and 2 heater hoses from the thermostat housing.
18. Detach the wiring harness retainer from the transaxle control cable bracket.

19. Disconnect the transaxle control cable from the control lever.

20. Detach the control cable from the bracket.

21. Disconnect the transaxle control electrical connector.

22. If equipped, detach the engine block heater harness retainers from the radiator support and the A/C suction tube.

23. Remove the nut and disconnect the A/C pressure tube fitting.

24. Discard the O-ring seal.

25. Remove the safety clip from the A/C fitting.

26. Disconnect the A/C suction tube fitting.

27. Disconnect the hose from the power steering reservoir.

28. Disconnect the fuel supply tube.

29. Disconnect the fuel hose routing clip from the transaxle stud and position the fuel hose aside.

30. Disconnect the 2 engine wiring harness electrical connectors.

31. Detach the electrical connector from the LH valve cover.

32. Remove the oil level indicator dipstick.

33. Detach the wiring harness retainer from the RH valve cover stud bolt.

34. Remove the bolt and the ground wire from the engine front cover.

35. Remove the nut, the ground wire and the radio interference capacitor wire from the engine front cover stud.

36. Loosen the exhaust flexible pipe clamp and disconnect the 2 exhaust hangers.

37. Remove the 4 nuts and the exhaust flexible pipe and Y-pipe as an assembly.

38. Discard the nuts and the gasket.

39. Remove the 3 pin-type retainers, the 7 screws and the radiator splash shield.

40. Remove the LH inner splash shield.

41. Remove the 2 secondary latches from the transmission fluid cooler tubes.

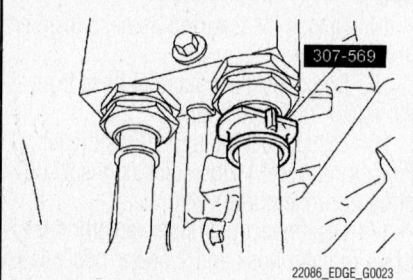

Fig. 200 Using the special tool shown, disconnect the transaxle cooling tubes

42. Using the special tool shown in the accompanying illustration, disconnect the transaxle cooling tubes.

43. Remove the 4 oil pan-to-transaxle bolts.

44. Remove the 2 fasteners and the inspection cover.

45. Remove and discard the 3 torque converter bolts.

46. Remove the drain plug and drain the engine oil. Install the drain plug and tighten to 27 Nm (20 ft. lbs.).

47. Remove and discard the engine oil filter.

48. Remove the power steering cooler bracket bolt from the RH side of the subframe.

49. For All Wheel Drive (AWD) vehicles, match mark the driveshaft for installation, then remove the 4 bolts and support the driveshaft with a piece of wire.

50. Remove and discard the RH front halfshaft nut.

51. Remove the 2 nuts and the roll restrictor heat shield.

52. Remove the engine roll restrictor-to-subframe through bolt.

53. Remove and discard the power steering pressure (PSP) tube-to-pump banjo bolt and the 2 seals.

✶✶ WARNING

Do not let the intermediate shaft rotate while it is disconnected from the gear or damage to the clockspring can occur. If there is evidence that the intermediate shaft has rotated, the clockspring must be removed and recentered, as outlined in the Chassis Electrical Section.

54. Remove and discard the steering intermediate shaft bolt.

55. Separate the steering intermediate shaft from the steering gear.

56. Remove and discard the cotter pins and tie-rod end nuts.

57. Using a suitable puller, separate the tie-rod ends from the wheel knuckles.

58. Remove the 2 stabilizer link-to-lower control arm nuts and separate the stabilizer bar links from the lower control arms.

59. Remove the lower control arm-to-knuckle pinch bolts and separate the lower control arms from the knuckles.

60. Remove the 3 RH subframe-to-lower bumper nuts.

61. Remove the 3 LH subframe-to-lower bumper nuts and separate the lower bumper from the subframe.

62. Position the special tool under the subframe assembly.

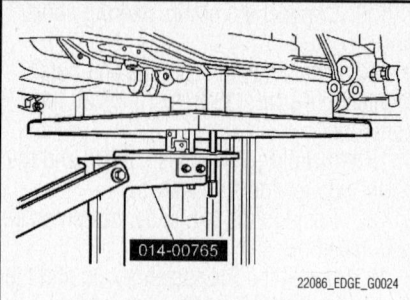

Fig. 201 Position the special tool under the subframe assembly

63. Remove the 2 nuts, 4 bolts and the subframe support brackets.

64. Remove the 2 front subframe nuts.

65. Remove the 2 middle subframe nuts.

66. Using the special tool, lower the subframe assembly from the vehicle.

67. If equipped, disconnect the oil cooler coolant hoses.

Fig. 202 Remove the 2 nuts, 4 bolts and the subframe support brackets

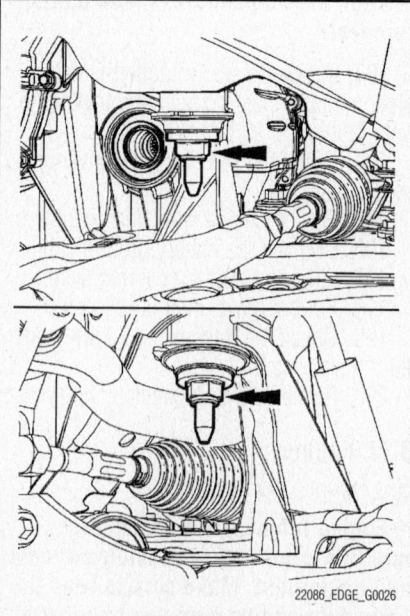

Fig. 203 Remove the 2 middle subframe nuts

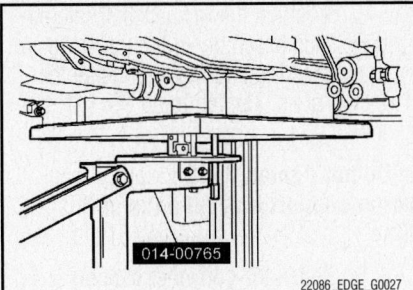

Fig. 204 Using the special tool, lower the subframe assembly from the vehicle

68. Using the special tools, or their equivalents, separate the LH halfshaft from the transaxle and support the halfshaft with a piece of wire.

69. Remove the 2 RH catalytic converter support bracket bolts.

70. Using a suitable puller, separate the RH halfshaft from the hub.

71. For Front wheel drive (FWD) vehicles, perform the following:

a. Remove the bolt, the nut and the RH catalytic converter support bracket.

b. Remove the 2 stud bolts and the RH halfshaft/intermediate shaft assembly.

72. For AWD vehicles, perform the following:

a. Remove the 2 RH halfshaft bearing support bracket bolts and the RH halfshaft/intermediate shaft assembly.

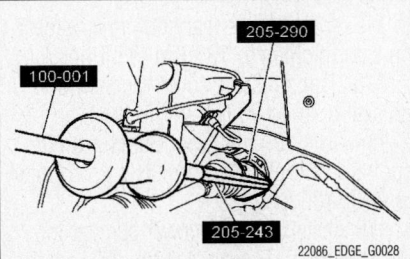

Fig. 205 Using the special tools, separate the LH halfshaft from the transaxle and support the halfshaft with a piece of wire

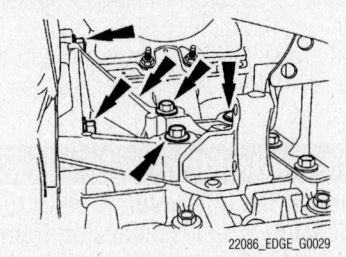

Fig. 206 Remove the 5 bolts and the Power Transfer Unit (PTU) support bracket—AWD models

b. Disconnect the RH catalyst monitor electrical connector.

c. Remove the 4 nuts and the RH catalytic converter.

d. Discard the gasket and the nuts.

e. Remove the 5 bolts and the Power Transfer Unit (PTU) support bracket.

f. Remove the 5 bolts and the PTU.

73. Position a block of wood under the transaxle. Install the special tools, or their equivalents, as shown in the accompanying illustration.

74. Remove the transaxle support insulator through bolt and nut.

75. Remove the 3 nuts, the bolt and the transaxle support insulator bracket.

76. Remove the nut, bolt and engine mount brace.

77. Remove the 4 engine mount nuts.

78. Remove the 3 bolts and the engine mount.

79. Lower the engine and transaxle assembly from the vehicle.

80. Position the starter cable boot back and remove the 2 nuts.

81. Detach the 2 wire terminals from the starter.

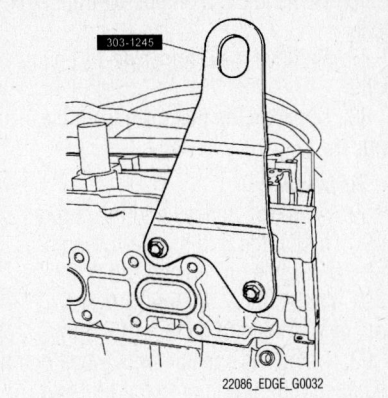

Fig. 208 Install the special tool on the LH cylinder head

82. Disconnect the wiring harness retainer from the starter motor stud bolt.

83. Remove the bolt, stud bolt and the starter.

84. Install the special tool on the LH cylinder head.

85. Using the special tools and a suitable engine crane, remove the engine and transaxle from the lift table.

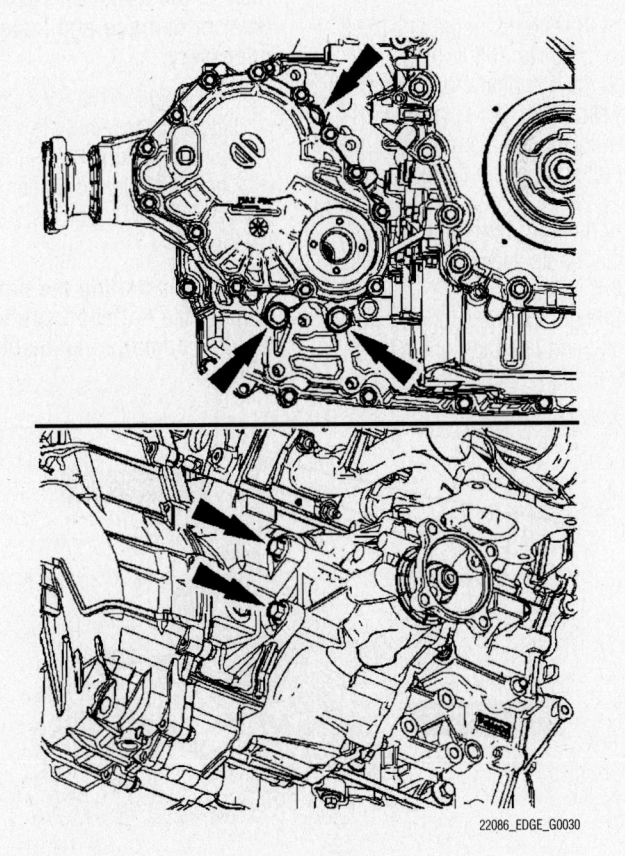

Fig. 207 Remove the 5 bolts and the PTU—AWD models

86. Remove the 2 engine-to-transaxle bolts.

87. Remove the 5 transaxle-to-engine bolts.

88. Separate the transaxle from the engine.

To install:

89. Align the transaxle to the engine.

90. Install the 5 transaxle-to-engine bolts and tighten to 48 Nm (35 ft. lbs.).

91. Install the 2 engine-to-transaxle bolts and tighten to 48 Nm (35 ft. lbs.).

92. Using the special tools, position the engine and transaxle onto the lift table.

93. Position a block of wood under the transaxle. Install the special tools, as shown.

94. Install the starter, the bolt and the stud bolt. Tighten to 27 Nm (20 ft. lbs.).

95. Connect the wiring harness retainer to the starter stud bolt.

96. Attach the starter motor wire terminals and install the 2 nuts. Tighten as follows:

    a. Tighten to 12 Nm (9 ft. lbs.).

    b. Tighten to 5 Nm (44 inch lbs.).

97. Position the starter terminal boot over the starter terminal.

98. Raise the engine and transaxle assembly into the vehicle.

99. Install the engine mount and the 3 bolts. Tighten to 90 Nm (66 ft. lbs.).

100. Install the 4 engine mount nuts and tighten to 63 Nm (46 ft. lbs.).

101. Install the engine mount brace, the nut and the bolt and tighten to 20 Nm (15 ft. lbs.).

102. Install the transaxle support insulator bracket, the 3 nuts and the bolt. Tighten to 63 Nm (46 ft. lbs.).

103. Install the transaxle support insulator through bolt and nut and tighten to 175 Nm (129 ft. lbs.).

104. For AWD vehicles, perform the following:

    a. Position the Power Transfer Unit (PTU) in place and install the 5 bolts. Tighten to 90 Nm (66 ft. lbs.).

    b. Position the PTU support bracket in place and install the 5 bolts. Tighten to 70 Nm (52 ft. lbs.).

➡**Do not tighten the 4 catalytic converter nuts at this time.**

    c. Using a new gasket, install the RH catalytic converter and 4 new nuts.

    d. Install the 2 catalytic converter-to-bracket bolts.

    e. Tighten the 4 catalytic converter nuts to 40 Nm (30 ft. lbs.).

    f. Tighten the 2 catalytic converter-to-bracket bolts to 20 Nm (15 ft. lbs.).

    g. Connect the RH catalyst monitor electrical connector.

❋❋ WARNING

A new PTU seal must be installed whenever the intermediate shaft is removed.

    h. Install a new PTU seal.

➡**Before installing the halfshaft, inspect the halfshaft sealing surface for wear or damage and install new, if necessary.**

    i. Position the RH halfshaft/intermediate shaft assembly in the PTU and in the steering knuckle and install the 2 bolts. Tighten to 40 Nm (30 ft. lbs.).

105. For FWD vehicles, perform the following:

➡**Before installing the halfshaft, inspect the halfshaft sealing surface for wear or damage and install new if necessary.**

    j. Position the RH halfshaft/intermediate shaft assembly in the transaxle and in the steering knuckle and install the 2 stud bolts. Tighten to 55 Nm (41 ft. lbs.).

➡**Do not tighten the 2 catalytic converter support bracket bolts at this time.**

    k. Install the converter support bracket and the 2 bolts.

    l. Install the catalytic converter bracket bolt and the nut. Tighten the nut to 40 Nm (30 ft. lbs.) and the bolt to 55 Nm (41 ft. lbs.).

    m. Tighten the 2 RH catalytic converter support bracket bolts to 20 Nm (15 ft. lbs.).

➡**Prior to installation of the halfshaft, inspect the halfshaft sealing surface for wear or damage and install new, if necessary.**

106. Install the LH halfshaft into the transaxle.

107. If equipped, connect the oil cooler coolant hoses.

108. Using the special tool, raise the subframe into the installed position.

109. Install the 2 middle subframe nuts and tighten to 133 Nm (98 ft. lbs.).

110. Install the 2 front subframe nuts and tighten to 133 Nm (98 ft. lbs.).

111. Position the subframe support brackets in place and loosely install the 4 bolts.

112. Install the 2 rear subframe bracket nuts and tighten to 133 Nm (98 ft. lbs.).

113. Tighten the 4 subframe support bracket bolts to 90 Nm (66 ft. lbs.).

114. Position the lower bumper on the subframe and install the 3 LH nuts. Tighten to 9 Nm (80 inch lbs.).

115. Install the 3 RH lower bumper-to-subframe nuts. Tighten to 9 Nm (80 inch lbs.).

116. Install the ball joints in the steering knuckles and install the pinch bolts. Tighten to 55 Nm (41 ft. lbs.).

117. Position the stabilizer bar links in the lower control arms and install the nuts. Tighten to 90 Nm (66 ft. lbs.).

118. Install the tie-rod ends and nuts and tighten to 48 Nm (35 ft. lbs.). Install new cotter pins.

❋❋ WARNING

Do not let the intermediate shaft to rotate while it is disconnected from the gear or damage to the clock-spring can occur. If there is evidence that the intermediate shaft has rotated, the clockspring must be

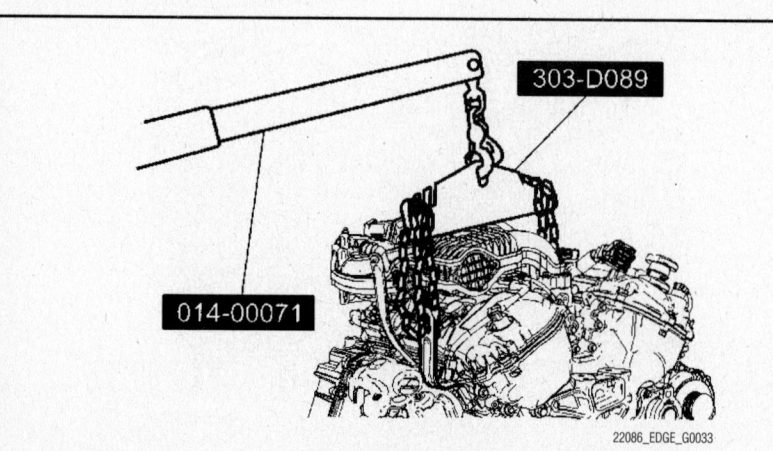

Fig. 209 Using the special tools and a suitable engine crane, remove the engine and transaxle from the lift table

removed and recentered, as outlined in the Chassis Electrical Section.

119. Install the intermediate shaft onto the steering gear and install a new bolt. Tighten to 23 Nm (17 ft. lbs.).

120. Using a new banjo bolt and 2 new seals, install the PSP tube. Tighten to 48 Nm (35 ft. lbs.).

121. Install the engine roll restrictor-to-subframe through bolt and tighten to 103 Nm (76 ft. lbs.).

122. Install the roll restrictor heat shield and the 2 nuts and tighten to 11 Nm (8 ft. lbs.).

➡**Apply the brake to keep the halfshaft from rotating.**

123. Install a new RH front halfshaft nut and tighten to 350 Nm (258 ft. lbs.).

124. For AWD vehicles, align the match-marks on the rear driveshaft to the index marks on the PTU flange made during removal and install the 4 bolts. Tighten the bolts to 70 Nm (52 ft. lbs.).

125. Install the power steering cooler bracket bolt to the RH side of the subframe. Tighten to 9 Nm (80 inch lbs.).

126. Connect the power steering cooler hose.

➡**Lubricate the engine oil filter gasket with clean engine oil before installing the oil filter.**

127. Install a new engine oil filter. Tighten to 5 Nm (44 inch lbs.) and then rotate an additional 180 degrees.

128. Install the 3 new torque converter bolts and tighten to 55 Nm (41 ft. lbs.).

129. Install the inspection cover and the 2 fasteners.

130. Install the 4 oil pan-to-transaxle bolts and tighten to 48 Nm (35 ft. lbs.).

131. Connect the 2 transmission fluid cooler tubes.

132. Install the 2 secondary latches onto the transmission fluid cooler tubes.

133. Install the LH inner splash shield.

134. Install the radiator splash shield, the 3 pin-type retainers and the 7 screws.

135. Using a new gasket, install the Y-pipe and exhaust flexible pipe assembly and 4 new nuts. Tighten to 40 Nm (30 ft. lbs.).

136. Install the 2 exhaust hangers and tighten the exhaust clamp. Tighten to 40 Nm (30 ft. lbs.).

137. Install the ground wire, the radio interference capacitor wire and the nut to the engine front cover stud. Tighten to 10 Nm (89 inch lbs.).

138. Install the ground wire and bolt to the engine front cover. Tighten to 10 Nm (89 inch lbs.).

139. Attach the wiring harness retainer to the RH valve cover stud bolt.

140. Install the oil level indicator.

141. Connect the 2 engine wiring harness electrical connectors.

142. Attach the electrical connector to the LH valve cover.

143. Connect the fuel hose routing clip to the transaxle stud.

144. Connect the fuel supply tube.

145. Connect the hose to the power steering reservoir.

146. Connect the A/C suction tube fitting. Install the safety clip onto the A/C fitting.

147. Using a new O-ring seal, connect the A/C tube fitting and install the nut. Tighten to 8 Nm (71 inch lbs.).

If equipped, attach the engine block heater harness retainers to the radiator support and the A/C suction tube.

148. Connect the transaxle control electrical connector.

149. Attach the control cable to the bracket.

150. Connect the transaxle control cable to the control lever.

151. Attach the wiring harness retainer to the transaxle control cable bracket.

152. Connect the upper radiator hose, lower radiator hose and 2 heater hoses to the thermostat housing.

153. Connect the upper EVAP tube quick connect coupling to the purge valve.

154. Connect the vacuum hose to the upper intake manifold.

155. Install the ground wire and the bolt and tighten to 10 Nm (89 inch lbs.).

156. Attach the 2 wiring harness retainers to the cowl.

157. Connect the power feed to the battery terminal and install the nut. Tighten to 8 Nm (71 inch lbs.).

158. Connect the battery harness electrical connector.

159. Install the battery tray and the battery.

160. Install the engine air cleaner and the air cleaner outlet pipe.

161. Install the degas bottle.

162. Install the accessory drive belt and the power steering belt, as outlined in this section.

163. Connect the positive, then the negative battery cables.

164. Fill the engine with clean engine oil.

165. Fill and bleed the cooling system.

166. Fill the power steering system.

167. Recharge the air conditioning system.

EXHAUST MANIFOLD

REMOVAL & INSTALLATION

2.3L Engine

See Figure 210.

1. Raise and safely support the vehicle.

2. Remove the generator air inlet duct.

3. Remove the Heated Oxygen Sensor (HO2S) and Catalyst Monitor Sensor (CMS).

4. Remove the wiring harness bracket from the valve cover stud and position it aside.

5. Remove the 2 catalytic converter manifold-to-exhaust flexible pipe nuts.

6. Discard the gasket and the 2 nuts.

7. Remove the 6 heat shield bolts and the heat shield.

8. Remove the 2 catalytic converter manifold shield bracket bolts and the bracket.

9. Loosen the 2 catalytic converter manifold bracket bolts.

10. Remove the 7 nuts and the catalytic converter manifold.

11. Discard the 7 nuts and the gasket.

12. Remove and discard the 7 catalytic converter manifold studs.

13. Clean and inspect the catalytic converter manifold.

To install:

14. Install the 7 new catalytic converter manifold studs. Tighten to 17 Nm (13 ft. lbs.).

15. Position a new catalytic converter manifold gasket on the studs.

❊❊ **WARNING**

Failure to tighten the catalytic converter manifold nuts to specification before installing the converter bracket bolts will cause the converter to develop an exhaust leak.

❊❊ **WARNING**

Failure to tighten the catalytic converter manifold nuts to specification a second time will cause the converter to develop an exhaust leak.

➡**Make sure to tighten the nuts in the sequence shown in 2 stages.**

16. Position the catalytic converter manifold and tighten the 7 new nuts in the sequence shown, in 2 stages:

a. Stage 1: Tighten to 55 Nm (41 ft. lbs.).

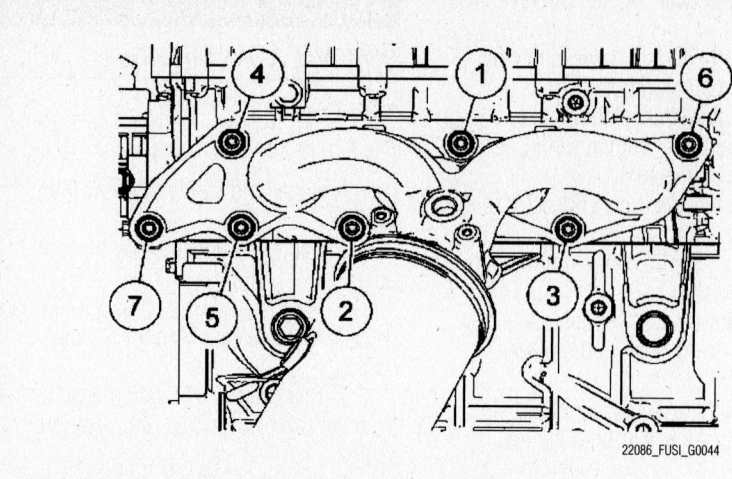

Fig. 210 Catalytic converter manifold tightening sequence—2.3L engine

b. Stage 2: Tighten to 55 Nm (41 ft. lbs.).

17. Install the 2 catalytic converter manifold shield bracket bolts and the bracket. Tighten to 20 Nm (15 ft. lbs.).

18. Tighten the 2 catalytic converter manifold bracket bolts. Tighten to 20 Nm (15 ft. lbs.).

19. Position the heat shield and install the 6 heat shield bolts. Tighten to 10 Nm (89 lb-in).

20. Install the 2 catalytic converter manifold-to-exhaust flexible pipe nuts. Install a new gasket. Tighten to 40 Nm (30 ft. lbs.).

21. Position the wiring harness bracket on the stud.

22. Install the HO2S and CMS.

23. Install the generator air inlet duct

3.0L Engine

Left Side

See Figure 211.

1. Raise and safely support the vehicle.

2. Remove and discard the oil filter.

3. Remove the oil level indicator and tube.

4. Remove the Heated Oxygen Sensor (HO2S) and the Catalyst Monitor Sensor (CMS).

5. Remove the 2 LH catalytic converter-to-exhaust flexible pipe nuts. Discard the gasket and the 2 nuts.

6. Remove the 4 bolts and the LH catalytic converter manifold shield.

7. Remove the 2 LH catalytic converter manifold shield bracket bolts and the shield bracket.

8. Loosen the 2 LH catalytic converter manifold bracket bolts.

9. Remove the 6 nuts and the LH catalytic converter manifold.

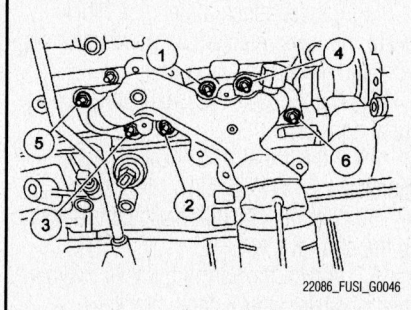

Fig. 211 Left side catalytic converter manifold bolt tightening sequence—3.0L engine

10. Discard the 6 LH catalytic converter manifold nuts and the gasket.

11. Remove and discard the 6 LH catalytic converter manifold studs.

12. Clean and inspect the manifold.

To install:

13. Install the 6 new LH catalytic converter manifold studs. Tighten to 11 Nm (8 ft. lbs.).

14. Position a new LH catalytic converter manifold gasket on the studs.

15. Position the LH catalytic converter manifold and finger tighten the 6 new nuts.

16. Install a new gasket and the 2 nuts at the LH catalytic converter-to-exhaust flexible pipe. Tighten to 40 Nm (30 ft. lbs.).

✳✳ WARNING

Failure to tighten the catalytic converter manifold nuts to specification before installing the converter bracket bolts will cause the converter to develop an exhaust leak.

✳✳ WARNING

Failure to tighten the catalytic converter manifold nuts to specification a second time will cause the converter to develop an exhaust leak.

➡ **Make sure to tighten the nuts in the sequence shown in 2 stages.**

17. Position the LH catalytic converter manifold and tighten the 6 new nuts in the sequence shown, in 2 stages:
   a. Stage 1: Tighten to 20 Nm (15 ft. lbs.).
   b. Stage 2: Tighten to 20 Nm (15 ft. lbs.).

18. Install the shield bracket and the 2 LH catalytic converter manifold shield bracket bolts. Tighten to 20 Nm (15 ft. lbs.).

19. Tighten the 2 LH catalytic converter manifold bracket bolts. To install, tighten to 20 Nm (15 ft. lbs.).

20. Position the LH catalytic converter manifold shield and install the 4 bolts. Tighten to 10 Nm (89 lb-in).

21. Install the 2 LH catalytic converter-to-exhaust flexible pipe nuts in 3 stages:
   a. Stage 1: Tighten the passenger side nut to 5 Nm (44 lb-in).
   b. Stage 2: Tighten the driver side nut to 40 Nm (30 ft. lbs.).
   c. Stage 3: Tighten the passenger side nut to 40 Nm (30 ft. lbs.).

22. Install the HO2S and the CMS.

23. Install the oil level indicator and tube.

24. Install a new oil filter. Tighten to 5 Nm (44 lb-in) and then rotate an additional 180 degrees.

Right Side—FWD Models

See Figure 212.

1. With the vehicle in NEUTRAL, position it on a hoist.

2. Remove the exhaust flexible pipe.

3. Remove the Exhaust Gas Recirculation (EGR) tube.

4. Disconnect the Heated Oxygen Sensor (HO2S) and Catalyst Monitor Sensor (CMS) electrical connectors.

5. Remove the 2 bolts and the RH catalytic converter manifold shield.

6. Remove the 2 RH catalytic converter manifold shield bracket bolts and the shield bracket.

7. Loosen the 2 RH catalytic converter manifold bracket bolts.

8. Remove the 6 nuts and the RH catalytic converter manifold.

9. Discard the 6 RH catalytic converter manifold nuts and gasket.

10. Remove the 6 RH catalytic converter manifold studs and discard.

➡**If installing a new RH catalytic converter manifold, remove and save the HO2S and CMS for installation in the new RH catalytic converter manifold.**

11. Using special tool 303-476, or equivalent, remove the RH catalytic converter manifold HO2S and CMS.

12. Clean and inspect the manifold.

To install:

➡**Apply anti-seize lubricant to the threads of the HO2S and CMS before installation.**

13. If installing a new RH catalytic converter manifold, install the HO2S and CMS using the special tool. Tighten to 47 Nm (35 ft. lbs.).

14. Install the 6 new RH catalytic converter manifold studs. Tighten to 11 Nm (8 ft. lbs.).

15. Position a new RH catalytic converter manifold gasket on the studs.

❋❋ WARNING

Failure to tighten the catalytic converter nuts to specification before installing the converter bracket bolts will cause the converter to develop an exhaust leak.

❋❋ WARNING

Failure to tighten the catalytic converter nuts to specification a second time will cause the converter to develop an exhaust leak.

➡**Make sure to tighten the nuts in the sequence shown in 2 stages.**

16. Position the RH catalytic converter manifold and tighten the 6 new nuts in the sequence shown, in 2 stages:

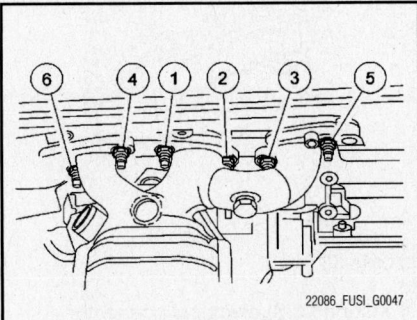

Fig. 212 Right side catalytic converter manifold bolt tightening sequence—3.0L engine, FWD models

   a. Stage 1: Tighten to 20 Nm (15 ft. lbs.).
   b. Stage 2: Tighten to 20 Nm (15 ft. lbs.).

17. Install the shield bracket and the 2 RH catalytic converter manifold shield bracket bolts. Tighten to 20 Nm (15 ft. lbs.).

18. Tighten the 2 RH catalytic converter manifold bracket bolts. Tighten to 20 Nm (15 ft. lbs.).

19. Position the RH catalytic converter manifold shield and install the 2 bolts. Tighten to 10 Nm (89 lb-in).

20. Connect the HO2S and CMS electrical connectors.

21. Install the EGR tube.

22. Install the exhaust flexible pipe

Right Side—AWD Models

See Figure 213.

1. Raise and safely support the vehicle.

2. Remove the Exhaust Gas Recirculation (EGR) tube.

3. Remove the RH catalytic converter.

➡**The heat shield that was unbolted from the exhaust manifold during removal of the RH catalytic converter, cannot be removed from the vehicle until the power steering rack heat shield is removed.**

4. Remove the 2 bolts and the power steering rack heat shield.

5. Remove the catalytic converter heat shield from the vehicle.

6. Remove the 6 nuts and the RH exhaust manifold. Discard the gasket and nuts.

7. Remove and discard the 6 RH catalytic converter studs.

To install:

8. Install 6 new RH catalytic converter studs. Tighten to 12 Nm (9 ft. lbs.).

➡**The catalytic converter heat shield must be positioned up into the engine**

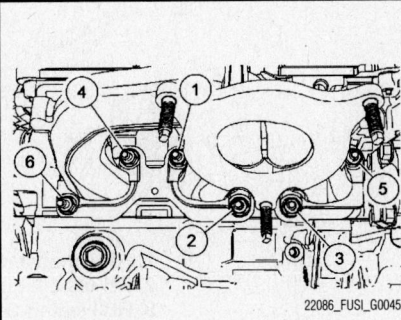

Fig. 213 Right side exhaust manifold tightening sequence—3.0L engine, AWD models

compartment prior to installing the power steering rack heat shield.

9. Position the catalytic converter heat shield into the engine compartment.

10. Install the power steering rack heat shield and the 2 bolts. Tighten to 15 Nm (11 ft. lbs.).

11. Install a new gasket, the RH exhaust manifold and 6 new nuts. Tighten to 20 Nm (15 ft. lbs.) in the sequence shown.

12. Install the RH catalytic converter.

13. Install the EGR tube

3.5L Engine

Left Side

See Figures 214 and 215.

1. Remove the LH catalytic converter, as follows:
   a. Raise and safely support the vehicle.
   b. Disconnect the catalyst monitor sensor electrical connector.
   c. Remove the exhaust Y-pipe.
   d. Remove the 2 catalytic converter support bracket-to-transmission bolts.
   e. Remove the 4 nuts and the LH catalytic converter.
   f. Discard the 4 LH catalytic converter nuts and gasket.

2. Remove the LH Heated Oxygen Sensor (HO2S).

3. Remove the 3 bolts and the LH exhaust manifold heat shield.

4. Remove the 6 nuts and the LH exhaust manifold. Discard the nuts and gasket.

5. Clean and inspect the LH exhaust manifold.

6. Remove and discard the 6 LH exhaust manifold studs.

❋❋ WARNING

Do not use metal scrapers, wire brushes, power abrasive discs or other abrasive means to clean the sealing surfaces. These may cause scratches and gouges resulting in leak paths. Use a plastic scraper to clean the sealing surfaces.

7. Clean the exhaust manifold mating surface of the cylinder head with metal surface prep. Follow the directions on the packaging.

To install:

8. Install 6 new LH exhaust manifold studs and tighten to 12 Nm (9 ft. lbs.).

9. Using a new gasket, install the LH exhaust manifold and 6 new nuts. Tighten in the sequence shown to 20 Nm (15 ft. lbs.).

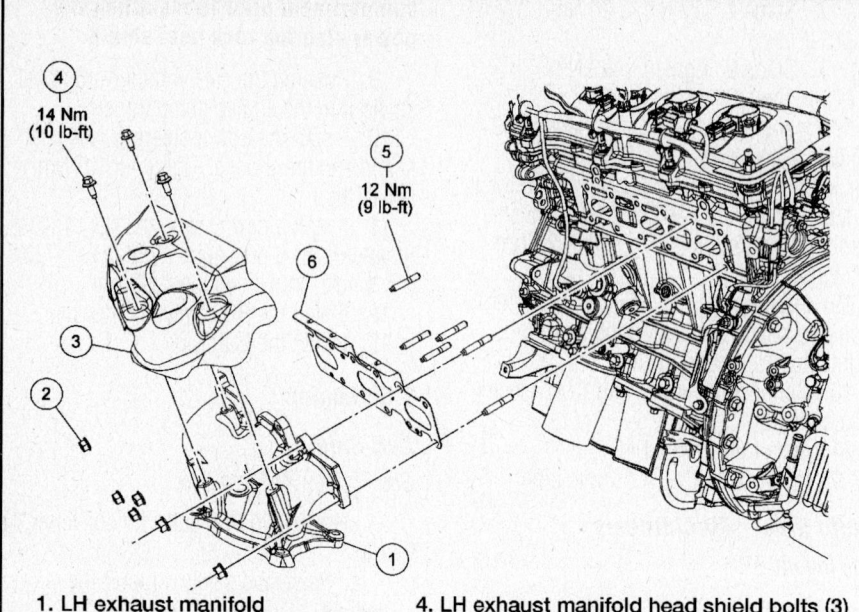

4 14 Nm (10 lb-ft)

5 12 Nm (9 lb-ft)

1. LH exhaust manifold
2. LH exhaust manifold nuts (6)
3. LH exhaust manifold heat shield
4. LH exhaust manifold head shield bolts (3)
5. LH exhaust manifold studs (6)
6. LH exhaust manifold gasket

22086_EDGE_G0050

Fig. 214 Exploded view of the left side exhaust manifold and related components

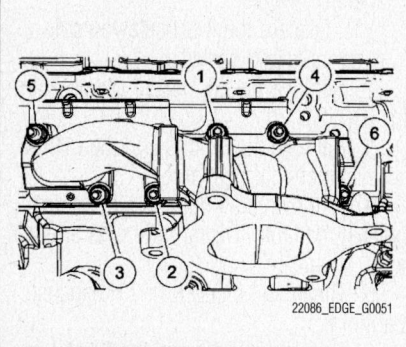

22086_EDGE_G0051

Fig. 215 Exhaust manifold tightening sequence—left side

10. Install the LH exhaust manifold heat shield and the 3 bolts and tighten to 14 Nm (10 ft. lbs.).

11. Install the LH HO2S.

➡ **When installing the catalytic converter, always install new fasteners and gaskets. Clean the flange faces prior to new gasket installation to ensure proper sealing.**

12. Install the LH catalytic converter, with new gaskets and nuts, in the reverse of the removal procedure. Tighten the retainers as follows:

  a. Catalytic converter nuts: 40 Nm (30 ft. lbs.)

  b. Catalytic converter support bracket-to-transmission bolts: 48 Nm (35 ft. lbs.)

Right Side

See Figures 216 and 217.

1. Remove the right side catalytic converter, as follows:

  a. Raise and safely support the vehicle.

  b. Remove the catalyst monitor sensor.

  c. Remove the exhaust Y-pipe.

  d. For All Wheel Drive (AWD) models,

Remove and discard the 4 universal joint (U-joint) flange bolts and separate the front driveshaft and secure it with a piece of wire.

  e. For AWD models, remove the RH halfshaft assembly. Remove the 2 catalytic converter support bracket-to-engine block bolts.

  f. For Front Wheel Drive (FWD) models, remove the 2 bolts and the power steering rack shield.

  g. For FWD models, remove the catalytic converter support bracket-to-engine block bolt and nut.

  h. Remove the 2 nuts and the roll restrictor shield.

  i. Remove the roll restrictor bolt and rotate the engine forward.

  j. Remove the 2 bracket-to-RH catalytic converter bolts.

  k. Remove the 4 nuts and the RH catalytic converter.

  l. Discard the 4 RH catalytic converter nuts and gasket.

2. Disconnect the RH Heated Oxygen Sensor (HO2S) electrical connector.

3. Remove the 6 nuts and the RH exhaust manifold. Discard the nuts and gasket.

4. Clean and inspect the RH exhaust manifold.

5. Remove and discard the 6 RH exhaust manifold studs.

※※ **WARNING**

NEVER use metal scrapers, wire brushes, power abrasive discs or

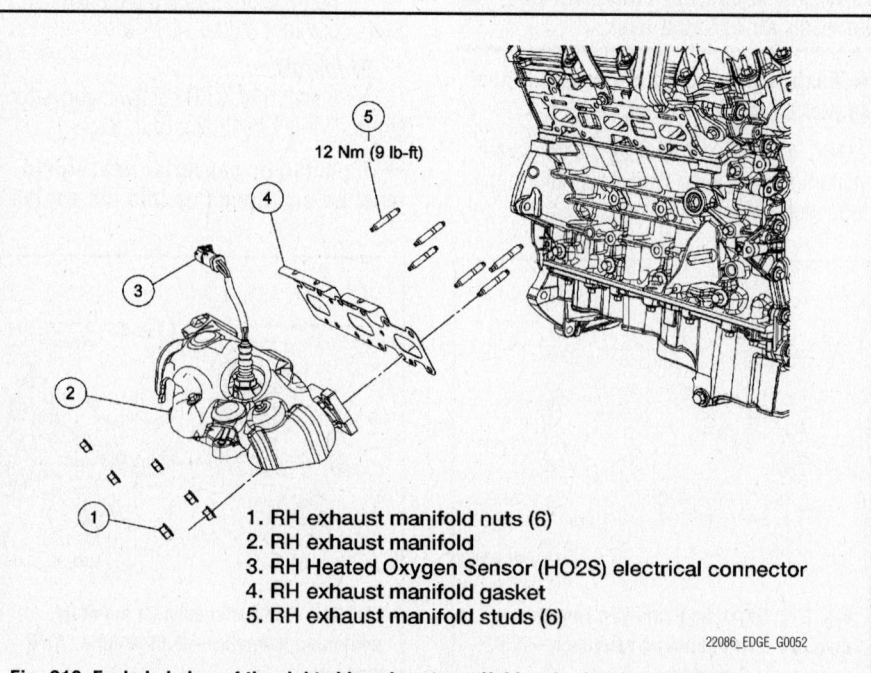

5 12 Nm (9 lb-ft)

1. RH exhaust manifold nuts (6)
2. RH exhaust manifold
3. RH Heated Oxygen Sensor (HO2S) electrical connector
4. RH exhaust manifold gasket
5. RH exhaust manifold studs (6)

22086_EDGE_G0052

Fig. 216 Exploded view of the right side exhaust manifold and related components

other abrasive means to clean the sealing surfaces. These may cause scratches and gouges resulting in leak paths. Use a plastic scraper to clean the sealing surfaces.

6. Clean the exhaust manifold mating surface of the cylinder head with metal surface prep. Follow the directions on the packaging.

To install:

7. Install 6 new RH exhaust manifold studs and tighten to 12 Nm (9 ft. lbs.).

8. Using a new gasket, install the RH exhaust manifold and 6 new nuts. Tighten in the sequence shown to 20 Nm (15 ft. lbs.).

9. Connect the RH HO2S electrical connector.

➡**When installing the catalytic converter, always install new fasteners and gaskets. Clean the flange faces prior to new gasket installation to ensure proper sealing.**

10. Install the right side catalytic converter, with new gaskets and nuts, in the reverse of the removal procedure. Tighten the retainers as follows:

  a. Catalytic converter nuts: 40 Nm (30 ft. lbs.)

  b. Bracket-to-RH catalytic converter bolts: 20 Nm (15 ft. lbs.)

  c. Roll restrictor bolt: 90 Nm (66 ft. lbs.)

  d. Roll restrictor shield: 8 ft. lbs. (11 Nm)

  e. Catalytic converter support bracket-to-engine block bolt and nut (FWD models): 40 Nm (30 ft. lbs.)

  f. Power steering rack shield (FWD models): 15 Nm (11 ft. lbs.)

  g. Catalytic converter support bracket-to-engine block bolts (AWD models): 40 Nm (30 ft. lbs.)

  h. U-joint flange bolts (AWD models): 70 Nm (52 ft. lbs.)

INTAKE MANIFOLD

REMOVAL & INSTALLATION

2.3L Engine

See Figure 218.

1. Raise and safely support the vehicle.
2. Disconnect the battery ground cable.
3. Remove the air cleaner outlet pipe.
4. Remove the bolt, 2 nuts and the generator air inlet duct.

  a. To install, tighten to 6 Nm (53 lb-in).

5. Depress the locking ring and disconnect the brake booster vacuum supply tube from the intake manifold.
6. Disconnect the evaporative emissions (EVAP) tube from the intake manifold.
7. Disconnect the 2 swirl control valve electrical connectors.
8. Detach the 2 wiring harness pin-type retainers and remove the fuel rail insulator.
9. Detach the electrical connector pin-type retainer.
10. If equipped, remove the 7 screws and the underbody cover.
11. On vehicles equipped with manual transaxle:

  a. Remove the 2 bolts and position the clutch slave cylinder aside.

  b. To install, tighten to 22 Nm (16 ft. lbs.).

12. On vehicles with secondary air injection (AIR):

  a. Disconnect the AIR pump electrical connector.

  b. Remove the 3 bolts and position the AIR pump aside.

  c. To install, tighten to 30 Nm (22 ft. lbs.).

  d. Disconnect the vacuum hose from the intake manifold.

13. Detach the radiator hose retaining clip from the intake manifold.
14. Remove the intake manifold lower bolt.

  a. To install, tighten to 18 Nm (13 ft. lbs.).

15. Disconnect the Manifold Absolute Pressure (MAP) sensor electrical connector.
16. Disconnect the Intake Manifold Runner Control (IMRC) actuator electrical connector.
17. Disconnect the oil pressure sender electrical connector.
18. Detach the wiring harness pin-type retainer and position the wiring harness aside.
19. Remove the nut and the S-terminal wire from the starter.

  a. To install, tighten to 12 Nm (9 ft. lbs.).

20. Disconnect the throttle body electrical connector.

➡**Discard the throttle body gasket.**

21. Remove the 4 bolts and position the throttle body aside.

  a. To install, tighten to 10 Nm (89 lb-in).

22. Detach the 2 pin-type retainers from the intake manifold.

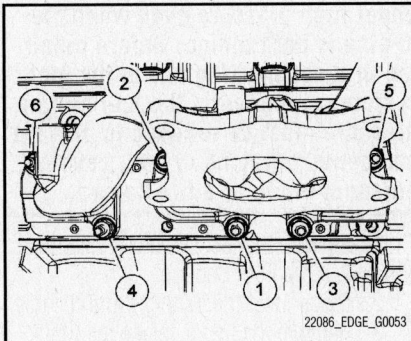

Fig. 217 Exhaust manifold tightening sequence—right side

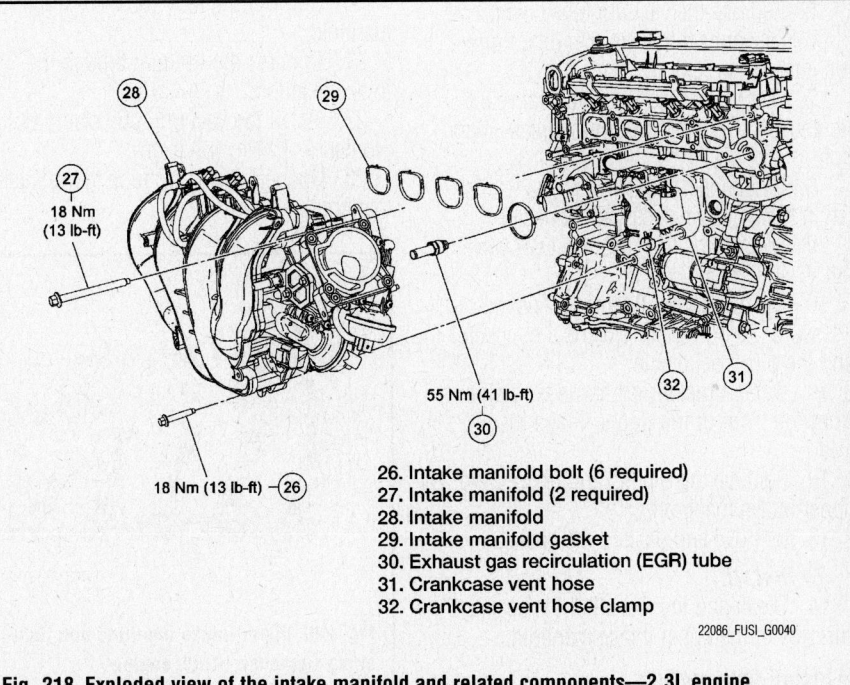

26. Intake manifold bolt (6 required)
27. Intake manifold (2 required)
28. Intake manifold
29. Intake manifold gasket
30. Exhaust gas recirculation (EGR) tube
31. Crankcase vent hose
32. Crankcase vent hose clamp

Fig. 218 Exploded view of the intake manifold and related components—2.3L engine

➡There are 2 different size bolts used. Mark the location of the bolts to make sure they are installed in their original locations.

23. Remove the 7 bolts and position the intake manifold aside to access the crankcase vent hose clamp and the EGR tube.

   a. To install, tighten to 18 Nm (13 ft. lbs.).

24. Release the clamp and disconnect the crankcase vent hose.

25. Detach the knock sensor (KS) electrical connector pin-type retainer.

26. Remove the exhaust gas recirculation (EGR) tube.

   a. To install, tighten to 55 Nm (41 ft. lbs.).

27. Remove the intake manifold and discard the gaskets.

   a. To install, tighten to 18 Nm (13 ft. lbs.).

28. To install, reverse the removal procedure. Install new throttle body and intake manifold gaskets

3.0L Engine

Upper Intake Manifold

See Figures 219 and 220.

1. Remove the air cleaner outlet pipe.
2. Disconnect the throttle body electrical connector.
3. Remove the 4 bolts and position the throttle body aside. Discard the gasket.
4. Disconnect the Evaporative emissions (EVAP) tube from the intake manifold.
5. Remove the vacuum tube clamp bolt.
6. Disconnect the vacuum tube from the intake manifold.
7. Disconnect the Positive Crankcase Ventilation (PCV) tube from the intake manifold.
8. Disconnect the Exhaust Gas Recirculation (EGR) valve electrical connector.
9. Loosen the EGR tube-to-EGR valve nut.
10. Disconnect the Manifold Absolute Pressure (MAP) sensor electrical connector and the pin-type retainer.
11. Detach the wiring harness retainer from the front of the upper intake manifold.
12. Remove the 8 bolts and remove the upper intake manifold.
13. Remove and discard the gaskets.

To install:

14. Clean and inspect all of the sealing surfaces of the upper intake manifold.

➡Install new gaskets.

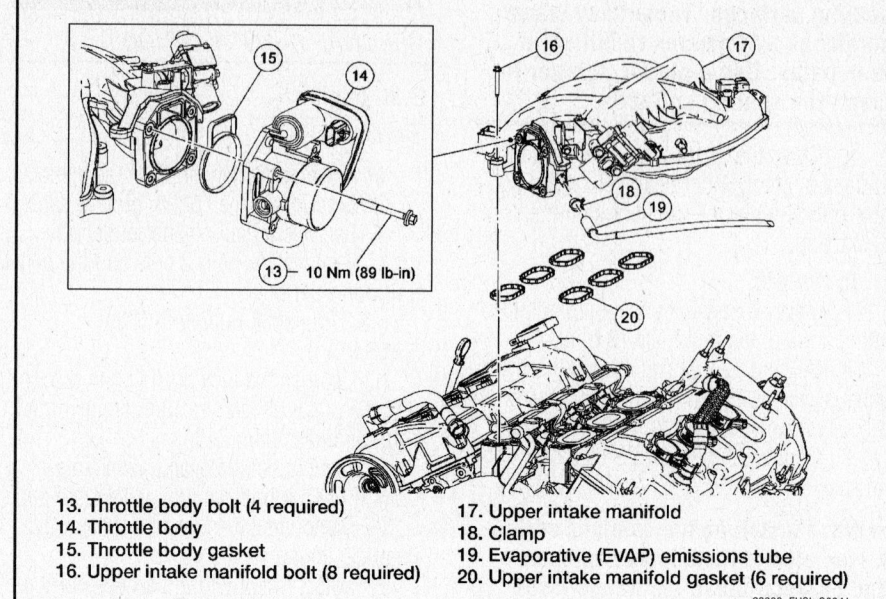

13. Throttle body bolt (4 required)
14. Throttle body
15. Throttle body gasket
16. Upper intake manifold bolt (8 required)
17. Upper intake manifold
18. Clamp
19. Evaporative (EVAP) emissions tube
20. Upper intake manifold gasket (6 required)

22086_FUSI_G0041

Fig. 219 Exploded view of the upper intake manifold—3.0L engine

15. Install the upper intake manifold, gaskets and the 8 bolts. Tighten in the sequence shown to 10 Nm (89 lb-in).
16. Attach the wiring harness retainer to the front of the upper intake manifold.
17. Connect the MAP sensor electrical connector and the pin-type retainer.
18. Install the EGR tube-to-EGR valve nut. Tighten to 40 Nm (30 ft. lbs.).
19. Connect the EGR valve electrical connector.
20. Connect the PCV tube to the intake manifold.
21. Connect the vacuum tube to the intake manifold.
22. Install the vacuum tube clamp bolt. Tighten to 10 Nm (89 lb-in).
23. Connect the EVAP tube to the intake manifold.

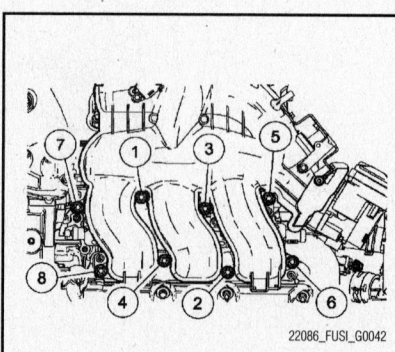

22086_FUSI_G0042

Fig. 220 Upper intake manifold bolt tightening sequence—3.0L engine

24. Install a new gasket. Install the gasket, throttle body and 4 bolts. Tighten to 10 Nm (89 lb-in).
25. Connect the throttle body electrical connector.
26. Install the air cleaner outlet pipe

Lower Intake Manifold

See Figure 221.

✳✳ CAUTION

Do not smoke or carry lighted tobacco or open flame of any type when working on or near any fuel-related component. Highly flammable mixtures are always present and may be ignited, resulting in possible personal injury.

✳✳ CAUTION

Fuel in the fuel system remains under high pressure even when the engine is not running. Before repairing or disconnecting any of the fuel system components, the fuel system pressure must be relieved to prevent accidental spraying of fuel, causing personal injury or a fire hazard.

1. Release the fuel system pressure, as outlined in the Fuel Section.
2. Disconnect the battery ground cable.
3. Remove the upper intake manifold.
4. Disconnect the fuel supply tube quick connect coupling from the fuel rail.

5. Detach the 2 wiring harness retainers from the LH valve cover stud bolts.

6. Detach the 3 pin-type retainers from the fuel rail.

7. Disconnect the 6 fuel injector electrical connectors.

8. Remove the 8 lower intake manifold bolts and the lower intake manifold.

9. Remove and discard the gaskets.

To install:

→Clean and inspect all sealing surfaces. Install new gaskets.

10. Position the lower intake manifold and install the 8 bolts. Tighten in the sequence shown to 10 Nm (89 lb-in).

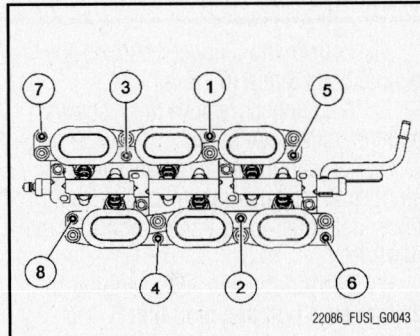

Fig. 221 Lower intake manifold bolt tightening sequence—3.0L engine

11. Connect the 6 fuel injector electrical connectors.

12. Attach the 3 pin-type retainers to the fuel rail.

13. Attach the 2 wiring harness retainers to the LH valve cover stud bolts.

14. Connect the fuel supply tube quick connect coupling at the fuel rail.

15. Install the upper intake manifold.

16. Connect the battery ground cable

3.5L Engine

Upper Intake Manifold

See Figures 222 through 224.

1. Disconnect the negative battery cable.

2. Remove the air cleaner outlet pipe.

3. Disconnect the throttle body electrical connector.

4. Disconnect the Evaporative Emissions (EVAP) tube from the intake manifold.

5. Disconnect the brake booster vacuum hose from the intake manifold.

6. Disconnect the Positive Crankcase Ventilation (PCV) tube from the PCV valve.

7. Disconnect the PCV fitting electrical connector.

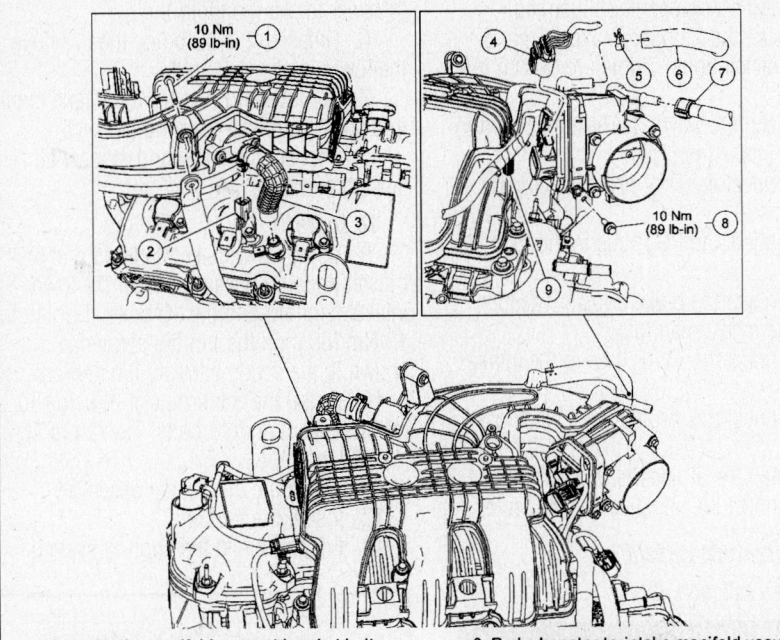

1. Upper intake manifold support bracket bolt
2. PCV fitting electrical connector
3. PCV hose
4. Throttle body electrical connector
5. Brake booster-to-intake manifold vacuum hose clamp
6. Brake booster-to-intake manifold vacuum hose
7. EVAP-to-intake manifold tube
8. Upper intake manifold support bracket bolt
9. Engine control wiring harness retainer

Fig. 222 Installed view of the upper intake manifold and related components—3.5L engine

8. Detach the wiring harness retainers from the upper intake manifold.

9. Remove the 2 upper intake manifold support bracket bolts.

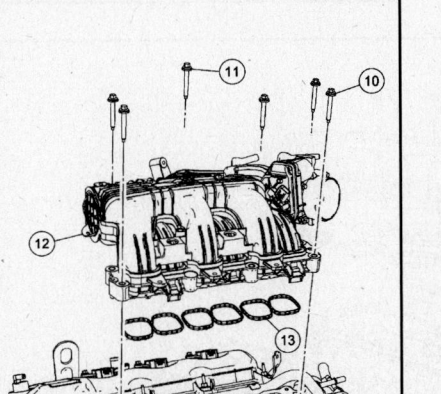

10. Upper intake manifold bolts (5)
11. Upper intake manifold bolt
12. Upper intake manifold
13. Upper intake manifold gaskets (3)

Fig. 223 Exploded view of the upper intake manifold and related components—3.5L engine

10. Remove the 6 bolts and remove the upper intake manifold.

11. Remove and discard the gaskets.

12. Clean and inspect all of the sealing surfaces of the upper and lower intake manifold.

To install:

13. Using new gaskets, install the upper intake manifold and the 6 bolts and tighten

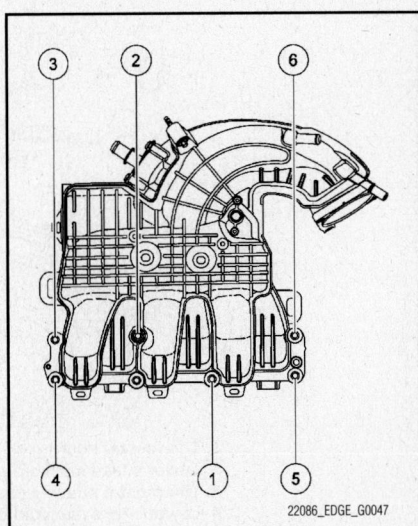

Fig. 224 Upper intake manifold bolt tightening sequence—3.5L engine

to 10 Nm (89 inch lbs.) in the sequence shown in the accompanying illustration.

14. Install the 2 upper intake manifold support bracket bolts. Tighten to 10 Nm (89 inch lbs.).

15. Attach the wiring harness retainers to the upper intake manifold.

16. Connect the PCV fitting electrical connector.

17. Connect the PCV tube to the PCV valve.

18. Connect the brake booster vacuum hose to the intake manifold.

19. Connect the EVAP tube to the intake manifold.

20. Connect the throttle body electrical connector.

21. Install the air cleaner outlet pipe.

22. Connect the negative battery cable.

Lower Intake Manifold

See Figures 225 and 226.

> ※※ **WARNING**
>
> **During engine repair procedures, cleanliness is extremely important. Any foreign material, including any material created while cleaning gasket surfaces that enters the oil passages, coolant passages or the oil pan, can cause engine failure.**

1. Raise and safely support the vehicle.
2. Drain the cooling system.
3. Remove the fuel rail, as outlined in the Fuel System Section.
4. Remove the air cleaner assembly.

5. Remove the 3 thermostat housing-to-lower intake manifold bolts.

6. Unfasten the 10 bolts, then remove the lower intake manifold.

7. Remove and discard the intake manifold and thermostat housing gaskets.

8. Thoroughly clean and inspect all sealing surfaces.

To install:

9. Using new intake manifold and thermostat housing gaskets, install the lower intake manifold and the 10 bolts. Tighten to 10 Nm (89 inch lbs.) in the sequence shown in the accompanying illustration.

10. Install the 3 thermostat housing-to-lower intake manifold bolts. Tighten to 10 Nm (89 inch lbs.).

11. Install the air cleaner assembly.

12. Install the fuel rail.

13. Fill and bleed the cooling system.

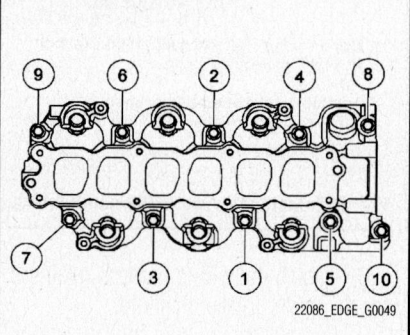

22086_EDGE_G0049

Fig. 226 Lower intake manifold bolt tightening sequence—3.5L engine

OIL PAN

REMOVAL & INSTALLATION

2.3L Engine

See Figure 227.

1. Raise and safely support the vehicles..
2. Remove the air cleaner.
3. If equipped with an A/T, remove the battery tray..

> ※※ **WARNING**
>
> **To prevent damage to the transmission, do not loosen the transmission-to-engine bolts more than 5 mm (0.19 in).**

4. Loosen the 3 upper transaxle-to-engine bolts 5 mm (0.19 in).

5. If equipped, remove the 7 screws and the underbody cover.

6. Loosen the 1 (automatic transmission) or 2 (manual transmission) front lower bellhousing-to-engine bolt(s) 5 mm (0.19 in).

7. Loosen the rear lower engine-to-bellhousing bolt and stud bolt 5 mm (0.19 in).

8. Remove the 2 oil pan-to-bellhousing bolts.

9. Remove the bellhousing-to-oil pan bolt.

10. Slide the transmission rearward 5 mm (0.19 in).

11. Drain the engine oil.

12. Install the drain plug and tighten to 28 Nm (21 ft. lbs.).

13. Remove the 4 engine front cover-to-oil pan bolts.

14. Remove the 13 bolts and the oil pan.

To install:

> ※※ **WARNING**
>
> **Do not use metal scrapers, wire brushes, power abrasive discs or other abrasive means to clean the sealing surfaces. These tools cause scratches and gouges, which make leak paths. Use a plastic scraping tool to remove traces of sealant.**

15. Clean and inspect all mating surfaces.

➡If the oil pan is not secured within 10 minutes of sealant application, the sealant must be removed and the sealing area cleaned with metal surface cleaner. Allow to dry until there is no sign of wetness, or 10 minutes,

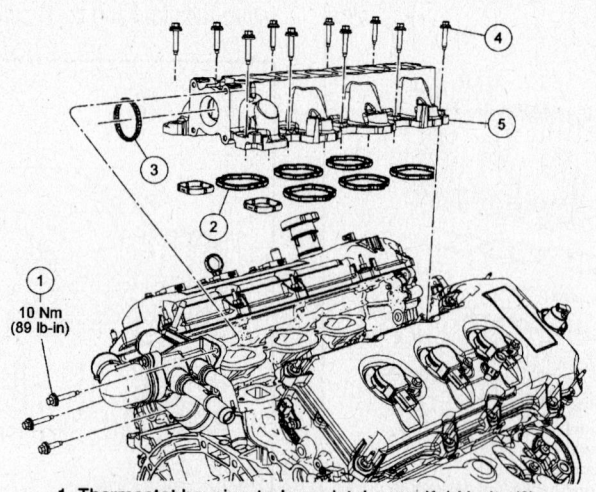

1. Thermostat housing-to-lower intake manifold bolts (3)
2. Lower intake manifold gaskets (8)
3. Thermostat housing gasket
4. Lower intake manifold bolts (10)
5. Lower intake manifold

10 Nm (89 lb-in)

22086_EDGE_G0048

Fig. 225 Exploded view of the lower intake manifold and related components—3.5L engine

whichever is longer. **Failure to follow this procedure can cause future oil leakage.**

16. Apply a 2.5 mm (0.09 in) bead of silicone gasket and sealant to the oil pan-to-engine block and to the oil pan-to-engine front cover mating surface.

17. Position the oil pan onto the engine and install the oil pan bolts finger-tight.

18. Install the 4 engine front cover-to-oil pan bolts. Tighten to 10 Nm (89 lb-in).

19. Tighten the oil pan bolts in the sequence shown to 25 Nm (18 ft. lbs.).

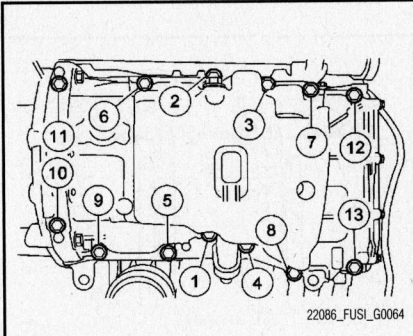

Fig. 230 Oil pan bolt tightening sequence—2.3L engine

20. Alternate tightening the 1 front and 1 rear lower bolts to slide the transmission and engine together. Tighten to 48 Nm (35 ft. lbs.).

21. Tighten the remaining front lower bolt (manual transmission) and rear lower stud bolt. Tighten to 48 Nm (35 ft. lbs.).

22. Install the bellhousing-to-oil pan bolt. Tighten to 48 Nm (35 ft. lbs.).

23. Install the 2 oil pan-to-bellhousing bolts. Tighten to 48 Nm (35 ft. lbs.).

24. If equipped, install the underbody cover and the 7 screws.

25. Tighten the 3 top bellhousing-to-engine bolts. Tighten to 48 Nm (35 ft. lbs.).

26. If equipped with an A/T, install the battery tray.

27. Install the air cleaner assembly.

28. Fill the engine with clean engine oil

3.0L Engine

See Figures 228 and 229.

1. Raise and safely support the vehicle..
2. Remove the LH catalytic converter.
3. Drain the engine oil and install the drain plug. Tighten to 26 Nm (19 ft. lbs.).
4. Remove the 2 oil pan-to-transaxle bolts.

➡**For reference during installation, mark the location of the stud bolts.**

5. Remove the 10 bolts, 5 stud bolts and the oil pan. Discard the gasket.

To install:

➡**Use a plastic scraping tool to remove all traces of the oil pan gasket.**

6. Clean all sealing surfaces with metal surface cleaner and install a new oil pan gasket.

➡**The oil pan must be installed and the bolts tightened within 4 minutes of sealant application.**

7. Apply a 10 mm (0.39 in) diameter dot of silicone sealant to the areas indicated.

8. Position the oil pan and install the 10 bolts and 5 stud bolts finger tight.

9. Install the 2 oil pan-to-transaxle bolts. Tighten to 48 Nm (35 ft. lbs.).

10. Tighten the oil pan-to-engine bolts

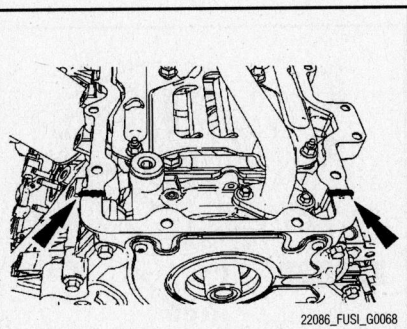

Fig. 228 Apply a 10mm (0.39 in) diameter dot of silicone sealant where indicated

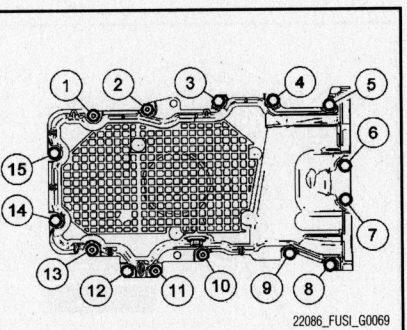

Fig. 229 Oil pan bolt tightening sequence—3.0L engine

and stud bolts in the sequence shown to 25 Nm (18 ft. lbs.).

11. Install the LH catalytic converter.
12. Fill the engine with clean engine oil

3.5L Engine

See Figures 230 through 253.

➡**This procedure requires engine removal, as well as a variety of specialized tools and equipment.**

1. Remove the engine from the vehicle, as outlined in this section.
2. Remove the 8 bolts and the flexplate.
3. Remove the crankshaft sensor ring.

4. Mount the engine on a suitable engine stand.

5. If equipped, remove the heat shield and disconnect the block heater electrical connector.

6. Detach all of the engine block heater harness retainers and remove the harness.

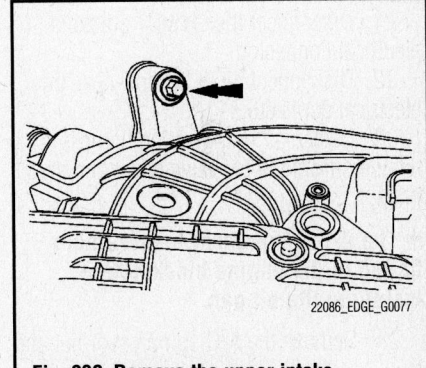

Fig. 230 Remove the upper intake manifold support bracket bolt

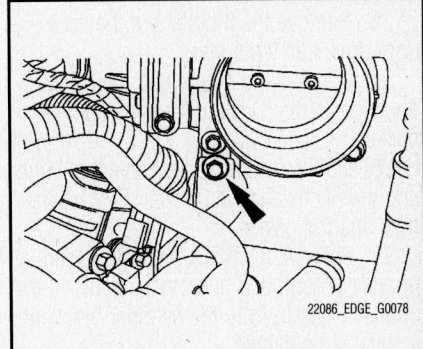

Fig. 231 Remove the upper intake manifold support bracket bolt

7. Disconnect the Positive Crankcase Ventilation (PCV) fitting electrical connector.

8. Disconnect the PCV hose from the PCV valve.

9. Disconnect the throttle body electrical connector.

10. Detach the wiring harness retainers from the upper intake manifold.

11. Remove the upper intake manifold support bracket bolt.

12. Remove the upper intake manifold support bracket bolt.

13. Remove the 6 bolts and the upper intake manifold. Discard the gaskets.

14. Disconnect the Power Steering Pressure (PSP) switch electrical connector.

15. On Front Wheel Drive (FWD) vehicles, disconnect the RH catalyst monitor sensor electrical connector.

16. Disconnect the RH Variable Camshaft Timing (VCT) solenoid electrical connector.

17. Disconnect the 3 RH coil-on-plug electrical connectors.

18. Disconnect the heated PCV valve electrical connector.

19. Detach all of the wiring harness retainers from the RH valve cover and stud bolts.

20. Disconnect the LH catalyst monitor sensor electrical connector.

21. Disconnect the LH VCT solenoid electrical connector.

22. Disconnect the 3 LH coil-on-plug electrical connectors.

23. Detach all of the wiring harness retainers from the LH valve cover and stud bolts.

➡**The A/C compressor must remain bolted to the engine block before installing the oil pan.**

24. Remove the A/C compressor nut and stud.

25. Remove the 3 bolts and the power steering pump. Do NOT disconnect the fluid lines.

26. Remove the 3 bolts and the accessory drive belt tensioner.

27. Remove the 4 nuts and the LH catalytic converter. Discard the nuts and the gasket.

28. On FWD vehicles, remove the 4 nuts and the RH catalytic converter. Discard the nuts and the gasket.

29. Remove the RH cylinder block drain plug or, if equipped, the block heater. Allow coolant to drain from the cylinder block into a suitable container.

30. Remove the LH cylinder block drain plug. Allow coolant to drain from the cylinder block into a suitable container.

31. Remove the 6 bolts and the 6 coil-on-plugs.

32. Remove the 11 stud bolts and the LH valve cover. Discard the gasket.

33. Remove the bolt, the 10 stud bolts and the RH valve cover. Discard the gasket.

➡**VCT solenoid seal removal shown, spark plug tube seal removal similar.**

34. Inspect the VCT solenoid seals and the spark plug tube seals. Remove any damaged seals.

   a. Using the special tools, remove the seal(s).

35. Using the special tool, remove the crankshaft bolt and washer. Discard the bolt.

36. Using the special tool, remove the crankshaft pulley.

37. Using the special tool, remove and discard the crankshaft front seal.

38. Remove the 2 bolts and the engine mount bracket.

39. Remove the 2 engine mount studs.

40. Remove the 3 bolts and the engine mount bracket.

41. Remove the 22 engine front cover bolts.

42. Install 6 of the engine front cover

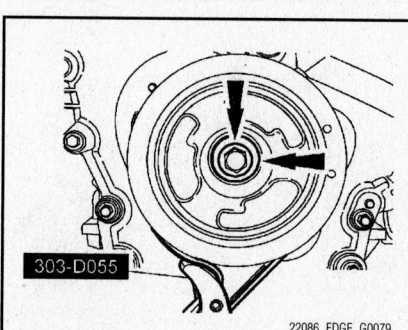

Fig. 232 Using the special tool, remove the crankshaft bolt and washer. Discard the bolt

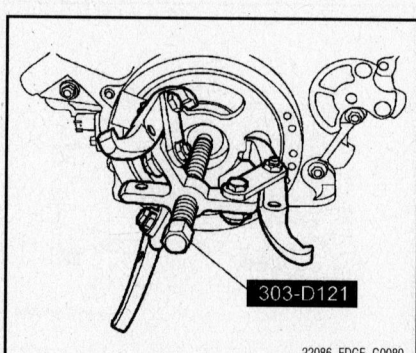

Fig. 233 Using the special tool, remove the crankshaft pulley

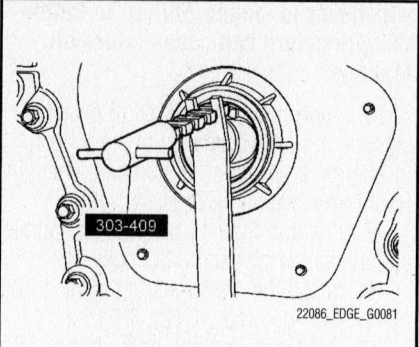

Fig. 234 Using the special tool, remove and discard the crankshaft front seal

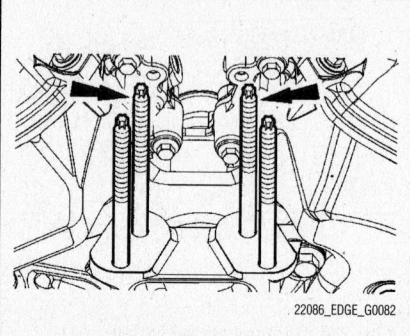

Fig. 235 Remove the 2 engine mount studs (arrows)

bolts (finger tight) into the 6 threaded holes in the engine front cover. Tighten the bolts one turn at a time in a criss-cross pattern until the engine front cover-to-cylinder block seal is released.

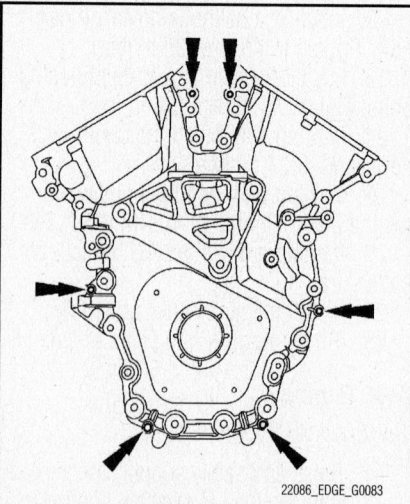

Fig. 236 Install 6 of the engine front cover bolts (finger tight) into the 6 threaded holes in the engine front cover. Tighten the bolts one turn at a time in a criss-cross pattern until the engine front cover-to-cylinder block seal is released

43. Remove the engine front cover.
44. Remove the 16 oil pan bolts.
45. Install 2 of the oil pan bolts (finger tight) into the 2 threaded holes in the oil pan. Alternately tighten the 2 bolts one turn at a time until the oil pan-to-cylinder block seal is released. Remove the oil pan.

✳ WARNING

Only use a 3M Roloc® Bristle Disk, (2 inch, white, part number 07528) to clean the engine front cover and oil pan. Do not use metal scrapers, wire brushes or any other power abrasive disk to clean the crankshaft rear seal retainer plate. These tools cause scratches and gouges that make leak paths.

46. Clean the engine front cover and oil pan using a 3M Roloc® Bristle Disk, (2 inch, white, part number 07528) in a suitable tool turning at the recommended speed of 15,000 rpm.
47. Thoroughly wash the engine front cover and oil pan to remove any foreign material, including any abrasive particles created during the cleaning process.

✳ WARNING

Place clean, lint free shop towels over all exposed engine cavities. Carefully remove the towels so foreign material is not dropped into the engine. Any foreign material (including any material created while clean-

ing gasket surfaces) that enters the oil passages or the oil pan, can cause engine failure.

✳ WARNING

Do not use metal scrapers, wire brushes, power abrasive discs or other abrasive means to clean the sealing surfaces. These tools cause scratches and gouges that make leak paths. Use a plastic scraping tool to remove all traces of sealant.

✳ WARNING

Observe all warnings or cautions and follow all application directions contained on the packaging of the silicone gasket remover and the metal surface prep.

48. Clean the sealing surfaces of the cylinder block.
49. Remove any large deposits of silicone or gasket material with a plastic scraper.
50. Apply silicone gasket remover, following package directions, and allow to set for several minutes. Remove the silicone gasket remover with a plastic scraper. A second application of silicone gasket remover may be required if residual traces of silicone or gasket material remain.
51. Apply metal surface prep, following package directions, to remove any remaining traces of oil or coolant and to prepare the surfaces to bond. Do not attempt to make the metal shiny. Some staining of the metal surfaces is normal.
52. Make sure the 2 locating dowel pins are seated correctly in the cylinder block.

To install:

✳ WARNING

Failure to use the correct RTV Silicone Sealant (TA-357) may cause the engine oil to foam excessively and result in serious engine damage.

➡ The oil pan and the 4 specified bolts must be installed and the oil pan aligned to the cylinder block and A/C compressor within 4 minutes of sealant application. Final tightening of the oil pan bolts must be carried out within 60 minutes of sealant application.

53. Apply a 3 mm (0.11 in) bead of RTV Silicone Sealant (TA-357) to the sealing surface of the oil pan.

54. Apply a 5.5 mm (0.21 in) bead of RTV Silicone Sealant (TA-357) to the 2 crankshaft seal retainer plate-to-cylinder block joint areas on the sealing surface of the oil pan.

➡ The oil pan and the 4 specified bolts must be installed within 4 minutes of the start of sealant application.

55. Install the oil pan and bolts 10, 11, 13 and 14, as shown in the accompanying illustration. Tighten the bolts in the sequence shown to 3 Nm (27 inch lbs.). Loosen the bolts 180 degrees.
56. Align the oil pan to the cylinder block and the A/C compressor.
57. Position the oil pan so the mounting boss is against the A/C compressor and using a straightedge, align the oil pan flush with the rear of the cylinder block at the 2 areas shown in the illustration.
58. Tighten bolts 10, 11, 13 and 14 in the sequence shown, to 3 Nm (27 inch lbs.).

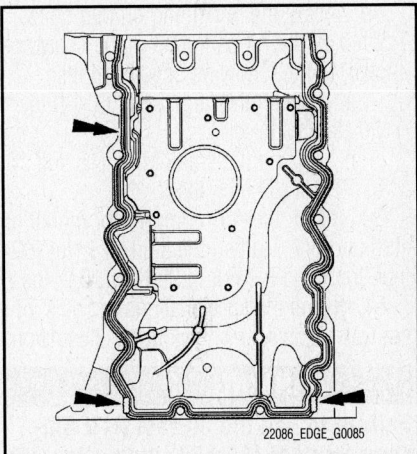

22086_EDGE_G0085

Fig. 238 Silicone sealant locations on the oil pan

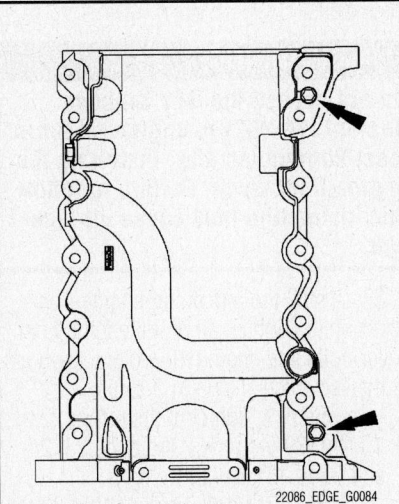

22086_EDGE_G0084

Fig. 237 Install 2 of the oil pan bolts (finger tight) into the 2 threaded holes in the oil pan. Alternately tighten the 2 bolts one turn at a time until the oil pan-to-cylinder block seal is released. Remove the oil pan

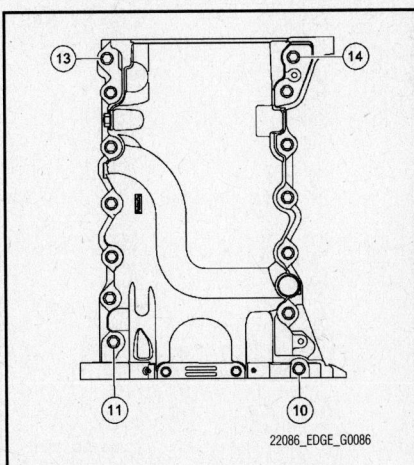

22086_EDGE_G0086

Fig. 239 Location of oil pan bolts 10, 11, 13 and 14

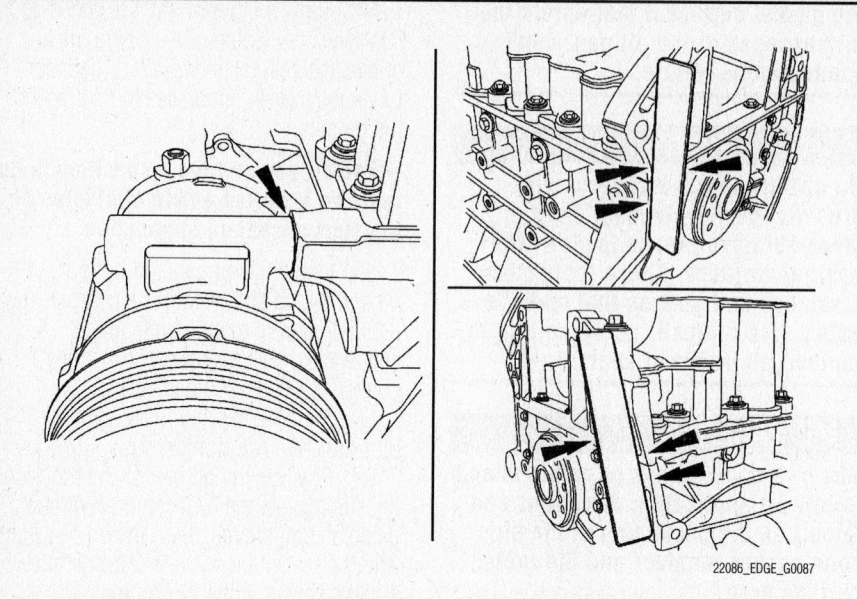

Fig. 240 Position the oil pan so the mounting boss is against the A/C compressor and using a straightedge, align the oil pan flush with the rear of the cylinder block at the 2 areas shown

59. Install the remaining oil pan bolts. Tighten all the oil pan bolts in the sequence shown, to the following specifications:

a. Tighten the large bolts (1-14) to 20 Nm (15 ft. lbs.).

b. Tighten the small bolts (15 and 16) to 10 Nm (89 inch lbs.).

60. Install the A/C compressor mounting stud and nut. Tighten the stud to 9 Nm (80 inch lbs.) and the nut to 25 Nm (18 ft. lbs.).

61. Install the special alignment pins, or equivalent tools, as shown in the illustration.

❉❉ WARNING

Failure to use the correct RTV Silicone Sealant (TA-357) may cause the

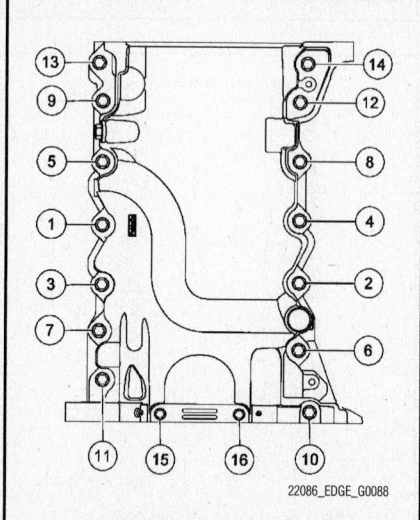

Fig. 241 Oil pan bolt locations and tightening sequence

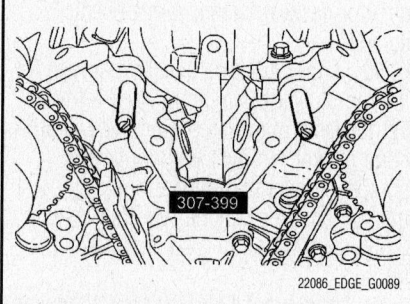

Fig. 242 Install the alignment pins, or equivalent special tools as shown

engine oil to foam excessively and result in serious engine damage.

➡ **The engine front cover and bolts 17, 18, 19 and 20 must be installed within 4 minutes of the initial sealant application. The remainder of the engine front cover bolts and the engine mount bracket bolts must be installed and tightened within 35 minutes of the initial sealant application. If the time limits are exceeded, the sealant must be removed, the sealing area cleaned and sealant reapplied. To clean the sealing area, use silicone gasket remover and metal surface prep. Follow the directions on the packaging. Failure to follow this procedure can cause future oil leakage.**

62. Apply a 3.0 mm (0.11 in) bead of RTV Silicone Sealant (TA-357) to the engine front cover sealing surfaces including the 3 engine mount bracket bosses.

63. Apply a 5.5 mm (0.21 in) bead of RTV Silicone Sealant (TA-357) to the oil pan-to-cylinder block joint and the cylinder head-to-cylinder block joint areas of the engine front cover in 5 places as indicated.

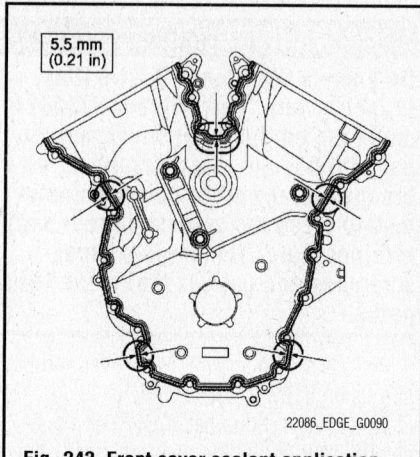

Fig. 243 Front cover sealant application locations

➡ **Make sure the 2 locating dowel pins are seated correctly in the cylinder block.**

64. Install the engine front cover and bolts 17, 18, 19 and 20. Tighten in sequence to 3 Nm (27 inch lbs.).

65. Remove the special tools (alignment pins).

➡ **Do not tighten the bolt at this time.**

66. Install the engine mount bracket and the 3 bolts.

❉❉ WARNING

Do not expose the RTV Silicone Sealant (TA-357) to engine oil for at least 90 minutes after installing the engine front cover. Failure to follow this instruction may cause oil leakage.

67. Install the remaining engine front cover bolts. Tighten all of the engine front cover bolts and engine mount bracket bolts in the sequence shown in 2 steps:

a. Step 1: Tighten bolts 1 thru 22 to 10 Nm (89 inch lbs.) and bolts 23, 24 and 25 to 15 Nm (11 ft. lbs.).

b. Step 2: Tighten bolts 1 thru 22 to 24 Nm (18 ft. lbs.) and bolts 23, 24 and 25 to 75 Nm (55 ft. lbs.).

68. Install the engine mount bracket and the 2 bolts. Tighten to 24 Nm (18 ft. lbs.).

69. Install the 2 engine mount studs. Tighten to 18 Nm (13 ft. lbs.).

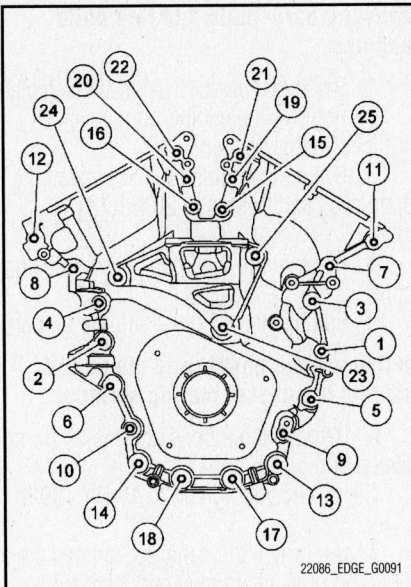

Fig. 244 Front cover bolt locations and tightening sequence

➡ **Apply clean engine oil to the crankshaft front seal bore in the engine front cover.**

70. Using the special tools, install a new crankshaft front seal.

➡ **Lubricate the outside diameter sealing surfaces with clean engine oil.**

71. Using the special tools, install the crankshaft pulley.

72. Using the special tool, install the crankshaft pulley washer and new bolt and tighten in 4 steps.

   a. Step 1: Tighten to 120 Nm (89 (ft. lbs.).

   b. Step 2: Loosen one full turn.

   c. Step 3: Tighten to 50 Nm (37 ft. lbs.).

   d. Step 4: Tighten an additional 90 degrees.

➡ **Installation of new seals is only required if damaged seals were**

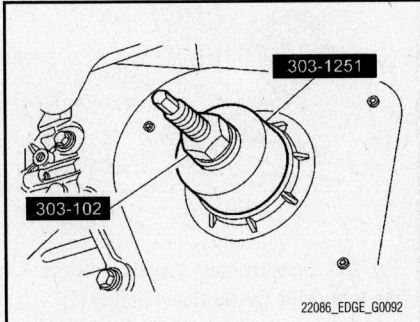

Fig. 245 Using the special tools, install a new crankshaft front seal

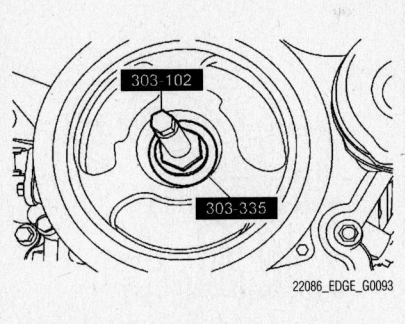

Fig. 246 Using the special tools, install the crankshaft pulley

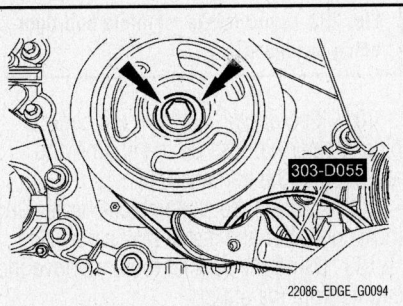

Fig. 247 Using the special tool, install the crankshaft pulley washer and new bolt and tighten in 4 steps

removed during disassembly of the engine.

73. Using the special tools, install new VCT solenoid and/or spark plug tube seals.

❋❋ **WARNING**

Failure to use the correct RTV Silicone Sealant (TA-357) may cause the engine oil to foam excessively and result in serious engine damage.

➡ **If the valve cover is not installed and the fasteners tightened within 4 minutes, the sealant must be removed and the sealing area cleaned. To clean the sealing area, use silicone gasket remover and metal surface prep. Follow the directions on the packaging. Failure to follow this procedure can cause future oil leakage.**

74. Apply a 8 mm (0.31 in) bead of RTV Silicone Sealant (TA-357) to the engine front cover-to-RH cylinder head joints.

75. Using a new gasket, install the RH valve cover, bolt and the 10 stud bolts. Tighten in the sequence shown to 10 Nm (89 inch lbs.).

76. Apply a 8 mm (0.31 in) bead of RTV Silicone Sealant (TA-357) to the engine front cover-to-LH cylinder head joints.

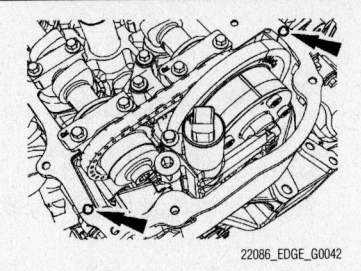

Fig. 248 Apply an 8 mm (0.31 in) bead of RTV Silicone Sealant (TA-357) to the engine front cover-to-RH cylinder head joints

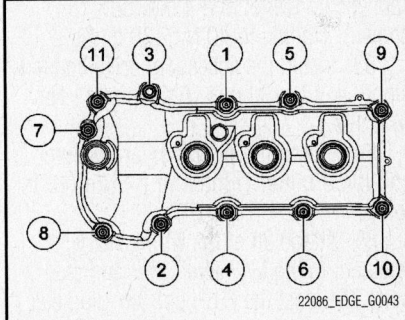

Fig. 249 Right side valve cover bolt tightening sequence

77. Using a new gasket, install the LH valve cover and 11 stud bolts. Tighten in the sequence shown to 10 Nm (89 inch lbs.).

78. Install the 6 coil-on-plug assemblies and the 6 bolts. Tighten to 7 Nm (62 inch lbs.).

79. Install the LH cylinder block drain plug. Tighten to 20 Nm (15 ft. lbs.) plus an additional 180 degrees.

80. Install the RH cylinder block drain plug or, if equipped, the block heater. Tighten to 40 Nm (30 ft. lbs.).

81. On FWD vehicles, using a new gasket, install the RH catalytic converter and 4 new nuts. Tighten to 40 Nm (30 ft. lbs.).

82. Using a new gasket, install the LH

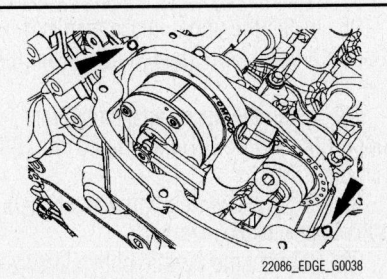

Fig. 250 Apply a 8mm (0.31 in) bead of RTV Silicone Sealant (TA-357, or equivalent) to the engine front cover-to-LH cylinder head joints

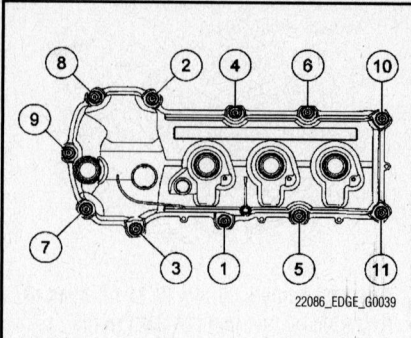

Fig. 251 Left side valve cover bolt tightening sequence

catalytic converter and 4 new nuts (3 shown). Tighten to 40 Nm (30 ft. lbs.).

83. Install the accessory drive belt tensioner and the 3 bolts. Tighten to 11 Nm (8 ft. lbs.).

84. Install the power steering pump and the 3 bolts. Tighten to 24 Nm (18 ft. lbs.).

85. Attach all of the wiring harness retainers to the LH valve cover and stud bolts. Connect the 3 LH coil-on-plug electrical connectors.

86. Connect the LH camshaft VCT solenoid electrical connector.

87. Connect the LH catalyst monitor sensor electrical connector.

88. Attach all of the wiring harness retainers to the RH valve cover and stud bolts.

89. Connect the heated PCV valve electrical connector.

90. Connect the 3 RH coil-on-plug electrical connectors.

91. Connect the RH VCT solenoid electrical connector.

92. On FWD vehicles, connect the RH catalyst monitor sensor electrical connector.

93. Connect the PSP switch electrical connector.

94. Using new gaskets, install the upper intake manifold and the 6 bolts. Tighten in the sequence shown to 10 Nm (89 inch lbs.).

95. Install the upper intake manifold support bracket bolt. Tighten to 10 Nm (89 inch lbs.).

96. Install the upper intake manifold support bracket bolt. Tighten to 10 Nm (89 inch lbs.).

97. Attach the wiring harness retainers to the upper intake manifold.

98. Connect the throttle body electrical connector.

99. Connect the PCV hose to the PCV valve.

100. Connect the PCV fitting electrical connector.

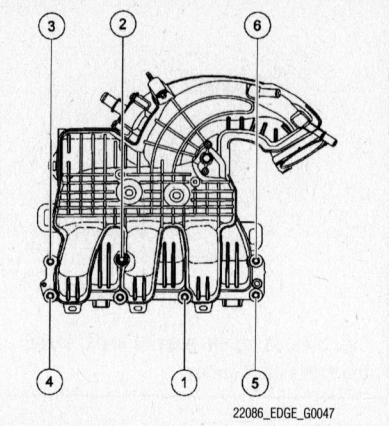

Fig. 252 Upper intake manifold bolt tightening sequence

101. If equipped, position the engine block heater harness on the engine and attach all of the harness retainers.

102. Connect the engine block heater electrical connector and install the heat shield.

103. Using the special tools, remove the engine from the stand.

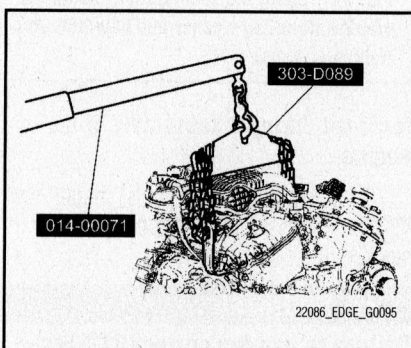

Fig. 253 Using the special tools, remove the engine from the stand

104. Install the crankshaft sensor ring.

105. Install the flexplate and the 8 bolts. Tighten to 80 Nm (59 ft. lbs.).

106. Install the engine in the vehicle, as outlined in this section.

OIL PUMP

REMOVAL & INSTALLATION

2.3L Engine

See Figures 254 through 257.

➡**Early build engines are equipped with an oil pump drive chain guide. Late build engines do not have an oil pump drive chain guide. Also, late build engines use an updated design for the oil pump drive chain and tensioner. Therefore, the oil pump drive components are not interchangeable**

between early build and late build engines.

1. Raise and safely support the vehicle.

2. Remove the engine front cover, as outlined in this section.

3. Drain the engine oil, then install the drain plug and tighten to 28 Nm (21 ft. lbs.).

4. Remove the 3 oil pan-to-bellhousing bolts.

5. Remove the 13 bolts and the oil pan.

➡**Discard the gasket and clean and inspect the gasket mating surfaces.**

6. Remove the 2 bolts and the oil pump screen and pickup tube.

a. To install, tighten to 10 Nm (89 lb-in).

7. On Early build vehicles, remove the oil pump drive chain tensioner and guide.

a. Release the tension on the tensioner spring (1).

b. Remove the 2 shoulder bolts and the tensioner (2).

c. Remove the 2 shoulder bolts and the guide (3).

8. On Late build vehicles, remove the oil pump drive chain tensioner:

a. Release the tension on the tensioner spring (1).

b. Remove the tensioner and the 2 shoulder bolts (2).

9. Remove the chain from the oil pump sprocket.

10. Remove the bolt and oil pump sprocket.

11. Remove the 4 bolts and the oil pump.

To install:

➡**Clean the oil pump and cylinder block mating surfaces with metal surface cleaner.**

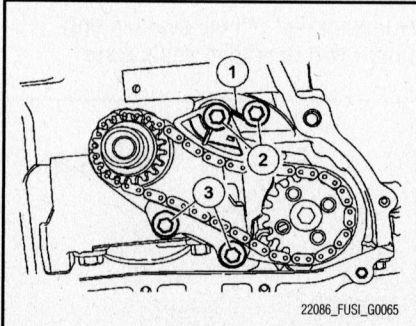

Fig. 254 On early build models, release the tension on the tensioner spring (1). Then remove the 2 shoulder bolts and the tensioner (2) and remove the 2 shoulder bolts and the guide (3).

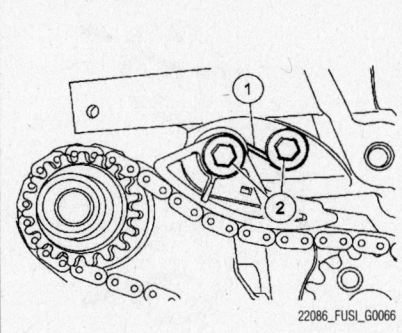

Fig. 255 On Late build vehicles, release the tension on the tensioner spring (1), then remove the tensioner and the 2 shoulder bolts. (2)

12. Install the oil pump assembly. Tighten the 4 bolts in the sequence shown in 2 stages:
    a. Stage 1: Tighten to 10 Nm (89 lb-in).
    b. Stage 2: Tighten to 20 Nm (15 ft. lbs.).

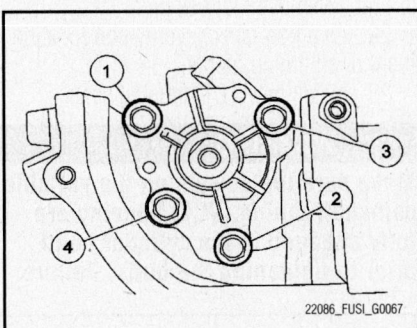

Fig. 256 Oil pump assembly bolt tightening sequence—2.3L engine

13. Install the oil pump sprocket and bolt. Tighten to 25 Nm (18 ft. lbs.).
14. Install the chain onto the oil pump sprocket.
15. On late build vehicles:
    a. Install the oil pump drive chain tensioner shoulder bolt.
    Tighten to 10 Nm (89 lb-in).
16. On early build vehicles:
    a. Install the oil pump drive chain guide and the shoulder bolts.
    b. Tighten to 10 Nm (89 lb-in).
17. Install the oil pump chain tensioner and bolt. Hook the tensioner spring around the shoulder bolt. Tighten to 10 Nm (89 lb-in).
18. Install the oil pump screen and pickup tube and the 2 bolts. Tighten to 10 Nm (89 lb-in).

✳✳ WARNING

Do not use metal scrapers, wire brushes, power abrasive discs or other abrasive means to clean the sealing surfaces. These tools cause scratches and gouges, which make leak paths. Use a plastic scraping tool to remove traces to sealant.

19. Clean all mating surfaces with metal surface cleaner.

➡If the oil pan is not secured within 10 minutes of sealant application, the sealant must be removed and the sealing area cleaned with metal surface cleaner. Allow to dry until there is no sign of wetness, or 10 minutes, whichever is longer. Failure to follow this procedure can cause future oil leakage.

20. Apply a 2.5 mm (0.09 in) bead of sealant gasket and sealant to the oil pan.
21. Position the oil pan onto the engine and install the 2 rear oil pan bolts finger-tight.
22. Using a suitable straight edge, align the front surface of the oil pan flush with the front surface of the engine block.
23. Install the remaining oil pan bolts. Tighten in the sequence shown to 25 Nm (18 ft. lbs.).

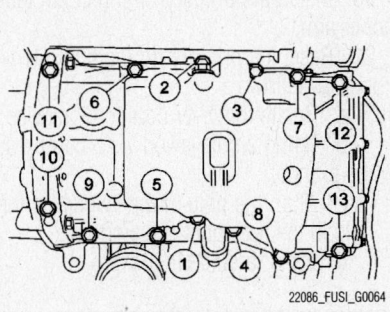

Fig. 257 Oil pan bolt tightening sequence—2.3L engine

24. Install the 3 oil pan-to-bellhousing bolts. Tighten to 48 Nm (35 ft. lbs.).
25. Install the engine front cover.
26. Fill the engine with clean engine oil

3.0L Engine

See Figures 258 and 259.

1. Raise and safely support the vehicle.
2. Remove the timing drive components.
3. Remove the oil pump screen and pickup tube.
4. Remove the 4 bolts in the sequence shown.

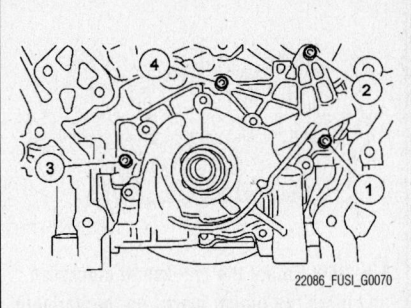

Fig. 258 Remove the 4 bolts in the sequence shown—3.0L engine

To install:

5. Position the oil pump and install the 4 bolts. Tighten in the sequence shown to 10 Nm (89 lb-in).

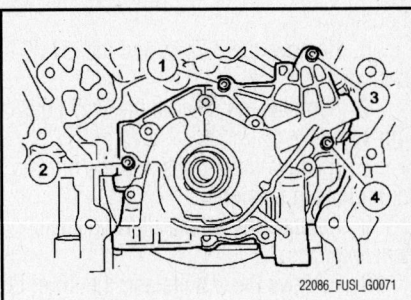

Fig. 259 Position the oil pump and install the 4 bolts. Tighten in the sequence shown to 10 Nm (89 lb-in)—3.0L engine

6. Install the oil pump screen and pickup tube.
7. Install the timing drive components

3.5L Engine

See Figures 260 through 268.

✳✳ WARNING

During engine repair procedures, cleanliness is extremely important. Any foreign material, including any material created while cleaning gasket surfaces, that enters the oil passages, coolant passages or the oil pan may cause engine failure.

1. Remove the engine front cover, as outlined in this section.
2. Rotate the crankshaft clockwise and align the timing marks on the Variable Camshaft Timing (VCT) assemblies as shown.

➡The special tool will hold the camshafts in the top dead center (TDC) position.

Fig. 260 Rotate the crankshaft clockwise and align the timing marks on the Variable Camshaft Timing (VCT) assemblies as shown

3. Install the special tool onto the flats of the LH camshafts.

4. Install the special tool onto the flats of the RH camshafts.

5. Remove the 3 bolts and the RH VCT housing.

6. Remove the 3 bolts and the LH VCT housing.

7. Remove and discard the VCT housing seals.

8. Remove the 2 bolts and the primary timing chain tensioner.

9. Remove the primary timing chain tensioner arm.

10. Remove the 2 bolts and the lower LH primary timing chain guide.

11. Remove the primary timing chain.

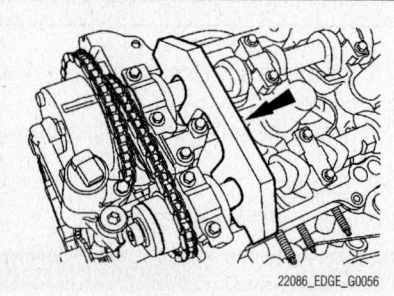

Fig. 261 Install the special tool onto the flats of the camshafts—left side shown, right side similar

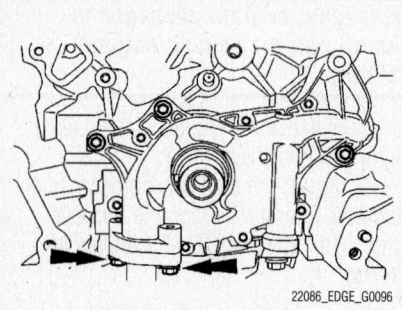

Fig. 262 Remove the 2 oil pump screen and pickup tube bolts

For more information, refer to the Timing Chain procedure in this section.

12. Remove the crankshaft timing chain sprocket.

13. Remove the 2 oil pump screen and pickup tube bolts.

14. Remove the 3 oil pump bolts. Rotate the oil pump clockwise and separate the oil pump from the oil pump screen and pickup tube. Remove the oil pump. Discard the oil pump screen and pickup tube O-ring seal.

To install:

➡ Install a new oil pump screen and pickup tube O-ring seal before installing the oil pump.

15. Position the oil pump onto the crankshaft and rotate counterclockwise to position the pump onto the oil pump screen and pickup tube. Install the 3 bolts and tighten to 10 Nm (89 inch lbs.).

16. Install the 2 oil pump screen and pickup tube bolts. Tighten to 10 Nm (89 inch lbs.).

17. Install the crankshaft timing chain sprocket.

18. Install the primary timing chain with the colored links aligned with the timing marks on the VCT assemblies and the crankshaft sprocket.

19. Install the LH primary timing chain guide and the 2 bolts. Tighten to 10 Nm (89 inch lbs.).

20. Install the primary timing chain tensioner arm.

21. Reset the primary timing chain tensioner, as follows:

    a. Rotate the lever counterclockwise.

    b. Using a soft-jawed vise, compress the plunger.

    c. Align the hole in the lever with the hole in the tensioner housing.

    d. Install a suitable lockpin.

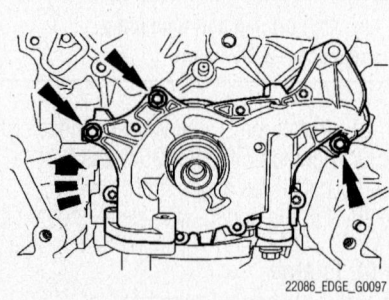

Fig. 263 Remove the 3 oil pump bolts. Rotate the oil pump clockwise and separate the oil pump from the oil pump screen and pickup tube. Remove the oil pump. Discard the oil pump screen and pickup tube O-ring seal

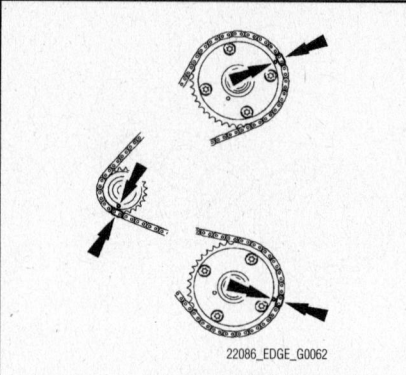

Fig. 264 Install the primary timing chain with the colored links aligned with the timing marks on the VCT assemblies and the crankshaft sprocket

➡ It may be necessary to rotate the crankshaft slightly to remove slack from the timing chain and install the tensioner.

    e. Install the primary tensioner and the 2 bolts. Tighten to 10 Nm (89 inch lbs.).

    f. Remove the lock pin.

22. As a post-check, verify correct alignment of all timing marks.

23. Install new VCT housing seals.

❋❋ WARNING

Make sure the dowels on the variable camshaft timing (VCT) housing are fully engaged in the cylinder head prior to tightening the bolts. Failure

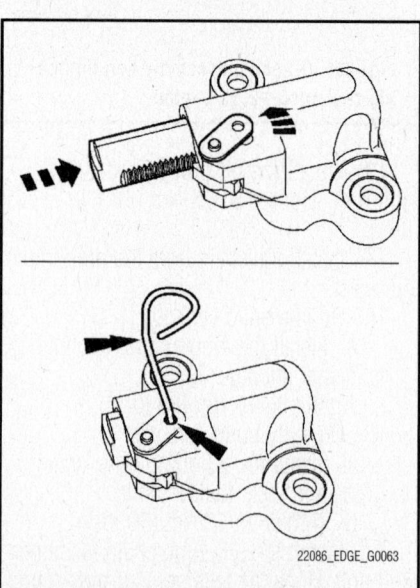

Fig. 265 Rotate the lever counterclockwise. Using a soft-jawed vise, compress the plunger. Align the hole in the lever with the hole in the tensioner housing, then insert a lock pin

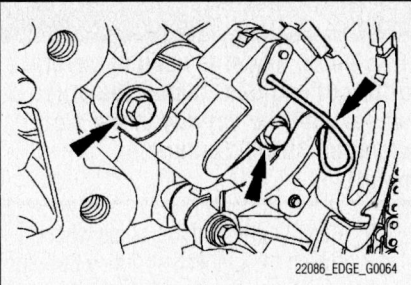

Fig. 266 Install the primary tensioner, secure with the 2 bolts, then remove the lock pin

to follow this process will result in severe engine damage.

24. Install the LH VCT housing and the 3 bolts. Tighten in the sequence shown to 10 Nm (89 inch lbs.).

✸✸ WARNING

Make sure the dowels on the VCT housing are fully engaged in the cylinder head prior to tightening the bolts.

25. Install the RH VCT housing and the 3 bolts. Tighten in the sequence shown to 10 Nm (89 inch lbs.).
26. Install the engine front cover, as outlined in this section.

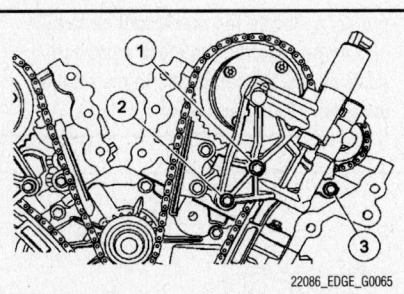

Fig. 267 Install the left side VCT housing and tighten the bolts in the sequence shown

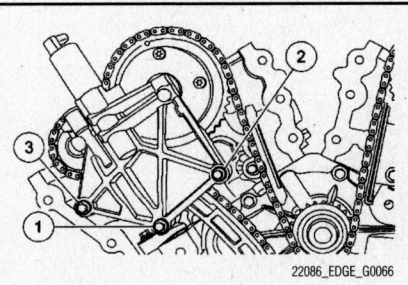

Fig. 268 Install the right side VCT housing and tighten the bolts in the sequence shown

REAR MAIN SEAL

REMOVAL & INSTALLATION

See Figures 269 through 271.

➡ **This procedure requires the use of the following special tools, or their equivalents:**

- Handle 205-153 (T80T-4000-W)
- Crankshaft Rear Seal Installer 303-1250
- Crankshaft Rear Seal Remover 303-519 (T95P-6701-EH)
- Slide Hammer 307-005 (T59L-100-B)

1. Raise and safely support the vehicle.
2. Remove the flexplate, as outlined in this section.
3. Remove the crankshaft sensor ring.
4. Using the special tools shown in the illustration, remove and discard the crankshaft rear seal.
5. Clean all sealing surfaces with metal surface cleaner.

To install:

➡ **Lubricate the seal lips and bore with clean engine oil prior to installation.**

6. Position the special tool onto the end of the crankshaft and slide a new crankshaft rear seal onto the tool.

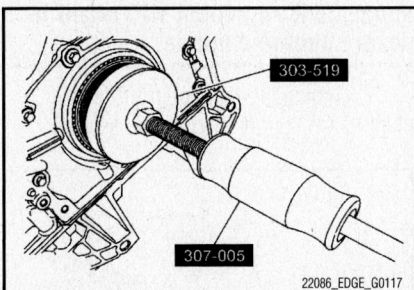

Fig. 269 Using the special tools shown in the illustration, remove and discard the crankshaft rear seal

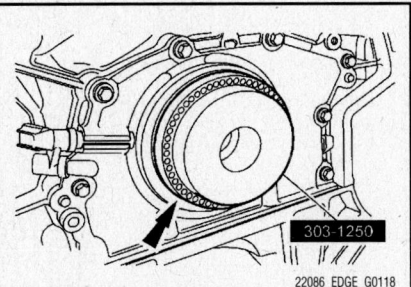

Fig. 270 Position the special tool onto the end of the crankshaft and slide a new crankshaft rear seal onto the tool

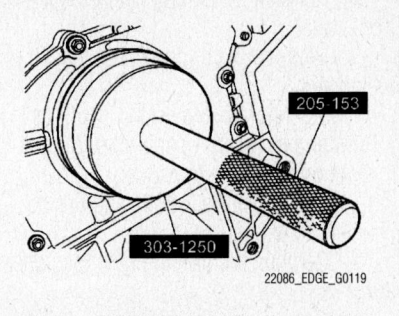

Fig. 271 Using the special tools, install the new crankshaft rear seal

7. Using the special tools, install the new crankshaft rear seal.
8. Install the crankshaft sensor ring.
9. Install the flexplate, as outlined in this section.

TIMING CHAIN, SPROCKETS, FRONT COVER AND SEAL

REMOVAL & INSTALLATION

2.3L Engine
See Figure 272.

✸✸ WARNING

Do not loosen or remove the crankshaft pulley bolt without first installing the special tools as instructed in this procedure. The crankshaft pulley and the crankshaft timing sprocket are not keyed to the crankshaft. The crankshaft, the crankshaft sprocket and the pulley are fitted together by friction, using diamond washers between the flange faces on each part. For that reason, the crankshaft sprocket is also unfastened if you loosen the pulley bolt. Before any repair requiring loosening or removal of the crankshaft pulley bolt, the crankshaft and camshafts must be locked in place by the special service tools, otherwise severe engine damage can occur.

✸✸ WARNING

During engine repair procedures, cleanliness is extremely important. Any foreign material, including any material created while cleaning gasket surfaces, that enters the oil passages, coolant passages or the oil pan can cause engine failure.

1. Raise and safely support the vehicle.

2. Remove the timing chain/engine front cover.

3. Remove the timing chain tensioner, as follows:

    a. Compress the timing chain tensioner and insert a paper clip into the hole to retain the tensioner.

    b. Remove the 2 bolts and timing chain tensioner.

4. Remove the timing chain tensioner arm.

5. Remove the timing chain.

6. Remove the 2 bolts and the timing chain guide.

✳✳ WARNING

The special tool 303-465 is for camshaft alignment only. Using this tool to prevent engine rotation can result in engine damage.

7. Using the flats on the camshaft to prevent camshaft rotation, remove the bolt and the exhaust camshaft sprocket.

✳✳ WARNING

The special tool 303-465 is for camshaft alignment only. Using this tool to prevent engine rotation can result in engine damage.

8. Using the flats on the camshaft to prevent camshaft rotation, remove the bolt and the camshaft phaser and sprocket.

To install:

9. Install the camshaft sprockets and the bolts. Do not tighten the bolts at this time.

10. Install the timing chain guide and the 2 bolts. To install, tighten to 10 Nm (89 lb-in).

11. Install the timing chain.

12. Install the timing chain tensioner arm.

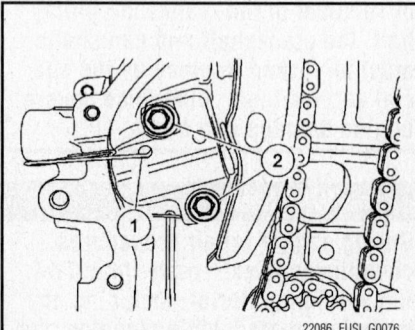

Fig. 272 Compress the timing chain tensioner and insert a paper clip into the hole to retain the tensioner (1). Then, remove the 2 bolts and timing chain tensioner (2)—2.3L engine

13. Install the timing chain tensioner and the 2 bolts. Remove the paper clip to release the piston. Tighten to 10 Nm (89 lb-in).

✳✳ WARNING

The special tool 303-465 is for camshaft alignment only. Using this tool to prevent engine rotation can result in engine damage.

14. Using the flats on the camshafts to prevent camshaft rotation, tighten the bolts. Tighten to 72 Nm (53 ft. lbs.).

15. Install the engine front/timing chain cover.

3.0L Engine

See Figures 273 through 287.

✳✳ WARNING

During engine repair procedures, cleanliness is extremely important. Any foreign material, including any material created while cleaning gasket surfaces that enters the oil passages, coolant passages or the oil pan, can cause engine failure.

✳✳ WARNING

Failure to verify correct timing drive component alignment will result in severe engine damage.

1. Remove the engine front/timing chain cover, as outlined in this section.

✳✳ WARNING

This pulse wheel is used in several different engines. Install the pulse wheel with the keyway in the slot stamped 30RFF (orange in color).

2. Remove the ignition pulse wheel.

3. Install the crankshaft pulley bolt and washer.

4. Remove the 6 spark plugs

5. Rotate the crankshaft clockwise to position the crankshaft keyway in the 11 o'clock position and position the camshafts in the correct position. This will position the No.1 cylinder at top dead center (TDC):

    a. Verify that the camshafts are correctly located. If not, rotate the crankshaft one additional turn and recheck.

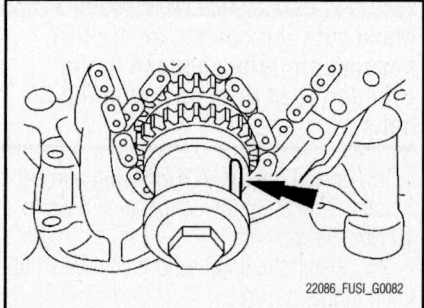

Fig. 274 Rotate the crankshaft clockwise 120 degrees to the 3 o'clock position to position the RH camshafts in the neutral position—3.0L engine

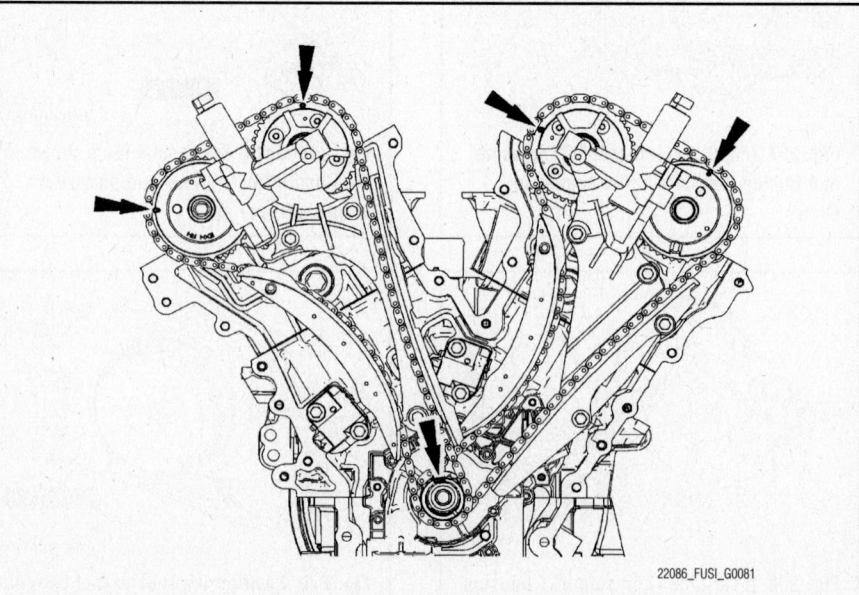

Fig. 273 Verify that the camshafts are correctly located. If not, rotate the crankshaft one additional turn and recheck—3.0L engine

6. Rotate the crankshaft clockwise 120 degrees to the 3 o'clock position to position the RH camshafts in the neutral position.

7. Verify that the RH camshafts are in the neutral position.

8. Remove the RH timing chain tensioner arm:

a. Remove the 2 bolts.

b. Remove the tensioner.

c. Remove the tensioner arm.

9. Remove the RH timing chain.

10. Remove the 3 bolts and the RH VCT assembly.

11. Rotate the crankshaft clockwise 600 degrees (1-2/3 turns) to position the crankshaft keyway in the 11 o'clock position. This will position the LH camshafts in the neutral position.

12. Verify the LH camshafts are in the neutral position.

13. Remove the LH timing chain tensioner and tensioner arm:

a. Remove the 2 bolts.

b. Remove the tensioner.

c. Remove the tensioner arm.

14. Remove the LH timing chain.

15. Remove the 4 bolts and the LH VCT assembly.

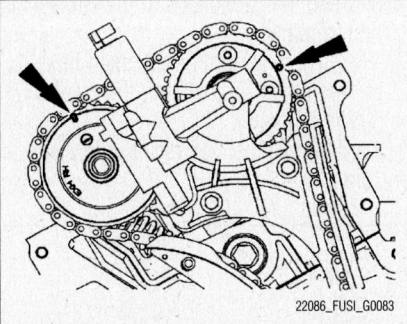

Fig. 275 Verify that the RH camshafts are in the neutral position—3.0L engine

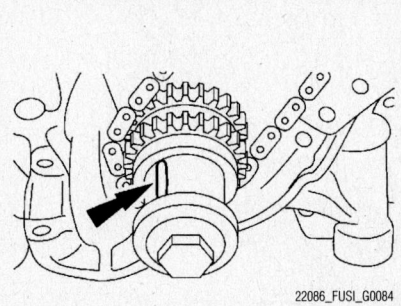

Fig. 276 Rotate the crankshaft clockwise 600 degrees (1-2/3 turns) to position the crankshaft keyway in the 11 o'clock position. This will position the LH camshafts in the neutral position—3.0L engine

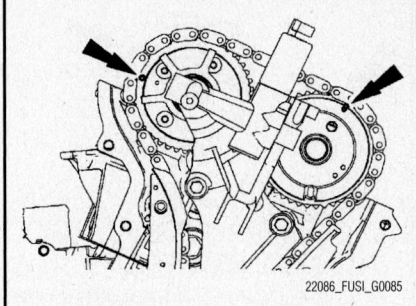

Fig. 277 Verify the LH camshafts are in the neutral position—3.0L engine

16. Remove the pulley bolt, washer and the crankshaft sprocket.

To install:

17. Install the crankshaft sprockets with the timing marks out.

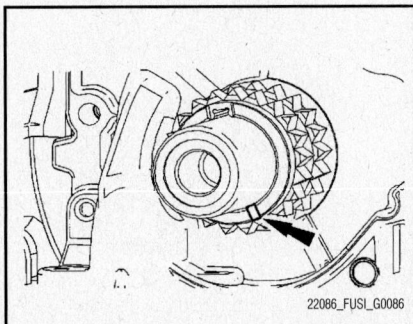

Fig. 278 Install the crankshaft sprockets with the timing marks out—3.0L engine

18. Position the chain tensioner in a soft-jawed vise.

19. Hold the chain tensioner ratchet lock mechanism away from the ratchet stem with a small pick.

※※ WARNING

During tensioner compression, do not release the ratchet stem until the tensioner piston is fully bottomed in

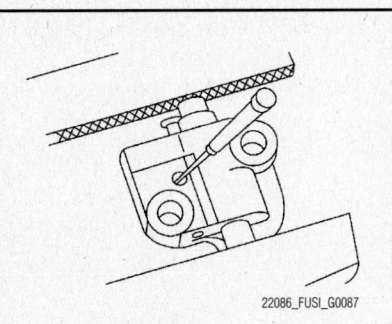

Fig. 279 Hold the chain tensioner ratchet lock mechanism away from the ratchet stem with a small pick

its bore or damage to the ratchet stem will result.

20. Slowly compress the timing chain tensioner.

21. Retain the tensioner piston with a 1.5 mm (0.05 in) wire or paper clip.

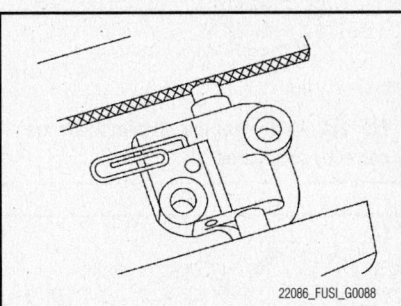

Fig. 280 Retain the tensioner piston with a 1.5 mm (0.05 in) wire or paper clip—3.0L engine

22. If timing marks in the timing chains are not evident, use a permanent-type marker to mark the crankshaft and camshaft timing marks on the LH and RH timing chains.

a. Mark any link to use as the crankshaft timing mark.

b. Starting with the crankshaft timing mark, count counterclockwise 29 links and mark the link.

c. Continue counting counterclockwise to link 42 and mark the link.

23. Verify that the LH camshafts are correctly positioned.

24. Install the variable camshaft timing (VCT) assembly and the 4 bolts. Tighten to 25 Nm (18 ft. lbs.).

25. Install the LH timing chain. Align the marks on the timing chain with the marks on the camshaft and crankshaft sprockets.

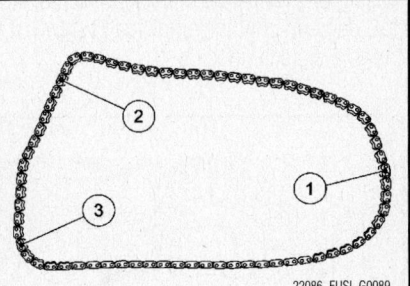

Fig. 281 Mark any link to use as the crankshaft timing mark (1). Starting with the crankshaft timing mark, count counterclockwise 29 links and mark the link (2). Continue counting counterclockwise to link 42 and mark the link (3)—3.0L engine

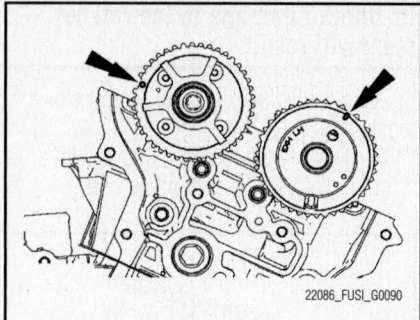

Fig. 282 Verify that the LH camshafts are correctly positioned

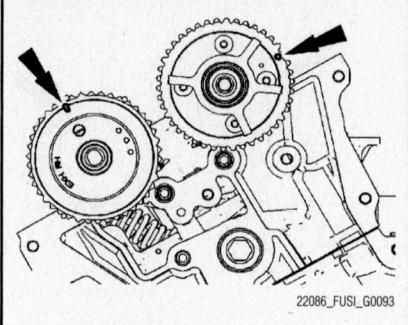

Fig. 285 Verify that the RH camshafts are correctly positioned

28. Verify that the RH camshafts are correctly positioned.

29. Install the RH VCT assembly and the 3 bolts. Tighten to 25 Nm (18 ft. lbs.).

30. Install the RH timing chain. Align the marks on the timing chain with the marks on the camshaft and crankshaft sprockets.

31. Install the RH timing chain tensioner and tensioner arm:

   a. Install the tensioner arm.

   b. Position the tensioner.

   c. Install the 2 bolts and tighten to 25 Nm (18 ft. lbs.).

32. Remove the LH and RH timing chain tensioner piston retaining wires.

33. Rotate the crankshaft counterclockwise 120 degrees to top dead center (TDC).

✳✳ WARNING

Failure to verify correct timing drive component alignment will result in severe engine damage.

34. Verify the timing with the following steps.

   a. There should be 12 chain links between the camshaft timing marks.

   b. There should be 27 chain links between the camshaft and the crankshaft timing marks.

   c. There should be 30 chain links between the camshaft and the crankshaft timing marks.

35. Remove the crankshaft pulley bolt and washer.

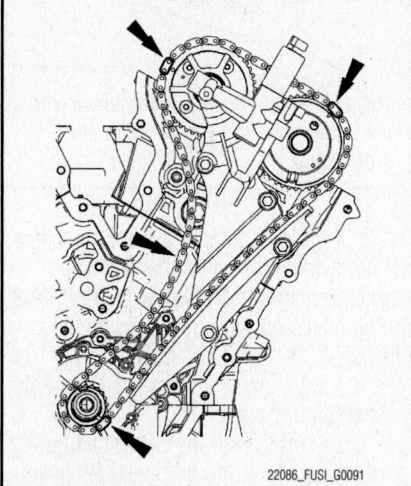

Fig. 283 Align the marks on the timing chain with the marks on the camshaft and crankshaft sprockets

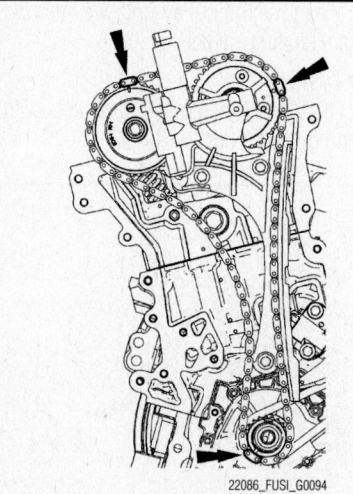

Fig. 286 Align the marks on the timing chain with the marks on the camshaft and crankshaft sprockets.

26. Install the LH timing chain tensioner arm and the LH timing chain tensioner:

   a. Install the tensioner arm.

   b. Position the tensioner.

   c. Install the 2 bolts and tighten to 25 Nm (18 ft. lbs.).

27. Install the crankshaft pulley bolt and washer and rotate the crankshaft clockwise 120 degrees until the crankshaft keyway is in the 3 o'clock position.

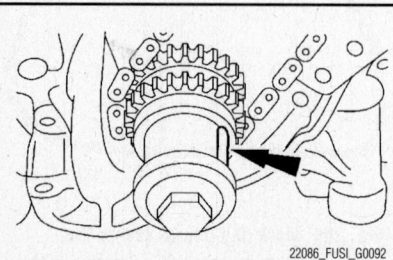

Fig. 284 Install the crankshaft pulley bolt and washer and rotate the crankshaft clockwise 120 degrees until the crankshaft keyway is in the 3 o'clock position

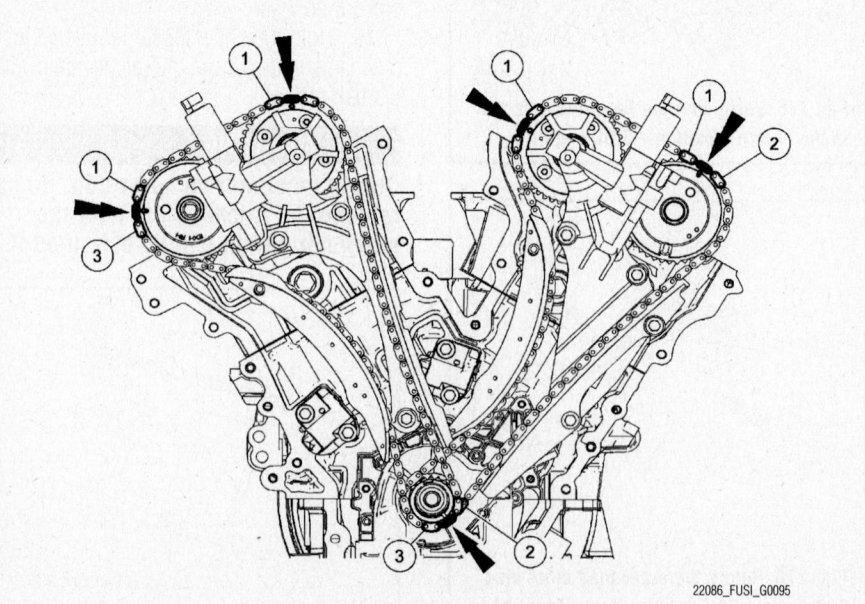

Fig. 287 There should be 12 chain links between the camshaft timing marks (1). There should be 27 chain links between the camshaft and the crankshaft timing marks (2). There should be 30 chain links between the camshaft and the crankshaft timing marks (3).

✳✳ WARNING

This pulse wheel is used in several different engines. Install the pulse wheel with the keyway in the slot stamped 30RFF only (orange in color).

36. Install the ignition pulse wheel.
37. Install the 6 spark plugs. Tighten to 15 Nm (11 ft. lbs.).
38. Install the engine front/timing chain cover, as outlined in this section.

3.5L Engine

See Figures 288 through 306.

✳✳ WARNING

During engine repair procedures, cleanliness is extremely important. Any foreign material, including any material created while cleaning gasket surfaces, that enters the oil passages, coolant passages or the oil pan may cause engine failure.

1. Remove the engine front (timing chain) front cover, as outlined in this section.
2. Rotate the crankshaft clockwise and align the timing marks on the Variable Camshaft Timing (VCT) assemblies as shown.

Fig. 288 Rotate the crankshaft clockwise and align the timing marks on the Variable Camshaft Timing (VCT) assemblies as shown

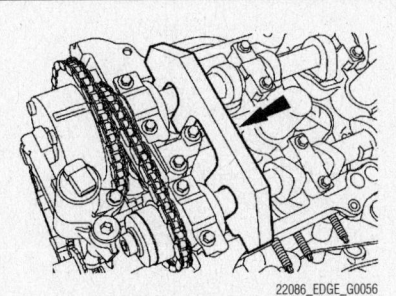

Fig. 289 Install the special tool onto the flats of the camshafts—left side shown, right side similar

➡ **The special tool will hold the camshafts in the Top Dead Center (TDC) position.**

3. Install the special tool onto the flats of the LH camshafts.
4. Install the special tool onto the flats of the RH camshafts.
5. Remove the 3 bolts and the RH VCT housing.
6. Remove the 3 bolts and the LH VCT housing.
7. Remove and discard the VCT housing seals.
8. Remove the 2 bolts and the primary timing chain tensioner.

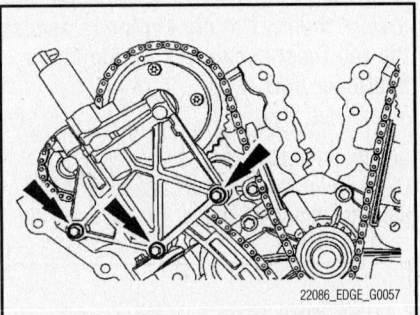

Fig. 290 Remove the 3 bolts and the VCT housing—right side shown, left side similar

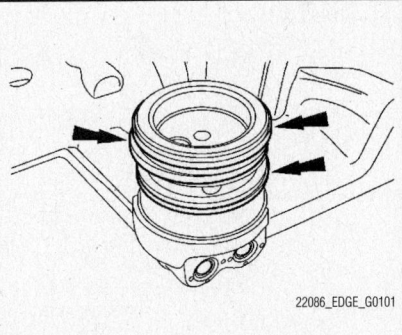

Fig. 291 Remove and discard the VCT housing seals

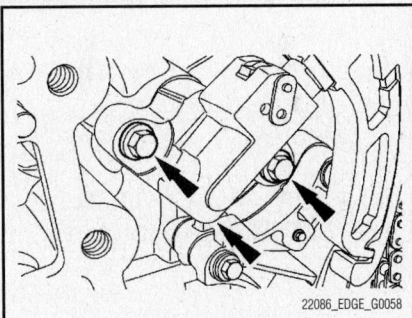

Fig. 292 Remove the 2 bolts and the primary timing chain tensioner

9. Remove the primary timing chain tensioner arm.
10. Remove the 2 bolts and the lower LH primary timing chain guide.
11. Remove the primary timing chain.
12. Remove the crankshaft timing chain sprocket.
13. Remove the 2 bolts and the upper LH primary timing chain guide.
14. Compress the LH secondary timing chain tensioner and install a suitable lock-pin to retain the tensioner in the collapsed position.

➡ **The VCT bolt and the exhaust camshaft bolt must be discarded and**

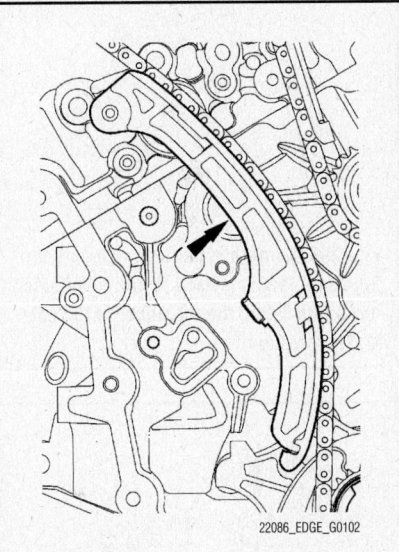

Fig. 293 Remove the primary timing chain tensioner arm

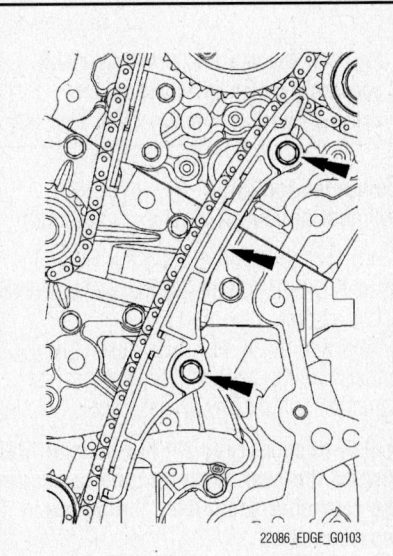

Fig. 294 Remove the 2 bolts and the lower LH primary timing chain guide

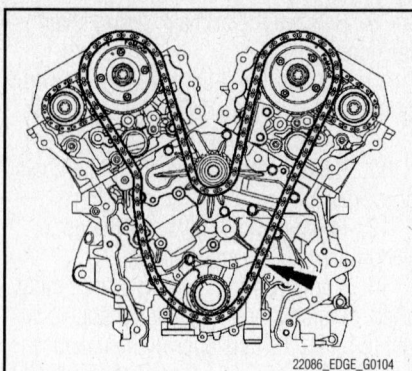

Fig. 295 Remove the primary timing chain

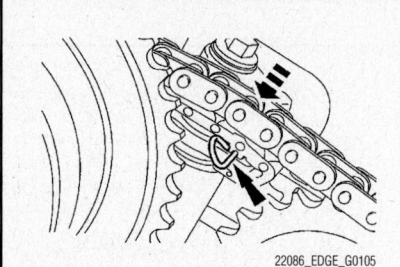

Fig. 296 Compress the LH secondary timing chain tensioner and install a suitable lockpin to retain the tensioner in the collapsed position

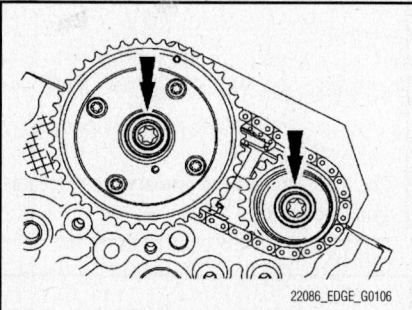

Fig. 297 Remove the LH VCT assembly, secondary timing chain and the LH exhaust camshaft sprocket as an assembly

new ones installed. However, the exhaust camshaft washer is reusable.

15. Remove and discard the LH VCT assembly bolt and the LH exhaust camshaft sprocket bolt.

16. Remove the LH VCT assembly, secondary timing chain and the LH exhaust camshaft sprocket as an assembly.

➥It is necessary to tilt the special tool toward the rear of the engine to access the rearmost secondary timing chain tensioner bolt.

17. Remove the 2 bolts and the LH secondary timing chain tensioner.

18. Compress the RH secondary timing chain tensioner and install a suitable lockpin to retain the tensioner in the collapsed position.

➥The VCT bolt and the exhaust camshaft bolt must be discarded and new ones installed. However, the exhaust camshaft washer is reusable.

19. Remove and discard the RH VCT assembly bolt and the RH exhaust camshaft sprocket bolt.

20. Remove the RH VCT assembly, secondary timing chain and the RH exhaust camshaft sprocket as an assembly.

➥It is necessary to tilt the special tool toward the rear of the engine to access the rearmost secondary timing chain tensioner bolt.

21. Remove the 2 bolts and the RH secondary timing chain tensioner.

22. Remove the 2 bolts and the RH primary timing chain guide.

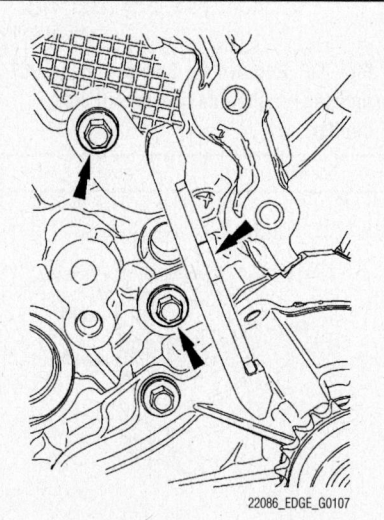

Fig. 298 Remove the 2 bolts and the RH primary timing chain guide

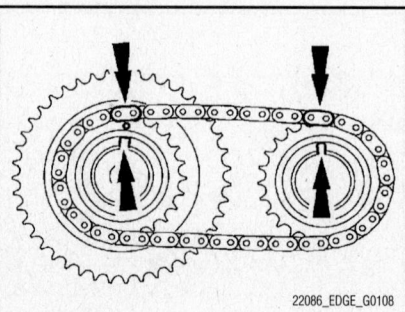

Fig. 299 Align the colored links with the timing marks

To install:

23. Install the RH primary timing chain guide and the 2 bolts. Tighten to 10 Nm (89 inch lbs.).

➥It is necessary to tilt the special tool toward the rear of the engine to access the rearmost secondary timing chain tensioner bolt.

24. Install the RH secondary timing chain tensioner and the 2 bolts. Tighten to 10 Nm (89 inch lbs.).

25. Assemble the RH VCT assembly, the RH exhaust camshaft sprocket and the RH secondary timing chain.

26. Align the colored links with the timing marks.

27. Position the RH secondary timing assembly onto the camshafts.

28. Install the new VCT bolt and new exhaust camshaft bolt and the original washers. Tighten in 4 steps, as follows:

  a. Step 1: Tighten to 40 Nm (30 ft. lbs.).

  b. Step 2: Loosen one full turn.

  c. Step 3: Tighten to 10 Nm (89 inch lbs.).

  d. Step 4: Tighten 90 degrees.

29. Remove the lockpin from the RH secondary timing chain tensioner.

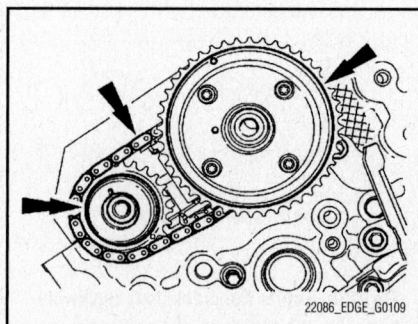

Fig. 300 Position the RH secondary timing assembly onto the camshafts

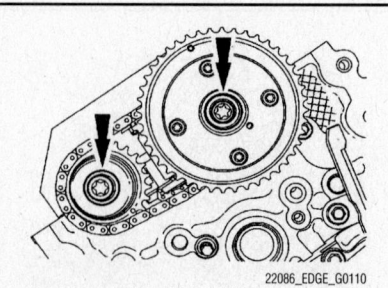

Fig. 301 Install the new VCT bolt and new exhaust camshaft bolt and the original washers

➡️**It is necessary to tilt the special tool toward the rear of the engine to access the rearmost secondary timing chain tensioner bolt.**

30. Install the LH secondary timing chain tensioner and the 2 bolts. Tighten to 10 Nm (89 inch lbs.).

31. Assemble the LH VCT assembly, the LH exhaust camshaft sprocket and the LH secondary timing chain.

32. Align the colored links with the timing marks.

33. Position the LH secondary timing assembly onto the camshafts.

34. Install the new VCT bolt and new exhaust camshaft bolt and the original washers. Tighten in 4 steps.

    a. Step 1: Tighten to 40 Nm (30 ft. lbs.).

    b. Step 2: Loosen one full turn.

    c. Step 3: Tighten to 10 Nm (89 inch lbs.).

    d. Step 4: Tighten 90 degrees.

35. Remove the lockpin from the LH secondary timing chain tensioner.

36. Install the crankshaft timing chain sprocket.

37. Install the primary timing chain with the colored links aligned with the timing marks on the VCT assemblies and the crankshaft sprocket.

38. Install the upper LH primary timing chain guide and the 2 bolts. Tighten to 10 Nm (89 inch lbs.).

39. Install the lower LH primary timing chain guide and the 2 bolts. Tighten to 10 Nm (89 inch lbs.).

40. Install the primary timing chain tensioner arm.

41. Reset the primary timing chain tensioner, as follows:

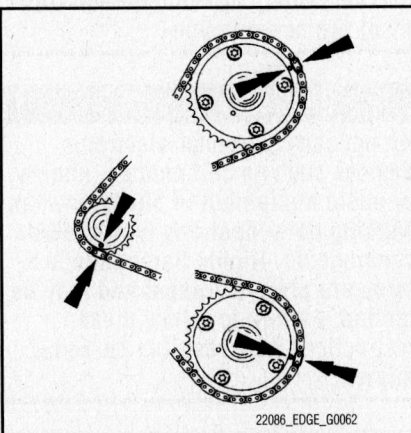

Fig. 302 Install the primary timing chain with the colored links aligned with the timing marks on the VCT assemblies and the crankshaft sprocket

    a. Rotate the lever counterclockwise.

    b. Using a soft-jawed vise, compress the plunger.

    c. Align the hole in the lever with the hole in the tensioner housing.

    d. Install a suitable lockpin.

➡️**It may be necessary to rotate the crankshaft slightly to remove slack from the timing chain and install the tensioner.**

    e. Install the primary tensioner and the 2 bolts. Tighten to 10 Nm (89 inch lbs.).

    f. Remove the lock pin.

42. As a post-check, verify correct alignment of all timing marks.

43. Install new VCT housing seals.

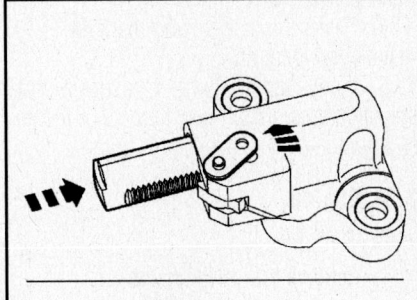

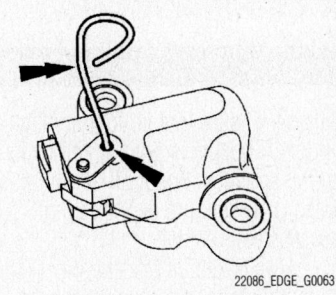

Fig. 303 Rotate the lever counterclockwise. Using a soft-jawed vise, compress the plunger. Align the hole in the lever with the hole in the tensioner housing, then insert a lock pin

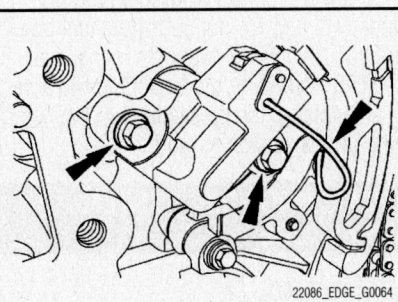

Fig. 304 Install the primary tensioner, secure with the 2 bolts, then remove the lock pin

✳✳ WARNING

Make sure the dowels on the variable camshaft timing (VCT) housing are fully engaged in the cylinder head prior to tightening the bolts. Failure to follow this process will result in severe engine damage.

44. Install the LH VCT housing and the 3 bolts. Tighten in the sequence shown to 10 Nm (89 inch lbs.).

✳✳ WARNING

Make sure the dowels on the VCT housing are fully engaged in the cylinder head prior to tightening the bolts.

45. Install the RH VCT housing and the 3 bolts. Tighten in the sequence shown to 10 Nm (89 inch lbs.).

46. Install the engine front (timing chain) cover, as outlined in this section.

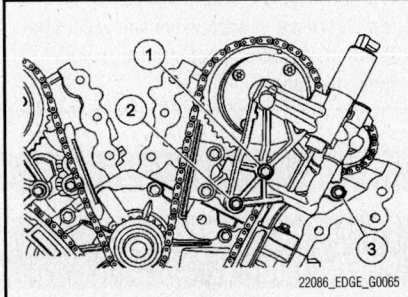

Fig. 305 Install the left side VCT housing and tighten the bolts in the sequence shown

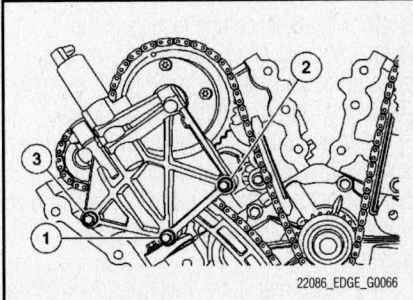

Fig. 306 Install the right side VCT housing and tighten the bolts in the sequence shown

VALVE LASH

ADJUSTMENT

2.3L Engine

See Figure 307.

1. Remove the valve cover.

Turn the engine clockwise only, and only use the crankshaft bolt.

➡Before removing the camshafts, measure the clearance of each valve at base circle, with the lobe pointed away from the tappet. Failure to measure all clearances prior to removing the camshafts will neces-

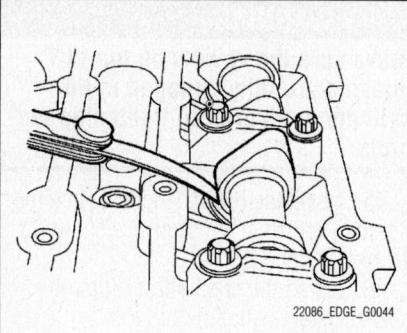

22086_EDGE_G0044

Fig. 307 Use a feeler gauge to measure the clearance of each valve and record its location. A midrange clearance is the most desirable

sitate repeated removal and installation and wasted labor time.

➡ **The number on the valve tappet only reflects the digits that follow the decimal. For example, a tappet with the number 0.650 has the thickness of 3.650 mm.**

2. Use a feeler gauge to measure the clearance of each valve and record its location. A midrange clearance is the most desirable:

　　a. Intake: 0.22–0.28 mm (0.008–0.011 in)
　　b. Exhaust: 0.27–0.33 mm (0.010–0.013 in)

3. Select tappets using this formula: tappet thickness = measured clearance + the base tappet thickness - most desirable thickness.

4. Select the tappets and mark the installation location.

5. If any tappets do not measure within specifications, install new tappets in these locations.

3.5L Engine

See Figure 307.

1. Remove the valve covers.

➡The valve clearance must be measured with the camshaft at base circle. The engine will have to be rotated with the crankshaft pulley bolt to bring each valve to base circle.

2. Use a feeler gauge to measure the clearance of each valve and record its location. A midrange clearance is the most desirable:

　　a. Intake: 0.15–0.25 mm (0.006–0.01 in)
　　b. Exhaust: 0.300–0.400 mm (0.0118–0.0157 in)

➡The number on the valve tappet reflects the thickness of the valve tappet. For example, a tappet with the number 3.310 has the thickness of 3.31 mm (0.13 in).

3. If any of the valve clearances are out of specification, select new tappets using this formula: tappet thickness = measured clearance + the base tappet thickness − most desirable thickness.

4. Select the tappets and mark the installation location.

5. If required, install the new selected valve tappets in the marked locations.

FUEL

GASOLINE FUEL INJECTION SYSTEM

FUEL SYSTEM SERVICE PRECAUTIONS

Safety is the most important factor when performing not only fuel system maintenance but any type of maintenance. Failure to conduct maintenance and repairs in a safe manner may result in serious personal injury or death. Maintenance and testing of the vehicle's fuel system components can be accomplished safely and effectively by adhering to the following rules and guidelines.

• To avoid the possibility of fire and personal injury, always disconnect the negative battery cable unless the repair or test procedure requires that battery voltage be applied.

• Always relieve the fuel system pressure prior to disconnecting any fuel system component (injector, fuel rail, pressure regulator, etc.), fitting or fuel line connection. Exercise extreme caution whenever relieving fuel system pressure to avoid exposing skin, face and eyes to fuel spray. Please be advised that fuel under pressure may penetrate the skin or any part of the body that it contacts.

• Always place a shop towel or cloth around the fitting or connection prior to loosening to absorb any excess fuel due to

spillage. Ensure that all fuel spillage (should it occur) is quickly removed from engine surfaces. Ensure that all fuel soaked cloths or towels are deposited into a suitable waste container.

• Always keep a dry chemical (Class B) fire extinguisher near the work area.

• Do not allow fuel spray or fuel vapors to come into contact with a spark or open flame.

• Always use a back-up wrench when loosening and tightening fuel line connection fittings. This will prevent unnecessary stress and torsion to fuel line piping.

• Always replace worn fuel fitting O-rings with new Do not substitute fuel hose or equivalent where fuel pipe is installed.

Before servicing the vehicle, make sure to also refer to the precautions in the beginning of this section as well.

RELIEVING FUEL SYSTEM PRESSURE

See Figure 308.

Observe all applicable safety precautions when working around

fuel. Whenever servicing the fuel system, always work in a well ventilated area. Do not allow fuel spray or vapors to come in contact with a spark or open flame. Keep a dry chemical fire extinguisher near the work area. Always keep fuel in a container specifically designed for fuel storage; also, always properly seal fuel containers to avoid the possibility of fire or explosion.

Do not carry personal electronic devices such as cell phones, pagers or audio equipment of any type when working on or near any fuel-related components. Highly flammable mixtures are always present and may be ignited. Failure to follow these instructions may result in personal injury.

Fuel in the fuel system remains under high pressure, even when the engine is not running. Before servic-

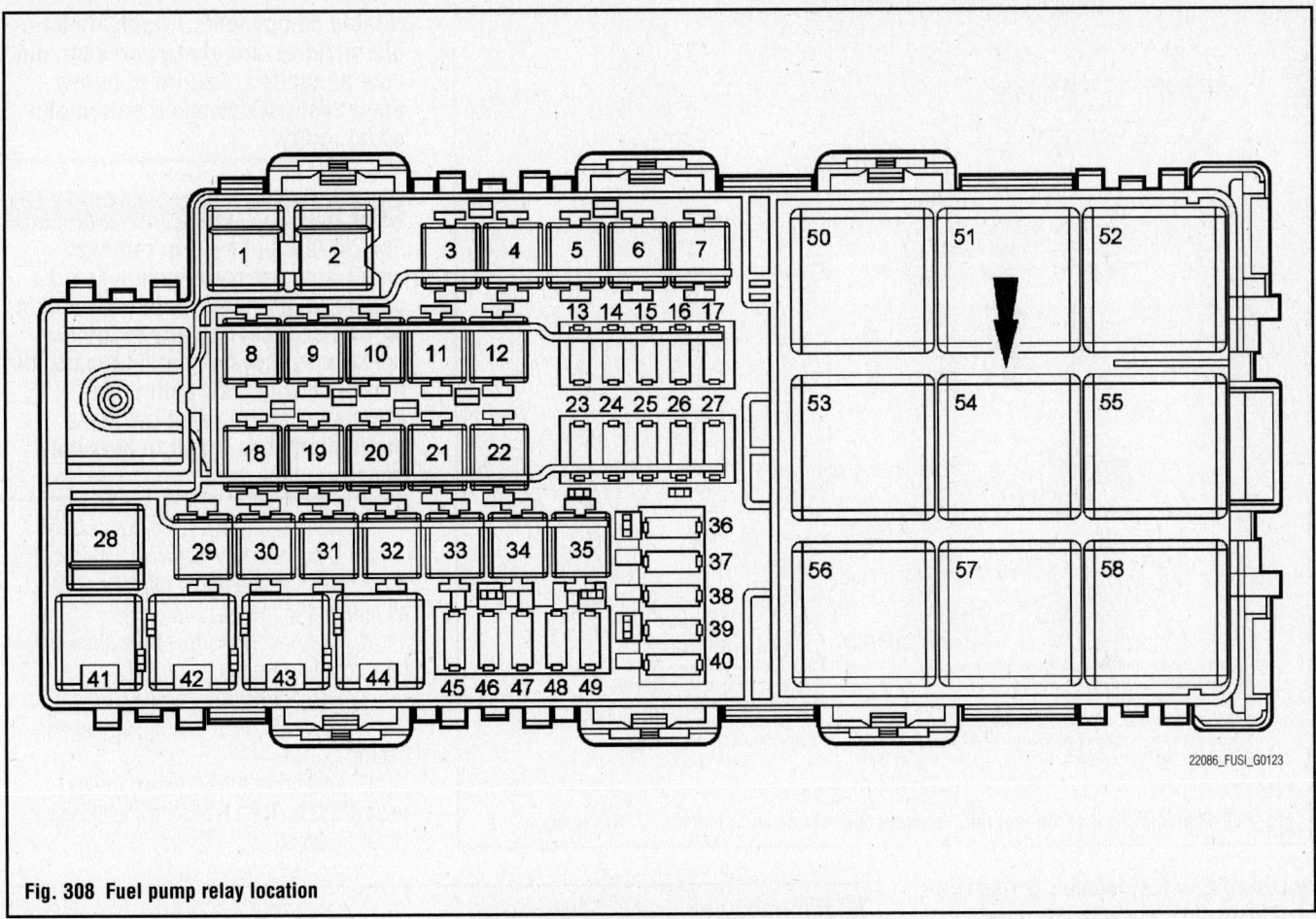

Fig. 308 Fuel pump relay location

ing or disconnecting any of the fuel lines or fuel system components, the fuel system pressure must be relieved to prevent accidental spraying of fuel, which may cause personal injury or a fire hazard.

➡The fuel pump relay is located in the battery junction box (BJB), relay number 54.

1. Remove the fuel pump relay.
2. Start the engine and allow it to idle until it stalls.
3. After the engine stalls, crank the engine for approximately 5 seconds to make sure the fuel injection supply manifold pressure has been released.
4. Turn the ignition switch to the **OFF** position.
5. When fuel system service is complete, install the fuel pump relay.

➡It may take more than one key cycle to pressurize the fuel system.

6. Cycle the ignition key and wait 3 seconds to pressurize the fuel system. Check for leaks before starting the engine.
7. Start the vehicle and check the fuel system for leaks

FUEL INJECTORS

REMOVAL & INSTALLATION

2.3L Engine

See Figure 309.

✳✳ CAUTION

Do not smoke or carry lighted tobacco or open flame of any type when working on or near any fuel-related components. Highly flammable mixtures are always present and may be ignited. Failure to follow these instructions can result in personal injury.

✳✳ CAUTION

Fuel in the fuel system remains under high pressure even when the engine is not running. Before working on or disconnecting any of the fuel tubes or fuel system components, the fuel system pressure must be relieved. Failure to follow these instructions can result in personal injury.

1. Relieve the fuel system pressure, as outlined in this section.
2. Disconnect the negative battery cable.
3. Remove the 2 nuts, the bolt and the generator air inlet duct.
4. Disconnect the fuel tube quick connect coupling from the fuel rail.
5. Detach the 2 wiring retainers from the fuel rail and remove the fuel rail insulator.
6. Disconnect the 2 swirl control valve electrical connectors.
7. Disconnect the 4 fuel injector electrical connectors.
8. Remove the 2 fuel rail bolts.
9. Remove the fuel rail and fuel injectors as an assembly.
10. Remove the 4 fuel injector retainer clips and the fuel injectors.
11. Remove and discard the 8 fuel injector O-ring seals.

To install:

✳✳ WARNING

Use O-ring seals that are made of special fuel-resistant material. Use of ordinary O-rings can cause the fuel system to leak. Do not reuse the O-ring seals.

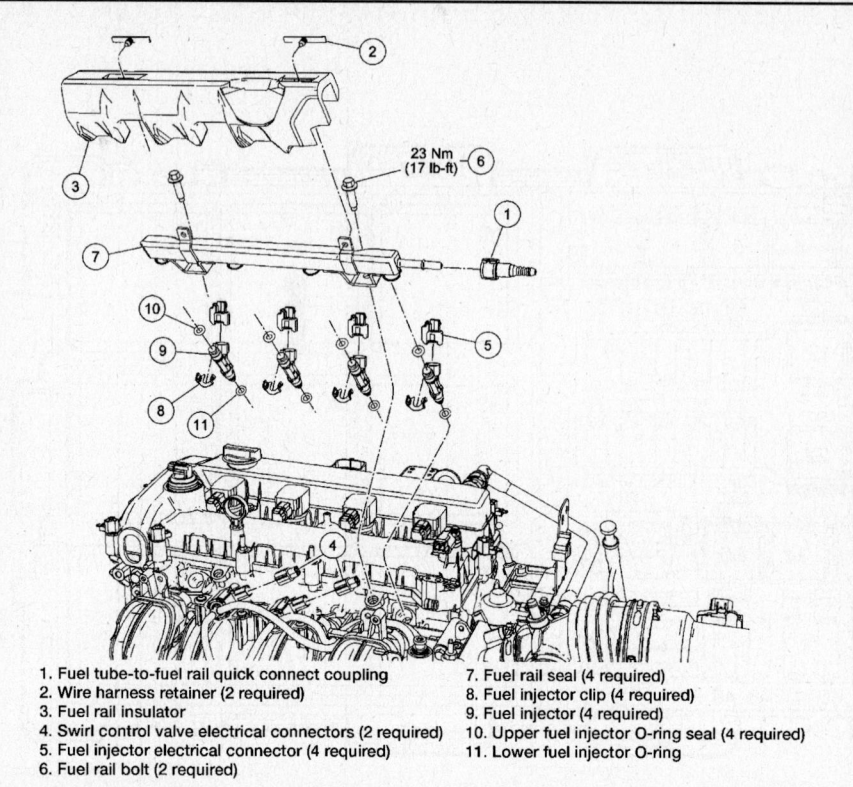

1. Fuel tube-to-fuel rail quick connect coupling
2. Wire harness retainer (2 required)
3. Fuel rail insulator
4. Swirl control valve electrical connectors (2 required)
5. Fuel injector electrical connector (4 required)
6. Fuel rail bolt (2 required)
7. Fuel rail seal (4 required)
8. Fuel injector clip (4 required)
9. Fuel injector (4 required)
10. Upper fuel injector O-ring seal (4 required)
11. Lower fuel injector O-ring

22086_FUSI_G0128

Fig. 309 Exploded view of the fuel rail, injectors and related components—2.3L engine

➡ Install new fuel injector O-ring seals and lubricate them with clean engine oil.

➡ Make sure the fuel rail clips snap back into place.

12. Install the fuel injectors and the retainer clips into the fuel rail.

13. Install the fuel rail and fuel injectors as an assembly.

14. Install the 2 fuel rail bolts. Tighten to 23 Nm (17 ft. lbs.).

15. Connect the 4 fuel injector electrical connectors.

16. Connect the 2 swirl control valve electrical connectors.

17. Install the fuel rail insulator and attach the 2 wiring harness retainers.

18. Connect the fuel tube quick connect coupling to the fuel rail.

19. Install the generator air inlet duct and the 2 nuts and the bolt. Tighten to 6 Nm (53 lb-in).

20. Connect the battery ground cable.

3.0L Engine

See Figure 310.

✳✳ CAUTION

Do not smoke or carry lighted tobacco or open flame of any type when working on or near any fuel-

related components. Highly flammable mixtures are always present and may be ignited. Failure to follow these instructions can result in personal injury.

✳✳ CAUTION

Fuel in the fuel system remains under high pressure even when the engine is not running. Before working on or disconnecting any of the fuel tubes or fuel system components, the fuel system pressure must be relieved. Failure to follow these instructions can result in personal injury.

1. Relieve the fuel system pressure.

2. Disconnect the negative battery cable.

3. Remove the upper intake manifold, as outlined in this section.

4. Disconnect the fuel tube quick connect coupling from the fuel rail.

5. Disconnect the Engine Coolant Temperature (ECT) sensor electrical connector.

6. Disconnect the 2 wire harness retainers from the LH side of the LH valve cover stud bolts.

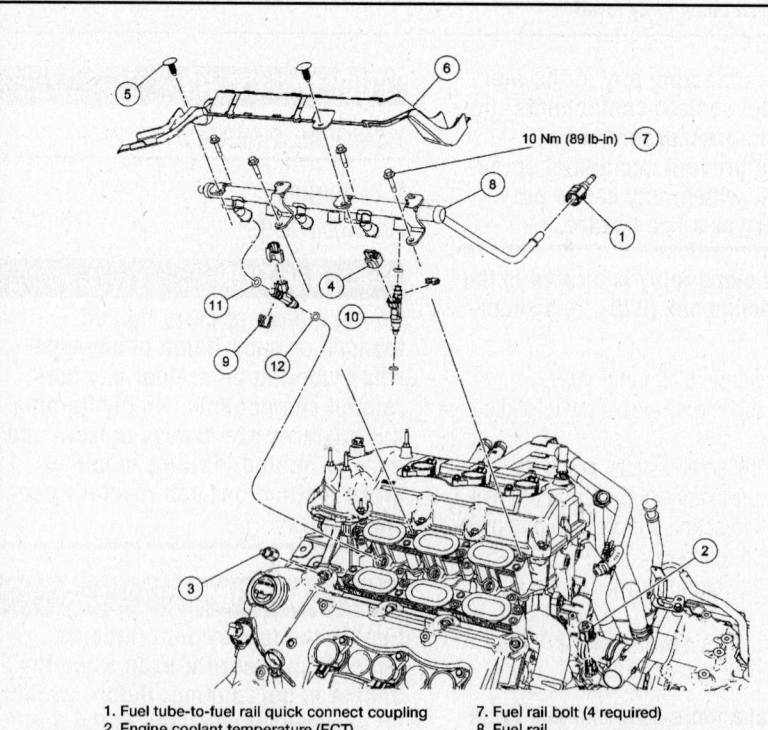

1. Fuel tube-to-fuel rail quick connect coupling
2. Engine coolant temperature (ECT) sensor electrical connector
3. Engine wiring harness retainer
4. Fuel injector electrical connector (6 required)
5. Pin-type retainer (2 required)
6. Wire harness cover seal
7. Fuel rail bolt (4 required)
8. Fuel rail
9. Fuel injector clip (6 required)
10. Fuel injector
11. Upper fuel injector O-ring (6 required)
12. Lower fuel injector O-ring (6 required)

22086_FUSI_G0129

Fig. 310 Exploded view of the fuel rail, injectors and related components—3.0L engine

7. Disconnect the 6 fuel injector electrical connectors.

8. Remove the 2 pin-type retainers from the wiring harness cover.

9. Remove the 4 fuel rail bolts.

10. Remove the fuel rail and injectors as an assembly.

11. Remove the 6 fuel injector clips and the 6 fuel injectors.

12. Remove and discard the 12 fuel injector O-ring seals.

To install:

✳✳ WARNING

Use O-ring seals that are made of special fuel-resistant material. The use of ordinary O-rings can cause the fuel system to leak. Do not reuse the O-ring seals.

➡️**Install new fuel injector O-ring seals and lubricate them with clean engine oil.**

13. Install the 6 fuel injectors and the 6 fuel injector clips into the fuel rail.

14. Install the fuel rail and fuel injectors as an assembly.

15. Install the 4 fuel rail bolts. Tighten to 10 Nm (89 lb-in).

16. Install the wiring harness cover and the 2 pin-type retainers.

17. Connect the 6 fuel injector electrical connectors.

18. Connect the 2 wire harness retainers to the LH valve cover stud bolts.

19. Connect the ECT sensor electrical connector.

20. Connect the fuel tube quick connect coupling to the fuel rail.

21. Install the upper intake manifold.

22. Connect the negative battery cable

3.5L Engine

See Figure 311.

✳✳ CAUTION

Observe all applicable safety precautions when working around fuel. Whenever servicing the fuel system, always work in a well ventilated area. Do not allow fuel spray or vapors to come in contact with a spark or open flame. Keep a dry chemical fire extinguisher near the work area. Always keep fuel in a container specifically designed for fuel storage; also, always properly seal fuel containers to avoid the possibility of fire or explosion.

1. Disconnect the negative battery cable.

2. Relieve the fuel system pressure, as outlined in this section.

3. Remove the upper intake manifold. Refer to the Intake Manifold procedure in the Engine Mechanical Section.

4. Disconnect the fuel tube-to-fuel rail quick connect coupling.

5. Disconnect the 6 fuel injector electrical connectors.

6. Remove the 4 fuel rail bolts.

7. Remove the fuel rail and injectors as an assembly.

8. Remove the 6 fuel injector clips and the 6 fuel injectors.

9. Remove and discard the 12 fuel injector O-ring seals.

To install:

✳✳ WARNING

Only use O-ring seals that are made of special fuel-resistant material. Using regular O-rings can cause the fuel system to leak. Do not reuse the O-ring seals.

✳✳ WARNING

The upper and lower O-ring seals are not interchangeable.

➡️**Install new fuel injector O-ring seals and lubricate them with clean engine oil.**

10. Install the 6 fuel injectors and the 6 fuel injector clips into the fuel rail.

11. Install the fuel rail and fuel injectors as an assembly.

12. Install the 4 fuel rail bolts. Tighten to 10 Nm (89 inch lbs.).

13. Connect the 6 fuel injector electrical connectors.

14. Connect the fuel tube-to-fuel rail quick connect coupling.

15. Install the upper intake manifold.

16. Connect the negative battery cable.

FUEL PUMP

REMOVAL & INSTALLATION

See Figures 312 and 313.

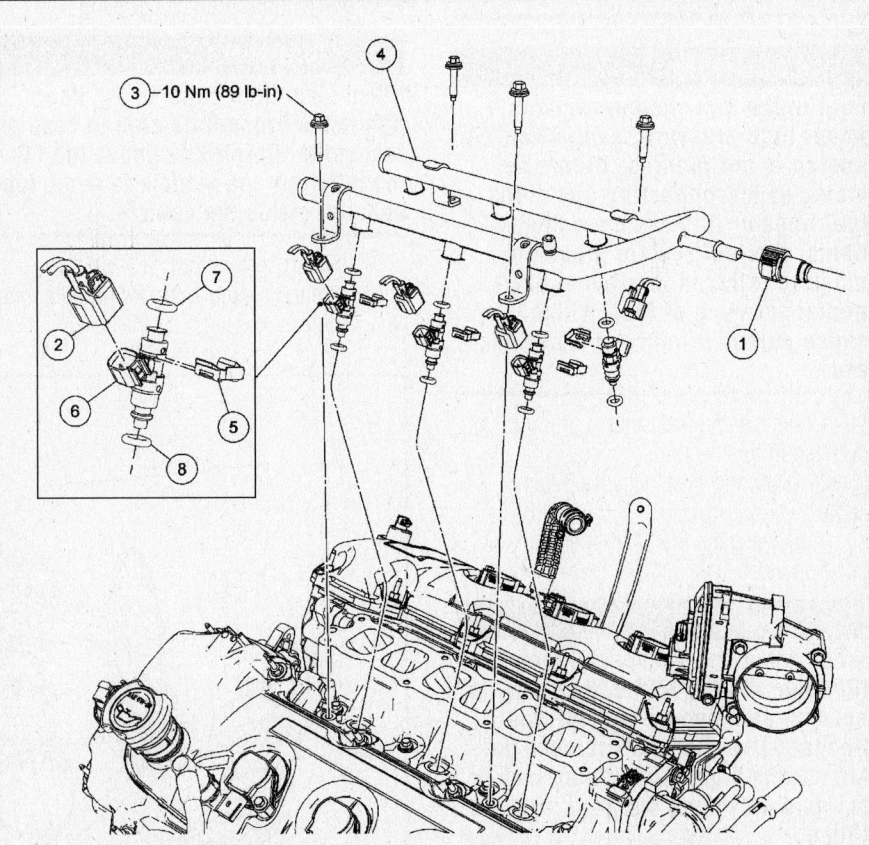

1. Fuel tube-to-fuel rail quick connect coupling
2. Fuel injector electrical connector (6 required)
3. Fuel rail bolt (4 required)
4. Fuel rail
5. Fuel injector clip (6 required)
6. Fuel injector (6 required)
7. Upper fuel injector O-ring seal (6 required)
8. Lower fuel injector O-ring seal (6 required)

22086_EDGE_G0124

Fig. 311 Exploded view of the fuel rail, injectors and related components—3.5L engine

⁑ CAUTION

Observe all applicable safety precautions when working around fuel. Whenever servicing the fuel system, always work in a well ventilated area. Do not allow fuel spray or vapors to come in contact with a spark or open flame. Keep a dry chemical fire extinguisher near the work area. Always keep fuel in a container specifically designed for fuel storage; also, always properly seal fuel containers to avoid the possibility of fire or explosion.

⁑ CAUTION

Do not carry personal electronic devices such as cell phones, pagers or audio equipment of any type when working on or near any fuel-related components. Highly flammable mixtures are always present and may be ignited. Failure to follow these instructions may result in personal injury.

⁑ CAUTION

Fuel in the fuel system remains under high pressure, even when the engine is not running. Before servicing or disconnecting any of the fuel lines or fuel system components, the fuel system pressure must be relieved to prevent accidental spraying of fuel, which may cause personal injury or a fire hazard.

1. Relieve the fuel system pressure, as outlined in this section.
2. Disconnect the negative battery cable.
3. Release the fuel tank filler cap and position aside.

⁑ WARNING

When removing the special tool, the fitting on the end of the hose can become detained by the one-way flapper valve. Carefully remove the hose using a gentle agitating motion to avoid detaching the hose from the fitting.

➡ The special tool must be inserted into the fuel tank filler pipe until the fitting on the end of the hose enters into the fuel tank spout, opening the one-way flapper valve.

4. Insert special tool 310-102, or equivalent fuel draining device into the fuel tank filler pipe.

➡ This step will remove approximately 1/8 tank of the fuel from a completely full fuel tank and the majority of any residual fuel in the fuel tank filler pipe.

5. Attach the fuel storage tanker to the special tool and remove as much fuel as possible from the fuel tank and fuel tank filler pipe.
6. Remove the rear seat lower cushion.
7. Position aside the carpet and/or any insulation covering the FP module access cover.
8. For Front Wheel Drive (FWD) vehicles, remove the 4 screws and the FP module access cover.
   a. To install, tighten to 2 Nm (18 lb-in).
9. For All Wheel Drive (AWD) vehicles, remove the 3 screws and the FP module access cover.
   a. To install, tighten to 2 Nm (18 lb-in).
10. Disconnect the FP module electrical connector.
11. Disconnect the fuel supply tube-to-FP module quick connect coupling.

⁑ WARNING

Place absorbent pads on the floor pan in the immediate area in case of fuel spills. Carefully remove the FP module from the vehicle to avoid fuel spillage inside the vehicle.

12. Using special tool 310-123, or equivalent tool, remove the FP module lock ring retainer.

13. For AWD vehicles. carefully lift the FP module out of the fuel tank enough to access and release the fuel crossover tube-to-FP module quick connect coupling.

⁑ WARNING

The FP module must be handled carefully to avoid damage to the float arm.

⁑ WARNING

The FP module will have residual fuel remaining internally, drain into a suitable container.

14. Completely remove the FP module from the fuel tank.

⁑ WARNING

Inspect the mating surfaces of the FP module flange and the fuel tank O-ring seal contact surfaces. Do not polish or adjust the O-ring seal contact area of the fuel tank flange or the fuel tank.

15. Install a new FP module or fuel tank if the O-ring seal contact area is bent, scratched or corroded.

⁑ WARNING

Make sure to install a new FP module O-ring seal. Install a new lock ring if it is bent, damaged or corroded.

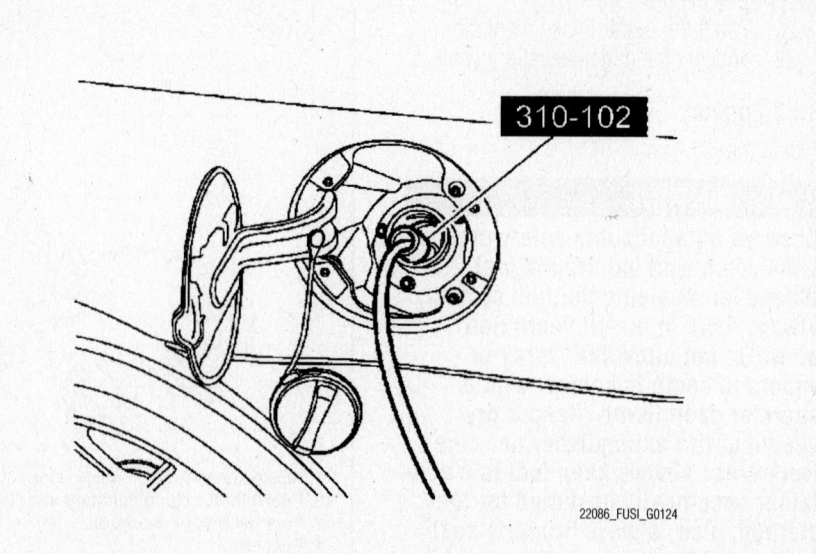

310-102

22086_FUSI_G0124

Fig. 312 Insert special tool 310-102, or equivalent fuel draining device into the fuel tank filler pipe.

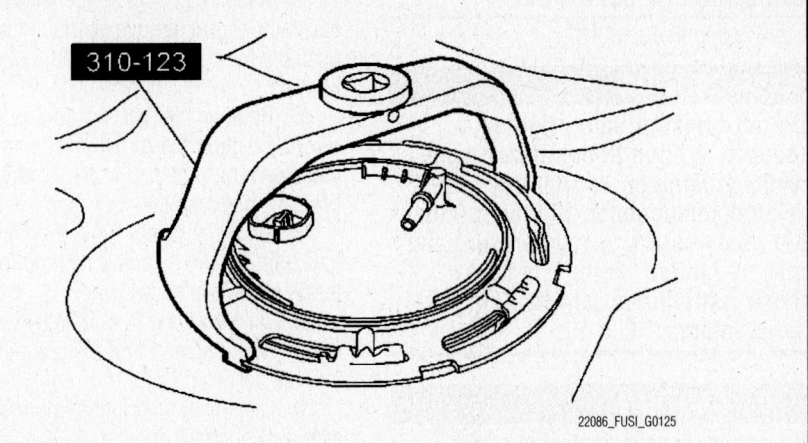

Fig. 313 Using special tool 310-123, or equivalent tool, remove the FP module lock ring retainer

➡ **To install, apply clean engine oil to the O-ring seal.**

16. Remove and discard the FP module O-ring seal.

17. To install, reverse the removal procedure. Make sure the alignment tab on the FP module and the fuel tank meet before tightening the FP module lock ring

FUEL TANK

REMOVAL & INSTALLATION

Front Wheel Drive (FWD) Models

❊❊ CAUTION

Do not smoke or carry lighted tobacco or open flame of any type when working on or near any fuel-related components. Highly flammable mixtures are always present and may be ignited. Failure to follow these instructions can result in personal injury.

❊❊ CAUTION

Do not carry personal electronic devices such as cell phones, pagers or audio equipment of any type when working on or near any fuel-related components. Highly flammable mixtures are always present and may be ignited. Failure to follow these instructions can result in personal injury.

❊❊ CAUTION

The evaporative emissions system contains fuel vapor and condensed fuel vapor. Although not present in large quantities, it still presents the danger of explosion or fire. Disconnect the battery ground cable from the battery to minimize the possibility of an electrical spark occurring, and possibly causing a fire or explosion if fuel vapor or liquid fuel are present in the area. Failure to follow these instructions can result in personal injury.

❊❊ CAUTION

Fuel in the fuel system remains under high pressure even when the engine is not running. Before repairing or disconnecting any of the fuel system components, the fuel system pressure must be relieved to prevent accidental spraying of fuel causing personal injury or a fire hazard.

1. Raise and safely support the vehicle.
2. Relieve the fuel system pressure.
3. Disconnect the battery ground cable.
4. Drain the fuel tank, as outlined in this section.

❊❊ WARNING

Some residual fuel may remain in the fuel tank filler pipe after draining the fuel tank. Carefully drain any remaining fuel into a suitable container.

5. Release the clamp and disconnect the fuel tank filler pipe hose from the fuel tank.

   a. To install, tighten to 4 Nm (35 lb-in).

6. Disconnect the fuel vapor tube assembly-to-fuel tank quick connect coupling.

7. Support the exhaust system with suitable jack stands.

8. Remove the 2 nuts and disconnect the catalytic converter from the exhaust flexible pipe.

   a. To install, tighten to 40 Nm (30 ft. lbs.).

9. Discard the catalytic converter flange gasket.

10. For vehicles with 2.3L engine, with the aid of an assistant, release the 4 exhaust hangers and remove the exhaust system.

11. For vehicles with 3.0L and 3.5L engines, with the aid of an assistant, release the 5 exhaust hangers and remove the exhaust system.

12. Remove the 4 nuts, 2 clips and 2 pin-type retainers from the fuel tank heat shield.

13. Remove the fuel tank heat shield.

14. Install a suitable lifting device below the fuel tank.

15. Remove the 4 bolts and the 2 fuel tank mounting straps.

   a. To install, tighten to 47 Nm (35 ft. lbs.).

16. Carefully lower the fuel tank from the vehicle.

17. To install, reverse the removal procedure. Install a new catalytic converter flange gasket.

All Wheel Drive (AWD) Models

❊❊ CAUTION

Do not smoke or carry lighted tobacco or open flame of any type when working on or near any fuel-related components. Highly flammable mixtures are always present and may be ignited. Failure to follow these instructions can result in personal injury.

❊❊ CAUTION

Do not carry personal electronic devices such as cell phones, pagers or audio equipment of any type when working on or near any fuel-related components. Highly flammable mixtures are always present and may be ignited. Failure to follow these instructions can result in personal injury.

✳ CAUTION

The evaporative emissions system contains fuel vapor and condensed fuel vapor. Although not present in large quantities, it still presents the danger of explosion or fire. Disconnect the battery ground cable from the battery to minimize the possibility of an electrical spark occurring, and possibly causing a fire or explosion if fuel vapor or liquid fuel are present in the area. Failure to follow these instructions can result in personal injury.

✳ CAUTION

Fuel in the fuel system remains under high pressure even when the engine is not running. Before repairing or disconnecting any of the fuel system components, the fuel system pressure must be relieved to prevent accidental spraying of fuel causing personal injury or a fire hazard.

1. Raise and safely support the vehicle.
2. Relieve the fuel system pressure.
3. Disconnect the battery ground cable.
4. Drain the fuel tank, as outlined in this section.
5. Remove the muffler and tailpipe.
6. Remove the driveshaft.
7. Position a suitable lifting device under the fuel tank.
8. Remove the 4 bolts and the 2 fuel tank mounting straps.
   a. To install, tighten to 47 Nm (35 ft. lbs.).
9. Partially lower the fuel tank enough to access the fuel tank filler pipe clamp.

✳ WARNING

Some residual fuel may remain in the fuel tank filler pipe after draining the fuel tank. Carefully drain any remaining fuel into a suitable container.

10. Release the clamp and disconnect the fuel tank filler pipe hose from the fuel tank.
    a. To install, tighten to 4 Nm (35 lb-in).
11. Disconnect the fuel vapor tube assembly-to-fuel tank quick connect coupling.
12. Carefully lower the fuel tank from the vehicle.
13. To install, reverse the removal procedure

DRAINING THE FUEL TANK
See Figures 315 and 316.

✳ CAUTION

Do not smoke or carry lighted tobacco or open flame of any type when working on or near any fuel-related components. Highly flammable mixtures are always present and may be ignited. Failure to follow these instructions can result in personal injury.

✳ CAUTION

Do not carry personal electronic devices such as cell phones, pagers or audio equipment of any type when working on or near any fuel-related components. Highly flammable mixtures are always present and may be ignited. Failure to follow these instructions can result in personal injury.

✳ CAUTION

This procedure involves fuel handling. Be prepared for spillage at all times and always observe fuel handling precautions. Failure to follow these instructions can result in personal injury.

1. Relieve the fuel system pressure, as outlined in this section.
2. Disconnect the negative battery cable.
3. Release the fuel tank filler cap and position it aside.

✳ WARNING

After removing the special tool, the fitting on the end of the hose can become detained by the one-way flapper valve. Carefully remove the hose using a gentle agitating motion to avoid detaching the hose from the fitting.

➡ The special tool must be inserted into the fuel tank filler pipe until the fitting on the end of the hose enters into the fuel tank spout, opening the one-way flapper valve.

4. Insert special tool 310-102, or equivalent fuel draining device into the fuel tank filler pipe.

➡ This step will remove approximately 1/8 tank of the fuel from a completely full fuel tank and the majority of any residual fuel in the fuel tank filler pipe.

5. Attach the fuel storage tanker to the special tool and remove as much fuel as possible from the fuel tank and fuel tank filler pipe.
6. Remove the rear seat lower cushion.
7. Position the carpet and/or any insulation covering the fuel pump module access cover aside.
8. On Front wheel Drive (FWD) vehicles, remove the 4 screws and the fuel pump module access cover.
9. On All Wheel Drive (AWD) vehicles, remove the 3 screws and the fuel pump module access cover.
10. Disconnect the fuel pump module electrical connector.
11. Disconnect the fuel supply tube-to-fuel pump module quick connect coupling.
12. Using the special tool, remove the fuel pump module lock ring retainer.
13. Position the fuel pump module aside and insert the tube from the fuel storage tanker into the fuel pump module aperture and drain as much fuel from the fuel tank as possible.
14. On AWD vehicles:
    a. Remove the 3 screws and the fuel level sensor access cover.
    b. Disconnect the fuel level sensor electrical connector.
    c. Release the lock tab, rotate the fuel level sensor counterclockwise approximately ¼ turn, lift and position aside.
    d. Insert the tube from the fuel storage tanker into the fuel level sensor aperture and drain the remainder of the fuel from the fuel tank.

IDLE SPEED

ADJUSTMENT

Idle speed is maintained by the Powertrain Control Module (PCM). No adjustment is necessary or possible.

THROTTLE BODY

REMOVAL & INSTALLATION
See Figures 314 through 316.

1. Remove the air cleaner outlet pipe.
2. Disconnect the electronic throttle control electrical connector.
3. Remove the 4 bolts and the throttle body. Discard the throttle body gasket.

To install:
4. Install a new throttle gasket.
5. Install the throttle body and tighten to 10 Nm (89 inch lbs.).
6. Attach the electronic throttle control electrical connector.
7. Install the air cleaner outlet pipe.

1. Electronic throttle control electrical connector
2. Coolant inlet hose-to-throttle body (TB) clamp
3. Coolant inlet hose to TB
4. Coolant outlet hose-to-TB clamp
5. Coolant outlet hose to TB
6. TB bolt (4 required)
7. TB
8. B gasket

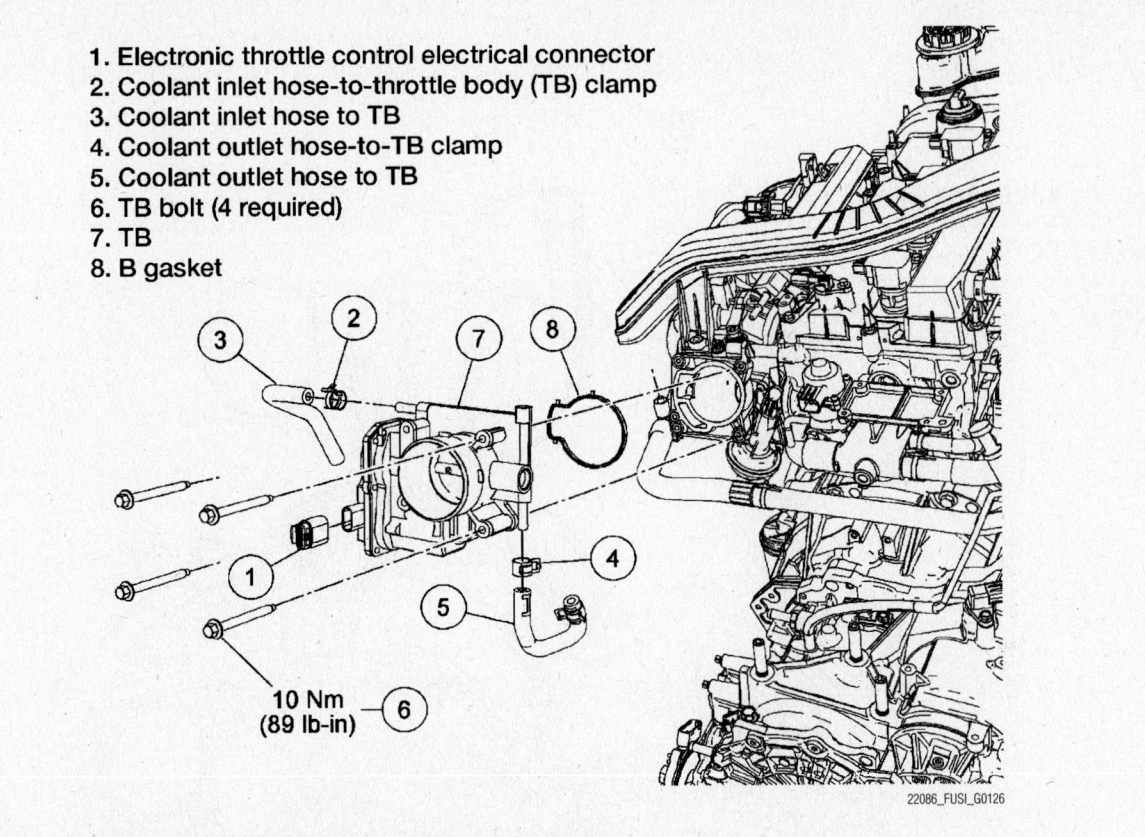

10 Nm
(89 lb-in)

22086_FUSI_G0126

Fig. 314 Exploded view of the throttle body and related components—2.3L engine

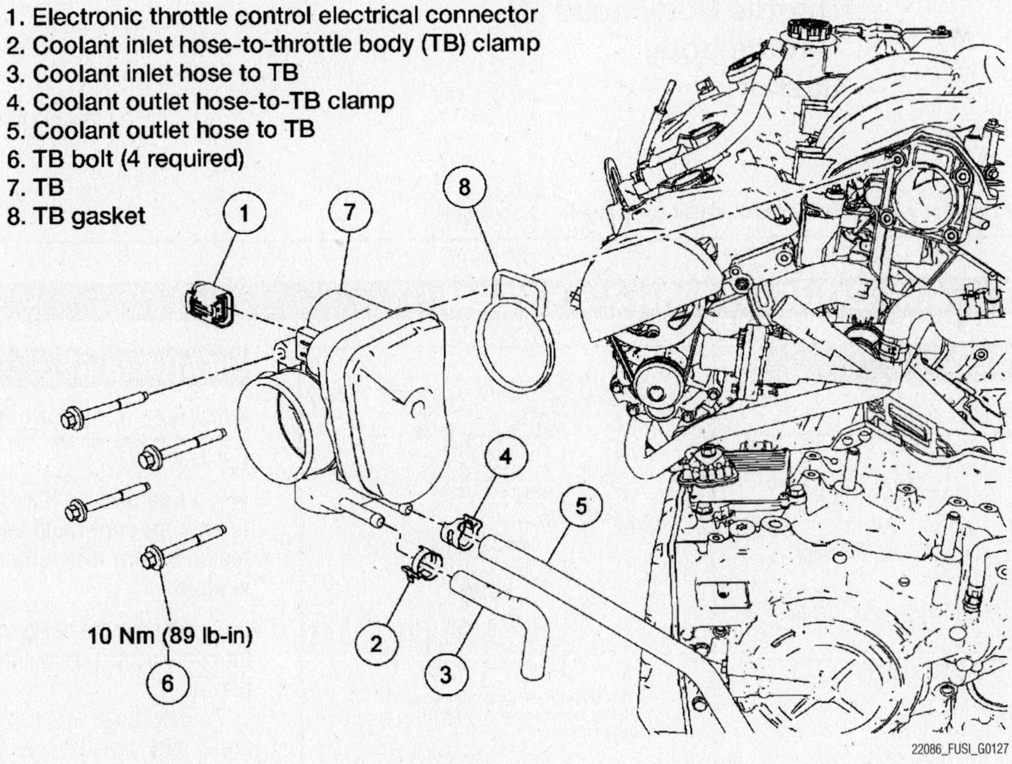

1. Electronic throttle control electrical connector
2. Coolant inlet hose-to-throttle body (TB) clamp
3. Coolant inlet hose to TB
4. Coolant outlet hose-to-TB clamp
5. Coolant outlet hose to TB
6. TB bolt (4 required)
7. TB
8. TB gasket

10 Nm (89 lb-in)

22086_FUSI_G0127

Fig. 315 Exploded view of the throttle body and related components—3.0L engine

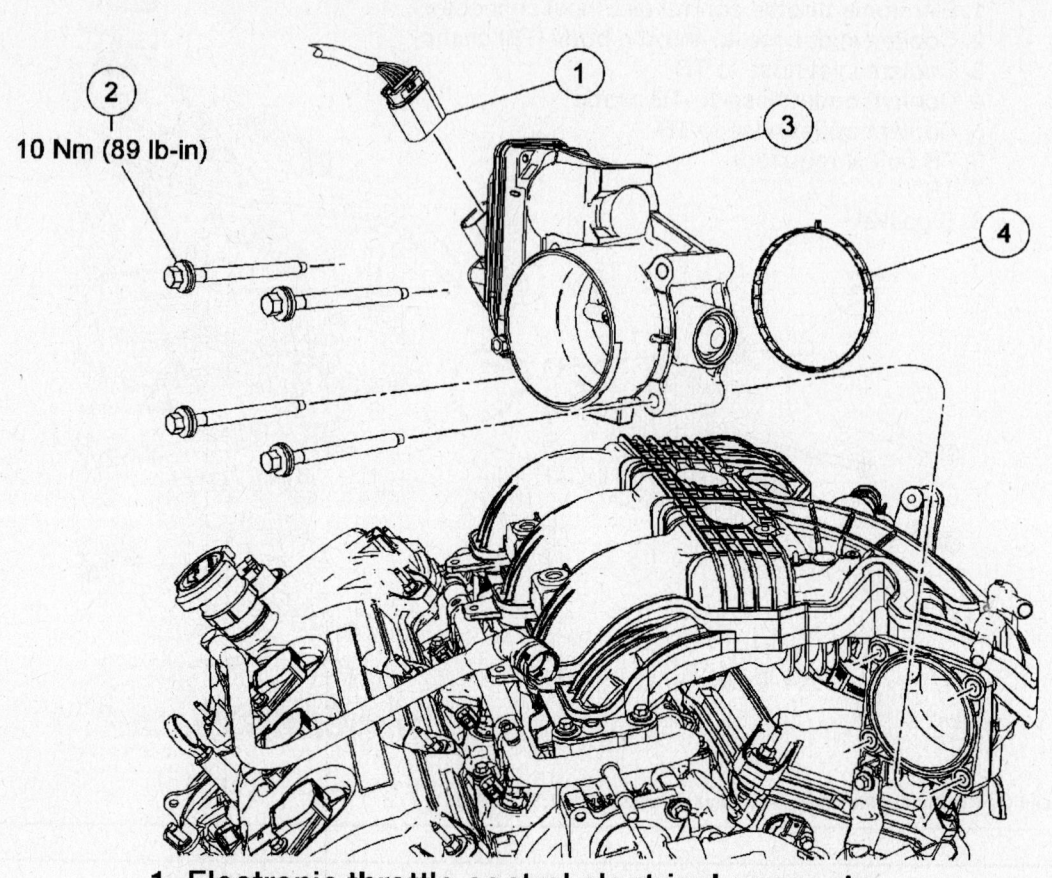

10 Nm (89 lb-in)

1, Electronic throttle control electrical connector
2. Throttle Body bolts (4)
3. Throttle body
4. Gasket

22086_EDGE_G0123

Fig. 316 Exploded view of the throttle body and related components—3.5L engine

HEATING & AIR CONDITIONING SYSTEM

BLOWER MOTOR

REMOVAL & INSTALLATION

See Figure 317.

1. Disconnect the negative battery cable.

2. For the MKZ, remove the RH lower instrument panel insulator.

3. Disconnect the blower motor electrical connector.

4. Remove the 3 blower motor screws.

5. Remove the blower motor.

6. Installation is the reverse of the removal procedure.

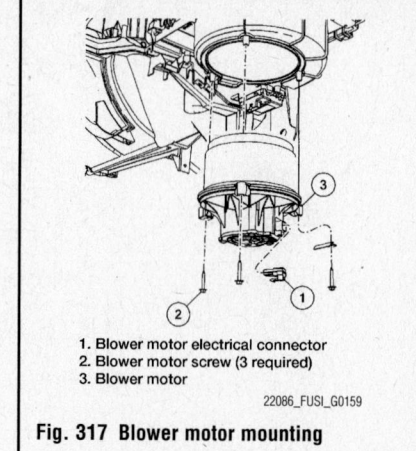

1. Blower motor electrical connector
2. Blower motor screw (3 required)
3. Blower motor

22086_FUSI_G0159

Fig. 317 Blower motor mounting

HEATER CORE

REMOVAL & INSTALLATION

See Figure 318.

→If a heater core leak is suspected, the heater core must be pressure leak tested before it is removed from the vehicle.

1. Remove the heater core and evaporator core housing, as outlined in this section.

2. Detach the wire harness from the heater core cover.

3. Remove the 8 heater core cover screws.

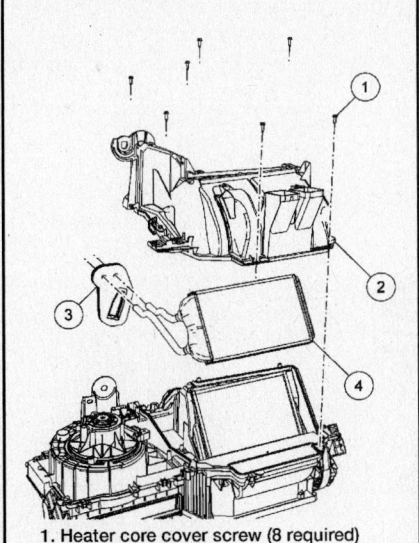

Fig. 318 Exploded view of the heater core

1. Heater core cover screw (8 required)
2. Heater core cover
3. Dash panel seal
4. Heater core

22086_FUSI_G0160

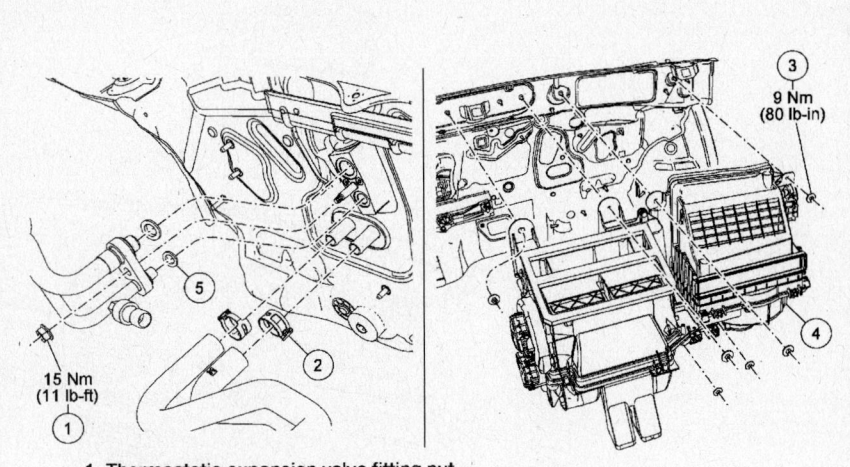

1. Thermostatic expansion valve fitting nut
2. Heater hose clamp (2 required)
3. Heater core and evaporator core housing nut (6 required)
4. Heater core and evaporator core housing
5. Gaskt seal (2 required)

22086_FUSI_G0161

Fig. 319 Exploded view of the heater core and evaporator core housing

4. Remove the heater core cover.
5. Remove the dash panel seal from the heater core tubes.
6. Remove the heater core.
7. To install, reverse the removal procedure

HEATER CORE AND EVAPORATOR CORE HOUSING

REMOVAL & INSTALLATION

See Figure 319.

1. For 3.0L or 3.5L engines, remove the lower cowl panel grille.

✳✳ WARNING

Only a MVAC-trained, EPA-certified, automotive technician should service the A/C system or its components.

2. Recover the refrigerant, using the proper equipment.
3. Drain the engine coolant.
4. Remove the instrument panel, as outlined in this section.
5. Disconnect the A/C pressure transducer electrical connector and detach the wire harness from the thermostatic expansion valve (TXV) stud.
6. Remove the TXV fitting nut and disconnect the fitting.
7. Discard the gasket seals.
8. Release the heater hoses clamps and disconnect the hoses from the heater core

9. Remove the 6 heater core and evaporator core housing nuts.
10. Remove the heater core and evaporator core housing.

To install:

11. To install, reverse the removal procedure, noting the following:
    a. Tighten the heater core and evaporator core housing nuts to 9 Nm (80 lb-in).
    b. Tighten the TXV fitting nut to 15 Nm (11 ft. lbs.).
    c. Install new gasket seals.
    d. Lubricate the refrigerant system with the correct amount of clean PAG oil.
    e. Fill the engine coolant level.
    f. Evacuate, leak test and charge the refrigerant system.

INSTRUMENT PANEL

REMOVAL & INSTALLATION

See Figures 320 through 323.

✳✳ WARNING

Electronic modules are sensitive to static charges. If exposed to these charges, damage may result.

1. Disarm the Supplemental Restraint System (SRS), as outlined in the Chassis Electrical Section.
2. Remove the floor console.
3. Remove the gearshift lever.

4. Remove the LH and RH instrument panel end trim panels.
5. Remove the weatherstripping from the front door openings near the instrument panel.
6. Remove the A-pillar trim panels.
7. Remove the RH and LH cowl kick panels.
8. If equipped, remove the RH instrument panel insulator.
9. From behind the LH kick panel, disconnect the 2 electrical connectors.
10. Remove the small gray connector and the large black connector from the smart junction box (SJB).
11. Remove the 2 screws and position the hood latch release handle aside.

✳✳ WARNING

To avoid damage to the bulkhead electrical connector, be sure the release handle is in the full upward position before disconnecting the electrical connector.

12. From behind the RH kick panel, disconnect the bulkhead electrical connector and the antenna lead-in cable.
13. From inside the glove box, disconnect the 2 A/C electrical connectors.
14. Disconnect the 2 electrical connector and retainer located on the floor between the 2 front seats.

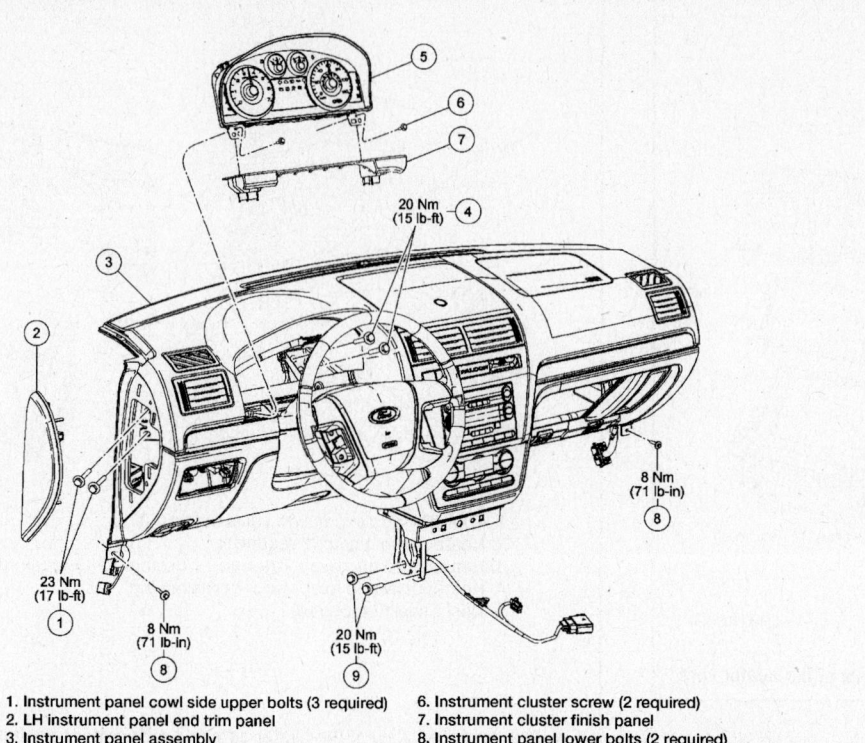

20 Nm
(15 lb-ft)

23 Nm
(17 lb-ft)

8 Nm
(71 lb-in)

20 Nm
(15 lb-ft)

8 Nm
(71 lb-in)

1. Instrument panel cowl side upper bolts (3 required)
2. LH instrument panel end trim panel
3. Instrument panel assembly
4. Instrument panel cluster opening bolts (2 required)
5. Instrument cluster
6. Instrument cluster screw (2 required)
7. Instrument cluster finish panel
8. Instrument panel lower bolts (2 required)
9. Instrument panel center brace bolts (2 required)

22086_FUSI_G0162

Fig. 320 Exploded view of the instrument panel—Fusion shown, Milan similar

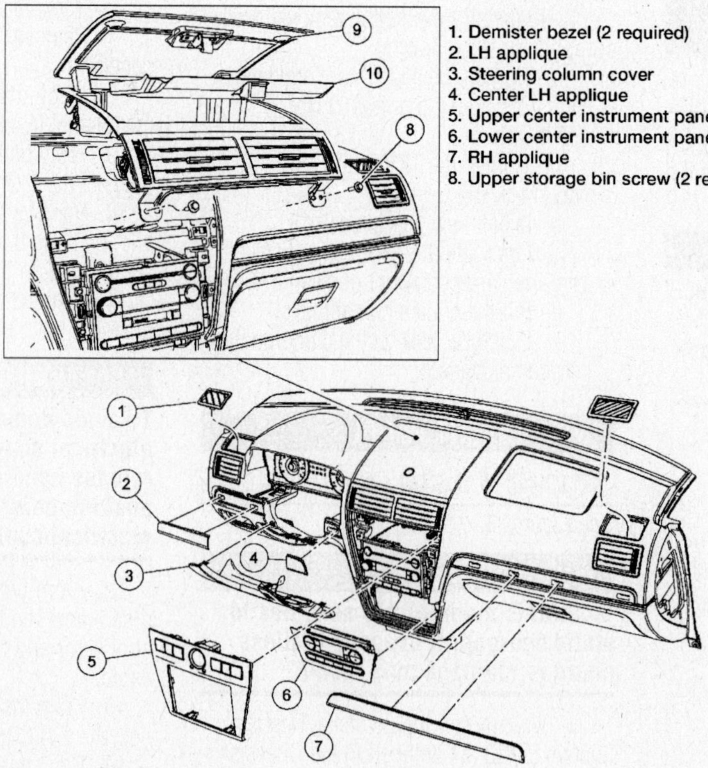

1. Demister bezel (2 required)
2. LH applique
3. Steering column cover
4. Center LH applique
5. Upper center instrument panel finish panel
6. Lower center instrument panel finish panel
7. RH applique
8. Upper storage bin screw (2 required)

22086_FUSI_G0163

Fig. 321 Exploded view of the instrument panel finish panels—Fusion and Milan

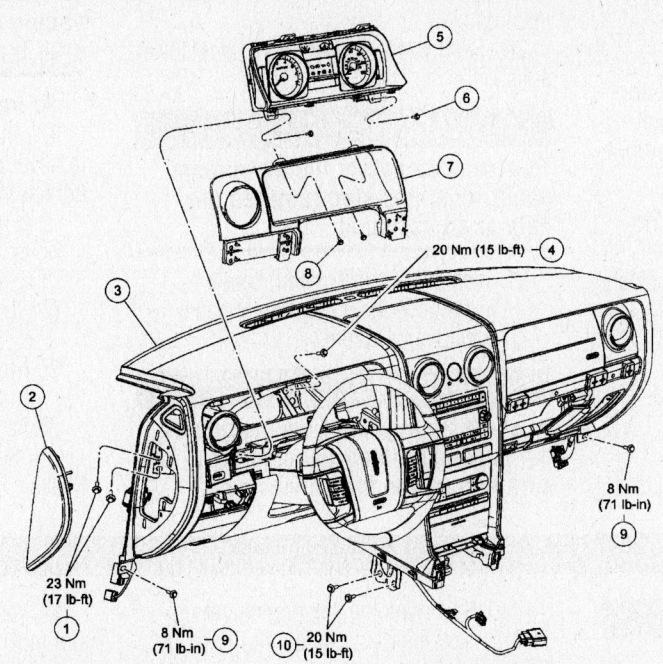

20 Nm (15 lb-ft)

8 Nm
(71 lb-in)

23 Nm
(17 lb-ft)

8 Nm
(71 lb-in)

20 Nm
(15 lb-ft)

1. Instrument panel cowl side upper bolts (3 required)
2. LH instrument panel end trim panel
3. Instrument panel assembly
4. Instrument panel cluster opening bolt (2 required)
5. Instrument cluster
6. Instrument cluster screw (2 required)
7. Instrument cluster finish panel
8. Instrument cluster finish panel screw (2 required)
9. Instrument panel lower bolts (2 required)
10. Instrument panel center brace bolts (2 required)

22086_FUSI_G0164

Fig. 322 Exploded view of the instrument panel—MKZ shown, Zephyr similar

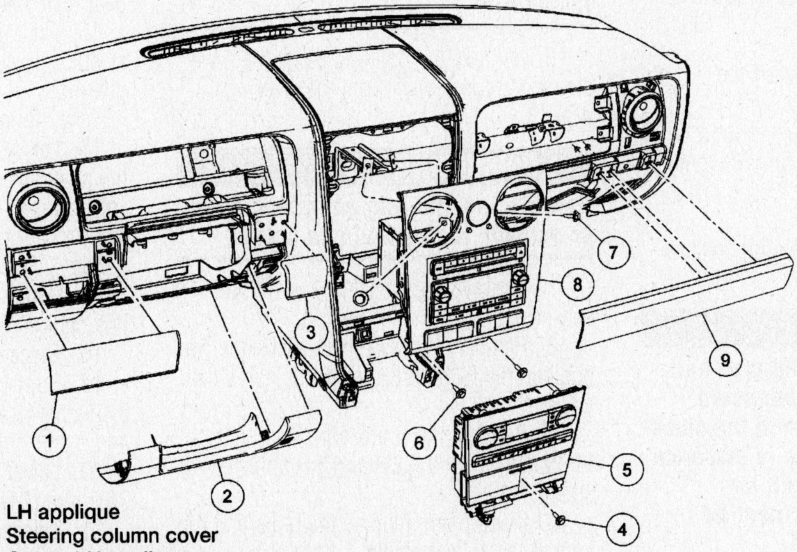

1. LH applique
2. Steering column cover
3. Center LH applique
4. Lower center instrument panel finish panel screw
5. Lower center instrument panel finish panel
6. Upper center instrument panel finish panel lower screw (2 required)
7. Upper center instrument panel finish panel upper screw (2 required)
8. Upper center instrument panel finish panel
9. RH applique

22086_FUSI_G0165

Fig. 323 Exploded view of the instrument panel finish panels—MKZ shown, Zephyr similar

15. Remove the 2 nuts and position the steering column pinch bolt cover aside.

➡To make sure of proper location during installation, index-mark the position of the steering column shaft before removing the pinch bolt.

16. Remove the steering column pinch bolt.

17. Remove the instrument cluster finish panel.

18. Remove the instrument cluster:
a. Remove the 2 screws.
b. Remove the instrument cluster.
c. Disconnect the electrical connector.

19. From through the instrument cluster opening, remove the 2 instrument cluster opening bolts.

20. Remove the 2 instrument panel lower bolts.

❋❋ WARNING

To avoid damage to the instrument panel, this next step requires the help of an assistant.

21. Remove the instrument panel:
a. Remove the 3 instrument panel cowl side upper bolts.

❋❋ WARNING

To avoid an improper connection at the bulkhead electrical connector, be sure to position the connector for

installation then push the release handle to the full downward position until it clicks.

To install:

22. Installation is the reverse of the removal procedure, noting the following tighten the specifications:
a. Instrument panel cowl side upper bolts: 23 Nm (17 ft. lbs.)
b. Instrument panel lower bolts: 8 Nm (71 lb-in)
c. Instrument cluster opening bolts: 20 Nm (15 ft. lbs.)
d. Steering column pinch bolt: 25 Nm (18 ft. lbs.)

23. Rearm the SRS, as outlined in the Chassis Electrical Section.

STEERING

POWER STEERING GEAR

REMOVAL & INSTALLATION

❋ WARNING

When repairing the power steering system, care should be taken to prevent the entry of contaminants or premature failure of the power steering components may result.

Front Wheel Drive (FWD) Models
See Figure 324.

1. Raise and safely support the vehicle.

2. Turn the steering wheel to the straight-ahead position and turn the ignition switch to the OFF position.

3. Remove the key.

4. Remove the lower steering column shaft joint cover bolts.

❋ WARNING

Do not allow the intermediate shaft to rotate while it is disconnected from the gear or damage to the clockspring can occur. If there is evidence that the intermediate shaft has rotated, the clockspring must be removed and recentered.

❋❋ WARNING

Make sure to correctly index-mark the steering gear-to-steering column shaft position or unequal right to left turns may occur, causing tire contact with the body and/or clockspring damage.

5. Matchmark the steering column shaft-to-steering gear position for reference during installation.

❋❋ WARNING

Do not allow the steering intermediate shaft to rotate while it is disconnected from the steering gear or damage to the clockspring may occur. If there is evidence that the intermediate shaft has rotated, the clockspring must be removed and recentered.

6. Remove the bolt and disconnect the steering column shaft from the steering gear.

❋❋ WARNING

Remove the steering gear/dash seal or damage to the seal can occur.

7. Remove the steering gear/dash seal.

8. Remove 4 screws from each side and position the RH and LH fender splash shield aside.

9. Remove the 6 pin-type retainers (4 shown) from the LH and RH splash shield.

10. If equipped, remove the bolts and the underbody splash shield.

11. Remove the 2 outer tie-rod end cotter pins and nuts. Discard the cotter pins.

❋❋ WARNING

Do not use a hammer to separate the outer tie-rod end from the wheel knuckle or damage to the wheel knuckle may result.

12. Using a suitable tie rod end removal tool tool, separate the outer tie-rod ends from the knuckle.

➡**Always install new fasteners and gaskets. Clean flange faces prior to new gasket installation to make sure of proper sealing.**

13. Remove and discard the 2 catalytic converter-to-exhaust flexible pipe nuts and separate the exhaust flexible pipe.

14. Remove the 2 bolts and the steering gear heat shield.

15. On 2.3L engines, remove the power steering pressure line bracket-to-steering gear bolt.
a. To install, tighten to 9 Nm (80 lb-in).

16. On 3.0L and 3.5L engines, remove the power steering pressure line bracket-to-steering gear bolt.
a. To install, tighten to 15 Nm (11 ft. lbs.).

17. Remove the power steering pressure line banjo bolt.

18. Discard the bolt and 2 seals.

19. Support the rear of the subframe with a suitable jack and remove the 4 rear bolts and 2 rear nuts.

20. Lower the rear of the front subframe 76.2 mm (3 in) with the support of the jack.

21. Release the clamp and disconnect the steering gear-to-fluid cooler return hose.

22. Remove the 3 steering gear bolts.

23. Remove the steering gear from the LH side of the vehicle.

To install:

❋❋ WARNING

While repairing the power steering system, care should be taken to

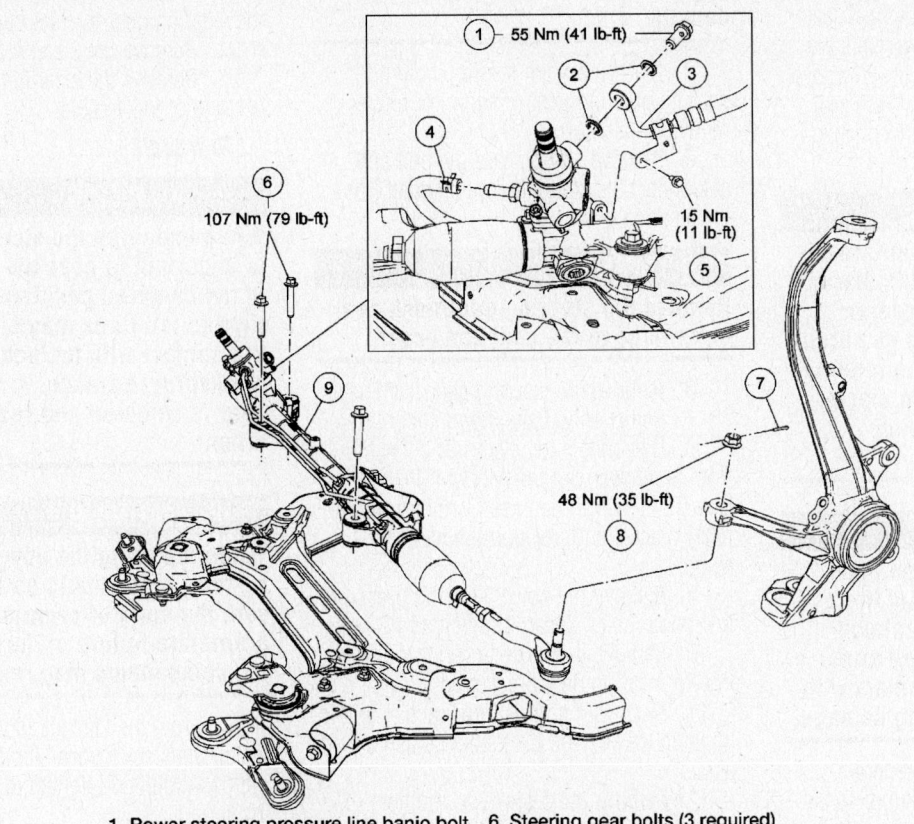

1 — 55 Nm (41 lb-ft)

107 Nm (79 lb-ft)

15 Nm (11 lb-ft)

48 Nm (35 lb-ft)

1. Power steering pressure line banjo bolt
2. Power steering pressure line seals
3. Power steering return hose
4. Power steering pressure line
5. Power steering pressure line bracket-to-steering gear bolt
6. Steering gear bolts (3 required)
7. Cotter pin (2 required)
8. Outer tie-rod end-to-wheel knuckle nut (2 required)
9. Steering gear

22086_FUSI_G0143

Fig. 324 Exploded view of the FWD power steering gear—3.0L engine shown, 3.5L engine similar

prevent the entry of contaminants or premature failure of the power steering components may result.

24. From the LH side of the vehicle, install the steering gear.

25. Install the 3 steering gear bolts.
   a. Tighten to 107 Nm (79 ft. lbs.).

26. Release the clamp and connect the steering gear-to-fluid cooler return hose.

27. Using a suitable jack, raise the rear of the front subframe.

28. Install the 4 rear bolts and 2 rear nuts. Tighten the bolts and nuts in 2 stages:
   a. Stage 1: Tighten the nuts to 150 Nm (111 ft. lbs.).
   b. Stage 2: Tighten the bolts to 103 Nm (76 ft. lbs.).

⁑ WARNING

New banjo bolts and new seals must be installed any time the power steering pressure line is disconnected from the power steering pump

and/or the steering gear or a fluid leak may occur.

29. Install the power steering pressure line banjo bolt. Install 2 new seals.
   a. Tighten to 55 Nm (41 ft. lbs.).

30. For 3.0L and 3.5L engines:
   a. Install the power steering pressure line bracket-to-steering gear bolt and tighten to 15 Nm (11 ft. lbs.).

31. For 2.3L engines, install the power steering pressure line bracket-to-steering gear bolt and tighten to 9 Nm (80 lb-in).

32. Install the steering gear heat shield and the 2 bolts. Tighten to 15 Nm (11 ft. lbs.).

➡Always install new fasteners and gaskets. Clean flange faces prior to new gasket installation to make sure of proper sealing.

33. Position the exhaust flexible pipe and install the 2 catalytic converter-to-exhaust flexible pipe nuts. Tighten to 40 Nm (30 ft. lbs.).

34. Install the 2 outer tie-rod end nuts. Tighten to 48 Nm (35 ft. lbs.).

35. Install 2 new cotter pins.

36. If equipped, install the underbody splash shield and bolts. Tighten to 7 Nm (62 lb-in).

37. Install the LH and RH splash shield and the 6 pin-type retainers (4 shown).

38. Install the RH and LH fender splash shield and the 4 screws from each side.

⁑ WARNING

The steering gear/dash seal must be fully seated in the steering gear valve tower groove before the retaining clips are fully engaged into the body. If the steering gear/dash seal is not seated to the steering gear valve tower groove and the clips are not fully engaged to the body, water and foreign material may enter the passengers compartment causing damage to the vehicle interior.

39. Applying hand force to the center of the seal, install the steering gear/dash seal onto the steering gear valve tower until the seal is fully seated in the valve tower groove.

40. Install the steering gear/dash seal until the retaining clips are fully engaged into the body.

❋❋ WARNING

Do not allow the steering intermediate shaft to rotate while it is disconnected from the steering gear or damage to the clockspring can occur. If there is evidence that the intermediate shaft has rotated, the clockspring must be removed and recentered.

❋❋ WARNING

Make sure to correctly align the index marks when installing the steering gear-to-steering column shaft or unequal right to left turns may occur, causing tire contact with the body and/or clockspring damage.

41. With the index marks properly aligned, connect the steering column shaft to the steering gear and install the bolt. Tighten to 25 Nm (18 ft. lbs.).

42. Install the lower steering column shaft joint cover and the 2 bolts.

43. Fill the power steering system.

44. Check and, if necessary, align the front end

All Wheel Drive (AWD) Models

See Figure 325.

1. Raise and safely support the vehicle.

2. Place the steering wheel in the straight-ahead position and the ignition key in the OFF position.

3. Remove the 2 lower steering column shaft joint cover bolts and cover.

❋❋ WARNING

Do not allow the intermediate shaft to rotate while it is disconnected from the gear or damage to the clockspring can occur. If there is evidence that the intermediate shaft has rotated, the clockspring must be removed and recentered.

❋❋ WARNING

Make sure to correctly index-mark the steering gear to steering column shaft position or unequal right to left turns may occur, causing tire contact

with the body and/or clockspring damage.

4. Matchmark the steering column shaft-to-steering gear position for reference during installation.

5. Remove and discard the bolt and disconnect the steering column shaft from the steering gear.

❋❋ WARNING

Remove the steering gear/dash seal or damage to the seal can occur.

6. Remove the steering gear/dash seal.

7. Remove the battery and battery tray.

8. Disconnect the electrical connectors from the Power Control Module (PCM). Detach the wiring harness retainer from the PCM bracket and position the harness aside.

9. Remove the power steering pressure line banjo bolt. Discard the bolt and 2 seals.

10. Remove the power steering pressure line-to-steering gear bracket bolt.

11. Remove 4 screws from each side and position the RH and LH fender splash shield aside.

12. Remove the 6 pin-type retainers (4 shown) from the LH and RH splash shield.

13. If equipped, remove the bolts and the underbody splash shield.

14. Remove the 2 outer tie-rod end cotter pins and nuts. Discard the cotter pins.

❋❋ WARNING

Do not use a hammer to separate the outer tie-rod end from the wheel knuckle or damage to the wheel knuckle may result.

15. Using a suitable tie rod end removal tool, separate the outer tie-rod ends from the knuckle.

➡Always install new fasteners and gaskets. Clean flange faces prior to new gasket installation to make sure of proper sealing.

16. Remove and discard the 2 catalytic converter-to-exhaust flexible pipe nuts and separate the exhaust flexible pipe.

17. Remove the 2 bolts and the steering gear heat shield.

18. Support the rear of the subframe with a suitable jack and remove the 4 rear bolts and 2 rear nuts. Lower the rear of the front subframe 76.2 mm (3 in) with the support of the jack.

19. On 3.5L engines, remove the power steering pressure line bracket-to-steering gear bolt.

20. Release the clamp and disconnect the steering gear-to-fluid cooler return hose.

21. Remove the 3 steering gear bolts.

22. Remove the steering gear from the LH side of the vehicle.

To install:

❋❋ WARNING

When installing the steering gear, it is important to have the steering gear in the centered position or unequal right to left turns may occur, causing tire contact with the body and/or clockspring damage. A new steering gear is centered and ready for installation.

❋❋ WARNING

When repairing the power steering system, care should be taken to prevent the entry of contaminants, or premature failure of the power steering components may result.

23. From the LH side of the vehicle, install the steering gear. Install the 3 steering gear bolts and tighten to 107 Nm (79 ft. lbs.).

24. Connect the steering gear-to-fluid cooler return hose and connect the clamp.

25. Using a suitable jack, raise the rear of the front subframe.

26. Install the 4 rear bolts and 2 rear nuts. Tighten the bolts and nuts in 2 stages:

   a. Stage 1: Tighten the nuts to 150 Nm (111 ft. lbs.).

   b. Stage 2: Tighten the bolts to 103 Nm (76 ft. lbs.).

27. Install the steering gear heat shield and the 2 bolts. Tighten to 15 Nm (11 ft. lbs.).

➡Always install new fasteners and gaskets. Clean flange faces prior to new gasket installation to make sure of correct sealing.

28. Position the exhaust flexible pipe and install the 2 catalytic converter-to-exhaust flexible pipe nuts. Tighten to 40 Nm (30 ft. lbs.).

29. Install the 2 outer tie-rod end nuts. Tighten to 48 Nm (35 ft. lbs.). Install 2 new cotter pins.

30. If equipped, install the underbody splash shield and bolts. Tighten to 7 Nm (62 lb-in).

31. Install the LH and RH splash shield and the 6 pin-type retainers (4 shown).

32. Install the RH and LH fender splash shield and the 4 screws from each side.

33. Install the power steering pressure

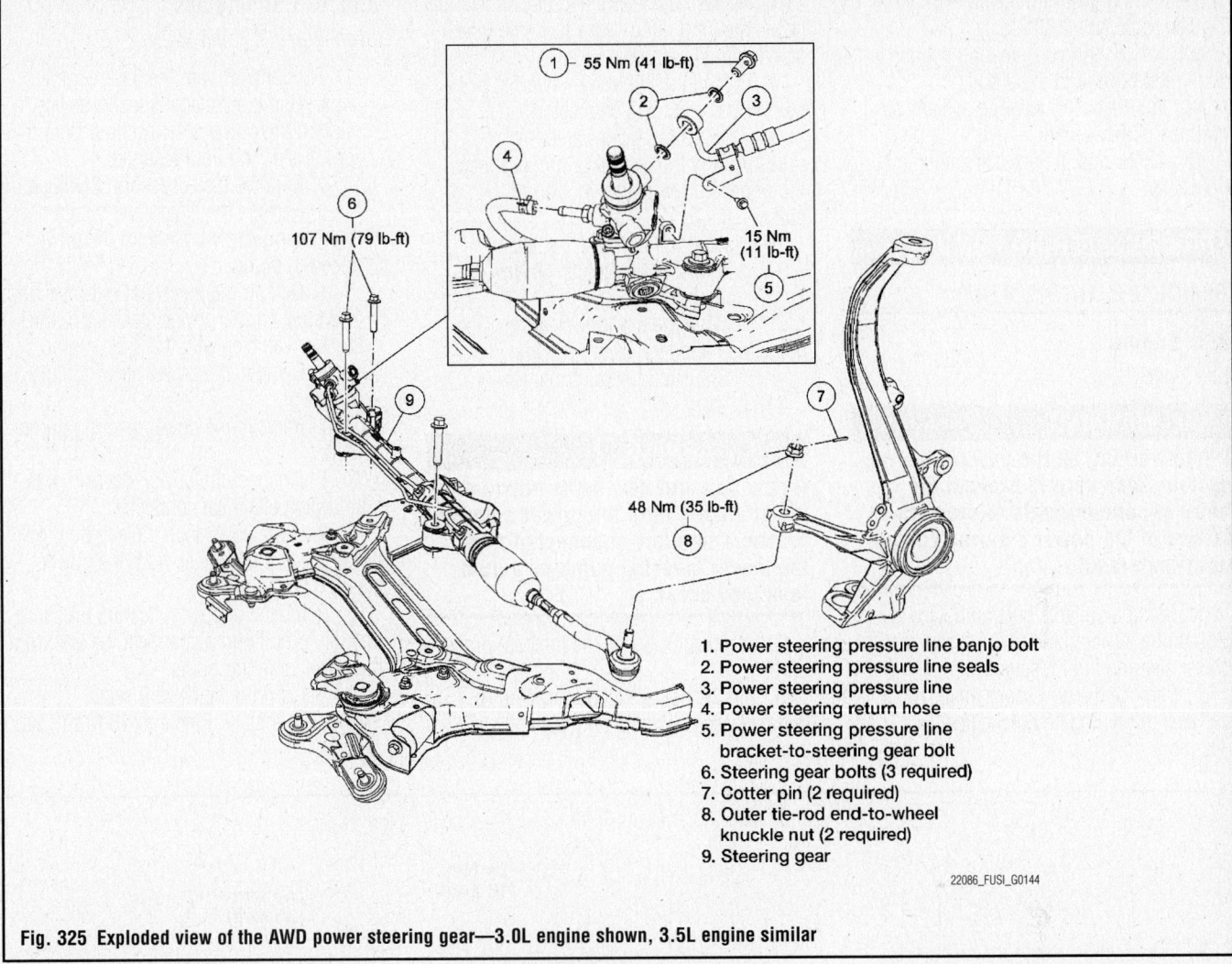

1. 55 Nm (41 lb-ft)
107 Nm (79 lb-ft)
15 Nm (11 lb-ft)
48 Nm (35 lb-ft)

1. Power steering pressure line banjo bolt
2. Power steering pressure line seals
3. Power steering pressure line
4. Power steering return hose
5. Power steering pressure line
   bracket-to-steering gear bolt
6. Steering gear bolts (3 required)
7. Cotter pin (2 required)
8. Outer tie-rod end-to-wheel
   knuckle nut (2 required)
9. Steering gear

22086_FUSI_G0144

Fig. 325 Exploded view of the AWD power steering gear—3.0L engine shown, 3.5L engine similar

line bracket-to-steering gear bolt. Tighten to 15 Nm (11 ft. lbs.).

❋❋ WARNING

New banjo bolts and new seals must be installed any time the power steering pressure line is disconnected from the power steering pump and/or the steering gear or a fluid leak may occur.

34. Install the power steering pressure line banjo bolt and seals. Tighten to 55 Nm (41 ft. lbs.).

35. Connect the electrical connectors to the power control module (PCM). Attach the wiring harness retainer to the PCM bracket.

36. Install the battery tray and battery.

❋❋ WARNING

The steering gear/dash seal must be fully seated in the steering gear valve tower groove before the retaining clips are fully engaged into the body. If the steering gear/dash seal

is not seated to the steering gear valve tower groove and the clips are not fully engaged to the body, water and foreign material may enter the passengers compartment causing damage to the vehicle interior.

37. Applying hand force to the center of the seal, install the steering gear/dash seal onto the steering gear valve tower until the seal is fully seated in the valve tower groove.

❋❋ WARNING

The steering gear/dash seal must be fully seated in the steering gear valve tower groove before the retaining clips are fully engaged into the body. If the steering gear/dash seal is not seated to the steering gear valve tower groove and the clips are not fully engaged to the body, water and foreign material may enter the passengers compartment and damage the vehicle interior.

38. Install the steering gear/dash seal until the retaining clips are fully engaged into the body.

❋❋ WARNING

Do not allow the steering intermediate shaft to rotate while it is disconnected from the steering gear or damage to the clockspring may occur. If there is evidence that the intermediate shaft has rotated, the clockspring must be removed and recentered.

❋❋ WARNING

Make sure to correctly align the index marks when installing the steering gear to steering column shaft or unequal right to left turns may occur, causing tire contact with the body and/or clockspring damage.

39. With the index marks correctly aligned, connect the steering column shaft

to the steering gear and install the bolt. Tighten to 25 Nm (18 ft. lbs.).

40. Install the lower steering column shaft joint cover and the 2 bolts.

41. Fill the power steering system, as outlined in this section.

42. Check and, if necessary, align the front end

POWER STEERING PUMP

REMOVAL & INSTALLATION

2.3L Engine

See Figure 326.

> **✳✳ WARNING**
>
> **When working on the power steering system, take care to prevent the entry of contaminants or premature failure of the power steering components can result.**

1. Using a suitable suction device, siphon the power steering fluid from the power steering fluid reservoir.

2. Remove the accessory drive belt, as outlined in the Engine Mechanical Section.

3. Release the clamp and disconnect the power steering return hose from the power steering fluid reservoir.

4. Disconnect the power steering pressure switch electrical connector.

5. Remove the power steering pressure line banjo bolt and disconnect the line from the power steering pump.

6. Discard the bolt and 2 seals.

   a. To install, tighten to 48 Nm (35 ft. lbs.).

7. Remove the 3 power steering pump bolts and the power steering pump.

   a. To install, tighten to 24 Nm (18 ft. lbs.).

> **✳✳ WARNING**
>
> **A new bolt and new seals must be installed any time the power steering pressure line is disconnected from the power steering pump or a fluid leak may occur.**

8. To install, reverse the removal procedure.

9. Fill the power steering system as outlined under Bleeding in this section.

3.0L & 3.5L Engines

See Figures 327 and 328.

1. For vehicles with the 3.0L engine:

   a. Using a suitable suction device, siphon the power steering fluid from the power steering fluid reservoir.

   b. Remove the accessory drive belt.

   c. Release the clamp and disconnect the pump supply hose from the power steering pump.

   d. Detach the electrical harness from the stud on the power steering pump.

2. For vehicles with the 3.5L engine:

   a. Remove the power steering fluid reservoir.

   b. Remove the power steering pump belt.

3. Disconnect the power steering pressure switch electrical connector.

4. If equipped, detach the engine block heater electrical harness from the power steering pressure line.

5. Remove the power steering pressure line banjo bolt and disconnect the line from the power steering pump.

6. Discard the bolt and 2 seals.

   a. To install, tighten to 48 Nm (35 ft. lbs.).

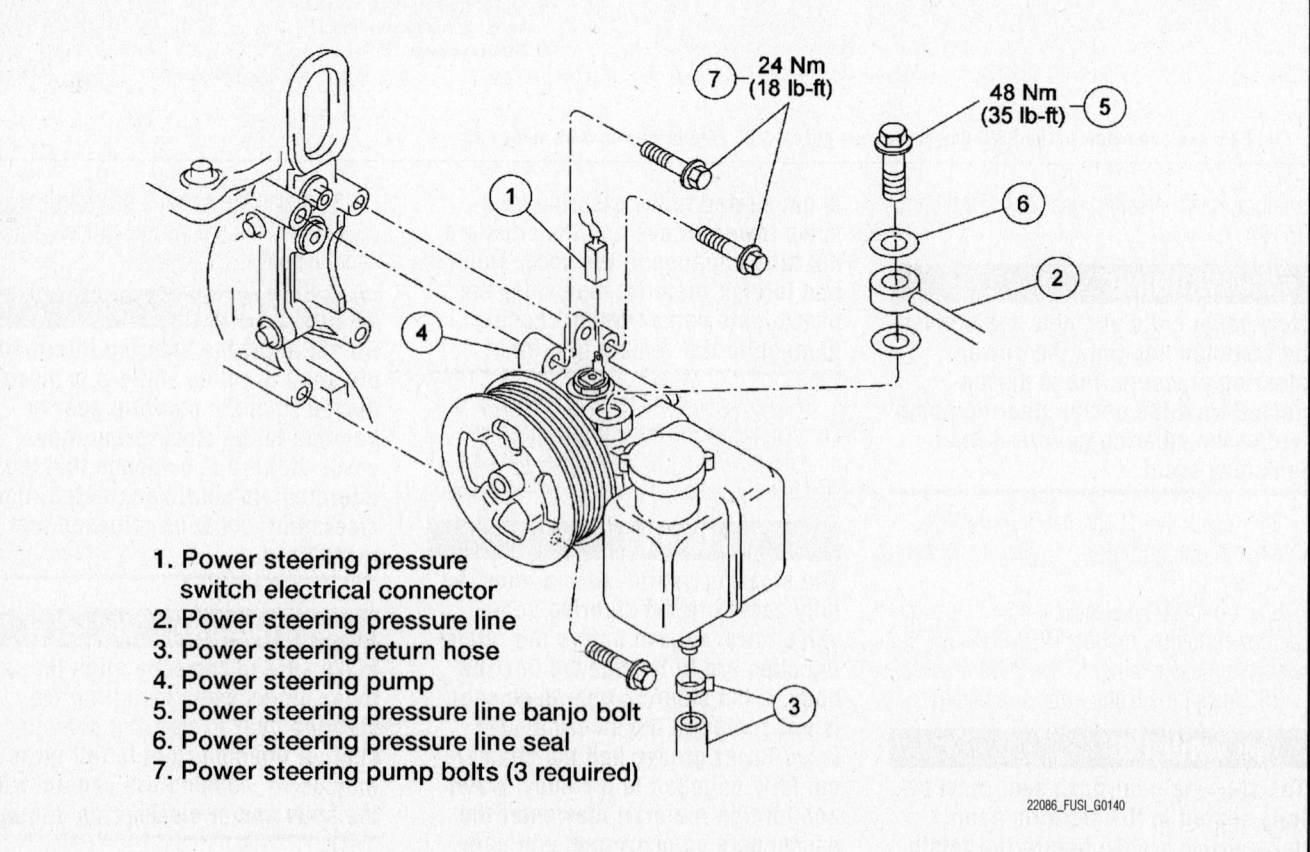

1. **Power steering pressure switch electrical connector**
2. **Power steering pressure line**
3. **Power steering return hose**
4. **Power steering pump**
5. **Power steering pressure line banjo bolt**
6. **Power steering pressure line seal**
7. **Power steering pump bolts (3 required)**

22086_FUSI_G0140

Fig. 326 Exploded view of the power steering pump and related components—2.3L engine

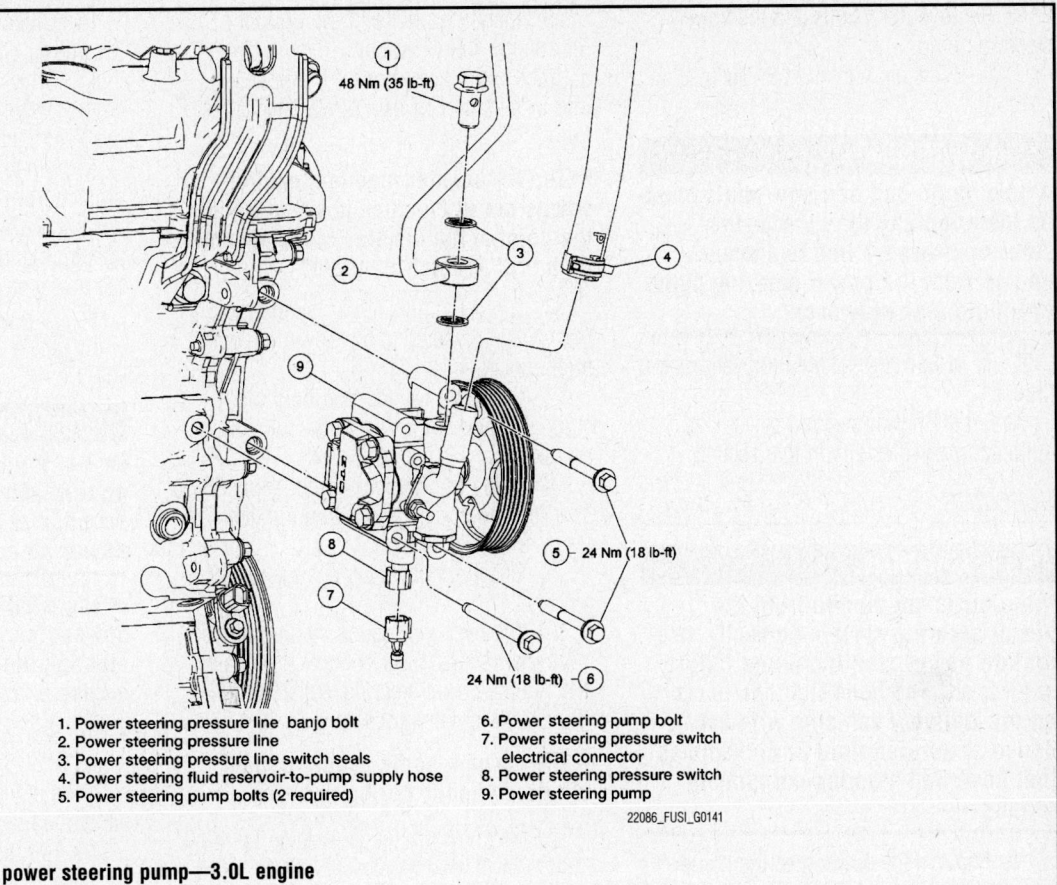

1. Power steering pressure line banjo bolt
2. Power steering pressure line
3. Power steering pressure line switch seals
4. Power steering fluid reservoir-to-pump supply hose
5. Power steering pump bolts (2 required)
6. Power steering pump bolt
7. Power steering pressure switch electrical connector
8. Power steering pressure switch
9. Power steering pump

22086_FUSI_G0141

Fig. 327 Exploded view of the power steering pump—3.0L engine

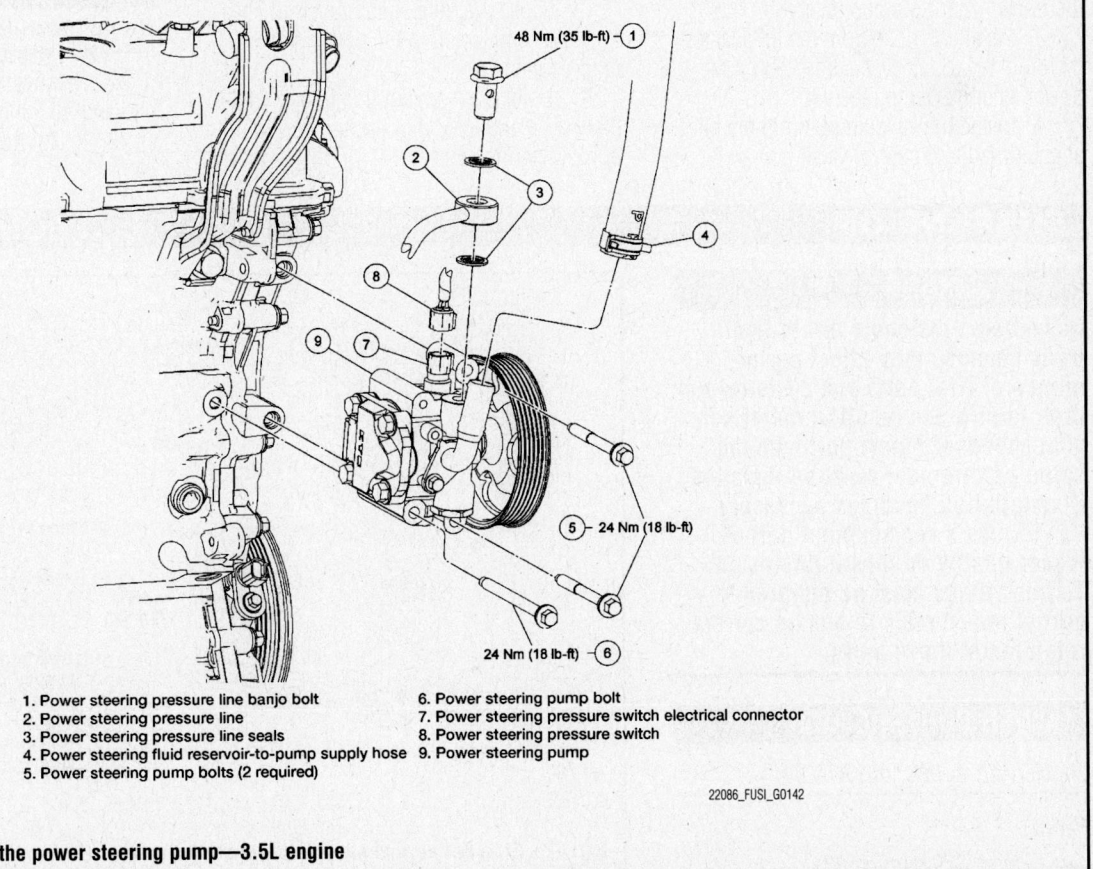

1. Power steering pressure line banjo bolt
2. Power steering pressure line
3. Power steering pressure line seals
4. Power steering fluid reservoir-to-pump supply hose
5. Power steering pump bolts (2 required)
6. Power steering pump bolt
7. Power steering pressure switch electrical connector
8. Power steering pressure switch
9. Power steering pump

22086_FUSI_G0142

Fig. 328 Exploded view of the power steering pump—3.5L engine

7. Remove the 3 bolts and the power steering pump.

    a. To install, tighten to 24 Nm (18 ft. lbs.).

> ✳✳ **WARNING**
>
> **A new banjo bolt and new seals must be installed any time the power steering pressure line is disconnected from the power steering pump or a fluid leak may occur.**

8. To install, reverse the removal procedure.

9. Fill the power steering system, as outlined under Bleeding in this section.

BLEEDING

> ✳✳ **WARNING**
>
> **If the air is not purged from the power steering system correctly, premature power steering pump failure can result. The condition can occur on pre-delivery vehicles with evidence of aerated fluid or on vehicles that have had steering component repairs.**

1. Remove the power steering pump reservoir cap.

2. Tightly install the evacuation cap to the power steering pump reservoir.

3. Install the hose from the fill adapter manifold tee to the evacuation cap on the power steering pump reservoir.

4. Install the vacuum pump to the fill adapter manifold control valve.

5. Install the hose to the opposite fill adapter manifold control valve and submerge the open end of the hose into a container of new power steering fluid.

➡ **The fill adapter manifold control valves are in the open position when the point of the handles face the center of the fill adapter manifold.**

6. Close the fill adapter manifold control valve connected to the power steering fluid container.

7. Open the fill adapter manifold control valve connected to the vacuum pump.

8. Using the vacuum pump, apply 68-85 kPa (20-25 in-Hg) of vacuum to the power steering system.

9. Observe the vacuum gauge for 30 seconds.

10. If the vacuum gauge reading drops more than 3 kPa (0.88 in-Hg), correct any leaks in the power steering system or the filling tools before proceeding.

➡ **The vacuum pump gauge reading will drop slightly during this step.**

11. Slowly open the fill adapter manifold control valve connected to the power steering fluid container until power steering fluid completely fills the hose.

12. Close the fill adapter manifold control valve connected to the power steering fluid container.

13. Using the vacuum pump, apply 68-85 kPa (20-25 in-Hg) of vacuum to the power steering system.

14. Close the fill adapter manifold control valve connected to the vacuum pump.

15. Slowly open the fill adapter manifold control valve connected to the power steering fluid container.

16. When the power steering fluid has drained from the hose connected to the power steering fluid container, close the fill adapter manifold control valve connected to the power steering fluid container.

17. Remove the tools from the vehicle.

18. Install the power steering reservoir cap.

> ✳✳ **WARNING**
>
> **Do not hold the steering wheel against the stops for more than 3 to 5 seconds at a time. Damage to the power steering pump can occur.**

➡ **There will be a slight drop in the power steering fluid level in the power steering fluid reservoir when the engine is started.**

19. Start the engine and turn the steering wheel from stop-to-stop.

20. If equipped with Hydro-Boost®, apply the brake pedal twice.

21. Turn the ignition switch to the **OFF** position.

> ✳✳ **WARNING**
>
> **Do not overfill the reservoir.**

22. Remove the power steering reservoir cap and fill the reservoir.

23. Install the power steering reservoir cap

SUSPENSION

> ✳✳ **WARNING**
>
> **Suspension fasteners are critical parts because they affect performance of vital parts and systems and their failure can result in major service expense. A new part with the same part number must be installed if installation becomes necessary. NEVER use a replacement part of lesser quality or substitute design. Torque values must be adhered to during reassembly to ensure correct retention of these parts.**

LOWER CONTROL ARM

REMOVAL & INSTALLATION

Front

See Figures 329 through 331.

FRONT SUSPENSION

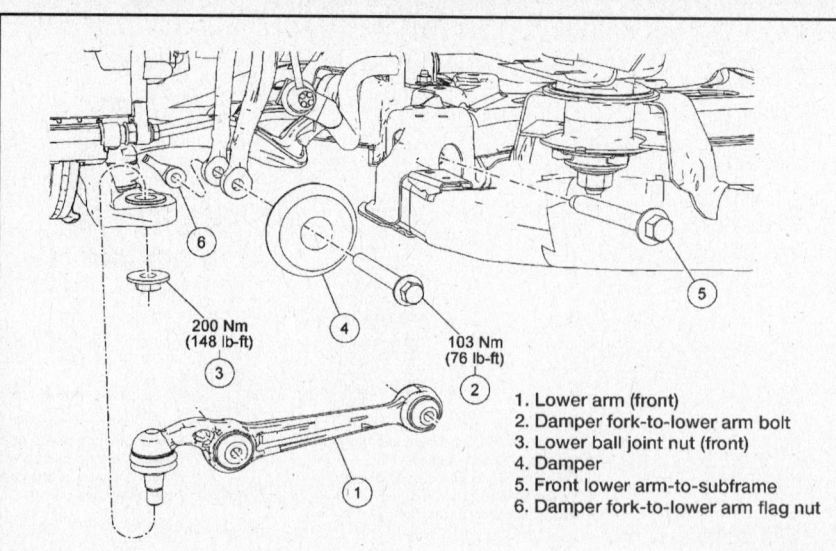

200 Nm (148 lb-ft)

103 Nm (76 lb-ft)

1. Lower arm (front)
2. Damper fork-to-lower arm bolt
3. Lower ball joint nut (front)
4. Damper
5. Front lower arm-to-subframe
6. Damper fork-to-lower arm flag nut

22086_FUSI_G0181

Fig. 329 Exploded view of the front lower control arm

1. Raise and safely support the vehicle.
2. Remove the wheel and tire assembly.
3. Using a suitable jack, support the front wheel knuckle at the rear lower ball joint.
4. Remove the front lower arm-to-subframe bolt and washer. Discard the bolt and washer.

   a. To install, tighten to 65 Nm (48 ft. lbs.), then tighten an additional 90 degrees with the suspension at the bushing fastener tightening position.

5. Remove the damper fork-to-lower arm bolt flag nut and damper. Discard the bolt and flag nut.

   a. To install, tighten to 103 Nm (76 ft. lbs.) with the suspension at the bushing fastener tightening position.

6. Remove and discard the front lower ball joint nut.

   a. To install, tighten to 200 Nm (148 ft. lbs.).

✳✳ WARNING

When the lower ball joint is separated from the wheel knuckle, the lower arm may strike the outer constant velocity (CV) joint boot with enough force to damage the boot clamp. This will result in a loss of grease from the outer CV joint. Place a block of wood, or similar item, between the lower arm and the outer CV joint to prevent the lower arm from striking the outer CV joint.

➡**Once pressure is applied to the ball joint with the special tool, it may be necessary to tap the wheel knuckle at the ball joint area to separate the ball joint from the wheel knuckle.**

7. Using the special tools, separate the front lower ball joint from the wheel knuckle and remove the front lower arm.

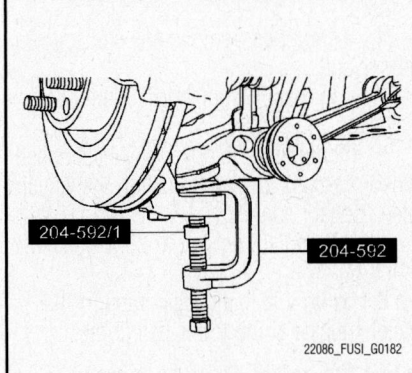

204-592/1   204-592

22086_FUSI_G0182

Fig. 330 Using the special tools, separate the front lower ball joint from the wheel knuckle and remove the front lower arm

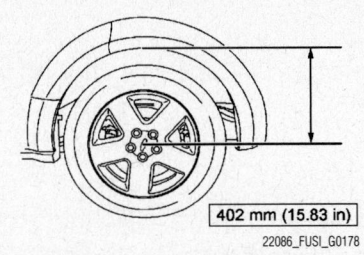

402 mm (15.83 in)

22086_FUSI_G0178

Fig. 331 Before tightening any suspension bushing fasteners, the suspension must be at the bushing fastener tightening position. Use a suitable jack to raise the suspension until the distance between the center of the hub and the lip of the fender is equal to 402 mm (15.83 in)

✳✳ WARNING

Before tightening any suspension bushing fasteners, the suspension must be at the bushing fastener tightening position. Use a suitable jack to raise the suspension until the distance between the center of the hub and the lip of the fender is equal to 402 mm (15.83 in).

8. To install, reverse the removal procedure.

Rear

See Figures 331 through 333.

1. Place the steering wheel in the straight-ahead position and the ignition key in the OFF position.

2. Remove the 2 lower steering column shaft joint cover bolts and cover.

✳✳ WARNING

Do not allow the steering column shaft to rotate while it is disconnected from the gear or damage to the clockspring can occur. If there is evidence that the steering column shaft has rotated, the clockspring must be removed and recentered.

➡**Matchmatch the steering column shaft position to the steering gear for reference during installation.**

3. Remove the bolt and disconnect the steering column shaft from the steering gear.

   a. To install, align the index marks and tighten to 20 Nm (15 ft. lbs.).

✳✳ WARNING

Remove the steering column shaft-to-dash seal or damage to the seal can occur.

✳✳ WARNING

Make sure that the dash seal is correctly installed on the steering gear and the retaining clips are fully engaged into the body or damage to the steering gear can result.

4. Remove the steering column shaft-to-dash seal.

5. Raise and safely support the vehicle.

6. Remove the 8 screws and position the LH and RH splash shields aside.

7. Remove the 6 pin-type retainers (4 shown) and the RH splash shield.

8. Remove the 6 pin-type retainers (4 shown) and the LH splash shield.

9. If equipped, remove the bolts and the underbody cover shield.

   a. To install, tighten 7 Nm (62 lb-in).

10. Remove and discard the 2 catalytic converter manifold-to-exhaust flexible pipe nuts and separate the exhaust flexible pipe.

   a. To install, tighten to 40 Nm (30 ft. lbs.).

11. Using 2 suitable jack stands, support the rear of the subframe assembly.

12. Remove and discard the 4 subframe bracket-to-body bolts, the 2 subframe bracket-to-subframe nuts and washers. Lower the rear of the subframe.

   a. To install, tighten the bolts to 103 Nm (76 ft. lbs.).

   b. To install, tighten the nuts to 150 Nm (111 ft. lbs.).

13. Remove and discard the rear lower ball joint nut.

   a. To install, tighten to 200 Nm (148 ft. lbs.).

✳✳ WARNING

When the lower ball joint is separated from the wheel knuckle, the lower arm may strike the outer constant velocity (CV) joint boot with enough force to damage the boot clamp. This will result in a loss of grease from the outer CV joint. Place a block of wood, or similar item, between the lower arm and the outer CV joint to prevent the lower arm from striking the outer CV joint.

➡**Once pressure is applied to the ball joint with the special tool, it may be necessary to tap the wheel knuckle at the ball joint area to separate the ball joint from the wheel knuckle.**

14. Using the special tools, separate the rear lower ball joint from the wheel knuckle.

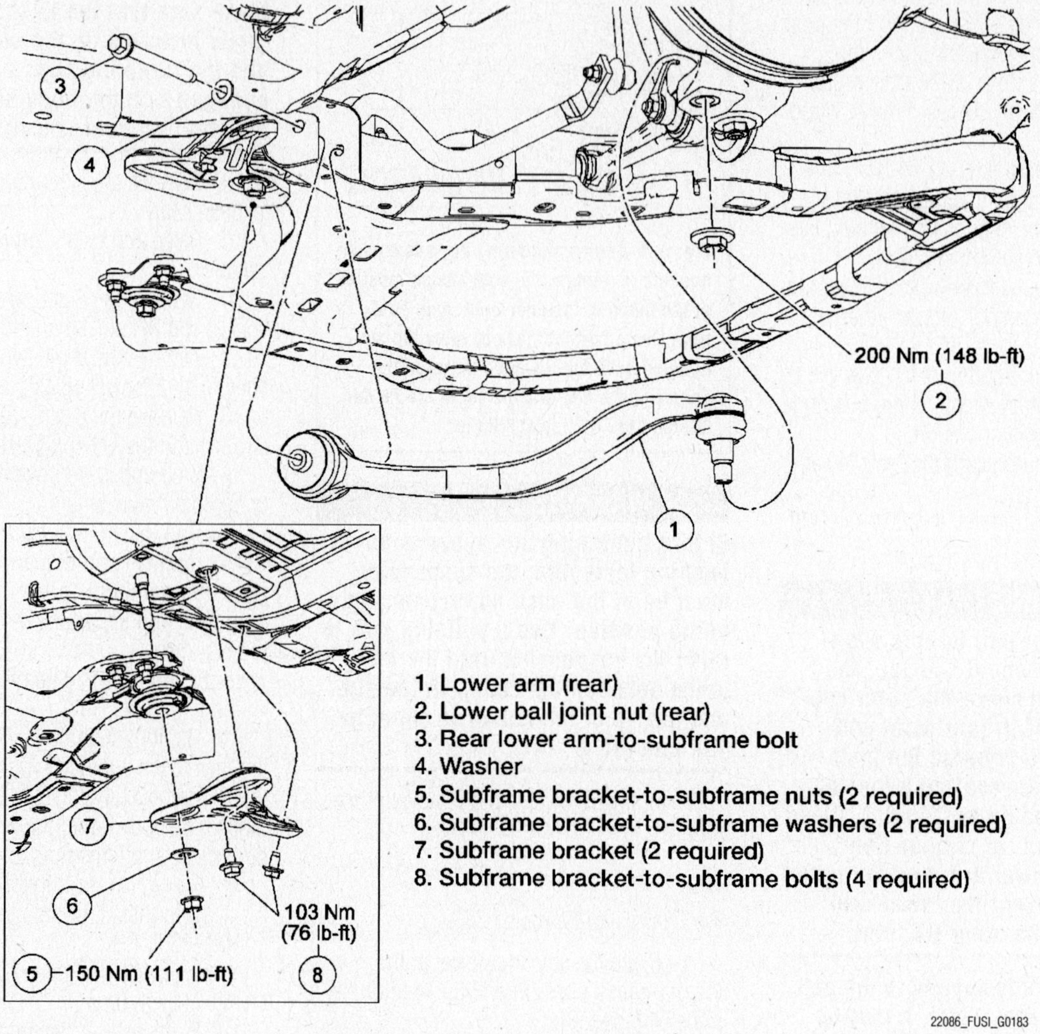

200 Nm (148 lb-ft)

1. Lower arm (rear)
2. Lower ball joint nut (rear)
3. Rear lower arm-to-subframe bolt
4. Washer
5. Subframe bracket-to-subframe nuts (2 required)
6. Subframe bracket-to-subframe washers (2 required)
7. Subframe bracket (2 required)
8. Subframe bracket-to-subframe bolts (4 required)

103 Nm (76 lb-ft)

5—150 Nm (111 lb-ft)

22086_FUSI_G0183

Fig. 332 Exploded view of the rear lower arm assembly

15. Remove the rear lower arm-to-subframe bolt and washer and remove the rear lower arm. Discard the bolt and washer.

a. To install, tighten to 65 Nm (48 ft. lbs.), then tighten an additional 90 degrees.

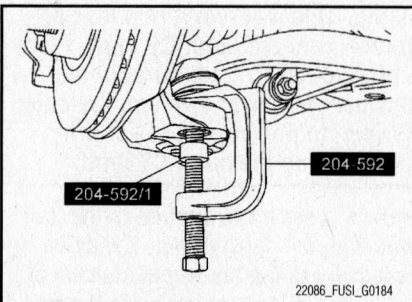

204-592

204-592/1

22086_FUSI_G0184

Fig. 333 Using the special tools, separate the rear lower ball joint from the wheel knuckle

❋ WARNING

Before tightening any suspension bushing fasteners, the suspension must be at the bushing fastener tightening position. Use a suitable jack to raise the suspension until the distance between the center of the hub and the lip of the fender is equal to 402 mm (15.83 in.).

16. To install, reverse the removal procedure

SHOCK ABSORBER & SPRING ASSEMBLY

REMOVAL & INSTALLATION

See Figures 331 and 334.

1. Remove and discard the 3 shock absorber upper mount nuts.

2. Remove the wheel and tire assembly.

3. Remove the brake line bracket bolt and position the brake line aside.

a. To install, tighten to 23 Nm (17 ft. lbs.).

4. If equipped, remove the wheel speed sensor bolt.

a. To install, tighten to 23 Nm (17 ft. lbs.).

5. If equipped, remove the wheel speed sensor harness bolt and position the wheel speed sensor aside.

a. To install, tighten to 23 Nm (17 ft. lbs.).

6. Using a suitable jack, support the wheel knuckle at the lower ball joints.

➡Use the holding feature to prevent the ball stud from turning while removing or installing the stabilizer bar link nut.

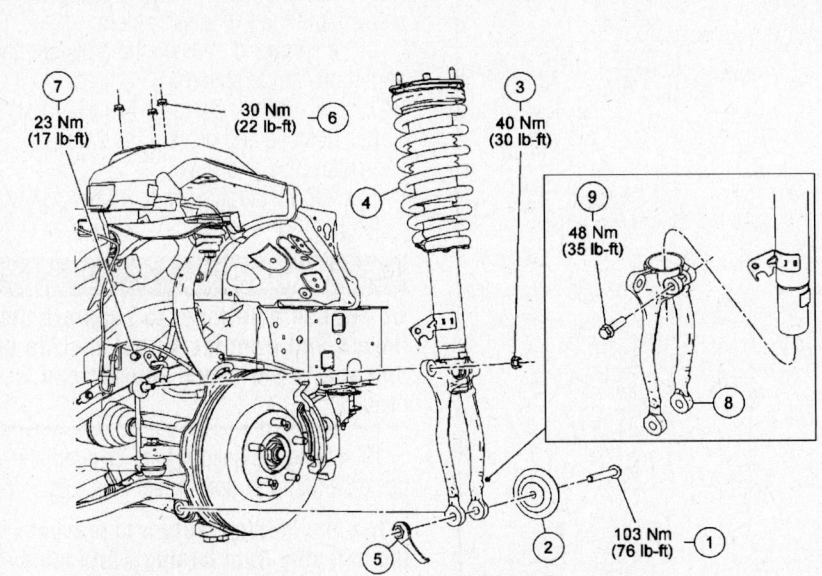

1. Damper fork-to-lower arm bolt
2. Damper
3. Stabilizer bar link upper nut
4. Shock absorber and spring assembly
5. Damper fork-to-lower arm flag nut
6. Shock absorber upper mount nut (3 required)
7. Brake line bracket bolt
8. Damper fork
9. Shock absorber-to-damper fork bolt

22086_FUSI_G0177

Fig. 334 Exploded view of the front shock absorber and spring assembly

7. Remove the stabilizer bar link upper nut.
    a. To install, tighten to 40 Nm (30 ft. lbs.).
8. Remove the shock absorber lower bolt, flag nut and damper. Discard the bolt and flag nut.
    a. To install, tighten to 103 Nm (76 ft. lbs.) with the suspension at the bushing fastener tightening position.
9. Remove the shock absorber-to-damper fork bolt and separate the damper fork from the shock absorber and spring assembly.
    a. To install, tighten to 48 Nm (35 ft. lbs.).
10. Lower the wheel knuckle and remove the shock absorber and spring assembly.

✳✳ WARNING

Before tightening any suspension bushing fasteners, the suspension must be at the bushing fastener tightening position. Use a suitable jack to raise the suspension until the distance between the center of the hub and the lip of the fender is equal to 402 mm (15.83 in).

11. To install, reverse the removal procedure.

OVERHAUL
See Figures 335 and 336.

✳✳ CAUTION

These vehicles are equipped with gas-pressurized shock absorbers which will extend unassisted. Do not apply heat or flame to the shock absorbers during removal or component servicing. Failure to follow these instructions may result in personal injury.

✳✳ CAUTION

The spring is under extreme compression, care must be taken at all times. Failure to follow this instruction may result in personal injury.

✳✳ CAUTION

The coil spring is coated with long-term corrosion protective paint. Do not damage the paint during component servicing.

✳✳ CAUTION

Suspension fasteners are critical parts because they affect perfor-

mance of vital parts and systems and their failure can result in major service expense. A new part with the same part number must be installed if installation becomes necessary. Do not use a replacement part of lesser quality or substitute design. Torque values must be used as specified during reassembly to make sure of correct retention of these parts.

1. Remove the shock absorber and spring assembly, as outlined in this section

✳✳ WARNING

Always wear safety goggles when using a spring compressor. Failure to follow these instructions may result in personal injury.

2. Position the shock and spring assembly in a suitable spring compressor.
3. Compress the spring enough to relieve the tension on the shock and spring assembly.
4. Remove the shock rod protective cap.

✳✳ WARNING

Do not use an impact wrench on the shock absorber rod nut.

➡ Use the holding feature to prevent the shock absorber rod from turning while removing or installing the nut.

5. While holding the shock absorber rod, remove and discard the nut.
    a. To assemble, tighten to 40 Nm (30 ft. lbs.).
6. Remove the shock absorber and lower mount assembly.
7. Remove the dust boot.
8. Remove the shock absorber upper mount and spring upper seat.
9. Carefully release the tension on the spring compressor and remove the spring.
10. Remove and discard the shock absorber-to-damper fork bolt, then separate the shock and damper fork.
    a. To assembly, tighten to 48 Nm (35 ft. lbs.).

➡ Before tightening the shock absorber rod nut, position the end of the spring within 0-10 mm (0-0.39 in) of the step on the spring mount.

11. To assemble, reverse the disassembly procedure.
12. Install the strut assembly

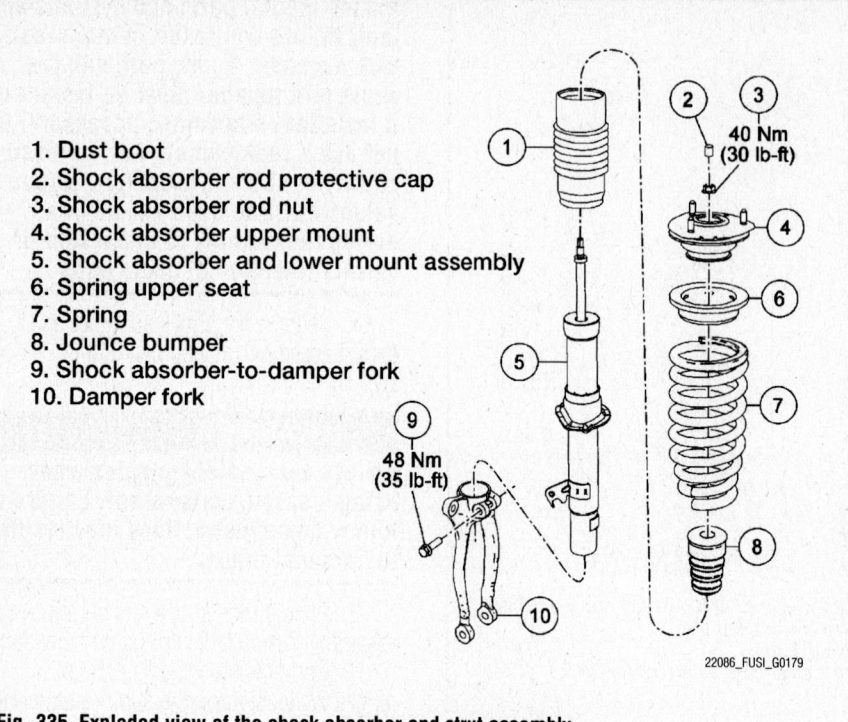

1. Dust boot
2. Shock absorber rod protective cap
3. Shock absorber rod nut
4. Shock absorber upper mount
5. Shock absorber and lower mount assembly
6. Spring upper seat
7. Spring
8. Jounce bumper
9. Shock absorber-to-damper fork
10. Damper fork

40 Nm (30 lb-ft)

48 Nm (35 lb-ft)

22086_FUSI_G0179

Fig. 335 Exploded view of the shock absorber and strut assembly

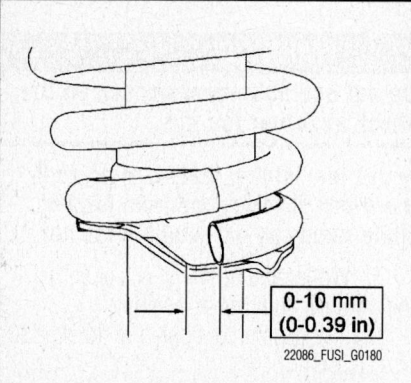

0-10 mm (0-0.39 in)

22086_FUSI_G0180

Fig. 336 Before tightening the shock absorber rod nut, position the end of the spring within 0-10 mm (0-0.39 in) of the step on the spring mount

STABILIZER BAR

REMOVAL & INSTALLATION

See Figures 331, 337 and 338.

1. Raise and safely support the vehicle.
2. Remove the wheel and tire assembly.
3. Place the steering wheel in the straight-ahead position and the ignition key in the OFF position.
4. Remove the 2 lower steering column shaft joint cover bolts and cover.

✳✳ WARNING

Do not allow the steering column shaft to rotate while it is discon- nected from the gear or damage to the clockspring can occur. If there is evidence that the steering column shaft has rotated, the clockspring must be removed and recentered.

➡Index the steering column shaft position to the steering gear for reference during installation.

5. Remove the bolt and disconnect the steering column shaft from the steering gear.
   a. To install, align the index marks, tighten to 25 Nm (18 ft. lbs.).

✳✳ WARNING

Remove the steering column shaft-to-dash seal or damage to the seal can occur.

✳✳ WARNING

Make sure that the dash seal is correctly installed on the steering gear and the retaining clips are fully engaged into the body or damage to the steering gear can result.

6. Remove the steering column shaft-to-dash seal.
7. Raise and safely support the vehicle.
8. Remove the 8 screws and position the LH and RH splash shields aside.
9. Remove the 6 pin-type retainers (4 shown) and the RH splash shield.

10. Remove the 6 pin-type retainers (4 shown) and the LH splash shield.
11. If equipped, remove the bolts and the underbody cover shield.
    a. To install, tighten 7 Nm (62 lb-in).
12. Remove and discard the 2 tie-rod end cotter pins and nuts.
    a. To install, tighten to 48 Nm (35 ft. lbs.).

✳✳ WARNING

Do not use a hammer to separate the tie-rod end from the wheel knuckle or damage to the wheel knuckle can result.

13. Using the special tool, separate the tie-rod ends from both wheel knuckles.

➡Use the holding feature to prevent the ball stud from turning while removing or installing the stabilizer bar link nuts.

14. Remove and discard the 2 stabilizer bar link lower nuts and disconnect both stabilizer bar links from the stabilizer bar.
    a. To install, tighten to 42 Nm (31 ft. lbs.).
15. Remove and discard the 2 catalytic converter manifold-to-exhaust flexible pipe nuts and separate the exhaust flexible pipe.
    a. To install, tighten to 40 Nm (30 ft. lbs.).
16. For All Wheel Drive (AWD) vehicles:
    a. Index the rear drive shaft-to-power transfer unit (PTU).
    b. Remove the 4 bolts (3 shown) and position the drive shaft aside.
    c. To install, tighten to 70 Nm (52 ft. lbs.).
17. Using 2 suitable jack stands, support the rear of the subframe assembly.
18. Remove and discard the 4 subframe bracket-to-body bolts, the 2 subframe bracket-to-subframe nuts and lower the rear of the subframe.

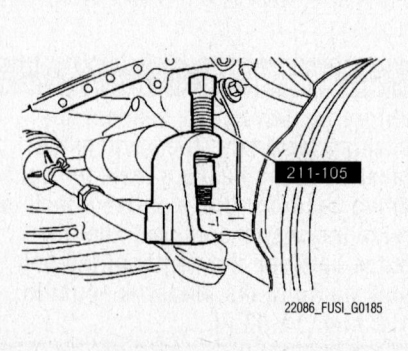

211-105

22086_FUSI_G0185

Fig. 337 Using the special tool, separate the tie-rod ends from both wheel knuckles

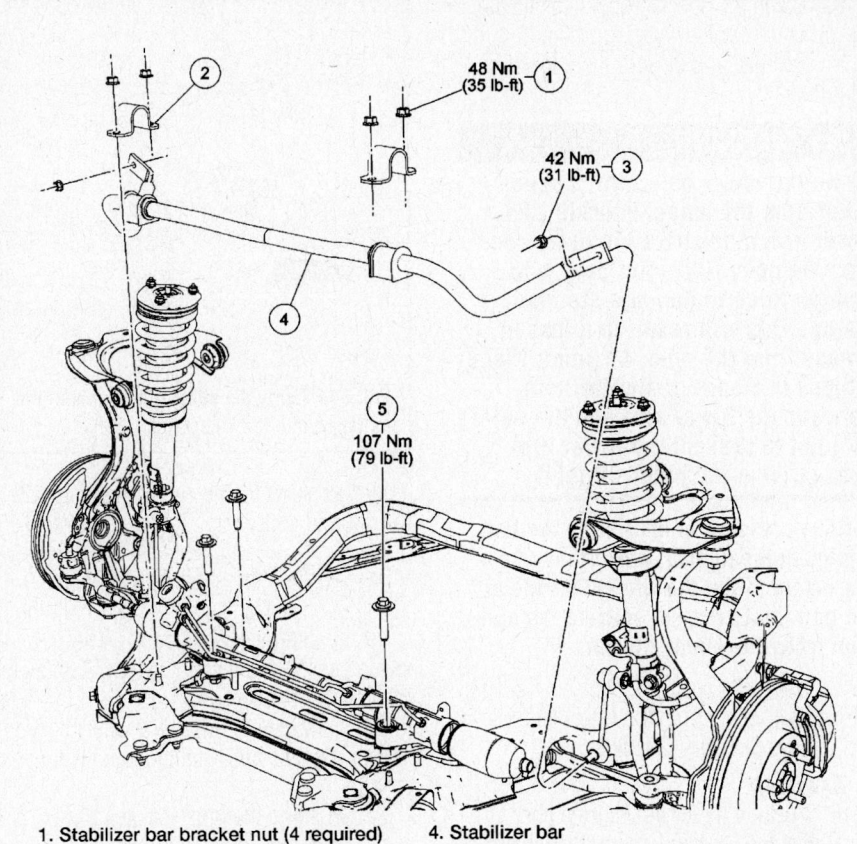

1. Stabilizer bar bracket nut (4 required)
2. Stablizer bar bracket (2 required)
3. Stabilizer bar link lower nut (2 required)
4. Stabilizer bar
5. Steering gear-to-subframe bolt (3 required)

22086_FUSI_G0186

Fig. 338 Exploded view of the stabilizer bar

a. To install, tighten the bolts to 103 Nm (76 ft. lbs.).

b. To install, tighten the nuts to 150 Nm (111 ft. lbs.).

19. Remove RH steering gear-to-subframe bolt.

a. To install, tighten to 107 Nm (79 ft. lbs.).

20. Remove the 2 LH steering gear-to-subframe bolts and position the steering gear to access the stabilizer bar LH bracket front nut.

a. To install, tighten to 107 Nm (79 ft. lbs.).

21. Remove and discard the 4 stabilizer bar bracket nuts and remove the 2 stabilizer bar brackets.

a. To install, tighten the bracket nuts to 48 Nm (35 ft. lbs.).

22. Remove the 2 stabilizer bar bushings.

23. Remove the stabilizer bar through the LH wheel opening.

⁂ WARNING

Before tightening the stabilizer bar bracket nuts, the suspension must be at the bushing fastener tightening position. Use a suitable jack to raise the suspension until the distance between the center of the hub and the lip of the fender is equal to 402 mm (15.83 in).

24. To install, reverse the removal procedure.

STEERING KNUCKLE

REMOVAL & INSTALLATION

See Figures 339 through 344.

1. Raise and safely support the vehicle.
2. Remove the wheel and tire assembly.
3. If equipped, remove the wheel speed sensor bolt.
4. If equipped, remove the wheel speed sensor harness bolt and position the wheel speed sensor aside.

➡**Apply the brake to keep the halfshaft from rotating.**

5. Remove and discard the halfshaft nut.

⁂ WARNING

Do not allow the caliper and anchor plate assembly to hang from the brake hose or damage to the hose can occur.

6. Remove the bolts and position the caliper and anchor plate assembly aside.
7. Support the caliper and anchor plate assembly using mechanic's wire.
8. Remove the 2 brake disc bolts and the brake disc.
9. Using the special tool, separate the halfshaft from the wheel hub.

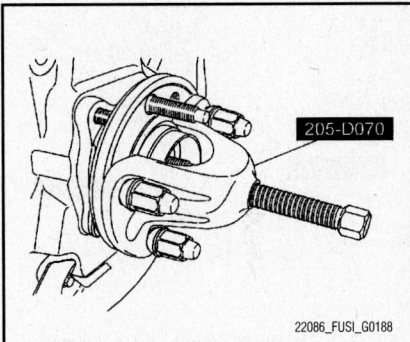

22086_FUSI_G0188

Fig. 339 Using the special tool, separate the halfshaft from the wheel hub

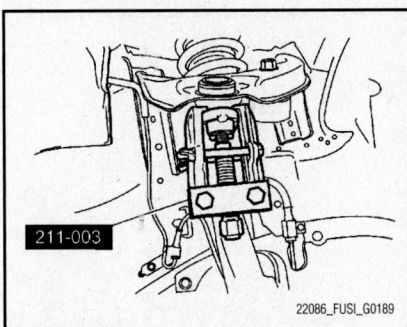

22086_FUSI_G0189

Fig. 340 Using the special tool, separate the upper ball joint from the wheel knuckle

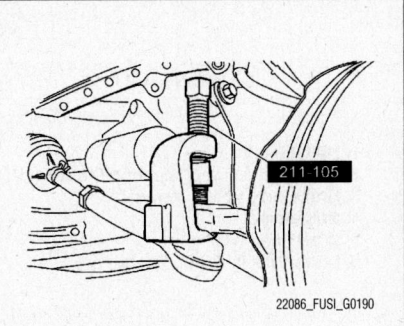

22086_FUSI_G0190

Fig. 341 Using the special tool, separate the tie-rod end from the wheel knuckle

10. Remove and discard the upper ball joint nut.

11. Using the special tool, separate the upper ball joint from the wheel knuckle.

12. Remove and discard the tie-rod end cotter pin and nut.

✱✱ WARNING

Do not use a hammer to separate the tie-rod end from the wheel knuckle or damage to the wheel knuckle can result.

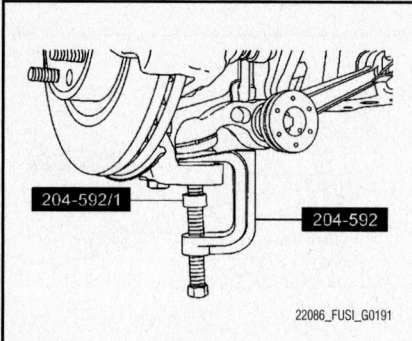

Fig. 342 Using the special tools, separate the 2 lower ball joints from the wheel knuckle and remove the wheel knuckle

13. Using the special tool, separate the tie-rod end from the wheel knuckle.

14. Remove and discard the 2 lower ball joint nuts.

✱✱ WARNING

When the lower ball joint is separated from the wheel knuckle, the lower arm may strike the outer constant velocity (CV) joint boot with enough force to damage the boot clamp. This will result in a loss of grease from the outer CV joint. Place a block of wood, or similar item, between the lower arm and the outer CV joint to prevent the lower arm from striking the outer CV joint.

➡Once pressure is applied to the ball joint with the special tool, it may be necessary to tap the wheel knuckle at the ball joint area to separate the ball joint from the wheel knuckle.

15. Using the special tools, separate the 2 lower ball joints from the wheel knuckle and remove the wheel knuckle.

To install:

16. Position the wheel knuckle and install the 2 lower ball joint nuts. Tighten the nuts to 200 Nm (148 ft. lbs.).

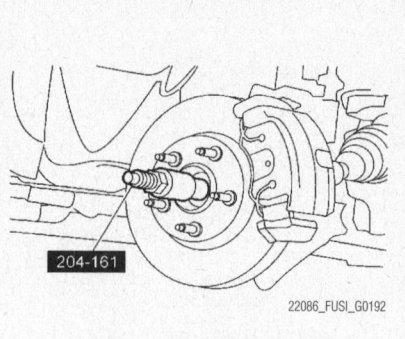

Fig. 344 Using the special tool, install the halfshaft into the wheel hub

17. Position the tie-rod end and install the nut and cotter pin. Tighten to 48 Nm (35 ft. lbs.).

18. Position the upper ball joint and install the nut. Tighten to 48 Nm (35 ft. lbs.).

19. If equipped, position the wheel speed sensor and install the bolt. Tighten to 23 Nm (17 ft. lbs.).

20. If equipped, install the wheel speed sensor harness bolt. Tighten to 23 Nm (17 ft. lbs.).

21. Position the brake caliper and anchor plate assembly and install the 2 bolts. Tighten to 90 Nm (66 ft. lbs.).

22. Install the brake disc and the 2 brake disc bolts. Tighten to 20 Nm (15 ft. lbs.).

23. Using the special tool, install the halfshaft into the wheel hub.

✱✱ WARNING

Do not tighten the halfshaft nut with the vehicle on the ground. The nut must be tightened to specification before the vehicle is lowered onto the wheels. Wheel bearing damage will occur if the wheel bearing is loaded with the weight of the vehicle applied.

➡Apply the brake to keep the halfshaft from rotating.

24. Install the halfshaft nut and tighten to 225 Nm (185 ft. lbs.).

WHEEL HUB AND BEARING

REMOVAL & INSTALLATION

See Figures 345 through 350.

➡If removing the wheel hub, the wheel bearing must be replaced.

1. Remove the steering knuckle, as outlined in this section.

2. Using the special tool, press the wheel hub from the wheel bearing.

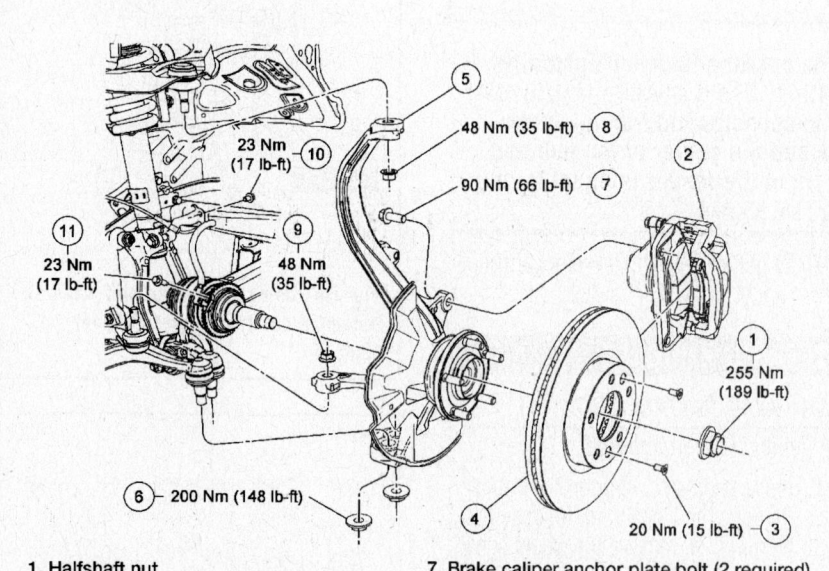

1. Halfshaft nut
2. Brake caliper and anchor plate assembly
3. Brake disc bolt (2 required)
4. Brake disc
5. Wheel knuckle
6. Lower ball joint nut (2 required)
7. Brake caliper anchor plate bolt (2 required)
8. Upper ball joint nut
9. Tie-rod end nut
10. Wheel speed sensor harness bolt
11. Wheel speed sensor bolt

Fig. 343 Exploded view of the wheel knuckle and related components

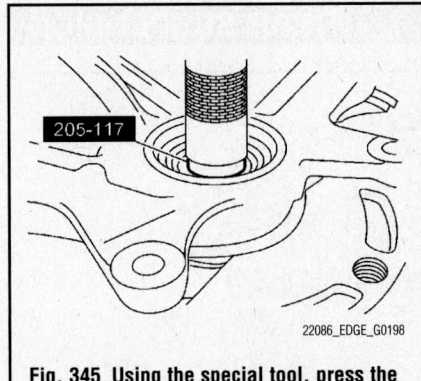

Fig. 345 Using the special tool, press the wheel hub from the wheel bearing

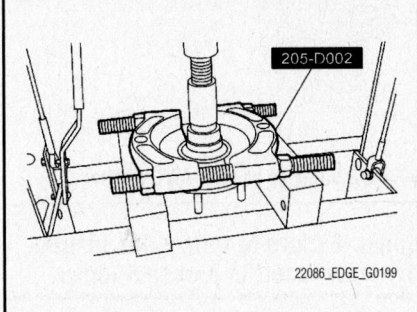

Fig. 346 Using the special tool, press the inner wheel bearing race from the wheel hub

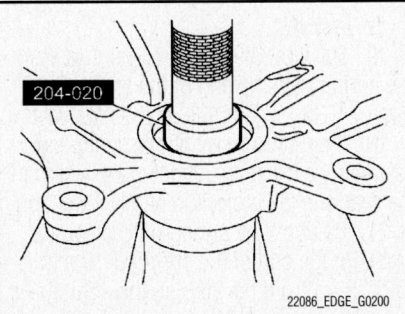

Fig. 347 Using the special tool, press the outer wheel bearing race from the wheel knuckle

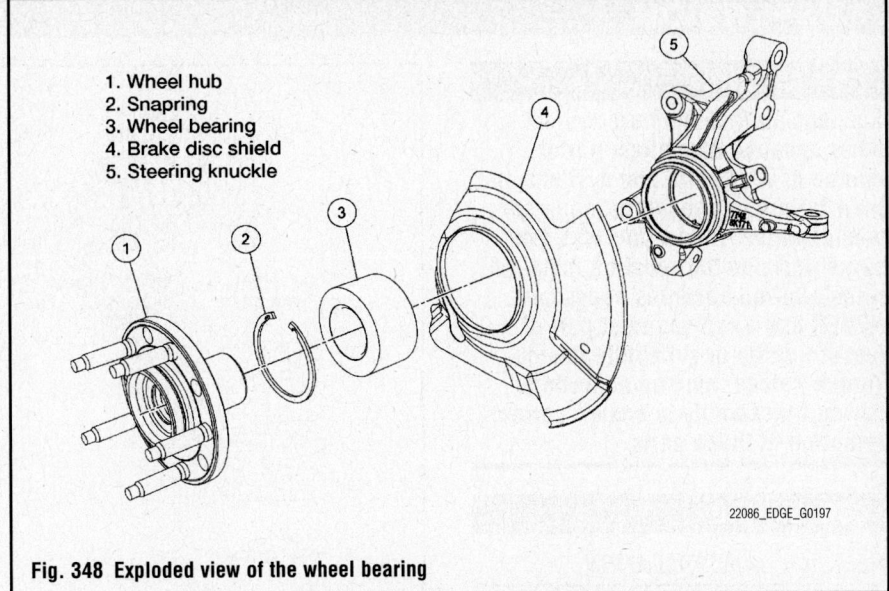

1. Wheel hub
2. Snapring
3. Wheel bearing
4. Brake disc shield
5. Steering knuckle

Fig. 348 Exploded view of the wheel bearing

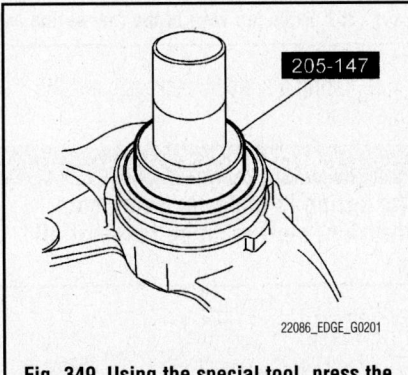

Fig. 349 Using the special tool, press the wheel bearing into the wheel knuckle

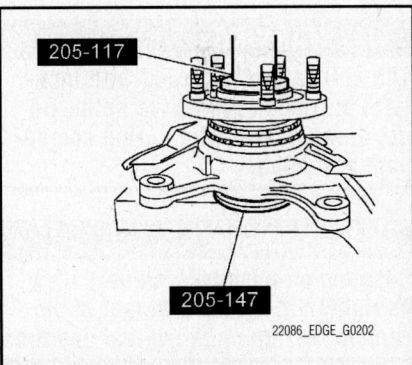

Fig. 350 Using the special tools, press the wheel hub into the wheel bearing

➡This step may not be necessary if the inner wheel bearing race remains in the wheel knuckle after removing the wheel hub.

3. Using the special tool, press the inner wheel bearing race from the wheel hub.
4. Remove the snap ring.
5. Using the special tool, press the outer wheel bearing race from the wheel knuckle.

To install:

6. Using the special tool, press the wheel bearing into the wheel knuckle.
7. Install the snap ring.
8. Using the special tools, press the wheel hub into the wheel bearing.
9. Install the steering knuckle, as outlined in this section.

SUSPENSION   **REAR SUSPENSION**

❋❋ WARNING

Suspension fasteners are critical parts because they affect performance of vital parts and systems and their failure can result in major service expense. A new part with the same part number must be installed if installation becomes necessary. NEVER use a replacement part of lesser quality or substitute design. Torque values must be adhered to during reassembly to ensure correct retention of these parts.

COIL SPRING

REMOVAL & INSTALLATION

See Figures 351 through 355.

❋ WARNING

The coil spring is coated with long-term corrosion protective paint. Do not damage the paint during component servicing.

❋❋ WARNING

Suspension bushing fasteners must be tightened with the weight of the vehicle resting on the wheel and tires

1. Raise and safely support the vehicle.
2. Remove the wheel and tire assembly.

❋ WARNING

Do not fully tighten the cam adjuster nut until the rear alignment has been checked and, if necessary, adjusted.

3. Matchmark the cam bolt and cam adjuster and then loosen the cam adjuster nut.
4. Remove the stabilizer bar link lower bolt.

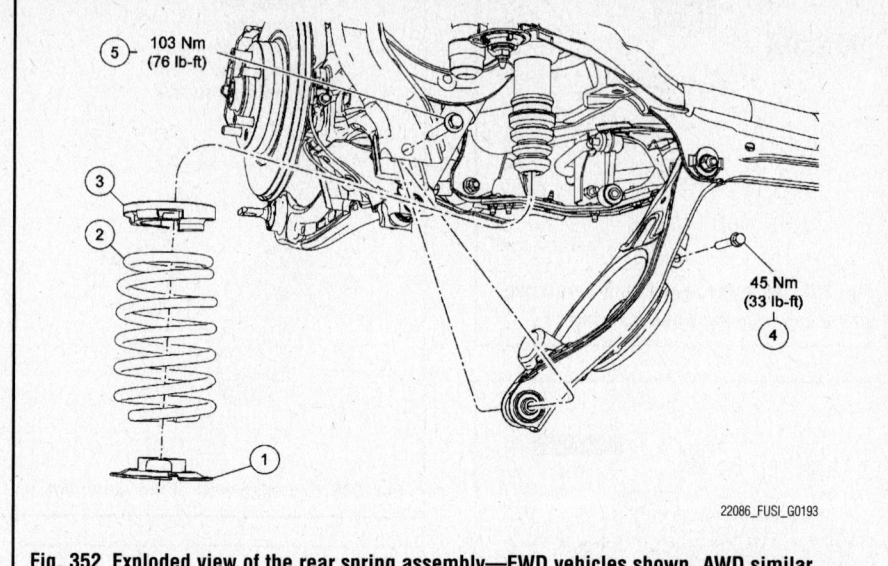

Fig. 352 Exploded view of the rear spring assembly—FWD vehicles shown, AWD similar

5. Using a suitable jack, support the lower arm.

❋❋ CAUTION

The spring is under extreme compression, care must be taken at all

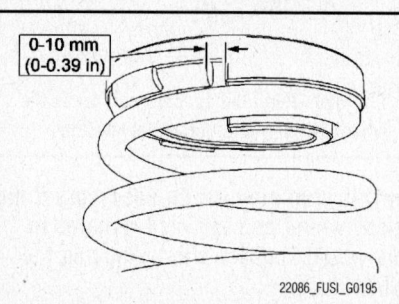

Fig. 353 Position the spring upper seat onto the spring with the end of the spring 0-10 mm (0-0.39 in) from the step on the seat

times. Failure to follow this instruction may result in personal injury.

6. Remove the lower arm outboard bolt.
7. Lower the lower arm and remove the spring.
8. Inspect the spring upper and lower seats, install new seats as necessary.

To install:

9. Position the spring upper seat onto the spring with the end of the spring 0-10 mm (0-0.39 in) from the step on the seat.
10. If removed, position the spring lower seat into the lower arm aligning the recess in the seat with the projection on the lower arm.
11. Position the spring onto the lower arm with the end of the spring 0-10 mm (0-0.39 in) from the step on the spring seat.

➡ Do not tighten the bolt at this time.

12. Using the jack, raise the lower arm and install the lower arm outboard bolt.

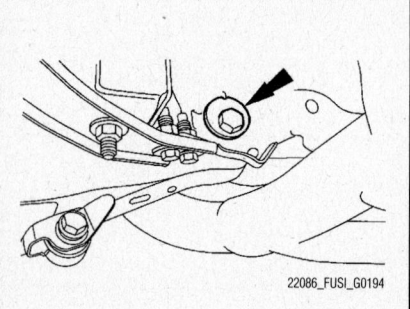

Fig. 351 Matchmark the cam bolt and cam adjuster and then loosen the cam adjuster nut

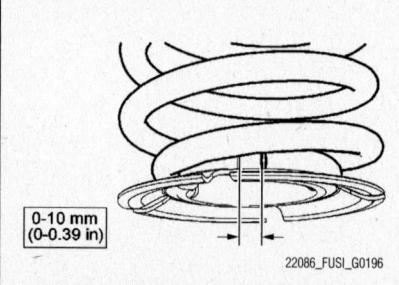

Fig. 354 Position the spring onto the lower arm with the end of the spring 0-10 mm (0-0.39 in) from the step on the spring seat

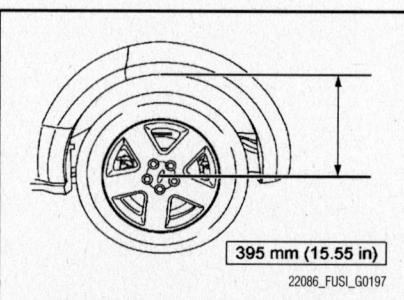

Fig. 355 Using the jack, raise the suspension until the distance between the center of the hub and the lip of the fender is equal to 395 mm (15.55 in)

> ❊❊ **WARNING**
>
> **Before tightening any suspension bushing fasteners, the suspension must be at the bushing fastener tightening position.**

13. Using the jack, raise the suspension until the distance between the center of the hub and the lip of the fender is equal to 395 mm (15.55 in).

14. Tighten the lower arm outboard bolt to 103 Nm (74 ft. lbs.).

15. Install the stabilizer bar link lower bolt. Tighten to 45 Nm (33 ft. lbs.).

16. Align the index mark on the cam bolt and cam adjuster with the index mark on the lower arm and tighten the cam adjuster nut to 101 Nm (74 ft. lbs.).

17. Check, and if necessary, align the vehicle.

CONTROL ARMS/LINKS

REMOVAL & INSTALLATION

Lower Arm

See Figure 355.

> ❊❊ **WARNING**
>
> **Suspension bushing fasteners must be tightened with the weight of the vehicle resting on the wheel and tires.**

1. Remove the Coil Spring, as outlined in this section.

2. Remove the cam adjuster nut, cam adjuster and cam bolt. Discard the cam bolt and nut.

3. Remove the lower arm.

To install:

> ❊❊ **WARNING**
>
> **Do not fully tighten the cam adjuster nut until the rear alignment has been checked and, if necessary, adjusted.**

➡ Install the cam bolt and the cam adjuster with the cam facing upward

4. Installation is the reverse of the removal procedure. Tighten the cam adjuster bolt and nut to 101 Nm (74 ft. lbs.).

> ❊❊ **WARNING**
>
> **Before tightening any suspension bushing fasteners, the suspension must be at the bushing fastener tightening position.**

5. Using the jack, raise the suspension until the distance between the center of the

hub and the lip of the fender is equal to 395 mm (15.55 in).

Upper Arm

See Figures 355, 356 and 357.

> ❊❊ **WARNING**
>
> **Suspension fasteners are critical parts because they affect performance of vital parts and systems and their failure can result in major service expense. A new part with the same part number must be installed**

if installation becomes necessary. NEVER use a replacement part of lesser quality or substitute design. Torque values must be adhered to during reassembly to ensure correct retention of these parts.

> ❊❊ **WARNING**
>
> **Suspension bushing fasteners must be tightened with the weight of the vehicle resting on the wheel and tires.**

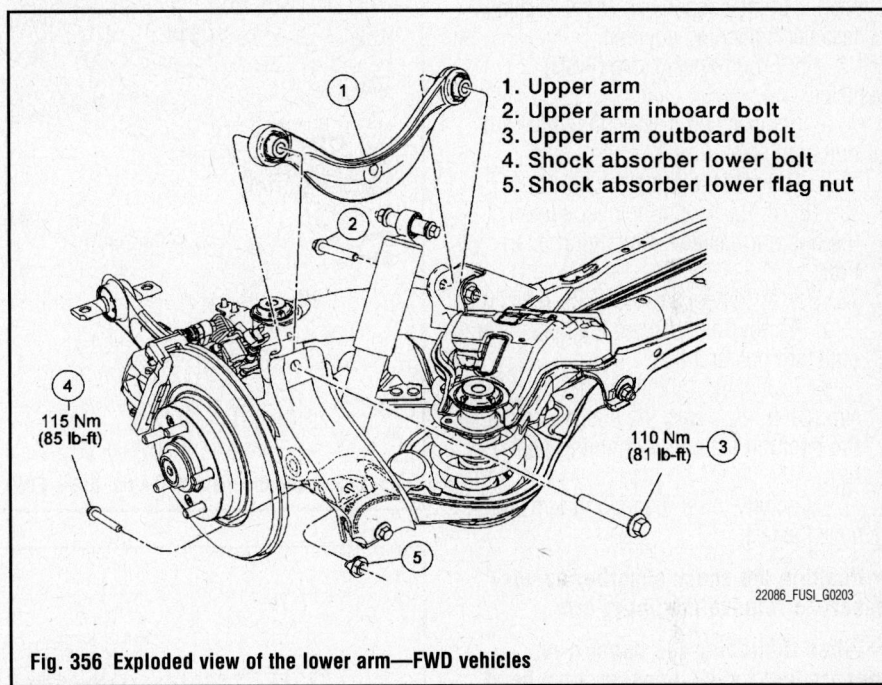

1. Upper arm
2. Upper arm inboard bolt
3. Upper arm outboard bolt
4. Shock absorber lower bolt
5. Shock absorber lower flag nut

115 Nm (85 lb-ft)

110 Nm (81 lb-ft)

22086_FUSI_G0203

Fig. 356 Exploded view of the lower arm—FWD vehicles

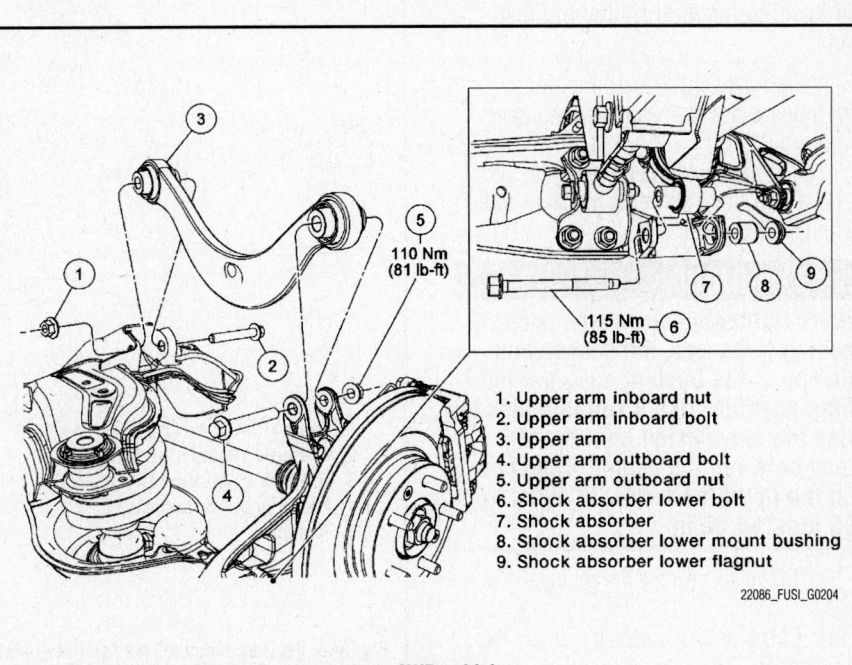

110 Nm (81 lb-ft)

115 Nm (85 lb-ft)

1. Upper arm inboard nut
2. Upper arm inboard bolt
3. Upper arm
4. Upper arm outboard bolt
5. Upper arm outboard nut
6. Shock absorber lower bolt
7. Shock absorber
8. Shock absorber lower mount bushing
9. Shock absorber lower flagnut

22086_FUSI_G0204

Fig. 357 Exploded view of the lower arm—AWD vehicles

1. Raise and safely support the vehicle.
2. Remove the wheel and tire assembly.
3. Using a suitable jack, support the trailing arm.

⁂ WARNING

Do not fully tighten the shock absorber lower nut until the suspension is at the bushing fastener tightening position.

4. Remove and discard the shock absorber lower bolt and flag nut.

   a. To install, tighten to 115 Nm (85 ft. lbs.) with the suspension at the bushing fastener tightening position.

5. For Front Wheel Drive (FWD) vehicles:

   a. Remove and discard the upper arm outboard bolt.

   b. To install, tighten the bolt to 110 Nm (81 ft. lbs.) with the suspension at the bushing fastener tightening position.

6. For All Wheel Drive (AWD) vehicles:

   a. Remove and discard the upper arm outboard bolt and nut.

   b. To install, tighten the nut to 110 Nm (81 ft. lbs.) with the suspension at the bushing fastener tightening position.

7. Carefully lower the trailing arm and remove the jack.

➡ Position the shock absorber as necessary to remove the upper arm.

➡ When tightening the upper arm inboard bolt the suspension must be at the bushing fastener tightening position.

8. Remove and discard the upper arm inboard bolt and remove the upper arm.

   a. To install, tighten the bolt to 100 Nm (74 ft. lbs.) and then rotate an additional 90 degrees.

⁂ WARNING

Before tightening any suspension bushing fasteners, the suspension must be at the bushing fastener tightening position. Use a suitable jack to raise the suspension until the distance between the center of the hub and the lip of the fender is equal to 395 mm (15.55 in).

9. To install, reverse the removal procedure.

10. Check and, if necessary, adjust the rear camber

Toe Link

See Figures 355, 358 and 359.

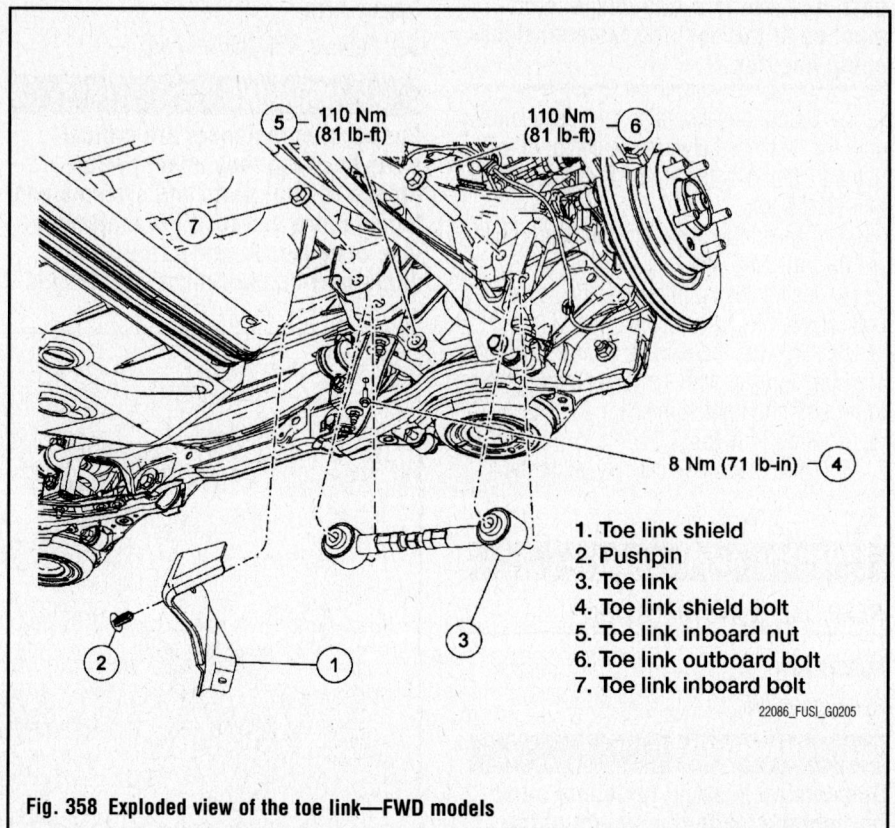

1. Toe link shield
2. Pushpin
3. Toe link
4. Toe link shield bolt
5. Toe link inboard nut
6. Toe link outboard bolt
7. Toe link inboard bolt

22086_FUSI_G0205

Fig. 358 Exploded view of the toe link—FWD models

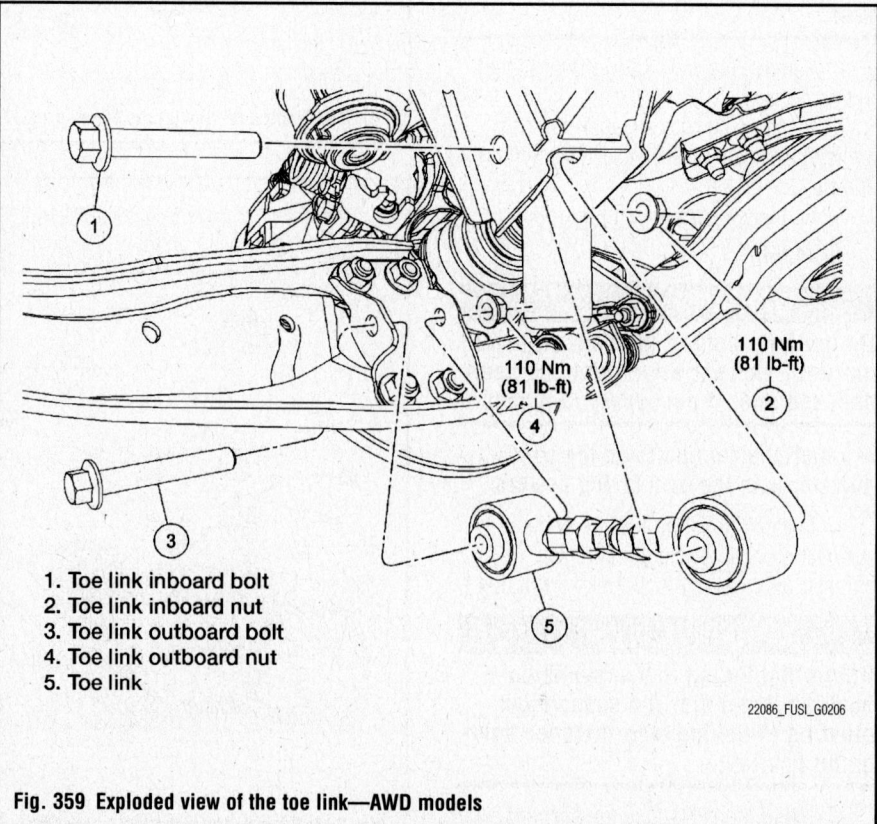

1. Toe link inboard bolt
2. Toe link inboard nut
3. Toe link outboard bolt
4. Toe link outboard nut
5. Toe link

22086_FUSI_G0206

Fig. 359 Exploded view of the toe link—AWD models

❊❊ WARNING

Suspension fasteners are critical parts because they affect performance of vital parts and systems and their failure can result in major service expense. A new part with the same part number must be installed if installation becomes necessary. NEVER use a replacement part of lesser quality or substitute design. Torque values must be adhered to during reassembly to ensure correct retention of these parts.

1. Raise and safely support the vehicle.
2. Remove the wheel and tire assembly.
3. For Front Wheel Drive (FWD) vehicles:

    a. Remove the toe link shield bolt.

    b. To install, tighten to 8 Nm (71 lb-in).

    c. Remove the pushpin and the shield.

4. Remove and discard the toe link inboard nut and bolt.

    a. To install, tighten the nut to 70 Nm (52 ft. lbs.) with the suspension at the bushing fastener tightening position.

5. Remove and discard the toe link outboard bolt and remove the toe link.

    a. To install, tighten to 70 Nm (52 ft. lbs.) with the suspension at the bushing fastener tightening position.

❊❊ WARNING

Before tightening any suspension bushing fasteners, the suspension must be at the bushing fastener tightening position. Use a suitable jack to raise the suspension until the distance between the center of the hub and the lip of the fender is equal to 395 mm (15.55 in).

6. To install, reverse the removal procedure.
7. Check and, if necessary, adjust the rear toe

KNUCKLE

REMOVAL & INSTALLATION

See Figures 360 through 363.

❊❊ WARNING

Suspension fasteners are critical parts because they affect performance of vital parts and systems and their failure can result in major service expense. A new part with the same part number must be installed

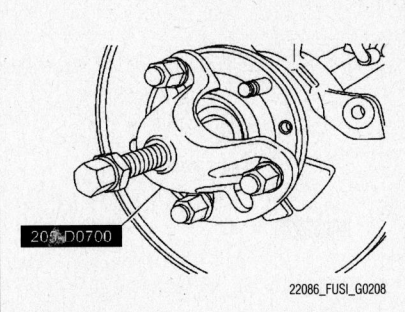

Fig. 360 Using the special tool, separate the halfshaft from the wheel hub

22086_FUSI_G0208

if installation becomes necessary. NEVER use a replacement part of lesser quality or substitute design. Torque values must be adhered to during reassembly to ensure correct retention of these parts.

❊❊ WARNING

Before tightening any suspension bushing fasteners, the suspension must be at the bushing fastener tightening position.

1. Raise and safely support the vehicle.
2. Remove the wheel and tire assembly.
3. If equipped, remove the wheel speed sensor bolt and position the sensor aside.
4. Disconnect the parking brake cable from the brake caliper:

    a. Remove the clip.

    b. Disconnect the parking brake cable from the brake caliper.

➡**Apply the brake to keep the halfshaft from rotating.**

5. Remove and discard the wheel hub nut.

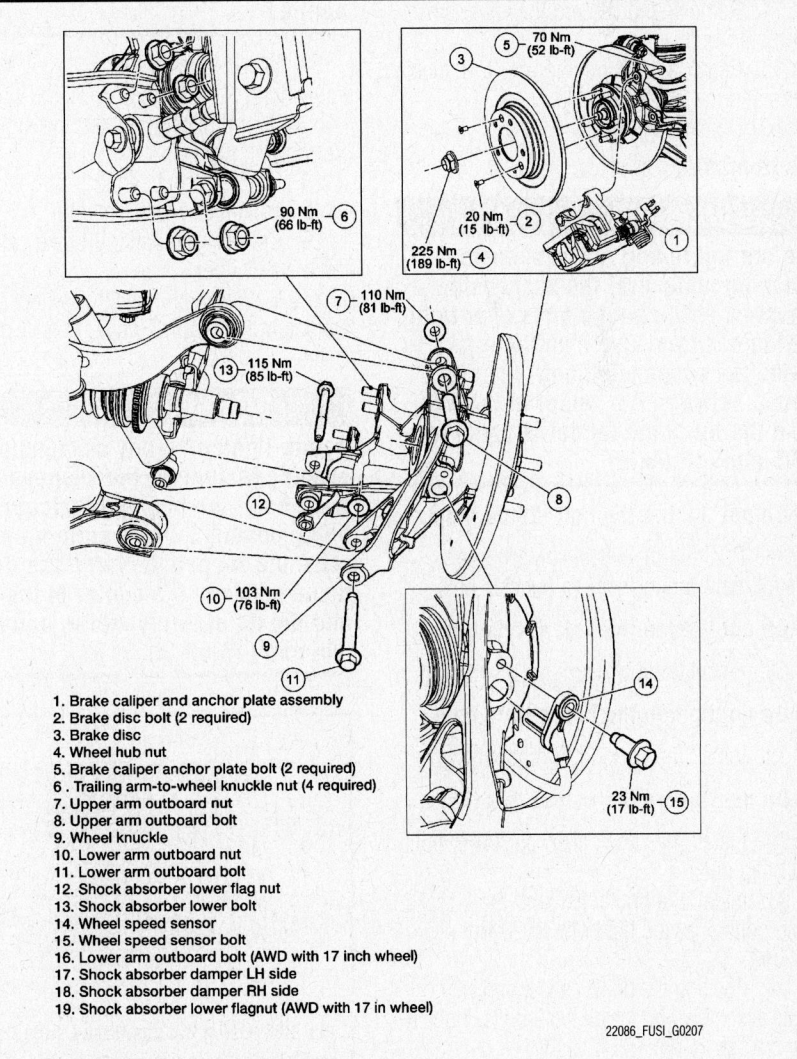

1. Brake caliper and anchor plate assembly
2. Brake disc bolt (2 required)
3. Brake disc
4. Wheel hub nut
5. Brake disc anchor plate bolt (2 required)
6. Trailing arm-to-wheel knuckle nut (4 required)
7. Upper arm outboard nut
8. Upper arm outboard bolt
9. Wheel knuckle
10. Lower arm outboard nut
11. Lower arm outboard bolt
12. Shock absorber lower flag nut
13. Shock absorber lower bolt
14. Wheel speed sensor
15. Wheel speed sensor bolt
16. Lower arm outboard bolt (AWD with 17 inch wheel)
17. Shock absorber damper LH side
18. Shock absorber damper RH side
19. Shock absorber lower flagnut (AWD with 17 in wheel)

22086_FUSI_G0207

Fig. 361 Exploded view of the rear knuckle and related components

✳✳ WARNING

Do not allow the brake caliper and anchor plate assembly to hang from the brake hose or damage to the hose can occur.

6. Remove the anchor plate bolts and position the brake caliper and anchor plate assembly aside.

7. Support the brake caliper and anchor plate assembly using mechanic's wire.

8. Remove the 2 brake disc bolts and the brake disc.

9. Using the special tool, separate the halfshaft from the wheel hub.

10. Remove and discard the shock absorber lower bolt and flag nut.

11. If equipped, remove the shock absorber damper.

12. Using a suitable jack, raise the lower arm.

13. Remove and discard the upper arm outboard bolt.

14. Remove and discard the lower arm outboard bolt.

15. Remove the 4 trailing arm-to-knuckle nuts and the wheel knuckle.

16. Discard the nuts.

To install:

✳✳ WARNING

Before tightening any suspension bushing fasteners, the suspension must be at the bushing fastener tightening position. Use a suitable jack to raise the suspension until the distance between the center of the hub and the lip of the fender is equal to 395 mm (15.55 in).

➡**Do not tighten the bolt at this time.**

17. Position the wheel knuckle and install the 4 trailing arm-to-knuckle nuts.

➡**Do not tighten the bolt at this time.**

18. Install the lower arm outboard bolt.

➡**Do not tighten the bolt at this time.**

19. Install the upper arm outboard bolt.

➡**Do not tighten the bolt at this time.**

20. Install the shock absorber lower bolt and flag nut.

21. Install the brake disc and the 2 brake disc bolts. Tighten the bolts to 20 Nm (15 ft. lbs.).

22. Position the brake caliper and anchor plate assembly and install the 2 bolts. Tighten the bolts to 70 Nm (52 ft. lbs.).

23. Using the special tool, install the halfshaft into the wheel hub.

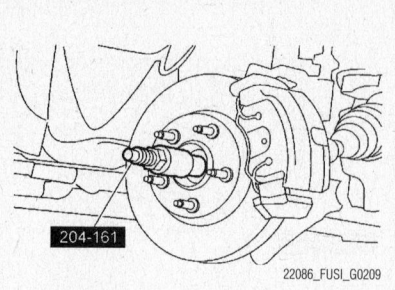

Fig. 362 Using the special tool, install the halfshaft into the wheel hub

✳✳ WARNING

Do not tighten the wheel hub nut with the vehicle on the ground. The nut must be tightened to specification before the vehicle is lowered onto the wheels. Wheel bearing damage will occur if the wheel bearing is loaded with the weight of the vehicle applied.

24. Install a new wheel hub nut. While applying the brakes to prevent the wheel hub nut from turning, tighten the nut to 225 Nm (185 ft. lbs.).

25. Connect the parking brake cable to the brake caliper. Install the clip.

26. Connect the parking brake cable to the brake caliper.

27. If equipped, install the wheel speed sensor and the bolt. Tighten to 23 Nm (17 ft. lbs.).

✳✳ WARNING

Before tightening any suspension bushing fasteners, the suspension must be at the bushing fastener tightening position. Use a suitable jack to raise the suspension until the distance between the center of the hub and the lip of the fender is equal to 395 mm (15.55 in).

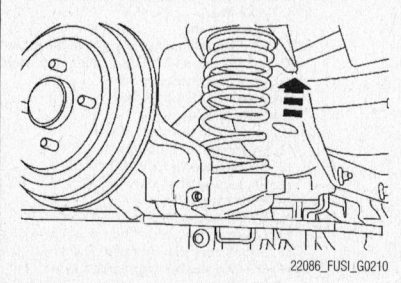

Fig. 363 Using the positioned suitable jack, raise the lower arm to bushing fastener tightening position

28. Using the positioned suitable jack, raise the lower arm to bushing fastener tightening position.

29. Tighten the 4 trailing arm-to-knuckle nuts to 90 Nm (66 ft. lbs.) with the suspension at the bushing fastener tightening position.

30. Tighten the lower arm outboard nut to 103 Nm (76 ft. lbs.) with the suspension at the bushing fastener tightening position.

31. Tighten the upper arm outboard bolt to 110 Nm (81 ft. lbs.) with the suspension at the bushing fastener tightening position.

32. Tighten the shock absorber lower bolt to 115 Nm (85 ft. lbs.) with the suspension at the bushing fastener tightening position.

33. Lower and remove the jack

STABILIZER BAR

REMOVAL & INSTALLATION

See Figures 364 and 365.

✳✳ WARNING

Suspension fasteners are critical parts because they affect performance of vital parts and systems and their failure can result in major service expense. A new part with the same part number must be installed if installation becomes necessary. NEVER use a replacement part of lesser quality or substitute design. Torque values must be adhered to during reassembly to ensure correct retention of these parts.

✳✳ WARNING

Before tightening any suspension bushing fasteners, the suspension must be at the bushing fastener tightening position.

1. For All Wheel Drive (AWD) vehicles:
   a. Remove the rear halfshafts
   b. Remove the RH side spring.

2. For Front Wheel Drive (FWD) vehicles:
   a. Raise and safely support the vehicle.

3. Remove the 2 stabilizer bar link upper nuts. Discard the nuts.
   a. To install, tighten to 40 Nm (30 ft. lbs.).

4. Remove the 2 stabilizer bar link lower bolts and the stabilizer bar links. Discard the bolts.

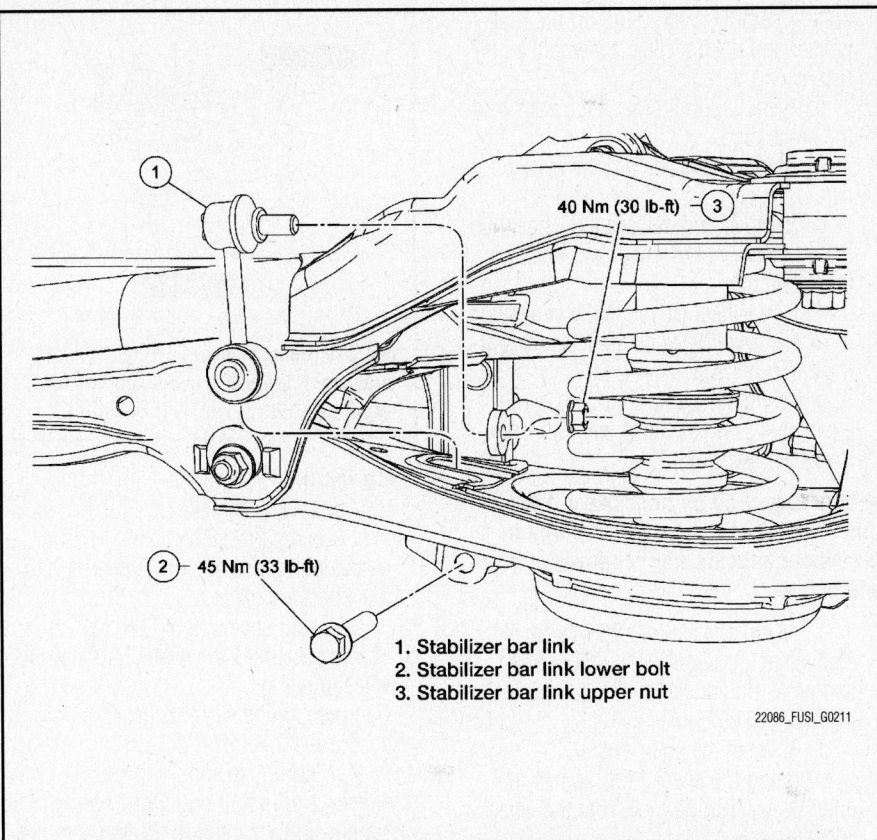

1. Stabilizer bar link
2. Stabilizer bar link lower bolt
3. Stabilizer bar link upper nut

22086_FUSI_G0211

Fig. 364 Stabilizer bar and related components (1 of 2)—FWD vehicles shown, AWD similar

a. To install, tighten to 45 Nm (33 ft. lbs.) with the suspension at the bushing fastener tightening position.

5. Remove the stabilizer bar bracket nuts. Discard the nuts.

a. To install, tighten to 40 Nm (30 ft. lbs.) with the suspension at the bushing fastener tightening position.

6. Remove the stabilizer bar bracket bolts and the brackets. Discard the bolts.

a. To install, tighten to 40 Nm (30 ft. lbs.) with the suspension at the bushing fastener tightening position.

7. For FWD vehicles, remove the stabilizer bar.

8. For AWD vehicles, remove the stabilizer bar from the RH side of the vehicle.

> ✳✳ **WARNING**
>
> **Be careful not to contact the fuel lines or wiring harness when removing and installing the stabilizer bar.**

9. Inspect the stabilizer bar bushings and install a new bushing(s) if necessary.

> ✳✳ **WARNING**
>
> **Before tightening any suspension bushing fasteners, the suspension must be at the bushing fastener tightening position.**

10. Installation is the reverse of the removal procedure

WHEEL HUB AND BEARING

REMOVAL & INSTALLATION

See Figures 366 through 370.

1. For Front Wheel Drive (FWD) vehicles:

a. Raise and safely support the vehicle.

b. If equipped, remove the wheel speed sensor bolt and position the sensor aside.

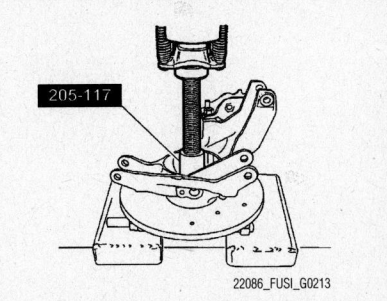

22086_FUSI_G0213

Fig. 366 Using special tool 205-117, or equivalent to press the wheel hub from the wheel bearing

1. Stabilizer bar bracket (2 required)
2. Stabilizer bar bushing (2 required)
3. Stabilzer bar
4. Stabilizer bar bracket nut (2 required)
5. Stabilizer bar bracket bolt (2 required)
6. Stabilizer bar link upper nut (2 required)

22086_FUSI_G0212

Fig. 365 Stabilizer bar and related components (2 of 2)—FWD vehicles shown, AWD similar

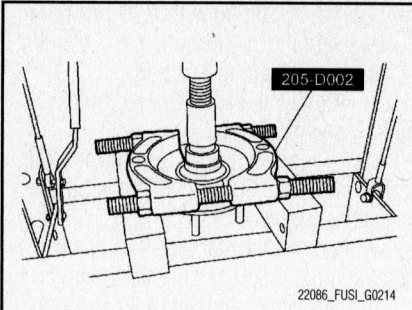

Fig. 367 Install the special tool, position in a suitable press and press the inner wheel bearing race from the wheel hub.

c. Disconnect the parking brake cable from the brake caliper, by removing the clip, then disconnecting the parking brake cable from the brake caliper.

❉❉ WARNING

Do not allow the brake caliper and anchor plate assembly to hang from the brake hose or damage to the hose can occur.

d. Remove the anchor plate bolts and position the brake caliper and anchor

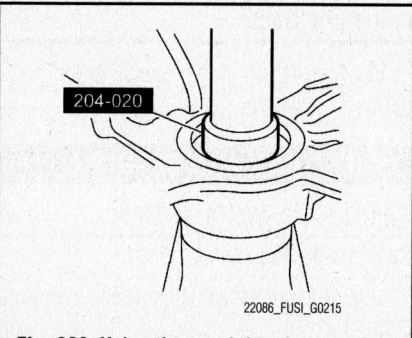

Fig. 368 Using the special tool, press the outer wheel bearing race from the wheel knuckle.

plate assembly aside. Support the brake caliper and anchor plate assembly using mechanic's wire.

e. Remove the 2 brake disc bolts and the brake disc.

f. Remove and discard the grease cap.

g. Remove and discard the wheel hub nut and remove the wheel hub and bearing assembly.

2. For All Wheel Drive (AWD) vehicles:

a. Remove the wheel knuckle, as outlined in this section.

b. Using special tool 205-117, or equivalent to press the wheel hub from the wheel bearing.

➡**This step may be necessary if the inner wheel bearing race remains in the wheel knuckle after removing the wheel hub.**

c. Install special tool 205-D002, or equivalent, position in a suitable press and press the inner wheel bearing race from the wheel hub.

d. Remove the span ring.

e. Using the special tool, press the outer wheel bearing race from the wheel knuckle.

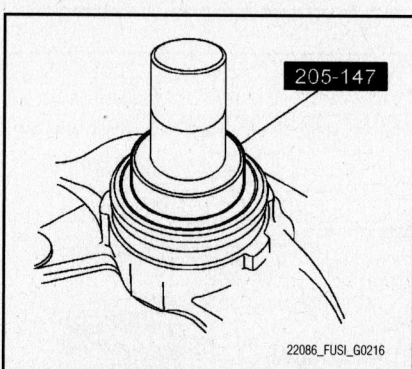

Fig. 369 Using the special tool, press the wheel bearing into the wheel knuckle

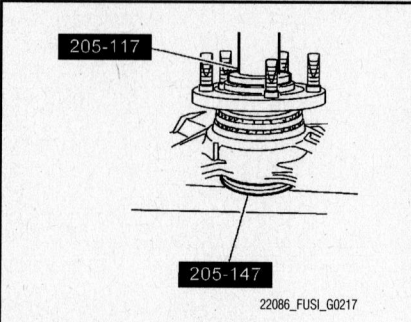

Fig. 370 Using special tool 205-117, or equivalent, press the wheel hub into the wheel bearing

To install:

3. For AWD vehicles:

a. Using special tool 205-147, or equivalent, press the wheel bearing into the wheel knuckle.

b. Using special tool 205-117, or equivalent, press the wheel hub into the wheel bearing.

c. Install the wheel knuckle.

4. For FWD vehicles:

a. If equipped, position the sensor and install the wheel speed sensor bolt. Tighten to 23 Nm (17 ft. lbs.).

b. Connect the parking brake cable to the brake caliper. Install the clip.

c. Connect the parking brake cable to the brake caliper.

d. Position the brake caliper and install the brake caliper anchor plate bolts. Tighten to 70 Nm (52 ft. lbs.).

e. Install the brake disc and the 2 brake disc bolts. Tighten to 20 Nm (15 ft. lbs.).

f. Install the grease cap.

g. Install the wheel hub and bearing assembly and the wheel hub nut. Tighten to 255 Nm (189 ft. lbs.).

LINCOLN

LS

14

SPECIFICATIONS AND MAINTENANCE CHARTS

ENGINE AND VEHICLE IDENTIFICATION

			Engine					Model Year	
Code ①	Liters (cc)	Cu. In.	Cyl.	Fuel Sys.	Type	Eng. Mfg.		Code ②	Year
S	3.0 (3049)	182	6	MFI	DOHC	Ford		5	2005
A	3.9 (3947)	238	8	MFI	DOHC	Ford		6	2006

MFI: Multi-Port Fuel Injection

DOHC: Double Overhead Camshaft

① 8th digit of the VIN

② 10th digit of the VIN

22086_LILS_C0001

GENERAL ENGINE SPECIFICATIONS

Year	Model	Engine Displacement Liters	Engine ID/VIN	Net Horsepower @ rpm	Net Torque @ rpm (ft. lbs.)	Bore x Stroke (in.)	Compression Ratio	Oil Pressure @ rpm
2005	LS	3.0	S	232@6500	220@4750	3.50x3.13	10.5:1	20-45@1500
	LS	3.9	A	280@6000	286@4000	3.38x3.34	10.75:1	61-73@400
2006	LS	3.9	A	280@6000	286@4000	3.38x3.34	10.75:1	61-73@400

22086_LILS_C0002

ENGINE TUNE-UP SPECIFICATIONS

Year	Engine Displacement Liters	Engine ID/VIN	Spark Plugs Gap (in.)	Ignition Timing (deg.) ① MT	AT	Fuel Pump (psi)	Idle Speed (rpm) ① MT	AT	Valve Clearance In.	Ex.
2005	3.0	S	0.051-0.057	—	12-17B	30-55	—	650-750	0.0069-0.0089	0.0128-0.0148
	3.9	A	0.039-0.043	—	10-20B	30-55	—	650-750	0.0069-0.0089	0.009-0.011
2006	3.9	A	0.039-0.043	—	10-20B	30-55	—	650-750	0.0069-0.0089	0.009-0.011

NOTE: The underhood specifications sticker often reflects tune-up specification changes in production. Sticker figures must be used if they disagree with those in this chart.

① Controlled by the engine computer

22086_LILS_C0003

CAPACITIES

Year	Model	Engine Displacement Liters	Engine ID/VIN	Engine Oil with Filter (qts.)	Transmission (pts.)		Drive Axle Rear (pts.)	Fuel Tank (gal.)	Cooling System (qts.)
					Manual	Auto.			
2005	LS	3.0	S	6.9	—	23.8	2.7	18.0	11.2
		3.9	A	6.9	—	23.8	2.7	18.0	12.0
2006	LS	3.9	A	6.9	—	23.8	2.7	18.0	12.0

22086_LILS_C0004

FLUID SPECIFICATIONS

Year	Model	Engine Displacement Liters	Engine ID/VIN	Engine Oil ①	Auto. Trans.	Drive Axle	Power Steering Fluid	Brake Master Cylinder
2005	LS	3.0	S	5W-20	MERCON V	75W-140	MERCON ②	DOT 3
		3.9	A	5W-20	MERCON V	75W-140	MERCON ②	DOT 3
2006	LS	3.9	A	5W-20	MERCON V	75W-140	MERCON ②	DOT 3

DOT: Department Of Transpotation

① Premium Synthetic Blend Motor Oil XO-5W20-QSP or equivalent

② MERCON Multi-Purpose ATF Transmission Fluid XT-2-QDX

22086_LILS_C0005

VALVE SPECIFICATIONS

Year	Engine Displacement Liters	Engine ID/VIN	Seat Angle (deg.)	Face Angle (deg.)	Spring Test Pressure (lbs. @ in.)	Spring Free Length (in.)	Stem-to-Guide Clearance (in.)		Stem Diameter (in.)	
							Intake	Exhaust	Intake	Exhaust
2005	3.0	S	44.75	45.5	153@1.18	1.740	0.0008-0.0026	0.0017-0.0037	0.2160-0.2150	0.2150
	3.9	A	NA	45	NA	NA	0.0010	0.0010	0.1960-0.1970	0.1950-0.1960
2006	3.9	A	NA	45	NA	NA	NA	NA	NA	NA

NA: Not Available

22086_LILS_C0009

CAMSHAFT AND BEARING SPECIFICATIONS CHART

All measurements are given in inches.

Year	Engine Displ. Liters	Engine ID/VIN	Journal Dia.	Brg. Oil Clearance	Shaft End-play	Runout	Journal Bore	Lobe Height Intake	Lobe Height Exhaust
2005	3.0	S	1.060	0.0009– 0.0033	0.002– 0.010	NA	1.062– 1.0630	NA	NA
	3.9	A	NA	NA	0.0003– 0.0070	NA	NA	NA	NA
2006	3.9	A	NA	NA	0.0003– 0.0070	NA	NA	NA	NA

NA: Not Available

22086_LILS_C0008

CRANKSHAFT AND CONNECTING ROD SPECIFICATIONS

All measurements are given in inches.

Year	Engine Displacement Liters	Engine ID/VIN	Crankshaft Main Brg. Journal Dia.	Crankshaft Main Brg. Oil Clearance	Crankshaft Shaft End-play	Crankshaft Thrust on No.	Connecting Rod Journal Diameter	Connecting Rod Oil Clearance	Connecting Rod Side Clearance
2005	3.0	S	2.4790– 2.4800	0.0009– 0.0018	0.0040 0.0090	4	1.9670– 1.9680	0.0010 0.0025	0.0039– 0.0118
	3.9	A	NA	NA	NA	NA	NA	NA	NA
2006	3.9	A	NA	NA	NA	NA	NA	NA	NA

NA: Not Available

22086_LILS_C0006

PISTON AND RING SPECIFICATIONS

All measurements are given in inches.

Year	Engine Displacement Liters	Engine ID/VIN	Piston Clearance	Ring Gap Top Compression	Ring Gap Bottom Compression	Ring Gap Oil Control	Ring Side Clearance Top Compression	Ring Side Clearance Bottom Compression	Ring Side Clearance Oil Control
2005	3.0	S	0.0005– 0.0009	0.0039– 0.0098	0.0106– 0.0165	0.0059– 0.0255	0.0015– 0.0029	0.0015– 0.0033	SNUG
	3.9	A	NA	NA	NA	NA	NA	NA	NA
2006	3.9	A	NA	NA	NA	NA	NA	NA	NA

NA: Not Available

22086_LILS_C0007

TORQUE SPECIFICATIONS
All readings in ft. lbs.

Year	Engine Displacement Liters	Engine ID/VIN	Cylinder Head Bolts	Main Bearing Bolts	Rod Bearing Bolts	Crankshaft Damper Bolts	Flywheel Bolts	Manifold		Spark Plugs	Oil Pan Drain Plug
								Intake	Exhaust		
2005	3.0	S	①	②	③	④	54-64	⑤	13-16	7-15	17
	3.9	A	⑥	NA	NA	⑦	⑧	15	18	20	17
2006	3.9	A	⑥	NA	NA	⑦	⑧	15	18	20	17

NA: Not Available

① Step 1: 22 ft. lbs.
Step 2: Plus 85-95 degrees
Step 3: Loosen one turn
Step 4: 22 ft. lbs.
Step 5: Plus 85-95 degrees
Step 6: Plus 85-95 degrees

② Step 1: Cap bolts 1-8 (outer) 17-20 ft. lbs.
Step 2: Cap bolts 9-16 (inner) 28-31 ft. lbs.
Step 3: Rotate bolts 1-16, 85-95 degrees
Step 4: Bolts 17-22; 15-22 ft. lbs.

③ Step 1: 30-33 ft. lbs.
Step 2: Plus 90-120 degrees

④ Step 1: 77-99 ft. lbs.
Step 2: Loosen 360 degrees
Step 3: Tighten to 35-39 ft. lbs.
Step 4: Plus 85-95 degrees

⑤ 71-106 inch lbs.

⑥ Step 1: Tighten M10 bolts to 15 ft. lbs.
Step 2: Tighten M10 bolts to 26 ft. lbs.
Step 3: Tighten M10 bolts to 33 ft. lbs.
Step 4: Tighten M10 bolts plus 90 degrees
Step 5: Tighten M10 bolts plus 90 degrees
Step 6: Tighten M8 bolts to 15 ft. lbs.
Step 7: Tighten M8 bolts plus 90 degrees

⑦ Step 1: 59 ft. lbs.
Step 2: Loosen bolt two full turns
Step 3: Tighten to 37 ft. lbs.
Step 4: Tighten an additional 90 degrees

⑧ Step 1: 11 ft. lbs.
Step 2: 81 ft. lbs.

22086_LILS_C0010

WHEEL ALIGNMENT

Year	Model		Caster		Camber		Toe-in (Deg.)
			Range (+/-Deg.)	Preferred Setting (Deg.)	Range (+/-Deg.)	Preferred Setting (Deg.)	
2005	LS	F	0.5	8.10	0.50	- 0.15	0.16 +/- 0.25
		R	—	—	0.75	-1.00	0.24 +/- 0.25
2006	LS	F	0.5	8.10	0.70	- 0.15	0.08 +/- 0.16
		R	—	—	0.75	-1.00	0.24 +/- 0.25

22086_LILS_C0011

TIRE, WHEEL AND BALL JOINT SPECIFICATIONS

| Year | Model | OEM Tires | | Tire Pressures (psi) | | Wheel Size | Ball Joint Inspection | Lug Nut (ft. lbs.) |
		Standard	Optional	Front	Rear			
2005	LS	P225/55R16	P235/50R17	①	①	②	U ③ L ③ ④	100
2006	LS	P225/55R16	P235/50R17	①	①	②	U ③ L ③ ④	100

OEM: Original Equipment Manufacturer

PSI: Pounds Per Square Inch

STD: Standard

OPT: Optional

L: Lower

U: Upper

① Refer to the safety certification sticker located on driver door jamb or tire inflation placard on the passenger door jamb.

② 16x7.5J or 17x7.5J

③ Replace if any measurable movement is found.

④ Do not lift car. Inspect the boss into which the grease fitting is threaded. Replace if the boss is flush or receded below the surface of the ball joint.

22086_LILS_C0012

BRAKE SPECIFICATIONS
All measurements in inches unless noted

| Year | Model | | Brake Disc | | | Minimum Lining Thickness | Brake Caliper | |
			Original Thickness	Minimum Thickness	Maximum Runout		Bracket Bolts (ft. lbs.)	Mounting Bolts (ft. lbs.)
2005	LS	F	1.180	1.120	0.004	0.118	76	26
		R	0.810	0.752	0.004	0.118	76	26
2006	LS	F	1.180	1.120	0.004	0.118	76	26
		R	0.810	0.752	0.004	0.118	76	26

22086_LILS_C0013

SCHEDULED MAINTENANCE INTERVALS
Lincoln—LS

TO BE SERVICED	TYPE OF SERVICE	VEHICLE MILEAGE INTERVAL (x1000)												
		5	10	15	20	25	30	35	40	45	50	55	60	65
Air cleaner filter	R						✓						✓	
Accessory drive belt	S/I												✓	
Brake system ①	S/I			✓			✓			✓			✓	
Clutch pedal operation	S/I						✓						✓	
Cooling system hoses and clamps	S/I			✓			✓			✓			✓	
CV-joint boots & axle seals	S/I						✓						✓	
Engine coolant	R	Ten years or 150,000 miles												
Engine oil & filter	R	✓	✓	✓	✓	✓	✓	✓	✓	✓	✓	✓	✓	✓
Exterior Lights	S/I	Check monthly												
PCV valve	S/I												✓	
Exhaust system & heat shields	S/I						✓						✓	
Parking brake system	S/I	Every 6 months												
Power steering fluid	S/I	Every 6 months												
Rotate tires	S/I	✓		✓		✓		✓		✓		✓		✓
Steering linkage	S/I						✓						✓	
Spark plugs	R	Change at 100,000 miles												
Suspension components	S/I						✓						✓	

R: Replace   S/I: Inspect and service, if necessary   L: Lubricate   A: Adjust   C: Clean

① Inspect the reservoir fluid level, rotor and or drum, brake lines, hoses, calipers and or wheel cylinders

FREQUENT OPERATION MAINTENANCE (SEVERE SERVICE)

If a vehicle is operated under any of the following conditions it is considered severe service:

- Extremely dusty areas.
- 50% or more of the vehicle operation is in 32°C (90°F) or higher temperatures, or constant operation in temps below 0°C (32°F).
- Prolonged idling (vehicle operation in stop and go traffic).
- Frequent short running periods (engine does not warm to normal operating temperatures).
- Police, taxi, delivery usage or trailer towing usage.

Oil & oil filter change: change every 3000 miles.

Air filter element: change every 15,000 miles.

22086_LILS_C0014

PRECAUTIONS

Before servicing any vehicle, please be sure to read all of the following precautions, which deal with personal safety, prevention of component damage, and important points to take into consideration when servicing a motor vehicle:

• Never open, service or drain the radiator or cooling system when the engine is hot; serious burns can occur from the steam and hot coolant.

• Observe all applicable safety precautions when working around fuel. Whenever servicing the fuel system, always work in a well-ventilated area. Do not allow fuel spray or vapors to come in contact with a spark, open flame, or excessive heat (a hot drop light, for example). Keep a dry chemical fire extinguisher near the work area. Always keep fuel in a container specifically designed for fuel storage; also, always properly seal fuel containers to avoid the possibility of fire or explosion. Refer to the additional fuel system precautions later in this section.

• Fuel injection systems often remain pressurized, even after the engine has been turned **OFF**. The fuel system pressure must be relieved before disconnecting any fuel lines. Failure to do so may result in fire and/or personal injury.

• Brake fluid often contains polyglycol ethers and polyglycols. Avoid contact with the eyes and wash your hands thoroughly after handling brake fluid. If you do get brake fluid in your eyes, flush your eyes with clean, running water for 15 minutes. If eye irritation persists, or if you have taken brake fluid internally, IMMEDIATELY seek medical assistance.

• The EPA warns that prolonged contact with used engine oil may cause a number of skin disorders, including cancer. You should make every effort to minimize your exposure to used engine oil. Protective gloves should be worn when changing oil. Wash your hands and any other exposed skin areas as soon as possible after exposure to used engine oil. Soap and water, or waterless hand cleaner should be used.

• All new vehicles are now equipped with an air bag system, often referred to as a Supplemental Restraint System (SRS) or Supplemental Inflatable Restraint (SIR) system. The system must be disabled before performing service on or around system components, steering column, instrument panel components, wiring and sensors. Failure to follow safety and disabling procedures could result in accidental air bag deployment, possible personal injury and unnecessary system repairs.

• Always wear safety goggles when working with, or around, the air bag system. When carrying a non-deployed air bag, be sure the bag and trim cover are pointed away from your body. When placing a non-deployed air bag on a work surface, always face the bag and trim cover upward, away from the surface. This will reduce the motion of the module if it is accidentally deployed. Refer to the additional air bag system precautions later in this section.

• Clean, high quality brake fluid from a sealed container is essential to the safe and proper operation of the brake system. You should always buy the correct type of brake fluid for your vehicle. If the brake fluid becomes contaminated, completely flush the system with new fluid. Never reuse any brake fluid. Any brake fluid that is removed from the system should be discarded. Also, do not allow any brake fluid to come in contact with a painted surface; it will damage the paint.

• Never operate the engine without the proper amount and type of engine oil; doing so WILL result in severe engine damage.

• Timing belt maintenance is extremely important. Many models utilize an interference-type, non-freewheeling engine. If the timing belt breaks, the valves in the cylinder head may strike the pistons, causing potentially serious (also time-consuming and expensive) engine damage. Refer to the maintenance interval charts for the recommended replacement interval for the timing belt, and to the timing belt section for belt replacement and inspection.

• Disconnecting the negative battery cable on some vehicles may interfere with the functions of the on-board computer system(s) and may require the computer to undergo a relearning process once the negative battery cable is reconnected.

• When servicing drum brakes, only disassemble and assemble one side at a time, leaving the remaining side intact for reference.

• Only an MVAC-trained, EPA-certified automotive technician should service the air conditioning system or its components.

BRAKES

GENERAL INFORMATION

The Four Wheel Anti-lock Brake System (4WABS) consists of the following components: anti-lock brake module, front anti-lock brake sensors, front anti-lock brake sensor indicators, Hydraulic Control Unit (HCU), rear anti-lock brake sensors, rear anti-lock brake sensor indicators, and a yellow anti-lock brake warning indicator.

SPEED SENSORS

REMOVAL & INSTALLATION

Front

1. Before servicing the vehicle, refer to the precautions in the beginning of this section.

ANTI-LOCK BRAKE SYSTEM (ABS)

2. Raise and support the vehicle.

3. Position the inner splash shield aside, disconnecting it via the pin-type retainers.

4. Disconnect the anti-lock brake sensor electrical connector.

5. Remove the anti-lock brake sensor harness from the brake hose clips.

6. Remove the anti-lock brake sensor clip.

7. Remove the anti-lock brake sensor.

To install:

➡ **Make sure the anti-lock brake sensor is fully seated before installation of the new clip.**

8. Apply a 0.1 inch (2.5mm) bead of silicone sealant to the outside diameter of the anti-lock brake sensor.

9. Install the anti-lock brake sensor.

10. Install the anti-lock brake sensor clip.

11. Install the anti-lock brake sensor harness to the brake hose clips.

12. Connect the anti-lock brake sensor electrical connector.

13. Attach the inner splash shield with the pin-type retainers.

Rear

1. Before servicing the vehicle, refer to the precautions in the beginning of this section.

2. Raise and support the vehicle.

3. Disconnect the rear anti-lock brake sensor electrical connector.

4. Remove the rear anti-lock brake sensor harness from the control arm clips.

➡ Clean off dirt and foreign material that may have collected around the rear anti-lock brake sensor before removal.

5. Remove the rear anti-lock brake sensor via the bolt.

To install:

6. Install the rear anti-lock brake sensor and the bolt.

a. Tightening torque 97 inch lbs. (11 Nm)

7. Replace the rear anti-lock brake sensor harness with the control arm clips.

8. Connect the rear anti-lock brake sensor electrical connector.

BRAKES   BLEEDING THE BRAKE SYSTEM

BLEEDING PROCEDURE

BLEEDING PROCEDURE

Manual Bleeding Procedure

> ❋ **WARNING**
>
> **Use of any other than approved DOT 3 or DOT 4 brake fluid will cause permanent damage to brake components and will render the brakes inoperative.**

> ❋ **WARNING**
>
> **Brake fluid contains polyglycol ethers and polyglycols. Avoid contact with eyes. Wash hands thoroughly after handling. If brake fluid contacts eyes, flush eyes with running water for 15 minutes. Get medical attention if irritation persists. If taken internally, drink water and induce vomiting. Get medical attention immediately.**

> ❋ **CAUTION**
>
> **Brake fluid is harmful to painted and plastic surfaces. If brake fluid is spilled onto a painted or plastic surface, immediately wash it with water.**

> ❋ **CAUTION**
>
> **Do not allow the brake master cylinder reservoir to run dry during the bleeding operation. Keep the brake master cylinder reservoir filled with the specified brake fluid. Never reuse the brake fluid that has been drained from the hydraulic system.**

➡ When any part of the hydraulic system has been disconnected for repair or installation of new components, air can get into the system and cause spongy brake pedal action. This requires bleeding of the hydraulic system after it has been correctly connected. The hydraulic system can be bled manually or with pressure bleeding equipment.

1. Before servicing the vehicle, refer to the precautions in the beginning of this section.

2. Clean all dirt from and remove the brake master cylinder filler cap and fill the brake master cylinder reservoir with the specified brake fluid.

3. Place a box end wrench on the right rear bleeder screw. Attach a rubber drain tube to the right rear bleeder screw and submerge the free end of the tube in a container partially filled with clean brake fluid.

4. Have an assistant hold firm pressure on the brake pedal.

5. Loosen the right rear bleeder screw until a stream of brake fluid comes out. While the assistant maintains pressure on the brake pedal, tighten the right rear bleeder screw.

6. Repeat until clear, bubble-free fluid comes out.

7. Refill the brake master cylinder reservoir as necessary.

8. Tighten the right rear bleeder screw.

9. Repeat Steps 3, 4, 5 and 6 for the left rear bleeder screw.

10. Place a box end wrench on the right front disc brake caliper bleeder screw. Attach a rubber drain tube to the right front disc brake caliper bleeder screw, and submerge the free end of the tube in a container partially filled with clean brake fluid.

11. Have an assistant hold firm pressure on the brake pedal.

12. Loosen the right front disc brake caliper bleeder screw until a stream of brake fluid comes out. While the assistant maintains pressure on the brake pedal, tighten the right front disc brake caliper bleeder screw.

13. Repeat until clear, bubble-free fluid comes out.

14. Refill the brake master cylinder reservoir as necessary.

15. Tighten the right front disc brake caliper bleeder screw. For additional information, refer to Specifications in this section.

16. Repeat Steps 8, 9, 10 and 11 for the left front disc brake caliper bleeder screw.

Pressure Bleeding Procedure

> ❋❋ **WARNING**
>
> **Use of any other than approved DOT 3 or DOT 4 brake fluid will cause permanent damage to brake components and will render the brakes inoperative.**

> ❋❋ **WARNING**
>
> **Brake fluid contains polyglycol ethers and polyglycols. Avoid contact with eyes. Wash hands thoroughly after handling. If brake fluid contacts eyes, flush eyes with running water for 15 minutes. Get medical attention if irritation persists. If taken internally, drink water and induce vomiting. Get medical attention immediately.**

> ❋❋ **CAUTION**
>
> **Brake fluid is harmful to painted and plastic surfaces. If brake fluid is spilled onto a painted or plastic surface, immediately wash it with water.**

> ❋❋ **CAUTION**
>
> **Do not allow the brake master cylinder reservoir to run dry during the bleeding operation. Keep the brake master cylinder reservoir filled with the specified brake fluid. Never reuse the brake fluid that has been drained from the hydraulic system.**

➡ Master cylinder pressure bleeder adapter tools are available from various manufacturers of pressure bleeding equipment. Follow the instructions of the manufacturer when installing the adapter.

1. Before servicing the vehicle, refer to the precautions in the beginning of this section.

2. Install the bleeder adapter to the brake master cylinder reservoir, and attach the bleeder tank hose to the fitting on the adapter.

➡**Bleed the longest line first. Make sure the bleeder tank contains enough specified brake fluid to complete the bleeding operation.**

3. Place a box end wrench on the right rear bleeder screw. Attach a rubber drain tube to the right rear bleeder screw, and submerge the free end of the tube in a container partially filled with clean brake fluid.

4. Open the valve on the bleeder tank.

5. Loosen the right rear bleeder screw. Leave open until clear, bubble-free brake fluid flows, then tighten the right rear bleeder screw and remove the rubber hose.

6. Continue bleeding the rear of the system, going in order from the left rear bleeder screw to the right front disc brake caliper bleeder screw ending with the left front disc brake caliper bleeder screw.

7. Close the bleeder tank valve. Remove the tank hose from the adapter, and remove the adapter.

BRAKES

❊❊ CAUTION

Dust and dirt accumulating on brake parts during normal use may contain asbestos fibers from production or aftermarket brake linings. Breathing excessive concentrations of asbestos fibers can cause serious bodily harm. Exercise care when servicing brake parts. Do not sand or grind brake lining unless equipment used is designed to contain the dust residue. Do not clean brake parts with compressed air or by dry brushing. Cleaning should be done by dampening the brake components with a fine mist of water, then wiping the brake components clean with a dampened cloth. Dispose of cloth and all residue containing asbestos fibers in an impermeable container with the appropriate label. Follow practices prescribed by the Occupational Safety and Health Administration (OSHA) and the Environmental Protection Agency (EPA) for the handling, processing, and disposing of dust or debris that may contain asbestos fibers.

BRAKE CALIPER

REMOVAL & INSTALLATION
See Figure 1.

1. Before servicing the vehicle, refer to the precautions in the beginning of this section.

2. Remove or disconnect the following:
  • Front wheel
  • Brake fluid hose
  • Caliper mounting bolts
  • Brake caliper

To install:

3. Install or connect the following:
  • Brake caliper. Tighten the mounting bolts to 26 ft. lbs. (35 Nm).

FRONT DISC BRAKES

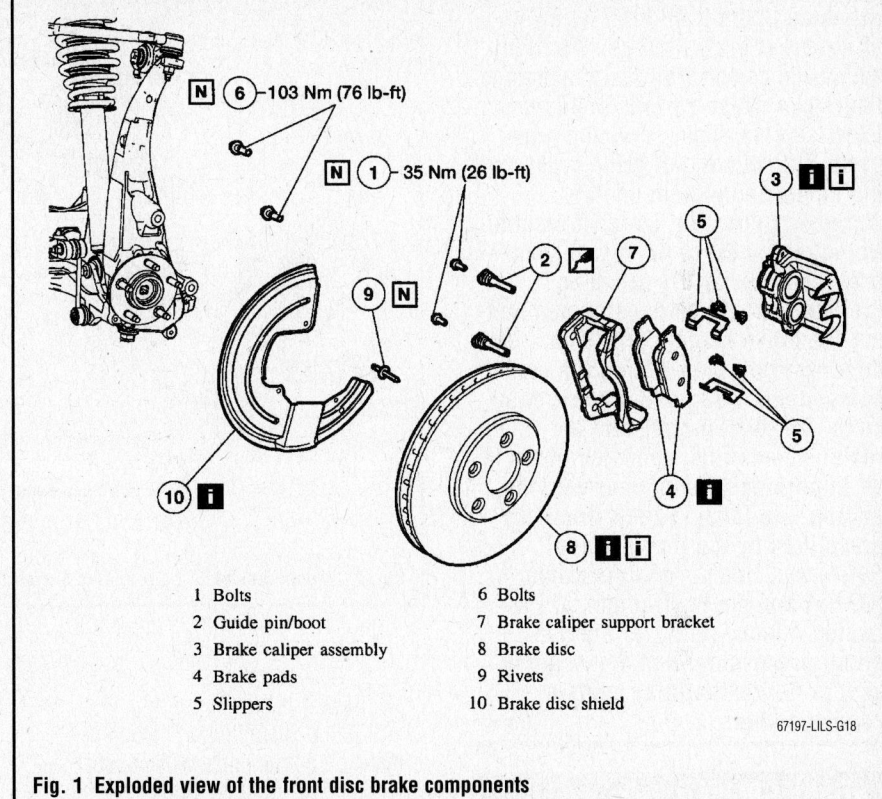

1 Bolts
2 Guide pin/boot
3 Brake caliper assembly
4 Brake pads
5 Slippers
6 Bolts
7 Brake caliper support bracket
8 Brake disc
9 Rivets
10 Brake disc shield

67197-LILS-G18

Fig. 1 Exploded view of the front disc brake components

  • Brake fluid hose. Use new copper washers and tighten the bolt to 35 ft. lbs. (47 Nm).
  • Front wheel

4. Bleed the brake system.

5. Before attempting to move the vehicle, pump the brake pedal to seat the pads against the rotors. Make sure the vehicle has a firm brake pedal. Check the level of the brake fluid and add DOT 3 or 4 brake fluid if necessary.

DISC BRAKE PADS

REMOVAL & INSTALLATION
See Figure 1.

1. Before servicing the vehicle, refer to the precautions in the beginning of this section.

2. Remove or disconnect the following:
  • Master cylinder reservoir cap and check the fluid level in the reservoir
  • Brake fluid until the reservoir is ½ full. Discard the removed fluid.
  • Wheel and tire assembly
  • Disc brake caliper locating pins. Lift the caliper assembly from the anchor plate and rotor.

3. Suspend the caliper inside the fender housing with wire. Do not allow the caliper to hang from the brake hose.
  • Inner and outer brake pads. Inspect the rotor braking surfaces for scoring and machine as necessary.

To install:

4. Use a C-clamp and an old brake pad or block of wood to seat the caliper piston in its bore.

5. Remove any rust buildup from the inside of the caliper in the brake pad contact area.

6. Install or connect the following:
- Inner pad in the caliper piston
- Outer pad onto the anchor plate.

Make sure the clips are properly seated.
- Disc brake caliper onto the anchor plate
- Caliper locating pins and torque to 26 ft. lbs. (35 Nm)
- Wheel and tire assembly

7. Pump the brake pedal several times prior to moving the vehicle to position the brake pads to the rotor.

8. Refill the master cylinder reservoir as necessary, using only clean DOT 3 or 4 brake fluid from a closed container.

BRAKES   REAR DISC BRAKES

❋❋ CAUTION

Dust and dirt accumulating on brake parts during normal use may contain asbestos fibers from production or aftermarket brake linings. Breathing excessive concentrations of asbestos fibers can cause serious bodily harm. Exercise care when servicing brake parts. Do not sand or grind brake lining unless equipment used is designed to contain the dust residue. Do not clean brake parts with compressed air or by dry brushing. Cleaning should be done by dampening the brake components with a fine mist of water, then wiping the brake components clean with a dampened cloth. Dispose of cloth and all residue containing asbestos fibers in an impermeable container with the appropriate label. Follow practices prescribed by the Occupational Safety and Health Administration (OSHA) and the Environmental Protection Agency (EPA) for the handling, processing, and disposing of dust or debris that may contain asbestos fibers.

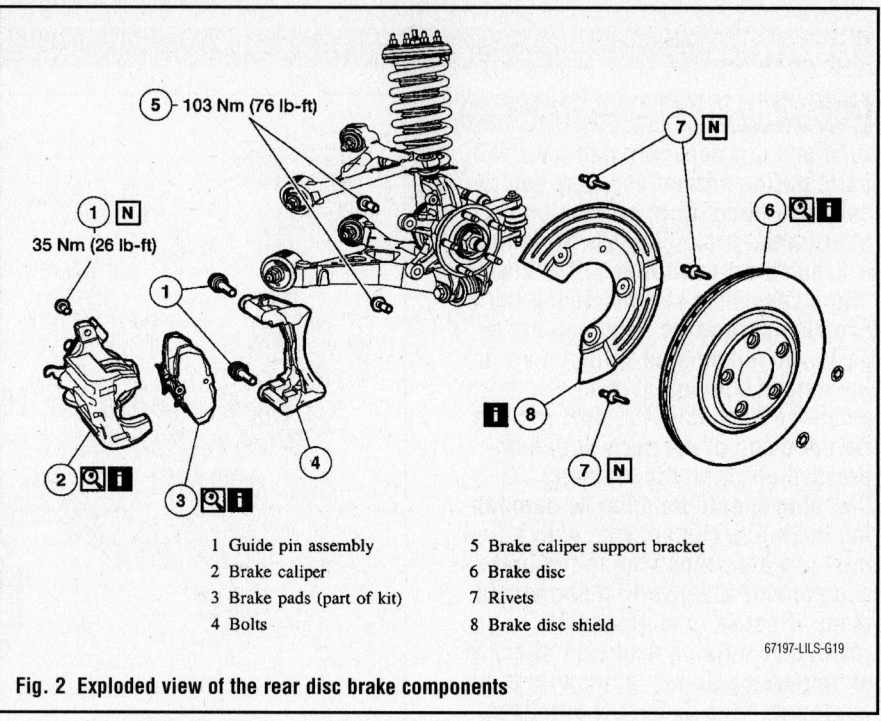

5 — 103 Nm (76 lb-ft)

35 Nm (26 lb-ft)

1 Guide pin assembly
2 Brake caliper
3 Brake pads (part of kit)
4 Bolts
5 Brake caliper support bracket
6 Brake disc
7 Rivets
8 Brake disc shield

67197-LILS-G19

Fig. 2 Exploded view of the rear disc brake components

BRAKE CALIPER

REMOVAL & INSTALLATION

See Figure 2.

1. Before servicing the vehicle, refer to the precautions in the beginning of this section.

2. Remove or disconnect the following:
- Rear wheel
- Parking brake cable
- Caliper mounting bolts
- Brake fluid hose
- Brake caliper

To install:

3. Install or connect the following:
- Brake caliper. Tighten the mounting bolts to 26 ft. lbs. (35 Nm).
- Brake fluid hose. Use new copper washers and tighten the bolt to 35 ft. lbs. (47 Nm).

- Parking brake cable
- Rear wheel
4. Bleed the brake system.
5. Before attempting to move the vehicle, pump the brake pedal to seat the pads against the rotors. Make sure the vehicle has a firm brake pedal. Check the level of the brake fluid and add DOT 3 or 4 brake fluid if necessary.

DISC BRAKE PADS

REMOVAL & INSTALLATION

See Figure 2.

1. Before servicing the vehicle, refer to the precautions in the beginning of this section.
2. Remove or disconnect the following:
- Master cylinder reservoir cap and check the fluid level in the reservoir
- Brake fluid until the reservoir is ½ full. Discard the removed fluid.
- Wheel and tire assembly
- Disc brake caliper locating pins at the support bracket
- Caliper
- Disc brake pads

3. Inspect the rotor braking surfaces for scoring and machine as necessary.

To install:

4. Using caliper compressor tool 206-026, compress the piston until it is fully seated. Position the notch in the caliper piston up and down to align with the alignment pin on the brake pad

5. Install or connect the following:
- Brake pads in the support bracket
- Caliper assembly over the rotor into position on the support bracket. Make sure the brake pads are installed correctly.
- Disc brake caliper locating pin, and tighten to 25 ft. lbs. (33 Nm)
- Wheel and tire assembly

6. Pump the brake pedal several times prior to moving the vehicle, to position the brake pads to the rotor.

7. Refill the master cylinder reservoir if necessary, using only clean DOT 3 or 4 brake fluid from a closed container.

8. Road test the vehicle and check the brake system for proper operation.

BRAKES   **PARKING BRAKE**

PARKING BRAKE CABLES

ADJUSTMENT

See Figure 3.

The parking brakes are applied and released electronically. No adjustment is necessary.

PARKING BRAKE SHOES

REMOVAL & INSTALLATION

The rear disc brake shoes serve as the parking brakes. Refer to the procedures under Rear Disc Brakes.

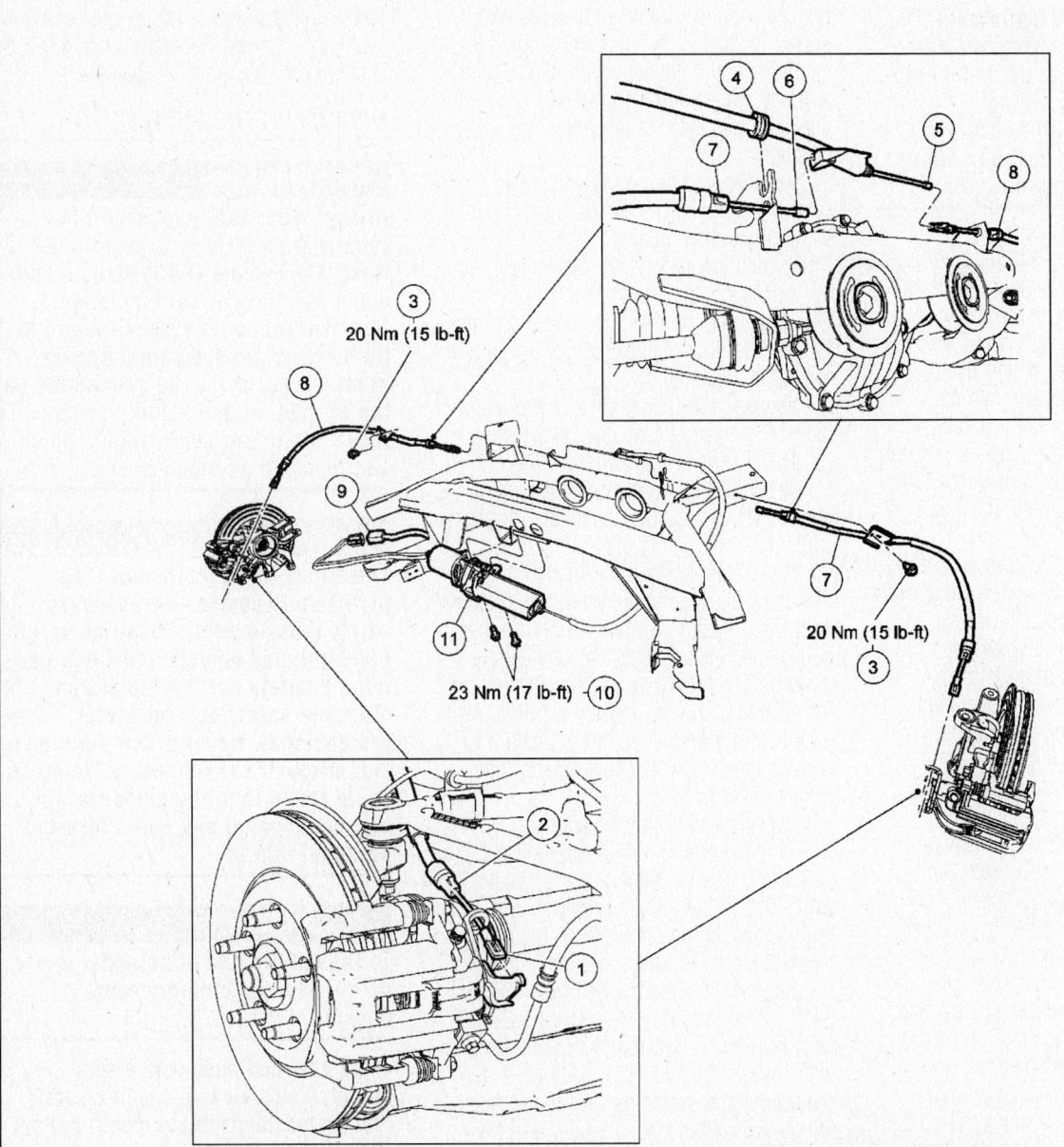

1. Parking brake cable end
2. Parking brake cable and conduit
3. Parking brake cable bracket bolts (2 required)
4. Electronic parking brake actuator cable grommet
5. Electronic parking brake actuator cable end
6. LH parking brake cable end
7. Parking brake cable and conduit (LH)
8. Parking brake cable and conduit (RH)
9. Electronic parking brake actuator assembly electrical connector
10. Electronic parking brake actuator assembly bolts (2 required)
11. Electronic parking brake actuator assembly

22086_LILS_G0007

Fig. 3 Parking brake exploded view

CHASSIS ELECTRICAL — AIR BAG (SUPPLEMENTAL RESTRAINT SYSTEM)

GENERAL INFORMATION

✳✳ CAUTION

These vehicles are equipped with an air bag system. The system must be disarmed before performing service on, or around, system components, the steering column, instrument panel components, wiring and sensors. Failure to follow the safety precautions and the disarming procedure could result in accidental air bag deployment, possible injury and unnecessary system repairs.

SERVICE PRECAUTIONS

Disconnect and isolate the battery negative cable before beginning any airbag system component diagnosis, testing, removal, or installation procedures. Allow system capacitor to discharge for two minutes before beginning any component service. This will disable the airbag system. Failure to disable the airbag system may result in accidental airbag deployment, personal injury, or death.

Do not place an intact undeployed airbag face down on a solid surface. The airbag will propel into the air if accidentally deployed and may result in personal injury or death.

When carrying or handling an undeployed airbag, the trim side (face) of the airbag should be pointing towards the body to minimize possibility of injury if accidental deployment occurs. Failure to do this may result in personal injury or death.

Replace airbag system components with OEM replacement parts. Substitute parts may appear interchangeable, but internal differences may result in inferior occupant protection. Failure to do so may result in occupant personal injury or death.

Wear safety glasses, rubber gloves, and long sleeved clothing when cleaning powder residue from vehicle after an airbag deployment. Powder residue emitted from a deployed airbag can cause skin irritation. Flush affected area with cool water if irritation is experienced. If nasal or throat irritation is experienced, exit the vehicle for fresh air until the irritation ceases. If irritation continues, see a physician.

Do not use a replacement airbag that is not in the original packaging. This may result in improper deployment, personal injury, or death.

The factory installed fasteners, screws and bolts used to fasten airbag components have a special coating and are specifically designed for the airbag system. Do not use substitute fasteners. Use only original equipment fasteners listed in the parts catalog when fastener replacement is required.

During, and following, any child restraint anchor service, due to impact event or vehicle repair, carefully inspect all mounting hardware, tether straps, and anchors for proper installation, operation, or damage. If a child restraint anchor is found damaged in any way, the anchor must be replaced. Failure to do this may result in personal injury or death.

Deployed and non-deployed airbags may or may not have live pyrotechnic material within the airbag inflator.

Do not dispose of driver/passenger/curtain airbags or seat belt tensioners unless you are sure of complete deployment. Refer to the Hazardous Substance Control System for proper disposal.

Dispose of deployed airbags and tensioners consistent with state, provincial, local, and federal regulations.

After any airbag component testing or service, do not connect the battery negative cable. Personal injury or death may result if the system test is not performed first.

If the vehicle is equipped with the Occupant Classification System (OCS), do not connect the battery negative cable before performing the OCS Verification Test using the scan tool and the appropriate diagnostic information. Personal injury or death may result if the system test is not performed properly.

Never replace both the Occupant Restraint Controller (ORC) and the Occupant Classification Module (OCM) at the same time. If both require replacement, replace one, then perform the Airbag System test before replacing the other.

Both the ORC and the OCM store Occupant Classification System (OCS) calibration data, which they transfer to one another when one of them is replaced. If both are replaced at the same time, an irreversible fault will be set in both modules and the OCS may malfunction and cause personal injury or death.

If equipped with OCS, the Seat Weight Sensor is a sensitive, calibrated unit and must be handled carefully. Do not drop or handle roughly. If dropped or damaged, replace with another sensor. Failure to do so may result in occupant injury or death.

If equipped with OCS, the front passenger seat must be handled carefully as well.

When removing the seat, be careful when setting on floor not to drop. If dropped, the sensor may be inoperative, could result in occupant injury, or possibly death.

If equipped with OCS, when the passenger front seat is on the floor, no one should sit in the front passenger seat. This uneven force may damage the sensing ability of the seat weight sensors. If sat on and damaged, the sensor may be inoperative, could result in occupant injury, or possibly death.

DISARMING THE SYSTEM

✳✳ WARNING

Always wear safety glasses when repairing an air bag Supplemental Restraint System (SRS) vehicle and when handling an air bag module. This will reduce the risk of injury in the event of an accidental deployment. Never probe the connectors on the air bag module. Doing so can result in air bag deployment, which can result in personal injury.

✳✳ WARNING

The safety belt pretensioner is a pyrotechnic device. Always wear safety glasses when repairing an air bag equipped vehicle and when handling a safety belt buckle pretensioner or safety belt retractor pretensioner. Never probe a pretensioner electrical connector. Doing so could result in pretensioner or air bag deployment and could result in personal injury.

✳✳ WARNING

To reduce the risk of personal injury, do not use any memory saver devices.

➡ If a seat equipped with a seat mounted side air bag and/or a safety belt pretensioner (if equipped) system is being serviced, the Supplemental Restraint System (SRS) must be depowered.

➡ The air bag warning lamp illuminates when the RCM fuse is removed and the ignition switch is ON. This is normal operation and does not indicate a SRS fault. The SRS must be fully operational and free of faults before releasing the vehicle to the customer.

1. Before servicing the vehicle, refer to the precautions in the beginning of this section.

2. Turn all vehicle accessories OFF.

3. Turn the ignition switch to OFF.

4. Remove the right hand kick panel cover and remove the restraints control module fuse F2.05 (10A) from the central junction box.

5. Turn the ignition ON and visually monitor the air bag indicator for at least 30 seconds. The air bag indicator will remain lit continuously (no flashing) if the correct RCM fuse has been removed. If the air bag indicator does not remain lit continuously, remove the correct RCM fuse before proceeding. Turn the ignition OFF.

❊❊ WARNING

To avoid accidental deployment and possible personal injury, the backup power supply must be depleted before repairing or replacing any front or side air bag (SRS) components and before servicing, replacing, adjusting or striking components near the front or side air bag sensors, such as doors, instrument panel, console, door latches, strikers, seats and hood latches.

6. The first row side impact sensors are located at or near the base of the B-pillars.

7. The second row side impact sensors, if equipped are located at or near the base of the C-pillars.

8. To deplete the backup power supply energy, disconnect the battery ground cable and wait at least 1 minute. Be sure to disconnect auxiliary batteries and power supplies, if equipped.

9. Disconnect the negative battery cable.

ARMING THE SYSTEM

❊❊ WARNING

The restraint system diagnostic tool is for restraint system service only.

Remove from vehicle prior to road use. Failure to remove could result in injury and possible violation of vehicle safety standards.

1. Make sure all restraint system diagnostic tool(s) that may have been installed during the repair have been removed from the vehicle and all SRS components are connected.

2. Turn the ignition switch from OFF to ON.

3. Install the restraints control module fuse F2.05 (10A) to the CJB and install the right hand kick panel cover.

❊❊ WARNING

Be sure that nobody is in the vehicle and that there is nothing blocking or set in front of any air bag module when the battery ground cable is connected.

4. Connect the negative battery cable.

5. Prove out the Supplemental Restraint System (SRS) as follows:

a. Turn the ignition key from ON to OFF. Wait 10 seconds, then turn the key back to ON and visually monitor the air bag indicator with the air bag modules installed. The air bag indicator will light continuously for approximately 6 seconds and then turn off. If an air bag Supplemental Restraint System (SRS) fault is present, the air bag indicator will either, fail to light, remain lit continuously or flash.

b. The flashing might not occur until approximately 30 seconds after the ignition switch has been turned from the OFF to the ON position. This is the time required for the RCM to complete the testing of the SRS.

c. If the air bag indicator is inoperative and a SRS fault exists, a chime will sound in a pattern of 5 sets of 5 beeps.

If this occurs, the air bag indicator and any SRS fault discovered must be diagnosed and repaired.

d. Clear all continuous DTCs from the restraints control module using a scan tool.

CLOCKSPRING CENTERING

❊❊ WARNING

Incorrect centralization may result in premature component failure. If in doubt when centralizing the clockspring, repeat the centralizing procedure. Failure to follow this instruction may result in personal injury.

❊❊ CAUTION

Make sure the road wheels are in the straight-ahead position.

❊❊ CAUTION

Overturning will destroy the clockspring. The internal ribbon wire acts as the stop and can be broken from its internal connection.

1. Before servicing the vehicle, refer to the precautions in the beginning of this section.

2. If the clockspring has rotated out of center, follow these steps to center the clockspring.

a. Hold the clockspring outer housing stationary.

b. While turning the rotor counterclockwise, carefully feel for the ribbon wire to run out of length and feel for a slight resistance. Stop turning at this point.

c. Turn the clockspring clockwise approximately 2-1/2 turns. This is the center point of the clockspring.

3. Do not allow the rotor to turn from this position.

DRIVE TRAIN

AUTOMATIC TRANSMISSION ASSEMBLY

REMOVAL & INSTALLATION
See Figure 4.

✲✲ WARNING

Secure the transmission to the transmission jack with a safety chain. Failure to follow these instructions can result in personal injury.

➡ **When the battery has been disconnected and reconnected, some abnormal drive symptoms can occur while the vehicle relearns its adaptive strategy. The customer needs to be notified that they can experience slightly different upshifts either (soft or firm) and that this is a temporary condition and will eventually return to normal operating condition.**

➡ **If transmission disassembly or installation of a new transmission is necessary, drain the transmission fluid. Install the drain plug when finished. If the transmission is to be removed for an extended period of time, support the engine with a safety stand and a wood block.**

1. Before servicing the vehicle, refer to the precautions in the beginning of this section.
2. Disconnect the negative battery cable.
3. Remove the complete exhaust system and front heat shields.
4. Remove the driveshaft.

✲✲ WARNING

Secure the transmission to the transmission jack with a safety chain. Failure to follow these instructions may result in personal injury.

5. Using a suitable transmission jack, support the transmission.
6. Disconnect the Heated Oxygen (HO2s) sensor connector and remove the sensor wire retaining clip from the right side of the transmission pan rail.
7. Remove the HO2s sensor connector from the front of the transmission pan rail.
8. Remove the transmission support center screw.
9. Remove the transmission support outer screws and remove the rear transmission support.

10. Disconnect the transmission shift cable retainer and position it aside.
11. Disconnect the transmission shift cable eyelet from the manual lever.
12. Disconnect the wire harness from the top of the transmission shift cable bracket.
13. Lower the transmission enough to gain access to the sensors. Disconnect the Turbine Shaft Speed (TSS) sensor, Output Shaft Speed (OSS) sensor and Intermediate Shaft Speed (ISS) sensor electrical connectors.
14. Remove the transmission shift cable bracket screws and bracket.

➡ **Clean the area around connector to prevent contamination of the solenoid body connector. Remove the screw from the solenoid body connector and disconnect the connector.**

15. Disconnect the wire harness retainers.
16. Remove and discard the tie strap from the digital Transmission Range (TR) sensor connector boot.
17. Slide the rubber boot back and disconnect the digital TR sensor connector.
18. Remove the screws and pushpins, then remove the splash shield.
19. Disconnect the wire harness from the cooler line bracket.
20. Disconnect the transmission cooler line bracket.

✲✲ CAUTION

Do not damage the cooler tubes. Hold the transmission case fittings with a wrench.

21. Disconnect the transmission cooler tubes.
22. Remove the torque converter access cover.
23. Remove the torque converter nuts.
24. Remove the transmission bellhousing-to-engine bolts.
25. Carefully lower the transmission from the vehicle. Make sure the transmission fluid cooler and cooler lines are cleaned at this time.

To install:

✲✲ WARNING

Secure the transmission to the transmission jack with a safety chain. Failure to follow these instructions can result in personal injury.

26. Secure the transmission to the transmission jack with a safety chain.

➡ **Rotate the torque converter so that the torque converter paint mark is in the 12 o'clock position.**

27. While raising and positioning the transmission to the engine, install the wire harness to the top of the transmission.
28. Carefully position the transmission in alignment with the engine and install the transmission bellhousing-to-engine bolts. Refer to the accompanying illustration for component location and torque specifications.
29. Install the torque converter nuts. Refer to the accompanying illustration for component location and torque specifications.
30. Install the converter access cover.

✲✲ CAUTION

Do not damage the cooler tubes. Hold the transmission case fitting with a wrench.

31. Connect the transmission cooler tubes. Refer to the accompanying illustration for component location and torque specifications.
32. Install the cooler line bracket. Refer to the accompanying illustration for component location and torque specifications.
33. Connect the wire harness to the cooler line bracket.
34. Install the splash shield, then install the screws and pushpin.
35. Reconnect the digital TR sensor connector.
36. Slide the boot over the digital TR sensor connector and install a new tie strap.
37. Connect the wire harness retainers to the transmission.

✲✲ CAUTION

Damage will occur to the solenoid body assembly if the screw is tightened above the specification.

➡ **Always install new O-ring seals on the vehicle harness connector. Use petroleum jelly to lubricate the O-ring seals to aid in the installation process.**

38. Install and lubricate new O-ring seals on the transmission connector and connect the connector. Tighten to 44 inch lbs. (5 Nm).
39. Install the shift cable bracket screws and bracket. Refer to the accompanying

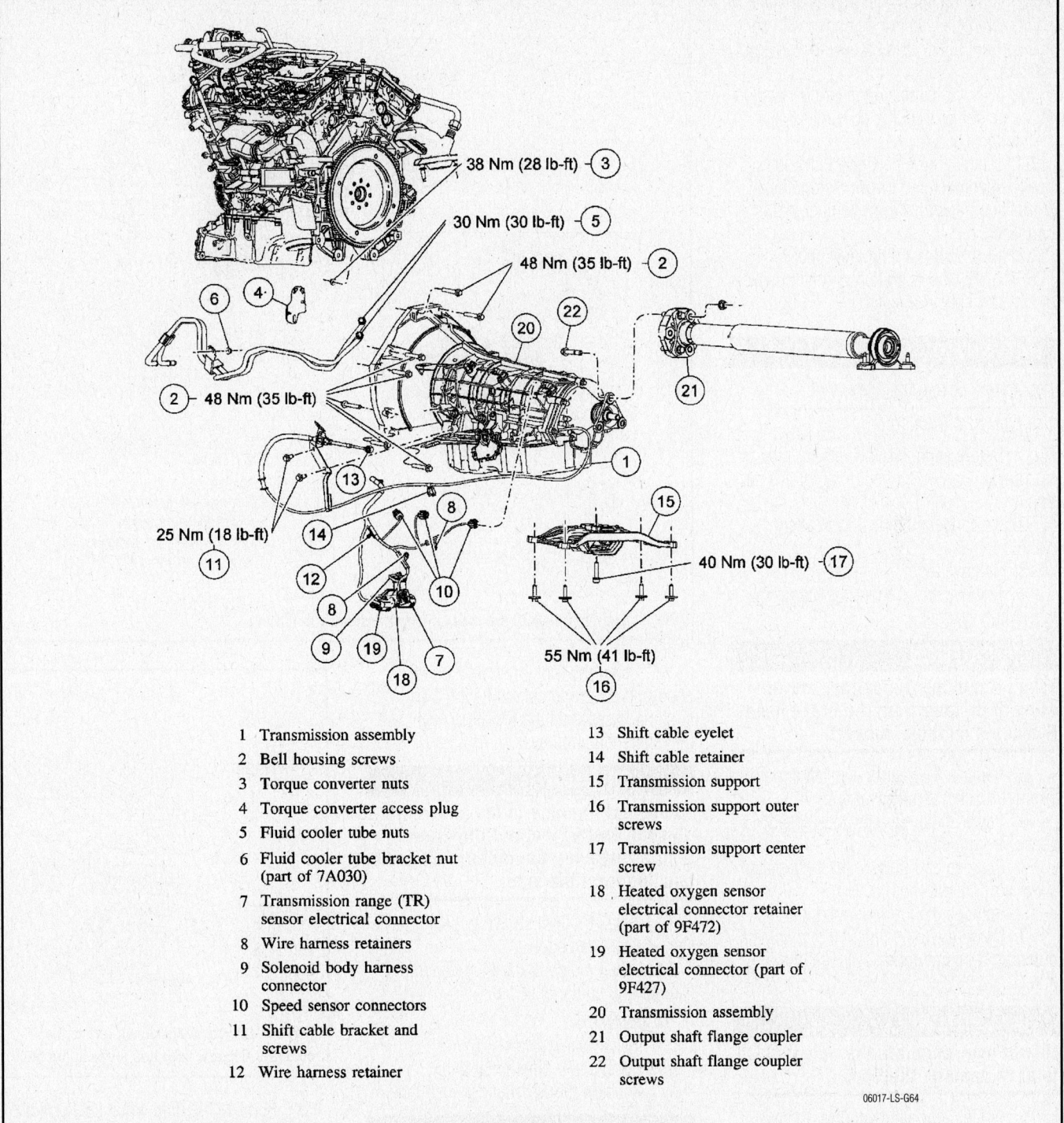

38 Nm (28 lb-ft) — 3

30 Nm (30 lb-ft) — 5

48 Nm (35 lb-ft) — 2

2 — 48 Nm (35 lb-ft)

25 Nm (18 lb-ft)

40 Nm (30 lb-ft) — 17

55 Nm (41 lb-ft)

1	Transmission assembly	13	Shift cable eyelet
2	Bell housing screws	14	Shift cable retainer
3	Torque converter nuts	15	Transmission support
4	Torque converter access plug	16	Transmission support outer screws
5	Fluid cooler tube nuts	17	Transmission support center screw
6	Fluid cooler tube bracket nut (part of 7A030)	18	Heated oxygen sensor electrical connector retainer (part of 9F472)
7	Transmission range (TR) sensor electrical connector	19	Heated oxygen sensor electrical connector (part of 9F427)
8	Wire harness retainers	20	Transmission assembly
9	Solenoid body harness connector	21	Output shaft flange coupler
10	Speed sensor connectors	22	Output shaft flange coupler screws
11	Shift cable bracket and screws		
12	Wire harness retainer		

06017-LS-G64

Fig. 4 Exploded view of the automatic transmission component locations and torque specifications

illustration for component location and torque specifications.

40. Connect the TSS, OSS and ISS electrical connectors.

41. Install the wire harness to the top of the transmission shift cable bracket.

42. Connect the transmission shift cable eyelet to the manual lever.

43. Install the shift cable to the rear transmission support.

44. Position the rear transmission support and install the screws. Refer to the accompanying illustration for component location and torque specifications.

45. Install the transmission support center screw. Refer to the accompanying illustration for component location and torque specifications.

46. Install the oxygen sensor connector on the front of the transmission pan rail.

47. Install the wire in the clip on the right side of the transmission pan rail and connect the heated oxygen sensors.

48. Install the driveshaft.

49. Install the exhaust system and front heat shields.

50. Connect the negative battery cable.

51. If the transmission was overhauled and the vehicle was equipped with an in-line fluid filter, install a new in-line fluid filter.

52. If the transmission was overhauled and the vehicle was not equipped with an in-line fluid filter, install a new in-line fluid filter kit.

53. If the transmission is being installed for a non-internal repair, do not install an in-line filter or filter kit.

54. If installing a new or a Ford-authorized remanufactured transmission, install the in-line transmission fluid filter that is supplied.

55. Carry out the fluid level check.

56. Check the operation of the transmission and inspect for leaks.

HALFSHAFT

REMOVAL & INSTALLATION

See Figures 5 through 8.

1. Before servicing the vehicle, refer to the precautions in the beginning of this section.

2. Disconnect the negative battery cable.

3. Remove the rear wheel.

4. Remove and discard the rear axle wheel hub retainer.

✳ CAUTION

When removing the caliper, never allow it to hang from the brake hose. Provide a suitable support.

5. Remove the rear brake caliper and support bracket as an assembly.

6. Remove the rear anti-lock speed sensor from the hub.

7. Remove and discard the suspension lower arm nut and bolt.

8. Remove the toe-link nut and bolt.

9. Using the tools illustrated, press the outboard CV joint until it is loose in the hub.

✳ CAUTION

Do not over-angulate the outboard CV joint or damage the boot.

10. While raising the knuckle, remove the CV joint from the hub.

11. Position the knuckle to gain clear access for the halfshaft removal.

✳ CAUTION

The crown of the tool forks must face away from the axle housing. Position the removal tool correctly between the CV joint and the axle housing so as not to damage the differential seal.

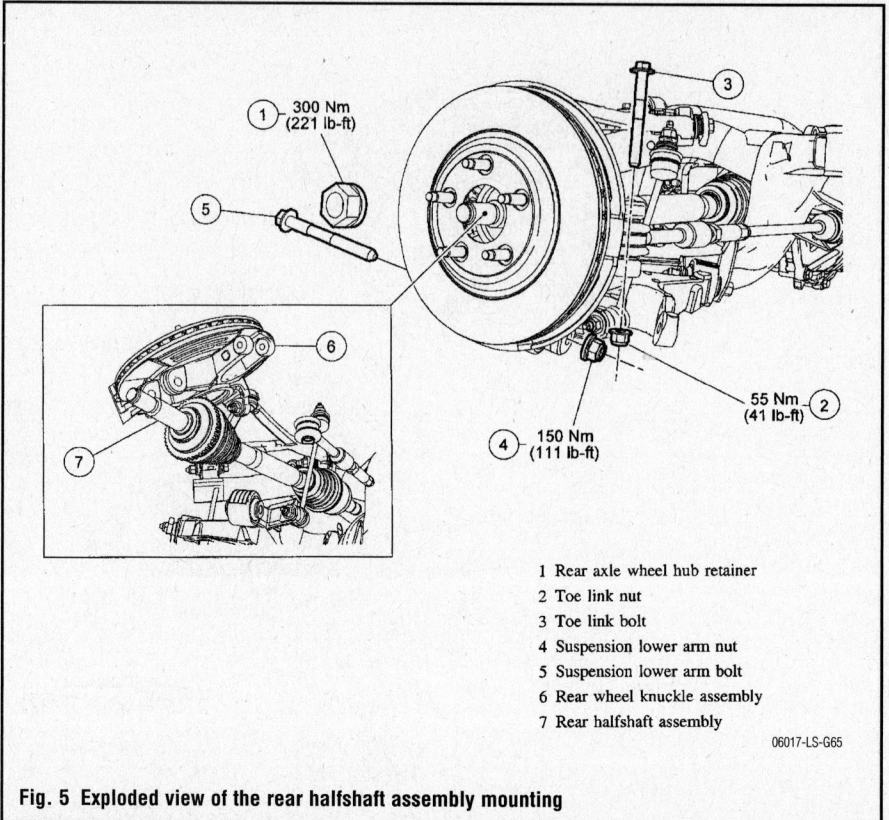

Fig. 5 Exploded view of the rear halfshaft assembly mounting

1 — 300 Nm (221 lb-ft)
5
6
7
4 — 150 Nm (111 lb-ft)
55 Nm (41 lb-ft) — 2
3

1 Rear axle wheel hub retainer
2 Toe link nut
3 Toe link bolt
4 Suspension lower arm nut
5 Suspension lower arm bolt
6 Rear wheel knuckle assembly
7 Rear halfshaft assembly

06017-LS-G65

12. Using the tool illustrated, exert enough pressure to overcome the axle circlip and separate the CV joint from the differential side gear.

✳ CAUTION

To prevent damage to the axle shaft oil seal, install the tool illustrated before removing the inboard CV joint housing from the axle.

13. Install the tool shown to prevent axle shaft oil seal damage.

14. Install a differential plug to avoid leakage and contamination.

To install:

15. Install a new axle circlip.

16. Remove the differential plug.

17. Position the halfshaft for installation.

✳ CAUTION

Differential seal damage will occur if installing the halfshaft without the special tool installed.

18. Install the differential seal protector tool.

19. Seat the CV joint in the differential side gear.

20. Slide the CV joint into the axle housing until the shaft splines are past the differential seal.

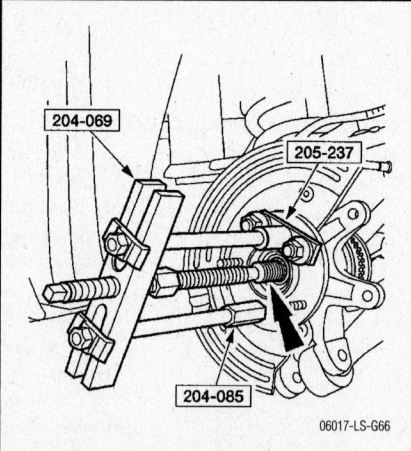

Fig. 6 Using the tools shown, press the outboard CV joint until it is loose in the hub

204-069
205-237
204-085
06017-LS-G66

21. Remove the differential seal protector tool.

22. Align the CV joint and side gear splines, and slide the joint into the gear until it seats.

23. When seated, the axle circlip will lock the CV joint in the differential side gear.

24. Check the axle circlip engagement by attempting to pull the inboard CV joint out of the differential side gear.

25. If the circlip is not seated, push the CV joint inward until the circlip is fully engaged in the differential side gear.

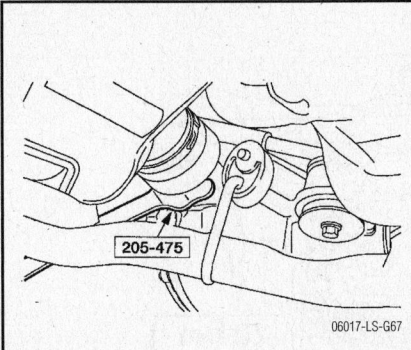

Fig. 7 Using the tool shown, exert enough pressure to overcome the axle circlip and separate the CV joint from the differential side gear

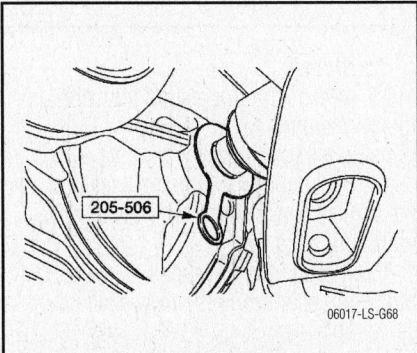

Fig. 8 Install the tool shown to prevent axle shaft oil seal damage

✶✶ CAUTION

Do not over-angulate the outboard CV joint or damage the boot.

26. While raising the knuckle, install the CV joint into the hub, then position the knuckle onto the lower control arm.

✶✶ CAUTION

Position the suspension at curb ride height before tightening the bolt and nut.

27. Install the new suspension lower arm bolt and nut. Tighten to 111 ft. lbs. (150 Nm).
28. Install the toe-link nut and bolt. Tighten to 41 ft. lbs. (55 Nm).
29. Install the rear brake caliper and bracket and the bolts. Tighten to 76 ft. lbs. (103 Nm).
30. Install the rear brake anti-lock sensor and the bolt. Tighten to 5 ft. lbs. (7 Nm).
31. Install the new rear axle wheel hub retainer. Tighten to 221 ft. lbs. (300 Nm).

32. Install the rear wheel and tire assembly
33. Connect the negative battery cable.

CV-JOINT

OVERHAUL

The CV-joints are serviced with the axle halfshaft as an assembly.

PINION SEAL

REMOVAL & INSTALLATION

See Figures 9 and 10.

1. Before servicing the vehicle, refer to the precautions in the beginning of this section.
2. Remove the pinion flange.
3. Force up the metal flange of the rear axle drive pinion seal.
4. Strike the pliers with a hammer to remove the rear axle drive pinion seal.

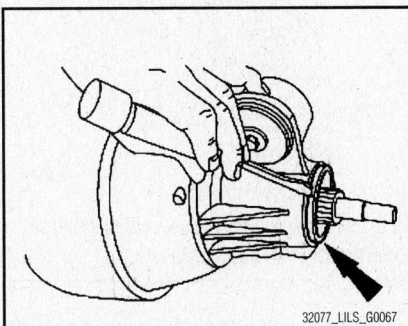

Fig. 9 Force up the metal flange of the rear axle drive pinion seal

To install:
5. Lubricate the lips of the new rear axle drive pinion seal.
6. Use Premium Long-Life Grease XG-1-C or equivalent.

✶✶ WARNING

Installation without the correct tool can result in early seal failure.

✶✶ WARNING

If the rear axle drive pinion seal becomes misaligned during installation, remove it and install a new one.

7. Using the special tool, install the rear axle drive pinion seal.
8. Install the pinion flange.

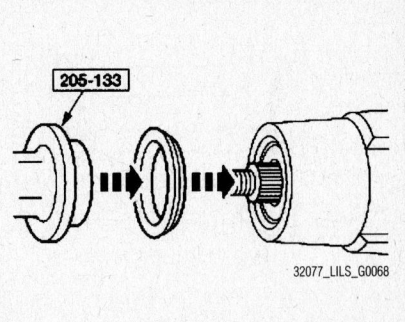

Fig. 10 Install the rear axle drive pinion seal

REAR AXLE HOUSING

REMOVAL & INSTALLATION

See Figures 11 through 14.

1. Before servicing the vehicle, refer to the precautions in the beginning of this section.
2. Remove the halfshafts.
3. Remove the heat shield underbody.

✶✶ WARNING

The driveshaft-to-pinion flange bolts, nuts and weighted nuts must be installed in the same locations from which they were removed.

4. Mark the pinion flange, the driveshaft flexible coupling and each of the three driveshaft-to-pinion flange bolts, nuts and weighted nuts with different color paint so that the driveshaft and differential may be realigned during installation.

✶✶ WARNING

Do not remove the flex coupling on the driveshaft flange. Make sure to remove only the driveshaft-to-pinion flange bolts and nuts.

5. Remove the three driveshaft-to-pinion flange bolts and nuts.
6. Support the driveshaft at the center and rear.
7. Loosen the driveshaft yoke adjuster nut.

➡There are shims between the center bearing mounting bracket and the body.

➡The shims must be installed in their original locations.

8. Remove the bolts and the shims.
9. Slide the rear driveshaft to the full forward position and tighten the adjuster nut.
10. Position a suitable jack under the axle housing.

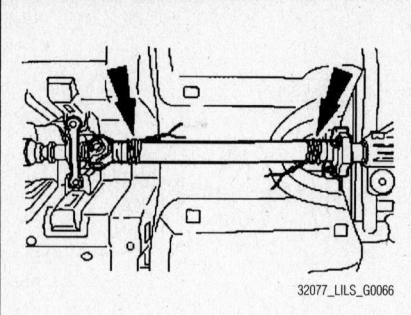

Fig. 11 Support the driveshaft at the center and rear

➡ **The front mount has a nut and shim on the top.**

11. Remove the three mounting bolts.
12. Lower the axle housing assembly from the vehicle.

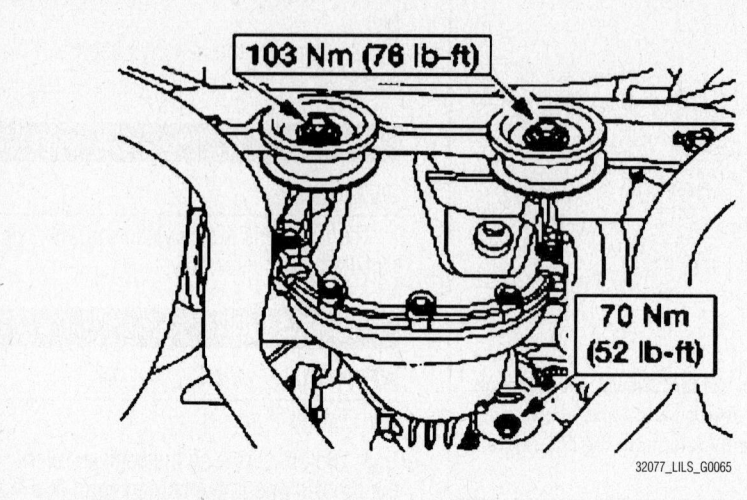

103 Nm (76 lb-ft)

70 Nm (52 lb-ft)

Fig. 13 The proper torque settings for the axle housing

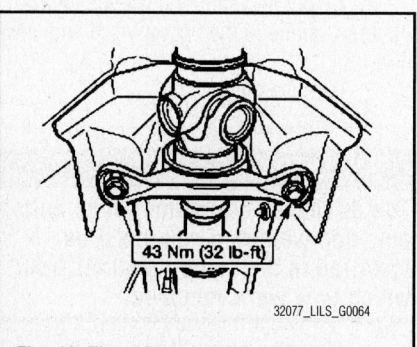

43 Nm (32 lb-ft)

Fig. 12 The shims must be installed in their original locations.

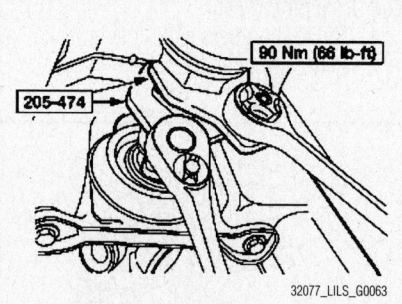

90 Nm (66 lb-ft)

205-474

Fig. 14 The proper torque settings for the driveshaft yoke adjuster nut

To install:

13. Make sure to position the shim on the front mount before raising the axle housing into position.
14. Raise the axle housing assembly into the vehicle and install it with the three mounting bolts.
15. Tighten the driveshaft yoke adjuster nut, while supporting the driveshaft at the center and rear
16. Install the three driveshaft-to-pinion flange bolts and nuts.
17. Install the heat shield underbody.
18. Install the halfshafts.

ENGINE COOLING

ENGINE FAN

REMOVAL & INSTALLATION

The Engine Fan is removed with the radiator. Refer to the Radiator procedure in this section.

RADIATOR

REMOVAL & INSTALLATION

1. Before servicing the vehicle, refer to the precautions in the beginning of this section.
2. Drain the engine cooling system.
3. Remove the upper radiator sight shield.
4. Remove the air cleaner outlet tube.
5. Remove the six bolts and the two radiator upper support brackets.
6. Remove the upper radiator hose.
7. Remove the bolt and position the receiver drier aside.

8. Disconnect the dual flow coolant valve electrical connector and the A/C line from the fan shroud.
9. 3.0L engine only:
   - Disconnect the Throttle Position (TP) sensor and the Idle Air Control (IAC) valve electrical connectors.
10. Remove the bolts.
11. Remove the bracket.
12. 3.9L engine only:
    - Remove the bolt and position the electric water pump aside.
13. Disconnect the high pressure cooling fan bracket and line.
14. Inspect the seal and install a new seal if necessary.
15. Disconnect the return hose from the cooling fan and shroud.
16. Separate the return hose from the fan shroud and position aside.
17. Remove the two bolts and the fan shroud assembly.
18. Remove the A/C condenser.

19. Remove the two bolts and position the multi-cooler assembly aside.
20. Remove the bolts and the condenser support brackets.
21. Remove the radiator.

To install:
22. Install the following:
    - Radiator
    - Condenser support brackets
    - Multi-cooler assembly
    - A/C condenser
    - Fan shroud assembly
23. Connect the return hose to the fan shroud
24. Connect the high pressure cooling fan bracket and line.
25. 3.9L engine only:
    - Replace the bolt and position the electric water pump aside.
26. 3.0L engine only:
    - Connect the Throttle Position (TP) sensor and the Idle Air Control (IAC) valve electrical connectors.

27. Replace the following
   - The upper radiator sight shield.
   - The air cleaner outlet tube.
   - The six bolts and the two radiator upper support brackets.
   - The upper radiator hose.
   - The bolt and position the receiver drier aside.

THERMOSTAT

REMOVAL & INSTALLATION

3.0L Engine

See Figure 15.

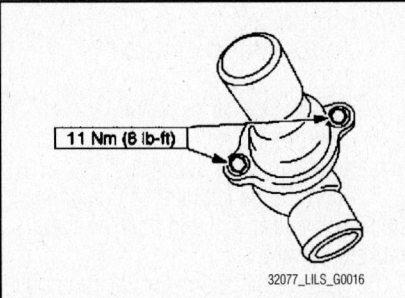

Fig. 15 Install the air cleaner outlet tube to the shown torque

1. Before servicing the vehicle, refer to the precautions in the beginning of this section.
2. Drain the engine cooling system.
3. Remove the air cleaner outlet tube.
4. Disconnect the hose.
5. Disconnect the hose and remove the thermostat housing assembly.
6. Remove the bolts, separate the housing and remove the thermostat and seal.

To install:

➡**Clean all the sealing surfaces and inspect the O-ring seals thoroughly.**

7. Install the bolts, separate the housing and remove the thermostat and seal.
8. Connect the hose and replace the thermostat housing assembly.
9. Connect the hose.
10. Install the air cleaner outlet tube to the shown torque.

3.9L Engine

See Figure 16.

1. Before servicing the vehicle, refer to the precautions in the beginning of this section.

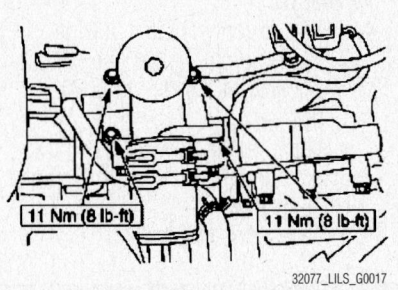

Fig. 16 Install the air cleaner outlet tube to the shown torque

2. Remove the air cleaner outlet tube.
3. Drain the cooling system.
4. Disconnect and position the lower radiator hose out of the way.

➡**Use care so that coolant does not get on the drive belt.**

5. Remove the bolts and the thermostat housing.
6. Remove the thermostat and the O-ring.

To install:

➡**Clean all the sealing surfaces and inspect the O-ring seals thoroughly.**

7. Replace the thermostat and the O-ring.
8. Install the bolts and the thermostat housing.
9. Connect the lower radiator hose.

WATER PUMP

REMOVAL & INSTALLATION

3.0L Engine

1. Before servicing the vehicle, refer to the precautions in the beginning of this section.
2. Drain the cooling system.
3. Remove the cooling fan motor and shroud.
4. Remove the accessory drive belt.
5. Remove the 3 bolts and the intake manifold support bracket.
6. Disconnect the coolant pump-to-radiator hose and position aside.
7. Disconnect the coolant pump-to-coolant inlet pipe hose and position aside.
8. Disconnect the coolant pump-to-thermostat housing hose and position aside.
9. Remove the 3 bolts and the coolant pump.

To install:

10. Installation is the reverse of removal. Please note the following torque specifications:
   a. Water pump. Tighten the bolts to 18 ft. lbs. (25 Nm).
   b. Bracket assembly. Tighten the fasteners to 89 inch lbs. (10 Nm).
11. Fill the cooling system.
12. Start the engine and check for leaks.

3.9L Engine

See Figure 17.

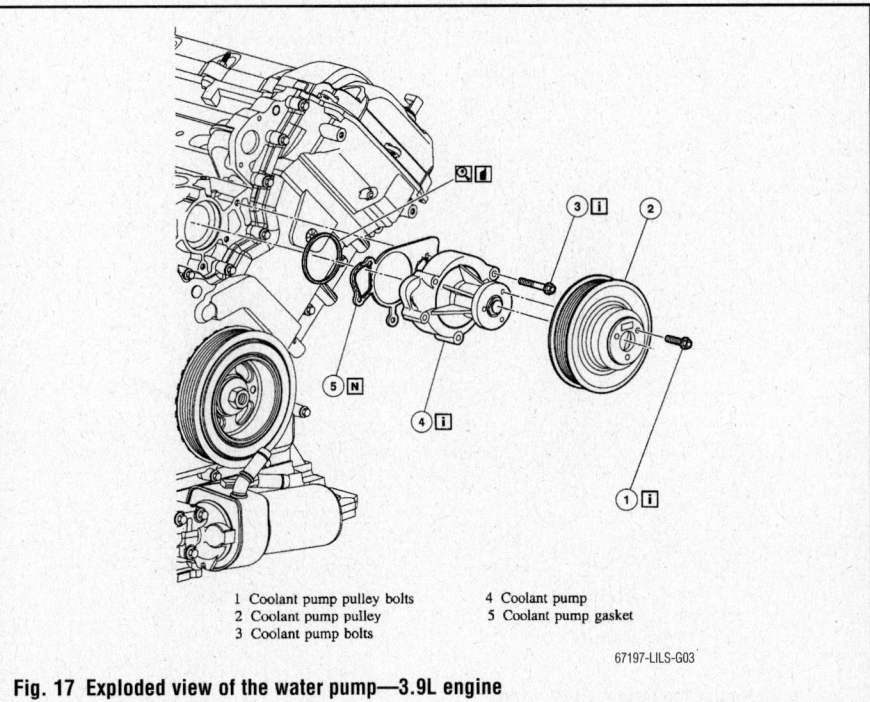

1 Coolant pump pulley bolts	4 Coolant pump
2 Coolant pump pulley	5 Coolant pump gasket
3 Coolant pump bolts	

Fig. 17 Exploded view of the water pump—3.9L engine

1. Before servicing the vehicle, refer to the precautions in the beginning of this section.
2. Drain the cooling system.
3. Remove or disconnect the following:
   - Thermostat housing
   - Accessory drive belt
   - Water pump pulley
   - Water pump

To install:

4. Install or connect the following:
   - Water pump. Tighten the bolts to 71 inch lbs. (8 Nm) plus 90 degrees.
   - Water pump pulley. Tighten the bolts to 89 inch lbs. (10 Nm) plus 45 degrees.
   - Accessory drive belt

- Install a new thermostat housing O-ring seal and lubricate with clean engine coolant.
- Thermostat housing. Tighten the retainers to 89 inch lbs. (10 Nm).
5. Fill the cooling system.
6. Start the engine and check for leaks.

ENGINE ELECTRICAL

ALTERNATOR

REMOVAL & INSTALLATION

3.0L Engine

See Figure 18.

1. Before servicing the vehicle, refer to the precautions in the beginning of this section.
2. Remove or disconnect the following:
   - Negative battery cable
   - Accessory drive belt
   - Lower splash shield
   - Alternator mounting bolts
   - Alternator harness connectors
   - Alternator

To install:

3. Before servicing the vehicle, refer to the precautions in the beginning of this section.

Install or connect the following:
- Alternator
- Alternator harness connectors. Tighten the battery cable terminal nut to 62 inch lbs. (7 Nm).
- Alternator mounting bolts. Tighten the bolts to 25 ft. lbs. (45 Nm).
- Lower splash shield
- Accessory drive belt
- Negative battery cable

3.9L Engine

See Figure 19.

1. Before servicing the vehicle, refer to the precautions in the beginning of this section.

➡ The A/C suction line may need to be positioned rearward to ease removal of the alternator.

CHARGING SYSTEM

2. Disconnect the negative battery cable.
3. Rotate the front end accessory drive belt tensioner counterclockwise and position the belt aside.
4. Remove the front valance panel.
5. Remove the air deflector.
6. Remove the A/C suction line clip from the radiator core support.
7. Remove the left hand A/C suction line lower bracket bolt and position the bracket rearward.
8. Remove the alternator upper mounting bolt.
9. Remove the alternator lower mounting nut and bolt.
10. Disconnect the alternator electrical connector.
11. Position the alternator B+ wire protective cover aside and remove the alternator B+ wire nut and cable end.
12. Remove the alternator.

To install:

13. Install the alternator harness connectors, then install the alternator. Tighten the bolts in sequence as follows:
    a. Step 1: Tighten bolt No. 1 to 35 ft. lbs. (48 Nm)
    b. Step 2: Tighten bolt No. 2 to 15 ft. lbs. (20 Nm) plus 90 degrees
    c. Step 3: Tighten bolt No. 3 to 35 ft. lbs. (48 Nm)
14. Install or connect the following:
    - Lower splash shield
    - Accessory drive belt
    - Air intake tube
    - Negative battery cable
15. Please note the following specifications:
    a. Alternator B+ wire nut to 71 inch lbs. (8 Nm).
    b. Alternator lower mounting nut and bolt. Tighten to 33 ft. lbs. (45 Nm).
    c. Alternator upper mounting bolt. Tighten to 15 ft. lbs. (21 Nm).
    d. Left hand A/C suction line lower bracket bolt. Tighten to 89 inch lbs. (10 Nm).

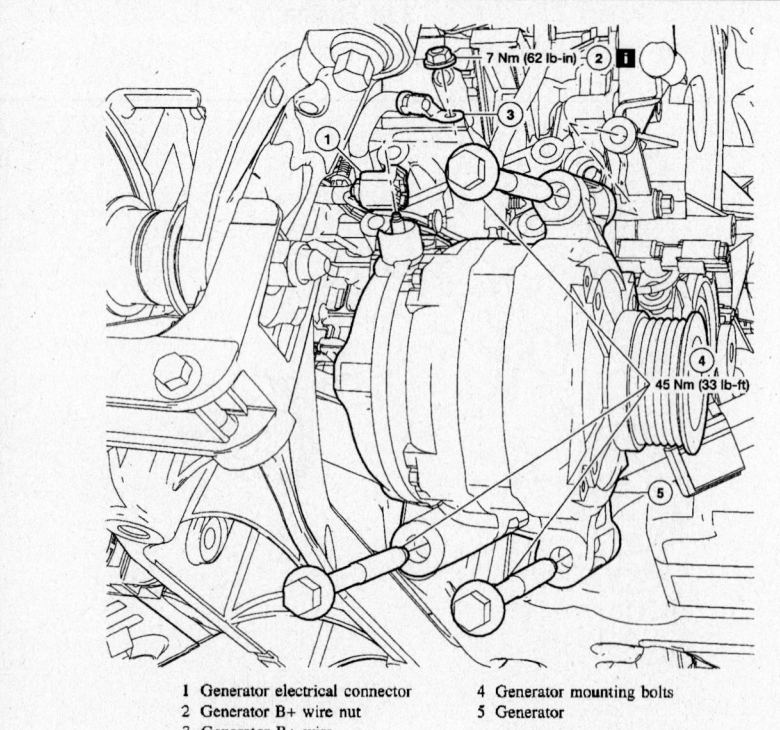

7 Nm (62 lb-in)
45 Nm (33 lb-ft)

1 Generator electrical connector
2 Generator B+ wire nut
3 Generator B+ wire
4 Generator mounting bolts
5 Generator

67197-LILS-G01

Fig. 18 Alternator mounting—3.0L engine

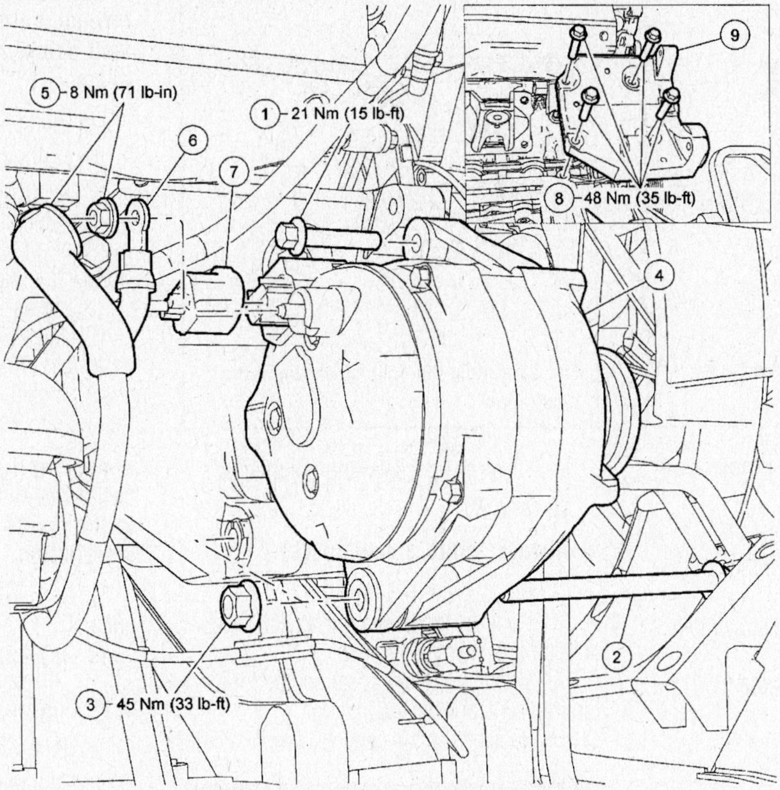

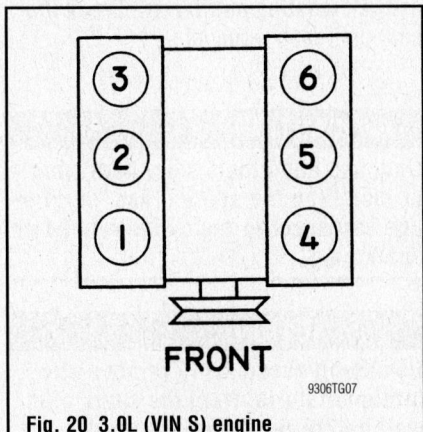

1 Generator upper bolt
2 Generator lower bolt
3 Generator lower nut
4 Generator
5 Generator B+ wire nut
6 Generator B+ wire
7 Generator electrical connector
8 Generator bracket bolts (4 required)
9 Generator bracket

06017-LS-G01

Fig. 19 Alternator torque sequence—3.9L engine

ENGINE ELECTRICAL

IGNITION SYSTEM

FIRING ORDER

See Figures 20 and 21.

Fig. 20 3.0L (VIN S) engine
Firing order:1–4–2–5–3–6
Distributorless ignition system
(one coil on each cylinder)

9306TG07

Fig. 21 3.9L (VIN A) engine
Firing order:1–5–4–2–6–3–7–8
Distributorless ignition system
(one coil on each cylinder)

93003G02

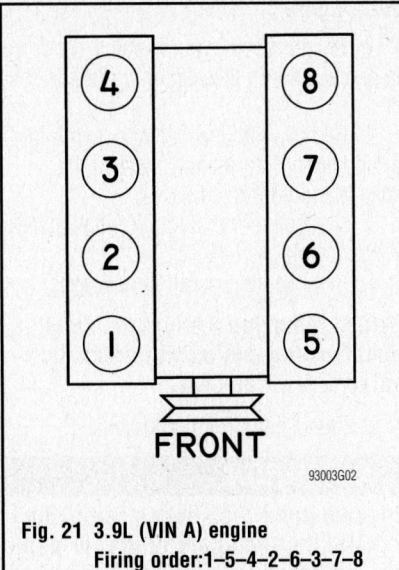

IGNITION COIL

REMOVAL & INSTALLATION

3.0L Engine

See Figure 22.

1. Before servicing the vehicle, refer to the precautions in the beginning of this section.

2. Remove the engine appearance cover.

3. To access the right bank ignition coils, remove the upper intake manifold..

4. Disconnect the electrical connector from the ignition coils.

5. Remove the bolts.

6. Remove the ignition coils.

To install:

➡Verify the ignition coils are seated and the boots are not damaged. If the

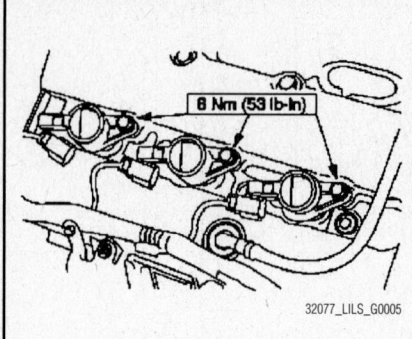

Fig. 22 Torque the bolts as shown in the illustration

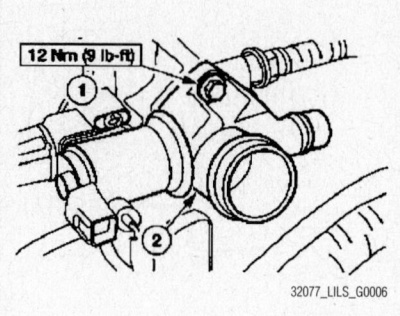

Fig. 23 Torque the bolts as shown in the illustration

boots are damaged, install a new ignition coil.

7. Replace the ignition coils.
8. Connect the electrical connector to the ignition coils.
9. Remove the upper intake manifold for the right bank ignition coils.
10. Replace the engine appearance cover.

3.9L Engine

See Figure 23.

1. Before servicing the vehicle, refer to the precautions in the beginning of this section.
2. Disconnect the battery ground cable.
3. Remove the pin-type retainers.
4. Disconnect the electrical connector from the Idle Air Control (IAC) valve.

❋❋ WARNING

In order to disconnect the Noma-type hose fittings, squeeze the tabs and pull the hose straight back. Failure to squeeze tabs may result in fitting damage.

5. Disconnect the hoses.
6. Disconnect the air assist hose.
7. Disconnect the idle air bypass hose.
8. Remove the IAC valve.
9. Remove the bolts from the IAC valve.
10. Lift and remove the IAC valve from the vehicle and discard the gasket.

❋❋ WARNING

Do not use carburetor cleaner or any other type of solvent as damage to the valve internal components may result.

➡ **The engine control sensor wiring cannot be cleaned. If necessary, new wiring must be installed.**

11. Clean the gasket mating surfaces.

To install:

➡ **Always install a new gasket.**

12. Remove the IAC valve.
13. Connect the hoses, air assist hose, and the idle air bypass hose.
14. Connect the electrical connector to the Idle Air Control (IAC) valve.
15. Replace the pin-type retainers.

IGNITION TIMING

ADJUSTMENT

This vehicle is equipped with a Distributorless Ignition System (DIS). The ignition timing is not adjustable. It is controlled by the PCM.

SPARK PLUGS

REMOVAL & INSTALLATION

3.0L Engine

1. Before servicing the vehicle, refer to the precautions in the beginning of this section.
2. Remove the upper intake manifold. For additional information, refer to the Intake Manifold procedure.
3. Disconnect the 6 ignition coil electrical connectors.
4. Remove the 6 ignition coil bolts.

➡ **When removing the ignition coils, a slight twisting motion will break the seal and ease removal.**

5. Remove the 6 ignition coils.

❋❋ CAUTION

Only use hand tools when removing or installing the spark plugs, or damage can occur to the cylinder head or spark plug.

➡ **Use compressed air to remove any foreign material from the spark plug well before removing the spark plugs.**

6. Remove the 6 spark plugs.

To install:

7. Inspect the spark plugs.
8. Clean the spark plugs with a wire brush or a professional spark plug cleaner (follow the manufacturer's instructions).
9. Adjust the plug gap as necessary.
10. Install the sparkplugs and tighten to 11 ft. lbs. (15 Nm).
11. Install the ignition coils and tighten the bolts to 44 inch lbs. (5 Nm).

➡ **Apply a light film of silicone brake caliper grease and dielectric compound to the inside of the coil boots before installation.**

12. Connect the coil wiring harness connectors.
13. Install the upper intake manifold.

3.9L Engine

1. Before servicing the vehicle, refer to the precautions in the beginning of this section.
2. Remove the evaporative emissions (EVAP) canister purge valve nuts and position the valve and bracket aside.
3. Remove the 12 bolts and the 2 ignition coil covers.
4. Remove all silicone sealant and residue from the coil cover.
5. Remove all silicone sealant and residue from the valve cover surface and ignition coil wiring harness.
6. Disconnect the 8 ignition coil electrical connectors.
7. Remove the 8 ignition coil bolts.

➡ **When removing the ignition coils, a slight twisting motion will break the seal and ease removal.**

8. Remove the 8 ignition coils.

❋❋ CAUTION

Only use hand tools when removing or installing the spark plugs, or damage can occur to the cylinder head or spark plug.

❋❋ CAUTION

Use compressed air to remove any foreign material from the spark plug well before removing the spark plugs.

9. Remove the 8 spark plugs.

To install:

10. Inspect the spark plugs. For additional information, refer to Section 303-00.

➡ **Clean the spark plugs with a wire brush or a professional spark plug cleaner (follow the manufacturer's instructions).**

11. Adjust the plug gap as necessary.

12. Install the spark plugs and tighten to 20 ft. lbs. (27 Nm).

13. Apply a light film of silicone brake caliper grease and dielectric compound to the inside of the coil boots before installation.

14. Install the 8 ignition coils and the bolts. Tighten the bolts to 44 inch lbs. (5 Nm).

15. Connect the 8 ignition coil electrical connectors.

➡ **Remove all dirt and moisture from the valve cover before applying silicone sealant.**

16. Lift up the wire harness and apply a 12.7 mm (0.5 in) bead of silicone sealant in the notch of the valve cover.

17. Set the ignition coil harness in the bead of silicone sealant and apply enough additional sealant to surround the wire harness and notch.

18. Install the ignition coil covers and the bolts. Tighten the bolts to 44 inch lbs. (5 Nm).

19. Position the EVAP canister purge valve bracket and tighten the nuts to 15 ft. lbs. (20 Nm).

ENGINE ELECTRICAL

STARTING SYSTEM

STARTER

REMOVAL & INSTALLATION

See Figures 24 and 25.

1. Before servicing the vehicle, refer to the precautions in the beginning of this section.

2. Remove or disconnect the following:
- Negative battery cable
- Starter motor wiring connectors
- Starter motor

To install:

3. Install or connect the following:
- Starter motor. Tighten the bolts to 18 ft. lbs. (25 Nm).
- Starter motor wiring connectors
- Negative battery cable

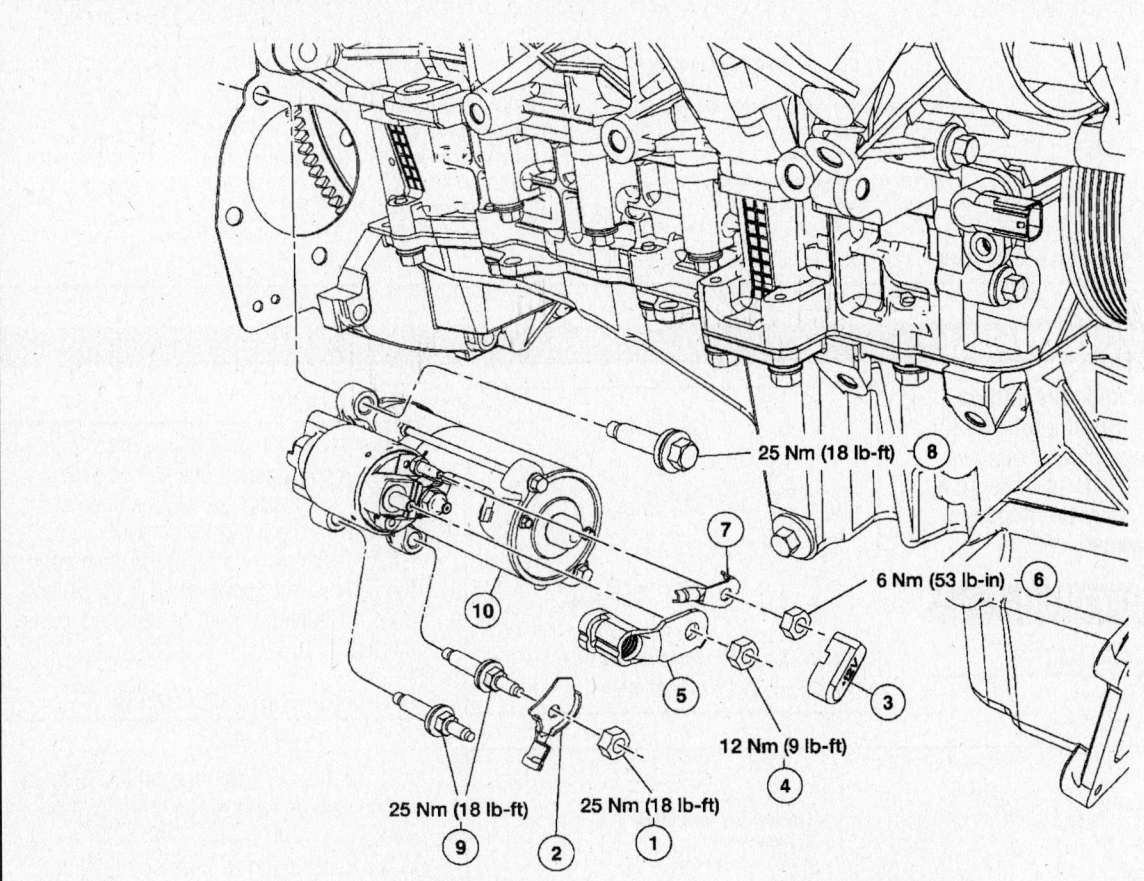

1 Ground strap nut
2 Ground strap
3 Starter motor solenoid terminal cover
4 Starter solenoid battery cable nut
5 Starter solenoid battery cable
6 Starter solenoid wire nut
7 Starter solenoid wire
8 Starter motor bolt
9 Starter motor stud bolts
10 Starter motor

67197-LILS-G07

Fig. 24 Starter motor mounting—3.0L engine

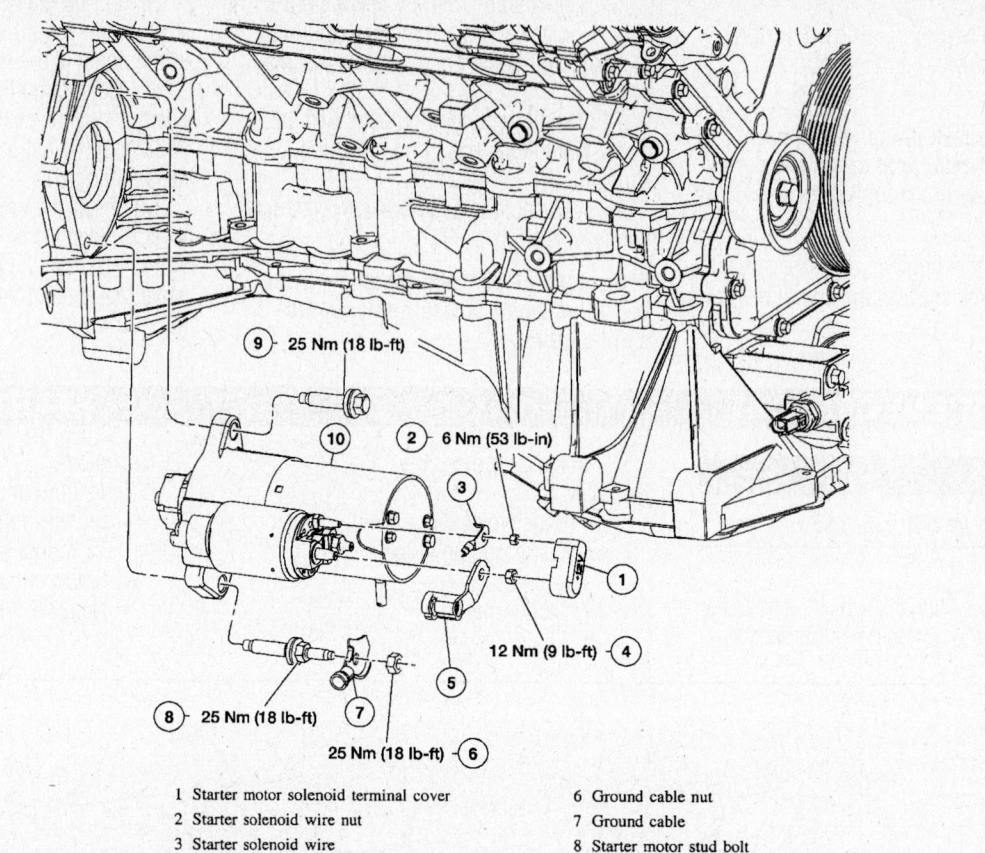

1 Starter motor solenoid terminal cover
2 Starter solenoid wire nut
3 Starter solenoid wire
4 Starter solenoid battery cable nut
5 Starter solenoid battery cable
6 Ground cable nut
7 Ground cable
8 Starter motor stud bolt
9 Starter motor bolt
10 Starter motor

67197-LILS-G08

Fig. 25 Starter motor mounting—3.9L engine

ENGINE MECHANICAL

➡ Disconnecting the negative battery cable may interfere with the functions of the on board computer systems and may require the computer to undergo a relearning process, once the negative battery cable is reconnected.

ACCESSORY DRIVE BELTS

ACCESSORY BELT ROUTING

See Figures 26 and 27.

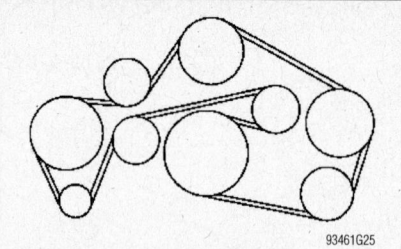

1. Power steering pump
2. Water pump
3. A/C compressor
4. Drive belt
5. Crankshaft pulley
6. Drive belt tensioner
7. Generator

79224G25

Fig. 26 Serpentine accessory drive belt routing—3.0L (VIN S) engine

93461G25

Fig. 27 Serpentine accessory drive belt routing—3.9L (VIN A) engine

INSPECTION

Inspect the drive belt for signs of glazing or cracking. A glazed belt will be perfectly smooth from slippage, while a good belt will have a slight texture of fabric visible. Cracks will usually start at the inner edge of the belt and run outward. All worn or damaged drive belts should be replaced immediately.

REMOVAL & INSTALLATION

See Figures 28 and 29.

1. Before servicing the vehicle, refer to the precautions in the beginning of this section.

2. Remove the air cleaner outlet tube.

3. Rotate the tensioner counterclockwise and remove the drive belt.

To install:

✳✳ CAUTION

Incorrect drive belt installation will cause premature drive belt failure.

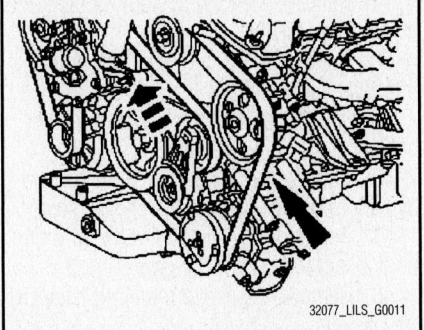

Fig. 28 Rotate the tensioner counterclockwise and remove the drive belt—3.0L engine

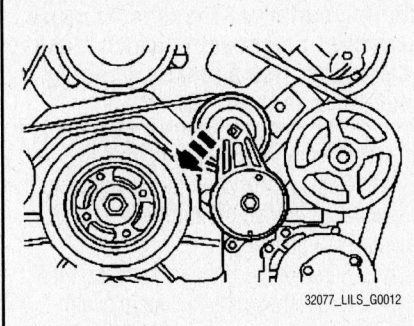

Fig. 29 Rotate the tensioner counterclockwise and remove the drive belt—3.9L engine

➡**Make sure the drive belt is correctly installed on each pulley.**

4. Install the air cleaner outlet tube.

CAMSHAFT AND VALVE LIFTERS

REMOVAL & INSTALLATION

3.0L Engine

See Figure 30.

1. Before servicing the vehicle, refer to the precautions in the beginning of this section.
2. Remove or disconnect the following:
   - Negative battery cable
   - Valve covers
   - Front cover
   - Timing chains

❋❋ WARNING

The camshaft journal thrust caps must be removed before loosening the remaining camshaft journal cap bolts to ensure that the camshaft journal thrust caps are not damaged.

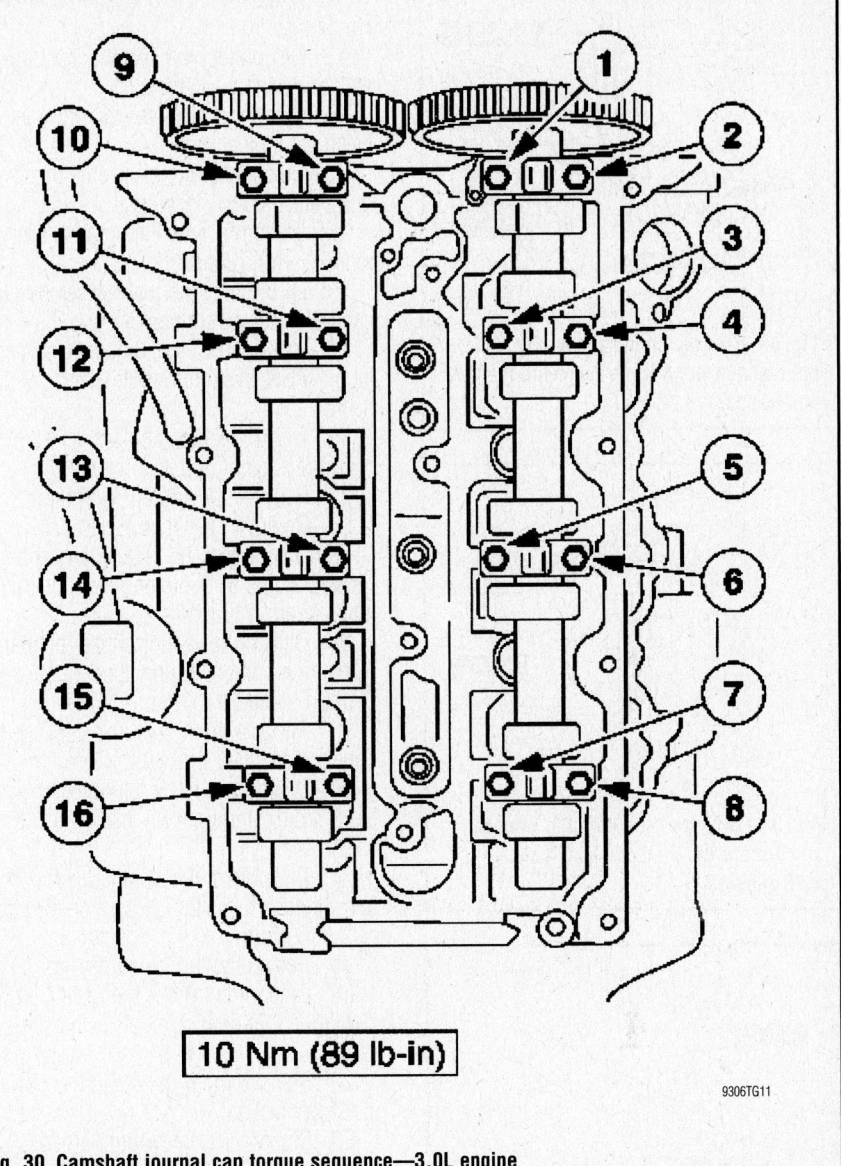

10 Nm (89 lb-in)

Fig. 30 Camshaft journal cap torque sequence—3.0L engine

➡**Keep all valvetrain components in order for assembly.**

- Camshaft journal thrust caps
- Remaining camshaft journal caps
- Camshafts
- Valve tappets and shims

To install:

3. Install or connect the following:
   - Valve tappets and shims in their original locations
   - Camshafts
   - Camshaft journal caps in their original positions. Install the thrust journal caps last. Tighten the bolts in sequence to 89 inch lbs. (10 Nm).
   - Timing chains
   - Front cover
   - Valve covers
   - Negative battery cable

4. Start the engine and check for leaks.

3.9L Engine

See Figures 31 through 49.

1. Before servicing the vehicle, refer to the precautions in the beginning of this section.
2. Disconnect the negative battery cable.
3. Remove the bolt and the accessory drive belt tensioner.
4. Remove the bolt and the accessory drive belt idler pulley.
5. Remove the 3 bolts and the coolant pump pulley.

➡**Hold the crankshaft pulley with the tool 303-D055 while removing the bolt and washer.**

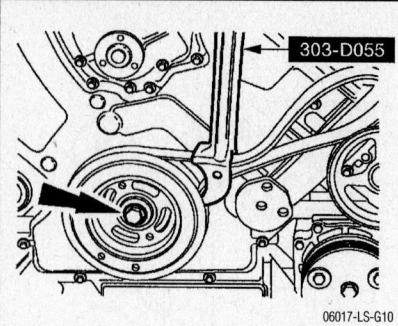

Fig. 31 Hold the crankshaft pulley with the tool 303-D055 while removing the bolt and washer—3.9L engine

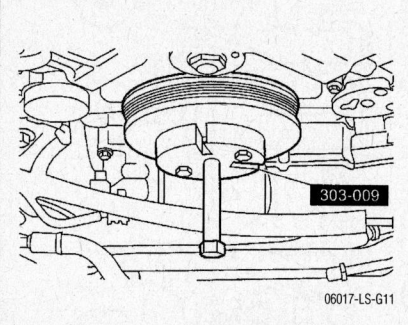

Fig. 32 Using the tool 303-009, remove and discard the front crankshaft seal—3.9L engine

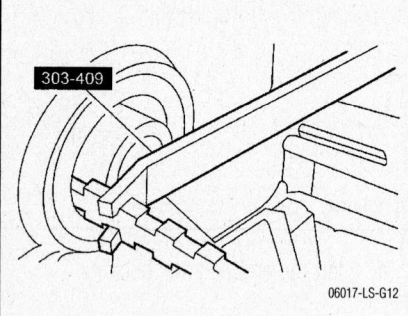

Fig. 33 Using the tool 303-409, remove and discard the front crankshaft seal—3.9L engine

6. Remove and discard the bolt and washer.

7. Using the puller tool 303-009, remove the crankshaft damper.

8. Using the tool 303-409, remove and discard the front crankshaft seal.

9. Remove the ignition coil covers.

10. Remove all silicone sealer and residue from the ignition coil covers.

11. Remove all silicone sealer and residue from the valve cover surface and ignition coil wiring harness.

12. Disconnect the 8 ignition coil electrical connectors.

13. Disconnect the Throttle Position (TP) sensor electrical connector.

14. Disconnect the fuel pressure sensor electrical connector.

15. Disconnect the electronic throttle body electrical connector.

16. Disconnect the Evaporative Emissions (EVAP) tube.

17. Disconnect the fuel rail temperature sensor electrical connector.

18. Disconnect the Exhaust Gas Recirculation (EGR) system module electrical connector.

19. Disconnect the coolant vent hose from the coolant outlet.

20. Remove the coolant vent hose.

21. Remove the vacuum harness.

22. Disconnect the engine wiring harness retainers from the engine appearance cover support brackets.

23. Detach the vacuum hose retainers from the left hand engine appearance cover support bracket.

24. Remove the 4 nuts and the 2 engine appearance cover brackets.

25. Disconnect the 8 fuel injector and the 2 radio interference capacitor electrical connectors

26. Disconnect the Knock Sensor (KS) and Camshaft Position (CMP) senor electrical connectors.

27. Detach the pin-type retainers.

28. Disconnect the 2 Variable Cam Timing (VCT) sensor electrical connectors.

29. Remove the 5 bolts and the power steering bracket.

30. Disconnect the wiring harness retainers from the left hand valve cover.

31. Detach the wiring harness from the engine front cover.

32. Disconnect the Crankshaft Position (CKP) sensor electrical connector and wiring harness retainers.

33. Disconnect the wiring harness retainers from the right hand valve cover.

34. Disconnect the alternator electrical connector and wiring harness retainers.

35. Remove the Heated Oxygen (HO2S) sensor electrical connectors from the brackets.

36. Remove the engine wiring harness from the engine.

37. Remove the nut and the oil level indicator tube. Discard the O-ring seal.

38. Remove the 8 bolts and the 8 ignition coils.

39. Remove the crankcase vent tube.

40. Remove the 2 EGR system module bolts and loosen the EGR tube nut.

41. Remove the EGR system module and discard the gasket.

42. Remove the 2 nuts and the radio interference capacitors.

43. Disconnect the throttle body heater hoses.

44. Remove the 4 bolts and the coolant bypass housing. Discard the O-ring seals.

45. Remove the 4 bolts and the throttle body adapter. Discard the gasket.

46. Remove the intake manifold. Discard the gaskets.

❉❉ CAUTION

Do not use metal scrapers, wire brushes, power abrasive discs, or other abrasive means to clean the sealing surfaces. These tools cause scratches and gouges, which make leak paths. Use a plastic scraping tool to clean the surfaces.

47. Clean the sealing surfaces.

48. Remove the bolts in the sequence shown and remove the right valve cover. Discard the gasket.

49. Remove the bolts in the sequence shown and remove the left valve cover.

❉❉ CAUTION

Do not use metal scrapers, wire brushes, power abrasive discs, or other abrasive means to clean the sealing surfaces. These tools cause scratches and gouges, which make leak paths. Use a plastic scraping tool to clean the surfaces.

50. Remove the gaskets and all silicone sealer. Clean the mating surfaces with silicone gasket remover.

51. Remove the engine front cover bolts in the sequence shown.

52. Remove the engine front cover. Discard the gaskets.

53. Do not use metal scrapers, wire brushes, power abrasive discs or other abrasive means to clean the sealing surfaces. These tools cause scratches and gouges, which make leak paths. Use a plastic scraping tool to remove all traces of sealant.

54. Clean the sealing surfaces.

55. Remove the right and left hand Variable Cam Timing (VCT) bush carriers.

56. Remove the bolt and the CKP sensor.

➡ **There is one window on the ignition pulse wheel that is unique to accept the tool 303-645.**

57. Install the tool 303-645.

58. Turn the crankshaft to 45 degrees

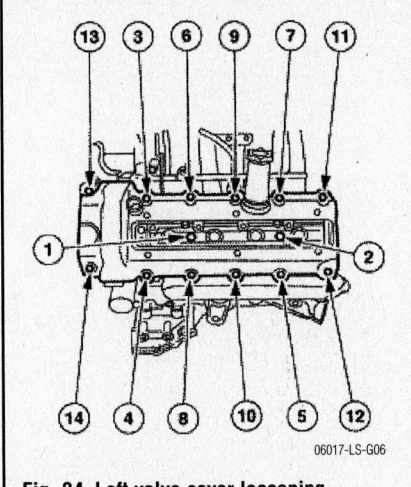

Fig. 34 Left valve cover loosening sequence—3.9L engine

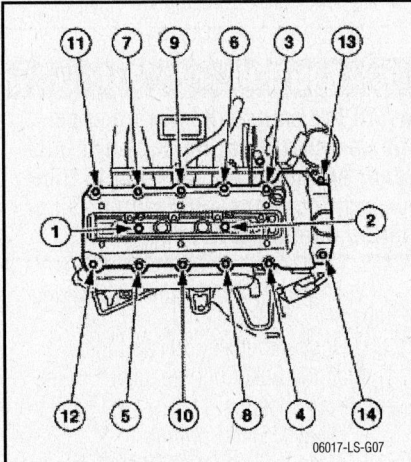

Fig. 35 Right valve cover loosening sequence—3.9L engine

After Top Dead Center (ATDC). The crankshaft keyway will be in the 6 o'clock position.

59. Make sure the flats of the camshaft are facing upward. If not, repeat the previous step.

✳✳ CAUTION

The flats on the camshaft must completely contact the special service tool or damage to the camshafts can occur. Slowly draw the special tool down evenly until it is fully seated on the camshaft flats.

60. Install the holding tool 303-530 on the right hand cylinder head.

✳✳ CAUTION

An open-end wrench must be used on the hex area of the camshaft or damage to the head will occur.

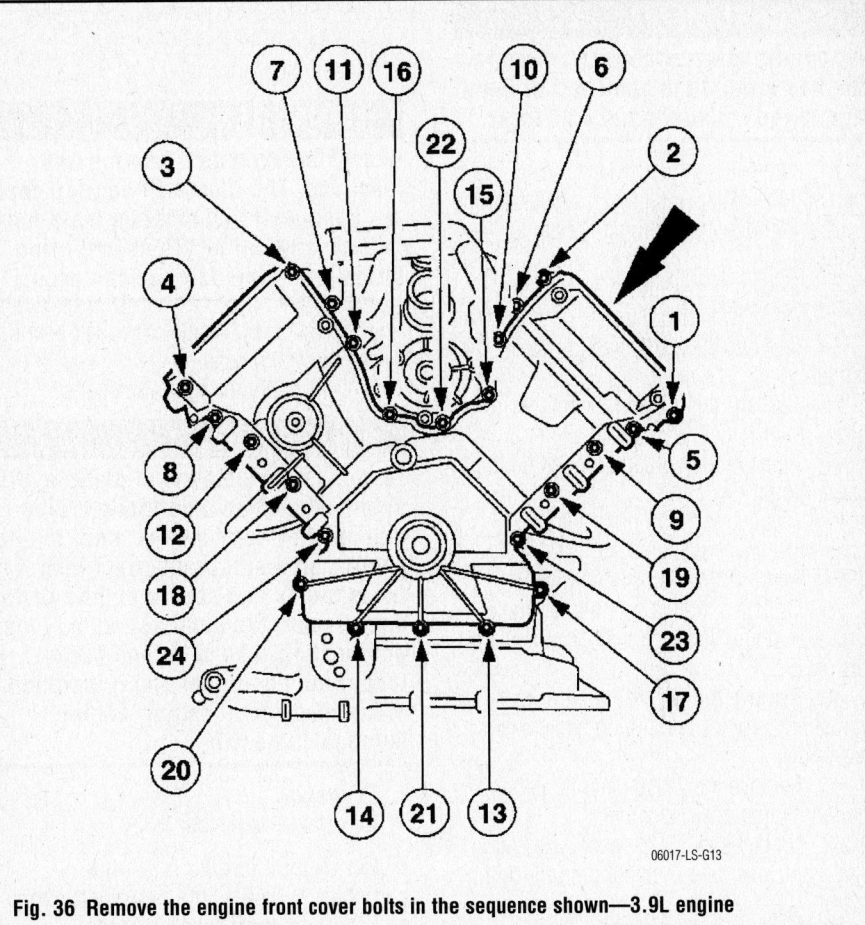

Fig. 36 Remove the engine front cover bolts in the sequence shown—3.9L engine

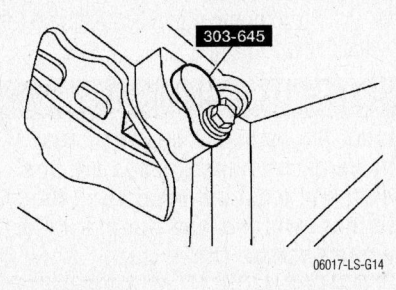

Fig. 37 There is one window on the ignition pulse wheel that is unique to accept the tool 303-645—3.9L engine

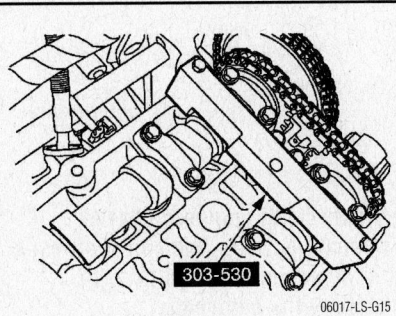

Fig. 38 Tool 303-530 is used to hold the camshafts during removal—3.9L engine

61. Remove and discard the exhaust camshaft sprocket bolt.

62. Remove and discard the variable VCT unit bolt.

63. Remove the right hand timing chain tensioner.

64. Push the lever down and install a drill rod to lock the piston.

65. Remove the 2 bolts and the tensioner.

66. Remove the bolt and the right tensioner arm.

67. Remove the bolt and the right timing chain guide.

68. Remove the right primary timing chain.

69. Remove the holding tool from the right cylinder head.

✳✳ CAUTION

The flats on the camshaft must completely contact the special service tool or damage to the camshafts can occur. Slowly draw the special tool down evenly until it is fully seated on the camshaft flats.

70. Install the holding tool on the left cylinder head.

✳✳ CAUTION

An open-end wrench must be used on the hex area of the camshaft or damage to the cylinder head will occur.

71. Remove and discard the left VCT unit bolt and the exhaust camshaft sprocket bolt.
72. Remove the left timing chain tensioner.
73. Push the lever down and install a drill rod to lock the piston.
74. Remove the 2 bolts and the tensioner.
75. Remove the nut and the left tensioner arm.
76. Remove the bolt and the left timing chain guide.
77. Remove the left primary timing chain.
78. Remove the crankshaft sprocket.
79. Collapse the left secondary timing chain tensioner and install a pin to lock the piston.
80. Remove the left VCT unit, exhaust camshaft sprocket and timing chain as an assembly.
81. Remove the 2 bolts and the left secondary timing chain tensioner.
82. Collapse the right secondary timing chain tensioner and install a pin to lock the piston.
83. Remove the right VCT unit, exhaust camshaft sprocket and timing chain as an assembly.
84. Remove the 2 bolts and the right secondary timing chain tensioner.
85. Remove the holding tool.
86. On the left side:

✳✳ CAUTION

Record the camshaft bearing cap locations. The camshaft bearing caps are positional and must be installed in their original locations and orientation or engine damage can occur.

  e. Remove the left camshaft bearing cap bolts and caps.
  f. Remove the left hand camshafts.

✳✳ CAUTION

Do not use any means of marking the shims other than a permanent-type marker. Any scratches or paint on the shims can result in incorrect lash adjustments and severe engine damage. Record the shim and bucket tappet location. The shim and bucket tappet are positional and if installed in the incorrect location, engine damage can occur.

  g. Record the location of the valve tappets and remove the tappets.
87. On the right side:

✳✳ CAUTION

Record the camshaft bearing cap locations. The camshaft bearing caps are positional and must be installed in their original locations and orientation or engine damage can occur.

  h. Remove the right camshaft bearing cap bolts and caps.
  i. Remove the right camshafts.

✳✳ CAUTION

Do not use any means of marking the shims other than a permanent-type marker. Any scratches or paint on the shims can result in incorrect lash adjustments and severe engine damage. Record the shim and bucket tappet location. The shim and bucket tappet are positional and if installed in the incorrect location, engine damage can occur.

To install:
88. On the right side:

➡ Apply clean engine oil to the camshaft journals, the camshaft caps and the camshaft lobes prior to installing the camshafts.

  j. Position the right camshafts on the camshaft journals.

✳✳ CAUTION

Install the camshaft bearing caps. The camshaft bearing caps are positional and must be installed in their original locations and orientation or engine damage can occur.

  k. Install the right camshaft bearing caps.
  l. Install the bearing cap bolts. Tighten the bolts in three stages in the sequence shown.
  m. Step 1: Hand-tighten.
  n. Step 2: Tighten to 53 inch lbs. (6 Nm).
  o. Step 3: Tighten an additional 90 degrees.
89. On the left side:

➡ Apply clean engine oil to the camshaft journals, the camshaft caps and the camshaft lobes prior to installing the camshafts.

  p. Position the right camshafts on the camshaft journals.

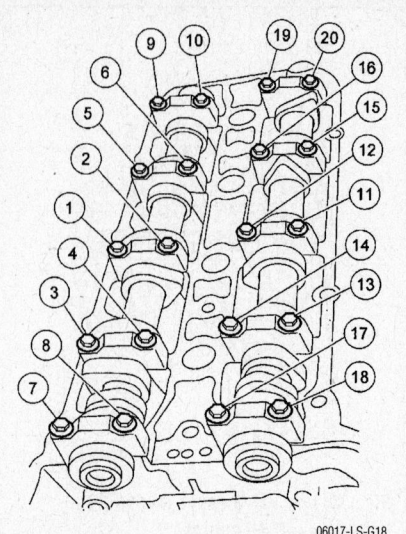

06017-LS-G18

Fig. 39 Right camshaft bearing cap tightening sequence—3.9L engine

✳✳ CAUTION

Install the camshaft bearing caps. The camshaft bearing caps are positional and must be installed in their original locations and orientation or engine damage can occur.

  q. Install the right camshaft bearing caps.
  r. Install the bearing cap bolts. Tighten the bolts in three stages in the sequence shown.
  s. Step 1: Hand-tighten.
  t. Step 2: Tighten to 53 inch lbs. (6 Nm).
  u. Step 3: Tighten an additional 90 degrees.

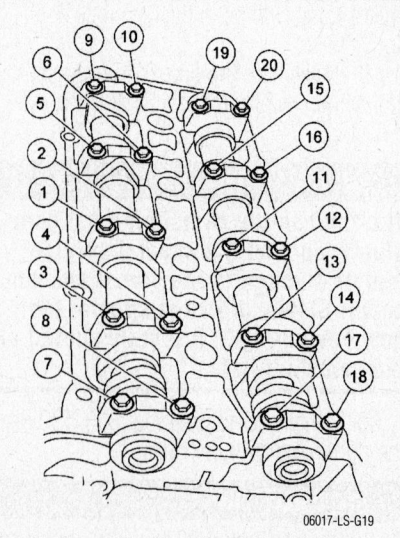

06017-LS-G19

Fig. 40 Left camshaft bearing cap tightening sequence—3.9L engine

If any components are installed new, the engine must be reshimmed or engine damage can occur.

90. Using a feeler gauge, confirm that the tappet and shim clearances are within specification.

91. If tappet and shim clearances are not within specification, adjust the clearance.

92. Turn the crankshaft to 45 degrees ATDC. The crankshaft keyway will be in the 6 o'clock position.

93. Install the tool 303-645.

94. Position all of the camshafts so the flats of the camshafts are facing upward.

95. Install the left secondary timing chain tensioner and 2 bolts. Tighten to 8 ft. lbs. (11 Nm).

96. Install the left VCT unit, exhaust camshaft sprocket and timing chain as an assembly.

97. Using new bolts, install the left VCT unit and exhaust camshaft sprocket bolts finger-tight.

98. Remove the locking pin from the left secondary timing chain tensioner.

99. Install the right secondary timing chain tensioner and 2 bolts. Tighten to 8 ft. lbs. (11 Nm).

100. Install the right VCT unit, exhaust camshaft sprocket and timing chain as an assembly.

101. Using new bolts, install the right VCT unit and exhaust camshaft sprocket bolts finger-tight.

102. Remove the locking pin from the right secondary timing chain tensioner.

103. Reset the timing chain tensioners by holding the lever toward the tensioner piston. Using finger pressure, compress the tensioner. Push the lever down and install a drill rod to lock the piston.

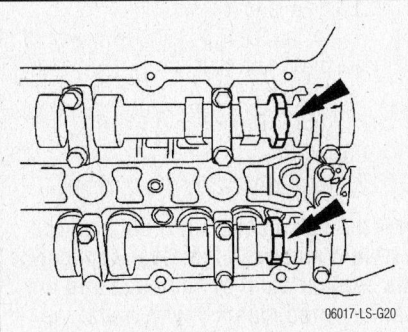

Fig. 41 Position all of the camshafts so the flats of the camshafts are facing upward—3.9L engine

The flats on the camshaft must completely contact the special service tool or damage to the camshafts can occur. Slowly draw the special tool down evenly until it is fully seated on the camshaft flats.

104. Install the holding tool on the left head.

105. Position the left timing chain and crankshaft gear.

106. Position the timing chain over the left intake camshaft sprocket.

107. Position the crankshaft gear in the timing chain.

108. Install the left timing chain guide and bolt. Tighten to 8 ft. lbs. (11 Nm).

109. Install the left timing chain tensioner arm and nut. Tighten to 8 ft. lbs. (11 Nm).

110. Install the left timing chain tensioner.

111. Install the timing chain tensioner and bolts, and remove the drill rod.

The exhaust camshaft sprocket bolt must be fully tightened before tightening the intake camshaft sprocket bolt. Using the tool, apply 89 inch lbs. (10 Nm) counterclockwise to the left exhaust camshaft sprocket.

112. Tighten the left exhaust camshaft sprocket and VCT unit bolts 26 ft. lbs. (35 Nm) then an additional 90 degrees.

113. Remove the holding tool.

The flats on the camshaft must completely contact the special service tool or damage to the camshafts can occur. Slowly draw the special tool downward evenly until it is fully seated on the camshaft flats.

114. Install the holding tool on the right cylinder head.

115. Position the right timing chain over the right intake camshaft sprocket and over the crankshaft gear.

116. Install the right timing chain guide and bolt. Tighten to 8 ft. lbs. (11 Nm).

117. Install the right timing chain tensioner arm. Tighten to 8 ft. lbs. (11 Nm).

118. Install the right timing chain tensioner.

119. Install the timing chain tensioner and bolts, and remove the drill rod.

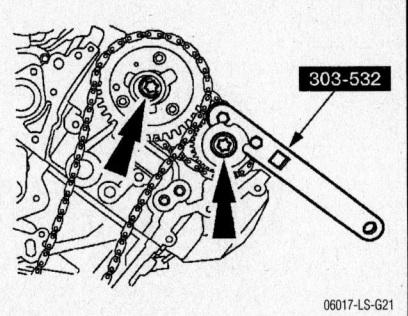

Fig. 42 Using the tool, apply 89 inch lbs. (10 Nm) counterclockwise to the camshaft sprocket—3.9L engine

The exhaust camshaft sprocket bolt must be fully tightened before tightening the intake camshaft sprocket bolt. Using the tool, apply 89 inch lbs. (10 Nm) counterclockwise to the left exhaust camshaft sprocket.

120. Tighten the right exhaust camshaft sprocket and VCT unit bolts 26 ft. lbs. (35 Nm) then an additional 90 degrees.

121. Remove the holding tool.

➡ Lubricate the VCT bush carrier seals with clean engine oil.

122. Carefully insert the bush carrier into the VCT unit, compress ring seals with fingers as required. Fully seat the bush carrier by hand before fitting the bolts and nut. Tighten the bolts to 15 ft. lbs. (20 Nm). Tighten the nut to 89 inch lbs. (10 Nm).

123. Install new engine front cover gaskets.

➡ If the front cover is not secured within 4 minutes of sealant application, the sealant must be removed and the sealing area cleaned with metal surface cleaner. Allow to dry until there is no sign of wetness, or 4 minutes, whichever is longer. Failure to follow this procedure can cause future oil leakage.

124. Apply silicone gasket and sealant in the 8 places shown.

125. Install the engine front cover. Loosely install the bolts.

126. Tighten the bolts in 2 stages in the sequence shown. Tighten to 44 inch lbs. (5 Nm) in sequence and then retighten in sequence to 89 inch lbs. (10 Nm).

➡ Lubricate the front oil seal and the engine front cover mating surface with clean engine oil.

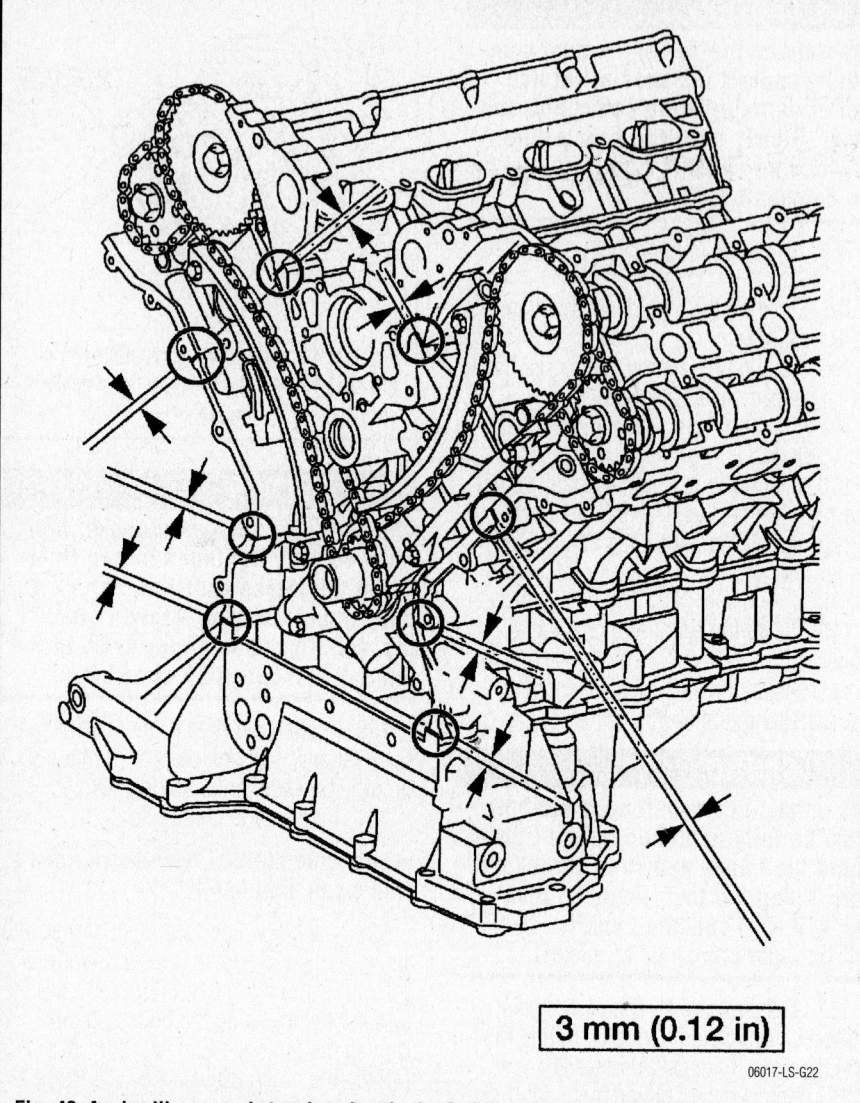

Fig. 43 Apply silicone gasket and sealant in the 8 places shown—3.9L engine

3 mm (0.12 in)

06017-LS-G22

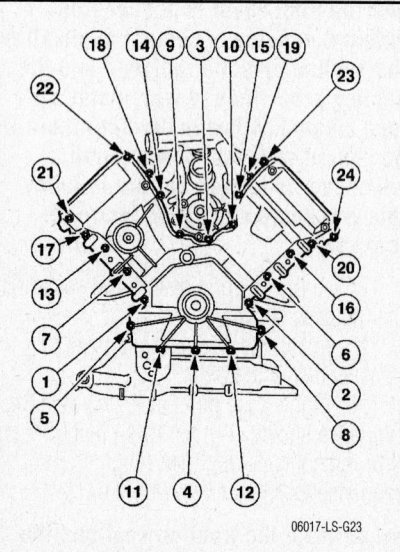

06017-LS-G23

Fig. 44 Engine front cover torque sequence—3.9L engine

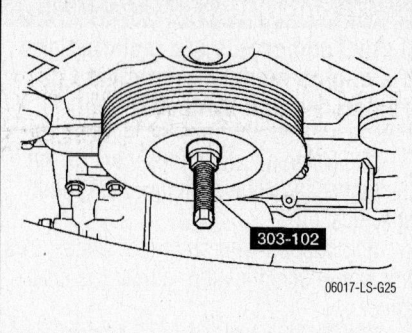

06017-LS-G25

Fig. 46 Using the tool 303-102, install the crankshaft pulley—3.9L engine

face cleaner. Allow to dry until there is no sign of wetness, or 4 minutes, whichever is longer. Failure to follow this procedure can cause future oil leakage.

128. Apply a bead of silicone gasket and sealant to the keyway.

129. Using the tool 303-102, install the crankshaft pulley.

130. Install a new bolt and using the special tool to hold the pulley, tighten as follows:.

a. Step 1: Tighten to 59 ft. lbs. (80 Nm).

b. Step 2: Loosen the bolt 2 complete turns.

c. Step 3: Tighten to 37 ft. lbs. (50 Nm).

d. Step 4: Tighten an additional 90 degrees.

131. On the left side:

a. Install a new gasket, left exhaust manifold, spacers and bolts.

b. Install the left exhaust manifold heat shield and 4 bolts.

c. Install the left exhaust manifold heat shield stud bolt.

132. On the right side:

a. Install a new gasket, right exhaust manifold, spacers and bolts.

b. Install the right exhaust manifold heat shield and 4 bolts.

c. Install the right exhaust manifold heat shield stud bolt.

d. Install a new gasket, EGR tube and 2 nuts. Tighten to 15 ft. lbs. (20 Nm).

133. Install new valve cover gaskets.

➡ If the valve covers are not secured within 4 minutes of sealant application the sealant must be removed and the sealing area cleaned with metal surface cleaner. Allow to dry until there is no sign of wetness, or 4 minutes, whichever is longer. Failure to follow this procedure can cause future oil leakage.

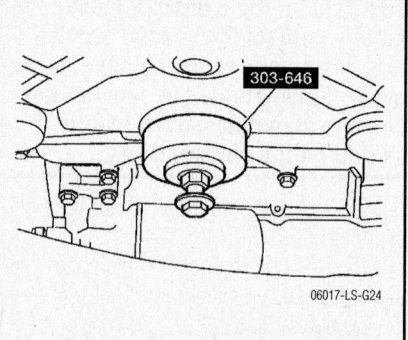

06017-LS-G24

Fig. 45 Using the tool 303-646, install a new front crankshaft seal—3.9L engine

127. Using the tool 303-646, install a new front crankshaft seal.

➡ If crankshaft pulley is not secured within 4 minutes of sealant application the sealant must be removed and the sealing area cleaned with metal sur-

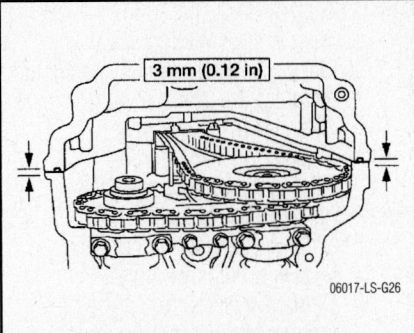

Fig. 47 Apply 4 beads of silicone gasket and sealant as shown—3.9L engine

134. Apply 4 beads of silicone gasket and sealant as shown.

135. Install the left valve cover and tighten the bolts in sequence to 89 inch lbs. (10 Nm).

136. Install the right valve cover and tighten the bolts in sequence to 89 inch lbs. (10 Nm).

137. Install new intake manifold gaskets and the manifold.

138. Install the intake manifold, the 7 bolts and the 3 studs.

139. Install a new gasket, the throttle body adapter and the 4 bolts. Tighten to 89 inch lbs. (10 Nm).

140. Install new O-ring seals, the coolant bypass housing and the 4 bolts. Tighten to 89 inch lbs. (10 Nm).

141. Connect the 2 throttle body coolant hoses.

142. Install the 2 radio interference ignition capacitors and the 2 nuts. Tighten to 89 inch lbs. (10 Nm).

143. Install a new gasket, the EGR system module and bolts. Tighten to 18 ft. lbs. (25 Nm).

144. Tighten the EGR tube nut to 30 ft. lbs. (40 Nm).

145. Install the crankcase vent tube.

146. Install the 8 ignition coils and bolts. Tighten to 44 inch lbs. (5 Nm).

❉❉ CAUTION

Make sure the O-ring seal remains in position and does not roll up the indicator tube during installation.

147. Install a new O-ring seal, oil level indicator tube and nut. Lubricate the O-ring seal with clean engine oil prior to installation and tighten the nut to 53 inch lbs. (6 Nm).

148. Install the crankshaft position sensor and bolt. Tighten to 89 inch lbs. (10 Nm).

149. Position the engine wiring harness onto the engine.

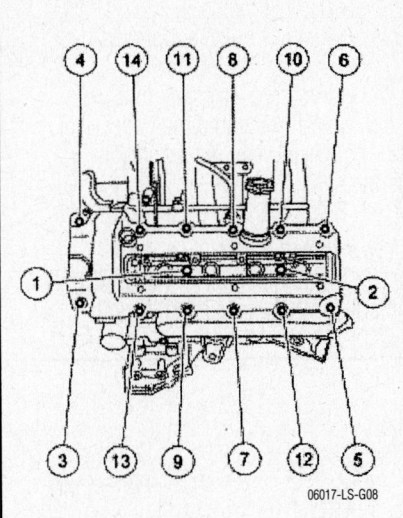

Fig. 48 Left valve cover torque sequence—3.9L engine

150. Attach the (HO2S) sensor electrical connectors onto the brackets.

151. Connect the alternator electrical connector and wiring harness retainers.

152. Connect the wiring harness retainers to the right valve cover.

153. Connect the crankshaft position sensor electrical connector and wiring harness retainers.

154. Attach the wiring harness onto the front cover.

155. Connect the wiring harness retainers to the left valve cover.

156. Install the power steering bracket and 5 bolts. Tighten to 18 ft. lbs. (25 Nm).

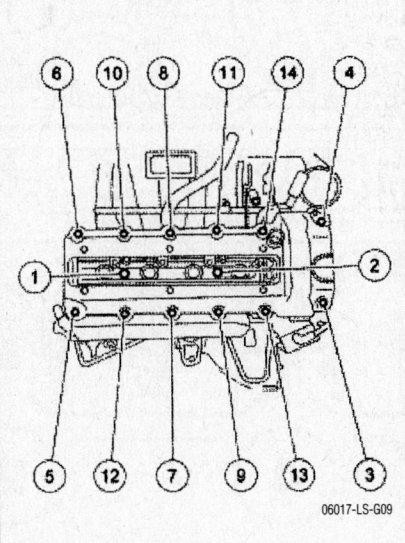

Fig. 49 Right valve cover torque sequence—3.9L engine

157. Connect the VCT sensor electrical connectors.

158. Connect the KS and CMP senor electrical connectors.

159. Attach the pin-type retainers.

160. Connect the 8 fuel injector and the 2 radio interference capacitor electrical connectors.

161. Install the 2 engine appearance cover brackets and the 4 nuts.

162. Attach the vacuum hose retainers onto the left engine appearance cover support bracket.

163. Connect the engine wiring harness retainers to the engine appearance cover support brackets.

164. Connect the 8 ignition coil electrical connectors.

➡**Remove all dirt and moisture from the valve cover before applying silicone sealer. Lift up the wire harness and apply a 0.5 inch (12.7 mm) bead of silicone sealer in the notch of the valve cover.**

165. Set the ignition coil harness in the bead of silicone sealer and apply enough additional sealer to surround the wire harness and notch. Tighten to 89 inch lbs. (10 Nm).

166. Install the ignition coil covers. 89 inch lbs. (10 Nm).

167. Install the vacuum harness.

168. Connect the coolant vent hose to the coolant outlet.

169. Connect the EGR system module electrical connector.

170. Connect the fuel rail temperature sensor electrical connector.

171. Connect the EVAP tube.

172. Connect the electronic throttle body electrical connector.

173. Connect the fuel pressure sensor electrical connector.

174. Connect the TP sensor electrical connector.

175. Install the coolant pump pulley and 3 bolts. Tighten to 89 inch lbs. (10 Nm).

176. Install the accessory drive belt idler pulley and bolt. Tighten to 18 ft. lbs. (25 Nm).

177. Install the accessory drive belt tensioner. Tighten to 18 ft. lbs. (25 Nm).

178. Fill the crankcase to the correct level.

179. Fill the cooling system.

180. Recharge the A/C system.

181. Connect the negative battery cable.

182. Start the engine and check for leaks.

CYLINDER HEAD

REMOVAL & INSTALLATION

3.0L Engine

See Figures 50 through 52.

1. Before servicing the vehicle, refer to the precautions in the beginning of this section.
2. Drain the cooling system.
3. Relieve the fuel system pressure.
4. Drain the engine oil.
5. Remove or disconnect the following:
   - Negative battery cable
   - Upper and lower intake manifolds
   - Valve covers
   - Accessory drive belts
6. Install a support fixture to the engine lifting eyes.
7. Remove or disconnect the following:
   - Motor mount nuts
   - Subframe bolts
   - Oil pan
   - Front cover
   - Timing chains
   - Camshafts
   - Exhaust manifolds
   - Ground strap
   - Positive Crankcase Ventilation (PCV) tube
   - Ignition noise suppressor
   - Coolant outlet tube
   - Engine oil dipstick tube
8. Install the subframe bolts and remove the engine support fixture.
9. Remove the cylinder heads.

To install:

10. Install the cylinder heads. Tighten the bolts in sequence as follows:

   a. Step 1: 22 ft. lbs. (30 Nm)
   b. Step 2: Plus 90 degrees
   c. Step 3: Loosen all bolts one full turn
   d. Step 4: 22 ft. lbs. (30 Nm)
   e. Step 5: Plus 90 degrees
   f. Step 6: Plus 90 degrees

11. Install the engine support fixture and remove the subframe bolts.
12. Install or connect the following:
   - Engine oil dipstick tube
   - Coolant outlet tube
   - Ignition noise suppressor

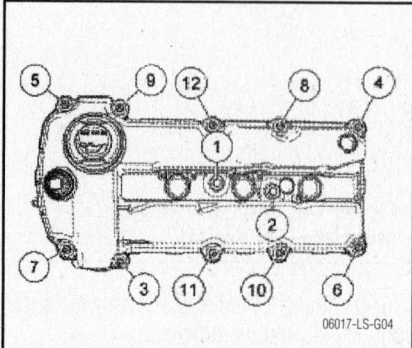

Fig. 51 Left valve cover torque sequence—3.0L engine

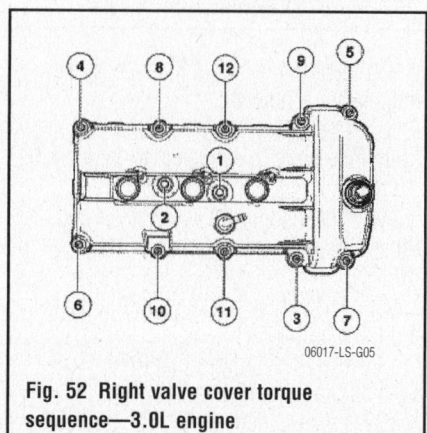

Fig. 52 Right valve cover torque sequence—3.0L engine

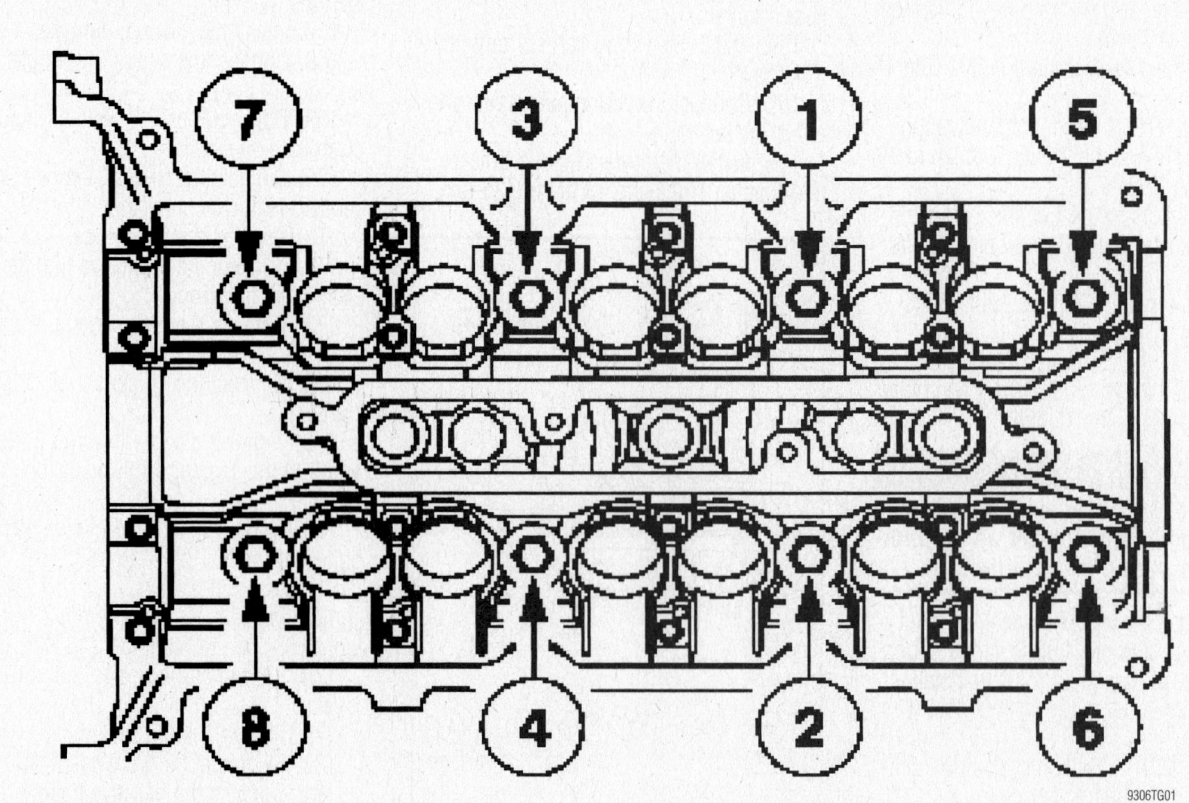

Fig. 50 Cylinder head torque sequence—3.0L engine

- PCV tube
- Ground strap
- Exhaust manifolds
- Camshafts
- Timing chains
- Front cover
- Oil pan
- Subframe bolts. Tighten the bolts to 76 ft. lbs. (103 Nm).
- Motor mount nuts. Tighten the nuts to 46 ft. lbs. (63 Nm).
- Accessory drive belts
- Valve covers and tighten to 89 inch lbs. (10 Nm) in the sequence illustrated.
- Upper and lower intake manifolds
- Negative battery cable

13. Fill the crankcase to the correct level.

14. Fill the cooling system.

15. Start the engine and check for leaks.

3.9L Engine

See Figures 53 through 75.

1. Before servicing the vehicle, refer to the precautions in the beginning of this section.

2. Remove the engine.

3. Install the engine on a suitable engine stand.

4. Remove the engine block plug to drain the engine coolant.

5. Disconnect the oil pressure and oil temperature sensor electrical connectors.

6. Remove and discard the oil filter.

�֍ CAUTION

A new oil cooler must be installed or severe damage to the engine can occur.

7. Remove the bolt and oil cooler.

8. Discard the oil cooler and gasket.

9. Remove the bolt and the accessory drive belt tensioner.

10. Remove the bolt and the accessory drive belt idler pulley.

11. Remove the 3 bolts and the coolant pump pulley.

➡ **Hold the crankshaft pulley with the tool 303-D055 while removing the bolt and washer.**

12. Remove and discard the bolt and washer.

13. Using the puller tool 303-009, remove the crankshaft damper.

14. Using the tool 303-409, remove and discard the front crankshaft seal.

15. Remove the ignition coil covers.

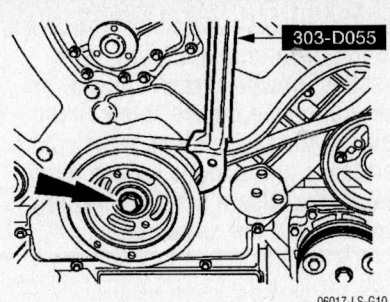

Fig. 53 Hold the crankshaft pulley with the tool 303-D055 while removing the bolt and washer—3.9L engine

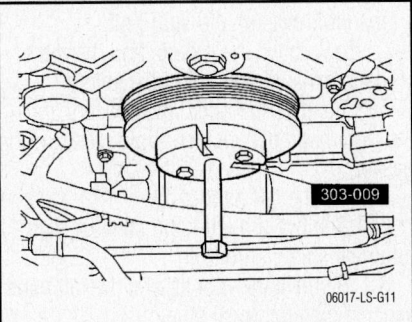

Fig. 54 Using the tool 303-009, remove and discard the front crankshaft seal—3.9L engine

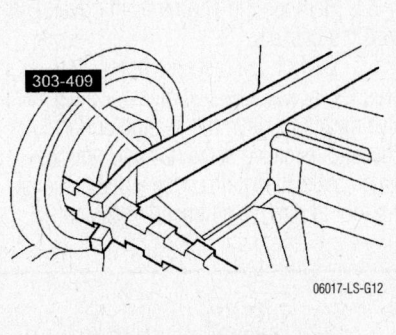

Fig. 55 Using the tool 303-409, remove and discard the front crankshaft seal—3.9L engine

16. Remove all silicone sealer and residue from the ignition coil covers.

17. Remove all silicone sealer and residue from the valve cover surface and ignition coil wiring harness.

18. Disconnect the 8 ignition coil electrical connectors.

19. Disconnect the Throttle Position (TP) sensor electrical connector.

20. Disconnect the fuel pressure sensor electrical connector.

21. Disconnect the electronic throttle body electrical connector.

22. Disconnect the Evaporative Emissions (EVAP) tube.

23. Disconnect the fuel rail temperature sensor electrical connector.

24. Disconnect the Exhaust Gas Recirculation (EGR) system module electrical connector.

25. Disconnect the coolant vent hose from the coolant outlet.

26. Remove the coolant vent hose.

27. Remove the vacuum harness.

28. Disconnect the engine wiring harness retainers from the engine appearance cover support brackets.

29. Detach the vacuum hose retainers from the left hand engine appearance cover support bracket.

30. Remove the 4 nuts and the 2 engine appearance cover brackets.

31. Disconnect the 8 fuel injector and the 2 radio interference capacitor electrical connectors

32. Disconnect the Knock Sensor (KS) and Camshaft Position (CMP) senor electrical connectors.

33. Detach the pin-type retainers.

34. Disconnect the 2 Variable Cam Timing (VCT) sensor electrical connectors.

35. Remove the 5 bolts and the power steering bracket.

36. Disconnect the wiring harness retainers from the left hand valve cover.

37. Detach the wiring harness from the engine front cover.

38. Disconnect the Crankshaft Position (CKP) sensor electrical connector and wiring harness retainers.

39. Disconnect the wiring harness retainers from the right hand valve cover.

40. Disconnect the alternator electrical connector and wiring harness retainers.

41. Remove the Heated Oxygen (HO2s) sensor electrical connectors from the brackets.

42. Remove the engine wiring harness from the engine.

43. Remove the nut and the oil level indicator tube. Discard the O-ring seal.

44. Remove the 8 bolts and the 8 ignition coils.

45. Remove the crankcase vent tube.

46. Remove the 2 EGR system module bolts and loosen the EGR tube nut.

47. Remove the EGR system module and discard the gasket.

48. Remove the 2 nuts and the radio interference capacitors.

49. Disconnect the throttle body heater hoses.

50. Remove the 4 bolts and the coolant bypass housing. Discard the O-ring seals.

51. Remove the 4 bolts and the throttle body adapter. Discard the gasket.

52. Remove the intake manifold. Discard the gaskets.

✳✳ CAUTION

Do not use metal scrapers, wire brushes, power abrasive discs, or other abrasive means to clean the sealing surfaces. These tools cause scratches and gouges, which make leak paths. Use a plastic scraping tool to clean the surfaces.

53. Clean the sealing surfaces.

54. Remove the bolts in the sequence shown and remove the right valve cover. Discard the gasket.

55. Remove the bolts in the sequence shown and remove the left valve cover.

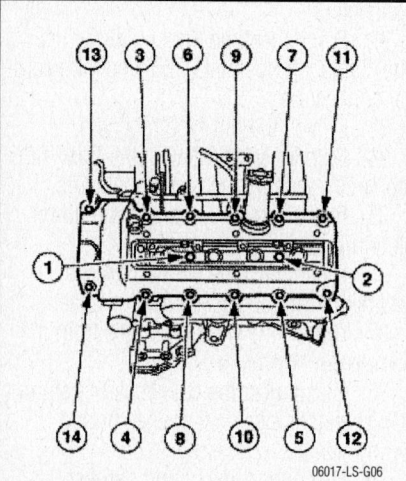

Fig. 56 Left valve cover loosening sequence—3.9L engine

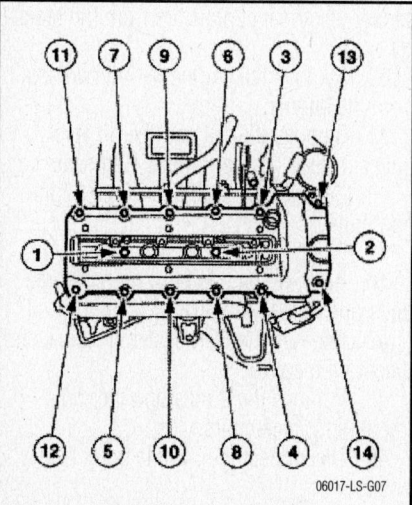

Fig. 57 Right valve cover loosening sequence—3.9L engine

✳✳ CAUTION

Do not use metal scrapers, wire brushes, power abrasive discs, or other abrasive means to clean the sealing surfaces. These tools cause scratches and gouges, which make leak paths. Use a plastic scraping tool to clean the surfaces.

56. Remove the gaskets and all silicone sealer. Clean the mating surfaces with silicone gasket remover.

57. On the right hand side:
  a. Remove the 2 nuts and the EGR tube. Discard the gasket.
  b. Remove the right hand exhaust manifold heat shield stud bolt.
  c. Remove the 4 bolts and the right hand exhaust manifold heat shield.

58. Remove the bolts, the spacers and the right hand exhaust manifold. Discard the gasket.

59. On the left hand side:

60. Remove the left hand exhaust manifold heat shield stud bolt.

61. Remove the 4 bolts and the left hand exhaust manifold heat shield.

62. Remove the bolts, the spacers and the left exhaust manifold. Discard the gasket.

63. Remove the engine front cover bolts in the sequence shown.

64. Remove the engine front cover. Discard the gaskets.

65. Do not use metal scrapers, wire brushes, power abrasive discs or other abrasive means to clean the sealing surfaces. These tools cause scratches and gouges, which make leak paths. Use a plastic scraping tool to remove all traces of sealant.

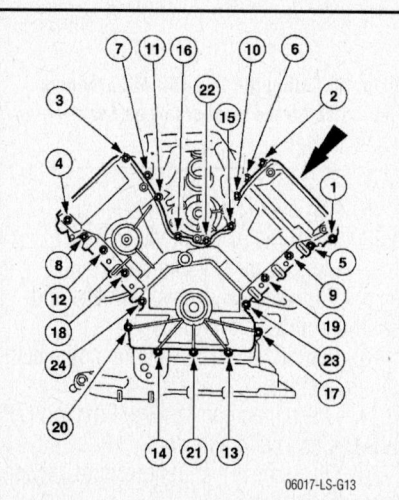

Fig. 58 Remove the engine front cover bolts in the sequence shown—3.9L engine

66. Clean the sealing surfaces.

67. Remove the right and left hand Variable Cam Timing (VCT) bush carriers.

68. Remove the bolt and the CKP sensor.

➡There is one window on the ignition pulse wheel that is unique to accept the tool 303-645.

69. Install the tool 303-645.

70. Turn the crankshaft to 45 degrees After Top Dead Center (ATDC). The crankshaft keyway will be in the 6 o'clock position.

71. Make sure the flats of the camshaft are facing upward. If not, repeat the previous step.

✳✳ CAUTION

The flats on the camshaft must completely contact the special service tool or damage to the camshafts can occur. Slowly draw the special tool down evenly until it is fully seated on the camshaft flats.

72. Install the holding tool 303-530 on the right hand cylinder head.

✳✳ CAUTION

An open-end wrench must be used on the hex area of the camshaft or damage to the head will occur.

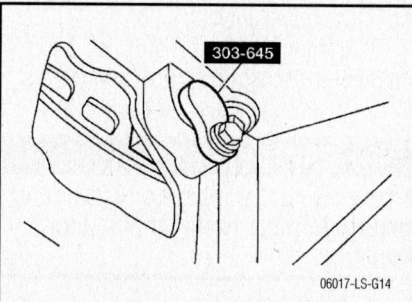

Fig. 59 There is one window on the ignition pulse wheel that is unique to accept the tool 303-645—3.9L engine

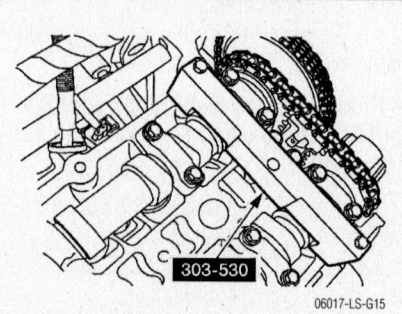

Fig. 60 Tool 303-530 is used to hold the camshafts during removal—3.9L engine

73. Remove and discard the exhaust camshaft sprocket bolt.

74. Remove and discard the variable VCT unit bolt.

75. Remove the right hand timing chain tensioner.

76. Push the lever down and install a drill rod to lock the piston.

77. Remove the 2 bolts and the tensioner.

78. Remove the bolt and the right tensioner arm.

79. Remove the bolt and the right timing chain guide.

80. Remove the right primary timing chain.

81. Remove the holding tool from the right cylinder head.

> ❋❋ **CAUTION**
>
> **The flats on the camshaft must completely contact the special service tool or damage to the camshafts can occur. Slowly draw the special tool down evenly until it is fully seated on the camshaft flats.**

82. Install the holding tool on the left cylinder head.

> ❋❋ **CAUTION**
>
> **An open-end wrench must be used on the hex area of the camshaft or damage to the cylinder head will occur.**

83. Remove and discard the left VCT unit bolt and the exhaust camshaft sprocket bolt.

84. Remove the left timing chain tensioner.

85. Push the lever down and install a drill rod to lock the piston.

86. Remove the 2 bolts and the tensioner.

87. Remove the nut and the left tensioner arm.

88. Remove the bolt and the left timing chain guide.

89. Remove the left primary timing chain.

90. Remove the crankshaft sprocket.

91. Collapse the left secondary timing chain tensioner and install a pin to lock the piston.

92. Remove the left VCT unit, exhaust camshaft sprocket and timing chain as an assembly.

93. Remove the 2 bolts and the left secondary timing chain tensioner.

94. Collapse the right secondary timing chain tensioner and install a pin to lock the piston.

95. Remove the right VCT unit, exhaust camshaft sprocket and timing chain as an assembly.

96. Remove the 2 bolts and the right secondary timing chain tensioner.

97. Remove the holding tool.

98. On the left side:

> ❋❋ **CAUTION**
>
> **Record the camshaft bearing cap locations. The camshaft bearing caps are positional and must be installed in their original locations and orientation or engine damage can occur.**

   d. Remove the left camshaft bearing cap bolts and caps.

   e. Remove the left hand camshafts.

> ❋❋ **CAUTION**
>
> **Do not use any means of marking the shims other than a permanent-type marker. Any scratches or paint on the shims can result in incorrect lash adjustments and severe engine damage. Record the shim and bucket tappet location. The shim and bucket tappet are positional and if installed in the incorrect location, engine damage can occur.**

   f. Record the location of the valve tappets and remove the tappets.

> ❋❋ **CAUTION**
>
> **The cylinder head must be cool before removing it from the engine. Cylinder head warpage can result if a warm or hot cylinder head is removed. Place clean shop towels over exposed engine cavities. Carefully remove the towels so foreign material is not dropped into the engine. The cylinder head bolts must be discarded and new bolts installed. They are tighten-to-yield designed and cannot be reused. Aluminum surfaces are soft and can be scratched easily. Never place the cylinder head gasket surface, unprotected, on a bench surface.**

   g. Remove the left hand cylinder head end bolts and discard the bolts.

   h. Remove and discard the bolts from left cylinder head in the sequence shown.

   i. Remove the cylinder head. Discard the gasket.

99. On the right side:

> ❋❋ **CAUTION**
>
> **Record the camshaft bearing cap locations. The camshaft bearing caps**

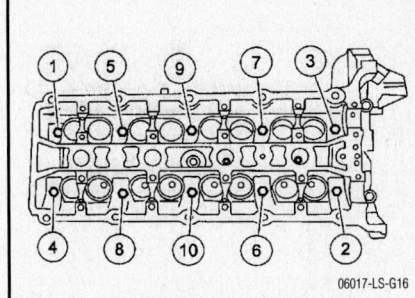

06017-LS-G16

Fig. 61 Left cylinder head bolt loosening sequence—3.9L engine

are positional and must be installed in their original locations and orientation or engine damage can occur.

   j. Remove the right camshaft bearing cap bolts and caps.

   k. Remove the right camshafts.

> ❋❋ **CAUTION**
>
> **Do not use any means of marking the shims other than a permanent-type marker. Any scratches or paint on the shims can result in incorrect lash adjustments and severe engine damage. Record the shim and bucket tappet location. The shim and bucket tappet are positional and if installed in the incorrect location, engine damage can occur.**

   l. Record the location of the valve tappets and remove the tappets.

> ❋❋ **CAUTION**
>
> **The cylinder head must be cool before removing it from the engine. Cylinder head warpage can result if a warm or hot cylinder head is removed. Place clean shop towels over exposed engine cavities. Carefully remove the towels so foreign material is not dropped into the engine. The cylinder head bolts must be discarded and new bolts installed. They are tighten-to-yield designed and cannot be reused. Aluminum surfaces are soft and can be scratched easily. Never place the cylinder head gasket surface, unprotected, on a bench surface.**

   m. Remove the right cylinder head end bolts. Discard the bolts.

   n. Remove and discard the bolts from right cylinder head in the sequence shown.

   o. Remove the cylinder head. Discard the gasket.

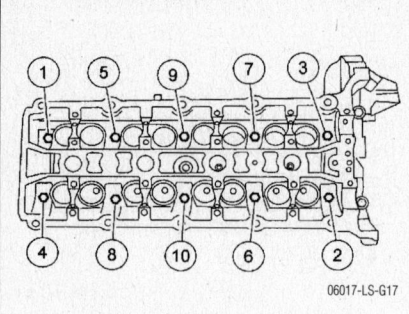

Fig. 62 Right cylinder head bolt loosening sequence—3.9L engine

✷✷ CAUTION

Do not use metal scrapers, wire brushes, power abrasive discs or other abrasive means to clean the sealing surfaces. These tools cause scratches and gouges, which make leak paths. Use a plastic scraping tool to remove all traces of sealant. Observe all warnings or cautions and follow all application directions contained on the packaging of the silicone gasket remover and the metal surface prep.

➡ **If there is no residual gasket material present, metal surface prep can be used to clean and prepare the surfaces.**

100. Clean the cylinder head-to-cylinder block mating surfaces of both the cylinder heads and the cylinder block.

101. Remove any large deposits of silicone or gasket material with a plastic scraper.

102. Apply silicone gasket remover, following package directions, and allow to set for several minutes.

103. Remove the silicone gasket remover with a plastic scraper. A second application of silicone gasket remover may be required if residual traces of silicone or gasket material remain.

104. Apply metal surface prep, following package directions, to remove any remaining traces of oil or coolant, and to prepare the surfaces to bond with the new gasket. Do not attempt to make the metal shiny. Some staining of the metal surfaces is normal.

➡ **The straightedge used must be flat within 0.0002 inch (0.0051 mm) per foot of tool length.**

105. Support the cylinder heads on a bench with the head gasket side up. Inspect all areas of the deck face with a straightedge, paying particular attention to the oil pressure feed area. The cylinder heads must not have depressions deeper than 0.001 inch (0.0254 mm) across a 1.5 inch (38.1 mm) square area, or scratches more than 0.001 inch (0.0254 mm).

To install:

✷✷ CAUTION

The gasket sealing surfaces on the cylinder head and cylinder block must be clean and dry. The use of sealing aids (aviation cement, copper spray and glue) is not permitted. The gasket must be installed dry. The new gasket has a film coating which is crucial to the gasket's ability to seal correctly. Do not scratch the gasket. Do not allow the dowels to scratch the sealing surface of the cylinder head during cylinder head installation.

106. On the right side:
   a. Lightly oil the new cylinder head bolts and allow to drain for a few minutes before installing.
   b. Install a new gasket and position the right cylinder head on the engine.

➡ **The cylinder head bolts are a torque-to-yield design and must not be reused. Always use new bolts.**

107. Install and tighten the right head bolts in stages in the sequence shown.
   a. Step 1: Tighten bolts 1 through 10 to 15 ft. lbs. (20 Nm).
   b. Step 2: Tighten bolts 1 through 10 to 26 ft. lbs. (35 Nm).
   c. Step 3: Tighten bolts 1 through 10 to 33 ft. lbs. (45 Nm).
   d. Step 4: Tighten bolts 1 through 10 an additional 90 degrees.
   e. Step 5: Tighten bolts 1 through 10 an additional 90 degrees.
   f. Step 6: Install the 2 end bolts and tighten to 15 ft. lbs. (20 Nm), then retighten an additional 90 degrees.
108. On the left side:
   a. Lightly oil the new cylinder head bolts and allow to drain for a few minutes before installing.
   b. Install a new gasket and position the right cylinder head on the engine.

➡ **The cylinder head bolts are a torque-to-yield design and must not be reused. Always use new bolts.**

109. Install and tighten the left head bolts in stages in the sequence shown.
   a. Step 1: Tighten bolts 1 through 10 to 15 ft. lbs. (20 Nm).

   b. Step 2: Tighten bolts 1 through 10 to 26 ft. lbs. (35 Nm).
   c. Step 3: Tighten bolts 1 through 10 to 33 ft. lbs. (45 Nm).
   d. Step 4: Tighten bolts 1 through 10 an additional 90 degrees.
   e. Step 5: Tighten bolts 1 through 10 an additional 90 degrees.
   f. Step 6: Install the 2 end bolts and tighten to 15 ft. lbs. (20 Nm), then retighten an additional 90 degrees.

➡ **Coat the valve tappets with clean engine oil prior to installing.**

110. Install the valve tappets and shims in their original locations.
111. On the right side:
   NOTE: Apply clean engine oil to the camshaft journals, the camshaft caps and the camshaft lobes prior to installing the camshafts.
   g. Position the right camshafts on the camshaft journals.

✷✷ CAUTION

Install the camshaft bearing caps. The camshaft bearing caps are positional and must be installed in their original locations and orientation or engine damage can occur.

   h. Install the right camshaft bearing caps.
   i. Install the bearing cap bolts. Tighten the bolts in three stages in the sequence shown.
   j. Step 1: Hand-tighten.
   k. Step 2: Tighten to 53 inch lbs. (6 Nm).
   l. Step 3: Tighten an additional 90 degrees.
112. On the left side:

➡ **Apply clean engine oil to the camshaft journals, the camshaft caps and the camshaft lobes prior to installing the camshafts.**

   m. Position the right camshafts on the camshaft journals.

✷✷ CAUTION

Install the camshaft bearing caps. The camshaft bearing caps are positional and must be installed in their original locations and orientation or engine damage can occur.

   n. Install the right camshaft bearing caps.
   o. Install the bearing cap bolts. Tighten the bolts in three stages in the sequence shown.

p. Step 1: Hand-tighten.
q. Step 2: Tighten to 53 inch lbs.
(6 Nm).
r. Step 3: Tighten an additional 90
degrees.

> **✳✳ CAUTION**
>
> **If any components are installed new,
> the engine must be reshimmed or
> engine damage can occur.**

113. Using a feeler gauge, confirm that
the tappet and shim clearances are within
specification.
114. If tappet and shim clearances are
not within specification, adjust the clearance.

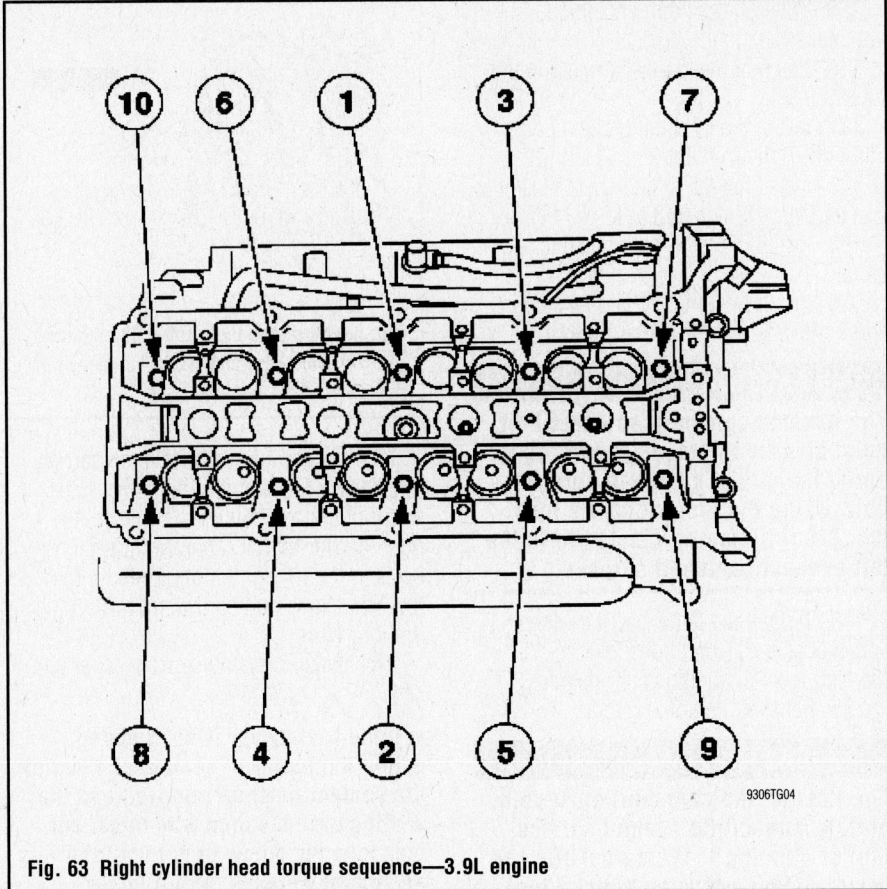

Fig. 63 Right cylinder head torque sequence—3.9L engine

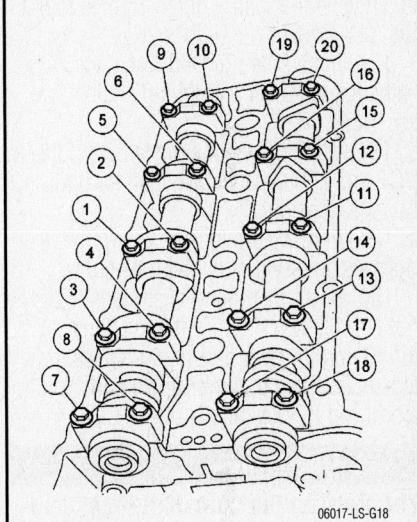

**Fig. 65 Right camshaft bearing cap tight-
ening sequence—3.9L engine**

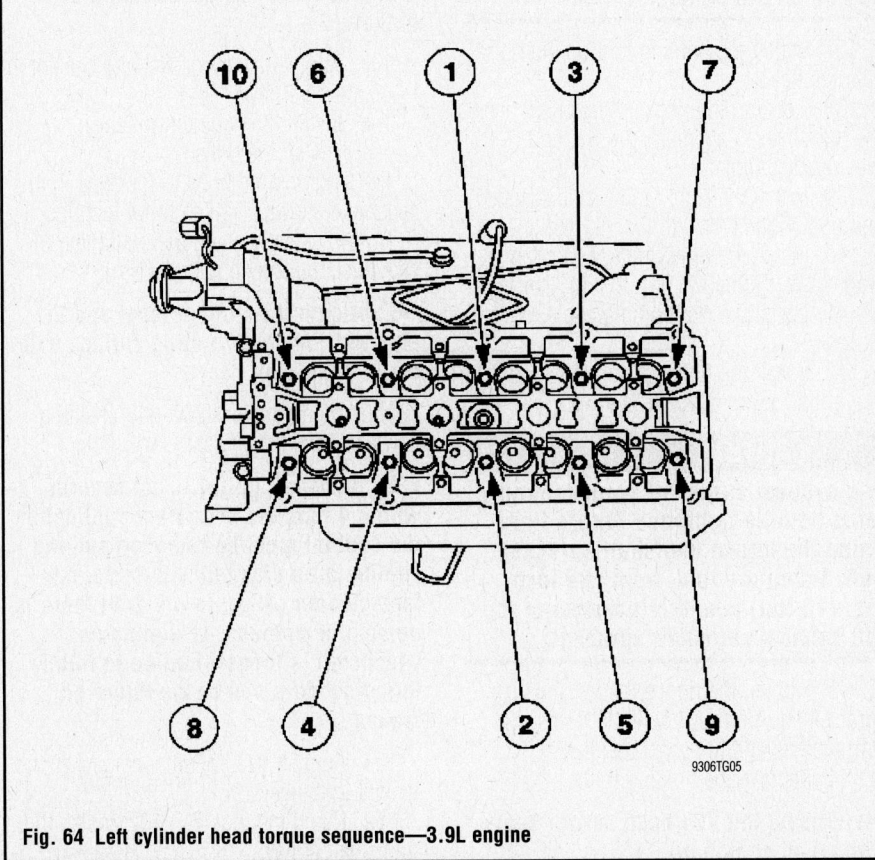

Fig. 64 Left cylinder head torque sequence—3.9L engine

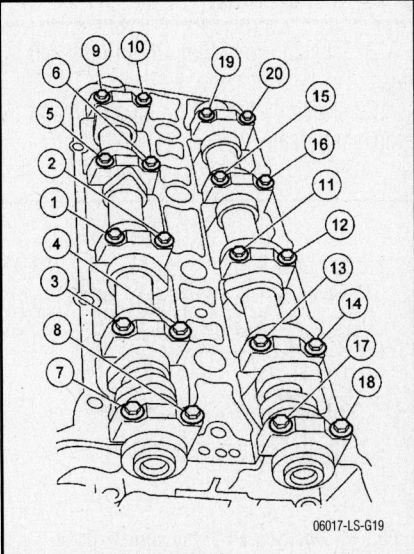

**Fig. 66 Left camshaft bearing cap tighten-
ing sequence—3.9L engine**

115. Turn the crankshaft to 45 degrees ATDC. The crankshaft keyway will be in the 6 o'clock position.

116. Install the tool 303-645.

117. Position all of the camshafts so the flats of the camshafts are facing upward.

118. Install the left secondary timing chain tensioner and 2 bolts. Tighten to 8 ft. lbs. (11 Nm).

119. Install the left VCT unit, exhaust camshaft sprocket and timing chain as an assembly.

120. Using new bolts, install the left VCT unit and exhaust camshaft sprocket bolts finger-tight.

121. Remove the locking pin from the left secondary timing chain tensioner.

122. Install the right secondary timing chain tensioner and 2 bolts. Tighten to 8 ft. lbs. (11 Nm).

123. Install the right VCT unit, exhaust camshaft sprocket and timing chain as an assembly.

124. Using new bolts, install the right VCT unit and exhaust camshaft sprocket bolts finger-tight.

125. Remove the locking pin from the right secondary timing chain tensioner.

126. Reset the timing chain tensioners by holding the lever toward the tensioner piston. Using finger pressure, compress the tensioner. Push the lever down and install a drill rod to lock the piston.

✳✳ CAUTION
The flats on the camshaft must completely contact the special service tool or damage to the camshafts can occur. Slowly draw the special tool down evenly until it is fully seated on the camshaft flats.

127. Install the holding tool on the left head.

128. Position the left timing chain and crankshaft gear.

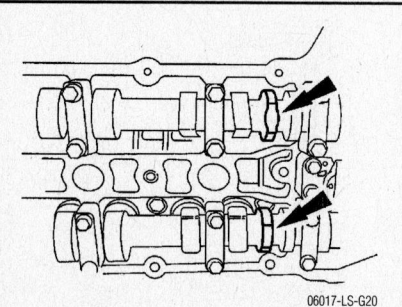

Fig. 67 Position all of the camshafts so the flats of the camshafts are facing upward—3.9L engine

129. Position the timing chain over the left intake camshaft sprocket.

130. Position the crankshaft gear in the timing chain.

131. Install the left timing chain guide and bolt. Tighten to 8 ft. lbs. (11 Nm).

132. Install the left timing chain tensioner arm and nut. Tighten to 8 ft. lbs. (11 Nm).

133. Install the left timing chain tensioner.

134. Install the timing chain tensioner and bolts, and remove the drill rod.

✳✳ CAUTION
The exhaust camshaft sprocket bolt must be fully tightened before tightening the intake camshaft sprocket bolt. Using the tool, apply 89 inch lbs. (10 Nm) counterclockwise to the left exhaust camshaft sprocket.

135. Tighten the left exhaust camshaft sprocket and VCT unit bolts 26 ft. lbs. (35 Nm) then an additional 90 degrees.

136. Remove the holding tool.

✳✳ CAUTION
The flats on the camshaft must completely contact the special service tool or damage to the camshafts can occur. Slowly draw the special tool downward evenly until it is fully seated on the camshaft flats.

137. Install the holding tool on the right cylinder head.

138. Position the right timing chain over the right intake camshaft sprocket and over the crankshaft gear.

139. Install the right timing chain guide and bolt. Tighten to 8 ft. lbs. (11 Nm).

140. Install the right timing chain tensioner arm. Tighten to 8 ft. lbs. (11 Nm).

141. Install the right timing chain tensioner.

142. Install the timing chain tensioner and bolts, and remove the drill rod.

✳✳ CAUTION
The exhaust camshaft sprocket bolt must be fully tightened before tightening the intake camshaft sprocket bolt. Using the tool, apply 89 inch lbs. (10 Nm) counterclockwise to the left exhaust camshaft sprocket.

143. Tighten the right exhaust camshaft sprocket and VCT unit bolts 26 ft. lbs. (35 Nm) then an additional 90 degrees.

144. Remove the holding tool.

➡ **Lubricate the VCT bush carrier seals with clean engine oil.**

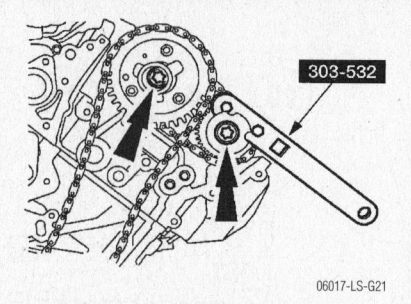

Fig. 68 Using the tool, apply 89 inch lbs. (10 Nm) counterclockwise to the camshaft sprocket—3.9L engine

145. Carefully insert the bush carrier into the VCT unit, compress ring seals with fingers as required. Fully seat the bush carrier by hand before fitting the bolts and nut. Tighten the bolts to 15 ft. lbs. (20 Nm). Tighten the nut to 89 inch lbs. (10 Nm).

146. Install new engine front cover gaskets.

➡ **If the front cover is not secured within 4 minutes of sealant application, the sealant must be removed and the sealing area cleaned with metal surface cleaner. Allow to dry until there is no sign of wetness, or 4 minutes, whichever is longer. Failure to follow this procedure can cause future oil leakage.**

147. Apply silicone gasket and sealant in the 8 places shown.

148. Install the engine front cover. Loosely install the bolts.

149. Tighten the bolts in 2 stages in the sequence shown. Tighten to 44 inch lbs. (5 Nm) in sequence and then retighten in sequence to 89 inch lbs. (10 Nm).

➡ **Lubricate the front oil seal and the engine front cover mating surface with clean engine oil.**

150. Using the tool 303-646, install a new front crankshaft seal.

➡ **If crankshaft pulley is not secured within 4 minutes of sealant application the sealant must be removed and the sealing area cleaned with metal surface cleaner. Allow to dry until there is no sign of wetness, or 4 minutes, whichever is longer. Failure to follow this procedure can cause future oil leakage.**

151. Apply a bead of silicone gasket and sealant to the keyway.

152. Using the tool 303-102, install the crankshaft pulley.

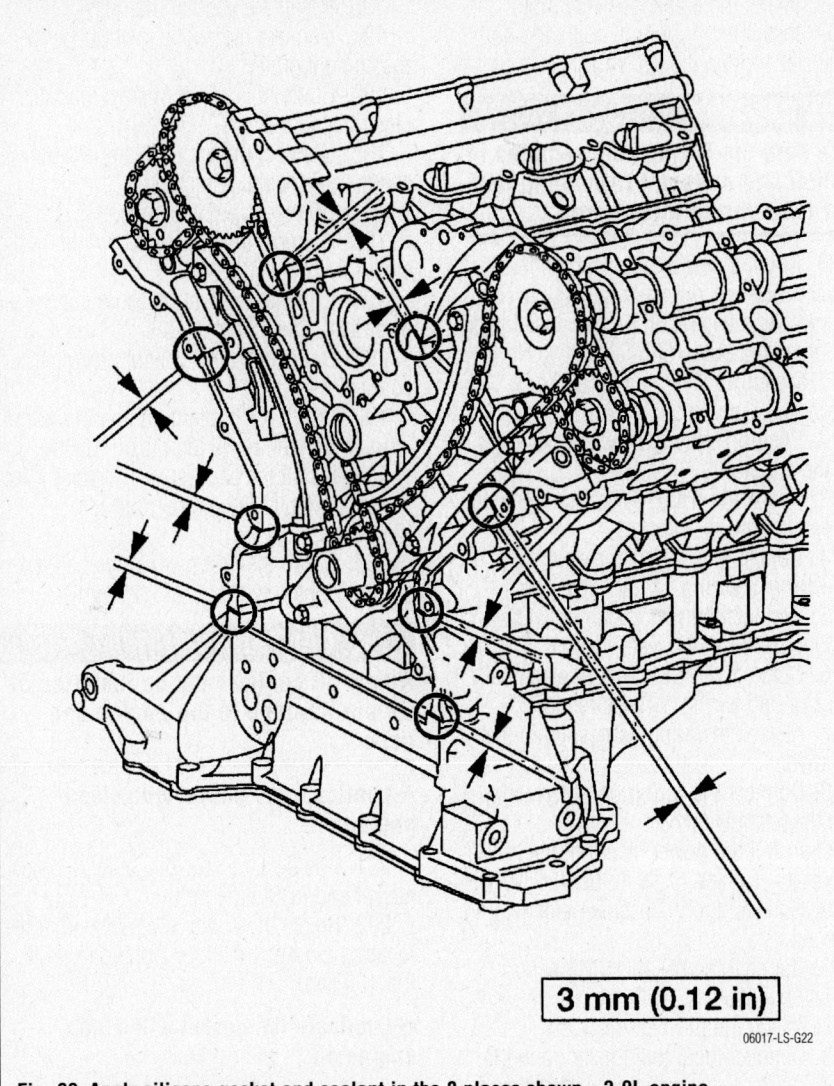

Fig. 69 Apply silicone gasket and sealant in the 8 places shown—3.9L engine

3 mm (0.12 in)

06017-LS-G22

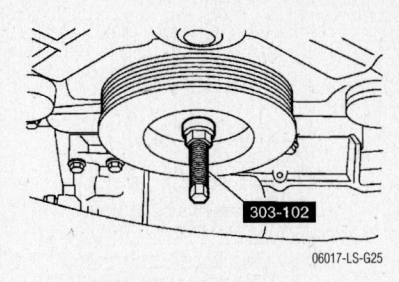

303-102

06017-LS-G25

Fig. 72 Using the tool 303-102, install the crankshaft pulley—3.9L engine

d. Step 4: Tighten an additional 90 degrees.

154. On the left side:

a. Install a new gasket, left exhaust manifold, spacers and bolts.

b. Install the left exhaust manifold heat shield and 4 bolts.

c. Install the left exhaust manifold heat shield stud bolt.

155. On the right side:

a. Install a new gasket, right exhaust manifold, spacers and bolts.

b. Install the right exhaust manifold heat shield and 4 bolts.

c. Install the right exhaust manifold heat shield stud bolt.

d. Install a new gasket, EGR tube and 2 nuts. Tighten to 15 ft. lbs. (20 Nm).

156. Install new valve cover gaskets.

➡**If the valve covers are not secured within 4 minutes of sealant application the sealant must be removed and the sealing area cleaned with metal surface cleaner. Allow to dry until there is no sign of wetness, or 4 minutes, whichever is longer. Failure to follow this procedure can cause future oil leakage.**

157. Apply 4 beads of silicone gasket and sealant as shown.

158. Install the left valve cover and tighten the bolts in sequence to 89 inch lbs. (10 Nm).

153. Install a new bolt and using the special tool to hold the pulley, tighten as follows:.

a. Step 1: Tighten to 59 ft. lbs. (80 Nm).

b. Step 2: Loosen the bolt 2 complete turns.

c. Step 3: Tighten to 37 ft. lbs. (50 Nm).

06017-LS-G23

Fig. 70 Engine front cover torque sequence—3.9L engine

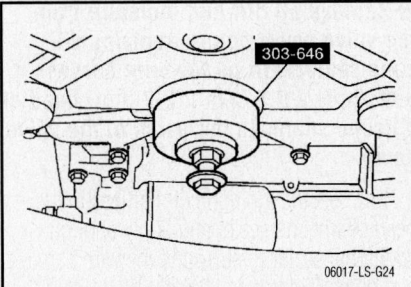

303-646

06017-LS-G24

Fig. 71 Using the tool 303-646, install a new front crankshaft seal—3.9L engine

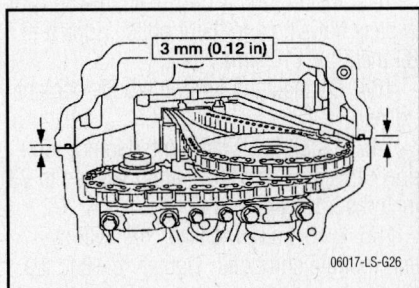

3 mm (0.12 in)

06017-LS-G26

Fig. 73 Apply 4 beads of silicone gasket and sealant as shown—3.9L engine

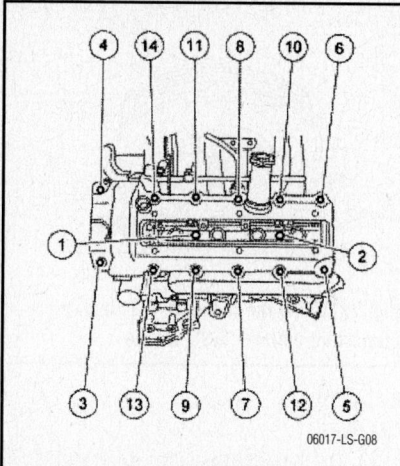

Fig. 74 Left valve cover torque sequence—3.9L engine

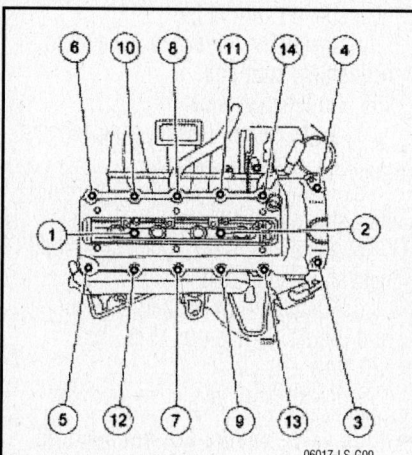

Fig. 75 Right valve cover torque sequence—3.9L engine

159. Install the right valve cover and tighten the bolts in sequence to 89 inch lbs. (10 Nm).

160. Install new intake manifold gaskets and the manifold.

161. Install the intake manifold, the 7 bolts and the 3 studs.

162. Install a new gasket, the throttle body adapter and the 4 bolts. Tighten to 89 inch lbs. (10 Nm).

163. Install new O-ring seals, the coolant bypass housing and the 4 bolts. Tighten to 89 inch lbs. (10 Nm).

164. Connect the 2 throttle body coolant hoses.

165. Install the 2 radio interference ignition capacitors and the 2 nuts. Tighten to 89 inch lbs. (10 Nm).

166. Install a new gasket, the EGR system module and bolts. Tighten to 18 ft. lbs. (25 Nm).

167. Tighten the EGR tube nut to 30 ft. lbs. (40 Nm).

168. Install the crankcase vent tube.

169. Install the 8 ignition coils and bolts. Tighten to 44 inch lbs. (5 Nm).

❊❊ CAUTION

Make sure the O-ring seal remains in position and does not roll up the indicator tube during installation.

170. Install a new O-ring seal, oil level indicator tube and nut. Lubricate the O-ring seal with clean engine oil prior to installation and tighten the nut to 53 inch lbs. (6 Nm).

171. Install the CKP sensor and bolt. Tighten to 89 inch lbs. (10 Nm).

172. Position the engine wiring harness onto the engine.

173. Attach the (HO22S) sensor electrical connectors onto the brackets.

174. Connect the alternator electrical connector and wiring harness retainers.

175. Connect the wiring harness retainers to the right valve cover.

176. Connect the CKP sensor electrical connector and wiring harness retainers.

177. Attach the wiring harness onto the front cover.

178. Connect the wiring harness retainers to the left valve cover.

179. Install the power steering bracket and 5 bolts. Tighten to 18 ft. lbs. (25 Nm).

180. Connect the VCT sensor electrical connectors.

181. Connect the KS and CMP senor electrical connectors.

182. Attach the pin-type retainers.

183. Connect the 8 fuel injector and the 2 radio interference capacitor electrical connectors.

184. Install the 2 engine appearance cover brackets and the 4 nuts.

185. Attach the vacuum hose retainers onto the left engine appearance cover support bracket.

186. Connect the engine wiring harness retainers to the engine appearance cover support brackets.

187. Connect the 8 ignition coil electrical connectors.

➥Remove all dirt and moisture from the valve cover before applying silicone sealer. Lift up the wire harness and apply a 0.5 inch (12.7 mm) bead of silicone sealer in the notch of the valve cover.

188. Set the ignition coil harness in the bead of silicone sealer and apply enough additional sealer to surround the wire harness and notch. Tighten to 89 inch lbs. (10 Nm).

189. Install the ignition coil covers. 89 inch lbs. (10 Nm).

190. Install the vacuum harness.

191. Connect the coolant vent hose to the coolant outlet.

192. Connect the EGR system module electrical connector.

193. Connect the fuel rail temperature sensor electrical connector.

194. Connect the EVAP tube.

195. Connect the electronic throttle body electrical connector.

196. Connect the fuel pressure sensor electrical connector.

197. Connect the TP sensor electrical connector.

198. Install the coolant pump pulley and 3 bolts. Tighten to 89 inch lbs. (10 Nm).

199. Install the accessory drive belt idler pulley and bolt. Tighten to 18 ft. lbs. (25 Nm).

200. Install the accessory drive belt tensioner. Tighten to 18 ft. lbs. (25 Nm).

❊❊ CAUTION

A new oil cooler must be installed or severe damage to the engine can occur.

➥Lubricate the gasket with clean engine oil.

201. Position the new oil cooler, the new gasket and install the bolt.

202. Rotate the cooler clockwise until the locating pin hits the stop. Tighten to 44 ft. lbs. (60 Nm).

➥Lubricate the gasket with clean engine oil.

203. Install a new oil filter and tighten until the seal makes contact. Using an oil filter strap wrench, tighten filter an additional 270 degrees.

204. Connect the oil pressure and oil temperature sensor electrical connectors.

205. Install the engine block drain plug. Tighten to 37 ft. lbs. (50 Nm).

206. Install the engine in the vehicle.

207. Fill the crankcase to the correct level.

208. Fill the cooling system.

209. Recharge the A/C system.

210. Connect the negative battery cable.

211. Start the engine and check for leaks.

ENGINE ASSEMBLY

REMOVAL & INSTALLATION

3.0L Engine

See Figures 76 and 77.

1. Before servicing the vehicle, refer to the precautions in the beginning of this section.

2. Drain the cooling system.

3. Relieve the fuel system pressure.

4. Recover the A/C refrigerant.

5. Drain the engine oil.

6. Disconnect the negative battery cable.

7. Remove the air cleaner outlet pipe and the air cleaner.

8. Remove the fresh air inlet duct.

9. Disconnect the fuel tube.

10. Remove the upper radiator sight shield.

11. Remove the 6 bolts and the 2 upper radiator support brackets.

12. Disconnect the A/C pressure switch electrical connector.

13. Remove the 2 power steering fluid reservoir bolts and secure the power steering fluid reservoir to the engine.

14. Disconnect the degas bottle coolant hose and the Positive Crankcase Ventilation (PCV) tube from the upper intake manifold.

15. Detach the retainer from the upper intake manifold and position the PCV tube and degas bottle coolant hose aside.

16. Disconnect the coolant hose and brake booster hose from the upper intake manifold. Detach the retainers and position the brake booster vacuum hose aside.

❋❋ CAUTION

To disconnect the quick release coupling, squeeze the tabs and pull straight out or damage to the coupling can occur.

17. Disconnect the Evaporative Emissions (EVAP) hose from the canister purge valve.

18. Remove the nut and disconnect the A/C manifold tube.

19. Remove the ground strap bolt.

20. Loosen the bolt and disconnect the main engine wiring harness connector.

21. Loosen the bolt and disconnect the main transmission wiring harness connector.

22. Disconnect the 2 engine wiring harness connectors.

23. Detach the wiring harness retainer from the bracket.

24. Disconnect the coolant valve electrical connector and detach the wiring retainer.

25. Remove the splash shields.

26. Remove the inner air deflector.

27. Remove the catalytic converters..

❋❋ CAUTION

Index-mark (color paint) the bolts, washers, nuts and the flex coupling to the transmission flange to make sure they are installed in the same

location. Components that are not assembled in their original locations can cause driveshaft imbalance. Do not remove the bolts retaining the flex coupling to the driveshaft.

28. Index-mark the front driveshaft pinion flange. Remove the 3 nuts, washers and bolts.

29. Slide the front shaft assembly rearward and support it.

➡**The top heater hose has a green identifying mark to match the hose on the dual coolant flow valve. If the mark is not visible, identify the hoses for location. This will aid in the correct installation of the hose assemblies.**

30. Disconnect the 3 quick-disconnect couplings from the coolant control valve hoses.

31. Remove the nut and disconnect the A/C high-pressure tube at the right frame rail.

32. Disconnect the A/C suction tube.

33. Remove the safety clip and disconnect the A/C tube.

34. Position the right and left hand inner fender splash shields aside.

35. Remove the 3 pin-type retainers and position the inner splash shields aside.

36. Disconnect the 2 anti-lock brake sensor electrical connectors.

37. Detach the right and left hand anti-lock brake sensor harnesses from the brake hose clips.

❋❋ CAUTION

Do not allow the brake caliper to hang from the brake hose or damage to the brake hose can occur.

38. Remove the 4 bolts and position the front brake calipers aside. Support the calipers using mechanic's wire.

➡**To remove the nut, first loosen the nut, then use the hex-holding feature to prevent the stabilizer bar link ball joint from turning while removing the nut.**

39. Remove the 2 nuts and disconnect the stabilizer bar links from the lower control arms.

➡**To remove the nut, first loosen the nut, then use the hex-holding feature to prevent the upper ball joint stud from turning while removing the nut.**

40. Remove the 2 nuts and disconnect the upper ball joints from the wheel knuckles.

41. Remove the 2 strut-to-control arm bolts and nuts.

42. Disconnect the shift cable from the shifter.

43. Remove the 2 shift cable bracket-to-body bolts.

44. Detach the shift cable pin-type retainer from the exhaust heat shield.

45. Disconnect the Variable Assist Power Steering (VAPS) actuator electrical connector.

46. Detach the power steering return tube from the Power Steering Pressure (PSP) tube clip.

47. Remove the steering intermediate shaft bolt.

❋❋ CAUTION

Do not allow the steering w heel to rotate while the steering column intermediate shaft is disconnected or damage to the clockspring can result. If there is evidence that the wheel has rotated, the clockspring must be removed and recentered.

48. Remove the bolt and detach the steering column intermediate shaft from the steering gear.

49. Remove the nut and detach the PSP tube bracket from the oil pan stud bolt.

50. Remove the bolt and detach the PSP tube bracket from the left hand frame rail.

51. If equipped, disconnect the block heater electrical connector.

52. Remove the nut and detach the ground strap.

53. Remove the starter motor terminal cover.

54. Remove the nuts and position the starter motor cables aside.

55. Remove the nut and disconnect the B+ terminal from the alternator.

56. Remove the torque converter access cover.

➡**Mark one stud and the flexplate for assembly reference.**

57. Remove the 4 torque converter nuts.

58. Remove the engine-to-transmission bolt.

59. Remove the 4 lower engine-to-transmission bolts.

60. Support the rear of the vehicle with suitable safety stands.

61. Using the tools in the accompanying illustration, support the engine, transmission, front and center crossmembers and the cooling system.

62. Remove the 5 transmission crossmember bolts.

63. Remove the 4 center crossmember I brace bolts.

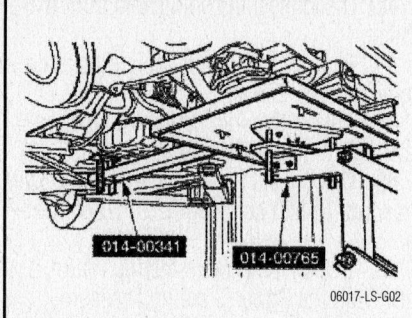

Fig. 76 Using the tools illustrated, support the engine, transmission, front and center crossmembers and the cooling system

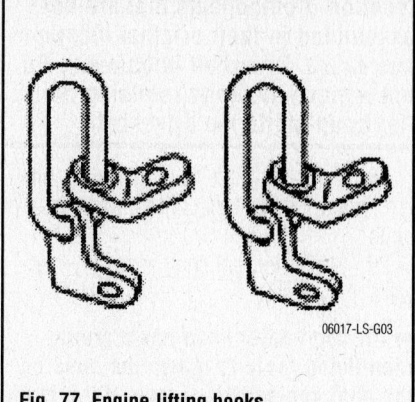

Fig. 77 Engine lifting hooks

64. Remove the 8 front and center crossmember bolts.

65. Using the tools illustrated, carefully lower the entire assembly from the vehicle.

66. Detach the 2 wire harness retainers and position the harness aside.

67. Remove the 2 bolts, the stud bolt and the starter motor.

68. Rotate the accessory drive belt tensioner counterclockwise and remove the accessory drive belt.

69. Disconnect the A/C compressor electrical connector.

70. Remove the 4 bolts and position the A/C compressor and manifold assembly aside.

71. Disconnect the Power Steering Pressure (PSP) switch electrical connector.

72. Remove the 3 bolts and position the power steering pump and reservoir aside.

73. Disconnect the coolant inlet hose.

74. Disconnect the heater hose and the lower radiator hose from the coolant pump.

75. If equipped, disconnect the oil cooler hoses.

76. Remove the nut and detach the transmission cooler tube bracket from the oil pan.

77. Install the lifting hook 303-050.

78. Using an engine crane support the engine and transmission.

79. Remove the right and left hand engine mount nut.

80. Remove the engine and transmission from the crossmember and cooling system assembly. Rest on the floor or on a bench.

81. Disconnect the transmission oil cooler tubes and plug the openings.

82. Remove the 5 transmission-to-engine bolts.

83. Using the special tools and a suitable engine crane, separate the engine from the transmission.

To install:

84. Using the special tools and a suitable engine crane, align the engine with the transmission.

85. Install the 5 transmission-to-engine bolts and tighten to 33 ft. lbs. (45 Nm).

86. Connect the transmission oil cooler tubes and tighten the fittings. Tighten to 15 ft. lbs (20 Nm).

87. Position the engine and transmission on the crossmember and cooling system assembly.

88. Install the right hand engine mount nut and tighten to 46 ft. lbs. (63 Nm).

89. Install the left hand engine mount nut and tighten to 46 ft. lbs. (63 Nm).

90. Attach the transmission cooler tube bracket to the oil pan and install the nut.

91. If equipped, connect the oil cooler hoses.

92. Connect the heater hose and the lower radiator hose to the coolant pump.

93. Connect the coolant inlet hose.

94. Position the power steering pump and install the 3 bolts. Tighten to 18 ft. lbs. (25 Nm).

95. Secure the power steering fluid reservoir to the engine.

96. Connect the PSP switch electrical connector.

97. Position the A/C compressor and manifold assembly. Install the 4 bolts and tighten to 18 ft. lbs. (25 Nm).

98. Connect the A/C compressor electrical connector.

99. Rotate the accessory drive belt tensioner counterclockwise and install the accessory drive belt.

100. Position the starter motor and install the 2 bolts and the stud bolt. Tighten to 18 ft. lbs. (25 Nm).

101. Position the wiring harness and attach the 2 retainers.

102. Carefully position the entire assembly into the vehicle.

103. Install the 8 front and center crossmember bolts. Tighten to 76 ft. lbs. (103 Nm).

104. Install the 4 center crossmember I brace bolts. Tighten to 76 ft. lbs. (103 Nm).

105. Install the 4 transmission crossmember bolts. Tighten to 41 ft. lbs. (55 Nm).

106. Install the 4 lower engine-to-transmission bolts. Tighten to 33 ft. lbs. (45 Nm).

107. Install the engine-to-transmission bolt. Tighten to 33 ft. lbs. (45 Nm).

108. Install the engine-to-transmission bolt. Tighten to 33 ft. lbs. (45 Nm).

109. Install the 4 torque converter nuts. Tighten to 28 ft. lbs. (38 Nm).

110. Install the torque converter access cover.

111. Connect the B+ terminal to the alternator and install the nut.

112. Position the starter motor cables and install the nuts.

113. Install the starter motor terminal cover.

114. Position the ground strap and install the nut. Tighten to 89 inch lbs. (10 Nm).

115. If equipped, connect the block heater electrical connector.

116. Position the PSP tube bracket and install the bolt.

117. Attach the PSP tube bracket to the oil pan stud bolt and install the nut. Tighten to 71 inch lbs. (8 Nm)

✸✸ CAUTION

Do not allow the steering wheel to rotate while the steering column intermediate shaft is disconnected or damage to the clockspring can result. If there is evidence that the wheel has rotated, the clockspring must be removed and recentered.

118. Attach the steering column intermediate shaft to the steering gear and install the bolt. Tighten to 26 ft. lbs. (35 Nm).

119. Install the steering intermediate shaft bolt. Tighten to 22ft. lbs. (30 Nm).

120. Attach the power steering return tube to the PSP tube clip.

121. Connect the VAPS actuator electrical connector.

122. Attach the shift cable pin-type retainer to the exhaust heat shield.

123. Position shift cable bracket and install the bolts. Tighten to 89 inch lbs. (10 Nm).

124. Connect the shift cable from the shifter.

125. Install the 2 strut-to-control arm bolts and nuts. Tighten to 129 ft. lbs. (175 Nm).

➡**To install the nut, first loosen the nut, then use the hex-holding feature to prevent the upper ball joint stud from turning while tightening the nut.**

126. Connect the upper ball joints to the wheel knuckles and install the 2 nuts. Tighten to 66 ft. lbs. (90 Nm).

127. To install the nut, first loosen the nut, then use the hex-holding feature to prevent the stabilizer bar link ball joint from turning while tightening the nut.

128. Connect the stabilizer bar links to the lower control arms and install the 2 nuts.

✳✳ CAUTION

Do not allow the brake caliper to hang from the brake hose or damage to the brake hose can occur.

129. Position the front brake calipers and install the 4 bolts. Tighten to 76 ft. lbs. (103 Nm).

130. Attach the right and left hand anti-lock brake sensor harnesses to the brake hose clips.

131. Connect the 2 anti-lock brake sensor electrical connectors.

132. Position the right and left hand inner fender splash shields aside.

133. Position the inner splash shields.

134. Install the 3 pin-type retainers.

135. Connect the A/C low pressure hose and install the safety clip.

136. Connect the A/C high-pressure tube at the right frame rail and install the nut. Tighten to 71 inch lbs. (8 Nm).

➡**Install the hoses to the marks made during the removal procedure.**

137. Connect the three quick-disconnect couplings to the coolant control valve hoses.

✳✳ CAUTION

Install the bolts, washers and nuts in their original positions or driveshaft NVH can occur. Install the driveshaft flex coupling bolts with the head of the bolt seated against the flange and the nuts seated against the flex coupling.

➡**The bolt heads are serrated. Hold the bolt and tighten the nut. Install the bolts, washers and nuts. Coat the nut and bolt threads with sealer. Tighten to 60 ft. lbs. (81 Nm).**

138. Install the catalytic converters.

139. Install the inner air deflector.

140. Install the splash shields.

141. Connect the coolant valve electrical connector and attach the wiring retainer.

142. Attach the wiring harness retainer to the bracket.

143. Connect the 2 engine wiring harness connectors.

144. Position the main transmission wiring harness connector and tighten the bolt. Tighten to 53 inch lbs. (6 Nm).

145. Position the main engine wiring harness connector and tighten the bolt. Tighten to 53 inch lbs. (6 Nm).

146. Position the ground strap and install the bolt. Tighten to 89 inch lbs. (10 Nm).

147. Position the A/C manifold tube and install the nut. Tighten to 71 inch lbs. (8 Nm).

148. Connect EVAP hose to the canister purge valve.

149. Position the brake booster vacuum hose and attach the retainers.

150. Connect the brake booster vacuum hose to the upper intake manifold.

151. Connect the coolant hose to the upper intake manifold.

152. Position the PCV tube and degas bottle coolant hose. Attach the retainer to the upper intake manifold.

153. Connect the degas bottle coolant hose and the PCV tube to the upper intake manifold.

154. Position power steering fluid reservoir and install the 2 bolts. Tighten to 89 inch lbs. (10 Nm).

155. Connect the A/C pressure switch electrical connector.

156. Install the 2 upper radiator support brackets and the 6 bolts.

157. Install the upper radiator sight shield.

158. Connect the fuel tube.

159. Install the clean air inlet duct.

160. Install the air cleaner assembly.

161. Install the air cleaner outlet pipe and the air cleaner.

162. Fill the crankcase to the correct level.

163. Fill the cooling system.

164. Recharge the A/C system.

165. Connect the negative battery cable.

166. Start the engine and check for leaks.

3.9L Engine

1. Before servicing the vehicle, refer to the precautions in the beginning of this section.

2. Drain the cooling system.

3. Relieve the fuel system pressure.

4. Recover the A/C refrigerant.

5. Drain the engine oil.

6. Disconnect the negative battery cable.

✳✳ CAUTION

The engine appearance cover is equipped with a noise suppressor. If the noise suppressor becomes separated from the engine appearance cover it must be positioned on the intake manifold prior to installing the engine appearance cover.

7. Remove the engine appearance cover and the noise suppressor, if detached.

8. Remove the air cleaner assembly and outlet pipe

9. Remove the fresh air inlet duct.

10. Disconnect the fuel supply tube.

11. Remove the upper radiator sight shield.

12. Remove the 6 bolts and the 2 upper radiator support brackets.

✳✳ CAUTION

To disconnect the quick release coupling, squeeze the tabs and pull straight out or damage to the coupling can occur.

13. Disconnect the Evaporative Emissions (EVAP) hose from the canister purge valve.

14. Disconnect the vacuum hose.

15. Disconnect the degas bottle hose.

16. Remove the 2 power steering reservoir bolts.

17. Remove the bolt and disconnect the ground strap.

18. Disconnect the engine wiring harness electrical connectors located on the backside of the right hand strut tower.

19. Disconnect the bulkhead electrical connectors.

20. Disconnect the coolant valve electrical connector, unclip from the radiator support and position the harness aside.

21. Disconnect the cooling fan electrical connector.

22. Disconnect the A/C pressure switch electrical connector.

23. Remove the splash shield.

24. Remove the inner air deflector.

25. Remove the catalytic converters.

✳✳ CAUTION

To make sure assembly will be in the exact location as when removed, index-mark the bolt, nut, washer and flex coupling to the pinion flange with paint or marker. Using a different color paint or marker, index-mark the second bolt, nut, washer and flex coupling to the pinion flange. These fasteners are balanced weights. Always assemble them in their original positions. Failure to do so can cause driveshaft Noise, Vibration and Harshness (NVH).

✳✳ CAUTION

Do not remove the bolts retaining the flex coupling to the driveshaft.

26. Index-mark the front driveshaft pinion flange. Remove the 3 nuts, washers and bolts. Slide the front shaft assembly rearward and support.

➡ **The top heater hose has a green identifying mark to match the hose on the dual coolant flow valve. If the mark is not visible, identify the hoses for location. This will aid in the correct installation of the hose assemblies.**

27. Disconnect the 3 heater hose quick release couplings.
28. Remove the nut and disconnect the A/C high pressure hose.
29. Disconnect the low pressure A/C hose.
30. Position the right and left hand inner splash shields aside.
31. Disconnect the right and left anti-lock brake sensor electrical connectors.
32. Detach the right and left anti-lock brake sensor harnesses from the brake hose clips.
33. Remove the 4 bolts and position the front brake calipers aside. Support the calipers using mechanic's wire.

➡ **To remove the nut, first loosen the nut, then use the hex-holding feature to prevent the stabilizer bar link ball joint from turning while removing the nut.**

34. Remove the 2 nuts and disconnect the stabilizer bar links from the lower control arms.

➡ **Use the hex-holding feature to prevent the stud from turning while removing the nut from ball joints and stabilizer bar links.**

35. Remove the 2 nuts and disconnect the upper ball joints from the wheel knuckles.
36. Remove the 2 strut-to-control arm bolts and nuts.
37. Disconnect the shift cable from the shifter.
38. Remove the 2 bolts and position the shift cable bracket aside.
39. Detach the shift cable pin-type retainer from the exhaust heat shield
40. Disconnect the Variable Assist Power Steering (VAPS) actuator electrical connector.
41. Release the power steering return hose from the pressure hose clip.
42. Remove the retaining bolt for the high pressure power steering hose bracket.
43. Disconnect the block heater electrical connector, if equipped.
44. Remove the steering shaft bolt.

✳✳ CAUTION

Do not allow the steering wheel to rotate while the steering column intermediate shaft is disconnected or damage to the clockspring can result. If there is evidence that the wheel has rotated, the clockspring must be removed and recentered.

45. Remove the bolt and disconnect the steering coupling.
46. Remove the nut and starter motor ground cable.
47. Remove the nuts and disconnect the starter motor wiring.
48. Disconnect the alternator electrical connector and pin-type retainer.
49. Remove the 6 lower transmission to engine bolts.
50. Remove the cover.

➡ **Make an identifying mark on the nut, the stud and adapter plate to allow for correct installation.**

51. Remove the 4 torque converter nuts.
52. Support the rear of the vehicle with suitable safety stands.
53. Support the engine, transmission, front and center crossmembers, and the cooling system with a powertrain lift and a transmission support bracket.
54. Remove the 4 transmission support bolts.
55. Remove the 4 right and left center crossmember I-brace bolts
56. Remove the 4 front crossmember and the 4 center crossmember bolts.
57. Carefully lower the entire assembly from the vehicle.

58. Remove the lower radiator hose bracket nut.
59. Disconnect the lower radiator, upper radiator and heater hose.
60. Disconnect the 2 oil cooler hoses, if equipped.
61. Rotate the tensioner and remove the accessory drive belt.
62. Disconnect the A/C compressor and Power Steering Pressure (PSP) switch electrical connectors.
63. Remove the 4 bolts and position the A/C compressor aside.
64. Remove the power steering tube bracket nut.
65. Remove the 4 bolts and position aside the power steering pump and reservoir.
66. Remove the transmission cooler tube bracket nut.
67. Disconnect the transmission cooler tubes.
68. Install the lifting hooks 303-050.
69. Using an engine crane, support the engine and transmission.
70. Remove the right and left hand upper engine mount nuts.
71. Using an engine hoist and the lifting hooks, move the engine and transmission from the crossmember and cooling system assembly to rest on the floor or on a bench.
72. Remove the nuts and position the wiring harness aside.
73. Remove the bolts and separate the engine from the transmission.

To install:
74. Align the flexplate to converter marks made during engine removal.
75. Install the engine to the transmission and install the bolts. Tighten to 35 ft. lbs. (47 Nm).
76. Position the wiring harness and install the 2 nuts.
77. Using the lifting hooks and an engine crane, move the engine and transmission onto the crossmember and cooling system assembly.
78. Install the right and left hand upper engine mount nuts. Tighten to 37 ft. lbs. (50 Nm).
79. Connect the transmission cooler tubes. Tighten to 26 ft. lbs. (35 Nm).
80. Install the transmission cooler tube bracket nut.
81. Install the power steering pump and 4 bolts. Tighten to 18 ft. lbs. (25 Nm).
82. Install the power steering tube bracket nut. Tighten to 13 ft. lbs. (18 Nm).
83. Install the A/C compressor and 4 bolts. Tighten to 18 ft. lbs. (25 Nm).
84. Connect the A/C compressor and PSP switch electrical connectors.

85. Install the accessory drive belt.

86. Connect the 2 oil cooler hoses, if equipped.

87. Connect the lower radiator, upper radiator and heater hose.

88. Install the lower radiator hose bracket nut.

89. Using the powertrain lift and the transmission support bracket, carefully raise the entire assembly into the vehicle.

90. Install the 4 front crossmember and the 4 center crossmember bolts. Tighten to 76 ft. lbs. (103 Nm).

91. Install the 4 right and left hand center crossmember I-brace bolts. Tighten to 76 ft. lbs. (103 Nm).

92. Install the 4 transmission support bolts. Tighten to 30 ft. lbs. (40 Nm).

93. Install the 4 torque converter nuts. Tighten to 28 ft. lbs. (38 Nm).

94. Install the cover.

95. Install the 6 lower transmission to engine bolts. Tighten to 35 ft. lbs. (47 Nm).

96. Connect the alternator electrical connector and pin-type retainer.

97. Connect the starter motor wiring and install the nuts.

98. Install the cover.

99. Install the starter motor ground cable and nut.

❋❋ CAUTION

Do not allow the steering wheel to rotate while the steering column intermediate shaft is disconnected or damage to the clockspring can result. If there is evidence that the wheel has rotated, the clockspring must be removed and recentered.

100. Connect the steering coupling and install the bolt. Tighten to 26 ft. lbs. (35 Nm).

101. Install the steering shaft bolt. Tighten to 22 ft. lbs. (30 Nm).

102. Connect the block heater electrical connector, if equipped.

103. Install the retaining bolt for the high pressure power steering hose bracket.

104. Attach the power steering return hose to the pressure hose clip.

105. Connect the VAPS actuator electrical connector.

106. Attach the shift cable pin-type retainer to the exhaust heat shield

107. Install the shift cable bracket and 2 bolts.

108. Connect the shift cable to the shifter.

109. Install the 2 strut-to-control arm bolts and nuts. Tighten to 129 ft. lbs. (175 Nm).

110. Position the upper ball joints into the wheel knuckles and install the 2 nuts. Tighten to 66 ft. lbs. (90 Nm).

111. Position the stabilizer bar links into the lower control arms and install the 2 nuts. Tighten to 41 ft. lbs. (55 Nm).

112. Install the front brake calipers and the 4 bolts. Tighten to 26 ft. lbs. (35 Nm).

113. Attach the right and left hand anti-lock brake sensor harnesses to the brake hose clips.

114. Connect the right and left hand anti-lock brake sensor electrical connectors.

115. Install the right and left hand inner splash shields.

116. Connect the low pressure A/C hose.

117. Connect the A/C high pressure hose and install the nut. Tighten to 71 inch lbs. (8 Nm).

➡**The top heater hose has a green identifying mark to match the hose on the dual coolant flow valve. This will aid in the correct installation of the hose assemblies.**

➡**Hose assemblies shown with components removed for clarity.**

118. Connect the 3 heater hose quick release couplings.

❋❋ CAUTION

Install the bolts, washers and nuts in their original positions or driveshaft NVH can occur. Install the driveshaft flex coupling bolts with the head of the bolt seated against the flange and the nuts seated against the flex coupling.

➡**The bolt heads are serrated. Hold the bolt and tighten the nut.**

119. Install the bolts, washers and nuts. Coat the nut and bolt threads with sealer. Tighten to 60 ft. lbs. (81 Nm).

120. Install the catalytic converters.

121. Install the inner air deflector.

122. Install the splash shields.

123. Connect the A/C pressure switch electrical connector.

124. Connect the cooling fan electrical connector.

125. Connect the coolant valve electrical connector and attach the wiring harness clip to the radiator support.

126. Connect the bulkhead electrical connectors.

127. Connect the engine wiring harness electrical connectors.

128. Position the ground strap and install the bolt. Tighten to 89 inch lbs. (10 Nm).

129. Install the power steering reservoir and 2 bolts. Tighten the top bolt to 53 inch lbs. (6 Nm) and the bottom bolt to 9 ft. lbs. (12 Nm).

130. Connect the degas bottle hose.

131. Connect the vacuum hose.

132. Connect the EVAP hose to the canister purge valve.

133. Install the 2 upper radiator support brackets and the 6 bolts.

134. Install the upper radiator sight shield.

135. Connect the fuel supply tube.

136. Install the fresh air inlet duct.

137. Install the air cleaner assembly and outlet pipe.

138. Connect the battery ground cable.

139. Fill and bleed the engine cooling system.

❋❋ CAUTION

The engine appearance cover is equipped with a noise suppressor. If the noise suppressor becomes separated from the engine appearance cover it must be positioned on the intake manifold prior to installing the engine appearance cover.

140. Install the noise suppressor and the engine appearance cover.

141. Fill the crankcase to the correct level.

142. Fill the cooling system.

143. Recharge the A/C system.

144. Connect the negative battery cable.

145. Start the engine and check for leaks.

EXHAUST MANIFOLD

REMOVAL & INSTALLATION

3.0L Engine

See Figures 78 and 79.

1. Before servicing the vehicle, refer to the precautions in the beginning of this section.

2. Remove or disconnect the following:
   • Negative battery cable
   • Heat shields
   • Lower splash shields
   • Exhaust front pipes
   • Secondary air tubes
   • Exhaust Gas Recirculation (EGR) tube
   • Exhaust manifolds

To install:

3. Install the exhaust manifolds. Tighten the fasteners in sequence as follows:
   a. Step 1: 15 ft. lbs. (20 Nm)
   b. Step 2: 15 ft. lbs. (20 Nm)

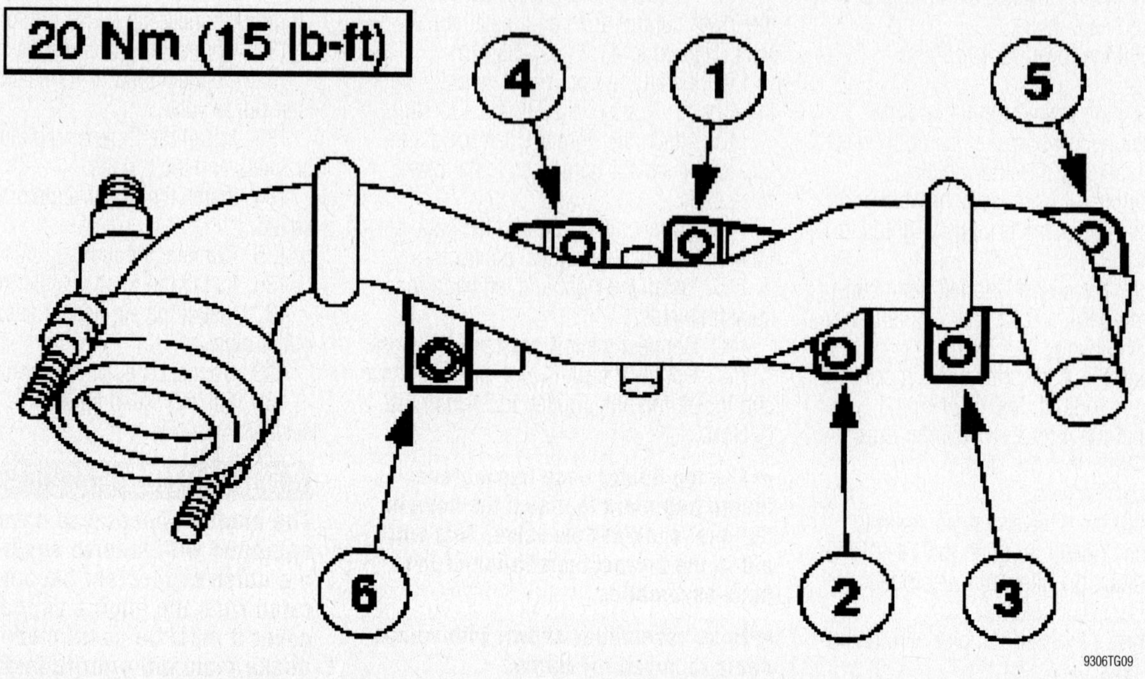
20 Nm (15 lb-ft)
4
1
5
6
2
3
9306TG09

Fig. 78 Right exhaust manifold torque sequence—3.0L engine

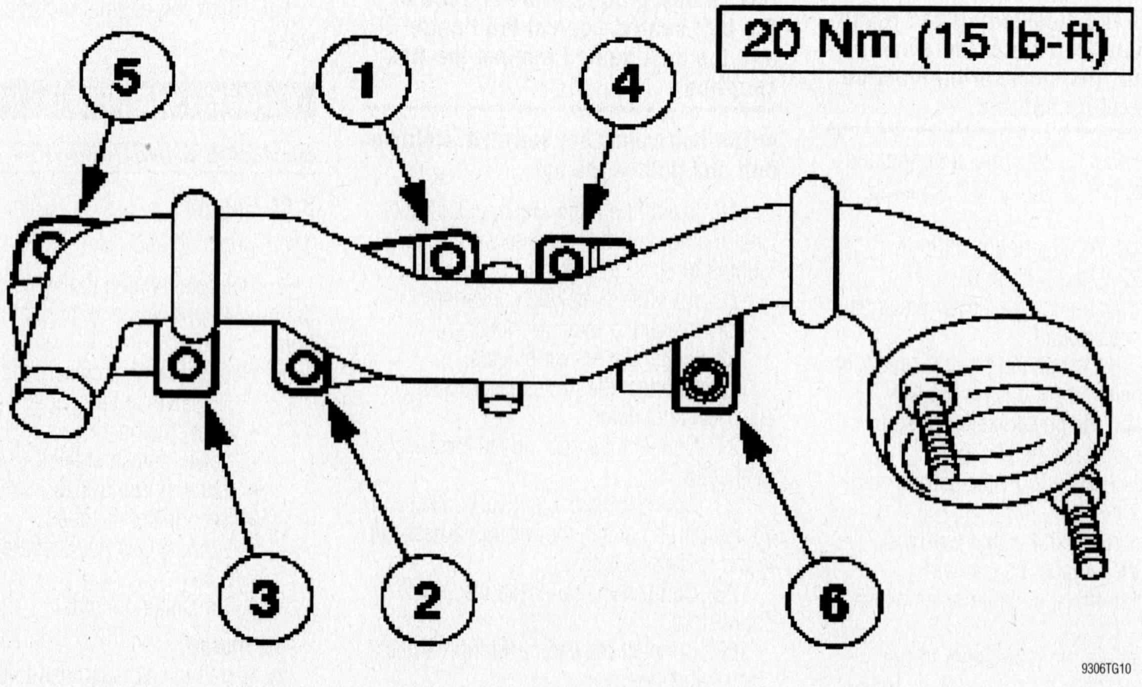
20 Nm (15 lb-ft)
5
1
4
3
2
6
9306TG10

Fig. 79 Left exhaust manifold torque sequence—3.0L engine

4. Install or connect the following:
- Exhaust Gas Recirculation (EGR) tube
- Secondary air tubes
- Exhaust front pipes
- Lower splash shields
- Heat shields
- Negative battery cable

5. Start the engine and check for leaks.

3.9L Engine

Right Side

See Figure 80.

1. Before servicing the vehicle, refer to the precautions in the beginning of this section.
2. Remove the catalytic converters.
3. Remove the starter motor.
4. Remove the screws and the lower right hand splash shield.
5. Remove the two Exhaust Gas Recirculation (EGR) tube flange nuts.
6. Remove the heat shield stud bolt.
7. Remove the four bolts and the heat shield.
8. Remove the eight bolts, spacers and the exhaust manifold.
9. Discard the exhaust manifold and EGR tube gaskets.

To install:

10. Position the new exhaust manifold gasket, the new EGR tube gasket and the exhaust manifold.
11. Install the spacers and exhaust manifold bolts hand-tight.
12. Install the EGR tube nuts and tighten to 15 ft. lbs. (20 Nm).
13. Tighten the manifold bolts to 18 ft. lbs. (25 Nm) in the sequence illustrated.
14. Install the heat shield and tighten the bolts.
15. Install the heat shield stud bolt and tighten to 37 ft. lbs. (50 Nm).
16. Install the lower splash shield and screws.

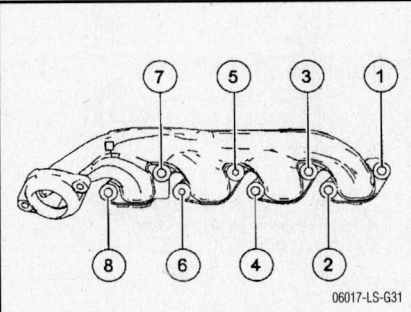

Fig. 80 Right side exhaust manifold tightening sequence—3.9L engine

17. Install the starter motor.
18. Install the catalytic converters.

Left Side

See Figure 81.

1. Before servicing the vehicle, refer to the precautions in the beginning of this section.
2. Remove the catalytic converters.
3. Remove the dipstick tube.
4. Remove the bolts and position the power steering reservoir aside
5. Remove the screws and the lower left hand splash shield.
6. Remove the heat shield stud bolt.
7. Remove the four bolts and the heat shield.
8. Remove the eight bolts, spacers and the exhaust manifold.
9. Discard the exhaust manifold and EGR tube gaskets.

To install:

10. Position the new exhaust manifold gasket and the exhaust manifold.
11. Install the spacers and tighten the manifold bolts to 18 ft. lbs. (25 Nm) in the sequence illustrated.
12. Install the heat shield and tighten the bolts.
13. Install the heat shield stud bolt and tighten to 37 ft. lbs. (50 Nm).
14. Install the lower splash shield and screws.
15. Position the power steering reservoir and tighten the upper bolt to 53 inch lbs. (6 Nm) and the lower bolt to 9 ft. lbs. (12 Nm).
16. Install the dipstick tube.
17. Install the catalytic converters.

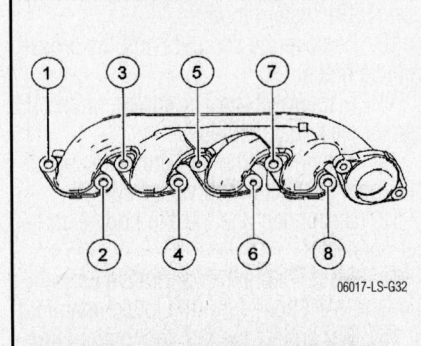

Fig. 81 Left side exhaust manifold tightening sequence—3.9L engine

INTAKE MANIFOLD

REMOVAL & INSTALLATION

3.0L Engine

See Figures 82 and 83.

1. Before servicing the vehicle, refer to the precautions in the beginning of this section.
2. Properly relieve the fuel system pressure.
3. Drain the cooling system.
4. Disconnect the negative battery cable.
5. Remove the air cleaner outlet pipe.
6. Remove the cowl panel grill.
7. Remove the seven bolts and the cross-vehicle brace.
8. Disconnect the Throttle Position (TP) sensor and electronic throttle control electrical connectors.
9. Disconnect the brake booster vacuum hose from the upper intake manifold.
10. Disconnect the Evaporative Emissions (EVAP) and Positive Crankcase Ventilation (PCV) tubes from the upper intake manifold.
11. Disconnect and plug the two coolant hoses from the upper intake manifold.
12. Detach the coolant hose and the PCV tube retainer from the upper intake manifold.
13. Disconnect the PCV tube from the PCV valve and position the PCV tube and coolant hose aside.
14. Remove the front upper intake manifold support brace-to-upper intake manifold bolt.
15. Disconnect the two Intake Manifold Tuning (IMT) valve electrical connectors.
16. Disconnect the fuel pressure sensor electrical connector and vacuum hose.
17. Remove three bolts and the fuel pressure sensor shield.
18. Remove the right hand upper intake manifold support brace-to-upper intake manifold bolt.
19. Remove the four upper intake manifold bolts and the upper intake manifold.
20. Remove the fuel line clip.
21. Install the tool 310-D005. Close the tool and push it into the open side of the cage.

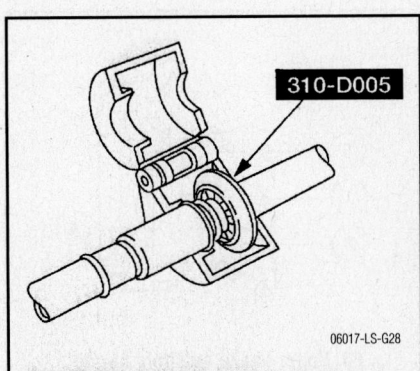

Fig. 82 Use tool 310-D005 to disconnect the fuel line coupling—3.0L engine

22. Separate the fitting and remove the tool.

23. Remove the fuel rail bracket bolt.

24. Disconnect the fuel pressure sensor vacuum tube.

25. Disconnect the fuel rail wiring harness electrical connector.

26. Remove the four bolts and the lower intake manifold.

To install:

➡ **Clean and inspect all sealing surfaces. Inspect and install new gaskets as necessary.**

27. Position the upper intake manifold and loosely install the 4 bolts.

28. Position the fuel pressure sensor shield and loosely install the two upper intake manifold bolts.

29. Tighten the upper intake manifold bolts in the sequence illustrated to 89 inch lbs. (10 Nm).

30. Install the right hand upper intake manifold support brace-to-upper intake manifold bolt. Tighten to 89 inch lbs. (10 Nm).

31. Install the fuel pressure sensor shield-to-upper intake manifold bolt. Tighten to 53 inch lbs. (6 Nm).

32. Connect the fuel pressure sensor electrical connector and vacuum hose.

33. Connect the two IMT valve electrical connectors.

34. Install the front upper intake manifold support brace-to-upper intake manifold bolt. Tighten to 89 inch lbs. (10 Nm).

35. Position the PCV tube and the coolant hose and attach the PCV tube to the PCV valve.

36. Attach the coolant hose and the PCV tube retainer to the upper intake manifold.

37. Connect the two coolant hoses to the upper intake manifold.

38. Connect the EVAP and PCV tubes to the upper intake manifold.

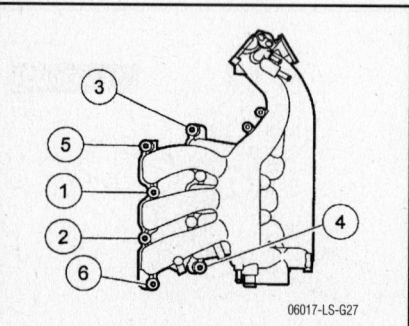

Fig. 83 Upper intake manifold torque sequence—3.0L engine

39. Connect the brake booster vacuum hose to the upper intake manifold.

40. Connect the TP sensor and electronic throttle control electrical connectors.

41. Position the cross-vehicle brace and install the seven bolts. Tighten to 15 ft. lbs. (20 Nm).

42. Install the cowl panel grill.

43. Install the air cleaner outlet pipe.

44. Fill the cooling system.

45. Connect the negative battery cable.

46. Start the engine and check for leaks.

3.9L Engine

See Figures 84 and 85.

1. Before servicing the vehicle, refer to the precautions in the beginning of this section.

2. Drain the cooling system.

3. Relieve the fuel system pressure.

4. Disconnect the negative battery cable.

✳✳ CAUTION

The engine appearance cover is equipped with a noise suppressor. If the noise suppressor becomes separated from the engine appearance cover it must be positioned on the intake manifold prior to installing the engine appearance cover.

5. Remove the engine appearance cover and the noise suppressor, if detached.

6. Remove the air cleaner outlet pipe.

7. Remove the cowl panel grille.

8. Disconnect the fuel supply tube spring lock coupling from the fuel rail.

9. Remove the Exhaust Gas Recirculation (EGR) system module.

10. Remove the six bolts and the cross-vehicle brace.

11. Disconnect the Throttle Position (TP) sensor electrical connector.

12. Disconnect the fuel pressure sensor electrical connector and vacuum hose.

13. Disconnect the throttle body electrical connector.

14. Disconnect the Evaporative Emissions (EVAP) hose from the intake manifold.

15. Disconnect the fuel rail temperature sensor electrical connector.

16. Remove the crankcase ventilation tube.

17. Disconnect the vacuum supply tube.

18. Detach the vacuum harness retainers from the left hand engine appearance cover bracket.

19. Detach the engine wiring harness from the engine appearance cover brackets.

20. Remove the four nuts and the two engine appearance cover brackets.

21. Disconnect the eight fuel injector electrical connectors.

22. Disconnect the radio interference ignition capacitor electrical connector.

23. Remove the two nuts and the engine wiring harness retainer.

24. Remove the nut and the radio interference ignition capacitor.

25. Remove the four fuel rail bolts.

26. Remove the fuel rail and injectors as an assembly.

27. Remove the clips and the 8 fuel injectors from the fuel rail.

28. Remove and discard the sixteen O-ring seals from the fuel injectors.

29. Disconnect and plug the 2 throttle body coolant tubes.

➡ **It is not necessary to remove the throttle body and adapter to remove the intake manifold.**

30. Remove the seven bolts and three studs in the sequence illustrated.

31. Remove the intake manifold and discard the gaskets.

To install:

✳✳ CAUTION

Do not use metal scrapers, wire brushes, power abrasive discs, or other abrasive means to clean the sealing surfaces. These tools cause scratches and gouges, which make leak paths. Use a plastic scraping tool to clean the surfaces.

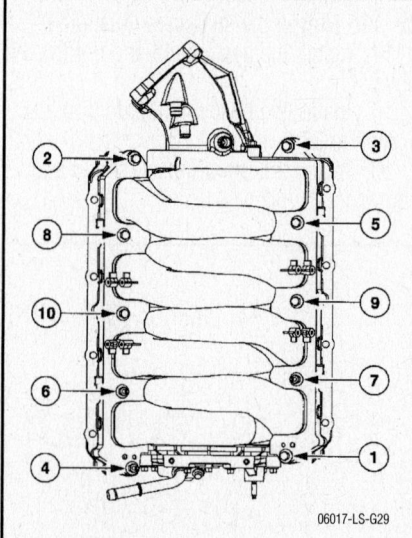

Fig. 84 Intake manifold loosening sequence—3.9L engine

32. Clean the gasket sealing surfaces.

33. Install new gaskets, the intake manifold, the seven bolts and the three studs. Tighten in the sequence illustrated to 15 ft. lbs. (20 Nm).

34. Unplug and connect the two throttle body coolant tubes.

❋❋ CAUTION

Use O-ring seals that are made of special fuel-resistant material. Use of ordinary O-rings can cause the fuel system to leak. Do not reuse the O-ring seals.

35. Install sixteen new O-ring seals onto the fuel injectors. Lubricate the O-ring seals with clean engine oil prior to installation.

36. Install the fuel injectors and clips onto the fuel rail.

37. Install the fuel rail and injectors as an assembly. Tighten the fuel rail bolts to 89 inch lbs. (10 Nm).

38. Install the radio interference ignition capacitors and nuts. Tighten to 89 inch lbs. (10 Nm).

39. Install the engine wiring harness retainer and the two nuts. Tighten to 89 inch lbs. (10 Nm).

40. Connect the radio interference ignition capacitor electrical connectors.

41. Connect the fuel injector electrical connectors.

42. Install the engine appearance cover brackets and the nuts.

43. Attach the engine wiring harness to the engine appearance cover brackets.

44. Attach the vacuum harness retainers to the left hand engine appearance cover bracket.

45. Connect the vacuum supply tube.

46. Install the crankcase ventilation tube.

47. Connect the fuel rail temperature sensor electrical connector.

48. Connect the EVAP hose to the intake manifold.

49. Connect the throttle body electrical connector.

50. Connect the fuel pressure sensor electrical connector and vacuum hose.

51. Connect the TP sensor electrical connector. Tighten to 15 ft. lbs. (20 Nm)

52. Install the six bolts and the cross-vehicle brace.

53. Install the EGR system module.

54. Install the air cleaner outlet pipe.

55. Connect the fuel supply tube spring lock coupling to the fuel rail.

❋❋ CAUTION

The engine appearance cover is equipped with a noise suppressor. If the noise suppressor becomes separated from the engine appearance cover it must be positioned on the intake manifold prior to installing the engine appearance cover.

56. Install the noise suppressor and the engine appearance cover.

57. Install the cowl panel grille.

58. Fill the cooling system.

59. Connect the negative battery cable.

60. Start the engine and check for leaks.

OIL PAN

REMOVAL & INSTALLATION

3.0L Engine

See Figure 86.

1. Before servicing the vehicle, refer to the precautions in the beginning of this section.

2. Drain the engine oil.

3. Install a support fixture to the engine lifting eyes.

4. Remove or disconnect the following:
- Negative battery cable
- Air cleaner outlet tube
- Accessory drive belt
- Alternator
- Center and right splash shields
- A/C compressor
- Electronic Thermactor Air (ETA) bracket, if equipped
- Rack and pinion steering gear
- Lower control arm through bolts
- Transmission cooler line bracket
- Engine mount nuts
- Left and right subframe bolts. Pry the subframe down for clearance.
- Wiring harness bracket
- Oil pan

To install:

5. Install or connect the following:
- Oil pan. Tighten the pan bolts in sequence to 18 ft. lbs. (25 Nm) and the transmission bolts to 35 ft. lbs. (47 Nm).
- Wiring harness bracket
- Left and right subframe bolts. Tighten the bolts to 76 ft. lbs. (103 Nm).

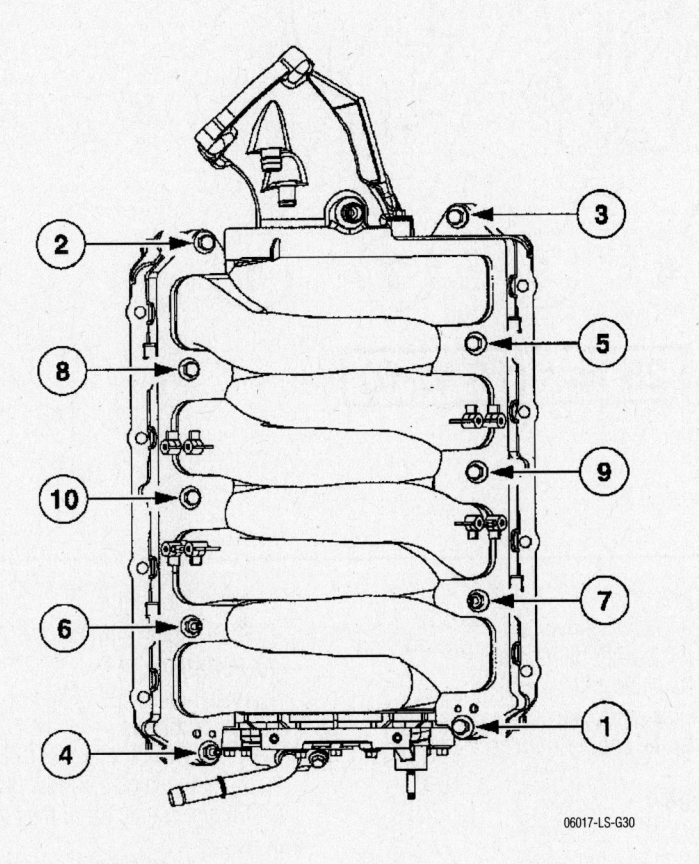

06017-LS-G30

Fig. 85 Intake manifold tightening sequence—3.9L engine

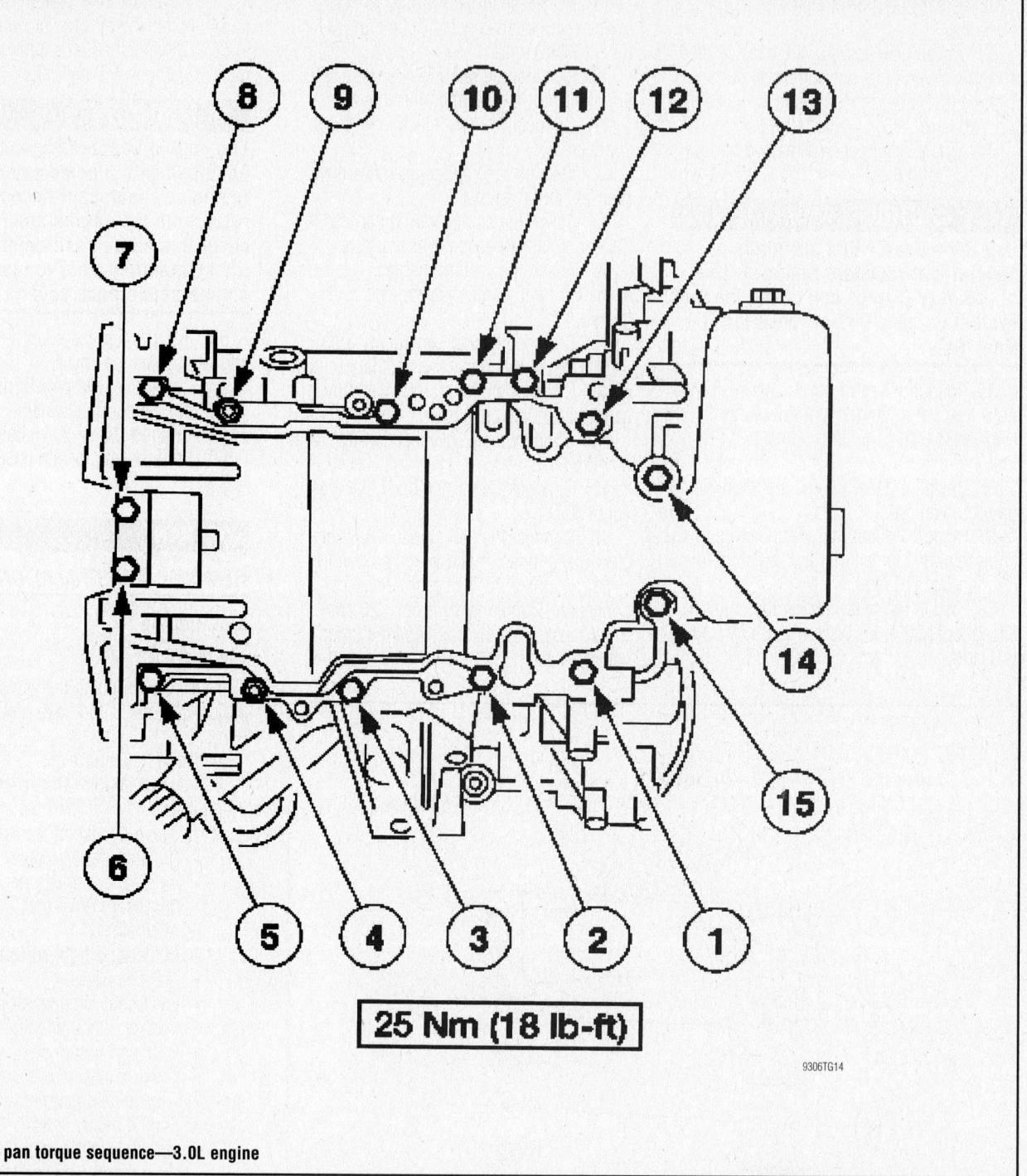

25 Nm (18 lb-ft)

9306TG14

Fig. 86 Oil pan torque sequence—3.0L engine

- Engine mount nuts. Tighten the nuts to 46 ft. lbs. (63 Nm).
- Transmission cooler line bracket
- Lower control arm through bolts. Tighten the bolts to 129 ft. lbs. (175 Nm).
- Rack and pinion steering gear. Tighten the nuts to 76 ft. lbs. (103 Nm).
- ETA bracket, if equipped
- A/C compressor
- Center and right splash shields

- Alternator
- Accessory drive belt
- Air cleaner outlet tube
- Negative battery cable
6. Fill the crankcase to the correct level.
7. Start the engine and check for leaks.

3.9L Engine

See Figure 87.

1. Before servicing the vehicle, refer to the precautions in the beginning of this section.

2. Drain the engine oil.
3. Remove the oil pan.

To install:

4. Install the oil pan. Tighten the bolts in sequence as follows:

    a. Step 1: 44 inch lbs. (5 Nm)

    b. Step 2: 108 inch lbs. (12 Nm)

5. Fill the crankcase to the correct level.

6. Start the engine and check for leaks.

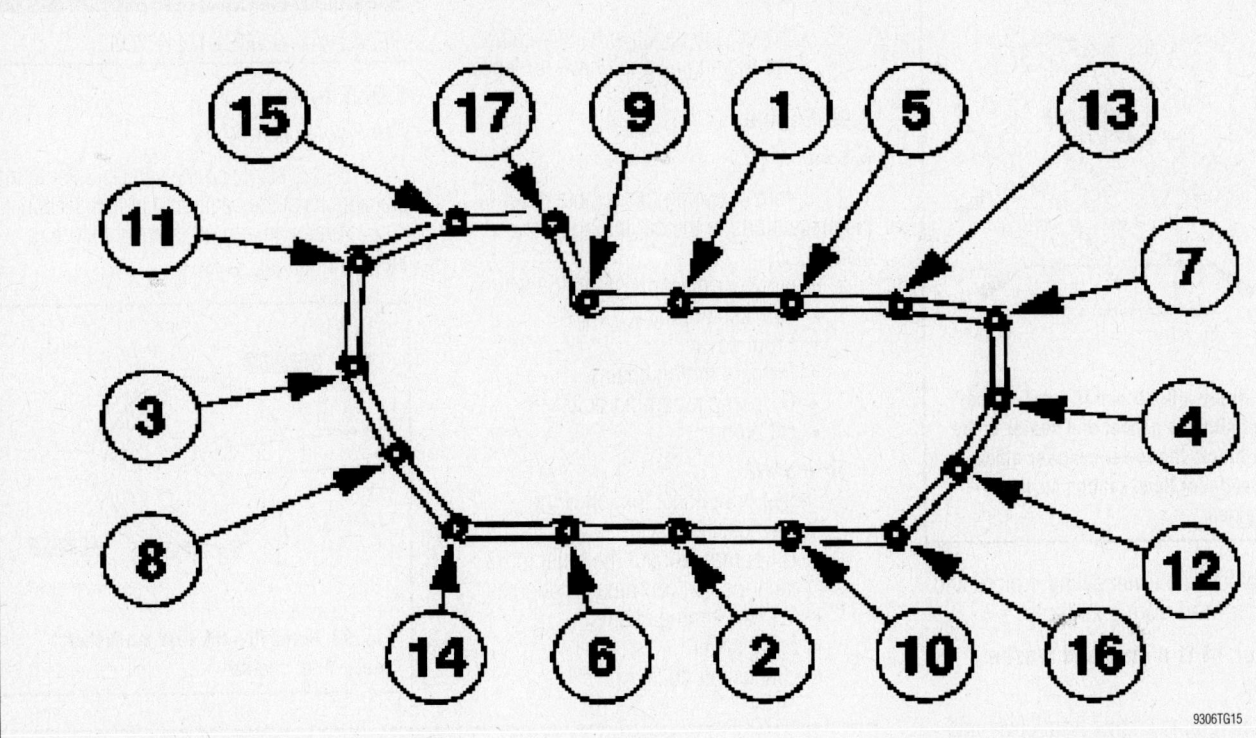

Fig. 87 Oil pan torque sequence—3.9L engine

OIL PUMP

REMOVAL & INSTALLATION

3.0L Engine

See Figures 88 through 91.

1. Before servicing the vehicle, refer to the precautions in the beginning of this manual.
2. Disconnect the negative battery cable.
3. Drain the cooling system.
4. Remove the valve covers.
5. Remove the accessory drive belt tensioner and idler pulleys.
6. Remove the water pump.
7. Disconnect the upper and lower radiator hoses.

8. Remove the oil pan.
9. Remove the power steering pump.
10. Remove the crankshaft front seal.
11. Disconnect the two Camshaft Position (CMP) sensors and the Crankshaft Position (CKP) sensor electrical connectors.
12. Remove fifteen bolts, the stud bolt and the engine front cover. Discard the gaskets.
13. Remove the timing chain components.
14. Remove the two bolts and the oil pump screen and pickup tube.
15. Remove the four oil pump bolts in the sequence illustrated. Remove the pump.

To install:

16. Position the oil pump and install the bolts. Tighten in the sequence shown to 89 inch lbs. (10 Nm).

➡Inspect and install a new oil pump screen and pickup tube O-ring seal as necessary. Lubricate the oil pump screen and pickup tube O-ring seal with clean engine oil.

17. Position the oil pump screen and pickup tube and install the bolts. Tighten to 89 inch lbs. (10 Nm).
18. Install the timing chain components.

❊❊ CAUTION

Do not use metal scrapers, wire brushes, power abrasive discs or other abrasive means to clean the sealing surfaces. These tools cause scratches and gouges which make leak paths.

19. Use a plastic scraping tool to remove all traces of sealant from the front cover. Clean all sealing surfaces with silicone gasket remover and metal surface prep.
20. Install a new gasket on the engine front cover.

➡The engine front cover must be installed and the bolts tightened within four minutes of applying sealant.

21. Apply a 0.23 inch (6 mm) diameter dot of silicone gasket and sealer to the

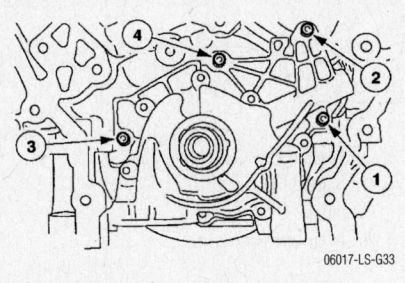

Fig. 88 Oil pump loosening sequence— 3.0L engines

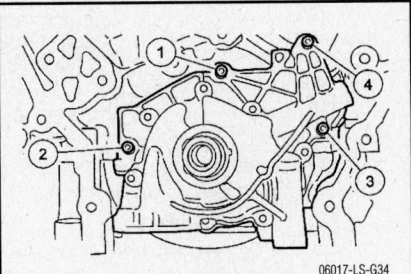

Fig. 89 Oil pump tightening sequence— 3.0L engines

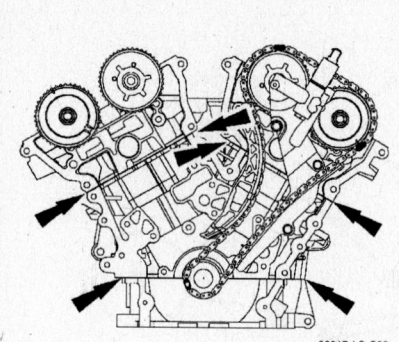

Fig. 90 Apply a 0.23 inch (6 mm) diameter dot of silicone gasket and sealer to the cylinder block, the lower cylinder block and the cylinder head mating surfaces— 3.0L engines

cylinder block, the lower cylinder block and the cylinder head mating surfaces.

➡**Number 14 is a stud and washer assembly.**

22. Position the engine front cover and install the bolts and the stud bolt. Tighten in the sequence illustrated to 18 ft. lbs (25 Nm).

23. Connect the CMP sensors and the CKP sensor electrical connectors.

24. Install the crankshaft front seal

25. Install the power steering pump.

26. Install the oil pan.

27. Connect the radiator hoses.

28. Install the water pump.

29. Install the accessory drive belt tensioner and idler pulleys.

30. Install the valve covers.

31. Fill and bleed the cooling system.

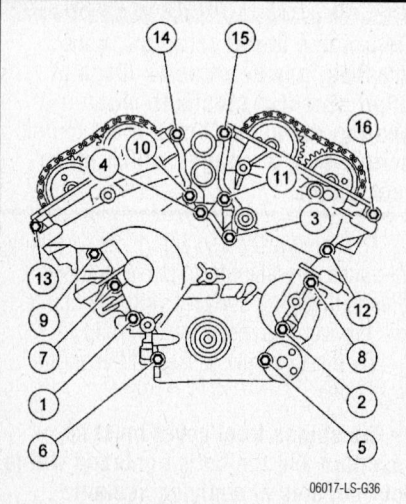

Fig. 91 Front cover torque sequence— 3.0L engines

32. Fill the engine with correct type and amount of oil.

33. Connect the negative battery cable.

34. Start the engine and check for leaks.

3.9L Engine

See Figure 92.

1. Before servicing the vehicle, refer to the precautions in the beginning of this manual.

2. Remove or disconnect the following:
   - Crankshaft pulley
   - Front cover
   - Primary timing chains
   - Oil pump mounting bolts
   - Oil pump

To install:

3. Install or connect the following:
   - New gasket
   - Oil pump. Tighten the bolts to 53 inch lbs. (6 Nm) plus 90 degrees.
   - Primary timing chains
   - Front cover
   - Crankshaft pulley

REAR MAIN SEAL

REMOVAL & INSTALLATION

3.0L Engine

See Figures 93 and 94.

1. Before servicing the vehicle, refer to the precautions at the beginning of this section.

2. Attach an engine support fixture to the engine lifting eyes.

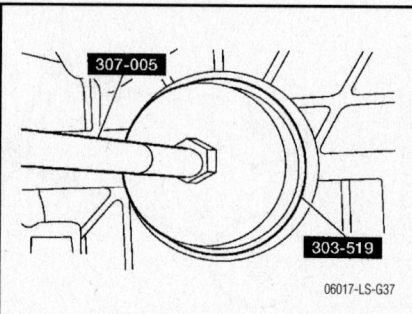

Fig. 93 Removing the rear crankshaft seal—3.0L engine

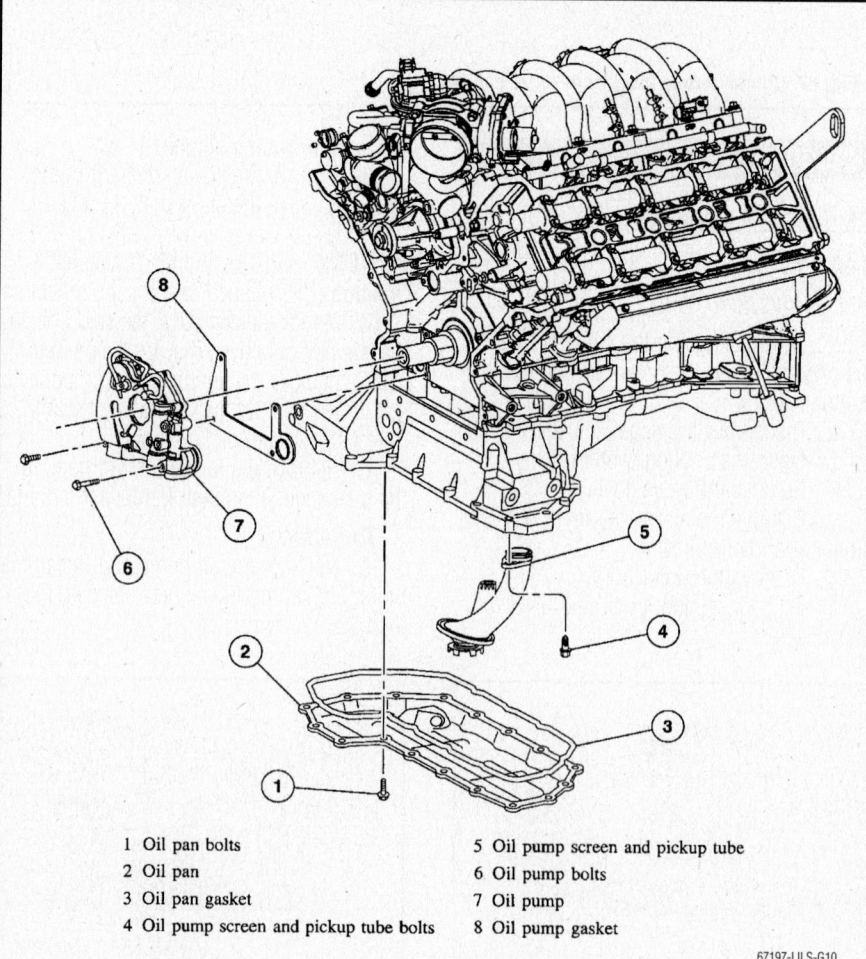

1 Oil pan bolts		5 Oil pump screen and pickup tube	
2 Oil pan		6 Oil pump bolts	
3 Oil pan gasket		7 Oil pump	
4 Oil pump screen and pickup tube bolts		8 Oil pump gasket	

Fig. 92 Oil pump mounting—3.9L engine

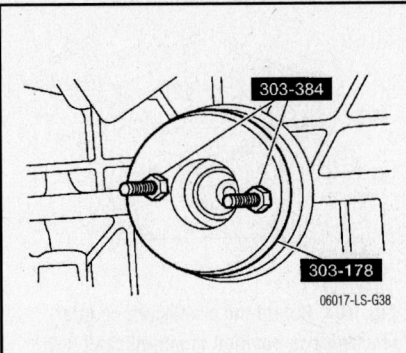

Fig. 94 Installing the rear crankshaft seal—3.0L engine

3. Remove or disconnect the following:
  • Negative battery cable
  • Transmission
  • Flywheel
  • Rear crankshaft seal using the tools illustrated.

To install:

4. Install or connect the following:
  • Rear main seal flush with the cylinder block surface using the tools illustrated
  • Flywheel. Tighten the bolts to 59 ft. lbs. (80 Nm).
  • Transmission
  • Negative battery cable
5. Start the engine and check for leaks.

3.9L Engine

See Figures 95 through 97.

1. Before servicing the vehicle, refer to the precautions at the beginning of this section.
2. Attach an engine support fixture to the engine lifting eyes.
3. Remove or disconnect the following:
  • Negative battery cable
  • Transmission
  • Flywheel
  • Rear crankshaft seal using the tools illustrated.

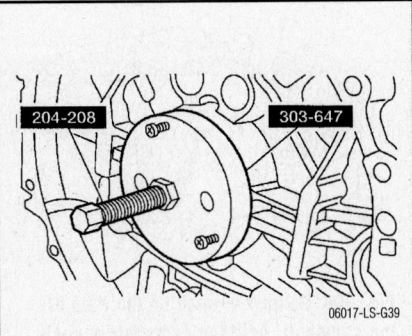

Fig. 95 Removing the rear crankshaft seal—3.9L engine

To install:
4. Install or connect the following:

> ※※ **CAUTION**

The plastic sleeve that comes with the new crankshaft rear oil seal, protects the seal while in transit and is also used as an installation tool to prevent lip seal roll when carrying out the repair. The sleeve must be used to prevent future seal concerns.

➡ Lubricate the cylinder block bore and the crankshaft with clean engine oil before installing seal.

  • Position the rear oil seal with the protective installer onto the end of the crankshaft
  • Rear main seal flush with the cylinder block surface using the tools illustrated
  • Flywheel
5. Tighten the flywheel bolts in a crossing pattern as follows:
  a. Step 1: 11 ft. lbs. (15 Nm)
  b. Step 2: 81 ft. lbs. (110 Nm)
6. Install or connect the following:
  • Transmission
  • Negative battery cable
7. Start the engine and check for leaks.

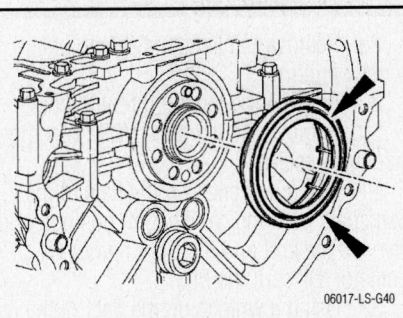

Fig. 96 Position the rear oil seal with the protective installer onto the end of the crankshaft—3.9L engine

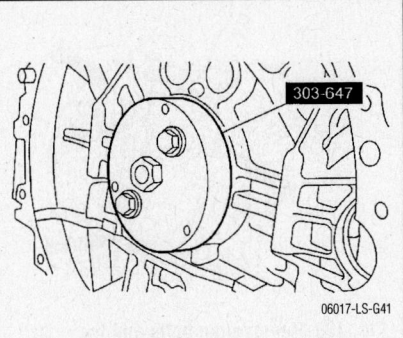

Fig. 97 Installing the rear crankshaft seal—3.9L engine

TIMING CHAIN, SPROCKETS, FRONT COVER AND SEAL

REMOVAL & INSTALLATION

3.0L Engine

See Figures 98 through 119.
See Figure 120.

1. Before servicing the vehicle, refer to the precautions in the beginning of this section.
2. Disconnect the negative battery cable.
3. Drain the cooling system.
4. Remove the valve covers.
5. Remove the accessory drive belt tensioner and idler pulleys.
6. Remove the water pump.
7. Disconnect the upper and lower radiator hoses.
8. Remove the oil pan.
9. Remove the power steering pump.
10. Remove the crankshaft front seal.
11. Disconnect the two Camshaft Position (CMP) sensors and the Crankshaft Position (CKP) sensor electrical connectors.
12. Remove fifteen bolts, the stud bolt and the engine front cover. Discard the gaskets.
13. Remove the ignition pulse wheel.
14. Install the crankshaft damper bolt and washer.
15. Rotate the crankshaft clockwise to position the crankshaft keyway to the 9 o'clock position.
16. Rotate the crankshaft clockwise to position the crankshaft keyway to the 3 o'clock position.
17. Verify that the front 2 intake camshaft lobes are pointing up.
18. Compress the right hand timing chain tensioner. Release the ratcheting pawl.
19. Compress the timing chain tensioner and install a stiff wire or paper clip.
20. Remove the bolts and the right hand timing chain tensioner.

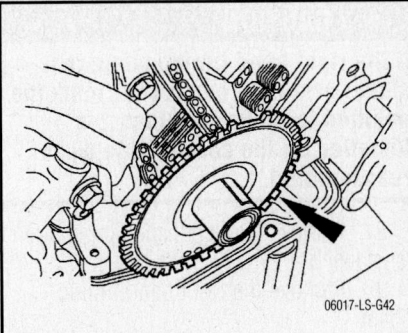

Fig. 98 Remove the ignition pulse wheel—3.0L engine

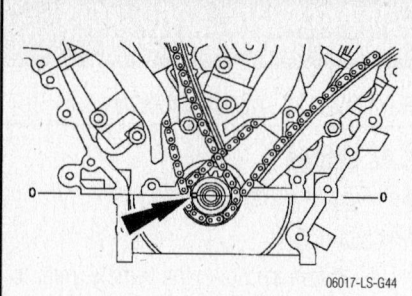

Fig. 99 Rotate the crankshaft clockwise to position the crankshaft keyway to the 9 o'clock position—3.0L engine

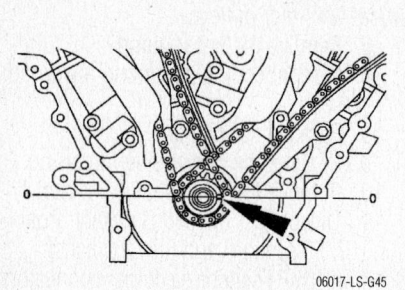

Fig. 100 Rotate the crankshaft clockwise to position the crankshaft keyway to the 3 o'clock position—3.0L engine

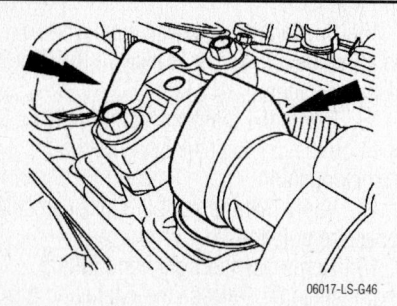

Fig. 101 Verify that the front 2 intake camshaft lobes are pointing up—3.0L engine

※※ CAUTION

If the right hand timing chain tensioner arm is to be reused, mark the position to make sure that it is installed on the correct side when reassembled.

21. Remove the right hand timing chain tensioner arm.
22. Remove the right hand timing chain.
23. Remove the bolts and the right hand Variable Camshaft Timing (VCT) solenoid housing assembly.

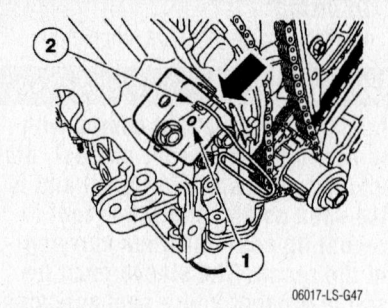

Fig. 102 Compress the timing chain tensioner and install a stiff wire or paper clip—3.0L engine

24. Rotate the crankshaft counterclockwise to position the crankshaft keyway to the 11 o'clock position.
25. Compress the left hand timing chain tensioner. Release the ratcheting pawl.
26. Compress the timing chain tensioner and install a stiff wire or paper clip.
27. Remove the bolts and the left hand timing chain tensioner.

※※ CAUTION

If the left hand timing chain tensioner arm is to be reused, mark the position to make sure that it is installed on the correct side when reassembled.

28. Remove the left hand timing chain tensioner arm.
29. Remove the left hand timing chain.
30. Remove the left hand VCT solenoid housing assembly.
31. Using a wrench on the flats of the camshaft, hold the camshaft in position and remove the bolt and the right hand VCT actuator. Discard the bolt.
32. Using a wrench on the flats of the camshaft, hold the camshaft in position and remove the bolt and the right hand exhaust camshaft sprocket. Discard the bolt.

Fig. 103 Remove the bolts and the right hand Variable Camshaft Timing (VCT) solenoid housing assembly—3.0L engine

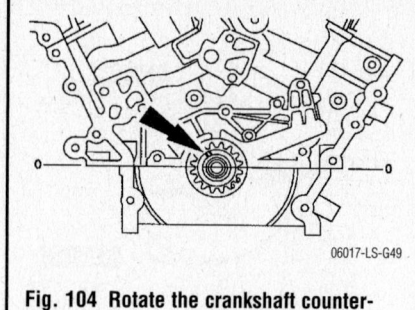

Fig. 104 Rotate the crankshaft counterclockwise to position the crankshaft keyway to the 11 o'clock position—3.0L engine

33. Using a wrench on the flats of the camshaft, hold the camshaft in position and remove the bolt and the left hand VCT actuator. Discard the bolt.
34. Using a wrench on the flats of the camshaft, hold the camshaft in position and

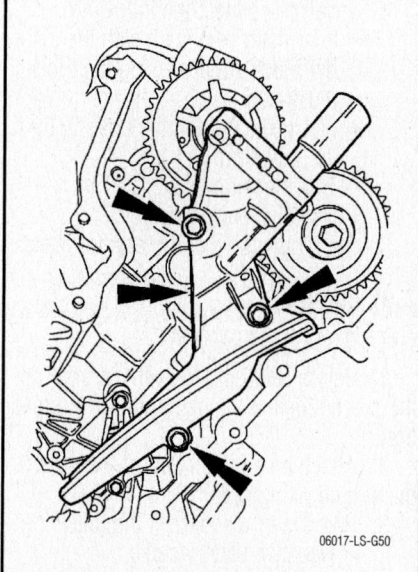

Fig. 105 Remove the left hand VCT solenoid housing assembly—3.0L engine

Fig. 106 Using a wrench on the flats of the camshaft, hold the camshaft in position and remove the bolt and the right hand VCT actuator—3.0L engine

Fig. 107 Using a wrench on the flats of the camshaft, hold the camshaft in position and remove the bolt and the right hand exhaust camshaft sprocket—3.0L engine

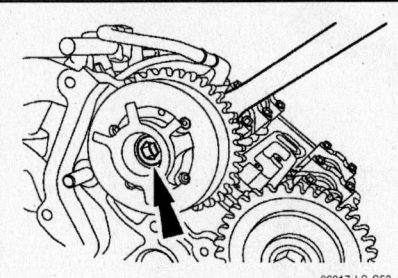

Fig. 108 Using a wrench on the flats of the camshaft, hold the camshaft in position and remove the bolt and the left hand VCT actuator—3.0L engine

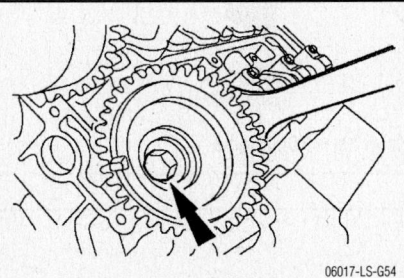

Fig. 109 Using a wrench on the flats of the camshaft, hold the camshaft in position and remove the bolt and the left hand exhaust camshaft sprocket—3.0L engine

remove the bolt and the left hand exhaust camshaft sprocket. Discard the bolt.

35. Remove the crankshaft sprockets.

To install:

36. Install the left hand VCT actuator and install a new bolt hand-tight. Use a wrench on the flats of the camshaft to hold it in position and tighten the bolt in 2 steps:

a. Step 1: Tighten the VCT actuator bolt to 15 ft. lbs. (20 Nm).

b. Step 2: Tighten an additional 90 degrees.

37. Install the left hand exhaust camshaft sprocket and install a new bolt hand-tight.

Using a wrench on the flats of the camshaft, hold the camshaft in position and tighten the bolt in 2 steps:

a. Step 1: Tighten the exhaust camshaft sprocket bolt to 15 ft. lbs. (20 Nm).

b. Step 2: Tighten an additional 90 degrees.

38. Install the right hand variable camshaft timing (VCT) actuator and install a new bolt hand-tight. Using a wrench on the flats of the camshaft, hold the camshaft in position and tighten the bolt in 2 steps:

a. Step 1: Tighten the VCT actuator bolt to 15 ft. lbs. (20 Nm).

b. Step 2: Tighten an additional 90 degrees.

39. Install the left hand exhaust camshaft sprocket and install a new bolt hand-tight. Using a wrench on the flats of the camshaft, hold the camshaft in position and tighten the bolt in 2 steps:

a. Step 1: Tighten the exhaust camshaft sprocket bolt to 15 ft. lbs. (20 Nm).

b. Step 2: Tighten an additional 90 degrees.

40. With the 2 keyways facing forward, install the crankshaft sprockets.

41. If timing marks in the timing chains are not evident, use a permanent-type marker to mark the crankshaft and camshaft timing marks on the left and right hand timing chains.

42. Mark any link to use as the exhaust camshaft timing mark.

43. Starting with the exhaust camshaft timing mark, count 16 links and mark the

link as the intake camshaft sprocket timing mark.

44. Starting with the intake camshaft timing mark, count 25 links and mark the link as the crankshaft sprocket timing mark.

45. Verify that the crankshaft keyway is in the 11 o'clock position.

✽✽ CAUTION

The crankshaft keyway must remain in the 11 o'clock position until the cams are located in the NEUTRAL position, or damage to the valves can occur.

46. Rotate the left and right hand intake and exhaust camshafts to locate them in their NEUTRAL positions.

➡ **The gold colored bolt must be installed in its original location.**

47. Install the left hand VCT solenoid housing assembly and the bolts. Tighten to 18 ft. lbs. (25 Nm).

48. Install the left hand timing chain, aligning the copper (or marked) link with the marks on the camshaft and crankshaft sprockets.

49. Install the left hand timing chain tensioner arm.

➡ **Be sure to position the tensioner so that the tensioner piston is fully engaged in the tensioner arm. Install the left hand timing chain tensioner and bolts.**

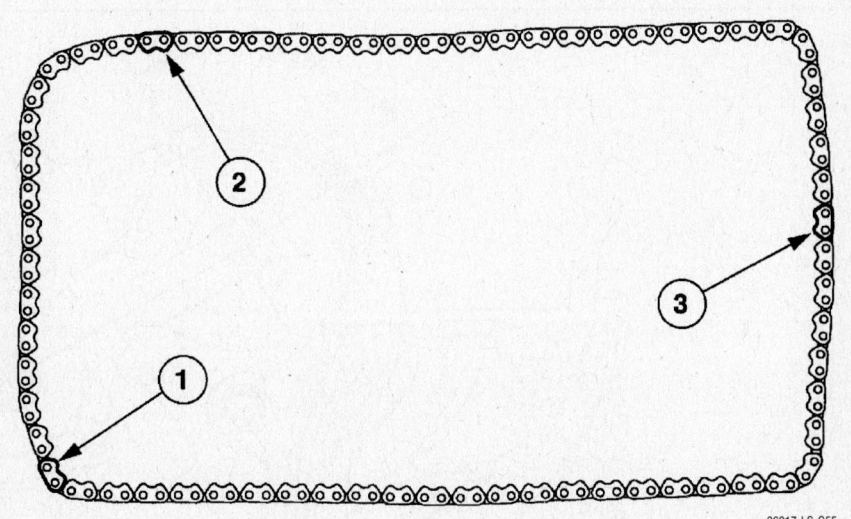

Fig. 110 If timing marks in the timing chains are not evident, use a permanent-type marker to mark the crankshaft and camshaft timing marks on the left and right hand timing chains—3.0L engine

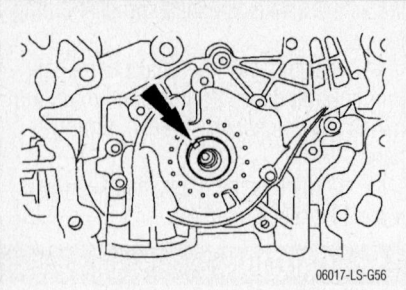

Fig. 111 Verify that the crankshaft keyway is in the 11 o'clock position—3.0L engine

06017-LS-G56

50. Remove the wire or paper clip from the tensioner.

51. Rotate the crankshaft clockwise and position the keyway at the 3 o'clock position for right hand timing chain installation.

52. Verify that the copper (or marked) links on the left hand timing chain are in alignment with the timing marks on the camshaft and crankshaft sprockets.

53. Install the right hand VCT solenoid housing assembly and bolts. Tighten to 18 ft. lbs. (25 Nm).

54. Install the right hand timing chain, aligning the copper or (marked) links with the marks on the camshaft and crankshaft sprockets.

55. Verify that the copper (or marked) links on the right hand timing chain are in alignment with the timing marks on the camshaft and crankshaft sprockets.

56. Install the right hand timing chain tensioner arm.

57. Install the right hand timing chain tensioner and bolts.

58. Remove the wire or paper clip from the right hand timing chain tensioner.

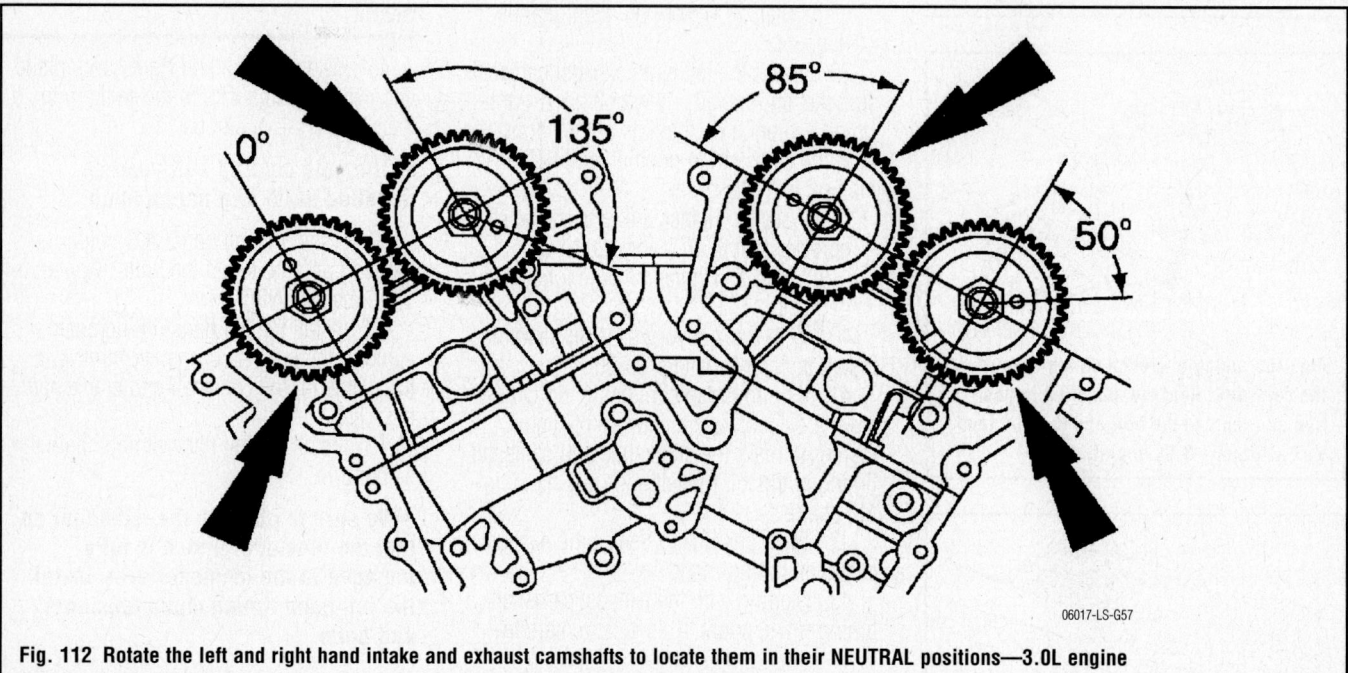

06017-LS-G57

Fig. 112 Rotate the left and right hand intake and exhaust camshafts to locate them in their NEUTRAL positions—3.0L engine

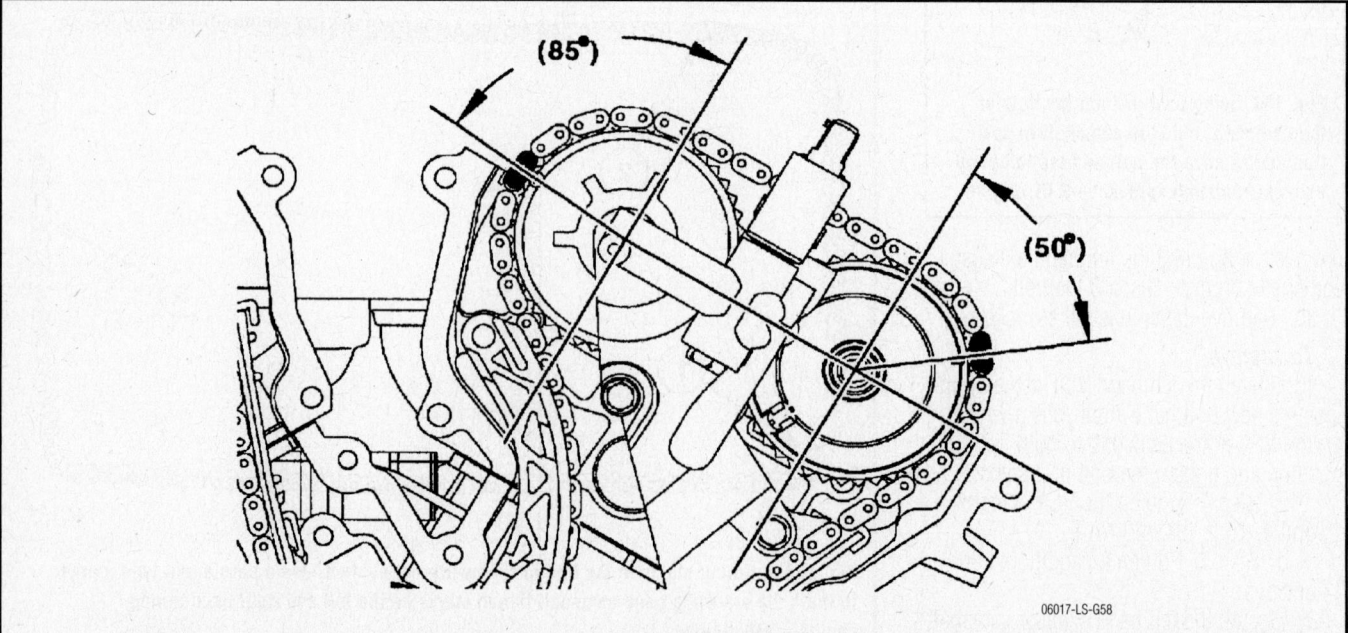

06017-LS-G58

Fig. 113 Install the left hand timing chain, aligning the copper (or marked) link with the marks on the camshaft and crankshaft sprockets—3.0L engine

82°
0
0
06017-LS-G59

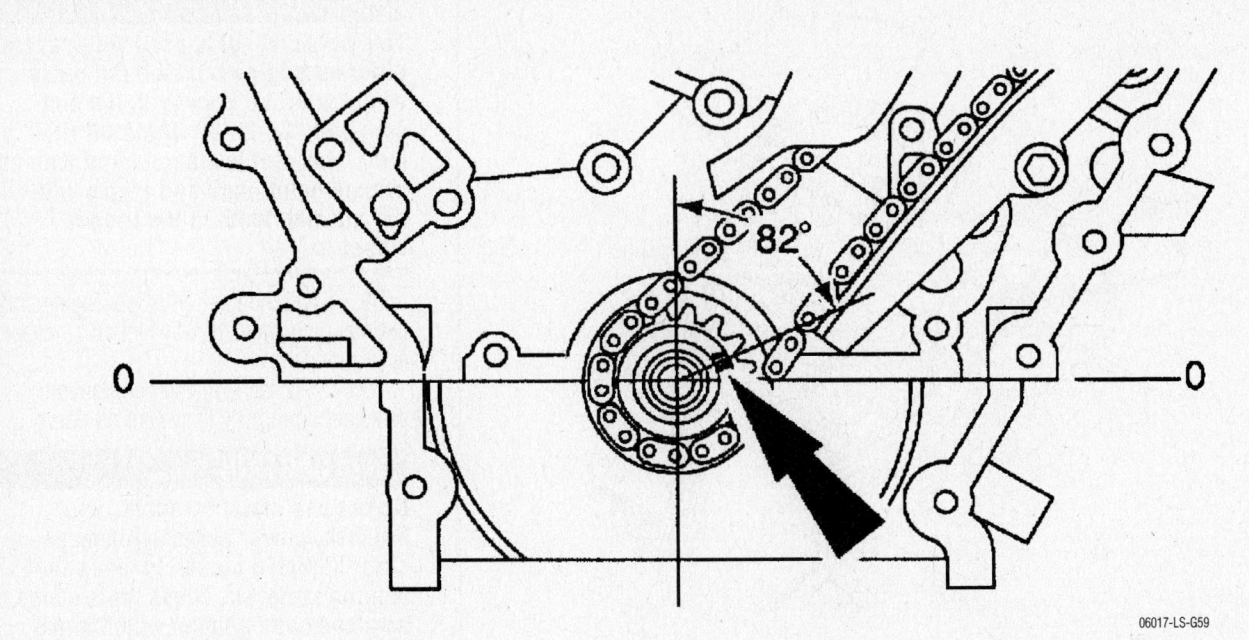

Fig. 114 Rotate the crankshaft clockwise and position the keyway at the 3 o'clock position for right hand timing chain installation—3.0L engine

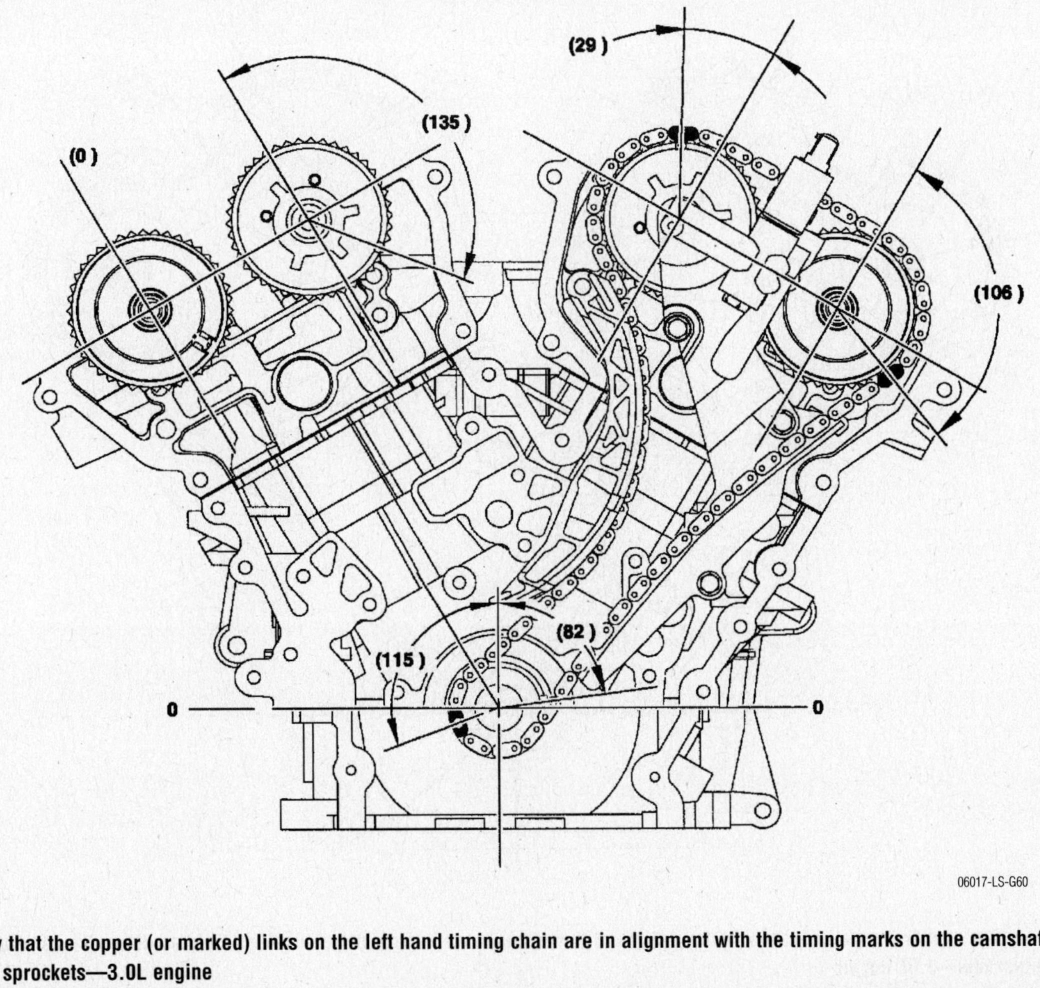

(29)
(135)
(0)
(106)
(82)
(115)
0
0
06017-LS-G60

Fig. 115 Verify that the copper (or marked) links on the left hand timing chain are in alignment with the timing marks on the camshaft and crankshaft sprockets—3.0L engine

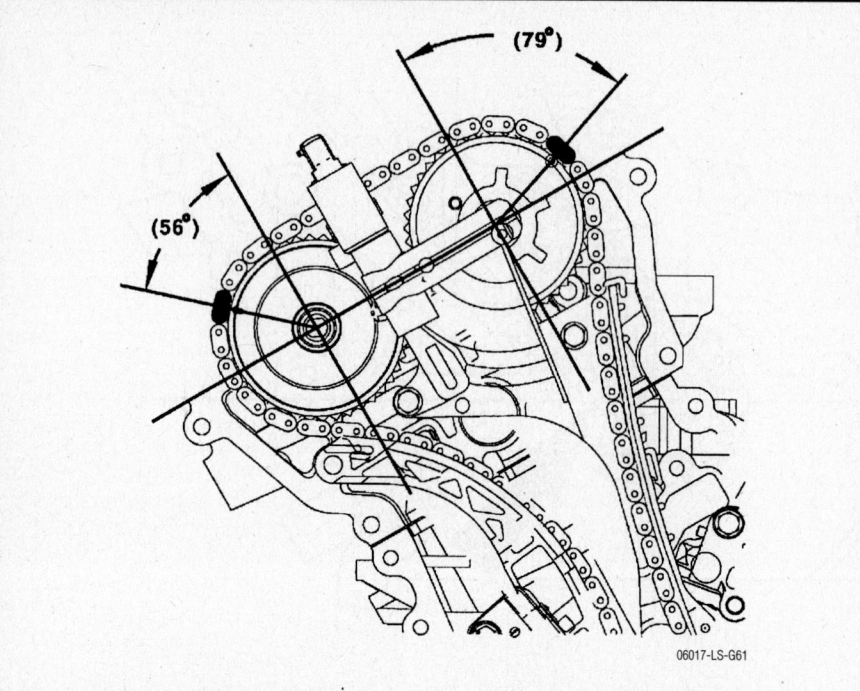

Fig. 116 Install the right hand timing chain, aligning the copper or (marked) links with the marks on the camshaft and crankshaft sprockets—3.0L engine

⁂ CAUTION

This pulse wheel is used with several different engines. Install the pulse wheel with the keyway in the slot stamped "20-25-30 DAMB 30 RFF" only. This slot is also marked with an orange paint mark and aligns with the missing tooth in the trigger wheel.

59. Install the ignition pulse wheel using the orange marked keyway slot and the teeth facing forward.

60. If necessary, install new variable camshaft timing (VCT) system oil filters

⁂ CAUTION

Do not use metal scrapers, wire brushes, power abrasive discs or other abrasive means to clean the sealing surfaces. These tools cause scratches and gouges which make leak paths.

61. Use a plastic scraping tool to remove all traces of sealant from the front cover.

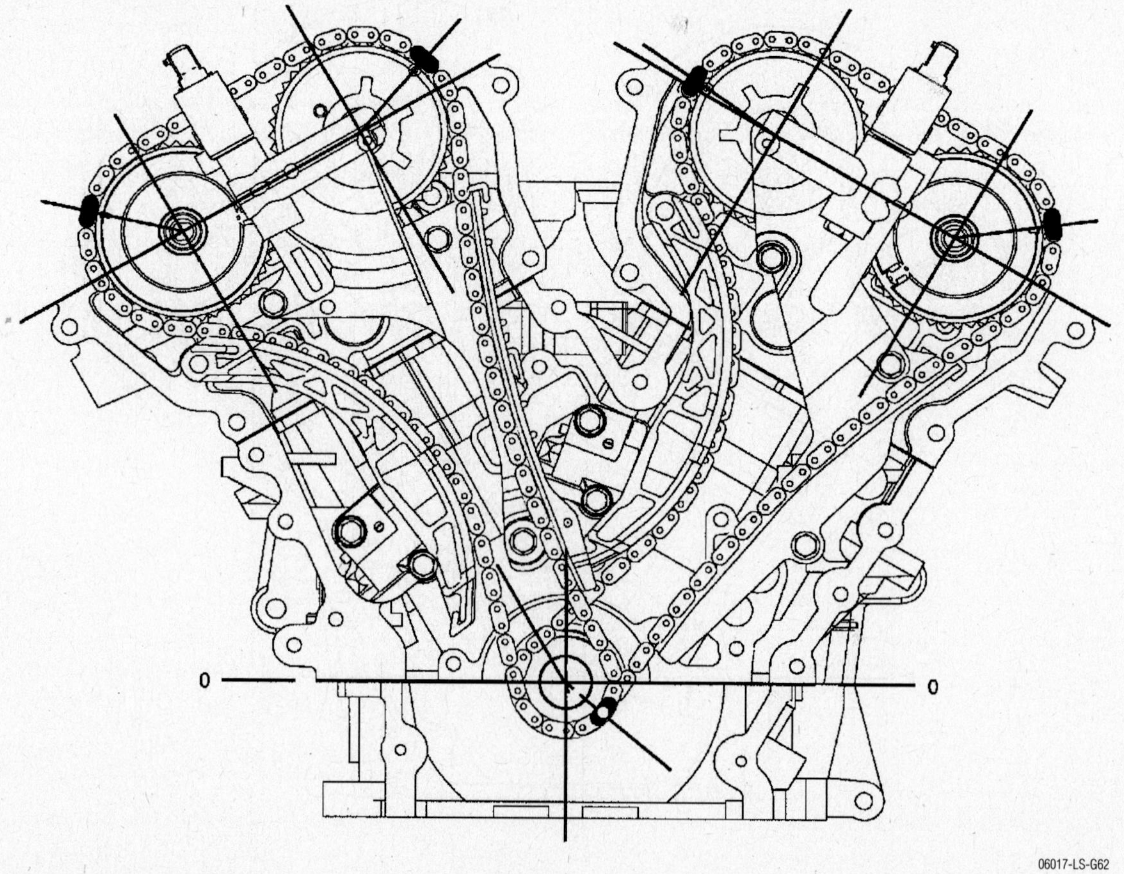

06017-LS-G62

Fig. 117 Verify that the copper (or marked) links on the right hand timing chain are in alignment with the timing marks on the camshaft and crankshaft sprockets—3.0L engine

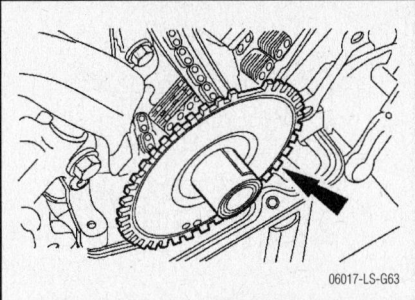

Fig. 118 Install the ignition pulse wheel using the orange marked keyway slot and the teeth facing forward—3.0L engine

Clean all sealing surfaces with silicone gasket remover and metal surface prep.

62. Install a new gasket on the engine front cover.

➡**The engine front cover must be installed and the bolts tightened within four minutes of applying sealant.**

63. Apply a 0.23 inch (6 mm) diameter dot of silicone gasket and sealer to the cylinder block, the lower cylinder block and the cylinder head mating surfaces.

➡**Number 14 is a stud and washer assembly.**

64. Position the engine front cover and install the bolts and the stud bolt. Tighten in the sequence illustrated to 18 ft. lbs (25 Nm).

65. Connect the CMP sensors and the CKP sensor electrical connectors.

66. Install the crankshaft front seal

67. Install the power steering pump.

68. Install the oil pan.

69. Connect the radiator hoses.

70. Install the water pump.

71. Install the accessory drive belt tensioner and idler pulleys.

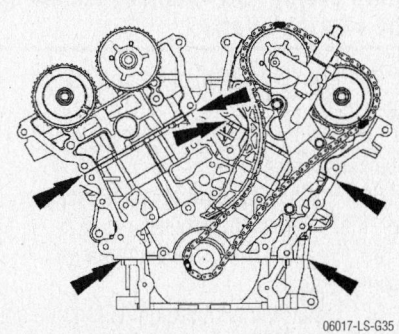

Fig. 119 Apply a 0.23 inch (6 mm) diameter dot of silicone gasket and sealer to the cylinder block, the lower cylinder block and the cylinder head mating surfaces—3.0L engine

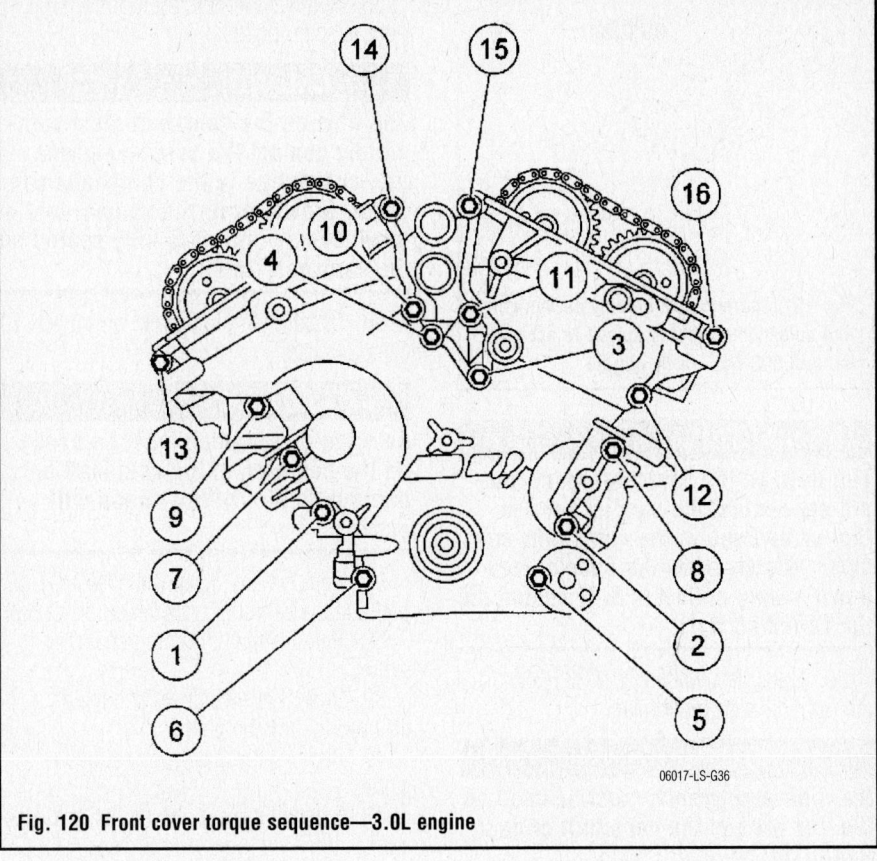

Fig. 120 Front cover torque sequence—3.0L engine

72. Install the valve covers.

73. Fill and bleed the cooling system.

74. Fill the engine with correct type and amount of oil.

75. Connect the negative battery cable.

76. Start the engine and check for leaks.

3.9L Engine

See Figures 121 through 130.

1. Before servicing the vehicle, refer to the precautions in the beginning of this section.

2. Disconnect the negative battery cable.

3. Drain and recycle the engine coolant.

4. Drain the engine oil.

5. Recover the AC refrigerant using approved equipment.

6. Remove the valve covers.

7. Remove the cooling fan assembly.

8. Remove the accessory drive belt idler pulley.

9. Remove the crankshaft front seal.

10. Remove the A/C compressor..

11. Remove the lower radiator hose bracket nut.

12. Disconnect the lower radiator, upper radiator and heater hose.

13. Disconnect the two oil cooler hoses, if equipped.

14. Disconnect the power steering reservoir hose.

15. Disconnect the Power Steering Pressure (PSP) switch.

➡**One bolt is blocked by the power steering pressure hose and must be removed with the power steering pump.**

16. Remove the four bolts and position the power steering pump aside.

17. Remove the five bolts and the power steering pump bracket.

18. Detach the wiring harness clips.

19. Remove the engine front cover bolts in the sequence illustrated.

20. Remove the engine front cover.

21. Remove the right and left hand Variable Cam Timing (VCT) bush carriers.

22. Remove the bolt and the Crankshaft Position (CKP) sensor.

➡**There is one window on the ignition pulse wheel that is unique to accept the tool 303-645.**

23. Install the tool 303-645.

24. Turn the crankshaft to 45 degrees After Top Dead Center (ATDC). The crankshaft keyway will be in the 6 o'clock position.

25. Make sure the flats of the camshaft are facing upward. If not, repeat the previous step.

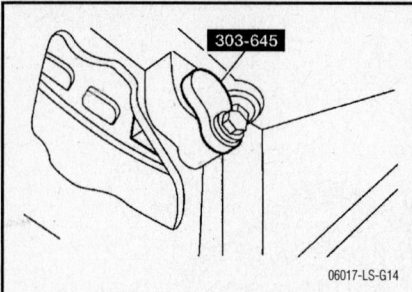

Fig. 121 There is one window on the ignition pulse wheel that is unique to accept the tool 303-645—3.9L engine

✳✳ CAUTION

The flats on the camshaft must completely contact the special service tool or damage to the camshafts can occur. Slowly draw the special tool down evenly until it is fully seated on the camshaft flats.

26. Install the holding tool 303-530 on the right hand cylinder head.

✳✳ CAUTION

An open-end wrench must be used on the hex area of the camshaft or damage to the head will occur.

27. Remove and discard the exhaust camshaft sprocket bolt.
28. Remove and discard the variable VCT unit bolt.
29. Remove the right hand timing chain tensioner.
30. Push the lever down and install a drill rod to lock the piston.
31. Remove the 2 bolts and the tensioner.
32. Remove the bolt and the right tensioner arm.
33. Remove the bolt and the right timing chain guide.
34. Remove the right primary timing chain.

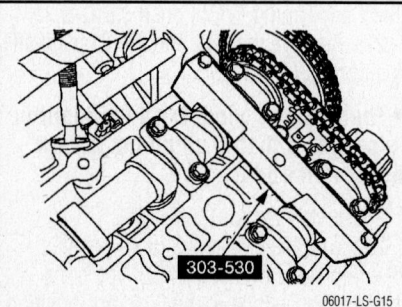

Fig. 122 Tool 303-530 is used to hold the camshafts during removal—3.9L engine

35. Remove the holding tool from the right cylinder head.

✳✳ CAUTION

The flats on the camshaft must completely contact the special service tool or damage to the camshafts can occur. Slowly draw the special tool down evenly until it is fully seated on the camshaft flats.

36. Install the holding tool on the left cylinder head.

✳✳ CAUTION

An open-end wrench must be used on the hex area of the camshaft or damage to the cylinder head will occur.

37. Remove and discard the left VCT unit bolt and the exhaust camshaft sprocket bolt.
38. Remove the left timing chain tensioner.
39. Push the lever down and install a drill rod to lock the piston.
40. Remove the 2 bolts and the tensioner.
41. Remove the nut and the left tensioner arm.
42. Remove the bolt and the left timing chain guide.
43. Remove the left primary timing chain.
44. Remove the crankshaft sprocket.
45. Collapse the left secondary timing chain tensioner and install a pin to lock the piston.
46. Remove the left VCT unit, exhaust camshaft sprocket and timing chain as an assembly.
47. Remove the 2 bolts and the left secondary timing chain tensioner.
48. Collapse the right secondary timing chain tensioner and install a pin to lock the piston.
49. Remove the right VCT unit, exhaust camshaft sprocket and timing chain as an assembly.
50. Remove the 2 bolts and the right secondary timing chain tensioner.

To install:
51. Turn the crankshaft to 45 degrees ATDC. The crankshaft keyway will be in the 6 o'clock position.
52. Install the tool 303-645.
53. Position all of the camshafts so the flats of the camshafts are facing upward.
54. Install the left secondary timing chain tensioner and 2 bolts. Tighten to 8 ft. lbs. (11 Nm).
55. Install the left VCT unit, exhaust

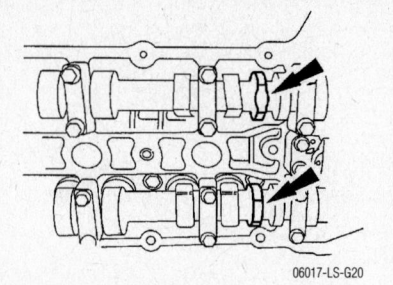

Fig. 123 Position all of the camshafts so the flats of the camshafts are facing upward—3.9L engine

camshaft sprocket and timing chain as an assembly.
56. Using new bolts, install the left VCT unit and exhaust camshaft sprocket bolts finger-tight.
57. Remove the locking pin from the left secondary timing chain tensioner.
58. Install the right secondary timing chain tensioner and 2 bolts. Tighten to 8 ft. lbs. (11 Nm).
59. Install the right VCT unit, exhaust camshaft sprocket and timing chain as an assembly.
60. Using new bolts, install the right VCT unit and exhaust camshaft sprocket bolts finger-tight.
61. Remove the locking pin from the right secondary timing chain tensioner.
62. Reset the timing chain tensioners by holding the lever toward the tensioner piston. Using finger pressure, compress the tensioner. Push the lever down and install a drill rod to lock the piston.

✳✳ CAUTION

The flats on the camshaft must completely contact the special service tool or damage to the camshafts can occur. Slowly draw the special tool down evenly until it is fully seated on the camshaft flats.

63. Install the holding tool on the left head.
64. Position the left timing chain and crankshaft gear.
65. Position the timing chain over the left intake camshaft sprocket.
66. Position the crankshaft gear in the timing chain.
67. Install the left timing chain guide and bolt. Tighten to 8 ft. lbs. (11 Nm).
68. Install the left timing chain tensioner arm and nut. Tighten to 8 ft. lbs. (11 Nm).
69. Install the left timing chain tensioner.
70. Install the timing chain tensioner and bolts, and remove the drill rod.

> ※ **CAUTION**
>
> The exhaust camshaft sprocket bolt must be fully tightened before tightening the intake camshaft sprocket bolt. Using the tool, apply 89 inch lbs. (10 Nm) counterclockwise to the left exhaust camshaft sprocket.

71. Tighten the left exhaust camshaft sprocket and VCT unit bolts 26 ft. lbs. (35 Nm) then an additional 90 degrees.
72. Remove the holding tool.

> ※ **CAUTION**
>
> The flats on the camshaft must completely contact the special service tool or damage to the camshafts can occur. Slowly draw the special tool downward evenly until it is fully seated on the camshaft flats.

73. Install the holding tool on the right cylinder head.
74. Position the right timing chain over the right intake camshaft sprocket and over the crankshaft gear.
75. Install the right timing chain guide and bolt. Tighten to 8 ft. lbs. (11 Nm).
76. Install the right timing chain tensioner arm. Tighten to 8 ft. lbs. (11 Nm).
77. Install the right timing chain tensioner.
78. Install the timing chain tensioner and bolts, tighten to 8 ft. lbs. (11 Nm) and remove the drill rod.

> ※ **CAUTION**
>
> The exhaust camshaft sprocket bolt must be fully tightened before tightening the intake camshaft sprocket bolt. Using the tool, apply 89 inch lbs. (10 Nm) counterclockwise to the left exhaust camshaft sprocket.

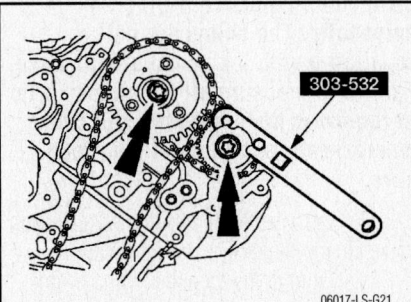

Fig. 124 Using the tool, apply 89 inch lbs. (10 Nm) counterclockwise to the camshaft sprocket—3.9L engine

79. Tighten the right exhaust camshaft sprocket and VCT unit bolts 26 ft. lbs. (35 Nm) then an additional 90 degrees.
80. Remove the holding tool.

➤ **Lubricate the VCT bush carrier seals with clean engine oil.**

81. Carefully insert the bush carrier into the VCT unit, compress ring seals with fingers as required. Fully seat the bush carrier by hand before fitting the bolts and nut. Tighten the bolts to 15 ft. lbs. (20 Nm). Tighten the nut to 89 inch lbs. (10 Nm).
82. Install new engine front cover gaskets.

➤ **If the front cover is not secured within 4 minutes of sealant application, the sealant must be removed and the sealing area cleaned with metal surface cleaner. Allow to dry until there is no sign of wetness, or 4 minutes, whichever is longer. Failure to follow this procedure can cause future oil leakage.**

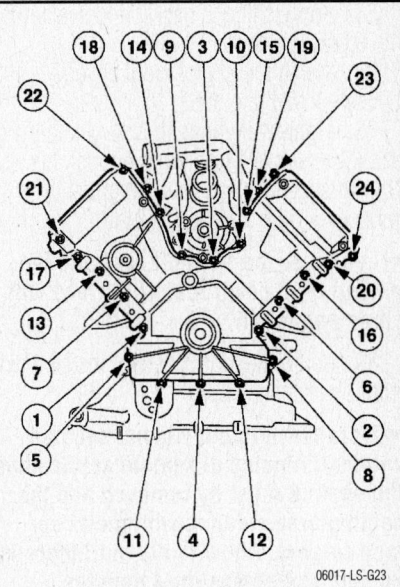

Fig. 126 Engine front cover torque sequence—3.9L engine

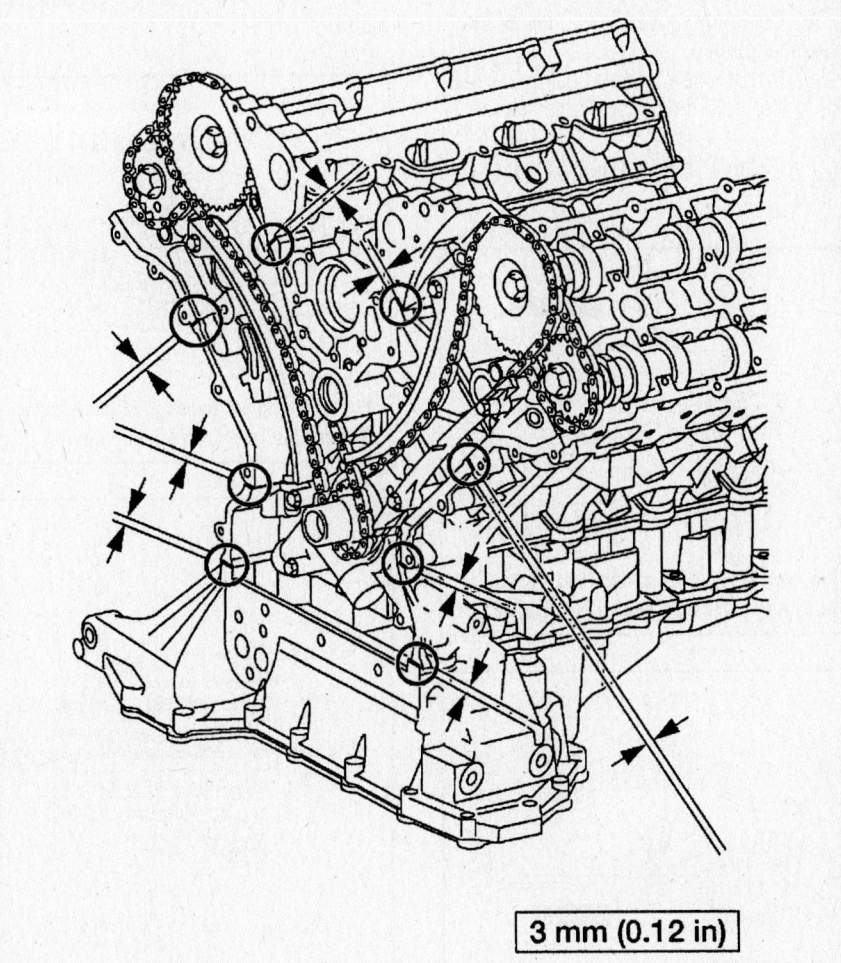

3 mm (0.12 in)

Fig. 125 Apply silicone gasket and sealant in the 8 places shown—3.9L engine

83. Apply silicone gasket and sealant in the 8 places shown.

84. Install the engine front cover. Loosely install the bolts.

85. Tighten the bolts in 2 stages in the sequence shown. Tighten to 44 inch lbs. (5 Nm) in sequence and then retighten in sequence to 89 inch lbs. (10 Nm).

➡**Lubricate the front oil seal and the engine front cover mating surface with clean engine oil.**

86. Using the tool 303-646, install a new front crankshaft seal.

➡**If crankshaft pulley is not secured within 4 minutes of sealant application the sealant must be removed and the sealing area cleaned with metal surface cleaner. Allow to dry until there is no sign of wetness, or 4 minutes, whichever is longer. Failure to follow this procedure can cause future oil leakage.**

87. Apply a bead of silicone gasket and sealant to the keyway.

88. Using the tool 303-102, install the crankshaft pulley.

89. Install a new bolt and using the special tool to hold the pulley, tighten as follows:.

   a. Step 1: Tighten to 59 ft. lbs. (80 Nm).

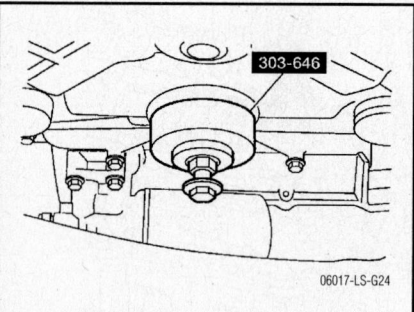

Fig. 127 Using the tool 303-646, install a new front crankshaft seal—3.9L engine

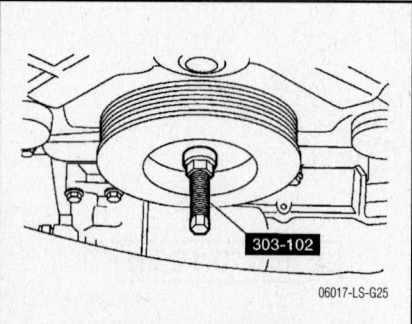

Fig. 128 Using the tool 303-102, install the crankshaft pulley—3.9L engine

   b. Step 2: Loosen the bolt 2 complete turns.

   c. Step 3: Tighten to 37 ft. lbs. (50 Nm).

   d. Step 4: Tighten an additional 90 degrees.

90. Install new valve cover gaskets.

➡**If the valve covers are not secured within 4 minutes of sealant application the sealant must be removed and the sealing area cleaned with metal surface cleaner. Allow to dry until there is no sign of wetness, or 4 minutes, whichever is longer. Failure to follow this procedure can cause future oil leakage.**

91. Apply 4 beads of silicone gasket and sealant as shown.

92. Install the left valve cover and tighten the bolts in sequence to 89 inch lbs. (10 Nm).

93. Install the right valve cover and tighten the bolts in sequence to 89 inch lbs. (10 Nm).

94. Install the accessory drive belt idler pulley.

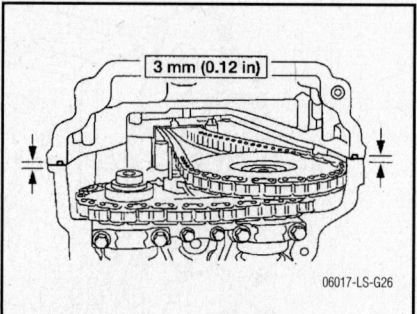

Fig. 129 Apply 4 beads of silicone gasket and sealant as shown—3.9L engine

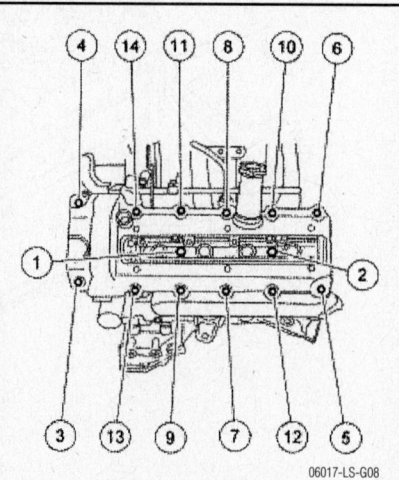

Fig. 130 Left valve cover torque sequence—3.9L engine

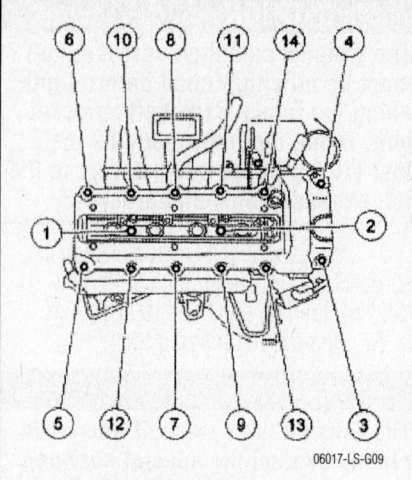

Fig. 131 Right valve cover torque sequence—3.9L engine

95. Install the cooling fan assembly.

96. Fill the engine with clean engine oil.

97. Connect the negative battery cable.

98. Fill and bleed the power steering system.

99. Fill and bleed the engine cooling system.

100. Evacuate and recharge the A/C system

101. Start the engine and check for leaks.

VALVE LASH

ADJUSTMENT

3.0L Engine

1. Before servicing the vehicle, refer to the precautions in the beginning of this section.

2. Disconnect the negative battery cable.

3. Remove the timing chains.

➡**Measure each valve clearance at base circle before removing the camshafts. The shims are not repairable with the camshafts in place. Failure to measure all clearances prior to removing the camshafts will cause unnecessary repetition of the procedure.**

4. Use a feeler gauge to measure each valve clearance and record its location.

5. Remove the camshafts and shims.

➡**The shims are marked for thickness; example: 2.22 mm = 222 on shim.**

6. The corrected shims allow the following valve clearances.

a. Intake valve clearance: 0.00709–0.00866 inch (0.18–0.22 mm).

b. Exhaust valve clearance: 0.0128–0.0148 inch (0.33–0.38 mm).

➡A midrange clearance of 0.00787 inch (0.20 mm) on the intake side and 0.014 inch (0.35 mm) is the most desirable:

➡Select shims using this formula: required shim thickness = measured clearance plus the base shim thickness minus most desirable clearance.

7. Select shims and mark the installation location.

8. Install new shims.

9. Install the camshafts.

10. Measure the new valve clearances.

11. Install the timing chains

12. Disconnect the negative battery cable.

3.9L Engine

1. Before servicing the vehicle, refer to the precautions in the beginning of this section.

2. Disconnect the negative battery cable.

3. Remove the timing chains.

➡Measure each valve clearance at base circle before removing the camshafts. The shims are not repairable with the camshafts in place. Failure to measure all clearances prior to removing the camshafts will cause unnecessary repetition of the procedure.

4. Use a feeler gauge to measure each valve clearance and record its location.

5. Remove the camshafts and shims.

➡The shims are marked for thickness; example: 2.22 mm = 222 on shim.

6. The corrected shims allow the following valve clearances.

a. Intake valve clearance: 0.00709–0.00866 inch (0.18–0.22 mm).

b. Exhaust valve clearance: 0.0128–0.0148 inch (0.33–0.38 mm).

➡A midrange clearance of 0.00787 inch (0.20 mm) on the intake side and 0.014 inch (0.35 mm) is the most desirable:

➡Select shims using this formula: required shim thickness = measured clearance plus the base shim thickness minus most desirable clearance.

7. Select shims and mark the installation location.

8. Install new shims.

9. Install the camshafts.

10. Measure the new valve clearances.

11. Install the timing chains

12. Disconnect the negative battery cable.

ENGINE PERFORMANCE & EMISSION CONTROL

COMPONENT LOCATIONS

See Figure 132.

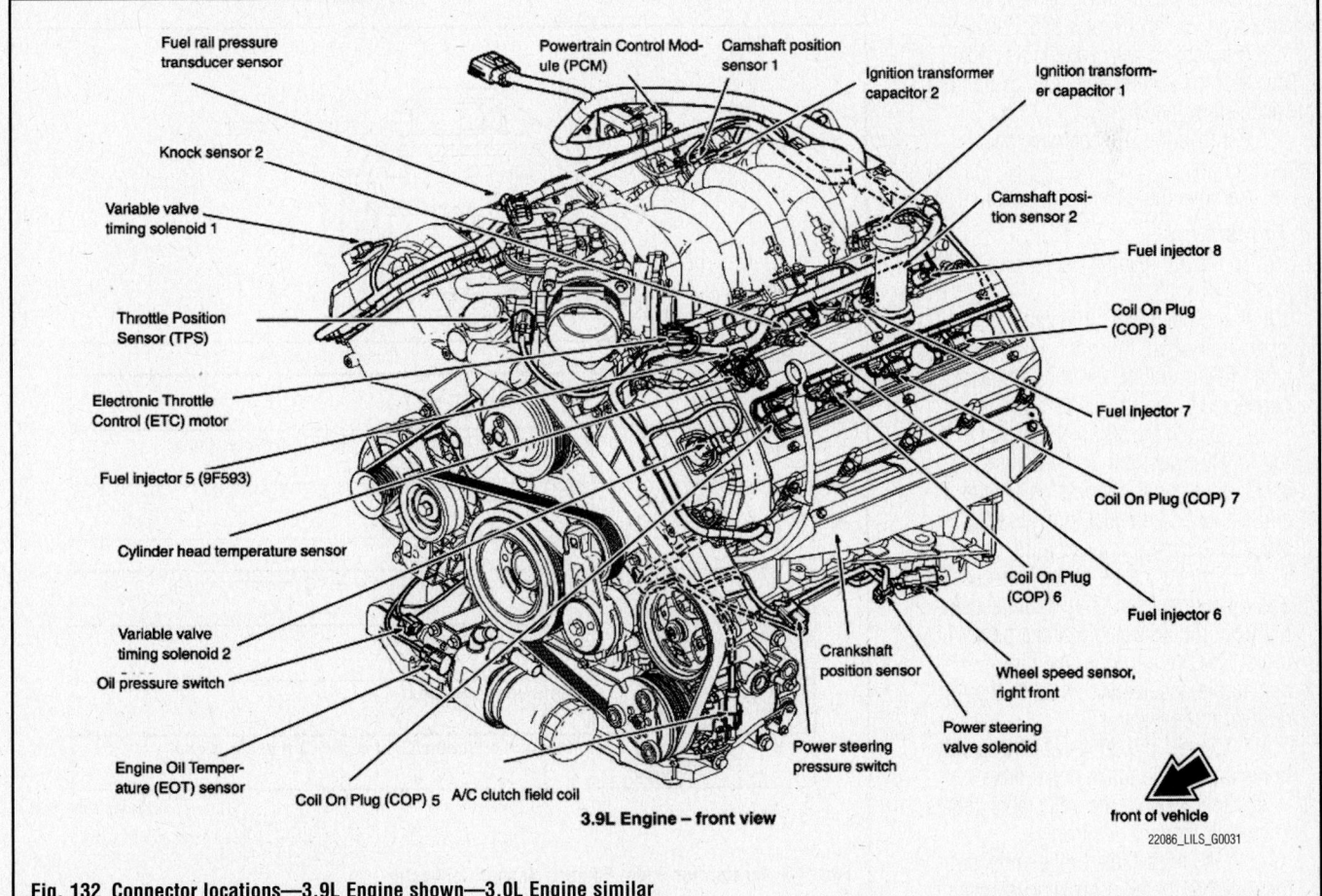

3.9L Engine – front view

front of vehicle

22086_LILS_G0031

Fig. 132 Connector locations—3.9L Engine shown—3.0L Engine similar

ACCELERATOR PEDAL POSITION (APP) SENSOR

LOCATION

Part of the accelerator pedal assembly.

REMOVAL & INSTALLATION

❊❊ CAUTION

The adjustable pedal system must be indexed whenever the brake pedal assembly or accelerator pedal assembly is serviced.

➡ **A new adjustable brake pedal or adjustable accelerator pedal assembly will be in the full forward (towards the front of the vehicle) position.**

1. Before servicing the vehicle, refer to the precautions in the beginning of this section.
2. Disconnect the battery ground cable.
3. Disconnect the accelerator pedal electrical connector.
4. Remove the accelerator pedal wiring harness retainer from the accelerator pedal bracket bolt.
5. If equipped with fixed pedal, remove the accelerator pedal wiring harness pin-type retainer from the accelerator pedal bracket.
6. If equipped with adjustable pedal, disconnect the accelerator drive cable from the accelerator pedal.
7. Remove the 3 accelerator pedal retaining nuts.
8. Remove the accelerator pedal.

To install:

9. To install, reverse the removal procedure.
10. If equipped with adjustable pedal, index the pedals as follows:

a. Make sure the electrical connector is connected to the adjustable pedal motor.

b. Operate the adjustable pedal to the full forward position. If the adjustable accelerator pedal bottoms before the adjustable brake pedal, operate both adjustable pedals full rearward.

c. Remove the tie-strap, if necessary, and disconnect the drive cable assembly from the adjustable brake pedal drive. Continue to operate the adjustable accelerator pedal to the full rearward position.

d. Connect the drive cable assembly to the adjustable brake pedal drive.

e. Operate both the adjustable pedals to the full forward position.

f. If the adjustable brake pedal bottoms before the adjustable accelerator

pedal, remove the tie-strap, if necessary, and disconnect the adjustable brake pedal drive cable.

g. Operate the accelerator pedal to the full forward position.

h. Connect the drive cable assembly to the adjustable brake pedal drive.

i. Operate both the adjustable pedals to the full forward position.

j. Check that the adjustable brake pedal and adjustable accelerator pedal can be adjusted fully forward, fully rearward, and they hit the forward and rearward stops at the same time.

TESTING

See Figure 133.

1. Before servicing the vehicle, refer to the precautions in the beginning of this section.

❊❊ WARNING

Use only a high-impedance multimeter, otherwise damage to the PCM and/or sensors can result.

2. With the key **ON** and the engine **OFF**, check pin 2 for reference voltage.
3. Turn the key **OFF** and disconnect the APP sensor connector.
4. Measure the resistance of the following APP sensor pins:
   - Pins 2 and 6: 400–1200 ohms
   - Pins 2 and 7: 400–1200 ohms
   - Pins 2 and 1: 900–2200 ohms
   - Pins 2 and 3: 900–2200 ohms
   - Pins 2 and 5: 2000–4800 ohms
   - Pins 2 and 8: 2000–4800 ohms
   - Pins 5 and 6: 1700–4100 ohms
   - Pins 5 and 7: 1700–4100 ohms
   - Pins 5 and 1: 1400–3500 ohms
   - Pins 5 and 3: 1400–3500 ohms
   - Pins 5 and 8: 2700–6500 ohms
   - Pins 8 and 6: 1700–4100 ohms
   - Pins 8 and 7: 1700–4100 ohms
   - Pins 8 and 1: 1300–3200 ohms
   - Pins 8 and 3: 1300–3200 ohms
   - Pins 6 and 1: 700–1700 ohms
   - Pins 6 and 3: 700–1700 ohms
   - Pins 7 and 1: 700–1700 ohms
   - Pins 7 and 3: 700–1700 ohms
5. If any measurement falls outside the range given, replace the APP sensor.

CAMSHAFT POSITION (CMP) SENSOR

LOCATION

See Figures 134 and 135.

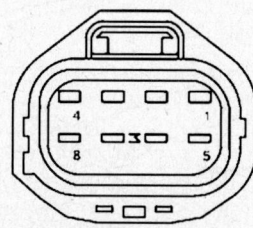

FEMALE

Pin	Circuit	Circuit function
1	9-RJ30 (BN)	Signal return
2	8-RJ30 (WH)	Electronic Throttle Control (ETC) module, signal
3	9-RJ35 (BN/RD)	Signal return
4	–	not used
5	8-RJ35 (WH/RD)	Electronic Throttle Control (ETC) module, signal
6	7-RJ30 (YE)	Reference voltage
7	7-RJ35 (YE/RD)	Reference voltage
8	8-RJ36 (WH/BU)	Electronic Throttle Control (ETC) module, signal

22086_LILS_G0030

Fig. 133 Accelerator Pedal Position Sensor Connector

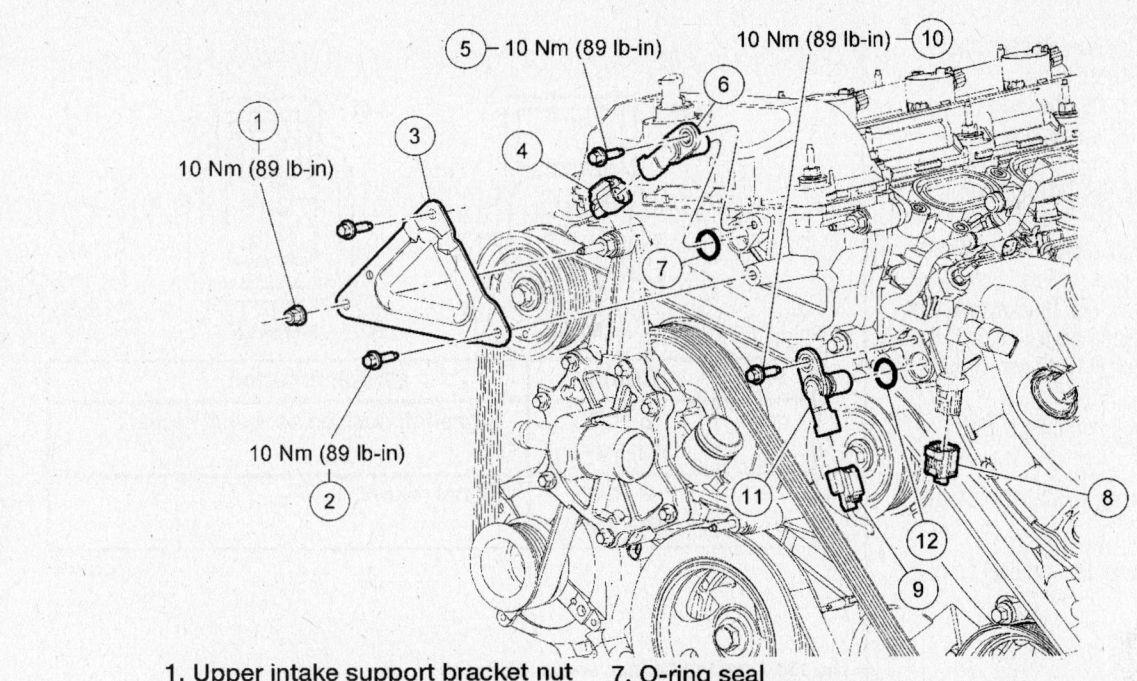

1. Upper intake support bracket nut
2. Upper intake support bracket bolt
3. Upper intake support bracket
4. RH camshaft position (CMP) sensor electrical connector
5. RH CMP sensor bolt
6. RH CMP sensor
7. O-ring seal
8. Fuel temperature sensor electrical connector
9. LH CMP sensor electrical connector
10. LH CMP sensor bolt
11. LH CMP sensor
12. O-ring seal

22086_LILS_G0033

Fig. 134 Camshaft Position Sensor location exploded view–3.0L Engine

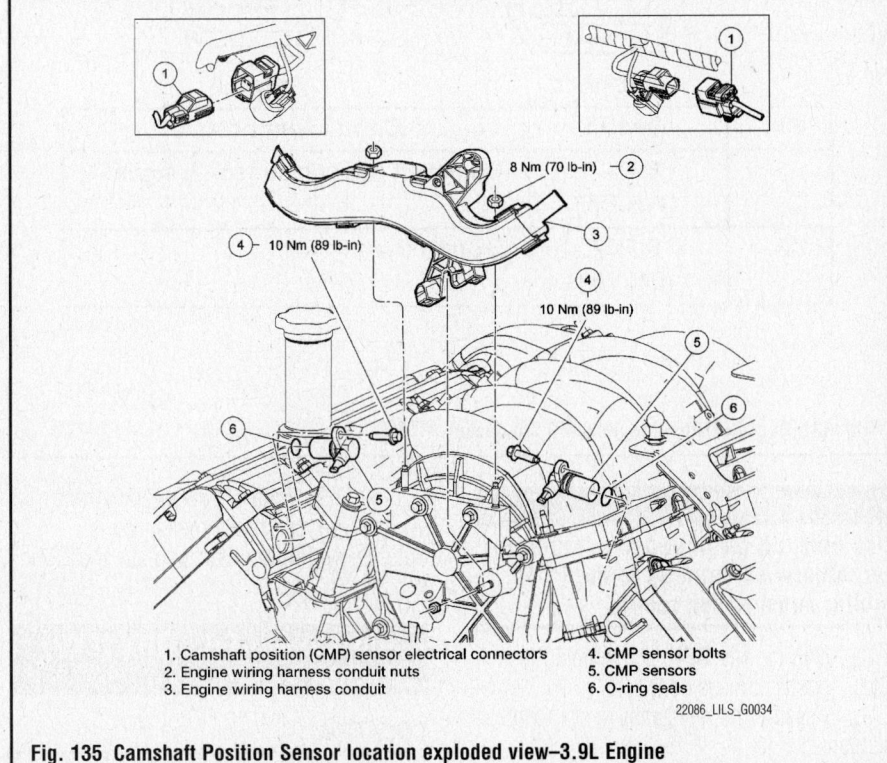

1. Camshaft position (CMP) sensor electrical connectors
2. Engine wiring harness conduit nuts
3. Engine wiring harness conduit
4. CMP sensor bolts
5. CMP sensors
6. O-ring seals

22086_LILS_G0034

Fig. 135 Camshaft Position Sensor location exploded view–3.9L Engine

OPERATION

The CMP sensor detects the position of the camshaft. The CMP sensor identifies when piston No. 1 is on its compression stroke. A signal is then sent to the PCM and used for synchronizing the sequential firing of the fuel injectors. Coil-on-plug (COP) ignition applications use the CMP signal to select the proper ignition coil to fire. The input circuit to the PCM is referred to as the CMP input or circuit. DTC P0340 is associated with this sensor.

Vehicles with 2 CMP sensors are equipped with variable camshaft timing (VCT). They use the second sensor to identify the position of the camshaft on bank 2 as an input to the PCM. DTC P0345 is associated with this sensor and it is referred to as CMP2.

REMOVAL & INSTALLATION

3.0L Engine

1. Before servicing the vehicle, refer to the precautions in the beginning of this section.

2. Disconnect the battery ground cable.

3. Remove the air cleaner assembly.

4. Remove the throttle body.

5. Remove the 2 bolts, the nut and the upper intake manifold support bracket.

6. Disconnect the RH CMP electrical connector.

7. Remove the bolt and the RH CMP sensor.

8. Remove the fuel tube bracket bolt and position the fuel tube aside.

9. Disconnect the LH CMP sensor electrical connector.

10. Remove the bolt and the LH CMP sensor.

➡**Lubricate the O-ring seals with clean engine oil.**

11. To install, reverse the removal procedure.

3.9L Engine

1. Before servicing the vehicle, refer to the precautions in the beginning of this section.

2. Disconnect the battery ground cable.

➡**The engine appearance cover is equipped with a noise suppressor. If the noise suppressor becomes separated from the engine appearance cover it must be positioned on the intake manifold prior to installing the engine appearance cover.**

3. Remove the engine appearance cover and the noise suppressor (if detached).

4. Disconnect the 2 CMP sensor electrical connectors.

5. Remove the ground strap nut and position the ground strap aside.

6. Remove the 3 nuts and position the wiring harness conduit aside.

7. Remove the 2 bolts and the LH and RH CMP sensors.

➡**Inspect and install new O-ring seals as necessary.**

➡**Lubricate the O-ring seals with clean engine oil.**

8. To install, reverse the removal procedure.

TESTING

See Figures 136 and 137.

1. Before servicing the vehicle, refer to the precautions in the beginning of this section.

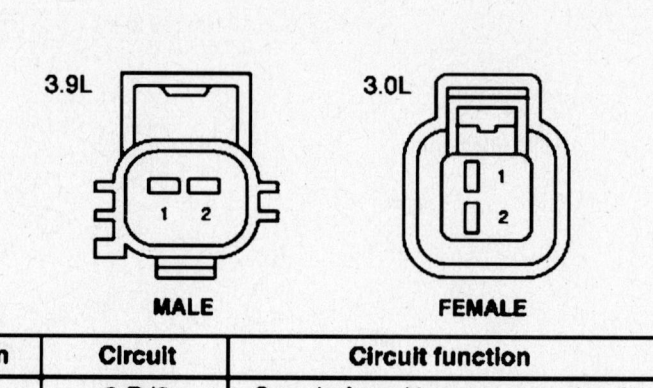

Pin	Circuit	Circuit function
1	8-RJ3 (WH/VT)	Camshaft position sensor 1, signal
2	9-RJ3 (BN/WH)	Signal return

22086_LILS_G0019

Fig. 136 Camshaft Position Sensor 1 Connector

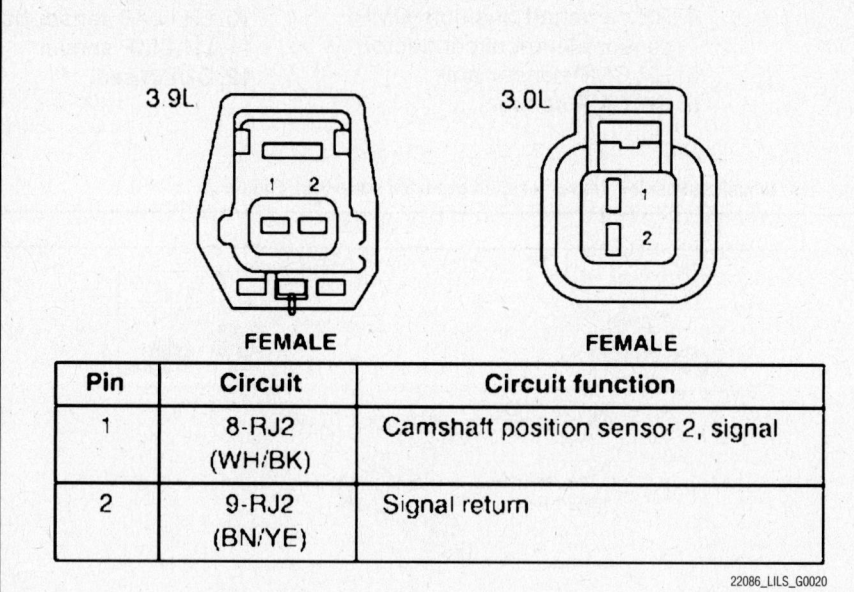

Pin	Circuit	Circuit function
1	8-RJ2 (WH/BK)	Camshaft position sensor 2, signal
2	9-RJ2 (BN/YE)	Signal return

22086_LILS_G0020

Fig. 137 Camshaft Position Sensor 2 Connector

※※ WARNING

Use only a high-impedance multimeter, otherwise damage to the PCM and/or sensors can result.

2. With the key **OFF**, disconnect the CMP sensor harness connector.

3. Measure the resistance of the CMP sensor.

• 3.0L Engine: 250–1000 ohms

• 3.9L Engine: 1850–2850 ohms

4. If the resistance measured is outside the limits given, replace the CMP sensor.

CRANKSHAFT POSITION (CKP) SENSOR

LOCATION

See Figures 138 and 139.

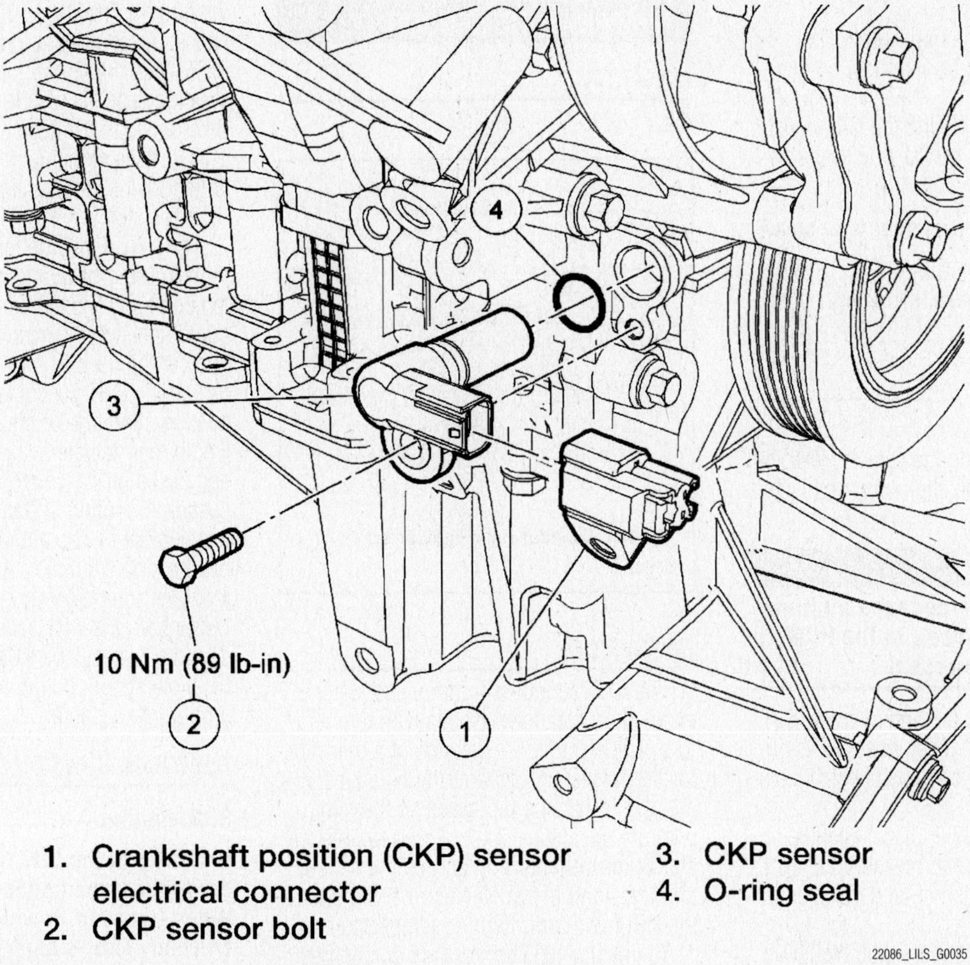

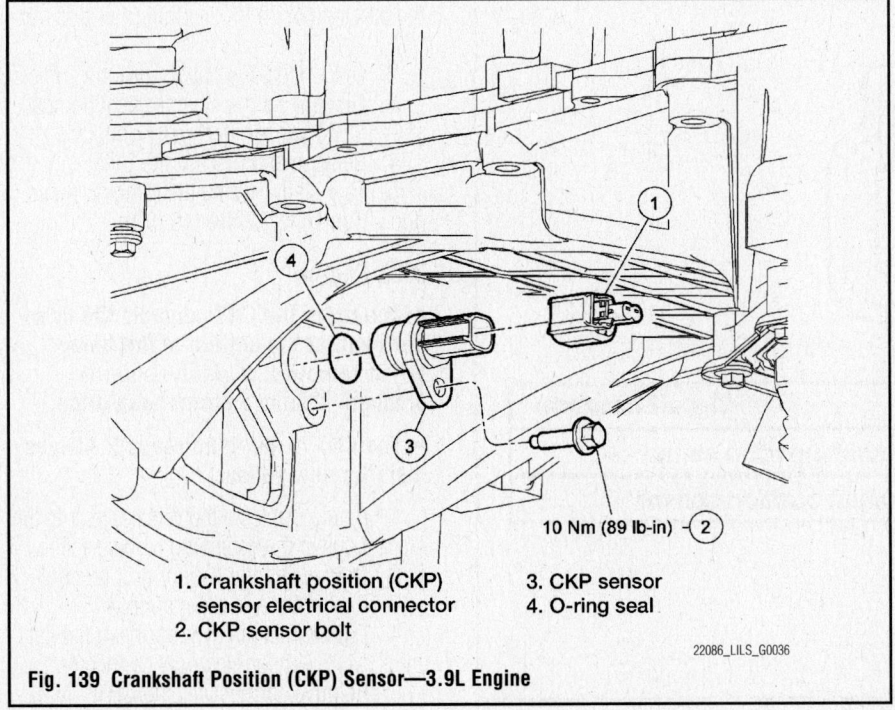

10 Nm (89 lb-in)
②

1. **Crankshaft position (CKP) sensor electrical connector**
2. **CKP sensor bolt**
3. **CKP sensor**
4. **O-ring seal**

22086_LILS_G0035

Fig. 138 Crankshaft Position (CKP) Sensor—3.0L Engine

10 Nm (89 lb-in) ②

1. **Crankshaft position (CKP) sensor electrical connector**
2. **CKP sensor bolt**
3. **CKP sensor**
4. **O-ring seal**

22086_LILS_G0036

Fig. 139 Crankshaft Position (CKP) Sensor—3.9L Engine

OPERATION

The CKP sensor is a magnetic transducer mounted on the engine block or timing cover and is adjacent to a pulse wheel located on the crankshaft. By monitoring the crankshaft mounted pulse wheel, the CKP is the primary sensor for ignition information to the PCM. The trigger wheel has a total of 35 teeth spaced 10 degrees apart with one empty space for a missing tooth. By monitoring the trigger wheel, the CKP indicates crankshaft position and speed information to the PCM. By monitoring the missing tooth, the PCM uses the CKP signal to synchronize the ignition system and track the rotation of the crankshaft.

REMOVAL & INSTALLATION

1. Before servicing the vehicle, refer to the precautions in the beginning of this section.

2. With the vehicle in NEUTRAL, position it on a hoist.

3. Disconnect the battery ground cable.

4. Disconnect the crankshaft position (CKP) sensor electrical connector.

5. Remove the bolt and the CKP sensor. Inspect and install a new O-ring seal as necessary.

➡**Lubricate the O-ring seal with clean engine oil.**

6. To install, reverse the removal procedure.

TESTING

See Figure 140.

1. Before servicing the vehicle, refer to the precautions in the beginning of this section.

✳✳ WARNING

Use only a high-impedance multimeter, otherwise damage to the PCM and/or sensors can result.

2. Visually check the timing cover, CKP sensor and external trigger wheel (outside the timing cover) for obvious physical damage.

3. With the key **OFF**, disconnect the CKP sensor harness and measure the resistance of the CKP sensor. Standard value is 250–1000 ohms.

4. If the resistance is outside the limits given, replace the CKP sensor.

FEMALE

Pin	Circuit	Circuit function
1	8-RJ4 (WH/RD)	Crankshaft position sensor +
2	10-RJ4 (GY/RD)	Crankshaft position sensor -

22086_LILS_G0022

Fig. 140 Crankshaft Position Sensor Connector

CYLINDER HEAD TEMPERATURE SENSOR

LOCATION

See Figure 141.

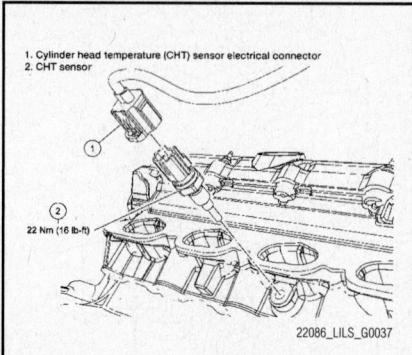

1. Cylinder head temperature (CHT) sensor electrical connector
2. CHT sensor

22 Nm (16 lb-ft)

22086_LILS_G0037

Fig. 141 Cylinder Head Temperature Sensor

OPERATION

The CHT sensor is a thermistor device in which resistance changes with temperature. The electrical resistance of a thermistor decreases as temperature increases, and the resistance increases as the temperature decreases. The varying resistance affects the voltage drop across the sensor terminals and provides electrical signals to the PCM corresponding to temperature.

Thermistor-type sensors are considered passive sensors. A passive sensor is connected to a voltage divider network so that varying the resistance of the passive sensor causes a variation in total current flow.

Voltage that is dropped across a fixed resistor in series with the sensor resistor determines the voltage signal at the PCM. This voltage signal is equal to the reference voltage minus the voltage drop across the fixed resistor.

The CHT sensor is installed in the aluminum cylinder head and measures the metal temperature. The CHT sensor can provide complete engine temperature information and can be used to infer coolant temperature. If the CHT sensor conveys an overheating condition to the PCM, the PCM would then initiate a fail-safe cooling strategy based on information from the CHT sensor. A cooling system failure such as low coolant or coolant loss could cause an overheating condition. As a result, damage to major engine components could occur. Using both the CHT sensor and fail-safe cooling strategy, the PCM prevents damage by allowing air cooling of the engine and limp home capability.

REMOVAL & INSTALLATION

3.0L Engine

➡**The tip of the CHT contacts the cylinder head at the bottom of the hole. When removed, it will be slightly crushed. This is a normal condition.**

➡**The CHT is not to be reused. Always install a new sensor.**

1. Before servicing the vehicle, refer to the precautions in the beginning of this section.

2. Disconnect the battery ground cable.

3. Disconnect the cylinder head temperature (CHT) sensor electrical connector.

4. Remove and discard the CHT.

5. To install, reverse the removal procedure. Tighten to 22 Nm (16 lb-ft).

3.9L Engine

➡**The tip of the CHT contacts the cylinder head at the bottom of the hole. When removed, it will be slightly crushed. This is a normal condition.**

➡**The CHT is not to be reused. Always install a new sensor.**

1. Before servicing the vehicle, refer to the precautions in the beginning of this section.

2. Disconnect the battery ground cable.

3. Remove the intake manifold.

4. Disconnect the cylinder head temperature (CHT) sensor electrical connector.

5. Remove and discard the CHT.

FEMALE

Pin	Circuit	Circuit function
1	8-RJ33 (WH/VT)	Cylinder-head temperature sensor, feed
2	9-RJ33 (BN/WH)	Signal return

22086_LILS_G0021

Fig. 142 Cylinder Head Temperature Sensor Connector

CYLINDER HEAD TEMPERATURE SENSOR EXPECTED VALUES

Temperature		CHT Sensor Values		
°C	°F	COLD END (volts)	HOT END (volts)	Resistance (K ohms)
-40	-40	4.89	-	965.808
-30	-22	4.81	-	513.019
-20	-4	4.67	-	283.664
-10	14	4.45	-	162.584
0	32	4.14	-	96.255
10	50	3.73	-	59.175
20	68	3.26	-	37.387
30	86	2.74	-	24.215
40	104	2.23	-	16.043
50	122	1.76	-	10.85
60	140	1.36	-	7.487
70	158	1.04	-	5.268
80	176	0.79	3.99	3.775
85	185	0.69	3.86	3.215
90	194	0.60	3.71	2.75
95	203	0.53	3.56	2.361
100	212	0.46	3.41	2.034
110	230	-	3.07	1.523
120	248	-	2.74	1.155
130	266	-	2.41	0.8866
140	284	-	2.10	0.6891
150	302	-	1.81	0.5417
160	320	-	1.55	0.4301
170	338	-	1.33	0.3449
180	356	-	1.13	0.2791
190	374	-	0.96	0.2278
200	392	-	0.82	0.1875
210	410	-	0.70	0.155
220	428	-	0.60	0.130
230	446	-	0.51	0.109
240	464	-	0.44	0.092
250	482	-	0.35	0.078
260	500	-	0.33	0.067

22086_LILS_G0032

Fig. 143 CHT Temperature, Resistance and Voltage Table

6. To install, reverse the removal procedure. Tighten to 22 Nm (16 lb-ft).

TESTING

See Figures 142 and 143.

➡The CHT sensor is used to determine the engine coolant temperature. To cover the entire temperature range of both the CHT and ECT sensors, the PCM has a dual switching resistor circuit on the CHT input. A graph showing the temperature switching from the COLD END line to the HOT END line, with increasing temperature and back with decreasing temperature is included. Note the temperature to voltage overlap zone. Within this zone it is possible to have either a COLD END or HOT END voltage at the same temperature. For example, at 90°C (194°F) the voltage could read either 0.60 volt or 3.71 volts. Refer to the table for the temperature to voltage expected values.

1. Before servicing the vehicle, refer to the precautions in the beginning of this section.

✳✳ WARNING

Use only a high-impedance multimeter, otherwise damage to the PCM and/or sensors can result.

2. With the key **OFF**, disconnect the CHT sensor harness connector and measure the resistance of the sensor. Compare the resistance and the temperature with the illustration.

3. Connect the CHT sensor harness and backprobe the connection.

4. With the key **ON**, compare the voltage measurement and the temperature with the illustration.

5. If the measurements are not as listed, replace the CHT sensor.

ENGINE OIL TEMPERATURE (EOT) SENSOR

LOCATION

On the engine near the oil filter.

OPERATION

The EOT sensor is a thermistor device in which resistance changes with temperature. The electrical resistance of a thermistor decreases as the temperature increases and the resistance increases as the temperature decreases. The varying resistance affects the voltage drop across the sensor terminals and provides electrical signals to the PCM corresponding to temperature.

Thermistor-type sensors are considered passive sensors. A passive sensor is connected to a voltage divider network so that varying the resistance of the passive sensor causes a variation in total current flow.

Voltage that is dropped across a fixed resistor in a series with the sensor resistor determines the voltage signal at the PCM. This voltage signal is equal to the reference voltage minus the voltage drop across the fixed resistor.

The EOT sensor measures the temperature of the engine oil. The sensor is typically threaded into the engine oil lubrication system. The PCM can use the EOT sensor input to determine the following:

• On variable cam timing (VCT) applications the EOT input is used to adjust the VCT control gains and logic for camshaft timing.

• The PCM can use EOT sensor input in conjunction with other PCM inputs to determine oil degradation.

• The PCM can use EOT sensor input to initiate a soft engine shutdown. To prevent engine damage from occurring as a result of high oil temperatures, the PCM has the ability to initiate a soft engine shutdown. Whenever engine RPM exceeds a calibrated level for a certain period of time, the PCM will begin reducing power by disabling engine cylinders.

TESTING

See Figure 144.

1. Before servicing the vehicle, refer to the precautions in the beginning of this section.
2. Measure the oil temperature.
3. With the oil temperature sensor disconnected, measure the resistance of the sensor and compare to the illustration.

HEATED OXYGEN (HO2S) SENSOR

LOCATION

In the exhaust, near the catalytic converters.

Temperature		Temperature Sensor Values	
°C	°F	Voltage	Resistance (K ohms)
120	248	0.28	1.18
110	230	0.36	1.55
100	212	0.47	2.07
90	194	0.61	2.80
80	176	0.80	3.84
70	158	1.05	5.37
60	140	1.37	7.70
50	122	1.77	10.97
40	104	2.23	16.15
30	86	2.74	24.27
20	68	3.26	37.30
10	50	3.73	58.75
0	32	4.14	95.85
-10	14	4.45	160.31

22086_LILS_G0038

Fig. 144 Oil Temperature Sensor specifications

OPERATION

The HO2S detects the presence of oxygen in the exhaust and produces a variable voltage according to the amount of oxygen detected. A high concentration of oxygen (lean air/fuel ratio) in the exhaust produces a voltage signal less than 0.4 volt. A low concentration of oxygen (rich air/fuel ratio) produces a voltage signal greater than 0.6 volt. The HO2S provides feedback to the PCM indicating air/fuel ratio in order to achieve a near stoichiometric air/fuel ratio of 14.7:1 during closed loop engine operation. The HO2S generates a voltage between 0.0 and 1.1 volts.

Embedded with the sensing element is the HO2S heater. The heating element heats the sensor to a temperature of 800°C (1400°F). At approximately 300°C (600°F) the engine can enter closed loop operation. The VPWR circuit supplies voltage to the heater. The PCM will turn on the heater by providing the ground when the proper conditions occur. The heater allows the engine to enter closed loop operation sooner. The use of this heater requires the HO2S heater control to be duty cycled, to prevent damage to the heater.

REMOVAL & INSTALLATION

1. Before servicing the vehicle, refer to the precautions in the beginning of this section.
2. Raise and support the vehicle.
3. Disconnect the wiring harness connector.
4. Using an oxygen sensor wrench or socket, remove the oxygen sensor.

To install:

➡ **Apply anti-seize to the sensor threads before installing the sensor.**

5. Install the oxygen sensor and tighten to 30 ft. lbs. (40 Nm).
6. Connect the wiring harness connector.

TESTING

See Figures 145 through 148.

1. Before servicing the vehicle, refer to the precautions in the beginning of this section.

❋❋ WARNING

Use only a high-impedance multimeter, otherwise damage to the PCM and/or sensors can result.

❋❋ WARNING

Do not measure resistance between pins 3 and 4. Damage to the HO2S will result.

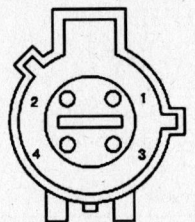

FEMALE

Pin	Circuit	Circuit function
1	15S-RJ14 (GN/YE)	Voltage supplied in Start and Run (overload protected)
2	91S-RJ14 (BN)	Heated Oxygen Sensor (HO2S) #11, heater
3	9-RJ14 (BN)	Signal return
4	8-RJ14 (WH)	Heated Oxygen Sensor (HO2S) #11, input

22086_LILS_G0025

Fig. 145 Heated Oxygen Sensor Connector—Bank 1 Sensor 1

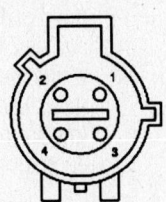

FEMALE

Pin	Circuit	Circuit function
1	15S-RJ15 (GN/BU)	Voltage supplied in Start and Run (overload protected)
2	91S-RJ15 (BN/RD)	Heated Oxygen Sensor (HO2S) #21, heater
3	9-RJ15 (BN/RD)	Signal return
4	8-RJ15 (WH/RD)	Heated Oxygen Sensor (HO2S) #21, input

22086_LILS_G0026

Fig. 146 Heated Oxygen Sensor Connector—Bank 2 Sensor 1

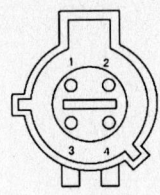

FEMALE

Pin	Circuit	Circuit function
1	91S-RJ25 (BN/BU)	Heated Oxygen Sensor (HO2S) #12, heater
2	15S-RJ25 (GN/RD)	Voltage supplied in Start and Run (overload protected)
3	8-RJ25 (WH/BU)	Heated Oxygen Sensor (HO2S) #12, input
4	9-RJ25 (BN/BU)	Signal return

22086_LILS_G0027

Fig. 147 Heated Oxygen Sensor Connector—Bank 1 Sensor 2

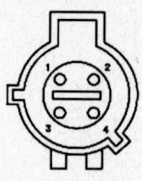

FEMALE

Pin	Circuit	Circuit function
1	91S-RJ26 (BN/GN)	Heated Oxygen Sensor (HO2S) #22, heater
2	15S-RJ26 (GN/BK)	Voltage supplied in Start and Run (overload protected)
3	8-RJ26 (WH/GN)	Heated Oxygen Sensor (HO2S) #22, input
4	9-RJ26 (BN/GN)	Signal return

22086_LILS_G0028

Fig. 148 Heated Oxygen Sensor Connector—Bank 2 Sensor 2

2. With the key **OFF**, disconnect the HO2S harness connector.

3. Measure the HO2S sensor resistances as follows:

- Pins 1 and 2: 3–30 ohms
- Pins 1 and 4: Greater than 10M ohms
- Pin 1 and battery negative: Greater than 10M ohms.

4. If any measurement is outside the range given, replace the HO2S.

INJECTION CONTROL PRESSURE (ICP) SENSOR

LOCATION

3.0L Engine

On the fuel rail, at the rear of the engine.

3.9L Engine

On the fuel rail, at the right front of the engine.

OPERATION

Also referred to as the Fuel Rail Pressure (FRP) sensor.

The FRP sensor is a diaphragm strain gauge device in which resistance changes with pressure. The electrical resistance of a strain gauge increases as pressure increases, and the resistance decreases as the pressure decreases. The varying resistance affects the voltage drop across the sensor terminals and provides electrical signals to the PCM corresponding to pressure.

Strain gauge type sensors are considered passive sensors. A passive sensor is connected to a voltage divider network so that varying the resistance of the passive sensor causes a variation in total current flow.

Voltage that is dropped across a fixed resistor in series with the sensor resistor determines the voltage signal at the PCM. This voltage signal is equal to the reference voltage minus the voltage drop across the fixed resistor.

The FRP sensor measures the pressure of the fuel near the fuel injectors. This signal is used by the PCM to adjust the fuel injector pulse width and meter fuel to each engine combustion cylinder.

REMOVAL & INSTALLATION

3.0L Engine

See Figure 149.

> **⁂ WARNING**
>
> Do not smoke or carry lighted tobacco or open flame of any type when working on or near any fuel-related components. Highly flammable mixtures are always present and can be ignited. Failure to follow these instructions may result in personal injury.

> **⁂ WARNING**
>
> Fuel in the fuel system remains under high pressure even when the engine is not running. Before working on or disconnecting any of the fuel lines or fuel system components the fuel system pressure must be relieved to prevent accidental spraying of fuel, which can cause personal injury or a fire hazard.

1. Before servicing the vehicle, refer to the precautions in the beginning of this section.

2. Disconnect the battery ground cable.

3. Release the fuel system pressure.

4. Remove the cowl vent screen.

5. Disconnect the fuel pressure sensor electrical connector and vacuum tube.

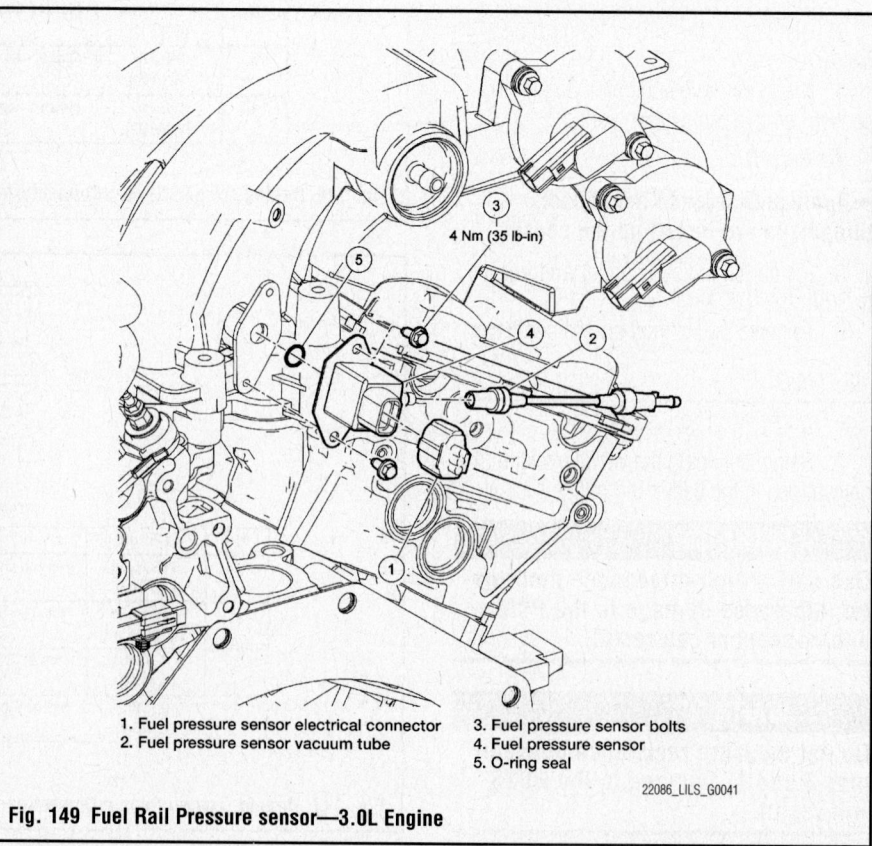

4 Nm (35 lb-in)

1. Fuel pressure sensor electrical connector
2. Fuel pressure sensor vacuum tube
3. Fuel pressure sensor bolts
4. Fuel pressure sensor
5. O-ring seal

22086_LILS_G0041

Fig. 149 Fuel Rail Pressure sensor—3.0L Engine

6. Remove the 2 bolts and the fuel pressure sensor.

7. To install, reverse the removal procedure. Tighten the FRP sensor bolts to 35 inch lbs. (4 Nm).

➡Lubricate the O-ring seal with clean engine oil.

3.9L Engine

See Figure 150.

☀ WARNING

Do not smoke or carry lighted tobacco or open flame of any type when working on or near any fuel-related components. Highly flammable mixtures are always present and can be ignited. Failure to follow these instructions may result in personal injury.

☀ WARNING

Fuel in the fuel system remains under high pressure even when the engine is not running. Before working on or disconnecting any of the fuel lines or fuel system components the fuel system pressure must be relieved to prevent accidental spraying of fuel, which can cause personal injury or a fire hazard.

1. Before servicing the vehicle, refer to the precautions in the beginning of this section.

2. Disconnect the battery ground cable.

☀ CAUTION

The engine appearance cover is equipped with a noise suppressor. If the noise suppressor becomes separated from the engine appearance cover it must be positioned on the intake manifold prior to installing the engine appearance cover.

3. Remove the engine appearance cover and the noise suppressor (if detached).

4. Release the fuel system pressure.

5. Disconnect the fuel pressure sensor electrical connector and vacuum tube.

6. Remove the 2 bolts and the fuel pressure sensor.

7. To install, reverse the removal procedure. Tighten the FRP sensor bolts to 44 inch lbs. (5 Nm).

➡Lubricate the O-ring seal with clean engine oil.

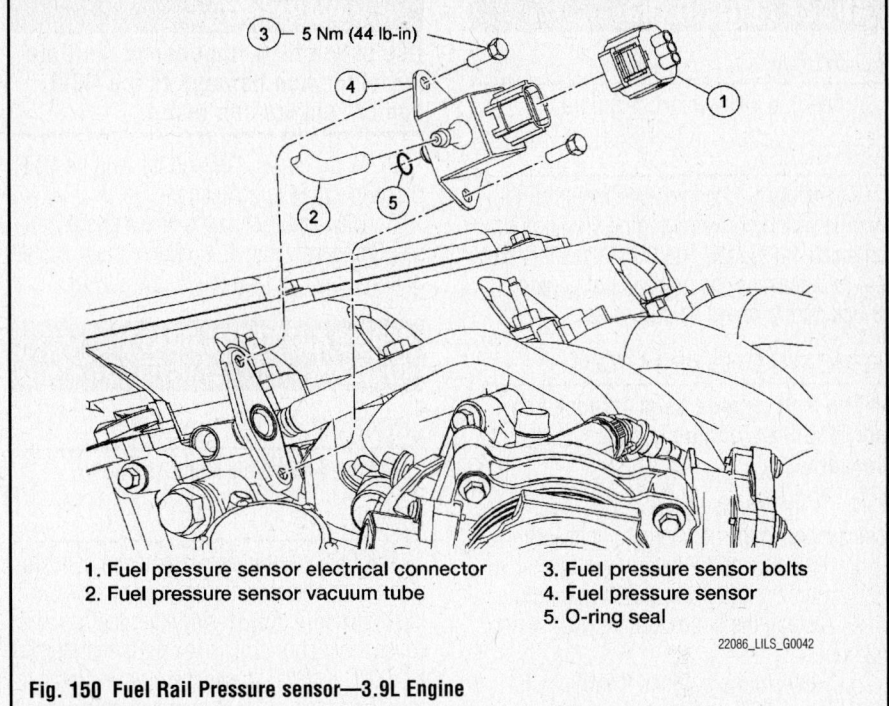

1. Fuel pressure sensor electrical connector
2. Fuel pressure sensor vacuum tube
3. Fuel pressure sensor bolts
4. Fuel pressure sensor
5. O-ring seal

22086_LILS_G0042

Fig. 150 Fuel Rail Pressure sensor—3.9L Engine

TESTING

See Figures 151 and 152.

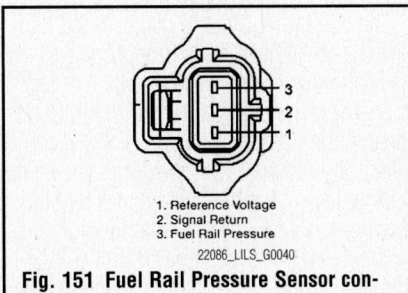

1. Reference Voltage
2. Signal Return
3. Fuel Rail Pressure

22086_LILS_G0040

Fig. 151 Fuel Rail Pressure Sensor connector

1. Before servicing the vehicle, refer to the precautions in the beginning of this section.

2. Connect a mechanical fuel pressure gauge.

3. With the key **ON**, backprobe the FRP sensor pins 2 and 3.

4. Compare the voltage and pressure readings with the specifications table.

INTAKE AIR TEMPERATURE (IAT) SENSOR

Part of the Mass Air Flow meter.

Voltage	Pressure (kPa)	Pressure (psi)
4.5	482	70
3.9	413	60
3.4	344	50
2.8	275	40
2.2	207	30
1.6	138	20
1.1	69	10
0.5	0	0

22086_LILS_G0039

Fig. 152 Fuel Rail Pressure sensor specification table

KNOCK SENSOR (KS)

LOCATION

Under the lower intake manifold.

OPERATION

The KS is a tuned accelerometer on the engine which converts engine vibration to an electrical signal. The PCM uses this signal to determine the presence of engine knock and to retard spark timing.

REMOVAL & INSTALLATION

➡ **The 3.0L engine uses 1 knock sensor. The 3.9L engine uses 2 knock sensors.**

1. Before servicing the vehicle, refer to the precautions in the beginning of this section.
2. Disconnect the battery ground cable.
3. Remove the lower intake manifold.
4. Detach the knock sensor (KS) wiring retainer.
5. Remove the bolt and the KS.
6. To install, reverse the removal procedure. Tighten the KS bolt to 15 ft. lbs. (20 Nm).

TESTING

See Figures 153 and 154.

1. Before servicing the vehicle, refer to the precautions in the beginning of this section.

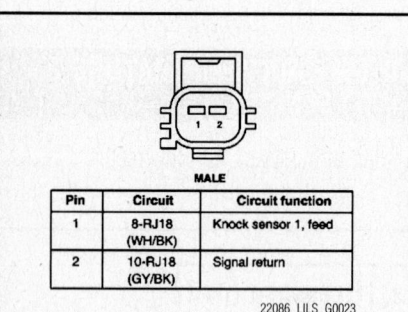

Pin	Circuit	Circuit function
1	8-RJ18 (WH/BK)	Knock sensor 1, feed
2	10-RJ18 (GY/BK)	Signal return

22086_LILS_G0023

Fig. 153 Knock Sensor 1 Connector–3.0L and 3.9L Engines

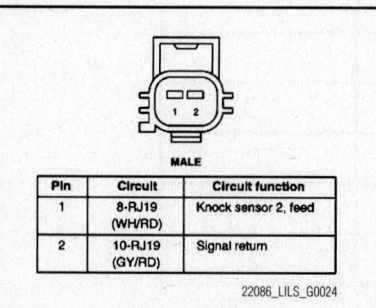

Pin	Circuit	Circuit function
1	8-RJ19 (WH/RD)	Knock sensor 2, feed
2	10-RJ19 (GY/RD)	Signal return

22086_LILS_G0024

Fig. 154 Knock Sensor 2 Connector–3.9L Engine

Use only a high-impedance multimeter, otherwise damage to the PCM and/or sensors can result.

2. With the key **ON** and the engine **OFF**, disconnect the knock sensor.
3. Measure resistance of the knock sensor. Standard value is 4.39M ohms—5.35M ohms. If not, replace the knock sensor.

MASS AIR FLOW (MAF) SENSOR

LOCATION

Attached to the air filter assembly.

OPERATION

The MAF sensor uses a hot wire sensing element to measure the amount of air entering the engine. Air passing over the hot wire causes it to cool. This hot wire is maintained at 200°C (392°F) above the ambient temperature as measured by a constant cold wire. If the hot wire electronic sensing element must be replaced, then the entire assembly must be replaced. Replacing only the element may change the air flow calibration.

The current required to maintain the temperature of the hot wire is proportional to the mass air flow. The MAF sensor then outputs an analog voltage signal to the PCM proportional to the intake air mass. The PCM calculates the required fuel injector pulse width in order to provide the desired air/fuel ratio. This input is also used in determining transmission electronic pressure control (EPC), shift and torque converter clutch scheduling.

REMOVAL & INSTALLATION

See Figure 155.

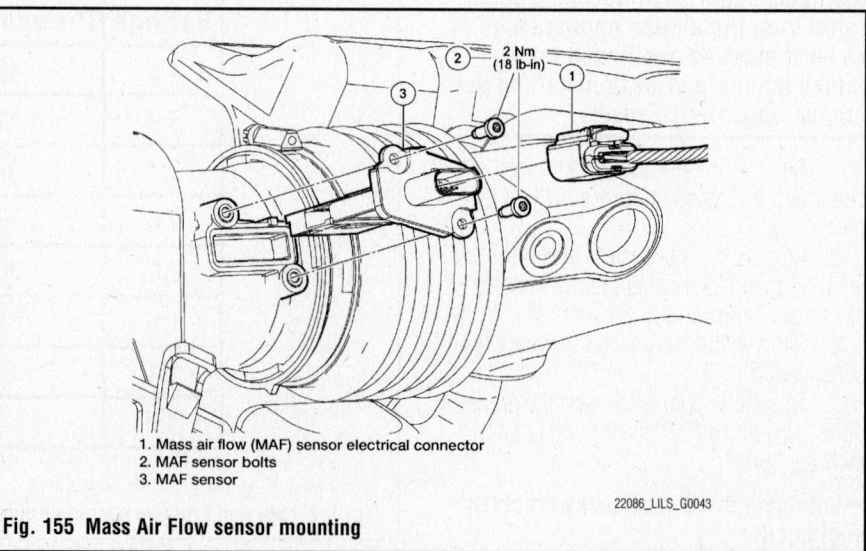

1. Mass air flow (MAF) sensor electrical connector
2. MAF sensor bolts
3. MAF sensor

22086_LILS_G0043

Fig. 155 Mass Air Flow sensor mounting

1. Before servicing the vehicle, refer to the precautions in the beginning of this section.
2. Disconnect the battery ground cable.
3. Disconnect the mass air flow (MAF) sensor electrical connector.
4. Remove the 2 bolts and the MAF sensor.
5. To install, reverse the removal procedure. Tighten the bolts to 18 inch lbs. (2 Nm).

TESTING

See Figure 156.

1. Before servicing the vehicle, refer to the precautions in the beginning of this section.

Use only a high-impedance multimeter, otherwise damage to the PCM and/or sensors can result.

2. Check the air inlet system (air cleaner, housing, ductwork) for obstructions or blockage.
3. Check for broken/loose air outlet tube clamps (throttle body and air cleaner assembly ends), cracks/holes in the air outlet tube, and worn gaskets between the MAF sensor and the air cleaner assembly. Check throttle body bore for sludge. Verify the MAF sensor is connected. Repair as necessary.
4. Disconnect the MAF harness connector.
5. With the key **ON** and engine **OFF**, check the following:
   - Pins 2, 4, and 5 should be ground.
   - Pin 6 should be B+ voltage.
6. Turn the key **OFF** and reconnect the MAF harness connector.

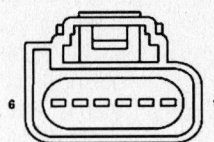

Pin	Circuit	Circuit function
1	8-RJ17 (WH/VT)	Intake Air Temperature (IAT) sensor, signal
2	9-RJ17 (BN/WH)	Intake Air Temperature (IAT) sensor, Signal return
3	8-RJ22 (WH/BU)	Mass Air Flow (MAF) sensor, signal
4	9-RJ22 (BN/BU)	Mass Air Flow (MAF) sensor, Signal return
5	31-RJ22 (BK/OG)	Ground
6	15S-RJ22 (GN/RD)	Voltage supplied in Start and Run (overload protected)

22086_LILS_G0029

Fig. 156 Mass Air Flow Sensor Connector

7. Start the engine and backprobe pin 1. This voltage should change with the intake air temperature.

8. Start the engine and backprobe pin 3. This voltage should rise with the engine rpm.

POWERTRAIN CONTROL MODULE (PCM)

LOCATION

Passenger side, near side cowl, behind the glove compartment.

OPERATION

The center of the electronic engine control (EEC) system is a microprocessor called the PCM. The PCM receives input from sensors and other electronic components (switches, relays). Based on the information received and programmed into its memory, the PCM generates output signals to control various relays, solenoids and actuators.

REMOVAL & INSTALLATION

1. Before servicing the vehicle, refer to the precautions in the beginning of this section.

2. Disconnect the battery ground cable.

3. Remove the fresh air inlet duct.

4. Remove the glove compartment.

5. Disconnect the 3 powertrain control module (PCM) electrical connectors.

6. Remove the 2 PCM nuts.

7. Remove the 2 PCM bracket bolts.

8. Remove the PCM and bracket as an assembly through the glove compartment opening.

9. To install, reverse the removal procedure.

THROTTLE POSITION SENSOR (TPS)

LOCATION

Mounted to the throttle body.

OPERATION

The TP sensor is a rotary potentiometer sensor that provides a signal to the PCM that is linearly proportional to the throttle plate/shaft position. The sensor housing has a 3-blade electrical connector that may be gold plated. The gold plating increases corrosion resistance on terminals and increases connector durability. The TP sensor is mounted on the throttle body. As the TP sensor is rotated by the throttle shaft, 4 operating conditions are determined by the PCM from the TP. Those conditions are closed throttle (includes idle or deceleration), part throttle (includes cruise or moderate acceleration), wide open throttle (includes maximum acceleration or dechoke on crank), and throttle angle rate.

REMOVAL & INSTALLATION

3.0L Engine

See Figure 157.

1. Before servicing the vehicle, refer to the precautions in the beginning of this section.

2. Disconnect the battery ground cable

3. Disconnect the throttle position (TP) sensor electrical connector.

✳✳ CAUTION

Failure to remove the TP sensor screws in the following manner will result in damage to the screws. First

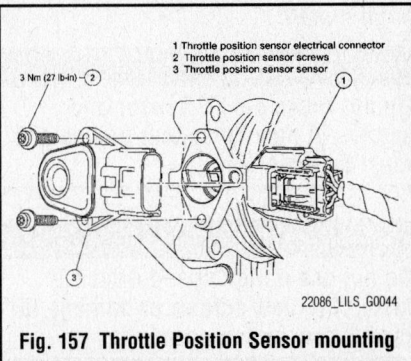

22086_LILS_G0044

Fig. 157 Throttle Position Sensor mounting

loosen the screws 1-2 full turns using a hand tool and then use a suitable high speed driver to complete the removal.

4. Remove and discard the 2 screws and the TP sensor.

To install:

✳✳ CAUTION

Do not reuse the TP sensor and screws. A new TP sensor and screws must be installed.

✳✳ CAUTION

Do not use a high speed driver to install the new screws or damage to the TP sensor can occur.

➡ **When installing the new TP sensor, make sure that the radial locator tab on the TP sensor is aligned with the radial locator hole on the throttle body.**

5. Position the new TP sensor and install the 2 new screws. Tighten to 3 Nm (27 lb-in).

6. Connect the TP sensor electrical connector.

7. Connect the battery ground cable.

3.9L Engine

See Figure 157.

1. Before servicing the vehicle, refer to the precautions in the beginning of this section.

2. Disconnect the battery ground cable.

3. Remove the throttle body.

✳✳ CAUTION

Failure to remove the TP sensor screws in the following manner will result in damage to the screws. First loosen the screws 1-2 full turns using a hand tool and then use a suitable high speed driver to complete the removal.

4. Remove and discard the 2 screws and the TP sensor.

To install:

> ❋❋ **CAUTION**
>
> **Do not reuse the TP sensor and screws. A new TP sensor and screws must be installed.**

> ❋❋ **CAUTION**
>
> **Do not use a high speed driver to install the new screws or damage to the TP sensor can occur.**

➡ **When installing the new TP sensor, make sure that the radial locator tab on the TP sensor is aligned with the radial locator hole on the throttle body.**

5. Position the new TP sensor and install the 2 new screws. Tighten to 3 Nm (27 lb-in).
6. Install the throttle body.
7. Connect the battery ground cable.

TESTING

See Figure 158.

1. Before servicing the vehicle, refer to the precautions in the beginning of this section.
2. With the key **ON** and the engine **OFF**, backprobe pins 2 and 3. Measure the voltage while slowly opening the throttle. The voltage should rise as the throttle opens.

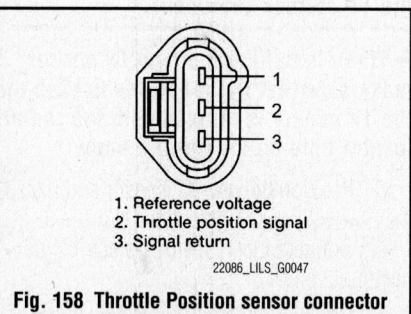

1. Reference voltage
2. Throttle position signal
3. Signal return

22086_LILS_G0047

Fig. 158 Throttle Position sensor connector

VARIABLE CAMSHAFT TIMING OIL CONTROL SOLENOID

LOCATION

Front of the cylinder head, under the valve cover.

OPERATION

The VCT solenoid valve is an integral part of the VCT system. The solenoid valve controls the flow of engine oil in the VCT actuator assembly. As the PCM controls the duty cycle of the solenoid valve, oil pressure/flow advances or retards the cam timing. Duty cycles near 0% or 100% represent rapid movement of the camshaft. Retaining a fixed camshaft position is accomplished by dithering (oscillating) the solenoid valve duty cycle.

The PCM calculates and determines the desired camshaft position. It will continually update the VCT solenoid duty cycle until the desired position is achieved. A difference between the desired and actual camshaft position represents a position error in the PCM VCT control loop. The PCM will disable the VCT and place the camshaft in a default position if a fault is detected. A related DTC will also be set when the fault is detected.

REMOVAL & INSTALLATION

See Figure 159.

1. Before servicing the vehicle, refer to the precautions in the beginning of this section.
2. Remove the LH or RH valve cover.
3. Remove the bolt and the variable camshaft timing (VCT) oil control solenoid.
4. To install, reverse the removal procedure. Tighten to 7 Nm (62 lb-in).

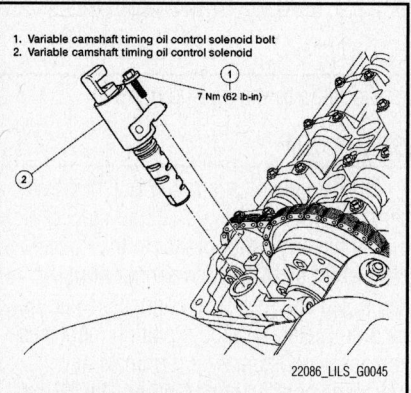

1. Variable camshaft timing oil control solenoid bolt
2. Variable camshaft timing oil control solenoid

7 Nm (62 lb-in)

22086_LILS_G0045

Fig. 159 Variable Camshaft Timing Oil Control Solenoid mounting

TESTING

See Figure 160.

1. Before servicing the vehicle, refer to the precautions in the beginning of this section.
2. With the key **OFF**, disconnect the VCT solenoid connector.

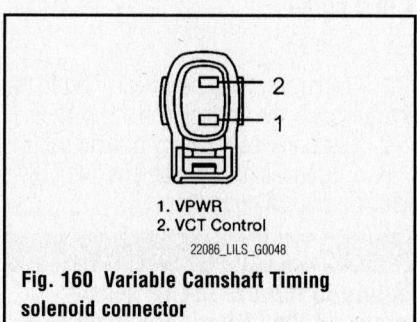

1. VPWR
2. VCT Control

22086_LILS_G0048

Fig. 160 Variable Camshaft Timing solenoid connector

3. Measure the resistance of the VCT solenoid. Specification is 5–14 ohms.
4. Measure the resistance between VTC solenoid pin 1 and ground. Specification is infinite resistance.
5. Replace the VCT solenoid if any tests are out of specifications.

VEHICLE SPEED SENSOR (VSS)

LOCATION

Rear of the transmission, near the output shaft.

OPERATION

Also called the Output Shaft Speed (OSS) Sensor.

The OSS sensor provides the PCM with information about the rotational speed of an output shaft. The PCM uses the information to control and diagnose powertrain behavior. The sensor is also used as the source of vehicle speed.

REMOVAL & INSTALLATION

1. Before servicing the vehicle, refer to the precautions in the beginning of this section.
2. Raise and support the vehicle.
3. Disconnect the OSS wiring connector.
4. Remove the OSS bolt and the OSS.
5. To install, reverse the removal procedure.

TESTING

See Figure 161.

1. Before servicing the vehicle, refer to the precautions in the beginning of this section.
2. Raise and support the vehicle.
3. Disconnect the OSS sensor wiring connector.
4. Measure the OSS sensor resistance and compare with the specification illustration. Replace if out of specification.

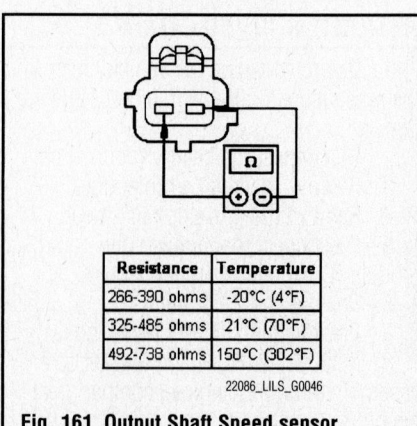

Resistance	Temperature
266-390 ohms	-20°C (4°F)
325-485 ohms	21°C (70°F)
492-738 ohms	150°C (302°F)

22086_LILS_G0046

Fig. 161 Output Shaft Speed sensor specifications

FUEL SYSTEM SERVICE PRECAUTIONS

Safety is the most important factor when performing not only fuel system maintenance but any type of maintenance. Failure to conduct maintenance and repairs in a safe manner may result in serious personal injury or death. Maintenance and testing of the vehicle's fuel system components can be accomplished safely and effectively by adhering to the following rules and guidelines.

• To avoid the possibility of fire and personal injury, always disconnect the negative battery cable unless the repair or test procedure requires that battery voltage be applied.

• Always relieve the fuel system pressure prior to disconnecting any fuel system component (injector, fuel rail, pressure regulator, etc.), fitting or fuel line connection. Exercise extreme caution whenever relieving fuel system pressure to avoid exposing skin, face and eyes to fuel spray. Please be advised that fuel under pressure may penetrate the skin or any part of the body that it contacts.

• Always place a shop towel or cloth around the fitting or connection prior to loosening to absorb any excess fuel due to spillage. Ensure that all fuel spillage (should it occur) is quickly removed from engine surfaces. Ensure that all fuel soaked cloths or towels are deposited into a suitable waste container.

• Always keep a dry chemical (Class B) fire extinguisher near the work area.

• Do not allow fuel spray or fuel vapors to come into contact with a spark or open flame.

• Always use a back-up wrench when loosening and tightening fuel line connection fittings. This will prevent unnecessary stress and torsion to fuel line piping.

• Always replace worn fuel fitting O-rings with new Do not substitute fuel hose or equivalent where fuel pipe is installed.

Before servicing the vehicle, make sure to also refer to the precautions in the beginning of this section as well.

RELIEVING FUEL SYSTEM PRESSURE

1. Before servicing the vehicle, refer to the precautions in the beginning of this section.
2. Remove the fuel pump relay.

3. Start the engine and allow it to idle until it stalls.
4. After the engine stalls, crank the engine for approximately 5 seconds to make sure the fuel injection supply manifold pressure has been released.
5. Turn the ignition switch to the OFF position.
6. Disconnect the negative battery cable.
7. When fuel system service is complete, install the fuel pump relay.

➡**It may take more than one key cycle to pressurize the fuel system.**

8. Cycle the ignition key and wait 3 seconds to pressurize the fuel system. Check for leaks before starting the engine.
9. Connect the negative battery cable.
10. Start the vehicle and check the fuel system for leaks.

FUEL FILTER

REMOVAL & INSTALLATION

1. Before servicing the vehicle, refer to the precautions in the beginning of this section.
2. Relieve the fuel system pressure.
3. Disconnect the negative battery cable.
4. Remove the left front wheel well rear splash shield.
5. Disconnect the fuel tube quick release fittings from both sides of the fuel filter.
6. Remove the fuel filter bracket mounting bolt, fuel filter bracket, and the fuel filter.

To install:

7. Install or connect the following:
• Fuel filter into the bracket making sure the flow direction is correct. Tighten the clamp to 15–25 inch lbs. (2–3 Nm).
• Fuel lines. Tighten the fittings to 22 ft. lbs. (30 Nm).
8. Tighten the bracket bolts to 62 inch lbs. (7 Nm).
9. Start the engine and check for leaks.

FUEL INJECTORS

REMOVAL & INSTALLATION

See Figure 162.

1. Before servicing the vehicle, refer to the precautions in the beginning of this section.
2. Disconnect the negative battery cable.

✳✳ CAUTION

The engine appearance cover is equipped with a noise suppressor. If the noise suppressor becomes separated from the engine appearance cover it must be positioned on the intake manifold prior to installing the engine appearance cover.

3. Remove the engine appearance cover and the noise suppressor, if detached.
4. Remove the air cleaner outlet pipe.
5. Release the fuel system pressure.
6. Remove the four engine appearance cover mounting bracket nuts and the brackets.
7. Disconnect the fuel pressure sensor electrical connector from the sensor.
8. Disconnect the fuel pressure sensor vacuum connector from the sensor.
9. Disconnect the eight fuel injector electrical connectors from the injectors.
10. Disconnect the fuel temperature sensor electrical connector from the sensor.
11. Disconnect the fuel supply tube retaining clip from the fuel injection supply manifold.
12. Disconnect the fuel supply tube spring lock coupling.
13. Remove the four bolts and the fuel injection supply manifold and fuel injectors as an assembly.
14. Remove the fuel injectors from the fuel injection supply manifold.

✳✳ CAUTION

Use O-ring seals that are made of special fuel-resistant material. Use of ordinary O-ring seals can cause the fuel system to leak. Do not reuse the O-ring seals.

15. Remove and discard the 16 O-ring seals from the fuel injectors.

To install:

16. Lubricate the new fuel injector O-ring seals with clean engine oil before installing.

✳✳ CAUTION

Use O-ring seals that are made of special fuel-resistant material. Use of ordinary O-rings can cause the fuel system to leak. Do not reuse the O-ring seals.

17. Install sixteen new O-ring seals onto the fuel injectors. Lubricate the O-ring seals with clean engine oil prior to installation.

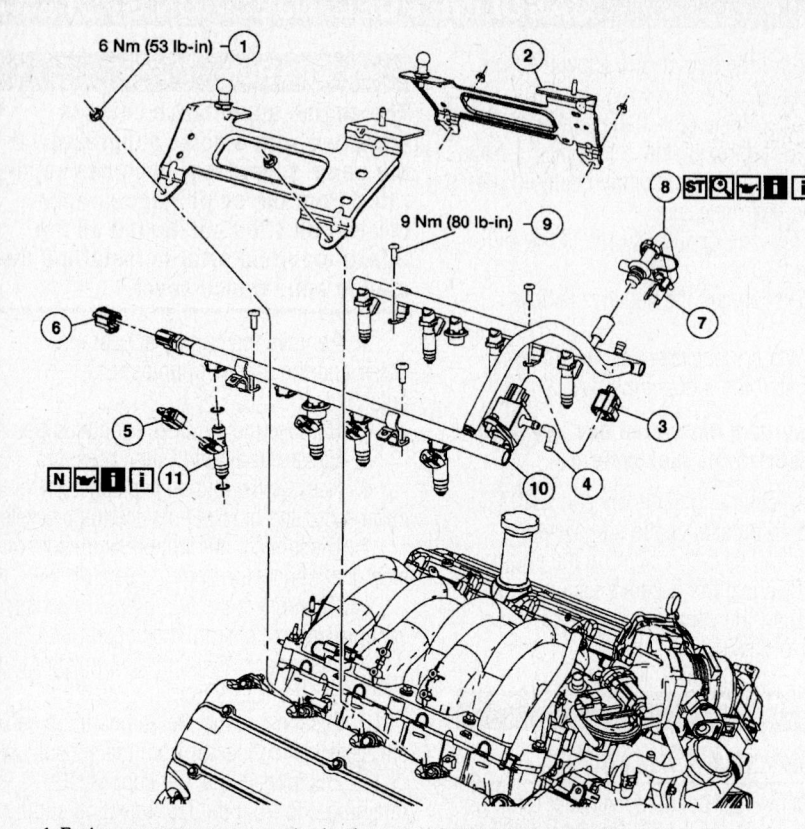

1 Engine appearance cover mounting bracket nuts
2 Engine appearance cover mounting brackets
3 Fuel pressure sensor electrical connector
4 Fuel pressure sensor vacuum connector
5 Fuel injector electrical connector
6 Fuel temperature sensor electrical connector
7 Fuel tube retaining clip
8 Fuel tube spring lock coupling
9 Fuel injection supply manifold bolts
10 Fuel injection supply manifold and fuel injectors
11 Fuel injectors

67197-LILS-G13

Fig. 162 Exploded view of the fuel injector mounting—3.9L engine shown

18. Install the fuel injectors and clips onto the fuel rail.

19. Install the fuel rail and injectors as an assembly. Tighten the fuel rail bolts to 89 inch lbs. (10 Nm).

20. Install the remaining components in the reverse order of removal.

FUEL PUMP

REMOVAL & INSTALLATION

1. Before servicing the vehicle, refer to the precautions in the beginning of this section.

2. Remove the rear seat cushion to and any insulation padding covering the access covers.

3. Drain the fuel tank.

4. Support the tank and loosen the straps to gain access to the pump.

5. Remove the access covers.

➡ **The routing of the internal fuel crossover tubes is critical to correct fuel system operation. Note the routing of the internal fuel crossover hoses at this time.**

6. Partially raise the fuel transfer pump and disconnect the internal fuel crossover tube quick release fittings.

7. Disconnect the fuel pump module tube quick release fitting from the fuel pump module and position aside.

❊❊ CAUTION

Drain the remaining fuel from the delivery module into the fuel tank prior to removal.

8. Before removal, attach a non-conductive material to the crossover tubes. Then remove the fuel pump module and crossover tubes as an assembly, using the non-conductive material to pull the crossover lines through the gas tank.

9. Remove and discard the fuel pump module gasket.

To install:

10. Install the fuel pump module and crossover tubes as an assembly.

11. Attaching the non-conductive material to the crossover tubes, pull the crossover tubes through the gas tank to install the fuel pump module.

12. Using tool 310-069, install the fuel pump module using a new gasket. Install the lock ring and tighten to 59 ft. lbs. (80 Nm).

➡ **Make sure that the fuel crossover tubes are routed correctly.**

13. Partially raise the fuel transfer pump and connect the internal fuel crossover hose quick disconnect fittings.

14. Using the tool 310-069, install the fuel transfer pump with a new gasket and lock ring. Tighten to 59 ft. lbs. (80 Nm).

15. Connect the fuel pump module tube quick release fitting at the fuel pump module.

16. Connect the fuel pump module and fuel transfer pump electrical connectors.

17. Install the fuel pump module and fuel transfer pump access covers.

18. Install the rear seat bottom and any insulation padding covering the access covers.

19. Tighten the 2 fuel tank support strap bolts to 26 ft. lbs. (35 Nm).

20. Connect the negative battery cable.

FUEL TANK

REMOVAL & INSTALLATION

See Figure 163.

1. Before servicing the vehicle, refer to the precautions in the beginning of this section.

2. With the vehicle in NEUTRAL, position it on a hoist.

3. Drain the fuel tank.

4. Remove the driveshaft.

5. Remove the 2 pin-type retainers and the bolt and position aside the fuel tube shield.

6. Disconnect the vapor tube and the fuel supply tube quick connect coupling. Disconnect the fuel filler pipe hose from the fuel tank.

7. Position a suitable lifting device to support the fuel tank.

8. Remove the 2 fuel tank strap mounting bolts and position aside the 2 fuel tank straps.

9. Disconnect the fuel tank electrical connector.

10. Partially lower the fuel tank and disconnect the vapor tube quick connect coupling.

11. Remove the fuel tank.

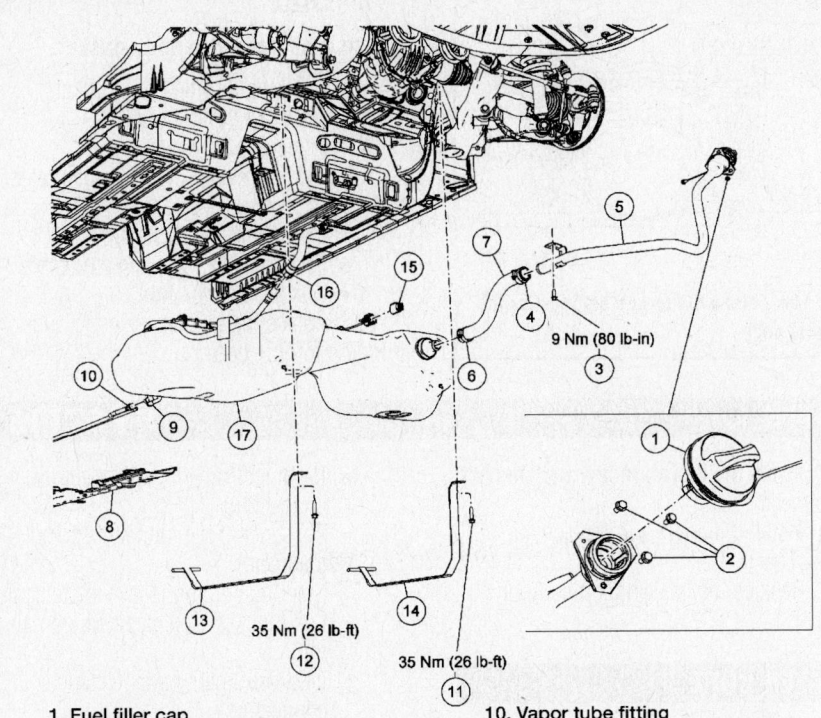

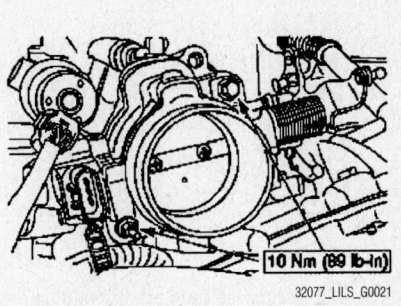

10 Nm (89 lb-in)

32077_LILS_G0021

Fig. 164 Torque settings for the throttle body bolts

9 Nm (80 lb-in)

35 Nm (26 lb-ft)

35 Nm (26 lb-ft)

1. Fuel filler cap
2. Fuel filler pipe mounting screws (3 required)
3. Fuel filler pipe mounting bolt
4. Fuel hose-to-filler pipe clamp
5. Fuel filler pipe
6. Fuel hose-to-tank clamp
7. Fuel hose and clamps
8. Fuel tube shield
9. Fuel supply quick release
10. Vapor tube fitting
11. Fuel tank strap mounting bolt
12. Fuel tank strap mounting bolt
13. Fuel tank strap
14. Fuel tank strap
15. Fuel tank electrical connector
16. Vapor tube quick release fitting
17. Fuel tank

22086_LILS_G0006

Fig. 163 Fuel tank mounting exploded view

To install:

12. To install, reverse the removal procedure. Tighten the fuel tank mounting strap bolts to 35 Nm (26 lb-ft).

13. Turn the ignition key to the ON position to pressurize the fuel system.

14. Visually inspect the fuel system for leaks.

IDLE SPEED

ADJUSTMENT

Idle speed is maintained by the Powertrain Control Module (PCM). No adjustment is necessary or possible.

THROTTLE BODY

REMOVAL & INSTALLATION

3.0L Engine

See Figure 164.

❊❊ CAUTION

Do not smoke or carry lighted tobacco or open flame of any type when working on or near any fuel-related components. Highly flammable mixtures are always present and may be ignited. Failure to follow these instructions may result in personal injury.

❊❊ WARNING

The throttle body bore and plate area have a special coating and cannot be cleaned.

1. Before servicing the vehicle, refer to the precautions in the beginning of this section.

2. Remove the air cleaner outlet tube from the throttle body.

3. Disconnect the throttle position sensor electrical connector and the wiring harness retainer.

4. Disconnect the accelerator cable and the speed control actuator cable from the throttle body.

➡**The throttle body (TB) gasket is reusable.**

5. Remove the bolts and the throttle body.

To install:

6. Replace the bolts and the throttle body.

7. Connect the accelerator cable and the speed control actuator cable to the throttle body.

8. Connect the throttle position sensor electrical connector and the wiring harness retainer.

9. Replace the air cleaner outlet tube from the throttle body.

3.9L Engine

See Figures 165 and 166.

❊❊ CAUTION

Do not smoke or carry lighted tobacco or open flame of any type when working on or near any fuel-related components. Highly flammable mixtures are always present and may be ignited. Failure to follow these instructions may result in personal injury.

❊❊ WARNING

Throttle body bore and plate area have a special coating and cannot be cleaned.

1. Before servicing the vehicle, refer to the precautions in the beginning of this section.

2. Remove the air cleaner outlet tube from the throttle body.

3. Disconnect the Throttle Position (TP) sensor electrical connector.

4. Disconnect the throttle body linkages.

5. Disconnect the speed control actuator cable.

6. Disconnect the accelerator cable.

➡**Discard the Throttle Body (TB) gasket.**

7. Remove the throttle body.

8. Remove the throttle body gasket.

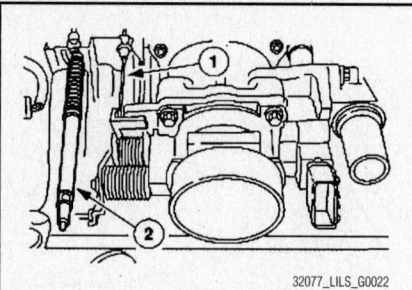

Fig. 165 Illustrated here are the throttle body linkage (1) and the accelerator cable

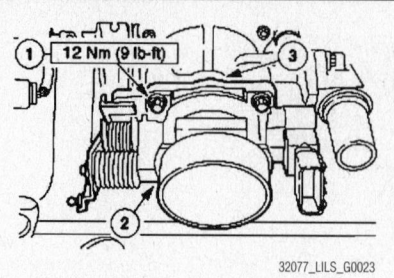

Fig. 166 Follow the torque settings for the throttle body

To install:

→Use a new throttle body gasket.

9. Install the throttle body gasket.
10. Install the throttle body.
11. Connect the following:
   • Throttle Position (TP) sensor electrical connector
   • The throttle body linkages
   • The speed control actuator cable
   • The accelerator cable
12. Replace the air cleaner outlet tube from the throttle body.

HEATING & AIR CONDITIONING   SYSTEM

BLOWER MOTOR

REMOVAL & INSTALLATION

See Figure 167.

1. Before servicing the vehicle, refer to the precautions in the beginning of this section.
2. Disconnect the battery ground cable.
3. Remove the passenger side floor duct.
4. Remove the screws and remove the cover.
5. Disconnect the connector and remove the blower motor.

✳✳ WARNING

Prior to removing a wheel that is to be reused, clean any corrosion from the blower motor shaft to prevent damage to the wheel mounting diameter.

6. Remove the wheel from the blower motor, by removing the push clip.

To install:

→Make sure to install the blower motor cover. It is necessary for correct cooling.

7. Install the wheel to the blower motor, by replacing the push clip.

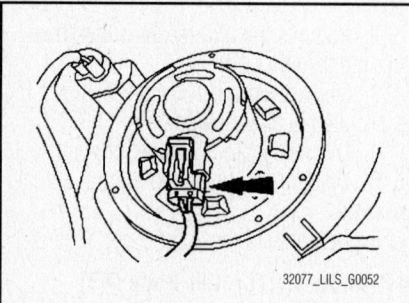

Fig. 167 The location of the blower motor and the connector

8. Install the blower motor and connect the connector.
9. Install the cover and replace the screws.
10. Replace the passenger side floor duct.

HEATER CORE

REMOVAL & INSTALLATION

See Figures 168 and 169.

1. Before servicing the vehicle, refer to the precautions in the beginning of this section.
2. Drain the cooling system.
3. Recover the A/C refrigerant.
4. Remove or disconnect the following:
   • Negative battery cable
   • Heater hose assembly
   • Cabin air filter plenum
   • Thermostatic expansion valve manifold and tube assembly
   • Driver's side air bag module
   • Floor console and A/C duct
   • Shift lever assembly, if equipped with automatic transmission
   • Left and right instrument panel insulators
   • Left and right door sill scuff plates
   • Left and right door weatherstrips
   • Left and right A pillar lower trim panels
   • Left and right windshield side garnish moldings
   • Instrument panel defroster opening grille assembly
   • Instrument panel cowl top screws
   • Instrument panel upper reinforcement bolts
   • Left and right instrument panel side finish panels
   • Hood release handle and cable
   • Upper right bulkhead electrical connector

   • Right instrument panel electrical connectors
   • Passenger side tunnel electrical connector
   • Steering column intermediate shaft
   • Left junction box electrical connectors
   • Left instrument panel electrical connectors
   • Ignition shift interlock connector, if equipped
   • 4 instrument panel tunnel brace bolts
   • Left outer instrument panel cowl side cover and reinforcement bolt
   • Left instrument panel cowl side bolt and nut
   • Right instrument panel cowl side bolt and nut
   • Instrument panel
   • Evaporator housing electrical connector
   • Cowl top attachment bolt
   • Evaporator housing attachment bolt
   • 3 evaporator nuts and washers in the engine compartment
   • Rear seat floor ducts
   • Evaporator core housing
   • Evaporator core housing air inlet
   • Bypass door harness connector
   • Heater core

To install:
5. Install or connect the following:
   • Heater core
   • Bypass door harness connector
   • Evaporator core housing air inlet
   • Evaporator core housing
   • Rear seat floor ducts
   • 3 evaporator nuts and washers in the engine compartment
   • Evaporator housing attachment bolt
   • Cowl top attachment bolt
   • Evaporator housing electrical connector
   • Instrument panel

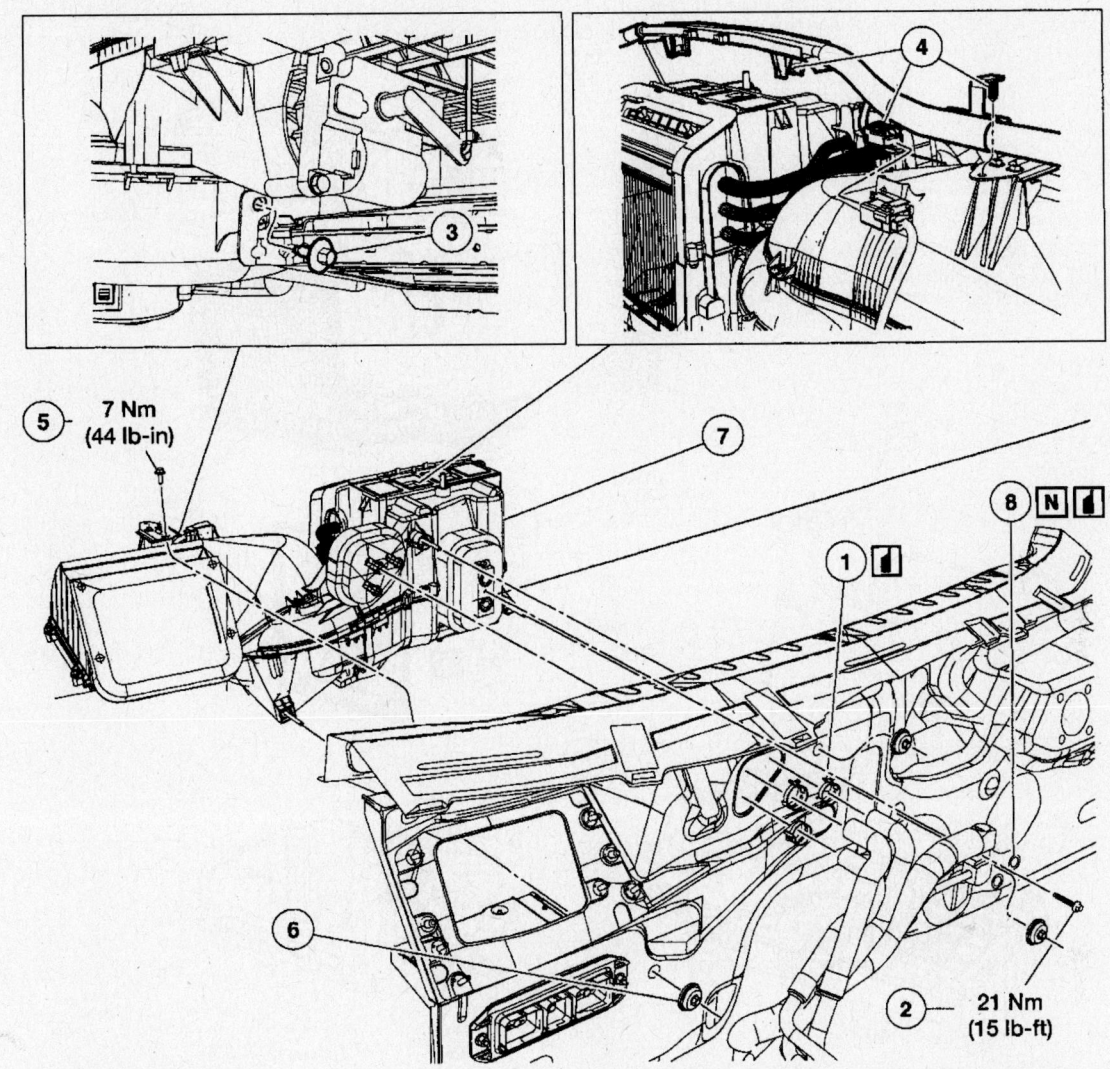

1 Heater hose clamp
2 Thermostatic expansion valve manifold bolt
3 PCM bracket bolt
4 Wire harness
5 Heater core and evaporator core housing bracket bolt
6 Heater core and evaporator core housing nut
7 Heater core and evaporator core housing
8 Thermostatic expansion valve O-ring

67197-LILS-G04

Fig. 168 Heater core and related components (1 of 2)

- Instrument panel cowl top screws. Tighten to 27 inch lbs. (3 Nm).
- Right instrument panel cowl side bolt and nut. Tighten the fasteners to 15 ft. lbs. (20 Nm).
- Left instrument panel cowl side bolt and nut. Tighten the fasteners to 15 ft. lbs. (20 Nm).
- Left outer instrument panel cowl side cover and reinforcement bolt. Tighten the bolt to 15 ft. lbs. (20 Nm).
- Instrument panel upper reinforcement bolts. Tighten the bolts to 15 ft. lbs. (20 Nm).

- 4 instrument panel tunnel brace bolts. Tighten the bolts to 15 ft. lbs. (20 Nm).
- Ignition shift interlock connector, if equipped
- Left instrument panel electrical connectors
- Left junction box electrical connectors
- Steering column intermediate shaft. Tighten the pinch bolt to 26 ft. lbs. (35 Nm).
- Passenger side tunnel electrical connector

- Right instrument panel electrical connectors
- Upper right bulkhead electrical connector
- Hood release handle and cable
- Left and right instrument panel side finish panels
- Instrument panel defroster opening grille assembly
- Left and right windshield side garnish moldings
- Left and right A pillar lower trim panels
- Left and right door weatherstrips

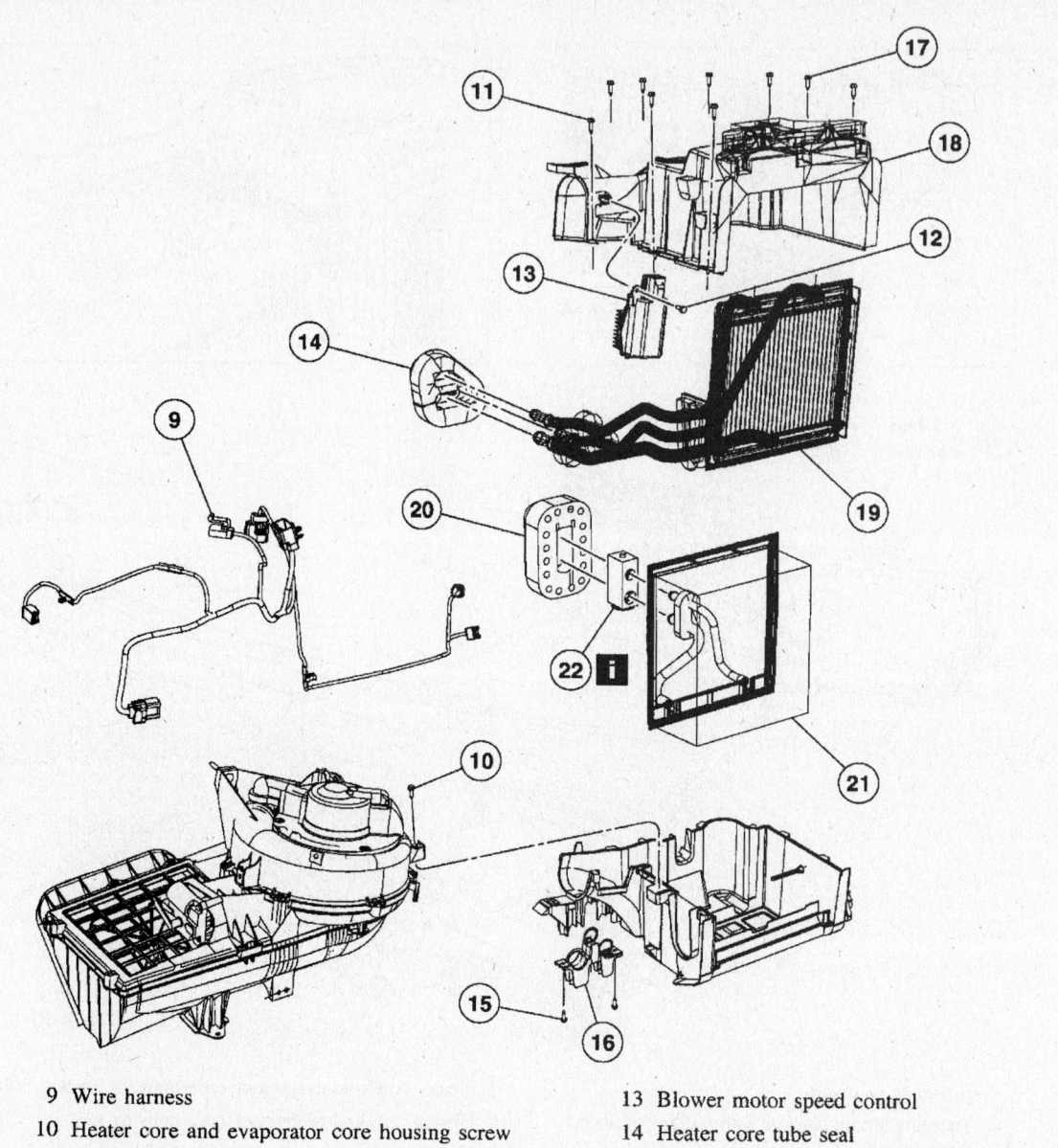

Fig. 169 Heater core and related components (2 of 2)

9 Wire harness

10 Heater core and evaporator core housing screw

11 Heater core and evaporator core housing screw

12 Blower motor speed control screw

13 Blower motor speed control

14 Heater core tube seal

15 Heater core tube bracket screw

67197-LILS-G05

- Left and right door sill scuff plates
- Left and right instrument panel insulators
- Shift lever assembly, if equipped with automatic transmission
- Floor console and A/C duct
- Driver's side air bag module
- Thermostatic expansion valve manifold and tube assembly
- Cabin air filter plenum
- Heater hose assembly
- Negative battery cable
6. Fill the cooling system.
7. Recharge the A/C system.
8. Start the engine and check for leaks.

STEERING

POWER STEERING GEAR

REMOVAL & INSTALLATION

See Figure 170.

1. Before servicing the vehicle, refer to the precautions in the beginning of this section.

✳✳ CAUTION

While repairing the power steering system, care should be taken to prevent the entry of contaminants or pre- mature failure of the power steering components can result. Do not allow the steering wheel to rotate while the intermediate shaft is disconnected or damage to the clockspring can result. If there is evidence that the shaft has rotated, the clockspring must be removed and recentered.

2. Before servicing the vehicle, refer to the precautions in the beginning of this section.

3. Disconnect the negative battery cable.

4. Hold the steering wheel in the straight-ahead position using a suitable holding device.

5. Remove the two tie-rod end nuts and separate the 2 tie-rod ends from the wheel knuckles.

6. Remove and discard the steering line clamp plate bolt and disconnect the steering lines from the steering gear.

7. Remove and discard the 2 O-ring seals.

8. Disconnect the VAPS actuator electrical connector.

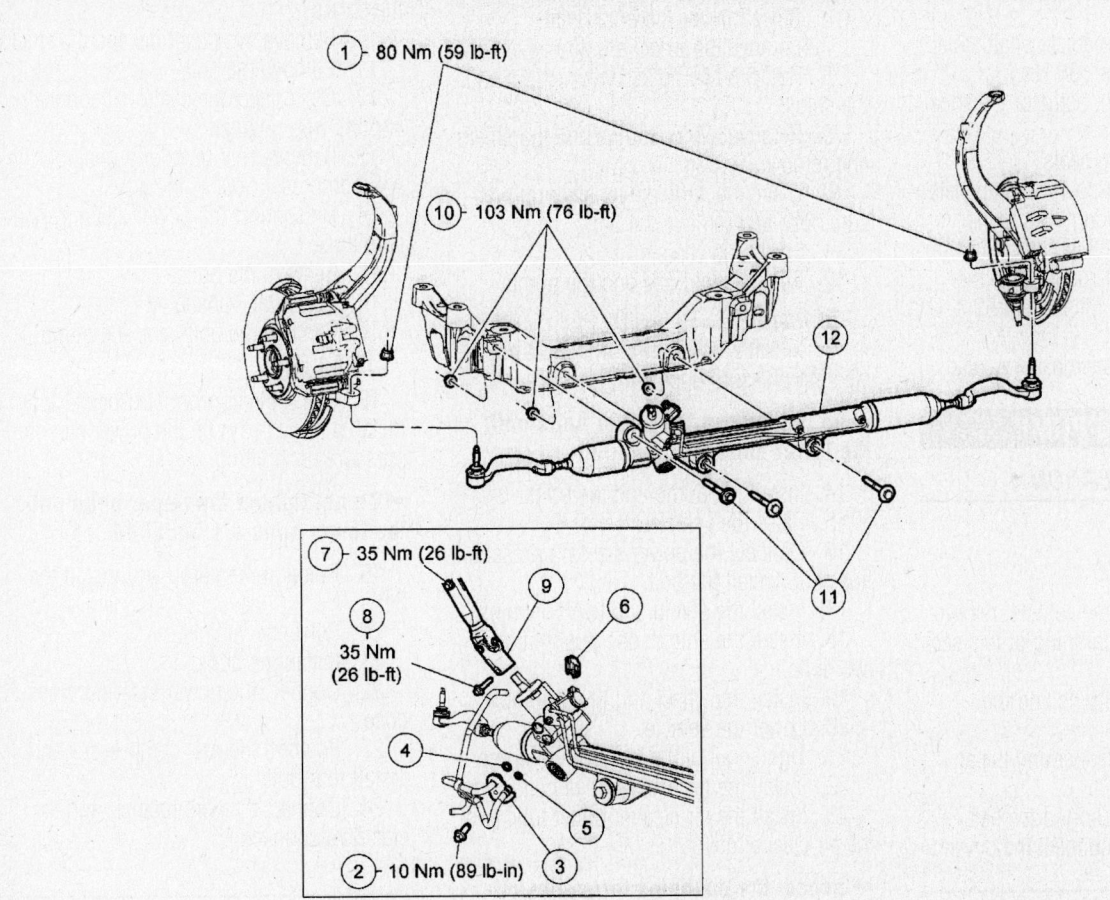

1   Tie-rod end nuts (2 required)
2   Steering line clamp plate bolt
3   Steering lines (pressure/return)
4   O-ring (pressure line)
5   O-ring (return line)
6   Variable assist power steering (VAPS) actuator electrical connector
7   Intermediate shaft slider bolt
8   Intermediate shaft-to-steering gear bolt
9   Intermediate shaft
10   Steering gear-to-crossmember nuts (3 required)
11   Steering gear-to-crossmember bolts (3 required)
12   Steering gear

06017-LS-G69

Fig. 170 Exploded view of the steering gear mounting

9. Loosen the intermediate shaft slider bolt.

10. Remove and discard the intermediate shaft-to-steering gear bolt and disconnect the intermediate shaft from the steering gear.

11. Remove the 3 steering gear-to-crossmember nuts and bolts.

12. Remove the steering gear.

To install:

13. Install the steering gear.

14. Install the 3 steering gear-to-crossmember nuts and bolts. Tighten to 76 ft. lbs. (103 Nm).

15. Install a new the intermediate shaft-to-steering gear bolt and connect the intermediate shaft to the steering gear. Tighten to 26 ft. lbs. (35 Nm).

16. Tighten the intermediate shaft slider bolt. Tighten to 26 ft. lbs. (35 Nm).

17. Connect the VAPS actuator electrical connector.

18. Install new O-ring seals.

19. Install a new steering line clamp plate bolt and connect the steering lines to the steering gear. Tighten to 89 inch lbs. (10 Nm).

20. Install the two tie-rod ends to the wheel knuckles. Tighten the nuts to 59 ft. lbs. (80 Nm).

21. Connect the negative battery cable.

POWER STEERING PUMP

REMOVAL & INSTALLATION

3.0L Engine

See Figures 171 and 172.

1. Before servicing the vehicle, refer to the precautions in the beginning of this section.

2. Remove four pushpins and the engine cover.

3. Remove the air cleaner and the air cleaner outlet tube.

4. Remove the accessory drive belt.

5. Unclamp and disconnect the power

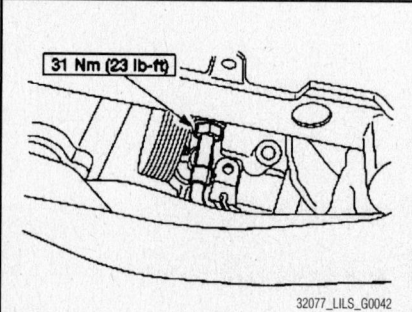

31 Nm (23 lb-ft)

32077_LILS_G0042

Fig. 171 Tighten the power steering pressure hose to the specified torque

25 Nm (18 lb-ft)

32077_LILS_G0041

Fig. 172 Tighten the pump bolts to the specified torque

steering reservoir-to-pump hose and drain the reservoir into a suitable container.

6. Raise the vehicle on a hoist.

7. Remove the wheel and tire assembly.

8. Remove two bolts, one pushpin and the shield.

9. Remove two pushpins and the shield and remove the bolt.

10. Disconnect the power steering pressure hose and remove the bolt.

11. Lower the vehicle.

12. Remove the bolts and the pump.

To install:

13. Install a new O-ring on the power steering pressure hose fitting.

➡ **Do not tighten the upper bolts until the lower bolts are installed.**

14. Install the pump and the bolts.

15. Raise the vehicle.

16. Connect the power steering pressure hose and install the bolt.

17. Install the shield and two pushpins.

18. Install the shield, one pushpin and two bolts.

19. Install the wheel and tire assembly.

20. Lower the vehicle.

21. Tighten all of the bolts of the pump.

22. Install the accessory drive belt.

23. Install the air cleaner outlet tube and the air cleaner cover.

➡ **Inspect the pushpins for cracks or other damage. Install new pushpins if necessary.**

24. Install the engine cover and four pushpins.

25. Fill and leak check the system.

3.9L Engine

See Figures 173 through 177.

1. Before servicing the vehicle, refer to the precautions in the beginning of this section.

2. Remove four pushpins and the engine cover.

3. Remove the air cleaner and the air cleaner outlet tube and remove the bolts.

4. Remove the accessory drive belt.

5. Unclamp and disconnect the power steering reservoir-to-pump hose (3691) and drain the reservoir into a suitable container.

6. Position the power steering reservoir out of the way by doing the following:

• Loosen the bolts.

• Rotate the reservoir from the insulator.

• Pull the reservoir down from the insulator and position the reservoir out of the way.

7. Raise the vehicle on a hoist.

8. Remove the wheel and tire assembly.

9. Remove two bolts, one pushpin and the shield.

10. Remove two pushpins and the shield.

11. Remove the bolt.

12. Disconnect the electrical connector and the wire retainer.

13. Remove four bolts and position the A/C compressor out of the way.

14. Disconnect the power steering pressure hose.

15. Remove the bolts.

16. Lower the vehicle.

17. Remove the bolts and the pump.

To install:

18. Using the appropriate special tool, install a new O-ring on the power steering pressure hose fitting.

➡ **Do not tighten the upper bolts until the lower bolts are installed.**

19. Position the pump and install the bolts.

20. Raise the vehicle.

21. Install the bolts.

22. Connect the power steering pressure hose.

23. Position the A/C compressor and install four bolts.

24. Connect the wire retainer and the electrical connector.

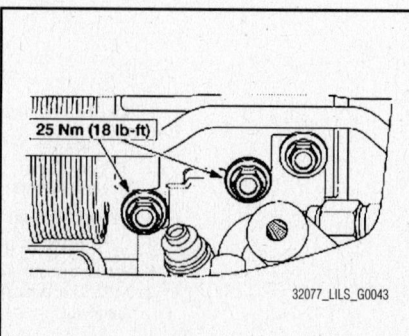

25 Nm (18 lb-ft)

32077_LILS_G0043

Fig. 173 Tighten the pump bolts to the specified torque

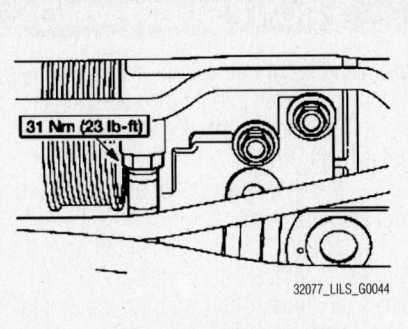

Fig. 174 Tighten the power steering pressure hose to the specified torque

Fig. 175 Tighten the bolts to the A/C compressor to the specified torque

25. Install the bolt.
26. Install the shield and two pushpins.
27. Install the shield, one pushpin and two bolts.
28. Install the wheel and tire assembly.
29. Lower the vehicle.
30. Tighten the bolts.
31. Connect the reservoir by doing the following:
 • Push the reservoir up on the insulator.
 • Rotate the reservoir on the insulator.
 • Tighten the bolts.
32. Connect and clamp the power steering reservoir-to-pump hose.

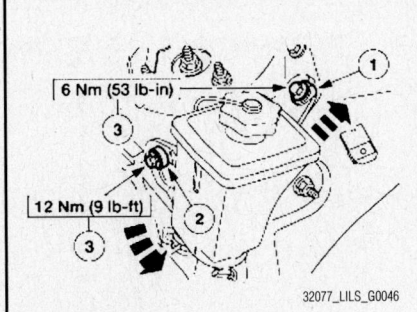

Fig. 176 Tighten the bolts to the reservoir to the specified torque

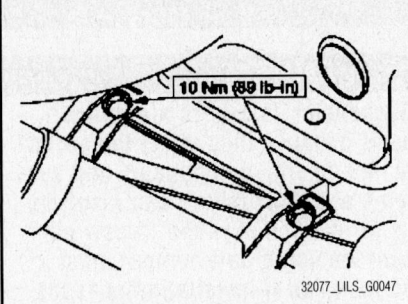

Fig. 177 Tighten the bolts to the air cleaner outlet tube to the specified torque

33. Install the accessory drive belt.
34. Install the bolts.
35. Install the air cleaner outlet tube and the air cleaner.

➡**Inspect the pushpins for cracks or other damage. Install new pushpins if necessary.**

36. Install the engine cover and four pushpins.
37. Fill and leak check the system.

BLEEDING

❊❊ **WARNING**

If the air is not purged from the power steering system correctly, premature power steering pump failure can result. The condition can occur on pre-delivery vehicles with evidence of aerated fluid or on vehicles that have had steering component repairs.

1. Before servicing the vehicle, refer to the precautions in the beginning of this section.
2. Remove the power steering pump reservoir cap.
3. Tightly install the evacuation cap to the power steering pump reservoir.
4. Install the hose from the fill adapter manifold tee to the evacuation cap on the power steering pump reservoir.
5. Install the vacuum pump to the fill adapter manifold control valve.
6. Install the hose to the opposite fill adapter manifold control valve and submerge the open end of the hose into a container of clean, fresh power steering fluid.

➡**The fill adapter manifold control valves are in the open position when the point of the handles face the center of the fill adapter manifold.**

7. Open the fill adapter manifold control valve connected to the power steering fluid container.
8. Close the fill adapter manifold control valve connected to the vacuum pump.
9. Using the vacuum pump, apply −30 inches-Hg (84–101 kPa) of vacuum to the power steering system.
10. Observe the vacuum gauge for 30 seconds.
11. If the vacuum gauge reading drops more than 1 inch-Hg (3 kPa), correct any leaks in the power steering system or the filling tools before proceeding.

➡**The vacuum pump gauge reading will drop slightly during this step.**

12. Slowly open the fill adapter manifold control valve connected to the power steering fluid container until power steering fluid completely fills the hose.
13. Close the fill adapter manifold control valve connected to the power steering fluid container.
14. Using the vacuum pump, apply 25–30 inches-Hg (84–101 kPa) of vacuum to the power steering system.
15. Close the fill adapter manifold control valve connected to the vacuum pump.
16. Slowly open the fill adapter manifold control valve connected to the power steering fluid container.
17. When the power steering fluid has drained from the hose connected to the power steering fluid container, close the fill adapter manifold control valve connected to the power steering fluid container.
18. Remove the tools from the vehicle.
19. Install the power steering reservoir cap.

❊❊ **WARNING**

Do not hold the steering wheel against the stops for more than 3 to 5 seconds at a time. Damage to the power steering pump can occur.

➡**There will be a slight drop in the power steering fluid level in the power steering fluid reservoir when the engine is started.**

20. Start the engine and turn the steering wheel from stop-to-stop 10 times.
21. Turn the ignition switch to **OFF**.

❊❊ **WARNING**

Do not overfill the reservoir.

22. Remove the power steering reservoir cap and fill the reservoir.
23. Install the power steering reservoir cap.

COIL SPRING

REMOVAL & INSTALLATION

1. Before servicing the vehicle, refer to the precautions in the beginning of this section.
2. Remove the strut assembly from the vehicle.
3. Compress the coil spring and remove the piston rod nut.
4. Remove or disconnect the following:
   - Upper strut mount
   - Spring upper seat
   - Coil spring

To install:

5. Install or connect the following:
   - Coil spring
   - Spring upper seat
   - Upper strut mount. Tighten the piston rod nut to 37 ft. lbs. (50 Nm).
6. Remove the spring compressor and install the strut assembly to the vehicle.

CONTROL LINKS

REMOVAL & INSTALLATION

➡ **The stabilizer bar nuts are of torque prevailing design. New nuts must be installed during assembly.**

1. Before servicing the vehicle, refer to the precautions in the beginning of this section.
2. With the vehicle in NEUTRAL, position it on a hoist.
3. Remove and discard the stabilizer bar link-to-lower arm nut, then disconnect the stabilizer bar link from the suspension lower arm.
4. Remove and discard the nut from the upper stabilizer bar link, then remove the stabilizer bar link.
5. To install, reverse the removal procedure. Tighten the stabilizer bar link nuts to 55 Nm (41 lb-ft).

LOWER BALL JOINT

REMOVAL & INSTALLATION

The lower ball joint is serviced with the lower control arm as an assembly.

LOWER CONTROL ARM

REMOVAL & INSTALLATION

See Figures 178 and 179.

1. Before servicing the vehicle, refer to the precautions in the beginning of this section.

✳✳ CAUTION

Suspension fasteners are critical parts because they affect the performance of vital components and systems and their failure can result in major service expense. A new part with the same part number must be installed if installation is necessary. Do not use a new part of lesser quality or substitute design. Torque values must be used as specified during reassembly to make sure of correct retention of these parts.

➡ **New cam bolts and lock nuts must be installed whenever the lower control arm is removed.**

2. Remove the splash shield.

➡ **The hex holding feature can be used to prevent turning of the stud while removing the nut.**

3. Remove and discard the stabilizer bar link-to-lower arm nut. While prying down on the stabilizer bar, disconnect the stabilizer bar link.
4. Remove and discard the shock absorber-to-lower arm nut and bolt. Disconnect the shock absorber and spring assembly from the lower arm.

➡ **The hex holding feature can be used to prevent turning of the stud while removing the nut. The tapered washer is reused with the new ball joint nut.**

5. Remove and discard the lower ball joint-to-knuckle nut. Separate the front suspension lower arm from the wheel knuckle.
6. Remove and discard the front nut and bolt.
7. Remove the power steering gear nuts and bolts. Discard the nuts.
8. Position the power steering gear to access the lower control arm rear bolt.
9. Remove and discard the lower control arm rear nut and bolt. Remove the front suspension lower arm.

To install:

10. Position the front suspension lower arm.
11. Install a new caster adjustment cam bolt and a new nut.
12. The bolt must be installed from the rear, as illustrated. Install the bolt with the cam lobe down. The cam must be seated

between the cam guides on the No. 1 crossmember. The nut should only be snugged up at this time to allow for wheel alignment adjustment.

13. Install a new camber adjustment cam bolt and a new nut.
14. The bolt must be installed from the rear as illustrated. Install the bolt with the cam lobe down. The cam must be seated in the groove in the No. 2 crossmember. The nut should only be snugged up at this time to allow for wheel alignment adjustment.

➡ **Make sure the tapered washer is installed on the ball joint before connecting the lower control arm to the knuckle. The hex holding feature can be used to prevent turning of the stud while tightening the nut.**

15. Connect the lower control arm to the knuckle. Install a new lower ball joint-to-knuckle nut and tighten to 148 ft. lbs. (200 Nm).

➡ **Make sure the shock absorber lower bushing end caps are in place before installing the bolt and nut. Connect the shock absorber and spring assembly to the lower control arm.**

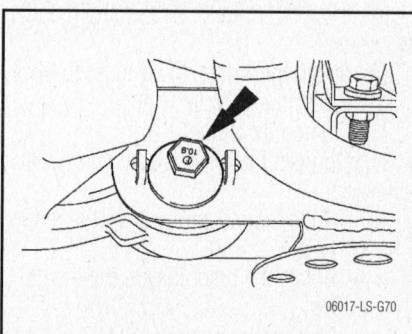

06017-LS-G70

Fig. 178 Position the caster adjustment cam bolt as shown

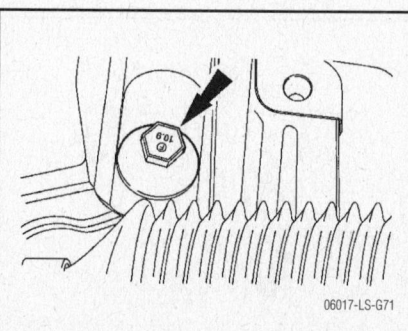

06017-LS-G71

Fig. 179 Position the camber adjustment cam bolt as shown

16. Install a new shock absorber-to-lower arm bolt and nut. Tighten to 129 ft. lbs. (175 Nm).

17. While prying down on the stabilizer bar, connect the stabilizer bar link to the stabilizer bar. Install a new stabilizer bar link-to-lower arm nut. Install the nut until snug using the hex-head feature, then tighten the nut using a socket and a torque wrench to 41 ft. lbs. (55 Nm).

18. Install the splash shield.

19. Position the power steering gear in place. Install the power steering gear bolts and new nuts and tighten to 76 ft. lbs. (103 Nm).

20. Final tighten the camber and caster bolts to 129 ft. lbs. (175 Nm).

21. Check the wheel alignment. Adjust as necessary.

CONTROL ARM BUSHING REPLACEMENT

The control arm bushings are serviced with the control arm as an assembly.

STABILIZER BAR

REMOVAL & INSTALLATION

See Figures 180 through 183.

✳✳ CAUTION

Suspension fasteners are critical parts because they affect the performance of vital components and systems and their failure can result in major service expense. A new part with the same part number must be installed if installation becomes necessary. Do not use a new part of lesser quality or substitute design. Torque values must be used as specified during reassembly to make sure of correct retention of these parts.

1. Before servicing the vehicle, refer to the precautions in the beginning of this section.

2. Remove the upper radiator sight shield.

3. Remove the air cleaner.

4. Drain the engine cooling system.

5. Disconnect the upper radiator hose.

6. Disconnect the lower radiator hose.

7. Disconnect the dual flow coolant valve electrical connector and the A/C line from the fan shroud.

8. For 3.0L engine: Disconnect the Throttle Position (TP) sensor and the Idle Air Control (IAC) valve electrical connectors.

9. Separate the return hose from the fan shroud and position aside.

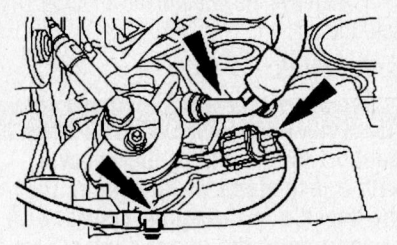

Fig. 180 Electrical connection points for the dual flow coolant valve and the A/C line from the fan shroud

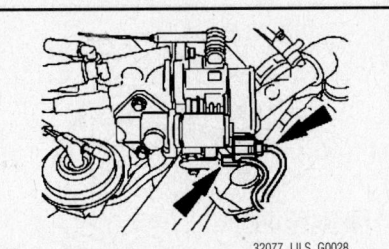

Fig. 181 Locations of the throttle position sensor and the idle air control valve and their electrical connectors on the 3.0L engine

10. Disconnect the lower radiator hose.

11. Remove the two bolts and position the multi-cooler assembly and fan shroud assembly aside.

12. Remove the front wheel and tire assemblies.

13. Remove two pushpins, four bolts and both splash shields.

➡ **To remove the nut, first loosen the nut, then use the hex holding feature to prevent the stabilizer bar link ball joint from turning while removing the nut.**

14. Remove the nut and disconnect the stabilizer bar link. Discard the nut.

➡ **To remove the nut, first loosen the nut, then use the hex holding feature to prevent the stabilizer bar link ball joint from turning while removing the nut.**

15. Remove and discard the nut and bolt. Disconnect the left shock absorber and spring assembly.

➡ **To remove the nut, first loosen the nut, then use the hex holding feature to prevent the lower control arm ball joint from turning while removing the nut.**

➡ **Make sure not to lose the tapered washer on the ball joint.**

16. Remove and discard the nut. Disconnect the left suspension lower arm and position the knuckle out of the way.

17. Remove the bolt and detach the A/C hose retainer. Position the A/C hose aside.

➡ **To ease removal of the right front bolt, remove it first.**

18. Remove the bolts and the stabilizer bar brackets and bushings.

➡ **Deflect the left lower control arm downward to ease removal of the stabilizer bar.**

19. Carefully remove the stabilizer bar through the left wheel well.

➡ **The replacement stabilizer bar includes the brackets and bushings as an assembly.**

To install:

20. Carefully replace the stabilizer bar through the left wheel well.

21. Replace the bolts and the stabilizer bar brackets and bushings.

22. Replace the bolt and attach the A/C hose retainer.

23. Connect the left suspension lower arm and reposition the knuckle.

24. Replace and discard the nut and bolt. Connect the left shock absorber and spring assembly.

25. Replace two pushpins, four bolts and both splash shields.

26. Replace the front wheel and tire assemblies.

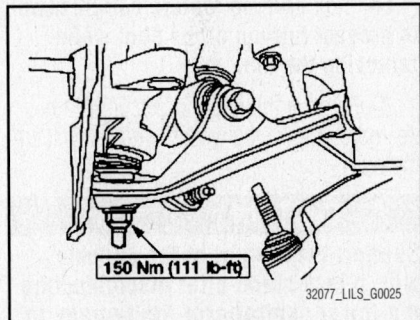

Fig. 182 Proper torque settings for the lower control arm and knuckle

150 Nm (111 lb-ft)

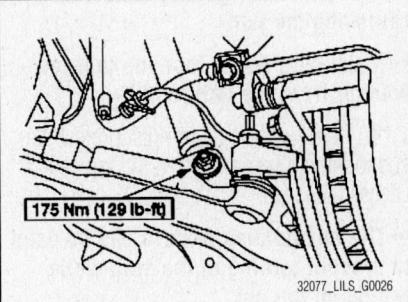

Fig. 183 Proper torque settings for the shock absorber and spring assembly

175 Nm (129 lb-ft)

27. For 3.0L engine: Connect the Throttle Position (TP) sensor and the Idle Air Control (IAC) valve electrical connectors.

28. Connect the upper and lower radiator hoses, the dual flow coolant valve electrical connector and the A/C line from the fan shroud.

29. Replace the upper radiator sight shield and the air cleaner.

STEERING KNUCKLE

REMOVAL & INSTALLATION

See Figures 184 through 186.

> ❊❊ **CAUTION**
>
> **Suspension fasteners are critical parts because they affect the performance of vital components and systems and their failure can result in major service expense. A new part with the same part number must be installed if installation becomes necessary. Do not use a new part of lesser quality or substitute design. Torque values must be used as specified during reassembly to make sure of correct retention of these parts.**

1. Before servicing the vehicle, refer to the precautions in the beginning of this section.

2. Remove the wheel bearing and hub.

➡ **The hex holding feature can be used to prevent turning of the stud while removing the nut.**

3. Remove the nut and disconnect the tie-rod end from the wheel knuckle. Discard the nut.

> ❊❊ **CAUTION**
>
> **Support the weight of the knuckle with a jack stand after disconnecting the lower control arm, or damage to the upper control arm can result.**

➡ **The hex holding feature can be used to prevent turning of the stud while removing the nut.**

➡ **Make sure not to lose the tapered washer from the ball joint.**

4. Remove the nut and disconnect the suspension lower arm from the knuckle. Discard the nut.

➡ **The hex holding feature can be used to prevent turning of the stud while removing the nut.**

➡ **Make sure not to lose the tapered washer from the ball joint.**

5. Remove the nut and the knuckle. Discard the nut.

To install:

> ❊❊ **CAUTION**
>
> **Support the weight of the knuckle with a jack stand while connecting the knuckle to the upper control arm or damage to the upper control arm can result.**

➡ **The upper arm-to-knuckle nut, lower arm-to-knuckle nut and the tie-rod-to-**

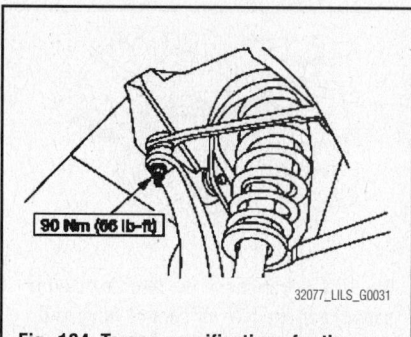

Fig. 184 Torque specifications for the knuckle

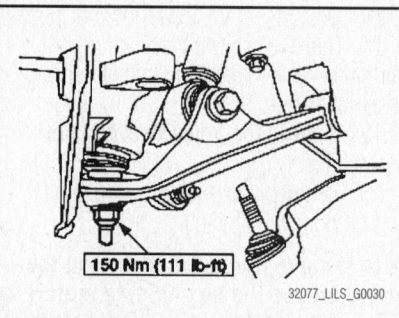

Fig. 185 Torque specifications for the lower control arm

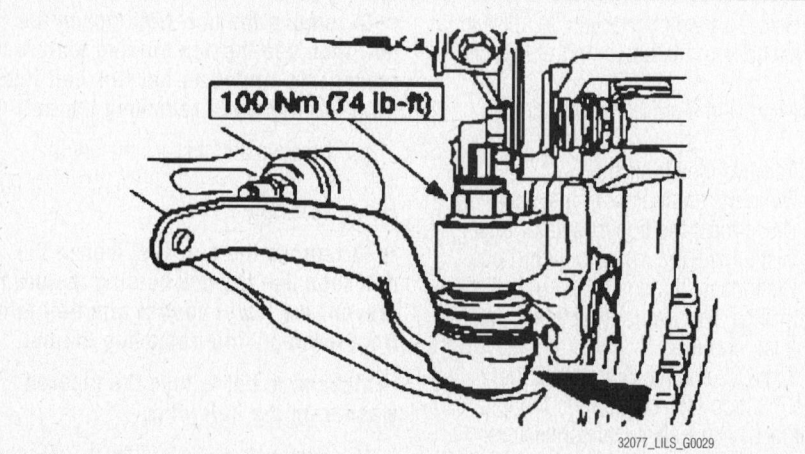

Fig. 186 Torque settings for the tie-rod end and its connection to the wheel knuckle

knuckle nut are of a torque prevailing design. New nuts must be installed.

➡ **Make sure the tapered washer is installed on the ball joints before connecting the upper and lower control arms to the knuckle.**

6. Install the nut and the knuckle.

7. Replace the nut and connect the suspension lower arm to the knuckle.

8. Replace the nut and disconnect the tie-rod end to the wheel knuckle.

9. Replace the wheel bearing and hub.

STRUT & SPRING ASSEMBLY

REMOVAL & INSTALLATION

See Figure 187.

1. Before servicing the vehicle, refer to the precautions in the beginning of this section.

2. Remove or disconnect the following:
   - Front wheel
   - Stabilizer bar link
   - Lower strut mounting bolt
   - Upper strut mount cover and fasteners
   - Strut and spring assembly

To install:

➡ **Use new fasteners for assembly.**

3. Install or connect the following:
   - Strut and spring assembly. Tighten the upper mount nuts to 21 ft. lbs. (29 Nm).
   - Upper strut mount cover
   - Lower strut mounting bolt. Tighten the bolts to 129 ft. lbs. (175 Nm).
   - Stabilizer bar link. Tighten the nut to 41 ft. lbs. (55 Nm).
   - Front wheel

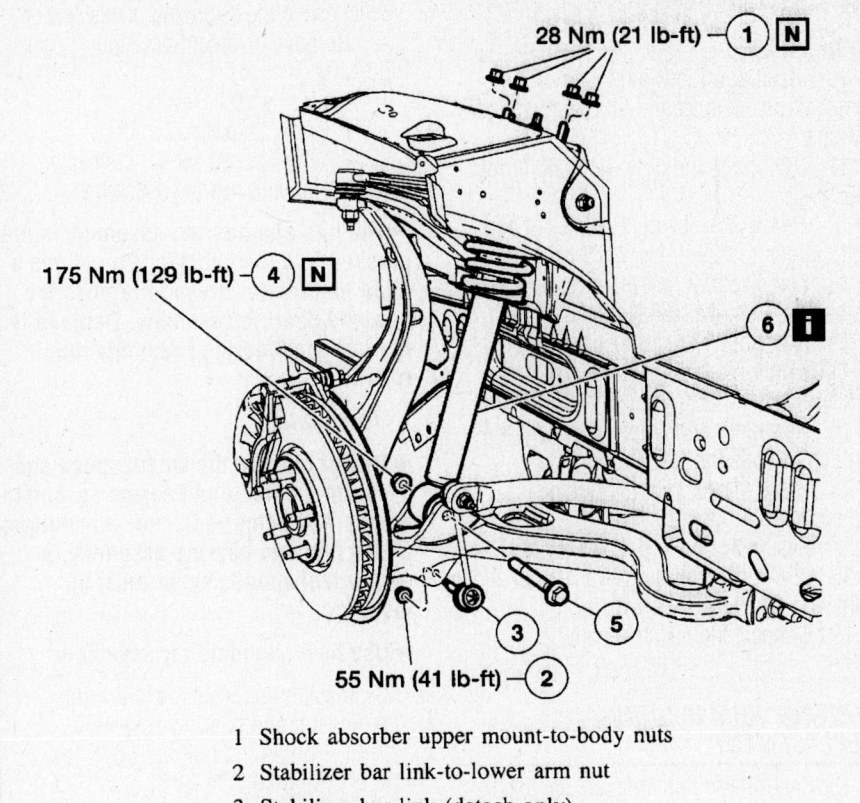

28 Nm (21 lb-ft) — (1) [N]

175 Nm (129 lb-ft) — (4) [N]

(6) [i]

55 Nm (41 lb-ft) — (2)

1 Shock absorber upper mount-to-body nuts
2 Stabilizer bar link-to-lower arm nut
3 Stabilizer bar link (detach only)
4 Shock absorber-to-lower arm nut
5 Shock absorber-to-lower arm bolt
6 Shock absorber and spring assembly

67197-LILS-G16

Fig. 187 Front strut mounting

DISASSEMBLY AND ASSEMBLY

> ⚠ **WARNING**
>
> All vehicles are equipped with gas pressurized shock absorbers which will extend unassisted. Do not apply heat or flame to the shock absorbers during removal or component servicing. Failure to follow these instructions can result in personal injury.

> ⚠ **CAUTION**
>
> The shock absorber and spring assembly is under extreme load. Do not attempt to disassemble the shock absorber and spring assembly without using a spring compressor. Failure to follow these instructions can result in personal injury.

> ⚠ **CAUTION**
>
> Suspension fasteners are critical parts because they affect performance of vital components and systems and their failure can result in major service expense. A new part with the same part number must be installed if installation is necessary. Do not use a new part of lesser quality or substitute design. Torque values must be used as specified during reassembly to make sure of correct retention of these parts.

1. Before servicing the vehicle, refer to the precautions in the beginning of this section.
2. Remove the shock absorber and spring assembly.

> ⚠ **CAUTION**
>
> Over-tightening the vise can damage the shock absorber tube.

3. Mount and mark the shock absorber and spring assembly.
4. Position the shock absorber and spring assembly in a suitable holding device.

5. Mark the upper mount, spring and shock absorber for assembly reference.

➡ **If installing a new spring, make sure the part number is correct. Refer to the Vehicle Certification (VC) label for the correct spring code.**

6. Compress the spring.
7. Install an appropriate spring compressor.
8. Compress the spring.
9. While holding the shock absorber rod, remove and discard the nut.
10. Remove the upper mount and dust boot as an assembly.
11. Carefully remove the spring and spring compressor.

To assemble:

➡ **If a new shock absorber, spring or upper mount is installed, the new part should be marked in the same place as the old part to make sure the assembly is correctly aligned.**

12. Inspect the lower and upper spring seats for damage.
13. Inspect the spring insulator for wear or damage. Install a new upper mount if necessary.

➡ **If installing a new spring, make sure the part number is correct. Refer to the Vehicle Certification (VC) label for the correct spring code.**

14. Inspect the spring for nicked or scratched paint. If the paint is nicked or scratched, install a new spring.
15. If removed, place the shock absorber into the vise.
16. Position the shock and spring compressor onto the strut.
17. Position the upper mount and dust boot onto the spring. Make sure the marks made during disassembly are lined up.
18. Install a new nut.
19. Remove the spring compressor.

UPPER BALL JOINT

REMOVAL & INSTALLATION

The upper ball joint is serviced with the upper control arm as an assembly.

UPPER CONTROL ARM

REMOVAL & INSTALLATION

1. Before servicing the vehicle, refer to the precautions in the beginning of this section.
2. Disconnect the negative battery cable.

3. If removing the left hand upper arm:

a. Remove and discard the power steering reservoir nut. Position the power steering reservoir aside.

b. Remove the retainers and the left upper shock mount cover, if equipped.

c. Remove the EVAP canister purge valve nuts and position the EVAP canister purge valve aside.

d. Disconnect the fluid level sensor connector.

e. Disconnect the brake master cylinder main pressure transducer electrical connector, if equipped.

f. Back out the reservoir bolt to give access to the master cylinder bolt. Tighten to 8 Nm (6 lb-ft).

g. Remove the 2 brake master cylinder nuts and position the brake master cylinder aside.

4. Remove and discard the inner and outer upper arm nuts.

✳✳ WARNING

Do not remove the center nut. This nut holds the upper spring mount in place and if this nut is removed the spring tension will be released. Failure to follow these instructions may result in personal injury.

5. Remove and discard 2 shock absorber upper mount-to-body nuts.

➡The hex-holding feature can be used to prevent turning of the stud while removing the nut. Remove the stabilizer bar link-to-lower arm nut. While prying down on the stabilizer bar, disconnect the stabilizer bar link from the stabilizer bar.

6. Remove and discard shock absorber lower nut and bolt, then remove the shock absorber and spring assembly.

➡Wire the top of the wheel knuckle to the body to prevent knuckle movement. To remove the nut, first loosen the nut, then use the hex-holding feature to prevent the upper control arm ball joint from turning while removing the nut. The tapered washer on the ball joint is reused with the new nut.

7. Remove and discard the suspension upper arm nut. Disconnect the suspension upper arm from the knuckle.

8. Remove and discard the inner and outer bolts and the suspension upper arm.

9. Remove the suspension upper arm.

To install:

10. Installation is the reverse of removal, please note the following specifications:

11. New inner and outer bolts 66 ft. lbs. (90 Nm).

12. New shock absorber lower nut and bolt, tighten to 129 ft. lbs. (175 Nm).

13. Stabilizer bar link-to-lower arm nut. Tighten to 41 ft. lbs. (55 Nm).

14. New shock absorber upper mount-to-body nuts. Tighten to 21 ft. lbs. (28 Nm).

15. New inner and outer upper arm nuts. Tighten to 35 ft. lbs. (48 Nm).

16. Brake master cylinder nuts and tighten to 18 ft. lbs. (25 Nm).

17. Reservoir bolt to 6 ft. lbs. (8 Nm).

18. EVAP canister purge valve nuts and tighten to 21 ft. lbs. (28 Nm).

19. Connect the negative battery cable.

CONTROL ARM BUSHING REPLACEMENT

The control arm bushings are serviced with the control arm as an assembly.

WHEEL BEARINGS

REMOVAL & INSTALLATION
See Figure 188.

1. Before servicing the vehicle, refer to the precautions in the beginning of this section.

2. Remove or disconnect the following:
- Front wheel
- Brake caliper and rotor
- Wheel speed sensor connector
- Hub and bearing assembly

➡**The hub and bearing assembly is not pressed into the knuckle. Do not use a slide hammer or press to remove the hub and bearing assembly. Damage to the hub and bearing assembly may result.**

To install:

➡**Do not remove the wheel speed sensor from the hub and bearing assembly unless it is being replaced. If installing a new hub and bearing assembly, a new wheel speed sensor must be installed.**

➡**Use new fasteners for assembly.**

3. Install or connect the following:
- Hub and bearing assembly. Tighten the bolts to 66 ft. lbs. (90 Nm).
- Wheel speed sensor connector
- Brake caliper and rotor
- Front wheel

ADJUSTMENT

The wheel bearings are not adjustable.

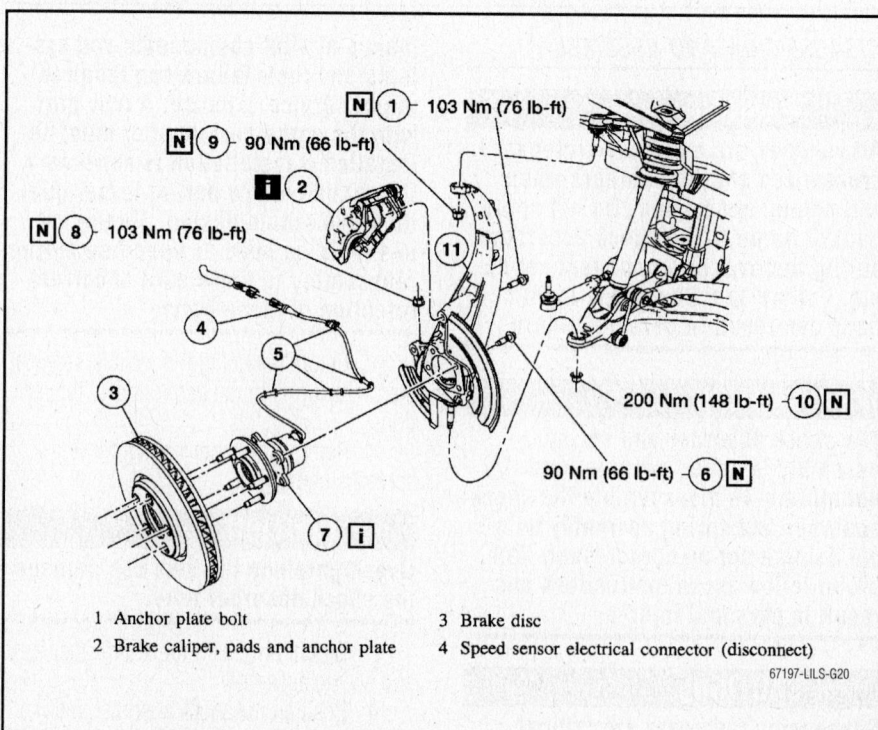

1 Anchor plate bolt
2 Brake caliper, pads and anchor plate
3 Brake disc
4 Speed sensor electrical connector (disconnect)

67197-LILS-G20

Fig. 188 Front hub and bearing exploded view

SUSPENSION   **REAR SUSPENSION**

COIL SPRING

REMOVAL & INSTALLATION

1. Before servicing the vehicle, refer to the precautions in the beginning of this section.
2. Remove the strut assembly from the vehicle.
3. Compress the coil spring and remove the piston rod nut.
4. Remove or disconnect the following:
   - Upper strut mount
   - Spring upper seat
   - Coil spring

To install:

5. Install or connect the following:
   - Coil spring
   - Spring upper seat
   - Upper strut mount. Tighten the piston rod nut to 37 ft. lbs. (50 Nm).
6. Remove the spring compressor and install the strut assembly to the vehicle.

LOWER CONTROL ARM

REMOVAL & INSTALLATION

1. Before servicing the vehicle, refer to the precautions in the beginning of this section.

※ CAUTION

Suspension fasteners are critical parts because they affect the performance of vital components and systems and their failure can result in major service expense. A new part with the same part number must be installed if installation is necessary. Do not use a new part of lesser quality or substitute design. Torque values must be used as specified during reassembly to make sure of correct retention of these parts.

➡ **The lower arm bushings are not serviced separately from the lower suspension arm. If the bushings require service, a new lower arm must be installed.**

2. With the vehicle in a static, level ground position, remove the hub cap and measure the distance from the center of the hub to the lip of the fender (curb height).
3. Remove the rear wheels.
4. Remove the rear brake rotor.
5. Disconnect the shock absorber and spring assembly.
6. Remove and discard the shock absorber-to-lower arm bolt.

7. Disconnect the shock absorber and spring assembly from the lower arm.

※ CAUTION

Do not use air tools to remove the nut. Damage to the boot can result.

➡ **Use the hex holding feature to prevent the stabilizer bar link ball joint from turning while removing the stabilizer bar link nut.**

8. Disconnect the stabilizer bar link from the suspension lower arm.
9. Remove and discard the stabilizer bar link-to-lower arm nut.
10. Disconnect the stabilizer bar link.
11. Disconnect the lower arm from the wheel knuckle.
12. Remove and discard the lower arm-to-wheel knuckle bolt. Disconnect the lower arm.
13. Remove and discard the lower arm-to-frame bolts. Remove the lower arm.

To install:

※※ CAUTION

Do not tighten the lower arm-to-subframe fasteners until the suspension is at curb height. Failure to do so can cause severe damage to the bushings resulting in poor ride quality and handling.

14. Install the lower arm. By positioning the suspension lower arm onto the subframe.
15. Install new lower arm-to-frame bolts and nuts. Do not tighten at this time.
16. Connect the lower arm to the knuckle. Install a new lower arm-to-wheel knuckle nut and bolt. Tighten to 111 ft. lbs. (150 Nm).

※※ CAUTION

Do not use air tools to install the nut. Damage to the boot can result.

➡ **Use the hex holding feature to prevent the stabilizer bar link ball joint from turning while installing the nut on the stabilizer bar link. Tighten the nut to specification using a socket and a torque wrench.**

17. Connect the stabilizer bar link to the suspension lower arm. Install a new stabilizer bar link nut. Tighten to 35 ft. lbs. (48 Nm).
18. Position the shock absorber and

spring assembly onto the suspension lower arm. Install a new shock absorber-to-lower arm bolt and tighten to 98 ft. lbs. (133 Nm).
19. Position a jack stand under the lower arm and raise the suspension until the measurement between the center of the hub and the lip of the fender is equal to the measurement taken prior to removal.
20. Tighten the lower arm-to-frame rear bolt and the lower arm-to-frame front nut to 111 ft. lbs. (150 Nm).
21. Lower the suspension and remove the jack stand.
22. Install the rear brake disc rotor and rear wheel.

STRUT & SPRING ASSEMBLY

REMOVAL & INSTALLATION

See Figure 189.

1. Before servicing the vehicle, refer to the precautions in the beginning of this section.
2. Remove or disconnect the following:
   - Trunk trim covers
   - Upper strut mount nuts
   - Lower strut mount bolt
   - Strut and spring assembly

To install:

➡ **Use new fasteners for assembly.**

3. Install or connect the following:
   - Strut and spring assembly. Tighten the lower bolt to 98 ft. lbs. (133 Nm) and the upper nuts to 21 ft. lbs. (28 Nm).
   - Trunk trim covers

UPPER CONTROL ARM

REMOVAL & INSTALLATION

1. Before servicing the vehicle, refer to the precautions in the beginning of this section.

※※ CAUTION

Suspension fasteners are critical parts because they affect the performance of vital components and systems and their failure can result in major service expense. A new part with the same part number must be installed if installation is necessary. Do not use a new part of lesser quality or substitute design. Torque values must be used as specified during reassembly to make sure of correct retention of these parts.

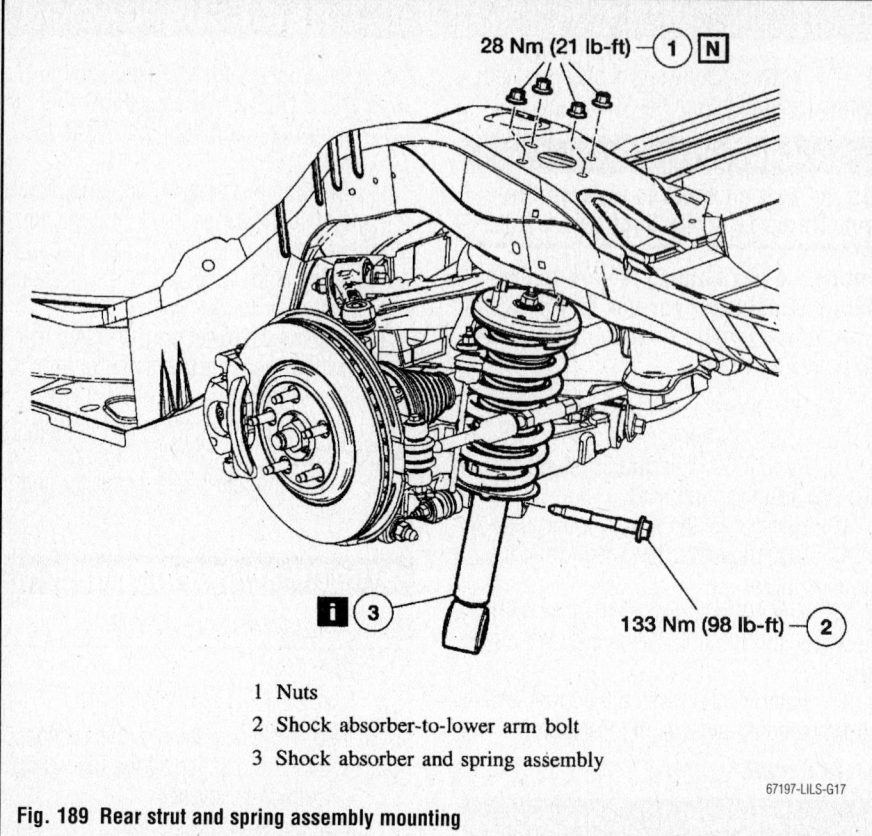

28 Nm (21 lb-ft) — ① N

133 Nm (98 lb-ft) — ②

i ③

1 Nuts
2 Shock absorber-to-lower arm bolt
3 Shock absorber and spring assembly

67197-LILS-G17

Fig. 189 Rear strut and spring assembly mounting

➡ The suspension upper arm bushings or ball joints are not serviced separately from the upper rear suspension arm. If the bushings or ball joints require service a new suspension upper arm must be installed.

2. Remove the hub cap. Measure the distance from the center of the hub to the lip of the fender with the vehicle in a level, static ground position.

3. Remove the rear wheels.

4. Unclip the wheel speed sensor wire retainer from the suspension upper arm.

5. Remove the speed sensor bolt and the sensor. Position the sensor aside.

✳✳ CAUTION

Use care not to damage the Anti-lock Brake System (ABS) sensor ring. A damaged sensor ring will result in incorrect ABS operation.

➡ Use the hex holding feature to prevent the ball joint from turning while removing the nut.

6. Remove and discard the upper ball joint-to-wheel knuckle nut, then disconnect the upper ball joint from the wheel knuckle.

7. Remove the suspension upper arm-to-subframe nuts and bolts. Discard the nuts and bolts.

8. Remove the suspension upper arm.

To install:

✳✳ CAUTION

Do not tighten the suspension upper arm-to-subframe nuts until the suspension is at curb height. Failure to do so can cause severe damage to the bushings resulting in poor ride quality and handling.

➡ The bolts and nuts retaining the suspension upper arm are of a torque prevailing design. New bolts and nuts must be used.

9. Install the suspension upper arm, install new upper arm-to-subframe nuts and bolts. Do not tighten at this time.

➡ Install the ball joint-to-wheel knuckle nut using the hex holding feature until snug. Final tighten the nut using a line-type crow's foot and a torque wrench.

10. Connect the ball joint to the wheel knuckle and hub assembly. Install a new ball joint-to-wheel knuckle nut and tighten to 66 ft. lbs. (90 Nm).

11. Clip the speed sensor wire to the suspension upper arm.

12. Position a jack stand under the suspension lower arm and raise the suspension until the distance between the center of the hub and the lip of the fender is equal to the measurement taken prior to removal.

13. Tighten the suspension upper arm nuts to 66 ft. lbs. (90 Nm).

14. Lower the suspension and remove the jack stand.

WHEEL BEARINGS

REMOVAL & INSTALLATION

See Figures 190 and 191.

✳✳ CAUTION

Suspension fasteners are important parts because they affect performance of vital components and systems and their failure can result in major service expense. A new part with the same part number must be installed if installation is necessary. Do not use a new part of lesser quality or substitute design. Torque values must be used as specified during reassembly to make sure of correct retention of these parts.

➡ The wheel knuckle/wheel hub is serviced as an assembly. Do not attempt to separate the wheel hub from the wheel knuckle.

1. Before servicing the vehicle, refer to the precautions in the beginning of this section.

2. For reference during the installation of an upper or lower arm, measure the distance between the center of the wheel hub and the lip of the fender with the weight of the vehicle resting on the wheel and tire assemblies.

3. Remove the rear wheel.

4. Remove the brake caliper and rotor.

✳✳ CAUTION

The axle shaft retaining nut is a one time use item and a new nut must be installed when removed. Failure to do so can cause the nut to loosen during vehicle operation resulting in loss of vehicle control.

5. Remove and discard the axle shaft retaining nut.

6. Disconnect the toe link from the knuckle by removing the toe link-to-wheel knuckle bolt. Discard the nut and bolt and disconnect the link.

7. Remove the ABS bolt and disconnect the ABS sensor.

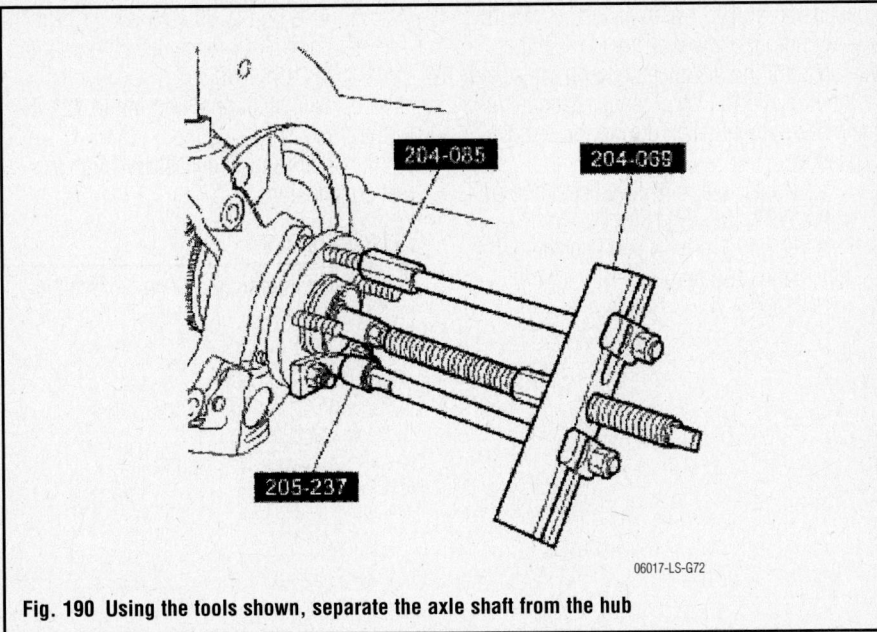

204-085 204-069

205-237

06017-LS-G72

Fig. 190 Using the tools shown, separate the axle shaft from the hub

⁂ CAUTION

Support the axle shaft after removing it from the hub. Failure to do so can damage the axle shaft.

8. Do not use a hammer to separate the outboard CV joint from the hub. Damage to the threads and internal CV joint components can result.

9. Using the tools illustrated, separate the axle shaft from the hub. Support the axle shaft.

10. Disconnect the lower arm from the wheel knuckle by removing the lower arm-to-wheel knuckle bolt and disconnecting the arm. Discard the nut.

11. Remove the wheel knuckle and hub assembly.

→Use the hex holding feature to prevent the upper arm ball joint from turning while removing the nut.

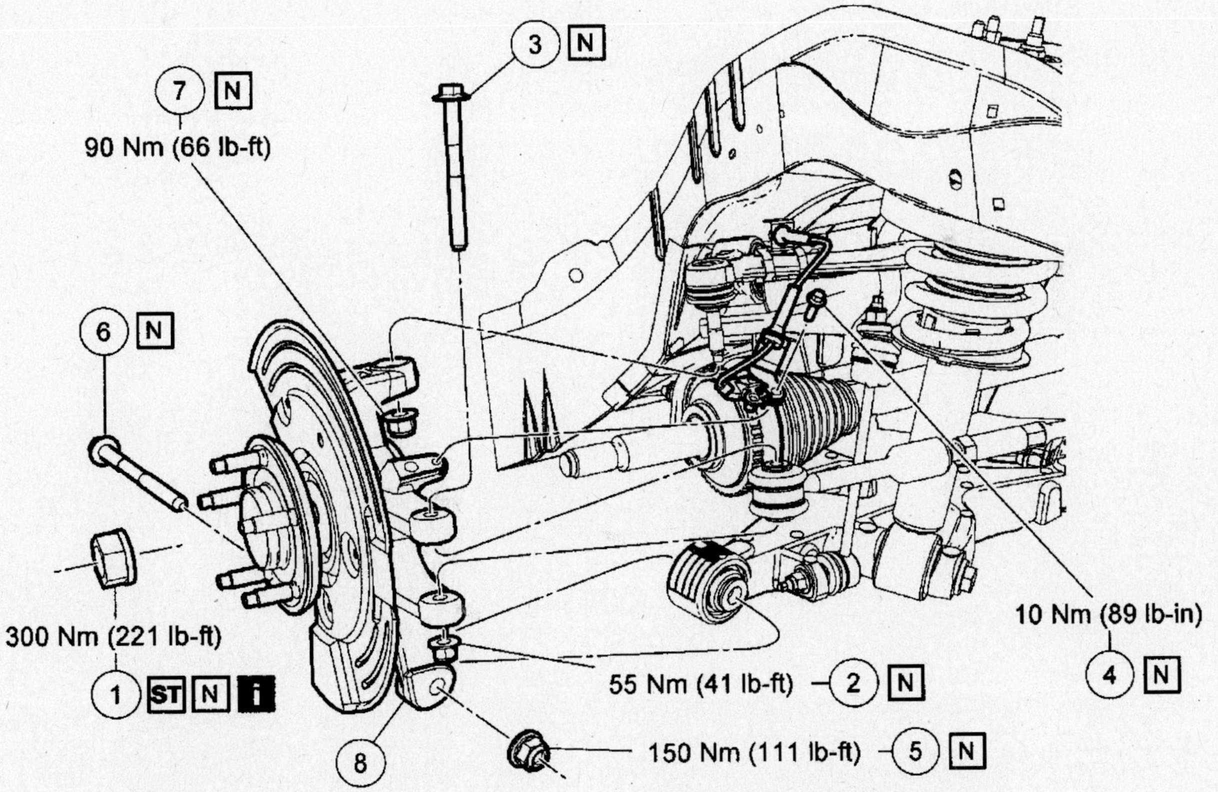

7 N 90 Nm (66 lb-ft)

3 N

6 N

300 Nm (221 lb-ft)

1 ST N i

8

55 Nm (41 lb-ft) 2 N

150 Nm (111 lb-ft) 5 N

10 Nm (89 lb-in)

4 N

1 Axle nut
2 Toe link-to-wheel knuckle nut
3 Toe link-to-wheel knuckle bolt
4 Speed sensor-to-wheel knuckle bolt
5 Lower arm-to-wheel knuckle nut
6 Lower arm-to-wheel knuckle bolt
7 Upper ball joint-to-wheel knuckle nut
8 Wheel knuckle

67197-LILS-G21

Fig. 191 Exploded view of the rear wheel bearing assembly

12. Remove and discard the upper ball joint-to-wheel knuckle nut. To install, tighten to 90 Nm (66 lb-ft).

13. Remove the wheel knuckle and hub assembly.

To install:

14. Installation is the reverse of removal, please note the following steps and torque specifications:

15. Before tightening the upper or lower suspension arm-to-frame fasteners, position a jack under the lower arm and raise the vehicle until the distance between the center of the hub and the lip of fender is equal to the measurement taken during the removal procedure.

   a. Upper ball joint-to-wheel knuckle nut to 66 ft. lbs. (90 Nm).

   b. Lower arm-to-wheel knuckle bolt to 111 ft. lbs (150 Nm).

   c. ABS bolt to 89 inch lbs. (10 Nm).

   d. Toe link-to-wheel knuckle bolt to 41 ft. lbs. (55 Nm).

   e. Axle shaft retaining nut to 221 ft. lbs. (300 Nm).

16. Check and, if necessary, align the rear suspension

ADJUSTMENT

The wheel bearings are not adjustable.

SPECIFICATIONS AND MAINTENANCE CHARTS

ENGINE AND VEHICLE IDENTIFICATION

| Code ① | Engine | | | | | | Model Year | |
	Liters (cc)	Cu. In.	Cyl.	Fuel Sys.	Engine Type	Eng. Mfg.	Code ②	Year
H	4.6 (4605)	281	8	SFI	SOHC	Ford	5	2005
N	4.0 (3999)	244	6	SFI	SOHC	Ford	6	2006
S	5.4 (5409)	330	8	SFI	DOHC	Ford	7	2007
							8	2008

SOHC: Single Overhead Camshaft

DOHC: Dual Overhead Camshaft

SFI: Sequential Fuel Injection

① 8th position of VIN

② 10th position of VIN

22086_MUST_C0001

GENERAL ENGINE SPECIFICATIONS
All measurements are given in inches.

Year	Model	Engine Displacement Liters	Engine Series (ID/VIN)	Net Horsepower @ rpm	Net Torque @ rpm (ft. lbs.)	Bore x Stroke (in.)	Com- pression Ratio	Oil Pressure @ rpm
2005	Mustang	4.0	N	210@5250	250@3500	3.95x3.32	9.7:1	15@2000
		4.6	H	300@5750	320@4500	3.55x3.54	9.8:1	75@2000
2006	Mustang	4.0	N	210@5250	250@3500	3.95x3.32	9.7:1	15@2000
		4.6	H	300@5750	320@4500	3.55x3.54	9.8:1	75@2000
2007	Mustang	4.0	N	210@5250	250@3500	3.95x3.32	9.7:1	15@2000
		4.6	H	300@5750	320@4500	3.55x3.54	9.8:1	75@2000
		5.4	S	500@6000	480@4500	3.55x4.23	8.4:1	50@2000
2008	Mustang	4.0	N	210@5250	250@3500	3.95x3.32	9.7:1	15@2000
		4.6	H	300@5750	320@4500	3.55x3.54	9.8:1	75@2000
		5.4	S	500@6000	480@4500	3.55x4.23	8.4:1	50@2000

22086_MUST_C0002

ENGINE TUNE-UP SPECIFICATIONS

Year	Engine Displacement Liters	Engine ID/VIN	Spark Plug Gap (in.)	Ignition Timing (deg.)		Fuel Pump (psi) ①	Idle Speed (rpm)		Valve Clearance	
				MT	AT		MT	AT	Intake	Exhaust
2005	4.0	N	0.052-0.056	NA	NA	27-37	②	②	HYD	HYD
	4.6	H	0.052-0.056	10B	10B	27-37	②	②	HYD	HYD
2006	4.0	N	0.052-0.056	NA	NA	27-37	②	②	HYD	HYD
	4.6	H	0.052-0.056	10B	10B	27-37	②	②	HYD	HYD
2007	4.0	N	0.052-0.056	NA	NA	27-37	②	②	HYD	HYD
	4.6	H	0.052-0.056	10B	10B	27-37	②	②	HYD	HYD
	5.4	S	0.041-0.047	NA	NA	25-40	②	②	HYD	HYD
2008	4.0	N	0.052-0.056	NA	NA	27-37	②	②	HYD	HYD
	4.6	H	0.052-0.056	10B	10B	27-37	②	②	HYD	HYD
	5.4	S	0.041-0.047	NA	NA	25-40	②	②	HYD	HYD

NOTE: The Vehicle Emission Control Information label often reflects specification changes made during production. The label figures must be used if they differ from those in this chart.

NA: Not available

B: Before Top Dead Center

HYD: Hydraulic

① Fuel pressure with engine running, pressure regulator vacuum hose connected

② Refer to Vehicle Emission Control Information label

22086_MUST_C0003

CAPACITIES

Year	Model	Engine Displacement Liters	Engine ID/VIN	Engine Oil with Filter (qts.)	Transmission (pts) Manual	Transmission (pts) Auto. ①	Drive Axle Rear (pts.)	Fuel Tank (gal.)	Cooling System (qts.)
2005	Mustang	4.0	N	5.0	②	23.8	③	16.0	16.0
		4.6	H	6.5	②	28.6	③	16.0	16.0
2006	Mustang	4.0	N	5.0	②	23.8	③	16.0	16.0
		4.6	H	6.5	②	28.6	③	16.0	16.0
2007	Mustang	4.0	N	5.0	②	23.8	③	16.0	16.0
		4.6	H	6.5	②	28.6	③	16.0	16.0
		5.4	S	6.5	②	NA	③	16.0	18.0
2008	Mustang	4.0	N	5.0	②	23.8	③	16.0	16.0
		4.6	H	6.5	②	28.6	③	16.0	16.0
		5.4	S	6.5	②	NA	③	16.0	18.0

NOTE: All capacities are approximate. Add fluid gradually and ensure a proper fluid level is obtained.

NA: Not Available

① Includes torque converter

② T50D 5-speed: 5.6 pts.

  TR3650 5-speed: 7.5 pts.

  T56 6-speed: 10.0 pts.

③ If equipped with 7.5 inch ring gear: 3.0 pts. + 4 oz. friction modifier.

  If equipped with 8.8 inch ring gear: 3.2 pts. + 4 oz. friction modifier.

22086_MUST_C0004

FLUID SPECIFICATIONS

Year	Model	Engine Displacement Liters	Engine ID/VIN	Engine Oil	Auto. Trans. ①	Manual Trans.	Drive Axle	Power Steering Fluid	Brake Master Cylinder
2005	Mustang	4.0	N	5W-30	Mercon V	Mercon V	80W-90	Mercon MP ATF	DOT 3
	Mustang	4.6	H	5W-20	Mercon V	Mercon V	80W-90	Mercon MP ATF	DOT 3
2006	Mustang	4.0	N	5W-30	Mercon V	Mercon V	80W-90	Mercon MP ATF	DOT 3
	Mustang	4.6	H	5W-20	Mercon V	Mercon V	80W-90	Mercon MP ATF	DOT 3
2007	Mustang	4.0	N	5W-30	Mercon V	Mercon V	80W-90	Mercon MP ATF	DOT 3
	Mustang	4.6	H	5W-20	Mercon V	Mercon V	80W-90	Mercon MP ATF	DOT 3
2008	Mustang	4.0	N	5W-30	Mercon V	Mercon V	80W-90	Mercon MP ATF	DOT 3
	Mustang	4.6	H	5W-20	Mercon V	Mercon V	80W-90	Mercon MP ATF	DOT 3
	Shelby GT500	5.4	S	5W-50	Mercon V	Mercon V	80W-90	Mercon MP ATF	DOT 3

① MERCON V = XT-5-QM or XT-5-QMC (US); CXT-5-LM12 (Canada)

22086_MUST_C0014

VALVE SPECIFICATIONS

Year	Engine Displacement Liters	Engine ID/VIN	Seat Angle (deg.)	Face Angle (deg.)	Spring Test Pressure (lbs. @ in.)	Spring Installed Height (in.)	Stem-to-Guide Clearance (in.)		Stem Diameter (in.)	
							Intake	Exhaust	Intake	Exhaust
2005	4.0	N	45	45	①	1.569-1.609	0.0010-0.0020	0.0010-0.0030	0.2742-0.2748	0.2736-0.2742
	4.6	H	45	44.5-45	79@1.22	1.660	0.0010-0.0030	0.0020-0.0040	0.2352-0.2360	0.2742-0.2350
2006	4.0	N	45	45	①	1.569-1.609	0.0010-0.0020	0.0010-0.0030	0.2742-0.2748	0.2736-0.2742
	4.6	H	45	44.5-45	79@1.22	1.660	0.0010-0.0030	0.0020-0.0040	0.2352-0.2360	0.2742-0.2350
2007	4.0	N	45	45	①	1.569-1.609	0.0010-0.0020	0.0010-0.0030	0.2742-0.2748	0.2736-0.2742
	4.6	H	45	44.5-45	79@1.22	1.660	0.0010-0.0030	0.0020-0.0040	0.2352-0.2360	0.2742-0.2350
	5.5	S	44.50-45	44.25-45.75	In: 320.9@1.25 Ex: 299.2@1.08	In: 1.692 Ex: 1.555	0.0009-0.0022	0.0015-0.0028	0.2754-0.2762	0.2748-0.2756
2008	4.0	N	45	45	①	1.569-1.609	0.0010-0.0020	0.0010-0.0030	0.2742-0.2748	0.2736-0.2742
	4.6	H	45	44.5-45	79@1.22	1.660	0.0010-0.0030	0.0020-0.0040	0.2352-0.2360	0.2742-0.2350
	5.5	S	44.50-45	44.25-45.75	In: 320.9@1.25 Ex: 299.2@1.08	In: 1.692 Ex: 1.555	0.0009-0.0022	0.0015-0.0028	0.2754-0.2762	0.2748-0.2756

① 202-225@1.413-1.445

22086_MUST_C0005

CAMSHAFT AND BEARING SPECIFICATIONS CHART

All measurements are given in inches.

Year	Engine Displ. Liters	Engine ID/VIN	Journal Dia.	Brg. Oil Clearance	Shaft End-play	Runout	Journal Bore	Lobe Height	
								Intake	Exhaust
2005	4.0	N	1.099-1.1010	0.0020-0.0040	0.0030-0.0070	0.0020	1.1020-1.1040	0.2590	0.2590
	4.6	H	1.1260 1.1270	0.0010-0.003	0.0002-0.0090	0.0010	1.1280-1.1290	0.2170	0.2170
2006	4.0	N	1.099-1.1010	0.0020-0.0040	0.0030-0.0070	0.0020	1.1020-1.1040	0.2590	0.2590
	4.6	H	1.1260 1.1270	0.0010-0.003	0.0002-0.0090	0.0010	1.1280-1.1290	0.2170	0.2170
2007	4.0	N	1.099-1.1010	0.0020-0.0040	0.0030-0.0070	0.0020	1.1020-1.1040	0.2590	0.2590
	4.6	H	1.1260 1.1270	0.0010-0.003	0.0002-0.0090	0.0010	1.1280-1.1290	0.2170	0.2170
	5.4	S	1.0605-1.0615	0.0010-0.0030	0.0011-0.0075	0.0035 (4 places)	1.0625-1.0635	0.2424	0.2597
2008	4.0	N	1.099-1.1010	0.0020-0.0040	0.0030-0.0070	0.0020	1.1020-1.1040	0.2590	0.2590
	4.6	H	1.1260 1.1270	0.0010-0.003	0.0002-0.0090	0.0010	1.1280-1.1290	0.2170	0.2170
	5.4	S	1.0605-1.0615	0.0010-0.0030	0.0011-0.0075	0.0035 (4 places)	1.0625-1.0635	0.2424	0.2597

22086_MUST_C0006

CRANKSHAFT AND CONNECTING ROD SPECIFICATIONS

All measurements are given in inches.

Year	Engine Displacement Liters	Engine ID/VIN	Crankshaft				Connecting Rod		
			Main Brg. Journal Dia.	Main Brg. Oil Clearance	Shaft End-play	Thrust on No.	Journal Diameter	Oil Clearance	Side Clearance
2005	4.0	N	2.2430-2.2440	0.0003-0.0024	0.0020-0.0126	5	2.125-2.1260	0.0003-0.0024	0.0036-0.0106
	4.6	H	2.6567-2.6576	0.0009-0.0019	0.0030-0.0148	5	2.0859-2.0867	0.0009-0.0026	0.0020-0.0060
2006	4.0	N	2.2430-2.2440	0.0003-0.0024	0.0020-0.0126	5	2.125-2.1260	0.0003-0.0024	0.0036-0.0106
	4.6	H	2.6567-2.6576	0.0009-0.0019	0.0030-0.0148	5	2.0859-2.0867	0.0009-0.0026	0.0020-0.0060
2007	4.0	N	2.2430-2.2440	0.0003-0.0024	0.0020-0.0126	5	2.125-2.1260	0.0003-0.0024	0.0036-0.0106
	4.6	H	2.6567-2.6576	0.0009-0.0019	0.0030-0.0148	5	2.0859-2.0867	0.0009-0.0026	0.0020-0.0060
	5.4	S	2.6567-2.6577	0.0009-0.0019	0.0030-0.0148	5	2.0859-2.0877	0.0010-0.0025	0.0049-0.0187
2008	4.0	N	2.2430-2.2440	0.0003-0.0024	0.0020-0.0126	5	2.125-2.1260	0.0003-0.0024	0.0036-0.0106
	4.6	H	2.6567-2.6576	0.0009-0.0019	0.0030-0.0148	5	2.0859-2.0867	0.0009-0.0026	0.0020-0.0060
	5.4	S	2.6567-2.6577	0.0009-0.0019	0.0030-0.0148	5	2.0859-2.0877	0.0010-0.0025	0.0049-0.0187

22086_MUST_C0008

PISTON AND RING SPECIFICATIONS

All measurements are given in inches.

Year	Engine Displacement Liters	Engine ID/VIN	Piston Clearance	Ring Gap			Ring Side Clearance		
				Top Compression	Bottom Compression	Oil Control	Top Compression	Bottom Compression	Oil Control
2005	4.0	N	0.0012-0.0020	0.0008-0.0018	0.0016-0.0024	NA	0.0016-0.0030	0.0012-0.0026	NA
	4.6	H	0.0007-0.0019	0.0006-0.0012	0.0098-0.0197	0.0059-0.0256	0.0008-0.0020	0.0008-0.0020	NA
2006	4.0	N	0.0012-0.0020	0.0008-0.0018	0.0016-0.0024	NA	0.0016-0.0030	0.0012-0.0026	NA
	4.6	H	0.0007-0.0019	0.0006-0.0012	0.0098-0.0197	0.0059-0.0256	0.0008-0.0020	0.0008-0.0020	NA
2007	4.0	N	0.0012-0.0020	0.0008-0.0018	0.0016-0.0024	NA	0.0016-0.0030	0.0012-0.0026	NA
	4.6	H	0.0007-0.0019	0.0006-0.0012	0.0098-0.0197	0.0059-0.0256	0.0008-0.0020	0.0008-0.0020	NA
	5.4	S	0.0002-0.0010	0.0051-0.0111	0.0098-0.0157	0.0059-0.0256	0.0012-0.0020	0.0012-0.0031	NA
2008	4.0	N	0.0012-0.0020	0.0008-0.0018	0.0016-0.0024	NA	0.0016-0.0030	0.0012-0.0026	NA
	4.6	H	0.0007-0.0019	0.0006-0.0012	0.0098-0.0197	0.0059-0.0256	0.0008-0.0020	0.0008-0.0020	NA
	5.4	S	0.0002-0.0010	0.0051-0.0111	0.0098-0.0157	0.0059-0.0256	0.0012-0.0020	0.0012-0.0031	NA

NA: Not Available

22086_MUST_C0007

TORQUE SPECIFICATIONS
All readings in ft. lbs.

Year	Engine Displacement Liters	Engine ID/VIN	Cylinder Head Bolts	Main Bearing Bolts	Rod Bearing Bolts	Crankshaft Damper Bolts	Flywheel Bolts	Manifold		Spark Plugs	Oil Pan Drain Plug
								Intake	Exhaust		
2005	4.0	N	①	②	③	④	⑤	⑥	16	13	18
	4.6	H	⑦	⑧	⑨	⑩	59	⑥	18	25	19
2006	4.0	N	①	②	③	④	⑤	⑥	16	13	18
	4.6	H	⑦	⑧	⑨	⑩	59	⑥	18	25	19
2007	4.0	N	①	②	③	④	⑤	⑥	16	13	18
	4.6	H	⑦	⑧	⑨	⑩	59	⑥	18	25	19
	5.4	S	⑪	⑫	⑬	⑩	59	⑥	15	13	19
2008	4.0	N	①	②	③	④	⑤	⑥	16	13	18
	4.6	H	⑦	⑧	⑨	⑩	59	⑥	18	25	19
	5.4	S	⑪	⑫	⑬	⑩	59	⑥	15	13	19

① M8 Bolts: 24 ft. lbs.
  M12 Bolts: Step 1: 9 ft. lbs.
  Step 2: 18 ft. lbs.
  Step 3: Tighten an additional 90 degrees
  Step 4: Tighten an additional 90 degrees

② Step 1: 35 ft. lbs.
  Step 2: Tighten an additional 57 degrees

③ Step 1: 15 ft. lbs.
  Step 2: Tighten an additional 90 degrees

④ Step 1: 33 ft. lbs.
  Step 2: Tighten an additional 85 degrees

⑤ Step 1: 10 ft, lbs.
  Step 2: 52 ft. lbs.

⑥ 89 INCH lbs.

⑦ Step 1: 30 ft. lbs.
  Step 2: Tighten an additional 90 degrees
  Step 3: Tighten an additional 90 degrees

⑧ Step 1: Bolts 1 through 10 to 18 ft. lbs.
  Step 2: Bolts 11 through 20 to 30 ft. lbs.
  Step 3: Bolts 1 through 20 an additional 90 degrees
  Step 4: Side mounted bolts to 30 ft. lbs.
  Step 5: Side bolts tighten an additional 90 degrees

⑨ Step 1: 32 ft. lbs.
  Step 2: Tighten an additional 105 degrees

⑩ Step 1: 66 ft. lbs.
  Step 2: Loosen all bolts one turn
  Step 3: 37 ft. lbs.
  Step 4: Tighten an additional 90 degrees

⑪ Step 1: 15 ft. lbs.
  Step 2: 37 ft. lbs.
  Step 3: 59 ft. lbs.
  Step 4: Tighten an additional 90 degrees
  Step 5: Tighten an additional 90 degrees

⑫ Step 1: 89 inch lbs.
  Step 2: 30 ft. lbs.
  Step 3: Tighten an additional 90 degrees

⑬ Step 1: 30 ft. lbs.
  Step 2: Tighten an additional 90 degrees

22086_MUST_C0009

WHEEL ALIGNMENT

Year	Model		Caster Range (+/-Deg.)	Caster Preferred Setting (Deg.)	Camber Range (+/-Deg.)	Camber Preferred Setting (Deg.)	Toe-in (in.)
2005	Mustang	F	0.70	7.1	0.70	0.75	0.10 +/- 0.20
		R	—	—	NA	NA	NA
2006	Mustang	F	0.70	7.1	0.70	0.75	0.10 +/- 0.20
		R	—	—	NA	NA	NA
2007	Mustang	F	0.70	7.1	0.70	0.75	0.10 +/- 0.20
		R	—	—	NA	NA	NA
2008	Mustang	F	0.70	7.1	0.70	0.75	0.10 +/- 0.20
		R	—	—	NA	NA	NA

NA: Not Available

22086_MUST_C0010

TIRE, WHEEL AND BALL JOINT SPECIFICATIONS

Year	Model	OEM Tires Standard	OEM Tires Optional	Tire Pressures (psi) Front	Tire Pressures (psi) Rear	Wheel Size	Ball Joint Inspection	Lug Nut Torque (ft. lbs.)
2005	Mustang	P215/65R16	P235/55ZR17	30	30	—	①	98
2006	Mustang	P215/65R16	P235/55ZR17	30	30	—	①	98
2007	Mustang	P215/65R16	P235/55ZR17	30	30	—	①	98
	Shelby	F: P255/45ZR18	NA	②	②	—	①	98
	GT500	R: P285/40/ZR18	NA	②	②	—	①	98
2008	Mustang	P215/65R16	P235/55ZR17	30	30	—	①	98
	Shelby	F: P255/45ZR18	NA	②	②	—	①	98
	GT500	R: P285/40/ZR18	NA	②	②	—	①	98

NA: Not Available

F: Front

R: Rear

OEM: Original Equipment Manufacturer

PSI: Pounds Per Square Inch

① Replace if movement exceeds the maximum measurement of 1/32 inches (0.8mm)

② Refer to recommended specifications of tire manufacturer

22086_MUST_C0011

BRAKE SPECIFICATIONS

All measurements in inches unless noted

Year	Model		Brake Disc Original Thickness	Brake Disc Minimum Thickness	Brake Disc Maximum Run-out	Brake Drum Diameter Original Inside Diameter	Brake Drum Diameter Max. Wear Limit	Brake Drum Diameter Maximum Machine Diameter	Minimum Lining Thickness	Brake Caliper Mounting Bolts (ft. lbs.)
2005	Mustang	F	NA	1.110	0.002	—	—	—	0.118	25
		R	NA	0.680	0.004	—	—	—	0.118	24
2006	Mustang	F	NA	1.110	0.002	—	—	—	0.118	25
		R	NA	0.680	0.004	—	—	—	0.118	24
2007	Mustang	F	NA	1.110	0.002	—	—	—	0.118	25
		R	NA	0.680	0.004	—	—	—	0.118	24
	Shelby	F	NA	1.118	0.002	—	—	—	0.118	85
	GT500	R	NA	0.680	0.004	—	—	—	0.118	50
2008	Mustang	F	NA	1.110	0.002	—	—	—	0.118	25
		R	NA	0.680	0.004	—	—	—	0.118	24
	Shelby	F	NA	1.118	0.002	—	—	—	0.118	85
	GT500	R	NA	0.680	0.004	—	—	—	0.118	50

NA: Not Available

F: Front

R: Rear

22086_MUST_C0012

SCHEDULED MAINTENANCE INTERVALS
2005-2008 FORD MUSTANG

TO BE SERVICED	TYPE OF SERVICE	VEHICLE MILEAGE INTERVAL (x1000)																	
		5	10	15	20	25	30	35	40	45	50	55	60	65	70	75	80	85	90
Engine oil & filter ①	R																		
Rotate tires	S/I	✓	✓	✓	✓	✓	✓	✓	✓	✓	✓	✓	✓	✓	✓	✓	✓	✓	✓
Engine coolant strength hoses & clamps	S/I			✓			✓			✓			✓				✓		✓
Air cleaner filter	R						✓						✓						✓
Automatic transmission fluid & filter	R						✓						✓						✓
Engine coolant ②	R																		
PCV valve	R												✓						✓
Spark plugs ③	R																		
Drive belts	S/I						✓						✓						✓
Exhaust system & heat shields	S/I						✓						✓						✓
Front & rear brakes	S/I	✓	✓	✓	✓	✓	✓	✓	✓	✓	✓	✓	✓	✓	✓	✓	✓	✓	✓
Fuel filter	R			✓			✓				✓		✓			✓			✓

R: Replace   S/I: Service or Inspect

① Engine oil and filter: replace every 3000 miles.

② Engine coolant: change initially at 100,000 miles or 5 years.

③ Spark plugs: replace every 100,000 miles.

Special Operating Condition Requirements

During extensive idling and/or low speed driving for long distances, as in heavy commercial use such as delivery, taxi, patrol car or livery:

Lube front lower control arm and steering linkage ball joints with

Zerk fittings (if equipped) every 4,800 km (3,000 miles) or 3 months.

Inspect brake system and check battery electrolyte level (Patrol cars) every 8,000 km (5,000 miles).

Install a new cabin air filter as required.

When operating in dusty conditions such as unpaved or dusty roads:

Install a new engine air filter as required.

Install a new cabin air filter as required.

When operating in off-road conditions:

Change automatic transmission fluid every 48,000 km (30,000 miles).

Install a new cabin air filter as required.

Inspect and lubricate U-joints.

Inspect and lubricate steering linkage ball joints with zerk fittings.

22086_MUST_C0013

PRECAUTIONS

Before servicing any vehicle, please be sure to read all of the following precautions, which deal with personal safety, prevention of component damage, and important points to take into consideration when servicing a motor vehicle:

• Never open, service or drain the radiator or cooling system when the engine is hot; serious burns can occur from the steam and hot coolant.

• Observe all applicable safety precautions when working around fuel. Whenever servicing the fuel system, always work in a well-ventilated area. Do not allow fuel spray or vapors to come in contact with a spark, open flame, or excessive heat (a hot drop light, for example). Keep a dry chemical fire extinguisher near the work area. Always keep fuel in a container specifically designed for fuel storage; also, always properly seal fuel containers to avoid the possibility of fire or explosion. Refer to the additional fuel system precautions later in this section.

• Fuel injection systems often remain pressurized, even after the engine has been turned **OFF**. The fuel system pressure must be relieved before disconnecting any fuel lines. Failure to do so may result in fire and/or personal injury.

• Brake fluid often contains polyglycol ethers and polyglycols. Avoid contact with the eyes and wash your hands thoroughly after handling brake fluid. If you do get brake fluid in your eyes, flush your eyes with clean, running water for 15 minutes. If eye irritation persists, or if you have taken brake fluid internally, IMMEDIATELY seek medical assistance.

• The EPA warns that prolonged contact with used engine oil may cause a number of skin disorders, including cancer. You should make every effort to minimize your exposure to used engine oil. Protective gloves should be worn when changing oil. Wash your hands and any other exposed skin areas as soon as possible after exposure to used engine oil. Soap and water, or waterless hand cleaner should be used.

• All new vehicles are now equipped with an air bag system, often referred to as a Supplemental Restraint System (SRS) or Supplemental Inflatable Restraint (SIR) system. The system must be disabled before performing service on or around system components, steering column, instrument panel components, wiring and sensors. Failure to follow safety and disabling procedures could result in accidental air bag deployment, possible personal injury and unnecessary system repairs.

• Always wear safety goggles when working with, or around, the air bag system. When carrying a non-deployed air bag, be sure the bag and trim cover are pointed away from your body. When placing a non-deployed air bag on a work surface, always face the bag and trim cover upward, away from the surface. This will reduce the motion of the module if it is accidentally deployed. Refer to the additional air bag system precautions later in this section.

• Clean, high quality brake fluid from a sealed container is essential to the safe and proper operation of the brake system. You should always buy the correct type of brake fluid for your vehicle. If the brake fluid becomes contaminated, completely flush the system with new fluid. Never reuse any brake fluid. Any brake fluid that is removed from the system should be discarded. Also, do not allow any brake fluid to come in contact with a painted surface; it will damage the paint.

• Never operate the engine without the proper amount and type of engine oil; doing so WILL result in severe engine damage.

• Timing belt maintenance is extremely important. Many models utilize an interference-type, non-freewheeling engine. If the timing belt breaks, the valves in the cylinder head may strike the pistons, causing potentially serious (also time-consuming and expensive) engine damage. Refer to the maintenance interval charts for the recommended replacement interval for the timing belt, and to the timing belt section for belt replacement and inspection.

• Disconnecting the negative battery cable on some vehicles may interfere with the functions of the on-board computer system(s) and may require the computer to undergo a relearning process once the negative battery cable is reconnected.

• When servicing drum brakes, only disassemble and assemble one side at a time, leaving the remaining side intact for reference.

• Only an MVAC-trained, EPA-certified automotive technician should service the air conditioning system or its components.

BRAKES

GENERAL INFORMATION

PRECAUTIONS

• Certain components within the ABS system are not intended to be serviced or repaired individually.

• Do not use rubber hoses or other parts not specifically specified for and ABS system. When using repair kits, replace all parts included in the kit. Partial or incorrect repair may lead to functional problems and require the replacement of components.

• Lubricate rubber parts with clean, fresh brake fluid to ease assembly. Do not use shop air to clean parts; damage to rubber components may result.

• Use only DOT 3 brake fluid from an unopened container.

• If any hydraulic component or line is removed or replaced, it may be necessary to bleed the entire system.

• A clean repair area is essential. Always clean the reservoir and cap thoroughly before removing the cap. The slightest amount of dirt in the fluid may plug an orifice and impair the system function. Perform repairs after components have been thoroughly cleaned; use only denatured alcohol to clean components. Do not allow ABS components to come into contact with any substance containing mineral oil; this includes used shop rags.

• The Anti-Lock control unit is a microprocessor similar to other computer units in the vehicle. Ensure that the ignition

ANTI-LOCK BRAKE SYSTEM (ABS)

switch is **OFF** before removing or installing controller harnesses. Avoid static electricity discharge at or near the controller.

• If any arc welding is to be done on the vehicle, the control unit should be unplugged before welding operations begin.

SPEED SENSORS

REMOVAL & INSTALLATION
See Figure 1.

1. With the vehicle in NEUTRAL, place it on a hoist.
2. Disconnect the wheel speed sensor electrical connector.
3. Disconnect the 3 wheel speed sensor harness pin type retainers.

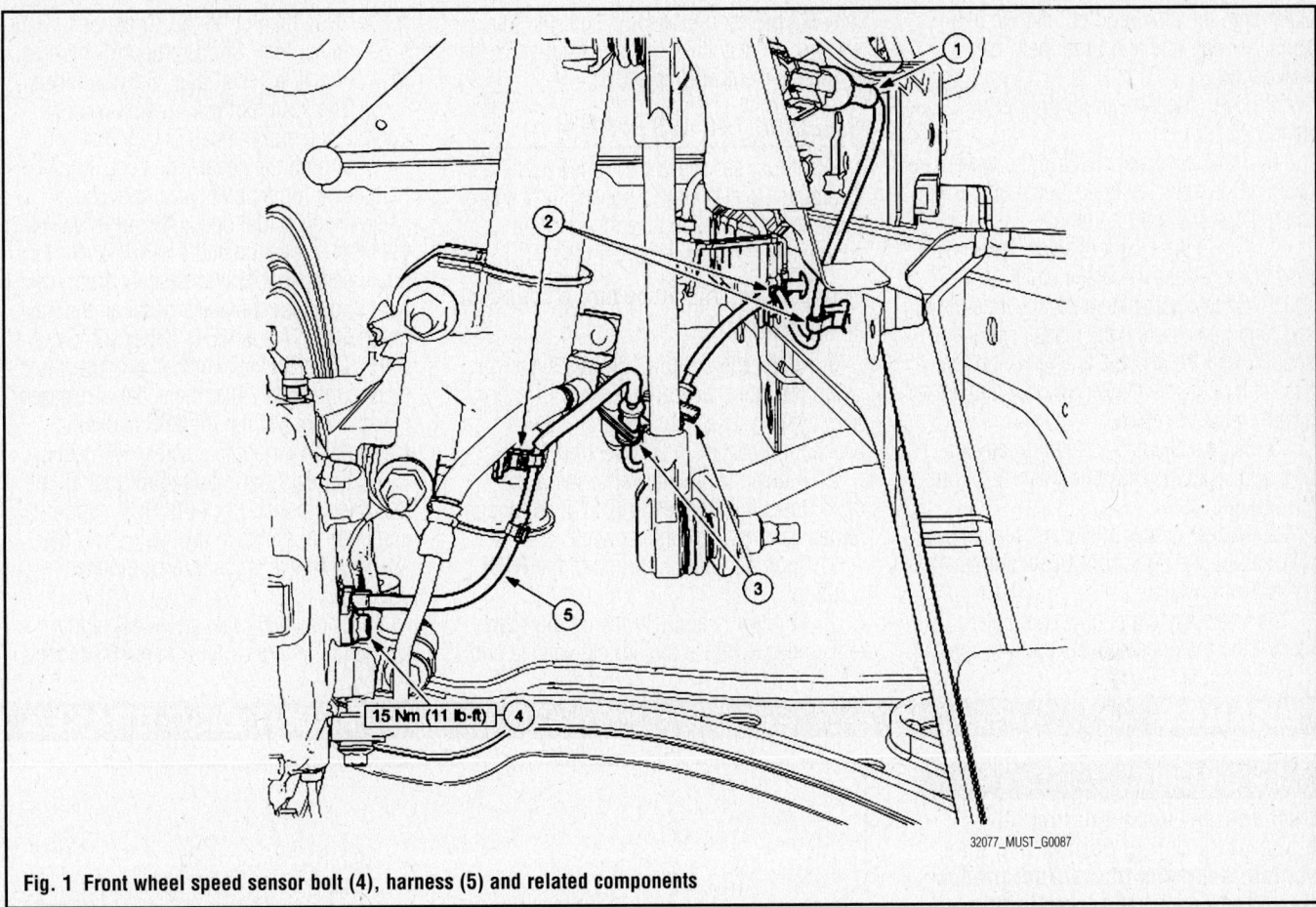

32077_MUST_G0087

Fig. 1 Front wheel speed sensor bolt (4), harness (5) and related components

4. Disconnect the 2 wheel speed sensor grommet retainers from the brake hose clips.

5. Remove the wheel speed sensor bolt.

6. Remove the wheel speed sensor and harness assembly.

To install:

7. Installation is the reverse of the removal procedure. Observe the following tightening torques:
- Wheel speed sensor bolt 11 ft. lbs (15 Nm).

BRAKES   BLEEDING THE BRAKE SYSTEM

BLEEDING PROCEDURE

BLEEDING PROCEDURE

✳✳ WARNING

Clean, high quality brake fluid is essential to the safe and proper operation of the brake system. You should always buy the highest quality brake fluid that is available. If the brake fluid becomes contaminated, drain and flush the system, then refill the master cylinder with new fluid. Never reuse any brake fluid. Any brake fluid that is removed from the system should be discarded. Also, do not allow any brake fluid to come in contact with a painted surface; it will damage the paint.

✳✳ CAUTION

Brake fluid contains polyglycol ethers and polyglycols. Avoid contact with the eyes and wash your hands thoroughly after handling brake fluid. If you do get brake fluid in your eyes, flush your eyes with clean, running water for 15 minutes. If eye irritation persists, or if you have taken brake fluid internally, IMMEDIATELY seek medical assistance.

➡ On models equipped with an Anti-lock Brake System (ABS), if during brake system service, or because of a fluid leak, the level of fluid in the system ever falls below that of the Hydraulic Control Unit (HCU), refer to the bleeding procedure in the ABS portion of this section. To properly bleed the HCU, an expensive scan tool is

necessary; take this into consideration when contemplating brake system service. However, if only the brake pads, calipers, master cylinder, and other non–ABS components are being removed and installed, bleeding the HCU is not necessary and, therefore, the scan tool is not necessary.

Bleed the right rear wheel first then the left rear wheel followed by the right front wheel and the front left wheel last.

1. Bleed the master cylinder if not already done.

2. Fill the master cylinder with clean, new DOT 3 brake fluid. Leave a clean shop rag on the master cylinder while bleeding it.

3. Raise and properly support the vehicle.

4. Position a box end wrench on the right rear caliper bleeder valve, then install a clear plastic tube on the bleeder valve nipple.

Submerge the other end of the tube in a container partially filled with new, clean brake fluid.

5. Open the bleeder valve approximately ¾ turn.

6. Have an assistant sit in the driver's seat and depress the brake pedal all the way to the floor and hold it there.

7. Close the bleeder valve, THEN have the helper release the brake pedal.

8. Check the brake master cylinder level and fill it if necessary; the master cylinder should never be allowed to empty of brake fluid. If it does, the master cylinder and brake system must be rebled.

9. Repeat Steps 5–8 until no air bubbles appear in the brake fluid emitted from the bleeder tube.

10. Repeat procedure for left rear wheel followed by the right front wheel and finally the left front wheel.

The brake system is now completely bled. If the brake pedal feels spongy, refer to the ABS bleeding procedure later in this section; air may have become trapped in the Hydraulic Control Unit (HCU).

BLEEDING THE ABS SYSTEM

Whenever service is performed to the Hydraulic Control Unit, a specific procedure must be performed to bleed the system to ensure that no air is trapped in the HCU.

➡ **To perform this procedure a scan tool is necessary.**

1. Bleed the entire hydraulic system using the same procedure used for a non-ABS system. (Refer to the brake bleeding procedure, earlier in this section.)

2. Attach the NGS tester to the under dash Data Link Connector (DLC), as though retrieving engine trouble codes.

3. Turn the ignition switch to the **RUN** position.

4. Follow the instructions on the scan tool screen. Choose the correct vehicle and model year, then go to the "Diagnostic Data Link" menu item. Choose the ABS module, then "Function Tests" and "Service Bleed."

5. The scan tool will instruct you to depress the brake pedal. Ensure that you push hard on the pedal. The pedal must be held down for approximately 5 seconds while the scan tool opens the outlet valves in the HCU. When the outlet valves open, the brake pedal should immediately drop; make sure to depress the brake pedal all the way to the floor. This is VERY important to do!

6. The scan tool will then prompt you to release the pedal. After the pedal is released, the scan tool will run the ABS hydraulic pump motor for approximately 15 seconds.

7. Repeat Step 5 to ensure that all air has been flushed from the HCU. Upon completion, the scan tool will show the "Service Bleed Procedure Completed" message.

8. Once again, bleed the rest of the hydraulic system as for a non-ABS model.

BRAKES — FRONT DISC BRAKES

❊❊ CAUTION

Dust and dirt accumulating on brake parts during normal use may contain asbestos fibers from production or aftermarket brake linings. Breathing excessive concentrations of asbestos fibers can cause serious bodily harm. Exercise care when servicing brake parts. Do not sand or grind brake lining unless equipment used is designed to contain the dust residue. Do not clean brake parts with compressed air or by dry brushing. Cleaning should be done by dampening the brake components with a fine mist of water, then wiping the brake components clean with a dampened cloth. Dispose of cloth and all residue containing asbestos fibers in an impermeable container with the appropriate label. Follow practices prescribed by the Occupational Safety and Health Administration (OSHA) and the Environmental Protection Agency (EPA) for the handling, processing, and disposing of dust or debris that may contain asbestos fibers.

BRAKE CALIPER

REMOVAL & INSTALLATION

See Figure 2.

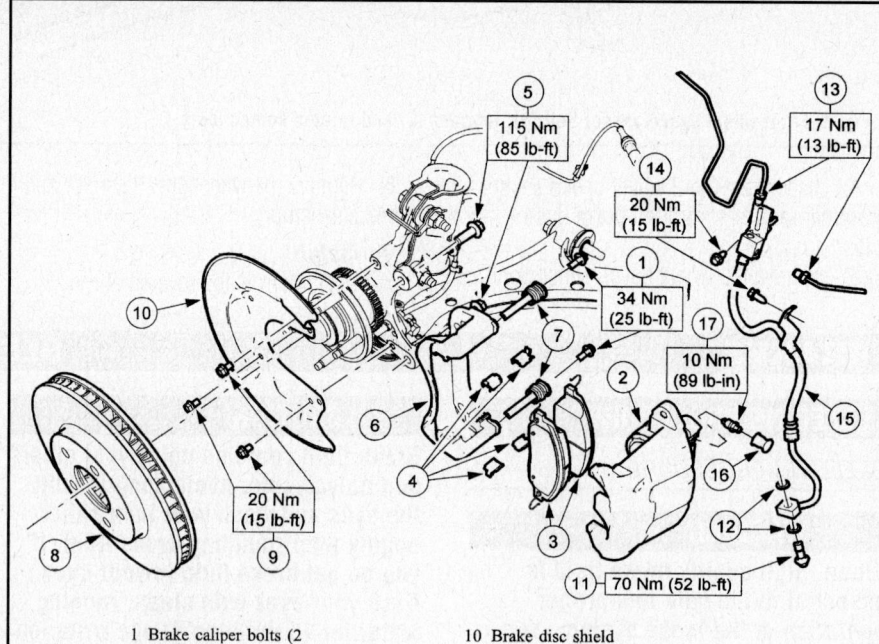

1. Brake caliper bolts (2 required)
2. Brake caliper RH/LH
3. Brake pads kit
4. Spring clips (4 required)
5. Brake caliper anchor plate bolts (2 required)
6. Brake caliper anchor plate
7. Guide pins
8. Brake disc
9. Brake disc shield bolts (3 required)
10. Brake disc shield
11. Brake caliper flow bolt
12. Copper washers (2 required)
13. Brake line fitting
14. Brake flexible hose bracket bolts
15. Brake flexible hose RH/LH
16. Bleeder screw cap (part of 2208)
17. Bleeder screw

115 Nm (85 lb-ft) — 5
17 Nm (13 lb-ft) — 13
20 Nm (15 lb-ft) — 14
34 Nm (25 lb-ft) — 1
10 Nm (89 lb-in) — 17
20 Nm (15 lb-ft) — 9
70 Nm (52 lb-ft) — 11

06017-TANG-G66

Fig. 2 Exploded view of the front disc brake assembly—Mustang

1. Before servicing the vehicle, refer to the precautions at the beginning of this section.

2. Remove the wheel and tire assembly.

3. Mark the disc brake caliper to ensure that it will be installed to the same side if both calipers are being removed.

4. Disconnect the caliper flow bolt and discard 2 copper sealing washers.

5. Remove lower brake caliper locating pin, if equipped.

6. Remove brake caliper mounting bolts and discard.

7. Rotate the brake caliper approximately 90° away from the anchor assembly.

8. Remove the disc brake caliper.

To install:

9. If required, compress the caliper piston(s) using a C-clamp and an old disc brake pad or block of wood.

10. Position the brake caliper assembly into place on the anchor plate and tighten the bolts to 25 ft. lbs. (34 Nm).

11. Connect the caliper flow bolt using new copper sealing washers and tighten the bolt to 52 ft. lbs. (70 Nm).

12. Install the wheel and tire assembly.

13. Pump the brake pedal several times to position the brake pads before the vehicle is moved.

14. Road test the vehicle and check for proper brake system operation.

DISC BRAKE PADS

REMOVAL & INSTALLATION

4.0L & 4.6L Engines

See Figure 3.

1. Before servicing the vehicle, refer to the precautions at the beginning of this section.

2. Remove and discard ½ of the brake fluid from the brake master cylinder reservoir. Properly dispose of the used brake fluid.

3. Remove the wheel and tire assembly.

4. Remove disc brake caliper assembly from anchor plate. Hang the disc brake caliper from the body with wire. Do not let the disc brake caliper hang by the brake hose.

5. Remove the outer and inner disc brake pads from the disc brake caliper.

6. Clean any residue from the caliper anchor plate and disc brake pad contact areas.

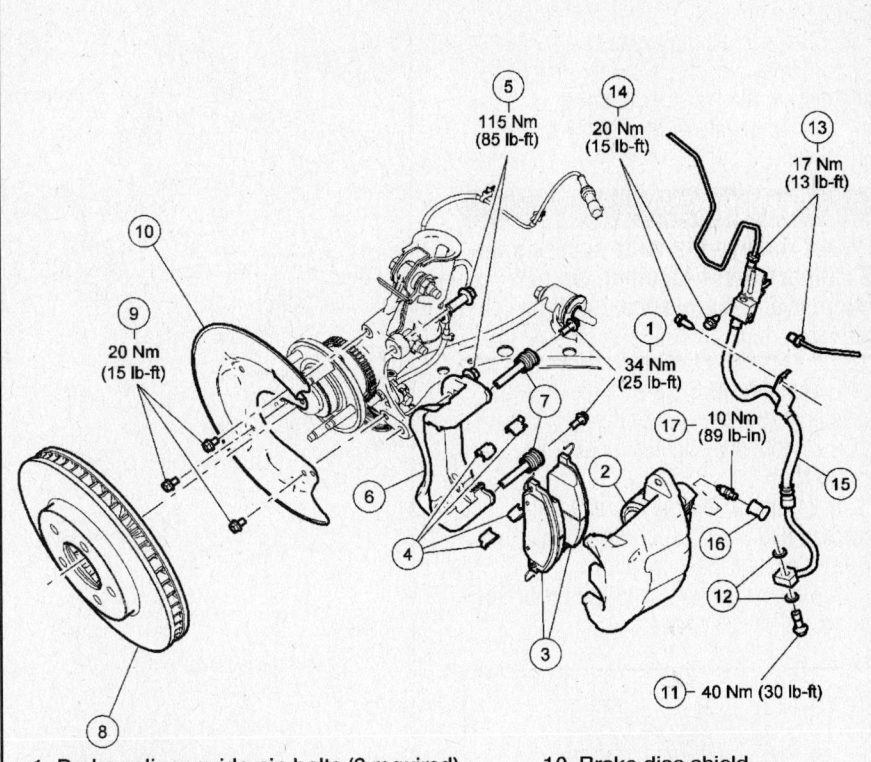

1. Brake caliper guide pin bolts (2 required)
2. Brake caliper
3. Brake pads kit
4. Spring clips (4 required))
5. Brake caliper anchor plate bolts (2 required)
6. Brake caliper anchor plate
7. Guide pins
8. Brake disc
9. Brake disc shield bolts (3 required)
10. Brake disc shield
11. Brake caliper flow bolt
12. Copper washers (2 required)
13. Brake tube fittings
14. Brake flexible hose bracket bolts
15. Brake flexible hose
16. Bleeder screw cap
17. Bleeder screw

22086_MUST_G0176

Fig. 3 Disc brake assembly view—4.0L and 4.6L engines

7. Inspect the disc brake rotor for scoring and wear. Replace or machine, as necessary.

8. Inspect the piston boots and the caliper pin boots for damage. Replace as necessary.

To install:

9. Use a large C-clamp and a wood block to push the caliper pistons back into their bores.

10. Remove the protective paper from the insulators on the back of the disc brake pads, if equipped.

11. Install the inner and outer disc brake pads in the disc brake caliper. Make sure the pads are seated properly.

12. Install the disc brake caliper and pads.

13. Install the wheel and tire assembly. Torque the lug nuts in a star pattern to 95 ft. lbs. (129 Nm).

14. Repeat the procedure for the opposite disc brake caliper assembly.

15. Pump the brake pedal prior to moving the vehicle to position the brake pads.

16. Fill the brake master cylinder reservoir with clean DOT 3 brake fluid from a closed container.

17. If the disc brake calipers were replaced or repaired, be sure to bleed the system.

18. Road test the vehicle and check the brake system for proper operation.

5.4L Engine

See Figures 4 and 5.

➡A revised part, with the same base part number, has been released for the RH brake hose. When installing a new RH brake hose, position the anti-rotation tab on the mounting bracket toward the front of the vehicle and install the bolt with the head toward the rear of the vehicle.

1. With the vehicle in NEUTRAL, position it on a hoist.

2. Remove the brake pads.

3. Remove the brake caliper flow bolt and discard the 2 copper washers.

    a. To install, tighten to 35 ft. lbs. (48 Nm).

✸✸ WARNING

Do not remove the bolts securing the 2 caliper halves together. Do not attempt to separate the 2 caliper halves.

4. Remove the 2 brake caliper anchor plate bolts and the brake caliper.

    a. To install, tighten to 30 ft. lbs. (40 Nm).

5. To install, reverse the removal procedure.

6. Bleed the brake system.

7. Check fluid level, and test the brakes for normal operation.

Fig. 4 Brake pad removal and installation

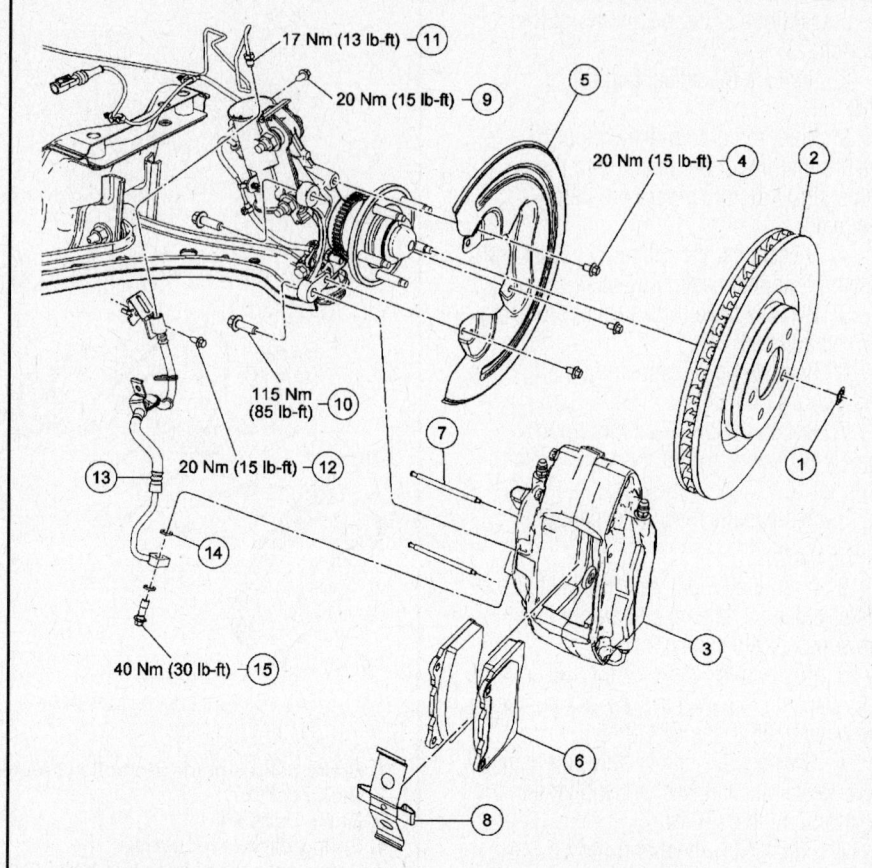

1. Retaining nut
2. Brake disc
3. Brake caliper
4. Brake disc shield bolt (3 required)
5. Brake disc shield
6. Brake pad (2 required)
7. Brake pad mounting pin (2 required)
8. Spring retainer clip
9. Brake hose to strut bolt
10. Brake caliper bolt (2 required)
11. Brake tube fitting
12. Brake flexible hose bracket bolt
13. Brake flexible hose
14. Copper washer (2 required)
15. Brake caliper flow bolt

22086_MUST_G0177

Fig. 5 Disc brake assembly view—5.4L engines

BRAKES

REAR DISC BRAKES

✸✸ CAUTION

Dust and dirt accumulating on brake parts during normal use may contain asbestos fibers from production or aftermarket brake linings. Breathing excessive concentrations of asbestos fibers can cause serious bodily harm. Exercise care when servicing brake parts. Do not sand or grind brake lining unless equipment used is designed to contain the dust residue. Do not clean brake parts with compressed air or by dry brushing. Cleaning should be done by dampening the brake components with a fine mist of water, then wiping the brake components clean with a dampened cloth. Dispose of cloth and all residue containing asbestos fibers in an impermeable container with the appropriate label. Follow practices prescribed by the Occupational Safety and Health Administration (OSHA) and the Environmental Protection Agency (EPA) for the handling, processing, and disposing of dust or debris that may contain asbestos fibers.

BRAKE CALIPER

REMOVAL & INSTALLATION

See Figure 6.

1. Remove wheel and tire assembly.

2. Remove the retaining clip and the parking brake cable and conduit from the caliper.

3. Disconnect the caliper flow bolt and discard 2 copper sealing washers.

4. Remove brake caliper mounting bolts and discard.

5. Rotate the brake caliper approximately 90° away from the anchor assembly.

6. Remove the disc brake caliper.

To install:

7. If required, compress the caliper piston(s) using a C-clamp and an old disc brake pad or block of wood.

8. Position the brake caliper assembly into place on the anchor plate and tighten the bolts to 24 ft. lbs. (33 Nm).

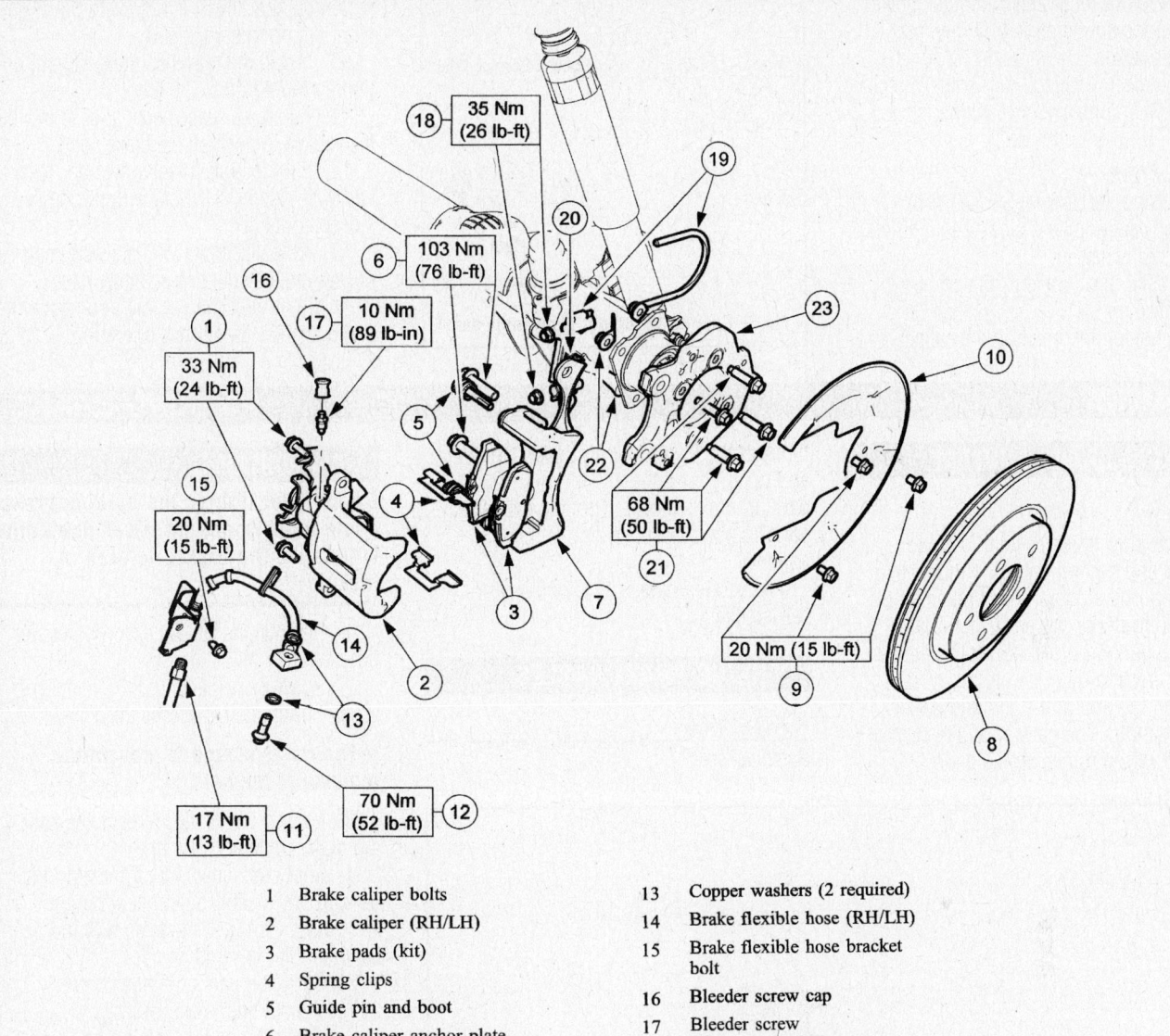

1   Brake caliper bolts
2   Brake caliper (RH/LH)
3   Brake pads (kit)
4   Spring clips
5   Guide pin and boot
6   Brake caliper anchor plate bolt kit (2 bolts each side)
7   Brake caliper anchor plate
8   Brake disc
9   Brake disc shield bolts (3 required)
10   Brake disc shield
11   Brake line fitting
12   Brake caliper flow bolt

13   Copper washers (2 required)
14   Brake flexible hose (RH/LH)
15   Brake flexible hose bracket bolt
16   Bleeder screw cap
17   Bleeder screw
18   Anti-moan bracket U-bolt nuts (2 required)
19   Anti-moan bracket U-bolt and clamp
20   Anti-moan bracket
21   Brake caliper support bracket bolts (4 required)
22   Brake caliper support bracket flag nuts (4 required)
23   Brake caliper support bracket

06017-TANG-G67

Fig. 6 Exploded view of the rear disc brake assembly—Mustang

9. Connect the caliper flow bolt using new copper sealing washers and tighten the bolt to 52 ft. lbs. (70 Nm).

10. Install the retaining clip and the parking brake cable and conduit to the caliper.

11. Install the wheel and tire assembly.

12. Pump the brake pedal several times to position the brake pads before the vehicle is moved.

13. Road test the vehicle and check for proper brake system operation.

DISC BRAKE PADS

REMOVAL & INSTALLATION

See Figure 7.

1. Before servicing the vehicle, refer to the precautions at the beginning of this section.

2. Remove ½ of the brake fluid from the brake master cylinder reservoir. Properly dispose of the used brake fluid.

3. Remove wheel and tire assembly.

4. Remove the rear disc brake caliper. Hang the caliper from the body with wire. Do not let the disc brake caliper hang by the brake hose.

5. Remove inner and outer disc brake pads and the spring clips from the disc support bracket.

6. Inspect the disc brake rotor for scoring and wear. Replace or machine, as necessary.

To install:

7. Using the Special Service Tool, rotate the caliper piston clockwise until the piston is fully seated.

8. Install disc brake pads and new spring clips.

9. Position the notch in the caliper

Fig. 7 Rear brake caliper piston adjuster

piston up and down to align with the alignment pin on the brake pad.

10. Install the rear disc brake caliper and tighten to 24 ft. lbs. (33 Nm).

11. Pump the brake pedal prior to moving the vehicle to position the brake pads.

12. Fill the brake master cylinder reservoir with clean DOT 3 brake fluid from a closed container.

13. If the disc brake calipers were replaced or repaired, be sure to bleed the system.

14. Road test the vehicle and check the brake system for proper operation.

BRAKES

PARKING BRAKE

PARKING BRAKE SYSTEM

See Figure 8.

The parking brake system is cable actuated and controlled by an independent hand operated parking brake control. The parking brake system is actuated when the parking brake control is pulled up and released by pressing the release button on the end of the parking brake control handle. The parking brake control applies tension to rear brake pads through the front parking brake cable and conduit and the LH and RH rear parking brake cables. The respective rear parking brake assemblies are then applied.

The parking brake cable tension is not self-adjusting.

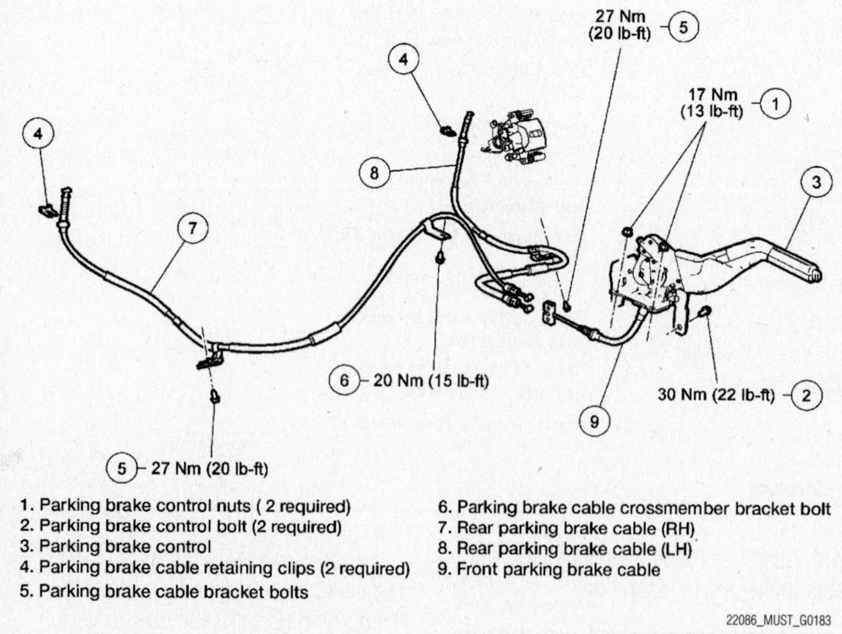

PARKING BRAKE CABLES

ADJUSTMENT

See Figure 9.

✹✹ WARNING

Do not over tighten the parking brake cable adjustment nut. Over tightening will cause the brakes to drag or lock up.

1. Remove the access cover inside the floor console bin.

2. Position the parking brake handle up at the fourth notch to access the adjuster nut.

➡ **The rod is staked to prevent the removal of the nut.**

3. Loosen but do not remove the parking brake cable adjuster nut.

4. Apply the tension by tightening the parking brake cable adjustment nut until there is no lash in the system with the handle in the lowered position.

5. Cycle the parking brake control 4 times and adjust as necessary.

6. Lower the parking brake handle and install the access cover.

7. Test the parking brake system for proper operation.

27 Nm (20 lb-ft) — 5

17 Nm (13 lb-ft) — 1

4

8

4

7

4

3

6 — 20 Nm (15 lb-ft)

30 Nm (22 lb-ft) — 2

9

5 — 27 Nm (20 lb-ft)

1. Parking brake control nuts (2 required)
2. Parking brake control bolt (2 required)
3. Parking brake control
4. Parking brake cable retaining clips (2 required)
5. Parking brake cable bracket bolts
6. Parking brake cable crossmember bracket bolt
7. Rear parking brake cable (RH)
8. Rear parking brake cable (LH)
9. Front parking brake cable

Fig. 8 Parking brake components—exploded view

Fig. 9 Parking brake cable adjuster nut

GENERAL INFORMATION

❊❊ CAUTION

These vehicles are equipped with an air bag system. The system must be disarmed before performing service on, or around, system components, the steering column, instrument panel components, wiring and sensors. Failure to follow the safety precautions and the disarming procedure could result in accidental air bag deployment, possible injury and unnecessary system repairs.

SERVICE PRECAUTIONS

Disconnect and isolate the battery negative cable before beginning any airbag system component diagnosis, testing, removal, or installation procedures. Allow system capacitor to discharge for two minutes before beginning any component service. This will disable the airbag system. Failure to disable the airbag system may result in accidental airbag deployment, personal injury, or death.

Do not place an intact undeployed airbag face down on a solid surface. The airbag will propel into the air if accidentally deployed and may result in personal injury or death.

When carrying or handling an undeployed airbag, the trim side (face) of the airbag should be pointing towards the body to minimize possibility of injury if accidental deployment occurs. Failure to do this may result in personal injury or death.

Replace airbag system components with OEM replacement parts. Substitute parts may appear interchangeable, but internal differences may result in inferior occupant protection. Failure to do so may result in occupant personal injury or death.

Wear safety glasses, rubber gloves, and long sleeved clothing when cleaning powder residue from vehicle after an airbag deployment. Powder residue emitted from a deployed airbag can cause skin irritation. Flush affected area with cool water if irritation is experienced. If nasal or throat irritation is experienced, exit the vehicle for fresh air until the irritation ceases. If irritation continues, see a physician.

Do not use a replacement airbag that is not in the original packaging. This may result in improper deployment, personal injury, or death.

The factory installed fasteners, screws and bolts used to fasten airbag components have a special coating and are specifically designed for the airbag system. Do not use substitute fasteners. Use only original equipment fasteners listed in the parts catalog when fastener replacement is required.

During, and following, any child restraint anchor service, due to impact event or vehicle repair, carefully inspect all mounting hardware, tether straps, and anchors for proper installation, operation, or damage. If a child restraint anchor is found damaged in any way, the anchor must be replaced. Failure to do this may result in personal injury or death.

Deployed and non-deployed airbags may or may not have live pyrotechnic material within the airbag inflator.

Do not dispose of driver/passenger/curtain airbags or seat belt tensioners unless you are sure of complete deployment. Refer to the Hazardous Substance Control System for proper disposal.

Dispose of deployed airbags and tensioners consistent with state, provincial, local, and federal regulations.

After any airbag component testing or service, do not connect the battery negative cable. Personal injury or death may result if the system test is not performed first.

If the vehicle is equipped with the Occupant Classification System (OCS), do not connect the battery negative cable before performing the OCS Verification Test using the scan tool and the appropriate diagnostic information. Personal injury or death may result if the system test is not performed properly.

Never replace both the Occupant Restraint Controller (ORC) and the Occupant Classification Module (OCM) at the same time. If both require replacement, replace one, then perform the Airbag System test before replacing the other.

Both the ORC and the OCM store Occupant Classification System (OCS) calibration data, which they transfer to one another when one of them is replaced. If both are replaced at the same time, an irreversible fault will be set in both modules and the OCS may malfunction and cause personal injury or death.

If equipped with OCS, the Seat Weight Sensor is a sensitive, calibrated unit and must be handled carefully. Do not drop or handle roughly. If dropped or damaged, replace with another sensor. Failure to do so may result in occupant injury or death.

If equipped with OCS, the front passenger seat must be handled carefully as well. When removing the seat, be careful when setting on floor not to drop. If dropped, the sensor may be inoperative, could result in occupant injury, or possibly death.

If equipped with OCS, when the passenger front seat is on the floor, no one should sit in the front passenger seat. This uneven force may damage the sensing ability of the seat weight sensors. If sat on and damaged, the sensor may be inoperative, could result in occupant injury, or possibly death.

DISARMING THE SYSTEM

1. Ensure the ignition and all accessories are off.
2. Remove the Smart Junction Box (SJB) cover located below the left side of the instrument panel. Remove the Restraints Control Module (RCM) fuse no. F2.17.
3. Turn the ignition on and watch the air bag indicator for 30 seconds. The indicator light will remain lit constantly if the correct fuse has been removed. If the light is not on steadily, remove the correct fuse and check the light again.
4. Turn the ignition switch off.
5. Disconnect the negative battery cable.

ARMING THE SYSTEM

1. Turn the ignition switch on.
2. Install Restraints Control Module (RCM) fuse no. F2.17 and the fuse cover.
3. Turn the ignition **OFF**.
4. Connect the negative battery cable.
5. Turn the ignition on and then off. Wait 10 seconds and turn the key back on. Watch the air bag indicator. The indicator light will remain lit constantly for 6 seconds and then go off. If the indicator does not turn on and then off, diagnose the air bag system
6. Clear all Diagnostic Trouble Codes (DTC) using a scan tool.

CLOCKSPRING CENTERING

Vehicles Receiving a New Clockspring

➡**A new clockspring is supplied in a centralized position and held there with a key.**

1. Remove the key from the clockspring, holding the rotor in its centralized position.
   a. Do not allow the clockspring rotor to turn.

Vehicles Requiring Clockspring Centering

> ### ✳ CAUTION
> **Incorrect centralization may result in premature component failure. If in doubt when centralizing the clockspring, repeat the centralizing procedure. Failure to follow this instruction may result in personal injury.**

> ### ✳ WARNING
> **Make sure the road wheels are in the straight ahead position.**

➡ If a clockspring has rotated out of center, follow through with this step.

Centralize the clockspring.

1. Hold the clockspring outer housing stationary.
2. Depress the clockspring locking tab to release the rotor.

> ### ✳ WARNING
> **Overturning will destroy the clockspring. The internal ribbon wire acts as the stop and can be broken from its internal connection.**

3. While holding the clockspring locking tab in the released position, turn the rotor counterclockwise, carefully feeling for the ribbon wire to run out of length, and a slight resistance is felt. Stop turning at this point.

4. While holding the clockspring locking tab in the released position, turn the clockspring clockwise approximately three turns. This is the center point of the clockspring.

   a. Release the clockspring locking tab. Do not allow the rotor to turn from this position.

All Vehicles

➡ Slight turning of the clockspring rotor is allowable for alignment purposes to the steering column.

1. With the flats of the clockspring aligned to the flats of the steering column, slide the clockspring onto the steering column engaging the retaining tabs.

DRIVETRAIN

AUTOMATIC TRANSMISSION ASSEMBLY

REMOVAL & INSTALLATION

1. Disconnect the negative battery cable.
2. Drain the transmission fluid.
3. Remove the driveshaft.
4. Remove the 5 transmission lower mount screws and remove the mount.
5. Disconnect shift cable.
6. Position the manual lever out of "P."
7. Remove the shift cable and bracket and position aside.
8. Remove the starter motor.
9. Remove the flexplate cover.
10. Remove the torque converter access cover and remove the 4 torque converter nuts.
11. Remove the lower transmission mounting bolts.
12. Disconnect all transmission electrical connectors.
13. Disconnect and plug transmission fluid cooler lines.
14. Remove the engine to transmission bolts.
15. Support the transmission with a jack.
16. Lower the transmission away from the vehicle.
17. Install Torque Converter Retainer tool 307–346 to retain the torque converter.

To install:

18. Rotate the torque converter and adapter plate so the orange or green paint mark is at the 12 o'clock position.
19. Raise the transmission into and install the engine to transmission bolts. Tighten the bolts to 35 ft. lbs. (48 Nm).
20. Install the torque converter nuts and tighten to 28 ft. lbs. (38 Nm).

21. Install the access cover.
22. Install the flexplate cover and tighten to 25 ft. lbs. (34 Nm).
23. Install the starter and tighten to 18 ft. lbs. (25 Nm).
24. Install the lower transmission mounting bolts and tighten to 35 ft. lbs. (48 Nm).
25. Install the transmission fluid cooler lines.
26. Connect all transmission electrical connectors.
27. Install the transmission crossmember and tighten the center bolt to 30 ft. lbs. (40 Nm).
28. Install the transmission crossmember outer bolts and tighten to 41 ft. lbs. (55 Nm).
29. Remove the transmission jack.
30. Install the driveshaft.
31. Install the shift cable and bracket.
32. Connect the negative battery cable.
33. Fill the transmission with fluid.
34. Check the shift cable adjustment.
35. Start the engine. Check for leaks and proper operation.

MANUAL TRANSMISSION ASSEMBLY

REMOVAL & INSTALLATION

T50D 5-Speed

➡ The transmission and clutch housing are removed as an assembly.

1. Disconnect the negative battery cable.
2. Raise the vehicle on a hoist.
3. Index mark the driveshaft to the output shaft flange.
4. Remove the driveshaft from the output shaft and wire it aside.

5. Disconnect the shift linkage.
6. Disconnect all transmission electrical connectors.
7. Remove the starter.
8. Support the transmission with a transmission jack.
9. Remove 4 crossmember nuts and the transmission mount nut.
10. Move the crossmember down and slide the exhaust isolators from the brackets.
11. Remove the crossmember.
12. Separate the clutch slave cylinder line.
13. Loosen 4 exhaust manifold nuts.
14. Remove the transmission to engine bolts.
15. Slide the transmission rearward until it clears the input shaft, then lower and remove the transmission.

To install:

16. Reverse the removal procedure, noting the following:

   a. Tighten the transmission to engine bolts to 33 ft. lbs. (45 Nm).
   b. Tighten the exhaust manifold nuts to 30 ft. lbs. (40 Nm).
   c. Tighten the crossmember bolts to 46 ft. lbs. (62 Nm).
   d. Tighten the starter bolts to 18 ft. lbs. (25 Nm).
   e. Tighten the driveshaft bolts to 76 ft. lbs. (103 Nm).

17. Connect the negative battery cable.

TR3650 5-Speed

1. Disconnect the negative battery cable.
2. Raise the vehicle on a hoist.
3. Remove the catalytic converter H pipe.

4. Index mark the driveshaft to the output shaft flange.

5. Remove the driveshaft from the output shaft and wire it aside.

6. Disconnect all transmission electrical connectors.

7. Remove the starter.

8. Support the transmission with a transmission jack.

9. Remove the crossmember to transmission bolt and crossmember to frame bolts.

10. Remove the crossmember.

11. Disconnect the shift linkage.

12. Separate the clutch slave cylinder line.

13. Remove the transmission to engine bolts.

14. Slide the transmission rearward until it clears the input shaft, then lower and remove the transmission.

To install:

15. Reverse the removal procedure, noting the following:

    a. Tighten the transmission to engine bolts to 33 ft. lbs. (45 Nm).

    b. Tighten the crossmember to frame bolts to 46 ft. lbs. (62 Nm).

    c. Tighten the crossmember to transmission bolts to 52 ft. lbs. (70 Nm).

    d. Tighten the starter bolts to 18 ft. lbs. (25 Nm).

    e. Tighten the driveshaft bolts to 76 ft. lbs. (103 Nm).

16. Connect the negative battery cable.

T56 6–Speed

1. Disconnect the negative battery cable.

2. Raise the vehicle on a hoist.

3. Remove the catalytic converter H pipe.

4. Index mark the driveshaft to the output shaft flange.

5. Remove the driveshaft from the output shaft and wire it aside.

6. Disconnect all transmission electrical connectors.

7. Remove the starter.

8. Support the transmission with a transmission jack.

9. Remove the crossmember to transmission bolt and crossmember to frame bolts.

10. Remove the crossmember.

11. Disconnect the shift linkage.

12. Remove the clutch slave cylinder.

13. Remove the transmission to engine bolts.

14. Slide the transmission rearward until it clears the input shaft, then lower and remove the transmission.

To install:

15. Reverse the removal procedure, noting the following:

    a. Tighten the transmission to engine bolts to 33 ft. lbs. (45 Nm).

    b. Tighten the crossmember to frame bolts to 46 ft. lbs. (62 Nm).

    c. Tighten the crossmember to transmission bolts to 52 ft. lbs. (70 Nm).

    d. Tighten the starter bolts to 18 ft. lbs. (25 Nm).

    e. Tighten the driveshaft bolts to 76 ft. lbs. (103 Nm).

16. Connect the negative battery cable.

CLUTCH

REMOVAL & INSTALLATION

4.0L & 4.6L Engines

See Figure 10.

1. Disconnect the negative battery cable.

2. Remove the transmission.

3. Remove pressure plate bolts, loosen them evenly in several passes to avoid distortion of the pressure plate.

4. Remove pressure plate and clutch disk.

To install:

5. Install clutch disk and pressure plate. Tighten the pressure plate bolts in a star pattern evenly to 26 ft. lbs. (35 Nm) for 4.0L engines or to 33 ft. lbs. (45 Nm)

plus an additional 60 degrees for 4.6L engines.

6. Install the transmission.

7. Connect the negative battery cable.

5.4L Engine

See Figures 11 and 12.

1. Disconnect the negative battery cable.

2. Remove the transmission.

✲✲ CAUTION

Loosen the bolts evenly to prevent damage to the pressure plate.

➡**If the pressure plate is to be reused, index mark the pressure plate to the flywheel.**

3. Remove the 9 pressure plate bolts, then remove the pressure plate and the clutch disc. Discard the pressure plate bolts.

To install:

➡**If installing the original plate and disc assembly, align it using the index marks made during removal.**

➡**Always install new pressure plate bolts.**

4. Using a suitable clutch aligner, position the clutch disc on the flywheel, then install the pressure plate and 10 new pressure plate bolts.

5. Tighten the bolts in 2 stages, in the sequence shown.

    a. Stage 1: Tighten to 89 inch lbs. (10 Nm) in a star pattern.

    b. Stage 2: Tighten an additional 90 degrees in a star pattern.

6. Remove the clutch aligner.

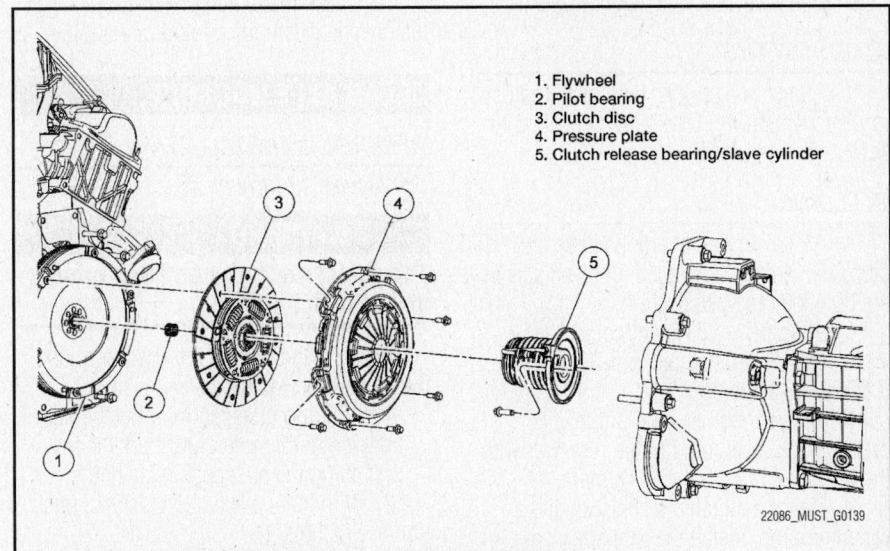

1. Flywheel
2. Pilot bearing
3. Clutch disc
4. Pressure plate
5. Clutch release bearing/slave cylinder

22086_MUST_G0139

Fig. 10 Clutch assembly exploded view—4.0L and 4.6L engines

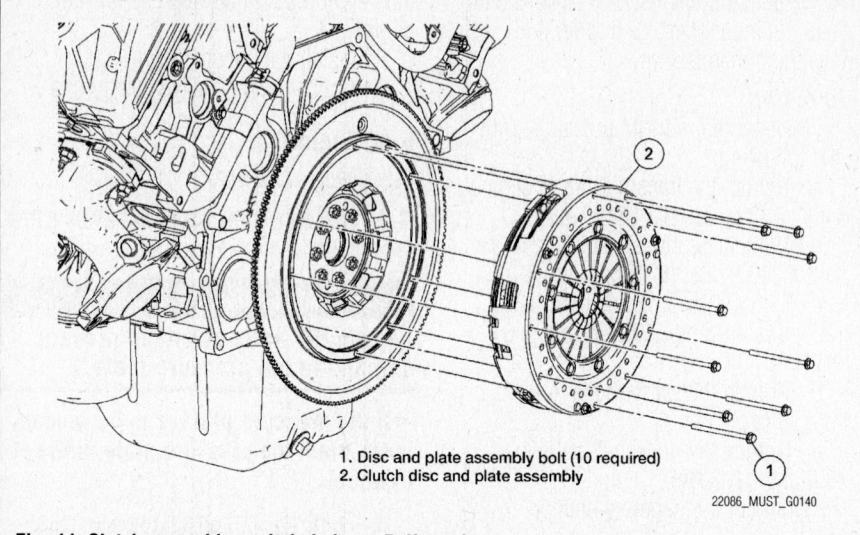

1. Disc and plate assembly bolt (10 required)
2. Clutch disc and plate assembly

22086_MUST_G0140

Fig. 11 Clutch assembly exploded view—5.4L engine

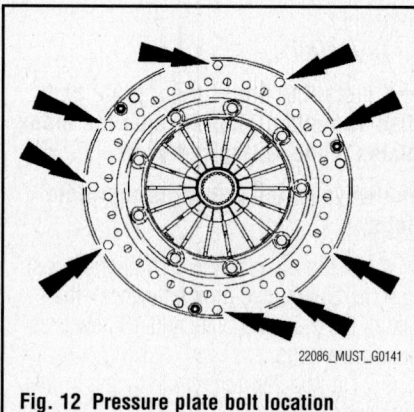

22086_MUST_G0141

Fig. 12 Pressure plate bolt location

➡**Before securing the transmission to the engine, connect the clutch hydraulic line to the slave cylinder.**

7. Install the transmission.
8. Bleed the clutch hydraulic system.

ADJUSTMENTS

The clutch is equipped with a self-adjusting mechanism. Pull the clutch pedal up to activate the adjuster.

BLEEDING

1. Make sure all hydraulic lines are correctly seated. Make sure all bleed screws are tightened to specification.
    a. Tighten to 71 inch lbs. (8 Nm).
2. Make sure the clutch pedal is in the most upward position.
3. Check the fluid level of the brake/clutch reservoir. Fill the reservoir with the specified fluid to the MAX mark.
4. Using a suitable bleeder kit and a vacuum pump, install the rubber stopper in the reservoir opening. Make sure the rubber stopper has a tight fit.

a. Alternate method: use a 1.96 inch (50mm) rubber stopper with an 0.31 inch (8mm) pipe inserted through the rubber stopper.
5. Holding the rubber stopper in place, operate the vacuum pump to 15–20 inches of vacuum. Hold the vacuum for 1 minute, then quickly relieve the vacuum. Remove the special tools.
6. Check the fluid level of the reservoir. Fill the reservoir with the specified fluid to the MAX mark. Install the reservoir cap.
7. Depress and release the clutch pedal 10 to 12 times or until clutch pedal effort is consistent and positive at top of clutch pedal travel.
8. Repeat the procedure two additional times or until clutch pedal effort is consistent and positive at top of clutch pedal travel.
9. Install the reservoir cap.
10. Check the clutch pedal reserve. Test the clutch system for normal operation.

REAR AXLE HOUSING

REMOVAL & INSTALLATION

See Figures 13 through 20.

✳✳ WARNING

The vehicle must be on level ground and at curb height.

1. Mark the rear shock absorbers relative to their protective sleeve (arrow).
    a. During installation, raise the suspension to this reference mark before tightening the suspension fasteners.
2. With the vehicle in NEUTRAL, position it on a hoist.
3. Remove the rear wheel and tire assemblies.

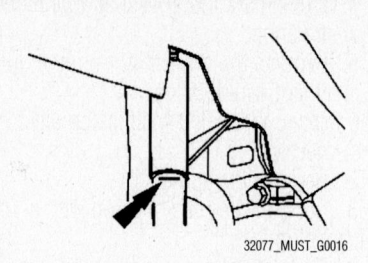

32077_MUST_G0016

Fig. 13 Mark the shock absorber (arrow) before removal. Raise suspension to this height before tightening the suspension fasteners

4. For convertible models, remove and discard the 4 rear support brace bolts.
    a. To install, tighten to 46 ft. lbs. (63 Nm).
5. For convertible models, remove and discard the 2 upper support brace bolts.
    a. To install, tighten to 46 ft. lbs. (63 Nm).
6. For convertible models, remove and discard the 4 front support brace bolts.
    a. To install, tighten to 46 ft. lbs. (63 Nm).
7. Remove the stabilizer bar bracket to frame bolts and disconnect the stabilizer bar from the axle.

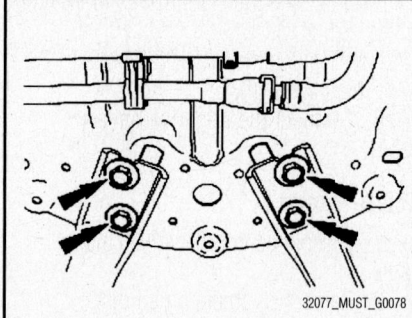

32077_MUST_G0078

Fig. 14 For convertible models, remove and discard the 4 rear support brace bolts.

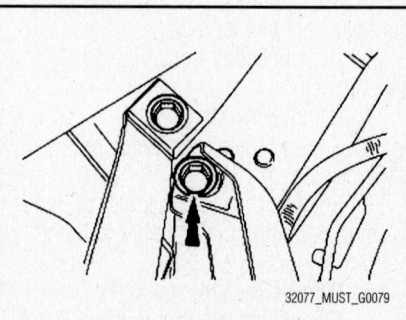

32077_MUST_G0079

Fig. 15 For convertible models, remove and discard the 2 upper support brace bolts

Fig. 16 For convertible models, remove and discard the 4 front support brace bolts

a. Discard the stabilizer bar bracket to frame bolts.

b. To install, tighten to 52 ft. lbs. (70 Nm).

➡**Using 2 screwdrivers through the access hole, depress the tabs of the track bar cover retaining clip.**

8. Remove the track bar cover.

➡**The suspension must be at ride height when tightening suspension components.**

9. Remove the track bar bolts and the track bar flag nuts, then the track bar.

a. Discard the track bar bolts and the track bar flag nuts.

b. To install, tighten to 129 ft. lbs. (175 Nm).

✳✳ WARNING

Secure the differential housing to the transmission jack with a suitable strap.

10. Support the differential housing with a suitable transmission jack.

11. Remove and discard the shock absorber nuts and shock absorber bolts.

a. To install, tighten to 85 ft. lbs. (115 Nm).

12. Remove and discard the upper suspension arm nut and upper suspension arm bolt.

a. To install, tighten to 129 ft. lbs. (175 Nm).

13. Lower the axle slightly and remove the springs.

14. Remove and discard the trailing arm nuts and trailing arm bolts.

a. To install, tighten to 129 ft. lbs (175 Nm).

15. Disconnect the lower suspension arms from the axle housing.

16. Lower the axle housing from the vehicle.

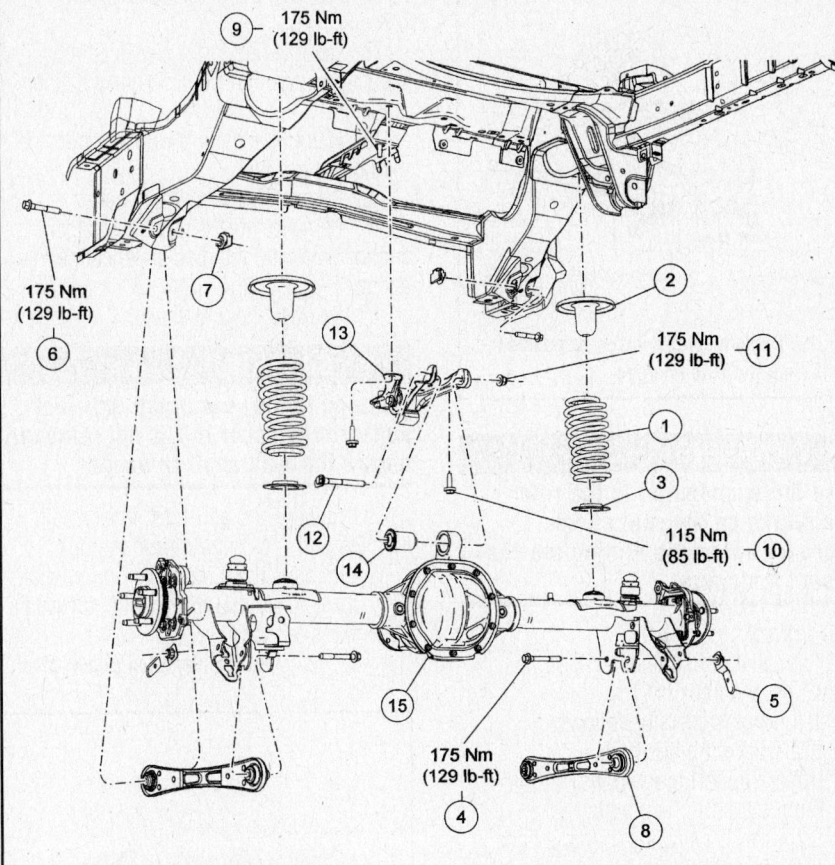

1 Spring (2 required)
2 Upper insulator (2 required)
3 Lower insulator (2 required)
4 Lower control arm rear bolt (2 required)
5 Lower control arm rear nut (2 required)
6 Lower control arm front bolt (2 required)
7 Lower control arm front nut (2 required)
8 Lower control arm (2 required)
9 Upper control arm front bolt
10 Upper control arm rear bolt (2 required)
11 Upper control arm rear nut
12 Upper control arm flag bolt
13 Upper control arm
14 Upper control arm bushing
15 Rear axle assembly

Fig. 17 Rear axle assembly—exploded view

Fig. 18 Remove and discard the upper suspension arm nut and upper suspension arm bolt

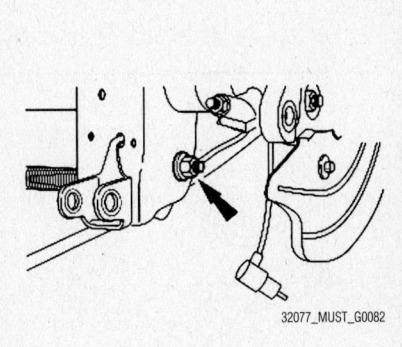

Fig. 19 Remove and discard the trailing arm nuts and trailing arm bolts

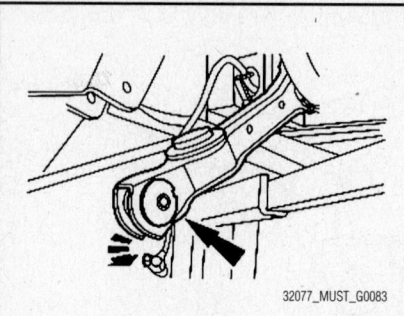

Fig. 20 Disconnect the lower suspension arms from the axle housing

✳✳ WARNING

Raise the suspension to the reference marks on the rear shock absorbers before tightening the suspension fasteners.

To install:

17. Installation is the reverse of the removal procedure.

Install new fasteners as follows:
- Rear support brace bolts
- Upper support brace bolts
- Front support brace bolts
- Stabilizer bar bracket to frame bolts
- Track bar bolts
- Track bar flag nuts
- Shock absorber bolts
- Shock absorber nuts
- Upper suspension arm bolts
- Upper suspension arm nuts
- Trailing arm bolts
- Trailing arm nuts

REAR AXLE SHAFT

REMOVAL & INSTALLATION

See Figures 21 through 24.

1. With the vehicle in NEUTRAL, position it on a hoist.
2. Remove the wheel and tire assembly.

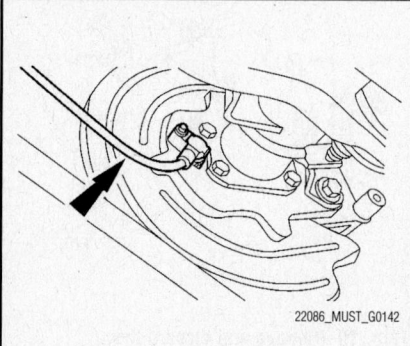

Fig. 21 Anti-lock sensor in axle hub

3. Remove the differential housing cover.
4. Remove the 2 disc brake caliper bolts, then position the disc brake caliper aside.
5. Using mechanic's wire, support the disc brake caliper.
6. Remove the disc brake pads.
7. Remove the 2 disc brake caliper anchor bolts and the disc brake caliper anchor.
8. Remove the brake disc.

✳✳ CAUTION

Damage to the rear brake anti-lock sensor may occur if it is not removed before the axle shaft U-washer.

9. Remove the anti-lock sensor bolt, then the anti-lock sensor from the hub.
10. Remove the differential pinion shaft.
   a. Remove and discard the differential pinion shaft lock bolt.
   b. Remove the differential pinion shaft.

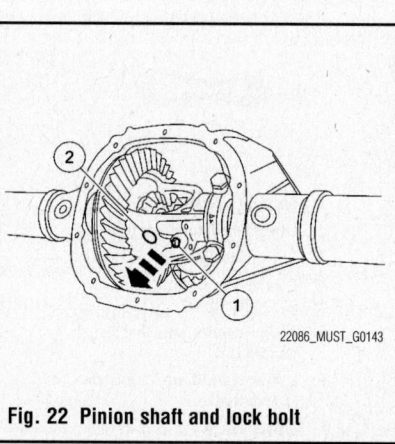

Fig. 22 Pinion shaft and lock bolt

✳✳ CAUTION

Do not damage the rubber O-ring in the axle shaft grooves.

11. Remove the axle shaft U-washer.
12. Push in on the axle shaft.
13. Remove the U-washer.

✳✳ CAUTION

Do not damage the axle shaft oil seal.

14. Remove the axle shaft.

To install:

15. Lubricate the lip of the axle shaft oil seal with grease.

✳✳ CAUTION

Do not damage the axle shaft oil seal when installing the axle shaft.

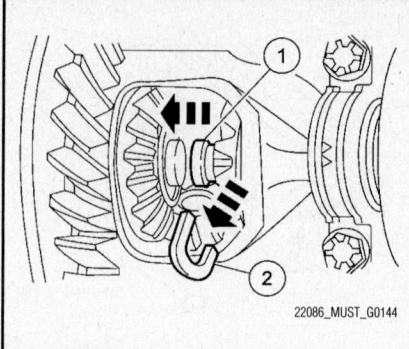

Fig. 23 Axle U-washer removal and installation

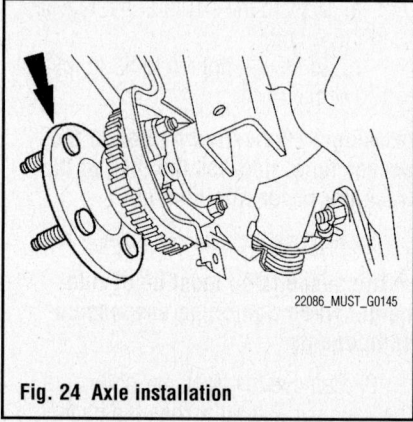

Fig. 24 Axle installation

16. Install the axle shaft.

✳✳ CAUTION

Do not damage the rubber O-ring in the U-washer groove.

17. Install the axle shaft U-washer.
18. Position the U-washer on the button end of the axle shaft.
19. Pull the axle shaft outward.

➡**If a new differential pinion shaft lock bolt is unavailable, coat the threads of the old differential pinion shaft lock bolt with Threadlock and Sealer.**

20. Install the differential pinion shaft.
21. Align the hole in the differential pinion shaft with the differential case lock bolt hole.
22. Install a new differential pinion shaft lock bolt.
   a. Tighten to 22 ft. lbs (30 Nm).

➡**Be sure to apply High Temperature Nickel Anti-Seize Lubricant.**

23. Install the anti-lock sensor and the anti-lock sensor bolt.
   a. Tighten to 62 inch lbs. (7 Nm).
24. Install the brake disc.
25. Install the disc brake caliper anchor, then install the 2 disc brake caliper anchor bolts.

a. Tighten to 76 ft. lbs. (103 Nm).

26. Install the disc brake pads.

27. Install the disc brake caliper and the 2 disc brake caliper bolts.

a. Tighten to 24 ft. lbs. (33 Nm).

28. Install the differential housing cover.

29. Install the tire and wheel assembly.

30. Fill the differential to the specified level.

31. Road test vehicle, and verify that there are no fluid leaks.

REAR AXLE SHAFT, BEARING & SEAL

REMOVAL & INSTALLATION

See Figure 25.

1. Before servicing the vehicle, refer to the precautions at the beginning of this section.

2. Place the transmission in neutral.

3. Raise the vehicle on a hoist

4. Remove rear wheel.

5. Remove disc brake caliper and rotor.

6. Remove wheel speed sensor.

7. Remove axle housing cover.

8. Remove differential pinion shaft lockbolt.

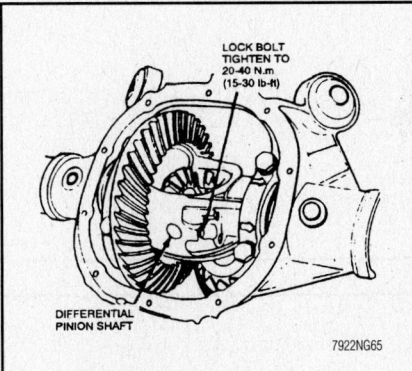

LOCK BOLT
TIGHTEN TO
20-40 N.m
(15-30 lb-ft)

DIFFERENTIAL
PINION SHAFT

7922NG65

Fig. 25 Differential pinion shaft and lockbolt

9. Remove differential pinion shaft.

10. Remove axle retaining U-washer.

11. Remove axle shaft.

12. Remove bearing and seal, using a slide hammer

To install:

13. Install bearing, so that it is fully seated in the axle tube.

14. Install axle seal.

15. Install axle shaft.

16. Install axle retaining U-washer.

17. Install differential pinion shaft. Tighten the lockbolt to 15–30 ft. lbs. (20–41 Nm).

18. Install axle housing cover. Tighten the cover bolts to 18–28 ft. lbs. (24–38 Nm).

19. Install wheel speed sensor.

20. Install disc brake rotor and caliper. Tighten the caliper mounting bolts to 65–87 ft. lbs. (87–119 Nm).

21. Install rear wheel.

22. Fill the differential with gear lubricant. Tighten the filler plug to 15–30 ft. lbs. (20–41 Nm).

REAR PINION SEAL

REMOVAL & INSTALLATION

1. Before servicing the vehicle, refer to the precautions at the beginning of this section.

2. Place the transmission in neutral.

3. Raise the vehicle on a hoist.

4. Index mark the driveshaft, then disconnect driveshaft and position it out of the way.

5. Disconnect driveshaft and position it out of the way.

6. Remove rear wheels.

7. Remove rear brake calipers.

➡**The rear brake calipers must be removed so that there is no additional drag when measuring pinion bearing preload.**

➡**Remember to index mark the driveshaft flange and pinion flange to maintain initial balance during installation.**

8. Use an inch lb. torque wrench and measure the amount of torque required to maintain pinion rotation through several revolutions.

9. Remove the pinion flange and remove the seal.

To install:

10. Install pinion seal and flange.

11. Install new pinion flange nut.

12. Rotate the pinion flange occasionally while tightening the flange nut to make sure the pinion bearings seat correctly.

13. Take frequent bearing preload torque readings.

14. If the preload recorded prior to disassembly is **lower** than the specification for used bearings, then tighten the pinion flange nut to specification. If the preload recorder prior to disassembly is **higher** than the specification for used bearings, then tighten the pinion flange nut to the original reading as recorded.

15. The pinion bearing preload specifications are as follows:

a. Used bearings: 8–14 inch lbs. (0.9–1.5 Nm).

b. New bearings: 16–29 inch lbs. (1.8–3.3 Nm).

✳✳ CAUTION

Never loosen the pinion nut to reduce bearing preload. If it is necessary to reduce bearing preload, install a new collapsible spacer and pinion nut.

16. Connect the driveshaft and install new bolts. Tighten the bolts to 83 ft. lbs. (112 Nm).

17. Install brake calipers.

18. Install rear wheels.

19. Fill the differential with gear lubricant and check for leaks.

ENGINE COOLING

ENGINE FAN

REMOVAL & INSTALLATION

✴✴ CAUTION

The cooling fan is automatic and may start anytime without warning. To avoid possible injury, always disconnect the negative battery cable when working near the electric cooling fan.

4.0L & 4.6L Engines

See Figures 26 and 27.

1. Disconnect the battery ground cable.
2. Remove the air cleaner outlet pipe.
3. Remove the bolt and position aside the power steering reservoir.
   a. To install, tighten to 71 inch lbs. (8 Nm).
4. Remove the 2 bolts and position the degas bottle aside.
   a. To install, tighten to 71 inch lbs. (8 Nm).
5. Detach the lower degas bottle hose and position aside.
6. Disconnect the cooling fan motor and shroud electrical connector.

7. Remove the 2 bolts and the cooling fan motor and shroud.
   a. To install, tighten to 80 inch lbs. (9 Nm).
8. To install, reverse the removal procedure.
9. Start the engine and verify proper fan operation.

5.4L Engine

See Figures 27 and 28.

1. Drain the cooling system.
2. Drain the supercharger cooling system.

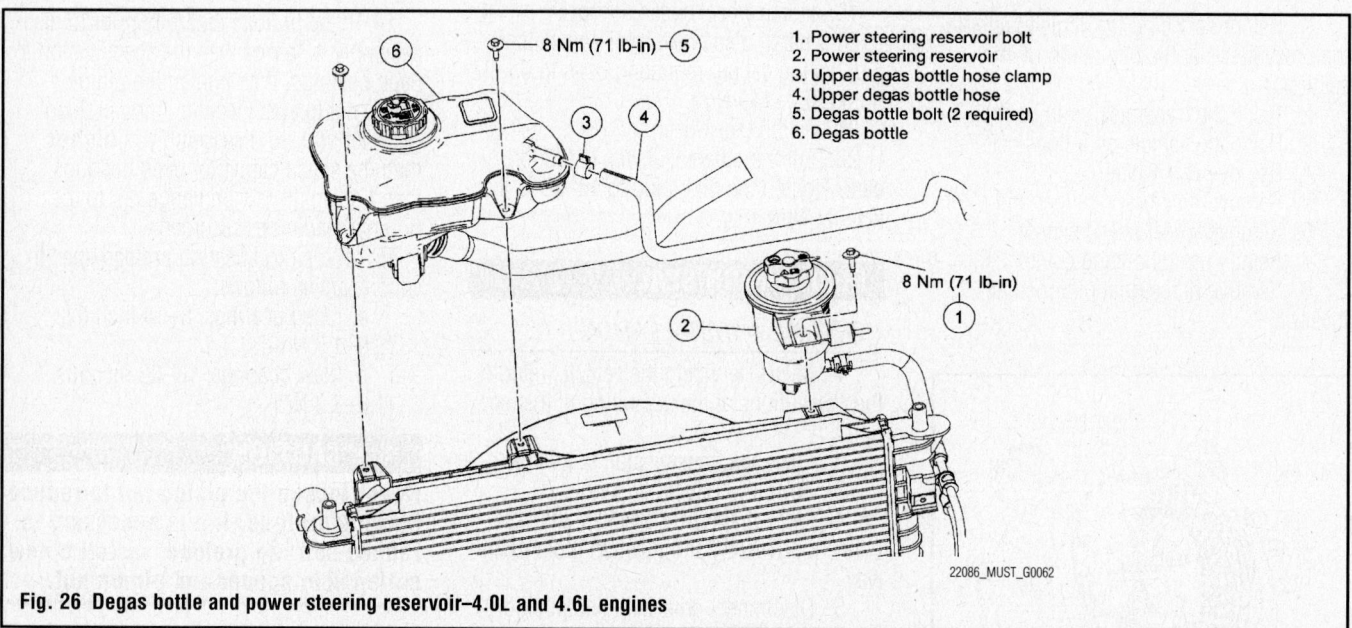

1. Power steering reservoir bolt
2. Power steering reservoir
3. Upper degas bottle hose clamp
4. Upper degas bottle hose
5. Degas bottle bolt (2 required)
6. Degas bottle

8 Nm (71 lb-in)

22086_MUST_G0062

Fig. 26 Degas bottle and power steering reservoir–4.0L and 4.6L engines

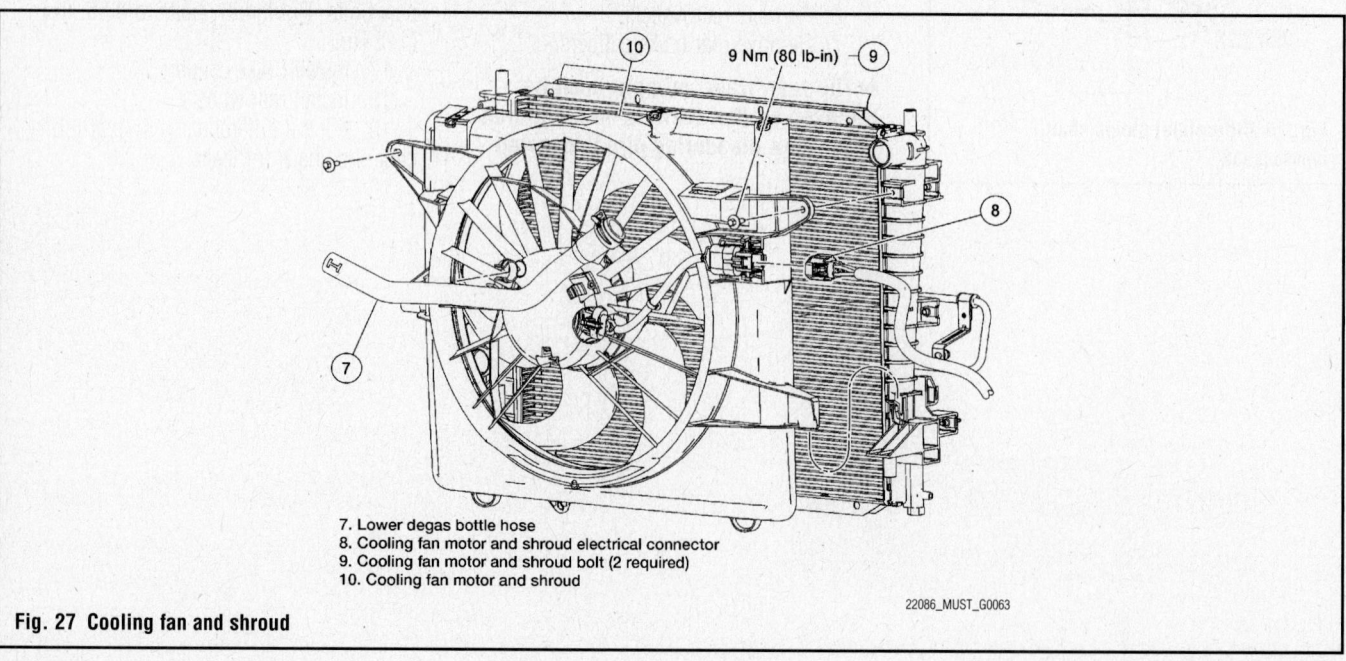

9 Nm (80 lb-in)

7. Lower degas bottle hose
8. Cooling fan motor and shroud electrical connector
9. Cooling fan motor and shroud bolt (2 required)
10. Cooling fan motor and shroud

22086_MUST_G0063

Fig. 27 Cooling fan and shroud

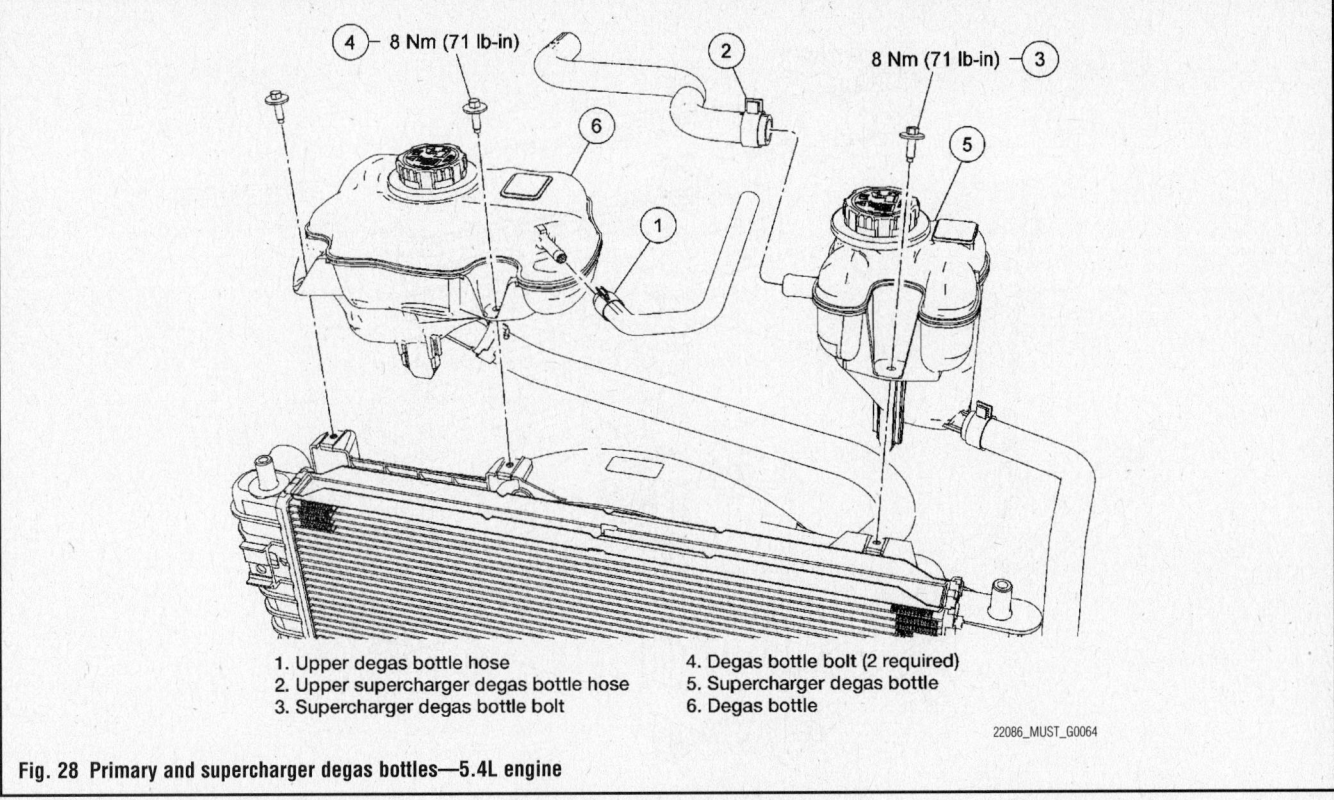

4 — 8 Nm (71 lb-in)   2   8 Nm (71 lb-in) — 3

1. Upper degas bottle hose
2. Upper supercharger degas bottle hose
3. Supercharger degas bottle bolt

4. Degas bottle bolt (2 required)
5. Supercharger degas bottle
6. Degas bottle

22086_MUST_G0064

Fig. 28 Primary and supercharger degas bottles—5.4L engine

3. Disconnect the battery ground cable.

4. Disconnect the upper supercharger degas bottle hose and position it aside.

5. Remove the bolt and position the supercharger degas bottle aside.

   a. To install, tighten to 71 inch lbs. (8 Nm).

6. Disconnect the upper degas bottle hose and position it aside.

7. Remove the 2 bolts and position the degas bottle aside.

   a. To install, tighten to 71 inch lbs. (8 Nm).

8. Disconnect the cooling fan motor and electrical connector.

9. Remove the 2 bolts, the cooling fan motor, and shroud.

   a. To install, tighten to 80 inch lbs. (9 Nm).

10. To install components, reverse the removal procedure.

11. Fill and bleed the cooling system.

12. Fill and bleed the supercharger cooling system.

13. Start the engine and verify proper fan operation.

RADIATOR

REMOVAL & INSTALLATION

See Figures 29 through 31.

1. Removal and Installation
2. Drain the cooling system.

22086_MUST_G0061

Fig. 29 Air deflector pushpin retainer locations

3. Remove the lower radiator air deflector.

4. Remove the 6 pushpin retainers and the air deflector.

5. Remove the cooling fan motor and shroud.

6. Disconnect the degas bottle to radiator hose and position aside.

7. Disconnect the upper radiator hose from the radiator and position aside.

8. Disconnect the lower radiator hose from the radiator and position aside.

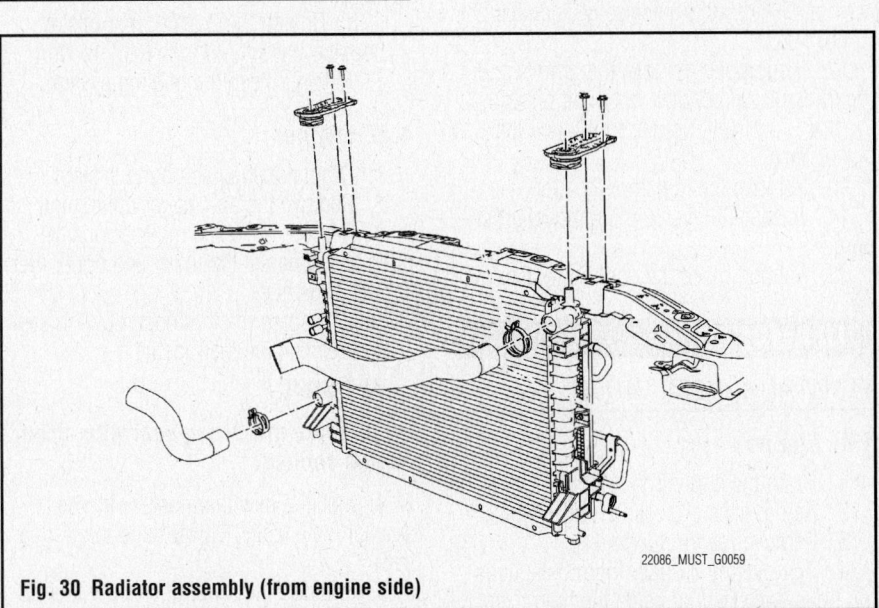

22086_MUST_G0059

Fig. 30 Radiator assembly (from engine side)

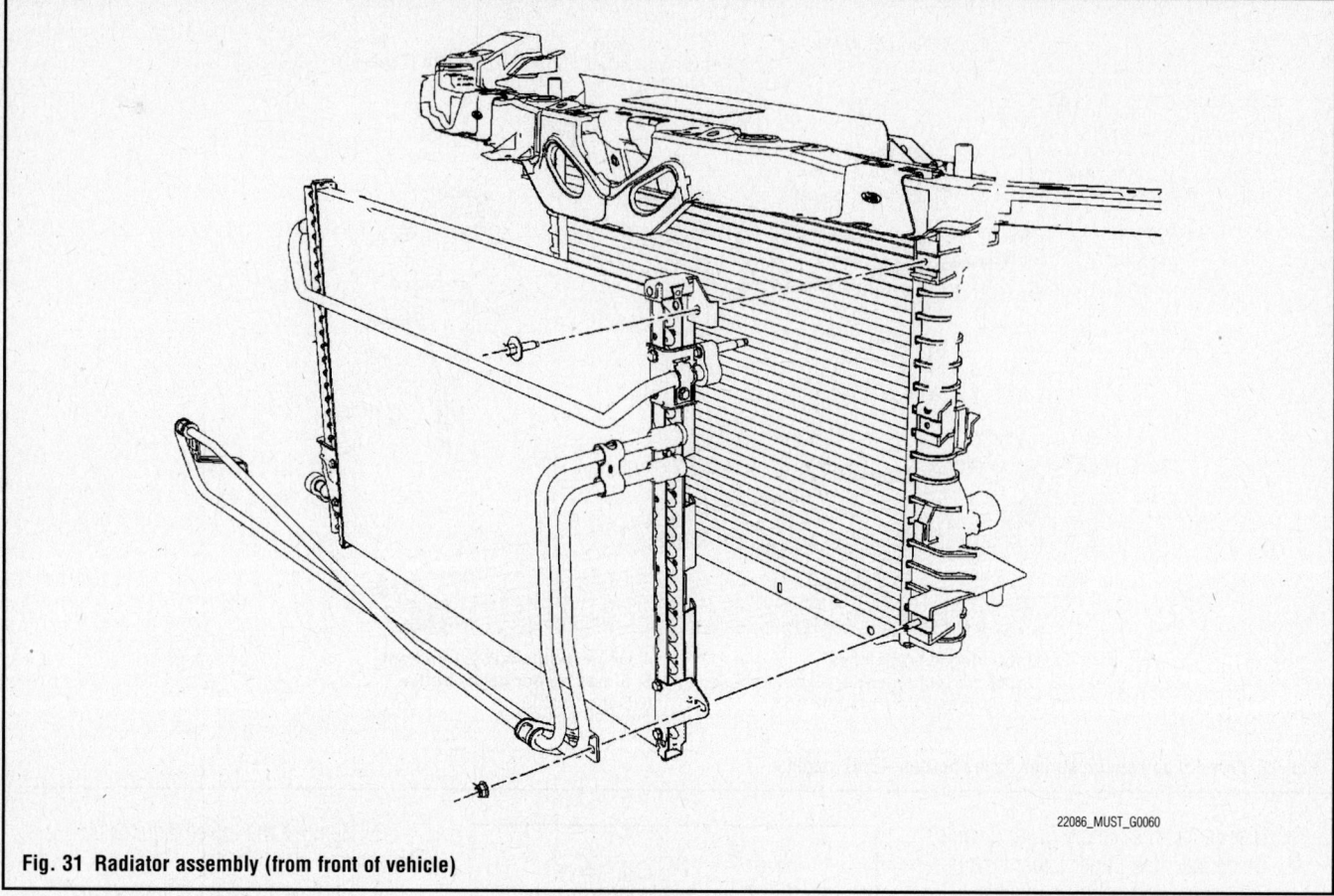

Fig. 31 Radiator assembly (from front of vehicle)

22086_MUST_G0060

9. Remove the 4 bolts and the radiator support brackets.

   a. To install, tighten to 89 inch lbs. (10 Nm).

10. Remove the 2 power steering tubes and A/C condenser retaining nuts and position aside the power steering tubes. To install, tighten to 71 inch lbs. (8 Nm).

11. Remove the 2 A/C condenser bolts.

   a. To install, tighten to 89 inch lbs. (10 Nm).

12. If equipped, remove the 2 bolts and the transmission cooler and position aside.

   a. To install, tighten to 89 inch lbs. (10 Nm).

13. Remove the radiator.

14. To install, reverse the removal procedure.

15. Fill and bleed the cooling system.

THERMOSTAT

REMOVAL & INSTALLATION

4.0L Engine

1. Drain the cooling system.
2. Remove the air cleaner outlet pipe.
3. Remove the throttle body.
4. Remove the 3 upper thermostat housing bolts and position aside the thermostat housing. Discard the thermostat O-ring seal.

5. Remove the thermostat.

To install:

6. Installation is the reverse the removal procedure. Please note the following:

   a. Install a new thermostat O-ring seal and lubricate with clean engine coolant.

   b. Tighten the 2 upper thermostat housing bolts to 89 inch lbs. (10 Nm).

7. Fill and bleed the cooling system.

4.6L Engine

1. Drain the engine cooling system.
2. Remove the air cleaner outlet pipe.
3. Remove the 2 thermostat housing bolts and separate the lower and upper thermostat housings.

   a. Discard the thermostat O-ring seal and remove the thermostat.

To install:

➡**Lubricate the O-ring seal with clean engine coolant.**

4. Install a new thermostat with the smaller plate facing upward and the O-ring seal.

5. Position the lower and upper thermostat housings together and install the 2 bolts.

   a. Tighten to 89 inch lbs. (10 Nm).

6. Install the air cleaner outlet pipe.

7. Fill and bleed the cooling system.

5.4L Engine

1. Drain the engine cooling system.
2. Remove the 2 bolts and position the thermostat housing cover and hose assembly aside.

   a. To install, tighten to 89 inch lbs. (10 Nm).

3. Remove the O-ring seal and the thermostat.

4. Discard the O-ring seal.

5. To install, reverse the removal procedure.

6. Lubricate the new O-ring seal with clean engine coolant.

7. Fill and bleed the cooling system.

8. Start the engine and verify that there are no coolant leaks.

WATER PUMP

REMOVAL & INSTALLATION

4.0L Engine

See Figure 32.

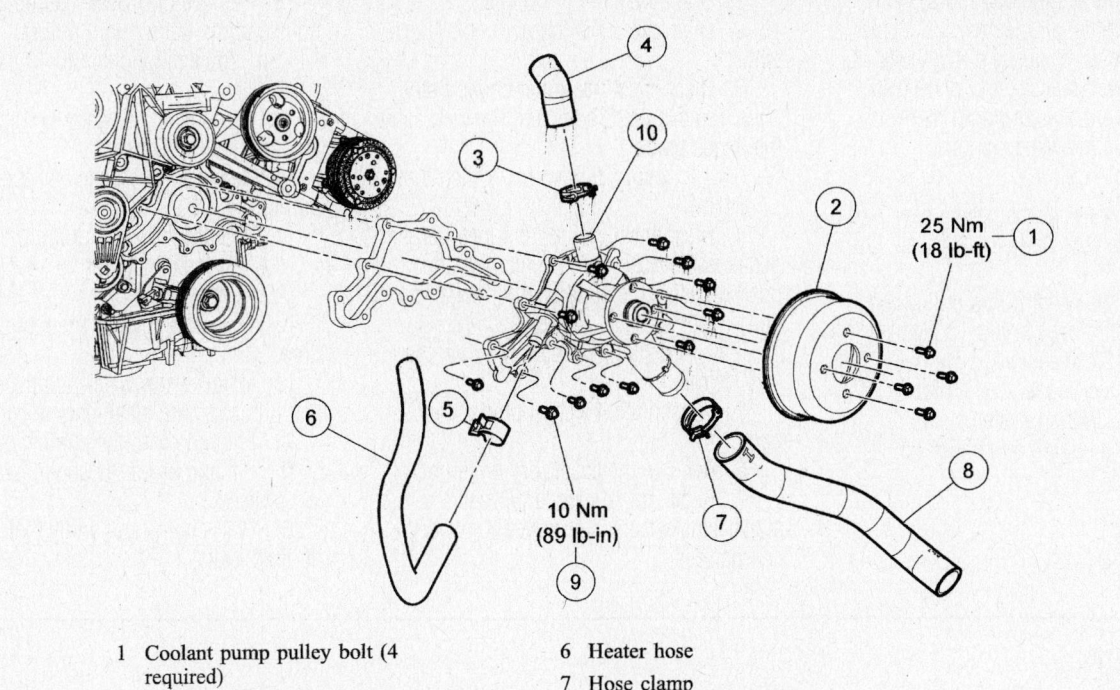

1 Coolant pump pulley bolt (4 required)	6 Heater hose
2 Coolant pump pulley	7 Hose clamp
3 Hose clamp	8 Radiator-to-coolant pump hose
4 Thermostat housing-to-coolant pump hose	9 Coolant pump bolt (12 required)
5 Hose clamp	10 Coolant pump

06017-TANG-G07

Fig. 32 Exploded view of the water pump mounting—4.0L engine

1. Drain the engine cooling system.
2. Remove the air cleaner outlet pipe.
3. Loosen water pump pulley bolts.
4. Remove the accessory drive belt.
5. Remove the water pump pulley.
6. Remove the upper and lower radiator hose.
7. Remove the heater hose.
8. Remove the 12 attaching bolt and remove the water pump. Clean and inspect gasket mating surfaces.

To install:

9. Install the water pump. Use a new gasket and tighten the bolts to 89 inch lbs. (10 Nm).
10. Install the heater hose.
11. Install the upper and lower radiator hose.
12. Install the water pump pulley.
13. Install the accessory drive belt.
14. Install water pump pulley bolts.
15. Install the air cleaner outlet pipe.
16. Fill the cooling system.
17. Start the engine and check for coolant leaks.

4.6L Engine

See Figure 33.

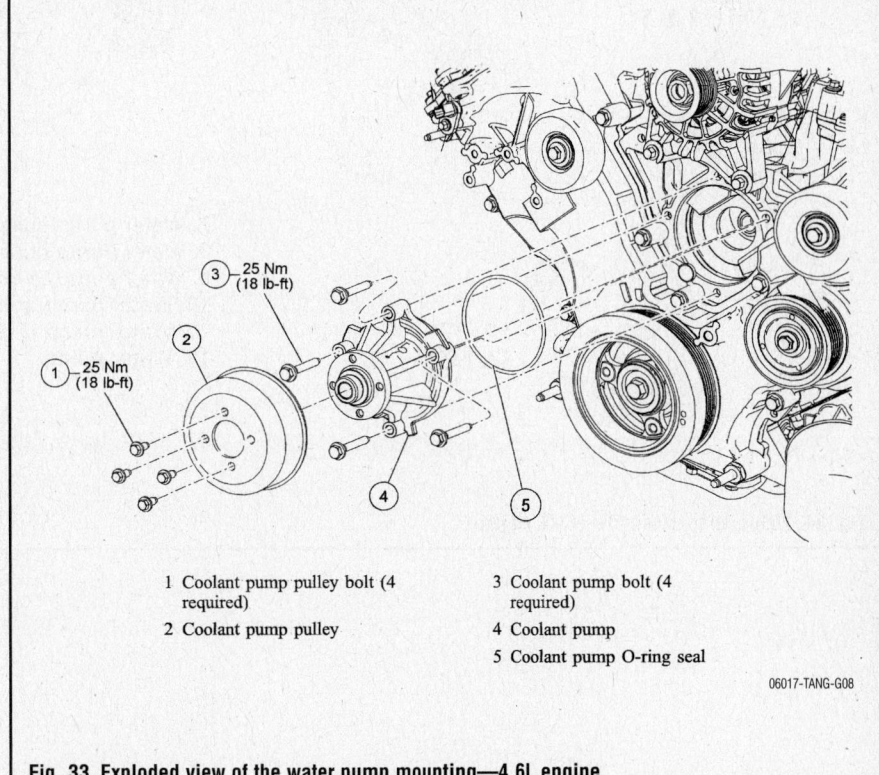

1 Coolant pump pulley bolt (4 required)	3 Coolant pump bolt (4 required)
2 Coolant pump pulley	4 Coolant pump
	5 Coolant pump O-ring seal

06017-TANG-G08

Fig. 33 Exploded view of the water pump mounting—4.6L engine

1. Drain the engine cooling system.
2. Remove the air cleaner outlet pipe.
3. Loosen water pump pulley bolts.
4. Remove the accessory drive belt.
5. Remove the water pump pulley.
6. Remove the water pump.

To install:

7. Install water pump. Use a new O-ring seal and tighten the bolts to 18 ft. lbs. (25 Nm).
8. Install the water pump pulley and tighten the bolts to 18 ft. lbs. (25 Nm).
9. Install the accessory drive belt.
10. Install air cleaner outlet pipe.
11. Fill the cooling system.
12. Start the engine and check for coolant leaks.

5.4L Engine

See Figures 28 and 34.

1. Drain the cooling system.
2. Drain the supercharger cooling system.
3. Disconnect the upper degas bottle hose, remove the 2 bolts and position aside the degas bottle.
   a. To install, tighten to 71 inch lbs. (8 Nm).
4. Disconnect the upper supercharger degas bottle hose, remove the bolt and position aside the supercharger degas bottle.
   a. To install, tighten to 71 inch lbs. (8 Nm).
5. Loosen the 4 water pump pulley bolts.
6. Remove the accessory drive belt.
7. Rotate the supercharger belt tensioner clockwise and remove the supercharger belt.

8. Remove the 4 water pump pulley bolts and the water pump pulley.
   a. To install, tighten to 18 ft. lbs. (25 Nm).
9. Disconnect the water pump to lower radiator hose assembly.
10. Remove the 4 bolts and the water pump.
11. Discard the water pump O-ring seal.
    a. To install, tighten to 18 ft. lbs. (25 Nm).
12. To install, reverse the removal procedure.
13. Install a new water pump O-ring seal and lubricate with clean engine coolant.
14. Fill and bleed the cooling system.
15. Fill and bleed the supercharger cooling system.
16. Start engine and verify that there are no fluid leaks.

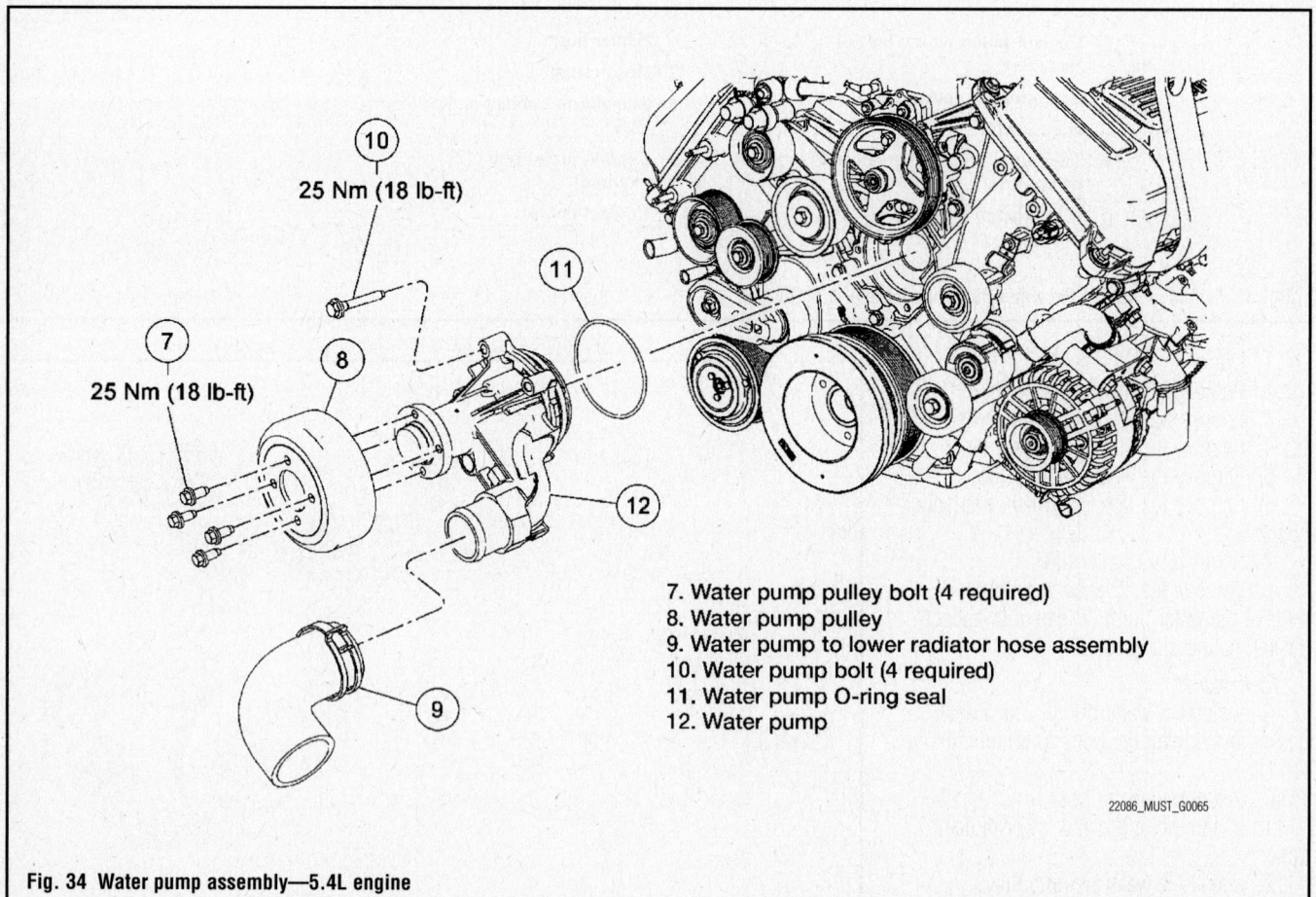

7. Water pump pulley bolt (4 required)
8. Water pump pulley
9. Water pump to lower radiator hose assembly
10. Water pump bolt (4 required)
11. Water pump O-ring seal
12. Water pump

22086_MUST_G0065

Fig. 34 Water pump assembly—5.4L engine

ALTERNATOR

REMOVAL & INSTALLATION

4.0L Engine

See Figure 35.

1. Before servicing the vehicle, refer to the precautions at the beginning of this section.
2. Disconnect the negative battery cable.
3. Remove the accessory drive belt.
4. Disconnect the alternator electrical connectors.
5. Remove the alternator shield (4.0L engine).
6. Remove the alternator mounting bolts.
7. Remove the alternator from the vehicle.
8. Installation is the reverse of the removal procedure.

To install:

9. Position the alternator onto engine. Tighten the lower bolt to 35 ft. lbs. (48 Nm).
10. Install the alternator shield.
11. Connect the alternator electrical connectors.
12. Install the main lead and tighten to 71 inch lbs (8 Nm).
13. Install the accessory drive belt.
14. Connect the negative battery cable.

4.6L Engines

See Figure 36.

1. Before servicing the vehicle, refer to the precautions at the beginning of this section.
2. Disconnect the negative battery cable.
3. Remove the air intake scoop bracket, if equipped.
4. Remove the accessory drive belt.
5. Remove the upper alternator bracket.

6. Disconnect the alternator electrical connectors.
7. Remove the alternator bolts.
8. Remove the alternator from the vehicle.
9. Installation is the reverse of the removal procedure.

To install:

10. Position the alternator onto engine. Tighten the mounting bolts to 18 ft. lbs. (25 Nm).
11. Connect the alternator electrical connectors.
12. Install the main lead and tighten to 71 inch lbs (8 Nm).
13. Install the upper alternator bracket. Tighten the bolts to 89 inch lbs. (10 Nm).
14. Install the accessory drive belt.
15. Install the air intake scoop bracket, if equipped.
16. Connect the negative battery cable.

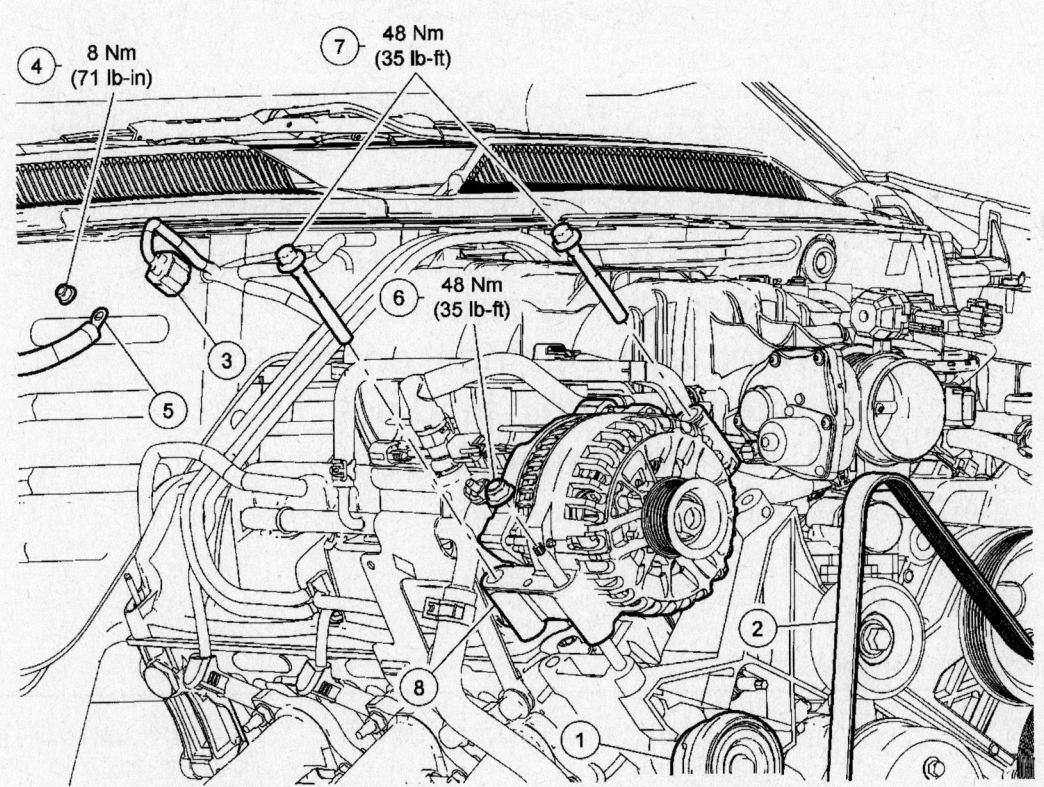

1. Accessory drive belt tensioner
2. Accessory drive belt
3. Alternator electrical connector
4. Main lead nut
5. Main lead
6. Alternator stud nut
7. Alternator bolts (2 required)
8. Alternator

22086_MUST_G0013

Fig. 35 Alternator location—4.0L engine

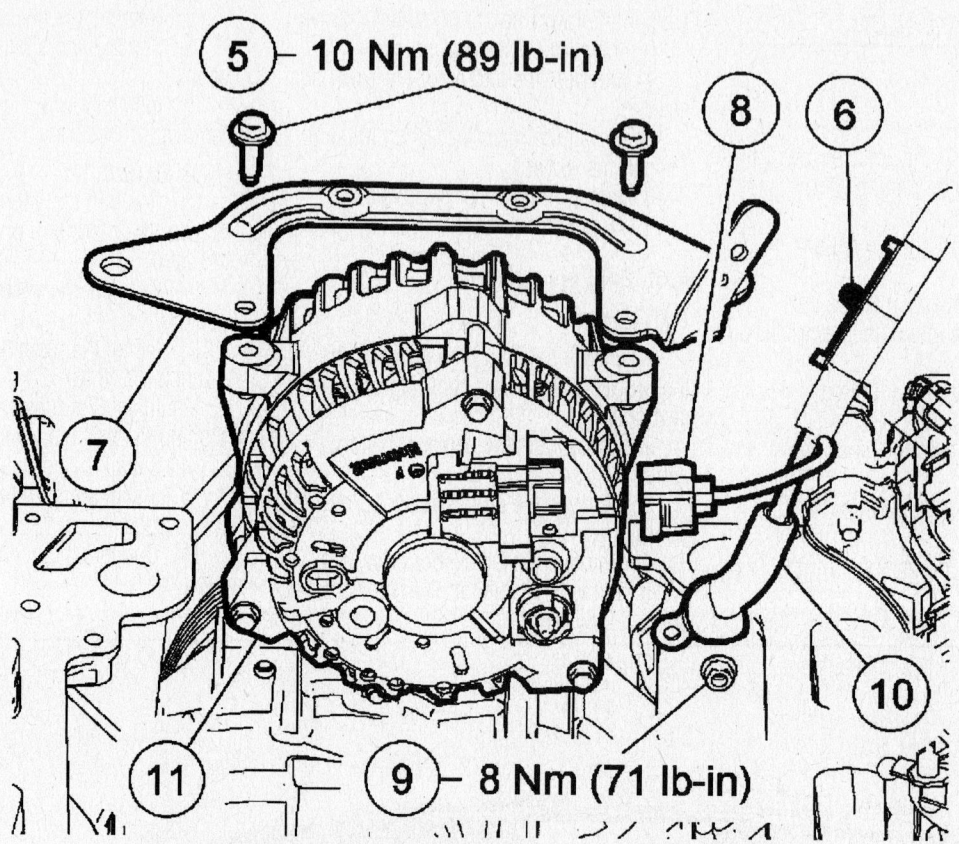

5 — 10 Nm (89 lb-in)

9 — 8 Nm (71 lb-in)

5. Upper alternator bracket bolts
6. Alternator electrical harness guide
7. Upper alternator bracket
8. Alternator electrical connector
9. Alternator main lead nut
10. Alternator main lead
11. Alternator

22086_MUST_G0014

Fig. 36 Alternator location—4.6L engine

5.4L Engine

See Figure 37.

1. Before servicing the vehicle, refer to the precautions at the beginning of this section.
2. Disconnect the negative battery cable.
3. Remove the accessory drive belt.
4. Raise the vehicle.

5. Disconnect the alternator electrical connectors.
6. Remove the alternator bolts.
7. Remove the alternator from the vehicle.
8. Installation is the reverse of the removal procedure.

To install:

9. Install alternator, and tighten the bolts to 35 ft. lbs. (48 Nm).

10. Install ATM cooling line, bracket, and nut; tighten the nut to 18 ft. lbs. (25 Nm).
11. Connect alternator main lead and tighten to 9 ft. lbs. (12 Nm).
12. Lower the vehicle.
13. Install the accessory drive belt.
14. Connect the negative battery cable.
15. Installation is the reverse of the removal procedure.

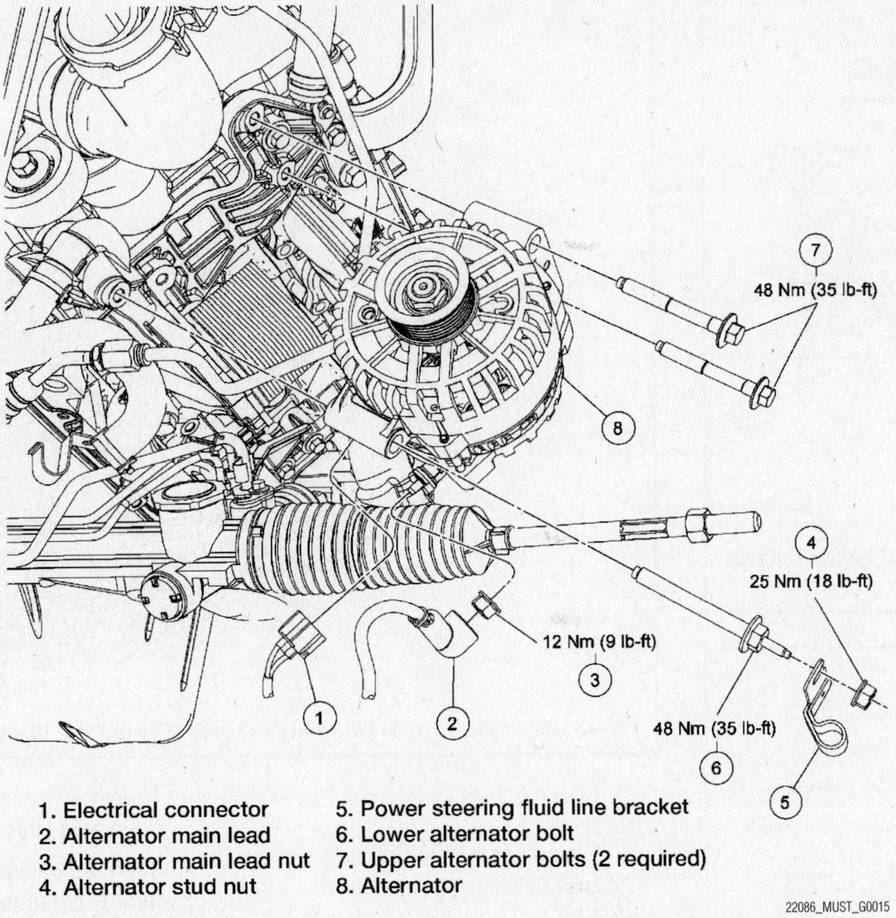

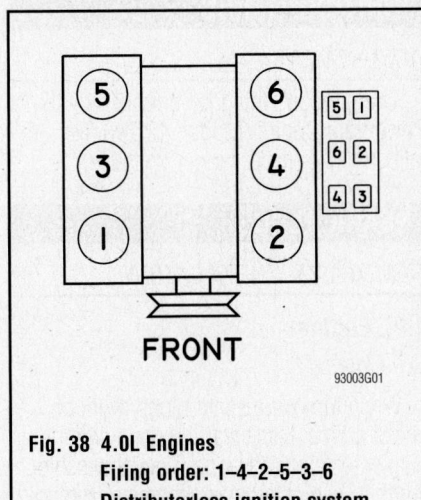

7
48 Nm (35 lb-ft)
8
4
25 Nm (18 lb-ft)
12 Nm (9 lb-ft)
3
1
2
48 Nm (35 lb-ft)
6
5
1. Electrical connector
2. Alternator main lead
3. Alternator main lead nut
4. Alternator stud nut
5. Power steering fluid line bracket
6. Lower alternator bolt
7. Upper alternator bolts (2 required)
8. Alternator
22086_MUST_G0015

Fig. 37 Alternator location—5.4L engine

ENGINE ELECTRICAL

FIRING ORDER

See Figures 38 and 39.

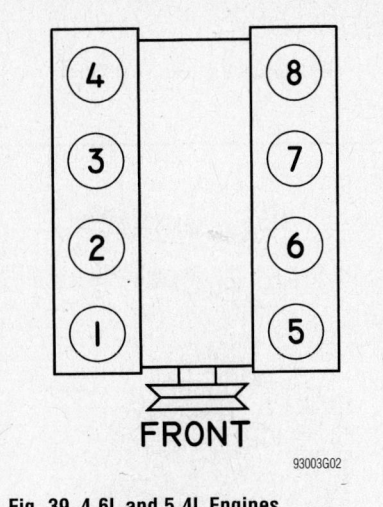

5
6
3
4
1
2
5 1
6 2
4 3
FRONT
93003G01

Fig. 38 4.0L Engines
Firing order: 1–4–2–5–3–6
Distributorless ignition system

4
8
3
7
2
6
1
5
FRONT
93003G02

Fig. 39 4.6L and 5.4L Engines
Firing order: 1–3–7–2–6–5–4–8
Distributorless ignition system—
One coil per cylinder

IGNITION SYSTEM

IGNITION COIL

REMOVAL & INSTALLATION

➡The 4.0L engines utilize one coil pack containing three separate coils. The 4.6L and 5.4L engines use a coil on plug, consisting of eight separate ignition coils (one for each spark plug).

4.0L Engine

See Figures 40 and 41.

1. Disconnect the negative battery cable.
2. Disconnect the electrical harness connector from the ignition coil pack.
3. Label and remove the spark plug wires from the ignition coil terminal towers by squeezing the locking tabs to release the coil boot retainers.
4. Disconnect the accelerator cable retaining clamp from the ignition coil stud bolt (if equipped).

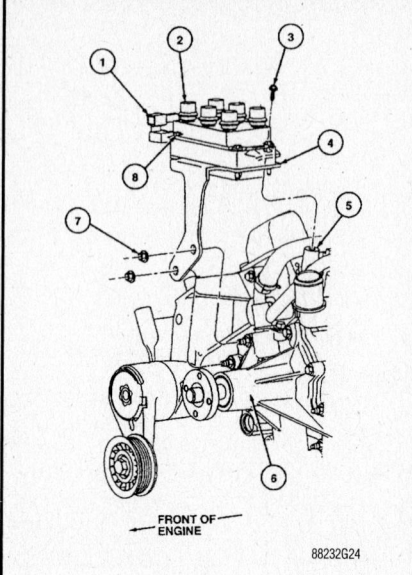

Fig. 40 Exploded view of ignition coil pack mounting—4.0L engine

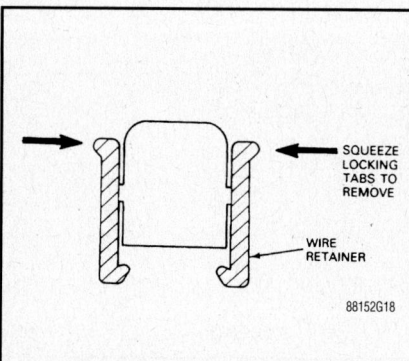

Fig. 41 The locking tabs on the ignition wire retainers must be released to be able to remove the wires from the coil

5. Remove the coil pack mounting screws and remove the coil pack.

To install:

6. Install the coil pack and the retaining screws. Tighten the retaining screws to 40–62 inch lbs. (4.5–7 Nm).

➡**Be sure to place some dielectric compound into each spark plug boot prior to installation of the spark plug wire.**

7. Attach the spark plug wires and electrical harness connector to the coil pack.

8. Connect the negative battery cable.

4.6L Engine

See Figure 42.

1. Disconnect the battery ground cable.

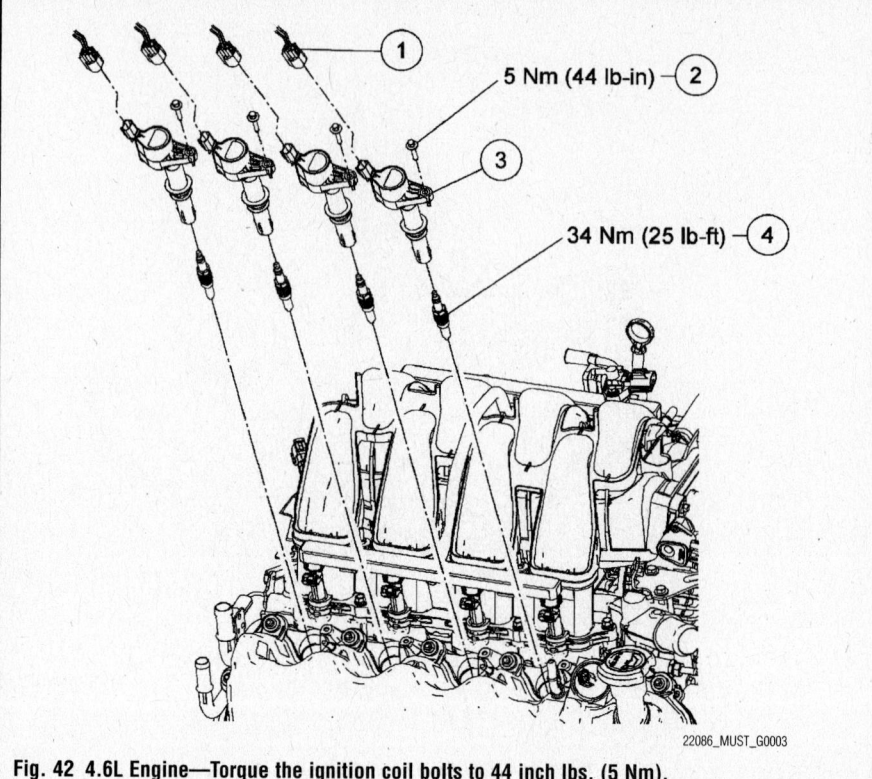

Fig. 42 4.6L Engine—Torque the ignition coil bolts to 44 inch lbs. (5 Nm).

2. Disconnect the ignition coil electrical connectors.

3. Remove the ignition coil bolts.
   a. Tightening torque 44 inch lbs. (5 Nm).

➡**When removing the ignition coils, a slight twisting motion will break the seal and ease removal.**

4. Remove the ignition coils.

5.4L Engine

See Figure 43.

1. Disconnect the battery ground cable.

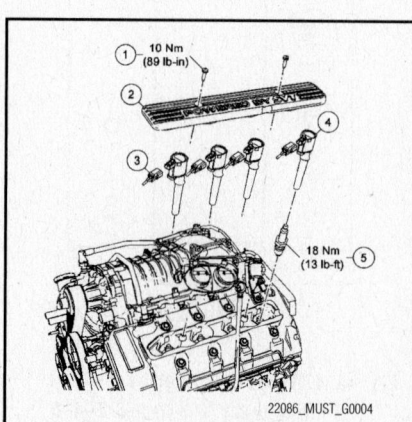

Fig. 43 5.4L engine—coil on plug ignition coils

2. Remove the ignition coil covers.

3. Remove ignition coils.

➡**When removing the ignition coils, a slight twisting motion will break the seal and ease removal.**

To install:

4. Installation is the reverse of the removal procedure.

➡**Apply a light film of silicone brake caliper grease and dielectric compound to the inside of the coil boots before installation.**

IGNITION TIMING

ADJUSTMENT

The ignition timing is controlled by the Powertrain Control Module (PCM). No adjustment is necessary or possible.

SPARK PLUGS

REMOVAL & INSTALLATION

4.0L Engine

See Figure 44.

When removing spark plugs, work on one at a time. Don't start by removing the plug wires all at once, because, unless you number them, they may become mixed up. Take a minute before you begin and number the wires with tape. The best location for numbering is near where the wires come out of the coil pack.

➡**Apply a small amount of silicone dielectric compound (D7AZ–19A331–A or equivalent) to the inside of the terminal boots whenever an ignition wire is disconnected from the plug or ignition coil.**

1. Disconnect the negative battery cable and, if the vehicle has been run recently, allow the engine to thoroughly cool.

2. Carefully twist the spark plug wire boot to loosen it, then pull upward and remove the boot from the plug. Be sure to pull on the boot and not on the wire, otherwise the connector located inside the boot may become separated.

3. Using compressed air, blow any water or debris from the spark plug well to assure that no harmful contaminants are allowed to enter the combustion chamber when the spark plug is removed. If compressed air is not available, use a rag or a brush to clean the area.

➡**Remove the spark plugs when the engine is cold, if possible, to prevent damage to the threads. If removal of the plugs is difficult, apply a few drops**

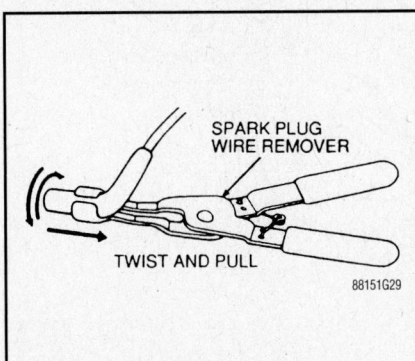

SPARK PLUG WIRE REMOVER

TWIST AND PULL

88151G29

Fig. 44 Use of a spark plug wire tool will help prevent damage to the wires

of penetrating oil or spray to the area around the base of the plug, and allow it a few minutes to permeate the threads.

4. Using a spark plug socket that is equipped with a rubber insert to properly hold the plug, turn the spark plug counterclockwise to loosen and remove it from the bore. Be sure to hold the socket straight on the plug; this will avoid breaking the plug or rounding off the hex flats on the plug.

✲✲ WARNING

Do not to use a universal joint, as shear force may unintentionally to be applied to the spark plug. Shear force could break the plug off in the cylinder head, leading to costly engine repairs.

5. Once the plug is out, inspect it for signs of wear, fouling or damage.

6. Loosen the plug with a spark plug socket and ratchet

7. Carefully unthread the plug from the cylinder head by hand

4.6L Engine

See Figure 42.

1. Carefully remove the ignition coils from each spark plug using a gentle twisting motion

2. Use compressed air to remove any foreign material from the spark plug well before removing the spark plugs

5.4L Engine

See Figure 43.

1. Remove the ignition coil cover

2. Carefully remove the ignition coils from each spark plug using a gentle twisting motion

3. Use compressed air to remove any foreign material from the spark plug well before removing the spark plugs

To install:

4. Inspect the spark plug boot for tears or damage. If a damaged boot is found, the spark plug wire must be replaced.

5. Using a wire feeler gauge, check and adjust the spark plug gap. When using a gauge, the proper size should pass between the electrodes with a slight drag. The next larger size should not be able to pass while the next smaller size should pass freely.

6. Apply a small amount of anti-seize compound to the threads of the new plug then carefully thread the plug into the bore by hand. If resistance is felt before the plug is almost completely threaded, back the plug out and begin threading again. In small, hard to reach areas, an old spark plug wire and boot could be used as a threading tool. The boot will hold the plug while you twist the end of the wire and the wire is supple enough to twist before it would allow the plug to cross thread.

✲✲ WARNING

Do not use the spark plug socket to thread the plugs. Always thread the plug carefully by hand or by using an old plug wire to prevent the possibility of cross threading and damaging the cylinder head bore.

7. Carefully tighten the spark plug. Refer to the Torque Specifications chart in the Engine Mechanical section of this manual for the correct torque specification.

8. Apply a small amount of silicone dielectric compound to the end of the spark plug lead or inside the spark plug boot to prevent sticking, then install the boot to the spark plug and push until it clicks into place. The click may be felt or heard, then gently pull back on the boot to assure proper contact.

STARTER

REMOVAL & INSTALLATION

4.0L Engine

See Figure 45.

1. Disconnect the negative battery cable.
2. Disconnect starter electrical connections.
3. Remove starter bolts.
4. Remove starter.

To install:

5. Install starter, and tighten the bolts to 18 ft. lbs. (25 Nm).

6. Connect starter main lead and tighten to 9 ft. lbs. (12 Nm).
7. Connect starter exciter lead and tighten to 44 inch lbs. (5 Nm).
8. Connect the negative battery cable.

4.6L and 5.4L Engines

See Figure 46.

1. Before servicing the vehicle, refer to the precautions at the beginning of this section.
2. Disconnect the negative battery cable.
3. Disconnect Heated Oxygen (HO2S)

sensor connector and bracket, if necessary.
4. Disconnect starter electrical connections.
5. Remove starter bolts.
6. Remove starter.

To install:

7. Install starter. Tighten the bolts to 17 ft. lbs. (23 Nm).
8. Connect starter electrical connections.
9. Connect HO2S sensor connector and bracket, if necessary.
10. Connect the negative battery cable.

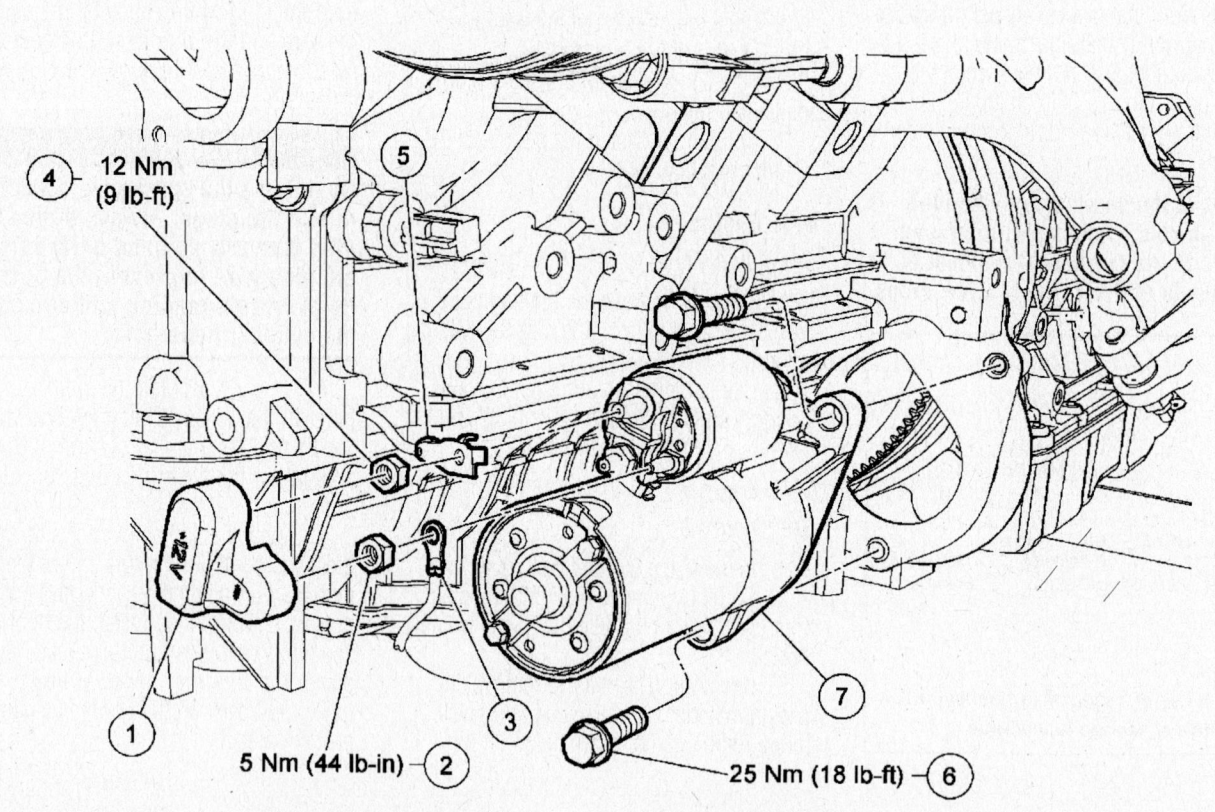

1. Solenoid terminal cover
2. Starter exciter lead nut
3. Starter exciter lead
4. Starter main lead nut
5. Starter main lead
6. Starter mounting bolt (2 required)
7. Starter motor

22086_MUST_G0006

Fig. 45 Starter mounting—4.0L engine

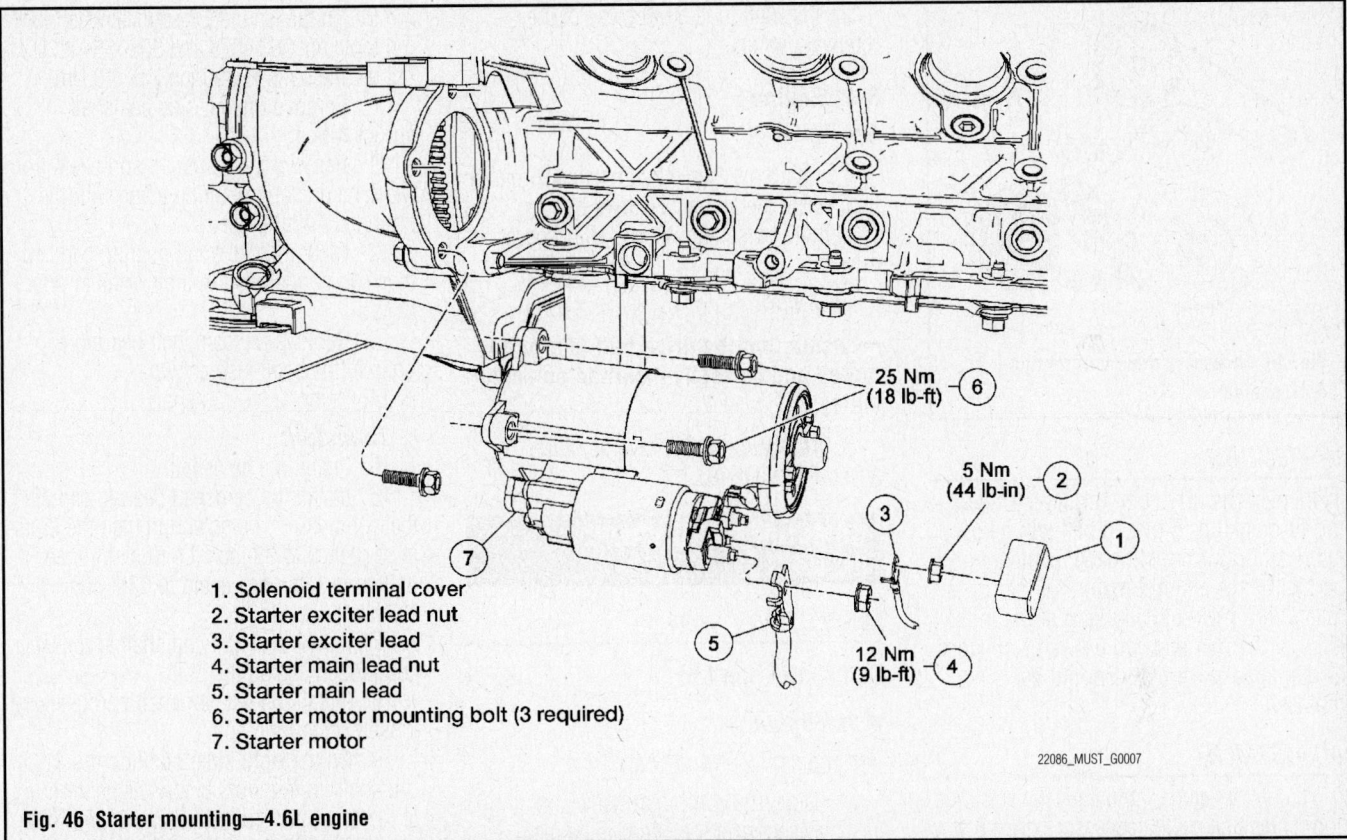

1. Solenoid terminal cover
2. Starter exciter lead nut
3. Starter exciter lead
4. Starter main lead nut
5. Starter main lead
6. Starter motor mounting bolt (3 required)
7. Starter motor

25 Nm
(18 lb-ft)

5 Nm
(44 lb-in)

12 Nm
(9 lb-ft)

22086_MUST_G0007

Fig. 46 Starter mounting—4.6L engine

ENGINE MECHANICAL

➡Disconnecting the negative battery cable may interfere with the functions of the on board computer systems and may require the computer to undergo a relearning process, once the negative battery cable is reconnected.

ACCESSORY DRIVE BELTS

ACCESSORY BELT ROUTING

See Figures 47 through 49.

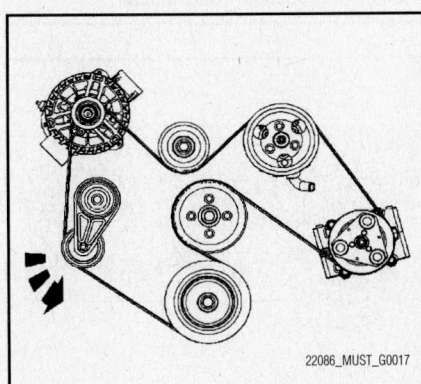

22086_MUST_G0017

Fig. 47 Accessory drive belt routing— 4.0L engine

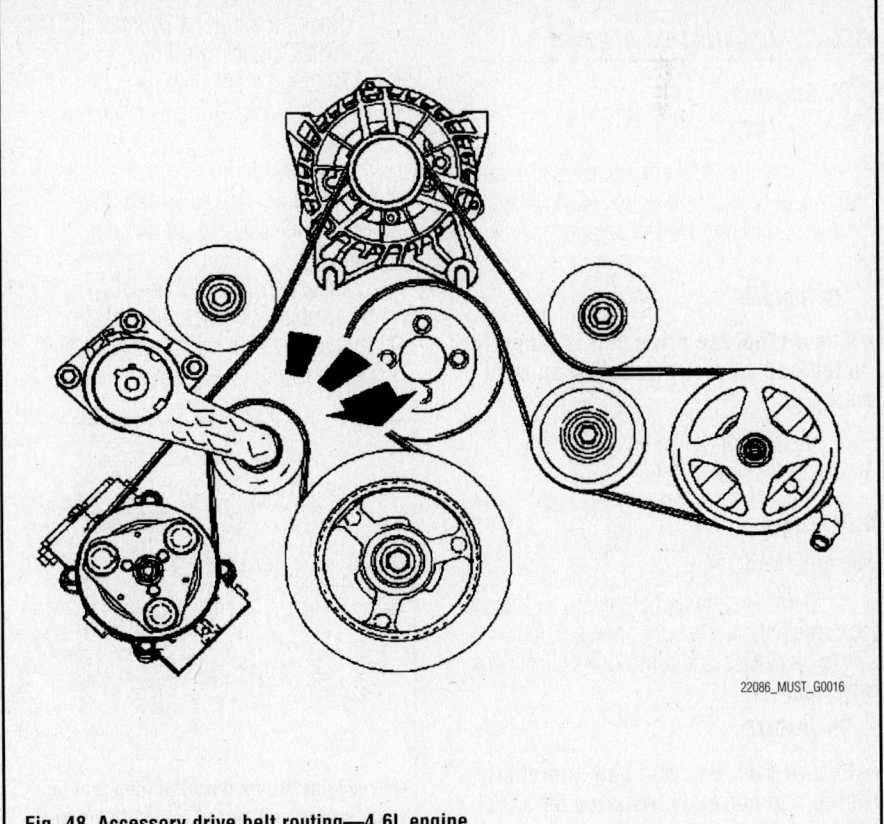

22086_MUST_G0016

Fig. 48 Accessory drive belt routing—4.6L engine

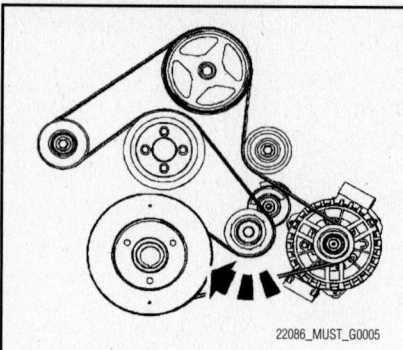

Fig. 49 Accessory drive belt routing—5.4L engine

INSPECTION

Inspect the drive belt for signs of glazing or cracking. A glazed belt will be perfectly smooth from slippage, while a good belt will have a slight texture of fabric visible. Cracks will usually start at the inner edge of the belt and run outward. All worn or damaged drive belts should be replaced.

ADJUSTMENT

The belt tensioner automatically sets the correct tension on the accessory drive belt. No adjustment is necessary. If tension is incorrect, check for proper mounting of all accessory drives and verify that the correct belt is being installed.

REMOVAL & INSTALLATION

4.0L Engines

See Figure 47.

1. Using a suitable belt tensioner release tool, rotate the accessory drive belt tensioner clockwise and remove the accessory drive belt.

To install:

➡️**Ensure that the drive belt is properly routed and correctly installed on each pulley.**

2. Installation is the reverse of the removal procedure.

4.6L Engine

See Figure 48.

1. Using a suitable belt tensioner release tool, rotate the accessory drive belt tensioner clockwise and remove the accessory drive belt.

To install:

➡️**Ensure that the drive belt is properly routed and correctly installed on each pulley.**

2. Installation is the reverse of the removal procedure.

5.4L Engine

See Figure 49.

1. Using a suitable belt tensioner release tool, rotate the accessory drive belt tensioner clockwise and remove the accessory drive belt.

To install:

➡️**Ensure that the drive belt is properly routed and correctly installed on each pulley.**

2. Installation is the reverse of the removal procedure.

CAMSHAFT AND VALVE LIFTERS

INSPECTION

Camshaft Lobe Lift

4.0L Engine

See Figures 50 through 53.

1. Drain the cooling system.
2. Disconnect the negative battery cable.
3. Remove the valve covers.
4. Remove the camshaft roller followers.
5. Position the no. 1 cylinder at TDC.
6. Install crankshaft timing tool no. 303–573 to the crankshaft damper so it contacts the block. This positions the engine at TDC.
7. On the right side, install camshaft locking tools no. 303–578 and 303–564 and tighten the bolts to 89 inch lbs. (10 Nm).
8. Install special tool no. 303–575 and using camshaft sprocket nut socket no. 303565, remove the right side camshaft sprocket bolt.

Fig. 50 Install crankshaft timing tool to position the engine at TDC—4.0L engine

9. On the left side, install camshaft locking tools no. 303–578 and 303–564 and tighten the bolts to 89 inch lbs. (10 Nm).
10. Remove the left side camshaft sprocket bolt.
11. Remove the camshaft sprockets from the camshaft and position aside with the timing chain in place.
12. Mark the camshaft bearing caps so they can be installed in their original positions.
13. Remove the camshaft bearing cap bolts in the sequence shown.
14. Remove the camshaft.

To install:

15. Install the camshaft.
16. Install the camshaft bearing caps in their original locations and tighten the bolts in sequence to 53 inch lbs. (6 Nm), then tighten in sequence again to 12 ft. lbs. (16 Nm).
17. Install the right camshaft sprocket and loosely install the bolt.
18. Install the left camshaft sprocket and loosely install the bolt.
19. On the right side, position the camshaft timing slots below the centerline of the camshaft and install camshaft timing tools 303–577 and 303–576 to the front of the cylinder head.

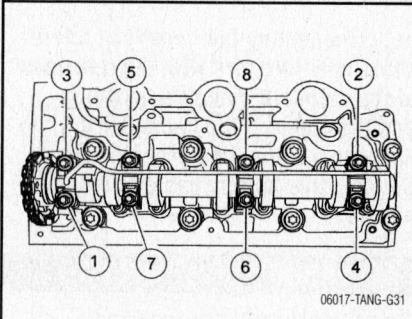

Fig. 51 Camshaft bearing cap bolt removal sequence—4.0L engine

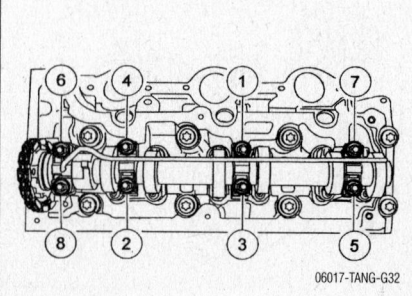

Fig. 52 Camshaft bearing cap bolt installation sequence—4.0L engine

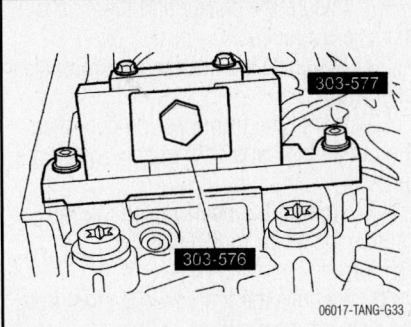

Fig. 53 Installing camshaft timing tools to the cylinder head—4.0L engine

20. Remove the right side camshaft tensioner bolt.

21. Install Timing Chain Tensioner tool no. 303–571 in the tensioner opening.

22. Tighten the camshaft locking tools no. 303–578 and 303–564 bolts to 89 inch lbs. (10 Nm).

23. Install special tool no. 303–575 and using camshaft sprocket nut socket no. 303–565, tighten the right side camshaft sprocket bolt to 63 ft. lbs. (85 Nm).

24. Remove timing tensioner tool and install the right side tensioner and tighten to 32 ft. lbs. (44 Nm).

25. Remove the tools from the right cylinder head and camshaft and install them on the left cylinder head and camshaft.

26. Repeat the timing procedure on the left side.

27. Remove the special tools.

28. Install the camshaft roller followers.

29. Install the valve covers.

30. Connect the negative battery cable.

4.6L Engine

See Figures 54 through 62.

> ※※ **CAUTION**
>
> **The procedure must be followed exactly or damage to the valves and pistons will result.**

➡ **If both camshafts are being removed, the right camshaft must be removed first.**

1. Disconnect the negative battery cable.

2. Position the crankshaft damper spoke at the 12 o'clock position and the timing mark indentation at the 1 o'clock position.

3. Remove the right side valve cover.

4. Loosen and back off the camshaft phaser bolt one full turn.

5. Disconnect the camshaft position sensor connector.

6. Remove the camshaft position sensor.

7. Position the camshaft lobes as shown so the no. 2 intake lobes and no. 1 exhaust lobe are in correct position..

➡ **The no. 1 cylinder must be coming up on the exhaust stroke with the crankshaft keyway in the 12 o'clock position.**

8. Remove the 3 camshaft roller followers as shown, using spring compressor 303–1039.

9. Remove the left side valve cover.

10. Loosen and back off the camshaft phaser bolt one full turn.

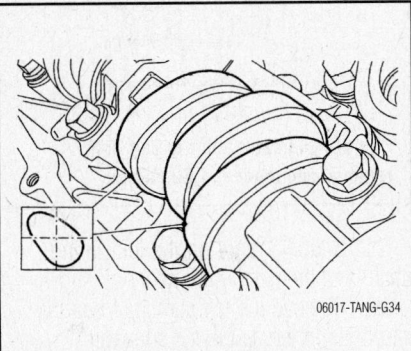

Fig. 54 Positioning camshaft lobes on right camshaft—4.6L engine

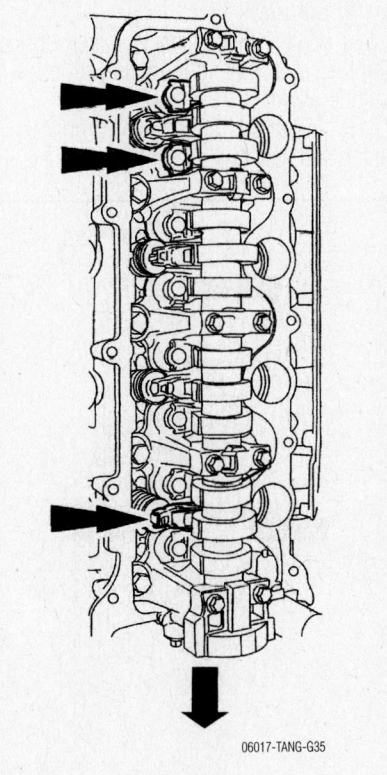

Fig. 55 Removing right cylinder head camshaft roller followers—4.6L engine

11. Disconnect the camshaft position sensor connector.

12. Remove the camshaft position sensor.

13. Position the camshaft lobes as shown so the no. 2 intake lobes and no. 5 exhaust lobe are in correct position..

➡ **The no. 5 cylinder must be coming up on the exhaust stroke with the crankshaft keyway in the 12 o'clock position.**

14. Remove the 3 camshaft roller followers as shown, using spring compressor 303–1039.

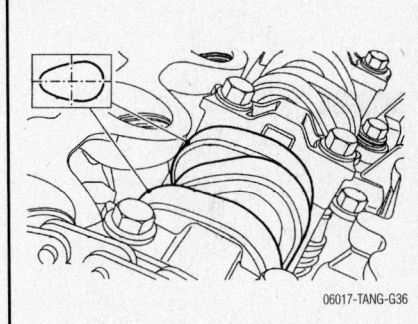

Fig. 56 Positioning camshaft lobes on left camshaft—4.6L engine

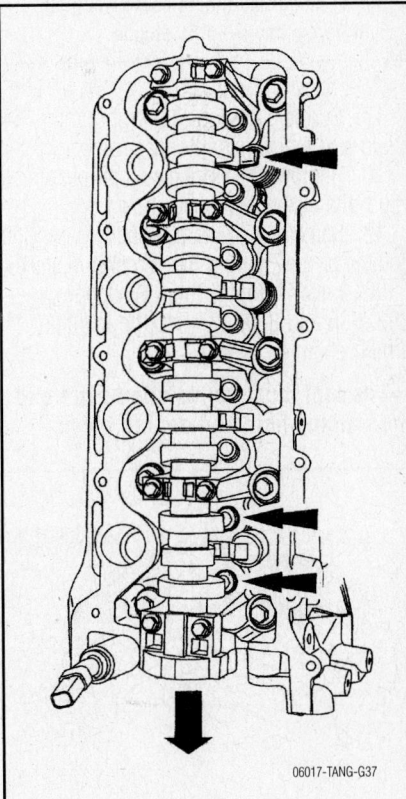

Fig. 57 Removing left cylinder head camshaft roller followers—4.6L engine

15. Rotate the crankshaft and position the crankshaft damper spoke at the 6 o'clock position and the timing mark indentation at the 7 o'clock position.

16. Install Timing Chain Wedge no. 303–636 and 303–637 into the right side timing chain as shown.

➡The tool must be installed square to the timing chain and engine block.

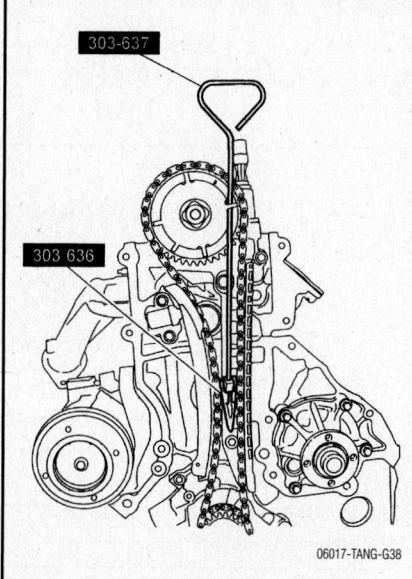

Fig. 58 Installing timing chain wedge in right timing chain—4.6L engine

17. Scribe a mark on the right timing chain and the camshaft phaser as shown.

18. Remove the right camshaft bearing cap bolts in the sequence shown.

19. Remove the right camshaft phaser bolt and the phaser, leaving the sprocket in place.

20. Install Timing Chain Wedge no. 303–636 and 303–637 into the left side timing chain as shown.

➡The tool must be installed square to the timing chain and engine block.

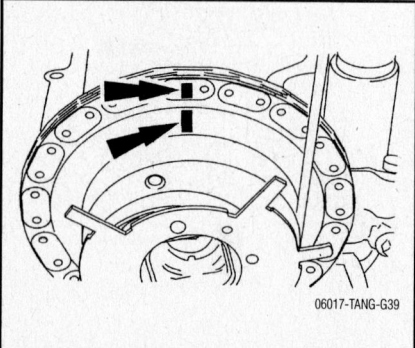

Fig. 59 Scribing a timing mark on timing chain and camshaft phaser—4.6L engine

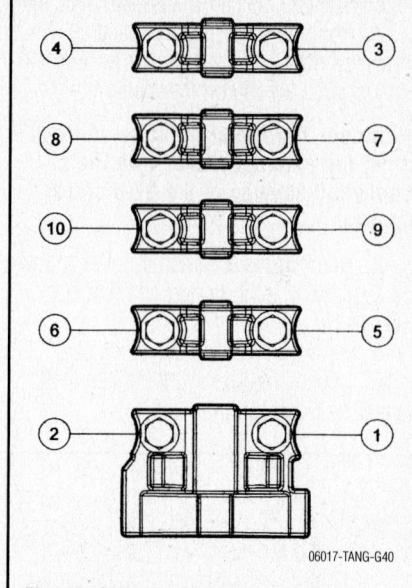

Fig. 60 Camshaft bearing cap bolt removal sequence—4.6L engine

21. Scribe a mark on the left timing chain and the camshaft phaser as shown.

22. Remove the left camshaft bearing cap bolts in the sequence shown.

23. Remove the left camshaft phaser bolt and the phaser, leaving the sprocket in place.

24. Remove the camshaft(s).

To install:

25. Install the camshaft(s) after lubricating the camshaft and journals with clean engine oil.

26. Install the right camshaft phaser using and new bolt. Hand tighten the bolt.

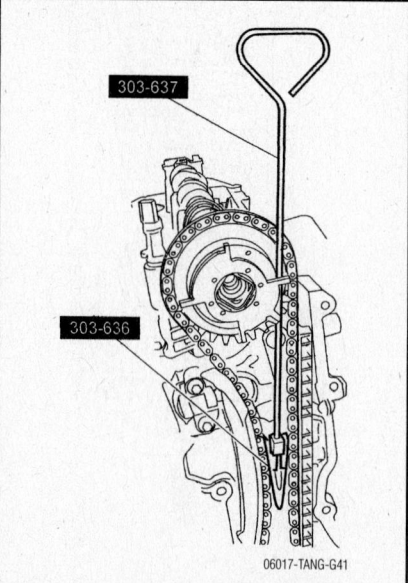

Fig. 61 Installing timing chain wedge in left timing chain—4.6L engine

27. Ensure the phaser and timing chain marks are aligned.

28. Lubricate the bearing caps with clean engine oil.

29. Install the front bearing cap, then the remaining caps and loosely install the bolts.

30. Tighten the bearing caps in the sequence shown to 89 inch lbs. (10 Nm).

31. Remove the timing wedge tool from the right timing chain.

32. Install the left camshaft phaser using and new bolt. Hand tighten the bolt.

33. Ensure the phaser and timing chain marks are aligned.

34. Lubricate the bearing caps with clean engine oil.

35. Install the front bearing cap, then the remaining caps and loosely install the bolts.

36. Tighten the bearing caps in the sequence shown to 89 inch lbs. (10 Nm).

37. Remove the timing wedge tool from the left timing chain.

38. Rotate the crankshaft damper so the spoke is at the 12 o'clock position and the timing mark indentation is at the 1 o'clock position.

39. Verify the camshaft lobes are in the correct position.

40. Install the 3 camshaft roller followers using the spring compressor.

41. Install the camshaft position sensor and connect the connector.

42. Tighten the camshaft phaser bolt to 30 ft. lbs. (40 Nm), then tighten an additional 90 degrees.

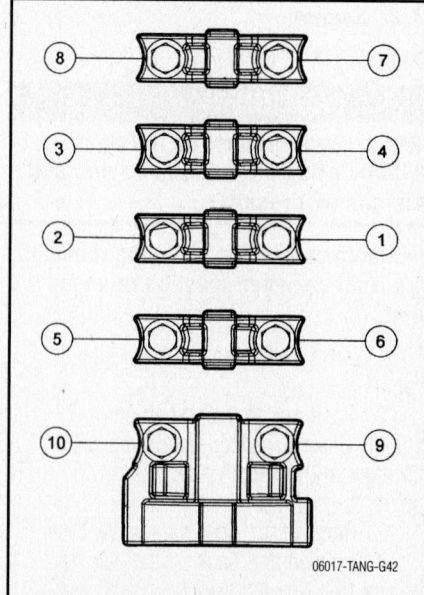

Fig. 62 Camshaft bearing cap bolt tightening sequence—4.6L engine

43. Install the right valve cover.
44. Verify the left camshaft lobes are in the correct position.
45. Install the 3 camshaft roller followers using the spring compressor.
46. Install the camshaft position sensor and connect the connector.
47. Tighten the camshaft phaser bolt to 30 ft. lbs. (40 Nm), then tighten an additional 90 degrees.
48. Install the left valve cover.
49. Connect the negative battery cable.
50. Start the engine and check for leaks.

5.4L Engine

See Figures 63 through 70.

1. Remove the timing drive components.
2. Install the camshaft holding tool.
3. Remove the bolt, washer and camshaft drive sprocket.
4. Remove the bolt, washer and camshaft sprocket spacer.
5. Compress the secondary timing chain tensioner and install a lock pin.
6. Remove the secondary timing chain and the 2 camshaft sprockets.
7. Remove the 2 bolts and the secondary timing chain tensioner.

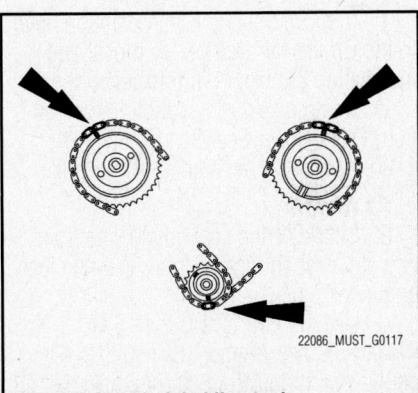

Fig. 63 Camshaft holding tool

Fig. 64 Camshaft holding tool installed

✳✳ CAUTION

The cam bearing cap bolts vary in length and head design and must be installed in their original position. Camshaft bearing caps are not interchangeable and must be installed in their original position.

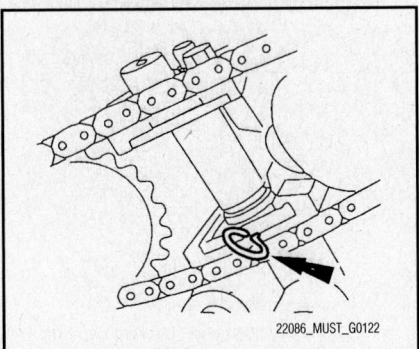

Fig. 65 Secondary chain tensioner with lock pin installed

8. Remove the camshaft bearing cap bolts in the sequence shown.
9. Remove the camshaft bearing caps.
10. Remove the camshafts.

To install:

➡ Lubricate the camshafts with clean engine oil prior to installation.

Install the camshafts.

✳✳ CAUTION

The cam bearing cap bolts vary in length and head design and must be installed in their original position. Camshaft bearing caps are not interchangeable and must be installed in their original position.

➡ Lubricate the camshaft bearing cap bearing surfaces with clean engine oil prior to installation.

11. Install the camshaft bearing caps.
12. Install the bearing cap bolts and

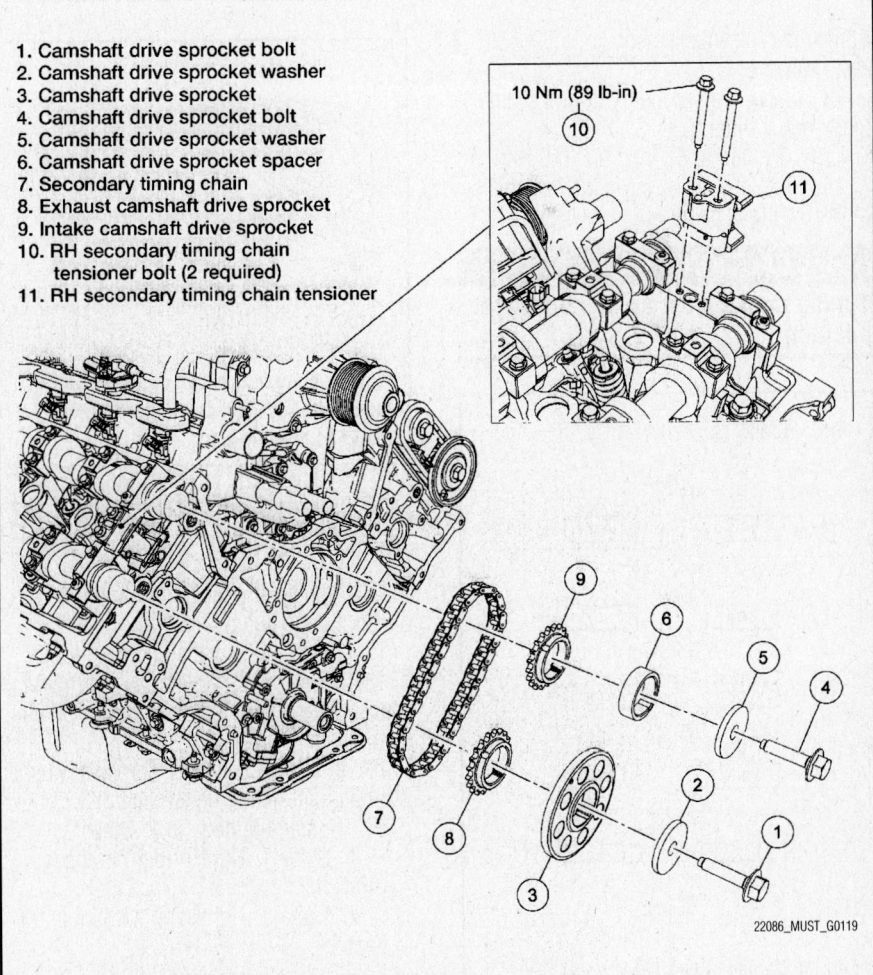

1. Camshaft drive sprocket bolt
2. Camshaft drive sprocket washer
3. Camshaft drive sprocket
4. Camshaft drive sprocket bolt
5. Camshaft drive sprocket washer
6. Camshaft drive sprocket spacer
7. Secondary timing chain
8. Exhaust camshaft drive sprocket
9. Intake camshaft drive sprocket
10. RH secondary timing chain tensioner bolt (2 required)
11. RH secondary timing chain tensioner

10 Nm (89 lb-in)

Fig. 66 RH timing drive components—exploded view—LH similar

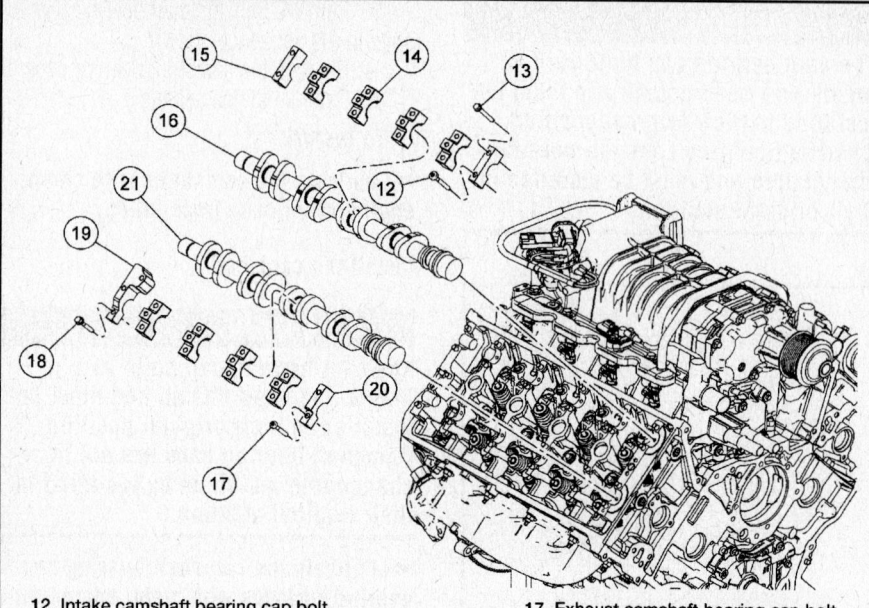

12. Intake camshaft bearing cap bolt
13. Intake/exhaust camshaft bearing cap bolt (22 required)
14. Intake/exhaust camshaft bearing cap (8 required)
15. Intake camshaft bearing cap (2 required)
16. RH intake camshaft
17. Exhaust camshaft bearing cap bolt
18. Exhaust camshaft bearing cap bolt
19. Exhaust camshaft bearing cap
20. Exhaust camshaft bearing cap
21. RH exhaust camshaft

22086_MUST_G0120

Fig. 67 RH camshaft main components—exploded view–LH similar

tighten in the sequence shown to 89 inch lbs. (10 Nm).

13. Install the secondary timing chain tensioner and the bolts.

    a. Tighten to 89 inch lbs. (10 Nm).

14. Index the keyways on the camshafts to the 6 o'clock position.

✳✳ CAUTION

Timing marks must be at 12 o'clock position.

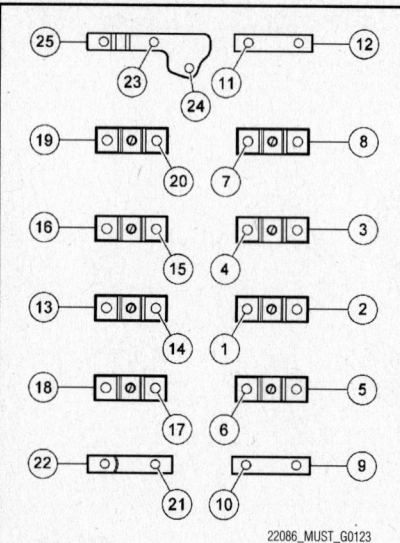

22086_MUST_G0123

Fig. 68 Camshaft bearing cap bolt sequence

22086_MUST_G0124

Fig. 69 Correct keyway and timing mark indexing—keyways at 6 o'clock; timing marks at 12 o'clock

15. Install the camshaft sprockets and the secondary timing chain as an assembly.

16. Remove the lockpin from the secondary timing chain tensioner.

17. Install the camshaft holding tool.

18. Install the camshaft drive sprocket spacer, washer and bolt, and hand tighten the bolt.

19. Install the camshaft sprocket, washer and bolt, and hand tighten the bolt.

20. Tighten the bolts in 2 stages:

    a. Stage 1: Tighten to 30 ft. lbs. (40 Nm).

    b. Stage 2: Tighten an additional 90 degrees.

21. Install the timing drive components.

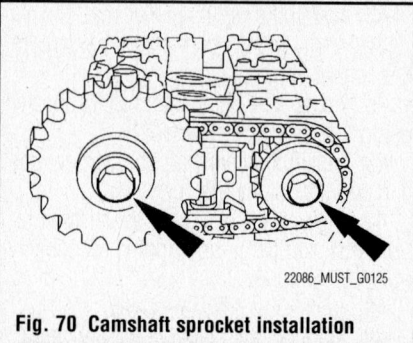

22086_MUST_G0125

Fig. 70 Camshaft sprocket installation

CRANKSHAFT FRONT SEAL

REMOVAL & INSTALLATION

This procedure provides oil seal replacement for the event that the engine front cover is not going to be removed from the engine. If the front engine cover is going to be removed, use the seal replacement steps in the Timing Chain, Sprockets, Front Cover and Seal procedure in this section.

➡**If the vibration damper is being replaced, it is strongly recommended that the crankshaft front seal be replaced at the same time.**

4.0L & 4.6L Engines

See Figure 71.

1. Remove the crankshaft damper. Refer to the Crankshaft Damper, Removal and Installation procedure in this section.

2. Using a seal removal tool, such as Ford Front Cover Seal Remover T74P–6700–A, remove the crankshaft oil seal.

To install:

3. Lubricate the seal bore in the front engine cover and the oil seal lip with clean engine oil.

4. Use the Ford Crankshaft Seal Replacer/Cover Aligner T88T–6701–A or equivalent, to install the front crankshaft oil seal.

5. Install the crankshaft damper. Refer to the Crankshaft Damper, Removal and Installation procedure in this section.

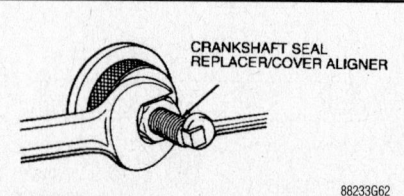

88233G62

Fig. 71 Use the appropriate tool, for example Ford Tool T88T–6701–A, to properly press the front oil seal into position in the engine front cover

5.4L Engines

See Figures 72 and 73.

1. Remove the crankshaft pulley.
2. Using a suitable seal puller, remove the crankshaft front seal.

To install:

3. Lubricate the engine front cover and the crankshaft front seal inner lip with clean engine oil.
4. Using suitable seal installing tool, install the crankshaft front seal.

Fig. 72 Lubrication of seal and engine cover

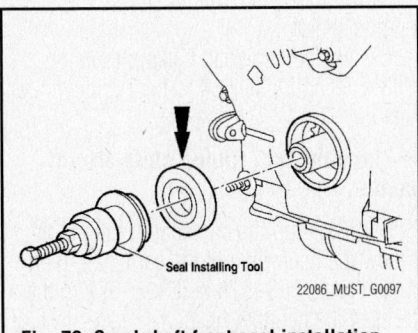

Fig. 73 Crankshaft front seal installation

5. Install the crankshaft pulley.
6. Install the accessory and super-charger drive belts.
7. Start the engine, and verify that there are no oil leaks.

CYLINDER HEAD

REMOVAL & INSTALLATION

4.0L Engine

See Figures 74 through 81.

1. Drain the cooling system.
2. Disconnect the negative battery cable.
3. Relieve the fuel system pressure.
4. Remove the intake manifold.
5. From the left valve cover remove or disconnect the following items:
- Ignition coil
- Fuel rail supply tube
- PCV tube

- Camshaft position sensor connector
- Fuel rail pressure and temperature sensor connector
- Fuel injector connectors
- Spark plug wire retainer
- Valve cover

6. From the right valve cover remove or disconnect the following items:
- PCV tube
- PCV connector
- Heater hose retainer
- Wiring harness bracket
- Valve cover

7. Remove the camshaft roller followers.
8. Loosen the drive belt tensioner and remove the accessory drive belt.
9. Disconnect the alternator electrical connectors.
10. Remove the accessory drive belt tensioner.
11. Remove the alternator mounting bracket.
12. Remove the heater hose from the thermostat housing.
13. Disconnect the coolant temperature sensor connector.
14. Remove the upper radiator hose.
15. Remove the thermostat housing.
16. From the left side cylinder head, remove or disconnect the following:
- Oil level indicator tube
- Power steering supply hose bracket

17. Remove the power steering pressure hose bracket from the crossmember.
18. Remove the power steering pump pulley, then the power steering pump, without disconnecting the lines, and position aside.
19. Remove the accessory drive belt bracket and then the A/C compressor, without disconnecting the lines, and position aside.
20. Remove the starter wiring bracket retainer.
21. Remove the ground strap and the wiring harness retainer from the rear of the cylinder head.
22. Remove the spark plug wires.
23. Remove the fuel rail and injectors and discard the O-ring seals.
24. Remove the catalytic converter to exhaust manifold nuts from both sides.
25. Remove the exhaust manifolds.
26. From the right side cylinder head, remove the hydraulic chain tensioner.
27. Install camshaft locking tools no. 303–578 and 303–564 and tighten the bolts to 89 inch lbs. (10 Nm).
28. Install special tool no. 303–575 and using camshaft sprocket nut socket no. 303565, remove the right side camshaft bolt.
29. Remove the right side camshaft cassette bolt.

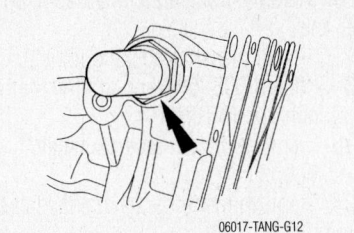

Fig. 74 Removing hydraulic chain tensioner bolt—4.0L engine—left side shown: right side similar

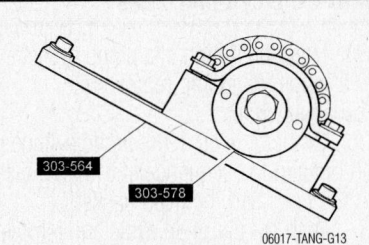

Fig. 75 Installing camshaft locking tools—4.0L engine—left side shown: right side similar

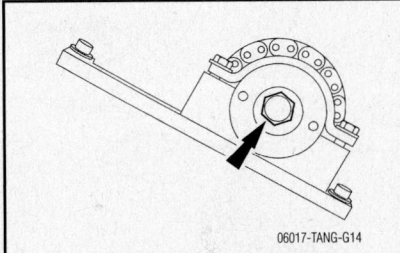

Fig. 76 Removing camshaft sprocket bolt—4.0L engine—left side shown: right side similar

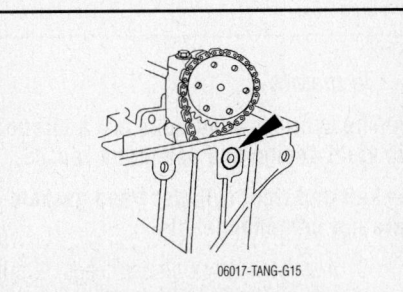

Fig. 77 Removing cassette bolt—4.0L engine—left side shown: right side similar

✲✲ CAUTION

Remove the camshaft sprocket from the timing chain to gain access to remove the cylinder head.

30. Hold the timing chain and cassette with a rubber band and remove the camshaft sprocket.

31. Remove the left side hydraulic chain tensioner.

32. Install camshaft locking tools no. 303–578 and 303–564 and tighten the bolts to 89 inch lbs. (10 Nm).

33. Remove the left side camshaft sprocket bolt.

34. Remove the left side camshaft cassette bolt.

✷✷ CAUTION

Remove the camshaft sprocket from the timing chain to gain access to remove the cylinder head.

35. Hold the timing chain and cassette with a rubber band and remove the camshaft sprocket.

36. On both sides, remove the cylinder head bolts in the sequence shown and discard the bolts and the head gasket.

37. With the aid of an assistant, remove the cylinder heads.

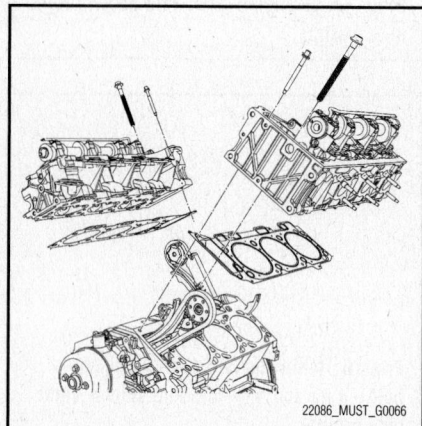

Fig. 78 Assembly of cylinder heads—4.0L engine

To install:

→**The cylinder head bolts are a torque to yield design and cannot be reused.**

→**Left and right cylinder head gaskets are not interchangeable.**

38. Install the new cylinder heads. Lubricate the new cylinder head bolt threads with clean oil and tighten them in sequence as follows:

   a. M12 bolts, Step 1: 9 ft. lbs. (12 Nm).

   b. Step 2: 18 ft. lbs. (25 Nm).

   c. M8 bolts Step 3: 24 ft. lbs. (32 Nm).

   d. Step 4: M12 bolts an additional 90 degrees.

   e. Step 5: M12 bolts an additional 90 degrees.

Fig. 79 Cylinder head bolt removal sequence—4.0L engine

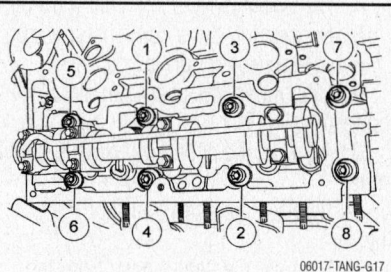

Fig. 80 Cylinder head bolt installation sequence—4.0L engine

39. On the right side, remove the rubber band and position the camshaft sprocket and chain in place.

40. Loosely install the sprocket bolt.

41. Install the right head cassette bolt and tighten to 9 ft. lbs. (12 Nm).

42. On the left side, remove the rubber band and position the camshaft sprocket and chain in place.

43. Loosely install the sprocket bolt.

44. Install the left head cassette bolt and tighten to 14 ft. lbs. (19 Nm).

45. Install the exhaust manifolds to both sides. See the procedure under exhaust manifolds.

46. Install the spark plug wires.

47. Install new o-rings on the fuel injectors and then install the injectors and fuel rail. Tighten the fuel rail bolts to 18 ft. lbs. (25 Nm).

48. Using a new gasket, install the thermostat housing and tighten the bolts to 8 ft. lbs. (11 Nm).

49. Install the coolant bypass hose clamp.

50. Install the upper radiator hose.

51. Connect the engine coolant temperature sensor connector.

52. Connect the heater hose to the thermostat housing.

53. Install the alternator bracket and tighten to 35 ft. lbs. (47 Nm).

54. Install the drive belt tensioner and tighten to 35 ft. lbs. (47 Nm).

55. Connect the alternator connectors.

56. Install the ground strap.

57. Connect the wiring harness retainer to the back of the left cylinder head.

58. Connect the starter wiring harness retainer.

59. Install the drive belt bracket and the A/C compressor and tighten the fasteners to 35 ft. lbs. (47 Nm).

60. Install the power steering pump and tighten the bolts to 18 ft. lbs. (25 Nm).

61. Install the power steering pump pulley and tighten the bolts to 18 ft. lbs. (25 Nm).

62. Install the power steering pressure tube bracket to the crossmember and tighten the bolt to 80 inch lbs. (10 Nm).

63. Install the power steering hose bracket.

64. Install the oil level indicator tube.

→**If the camshaft have been moved, the engine will require re-timing.**

65. Rotate the crankshaft until the no. 1 cylinder is at TDC.

66. Install crankshaft timing tool no. 303–573 to the crankshaft damper so it contacts the block. This positions the engine at TDC.

67. Install camshaft locking tools no. 303–578 and 303–564 to the right cylinder head.

→**The camshaft timing slots are off center.**

68. Position the camshaft timing slots below the centerline of the camshaft, then install tools 303–576 and 303–577 to the front of the cylinder head.

69. Tighten the bolts on tool 303–578 to 89 inch lbs. (10 Nm).

✷✷ CAUTION

The right camshaft sprocket bolt uses a left–hand thread.

70. Use camshaft sprocket nut socket 303–565 and tighten the sprocket bolt to 63 ft. lbs. (85 Nm).

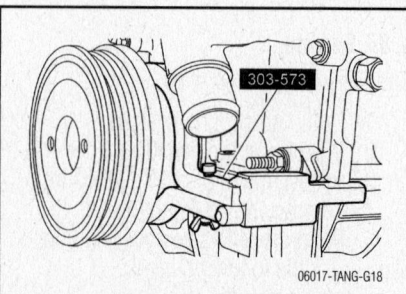

Fig. 81 Install crankshaft timing tool to position the engine at TDC—4.0L engine

71. Install the right camshaft tensioner and tighten the bolt to 32 ft. lbs. (44 Nm).

72. Remove the special tools from the right cylinder head and install them on the left cylinder head and repeat the previous procedure to tighten the left camshaft sprocket bolt.

73. Install the accessory drive belt.

74. Install the camshaft roller followers.

75. Install the intake manifold.

76. Install the valve covers and tighten the bolts in a criss–cross pattern to 89 inch lbs. (10 Nm).

77. Install the valve cover components and spark plug wires.

78. Connect the negative battery cable.

79. Fill the cooling system.

80. Start the engine and check for leaks.

81. Recharge the A/C system.

4.6L Engine

See Figures 82 through 87.

1. Drain the cooling system.

2. Relieve the fuel system pressure.

3. Disconnect the negative battery cable.

4. Drain the engine oil.

5. Remove the engine from the vehicle.

6. Install the engine on a suitable work stand.

7. Disconnect both camshaft position sensor connectors.

8. Disconnect both Variable Camshaft Timing (VCT) connectors.

9. Disconnect the engine wiring harness retainers.

10. Disconnect the radio interference capacitor.

11. Remove the PCV tubes from both valve covers.

12. Disconnect the ignition coil connectors.

13. Disconnect the engine wiring harness retainers from each valve cover.

14. Disconnect the cylinder head temperature sensor connector, and jumper harness connector retainer.

15. Disconnect the knock sensor connector retainer.

16. Disconnect the left side heated oxygen sensor connector.

17. Disconnect the oil pressure sender connector.

18. Remove the engine wiring harness.

19. Remove the oil filter.

20. Remove the oil level indicator tube.

21. Remove both camshaft position sensors.

22. Remove the crankshaft position sensor near the crankshaft damper.

23. Remove the ignition coils.

24. Remove both valve covers.

25. Remove the water pump pulley and the right side drive belt idler pulley.

26. Using a puller, remove the crankshaft pulley.

27. Remove the crankshaft oil seal.

28. Remove 4 engine front cover to oil pan bolts.

29. Remove the engine front cover.

30. Remove the timing chains. See the procedure under Timing Chain.

31. Remove the camshafts. See the procedure under Camshafts.

32. Remove the camshaft roller followers and hydraulic lash adjusters.

33. Install the cylinder head removal tool 303–572 to the left cylinder head.

34. Remove the left exhaust manifold.

35. Remove the ground strap from the left cylinder head.

36. Install the cylinder head removal tool 303–572 to the right cylinder head.

37. Remove the right exhaust manifold.

38. Remove the coolant tube from the right cylinder head.

39. Remove the cylinder heads.

To install:

40. Inspect the cylinder head for paying special attention to the areas around the oil pressure feed areas. Flatness should not exceed 0.002 inch (0.005mm) per running foot length.

➡**The cylinder head bolts are a torque to yield design and cannot be reused.**

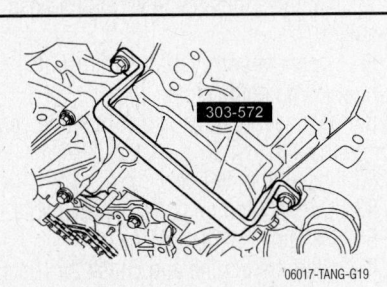

Fig. 82 Installing cylinder head removal tool to the left cylinder head—4.6L engine

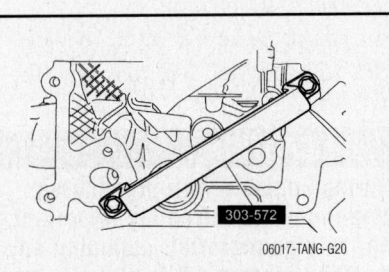

Fig. 83 Installing cylinder head removal tool to the right cylinder head—4.6L engine

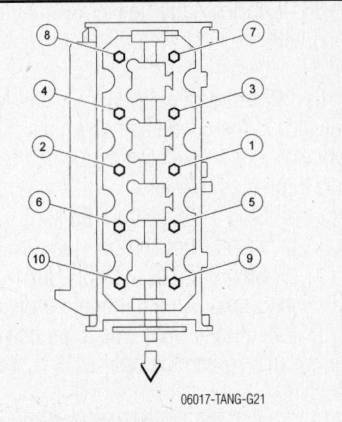

Fig. 84 Cylinder head bolt tightening sequence—4.6L engine

41. Install the cylinder head gasket and the cylinder head.

42. Tighten the cylinder head bolts in sequence as follows:

    a. Step 1: 30 ft. lbs. (40 Nm).

    b. Step 2: Plus 90 degrees.

    c. Step 3: Plus 90 degrees.

43. Remove the special tool from the left cylinder head.

44. Install the hydraulic lash adjusters. After lubricating them with clean engine oil.

45. Install the left exhaust manifold.

46. Install the ground strap to the left cylinder head.

47. Remove the special tool from the right cylinder head.

48. Install the right exhaust manifold.

49. Install new O-rings on the coolant tube and slide the tube into the cylinder block.

50. Install the coolant tube bolt and tighten to 89 inch lbs. (10 Nm).

51. Install the camshaft roller followers.

52. Install the camshafts. See the procedure under Camshafts.

53. Install the timing chains. See the procedure under Timing Chain.

54. Install the engine front cover.

55. Install 4 engine front cover to oil pan bolts and tighten in sequence to 15 ft. lbs. (20 Nm), plus an additional 60 degrees.

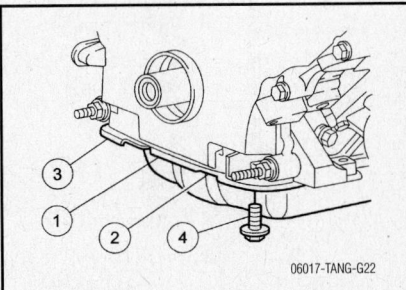

Fig. 85 Oil pan to front cover bolt tightening sequence—4.6L engine

56. Lubricate the new crankshaft oil seal with clean engine oil and install the seal.

57. Install gasket sealant to the Woodruff key slot in the crankshaft pulley and using tool 303–102 install the crankshaft pulley and tighten as follows:

   a. Step 1: 66 ft. lbs. (90 Nm).
   b. Step 2: Loosen one full turn.
   c. Step 3: 37 ft. lbs. (50 Nm).
   d. Step 4: An additional 90 degrees.

58. Install the right side drive belt idler pulley and tighten the bolt to 18 ft. lbs. (25 Nm).

59. Install the crankshaft position sensor and tighten to 89 inch lbs. (10 Nm).

60. Install both camshaft position sensors after lubricating the new O-ring seal with clean engine oil, and tighten to 89 inch lbs. (10 Nm).

61. Apply sealant to the 2 areas where the cylinder head meets the engine front cover on the right side.

62. Install the right side valve cover and tighten the bolts in sequence to 89 inch lbs. (10 Nm).

63. Apply sealant to the 2 areas where the cylinder head meets the engine front cover on the left side.

64. Install the left side valve cover and tighten the bolts in sequence to 89 inch lbs. (10 Nm).

65. Install the oil filter.

66. Install the ignition coils.

67. Install the engine wiring harness.

68. Connect the oil pressure sender connector.

69. Connect the left side heated oxygen sensor connector.

70. Connect the knock sensor connector retainer.

71. Install the oil level indicator tube.

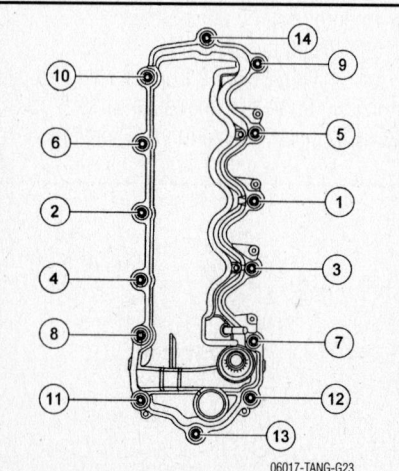

Fig. 86 Right side valve cover bolt tightening sequence—4.6L engine

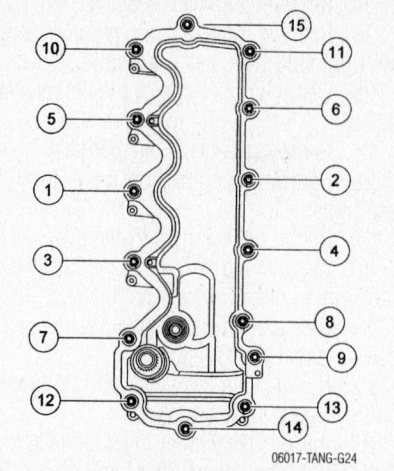

Fig. 87 Left side valve cover bolt tightening sequence—4.6L engine

72. Connect the left side heated oxygen sensor connector.

73. Connect the knock sensor connector retainer.

74. Connect the cylinder head temperature sensor connector, and jumper harness connector retainer.

75. Connect the engine wiring harness retainers from each valve cover.

76. Connect the ignition coil connectors.

77. Install the PCV tubes from both valve covers.

78. Connect the radio interference capacitor.

79. Connect the engine wiring harness retainers.

80. Connect both Variable Camshaft Timing (VCT) connectors.

81. Connect both camshaft position sensor connectors.

82. Install the engine.

83. Connect the negative battery cable.

84. Fill the cooling system.

85. Start the engine and check for leaks.

5.4L Engine

See Figures 88 through 90.

See Figures 91 through 93.

See Figures 94, 95, 96, 97, 98, 99, 100, 101, 102, 103, 104, 105, 106, 107, 108, and 109.

❋❋ CAUTION

During engine repair procedures, cleanliness is extremely important. Any foreign material, including any material created while cleaning gasket surfaces that enters the oil passages, coolant passages or the oil pan, can cause engine failure.

1. Drain the engine oil.

2. Drain the engine and supercharger cooling systems.

3. Disconnect the negative battery cable.

4. Disconnect the negative battery cable.

5. Remove the engine from the vehicle.

6. Remove the 8 bolts and the flywheel.

7. Remove the engine/transmission spacer plate.

8. Mount the engine on a suitable work stand.

9. Disconnect the coolant hose from the thermostat housing.

10. Remove the coolant tube bracket nut.

11. Disconnect the 2 coolant vent hoses from the intake manifold.

12. Disconnect the 2 upper radiator hoses from the intake manifold.

13. Disconnect the Engine Coolant Temperature (ECT) sensor electrical connector.

14. Remove the 2 nuts and the thermostat housing assembly.

15. Disconnect the coolant hose from the Charge Air Cooler (CAC).

16. Loosen the 4 water pump pulley bolts.

17. Rotate the accessory drive belt tensioner clockwise and remove the accessory drive belt.

18. Remove the bolt, supercharger (SC) drive belt tensioner and the SC drive belt.

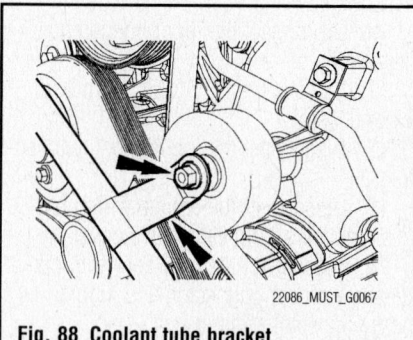

Fig. 88 Coolant tube bracket

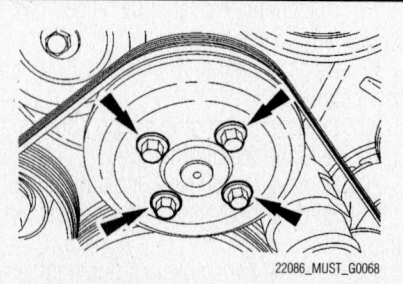

Fig. 89 Loosen, but do not remove water pump pulley bolts

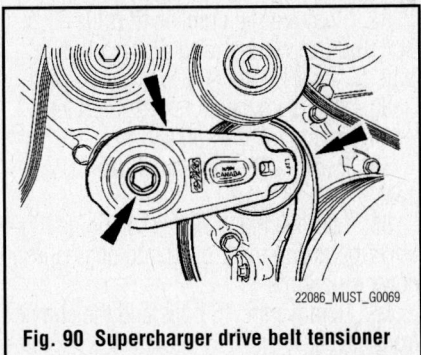

Fig. 90 Supercharger drive belt tensioner

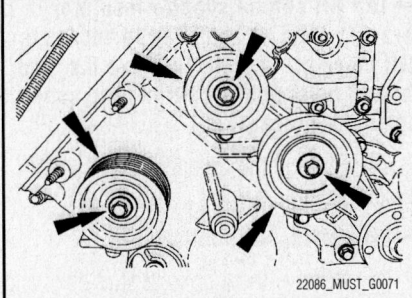

Fig. 92 SC drive belt idler pulleys

19. Remove the power steering tube bracket nut.

20. Disconnect the Power Steering Pressure (PSP) switch electrical connector.

21. Remove the power steering tube bracket bolt.

22. Remove the 2 power steering reservoir bracket bolts.

23. Remove the 3 bolts and the power steering pump and reservoir assembly.

24. Disconnect the generator electrical connector.

25. Detach the 2 wiring harness pin type retainers from the generator.

26. Remove the stud bolt, 2 bolts and the alternator.

27. Remove the bolt and the accessory drive belt tensioner.

28. Remove the stud bolt and the accessory drive belt idler pulley (smooth).

29. Remove the bolt and the accessory drive belt idler pulley (grooved).

30. Remove the 4 bolts and the water pump pulley.

31. Remove the 3 bolts and the 3 SC drive belt idler pulleys.

32. Disconnect the 2 Exhaust Gas Recirculation (EGR) tube fittings, and remove the EGR tube.

33. Disconnect and remove the crankcase ventilation tube.

34. Disconnect the Throttle Position (TP) sensor electrical connector.

35. Disconnect the Throttle Body (TB) control electrical connector.

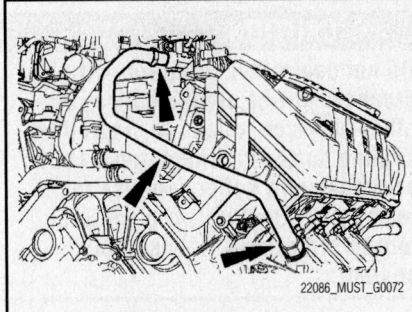

Fig. 93 EGR tube location

36. Remove the 4 bolts and the TB and spacer assembly, and discard the gasket.

37. Disconnect the Cylinder Head Temperature (CHT) sensor electrical connector.

38. Detach the wiring harness pin type retainer from the coolant tube assembly bracket.

39. Disconnect the LH Heated Oxygen Sensor (HO2S) electrical connector and pin type retainer.

40. Detach the wiring harness pin type retainer from the LH cylinder head.

41. Disconnect the bubbler tube from the SC.

42. Remove the 2 bolts and the wiring harness retaining bracket.

43. Detach the 3 wiring harness pin type retainers.

44. Disconnect the Positive Crankcase Ventilation (PCV) valve electrical connector.

45. Disconnect the 4 RH fuel injector electrical connectors.

46. Disconnect the fuel rail pressure and temperature sensor electrical connector.

47. Remove the nut and the RH radio interference capacitor.

48. Disconnect the EGR valve electrical connector.

49. Detach the wiring harness from the RH coil-on-plug cover stud bolt.

50. Detach the wiring harness retainers from the RH valve cover stud bolts.

51. Remove the bolt, stud bolt and the RH coil-on-plug cover.

52. Disconnect the 4 RH coil-on-plug electrical connectors.

53. Remove the 4 RH coil-on-plugs.

54. Disconnect the Engine Oil Pressure (EOP) sensor electrical connector.

55. Disconnect the Camshaft Position (CMP) sensor electrical connector.

56. Disconnect the Intake Air Temperature (IAT) sensor electrical connector.

57. Disconnect the 4 LH fuel injector electrical connectors.

58. Remove the nut and the LH radio interference capacitor.

59. Detach the wiring harness retainers from the LH valve cover stud bolts.

60. Remove the 2 bolts and the LH coil-on-plug cover.

61. Disconnect the 4 LH coil-on-plug electrical connectors.

62. Remove the 4 LH coil-on-plugs.

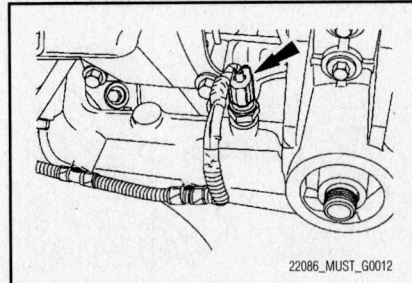

Fig. 95 Oil pressure (EOP) sensor electrical connector

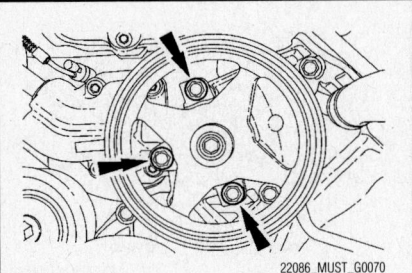

Fig. 91 Power steering pump and reservoir

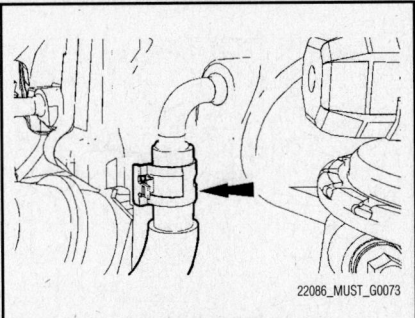

Fig. 94 Supercharger bubbler tube

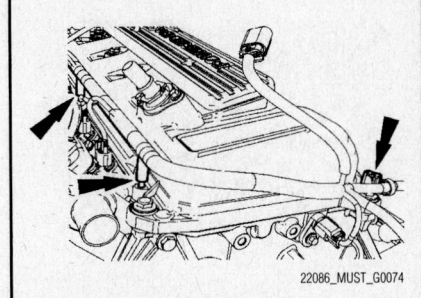

Fig. 96 Wiring harness retainers

63. Remove the wiring harness assembly from the engine.

64. Disconnect the intake manifold to coolant tube assembly hose.

65. Remove the 14 bolts and the intake manifold assembly.

66. Remove and discard the 2 intake manifold gaskets.

67. Remove the 3 coolant tube assembly bolts.

68. Remove the 6 bolts and the oil cooler.

69. Remove and discard the oil cooler gasket.

70. Remove the 8 bolts and the oil filter adapter.

71. Remove and discard the oil filter adapter gasket.

72. Remove the oil dipstick, the bolt, and the oil dipstick tube.

73. Remove and discard the oil dipstick tube O-ring seal.

➡The RH engine support insulator bracket must be removed to access the RH block drain plug. Remove the stud bolt, 3 bolts and the RH engine support insulator bracket.

74. Remove the LH and RH block drain plugs.

➡LH shown, RH similar.

75. Remove the 8 bolts, 2 stud bolts and the valve covers.

76. Remove and discard the gaskets.

✳✳ CAUTION

Do not use metal scrapers, wire brushes, power abrasive discs or other abrasive means to clean the sealing surfaces. These tools cause scratches and gouges, which make leak paths. Use a plastic scraping tool to remove all traces of old sealant.

77. Clean the mating surfaces with silicone gasket remover and metal surface prep. Follow the directions on the packaging.

78. Inspect the mating surfaces for damage.

79. Remove the bolt and the Crankshaft Position (CKP) sensor.

80. Remove the bolt and the CMP sensor.

81. Remove the 4 bolts and the water pump.

82. Remove the crankshaft pulley bolt and the washer, and discard the bolt.

83. Using a suitable bolt-grip puller, remove the crankshaft pulley.

84. Remove the crankshaft front seal.

85. Remove the 2 oil pan to engine front cover bolts and the 2 oil pan to engine front cover stud bolts.

86. Remove the 16 bolts and the engine front cover.

87. Remove and discard the engine front cover gaskets.

✳✳ CAUTION

Do not use metal scrapers, wire brushes, power abrasive discs or other abrasive means to clean the sealing surfaces. These tools cause scratches and gouges, which make leak paths. Use a plastic scraping

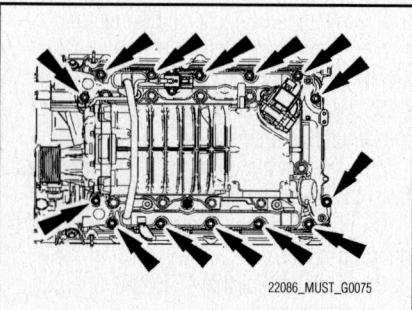

Fig. 97 Intake manifold bolt locations

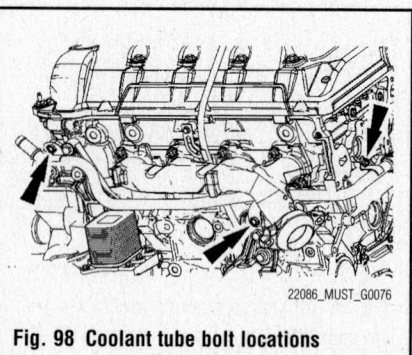

Fig. 98 Coolant tube bolt locations

Fig. 99 Oil filter adapter housing

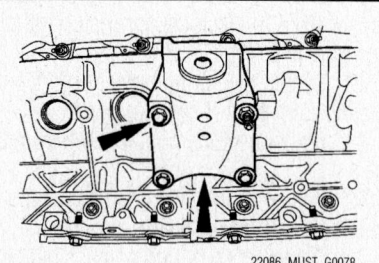

Fig. 100 RH engine support insulator bracket

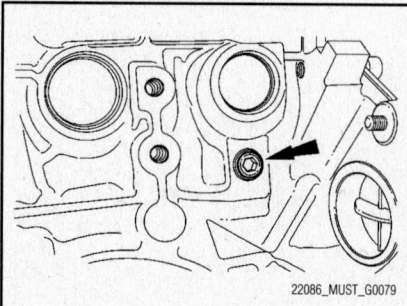

Fig. 101 LH engine block drain plug

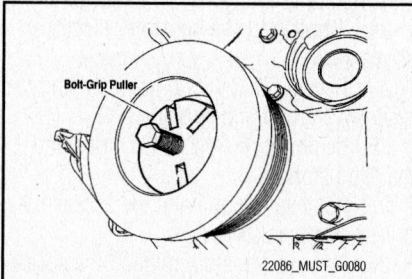

Fig. 102 Crankshaft pulley with bolt-grip puller installed

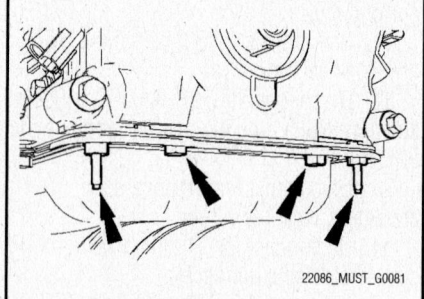

Fig. 103 Oil pan front cover bolts

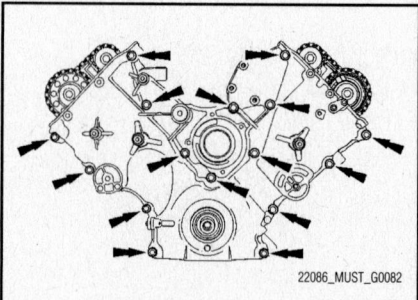

Fig. 104 Front engine cover bolt locations

tool to remove all traces of old sealant.

88. Clean the mating surfaces with silicone gasket remover and metal surface prep. Follow the directions on the packaging.

89. Inspect the mating surfaces for damage.

➡**RH shown, LH similar.**

90. Remove the 8 spark plugs.

❊❊ CAUTION

If the components are to be reinstalled, they must be installed in the same positions. Mark the components for installation into their original locations.

91. Using the special tool, compress the valve spring and remove the roller followers.

92. Repeat the previous step to remove

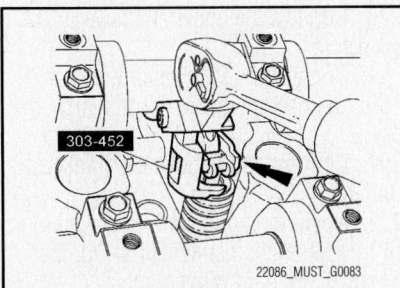

Fig. 105 Valve spring compressor—Ford part number 303–452

all the roller followers. Inspect roller followers for damage or excessive wear.

❊❊ CAUTION

If the components are to be reinstalled, they must be installed in the same positions. Mark the components for installation into their original locations.

93. Remove the hydraulic lash adjusters.

94. Inspect the hydraulic lash adjusters.

95. Remove the crankshaft sensor ring.

96. Remove the 2 bolts and the RH primary timing chain tensioner.

97. Remove the RH primary timing chain tensioner arm.

98. Remove the RH primary timing chain.

99. Remove the 2 bolts and the RH primary timing chain guide.

100. Remove the 2 bolts and the LH primary timing chain tensioner.

101. Remove the LH primary timing chain tensioner arm.

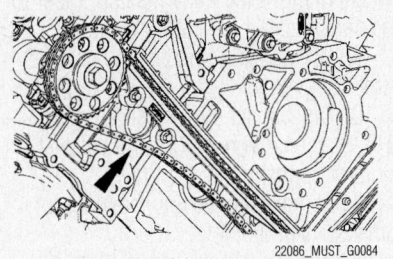

Fig. 106 RH primary timing chain; LH is similar

102. Remove the LH primary timing chain.

103. Remove the 2 bolts and the LH primary timing chain guide.

104. Remove the crankshaft sprocket.

105. Remove 8 nuts and the LH exhaust manifold.

106. Discard the nuts and gaskets.

107. Clean and inspect the LH exhaust manifold.

108. Remove 8 nuts and the RH exhaust manifold.

109. Discard the nuts and gaskets.

110. Clean and inspect the RH exhaust manifold.

111. Remove the 3 coolant tube assembly bolts.

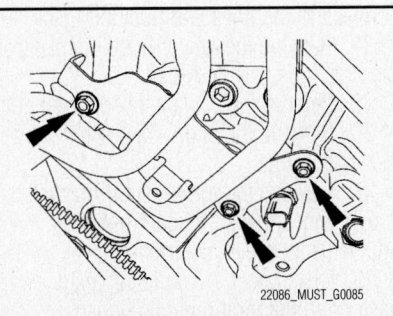

Fig. 107 Coolant tube assembly

❊❊ CAUTION

The cylinder head must be cool before removing it from the engine. Cylinder head warpage can result if a warm or hot cylinder head is removed.

❊❊ CAUTION

Place clean shop towels over exposed engine cavities. Carefully remove the towels so foreign material is not dropped into the engine.

❊❊ CAUTION

The cylinder head bolts must be discarded and new bolts must be

installed. They are tighten to yield designed and cannot be reused.

❊❊ CAUTION

Aluminum surfaces are soft and can be scratched easily. Never place the cylinder head gasket surface, unprotected, on a bench surface.

➡**LH shown, RH similar.**

112. Remove the 10 bolts and the cylinder head.

113. Discard the bolts.

114. Remove and discard the cylinder head gaskets.

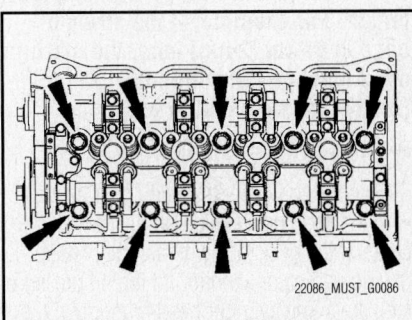

Fig. 108 Cylinder head bolt locations

❊❊ CAUTION

Do not use metal scrapers, wire brushes, power abrasive discs or other abrasive means to clean the sealing surfaces. These tools cause scratches and gouges that make leak paths. Use a plastic scraping tool to remove all traces of the head gasket.

❊❊ CAUTION

Observe all warnings or cautions and follow all application directions contained on the packaging of the silicone gasket remover and the metal surface prep.

➡**If there is no residual gasket material present, metal surface prep can be used to clean and prepare the surfaces.**

Clean the cylinder head to cylinder block mating surfaces of both the cylinder head and the cylinder block. Remove any large deposits of silicone or gasket material with a plastic scraper.

Apply silicone gasket remover, following package directions and allow it to set for several minutes.

Remove the silicone gasket remover with a plastic scraper. A second application of silicone gasket remover may be required if residual traces of silicone or gasket material remain.

Apply metal surface prep, following package directions, to remove any remaining traces of oil or coolant and to prepare the surfaces to bond with the new gasket. Do not attempt to make the metal shiny. Some staining of the metal surfaces is normal.

➡**Make sure all cylinder head surfaces are clear of any gasket material, RTV, oil and coolant. The cylinder head surface must be clean and dry before running a flatness check.**

➡**Use a straightedge that is calibrated by the manufacturer to be flat within 0.005 mm (0.0002 in) per running foot length. For example, if the straightedge is 61 cm (24 in) long, the machine edge must be flat within 0.010 mm (0.0004 in) from end to end.**

➡**LH shown, RH similar.**

Support the cylinder heads on a bench with the head gasket side up. Inspect all areas of the deck face with a straightedge, paying particular attention to the oil pressure feed area. The cylinder head must not have depressions deeper than 0.0254 mm (0.001 in) across a 38.1 mm (1.5 in) square area, or scratches more than 0.0254 mm (0.001 in).

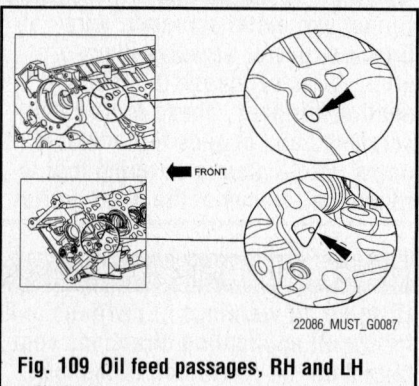

22086_MUST_G0087

Fig. 109 Oil feed passages, RH and LH cylinder heads

ENGINE ASSEMBLY

REMOVAL & INSTALLATION

4.0L Engine

1. Discharge the air conditioning system.
2. Drain the engine cooling system.
3. Drain the engine oil and remove the oil filter.
4. Disconnect the battery cables.
5. Relieve the fuel system pressure.
6. Remove the hood.
7. Remove the air cleaner assembly.

8. Remove the transmission. Refer to the transmission removal procedure.
9. On manual transmission models, remove the clutch.
10. Disconnect the Heated Oxygen (HO2S) sensor connectors and catalyst monitor connectors.
11. Remove 4 catalytic converter to exhaust manifold nuts.
12. Remove the ground strap.
13. Remove the radiator hoses.
14. Remove the power steering supply hose bracket.
15. Remove the power steering pressure tube bracket from the crossmember.
16. Remove the power steering pressure switch connector.
17. Remove the A/C pressure switch and compressor connectors.
18. Remove 2 wiring retainers from the accessory drive bracket.
19. Disconnect the fuel supply tube coupling.
20. Remove the accessory drive belt.
21. Remove the power steering pump pulley.
22. Remove the power steering pump and position aside.
23. Remove the accessory drive bracket, then remove A/C compressor without disconnecting the lines and position aside.
24. Remove the heater hose bracket from the right side valve cover.
25. Remove the coolant tube bracket bolts.
26. Remove the spark plug wires from the spark plugs.
27. Remove the ignition coil bracket.
28. Disconnect the spark plug with retainer from the intake manifold.
29. Disconnect the radio capacitor connector and the ignition coil connector.
30. Remove the upper and lower ignition coil bracket bolts, then remove the ignition coil and spark plug wires.
31. Disconnect and remove the crankcase vent tube.
32. Disconnect the brake booster vacuum hose.
33. Disconnect the PCV vapor tube.
34. Disconnect the upper and lower PCM connectors.
35. Disconnect all necessary wiring retainers.
36. Remove the power distribution box cover then remove the battery power terminal from the box.
37. Disconnect the upper and lower power distribution box covers and disconnect the 68–pin connector from the box.
38. Disconnect the ground cable from the right strut tower.

39. Attach lifting links to the cylinder head lifting eyes.
40. Remove the left and right engine mount nuts.
41. Attach an engine hoist and remove the engine from the vehicle.

To install:

42. Lower the engine into the vehicle.
43. Install left and right engine mount nuts and tighten the nuts to 37 ft. lbs. (50 Nm).
44. Connect the ground cable to the right strut tower and tighten to 89 inch lbs. (10 Nm).
45. Disconnect the upper and lower power distribution box covers and disconnect the 68–pin connector from the box.
46. Remove the power distribution box cover then remove the battery power terminal from the box.
47. Connect all necessary wiring retainers.
48. Connect the upper and lower PCM connectors.
49. Connect the PCV vapor tube.
50. Connect the brake booster vacuum hose.
51. Connect and remove the crankcase vent tube.
52. Install the upper and lower ignition coil bracket bolts, then install the ignition coil and spark plug wires.
53. Connect the radio capacitor connector and the ignition coil connector.
54. Connect the spark plug with retainer to the intake manifold.
55. Install the ignition coil bracket.
56. Install the coolant tube bracket bolts.
57. Install the heater hose bracket to the right side valve cover.
58. Install the accessory drive bracket and tighten the bolts to 35 ft. lbs. (47 Nm).
59. Install the A/C compressor.
60. Install the power steering pump and tighten the bolts to 18 ft. lbs. (25 Nm).
61. Install the power steering pump pulley and tighten the bolts to 18 ft. lbs. (25 Nm).
62. Install the accessory drive belt.
63. Connect the fuel supply tube coupling.
64. Install 2 wiring retainers from the accessory drive bracket.
65. Connect the A/C pressure switch and compressor connectors.
66. Connect the power steering pressure switch connector.
67. Install the power steering pressure tube bracket from the crossmember.
68. Install the power steering supply hose bracket.
69. Install the radiator hoses.

70. Install the ground strap.

71. Install 4 catalytic converter to exhaust manifold nuts and tighten to 30 ft. lbs. (40 Nm).

72. Connect the Heated Oxygen (HO2S) sensor connectors and catalyst monitor connectors.

73. On manual transmission models, install the clutch.

74. Install the transmission.

75. Install the air cleaner assembly.

76. Install hood.

✳✳ WARNING

Be sure to check engine to see that all electrical connectors, hoses and cables are properly connected and secure.

77. Install new oil filter and fill engine with fresh oil.

78. Connect the negative battery cable.

79. Fill the cooling system.

80. Recharge A/C system.

81. Start the engine and check for leaks.

4.6L Engine

1. Discharge the air conditioning system.

2. Drain the engine cooling system.

3. Drain the engine oil and remove the oil filter.

4. Relieve the fuel system pressure.

5. Disconnect the negative battery cable.

6. Remove the hood.

7. Remove the cowl vent screen.

8. Remove the air cleaner and outlet pipe.

9. Remove the engine coolant crossover.

10. Remove the degas bottle.

11. Remove the radiator sight shield.

12. Remove the accessory drive belt.

13. Disconnect the A/C pressure transducer connector.

14. Disconnect the coolant hose from the oil filter adapter.

15. Remove the degas hose from the cooling fan assembly.

16. Disconnect the lower radiator hose, then remove the thermostat housing and cooling hoses as an assembly.

17. Disconnect the oil temperature sensor connector.

18. Remove the ground wire.

19. Disconnect the pin retainer from the A/C compressor.

20. Disconnect the A/C clutch and crankshaft position sensor connectors.

21. Remove the A/C compressor without disconnecting the lines and position aside.

22. Remove the power steering pulley shield.

23. Disconnect the wiring harness retainer, then remove the power steering pump without disconnecting the lines, and position aside.

24. Install a lifting bracket to the threaded hole at the left side of the cylinder block.

25. Place a suitable jack to support the rear of the engine.

26. Install a 3 bar engine support to the lifting bracket on one side and the body structure near the suspension strut tower.

✳✳ WARNING

DO NOT place the 3 bar engine support leg on the vehicle fender.

27. On automatic transmission models, disconnect the transmission cooler tube and position aside.

28. Remove the transmission. Refer to the transmission procedure in this section.

29. On manual transmission models, remove the clutch.

30. Remove the catalytic converter flange nuts on both sides.

31. Disconnect the right side heated oxygen sensor connector.

32. Disconnect the catalyst monitor sensor connector on both sides.

33. Remove the engine to transmission spacer plate.

34. Disconnect the heater hoses.

35. Remove the ground strap from the cowl.

36. Disconnect the alternator jumper harness connector.

37. Remove the alternator harness and position aside.

38. Disconnect the upper and lower PCM connectors.

39. Disconnect all necessary wiring retainers.

40. Remove the power distribution box cover then remove the battery power terminal from the box.

41. Disconnect the upper and lower power distribution box covers and disconnect the 68–pin connector from the box.

42. Remove the nut, radio interference capacitor and J–bracket from the engine front cover stud bolt.

43. Remove both left and right engine insulator nuts.

44. Install an engine lifting bar on the engine.

45. Install an engine hoist to the lifting bar.

46. Remove the 3 bar support tool.

47. Remove the engine from the vehicle.

To install:

48. Install a lifting bracket to the threaded hole at the left side of the cylinder block.

49. Place a suitable jack to support the rear of the engine.

50. Lower the engine into the vehicle.

51. Install a 3 bar engine support to the lifting bracket on one side and the body structure near the suspension strut tower.

✳✳ WARNING

DO NOT place the 3 bar engine support leg on the vehicle fender.

52. Remove the engine hoist.

53. Install left and right engine support insulators nuts and tighten to 46 ft. lbs. (63 Nm).

54. Install the J–bracket nut and radio interference capacitor to the engine front cover stud bolt.

55. Connect the 68–pin connector and then the upper and lower power distribution box covers.

56. Install the battery power terminal and the power distribution box cover.

57. Connect all necessary wiring retainers.

58. Connect the upper and lower PCM connectors.

59. Install the alternator harness.

60. Connect the alternator jumper harness connector.

61. Install the ground strap from the cowl.

62. Connect the heater hoses.

63. Install the engine to transmission spacer plate.

64. Connect the catalyst monitor sensor connector on both sides.

65. Connect the right side heated oxygen sensor connector.

66. Install the catalytic converter flange nuts on both sides and tighten to 30 ft. lbs. (40 Nm).

67. On manual transmission models, install the clutch.

68. Install the transmission. Refer to the transmission procedure in this section.

69. On automatic transmission models, connect the transmission cooler tube.

70. Remove the 3 bar engine support, chain and lifting eye.

71. Install the power steering pump and tighten the bolts to 18 ft. lbs. (25 Nm).

72. Connect the power steering tube clip and the wiring harness retainer.

73. Install the power steering pulley shield.

74. Install the A/C compressor and tighten the nuts to 18 ft. lbs. (25 Nm).

75. Connect the A/C clutch and crankshaft position sensor connectors.

76. Connect the pin retainer to the A/C compressor.

77. Install the ground wire.

78. Connect the oil temperature sensor connector.

79. Install the thermostat housing, lower radiator hose and cooling hoses as an assembly.

80. Install the degas hose to the cooling fan assembly.

81. Connect the coolant hose to the oil filter adapter.

82. Connect the A/C pressure transducer connector.

83. Install the accessory drive belt.

84. Install the radiator sight shield.

85. Install the degas bottle.

86. Install the engine coolant crossover.

87. Install the air cleaner and outlet pipe.

88. Install the cowl vent screen.

89. Install the hood.

❊❊ WARNING

Be sure to check engine to see that all electrical connectors, hoses and cables are properly connected and secure.

90. Install a new oil filter and fill engine with fresh oil.

91. Fill the cooling system.

92. Connect the negative battery cable.

93. Recharge the air conditioning.

94. Start the engine and check for leaks.

5.4L Engine

See Figures 110 through 129.

❊❊ WARNING

Do not smoke or carry lighted tobacco or open flame of any type when working on or near any fuel related component. Highly flammable mixtures are always present and may be ignited, resulting in possible personal injury.

❊❊ WARNING

Fuel in the fuel system remains under high pressure even when the engine is not running. Before repairing or disconnecting any of the fuel system components,

the fuel system pressure must be relieved to prevent accidental spraying of fuel, causing personal injury or a fire hazard.

1. Before servicing the vehicle, refer to the precautions at the beginning of this section.

2. With the vehicle in NEUTRAL, position it on a hoist.

3. Release the 2 windshield washer hose retainers and the one hood insulation pin type retainer.

4. Position the hood insulation aside and disconnect the windshield washer hose.

5. Index mark the hood hinge location to aid in hood installation. Remove the 4 bolts and the hood.

6. Release the fuel system pressure.

7. Remove the 4 nuts and the strut tower cross brace.

8. Remove the battery and tray.

9. Remove the air cleaner and air cleaner outlet pipe.

10. Remove the 2 steering column dash boot nuts.

11. Remove the engine coolant degas bottle.

12. Remove the supercharger (SC) coolant degas bottle.

13. Disconnect the upper radiator hose from the thermostat housing.

14. Disconnect the cooling fan electrical connector.

15. Remove the 2 bolts and the cooling fan assembly.

16. Disconnect the coolant hose from the Charge Air Cooler (CAC).

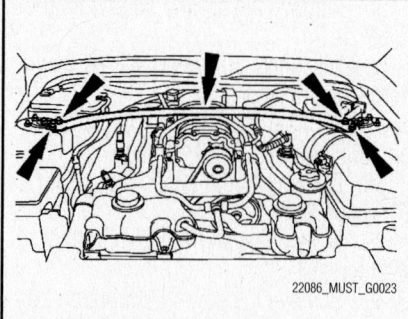

Fig. 110 Strut tower cross brace

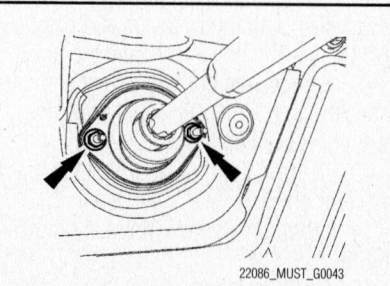

Fig. 111 Steering column dash boot removal

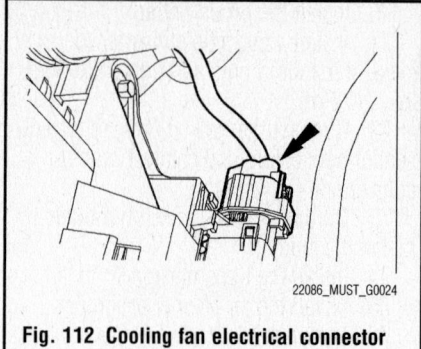

Fig. 112 Cooling fan electrical connector

17. Disconnect the coolant hose from the coolant tube assembly (above the generator).

18. Disconnect the coolant hose from the thermostat housing.

19. Disconnect the coolant hose from the coolant pump.

20. Disconnect the fuel supply tube.

21. Disconnect the Evaporative Emissions (EVAP) tube and brake booster vacuum supply tube from the Throttle Body (TB) spacer.

22. Disconnect the lower EVAP tube and electrical connector from the EVAP canister purge valve.

23. Remove the EVAP canister purge valve.

24. Disconnect the 2 heater hoses from the coolant tube assembly at the rear of the engine.

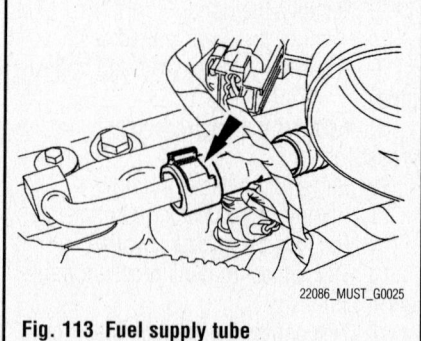

Fig. 113 Fuel supply tube

Fig. 114 Evap canister purge valve

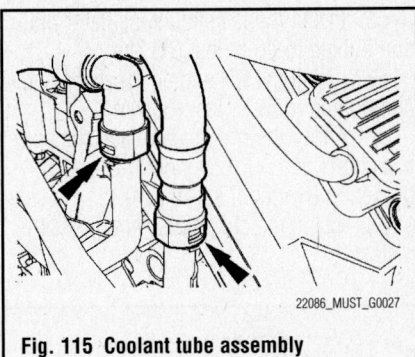
Fig. 115 Coolant tube assembly

25. Detach the pin type wire harness retainer from the cowl.

26. Detach the pin type wiring harness retainers.

27. Remove the power distribution box cover.

28. Detach the power distribution box upper housing from the lower housing, loosen the
bolt, then disconnect the 68–pin connector from the power distribution box.

29. Disconnect the jumper harness electrical connector.

30. Disconnect the upper and lower Powertrain Control Module (PCM) electrical connectors.

31. Disconnect the 16–pin electrical connector and detach the 2 wiring retainers.

32. Disconnect the hose from the power steering reservoir, and drain the power steering fluid into a suitable container.

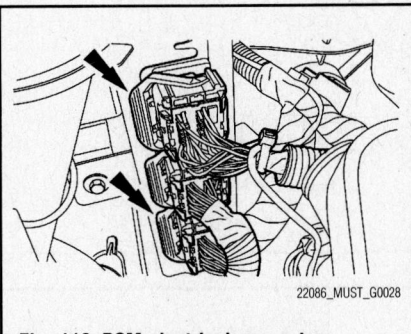
Fig. 116 PCM electrical connectors

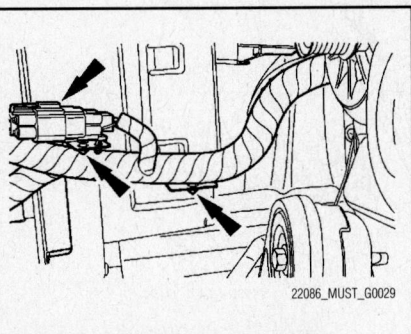
Fig. 117 16–pin electrical connector

33. Disconnect the A/C pressure transducer electrical connector.

34. Rotate the SC drive belt tensioner clockwise, and remove the drive belt from the SC drive pulley.

35. Disconnect the coolant hose from the oil cooler.

36. Disconnect the lower radiator hose from the radiator, and remove the lower radiator hose assembly from the vehicle.

37. Disconnect the Power Steering Pressure (PSP) tube fitting, and discard the Teflon® seal.

38. Disconnect the power steering return hose.

39. Remove the nut and disconnect the B+ wire from the generator.

40. Detach the wiring harness retainer from the oil pan stud bolt.

41. Remove the nut and wire harness bracket from the oil pan stud bolt.

42. Disconnect the Crankshaft Position (CKP) sensor electrical connector.

43. Detach the wire harness retainer from the A/C compressor stud bolt.

44. Disconnect the A/C compressor electrical connector.

45. Detach the wiring harness pin type retainer from the back of the A/C compressor.

46. Position the SC drive belt away from the A/C compressor and detach the 2 wiring

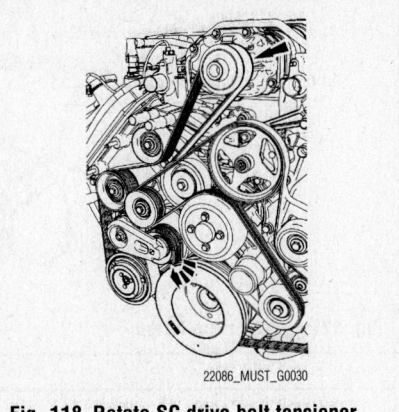
Fig. 118 Rotate SC drive belt tensioner as shown

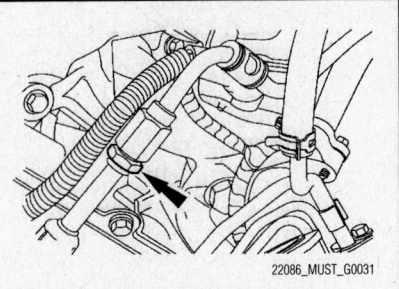
Fig. 119 Power steering pressure hose fitting

harness retainers from the A/C compressor stud bolts.

47. Remove the 3 stud bolts and position the A/C compressor aside.

48. Remove the nut and the ground wire from the RH engine support insulator bracket stud bolt.

49. Detach the 2 wiring harness pin type retainers from the oil pan.

50. Remove the starter solenoid terminal cover.

51. Remove the 2 nuts and disconnect the 2 wires from the starter solenoid.

52. Remove the 3 bolts and the starter.

53. Drain the engine oil.

54. Remove and discard the engine oil filter.

55. Install the drain plug, and tighten to 19 ft. lbs. (26 Nm)

56. Remove the upper bolt from the intermediate steering shaft.

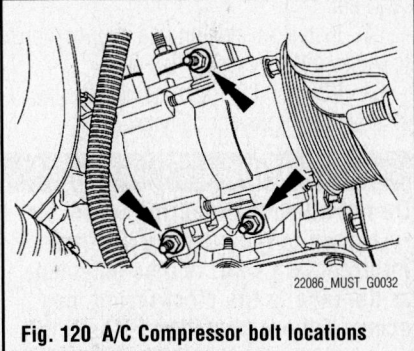
Fig. 120 A/C Compressor bolt locations

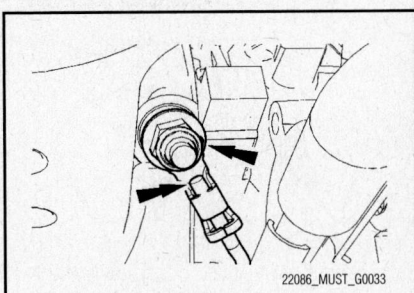
Fig. 121 Ground wire on RH engine support insulator

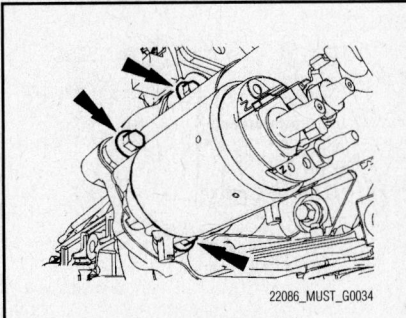
Fig. 122 Starter bolt locations

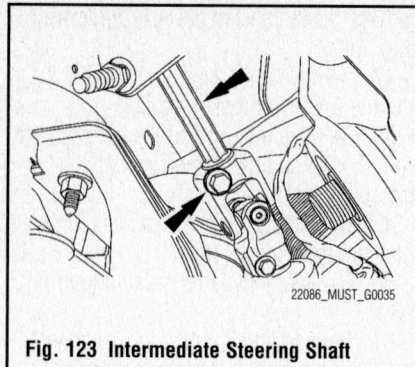

Fig. 123 Intermediate Steering Shaft

57. Remove the clutch disc and pressure plate.
58. Remove the bolt and the ground wire from the rear of the LH cylinder head.
59. Remove the RH engine support insulator nut.
60. Remove the LH engine support insulator nut.
61. Install suitable engine support hooks to the cylinder heads.
62. Position the intermediate steering shaft aside to prevent damage.

❋❋ CAUTION

Do not allow the steering wheel to rotate while the steering column intermediate shaft is disconnected, or damage to the clockspring may occur. If there is evidence that the

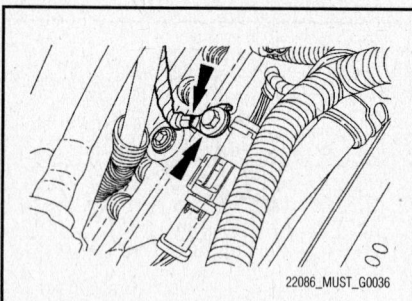

Fig. 124 Ground wire location on LH Cylinder Head

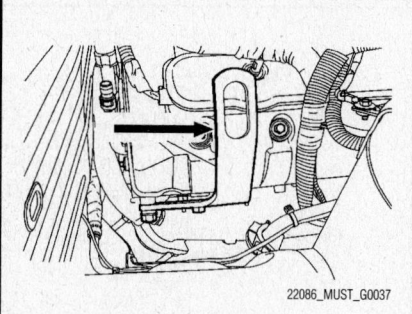

Fig. 125 Engine support hook

wheel has rotated, the clockspring must be removed, inspected, and centered.

63. Safely attach a suitable engine hoist, and remove the engine from the vehicle.

To install:

64. Using a suitable engine hoist, install the engine into the vehicle.

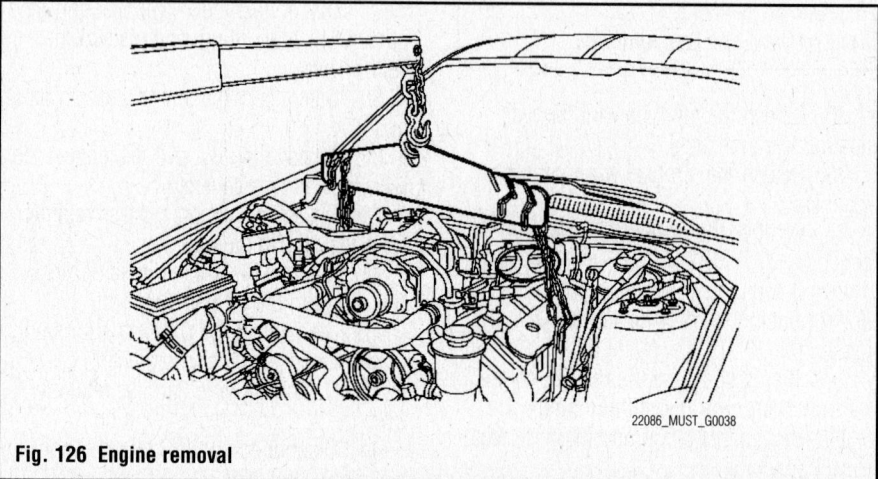

Fig. 126 Engine removal

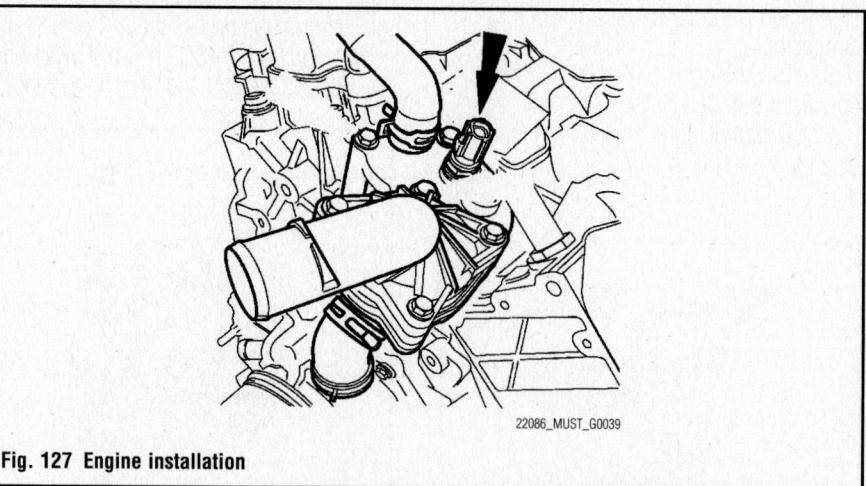

Fig. 127 Engine installation

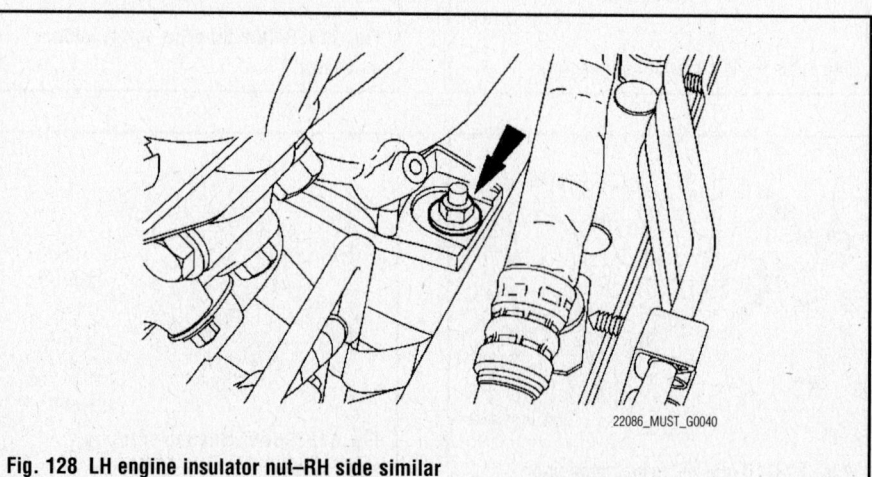

Fig. 128 LH engine insulator nut–RH side similar

65. Install the LH engine insulator nut, and tighten to 46 ft. lbs. (63 Nm).
66. Install the RH engine insulator nut, and tighten to 46 ft. lbs. (63 Nm).
67. Install the ground wire and the bolt to the rear of the LH cylinder head, and tighten to 89 inch lbs. (10 Nm).
68. Install the clutch disc and pressure plate.

Do not allow the steering wheel to rotate while the steering column intermediate shaft is disconnected, or damage to the clockspring may occur. If there is evidence that the wheel has rotated, the clockspring must be removed, inspected, and centered.

69. Install the intermediate steering shaft and the upper bolt, and tighten to 35 ft. lbs. (47 Nm).
70. Install a new engine oil filter.

For correct starter installation, the upper bolt must be tightened first.

➡Clean the starter motor mounting flange and mating surface of the starter motor to make sure there is a correct ground connection.

71. Install the starter and the 3 bolts finger tight.
72. Tighten the upper bolt to 18 ft. lbs (25 Nm).
73. Tighten the 2 lower bolts to 18 ft. lbs. (25 Nm).
74. Connect the 2 wires and install the 2 nuts on the starter solenoid.
75. Tighten the B+ terminal to 9 ft. lbs. (12 Nm).
76. Tighten the S terminal to 44 inch lbs. (5 Nm).
77. Install the starter solenoid terminal cover.
78. Attach the 2 wiring harness pin type retainers to the oil pan.
79. Install the ground wire and the nut to the RH engine insulator bracket stud bolt, and tighten to 18 ft. lbs. (25 Nm).
80. Install the A/C compressor and the 3 bolts, then tighten to 18 ft. lbs. (25 Nm).
81. Position the SC drive onto the A/C compressor and attach the 2 wiring harness retainers onto the A/C compressor stud bolts.

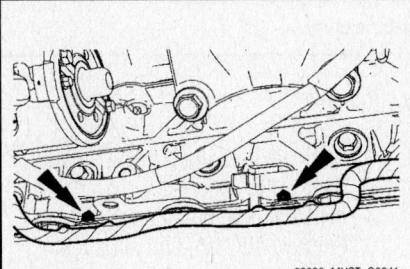

Fig. 129 Oil pan pin-type retainers

22086_MUST_G0041

82. Attach the wiring harness pin type retainer to the back of the A/C compressor.
83. Connect the A/C compressor electrical connector.
84. Attach the wire harness retainer to the A/C compressor stud bolt.
85. Connect the Crankshaft Position (CKP) sensor electrical connector.
86. Install the wire harness bracket to the oil pan stud bolt and install the nut, and tighten to 89 inch lbs. (10 Nm).
87. Attach the wiring harness retainer to the oil pan stud bolt.
88. Connect the B+ wire to the generator and install the nut, and tighten to 71 inch lbs (8 Nm).
89. Connect the power steering return hose.

➡A new Teflon® seal must be installed.

90. Using the special tool, install a new Teflon® seal on the Power Steering Pressure (PSP) tube fitting.
91. Connect the pressure PSP tube fitting, and tighten to 48 ft. lbs. (65 Nm).
92. Position the lower radiator hose assembly into the vehicle.
93. Connect the lower radiator hose to the radiator.
94. Connect the coolant hose to the oil cooler.
95. Rotate the supercharger (SC) drive belt tensioner clockwise and install the drive belt onto the SC drive pulley.
96. Connect the A/C pressure transducer electrical connector.
97. Connect the hose to the power steering reservoir.
98. Connect the 16–pin electrical connector and attach the 2 wiring retainers
99. Connect the upper and lower Powertrain Control Module (PCM) electrical connectors.
100. Connect the jumper harness electrical connector.
101. Connect the 68–pin connector to the power distribution box, and tighten bolts to 53 inch lbs. (6 Nm).
102. Attach the power distribution box upper housing to the lower housing.
103. Install the power distribution box cover.
104. Attach the 2 wiring harness pin type retainers.
105. Attach the pin type wire harness retainer to the cowl.
106. Connect the 2 heater hoses to the coolant tube assembly at the rear of the engine.
107. Install the Evaporative Emissions (EVAP) canister purge valve.

108. Connect the lower EVAP tube and electrical connector to the EVAP canister purge valve.
109. Connect the EVAP tube and brake booster vacuum supply tube to the Throttle Body (TB) spacer.
110. Connect the fuel supply tube.
111. Connect the coolant hose to the coolant pump.
112. Connect the coolant hose to the thermostat housing.
113. Connect the coolant hose to the coolant tube assembly (above the generator).
114. Connect the coolant hose from the Charge Air Cooler (CAC).
115. Install the cooling fan assembly and the 2 bolts, and then tighten to 80 inch lbs. (9 Nm).
116. Connect the cooling fan electrical connector.
117. Connect the upper radiator hose from the thermostat housing.
118. Install the SC coolant degas bottle.
119. Install the engine coolant degas bottle.
120. Install the 2 steering column dash boot nuts, and tighten to 80 inch lbs. (9 Nm).
121. Install the air cleaner and air cleaner outlet pipe.
122. Install the battery tray and battery.

➡Use the hood hinge location index marks made during removal to aid in hood installation.

123. Install the hood and 4 bolts, and tighten to 9 ft. lbs. (12 Nm).
124. Connect the windshield washer hose and position the hood insulation.
125. Install the hood insulation pin type retainer and attach the 2 windshield washer hose retainers.
126. Install the strut tower cross brace and the 4 nuts, and tighten to 26 ft. lbs. (35 Nm).
127. Fill the engine with clean engine oil.
128. Install the battery and tray.
129. Fill and bleed the engine cooling system.
130. Fill and bleed the SC cooling system.
131. Fill and bleed the power steering system.
132. Start the engine and check for fluid leaks.

EXHAUST MANIFOLD

REMOVAL & INSTALLATION

4.0L Engine

Left-Hand Manifold

See Figure 130.

1. Disconnect the negative battery cable.

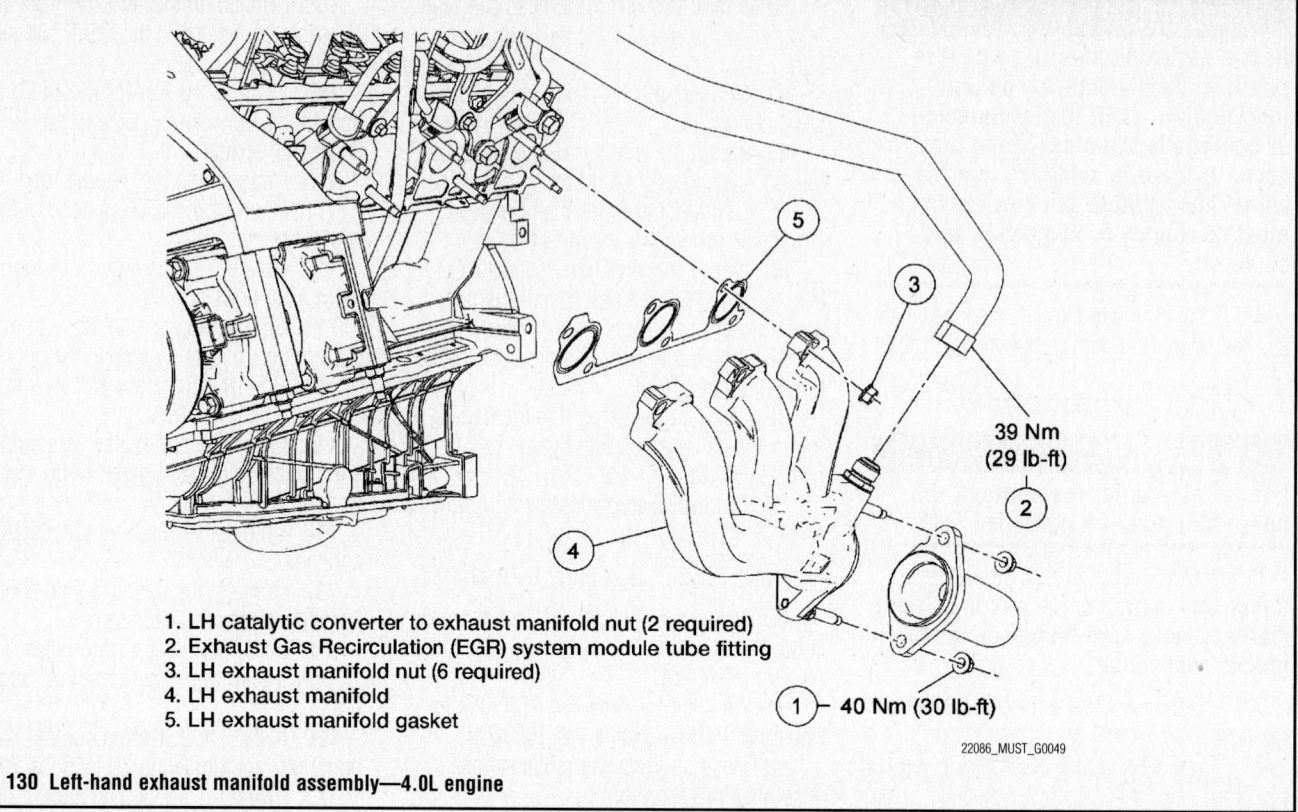

1. LH catalytic converter to exhaust manifold nut (2 required)
2. Exhaust Gas Recirculation (EGR) system module tube fitting
3. LH exhaust manifold nut (6 required)
4. LH exhaust manifold
5. LH exhaust manifold gasket

22086_MUST_G0049

Fig. 130 Left-hand exhaust manifold assembly—4.0L engine

2. Remove the catalytic converter to exhaust manifold nuts.

3. Disconnect the EGR tube from the manifold.

4. Remove the exhaust manifold nuts, and remove the exhaust manifold.

To install:

5. Install the exhaust manifold and nuts, then tighten the bolts to 17 ft. lbs. (23 Nm).

6. Connect the EGR tube to the manifold and tighten to 29 ft. lbs. (39 Nm).

7. Install the catalytic converter to exhaust manifold nuts and tighten to 30 ft. lbs. (40 Nm).

Right-Hand Manifold

See Figure 131.

1. Disconnect the negative battery cable.

2. Remove the catalytic converter to exhaust manifold nuts.

3. Remove the exhaust manifold nuts.

4. Remove the exhaust manifold.

To install:

5. Install the right exhaust manifold and nuts, then tighten the nuts to 17 ft. lbs. (23 Nm).

6. Install the catalytic converter to exhaust manifold nuts and tighten to 30 ft. lbs. (40 Nm).

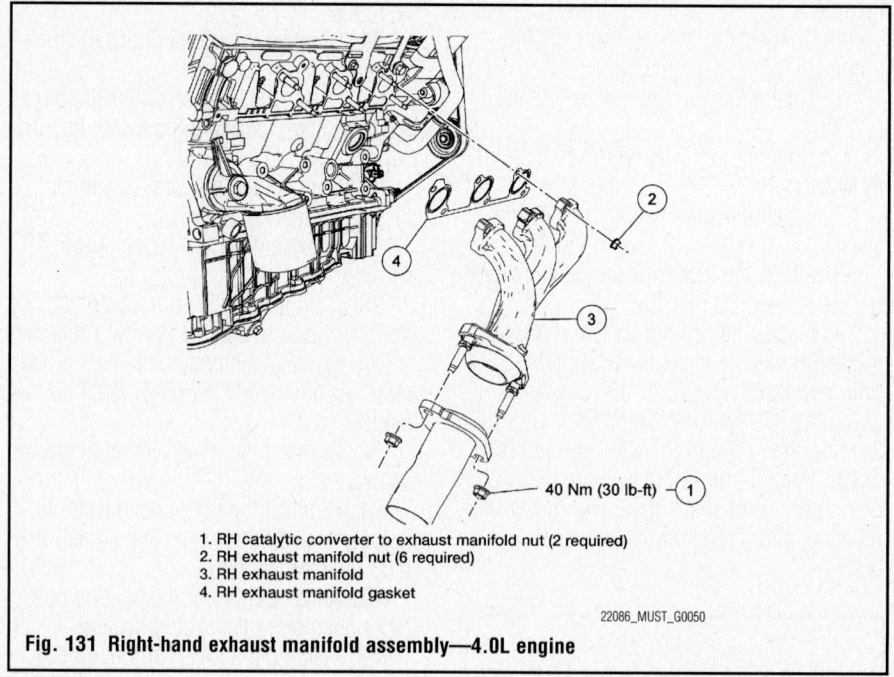

1. RH catalytic converter to exhaust manifold nut (2 required)
2. RH exhaust manifold nut (6 required)
3. RH exhaust manifold
4. RH exhaust manifold gasket

22086_MUST_G0050

Fig. 131 Right-hand exhaust manifold assembly—4.0L engine

4.6L Engine

See Figures 132 through 134.

1. Disconnect the negative battery cable.

2. Remove the air cleaner assembly.

3. Remove the throttle body.

4. Remove the starter.

5. On the both sides, remove the cat-alytic converter to exhaust manifold nuts.

6. Remove the radiator sight shield.

7. Remove the alternator.

8. Install an engine lifting device.

9. Remove the right and left engine support insulator nuts.

10. Raise the engine approximately 1–½ inches.

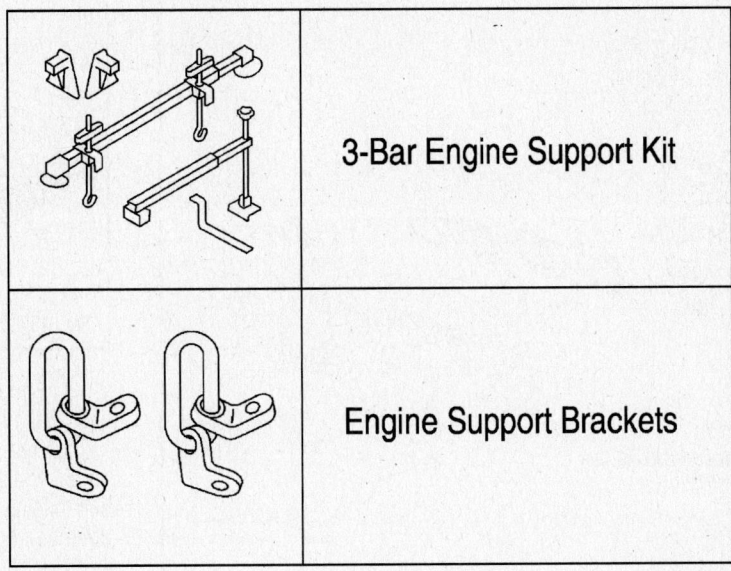

3-Bar Engine Support Kit

Engine Support Brackets

22086_MUST_G0051

Fig. 132 Special Service Tools—4.6L engine

11. Remove the steering column to steering gear pinch bolt.

12. On automatic transmission models, disconnect the transmission cooler tube bracket.

13. Remove the exhaust manifold(s).

To install:

14. Install the exhaust manifolds. Use new gaskets and tighten the nuts in sequence to 18 ft. lbs. (25 Nm).

15. On automatic transmission models, connect the transmission cooler tube bracket.

16. Install the steering column to steering gear pinch bolt and tighten to 18 ft. lbs. (25 Nm).

17. Lower the engine about 1–½ inches.

18. Install the right and left engine support insulator nuts and tighten to 46 ft. lbs. (63 Nm).

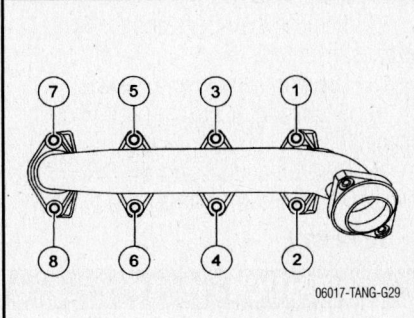

06017-TANG-G29

Fig. 133 Left exhaust manifold torque sequence—4.6L engine

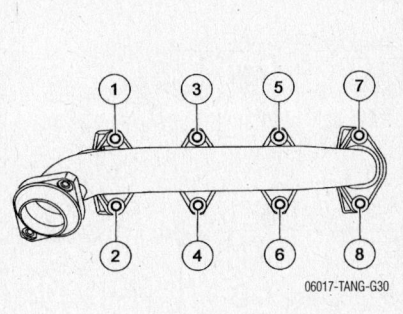

06017-TANG-G30

Fig. 134 Right exhaust manifold torque sequence—4.6L engine

19. Remove the engine lifting device.

20. Install the alternator.

21. Install the radiator sight shield.

22. On the both sides, install the catalytic converter to exhaust manifold nuts and tighten to 30 ft. lbs. (40 Nm).

23. Install the starter.

24. Install the throttle body.

25. Install the air cleaner assembly.

26. Connect the negative battery cable.

5.4L Engine

Left-Hand Manifold

See Figures 135 and 136.

1. With the vehicle in NEUTRAL, position it on a hoist.

2. Remove the Evaporative Emissions (EVAP) canister purge valve.

3. Remove the 2 dash boot nuts.

   a. To install, tighten to 80 inch lbs. (9 Nm).

4. Remove the catalytic converter.

5. Disconnect the LH Heated Oxygen Sensor (HO2S) electrical connector.

6. Remove and discard the engine oil filter.

7. Remove the upper bolt from the intermediate steering shaft and position the intermediate steering shaft aside.

✳✳ CAUTION

Do not allow the steering wheel to rotate while the steering column intermediate shaft is disconnected or damage to the clockspring can result. If there is evidence that the wheel has rotated, the clockspring must be removed and centered.

8. Remove the 8 nuts and the LH exhaust manifold.

9. Discard the nuts and gaskets.

10. Clean and inspect the LH exhaust manifold.

✳✳ CAUTION

Do not use metal scrapers, wire brushes, power abrasive discs or other abrasive means to clean the sealing surfaces. These tools cause scratches and gouges, which make leak paths. Use a plastic scraping tool to remove all traces of old sealant.

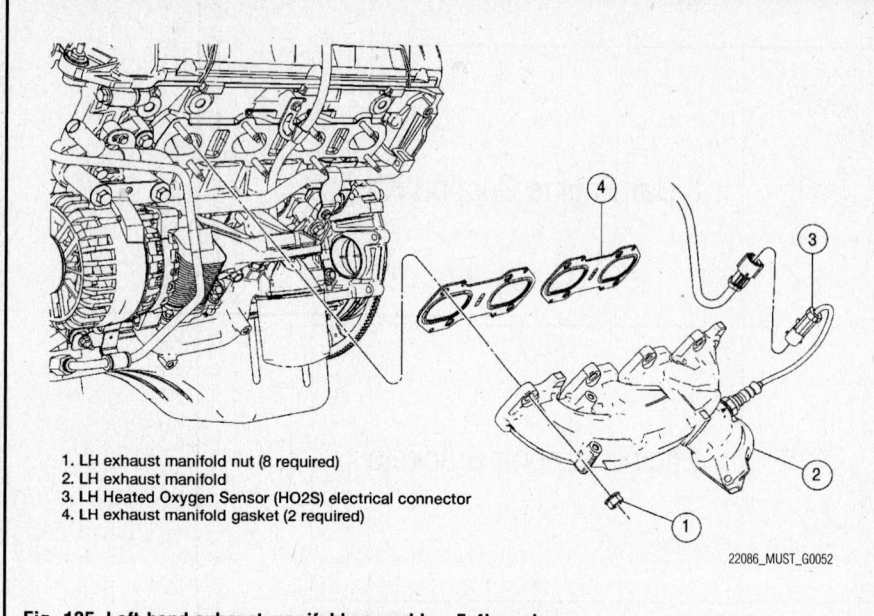

1. LH exhaust manifold nut (8 required)
2. LH exhaust manifold
3. LH Heated Oxygen Sensor (HO2S) electrical connector
4. LH exhaust manifold gasket (2 required)

22086_MUST_G0052

Fig. 135 Left-hand exhaust manifold assembly—5.4L engine

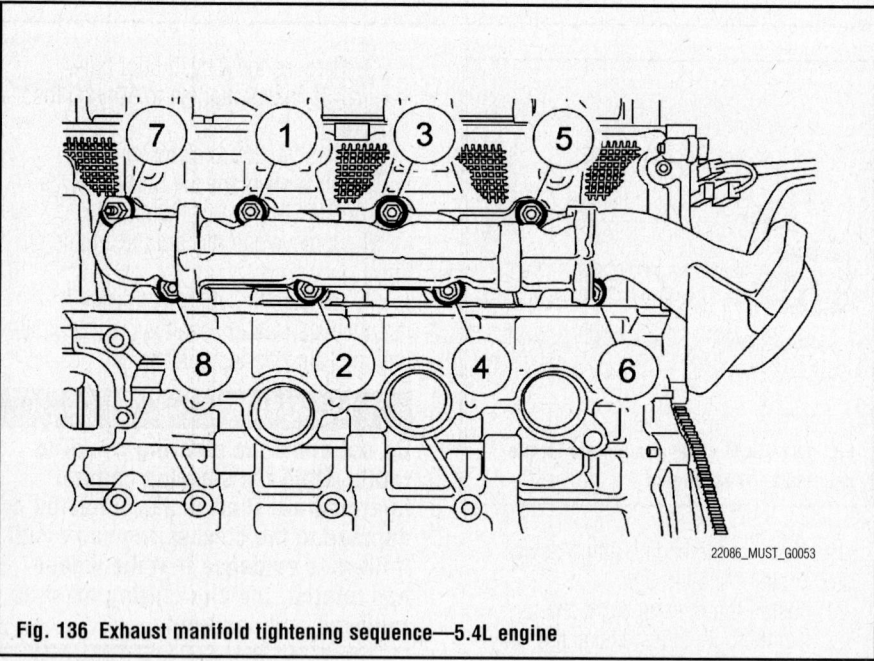

22086_MUST_G0053

Fig. 136 Exhaust manifold tightening sequence—5.4L engine

To install:

11. Clean the exhaust manifold mating surface of the cylinder head with metal surface prep. Follow the directions on the packaging.

12. Install new gaskets, the LH exhaust manifold and 8 new nuts.

13. Tighten in the sequence shown to 15 ft. lbs. (20 Nm).

14. Install a new engine oil filter.

15. Lubricate the oil filter gasket with clean engine oil and tighten until the seal makes contact.

16. Using an oil filter strap wrench, tighten the filter an additional 270 degrees.

17. Connect the LH HO2S electrical connector.

18. Install the catalytic converter.

19. Install the 2 dash boot nuts, and tighten to 80 inch lbs. (90 Nm).

20. Install the EVAP canister purge valve.

Right-Hand Manifold

See Figures 125, 132 and 137 through 139.

1. With the vehicle in NEUTRAL, position it on a hoist.

2. Remove the 4 nuts and the strut tower cross brace.

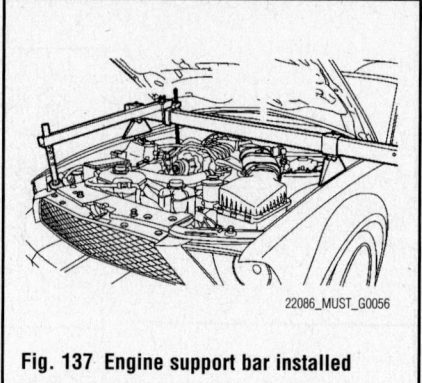

22086_MUST_G0056

Fig. 137 Engine support bar installed

3. Remove the Exhaust Gas Recirculation (EGR) tube.

4. Remove the catalytic converter.

5. Rotate the Supercharger (SC) drive belt tensioner clockwise and remove the drive belt from the SC drive pulley.

6. Install the special tool.

➡The heavy duty 3 bar support (303–F070) must be used with the draw screws from the light duty 3 bar support (303–F072). This will provide enough clearance between the supercharger (SC) and the 3 bar support, and enough clearance between the draw screw and the vehicle hood.

Install the special tools.

7. Remove the RH engine support insulator nut.

8. Install the engine support bar kit, and raise the RH side of the engine.

9. Remove the SC drive belt from the A/C compressor pulley.

10. Remove the wiring harness retainers from the A/C compressor stud bolts and position the wiring harness aside.

➡The A/C compressor stud bolts must be loosened to gain access to the RH exhaust manifold nuts.

11. Loosen the A/C compressor stud bolts 25 mm (0.98 in).

12. Remove the 8 nuts and the RH exhaust manifold.

13. Discard the nuts and gaskets.

14. Clean and inspect the RH exhaust manifold.

15. Remove and discard the 8 RH exhaust manifold-to-cylinder head studs.

To install:

❊❊ CAUTION

Do not use metal scrapers, wire brushes, power abrasive discs or other abrasive means to clean the sealing surfaces. These tools cause

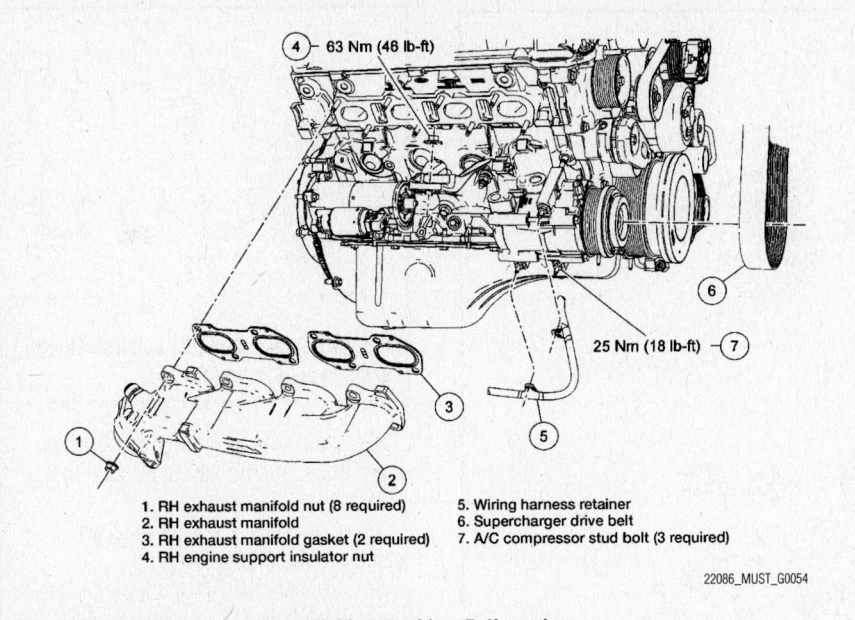

1. RH exhaust manifold nut (8 required)
2. RH exhaust manifold
3. RH exhaust manifold gasket (2 required)
4. RH engine support insulator nut
5. Wiring harness retainer
6. Supercharger drive belt
7. A/C compressor stud bolt (3 required)

22086_MUST_G0054

Fig. 138 Right-hand exhaust manifold assembly—5.4L engine

scratches and gouges, which make leak paths. Use a plastic scraping tool to remove all traces of old sealant.

16. Clean the exhaust manifold mating surface of the cylinder head with a suitable metal surface preparation solution.

17. Install the 8 new RH exhaust manifold to cylinder head studs.

   a. Tighten to 9 ft. lbs. (12 Nm).

18. Install new manifold gaskets, the RH exhaust manifold, and 8 new nuts.

   a. Tighten to 15 ft. lbs. (20 Nm) in the sequence shown.

19. Tighten the A/C compressor stud bolts to 18 ft. lbs. (25 Nm).

20. Install the wiring harness retainers onto the A/C compressor stud bolts.

21. Position the SC drive belt onto the A/C compressor pulley.

22. Using the special tools, lower the engine onto the engine support insulator.

23. Install the RH engine support insulator nut, and tighten to 46 ft. lbs. (63 Nm)

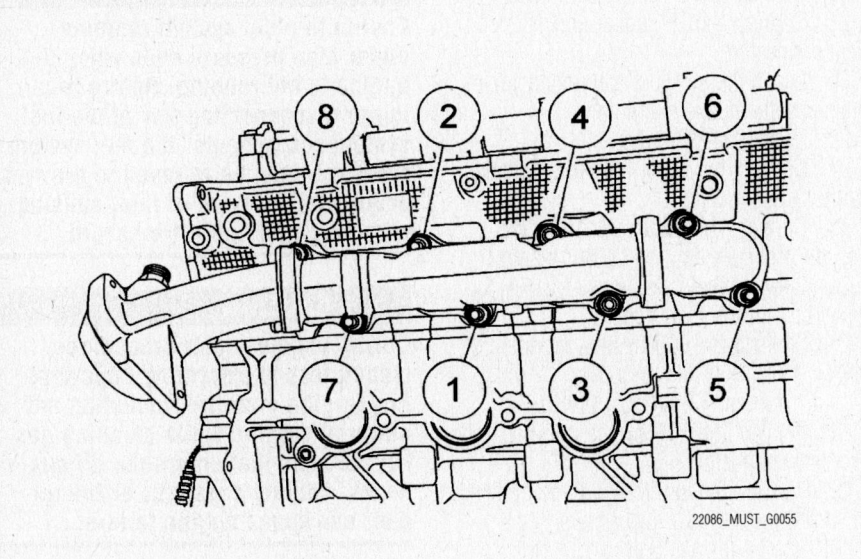

22086_MUST_G0055

Fig. 139 Exhaust manifold tightening sequence—5.4L engine

24. Rotate the SC drive belt tensioner clockwise and install the drive belt onto the SC drive pulley.

25. Install the catalytic converter.

26. Install the EGR tube.

27. Install the strut tower cross brace and the 4 nuts, and tighten to 26 ft. lbs. (35 Nm).

INTAKE MANIFOLD

REMOVAL & INSTALLATION

4.0L Engine

See Figures 140 and 141.

⁂ WARNING

Do not smoke or carry lighted tobacco or open flame of any type when working on or near any fuel related component. Highly flammable mixtures are always present and may be ignited, resulting in possible personal injury.

⁂ WARNING

Fuel in the fuel system remains under high pressure even when the engine is not running. Before repairing or disconnecting any of the fuel system components, the fuel system pressure must be relieved to prevent accidental spraying of fuel, causing personal injury or a fire hazard.

⁂ CAUTION

During engine repair procedures, cleanliness is extremely important. Any foreign material, including any material created while cleaning gasket surfaces that enters the oil passages, coolant passages or the oil pan, can cause engine failure.

⁂ CAUTION

During engine repair procedures, cleanliness is extremely important. Any foreign material, including any material created while cleaning gasket surfaces that enters the oil passages, coolant passages or the oil pan, can cause engine failure.

1. Disconnect the battery ground cable.

2. Remove the air cleaner outlet pipe.

3. Drain the cooling system.

4. Disconnect the RH spark plug wires from the ignition coil.

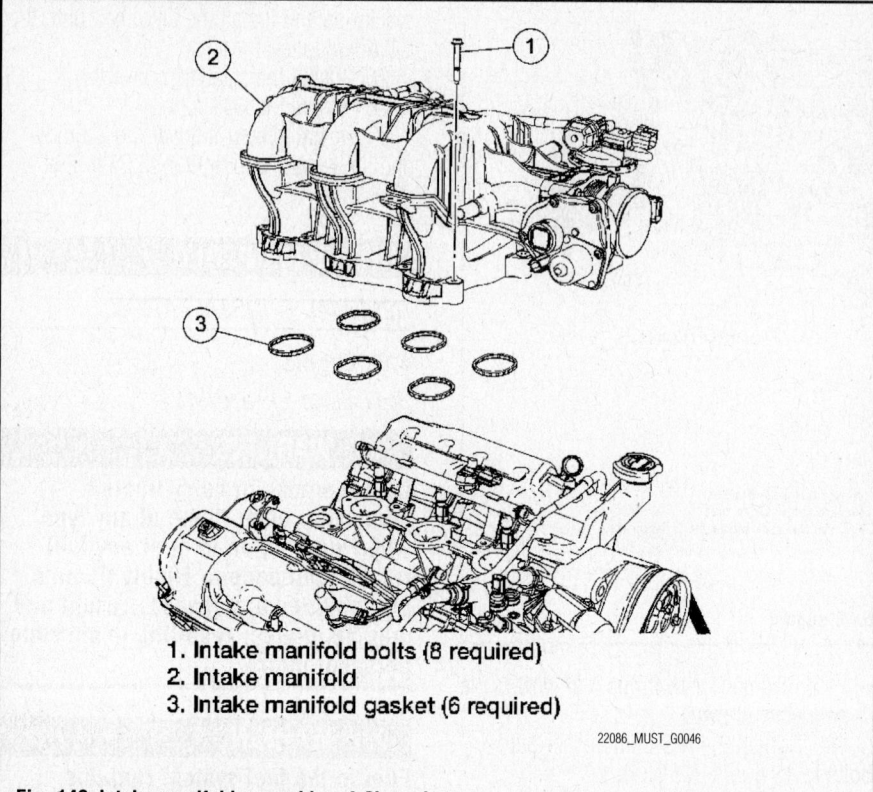

1. Intake manifold bolts (8 required)
2. Intake manifold
3. Intake manifold gasket (6 required)

22086_MUST_G0046

Fig. 140 Intake manifold assembly—4.0L engine

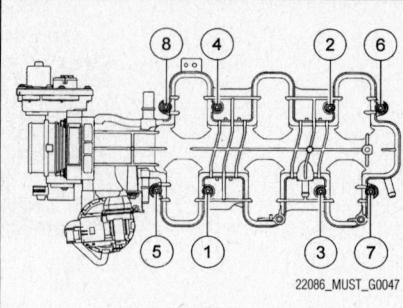

22086_MUST_G0047

Fig. 141 Intake manifold bolt tightening sequence—4.0L engine

5. Detach the RH spark plug wire retainer from the intake manifold.

6. Remove the 2 ignition coil bracket upper bolts.

7. Remove the 2 ignition coil lower bolts.

8. Position the ignition coil and bracket assembly aside.

9. Disconnect the Exhaust Gas Recirculation (EGR) system module electrical connector.

10. Disconnect the EGR system module tube from the EGR system module.

11. Disconnect the brake booster vacuum hose from the intake manifold.

12. Disconnect the vacuum tube from the fuel rail pressure and temperature sensor.

13. Disconnect the vapor tube from the intake manifold.

14. Remove the positive Crankcase Ventilation (PCV) tube.

15. Detach the Knock Sensor (KS) electrical connector retainer from the intake manifold.

16. Disconnect the Throttle Position (TP) sensor and Throttle Body (TB) electrical connectors.

17. Disconnect the 2 TB coolant hoses.

18. Remove the 8 bolts and the intake manifold.

To install:

→Clean and inspect all sealing surfaces. Inspect and install new gaskets as necessary.

19. Position the intake manifold and install the 8 bolts.
Tighten in the sequence shown to 89 inch lbs. (10Nm).

20. Connect the 2 TB coolant hoses.

21. Connect the TP sensor and TB electrical connectors.

22. Attach the KS electrical connector retainer to the intake manifold.

23. Install the PCV tube.

24. Connect the vapor tube to the intake manifold.

25. Connect the vacuum tube to the fuel rail pressure and temperature sensor.

26. Connect the brake booster vacuum hose to the intake manifold.

27. Connect the EGR system module tube to the EGR system module.
   a. Tighten to 29 ft. lbs. (39Nm).

28. Connect the EGR system module electrical connector.

29. Position the ignition coil and bracket assembly. Install the 2 lower bolts.

30. Tighten the M8 bolt to 18 ft. lbs. (24Nm).

31. Tighten the M12 bolt to 25 ft. lbs. (34Nm).

32. Install the 2 ignition coil bracket upper bolts, and tighten to 80 inch lbs. (9 Nm).

33. Attach the RH spark plug wire retainer to the intake manifold.

34. Connect the RH spark plug wires to the ignition coil.

35. Install the air cleaner outlet pipe.

36. Connect the battery ground cable.

37. Fill and bleed the cooling system.

4.6L Engine

See Figure 142.

>※※ **WARNING**

Do not smoke or carry lighted tobacco or open flame of any type when working on or near any fuel related component. Highly flammable mixtures are always present and may be ignited, resulting in possible personal injury.

>※※ **WARNING**

Fuel in the fuel system remains under high pressure even when the engine is not running. Before repairing or disconnecting any of the fuel system components, the fuel system pressure must be relieved to prevent accidental spraying of fuel, causing personal injury or a fire hazard.

>※※ **CAUTION**

During engine repair procedures, cleanliness is extremely important. Any foreign material, including any material created while cleaning gasket surfaces that enters the oil passages, coolant passages or the oil pan, can cause engine failure.

1. Relieve the fuel system pressure.
2. Disconnect the negative battery cable.

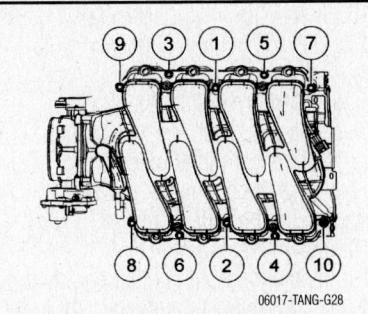

Fig. 142 Intake manifold tightening sequence—4.6L engine

3. Remove the air cleaner outlet pipe.
4. Remove the fuel rail and injectors.
5. Disconnect the EVAP tube and position aside.
6. Disconnect the PCV tube and position aside.
7. Disconnect the throttle body and throttle position sensor connectors.
8. Disconnect the charge motion control valve connector.
9. Disconnect the wiring harness from the manifold.
10. Disconnect the vacuum hose.
11. Remove the intake manifold.

To install:

12. Install the intake manifold. Use new gaskets and tighten the bolts, in sequence, to 89 inch lbs. (10 Nm).
13. Connect the vacuum hose.
14. Connect the wiring harness from the manifold.
15. Connect the charge motion control valve connector.
16. Connect the throttle body and throttle position sensor connectors.
17. Connect the PCV tube and position aside.
18. Connect the EVAP tube and position aside.
19. Install the fuel rail and injectors.
20. Install the air cleaner outlet pipe.
21. Connect the negative battery cable.
22. Start the engine and check for leaks.

5.4L Engine

See Figure 143.

⁂ **WARNING**

Do not smoke or carry lighted tobacco or open flame of any type when working on or near any fuel related component. Highly flammable mixtures are always present and may be ignited, resulting in possible personal injury.

⁂ **WARNING**

Fuel in the fuel system remains under high pressure even when the engine is not running. Before repairing or disconnecting any of the fuel system components, the fuel system pressure must be relieved to prevent accidental spraying of fuel, causing personal injury or a fire hazard.

⁂ **CAUTION**

During engine repair procedures, cleanliness is extremely important. Any foreign material, including any material created while cleaning gasket surfaces that enters the oil passages, coolant passages or the oil pan, can cause engine failure.

1. Release the fuel system pressure.
2. Drain the engine cooling system.
3. Drain the supercharger (SC) cooling system.
4. Remove the 4 nuts and the strut tower cross brace.
5. Remove the air cleaner outlet pipe.
6. Disconnect the battery ground cable.
7. Remove the Exhaust Gas Recirculation (EGR) tube.
8. Disconnect the Throttle Position (TP) sensor electrical connector.
9. Remove the 4 bolts and position the Throttle Body (TB) and spacer assembly aside.
10. Disconnect the Intake Air Temperature 2 (IAT2) sensor electrical connector.
11. Disconnect the fuel supply tube.
12. Disconnect the 4 LH fuel injector electrical connectors.
13. Remove the 2 bolts and the wiring harness retainer from the rear of the intake manifold.
14. Detach the 2 wiring harness pin type retainers from the rear of the intake manifold.
15. Disconnect the fuel rail pressure and temperature sensor electrical connector.
16. Disconnect the 4 RH fuel injector electrical connectors.
17. Disconnect the EGR system module electrical connector.
18. Disconnect the crankcase ventilation tube from the RH side of the SC.
19. Disconnect the SC bubbler hose from the rear of the SC.
20. Rotate the SC drive belt tensioner clockwise and remove the drive belt from the SC drive pulley.

21. Disconnect the 2 upper radiator hoses and the 2 coolant vent hoses from the intake manifold.
22. Disconnect the 2 coolant hoses from the Charge Air Cooler (CAC).
23. Disconnect the heater hose located below the rear of the intake manifold.
24. Remove the 14 bolts and the intake manifold assembly.
25. Discard the gaskets.

To install:

→ **Clean the sealing surfaces with metal surface prep. Follow the directions on the packaging. Inspect the mating surfaces.**

26. Using new intake manifold gaskets, position the intake manifold.
27. Install the 14 bolts.
28. Tighten in the sequence shown to 89 inch lbs. (10Nm).
29. Connect the heater hose located below the rear of the intake manifold.
30. Connect the 2 coolant hoses to the CAC.
31. Connect the 2 upper radiator hoses and the 2 coolant vent hoses to the intake manifold.
32. Rotate the SC drive belt tensioner clockwise and install the drive belt onto the SC drive pulley.
33. Connect the SC bubbler hose to the rear of the SC.
34. Connect the crankcase ventilation tube to the RH side of the SC.
35. Connect the EGR system module electrical connector.
36. Connect the 4 RH fuel injector electrical connectors.
37. Connect the fuel rail pressure and temperature sensor electrical connector.
38. Attach the 2 wiring harness pin type retainers to the rear of the intake manifold.
39. Install the wiring harness retainer and the 2 bolts onto the rear of the intake manifold.
40. Connect the 4 LH fuel injector electrical connectors.
41. Connect the fuel supply tube.
42. Connect the IAT2 sensor electrical connector.
43. Install the TB and spacer assembly and the 4 bolts.
   a. Tighten to 89 inch lbs. (10Nm).
44. Connect the TP sensor electrical connector.
45. Install the EGR tube.
46. Install the air cleaner outlet pipe.
47. Connect the battery ground cable.

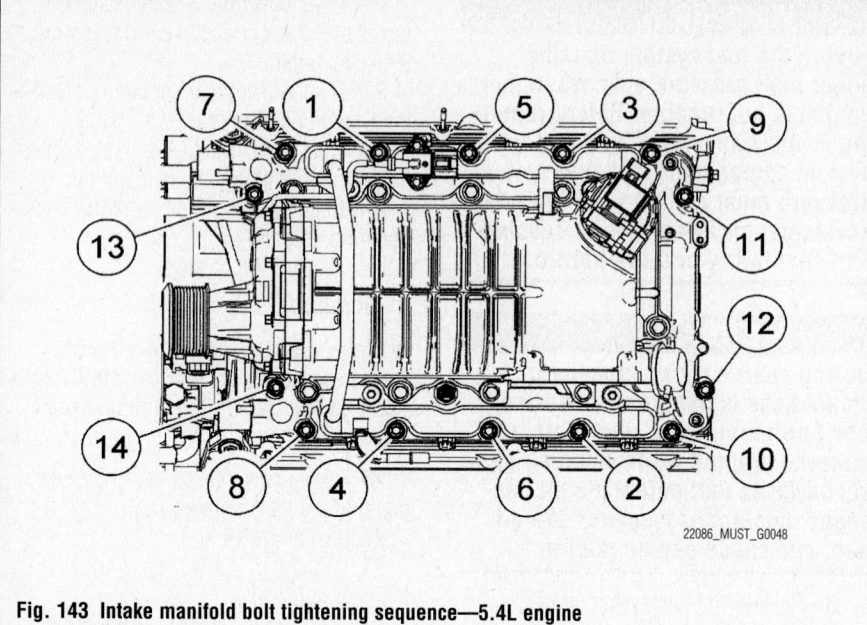

Fig. 143 Intake manifold bolt tightening sequence—5.4L engine

48. Install the strut tower cross brace and the 4 nuts.
   a. Tighten to 26 ft. lbs. (35Nm).
49. Fill and bleed the SC cooling system.
50. Fill and bleed the engine cooling system.

OIL PAN

REMOVAL & INSTALLATION

4.0L Engine

1. Drain the engine oil.
2. Disconnect the negative battery cable.
3. Raise the vehicle on a hoist.
4. Remove the oil pan.

To install:
5. Install a new gasket and the oil pan. Tighten the bolts to 80 inch lbs. (9 Nm).
6. Lower the vehicle.
7. Connect the negative battery cable.
8. Fill the engine with oil.
9. Run the engine and check for leaks.

4.6L Engine

See Figure 144.

1. Drain the engine oil.
2. Disconnect the negative battery cable.
3. Remove the air cleaner assembly.
4. Remove the throttle body.
5. Remove the radiator sight shield.
6. Remove the alternator.
7. Install an engine lifting device.
8. Remove the right and left engine support insulator nuts.
9. Raise the engine approximately 1 to 1½ inches.

10. Place a suitable jack under the subframe.
11. Remove the subframe bolts and nuts.
12. Lower the subframe about 2 inches.
13. Disconnect the oil temperature sensor connector.
14. Remove the oil pan.

To install:
15. Apply a bead of sealant at the crankshaft rear seal retainer plate to cylinder block surface and the engine front cover to cylinder block surface.

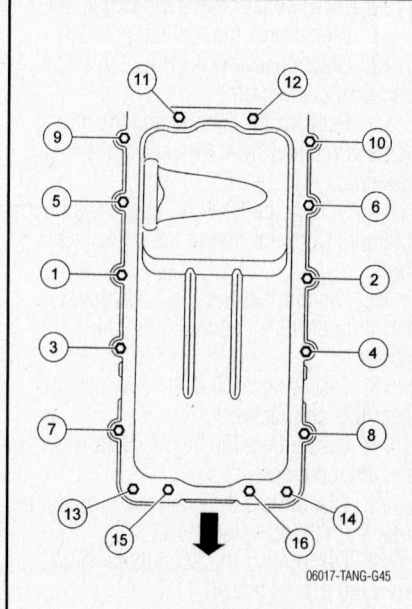

Fig. 144 Oil pan torque sequence—4.6L engines

16. Install the oil pan. Use a new gasket and tighten the bolts in sequence as follows:
   a. Step 1: 18 inch lbs. (2 Nm).
   b. Step 2: 15 ft. lbs. (20 Nm).
   c. Step 3: Plus 60 degrees.
17. Raise the subframe into position and tighten the bolts to 85 ft. lbs. (115 Nm).
18. Lower the engine.
19. Install the right and left engine support insulator nuts and tighten to 46 ft. lbs. (63 Nm).
20. Install an engine lifting device.
21. Install the alternator.
22. Install the radiator sight shield.
23. Install the throttle body.
24. Install the air cleaner assembly.
25. Connect the negative battery cable.
26. Fill the engine with oil.
27. Start the engine and check for leaks.

5.4L Engine

See Figures 111, 125 and 145 through 148.

1. Remove the 2 dash boot nuts.
2. Hold the steering wheel in the straight ahead position, using a suitable holding device.
3. Remove the 4 nuts and the strut tower cross brace.
4. Remove the battery and tray.
5. Remove the air cleaner outlet pipe.
6. Install the engine support hooks to each cylinder head.
7. Remove the RH and RH engine support insulator nuts.

➡The heavy duty 3 bar support (303–F070) must be used with the draw screws from the light duty 3 bar support (303–F072). This will provide enough clearance between the supercharger (SC) and the 3 bar support, and enough clearance between the draw screw and the vehicle hood. Install the special tools and raise the engine.

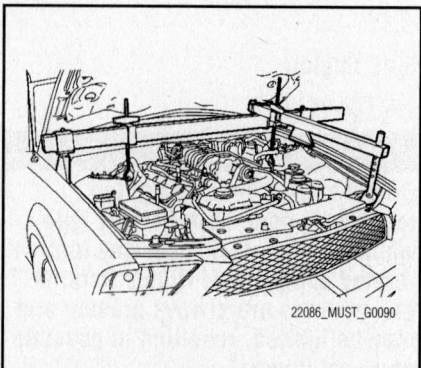

Fig. 145 3 bar engine support

8. Drain the engine oil.

9. Tighten the drain plug to 19 ft. lbs. (26 Nm).

10. Remove the 4 nuts and the sub-frame cross brace.

11. Position a suitable adjustable jack stand under the sub-frame.

☀☀ CAUTION

Do not allow the steering wheel to rotate while the steering column intermediate shaft is disconnected or damage to the clockspring can result. If there is evidence that the wheel has rotated, the clockspring must be removed and centered.

12. Remove the upper bolt from the intermediate steering shaft.

13. Mark the position of the 4 sub-frame nuts and 4 sub-frame bolts for referencing during assembly.

14. Remove the 4 sub-frame nuts and 4 sub-frame bolts.

15. Using the adjustable jack stand, lower the sub-frame 1.96 inch (50 mm).

16. Detach the 2 wiring harness retainers from the oil pan.

17. Detach the wiring harness retainer from the oil pan stud bolt.

18. Remove the nut and the wire harness retainer bracket from the oil pan stud bolt.

19. Remove the 14 bolts, 2 stud bolts, and the oil pan.

20. Discard the gasket.

To install:

☀☀ CAUTION

Do not use metal scrapers, wire brushes, power abrasive discs or other abrasive means to clean the sealing surfaces. These tools cause scratches and gouges, which make leak paths. Use a plastic scraping tool to remove all traces of old sealant.

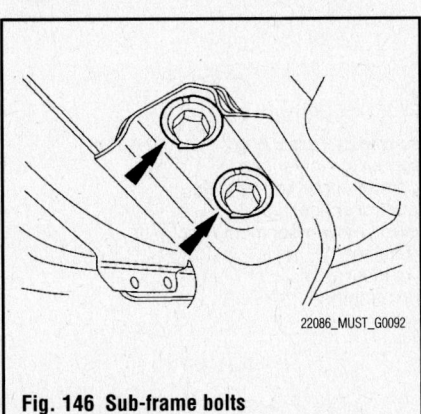

Fig. 146 Sub-frame bolts

➡Clean the sealing surfaces with silicone gasket remover and metal surface prep. Follow the directions on the packaging. Failure to follow this procedure can cause future oil leakage. Clean and inspect the mating surfaces of the engine block and oil pan.

☀☀ CAUTION

If not secured within 4 minutes, the sealant must be removed and the sealing area cleaned. To clean the sealing area, use silicone gasket remover and metal surface prep. Follow the directions on the packaging. Failure to follow this procedure can cause future oil leakage.

21. Apply silicone gasket and sealant at the engine front cover to cylinder block sealing joints and the crankshaft rear seal retainer plate-to-cylinder block sealing joints.

22. Using a new gasket, install the oil pan, 14 bolts and 2 stud bolts.

23. Tighten in the sequence shown to 18 ft. lbs. (25 Nm).

24. Install the wire harness retainer bracket on the oil pan stud bolt and install the nut, and tighten to 89 inch lbs. (10 Nm).

25. Attach the wiring harness retainer to the oil pan stud bolt.

26. Attach the 2 wiring harness retainers to the oil pan.

27. Using the adjustable jack stand, raise the sub-frame.

28. Install the steering intermediate shaft into the steering coupler.

☀☀ CAUTION

Do not allow the steering wheel to rotate while the steering column intermediate shaft is disconnected or damage to the clockspring can result. If there is evidence that the wheel has rotated, the clockspring must be removed and centered.

29. Position the intermediate steering shaft and install the upper bolt, and tighten to 35 ft. lbs. (47 Nm).

➡Do not tighten the sub-frame nuts and bolts at this time.

30. Install the 4 sub-frame nuts and 4 sub-frame bolts.

31. Align the sub-frame nuts and bolts with the reference marks made during removal.

32. Tighten the nuts to 85 ft. lbs. (115 Nm).

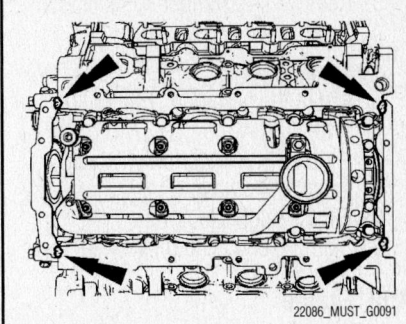

Fig. 147 Retainer plate–to–cylinder block sealing joints

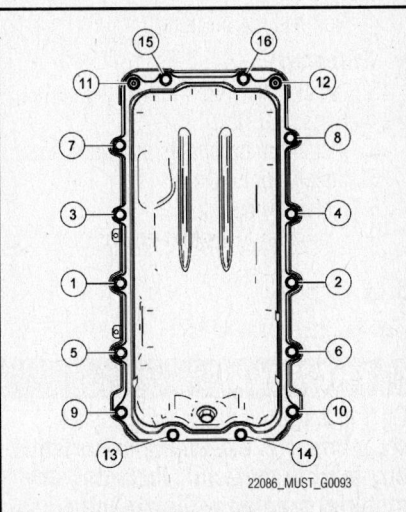

Fig. 148 Oil pan bolt tightening sequence

33. Tighten the bolts to 85 ft. lbs. (115 Nm).

34. Install the sub-frame cross brace and the 4 nuts, and tighten to 35 ft. lbs. (48 Nm).

35. Carefully lower the engine onto the engine support insulators.

36. Install the RH and RH engine support insulator nuts, and tighten to 46 ft. lbs. (63 Nm).

37. Install the air cleaner outlet pipe.

38. Install the battery and tray.

39. Install the strut tower cross brace and the 4 nuts, and tighten to 26 ft. lbs. (35 Nm).

40. Fill the engine with clean engine oil.

41. Install the dash boot and the 2 nuts, and tighten to 80 inch lbs. (9 Nm).

42. Start the engine, and verify that there are no oil leaks.

OIL PUMP

REMOVAL & INSTALLATION

4.0L Engine

1. Drain the engine oil.
2. Remove the oil pan.

3. Remove the cylinder block cradle.
4. Remove oil pump.

To install:

5. Install the oil pump. Tighten the bolts to 15 ft. lbs. (20 Nm).
6. Install the cylinder block cradle.
7. Install the oil pan.
8. Fill the engine with oil.
9. Start the engine and check for leaks.

4.6L Engine

1. Remove the oil pan.
2. Remove the front cover.
3. Remove the timing chains and sprockets.
4. Remove the oil pump.

To install:

5. Install oil pump. Tighten the bolts to 79 inch lbs. (10 Nm).
6. Install timing chains and sprockets.
7. Install front cover.
8. Install oil pan.
9. Check for leaks and proper operation.

5.4L Engine

See Figures 149 and 150.

> ❊❊ **CAUTION**
>
> **During engine repair procedures, cleanliness is extremely important. Any foreign material, including any material created while cleaning gasket surfaces that enters the oil passages, coolant passages or the oil pan, can cause engine failure.**

1. With the vehicle in NEUTRAL, position it on a hoist.
2. Remove the timing drive components.
3. Remove the oil pump screen and pickup tube.
4. Remove the 3 bolts and the oil pump.

> ❊❊ **CAUTION**
>
> **Do not use metal scrapers, wire brushes, power abrasive discs or**

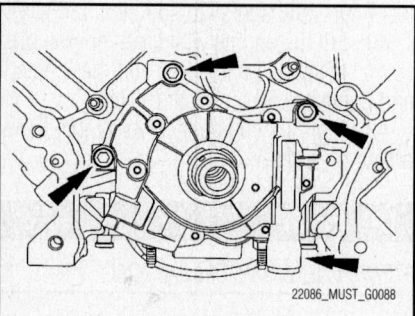

Fig. 149 Oil pump bolt locations—5.4L engine

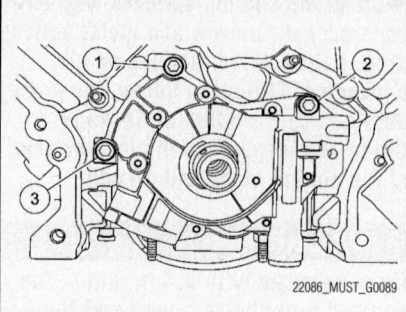

Fig. 150 Oil pump bolt tightening sequence—5.4L engine

other abrasive means to clean the sealing surfaces. These tools cause scratches and gouges, which make leak paths.**

5. Clean the sealing surfaces with metal surface prep. Follow the directions on the packaging.
6. Inspect the mating surfaces for damage or wear.
7. Install the oil pump and 3 bolts.
8. Tighten the bolts in the sequence shown to 89 inch lbs. (10 Nm).
9. Install the oil pump screen and pickup tube.
10. Install the timing drive components.

PISTON AND RING

POSITIONING

See Figures 151 and 152.

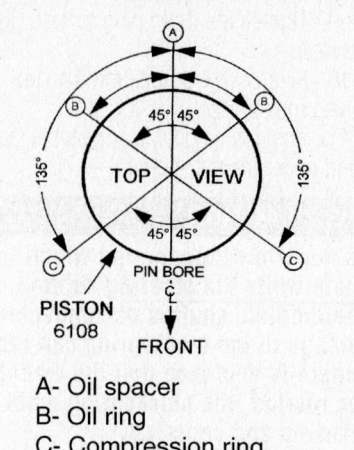

A- Oil spacer
B- Oil ring
C- Compression ring

Fig. 152 Piston ring positioning—All engines

REAR MAIN SEAL

REMOVAL & INSTALLATION

4.0L Engine

1. Disconnect the negative battery cable.
2. Remove transmission.
3. Remove clutch pressure plate and disc, if equipped.
4. Remove flywheel.
5. Remove engine rear plate, if equipped.
6. Remove rear main seal. Use Crankshaft Rear Seal Remover T92C–6700–CH.

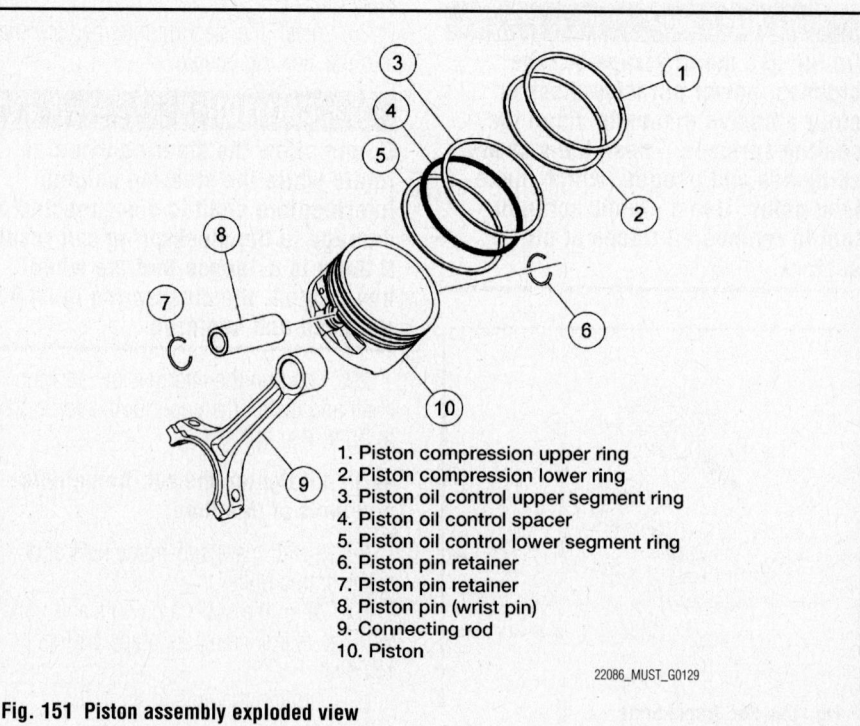

1. Piston compression upper ring
2. Piston compression lower ring
3. Piston oil control upper segment ring
4. Piston oil control spacer
5. Piston oil control lower segment ring
6. Piston pin retainer
7. Piston pin retainer
8. Piston pin (wrist pin)
9. Connecting rod
10. Piston

Fig. 151 Piston assembly exploded view

To install:

7. Place clean engine oil around the seal and install the seal. Use Rear Crankshaft Seal Installer 303–S524.

8. Install engine rear plate, if equipped.

9. Install flywheel.

10. Install clutch pressure plate and disc, if equipped.

11. Install transmission.

12. Connect the negative battery cable.

4.6L Engine

See Figure 153.

1. Disconnect the negative battery cable.

2. Remove transmission.

3. Remove clutch pressure plate and disc, if equipped.

4. Remove flywheel.

5. Remove the spacer plate.

6. Remove the oil slinger. Use Rear Crankshaft Oil Slinger Remover 303–514.

7. Remove rear oil seal.

8. Remove the seal retainer plate.

To install:

9. Apply sealer around the seal retainer plate on Essex built engines, or to the plate mating surface on the block on Romeo built engines.

10. Install the rear oil seal retainer. Tighten the bolts in sequence to 89 inch lbs. (10 Nm).

11. Install rear oil seal. Use Rear Crankshaft Seal Replacer 303–516 and 303–518.

12. Install oil slinger.

13. Install flywheel.

14. Install clutch pressure plate and disc, if equipped.

15. Install transmission.

16. Connect the negative battery cable.

17. Run the engine and check for leaks.

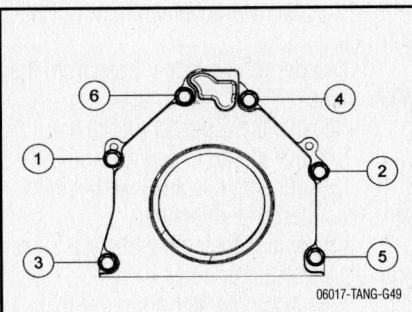

Fig. 153 Oil seal retainer torque sequence—4.6L engines

5.4L Engine

See Figures 154 through 156.

1. Disconnect the negative battery cable.

2. Remove transmission.

3. Remove clutch pressure plate and disc.

4. Remove flywheel.

5. Using the special tools, remove the crankshaft rear seal oil slinger.

6. Using the special tools, remove the crankshaft rear seal.

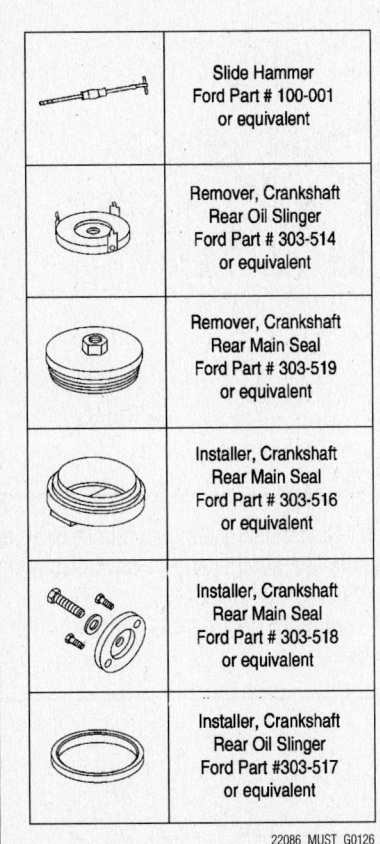

	Slide Hammer Ford Part # 100-001 or equivalent
	Remover, Crankshaft Rear Oil Slinger Ford Part # 303-514 or equivalent
	Remover, Crankshaft Rear Main Seal Ford Part # 303-519 or equivalent
	Installer, Crankshaft Rear Main Seal Ford Part # 303-516 or equivalent
	Installer, Crankshaft Rear Main Seal Ford Part # 303-518 or equivalent
	Installer, Crankshaft Rear Oil Slinger Ford Part #303-517 or equivalent

Fig. 154 Special Service Tools

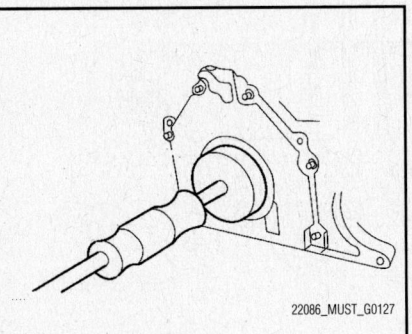

Fig. 155 Removal tools installed

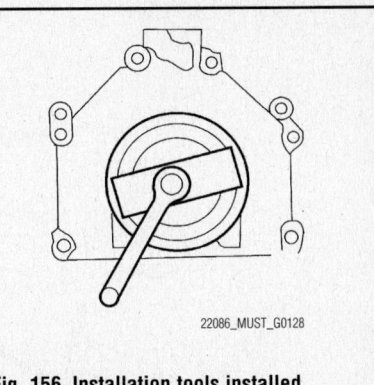

Fig. 156 Installation tools installed

To install:

➡ **Lubricate the inner lip of the crankshaft rear seal with clean engine oil.**

7. Using the special tools, install the crankshaft rear seal.

8. Using the special tools, install the crankshaft rear oil slinger.

9. Install flywheel, clutch assembly, and transmission

10. Start the vehicle, and verify that there are no fluid leaks.

SUPERCHARGER

REMOVAL & INSTALLATION

See Figures 157 through 159.

1. Release the fuel system pressure.

2. Disconnect the battery ground cable.

3. Remove the 4 nuts and the strut tower cross brace.

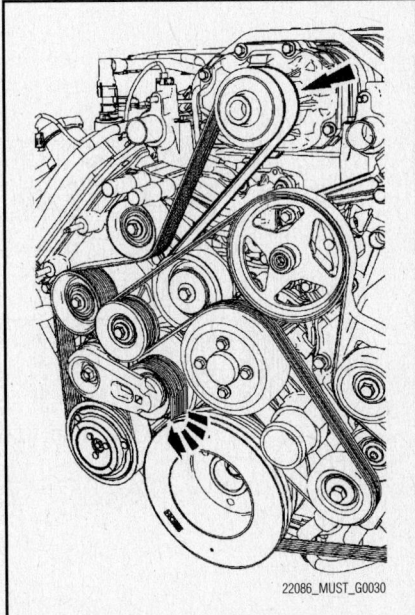

Fig. 157 Rotate SC drive belt tensioner as shown

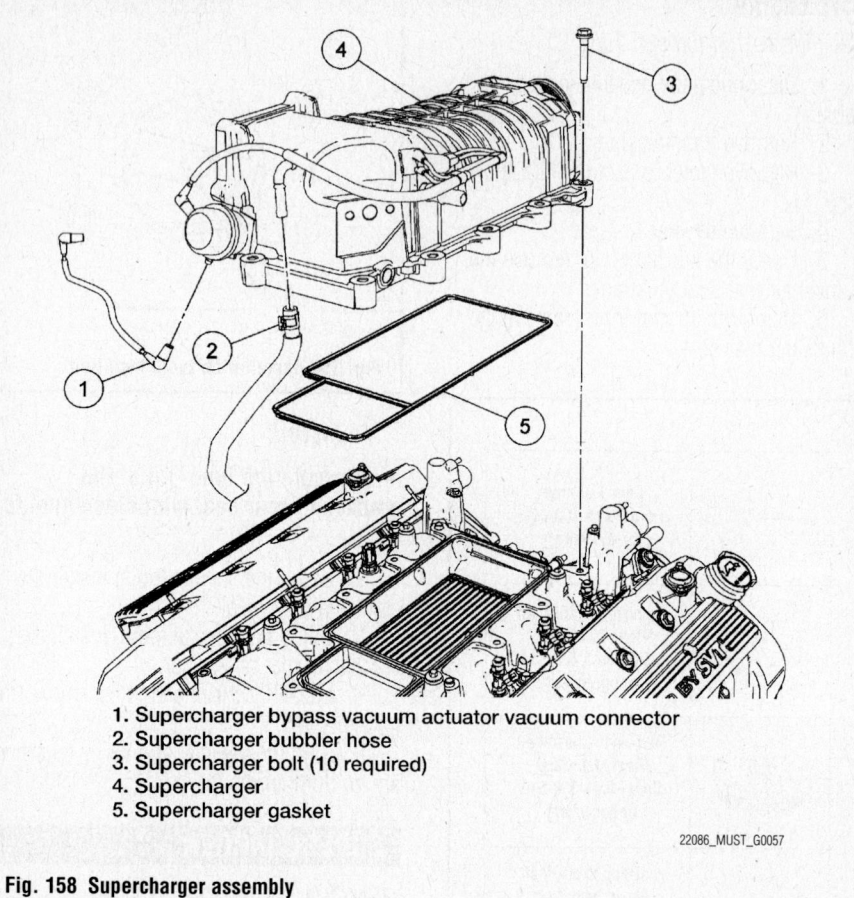

1. Supercharger bypass vacuum actuator vacuum connector
2. Supercharger bubbler hose
3. Supercharger bolt (10 required)
4. Supercharger
5. Supercharger gasket

22086_MUST_G0057

Fig. 158 Supercharger assembly

4. Rotate the drive belt tensioner clockwise and detach the drive belt from the supercharger pulley.

5. Remove the Exhaust Gas Recirculation (EGR) system module. Remove the fuel rail.

6. Disconnect the supercharger bubbler hose and the supercharger bypass vacuum actuator vacuum connector.

7. Remove the 10 bolts and the supercharger.

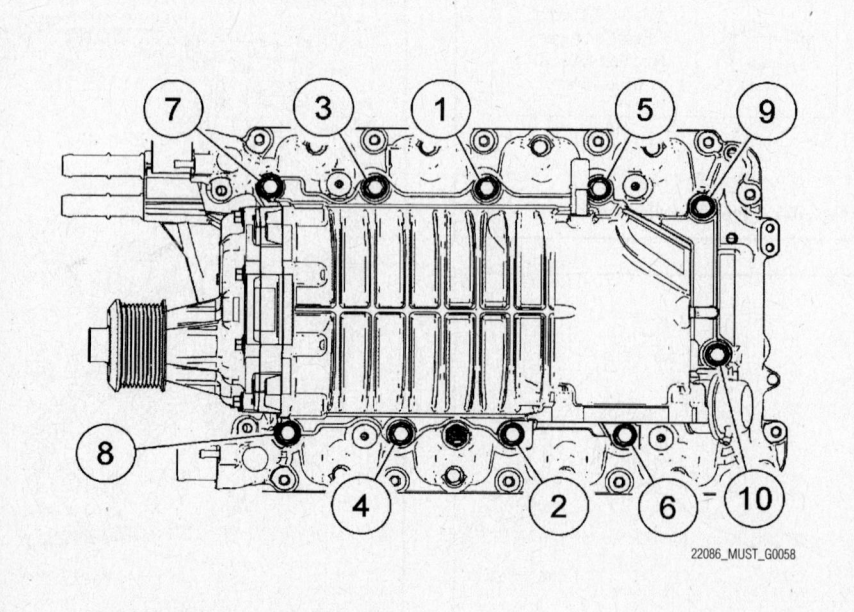

22086_MUST_G0058

Fig. 159 Supercharger bolt torque sequence

8. Remove and discard the supercharger gasket.

9. Cover the lower intake manifold with a shop towel to prevent foreign material from falling into the engine.

To install:

➡ **Always install a new gasket.**

10. Position the supercharger gasket on the lower intake manifold dowels.

11. Position the supercharger and install the bolts.

12. Tighten the bolts in the sequence shown in 2 stages:

   a. Stage 1: Tighten to 44 inch lbs. (5 Nm).

   b. Stage 2: Tighten to 18 ft. lbs. (25 Nm).

13. Connect the supercharger bubbler hose and the supercharger bypass vacuum actuator vacuum connector.

14. Install the fuel rail.

15. Install the EGR system module.

16. Rotate the drive belt tensioner clockwise and attach the drive belt to the supercharger pulley.

17. Install the strut tower cross brace and the 4 nuts, and tighten to 26 ft. lbs. (35 Nm)

18. Connect the battery ground cable.

TIMING CHAIN, SPROCKETS, FRONT COVER AND SEAL

REMOVAL & INSTALLATION

4.0L Engine

See Figure 160.

1. Drain the cooling system and the engine oil.

2. Disconnect the negative battery cable.

3. Remove the intake manifold.

4. Remove the crankshaft pulley bolt and the crankshaft damper using a puller.

5. Remove the crankshaft front oil seal using a puller.

6. Disconnect the upper and lower radiator hoses.

7. Disconnect the heater hose from the water pump.

8. Remove the accessory drive belt.

9. Remove the drive belt idler pulley.

10. Disconnect the crankshaft position sensor connector and retainer.

11. Disconnect the coolant bypass hose from the water pump.

12. Remove 5 engine front cover to engine block cradle bolts.

13. Remove 5 bolts and 4 stud bolts and remove the front cover.

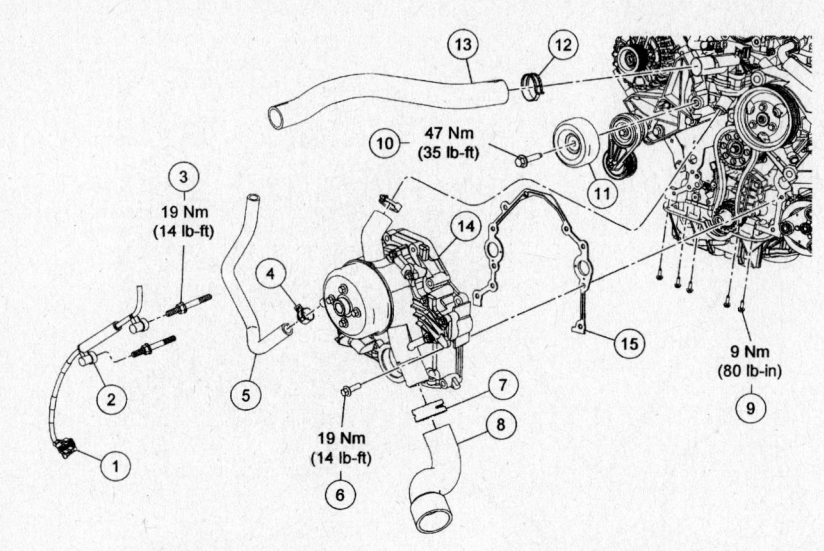

1	Crankshaft position (CKP) sensor electrical connector	9	Block cradle-to-engine front cover bolts (5 required)
2	Wiring retainers	10	Accessory drive belt idler pulley bolt
3	Engine front cover stud bolt (4 required)	11	Accessory drive belt idler pulley
4	Clamp	12	Clamp
5	Coolant hose	13	Upper radiator hose
6	Engine front cover bolt (5 required)	14	Engine front cover
7	Clamp	15	Engine front cover gasket
8	Lower radiator hose		

06017-TANG-G50

Fig. 160 Exploded view of the engine front cover—4.0L engine

14. Remove the camshaft roller followers.

15. Rotate the crankshaft so that the No. 1 cylinder is at Top Dead Center (TDC) of the compression stroke.

16. Remove the right side chain tensioner.

17. Install the special tools and remove the right camshaft sprocket bolt. See the procedure under Camshaft.

18. Hold the crankshaft from turning and remove the jackshaft sprocket bolt.

19. Remove the primary chain tensioner.

20. Remove the primary chain and sprockets as an assembly.

21. Remove the right side cassette upper and lower bolts and remove the cassette.

22. Remove the left side chain tensioner.

23. Install the special tools and remove the left camshaft sprocket bolt. See the procedure under Camshaft.

24. Remove the left side cassette upper and lower bolts and remove the cassette.

25. Remove the timing chains.

To install:

26. Install the timing chains.

27. Install the left side cassette lower bolt and tighten to 9 ft. lbs. (12 Nm).

28. Install the left side cassette upper bolt and tighten to 14 ft. lbs. (19 Nm).

29. Install the right side cassette lower bolt and tighten to 9 ft. lbs. (12 Nm).

30. Install the right side cassette upper bolt and tighten to 14 ft. lbs. (19 Nm).

31. Install the primary chain and sprockets as an assembly.

32. Install the primary chain tensioner and tighten to 80 inch lbs. (10 Nm).

33. Hold the crankshaft from turning and tighten the jackshaft sprocket bolt to 33 ft. lbs. (45 Nm), plus an additional 90 degrees.

34. Loosely install the camshaft sprocket bolts.

35. Perform the camshaft timing procedure. See the procedure under Camshaft.

36. Install the camshaft roller followers.

37. Apply sealant to the front cover in 2 spots near the top center of the cover.

38. Apply thread sealant to the front cover stud bolts.

39. Install the front cover and loosely tighten the bolts and stud bolts.

40. Use front cover alignment tool 303–107 and align the front cover.

41. Tighten the front cover bolts to 14 ft. lbs. (19 Nm).

42. Install the front cover to engine cradle bolts and tighten to 80 inch lbs. (10 Nm).

43. Connect the coolant bypass to from the water pump.

44. Connect the crankshaft position sensor connector and retainer.

45. Install the drive belt idler pulley and tighten to 35 ft. (47 Nm).

46. Install the accessory drive belt.

47. Connect the heater hose to the water pump.

48. Connect the upper and lower radiator hoses.

49. Install the crankshaft front oil seal using a seal installer.

50. Install the crankshaft damper and the pulley bolt. Tighten the pulley bolt to 33 ft. lbs. (45 Nm), plus an additional 85 degrees.

51. Install the intake manifold.

52. Connect the negative battery cable.

53. Fill the cooling system.

54. Fill the crankcase with clean engine oil.

55. Run the engine. Check for leaks and proper operation.

4.6L Engine

See Figures 161 through 165.

1. Disconnect the negative battery cable.

2. Drain the engine oil.

3. Raise the vehicle on a hoist.

4. Remove the coolant degas bottle.

5. Remove the accessory drive belt.

6. Remove the right side idler pulley.

7. Remove the valve covers. See the procedure under Cylinder Head.

8. Disconnect the hoses from the coolant crossover.

9. Remove both left and right radio interference capacitors and position aside.

10. Remove both left and right camshaft position sensor connectors.

11. Remove the J bracket from the engine front cover stud bolt.

12. Remove the water pump pulley.

13. Remove the power steering pump pulley shield.

14. Remove the wiring harness retainer from the power steering stud bolt.

15. Remove the power steering pump and position aside.

16. Disconnect the crankshaft position sensor connector.

17. Remove the crankshaft pulley bolt and washer.

18. Using a 3 jaw puller, remove the crankshaft pulley.

19. Use a seal remover and remove the front oil seal.

20. Remove the 4 front oil pan bolts.

21. Remove the front cover stud bolts and bolts and remove the front cover.

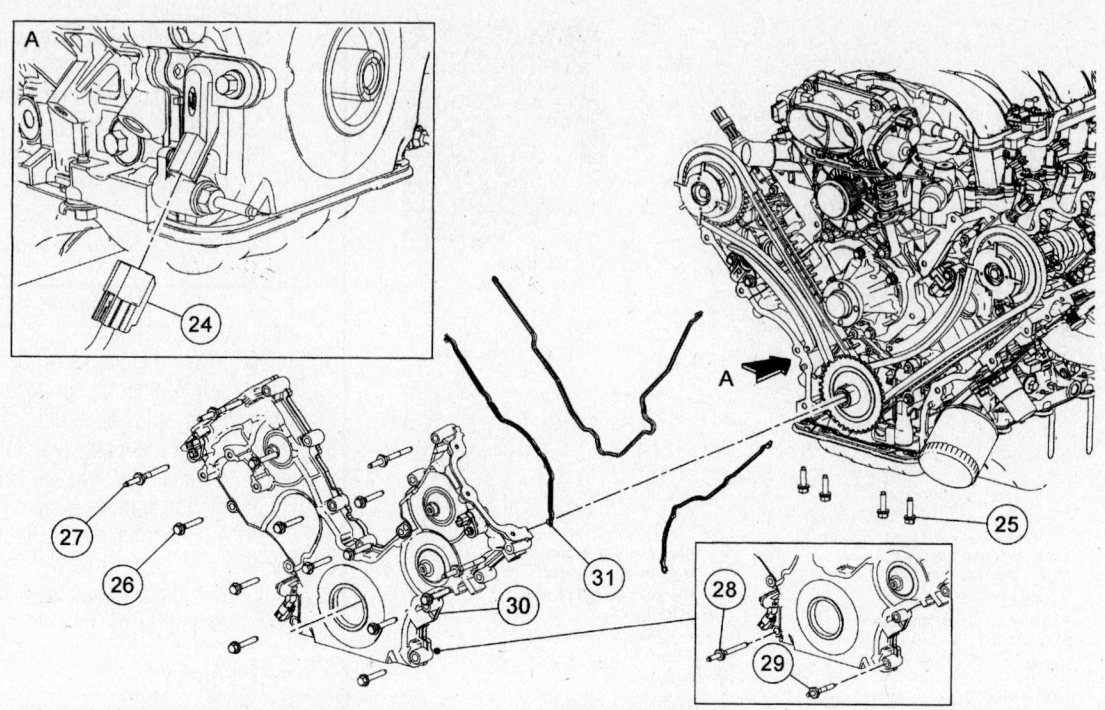

24 Crankshaft position (CKP) sensor electrical connector	28 Engine front cover stud bolt (Romeo engine only)
25 Oil pan bolts (4 required)	29 Engine front cover stud bolt (Romeo engine only)
26 Engine front cover bolts (11 required for Essex engine) (9 required for Romeo engine)	30 Engine front cover
27 Engine front cover studs (4 required)	31 Engine front cover gaskets (3 required)

06017-TANG-G51

Fig. 161 Exploded view of the engine front cover—4.6L engine

22. Remove the crankshaft sensor ring from the crankshaft.

23. Place the crankshaft keyway at the 12 o'clock position.

24. Remove the camshaft roller followers and camshaft sprocket bolts. See the procedure under Camshaft.

25. Remove the left side timing chain tensioner and arm.

26. Remove the right side timing chain tensioner and arm.

27. Remove the right and then the left timing chain and crankshaft sprockets.

28. Remove the left and right timing chain guides.

To install:

29. Compress the timing chain tensioner plunger in a soft jaw vise and install a retaining clip to hold the plunger in place.

30. Remove the tensioner.

31. If the copper links are not visible on the timing chains, mark one link on each end of the chain.

32. Install the left and right timing chain guides and tighten the bolts to 89 inch lbs. (10 Nm).

33. Position the lower end of the left timing chain on the crankshaft sprocket, aligning the copper link with the timing mark on the outer flange of the crankshaft sprocket.

34. Position the timing chain on the left camshaft sprocket with the camshaft sprocket timing mark aligned with the copper link.

35. Position the left timing chain tensioner arm on the dowel pin and install the timing chain tensioner. Tighten the bolts to 18 ft. lbs. (25 Nm).

36. Remove the retaining clip from the tensioner plunger.

37. Position the lower end of the right timing chain on the crankshaft sprocket, aligning the copper link with the timing mark on the outer flange of the crankshaft sprocket.

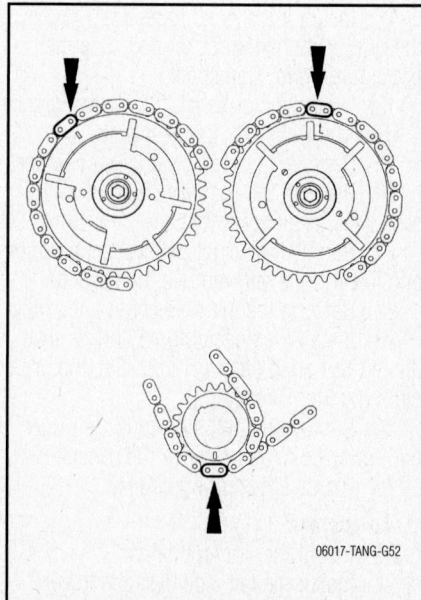

06017-TANG-G52

Fig. 162 Timing chain link and sprocket timing mark alignment—4.6L engine

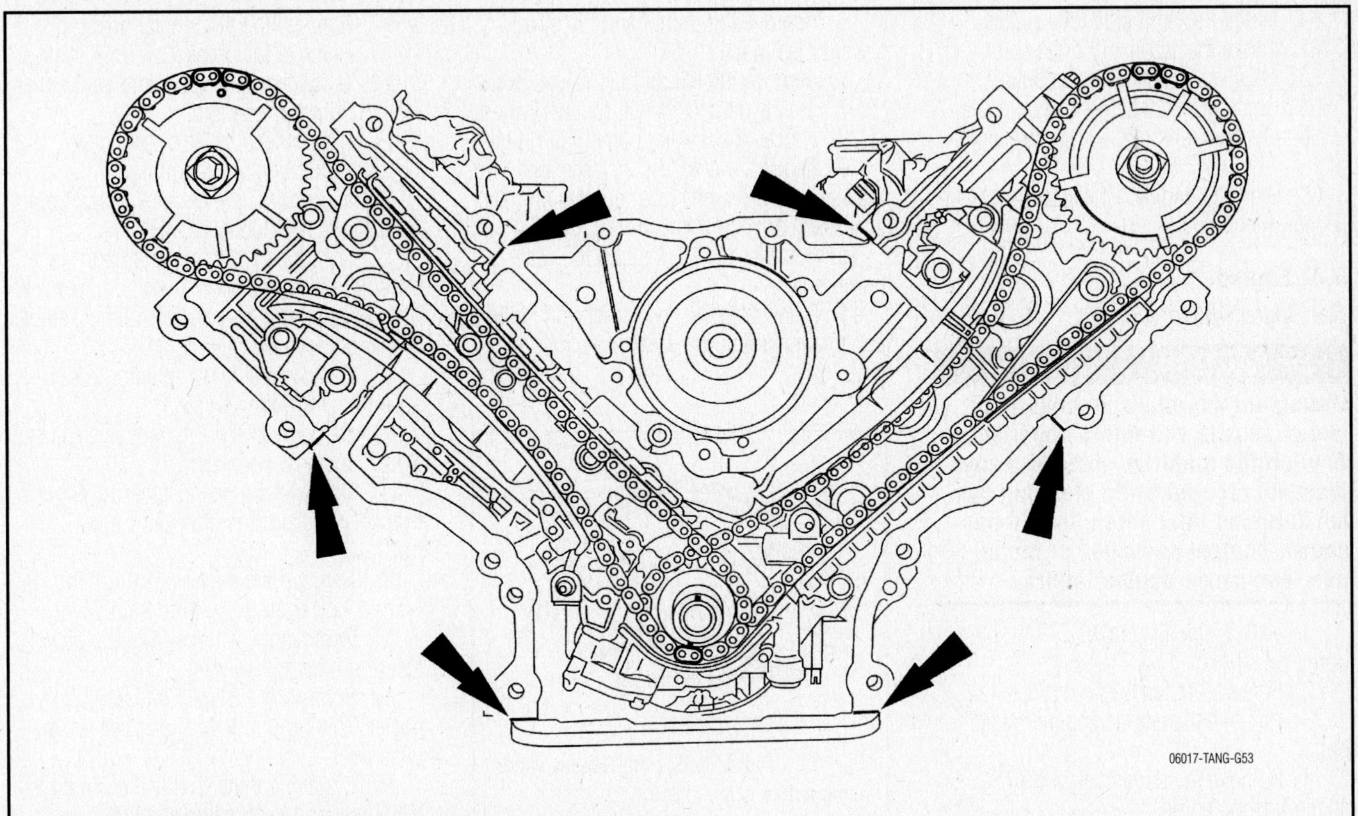

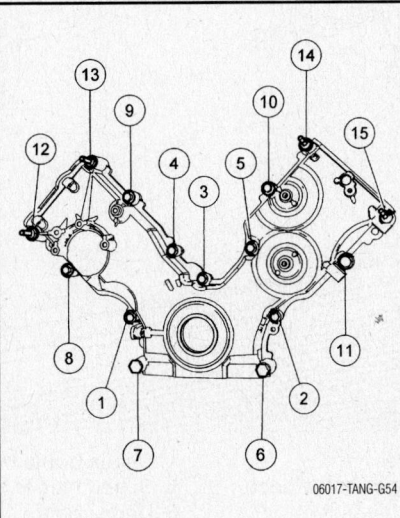

Fig. 163 Sealant application to the front cover mating surface—4.6L engine

38. Position the timing chain on the right camshaft sprocket with the camshaft sprocket timing mark aligned with the copper link.

39. Position the left timing chain tensioner arm on the dowel pin and install the timing chain tensioner. Tighten the bolts to 18 ft. lbs. (25 Nm).

40. Remove the retaining clip from the tensioner plunger.

41. Ensure correct alignment of all timing chain links and sprocket timing marks.

42. Install the camshaft roller followers and tighten the camshaft sprocket bolts. See the procedure under Camshaft.

43. Install the crankshaft sensor ring on the crankshaft.

44. Apply sealant to the front cover mating surface as shown.

45. Install a new gasket on the front cover, then install the front cover and hand tighten the bolts.

46. Tighten the front cover bolts in the sequence shown to 18 ft. lbs. (25 Nm).

47. Tighten the front cover to oil pan bolts in the sequence shown to 15 ft. lbs. (20 Nm), plus an additional 60 degrees.

48. Lubricate the engine front cover and oil seal lip with clean engine oil and install the seal using a seal installer.

49. Apply sealant to the Woodruff key

slot in the crankshaft pulley, then press on the crankshaft damper.

50. Tighten the crankshaft damper as follows:
   a. Step 1: 66 ft. lbs. (90 Nm).
   b. Step 2: Loosen the bolt one full turn.
   c. Step 3: 37 ft. lbs. (50 Nm).
   d. Step 4: 90 degrees.

51. Connect the crankshaft position sensor connector.

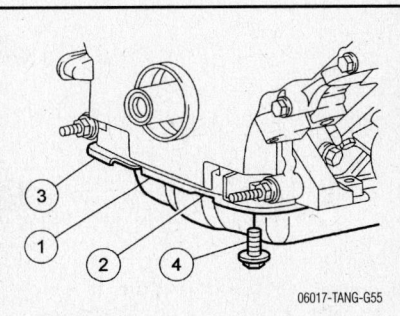

06017-TANG-G55

Fig. 165 Front cover to oil pan bolt tightening sequence—4.6L engine

52. Install the power steering pump and tighten the bolts to 18 ft. lbs. (25 Nm).

53. Install the wiring harness retainer to the power steering stud bolt.

54. Install the power steering pump pulley shield.

55. Install the water pump pulley.

56. Install the J bracket to the engine front cover stud bolt.

57. Install both left and right camshaft position sensor connectors.

58. Install both left and right radio interference capacitors.

59. Connect the hoses from the coolant crossover.

60. Install the valve covers. See the procedure under Cylinder Head.

06017-TANG-G54

Fig. 164 Front cover bolt tightening sequence—4.6L engine

61. Install the right side idler pulley.
62. Install the accessory drive belt.
63. Install the coolant degas bottle.
64. Connect the negative battery cable.
65. Fill the crankcase with clean engine oil.
66. Start the engine. Check for leaks and proper operation.

5.4L Engine

See Figures 166 through 191.

> **✳✳ CAUTION**
>
> **During engine repair procedures, cleanliness is extremely important. Any foreign material, including any material created while cleaning gasket surfaces, that enters the oil passages, coolant passages or the oil pan, can cause engine failure.**

1. With the vehicle in NEUTRAL, position it on a hoist.
2. Release the fuel system pressure.
3. Remove the engine coolant degas bottle.
4. Remove the supercharger (SC) coolant degas bottle.

5. Remove the 4 nuts and the strut tower cross brace.
6. Remove the RH and LH valve covers.
7. Remove the camshaft roller followers.
8. Loosen the 4 water pump pulley bolts.
9. Remove the accessory drive belt, the 2 accessory drive belt idler pulleys and the accessory drive belt tensioner.
10. Remove the 4 bolts and the water pump pulley.
11. Remove the SC drive belt, SC drive belt tensioner and the 3 SC drive belt idler pulleys.

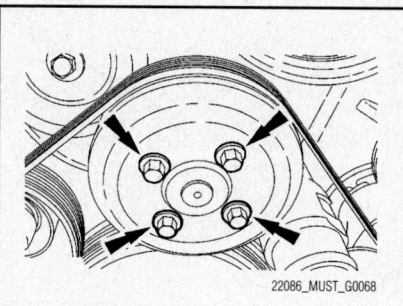

22086_MUST_G0068

Fig. 167 Loosen, but do not remove water pump pulley bolts

12. Remove the thermostat housing.
13. Remove the crankshaft front seal.
14. Disconnect the 2 coolant vent hoses from the intake manifold.
15. Disconnect the 2 upper radiator hoses from the intake manifold.
16. Disconnect the coolant hoses from the Charge Air Cooler (CAC).
17. Disconnect the lower radiator hose assembly from the water pump, radiator, oil filter adapter and the coolant tube assembly (located above the alternator).
18. Remove the lower radiator hose assembly from the vehicle.
19. Disconnect the A/C pressure transducer electrical connector.
20. Remove the power steering tube bracket nut from the alternator stud bolt.
21. Remove the power steering tube bracket bolt from the engine front cover.
22. Remove the 2 bolts from the power steering reservoir bracket.
23. Remove the 3 bolts and position the power steering pump and reservoir assembly aside.
24. Disconnect the Crankshaft Position (CKP) sensor electrical connector.

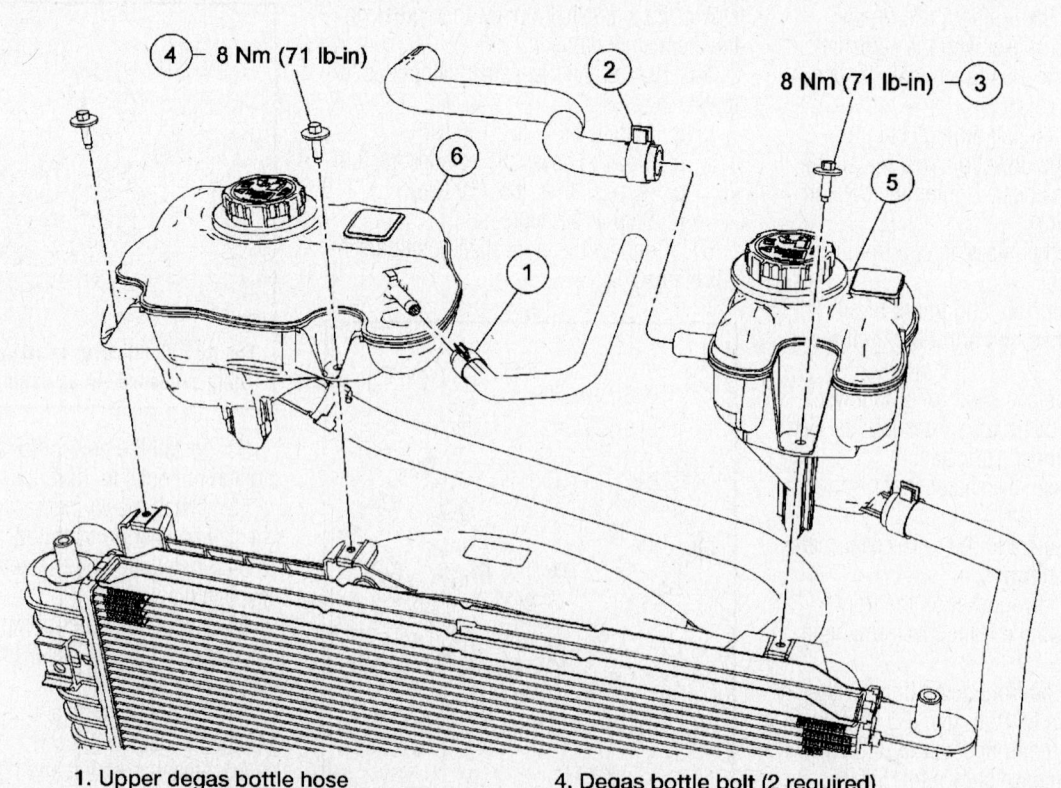

1. Upper degas bottle hose
2. Upper supercharger degas bottle hose
3. Supercharger degas bottle bolt
4. Degas bottle bolt (2 required)
5. Supercharger degas bottle
6. Degas bottle

22086_MUST_G0064

Fig. 166 Primary and supercharger degas bottles—5.4L engine

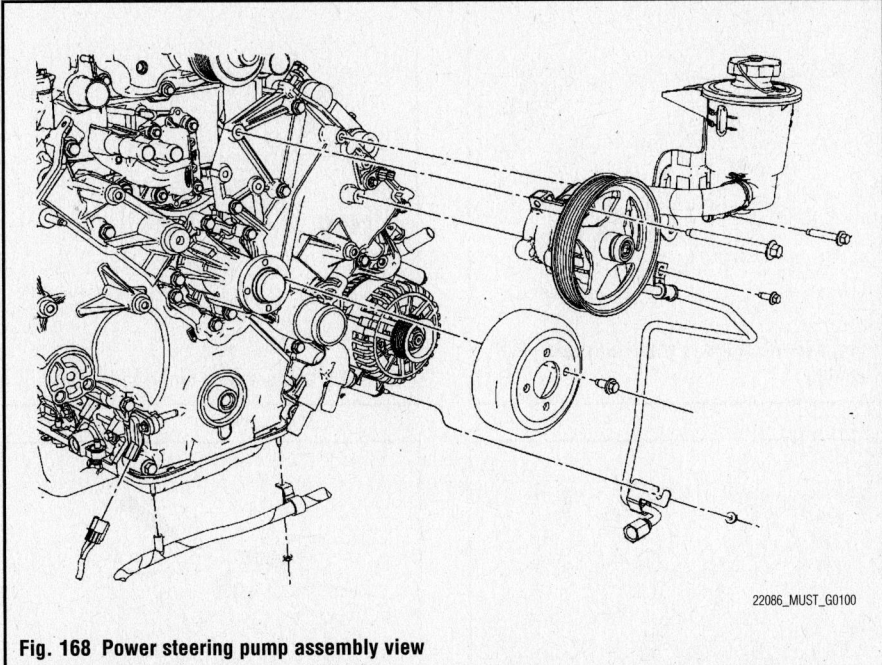

Fig. 168 Power steering pump assembly view

25. Install the engine support hooks to each cylinder head.

➡️ **The heavy duty 3 bar support (303–F070) must be used with the draw screws from the light duty 3 bar support (303–F072). This will provide enough clearance between the supercharger (SC) and the 3 bar support, and enough clearance between the draw screw and the vehicle hood.**

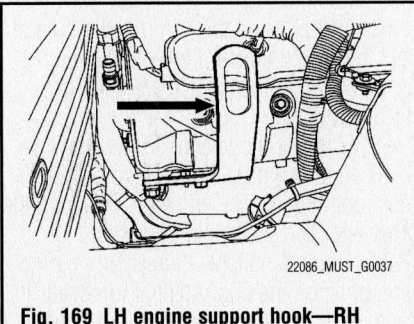

Fig. 169 LH engine support hook—RH similar

Fig. 170 3 bar engine support

Install the special tools and raise the engine.

26. Remove the nut and disconnect the B+ wire terminal from the alternator.

27. Disconnect the alternator electrical connector.

28. Detach the wiring harness retainer from the oil pan stud bolt.

29. Remove the nut and the wire harness retainer bracket from the oil pan stud bolt.

30. Detach the 2 wiring harness pin type retainers from the alternator.

31. Remove the stud bolt, 2 bolts and the alternator.

32. Disconnect the coolant hose from the oil filter adapter.

❋❋ CAUTION

If metal or aluminum foreign material is present in the oil cooler, mechanical concerns exist.

33. Remove the 6 bolts and the oil cooler.

34. Discard the gaskets.

35. Inspect the oil cooler for contamination or damage.

36. Drain the engine oil.

37. Tighten the drain plug to 19 ft. lbs. (26 Nm).

38. Remove and discard the engine oil filter.

39. Remove the 3 coolant tube assembly bolts.

40. Disconnect the Engine Oil Pressure (EOP) sensor electrical connector and the 2 wiring harness pin type retainers.

41. Remove the 8 bolts and the oil filter adapter.

42. Discard the gasket.

43. Remove the 2 oil pan to engine front cover bolts and the 2 oil pan to engine front cover stud bolts.

44. Remove the 4 bolts and the water pump.

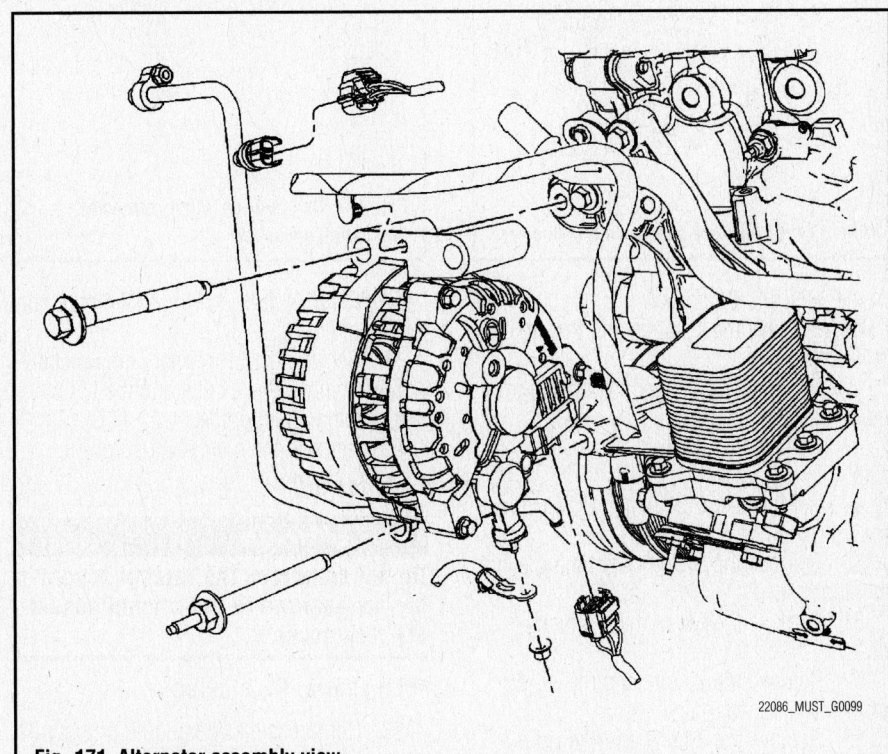

Fig. 171 Alternator assembly view

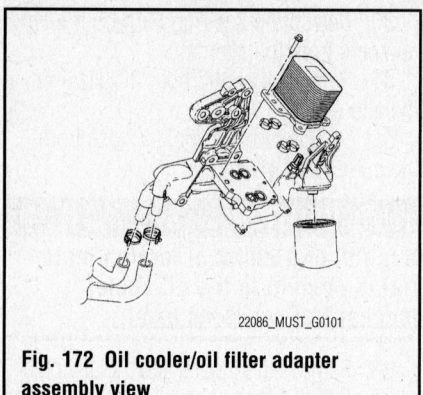

Fig. 172 Oil cooler/oil filter adapter assembly view

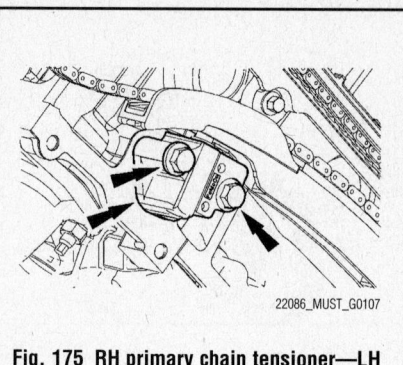

Fig. 175 RH primary chain tensioner—LH similar

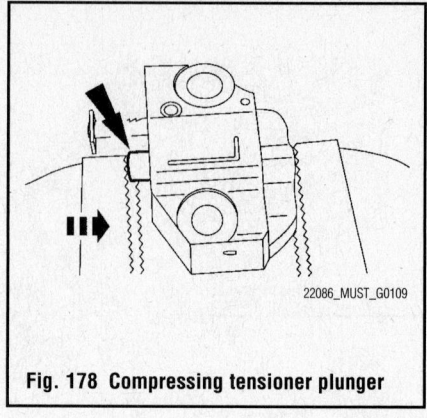

Fig. 178 Compressing tensioner plunger

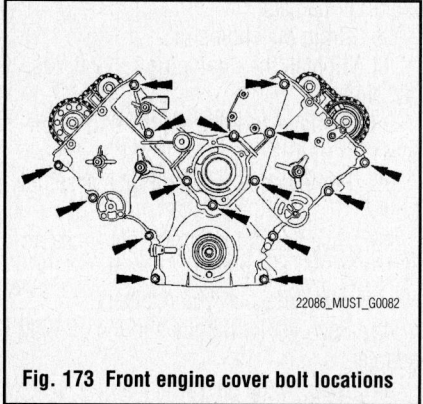

Fig. 173 Front engine cover bolt locations

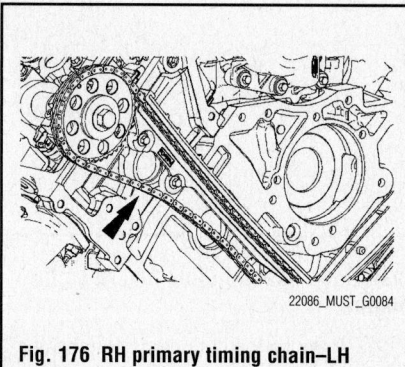

Fig. 176 RH primary timing chain–LH similar

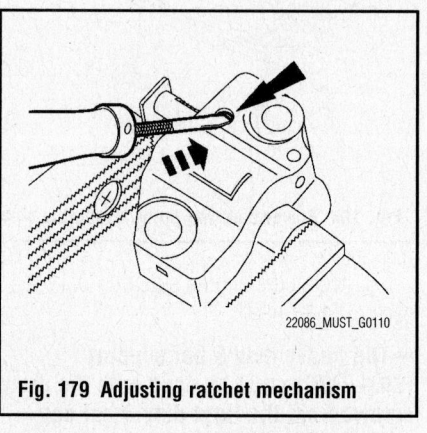

Fig. 179 Adjusting ratchet mechanism

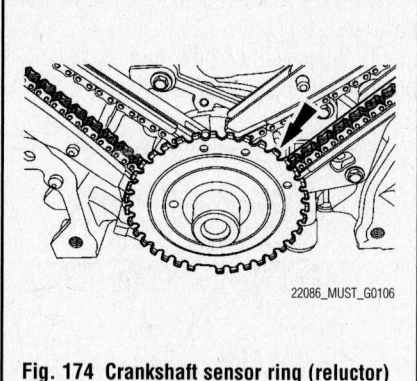

Fig. 174 Crankshaft sensor ring (reluctor)

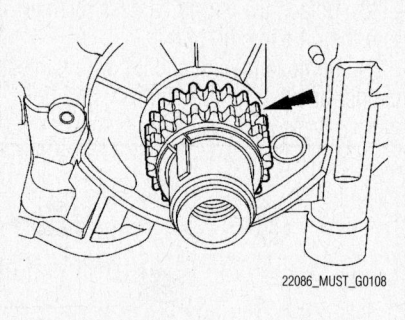

Fig. 177 Use caution when removing crankshaft sprocket

45. Discard the gasket.
46. Remove the 16 bolts and the engine front cover.
47. Remove and discard the engine front cover gaskets.
48. Remove the crankshaft sensor ring.
49. Remove the 2 bolts and the RH primary timing chain tensioner.
50. Remove the RH primary timing chain tensioner arm.
51. Remove the RH primary timing chain.
52. Remove the 2 bolts and the RH primary timing chain guide.
53. Remove the 2 bolts and the LH primary timing chain tensioner.

54. Remove the LH primary timing chain tensioner arm.
55. Remove the LH primary timing chain.
56. Remove the 2 bolts and the LH primary timing chain guide.
57. Remove the crankshaft sprocket.

To install:

☀ CAUTION

Do not compress the ratchet assembly, as damage to the ratchet assembly may occur.

➡ **LH shown, RH similar.**

58. Compress each tensioner plunger, using a standard bench vise.

59. Using a small screwdriver or pick, push back and hold the ratchet mechanism
60. While holding the ratchet mechanism, push the ratchet arm back into the tensioner housing.
61. Install a suitable pin into the hole of each tensioner housing to hold the ratchet assembly and plunger in place during installation.
62. Remove the tensioner from the vise.
63. If the colored links are not visible, mark one link on one end and 2 links on the other end, and use as timing marks.
64. Using a suitable crankshaft holding tool, position the crankshaft at top dead center. Install the crankshaft sprocket with the flange facing forward.
65. Install the LH primary timing chain guide and the 2 bolts.
   a. Tighten to 89 inch lbs. (10 Nm).
66. Position the camshaft sprocket timing marks as shown.
67. Position the LH (inner) timing chain onto the crankshaft sprocket, aligning the one colored link on the timing chain with the slot on the crankshaft sprocket.
68. Install the LH timing chain on the camshaft sprocket, aligning the 2 colored links with the timing mark on the sprocket.

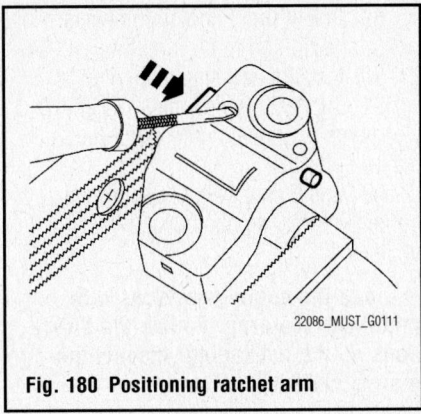

Fig. 180 Positioning ratchet arm

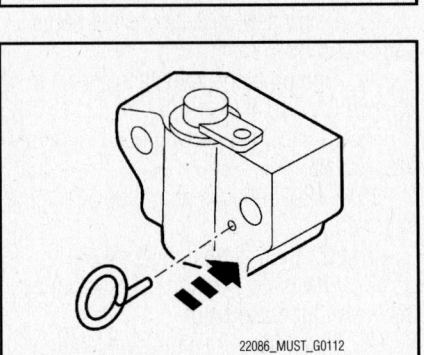

Fig. 181 Insert pin into tensioner as shown in illustration

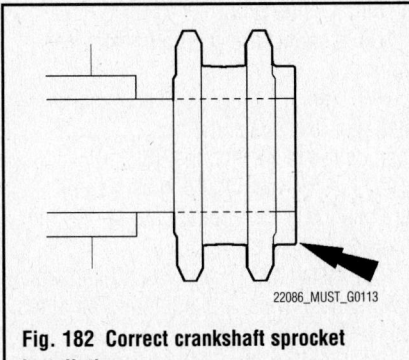

Fig. 182 Correct crankshaft sprocket installation

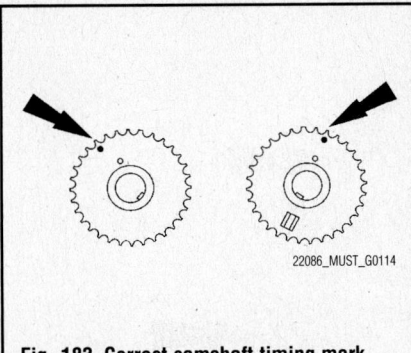

Fig. 183 Correct camshaft timing mark alignment

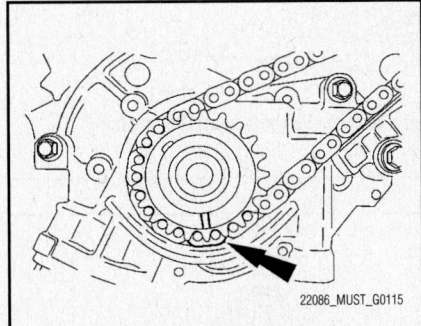

Fig. 184 Correct timing chain alignment on crankshaft—LH shown, RH similar.

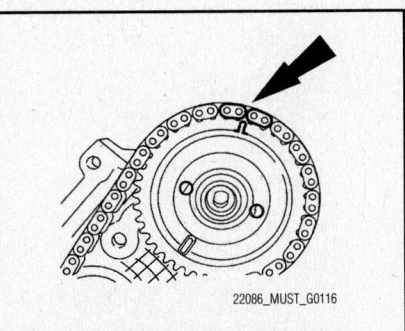

Fig. 185 Correct timing chain alignment on camshaft—LH shown, RH similar

75. Install the RH primary timing chain tensioner arm.

76. Install the RH primary timing chain tensioner and the 2 bolts.

   a. Tighten to 18 ft. lbs. (25 Nm).

77. Remove the pin from the tensioner.

78. Verify correct alignment of all timing marks. Make sure that the colored links are lined up with the marks on the crankshaft sprocket and the camshaft sprockets.

79. Install the crankshaft sensor ring.

80. Install the engine front cover.

81. Install the camshaft roller followers.

82. Install the valve covers.

➥**If the engine front cover is not secured within 4 minutes, the sealant must be removed and the sealing area cleaned with metal surface cleaner. Allow to dry until there is no sign of wetness or 4 minutes, whichever is longer. Failure to follow this procedure can result in future oil leakage.**

Timing cover bolts
- 1–14 Bolt, hex head pilot, M8 x 1.25 x 53 (14 required)
- 14–15 Bolt, hex flange head pilot, M10 x 1.50 x 55 (2 required)

83. Using new gaskets, install the engine front cover and the 16 bolts. Tighten the bolts in the sequence shown:

- Bolts 1 through 14: 18 ft. lbs. (25 Nm).
- Bolts 15 and 16: 37 ft. lbs. (50 Nm).

84. Install the 2 oil pan to engine front cover bolts and the 2 oil pan to engine front cover stud bolts.

   a. Tighten to 18 ft. lbs. (25 Nm).

69. Install the LH primary timing chain tensioner arm.

70. Install the LH primary timing chain tensioner and the 2 bolts.

   a. Tighten to 18 ft. lbs. (25 Nm).

71. Remove the pin from the tensioner.

72. Install the RH primary timing chain guide and the 2 bolts.

   a. Tighten to 89 inch lbs. (10 Nm).

73. Position the RH (outer) timing chain on the crankshaft sprocket, aligning the colored link with the timing marks on the sprocket.

74. Install the RH timing chain on the camshaft sprocket, aligning the 2 colored links with the timing mark on the sprocket.

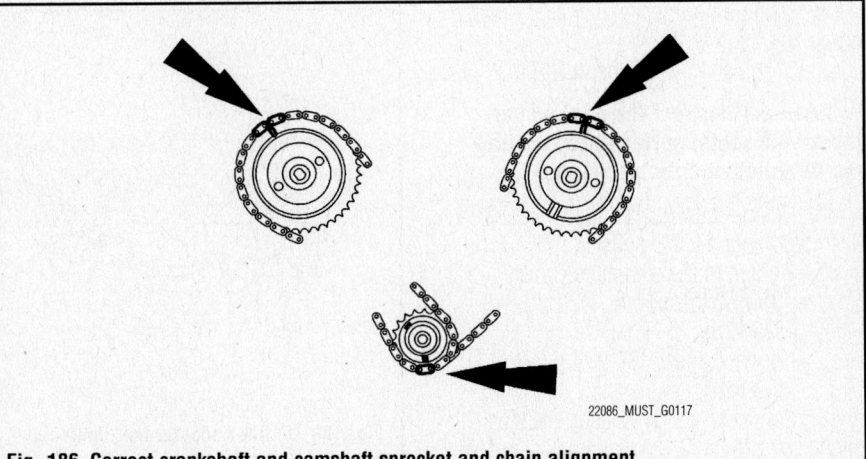

Fig. 186 Correct crankshaft and camshaft sprocket and chain alignment

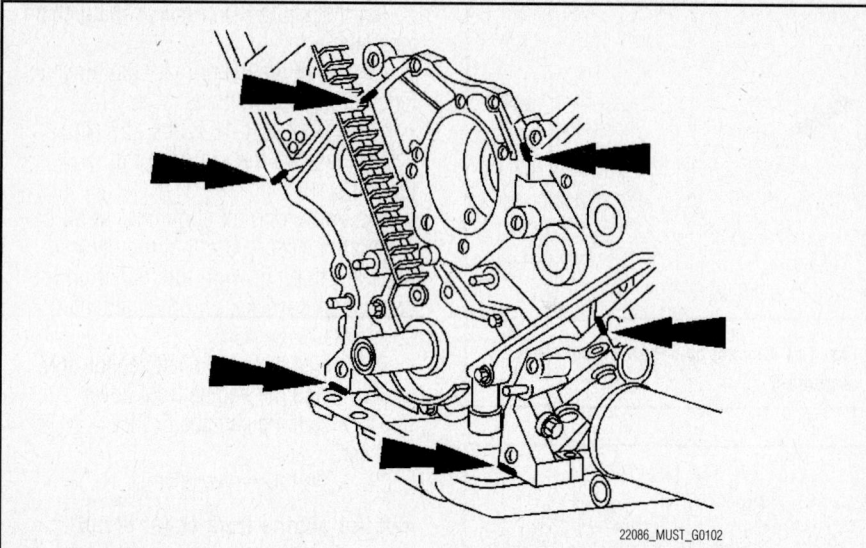

Fig. 187 Apply silicone gasket sealant in the locations shown. Sealant bead thickness should be 0.32"(8.0mm)

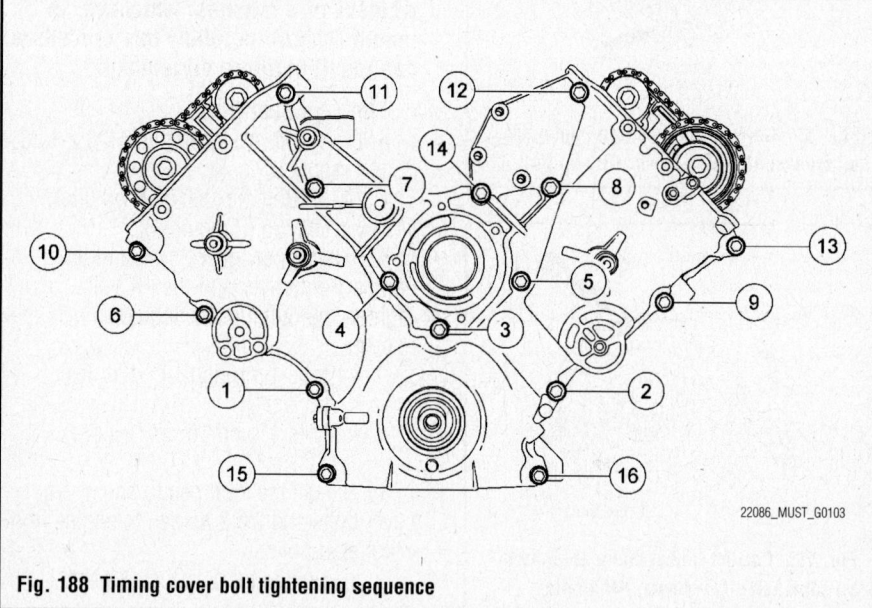

Fig. 188 Timing cover bolt tightening sequence

85. Using a new gasket, install the water pump and the 4 bolts.
   a. Tighten to 18 ft. lbs. (25 Nm).

➡**Clean and inspect the sealing surfaces with metal surface prep. Follow the directions on the packaging.**

86. Using a new gasket, install the oil filter adapter and the 8 bolts.
87. Tighten in the sequence shown:
   • Bolts 1 through 6: 18 ft. lbs. (25 Nm).
   • Bolts 7 and 8: 37 ft. lbs. (50 Nm).
88. Connect the EOP sensor electrical connector and the 2 wiring harness pin type retainers.

89. Install the 3 coolant tube assembly bolts, and tighten to 89 inch lbs. (10 Nm).
90. Install a new engine oil filter.
91. Lubricate the oil filter gasket with clean engine oil and tighten until the seal makes contact.
92. Using an oil filter strap wrench, tighten the filter an additional 270 degrees.

➡**Clean the sealing surfaces with metal surface prep. Follow the directions on the packaging. Inspect the mating surfaces.**

93. Using new gaskets, install the oil cooler and the 6 bolts.
94. Tighten in the sequence shown to 89 inch lbs. (10 Nm).
95. Connect the coolant hose to the oil filter adapter.
96. Install the alternator, 2 bolts and the stud bolt.
   a. Tighten to 37 ft. lbs. (50 Nm).
97. Attach the 2 wiring harness pin type retainers to the alternator.
98. Install the wire harness retainer bracket on the oil pan stud bolt and install the nut.
   a. Tighten to 89 inch lbs. (10 Nm).
99. Attach the wiring harness retainer to the oil pan stud bolt.
100. Connect the alternator electrical connector.
101. Connect the B+ wire terminal to the alternator and install the nut.
   a. Tighten to 71 inch lbs. (8 Nm).
102. Using the 3 bar engine support, carefully lower the engine onto the engine support insulators.
103. Install the LH and RH engine support insulator nuts, and tighten to 46 ft. lbs. (63 Nm).
104. Connect the CKP sensor electrical connector.

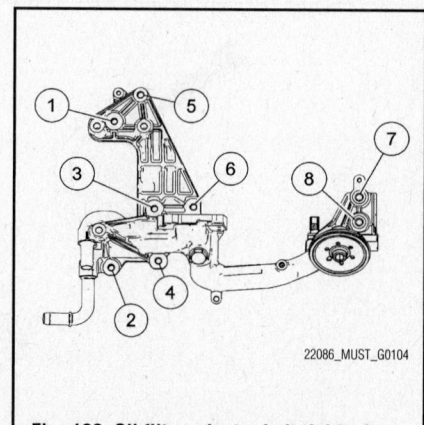

Fig. 189 Oil filter adapter bolt tightening sequence

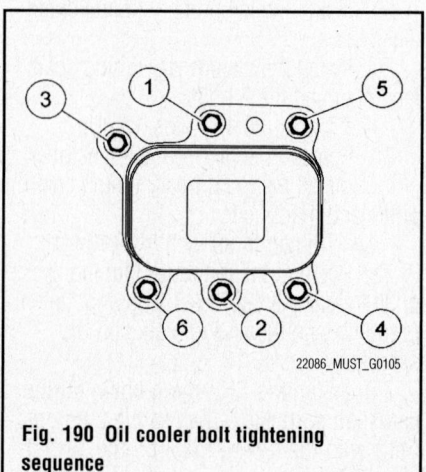

Fig. 190 Oil cooler bolt tightening sequence

105. Install the power steering pump and reservoir assembly and the 3 bolts, and tighten to 18 ft. lbs. (25 Nm).

106. Install the 2 power steering reservoir bracket bolts, and tighten to 18 ft. lbs. (25 Nm).

107. Install the power steering tube bracket bolt, and tighten to 89 inch lbs. (10 Nm).

108. Install the power steering tube bracket nut to the alternator stud bolt, and tighten to 89 inch lbs. (10 Nm).

109. Connect the A/C pressure transducer electrical connector.

110. Install the lower radiator hose assembly to the water pump, radiator, oil filter adapter and the coolant

111. tube assembly (located above the alternator).

112. Connect the coolant hoses from the CAC.

113. Connect the 2 upper radiator hoses to the intake manifold.

114. Connect the 2 coolant vent hoses to the intake manifold.

115. Install the crankshaft front seal.

116. Install the thermostat housing.

117. Install the 3 supercharger (SC) drive belt idler pulleys, SC drive belt and the SC drive belt tensioner.

118. Install the water pump pulley and the 4 bolts.

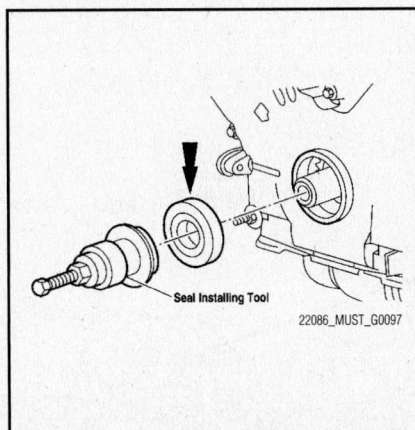

Fig. 191 Crankshaft front seal installation

119. Install the 2 accessory drive belt idler pulleys, the accessory drive belt tensioner and the accessory drive belt.

120. Tighten the 4 water pump pulley bolts to 18 ft. lbs. (25 Nm).

121. Install the RH and LH valve covers.

122. Install the SC coolant degas bottle.

123. Install the engine coolant degas bottle.

124. Install the strut tower cross brace and the 4 nuts, and tighten to 26 ft. lbs. (35 Nm).

125. Fill and bleed the SC cooling system.

126. Fill and bleed the engine cooling system.

127. Start the engine, and verify that there are no fluid leaks.

VALVE LASH

ADJUSTMENT

All vehicles are equipped with hydraulic lash adjusters. Valve clearance is not adjustable.

ENGINE PERFORMANCE & EMISSION CONTROL

→A high–impedance digital multi–meter is required for the following test procedures. Never use a low–impedance analog multi–meter or low–impedance test light, as damage to electronic components may occur

COMPONENT LOCATIONS

See Figures 192 through 201.

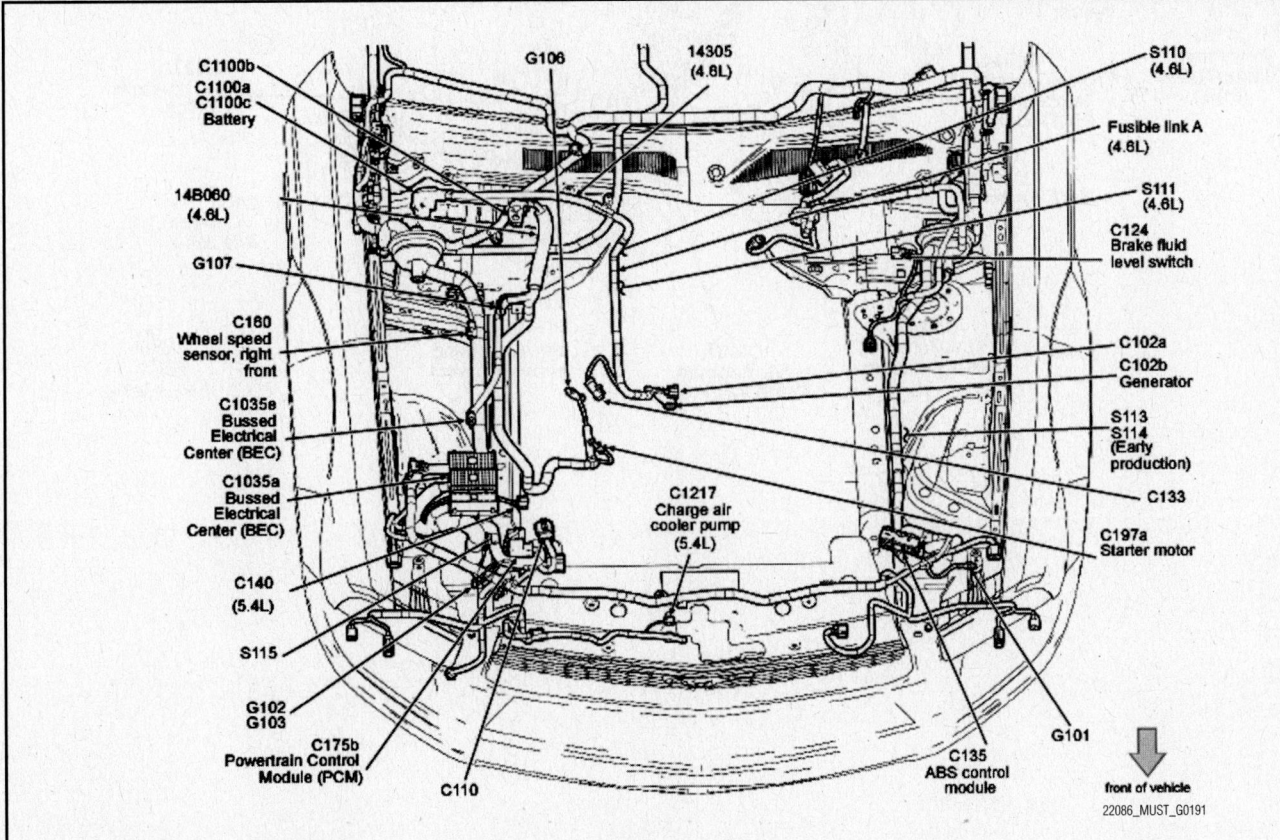

Fig. 192 Mustang engine control component locations (Engine Compartment, All Models)

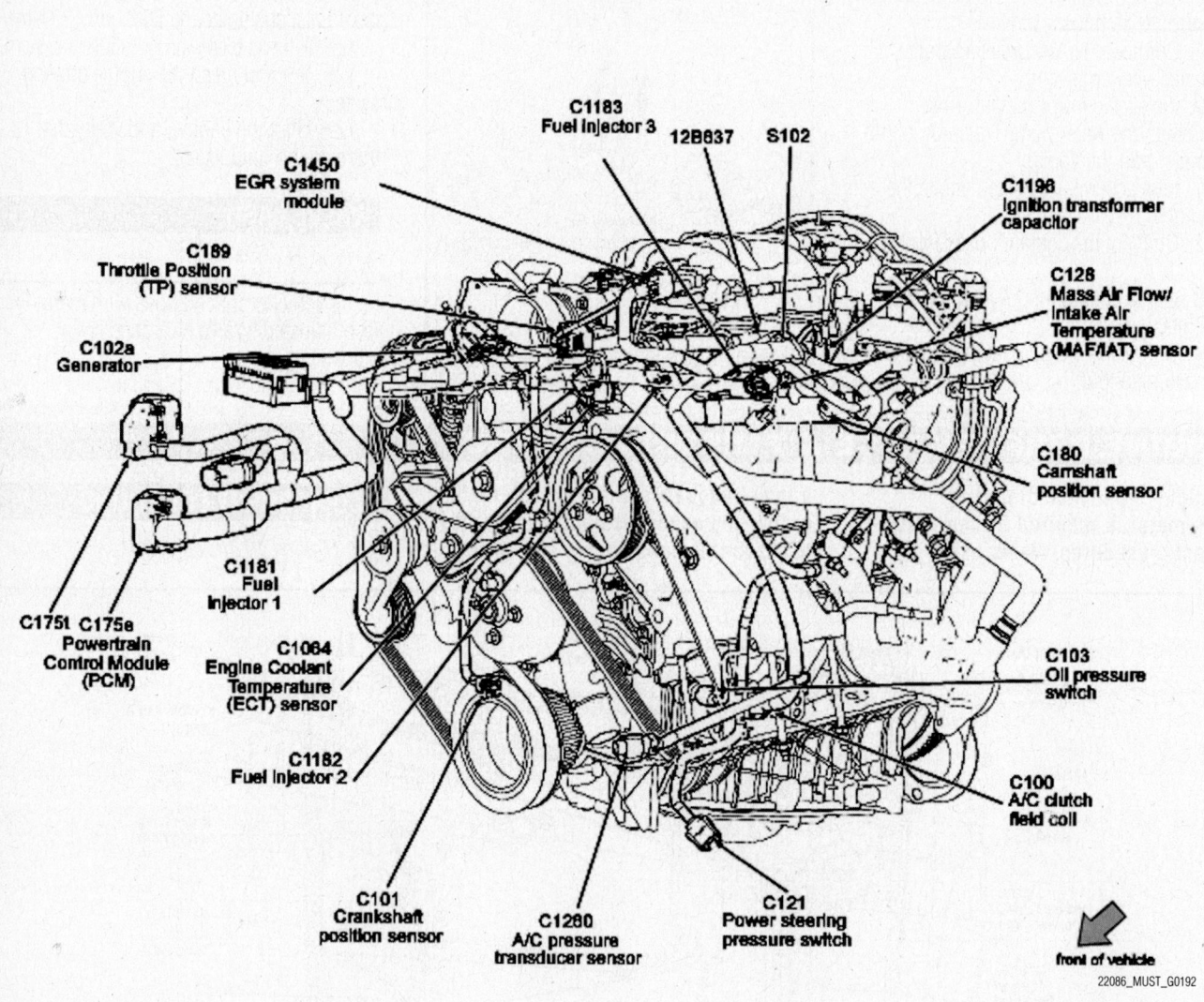

C1183
Fuel Injector 3   12B637   S102

C1450
EGR system
module

C1196
Ignition transformer
capacitor

C189
Throttle Position
(TP) sensor

C128
Mass Air Flow/
Intake Air
Temperature
(MAF/IAT) sensor

C102a
Generator

C180
Camshaft
position sensor

C1181
Fuel
Injector 1

C175t C175e
Powertrain
Control Module
(PCM)

C1064
Engine Coolant
Temperature
(ECT) sensor

C103
Oil pressure
switch

C1182
Fuel Injector 2

C100
A/C clutch
field coil

C101
Crankshaft
position sensor

C1280
A/C pressure
transducer sensor

C121
Power steering
pressure switch

front of vehicle

22086_MUST_G0192

Fig. 193 Mustang engine control component locations (4.0L Engine)

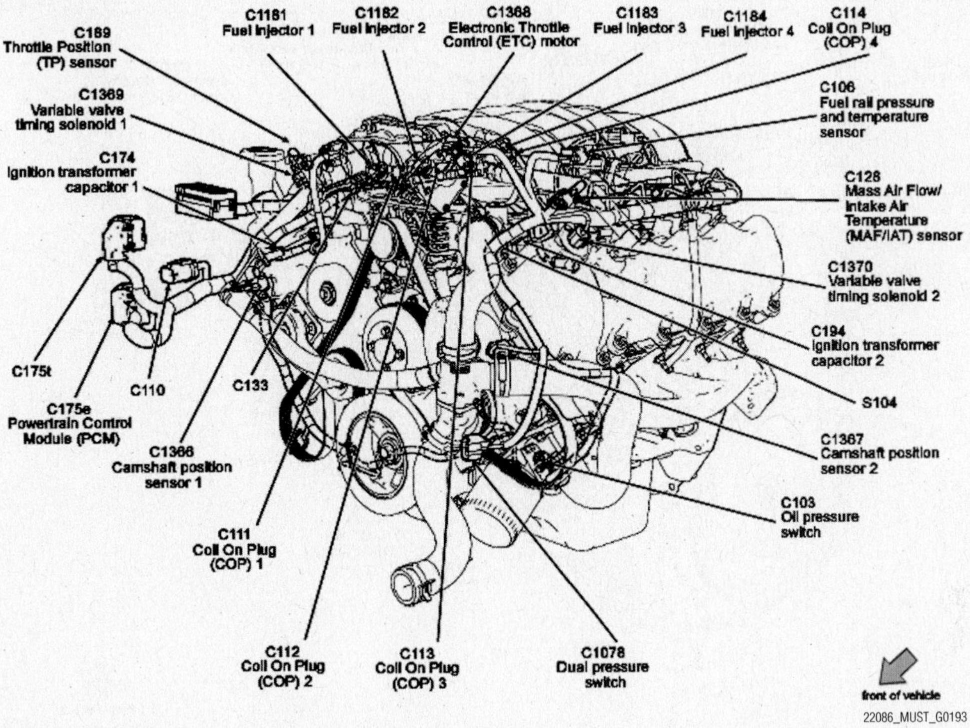

C189
Throttle Position
(TP) sensor

C1369
Variable valve
timing solenoid 1

C174
Ignition transformer
capacitor 1

C175t

C175e
Powertrain Control
Module (PCM)

C110

C133

C1366
Camshaft position
sensor 1

C1181
Fuel injector 1

C1182
Fuel injector 2

C1368
Electronic Throttle
Control (ETC) motor

C1183
Fuel injector 3

C1184
Fuel injector 4

C114
Coil On Plug
(COP) 4

C106
Fuel rail pressure
and temperature
sensor

C128
Mass Air Flow/
Intake Air
Temperature
(MAF/IAT) sensor

C1370
Variable valve
timing solenoid 2

C194
Ignition transformer
capacitor 2

S104

C1367
Camshaft position
sensor 2

C103
Oil pressure
switch

C111
Coil On Plug
(COP) 1

C112
Coil On Plug
(COP) 2

C113
Coil On Plug
(COP) 3

C1078
Dual pressure
switch

front of vehicle
22086_MUST_G0193

Fig. 194 Mustang engine control component locations (4.6L Engine)

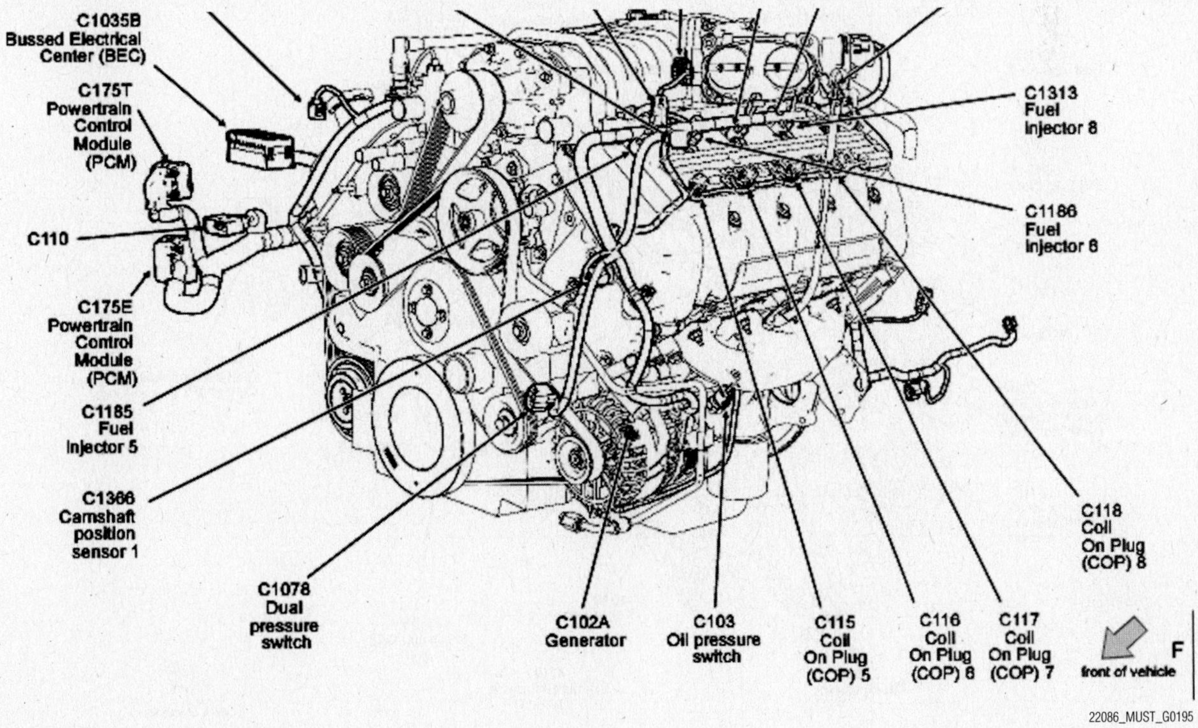

C1035B
Bussed Electrical
Center (BEC)

C175T
Powertrain
Control
Module
(PCM)

C110

C175E
Powertrain
Control
Module
(PCM)

C1185
Fuel
Injector 5

C1366
Camshaft
position
sensor 1

C1078
Dual
pressure
switch

C102A
Generator

C103
Oil pressure
switch

C115
Coil
On Plug
(COP) 5

C116
Coil
On Plug
(COP) 6

C117
Coil
On Plug
(COP) 7

C118
Coil
On Plug
(COP) 8

C1313
Fuel
Injector 8

C1186
Fuel
Injector 6

front of vehicle F
22086_MUST_G0195

Fig. 195 Mustang engine control component locations (5.4L Engine, S/C)

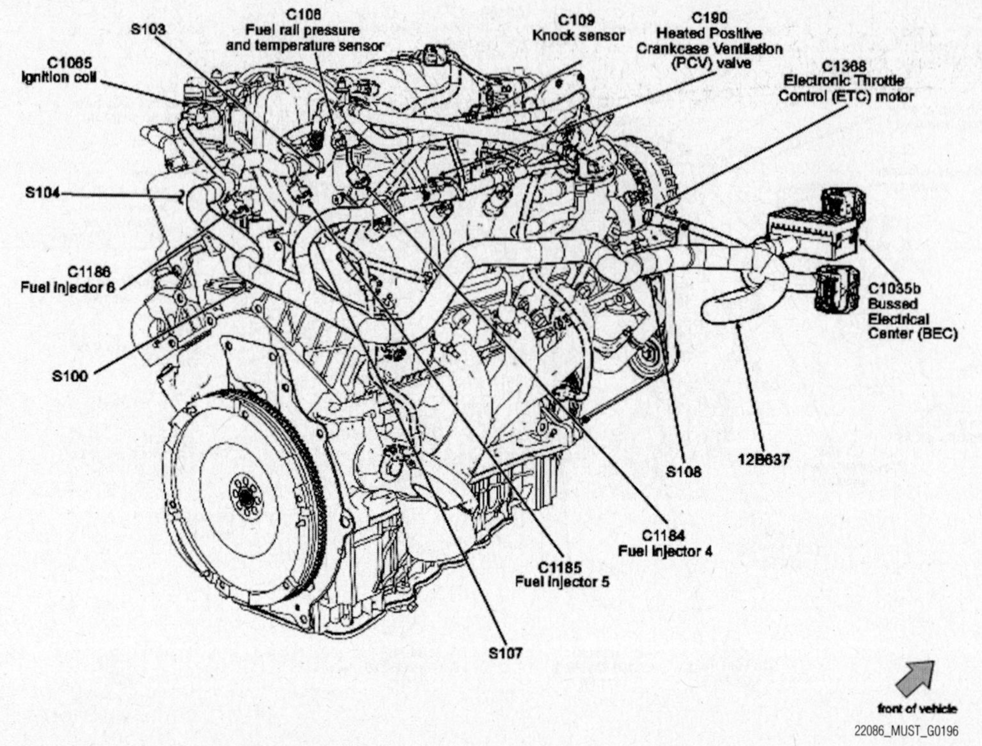

C1065
Ignition coil

S103

C108
Fuel rail pressure
and temperature sensor

C109
Knock sensor

C190
Heated Positive
Crankcase Ventilation
(PCV) valve

C1368
Electronic Throttle
Control (ETC) motor

S104

C1186
Fuel injector 6

S100

C1035b
Bussed
Electrical
Center (BEC)

S108

12B637

C1184
Fuel injector 4

C1185
Fuel injector 5

S107

front of vehicle
22086_MUST_G0196

Fig. 196 Mustang engine control component locations (5.4L Engine, S/C)

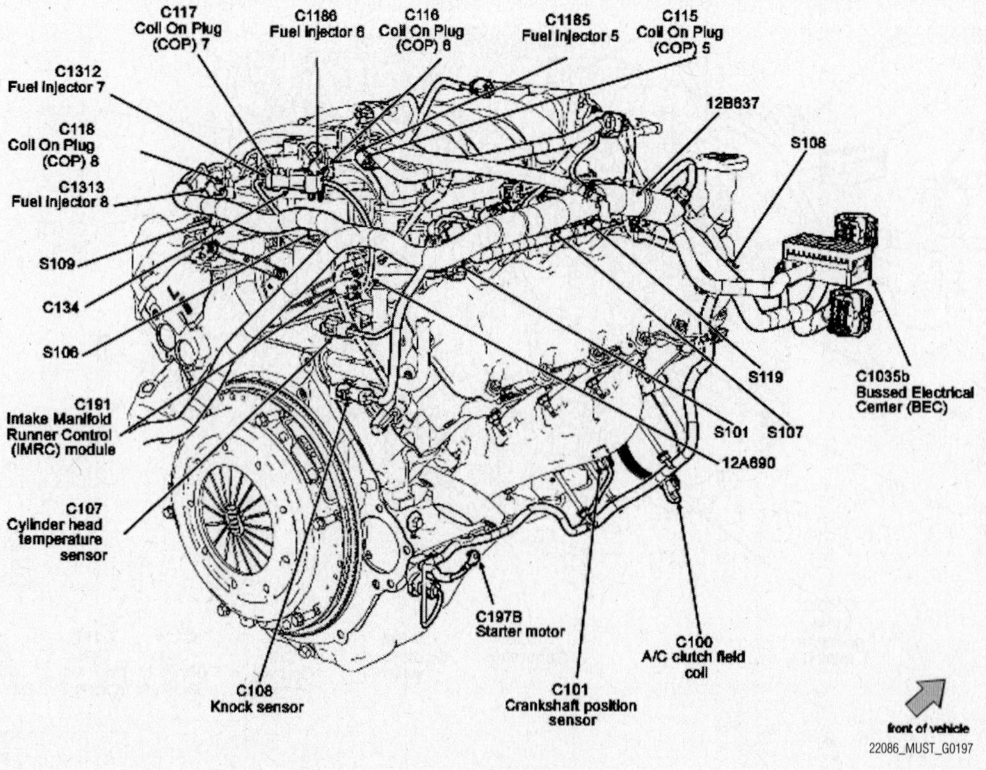

C117
Coil On Plug
(COP) 7

C1186
Fuel injector 6

C116
Coil On Plug
(COP) 6

C1185
Fuel injector 5

C115
Coil On Plug
(COP) 5

C1312
Fuel Injector 7

C118
Coil On Plug
(COP) 8

C1313
Fuel Injector 8

S109

C134

S106

C191
Intake Manifold
Runner Control
(IMRC) module

C107
Cylinder head
temperature
sensor

12B637

S108

S119

C1035b
Bussed Electrical
Center (BEC)

S101   S107

12A690

C197B
Starter motor

C100
A/C clutch field
coil

C108
Knock sensor

C101
Crankshaft position
sensor

front of vehicle
22086_MUST_G0197

Fig. 197 Mustang engine control component locations (4.0L and 4.6L Engines, M/T)

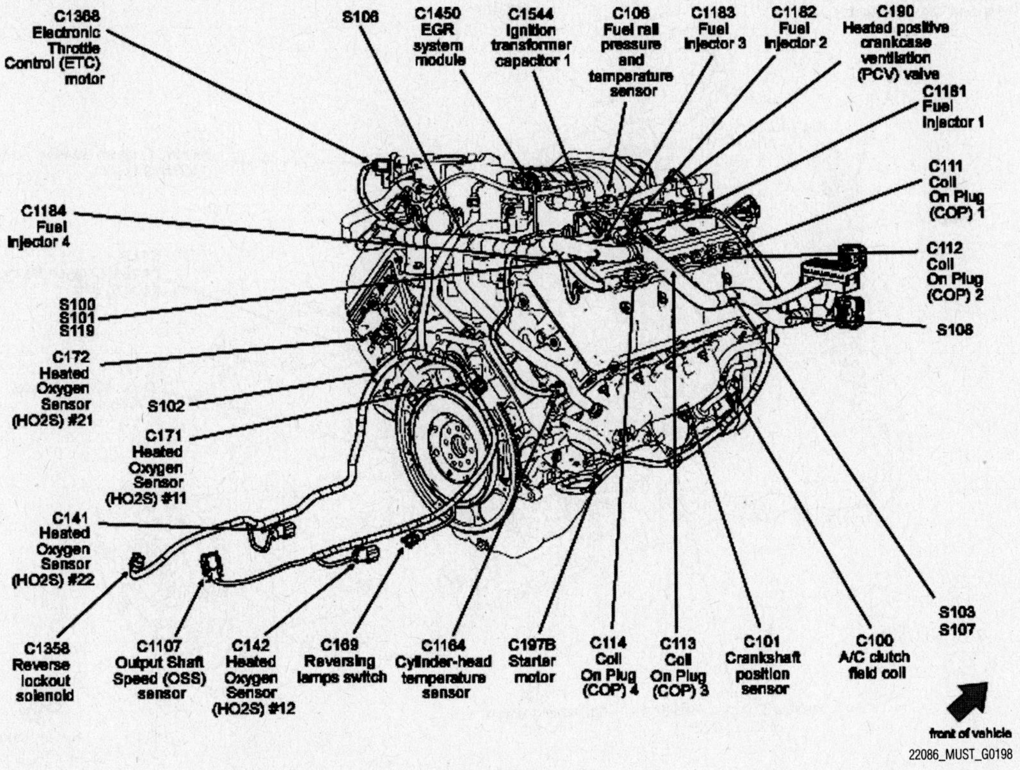

C1368
Electronic
Throttle
Control (ETC)
motor

S106

C1450
EGR
system
module

C1544
Ignition
transformer
capacitor 1

C106
Fuel rail
pressure
and
temperature
sensor

C1183
Fuel
Injector 3

C1182
Fuel
Injector 2

C190
Heated positive
crankcase
ventilation
(PCV) valve

C1181
Fuel
Injector 1

C111
Coil
On Plug
(COP) 1

C112
Coil
On Plug
(COP) 2

S108

C1184
Fuel
Injector 4

S100
S101
S119

C172
Heated
Oxygen
Sensor
(HO2S) #21

S102

C171
Heated
Oxygen
Sensor
(HO2S) #11

C141
Heated
Oxygen
Sensor
(HO2S) #22

C1358
Reverse
lockout
solenoid

C1107
Output Shaft
Speed (OSS)
sensor

C142
Heated
Oxygen
Sensor
(HO2S) #12

C169
Reversing
lamps switch

C1164
Cylinder-head
temperature
sensor

C197B
Starter
motor

C114
Coil
On Plug
(COP) 4

C113
Coil
On Plug
(COP) 3

C101
Crankshaft
position
sensor

C100
A/C clutch
field coil

S103
S107

front of vehicle

22086_MUST_G0198

Fig. 198 Mustang engine control component locations (4.0L and 4.6L Engines, A/T)

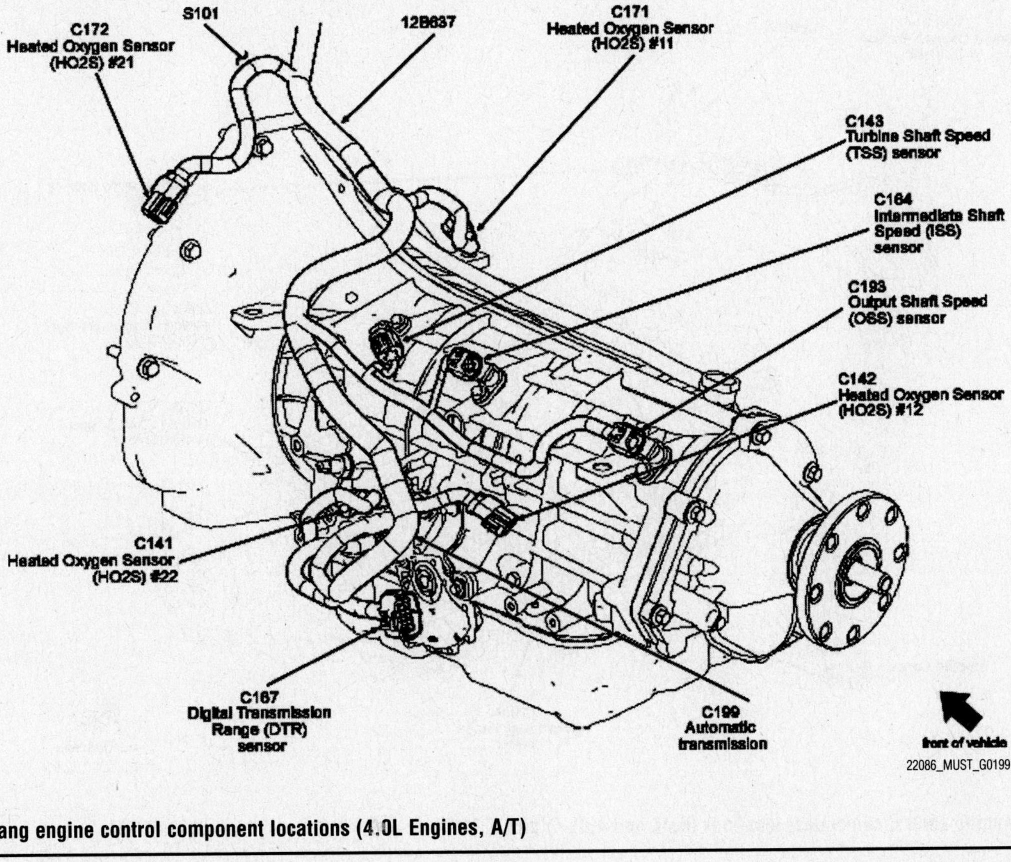

C172
Heated Oxygen Sensor
(HO2S) #21

S101

12B637

C171
Heated Oxygen Sensor
(HO2S) #11

C143
Turbine Shaft Speed
(TSS) sensor

C164
Intermediate Shaft
Speed (ISS)
sensor

C193
Output Shaft Speed
(OSS) sensor

C142
Heated Oxygen Sensor
(HO2S) #12

C141
Heated Oxygen Sensor
(HO2S) #22

C167
Digital Transmission
Range (DTR)
sensor

C199
Automatic
transmission

front of vehicle

22086_MUST_G0199

Fig. 199 Mustang engine control component locations (4.0L Engines, A/T)

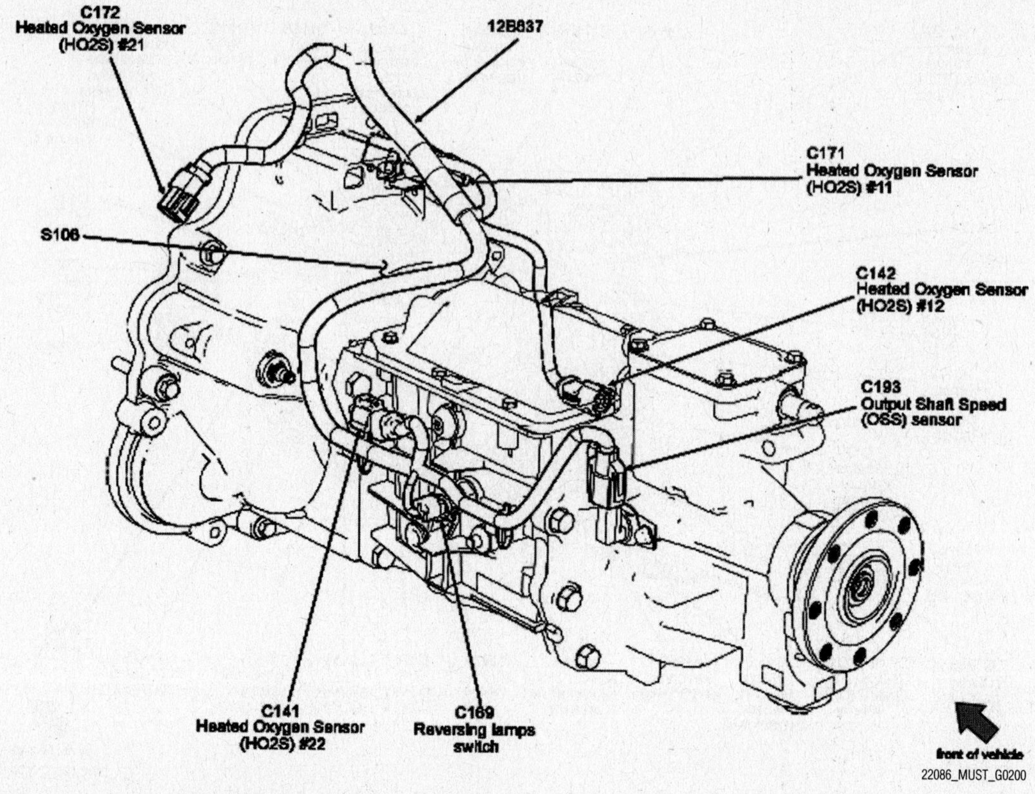

C172
Heated Oxygen Sensor
(HO2S) #21

12B837

C171
Heated Oxygen Sensor
(HO2S) #11

S106

C142
Heated Oxygen Sensor
(HO2S) #12

C193
Output Shaft Speed
(OSS) sensor

C141
Heated Oxygen Sensor
(HO2S) #22

C169
Reversing lamps
switch

front of vehicle
22086_MUST_G0200

Fig. 200 Mustang engine control component locations (4.0L Engine, M/T)

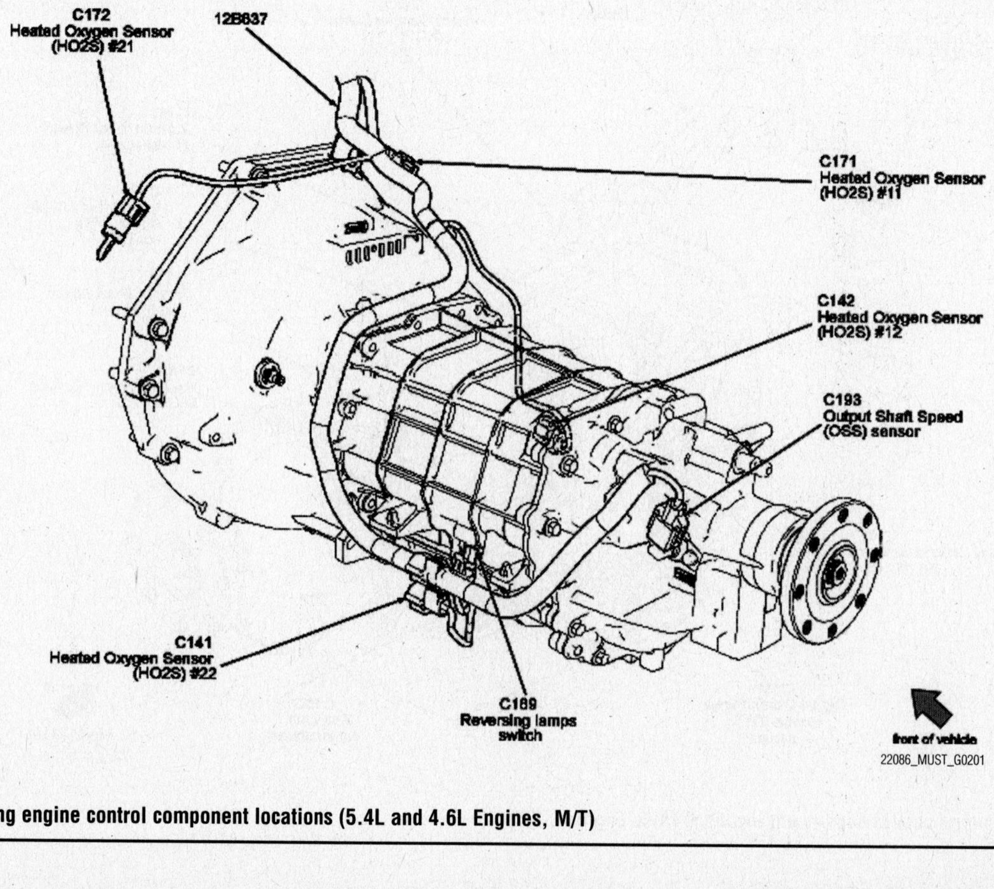

C172
Heated Oxygen Sensor
(HO2S) #21

12B837

C171
Heated Oxygen Sensor
(HO2S) #11

C142
Heated Oxygen Sensor
(HO2S) #12

C193
Output Shaft Speed
(OSS) sensor

C141
Heated Oxygen Sensor
(HO2S) #22

C169
Reversing lamps
switch

front of vehicle
22086_MUST_G0201

Fig. 201 Mustang engine control component locations (5.4L and 4.6L Engines, M/T)

ACCELERATOR PEDAL POSITION (APP) SENSOR

LOCATION

See Figure 202.

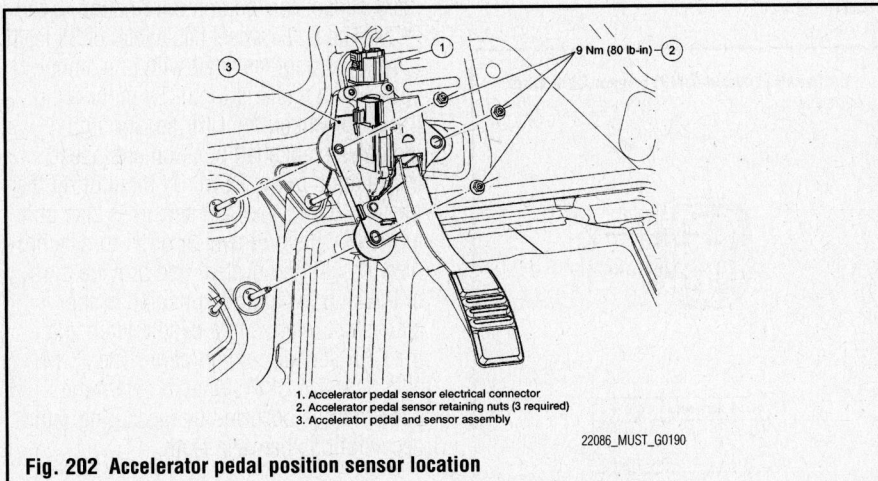

1. Accelerator pedal sensor electrical connector
2. Accelerator pedal sensor retaining nuts (3 required)
3. Accelerator pedal and sensor assembly

22086_MUST_G0190

Fig. 202 Accelerator pedal position sensor location

The Accelerator Pedal Position Sensor is located on top of the accelerator pedal assembly.

OPERATION

The APP sensor is an input to the Powertrain Control Module (PCM) and is used to determine the torque demand. There are 3 pedal position signals in the sensor. Signal 1, APPS1, has a negative slope (increasing angle, decreasing voltage) and signals 2 and 3, APPS2 and APPS3, both have a positive slope (increasing angle, increasing voltage). During normal operation APPS1 is used as the indication of pedal position by the strategy. The 3 pedal position signals make sure the PCM receives a correct input even if 1 signal has a concern. There are 2 reference voltage circuits and 2 signal return circuits for the sensor.

REMOVAL & INSTALLATION

1. Disconnect the battery ground cable.
2. Disconnect the accelerator pedal motor electrical connector.
3. Remove the two bolts and the accelerator pedal assembly.
   a. To install, reverse the removal procedure.

TESTING

See Figures 203 and 204.

Check the APP Sensor signal output voltage ranges for the accelerator pedal fully applied and released positions.

APPS1 (Pin #2)
APPS2 (Pin #5)
APPS3 (Pin #8)
  • Monitor the voltage readings between pins APPS1, APPS2, APPS3, and body ground.
  • Press the accelerator pedal fully to the floor and release.

➡ **After clearing an APP sensor Diagnostic Trouble Code (DTC) to verify a repair or an intermittent concern, apply the accelerator pedal before carrying out the self–test. Take 10 seconds to carry out a full sweep of the accelerator pedal from fully released to fully applied and back to fully released.**

APP Sensor Pin Testing

➡ **For reference values, refer to PCM testing—PCM reference voltage pin chart**

This pinpoint test is intended to diagnose the following:

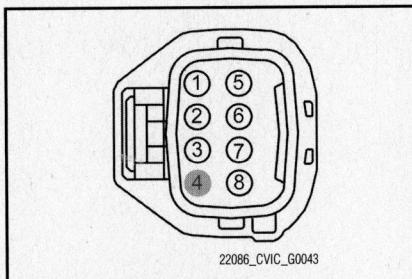

22086_CVIC_G0043

Fig. 203 Accelerator Pedal Position Sensor connector

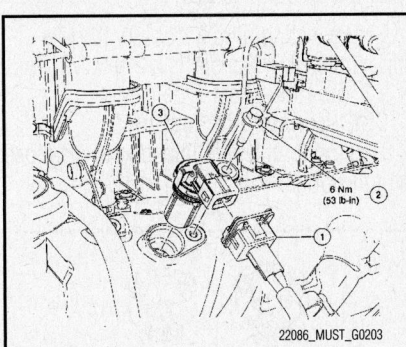

Accelerator Pedal Position Sensor

B

Vehicle	Connector	Pin	Circuit
Mustang	B	8	APPS3
		5	APPS2
		2	APPS1
		1, 3	ETCRTN
		6, 7	ETCREF

22086_MUST_G0189

Fig. 204 APPS connector view

  • Accelerator Pedal Position (APP) sensor (9F836)
  • Harness circuits: ETCRTN, SIGRTN, ETCREF, APP1, APP2, and APP3
  • Powertrain control module (PCM) (12A650)

CAMSHAFT POSITION (CMP) SENSOR

LOCATION

See Figures 205 and 206.

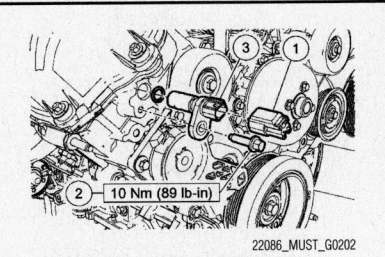

22086_MUST_G0203

Fig. 205 Camshaft Position Sensor—4.0L Engine

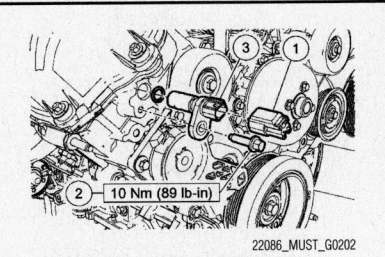

22086_MUST_G0202

Fig. 206 Camshaft Position Sensor—4.6L and 5.4L engines

The Camshaft Position Sensors are located on the timing cover, just below each valve cover on the 4.6L and 5.4L engines, and in the top of the valve cover on the 4.0L engine.

OPERATION

The CMP sensor detects the position of the camshaft. The CMP sensor identifies when piston number 1 is on its compression stroke. A signal is then sent to the PCM and used for synchronizing the sequential firing of the fuel injectors. Coil–On–Plug (COP) ignition applications use the CMP signal to select the correct ignition coil to fire.

There are 2 types of CMP sensors: the 3–pin connector Hall–effect type sensor and the 2–pin connector variable reluctance type sensor.

REMOVAL & INSTALLATION

See Figures 205 and 206.

1. Disconnect the battery ground cable.
2. Disconnect the Camshaft Position (CMP) sensor electrical connector.
3. Remove the CMP bolt.
4. Remove the CMP sensor.
5. To install, reverse the removal procedure, and tighten CMP bolt to 89 inch lbs. (10 Nm).

TESTING

See Figures 207 and 208.

Before testing, it is necessary to determine if the CMP Sensor is a 2–pin VR type, or a 3–pin Hall–effect Type.

CMP Sensor Pin Testing

This pinpoint test is intended to diagnose the following:

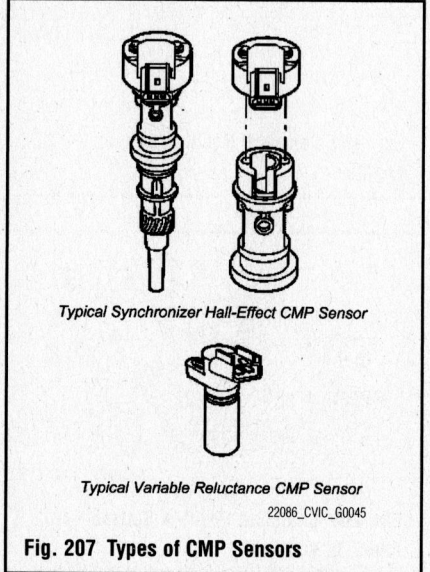

Typical Synchronizer Hall-Effect CMP Sensor

Typical Variable Reluctance CMP Sensor

22086_CVIC_G0045

Fig. 207 Types of CMP Sensors

- Camshaft Position (CMP) sensor (6B288)
- Harness circuits: CMP, CMP2, SIGRTN, VBPWR, VRSRTN, and VRSRTN2

➡**For reference values, refer to PCM testing—PCM reference voltage pin chart**

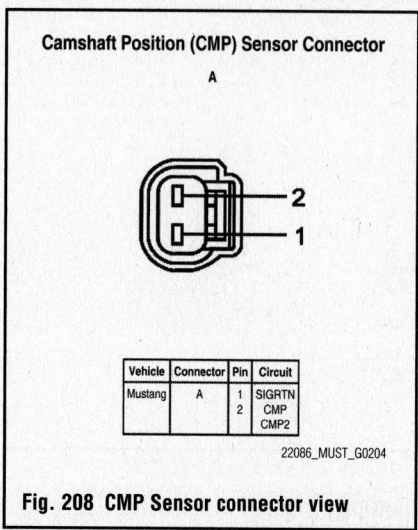

Camshaft Position (CMP) Sensor Connector

A

Vehicle	Connector	Pin	Circuit
Mustang	A	1	SIGRTN
		2	CMP
			CMP2

22086_MUST_G0204

Fig. 208 CMP Sensor connector view

CRANKSHAFT POSITION (CKP) SENSOR

LOCATION

See Figure 209.

Refer to the accompanying illustration for Crankshaft Position (CKP) sensor location.

OPERATION

The CKP sensor is a magnetic transducer mounted on the engine block adjacent to a pulse wheel located on the crankshaft. By monitoring the crankshaft mounted pulse wheel, the CKP is the primary sensor for ignition information to the PCM. The pulse wheel has a total of 35 teeth spaced 10 degrees apart with one empty space for a missing tooth. By monitoring the pulse wheel, the CKP sensor signal indicates crankshaft position and speed information to the PCM. By monitoring the missing tooth, the CKP sensor is also able to identify piston travel in order to synchronize the ignition system and provide a way of tracking the angular position of the crankshaft relative to a fixed reference for the CKP sensor configuration. The PCM also uses the CKP signal to determine if a misfire has occurred by measuring rapid decelerations between teeth.

REMOVAL & INSTALLATION

4.0L Engine

See Figure 210.

1. Disconnect the battery ground cable.
2. Disconnect the crankshaft position (CKP) sensor electrical connector.
3. Remove the CKP sensor bolt. To install, tighten to 89 inch lbs. (10 Nm).
4. Remove the CKP sensor.
5. To install, reverse the removal procedure.

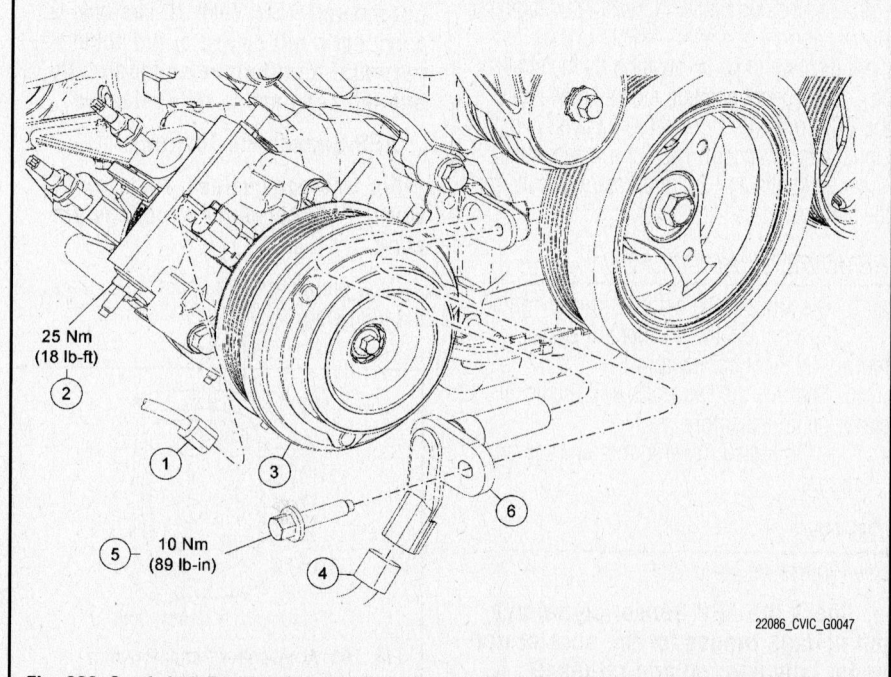

25 Nm (18 lb-ft)

10 Nm (89 lb-in)

22086_CVIC_G0047

Fig. 209 Crankshaft Position Sensor (6), connector (5), bolts (4) and related components

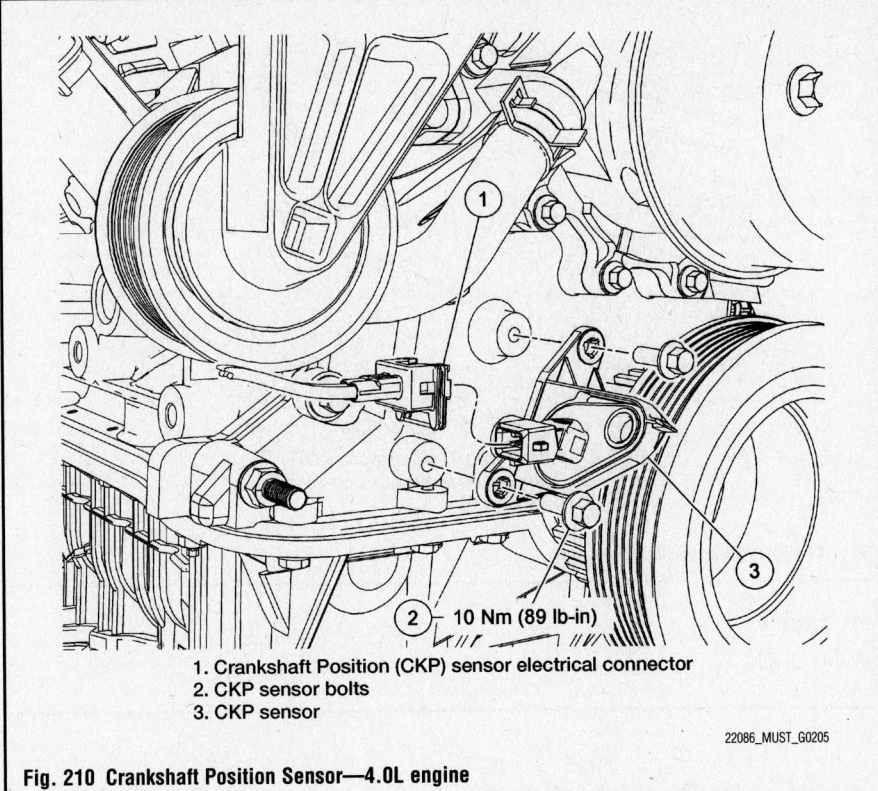

1. Crankshaft Position (CKP) sensor electrical connector
2. CKP sensor bolts
3. CKP sensor

22086_MUST_G0205

Fig. 210 Crankshaft Position Sensor—4.0L engine

4.6L and 5.4L Engines

See Figure 211.

1. With the vehicle in NEUTRAL, position it on a hoist.

2. Remove the supercharger (SC) belt (5.4L engine only).

3. Remove the accessory drive belt.

4. Detach the wiring harness retainers from the A/C compressor stud bolts.

5. Disconnect the A/C compressor field coil and the Crankshaft Position (CKP) sensor electrical connectors.

6. Remove the 3 stud bolts and position the A/C compressor aside.

   a. To install, tighten to 18 ft. lbs. (25 Nm).

7. Remove the CKP sensor bolt and sensor.

   a. To install, tighten to 89 inch lbs. (10 Nm).

8. To install, reverse the removal procedure.

TESTING

See Figures 212 and 213.

Check the CKP Sensor resistance
- Key in OFF position
- Measure the resistance between: CKP+—CKP-

If the CKP sensor resistance is between 250—1,000 ohms, sensor resistance is within acceptable limits, proceed to pin test.

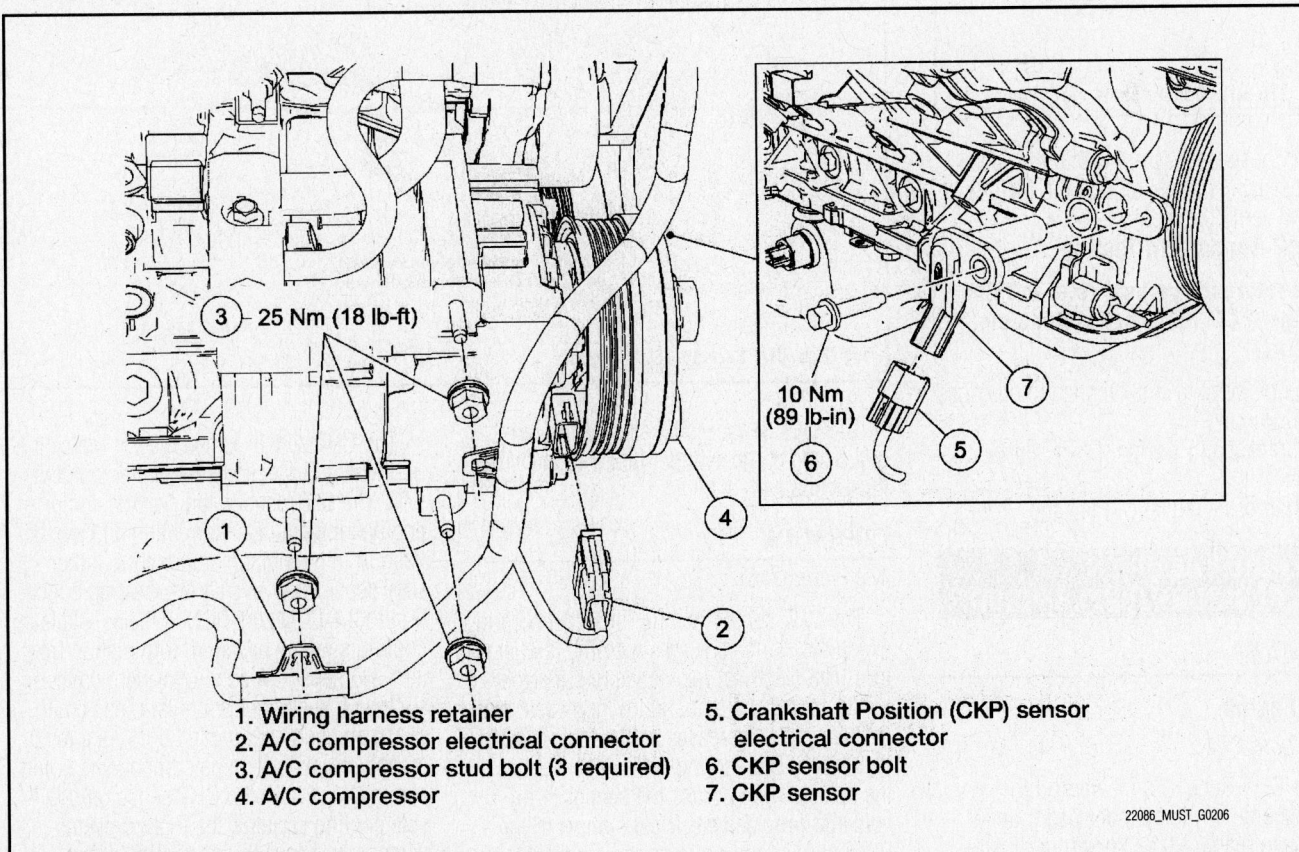

1. Wiring harness retainer
2. A/C compressor electrical connector
3. A/C compressor stud bolt (3 required)
4. A/C compressor
5. Crankshaft Position (CKP) sensor electrical connector
6. CKP sensor bolt
7. CKP sensor

22086_MUST_G0206

Fig. 211 Crankshaft Position Sensor—4.6L and 5.4L engines

Fig. 212 Crankshaft Position Sensor connector

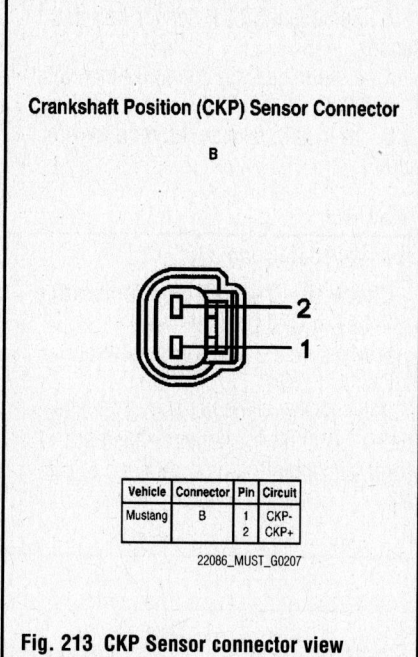

Fig. 213 CKP Sensor connector view

If the resistance is not within the specified resistance range, replace the CKP Sensor and verify the repair.

CMP Sensor Pin Testing

➡**For reference values, refer to PCM testing—PCM reference voltage pin chart**

This pinpoint test is intended to diagnose the following:

- Crankshaft Position (CKP) sensor (6C315)
- Harness circuits: CKP(+) and CKP(-)

CYLINDER HEAD TEMPERATURE (CHT) SENSOR

LOCATION

4.6L Engine

See Figure 214.

The CHT Sensor is located on the inboard side of the cylinder head, under the intake manifold, as shown in illustration.

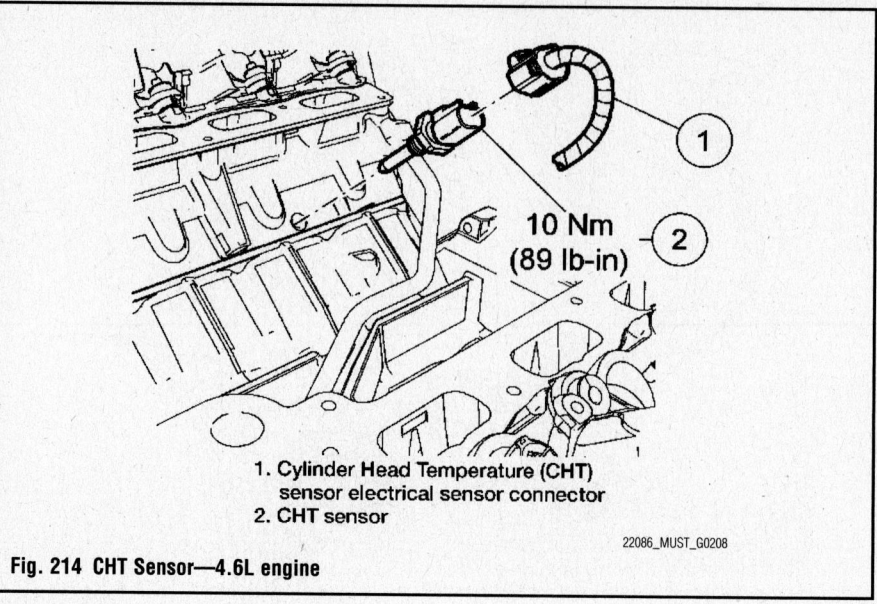

1. Cylinder Head Temperature (CHT) sensor electrical sensor connector
2. CHT sensor

Fig. 214 CHT Sensor—4.6L engine

5.4L Engine

See Figure 215.

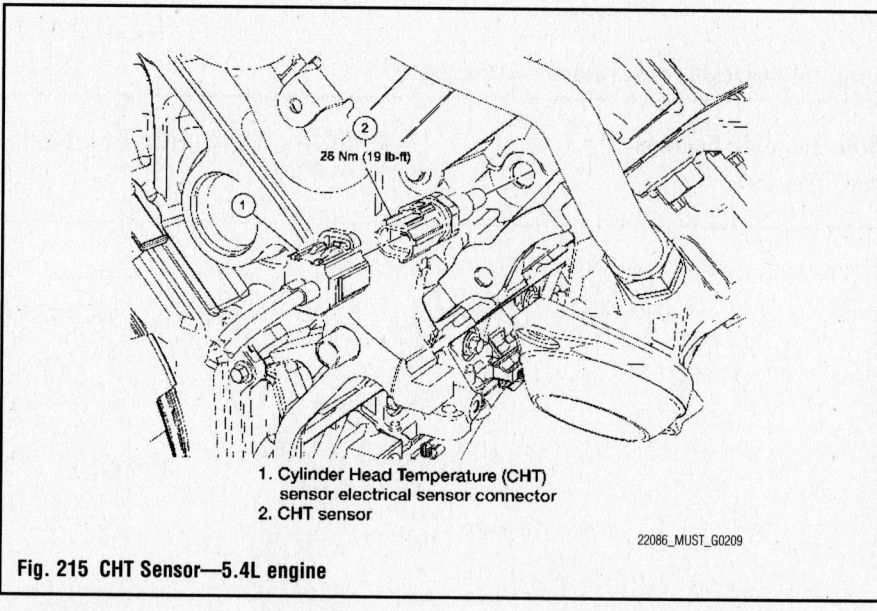

1. Cylinder Head Temperature (CHT) sensor electrical sensor connector
2. CHT sensor

Fig. 215 CHT Sensor—5.4L engine

The CHT Sensor is located on the outboard side of the cylinder head, as shown in illustration.

OPERATION

See Figure 216.

The CHT sensor is a thermistor device in which resistance changes with the temperature. The electrical resistance of a thermistor decreases as temperature increases, and the resistance increases as the temperature decreases. The varying resistance affects the voltage drop across the sensor terminals and provides electrical signals to the PCM corresponding to temperature.

The CHT sensor is installed in the cylinder head and measures the metal temperature. The CHT sensor can provide complete engine temperature information and can be used to infer coolant temperature. If the CHT sensor conveys an overheating condition to the PCM, the PCM initiates a failsafe cooling strategy based on information from the CHT sensor. A cooling system concern such as low coolant or coolant loss could cause an overheating condition. As a result, damage to major engine components could occur. Using both the CHT sensor and failsafe cooling strategy, the PCM prevents damage by allowing air-cooling of the engine and limp home capability.

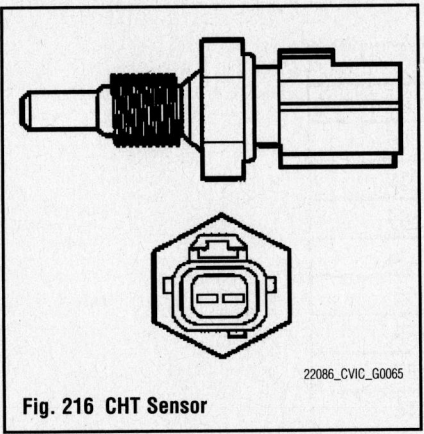

Fig. 216 CHT Sensor

The CHT sensor is mounted into the wall of the cylinder head and is not connected to any coolant passages, and it sends a signal to the PCM indicating the cylinder head temperature.

If the temperature exceeds approximately 121°C (250°F), the PCM disables 4 fuel injectors at a time. The PCM will alternate which fuel injectors are disabled every 32 engine cycles. The 4 cylinders that are not being fuel injected act as air pumps to aid in cooling the engine.

If the temperature exceeds approximately 166°C (330°F), the PCM disables all of the fuel injectors until the engine temperature drops below approximately 154°C (310°F).

If the engine reaches critical temperature, the coolant temperature gauge pointer will read fully hot at approximately 121°C (250°F).

REMOVAL & INSTALLATION

4.6L Engine
See Figure 214.

1. Release the fuel system pressure.
2. Disconnect the battery ground cable.
3. Remove the intake manifold. For additional information, refer to **Intake Manifold Removal and Installation** in the **Engine Repair** section.
4. Disconnect the Cylinder Head Temperature (CHT) sensor electrical connector.
5. Remove and discard the CHT sensor.
   a. To install, tighten to 89 inch lbs. (10 Nm).
6. To install, reverse the removal procedure.
   a. Do not reuse the CHT sensor, install a new sensor.

➡**The CHT sensor is not to be reused. Always install a new sensor.**

To install a new sensor, reverse the removal procedure.

5.4L Engine
See Figure 215.

1. Remove the battery, and the battery tray.
2. Disconnect the Cylinder Head Temperature (CHT) sensor electrical connector.
3. Remove and discard the CHT sensor.
   a. To install, tighten to 19 ft. lbs. (26 Nm).
4. To install, reverse the removal procedure.

Do not reuse the CHT sensor, install a new sensor.

TESTING

See Figures 217 and 218.

On applications that do not use an Engine Coolant Temperature (ECT) sensor, the CHT sensor is used to determine the engine coolant temperature. To cover the entire temperature range of both the CHT and ECT sensors, the PCM has a dual switching resistor circuit on the CHT input. A graph showing the temperature switching from the COLD END line to the HOT END line, with increasing temperature and back with decreasing temperature is included. Note the temperature to voltage overlap zone. Within this zone it is possible to have either a COLD END or HOT END voltage at the same temperature. For example, at 90°C (194°F) the voltage could read either 0.60 volt or 3.71 volts. Refer to the table for the temperature to voltage expected values.

Voltage values calculated for VREF = 5 volts. These values can vary by 15% due to sensor and VREF variations.

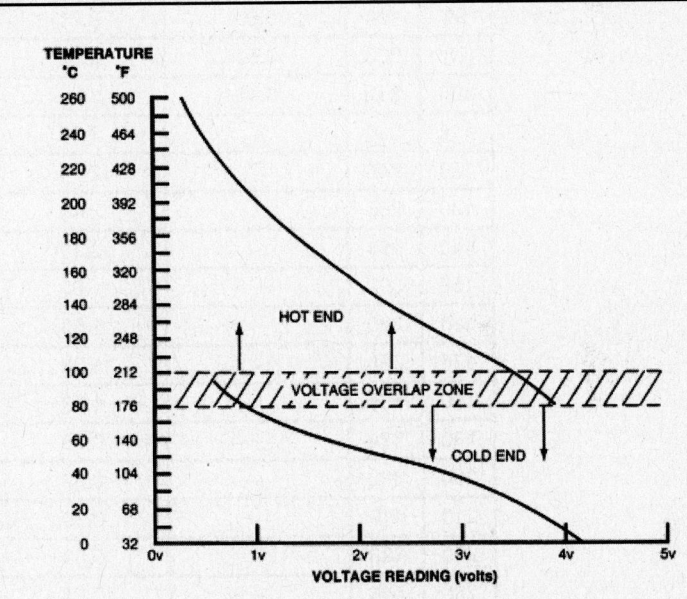

Cylinder Head Temperature (CHT) Sensor Connector

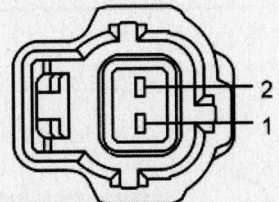

Pin	Circuit
2	SIGRTN (Signal Return)
1	CHT (Cylinder Head Temperature)

Fig. 217 CHT Sensor range chart

Temperature		CHT Sensor Values		
°C	°F	Cold End (volts)	Hot End (volts)	Resistance (K ohms)
-40	-40	4.89	-	965.808
-30	-22	4.81	-	513.019
-20	-4	4.67	-	283.664
-10	14	4.45	-	162.584
0	32	4.14	-	96.255
10	50	3.73	-	59.175
20	68	3.26	-	37.387
30	86	2.74	-	24.215
40	104	2.23	-	16.043
50	122	1.76	-	10.85
60	140	1.36	-	7.487
70	158	1.04	-	5.268
80	176	0.79	3.99	3.775
85	185	0.69	3.86	3.215
90	194	0.60	3.71	2.75
95	203	0.53	3.56	2.361
100	212	0.46	3.41	2.034
110	230	-	3.07	1.523
120	248	-	2.74	1.155
130	266	-	2.41	0.8866
140	284	-	2.10	0.6891
150	302	-	1.81	0.5417
160	320	-	1.55	0.4301
170	338	-	1.33	0.3449
180	356	-	1.13	0.2791
190	374	-	0.96	0.2278
200	392	-	0.82	0.1875
210	410	-	0.70	0.155
220	428	-	0.60	0.130
230	446	-	0.51	0.109
240	464	-	0.44	0.092
250	482		0.35	0.078
260	500		0.33	0.067

22086_CVIC_G0067

Fig. 218 CHT Sensor Expected Values

CHT Sensor Pin Testing

➡**For reference values, refer to PCM testing—PCM reference voltage pin chart**

This pinpoint test is intended to diagnose the following:

• Cylinder Head Temperature (CHT) sensor (6G004)

• Harness circuits: CHT, VREF, and SIGRTN

✷✷ WARNING

The CHT sensor is not to be reused. Always install a new sensor.

EXHAUST GAS RECIRCULATION (EGR) SYSTEM MODULE (ESM)

LOCATION

4.0L Engine

See Figure 219.

Refer to the accompanying illustration for the Exhaust Gas Recirculation (EGR) System Module (ESM) location.

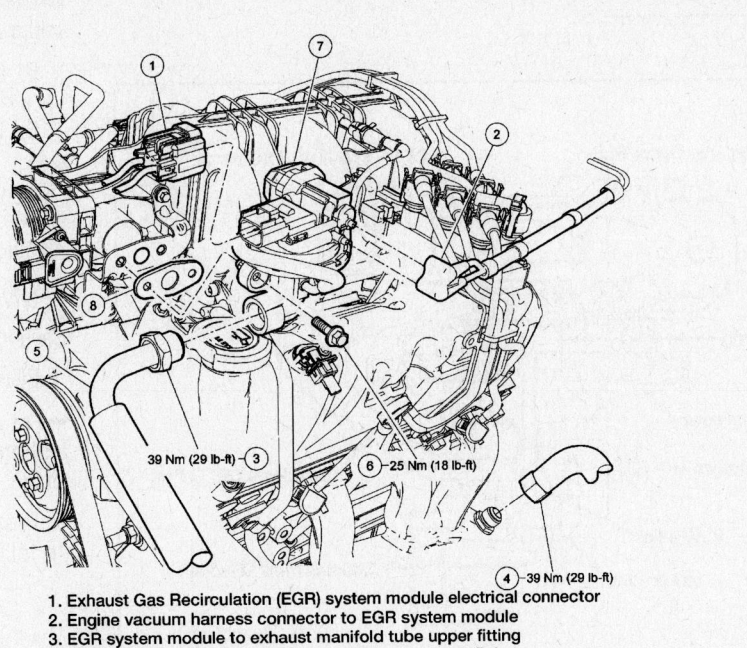

1. Exhaust Gas Recirculation (EGR) system module electrical connector
2. Engine vacuum harness connector to EGR system module
3. EGR system module to exhaust manifold tube upper fitting
4. EGR system module to exhaust manifold tube lower fitting
5. EGR system module tube
6. EGR system module bolts (2 required)
7. EGR system module
8. EGR system module gasket

22086_MUST_G0210

Fig. 219 EGR system components—4.0L and 4.6L engines

5.4L Engine

See Figure 220.

Refer to the accompanying illustration for the Exhaust Gas Recirculation (EGR) System Module (ESM) location.

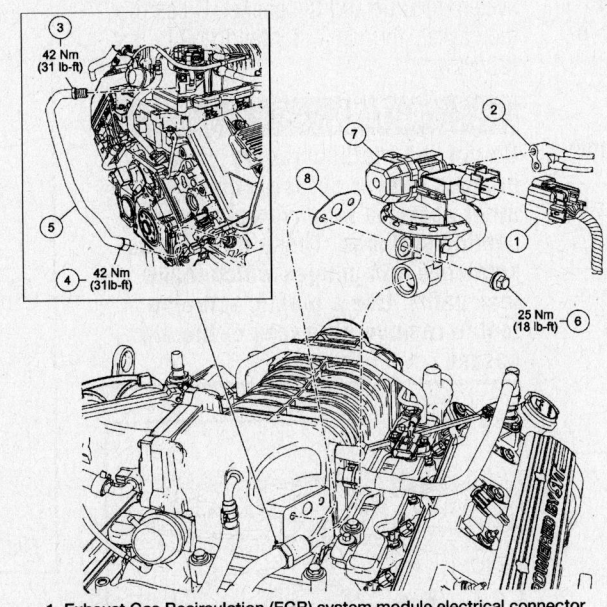

1. Exhaust Gas Recirculation (EGR) system module electrical connector
2. Engine vacuum harness connector to EGR system module
3. EGR system module to exhaust manifold tube upper fitting
4. EGR system module to exhaust manifold tube lower fitting
5. EGR system module tube
6. EGR system module bolts (2 required)
7. EGR system module
8. EGR system module gasket

22086_MUST_G0211

Fig. 220 EGR system components—5.4L engine

OPERATION

See Figure 221.

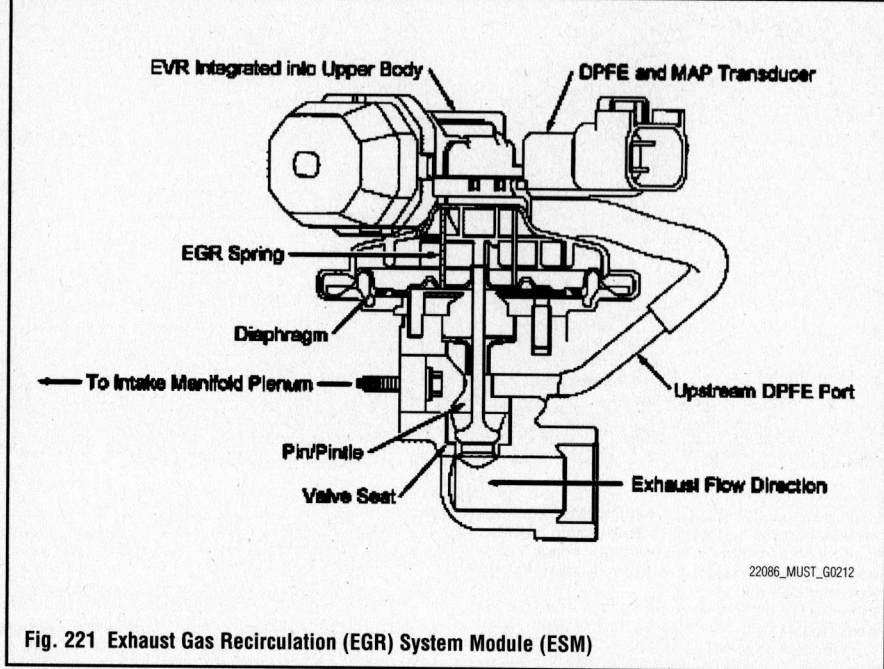

Fig. 221 Exhaust Gas Recirculation (EGR) System Module (ESM)

The ESM is an integrated Differential Pressure Feedback EGR (DPFE) system. It functions in the same manner as the conventional DPFE system, however the various system components have been integrated into a single component called the ESM. The flange of the valve portion of the ESM bolts directly to the intake manifold with a metal gasket that forms the measuring orifice. This arrangement increases system reliability, response time, and system precision. By relocating the EGR orifice from the exhaust to the intake side of the EGR valve, the downstream pressure signal measures Manifold Absolute Pressure (MAP). The system provides the Powertrain Control Module (PCM) with a differential DPFE signal, identical to a traditional DPFE system.

REMOVAL & INSTALLATION

See Figures 219, 220 and 222.

1. Disconnect the battery ground cable.
2. Disconnect the Exhaust Gas Recirculation (EGR) system module vacuum tube and electrical connector.
3. Disconnect the EGR system module to exhaust manifold tube upper fitting.
   a. To install, tighten to 29 ft. lbs. (39 Nm).

➡**Upon installation, make sure to install the correct EGR system module** mounting gasket. Even though varying gaskets may be very similar, orifice sizes may differ thus causing performance issues.

4. Remove the 2 bolts, the EGR system module and the gasket. Discard the gasket. To install, tighten to 18 ft. lbs. (25 Nm).

✳✳ CAUTION

Do not use metal scrapers, wire brushes, power abrasive disc or other abrasive means to clean the sealing surfaces. These tools cause scratches and gouges which make leak paths. Use a plastic scraping tool to remove all traces of the old gasket.

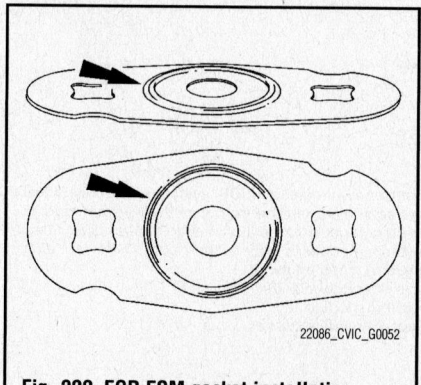

Fig. 222 EGR ESM gasket installation

➡**The EGR system module sealing surfaces are soft metals.**

5. Carefully clean the EGR system module sealing surfaces.
6. To install, reverse the removal procedure.
7. Install a new gasket with the raised circle facing away from the EGR system module.

TESTING

See Figure 223.

EGR ESM Pin Testing

➡**For reference values, refer to PCM testing—PCM reference voltage pin chart**

This pinpoint test is intended to diagnose the following:
- ESM (9Y456)
- Orifice tube assembly (9D477)
- Differential pressure feedback Exhaust Gas Recirculation (EGR) sensor pressure hoses
- Vacuum lines
- Harness circuits: VREF, DPFE, SIGRTN, EVR, VPWR and VREF

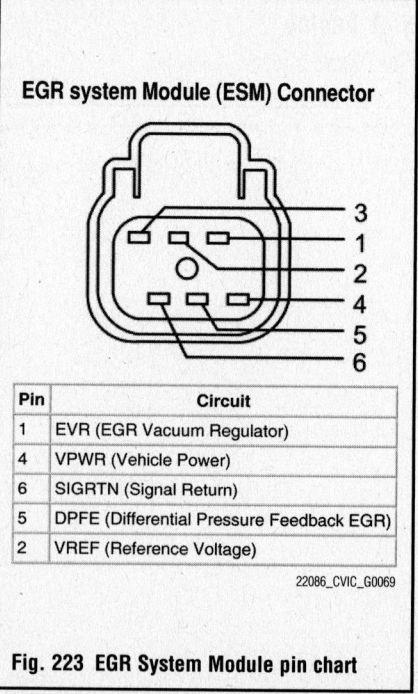

EGR system Module (ESM) Connector

Pin	Circuit
1	EVR (EGR Vacuum Regulator)
4	VPWR (Vehicle Power)
6	SIGRTN (Signal Return)
5	DPFE (Differential Pressure Feedback EGR)
2	VREF (Reference Voltage)

Fig. 223 EGR System Module pin chart

ENGINE COOLANT TEMPERATURE (ECT) SENSOR

LOCATION

4.0L Engine

See Figure 224.

Fig. 224 ECT Sensor—4.0L engine

Refer to the accompanying illustration for the Engine Coolant Temperature (ECT) sensor location.

5.4L Engine

See Figure 225.

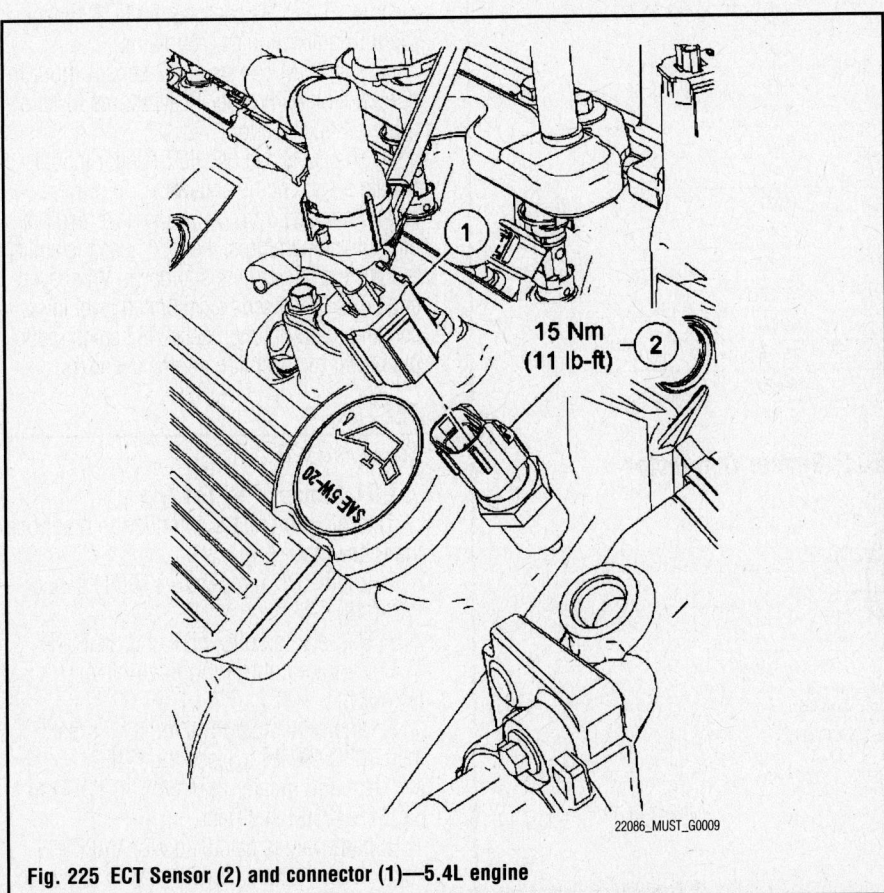

15 Nm
(11 lb-ft)

Fig. 225 ECT Sensor (2) and connector (1)—5.4L engine

Refer to the accompanying illustration for the Engine Coolant Temperature (ECT) sensor location.

OPERATION

See Figure 226.

The ECT sensor is a thermistor device in which resistance changes with temperature. The electrical resistance of a thermistor decreases as the temperature increases, and the resistance increases as the temperature decreases. The varying resistance changes the voltage drop across the sensor terminals and provides electrical signals to the PCM corresponding to temperature.

Thermistor–type sensors are considered passive sensors. A passive sensor is connected to a voltage divider network so that varying the resistance of the passive sensor causes a variation in total current flow. Voltage that is dropped across a fixed resistor in a series with the sensor resistor determines the voltage signal at the PCM. This voltage signal is equal to the reference voltage minus the voltage drop across the fixed resistor.

The ECT measures the temperature of the engine coolant. The PCM uses the ECT input for fuel control and for cooling fan control. There are 3 types of ECT sensors, threaded,

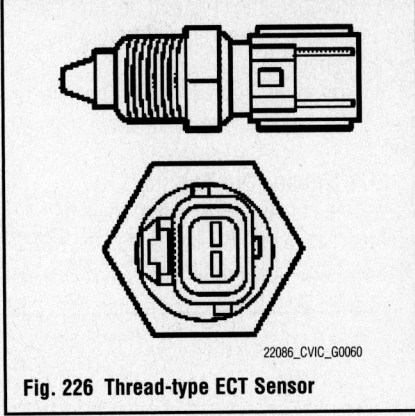

Fig. 226 Thread-type ECT Sensor

push–in, and twist–lock. The ECT sensor is located in an engine coolant passage.

REMOVAL & INSTALLATION

4.0L Engine

See Figure 224.

1. Drain the cooling system.
2. Disconnect the Engine Coolant Temperature (ECT) sensor electrical connector.
3. Remove the retaining clip and the ECT sensor.
  a. To install, reverse the removal procedure.
4. Fill and bleed the cooling system, and verify that there are no fluid leaks.

5.4L Engine

See Figure 225.

1. Drain the cooling system.
2. Disconnect the Engine Coolant Temperature (ECT) sensor electrical connector.
3. Remove the ECT sensor.
  a. To install, tighten to 11 ft. lbs. (15 Nm).
4. To install, reverse the removal procedure.
5. Fill and bleed the cooling system, and verify that there are no fluid leaks.

TESTING

See Figure 227.

1. Locate and disconnect the ECT sensor.
2. Connect a digital multi–meter between the ECT sensor terminals.
3. With the engine cold and the ignition switch in the ON position, measure and note the ECT sensor resistance.
4. Start the engine and allow the engine to reach normal operating temperature.
5. Monitor and note the ECT sensor resistance through the temperature range, and with the engine hot.

6. Compare the cold and hot ECT sensor resistance measurements with the accompanying chart.

7. If readings do not approximate those in the chart, proceed to the ECM voltage pin test.

ECT Sensor Pin Testing

Engine coolant temperature must be greater than 10°C (50°F) to pass the KOEO self–test and greater than 82°C (180°F) to pass the KOER self–test. to accomplish this, the engine must be at normal operating temperature.

ECT Sensor Pin Testing

This pinpoint test is intended to diagnose the following:
• Engine Coolant Temperature (ECT) sensor
• Harness circuits: ECT and SIGRTN
• Powertrain control module (PCM)

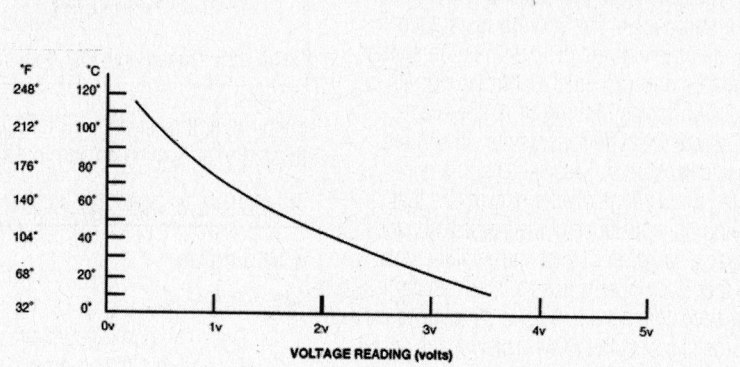

TEMPERATURE SENSOR VOLTAGE AND RESISTANCE SPECIFICATIONS			
Temperature		Temperature Sensor Values	
°C	°F	Voltage	Resistance (K ohms)
120	248	0.28	1.18
110	230	0.36	1.55
100	212	0.47	2.07
90	194	0.61	2.80
80	176	0.80	3.84
70	158	1.05	5.37
60	140	1.37	7.70
50	122	1.77	10.97
40	104	2.23	16.15
30	86	2.74	24.27
20	68	3.26	37.30
10	50	3.73	58.75
0	32	4.14	95.85
-10	14	4.45	160.31

Engine Coolant Temperature (ECT) Sensor Connector

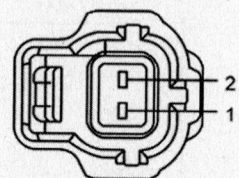

Vehicle	Connector	Pin	Circuit
Mustang	A	2	SIGRTN
		1	ECT

22086_MUST_G0213

Fig. 227 ECT resistance specification chart

Voltage values calculated for VREF = 5 volts. These values can vary by 15% due to sensor and VREF variations.

ENGINE OIL TEMPERATURE (EOT) SENSOR

OPERATION

The EOT sensor is a thermistor device in which resistance changes with temperature. The electrical resistance of a thermistor decreases as the temperature increases and the resistance increases as the temperature decreases. The varying resistance changes the voltage drop across the sensor terminals and provides electrical signals to the PCM corresponding to temperature.

Thermistor–type sensors are considered passive sensors. A passive sensor is connected to a voltage divider network so that varying the resistance of the passive sensor causes a variation in total current flow. Voltage that is dropped across a fixed resistor in a series with the sensor resistor determines the voltage signal at the PCM. This voltage signal is equal to the reference voltage minus the voltage drop across the fixed resistor.

The EOT sensor measures the temperature of the engine oil. The sensor is typically threaded into the engine oil lubrication system. The PCM can use the EOT sensor input to determine the following:
• The PCM can use EOT sensor input in conjunction with other PCM inputs to determine oil degradation.
• The PCM can use EOT sensor input to initiate a soft engine shutdown. To prevent engine damage from occurring as a result of high oil temperatures, the PCM has the ability to initiate a soft engine shutdown. Whenever engine RPM exceeds a calibrated level for a certain period of time, the PCM begins reducing power by disabling engine cylinders.

TESTING

See Figure 228.

EOT Sensor Pin Testing

This pinpoint test is intended to diagnose the following:
• Engine Oil Temperature (EOT) sensor (12A648)
• Harness circuits: EOT and SIGRTN Powertrain control module (PCM) (12A650)

Engine oil temperature must be greater than 10°C (50°F) to pass the KOEO self–test and greater than 66°C (150°F) to pass the KOER self–test.

Voltage values calculated for VREF = 5 volts. These values can vary by 15% due to sensor and VREF variations.

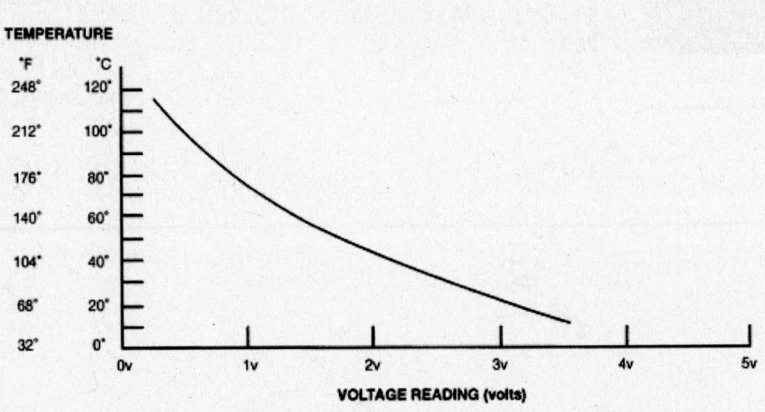

TEMPERATURE SENSOR VOLTAGE AND RESISTANCE SPECIFICATIONS			
Temperature		Temperature Sensor Values	
°C	°F	Voltage	Resistance (K ohms)
120	248	0.28	1.18
110	230	0.36	1.55
100	212	0.47	2.07
90	194	0.61	2.80
80	176	0.80	3.84
70	158	1.05	5.37
60	140	1.37	7.70
50	122	1.77	10.97
40	104	2.23	16.15
30	86	2.74	24.27
20	68	3.26	37.30
10	50	3.73	58.75
0	32	4.14	95.85
-10	14	4.45	160.31

Engine Oil Temperature (EOT) Sensor Connector

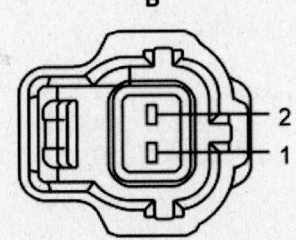

Vehicle	Connector	Pin	Circuit
Mustang	B	2 1	SIGRTN EOT

22086_MUST_G0214

Fig. 228 EOT Sensor resistance specification chart

LOCATION

4.0L Engine

See Figures 229 and 230.

Refer to the accompanying illustrations for Heated Oxygen (HO2S) Sensor and Catalyst Monitor Sensor (CMS) locations.

4.6L and 5.4L Engines

See Figures 231 and 232.

Refer to the accompanying illustrations for Heated Oxygen (HO2S) Sensor and Catalyst Monitor Sensor (CMS) locations.

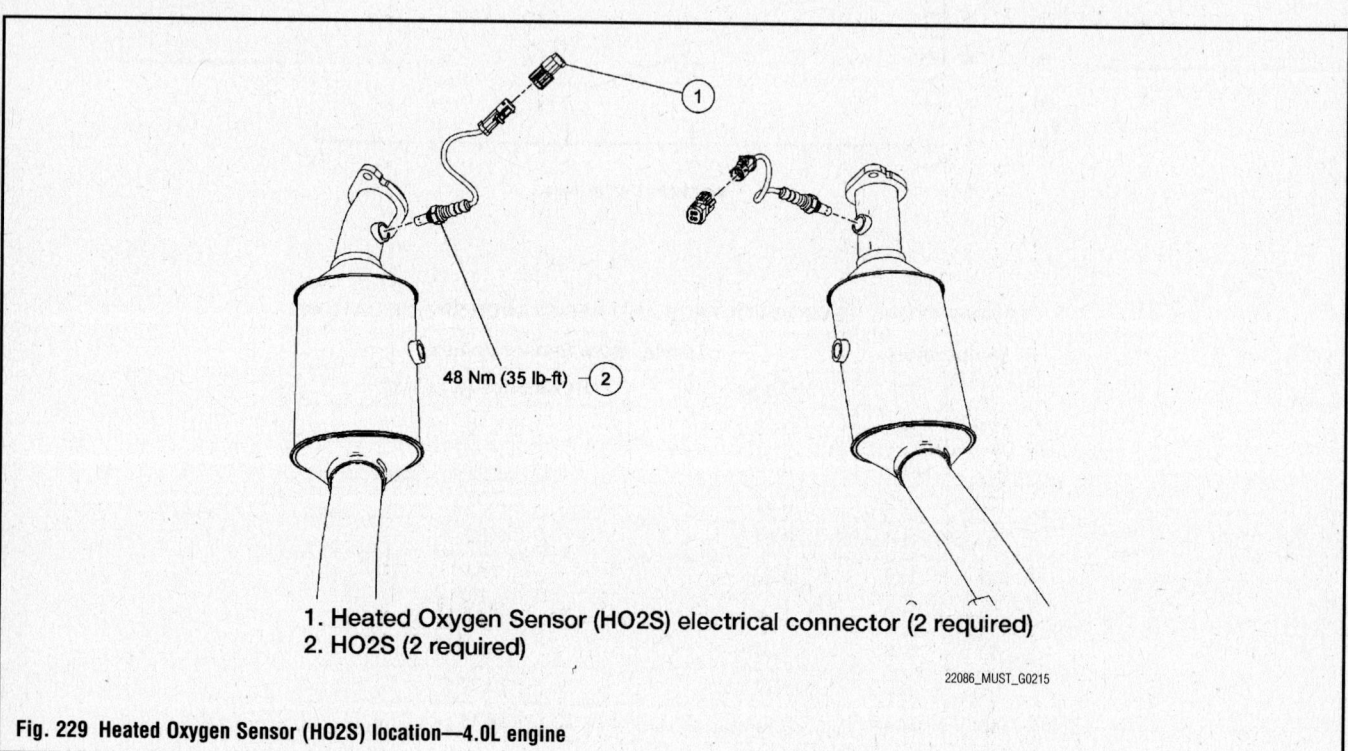

1. Heated Oxygen Sensor (HO2S) electrical connector (2 required)
2. HO2S (2 required)

22086_MUST_G0215

Fig. 229 Heated Oxygen Sensor (HO2S) location—4.0L engine

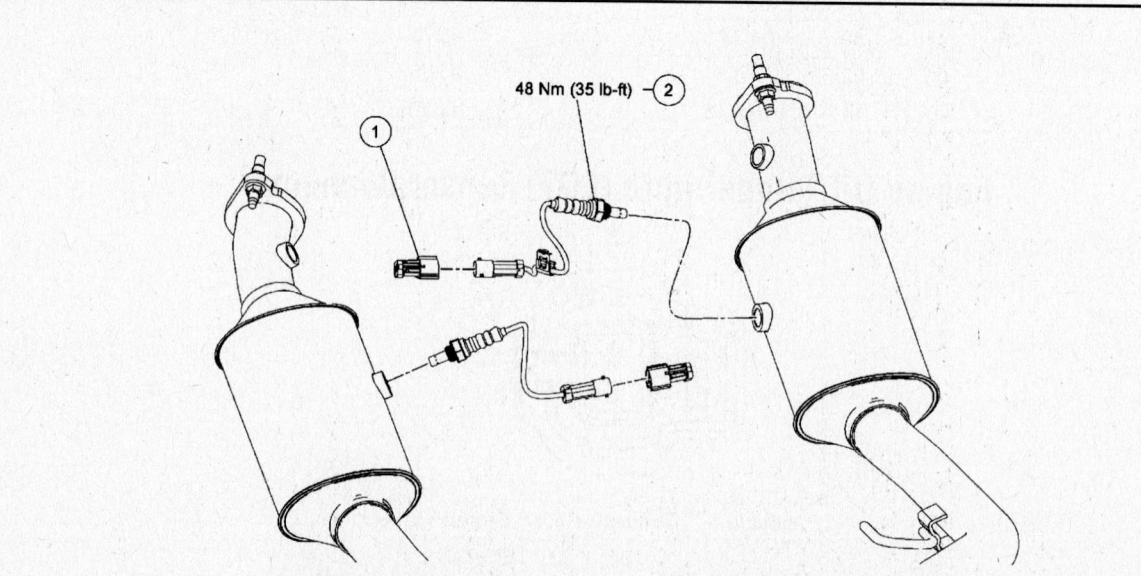

1. Catalyst Monitor Sensor (CMS) electrical connector (2 required)
2. CMS (2 required)

22086_MUST_G0216

Fig. 230 Catalyst Monitor Sensor location—4.0L engine

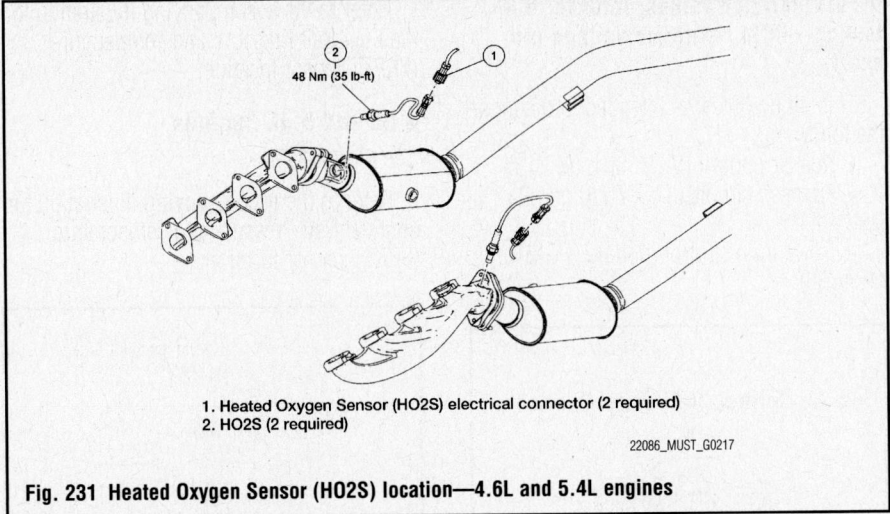

1. Heated Oxygen Sensor (HO2S) electrical connector (2 required)
2. HO2S (2 required)

22086_MUST_G0217

Fig. 231 Heated Oxygen Sensor (HO2S) location—4.6L and 5.4L engines

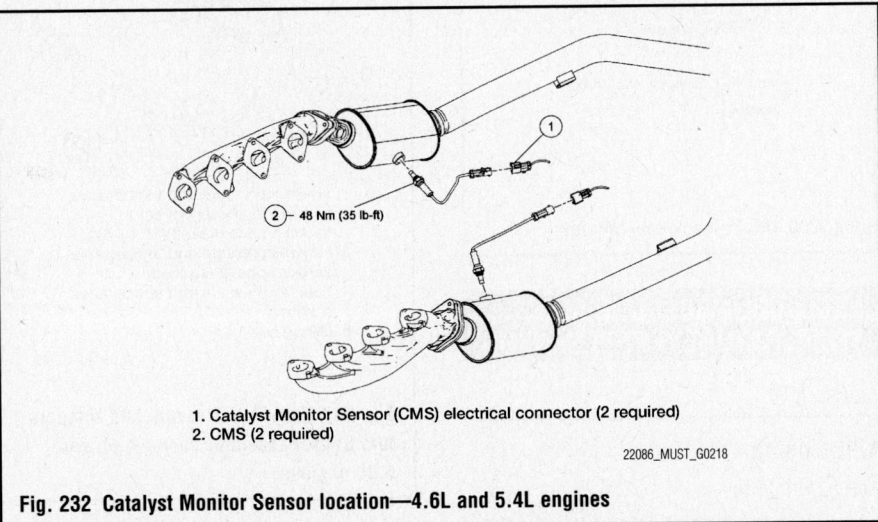

1. Catalyst Monitor Sensor (CMS) electrical connector (2 required)
2. CMS (2 required)

22086_MUST_G0218

Fig. 232 Catalyst Monitor Sensor location—4.6L and 5.4L engines

OPERATION

See Figure 233.

The HO2S detects the presence of oxygen in the exhaust and produces a variable voltage according to the amount of oxygen detected. A high concentration of oxygen (lean air/fuel ratio) in the exhaust produces a voltage signal less than 0.4 volt. A low concentration of oxygen (rich air/fuel ratio) produces a voltage

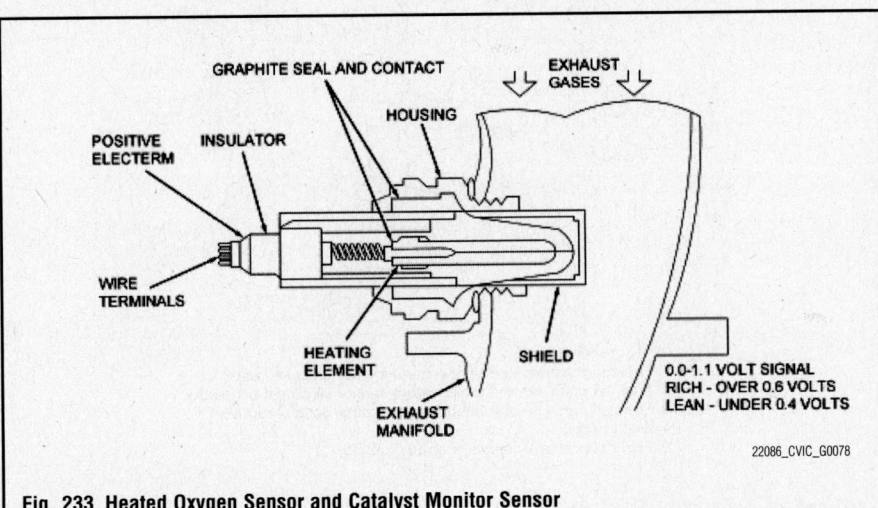

Fig. 233 Heated Oxygen Sensor and Catalyst Monitor Sensor

signal greater than 0.6 volt. The HO2S provides feedback to the PCM indicating air/fuel ratio in order to achieve a near stoichiometric air/fuel ratio of 14.7:1 during closed loop engine operation. The HO2S generates a voltage between 0.0 and 1.1 volts.

Embedded with the sensing element is the HO2S heater. The heating element heats the sensor to a temperature of 800°C (1,472°F). At approximately 300°C (572°F) the engine can enter closed loop operation. The VPWR circuit supplies voltage to the heater. The PCM turns the heater on by providing the ground when the correct conditions occur. The heater allows the engine to enter closed loop operation sooner. The use of this heater requires the HO2S heater control to be duty cycled, to prevent damage to the heater.

REMOVAL & INSTALLATION

Heated Oxygen Sensor

1. Disconnect the battery ground cable.
2. Disconnect the right side Heated Oxygen Sensor (HO2S) electrical connector.
3. Disconnect the left side HO2S electrical connector.
4. Remove the R/H or L/H HO2S as necessary. To install, tighten to 30 ft. lbs. (41 Nm).
5. To install, reverse the removal procedure. Apply a light coat of ant–seize lubricant to the threads of the HO2S.

Catalyst Monitor

6. Disconnect the battery ground cable.
7. Disconnect the right side Catalyst Monitor Sensor (CMS) electrical connector.
8. Disconnect the left side CMS electrical connector.
9. Remove the R/H or L/H CMS as necessary. To install, tighten to 30 ft. lbs. (41 Nm).
10. To install, reverse the removal procedure. Apply a light coat of ant–seize lubricant to the threads of the HO2S.

TESTING

See Figure 234.

HO2 Sensor Pin Testing

➡**For reference values, refer to PCM testing—PCM reference voltage pin chart**

This pinpoint test is intended to diagnose the following:
- HO2S/O2S (9F472)
- HO2S/O2S (9G444)
- Harness circuits: HO2S, HO2S Heater, VPWR, and SIGRTN

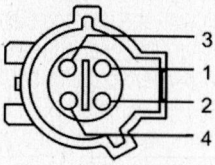

Heated Oxygen Sensor (HO2S) and Catalyst Mobitor Sensor (CMS) Connector

Vehicle	Connector	Pin	Circuit
Mustang	D	1	HO2S Heater
		4	SIGRTN
		2	VPWR
		3	HO2S Signal

22086_MUST_G0219

Fig. 234 HO2S and CMS connector view with pin identification

IDLE AIR CONTROL (IAC) VALVE

OPERATION

➡ **The IAC valve assembly is not adjustable and cannot be cleaned, also some IAC valves are normally open and others are normally closed. Some IAC valves require engine vacuum to operate.**

The IAC valve assembly controls the engine idle speed and provides a dashpot function. The IAC valve assembly meters intake air around the throttle plate through a bypass within the IAC valve assembly and throttle body. The PCM determines the desired idle speed or bypass air and signals the IAC valve assembly through a specified duty cycle. The IAC valve responds by positioning the IAC valve to control the amount of bypassed air. The PCM monitors engine RPM, and increases or decreases the IAC duty cycle in order to achieve the desired RPM.

The PCM uses the IAC valve assembly to control:
- No touch start
- Cold engine fast idle for rapid warm-up
- Idle (corrects for engine load)
- Stumble or stalling on deceleration (provides a dashpot function)
- Over-temperature idle boost

TESTING

See Figure 235.

IAC Valve Pin Testing

➡ **For reference values, refer to PCM testing—PCM reference voltage pin chart**

This pinpoint test is intended to diagnose the following:
- Idle air control (IAC) valve (9F715)
- Harness circuits: IAC, PWR and B+ (IAC-RC)
- Powertrain control module (PCM) (12A650)

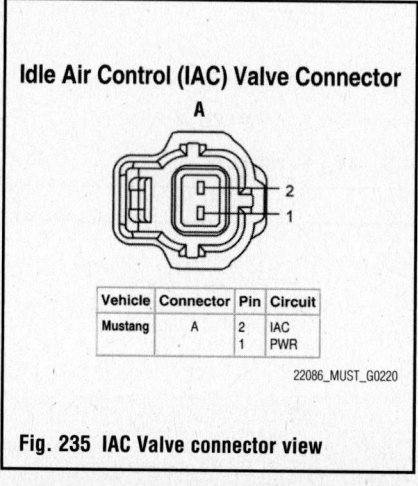

Idle Air Control (IAC) Valve Connector A

Vehicle	Connector	Pin	Circuit
Mustang	A	2	IAC
		1	PWR

22086_MUST_G0220

Fig. 235 IAC Valve connector view

FUEL RAIL PRESSURE AND TEMPERATURE (FRPT) SENSOR

LOCATION

4.0L Engine

See Figure 236.

Refer to the accompanying illustration for the Fuel Rail Pressure and Temperature (FRPT) sensor location.

4.6L and 5.4L Engines

See Figure 237.

Refer to the accompanying illustration for the Fuel Rail Pressure and Temperature (FRPT) sensor location.

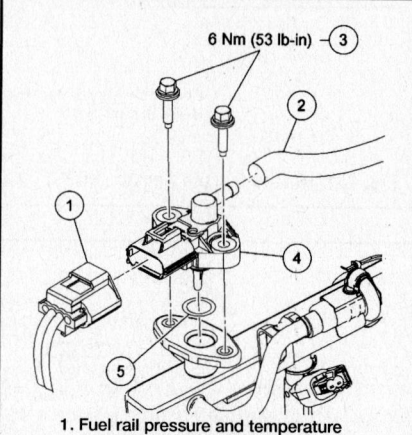

1. Fuel rail pressure and temperature sensor electrical connector
2. Vacuum hose (4.6L-3V/ 5.4L-4V)
3. Fuel rail pressure and temperature sensor bolts (2 required)
4. Fuel rail pressure and temperature sensor
5. O-ring seal

22086_MUST_G0222

Fig. 237 Fuel Rail Pressure and Temperature Sensor assembly view—4.6L and 5.4L engines

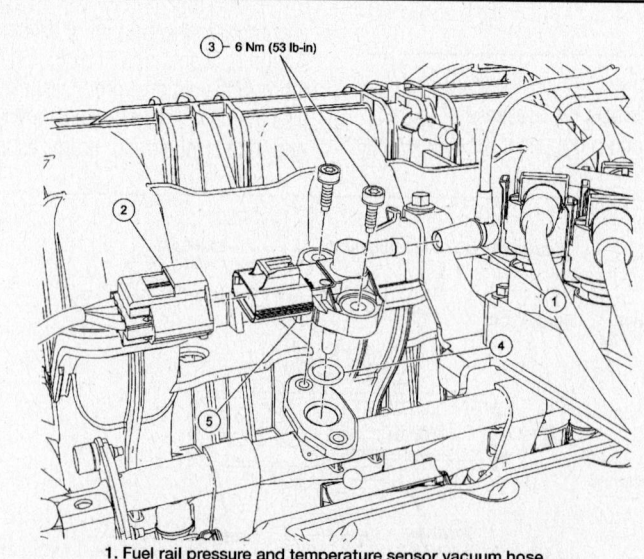

1. Fuel rail pressure and temperature sensor vacuum hose
2. Fuel rail pressure and temperature sensor electrical connector
3. Fuel rail pressure and temperature sensor bolts (2 required)
4. O-ring seal
5. Fuel rail pressure and temperature sensor

22086_MUST_G0221

Fig. 236 Fuel Rail Pressure and Temperature Sensor assembly view—4.0L engine

OPERATION

See Figure 238.

The FRPT sensor is a diaphragm strain gauge device in which resistance changes with pressure. The electrical resistance of a strain gauge increases as pressure increases, and the resistance decreases as the pressure decreases. The varying resistance affects the voltage drop across the sensor terminals and provides electrical signals to the PCM corresponding to pressure.

Strain gauge type sensors are considered passive sensors. A passive sensor is connected to a voltage divider network so that varying the resistance of the passive sensor causes a variation in total current flow. Voltage that is dropped across a fixed resistor in series with the sensor resistor determines the voltage signal at the PCM. This voltage signal is equal to the reference voltage minus the voltage drop across the fixed resistor.

The FRPT sensor measures the pressure of the fuel near the fuel injectors. This signal is used by the PCM to adjust the fuel injector pulse width and meter fuel to each engine combustion cylinder.

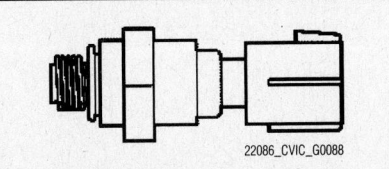

22086_CVIC_G0088

Fig. 238 Fuel Rail Pressure and Temperature (FRPT) Sensor

REMOVAL & INSTALLATION

✳✳ WARNING

Do not smoke, carry lighted tobacco or have an open flame of any type when working on or near any fuel-related component. Highly flammable mixtures are always present and may be ignited. Failure to follow these instructions may result in serious personal injury.

✳✳ WARNING

Before working on or disconnecting any of the fuel tubes or fuel system components, relieve the fuel system pressure to prevent accidental spraying of fuel. Fuel in the fuel system remains under high pressure, even when the engine is not running. Failure to follow this instruction may result in serious personal injury.

1. Release the fuel system pressure.
2. Disconnect the battery ground cable.
3. Disconnect the fuel rail pressure and temperature sensor electrical connector.
4. Disconnect the vacuum hose from the fuel rail pressure and temperature sensor.
5. Remove the 2 bolts and the fuel rail pressure and temperature sensor.
   a. To install, tighten to 53 inch lbs. (6 Nm).
6. To install, reverse the removal procedure.
7. Inspect the O-ring seal and install new as necessary.
8. Lubricate the O-ring seal with clean engine oil.

TESTING

See Figure 239.

➡With the engine running, the FRPT PID value may be 48–70 kPa (7–10 psi) higher than a fuel pressure reading taken with a mechanical gauge.

FRPT Sensor Pin testing

➡For reference values, refer to PCM testing—PCM reference voltage pin chart

This pinpoint test is intended to diagnose the following:
- Fuel Rail Pressure Temperature (FRPT) sensor (9G756)
- Harness circuits: FRPT

INTAKE AIR TEMPERATURE (IAT) SENSOR

LOCATION

See Figure 240.

Tables and Graphs

FRP AND FRPT SENSOR VOLTAGE AND PRESSURE SPECIFICATIONS

Voltage	Pressure (kPa)	Pressure (psi)
4.5	482	70
3.9	413	60
3.4	344	50
2.8	275	40
2.2	207	30
1.6	138	20
1.1	69	10
0.5	0	0

FRPT SENSOR TEMPERATURE, VOLTAGE, AND RESISTANCE SPECIFICATIONS

Temperature		Sensor	
°C	°F	Volts	K Ohms
100	212	0.47	2.073
95	203	0.54	2.405
90	194	0.61	2.800
85	185	0.70	3.273
80	176	0.80	3.840
75	167	0.92	4.524
70	158	1.06	5.351
65	149	1.21	6.356
60	140	1.38	7.584
55	131	1.56	9.091
50	122	1.77	10.949
45	113	1.99	13.252
40	104	2.23	16.123
35	95	2.48	19.720
30	86	2.74	24.253
25	77	3.00	30.000
20	68	3.26	37.332
15	59	3.50	46.745
10	50	3.73	58.911
5	41	3.95	74.745
0	32	4.13	95.501

Fuel Rail Pressure Temperature (FRPT) Sensor Connector

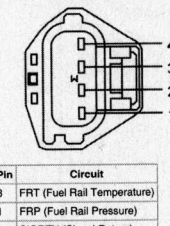

Pin	Circuit
3	FRT (Fuel Rail Temperature)
1	FRP (Fuel Rail Pressure)
4	SIGRTN (Signal Return)
2	VREF (Reference Voltage)

22086_MUST_G0223

Fig. 239 FRPT Sensor tables and graphs

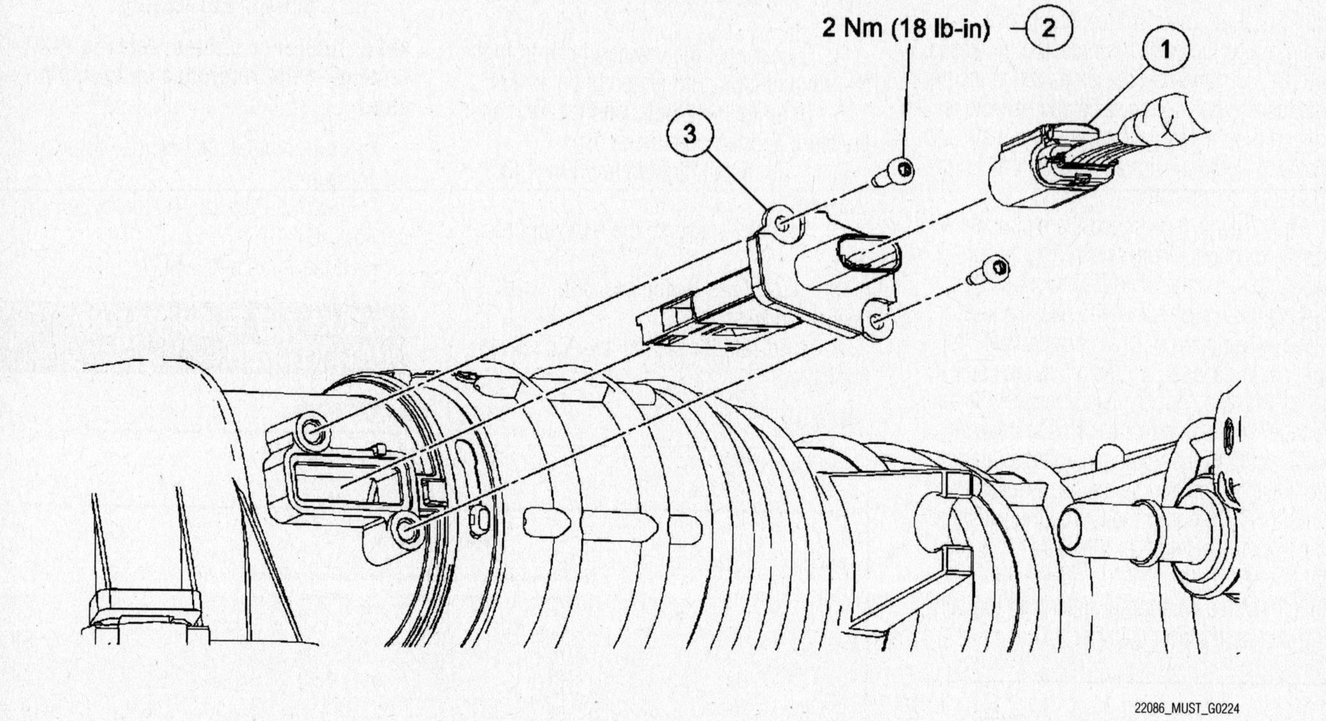

Fig. 240 Intake Air Temperature (IAT) sensor (3), connector (1) and retaining screws (2)

The Intake Air Temperature (IAT) Sensor is integrated with the Mass Air Flow (MAF) Sensor, and is located on the inboard side of the air cleaner housing.

OPERATION

See Figure 241.

The Intake Air Temperature (IAT) sensor determines the air temperature inside the intake manifold. Resistance changes in response to the ambient air temperature. The sensor has a negative temperature coefficient. As the temperature of the sensor rises the resistance across the sensor decreases. This provides a signal to the PCM indicating the temperature of the incoming air charge. This sensor helps the PCM to determine spark timing and air/fuel ratio. Information from this sensor is added to the pressure sensor information to calculate the air mass being sent to the cylinders. The IAT is a two wire sensor, a 5 volt reference signal is sent to the sensor and the signal return is based upon the change in the measured resistance due to temperature.

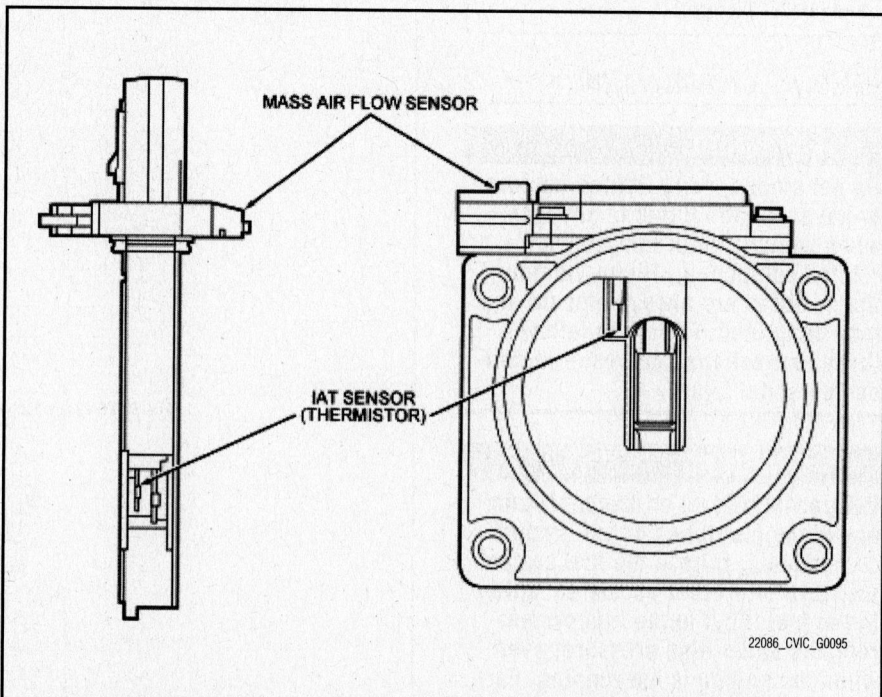

Fig. 241 Integrated Intake Air Temperature (IAT) Sensor is incorporated into a drop–in or flange–type MAF sensor

REMOVAL & INSTALLATION

See Figures 242 through 244.

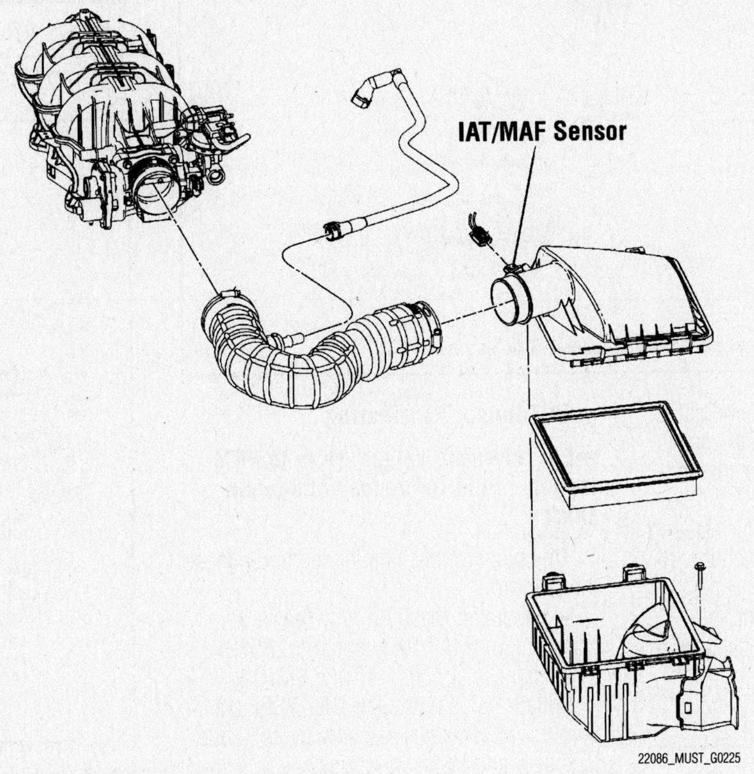

IAT/MAF Sensor

22086_MUST_G0225

Fig. 242 Intake air system component assembly view—4.0L engine

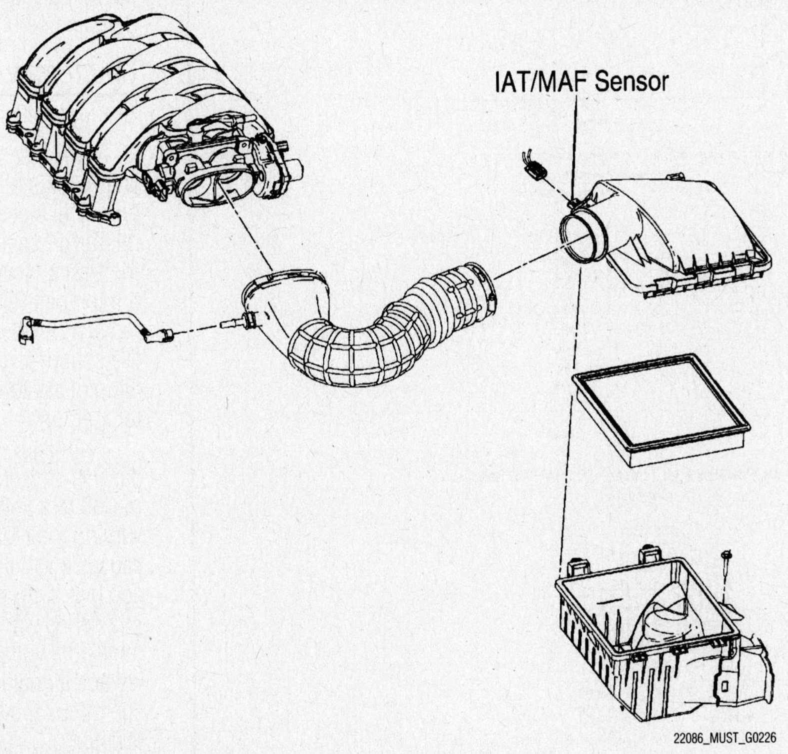

IAT/MAF Sensor

22086_MUST_G0226

Fig. 243 Intake air system component assembly view—4.6L engine

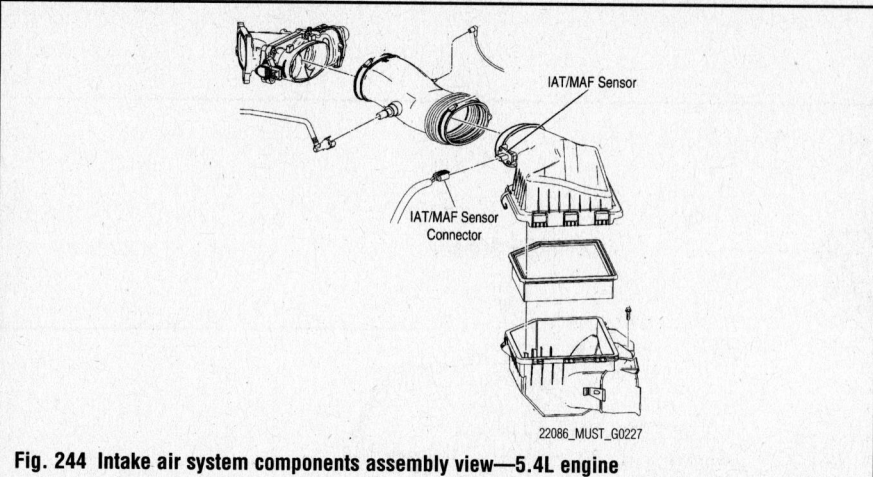

Fig. 244 Intake air system components assembly view—5.4L engine

1. Disconnect the battery ground cable.
2. Disconnect the Intake Air Temperature/Mass Air Flow (IAT/MAF) sensor electrical connector.
3. Remove the IAT/MAF sensor retaining screws. To install, tighten to 53 inch lbs. (6 Nm).
4. Remove the IAT/MAF sensor.
5. To install, reverse the removal procedure.

TESTING

See Figure 245.

IAT Sensor Pin Testing

➡**For reference values, refer to PCM testing—PCM reference voltage pin chart**

This pinpoint test is intended to diagnose the following:
- Integrated Mass Air Flow/Intake Air Temperature (MAF/IAT) sensor (12B579)
- Harness circuits: IAT and SIGRTN Voltage values calculated for VREF equal 5 volts. These values can vary by 15% due to sensor and VREF variations.

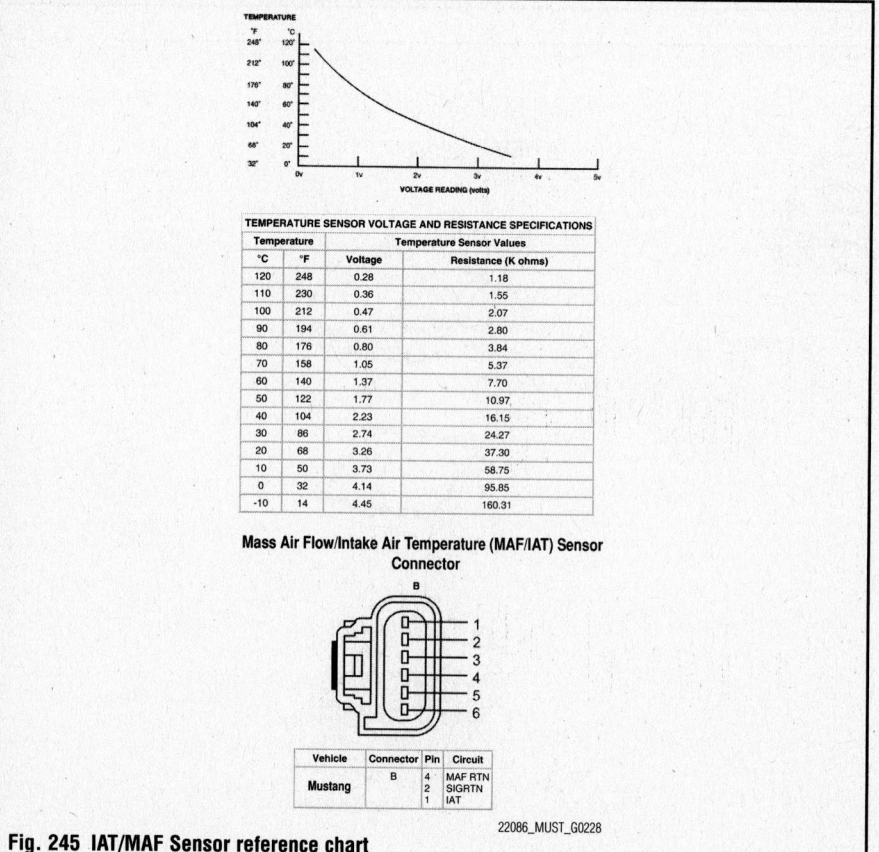

TEMPERATURE SENSOR VOLTAGE AND RESISTANCE SPECIFICATIONS

Temperature		Temperature Sensor Values	
°C	°F	Voltage	Resistance (K ohms)
120	248	0.28	1.18
110	230	0.36	1.55
100	212	0.47	2.07
90	194	0.61	2.80
80	176	0.80	3.84
70	158	1.05	5.37
60	140	1.37	7.70
50	122	1.77	10.97
40	104	2.23	16.15
30	86	2.74	24.27
20	68	3.26	37.30
10	50	3.73	58.75
0	32	4.14	95.85
-10	14	4.45	160.31

Mass Air Flow/Intake Air Temperature (MAF/IAT) Sensor Connector

Vehicle	Connector	Pin	Circuit
Mustang	B	4	MAF RTN
		2	SIGRTN
		1	IAT

Fig. 245 IAT/MAF Sensor reference chart

INTAKE AIR TEMPERATURE 2 (IAT2) SENSOR—(5.4L ENGINE ONLY)

LOCATION

See Figure 246.

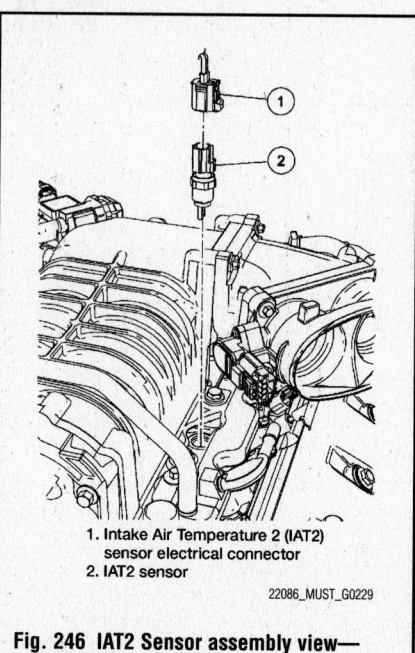

1. Intake Air Temperature 2 (IAT2) sensor electrical connector
2. IAT2 sensor

Fig. 246 IAT2 Sensor assembly view— 5.4L engine

Refer to the accompanying illustration for the IAT2 sensor. This sensor is used on the 5.4L engine only.

OPERATION

See Figure 247.

The IAT sensor is a thermistor device in which resistance changes with temperature. The electrical resistance of a thermistor decreases as the temperature increases, and the resistance increases as the temperature decreases. The varying resistance affects the voltage drop across the sensor terminals and provides electrical signals to the PCM corresponding to temperature.

Thermistor–type sensors are considered passive sensors. A passive sensor is connected to a voltage divider network so that varying the resistance of the passive sensor causes a variation in total current flow. Voltage that is dropped across a fixed resistor in a series with the sensor resistor determines the voltage signal at the PCM. This voltage signal is equal to the reference voltage minus the voltage drop across the fixed resistor.

The IAT provides air temperature information to the PCM. The PCM uses the air

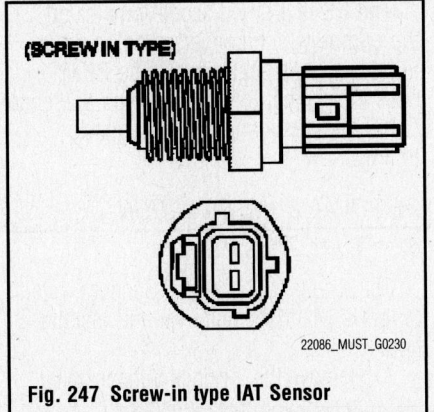

Fig. 247 Screw-in type IAT Sensor

temperature information as a correction factor in the calculation of fuel, spark, and air flow. The IAT sensor provides a quicker temperature change response time than the ECT or CHT sensor. Currently there are 2 design types of IAT sensors used, a stand alone/non–integrated type and a integrated type. Both types function the same, however the integrated type is incorporated into the mass air flow (MAF) sensor instead of being a stand alone sensor.

Supercharged vehicles use 2 IAT sensors. Both sensors are thermistor type devices and operate as described above. One is located before the supercharger at the air cleaner for standard OBD/cold weather input, while a second sensor (IAT2) is located after the super-charger in the intake manifold. The IAT2 sensor located after the super-charger provides air temperature information to the PCM to control spark and to help determine Charge Air Cooler (CAC) efficiency.

REMOVAL & INSTALLATION

See Figure 246.

1. Disconnect the Intake Air Temperature 2 (IAT2) sensor electrical connector.
2. Remove the IAT2 sensor.

To install:

3. Install the IAT2 sensor. Tighten the IAT2 sensor in 2 stages:
   a. Stage 1: Tighten the IAT2 sensor to 11 ft. lbs. (15 Nm).

➡**During Stage 2, do not tighten the IAT2 sensor more than one full turn and do not rotate the IAT2 sensor counter clockwise after tightening.**

   b. Stage 2: Tighten the IAT2 sensor until it is aligned as shown.
4. Connect the IAT2 sensor electrical connector.

TESTING
See Figure 248.

IAT Sensor Pin Testing

➡**For reference values, refer to PCM testing—PCM reference voltage pin chart**

This pinpoint test is intended to diagnose the following:
- Intake Air Temperature 2 (IAT2) sensor (12A697)
- Harness circuits: IAT2 and SIGRTN
- Powertrain control module (PCM) (12A650)

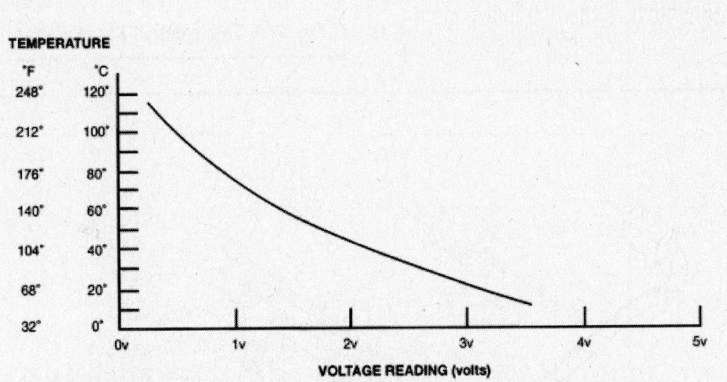

Temperature		Temperature Sensor Values	
°C	°F	Voltage	Resistance (K ohms)
120	248	0.28	1.18
110	230	0.36	1.55
100	212	0.47	2.07
90	194	0.61	2.80
80	176	0.80	3.84
70	158	1.05	5.37
60	140	1.37	7.70
50	122	1.77	10.97
40	104	2.23	16.15
30	86	2.74	24.27
20	68	3.26	37.30
10	50	3.73	58.75
0	32	4.14	95.85
-10	14	4.45	160.31

TEMPERATURE SENSOR VOLTAGE AND RESISTANCE SPECIFICATIONS

Intake Air Temperature 2 (IAT2) Sensor Connector

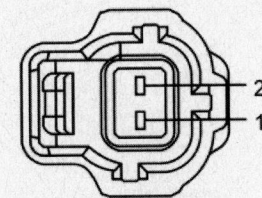

Pin	Circuit
2	SIGRTN (Signal Return)
1	IAT2 (Intake Air Temperature 2)

22086_MUST_G0231

Fig. 248 IAT2 connector view and reference chart

Voltage values calculated for VREF = 5 volts. These values can vary by 15% due to sensor and VREF variations.

KNOCK SENSOR (KS)

LOCATION

See Figures 249 and 250.

The Knock Sensors are located in the top of the engine block, under the intake manifold.

OPERATION

See Figure 251.

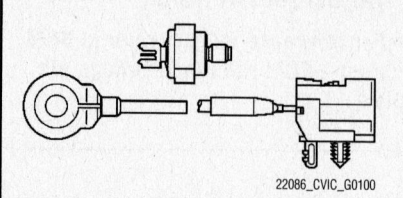

22086_CVIC_G0100

Fig. 251 Two types of Knock Sensor

The KS is a tuned accelerometer on the engine which converts engine vibration to an electrical signal. The PCM uses this signal to determine the presence of engine knock and to retard spark timing.

REMOVAL & INSTALLATION

See Figures 249 and 250.

For access to the Knock Sensors, refer to Intake Manifold Removal and Installation.

1. Remove the 2 Knock Sensor bolts, and remove the Knock Sensors.
   a. To install, tighten the Knock Sensor bolts to 15 ft. lbs. (20 Nm).
2. To install, reverse the removal procedure.

TESTING

See Figure 252.

Knock Sensor Pin Testing

➡ **For reference values, refer to PCM testing—PCM reference voltage pin chart**

This pinpoint test is intended to diagnose the following:
- Knock Sensors KS1, KS2 (12A699)
- Harness circuits: KS1+, KS1-, KS2+, and KS2-
- Powertrain control module (PCM) (12A650)

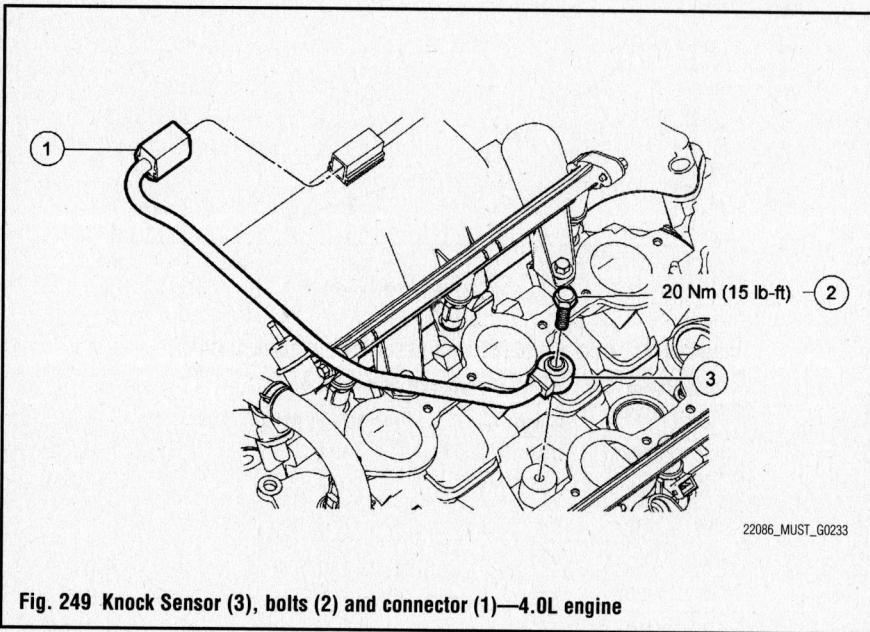

20 Nm (15 lb-ft)

22086_MUST_G0233

Fig. 249 Knock Sensor (3), bolts (2) and connector (1)—4.0L engine

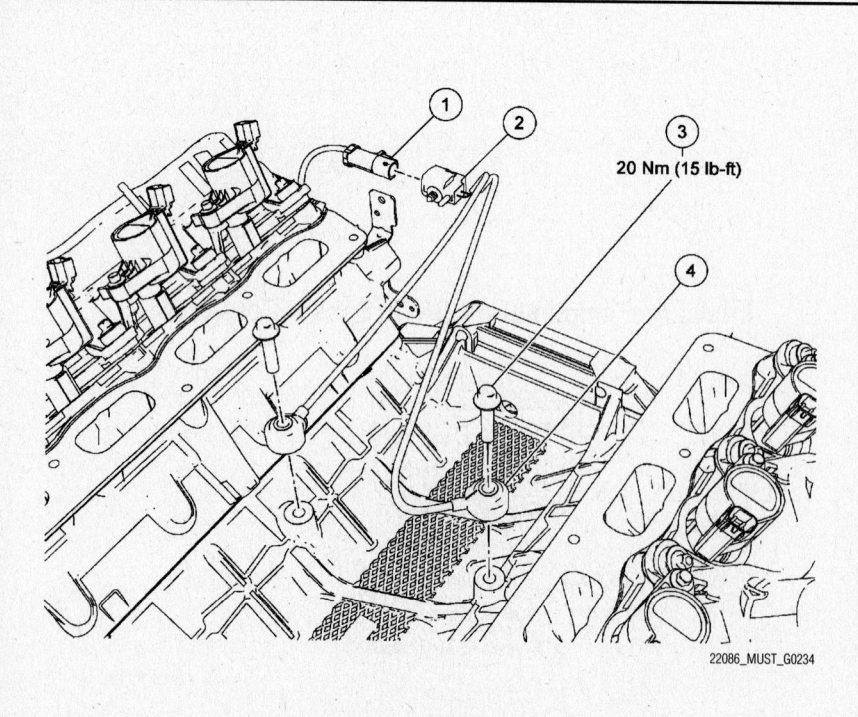

20 Nm (15 lb-ft)

22086_MUST_G0234

Fig. 250 Knock Sensor location (4) and related components—4.6L engine

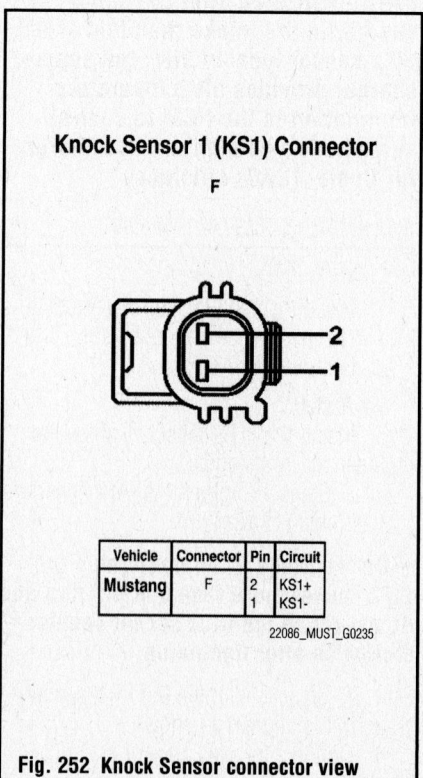

Knock Sensor 1 (KS1) Connector

F

Vehicle	Connector	Pin	Circuit
Mustang	F	2	KS1+
		1	KS1-

22086_MUST_G0235

Fig. 252 Knock Sensor connector view

MANIFOLD ABSOLUTE PRESSURE (MAP) SENSOR

OPERATION

See Figure 253.

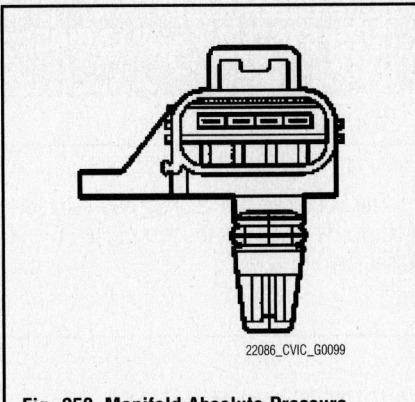

22086_CVIC_G0099

Fig. 253 Manifold Absolute Pressure (MAP) Sensor

The MAP sensor measures intake manifold absolute pressure. The PCM uses information from the MAP sensor to measure how much exhaust gas is introduced into the intake manifold.

TESTING

See Figure 254.

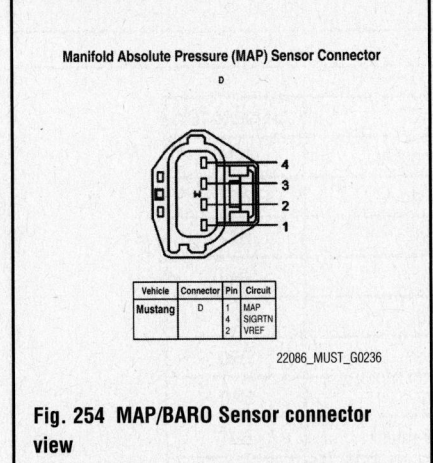

Manifold Absolute Pressure (MAP) Sensor Connector

Vehicle	Connector	Pin	Circuit
Mustang	D	1	MAP
		4	SIGRTN
		2	VREF

22086_MUST_G0236

Fig. 254 MAP/BARO Sensor connector view

MAP Sensor Pin Testing

➡**For reference values, refer to PCM testing—PCM reference voltage pin chart**

This pinpoint test is intended to diagnose the following:
- Manifold Absolute Pressure (MAP) sensor (9F479)
- Harness circuits: MAP, SIGRTN, VREF

- Powertrain Control Module (PCM) (12A650)

POWERTRAIN CONTROL MODULE (PCM)

LOCATION

See Figures 255 and 256.

The Powertrain Control Module is located in the engine compartment, on the passenger's side, front.

OPERATION

The center of the Electronic Engine Control (EEC) system is a microprocessor called the PCM. The PCM receives input from sensors and other electronic components (switches, relays). Based on the information received and programmed into its memory, the PCM generates output signals to control various relays, solenoids and actuators. There are several different types of PCMs in use for this model year. Refer to the Vehicle

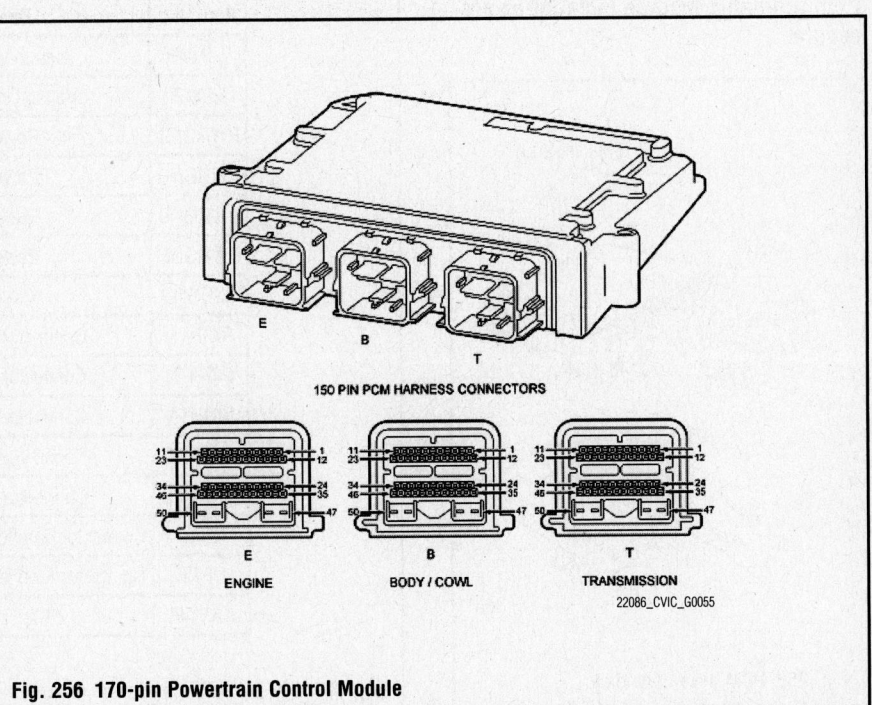

22086_MUST_G0237

Fig. 255 Powertrain Control Module location

Fig. 256 170-pin Powertrain Control Module

PCM Application Table below for PCM types and their applications.

REMOVAL & INSTALLATION

See Figures 257 and 258.

1. Release the clips and disconnect the 3 PCM electrical connectors.

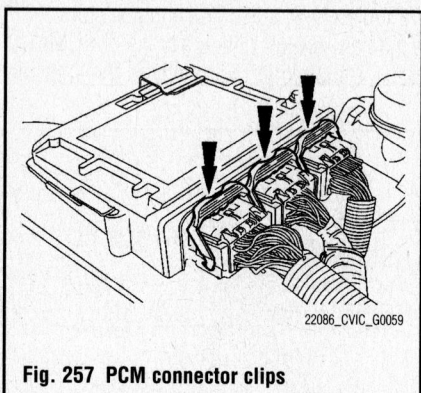

Fig. 257 PCM connector clips

2. Carefully disengage the three (3) PCM connectors clips, and remove the connectors.
3. Remove the PCM bolts.
4. Remove the PCM.

➡**Any Powertrain Control Module (PCM) replacement will require that ALL customer keys are available to be programmed at the time of installation. PCM replacement DOES NOT require new keys. Retrieve the module configuration. Carry out the module configuration retrieval steps of the Programmable Module Installation procedure.**

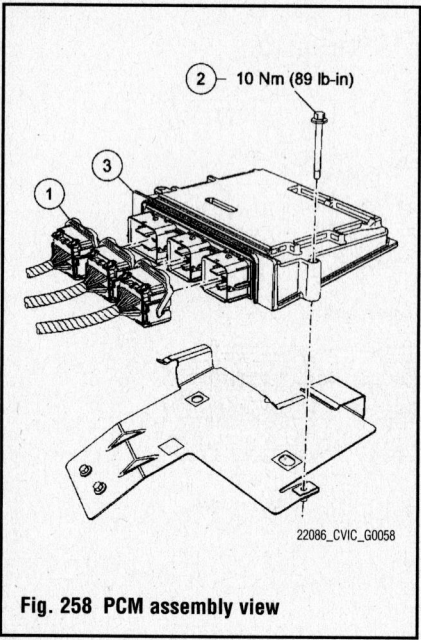

Fig. 258 PCM assembly view

To install:
5. Install the PCM and the bolts.
6. Tighten to 89 ft. lbs. (10 Nm).
7. Connect the 3 PCM electrical connectors and install the clips.
8. Restore the module configuration. Carry out the module configuration restore steps of the Programmable Module Installation procedure.
9. Reprogram the Passive Anti-Theft System (PATS). Carry out the Key Programming Using Two Programmed Keys procedure.

TESTING

See Figures 259 and 260.

Using a high–impedance digital multi–meter, test the PCM for correct power and ground inputs and outputs, according to the pin location chart.

➡**For component—specific reference values, refer to the PCM reference data pin chart**

SUPERCHARGER BYPASS (SCB) SYSTEM—5.4L ENGINE ONLY

LOCATION

See Figure 261.

The Supercharger (SC) Bypass Vacuum Actuator is located at the rear of the SC assembly.

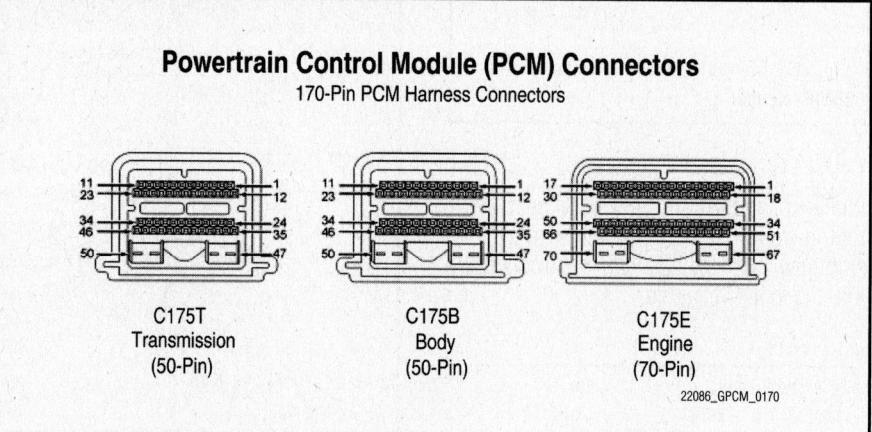

Fig. 259 170-pin PCM connector view—all models.

Function	Description	Connector/Pin
VPWR	Voltage input to module	B35
VPWR	Voltage input to module	B36
PWRGND	Power ground	B47
PWRGND	Power ground	B48
PWRGND	Power ground	B49
PWRGND	Power ground	B50
CSEGND	Case ground	B10
SIGRTN	Connector B signal return	B41
SIGRTN	Connector B signal return	B43
SIGRTN	Connector E signal return	E33
SIGRTN	Connector E signal return	E58
SIGRTN	Connector T signal return	T41
VREF	Connector B buffered 5.0-volt reference	B40
VREF	Connector E buffered 5.0-volt reference	E57
KAPWR	Keep alive power	B45

Fig. 260 170-pin PCM power and ground pin assignments—all models.

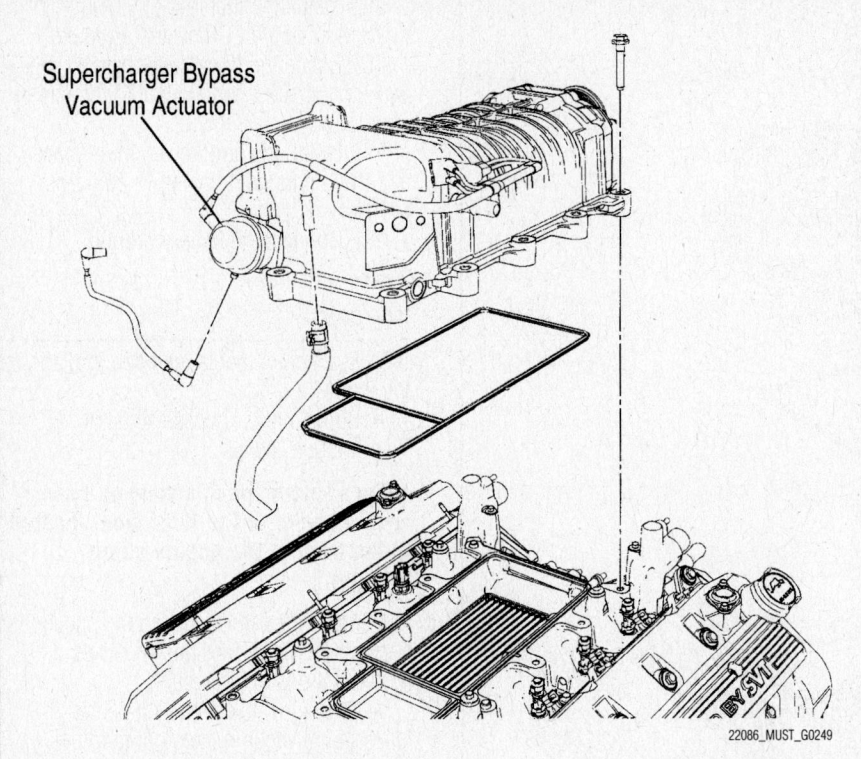

Fig. 261 Supercharger bypass system location

5. Remove the Exhaust Gas Recirculation (EGR) system module. Remove the fuel rail.

6. Disconnect the supercharger bubbler hose and the supercharger bypass vacuum actuator vacuum connector.

7. Remove the 10 bolts and the supercharger.

8. Remove and discard the supercharger gasket.

9. Cover the lower intake manifold with a shop towel to prevent foreign material from falling into the engine.

To install:

➡ **Always install a new gasket.**

10. Position the supercharger gasket on the lower intake manifold dowels.

11. Position the supercharger and install the bolts.

12. Tighten the bolts in the sequence shown in 2 stages:

    a. Stage 1: Tighten to 44 inch lbs. (5 Nm).

    b. Stage 2: Tighten to 18 ft. lbs. (25 Nm).

13. Connect the supercharger bubbler hose and the supercharger bypass vacuum actuator vacuum connector.

OPERATION

The SCB system allows the high pressure air at the outlet of the supercharger to vent back into the inlet of the supercharger, equalizing the pressure. This eliminates the boost (increased pressure that the supercharger produces) for times when supercharger function is undesirable. The system uses a vacuum bypass actuator, which controls the bypass valve inside the supercharger. The system normally operates with engine vacuum applied to the upper port of the vacuum bypass actuator, while the lower port references the air pressure in the clean air tube to cancel out any pressure difference in the intake air system. The actuator is set to open (bypassing the supercharger) during high vacuum engine conditions. As the throttle is opened and engine vacuum decreases, the actuator closes to allow the supercharger to pressurize the air in the manifold.

REMOVAL & INSTALLATION

See Figures 262 through 264.

1. Release the fuel system pressure.
2. Disconnect the battery ground cable.
3. Remove the 4 nuts and the strut tower cross brace.
4. Rotate the drive belt tensioner clockwise and detach the drive belt from the supercharger pulley.

Fig. 262 Rotate SC drive belt tensioner as shown

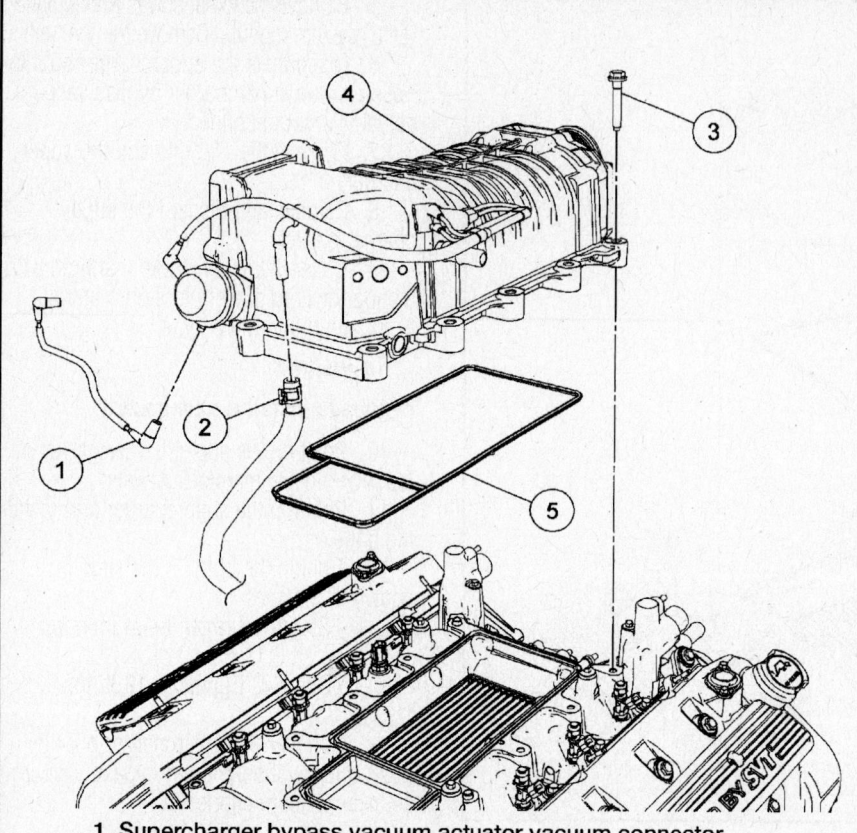

1. Supercharger bypass vacuum actuator vacuum connector
2. Supercharger bubbler hose
3. Supercharger bolt (10 required)
4. Supercharger
5. Supercharger gasket

22086_MUST_G0057

Fig. 263 Supercharger assembly

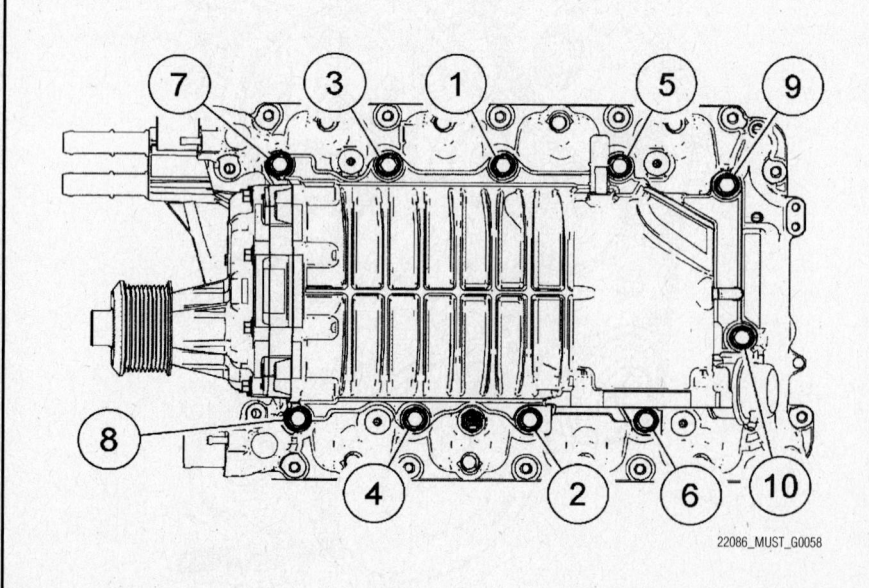

22086_MUST_G0058

Fig. 264 Supercharger bolt torque sequence

14. Install the fuel rail.

15. Install the EGR system module.

16. Rotate the drive belt tensioner clockwise and attach the drive belt to the supercharger pulley.

17. Install the strut tower cross brace and the 4 nuts, and tighten to 26 ft. lbs. (35 Nm).

18. Connect the battery ground cable.

TESTING

This pinpoint test is intended to diagnose the following:

- Supercharger bypass actuator
- Vacuum hoses

➡**For vehicle specific vacuum hose routing, refer to the VECI label located in the front of the engine comp artment.**

Perform the following visual inspections. Repair or replace lines and hoses as required if a fault is present.

- Check for holes, cracks, bends or kinks in the vacuum lines going to the supercharger bypass actuator.
- Check for any disconnected hoses at the supercharger bypass actuator.

➡**Additional DTCs may set as a result of disconnecting the vacuum line in this step.**

- Visually inspect the bypass valve actuator for damage.
- Key in OFF position.
- Note the position of the supercharger bypass actuator linkage.
- Key ON, engine running.
- Note the position of the supercharger bypass actuator linkage.
- Disconnect the supercharger bypass actuator upper vacuum hose.

Verify that the Supercharger Bypass Actuator linkage moves when the engine is started, and that it returns to the original position when the supercharger bypass actuator vacuum line is disconnected.

- If the conditions are not met, replace the Supercharger Bypass Actuator, clear all DTCs, and repeat the self–test.

THROTTLE POSITION SENSOR (TPS)

LOCATION

See Figure 265.

The Throttle Position Sensor (TPS) is located on the throttle body.

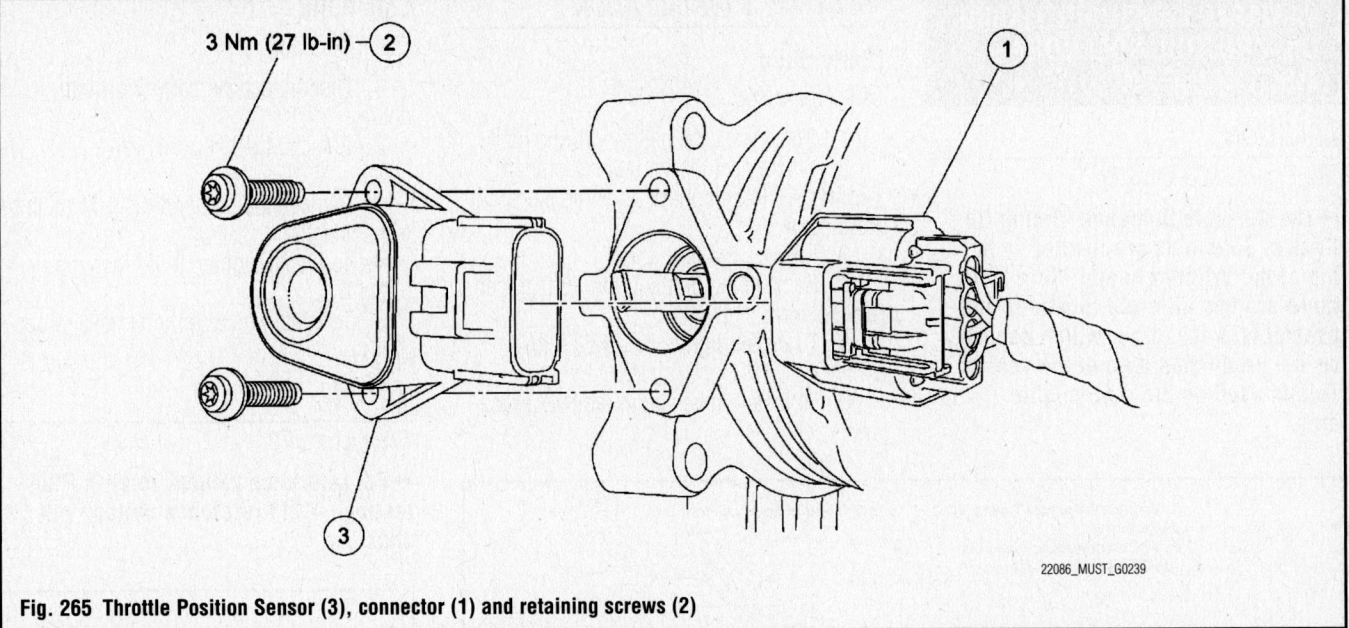

Fig. 265 Throttle Position Sensor (3), connector (1) and retaining screws (2)

22086_MUST_G0239

OPERATION

See Figure 266.

The TPS is a rotary potentiometer sensor that provides a signal to the PCM that is linearly proportional to the throttle plate/shaft position. The sensor housing has a 3–blade electrical connector that may be gold plated. The gold plating increases the corrosion resistance on the terminals and increases the connector durability. The TPS is mounted on the throttle body. As the TPS is rotated by the throttle shaft, 4 operating conditions are determined by the PCM from the TP.

The operating conditions are:
- Closed throttle (includes idle or deceleration)
- Part throttle (includes cruise or moderate acceleration)
- Wide open throttle (includes maximum acceleration or de–choke on crank) throttle angle rate

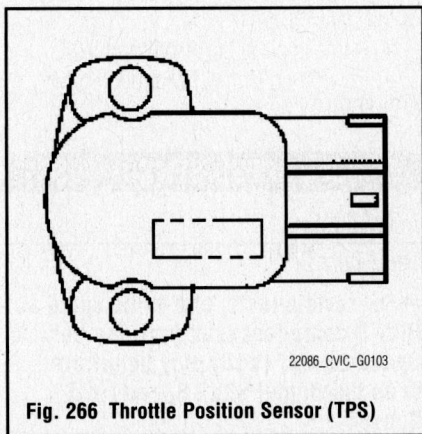

22086_CVIC_G0103

Fig. 266 Throttle Position Sensor (TPS)

REMOVAL & INSTALLATION

See Figure 265.

1. Disconnect the battery ground cable.
2. Disconnect the Throttle Position Sensor (TPS) the throttle body electrical connector.

❈❈ CAUTION

Failure to remove the TPS screws in the following manner will result in damage to the screws.

3. First loosen the screws 1–2 full turns using a hand tool, and then use a suitable high speed driver to complete the removal.
4. Remove and discard the 2 screws and the TPS.

❈❈ CAUTION

Do not reuse the TPS and screws. A new TPS and screws must be installed.

To install:

❈❈ CAUTION

Do not use a high speed driver to install the new screws or damage to the TPS can occur.

➡ **When installing the new TPS, make sure that the radial locator tab on the TP sensor is aligned with the radial locator hole on the throttle body.**

5. Position the new TPS and install the 2 new screws. Tighten to 27 inch lbs. (3 Nm).
6. Connect the TPS electrical connector.

TESTING

See Figure 267.

TPS Pin Testing

➡ **For reference values, refer to PCM testing—PCM reference voltage pin chart**

This pinpoint test is intended to diagnose the following:
- TPS (9B989)
- Binding or sticking throttle linkage
- Harness circuits: TP, SIGRTN, VREF, VPWR, and PWRGND

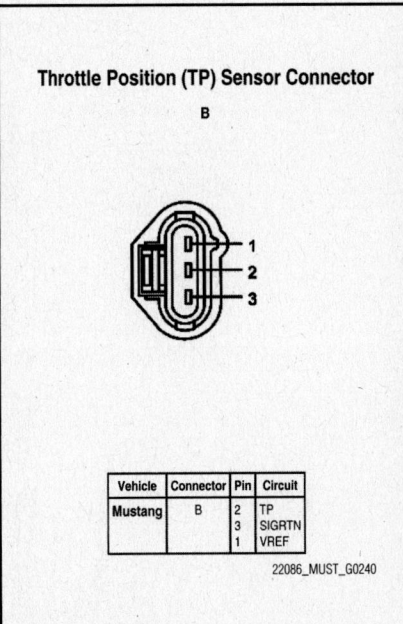

Throttle Position (TP) Sensor Connector

Vehicle	Connector	Pin	Circuit
Mustang	B	2	TP
		3	SIGRTN
		1	VREF

22086_MUST_G0240

Fig. 267 Throttle Position Sensor (TPS) connector view

VARIABLE CAMSHAFT TIMING OIL CONTROL SOLENOID— 4.6L ENGINE ONLY

LOCATION

See Figures 268 and 269.

➡The Variable Camshaft Timing Oil Control Solenoids are located in the top of the cylinder heads. Note that there are two different locations and assembly procedures, which depend on the production date of the vehicle. This is used on the 4.6L engine only.

REMOVAL & INSTALLATION

Early Build

See Figure 268.

1. Disconnect the battery ground cable.
2. Disconnect the Variable Camshaft Timing (VCT) oil control solenoid electrical connector.
3. Remove the grommet.
4. Remove the bolt and the VCT oil control solenoid.
5. To install, tighten to 44 inch lbs. (5 Nm).
6. To install, reverse the removal procedure.

Late Build

See Figure 269.

1. Disconnect the battery ground cable.
2. Remove the LH or RH valve cover.
3. Remove the bolt and the VCT oil control solenoid.
4. To install, tighten to 44 inch lbs. (5 Nm).
5. To install, reverse the removal procedure.

TESTING

See Figure 270.

➡For reference values, refer to PCM testing—PCM reference voltage pin chart

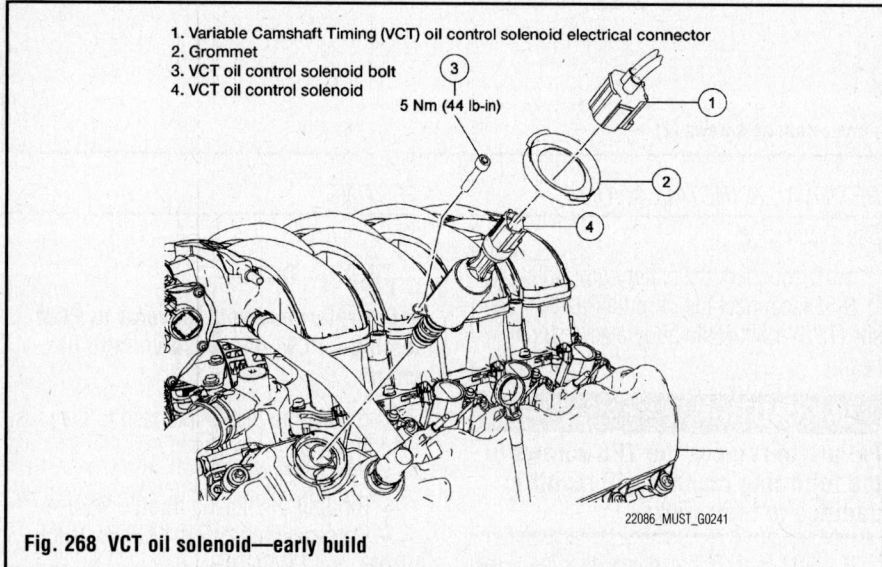

1. Variable Camshaft Timing (VCT) oil control solenoid electrical connector
2. Grommet
3. VCT oil control solenoid bolt
4. VCT oil control solenoid

5 Nm (44 lb-in)

Fig. 268 VCT oil solenoid—early build

22086_MUST_G0241

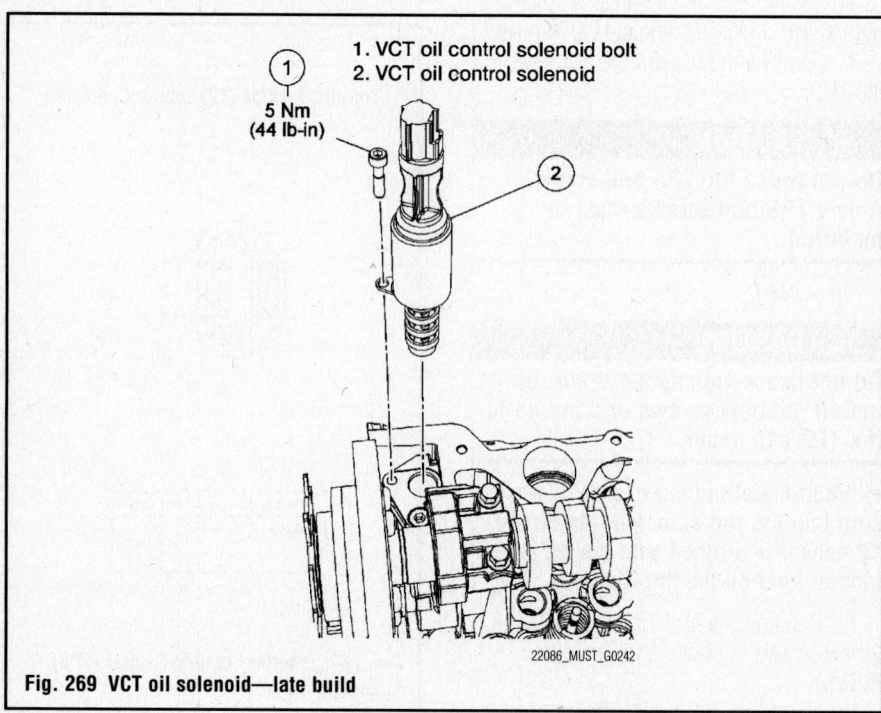

1. VCT oil control solenoid bolt
2. VCT oil control solenoid

5 Nm (44 lb-in)

Fig. 269 VCT oil solenoid—late build

22086_MUST_G0242

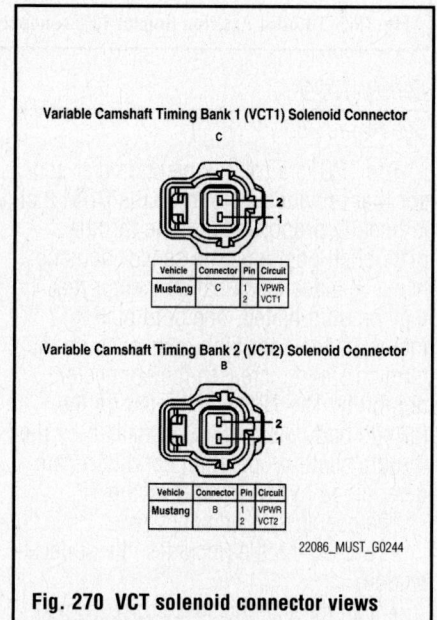

Variable Camshaft Timing Bank 1 (VCT1) Solenoid Connector
C

Vehicle	Connector	Pin	Circuit
Mustang	C	1	VPWR
		2	VCT1

Variable Camshaft Timing Bank 2 (VCT2) Solenoid Connector
B

Vehicle	Connector	Pin	Circuit
Mustang	B	1	VPWR
		2	VCT2

22086_MUST_G0244

Fig. 270 VCT solenoid connector views

This pinpoint test is intended to diagnose the following:
- VCT solenoid (6L713) or (6B297)
- Spider assembly right bank (6C260), or left bank (6C261)
- Harness circuits: VPWR and VCT
- Powertrain Control Module (PCM) (12A650)

VEHICLE SPEED SENSOR (VSS)

LOCATION

See Figure 271.

➡For certain tests, and while using an OBD-II compliant scan tool, the Vehicle Speed Sensor (VSS) may be referred to as the Output Shaft Speed (OSS) Sensor

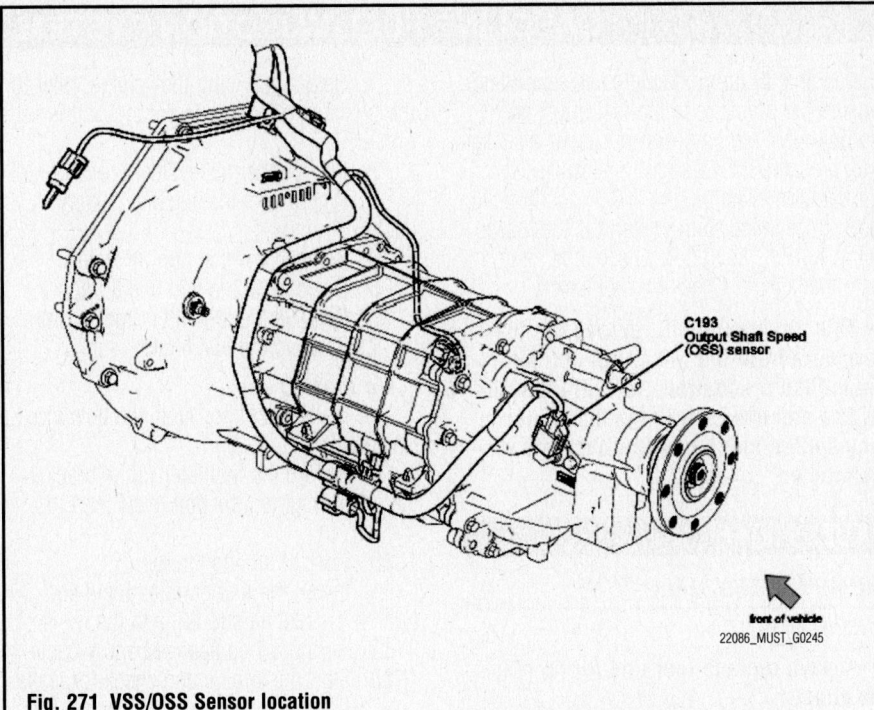

C193
Output Shaft Speed
(OSS) sensor

front of vehicle
22086_MUST_G0245

Fig. 271 VSS/OSS Sensor location

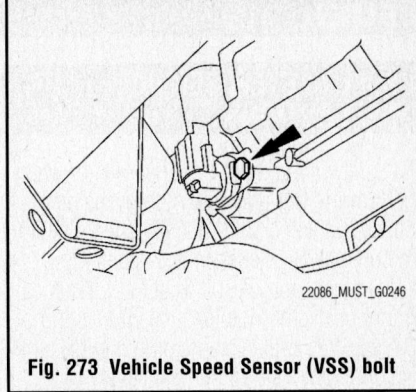

22086_MUST_G0246

Fig. 273 Vehicle Speed Sensor (VSS) bolt

2. Disconnect the Vehicle Speed (VSS) sensor electrical connector.

3. Remove the VSS sensor bolt and the sensor. To install, tighten to 9 ft. lbs (12 Nm).

4. To install, reverse the removal procedure.

TESTING

See Figure 274.

➡**For certain tests, and while using an OBD-II compliant scan tool, the Vehicle Speed Sensor (VSS) may be referred to as the Output Shaft Speed (OSS) Sensor**

Vehicle Speed (VSS) Sensor Pin Testing

➡**For reference values, refer to PCM testing—PCM reference voltage pin chart**

OPERATION

The VSS is a variable reluctance or hall–effect sensor that generates a waveform with a frequency that is proportional to the speed of the vehicle. If the vehicle is moving at a relatively low velocity, the sensor produces a signal with a low frequency. As the vehicle velocity increases, the sensor generates a signal with a higher frequency. The PCM uses the frequency signal generated by the VSS (and other inputs) to control such parameters as fuel injection, ignition control, transmission/transaxle shift scheduling, and torque converter clutch scheduling.

The VSS provides the PCM with information about the rotational speed of an output shaft. The PCM uses the information to control and diagnose Powertrain behavior. In some applications, the sensor is also used as the source of vehicle speed. The sensor may be physically located in different places on the vehicle, depending upon the specific application. The design of each speed sensor is unique and depends on which Powertrain control feature uses the information that is generated.

REMOVAL & INSTALLATION

See Figures 272 and 273.

1. Position the vehicle on a hoist, and place the automatic transmission selector into the NEUTRAL position.

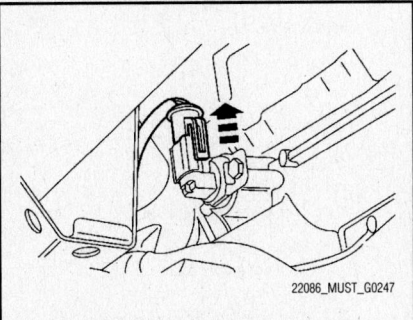

22086_MUST_G0247

Fig. 272 Vehicle Speed Sensor (VSS) connector

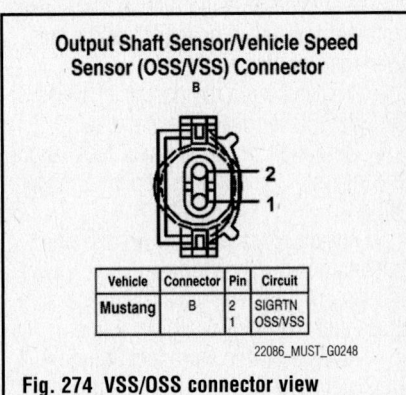

Output Shaft Sensor/Vehicle Speed Sensor (OSS/VSS) Connector
B

2
1

Vehicle	Connector	Pin	Circuit
Mustang	B	2	SIGRTN
		1	OSS/VSS

22086_MUST_G0248

Fig. 274 VSS/OSS connector view

FUEL   **GASOLINE FUEL INJECTION SYSTEM**

FUEL SYSTEM SERVICE PRECAUTIONS

Safety is the most important factor when performing not only fuel system maintenance but any type of maintenance. Failure to conduct maintenance and repairs in a safe manner may result in serious personal injury or death. Maintenance and testing of the vehicle's fuel system components can be accomplished safely and effectively by adhering to the following rules and guidelines.

• To avoid the possibility of fire and personal injury, always disconnect the negative battery cable unless the repair or test procedure requires that battery voltage be applied.

• Always relieve the fuel system pressure prior to disconnecting any fuel system component (injector, fuel rail, pressure regulator, etc.), fitting or fuel line connection. Exercise extreme caution whenever relieving fuel system pressure to avoid exposing skin, face and eyes to fuel spray. Please be advised that fuel under pressure may penetrate the skin or any part of the body that it contacts.

• Always place a shop towel or cloth around the fitting or connection prior to loosening to absorb any excess fuel due to spillage. Ensure that all fuel spillage (should it occur) is quickly removed from engine surfaces. Ensure that all fuel soaked cloths or towels are deposited into a suitable waste container.

• Always keep a dry chemical (Class B) fire extinguisher near the work area.

• Do not allow fuel spray or fuel vapors to come into contact with a spark or open flame.

• Always use a back-up wrench when loosening and tightening fuel line connection fittings. This will prevent unnecessary stress and torsion to fuel line piping.

• Always replace worn fuel fitting O-rings with new Do not substitute fuel hose or equivalent where fuel pipe is installed.

Before servicing the vehicle, make sure to also refer to the precautions in the beginning of this section as well.

RELIEVING FUEL SYSTEM PRESSURE

Remove the fuel pump relay; located in the bussed electrical center, relay C051. Start the engine and allow it to run at idle until it stalls. After the engine stalls, crank the engine for approximately five seconds to ensure the pressure in the fuel injection supply manifold has been released. After the fuel pressure has been fully released, turn the ignition switch to the "OFF" position. To pressurize the system, install the fuel pump relay, turn the key on for 3 seconds, then turn the key off. Check for fuel leaks.

➡This procedure will remove the fuel pressure from the lines, but not the fuel. Take precautions to avoid the risk of fire and use clean rags to soak up any spilled fuel when the lines are disconnected.

FUEL FILTER

REMOVAL & INSTALLATION
See Figure 275.

➡Always replace fuel line fitting plastic clips.

1. Before servicing the vehicle, refer to the precautions at the beginning of this section.
2. Relieve the fuel system pressure.
3. Disconnect the negative battery cable.
4. Remove the fuel bundle shield.
5. Disconnect the fuel line fittings.
6. Remove the fuel filter bracket bolt.
7. Remove the fuel filter.

To install:
8. Install fuel filter. Note the flow direction arrow.
9. Secure the fuel filter in the bracket clamp and tighten the bolt to 44 inch lbs. (5 Nm).
10. Install fuel line fittings.
11. Install the fuel bundle shield and tighten the retainers to 62 inch lbs. (7 Nm).
12. Connect the negative battery cable.
13. Start the engine and check for leaks.

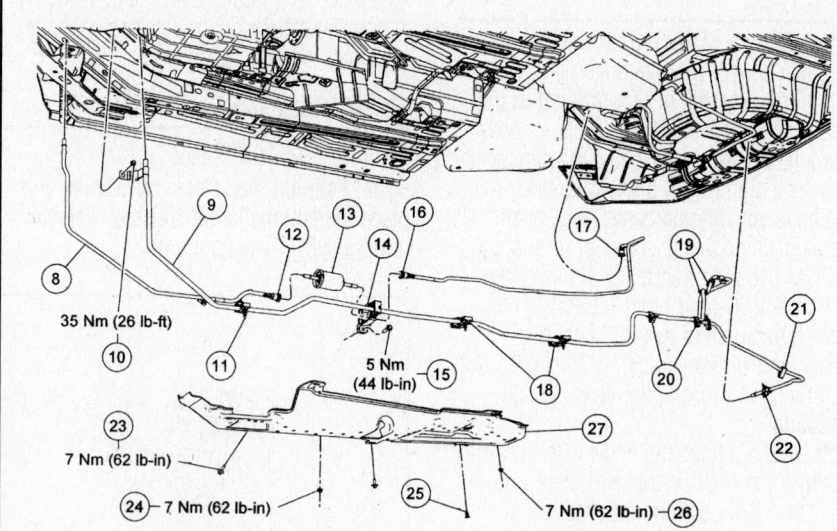

8	Fuel supply tube
9	Vapor tube
10	Vapor tube bracket retaining bolt
11	Fuel tube bundle retainer clip
12	Fuel supply tube quick connect coupling
13	Fuel filter
14	Fuel filter bracket
15	Fuel filter bracket retaining bolt
16	Fuel supply tube quick connect coupling
17	Fuel supply tube quick connect coupling
18	Fuel tube bundle retainer clip (2 required)
19	Tube spacers
20	Fuel tube bundle pin-type retainer clip (2 required)
21	Fuel tube bundle retainer clip
22	Fuel tube bundle pin-type retainer clip (2 required)
23	Fuel bundle shield retainer bolt (2 required)
24	Shield retainer nuts (2 required)
25	Fuel bundle shield pin-type retainer
26	Fuel bundle shield retainer nuts (2 required)
27	Fuel bundle shield

06017-TANG-G57

Fig. 275 Exploded view of fuel filter and fuel lines

FUEL INJECTORS

REMOVAL & INSTALLATION

4.0L Engine

See Figure 276.

1. Relieve the fuel system pressure.
2. Disconnect the negative battery cable.
3. On the right side, remove the wiring harness retainer from the valve cover and position aside.
4. Disconnect the injector connectors.
5. Remove the 2 fuel rail supply tube bolts.
6. Remove 2 bolts and the right side fuel rail.
7. On the left side, disconnect the fuel pressure and temperature sensor vacuum hose.
8. Disconnect the fuel pressure and temperature sensor connectors.
9. Remove the wiring harness retainer from the valve cover and position aside.
10. Disconnect the injector connectors.
11. Remove the 2 fuel rail supply tube bolts.
12. Remove 2 bolts and the left side fuel rail.
13. On both sides, remove the fuel injectors from the fuel rail and discard the O-ring seals.

To install:

14. Install new O-rings on the injectors and fuel supply tube.
15. Install the injectors.
16. Install 2 bolts and the left side fuel rail. Tighten the bolts to 17 ft. lbs. (23 Nm).
17. Install the 2 fuel rail supply tube bolts and tighten to 53 inch lbs. (6 Nm).
18. Connect the injector connectors.
19. Install the wiring harness retainer to the valve cover.

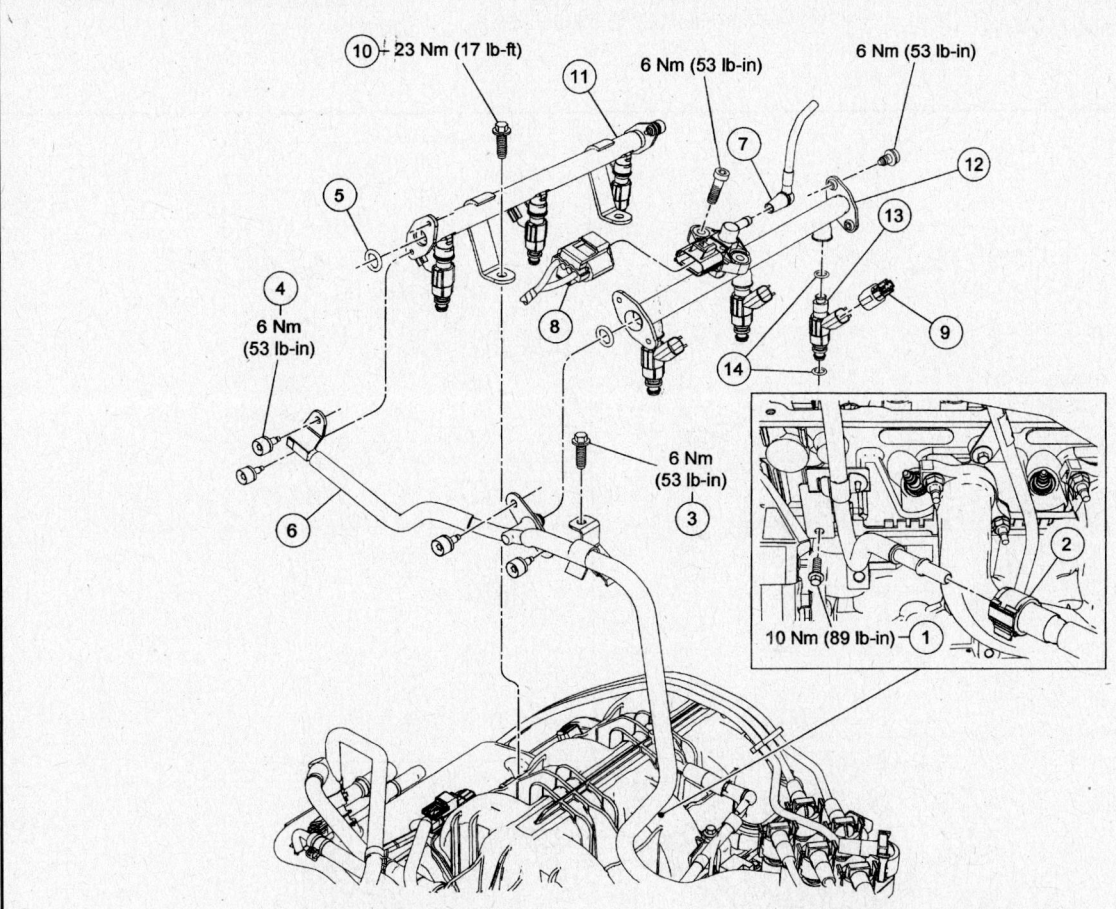

1 Lower fuel rail supply tube bracket bolt

2 Fuel rail supply tube quick connect coupling

3 Upper fuel rail supply tube bracket bolt

4 Fuel rail supply tube bolts (4 required)

5 O-ring seals (2 required)

6 Fuel rail supply tube

7 Fuel rail pressure and temperature sensor vacuum hose

8 Fuel rail pressure and temperature sensor electrical connector

9 Fuel injector electrical connector (6 required)

10 Fuel rail bolt (4 required)

11 RH fuel rail

12 LH fuel rail

13 Fuel injector (6 required)

14 O-ring seal (12 required)

06017-TANG-G58

Fig. 276 Exploded view of fuel rail and injectors—4.0L engine

20. Connect the fuel pressure and temperature sensor connectors.

21. Connect the fuel pressure and temperature sensor vacuum hose.

22. Install 2 bolts and the right side fuel rail. Tighten the bolts to 17 ft. lbs. (23 Nm).

23. Install the 2 fuel rail supply tube bolts and tighten to 53 inch lbs. (6 Nm).

24. Install the wiring harness retainer to the valve cover.

25. Connect the negative battery cable.

26. Start the engine and check for leaks.

4.6L Engine

See Figure 277.

1. Relieve the fuel system pressure.
2. Disconnect the negative battery cable.

3. Disconnect the fuel supply line.

4. Disconnect 2 wiring harness retainers from the fuel rail stud bolts and position the harness aside.

5. Disconnect the fuel pressure and temperature sensor connectors and vacuum hose.

6. Disconnect the injector connectors.
7. Remove the fuel rail stud bolts.
8. Remove the fuel rail; and injectors as an assembly.
9. Remove the injectors from the fuel rail.

To install:

10. Install new O-rings.
11. Install fuel injectors to the fuel rail.
12. Install the fuel rail with injectors attached. Tighten the bolts to 89 inch lbs. (10 Nm).

13. Connect the injector connectors.

14. Connect the fuel pressure and temperature sensor connectors and vacuum hose.

15. Connect 2 wiring harness retainers from the fuel rail stud bolts and position the harness aside.

16. Connect the fuel supply line.
17. Connect the negative battery cable.
18. Start the engine and check for leaks.

5.4L Engine

See Figure 278.

1. Relieve the fuel system pressure.
2. Disconnect the negative battery cable.
3. Disconnect the fuel supply line.

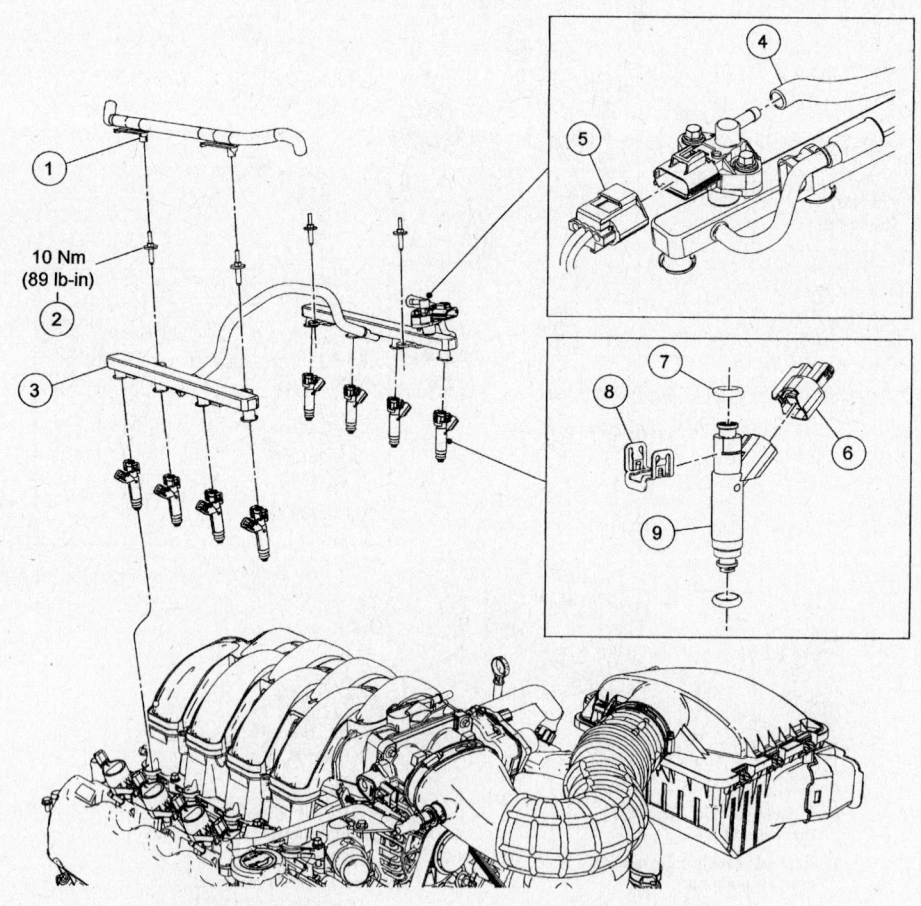

1 Wiring harness retainer (2 required)

2 Fuel rail stud bolt (4 required)

3 Fuel rail

4 Vacuum hose

5 Fuel rail pressure and temperature sensor electrical connector

6 Fuel injector electrical connector (8 required)

7 O-ring seal (16 required)

8 Fuel injector retaining clip (8 required)

9 Fuel injector

06017-TANG-G59

Fig. 277 Exploded view of fuel rail and injectors—4.6L engine

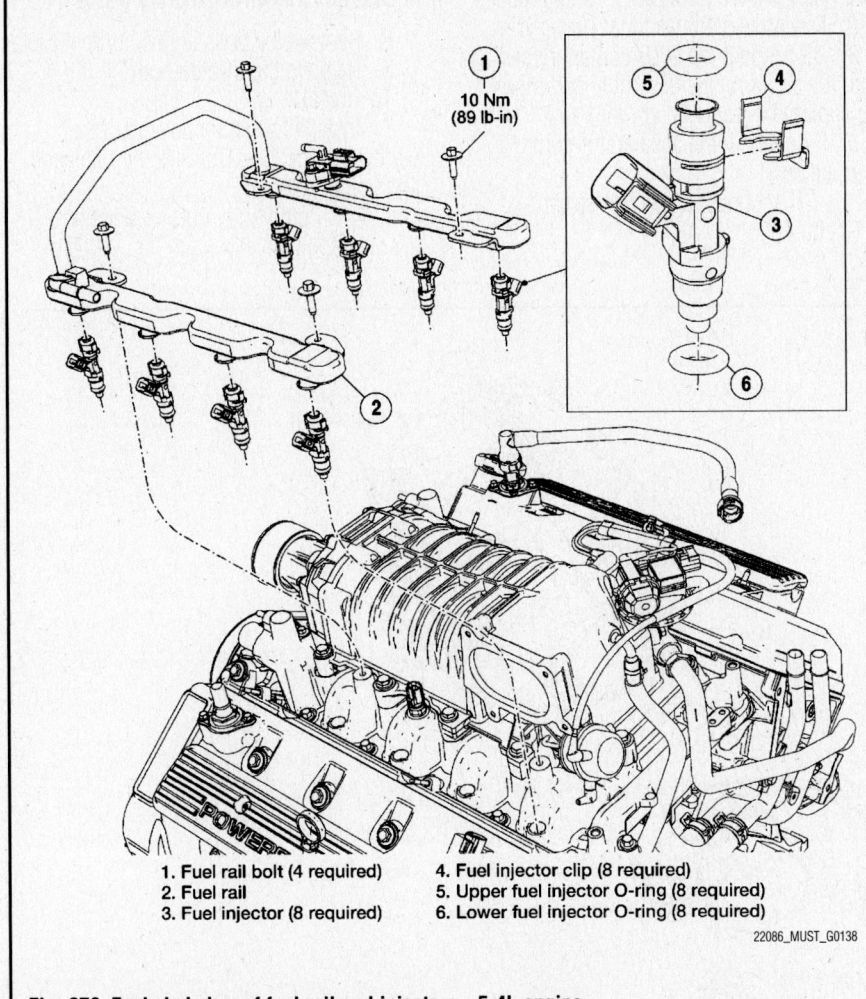

1. Fuel rail bolt (4 required)
2. Fuel rail
3. Fuel injector (8 required)
4. Fuel injector clip (8 required)
5. Upper fuel injector O-ring (8 required)
6. Lower fuel injector O-ring (8 required)

22086_MUST_G0138

Fig. 278 Exploded view of fuel rail and injectors—5.4L engine

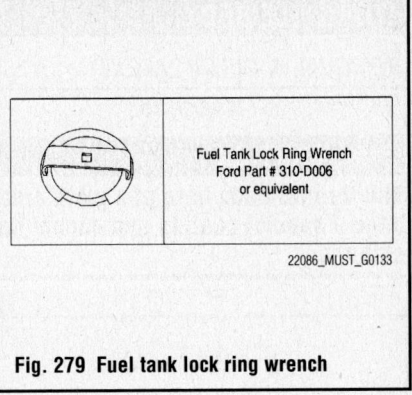

22086_MUST_G0133

Fig. 279 Fuel tank lock ring wrench

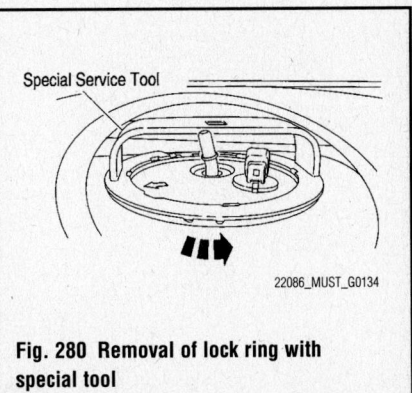

22086_MUST_G0134

Fig. 280 Removal of lock ring with special tool

4. Disconnect 2 wiring harness retainers from the fuel rail stud bolts and position the harness aside.
5. Disconnect the fuel pressure and temperature sensor connectors and vacuum hose.
6. Disconnect the injector connectors.
7. Remove the fuel rail stud bolts.
8. Remove the fuel rail; and injectors as an assembly.
9. Remove the injectors from the fuel rail.

To install:
10. Install new O-rings.
11. Install fuel injectors to the fuel rail.
12. Install the fuel rail with injectors attached. Tighten the bolts to 89 inch lbs. (10 Nm).
13. Connect the injector connectors.
14. Connect the fuel pressure and temperature sensor connectors and vacuum hose.
15. Connect 2 wiring harness retainers from the fuel rail stud bolts and position the harness aside.

16. Connect the fuel supply line.
17. Connect the negative battery cable.
18. Start the engine and check for leaks.

FUEL PUMP

REMOVAL & INSTALLATION

See Figures 279 and 280.

1. Before servicing the vehicle, refer to the precautions at the beginning of this section.
2. Relieve the fuel system pressure.
3. Disconnect the negative battery cable.
4. Remove the gas cap.
5. Drain the fuel tank.
6. Remove the rear seat bottom cushion.
7. Remove the fuel pump access cover.
8. Disconnect fuel pump module electrical connector.
9. Use tool 303–D006 and remove fuel pump module locking ring.

10. Raise the fuel pump module to access quick connect fitting. Disconnect the fitting and remove the fuel pump module from the fuel tank.

To install:
11. Apply clean engine oil to the fuel pump O-ring seal.
12. Connect the quick connect fitting.
13. Install the fuel pump module into the opening and ensure the alignment arrows on the fuel pump and tank are aligned.
14. Tighten the fuel pump locking ring.
15. Connect fuel pump module electrical connector.
16. Install the fuel pump access cover.
17. Install the rear seat bottom cushion.
18. Add fuel (10 gallons minimum) to the tank.
19. Install the gas cap.
20. Connect the negative battery cable.
21. Start the engine and check for leaks.

IDLE SPEED

ADJUSTMENT

Idle speed is maintained by the Powertrain Control Module (PCM). No adjustment is necessary or possible.

THROTTLE BODY

REMOVAL & INSTALLATION

See Figures 281 through 283.

✷✷ CAUTION

The throttle body bore and plate area have a special coating and cannot be cleaned.

1. Remove the air cleaner outlet tube.
2. Disconnect all electrical connectors.
3. Disconnect the 2 TB coolant hoses from the coolant tube assembly and plug the coolant hoses (4.0L engine).
4. Disconnect the accelerator controls (if equipped).
   a. Disconnect the return spring. (if equipped).

➡**Discard the throttle body gasket.**

5. Remove the bolts or nuts as applicable.
6. Remove the throttle body.

To install:

7. Installation is the reverse of the removal procedure. Observe the following tightening torques:
   • Throttle body nuts or bolts as applicable 89 inch lbs. (10 Nm)

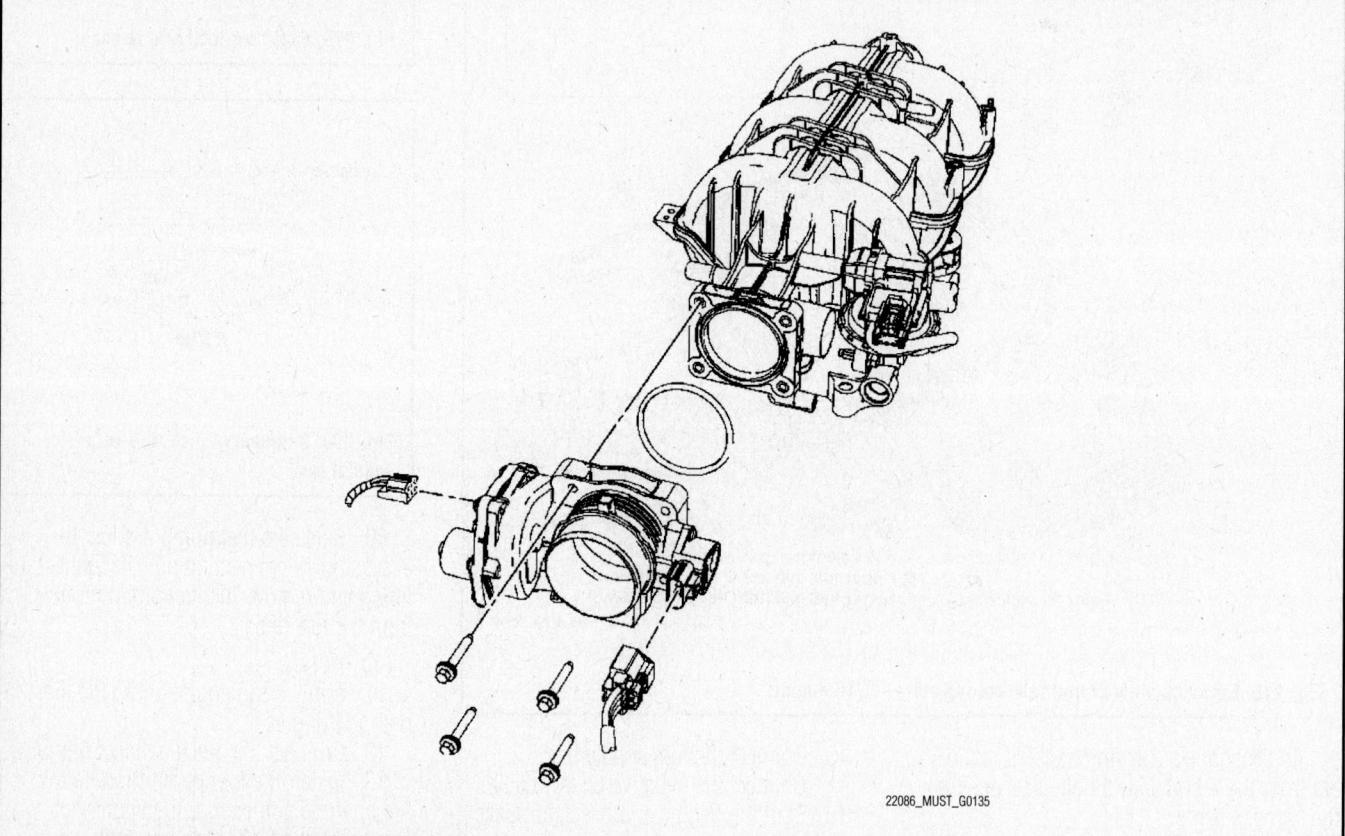

22086_MUST_G0135

Fig. 281 Throttle body assembly view—4.0L engine

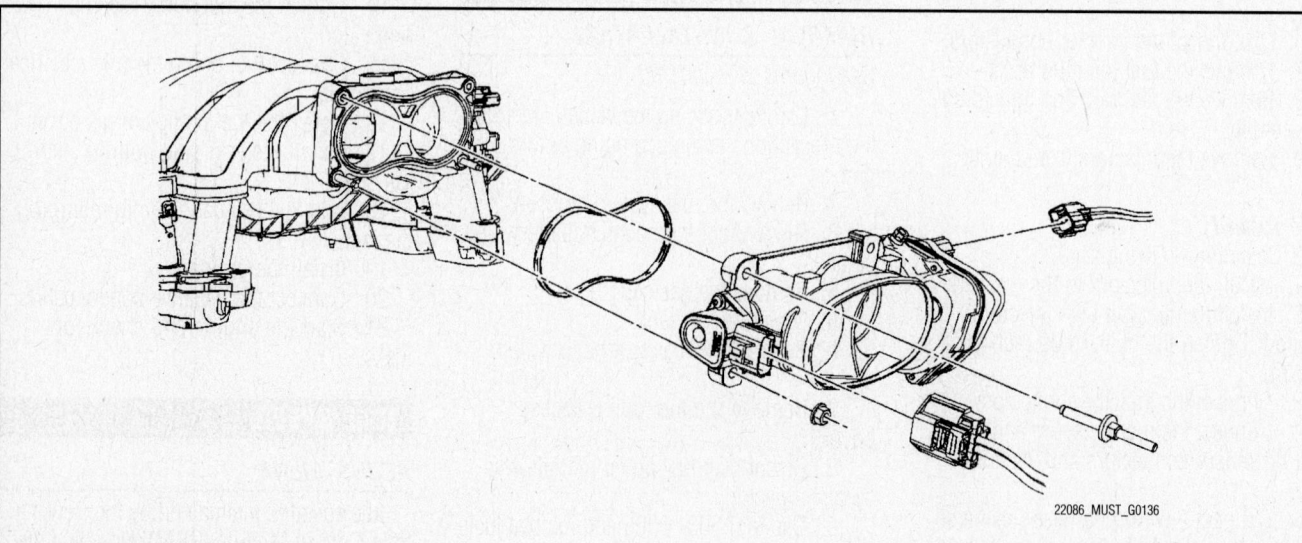

22086_MUST_G0136

Fig. 282 Throttle body assembly view—4.6L engine

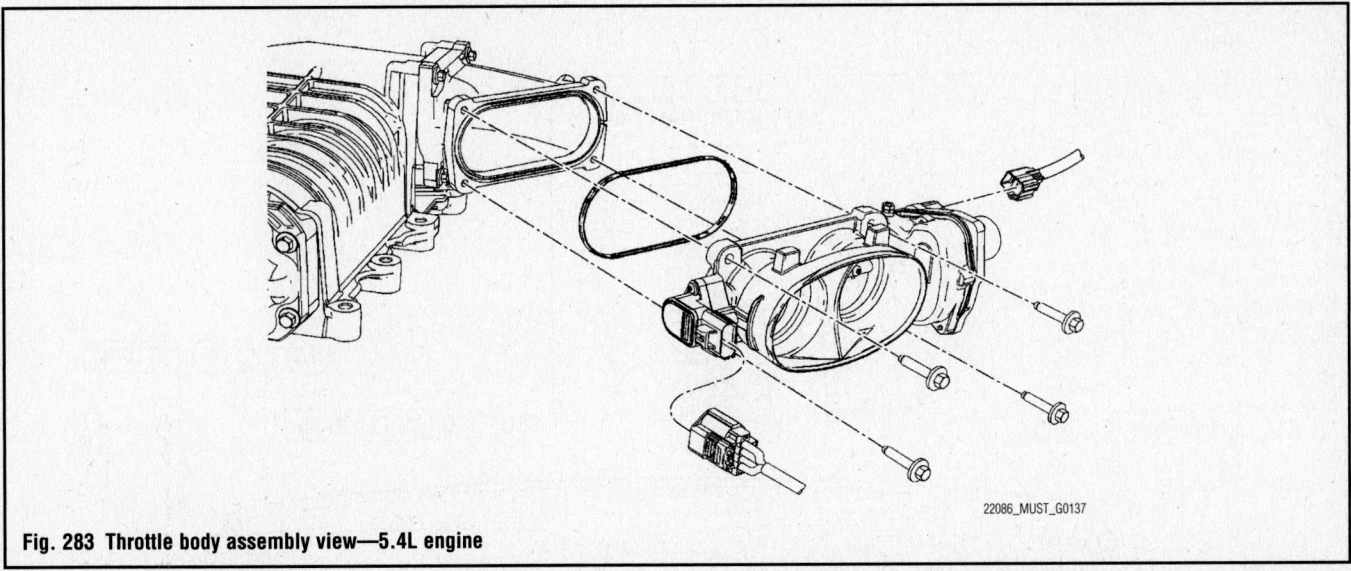

Fig. 283 Throttle body assembly view—5.4L engine

HEATING & AIR CONDITIONING SYSTEM

BLOWER MOTOR

REMOVAL & INSTALLATION
See Figure 284.

➡The heater/air conditioning blower motor is mounted in the heater case assembly, under the instrument panel on the passenger's side of the vehicle.

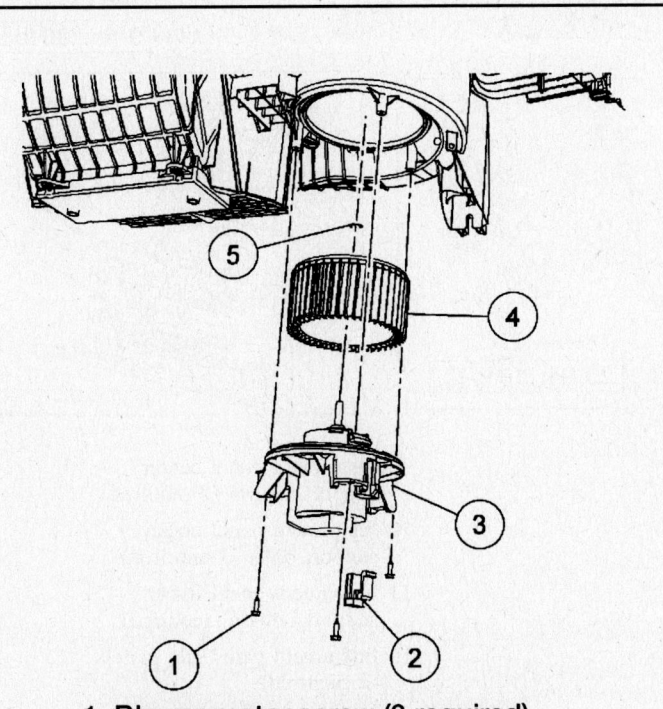

1. Blower motor screw (3 required)
2. Blower motor electrical connector
3. Blower motor
4. Blower motor wheel
5. Blower motor wheel clip

22086_MUST_G0184

Fig. 284 Blower motor assembly view

1. Disconnect the blower motor electrical connector.
2. Remove the 3 blower motor screws.
3. Remove the blower motor.
4. Remove the blower motor wheel clip.
5. Remove the blower motor wheel.
6. To install, reverse the removal procedure.

HEATER CORE

REMOVAL & INSTALLATION
See Figures 285 through 287.

➡The heater core and evaporator core are not serviced individually. The entire housing must be replaced if either component is defective.

1. Drain the cooling system.
2. Recover the A/C refrigerant, if equipped.
3. Disconnect the negative battery cable.
4. Disable the air bag system.
5. Remove the floor console.
6. Remove the 2 door scuff plates.
7. Remove the 2 lower A-pillar upper and lower trim panels.
8. Remove the instrument cluster.
9. Secure the steering wheel in the straight ahead position, then disconnect the steering shaft to steering column pinch bolt.
10. Disconnect the left side instrument panel bulkhead connector and remove the instrument panel support bolt.
11. Disconnect the antenna inline connector and the 4 instrument panel electrical connectors from the right side.

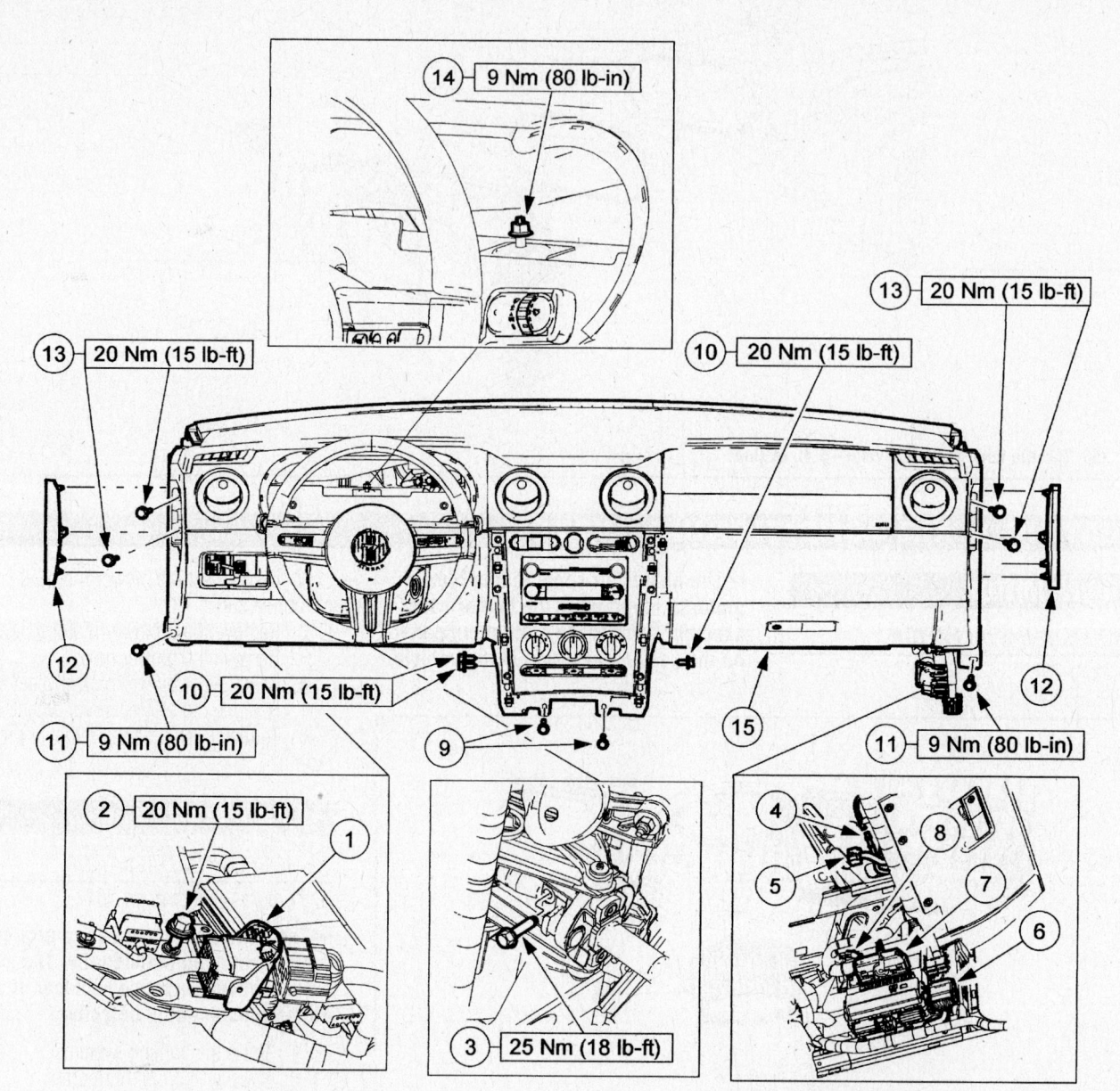

1 Bulkhead electrical connector

2 Instrument panel support bolt

3 Steering column shaft bolt

4 Antenna connector

5 Defrost mode actuator
   electrical connector

6 Bulkhead electrical connector

7 Smart junction box (SJB)
   electrical connector

8 SJB electrical connector

9 Instrument panel center
   support screws (2 required)

10 Instrument panel center
    support bolts (3 required)

11 Instrument panel lower
    support bolts (2 required)

12 Instrument panel end panels
    (2 required)

13 Instrument panel upper
    support bolts (4 required)

14 Instrument panel cowl top
    bracket nut

15 Instrument panel

06017-TANG-G09

Fig. 285 Exploded view of the instrument panel—Mustang

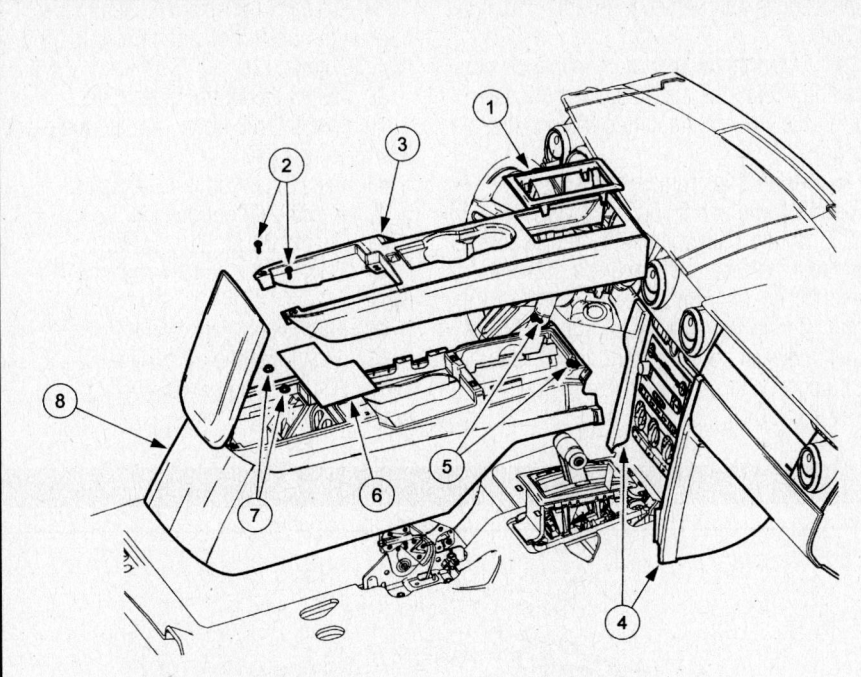

1 Shift lever bezel (if equipped)
2 Floor console finish panel screws (2 required)
3 Floor console finish panel
4 Center stack wings (2 required)
5 Floor console screws (2 required)
6 Floor console mat
7 Floor console nuts (2 required)
8 Floor console

06017-TANG-G10

Fig. 286 Removing the floor console—Mustang

12. Remove 2 instrument panel center support screws and 3 support bolts.

13. Through the instrument panel cluster opening, remove the instrument panel cowl top bracket nut.

14. Remove the 2 lower instrument panel support bolts.

15. Remove the 2 instrument panel end panels.

16. Remove the 4 instrument panel upper support bolts.

17. Using the help of an assistant, remove the instrument panel.

18. Clamp off and disconnect the 2 heater hoses at the heater core.

19. Disconnect the 2 evaporator core nuts and disconnect the fitting.

20. Remove the 2 heater core housing nuts at the dash panel.

21. Disconnect the antenna cable from the housing.

22. Remove the inside evaporator housing nuts.

23. Remove the heater core/evaporator housing.

To install:

24. Install the heater core/evaporator housing.

25. Install the inside evaporator housing nuts and tighten to 44 inch lbs. (5 Nm).

26. Connect the antenna cable from the housing.

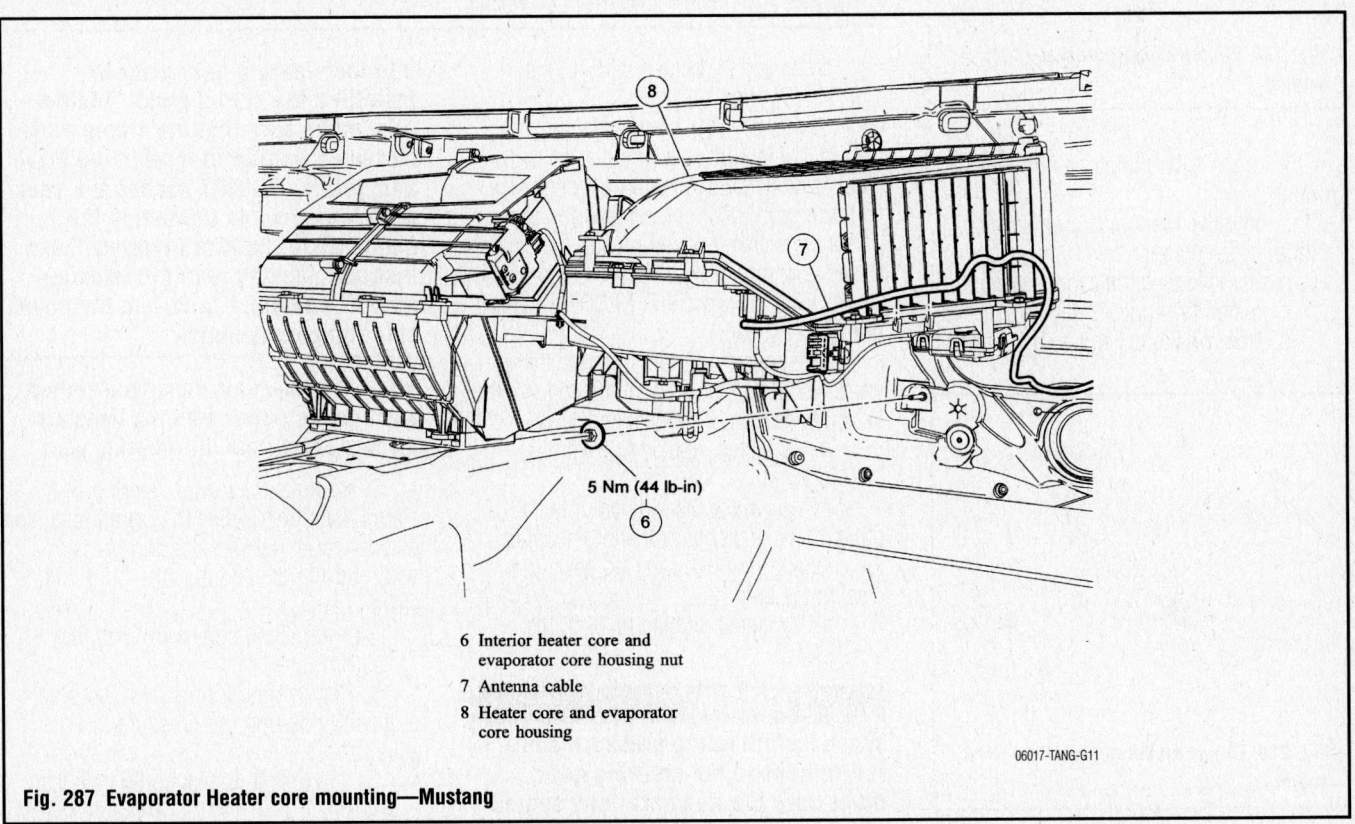

5 Nm (44 lb-in)

6 Interior heater core and evaporator core housing nut
7 Antenna cable
8 Heater core and evaporator core housing

06017-TANG-G11

Fig. 287 Evaporator Heater core mounting—Mustang

27. Install the 2 heater core housing nuts at the dash panel and tighten to 62 inch lbs. (7 Nm).

28. Connect the 2 evaporator core nuts and connect the fitting.

29. Connect the 2 heater hoses at the heater core.

30. Using the help of an assistant, install the instrument panel.

31. Install the 4 instrument panel upper support bolts and tighten to 15 ft. lbs. (20 Nm).

32. Install the 2 instrument panel end panels.

33. Install the 2 lower instrument panel support bolts and tighten to 80 inch lbs. (9 Nm).

34. Through the instrument panel cluster opening, install the instrument panel cowl top bracket nut and tighten to 80 inch lbs. (9 Nm).

35. Install 2 instrument panel center support screws and 3 support bolts.

36. Connect the antenna inline connector and the 4 instrument panel electrical connectors from the right side.

37. Connect the left side instrument panel bulkhead connector and install the instrument panel support bolt and tighten to 15 ft. lbs. (20 Nm).

38. Connect the steering shaft to steering column pinch bolt and tighten to 18 ft. lbs. (25 Nm).

39. Install the instrument cluster.

40. Install the 2 lower A-pillar upper and lower trim panels.

41. Install the 2 door scuff plates.

42. Install the floor console.

43. Enable the air bag system.

44. Connect the negative battery cable.

45. Fill the cooling system.

46. Recharge the A/C system.

47. Start the engine and check for leaks.

STEERING

POWER STEERING GEAR

REMOVAL & INSTALLATION

See Figures 288 through 293.

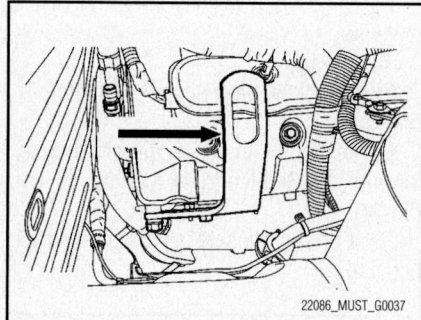

Fig. 288 Engine support bracket—5.4L engine

1. For the 5.4L engine, perform the following:

   a. Remove the 4 nuts and the strut tower cross brace.

   b. Remove the air cleaner outlet pipe.

   c. Install the engine support brackets.

   d. Remove the LH engine mount nut.

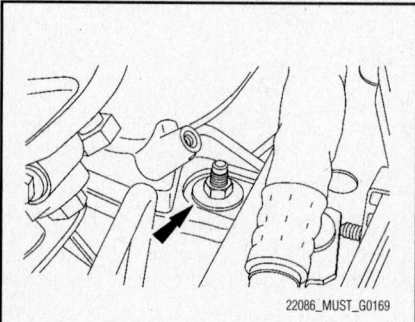

Fig. 289 Engine mount nut location—5.4L engine

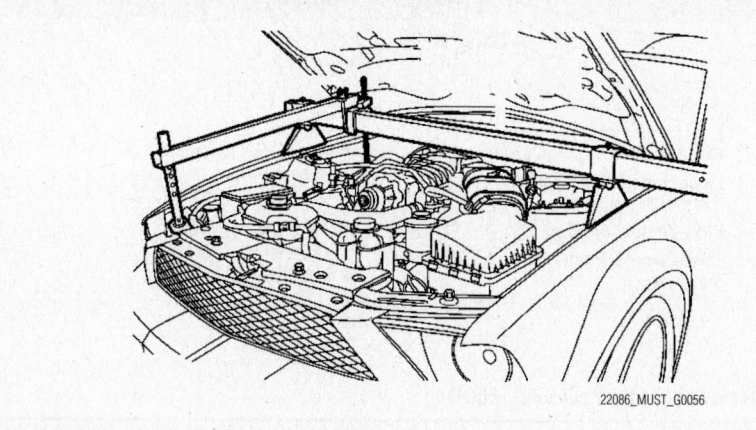

Fig. 290 3-bar engine support—5.4L engine

   • To install, tighten to 46 ft. lbs. (63 Nm).

   e. Install the 3-bar engine support.

   f. Using the special tools, raise the LH side of the engine to gain clearance for removal of the power steering pressure line clamp plate bolt and the steering gear mounting bolt.

2. With the vehicle in NEUTRAL, position it on a hoist.

3. Remove the 2 nuts from the tie rod ends. Using the special tool, disconnect the tie rod ends from the wheel knuckles.

   a. To install, tighten to 59 ft. lbs. (80 Nm).

4. Remove the steering column coupling to steering gear bolt and disconnect the coupling from the steering gear, and discard the bolt.

   a. To install, tighten to 18 ft. lbs. (25 Nm).

✳✳ CAUTION

When installing the pressure and return lines to the steering gear, make sure the lines are fully seated into the steering gear prior to installing the clamp plate. Additionally, make sure that the clamp plate surfaces are free of foreign material and debris. DO NOT exceed the specified torque when tightening the clamp plate. Failure to follow these instructions may result in leakage and/or premature failure of the power steering components.

➡ **New O-ring seals must be installed anytime the power steering lines are disconnected from the steering gear.**

5. Remove the power steering line clamp plate bolt, rotate the clamp plate and disconnect the power steering pressure and return lines, and discard the O-ring seals.

   a. To install, tighten to 17 ft. lbs. (23 Nm).

6. Remove the 2 pressure line bracket bolts and position the pressure line aside.

   a. To install, tighten to 80 inch lbs. (9 Nm).

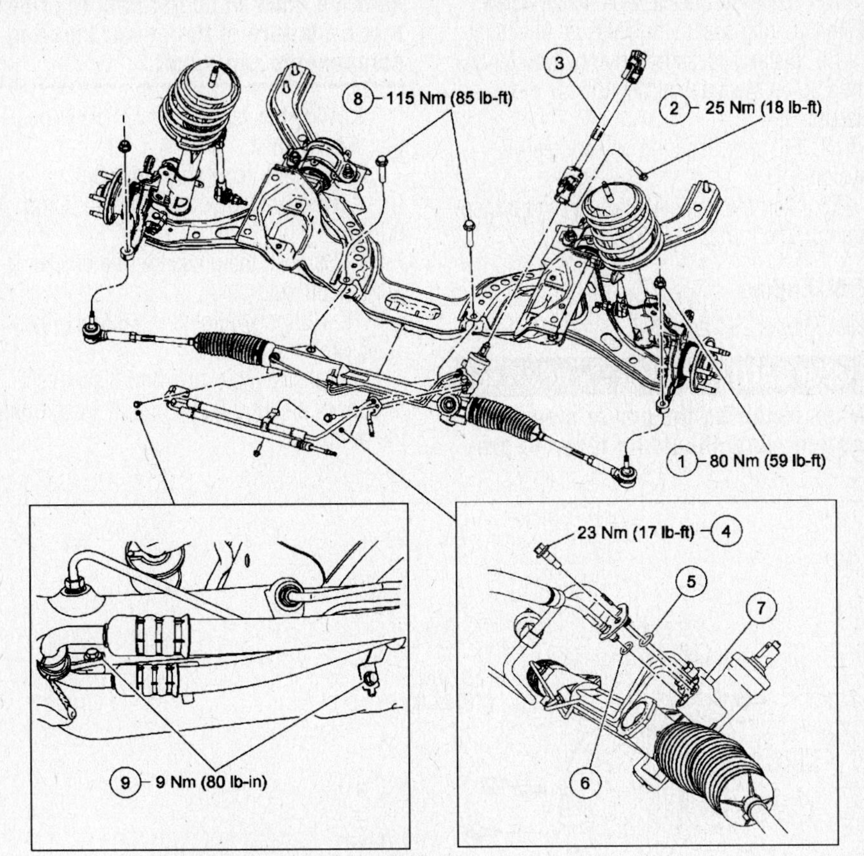

Fig. 291 Power rack and pinion steering gear—assembly view

1. Tie rod end nut (2 required)
2. Steering column coupling to steering gear bolt
3. Steering column lower shaft
4. Power steering line clamp plate bolt
5. Power steering pressure line to steering gear O-ring seal
6. Power steering return line to steering gear O-ring seal
7. Steering gear
8. Steering gear bolts (2 required)
9. Power steering pressure line bracket bolts (2 required)

22086_MUST_G0168

7. Remove the 2 bolts and the steering gear.
   a. To install, tighten to 85 ft. lbs. (115 Nm).
8. To install, reverse the removal procedure.

9. Fill and bleed the power steering system.
10. Perform wheel alignment, and road test vehicle to verify that there no handling or noise concerns exist.

POWER STEERING PUMP

REMOVAL & INSTALLATION

4.0L Engine
See Figures 294 through 296.

✳✳ CAUTION

When repairing the power steering system, care should be taken to prevent the entry of contaminants or premature failure of the power steering components can result.

1. Remove the air cleaner outlet pipe.
2. Loosen the 3 power steering pump pulley bolts.
3. Rotate the tensioner and remove the accessory drive belt from the power steering pump pulley.
4. Remove the 3 power steering pump pulley bolts.
   a. To install, tighten to 18 ft. lbs. (25 Nm).
5. Release the clamp and disconnect the power steering pump supply hose from the power steering pump.
6. Remove the pressure line bracket to alternator stud nut.
   a. To install, tighten to 62 inch lbs. (7 Nm).
7. Remove the power steering fluid reservoir to pump hose bracket bolt.
   a. To install, tighten to 71 inch lbs. (8 Nm).
8. Disconnect the pressure line from the power steering pump.
   a. Discard the Teflon® O-ring seal.
   b. To install, tighten to 48 ft. lbs. (65 Nm).
9. Remove the 3 bolts and the power steering pump.
   a. To install, tighten to 18 ft. lbs. (25 Nm).

➡A new Teflon® O-ring seal must be installed.

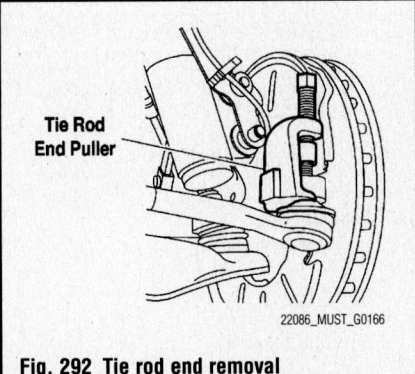

Tie Rod End Puller

22086_MUST_G0166

Fig. 292 Tie rod end removal

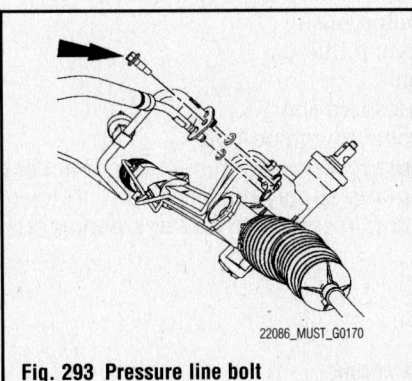

22086_MUST_G0170

Fig. 293 Pressure line bolt

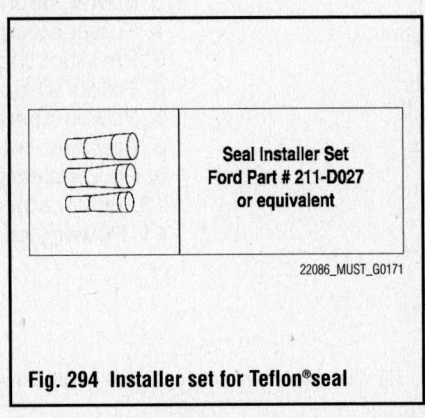

Seal Installer Set
Ford Part # 211-D027
or equivalent

22086_MUST_G0171

Fig. 294 Installer set for Teflon® seal

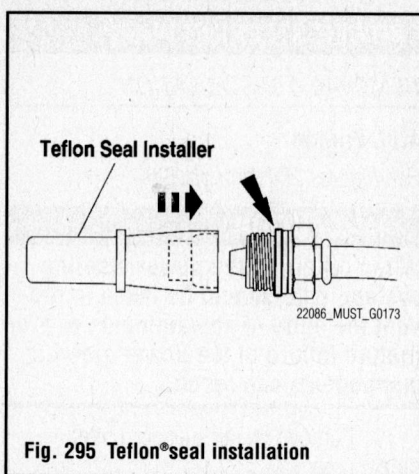

Teflon Seal Installer

22086_MUST_G0173

Fig. 295 Teflon®seal installation

10. Using the special tool, install a new Teflon® O-ring seal to the pressure line fitting.

11. Install accessory drive belt. Refer to the Engine Mechanical Section for more details.

12. Fill and bleed the power steering system.

13. Start the vehicle, and verify that there are no fluid leaks.

4.6L Engine

See Figures 294 and 297.

❋❋ CAUTION

When repairing the power steering system, care should be taken to pre- vent the entry of contaminants or pre- mature failure of the power steering components can result.

1. With the vehicle in NEUTRAL, posi- tion it on a hoist.

2. Remove accessory drive belt.

3. Remove the power steering pump pulley.

4. Remove the pressure line bracket to pump stud nut.

   a. To install, tighten to 62 inch lbs. (7 Nm).

5. Release the clamp and disconnect the power steering pump supply hose from the pump.

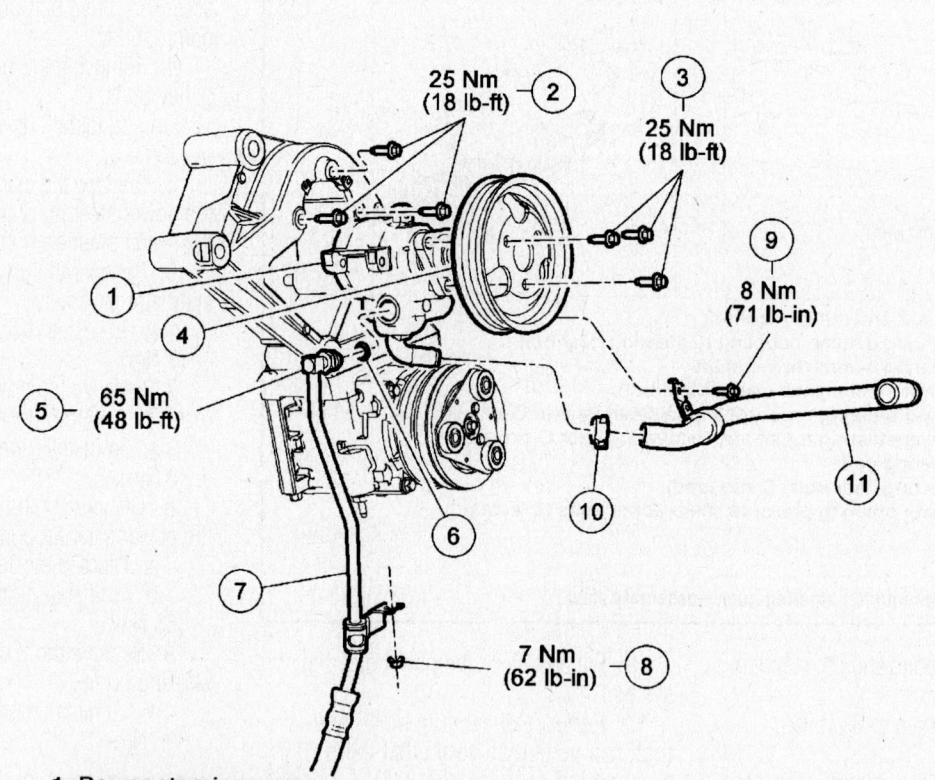

1. Power steering pump
2. Power steering pump bolts (3 required)
3. Power steering pump pulley bolts (3 required)
4. Power steering pump pulley
5. Pressure line to pump fitting
6. Teflon® O-ring seal
7. Power steering pressure line
8. Pressure line bracket to engine bolt
9. Power steering fluid reservoir to pump hose bracket bolt
10. Power steering pump supply hose clamp
11. Power steering fluid reservoir to power steering pump supply hose

22086_MUST_G0172

Fig. 296 Power steering pump assembly view—4.0L engine

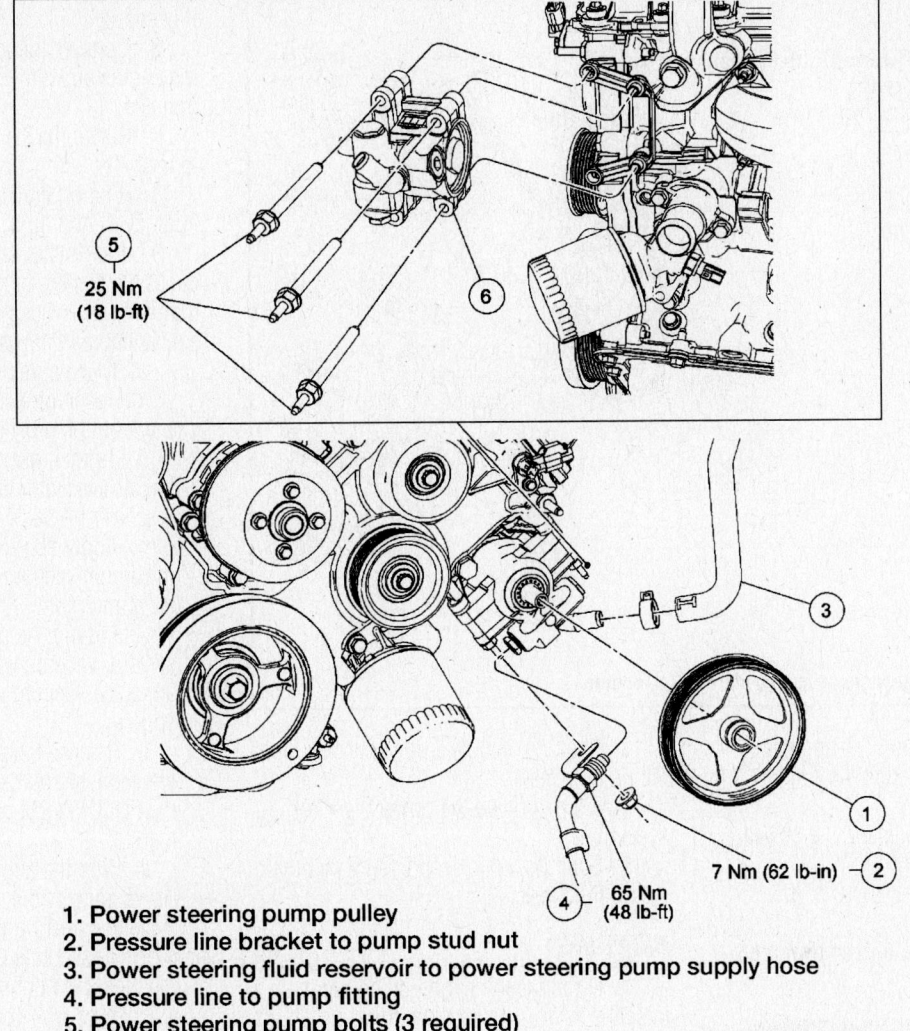

1. Power steering pump pulley
2. Pressure line bracket to pump stud nut
3. Power steering fluid reservoir to power steering pump supply hose
4. Pressure line to pump fitting
5. Power steering pump bolts (3 required)
6. Power steering pump

22086_MUST_G0174

Fig. 297 Power steering pump assembly view—4.6L engine

6. Disconnect the pressure line from the power steering pump.

a. Discard the Teflon® O-ring seal.

b. To install, tighten to 48 ft. lbs. (65 Nm).

7. Remove the 3 bolts and the power steering pump.

c. To install, tighten to 18 ft. lbs. (25 Nm).

➡**A new Teflon®O-ring seal must be installed.**

8. To install, reverse the removal procedure.

9. Using the special tool, install a new Teflon® O-ring seal to the pressure line fitting.

10. Install accessory drive belt. Refer to the Engine Mechanical Section for more details.

11. Fill and bleed the power steering system.

12. Start the vehicle, and verify that there are no fluid leaks.

5.4L Engine

See Figures 295 and 298.

✳✳ CAUTION

When repairing the power steering system, care should be taken to prevent the entry of contaminants or premature failure of the power steering components can result.

1. Remove accessory drive belt.
2. Remove the power steering pump pulley.

✳✳ CAUTION

Make sure to remove the power steering reservoir bolt and separate

the reservoir from the bracket or damage to the power steering reservoir will occur.

3. Remove the power steering fluid reservoir bolt and separate the reservoir from the power steering reservoir bracket.

a. To install, tighten to 80 inch lbs. (9 Nm).

4. Release the clamp and disconnect the power steering pump supply hose from the power steering pump.

5. Position the power steering fluid reservoir aside.

6. Remove the pressure line bracket to engine bolt.

a. To install, tighten to 62 inch lbs. (7 Nm).

7. Disconnect the pressure line from the power steering pump.

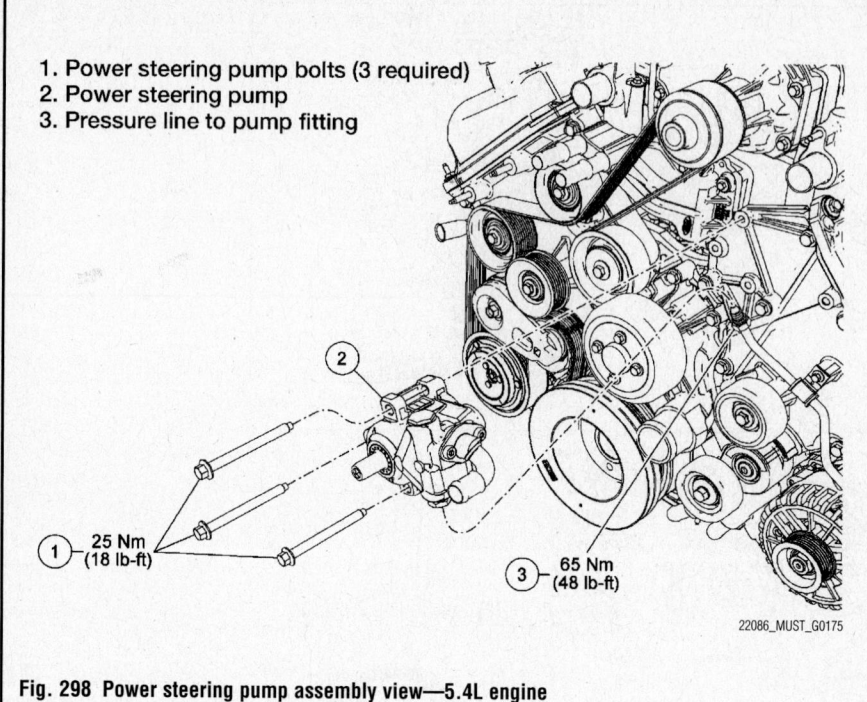

1. Power steering pump bolts (3 required)
2. Power steering pump
3. Pressure line to pump fitting

① 25 Nm (18 lb-ft)

③ 65 Nm (48 lb-ft)

22086_MUST_G0175

Fig. 298 Power steering pump assembly view—5.4L engine

a. Discard the Teflon® O-ring seal.

b. To install, tighten to 48 ft. lbs. (65 Nm).

8. Remove the 3 bolts and the power steering pump.

a. To install, tighten to 18 ft. lbs. (25 Nm).

9. To install, reverse the removal procedure.

➡ **A new Teflon® O-ring seal must be installed.**

10. Using the special tool, install a new Teflon® O-ring seal to the pressure line fitting.

11. Install accessory drive belt. Refer to the Engine Mechanical Section for more details.

12. Fill and bleed the power steering system.

13. Start the vehicle, and verify that there are no fluid leaks.

14. Fill and bleed the power steering system.

15. Start the vehicle, and verify that there are no fluid leaks.

BLEEDING

1. Disconnect the ignition coil and raise the front wheels off the floor.

2. Fill the power steering fluid reservoir.

3. Crank the engine with the starter and add fluid until the level remains constant.

4. While cranking the engine, rotate the steering wheel from lock to lock.

➡ **The front wheels must be off the floor during lock to lock rotation of the steering wheel.**

5. Check the fluid level and add fluid, if necessary.

6. Connect the ignition coil wire. Start the engine and allow it to run for several minutes.

7. Rotate the steering wheel from lock to lock.

8. Shut off the engine and check the fluid level. Add fluid, if necessary.

9. If air is still present in the system, purge the system of air using power steering pump air evacuator tool 021–00014 or equivalent, as follows:

a. Make sure the power steering pump reservoir is full to the FULL COLD mark on the dipstick.

b. Tightly insert the rubber stopper of the air evacuator assembly into the pump reservoir fill neck.

c. Apply 20–25 in. Hg (68–85 kPa) maximum vacuum on the pump reservoir for a minimum of three minutes with the engine idling. As air purges from the system, vacuum will fall off. Maintain adequate vacuum with the vacuum source.

d. Release the vacuum and remove the vacuum source. Fill the reservoir to the FULL WARM or center reservoir mark.

e. With the engine idling, apply 15 in. Hg vacuum to the pump reservoir. Slowly cycle the steering wheel from lock to lock every 30 seconds for approximately five minutes. Do not hold the steering wheel at its stops while cycling. Maintain adequate vacuum with the vacuum source as the air purges.

f. Release the vacuum and remove the vacuum source.

10. Lower the front end of the vehicle, and fill the reservoir until full.

11. Start the engine and cycle the steering wheel. Check for oil leaks at all connections.

LOWER BALL JOINT

REMOVAL & INSTALLATION

The lower ball joint is integrated with the lower control arm on all 2005–2008 Mustang models.

LOWER CONTROL ARM

REMOVAL AND & INSTALLATION

See Figure 299.

✳✳ CAUTION

Suspension fasteners are critical parts because they affect performance of vital components and systems and their failure can result in major service expense. A new part with the same part number or an equivalent part must be installed, if installation is necessary. Do not use a part of lesser quality or substitute design. Torque values must be used as specified during reassembly to make sure of correct retention of these parts.

1. With the vehicle in NEUTRAL, position it on a hoist.

✳✳ CAUTION

Note the orientation of the lower ball joint nut and bolt. They must be installed using the same orientation.

2. Remove the lower ball joint nut and bolt.
3. To install, tighten the nut to 76 ft. lbs. (103 Nm).
4. Separate the lower control arm and the wheel spindle.
5. Remove the steering gear bolts. Position the steering gear to gain access to the lower control arm forward bolt.
   a. To install, tighten to 85 ft. lbs. (115 Nm).

✳✳ CAUTION

Do not damage the steering gear boot while removing or installing the lower control arm forward bolt.

6. Remove the lower control arm forward bolt.
   a. To install, tighten to 129 ft. lbs. (175 Nm).

➡ **To ease installation, the position of the lower control arm nut and flag bolt**

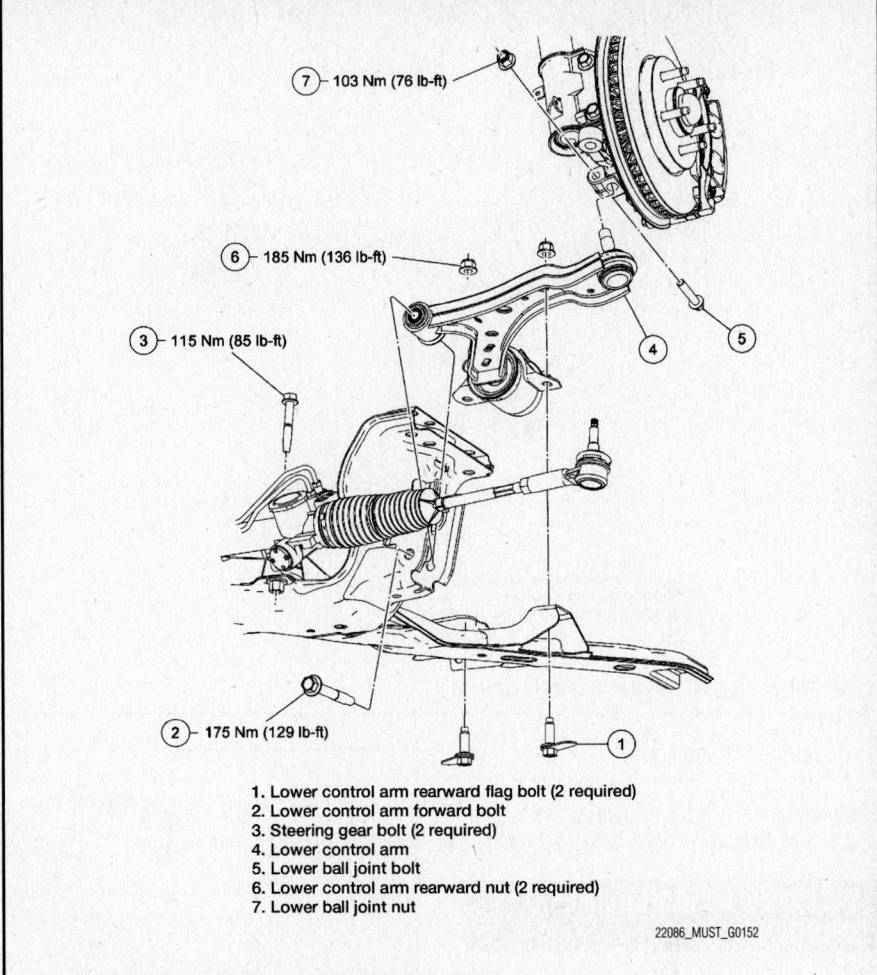

Fig. 299 Lower control arm assembly—exploded view

7 — 103 Nm (76 lb-ft)
6 — 185 Nm (136 lb-ft)
3 — 115 Nm (85 lb-ft)
2 — 175 Nm (129 lb-ft)

1. Lower control arm rearward flag bolt (2 required)
2. Lower control arm forward bolt
3. Steering gear bolt (2 required)
4. Lower control arm
5. Lower ball joint bolt
6. Lower control arm rearward nut (2 required)
7. Lower ball joint nut

22086_MUST_G0152

can be reversed to allow installation of the nut from underneath the vehicle.

7. Remove the lower control arm rearward nuts and flag bolts.
   a. To install, tighten to 136 ft. lbs. (185 Nm).
8. Remove the lower control arm and bracket assembly.

✳✳ CAUTION

Tighten the lower control arm and lower ball joint nuts with the suspension at curb height.

✳✳ CAUTION

The lower ball joint seal must be fully seated against the knuckle or premature damage to the ball joint can occur.

9. To install, reverse the removal procedure.
10. Perform wheel alignment on vehicle.

11. Perform a road test of the vehicle and verify that no handling or noise issues are present.

STABILIZER BAR

REMOVAL & INSTALLATION

See Figure 300.

1. Raise the vehicle on a hoist
2. Remove the front wheels.
3. Remove and discard the stabilizer bar link bolts and nuts.
4. Remove and discard the stabilizer bar clamp bolts.
5. Remove the stabilizer bar.

To install:

6. Install the stabilizer bar.
7. Install new stabilizer bar clamp bolts and tighten to 52 ft. lbs. (70 Nm).
8. Install the stabilizer bar link and tighten the new bolts and nuts to 85 ft. lbs. (115 Nm).
9. Install the front wheels.

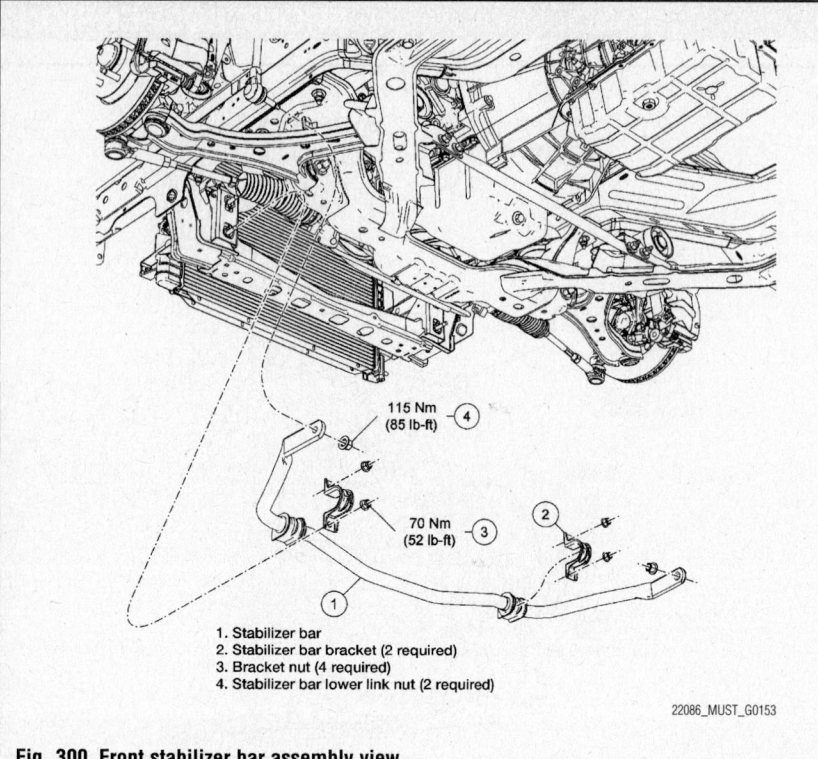

115 Nm (85 lb-ft) — ④

70 Nm (52 lb-ft) — ③   ②

1. Stabilizer bar
2. Stabilizer bar bracket (2 required)
3. Bracket nut (4 required)
4. Stabilizer bar lower link nut (2 required)

22086_MUST_G0153

Fig. 300 Front stabilizer bar assembly view

10. Lower the vehicle.

11. Road test vehicle, and verify that no handling or noise concerns are present.

12. If necessary, perform wheel alignment.

STEERING KNUCKLE AND SPINDLE

REMOVAL & INSTALLATION

See Figure 301.

1. Place the transmission in neutral.
2. Raise the vehicle on a hoist.
3. Remove the front wheel.
4. Remove the front wheel hub.
5. Remove the brake disc shield.
6. Remove the ABS sensor.
7. Remove and discard the outer tie rod end nut.
8. Press the tie rod end from the wheel spindle.
9. Place a jack under the lower control arm.
10. Remove the control arm pinch bolt and nut.
11. Separate the control arm from the spindle.
12. Index mark the spindle to strut bolts, then remove the bolts.
13. Remove the wheel spindle.

To install:

14. Install the wheel spindle.
15. Install the spindle to strut bolts and tighten to 148 ft. lbs. (200 Nm).

16. Attach the control arm to the spindle.
17. Install the control arm pinch bolt and nut and tighten to 76 ft. lbs. (103 Nm).
18. Attach the tie rod end to the wheel spindle.
19. Install the outer tie rod end nut and tighten to 59 ft. lbs. (80 Nm).
20. Install the ABS sensor.
21. Install the brake disc shield.
22. Install the front wheel hub.
23. Install the front wheel.
24. Lower the vehicle.

STRUT & SPRING ASSEMBLY

REMOVAL & INSTALLATION

See Figures 302 and 303.

❋❋ WARNING

All vehicles are equipped with gas–pressurized struts which will extend unassisted. Do not apply heat or flame to the struts during removal or component servicing. Failure to follow these instructions can result in personal injury.

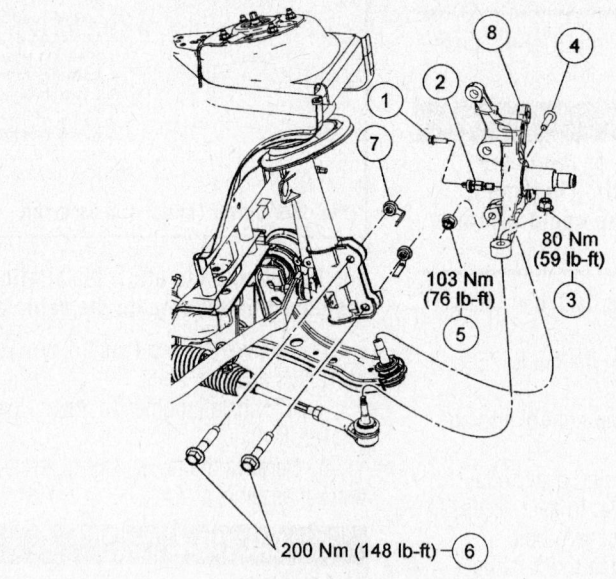

⑧   ④

②

①

⑦   80 Nm (59 lb-ft)

103 Nm (76 lb-ft)   ③

⑤

200 Nm (148 lb-ft) — ⑥

1 Wheel speed sensor bolt
2 Wheel speed sensor
3 Outer tie rod end nut
4 Wheel spindle pinch bolt
5 Wheel spindle pinch nut
6 Strut-to-wheel spindle bolt (2 required)
7 Strut-to-wheel spindle flag nut (2 required)
8 Wheel spindle (RH/LH)

06017-TANG-G65

Fig. 301 Exploded view of the front wheel spindle—Mustang

1. Place the vehicle in NEUTRAL, and position it on a hoist.

2. Remove the 4 strut upper mount nuts.

   a. To install, tighten to 26 ft. lbs. (35 Nm).

3. Remove the wheel speed sensor bolt and position the sensor aside.

   a. To install, tighten to 11 ft. lbs. (15 Nm).

4. Remove the brake line bracket bolt and disconnect the wheel speed sensor wire from the bracket.

   a. To install, tighten to 15 ft. lbs. (20 Nm).

※ CAUTION

Use the holding feature to prevent the studs from turning while removing or installing the stabilizer bar link nuts.

5. Remove and discard the stabilizer bar link upper nut and disconnect the link from the strut.

   a. To install, tighten to 85 ft. lbs. (115 Nm).

6. Using a suitable jack stand, support the lower control arm.

Fig. 302 Indexing strut to spindle cam bolts

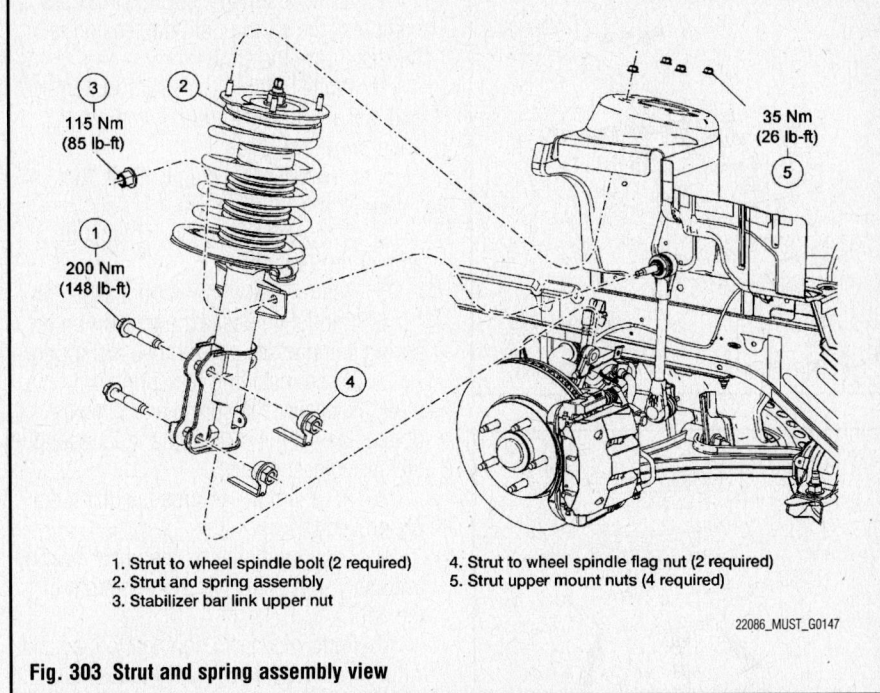

③ 115 Nm (85 lb-ft)

① 200 Nm (148 lb-ft)

35 Nm (26 lb-ft) ⑤

1. Strut to wheel spindle bolt (2 required)
2. Strut and spring assembly
3. Stabilizer bar link upper nut
4. Strut to wheel spindle flag nut (2 required)
5. Strut upper mount nuts (4 required)

22086_MUST_G0147

Fig. 303 Strut and spring assembly view

7. If equipped, index mark the 2 strut to spindle cam bolts.

※ WARNING

All vehicles are equipped with gas–pressurized struts which will extend unassisted. Do not apply heat or flame to the struts during removal or component servicing. Failure to follow these instructions can result in personal injury.

➡ **If equipped, do not discard the strut to spindle cam nuts and bolts.**

Remove and discard the strut to spindle bolts and flag nuts.

   b. To install, tighten to 148 ft. lbs. (200 Nm).

※ CAUTION

Damage to the lower control arm bushings may occur if the lower control arm is not supported.

8. Carefully lower the lower control arm and remove the strut and spring assembly.

9. To install, the notch and the arrow etched into the upper bearing assembly must face the outboard side of the vehicle.

10. If necessary, disassemble the strut and spring assembly as required.

11. To install, reverse the removal procedure.

12. Check and, if necessary, adjust the front end alignment.

DISASSEMBLY & REASSEMBLY

See Figures 304 through 306.

※ WARNING

All vehicles are equipped with gas–pressurized struts which will extend unassisted. Do not apply heat or flame to the struts during removal or component servicing. Failure to follow these instructions may result in personal injury.

※ WARNING

The strut and spring assembly is under extreme load. Do not attempt to disassemble the strut and spring assembly without using a spring compressor. Failure to follow these instructions may result in personal injury.

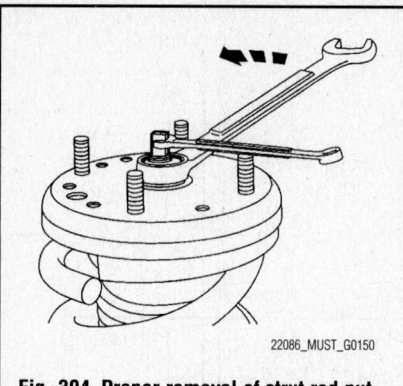

Fig. 304 Proper removal of strut rod nut

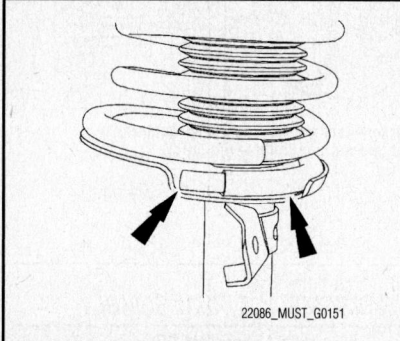

Fig. 305 Correct alignment of spring in seat pocket

1. Remove the strut and spring assembly.

➡️**If installing a new spring, make sure the part number is correct. Refer to the Vehicle Certification (VC) label for the correct spring code.**

2. Using a suitable spring compressor, compress the spring until the tension is released from the strut.

3. While holding the strut rod, remove and discard the strut rod nut and washer and remove the strut.

   a. To install, tighten to 59 ft. lbs. (80 Nm).

4. If necessary, remove the dust boot and jounce bumper.

5. Remove the upper mount assembly.

6. Carefully release the tension on the spring compressor and remove the spring.

7. When installing the spring onto the strut, make sure the spring end is positioned against the seat stop and is resting in the spring seat pocket.

8. To assemble, reverse the disassembly procedure.

9. Align the notch on the upper bearing assembly with the clevis at the bottom of the strut.

10. Perform wheel alignment on vehicle.

11. Perform a road test of the vehicle and verify that no handling or noise issues are present.

WHEEL BEARINGS

REMOVAL & INSTALLATION

See Figure 307.

1. Before servicing the vehicle, refer to the precautions at the beginning of this section.

2. Remove front wheel.

3. Remove disc brake caliper and rotor.

4. Remove grease cap.

5. Remove spindle retainer nut.

6. Remove hub and bearing assembly.

To install:

7. Install hub and bearing assembly. Tighten the spindle retainer nut to 221–295 ft. lbs. (300–400 Nm).

8. Install grease cap.

9. Install disc brake caliper and rotor.

10. Install front wheel

ADJUSTMENT

The front wheel bearings are an integral part of the hub assembly. They require no periodic maintenance or adjustment. If the bearings are found to be defective, they must be replaced along with the hub assembly.

INSPECTION

See Figure 308.

➡️**Be sure not to confuse the lower ball joint looseness with wheel bearing looseness.**

Wheel bearings that need replacing may be indicated by a noise that occurs only during turning. Diagnose the wheel bearings as follows:

1. Road test the vehicle on a smooth road. Make sharp turns to the right and left.

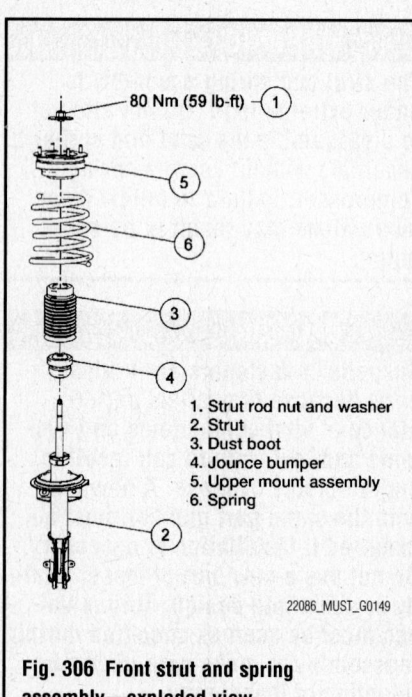

1. Strut rod nut and washer
2. Strut
3. Dust boot
4. Jounce bumper
5. Upper mount assembly
6. Spring

Fig. 306 Front strut and spring assembly—exploded view

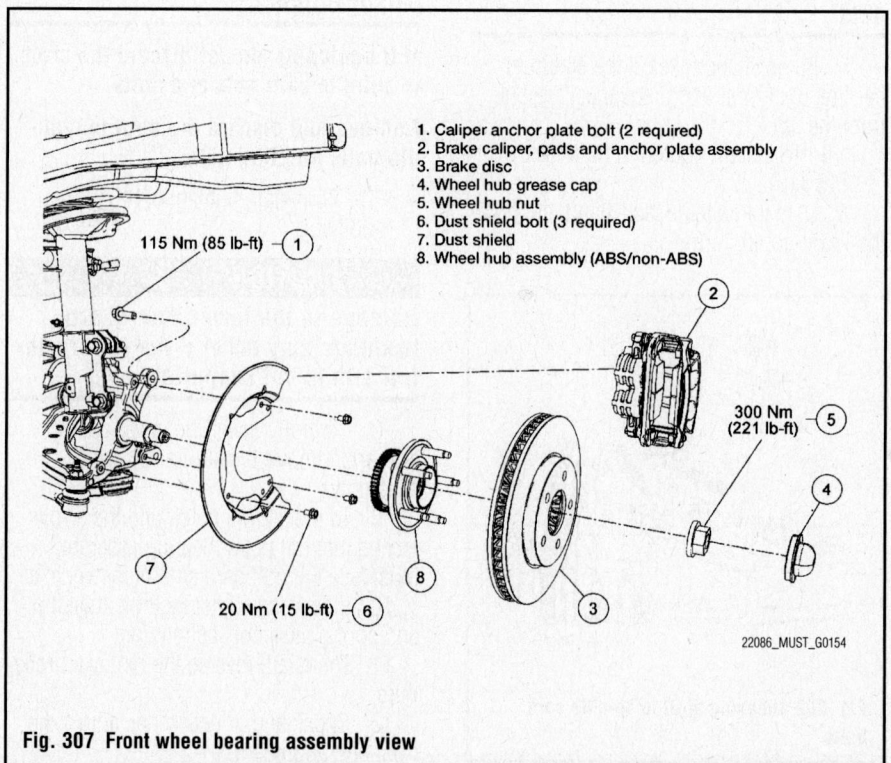

1. Caliper anchor plate bolt (2 required)
2. Brake caliper, pads and anchor plate assembly
3. Brake disc
4. Wheel hub grease cap
5. Wheel hub nut
6. Dust shield bolt (3 required)
7. Dust shield
8. Wheel hub assembly (ABS/non-ABS)

Fig. 307 Front wheel bearing assembly view

a. If the vehicle makes noises on right turns, the left wheel bearing may need to be replaced.

b. If the vehicle makes noises on left turns, the right wheel bearing may need to be replaced.

2. Raise and safely support the vehicle.

3. Using one hand on top of the tire and one hand on the bottom, rock the wheel assembly to check for wheel bearing looseness.

4. Spin the tire quickly by hand and be sure that the tire rotates smoothly and without noise from the wheel bearings.

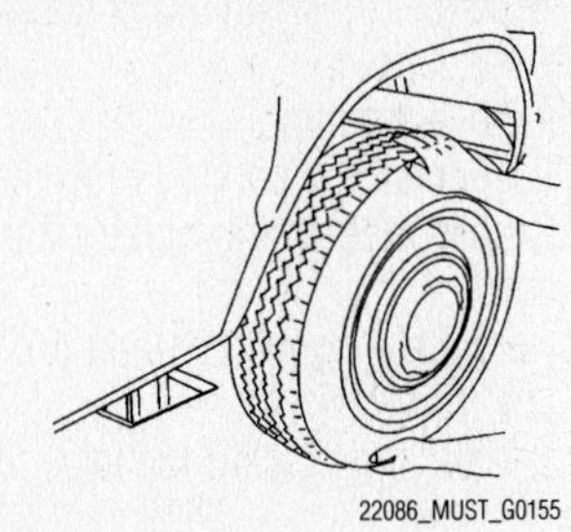

Fig. 308 Checking wheel bearing for looseness

5. Remove the wheel and disc brake caliper.

6. Position a dial indicator, such as Ford Position Dial Indicator with Bracket TOOL–4201–C, against the wheel bearing hub. Push and pull on the hub and read the hub movement range on the dial indicator. The maximum allowable hub play is 0.002 in. (0.05mm). If end play exceeds the specified value, replace the wheel hubs.

SUSPENSION

REAR SUSPENSION

COIL SPRING

REMOVAL & INSTALLATION

See Figure 309.

1. Raise the vehicle on a hoist.

2. Use a hi-lift jack and support the rear axle.

3. If equipped with a stabilizer bar, remove the stabilizer bar link bolts.

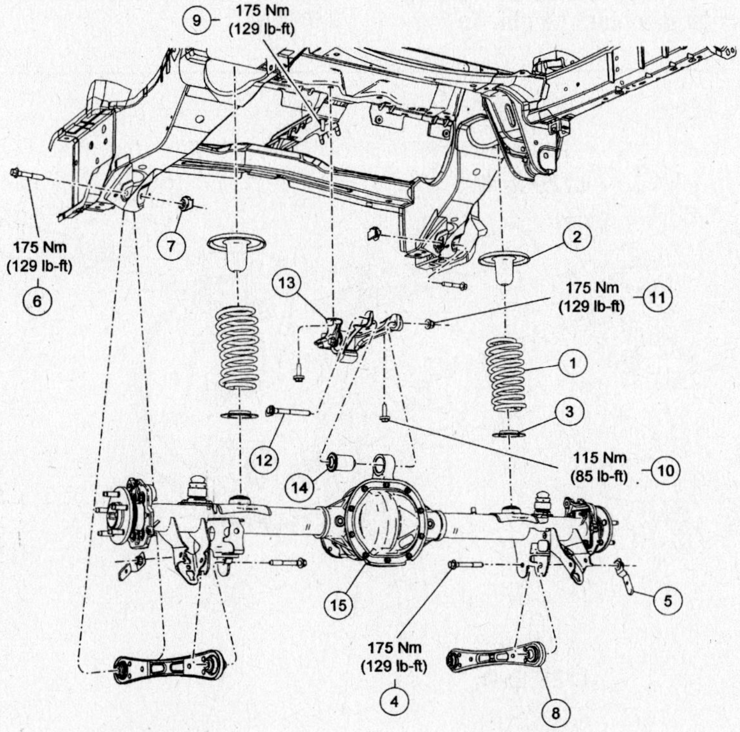

1 Spring (2 required)
2 Upper insulator (2 required)
3 Lower insulator (2 required)
4 Lower control arm rear bolt (2 required)
5 Lower control arm rear nut (2 required)
6 Lower control arm front bolt (2 required)
7 Lower control arm front nut (2 required)
8 Lower control arm (2 required)
9 Upper control arm front bolt
10 Upper control arm rear bolt (2 required)
11 Upper control arm rear nut
12 Upper control arm flag bolt
13 Upper control arm
14 Upper control arm bushing
15 Rear axle assembly

06017-TANG-G63

Fig. 309 Exploded view of the rear coil spring mounting

4. Remove lower shock absorber bolt.

5. Remove the brake hose bracket bolt.

6. Use the jack to lower the rear axle until the spring can be removed.

To install:

7. Place the upper spring insulator on top of the spring. Place the lower spring insulator on the lower arm.

8. Position the coil spring on the lower arm spring seat with the tag facing toward the rear axle.

9. Slowly raise the jack until the spring is in place.

10. Install the brake hose bracket bolt.

11. Install the lower shock absorber bolts and tighten to 85 ft. lbs. (115 Nm).

12. If equipped with a stabilizer bar, install new stabilizer bar link bolts and tighten to 85 ft. lbs. (115 Nm).

13. Remove the jack.

14. Lower the vehicle.

LOWER CONTROL ARM

REMOVAL & INSTALLATION

See Figures 310 through 312.

⁂ CAUTION

Suspension fasteners are critical parts because they affect performance of vital parts and systems and their failure can result in major service expense. A new part with the same part number must be installed if installation becomes necessary. Torque values must be used as specified during reassembly to make sure of correct retention of these parts.

1. With the vehicle in NEUTRAL, position it on a hoist.

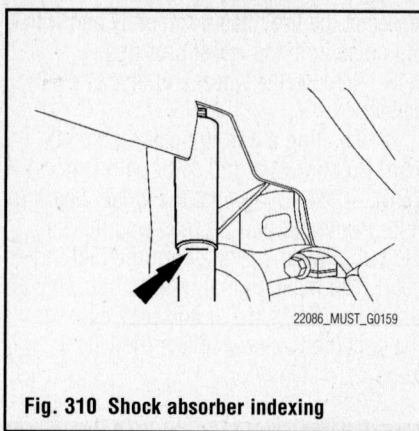

Fig. 310 Shock absorber indexing

✳✳ CAUTION

Do not support the rear axle at the differential housing.

2. Using 2 suitable jack stands, support the rear axle.

3. Raise the rear axle so the mark made on the rear shock absorber in Step 1 lines up with the protective sleeve.

4. Disconnect the parking brake cable from the rear caliper.

5. Remove the clip.

6. Disconnect the parking brake cable.

7. Remove the parking brake cable bracket bolt.
   - To install, tighten the bolt to 20 ft. lbs. (27 Nm).

8. Remove and discard the lower arm front bolt.
   c. To install, tighten to 129 ft. lbs. (175 Nm).

9. Remove and discard the lower arm front nut.

10. Rotate the nut clockwise.

11. Remove and discard the nut.

12. Remove and discard the lower arm rear bolt and flag nut and then remove the lower arm.
   a. To install, tighten to 129 ft. lbs. (175 Nm).

✳✳ CAUTION

Tighten the lower arm bolts while the suspension is at curb height. To

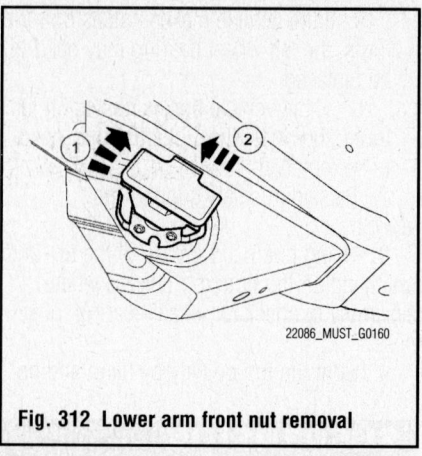

Fig. 312 Lower arm front nut removal

install, reverse the removal procedure.

CONTROL ARM BUSHING REPLACEMENT

The lower control arm bushings are serviced with the lower control arm as an assembly.

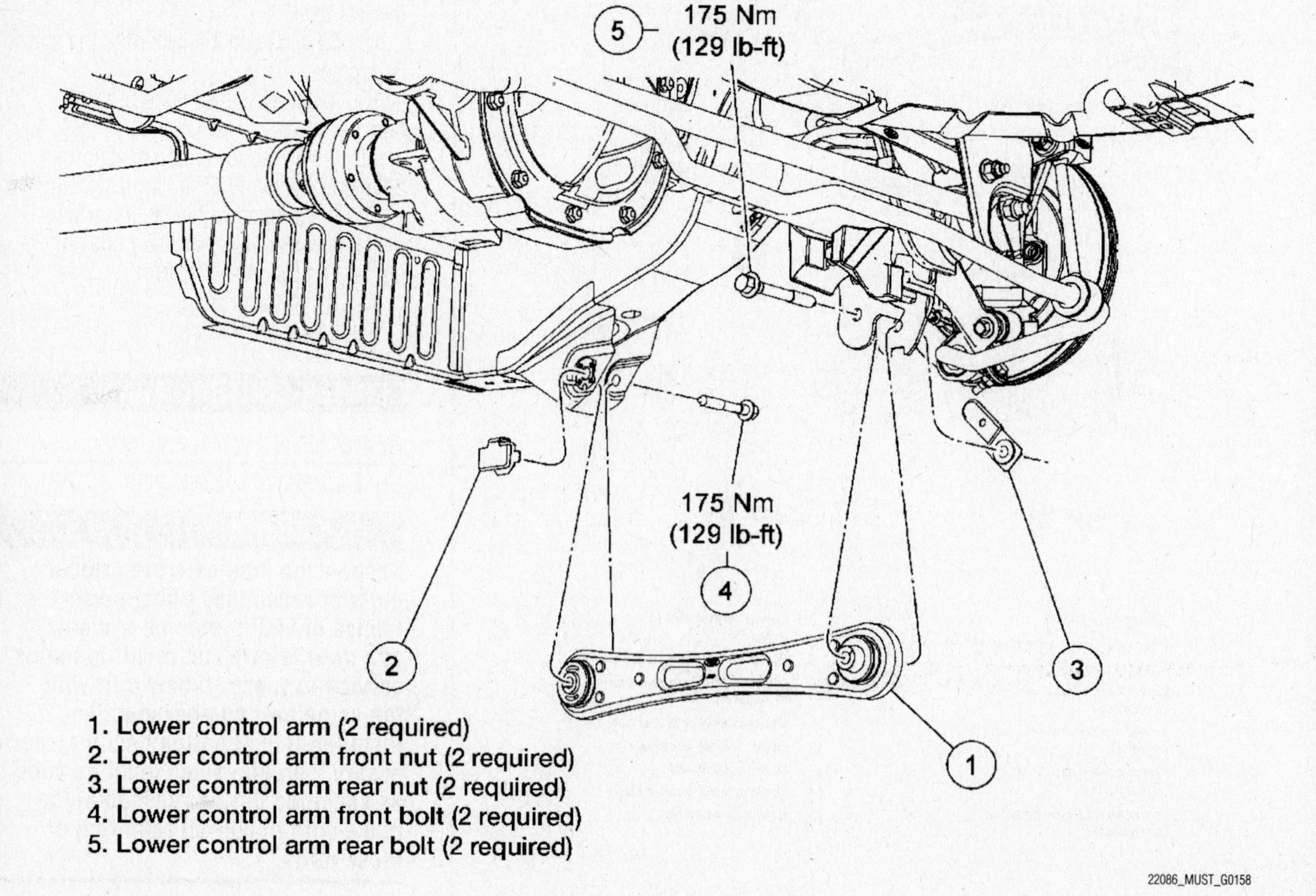

---

175 Nm
(129 lb-ft)
⑤

175 Nm
(129 lb-ft)
④

1. Lower control arm (2 required)
2. Lower control arm front nut (2 required)
3. Lower control arm rear nut (2 required)
4. Lower control arm front bolt (2 required)
5. Lower control arm rear bolt (2 required)

Fig. 311 Rear lower arm assembly view

SHOCK ABSORBER

REMOVAL & INSTALLATION

See Figure 313.

1. Pull aside the rear compartment carpet.

2. Support the rear axle with jack stands.

3. Remove upper shock absorber retaining nut.

4. If equipped with a stabilizer bar, remove the stabilizer bar link bolts.

5. Remove lower shock absorber bolt.

6. Remove shock absorber.

To install:

7. Install the shock absorber and tighten the lower bolt to 85 ft. lbs. (115 Nm).

8. If equipped with a stabilizer bar, install new stabilizer bar link bolts and tighten to 85 ft. lbs. (115 Nm).

9. Install upper shock absorber nut. Tighten it to 30 ft. lbs. (40 Nm).

10. Remove the jack stands.

11. Reinstall the carpet.

STABILIZER BAR

REMOVAL & INSTALLATION

See Figure 314.

1. Raise the vehicle on a hoist
2. Remove the appropriate wheel.
3. Remove and discard the stabilizer bar link bolts and nuts.

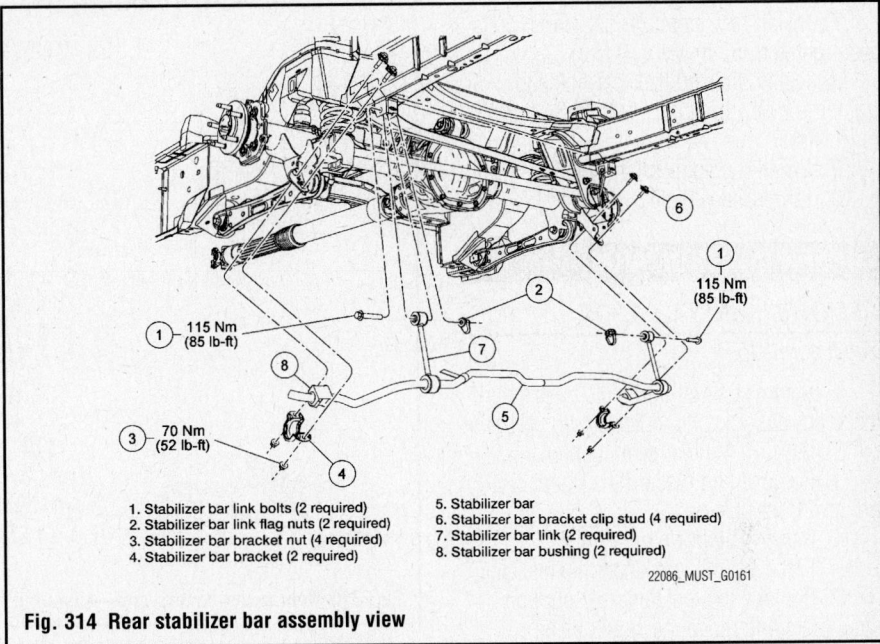

1. Stabilizer bar link bolts (2 required)
2. Stabilizer bar link flag nuts (2 required)
3. Stabilizer bar bracket nut (4 required)
4. Stabilizer bar bracket (2 required)
5. Stabilizer bar
6. Stabilizer bar bracket clip stud (4 required)
7. Stabilizer bar link (2 required)
8. Stabilizer bar bushing (2 required)

22086_MUST_G0161

Fig. 314 Rear stabilizer bar assembly view

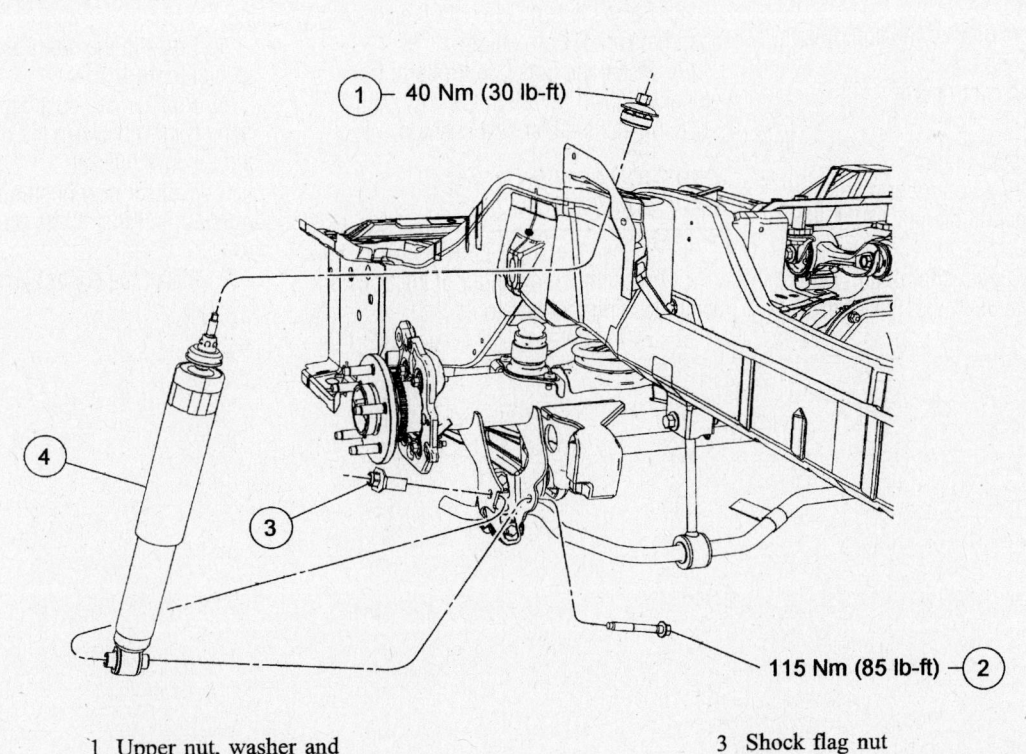

1 Upper nut, washer and insulator
2 Shock lower bolt
3 Shock flag nut
4 Shock

06017-TANG-G62

Fig. 313 Exploded view of the rear shock absorber mounting—Mustang

4. Remove and discard the stabilizer bar clamp bolts.

5. Remove the stabilizer bar.

To install:

6. Install the stabilizer bar.

7. Install new stabilizer bar clamp bolts and tighten to 52 ft. lbs. (70 Nm).

8. Install the stabilizer bar link and tighten the new bolts and nuts to 85 ft. lbs. (115 Nm).

9. Install the appropriate wheel.

10. Lower the vehicle.

UPPER CONTROL ARM

REMOVAL & INSTALLATION

See Figure 315.

1. Before raising the vehicle, matchmark the shock absorbers to indicate curb height.

2. Remove the rear seat cushion.

3. Remove and discard the upper control arm front bolt.

4. Raise the vehicle on a hoist.

5. Place a hi-lift jack under the fuel tank.

6. Remove the fuel tank rear support strap bolts and move the straps aside.

7. Partially lower the fuel tank.

8. Remove and discard the upper control arm rear bolts.

9. Remove and discard the control arm bushing flag bolt and nut.

10. Remove the control arm.

To install:

11. Install the control arm.

12. Install the new control arm bushing flag bolt and nut and tighten to 129 ft. lbs. (175 Nm).

13. Install new upper control arm rear bolts and tighten to 85 ft. lbs. (115 Nm).

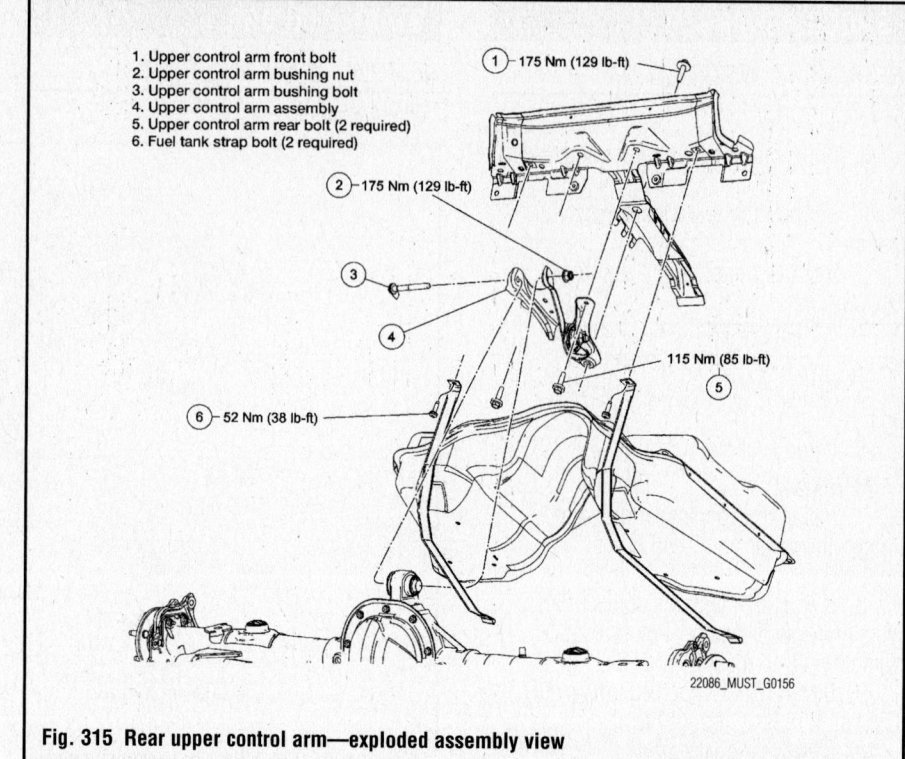

1. Upper control arm front bolt
2. Upper control arm bushing nut
3. Upper control arm bushing bolt
4. Upper control arm assembly
5. Upper control arm rear bolt (2 required)
6. Fuel tank strap bolt (2 required)

1 — 175 Nm (129 lb-ft)
2 — 175 Nm (129 lb-ft)
115 Nm (85 lb-ft)
6 — 52 Nm (38 lb-ft)

22086_MUST_G0156

Fig. 315 Rear upper control arm—exploded assembly view

14. Raise the fuel tank.

15. Attach the fuel tank straps.

16. Raise the rear axle until the shock absorbers are at curb height.

17. Install the upper control arm front bolt and tighten to 129 ft. lbs. (175 Nm).

18. Install the rear seat cushion.

CONTROL ARM BUSHING REPLACEMENT

1. Remove the upper control arm.

2. Press the bushing out of the housing using bushing remover tools.

3. Position the new bushing so the voids are at the top and bottom of the housing.

4. Press in the new bushing using the special tools.

5. Position the bushing so there is 0.47 inch (12mm) between the bushing flange and the axle bracket.

6. Press a new bushing into the axle housing and install the upper control arm.

7. Install the control arm.

FORD

Ranger

SPECIFICATIONS AND MAINTENANCE CHARTS

ENGINE AND VEHICLE IDENTIFICATION

			Engine						Model Year	
Code ①	Liters (cc)	Cu. In.	Cyl.	Fuel Sys.	Type	Eng. Mfg.		Code ②		Year
D	2.3 (2261)	138	4	MFI	DOHC	Ford		5		2005
U	3.0 (2999)	183	6	MFI	OHV	Ford		6		2006
E	4.0 (4000)	244	6	MFI	SOHC	Ford		7		2007

MFI: Multi-port Fuel Injection

OHV: Overhead Valve

DOHC: Dual Overhead Camshafts

SOHC: Single Overhead Camshaft

① 8th digit of the Vehicle Identification Number (VIN)

② 10th digit of the Vehicle Identification Number (VIN)

22086_RANG_C0001

GENERAL ENGINE SPECIFICATIONS

Year	Model	Engine Displacement Liters (cc)	Engine Series (ID/VIN)	Fuel System Type	Net Horsepower @ rpm	Net Torque @ rpm (ft. lbs.)	Bore x Stroke (in.)	Compression Ratio	Oil Pressure @ rpm
2005	Ranger	2.3 (2261)	D	MFI	143@5200	154@3750	3.44x3.70	NA	29-39@3000
	Ranger	3.0 (2982)	U	MFI	147@5000	147@5000	3.50x3.14	9.3:1	40-60@2500
	Ranger	4.0 (4000)	E	MFI	160@4000	225@2500	3.81x3.39	9.0:1	40-60@2000
2006	Ranger	2.3 (2261)	D	MFI	143@5200	154@3750	3.44x3.70	NA	29-39@3000
	Ranger	3.0 (2982)	U	MFI	147@5000	147@5000	3.50x3.14	9.3:1	40-60@2500
	Ranger	4.0 (4000)	E	MFI	160@4000	225@2500	3.81x3.39	9.0:1	40-60@2000
2007	Ranger	2.3 (2261)	D	MFI	143@5200	154@3750	3.44x3.70	NA	29-39@3000
	Ranger	3.0 (2982)	U	MFI	147@5000	147@5000	3.50x3.14	9.3:1	40-60@2500
	Ranger	4.0 (4000)	E	MFI	160@4000	225@2500	3.81x3.39	9.0:1	40-60@2000

MFI: Multi-port Fuel Injection

22086_RANG_C0002

GASOLINE ENGINE TUNE-UP SPECIFICATIONS

Year	Engine Displacement Liters	Engine ID/VIN	Spark Plug Gap (in.)	Ignition Timing (deg.) MT	AT	Fuel Pump (psi)	Idle Speed (rpm) MT	AT	Valve Clearance In.	Ex.
2005	2.3	D	0.041-0.045	10B	10B	64-72	①	①	HYD	HYD
	3.0	U	0.042-0.046	10B	10B	64-72	①	①	HYD	HYD
	4.0	E	0.062-0.068	10B	10B	64-72	①	①	HYD	HYD
2006	2.3	D	0.041-0.045	10B	10B	64-72	①	①	HYD	HYD
	3.0	U	0.042-0.046	10B	10B	64-72	①	①	HYD	HYD
	4.0	E	0.062-0.068	10B	10B	64-72	①	①	HYD	HYD
2007	2.3	D	0.041-0.045	10B	10B	60-65	①	①	HYD	HYD
	3.0	U	0.042-0.046	10B	10B	60-65	①	①	HYD	HYD
	4.0	E	0.062-0.068	10B	10B	60-65	①	①	HYD	HYD

NOTE: The Vehicle Emission Control Information label often reflects specification changes changes made during production. The label figures must be used if they differ from those in this chart.

B: Before top dead center

HYD: Hydraulic

① Electronically controlled and cannot be adjusted

22086_RANG_C0003

CAPACITIES

Year	Model	Engine Displacement Liters	Engine ID/VIN	Engine Oil with Filter (qts.)	Transmission (pts.)		Transfer Case (pts.)	Drive Axle		Fuel Tank (gal.)	Cooling System (qts.)
					5-Spd	Auto.		Front (pts.)	Rear (pts.)*		
2005	Ranger	2.3	D	4.0	3.0	19.8	—	—	5.0	④	⑤
	Ranger	3.0	U	4.5	3.0	①	2.5	2.7	5.0	④	②
	Ranger	4.0	E	5.0	3.0	①	2.5	2.7	5.0	④	③
2006	Ranger	2.3	D	4.0	3.0	19.8	—	—	5.0	④	⑤
	Ranger	3.0	U	4.5	3.0	①	2.5	3.25	5.0	④	②
	Ranger	4.0	E	5.0	3.0	①	2.5	3.25	5.0	④	③
2007	Ranger	2.3	D	4.0	3.6	19.8	—	—	5.0	④	⑤
	Ranger	3.0	U	4.5	3.6	①	2.5	3.60	5.0	④	②
	Ranger	4.0	E	5.0	3.6	①	2.5	3.60	5.0	④	③

NOTE: All capacities are approximate. Add fluid gradually and check to be sure a proper fluid level is obtained.

* For limited slip axles, add 4 oz. of friction modifier, exc. for 1-ton models

① 2WD: 20.0
   4WD: 20.6

② w/MT: 15.2
   w/AT: 14.8

③ w/MT: 13.5
   w/AT: 13.2

④ w/MT: 11.2
   w/AT: 10.9

⑤ w/MT: 15.2
   w/AT: 14.8

22086_RANG_C0004

FLUID SPECIFICATIONS

Year	Model	Engine Displacement Liters	Engine ID/VIN	Engine Oil	Auto. Trans.	Drive Axle	Power Steering Fluid	Brake Master Cylinder
2005	Ranger	2.3	D	5W-20 ①	Mercon® V	80W-90 ② ③	Mercon®	DOT 3
		3.0	U	5W-20 ①	Mercon® V	80W-90 ② ③	Mercon®	DOT 3
		4.0	E	5W-30 ①	Mercon® V	80W-90 ② ③	Mercon®	DOT 3
2006	Ranger	2.3	D	5W-20 ①	Mercon® V	80W-90 ② ③	Mercon®	DOT 3
		3.0	U	5W-20 ①	Mercon® V	80W-90 ② ③	Mercon®	DOT 3
		4.0	E	5W-30 ①	Mercon® V	80W-90 ② ③	Mercon®	DOT 3
2007	Ranger	2.3	D	5W-20 ①	Mercon® V	80W-90 ② ③	Mercon®	DOT 3
		3.0	U	5W-20 ①	Mercon® V	80W-90 ② ③	Mercon®	DOT 3
		4.0	E	5W-30 ①	Mercon® V	80W-90 ② ③	Mercon®	DOT 3

DOT: Department Of Transportation

® Registered trademark

① Synthetic motor oil is recommended

② 8.8 inch. ring gear high torque 75W-140 synthetic lubricant

③ Friction modifier XL-3

22086_RANG_C0012

VALVE SPECIFICATIONS

Year	Engine Displacement Liters	Engine ID/VIN	Seat Angle (deg.)	Face Angle (deg.)	Spring Test Pressure (lbs. @ in.)	Spring Installed Height (in.)	Stem-to-Guide Clearance (in.)		Stem Diameter (in.)	
							Intake	Exhaust	Intake	Exhaust
2005	2.3	D	45	45	①	1.492	0.0009	0.0011	0.2153-0.2159	0.2151-0.2157
	3.0	U	45	44	185@1.16	1.580-1.610	0.0010-0.0027	0.0015-0.0032	0.3126-0.3134	0.3121-0.3129
	4.0	E	45	45	202-225@1.413-1.445	1.569-1.601	0.0010-0.0020	0.0010-0.0030	0.2742-0.2748	0.2736-0.2742
2006	2.3	D	45	45	①	1.492	0.0009	0.0011	0.2153-0.2159	0.2151-0.2157
	3.0	U	45	44	185@1.16	1.580-1.610	0.0010-0.0027	0.0015-0.0032	0.3126-0.3134	0.3121-0.3129
	4.0	E	45	45	202-225@1.413-1.445	1.569-1.601	0.0010-0.0020	0.0010-0.0030	0.2742-0.2748	0.2736-0.2742
2007	2.3	D	45	45	①	1.492	0.0009	0.0011	0.2153-0.2159	0.2151-0.2157
	3.0	U	45	44	185@1.16	1.580-1.610	0.0010-0.0027	0.0015-0.0032	0.3126-0.3134	0.3121-0.3129
	4.0	E	45	45	202-225@1.413-1.445	1.569-1.601	0.0010-0.0020	0.0010-0.0030	0.2742-0.2748	0.2736-0.2742

① Intake: 97.0@1.201
Exhaust: 93.3@1.201

22086_RANG_C0005

CAMSHAFT AND BEARING SPECIFICATIONS CHART
All measurements are given in inches.

Year	Engine Displ. Liters	Engine ID/VIN	Journal Dia.	Brg. Oil Clearance	Shaft End-play	Runout	Journal Bore	Lobe Height	
								Intake	Exhaust
2005	2.3	D	0.982-0.983	0.001-0.003	0.003-0.009	0.001	0.001-0.003	0.324	0.307
	3.0	U	2.0074-2.0084	0.001-0.003	0.003-0.007	0.002	NA	0.260	0.260
	4.0	E	1.099-1.101	0.002-0.004	0.003-0.007	0.002	1.102-1.104	0.259	0.259
2006	2.3	D	0.982-0.983	0.001-0.003	0.003-0.009	0.001	0.001-0.003	0.324	0.307
	3.0	U	2.0074-2.0084	0.001-0.003	0.003-0.007	0.002	NA	0.260	0.260
	4.0	E	1.099-1.101	0.002-0.004	0.003-0.007	0.002	1.102-1.104	0.259	0.259
2007	2.3	D	0.982-0.983	0.001-0.003	0.003-0.009	0.001	0.001-0.003	0.324	0.307
	3.0	U	2.0074-2.0084	0.001-0.003	0.003-0.007	0.002	NA	0.260	0.260
	4.0	E	1.099-1.101	0.002-0.004	0.003-0.007	0.002	1.102-1.104	0.259	0.259

NA: Not Available

22086_RANG_C0014

CRANKSHAFT AND CONNECTING ROD SPECIFICATIONS

All measurements are given in inches.

Year	Engine Displacement Liters	Engine ID/VIN	Crankshaft				Connecting Rod		
			Main Brg. Journal Dia.	Main Brg. Oil Clearance	Shaft End-play	Thrust on No.	Journal Diameter	Oil Clearance	Side Clearance
2005	2.3	D	2.0465-2.2059	0.0007-0.0013	0.0080-0.0160	3	1.9606-1.9685	0.0010-0.0020	0.0767-0.1200
	3.0	U	2.5190-2.2059	0.0010-0.0015	0.0040-0.0080	3	2.1253-2.0472	0.0010-0.0015	0.0060-0.0115
	4.0	E	2.2430-2.2440	0.0008-0.0015	0.0020-0.0125	3	2.7252-2.7260	0.0003-0.0024	0.0036-0.0106
2006	2.3	D	2.0465-2.2059	0.0007-0.0013	0.0080-0.0160	3	1.9606-1.9685	0.0010-0.0020	0.0767-0.1200
	3.0	U	2.5190-2.2059	0.0010-0.0015	0.0040-0.0080	3	2.1253-2.0472	0.0010-0.0015	0.0060-0.0115
	4.0	E	2.2430-2.2440	0.0008-0.0015	0.0020-0.0125	3	2.7252-2.7260	0.0003-0.0024	0.0036-0.0106
2007	2.3	D	2.0465-2.2059	0.0007-0.0013	0.0080-0.0160	3	1.9606-1.9685	0.0010-0.0020	0.0767-0.1200
	3.0	U	2.5190-2.2059	0.0010-0.0015	0.0040-0.0080	3	2.1253-2.0472	0.0010-0.0015	0.0060-0.0115
	4.0	E	2.2430-2.2440	0.0008-0.0015	0.0020-0.0125	3	2.7252-2.7260	0.0003-0.0024	0.0036-0.0106

22086_RANG_C0007

PISTON AND RING SPECIFICATIONS

All measurements are given in inches.

Year	Engine Displacement Liters	Engine ID/VIN	Piston Clearance	Ring Gap			Ring Side Clearance		
				Top Compression	Bottom Compression	Oil Control	Top Compression	Bottom Compression	Oil Control
2005	2.3	D	0.0009-0.0017	0.006-0.0012	0.012-0.0180	0.007-0.0270	0.0008-0.0013	0.0004-0.0011	0.0025-0.0054
	3.0	U	0.0012-0.0023	0.010-0.020	0.010-0.020	0.010-0.049	0.0602-0.0612	0.0602-0.0612	SNUG
	4.0	E	0.0008-0.0019	0.015-0.023	0.015-0.023	0.015-0.055	0.0010-0.0030	0.0010-0.0030	SNUG
2006	2.3	D	0.0009-0.0017	0.006-0.0012	0.012-0.0180	0.007-0.0270	0.0008-0.0013	0.0004-0.0011	0.0025-0.0054
	3.0	U	0.0012-0.0023	0.010-0.020	0.010-0.020	0.010-0.049	0.0602-0.0612	0.0602-0.0612	SNUG
	4.0	E	0.0008-0.0019	0.015-0.023	0.015-0.023	0.015-0.055	0.0010-0.0030	0.0010-0.0030	SNUG
2007	2.3	D	0.0009-0.0017	0.006-0.0012	0.012-0.0180	0.007-0.0270	0.0008-0.0013	0.0004-0.0011	0.0025-0.0054
	3.0	U	0.0012-0.0023	0.010-0.020	0.010-0.020	0.010-0.049	0.0602-0.0612	0.0602-0.0612	SNUG
	4.0	E	0.0008-0.0019	0.015-0.023	0.015-0.023	0.015-0.055	0.0010-0.0030	0.0010-0.0030	SNUG

22086_RANG_C0006

TORQUE SPECIFICATIONS
All readings in ft. lbs.

	Engine Displacement Liters	Engine ID/VIN	Cylinder Head Bolts	Main Bearing Bolts	Rod Bearing Bolts	Crankshaft Damper Bolts	Flywheel Bolts	Manifold Intake *	Manifold Exhaust	Spark Plugs	Oil Drain Plug
2005	2.3	D	①	NA	NA	②	③	13	40	9	21
	3.0	U	④	59	26	107	59	21	⑤	11	NA
	4.0	E	⑥	72	⑦	⑧	⑨	7	16	13	18
2006	2.3	D	①	NA	NA	②	③	13	40	9	21
	3.0	U	④	59	26	107	59	21	⑤	11	NA
	4.0	E	⑥	72	⑦	⑧	⑨	7	16	13	18
2007	2.3	D	①	NA	NA	②	③	13	40	9	21
	3.0	U	④	59	26	107	59	21	⑤	11	NA
	4.0	E	⑥	72	⑦	⑧	⑨	7	16	13	18

NA: Information not available

* NOTE: Applies to Lower Manifold only.

① Step 1: 44 inch. lbs.
Step 2: 11 ft. lbs.
Step 3: 33 ft. lbs.
Step 4: +90 degrees
Step 5: +90 degrees

② Step 1: 51-59 ft. lbs.
Step 2: 76-84 ft. lbs.
Step 3: +90 degrees

③ Step 1: 26-30 ft. lbs.
Step 2: 31-36 ft. lbs.

④ Step 1: 37 ft. lbs.
Step 2: back off 1 full turn
Step 3: 22 ft. lbs.
Step 4: plus 90 degrees
Step 5: plus 90 degrees more

⑤ Step 1: 89 inch. lbs.
Step 2: 17 ft. lbs.

⑥ 8mm bolts: 24 ft. lbs.
12mm bolts: 24 ft. lbs. +160 degrees

⑦ Step 1: 15 ft. lbs.
Step 2: +90 degrees

⑧ Step 1: 37 ft. lbs.
Step 2: plus 90 degrees

⑨ Step 1: 10 ft.lbs.
Step 2: 52 ft. lbs.

22086_RANG_C0008

WHEEL ALIGNMENT

Year	Model		Caster Range (+/-Deg.)	Caster Preferred Setting (Deg.)	Camber Range (+/-Deg.)	Camber Preferred Setting (Deg.)	Toe-in (in.)
2005	Ranger	2WD	1.0	①	0.70	-0.50	0.06+/-0.25
		4WD	1.0	②	0.70	-0.50	0.12+/-0.25
		Rear	—	—	0.75	0	0+/-0.30
2006	Ranger	2WD	1.0	①	0.70	-0.50	0.06+/-0.25
		4WD	1.0	②	0.70	-0.50	0.12+/-0.25
		Rear	—	—	0.75	0	0+/-0.30
2007	Ranger	2WD	1.0	①	0.70	-0.50	0.06+/-0.25
		4WD	1.0	②	0.70	-0.50	0.12+/-0.25
		Rear	—	—	0.75	0	0+/-0.30

① Left: +3.5
Right: +3.9

② Left: +2.8
Right: +3.5

22086_RANG_C0011

TIRE, WHEEL AND BALL JOINT SPECIFICATIONS

Year	Model	OEM Tires Standard	OEM Tires Optional	Tire Pressures (psi) Front	Tire Pressures (psi) Rear	Wheel Size	Ball Joint Inspection	Lug Nut Torque (ft. lbs.)
2005	Edge Reg. Cab	P235/75R15	P235/70R16	①	①	7-JJ	0.030 in. ②	100
	Edge SuperCab 2wd	P235/75R15	P235/70R16	①	①	7-JJ	0.030 in. ②	100
	FX4 Level II	31x10.50R15LT	none	①	①	NA	0.030 in. ②	100
	FX4 Off Road	P255/70R16	none	①	①	7-JJ	0.030 in. ②	100
	STX Reg. Cab	P225/70R15	none	①	①	6-JJ	0.030 in. ②	100
	STX SuperCab	P225/70R15	none	①	①	6-JJ	0.030 in. ②	100
	XL Reg. Cab	P235/75R15	none	①	①	6-JJ	0.030 in. ②	100
	XL SuperCab	P235/75R15	none	①	①	7-JJ	0.030 in. ②	100
	XLT Reg. Cab 2wd	P225/70R15	none	①	①	7-JJ	0.030 in. ②	100
	XLT SuperCab 2wd	P225/70R15	none	①	①	7-JJ	0.030 in. ②	100
	XLT Reg. Cab 4wd	P235/75R15	none	①	①	6-JJ	0.030 in. ②	100
	XLT SuperCab 4wd	P255/70R16	none	①	①	7-JJ	0.030 in. ②	100
	Tremor 2wd	P235/75R16	none	①	①	7-JJ	0.030 in. ②	100
	Tremor 4wd	P245/75R16	none	①	①	7-JJ	0.030 in. ②	100
2006	FX4 4X4 Super Cab	P255/70R16	31x10.50R15LT	①	①	7-J	0.030 in. ②	100
	FX4 Level II	P255/70R16	31x10.50R15LT	①	①	7-J	0.030 in. ②	100
	STX 4X2 Reg. Cab	P225/70R15	none	①	①	7-J	0.030 in. ②	100
	STX 4X2 Super Cab	P225/70R15	none	①	①	7-J	0.030 in. ②	100
	Sport 4X2 Reg. Cab	P235/75R15	none	①	①	7-J	0.030 in. ②	100
	Sport 4X2 Super Cab	P235/75R15	P235/70R16	①	①	7-J	0.030 in. ②	100
	Sport 4X4 Reg. Cab	P235/75R15	none	①	①	7-J	0.030 in. ②	100
	Sport 4X4 SuperCab	P255/70R16	none	①	①	7-J	0.030 in. ②	100
	XL 4X2 Reg. Cab	P225/70R15	none	①	①	6J/7J	0.030 in. ②	100
	XL 4X2 Super Cab	P225/70R15	none	①	①	6J/7J	0.030 in. ②	100
	XL 4X4 Reg. Cab	P235/75R15	none	①	①	7-J	0.030 in. ②	100
	XL 4X4 Super Cab	P235/75R15	none	①	①	7-J	0.030 in. ②	100
	XLT 4X2 Reg. Cab	P225/70R15	none	①	①	7-J	0.030 in. ②	100
	XLT 4X2 Super Cab	P225/70R15	none	①	①	7-J	0.030 in. ②	100
	XLT 4X4 Reg. Cab	P235/75R15	none	①	①	7-J	0.030 in. ②	100
	XLT 4X4 Super Cab	P255/70R16	none	①	①	7-J	0.030 in. ②	100
2007	FX4 4X4 Super Cab	P255/70R16	31x10.50R15LT	①	①	7-J	0.030 in. ②	100
	FX4 Level II	P255/70R16	31x10.50R15LT	①	①	7-J	0.030 in. ②	100
	STX 4X2 Reg. Cab	P225/70R15	none	①	①	7-J	0.030 in. ②	100
	STX 4X2 Super Cab	P225/70R15	none	①	①	7-J	0.030 in. ②	100
	Sport 4X2 Reg. Cab	P235/75R15	none	①	①	7-J	0.030 in. ②	100
	Sport 4X2 Super Cab	P235/75R15	P235/70R16	①	①	7-J	0.030 in. ②	100
	Sport 4X4 Reg. Cab	P235/75R15	none	①	①	7-J	0.030 in. ②	100
	Sport 4X4 SuperCab	P255/70R16	none	①	①	7-J	0.030 in. ②	100
	XL 4X2 Reg. Cab	P225/70R15	none	①	①	6J/7J	0.030 in. ②	100
	XL 4X2 Super Cab	P225/70R15	none	①	①	6J/7J	0.030 in. ②	100
	XL 4X4 Reg. Cab	P235/75R15	none	①	①	7-J	0.030 in. ②	100
	XL 4X4 Super Cab	P235/75R15	none	①	①	7-J	0.030 in. ②	100
	XLT 4X2 Reg. Cab	P225/70R15	none	①	①	7-J	0.030 in. ②	100
	XLT 4X2 Super Cab	P225/70R15	none	①	①	7-J	0.030 in. ②	100
	XLT 4X4 Reg. Cab	P235/75R15	none	①	①	7-J	0.030 in. ②	100
	XLT 4X4 Super Cab	P255/70R16	none	①	①	7-J	0.030 in. ②	100

OEM: Original Equipment Manufacturer

PSI: Pounds Per Square Inch

STD: Standard

OPT: Optional

① See placard on door post

② Both upper and lower

BRAKE SPECIFICATIONS

All measurements in inches unless noted

| Year | Model | Brake Disc | | | Brake Drum Diameter | | | Minimum Lining Thickness | Brake Caliper | |
		Original Thickness	Minimum Thickness	Maximum Runout	Original Inside Diameter	Max. Wear Limit	Maximum Machine Diameter		Bracket Bolts (ft. lbs.)	Mounting Bolts (ft. lbs.)
2005	Ranger	NA	0.965	NA	NA	NA	①	②	85	24
2006	Ranger	NA	0.965	NA	NA	NA	①	②	85	27
2007	Ranger	NA	0.965	NA	NA	NA	①	②	85	27

NOTE: Due to changes made during production, refer to manufacturer's specifications if they differ from those in this chart

NA: Not Available

F: Front

R: Rear

① Molded into the drum

② Front: 0.118 in.

　Rear: 0.03 in.

22086_RANG_C0009

SCHEDULED MAINTENANCE INTERVALS
2005-07 FORD RANGER

TO BE SERVICED	TYPE OF SERVICE	VEHICLE MILEAGE INTERVAL (x1000)												
		5	10	15	20	25	30	35	40	45	50	55	60	65
Engine oil & filter	R	✓	✓	✓	✓	✓	✓	✓	✓	✓	✓	✓	✓	✓
Tires	Rotate	✓	✓	✓	✓	✓	✓	✓	✓	✓	✓	✓	✓	✓
Auto trans. fluid	I									✓				
Brake pads/shoes	I			✓			✓			✓			✓	
Wheel ends ①	I			✓			✓			✓			✓	
Coolant hoses	S/I			✓			✓			✓			✓	
Steering linkage	I/L			✓			✓			✓			✓	
Suspension and driveshaft	I			✓			✓			✓			✓	
Cabin air filter	R			✓			✓			✓			✓	
Ball joints (2wd)	I/L			✓			✓			✓			✓	
Exhaust system	I						✓						✓	
Engine air filter	R						✓						✓	
Fuel filter	R						✓						✓	
Manual trans fluid	R												✓	
Wheel bearings (2wd)	R	at 150,000 miles, if not previously replaced, including seals												
Premium Gold coolant ②	R	at 5 years or 100,000 miles												
Spark plugs	R	every 100,000 miles												
PCV valve	R	every 100,000 miles												
Auto trans fluid	R	every 150,000 miles, if not previously replaced												
Rear axle fluid	R	every 150,000 miles												
Accessory drive belts	I	every 100,000 miles												
Accessory drive belts	R	every 150,000 miles, if not previously replaced												

R: Replace   S: Service   I: Inspect   L: Lubricate

① Check for play and noise

② After the initial change, every 3 years or 50,000 miles

Special Operating Condition Requirements

When towing a trailer or using a camper or car-top carrier:

Change engine oil and install a new oil filter every 4,800 km (3,000 miles), 3 months or 200 hours of engine operation (whichever occurs first).

Change transfer case fluid every 96,000 km (60,000 miles).

Change manual transmission fluid as required.

Inspect and lubricate U-joints as required.

During extensive idling and/or low speed driving for long distances, as in heavy commercial use such as delivery, taxi, patrol car or livery:

Change engine oil and install a new oil filter every 4,800 km (3,000 miles), 3 months or 200 hours of engine operation (whichever occurs first).

Lube front lower control arm and steering linkage ball joints with zerk fittings (if equipped) every 4,800 km (3,000 miles) or 3 months.

Inspect brake system and check battery electrolyte level (Patrol cars) every 8,000 km (5,000 miles).

Install a new fuel filter every 24,000 km (15,000 miles).

Change automatic transmission fluid, lubricate 4x2 wheel bearings, install new grease seals and adjust bearings every 48,000 km (30,000 miles). If equipped, change the in-line service installed transmission fluid filter.

Install new spark plugs and change transfer case fluid every 96,000 km (60,000 miles).

Install a new cabin air filter as required.

When operating in dusty conditions such as unpaved or dusty roads:

Change engine oil and install a new oil filter every 4,800 km (3,000 miles) or 3 months.

Install a new fuel filter every 24,000 km (15,000 miles).

Change automatic transmission fluid every 48,000 km (30,000 miles). If equipped, change the in-line service installed transmission fluid filter.

Change transfer case fluid every 96,000 km (60,000 miles).

Install a new engine air filter as required.

Install a new cabin air filter as required.

When operating in off-road conditions:

Change automatic transmission fluid every 48,000 km (30,000 miles). If equipped, change the in-line service installed transmission fluid filter.

Change transfer case fluid every 96,000 km (60,000 miles).

Install a new cabin air filter as required.

Inspect and lubricate U-joints.

Inspect and lubricate steering linkage ball joints with zerk fittings.

PRECAUTIONS

Before servicing any vehicle, please be sure to read all of the following precautions, which deal with personal safety, prevention of component damage, and important points to take into consideration when servicing a motor vehicle:

• Never open, service or drain the radiator or cooling system when the engine is hot; serious burns can occur from the steam and hot coolant.

• Observe all applicable safety precautions when working around fuel. Whenever servicing the fuel system, always work in a well-ventilated area. Do not allow fuel spray or vapors to come in contact with a spark, open flame, or excessive heat (a hot drop light, for example). Keep a dry chemical fire extinguisher near the work area. Always keep fuel in a container specifically designed for fuel storage; also, always properly seal fuel containers to avoid the possibility of fire or explosion. Refer to the additional fuel system precautions later in this section.

• Fuel injection systems often remain pressurized, even after the engine has been turned **OFF**. The fuel system pressure must be relieved before disconnecting any fuel lines. Failure to do so may result in fire and/or personal injury.

• Brake fluid often contains polyglycol ethers and polyglycols. Avoid contact with the eyes and wash your hands thoroughly after handling brake fluid. If you do get brake fluid in your eyes, flush your eyes with clean, running water for 15 minutes. If eye irritation persists, or if you have taken brake fluid internally, IMMEDIATELY seek medical assistance.

• The EPA warns that prolonged contact with used engine oil may cause a number of skin disorders, including cancer. You should make every effort to minimize your exposure to used engine oil. Protective gloves should be worn when changing oil. Wash your hands and any other exposed skin areas as soon as possible after exposure to used engine oil. Soap and water, or waterless hand cleaner should be used.

• All new vehicles are now equipped with an air bag system, often referred to as a Supplemental Restraint System (SRS) or Supplemental Inflatable Restraint (SIR) system. The system must be disabled before performing service on or around system components, steering column, instrument panel components, wiring and sensors. Failure to follow safety and disabling procedures could result in accidental air bag deployment, possible personal injury and unnecessary system repairs.

• Always wear safety goggles when working with, or around, the air bag system. When carrying a non-deployed air bag, be sure the bag and trim cover are pointed away from your body. When placing a non-deployed air bag on a work surface, always face the bag and trim cover upward, away from the surface. This will reduce the motion of the module if it is accidentally deployed. Refer to the additional air bag system precautions later in this section.

• Clean, high quality brake fluid from a sealed container is essential to the safe and proper operation of the brake system. You should always buy the correct type of brake fluid for your vehicle. If the brake fluid becomes contaminated, completely flush the system with new fluid. Never reuse any brake fluid. Any brake fluid that is removed from the system should be discarded. Also, do not allow any brake fluid to come in contact with a painted surface; it will damage the paint.

• Never operate the engine without the proper amount and type of engine oil; doing so WILL result in severe engine damage.

• Timing belt maintenance is extremely important. Many models utilize an interference-type, non-freewheeling engine. If the timing belt breaks, the valves in the cylinder head may strike the pistons, causing potentially serious (also time-consuming and expensive) engine damage. Refer to the maintenance interval charts for the recommended replacement interval for the timing belt, and to the timing belt section for belt replacement and inspection.

• Disconnecting the negative battery cable on some vehicles may interfere with the functions of the on-board computer system(s) and may require the computer to undergo a relearning process once the negative battery cable is reconnected.

• When servicing drum brakes, only disassemble and assemble one side at a time, leaving the remaining side intact for reference.

• Only an MVAC-trained, EPA-certified automotive technician should service the air conditioning system or its components.

BRAKES

GENERAL INFORMATION

PRECAUTIONS

• Certain components within the ABS system are not intended to be serviced or repaired individually.

• Do not use rubber hoses or other parts not specifically specified for and ABS system. When using repair kits, replace all parts included in the kit. Partial or incorrect repair may lead to functional problems and require the replacement of components.

• Lubricate rubber parts with clean, fresh brake fluid to ease assembly. Do not use shop air to clean parts; damage to rubber components may result.

• Use only DOT 3 brake fluid from an unopened container.

• If any hydraulic component or line is removed or replaced, it may be necessary to bleed the entire system.

• A clean repair area is essential. Always clean the reservoir and cap thoroughly before removing the cap. The slightest amount of dirt in the fluid may plug an orifice and impair the system function. Perform repairs after components have been thoroughly cleaned; use only denatured alcohol to clean components. Do not allow ABS components to come into contact with any substance containing mineral oil; this includes used shop rags.

• The Anti-Lock control unit is a microprocessor similar to other computer units in the vehicle. Ensure that the ignition switch is **OFF** before removing or installing controller harnesses. Avoid static electricity discharge at or near the controller.

ANTI-LOCK BRAKE SYSTEM (ABS)

• If any arc welding is to be done on the vehicle, the control unit should be unplugged before welding operations begin.

SPEED SENSORS

REMOVAL & INSTALLATION

Front

2-Wheel Drive Models

See Figure 1.

1. Before servicing the vehicle, refer to the Precautions Section.
2. Disconnect the negative battery cable.
3. Raise and support the vehicle.
4. Disconnect the wheel speed sensor electrical connector.

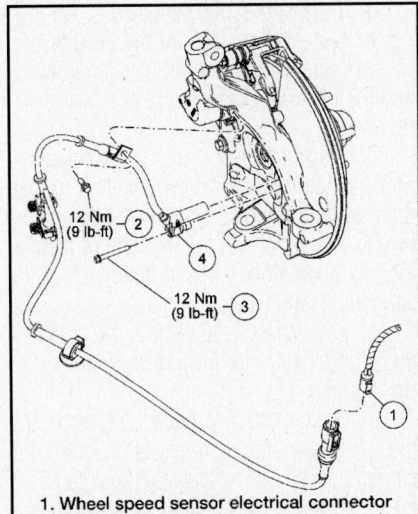

1. Wheel speed sensor electrical connector
2. Wheel speed sensor harness bolt
3. Wheel speed sensor bolt
4. Wheel speed sensor

22086_RANG_G0032

Fig. 1 Front speed sensor view—2-wheel drive model

5. Remove the wheel speed sensor harness bolt and unclip the retainers.

6. Remove the wheel speed sensor bolt and the wheel speed sensor.

➡**Plug the sensor cavity and thoroughly clean the sensor mounting surface. Apply wheel bearing grease to the mounting surface.**

7. To install, reverse the removal procedure and note the following:
- Tighten the wheel speed sensor bolt to 9 ft. lbs. (12 Nm).
- Tighten speed sensor harness bolt to 9 ft. lbs. (12 Nm).

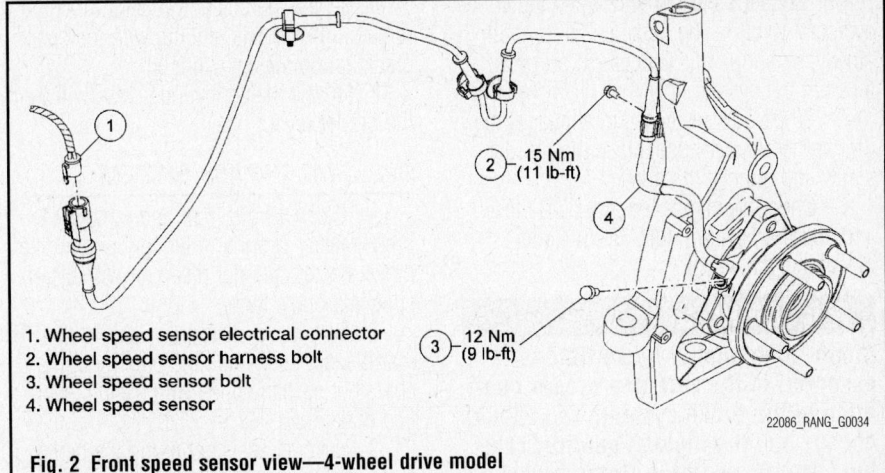

1. Wheel speed sensor electrical connector
2. Wheel speed sensor harness bolt
3. Wheel speed sensor bolt
4. Wheel speed sensor

22086_RANG_G0034

Fig. 2 Front speed sensor view—4-wheel drive model

4-Wheel Drive Models

See Figure 2.

1. Remove the brake disc shield.
2. Disconnect the battery ground cable.
3. Disconnect the wheel speed sensor electrical connector.
4. Remove the wheel speed sensor harness bolt and unclip the retainers.
5. Remove the wheel speed sensor bolt and the wheel speed sensor.
6. To install, reverse the removal procedure and note the following:
- Tighten wheel speed sensor bolt to 9 ft. lbs. (12 Nm).
- Tighten wheel speed sensor harness bolt to 11 ft. lbs. (15 Nm).

Rear

See Figure 3.

1. Before servicing the vehicle, refer to the Precautions Section.

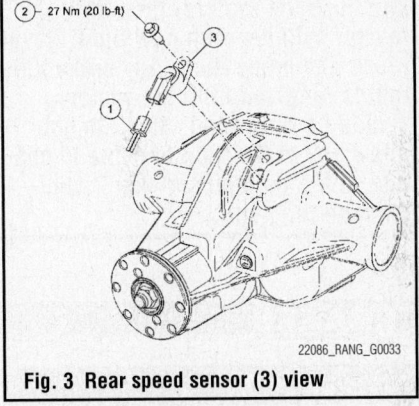

22086_RANG_G0033

Fig. 3 Rear speed sensor (3) view

2. Disconnect the negative battery cable
3. Raise and support vehicle.
4. Disconnect the electrical connector, remove the bolt and remove the sensor.
5. To install, reverse the removal procedure and tighten speed sensor mounting bolt to 20 ft. lbs. (27 Nm).

BRAKES   BLEEDING THE BRAKE SYSTEM

BLEEDING PROCEDURE

BRAKE LINE BLEEDING

❋❋ CAUTION

Brake fluid contains polyglycol ethers and polyglycols. Avoid contact with the eyes and wash your hands thoroughly after handling brake fluid. If you do get brake fluid in your eyes, flush your eyes with clean, running water for 15 minutes. If eye irritation persists, or if you have taken brake fluid internally, IMMEDIATELY seek medical assistance.

When any part of the hydraulic system has been disconnected for repair or replacement, air may get into the lines and cause spongy pedal action (because air can be compressed and brake fluid cannot). To correct this condition, it is necessary to bleed the hydraulic system so to be sure all air is purged.

When bleeding the brake system, bleed one brake cylinder at a time, beginning at the cylinder with the longest hydraulic line (farthest from the master cylinder) first. ALWAYS Keep the master cylinder reservoir filled with brake fluid during the bleeding operation. Never use brake fluid that has been drained from the hydraulic system, no matter how clean it is.

The primary and secondary hydraulic brake systems are separate and are bled independently. During the bleeding operation, do not allow the reservoir to run dry.

Keep the master cylinder reservoir filled with brake fluid.

1. Clean all dirt from around the master cylinder fill cap, remove the cap and fill the master cylinder with brake fluid until the level is within ¼ in. (6mm) of the top edge of the reservoir.

2. Clean the bleeder screws at all 4 wheels. The bleeder screws are located on the back of the brake backing plate (drum brakes) and on the top of the brake calipers (disc brakes).

3. Attach a length of rubber hose over the bleeder screw and place the other end of the hose in a glass jar, submerged in brake fluid.

4. Open the bleeder screw ½–¾ turn. Have an assistant slowly depress the brake pedal.

5. Close the bleeder screw and tell your assistant to allow the brake pedal to return slowly. Continue this process to purge all air from the system.

6. When bubbles cease to appear at the end of the bleeder hose, close the bleeder screw and remove the hose.

7. Check the master cylinder fluid level and add fluid accordingly. Do this after bleeding each wheel.

❋ WARNING

Clean, high quality brake fluid is essential to the safe and proper operation of the brake system. You should always buy the highest quality brake fluid that is available. If the brake fluid becomes contaminated, drain and flush the system, then refill the master cylinder with new fluid. Never reuse any brake fluid. Any brake fluid that is removed from the system should be discarded. Also, do not allow any brake fluid to come in contact with a painted surface; it will damage the paint.

8. Repeat the bleeding operation at the remaining 3 wheels, ending with the one closet to the master cylinder.

9. Fill the master cylinder reservoir to the proper level.

BLEEDING THE ABS SYSTEM

1. Clean all dirt from and remove the brake master cylinder filler cap, and fill the brake master cylinder reservoir with clean, specified brake fluid.

2. Connect a clear drain tube to the RH rear bleeder screw and the other end in a container partially filled with clean, specified brake fluid.

3. Have an assistant pump the brake pedal and then hold firm pressure on the brake pedal.

4. Loosen the RH rear bleeder screw until a stream of brake fluid comes out. While the assistant maintains pressure on the brake pedal, tighten the bleeder screw.

5. Repeat until clear, bubble-free fluid comes out.

➡️**Refill the brake master cylinder reservoir as necessary.**

6. Tighten the bleeder screw.

7. Repeat Steps 3-5 for the LH rear bleeder screw, the RH front bleeder screw and the LH front bleeder screw, in that order.

8. Place a box-end wrench on the disc brake caliper bleeder screw. Attach a rubber drain tube to the disc brake caliper bleeder screw, and submerge the free end of the tube in a container partially filled with clean, specified brake fluid.

9. Have an assistant pump the brake pedal and then hold firm pressure on the brake pedal.

10. Loosen the disc brake caliper bleeder screw until a stream of brake fluid comes out. While the assistant maintains pressure on the brake pedal, tighten the disc brake caliper bleeder screw.

11. Repeat until clear, bubble-free fluid comes out.

➡️**Refill the brake master cylinder reservoir as necessary.**

12. Tighten the disc brake caliper bleeder screw.

BRAKES

FRONT DISC BRAKES

❋❋ CAUTION

Dust and dirt accumulating on brake parts during normal use may contain asbestos fibers from production or aftermarket brake linings. Breathing excessive concentrations of asbestos fibers can cause serious bodily harm. Exercise care when servicing brake parts. Do not sand or grind brake lining unless equipment used is designed to contain the dust residue. Do not clean brake parts with compressed air or by dry brushing. Cleaning should be done by dampening the brake components with a fine mist of water, then wiping the brake components clean with a dampened cloth. Dispose of cloth and all residue containing asbestos fibers in an impermeable container with the appropriate label. Follow practices prescribed by the Occupational Safety and Health Administration (OSHA) and the Environmental Protection Agency (EPA) for the handling, processing, and disposing of dust or debris that may contain asbestos fibers.

BRAKE CALIPER

REMOVAL & INSTALLATION

See Figures 4 through 7.

1. Before servicing the vehicle, refer to the Precautions Section.

2. Loosen the wheel lug nuts.

3. Raise and safely support the front of the vehicle. Remove the wheel.

4. Place an 8 in. (203mm) C-clamp on the caliper and tighten the clamp to bottom the caliper pistons in their bores. Remove the clamp.

5. Remove the two caliper slide pin bolts and lift the caliper from the anchor plate.

➡️**Use care to retain as much of the original caliper slide pin grease as possible.**

6. Position the caliper on a frame member or suspend it with some wire. Do not allow the caliper to hang by the brake hose.

7. Disconnect and plug the brake hose at the caliper. Remove the caliper from the rotor.

To install:

8. Position the caliper over the brake pads and align the slide pin mounting holes.

9. Install the slide pin bolts and tighten them to 27 ft. lbs. (36 Nm).

10. Install the caliper brake hose using new washers. Tighten the bolt to 25 ft. lbs. (34 Nm)

11. Install the wheel and snug the lug nuts.

12. Lower the vehicle and tighten the lug nuts to 100 ft. lbs. (135 Nm).

➡️**The first couple of times you apply the brakes, the pedal may go to the floor. Continue to pump the brake pedal until it feels firm.**

13. Start the engine and apply the brakes several times to readjust the caliper pistons. Ensure that the pedal feels firm before operating the vehicle.

DISC BRAKE PADS

REMOVAL AND INSTALLATION

See Figures 4 through 7.

1. Before servicing the vehicle, refer to the Precautions Section.

2. Raise and safely support the front of the vehicle. Remove the wheel.

3. Place an 8 in. (203mm) C-clamp on the caliper and tighten the clamp to bottom the caliper pistons in their bores. Remove the clamp.

4. Remove the two caliper slide pin

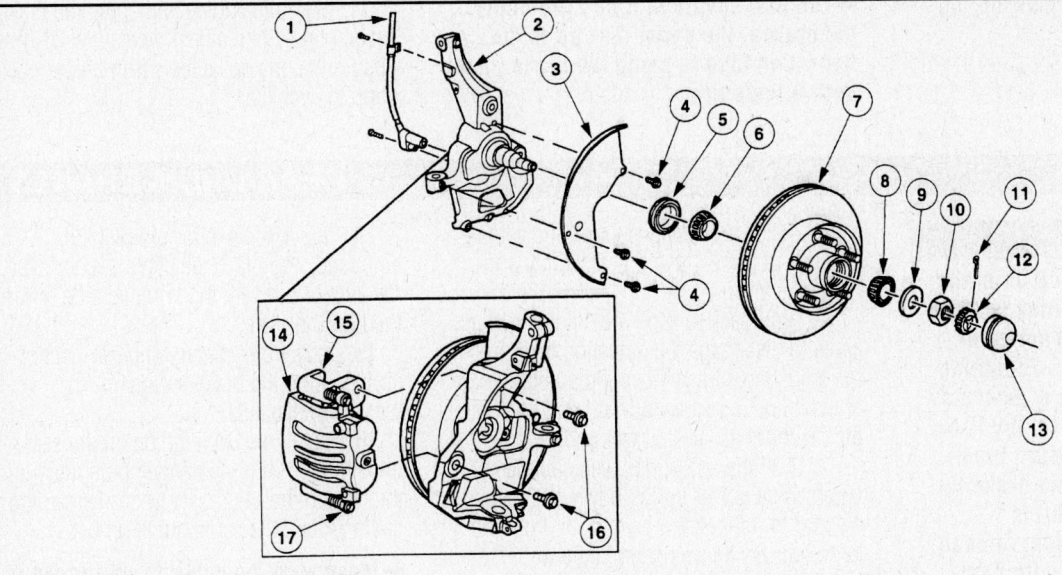

1 Front Brake Anti-Lock Sensor
2 Front Wheel Spindle
3 Front Disc Brake Rotor Shield
4 Rotor Shield Bolt
5 Grease Seal
6 Front Wheel Bearing

7 Front Disc Brake Hub and Rotor
8 Front Wheel Bearing
9 Front Wheel Outer Bearing Retainer Washer
10 Hub Spindle Nut
11 Cotter Pin

12 Nut Retainer
13 Hub Grease Cap
14 Disc Brake Caliper
15 Front Disc Brake Caliper Anchor Plate
16 Caliper Anchor Plate Bolts
17 Disc Brake Caliper Bolt

93026G22

Fig. 4 Exploded view of the 2WD front disc brake assembly

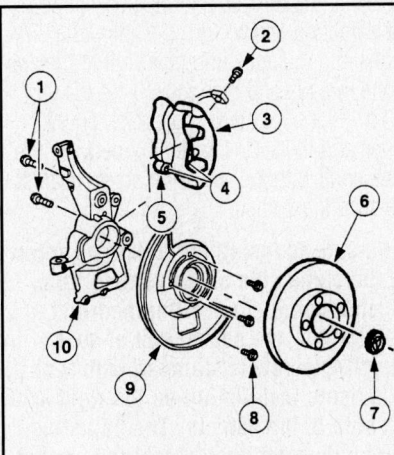

1 Front Disc Brake Caliper Anchor Plate Bolt (2 Req'd)
2 Front Brake Hose Bolt
3 Disc Brake Caliper
4 Pads
5 Front Disc Brake Caliper Anchor Plate
6 Front Disc Brake Rotor
7 Front Axle Wheel Hub Retainer
8 Front Disc Brake Rotor Shield Bolt (3 Req'd)
9 Front Disc Brake Rotor Shield
10 Front Wheel Knuckle

93026G23

Fig. 5 Exploded view of the 4WD front disc brake assembly

bolts and lift the caliper from the anchor plate.

➡**Use care to retain as much of the original caliper slide pin grease as possible.**

5. Position the caliper on a frame member or suspend it with some wire. Do not allow the caliper to hang by the brake hose.

6. Remove the brake pads and, if necessary, the anti-rattle clips from the anchor plate.

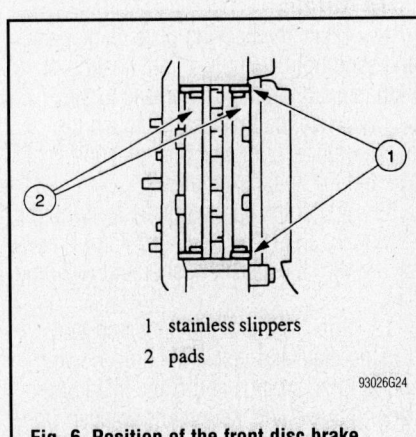

1 stainless slippers
2 pads

93026G24

Fig. 6 Position of the front disc brake components

7. Remove the shims, if any, from the brake pads for re-use.

To install:

8. If removed, install the anti-rattle clips.

9. Install the brake pads to the anchor plate.

10. Position the caliper over the brake pads and align the slide pin mounting holes.

11. Install the slide pin bolts and tighten them to 24 ft. lbs. (32 Nm).

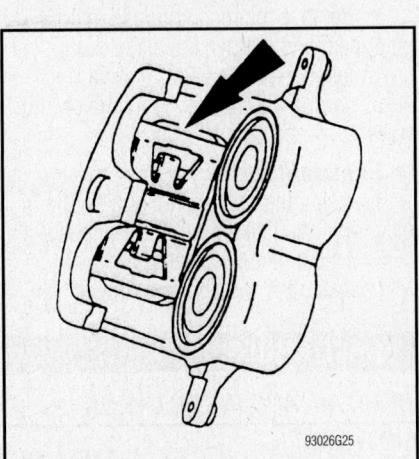

93026G25

Fig. 7 View of the front disc brake anti-rattle spring

12. Install the wheel and snug the lug nuts.

13. Lower the vehicle and tighten the lug nuts to 100 ft. lbs. (135 Nm).

➡The first couple of times you apply the brakes, the pedal may go to the floor. Continue to pump the brake pedal until it feels firm.

14. Start the engine and apply the brakes several times to readjust the caliper pistons. Ensure that the pedal feels firm before operating the vehicle.

BRAKES

REAR DRUM BRAKES

❋❋ CAUTION

Dust and dirt accumulating on brake parts during normal use may contain asbestos fibers from production or aftermarket brake linings. Breathing excessive concentrations of asbestos fibers can cause serious bodily harm. Exercise care when servicing brake parts. Do not sand or grind brake lining unless equipment used is designed to contain the dust residue. Do not clean brake parts with compressed air or by dry brushing. Cleaning should be done by dampening the brake components with a fine mist of water, then wiping the brake components clean with a dampened cloth. Dispose of cloth and all residue containing asbestos fibers in an impermeable container with the appropriate label. Follow practices prescribed by the Occupational Safety and Health Administration (OSHA) and the Environmental Protection Agency (EPA) for the handling, processing, and disposing of dust or debris that may contain asbestos fibers.

BRAKE DRUM

REMOVAL & INSTALLATION

1. Before servicing the vehicle, refer to the Precautions Section.

2. Raise and safely support the vehicle. Remove the wheel and tire assembly.

3. Remove the retaining nuts, if equipped, and remove the brake drum.

4. Inspect the brake drum surface for wear, scoring and runout. Machine or replace, as necessary.

To install:

5. Install the brake drum and secure in place with the retainer nuts, if equipped.

6. Adjust the rear brakes.

7. Install the wheel. Lower the vehicle.

BRAKE SHOES

REMOVAL AND INSTALLATION

See Figure 8.

1. Before servicing the vehicle, refer to the Precautions Section.

2. Raise and safely support the vehicle. Remove the wheel and tire assembly and the brake drum.

3. Pull backward on the adjusting lever cable to disengage the adjusting lever from the adjusting screw. Move the outboard side of the adjusting screw upward and back off the pivot nut as far as it will go.

4. Pull the adjusting lever, cable and automatic adjuster spring down and toward the rear to unhook the pivot hook from the large hole in the secondary shoe web. Do not pry the pivot hook from the hole.

5. Remove the automatic adjuster spring and adjusting lever.

6. Remove the secondary shoe-to-anchor spring using a suitable brake spring removal/installation tool. Using the tool, remove the primary shoe-to-anchor spring and unhook the cable anchor. Remove the anchor pin plate, if equipped.

7. Remove the cable guide from the secondary shoe.

8. Remove the shoe hold-down springs, shoes, adjusting screw, pivot nut and socket. Note the color and position of each hold-down spring so they can be reassembled in the same position.

9. Remove the parking brake link and spring. Disconnect the parking brake cable from the parking brake lever.

10. Remove the secondary brake shoe. On 9 in. (22.8cm) rear brakes, remove the parking brake lever from the shoe. On 10 in. (25.4cm) rear brakes, remove the retainer clip and spring washer and remove the parking brake lever.

To install:

11. Clean the backing plate ledge pads and sand lightly. Apply a light coating of high temperature lithium grease to the points where the brake shoes touch the backing plate. Lubricate the adjusting cable eye and the anchor pin area.

12. Install the parking brake lever on the secondary shoe. On 10 in. (25.4cm) brakes, secure with the spring washer and retaining clip.

13. Position the brake shoes on the backing plate and install the hold-down spring pins, springs and cups. Install the parking brake link, spring and washer. Connect the parking brake cable to the parking brake lever.

14. Install the anchor pin plate, if equipped, and place the cable anchor over the anchor pin with the crimped side toward the backing plate.

15. Install the primary shoe-to-anchor spring using the brake spring removal/installation tool.

16. Install the cable guide on the secondary shoe with the flanged hole fitted into the hole in the secondary shoe. Thread the cable around the cable guide groove.

➡Make sure the cable is positioned in the groove and not between the guide and shoe web.

17. Install the secondary shoe-to-anchor (long) spring.

➡Make sure the cable end is not cocked or binding on the anchor pin when installed. All parts should be flat on the anchor pin.

18. Apply high temperature lithium grease to the threads and the socket end of the adjusting screw. Turn the adjusting screw into the adjusting pivot nut to the end of the threads and then loosen, ½ turn.

19. Place the adjusting socket on the screw and install the assembly between the shoe ends with the adjusting screw nearest the secondary shoe.

➡Be sure to install the adjusting screw on the same side of the vehicle from which it came. To prevent incorrect installation, the socket end of each adjusting screw is stamped with R or L, to indicate installation on the right or left side of the vehicle. The adjusting pivot nuts have lines machined around the body of the nut, 2 lines indicating the right side nut and 1 line indicating the left side nut.

20. Hook the cable hook into the hole in the adjusting lever from the outboard plate side. The adjusting levers are also stamped with an **R** or **L** to indicate right or left side installation.

21. Place the hooked end of the adjuster spring in the large hole in the primary shoe web and connect the loop end of the spring to the adjuster lever hole.

22. Pull the adjuster lever, cable and automatic adjuster spring down toward the

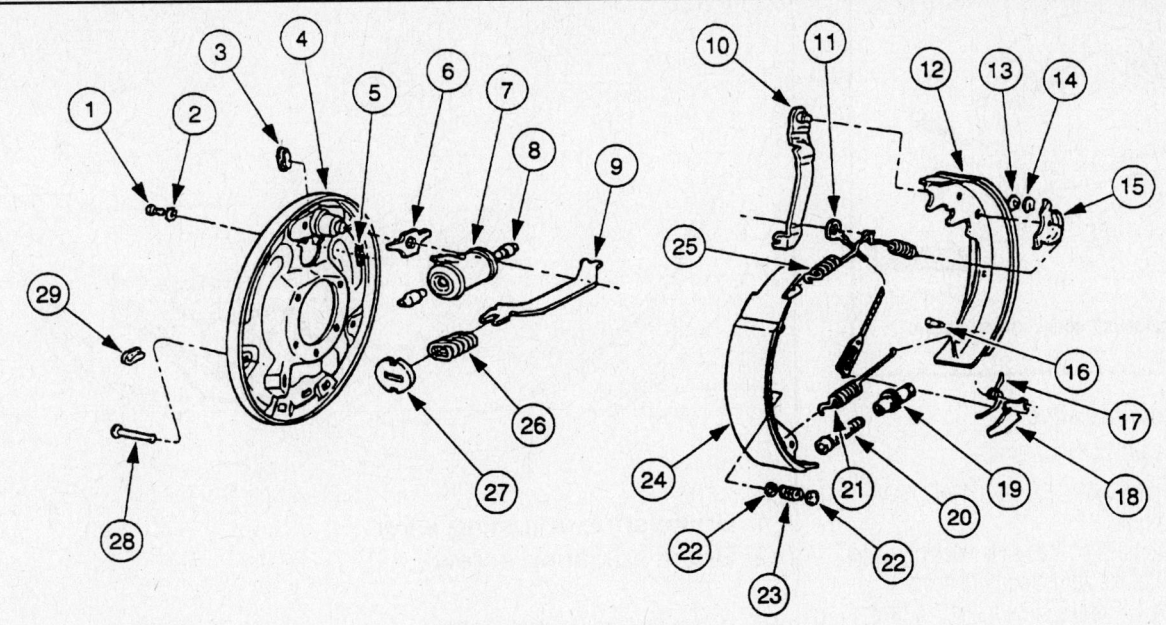

1	Wheel Cylinder-to-Backing Plate Bolt (2 Req'd)	12	Rear Brake Shoe and Lining, Secondary	22	Brake Shoe Hold-Down Spring Cup
2	Washer	13	Washer	23	Brake Shoe Hold-Down Spring
3	Inspection Hole Cover	14	Parking Brake Lever Pin Retainer	24	Rear Brake Shoe and Lining, Primary
4	Brake Backing Plate	15	Cable Guide	25	Brake Shoe Retracting Spring, Short
5	Lining Inspection Hole	16	Adjusting Lever Pin		
6	Anchor Pin Guide Plate	17	Adjusting Lever Return Spring	26	Parking Brake Link Spring
7	Rear Wheel Cylinder	18	Brake Shoe Adjusting Lever	27	Parking Brake Spring Retainer
8	Wheel Cylinder Brake Shoe Link	19	Brake Shoe Adjusting Screw Nut	28	Brake Shoe Hold-Down Spring Pin
9	Parking Brake Strut	20	Brake Adjuster Screw	29	Brake Adjusting Hole Cover
10	Parking Brake Lever	21	Brake Shoe Adjusting Screw Spring		
11	Brake Shoe Adjusting Lever Cable				

93026G21

Fig. 8 Exploded view of the rear brake shoes and components

rear to engage the pivot hook in the large hole in the secondary shoe web.

23. After installation, check the action of the adjuster by pulling the section of the cable between the cable guide and the adjusting lever toward the secondary shoe web far enough to lift the lever past a tooth on the adjusting screw wheel. The lever should snap into position behind the next tooth and releasing the cable should cause the adjuster spring to return the lever to its original position. This return action will turn the adjusting screw 1 tooth.

24. If pulling the cable does not produce the action described previously, or if lever action is sluggish instead of positive and sharp, check the position of the lever on the adjusting screw toothed wheel. With the brake in a vertical position, anchor at the top, the lever should contact the adjusting wheel 1 tooth above the centerline of the adjusting screw. If the contact point is below the centerline, the lever will not lock on the adjusting screw wheel teeth and the screw will not turn, since the lever is actuated by the cable.

25. Adjust the brake shoes using either a brake adjustment gauge or manually with the drums installed.

26. Install the wheels, and lower the vehicle.

ADJUSTMENT

Brake Drum Removed

See Figures 9 and 10.

1. Using the special tool or equivalent, measure the brake drum inside diameter.

2. Rotate the brake adjusting screw until the brake shoes and linings touch the tool.

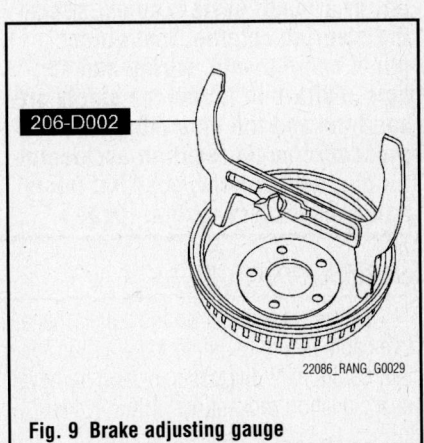

206-D002

22086_RANG_G0029

Fig. 9 Brake adjusting gauge

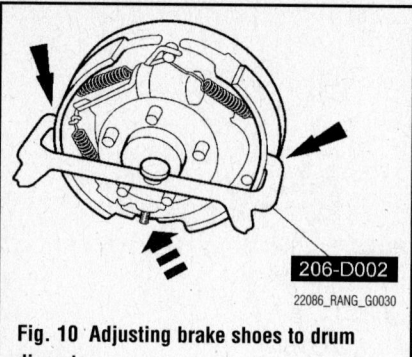

Fig. 10 Adjusting brake shoes to drum diameter

206-D002

22086_RANG_G0030

Brake Drum Installed

See Figure 11.

1. With the vehicle in NEUTRAL, position it on a hoist.
2. At the back of the brake backing plate, remove the brake adjusting hole cover.
3. Move the brake shoe adjusting lever off the brake shoe adjusting screw.
4. Using the special tool or equivalent, turn the adjusting screw until the brake drum

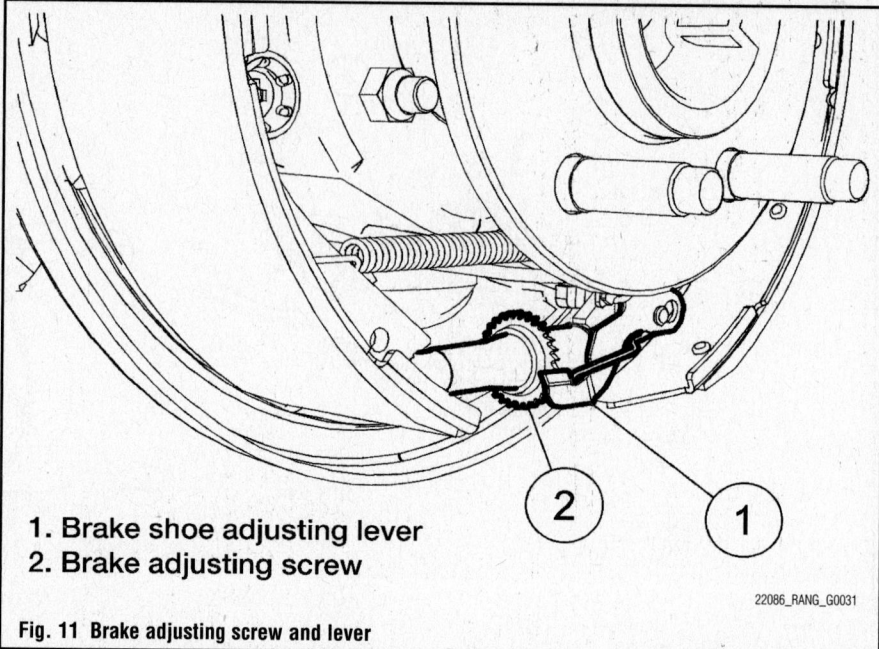

1. Brake shoe adjusting lever
2. Brake adjusting screw

Fig. 11 Brake adjusting screw and lever

22086_RANG_G0031

begins to drag. Then loosen the brake adjusting screw until the brake drum rotates freely.

5. Install the brake backing plate adjusting hole cover.

BRAKES   PARKING BRAKE

PARKING BRAKE CABLES

ADJUSTMENT

The rear drum brake shoes serve as the parking brakes. Refer to the procedures under Rear Drum Brakes.

PARKING BRAKE SHOES

REMOVAL & INSTALLATION

The rear drum brake shoes serve as the parking brakes. Refer to the procedures under Rear Drum Brakes.

CHASSIS ELECTRICAL   AIR BAG (SUPPLEMENTAL RESTRAINT SYSTEM)

GENERAL INFORMATION

✳✳ CAUTION

These vehicles are equipped with an air bag system. The system must be disarmed before performing service on, or around, system components, the steering column, instrument panel components, wiring and sensors. Failure to follow the safety precautions and the disarming procedure could result in accidental air bag deployment, possible injury and unnecessary system repairs.

SERVICE PRECAUTIONS

Disconnect and isolate the battery negative cable before beginning any airbag system component diagnosis, testing, removal, or installation procedures. Allow system

capacitor to discharge for two minutes before beginning any component service. This will disable the airbag system. Failure to disable the airbag system may result in accidental airbag deployment, personal injury, or death.

Do not place an intact undeployed airbag face down on a solid surface. The airbag will propel into the air if accidentally deployed and may result in personal injury or death.

When carrying or handling an undeployed airbag, the trim side (face) of the airbag should be pointing towards the body to minimize possibility of injury if accidental deployment occurs. Failure to do this may result in personal injury or death.

Replace airbag system components with OEM replacement parts. Substitute parts may appear interchangeable, but internal differences may result in inferior occupant protection. Failure to do so may result in occupant personal injury or death.

Wear safety glasses, rubber gloves, and long sleeved clothing when cleaning powder residue from vehicle after an airbag deployment. Powder residue emitted from a deployed airbag can cause skin irritation. Flush affected area with cool water if irritation is experienced. If nasal or throat irritation is experienced, exit the vehicle for fresh air until the irritation ceases. If irritation continues, see a physician.

Do not use a replacement airbag that is not in the original packaging. This may result in improper deployment, personal injury, or death.

The factory installed fasteners, screws and bolts used to fasten airbag components have a special coating and are specifically designed for the airbag system. Do not use substitute fasteners. Use only original equipment fasteners listed in the parts catalog when fastener replacement is required.

During, and following, any child restraint anchor service, due to impact event or vehicle repair, carefully inspect all mounting hardware, tether straps, and anchors for proper installation, operation, or damage. If a child restraint anchor is found damaged in any way, the anchor must be replaced. Failure to do this may result in personal injury or death.

Deployed and non-deployed airbags may or may not have live pyrotechnic material within the airbag inflator.

Do not dispose of driver/passenger/curtain airbags or seat belt tensioners unless you are sure of complete deployment. Refer to the Hazardous Substance Control System for proper disposal.

Dispose of deployed airbags and tensioners consistent with state, provincial, local, and federal regulations.

After any airbag component testing or service, do not connect the battery negative cable. Personal injury or death may result if the system test is not performed first.

If the vehicle is equipped with the Occupant Classification System (OCS), do not connect the battery negative cable before performing the OCS Verification Test using the scan tool and the appropriate diagnostic information. Personal injury or death may result if the system test is not performed properly.

Never replace both the Occupant Restraint Controller (ORC) and the Occupant Classification Module (OCM) at the same time. If both require replacement, replace one, then perform the Airbag System test before replacing the other.

Both the ORC and the OCM store Occupant Classification System (OCS) calibration data, which they transfer to one another when one of them is replaced. If both are replaced at the same time, an irreversible fault will be set in both modules and the OCS may malfunction and cause personal injury or death.

If equipped with OCS, the Seat Weight Sensor is a sensitive, calibrated unit and must be handled carefully. Do not drop or handle roughly. If dropped or damaged, replace with another sensor. Failure to do so may result in occupant injury or death.

If equipped with OCS, the front passenger seat must be handled carefully as well. When removing the seat, be careful when setting on floor not to drop. If dropped, the sensor may be inoperative, could result in occupant injury, or possibly death.

If equipped with OCS, when the passenger front seat is on the floor, no one should sit in the front passenger seat. This uneven force may damage the sensing ability of the seat weight sensors. If sat on and damaged, the sensor may be inoperative, could result in occupant injury, or possibly death.

DISARMING THE SYSTEM

1. Before servicing the vehicle, refer to the Precautions Section.
2. Turn all vehicle accessories OFF.
3. Turn the ignition switch to OFF.
4. At the smart junction box (SJB), located below the RH side of the instrument panel, remove the RH lower cowl trim panel and remove the restraints control module (RCM) fuse from the SJB. For additional information, refer to the Owner's Manual.
5. Turn the ignition ON and visually monitor the air bag indicator for at least 30 seconds. The air bag indicator will remain lit continuously (no flashing) if the correct RCM fuse has been removed. If the air bag indicator does not remain lit continuously, remove the correct RCM fuse before proceeding.
6. Turn the ignition OFF.

❊❊ CAUTION

To avoid accidental deployment and possible personal injury, the backup power supply must be depleted before repairing or replacing any front or side air bag supplemental restraint system (SRS) components and before servicing, replacing, adjusting or striking components near the front or side air bag sensors or RCM, such as doors, instrument panel, console, door latches, strikers, seats and hood latches.

7. To deplete the backup power supply energy, disconnect the battery ground cable and wait at least one minute. Be sure to disconnect auxiliary batteries and power supplies (if equipped).
8. Disconnect the battery ground cable (14301) and wait at least one minute.

ARMING THE SYSTEM

1. Before servicing the vehicle, refer to the Precautions Section.

❊❊ CAUTION

The restraint system diagnostic tool is for restraint system service only. Remove from vehicle prior to road use. Failure to remove could result in injury and possible violation of vehicle safety standards. Make sure all restraint system diagnostic tool(s) that may have been installed during the repair have been removed from the vehicle and all SRS components are connected.

2. Turn the ignition switch from OFF to ON.
3. Install the RCM fuse to the SJB and install the RH lower cowl trim panel.

❊❊ CAUTION

Be sure that nobody is in the vehicle and that there is nothing blocking or set in front of any air bag module when the battery ground cable is connected.

4. Connect the battery ground cable.
5. Prove out the supplemental restraint system (SRS) as follows:

a. Turn the ignition key from ON to OFF. Wait 10 seconds, then turn the key back to ON and visually monitor the air bag indicator with the air bag modules installed. The air bag indicator will light continuously for approximately six seconds and then turn off. If an air bag supplemental restraint system (SRS) fault is present, the air bag indicator will either:

- fail to light.
- remain lit continuously.
- flash.

b. The flashing might not occur until approximately 30 seconds after the ignition switch has been turned from the OFF to the ON position. This is the time required for the restraints control module (RCM) to complete the testing of the SRS. If the air bag indicator is inoperative and a SRS fault exists, a chime will sound in a pattern of five sets of five beeps. If this occurs, the air bag indicator and any SRS fault discovered must be diagnosed and repaired.

c. Clear all continuous DTCs from the restraints control module using a scan tool.

AUTOMATIC TRANSMISSION ASSEMBLY

REMOVAL & INSTALLATION

1. Before servicing the vehicle, refer to the Precautions Section.

➡ **If the transmission is to be removed for a period of time, support the engine with a safety stand and a wood block.**

2. With the vehicle in NEUTRAL, position it on a hoist.

➡ **When the battery has been disconnected and reconnected, some abnormal drive symptoms can occur while the vehicle relearns its adaptive strategy.**

3. Disconnect the battery ground cable
4. On 4.0L vehicles, remove the fluid level indicator tube bolt and remove the tube and indicator.
5. If transmission disassembly is required, drain the transmission fluid.
6. On 4-wheel drive vehicles, remove the transfer case.
7. To maintain initial driveshaft balance, mark the driveshaft yoke and axle flange so they can be installed in their original alignment.
8. Remove the rear driveshaft.
    a. Remove the four bolts.
    b. Remove the driveshaft.
9. Remove the starter motor.
10. With a 2.3L engine:
    a. When removing the torque converter nuts, the crankshaft must be rotated only in the clockwise direction, otherwise engine damage can occur. The crankshaft, crankshaft sprocket and the pulley are fitted together by friction between the flange faces on each part. For that reason, the crankshaft sprocket can also be moved when the crankshaft pulley is turned in the counterclockwise direction.
    b. It may be necessary to gain access to the flexplate nuts through the wheel well.
    c. Mark the torque converter and the flexplate for correct alignment at reinstallation.
    d. Remove and discard the four torque converter nuts. Rotate the flexplate to access to all the nuts.
11. With 3.0L and 4.0L engines:
    a. Mark the torque converter and the flexplate for correct alignment at rein-

stallation. Remove the four nuts. Rotate the flexplate to access to all the nuts.
    b. Disconnect the shift cable.
    c. Disconnect the transmission wiring harness from the case.
12. Disconnect the transmission wiring harness. Remove the three way catalytic converter.
13. With a 2.3L engine, remove the rear engine cover plate.

➡ **Care should be taken not to bend or damage the cooler lines.**

14. Hold the case fitting and remove the transmission cooler lines.
15. Remove the nuts.
16. Position a transmission jack under the transmission. Raise and support the transmission.
17. Remove the crossmember.
18. Remove the transmission mount.
19. With a 2.3L engine, remove the rear vibration damper.
20. 2.3L and 3.0L engines, remove the transmission upper fill tube.
21. Lower the jack to gain access to screws. Remove the transmission-to-engine bolts.
22. With a 2.3L engine, remove the lower screws.
23. Remove the HO2S connector bracket from the transmission.
24. On 4-wheel drive vehicles, remove the vent tube assembly.

❋❋ CAUTION

The torque converter is heavy and may result in injury if it falls out of the transmission. Secure the torque converter in the transmission. Failure to follow these instructions may result in personal injury. Install a converter locking tool before lowering the transmission from the vehicle.

❋❋ CAUTION

Secure the transmission to the transmission jack with a safety chain. Failure to follow these instructions may result in personal injury.

25. Lower the transmission.
26. If the transmission is being overhauled or if installing a new or remanufactured transmission, carry out transmission fluid cooler backflushing and cleaning.

To install:

27. On 4-wheel drive vehicles, install the vent tube assembly.

❋❋ CAUTION

Secure the transmission to the transmission jack with a safety chain. Failure to follow these instructions may result in personal injury.

28. Raise and position the transmission.
29. Remove the holding tool.
30. With the 4.0L engine:
    a. Align the flexplate to the converter marks made at removal.
    b. Install the transmission-to-engine screws. Torque to 35 ft. lbs. (48 Nm).
31. With the 2.3L and 3.0L engines
    a. Align the flexplate to the converter marks made at removal.
    b. Install the transmission-to-engine screws. Torque to 35 ft. lbs. (48 Nm).
    c. Install the upper fluid filler tube and bracket screw.
32. With the 2.3L engine:
    a. Install the lower transmission-to-engine screws. Torque to 35 ft. lbs. (48 Nm).
    b. Install the HO2S connector bracket.
    c. Install the rear engine cover plate.
33. On 4-wheel drive vehicles, install the transfer case.
34. Install the exhaust bracket. Torque the bolts to 73 ft. lbs. (99 Nm).
35. Install the crossmember. Tighten the bolts to 74 ft. lbs. (101 Nm).
36. Install the transmission mount into the crossmember and torque the nuts to 73 ft. lbs. (99 Nm).
37. With 3.0L engines, install the rear vibration damper. Torque the nuts to 22 ft. lbs. (30 Nm).
38. With 3.0L and 4.0L engines:

➡ **Prior to installing the cooler lines to the case, inspect the O-rings. If damaged new O-rings will need to be installed.**

    d. Hold the case fitting and install the transmission cooler lines. Torque to 19 ft. lbs. (28 Nm).
    e. Install four new torque converter nuts. Rotate the crankshaft as needed to gain access to all the nuts. Torque to 26 ft. lbs. (35 Nm).
39. With the 2.3L vehicles: Install four new torque converter nuts. Rotate the crankshaft as needed to gain access to all the nuts. Torque to 26 ft. lbs. (35 Nm).

➡️**When installing the torque converter nuts, the crankshaft must be rotated only in the clockwise direction, otherwise engine damage can occur. The crankshaft, the crankshaft sprocket and the pulley are fitted together by friction between the flange faces on each part. For that reason, the crankshaft sprocket can also be moved when the crankshaft pulley is turned in the counterclockwise direction.**

40. Install the starter motor.

41. Install the catalytic converter assembly.

42. Position the transmission wiring harness in place.

43. Connect the transmission wiring harness.

44. Install the shift cable.

45. Align the driveshaft yoke and the axle shaft marks made at removal to maintain driveline balance. Install the rear driveshaft. Install the driveshaft bolts. Torque to 83 ft. lbs. (112 Nm).

46. Use the following guidelines for installing the in-line transmission fluid filter:

   a. If the transmission was overhauled and the vehicle was equipped with an in-line fluid filter, install a new in-line fluid filter.

   b. If the transmission was overhauled and the vehicle was not equipped with an in-line fluid filter, install a new in-line fluid filter kit.

   c. If the transmission is being installed for a non-internal repair, do not install an in-line filter or filter kit.

   d. If installing a new or re-manufactured transmission, install the in-line transmission fluid filter that is supplied.

   e. Prior to lowering the vehicle, install a new in-line transmission filter or a filter kit.

47. With the 4.0L engine, install the transmission fill tube and indicator as an assembly.

➡️**When the battery has been disconnected and reconnected, some abnormal drive symptoms can occur while the vehicle relearns its adaptive strategy.**

48. Connect the battery ground cable.

49. Fill the transmission with clean automatic transmission fluid to the specified level.

50. Check the transmission for correct operation.

51. Verify that the shift cable is correctly adjusted.

MANUAL TRANSMISSION ASSEMBLY

REMOVAL & INSTALLATION

2-Wheel Drive Models

1. Remove the upper gearshift lever, the outer gearshift lever boot and the console as an assembly.

2. With the vehicle in NEUTRAL, position it on a hoist.

3. If transmission disassembly is required, remove the drain plug and drain the transmission fluid. Install the drain plug after draining all the fluid.

4. To maintain initial driveshaft balance, index-mark the driveshaft yoke to the axle flange, so they can be installed in their original positions. Remove the rear driveshaft.

5. Disconnect the wire harness from the crossmember.

6. Place a suitable jack under the transmission. Secure the transmission to the jack with a safety strap.

7. Remove the six crossmember bolts.

8. Remove the transmission mount nuts and the crossmember.

9. Remove the heated oxygen sensor (HO2S) bracket nut and the bracket from the extension housing.

10. Remove the transmission mount bolts and the transmission mount.

11. For 3.0L and 4.0L engines, remove the catalytic converter Y-pipe.

12. Disconnect the vehicle speed sensor (VSS) electrical connector and the reverse lamp switch electrical connector. Then unclip the wiring harness from the transmission.

13. Remove the starter motor. Using mechanics wire, position the starter aside.

14. Using the special tool, disconnect the clutch hydraulic line.

15. Using a suitable jack, support the engine.

16. Lower the transmission enough to gain access to the upper transmission-to-engine bolts. Remove the nine transmission-to-engine bolts.

17. Pull the transmission rearward until the input shaft is clear of the pressure plate, then lower the transmission from the vehicle.

To install:

18. Before securing the engine to the transmission, connect the hydraulic line to the clutch slave cylinder.

19. Install the rear driveshaft with new bolts.

20. Align the index marks when installing the rear driveshaft.

21. Check and, if necessary, fill the transmission with the specified type and quantity of fluid.

22. To install, reverse the removal procedure. Observe the following torques:
   - Drain plug: 35 ft. lbs. (48 Nm)
   - Crossmember bolts: 74 ft. lbs. (101 Nm)
   - Transmission mount nuts: 72 ft. lbs. (98 Nm)
   - Oxygen sensor bracket nut: 29 ft. lbs. (39 Nm)
   - Transmission mount bolts: 73 ft. lbs. (99 Nm)
   - Transmission-to-engine bolts: 41 ft. lbs. (55 Nm)

4-Wheel Drive Models

1. Remove the upper gearshift lever, the outer gearshift lever boot and the console as an assembly.

2. With the vehicle in NEUTRAL, position it on a hoist.

3. Remove the skid plate, if equipped.

4. If transmission disassembly is required, remove the drain plug and drain the transmission fluid. Install the drain plug after draining all the fluid.

5. To maintain initial driveshaft balance, index-mark the front output shaft and the front driveshaft constant velocity (CV) joint. Index-mark the rear driveshaft yokes to the axle flange and on the transfer case flange.

6. Remove the transfer case.

7. Disconnect the wire harness from the crossmember.

8. Position a suitable jack under the transmission. Secure the transmission to the jack with a safety strap.

9. Remove the six crossmember bolts.

10. Remove the transmission mount nuts and the crossmember

11. Remove the heated oxygen sensor (HO2S) bracket nut and the bracket from the extension housing.

12. Remove the catalytic converter Y-pipe.

13. Disconnect the vehicle speed sensor (VSS) electrical connector and the reverse lamp switch electrical connector. Then unclip the wiring harness from the transmission.

14. Remove the starter motor. Using mechanics wire, position the starter aside.

15. Using the special tool, disconnect the clutch hydraulic line.

16. Using a suitable jack, support the engine.

17. Lower the transmission enough to gain access to the upper transmission-to-engine bolts. Remove the nine transmission-to-engine bolts.

18. Pull the transmission rearward until the input shaft is clear of the pressure plate, then lower the transmission from the vehicle.

To install:

19. Before securing the engine to the transmission, connect the hydraulic line to the clutch slave cylinder.

20. Install the transfer case with a new gasket.

21. Tighten the bolts that retain the transfer case to the extension housing in a clockwise direction beginning with the upper LH bolt.

22. Install the front driveshaft with new bolts and washers and the rear driveshaft with new bolts.

23. Align the index marks when installing the front and rear driveshafts.

24. Check and, if necessary, fill the transmission with the specified type and quantity of fluid.

25. To install, reverse the removal procedure. Observe the following torques:

- Skid plate: 18 ft. lbs. (24 Nm)
- Drain plug: 35 ft. lbs. (48 Nm)
- Crossmember bolts: 46 ft. lbs. (63 Nm)
- Transmission mount nuts: 72 ft. lbs. (98 Nm)
- Oxygen sensor bracket: 29 ft. lbs. (39 Nm)
- Transmission-to-engine bolts: 44 ft. lbs. (60 Nm)

CLUTCH

REMOVAL & INSTALLATION

See Figures 12 12

1. Before servicing the vehicle, refer to the Precautions Section.

2. Remove or disconnect the following:

- Negative battery cable
- Transmission

➡**If the clutch disc and pressure plate are to be reinstalled, bolts must be removed evenly or permanent damage to the diaphragm spring will occur resulting in complete clutch release.**

- Bolts, clutch pressure plate and the clutch disc.

➡**If the parts are to be reused, index-mark the clutch pressure plate to the flywheel.**

To install:

3. Lubricate the transmission input shaft pilot bearing with front axle grease.

4. Using a suitable press, press down-

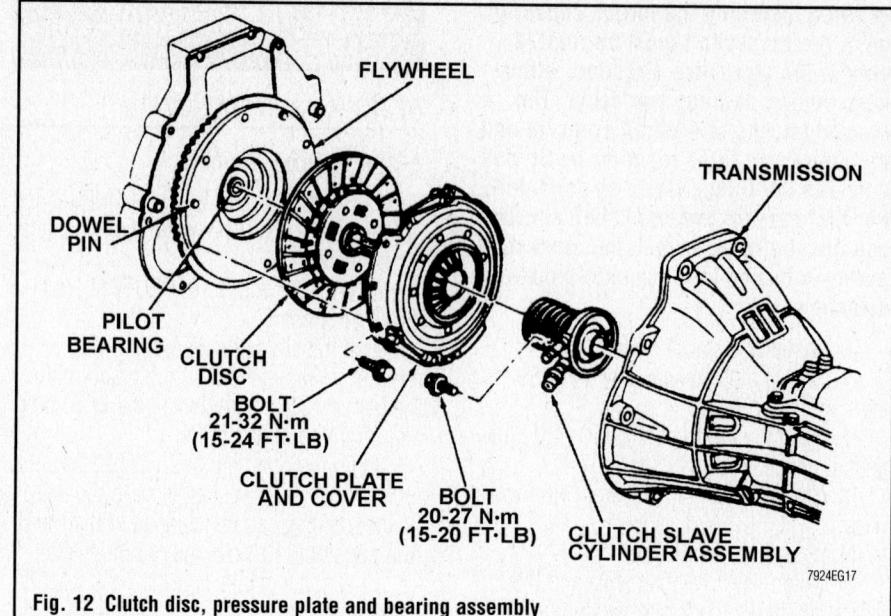

Fig. 12 Clutch disc, pressure plate and bearing assembly

ward on the pressure plate fingers until the adjusting ring moves freely.

5. Rotate the adjusting ring counter-clockwise to compress the tension springs. Hold the adjusting ring in this position.

6. Release the pressure on the fingers. The adjusting ring will stay in the reset position.

7. Position the clutch disc on the flywheel.

➡**If reusing the clutch pressure plate and flywheel, align the marks made during removal.**

8. Align the clutch disc and the clutch pressure plate. Install the bolts and tighten in a star pattern sequence to 20 ft. lbs. (27 Nm)

- Install the transmission.

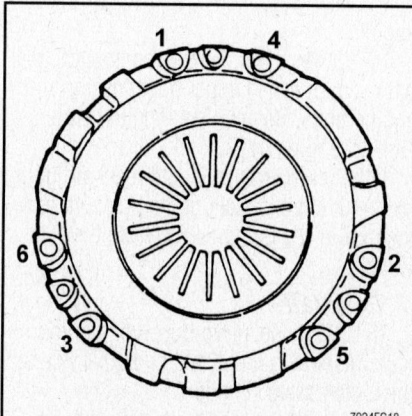

Fig. 13 Tighten the bolts gradually in the correct sequence to avoid warping the pressure plate

ADJUSTMENTS

1. Before servicing the vehicle, refer to the Precautions Section.

Because the clutch is hydraulically driven, there is no adjustment required.

In the event the clutch pedal develops a squeak or uneven feel when depressing, spray the pedal bushing assembly with penetrating oil and work the pedal back-and-forth.

HYDRAULIC CLUTCH SYSTEM

BLEEDING

The following procedure is recommended for bleeding the clutch hydraulic system installed on the vehicle. It is recommended that the original clutch tube, with quick-connect fitting be replaced when servicing the hydraulic system, because air can be trapped in the quick-connect fitting and prevent complete bleeding of the system. The replacement tube does not include a quick-connect fitting.

1. Before servicing the vehicle, refer to the Precautions Section.

2. Clean the dirt and grease from the dust cap.

3. Remove the cap and diaphragm and fill the reservoir to the top with approved brake fluid C6AZ-19542-AA or BA, (ESA-M6C25-A).

➡**To keep brake fluid from entering the clutch housing, route a suitable rubber tube of appropriate inside diameter from the bleed screw to a container.**

4. Loosen the bleed screw, located in the slave cylinder body, next to the inlet

connection. Fluid will now begin to move from the master cylinder down the tube to the slave cylinder.

➡️**The reservoir must be kept full at all times during the bleeding operation, to ensure no additional air enters the system.**

5. Observe the bleed screw outlet. When the slave cylinder is full, a steady stream of fluid will flow from the outlet port. Tighten the bleed screw.

6. Depress the clutch pedal to the floor and hold for 1–2 seconds. Release the pedal as rapidly as possible. The pedal must be released completely. Pause for 1–2 seconds. Repeat 10 times.

7. Check the fluid level in the reservoir. The fluid should be level with the step when the diaphragm is removed.

8. Hold the pedal to the floor, slightly open the bleed screw to allow any additional air to escape. Close the bleed screw, then release the pedal.

9. Check the fluid in the reservoir. The hydraulic system should now be fully bled, and should actuate the clutch.

10. Check the vehicle by starting, pushing the clutch pedal to the floor and selecting reverse gear. There should be no grating of gears. If there is, and the hydraulic system still contains air; repeat the bleeding procedure.

TRANSFER CASE ASSEMBLY

REMOVAL & INSTALLATION

1. Before servicing the vehicle, refer to the Precautions Section.

2. With the vehicle in NEUTRAL, raise and support the vehicle.

3. Remove the skid plate.

4. Remove the damper, if so equipped.

5. Disconnect the transfer case harness connector and position it aside.

6. If transfer case disassembly is necessary, remove the drain plug and drain the fluid. Install the drain plug when all of the fluid has drained.

➡️**Index-mark the front output shaft assembly and the front driveshaft constant velocity (CV) joint.**

✳️ WARNING

Always disconnect the front driveshaft from the transfer case first. Otherwise, the weight of the driveshaft can pinch the boot between the shaft and the boot can and cause the boot to tear.

7. Index-mark the front output shaft assembly and the front driveshaft constant velocity (CV) joint.

8. Remove and discard the bolts and washers.

9. Disconnect the front driveshaft from the transfer case and position the driveshaft aside.

➡️**Index-mark the front flange on the rear driveshaft and the flange on the transfer case.**

10. Remove the rear driveshaft.

✳️ CAUTION

Secure the transfer case to the jack with safety straps.

11. Position a high lift jack under the transfer case.

12. Remove the five bolts retaining the transfer case to the extension housing.

13. Slide the transfer case rearward and off of the transmission output shaft.

14. Remove and discard the front extension housing gasket, and clean the mating surfaces.

To install:

15. Install the transfer case with a new gasket.

16. Tighten the bolts that retain the transfer case to the extension housing in a clockwise direction beginning with the upper LH bolt. Torque to 40 ft. lbs. (54 Nm).

17. Install the front driveshaft with new bolts and washers and the rear driveshaft with new bolts. If new bolts are not available, coat the threads of the original bolts with Threadlock and Sealer E0AZ-19554-AA, or equivalent.

➡️**When installing the front driveshaft, always connect it to the axle first and then connect it to the transfer case.**

➡️**Align the index marks when installing the front and rear driveshafts.**

18. The remainder of installation is the reverse of the removal procedure.

19. Check and, if necessary, fill the transfer case with the specified type and quantity of fluid.

TRANSFER CASE SHIFT MOTOR

REMOVAL & INSTALLATION
See Figure 14.

1. Before servicing the vehicle, refer to the Precautions Section.

2. Set the mode select switch to the 4x4 HIGH position.

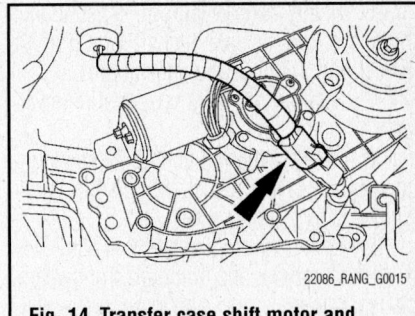

22086_RANG_G0015

Fig. 14 Transfer case shift motor and electrical connector

3. With the vehicle in NEUTRAL, position it on a hoist.

4. Disconnect the transfer case shift motor connector.

5. Remove the bracket bolt and the transfer case shift motor bolts, then remove the transfer case shift motor.

6. Remove the grease from the motor adapter and check for any nicks or burrs. If any damage is found, repair or install a new transfer case shift motor as necessary.

7. To install, reverse the removal procedure and tighten shift motor mounting bolts to 89 inch. lbs. (10 Nm).

HALFSHAFT

REMOVAL & INSTALLATION

See Figures 15 through 17.

1. With the vehicle in NEUTRAL, raise and support the vehicle.

2. Remove the front wheel and tire assembly.

➡️**Do not reuse the torque prevailing design hub nut and washer assembly.**

3. Remove and discard the hub nut and washer assembly.

✳️ WARNING

Do not allow the disc brake caliper to hang suspended from the brake hose. Provide a suitable support.

4. Remove the front disc brake caliper, anchor plate, and pads as an assembly, and position the assembly aside.

5. Remove the brake disc.

✳️ WARNING

Do not use a hammer to separate the outboard front wheel halfshaft joint from the wheel hub. Damage to the outboard CV joint stub shaft threads and internal CV joint components may result.

6. Using the special tool, separate the outboard front wheel halfshaft joint from the wheel hub. Remove the special tool.

7. Support the front suspension lower arm.

8. Remove the nut and bolt retaining the upper ball joint to the front wheel knuckle.

9. Rotate the front wheel knuckle.

10. Compress the outboard front wheel halfshaft joint.

11. Remove the outboard front wheel halfshaft joint from the wheel hub.

12. Using the special tools, 205-241 and 100-001, or equivalent, separate the inboard front wheel halfshaft joint from the front axle housing.

13. Remove the halfshaft assembly from the vehicle with both hands. Do not damage the axle seal.

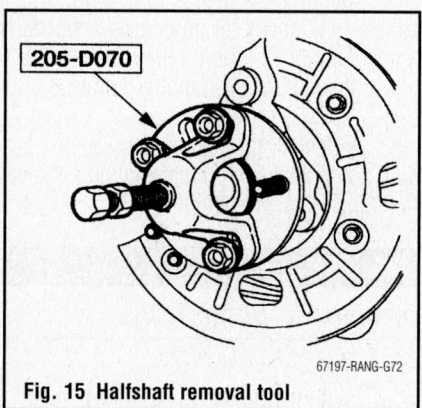

Fig. 15 Halfshaft removal tool

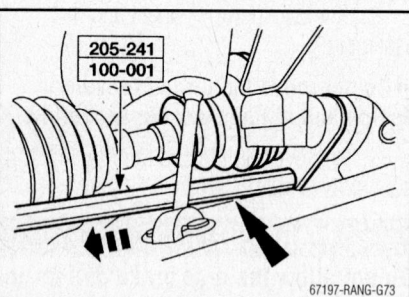

Fig. 16 Separating the halfshaft from the axle housing

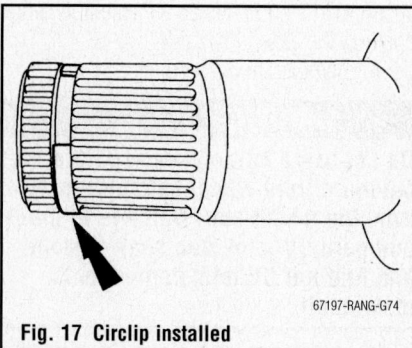

Fig. 17 Circlip installed

To install:

✳✳✳ WARNING

Install the halfshaft with a new hub nut and washer assembly. Do not use power or impact tools to tighten the hub nut and washer assembly.

→Install a new retainer circlip in the groove in the LH inboard CV joint housing stub shaft before installing the halfshaft in the vehicle. To prevent the new retainer circlip from over-expanding when installing it, start one end in the groove and work the circlip over the shaft and into the groove.

14. To install, reverse the removal procedure. Observe the following torques:
- Hub nut: 162 ft. lbs. (220 Nm)
- Upper ball joint-to-knuckle nut: 41 ft. lbs. (55 Nm)

CV-JOINTS

OVERHAUL

See Figures 18 through 21.

1. Remove the front wheel halfshaft. Do not damage the halfshaft boot.

2. Remove the two inboard boot clamps.

3. Slide the inboard halfshaft boot off the inboard CV joint housing.

4. Separate the CV joint from the CV joint housing.

5. Index-mark the shaft and the inboard CV joint for correct alignment during assembly.

6. Remove the snap ring.

7. Remove the CV joint.

8. Remove the inboard halfshaft boot from the shaft assembly.

9. Remove the front wheel excluder seal, if necessary. Discard the seal. Tap uniformly around the seal to separate it from the joint.

10. Remove the two outboard boot clamps.

11. Remove the outboard halfshaft boot.

12. If the grease is contaminated, clean

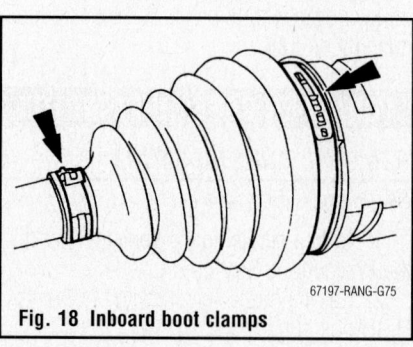

Fig. 18 Inboard boot clamps

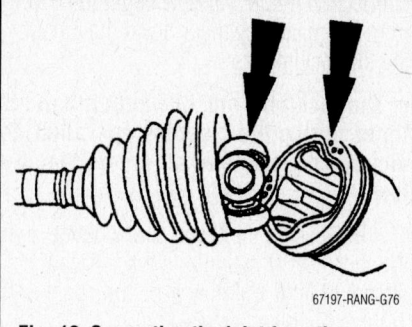

Fig. 19 Separating the joint from the housing

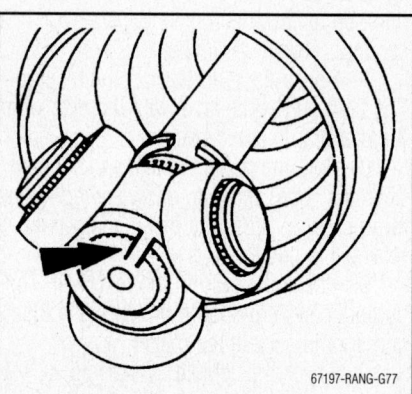

Fig. 20 Make an alignment mark for reassembly

and inspect the joint for wear. Install a new outboard CV joint and shaft assembly if worn/damaged.

13. Inspect the assembly for contaminated grease.

To assemble:

14. Pack the outboard CV joint with grease. Use Ford High Temp Constant Velocity Joint Grease E43Z-19590-A or equivalent meeting Ford specification ESP-M1C207-A. Spread any remaining grease from the service kit evenly inside the outboard halfshaft boot.

15. Clean the halfshaft boot mounting surfaces of excess grease before positioning the halfshaft boot into place.

16. Position the outboard halfshaft boot.

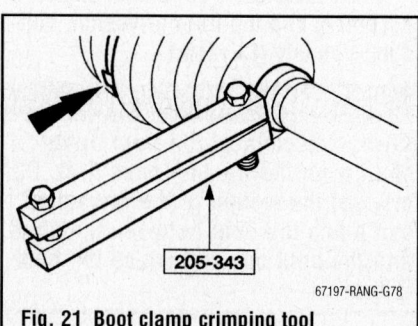

Fig. 21 Boot clamp crimping tool

17. Position the boot clamps on the outboard halfshaft boot.

18. Tighten the through-bolt until the installer is in the closed position.

19. Install the outboard CV joint boot clamps. There are special tools made for this procedure.

20. Position the boot clamp on the halfshaft.

21. Position the inboard halfshaft boot.

22. Align the index marks on the halfshaft and the CV joint.

23. Install the CV joint on the halfshaft.

24. Install the snap ring.

25. Lubricate the three CV joint needle bearings. Use Ford High Temp Constant Velocity Joint Grease E43Z-19590-A or equivalent meeting Ford specification ESP-M1C207-A.

26. Fill the inboard CV joint housing with 235 grams (8.3 oz.) of grease. Use Ford High Temp Constant Velocity Joint Grease E43Z-19590-A or equivalent meeting Ford specification ESP-M1C207-A.

27. Position the CV joint housing onto the CV joint.

28. Remove any excess grease from the inboard halfshaft boot mating surface before positioning it into place.

29. Position the inboard halfshaft boot into place.

30. Position the boot clamp.

31. Insert a dulled screwdriver blade to relieve built-up air pressure in the halfshaft boot.

32. Using the special tool, install the inboard boot clamps.

33. Using the special tool, install the new front wheel excluder seal, if removed. Seat the metal ring at the seal's inner diameter flat against the CV joint housing.

34. Install the front wheel halfshaft.

FRONT AXLE TUBE BEARING

REMOVAL & INSTALLATION

See Figures 22 through 28.

1. Before servicing the vehicle, refer to the Precautions Section.

2. Remove or disconnect the following:
   - Right-hand halfshaft
   - Right-hand axle shaft
   - Axle seal, with a slide hammer
   - Axle tube bearing, with a slide hammer

3. Clean the bearing and seal surfaces of any foreign debris.

To install:

4. Use an axle bearing replacer and the handle to replace the RH axle tube bearing.

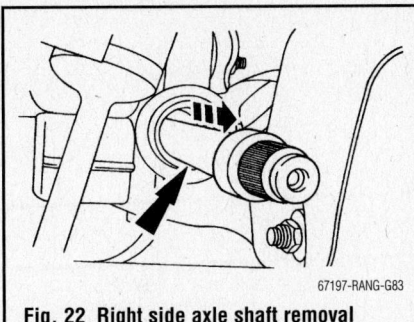
67197-RANG-G83
Fig. 22 Right side axle shaft removal

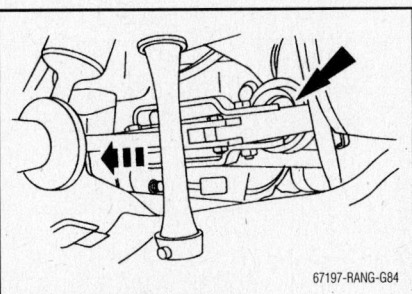
67197-RANG-G84
Fig. 23 Axle seal removal

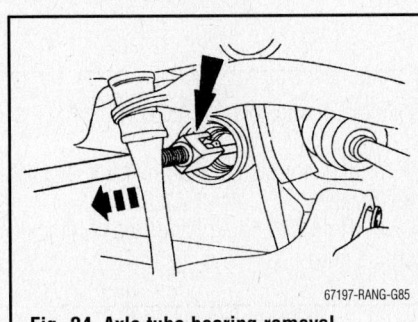
67197-RANG-G85
Fig. 24 Axle tube bearing removal

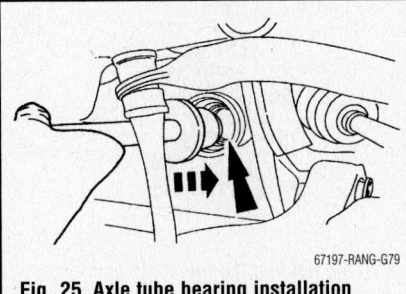
67197-RANG-G79
Fig. 25 Axle tube bearing installation

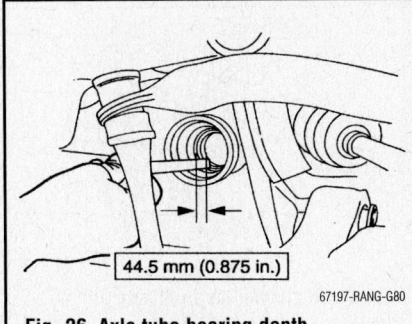
44.5 mm (0.875 in.)
67197-RANG-G80
Fig. 26 Axle tube bearing depth

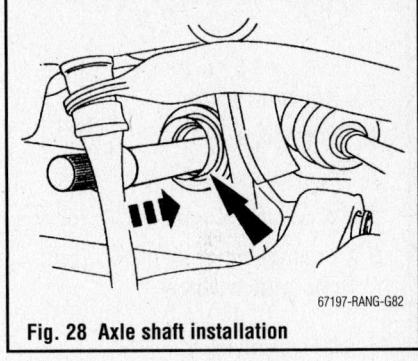
67197-RANG-G81
Fig. 27 Axle tube seal installation

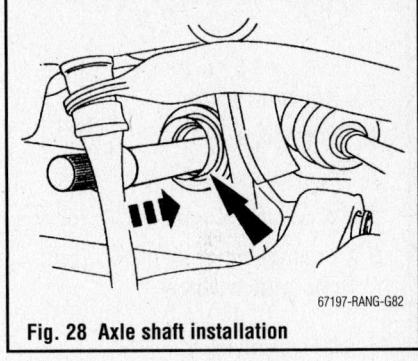
67197-RANG-G82
Fig. 28 Axle shaft installation

5. Check the bearing depth as shown.

6. Use an axle seal replacer and the handle to replace the axle tube seal.

➡**Care should be taken not to damage the axle seal surface.**

7. Install the axle shaft.

8. Refill the front drive axle to proper level using SAE 80W90.

9. Install the RH halfshaft.

FRONT DRIVESHAFT

REMOVAL & INSTALLATION

See Figure 29.

1. Before servicing the vehicle, refer to the Precautions Section.

2. With the vehicle in NEUTRAL, raise and support the vehicle.

3. Index the front axle pinion flange to the front driveshaft.

4. Index the transfer case pinion flange to the front driveshaft.

5. Remove the front driveshaft-to-transfer case bolts and retainers.

6. Remove the front driveshaft-to-front axle bolts.

7. Remove the front driveshaft.

8. To install, reverse the removal procedure. Torque the bolts at the axle end to 15 ft. lbs. (20 Nm); the transfer case end bolts to 22 ft. lbs. (30 Nm).

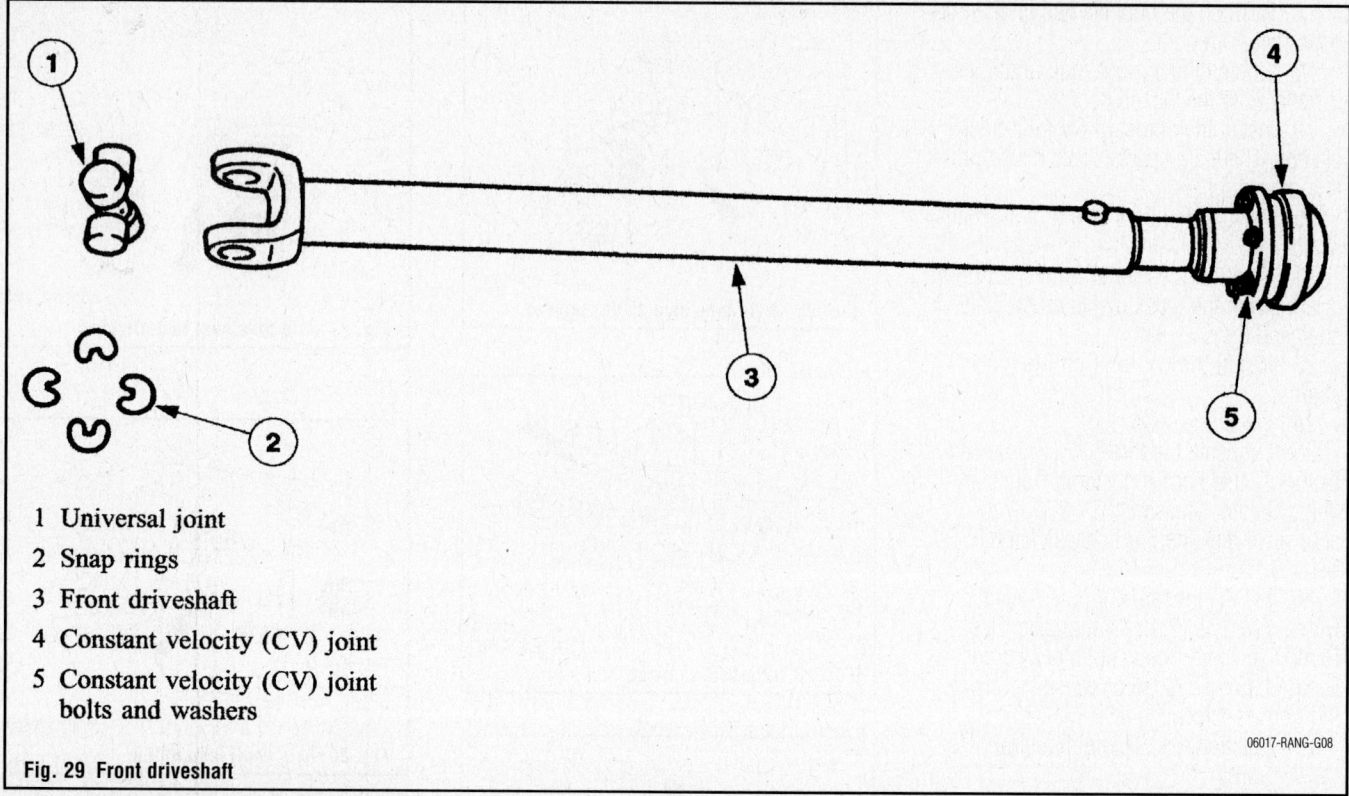

1 Universal joint
2 Snap rings
3 Front driveshaft
4 Constant velocity (CV) joint
5 Constant velocity (CV) joint
   bolts and washers

06017-RANG-G08

Fig. 29 Front driveshaft

FRONT PINION SEAL

REMOVAL & INSTALLATION

See Figures 30 through 32.

➡**This operation disturbs the differential pinion bearing preload. Carefully reset the preload during assembly.**

✳✳ CAUTION

The electrical power to the air suspension system must be shut off prior to hoisting, jacking or towing an air suspension vehicle. This can be accomplished by turning off the air suspension switch located in the rear jack storage area. Failure to do so can result in unexpected inflation or deflation of the air springs, which can result in shifting of the vehicle during these operations.

1. Before servicing the vehicle, refer to the Precautions Section.
2. Index-mark the front driveshaft and pinion flange.
3. Remove or disconnect the following:
   • Front driveshaft from the pinion flange, and position it aside

➡**Do not allow the driveshaft to hang unsupported.**

4. Using a Nm (inch-pound) torque wrench, measure the torque required to maintain pinion rotation. Record the measurement.
5. Index-mark the pinion flange and the pinion stem.
6. Hold the pinion flange while removing the nut.

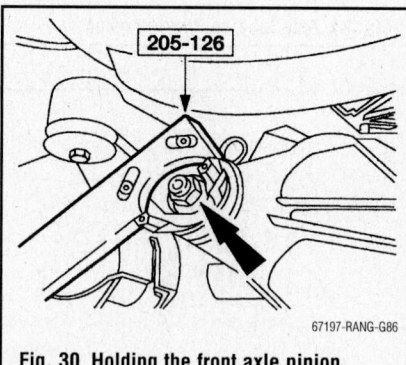

205-126

67197-RANG-G86

Fig. 30 Holding the front axle pinion flange

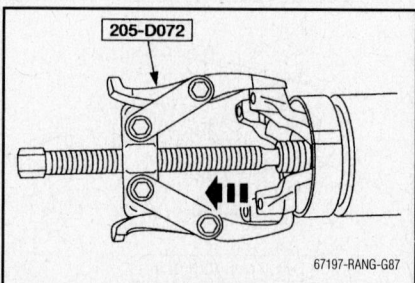

205-D072

67197-RANG-G87

Fig. 31 Removing the front axle pinion flange

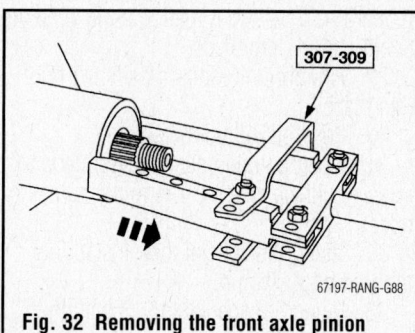

307-309

67197-RANG-G88

Fig. 32 Removing the front axle pinion seal

7. Place a drain pan under the differential housing.
8. Using a puller, remove the pinion flange.
9. Inspect the pinion flange for burrs and damage. Inspect the end of the pinion flange that contacts the bearing cone, the nut counterbore, and the seal surface for nicks. Discard the pinion flange as necessary.
10. Using a seal remover and impact slide hammer, remove the pinion seal.
11. Remove the front axle drive pinion shaft oil slinger and the differential pinion bearing.
12. Remove and discard the collapsible spacer.

To install:
13. Verify that the splines on the pinion stem are free of burrs. If burrs are evident,

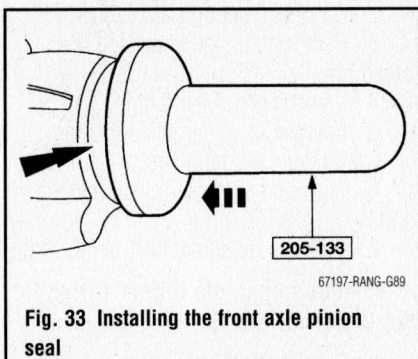

Fig. 33 Installing the front axle pinion seal

remove them with a fine crocus cloth. Work in a rotating motion to wipe the pinion clean.

14. Clean the pinion seal bore.

15. Install a new collapsible spacer.

16. Install the original differential pinion bearing and the front axle drive pinion shaft oil slinger.

17. Lubricate the pinion seal. Use Motorcraft® SAE 80W90 Thermally Stable 4x4 Axle Lubricant meeting Ford specification WSP-M2C197-A.

18. Install the pinion seal.

19. Lubricate the pinion flange splines. Use Motorcraft® SAE 80W90 Thermally Stable 4x4 Axle Lubricant meeting Ford specification WSP-M2C197-A.

➡**Never use a metal hammer on the pinion flange or install the flange with power tools. If necessary, use a plastic hammer to tap on a tight fitting flange.**

- Align the index marks and install the pinion flange.
- Install the new nut hand-tight.

➡**Do not loosen the nut to reduce preload. Install a new collapsible spacer and nut if preload reduction is necessary.**

20. Use the special tool to hold the pinion flange while tightening the nut to set the preload.

21. Tighten the nut, rotating the pinion occasionally to ensure the differential pinion bearings are seating correctly. Take frequent differential pinion bearing preload readings by rotating the pinion with a Nm (inch-pound) torque wrench. The final reading must be 5 inch lbs. (0.56 Nm) more than the initial reading taken during removal.

22. Align the index marks and position the front driveshaft.

23. Install the universal joint spider retainers and bolts.

24. Check the fluid level and, if necessary, fill the axle to specification. Use Motorcraft® SAE 80W90 Thermally Stable

4x4 Axle Lubricant meeting Ford specification WSP-M2C197-A.

25. Lower the vehicle.

26. If so equipped, reactivate the air suspension.

REAR AXLE HOUSING

REMOVAL & INSTALLATION

See Figures 34 and 35.

1. Before servicing the vehicle, refer to the Precautions Section.

2. With the vehicle in NEUTRAL, position it on a hoist.

3. Remove the wheel and tire assembly.

4. Remove the rear stabilizer bar on vehicles equipped with rear stabilizer bars.

5. Remove the rear stabilizer bar link nuts and bolt.

6. Remove the rear stabilizer bar link.

7. Remove the rear stabilizer bar mounting bracket bolts and remove the brackets.

8. Remove the rear stabilizer bar.

9. Remove the axle shafts. For additional information, refer to axle shaft bearing and seal in this section.

10. Disconnect the rear brake anti-lock sensor electrical connector from the sensor.

11. Separate the wiring harness from the clips and position the harness aside.

12. Disconnect the vent hose from the axle.

13. Separate the brake lines from the retaining clips on the axle.

➡**Do not disconnect the brake lines from the brake hose junction block.**

14. Disconnect the brake hose junction block from the differential housing.

15. Disconnect the rear brake backing plates from the axle. Wire the assemblies aside.

16. Position a suitable jack under the differential housing and strap it securely in place.

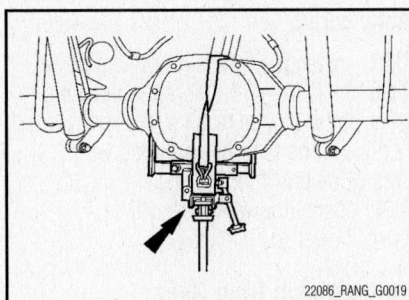

22086_RANG_G0019

Fig. 34 Differential housing and support jack

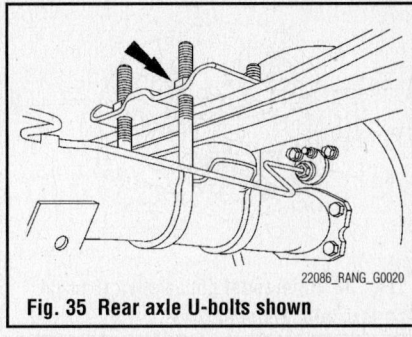

22086_RANG_G0020

Fig. 35 Rear axle U-bolts shown

17. Remove the nuts and bolts retaining the shock absorbers to the axle.

18. Remove the nuts, the rear axle U-bolts and the rear spring plates.

19. Lower the rear axle from the vehicle.

To install:

20. Support and raise axle housing to the vehicle.

21. Install rear axle U-bolts and spring plates being careful to line up dowels on springs to rear axle housing.

22. Install the rear axle U-bolts and the rear spring plates and tighten U-bolts to 76 ft. lbs. (103 Nm).

➡**Make sure dowels on leaf springs are properly lined up to spring plates and axle housing.**

23. Install rear shocks and tighten mounting bolts to 50 ft. lbs. (68 Nm).

24. Install rear axle housing brake backing plates.

25. Reconnect the rear brake junction block to axle housing and tighten mounting bolt to 13 ft. lbs. (18 Nm).

26. Secure rear brake lines to axle housing.

27. Reconnect the rear brake anti-lock sensor electrical connector to the sensor.

28. Install axle shafts.

29. Install the rear stabilizer bar and related parts if previously removed.

30. Check rear axle for gear lubricant and add as needed.

31. Bleed and adjust brakes if needed.

32. Install the tire and wheel assembly.

33. Lower vehicle.

REAR AXLE SHAFT, BEARING & SEAL

REMOVAL & INSTALLATION

Ford 7½ Inch Ring Gear

See Figures 36 and 37.

1. Before servicing the vehicle, refer to the Precautions Section.

2. Raise and support the vehicle.

3. Remove the wheel and tire assembly.

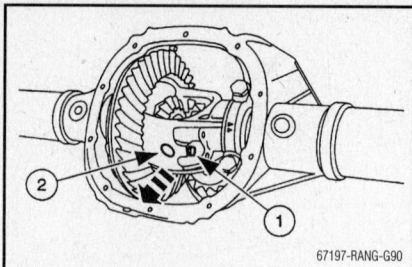

Fig. 36 Differential pinion shaft removal. 1-lock bolt; 2-pinion shaft

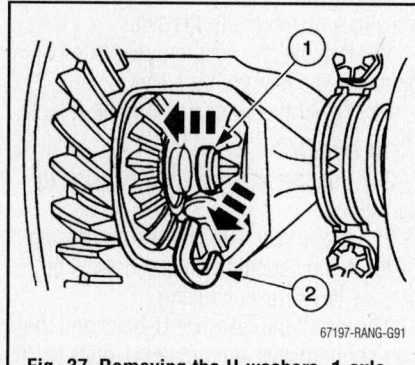

Fig. 37 Removing the U-washers. 1-axle shaft; 2-U-washer

4. Remove the 10 differential housing cover bolts and drain the lubricant from the rear axle housing.

5. Remove the differential housing cover.

6. Remove the rear brake drums.

7. Remove and discard the differential pinion shaft lock bolt.

8. Remove the differential pinion shaft.

➡️**Do not damage the rubber O-rings in the axle shaft grooves.**

9. Push the axle shafts inboard.

10. Remove the U-washers.

➡️**Do not damage the wheel bearing oil seal.**

11. Remove the two axle shafts.

➡️**If only a new seal needs to be installed, use care to avoid damaging the seal bore.**

12. Using a suitable seal remover, remove the axle shaft oil seal. Discard the oil seal.

13. Inspect the rear wheel bearing and axle shaft for wear or damage.

14. If necessary, using a slide hammer, remove the rear wheel bearing.

To install:

15. Lubricate the new rear wheel bearing with lubricant.

16. Using a driver, install the rear wheel bearing.

17. Lubricate the lip of the new wheel bearing oil seal with grease.

18. Using a driver, install the wheel bearing oil seal.

➡️**Make sure the machined surfaces on both the rear axle housing and the differential housing cover are clean and free of oil before installing the new silicone sealant. The inside of the rear axle must be covered when cleaning the machined surface to prevent contamination.**

19. Clean the gasket mating surface of the rear axle and the differential housing cover.

20. Lubricate the lip of the wheel bearing oil seal with grease.

➡️**Do not damage the wheel bearing oil seal.**

21. Install the axle shafts.

➡️**Do not damage the rubber O-rings in the axle shaft grooves.**

22. Position the two U-washers on the button end of the axle shafts.

23. Pull the axle shafts outward.

➡️**If a new pinion shaft lock bolt is unavailable, coat the threads with threadlock and sealer prior to installation.**

24. Install the differential pinion shaft.

   a. Align the hole in the differential pinion shaft with the case lock bolt hole.

   b. Install a new differential pinion shaft lock bolt. Torque to 22 ft. lbs. (30 Nm).

25. Install the rear brake drums.

26. Apply a new continuous bead of sealant of the specified thickness to the differential housing cover.

➡️**The differential housing cover must be installed within 15 minutes of application of the silicone, or new sealant must be applied. If possible, allow one hour before filling with lubricant to make sure the silicone sealant has correctly cured.**

27. Install the different housing cover.

28. Install the 10 differential housing cover bolts. Torque to 33 ft. lbs. (45 Nm).

29. Fill the rear axle housing with 2.4 liters (5 pints) of lubricant.

30. Install the wheels and tires.

31. Lower the vehicle.

Ford 8.8 Inch Ring Gear

1. Before servicing the vehicle, refer to the Precautions Section.

2. Raise and support the vehicle.

3. Remove the rear wheel and tire assembly.

4. Remove the brake drum.

5. Remove the differential housing cover and drain the lubricant.

6. Remove and discard the pinion shaft bolt.

7. Remove the differential pinion shaft.

➡️**Do not damage the rubber O-ring in the U-washer groove.**

8. Push the axle shaft inboard.

9. Remove the U-washer.

10. Do not damage the wheel bearing oil seal.

11. Remove the axle shaft.

➡️**If only a new seal needs to be installed, use care to avoid damaging the seal bore. If the wheel bearing oil seal is leaking, the differential housing vent may be plugged with foreign material.**

12. Using a suitable seal remover, remove the axle shaft oil seal. Discard the oil seal.

13. Inspect the rear wheel bearing and axle shaft for wear or damage.

14. Using the special tools, remove the rear wheel bearing.

To install:

15. Lubricate the new rear wheel bearing with rear axle lubricant.

16. Using the special tools, install the rear wheel bearing.

17. Lubricate the lip of the new wheel bearing oil seal with grease.

18. Using the special tools, install the wheel bearing oil seal.

19. Install the axle shaft.

20. Lubricate the lip of the wheel bearing oil seal with grease.

➡️**Do not damage the wheel bearing oil seal.**

21. Install the axle shaft.

22. Do not damage the rubber O-ring in the U-washer groove.

23. Position the U-washer on the button end of the axle shaft.

24. Pull the axle shaft outward.

➡️**If a new bolt is unavailable, coat the bolt threads with threadlock prior to installation.**

25. Align the bolt hole in the differential pinion shaft with the bolt hole in the case.

26. Install the new bolt. Torque to 22 ft. lbs. (33 Nm).

27. Install the brake drum.

28. Install the differential housing cover

and fill the differential housing with the specified lubricant.

29. Install the rear wheel and tire assembly.

30. Lower the vehicle.

Ford 8.8 Inch Ring Gear High Torque

See Figures 38 through 40.

1. With the vehicle in NEUTRAL, position it on a hoist.

2. Remove the wheel and tire assembly.

3. Remove the 10 differential housing cover bolts and drain the lubricant from the rear axle housing.

4. Remove the differential housing cover.

5. Remove the rear brake drums.

6. Remove and discard the differential thrust plate lock bolt.

7. Remove the differential thrust plate.

✳✳ WARNING

Do not damage the rubber O-rings in the axle shaft grooves.

8. Push the axle shafts inboard.

9. Remove the U-washers.

10. Remove the 2 axle shafts.

11. Using a suitable seal remover, remove the axle shaft oil seal.

12. Using a slide hammer, remove the rear wheel bearing.

To install:

13. Lubricate the new rear wheel bearing with rear axle lubricant

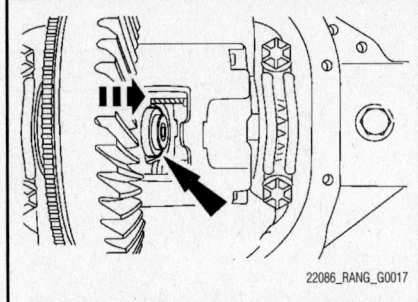

Fig. 39 Differential view of axle shaft and U-washers

22086_RANG_G0017

14. Using a suitable tool, install the rear wheel bearing.

15. Lubricate the lip of the new wheel bearing oil seal with grease.

16. Using the suitable tool, install the wheel bearing oil seal.

17. Carefully install the 2 axle shafts.

18. Position the 2 U-washers on the button end of the axle shafts.

19. Pull the axle shafts outward.

➡**If a new thrust plate lock bolt is unavailable, coat the threads with threadlock and sealer prior to installation.**

20. Align the hole in the thrust plate shaft with the case lock bolt hole.

21. Install a new differential pinion shaft lock bolt and tighten to 22 ft. lbs. (30 Nm).

22. Install the rear brake drums.

23. Clean the gasket mating surface of

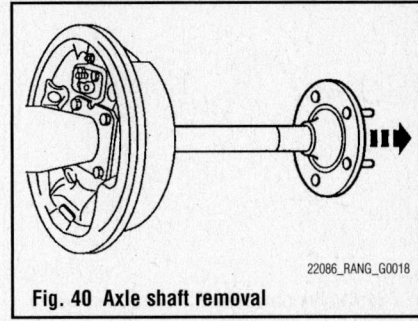

Fig. 40 Axle shaft removal

22086_RANG_G0018

the rear axle and the differential housing cover.

24. Apply a continuous bead of sealant to the differential housing cover.

➡**The differential housing cover must be installed within 15 minutes of application of the silicone, or new sealant must be applied. If possible, allow one hour before filling with lubricant to make sure the silicone sealant has correctly cured.**

25. Install the differential housing cover.

26. Install the differential housing cover bolts and tighten to 33 ft. lbs. (45 Nm).

27. Fill the rear axle housing with 5.37 pints (2.54 liters) of 74W-140 Synthetic Rear Axle Lubricant.

28. Clean the wheel hub and mounting surfaces.

29. Install the tire and wheel assembly.

REAR DRIVESHAFT

REMOVAL & INSTALLATION

2-Wheel Drive Models

See Figures 41 and 42.

1. Before servicing the vehicle, refer to the Precautions Section.

2. With the vehicle in NEUTRAL, raise and support the vehicle.

3. Index-mark the driveshaft flange and rear axle pinion flange.

4. Index-mark the driveshaft and the extension housing.

5. Remove the four bolts.

✳✳ WARNING

The driveshaft flange fits tightly on the rear axle pinion flange pilot. Never hammer on the driveshaft or any of its components to disconnect the driveshaft flange from the pinion flange. Pry only in the area shown, with a suitable tool, to disconnect the driveshaft flange from the pinion flange.

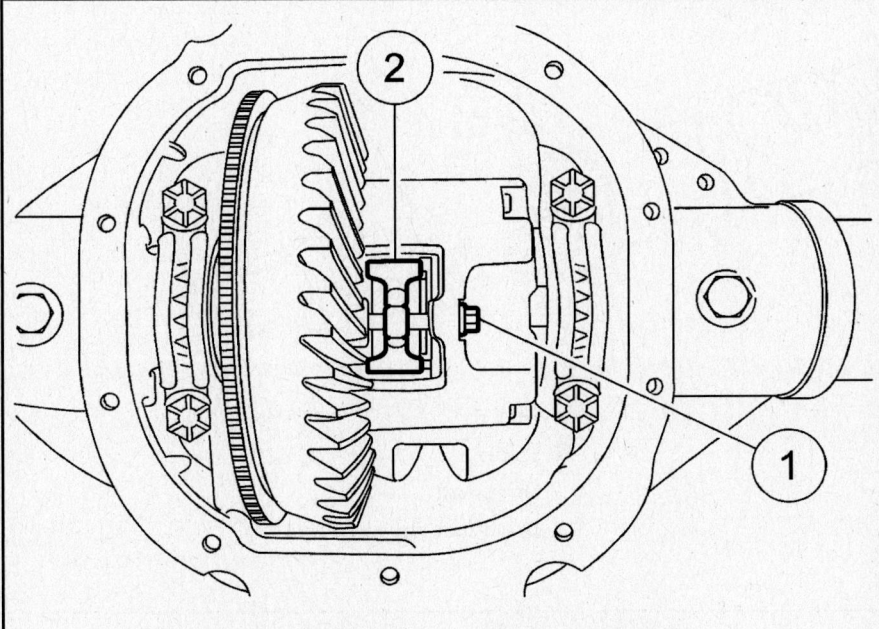

1. Thrust plate lock bolt   2. Thrust plate

22086_RANG_G0016

Fig. 38 Differential view 8.8 inch. ring gear high torque

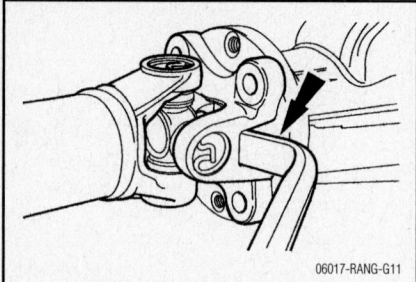

Fig. 41 Pry only in the area shown, with a suitable tool, to disconnect the driveshaft flange from the pinion flange

6. Using a suitable tool as shown, disconnect the driveshaft flange from the rear axle pinion flange.

7. Lower the driveshaft and slide it off the output shaft.

8. Plug the extension housing to prevent fluid loss.

✳✳ WARNING

If new bolts to retain the driveshaft to the axle are not available, coat the threads of the original bolts with Threadlock and Sealer EOAZ-19554-AA or equivalent meeting Ford specification WSK-M2G351-A5.

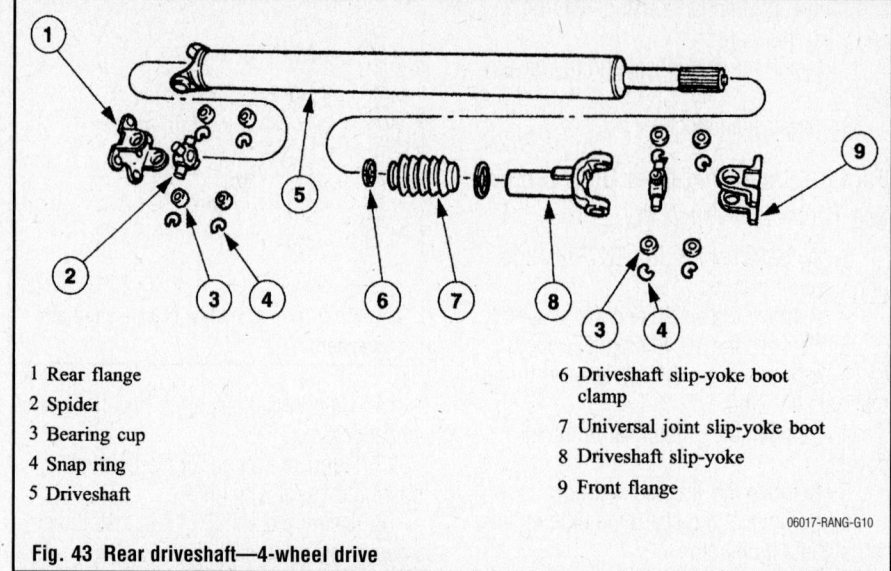

1 Rear flange
2 Spider
3 Bearing cup
4 Snap ring
5 Driveshaft

6 Driveshaft slip-yoke boot clamp
7 Universal joint slip-yoke boot
8 Driveshaft slip-yoke
9 Front flange

06017-RANG-G10

Fig. 43 Rear driveshaft—4-wheel drive

✳✳ WARNING

The driveshaft flange fits tightly on the rear axle pinion flange pilot. To make sure that the driveshaft flange seats squarely on the pinion flange, tighten the bolts evenly in a cross pattern as shown.

9. To install, reverse the removal procedure. Torque the bolts to 83 ft. lbs. (112 Nm).

4-Wheel Drive Models

See Figure 43.

1. Before servicing the vehicle, refer to the Precautions Section.

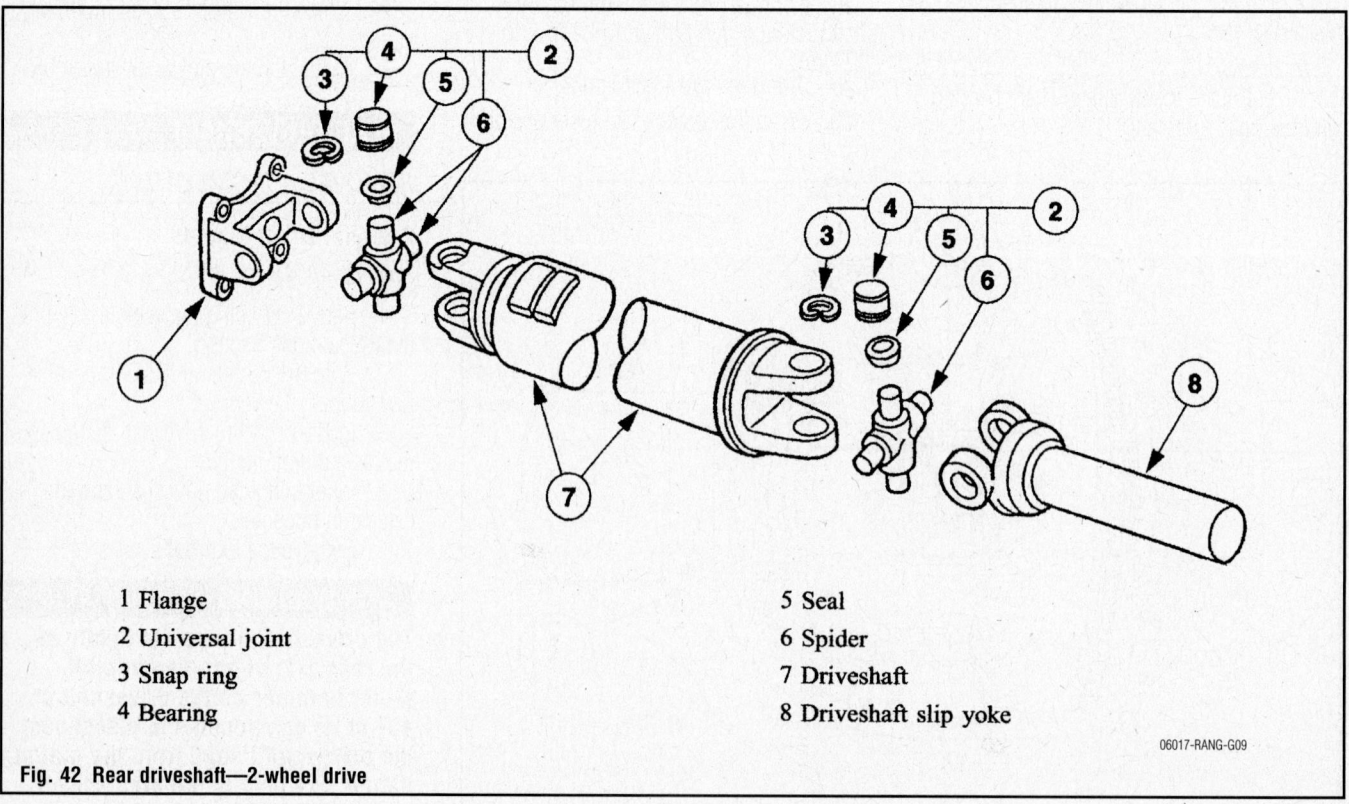

1 Flange
2 Universal joint
3 Snap ring
4 Bearing

5 Seal
6 Spider
7 Driveshaft
8 Driveshaft slip yoke

06017-RANG-G09

Fig. 42 Rear driveshaft—2-wheel drive

2. With the vehicle in NEUTRAL, raise and support the vehicle.

3. Index-mark the driveshaft flange to the rear axle pinion flange.

4. Remove the four rear axle flange bolts.

5. Index-mark the driveshaft and the extension housing.

☀ WARNING

The driveshaft flange fits tightly on the rear axle pinion flange pilot. Never hammer on the driveshaft or any of its components to disconnect the driveshaft flange from the pinion flange. Pry only in the area shown, with a suitable tool, to disconnect the driveshaft flange from the pinion flange.

6. Using a suitable tool as shown, disconnect the driveshaft flange from the rear axle pinion flange.

➡**Make sure the index marks on the extension housing and driveshaft are aligned before separation.**

7. Lower the driveshaft and separate it from the transmission.

☀ WARNING

If new bolts to retain the driveshaft to the axle are not available, coat the threads of the original bolts with Threadlock and Sealer E0AZ-19554-AA or equivalent meeting Ford specification WSK-M2G351-A5.

☀ WARNING

The driveshaft flange fits tightly on the rear axle pinion flange pilot. To make sure that the driveshaft flange seats squarely on the pinion flange, tighten the bolts evenly in a cross pattern as shown.

8. To install, reverse the removal procedure. Torque the bolts at each end to 83 ft. lbs. (112 Nm).

REAR PINION SEAL

REMOVAL & INSTALLATION

1. Before servicing the vehicle, refer to the Precautions Section.

2. Drain the axle housing fluid.

3. Remove or disconnect the following:

- Negative battery cable
- Rear wheels
- Driveshaft
- Brake calipers and pads or brake drum

➡**The brake calipers and pads or brake drum must be removed so that there is no additional drag when measuring pinion bearing preload.**

4. Use an inch lb. torque wrench and measure and record the amount of torque required to maintain pinion rotation through several revolutions.

5. Remove or disconnect the following:

- Pinion flange
- Pinion seal
- Pinion bearing
- Collapsible spacer

To install:

➡**Use a new collapsible spacer and flange nut for assembly.**

6. Install or connect the following:

- Collapsible spacer
- Pinion bearing
- Pinion seal
- Pinion flange

7. Rotate the pinion flange occasionally while tightening the flange nut to make sure the pinion bearings seat correctly.

8. Take frequent bearing preload torque readings. Tighten the flange nut to achieve the preload torque readings originally recorded.

☀ CAUTION

Never loosen the pinion nut to reduce bearing preload. If it is necessary to reduce bearing preload, install a new collapsible spacer and pinion nut.

9. Install or connect the following:

- Driveshaft
- Brake calipers and pads or brake drum
- Wheels
- Negative battery cable

10. Fill the differential with gear lubricant and check for leaks.

ENGINE COOLING   COMPONENTS

ENGINE FAN

REMOVAL & INSTALLATION

2.3L Engine

1. Remove the air cleaner outlet pipe.
2. Remove the accessory drive belt.
3. Loosen the mechanical fan nut.
4. Remove the fan and clutch assembly.
5. To install, reverse the removal procedure. Tighten the bolt to 41 ft. lbs. (55 Nm).

3.0L and 4.0L Engines

1. Remove fan shroud.
2. Remove the bolts.
3. Separate the fan blade from the fan clutch.
4. To install, reverse the removal procedure. Tighten the fan bolts to 52 inch lbs. (7 Nm).

RADIATOR

REMOVAL & INSTALLATION

2.3L Engine

See Figure 44.

1. Drain the cooling system.
2. Disconnect the coolant overflow hose from the radiator, position the hose away from the radiator.
3. Disconnect the upper radiator hose.
4. Remove the cooling fan and shroud.
5. Disconnect the lower radiator hose.
6. Remove the bolts, tilt the radiator back and lift it directly upward.
7. Remove the three pushpins and the plastic cap from the top of the radiator channel.

To install:

8. Install the plastic cap and the three pushpins on the top of the radiator channel.

9. Position the radiator into the engine compartment and install the bolts.

10. Install the lower radiator hose to the radiator.

11. Install the cooling fan and shroud.

12. Install the upper radiator hose to the radiator.

13. Position the coolant overflow hose in the channel on top of the radiator, then connect the hose to the radiator.

14. Fill the cooling system.

15. Operate the engine for several minutes and check the hoses and connections for leaks.

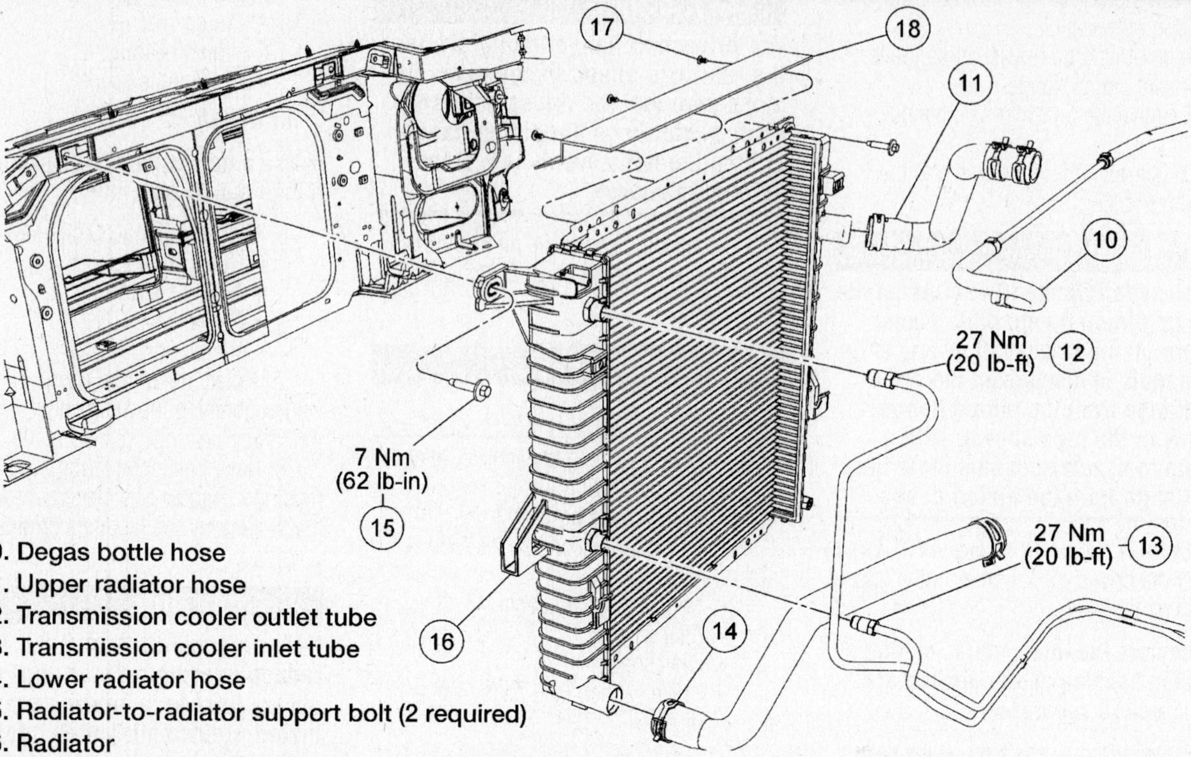

10. Degas bottle hose
11. Upper radiator hose
12. Transmission cooler outlet tube
13. Transmission cooler inlet tube
14. Lower radiator hose
15. Radiator-to-radiator support bolt (2 required)
16. Radiator
17. Pushpin (3 required)
18. Seal

22086_RANG_G0063

Fig. 44 View of the radiator—2.3L engine

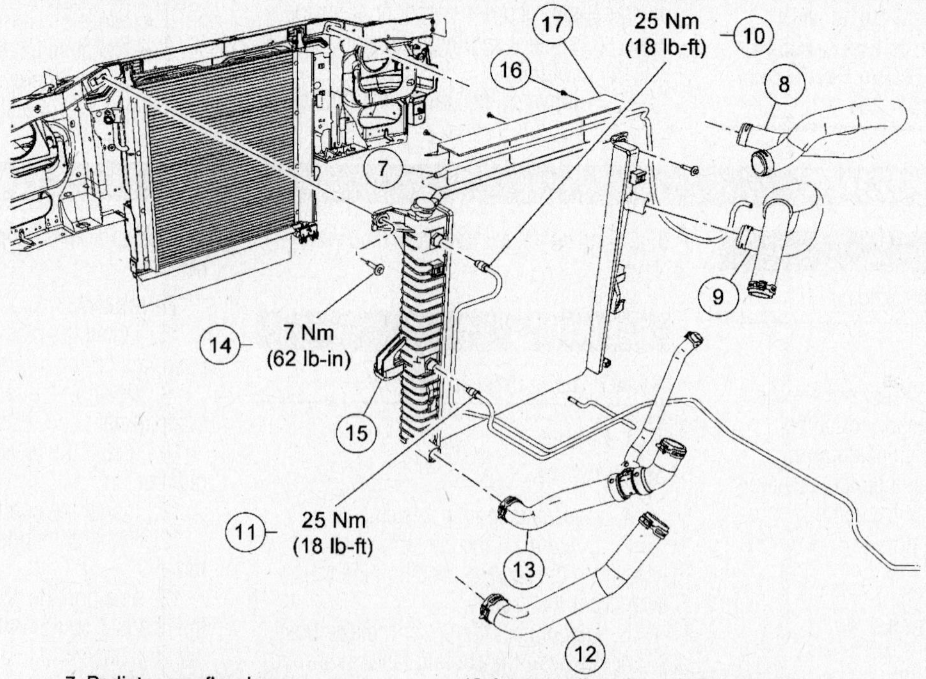

7. Radiator overflow hose
8. Upper radiator hose (4.0L engines)
9. Upper radiator hose (3.0L engines)
10. Transmission cooler outlet hose
11. Transmission cooler inlet hose
12. Lower radiator hose (4.0L engines)
13. Lower radiator hose (3.0L engines)
14. Radiator-to-radiator support bolts (2 required)
15. Radiator
16. Pushpin
17. Seal

22086_RANG_G0064

Fig. 45 Radiator view—3.0L and 4.0L engines

3.0L and 4.0L Engines

See Figure 45.

1. Drain the cooling system.
2. Remove the air cleaner outlet pipe.
3. Remove the two screws. Lift the fan shroud out of the lower retaining clips and drape it on the fan blade
4. Remove the rubber radiator overflow hose or radiator vent hose.
5. Remove the cooling fan shroud.
6. On all models, remove the upper and lower radiator hoses.
7. Disconnect the two transmission cooling lines, if equipped.
8. Remove the screws and tilt the radiator back and lift it directly upward.

To install:

9. Position the radiator into the engine compartment and install the bolts.
10. Connect the two transmission cooling lines to the radiator oil cooler fittings if equipped.
11. Reinstall the constant tension clamps in the same position from where they were removed.
12. Install the upper and lower radiator hoses.
13. Install the cooling fan shroud.
14. Install the fan shroud and the two screws.
15. Connect the electro-drive fan wiring connector, if equipped.
16. Install the air cleaner outlet pipe.
17. Refill the engine with coolant.
18. Start the vehicle and check for leaks.

THERMOSTAT

REMOVAL & INSTALLATION

2.3L Engine

1. Drain the cooling system.
2. Disconnect the radiator hose and the electrical connector.
3. Disconnect the radiator lower hose.
4. Remove the bolts and the thermostat housing.
5. To install, reverse the removal procedure. Tighten the housing bolts to 89 inch lbs. (10 Nm).

3.0L and 4.0L Engines

1. Drain the cooling system.
2. Remove the upper radiator hose from the water outlet connection.
3. On 4.0L engines, remove the air cleaner outlet tube.
4. Remove the generator wiring harness bracket nut and position the wiring harness aside.

5. On all engines, remove the bolts, the water outlet connection and the water thermostat.
6. Discard the gasket and clean the sealing surfaces.
7. To install, reverse the removal procedure. Tighten the bolts to 89 inch lbs. (10 Nm).
8. Start the engine and check for coolant leaks.

WATER PUMP

REMOVAL & INSTALLATION

2.3L Engine

See Figure 46.

1. Before servicing the vehicle, refer to the precautions in the beginning of this section.
2. Drain the cooling system.
3. Remove the drive belt.
4. Remove the water pump pulley.
5. Remove the water pump.

➡**Lubricate the water pump O-ring, with MERPOL®.**

6. To install, reverse the removal procedure. Torque the water pump mount bolts to 89 inch lbs. (10 Nm). Torque the pulley bolts to 18 ft. lbs. (25 Nm).

3.0L Engine

See Figure 47.

1. Before servicing the vehicle, refer to the precautions in the beginning of this section.

2. Drain the cooling system.
3. Remove or disconnect the following:
- Negative battery cable
- Air cleaner outlet tube
- Fan and radiator shroud
- Water bypass tube
- Drive belt
- Heater hose
- Water pump pulley
- Lower radiator hose
- Air conditioning compressor and bracket assembly and move them aside
- Water pump

To install:

4. Clean the mating surfaces where the water pump attaches to the engine.
5. Install or connect the following:
- Water pump. Torque the bolts to 106 in lbs. (12 Nm).
- Air conditioning compressor mounting bracket. Torque the bolts to 44 ft. lbs. (61 Nm).
- Water pump pulley. Torque the bolts to 20 ft. lbs. (28 Nm).
- Drive belt
- Heater hose
- Lower radiator hose
- Fan and shroud
- Air cleaner outlet tube
- Negative battery cable
6. Fill the cooling system.
7. Start the vehicle and check for leaks, repair if necessary.

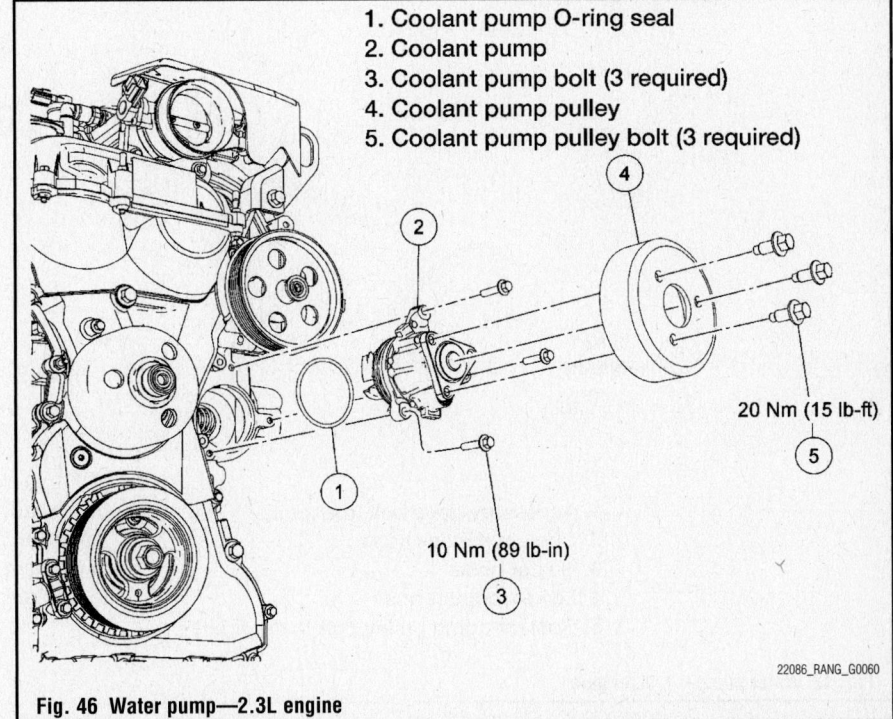

1. Coolant pump O-ring seal
2. Coolant pump
3. Coolant pump bolt (3 required)
4. Coolant pump pulley
5. Coolant pump pulley bolt (3 required)

20 Nm (15 lb-ft)

10 Nm (89 lb-in)

Fig. 46 Water pump—2.3L engine

22086_RANG_G0060

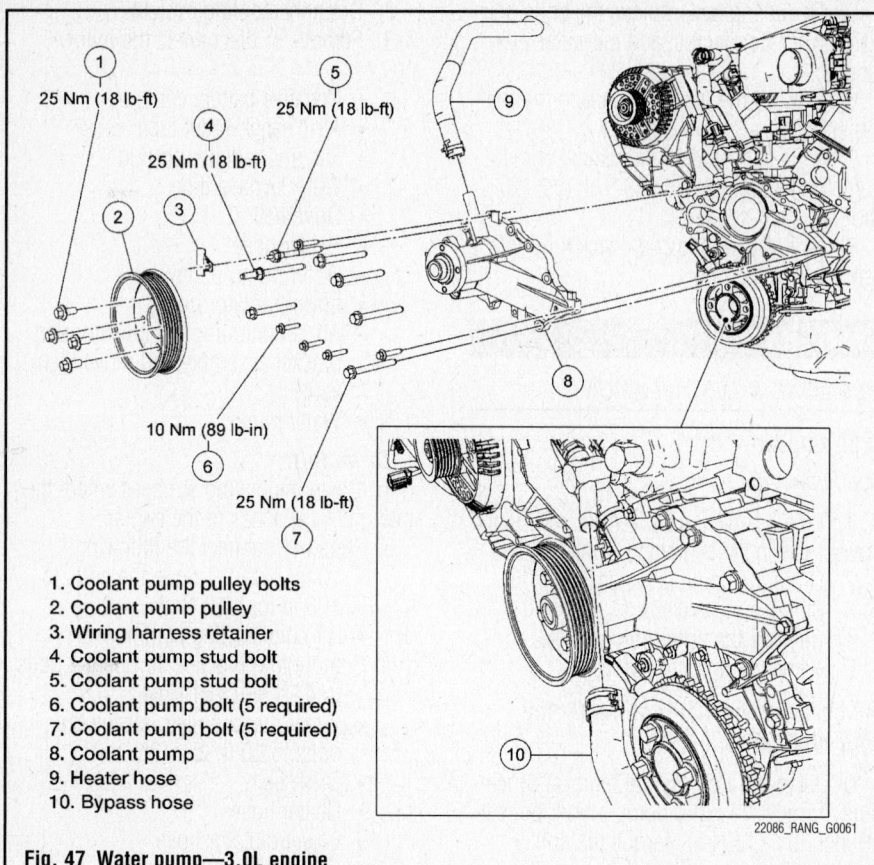

1. Coolant pump pulley bolts
2. Coolant pump pulley
3. Wiring harness retainer
4. Coolant pump stud bolt
5. Coolant pump stud bolt
6. Coolant pump bolt (5 required)
7. Coolant pump bolt (5 required)
8. Coolant pump
9. Heater hose
10. Bypass hose

25 Nm (18 lb-ft)
25 Nm (18 lb-ft)
25 Nm (18 lb-ft)
10 Nm (89 lb-in)
25 Nm (18 lb-ft)

22086_RANG_G0061

Fig. 47 Water pump—3.0L engine

4.0L Engine

See Figure 48.

1. Before servicing the vehicle, refer to the precautions in the beginning of this section.

2. Drain the cooling system.

3. Remove or disconnect the following:

- Fan shroud
- Accessory drive belt
- Idler pulley
- Water bypass hose
- Heater hose
- Lower radiator hose
- Water pump pulley
- Water pump

> ❄❄ **WARNING**
>
> **Use care when scraping the water pump-to-engine block mating surfaces. Gouges in the aluminum could form leak paths.**

4. Clean all the sealing surfaces.

5. To install, reverse the removal procedure. Torque the water pump bolts to 89 inch lbs. (10 Nm). Torque the pulley bolts to 18 ft. lbs. (25 Nm).

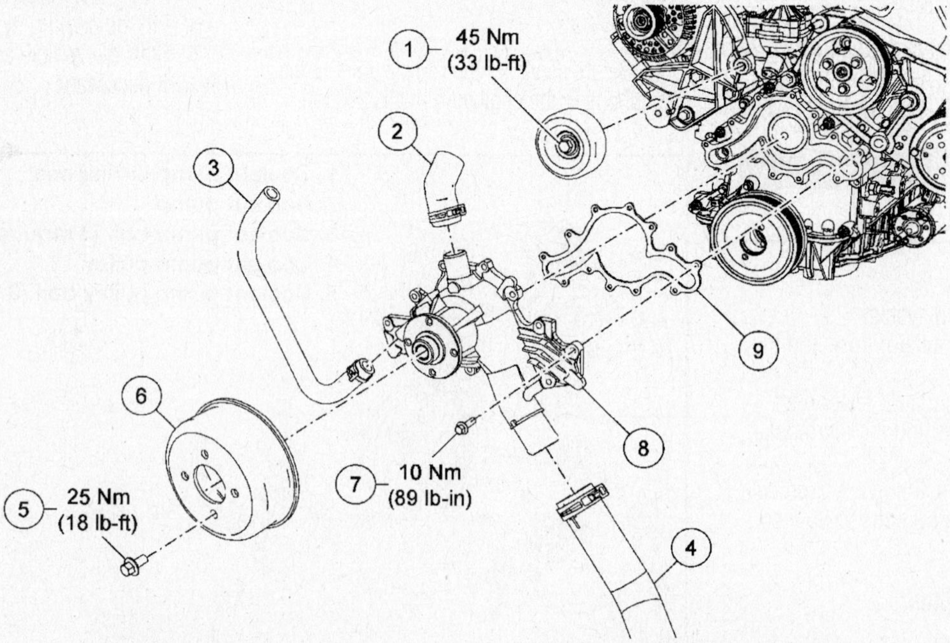

45 Nm (33 lb-ft)

10 Nm (89 lb-in)

25 Nm (18 lb-ft)

1. Accessory drive belt idler pulley
2. Coolant bypass hose
3. Heater hose
4. Lower radiator hose
5. Coolant pump pulley bolt (4 required)
6. Coolant pump pulley
7. Coolant pump bolts (12 required)
8. Coolant pump
9. Coolant pump gasket

22086_RANG_G0062

Fig. 48 Water pump—4.0L engine

ENGINE ELECTRICAL

CHARGING SYSTEM

ALTERNATOR

REMOVAL & INSTALLATION

2.3L Engine

See Figures 49 and 50.

1. Before servicing the vehicle, refer to the Precautions Section.
2. Remove or disconnect the following:
   - Battery ground cable
   - Air cleaner outlet tube
   - Accessory drive belt
   - Mounting bolts and alternator
   - Nut and the electrical connectors.
3. To install, reverse the removal procedure. Torque all mounting bolts to 18 ft. lbs. (25 Nm).

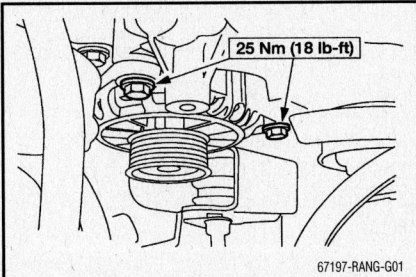

Fig. 49 Alternator mounting bolts—2.3L engine

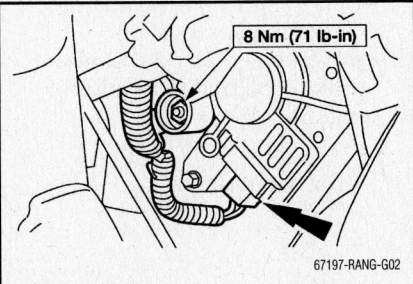

Fig. 50 Alternator wiring connections—2.3L engine

3.0L Engine

See Figures 51 through 53.

1. Before servicing the vehicle, refer to the Precautions Section.
2. Remove or disconnect the following:
   - Negative battery cable
   - Air cleaner outlet tube
   - Drive belt
   - Electrical connectors from the alternator
   - Wiring harness to alternator push pin
   - Alternator

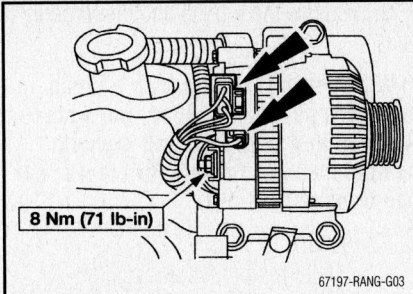

Fig. 51 Alternator wiring connections—3.0L engine

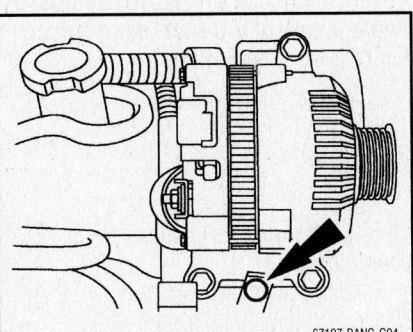

Fig. 52 Wiring harness pin-type retainer—3.0L engine

To install:

3. Install or connect the following:
   - Alternator. Torque the bolts to 35 ft. lbs (48 Nm).
   - Pushpin for the alternator wiring harness
   - Electrical connectors to the alternator
   - Drive belt
   - Air cleaner outlet tube
   - Negative battery cable

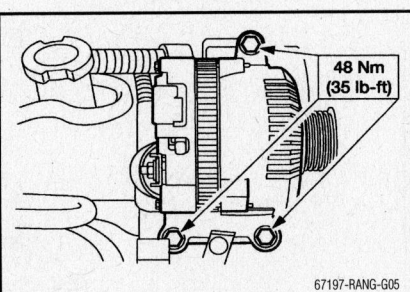

Fig. 53 Alternator mounting bolts—3.0L engine

4.0L Engine

See Figures 54 through 56.

1. Before servicing the vehicle, refer to the Precautions Section.

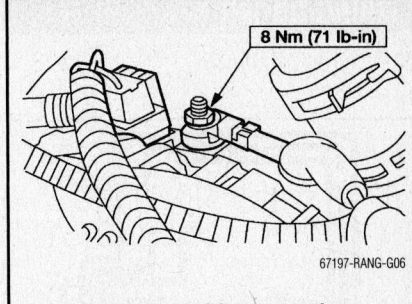

Fig. 54 Alternator wiring connections—4.0L engine

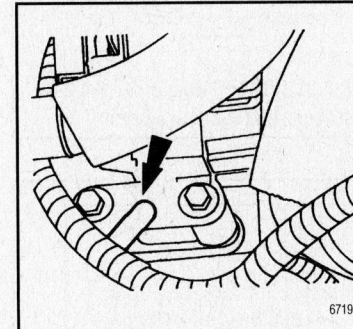

Fig. 55 Alternator wiring pin-type retainer—4.0L engine

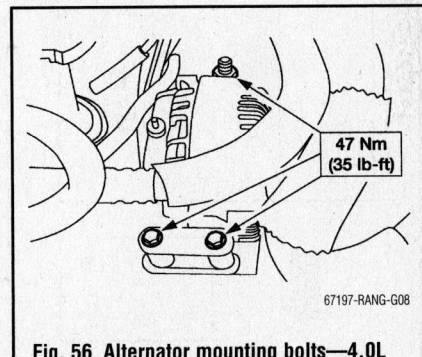

Fig. 56 Alternator mounting bolts—4.0L engine

2. Remove or disconnect the following:
   - Negative battery cable
   - Air cleaner outlet tube
   - Accessory drive belt
   - Electrical connectors
   - Wiring harness-to-generator pin-type retainer
   - Stud bolt, the bolts and the alternator
3. To install, reverse the removal procedure. Torque all mounting bolts to 35 ft. lbs. (47 Nm).

FIRING ORDER

See Figures 57 and 58.

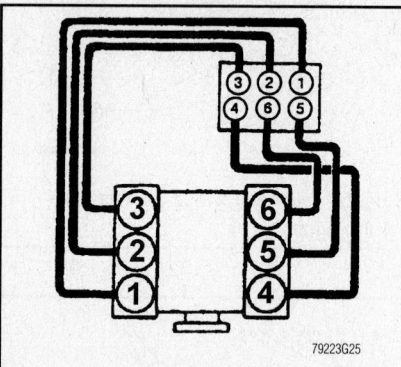

Fig. 57 3.0L (VIN U) Firing order 1-4-2-5-3-6 Distributorless ignition system

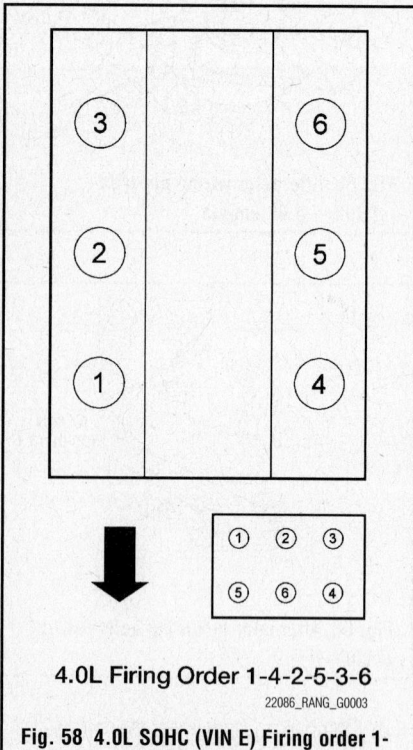

4.0L Firing Order 1-4-2-5-3-6

22086_RANG_G0003

Fig. 58 4.0L SOHC (VIN E) Firing order 1-4-2-5-3-6 Distributorless ignition system

IGNITION COIL

REMOVAL & INSTALLATION

2.3L Engine

See Figure 59.

1. Remove the spark plug wires by slightly twisting while pulling upwards.
2. Disconnect the ignition coil electrical connector.

3. Remove the 4 bolts and the ignition coil.

➡ Wipe the coil towers with a clean cloth dampened with soap and water. Remove any soap film and dry with compressed air. Inspect for cracks, carbon tracking and dirt.

To install:

4. Install ignition coil and tighten mounting bolts to 53 inch. lbs. (6 Nm).
5. Reconnect ignition coil electrical connector.

➡ Apply silicone dielectric compound to the inside of the spark plug wire boots prior to installation.

6. Install spark plug wires.

3.0L Engine

See Figure 60.

1. Disconnect the ignition coil electrical connector.
2. Disconnect the spark plug wires by twisting while pulling upward.
3. Disconnect the heater hose support from the stud.

4. Remove the 2 bolts, the stud bolt and the ignition coil.

To install:

5. Install ignition coil and tighten mounting bolts to 53 inch. lbs. (6 Nm).
6. Use a small, clean tool to coat the entire interior surface of the boot with silicone brake caliper grease.
7. Reconnect ignition coil electrical connector.
8. Install spark plug wires.

4.0L Engine

1. Disconnect the battery ground cable.
2. Disconnect the ignition coil electrical connector.
3. Squeeze the locking tabs and twist while pulling upward, to disconnect the 6 spark plug wires from the ignition coil.
4. Remove the 4 bolts and the ignition coil.

To install:

5. Install ignition coil and tighten mounting bolts to 53 inch. lbs. (6 Nm).
6. Reconnect ignition coil electrical connector.

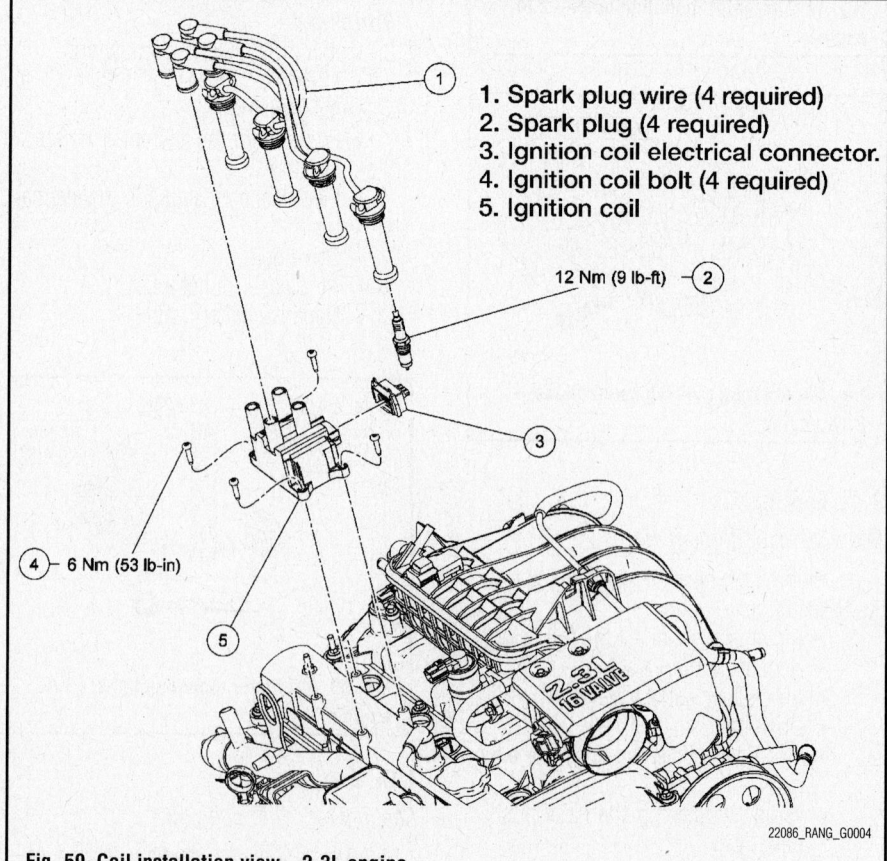

1. Spark plug wire (4 required)
2. Spark plug (4 required)
3. Ignition coil electrical connector.
4. Ignition coil bolt (4 required)
5. Ignition coil

12 Nm (9 lb-ft) – 2

4 – 6 Nm (53 lb-in)

22086_RANG_G0004

Fig. 59 Coil installation view—2.3L engine

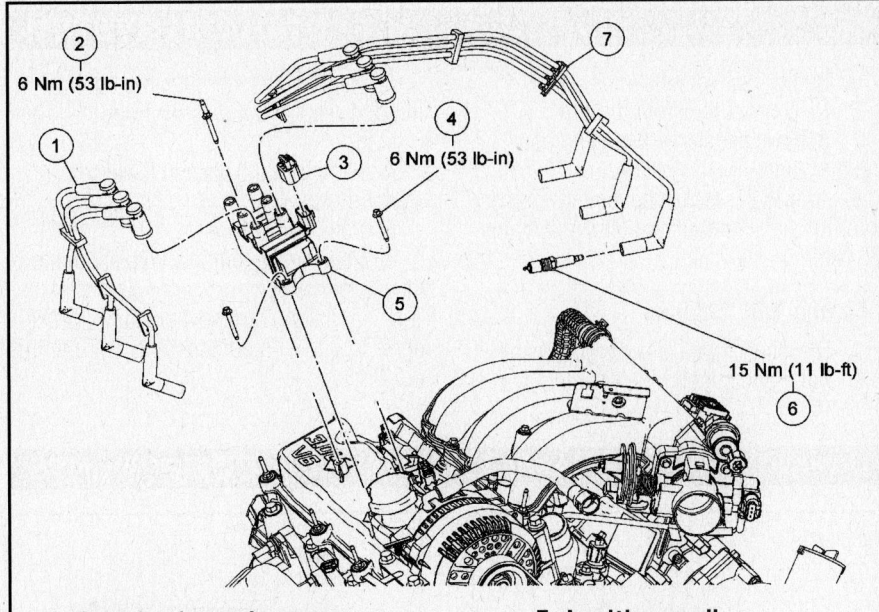

1. Spark plug wire set
2. Ignition coil stud bolt
3. Ignition coil electrical connector
4. Ignition coil bolt
   (3 required)
5. Ignition coil
6. Spark plug
   (6 required)
7. Spark plug wire retainer
   (7 required)

6 Nm (53 lb-in)
6 Nm (53 lb-in)
15 Nm (11 lb-ft)

22086_RANG_G0005

Fig. 60 Coil installation view—3.0L engine

7. Apply silicone dielectric compound to the inside of the spark plug wire coil boots.

8. Install spark plug wires.

➡**Be sure to reinstall the radio ignition interference capacitor under the correct ignition coil mounting bolt**

IGNITION TIMING

INSPECTION

1. Place the vehicle in **P** or **N** with the parking brake applied and the drive wheels blocked.

2. Start the engine and allow it reach normal operating temperature. Make sure all accessories are off.

3. Connect a suitable tachometer and timing light to the engine, as per the manufacturer's instructions.

4. Check that the idle speed is within the specified rpm range.

5. Disconnect the SPOUT (spark output) connector to set the engine to base timing, so the PCM cannot adjust timing electronically.

6. Following the manufacturer's instructions, aim the timing light and check the ignition timing. As the light flashes, note the position of the mark on the crankshaft pulley against the scale on the timing cover. Timing should be 10 degrees BTDC.

7. If ignition timing is not within specification, there is a fault in the engine control system. Diagnose and repair the problem as necessary.

8. Plug the SPOUT connector in.

9. Stop the engine and remove the tachometer and timing light.

ADJUSTMENT

The ignition timing is controlled by the Powertrain Control Module (PCM). No adjustment is necessary or possible.

SPARK PLUGS

REMOVAL & INSTALLATION

2.3L and 3.0L Engines

1. Use a Spark Plug Wire Remover to grasp and twist the spark plug wire boot back and forth on the spark plug insulator to release the connectors.

✳✳ WARNING

Do not pull on the spark plug wire as it may separate from the spark plug wire connector inside the spark plug wire boot.

2. Remove any foreign material from the spark plug areas of the cylinder head with compressed air.

3. Remove the spark plugs.

To install:

4. Inspect the spark plugs.

5. Adjust the spark plug gap as necessary.

6. Install and tighten spark plugs to 9 ft. lbs. (12 Nm) for 2.3L engine and 11 ft. lbs. (15 Nm) for 3.0L engine.

7. Apply silicone dielectric compound to the inside of the spark plug wire boots prior to installation.

8. Install Spark plug wires.

4.0L Engine

1. With the vehicle in NEUTRAL, position it on a hoist.

2. Remove the right front tire and wheel.

3. Remove the right front fenderwell splash shield

✳✳ WARNING

It is important to twist the spark plug wire boots while pulling upward, to avoid possible damage to the spark plug wires.

4. Remove the spark plug wires from the right side of the engine.

5. Use compressed air to remove any foreign material in the spark plug wells before removing the spark plugs.

6. Remove the RH spark plugs.

7. Remove LH spark plugs.

8. Inspect the spark plugs.

To install:

9. Use a suitable spark plug gap tool to check and adjust the spark plug gap.

10. Install and tighten spark plugs to 13 ft. lbs. (17 Nm).

11. Apply silicone dielectric compound to the inside of the spark plug wire boots prior to installation.

12. Install the spark plug wires.

ENGINE ELECTRICAL

STARTER

REMOVAL & INSTALLATION

2.3L Engine

1. Disconnect the battery ground cable.
2. Raise and support the vehicle.
3. Remove the left front inner fender splash shield.
4. Remove the protective cap from the terminals.

5. Remove the terminal nuts
6. Disconnect the ground cable.
7. Remove the starter mounting bolts and the starter.
8. To install, reverse the removal procedure. Torque all mounting bolts to 18 ft. lbs. (25 Nm).

3.0L and 4.0L Engines

1. Disconnect the battery ground cable.
2. Raise and support the vehicle.

STARTING SYSTEM

3. Remove the starter cable retainer nut and release the retainer from the stud.
4. Remove the bolts and lower the starter motor.
5. Remove the cap.
6. Remove the terminal nuts and remove the starter motor.
7. To install, reverse the removal procedure. Torque all mounting bolts to 18 ft. lbs. (25 Nm).

ENGINE MECHANICAL

➡**Disconnecting the negative battery cable may interfere with the functions of the on board computer systems and may require the computer to undergo a relearning process, once the negative battery cable is reconnected.**

ACCESSORY DRIVE BELTS

ACCESSORY BELT ROUTING

See Figures 61 through 66.

INSPECTION

Inspect the drive belt for signs of glazing or cracking. A glazed belt will be perfectly smooth from slippage, while a good belt will have a slight texture of fabric visible. Cracks will usually start at the inner edge of the belt and run outward. All worn or damaged drive belts should be replaced immediately.

COMPONENTS

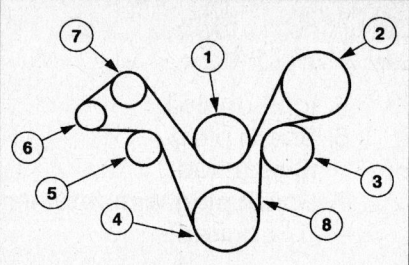

1 Fan pulley
2 Power steering pump pulley
3 Water pump pulley
4 Crankshaft pulley
5 Belt tensioner pulley
6 Generator pulley
7 Belt idler pulley
8 Drive belt

67197-RANG-G98

Fig. 62 Accessory drive belt routing—2.3L engine without A/C

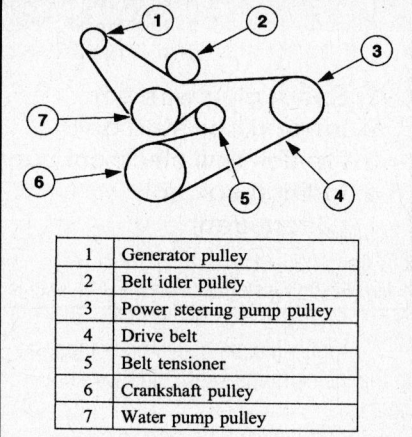

1	Generator pulley
2	Belt idler pulley
3	Power steering pump pulley
4	Drive belt
5	Belt tensioner
6	Crankshaft pulley
7	Water pump pulley

67197-RANG-G00

Fig. 64 Accessory drive belt routing—3.0L without A/C

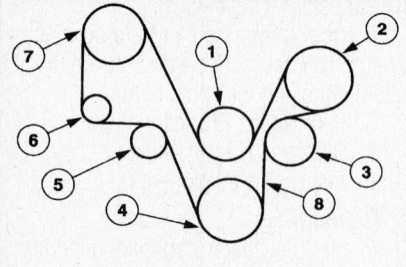

1 Fan pulley
2 Power steering pump pulley
3 Water pump pulley
4 Crankshaft pulley
5 Belt tensioner pulley
6 Generator pulley
7 A/C clutch pulley
8 Drive belt

67197-RANG-G97

Fig. 61 Accessory drive belt routing—2.3L engine with A/C

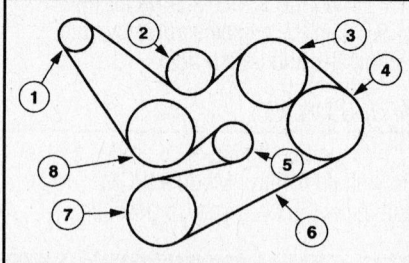

1 Generator pulley
2 Belt idler pulley
3 A/C clutch pulley
4 Power steering pump pulley
5 Belt tensioner
6 Drive belt
7 Crankshaft pulley
8 Water pump pulley

67197-RANG-G99

Fig. 63 Accessory drive belt routing—3.0L with A/C

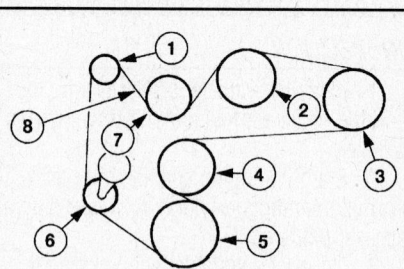

1	Generator pulley
2	Power steering pump pulley
3	A/C clutch pulley
4	Water pump pulley
5	Crankshaft pulley
6	Drive belt tensioner
7	Belt idler pulley
8	Drive belt

67197-RANG-G1A

Fig. 65 Accessory drive belt routing—4.0L with A/C

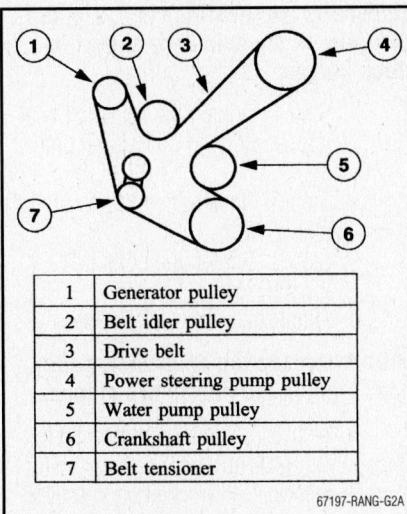

1	Generator pulley
2	Belt idler pulley
3	Drive belt
4	Power steering pump pulley
5	Water pump pulley
6	Crankshaft pulley
7	Belt tensioner

67197-RANG-G2A

Fig. 66 Accessory drive belt routing—4.0L without A/C

REMOVAL & INSTALLATION

On 2.3L and 3.0L engines, rotate the tensioner bolt clockwise and remove the belt. On 4.0L engines, rotate the tensioner bolt counterclockwise and remove the belt.

CAMSHAFT AND VALVE LIFTERS

➡**Although Ford suggests that this component is removable while the engine is installed in the vehicle, depending on the particular options with which your truck is equipped, working clearance may be extremely tight and this procedure may be much easier to perform with the engine removed. Before commencing, read through this procedure and make certain enough clearance, or working room, exists with the engine in the vehicle; if there is not enough space, the engine should be removed.**

INSPECTION

Camshaft Lobe Lift

Camshaft lobe lift is the amount (measured in inches or millimeters) that the camshaft is capable of LIFTING the valve train components in order to open the valves. The lobe lift is a measure of how much taller the "egg shaped" portion of the camshaft lobe is above the base or circular portion of the shaft lobe. Lift is directly proportional to how far the valves can open and a worn camshaft (with poor lobe lift) cannot fully open the valves. The lobe lift therefore can be directly responsible for proper or poor engine performance.

Lobe lift can be measured in 2 ways, depending on what tools are available and whether or not the camshaft has been removed from the engine. A dial gauge can be used to measure the lift with the camshaft installed, while a micrometer is normally only used once the shaft has been removed from the engine.

Dial Gauge Method

Lobe lift may be checked with the camshaft installed. In all cases, a dial gauge is positioned somewhere on the valve train (pushrod, lifter, or camshaft itself) and the camshaft is then turned to measure the lift.

Check the lift of each lobe in consecutive order and make a note of the reading.

1. Remove the valve cover for access to the camshaft.

2. Install a dial indicator so that the actuating point of the indicator is directly placed on the camshaft.

➡**A remote starter can be used to turn the engine over during the next steps. If a remote starter is not available, remove the spark plugs in order to relieve engine compression, and turn the engine over using a large wrench or socket on the crankshaft damper bolt. BE SURE to only turn the engine in the normal direction of rotation.**

3. Turn the crankshaft over until the tappet is on the base circle of the camshaft lobe.

4. Zero the dial indicator. Continue to rotate the crankshaft slowly until the pushrod (or camshaft lobe) is in the fully raised position.

5. Compare the total lift recorded on the dial indicator with the elevation specification.

To check the accuracy of the original indicator reading, continue to rotate the crankshaft until the indicator reads zero. If the lift on any lobe is below specified wear limits listed, the camshaft and the valve tappets must be replaced.

6. Install the valve cover(s).

Micrometer

See Figure 67.

A micrometer may used to measure camshaft lobe lift, but this is usually only after it has been removed from the engine. Once the valve cover is removed from the, access may be possible (though a little awkward) to measure the camshaft lobes using a micrometer.

In any case, two measurements are necessary for each lobe. Measurement **Y** or the total LOBE HEIGHT and measurement **X** or

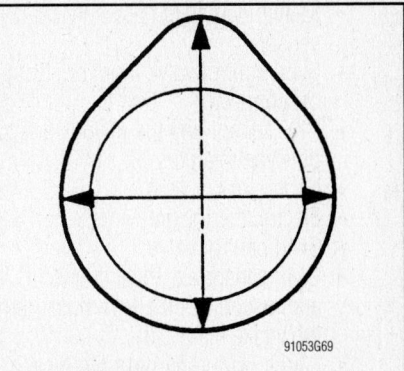

91053G69

Fig. 67 Camshaft lobe lift is measured in two places

the total LOBE WIDTH. To find the lobe lift, you simply subtract **X** from **Y** (subtract the width from the height).

Note each measurement, then make your calculation to determine the lift. Note the final results and repeat the process on the remaining camshaft lobes. Finally, you should compare your results to the specifications and decide if a new camshaft is in your future.

REMOVAL & INSTALLATION

2.3L Engine

See Figures 68 and 69

1. Before servicing the vehicle, refer to the precautions in the beginning of this section.

2. Relieve the fuel system pressure.

3. Drain the cooling system.

4. Properly discharge the air conditioning system.

5. Remove or disconnect the following:
   - Negative battery cable
   - Drive belt.
   - Engine oil level indicator assembly.
   - Engine oil level indicator.
   - Engine oil level indicator tube.
   - Water outlet tube.
   - Water outlet tube.
   - Air conditioning compressor.

➡**The generator will be removed with the accessory bracket.**

   - Accessory bracket.
   - Right motor mount.
   - Coolant hose from the thermostat.
   - Coolant hose from the EGR valve.
   - Coolant tube assembly.
   - Exhaust manifold and gasket.
   - Block heater (if so equipped).
   - Water outlet.
   - EGR valve.
   - Power steering pump and reservoir as an assembly.
   - Idle air control (IAC) valve.
   - Throttle position (TP) sensor.

- Manifold absolute pressure (MAP) sensor.
- Swirl control valve monitor electrical connector.
- CKP sensor and the wiring harness pin-type retainers.
- Knock sensor (KS).
- Electric thermostat.
- Swirl control valve.
- CMP sensor electrical connector and disconnect the PCV hose from the intake manifold.
- Engine wiring harness pin-type retainers from the intake manifold.
- Engine wiring harness connector bracket. Position the engine wiring harness aside.
- EGR tube.
- Fuel supply line clip from the front of the intake manifold. Disconnect the vacuum hose from the intake manifold.
- Intake manifold assembly.
- Fuel injector electrical connectors. Detach the wiring harness pin-type retainers.
- Ignition coil and the cylinder head temperature (CHT) sensor electrical connectors.
- Engine wiring harness anchors from the valve cover studs. Remove the engine wiring harness.
- Ignition coil.
- Bypass hose.
- Thermostat housing.
- Knock sensor and the engine vent cover.
- Left motor mount.
- Fuel injector supply manifold with the injectors and the ground strap.
- Water pump pulley.
- Water pump.
- CMP sensor.
- CHT sensor.
- Spark plugs.
- Valve cover.
- CKP sensor.
- Crankshaft vibration damper

➡**There is one front cover bolt behind the cooling fan drive pulley. To remove this bolt, align one of the cooling fan drive pulley access holes with the bolt head to access the bolt.**

- Front cover.
- Timing chain tensioner.
- Timing chain guides.
- Timing chain assembly.

➡**Use a wrench on the flats between cylinders No. 1 and No. 2 to hold the camshaft in place.**

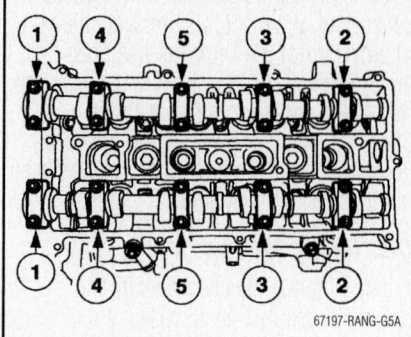

Fig. 68 Camshaft cap loosening sequence—2.3L engine

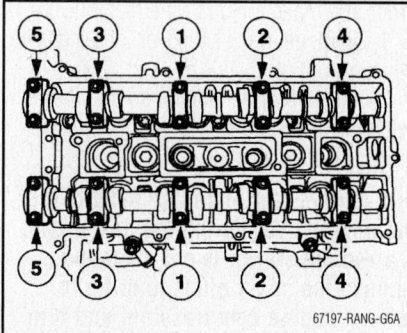

Fig. 69 Camshaft cap torque sequence— 2.3L engine

- Camshaft drive sprockets.
- Oil pump chain tensioner and guide.

➡**The oil pump chain sprocket must be held in place.**

- Oil pump chain and sprockets.

➡**Note the position of the lobes on the No. 1 cylinder before removing the camshafts for assembly reference.**

6. Loosen the camshaft bearing cap bolts in sequence, one turn at a time. Repeat the first step until all tension is released from the camshaft bearing caps. Remove the camshaft bearing caps.

7. Remove the camshafts.

8. Installation is the reverse of removal.

➡**Install the camshafts with the alignment notches in the camshaft lined up so the camshaft alignment plate can be installed without rotating the camshafts. Make sure the lobes on the No. 1 cylinder are in the same position as noted in the disassembly procedure. Rotating the camshafts, or installing the camshafts 180 degrees out of position can cause severe damage to the valves and pistons. Lubricate the camshaft journals and bearing caps with clean engine oil. Install the**

camshafts and bearing caps. Tighten the bolts in the sequence shown in three stages.

- Step 1: Tighten the camshaft bearing caps one turn at a time until tight.
- Step 2: Tighten the bolts to 62 inch lbs. (7 Nm)
- Step 3: Tighten the bolts to 12 ft. lbs. (16 Nm)

c. Crankshaft vibration damper:

➡**Do not reuse the crankshaft pulley bolt. Tighten the bolt in two stages.**

- Step 1: Tighten the bolt to 30 ft. lbs. (40 Nm)
- Step 2: Tighten the bolt and additional 90 degrees (1/4 turn).

3.0L Engine

1. Before servicing the vehicle, refer to the precautions in the beginning of this section.

2. Properly relieve the fuel system pressure.

3. Drain the cooling system.

4. Drain the engine oil.

5. Evacuate the air conditioning system.

6. Remove or disconnect the following:

- Negative battery cable
- Air cleaner hoses
- Fan, spacer and shroud
- Radiator

7. Rotate the crankshaft so that No. 1 piston is at Top Dead Center (TDC) on the compression stroke.

- Air conditioning condenser
- Fuel lines from the fuel supply manifold
- Vacuum hoses
- Electrical wiring
- Engine front cover
- Water pump
- Alternator
- Power steering pump. Do not disconnect the hoses
- Air conditioning compressor. Do not disconnect the hoses
- Throttle body
- Fuel injection wire harness

8. Turn the engine by hand to TDC of the power stroke on No. 1 cylinder.

- Spark plug wires from the plugs
- Distributor cap with the spark plug wires as an assembly, if equipped

9. Matchmark the rotor, distributor body and engine. Disconnect the distributor wiring harness and remove the distributor, if equipped.

- Rocker arm covers
- Intake manifold

- Loosen the rocker arm bolts enough to pivot the rocker arms out of the way and remove the pushrods. Identify them for installation
- Lifters and identify them for installation
- Crankshaft pulley/damper
- Starter
- Oil pan
- Camshaft gear attaching bolt and washer, then slide the gear off the camshaft
- Camshaft thrust plate

10. Carefully slide the camshaft out of the engine block, using caution to avoid any damage to the camshaft bearings.

To install:

11. Oil the camshaft journals and cam lobes with heavy SJ engine oil (50W). Install the spacer ring with the chamfered side toward the camshaft, then insert the camshaft key.

12. Install or connect the following:
- Camshaft using caution to avoid any damage to the camshaft bearings
- Thrust plate. Torque the screws to 84 inch lbs. (10 Nm).

13. Rotate the camshaft and crankshaft as necessary to align the timing marks. Install the camshaft gear and chain. Torque the bolt to 46 ft. lbs. (62 Nm).

14. Coat the tappets with 50W engine oil and place them in their original locations.

15. Apply 50W engine oil to both ends of the pushrods. Install the pushrods in their original locations.

16. Pivot the rocker arms into position. Torque the fulcrum bolts to 96 inch lbs. (11 Nm).

17. Rotate the engine until both timing marks are at the top of their sprockets and aligned. Torque the following fulcrum bolts to 18 ft. lbs. (24 Nm):
- a. No.1 intake.
- b. No.2 exhaust.
- c. No.4 intake.
- d. No.5 exhaust.

18. Rotate the engine until the camshaft timing mark is at the bottom of the sprocket and the crankshaft timing mark is at the top of the sprocket, and both are aligned. Torque the following fulcrum bolts to 18 ft. lbs. (24 Nm):
- a. No.1 exhaust.
- b. No.2 intake.
- c. No.3 intake and exhaust.
- d. No.4 exhaust.
- e. No.5 intake.
- f. No.6 intake and exhaust.

19. Torque all the bolts to 24 ft. lbs. (33 Nm).

20. Turn the engine by hand to 0 degrees Before Top Dead center (BTDC) of the power stroke on No. 1 cylinder.

21. Install or connect the following:
- Engine front cover and water pump assembly
- Oil pan
- Crankshaft damper/pulley and tighten the retaining bolt to 107 ft. lbs. (145 Nm).
- Intake manifold
- Starter
- Crankshaft pulley and damper
- Rocker arm covers
- Rotor and distributor cap, if equipped
- Spark plug wires
- Fuel lines to the fuel supply manifold
- Fuel injection wire harness
- Throttle body
- Air conditioning compressor
- Power steering pump
- Alternator
- Water pump
- Engine front cover
- All electrical connectors and vacuum lines
- Air conditioning condenser
- Radiator
- Fan, spacer and shroud
- Air cleaner hoses
- Negative battery cable

22. Recharge the air conditioning system.

23. Refill the cooling system.

24. Replace the oil filter and refill the engine with the specified amount of engine oil.

25. Start the engine and check the ignition timing and idle speed. Adjust if necessary. Run the engine at fast idle and check for coolant, fuel, vacuum or oil leaks.

4.0L Engine

See Figures 70 and 71.

1. Before servicing the vehicle, refer to the precautions in the beginning of this section.

2. Remove or disconnect the following:
- Negative battery cable for safety
- Valve cover
- Hydraulic camshaft tensioner

➡**The right-hand camshaft sprocket bolt uses left-hand threads.**

3. For the right-hand camshaft use the Cam Gear Torque Adapter tool T97T-6256-F, to remove the camshaft sprocket bolt.

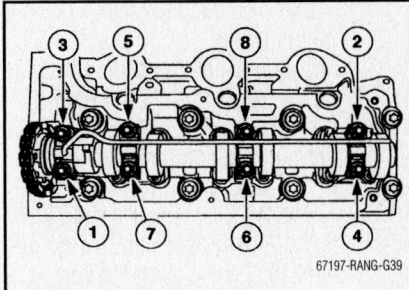

Fig. 70 Camshaft bolt removal sequence—4.0L engine

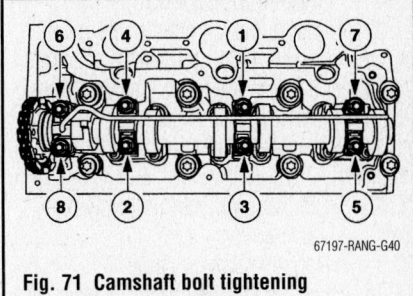

Fig. 71 Camshaft bolt tightening sequence—4.0L engine

4. For the left-hand camshaft, remove the sprocket bolt.

➡**When removing the followers, label them so that they may be returned to their original positions.**

5. Using the Valve Spring Compressor tool ST1330-A, remove the camshaft roller followers.

6. Remove or disconnect the following:
- Camshaft bearing cap bolts and the oil rail
- Camshaft

To install:

7. Lubricate all of the moving parts with SAE 50W engine oil.

8. Install camshaft onto the cylinder head.

9. Position the oil rail and install the bearing caps and bolts. Torque the bolts in 2 steps:
- a. Step 1—53.5 inch lbs. (6 Nm).
- b. Step 2—11–12.5 ft. lbs. (15–17 Nm).

10. Install or connect the following:
- Camshaft followers
- Camshaft sprocket bolt and hand tighten the bolt
- Camshaft Chain Tensioner T97T-6K254-A in the hole that the hydraulic chain tensioner was in

11. Turn the crankshaft one revolution clockwise until No. 1 piston is Top Dead Center (TDC).

12. Install or connect the following:
- Crankshaft Holding tool T97T-

6303-A on the crankshaft to keep it from turning
- Position the timing slot on the rear of the camshaft to fit Camshaft Holding tool T97T-6256-C and install the holding tool on the rear of the head
- Camshaft Gear Holding tool T97T-6256-B and Camshaft Gear Holding tool T97T-6256-A on the front of the cylinder head to securely hold the camshaft gear
- Tighten the camshaft sprocket bolt to 63 ft. lbs. (85 Nm).

13. Remove the Camshaft Chain Tensioner tool and install the hydraulic chain tensioner, tighten the tensioner to 35–39 ft. lbs. (47–53 Nm).
14. Remove the special tools from the engine.
15. Install or connect the following:
- Valve cover
- Negative battery cable

16. Start the engine check for leaks and repair if necessary.

CRANKSHAFT FRONT SEAL

REMOVAL & INSTALLATION

2.3L Engine

See Figures 72 and 73.

1. Before servicing the vehicle, refer to the precautions in the beginning of this section.
2. Remove or disconnect the following:
- Negative battery cable
- Crankshaft pulley

✷✷ WARNING

Use care not to damage the engine front cover or the crankshaft when removing the seal.

- Crankshaft front oil seal by prying the seal out of the front cover

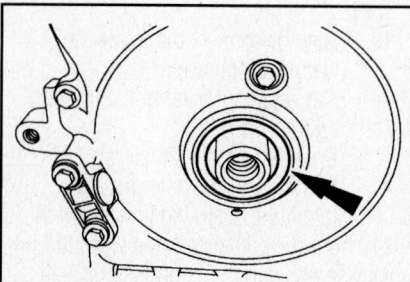

Fig. 72 Front crankshaft seal—2.3L engine

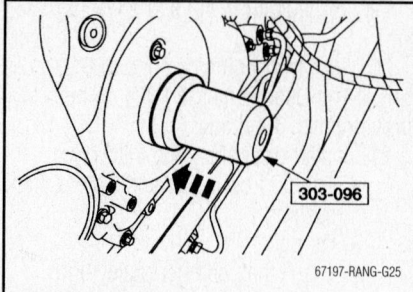

Fig. 73 Front crankshaft seal installation—2.3L engine

To install:

3. Using the special tool, install the crankshaft front oil seal.
4. Install the crankshaft pulley.
5. Tighten the crankshaft damper in two stages:
- Step 1: Tighten to 74 ft. lbs. (100 Nm)
- Step 2: Tighten an additional 90 degrees

3.0L Engine

See Figure 74.

1. Before servicing the vehicle, refer to the precautions in the beginning of this section.
2. Remove the crankshaft vibration damper.
3. Remove the crankshaft front seal.

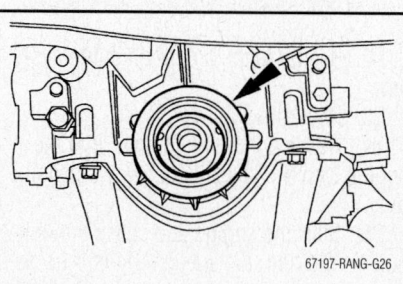

Fig. 74 Front crankshaft seal—3.0L engine

To install:

4. Install the crankshaft front seal.
    a. Lubricate the seal lip with clean engine oil.
    b. Using a seal installer, install the crankshaft front seal.
5. Install the crankshaft damper. Torque to 107 ft. lbs. (145 Nm).

4.0L Engine

See Figures 75 and 76.

1. Before servicing the vehicle, refer to the precautions in the beginning of this section.

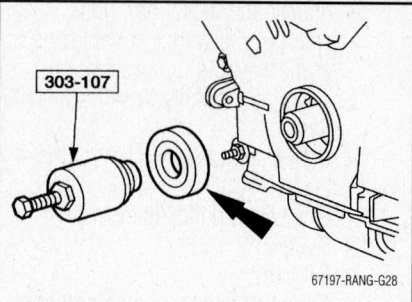

Fig. 75 Front crankshaft seal removal—4.0L engine

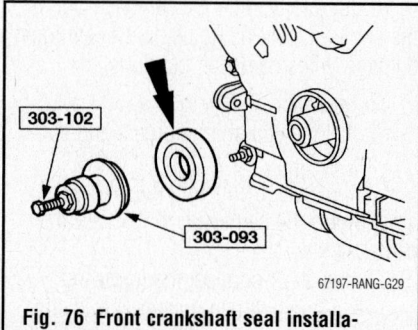

Fig. 76 Front crankshaft seal installation—4.0L engine

2. Remove or disconnect the following:
- Negative battery cable
- Crankshaft pulley

3. Using a seal remover, remove the crankshaft front oil seal.

To install:

4. Lubricate the seal lip with clean engine oil.
5. Using a seal driver, install the crankshaft front oil seal.
6. Install the crankshaft pulley. Torque to 37 ft. lbs. (50 Nm), then 90 degrees more.

CYLINDER HEAD

REMOVAL & INSTALLATION

2.3L Engine

See Figures 77 and 78.

1. Before servicing the vehicle, refer to the precautions in the beginning of this section.
2. Relieve the fuel system pressure.
3. Drain the cooling system.
4. Properly discharge the air conditioning system.
5. Remove or disconnect the following:
- Negative battery cable
- Drive belt
- Engine oil level indicator assembly
- Engine oil level indicator
- Engine oil level indicator tube
- Water outlet tube

- Water outlet tube
- Air conditioning compressor

➡️ **The generator will be removed with the accessory bracket**

- Accessory bracket
- Right motor mount
- Coolant hose from the thermostat
- Coolant hose from the EGR valve
- Coolant tube assembly
- Exhaust manifold and gasket
- Block heater (if so equipped)
- Water outlet
- EGR valve
- Power steering pump and reservoir as an assembly
- Idle air control (IAC) valve
- Throttle position (TP) sensor
- Manifold absolute pressure (MAP) sensor
- Swirl control valve monitor electrical connector
- CKP sensor and the wiring harness pin-type retainers
- Knock sensor (KS)
- Electric thermostat
- Swirl control valve
- CMP sensor electrical connector and disconnect the PCV hose from the intake manifold
- Engine wiring harness pin-type retainers from the intake manifold
- Engine wiring harness connector bracket. Position the engine wiring harness aside
- EGR tube
- Fuel supply line clip from the front of the intake manifold. Disconnect the vacuum hose from the intake manifold
- Intake manifold assembly
- Fuel injector electrical connectors. Detach the wiring harness pin-type retainers.
- Ignition coil and the cylinder head temperature (CHT) sensor electrical connectors.
- Engine wiring harness anchors from the valve cover studs. Remove the engine wiring harness.
- Ignition coil.
- Bypass hose.
- Thermostat housing.
- Knock sensor and the engine vent cover.
- Left motor mount.
- Fuel injector supply manifold with the injectors and the ground strap.
- Water pump pulley.
- Water pump.
- CMP sensor.
- CHT sensor.

- Spark plugs.
- Valve cover.
- CKP sensor.
- Crankshaft vibration damper

➡️ **There is one front cover bolt behind the cooling fan drive pulley. To remove this bolt, align one of the cooling fan drive pulley access holes with the bolt head to access the bolt.**

- Front cover.
- Timing chain tensioner.
- Timing chain guides.
- Timing chain assembly.

➡️ **Use a wrench on the flats between cylinders No. 1 and No. 2 to hold the camshaft in place.**

- Camshaft drive sprockets.
- Oil pump chain tensioner and guide.

➡️ **The oil pump chain sprocket must be held in place.**

- Oil pump chain and sprockets.

➡️ **Note the position of the lobes on the No. 1 cylinder before removing the camshafts for assembly reference.**

6. Loosen the camshaft bearing cap bolts in sequence, one turn at a time. Repeat the first step until all tension is released from the camshaft bearing caps. Remove the camshaft bearing caps.

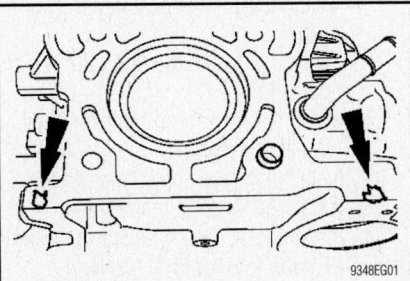

9348EG01

Fig. 77 RTV sealer application—2.3L engine cylinder head

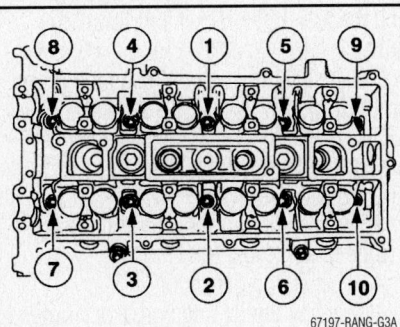

67197-RANG-G3A

Fig. 78 Head bolt torque sequence—2.3L engine

7. Remove or disconnect the following:
- Camshafts.
- Cylinder head bolts and the cylinder head.
- Cylinder head gasket.

8. Installation is the reverse of removal. Apply RTV sealer to the places shown. The head must be installed within 4 minutes of application. Observe the following torques:
   a. Cylinder head:
   - Step 1: Tighten the bolts to 44 inch lbs. (5 Nm)
   - Step 2: Tighten the bolts to 11 ft. lbs. (15 Nm)
   - Step 3: tighten the bolts to 33 ft. lbs. (45 Nm)
   - Step 4: Tighten the bolts an additional 90 degrees (¼ turn)
   - Step 5: Tighten the bolts an additional 90 degrees (¼ turn)
   b. Camshafts:

➡️ **Install the camshafts with the alignment notches in the camshaft lined up so the camshaft alignment plate can be installed without rotating the camshafts. Make sure the lobes on the No. 1 cylinder are in the same position as noted in the disassembly procedure. Rotating the camshafts, or installing the camshafts 180 degrees out of position can cause severe damage to the valves and pistons. Lubricate the camshaft journals and bearing caps with clean engine oil. Install the camshafts and bearing caps. Tighten the bolts in the sequence shown in three stages.**

- Step 1: Tighten the camshaft bearing caps one turn at a time until tight.
- Step 2: Tighten the bolts to 62 inch lbs. (7 Nm)
- Step 3: Tighten the bolts to 12 ft. lbs. (16 Nm)
   c. Crankshaft vibration damper:

➡️ **Do not reuse the crankshaft pulley bolt. Tighten the bolt in two stages.**

- Step 1: Tighten the bolt to 30 ft. lbs. (40 Nm)
- Step 2: Tighten the bolt and additional 90 degrees (¼ turn).

3.0L Engine

See Figure 79.

1. Before servicing the vehicle, refer to the Precautions Section.
2. With the vehicle in NEUTRAL, position it on a hoist.
3. Disconnect the battery ground cable.
4. Remove the lower intake manifold.

⁂⁂ WARNING

Refrigerant compressor oil (mineral oil) F73Z-19577-AA (Motorcraft® YN-9-A) should be used to lubricate R-134a refrigerant system O-ring seals only and should not be added to the R-134a refrigerant system as an A/C compressor lubricant. PAG refrigerant compressor oil F7AZ-19D589-DA (Motorcraft® YN-12-C) or equivalent meeting Ford specification WSH-M1C231-B only should be used as an A/C compressor lubricant.

➡Installation of a new suction accumulator is not required when repairing the air conditioning system except when there is physical evidence of system contamination from a failed A/C compressor or damage to the suction accumulator.

5. If flushing of the refrigerant system has not been carried out, recover the refrigerant.

6. Position the air cleaner outlet tube aside.

7. Remove the drive belt from the A/C compressor pulley.

8. Disconnect the electrical connector.

9. Remove the clamp nut on the compressor manifold and tube assembly.

10. Loosen the bolt and disconnect the compressor manifold and tube assembly from the A/C compressor.

11. Remove the bolts and the A/C compressor. Discard the O-ring seals.

12. Remove the generator.

13. Remove the power steering pump pulley.

14. Disconnect the power steering pressure hose. Remove and discard the seal.

15. Disconnect the power steering return hose.

16. Disconnect the power steering return line hose.

17. Remove the bolts and the power steering pump.

18. Remove the generator mounting bracket.

19. Remove the rocker arms and the push rods.

20. Remove the nuts and detach the fuel tube bracket and the wiring harness bracket.

21. Remove the two stud bolts from the rear of the A/C compressor mounting bracket.

22. Remove the bolts and remove the front of the A/C compressor mounting bracket.

23. Remove the exhaust manifolds.

24. Remove and discard the eight cylinder head bolts.

25. Remove the cylinder heads.

26. Remove and discard the cylinder head gaskets.

To install:

27. Clean all the sealing surfaces.

28. Check the cylinder head for flatness.

➡The "V" notch in the head gasket faces the front of the engine.

29. Install new cylinder head gaskets.

30. Install the cylinder heads.

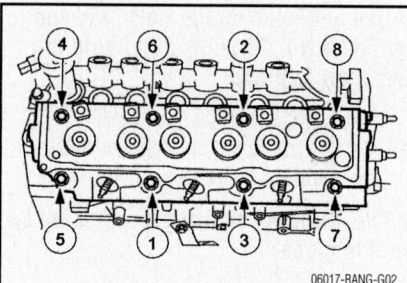

06017-RANG-G02

Fig. 79 Cylinder head bolt torque sequence—2005 3.0L engine

31. Install the bolts. Tighten the bolts in five steps in the sequence shown.
- Step 1: Tighten to 37 ft. lbs. (50 Nm).
- Step 2: Loosen the bolts one full turn.
- Step 3: Tighten to 22 ft. lbs. (30 Nm).
- Step 4: Tighten the bolts 90 degrees.
- Step 5: Tighten the bolts an additional 90 degrees.

32. Install the lower intake manifold.

33. Install the exhaust manifolds.

34. Install the A/C compressor mounting bracket. Torque to 34 ft. lbs. (46 Nm).

35. Install the stud bolts to the A/C compressor mounting bracket. Torque to 35 ft. lbs. (48 Nm).

36. Position the wiring harness bracket and the fuel tube bracket and install the nuts.

37. Install the push rods and the rocker arms. Torque to 24 ft. lbs. (32 Nm).

38. Install the generator mounting bracket. Install the bolts. Torque to 34 ft. lbs. (46 Nm).

39. Install the power steering pump. Torque to 35 ft. lbs. (48 Nm).

40. Install the generator.

41. Install the A/C compressor. Torque to 18 ft. lbs. (25 Nm).

42. Connect the battery ground cable.

43. Drain the engine oil.

44. Fill the engine with clean engine oil.

45. Fill and bleed the cooling system.

46. Fill the power steering system.

47. Charge the A/C system.

4.0L Engine

See Figures 80 and 81.

1. Before servicing the vehicle, refer to the precautions in the beginning of this section.

➡If only one cylinder head is to be removed, only follow the procedures that apply. The following tools, or their equivalents are absolutely necessary to properly perform this procedure:

- Cam Chain Tensioner tool T97T-6K254-A
- Cam Gear Removal tool T97T-6256-F
- Cam Gear Torque adapter T97T-6256-G
- Camshaft Gear Positioning/Holding tool T97T-6256-B
- Camshaft Gear Positioning/Holding tool adapter T97T-6256-A
- Camshaft holding tool T97T-6256-C
- Crankshaft holding tool T97T-6303-A
- Camshaft holding tool adapter T97T-6256-D

2. Before servicing the vehicle, refer to the Precautions Section.

3. Properly relieve the fuel system pressure.

4. Drain the cooling system.

5. Remove or disconnect the following:
- Negative battery cable
- Lower intake manifold
- Fan blade and shroud
- Valve cover
- Roller followers, if equipped
- Drive belt
- Upper radiator hose and tube
- Alternator electrical connectors
- Alternator mounting bracket
- Engine accessory bracket and move it aside
- Camshaft Position (CMP) electrical connector
- Crankshaft Position (CKP) sensor electrical connector
- Engine Coolant Temperature (ECT) sensor electrical connector
- Coil pack electrical connector
- Exhaust Gas Recirculation (EGR) valve electrical connector
- EGR valve bracket and move it aside

Fig. 80 The correct cylinder head bolt loosening sequence must be used to prevent warpage—4.0L engine

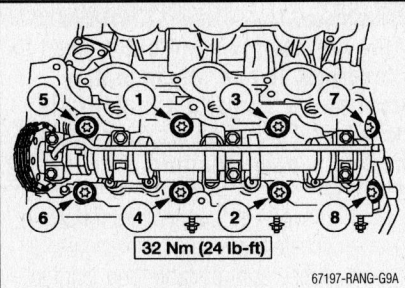

`32 Nm (24 lb-ft)`

67197-RANG-G9A

Fig. 81 Cylinder head bolt torque sequence 4.0L engine

- Heater hoses
- Fuel injector electrical connectors
- Water bypass hose
- Thermostat housing
- Spark plug wires
- Fuel injection supply manifold
- Fuel injectors
- Crankcase vent separator spring
- Oil dipstick housing
- Exhaust manifold
- Hydraulic chain tensioner
- Cassette retaining bolt
- Camshaft sprocket
- Cylinder head and discard the gasket

To install:

6. Thoroughly clean all gasket mating surfaces. Remove all traces of old gasket material, oil, grease or dirt.

7. Insure that the rubber band is holding the right-hand chain to the cassette.

8. Install a new head gasket and the cylinder head.

9. Torque the new cylinder head bolts in sequence as follows:

  a. Install bolts 1, 2, 3, 4, 7, and 8 (12mm) and torque, in sequence to:
  - Step 1: 24 ft. lbs. (32 Nm).
  - Step 2: Plus 80 degrees.
  - Step 3: Plus an additional 80 degrees.
  - Install bolts 5 and 6 (8mm), and torque to 24 ft. lbs. (32 Nm).

10. Install or connect the following:

- Camshaft sprocket in the cassette and make certain that the camshaft sprocket turns freely on the camshaft
- Cassette retaining bolt. Torque the bolt to 89 inch lbs. (10 Nm).
- Exhaust manifold
- Oil level indicator tube. Torque the bolt to 18 ft. lbs. (25 Nm).
- Crankcase vent separator and spring
- Thermostat housing. Torque the bolts to 8 ft. lbs. (11 Nm).
- Water bypass hose
- Heater hoses
- EGR bracket. Torque the bolt to 89 inch lbs. (10 Nm).
- EGR tube. Torque the nut to 30 ft. lbs. (40 Nm).
- ECT sensor electrical connector
- Electrical harness retainer. Torque the bolt to 89 inch lbs. (10 Nm).
- CKP and CMP electrical connectors
- Accessory bracket. Torque the bolts to 31 ft. lbs. (42 Nm).
- Alternator mounting bracket. Torque the bolts to 31 ft. lbs. (42 Nm).
- Alternator and electrical connectors
- Drive belt
- Fan shroud
- Roller followers
- Valve cover
- Lower intake manifold
- Negative battery cable

11. Change the engine oil and filter.
12. Refill the cooling system.
13. Start the engine and check for leaks, repair if necessary.

ENGINE ASSEMBLY

REMOVAL & INSTALLATION

2.3L Engine

See Figure 82.

1. Before servicing the vehicle, refer to the precautions in the beginning of this section.
2. Relieve the fuel system pressure.
3. Drain the cooling system.
4. Drain the engine oil.
5. Properly discharge the air conditioning system.
6. Remove or disconnect the following:
- Hood
- Accelerator control snow shield
- Air cleaner tube
- Upper radiator hose
- Lower radiator hose
- Fan and shroud

- PCM electrical connector. Remove the retaining nut on the harness clamp. Position the harness on the engine.
- Ground stud for the PCM
- Heater hoses
- All vacuum hoses
- Coolant reservoir hoses
- Air conditioning compressor clutch
- MAF electrical connector
- Air conditioning compressor manifold, plug the lines and the compressor ports
- Accelerator and speed control cables
- Power steering return hose
- PSP switch electrical connector
- High pressure power steering hose
- Fuel supply hose
- 42-pin electrical connector
- VMV vacuum regulator solenoid supply hose
- Evaporative purge hose
- Brake booster vacuum hose and the engine ground strap
- Positive battery cable
- Solenoid control wire at the starter
- Starter wiring harness clamp bolt and position it out of the way.
- RH splash shield
- Alternator electrical connections
- Block heater electrical connector
- Front heated oxygen sensor electrical connector at the bell housing
- Oil pressure sensor electrical connector
- Engine wiring pushpins and position the engine wiring harnesses out of the way.
- Oil filter
- With automatic transmission, the bolt retaining the transmission cooling tubes to the engine. Remove the bracket.
- Transmission dust shield
- Starter motor
- Heated oxygen sensor electrical connector at the rear of the transmission
- Transmission wiring harness
- Vehicle speed sensor, transmission range sensor, backup light switch and the transmission electrical connectors. Disconnect the pushpins and position the harness forward to the engine.
- Oil filter adapter

➡**Leave two side bolts in until the engine is ready to be removed.**

- Nine of the transmission-to-engine bolts

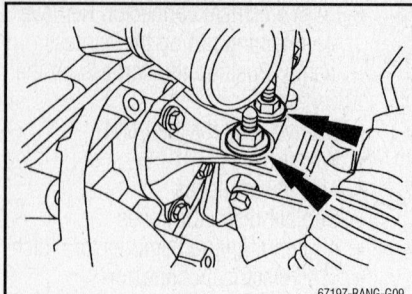

Fig. 82 Engine support insulator nuts, left side shown, right side similar—2.3L engine

- With automatic transmission, the transmission fluid indicator and tube assembly
- Starter dust shield

➡ **Mark one stud and the flex plate for assembly reference.**

- With automatic transmission, the four torque converter nuts

7. Support the transmission with a floor jack.

8. Support the engine with a floor crane using a spreader bar.

9. Remove the two side transmission-to-engine bolts.

10. Remove the four engine support insulator.

11. Remove the engine from the vehicle.

12. Installation is the reverse of removal. Observe the following torques:
- Torque converter bolts: 26 ft. lbs. (35 Nm)
- Nine transmission-to-engine bolts 35 ft. lbs. (48 Nm)
- Oil filter adapter: 18 ft. lbs. (25 Nm)
- Starter: 30 ft. lbs. (40 Nm)
- Engine support nuts: 75 ft. lbs. (102 Nm)

3.0L Engine

See Figure 83.

1. Before servicing the vehicle, refer to the precautions in the beginning of this section.

2. Relieve the fuel system pressure.
3. Drain the cooling system.
4. Drain the engine oil.
5. Properly discharge the air conditioning system.
6. Remove or disconnect the following:
- Hood
- Air cleaner outlet tube

- Upper and the lower radiator hoses

✳✳ WARNING

The fan clutch has left-hand threads.

- The fan clutch and blade as an assembly
- Drive belt
- Fan shroud
- Radiator
- Air conditioning manifold and tube. Remove the nut and position the line aside.
- Air conditioning compressor wiring
- Air conditioning compressor and the air conditioning compressor mounting bracket
- Heater hoses
- Ground cable
- Fuel lines
- Snow shield
- Accelerator cable and the speed control actuator cable
- All vacuum lines
- 42-pin connector
- Powertrain control module connector
- Nut from the powertrain control module harness
- Stud bolt and the powertrain control module ground strap
- Alternator wiring and position aside
- Both heated oxygen sensors
- Transmission harness connectors
- MAF sensor
- LH heated oxygen sensor
- Dual converter Y pipe
- Starter motor and the starter grounding stud bolt
- Torque converter nuts
- 8 transmission-to-engine bolts

7. Install the lifting eyes.
8. Remove the four nuts.
9. Support the transmission.
10. Remove the engine from the vehicle.
11. Installation is the reverse of removal.

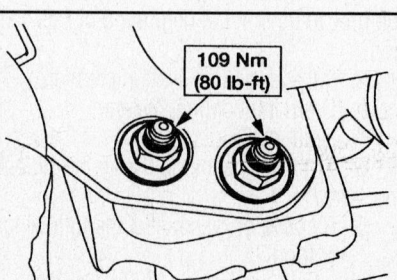

Fig. 83 Engine support nuts, one side shown—3.0L engine

Observe the following torques:
- Engine mount nuts: 80 ft. lbs. (109 Nm)
- Transmission-to-engine bolts: 33 ft. lbs. (45 Nm)
- Torque converter nuts: 35 ft. lbs. (47 Nm).

4.0L Engine

See Figures 84 and 85.

1. Before servicing the vehicle, refer to the precautions in the beginning of this section.

✳✳ CAUTION

If the fuel supply manifold is used as a leverage device, damage may occur to the supply manifold. Care must be taken when working around the fuel supply manifold.

2. Remove or disconnect the following:
- Accelerator cable from engine
- Speed control cable from engine
- Radiator, the fan blade, and the fan shroud
- Accessory bracket bolts and position bracket aside
- Alternator wiring
- Wiring harness retainer and position generator wiring away from engine
- Engine electrical connector
- PCM connector
- PCM ground wire
- Engine ground wire
- Brake booster vacuum hose
- Air conditioning high pressure switch electrical connector
- Bolt and position the air conditioning lines aside

➡ **Heater hose will be removed with engine.**

- Heater hoses
- Fuel line
- Starter motor
- Engine oil
- Oil drain plug
- Transmission portion of wiring harness
- RH and LH heated oxygen sensor connectors
- Transmission control connector
- Output shaft speed sensor connector
- Digital transmission range sensor connector
- Catalyst monitor sensor electrical connector

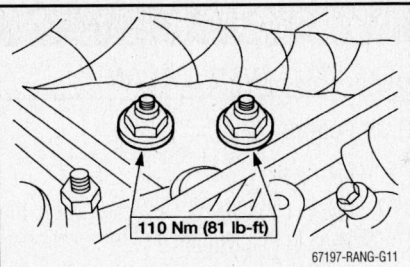

Fig. 84 Left side engine insulator nuts—4.0L engine

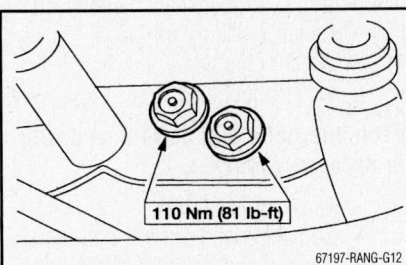

Fig. 85 Right side engine insulator nuts—4.0L engine

- Transmission/transfer case portion of the wiring harness from any routing clips or pushpins. Route transmission/transfer case portion of the wiring harness to top of engine.
- Bolt, and position the transmission cooling line bracket aside
- Air conditioning line bracket nut and position it aside
- Power steering return hose
- Power steering pressure hose
- Vapor management valve hose connector
- Eight bolts and the LH and the RH engine support insulator nuts

➡**The lifting eyes should be installed on the exhaust manifold studs for number three and number four cylinders.**

3. Install the lifting eyes.
4. Install the spreader bar to the lifting eyes.
5. Attach a floor crane to the spreader bar and remove the engine.
6. Installation is the reverse of removal. Observe the following torques:
- Left and right engine insulator nuts: 81 ft. lbs. (110 Nm)
- Engine mount nuts: 59 ft. lbs. (80 Nm)
- Transmission-to-engine bolts: 35 ft. lbs. (47 Nm)
- Torque converter nuts: 35 ft. lbs. (47 Nm)

EXHAUST MANIFOLD

REMOVAL & INSTALLATION

2.3L Engine

See Figures 86 and 87.

1. Before servicing the vehicle, refer to the precautions in the beginning of this section.
2. Remove or disconnect the following:
- Negative battery cable
- Exhaust flange nuts
- Drive belt
- Coolant
- Upper radiator hose and the engine reservoir hose
- Air conditioning compressor
- Heater hose
- Oil indicator and the upper bolt for the tube assembly
- Lower bolt and remove the oil indicator tube assembly
- Front radiator tube
3. Remove the pushpins and position the right inner fender splash shield out of the way.
4. Remove or disconnect the following:
- Alternator electrical connectors
- Lower front end accessory drive (FEAD) mounting bolts
- Upper mounting bolt and the FEAD assembly
- Two nuts and position the coolant tube out of the way
- Exhaust manifold
- Exhaust manifold gasket

To install:

5. Install or connect the following:
- Exhaust manifold gasket
- Exhaust manifold and the nuts
- Coolant tube and the nuts
- FEAD assembly and the upper mounting bolts, finger tight.
- Lower FEAD mounting bolts, finger tight. Then, torque all FEAD bolts, in the sequence shown, to 35 ft. lbs. (47 Nm).
- Alternator electrical connectors

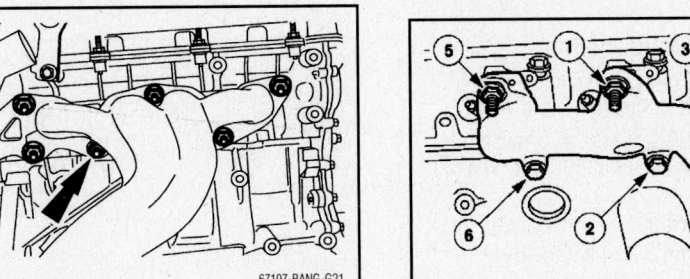

Fig. 86 Exhaust manifold retaining nuts—2.3L engine

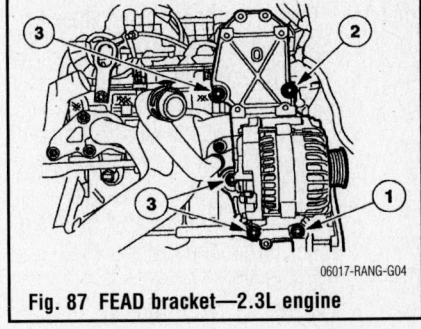

Fig. 87 FEAD bracket—2.3L engine

- Right inner splash shield and pushpins
- Upper radiator tube and install the bolts
- Oil indicator tube assembly and the lower bolt
- Oil indicator tube upper bolt and the oil indicator
- Heater water hose
- Air conditioning compressor
- Upper radiator hose and the engine reservoir hose
6. Fill the cooling system.
7. Install the serpentine drive belt.
8. Install the exhaust flange nuts.
9. Connect the battery ground cable.

3.0L Engine

Left Side

See Figure 88.

1. Before servicing the vehicle, refer to the precautions in the beginning of this section.
2. Install or connect the following:
- Negative battery cable
- Exhaust flange nuts
- Exhaust Gas Recirculation (EGR) valve from the exhaust manifold tube
- Oil lever indicator and bracket
- Exhaust manifold and discard the gasket

To install:

3. Clean the mating surfaces for the exhaust manifold and cylinder head.

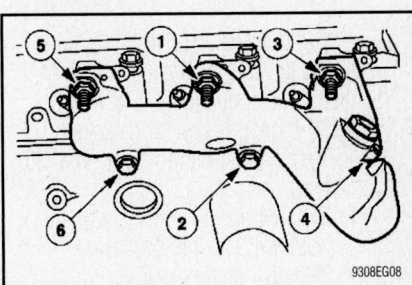

Fig. 88 Tighten the exhaust manifold bolts in sequence—3.0L engine, left side

4. Install a new gasket and the exhaust manifold. Torque the bolts in sequence to:
   a. 89 inch lbs. (10 Nm).
   b. 15 ft. lbs. (20 Nm).
5. Install or connect the following:
   - Oil lever indicator tube and bracket. Torque the bolt to 12 ft. lbs. (16 Nm).
   - EGR valve to the exhaust manifold tube. Torque the fastener to 26 ft. lbs. (35 Nm).
   - Exhaust flange. Torque the nuts to 25 ft. lbs. (34 Nm).
   - Negative battery cable
6. Start the vehicle and check for leaks, repair if necessary.

Right Side

See Figure 89.

1. Before servicing the vehicle, refer to the precautions in the beginning of this section.
2. Remove or disconnect the following:
   - Negative battery cable
   - Exhaust manifold flange
   - Ignition coil support bracket
   - Exhaust manifold and discard the gasket

To install:

3. Clean the mating surfaces for the exhaust manifold and cylinder head

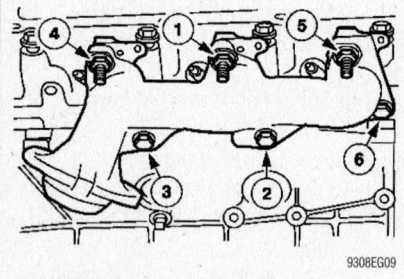

Fig. 89 Tighten the right side exhaust manifold bolts in the proper sequence—3.0L engine

9308EG09

4. Install a new gasket and the exhaust manifold. Torque the bolts is sequence to:
   a. 89 inch lbs. (10 Nm).
   b. 18 ft. lbs. (25 Nm).
5. Install or connect the following:
   - Ignition coil support bracket. Torque the bolts to 15 ft. lbs. (20 Nm).
   - Exhaust flange nuts. Torque the nuts to 33 ft. lbs. (46 Nm).
   - Negative battery cable
6. Start the vehicle and check for leaks, repair if necessary.

4.0L Engine

See Figures 90 and 91.

1. Before servicing the vehicle, refer to the precautions in the beginning of this section.
2. Remove or disconnect the following:
   - Negative battery cable
   - Exhaust inlet pipe-to-manifold attaching bolts
   - Differential Pressure Feedback EGR (DPFE) transducer hoses, left side manifold only
   - Exhaust Gas Recirculation (EGR) tube from the manifold and valve, left side manifold only
   - Exhaust manifold and discard the gasket

To install:

3. Clean the gasket mating surfaces.
4. Install or connect the following:
   - New gasket and the exhaust manifold. Torque the bolts to 16 ft. lbs. (22 Nm).
   - EGR tube to the manifold. Torque the fastener to 30 ft. lbs. (40 Nm) left side manifold only
   - DPFE transducer hoses, left side manifold only
   - Exhaust inlet pipe-to-manifold attaching bolts. Torque the bolts to 30 ft. lbs. (40 Nm).
   - Negative battery cable
5. Start the vehicle and check for leaks, repair if necessary.

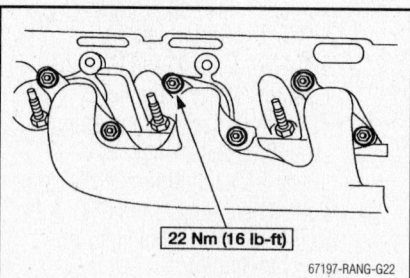

22 Nm (16 lb-ft)

67197-RANG-G22

Fig. 90 Left side exhaust manifold retaining nuts—4.0L engine

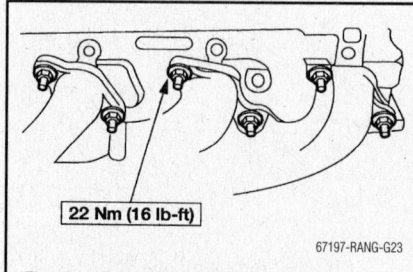

22 Nm (16 lb-ft)

67197-RANG-G23

Fig. 91 Right side exhaust manifold retaining nuts—4.0L engine

INTAKE MANIFOLD

REMOVAL & INSTALLATION

2.3L Engine

See Figure 92.

1. Before servicing the vehicle, refer to the precautions in the beginning of this section.
2. Relieve the fuel system pressure.
3. Drain the cooling system.
4. Properly discharge the air conditioning system.
5. Remove or disconnect the following:
   - Negative battery cable
   - Water outlet tube.
   - Water outlet tube.

➡ **The alternator will be removed with the accessory bracket.**

   - Accessory bracket.
   - Coolant hose from the thermostat.
   - Coolant hose from the EGR valve.
   - Coolant tube assembly.
   - Block heater (if so equipped).
   - Water outlet.
   - EGR valve.
   - Idle air control (IAC) valve.
   - Throttle position (TP) sensor.
   - Manifold absolute pressure (MAP) sensor.
   - Swirl control valve monitor electrical connector.
   - Electric thermostat.
   - Swirl control valve.
   - CMP sensor electrical connector and disconnect the PCV hose from the intake manifold.
   - Engine wiring harness pin-type retainers from the intake manifold.
   - Engine wiring harness connector bracket. Position the engine wiring harness aside.
   - EGR tube.
   - Fuel supply line clip from the front of the intake manifold. Disconnect the vacuum hose from the intake manifold.
   - Intake manifold assembly.
6. Installation is the reverse of removal.

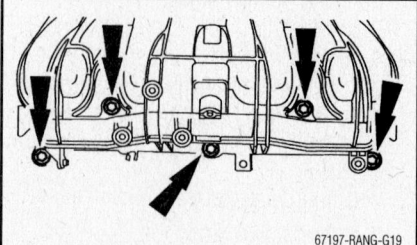

67197-RANG-G19

Fig. 92 Intake manifold bolts—2.3L engine

Torque the bolts to 13 ft. lbs. (18 Nm). There is no special torque sequence.

3.0L Engine

Upper Manifold

See Figure 93.

1. Before servicing the vehicle, refer to the precautions in the beginning of this section.
2. Disconnect the battery ground cable.
3. Remove the air cleaner outlet pipe.
4. Remove the bolt and the snow shield.
5. Disconnect the accelerator cable, speed control cable and the return spring.
6. Disconnect the accelerator cable and speed control cable from the accelerator bracket.
7. Disconnect the throttle position (TP) sensor and idle air control (IAC) valve electrical connectors.
8. Disconnect the two vacuum hoses.
9. Detach the 42-pin wiring harness retainer from the stud bolt.
10. Remove the nut and the stud bolt. Position the 42-pin wiring harness and bracket aside.
11. Remove the oil indicator tube bracket nut and the upper intake manifold support bracket stud bolt.
12. Disconnect the brake booster vacuum hose and the positive crankcase ventilation (PCV) valve tube.

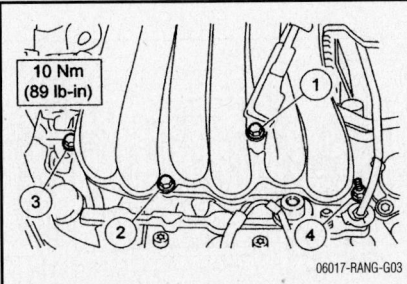

Fig. 93 Upper intake manifold torque sequence—3.0L engine

13. Remove the bolts, the stud bolt and the upper intake manifold. Remove and discard the gaskets. Clean and inspect all mating surfaces.
14. To install, reverse the removal procedure. Install new gaskets and tighten the upper intake manifold bolts and stud bolt in the sequence shown, to 89 inch lbs. (10 Nm).

Lower Manifold

See Figure 94.

1. Before servicing the vehicle, refer to the precautions in the beginning of this section.

2. Drain the engine cooling system.
3. Remove both the valve covers.
4. Disconnect the upper radiator hose, heater hose and coolant bypass hose.
5. Disconnect the engine coolant temperature (ECT) sensor and coolant temperature sender electrical connectors.
6. Disconnect the crankshaft position (CKP) sensor and detach the wiring from the stud bolt.
7. Disconnect the fuel injector electrical connectors and position the engine control wiring aside.
8. Release the fuel pressure and disconnect the fuel tube.
9. Loosen the rocker arm bolts.

➡ **Identify the location of each pushrod. Each pushrod is to be installed in the original location to prevent premature wear.**

10. Remove all the pushrods.
11. Remove the bolts from the lower intake manifold.

➡ **Gently loosen the intake manifold to separate the silicone sealant from the cylinder block.**

12. Remove the lower intake manifold.
13. Remove and discard the intake manifold gaskets and end seals.

To install:

➡ **Clean and inspect all mating surfaces.**

➡ **If the lower intake manifold is not installed within four minutes, remove the sealant and reapply.**

14. Apply a drop of silicone gasket and sealant at the four cylinder block-to-cylinder head seams.
15. Install the intake manifold gaskets and end seals.
16. Position the lower intake manifold.
17. Install the bolts and tighten in the sequence shown to 21 ft. lbs. (29 Nm).
18. Install the pushrods.

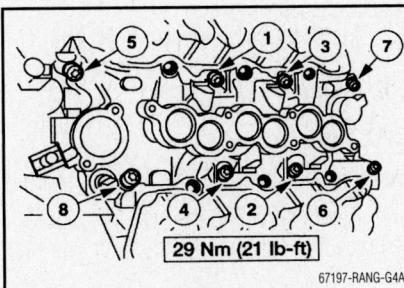

Fig. 94 Lower intake manifold torque sequence—3.0L engine

19. Tighten the rocker arms to 24 ft. lbs. (32 Nm).
20. Connect the fuel tube.
21. Connect the fuel injector electrical connectors.
22. Connect the crankshaft position (CKP) sensor and attach the wiring from the stud bolt.
23. Connect the engine coolant temperature (ECT) sensor and coolant temperature sender electrical connectors.
24. Connect the upper radiator hose, heater hose and coolant bypass hose.
25. Install both valve covers.
26. Fill and bleed the engine cooling system.

4.0L Engine

See Figure 95.

1. Before servicing the vehicle, refer to the precautions in the beginning of this section.
2. Disconnect the battery ground cable.
3. Remove the bolts and the shield.
4. Remove the air cleaner outlet pipe.
5. Disconnect the idle air control (IAC) valve, throttle position (TP) sensor electrical connectors and the TP sensor wiring pin-type retainer.
6. Disconnect the MAF sensor wiring pin-type retainer.
7. Detach the accelerator and speed control cables from the throttle body.
8. Detach the accelerator and speed control cables from the bracket, and position the cables aside.
9. Disconnect the exhaust gas recirculation (EGR) valve vacuum hose and tube fitting.
10. Disconnect the EGR vacuum regulator solenoid valve electrical connector and vacuum hose.
11. Disconnect the hose.
12. Loosen the clamp and disconnect the brake booster vacuum hose.

❊❊ CAUTION

It is important to twist the spark plug wire boots while pulling upward to avoid possible damage to the spark plug wire.

➡ **Mark the spark plug wire locations before removing them.**

13. Disconnect the RH spark plug wires from the coil. Remove the spark plug wire routing clip pin-type retainer and position the wires aside.
14. Remove the wiring harness bracket retainer, then position the wiring harness aside.

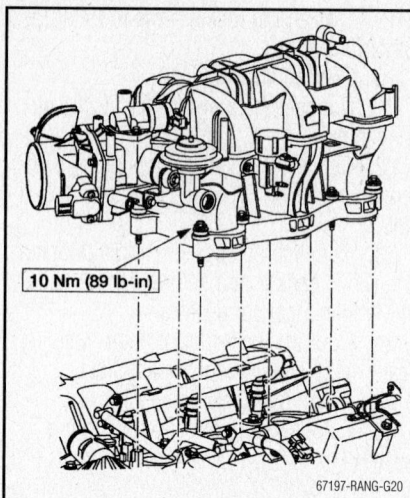

10 Nm (89 lb-in)

67197-RANG-G20

Fig. 95 Intake manifold installation—4.0L engine

15. Remove the accelerator cable routing clip pin-type retainer and the wiring harness pin-type retainer.

16. Remove the bolts.

17. Remove the bolts and position the coil and bracket aside.

18. Disconnect the vacuum hoses.

19. Remove the nut.

20. Disconnect the Powertrain Control Module (PCM) electrical connector.

21. Remove the retainer and position the ground wires aside.

22. Detach the electrical connector retainer.

23. Remove the intake manifold bolts and lift up the intake manifold.

24. Remove the heated positive crankcase ventilation (PCV) hose retainers and remove the heated PCV fitting.

25. Remove the intake manifold.

26. To install, reverse the removal procedure. Torque the fasteners to 89 inch lbs. (10 Nm).

MAIN BEARING TORQUE SEQUENCE

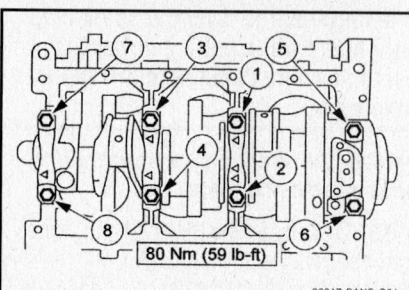

80 Nm (59 lb-ft)

06017-RANG-G01

Fig. 96 Crankshaft main bearing torque sequence—3.0L engine

OIL PAN

REMOVAL & INSTALLATION

2.3L Engine

See Figure 97.

1. Before servicing the vehicle, refer to the precautions in the beginning of this section.

2. Drain the engine oil.

3. Remove or disconnect the following:
   • Engine from the vehicle
   • Engine oil level indicator assembly
   • Engine oil pan bolts and oil pan

To install:

4. Clean and inspect all mating surfaces.

➡**The oil pan must be installed and the bolts tightened with four minutes of applying the silicone gasket and sealant.**

5. Apply a 2.5 mm bead of silicone gasket and sealant to the oil pan. Install the oil pan. Tighten the oil pan in the sequence shown.

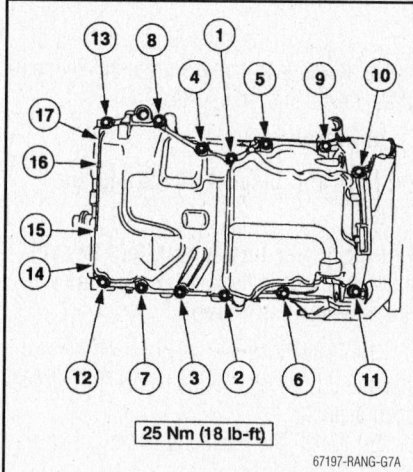

25 Nm (18 lb-ft)

67197-RANG-G7A

Fig. 97 Oil pan torque sequence—2.3L engine

6. Lubricate the O-ring with clean engine oil and install the engine oil level indicator assembly.

7. Install the engine into the vehicle.

3.0L Engine

2WD Models

See Figures 98 and 99.

1. Before servicing the vehicle, refer to the precautions in the beginning of this section.

2. Drain the engine oil.

3. Remove or disconnect the following:
   • Negative battery cable

   • Oil level dipstick tube
   • Fan shroud. Leave the fan shroud over the fan assembly
   • Motor mount nuts from the frame

On models equipped with distributor ignition, failure to remove the distributor will damage or break it when the engine is lifted.

   • Starter
   • Transmission inspection cover
   • Right hand axle I-beam. The brake caliper must be removed and secured out of the way.
   • Oil pan attaching bolts, using a suitable lifting device, raise the engine about 2 in. (5cm)
   • Oil pan and discard the gasket

➡**The oil pan fits tightly between the transmission spacer plate and oil pump pick-up tube. Use care when removing the oil pan from the engine.**

4. Clean all gasket surfaces on the engine and oil pan. Remove all traces of old gasket and/or sealer.

To install:

5. Apply a ⅛ (4mm) bead of RTV sealer to the junctions of the rear main bearing cap and block, and the front cover and block. The sealer sets in 15 minutes, so work quickly!

6. Apply adhesive to the gasket surfaces and install the oil pan gasket.

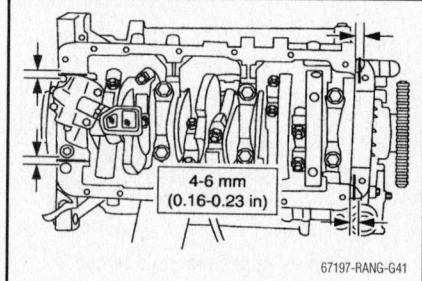

4-6 mm (0.16-0.23 in)

67197-RANG-G41

Fig. 98 Oil pan sealer application—3.0L engine

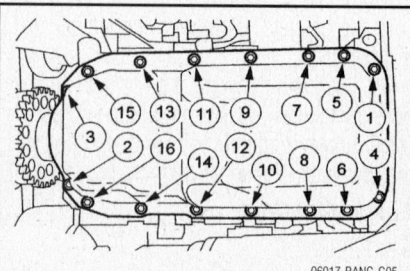

06017-RANG-G05

Fig. 99 Oil pan bolt torque sequence—3.0L engine with 2-wheel drive

7. Install or connect the following:
- Oil pan on the engine block. Torque the bolts EVENLY to 9 ft. lbs. (12 Nm) working from the center to the end position on the oil pan.
- Right hand axle I-beam
- Brake caliper
- Transmission inspection cover
- Starter
- Fan shroud
- Motor mount retaining nuts
- Oil level dipstick tube
- Negative battery cable

8. Fill the engine with clean oil.

9. Start the vehicle and check for leaks, repair if necessary.

4WD Models

See Figure 100.

1. Before servicing the vehicle, refer to the precautions in the beginning of this section.

2. Drain the engine oil.

3. Remove or disconnect the following:
- Negative battery cable
- Engine from the vehicle and place it on a suitable engine stand
- Oil pan and discard the gasket

To install:

4. Install or connect the following:
- New oil pan gasket and secure the gasket with trim adhesive
- Oil pan. Torque the bolts to 9 ft. lbs. (12 Nm).

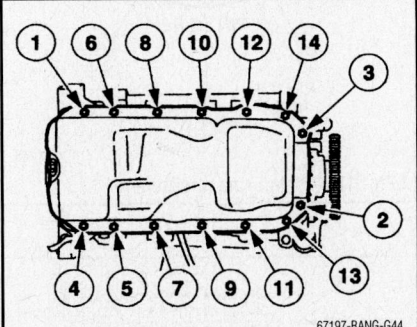

Fig. 100 Oil pan bolts—3.0L engine with 4-wheel drive

- Engine
- Negative battery cable

5. Fill the engine with clean oil.

6. Start the vehicle and check for leaks, repair if necessary.

4.0L Engine

See Figure 101.

➡**The 4.0L engine does not use an oil pan in the conventional sense. There is**

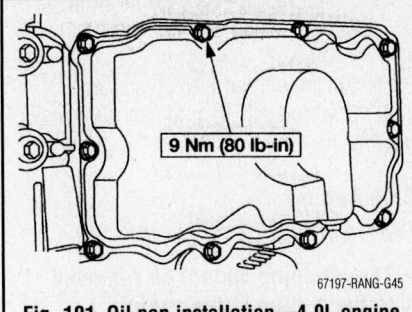

Fig. 101 Oil pan installation—4.0L engine

a separate access panel that unbolts from what would be considered the oil pan (which is now known as the ladder frame).

1. Before servicing the vehicle, refer to the precautions in the beginning of this section.

2. Drain the engine oil.

3. Remove or disconnect the following:
- Negative battery cable
- Oil pan and discard the gasket

To install:

4. Install or connect the following:
- New gasket and oil pan. Torque the bolts to 80 inch lbs. (9 Nm).

- Negative battery cable

5. Fill the engine with clean oil.

6. Start the vehicle and check for leaks, repair if necessary.

OIL PUMP

REMOVAL & INSTALLATION

2.3L Engine

See Figures 102 and 103.

1. Before servicing the vehicle, refer to the precautions in the beginning of this section.

2. Remove or disconnect the following:
- Negative battery cable
- Timing chain
- Oil pump chain and sprockets
- Oil pan
- Oil pump pickup tube and gasket
- Oil pump assembly and gasket

To install:

3. Turn the crankshaft clockwise to position the No. 1 piston.

4. Remove the plug bolt.

5. Install the Engine Timing Peg 303-507.

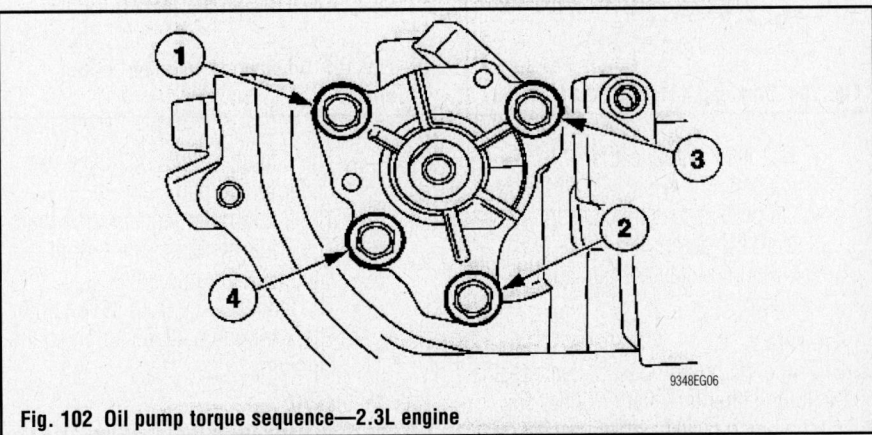

Fig. 102 Oil pump torque sequence—2.3L engine

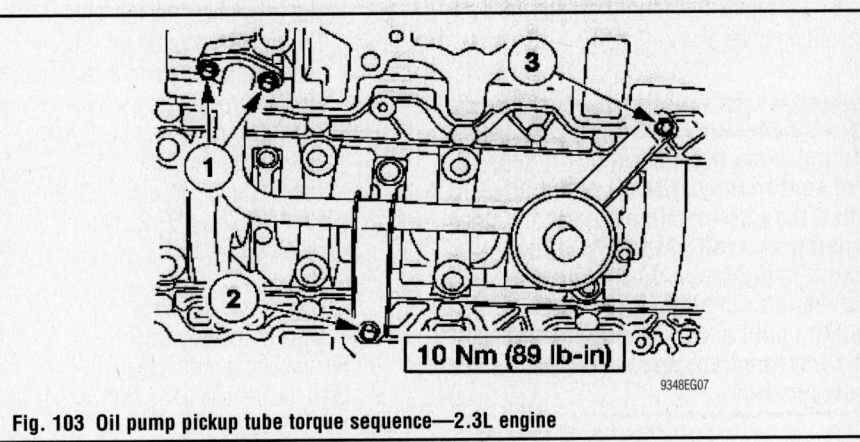

Fig. 103 Oil pump pickup tube torque sequence—2.3L engine

➡**Clean the gasket surface with metal surface cleaner.**

6. Install a new gasket and the oil pump assembly. Tighten the bolts in the sequence shown in two stages.
   - Step 1: Tighten the bolts to 80 inch lbs. (10 Nm)
   - Step 2: Tight the bolts to 17 ft. lbs. (23 Nm)

7. Install a new oil pump pickup tube gasket and the pickup tube. Tighten the bolts in the sequence shown

3.0L Engine

See Figure 104.

1. Before servicing the vehicle, refer to the precautions in the beginning of this section.
2. Drain the engine oil.
3. Remove or disconnect the follow-ing:

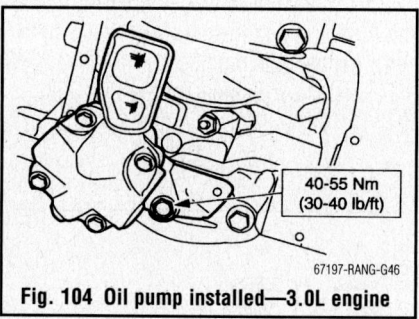

Fig. 104 Oil pump installed—3.0L engine

- Negative battery cable
- Oil pan
- Oil pick-up and tube assembly from the pump
- Oil pump retainer bolts and the oil pump

To install:

4. Prime the oil pump with clean engine oil by filling either the inlet or outlet port. Rotate the pump shaft to distribute the oil within the pump body.

5. Install the oil pump and tighten the mounting bolts to 30–40 ft. lbs. (41–54 Nm).

❄❄ WARNING

Do not force the oil pump if it does not seat readily. The oil pump drive-shaft may be misaligned with the dis-tributor or shaft assembly. If the pump is tightened down with the driveshaft misaligned, damage to the pump could occur. To align, rotate the intermediate driveshaft into a new position.

6. Install or connect the following:
   - Oil pick-up and tube assembly
   - Oil pan

7. Fill the engine with clean oil.

8. Start the vehicle and check for leaks, repair if necessary.

4.0L Engine

See Figure 105.

➡**The oil pump cannot be removed with the engine in the vehicle.**

1. Before servicing the vehicle, refer to the precautions in the beginning of this section.
2. Drain the engine oil.
3. Remove or disconnect the following:
   - Engine from the vehicle
   - Oil pan
   - Unbolt the oil pick-up tube

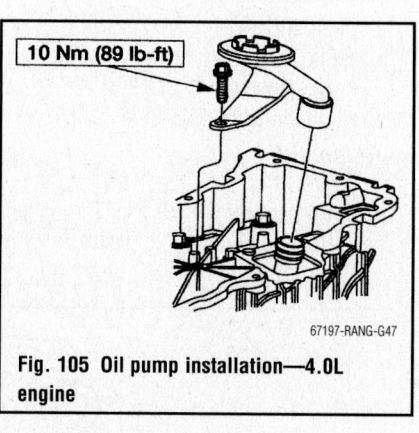

Fig. 105 Oil pump installation—4.0L engine

- The 8 ladder frame bolts that were under the oil pan
- The 2 rear outer ladder frame bolts
- The 7 left-hand and the 8 right-hand ladder frame bolts
- The ladder frame from the engine
- The 2 oil pump attaching bolts and the pump.

To install:

4. Submerge the pump in clean engine oil to prime it.
5. Install or connect the following:
   - The ladder frame on the engine
   - The 8 right-hand and 7 left-hand ladder frame bolts
   - The 2 rear outer and the 8 frame bolts under the pan
   - The oil pump. Torque the bolts to 13–15 ft. lbs. (17–21 Nm).
   - Oil pick-up tube
   - Oil pan
   - Engine to the vehicle
   - Negative battery cable

6. Fill the engine with clean oil.
7. Start the vehicle and check for leaks, repair if necessary.

PISTON AND RING

POSITIONING

See Figures 106 through 109.

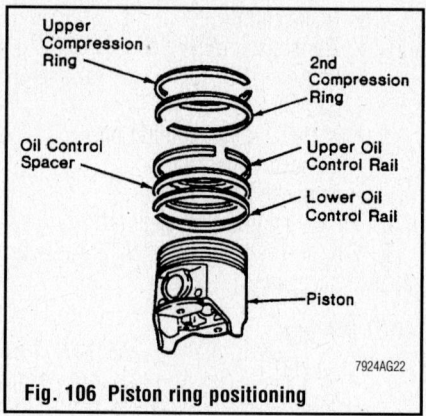

Fig. 106 Piston ring positioning

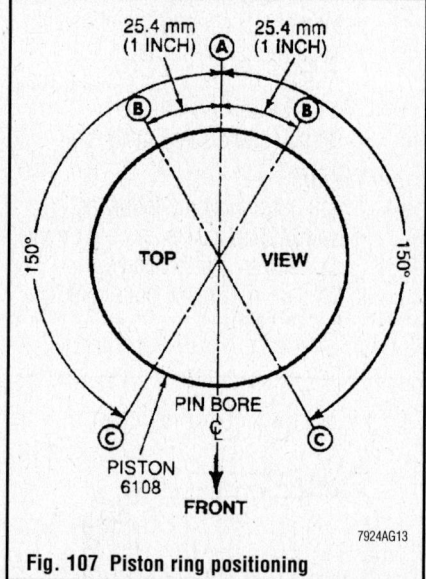

Fig. 107 Piston ring positioning

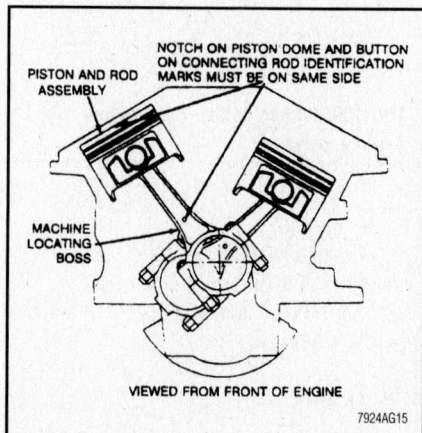

Fig. 108 Piston and connecting rod posi-tioning—3.0L engine

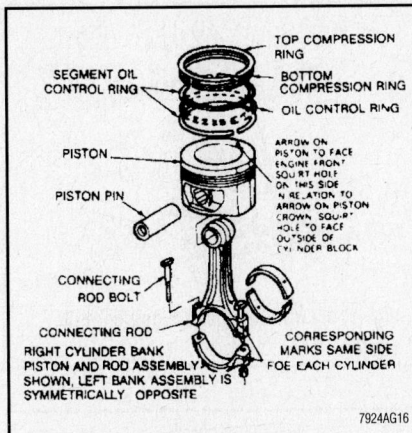

Fig. 109 Piston and connecting rod positioning—4.0L engine

REAR MAIN SEAL

REMOVAL & INSTALLATION

2.3L Engine

See Figure 110.

1. Before servicing the vehicle, refer to the precautions in the beginning of this section.
2. Remove or disconnect the following:
   - Flywheel or flexplate
   - Bolts and the crankshaft rear oil seal

To install:

3. Install or connect the following:
   - Rear oil seal on the Crankshaft Rear Main Oil Seal Installer
   - Crankshaft Rear Main Oil Seal Installer and the crankshaft rear oil seal on the crankshaft
4. Tighten the bolts in the sequence shown to 89 inch lbs. (10 Nm)
5. Remove the Crankshaft Rear Main Oil Seal Installer.
6. Install the flywheel or flexplate.

3.0L Engine

See Figures 111 and 112.

1. Before servicing the vehicle, refer to the precautions in the beginning of this section.
2. Remove the flexplate or flywheel.

⁂ WARNING

Use care to avoid scratching or damaging the oil seal surface or leakage may occur.

3. Using a sharp awl, punch one hole into the crankshaft rear oil seal metal surface between the seal lip and the cylinder block.

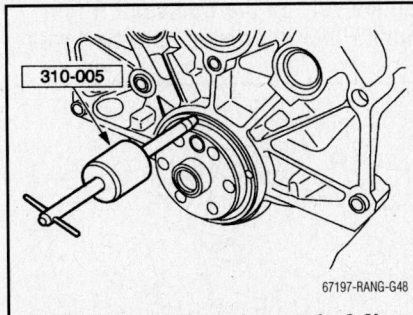

Fig. 111 Rear main seal removal—3.0L engine

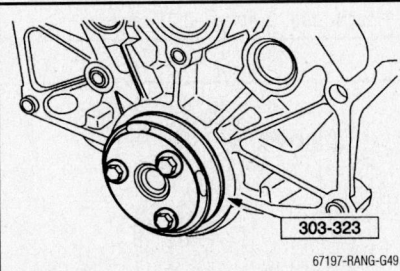

Fig. 112 Rear main seal installation—3.0L engine

4. Screw the threaded end of the special tool into the oil seal. Use the special tool to remove the crankshaft rear oil seal.

To install:

5. Lubricate the outer lips and the inner seal on the crankshaft rear oil seal with clean engine oil.
6. Using the special tool, install the crankshaft rear oil seal. Alternate bolt tightening to correctly seat the crankshaft rear oil seal.
7. Install the flexplate or flywheel.

4.0L Engine

See Figures 113, 114 115

1. Before servicing the vehicle, refer to the precautions in the beginning of this section.
2. Remove the flexplate or flywheel.

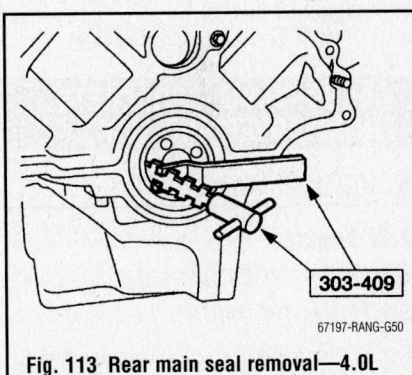

Fig. 113 Rear main seal removal—4.0L engine

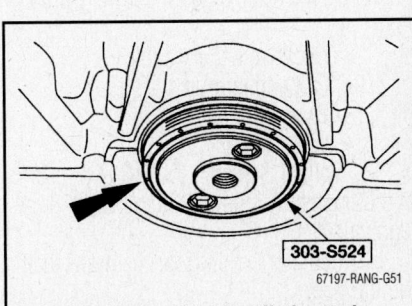

Fig. 114 Front part of installation tool—4.0L engine

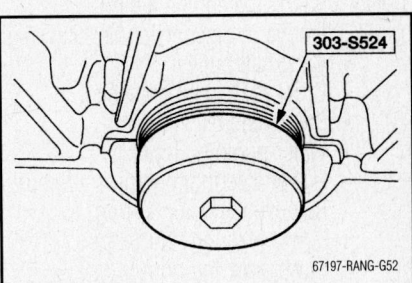

Fig. 115 Rear main seal installation—4.0L engine

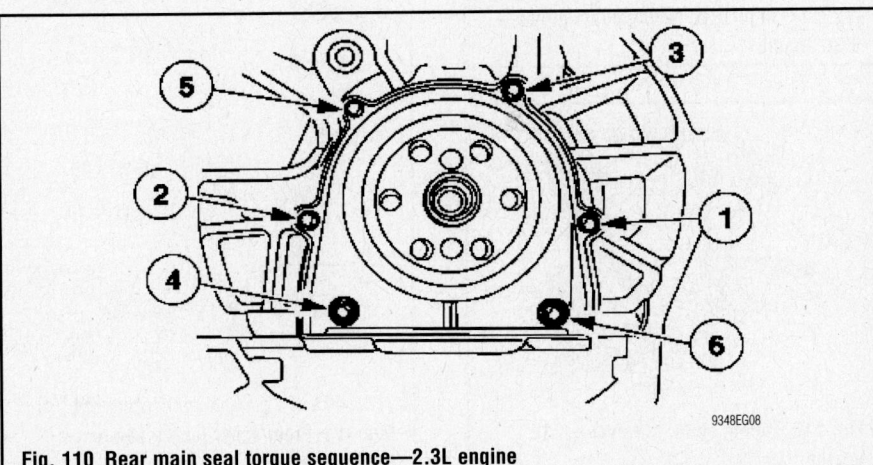

Fig. 110 Rear main seal torque sequence—2.3L engine

✳✳ WARNING

Avoid scratching or damaging the oil crankshaft seal running surface during removal of the crankshaft rear oil seal.

3. Using the special tool, remove the crankshaft rear oil seal.

To install:

➡ Be sure the crankshaft rear sealing surface is clean and free of any rust or corrosion. To clean the crankshaft rear sealing surface, use extra-fine emery cloth or extra-fine 0000 steel wool with metal surface cleaner.

4. Lubricate the crankshaft rear oil seal with clean engine oil and install on the special tool.

5. Using the special tool, install the crankshaft rear oil seal.

6. Install the flexplate or flywheel.

TIMING CHAIN, SPROCKETS, FRONT COVER AND SEAL

REMOVAL & INSTALLATION

2.3L Engine

See Figures 116 through 119.
See Figures 120 and 121.

1. Before servicing the vehicle, refer to the precautions in the beginning of this section.

2. Remove or disconnect the following:

- Negative battery cable
- Fan and shroud
- Drive belt
- Valve cover

3. Set No. 1 piston to TDC and install the Camshaft Alignment Plate 303-376, or equivalent.

4. Remove the plug for the crankshaft timing peg.

5. Install the Crankshaft Timing Peg 303-507, or equivalent.

6. Install an M6 bolt into the crankshaft pulley to verify the engine timing.

7. Remove or disconnect the following:

- Camshaft pulley
- Crankshaft position sensor
- Belt tensioner
- Water pump pulley
- Power steering high pressure hose. Remove the nylon O-ring.
- Power steering return hose
- Power steering pump

➡ This step is needed only if a new front cover is being installed.

8. Using a three-jaw puller, remove the fan drive pulley.

➡ There is one bolt behind the cooling fan drive pulley. This bolt can be accessed by lining up one of the holes in the pulley with the bolt.

9. Remove the bolts and the engine front cover.

10. Compress the timing chain tensioner and remove the tensioner.

11. Remove the right-hand timing chain guide.

12. Remove the timing chain.

13. Remove the bolts and the left-hand timing chain guide.

✳✳ WARNING

Do not rely on the Camshaft Alignment Plate to prevent camshaft rota-

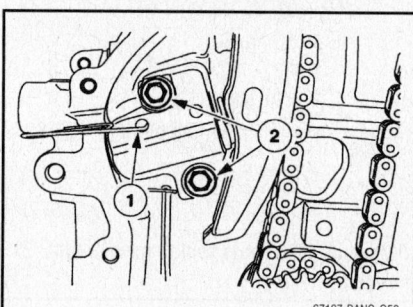

Fig. 116 Timing chain tensioner removal; 1-paper clip, 2-bolts—2.3L engine

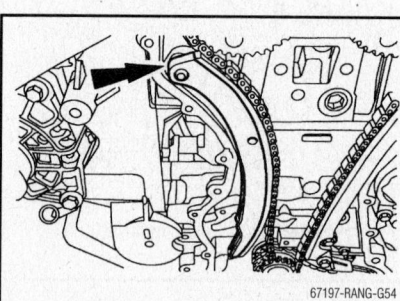

Fig. 117 Right side timing chain guide—2.3L engine

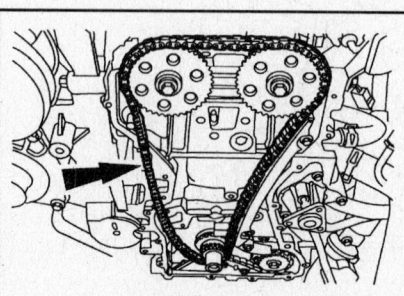

Fig. 118 Timing chain removal—2.3L engine

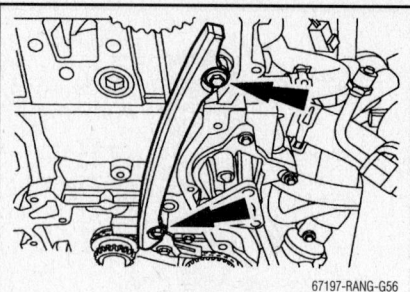

Fig. 119 Left timing chain guide—2.3L engine

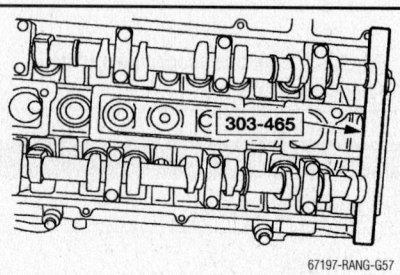

Fig. 120 Camshaft alignment plate installed—2.3L engine

tion. Damage to the tool or the camshaft can occur.

14. If necessary, remove the bolts and the camshaft sprockets. Use the flats on the camshaft to prevent camshaft rotation.

To install:

15. Remove the special tool.

✳✳ WARNING

Do not rotate the camshafts. Damage to the valves and pistons can occur.

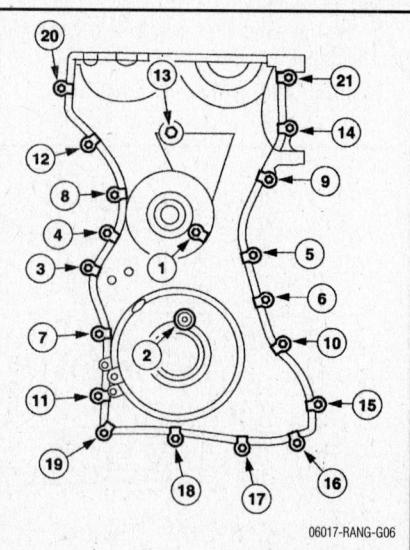

Fig. 121 Front cover torque sequence—2.3L engine

If the camshaft sprockets were not removed, use the flats on the camshafts to prevent camshaft rotation and loosen the sprocket bolts.

16. If removed, install the camshaft sprockets and the bolts. Do not tighten the bolts at this time.

17. Install or connect the following:
- Left-hand timing chain guide and bolts
- Timing chain
- Right-hand timing chain guide
- Timing chain tensioner and release the piston
- Timing chain tensioner and the bolts

18. Remove the drill rod to release the piston.

19. Install the special tool.

❊❊ WARNING

Do not rely on the Camshaft Alignment Plate to prevent camshaft rotation. Damage to the tool or the camshafts can result. Using the flats on the camshafts to prevent camshaft rotation, tighten the bolts.

➡**This step is needed only if a new front cover is being installed.**

20. Install the fan drive pulley using a nut and bolt with flat washers.

21. Clean and inspect the mounting surfaces of the engine and the front cover.

➡**The engine front cover must be installed and the bolts tightened within four minutes of applying the silicone gasket and sealant.**

22. Apply a 2.5 mm bead of silicone gasket and sealant to the cylinder head and oil pan joint areas. Apply a 2.5 mm bead of silicone gasket and sealant to the front cover.

23. Install the front cover. Tighten the bolts in the sequence shown, to the following specifications:
- Step 1: 8 mm bolts to 89 inch lbs. (10 Nm)
- Step 2: 10 mm bolts to 18 ft. lbs. (25 Nm)
- Step 3: 13 mm bolts to 35 ft. lbs. (48 Nm)

24. Install or connect the following:
- Power steering pump and lower retaining bolt
- Power steering return hose
- New nylon O-ring and install the high pressure line.
- Water pump pulley
- Belt tensioner

➡**Do not reuse the crankshaft damper bolt.**

- Crankshaft pulley and hand-tighten the bolt

25. Install an M6 bolt in the crankshaft pulley. Tighten the crankshaft retaining bolt in two stages.
- Step 1: 30 ft. lbs. (40 Nm)
- Step 2: Rotate the bolt an additional 90 degrees.

26. Install the crankshaft position sensor, do not tighten the bolts at this time.

27. Adjust the crankshaft position sensor with the Alignment Tool, and tighten the mounting bolts.

28. Connect the crankshaft position sensor electrical connector.

29. Remove the M6 bolt from the crankshaft pulley.

30. Remove the Crankshaft Timing Peg 303-507.

31. Install the plug.

32. Remove the Camshaft Alignment Plate 303-376.

33. Install the valve cover.

34. Install the drive belt.

35. Install the fan and shroud.

36. Connect the battery ground cable.

3.0L Engine

See Figure 122.

1. Before servicing the vehicle, refer to the precautions in the beginning of this section.

2. Remove or disconnect the following:
- Negative battery cable
- Engine front cover
- Rotate the crankshaft and align the timing marks
- Timing chain tensioner, 4.0L engine only
- Sprocket bolt
- Timing chain, camshaft sprocket

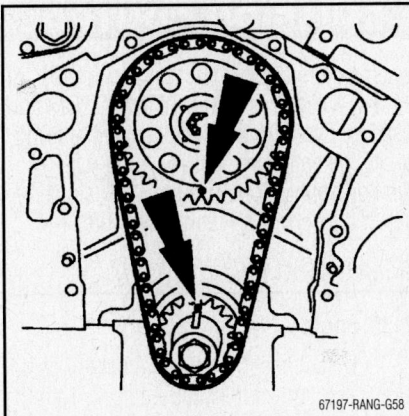

Fig. 122 Timing mark alignment—3.0L engine

and crankshaft sprocket as an assembly

To install:

3. Install or connect the following:
- Timing chain, camshaft and crankshaft sprockets as an assembly

4. Align the timing marks.

5. Install or connect the following:
- Timing chain tensioner
- Sprocket bolt. Torque the bolt to 51 ft. lbs. (70 Nm).
- Engine front cover
- Negative battery cable

4.0L Engine

See Figures 123 through 126.

1. Before servicing the vehicle, refer to the precautions in the beginning of this section.

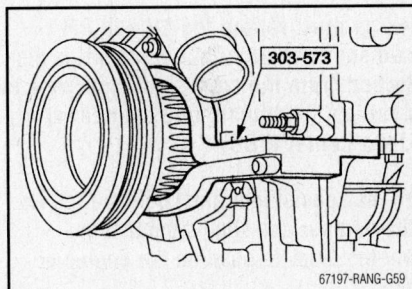

Fig. 123 TDC positioning tool installed—4.0L engine

Fig. 124 Loosening the right side camshaft sprocket bolt—4.0L engine

Fig. 125 Camshaft holding tool installed—4.0L engine

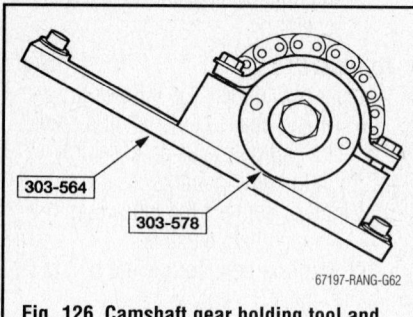

303-564
303-578

67197-RANG-G62

Fig. 126 Camshaft gear holding tool and adapter—4.0L engine

2. With the vehicle in neutral, position it on a hoist.
3. Remove the intake manifold.
4. Remove the fuel supply manifold.
5. Remove the accessory drive belt.
6. Remove the thermostat housing.
7. Remove the roller followers.

➡️**You must retime the LH and RH camshafts when either camshaft is disturbed. Turn the crankshaft clockwise to position the number one cylinder at Top Dead Center (TDC).**

➡️**The special tool must be installed on the damper and should contact the engine block to position the engine at TDC.**

8. Install the special tool.

➡️**The right-hand camshaft sprocket bolt is a left-hand threaded bolt.**

➡️**If necessary, use camshaft gear torque adapter to loosen the camshaft sprocket bolt.**

9. Using the special tool, loosen the RH camshaft sprocket bolt.

➡️**The camshaft timing slots are off-center.**

10. Position the camshaft timing slots below the centerline of the camshaft to correctly fit the special tools. Install the special tools on the front of the RH cylinder head.
11. Remove the RH lower splash shield.
12. Remove the RH camshaft tensioner.

➡️**Leave the top two special tool clamp bolts loose.**

13. Install the special tools on the rear of the RH cylinder head.
14. Install the special tool.

➡️**The right-hand camshaft sprocket bolt is a left-hand threaded bolt.**

➡️**If necessary, use camshaft gear torque adapter to tighten the camshaft sprocket bolt.**

15. Tighten the bolts.
16. Tighten the special tool top two clamp bolts to 89 inch lbs. (10 Nm).
17. Tighten the camshaft bolt.
18. Install the RH camshaft tensioner.
19. Install the RH lower splash shield.
20. Remove the LH camshaft tensioner.
21. Install the special tools on the front of the LH cylinder head and tighten the top two clamp bolts to 89 inch lbs. (10 Nm).
22. Loosen the LH camshaft sprocket bolt.
23. Loosen the top two clamp bolts on the special tool to allow the camshaft sprocket to rotate freely.

➡️**The camshaft timing slots are off-center.**

24. Position the camshaft timing slots below the centerline of the camshaft to correctly fit the special tools. Install the special tools on the rear of the LH cylinder head.
25. Install the special tool.
26. Tighten the bolts.

27. Tighten the special tool top two clamp bolts to 89 inch lbs. (10 Nm).
28. Tighten the camshaft bolt.
29. Install the LH camshaft tensioner.
30. Install the roller followers.
31. Install the thermostat housing.
32. Install the accessory drive belt.
33. Install the fuel supply manifold.
34. Install the intake manifold.
35. Install the RH valve cover.
36. Install the LH valve cover.

VALVE LASH

INSPECTION

1. Remove the valve cover.

✳✳ CAUTION

Turn the engine clockwise only, and use the crankshaft bolt only.

2. Measure each valve's clearance at base circle with the lobe pointed away from the tappet, before removing the camshafts. Failure to measure all clearances prior to removing the camshafts will necessitate repeated removal and installation and wasted labor time.
3. Use a feeler gauge to measure each valve's clearance and record its location.
4. A midrange clearance is the most desirable: intake: 0.008-0.011 in. (0.22-0.28mm), exhaust 0.010-0.013 in (0.27-0.33mm).
5. Select tappets using this formula: tappet thickness = measured clearance plus the base tappet thickness minus most desirable thickness.
6. Select tappets and mark installation location.
7. If any tappets do not measure within specifications, install new tappets in those locations

ENGINE PERFORMANCE & EMISSION CONTROL   COMPONENTS

COMPONENT LOCATIONS

See Figures 127 through 133.

CAMSHAFT POSITION (CMP) SENSOR

LOCATION

See Figures 134 through 136.

OPERATION

The CMP sensor detects the position of the camshaft. The CMP sensor identifies when piston number 1 is on its compression stroke. A signal is then sent to the PCM and used for synchronizing the sequential firing of the fuel injectors. Coil-on-plug (COP) ignition applications use the CMP signal to select the correct ignition coil to fire.

REMOVAL & INSTALLATION

2.3L Engine

1. Disconnect the negative battery cable.
2. Disconnect the vacuum hose from the intake manifold.
3. Disconnect the Camshaft Position Sensor (CMP) electrical connector.

4. Remove the bolt, the CMP sensor and discard the O-ring seal.

➡️**Lubricate the new O-ring seal with clean engine oil prior to installation.**

5. To install, reverse the removal procedure and note the following:
6. Tighten the CMP sensor mounting bolt to 62 inch. lbs. (7 Nm).

3.0L Engine

1. Disconnect the negative battery cable.
2. Disconnect the Camshaft Position (CMP) sensor electrical connector.

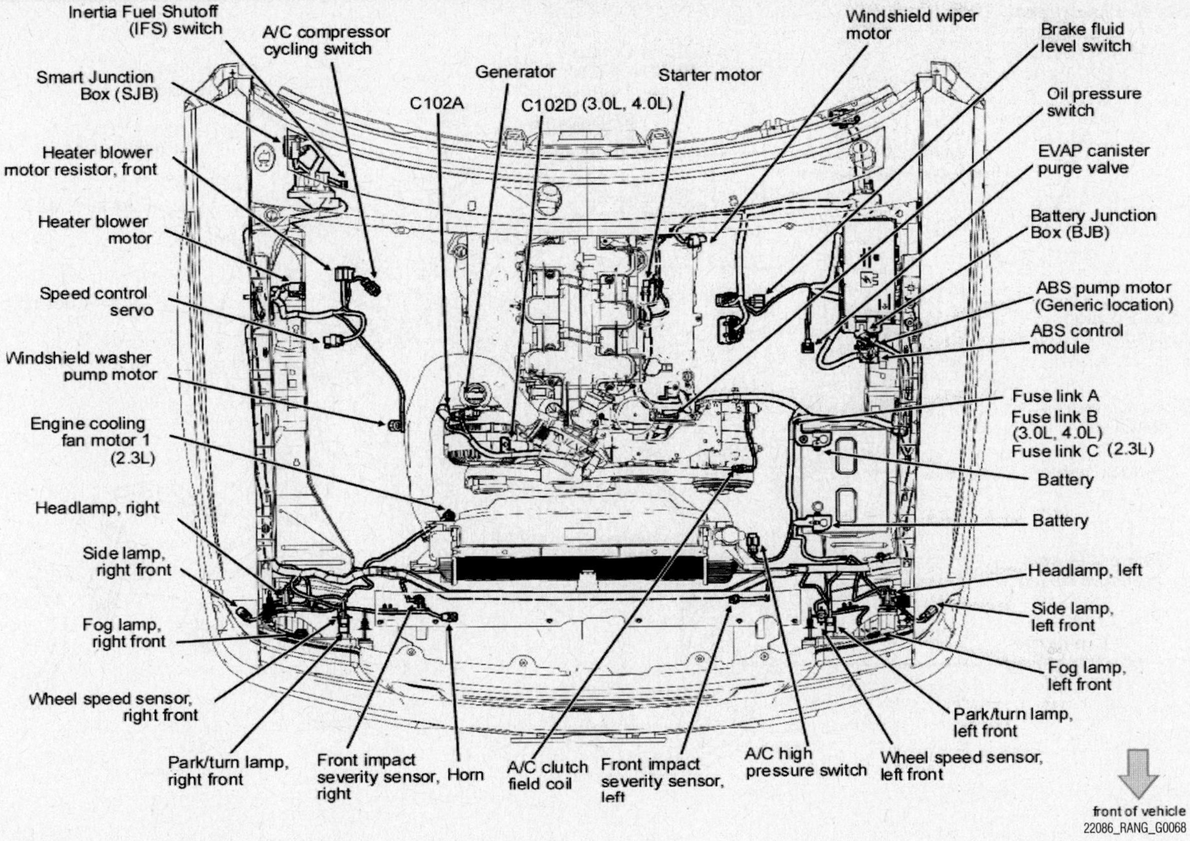

Fig. 127 Underhood component view—Ranger

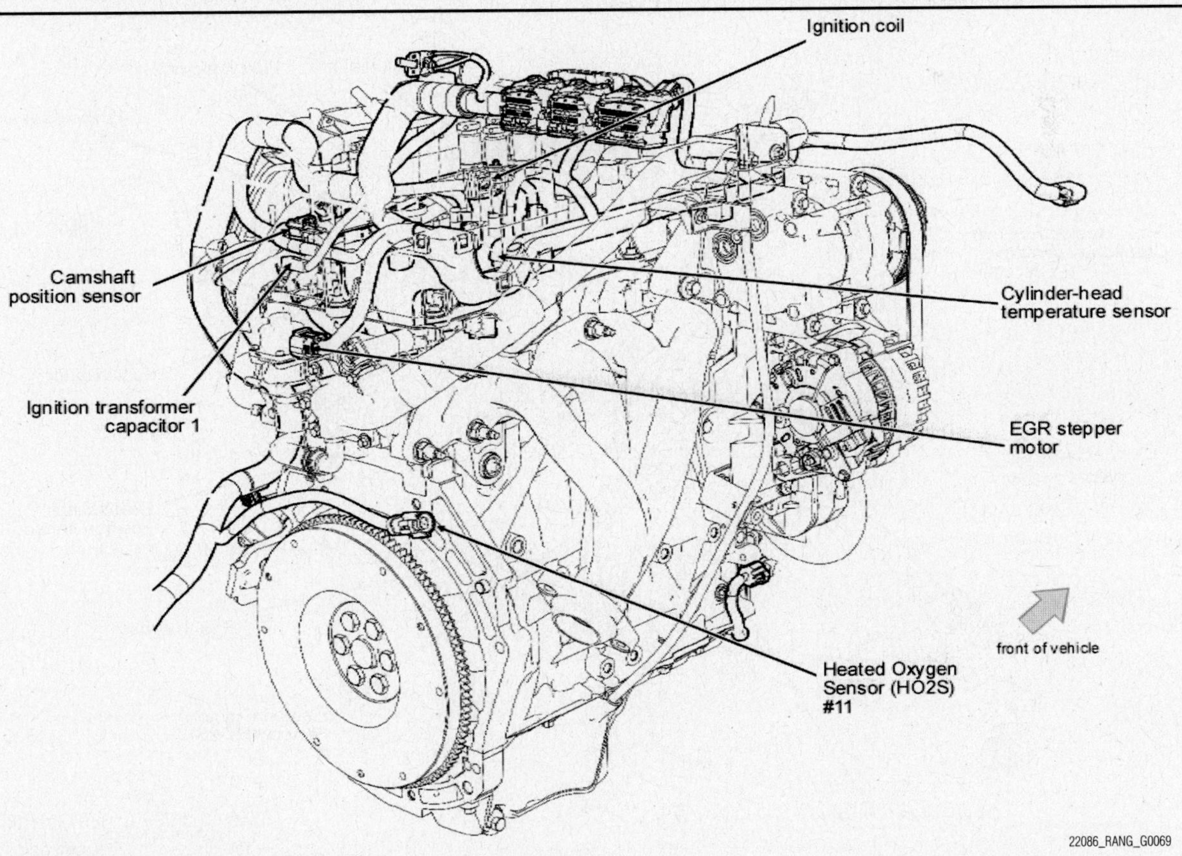

Inertia Fuel Shutoff (IFS) switch
A/C compressor cycling switch
Smart Junction Box (SJB)
Heater blower motor resistor, front
Heater blower motor
Speed control servo
Windshield washer pump motor
Engine cooling fan motor 1 (2.3L)
Headlamp, right
Side lamp, right front
Fog lamp, right front
Wheel speed sensor, right front
C102A
Generator
C102D (3.0L, 4.0L)
Starter motor
Windshield wiper motor
Brake fluid level switch
Oil pressure switch
EVAP canister purge valve
Battery Junction Box (BJB)
ABS pump motor (Generic location)
ABS control module
Fuse link A
Fuse link B (3.0L, 4.0L)
Fuse link C (2.3L)
Battery
Battery
Headlamp, left
Side lamp, left front
Fog lamp, left front
Park/turn lamp, left front
Wheel speed sensor, left front
Park/turn lamp, right front
Front impact severity sensor, Horn right
A/C clutch field coil
Front impact severity sensor, left
A/C high pressure switch
front of vehicle
22086_RANG_G0068

Fig. 128 Ranger engine electrical connectors (view 1)—2.3L engine

Ignition coil
Camshaft position sensor
Ignition transformer capacitor 1
Cylinder-head temperature sensor
EGR stepper motor
Heated Oxygen Sensor (HO2S) #11
front of vehicle
22086_RANG_G0069

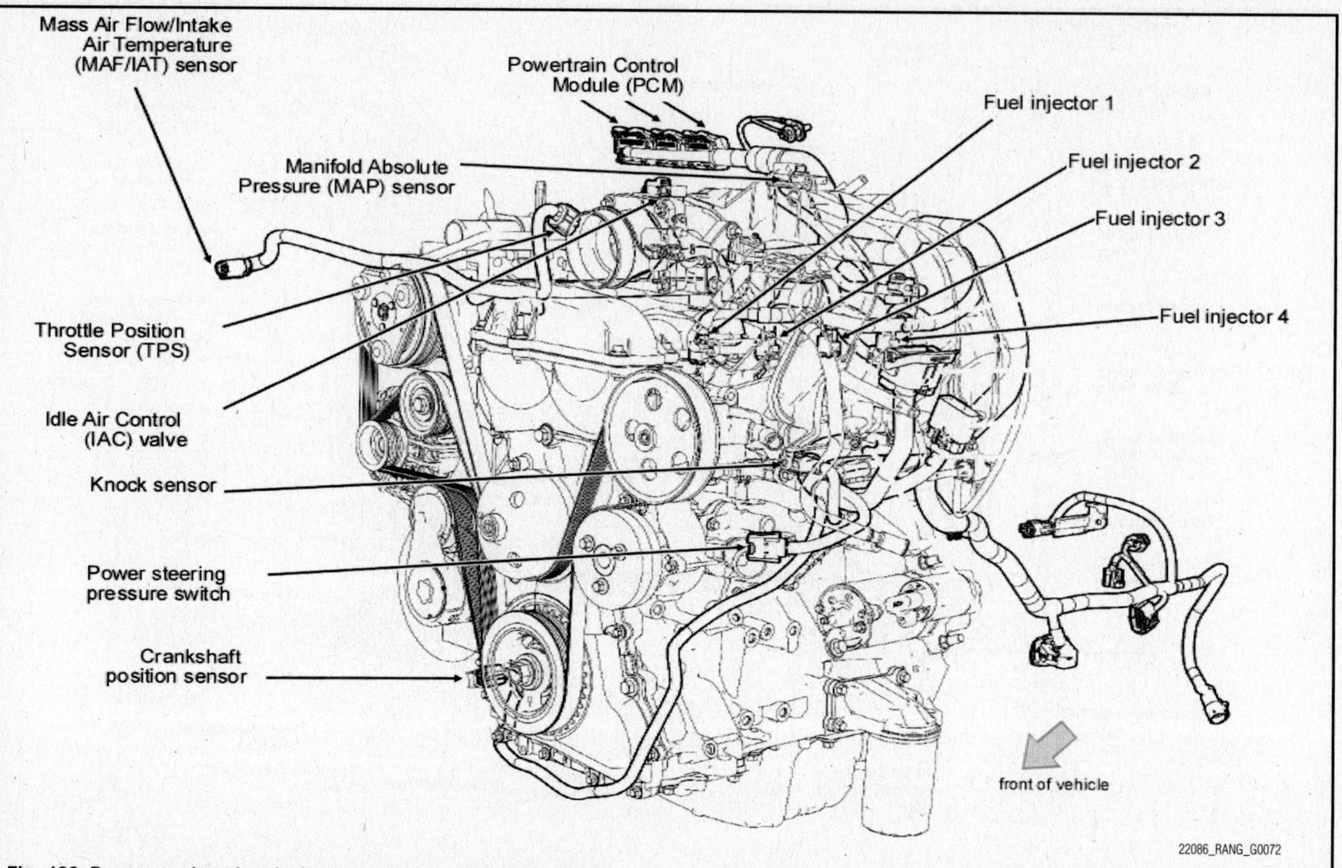

Fig. 129 Ranger engine electrical connectors (view 2)—2.3L engine

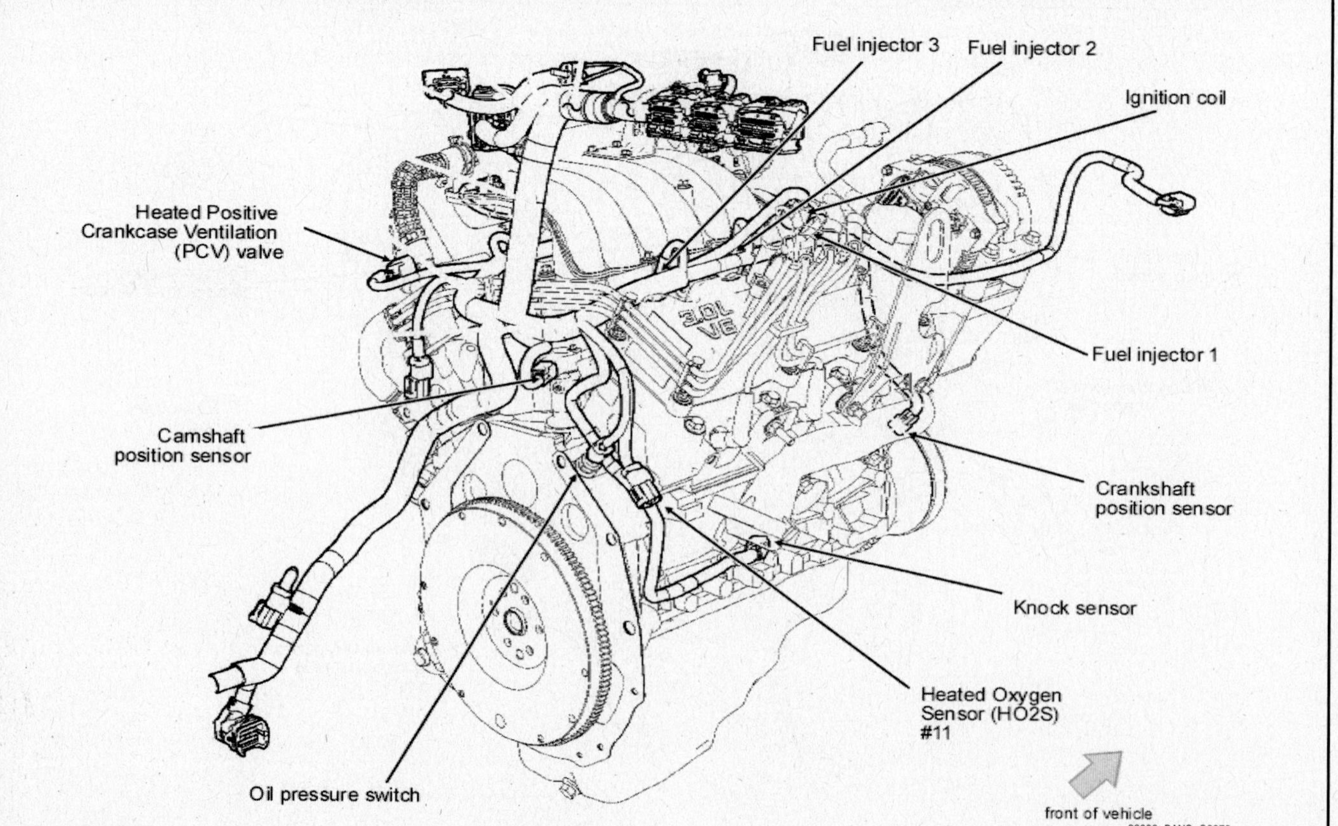

Mass Air Flow/Intake Air Temperature (MAF/IAT) sensor

Powertrain Control Module (PCM)

Fuel injector 1

Fuel injector 2

Fuel injector 3

Manifold Absolute Pressure (MAP) sensor

Fuel injector 4

Throttle Position Sensor (TPS)

Idle Air Control (IAC) valve

Knock sensor

Power steering pressure switch

Crankshaft position sensor

front of vehicle

22086_RANG_G0072

Fig. 130 Ranger electrical connectors (view 1)—3.0L engine

Fuel injector 3

Fuel injector 2

Ignition coil

Heated Positive Crankcase Ventilation (PCV) valve

Fuel injector 1

Camshaft position sensor

Crankshaft position sensor

Knock sensor

Heated Oxygen Sensor (HO2S) #11

Oil pressure switch

front of vehicle

22086_RANG_G0070

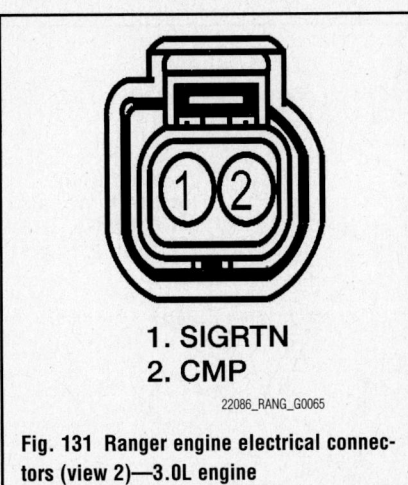

1. SIGRTN
2. CMP

22086_RANG_G0065

Fig. 131 Ranger engine electrical connectors (view 2)—3.0L engine

3. Remove the 2 bolts and the CMP sensor.

4. To install, reverse the removal procedure and note the following:

5. Tighten the CMP sensor mounting bolt to 27 inch. lbs. (3 Nm).

4.0L Engine

1. Disconnect the Camshaft Position (CMP) sensor electrical connector.

2. Remove the bolt, the CMP sensor and discard the O-ring seal.

➡**Lubricate the new O-ring seal with clean engine oil prior to installation.**

3. To install, reverse the removal procedure and note the following:

4. Tighten the Mounting bolt to 71 inch. lbs. (8 Nm).

TESTING

See Figures 137 through 139.

1. Check for any related diagnostic trouble codes.

2. Check the alternator for excessive electrical noise.

3. Verify the correct installation of the Camshaft Position (CMP) sensor.

4. Determine the CMP sensor electronic type.

➡**The Variable Reluctance (VR) sensors have 2-wire connectors, Hall-effect sensors have 3-wire connectors.**

5. Check the CMP sensor resistance.

6. To check the CMP sensor resistance turn the ignition to the **OFF** position.

7. Disconnect the CMP sensor electrical connector.

8. Check the resistance on sensor side between CMP and SIGRTN.

9. The sensor should read between 250—1000 ohms, if not suspect a faulty sensor.

10. Check the CMP sensor output.

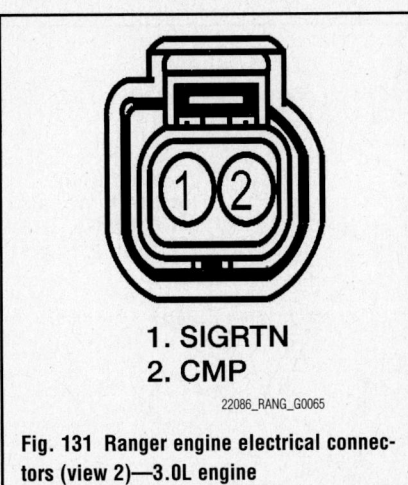

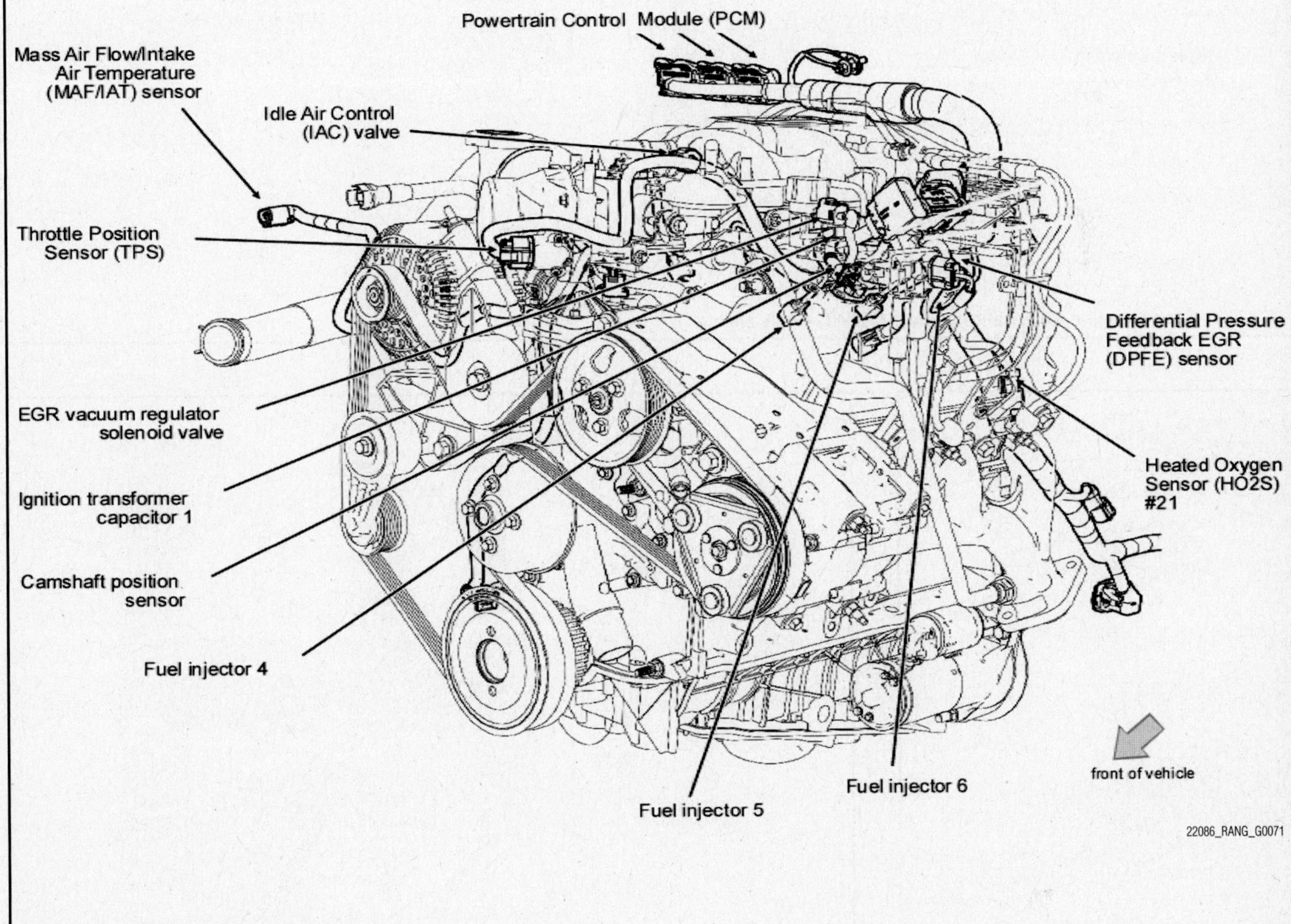

Mass Air Flow/Intake
Air Temperature
(MAF/IAT) sensor

Idle Air Control
(IAC) valve

Powertrain Control Module (PCM)

Throttle Position
Sensor (TPS)

Differential Pressure
Feedback EGR
(DPFE) sensor

EGR vacuum regulator
solenoid valve

Ignition transformer
capacitor 1

Camshaft position
sensor

Heated Oxygen
Sensor (HO2S)
#21

Fuel injector 4

Fuel injector 5

Fuel injector 6

front of vehicle

22086_RANG_G0071

Fig. 132 Ranger electrical connectors (view 1)—4.0L engine

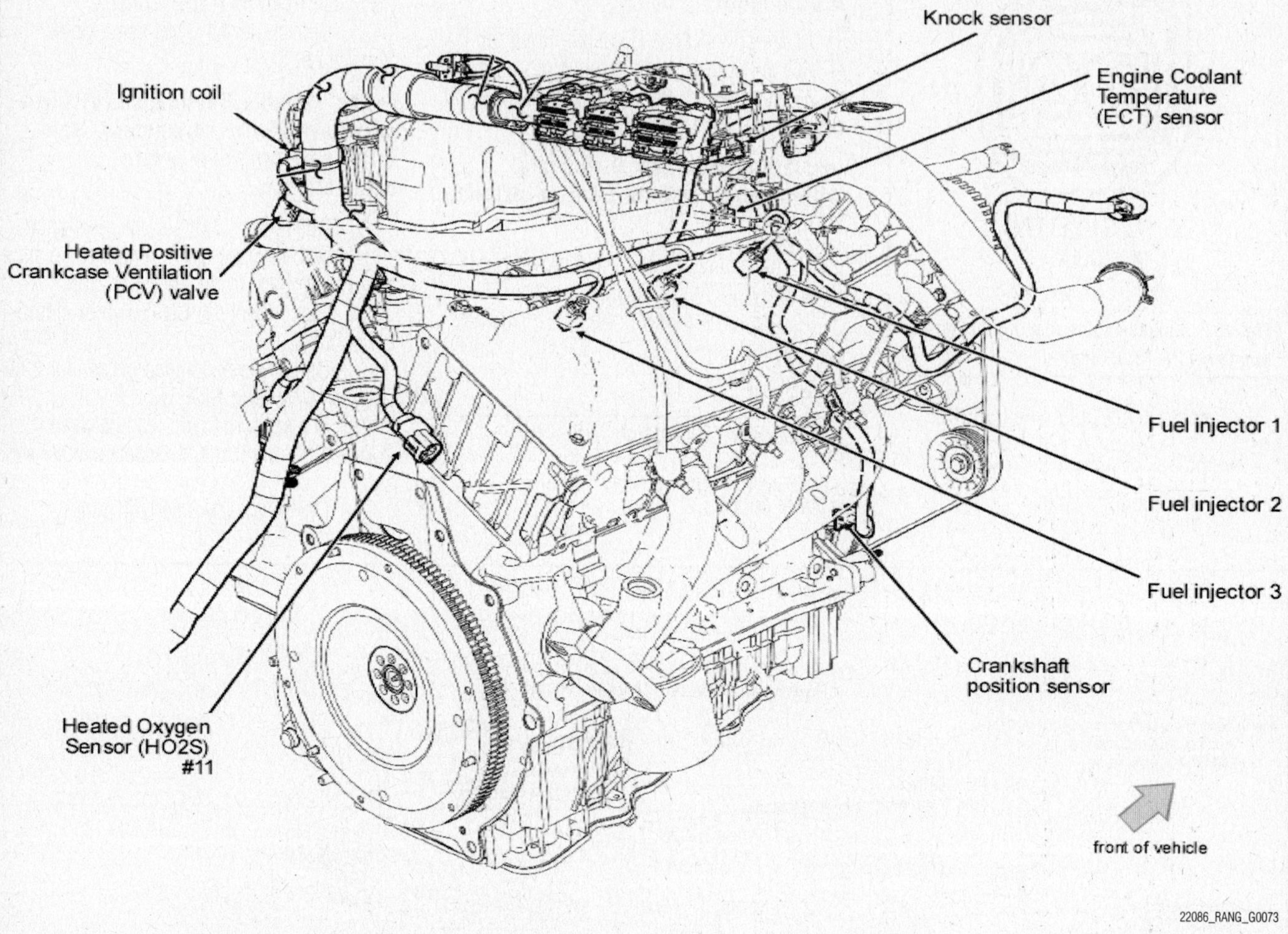

Knock sensor
Ignition coil
Engine Coolant Temperature (ECT) sensor
Heated Positive Crankcase Ventilation (PCV) valve
Fuel injector 1
Fuel injector 2
Fuel injector 3
Crankshaft position sensor
Heated Oxygen Sensor (HO2S) #11
front of vehicle
22086_RANG_G0073

Fig. 133 Ranger engine electrical connectors (view 2)—4.0L engine

7 Nm (62 lb-in)
2
1
3
4
22086_RANG_G0075

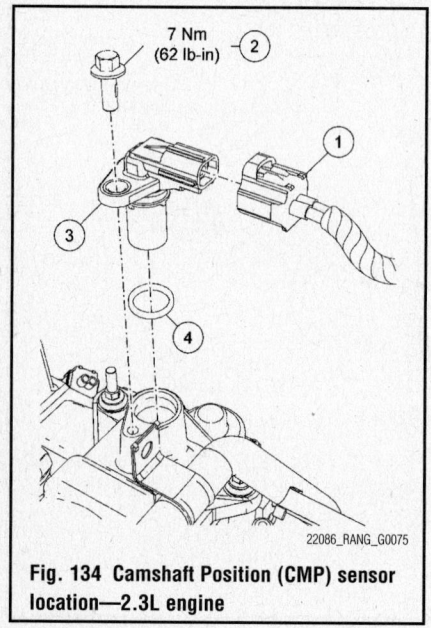

Fig. 134 Camshaft Position (CMP) sensor location—2.3L engine

3 Nm (27 lb-in)
2
3
1
5
4
30 Nm (22 lb-ft)
3.0L V6
22086_RANG_G0076

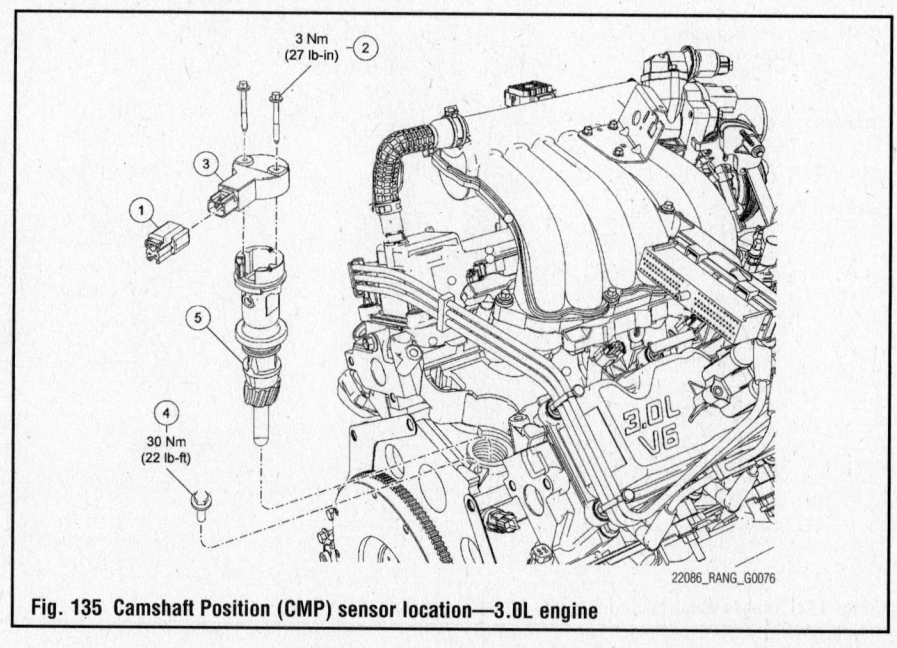

Fig. 135 Camshaft Position (CMP) sensor location—3.0L engine

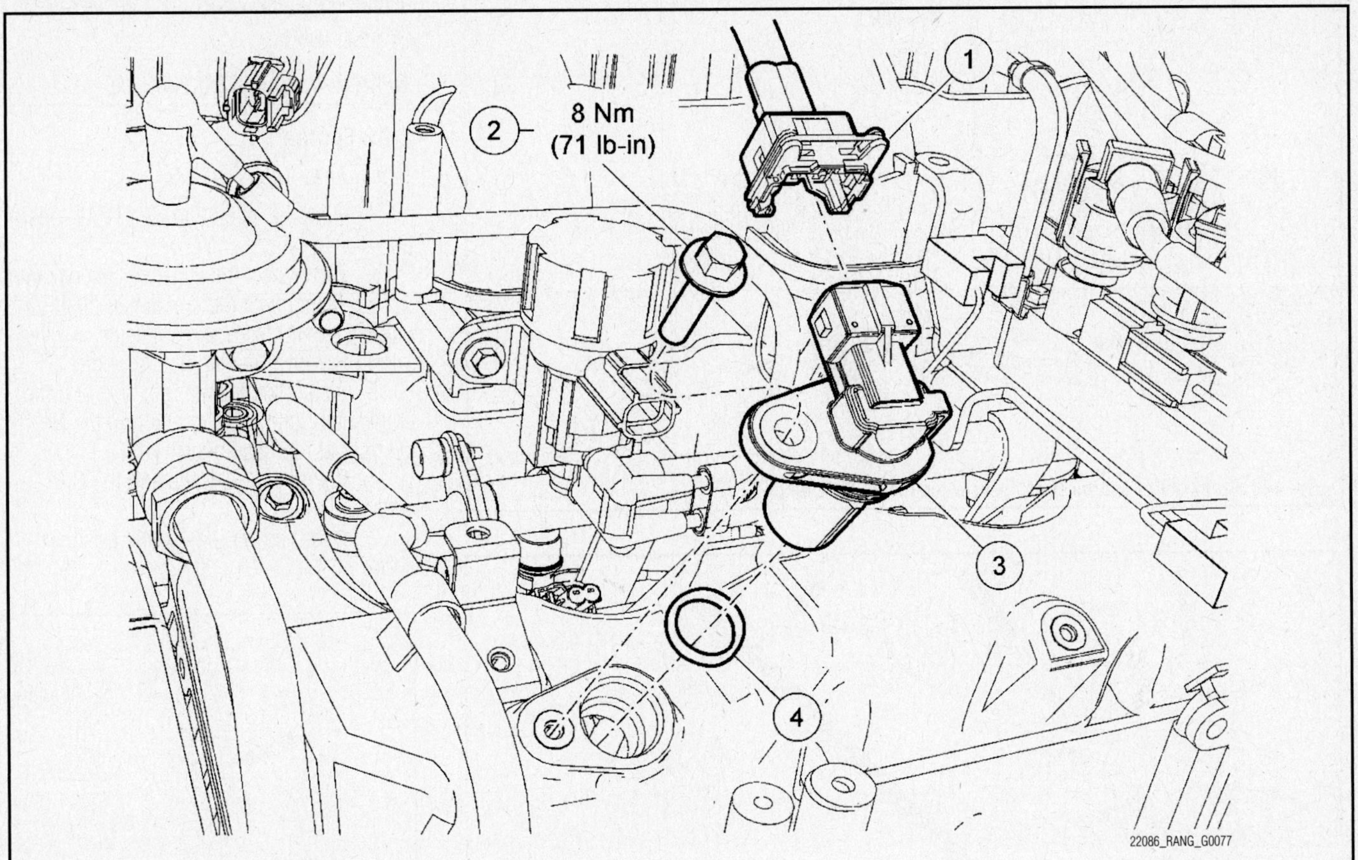

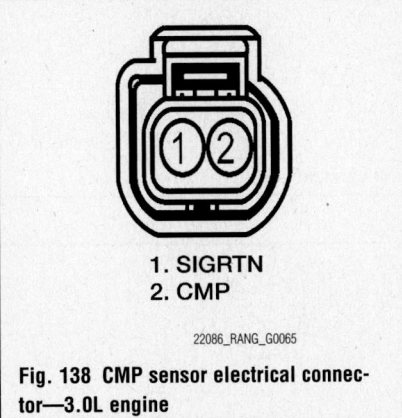

Fig. 136 Camshaft Position (CMP) sensor location—4.0L engine

8 Nm
(71 lb-in)

11. To check CMP sensor output, turn the ignition to the off position.

12. Alternator/regulator B+ connector connected.

13. Disconnect the CMP sensor connector.

14. With the engine running connect a Digital multimeter (DMM).

15. Measure the voltage reading with the DMM set on AC low voltage scale.

16. Run the engine at approximately 2,500 RPM.

17. Measure for voltage at the component side, between CMP and SIGRTN connectors.

**1. SIGRTN
2. CMP**

Fig. 138 CMP sensor electrical connector—3.0L engine

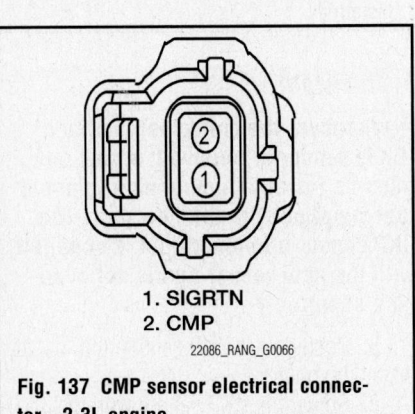

**1. SIGRTN
2. CMP**

Fig. 137 CMP sensor electrical connector—2.3L engine

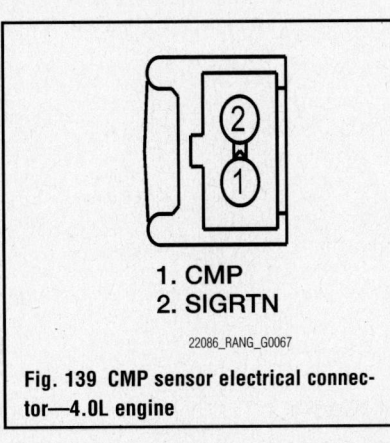

**1. CMP
2. SIGRTN**

Fig. 139 CMP sensor electrical connector—4.0L engine

18. The reading should be greater than 0.25 volts. If not suspect a faulty sensor.

CRANKSHAFT POSITION (CKP) SENSOR

LOCATION

See Figures 140 through 142.

OPERATION

The CKP sensor is a magnetic transducer mounted on the engine block adjacent to a pulse wheel located on the crankshaft. By monitoring the crankshaft mounted pulse wheel, the CKP is the primary sensor for ignition information to the PCM. The pulse wheel has a total of 35 teeth spaced 10 degrees apart with one empty space for a missing tooth. By monitoring the pulse wheel, the CKP sensor signal indicates crankshaft position and speed information to the PCM. By monitoring the missing tooth, the CKP sensor is also able to identify piston travel in order to synchronize the ignition system and provide a way of tracking the angular position of the crankshaft relative to a fixed reference for the CKP sensor configuration. The PCM also uses the CKP signal to determine if a misfire has

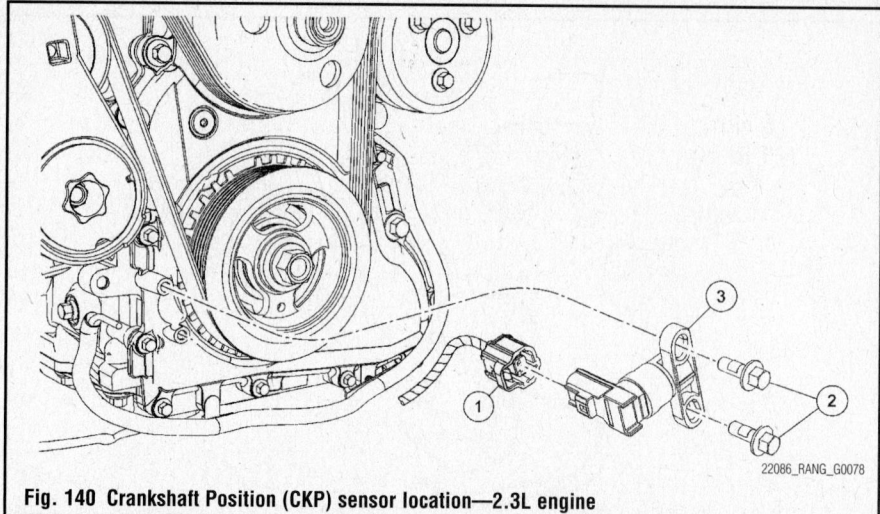

Fig. 140 Crankshaft Position (CKP) sensor location—2.3L engine

22086_RANG_G0078

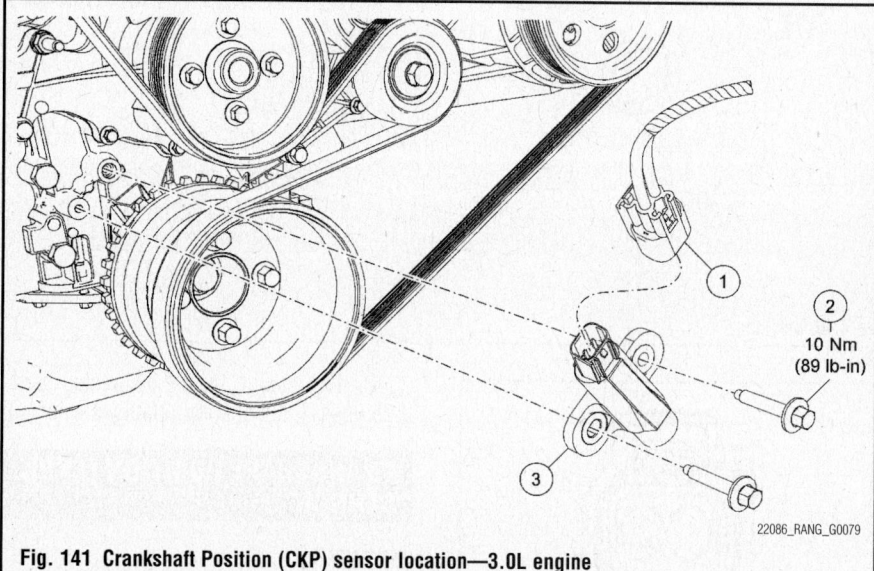

10 Nm
(89 lb-in)

Fig. 141 Crankshaft Position (CKP) sensor location—3.0L engine

22086_RANG_G0079

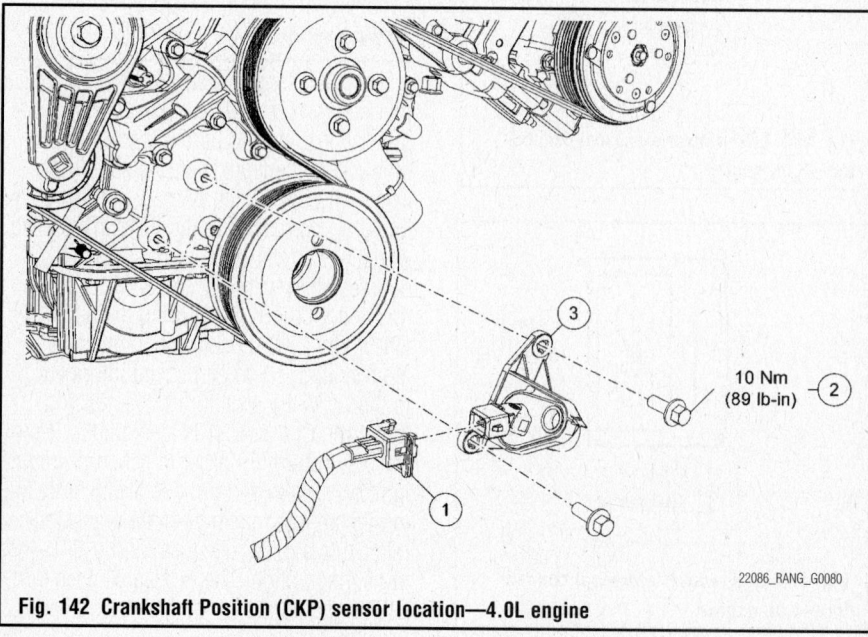

10 Nm
(89 lb-in)

Fig. 142 Crankshaft Position (CKP) sensor location—4.0L engine

22086_RANG_G0080

occurred by measuring rapid decelerations between teeth.

REMOVAL & INSTALLATION

2.3L Engine

See Figures 143, 144, 145

1. With the vehicle in NEUTRAL, position it on a hoist.
2. Disconnect the negative battery cable.
3. Disconnect the crankshaft position (CKP) sensor electrical connector.
4. Remove the engine plug bolt.
5. Install the special tool and turn the crankshaft pulley bolt to position the No. 1 cylinder at top dead center (TDC).
6. Remove the 2 bolts and the CKP sensor.
7. Install an M6 bolt in the position shown.

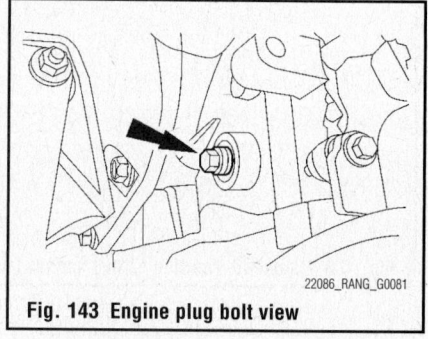

22086_RANG_G0081

Fig. 143 Engine plug bolt view

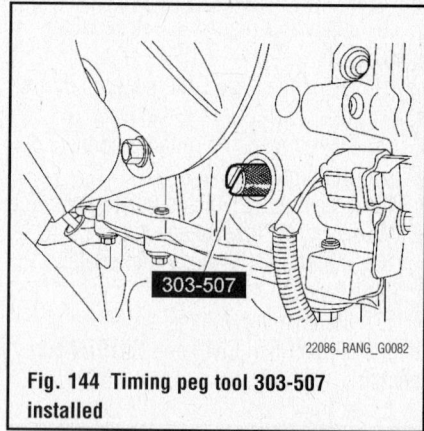

303-507

22086_RANG_G0082

Fig. 144 Timing peg tool 303-507 installed

To install:

➡ Whenever the crankshaft position (CKP) sensor is removed, a new one must be installed using the alignment tool supplied with the new part. The CKP sensor alignment tool is supplied with the new sensor and is not available separately.

8. Position the CKP sensor and loosely install the bolts.
9. Adjust the CKP sensor with the

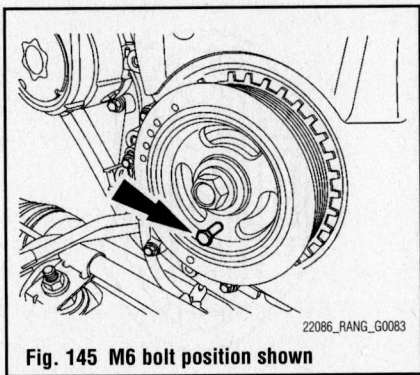

Fig. 145 M6 bolt position shown

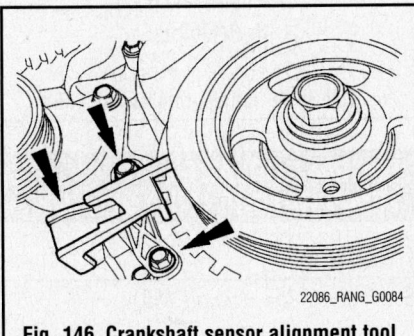

Fig. 146 Crankshaft sensor alignment tool shown

alignment tool and tighten the bolts to 62 inch. lbs. (7 Nm).

10. Connect the CKP sensor electrical connector.

11. Remove the M6 bolt

12. Remove the special tool.

13. Install the engine plug bolt and tighten to 15 ft. lbs. (20 Nm).

3.0L and 4.0L Engines

1. With the vehicle in NEUTRAL, position it on a hoist.

2. Disconnect the battery ground cable.

3. Disconnect the crankshaft position (CKP) sensor electrical connector.

4. Remove the 2 bolts and the CKP sensor.

5. To install, reverse the removal procedure and tighten the CKP sensor bolts to 89 inch. lbs. (10 Nm).

TESTING

See Figures 147, 148, and 149

➡**The battery should be fully charged and the starting system should be functioning properly.**

1. Install scan tool.

2. Disable the inertia switch and crank engine

3. Access the PCM and monitor the RPM PID.

4. The reading should be greater than

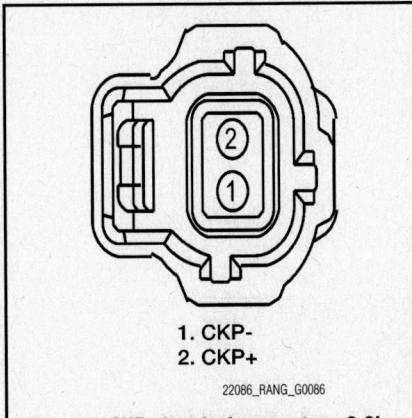

1. CKP-
2. CKP+

Fig. 147 CKP electrical connector—2.3L engine

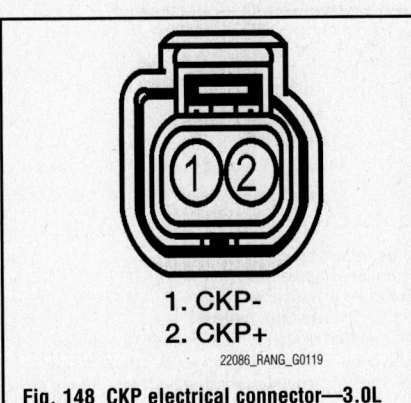

1. CKP-
2. CKP+

Fig. 148 CKP electrical connector—3.0L engine

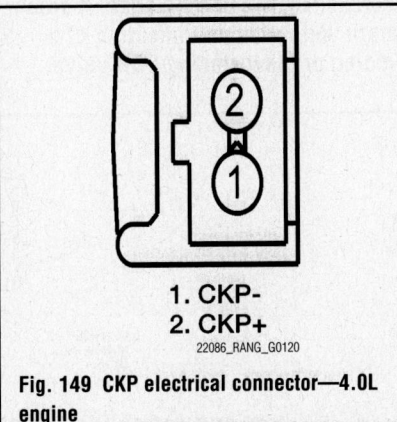

1. CKP-
2. CKP+

Fig. 149 CKP electrical connector—4.0L engine

150 RPM. If so the CKP, harness and PCM are working properly.

5. Check the sensor and connector for any obvious physical external damage.

6. Check the CKP sensor for resistance.

7. To check the CKP sensor for resistance, turn the ignition to the off position.

8. Measure the resistance between the terminals on the component side. (CKP+ and CKP-)

9. If the resistance is between 250—1000k ohms. The CKP sensor is okay.

DIFFERENTIAL PRESSURE FEEDBACK EGR (DPFE)

LOCATION

See Figure 150.

The Differential Pressure Feedback EGR (DPFE) sensor is located above the left exhaust manifold and EGR valve tube.

OPERATION

2.3L Engine

The 2.3L engine incorporates a stepper motor-controlled EGR valve which receives its signal from the Powertrain Control Module (PCM). Engine coolant is used to cool the EGR valve. The EGR valve and stepper motor are serviced as an assembly.

3.0L and 4.0L Engines

The Differential Pressure Feedback EGR (DPFE) sensor is a ceramic, capacitive-type pressure transducer that monitors the differential pressure across a metering orifice located in the orifice tube assembly. The DPFE sensor receives this signal through 2 hoses referred to as the downstream pressure hose (REF SIGNAL) and upstream pressure hose (HI SIGNAL). The HI and REF hose connections are marked on the differential pressure feedback EGR sensor housing for identification (note that the HI signal uses a larger diameter hose). The DPFE sensor outputs a voltage proportional to the pressure drop across the metering orifice and supplies it to the PCM as EGR flow rate feedback.

The PCM controls the EGR vacuum regulator solenoid. The EGR vacuum regulator solenoid controls the vacuum to the EGR valve. When the EGR valve opens, exhaust gas flows to the intake manifold to be returned to the combustion cycle. The differential pressure feedback EGR system monitors the flow and returns a signal to the PCM.

The amount of recirculated exhaust gas depends upon:
- Engine rpm
- Intake manifold vacuum
- Exhaust backpressure
- Engine coolant temperature
- Throttle position

REMOVAL & INSTALLATION

3.0L and 4.0L Engines

1. Disconnect the negative battery cable.

2. Disconnect the pushpin retainer from

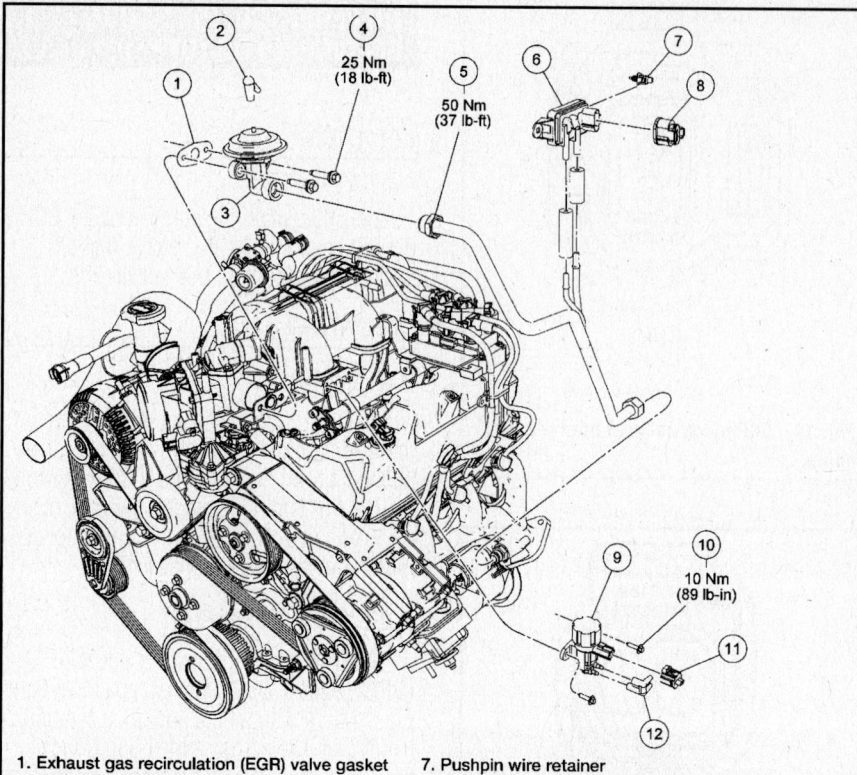

1. Exhaust gas recirculation (EGR) valve gasket
2. EGR valve vacuum connector
3. EGR valve assembly
4. EGR valve bolt (2 required)
5. EGR tube
6. Differential pressure feedback EGR sensor
7. Pushpin wire retainer
8. Differential pressure feedback EGR sensor electrical connector
9. EGR vacuum regulator solenoid
10. EGR vacuum regulator solenoid bolt (2 required)
11. EGR vacuum regulator solenoid electrical connector
12. EGR vacuum regulator solenoid vacuum connector

22086_RANG_G0098

Fig. 150 DPFE sensor and related EGR components—4.0L engine shown, 3.0L engine similar

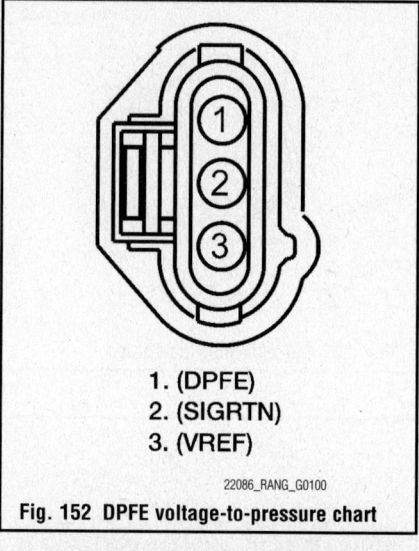

1. (DPFE)
2. (SIGRTN)
3. (VREF)

22086_RANG_G0100

Fig. 152 DPFE voltage-to-pressure chart

the Differential Pressure Feedback EGR (DPFE) sensor.

3. Disconnect the DPFE sensor electrical connector.

4. Remove the DPFE sensor from the hoses.

5. To install, reverse the removal procedure.

TESTING

3.0L and 4.0L Engines

See Figures 151 and 152.

1. Disconnect the DPFE sensor harness connector. With the ignition on and engine off, measure the voltage between VREF and SIGRTN terminals of the DPFE harness connector. If the voltage is 4 —5.5V, the power circuits to the sensor are okay.

➡ **Typical sensor voltage with no EGR flow is between 0.25 volt and 1.3 volts. A higher voltage at idle may be due to a non-seating or heavily carboned EGR valve pintle. DPFEGR PID voltage must increase as the valve opens and decrease as the valve closes. A slow return voltage is an indication of a binding or slow closing EGR valve.**

ENGINE COOLANT TEMPERATURE (ECT) SENSOR

LOCATION

See Figures 153 through 155.

The Cylinder Head Temperature (CHT) sensor for the 2.3L engine is located between the two center ignition coils.

The Engine Coolant Temperature (ECT) sensor for the 3.0L engine is located in the intake manifold to the right of the thermostat housing.

The Engine Coolant Temperature (ECT) sensor for the 4.0L engine is located in the intake manifold behind the thermostat housing.

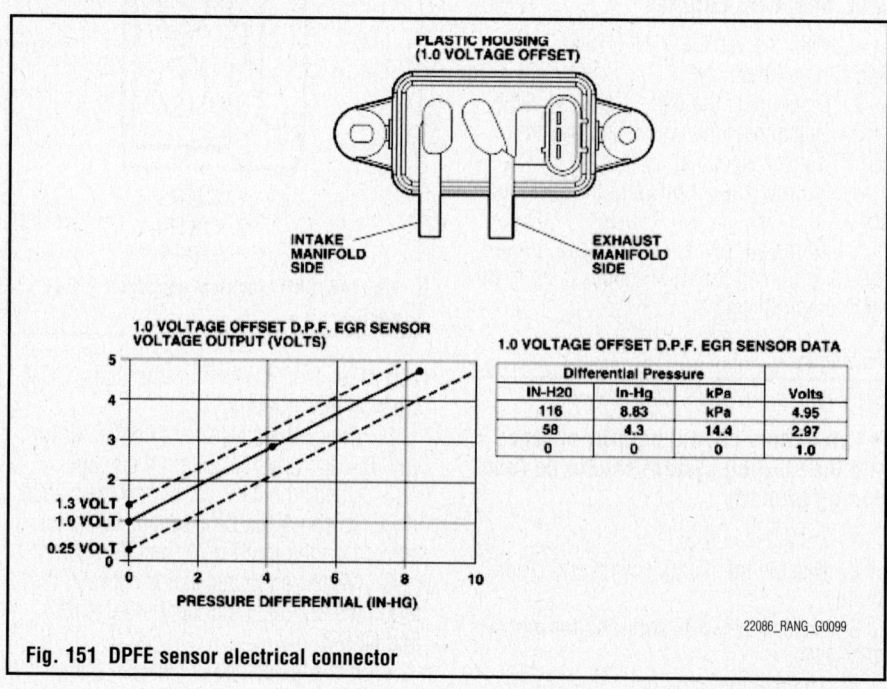

Differential Pressure			
IN-H20	In-Hg	kPa	Volts
116	8.83	kPa	4.95
58	4.3	14.4	2.97
0	0	0	1.0

22086_RANG_G0099

Fig. 151 DPFE sensor electrical connector

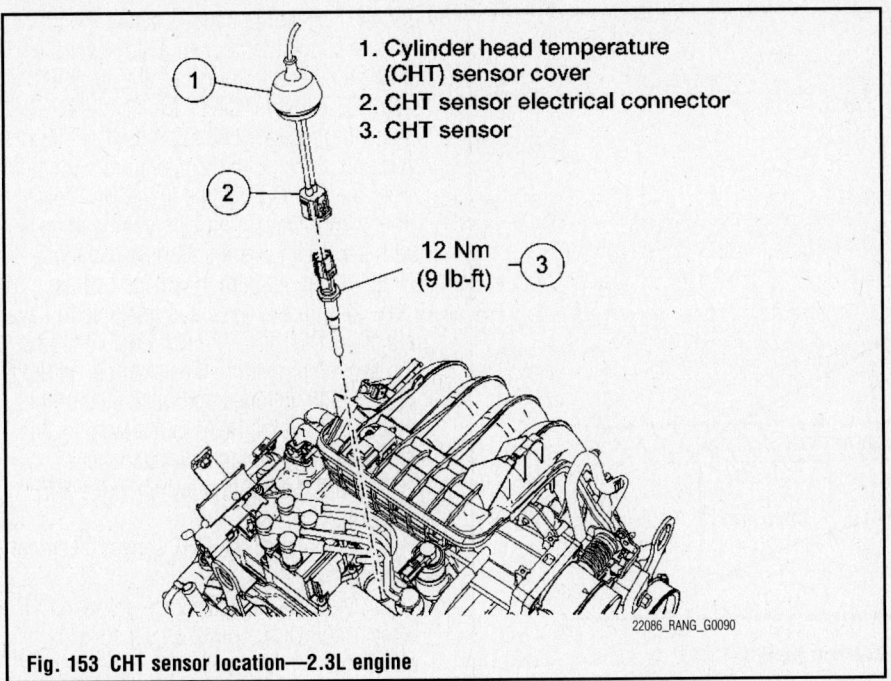

1. Cylinder head temperature (CHT) sensor cover
2. CHT sensor electrical connector
3. CHT sensor

12 Nm (9 lb-ft)

22086_RANG_G0090

Fig. 153 CHT sensor location—2.3L engine

OPERATION

CHT Sensor

The CHT sensor is a thermistor device in which resistance changes with the temperature. The electrical resistance of a thermistor decreases as temperature increases, and the resistance increases as the temperature decreases. The varying resistance affects the voltage drop across the sensor terminals and provides electrical signals to the PCM corresponding to temperature.

The CHT sensor is installed in the cylinder head and measures the metal temperature. The CHT sensor can provide complete engine temperature information and can be used to infer coolant temperature. If the CHT sensor conveys an overheating condition to the PCM, the PCM initiates a fail-safe cooling strategy based on information from the CHT sensor. A cooling system concern such as low coolant or coolant loss could cause an overheating condition. As a result, damage to major engine components could occur. Using both the CHT sensor and fail-safe cooling strategy, the PCM prevents damage by allowing air cooling of the engine and limp home capability.

ECT Sensor

The ECT sensor is a thermistor device in which resistance changes with temperature.

The electrical resistance of a thermistor decreases as the temperature increases, and the resistance increases as the temperature decreases. The varying resistance changes the voltage drop across the sensor terminals and provides electrical signals to the PCM corresponding to temperature.

Thermistor-type sensors are considered passive sensors. A passive sensor is connected to a voltage divider network so that varying the resistance of the passive sensor causes a variation in total current flow. Voltage that is dropped across a fixed resistor in a series with the sensor resistor determines the voltage signal at the PCM. This voltage signal is equal the reference voltage minus the voltage drop across the fixed resistor.

The ECT measures the temperature of the engine coolant. The PCM uses the ECT input for fuel control and for cooling fan control. There are 3 types of ECT sensors, threaded, push-in, and twist-lock. The ECT sensor is located in an engine coolant passage.

REMOVAL & INSTALLATION

2.3L Engine

1. Disconnect the negative battery cable.
2. Pull back the Cylinder Head Temperature (CHT) sensor cover and disconnect the electrical connector.
3. Remove the CHT sensor.
4. To install, reverse the removal procedure and tighten sensor to 9 ft. lbs. (12 Nm).

3.0L Engine

1. Drain the cooling system.
2. Disconnect the Engine Coolant Temperature (ECT) sensor electrical connector.
3. Remove the ECT sensor.
4. To install, reverse the removal procedure and tighten ECT sensor to 15 ft. lbs. (20 Nm).

4.0L Engine

1. Drain the cooling system.
2. Disconnect the battery ground cable.
3. Disconnect the Engine Coolant Temperature (ECT) sensor electrical connector.
4. Remove the clip and the ECT sensor. Discard the O-ring seal.
5. To install, reverse the removal procedure. Install a new O-ring seal.

TESTING

2.3L Engine

See Figures 156 through 158.

On applications that do not use an Engine Coolant Temperature (ECT) sensor,

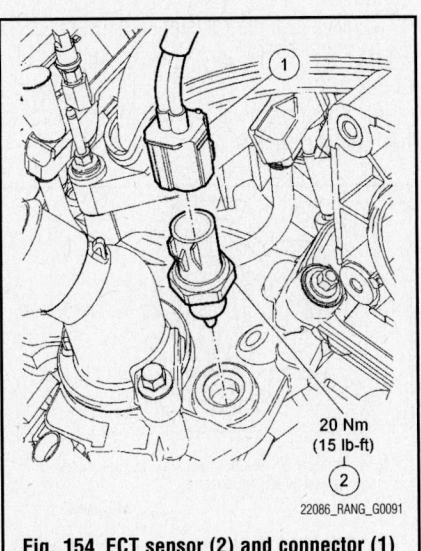

1. Engine coolant temperature (ECT) sensor electrical connector
2. ECT sensor clip
3. ECT sensor
4. ECT sensor O-ring seal

20 Nm (15 lb-ft)

22086_RANG_G0091

Fig. 154 ECT sensor (2) and connector (1) locations—3.0L engine

22086_RANG_G0092

Fig. 155 ECT sensor location—4.0L engine

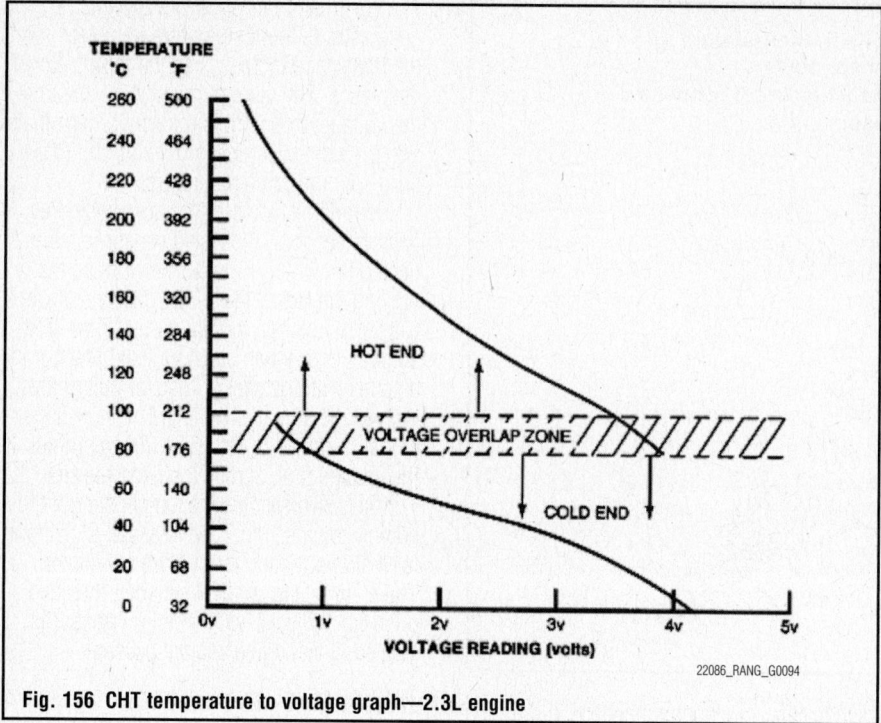

Fig. 156 CHT temperature to voltage graph—2.3L engine

Cylinder Head Temperature Sensor Expected Values				
Temperature		CHT Sensor Values		
°C	°F	Cold End (volts)	Hot End (volts)	Resistance (K ohms)
-40	-40	4.89	-	965.808
-30	-22	4.81	-	513.019
-20	-4	4.67	-	283.664
-10	14	4.45	-	162.584
0	32	4.14	-	96.255
10	50	3.73	-	59.175
20	68	3.26	-	37.387
30	86	2.74	-	24.215
40	104	2.23	-	16.043
50	122	1.76	-	10.85
60	140	1.36	-	7.487
70	158	1.04	-	5.268
80	176	0.79	3.99	3.775
85	185	0.69	3.86	3.215
90	194	0.60	3.71	2.75
95	203	0.53	3.56	2.361
100	212	0.46	3.41	2.034
110	230	-	3.07	1.523
120	248	-	2.74	1.155
130	266	-	2.41	0.8866
140	284	-	2.10	0.6891
150	302	-	1.81	0.5417
160	320	-	1.55	0.4301
170	338	-	1.33	0.3449
180	356	-	1.13	0.2791
190	374	-	0.96	0.2278
200	392	-	0.82	0.1875
210	410	-	0.70	0.155
220	428	-	0.60	0.130
230	446	-	0.51	0.109
240	464	-	0.44	0.092
250	482	-	0.35	0.078
260	500	-	0.33	0.067

Fig. 157 CHT sensor expected values chart—2.3L engine

the CHT sensor is used to determine the engine coolant temperature. To cover the entire temperature range of both the CHT and ECT sensors, the PCM has a dual switching resistor circuit on the CHT input. A graph showing the temperature switching from the COLD END line to the HOT END line, with increasing temperature and back with decreasing temperature is included. Note the temperature to voltage overlap zone. Within this zone it is possible to have either a COLD END or HOT END voltage at the same temperature. For example, at 90°C (194°F) the voltage could read either 0.60 volt or 3.71 volts. Refer to the table for the temperature to voltage expected values.

1. Turn the ignition switch to the **OFF** position.

2. Disconnect the CHT sensor electrical connector.

3. Measure the resistance between CHT + pin 1 and CHT - pin 2 on sensor side of connector.

4. If resistance is not within specification replace sensor.

3.0L and 4.0L Engines

See Figures 158, 159 and 160.

➡️**Engine coolant temperature must be greater than 10°C (50°F) to pass the KOEO self-test and greater than 82°C (180°F) to pass the KOER self-test. to accomplish this, the engine must be at normal operating temperature. Voltage values calculated for VREF = 5 volts. These values can vary by 15% due to sensor and VREF variations.**

1. Turn the ignition switch to the **OFF** position.

2. Disconnect the CHT sensor electrical connector.

3. Measure the resistance between CHT + pin 1 and CHT - pin 2 on sensor side of connector.

4. If resistance is not within specification replace sensor.

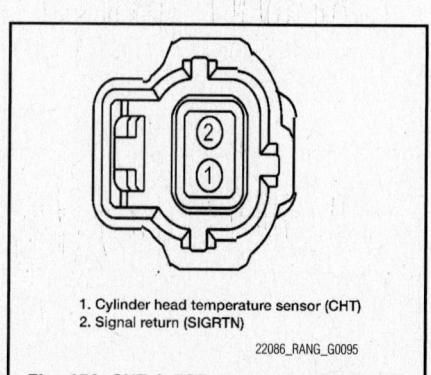

1. Cylinder head temperature sensor (CHT)
2. Signal return (SIGRTN)

Fig. 158 CHT & ECT sensor electrical connector

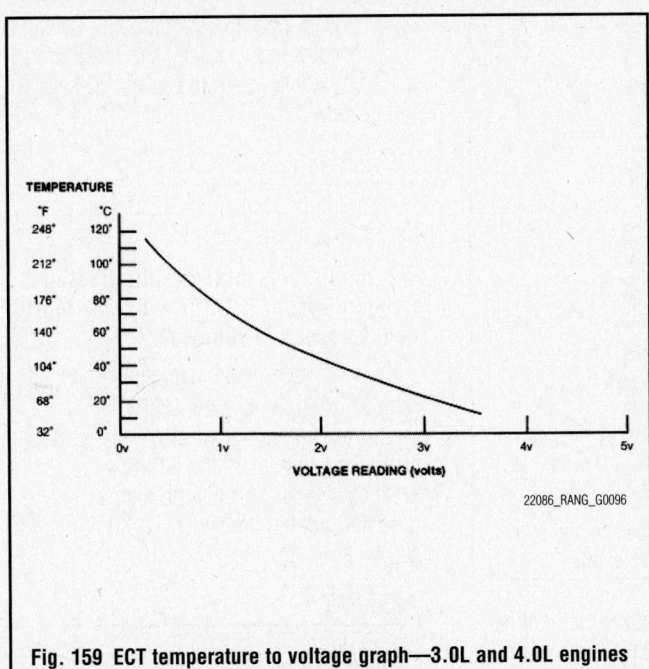

Fig. 159 ECT temperature to voltage graph—3.0L and 4.0L engines

TEMPERATURE SENSOR VOLTAGE AND RESISTANCE SPECIFICATIONS

Temperature		Temperature Sensor Values	
°C	°F	Voltage	Resistance (K ohms)
120	248	0.28	1.18
110	230	0.36	1.55
100	212	0.47	2.07
90	194	0.61	2.80
80	176	0.80	3.84
70	158	1.05	5.37
60	140	1.37	7.70
50	122	1.77	10.97
40	104	2.23	16.15
30	86	2.74	24.27
20	68	3.26	37.30
10	50	3.73	58.75
0	32	4.14	95.85
-10	14	4.45	160.31

Fig. 160 ECT temperature sensor voltage and resistance chart— 3.0L and 4.0L engines

EXHAUST BACKPRESSURE REGULATOR

LOCATION

See Figure 161.

The EGR vacuum regulator is located on the left side of engine and above the valve cover.

OPERATION

The EGR vacuum regulator solenoid is an electromagnetic device used to regulate the vacuum supply to the EGR valve. The solenoid contains a coil which magnetically controls the position of a disc to regulate the vacuum. As the duty cycle to the coil increases, the vacuum signal passed through the solenoid to the EGR valve also increases. Vacuum not directed to the EGR valve is vented through the solenoid vent to atmosphere. Note that at 0% duty cycle (no electrical signal applied), the EGR vacuum regulator solenoid allows some vacuum to pass, but not enough to open the EGR valve.

REMOVAL & INSTALLATION

3.0L and 4.0L Engines

1. Disconnect the negative battery cable.
2. Disconnect the electrical and vacuum connectors from the Exhaust Gas Recirculation (EGR) vacuum regulator solenoid.
3. Remove the retaining bolts and the EGR vacuum regulator solenoid.

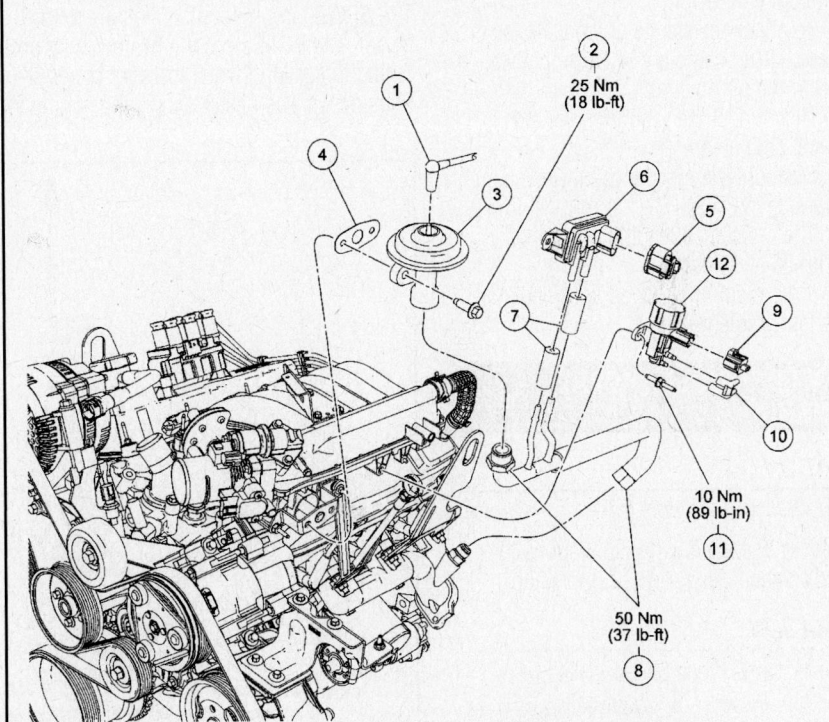

1. Exhaust gas recirculation (EGR) vacuum hose fitting
2. EGR valve bolt (2 required)
3. EGR valve
4. EGR valve gasket
5. Differential pressure feedback EGR sensor electrical connector
6. Differential pressure feedback EGR sensor
7. Differential pressure feedback EGR sensor hoses
8. Exhaust manifold-to-EGR valve tube
9. EGR vacuum regulator solenoid electrical connector
10. EGR vacuum regulator solenoid vacuum hose fitting
11. EGR vacuum regulator solenoid stud bolt
12. EGR vacuum regulator solenoid

Fig. 161 EGR vacuum regulator solenoid and related EGR components—3.0L engine shown, 4.0L engine similar

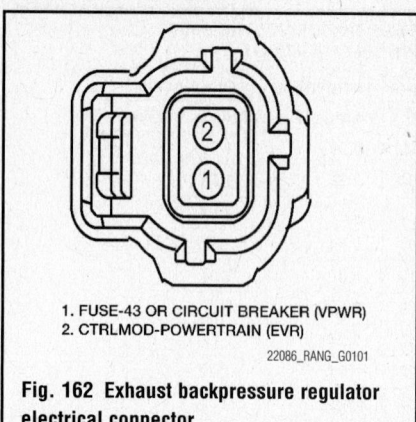

1. FUSE-43 OR CIRCUIT BREAKER (VPWR)
2. CTRLMOD-POWERTRAIN (EVR)

22086_RANG_G0101

Fig. 162 Exhaust backpressure regulator electrical connector

4. To install, reverse the removal procedure and tighten vacuum regulator mounting bolts to 89 inch. lbs. (10 Nm).

TESTING

3.0L and 4.0L Engines

See Figure 162.

1. Check the voltage signal and ground at solenoid connector.
2. To check resistance of the EGR vacuum regulator solenoid coil. Turn ignition switch to the off position.
3. Disconnect the vacuum solenoid electrical connector.
4. Measure the resistance between component side (VPWR) Pin-1 and (EVR) Pin-2.
5. The resistance reading should be between 26—40 ohms.
6. If the reading is not as specified suspect a faulty solenoid.

HEATED OXYGEN (HO2S) SENSOR

LOCATION

See Figures 163 through 165.

Refer to accompanying illustrations for Heated Oxygen Sensor (HO2S) location.

OPERATION

The Heated Oxygen Sensor (HO2S) detects the presence of oxygen in the exhaust and produces a variable voltage according to the amount of oxygen detected. A high concentration of oxygen (lean air/fuel ratio) in the exhaust produces a voltage signal less than 0.4 volt. A low concentration of oxygen (rich air/fuel ratio) produces a voltage signal greater than 0.6 volt. The HO2S provides feedback to the PCM indicating air/fuel ratio in order to achieve a near stoichiometric air/fuel ratio of 14.7:1 during closed loop engine operation. The HO2S generates a voltage between 0.0 and 1.1 volts.

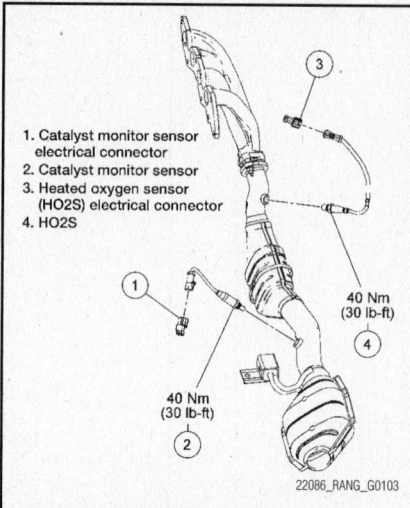

1. Catalyst monitor sensor electrical connector
2. Catalyst monitor sensor
3. Heated oxygen sensor (HO2S) electrical connector
4. HO2S

40 Nm (30 lb-ft)

40 Nm (30 lb-ft)

22086_RANG_G0103

Fig. 163 Engine Heated oxygen and catalyst monitor sensors—2.3L engine

Embedded with the sensing element is the HO2S heater. The heating element heats the sensor to a temperature of 800°C (1,472°F). At approximately 300°C (572°F) the engine can enter closed loop operation. The VPWR circuit supplies voltage to the heater. The PCM turns the heater on by providing the ground when the correct conditions occur. The heater allows the engine to enter closed loop operation sooner. The use of this heater requires the HO2S heater control to be duty cycled, to prevent damage to the heater.

REMOVAL & INSTALLATION

1. With the vehicle in NEUTRAL, position it on a hoist.

➡ **If necessary, lubricate the Heated Oxygen Sensor (HO2S) with lock lubricant to assist in removal.**

2. Using a suitable oxygen sensor removal tool, remove the HO2S.
3. Apply a light coat of anti-seize lubricant to the threads of the HO2S.
4. To install, reverse the removal procedure and tighten the sensor to 30 ft. lbs. (40 Nm).

TESTING

See Figures 166 and 167.

1. Scan and monitor HO2S signal pid.
2. Check for clean and secure connections at harness.
3. Check the internal resistance of the HO2S heater by disconnecting the sensor connector.

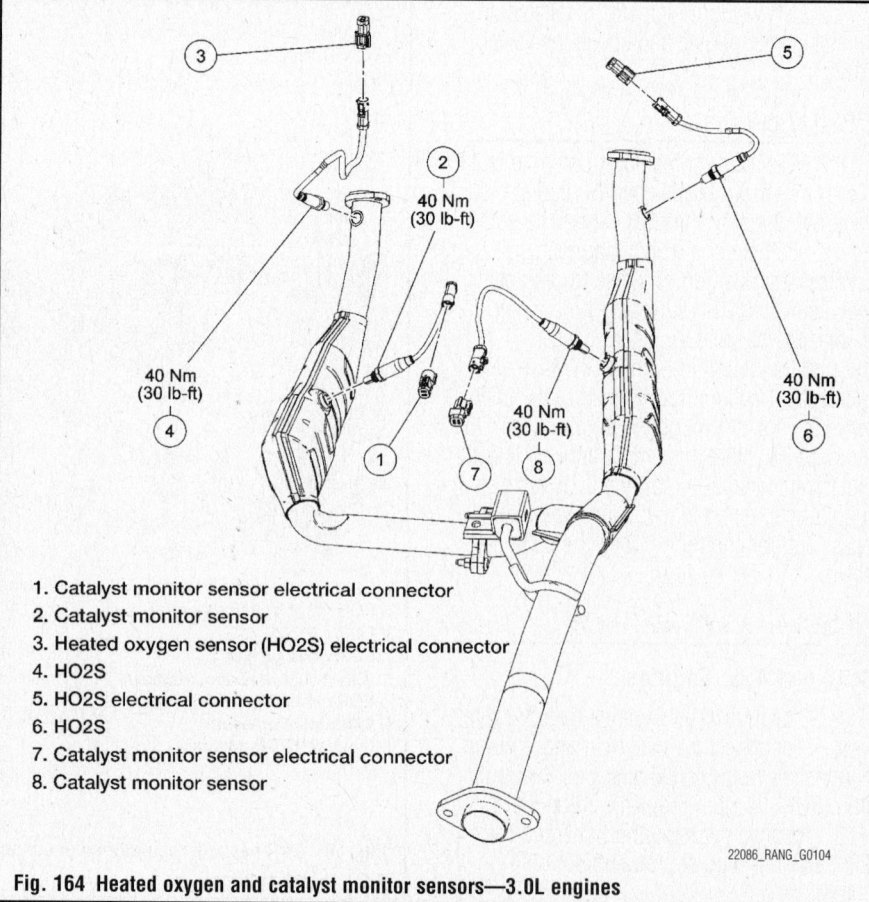

40 Nm (30 lb-ft)

40 Nm (30 lb-ft)

40 Nm (30 lb-ft)

40 Nm (30 lb-ft)

1. Catalyst monitor sensor electrical connector
2. Catalyst monitor sensor
3. Heated oxygen sensor (HO2S) electrical connector
4. HO2S
5. HO2S electrical connector
6. HO2S
7. Catalyst monitor sensor electrical connector
8. Catalyst monitor sensor

22086_RANG_G0104

Fig. 164 Heated oxygen and catalyst monitor sensors—3.0L engines

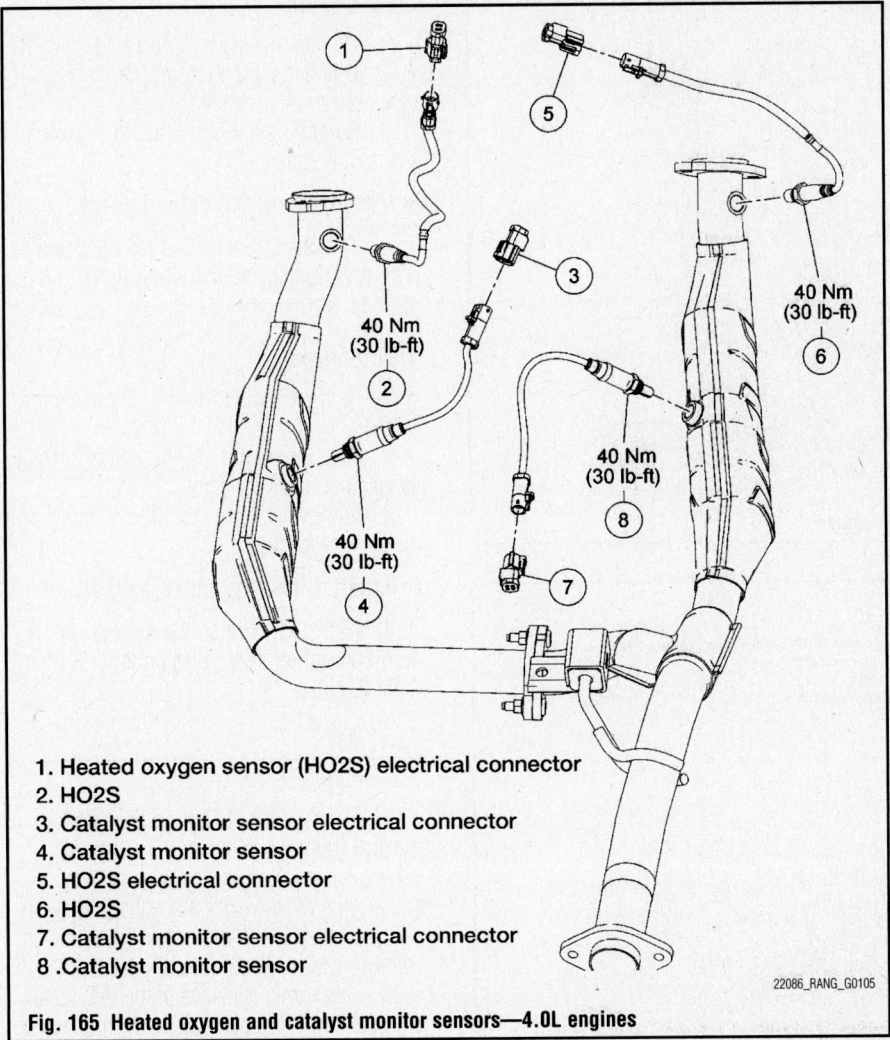

1. Heated oxygen sensor (HO2S) electrical connector
2. HO2S
3. Catalyst monitor sensor electrical connector
4. Catalyst monitor sensor
5. HO2S electrical connector
6. HO2S
7. Catalyst monitor sensor electrical connector
8. Catalyst monitor sensor

22086_RANG_G0105

Fig. 165 Heated oxygen and catalyst monitor sensors—4.0L engines

4. Measure the resistance on the component side of the harness between (HO2S heater) Pin-1 and (VPWR) Pin-2

5. The resistance should read between 3—30 ohms.
6. If the reading is not as specified suspect a faulty HO2S.

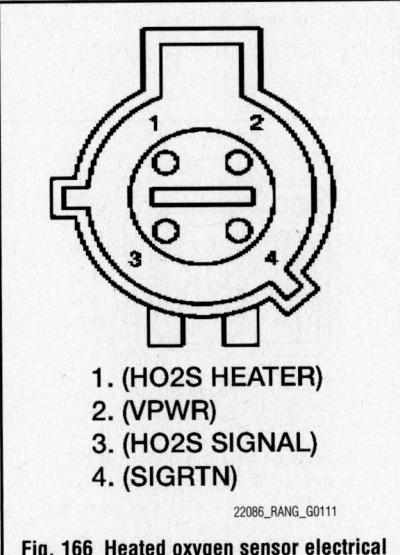

1. (HO2S HEATER)
2. (VPWR)
3. (HO2S SIGNAL)
4. (SIGRTN)

22086_RANG_G0111

Fig. 166 Heated oxygen sensor electrical connector—2005–06 models

1. (HO2S HEATER)
2. (VPWR)
3. (HO2S SIGNAL)
4. (SIGRTN)

22086_RANG_G0106

Fig. 167 Heated oxygen sensor electrical connector—2007 models

IDLE AIR CONTROL (IAC) VALVE

LOCATION

2.3L Engine

See Figure 168.

The Idle Air Control (IAC) valve is located just behind the throttle body on the intake manifold.

3.0L Engine

See Figure 169.

The Idle Air Control (IAC) valve is located just behind the throttle body on the intake manifold.

4.0L Engine

See Figure 170.

The Idle Air Control (IAC) valve is located just behind the throttle body on the intake manifold.

OPERATION

The IAC valve assembly controls the engine idle speed and provides a dashpot function. The IAC valve assembly meters intake air around the throttle plate through a bypass within the IAC valve assembly and throttle body. The PCM determines the desired idle speed or bypass air and signals the IAC valve assembly through a specified duty cycle. The IAC valve responds by positioning the IAC valve to control the amount of bypassed air. The PCM monitors engine RPM and increases or decreases the IAC duty cycle in order to achieve the desired RPM.

The PCM uses the IAC valve assembly to control:

- No touch start
- Cold engine fast idle for rapid warm-up
- Idle (corrects for engine load)
- Stumble or stalling on deceleration (provides a dashpot function)
- Over-temperature idle boost

REMOVAL & INSTALLATION

2.3L Engine

1. Disconnect the battery ground cable.
2. Disconnect the Idle Air Control (IAC) valve electrical connector.
3. Remove the 2 bolts, the IAC valve and discard the gasket.
4. To install, reverse the removal procedure and tighten mounting bolts to 89 inch. lbs. (10 Nm). Install new gasket.

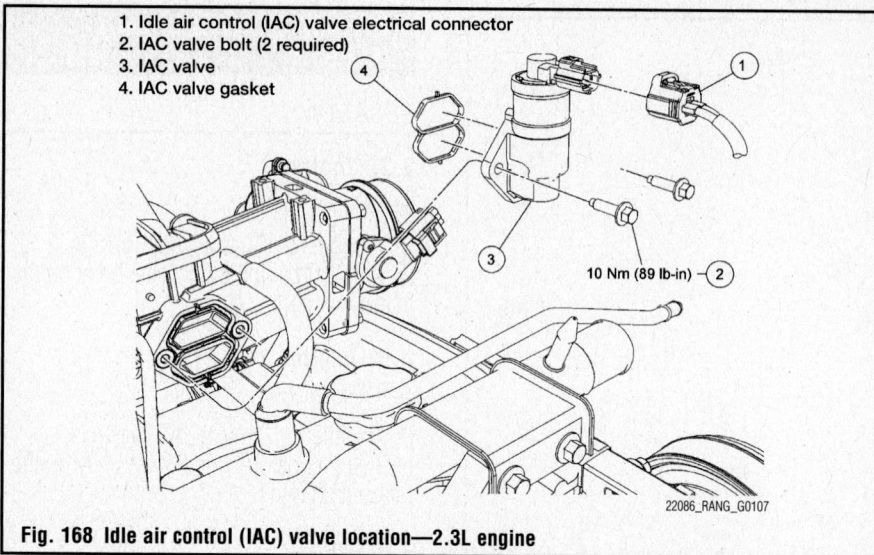

1. Idle air control (IAC) valve electrical connector
2. IAC valve bolt (2 required)
3. IAC valve
4. IAC valve gasket

10 Nm (89 lb-in)

Fig. 168 Idle air control (IAC) valve location—2.3L engine

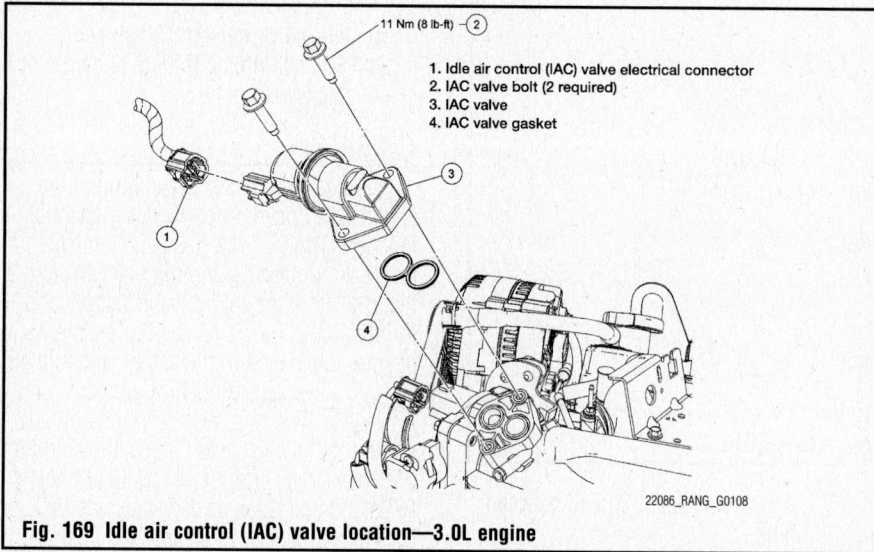

11 Nm (8 lb-ft)

1. Idle air control (IAC) valve electrical connector
2. IAC valve bolt (2 required)
3. IAC valve
4. IAC valve gasket

Fig. 169 Idle air control (IAC) valve location—3.0L engine

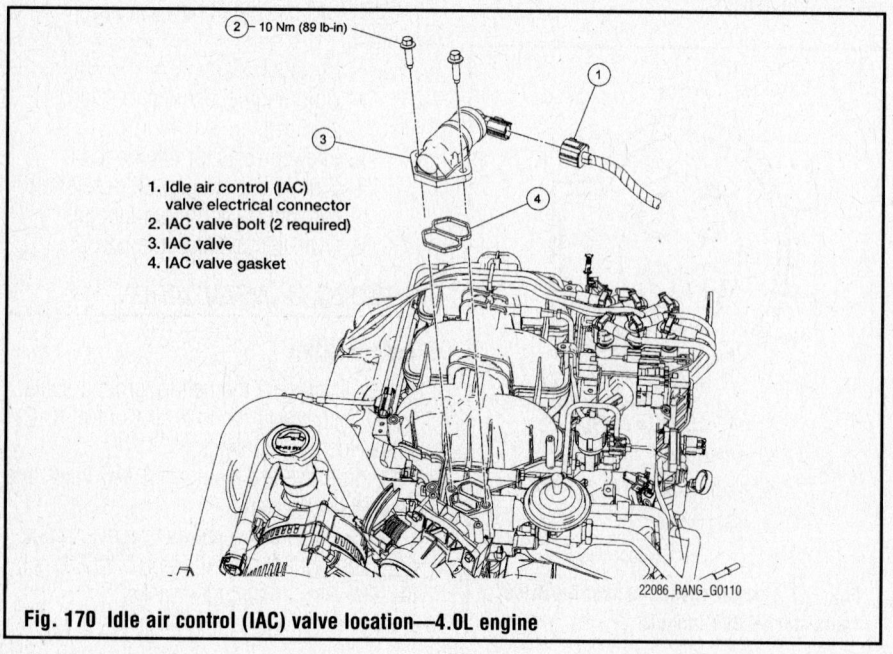

10 Nm (89 lb-in)

1. Idle air control (IAC) valve electrical connector
2. IAC valve bolt (2 required)
3. IAC valve
4. IAC valve gasket

Fig. 170 Idle air control (IAC) valve location—4.0L engine

3.0L Engine

1. Disconnect the negative battery cable.
2. Disconnect the Idle Air Control (IAC) valve electrical connector.
3. Remove the 2 bolts, the IAC valve and discard the gasket.

➡ **Install a new IAC valve gasket.**

4. To install, reverse the removal procedure and tighten the mounting bolts to 8 ft. lbs. (11 Nm).

4.0L Engine

1. Remove the accelerator control snow shield.
2. Disconnect the Idle Air Control (IAC) valve electrical connector.
3. Remove the 2 bolts, the IAC valve and discard the gasket

➡ **Install a new IAC valve gasket.**

4. To install, reverse the removal procedure and tighten mounting bolts to 89 inch. lbs. (10 Nm).

TESTING

See Figure 171.

1. To check for voltage to the Idle Air Control (IAC) valve, disconnect the IAC valve electrical connector. With the key on and engine off measure the voltage between (IAC) harness PWR and battery ground. The voltage reading should be greater than 10V.
2. Check the resistance of the IAC valve. With the key in the off position disconnect the (IAC) valve harness connector. Measure the resistance PWR and IAC (GRD) at the sensor. If the reading is not within specification 6—15 ohms suspect a faulty (IAC) valve.
3. With the engine running at idle (if possible), listen for vacuum leaks. Inspect the entire intake air system from the Mass Air Flow (MAF) sensor to the intake manifold for leaks.

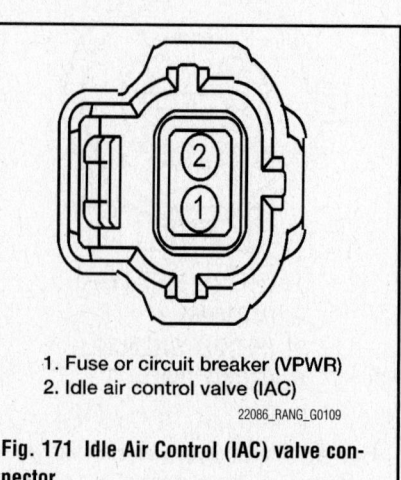

1. Fuse or circuit breaker (VPWR)
2. Idle air control valve (IAC)

Fig. 171 Idle Air Control (IAC) valve connector

KNOCK SENSOR (KS)

LOCATION

2.3L Engine

See Figure 172.

The Knock Sensor (KS) is located on the left side of the engine block, just below the intake manifold.

3.0L Engine

See Figure 173.

The Knock Sensor (KS) is located on left side of the engine block, just above the oil pan.

4.0L Engine

See Figure 174.

The Knock Sensor (KS) is located under the upper intake manifold. The manifold must be removed to replace the sensor.

OPERATION

The Knock Sensor (KS) is a tuned accelerometer on the engine which converts engine vibration to an electrical signal. The PCM uses this signal to determine the presence of engine knock and to retard spark timing.

REMOVAL & INSTALLATION

2.3L Engine

1. Disconnect the negative battery cable.
2. Disconnect the Knock Sensor (KS) electrical connector.
3. Remove the bolt and remove KS.

➡**The KS is a one-time use item and, if serviced, a new KS must be installed.**

4. To install, reverse the removal procedure and tighten the mounting bolt to 15 ft. lbs. (20 Nm).

3.0L Engine

1. Disconnect the negative battery cable.
2. With the vehicle in NEUTRAL, position it on a hoist.
3. Disconnect the Knock Sensor (KS) electrical connector.
4. Remove the bolt and the KS.
5. To install, reverse the removal procedure and tighten mounting bolt to 18 ft. lbs. (25 Nm).

4.0L Engine

1. Disconnect the negative battery cable.
2. Remove the intake manifold.
3. Disconnect the Knock Sensor (KS) electrical connector.
4. Remove the bolt and the KS.

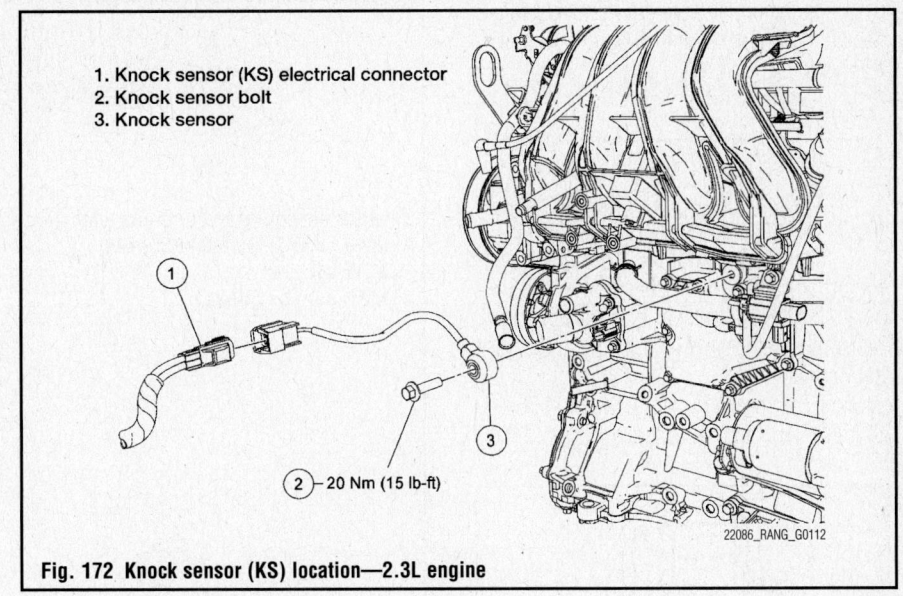

1. Knock sensor (KS) electrical connector
2. Knock sensor bolt
3. Knock sensor

2 — 20 Nm (15 lb-ft)

22086_RANG_G0112

Fig. 172 Knock sensor (KS) location—2.3L engine

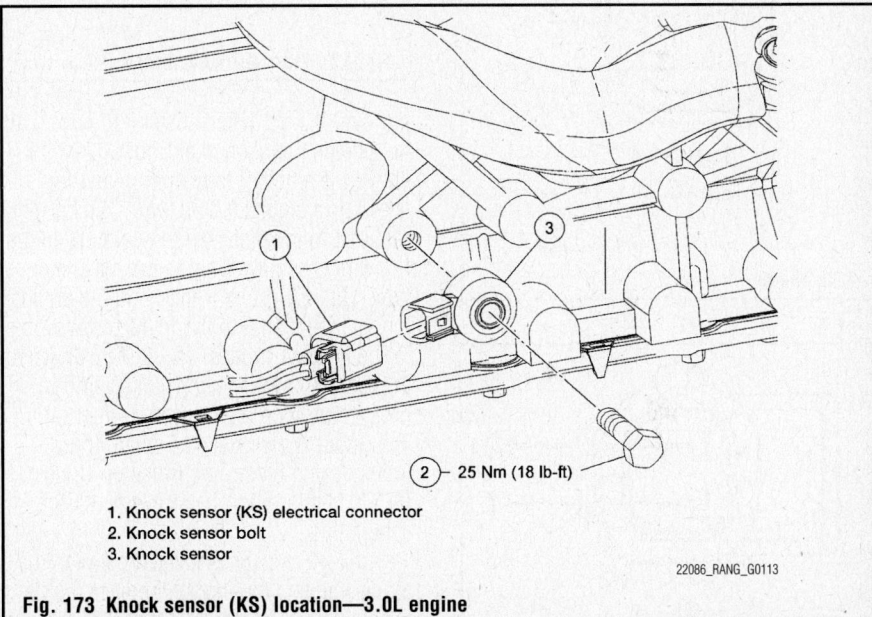

2 — 25 Nm (18 lb-ft)

1. Knock sensor (KS) electrical connector
2. Knock sensor bolt
3. Knock sensor

22086_RANG_G0113

Fig. 173 Knock sensor (KS) location—3.0L engine

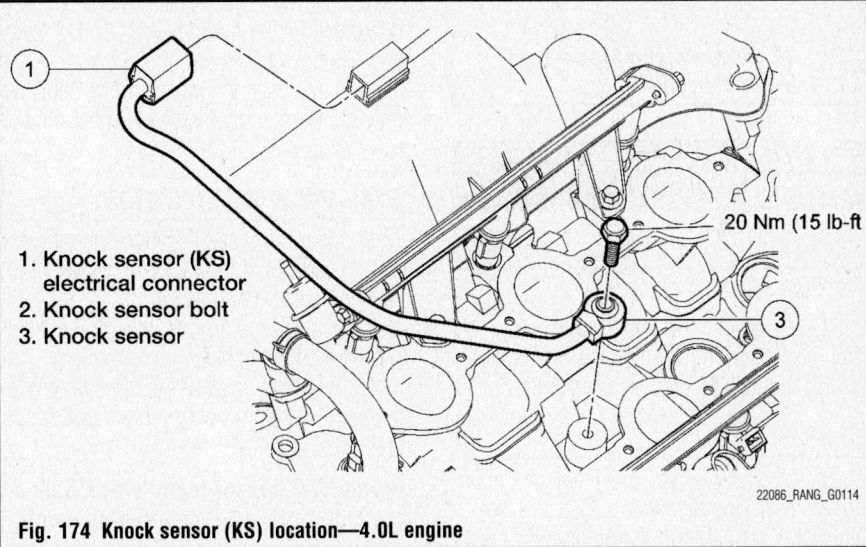

20 Nm (15 lb-ft

1. Knock sensor (KS) electrical connector
2. Knock sensor bolt
3. Knock sensor

22086_RANG_G0114

Fig. 174 Knock sensor (KS) location—4.0L engine

5. To install, reverse the removal procedure and tighten mounting bolt to 15 ft. lbs. (20 Nm).

TESTING

See Figures 175 and 176.

1. Disconnect the Knock Sensor (KS) electrical connector.

2. Check connector for any signs of corrosion or damaged pin connectors.

3. On the component side measure the resistance between KS+ and KS- of the sensor connector.

4. If the reading is not between 4.39—5.35 mohms, suspect a faulty knock sensor.

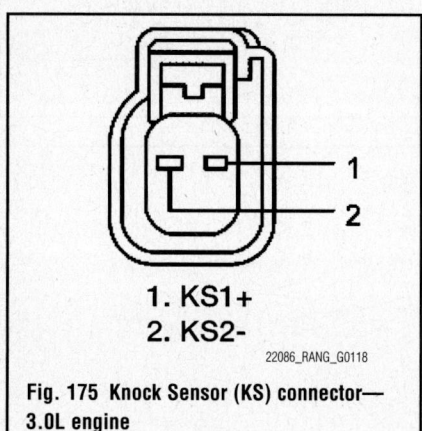

1. KS1+
2. KS2-

Fig. 175 Knock Sensor (KS) connector—3.0L engine

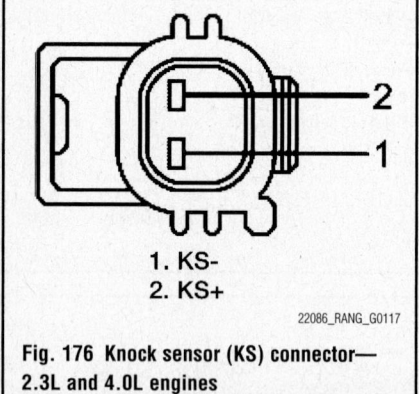

1. KS-
2. KS+

Fig. 176 Knock sensor (KS) connector—2.3L and 4.0L engines

MASS AIR FLOW (MAF) SENSOR

LOCATION

See Figure 177.

The Mass Air Flow (MAF) sensor is mounted between the air filter housing and air intake tube. All engines are similar.

OPERATION

The Mass Air Flow (MAF) sensor uses a hot wire sensing element to measure the amount of air entering the engine. Air pass-

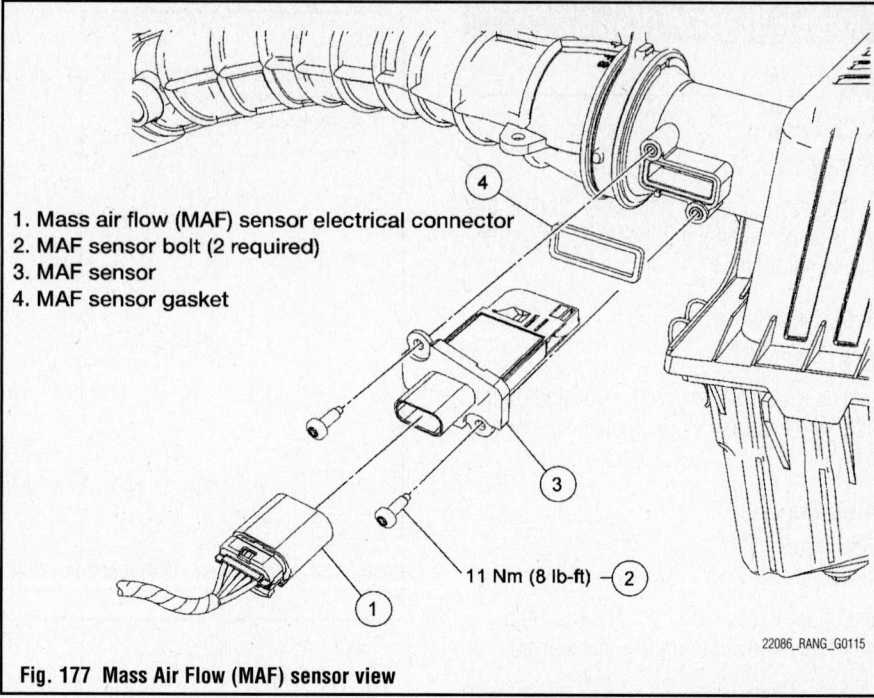

1. Mass air flow (MAF) sensor electrical connector
2. MAF sensor bolt (2 required)
3. MAF sensor
4. MAF sensor gasket

11 Nm (8 lb-ft)

Fig. 177 Mass Air Flow (MAF) sensor view

ing over the hot wire causes it to cool. This hot wire is maintained at 200°C (392°F) above the ambient temperature as measured by a constant cold wire. The current required to maintain the temperature of the hot wire is proportional to the mass air flow. The MAF sensor then outputs an analog voltage signal to the PCM proportional to the intake air mass. The PCM calculates the required fuel injector pulse width in order to provide the desired air/fuel ratio. This input is also used in determining transmission Electronic Pressure Control (EPC), shift and torque converter clutch scheduling.

The MAF sensor is located between the air cleaner and the throttle body or inside the air cleaner assembly. Most MAF sensors have integrated bypass technology with an integrated Intake Air Temperature (IAT) sensor. The hot wire electronic sensing element must be replaced as an assembly. Replacing only the element may change the air flow calibration.

REMOVAL & INSTALLATION

1. Disconnect the negative battery cable.

2. Disconnect the Mass Air Flow (MAF) sensor electrical connector

3. Remove the 2 bolts, the MAF sensor and discard the gasket.

4. To install, reverse the removal procedure and tighten mounting bolts to 8 ft. lbs. (11 Nm).

➥The MAF sensor module and body are calibrated and installed as a unit.

❊❊ WARNING

Do not tamper with the MAF sensing elements located in the airflow bypass. Tampering may result in failure.

TESTING

See Figure 178.

1. To check voltage power to the Mass Air Flow (MAF) sensor, first turn the ignition to the **OFF** position.

2. Disconnect the MAF sensor connector.

3. Turn the ignition switch to the **ON** position with the engine off.

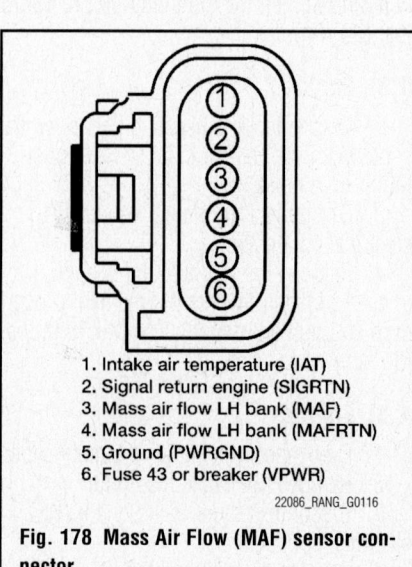

1. Intake air temperature (IAT)
2. Signal return engine (SIGRTN)
3. Mass air flow LH bank (MAF)
4. Mass air flow LH bank (MAFRTN)
5. Ground (PWRGND)
6. Fuse 43 or breaker (VPWR)

Fig. 178 Mass Air Flow (MAF) sensor connector

4. Measure the voltage with a digital multi-meter between (VPWR) and negative battery terminal.

5. The voltage reading should be greater than 10v. If not, check for an open wire, a blown fuse or faulty circuit breaker.

6. To check ground circuit measure the voltage between (PWRGND) and positive battery terminal.

7. The voltage reading should be greater than 10v. If not, suspect an open circuit.

MANIFOLD ABSOLUTE PRESSURE (MAP) SENSOR

LOCATION

See Figure 179.

The Manifold Absolute Pressure (MAP) sensor is located on top of the intake manifold, directly behind the throttle body.

OPERATION

The Manifold Absolute Pressure (MAP) sensor measures intake manifold absolute pressure. The PCM uses information from the MAP sensor to measure how much exhaust gas is introduced into the intake manifold.

REMOVAL & INSTALLATION

1. Disconnect the negative battery cable.
2. Disconnect the Manifold Absolute Pressure (MAP) sensor electrical connector.
3. Remove the bolt and lift the MAP sensor out of the intake manifold.
4. Discard the O-ring seal.
5. To install, reverse the removal procedure.

TESTING

See Figure 180.

1. Disconnect the Manifold Absolute Pressure (MAP) sensor electrical connector.

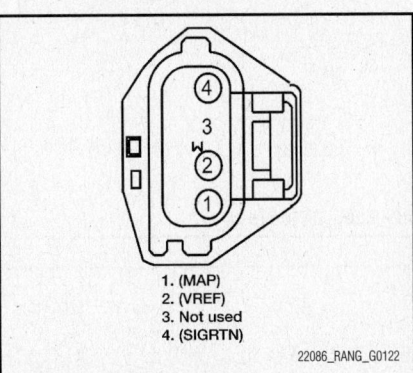

1. (MAP)
2. (VREF)
3. Not used
4. (SIGRTN)

22086_RANG_G0122

Fig. 180 MAP sensor connector—2.3L engine

2. Turn the ignition switch to the **ON** position with the engine off.

3. Measure the voltage on the harness side of connector.

4. With a multi-meter measure the voltage reading between (VREF) and (SIGRTN).

5. The reading should be between 4.5–5.5v if not, measure the voltage between (VREF) and the negative battery terminal.

6. If the voltage reading is between 4.5–5.5v check for an open (SIGRTN) circuit. Repair as needed.

POWERTRAIN CONTROL MODULE (PCM)

LOCATION

2005–06 Models

See Figure 181.

2007 Models

See Figure 182.

The Powertrain Control Module (PCM) is located behind the instrument panel (cowl), center to both driver and passenger sides (access from the engine compartment).

OPERATION

1. The center of the Electronic Engine Control (EEC) system is a microprocessor called the Powertrain Control Module (PCM). The PCM receives input from sensors and other electronic components (switches, relays). Based on the information received and programmed into its memory, the PCM generates output signals to control various relays, solenoids and actuators. A 170-Pin PCM is used for the Ranger model.

REMOVAL & INSTALLATION

2005–06 Models

➡**Any Powertrain Control Module (PCM) replacement will require that ALL customer keys are available to be programmed at the time of installation. PCM replacement DOES NOT require new keys.**

1. Retrieve the module configuration. Carry out the module configuration retrieval steps of the Programmable Module Installation procedure.

2. Remove the PCM wiring harness retainer nut.

3. Loosen the bolt and remove the PCM connector.

4. Remove the stud bolt. Position the ground cable and PCM wiring harness aside.

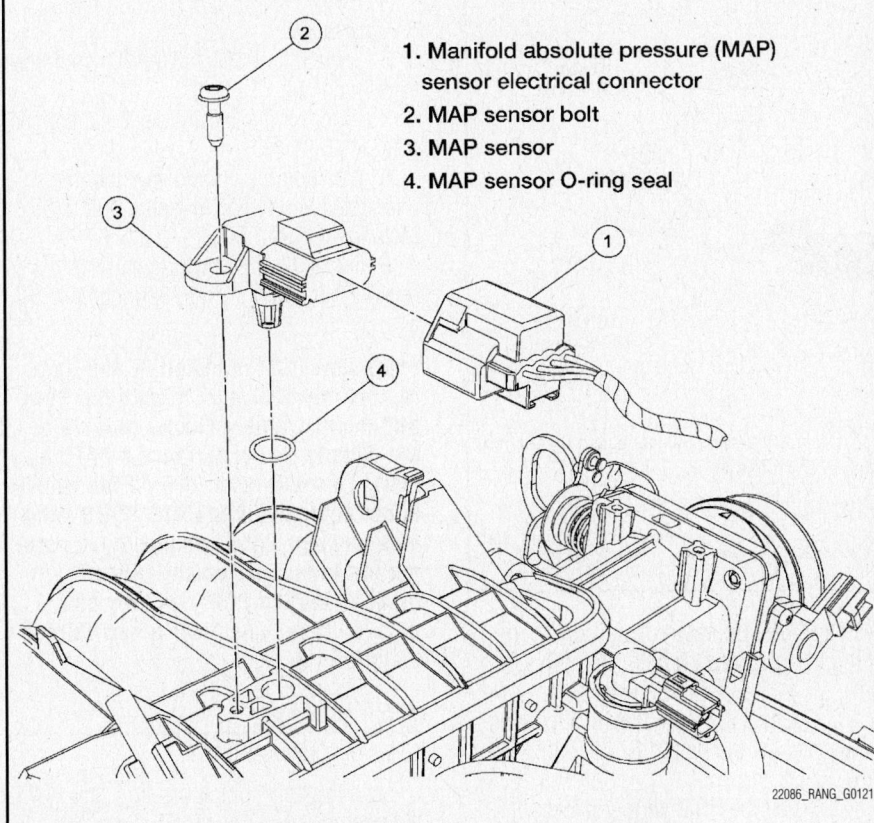

1. Manifold absolute pressure (MAP) sensor electrical connector
2. MAP sensor bolt
3. MAP sensor
4. MAP sensor O-ring seal

22086_RANG_G0121

Fig. 179 Manifold Absolute Pressure (MAP) sensor location—2.3L engine

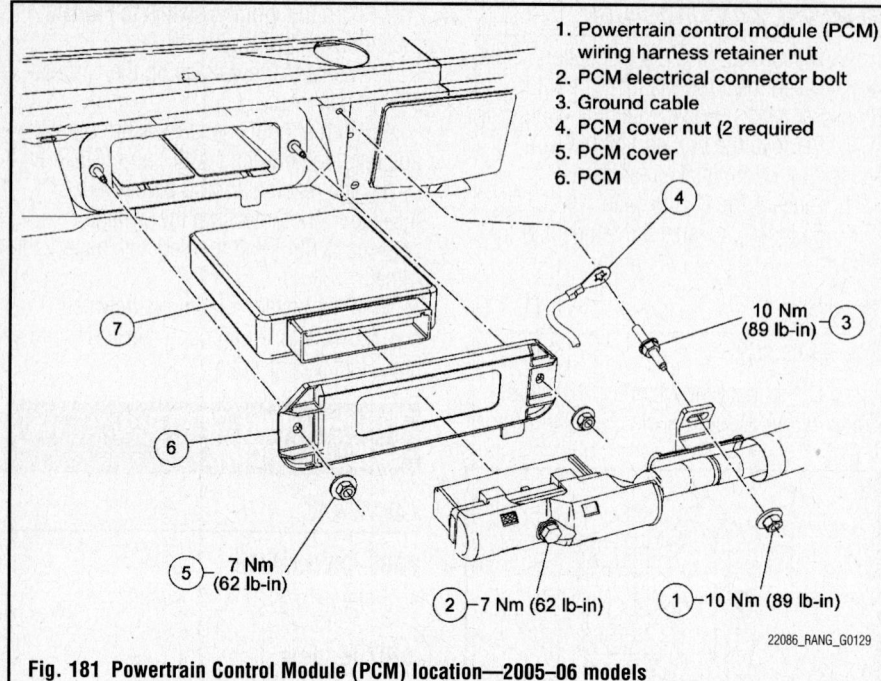

1. Powertrain control module (PCM) wiring harness retainer nut
2. PCM electrical connector bolt
3. Ground cable
4. PCM cover nut (2 required)
5. PCM cover
6. PCM

10 Nm (89 lb-in) — 3

7 Nm (62 lb-in) — 5

2 — 7 Nm (62 lb-in)

1 — 10 Nm (89 lb-in)

22086_RANG_G0129

Fig. 181 Powertrain Control Module (PCM) location—2005–06 models

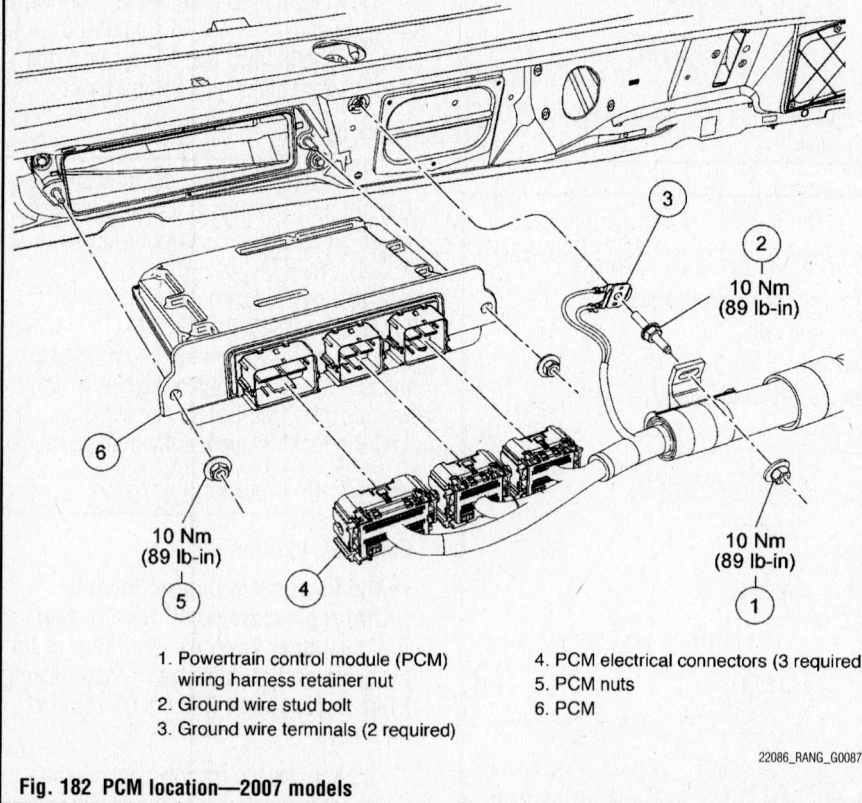

3

2

10 Nm (89 lb-in)

10 Nm (89 lb-in) — 5

4

10 Nm (89 lb-in) — 1

1. Powertrain control module (PCM) wiring harness retainer nut
2. Ground wire stud bolt
3. Ground wire terminals (2 required)
4. PCM electrical connectors (3 required)
5. PCM nuts
6. PCM

22086_RANG_G0087

Fig. 182 PCM location—2007 models

5. Remove the 2 nuts and the PCM cover.

6. Remove the PCM

To install:

7. Install the PCM.

8. Install the PCM cover and 2 nuts. Tighten to 62 inch. lbs. (7 Nm).

9. Position back the PCM wiring har-ness and ground cable. Install the stud bolt and tighten to 89 inch. lbs. (10 Nm).

10. Connect the PCM electrical connec-tor and tighten the bolt to 62 inch. lbs. (7 Nm).

11. Install the PCM wiring harness retainer nut.

➡️If a new PCM is installed, the para-meters must be reset in both the PCM and the instrument cluster module or the vehicle will experience a passive anti-theft system (PATS) no-start. This will occur even if the vehicle is not equipped with PATS. PATS vehicles and non-PATS vehicles have parame-ters in the instrument cluster module and the PCM and they both must be reset whenever a new PCM is installed.

12. Restore the module configuration. Carry out the module configuration restore steps of the Programmable Module Installa-tion procedure.

13. Reprogram the passive anti-theft system (PATS). Carry out the Key Program-ming Using Two Programmed Keys proce-dure.

2007 Models

1. Retrieve the module configuration. Carry out the module configuration retrieval steps of the Programmable Module Installa-tion procedure.

2. Remove the PCM wiring harness retainer nut.

3. Remove the ground wire stud bolt.

4. Disconnect the 3 PCM electrical con-nectors.

5. Remove the 2 nuts and the PCM.

To install:

6. Install the PCM and the 2 nuts tighten to 89 inch. lbs. (10 Nm).

7. Connect the 3 PCM electrical connec-tors.

8. Position the ground wire terminals and install and tighten the stud bolt to 89 inch. lbs. (10 Nm).

9. Install the PCM wiring harness retainer nut and tighten to 89 inch. lbs. (10 Nm).

➡️If a new PCM is installed, the para-meters must be reset in both the PCM and the instrument cluster module or the vehicle will experience a PATS no-start. This will occur even if the vehicle is not equipped with PATS. PATS vehi-cles and non-PATS vehicles have para-meters in the instrument cluster module and the PCM and they both must be reset whenever a new PCM is installed.

TESTING

See Figures 183 and 184.

Scan to verify communication with PCM. If no communication, check power and grounds to the PCM.

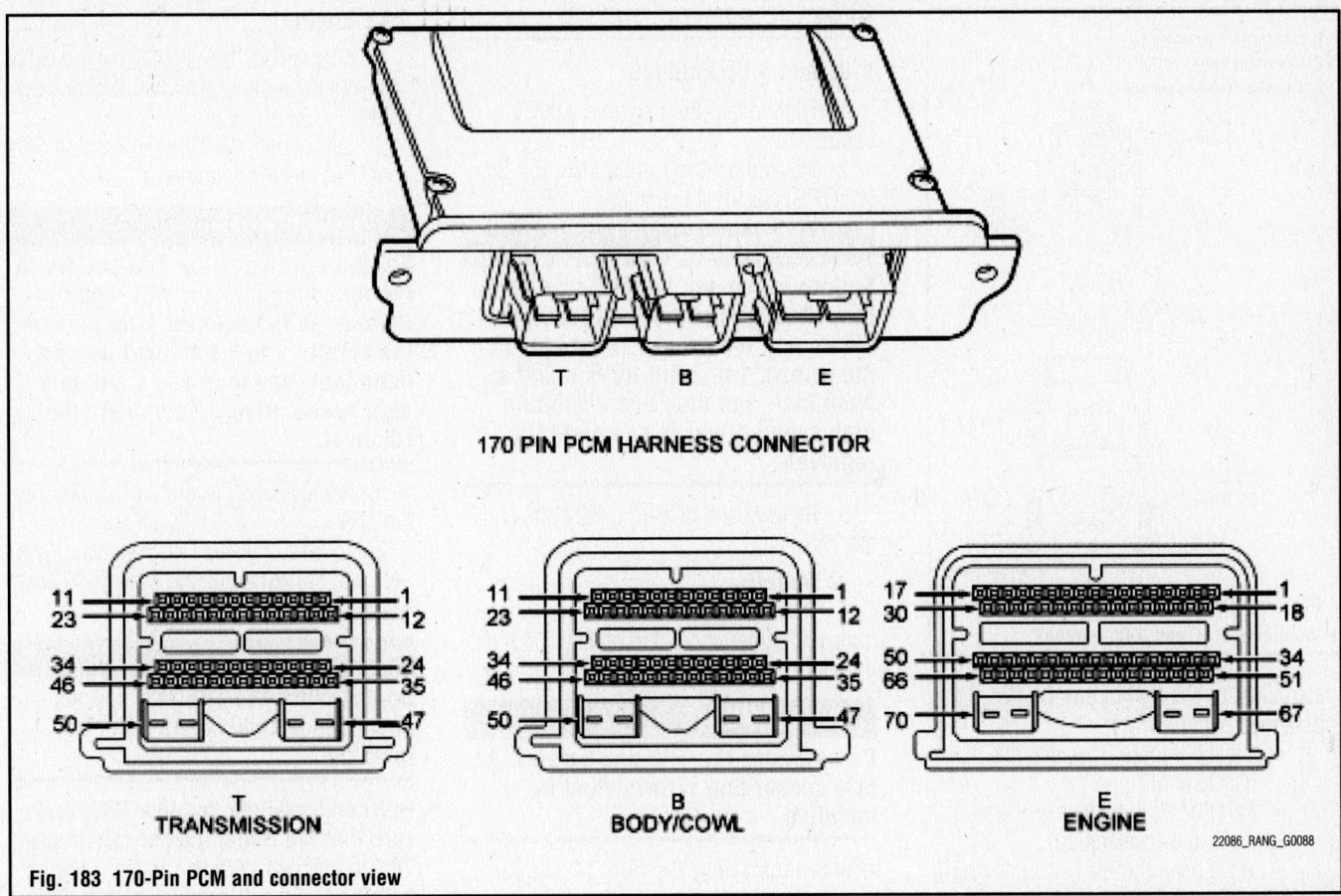

170 PIN PCM HARNESS CONNECTOR

T
TRANSMISSION

B
BODY/COWL

E
ENGINE

22086_RANG_G0088

Fig. 183 170-Pin PCM and connector view

Function	Description	Connector/Pin
VPWR	Voltage input to module	B35
VPWR	Voltage input to module	B36
PWRGND	Power ground	B47
PWRGND	Power ground	B48
PWRGND	Power ground	B49
PWRGND	Power ground	B50
CSEGND	Case ground	B10
SIGRTN	Connector B signal return	B41
SIGRTN	Connector B signal return	B43
SIGRTN	Connector E signal return	E33
SIGRTN	Connector E signal return	E58
SIGRTN	Connector T signal return	T41
VREF	Connector B buffered 5.0-volt reference	B40
VREF	Connector E buffered 5.0-volt reference	E57
KAPWR	Keep alive power	B45

22086_RANG_G0089

Fig. 184 170-Pin PCM power and grounds chart

THROTTLE POSITION SENSOR (TPS)

LOCATION

2.3L and 3.0L Engines
See Figure 185.

The Throttle Position Sensor (TPS) is located to the right of throttle plate.

4.0L Engine
See Figure 186.

The Throttle Position Sensor (TPS) is located to the left of throttle plate.

OPERATION

The Throttle Position Sensor (TPS) is a rotary potentiometer sensor that provides a signal to the PCM that is linearly proportional to the throttle plate/shaft position. The sensor housing has a 3-blade electrical connector that may be gold plated. The gold plating increases the corrosion resistance on the terminals and increases the connector durability. The TPS is mounted on the throttle body. As the TPS is rotated by the throttle shaft, 4 operating conditions are

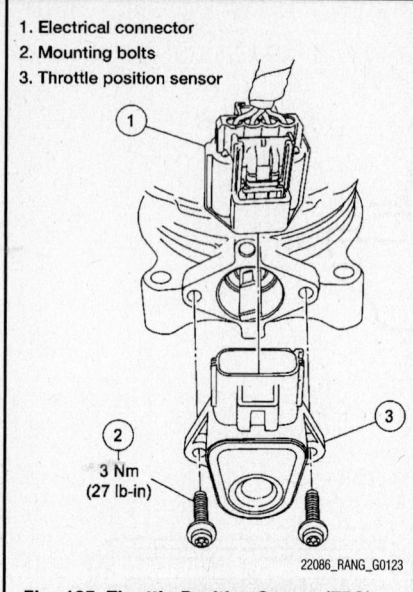

1. Electrical connector
2. Mounting bolts
3. Throttle position sensor

3 Nm
(27 lb-in)

22086_RANG_G0123

Fig. 185 Throttle Position Sensor (TPS) location—2.3L and 3.0L engines

determined by the PCM from the TPS. The operating conditions are:

- Closed throttle (includes idle or deceleration)
- Part throttle (includes cruise or moderate acceleration)
- Wide open throttle (includes maximum acceleration or de-choke on crank)
- Throttle angle rate

REMOVAL & INSTALLATION

2.3L and 3.0L Engines

1. Disconnect the negative battery cable.
2. Disconnect the Throttle Position Sensor (TPS) electrical connector.

✳ WARNING

Failure to remove the TPS screws in the following manner will result in damage to the screws. First loosen the screws 1 to 2 full turns using a hand tool, and then use a suitable high speed driver to complete the removal.

3. Remove and discard the 2 bolts and the TPS.

To install:

4. To install, reverse the removal procedure and tighten mounting bolts to 27 inch. lbs. (3 Nm).

✳ WARNING

Do not reuse the TPS and screws. A new sensor and screws must be installed.

➡When installing the new TP sensor, make sure that the radial locator tab on the TPS is aligned with the radial locator hole on the throttle body.

4.0L Engine

1. Disconnect the negative battery cable.
2. Remove the accelerator control snow shield.
3. Disconnect the Throttle Position Sensor (TPS) electrical connector.

✳ WARNING

Failure to remove the TPS screws in the following manner will result in damage to the screws. First loosen the screws 1 to 2 full turns using a hand tool, and then use a suitable high speed driver to complete the removal.

4. Remove and discard the 2 bolts and the TPS.
5. To install, reverse the removal procedure and tighten mounting bolts to 27 inch. lbs. (3 Nm).

✳ WARNING

Do not reuse the TPS and screws. A new sensor and screws must be installed.

➡When installing the new TPS, make sure that the radial locator tab on the TPS is aligned with the radial locator hole on the throttle body.

TESTING

See Figures 187 and 188

1. Check for voltage between VREF and SIGRTN at the TPS harness. With the harness connector unplugged from sensor and the ignition switch on engine off. The voltage reading should be between 4.5v—5.5v. If not check the circuits for power and or ground problems.
2. With the ignition **ON** and engine

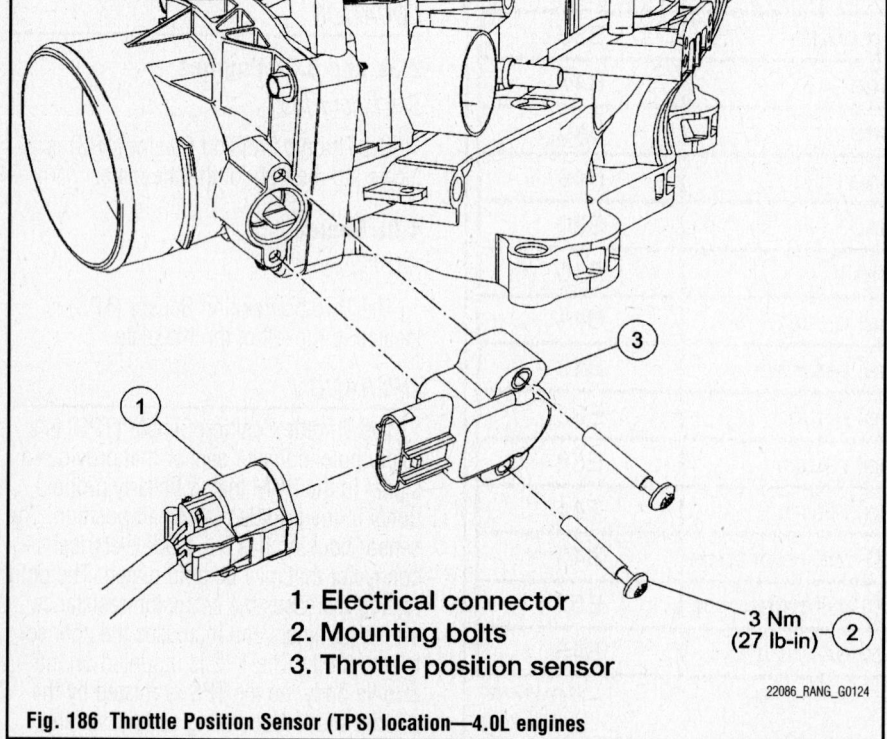

1. Electrical connector
2. Mounting bolts
3. Throttle position sensor

3 Nm
(27 lb-in)

22086_RANG_G0124

Fig. 186 Throttle Position Sensor (TPS) location—4.0L engines

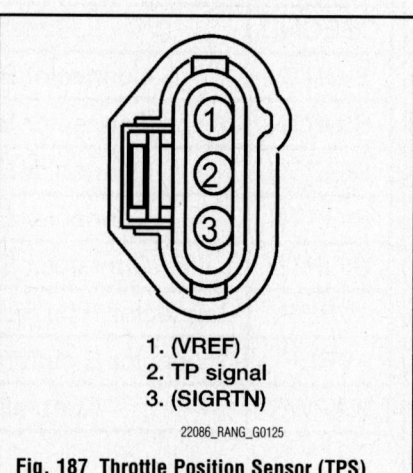

1. (VREF)
2. TP signal
3. (SIGRTN)

22086_RANG_G0125

Fig. 187 Throttle Position Sensor (TPS) connector—2.3L engine

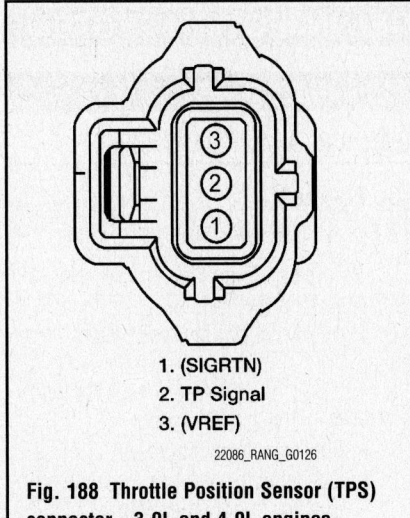

1. (SIGRTN)
2. TP Signal
3. (VREF)

22086_RANG_G0126

Fig. 188 Throttle Position Sensor (TPS) connector—3.0L and 4.0L engines

OFF, check the voltage at the SIGRTN circuit of the TPS by carefully back probing the connector using a multi-meter. The voltage should be between 0.2 and 1.4 volts at idle. Slowly open the throttle plate and carefully watch the readings. The voltage should rise to approximately 4.8v at wide open throttle, and should not jump erratically but in a smooth motion.

VEHICLE SPEED SENSOR (VSS)

LOCATION

See Figure 189.

➡**The Vehicle Speed Sensor (VSS) is also referred to as the Output Shaft Speed sensor (OSS).**

OPERATION

The Vehicle Speed Sensor (VSS) is a variable reluctance or hall-effect sensor that generates a waveform with a frequency that is proportional to the speed of the vehicle. If the vehicle is moving at a relatively low

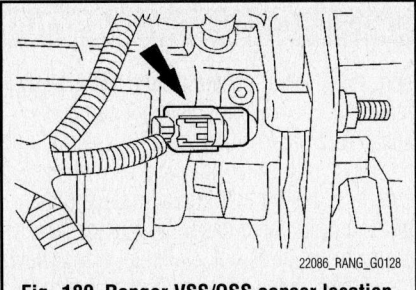

22086_RANG_G0128

Fig. 189 Ranger VSS/OSS sensor location

velocity, the sensor produces a signal with a low frequency. As the vehicle velocity increases, the sensor generates a signal with a higher frequency. The PCM uses the frequency signal generated by the VSS (and other inputs) to control such parameters as fuel injection, ignition control, transmission/transaxle shift scheduling, and torque converter clutch scheduling. This sensor may also be referred to as the Output Shaft Speed sensor (OSS)

The OSS sensor provides the PCM with information about the rotational speed of an output shaft. The PCM uses the information to control and diagnose powertrain behavior. In some applications, the sensor is also used as the source of vehicle speed. The sensor may be physically located in different places on the vehicle, depending upon the specific application. The design of each speed sensor is unique and depends on which powertrain control feature uses the information that is generated.

REMOVAL & INSTALLATION

1. With the vehicle in NEUTRAL, position it on a hoist.
2. Disconnect the Vehicle Speed Sensor (VSS)/Output Shaft Speed (OSS) sensor electrical connector
3. Remove the VSS/OSS sensor screw.

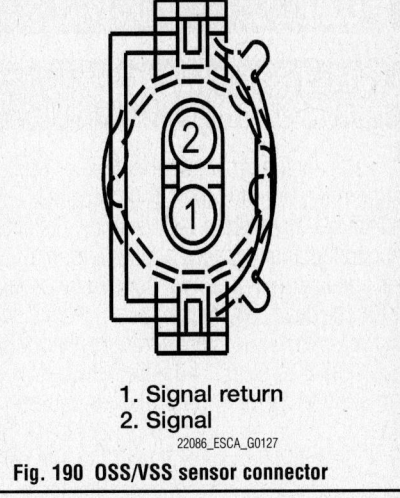

1. Signal return
2. Signal

22086_ESCA_G0127

Fig. 190 OSS/VSS sensor connector

4. Remove the VSS/OSS sensor from the transmission.
5. To install, reverse the removal procedure and tighten mounting bolt to 89 inch. lbs. (10 Nm).

TESTING

See Figure 190.

1. Check the voltage to the OSS/VSS sensor:
   a. Turn the ignition switch **OFF**, then disconnect the sensor connector.
   b. Turn the ignition **ON**, with engine off measure the voltage between VPWR and battery ground. Voltage should read 10v or more if not repair power circuit.
2. Check the VPWR ground to the OSS/VSS sensor by measuring the resistance between PWRGND and battery ground. If the resistance is less than 5 ohms ground circuit should be okay.
3. Inspect the OSS/VSS vehicle harness connector for damage and proper seating.
4. If possible, carry out a wiggle test.

FUEL SYSTEM SERVICE PRECAUTIONS

Safety is the most important factor when performing not only fuel system maintenance but any type of maintenance. Failure to conduct maintenance and repairs in a safe manner may result in serious personal injury or death. Maintenance and testing of the vehicle's fuel system components can be accomplished safely and effectively by adhering to the following rules and guidelines.

- To avoid the possibility of fire and personal injury, always disconnect the negative battery cable unless the repair or test procedure requires that battery voltage be applied.
- Always relieve the fuel system pressure prior to disconnecting any fuel system component (injector, fuel rail, pressure regulator, etc.), fitting or fuel line connection. Exercise extreme caution whenever relieving fuel system pressure to avoid exposing skin, face and eyes to fuel spray. Please be advised that fuel under pressure may penetrate the skin or any part of the body that it contacts.
- Always place a shop towel or cloth around the fitting or connection prior to loosening to absorb any excess fuel due to spillage. Ensure that all fuel spillage (should it occur) is quickly removed from engine surfaces. Ensure that all fuel soaked cloths or towels are deposited into a suitable waste container.
- Always keep a dry chemical (Class B) fire extinguisher near the work area.
- Do not allow fuel spray or fuel vapors to come into contact with a spark or open flame.
- Always use a back-up wrench when loosening and tightening fuel line connection fittings. This will prevent unnecessary stress and torsion to fuel line piping.
- Always replace worn fuel fitting O-rings with new Do not substitute fuel hose or equivalent where fuel pipe is installed.

Before servicing the vehicle, make sure to also refer to the precautions in the beginning of this section as well.

RELIEVING FUEL SYSTEM PRESSURE

All Sequential Fuel Injection (SFI) fuel injected engines are equipped with a pressure relief valve located on the fuel supply manifold. Remove the fuel tank cap and attach fuel pressure gauge T80L-9974-B, to the valve to release the fuel pressure. Be sure to drain the fuel into a suitable container and to avoid gasoline spillage. If a pressure gauge is not available, disconnect the vacuum hose from the fuel pressure regulator and attach a hand-held vacuum pump. Apply about 25 in. Hg (84 kPa) of vacuum to the regulator to vent the fuel system pressure into the fuel tank through the fuel return hose. Note that this procedure will remove the fuel pressure from the lines, but not the fuel. Take precautions to avoid the risk of fire and use clean rags to soak up any spilled fuel when the lines are disconnected.

An alternate method of relieving the fuel system pressure involves disconnecting the inertia switch.

FUEL FILTER

REMOVAL & INSTALLATION

See Figure 191.

1. Before servicing the vehicle, refer to the Precautions Section.
2. Properly relieve the fuel system pressure.
3. Remove or disconnect the following:

- Negative battery cable
- Push connect and R-clip fittings from the fuel filter
- Fuel filter

To install:

4. Install or connect the following:

- Fuel filter. Torque the nut to 17 ft. lbs. (23 Nm).
- R-clip and push connect fittings
- Negative battery cable

5. Start the vehicle, check for leaks and repair if necessary.

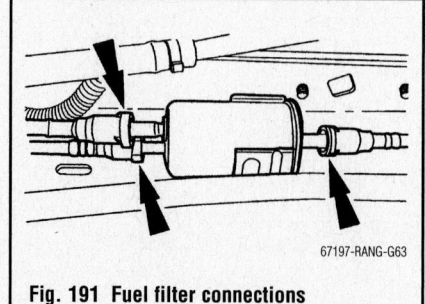

Fig. 191 Fuel filter connections

FUEL INJECTORS

REMOVAL & INSTALLATION

2.3L Engine

See Figures 192 and 193.

1. Before servicing the vehicle, refer to the Precautions Section.
2. Properly relieve the fuel system pressure.
3. Remove or disconnect the following:

- Negative battery cable
- Fuel injector connectors
- Fuel injector harness from the fuel injector supply manifold
- Fuel line spring lock
- Fuel line
- Fuel injection supply manifold
- Fuel injector retaining clip
- Fuel injector

✳ WARNING

Use O-ring seals that are made of special fuel-resistant material. Use of ordinary O-ring seals can cause the fuel system to leak. Do not reuse the O-ring seals.

4. Installation is the reverse of removal. Install new O-rings. Lubricate the O-rings

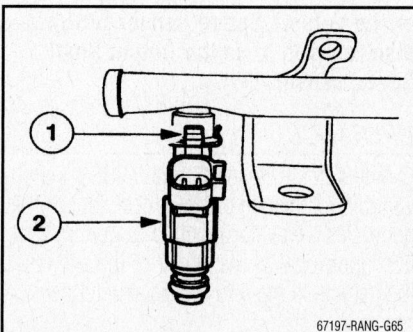

Fig. 192 Fuel injector-to-fuel rail installation. 1-retaining clip; 2-injector—2.3L engine

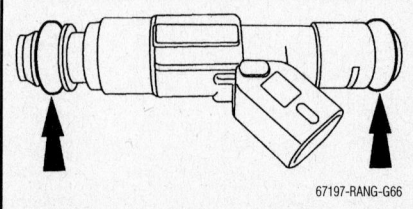

Fig. 193 Fuel injector O-rings—2.3L engine

with clean engine oil. Torque the supply manifold bolts to 18 ft. lbs. (25 Nm).

3.0L and 4.0L Engines

See Figures 194 through 198.

1. Before servicing the vehicle, refer to the Precautions Section.
2. Properly relieve the fuel system pressure.
3. Remove or disconnect the following:
   - Negative battery cable
   - Upper intake manifold
   - Engine control sensor wiring from the fuel injectors
   - Fuel lines
   - Fuel injection supply manifold and injectors as an assembly
   - Vacuum line
   - Fuel injectors from the supply manifold
   - Inspect the O-rings and replace them as needed

Fig. 194 Fuel injector wiring connectors—3.0L engine

Fig. 195 Fuel rail bolts—3.0L engine

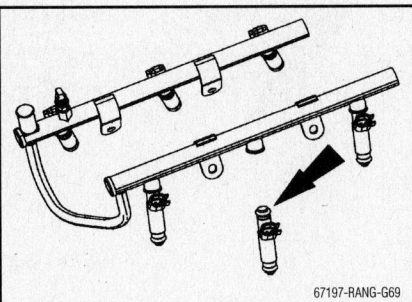

Fig. 196 Fuel rail and injectors—3.0L engine

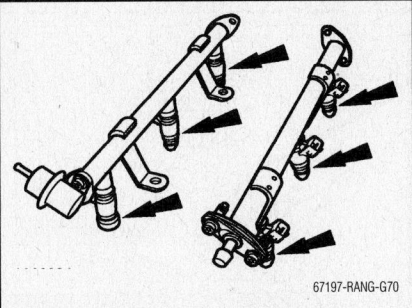

Fig. 197 Fuel rail and injectors—4.0L engine

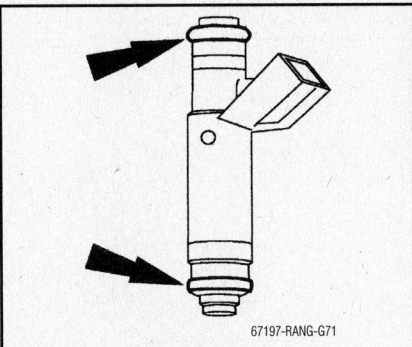

Fig. 198 Fuel injector O-rings—4.0L shown; 3.0L similar

To install:

4. Install or connect the following:
   - Fuel injectors
   - Vacuum line
   - Fuel injection supply manifold. Torque the bolts to 89 inch lbs. (10 Nm).
   - Fuel line
   - Engine control sensor wiring to the fuel injectors
   - Upper intake manifold
   - Negative battery cable
5. Start the vehicle, check for leaks and repair if necessary.

FUEL PUMP

REMOVAL & INSTALLATION

See Figure 199.

1. Before servicing the vehicle, refer to the Precautions Section.
2. Remove the fuel tank.
3. Clean the area around the fuel pump mounting flange.
4. Using the special tool, remove the fuel tank pump assembly locking retainer ring.

✳✳ WARNING

The fuel pump assembly must be removed and handled carefully to avoid damage to the float arm and filter.

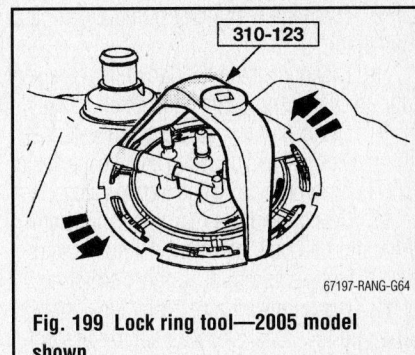

Fig. 199 Lock ring tool—2005 model shown

5. Remove the fuel pump assembly.
6. Remove and discard the fuel pump mounting gasket.

To install:

7. Clean the fuel pump mounting flange and the fuel tank mounting surface.
8. Install a new fuel pump mounting gasket.
9. Install the fuel pump and sender assembly with the float toward the rear of the tank. Align the arrows molded into the tank and flange.
10. Install the locking ring while compressing the pump assembly into the tank.
11. Using the special tool, tighten the fuel pump assembly locking ring retainer ring until it locks in place.
12. Install the fuel tank.

FUEL TANK

REMOVAL & INSTALLATION

✳✳ CAUTION

Fuel in the fuel system remains under high pressure even when the engine is not running. Before repairing or disconnecting any of the fuel lines or fuel system components, the fuel system pressure must be relieved to prevent accidental spraying of fuel, causing a fire hazard. Failure to follow these instructions may result in personal injury.

1. With vehicle in NEUTRAL, position it on a hoist.
2. Release the fuel system pressure.
3. Drain the fuel tank.
4. Loosen the main fuel tank filler pipe hose clamp on the fuel tank. Remove the fuel tank filler pipe hose from the fuel tank.
5. If equipped, remove the 4 skid plate nuts and the skid plate.
6. Remove the fuel tank support straps.
7. Partially lower the fuel tank for ease of access.

8. Disconnect the fuel pump electrical connector.

9. Disconnect the fuel tank filler pipe vent tube-to-fuel pump quick connect coupling.

10. Disconnect the fuel supply tube-to-fuel pump quick connect coupling and the fuel return tube-to-fuel pump quick connect coupling.

11. Disconnect the rear fuel tank vapor tube and fuel tank pressure sensor assembly-to-fuel pump quick connect coupling.

12. Disconnect the rear fuel tank vapor tube and fuel tank pressure sensor assembly-to-fuel tank vent valve quick connect coupling at the rear of the fuel tank.

13. Lower the fuel tank.

14. To install, reverse the removal procedure and note the following:

a. Tighten fuel tank support strap bolts to 35 ft. lbs. (47 Nm).

b. If removed install skid plate and nuts, tighten to 22 ft. lbs. (30 Nm).

IDLE SPEED

ADJUSTMENT

Idle speed is maintained by the Powertrain Control Module (PCM). No adjustment is necessary or possible.

THROTTLE BODY

REMOVAL & INSTALLATION

2.3L Engine

See Figure 200.

1. Before servicing the vehicle, refer to the Precautions Section.

2. Remove the accelerator control splash shield.

3. Disconnect the wiring harness and engine vent tube from the air cleaner outlet tube.

4. Loosen the clamps and remove the engine air cleaner intake tube and duct.

5. Remove the accelerator cable and the speed control cable (if equipped).

6. Disconnect the Throttle Position (TP) sensor electrical connector.

7. Remove the bolts and the throttle body.

8. To install, reverse the removal procedure. Tighten the throttle body bolts in a criss-cross pattern to 89 inch lbs. (10 Nm).

3.0L Engine

See Figure 201.

1. Before servicing the vehicle, refer to the Precautions Section.

2. Disconnect the battery ground cable.

3. Remove the air cleaner outlet tube.

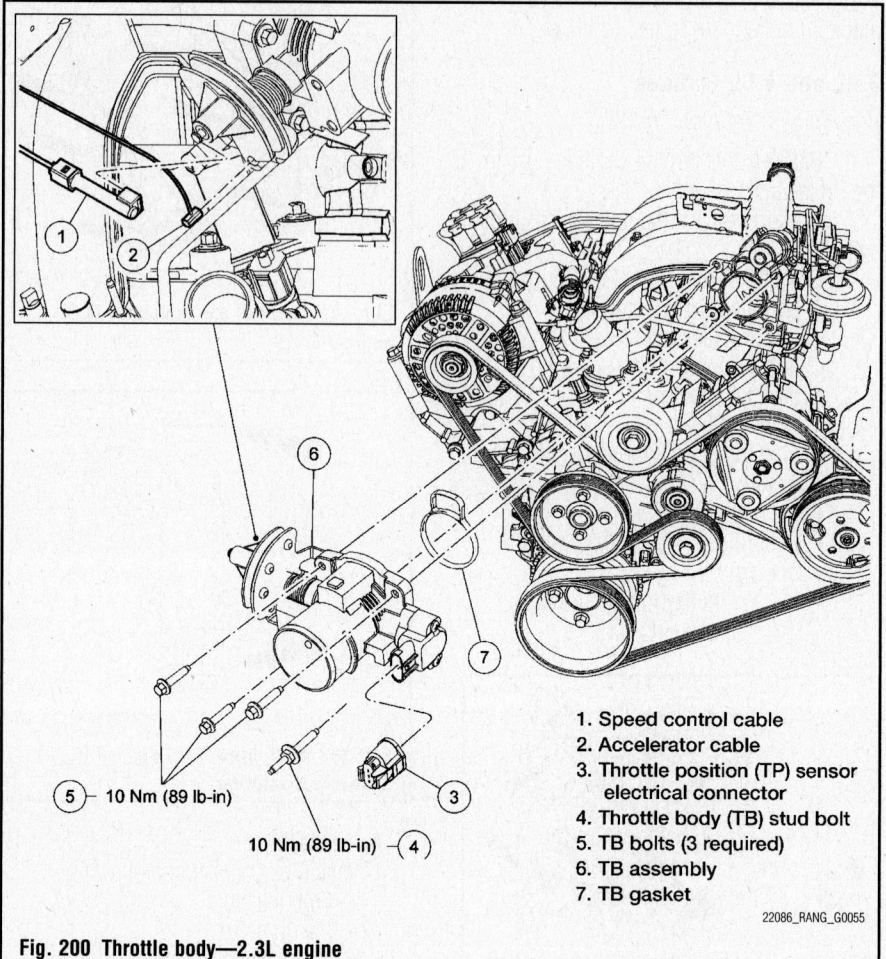

1. Speed control cable
2. Accelerator cable
3. Throttle position (TP) sensor electrical connector
4. Throttle body (TB) stud bolt
5. TB bolts (3 required)
6. TB assembly
7. TB gasket

5 — 10 Nm (89 lb-in)

10 Nm (89 lb-in) — 4

22086_RANG_G0055

Fig. 200 Throttle body—2.3L engine

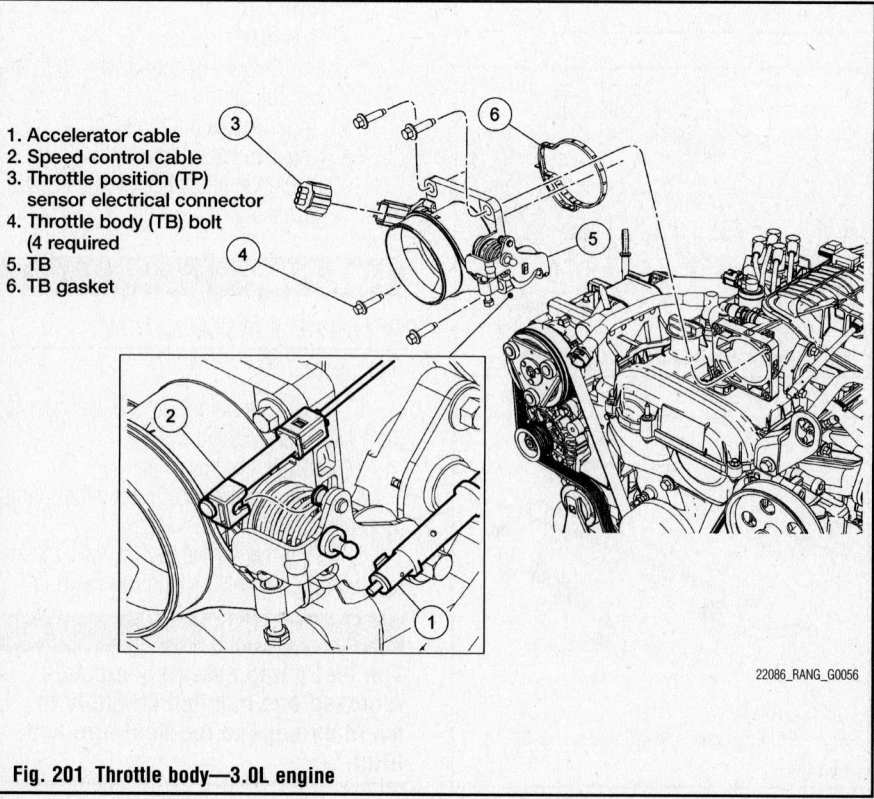

1. Accelerator cable
2. Speed control cable
3. Throttle position (TP) sensor electrical connector
4. Throttle body (TB) bolt (4 required
5. TB
6. TB gasket

22086_RANG_G0056

Fig. 201 Throttle body—3.0L engine

4. Remove the two bolts and the snow shield.

5. Disconnect the engine control sensor wiring from the Idle Air Control (IAC) valve and the Throttle Position (TP) sensor.

6. Disconnect the accelerator cable and speed control actuator cable.

7. Remove the throttle body.

8. If required, remove the throttle body gasket.

9. To install, reverse the removal procedure. Tighten the throttle body bolts to 89 inch lbs. (10 Nm).

4.0L Engine

1. Before servicing the vehicle, refer to the Precautions Section.

2. Disconnect the battery ground cable.

3. Remove the accelerator cable and the speed control cable (if equipped).

4. Disconnect the Throttle Position (TP) sensor electrical connector.

5. Remove the bolts and the throttle body.

6. To install, reverse the removal procedure. Tighten the throttle body bolts in a criss cross pattern to 80 inch lbs. (9 Nm).

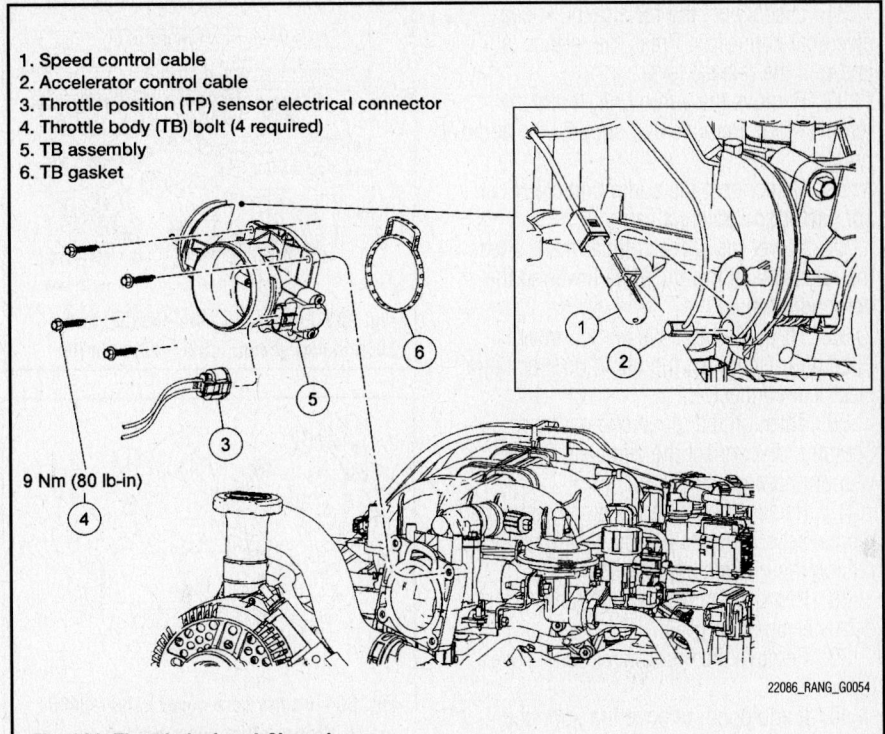

1. Speed control cable
2. Accelerator control cable
3. Throttle position (TP) sensor electrical connector
4. Throttle body (TB) bolt (4 required)
5. TB assembly
6. TB gasket

9 Nm (80 lb-in)

22086_RANG_G0054

Fig. 202 Throttle body—4.0L engine

HEATING & AIR CONDITIONING   COMPONENTS

BLOWER MOTOR

REMOVAL & INSTALLATION

1. Disconnect the connector from the speed control servo.

2. Remove the screw and reposition the speed control servo.

3. Disconnect the blower motor wire harness connector.

4. Remove the blower motor housing tube.

5. Remove the screws and the blower motor.

6. To install, reverse the removal procedure.

HEATER CORE

REMOVAL & INSTALLATION

See Figures 203 through 205.

1. Before servicing the vehicle, refer to the Precautions Section.

2. Recover the refrigerant.

3. Remove the suction accumulator.

4. On trucks with the 2.3L engine:
   a. Remove the A/C compressor.
   b. Remove the engine oil indicator and tube.

5. On vehicles with the 3.0L or 4.0L engine, position the coolant reservoir and windshield washer reservoir aside.

6. Detach the speed control servo.

7. Disconnect the blower motor and blower motor resistor electrical connectors.

8. Disconnect the heater hoses. Using suitable tools, clamp-off the heater

9. Detach the pin-type retainer and position aside the windshield washer hose.

10. Disconnect and detach the heater control valve vacuum hose.

11. Disconnect the vacuum supply hose near the evaporator core housing.

12. Disconnect the condenser to evaporator line spring lock coupling from the passenger compartment evaporator core inlet.

13. Disconnect the vacuum hose connector and remove the nut.

14. Remove the nuts and the evaporator core housing.

15. Remove the driver side and passenger side air bag modules.

16. Remove the front seats.

17. Remove the screws and position the parking brake release handle aside.

18. Remove the left and right lower cowl kick panels.

19. Position the parking brake assembly aside.

20. Remove the screws and position the hood release handle aside.

21. Remove the instrument panel steering column cover.

22. Remove the instrument panel steering column opening cover reinforcement.

23. Disconnect the Brake Pedal Position (BPP) switch electrical connector from the steering column shaft.

24. If equipped, disconnect the Clutch Pedal Position (CPP) switch electrical connector.

25. If equipped, disconnect the shift cable from the steering column.

26. Disconnect the upper intermediate steering shaft.

27. Remove the left and right side garnish moldings.
   a. Remove the bolt covers and remove the bolts.
   b. Remove the assist handle.
   c. Remove the windshield side garnish molding.

28. Remove the door moldings.

29. On regular cab vehicles
   a. Remove the screws.
   b. Remove the scuff plate.

30. Disconnect the electrical connectors and the ground wire from the RH side lower kick panel.

➡**To avoid damaging the bulkhead electrical connectors, be sure the release tab is fully depressed before pulling release lever into the disconnect position.**

31. Disconnect the LH side bulkhead electrical connector. Press the release tab and pull the release lever.

32. Remove the audio unit. Insert the removal tool. Remove and support the audio unit.

33. Disconnect the audio unit electrical connector and antenna cable.

34. Lower the glove compartment. Press the release tabs inward while lowering the compartment.

35. Through the glove compartment opening, disconnect the blend door actuator electrical connector.

36. Through the glove compartment opening, disconnect the climate control vacuum harness connector.

37. Raise and secure the glove compartment. Press the release tabs inward while raising the glove compartment.

38. Remove the instrument panel defroster opening grille.

39. Remove the instrument panel cowl top bolts.

40. If equipped, remove the floor console.

41. If not equipped with the high-series floor console, remove the cup holders.

42. Release the clips and remove the restraints control module (RCM) cover.

43. If not equipped with high-series floor console, remove the consolette mat.

44. Remove the screws and remove the restraints control module (RCM) cover.

45. Remove the consolette base.

46. Remove the gearshift lever.

47. Remove the screws and remove the manual transmission consolette.

48. Disconnect the RCM electrical connector.

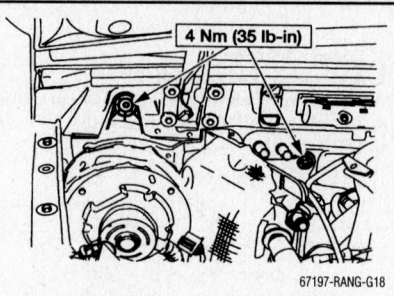

Fig. 203 Evaporator core housing bolts—2005 model shown, other years similar

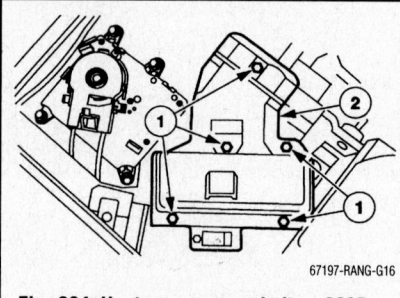

Fig. 204 Heater core cover bolts—2005 model shown, other years similar

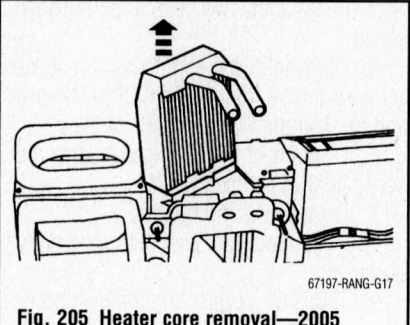

Fig. 205 Heater core removal—2005 model shown, other years similar

49. Pull the floor carpeting back.

50. On 2-wheel drive vehicles disconnect the instrument panel main harness.

51. On 4-wheel drive vehicles disconnect the instrument panel main harness. From underneath the vehicle, release the instrument panel main harness at the transfer case.

52. Remove the instrument panel side finish panel.

53. Disconnect the door harness electrical connector.

54. Remove the RH side instrument

panel bolt. If necessary, transfer the components to the new instrument panel.

55. Remove the LH instrument panel cowl side bolts.

56. Remove the instrument panel.

57. Remove the Powertrain Control Module (PCM).

58. Remove the PCM heat sink.

59. Remove the four nuts from the engine side of the dash panel. Position the plenum chamber on the vehicle floor.

60. Remove the heater core cover.

61. Remove the heater core.

62. To install, reverse the removal procedure. During installation, be sure to install a new oval foam seal around the heater core inlet and outlet tubes.

63. Lubricate the refrigerant system with the correct amount of clean PAG oil or equivalent. Install new O-ring seals lubricated in clean mineral oil. Lubricate the coolant hoses with plain water only, if needed.

64. Evacuate, leak test, and charge the refrigerant system.

STEERING

POWER STEERING GEAR

REMOVAL & INSTALLATION

2-Wheel Drive Models

See Figure 206.

1. Before servicing the vehicle, refer to the Precautions Section.

2. Turn the wheel to the straight-ahead position and turn the ignition switch to the OFF position.

3. Remove the front wheel and tire assemblies.

4. Remove the fluid cooler.

5. Remove and discard the cotter pins and nuts.

➡**Do not damage the tie-rod boot when installing the special tool.**

6. Using special tool, separate the tie-rod ends from the wheel knuckles.

➡**Do not allow the intermediate shaft to rotate while it is disconnected from the steering gear or damage to the clockspring can result. If there is evidence that the intermediate shaft has rotated, the clockspring must be removed and recentered.**

7. Remove the pinch bolt and detach the intermediate shaft from the gear. Discard the bolt.

8. Remove the nut and disconnect the lines.

9. Plug or cap the power steering return hose, power steering pressure hose, and the steering gear ports to prevent the entry of dirt.

COMPONENTS

➡**Hold the tops of the steering gear to crossmember stud bolts to avoid damaging the steering gear fluid transfer tubes.**

10. Remove the rack mounting nuts.

11. Remove the mounting stud, nut, washer and stop assemblies.

12. Remove the steering gear. Clean the mounting surfaces.

To install:

13. To install, reverse the removal procedure.

   a. Install new seals on the power steering return hose and power steering pressure hose.

   b. The dished side of the washer faces downward.

   c. Install a new intermediate shaft pinch bolt.

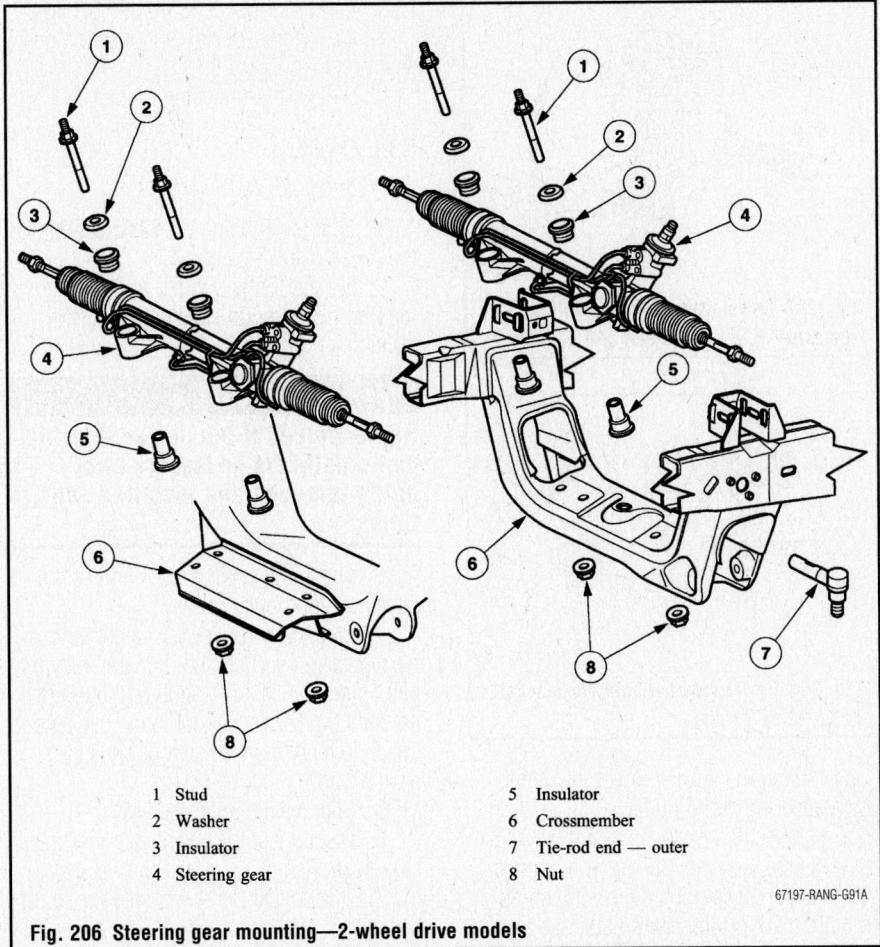

1	Stud	5	Insulator
2	Washer	6	Crossmember
3	Insulator	7	Tie-rod end — outer
4	Steering gear	8	Nut

67197-RANG-G91A

Fig. 206 Steering gear mounting—2-wheel drive models

14. Observe the following torques:
- Pinch bolt: 35 ft. lbs. (48 Nm)
- Pressure line bracket nut: 18 ft. lbs. (25 Nm)
- Rack retaining nuts: 111 ft. lbs. (150 Nm)

15. Fill and leak check the power steering system.

16. Check and, if necessary, adjust the wheel alignment.

4-Wheel Drive Models

1. Before servicing the vehicle, refer to the Precautions Section.

2. Turn the wheel to the straight-ahead position and turn the ignition switch to the OFF position.

3. Remove the wheel and tire assemblies.

4. Remove the fluid cooler.

5. Remove the four air deflector retaining screws.

6. Pull downward on the air deflector to disengage the retaining pins.

7. Loosen the LH tie-rod end jam nut.

8. Remove and discard the cotter pins and nuts.

➡**Do not damage the tie-rod boot when installing the special tool.**

9. Using a separator, separate the tie-rod ends from the wheel knuckles

10. Remove the LH tie-rod end. Count and record the number of turns required to remove the tie-rod end.

11. Remove the front stabilizer bar. Note or mark the driver side end of the sway bar for correct installation.

➡**Do not allow the intermediate shaft to rotate while it is disconnected from the steering gear or damage to the clockspring can result. If there is evidence that the intermediate shaft has rotated, the clockspring must be removed and recentered.**

12. Remove the pinch bolt and detach the intermediate shaft from the gear.

13. Remove the nut and disconnect the lines.

14. Plug the ends of all fluid lines removed and ports in the steering gear to prevent entry of dirt.

➡**Hold the tops of the steering gear to crossmember stud bolts to avoid damaging the steering gear fluid transfer tubes.**

15. Remove the steering rack nuts.

16. Remove the stud bolts and washers.

17. Remove the steering gear to crossmember insulator bushings.

18. Rotate the steering gear control valve housing toward the front of the vehicle.

19. Turn the steering gear input shaft to the right until the stop is reached.

20. Move the steering gear as far to the RH side of the vehicle as possible.

21. Move the LH front wheel spindle tie-rod forward to clear the frame crossmember.

22. Remove the steering gear from the vehicle.

To install:

23. Using special tool 211-027, install new seals on the power steering return hose and power steering pressure hose.

➡**Make sure the steering gear input shaft is turned to the left until the stop is reached.**

➡**Handle the steering gear with caution to avoid damage to fluid transfer tubes and to avoid dimples in tie-rod boots.**

24. Turn the steering gear input shaft to the right until the stop is reached. Note the number of turns required.

➡**Make sure the steering gear control valve housing is turned toward the front of the vehicle.**

25. Install the steering gear into the RH opening of the crossmember.

26. Move the steering gear as far to the RH side of the vehicle as possible.

27. Move the LH front wheel spindle tie-rod into the opening in the crossmember and move the steering gear into position.

28. To place the steering gear in the straight ahead position, turn the steering gear input shaft to the left by half the number of turns recorded previously.

29. Rotate the steering gear control valve housing toward the rear of the vehicle.

30. Install the steering gear to crossmember insulator bushings.

   a. The large end of the metal sleeve must be positioned downward.

   b. Check that the mounting surfaces on the crossmember are clean and free of foreign material.

31. Install the steering gear to crossmember washers and stud bolts. The dished side of the washer faces downward.

➡Hold the tops of the steering gear to crossmember stud bolts to avoid damaging the steering gear fluid transfer tubes.

32. Install the rack mounting nuts. Torque to 111 ft. lbs. (150 Nm).

33. Install the lines and tighten the pressure line bracket nut to 18 ft. lbs. (25 Nm).

➡Do not allow the intermediate shaft to rotate while it is disconnected from the steering gear or damage to the clockspring can result. If there is evidence that the intermediate shaft has rotated, the clockspring must be removed and recentered.

34. Connect the intermediate shaft to the steering gear input shaft. Install a new lower steering column pinch bolt. Torque to 35 ft. lbs. (48 Nm).

35. Install the power steering fluid cooler.

36. Install the front stabilizer bar. Orient the front stabilizer bar as noted during removal.

37. Install the LH tie-rod end on the front wheel spindle tie-rod. Rotate the tie-rod end the number of turns recorded during removal.

38. Position the tie-rod ends on the steering knuckles. Install the castellated nuts and new cotter pins. Check that the brake dust shields are not bent and are not in contact with the outer tie-rod boot seals. Torque to 52 ft. lbs. (70 Nm).

39. Tighten the tie-rod end jam nut. Torque to 59 ft. lbs. (80 Nm).

40. Position the air deflector, and install the retaining screws.

41. Install the front wheel and tire assemblies.

42. Fill and leak check the system.

43. Check and, if necessary, adjust the wheel alignment.

POWER STEERING PUMP

REMOVAL & INSTALLATION

2.3L Engine

See Figures 207 through 209.

1. Before servicing the vehicle, refer to the Precautions Section.

2. Remove the air cleaner outlet pipe.

3. Rotate the tensioner counterclockwise and remove the belt from the power steering pump pulley.

❊❊ WARNING

Replacement of the power steering pump pulley is necessary after being removed and installed two times.

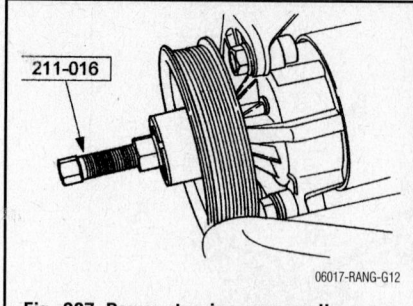

Fig. 207 Power steering pump pulley removal—2.3L engine and 3.0L engines

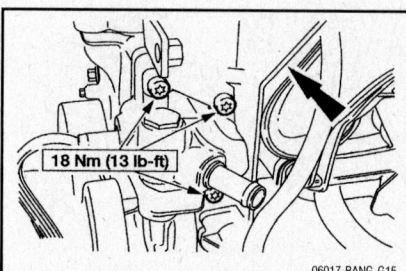

Fig. 208 Power steering pump-to-bracket bolts—2.3L engine

4. Using the special tool, remove the power steering pump pulley.

5. Inspect the pulley for paint marks in the web area near the hub. If there are two paint marks, discard the pulley. If there is no paint mark or one paint mark, use a paint pencil to mark the web area of the pulley near the hub.

6. Loosen the clamp and remove the hose.

7. Disconnect the pressure line. Remove and discard the seal.

8. Remove the bolts and the bracket.

9. Remove the bolt and the power steering pump.

To install:

10. To install, reverse the removal procedure. Rotate the tensioner clockwise, and install the belt to the power steering pump pulley. Observe the following torques:

• Mounting bolts: 13 ft. lbs. (18 Nm)

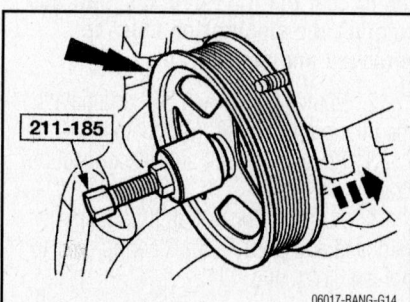

Fig. 209 Power steering pump pulley installation—2.3L engine

• Pressure line: 48 ft. lbs. (65 Nm)

11. Using the special tool, install a new seal on the pressure line.

12. Fill and leak test the system.

3.0L Engine

See Figures 207, 210 and 211.

1. Before servicing the vehicle, refer to the Precautions Section.

2. Rotate the tensioner, and remove the belt from the power steering pump pulley.

❊❊ WARNING

Replacement of the power steering pump pulley is necessary after being removed and installed two times.

3. Using the special tool, remove the power steering pump pulley.

4. Inspect the pulley for paint marks in the web area near the hub. If there are two paint marks, discard the pulley. If there is no paint mark or one paint mark, use a paint pencil to mark the web area of the pulley near the hub.

5. Remove the pump pulley.

6. Disconnect the power steering pressure hose. Remove and discard the seal.

7. Disconnect the power steering return hose.

8. Disconnect the power steering return line hose.

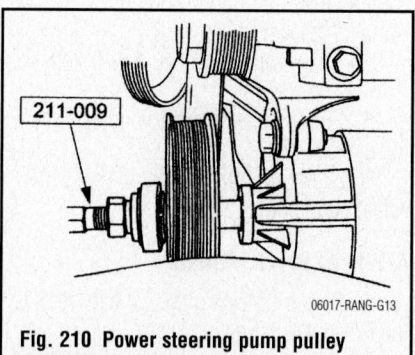

Fig. 210 Power steering pump pulley installation—3.0L engine

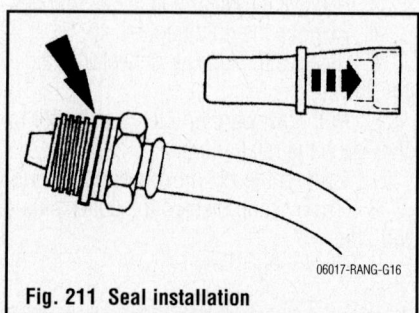

Fig. 211 Seal installation

9. Remove the bolts and the power steering pump.

10. To install, reverse the removal procedure. Using the special tool, install the power steering pump pulley. Torque the mounting bolts and pressure line to 35 ft. lbs. (48 Nm).

11. Using the special tool, install a new seal on the power steering pressure hose.

12. Fill and leak test the system.

4.0L Engine

See Figure 212.

1. Before servicing the vehicle, refer to the Precautions Section.

2. Remove the engine cooling fan.

3. Loosen the power steering pump pulley bolts.

4. Rotate the tensioner counterclockwise and remove the belt from the power steering pump pulley.

5. Remove the bolts. Remove the power steering pump pulley.

6. Disconnect the power steering return line hose at the power steering fluid reservoir. Allow the system to drain.

7. Disconnect the power steering pressure hose from the power steering pump.

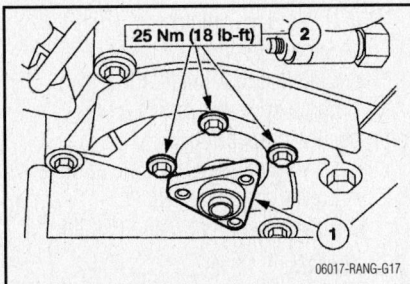

Fig. 212 Power steering pump mounting—4.0L engine

8. Compress and move the power steering fluid reservoir outlet hose clamp.

9. Disconnect the power steering fluid reservoir outlet hose from the power steering pump.

10. Remove the bolts. Remove the power steering pump.

To install:

11. Position the power steering pump.

12. Install the bolts. Torque to 18 ft. lbs. (25 Nm).

13. Connect the power steering fluid reservoir outlet hose to the power steering pump.

14. Connect the power steering fluid reservoir outlet hose to the power steering pump.

15. Compress and move the power steering fluid reservoir outlet hose clamp into place.

16. Using the special tool, install a new seal on the power steering pressure hose.

17. Connect the power steering pressure hose to the power steering pump. Torque to 48 ft. lbs. (65 Nm).

18. Connect the power steering return line hose to the power steering fluid reservoir.

19. Position the power steering pump pulley.

20. Install the bolts.

21. Install the drive belt.

22. Tighten the power steering pump pulley bolts to 18 ft. lbs. (25 Nm).

23. Install the engine cooling fan.

24. Fill and leak check the system.

BLEEDING

➡A whine heard from the power steering pump can be caused by air in the system. The power steering purge procedure must be carried out prior to any component repair for which power steering noise complaints are accompanied by evidence of aerated fluid.

1. Remove the power steering pump reservoir cap. Check the fluid.

2. Raise the front wheels off the floor.

3. Tightly insert the stopper of the vacuum pump into the reservoir.

4. Start the engine.

5. Install the vacuum pump, apply vacuum and maintain the maximum vacuum of 68-85 kPa (20-25 in-Hg).

6. If equipped with Hydro-Boost®, apply the brake pedal twice.

❋❋ WARNING

Do not hold the steering wheel against the stops for more than 3 to 5 seconds at a time. Damage to the power steering pump can occur.

7. Cycle the steering wheel fully from stop-to-stop 10 times.

8. Stop the engine.

9. Release the vacuum and remove the vacuum pump.

10. Fill the reservoir with approved transmission fluid.

11. Start the engine.

12. Install the vacuum pump. Apply and maintain the maximum vacuum of 68-85 kPa (20-25 in-Hg).

13. Cycle the steering wheel fully from stop-to-stop 10 times.

14. Stop the engine, release the vacuum and remove the vacuum pump.

➡**Do not overfill the reservoir.**

15. Fill the reservoir as needed and visually inspect the power steering system for leaks.

16. Install the reservoir cap.

COIL SPRING

REMOVAL & INSTALLATION

1. Before servicing the vehicle, refer to the Precautions Section.
2. Remove or disconnect the following:
   - Wheel and tire assembly
   - Shock absorber
   - Front stabilizer bar link nut
3. Use a coil spring compressor to compress the coil spring.
4. Remove the cotter pin and castellated nut.
5. Separate the lower ball joint from the front wheel spindle.
6. Position the front wheel spindle out of the way and remove the coil spring.

To install:

➡**The end of the coil spring must cover the first hole and should not be visible in the second hole.**

7. Install the coil spring in the lower arm.

✶ WARNING

Always install the cotter pin into the lower ball joint castellated nut from outboard to inboard. Failure to do so will result in damage to the wheel and tire assembly.

8. Install the lower ball joint.
9. Install the front stabilizer bar link nut.
10. Remove the Coil Spring Compressor.
11. Install the front shock absorber and the two lower nuts.
12. Install the upper shock absorber bushing and nut/washer assembly.
13. Install the wheel and tire assembly.

CONTROL LINKS

REMOVAL & INSTALLATION

1. Before servicing the vehicle, refer to the Precautions Section.
2. Raise the vehicle on a hoist.
3. Remove the wheel and tire assembly.
4. Remove the front stabilizer bar link nuts from the front suspension lower arms.
5. Remove the front stabilizer bar link bolts and the front stabilizer bar links and grommets.

To install:

6. Install the front stabilizer bar link bolts and the front stabilizer bar links and grommets.

7. Install the stabilizer link nuts and tighten to 18 ft. lbs. (25 Nm).
8. Install the wheel and tire assembly.
9. Lower vehicle.

LOWER BALL JOINT

REMOVAL & INSTALLATION

1. Before servicing the vehicle, refer to the Precautions Section.
2. With the vehicle in NEUTRAL, position it on a hoist.
3. Remove the wheel and tire assembly.

✶✶ WARNING

Do not allow the disc brake caliper to hang suspended from the brake hose. Provide a suitable support.

4. Remove the caliper support bracket bolts, then position the caliper and support bracket aside.
5. Disconnect the front anti-lock brake sensor (ABS) wire from the vehicle frame.
6. Using a suitable jack, support the front suspension lower arm.
7. Remove the tie-rod end castellated nut. Remove and discard the cotter pin and the castellated nut.

✶✶ WARNING

Do not use a hammer to separate the tie-rod from the wheel knuckle or damage to the wheel knuckle will result. Do not damage the tie-rod boot when installing the special tool.

8. Using the special tool, separate the tie-rod end from the front wheel knuckle.
9. Remove the lower ball joint castellated nut. Remove and discard the cotter pin and the castellated nut.
10. Separate the front wheel knuckle from the front suspension lower arm. Then, loosely install the lower ball joint castellated nut.
11. Remove the pinch bolt and nut.
12. Remove the hand-tightened lower ball joint castellated nut, then remove the front wheel knuckle.
13. Remove the snaring from the ball joint. Discard the snap ring.
14. Using a suitable ball joint remover tool, remove the ball joint.

✶✶ WARNING

Do not damage the ball joint boot when installing the special tool.

➡**Clean and inspect the control arm ball joint bore for damage before installing a new ball joint.**

➡**Make sure the new ball joint snap ring is fully seated.**

15. To install, reverse the removal procedure. Always install new castellated nuts and cotter pins. Observe the following torques:
   - Pinch bolt and nut: 41 ft. lbs. (55 Nm)
   - Lower ball stud nut: 98 ft. lbs. (133 Nm)
   - Tie rod stud nut: 52 ft. lbs. (70 Nm)
   - Caliper support bracket bolts: 83 ft. lbs. (112 Nm)

LOWER CONTROL ARM

REMOVAL AND & INSTALLATION

Coil Spring Suspension

1. Before servicing the vehicle, refer to the Precautions Section.
2. Remove or disconnect the following:
   - Negative battery cable
   - Front wheel
   - Brake rotor shield
   - Shock absorber
   - Stabilizer bar link hardware
3. Using a spring compressor tool, compress the coil spring.
   - Lower ball joint from the spindle
   - Lower control arm bolts
   - Lower control arm and coil spring

To install:
4. Install or connect the following:
   - Coil spring to the lower control arm

➡**The end of the coil spring must cover the first hole and should not be visible in the second hole.**

   - Lower arm and front coil spring
   - The two front suspension lower arm bolts and nuts. Do not tighten the nuts at this time.

➡**On the RH front suspension lower arm, install the rear bolt adjustment cam, and nut in the center of the frame slot.**

✶✶ CAUTION

Always install the cotter pin into the lower ball joint castellated nut from outboard to inboard, with the fingers bent together at a right angle. Failure

to do so will result in damage to the wheel and tire assembly.

- Lower ball joint. Torque the nut to 113 ft. lbs. (153 Nm).
5. Remove the Coil Spring Compressor.
6. Install or connect the following:
- Front stabilizer bar link nut. Torque the nut to 21 ft. lbs. (29 Nm).
- Shock absorber and the two lower nuts
- Upper shock absorber bushing and nut/washer assembly
7. Support the lower control arm with a jackstand. Torque the bolts to 129 ft. lbs. (175 Nm).
- Brake disc shield
- Wheel and tire assembly
8. Inspect and adjust the front end alignment.

Torsion Bar Suspension

1. Before servicing the vehicle, refer to the Precautions Section.
2. Raise the vehicle on a hoist.
3. Remove the wheel and tire assembly.
4. Remove the stabilizer link nut, washer and bushing.
5. Remove the front shock absorber-to-front suspension lower arm nuts.
6. Remove the torsion bar
7. Remove the lower ball joint castellated nut.

➡Do not use a hammer to separate the ball joint from the wheel knuckle or damage to the wheel knuckle will result. Do not damage the ball joint boot while installing the special tool.

8. Using the special tool, separate the front suspension lower arm from the front wheel knuckle/spindle.
9. Remove the front suspension lower arm bolts and nuts.
10. Remove the front suspension lower arm.

To install:

➡Tighten the front suspension lower arm pivot bolts and nuts until snug. Do not tighten to specification until the installation procedure is complete.

11. Position the front suspension lower arm to the front suspension crossmember.
12. Install the pivot bolts and nuts and tighten until snug.

✽✽ WARNING

Install the cotter pin into the lower ball joint from outboard to inboard with the fingers bent together at a

right angle. Failure to do so will cause damage to the wheel and tire assembly.

13. Position the lower ball joint into the front wheel knuckle/spindle.
14. Install the new castellated nut. Torque to 98 ft. lbs. (133 Nm).
15. Install a new cotter pin.
16. Install the front shock absorber-to-front suspension lower arm nuts. Torque to 18 ft. lbs. (25 Nm).
17. Install the stabilizer link bushing, washer, and nut. Torque to 18 ft. lbs. (25 Nm).

➡Whenever the torsion bar or torsion bar adjuster is removed, the vehicle ride height must be checked.

18. Install the torsion bar.
19. Install the tire and wheel assembly.
20. Lower the vehicle.
21. Tighten the front suspension lower arm nuts. Torque to 148 ft. lbs. (200 Nm).
22. Inspect and adjust the front end alignment.

SHOCK ABSORBERS

REMOVAL & INSTALLATION

➡Low pressure gas shocks are charged with nitrogen gas. Do not attempt to open, puncture or apply heat to them. Prior to installing a new shock absorber, hold it upright and extend it fully. Invert it and fully compress and extend it at least 3 times. This will bleed trapped air.

1. Before servicing the vehicle, refer to the Precautions Section.
2. Remove or disconnect the following:
- Negative battery cable
- Upper shock-to-frame attaching nut, washer and insulator assembly
- Lower shock-to-control arm attaching nuts
- Slightly compress the shock absorber by hand and remove it from the vehicle

To install:
3. Install or connect the following:
- Position the lower washer and insulator on the shock absorber rod and position the shock absorber to the upper frame bracket mount
- Position the upper insulator and washer on the shock absorber rod and install the attaching nut loosely.
- Position the lower shock absorber mounting studs into the control

arm and install the attaching nuts loosely.
- Torque the lower shock attaching nuts to 18 ft. lbs. (25 Nm), and the upper shock attaching bolts to 35 ft. lbs. (48 Nm).
- Negative battery cable

STABILIZER BAR

REMOVAL & INSTALLATION

1. Before servicing the vehicle, refer to the Precautions Section.
2. Raise the vehicle on a hoist.
3. Remove the wheel and tire assembly.
4. Remove the front stabilizer bar link nuts from the front suspension lower arms.
5. Remove the front stabilizer bar link bolts and the front stabilizer bar links.
6. Remove the four bolts and two brackets.
7. Remove the front stabilizer bar.
8. Remove the stabilizer bar insulator.
9. Installation is the reverse of removal. Observe the following torques:
- End link nuts: 18 ft. lbs. (25 Nm)
- Bracket bolts: 30 ft. lbs. (40 Nm)

➡In the event the self-tapping bolts cannot be installed in the frame, there is a kit available with flag nuts.

STEERING KNUCKLE

REMOVAL & INSTALLATION

2-Wheel Drive Models
See Figure 213.

1. Before servicing the vehicle, refer to the Precautions Section.
2. Put the vehicle in NEUTRAL and position on a hoist.
3. Remove tire and wheel assembly.
4. Remove the hub grease cap.
5. Remove the cotter pin.
6. Remove the hub spindle nut retainer.
7. Remove the hub spindle nut.
8. Remove the outer wheel bearing retaining washer.
9. Remove the outer wheel bearing.
10. Remove the brake disc and hub.
11. Remove the disc brake shield.
12. Remove and discard the wheel speed sensor harness bracket bolt.
13. Remove and discard the wheel speed sensor bolt and disconnect the wheel speed sensor from the wheel spindle.
14. Remove and discard the outer tie-rod end nut.
15. Using the special tool, separate the outer tie-rod end from the wheel spindle.

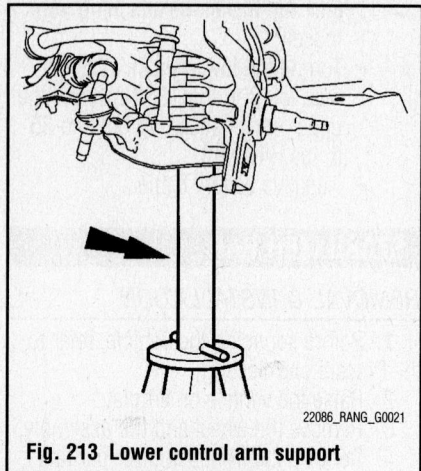

Fig. 213 Lower control arm support stand—2-wheel drive models

16. Use suitable jack to support the front suspension lower arm.

17. Disconnect the upper ball joint from the wheel spindle.

18. Remove and discard the lower ball joint cotter pin and nut.

19. Using the special tool, separate the lower ball joint from the wheel spindle and remove the front wheel spindle.

To install:

20. To install, reverse the removal procedure and note the following:

- Tighten lower ball joint nut to 98 ft. lbs. (133 Nm), install cotter pin.
- Tighten upper ball joint mounting bolt to 46 ft. lbs. (63 Nm).
- Tighten tie-rod end nut to 59 ft. lbs. (80 Nm), install cotter pin.
- Tighten speed sensor bracket bolt to 9 ft. lbs. (12 Nm).
- Repack wheel bearings and install new grease seal.

4-Wheel Drive Models

See Figure 214.

1. Loosen the wheel hub nut.

2. Put the vehicle in NEUTRAL and position on a hoist.

3. Remove the wheel hub nut and the washer. Discard the wheel hub nut.

4. Remove the brake disc.

5. Using special tool 205-D070, separate the outboard front wheel halfshaft joint from the wheel hub.

6. Remove the brake shield.

7. Remove the bolt and disconnect the wheel speed sensor from the wheel hub.

8. Remove the three bolts and the wheel hub.

9. Remove the tie-rod end castellated nut.

10. Using a tie-rod remover separate the tie-rod end from the front wheel knuckle.

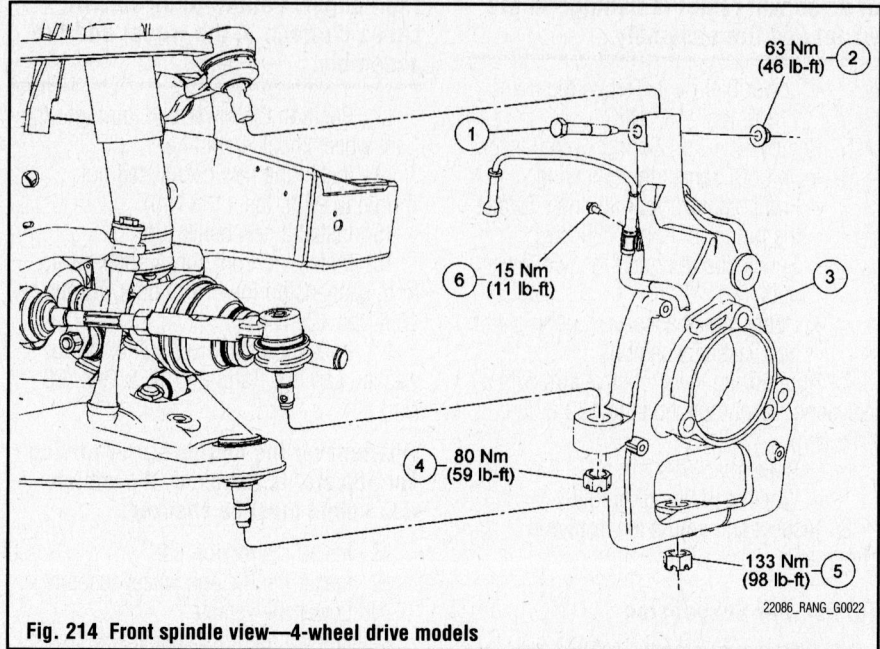

Fig. 214 Front spindle view—4-wheel drive models

11. Using a suitable jack, support the front suspension lower arm.

12. Remove the lower ball joint castellated nut.

13. Separate the front wheel knuckle from the front suspension lower arm.

14. Remove the pinch bolt and remove the wheel knuckle.

To install:

15. Install the wheel knuckle and the pinch bolt and tighten to 41 ft. lbs. (55 Nm).

16. Connect the front wheel knuckle to the front suspension lower arm.

17. Install the lower ball joint castellated nut and tighten to 98 ft. lbs. (133 Nm).

18. Connect the tie-rod end to the front wheel knuckle.

19. Install the tie-rod end castellated nut.

20. Install the three bolts and the wheel hub and tighten to 85 ft. lbs. (115 Nm).

21. Install the bolt and connect the wheel speed sensor to the wheel hub.

22. Install the brake shield.

23. Connect the outboard front wheel halfshaft joint to the wheel hub.

24. Install the brake disc.

25. Install the wheel hub nut and the washer. Tighten the new nut to 162 ft. lbs. (220 Nm).

TORSION BAR

REMOVAL & INSTALLATION

See Figures 215 through 217.

1. Before servicing the vehicle, refer to the Precautions Section.

2. Remove the torsion bar cover plate.

➡**Before relieving the torsion bar tension, measure and record the measurement of the torsion bar adjustment bolt. This measurement will be used as the preset depth for the new torsion bar adjustment bolt during installation.**

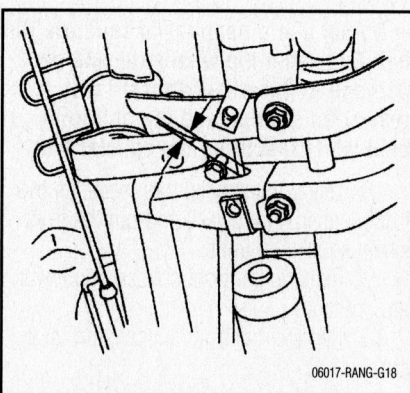

Fig. 215 Measure and record the measurement of the torsion bar adjustment bolt

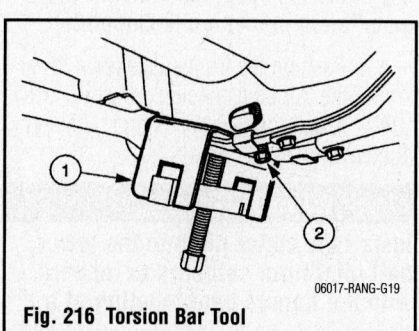

Fig. 216 Torsion Bar Tool

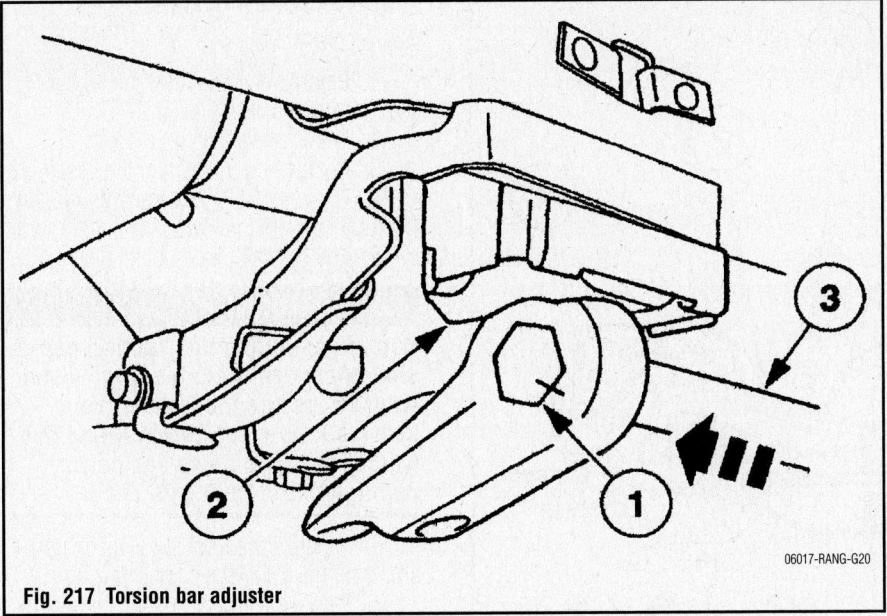

Fig. 217 Torsion bar adjuster

3. Relieve the torsion bar tension, as follows:

c. Position the Torsion Bar Tool and adapters.

d. Tighten the Torsion Bar Tool until the torsion bar adjuster lifts off the adjustment bolt.

❋❋ CAUTION

The torsion bar adjustment bolt is coated with dry adhesive; and must be replaced if it is backed off or removed. Failure to do so can cause the adjustment bolt to loosen during operation and cause a loss of vehicle alignment.

e. Remove the torsion bar adjustment bolt and nut.

f. Loosen the Torsion Bar Tool until the tension is removed from the torsion bar.

4. Mark the torsion bar and the adjuster for proper installation.

5. Remove the torsion bar insulator.

6. Grasp the torsion bar, and pull it free from the front suspension lower arm.

To install:

7. Position the torsion bar and the torsion bar adjuster.

8. Align the marks on the torsion bar and the torsion bar adjuster, then install the torsion bar adjuster.

9. Position the torsion bar insulator.

10. Install the Torsion Bar Tool and the adapters.

11. Tighten the Torsion Bar Tool until the new adjustment bolt and nut can be installed.

12. Turn the adjustment bolt until the preliminary adjustment measurement (recorded length of the old adjustment bolt) is reached.

13. Install the torsion bar cover plate. Torque the bolts to 46 ft. lbs. (63 Nm).

14. If equipped with air suspension, reactivate the system by turning on the air suspension switch.

15. Lower the vehicle.

16. Adjust the ride height.

17. Check the alignment.

UPPER BALL JOINT

REMOVAL & INSTALLATION

The ball joints are integral with the control arm. If the ball joint is defective, the entire control arm must be replaced. Refer to upper control arm removal and installation.

UPPER CONTROL ARM

REMOVAL & INSTALLATION

Coil Spring Suspension

1. Before servicing the vehicle, refer to the Precautions Section.

2. Remove or disconnect the following:
   • Wheel and tire assembly
   • Brake disc shield

3. Use a jack to support the front suspension lower arm.

4. Mark the position of the front suspension upper arm adjustment cams.

5. Remove the upper ball joint retaining nut and pinch bolt.

6. Separate the ball joint from the front wheel spindle.

7. Remove the front suspension upper arm.

8. Installation is the reverse of removal. Align the marks made during removal on the front suspension upper arm adjustment cam. The forward front suspension upper arm nut must be tightened first while the arm is held at the curb position ride height. Observe the following torques:

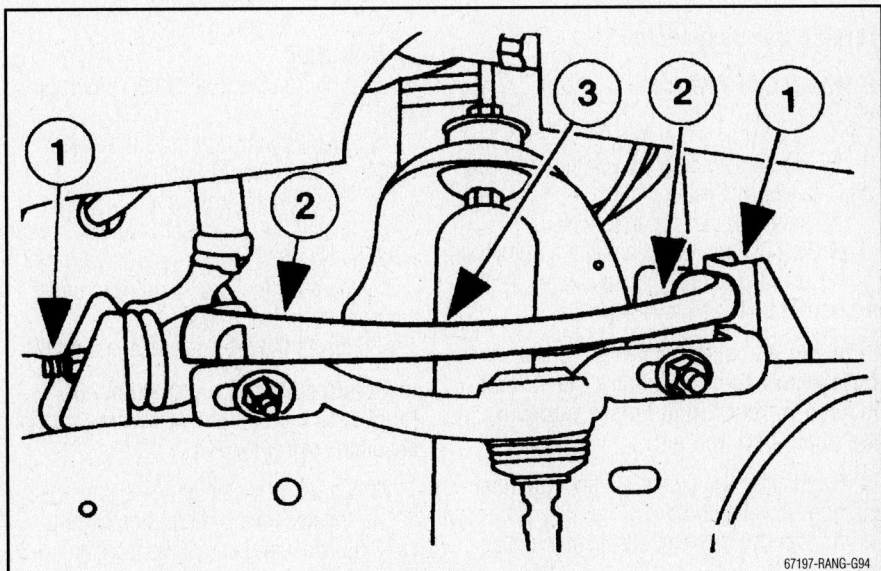

Fig. 218 Upper control arm—2-wheel drive torsion bar suspension; 1-nuts; 2-bolts; 3-arm

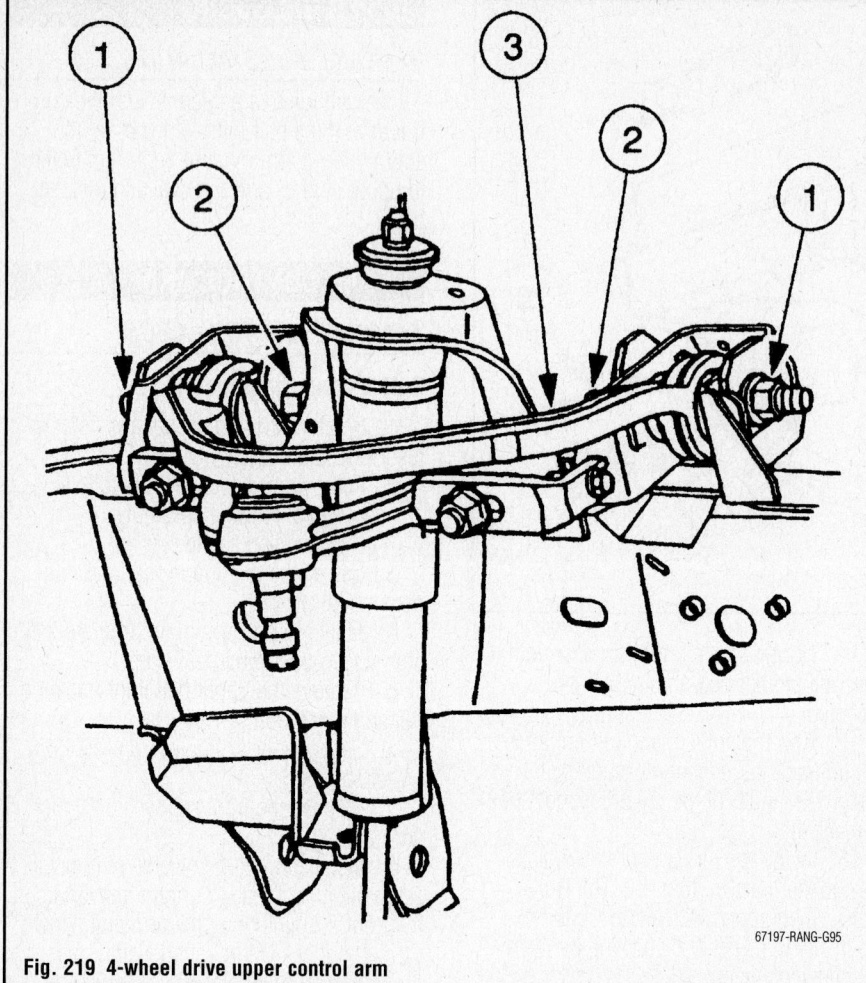

Fig. 219 4-wheel drive upper control arm

67197-RANG-G95

- Control arm attaching nuts: 98 ft. lbs. (133 Nm)
- Pinch bolt: 46 ft. lbs. (63 Nm)

Torsion Bar Suspension

2-Wheel Drive Models

See Figure 218.

1. Before servicing the vehicle, refer to the Precautions Section.
2. Raise the vehicle on a hoist.
3. Remove the wheel and tire assembly
4. Use a suitable jack stand to support the front suspension lower arm.

➡**To avoid possible damage to the front wheel spindle, secure the spindle to keep it from tilting before removing the pinch bolt and nut.**

5. Remove the pinch bolt and nut from the front wheel spindle.
6. Remove the front suspension upper arm:

a. Remove the two nuts.
b. Remove the two bolts.
c. Remove the front suspension upper arm.

To install:

7. Position the front suspension upper arm.
8. Install the two bolts and two nuts. Torque to 98 ft. lbs. (133 Nm).
9. Position the front wheel spindle.
10. Install the pinch bolt and nut. Torque to 46 ft. lbs. (63 Nm).
11. Remove the jack stand from under the front suspension lower arm.
12. Install the tire and wheel assembly

➡**If equipped with air suspension, reactivate the system by turning on the air suspension switch.**

13. Lower the vehicle.
14. Inspect the front end ride height.
15. Inspect and adjust the front end alignment .

4-Wheel Drive Models

See Figure 219.

1. Before servicing the vehicle, refer to the Precautions Section.
2. Raise the vehicle on a hoist.
3. Remove the wheel and tire assembly.
4. Use a suitable jack stand to support the front suspension lower arm.
5. Remove the pinch bolt.

✳✳ WARNING

Before separating the front suspension upper arm from the front wheel knuckle, secure the front wheel knuckle to prevent it from tilting outward. Failure to do so can cause damage to the front axle shaft.

6. Separate the front suspension upper arm from the front wheel knuckle.
7. Remove the front suspension upper arm:

a. Remove the two nuts and alignment plates.
b. Remove the two bolts and the cams.
c. Remove the front suspension upper arm.

To install:

➡**When installing the front suspension upper arm, replace the alignment plates with new alignment cams.**

8. Install the front suspension upper arm.

a. Position the front suspension arm bushing joint.
b. Install the two bolts, four cams and two nuts. Torque to 98 ft. lbs. (133 Nm).
9. Install the pinch bolt and nut.

a. Position the upper arm into the front wheel knuckle.
b. Install the pinch bolt and nut. Torque to 41 ft. lbs. (55 Nm).
10. Remove the jack stand from under the front suspension lower arm.
11. Install the wheel and tire assembly.
12. Lower the vehicle.
13. Check the wheel alignment.

WHEEL BEARINGS

REMOVAL & INSTALLATION

2-Wheel Drive Models

1. Before servicing the vehicle, refer to the Precautions Section.

2. Remove or disconnect the following:
- Disc brake caliper anchor plate
- Hub grease cap
- Cotter pin
- Nut retainer
- Spindle nut
- Wheel outer bearing retainer washer
- Outer front wheel bearing
- Brake disc and hub
- Hub grease seal
- Inner wheel bearing

To install:

3. Thoroughly clean and inspect the front wheel bearings and the brake disc and hub.
4. Lubricate the front wheel bearings.
5. Install the inner front wheel bearing.
6. Install a new wheel hub grease seal.
7. Position the brake disc and hub.
8. Assemble all parts and adjust the bearings.

4-Wheel Drive Models

1. Before servicing the vehicle, refer to the Precautions Section.
2. Remove the brake disc.
3. Remove and discard the nut and washer assembly.

✳✳ WARNING

Do not use a hammer to separate the outboard CV joint from the hub. Damage to the outboard CV threads and to internal components may result.

4. Using the special tool, separate the outboard CV joint from the hub.
5. Remove the dust shield.
6. Remove the bolt and detach the anti-lock sensor from the wheel hub.

✳✳ WARNING

Do not overextend the CV joint and boots when removing the hub and bearing assembly.

7. Remove the bolts and the wheel hub.
8. To install, reverse the removal procedure. Observe the following torques:
- Hub/bearing bolts: 85 ft. lbs. (115 Nm)
- Dust shield: 9 ft. lbs. (12 Nm)
- Halfshaft nut: 162 ft. lbs. (220 Nm)

ADJUSTMENT

1. The wheel bearings on 2-wheel drive models can be adjusted by tightening the spindle nut. Make sure bearings are properly packed before tightening. Tighten the spindle nut until no play is felt. Do not over tighten or bearing failure will result.

4-wheel drive models have a sealed bearing assembly that cannot be adjusted. If play is felt replace bearing assembly.

REPACKING

1. To repack 2-wheel drive front bearings, remove spindle nut outer bearing and rotor.
2. Remove grease seal and inner bearing.
3. Clean and inspect wheel bearings and races for signs of pitting and discoloration.
4. Repack using wheel bearing packer, clean mating surfaces.
5. Install wheel bearings and a new grease seal.
6. Tighten wheel bearings by adjusting spindle nut.

➡**Be careful not to over-tighten bearings, double check your adjustment.**

4-wheel drive models have a sealed bearing assembly that cannot be re-packed.

SUSPENSION

LEAF SPRING

REMOVAL & INSTALLATION

1. Before servicing the vehicle, refer to the Precautions Section.
2. Remove or disconnect the following:
- Negative battery cable
- Rear wheels
- U-bolts from the rear spring plate
- Hardware from the spring to bracket at the front of the rear spring
- Upper and lower shackle bolts at the rear of the spring
- Spring and shackle from the bracket

To install:

3. Install or connect the following:
- Spring and shackle to the bracket
- Upper and lower shackle bolts at the rear of the spring. Torque the nuts to 85 ft. lbs. (115 Nm).
- U-bolts to the spring plate. Torque the nuts 76 ft. lbs. (103 Nm).
- Rear wheels
- Negative battery cable

SHOCK ABSORBER

REMOVAL & INSTALLATION

➡**Low pressure gas shocks are charged with nitrogen gas. Do not attempt to open, puncture or apply heat to them. Prior to installing a new shock absorber, hold it upright and extend it fully. Invert it and fully compress and extend it at least 3 times. This will bleed trapped air.**

1. Before servicing the vehicle, refer to the Precautions Section.
2. Remove or disconnect the following:
- Upper shock-to-frame attaching nut
- Lower shock nut
- Slightly compress the shock absorber by hand and remove it from the vehicle

To install:

3. Install or connect the following:
- Shock absorber upper end and nut

REAR SUSPENSION

- Shock absorber lower end and nut
- Torque the upper and lower shock attaching nuts to 53 ft. lbs. (72 Nm)

TESTING

1. Test drive vehicle.
2. Inspect each shock absorber for external fluid leakage.
3. Use your hands in order to lift up and push down each corner of the vehicle 3 times.
4. Remove your hands from the vehicle.
5. Replace any shock that exceeds more than two bounces.

STABILIZER BAR

REMOVAL & INSTALLATION

See Figure 220.

1. Before servicing the vehicle, refer to the Precautions Section.

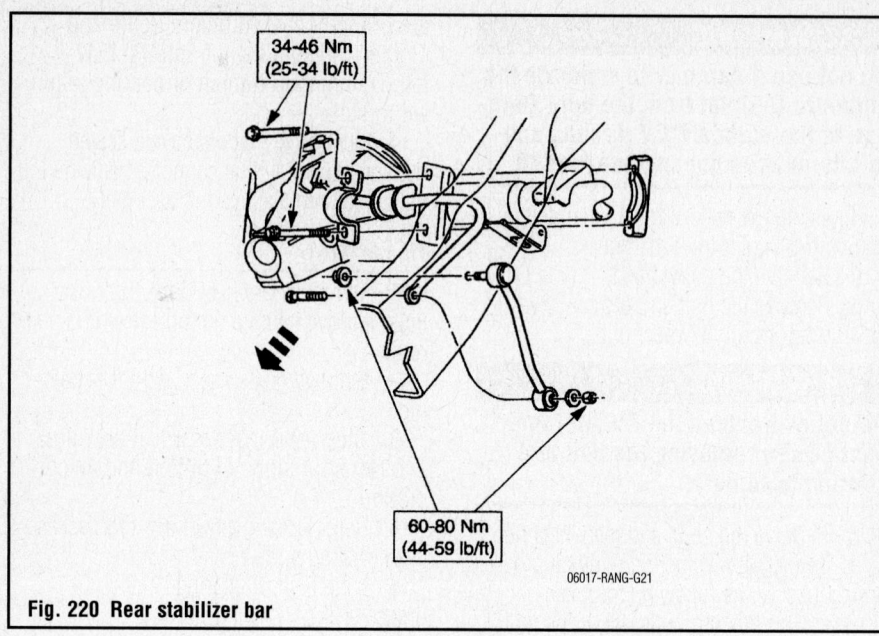

34-46 Nm
(25-34 lb/ft)

60-80 Nm
(44-59 lb/ft)

06017-RANG-G21

Fig. 220 Rear stabilizer bar

2. Raise the vehicle and install safety stands.

3. Remove the wheel and tire assembly.

4. Remove the rear stabilizer bar link nuts and bolt.

5. Remove the rear stabilizer bar link.

6. Remove the rear stabilizer bar mounting bracket bolts and remove the brackets.

7. Remove the rear stabilizer bar.

8. Installation is the reverse of removal. Observe the following torques:

- End link nuts: 59 ft. lbs. (80 Nm)
- Bracket bolts: 34 ft. lbs. (46 Nm)

WHEEL BEARINGS

REMOVAL & INSTALLATION

Refer to the Drive Train Section, Rear Axle, Bearing Axle and Seals.

FORD AND MERCURY

Sable • Taurus

17

FUEL 17-70

GASOLINE FUEL
INJECTION SYSTEM 17-70

HEATING & AIR CONDITIONING
SYSTEM 17-73

PRECAUTIONS..............17-11

SPECIFICATIONS AND
MAINTENANCE CHARTS.....17-3

STEERING 17-78

SUSPENSION 17-81

FRONT SUSPENSION 17-81

REAR SUSPENSION 17-86

SPECIFICATIONS AND MAINTENANCE CHARTS

ENGINE AND VEHICLE IDENTIFICATION

Code ①	Liters (cc)	Cu. In.	Cyl.	Fuel Sys.	Engine Type	Eng. Mfg.	Code ②	Year
			Engine				**Model Year**	
S	3.0 (3049)	182	6	MFI	DOHC	Ford	5	2005
U	3.0 (2982)	181	6	MFI	OHV	Ford	6	2006
2 ③	3.0 (2982)	181	6	MFI	OHV	Ford	7	2007

OHV: Overhead Valves

DOHC: Double Overhead Camshafts

MFI: Multiport Fuel Injection

① 8th digit of the Vehicle Identification Number (VIN)

② 10th digit of the Vehicle Identification Number (VIN)

③ Flex Fuel

22086_TAUR_C0001

GENERAL ENGINE SPECIFICATIONS

Year	Model	Engine Displacement Liters	Engine ID/VIN	Net Horsepower @ rpm	Net Torque @ rpm (ft. lbs.)	Bore x Stroke (in.)	Compression Ratio	Oil Pressure @ rpm
2005	Sable	3.0	U	153@5800	186@3250	3.50x3.10	9.4:1	40-60@2500
		3.0	2	153@5800	186@3250	3.50x3.10	9.4:1	40-60@2500
		3.0	S	201@5500	207@4500	3.50x3.13	10.0:1	11@1500
	Taurus	3.0	U	153@5800	186@3250	3.50x3.10	9.4:1	40-60@2500
		3.0	2	153@5800	186@3250	3.50x3.10	9.4:1	40-60@2500
		3.0	S	201@5500	207@4500	3.50x3.13	10.0:1	11@1500
2006	Taurus	3.0	U	153@5800	186@3250	3.50x3.10	9.4:1	40-60@2500
		3.0	2	153@5800	186@3250	3.50x3.10	9.4:1	40-60@2500
2007	Taurus	3.0	U	153@5800	186@3250	3.50x3.10	9.4:1	40-60@2500

22086_TAUR_C0002

ENGINE TUNE-UP SPECIFICATIONS

Year	Engine Displacement Liters	Engine ID/VIN	Spark Plug Gap (in.)	Ignition Timing (deg.)	Fuel Pump (psi) ①	Idle Speed (rpm)	Valve Clearance Intake	Valve Clearance Exhaust
2005	3.0	U	0.042-0.046	10B	26-45	②	HYD	HYD
	3.0	2	0.042-0.046	10B	26-45	②	HYD	HYD
	3.0	S	0.052-0.056	10B	26-45	②	HYD	HYD
2006	3.0	U	0.042-0.046	10B	26-45	②	HYD	HYD
	3.0	2	0.042-0.046	10B	26-45	②	HYD	HYD
2007	3.0	U	0.042-0.046	10B	26-45	②	HYD	HYD

NOTE: The Vehicle Emission Control Information label often reflects specification changes made during production. The label figures must be used if they differ from those in this chart.

B: Before Top Dead Center

HYD: Hydraulic

① Fuel pressure with engine running, pressure regulator vacuum hose connected

② Refer to Vehicle Emission Control Information label

22086_TAUR_C0003

CAPACITIES

Year	Model	Engine Displacement Liters	Engine ID/VIN	Engine Oil with Filter (qts.)	Transaxle (pts.) Auto. ①	Drive Axle (pts.)	Fuel Tank (gal.)	Cooling System (qts.)
2005	Sable	3.0	U	4.5	26.8	②	18.0	11.6
		3.0	2	4.5	26.8	②	18.0	11.6
		3.0	S	6.0	27.0	②	18.0	10.6
	Taurus	3.0	U	4.5	26.8	②	18.0	11.6
		3.0	2	4.5	26.8	②	18.0	11.6
		3.0	S	6.0	27.0	②	18.0	10.6
2006	Taurus	3.0	U	4.5	26.8	②	18.0	11.6
		3.0	2	4.5	26.8	②	18.0	11.6
2007	Taurus	3.0	U	4.5	26.8	②	18.0	11.6

NOTE: All capacities are approximate. Add fluid gradually and ensure a proper fluid level is obtained.

① Includes torque converter

② Included in transaxle capacity

22086_TAUR_C0004

FLUID SPECIFICATIONS

Year	Model	Engine Displacement Liters	Engine ID/VIN	Engine Oil ①	Auto. Trans.	Drive Axle	Power Steering Fluid	Brake Master Cylinder
2005	Taurus	3.0	U	5W-20	MERCON V	75W-140	MERCON ②	DOT 3
		3.0	2	5W-20	MERCON V	75W-140	MERCON ②	DOT 3
		3.0	S	5W-20	MERCON V	75W-140	MERCON ②	DOT 3
	Sable	3.0	U	5W-20	MERCON V	75W-140	MERCON ②	DOT 3
		3.0	2	5W-20	MERCON V	75W-140	MERCON ②	DOT 3
		3.0	S	5W-20	MERCON V	75W-140	MERCON ②	DOT 3
2006	Taurus	3.0	U	5W-20	MERCON V	75W-140	MERCON ②	DOT 3
		3.0	2	5W-20	MERCON V	75W-140	MERCON ②	DOT 3
2007	Taurus	3.0	U	5W-20	MERCON V	75W-140	MERCON ②	DOT 3

DOT: Department Of Transpotation

① Premium Synthetic Blend Motor Oil XO-5W20-QSP or equivalent

② MERCON Multi-Purpose ATF Transmission Fluid XT-2-QDX

22086_TAUR_C0005

VALVE SPECIFICATIONS

Year	Engine Displacement Liters	Engine ID/VIN	Seat Angle (deg.)	Face Angle (deg.)	Spring Test Pressure (lbs. @ in.)	Spring Installed Height (in.)	Stem-to-Guide Clearance (in.)		Stem Diameter (in.)	
							Intake	Exhaust	Intake	Exhaust
2005	3.0	U	45	44	193@1.17	1.650-1.736	0.0010-0.0028	0.0015-0.0033	0.2744-0.2752	0.2740-0.2748
	3.0	2	45	44	193@1.17	1.650-1.736	0.0010-0.0028	0.0015-0.0033	0.2744-0.2752	0.2740-0.2748
	3.0	S	44.75	45.5	156@1.18	1.570	0.0007-0.0027	0.0017-0.0037	0.2350-0.2358	0.2343-0.2350
2006	3.0	U	45	44	193@1.17	1.650-1.736	0.0010-0.0028	0.0015-0.0033	0.2744-0.2752	0.2740-0.2748
	3.0	2	45	44	193@1.17	1.650-1.736	0.0010-0.0028	0.0015-0.0033	0.2744-0.2752	0.2740-0.2748
2007	3.0	U	45	44	193@1.17	1.650-1.736	0.0010-0.0028	0.0015-0.0033	0.2744-0.2752	0.2740-0.2748

22086_TAUR_C0009

CAMSHAFT AND BEARING SPECIFICATIONS CHART
All measurements are given in inches.

Year	Engine Displ. Liters	Engine ID/VIN	Journal Dia.	Brg. Oil Clearance	Shaft End-play	Runout	Journal Bore	Lobe Height	
								Intake	Exhaust
2005	3.0	S	1.060-1.061	0.0010-0.0029	0.0075	—	1.062-1.063	NA	NA
	3.0	2	2.0074-2.0084	0.001-0.003	0.0070	0.002	①	NA	NA
	3.0	U	2.0074-2.0084	0.001-0.003	0.0070	0.002	①	NA	NA
2006	3.0	2	2.0074-2.0084	0.001-0.003	0.0070	0.002	①	NA	NA
	3.0	U	2.0074-2.0084	0.001-0.003	0.0070	0.002	①	NA	NA
2007	3.0	U	2.0074-2.0084	0.001-0.003	0.0070	0.002	①	NA	NA

NA: Not Available

① Journals 1 and 4: 2.1531-2.1541
 Journals 2 and 3: 2.1334-2.1344

22086_TAUR_C0008

CRANKSHAFT AND CONNECTING ROD SPECIFICATIONS

All measurements are given in inches.

Year	Engine Displacement Liters	Engine ID/VIN	Crankshaft				Connecting Rod		
			Main Brg. Journal Dia.	Main Brg. Oil Clearance	Shaft End-play	Thrust on No.	Journal Diameter	Oil Clearance	Side Clearance
2005	3.0	U	2.5190-2.5198	0.0009 0.0027	0.004-0.0080	3	2.1253-2.1261	0.0009 0.0027	0.0060 0.0140
	3.0	2	2.5190-2.5198	0.0009 0.0027	0.004-0.0080	3	2.1253-2.1261	0.0009 0.0027	0.0060 0.0140
	3.0	S	2.4790-2.4800	0.0009-0.0018	0.0050-0.0010	4	1.9670-1.9680	0.0010 0.0025	0.0039-0.0118
2006	3.0	U	2.5190-2.5198	0.0009 0.0027	0.004-0.0080	3	2.1253-2.1261	0.0009 0.0027	0.0060 0.0140
	3.0	2	2.5190-2.5198	0.0009 0.0027	0.004-0.0080	3	2.1253-2.1261	0.0009 0.0027	0.0060 0.0140
2007	3.0	U	2.5190-2.5198	0.0009 0.0027	0.004-0.0080	3	2.1253-2.1261	0.0009 0.0027	0.0060 0.0140

22086_TAUR_C0006

PISTON AND RING SPECIFICATIONS

All measurements are given in inches.

Year	Engine Displacement Liters	Engine ID/VIN	Piston Clearance	Ring Gap			Ring Side Clearance		
				Top Compression	Bottom Compression	Oil Control	Top Compression	Bottom Compression	Oil Control
2005	3.0	U	0.0012-0.0022	0.010-0.020	0.010-0.020	0.010-0.049	0.0602-0.0612	0.0602-0.0612	SNUG
	3.0	2	0.0012-0.0022	0.010-0.020	0.010-0.020	0.010-0.049	0.0602-0.0612	0.0602-0.0612	SNUG
	3.0	S	0.0005-0.0009	0.004-0.010	0.0005-0.017	0.006-0.026	0.0015-0.0029	0.0015-0.0033	SNUG
2006	3.0	U	0.0012-0.0022	0.010-0.020	0.010-0.020	0.010-0.049	0.0602-0.0612	0.0602-0.0612	SNUG
	3.0	2	0.0012-0.0022	0.010-0.020	0.010-0.020	0.010-0.049	0.0602-0.0612	0.0602-0.0612	SNUG
2007	3.0	U	0.0012-0.0022	0.010-0.020	0.010-0.020	0.010-0.049	0.0602-0.0612	0.0602-0.0612	SNUG

22086_TAUR_C0007

TORQUE SPECIFICATIONS
All readings in ft. lbs.

Year	Engine Displacement Liters	Engine ID/VIN	Cylinder Head Bolts	Main Bearing Bolts	Rod Bearing Bolts	Crankshaft Damper Bolts	Flywheel Bolts	Manifold Intake	Manifold Exhaust	Spark Plugs	Oil Pan Drain Plug
2005	3.0	U	①	59	26	107	59	②	③	11	10
	3.0	2	①	59	26	107	59	②	③	11	10
	3.0	S	④	⑤	⑥	⑦	59	⑧	15	7-15	11
2006	3.0	U	①	59	26	107	59	②	③	11	10
	3.0	2	①	59	26	107	59	②	③	11	10
2007	3.0	U	①	59	26	107	59	②	③	11	10

① Step 1: 35-39 ft. lbs.
Step 2: Loosen one turn
Step 3: 20-24 ft. lbs.
Step 4: Rotate 85-95 degrees
Step 5: Repeat Step 4

② Upper intake:
Step 1: Hand tighten all bolts
Step 2: 89 inch lbs.
Lower Intake:
Step 1: 1 ft. lbs.
Step 2: 24 ft. lbs.

③ Step 1: 8 ft. lbs.
Step 2: 16 ft. lbs.

④ Step 1: 30 ft. lbs.
Step 2: Rotate 90 degrees
Step 3: Loosen one turn
Step 4: 30 ft. lbs.
Step 5: Rotate 90 degrees
Step 6: Repeat Step 5

⑤ Step 1: Cap bolts 1-8 (outer) 18 ft. lbs.
Step 2: Cap bolts 9-16 (inner) 30 ft. lbs.
Step 3: Rotate bolts 1-16, 90 degrees
Step 4: Bolts 17-22; 18 ft. lbs.

⑥ Step 1: 17 ft. lbs.
Step 2: 32 ft. lbs.

⑦ Step 1: 89 ft. lbs.
Step 2: Loosen 360 degrees
Step 3: Tighten to 37 ft. lbs.
Step 4: Rotate 90 degrees

⑧ Upper and lower intake: 89 inch lbs.

22086_TAUR_C0010

WHEEL ALIGNMENT

Year	Model		Caster Range (+/-Deg.)	Caster Preferred Setting (Deg.)	Camber Range (+/-Deg.)	Camber Preferred Setting (Deg.)	Toe-in (Deg.)
2005	Taurus Sedan	F	1.0	3.8	0.60	-0.5	-0.20 +/- 0.25
		R	—	—	0.70	-1.0	0.36 +/- 0.25
	Taurus Wagon	F	1.0	3.8	0.60	-0.5	-0.20 +/- 0.25
		R	—	—	1.20	-0.6	0.36 +/- 0.25
	Sable	F	1.0	3.8	0.60	-0.5	-0.20 +/- 0.25
		R	—	—	0.70	-1.0	0.36 +/- 0.25
	Sable Wagon	F	1.0	3.8	0.60	-0.5	-0.20 +/- 0.25
		R	—	—	0.70	-0.6	0.36 +/- 0.25
2006	Taurus Sedan	F	1.0	3.8	0.60	-0.5	-0.20 +/- 0.25
		R	—	—	0.70	-1.0	0.36 +/- 0.25
2007	Taurus Sedan	F	1.0	3.8	0.60	-0.5	-0.20 +/- 0.25
		R	—	—	0.70	-1.0	0.36 +/- 0.25

22086_TAUR_C0011

TIRE, WHEEL AND BALL JOINT SPECIFICATIONS

Year	Model	OEM Tires Standard	OEM Tires Optional	Tire Pressure (psi) Front	Tire Pressure (psi) Rear	Wheel Size	Ball Joint Inspection	Lug Nut Torque (ft. lbs.)
2005	Sable	P215/60R16	None	33	33	6.5-JJ	0.030 in. ①	95
	Taurus	P215/60R16	None	33	33	6.5-JJ	0.030 in. ①	95
2006	Taurus	P215/60R16	None	33	33	6.5-JJ	0.030 in. ①	95
2007	Taurus	P215/60R16	None	33	33	6.5-JJ	0.030 in. ①	95

OEM: Original Equipment Manufacturer

PSI: Pounds Per Square Inch

① Maximum radial tolerance in inches

22086_TAUR_C0012

BRAKE SPECIFICATIONS
All measurements in inches unless noted

Year	Model		Brake Disc Original Thickness	Brake Disc Minimum Thickness	Brake Disc Maximum Run-out	Brake Drum Original Inside Diameter	Brake Drum Max. Wear Limit	Brake Drum Maximum Machine Diameter	Minimum Lining Thickness	Brake Caliper Bracket Bolts (ft. lbs.)	Brake Caliper Mounting Bolts (ft. lbs.)
2005	Sable	F	1.020	0.970	0.002	—	—	—	0.039	76	26
		R	0.550	0.504	0.004	8.85	0.05	8.92	0.039	76	24
	Taurus	F	1.020	0.970	0.002	—	—	—	0.039	76	26
		R	0.550	0.504	0.002	8.85	0.05	8.92	0.039	76	24
2006	Taurus	F	1.020	0.970	0.002	—	—	—	0.039	76	26
		R	0.550	0.504	0.002	8.85	0.05	8.92	0.039	76	24
2007	Taurus	F	1.020	0.970	0.002	—	—	—	0.039	76	26
		R	0.550	0.504	0.002	8.85	0.05	8.92	0.039	76	24

NOTE: Follow specifications stamped on rotor or drum if figures differ from those in this chart.

F: Front

R: Rear

22086_TAUR_C0013

SCHEDULED MAINTENANCE INTERVALS
Ford—Taurus & Mercury—Sable

TO BE SERVICED	TYPE OF SERVICE	VEHICLE MILEAGE INTERVAL (X1000)																			
		5	10	15	20	25	30	35	40	45	50	55	60	65	70	75	80	85	90	95	100
Engine oil & filter	R	✓	✓	✓	✓	✓	✓	✓	✓	✓	✓	✓	✓	✓	✓	✓	✓	✓	✓	✓	✓
Rotate tires	S/I	✓		✓		✓		✓		✓		✓		✓		✓		✓		✓	
Engine coolant protection, hoses & clamps	S/I			✓			✓			✓			✓			✓			✓		
Passenger compartment air filter	R				✓				✓				✓				✓				✓
Air cleaner filter	R						✓						✓						✓		
Automatic transaxle fluid & filter	R						✓						✓						✓		
Brake lines & connections	S/I						✓						✓						✓		
Exhaust heat shields	S/I						✓						✓						✓		
Front and rear disc brake pads & rotors	S/I						✓						✓						✓		
Accessory drive belt(s)	S/I												✓								
Engine coolant	R	At 5 years or 100,000 miles																			
Spark plugs (exc. 3.0L FF) ①	R																				✓
Spark plugs (3.0L FF)	R						✓						✓								
PCV valve (except 3.0L 4-valve)	R												✓								
PCV valve (3.0L 4-valve)	R																				✓

① Platinum tip spark plugs: change every 100,000 miles

R: Replace   S/I: Service and Inspect

FREQUENT OPERATION MAINTENANCE (SEVERE SERVICE)

If a vehicle is operated under any of the following conditions it is considered severe service:
- Extremely dusty areas.
- 50% or more of operation is in 32°C (90°F) or higher temperatures, or constant operation in temperatures below 0°C (32°F).
- Prolonged idling (vehicle operation in stop and go traffic).
- Frequent short running periods (engine does not warm to normal operating temperatures).
- Police, taxi, delivery usage or trailer towing usage.

Oil & oil filter: change every 3000 miles
Rotate tires at 6000 miles & every 9000 miles thereafter
Air cleaner element service or inspect every 15,000 miles
Automatic transaxle fluid & filter: change every 21,000 miles

SEVERE SCHEDULED MAINTENANCE INTERVALS
Ford—Taurus & Mercury—Sable

TO BE SERVICED	TYPE OF SERVICE	VEHICLE MILEAGE INTERVAL (X1000)																			
		3	6	9	12	15	18	21	24	27	30	33	36	39	42	45	48	51	54	57	60
Engine oil & filter	R	✓	✓	✓	✓	✓	✓	✓	✓	✓	✓	✓	✓	✓	✓	✓	✓	✓	✓	✓	✓
Rotate tires	S/I		✓			✓			✓			✓			✓			✓			✓
Engine coolant protection, hoses & clamps	S/I	✓	✓	✓	✓	✓	✓	✓	✓	✓	✓	✓	✓	✓	✓	✓	✓	✓	✓	✓	✓
Passenger compartment air filter ①	R																				
Air cleaner filter ①	R																				
Automatic transaxle fluid & filter	R										✓										✓
Brake lines & connections ②	S/I																				
Exhaust heat shields	S/I										✓										✓
Front and rear disc brake pads & rotors ②	S/I						✓						✓						✓		
Accessory drive belt(s)	S/I										✓										✓
Engine coolant	R	At 5 years or 100,000 miles																			
Spark plugs (exc. 3.0L FF) ②	R										✓										✓
Spark plugs (3.0L FF)	R										✓										✓
PCV valve (except 3.0L 4-valve)	R										✓										✓
PCV valve (3.0L 4-valve)	R										✓										✓

① Change as required

② Every 5000 miles

R: Replace   S/I: Service and Inspect

FREQUENT OPERATION MAINTENANCE (SEVERE SERVICE)

If a vehicle is operated under any of the following conditions it is considered severe service:

- Extremely dusty areas.
- 50% or more of the vehicle operation is in 32°C (90°F) or higher temperatures, or constant operation in temperatures below 0°C (32°F).
- Prolonged idling (vehicle operation in stop and go traffic)..
- Frequent short running periods (engine does not warm to normal operating temperatures).
- Police, taxi, delivery usage or trailer towing usage.

Oil & oil filter: change every 3000 miles

Rotate tires at 6000 miles & every 9000 miles thereafter

Air cleaner element service or inspect every 15,000 miles

Automatic transaxle fluid & filter: change every 21,000 miles

22086_TAUR_C0015

PRECAUTIONS

Before servicing any vehicle, please be sure to read all of the following precautions, which deal with personal safety, prevention of component damage, and important points to take into consideration when servicing a motor vehicle:

• Never open, service or drain the radiator or cooling system when the engine is hot; serious burns can occur from the steam and hot coolant.

• Observe all applicable safety precautions when working around fuel. Whenever servicing the fuel system, always work in a well-ventilated area. Do not allow fuel spray or vapors to come in contact with a spark, open flame, or excessive heat (a hot drop light, for example). Keep a dry chemical fire extinguisher near the work area. Always keep fuel in a container specifically designed for fuel storage; also, always properly seal fuel containers to avoid the possibility of fire or explosion. Refer to the additional fuel system precautions later in this section.

• Fuel injection systems often remain pressurized, even after the engine has been turned **OFF**. The fuel system pressure must be relieved before disconnecting any fuel lines. Failure to do so may result in fire and/or personal injury.

• Brake fluid often contains polyglycol ethers and polyglycols. Avoid contact with the eyes and wash your hands thoroughly after handling brake fluid. If you do get brake fluid in your eyes, flush your eyes with clean, running water for 15 minutes. If eye irritation persists, or if you have taken

brake fluid internally, IMMEDIATELY seek medical assistance.

• The EPA warns that prolonged contact with used engine oil may cause a number of skin disorders, including cancer. You should make every effort to minimize your exposure to used engine oil. Protective gloves should be worn when changing oil. Wash your hands and any other exposed skin areas as soon as possible after exposure to used engine oil. Soap and water, or waterless hand cleaner should be used.

• All new vehicles are now equipped with an air bag system, often referred to as a Supplemental Restraint System (SRS) or Supplemental Inflatable Restraint (SIR) system. The system must be disabled before performing service on or around system components, steering column, instrument panel components, wiring and sensors. Failure to follow safety and disabling procedures could result in accidental air bag deployment, possible personal injury and unnecessary system repairs.

• Always wear safety goggles when working with, or around, the air bag system. When carrying a non-deployed air bag, be sure the bag and trim cover are pointed away from your body. When placing a non-deployed air bag on a work surface, always face the bag and trim cover upward, away from the surface. This will reduce the motion of the module if it is accidentally deployed. Refer to the additional air bag system precautions later in this section.

• Clean, high quality brake fluid from a sealed container is essential to the safe and proper operation of the brake system. You should always buy the correct type of brake fluid for your vehicle. If the brake fluid becomes contaminated, completely flush the system with new fluid. Never reuse any brake fluid. Any brake fluid that is removed from the system should be discarded. Also, do not allow any brake fluid to come in contact with a painted surface; it will damage the paint.

• Never operate the engine without the proper amount and type of engine oil; doing so WILL result in severe engine damage.

• Timing belt maintenance is extremely important. Many models utilize an interference-type, non-freewheeling engine. If the timing belt breaks, the valves in the cylinder head may strike the pistons, causing potentially serious (also time-consuming and expensive) engine damage. Refer to the maintenance interval charts for the recommended replacement interval for the timing belt, and to the timing belt section for belt replacement and inspection.

• Disconnecting the negative battery cable on some vehicles may interfere with the functions of the on-board computer system(s) and may require the computer to undergo a relearning process once the negative battery cable is reconnected.

• When servicing drum brakes, only disassemble and assemble one side at a time, leaving the remaining side intact for reference.

• Only an MVAC-trained, EPA-certified automotive technician should service the air conditioning system or its components.

BRAKES

ANTI-LOCK BRAKE SYSTEM (ABS)

GENERAL INFORMATION

See Figures 1 and 2.

The 4-Wheel Anti-lock Brake System (ABS) is an electronically operated, all wheel brake control system. Major components include the vacuum power brake booster, master cylinder, the wheel speed sensors, and the Hydraulic Control Unit (HCU) which contains the control module, a relay, and the pressure control valves.

The system is designed to retard wheel lockup during periods of high wheel slip when braking. Retarding wheel lockup is accomplished by modulating fluid pressure to the wheel brake units. When the control module detects a variation in voltage across the wheel speed sensors, the

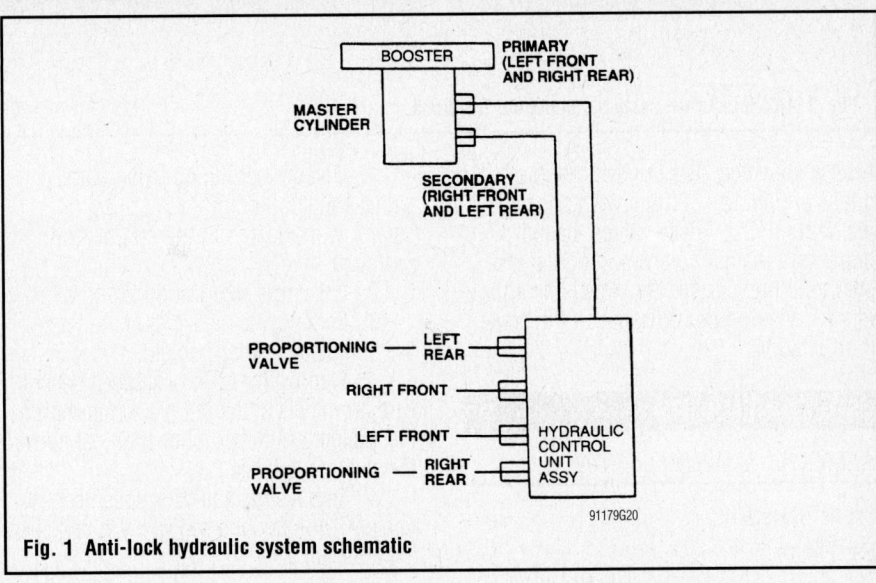

Fig. 1 Anti-lock hydraulic system schematic

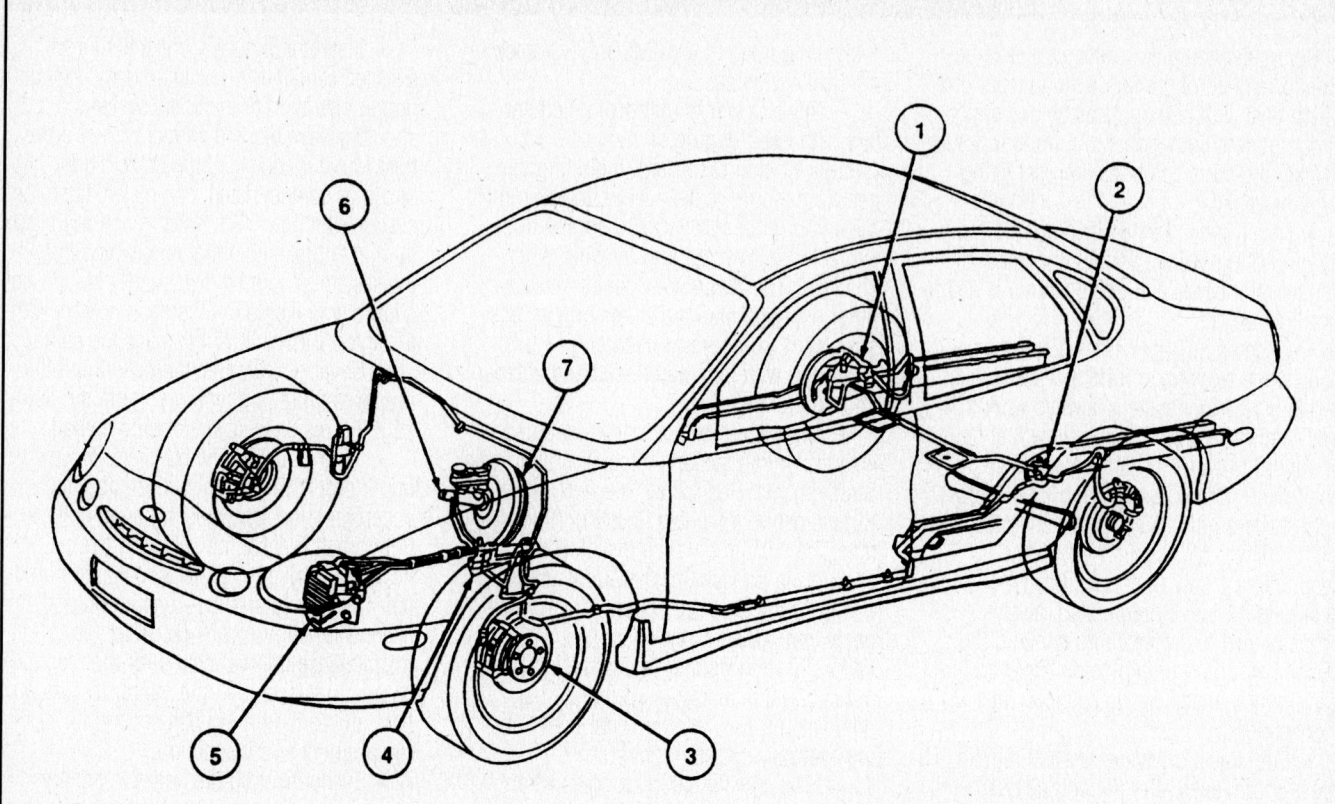

Item	Description
1	Rear Brake Anti-Lock Sensor
2	Brake Load Sensor Proportioning Valve (Sedan Only)
3	Front Brake Anti-Lock Sensor

Item	Description
4	Brake Pressure Control Valve (Station Wagon Only)
5	Anti-Lock Brake Control Module
6	Brake Master Cylinder
7	Power Brake Booster

91179G21

Fig. 2 Anti-lock brake system component locations

ABS is activated. The control module opens and closes various valves located inside the HCU. These valves, called dump and isolation valves, modulate the hydraulic pressure to the wheels by applying and venting the pressure to the brake fluid circuits.

SPEED SENSORS

REMOVAL & INSTALLATION

Front Sensor

See Figure 3.

1. Disconnect the negative battery cable. Detach the anti-lock speed sensor wire located in the engine compartment.
2. Raise and safely support the vehicle.
3. Remove the plastic studs to loosen the front fender splash shield.
4. Remove the anti-lock speed sensor wire grommets at the rail bracket and from the retainer on the strut housing just above the steering knuckle.
5. Remove the anti-lock speed sensor retaining bolt and the sensor from the steering knuckle.

To install:

6. Install the anti-lock speed sensor and the retaining bolt. Tighten the retaining bolt to 90–120 inch lbs. (10.2–13.8 Nm).
7. Install the grommets at the rail bracket and the retainer at the strut housing.
8. Install the plastic studs in the front fender splash shield.
9. Lower the vehicle.
10. Connect the sensor wire to the wire harness in the wheel opening at the frame rail.
11. Connect the negative battery cable. Road test the vehicle and check for proper operation.

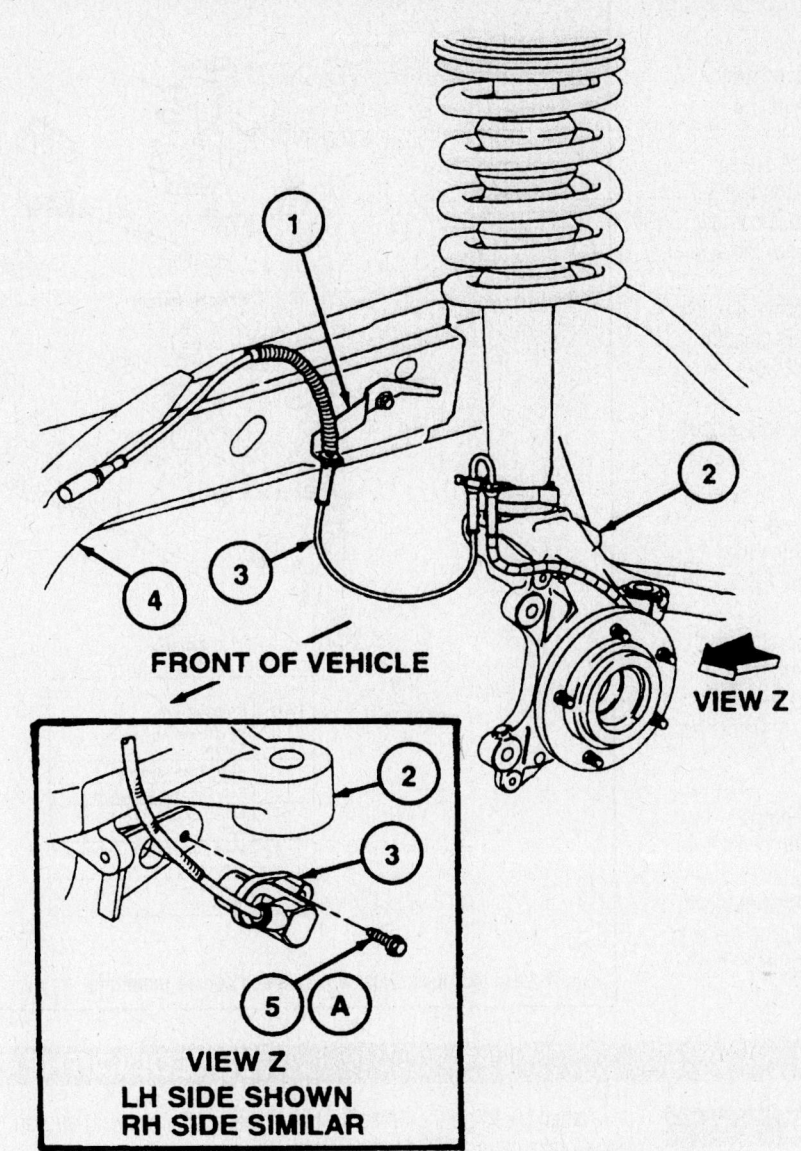

FRONT OF VEHICLE

VIEW Z

VIEW Z
LH SIDE SHOWN
RH SIDE SIMILAR

Item	Description
1	Front Brake Anti-Lock Sensor Support
2	Front Wheel Knuckle
3	Front Brake Anti-Lock Sensor
4	Sidemember
5	Bolt
A	Tighten to 10.2-13.8 N·m (91-122 Lb-In)

91179G26

Fig. 3 Front anti-lock brake wheel speed sensor mounting

Rear Sensor

See Figure 4.

1. Disconnect the negative battery cable. Raise and safely support the vehicle.

2. Disconnect the anti-lock speed sensor from the mating body connector located in the center of the crossmember.

3. Disconnect the clips from the suspension arm and crossmember.

4. On station wagons, remove the sensor retaining bolt from the brake adapter and on sedans remove the bolt from the spindle.

5. Remove the anti-lock speed sensor assembly.

To install:

6. Install the anti-lock speed sensor and retaining bolt. Tighten the retaining bolt 62–98 inch. lbs. (7.6–10.4 Nm).

7. Install the sensor wiring clips to the suspension arm and crossmember.

8. Connect the anti-lock speed sensor to the mating body connector in the center of the crossmember.

9. Lower the vehicle.

10. Connect the negative battery.

11. Road test the vehicle and check for proper operation.

12. If the amber or red brake indicator lamps illuminate at any time during the road test, check the brake system for possible faults.

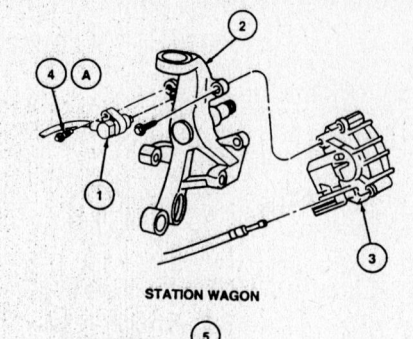

STATION WAGON

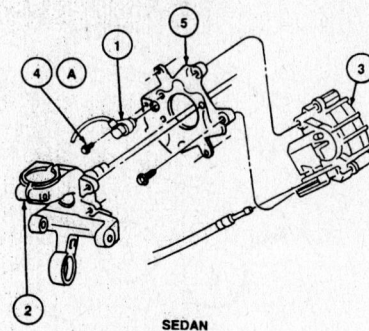

SEDAN

Item	Description
1	Rear Brake Anti-Lock Sensor
2	Rear Wheel Spindle
3	Rear Disc Brake Caliper
4	Anti-Lock Sensor Mounting Bolt
5	Right Hand Rear Disc Brake Adapter
A	Tighten to 7.6-10.4 N-m (68-92 Lb-In)

91179G27

Fig. 4 Rear anti-lock brake wheel speed sensor mounting

BRAKES

BLEEDING THE BRAKE SYSTEM

BLEEDING PROCEDURE

BLEEDING PROCEDURE

✳ CAUTION

Brake fluid contains polyglycol ethers and polyglycols. Avoid contact with the eyes and wash your hands thoroughly after handling brake fluid. If you do get brake fluid in your eyes, flush your eyes with clean, running water for 15 minutes. If eye irritation persists, or if you have taken brake fluid internally, IMMEDIATELY seek medical assistance.

When any part of the hydraulic system has been disconnected for repair or replacement, air may get into the lines and cause spongy pedal action (because air can be compressed and brake fluid cannot). To correct this condition, it is necessary to bleed the hydraulic system so to be sure all air is purged.

When bleeding the brake system, bleed one brake cylinder at a time, beginning at the cylinder with the longest hydraulic line (farthest from the master cylinder) first. ALWAYS Keep the master cylinder reservoir filled with brake fluid during the bleeding operation. Never use brake fluid that has been drained from the hydraulic system, no matter how clean it is.

The primary and secondary hydraulic brake systems are separate and are bled independently. During the bleeding operation, do not allow the reservoir to run dry. Keep the master cylinder reservoir filled with brake fluid.

1. Clean all dirt from around the master cylinder fill cap, remove the cap and fill the master cylinder with brake fluid until the level is within ¼ in. (6mm) of the top edge of the reservoir.

2. Clean the bleeder screws at all 4 wheels. The bleeder screws are located on the back of the brake backing plate (drum brakes) and on the top of the brake calipers (disc brakes).

3. Attach a length of rubber hose over the bleeder screw and place the other end of the hose in a glass jar, submerged in brake fluid.

4. Open the bleeder screw ½–¾ turn. Have an assistant slowly depress the brake pedal.

5. Close the bleeder screw and tell your assistant to allow the brake pedal to return slowly. Continue this process to purge all air from the system.

6. When bubbles cease to appear at the end of the bleeder hose, close the bleeder screw and remove the hose.

7. Check the master cylinder fluid level and add fluid accordingly. Do this after bleeding each wheel.

✳ WARNING

Clean, high quality brake fluid is essential to the safe and proper operation of the brake system. You should

always buy the highest quality brake fluid that is available. If the brake fluid becomes contaminated, drain and flush the system, then refill the master cylinder with new fluid. Never reuse any brake fluid. Any brake fluid that is removed from the system should be discarded. Also, do not allow any brake fluid to come in contact with a painted surface; it will damage the paint.

8. Repeat the bleeding operation at the remaining 3 wheels, ending with the one closet to the master cylinder.

9. Fill the master cylinder reservoir to the proper level.

BLEEDING THE ABS SYSTEM

If a spongy brake pedal is present and air in the hydraulic control unit is suspected, use the following procedure:

1. Bleed the brake system.

2. Connect a New Generation Star (NGS) tester or equivalent scan tool, to the serial data link connector below the instrument panel as though retrieving codes.

3. Make sure the ignition switch is in the **RUN** position.

4. Follow the instructions on the NGS screen. Verify correct vehicle and model year go to the "Diagnostic Data Link" menu item, choose ABS Module, choose "Function Tests", and choose "Service Bleed".

5. Bleed the right front wheel as follows:

a. Open the caliper bleed screw and pump the brake pedal for 3 seconds. Repeat the procedure again.

b. When the fluid runs clear, begin the program and continue to pump the brake pedal.

c. Continue bleeding for approximately 1–2 minutes after the program ends and then tighten the bleed screw.

6. Repeat the bleeding procedure to the left front, left rear and finally the right rear wheel.

7. Remove the pressure bleeding device and adjust the brake fluid level.

BRAKES   FRONT DISC BRAKES

✳ CAUTION

Dust and dirt accumulating on brake parts during normal use may contain asbestos fibers from production or aftermarket brake linings. Breathing excessive concentrations of asbestos fibers can cause serious bodily harm. Exercise care when servicing brake parts. Do not sand or grind brake lining unless equipment used is designed to contain the dust residue. Do not clean brake parts with compressed air or by dry brushing. Cleaning should be done by dampening the brake components with a fine mist of water, then wiping the brake components clean with a dampened cloth. Dispose of cloth and all residue containing asbestos fibers in an impermeable container with the appropriate label. Follow practices prescribed by the Occupational Safety and Health Administration (OSHA) and the Environmental Protection Agency (EPA) for the handling, processing, and disposing of dust or debris that may contain asbestos fibers.

BRAKE CALIPER

REMOVAL & INSTALLATION

See Figure 5.

1. Before servicing the vehicle, refer to the precautions section.

2. Remove brake fluid from the brake master cylinder reservoir until the reservoir is ½ full.

3. Remove the wheel and tire assembly.

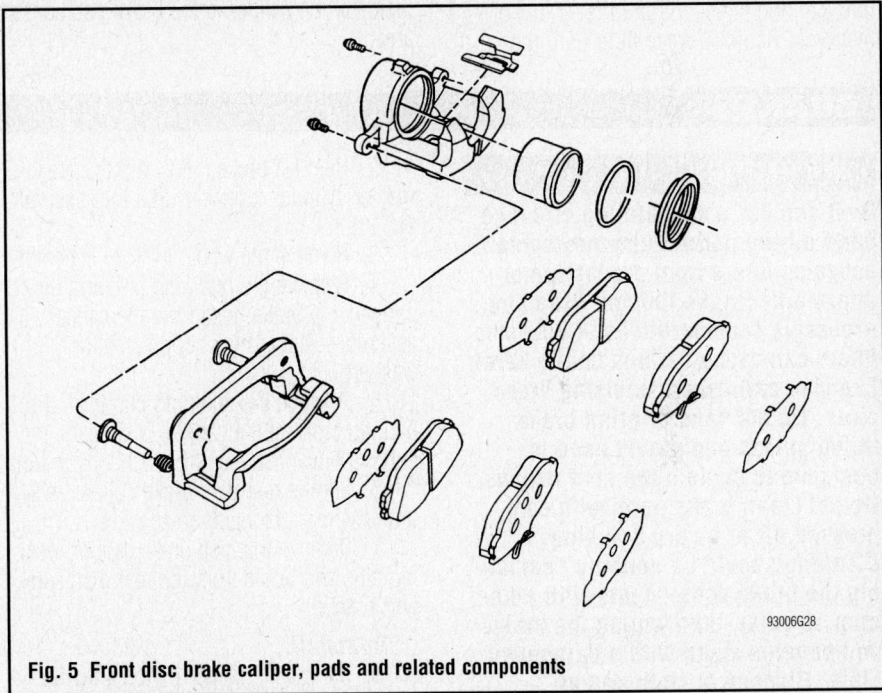

Fig. 5 Front disc brake caliper, pads and related components

93006G28

4. Mark the disc brake caliper to ensure that it is reinstalled in the correct location.

5. Remove the hollow bolt connecting the brake hose to the disc brake caliper and plug the brake hose. Discard the 2 copper sealing washers.

6. Remove the caliper locating pins and lift the caliper off the rotor using a rotating motion.

To install:

7. Retract the disc brake caliper piston fully in the piston bore, using an old brake pad or block of wood and a C-clamp.

➡**Make sure the clip-on insulators are attached to the brake pads.**

8. Install the disc brake pads to the caliper. Make sure the brake pad insulators are correctly attached to the brake pad plate.

9. Position the disc brake caliper and pad assembly above the rotor and install it with a rotating motion. Make sure the inner and outer pads are properly positioned and the outer anti-rattle spring is properly positioned.

10. Lubricate the locating pins and the inside of the insulators with silicone grease. Torque the locating pins to 26 ft. lbs. (35 Nm).

11. Remove the plug and install the brake hose to the disc brake caliper. Use

2 new copper washers and torque the hollow bolt to 35 ft. lbs. (48 Nm).

12. Bleed the brake system, filling the master cylinder as required.

13. Install the wheel and tire assembly; torque the nuts to 85–104 ft. lbs. (115–142 Nm).

14. Pump the brake pedal several times to position the brake pads prior to moving the vehicle.

15. Road test the vehicle and check for proper brake system operation.

DISC BRAKE PADS

REMOVAL & INSTALLATION

See Figure 5.

1. Before servicing the vehicle, refer to the precautions section.

2. Remove the master cylinder reservoir cap and check the fluid level in the reservoir. Remove brake fluid until the reservoir is ½ full. Discard the removed fluid.

3. On Continentals, turn the air suspension switch, located in the left side of the luggage compartment, to the **OFF** position.

4. Remove the wheel and tire assembly.

5. Remove the disc brake caliper locating pins. Lift the caliper assembly from the anchor plate and rotor using a rotating motion.

6. Suspend the caliper inside the fender housing with wire. Do not allow the caliper to hang from the brake hose.

7. Remove the inner and outer brake pads. Inspect the rotor braking surfaces for scoring and machine as necessary.

To install:

8. Use a C-clamp and an old brake pad or block of wood to seat the caliper piston in its bore.

9. Remove any rust buildup from the inside of the caliper in the brake pad contact area.

10. Install the inner pad in the caliper piston.

11. Install the outer pad onto the anchor plate. Make sure the clips are properly seated.

➡**Make sure the insulators are installed on the brake pads.**

12. Install the disc brake caliper onto the anchor plate.

13. Install caliper locating pins and torque to 26 ft. lbs. (35 Nm).

14. Install wheel and tire assembly.

15. Pump the brake pedal several times prior to moving the vehicle to position the brake pads to the rotor.

16. Refill the master cylinder reservoir as necessary, using only clean DOT 3 brake fluid from a closed container.

17. Road test the vehicle and check the brake system for proper operation.

BRAKES

✳✳ CAUTION

Dust and dirt accumulating on brake parts during normal use may contain asbestos fibers from production or aftermarket brake linings. Breathing excessive concentrations of asbestos fibers can cause serious bodily harm. Exercise care when servicing brake parts. Do not sand or grind brake lining unless equipment used is designed to contain the dust residue. Do not clean brake parts with compressed air or by dry brushing. Cleaning should be done by dampening the brake components with a fine mist of water, then wiping the brake components clean with a dampened cloth. Dispose of cloth and all residue containing asbestos fibers in an impermeable container with the appropriate label. Follow practices prescribed by the Occupational Safety and Health Administration (OSHA) and the Environmental Protection Agency (EPA) for the handling, processing, and disposing of dust or debris that may contain asbestos fibers.

BRAKE CALIPER

REMOVAL & INSTALLATION

1. Before servicing the vehicle, refer to the precautions section.

2. Remove brake fluid from the brake master cylinder reservoir until the reservoir is ½ full.

3. Remove the wheel and tire assembly.

4. Remove the retaining bolt and disconnect the brake hose from the caliper assembly. Discard the copper sealing washers.

5. Remove the retaining clip from the parking brake at the caliper. Disengage the parking brake cable end from the lever arm.

6. Lift the rear disc brake caliper away from the rear disc support bracket.

7. Remove the disc brake caliper locating pins and boots from the rear disc support bracket.

To install:

8. Using rear caliper piston adjuster tool T87P-2588-A, rotate the rear disc brake piston and adjuster clockwise until fully seated.

➡**Make sure one of the 2 slots in the rear disc brake piston and adjuster face is positioned so it will engage the nib on the disc brake pad.**

9. Apply silicone dielectric compound to the inside of the slider pin boots and the slider pins.

10. Position the slider pins and boots in the support bracket. Position the caliper assembly on the support bracket. Make sure the brake pads are installed correctly.

11. Remove the residue from the pin retainer threads and apply 1 drop of thread-lock and sealer. Install the pin retainers and torque to 24 ft. lbs. (33 Nm).

12. Attach the cable end to the parking brake lever. Install the cable retaining clip on the caliper assembly.

13. Using new washers, connect the brake flex hose to the caliper. Torque the retaining bolt to 41 ft. lbs. (55 Nm).

14. Bleed the brake system, filling the master cylinder as required.

15. Install the wheel and tire assembly; torque the nuts to 85–104 ft. lbs. (115–142 Nm).

16. Pump the brake pedal several times to position the brake pads prior to moving the vehicle.

17. Road test the vehicle and check for proper brake system operation.

DISC BRAKE PADS

REMOVAL AND INSTALLATION

✳✳ CAUTION

Dust and dirt accumulating on brake parts during normal use may contain asbestos fibers from production or aftermarket brake linings. Breathing excessive concentrations of asbestos fibers can cause serious bodily harm. Exercise care when servicing brake parts. Do not sand or grind brake lining unless equipment used is designed to contain the dust residue. Do not clean brake parts with com-

REAR DISC BRAKES

pressed air or by dry brushing. Cleaning should be done by dampening the brake components with a fine mist of water, then wiping the brake components clean with a dampened cloth. Dispose of cloth and all residue containing asbestos fibers in an impermeable container with the appropriate label. Follow practices prescribed by the Occupational Safety and Health Administration (OSHA) and the Environmental Protection Agency (EPA) for the handling, processing, and disposing of dust or debris that may contain asbestos fibers.

1. Before servicing the vehicle, refer to the precautions section.

2. Remove the master cylinder reservoir cap and check the fluid level in the reservoir. Remove brake fluid until the reservoir is ½ full. Discard the removed fluid.

3. Remove the wheel and tire assembly.

4. Remove the screw retaining the brake hose bracket to the frame side rail.

5. Remove the retaining clip from the parking brake cable at the disc brake caliper. Remove the cable end from the parking brake lever.

6. Remove the upper disc brake caliper locating pin at the support bracket. Rotate the caliper away from the rotor.

7. Remove the disc brake pads.

8. Inspect the rotor braking surfaces for scoring and machine as necessary.

To install:

9. Using Rear Caliper Piston Adjuster T87P-2588-A, rotate the piston clockwise until it is fully seated. Make sure one of the slots in the piston face is positioned so it will engage the nib on the brake pad.

10. Install the brake pads in the support bracket. Rotate the caliper assembly over

the rotor into position on the support bracket. Make sure the brake pads are installed correctly.

11. Remove the residue from the rear brake pin retainer bolt threads and apply 1 drop of a suitable threadlock sealer. Install and torque the disc brake caliper locating pin to 24 ft. lbs. (33 Nm).

12. Attach the cable end to the parking brake lever. Install the cable retaining clip on the caliper assembly. Position the brake flex hose and bracket assembly to the side rail, and install the retaining screw. Torque to 11 ft. lbs. (16 Nm).

13. Install the wheel and tire assembly.

14. Pump the brake pedal several times prior to moving the vehicle, to position the brake pads to the rotor.

15. Refill the master cylinder reservoir if necessary, using only clean DOT 3 brake fluid from a closed container.

16. Road test the vehicle and check the brake system for proper operation.

BRAKES

✳✳ CAUTION

Dust and dirt accumulating on brake parts during normal use may contain asbestos fibers from production or aftermarket brake linings. Breathing excessive concentrations of asbestos fibers can cause serious bodily harm. Exercise care when servicing brake parts. Do not sand or grind brake lining unless equipment used is designed to contain the dust residue. Do not clean brake parts with compressed air or by dry brushing. Cleaning should be done by dampening the brake components with a fine mist of water, then wiping the brake components clean with a dampened cloth. Dispose of cloth and all residue containing asbestos fibers in an impermeable container with the appropriate label. Follow practices prescribed by the Occupational Safety and Health Administration (OSHA) and the Environmental Protection Agency (EPA) for the handling, processing, and disposing of dust or debris that may contain asbestos fibers.

BRAKE DRUM

REMOVAL & INSTALLATION

See Figure 6.

1. Before servicing the vehicle, refer to the precautions section.

2. Remove the wheel and tire assembly.

3. Remove the brake drum.

➡ **If the brake drum cannot be removed easily, remove the brake tube-to-axle retention bracket and pry rubber plug from rear brake backing plate inspection hole. This will allow sufficient room for insertion of a screwdriver and brake tools to disengage brake shoe adjusting lever and back off the brake adjuster screw.**

REAR DRUM BRAKES

4. Inspect the drum for scoring and/or other wear. Machine or replace, as necessary.

To install:

5. Measure the brake drum inside diameter using a brake adjustment gauge.

6. Using the brake adjustment gauge, adjust the brake shoes to the same dimensions as the brake drum.

7. Position the brake drum over the brake shoes on the axle hub.

8. Install the wheel and tire assembly.

9. Pump the brake pedal several times

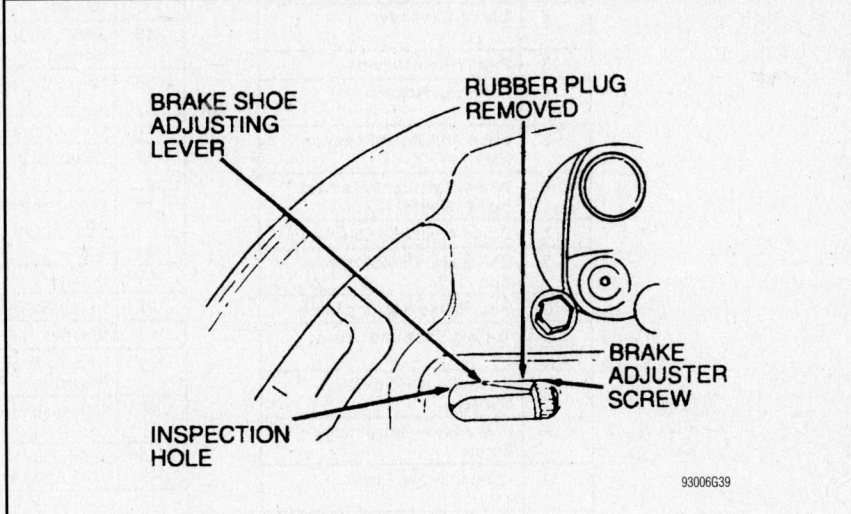

BRAKE SHOE ADJUSTING LEVER

RUBBER PLUG REMOVED

INSPECTION HOLE

BRAKE ADJUSTER SCREW

93006G39

Fig. 6 Retracting the brake shoes to allow drum removal

to position the brake shoes and complete the adjustment.

10. Road test the vehicle and check for proper brake system operation.

BRAKE SHOES

REMOVAL & INSTALLATION

See Figure 7.

1. Before servicing the vehicle, refer to the precautions section.

2. Remove the wheel and tire assembly.
3. Remove the brake drum.
4. Remove the parking brake cable from the parking brake lever.
5. Remove the 2 brake shoe hold-down springs and pins.
6. Lift the brake shoes, springs and adjuster assembly off the backing plate and wheel cylinder assembly. When removing the assembly, be careful not to bend the adjusting lever.

7. Remove the retracting springs from the lower brake attachments and upper shoe-to-adjusting lever attachment points.

8. Remove the horseshoe retaining clip and spring washer and slide the lever off the parking brake lever pin on the trailing shoe. Discard the horseshoe clip.

To install:

9. Apply a light coating of disc brake caliper slide grease at the points where the brake shoes contact the backing plate.

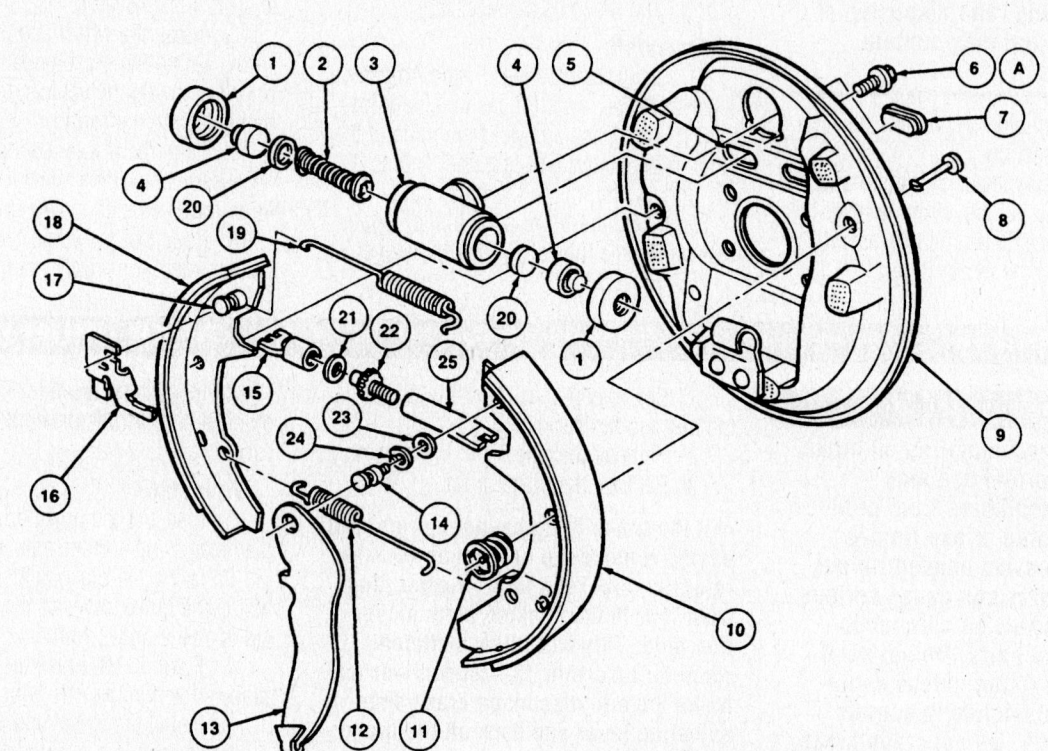

1	Boot		14	Parking Brake Lever Pin (Inner)
2	Spring Expander		15	Brake Shoe Adjusting Screw Socket
3	Rear Wheel Cylinder		16	Brake Shoe Adjusting Lever
4	Piston and Insert		17	Parking Brake Lever Pin
5	Shoe Adjustment Access Hole		18	Leading Shoe and Lining
6	Wheel Cylinder Retaining Bolt (2 Req'd)		19	Brake Shoe Adjusting Screw Spring
7	Brake Adjusting Hole Cover		20	Cup
8	Brake Shoe Hold-Down Spring Pin		21	Washer
9	Rear Brake Backing Plate		22	Brake Adjuster Screw
10	Trailing Shoe and Lining		23	Washer
11	Brake Shoe Hold-Down Spring		24	Parking Brake Lever Pin Retainer
12	Brake Shoe Retracting Spring		25	Adjusting Pivot Nut
13	Parking Brake Lever		A	Tighten to 12-18 N·m (107-159 Lb-In)

93006G56

Fig. 7 Brake shoes and related components

10. Apply a thin coat of lubricant to the adjuster screw threads and socket end of the adjusting screw. Install the stainless steel washer over the socket end of the adjusting screw and install the socket. Turn the adjusting screw into the adjusting pivot nut to the limit of the threads and then back off ½ turn.

11. Assemble the parking brake lever to the trailing shoe by installing the spring washer and a new horseshoe retaining clip. Crimp the clip until it retains the lever to the shoe securely.

12. Position the trailing shoe on the backing plate and attach the rear parking brake cable.

13. Position the leading shoe on the backing plate and attach the lower brake shoe adjusting spring to the brake shoes.

14. Install the adjuster assembly in the slots on the brake shoes. The wide slot on the dual slotted end must fit into the leading shoe. The narrow slot on the dual slotted end fits into the shoe adjusting lever. The single slotted side of the adjuster assembly must fit into the slots on the trailing shoe and the rear parking brake cable bracket.

➡ **The adjuster socket blade is marked R for the right or L for the left brake assemblies. The adjuster blade must be installed with the letter R or L in the upright position, facing the wheel cylinder. Make sure the adjuster socket fits into the parking brake lever.**

15. Complete the installation by reversing the removal procedures.

16. Pump the brake pedal several times to position the brake shoes and finish the brake shoe adjustment.

17. Road test the vehicle and check the brake system for proper operation.

ADJUSTMENT

See Figure 8.

The rear brakes are automatically adjusted while driving the vehicle. The brakes are also adjusted each time the parking brake is applied. Manual brake adjustment is only required after the brake shoes or hardware has been replaced, or the adjuster has been replaced.

1. Remove the brake drum as described in this section..

2. Remove any excessive dust and dirt present on the brakes using the appropriate methods.

3. Using a brake adjustment gauge, measure the inside diameter of the brake drum.

4. Line up the brake shoes vertically so the flats on the bottom of the brake shoes are aligned approximately 0.05 inch (1.5mm) above the bottom of the abutment plate.

5. Adjust the brake shoes to the same diameter as the drum by placing the brake adjustment gauge on the shoes and holding the adjusting lever out of engagement of the adjusting screw.

➡ **If the adjusting screw does not rotate freely, remove it, lubricate the threads, reinstall it and repeat the adjustment procedure.**

6. Install the brake drum.

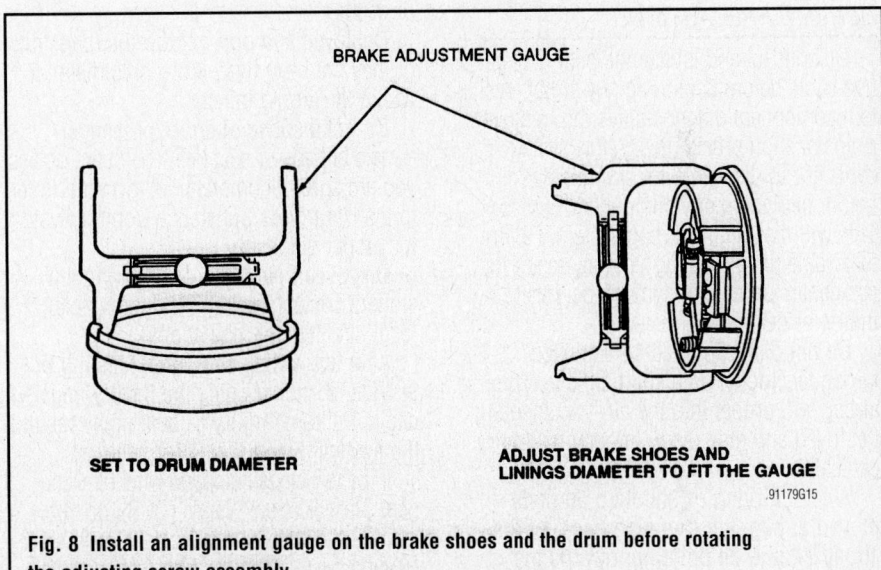

BRAKE ADJUSTMENT GAUGE

SET TO DRUM DIAMETER

ADJUST BRAKE SHOES AND LININGS DIAMETER TO FIT THE GAUGE

.91179G15

Fig. 8 Install an alignment gauge on the brake shoes and the drum before rotating the adjusting screw assembly

BRAKES

PARKING BRAKE

PARKING BRAKE CABLES

ADJUSTMENT

1. Make sure the parking brake is fully released.

2. Place the transaxle in **N**.

3. Partially raise and safely support the vehicle.

4. Place jackstands under the rear suspension.

5. Using Cable Tension Gauge 021-00018 or equivalent, tighten the adjusting nut against the rear parking brake cable adjuster until the cable tension is 18–26 lbs. for 1996 (8.1–11.7 Kg) and 34–46 lbs. (15.8–20.8 Kg) for 1997–98

6. Apply the parking brake control fully and then release.

7. Verify the cable tension is still as specified and no drag is present on the rear brakes.

8. Remove the jackstands.

9. Lower the vehicle.

10. Check the parking brake for proper operation.

CHASSIS ELECTRICAL — AIR BAG (SUPPLEMENTAL RESTRAINT SYSTEM)

GENERAL INFORMATION

✴ CAUTION

These vehicles are equipped with an air bag system. The system must be disarmed before performing service on, or around, system components, the steering column, instrument panel components, wiring and sensors. Failure to follow the safety precautions and the disarming procedure could result in accidental air bag deployment, possible injury and unnecessary system repairs.

SERVICE PRECAUTIONS

Disconnect and isolate the battery negative cable before beginning any airbag system component diagnosis, testing, removal, or installation procedures. Allow system capacitor to discharge for two minutes before beginning any component service. This will disable the airbag system. Failure to disable the airbag system may result in accidental airbag deployment, personal injury, or death.

Do not place an intact undeployed airbag face down on a solid surface. The airbag will propel into the air if accidentally deployed and may result in personal injury or death.

When carrying or handling an undeployed airbag, the trim side (face) of the airbag should be pointing towards the body to minimize possibility of injury if accidental deployment occurs. Failure to do this may result in personal injury or death.

Replace airbag system components with OEM replacement parts. Substitute parts may appear interchangeable, but internal differences may result in inferior occupant protection. Failure to do so may result in occupant personal injury or death.

Wear safety glasses, rubber gloves, and long sleeved clothing when cleaning powder residue from vehicle after an airbag deployment. Powder residue emitted from a deployed airbag can cause skin irritation. Flush affected area with cool water if irritation is experienced. If nasal or throat irritation is experienced, exit the vehicle for fresh air until the irritation ceases. If irritation continues, see a physician.

Do not use a replacement airbag that is not in the original packaging. This may result in improper deployment, personal injury, or death.

The factory installed fasteners, screws and bolts used to fasten airbag components have a special coating and are specifically designed for the airbag system. Do not use substitute fasteners. Use only original equipment fasteners listed in the parts catalog when fastener replacement is required.

During, and following, any child restraint anchor service, due to impact event or vehicle repair, carefully inspect all mounting hardware, tether straps, and anchors for proper installation, operation, or damage. If a child restraint anchor is found damaged in any way, the anchor must be replaced. Failure to do this may result in personal injury or death.

Deployed and non-deployed airbags may or may not have live pyrotechnic material within the airbag inflator.

Do not dispose of driver/passenger/curtain airbags or seat belt tensioners unless you are sure of complete deployment. Refer to the Hazardous Substance Control System for proper disposal.

Dispose of deployed airbags and tensioners consistent with state, provincial, local, and federal regulations.

After any airbag component testing or service, do not connect the battery negative cable. Personal injury or death may result if the system test is not performed first.

If the vehicle is equipped with the Occupant Classification System (OCS), do not connect the battery negative cable before performing the OCS Verification Test using the scan tool and the appropriate diagnostic information. Personal injury or death may result if the system test is not performed properly.

Never replace both the Occupant Restraint Controller (ORC) and the Occupant Classification Module (OCM) at the same time. If both require replacement, replace one, then perform the Airbag System test before replacing the other.

Both the ORC and the OCM store Occupant Classification System (OCS) calibration data, which they transfer to one another when one of them is replaced. If both are replaced at the same time, an irreversible fault will be set in both modules and the OCS may malfunction and cause personal injury or death.

If equipped with OCS, the Seat Weight Sensor is a sensitive, calibrated unit and must be handled carefully. Do not drop or handle roughly. If dropped or damaged, replace with another sensor. Failure to do so may result in occupant injury or death.

If equipped with OCS, the front passenger seat must be handled carefully as well. When removing the seat, be careful when setting on floor not to drop. If dropped, the sensor may be inoperative, could result in occupant injury, or possibly death.

If equipped with OCS, when the passenger front seat is on the floor, no one should sit in the front passenger seat. This uneven force may damage the sensing ability of the seat weight sensors. If sat on and damaged, the sensor may be inoperative, could result in occupant injury, or possibly death.

DISARMING THE SYSTEM

1. Before servicing the vehicle, refer to the precautions section.

✴ WARNING

Always wear safety glasses when repairing an air bag supplemental restraint system (SRS) vehicle and when handling an air bag module. This will reduce the risk of injury in the event of an accidental deployment.

✴ WARNING

Never probe the connectors on the air bag module. Doing so can result in air bag deployment, which can result in personal injury.

✴ WARNING

The safety belt pretensioner is a pyrotechnic device. Always wear safety glasses when repairing an air bag equipped vehicle and when handling a safety belt buckle pretensioner or safety belt retractor pretensioner. Never probe a pretensioner electrical connector. Doing so could result in pretensioner or air bag deployment and could result in personal injury.

✴ WARNING

To reduce the risk of personal injury, do not use any memory saver devices.

➡ The air bag warning lamp illuminates when the RCM fuse is removed and the ignition switch is ON. This is normal operation and does not indicate a supplemental restraint system (SRS) fault.

➡**The SRS must be fully operational and free of faults before releasing the vehicle to the customer.**

2. Turn all vehicle accessories OFF.

3. Turn the ignition switch to OFF.

4. At the Smart Junction Box (SJB), located below the left hand side of the instrument panel, remove the cover and the Restraints Control Module (RCM) fuse (10A) from the SJB.

5. Turn the ignition ON and visually monitor the air bag indicator for at least 30 seconds. The air bag indicator will remain lit continuously (no flashing) if the correct RCM fuse has been removed. If the air bag indicator does not remain lit continuously, remove the correct RCM fuse before proceeding

6. Turn the ignition switch to OFF.

✳✳ WARNING

To avoid accidental deployment and possible personal injury, the backup power supply must be depleted before repairing or replacing any front or side air bag supplemental restraint system (SRS) components and before servicing, replacing, adjusting or striking components near the front or side air bag sensors, such as doors, instrument panel, console, door latches, strikers, seats and hood latches.

➡**To deplete the backup power supply energy, disconnect the battery ground cable and wait at least one minute. Be sure to disconnect auxiliary batteries and power supplies (if equipped).**

7. Disconnect the battery ground cable and wait at least one minute.

ARMING THE SYSTEM

1. Before servicing the vehicle, refer to the precautions section.

✳✳ WARNING

The restraint system diagnostic tool is for restraint system service only. Remove from vehicle prior to road use. Failure to remove could result in injury and possible violation of vehicle safety standards.

2. Make sure all restraint system diagnostic tool(s) that may have been installed during the repair have been removed from the vehicle and all SRS components are connected.

3. Turn the ignition switch from OFF to ON.

4. Install the RCM fuse (10A) to the SJB and install the cover.

✳✳ WARNING

Be sure that nobody is in the vehicle and that there is nothing blocking or set in front of any air bag module when the battery ground cable is connected.

5. Connect the battery ground cable.

6. Prove out the supplemental restraint system (SRS) as follows:

a. Turn the ignition key from ON to OFF. Wait 10 seconds, then turn the key back to ON and visually monitor the air bag indicator with the air bag modules installed. The air bag indicator will light continuously for approximately six seconds and then turn off. If an air bag supplemental restraint system (SRS) fault is present, the air bag indicator will fail to light, remain lit continuously or flash.

b. The flashing might not occur until approximately 30 seconds after the ignition switch has been turned from the OFF to the ON position. This is the time required for the restraints control module (RCM) to complete the testing of the SRS. If the air bag indicator is inoperative and a SRS fault exists, a chime will sound in a pattern of 5 sets of 5 beeps. If this occurs, the air bag indicator and any SRS fault discovered must be diagnosed and repaired.

c. Clear all continuous DTCs from the restraints control module using a diagnostic tool.

CLOCKSPRING CENTERING

✳✳ WARNING

Incorrect centralization may result in premature component failure. If in doubt when centralizing the clockspring, repeat the centralizing procedure. Failure to follow this instruction may result in personal injury.

✳✳ CAUTION

Make sure the road wheels are in the straight ahead position.

1. Before servicing the vehicle, refer to the precautions in the beginning of this section.

2. Hold the clockspring outer housing stationary.

✳✳ WARNING

Overturning will destroy the clockspring. The internal ribbon wire acts as the stop and can be broken from its internal connection.

3. While turning the rotor counterclockwise, carefully feel for the ribbon wire to run out of length and for a slight resistance. Stop turning at this point.

4. Turn the clockspring clockwise approximately three turns. This is the center point of the clockspring. Do not allow the rotor to turn from this position.

DRIVETRAIN

AUTOMATIC TRANSAXLE ASSEMBLY

REMOVAL & INSTALLATION

3.0L (VIN U, 2) Engines

See Figures 9 through 13.

1. Before servicing the vehicle, refer to the precautions section.
2. Disconnect the battery cables, negative cable first.
3. Remove the battery.
4. Disconnect the Mass Air Flow (MAF) sensor and the two breather tubes.
5. Remove the engine air cleaner cover and tube assembly.
6. Remove the two bolts and the air filter assembly.
7. Remove the relay box and the battery tray.
8. Disconnect the electrical connector.
9. Remove the nut from the power steering line bracket.
10. Remove the electrical connector bracket.
11. Disconnect the Output Shaft Speed (OSS) sensor.

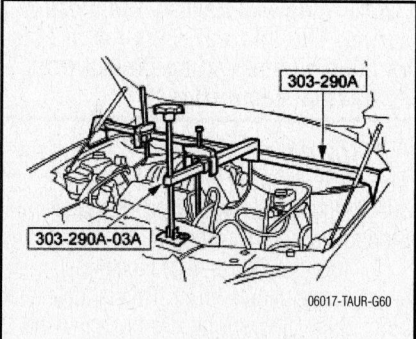

Fig. 9 Install an engine support device

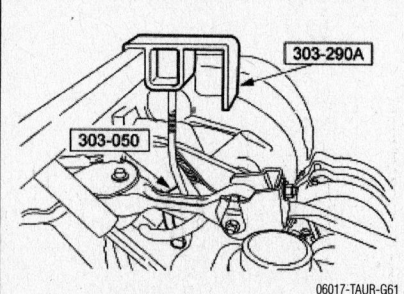

Fig. 10 Install the tools shown on the right (back) hand side of the engine

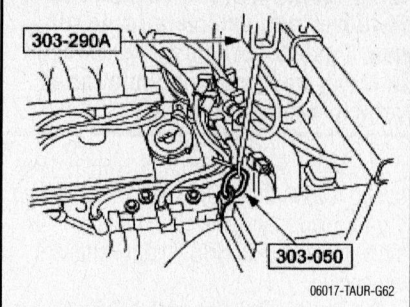

Fig. 11 Install the tools shown on the left (front) hand side of the engine

12. Disconnect the Turbine Shaft Speed (TSS) sensor.
13. Remove the manual control lever cable by removing the nut, then remove the shift actuator cable fitting from the shift cable and bracket.
14. Remove the ground cable and bracket.
15. Remove the cooler line retaining clips. Depress the tabs on the plastic insert retainer and remove cooler lines from fitting.
16. Remove the upper transmission bolts.
17. Install an engine support device such as the one illustrated.
18. Install the tools shown on the right (back) hand side of the engine.
19. Install the tools shown on the left (front) hand side of the engine.
20. Drain the transmission fluid by lowering the transaxle pan. Once the fluid has drained re-install the pan

> **✳✳ CAUTION**
>
> **If the steering gear is removed with the subframe, do not allow the steering wheel to rotate while the steering column intermediate is disconnected or damage to the clockspring can result. If there is evidence that the shaft has rotated, the clockspring must be recentered before the vehicle is driven.**

21. Remove the subframe assembly as follows:
    a. If equipped, remove the roll-restrictor bolt and nut.
    b. Remove the downstream catalytic converter and support the exhaust system to one side under the vehicle.
    c. If equipped, remove the five pin-type retainers from the chin spoiler.
    d. Remove the air dam.

e. Remove the front tires and wheels.
f. Remove the two lower ball joint nuts.
22. Disconnect the ball joint from the lower arm.
23. Push the lower arm downward until the ball joint is free of the arm.

> **✳✳ CAUTION**
>
> **Use extreme care not to damage boot seal. Do not use power tools to tighten the nut, or bearing and seal damage can result. Install nut using the hex hold feature to prevent the stud from rotating.**

g. Remove the two nuts and disconnect the front stabilizer bar links.
h. Support the steering gear to prevent damage to the steering shaft and remove the steering gear nuts.
i. Remove the four bolts holding the power steering line to the frame.
j. Remove the right hand front and rear engine mount nuts.
k. Remove the transmission insulator support bracket bolts from the frame.
24. Remove the pin-type retainers from the right hand subframe splash shield.
    a. Using a suitable support table, support the subframe.

> **✳✳ CAUTION**
>
> **Make sure all hoses and the steering gear assembly are clear of subframe to prevent damage to these components when lowering the subframe.**

b. Remove the four subframe bolts and lower the subframe from the vehicle.

➡ **The use of mechanic's wire will aid in positioning the halfshaft out of the way.**

25. Remove the halfshafts from the transaxle and position out of the way.
26. Remove the starter motor.
27. Remove the transaxle housing cover.
28. Remove and discard the four torque converter to flexplate nuts.
29. Position a transmission jack under the transaxle.
30. Remove the transaxle retaining bolts.
31. Lower the transaxle assembly from the engine compartment.

To install:

➡ **Locate and align the orange dot adjacent to the stud on the torque con-**

verter and place it in the 6 o'clock position.

32. Position the transaxle on a suitable transmission jack.

33. Apply multi-purpose grease to the torque converter pilot hub.

34. Raise the transmission into position and install the bolts. Tighten the bolts to 46 ft. lbs. (62 Nm).

35. Install new torque to flexplate nuts and tighten to 26 ft. lbs. (35 Nm).

36. Install the transmission housing cover.

37. Install the starter motor

38. Install the halfshafts.

❋ CAUTION

If the steering gear was removed with the subframe and there is evidence that the steering column intermediate shaft has rotated, the clockspring must be recentered before the vehicle is driven or damage to the clockspring can result.

❋ WARNING

Incorrect centralization may result in premature component failure. If in doubt when centralizing the clockspring, repeat the centralizing procedure. Failure to follow this instruction may result in personal injury.

❋ CAUTION

Make sure the road wheels are in the straight ahead position.

39. If a clockspring has rotated out of center, perform the following:

   a. Centralize the clockspring.

   b. Hold the clockspring outer housing (1) stationary.

❋ CAUTION

Overturning will destroy the clockspring. The internal ribbon wire acts as the stop and can be broken from its internal connection.

   c. While turning the rotor (2) counterclockwise, carefully feel for the ribbon wire to run out of length and for a slight resistance. Stop turning at this point.

   d. Turn the clockspring clockwise (3) approximately three turns. This is the center point of the clockspring. Do not allow the rotor to turn from this position.

40. Install the subframe assembly as follows:

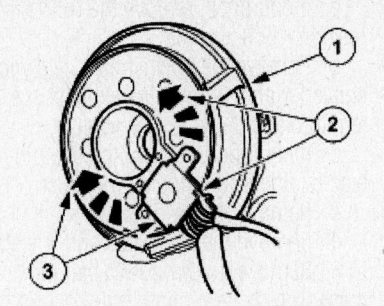

Fig. 12 Make sure the clockspring is properly centralized. Refer to the procedure for the accompanying steps.

06017-TAUR-G63

   a. Raise the subframe into the vehicle. Install the bolts and tighten to 76 ft. lbs. (103 Nm).

❋ CAUTION

Make sure all hoses and the steering gear assembly are clear of subframe to prevent damage to these components when lowering the subframe.

   b. Install the splash shield.

   c. Install the transmission insulator support bracket bolts to the frame and tighten to 65 ft. lbs. (88 Nm).

   d. Install the right hand engine mount nuts and tighten to 66 ft. lbs. (90 Nm).

   e. Install the four bolts holding the power steering line to the frame.

   f. Install the steering gear nuts and tighten to 91 ft. lbs. (123 Nm).

   g. Connect the front stabilizer bar links and tighten the nuts to 59 ft. lbs. (80 Nm).

   h. Connect the ball joint to the lower arm. Use new nuts and tighten to 59 ft. lbs. (80 Nm).

   i. Install the front wheels.

   j. Install the air dam.

   k. Install the downstream catalytic converter.

   l. If equipped, install the roll-restrictor bolt and nut. Tighten to 46 ft. lbs. (62 Nm).

41. Remove the engine lifting brackets.

42. Remove the engine support tools.

43. Install the upper transmission bolts and tighten to 46 ft. lbs. (62 Nm).

44. Reconnect the transmission fluid cooler tubes.

45. Install the retaining clips.

46. Install the bracket and ground cable.

47. Verify that the digital Transmission Range (TR) sensor is correctly adjusted as follows:

   a. Verify that the shift selector lever is in NEUTRAL.

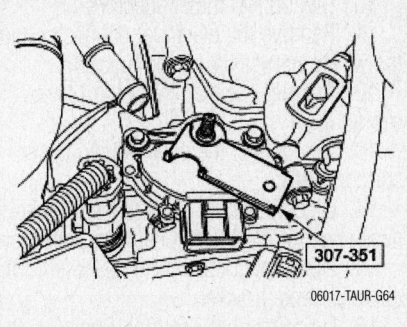

Fig. 13 Using the tool illustrated, align the digital TR sensor and tighten the bolts

06017-TAUR-G64

307-351

   b. Install the digital TR sensor and loosely install the bolts.

   c. Using the tool illustrated, align the digital TR sensor and tighten the bolts.

   d. Connect the connector.

48. Install the manual control lever cable onto the bracket and tighten the nut to 10 ft. lbs. (13 Nm).

49. Connect the TSS sensor.

50. Connect the OSS sensor.

51. Install the electrical connector bracket.

52. Install the power steering line bracket.

53. Reconnect the connector.

54. Install the battery tray.

55. Install the air filter assembly.

56. Install the engine air cleaner.

57. Reconnect the MAF sensor and the breather tubes.

58. Install the battery.

59. Connect the battery cables.

60. Fill the transaxle using clean automatic transmission fluid.

61. Start the engine.

62. Move the transaxle range selector lever through all positions.

63. Check the fluid level.

64. Check and adjust the wheel alignment.

3.0L (VIN S) Engine

See Figures 13 and 14.

1. Before servicing the vehicle, refer to the precautions section.

2. Disconnect the battery cables, negative cable first.

3. Remove the battery.

4. Disconnect the Mass Air Flow (MAF) sensor and the two breather tubes.

5. Remove the engine air cleaner cover and tube assembly.

6. Disconnect the breather tubes.

7. Remove the engine air cleaner.

8. Remove the air filter assembly.

9. Remove the battery tray.

10. Disconnect the connectors.

11. Remove the electrical connector and the wiring harness from the bracket.

12. Remove the manual control lever cable.

13. Disconnect the power steering sensor connector.

14. Disconnect the power steering harness and Output Shaft Speed (OSS) sensor.

15. Disconnect the wiring harness from the shift cable bracket.

16. Disconnect the Turbine Shaft Speed (TSS) sensor.

17. Remove the bolt from the coolant pipe bracket.

18. Remove the nut from the coolant pipe bracket.

19. Remove the left hand upper flange bolts.

20. Remove the cooler tube bolt for the cooling tube.

21. Install an engine lifting bracket.

22. Remove the right hand wiper, clips and upper cowl assembly.

23. Remove the right hand lower cowl assembly.

24. Remove the rear support brace.

25. Install the rear engine lifting bracket in the same location where the top bolt was removed from the rear support brace.

26. Install an engine support tool.

➡ It may be easier to access the nuts for the exhaust flange from the engine compartment.

27. Remove the front nuts from the front catalytic converter assembly.

28. Drain the transmission fluid by lowering the transaxle pan.

29. Disconnect the front Heated Oxygen Sensor (HO2S) .

30. Disconnect the rear HO2S sensor.

31. Remove the rear bolts from the front catalytic converter assembly.

32. Remove the nut from the rear catalytic converter assembly.

33. Remove the rear catalytic converter and cross over pipe assembly.

❈❈ CAUTION

If the steering gear is removed with the subframe, do not allow the steering wheel to rotate while the steering column intermediate is disconnected or damage to the clockspring can result. If there is evidence that the shaft has rotated, the clockspring must be recentered before the vehicle is driven.

34. Remove the subframe assembly as follows:

a. If equipped, remove the roll-restrictor bolt and nut.

b. Remove the downstream catalytic converter and support the exhaust system to one side under the vehicle.

c. If equipped, remove the five pin-type retainers from the chin spoiler.

d. Remove the air dam.

e. Remove the front tires and wheels.

f. Remove the two lower ball joint nuts.

35. Disconnect the ball joint from the lower arm.

36. Push the lower arm downward until the ball joint is free of the arm.

❈❈ CAUTION

Use extreme care not to damage boot seal. Do not use power tools to tighten the nut, or bearing and seal damage can result. Install nut using the hex hold feature to prevent the stud from rotating.

g. Remove the two nuts and disconnect the front stabilizer bar links.

h. Support the steering gear to prevent damage to the steering shaft and remove the steering gear nuts.

i. Remove the four bolts holding the power steering line to the frame.

j. Remove the right hand front and rear engine mount nuts.

k. Remove the transmission insulator support bracket bolts from the frame.

➡ The use of mechanic's wire will aid in positioning the halfshaft out of the way.

37. Remove the halfshafts from the transaxle and position out of the way.

38. Remove the nut and the battery ground cable.

39. Remove the starter motor.

40. Remove the cooler line retaining clips.

41. Depress the tabs on the plastic insert retainer and remove the cooler lines from the fitting.

42. Remove the transmission housing cover.

43. Remove and discard the four torque converter to flexplate nuts.

44. Position a transmission jack under the transaxle.

45. Remove the transaxle retaining bolts.

46. Remove the support bracket.

47. Lower the transaxle assembly from the engine compartment.

To install:

➡ Locate and align the orange dot adjacent to the stud on the torque converter and place it in the 6 o'clock position.

48. Position the transaxle on a suitable transmission jack.

49. Apply multi-purpose grease to the torque converter pilot hub.

50. Raise the transmission into position and install the bolts. Tighten the bolts to 30 ft. lbs. (40 Nm).

51. Install the transaxle retaining bracket. Tighten the retainers as shown in the accompanying illustration.

52. Install new torque to flexplate nuts and tighten to 26 ft. lbs. (35 Nm).

53. Install the transmission housing cover.

54. Install the cooler lines.

55. Install the starter motor.

56. Install the ground cable.

57. Install the halfshafts.

❈❈ CAUTION

If the steering gear was removed with the subframe and there is evidence that the steering column intermediate shaft has rotated, the clockspring must be recentered before the vehicle is driven or damage to the clockspring can result.

❈❈ WARNING

Incorrect centralization may result in premature component failure. If in doubt when centralizing the clockspring, repeat the centralizing procedure. Failure to follow this instruction may result in personal injury.

❈❈ CAUTION

Make sure the road wheels are in the straight ahead position.

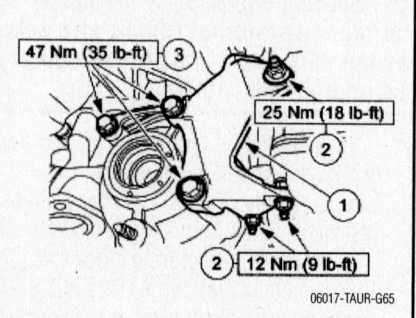

06017-TAUR-G65

Fig. 14 Install the transaxle retaining bracket—3.0L (VIN S) model

58. If a clockspring has rotated out of center, perform the following:

a. Centralize the clockspring.

b. Hold the clockspring outer housing (1) stationary.

❋ CAUTION

Overturning will destroy the clockspring. The internal ribbon wire acts as the stop and can be broken from its internal connection.

c. While turning the rotor (2) counterclockwise, carefully feel for the ribbon wire to run out of length and for a slight resistance. Stop turning at this point.

d. Turn the clockspring clockwise (3) approximately three turns. This is the center point of the clockspring. Do not allow the rotor to turn from this position.

59. Install the subframe assembly as follows:

a. Raise the subframe into the vehicle. Install the bolts and tighten to 76 ft. lbs. (103 Nm).

❋ CAUTION

Make sure all hoses and the steering gear assembly are clear of subframe to prevent damage to these components when lowering the subframe.

b. Install the splash shield.

c. Install the transmission insulator support bracket bolts to the frame and tighten to 65 ft. lbs. (88 Nm).

d. Install the right hand engine mount nuts and tighten to 66 ft. lbs. (90 Nm).

e. Install the four bolts holding the power steering line to the frame.

f. Install the steering gear nuts and tighten to 91 ft. lbs. (123 Nm).

g. Connect the front stabilizer bar links and tighten the nuts to 59 ft. lbs. (80 Nm).

h. Connect the ball joint to the lower arm. Use new nuts and tighten to 59 ft. lbs. (80 Nm).

i. Install the front wheels.

j. Install the air dam.

k. Install the downstream catalytic converter.

l. If equipped, install the roll-restrictor bolt and nut. Tighten to 46 ft. lbs. (62 Nm).

60. Install the rear catalytic converter and cross over pipe assembly. Tighten the retainers to 30 ft. lbs. (40 Nm).

61. Install the nut for the rear catalytic converter assembly. Tighten the retainers to 30 ft. lbs. (40 Nm).

62. Install the bolts for the front catalytic converter assembly. Tighten the retainers to 30 ft. lbs. (40 Nm).

63. Connect the rear HO2S sensor.

64. Connect the front HO2S sensor.

➡ **It may be easier to access the nuts from the engine compartment.**

65. Install the nuts for the front catalytic converter assembly. Tighten the retainers to 30 ft. lbs. (40 Nm).

66. Remove the engine support tool and lifting brackets.

67. Install the rear support brace. Tighten the retainers to 35 ft. lbs. (47 Nm).

68. Install the lower cowl assembly.

69. Install the wiper, upper cowl assembly and clips.

70. Install the nut for the cooling tube.

71. Install the left hand upper flange bolts. Tighten the retainers to 46 ft. lbs. (62 Nm).

72. Install the nut for the coolant pipe bracket.

73. Install the bolt for the coolant pipe bracket.

74. Connect the TSS sensor.

75. Connect the wiring harness to the shift cable bracket.

76. Connect the OSS sensor.

77. Connect the power steering sensor connector.

78. Verify that the digital Transmission Range (TR) sensor is correctly adjusted as follows:

a. Verify that the shift selector lever is in NEUTRAL.

b. Install the digital TR sensor and loosely install the bolts.

c. Using the tool illustrated, align the digital TR sensor and tighten the bolts.

d. Connect the connector.

79. Install the manual control lever cable onto the bracket and tighten the nut to 18 ft. lbs. (25 Nm).

80. Install the electrical connector and wiring harness to the bracket.

81. Connect the connector.

82. Install the battery tray.

83. Install the air filter assembly.

84. Install the engine air cleaner.

85. Reconnect the breather tubes.

86. Reconnect the MAF sensor and the breather tubes.

87. Install the battery.

88. Connect the battery cables.

89. Fill the transaxle using clean automatic transmission fluid.

90. Start the engine.

91. Move the transaxle range selector lever through all positions.

92. Check the fluid level.

93. Check and adjust the wheel alignment.

HALFSHAFTS

REMOVAL & INSTALLATION

1. Before servicing the vehicle, refer to the precautions section.

2. The following are required when performing this procedure:

a. A new front axle wheel hub retainer.

b. A new nut to retain the knuckle to the strut.

c. A new nut to retain the front suspension lower arm to the ball joint.

d. A new circlip.

➡ **Do not reuse these parts during assembly. Their torque retention capability diminishes during removal.**

3. Remove the center hub cap from the wheel.

4. Loosen the axle nut.

5. Remove the front wheel and tire assembly.

6. Remove the axle nut and washer.

7. Remove the front brake anti-lock sensor harness from the clip.

8. Remove and position the front brake anti-lock sensor aside.

9. Remove and discard lower control arm to strut nut.

10. Remove the strut to knuckle nut and bolt. Discard the nut.

11. Press the ball joint stud until it is loose in the knuckle.

❋❋ WARNING

Wire the knuckle to the strut. This will prevent the knuckle from falling off of the strut while the knuckle and lower ball joint are separated. Failure to follow these instructions may result in personal injury.

➡ **Failure to reposition the knuckle on the strut body will prevent separation of the front suspension lower arm from the knuckle.**

12. Reposition the knuckle, and secure it to the strut.

13. Pull upward on the knuckle to raise it approximately 0.5 inch (12.7 mm) on the strut body. Wire the knuckle to the strut.

14. Disconnect the front suspension lower arm from the knuckle.

❋❋ CAUTION

Never use a hammer to separate the front wheel driveshaft joint from the wheel hub. Damage to the joint threads and internal components can result.

15. Press the front wheel driveshaft joint until it is loose in the wheel hub.

> ❋ **CAUTION**
>
> **Do not allow the halfshaft to hang unsupported. Damage to the CV joints and boots can result. Do not damage the front wheel driveshaft joint boot or the clamps.**

16. Remove the front wheel driveshaft joint from the wheel hub.

> ❋ **CAUTION**
>
> **Do not damage the crank sensor when removing the right hand half-shaft assembly.**

17. Separate the inboard CV joint housing assembly from the transaxle.

> ❋ **CAUTION**
>
> **Do not damage the differential seal.**

18. Carefully remove the halfshaft assembly with both hands.

To install:
19. Lubricate the differential seal.
20. Use Ford Synthetic MERCON® Multi-Purpose Automatic Transmission Fluid E6AZ-19582-B or equivalent meeting Ford specification ESR-M2C 163-A2.

> ❋ **CAUTION**
>
> **Install a new circlip every time you remove the halfshaft from the vehicle.**

21. On the right hand side only, install a new circlip.
22. Start one end in the groove and work the circlip over the shaft and into the groove. This will prevent the circlip from over-expanding.

> ❋ **CAUTION**
>
> **Do not damage the inboard CV joint housing assembly and the differential seal.**

➡If necessary, use a non-metallic mallet to aid in seating the circlip in the differential side gear groove (right hand) or inboard CV joint housing (left). Tap only on the outboard front wheel driveshaft joint.

23. Align the inboard CV joint housing splines with the differential side gear splines (right hand) or output shaft splines (left hand), and push the inboard CV joint housing assembly inward until the circlip seats in the differential side gear (right hand) or inboard CV joint housing (left hand).

24. Align the front wheel driveshaft joint splines and the wheel hub splines, and push the joint into the wheel hub as far as possible.
25. Connect the suspension lower arm to the knuckle.
26. Using the old nut, seat the front wheel driveshaft joint in the hub. Remove the old nut and discard it.
27. Install a new lower control arm nut and tighten to 59 ft. lbs. (80 Nm).
28. Remove the wire. Install the strut to knuckle bolt and nut tighten to 85 ft. lbs. (115 Nm).
29. Position the brake hose bracket and install the bolt.
30. Install the front brake anti-lock sensor.
31. Install the front brake anti-lock sensor harness in the clip.
32. Install the wheel and tire assembly.

> ❋ **CAUTION**
>
> **Install and tighten the new front axle wheel hub retainer to specification in a continuous rotation. Stopping the rotation during installation will cause the nylon lock to set incorrectly. This will cause incorrect torque readings while tightening the retainer, and lead to bearing failure. Install a new front axle wheel hub retainer every time after loosening the retainer or not installing the retainer to specification in a continuous rotation.**

33. Tighten the new axle nut to 184 ft. lbs. (250 Nm) in a continuous rotation.
34. Check and, if necessary, fill the transaxle to the correct level.
35. Check and adjust the wheel alignment.

CV-JOINTS OVERHAUL

These vehicles use several different types of joints. Engine size, transaxle type, whether the joint is an inboard or outboard joint, even which side of the vehicle is being serviced could make a difference in joint type. Be sure to properly identify the joint before attempting joint or boot replacement. Look for identification numbers at the large end of the boots and/or on the end of the metal retainer bands.

The 3 types of joints used are the Birfield Joint, (B.J.), the Tripod Joint (T.J.) and the Double Offset Joint (D.O.J.).

➡**Do not disassemble a Birfield joint. Service with a new joint or clean and repack using a new boot kit.**

The distance between the large and small boot bands is important and should be checked prior to and after boot service. This is so the boot will not be installed either too loose or too tight, which could cause early wear and cracking, allowing the grease to get out and water and dirt in, leading to early joint failure.

➡**The driveshaft joints use special grease; do not add any grease other than that supplied with the kit.**

Double Offset Joint

The Double Offset Joint (D.O.J.) is bigger than other joints and, in these applications, is normally used as an inboard joint.

1. Remove the halfshaft from the vehicle.
2. Side cutter pliers can be used to cut the metal retaining bands. Remove the boot from the joint outer race.
3. Locate and remove the large circlip at the base of the joint. Remove the outer race (the body of the joint).
4. Remove the small snap-ring and take off the inner race, cage and balls as an assembly. Clean the inner race, cage and balls without disassembling.
5. If the boot is to be reused, wipe the grease from the splines and wrap the splines in vinyl tape before sliding the boot from the shaft.
6. Remove the inner (D.O.J.) boot from the shaft. If the outer (B.J.) boot is to be replaced, remove the boot retainer rings and slide the boot down and off of the shaft at this time.

To install:
7. Be sure to tape the shaft splines before installing the boots. Fill the inside of the boot with the specified grease. Often the grease supplied in the replacement parts kit is meant to be divided in half, with half being used to lubricate the joint and half being used inside the boot.
8. Install the cage onto the halfshaft so the small diameter side of the cage is installed first. With a brass drift pin, tap lightly and evenly around the inner race to install the race until it comes into contact with the rib of the shaft. Apply the specified grease to the inner race and cage and fit them together. Insert the balls into the cage.
9. Install the outer race (the body of the joint) after filling with the specified grease. The outer race should be filled with this grease.

10. Tighten the boot bands securely. Make sure the distance between the boot bands is correct.

11. Install the halfshaft to the vehicle.

Except Double Offset Joint

1. Disconnect the negative battery cable. Remove the halfshaft.

2. Use side cutter pliers to remove the metal retaining bands from the boot(s) that will be removed. Slide the boot from the T.J. case.

3. Remove the snap-ring and the tripod joint spider assembly from the halfshaft. Do not disassemble the spider and use care in handling.

4. If the boot is be reused, wrap vinyl tape around the splined part of the shaft so the boot(s) will not be damaged when removed. Remove the dynamic damper, if used, and the boots from the shaft.

To install:

5. Double check that the correct replacement parts are being installed. Wrap vinyl tape around the splines to protect the boot and install the boots and damper, if used, in the correct order.

6. Install the joint spider assembly to the shaft and install the snap-ring.

7. Fill the inside of the boot with the specified grease. Often the grease supplied in the replacement parts kit is meant to be divided in half, with half being used to lubricate the joint and half being used inside the boot. Keep grease off the rubber part of the dynamic damper (if used).

8. Secure the boot bands with the halfshaft in a horizontal position. Make sure distance between boot bands is correct.

9. Install the halfshaft to the vehicle and reconnect the negative battery cable.

ENGINE COOLING

ENGINE FAN

REMOVAL & INSTALLATION

See Figure 15.

➡ **Only an MVAC-trained, EPA-certified, automotive technician should service the A/C system or its components.**

1. If your vehicle is equipped with A/C evacuate the system using an approved recovery/recycling station.

2. Remove the engine air cleaner assembly.

3. Disconnect the battery cables, negative cable first.

4. Remove the battery and battery tray.

5. Raise the vehicle and support it with jackstands.

❄ CAUTION

Never open, service or drain the radiator or cooling system when hot; serious burns can occur from the steam and hot coolant. Also, when draining engine coolant, keep in mind that cats and dogs are attracted to ethylene glycol antifreeze and could drink any that is left in an uncovered container or in puddles on the ground. This will prove fatal in sufficient quantities. Always drain coolant into a sealable container. Coolant should be reused unless it is contaminated or is several years old.

6. Drain the cooling system into a suitable container.

7. Unfasten the bolts retaining the lower radiator hose shield and remove the shield.

8. Disconnect the lower radiator hose from the radiator.

9. Disconnect the A/C evaporator muffler and hoses from the A/C condenser core.

Cap all openings immediately to avoid system contamination.

10. Using a ³⁄₈ inch fuel line disconnect tool T90T-9550-S or its equivalent, disconnect the lower transaxle oil cooler tube from the radiator.

11. Unfasten the two screws from the lower transaxle oil cooler tube and allow the transaxle oil cooler tube to hang.

12. Remove both of the transaxle oil cooler tubes from the left end of the power steering/transaxle oil cooler.

13. Remove the lower radiator mounts and lower the vehicle.

14. Unfasten the four bolts retaining the hood latch support and position the latch support to one side.

15. Remove the front bumper cover and the upper radiator support.

16. Disconnect the radiator overflow hose from the radiator.

17. Remove the power distribution box, harness and bracket, then position the box and harness aside.

18. Tag and unplug the wiring from the fan motor.

19. Unfasten the screws retaining the engine control sensor wiring and position the wiring aside.

20. Disconnect the power steering fluid cooler from the power steering pump.

21. Support the fan blade and fan shroud assembly.

22. Unfasten the fan assembly brackets-to-sub-frame bolts.

23. Remove the cooling fan assembly from the vehicle.

To install:

24. Place the fan assembly in position and install the fan assembly-to-frame rail retainers. Tighten the retainers to 15–22 ft. lbs. (20–30 Nm).

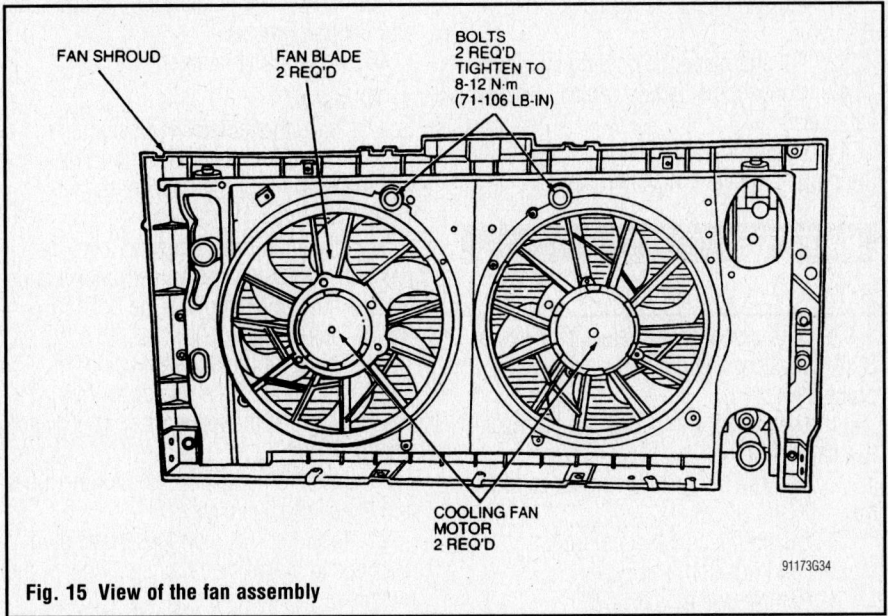

Fig. 15 View of the fan assembly

25. Connect the power steering fluid cooler to the power steering pump.

26. Place the engine wiring into position and install the retaining screws.

27. Attach the wiring to the power steering pump.

28. Place the power distribution box and bracket in position and install the retainers to 18–25 ft. lbs. (25–35 Nm).

29. Connect the upper radiator hose and the overflow hose to the radiator and tighten the hose clamps.

30. Install the upper radiator support and the front bumper cover.

31. Place the hood latch support assembly in position and install the retaining bolts. Tighten the bolts to 18–25 ft. lbs. (25–35 Nm).

32. Raise the vehicle and support it with jackstands.

33. Connect both of the transaxle oil cooler tubes to the left end of the power steering/transaxle oil cooler.

34. Install the power steering transaxle cooler and its retaining bolt and nut. Tighten the bolt and nut to 45–61 ft. lbs. (5–7 Nm).

35. Connect the lower transaxle oil cooler tube.

36. Connect the A/C evaporator muffler and hoses to the condenser core.

37. Connect the lower radiator hose to the radiator and tighten the clamp.

38. Install the lower radiator hose shield and its retainers. Tighten the retainers to 45–61 inch lbs. (5–7 Nm).

39. Lower the vehicle and install the battery tray and battery.

40. Install the engine air cleaner assembly.

41. Fill and bleed the power steering reservoir.

42. Fill and bleed the cooling system.

43. Connect the battery cables, negative cable last.

44. Evacuate and recharge the A/C using the proper recovery/recycling station.

RADIATOR

REMOVAL & INSTALLATION

Fuel line disconnect tool set T90T-9550-S or equivalent is required to perform this procedure.

1. Disconnect the battery cables, negative cable first.

2. Remove the battery and the battery tray.

3. Unclip the constant control relay module and position it aside.

4. Remove the radiator cap.

5. Raise the vehicle and support it with jackstands.

6. Remove the radiator splash shields.

⁑ CAUTION

Never open, service or drain the radiator or cooling system when hot; serious burns can occur from the steam and hot coolant. Also, when draining engine coolant, keep in mind that cats and dogs are attracted to ethylene glycol antifreeze and could drink any that is left in an uncovered container or in puddles on the ground. This will prove fatal in sufficient quantities. Always drain coolant into a sealable container. Coolant should be reused unless it is contaminated or is several years old.

7. Drain the cooling system into a suitable container.

8. Remove the radiator mounting bracket assembly.

9. Disconnect the lower and upper radiator hoses and the overflow hose from the radiator.

10. Remove the A/C condenser retaining bolts.

11. Remove the transaxle cooler line clips.

12. Using a ⅜ inch fuel line disconnect tool T90T-9550-S or its equivalent, disconnect the transaxle oil cooler tubes from the radiator.

13. Remove the transaxle oil cooler line bracket and position the oil cooler aside.

14. Remove the A/C condenser bracket and position the A/C condenser core aside.

15. Remove the retaining bolts and radiator support bracket.

16. Remove the radiator.

To install:

17. Place the radiator in position.

18. Install the radiator support bracket and the retaining nuts. Tighten the nuts to 71–106 inch lbs. (8–12 Nm).

19. Place the A/C condenser core into position, install the condenser bracket and the retaining bolts. Tighten the bolts to 45–61 inch lbs. (5–7 Nm).

20. Place the transaxle oil cooler in position and install the oil cooler tube bracket. Tighten the retainers to 45–61 inch lbs. (5–7 Nm).

21. Install the transaxle cooler line tubes and the cooler line clips.

22. Place the A/C condenser retaining bracket and install the retainers. Tighten the retainers to 45–61 inch lbs. (5–7 Nm).

23. Attach the radiator overflow hose and the radiator hoses to the radiator. Tighten the hose clamps securely.

24. Install the radiator mounting bracket and its retainers. Tighten the retainers to 81–106 inch lbs. (8–12 Nm).

25. Install the radiator splash shields and lower the vehicle.

26. Place the constant control relay module in position and install the retaining clip.

27. Install the battery tray and battery.

28. Connect the battery cables, negative cable last.

29. Fill and bleed the cooling system.

30. Start the engine and check for coolant and transmission fluid leaks.

THERMOSTAT

REMOVAL & INSTALLATION

⁑ CAUTION

Never open, service or drain the radiator or cooling system when hot; serious burns can occur from the steam and hot coolant. Also, when draining engine coolant, keep in mind that cats and dogs are attracted to ethylene glycol antifreeze and could drink any that is left in an uncovered container or in puddles on the ground. This will prove fatal in sufficient quantities. Always drain coolant into a sealable container. Coolant should be reused unless it is contaminated or is several years old.

3.0L (VIN U, 2) Engine
See Figure 16.

1. Drain the coolant until the level of the coolant is below the level of the thermostat.

2. Disconnect the upper radiator hose from the water hose connection.

3. Unfasten the three water inlet connection retaining bolts and remove the water hose connection.

4. Remove the gasket and thermostat from the water hose connection. Discard the gasket.

To install:

5. Clean the water inlet connection mating surfaces.

➡**The jiggle valve on the thermostat must be in the up position.**

6. Place the thermostat in the water hose connection making sure the thermostat jiggle valve is facing up.

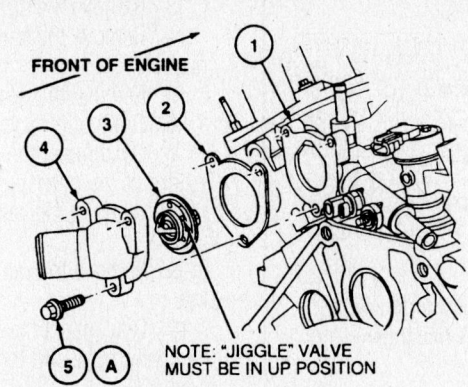

Item	Part Number	Description
1	9424	Intake Manifold (Lower)
2	8255	Water Hose Connection Gasket
3	8575	Water Thermostat
4	8592	Water Hose Connection
5	—	Bolt (3 Req'd)
A	—	Tighten to 10-14 N·m (89-124 Lb-In)

91173G18

Fig. 16 Exploded view of the water hose connection and the thermostat assembly—3.0L (VIN U, 2) engines

7. Install the new gasket and place the water hose connection assembly into position.

8. Install the water hose connection assembly retainers and tighten them to 89–124 inch lbs. (10–14 Nm).

9. Connect the upper radiator hose to the water hose connection.

10. Fill the engine with coolant, start the engine and check for leaks.

11. Stop the engine and top off the coolant recovery reservoir as necessary.

3.0L (VIN S) Engine

See Figure 17.

1. Drain the coolant until the level of the coolant is below the level of the thermostat.

2. Raise the vehicle and support it with jackstands.

3. Disconnect the lower radiator hose from the water inlet connection.

4. Unfasten the two water inlet connection retaining bolts and remove the water inlet connection.

5. Remove the O-ring seal and thermostat from the water inlet connection. Inspect the O-ring for damage and replace as necessary.

To install:

6. Clean the water inlet connection mating surfaces.

7. Install the O-ring, thermostat and the water inlet connection. Refer to the accom-panying illustration If you can't remember how the O-ring and thermostat are positioned.

8. Install the water inlet connection assembly retainers and tighten them to 71–106 inch lbs. (8–12 Nm).

9. Connect the lower radiator hose to the water inlet connection.

10. Fill the engine with coolant, start the engine and check for leaks.

11. Stop the engine and top off the coolant recovery reservoir as necessary.

WATER PUMP

REMOVAL & INSTALLATION

3.0L (VIN U, 2) Engines

See Figures 18 through 20.

1. Before servicing the vehicle, refer to the precautions section.

2. Disconnect the negative battery cable.

3. Drain the engine cooling system.

4. Loosen the water pump pulley.

5. Remove the accessory drive belt.

6. Remove the degas bottle.

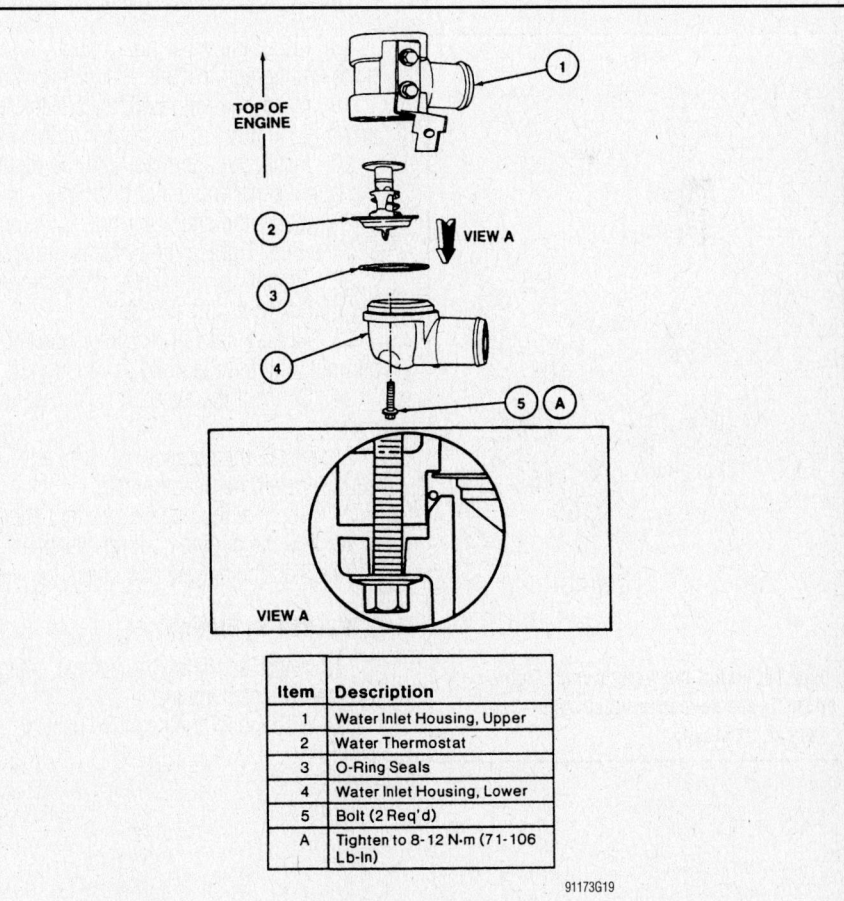

Item	Description
1	Water Inlet Housing, Upper
2	Water Thermostat
3	O-Ring Seals
4	Water Inlet Housing, Lower
5	Bolt (2 Req'd)
A	Tighten to 8-12 N·m (71-106 Lb-In)

91173G19

Fig. 17 Exploded view of the water inlet connection and the thermostat assembly—3.0L (VIN S) engines

7. Remove the alternator.

8. Remove the bolt and the nut, and position the roll restrictor bracket out of the way.

9. Remove the bolt and the accessory drive belt tensioner.

10. Remove the nut, the bolt and the support bracket.

11. Remove the bolts and the water pump pulley.

12. Disconnect the water pump inlet hose and the Crankshaft Position (CKP) sensor electrical connector.

13. Remove the bolts and the water pump, and clean the sealing surfaces.

To install:

14. Install the water pump. Tighten bolts in the sequence illustrated as follows:

    a. Bolts 1-7 to 18 ft. lbs. (25 Nm).

    b. Bolts 8-12 to 89 inch lbs. (10 Nm).

15. Connect the CKP sensor electrical connector and the water pump inlet hose.

16. Install the support bracket, the nut and the bolt and tighten to 18 ft. lbs. (25 Nm).

17. Install the accessory drive belt tensioner and the bolt and tighten to 18 ft. lbs. (25 Nm).

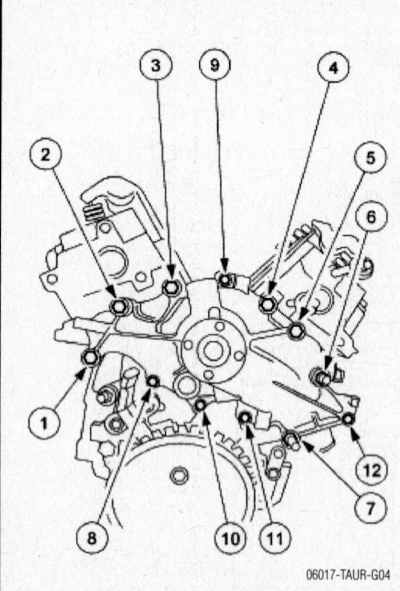

Fig. 18 Install the water pump. Tighten bolts in the sequence illustrated—3.0L (VIN U, 2) models

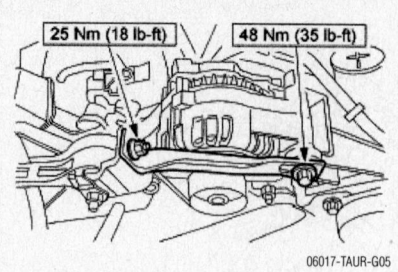

Fig. 19 Install the alternator brace, tighten the retainers as illustrated—3.0L (VIN U, 2) models

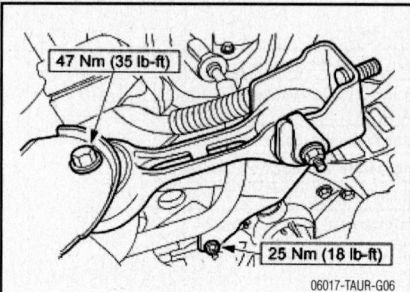

Fig. 20 Tighten the roll restrictor bracket bolt and nut as illustrated—3.0L (VIN U, 2) models

18. Install the water pump pulley and the bolts and tighten to 18 ft. lbs. (25 Nm).

19. Install the roll restrictor bracket, the bolt and the nut. Do not tighten at this time.

20. Install the alternator and the mounting bolt. Do not tighten at this time.

21. Install the alternator brace, the nut and the bolt. Tighten the bolts as illustrated.

22. Tighten the alternator lower mounting bolt to 18 ft. lbs. (25 Nm).

23. Tighten the roll restrictor bracket bolt and nut. Tighten the bolts as illustrated

24. Connect the alternator electrical connectors.

25. Install the accessory drive belt.

26. Install the degas bottle.

27. Connect the negative battery cable.

28. Fill the engine cooling system.

29. Start the engine and check for leaks.

3.0L (VIN S) Engine

1. Before servicing the vehicle, refer to the precautions section.

2. Disconnect the negative battery cable.

3. Remove the air cleaner assembly.

4. Remove the battery and the battery tray.

5. Remove the water pump belt.

6. Drain and recycle the engine coolant.

7. Disconnect the heater hose from the bottom of the water pump.

8. Remove the radiator lower tube bolt.

9. Remove the radiator upper front tube bolt.

10. Disconnect the upper radiator hose, the heater hose and the thermostat housing hose.

11. Remove the radiator bypass hose assembly.

12. Remove the pin-type retainer, disconnect the Engine Coolant Temperature (ECT) sensor electrical connector and position the harness aside.

13. Remove the three bolts, and reposition the water pump to access the remaining hoses.

14. Loosen the clamps, disconnect the hoses and remove the water pump.

To install:

15. Connect the hoses to the water pump.

16. Position the water pump and install the mounting bolts. Tighten the bolts in two steps:

    a. Step 1: Tighten to 89 inch lbs. (10 Nm).

    b. Step 2: Tighten an additional 90 degrees.

17. Install the radiator bypass hose assembly.

18. Connect the ECT sensor electrical connector and attach the pin-type retainer.

19. Connect the upper radiator hose, the heater hose and thermostat housing hose.

20. Install the radiator upper front cooling tube bolt.

21. Install the lower cooling tube bolt.

22. Connect the heater hose to the bottom of the water pump.

23. Install the water pump belt.

24. Install the battery and the battery tray.

25. Install the air cleaner assembly.

26. Fill and bleed the engine cooling system.

27. Connect the negative battery cable.

28. Start the engine and check for leaks.

ENGINE ELECTRICAL

CHARGING SYSTEM

ALTERNATOR

REMOVAL & INSTALLATION

3.0L (VIN U, 2) Engines

See Figure 21.

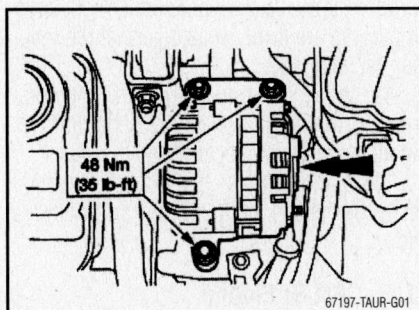

**Fig. 21 Alternator and mounting bolts—
2003–05 3.0L (VIN U, 2) Engines**

1. Before servicing the vehicle, refer to the precautions section.
2. Disconnect the battery ground cable.
3. Release the accessory drive belt tension and remove the belt from the alternator pulley.
4. Remove the alternator B+ nut and the B+ cable.
5. Position the B+ cable cover aside.
6. Position the wiring harness aside.
7. Remove the bolts and the alternator.
8. Disconnect the voltage regulator electrical connector.

To install:

9. Connect the voltage regulator electrical connector.

10. Install the alternator and tighten the bolts to 35 ft. lbs. (48 Nm).
11. Install the B+ cable and tighten the nut to 71 inch lbs. (8 Nm).
12. Install the accessory drive belt.

3.0L (VIN S) Engine

1. Before servicing the vehicle, refer to the precautions section.
2. Disconnect the negative battery cable.
3. Release the accessory drive belt tension and remove the belt from the alternator pulley.
4. Remove the power steering hose bracket nut from the alternator mounting bolt.

➡**The left side bolt will come out with the alternator.**

5. Remove the upper alternator bolts.
6. Remove the right hand front wheel and tire assembly and front fender splash shield.
7. Remove the screws and the alternator splash shield.
8. Remove the torque converter inspection cover.
9. Install a flywheel holding tool.

➡**The crankshaft pulley bolt has a reverse thread. The crankshaft pulley and bolt are a molded composite and are one piece.**

10. Remove the bolt and the crankshaft pulley.
11. Lower the alternator to allow access to the electrical connectors.

12. Disconnect the Crankshaft Position (CKP) sensor.
13. Release the Oxygen (O2s) sensor connector locator from the bracket.
14. Remove the lower alternator bolt.
15. Disconnect the regulator electrical connector.
16. Remove the alternator from the vehicle and disconnect the B+ connector nut.

To install:

17. Connect the B+ connector and tighten the nut to 71 inch lbs. (8 Nm).
18. Install the alternator and tighten the lower bolt to 18 ft. lbs. (25 Nm).
19. Connect the regulator electrical connector.
20. Connect the O2s sensor connector locator.
21. Connect the CKP sensor.

➡**The crankshaft pulley bolt has a reverse thread. The crankshaft pulley and bolt are a molded composite and are one piece.**

22. Install the crankshaft pulley and tighten the bolt to 74 ft. lbs. (100 Nm).
23. Install the torque converter inspection cover.
24. Install the alternator splash shield.
25. Install the right hand front fender splash shield and wheel assembly.
26. Install the upper alternator bolts and tighten to 18 ft. lbs. (25 Nm).
27. Install the power steering hose bracket nut and tighten to 13 ft. lbs. (18 Nm).
28. Install the accessory drive belt.
29. Connect the negative battery cable.

ENGINE ELECTRICAL

IGNITION SYSTEM

FIRING ORDER

See Figures 22 and 23.

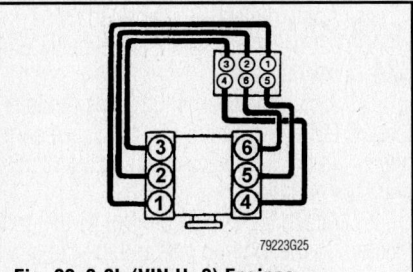

**Fig. 22 3.0L (VIN U, 2) Engines
Firing order: 1–4–2–5–3–6
Distributorless ignition system**

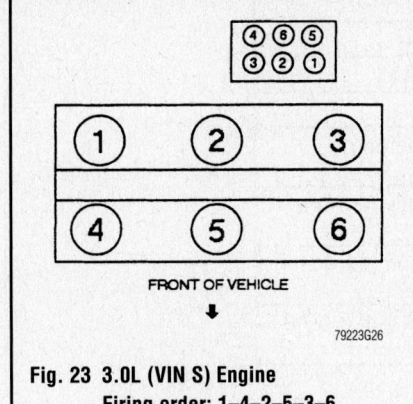

FRONT OF VEHICLE

**Fig. 23 3.0L (VIN S) Engine
Firing order: 1–4–2–5–3–6
Distributorless ignition system**

IGNITION COIL

REMOVAL & INSTALLATION

3.0L (VIN U, 2) Engines

See Figure 24.

1. Disconnect the negative battery cable.
2. Unplug the fuel charging wiring connectors from the ignition coil and the radio ignition interference capacitor.
3. Tag and disconnect the spark plug wires from the coil by squeezing the locking tabs, then twist the tab and pull upwards.
4. Unfasten the four ignition coil retaining screws and remove the coil and the

radio ignition interference capacitor as an assembly.

5. If you are replacing the coil, unfasten the radio ignition interference capacitor retaining screw and remove the capacitor.

6. Wipe the coil towers with a clean cloth dampened with soap and water. Remove any soap film and dry with com-

pressed air. Inspect the coil for cracks, carbon tracking, dirt or damage and replace as necessary.

To install:

7. If removed, place the capacitor in position and install its retaining screw. Tighten the screw to 45–61 inch lbs. (5–7 Nm).

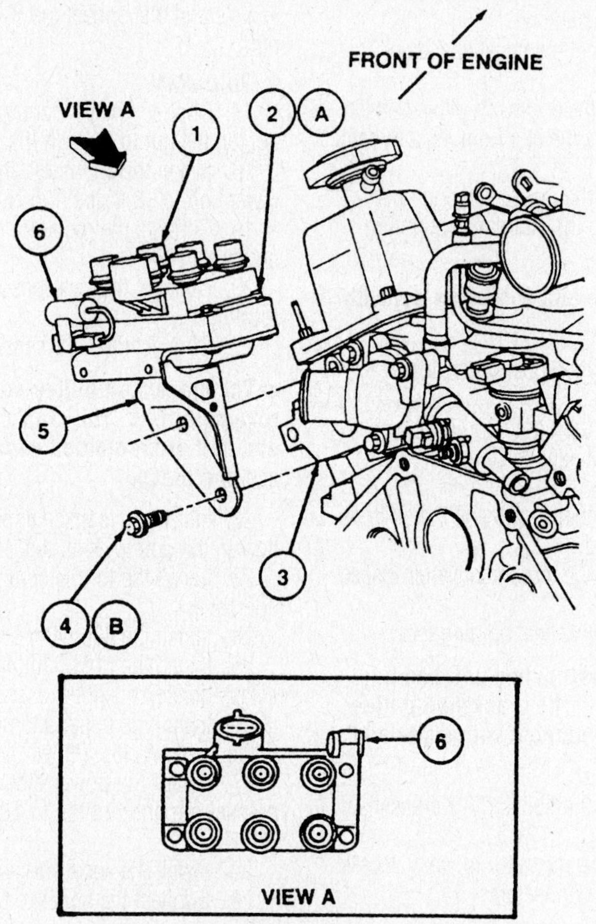

8. Place the coil and capacitor assembly into position on the bracket.

9. Install the coil assembly retaining screws and tighten to 45–61 inch lbs. (5–7 Nm).

10. Apply dielectric compound D7AZ-19A331-A or its equivalent to the spark plug wire boots.

11. Attach the spark plug wires to their proper terminals on the coil and make sure the boots are firmly seated so that the locking tabs engage.

12. Attach the fuel charging wiring connectors to the ignition coil and the radio ignition interference capacitor.

13. Connect the negative battery cable, start the vehicle and check for proper operation.

3.0L (VIN S) Engine

See Figure 25.

1. Disconnect the negative battery cable.

2. Unplug the engine control sensor wiring connectors from the ignition coil and the radio ignition interference capacitor.

3. Tag and disconnect the spark plug wires from the coil by squeezing the locking tabs, then twist the tab and pull upwards.

4. Unfasten the four ignition coil retainers and remove the coil and the coil ground wire the radio ignition interference capacitor. Save the capacitor and coil ground wire for re-installation of the coil assembly.

5. Wipe the coil towers with a clean cloth dampened with soap and water. Remove any soap film and dry with compressed air. Inspect the coil for cracks, carbon tracking, dirt or damage and replace as necessary.

To install:

6. Place the coil, capacitor and the coil ground wire onto its mounting location on the right hand valve cover.

7. Install the coil assembly retainers and tighten to 45–61 inch lbs. (5–7 Nm).

8. Apply dielectric compound D7AZ-19A331-A or its equivalent to the spark plug wire boots.

9. Attach the spark plug wires to their proper terminals on the coil and make sure the boots are firmly seated so that the locking tabs engage.

10. Attach the engine control wiring connectors to the ignition coil and the radio ignition interference capacitor.

11. Connect the negative battery cable, start the vehicle and check for proper operation.

Item	Description
1	Ignition Coil
2	Bolt (4 Req'd)
3	Cylinder Head (LH)
4	Bolt (2 Req'd)
5	Ignition Coil Mounting Bracket
6	Radio Ignition Interference Capacitor
A	Tighten to 5-7 N·m (45-61 Lb-In)
B	Tighten to 40-55 N·m (30-40 Lb-Ft)

91172G08

Fig. 24 Ignition coil and bracket mounting—3.0L OHV engines

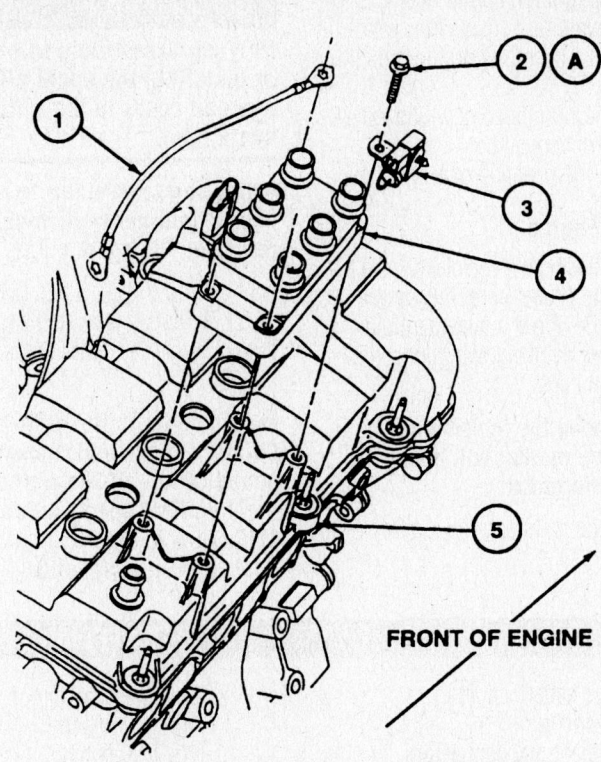

Item	Description
1	Ignition Coil Ground Cable
2	Bolt (4 Req'd)
3	Radio Ignition Interference Capacitor
4	Ignition Coil
5	Valve Cover
A	Tighten to 5-7 N·m (45-61 Lb-In)

FRONT OF ENGINE

91172G09

Fig. 25 Ignition coil assembly mounting—3.0L DOHC engines

IGNITION TIMING

ADJUSTMENT

The ignition timing is controlled by the Powertrain Control Module (PCM). No adjustment is necessary or possible.

SPARK PLUGS

REMOVAL & INSTALLATION

3.0L (VIN U, 2) Engines

On 3.0L OHV engines, if a spark plug is removed for inspection, it must be reinstalled in the same cylinder. Cylinders 1, 2 and 3 have a PG suffix and cylinders 4, 5 and 6 have a P suffix. If a spark plug has to be replaced, use only plugs with the service part number suffix letter PP as shown on the engine decal.

1. Disconnect the negative battery cable, and if the vehicle has been run recently, allow the engine to thoroughly cool.

2. Remove the right hand side of the cowl vent screen and the right hand cowl top extension.

3. Unplug the engine control sensor wiring from the ignition coil, then unfasten the four ignition coil hold-down screws and remove the coil so that access to the spark plugs located at cylinder 1, 2 and 3 is possible.

4. Unplug the electrical connection from the Intake Manifold Runner Control (IMRC) actuator, unfasten the actuator retaining screws and lay the actuator to one side so that access to the sparks plugs at cylinders 4, 5 and 6 is possible.

5. Carefully twist the spark plug wire boot to loosen it, then pull upward and remove the boot from the plug. Be sure to pull on the boot and not on the wire, otherwise the connector located inside the boot may become separated.

6. Loosen the spark plugs ¼ turn , then using compressed air, blow any water or debris from the spark plug well to assure that no harmful contaminants are allowed to enter the combustion chamber when the spark plug is removed. If compressed air is not available, use a rag or a brush to clean the area.

➡Remove the spark plugs when the engine is cold, if possible, to prevent damage to the threads. If removal of the plugs is difficult, apply a few drops of penetrating oil or silicone spray to the area around the base of the plug, and allow it a few minutes to work.

7. Using a spark plug socket that is equipped with a rubber insert to properly hold the plug, turn the spark plug counter-clockwise to loosen and remove the spark plug from the bore.

※※ WARNING

Be sure not to use a flexible extension on the socket. Use of a flexible extension may allow a shear force to be applied to the plug. A shear force could break the plug off in the cylinder head, leading to costly and frustrating repairs.

To install:

8. Inspect the spark plug boot for tears or damage. If a damaged boot is found, the spark plug wire must be replaced.

9. Using a wire feeler gauge, check and adjust the spark plug gap. When using a gauge, the proper size should pass between the electrodes with a slight drag. The next larger size should not be able to pass while the next smaller size should pass freely.

10. Carefully thread the plug into the bore by hand. If resistance is felt before the plug is almost completely threaded, back the plug out and begin threading again. In small, hard to reach areas, an old spark plug wire and boot could be used as a threading tool. The boot will hold the plug while you twist the end of the wire and the wire is supple enough to twist before it would allow the plug to crossthread.

✳✳ WARNING

Do not use the spark plug socket to thread the plugs. Always carefully thread the plug by hand or using an old plug wire to prevent the possibility of crossthreading and damaging the cylinder head bore.

11. Carefully tighten the spark plug to 80–177 inch lbs. (9–20 Nm).

12. Apply a small amount of silicone dielectric compound to the end of the spark plug lead or inside the spark plug boot to prevent sticking, then install the boot to the spark plug and push until it clicks into place. The click may be felt or heard, then gently pull back on the boot to assure proper contact.

13. Place the IMRC actuator into position and install its retaining screws, then attach the electrical connection to the actuator.

14. Place the ignition coil in position and install its retaining screws, then attach the engine control sensor wiring to the ignition coil.

15. Install the right hand cowl top extension and the cowl vent screen.

16. Connect the negative battery cable.

3.0L (VIN S) Engine

1. Before servicing the vehicle, refer to the precautions in the beginning of this section.

2. Remove the upper intake manifold.

3. Disconnect the electrical connectors from the ignition coils.

➡ **When removing the ignition coils, a slight twisting motion will break the seal and ease removal.**

4. Remove the bolts and the ignition coils.

✳✳ CAUTION

Only use hand tools when removing or installing the spark plugs, or damage can occur to the cylinder head or spark plug.

➡ **Use compressed air to remove any debris from the spark plug well before removing the spark plugs.**

5. Remove the LH and RH spark plugs.

6. To install, reverse the removal procedure. Tighten the spark plugs to 11 ft. lbs. (15 Nm).

➡ **Apply a light film of Silicone Brake Caliper Grease and Dielectric compound D7AZ-19A331-A or equivalent meeting Ford specifications ESE-M1C171-A to the inside of the coil boots before installation.**

ENGINE ELECTRICAL

STARTER

REMOVAL & INSTALLATION

See Figures 26 through 28.

1. Before servicing the vehicle, refer to the precautions section.

2. Remove or disconnect the following:

- Negative battery cable
- Splash shield
- Starter electrical connectors
- Starter

To install:

3. Install or connect the following:
- Starter and tighten the bolts to 18 ft. lbs. (25 Nm)

STARTING SYSTEM

- Starter electrical connectors and tighten the battery cable nut to 80–123 inch lbs. (9–14 Nm)
- Splash shield
- Negative battery cable

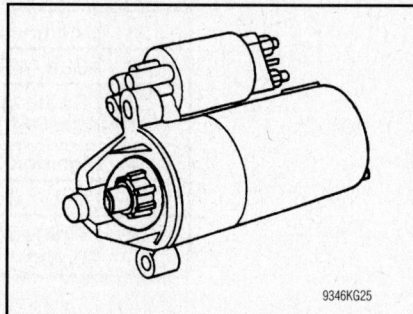

Fig. 27 Starter motor—3.0L (VIN U, 2) Engines

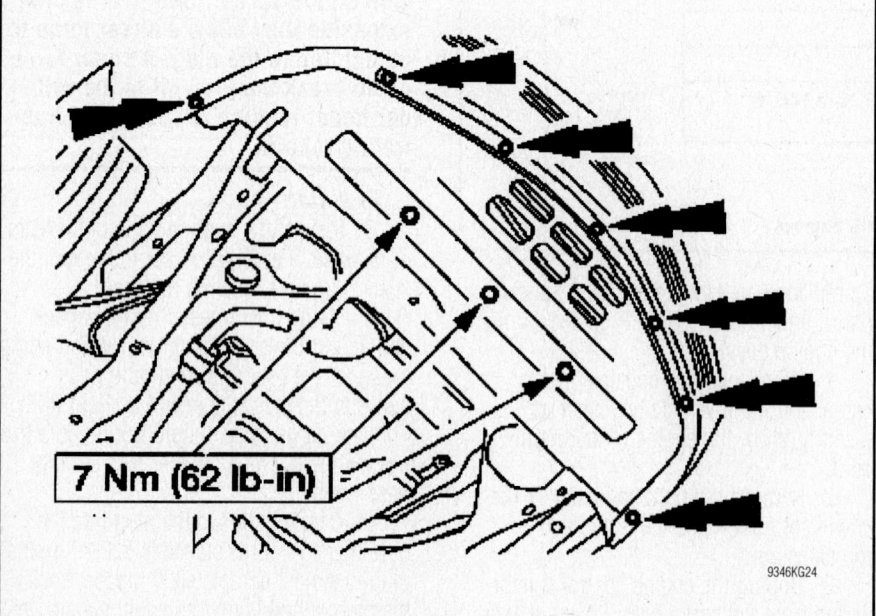

7 Nm (62 lb-in)

Fig. 26 Remove the front splash shield for access

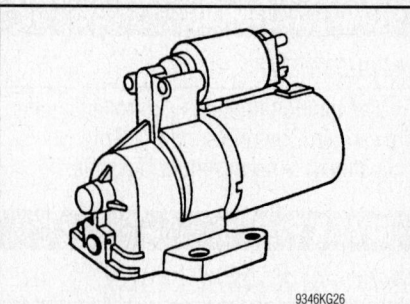

Fig. 28 Starter motor—3.0L (VIN S) Engine

ENGINE MECHANICAL

➠Disconnecting the negative battery cable may interfere with the functions of the on board computer systems and may require the computer to undergo a relearning process, once the negative battery cable is reconnected.

ACCESSORY DRIVE BELTS

ACCESSORY BELT ROUTING

See Figures 29 and 30.

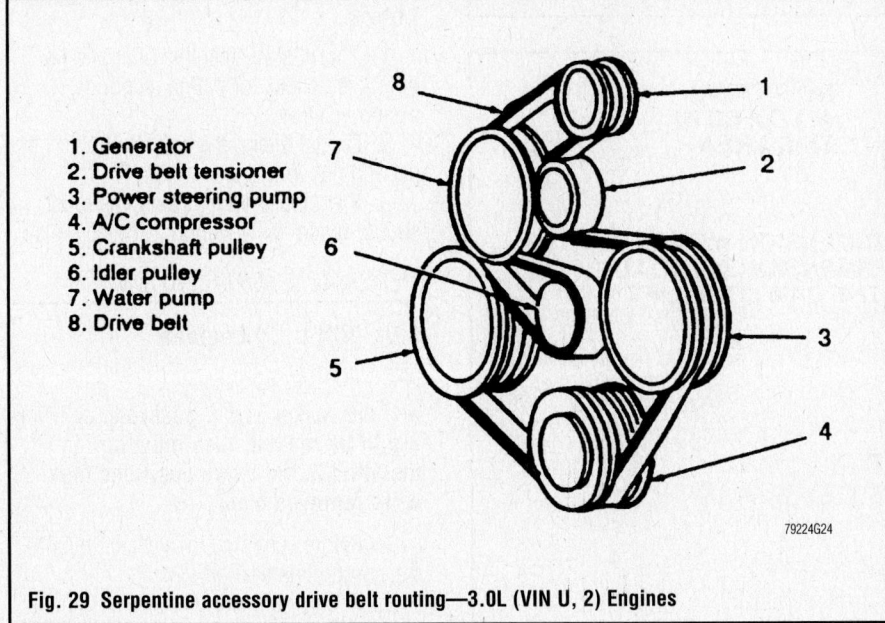

1. Generator
2. Drive belt tensioner
3. Power steering pump
4. A/C compressor
5. Crankshaft pulley
6. Idler pulley
7. Water pump
8. Drive belt

79224G24

Fig. 29 Serpentine accessory drive belt routing—3.0L (VIN U, 2) Engines

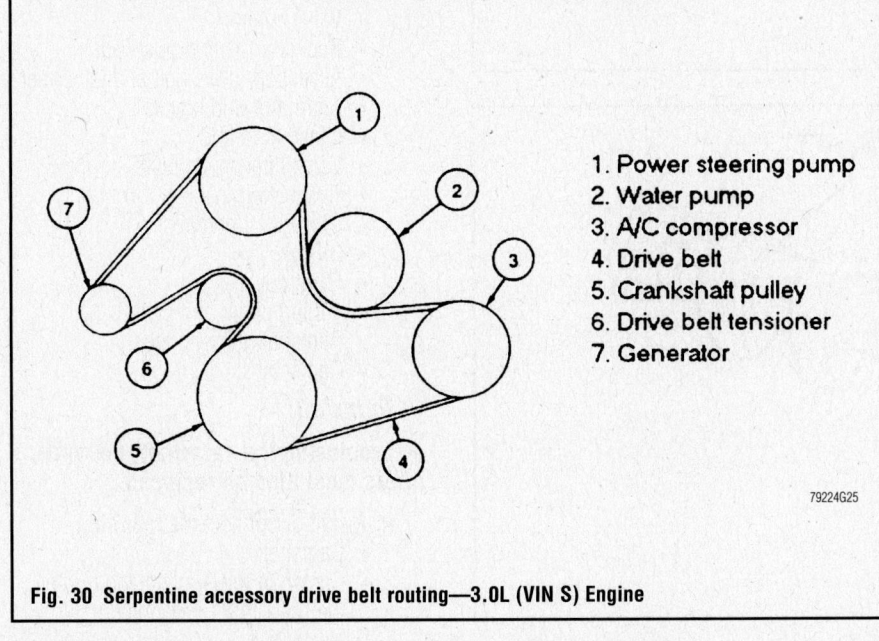

1. Power steering pump
2. Water pump
3. A/C compressor
4. Drive belt
5. Crankshaft pulley
6. Drive belt tensioner
7. Generator

79224G25

Fig. 30 Serpentine accessory drive belt routing—3.0L (VIN S) Engine

INSPECTION

Inspect the drive belt for signs of glazing or cracking. A glazed belt will be perfectly smooth from slippage, while a good belt will have a slight texture of fabric visible. Cracks will usually start at the inner edge of the belt and run outward. All worn or damaged drive belts should be replaced immediately.

ADJUSTMENT

The drive belt tension is maintained by an automatic belt tensioner and does not require adjustment.

REMOVAL & INSTALLATION

➠When installing the drive belt on the pulleys, make sure all the V-grooves make proper contact with the pulleys.

✷✷ WARNING

Use caution when removing or installing the belt and make sure the tool does not slip from the drive belt tensioner or personal injury or damage to the belt tensioner and the belt may occur.

1. Attach a 15mm socket or wrench to the bolt attaching the tensioner pulley.
2. On all 3.0L (OHV) engines, rotate the drive belt tensioner clockwise to relieve belt tension and slide the belt off the pulleys.
3. On 3.0L (DOHC) engines, rotate the tensioner counterclockwise to relieve belt tension and slide the belt off the pulleys.

To install:

4. Install the drive belt on all the pulleys except the tensioner pulley.
5. Rotate the belt tensioner as outlined in the removal procedure to relieve belt tension and install the belt onto the tensioner pulley. Make sure the V-grooves make proper contact with the pulleys. Make sure the spring keeper releases or improper belt tension will occur.

CAMSHAFT AND VALVE LIFTERS

INSPECTION

Camshaft

See Figures 31, 32 and 33.

Degrease the camshaft using safe solvent, clean all oil grooves. Visually inspect the cam lobes and bearing journals for excessive wear. If a lobe is questionable, check all lobes and journals with a micrometer.

Measure the lobes from nose to base and again at 90°. The lift is determined by subtracting the second measurement from the first. If all exhaust lobes and all intake lobes are not identical, the camshaft must be reground or replaced. Measure the bearing journals and compare to the specifications. If a journal is worn there is a good chance that the cam bearings are worn too, requiring replacement.

If the lobes and journals appear intact, place the front and rear camshaft journals in V-blocks and rest a dial indicator on the

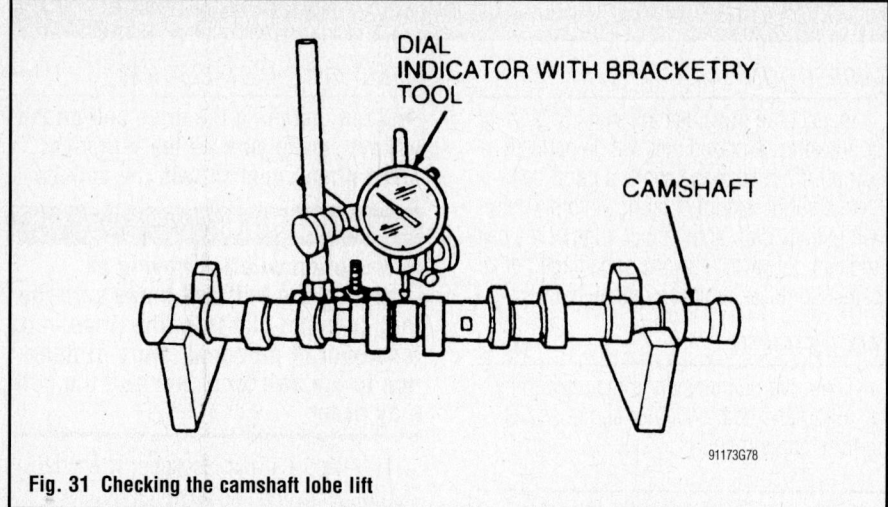

Fig. 31 Checking the camshaft lobe lift

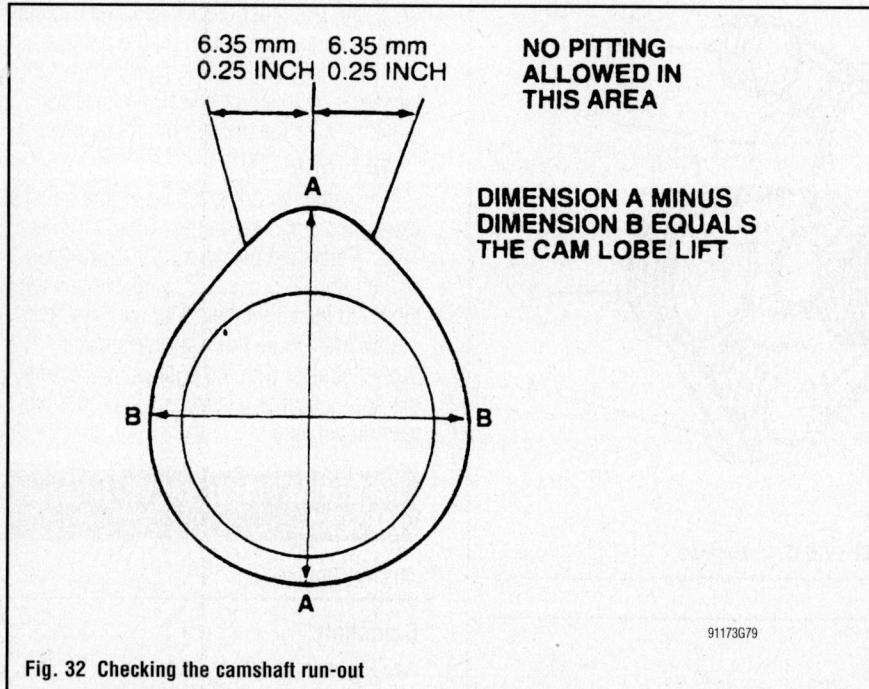

6.35 mm 6.35 mm
0.25 INCH 0.25 INCH

NO PITTING ALLOWED IN THIS AREA

DIMENSION A MINUS DIMENSION B EQUALS THE CAM LOBE LIFT

Fig. 32 Checking the camshaft run-out

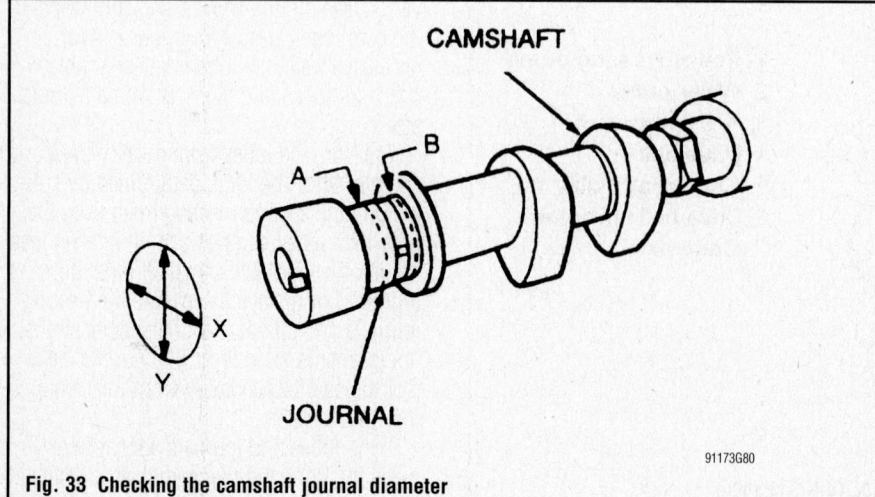

Fig. 33 Checking the camshaft journal diameter

center journal. Rotate the camshaft to check for run-out, if deviation exceeds specification, replace the camshaft.

Measure the camshaft journal diameter at the points shown in the accompanying illustration. If the If the diameters do not conform to specifications, replace the camshaft.

Bearings and Journals

Check the camshaft bores for size, taper, roundness, alignment and finish. If any of these exceed the specifications given in the engine rebuilding chart at the end of this section, install new bearings or cylinder heads.

Lifters

1. Thoroughly clean the lifter and its bore, then check for pitting, scoring or excessive wear.
2. On flat lifters, the bottom should be flat and not concave.
3. If equipped with a roller, the roller should rotate freely without excessive play.

REMOVAL & INSTALLATION

3.0L (VIN U, 2) Engines

See Figure 34.

➡ **If the rocker arms, pushrods or lifters are to be reused, they must be installed in the same positions they were removed from.**

1. Before servicing the vehicle, refer to the precautions section.
2. Remove the engine from the vehicle and mount it on an engine stand.
3. Remove or disconnect the following:
   • Valve covers
   • Rocker arms and pushrods
   • Accessory drive belt and tensioner
   • Alternator and brackets
   • Intake manifold
   • Valve lifter guide plate
   • Valve lifters
   • Crankshaft damper
   • Oil pan
   • Front cover
   • Timing chain and gears
   • Camshaft thrust plate
   • Camshaft

To install:

➡ **If replacing the camshaft, the valve lifters must also be replaced.**

4. Install or connect the following:
   • Camshaft
   • Camshaft thrust plate and tighten the bolts to 84 inch lbs. (10 Nm)

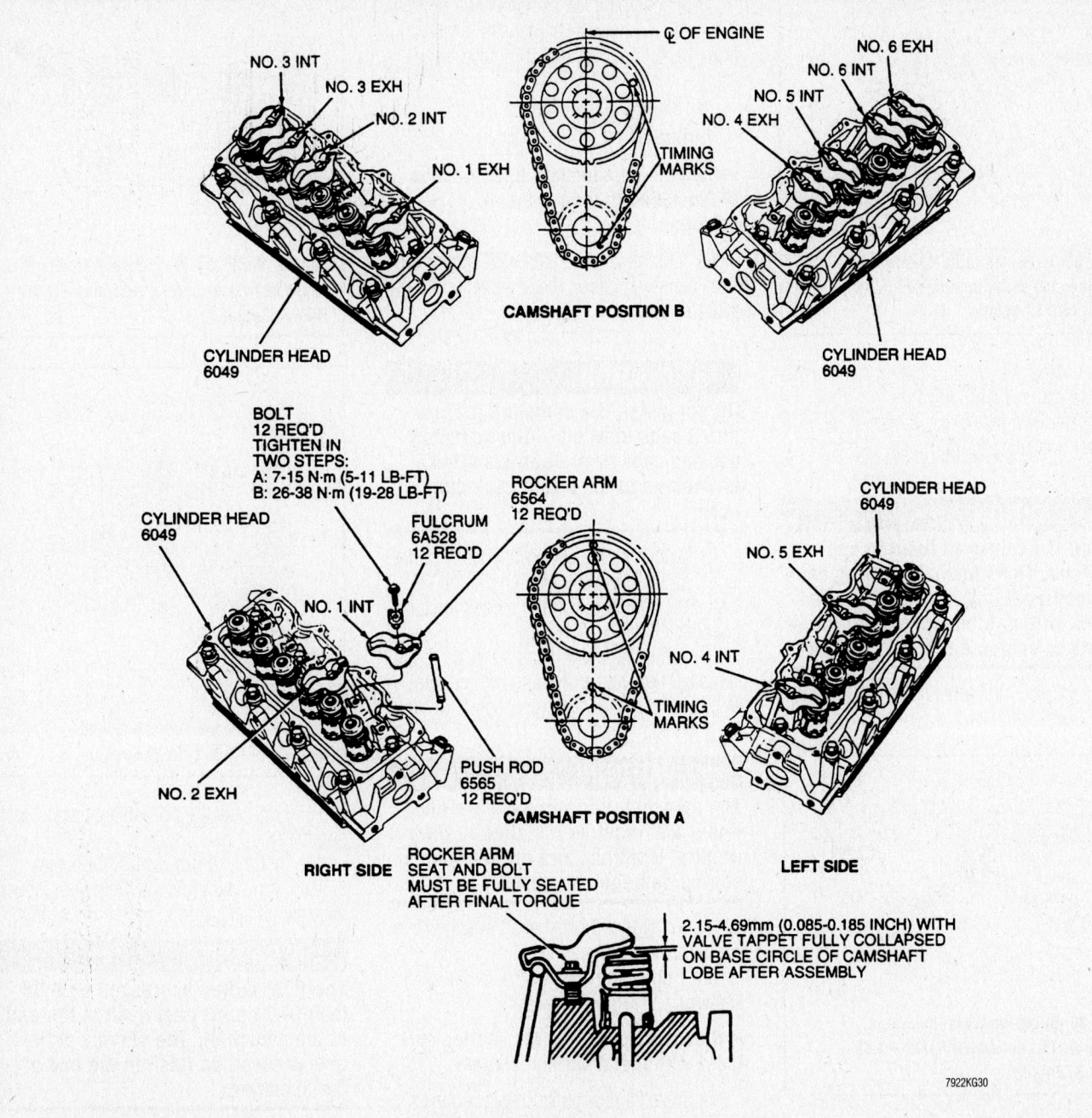

Fig. 34 Tighten the rocker arm nuts according to the position of the camshaft—3.0L (VIN U, 2) Engines

- Timing chain and gears. Align the timing marks on the sprockets.
- Front cover
- Oil pan
- Crankshaft damper
- Valve lifters
- Valve lifter guide plate
- Intake manifold
- Alternator and brackets
- Accessory drive belt and tensioner
- Rocker arms and pushrods
- Valve covers

5. Install the engine assembly into the vehicle.

6. Start the engine and check for leaks and proper engine operation.

3.0L (VIN S) Engine

Left Side

See Figures 35 through 42.

1. Before servicing the vehicle, refer to the precautions section.

2. Remove the timing drive components.

3. Remove the water pump belt.

> ※ **CAUTION**
>
> The OEM pulley is pressed on 0.18 inch (4.74 mm) past flush of the camshaft. The service pulley gets pressed on flush to the end of the camshaft.

4. Using the tools illustrated, remove the water pump drive pulley and discard.

> ※ **CAUTION**
>
> In order to make sure of correct sealing, do not scratch the camshaft.

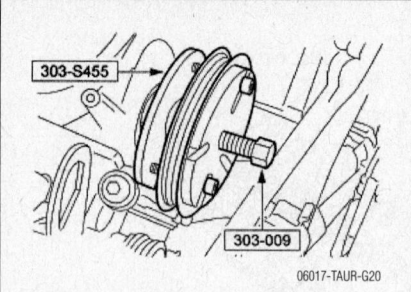

Fig. 35 Using the tools illustrated, remove the water pump drive pulley— 3.0L (VIN S) Engine

5. Using the tool illustrated, remove the camshaft oil seal and discard.

6. Remove the intake camshaft oil seal retainer and discard the press-in-place gasket.

❋❋ CAUTION

Record the camshaft bearing cap locations. The camshaft bearing caps are positional and must be installed in their original locations and orientations or engine damage can occur.

7. Loosen the bolts for the left camshaft thrust caps.

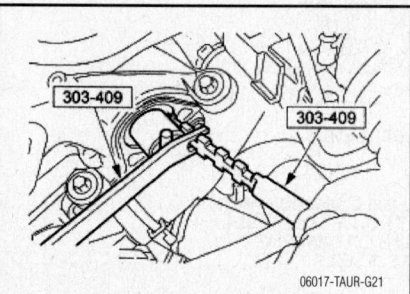

Fig. 36 Using the tools illustrated, remove the camshaft oil seal—3.0L (VIN S) Engine

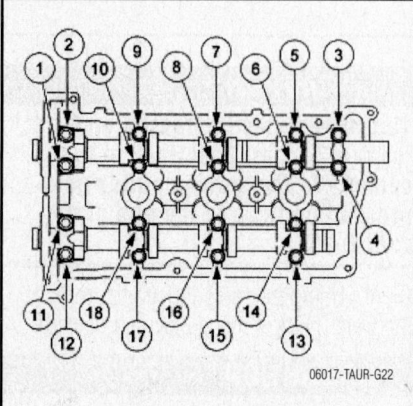

Fig. 37 Left camshaft cap loosening sequence—3.0L (VIN S) Engine

8. Loosen the left camshaft cap bolts in sequence to allow the camshafts to rise from the cylinder head and remove the caps.

9. Remove the camshafts.

To install:

➡ **Be sure the camshaft bearing caps are installed in their original positions.**

10. Lubricate camshafts with engine oil and carefully position the camshafts into the cylinder head.

11. Align the camshafts as illustrated

❋❋ CAUTION

Do not install the camshaft journal thrust caps until all of the camshaft bearing caps have been installed, or damage to the thrust caps can occur.

12. Lubricate the bearing surfaces of the camshaft bearing caps with engine oil. Install the bearing caps and loosely install the bolts.

13. Lubricate the bearing surfaces of the camshaft bearing thrust caps with engine oil. Install the bearing thrust caps and loosely install the bolts.

❋❋ CAUTION

The camshaft bearing caps are positional and must be installed in their original locations and orientations or engine damage can occur.

14. Verify that the camshaft bearing caps are in the correct locations.

15. Tighten the bolts in the sequence shown.

➡ **Clean and degrease the sealing surfaces with metal surface cleaner.**

16. Install a new press-in-place gasket and install the camshaft oil seal retainer. Tighten to 89 inch lbs. (10 Nm).

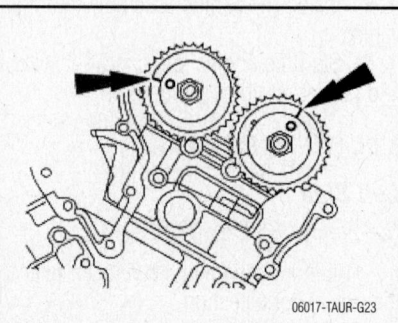

Fig. 38 Left camshaft alignment—3.0L (VIN S) Engine

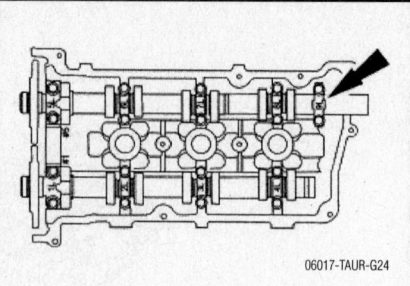

Fig. 39 Verify the left camshaft bearing caps are in their correct locations—3.0L (VIN S) Engine

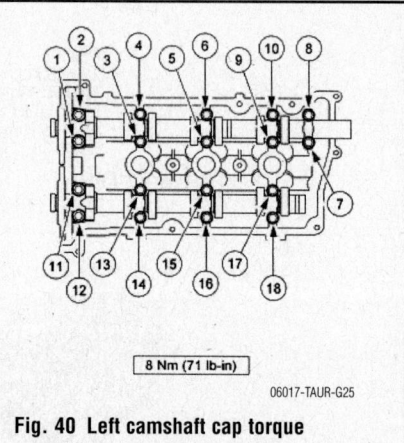

8 Nm (71 lb-in)

Fig. 40 Left camshaft cap torque sequence—3.0L (VIN S) Engine

17. Lubricate the camshaft oil seal with engine oil.

18. Install the new camshaft oil seal.

19. Using the tools illustrated positioned over the oil seal, turn to install the seal.

❋❋ CAUTION

The OEM pulley is pressed on 0.18 inch (4.74 mm) past flush of the end of the camshaft. The service pulley gets pressed on flush to the end of the camshaft.

20. Using the tool illustrated, install the water pump drive pulley.

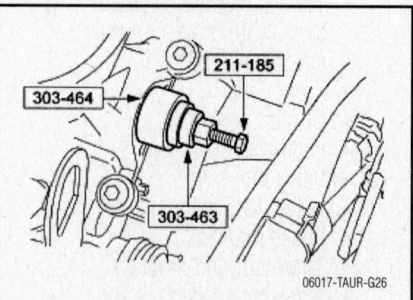

Fig. 41 Using the tools illustrated positioned over the oil seal, turn to install the seal—3.0L (VIN S) Engine

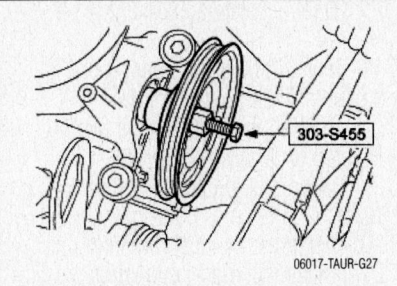

Fig. 42 Using the tools illustrated, install the water pump drive pulley—3.0L (VIN S) Engine

21. Install the water pump belt.
22. Install the timing drive components.

Right Side

See Figures 43 through 45.

1. Before servicing the vehicle, refer to the precautions section.
2. Remove the timing drive components.

> **❊❊ CAUTION**
>
> **Record the camshaft bearing cap location. The camshaft bearing caps are positional and must be installed in their original locations and orientations or engine damage can occur.**

3. Loosen the right hand camshaft thrust cap bolts.
4. Loosen the right hand camshaft cap bolts in sequence to allow the camshafts to rise from the cylinder head and remove the caps.
5. Remove the camshafts.

To install:

➥ **Be sure the camshaft bearing caps are installed in their original positions.**

6. Lubricate camshafts with engine oil and carefully position the camshafts into the cylinder head.
7. Align the camshafts as illustrated

> **❊❊ CAUTION**
>
> **Do not install the camshaft journal thrust caps until all of the camshaft bearing caps have been installed, or damage to the thrust caps can occur.**

8. Lubricate the bearing surfaces of the camshaft bearing caps with engine oil. Install the bearing caps and loosely install the bolts.
9. Lubricate the bearing surfaces of the camshaft bearing thrust caps with engine

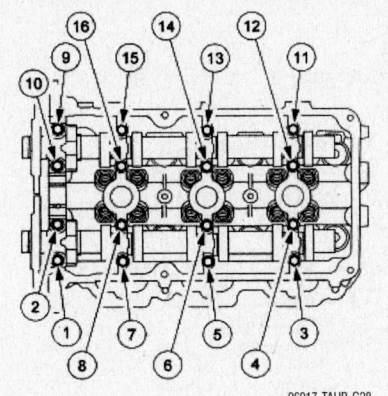

Fig. 43 Right camshaft cap loosening sequence—3.0L (VIN S) Engine

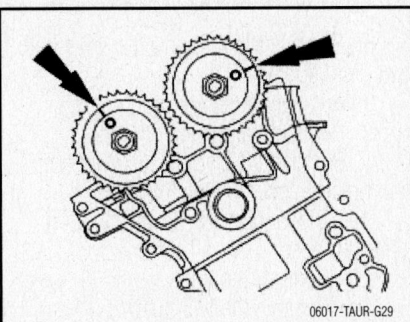

Fig. 44 Right camshaft alignment—3.0L (VIN S) Engine

oil. Install the bearing thrust caps and loosely install the bolts.

> **❊❊ CAUTION**
>
> **The camshaft bearing caps are positional and must be installed in their original locations and orientations or engine damage can occur.**

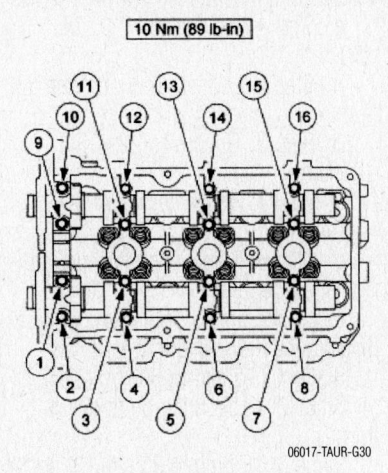

Fig. 45 Right camshaft cap torque sequence—3.0L (VIN S) Engine

10. Verify that the camshaft bearing caps are in the correct locations.
11. Tighten the right camshaft bolts in the sequence shown to 89 inch lbs. (10 Nm).
12. Install the timing drive components

CYLINDER HEAD

REMOVAL & INSTALLATION

3.0L (VIN U, 2) Engines

Right Side

1. Before servicing the vehicle, refer to the precautions section.
2. Remove the lower intake manifold.
3. Disconnect the Crankshaft Position (CKP) sensor connector.
4. Disconnect the Heated Oxygen Sensor (HO$_2$S) connector.
5. Remove the nut and disconnect the wiring harness ground connections.
6. Loosen the bolt and disconnect the Powertrain Control Module (PCM) electrical connector.
7. Disconnect the Evaporative Emissions (EVAP) canister purge valve electrical connector.
8. Disconnect the spark plug wires and position the wires aside.
9. Loosen the nut and disconnect the Exhaust Gas Recirculation (EGR) tube.
10. Remove the three bolts and the exhaust manifold heat shield.
11. Loosen the exhaust manifold-to-catalytic converter bolts.
12. Remove the six exhaust manifold-to-cylinder head bolts.
13. Disconnect the engine wire harness locator.
14. Remove the bolt and separate the catalytic converter heat shield from the cylinder head.
15. Remove the eight cylinder head bolts.
16. Remove the cylinder head.
17. Remove and discard the head gasket.

To install:

18. Using metal surface cleaner, clean the cylinder head sealing surfaces.

➥ **The "V" notch in the cylinder head gasket faces the front of the engine.**

19. Install a new cylinder head gasket.
20. Install the cylinder head.
21. Install the bolts. Tighten the bolts in five steps in the sequence shown.
　a. Step 1: Tighten to 37 ft. lbs. (50 Nm).
　b. Step 2: Loosen the bolts one full turn.

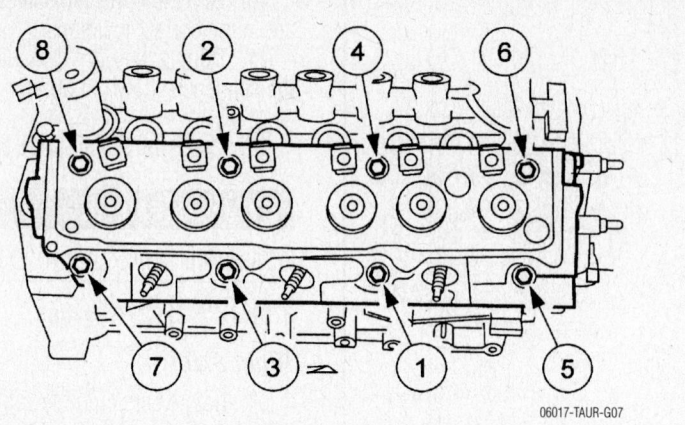

Fig. 46 Cylinder head torque sequence, right side show, left side similar—3.0L (VIN U, 2) models

c. Step 3: Tighten to 22 ft. lbs (30 Nm).

d. Step 4: Rotate each bolt 90 degrees.

e. Step 5: Rotate each bolt an additional 90 degrees.

22. Install the catalytic converter heat shield and wire harness ground connection.

23. Position the wiring harness and install the harness locator.

24. Install the exhaust manifold.

25. Tighten the exhaust manifold-to-catalytic converter bolts to 30 ft. lbs. (40 Nm).

26. Install the exhaust manifold heat shield.

27. Install the EGR tube and tighten to 37 ft. lbs. (50 Nm).

28. Connect the spark plug wires.

29. Connect the EVAP canister purge valve electrical connector.

30. Connect the PCM electrical connector.

31. Connect the wire harness ground connections.

32. Connect the HO2S sensor electrical connector.

33. Connect the CKP electrical connector.

34. Install the lower intake manifold.

Left Side

1. Before servicing the vehicle, refer to the precautions section.

2. Remove the lower intake manifold.

3. Remove the accessory drive belt.

4. Remove the retainers and the engine anti-roll strut brace.

5. Disconnect the alternator electrical connections.

6. Remove the retainers and the alternator.

7. Remove the bolt and the drive belt idler pulley.

8. Remove the bolt and the drive belt tensioner pulley.

9. Remove the spark plug wires.

10. Remove the exhaust manifold.

11. Remove the power steering pump and bracket assembly as follows:.

a. Disconnect the power steering return hose.

b. Remove the bolt.

c. Remove the two nuts.

12. Remove the eight cylinder head bolts.

13. Remove the cylinder heads.

14. Remove and discard the head gasket.

To install:

15. Using metal surface cleaner, clean the cylinder head sealing surfaces.

➡**The "V" notch in the cylinder head gasket faces the front of the engine.**

16. Install a new cylinder head gasket.

17. Install the cylinder head.

18. Install the bolts. Tighten the bolts in five steps in the sequence shown.

a. Step 1: Tighten to 37 ft. lbs. (50 Nm).

b. Step 2: Loosen the bolts one full turn.

c. Step 3: Tighten to 22 ft. lbs (30 Nm).

d. Step 4: Rotate each bolt 90 degrees.

e. Step 5: Rotate each bolt an additional 90 degrees.

Install the bolts. Tighten the bolts in five stages in the sequence shown.

Stage 1: Tighten to 50 Nm (37 lb-ft).

Stage 2: Loosen the bolts one full turn.

Stage 3: Tighten to 30 Nm (22 lb-ft).

Stage 4: Rotate an additional 90 degrees.

Stage 5: Rotate an additional 90 degrees.

19. Install the power steering pump and bracket assembly as follows:

a. Install the bolt and the two nuts. Tighten to 35 ft. lbs. (48 Nm).

b. Connect the power steering return hose.

20. Install the exhaust manifold.

21. Install the spark plug wires.

22. Install the drive belt tensioner and bolt. Tighten to 35 ft. lbs. (48 Nm).

23. Install the drive belt idler pulley and bolt. Tighten to 35 ft. lbs. (48 Nm).

24. Install the alternator and the retainers.

25. Connect the alternator electrical connections.

26. Install the engine anti-roll strut brace and the retainers. Tighten to 35 ft. lbs. (48 Nm).

27. Install the accessory drive belt.

28. Install the lower intake manifold.

3.0L (VIN S) Engine

Left Side

1. Before servicing the vehicle, refer to the precautions section.

2. Release the fuel system pressure.

3. Drain and recycle the engine coolant.

4. Remove the water pump bypass tube.

5. Remove the exhaust manifold-to-pipe nuts.

6. Remove the water pump.

7. Remove the lower intake manifold.

8. Remove the camshafts.

9. Install and engine support tool and lower the engine until it is aligned with the A/C compressor bracket, and finger-tighten the four bolts.

10. Remove the engine support tool.

11. Remove the camshaft followers.

12. Remove the hydraulic lash adjusters.

13. Remove the nuts and remove the exhaust manifold and discard the gasket.

14. Remove the dipstick tube.

15. Inspect and, if necessary, install a new O-ring seal.

16. Remove the left hand cylinder block drain plug.

➡**New cylinder head bolts must be installed. They are torque-to-yield designed and cannot be reused.**

17. Remove the bolts in the sequence shown and remove the cylinder head.

18. Discard the gasket and the bolts.

To install:

19. Position the cylinder head, gasket and install the bolts in the sequence shown in six steps:

a. Step 1: Tighten to 30 ft. lbs. (40 Nm).

b. Step 2: Tighten bolts 90 degrees.

c. Step 3: Loosen one full turn.

d. Step 4: Tighten to 30 ft. lbs. (40 Nm).

e. Step 5: Tighten 90 degrees.

f. Step 6: Tighten 90 degrees.

20. Install the cylinder block drain plug and tighten to 49 ft. lbs. (67 Nm).

➡**Lubricate the oil dipstick tube O-ring with clean engine oil.**

21. Install the oil dipstick tube and the nut.

22. Position a new gasket and install the exhaust manifold nuts.

23. Install the hydraulic lash adjusters. Lubricate the hydraulic lash adjusters with clean engine oil prior to installation.

24. Install the camshaft followers. Lubricate the camshaft followers with clean engine oil prior to installation

25. Install the engine support tool.

26. Remove the four A/C compressor bracket bolts.

27. Using the engine support tool, raise the engine away from the A/C compressor bracket.

28. Install the camshafts.

29. Install the lower intake manifold.

30. Install the water pump.

31. Install the exhaust manifold-to-pipe nuts.

32. Install the water pump bypass tube.

33. Run the engine and check for leaks.

Right Side

1. Before servicing the vehicle, refer to the precautions section.

2. Release the fuel system pressure.

3. Remove the water pump bypass tube.

4. Remove the rear support brace.

5. Remove the lower intake manifold.

6. Remove the camshafts.

7. Install and engine support tool and lower the engine until it is aligned with the A/C compressor bracket, and finger-tighten the four bolts.

8. Remove the engine support tool.

9. Remove the exhaust manifold-to-pipe bolts.

10. Disconnect the Exhaust Gas Recirculation (EGR) tube from the exhaust manifold.

11. Remove the bolt and the ground wire.

12. Remove the camshaft followers.

13. Remove the hydraulic lash adjusters.

14. Remove the nuts and remove the exhaust manifold and discard the gasket.

15. Remove the right hand cylinder block drain plug.

➡**New cylinder head bolts must be installed. They are torque-to-yield designed and cannot be reused.**

16. Remove the bolts in the sequence shown and remove the cylinder head.

17. Discard the gasket and the bolts.

To install:

18. Position the cylinder head, gasket and install the bolts in the sequence shown in six steps:

Tighten the bolts in six Steps.

g. Step 1: Tighten to 30 ft. lbs. (40 Nm).

h. Step 2: Tighten bolts 90 degrees.

i. Step 3: Loosen one full turn.

j. Step 4: Tighten to 30 ft. lbs. (40 Nm).

k. Step 5: Tighten 90 degrees.

l. Step 6: Tighten 90 degrees.

19. Install the cylinder block drain plug and tighten to 49 ft. lbs. (67 Nm).

20. Position a new gasket and install the exhaust manifold nuts.

21. Install the hydraulic lash adjusters. Lubricate the hydraulic lash adjusters with clean engine oil prior to installation.

22. Install the camshaft followers. Lubricate the camshaft followers with clean engine oil prior to installation.

23. Install the ground wire and bolt.

24. Connect the EGR tube to the exhaust manifold. Tighten to 30 ft. lbs. (40 Nm).

25. Install the exhaust manifold-to-pipe bolts. Tighten to 30 ft. lbs. (40 Nm).

26. Install the engine support tool.

27. Remove the four A/C compressor bracket bolts.

28. Using the engine support tool, raise the engine away from the A/C compressor bracket.

29. Install the camshafts.

30. Install the lower intake manifold.

31. Install the rear support brace. Tighten to 35 ft. lbs. (47 Nm).

32. Install the water pump bypass tube.

33. Run the engine and check for leaks.

ENGINE ASSEMBLY

REMOVAL & INSTALLATION

3.0L (VIN U, 2) Engines

See Figures 47 through 49.

1. Before servicing the vehicle, refer to the precautions section.

2. Disconnect the negative battery cable.

3. Drain the engine oil.

4. Drain the cooling system.

5. Recover the A/C refrigerant.

6. Remove the battery.

7. Remove the cowl vent screen and cowl extension.

8. Remove the halfshafts.

9. Remove the nuts and position the steering column input shaft coupling boot aside.

10. Remove the pinch bolt and slide the coupling off the steering gear input shaft.

11. Disconnect the tubes, loosen the clamps and remove the air cleaner outlet pipe.

12. Remove the pin-type retainers and the snow shield.

13. Disconnect the accelerator cable, speed control actuator cable and the throttle return spring from the throttle body.

14. Remove the bolts and position the accelerator cable bracket aside.

15. Disconnect the vacuum hose and the Evaporative Emissions (EVAP) return tube.

16. Remove the nut and disconnect the manual control lever cable.

17. Disconnect the manual control lever cable from the bracket and position aside.

18. Loosen the bolt and disconnect the 42-pin and Transmission Range (TR) sensor electrical connectors.

19. Disconnect the upper radiator hose and the heater hose from the thermostat housing.

20. Remove the nut and disconnect the ground strap electrical connector.

21. Disconnect the power steering return hose.

22. Disconnect the alternator electrical connectors and position the wire harness aside.

23. Disconnect the A/C suction tube from the accumulator drier.

24. Disconnect the fuel supply hose.

25. Disconnect the degas bottle hoses.

26. Remove the nut, the bolt and the engine roll restrictor brace.

27. Remove the bolts and the engine roll restrictor.

28. Disconnect the heater hose.

29. Remove the bolt and disconnect the ground electrical connectors.

30. Disconnect the EVAP canister purge valve electrical connector.

31. Loosen the bolt disconnect the Powertrain Control Module (PCM) electrical connector.

➡**Support the exhaust with mechanic's wire.**

32. Remove the nuts and disconnect the three-way catalytic converter from the dual converter Y-pipe.

33. Remove the nuts and the muffler clamp.

34. Separate and remove the three-way catalytic converter from the muffler pipe.

35. Remove the nut and disconnect the A/C discharge tube.

36. Remove the radiator support bracket.

37. Disconnect the lower radiator hose from the radiator and degas bottle supply hose.

38. Disconnect the transmission oil cooler hose.

39. If equipped, disconnect the wire harness electrical connector.

40. Disconnect the auxiliary oil cooler assembly.

41. Disconnect the transmission oil cooler hose, if equipped.

42. Disconnect the power steering return hose.

43. Remove the oil pan drain plug and drain the engine oil. Install the drain plug when finished and torque to 10 ft. lbs. (13 Nm).

44. Remove the starter motor.

45. Remove the bolt and the engine inspection cover.

46. Remove the four torque converter nuts.

47. Remove the nuts and disconnect both stabilizer links from the stabilizer bar.

48. Remove the nuts and separate both tie-rod ends from the steering knuckles.

49. Position engine dolly/support tool 014-00765.

50. Remove the four front subframe-to-body bolts.

51. Using the engine dolly/support tool 014-00765, lower the powertrain and sub-frame assembly out of the vehicle.

52. Remove the nut and detach the Power Steering Pressure (PSP) line bracket.

53. Remove the nut and detach the PSP line bracket.

54. Disconnect the PSP line from the power steering pump.

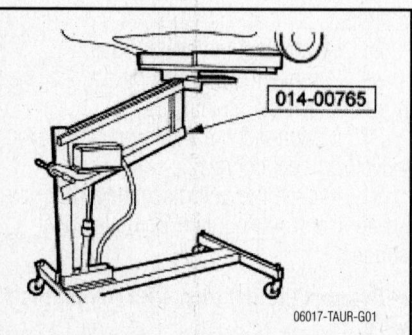

Fig. 47 Position engine dolly/support tool 014-00765—3.0L (VIN U, 2) models

55. Disconnect the spark plug wires.

56. Disconnect the ignition coil electrical connector.

57. Disconnect the Output Shaft Speed (OSS) sensor electrical connector and position the wire harness aside.

58. Disconnect the Turbine Shaft Speed (TSS) sensor electrical connector.

59. Disconnect the transaxle harness electrical connector and position the wire harness aside.

60. Remove the bolt, the nuts and the right hand catalytic converter heat shield.

61. Install lifting eye tool 303-D030 to the left and right side of the engine.

62. Attach a hoist to the lifting hooks and support the engine.

63. Remove the two right hand engine support insulator-to-transmission bolts.

64. Remove the left hand engine support insulator-to-subframe nut.

65. Remove the right hand engine support insulator through bolt.

66. Disconnect the catalyst monitor sensor electrical connector.

67. Remove the bolts and the Y-pipe.

68. Disconnect the lower radiator hose from the coolant pump.

69. Remove the five transmission-to-engine bolts and one stud bolt.

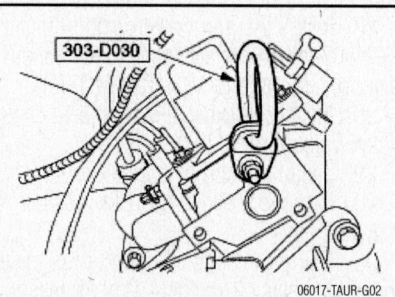

Fig. 48 Install lifting eye tool 303-D030 to the right side of the engine—3.0L (VIN U, 2) models

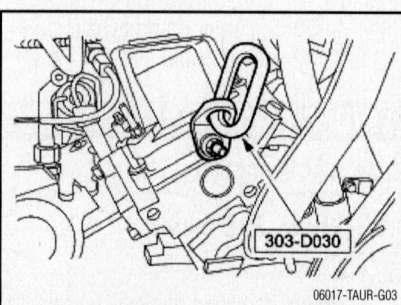

Fig. 49 Install lifting eye tool 303-D030 to the left side of the engine—3.0L (VIN U, 2) models

70. Separate the engine from the transmission.

To install:

71. Position the engine on the subframe and transmission assembly.

72. Install the transmission-to-engine bolts and tighten to 37 ft. lbs. (50 Nm).

73. Connect the lower radiator hose to the coolant pump.

74. Install the right hand engine support insulator through bolt and tighten to 89 ft. lbs. (120 Nm).

75. Install the dual converter Y-pipe and the bolts and tighten to 30 ft. lbs. (40 Nm).

76. Connect the catalyst monitor sensor electrical connector.

77. Install the left hand engine support insulator-to-subframe nut and tighten to 66 ft. lbs. (90 Nm).

78. Install the two right hand engine support insulator-to-transmission bolts and tighten to 44 ft. lbs. (60 Nm).

79. Using the lifting eyes, secure the engine to the hoist.

80. Install the right hand catalytic converter heat shield and install the two nuts.

81. Position the ground strap and install the bolt and tighten to 15 ft. lbs. (20 Nm).

82. Position the 42-pin connector on the bracket and connect the transaxle harness electrical connector.

83. Connect the TSS sensor electrical connector.

84. Connect the OSS electrical connector.

85. Install the ignition coil and the bolts.

86. Connect the ignition coil electrical connector.

87. Connect the spark plug wires to the ignition coil.

88. Connect the PSP tube to the power steering pump and tighten to 35 ft. lbs. (48 Nm).

89. Install the PSP tube bracket and the nut and tighten to 20 ft. lbs. (27 Nm).

90. Using the dolly/support tool, raise the engine, transmission and subframe into the vehicle.

91. Install the four front subframe-to-body bolts and tighten to 76 ft. lbs. (103 Nm).

92. Connect the tie-rod ends to the steering knuckles. Install the nuts and tighten to 41 ft. lbs. (55 Nm) and install new cotter pins.

93. Connect the stabilizer links to the stabilizer bar and tighten to 41 ft. lbs. (55 Nm).

94. Install the four torque converter nuts and tighten to 27 ft. lbs. (36 Nm).

95. Install the engine rear plate.

96. Install the starter motor.

97. Connect the auxiliary oil cooler assembly.

98. If equipped, connect the transmission oil cooler hose.

99. Connect the power steering return hose.

100. If equipped, connect the wiring harness electrical connector.

101. Connect the transmission oil cooler hose.

102. Connect the lower radiator hose to the radiator and the degas bottle supply hose.

103. Install the radiator support bracket.

→**Replace and lubricate the O-ring with PAG oil.**

104. Connect the A/C discharge tube and tighten to 89 inch lbs. (10 Nm).

105. Install a new gasket into the Y-pipe flange.

106. Connect the three-way converter to the dual converter Y-pipe and the muffler pipe and install the nuts and tighten to 30 ft. lbs. (40 Nm).

107. Install the exhaust clamp and tighten to 30 ft. lbs. (40 Nm).

108. Connect the PCM electrical connector.

109. Connect the EVAP canister purge valve electrical connector.

110. Connect the ground electrical connectors and install the bolt and tighten to 89 inch lbs. (10 Nm).

111. Connect the heater water hose.

112. Install the engine roll restrictor and the bolts and tighten to 35 ft. lbs. (48 Nm).

113. Install the engine roll restrictor brace and the nut and bolt and tighten to 35 ft. lbs. (48 Nm).

114. Connect the hoses to the degas bottle.

115. Connect the fuel tube spring lock coupling.

116. Connect the A/C suction tube to the accumulator drier.

117. Connect the alternator electrical connections.

118. Connect the power steering return hose.

119. Connect the ground strap electrical connector. and tighten to 18 ft. lbs. (25 Nm).

120. Connect the upper radiator hose and heater hose to the thermostat housing.

121. Connect the TR sensor and the 42-pin electrical connectors.

122. Install the manual control lever cable in the bracket.

123. Connect the manual control lever cable to the manual control lever and install the nut and tighten to 13 ft. lbs. (17 Nm).

124. Connect the vacuum hose and the EVAP return tube.

125. Position the accelerator cable and bracket and install the bolts and tighten to 13 ft. lbs. (17 Nm).

126. Connect the accelerator cable, speed control cable and throttle return spring.

127. Install the snow shield.

128. Position the air cleaner outlet pipe, connect the tubes and tighten the clamps.

129. Connect the steering column to the steering gear input shaft and install the bolt and tighten to 18 ft. lbs. (25 Nm).

130. Position the steering column input shaft coupling boot and install the nuts.

131. Install the halfshafts.

132. Install the cowl extension and cowl vent screen.

133. Install the battery and connect the negative battery cable.

134. Fill the engine with clean engine oil.

135. Fill and bleed the engine cooling system.

136. Charge the A/C system using approved equipment.

137. Fill and bleed the power steering system.

138. Start the vehicle and inspect the engine and cooling system for leaks.

3.0L (VIN S) Engine

See Figures 50 through 53.

1. Before servicing the vehicle, refer to the precautions section.

2. Disconnect the negative battery cable.

3. Drain the engine oil.

4. Drain the cooling system.

5. Recover the A/C refrigerant.

6. Remove the air cleaner and air cleaner outlet pipe.

7. Remove the cowl vent screen and cowl extension.

8. Remove the halfshafts.

9. Remove the pinch bolt and slide the coupling off the steering gear input shaft.

10. Remove the ground strap bolt.

11. Loosen the bolt and disconnect the Powertrain Control Module (PCM) electrical connector.

12. Disconnect the Evaporative Emission (EVAP) system hoses.

13. Remove the pin-type retainers and the accelerator cable splash shield.

14. Disconnect the accelerator cable and the cruise control cable.

15. Detach the cables from the bracket.

16. Disconnect the Transaxle Range (TR) sensor electrical connector.

17. Remove the nut and unclip the shifter cable from the bracket.

18. Loosen the bolt and disconnect the harness connector.

19. Disconnect the low pressure A/C tube spring lock coupling at the accumulator/drier.

20. Remove the heater hose bracket nut.

21. Disconnect the heater hoses.

22. Remove the heater hose bracket nut.

23. Disconnect the coolant recovery bottle hose.

24. Remove the nut and disconnect the starter motor ground cable.

25. Disconnect the upper radiator hose.

26. Disconnect the power steering fluid hose from the reservoir.

27. Remove the two left hand exhaust manifold-to-pipe nuts.

28. Remove the front splash shield.

29. Remove the inner fender splash shields.

30. Remove the starter cable cover.

31. Remove the nut and disconnect the cable from the starter.

32. Remove the stabilizer bar end link nuts.

33. Remove the tie-rod end cotter pin and nut.

34. Using the tool 211-001, separate the tie-rod end from the knuckle.

35. Remove the right hand exhaust manifold-to-pipe bolts.

36. Remove the nuts and the dual converter Y-pipe.

37. Disconnect the power steering and transaxle hoses from the cooler.

38. Disconnect the transaxle cooler hose.

39. Remove the nut and disconnect the A/C high pressure line at the condenser.

40. Remove four bolts and remove the radiator support bracket.

41. Disconnect the lower radiator hose and the reservoir supply hose.

42. If equipped, disconnect the engine block heater electrical connector.

43. If equipped, unclip the engine block heater harness.

44. Remove the torque converter inspection cover.

→**Index the flexplate and torque converter by marking one stud.**

45. Remove the four torque converter-to-flexplate nuts.

46. Using the dolly support tool 104-00765, support the subframe.

47. Remove the four subframe bolts and lower the subframe engine/transaxle assembly.

48. Remove the coolant tube lower mounting bolt.

49. Remove the coolant tube mounting bolt and position the tube away from the cylinder head.

50. Remove the engine support brace.

51. Install lift eye tools 303-050.

52. Using the lift eye tools and a suitable engine hoist, support the engine and transaxle at the cylinder heads.

53. Disconnect the power steering pressure tube and remove the clamp bolt.

54. Remove the left hand engine mount-to-frame nut.

55. Remove the right hand engine mount-to-frame nut.

56. Remove the engine bracket-to-transaxle bolts.

57. Remove the bolts and separate the engine from transaxle.

58. Remove the oil pan, if necessary.

To install:

➡**The studs from the torque converter must align with the engine flexplate holes to assemble the engine/transaxle. Install the indexed stud to the indexed hole in the flexplate.**

59. Using the lift hooks and a suitable engine hoist, support the engine and assemble with the transaxle.

60. Install the five engine-to-transaxle bolts and tighten to 30 ft. lbs. (40 Nm).

61. Install the right and left engine mount nut and tighten to 66 ft. lbs. (90 Nm).

62. Using the tool 211-D027, install new seals on the power steering hose fitting.

63. Connect the power steering pressure line and install the clamp bolt.

64. Install the engine support brace and tighten the bolts as illustrated.

65. Position the coolant tube to the head and install the coolant tube mounting bolt.

66. Install the coolant tube lower mounting bolt.

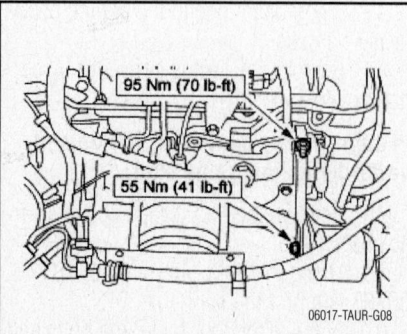

Fig. 50 Tighten the engine support brace bolts as shown—3.0L (VIN S) Engine

67. Using the dolly, raise the engine/transaxle assembly into the vehicle and loosely install the four subframe bolts.

68. Align the subframe with the body. Install a 0.75 inch (19 mm) rod into the front left and right hand subframe-to-body alignment hole.

69. Hand-tighten the bolts.

70. Verify the subframe-to-body alignment at both of the alignment holes.

71. Tighten the four subframe bolts to 76 ft. lbs. (103 Nm).

➡**Clean and degrease all sealing surfaces with metal surface cleaner. The oil pan must be installed and the bolts tightened within four minutes of the sealant application.**

72. Apply a 0.4 inch (10 mm) dot of silicone gasket and sealant to the front cover-to-cylinder block mating surface.

73. Install a new gasket, position the oil pan and loosely install the bolts and the studs in the sequence illustrated.

74. Install the oil pan to transaxle housing bolts and tighten to 30 ft. lbs. (40 Nm).

75. Tighten the oil pan bolts and studs in sequence to 18 ft. lbs. (25 Nm).

76. Position the engine-to-transaxle bracket and install the nuts and the bolt.

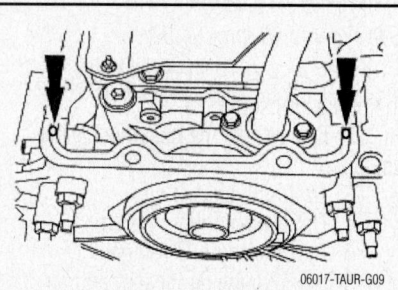

Fig. 51 Apply a 0.4 inch (10 mm) dot of silicone gasket and sealant to the front cover-to-cylinder block mating surface—3.0L (VIN S) Engine

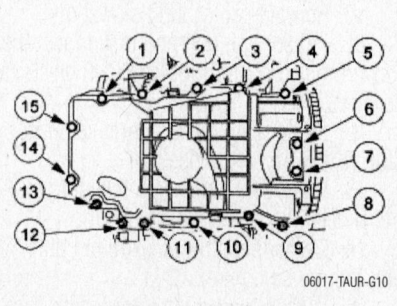

Fig. 52 Loosely install the oil pan bolts and the studs in the sequence shown—3.0L (VIN S) Engine

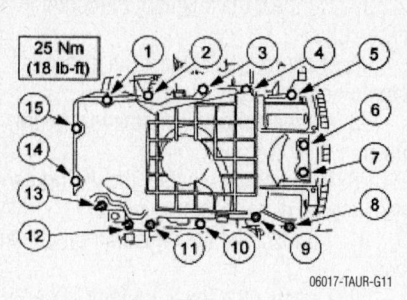

Fig. 53 Tighten the oil pan bolts and the studs in the sequence shown—3.0L (VIN S) Engine

Tighten the bolts to 18 ft. lbs. (25 Nm) and the nuts to 89 inch lbs. (10 Nm).

77. Install the four torque converter-to-flexplate nuts and tighten to 27 ft. lbs. (37 Nm).

78. Install the torque converter inspection cover.

79. Clip the engine block heater harness to the engine block.

80. If equipped, connect the engine block heater electrical connector.

81. If equipped, connect the lower radiator hose and reservoir supply hose.

82. Install the radiator support bracket and bolts.

83. Connect the A/C high pressure tube to the condenser and install the nut.

84. Connect the transaxle cooler hose.

85. Connect the power steering and transaxle hoses to the cooler.

86. Position the dual converter Y-pipe and install the nuts and tighten to 30 ft. lbs. (40 Nm).

87. Install the right hand exhaust manifold-to-pipe bolts and tighten to 30 ft. lbs. (40 Nm).

88. Connect the tie-rod ends and tighten the nuts to 41 ft. lbs. (55 Nm). Install new cotter pins.

89. Install the sway bar end link nuts and tighten to 41 ft. lbs. (55 Nm).

90. Position the starter cable and install the nut.

91. Install the starter cable cover.

92. Install the inner fender splash shield.

93. Install the front splash shield.

94. Install the two left hand exhaust manifold-to-pipe nuts and tighten to 30 ft. lbs. (40 Nm).

95. Connect the power steering fluid hose to the reservoir.

96. Connect the upper radiator hose.

97. Position the starter motor ground cable and tighten the nut to 18 ft. lbs. (25 Nm).

98. Connect the coolant recovery bottle hose.

99. Connect the heater hoses.

100. Install the heater hose bracket nut.

101. Connect the low pressure A/C tube spring lock coupling at the accumulator/drier.

102. Connect the harness and tighten the bolt.

103. Clip the shifter cable to the bracket and install the nut.

104. Connect the TR sensor electrical connector.

105. Install the accelerator and cruise control cables in the bracket.

106. Connect the cables and the throttle return spring.

107. Install the accelerator cable splash shield.

108. Connect the EVAP system hoses.

109. Connect the PCM electrical connector and tighten the bolt to 53 inch lbs. (6 Nm).

110. Position the ground strap and install the bolt.

111. Install the steering shaft pinch bolt and tighten to 18 ft. lbs. (25 Nm).

112. Install the halfshafts.

113. Install the cowl vent screen.

114. Install the air cleaner and the air cleaner outlet pipe.

115. Evacuate, leak test, and charge the A/C system using approved equipment.

116. Fill and bleed the cooling system.

117. Fill and bleed the power steering system.

118. Fill the engine with clean engine oil.

119. Connect the negative battery cable.

EXHAUST MANIFOLD

REMOVAL & INSTALLATION

3.0L (VIN U, 2) Engines

Right Side

See Figures 54 and 55.

1. Before servicing the vehicle, refer to the precautions section.

2. Remove or disconnect the following:
   - Negative battery cable
   - Cowl vent screen and extension
   - Heated Oxygen Sensor (HO2S) connector
   - Exhaust Gas Recirculation (EGR) tube
   - Exhaust manifold heat shield
   - Catalytic converter
   - Exhaust manifold

To install:

3. Install the exhaust manifold with

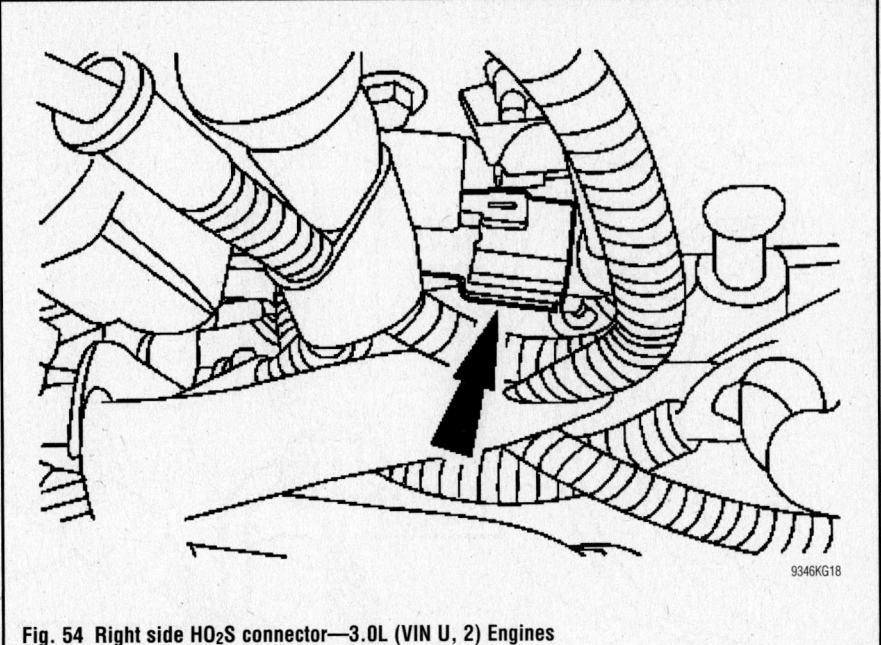

Fig. 54 Right side HO2S connector—3.0L (VIN U, 2) Engines

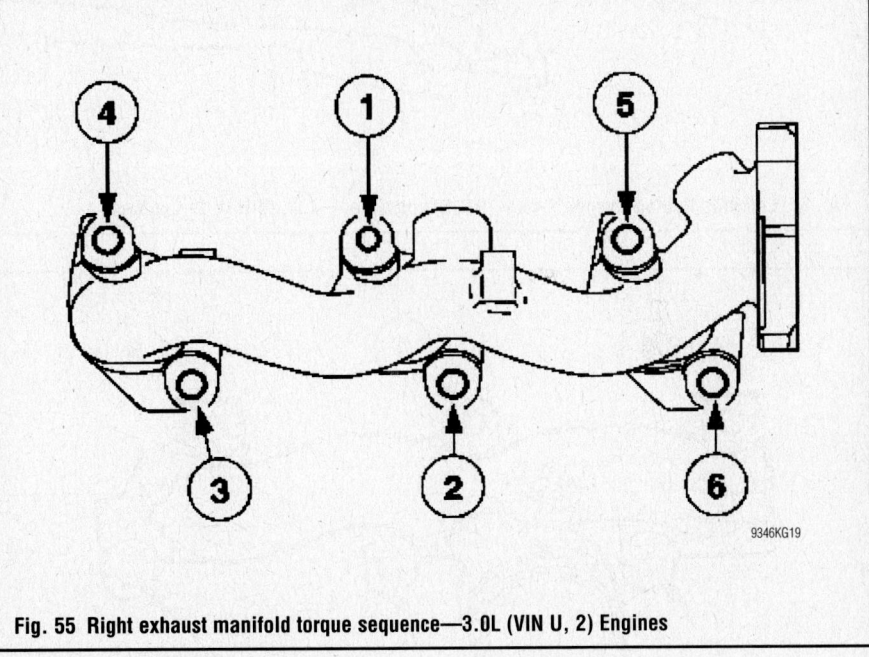

Fig. 55 Right exhaust manifold torque sequence—3.0L (VIN U, 2) Engines

a new gasket. Tighten the bolts in sequence as follows:
  a. Step 1: 89 inch lbs. (10 Nm)
  b. Step 2: 16 ft. lbs. (22 Nm)

4. Install or connect the following:
   - Catalytic converter and tighten the bolts to 30 ft. lbs. (40 Nm)
   - Exhaust manifold heat shield and tighten the bolts to 89 inch lbs. (10 Nm)
   - EGR tube
   - HO2S sensor connector
   - Cowl vent screen and extension
   - Negative battery cable

5. Start the engine and check for leaks.

Left Side

See Figures 56 and 57.

1. Before servicing the vehicle, refer to the precautions section.

2. Remove or disconnect the following:
   - Negative battery cable
   - Heated Oxygen Sensor (HO2S) connector
   - Oil dipstick tube
   - Power steering pressure line

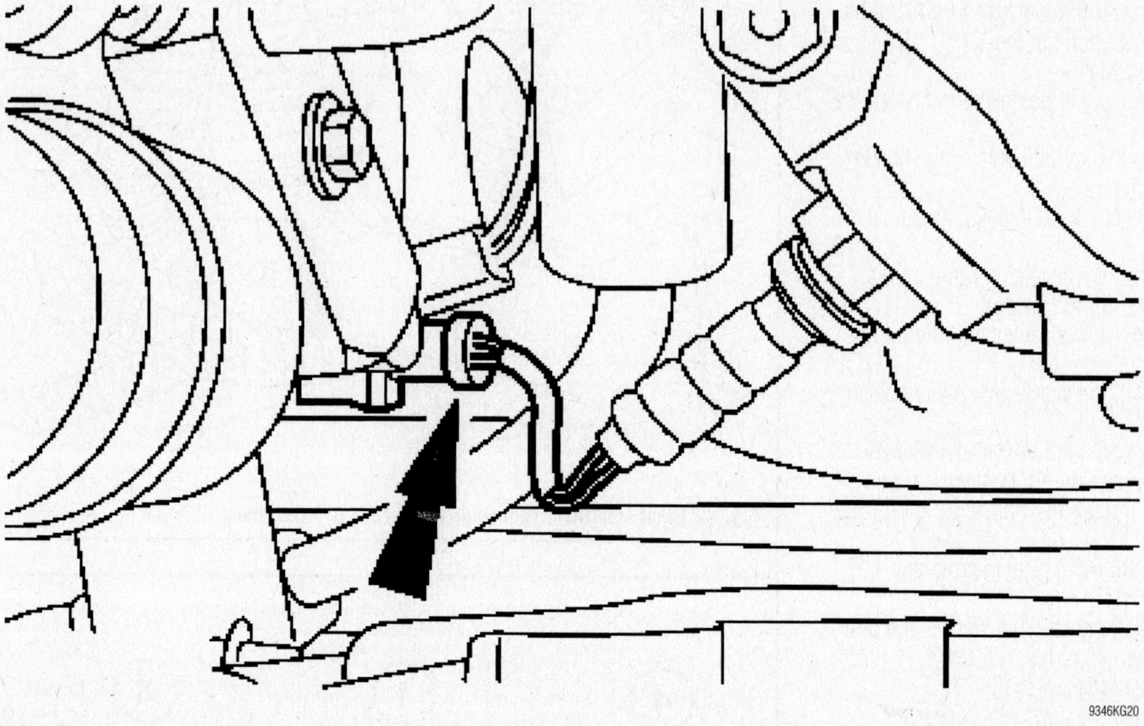

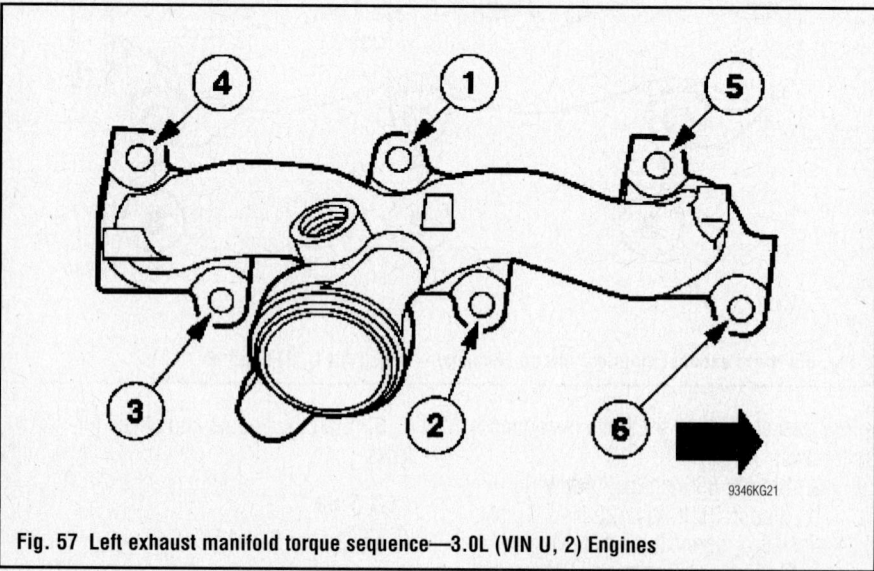

Fig. 56 Left side Heated Oxygen Sensor (HO$_2$S) connector—3.0L (VIN U, 2) Engines

Fig. 57 Left exhaust manifold torque sequence—3.0L (VIN U, 2) Engines

- Secondary air injection tube, if equipped
- Dual converter Y-pipe
- Exhaust manifold

To install:

3. Install the exhaust manifold with a new gasket. Tighten the bolts in sequence as follows:

a. Step 1: 89 inch lbs. (10 Nm)
b. Step 2: 16 ft. lbs. (22 Nm)

4. Install or connect the following:
- Dual converter Y-pipe and tighten the bolts to 30 ft. lbs. (40 Nm)
- Secondary air injection tube, if equipped
- Power steering pressure line

- Oil dipstick tube
- HO$_2$S sensor connector
- Negative battery cable

5. Start the engine and check for leaks.

3.0L (VIN S) Engine

Left Side

See Figure 58.

1. Before servicing the vehicle, refer to the precautions section.
2. Remove the coolant tube bracket bolt.
3. Disconnect and unclip the Heated Oxygen Sensor (HO$_2$S) electrical connector from the coolant tube.
4. Remove the dual converter Y-pipe.
5. Remove the front splash shield.
6. Remove the coolant tube lower bracket bolt.
7. Remove the nuts and the exhaust manifold.
8. Discard the gasket.

To install:

9. Installation is the reverse of removal. Tighten the manifold bolts in the sequence illustrated to 15 ft. lbs. (20 Nm).

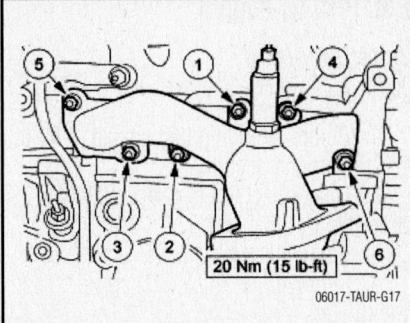

Fig. 58 Left exhaust manifold tightening sequence—3.0L (VIN S) Engine

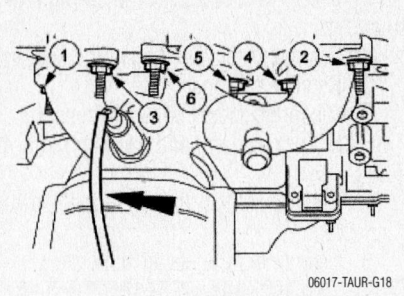

Fig. 59 Right exhaust manifold loosening sequence—3.0L (VIN S) Engine

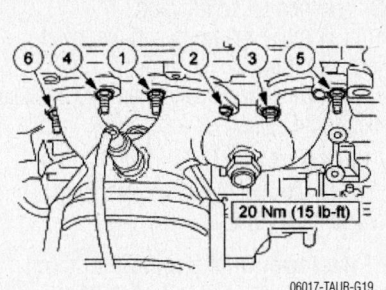

Fig. 60 Right exhaust manifold tightening sequence—3.0L (VIN S) Engine

Right Side

See Figures 59 and 60.

1. Before servicing the vehicle, refer to the precautions section.
2. Disconnect the negative battery cable.
3. Remove the wiper mounting arm and pivot shaft.
4. Remove the air cleaner outlet pipe.
5. Remove the three retaining screws and the right hand cowl top inner panel.
6. Remove the two retaining nuts and position the vacuum outlet manifold assembly aside.
7. Unseat the windshield wiper motor wiring harness grommet. Pull the wiring harness through the grommet.
8. Disconnect the cowl drain tube, remove the three retaining screws and the left hand cowl top inner panel.
9. Disconnect the differential pressure feedback Exhaust Gas Recirculation (EGR) sensor and the Heated Oxygen Sensor (HO2S) electrical connectors.
10. Remove the differential pressure feedback EGR sensor tube and bracket as follows:
    a. Detach the electrical connector pin-type retainer.
    b. Remove the bolts from the differential pressure feedback EGR bracket.
    c. Disconnect and remove the differential pressure feedback EGR and bracket from the vacuum tubes.
11. Remove the rear support brace.
12. Remove the steering gear heat shield.
13. Remove the EGR tube.
14. Remove the dual converter Y-pipe.
15. Remove the nuts in the sequence shown and remove the exhaust manifold.
16. Discard the gasket.

To install:

17. Position a new gasket and install the exhaust manifold nuts in the sequence shown. Tighten to 15 ft. lbs. (20 Nm).

18. Install the dual converter Y-pipe.
19. Install the EGR tube.
20. Install the steering gear heat shield.
21. Install the rear support brace. Position the rear support brace and tighten the retainers to 35 ft. lbs. (47 Nm).
22. Install the differential pressure feedback EGR valve sensor and bracket.
23. Attach the HO2S electrical connector.
24. Connect the differential pressure feedback EGR sensor and the HO2S electrical connectors.
25. Connect the negative battery cable.

INTAKE MANIFOLD

REMOVAL & INSTALLATION

3.0L (VIN U, 2) Engines

Upper Manifold

See Figure 61.

1. Before servicing the vehicle, refer to the precautions section.
2. Disconnect the negative battery cable.
3. Disconnect the tubes, loosen the clamps and remove the air cleaner outlet pipe.
4. Remove the snow shield.
5. Disconnect the accelerator cable, cruise control cable and throttle return spring from the throttle body.

6. Remove the bolts and position the accelerator cables and bracket aside.
7. Disconnect the Throttle Position (TP) sensor and the Intake Air Control (IAC) electrical connectors.
8. Detach the harness retainer from the throttle body stud bolt.
9. Disconnect the vacuum hose and the Evaporative Emissions (EVAP) return tube.
10. Remove the upper intake manifold support bracket bolt and nut.
11. Position the bracket and harness aside.
12. Loosen the nut and disconnect the Exhaust Gas Recirculation (EGR) tube from the EGR valve.
13. Disconnect the Positive Crankcase Ventilation (PCV) tube from the upper intake manifold.
14. Disconnect the fuel supply manifold pressure sensor vacuum tube.
15. Disconnect the PCV tube from the PCV valve and remove the tube.
16. Disconnect the EGR vacuum regulator solenoid and Intake Manifold Tuning valve (IMTV) electrical connectors.
17. Detach the pin-type harness retainer from the upper intake manifold.
18. Detach the spark plug wire holder from the valve cover stud and disconnect the radio interference capacitor electrical connector.
19. Remove the two nuts and position the EGR vacuum regulator solenoid and bracket aside.
20. Remove the bolts and the upper intake manifold.

To install:

→Clean all of the sealing surfaces. Inspect the upper intake manifold gaskets and install new gaskets as necessary.

21. Install the upper intake manifold. Tighten bolts in 2 steps in the sequence shown:
    a. Step 1: hand-tighten the bolts.
    b. Step 2: Tighten the bolts to 89 inch lbs. (10 Nm).
22. Position the EGR vacuum regulator solenoid and bracket and install the nuts.
23. Attach the spark plug wire holder to the valve cover stud and connect the radio interference capacitor electrical connector.
24. Connect the EGR vacuum regulator solenoid and IMRC electrical connectors.
25. Attach the pin-type harness retainer to the upper intake manifold.
26. Connect the PCV tube to the PCV valve.

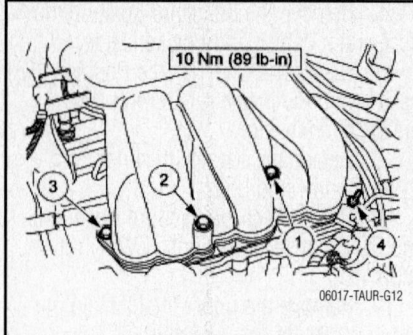

Fig. 61 Upper intake manifold torque sequence—3.0L (VIN U, 2) Engines

27. Connect the fuel supply manifold pressure sensor vacuum tube.

28. Connect the PCV tube to the upper intake manifold.

29. Connect the EGR tube to the EGR valve and tighten the fitting to 41 ft. lbs. (55 Nm).

30. Position the upper intake manifold support bracket and install bolt and nut.

31. Connect the vacuum hose and the EVAP return tube.

32. Connect the TP sensor and the IAC electrical connectors.

33. Attach the harness retainer from the throttle body stud bolt.

34. Position the accelerator cable bracket and install the bolts.

35. Connect the accelerator cable, cruise control cable and throttle return spring to the throttle body.

36. Install the snow shield.

37. Install the air cleaner outlet pipe, connect the tubes and tighten the clamps.

38. Connect the negative battery cable.

Lower Manifold

See Figure 62.

1. Before servicing the vehicle, refer to the precautions section.

2. Remove the upper intake manifold.

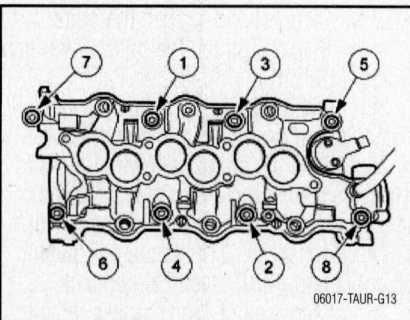

Fig. 62 Lower intake manifold torque sequence—3.0L (VIN U, 2) Engines

3. Disconnect the fuel tube spring lock coupling.

4. Drain and recycle the engine coolant.

5. Remove the push rods.

6. Disconnect the Fuel Rail Pressure (FRP) sensor electrical and vacuum connections.

7. Disconnect the fuel injector electrical connectors.

8. Disconnect the heater hose and Engine Coolant Temperature (ECT) sender electrical connector.

9. Disconnect the ECT sensor electrical connector and the degas bottle hose.

10. Disconnect the upper radiator hose from the thermostat housing.

11. Remove the bolts and the lower intake manifold.

12. Remove the intake manifold gaskets and the end seals.

To install:

13. Using metal surface cleaner, clean all the sealing surfaces.

➡ **If the lower intake manifold is not secured within four minutes, the sealant must be removed and the sealing area cleaned with metal surface cleaner. Allow to dry until there is no sign of wetness or four minutes, whichever is longer. Failure to follow this procedure can cause future oil leakage.**

14. Apply a 0.20–0.23 inch (5–6 mm) bead of silicone gasket and sealant at the four cylinder block-to-cylinder head seams.

15. Install the lower intake manifold gaskets and end seals.

16. Install the intake manifold. Tighten the bolts in two steps in the sequence shown:

    a. Step 1: Tighten to 15 Nm (11 lb-ft).

    b. Step 2: Tighten to 24 ft. lbs. (32 Nm.

17. Connect the upper radiator hose to the thermostat housing.

18. Connect the ECT sensor electrical connector and the degas bottle hose.

19. Connect the heater hose and the ECT sender electrical connector.

20. Connect the fuel injector electrical connectors.

21. Connect the FRP sensor electrical and vacuum connections.

22. Install the push rods.

23. Connect the fuel tube spring lock coupling.

24. Install the upper intake manifold.

25. Fill and bleed the engine cooling system.

3.0L (VIN S) Engine

Upper Manifold

See Figure 63.

1. Before servicing the vehicle, refer to the precautions section.

2. Disconnect the negative battery cable.

3. Remove the air cleaner outlet pipe.

4. Remove the accelerator cable splash shield.

5. Disconnect the accelerator cable, the cruise control cable and the throttle return spring.

6. Remove the bolts and position the bracket and cables aside.

7. Disconnect the Throttle Position (TP) sensor and the Idle Air Control (IAC) valve electrical connectors.

8. Detach the harness retainer from the throttle body stud bolt.

9. Disconnect the heated throttle body coolant tubes.

10. Disconnect the Positive Crankcase Ventilation (PCV) hose.

11. Disconnect the vacuum supply hose.

12. Disconnect the brake booster and Evaporative Emissions (EVAP) vacuum hoses.

13. Remove the Exhaust Gas Recirculation (EGR) valve as follows:

    a. Disconnect the vacuum hose.

    b. Remove the nuts and bolts.

    c. Remove the EGR valve.

14. Remove the EGR Vacuum Regulator (EVR) valve as follows:

    a. Disconnect the vacuum hose.

    b. Disconnect the electrical connector.

    c. Remove the bolts.

    d. Remove the valve.

15. Remove the eight bolts and the upper intake manifold.

16. Remove and discard the gaskets.

17. Clean all mating surfaces.

To install:

18. Position new gaskets in the upper intake manifold.

19. Position the upper intake manifold and install the bolts in the sequence shown. Tighten to 89 inch lbs. (10 Nm).

20. Install the EGR vacuum regulator valve and tighten the retainers to 53 inch lbs. (6 Nm).

21. Install the EGR valve. Tighten the bolts to 18 ft. lbs. (25 Nm) and the nuts to 89 inch lbs. (10 Nm).

22. Connect the brake booster and PCV vacuum hoses.

23. Connect the vacuum supply hose.

24. Connect the PCV valve hose.

25. Connect the TP and IAC valve electrical connectors.

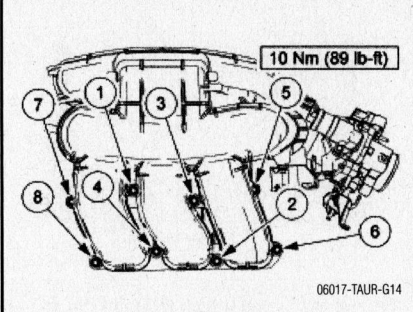

Fig. 63 Upper intake manifold torque sequence—3.0L (VIN S) Engine

26. Attach the harness retainer to the throttle body stud bolt.

27. Connect the heated throttle body coolant tubes.

28. Position the bracket and cables and install the bolts.

29. Connect the throttle return spring, accelerator cable and the cruise control cable.

30. Install the accelerator cable splash shield.

31. Install the air cleaner outlet pipe.

32. Connect the negative battery cable.

Lower Manifold

See Figures 64 and 65.

1. Before servicing the vehicle, refer to the precautions section.

2. Release the fuel system pressure.

3. Disconnect the fuel hose quick release coupling from the fuel supply manifold.

4. Remove the upper intake manifold.

5. Disconnect the fuel injection pres-

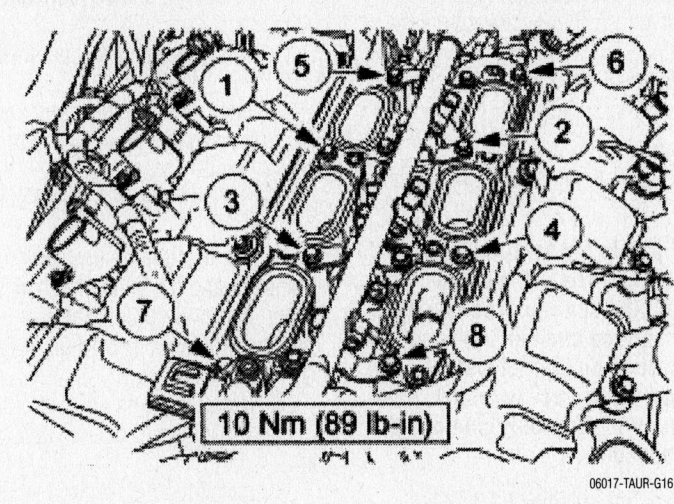

Fig. 65 Lower intake manifold tightening sequence—3.0L (VIN S) Engine

sure and temperature sensor vacuum tube and the electrical connector.

6. Disconnect the fuel injector electrical connectors.

7. Remove the intake manifold bolts in the sequence shown, and remove the lower intake manifold.

8. Remove and discard the gaskets from the lower intake manifold.

To install:

➡**Clean and inspect all mating surfaces and install new gaskets in the lower intake manifold.**

9. Install the lower intake manifold and tighten the bolts in the sequence shown to 89 inch lbs. (10 Nm).

10. Connect the fuel injector electrical connectors.

11. Connect the fuel injection pressure and temperature sensor vacuum tube and the electrical connector.

12. Connect the fuel hose quick release coupling to the fuel supply manifold.

13. Install the upper intake manifold.

OIL PAN

REMOVAL & INSTALLATION

3.0L (VIN U, 2) Engines

See Figures 66 and 67.

1. Before servicing the vehicle, refer to the precautions section.

2. Disconnect the negative battery cable.

3. Remove the bolts and engine roll restrictor.

4. Remove the bolt, ground strap and nut.

5. Remove the nuts from the front exhaust manifold.

6. Remove the bolt from the rear upper manifold.

7. Remove the nut and disconnect the ground strap electrical connector.

8. Remove the nut and position the heat shield aside.

9. Loosen the rear lower exhaust manifold bolt and position the Y-pipe aside.

10. Remove the bolts and position the starter aside.

11. Remove the bolt and the engine rear plate.

12. Remove the oil pan drain plug and drain the engine oil.

13. Install the drain plug when finished and tighten to 10 ft. lbs. (13 Nm).

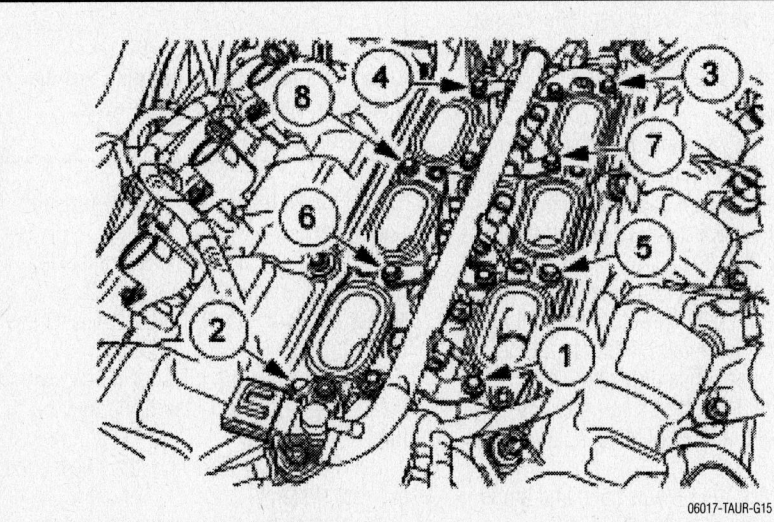

Fig. 64 Lower intake manifold loosening sequence—3.0L (VIN S) Engine

14. Remove the bolts and the oil pan.

15. Remove the oil pan gasket from the oil pan.

16. Using metal surface cleaner, clean the oil pan sealing surfaces.

To install:

17. Install the oil pan gasket onto the oil pan.

➡️If the oil pan is not secured within four minutes, the sealant must be removed and the sealing area cleaned with metal surface cleaner. Allow to dry until there is no sign of wetness or four minutes, whichever is longer. Failure to follow this procedure can cause future oil leakage.

18. Apply a bead of silicone gasket and sealant in two places where the cylinder block meets the front cover and in two places where the rear main bearing cap meets the cylinder block.

➡️Make sure the fasteners are clean and dry prior to installation.

19. Tighten the oil pan bolts in sequence to 9 ft. lbs. (12 Nm).

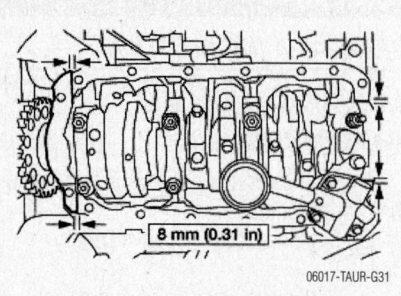

Fig. 66 Apply a bead of silicone gasket and sealant in two places where the cylinder block meets the front cover and in two places where the rear main bearing cap meets the cylinder block—3.0L (VIN U, 2) Engines

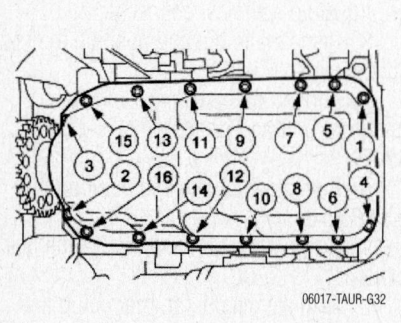

Fig. 67 Oil pan bolt torque sequence—3.0L (VIN U, 2) Engines

20. Install the engine rear plate and the bolt.

21. Position the starter and install the bolts.

22. Position the Y-pipe and tighten the rear lower exhaust manifold bolt to 35 ft. lbs. (48 Nm).

23. Position the heat shield and install the nut.

24. Connect the ground strap electrical connector and install the nut.

25. Install the bolt in the rear upper manifold tighten to bolt to 35 ft. lbs. (48 Nm).

26. Install the nuts on the front exhaust manifold. Tighten to bolt to 30 ft. lbs. (40 Nm).

27. Install the nut, ground strap and bolt.

28. Install the engine roll restrictor and the bolts. Tighten to bolt to 35 ft. lbs. (48 Nm).

29. Connect the negative battery cable.

30. Fill the engine with clean engine oil.

31. Start the engine and check for oil leaks around the oil pan.

3.0L (VIN S) Engine

See Figures 68 through 70.

1. Before servicing the vehicle, refer to the precautions section.

2. Disconnect the negative battery cable.

3. Remove the right front inner wheel splash shield.

4. Remove the dual converter Y-pipe.

5. Secure the exhaust system and remove the jackstand.

6. Drain the engine oil. Install and tighten the drain plug to 20 ft. lbs. (27 Nm).

7. Remove and discard the oil filter.

8. Remove the bolts, nuts and the engine-to-transaxle bracket.

9. Remove the torque converter inspection cover.

10. Remove the 18 bolts and the oil pan.

To install:

11. Clean all sealing surfaces on the engine and the oil pan with metal surface cleaner. Install a new gasket on the oil pan.

12. Apply a 0.4 inch (10 mm) dot of silicone gasket and sealant to the front cover-to-cylinder block mating surface.

13. Install a new gasket, position the oil pan and loosely install the bolts and the studs in the sequence illustrated.

14. Install the oil pan to transaxle housing bolts and tighten to 30 ft. lbs. (40 Nm).

15. Tighten the oil pan bolts and studs in sequence to 18 ft. lbs. (25 Nm).

16. Tighten the oil pan-to-transaxle bolts to 30 ft. lbs. (40 Nm).

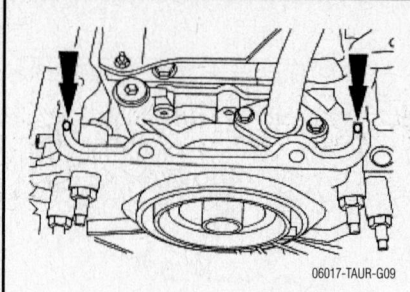

Fig. 68 Apply a 0.4 inch (10 mm) dot of silicone gasket and sealant to the front cover-to-cylinder block mating surface—3.0L (VIN S) Engine

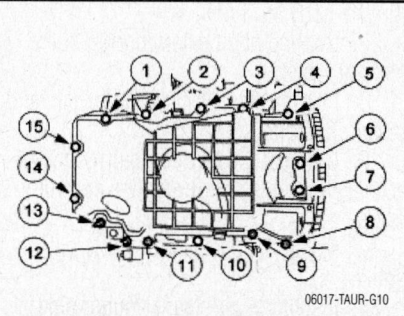

Fig. 69 Loosely install the oil pan bolts and the studs in the sequence shown—3.0L (VIN S) Engine

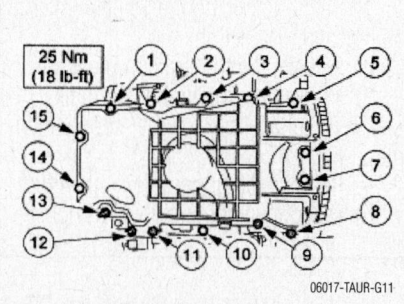

Fig. 70 Tighten the oil pan bolts and the studs in the sequence shown—3.0L (VIN S) Engine

17. Install the torque converter inspection cover.

18. Position the engine-to-transaxle bracket and install the nuts and the bolt. Tighten the bolts to 18 ft. lbs. (25 Nm) and the nuts to 89 inch lbs. (10 Nm).

19. Lubricate the oil filter O-ring with clean engine oil and install the new oil filter.

20. Position a jackstand and release the exhaust system.

21. Install the dual converter Y-pipe.

22. Install the front inner wheel splash shield.

23. Install the exhaust manifold-to-pipe nuts and tighten to 30 ft. lbs. (40 Nm).

24. Fill the crankcase with clean engine oil.

OIL PUMP

REMOVAL & INSTALLATION

3.0L (VIN U, 2) Engines

1. Before servicing the vehicle, refer to the precautions section.
2. Remove the oil pan.
3. Remove the bolts and the oil pump.
4. Clean all the sealing surfaces.
5. Installation is the reverse of removal, tighten the oil pump bolts to 35 ft. lbs. (48 Nm).

3.0L (VIN S) Engine

See Figures 71 and 72.

1. Before servicing the vehicle, refer to the precautions section.
2. Remove the oil pan.
3. Remove the nut, bolts and the oil pump screen and pick-up tube.
4. Remove and inspect the O-ring seal.
5. Remove the pump bolts in the sequence shown and remove the oil pump.

To install:

6. Position the oil pump and install the bolts in the sequence shown. Tighten to 89 inch lbs. (10 Nm).

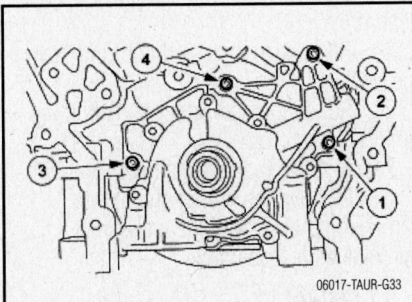

Fig. 71 Oil pump loosening sequence—3.0L (VIN S) Engine

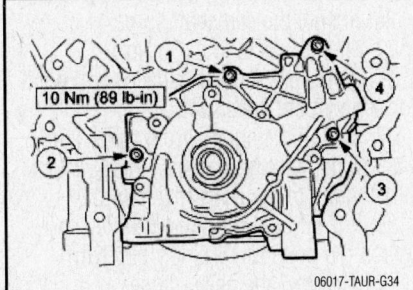

Fig. 72 Oil pump tightening sequence—3.0L (VIN S) Engine

7. Install a new O-ring seal.
8. Install the oil pump screen and pick-up tube. Tighten the nut in two steps:
    a. Step 1: Tighten to 89 inch lbs. (10 Nm).
    b. Step 2: Tighten an additional 45 degrees.
9. Install the oil pan.

PISTON AND RING

POSITIONING

See Figures 73 and 74.

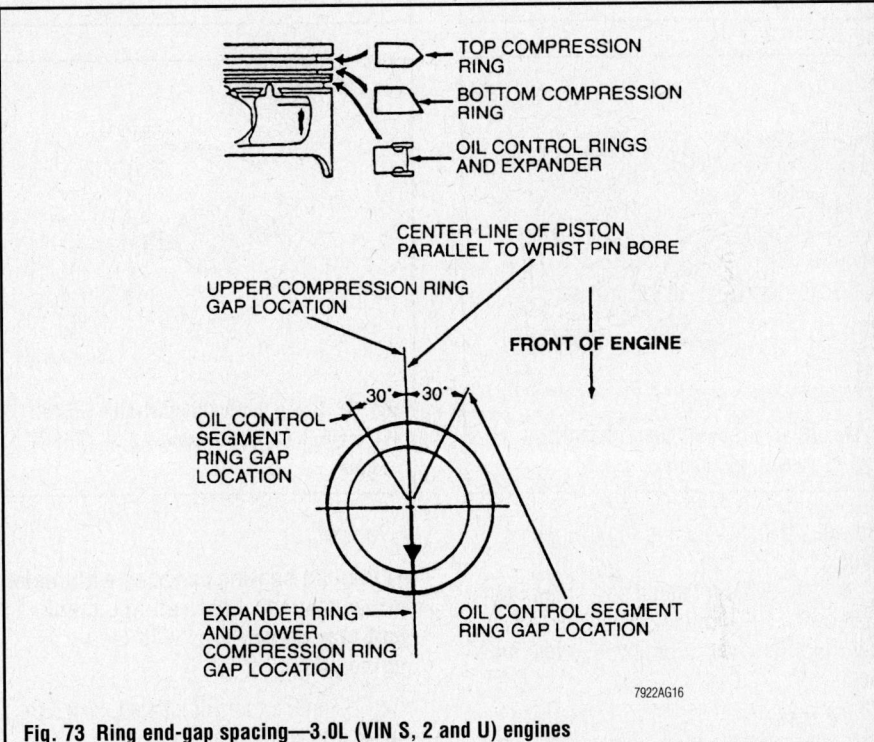

Fig. 73 Ring end-gap spacing—3.0L (VIN S, 2 and U) engines

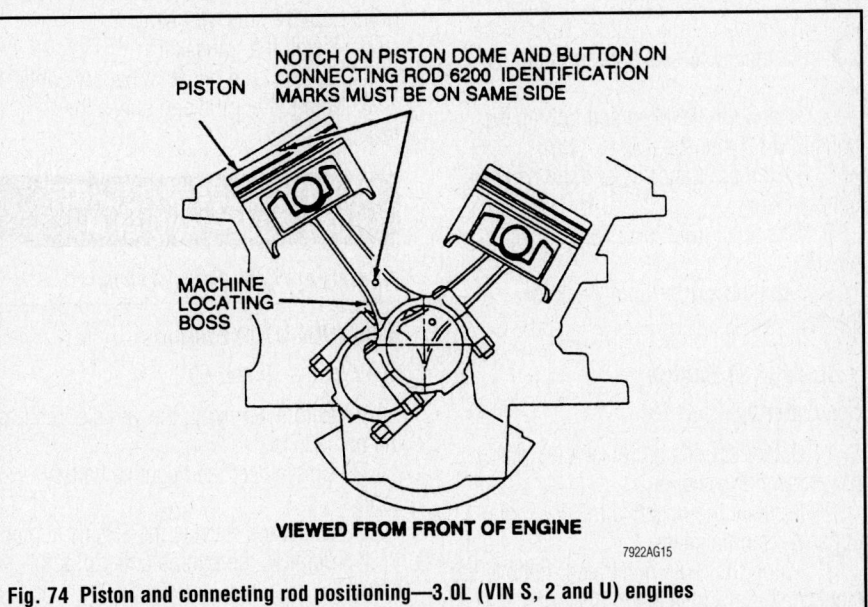

Fig. 74 Piston and connecting rod positioning—3.0L (VIN S, 2 and U) engines

REAR MAIN SEAL

REMOVAL & INSTALLATION

3.0L (VIN U, 2) Engines

See Figures 75 and 76.

1. Before servicing the vehicle, refer to the precautions section.
2. Remove the negative battery cable, transaxle and flexplate.
3. Use a sharp awl and punch a hole into the rear main seal metal surface

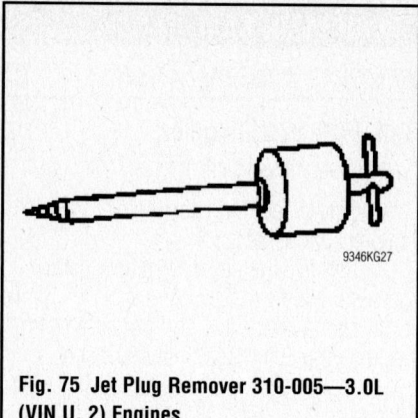

Fig. 75 Jet Plug Remover 310-005—3.0L (VIN U, 2) Engines

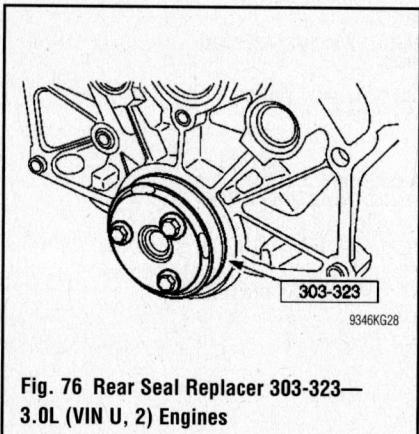

Fig. 76 Rear Seal Replacer 303-323— 3.0L (VIN U, 2) Engines

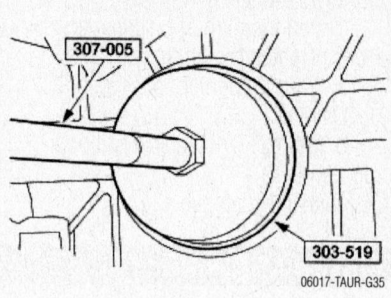

Fig. 77 Using the tools illustrated, remove the crankshaft rear oil seal—3.0L (VIN S) Engine

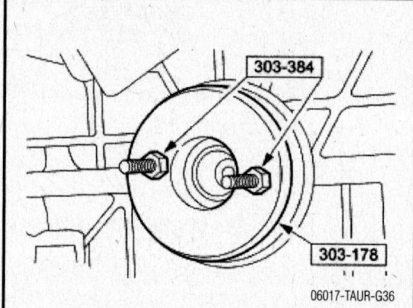

Fig. 78 Using the tools illustrated, install the crankshaft rear oil seal—3.0L (VIN S) Engine

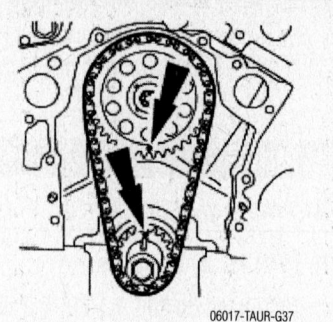

Fig. 79 Rotate the crankshaft and align the timing marks—3.0L (VIN U, 2) Engines

between the seal lip and the cylinder block.

4. Screw the threaded end of Jet Plug Remover 310-005 into the seal. Use the Jet Plug Remover to remove the rear main seal.

To install:

5. Position the rear oil seal on Rear Seal Replacer 303-323. Position the tool and seal on the rear of the engine. Tighten the bolts alternately to seat the rear main oil seal.
6. Install the flexplate and tighten the bolts to 54–64 ft. lbs. (73–87 Nm).
7. Install the transaxle and the negative battery cable.
8. Check all fluid levels and fill as needed.
9. Start the engine and check for leaks.

3.0L (VIN S) Engine

See Figures 77 and 78.

1. Before servicing the vehicle, refer to the precautions section.
2. Remove the negative battery cable, transaxle and flexplate.
3. Using the tools illustrated, remove the crankshaft rear oil seal and discard.

To install:

➡Clean all sealing surfaces with metal surface cleaner. Lubricate the crankshaft rear oil seal lips with clean engine oil.

4. Using the tools illustrated, install the crankshaft rear oil seal.
5. Install the flexplate and tighten the bolts to 549 ft. lbs. (80 Nm)
6. Install the transaxle.
7. Connect the negative battery cable.
8. Run the engine and check for leaks.

TIMING CHAIN, SPROCKETS, FRONT COVER AND SEAL

REMOVAL & INSTALLATION

3.0L (VIN U, 2) Engines

See Figures 79 and 80.

1. Before servicing the vehicle, refer to the precautions section.
2. Disconnect the negative battery cable.
3. Drain and recycle the engine coolant.
4. Remove the engine anti-roll strut brace.

5. Remove the engine anti-roll strut.
6. Remove the coolant expansion tank.
7. Loosen the four water pump pulley bolts.
8. Remove the crankshaft damper.
9. Disconnect the lower radiator hose.
10. Remove the Crankshaft Position (CKP) sensor.
11. Remove the oil pan.
12. Remove the alternator.
13. Remove the accessory drive belt idler pulley.
14. Remove the accessory drive belt tensioner.
15. Remove the A/C compressor bracket.
16. Disconnect the heater hose.
17. Remove the water pump pulley.
18. Remove the engine front cover bolts, cover and the water pump as an assembly.
19. Remove and discard the front cover gasket.
20. Rotate the crankshaft and align the timing marks.
21. Remove the camshaft sprocket bolt.
22. Remove the timing chain, the camshaft sprocket and the crankshaft sprocket as an assembly.

To install:

23. Align the timing marks.
24. Install the timing chain, the camshaft sprocket and the crankshaft sprocket as an assembly.
25. Install the camshaft sprocket bolt and tighten to 46 ft. lbs. (63 Nm).
26. Clean all sealing surfaces and position a new front cover gasket.
27. Install the engine front cover and water pump assembly. Apply Pipe Sealant with Teflon® to the bolts illustrated.
28. Install the water pump pulley and tighten the bolts to 18 ft. lbs. (25 Nm).
29. Connect the heater hose.
30. Install the A/C compressor bracket and tighten the bolts to 18 ft. lbs. (25 Nm).

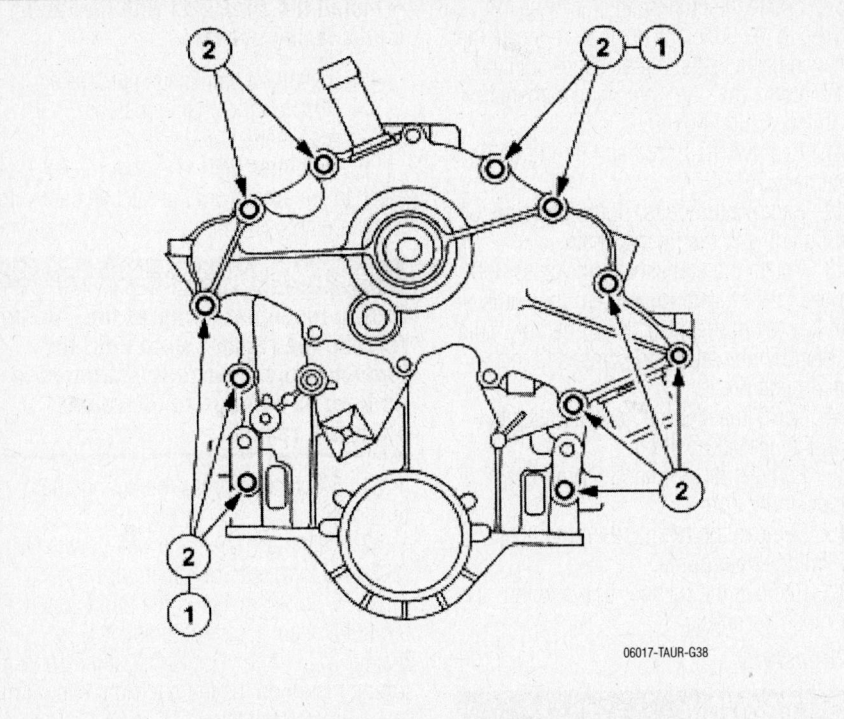

Fig. 80 Install the engine front cover and water pump assembly. Apply Pipe Sealant with Teflon® to the bolts illustrated—3.0L (VIN U, 2) Engines

31. Install the accessory drive belt tensioner and tighten the bolts to 35 ft. lbs. (48 Nm).

32. Install the accessory drive belt idler pulley and tighten the bolts to 35 ft. lbs. (48 Nm).

33. Install the alternator.

34. Install the CKP sensor.

35. Connect the lower radiator hose.

36. Install the oil pan.

37. Install the crankshaft damper.

38. Install the coolant expansion tank.

39. Install the engine anti-roll strut and tighten the bolts to 35 ft. lbs. (48 Nm).

40. Install the engine anti-roll strut brace and tighten the bolts to 35 ft. lbs. (48 Nm).

41. Connect the negative battery cable.

42. Fill and bleed the cooling system.

3.0L (VIN S) Engine

See Figures 81 through 99.

1. Before servicing the vehicle, refer to the precautions section.

2. Disconnect the negative battery cable.

3. Remove the valve covers.

4. Remove the power steering pump.

5. Remove the oil pan.

6. Remove the retaining nut and position the power steering pressure line and muffler out of the way.

7. Remove the upper retaining bolts from the alternator.

8. Remove the bolts, nuts and the engine-to-transaxle bracket.

9. Remove the torque converter inspection cover.

10. Remove the retainers and position the front rocker panel moulding aside.

11. Remove the rear portion of the front fender splash shield.

12. Remove the two screws and the alternator splash shield.

13. Install a Flywheel Holding Tool.

➡**The pulley bolt has a reverse thread.**

14. Remove the crankshaft damper pulley.

15. Remove the crankshaft damper bolt and washer.

16. Using the tool illustrated, remove the crankshaft damper.

17. Remove the Flywheel Holding Tool.

18. Disconnect the Crankshaft Position (CKP) sensor.

19. Remove the alternator bolt and position the alternator to gain access to the electrical connector and terminal nut.

20. Disconnect the alternator electrical connectors.

21. Remove the bolts and the A/C compressor to front cover bracket.

22. Disconnect the Camshaft Position (CMP) sensor

23. Remove the tie strap from the power steering hose.

24. Remove the retaining nut and position the A/C low-pressure hose out of the way.

25. Remove the bolts and position the A/C high-pressure hose on top of the belt tensioner.

26. Remove the bolt and remove the belt tensioner.

27. Disconnect the engine cooling fan electrical connector and unclip the wiring harness.

28. Remove the bolt and the engine cooling fan.

29. Install the lift eye hooks to support the engine.

30. Remove the two upper A/C compressor bolts.

31. Remove the two lower A/C compressor bolts and position the A/C compressor aside.

32. Remove the bolts from the A/C bracket.

33. Raise the engine away from the A/C bracket using an engine support tool.

34. Remove the bolts, studs and the engine front cover.

✸✸ CAUTION

This pulse wheel is used with several different engines. Install the pulse wheel with the keyway in the slot stamped "30" or "30 RFF" only (orange in color).

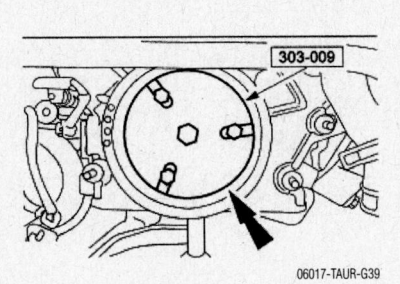

Fig. 81 Using the tool illustrated, remove the crankshaft damper—3.0L (VIN S) Engine

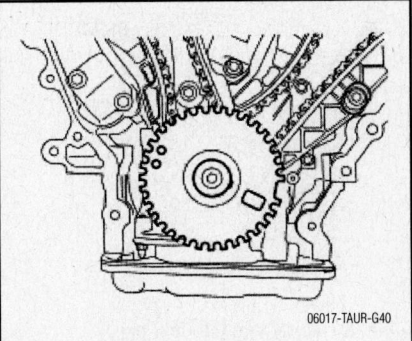

Fig. 82 Remove the ignition pulse wheel—3.0L (VIN S) Engine

35. Remove the ignition pulse wheel.

36. Install the damper bolt.

37. Remove the spark plugs.

38. Rotate the crankshaft clockwise to position the crankshaft keyway in the 11 o'clock position and position the camshafts in the correct position. This will position the number one cylinder at Top Dead Center (TDC). Verify that the camshafts are correctly located. If not, rotate the crankshaft one additional turn and recheck.

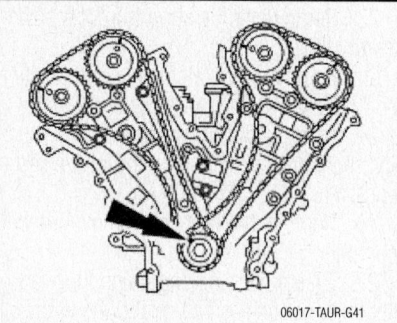

Fig. 83 Rotate the crankshaft clockwise to position the crankshaft keyway in the 11 o'clock position and position the camshafts in the correct position—3.0L (VIN S) Engine

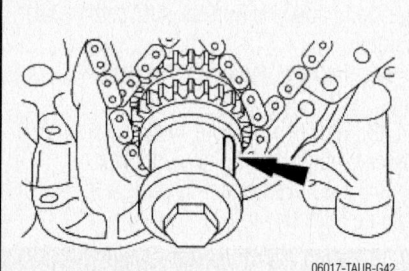

Fig. 84 Rotate the crankshaft clockwise 120 degrees to the 3 o'clock position to locate the right hand camshafts in the neutral position —3.0L (VIN S) Engine

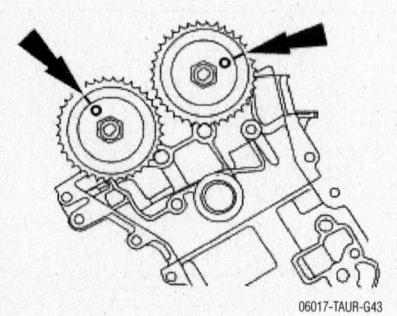

Fig. 85 Verify that the right hand camshafts are in the neutral position—3.0L (VIN S) Engine

39. Rotate the crankshaft clockwise 120 degrees to the 3 o'clock position to locate the right hand camshafts in the neutral position.

40. Verify that the right hand camshafts are in the neutral position.

41. Remove the right hand timing chain tensioner arm.

42. Remove the bolts, right hand timing chain guide and the timing chain.

43. Rotate the crankshaft clockwise 600 degrees (1-⅔ turns) to position the crankshaft keyway in the 11 o'clock position. This will position the left hand camshafts in the neutral position.

44. Verify that the left hand camshafts are in the neutral position.

45. Remove the left hand timing chain and tensioner arm.

46. Remove the left hand timing chain and timing chain guide.

47. Remove the damper bolt and the crankshaft sprockets.

To install:

⁕⁕ CAUTION

Failure to verify correct timing drive component alignment will result in severe engine damage.

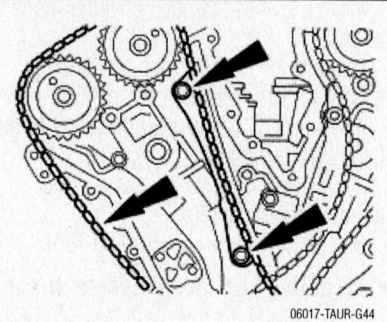

Fig. 86 Remove the bolts, right hand timing chain guide and the timing chain—3.0L (VIN S) Engine

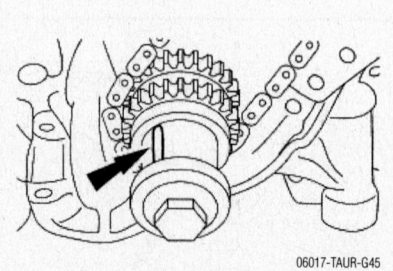

Fig. 87 Rotate the crankshaft clockwise 600 degrees (1⅔ turns) to position the crankshaft keyway in the 11 o'clock position—3.0L (VIN S) Engine

➡**Install the sprockets with the timing marks facing outward.**

48. Install the crankshaft sprockets.

49. Position the chain tensioner in a soft-jawed vise.

50. Hold the chain tensioner ratchet lock mechanism away from the ratchet stem with a small pick.

⁕⁕ CAUTION

During tensioner compression, do not release the ratchet stem until the tensioner piston is fully bottomed in its bore or damage to the ratchet stem will result.

51. Slowly compress the timing chain tensioner.

52. Retain the tensioner piston with a 0.06 (1.5 mm) wire or paper clip.

53. If timing marks in the timing chains are not evident, use a permanent-type marker to mark the crankshaft and camshaft timing marks on the left and right hand timing chains as follows:

　a. Mark any link to use as the crankshaft timing mark (1).

　b. Starting with the crankshaft timing mark, count 29 links and mark the link (2).

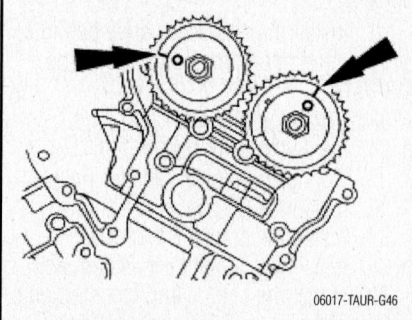

Fig. 88 Verify that the left hand camshafts are in the neutral position—3.0L (VIN S) Engine

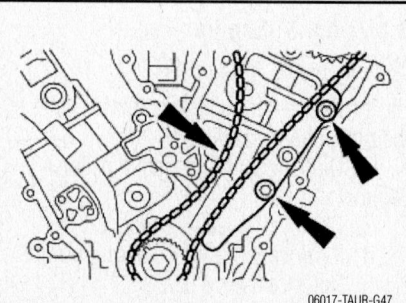

Fig. 89 Remove the left hand timing chain and timing chain guide—3.0L (VIN S) Engine

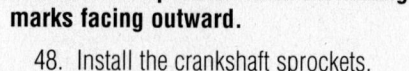

c. Continue counting to 42 and mark the link (3).

54. Position the left timing chain and guide and install the bolts.

55. Align the marks on the timing chain with the marks on the camshaft and crankshaft sprockets.

56. Install the left hand timing chain tensioner and tensioner arm. Tighten the bolts to 18 ft. lbs. (25 Nm).

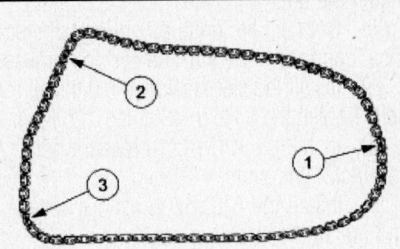

06017-TAUR-G48

Fig. 90 If timing marks in the timing chains are not evident, use a permanent-type marker to mark the crankshaft and camshaft timing marks on the left and right hand timing chains—3.0L (VIN S) Engine

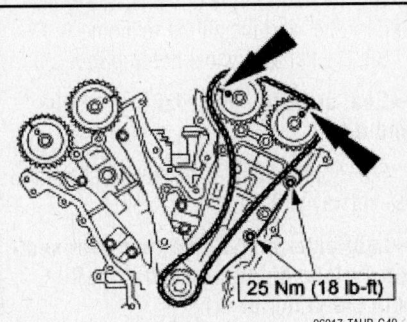

25 Nm (18 lb-ft)

06017-TAUR-G49

Fig. 91 Align the marks on the left hand timing chain with the marks on the camshaft and crankshaft sprockets—3.0L (VIN S) Engine

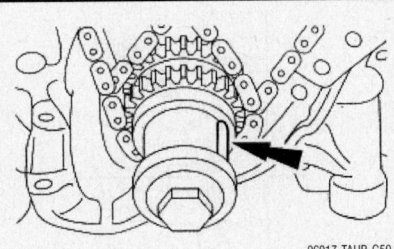

06017-TAUR-G50

Fig. 92 Install the crankshaft damper bolt and rotate the crankshaft clockwise 120 degrees until the crankshaft keyway is in the 3 o'clock position—3.0L (VIN S) Engine

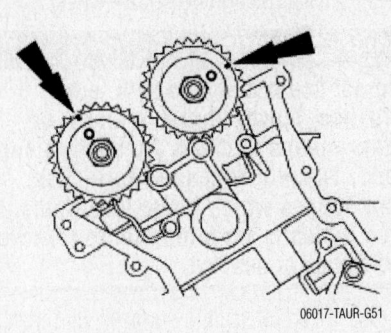

06017-TAUR-G51

Fig. 93 Verify that the right hand camshafts are correctly positioned—3.0L (VIN S) Engine

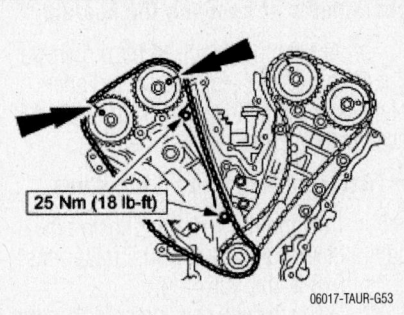

25 Nm (18 lb-ft)

06017-TAUR-G53

Fig. 94 Align the marks on the right hand timing chain with the marks on the camshaft and crankshaft sprockets—3.0L (VIN S) Engine

57. Install the crankshaft damper bolt and rotate the crankshaft clockwise 120 degrees until the crankshaft keyway is in the 3 o'clock position.

58. Verify that the right hand camshafts are correctly positioned.

59. Position the right timing chain and chain guide and install the bolts. Tighten the bolts to 18 ft. lbs. (25 Nm).

60. Align the marks on the timing chain with the marks on the camshaft and crankshaft sprockets.

61. Install the right hand timing chain tensioner and tensioner arm. Tighten the bolts to 18 ft. lbs. (25 Nm).

62. Remove the right and left hand timing chain tensioner piston retaining wires.

63. Rotate the crankshaft counterclockwise 120 degrees to top dead center (TDC).

✳✳ CAUTION

Failure to verify correct timing drive component alignment will result in severe engine damage.

64. Verify the timing drive component alignment with the following steps.

a. There should be 12 chain links between the front camshaft timing marks.

b. There should be 27 chain links between the camshaft and crankshaft timing marks.

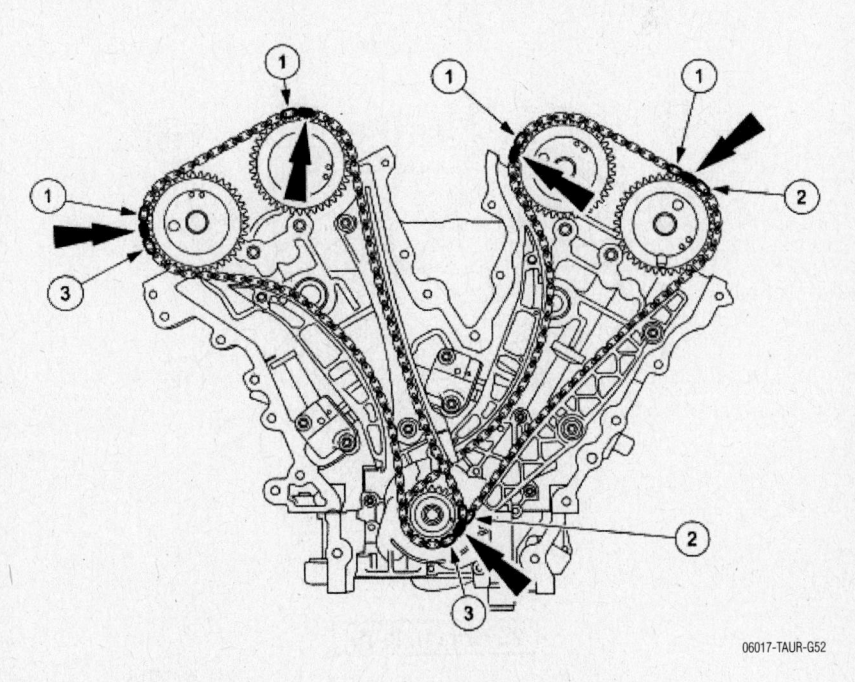

06017-TAUR-G52

Fig. 95 Refer to the procedure to verify the timing drive component alignment—3.0L (VIN S) Engine

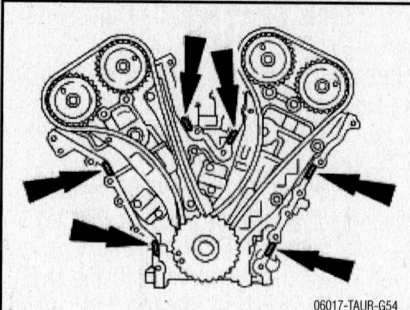

Fig. 96 Apply a 0.24 inch (6 mm) diameter dot of gasket and sealer to the cylinder block to lower cylinder block and cylinder head mating surfaces—3.0L (VIN S) Engine

c. There should be 30 chain links between the camshaft and crankshaft timing marks.

65. Remove the crankshaft damper bolt.

66. Install the spark plugs.

❊❊ CAUTION

This pulse wheel is used with several different engines. Install the pulse wheel with the keyway in the slot stamped "30" or "30 RFF" only (orange in color).

67. Install the ignition pulse wheel.

❊❊ CAUTION

Do not use metal scrapers, wire brushes, power abrasive discs, or other means to clean the sealing surface. These tools cause scratches and gouges which make leak paths. Use a plastic scraping tool to remove all traces of sealant.

68. Clean all sealing surfaces with metal surface cleaner.

69. Install three new gaskets in the front cover.

➡**The engine front cover must be installed and the bolts tightened within six minutes of applying the sealant.**

70. Apply a 0.24 inch (6 mm) diameter dot of gasket and sealer to the cylinder block to lower cylinder block and cylinder head mating surfaces.

➡**Fasteners No. 1 and 6 are studs.**

71. Position the cover and install the bolts in the sequence shown. Tighten the bolts to 18 ft. lbs. (25 Nm).

72. Using the engine support tool, lower the engine back together with the A/C bracket.

73. Install the bolts and tighten the bolts in two steps:

a. Step 1: Tighten to 18 ft. lbs. (25 Nm).

b. Step 2: Tighten an additional 90 degrees.

74. Position the A/C compressor and install the two lower bolts. Tighten the bolts to 18 ft. lbs. (25 Nm).

75. Install the two upper A/C compressor bolts. Tighten the bolts to 18 ft. lbs. (25 Nm).

76. Remove the lifting hooks.

77. Install the engine cooling fan and install the bolt.

78. Connect the engine cooling fan electrical connector and clip the wiring harness.

79. Install the belt tensioner and install the bolt. Tighten the bolts to 18 ft. lbs. (25 Nm).

80. Install the A/C high-pressure hose and install the bolts.

81. Install the A/C low-pressure hose and install the retaining nut.

82. Install the tie strap to the power steering hose.

83. Install the CMP sensor

84. Position the A/C compressor to front cover bracket and install the bolts. Tighten the bolts to 18 ft. lbs. (25 Nm).

85. Install the alternator.

86. Install the CKP sensor.

87. Reposition the power steering line and muffler and install the retaining nut.

88. Install a flywheel holding tool.

➡**Seal surfaces must be free of dirt and oil.**

89. Apply silicone gasket and sealant to the keyway slot.

➡**Lubricate the outside diameter sealing surface of the crankshaft pulley with clean motor oil.**

90. Using the tool illustrated, install the crankshaft damper.

91. Install the damper bolt and washer and tighten in four steps:

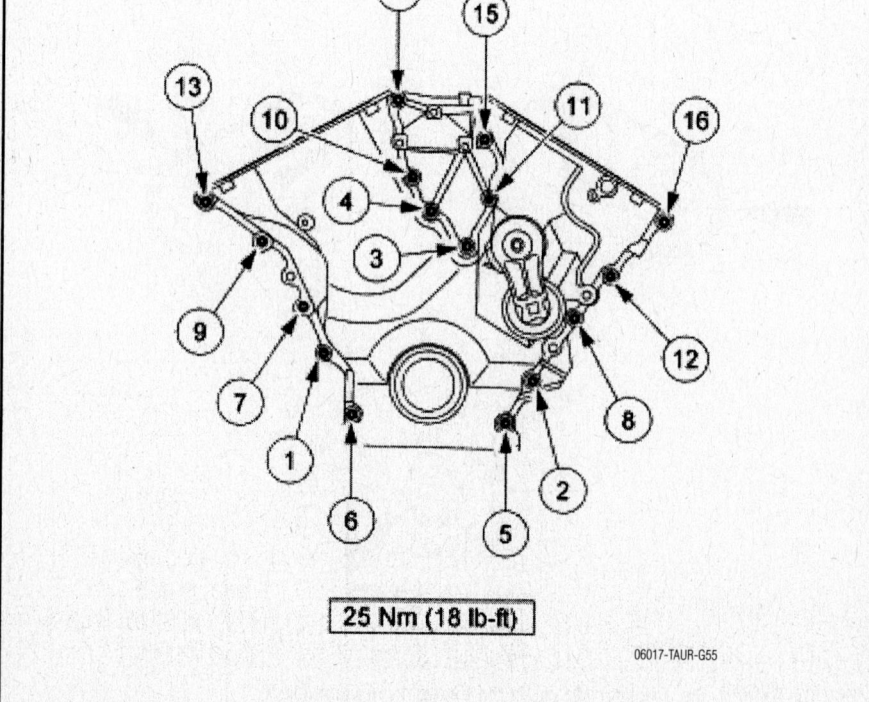

25 Nm (18 lb-ft)

06017-TAUR-G55

Fig. 97 Engine front cover torque sequence—3.0L (VIN S) Engine

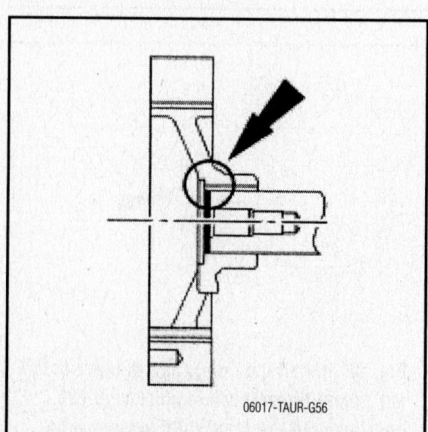

06017-TAUR-G56

Fig. 98 Apply silicone gasket and sealant to the keyway slot—3.0L (VIN S) Engine

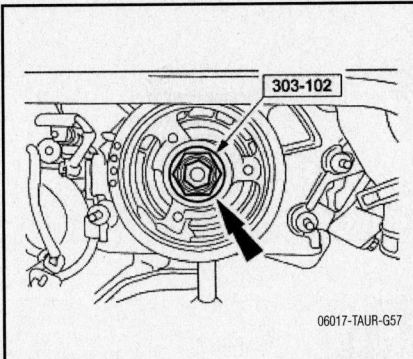

Fig. 99 Using the tool illustrated, install the crankshaft damper—3.0L (VIN S) Engine

303-102

06017-TAUR-G57

a. Step 1: Tighten to 89 ft. lbs. (120 Nm).

b. Step 2: Loosen 360 degrees.

c. Step 3: Tighten to 37 ft. lbs. (50 Nm).

d. Step 4: Tighten 90 degrees.

➡**The pulley has reverse threads.**

92. Install the crankshaft pulley. Tighten the bolt to 74 ft. lbs. (100 Nm).

93. Remove the Flywheel Holding Tool.

94. Install the alternator splash shield.

95. Install the rear portion of the front fender splash shield.

96. Install the front rocker panel moulding.

97. Install the torque converter inspection cover.

98. install the engine-to-transaxle bracket and install the nuts and bolts. Tighten the bolts to 18 ft. lbs. (25 Nm).

99. Install the oil pan.

100. Install the valve covers.

101. Connect the negative battery cable.

102. Install the power steering pump.

103. Start the engine and check for leaks.

VALVE LASH

ADJUSTMENT

The lash adjusters (valve tappets), are hydraulic and are not adjustable.

ENGINE PERFORMANCE & EMISSION CONTROL

COMPONENT LOCATIONS

See Figures 100 through 103.

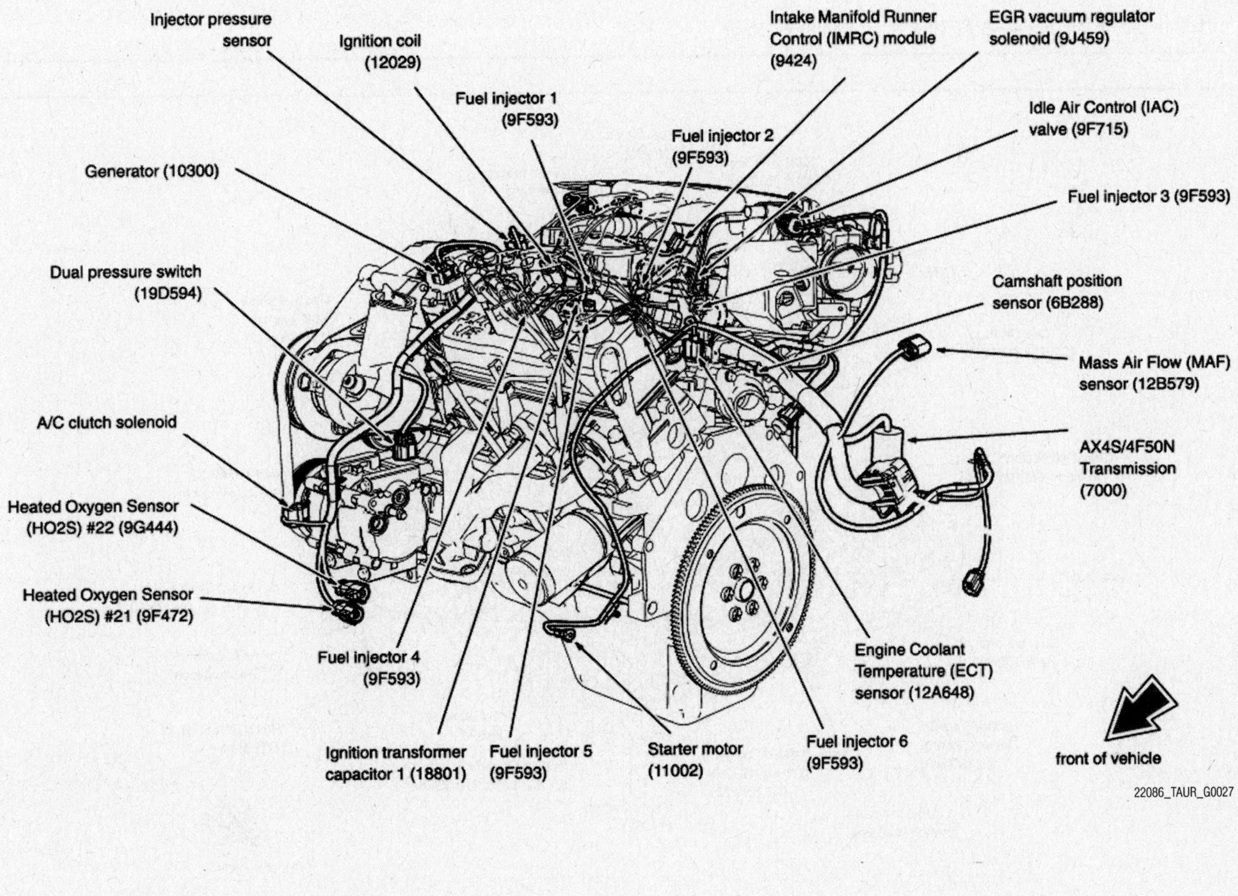

Injector pressure sensor

Ignition coil (12029)

Fuel injector 1 (9F593)

Fuel injector 2 (9F593)

Intake Manifold Runner Control (IMRC) module (9424)

EGR vacuum regulator solenoid (9J459)

Idle Air Control (IAC) valve (9F715)

Fuel injector 3 (9F593)

Generator (10300)

Dual pressure switch (19D594)

Camshaft position sensor (6B288)

Mass Air Flow (MAF) sensor (12B579)

A/C clutch solenoid

AX4S/4F50N Transmission (7000)

Heated Oxygen Sensor (HO2S) #22 (9G444)

Heated Oxygen Sensor (HO2S) #21 (9F472)

Fuel injector 4 (9F593)

Ignition transformer capacitor 1 (18801)

Fuel injector 5 (9F593)

Starter motor (11002)

Fuel injector 6 (9F593)

Engine Coolant Temperature (ECT) sensor (12A648)

front of vehicle

22086_TAUR_G0027

Fig. 100 Connector locations—3.0L (VIN U, 2) Engines—Front

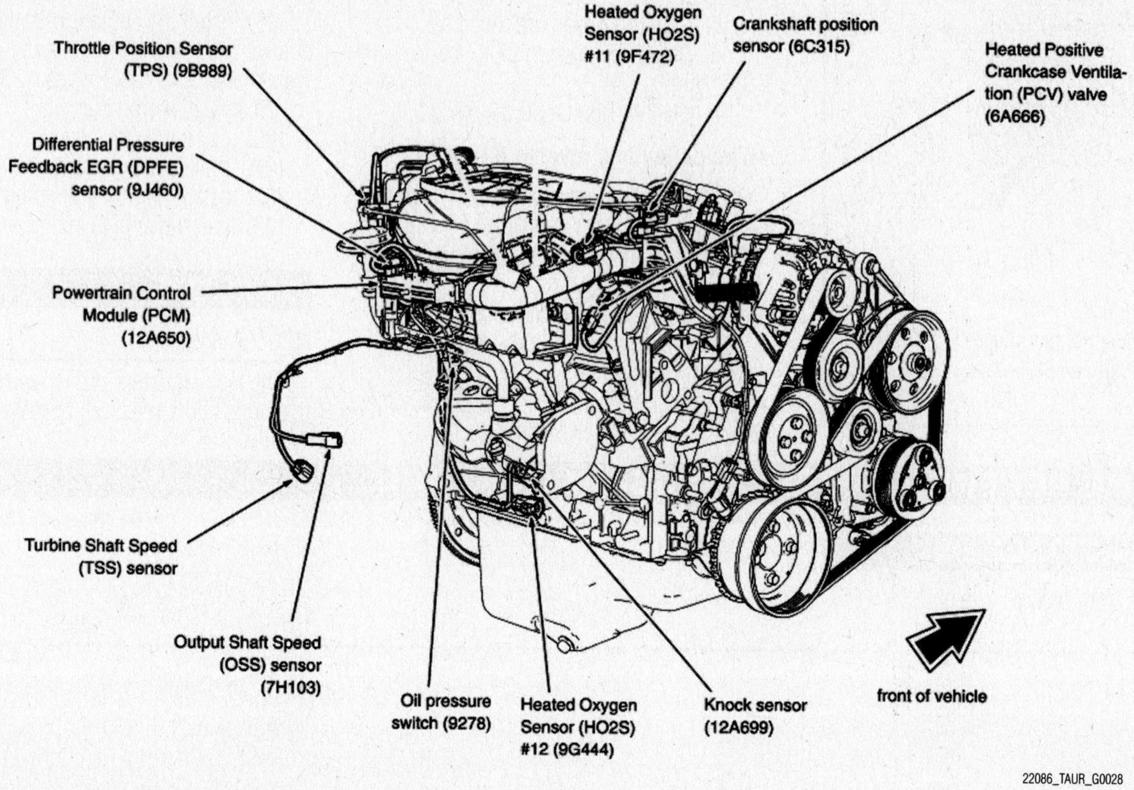

Heated Oxygen
Sensor (HO2S)
#11 (9F472)

Crankshaft position
sensor (6C315)

Heated Positive
Crankcase Ventila-
tion (PCV) valve
(6A666)

Throttle Position Sensor
(TPS) (9B989)

Differential Pressure
Feedback EGR (DPFE)
sensor (9J460)

Powertrain Control
Module (PCM)
(12A650)

Turbine Shaft Speed
(TSS) sensor

Output Shaft Speed
(OSS) sensor
(7H103)

Oil pressure
switch (9278)

Heated Oxygen
Sensor (HO2S)
#12 (9G444)

Knock sensor
(12A699)

front of vehicle

22086_TAUR_G0028

Fig. 101 Connector locations—3.0L (VIN U, 2) Engines—Rear

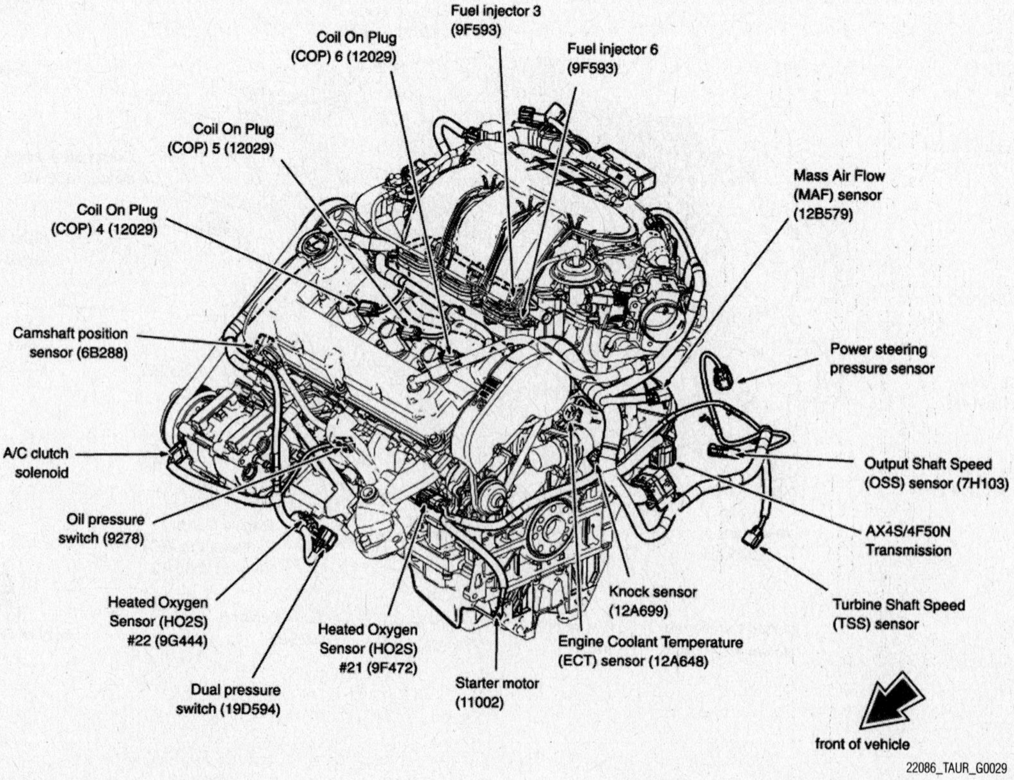

Fuel injector 3
(9F593)

Coil On Plug
(COP) 6 (12029)

Fuel injector 6
(9F593)

Coil On Plug
(COP) 5 (12029)

Mass Air Flow
(MAF) sensor
(12B579)

Coil On Plug
(COP) 4 (12029)

Camshaft position
sensor (6B288)

Power steering
pressure sensor

A/C clutch
solenoid

Output Shaft Speed
(OSS) sensor (7H103)

Oil pressure
switch (9278)

AX4S/4F50N
Transmission

Turbine Shaft Speed
(TSS) sensor

Heated Oxygen
Sensor (HO2S)
#22 (9G444)

Heated Oxygen
Sensor (HO2S)
#21 (9F472)

Knock sensor
(12A699)

Engine Coolant Temperature
(ECT) sensor (12A648)

Dual pressure
switch (19D594)

Starter motor
(11002)

front of vehicle

22086_TAUR_G0029

Fig. 102 Connector locations—3.0L (VIN S) Engine—Front

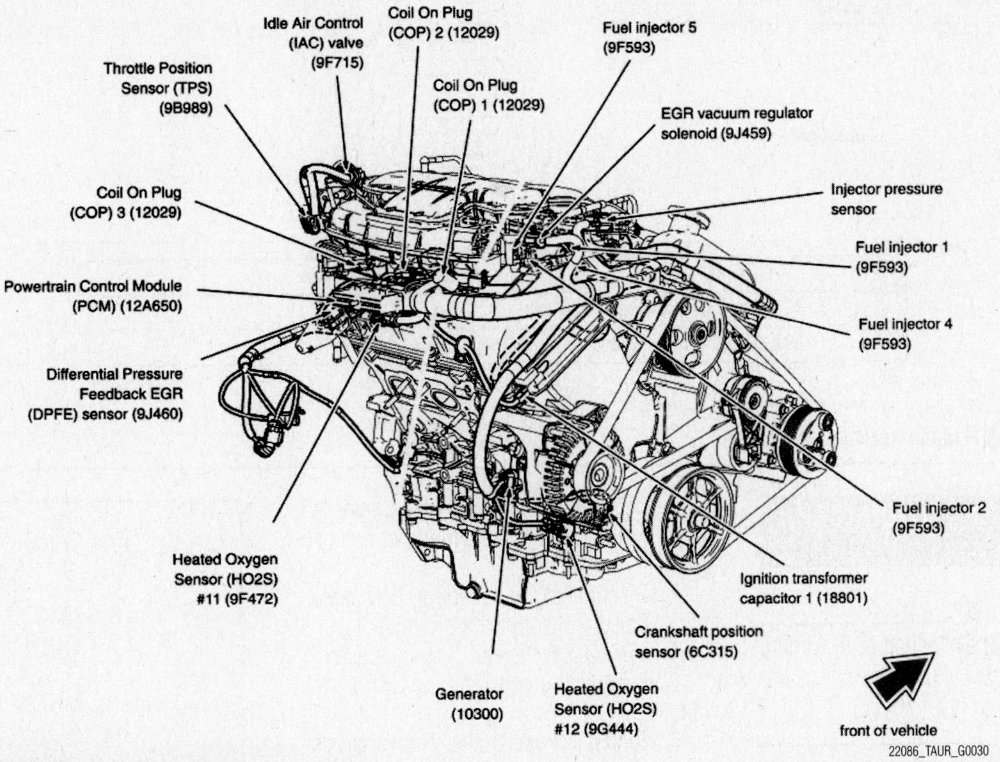

Throttle Position
Sensor (TPS)
(9B989)

Idle Air Control
(IAC) valve
(9F715)

Coil On Plug
(COP) 2 (12029)

Coil On Plug
(COP) 1 (12029)

Fuel injector 5
(9F593)

EGR vacuum regulator
solenoid (9J459)

Coil On Plug
(COP) 3 (12029)

Injector pressure
sensor

Powertrain Control Module
(PCM) (12A650)

Fuel injector 1
(9F593)

Differential Pressure
Feedback EGR
(DPFE) sensor (9J460)

Fuel injector 4
(9F593)

Fuel injector 2
(9F593)

Heated Oxygen
Sensor (HO2S)
#11 (9F472)

Ignition transformer
capacitor 1 (18801)

Crankshaft position
sensor (6C315)

Generator
(10300)

Heated Oxygen
Sensor (HO2S)
#12 (9G444)

front of vehicle

22086_TAUR_G0030

Fig. 103 Connector locations—3.0L (VIN S) Engine—Rear

CAMSHAFT POSITION (CMP) SENSOR

LOCATION

3.0L (VIN U, 2) Engines

At the rear of the engine between the cylinder banks.

3.0L (VIN S) Engine

Front of the engine attached to the forward cylinder head.

OPERATION

The CMP sensor detects the position of the camshaft. The CMP sensor identifies when piston No. 1 is on its compression stroke. A signal is then sent to the PCM and used for synchronizing the sequential firing of the fuel injectors. Coil-on-plug (COP) ignition applications use the CMP signal to select the proper ignition coil to fire. The input circuit to the PCM is referred to as the CMP input or circuit. DTC P0340 is associated with this sensor.

REMOVAL & INSTALLATION

3.0L (VIN U, 2) Engines

1. Before servicing the vehicle, refer to the precautions in the beginning of this section.

2. Disconnect the battery ground cable.

3. Remove the pin-type retainers and remove the accelerator cable snow shield.

4. Detach the spark plug wire retainer.

5. Detach the wiring harness from the intake manifold support.

6. Release the fuel charging wiring harness from the valve cover studs. Position the wiring harness away from the camshaft position sensor.

7. Disconnect the electrical connector.

8. Remove the screws and the CMP.

9. To install, reverse the removal procedure.

➡ **Make sure that the fuel charging wiring harness is fully secured to the valve cover studs.**

3.0L (VIN S) Engine

See Figure 104.

1. Before servicing the vehicle, refer to the precautions in the beginning of this section.

2. Disconnect the battery ground cable.

3. Remove the electrical connector.

4. Remove the bolt and the CMP sensor.

5. To install, reverse the removal procedure.

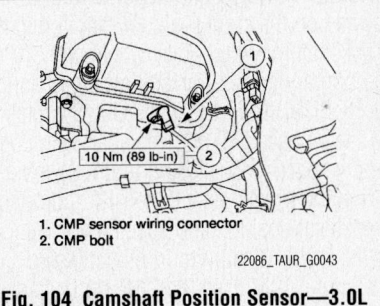

10 Nm (89 lb-in)

1. CMP sensor wiring connector
2. CMP bolt

22086_TAUR_G0043

Fig. 104 Camshaft Position Sensor—3.0L (VIN S) Engine

TESTING

See Figure 105.

1. Before servicing the vehicle, refer to the precautions in the beginning of this section.

❋❋ WARNING

Use only a high-impedance multimeter, otherwise damage to the PCM and/or sensors can result.

2. With the key **OFF**, disconnect the CMP sensor harness connector.

3. Measure the resistance of the CMP sensor:
   • 3.0L Engine: 250–1000 ohms

4. If the resistance measured is outside the limits given, replace the CMP sensor.

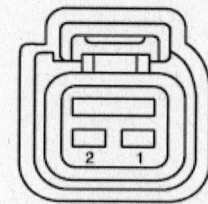

C180 (BK)

Camshaft position
sensor (6B288)

FEMALE

Pin	Circuit	Circuit function
1	359 (GY/RD)	signal, return
2	282 (DB/OG)	Camshaft position sensor, input

22086_TAUR_G0031

Fig. 105 Camshaft Position Sensor Connector

CRANKSHAFT POSITION (CKP) SENSOR

LOCATION

Front of the engine attached to the timing cover near the crankshaft pulley.

OPERATION

The CKP sensor is a magnetic transducer mounted on the engine block or timing cover and is adjacent to a pulse wheel located on the crankshaft. By monitoring the crankshaft mounted pulse wheel, the CKP is the primary sensor for ignition information to the PCM. The trigger wheel has a total of 35 teeth spaced 10 degrees apart with one empty space for a missing tooth. By monitoring the trigger wheel, the CKP indicates crankshaft position and speed information to the PCM. By monitoring the missing tooth, the PCM uses the CKP signal to synchronize the ignition system and track the rotation of the crankshaft.

REMOVAL & INSTALLATION

3.0L (VIN U, 2) Engines

See Figure 106.

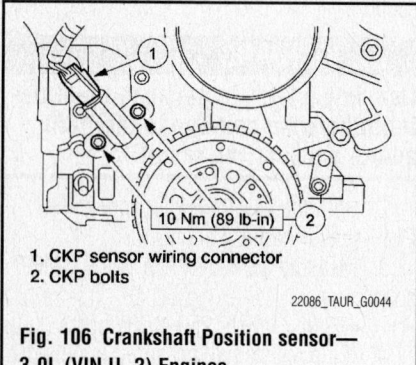

1. CKP sensor wiring connector
2. CKP bolts

22086_TAUR_G0044

Fig. 106 Crankshaft Position sensor— 3.0L (VIN U, 2) Engines

1. Before servicing the vehicle, refer to the precautions in the beginning of this section.
2. Disconnect the battery ground cable.
3. Raise and support the vehicle.
4. Disconnect the electrical connector.
5. Remove the bolts and the CKP sensor.
6. To install, reverse the removal procedure.

3.0L (VIN S) Engine

See Figures 107 and 108.

1. Before servicing the vehicle, refer to the precautions in the beginning of this section.
2. With vehicle in NEUTRAL, position it on a hoist.
3. Disconnect the battery ground cable.
4. Remove the accessory drive belt.
5. Remove the nut and position the power steering pressure line, muffler and bracket assembly out of the way.
6. Remove the right front fender splash shield.
7. Remove the screws and the generator splash shield.

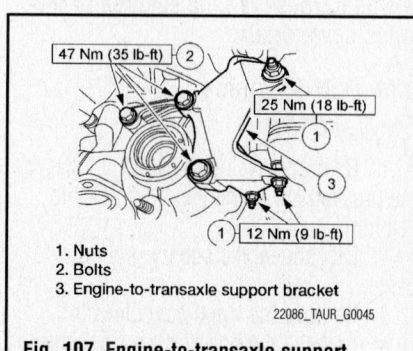

1. Nuts
2. Bolts
3. Engine-to-transaxle support bracket

22086_TAUR_G0045

Fig. 107 Engine-to-transaxle support bracket—3.0L (VIN S) Engine

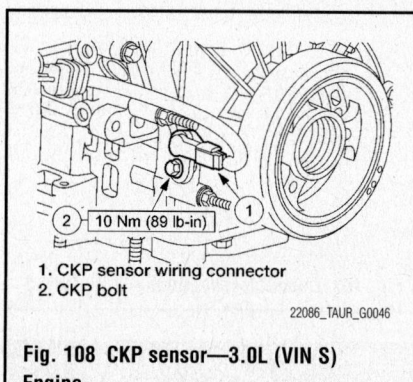

1. CKP sensor wiring connector
2. CKP bolt

22086_TAUR_G0046

Fig. 108 CKP sensor—3.0L (VIN S) Engine

8. Remove the left-hand upper stud bolt and the lower generator bolt. Loosen the right upper stud bolt.
9. Pivot the generator away from the engine block.
10. Remove the engine-to-transaxle support bracket.
11. Disconnect the electrical connector.
12. Remove the bolt and the CKP sensor.
13. To install, reverse the removal procedure.

TESTING

See Figure 109.

1. Before servicing the vehicle, refer to the precautions in the beginning of this section.

✳✳ WARNING

Use only a high-impedance multimeter, otherwise damage to the PCM and/or sensors can result.

2. Visually check the timing cover, CKP sensor and external trigger wheel (outside the timing cover) for obvious physical damage.
3. With the key OFF, disconnect the CKP sensor harness and measure the resis-

C101 (BK)

Crankshaft position
sensor (6C315)

FEMALE

Pin	Circuit	Circuit function
1	349 (DB)	Crankshaft position sensor -
2	350 (GY)	Crankshaft position sensor +

22086_TAUR_G0032

Fig. 109 Crankshaft Position Sensor Connector

tance of the CKP sensor. Standard value is 250–1000 ohms.

4. If the resistance is outside the limits given, replace the CKP sensor.

ENGINE COOLANT TEMPERATURE (ECT) SENSOR

LOCATION

At the rear of the engine between the cylinder banks.

OPERATION

The ECT sensor is a thermistor device in which resistance changes with temperature. The electrical resistance of a thermistor decreases as the temperature increases, and the resistance increases as the temperature decreases. The varying resistance affects the voltage drop across the sensor terminals and provides electrical signals to the PCM corresponding to temperature.

Thermistor-type sensors are considered passive sensors. A passive sensor is connected to a voltage divider network so that varying the resistance of the passive sensor causes a variation in total current flow.

Voltage that is dropped across a fixed resistor in a series with the sensor resistor determines the voltage signal at the PCM. This voltage signal is equal to the reference voltage minus the voltage drop across the fixed resistor.

The ECT measures the temperature of the engine coolant. The sensor is threaded into an engine coolant passage.

REMOVAL & INSTALLATION

3.0L (VIN U, 2) Engines

1. Before servicing the vehicle, refer to the precautions in the beginning of this section.
2. Disconnect the battery ground cable.

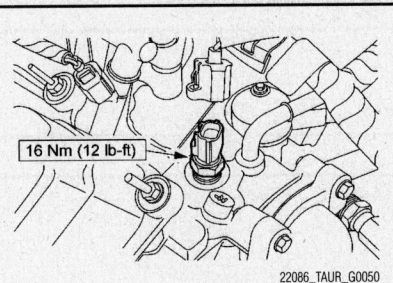

16 Nm (12 lb-ft)

22086_TAUR_G0050

Fig. 110 Engine Coolant Temperature sensor—3.0L (VIN U, 2) Engines

3. Drain the cooling system.
4. Disconnect the ECT sensor electrical connector.
5. Remove the ECT sensor.
6. To install, reverse the removal procedure.

3.0L (VIN S) Engine

See Figures 111 and 112.

1. Before servicing the vehicle, refer to the precautions in the beginning of this section.
2. Drain the cooling system.
3. Remove the air cleaner assembly.
4. Remove the battery tray.

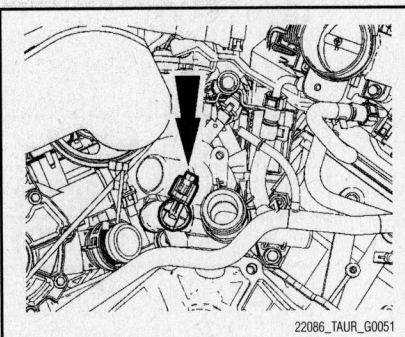

22086_TAUR_G0051

Fig. 111 Engine Coolant Temperature Sensor—3.0L (VIN S) Engine—Engine shown partially disassembled for clarity

5. Disconnect the ECT sensor electrical connector.
6. Pull upward on the locking tab.
7. Rotate the ETC sensor counterclockwise and remove.
8. To install, reverse the removal procedure.

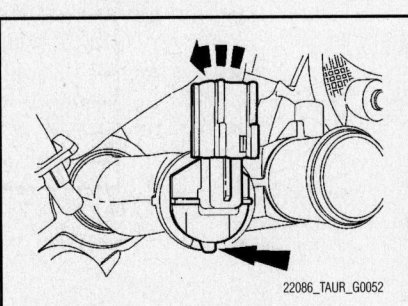

22086_TAUR_G0052

Fig. 112 Engine Coolant Temperature Sensor removal

TESTING

See Figures 113 and 114.

1. Before servicing the vehicle, refer to the precautions in the beginning of this section.

✳✳ WARNING

Use only a high-impedance multimeter, otherwise damage to the PCM and/or sensors can result.

2. With the engine running, backprobe the ECT sensor connector and measure the voltage. Compare readings with the values given in the illustration.

HEATED OXYGEN (HO2S) SENSOR

LOCATION

In the exhaust manifolds (Bank 1 and 2, Sensor 1) or after the catalytic converters (Bank 1 and 2, Sensor 2).

OPERATION

The HO2S detects the presence of oxygen in the exhaust and produces a variable voltage according to the amount of oxygen detected. A high concentration of oxygen (lean air/fuel ratio) in the exhaust produces a voltage signal less than 0.4 volt. A low concentration of oxygen (rich air/fuel ratio) produces a voltage signal greater than 0.6 volt. The HO2S provides feedback to the PCM indicating air/fuel ratio in order to achieve a near stoichiometric air/fuel ratio

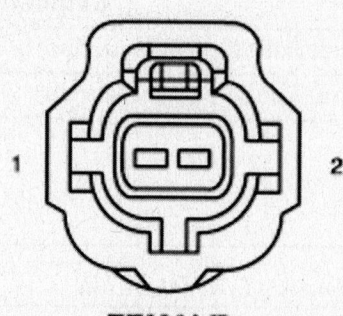

C1064 (GY)

Engine Coolant Temperature (ECT) sensor (12A648)

FEMALE

Pin	Circuit	Circuit function
1	354 (LG/RD)	Engine Coolant Temperature (ECT) sensor, input
2	359 (GY/RD)	signal, return

22086_TAUR_G0033

Fig. 113 Engine Coolant Temperature Sensor Connector

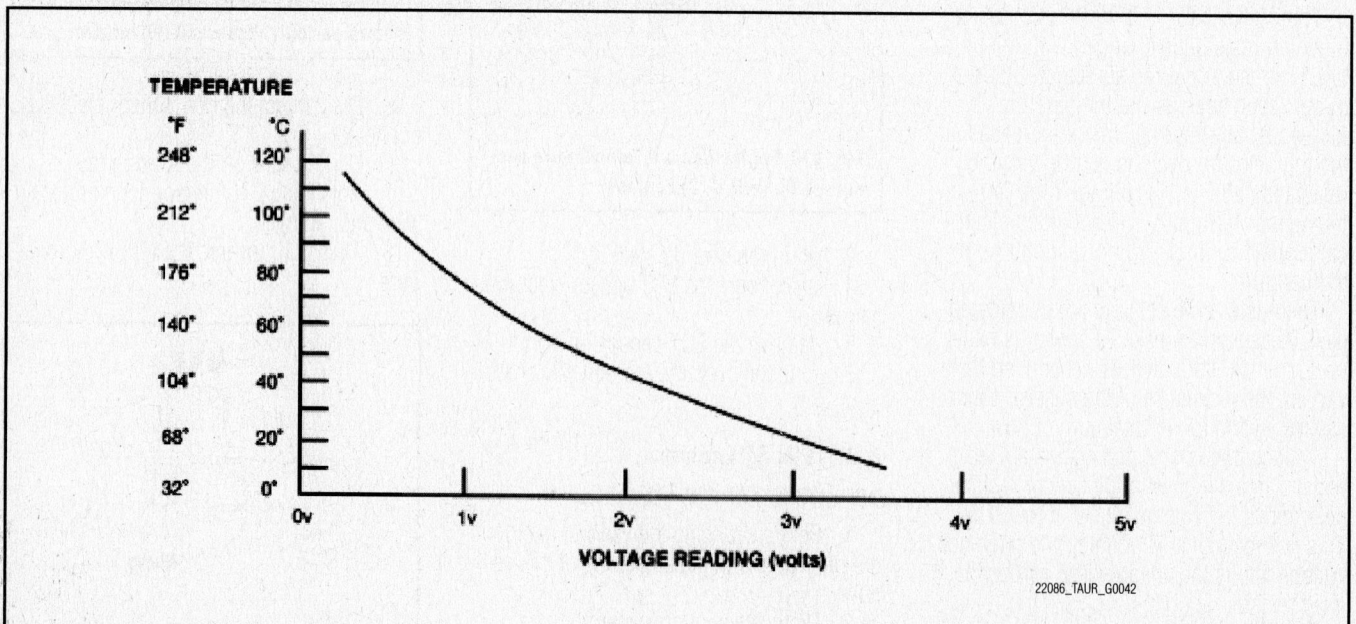

22086_TAUR_G0042

Fig. 114 ECT Temperature and Voltage Chart

of 14.7:1 during closed loop engine operation. The HO2S generates a voltage between 0.0 and 1.1 volts.

Embedded with the sensing element is the HO2S heater. The heating element heats the sensor to a temperature of 800°C (1400°F). At approximately 300°C (600°F) the engine can enter closed loop operation. The VPWR circuit supplies voltage to the heater. The PCM will turn on the heater by providing the ground when the proper conditions occur. The heater allows the engine to enter closed loop operation sooner. The use of this heater requires the HO2S heater control to be duty cycled, to prevent damage to the heater.

REMOVAL & INSTALLATION

See Figure 115.

1. Before servicing the vehicle, refer to the precautions in the beginning of this section.
2. Raise and support the vehicle.
3. Disconnect the wiring harness connector.
4. Using an oxygen sensor wrench or socket, remove the oxygen sensor.

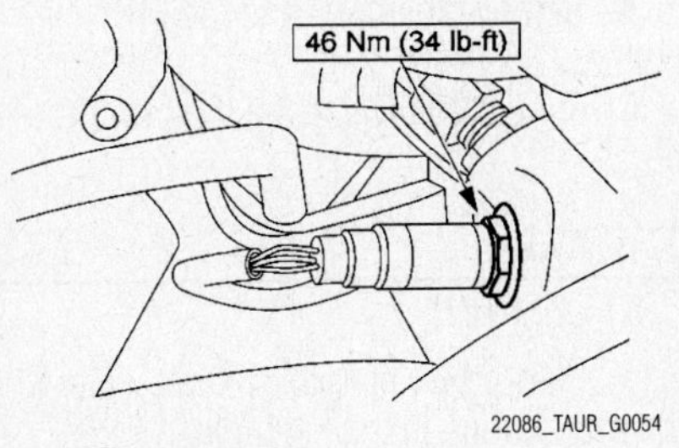
46 Nm (34 lb-ft)
22086_TAUR_G0054

Fig. 115 Heated Oxygen Sensor

To install:

➡Apply anti-seize to the sensor threads before installing the sensor.

5. Install the oxygen sensor and tighten to 34 ft. lbs. (46 Nm).
6. Connect the wiring harness connector.

TESTING

See Figures 116 through 119.

1. Before servicing the vehicle, refer to the precautions in the beginning of this section.

⁂ WARNING

Use only a high-impedance multimeter, otherwise damage to the PCM and/or sensors can result.

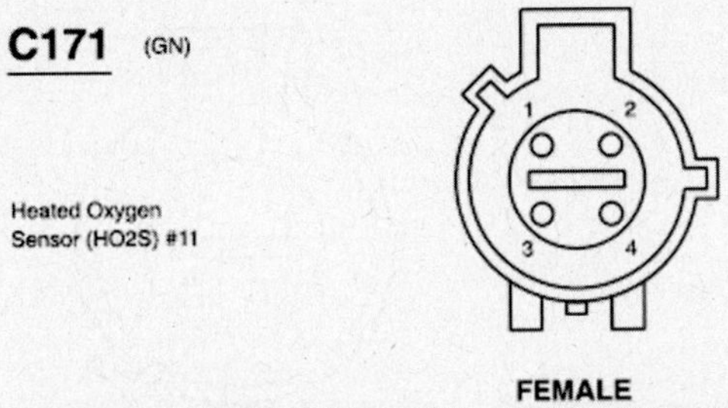
C171 (GN)
Heated Oxygen
Sensor (HO2S) #11
1
2
3
4
FEMALE

Pin	Circuit	Circuit function
1	387 (RD/WH)	Heated Oxygen Sensor (HO2S) #11, heater
2	361 (RD)	Voltage supplied in Start and Run (overload protected)
3	74 (GY/LB)	Heated Oxygen Sensor (HO2S) #11, input
4	359 (GY/RD)	signal, return

22086_TAUR_G0036

Fig. 116 Heated Oxygen Sensor Connector—Bank 1 Sensor 1

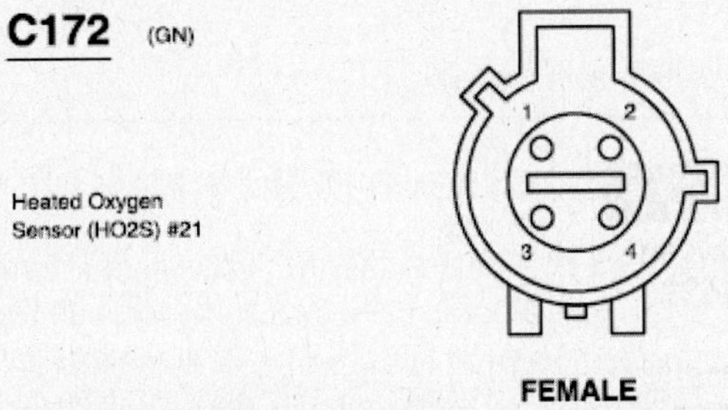
C172 (GN)
Heated Oxygen
Sensor (HO2S) #21
1
2
3
4
FEMALE

Pin	Circuit	Circuit function
1	389 (WH/BK)	Heated Oxygen Sensor (HO2S) #21, heater
2	361 (RD)	Voltage supplied in Start and Run (overload protected)
3	392 (RD/LG)	Heated Oxygen Sensor (HO2S) #21, input
4	359 (GY/RD)	signal, return

22086_TAUR_G0037

Fig. 117 Heated Oxygen Sensor Connector—Bank 2 Sensor 1

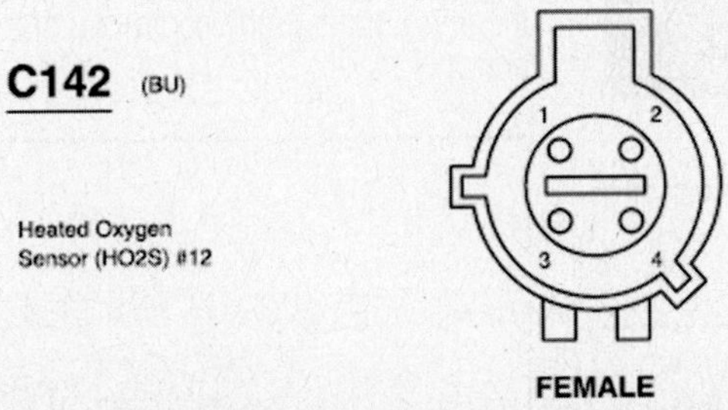
C142 (BU)
Heated Oxygen
Sensor (HO2S) #12
1
2
3
4
FEMALE

Pin	Circuit	Circuit function
1	388 (YE/LB)	Heated Oxygen Sensor (HO2S) #12, heater
2	361 (RD)	Voltage supplied in Start and Run (overload protected)
3	94 (RD/BK)	Heated Oxygen Sensor (HO2S) #12, input
4	359 (GY/RD)	signal, return

22086_TAUR_G0035

Fig. 118 Heated Oxygen Sensor Connector—Bank 1 Sensor 2

C141 (BU)

Heated Oxygen
Sensor (HO2S) #22

FEMALE

Pin	Circuit	Circuit function
1	390 (TN/YE)	Heated Oxygen Sensor (HO2S) #22, heater
2	361 (RD)	Voltage supplied in Start and Run (overload protected)
3	393 (VT/LG)	Heated Oxygen Sensor (HO2S) #22, input
4	359 (GY/RD)	signal, return

22086_TAUR_G0034

Fig. 119 Heated Oxygen Sensor Connector—Bank 2 Sensor 2

❊❊ WARNING

Do not measure resistance between pins 3 and 4. Damage to the HO2S will result.

2. With the key **OFF**, disconnect the HO2S harness connector.

3. Measure the HO2S sensor resistances as follows:

- Pins 1 and 2: 3–30 ohms.
- Pins 1 and 4: Greater than 10 Mohms.
- Pin 1 and battery negative: Greater than 10 Mohms.

4. If any measurement is outside the range given, replace the HO2S.

IDLE AIR CONTROL (IAC) VALVE

LOCATION

Attached to the throttle body.

OPERATION

The throttle body system meters air to the engine during idle, part throttle, and wide open throttle (WOT) conditions. The throttle body system consists of an idle air control (IAC) valve assembly, an idle air orifice, single or dual bores with butterfly valve throttle plates, and a throttle position (TP) sensor. One other source of idle air flow is the positive crankcase ventilation (PCV) system. The combined idle air flow (from idle air orifice IAC flow and PCV flow) is measured by the MAF sensor on all applications.

During idle, the throttle body assembly provides a set amount of air flow to the engine through the idle air passage and the PCV valve. The IAC valve assembly provides additional air when commanded by the PCM to maintain the proper engine idle speed under varying conditions. The IAC valve assembly mounts directly to the intake manifold assembly in most applications. Idle speed is controlled by the PCM and cannot be adjusted.

REMOVAL & INSTALLATION

See Figure 120.

1. Before servicing the vehicle, refer to the precautions in the beginning of this section.

2. Disconnect the battery ground cable.

3. Disconnect the electrical connector.

4. Remove the bolts and the IAC solenoid.

5. To install, reverse the removal procedure.

TESTING

See Figure 121.

1. Before servicing the vehicle, refer to the precautions in the beginning of this section.

❊❊ WARNING

Use only a high-impedance multimeter, otherwise damage to the PCM and/or sensors can result.

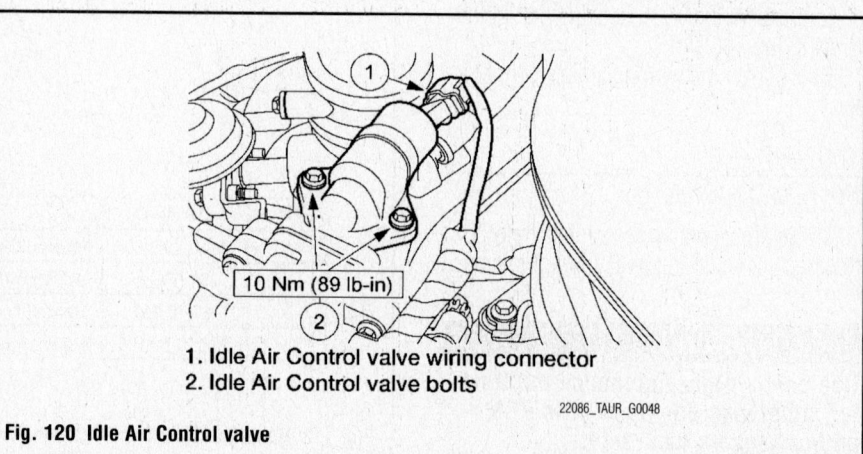

10 Nm (89 lb-in)

1. Idle Air Control valve wiring connector
2. Idle Air Control valve bolts

22086_TAUR_G0048

Fig. 120 Idle Air Control valve

C1066 (BK)

Idle Air Control (IAC) valve

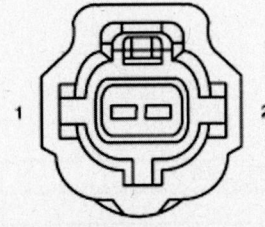

FEMALE

Pin	Circuit	Circuit function
1	883 (PK/LB)	Voltage supplied in Start and Run (overload protected)
2	264 (WH/LB)	Idle Air Control (IAC) valve, control

22086_TAUR_G0058

Fig. 121 IAC valve connector

2. With the key **OFF**, disconnect the IAC valve connector.

3. Measure the resistance of the IAC valve. Specification is 6–15 ohms.

4. Replace if out of specification.

INJECTION CONTROL PRESSURE (ICP) SENSOR

LOCATION

Front of the engine attached to the fuel rail.

OPERATION

Also referred to as the Fuel Rail Pressure (FRP) sensor.

The FRP sensor is a diaphragm strain gauge device in which resistance changes with pressure. The electrical resistance of a strain gauge increases as pressure increases, and the resistance decreases as the pressure decreases. The varying resistance affects the voltage drop across the sensor terminals and provides electrical signals to the PCM corresponding to pressure.

Strain gauge type sensors are considered passive sensors. A passive sensor is connected to a voltage divider network so that varying the resistance of the passive sensor causes a variation in total current flow.

Voltage that is dropped across a fixed resistor in series with the sensor resistor determines the voltage signal at the PCM. This voltage signal is equal to the reference voltage minus the voltage drop across the fixed resistor.

The FRP sensor measures the pressure of the fuel near the fuel injectors. This signal is used by the PCM to adjust the fuel injector pulse width and meter fuel to each engine combustion cylinder.

REMOVAL & INSTALLATION

See Figure 122.

1. Before servicing the vehicle, refer to the precautions in the beginning of this section.

2. Release the fuel system pressure.

3. Disconnect the battery ground cable.

4. Disconnect the fuel injection pressure and temperature sensor electrical connector and the vacuum hose.

5. Remove the bolts and the fuel injection pressure and temperature sensor.

➡Before installing the fuel injection pressure and temperature sensor, inspect and lubricate the O-ring seal with clean engine oil.

➡Hand-tighten both bolts before tightening to specification.

6. To install, reverse the removal procedure.

TESTING

See Figures 123 and 124.

1. Before servicing the vehicle, refer to the precautions in the beginning of this section.

2. Connect a mechanical fuel pressure gauge.

3. With the key **ON**, backprobe the FRP sensor pins 2 and 3.

4. Compare the voltage and pressure readings with the specifications table.

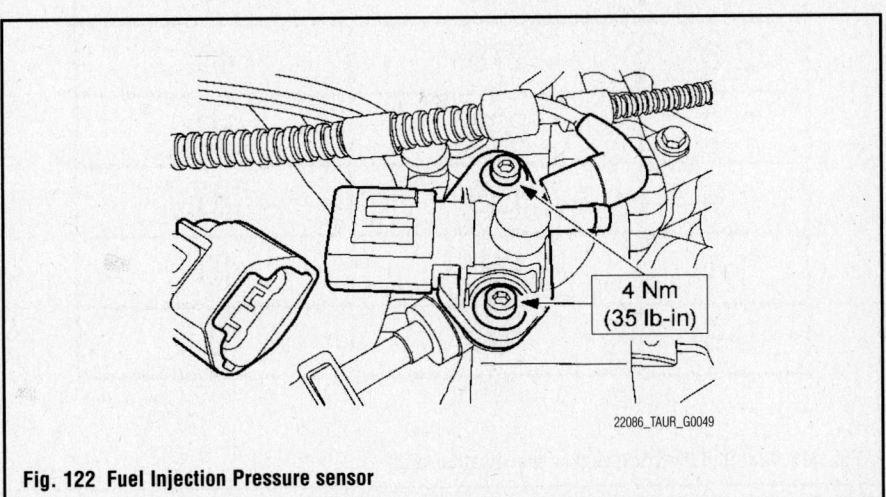

4 Nm (35 lb-in)

22086_TAUR_G0049

Fig. 122 Fuel Injection Pressure sensor

C1073 (BK)

Injector pressure
sensor

3.0L 2V

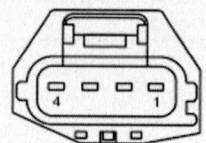

FEMALE

Pin	Circuit	Circuit function
1	351 (BN/WH)	Reference, voltage
2	359 (GY/RD)	signal, return
3	925 (WH/YE)	Injector pressure sensor, input

3.0L 4V

FEMALE

Pin	Circuit	Circuit function
1	925 (WH/YE)	Injector pressure sensor, input
2	351 (BN/WH)	Reference voltage
3	241 (LB/WH)	Injector pressure sensor signal (FRT)
4	359 (GY/RD)	Signal return

22086_TAUR_G0056

Fig. 123 Fuel Rail Pressure Sensor connector

Voltage	Pressure (kPa)	Pressure (psi)
4.5	482	70
3.9	413	60
3.4	344	50
2.8	275	40
2.2	207	30
1.6	138	20
1.1	69	10
0.5	0	0

22086_TAUR_G0057

Fig. 124 Fuel Rail Pressure sensor specification table

KNOCK SENSOR (KS)

LOCATION

On the engine block below the exhaust manifold.

OPERATION

The KS is a tuned accelerometer on the engine which converts engine vibration to an electrical signal. The PCM uses this signal to determine the presence of engine knock and to retard spark timing.

REMOVAL & INSTALLATION

See Figure 125.

1. Before servicing the vehicle, refer to the precautions in the beginning of this section.
2. With the vehicle in NEUTRAL, position it on a hoist.
3. Disconnect the battery ground cable.
4. Disconnect the KS electrical connector.

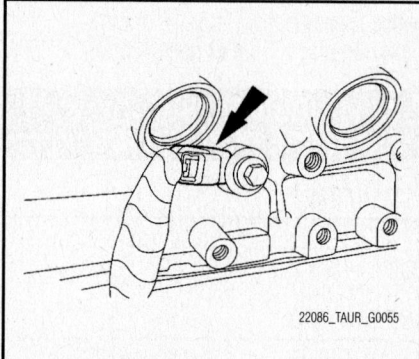

22086_TAUR_G0055

Fig. 125 Knock Sensor

5. Remove the bolt and the KS.
6. To install, reverse the removal procedure.

TESTING

See Figures 126 and 127.

1. Before servicing the vehicle, refer to the precautions in the beginning of this section.

✳✳ WARNING

Use only a high-impedance multimeter, otherwise damage to the PCM and/or sensors can result.

2. With the key **ON** and the engine **OFF**, disconnect the knock sensor.
3. Measure resistance of the knock sensor. Standard value is 4.39 Mohms–5.35 Mohms. If not, replace the knock sensor.

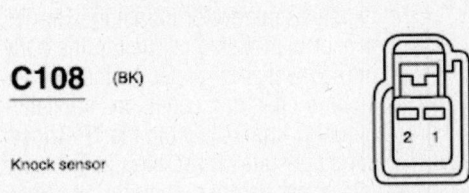

Pin	Circuit	Circuit function
1	310 (YE/RD)	Knock sensor +
2	1273 (YE)	Knock sensor −

22086_TAUR_G0038

Fig. 126 Knock Sensor Connector–3.0L (VIN U, 2) Engines

Pin	Circuit	Circuit function
1	310 (YE/RD)	Knock sensor +
2	1273 (YE)	Knock sensor −

22086_TAUR_G0039

Fig. 127 Knock Sensor Connector–3.0L (VIN S) Engine

MASS AIR FLOW (MAF) SENSOR

LOCATION

Attached to the air filter assembly.

OPERATION

The MAF sensor uses a hot wire sensing element to measure the amount of air entering the engine. Air passing over the hot wire causes it to cool. This hot wire is maintained at 200°C (392°F) above the ambient temperature as measured by a constant cold wire. If the hot wire electronic sensing element must be replaced, then the entire assembly must be replaced. Replacing only the element may change the air flow calibration.

The current required to maintain the temperature of the hot wire is proportional to the mass air flow. The MAF sensor then outputs an analog voltage signal to the PCM proportional to the intake air mass. The PCM calculates the required fuel injector pulse width in order to provide the desired air/fuel ratio. This input is also used in determining transmission electronic pressure control (EPC), shift and torque converter clutch scheduling.

REMOVAL & INSTALLATION

See Figure 128.

1. Before servicing the vehicle, refer to the precautions in the beginning of this section.

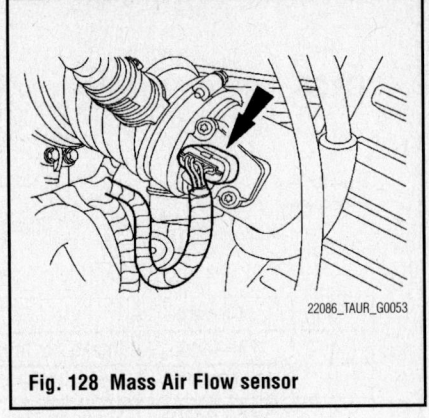

22086_TAUR_G0053

Fig. 128 Mass Air Flow sensor

2. Disconnect the battery ground cable.

3. Disconnect the MAF sensor electrical connector.

4. Remove the two retaining screws and the MAF sensor.

5. To install, reverse the removal procedure.

TESTING

See Figure 129.

1. Before servicing the vehicle, refer to the precautions in the beginning of this section.

⁂ WARNING

Use only a high-impedance multimeter, otherwise damage to the PCM and/or sensors can result.

2. Check the air inlet system (air cleaner, housing, ductwork) for obstructions or blockage.

3. Check for broken/loose air outlet tube clamps (throttle body and air cleaner assembly ends), cracks/holes in the air outlet tube, and worn gaskets between the MAF sensor and the air cleaner assembly. Check throttle body bore for sludge. Verify the MAF sensor is connected. Repair as necessary.

4. Disconnect the MAF harness connector.

5. With the key **ON** and engine **OFF**, check the following connector pin values:
- Pins 2, 4, and 5 should be ground.
- Pin 6 should be B+ voltage.

6. Turn the key **OFF** and reconnect the MAF harness connector.

7. Start the engine and backprobe pin 1. This voltage should change with the intake air temperature.

8. Start the engine and backprobe pin 3. This voltage should rise with the engine rpm.

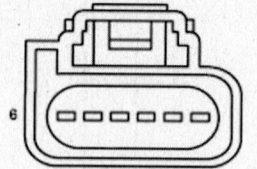

C128 (BK)

Mass Air Flow (MAF) sensor

6 [□ □ □ □ □ □] 1

FEMALE

Pin	Circuit	Circuit function
1	743 (GY)	Intake Air Temperature (IAT) sensor, input
2	359 (GY/RD)	signal, return
3	967 (LB/RD)	Mass Air Flow (MAF) sensor, signal
4	968 (TN/LB)	Mass Air Flow (MAF) sensor, signal return
5	570 (BK/WH)	Ground
6	361 (RD)	Voltage supplied in Start and Run (overload protected)

22086_TAUR_G0040

Fig. 129 Mass Air Flow Sensor Connector

POWERTRAIN CONTROL MODULE (PCM)

LOCATION

Under the right cowl panel.

OPERATION

The center of the electronic engine control (EEC) system is a microprocessor called the PCM. The PCM receives input from sensors and other electronic components (switches, relays). Based on the information received and programmed into its memory, the PCM generates output signals to control various relays, solenoids and actuators.

REMOVAL & INSTALLATION

3.0L (VIN U, 2) Engines

1. Before servicing the vehicle, refer to the precautions in the beginning of this section.
2. Park the wiper pivot arms in the highest position on the glass.
3. Disconnect the battery ground cable.
4. Remove the three RH cowl panel clips and remove the RH cowl panel.
5. Remove the clip on the water shield.
6. Remove the three RH water shield screws and remove the RH water shield.
7. Disconnect the evaporative emission (EVAP) canister purge valve return tube at the intake manifold and position aside.
8. Disconnect the powertrain control module (PCM) electrical connector and remove the gasket.

9. Remove the retaining bolts and the PCM.
10. To install, reverse the removal procedure.

3.0L (VIN S) Engine

1. Before servicing the vehicle, refer to the precautions in the beginning of this section.
2. Park the wiper pivot arms in the highest position on the glass.
3. Disconnect the battery ground cable.
4. Remove the three RH cowl panel clips and remove the RH cowl panel.
5. Remove the clip on the water shield.
6. Remove the three RH water shield screws and remove the RH water shield.
7. Disconnect the powertrain control module (PCM) electrical connector and remove the gasket.
8. Remove the retaining bolts and the PCM.
9. To install, reverse the removal procedure.

THROTTLE POSITION SENSOR (TPS)

LOCATION

Mounted to the throttle body.

OPERATION

The TP sensor is a rotary potentiometer sensor that provides a signal to the PCM that is linearly proportional to the throttle plate/shaft position. The sensor housing has a 3-blade electrical connector that may be gold plated. The gold plating increases corrosion resistance on terminals and increases connector durability. The TP sensor is mounted on the throttle body. As the TP sensor is rotated by the throttle shaft, 4 operating conditions are determined by the PCM from the TP. Those conditions are closed throttle (includes idle or deceleration), part throttle (includes cruise or moderate acceleration), wide open throttle (includes maximum acceleration or de-choke on crank), and throttle angle rate.

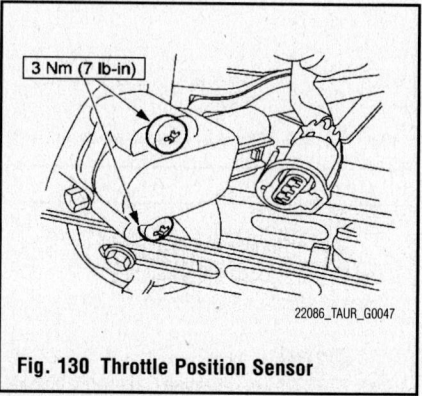

3 Nm (7 lb-in)

22086_TAUR_G0047

Fig. 130 Throttle Position Sensor

REMOVAL & INSTALLATION

See Figure 130.

1. Before servicing the vehicle, refer to the precautions in the beginning of this section.
2. Disconnect the battery ground cable.
3. Disconnect the TP sensor electrical connector.
4. Remove the screws and the TP sensor.
5. To install, reverse the removal procedure.

TESTING

See Figure 131.

1. Before servicing the vehicle, refer to the precautions in the beginning of this section.

✳✳ WARNING

Use only a high-impedance multimeter, otherwise damage to the PCM and/or sensors can result.

2. With the key **ON** and engine **OFF**, backprobe the TPS connector and check for the following values:
- Pin 1: 5 volt reference voltage
- Pin 2: Varies with throttle position
- Pin 3: Signal ground

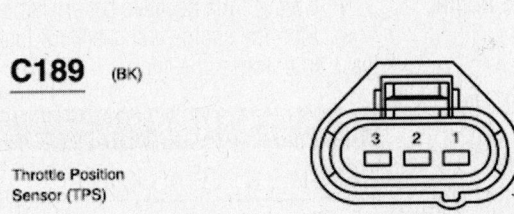

C189 (BK)

Throttle Position
Sensor (TPS)

FEMALE

Pin	Circuit	Circuit function
1	351 (BN/WH)	Reference, voltage
2	355 (GY/WH)	Throttle Position Sensor (TPS), input
3	359 (GY/RD)	signal, return

22086_TAUR_G0041

Fig. 131 Throttle Position Sensor Connector

VEHICLE SPEED SENSOR (VSS)

LOCATION

On top of the transaxle, under the RH exhaust manifold.

OPERATION

Also called the Output Shaft Speed (OSS) Sensor.

The OSS sensor provides the PCM with information about the rotational speed of an output shaft. The PCM uses the information to control and diagnose powertrain behavior. The sensor is also used as the source of vehicle speed.

REMOVAL & INSTALLATION

3.0L (VIN U, 2) Engines

See Figure 132.

1. Before servicing the vehicle, refer to the precautions in the beginning of this section.
2. Disconnect the output shaft speed (OSS) sensor connector.

➡**The OSS sensor is located under the RH exhaust manifold.**

3. Remove the connector.
4. Remove the bolt.
5. Remove the cover.
6. Remove the OSS sensor.

➡**Lubricate the OSS O-ring before installing the sensor.**

7. To install, reverse the removal procedure.

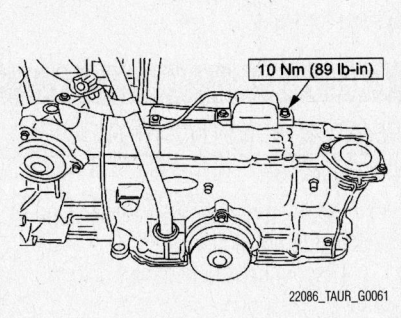

10 Nm (89 lb-in)

22086_TAUR_G0061

Fig. 132 OSS sensor—3.0L (VIN U, 2) Engines

3.0L (VIN S) Engine

See Figures 133 and 134.

1. Before servicing the vehicle, refer to the precautions in the beginning of this section.
2. Disconnect the output shaft speed (OSS) sensor connector.
3. Rotate the belt tensioner clockwise and remove the drive belt.
4. Raise and support the vehicle.
5. Remove the RH front wheel.
6. Remove the RH front inner fender splash shield.
7. Remove the torque converter inspection cover.
8. Use the special tool 303-544 to hold the flexplate.

➡**The crankshaft pulley has a reverse thread.**

9. Remove the crankshaft pulley.
10. Remove the stator and voltage regulator connectors.
11. Remove the generator mounting bolts and remove the generator.

➡**To remove the sensor, you must access from the passenger side of the vehicle.**

12. Remove the connector.
13. Remove the bolt.
14. Remove the cover.
15. Remove the OSS sensor.
16. To install, reverse the removal procedure.

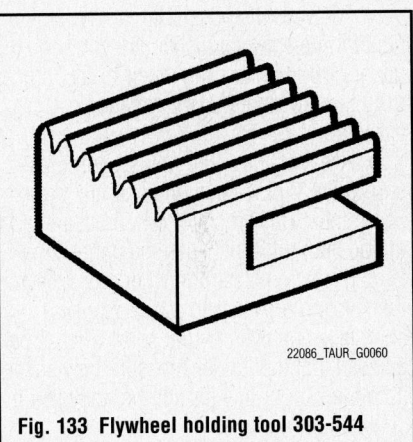

22086_TAUR_G0060

Fig. 133 Flywheel holding tool 303-544

TESTING

1. Before servicing the vehicle, refer to the precautions in the beginning of this section.
2. Raise and support the vehicle.
3. Disconnect the OSS sensor wiring connector.
4. Measure the OSS sensor resistance. Specification is 400–1250 ohms.
5. Replace if out of specification.

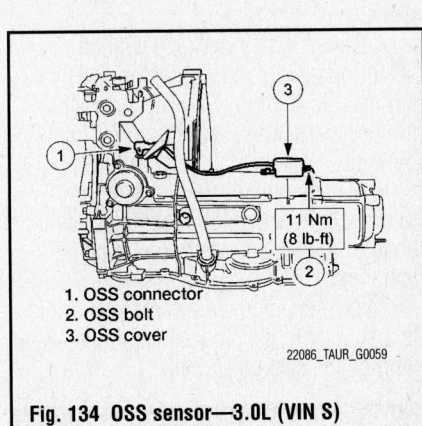

11 Nm (8 lb-ft)

1. OSS connector
2. OSS bolt
3. OSS cover

22086_TAUR_G0059

Fig. 134 OSS sensor—3.0L (VIN S) Engine

FUEL SYSTEM SERVICE PRECAUTIONS

Safety is the most important factor when performing not only fuel system maintenance but any type of maintenance. Failure to conduct maintenance and repairs in a safe manner may result in serious personal injury or death. Maintenance and testing of the vehicle's fuel system components can be accomplished safely and effectively by adhering to the following rules and guidelines.

• To avoid the possibility of fire and personal injury, always disconnect the negative battery cable unless the repair or test procedure requires that battery voltage be applied.

• Always relieve the fuel system pressure prior to disconnecting any fuel system component (injector, fuel rail, pressure regulator, etc.), fitting or fuel line connection. Exercise extreme caution whenever relieving fuel system pressure to avoid exposing skin, face and eyes to fuel spray. Please be advised that fuel under pressure may penetrate the skin or any part of the body that it contacts.

• Always place a shop towel or cloth around the fitting or connection prior to loosening to absorb any excess fuel due to spillage. Ensure that all fuel spillage (should it occur) is quickly removed from engine surfaces. Ensure that all fuel soaked cloths or towels are deposited into a suitable waste container.

• Always keep a dry chemical (Class B) fire extinguisher near the work area.

• Do not allow fuel spray or fuel vapors to come into contact with a spark or open flame.

• Always use a back-up wrench when loosening and tightening fuel line connection fittings. This will prevent unnecessary stress and torsion to fuel line piping.

• Always replace worn fuel fitting O-rings with new Do not substitute fuel hose or equivalent where fuel pipe is installed.

Before servicing the vehicle, make sure to also refer to the precautions in the beginning of this section as well.

RELIEVING FUEL SYSTEM PRESSURE

1. Before servicing the vehicle, refer to the precautions section.

➡ **The fuel pump relay is located in the engine compartment fuse box.**

2. Remove the fuel pump relay.
3. Start the engine and allow it to idle until it stalls.
4. After the engine stalls, crank the engine for approximately 5 seconds to make sure the fuel injection supply manifold pressure has been released.
5. Turn the ignition switch to the OFF position.
6. When fuel system service is complete, install the fuel pump relay.

➡ **It may take more than one key cycle to pressurize the fuel system.**

7. Cycle the ignition key and wait three seconds to pressurize the fuel system. Check for leaks before starting the engine.
8. Start the vehicle and check the fuel system for leaks.

FUEL FILTER

REMOVAL & INSTALLATION
See Figure 135.

1. Before servicing the vehicle, refer to the precautions section.
2. Disconnect the negative battery cable.
3. Relieve the fuel system pressure.
4. Disconnect the fuel lines.
5. Loosen the filter retaining clamp and remove the fuel filter.

To install:
6. Install the fuel filter with the flow arrow facing the proper direction and tighten the filter retaining clamp.
7. Push the fuel lines on to the filter fittings until an audible click is heard.

8. Connect the negative battery cable.
9. Start the engine and check for fuel leaks and proper operation.

FUEL INJECTORS

REMOVAL & INSTALLATION

3.0L (VIN U, 2) Engines
See Figure 136.

1. Before servicing the vehicle, refer to the precautions section.
2. Relieve fuel system pressure.
3. Remove or disconnect the following:
• Negative battery cable
• Air cleaner outlet tube
• Fuel lines
• Upper intake manifold
• Fuel injector electrical connectors
• Fuel pressure regulator vacuum line
• Fuel supply manifold with the injectors attached
• Injectors from the supply manifold

To install:
4. Install or connect the following:
• Fuel injectors. Use new O-ring seals.
• Fuel supply manifold with the injectors attached and tighten the bolts to 89 inch lbs. (10 Nm)
• Fuel pressure regulator vacuum line
• Fuel injector electrical connectors
• Upper intake manifold
• Fuel lines
• Air cleaner outlet tube
• Negative battery cable
5. Start the engine and check for leaks.

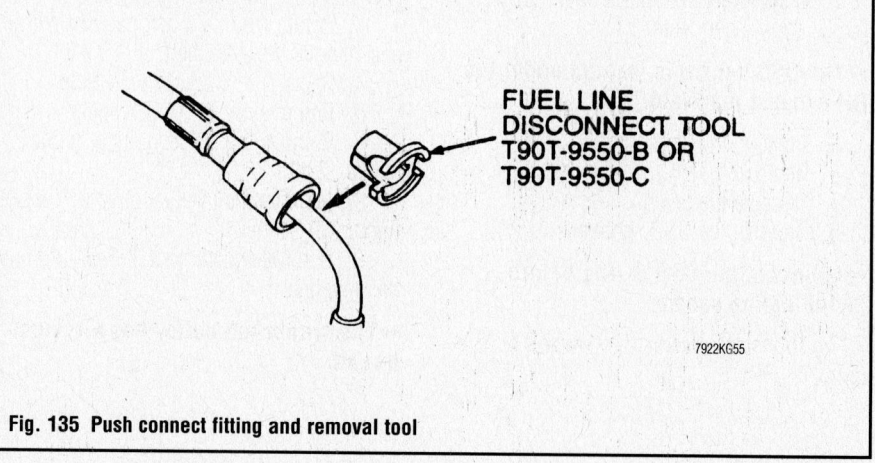

FUEL LINE
DISCONNECT TOOL
T90T-9550-B OR
T90T-9550-C

7922KG55

Fig. 135 Push connect fitting and removal tool

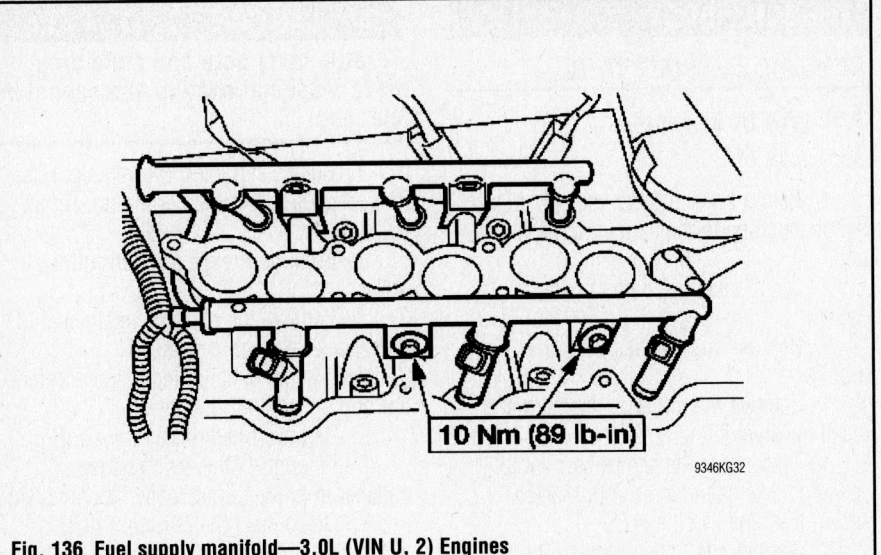

Fig. 136 Fuel supply manifold—3.0L (VIN U, 2) Engines

3.0L (VIN S) Engine

See Figure 137.

1. Before servicing the vehicle, refer to the precautions section.
2. Relieve fuel system pressure.
3. Remove or disconnect the following:
   - Negative battery cable
   - Air cleaner outlet tube
   - Fuel lines
   - Upper intake manifold
   - Fuel injector electrical connectors
   - Fuel pressure regulator vacuum line
   - Fuel supply manifold
   - Injectors from the lower intake manifold

To install:

4. Install or connect the following:
   - Fuel injectors. Use new O-ring seals.
   - Fuel supply manifold and tighten the bolts 89 inch lbs. (10 Nm)
   - Fuel pressure regulator vacuum line
   - Fuel injector electrical connectors
   - Upper intake manifold

- Fuel lines
- Air cleaner outlet tube
- Negative battery cable

5. Start the engine and check for leaks.

FUEL PUMP

REMOVAL & INSTALLATION

See Figures 138 and 139.

1. Before servicing the vehicle, refer to the precautions section.
2. Properly relieve the fuel system pressure.
3. Disconnect the negative battery cable.
4. Using suitable hose pinching pliers, clamp the fuel tank filler hose in the location illustrated.
5. Release the clamp to the fuel tank filler tube and remove. Disconnect the three quick release couplings from the fuel tank tubes.
6. Disconnect the fuel pump electrical connector.
7. Disconnect the fuel filter inlet tube.

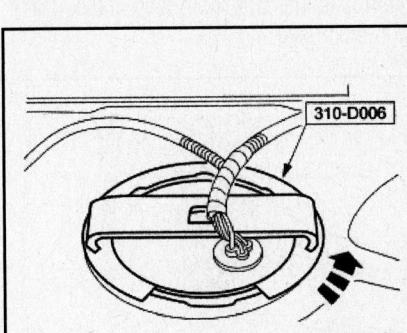

Fig. 138 Using suitable hose pinching pliers, clamp the fuel tank filler hose in the location illustrated

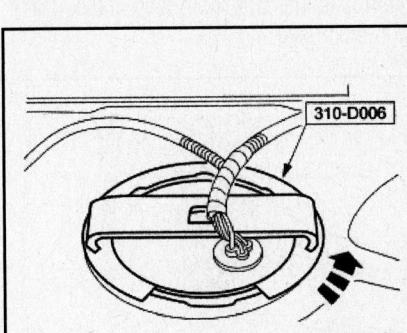

(310-D006)

Fig. 139 Using the tool illustrated, remove the fuel pump module retaining ring

8. Position a suitable lifting device under the fuel tank.
9. Remove the two fuel tank support strap bolts (one shown).
10. Lower the fuel tank to access the fuel pump module while swinging the fuel tank support straps away from the fuel tank.
11. Clean the area around the fuel pump mounting flange.
12. Disconnect the fuel pump module electrical connector and the fuel pump module fuel outlet tube.
13. Using the tool illustrated, remove the fuel pump module retaining ring.

※ CAUTION

The fuel pump module must be handled carefully to avoid damage to the float arm, filter and convolute hoses.

14. Turn the fuel pump module counterclockwise and the fuel pump module will release from the locking tabs.
15. Remove the fuel pump module from the fuel tank.
16. Drain the fuel from the fuel tank.

To install:

17. Installation is the reverse of removal.

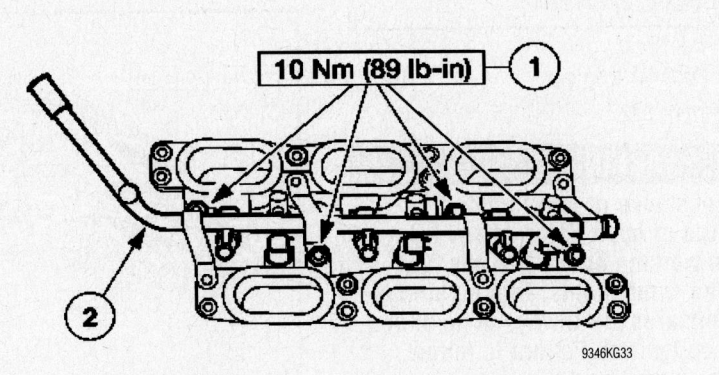

Fig. 137 Retaining bolts (1) and Fuel supply Manifold (2)—3.0L (VIN S) Engine

18. Tighten the fuel tank strap bolts to 26 ft. lbs. (35 Nm).

19. Start the engine and check for leaks.

FUEL TANK

REMOVAL & INSTALLATION

See Figure 140.

1. Before servicing the vehicle, refer to the precautions section.

2. Properly relieve the fuel system pressure.

3. Disconnect the negative battery cable.

4. Using suitable hose pinching pliers, clamp the fuel tank filler hose in the location illustrated.

06017-TAUR-G58

Fig. 140 Using suitable hose pinching pliers, clamp the fuel tank filler hose in the location illustrated

5. Release the clamp to the fuel tank filler tube and remove. Disconnect the three quick release couplings from the fuel tank tubes.

6. Disconnect the fuel pump electrical connector.

7. Disconnect the fuel filter inlet tube.

8. Position a suitable lifting device under the fuel tank.

9. Remove the two fuel tank support strap bolts.

10. Lower the fuel tank to access the fuel pump module while swinging the fuel tank support straps away from the fuel tank.

11. Disconnect the fuel pump module electrical connector and the fuel pump module fuel outlet tube.

To install:

12. Installation is the reverse of removal.

13. Tighten the fuel tank strap bolts to 26 ft. lbs. (35 Nm).

14. Start the engine and check for leaks.

IDLE SPEED

ADJUSTMENT

Idle speed is maintained by the Powertrain Control Module (PCM). No adjustment is necessary or possible.

THROTTLE BODY

REMOVAL & INSTALLATION

3.0L (VIN U, 2) Engines

See Figure 141.

1. Before servicing the vehicle, refer to the precautions in the beginning of this section.

2. Disconnect the battery ground cable.

3. Remove the air cleaner outlet tube.

4. Remove the pin-type retainers and the snow shield.

5. Disconnect the accelerator cable, speed control cable and throttle return spring from the throttle body.

6. Remove the bolts and position the accelerator cable bracket aside.

7. Disconnect the throttle position (TP) sensor electrical connector.

8. Remove the throttle body retaining bolts and remove the throttle body.

9. Remove and discard the throttle body gasket.

10. To install, reverse the removal procedure.

11. Clean all sealing surfaces and install a new throttle body gasket. Tighten the throttle body bolts to 89 inch lbs. (10 Nm).

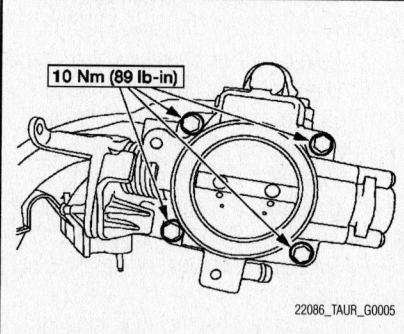

10 Nm (89 lb-in)

22086_TAUR_G0005

Fig. 141 Throttle body mounting bolts—3.0L (VIN U, 2) Engines

3.0L (VIN S) Engine

See Figure 142.

✴✴ WARNING

Do not smoke or carry lighted tobacco or open flame of any type when working on or near any fuel-related components. Highly flammable mixtures are always present and may be ignited. Failure to follow these instructions may result in personal injury.

✴✴ CAUTION

Throttle body bore and plate area have a special coating and cannot be cleaned.

1. Before servicing the vehicle, refer to the precautions in the beginning of this section.

2. Remove the air cleaner outlet tube.

3. Remove the pin-type retainers and the accelerator cable cover.

4. Disconnect and unclip the accelerator and speed control cables.

5. Remove the throttle return spring.

6. Disconnect the wiring harness retainer from the throttle body mounting stud.

7. Disconnect the Throttle Position (TPS) Sensor electrical connector.

8. Remove the accelerator cable bracket and position aside.

9. Disconnect the throttle body coolant feed and return hoses as follows:

   a. Push the connector toward the hose to release pressure.

   b. Press the coolant hose quick-release coupling button and pull the coolant hose to disconnect.

10. Remove the bolts, stud bolt and the throttle body.

11. Remove and discard the throttle body gasket.

12. Clean and inspect the sealing surfaces.

✴✴ CAUTION

Upon installation of the throttle body coolant feed and return hoses, make sure the tube clicks into place. Pull on the hose to verify seating.

13. To install, reverse the removal procedure. Use a new throttle body gasket and tighten the bolts to 89 inch lbs. (10 Nm).

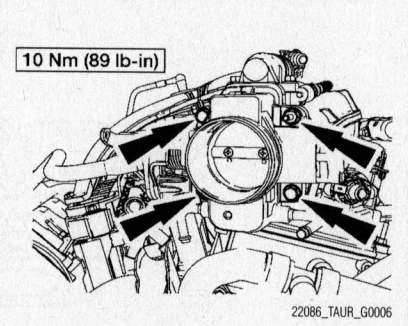

10 Nm (89 lb-in)

22086_TAUR_G0006

Fig. 142 Throttle body mounting bolts—3.0L (VIN S) Engine

HEATING & AIR CONDITIONING   SYSTEM

BLOWER MOTOR

REMOVAL & INSTALLATION

See Figures 143 and 144.

1. Before servicing the vehicle, refer to the precautions in the beginning of this section.

2. Disconnect the negative battery cable.

3. Disengage the instrument panel insulator from the instrument panel.

4. Detach the wiring connector at the blower motor.

5. Unsnap the instrument panel upper finish panel from the instrument panel.

6. On vehicles equipped with autolamp, Detach the electrical connector from the light sensor amplifier.

7. Unsnap and remove the instrument panel finish end panel from the right side of the instrument panel.

8. Remove the 3 screws retaining the instrument panel to the upper cowl top panel.

9. Remove the 2 screws at each right side of the instrument panel.

10. Remove the 3 screws retaining the blower motor to the evaporator housing.

11. Pull the instrument panel away from the cowl and remove the blower motor from the A/C evaporator housing.

12. If required, separate the blower motor wheel from the blower motor by removing the retainer from the blower motor shaft and sliding the blower motor wheel off the blower motor shaft.

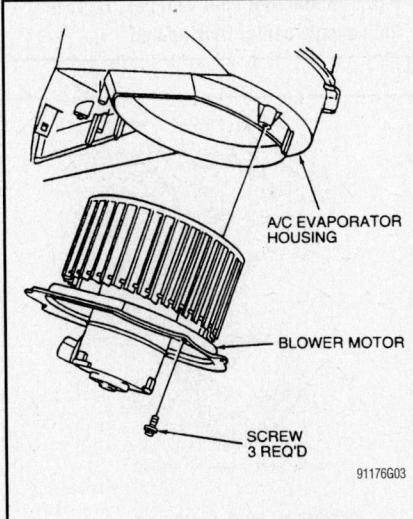

Fig. 143 The blower motor-to-evaporator housing mounting

A/C EVAPORATOR HOUSING

BLOWER MOTOR

SCREW 3 REQ'D

91176G03

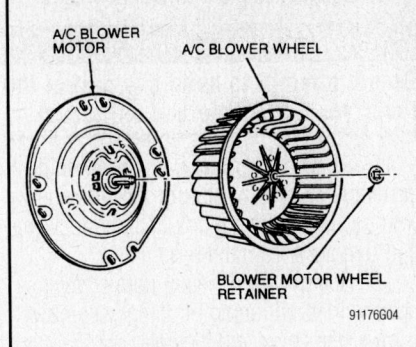

A/C BLOWER MOTOR

A/C BLOWER WHEEL

BLOWER MOTOR WHEEL RETAINER

91176G04

Fig. 144 The blower wheel is held to the motor by a retaining clip

To install:

13. If the blower motor wheel was removed, align the flats on the inside diameter of the wheel hub with the flat surface on the blower motor shaft and slide the blower motor wheel onto the blower motor shaft. Install a new blower motor wheel retainer onto the shaft.

14. Install the blower motor and wheel assembly into the evaporator housing and firmly tighten the 3 retaining screws.

15. Reposition the instrument panel and install the 2 screws at each right side of the instrument panel.

16. Install the 3 screws retaining the instrument panel to the upper cowl top panel.

17. Install the instrument panel finish end panel to the right side of the instrument panel.

18. On vehicles equipped with autolamp, Attach the electrical connector to the light sensor amplifier.

19. Snap the instrument panel upper finish panel to the instrument panel.

20. Attach the wiring connector at the blower motor.

21. Engage the instrument panel insulator to the instrument panel.

22. Connect the negative battery cable. Check for proper blower motor operation.

HEATER CORE

REMOVAL & INSTALLATION

See Figures 145 through 161.

1. Before servicing the vehicle, refer to the precautions in the beginning of this section.

2. Disconnect the negative battery cable.

✷✷ CAUTION

After disconnecting the negative battery cable, wait for at least 1 minute for the SRS or air bag module to deplete its energy.

3. Place the front wheels in the straight-ahead position.

4. Lock the steering column.

5. Remove or disconnect the following:
- SRS bolt covers from both sides of the steering wheel
- SRS module-to-steering wheel bolts
- SRS module and disconnect the electrical connector
- Steering wheel bolt and discard it

6. Press the steering wheel from the steering column.
- Lower steering column shaft bolt
- 2 lower instrument panel cover-to-instrument panel screws and unsnap the lower cover from the instrument panel

7. Turn ignition switch to the RUN position

8. Insert a ⅛ in. (3mm) wire or pin punch in the lower steering column shroud hole, under the ignition switch; then, press on the pin while pulling out on the ignition switch lock cylinder and remove it from the steering column lock cylinder housing.

9. Remove or disconnect the following:
- 3 steering column shroud screws and the shrouds
- Shift control selector lever boot
- Gearshift lever pin from the manual control lever and remove the lever
- Wiring connector at the bottom of the steering column and remove the wiring from the column, (if equipped with an overdrive lockout switch on the manual control lever)
- Electrical connectors
- Multi-function switch screws and move it aside
- Shift indicator cable from the shifter tube
- Shifter indicator-to-column adjustment cable screw
- Interlock cable and actuator (if equipped with a column shift)
- 4 steering column-to-instrument panel bracket nuts and steering column
- Push pins and the lower instrument cover from the instrument panel reinforcement (at the passenger's side)
- Console finish panel

10. Under the steering column, 2 instrument panel brace screws, the courtesy lamp socket, the 2 Diagnostic Link Connector (DLC) screws and the instrument panel brace.

11. If not equipped with an Electronic Automatic Temperature Control (EATC), disconnect the electrical connectors and the vacuum harness from the evaporator housing and the blower motor.

12. If equipped with an Electronic Automatic Temperature Control (EATC), remove the sensor hose/elbow and disconnect the electrical harness connectors and the vacuum hose harness from the evaporator housing.

13. Insert the Radio Removing tools 415-001 into the integrated control panel faceplate; then, push the tools in approximately 1½ in. (38mm) to release the retaining clips. Spread the tools slightly and pull the integrated control panel from the instrument panel.

14. Remove or disconnect the following:
- Electrical connectors and the automatic temperature control sensor hose and elbow, if equipped
- 6 console center finish panel screws and the panel, (if equipped with a floor shift)
- 4 instrument panel finish panel screws and panel, located at the right side of the steering column, (if equipped with a column shift)
- Instrument cluster finish panel-to-instrument panel clips and pull the finish panel straight out
- 4 instrument cluster-to-instrument panel screws, the electrical connectors and the instrument cluster
- Upper finish panel (located at the top of the instrument panel)
- Light sensor amplifier connector, (if equipped with an autolamp)
- Instrument panel finish end panels on both sides of the instrument panel
- Front scuff plates and pull the door weatherstrip away from the instrument panel (on both sides of the instrument panel)
- 3 instrument panel-to-upper cowl top panel screws
- 2 screws at each end of the instrument panel
- Instrument panel electrical connectors and the parking brake switch
- Instrument panel

15. Drain the cooling system into a clean container for reuse

16. Remove or disconnect the following:
- Heater hoses from the heater core and plug the openings
- 4 air conditioning electronic blend door actuator-to-heater/air conditioning housing assembly screws and the actuator
- Metal cover, disengage the spring from the heater core cover and from the lever

- Gently, depress the locking ramp and remove the lever from the secondary air temperature control door end

17. Rotate the primary air conditioning air temperature control door shaft downward, swing the metal link counterclockwise and remove it from the pin.

18. Remove the 3 heater core cover-to-heater/air conditioning housing assembly screws, the cover and the seal.

19. Press on the heater core tubes and remove the heater core from the heater/air conditioning housing assembly.

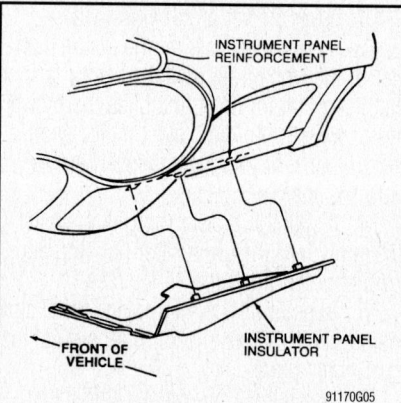

Fig. 145 Remove the instrument panel insulator from the instrument panel reinforcement

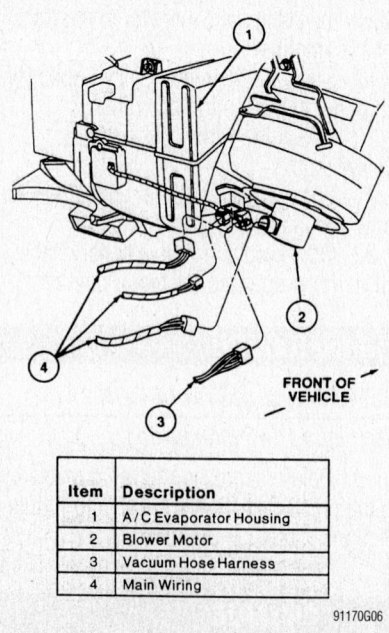

Item	Description
1	A/C Evaporator Housing
2	Blower Motor
3	Vacuum Hose Harness
4	Main Wiring

Fig. 146 Manual air conditioning/heater equipped vehicles disconnection points

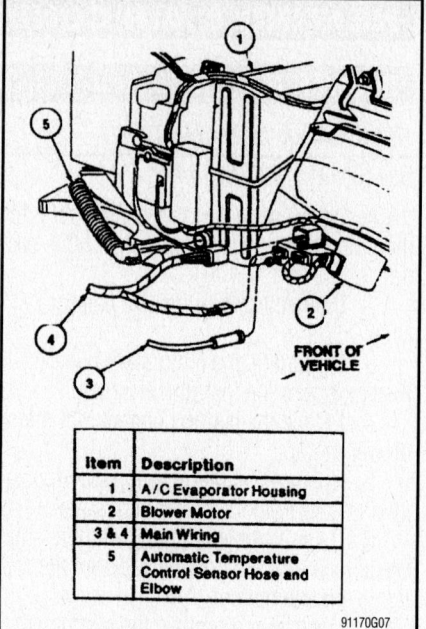

Item	Description
1	A/C Evaporator Housing
2	Blower Motor
3 & 4	Main Wiring
5	Automatic Temperature Control Sensor Hose and Elbow

Fig. 147 EATC equipped vehicles disconnection points

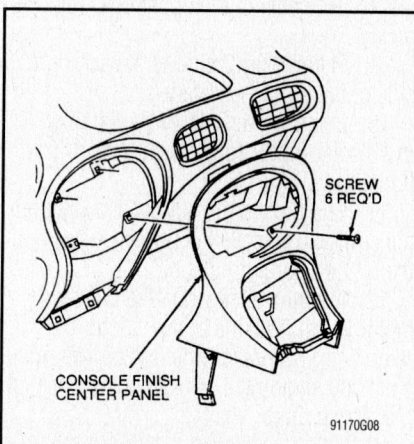

Fig. 148 On floor shift vehicles, remove the console center finish panel

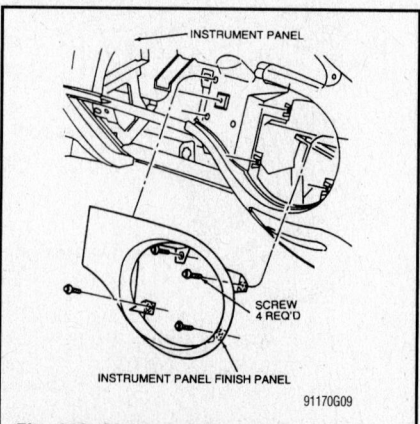

Fig. 149 On floor shift vehicles, remove the finish panel from around the integrated control panel

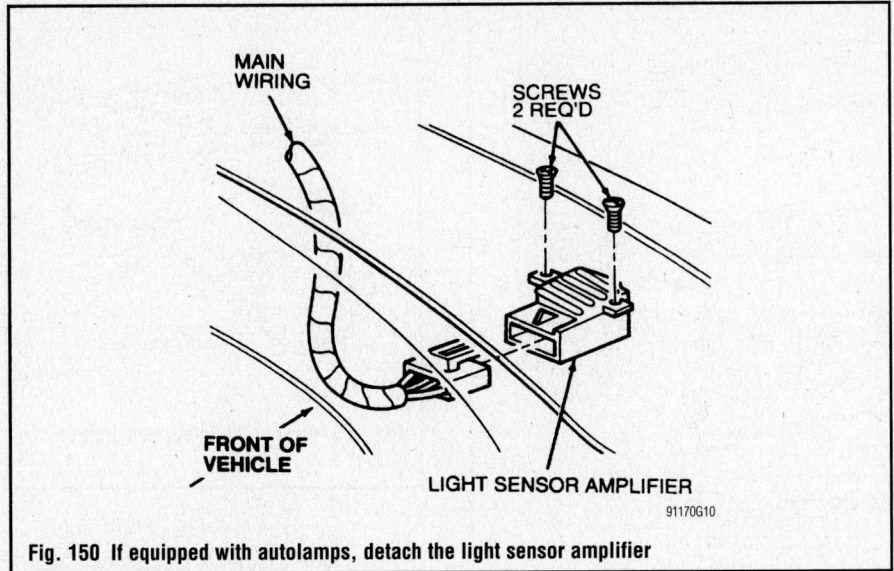

Fig. 150 If equipped with autolamps, detach the light sensor amplifier

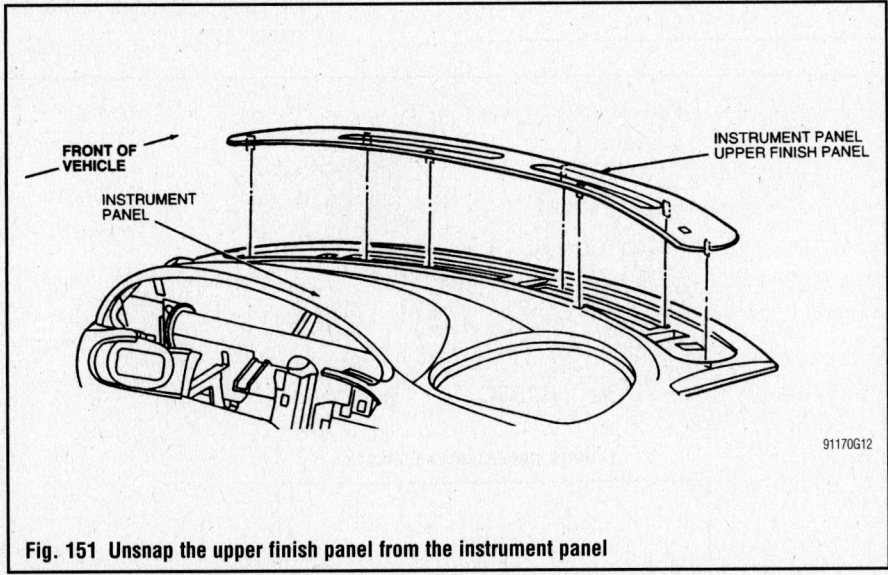

Fig. 151 Unsnap the upper finish panel from the instrument panel

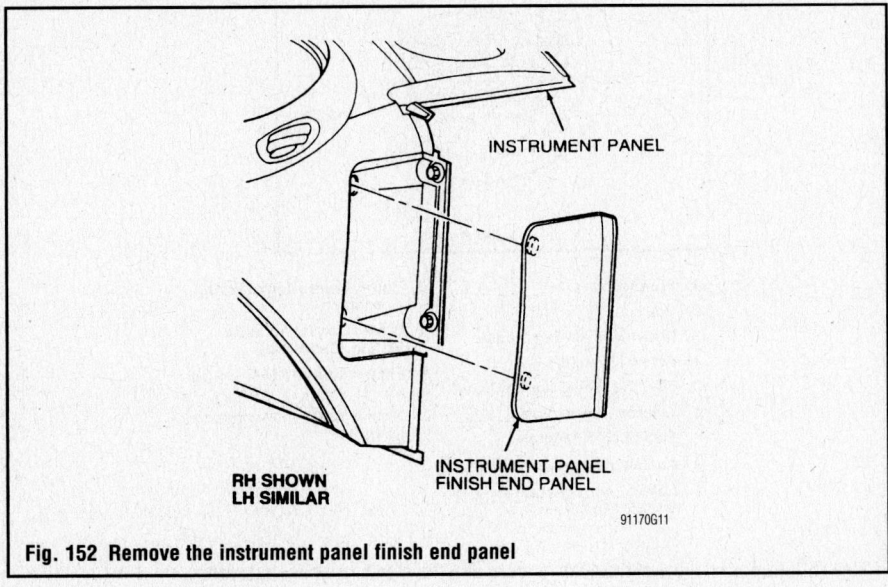

**RH SHOWN
LH SIMILAR**

Fig. 152 Remove the instrument panel finish end panel

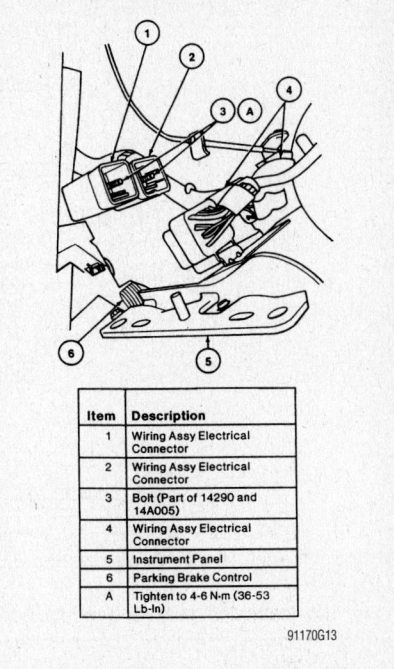

Item	Description
1	Wiring Assy Electrical Connector
2	Wiring Assy Electrical Connector
3	Bolt (Part of 14290 and 14A005)
4	Wiring Assy Electrical Connector
5	Instrument Panel
6	Parking Brake Control
A	Tighten to 4-6 N·m (36-53 Lb-In)

Fig. 153 Detach the electrical connectors

To install:

20. Install or connect the following:
    - Heater core to the heater/air conditioning housing assembly
    - Heater core cover, the seal and the 3 heater core cover-to-heater/air conditioning housing assembly screws
    - Lever to the secondary air conditioning air temperature control door end
    - Spring to the lever, engage the spring to the heater core cover and install the metal cover
    - Air conditioning electronic blend door actuator and the 4 actuator-to-heater/air conditioning housing assembly screws
    - Heater hoses to the heater core
    - Instrument panel with the help of an assistant
    - Instrument panel electrical connectors and the parking brake switch
    - 2 screws at each end of the instrument panel with the help of an assistant
    - 3 instrument panel-to-upper cowl top panel screws
    - Front scuff plates and the door weatherstrip (on both sides of the instrument panel)
    - Instrument panel finish end panels (on both sides of the instrument panel)

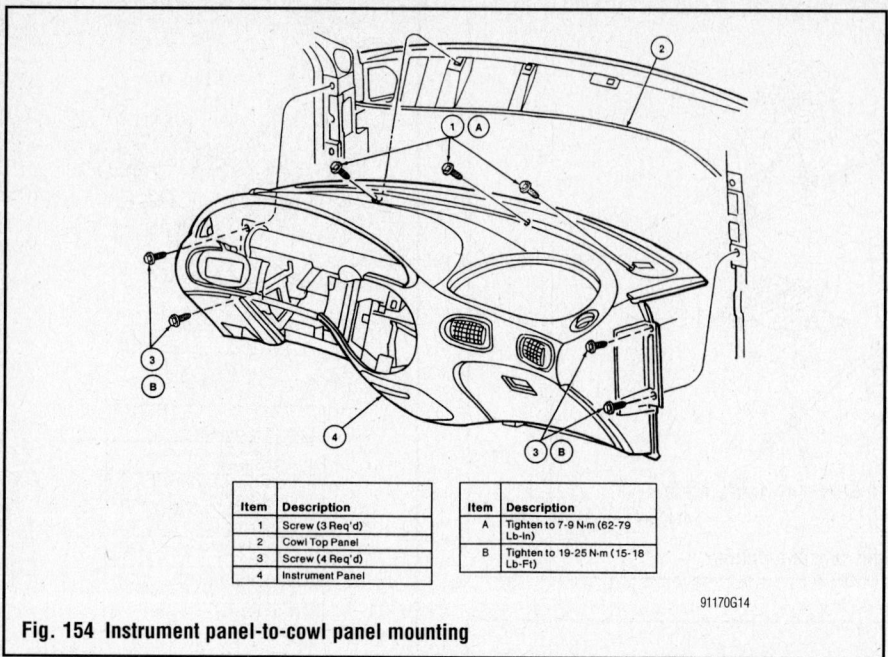

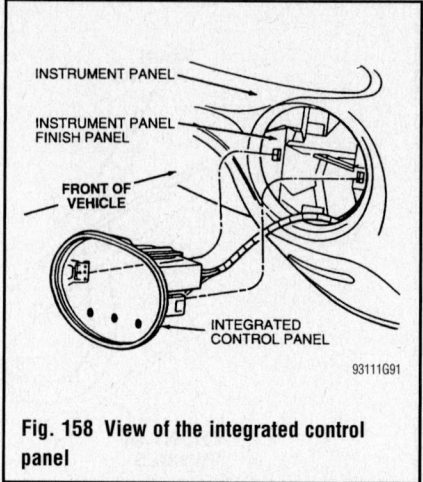

Item	Description
1	Screw (3 Req'd)
2	Cowl Top Panel
3	Screw (4 Req'd)
4	Instrument Panel

Item	Description
A	Tighten to 7-9 N·m (62-79 Lb-In)
B	Tighten to 19-25 N·m (15-18 Lb-Ft)

91170G14

Fig. 154 Instrument panel-to-cowl panel mounting

Fig. 158 View of the integrated control panel

- Electrical connector to the light sensor amplifier (if equipped with an autolamp)
- Upper finish panel (at the top of the instrument panel)

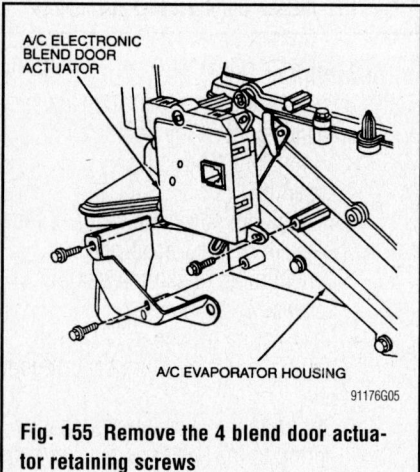

91176G05

Fig. 155 Remove the 4 blend door actuator retaining screws

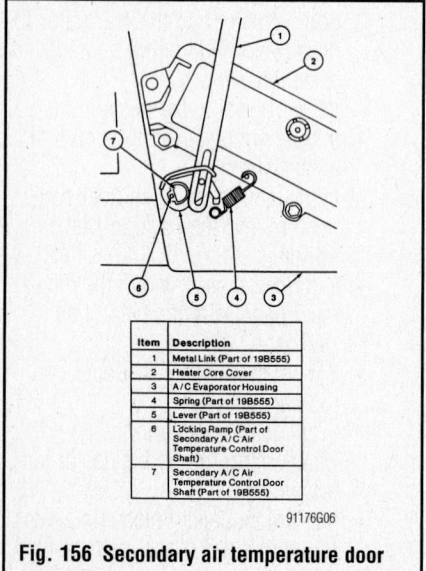

Item	Description
1	Metal Link (Part of 19B555)
2	Heater Core Cover
3	A/C Evaporator Housing
4	Spring (Part of 19B555)
5	Lever (Part of 19B555)
6	Locking Ramp (Part of Secondary A/C Air Temperature Control Door Shaft)
7	Secondary A/C Air Temperature Control Door Shaft (Part of 19B555)

91176G06

Fig. 156 Secondary air temperature door connections

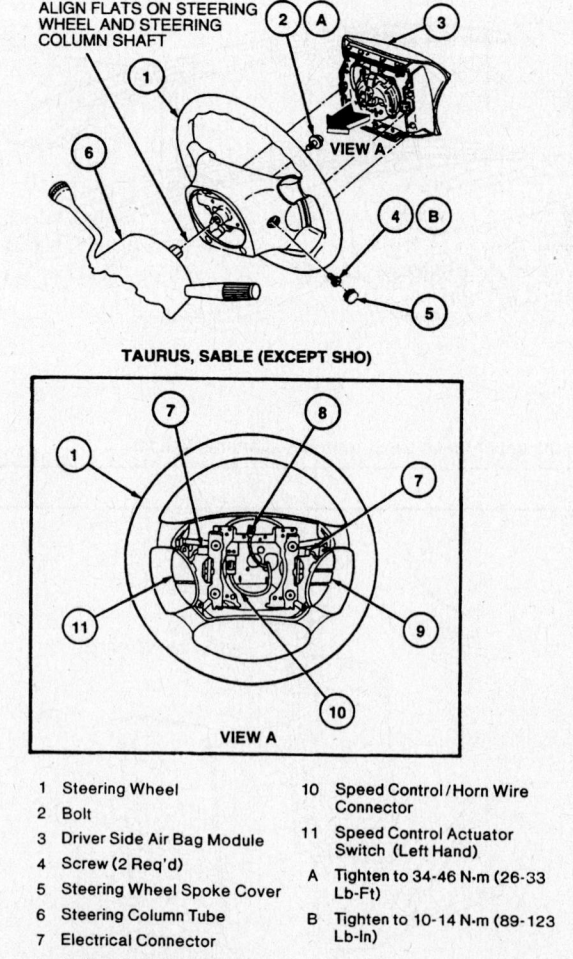

TAURUS, SABLE (EXCEPT SHO)

VIEW A

1 Steering Wheel	10 Speed Control / Horn Wire Connector
2 Bolt	11 Speed Control Actuator Switch (Left Hand)
3 Driver Side Air Bag Module	A Tighten to 34-46 N·m (26-33 Lb-Ft)
4 Screw (2 Req'd)	
5 Steering Wheel Spoke Cover	B Tighten to 10-14 N·m (89-123 Lb-In)
6 Steering Column Tube	
7 Electrical Connector	
8 Air Bag Electrical Connector	
9 Speed Control Actuator Switch (Right Hand)	

93111G90

Fig. 157 Exploded view of the SRS module and the steering wheel assembly

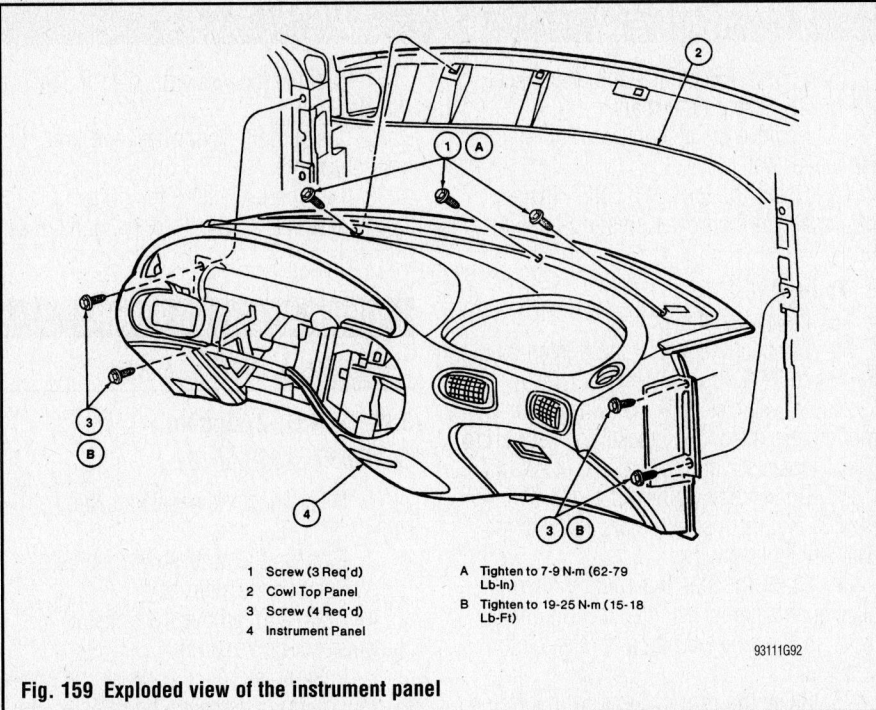

1 Screw (3 Req'd)
2 Cowl Top Panel
3 Screw (4 Req'd)
4 Instrument Panel

A Tighten to 7-9 N·m (62-79 Lb-In)
B Tighten to 19-25 N·m (15-18 Lb-Ft)

93111G92

Fig. 159 Exploded view of the instrument panel

- Instrument cluster, electrical connectors and the 4 instrument cluster-to-instrument panel screws
- Instrument cluster finish panel and engage the finish panel-to-instrument panel clips
- Instrument panel finish panel and 4 panel screws, located at the right side of the steering column (if equipped with a column shift)
- Console center finish panel and the

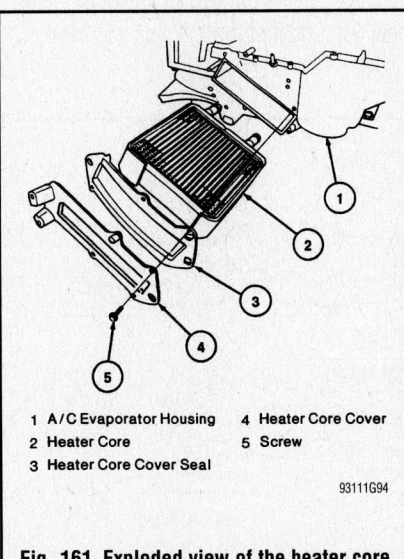

1 A/C Evaporator Housing
2 Heater Core
3 Heater Core Cover Seal
4 Heater Core Cover
5 Screw

93111G94

Fig. 161 Exploded view of the heater core

- 6 panel screws (if equipped with a floor shift)
- Electrical connectors and the automatic temperature control sensor hose and elbow, if equipped
- Integrated control panel faceplate

✳✳ WARNING

Do not use excessive force when installing the radio, the retaining clips can become damaged.

- Sensor hose/elbow, the electrical harness connectors and the vacuum hose harness to the evaporator housing (if equipped with an

Electronic Automatic Temperature Control (EATC)

- Connect the electrical connectors and the vacuum harness to the evaporator housing and the blower motor (if not equipped with an EATC)
- Instrument panel brace and the 2 Diagnostic Link Connector (DLC) screws
- Courtesy lamp socket and install the 2 instrument panel brace screws
- Console finish panel (if equipped with a floor shift)
- Lower instrument cover to the instrument panel reinforcement (located on the passenger's side)
- Steering column and torque the 4 steering column-to-instrument panel bracket nuts to 10–13 ft. lbs. (13–17 Nm)
- Interlock cable and actuator (if equipped with a column shift)
- Shifter indicator-to-column adjustment cable screw
- Shift indicator cable to the shifter tube
- Multi-function switch and the screws
- Electrical connectors
- Wiring connector at the bottom of the steering column and install the wiring to the column (if equipped with an overdrive lockout switch on the manual control lever)
- Gearshift lever and the lever pin to the manual control lever
- 3 steering column shroud screws and the shrouds
- Ignition switch to the steering column lock cylinder housing
- Lower instrument panel cover and the 2 lower cover-to-instrument panel screws
- Lower steering column shaft bolt and torque it to 17–20 ft. lbs. (22–26 Nm)
- Steering wheel to the steering column
- New steering wheel bolt and torque it to 26–33 ft. lbs. (34–46 Nm)
- SRS module and connect the electrical connector
- SRS module-to-steering wheel bolts and torque the bolts to 89–123 inch lbs. (10–14 Nm)
- SRS bolt covers
- Negative battery cable

21. Fill the cooling system.
22. Operate the engine to normal operating temperatures; then, check the climate control operation and check for leaks.

Fig. 160 temperature control mechanism labels

1 Metal Link
2 Heater Core Cover
3 A/C Evaporator Housing
4 Spring
5 Lever
6 Locking Ramp (Part of Secondary A/C Air Temperature Control Door Shaft)
7 Secondary A/C Air Temperature Control Door Shaft

93111G93

Fig. 160 View of the temperature control mechanism

STEERING

POWER STEERING GEAR

REMOVAL & INSTALLATION

See Figure 162.

1. Before servicing the vehicle, refer to the precautions section.
2. Turn the steering wheel 1/4 turn to the right and turn the ignition switch to the OFF position.
3. Remove both front wheel and tire assemblies.
4. Loosen the tie-rod end jam nuts.
5. Remove and discard the cotter pins and nuts.

⁑ CAUTION

Do not damage the tie rod end boot when installing the special tool.

6. Disconnect the tie-rod ends.

➡**Note the number of times the tie-rod ends turn for assembly reference.**

7. Remove the tie-rod ends.
8. Position the boot out of the way.
9. Remove the bolt and disconnect the intermediate shaft coupling. Discard the bolt.
10. Remove and discard the subframe nuts as shown.
11. Support the rear of the front subframe with jack stands.
12. Remove and discard the bolts. Lower the rear of the front subframe approximately 4 inches (102 mm).
13. On vehicles equipped with a 3.0L 4V (VIN S) engine, remove the bolts and the bracket with the heat shield attached.
14. On vehicles equipped with a 3.0L 2V MFI engine, remove the bolt and detach the bracket from the steering gear.

15. Loosen the fittings and disconnect the hoses. Discard the seals.
16. Remove the steering gear out of the left fender well.
17. Using the tool 211-D027, install new seals on the power steering hose fittings.

To install:

18. Install the steering gear.
19. Connect the hoses and tighten the fittings to 27 ft. lbs. (37 Nm).
20. On vehicles equipped with a 3.0L 2V MFI engine, attach the bracket to the steering gear. Tighten the bolt to 8 ft. lbs. (11 Nm).
21. On vehicles equipped with a 3.0L 4V (VIN S) engine, install the bracket with the heat shield attached.
22. Guide the steering column intermediate shaft coupling on the steering gear input shaft as the subframe is raised into position.
23. Raise the rear of the front subframe approximately 4 inches (102 mm). Tighten the bolts to 85 ft. lbs. (115 Nm).
24. Remove the jack stands.
25. Install new subframe nuts as shown in the earlier illustration and tighten the bolts to 85 ft. lbs. (115 Nm).
26. Center, and then turn the steering gear input shaft 1/4 turn to the right to make sure the intermediate shaft coupling will fit correctly on the input shaft.
27. Connect the intermediate shaft coupling. Install a new bolt and tighten to 35 ft. lbs. (47 Nm).
28. Install the boot.
29. Install the tie-rod ends and tighten the same number of turns as noted during removal.
30. Connect the tie rod ends and using new nuts, tighten to 41 ft. lbs. (55 Nm). Install a new cotter pin.

31. Tighten the jam nuts to 41 ft. lbs. (55 Nm).
32. Install both front wheel and tire assemblies.
33. Fill and leak check the system.
34. Check and adjust front alignment as necessary.

POWER STEERING PUMP

REMOVAL & INSTALLATION

3.0L (VIN U, 2) Engine

See Figures 163 and 164.

1. Disconnect the negative battery cable.
2. Remove the accessory drive belt.
3. Remove the alternator.
4. Drain and remove the radiator coolant recovery reservoir.
5. Position a drain pan under the power steering pump underneath the vehicle. Disconnect the hydraulic pressure and return lines and allow to drain.
6. Remove the idler pulley from the power steering pump support.
7. Remove the bracket mounting bolt located under the belt tensioner mounting.
8. Remove 2 retaining nuts from the bracket mounting studs. Remove both mounting studs, and pull off the power steering pump support with the pump attached.
9. Clamp the pump support bracket in a suitable vise.
10. Remove the power steering pump pulley from the pump shaft using Pump Pulley Remover T69L-10300-B, or equivalent. Remove the 3 bolts retaining the power steering pump to the power steering pump support and remove the power steering pump.

To install:

11. Install the power steering pump to the power steering pump support.
12. Install the power steering pump pulley using Steering Pump Pulley Replacer T65P-3A733-C, or equivalent; the pulley face must be flush within 0.010 inch (0.25mm) of the pump shaft.
13. Install the power steering pump/pump support and torque nuts/bolt to 17–24 ft. lbs. (23–32 Nm).
14. Complete the installation by reversing the removal procedure.
15. Fill the power steering reservoir with power steering fluid.

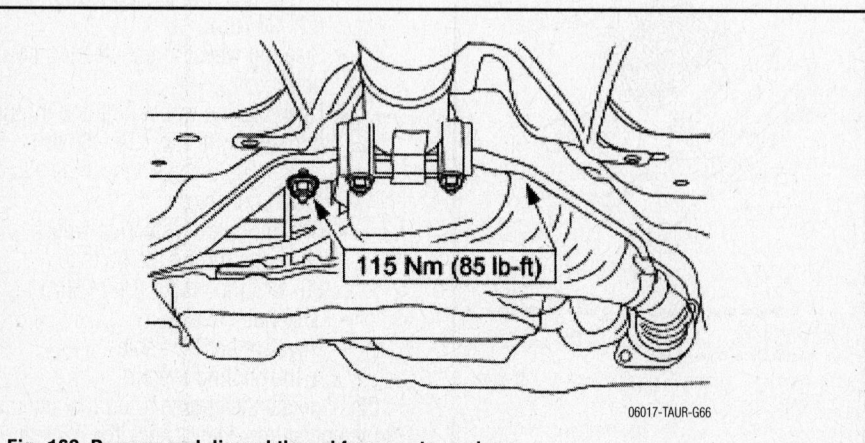

115 Nm (85 lb-ft)

06017-TAUR-G66

Fig. 162 Remove and discard the subframe nuts as shown

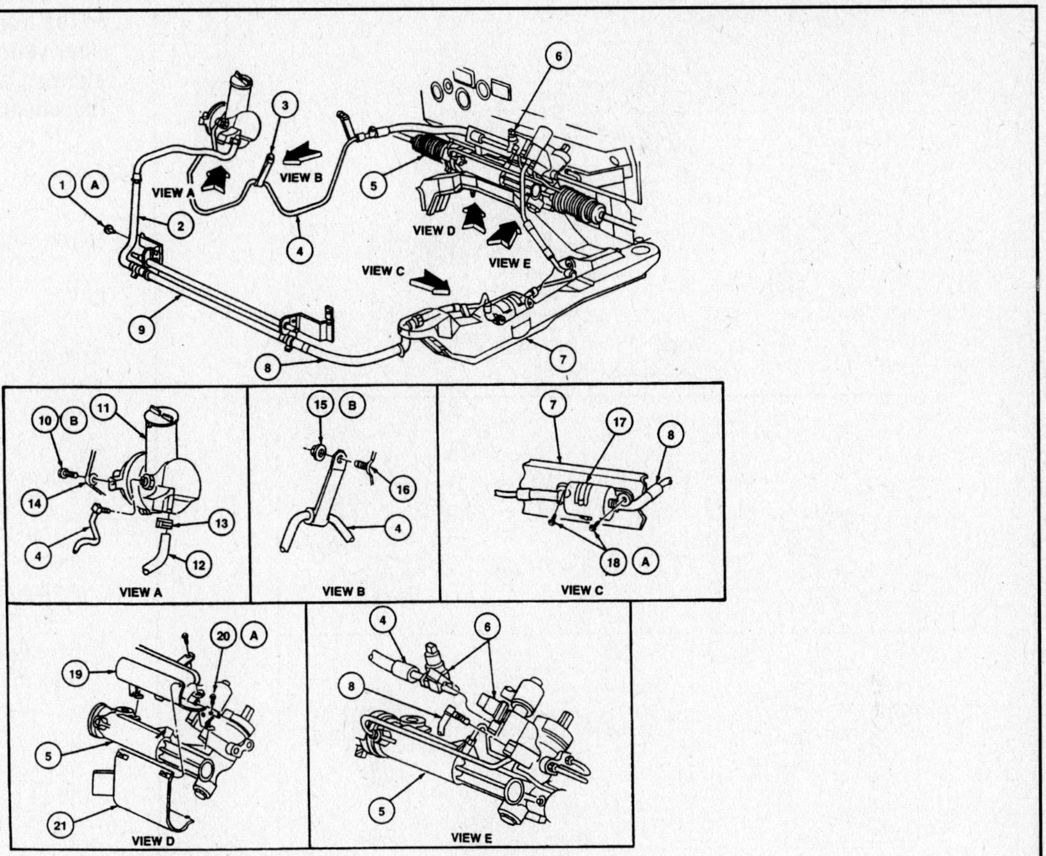

Fig. 163 Power steering system—3.0L (VIN U, 2)

Item	Description
1	Screw (4 Req'd)
2	Power Steering Return Line (Cooler-To-Pump)
3	Retainer (Part of 3F524)
4	Power Steering Left Turn Pressure Hose
5	Power Rack and Pinion Steering Gear
6	Power Steering Pressure Switch
7	Side Rail
8	Power Steering Return Hose
9	Power Steering Fluid Cooler
10	Bolt (3 Req'd)
11	Power Steering Pump
12	Power Steering Return Line

Item	Description
13	Power Steering Return Line Clamp
14	Power Steering Pump Support
15	Nut
16	Engine Reference
17	Bracket
18	Bolt (2 Req'd)
19	Power Steering Hose Bracket
20	Screw
21	Steering Shaft U-Joint Shield
A	Tighten to 9-12 N·m (80-106 Lb-In)
B	Tighten to 23-32 N·m (17-23 Lb-Ft)

91178G15

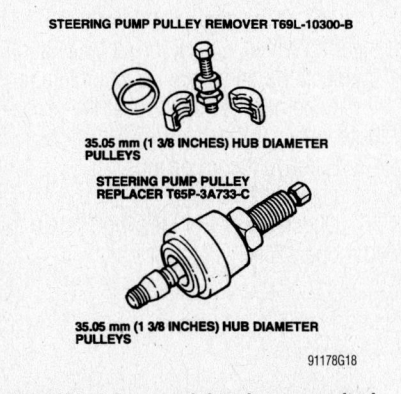

STEERING PUMP PULLEY REMOVER T69L-10300-B

35.05 mm (1 3/8 INCHES) HUB DIAMETER PULLEYS

STEERING PUMP PULLEY REPLACER T65P-3A733-C

35.05 mm (1 3/8 INCHES) HUB DIAMETER PULLEYS

91178G18

Fig. 164 A few special tools are required to remove and install the pulley on the power steering pump

16. Connect the negative battery cable.

17. Run the engine and check for leaks and proper operation. Bleed the power steering system if needed.

3.0L (VIN S) Engine

See Figure 165.

1. Disconnect the negative battery cable.

2. Remove the accessory drive belt.

3. Drain and remove the radiator coolant recovery reservoir.

4. Position a drain pan under the power steering pump. Disconnect the power steering pump reservoir hose and allow it to drain.

5. Using Pulley Remover T69L-10300-B, or equivalent, remove the pulley from the power steering pump shaft.

6. Disconnect the left turn pressure hose from the power steering pump and allow it to drain.

7. Remove the power steering pump retaining bolts and the pump.

To install:

8. Install the power steering pump and tighten bolts to 15–22 ft. lbs. (20–30 Nm).

9. Connect the left turn pressure hose and secure clamp.

10. Using a Steering Pump Pulley Replacer T65P-3A733-C, or equivalent, install the power steering pump pulley: the pulley face must be flush with the pump shaft or within 0.010 inch (0.25mm).

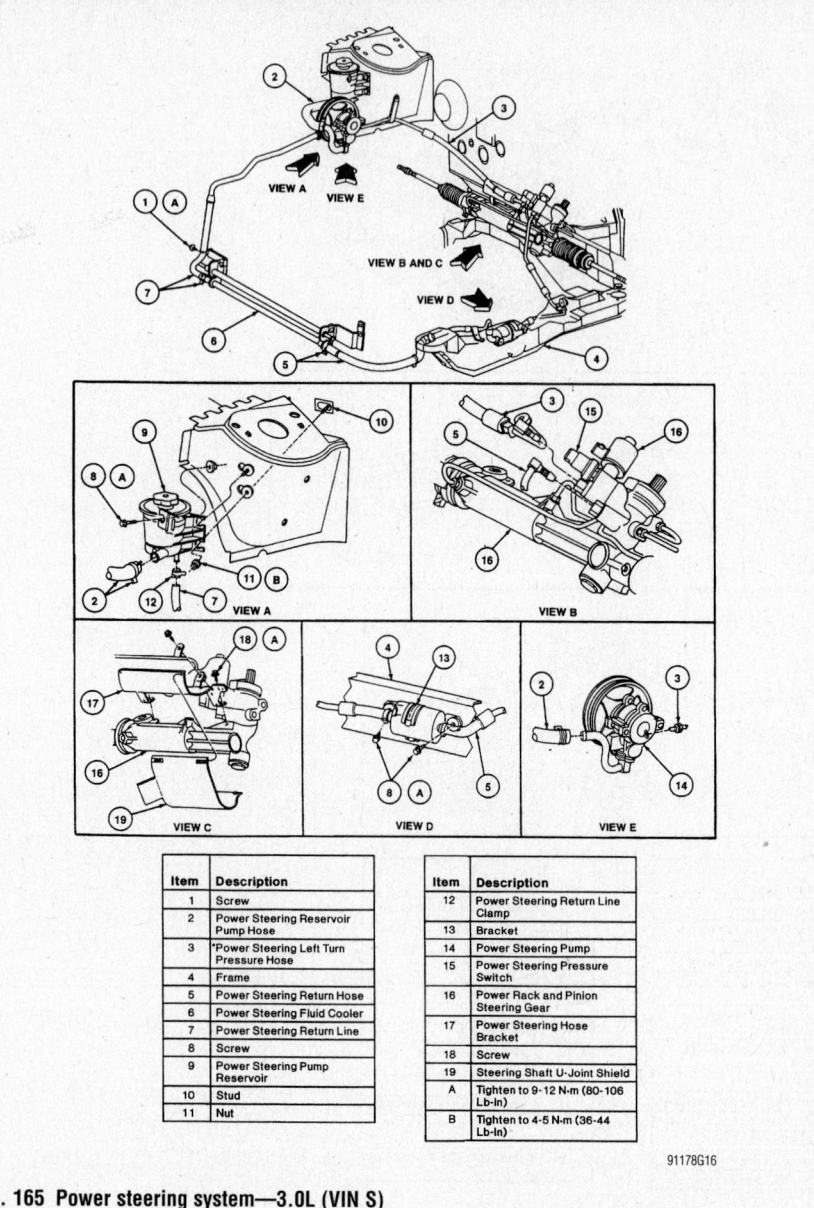

Item	Description
1	Screw
2	Power Steering Reservoir Pump Hose
3	*Power Steering Left Turn Pressure Hose
4	Frame
5	Power Steering Return Hose
6	Power Steering Fluid Cooler
7	Power Steering Return Line
8	Screw
9	Power Steering Pump Reservoir
10	Stud
11	Nut

Item	Description
12	Power Steering Return Line Clamp
13	Bracket
14	Power Steering Pump
15	Power Steering Pressure Switch
16	Power Rack and Pinion Steering Gear
17	Power Steering Hose Bracket
18	Screw
19	Steering Shaft U-Joint Shield
A	Tighten to 9-12 N·m (80-106 Lb-in)
B	Tighten to 4-5 N·m (36-44 Lb-in)

91178G16

Fig. 165 Power steering system—3.0L (VIN S)

11. Fill the power steering reservoir with power steering fluid. Connect the negative battery cable.

12. Start the engine and check for leaks and proper operation. Bleed the power steering system if needed.

BLEEDING

1. Disable the ignition by disconnecting the ignition module or disconnecting the camshaft position sensor.

2. Raise and safely support the vehicle so the front wheels are off the floor.

3. Place jackstands under the front of the vehicle.

4. Fill the power steering fluid reservoir.

5. Crank the engine with the starter motor and add fluid until the level remains constant.

6. While cranking the engine, rotate the steering wheel from lock-to-lock.

➡ **The front wheels must be off the floor during lock-to-lock rotation of the steering wheel. Do not hold the steering wheel on the stops.**

7. Check the fluid level and add fluid, if necessary.

8. Enable the ignition system. Start the engine and allow it to run for several minutes.

9. Rotate the steering wheel from lock-to-lock.

10. Stop the engine and check the fluid level. Add fluid, if necessary.

11. If air is still present in the system, purge the system of air using Power Steering Air Evacuator 021–00014 or equivalent, as follows:

a. Make sure the power steering pump reservoir is full to the COLD FULL mark on the dipstick or to just above the minimum indication on the reservoir.

b. Tightly insert the rubber stopper of the air evacuator assembly into the pump reservoir fill neck.

c. Apply 20 inch Hg maximum vacuum on the pump reservoir for a minimum of 3 minutes with the engine idling. As air purges from the system, vacuum will fall off. Maintain adequate vacuum with the vacuum source.

d. Release the vacuum and remove the vacuum source. Fill the reservoir to the COLD FULL mark or to just above the minimum indication on the reservoir. Install the evacuator tool again.

e. With the engine idling, apply 20 inch Hg vacuum to the pump reservoir. Slowly cycle the steering wheel from lock-to-lock every 30 seconds for approximately 5 minutes. Do not hold the steering wheel on the stops while cycling. Maintain adequate vacuum with the vacuum source as the air purges.

f. Release the vacuum and remove the vacuum source. Add fluid, if necessary.

g. Start the engine and cycle the steering wheel. Check for oil leaks at all connections. In severe cases of aeration, it may be necessary to repeat the procedure.

12. Remove the jackstands.

13. Lower the vehicle.

14. Check the power steering system for proper operation.

SUSPENSION   **FRONT SUSPENSION**

COIL SPRING

REMOVAL & INSTALLATION

See Figure 166.

1. Before servicing the vehicle, refer to the precautions section.
2. Remove the strut from the vehicle.
3. Compress the coil spring using a suitable spring compressor until the spring comes away from the seat.
4. Remove the large center nut and slowly release the spring compressor.

To install:

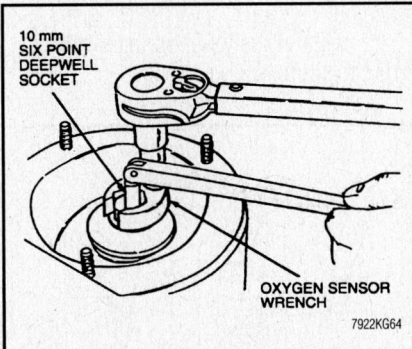

10 mm
SIX POINT
DEEPWELL
SOCKET

OXYGEN SENSOR
WRENCH

7922KG64

Fig. 166 Hold the strut rod while loosening or tightening the nut

5. Compress the spring and install it on the strut.
6. Install the lower washer and mounting bracket.
7. Install the upper washer and a new nut. Tighten the nut to 46 ft. lbs. (62 Nm).
8. Install the strut assembly in the vehicle.

LOWER BALL JOINT

REMOVAL & INSTALLATION

The lower ball joint is an integral part of the steering knuckle. If the lower ball joint is found to be defective, the entire steering knuckle must be replaced.

LOWER CONTROL ARM

REMOVAL & INSTALLATION

1. Before servicing the vehicle, refer to the precautions section.
2. Remove or disconnect the following:
   - Front wheel
   - Wheel speed sensor wiring harness
   - Lower ball joint
   - Lower control arm

To install:

3. Install or connect the following:
   - Lower control arm. Tighten the front bolt to 98 ft. lbs. (133 Nm), and the rear bolt to 85 ft. lbs. (115 Nm).
   - Lower ball joint. Use a new nut and tighten to 59 ft. lbs. (80 Nm).
   - Wheel speed sensor wiring harness
   - Front wheel
4. Check the wheel alignment and adjust as necessary.

MACPHERSON STRUT

REMOVAL & INSTALLATION

See Figures 167 through 169.

1. Before servicing the vehicle, refer to the precautions section.

※※ WARNING

All vehicles are equipped with gas-pressurized front shock absorbers which will extend unassisted. Do not apply heat or flame to the front shock absorber during removal or disassembly. Failure to follow these instructions may result in personal injury.

※※ CAUTION

Suspension fasteners are critical parts because they affect performance of vital components and systems and their failure can result in major service expense. A new part with the same part number must be installed if installation is necessary. Do not use a new part of lesser quality or substitute design. Torque values must be used as specified during reassembly to make sure of correct retention of these parts.

➡ Turn the ignition switch to position 1.

➡ It is not necessary to remove the wheel hub and bearing or the disc brake dust shield from the knuckle.

2. Remove the wheel knuckle as follows:

※※ CAUTION

Discard the wheel hub retainer. It is a torque prevailing design and cannot be reused. If loosened, the retainer must be removed and a new one installed.

➡ Make sure the steering wheel is in the unlocked position.

h. Remove the hub cap or wheel cover, the wheel hub retainer, and the washer. Discard the retainer.
i. Remove the front brake rotor.
j. Remove and discard the tie rod cotter pin and nut.

※※ CAUTION

Do not damage the tie-rod end boot when installing the removal tool 211-001.

➡ Remove the adapter from the ball end of the removal tool. Apply a small amount of grease to the tie-rod end stud and the ball of the special tool.

k. Using the removal tools illustrated, disconnect the tie-rod end.
l. Remove the bolt and detach the ABS sensor, if equipped. Unclip the ABS sensor wire retainer and position the sensor out of the way.
m. Remove and discard the strut to knuckle nut.
n. Remove and discard the ball joint nut.

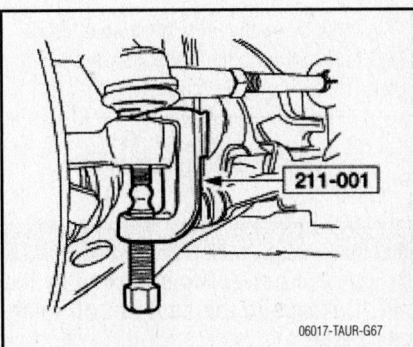

211-001

06017-TAUR-G67

Fig. 167 Using the removal tools illustrated, disconnect the tie-rod end

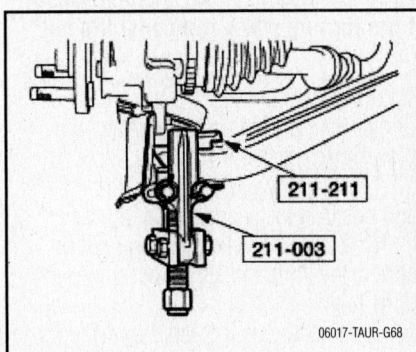

211-211

211-003

06017-TAUR-G68

Fig. 168 Using the tools illustrated, disconnect the ball joint from the lower arm

o. Using the tools illustrated, disconnect the ball joint from the lower arm.

p. Using a pry bar, push the lower arm down until the ball joint is free of the arm.

> **✳✳ CAUTION**
>
> **Do not allow the halfshaft to move outboard. Over-extension of the tripod CV joint can result in separation of internal parts, causing failure of the halfshaft.**

➡ **Hold the threaded rod while turning the nut.**

q. Using the tools illustrated, press the halfshaft from the wheel bearing and hub. Wire the halfshaft in a level position.

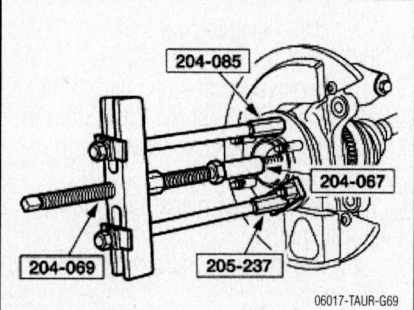

Fig. 169 Using the tools illustrated, press the halfshaft from the wheel bearing and hub

r. Remove the flag bolt and the knuckle.

> **✳✳ CAUTION**
>
> **Do not use power tools to remove the nut. Damage to the boot or ball joint can result.**

➡ **To remove the nut, first loosen the nut, then use the hex holding feature to keep the stabilizer bar link ball joint from turning while removing the nut.**

3. Remove the nut and disconnect the stabilizer bar link. Discard the nut.
4. Remove the bolt and detach the brake hose bracket.
5. Unclip the ABS sensor wire retainer and position the sensor out of the way.
6. Lower the vehicle far enough to access the strut and spring assembly-to-body nuts.
7. If necessary, detach the washer hose retainer.
8. Remove the nuts and the strut and spring assembly. Discard the nuts.

To install:

➡ **Make sure the spring is correctly seated in both spring seats**

9. Install the spring assembly and tighten the nuts to 26 ft. lbs. (35 Nm).
10. If removed, attach the washer hose retainer.
11. Install the ABS sensor.
12. Attach the brake hose bracket.

➡ **Use the hex holding feature to keep the stabilizer bar link ball joint from turning while installing the nut.**

13. Connect the stabilizer bar link. Install a new nut and tighten to 66 ft. lbs. (90 Nm).
14. Position the knuckle on the strut and install the flag bolt.
15. Using the tools used during removal, press the halfshaft into the wheel bearing and hub.
16. Using a pry bar, push the lower arm down until the ball joint can be installed.
17. Install a new nut and tighten to 59 ft. lbs. (80 Nm).
18. Install a new strut to knuckle nut and tighten to 85 ft. lbs. (115 Nm).
19. Install the ABS sensor wire retainer and sensor, if equipped.

➡ **Make sure the ABS sensor mounting hole does not have debris or corrosion build up, or false ABS activation can occur.**

➡ **If the hole in the tie-rod end does not line up with the slots in the nut, continue tightening the nut. Do not loosen the nut to align the slots in the nut with the hole in the outer tie-rod end.**

20. Connect the tie-rod end to the knuckle and install a new nut and cotter pin. Tighten the nut to 41 ft. lbs. (55 Nm).
21. Install the brake rotor.

> **✳✳ CAUTION**
>
> **The front axle wheel hub retainer must be tightened to specification immediately during installation. If the retainer is not tightened immediately, the nylon lock will set incorrectly, leading to incorrect torque readings and bearing failure. Any front wheel hub retainer that is not immediately tightened to specification or is loosened must be removed and a new retainer installed.**

22. Install the washer, the wheel hub retainer, tighten to 184 ft. lbs. (250 Nm). Install the hub cap or wheel cover.

OVERHAUL

See Figures 170 and 171.

> **✳✳ CAUTION**
>
> **Do not remove the strut rod nut until the spring has been compressed until it comes away from the seat.**

1. Remove the strut from the vehicle.
2. Compress the coil spring using a suitable spring compressor until the spring comes away from the seat.
3. Remove the large center nut and slowly release the spring compressor.
4. Remove the upper bearing from the strut assembly.
5. Remove the spring from the strut assembly.
6. Remove the lower spring insulator from the strut.

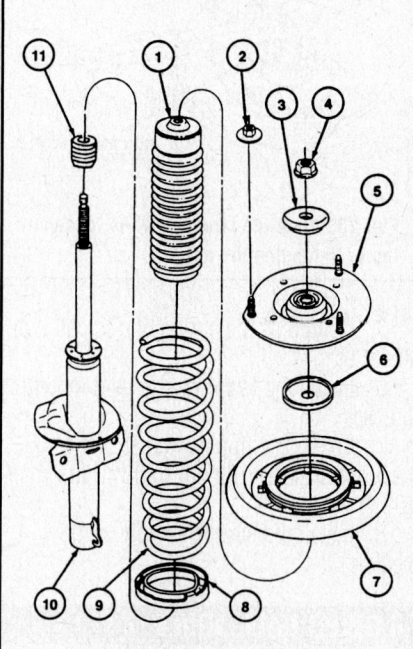

Item	Description
1	Dust Boot (Part of 18124)
2	Nut (3 Req'd)
3	Washer
4	Nut
5	Front Shock Absorber Mounting Bracket
6	Washer
7	Front Suspension Bearing and Seal
8	Front Spring Insulator (Part of 18124)
9	Front Coil Spring
10	Front Shock Absorber
11	Jounce Bumper (Part of 18124)

Fig. 170 Exploded view of the front strut and coil spring assembly

To install:

7. If replacing the strut, transfer any necessary components from the old strut.

8. Install the lower spring insulator onto the strut.

9. Compress the spring and install it on the strut.

10. Install the lower washer and upper bearing assembly.

11. Install the upper washer and a new nut. Tighten the nut to 39–53 ft. lbs. (53–72 Nm) while holding the rod with a T-50 size Torx® socket.

12. Install the strut assembly in the vehicle.

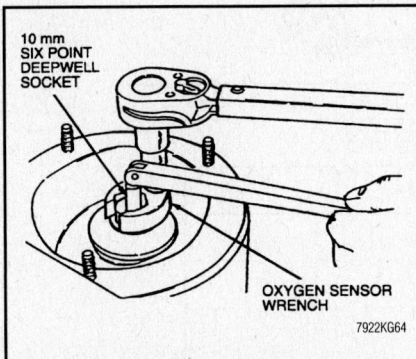

Fig. 171 Hold the strut rod while loosening or tightening the nut

STABILIZER BAR

REMOVAL & INSTALLATION

See Figures 172 and 173.

➡️**Make sure 4 new sway bar link retaining nuts, 2 sway bar insulators, 4 sway bar U-bracket bolts and 2 subframe to body retaining bolts are available. These parts lose their torque holding/retention capabilities during removal and must not be reused.**

1. Raise and safely support the vehicle.
2. On the SHO vehicles:
   a. Detach the height sensor wiring connector.
   b. Remove the wiring harness from the routing clip on the front shock absorber.
   c. Remove air suspension height sensor from the height sensor ball studs.
3. On SHO vehicles, remove the vinyl cover from the upper link stud.

➡️**Do not raise the vehicle on the lower control arms or subframe.**

4. Remove the sway bar (stabilizer bar) link-to-sway bar nuts at each strut assembly by holding the link stud with an 8 mm box wrench while removing the retaining nut

with an 18mm open end wrench. Discard the sway bar link nuts.

5. Remove the sway bar link-to-strut nuts and the links; discard the nuts.

➡️**Use care not to damage the boot seals on the sway bar links. Do not use power tools for removal or installation.**

6. Remove the rack and pinion-to-subframe nuts and move the rack and pinion assembly off the subframe to allow for removal of the sway bar.

7. Place a set of jackstands under the rear of the subframe and remove the rear subframe-to-body bolts.

8. Lower the rear of the subframe enough to gain access to the sway bar brackets.

9. Remove the sway bar U-bracket bolts, 2 per side and remove the U-brackets. Discard the 4 U-bracket bolts.

10. Remove the sway bar from the vehicle.

11. Remove the 2 sway bar insulators and discard.

To install:

12. Clean the sway bar of contamination in the areas that the sway bar insulators are positioned.

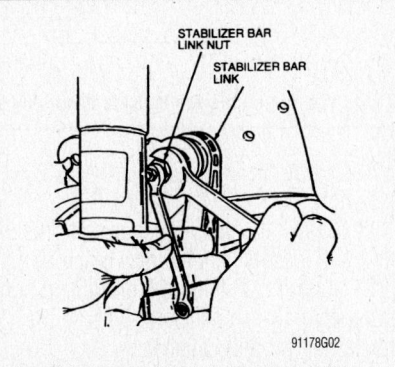

Fig. 172 Remove the stabilizer bar link from the stabilizer bar

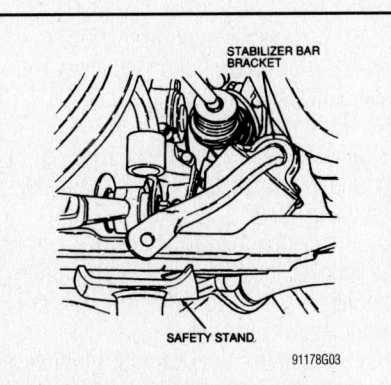

Fig. 173 The stabilizer bar bracket and bushing location

13. Lubricate the inside diameter of the new sway bar insulators with a lubricant designed for rubber suspension insulators.

14. Install the new sway bar insulators onto the sway bar and position the insulators in their approximate locations. Make sure the slits are positioned towards the front of the vehicle.

15. Install the sway bar onto the vehicle.

16. Install the U-brackets and 4 new retaining bolts securing the sway bar to the subframe. Tighten the bolts to 22–29 ft. lbs. (30–40 Nm).

17. Raise the subframe and install 2 new subframe to body retaining bolts. Tighten the bolts to 57–76 ft. lbs. (77–103 Nm).

18. Place the rack and pinion assembly in position on the subframe and install 2 retaining nuts. Tighten the retaining nuts to 85–99 ft. lbs. (115–135 Nm).

19. Install the sway bar links to the sway bar and struts. Note the letters TOP LH and TOP RH on each link for correct positioning. Install new nuts. Hold each link stud with an 8 mm box wrench while installing the new retaining nut with an 18mm open end wrench. Tighten the nuts at the strut to 57–75 ft. lbs. (77–103 Nm) and the nuts at the sway bar to 35–46 (47–63 Nm).

➡️**Use care not to damage the boot seals on the sway bar links. Do not use power tools for removal or installation.**

20. On SHO vehicles, install the vinyl cover to the upper link stud.
21. On the SHO vehicles:
   a. Install air suspension height sensor to the height sensor ball studs.
   b. Install the wiring harness to the routing clip on the front shock absorber.
   c. Attach the height sensor wiring connector.
22. Remove the jackstands.
23. Lower the vehicle. Check the front wheel alignment.

➡️**Whenever the vehicles subframe is removed or lowered, the wheel alignment should be checked.**

24. Road test the vehicle and check for proper operation.

STEERING KNUCKLE

REMOVAL & INSTALLATION

See Figure 174.

➡️**Be sure new wheel hub retainer nuts, tie rod end castellated nuts, hub-to-knuckle retaining bolts, knuckle-to-strut pinch bolt/nut and inboard halfshaft circlips are available. These parts lose** their torque holding/retention capabilities during removal and must not be reused.

1. Turn the ignition switch to the **OFF** position. Place the steering column in the UNLOCKED position.

2. Remove the wheel hub retainer nut before raising the vehicle off the ground. Discard the wheel hub retainer nut.

3. Raise and safely support the vehicle. Remove the wheel and tire assembly.

➡When raising the vehicle, do not lift by using the lower control arms.

4. Remove the wheel and tire assembly.

5. Remove the cotter pin and the castellated nut from the tie rod end. Discard the cotter pin and nut.

6. Separate the tie rod end from the steering knuckle using Remover tool 3290-D and adapter T81P-3504-W, or equivalents.

7. On SHO vehicles, remove the vinyl cover from the upper link stud.

8. Remove the stabilizer link from the strut. Remove the disc brake caliper and hang it aside.

9. Remove the disc brake rotor.

10. Remove the anti-lock sensor and move it aside.

11. Remove and discard the lower ball joint retaining nut. Using Ball Joint Remover T96P-3010-A or equivalent, separate the ball joint from the lower control arm.

12. Using Rotunda Spring Compressor 164-R-3571 or equivalent, compress the coil spring until the ball joint clears the lower control arm.

13. Remove and discard the steering knuckle-to-strut pinch bolt and nut.

14. Separate the halfshaft from the wheel hub using Front Hub Remover/Replacer T81P-1104-C or equivalent and adapters.

15. Support the halfshaft with wire in a level position to prevent it from hanging by the inner CV-joint.

➡Do not let the halfshaft hang by the inner CV-joint or move too far outward. The internal parts of the tripod CV-joint could be pulled apart.

16. Separate the steering knuckle from the strut assembly and remove it from the vehicle.

To install:

17. Install the disc brake rotor shield using new rivets, if removed.

18. Position the steering knuckle assembly to the vehicle.

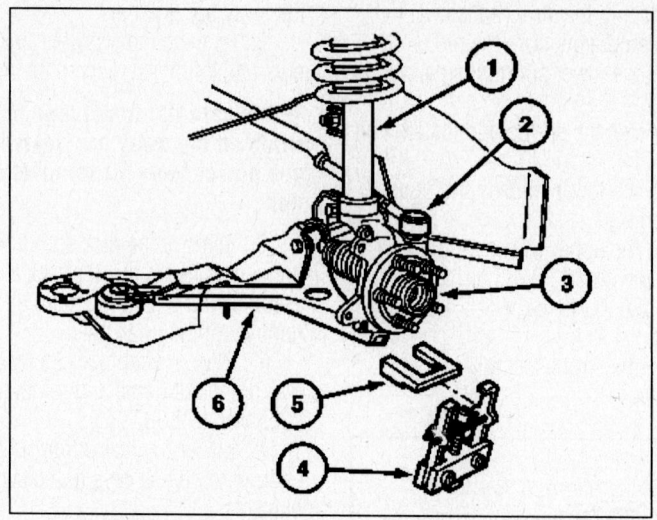

Item	Description
1	Front Shock Absorber
2	Tie Rod End
3	Wheel Hub
4	Pitman Arm Puller
5	Ball Joint Remover
6	Front Suspension Lower Arm

91178G19

Fig. 174 Front steering knuckle assembly and related components

19. Place the halfshaft into the hub assembly.

20. Install the steering knuckle to the strut and loosely install a new pinch bolt.

21. Install the steering knuckle and hub assembly onto the halfshaft. Be sure the splines are properly aligned.

22. Slowly release Rotunda Spring Compressor 164-R-3571 or equivalent, while guiding the lower ball joint into the lower control arm.

23. Remove the spring compressor.

24. Install a new nut on the lower ball joint stud and tighten to 50–67 ft. lbs. (68–92 Nm).

25. Install a new nut on the steering knuckle-to-strut pinch bolt. Tighten the pinch bolt nut to 72–97 ft. lbs. (98–132 Nm).

26. Position the tie rod end to the steering knuckle. Install a new castellated nut and tighten to 35–46 ft. lbs. (47–63 Nm). Install a new cotter pin.

27. Install the sway bar link and tighten the nut to 57–75 ft. lbs. (77–103 Nm).

28. On SHO vehicles, install the vinyl cover to the upper link stud.

➡Use care not to damage the sway bar link boot seals. Do not use power tools to tighten the nuts or seal damage will result.

29. Install the disc brake rotor and disc brake caliper. Tighten the caliper anchor bracket bolts to 65–87 ft. lbs. (88–118 Nm).

30. Install the wheel and tire assembly.

31. Lower the vehicle.

32. Install a new wheel hub retainer nut. Tighten the nut to 170–202 ft. lbs. (230–275 Nm).

33. Pump the brake pedal several times prior to moving the vehicle, to position the brake pads.

34. Road test the vehicle and check for proper operation.

WHEEL BEARINGS

REMOVAL & INSTALLATION

See Figures 175 through 177.

1. Before servicing the vehicle, refer to the precautions section.

> ❊❊ **CAUTION**
>
> **Discard the wheel hub retainer. It is a torque prevailing design and cannot be reused. If loosened, the retainer must be removed and a new one installed.**

➡ **Make sure the steering wheel is in the unlocked position.**

2. Remove the hub cap or wheel cover, the wheel hub retainer, and the washer. Discard the retainer.

3. Remove the front brake rotor.

  a. Remove and discard the tie rod cotter pin and nut.

> ❊❊ **CAUTION**
>
> **Do not damage the tie-rod end boot when installing the removal tool 211-001.**

➡ **Remove the adapter from the ball end of the removal tool. Apply a small amount of grease to the tie-rod end stud and the ball of the special tool.**

4. Using the removal tools illustrated, disconnect the tie-rod end.

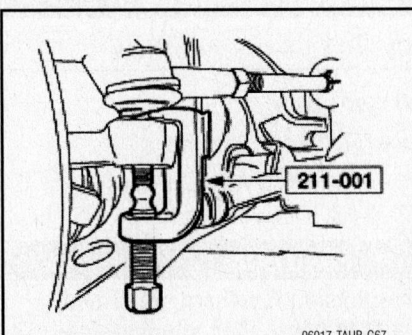

06017-TAUR-G67

Fig. 175 Using the removal tools illustrated, disconnect the tie-rod end

5. Remove the bolt and detach the ABS sensor, if equipped. Unclip the ABS sensor wire retainer and position the sensor out of the way.

6. Remove and discard the strut to knuckle nut.

7. Remove and discard the ball joint nut.

8. Using the tools illustrated, disconnect the ball joint from the lower arm.

9. Using a pry bar, push the lower arm down until the ball joint is free of the arm.

> ❊❊ **CAUTION**
>
> **Do not allow the halfshaft to move outboard. Over-extension of the tripod CV joint can result in separation**

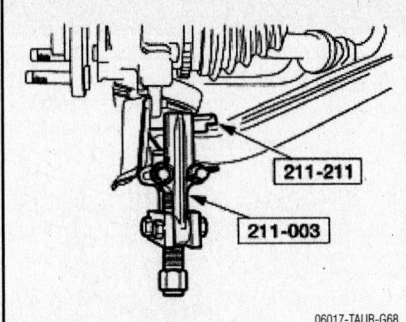

06017-TAUR-G68

Fig. 176 Using the tools illustrated, disconnect the ball joint from the lower arm

of internal parts, causing failure of the halfshaft.

➡ **Hold the threaded rod while turning the nut.**

10. Using the tools illustrated, press the halfshaft from the wheel bearing and hub. Wire the halfshaft in a level position.

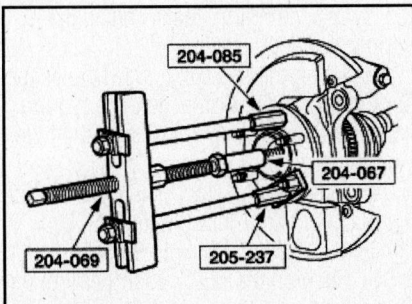

06017-TAUR-G69

Fig. 177 Using the tools illustrated, press the halfshaft from the wheel bearing and hub

11. Remove the flag bolt and the steering knuckle.

> ❊❊ **CAUTION**
>
> **The wheel bearing and hub is not pressed into the knuckle. Do not use a slide hammer or strike the inner race of the bearing. Damage to the bearing can result.**

➡ **If necessary, lubricate the knuckle and bearing with a rust inhibitor.**

12. Remove the bolts and the wheel hub and bearing. Discard the bolts.

> ❊❊ **CAUTION**
>
> **The knuckle bore must be clean enough to allow the wheel bearing and hub to seat completely by hand. Do not press or draw the wheel hub and bearing into place.**

13. Clean and inspect the knuckle bearing bore. If the knuckle is cracked, install a new knuckle.

To install:

14. Lubricate the knuckle bearing bore with anti-seize lubricant

15. Install the wheel bearing and hub and tighten to 70 ft. lbs. (95 Nm).

16. Position the knuckle on the strut and install the flag bolt.

17. Using the tools used during removal, press the halfshaft into the wheel bearing and hub.

18. Using a pry bar, push the lower arm down until the ball joint can be installed.

19. Install a new nut and tighten to 59 ft. lbs. (80 Nm).

20. Install a new strut to knuckle nut and tighten to 85 ft. lbs. (115 Nm).

21. Install the ABS sensor wire retainer and sensor, if equipped.

➡ **Make sure the ABS sensor mounting hole does not have debris or corrosion build up, or false ABS activation can occur.**

➡ **If the hole in the tie-rod end does not line up with the slots in the nut, continue tightening the nut. Do not loosen the nut to align the slots in the nut with the hole in the outer tie-rod end.**

22. Connect the tie-rod end to the knuckle and install a new nut and cotter pin. Tighten the nut to 41 ft. lbs. (55 Nm).

23. Install the brake rotor.

> ❊❊ **CAUTION**
>
> **The front axle wheel hub retainer must be tightened to specification immediately during installation. If the retainer is not tightened immediately, the nylon lock will set incorrectly, leading to incorrect torque readings and bearing failure. Any front wheel hub retainer that is not immediately tightened to specification or is loosened must be removed and a new retainer installed.**

24. Install the washer, the wheel hub retainer, tighten to 184 ft. lbs. (250 Nm). Install the hub cap or wheel cover.

ADJUSTMENT

There is no adjustment for the front wheel bearings due to the nature of their design. These bearings are permanently lubricated and require no periodic maintenance.

COIL SPRING

REMOVAL & INSTALLATION

Wagons Only

See Figures 178 through 180.

1. Raise and safely support the vehicle.
2. Remove the wheel and tire assembly.
3. Position a floor jack under the lower suspension control arm.

✳✳ WARNING

The lower control arm must be supported before removal of the upper or lower shock absorber mounts to prevent injury or damage to the related components due to tension applied by the coil spring.

4. Remove the bolt retaining the rear brake hose bracket to the body.
5. Remove the shock absorber. Refer to the procedure in this Section.
6. Remove the stabilizer bar and bracket from the lower control arm.
7. Using the floor jack, slowly raise the lower control arm to normal curb height.
8. Install Spring Cage 164-R3555 or equivalent, on the coil spring.
9. Remove and discard the upper ball joint nut. Separate the upper ball joint from the wheel spindle.
10. Slowly lower the lower control arm using the floor jack until the tension is relaxed on the coil spring. Remove the coil spring and the upper and lower spring insulators.

To install:

11. Place the lower spring insulator on the lower control arm. Press the insulator

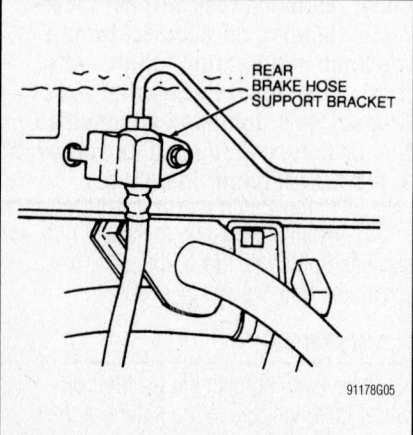

Fig. 178 Remove the bolt retaining the rear brake hose bracket to the body

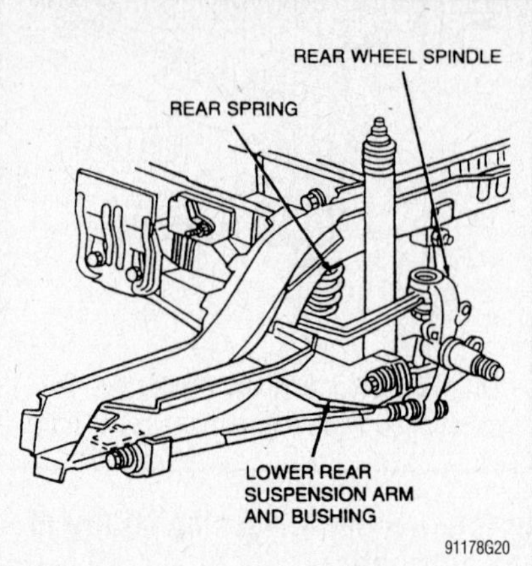

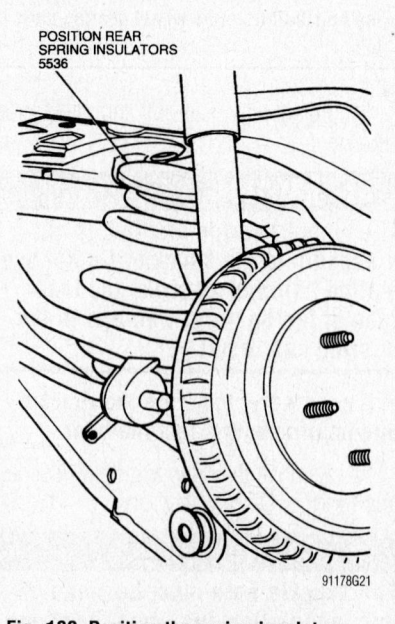

Fig. 179 Rear coil spring assembly mounting—wagon only

downward into place, making certain that the insulator is properly seated.

12. Position the upper insulator on top of the coil spring. Install the coil spring on the lower control arm. Make certain the spring is properly seated.
13. Using the floor jack, slowly raise the lower control arm. Guide the upper spring insulator onto the upper spring seat on the underbody.
14. Position the upper ball joint into the upper control arm. Install a new nut and tighten to 50–68 ft. lbs. (68–92 Nm).
15. Position the shock absorber into the tower opening with a new washer and insu-

Fig. 180 Position the spring insulators on installation before compressing the spring

lator installed. Push on the lower end of the shock until the lower bracket is lined up with the mounting holes in the lower control arm. Install a new lower retaining bolt and nut. Tighten to 50–68 ft. lbs. (68–92 Nm).

16. From inside the vehicle, install a new upper shock absorber insulator and washer. Tighten the nut to 19–25 ft. lbs. (25–34 Nm).
17. Install the rear compartment access panel.
18. Install the stabilizer bar and bracket to the lower control arm. Tighten to 15–19 ft. lbs. (19–26 Nm).
19. Install the brake hose support bracket to the body and install the retaining bolt.
20. Install the wheel and tire assembly. Tighten the lug nuts to 85–105 ft. lbs. (115–142 Nm).
21. Remove the floor jack.
22. Lower the vehicle.
23. Check the rear wheel alignment and adjust if necessary.
24. Road test the vehicle and check for proper operation.

CONTROL ARMS/LINKS

REMOVAL & INSTALLATION

Wagons Only

See Figure 181.

1. Before servicing the vehicle, refer to the precautions section.

✳✳ CAUTION

Suspension fasteners are critical parts because they affect performance of vital components and systems and their failure can result in major service expense. A new part with the same part number, or an equivalent part, must be installed if installation is necessary. Do not use a new part of lesser quality or substitute design. Torque values must be used as specified to make sure of correct retention of these parts.

2. Remove the hub cap or wheel cover.
3. Measure the distance from the center of the hub to the lip of the fender with the vehicle in a level, static ground position (curb height).
4. Remove the wheel and tire assembly.
5. Position a jack stand under the lower control arm and raise the suspension slightly.
6. Remove the bolt and detach the shock absorber. Discard the bolt.

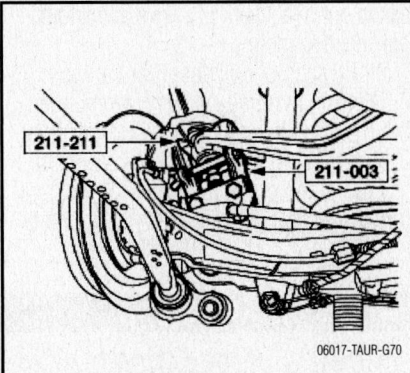

Fig. 181 Using the tools illustrated, separate the upper control arm from the ball joint—wagon models.

7. Remove the ball joint stud nut. Discard the nut.

8. Using the tools illustrated, separate the upper control arm from the ball joint.

9. Remove and discard the two flag nuts and bolts.

10. Remove the upper control arm.

To install:

11. Position the upper control arm and install two new bolts and flag nut but do not tighten the bolts at this time.

12. Attach the upper control arm and install a new nut. Tighten the nut to 59 ft. lbs. (80 Nm).

13. Using a jack stand, raise the suspension until the distance between the center of the hub and the lip of the fender is equal to the measurement taken in the removal procedure (curb height).

14. Tighten the two upper bolts to 85 ft. lbs. (115 Nm).

15. Attach the shock absorber. Install a new bolt and tighten to 59 ft. lbs. 80 Nm).

16. Lower the suspension and remove the jack stand.

17. Install the wheel and tire assembly.

18. Check and adjust the wheel alignment as necessary

MACPHERSON STRUTS

REMOVAL & INSTALLATION

Sedans Only

1. Before servicing the vehicle, refer to the precautions section.

2. Measure the distance from the center of the hub to the lip of the fender with the vehicle in a level, static ground position (curb height).

3. Remove the parcel tray.

4. Loosen the upper strut nuts.

5. Remove the wheel and tire assembly.

➡**It is not necessary to remove the stabilizer bar links from the stabilizer bar.**

6. Position a jackstand at the front of the vehicle under the subframe.

7. Detach the front muffler insulator from the muffler.

8. Position jackstands under the rear suspension and raise the suspension until the distance between the center of the hub and the lip of the fender is equal to the measurement taken previously (curb height).

9. Remove the nuts, washers, bushings, and bolts. Detach the stabilizer bar assembly from the body and the links. Discard the nuts and bolts.

10. Lower the suspension and remove the jack stands.

11. Carefully remove the stabilizer bar assembly out of the right wheel well.

12. Remove the bolt and detach the rear wheel brake hose.

13. Remove the nut, washer and bushing. Detach the tension strut from the spindle and discard the nut.

❈❈ CAUTION

Care should be taken when removing the strut and spring assembly so the rear wheel brake hose is not stretched.

14. Remove and discard the pinch bolt. Detach the spindle from the strut and spring assembly. To aid in removal, use a large prytool to spread the pinch joint.

15. Partially lower the vehicle.

16. Remove the nuts and the strut and spring assembly and discard the nuts.

To install:

17. Position the strut and spring assembly and install new nuts but do not tighten the nuts at this time.

18. Partially raise the vehicle.

19. Position the spindle on the strut and install a new pinch bolt. Tighten to 59 ft. lbs. (80 Nm).

➡**Make sure the cupped side of the washer is facing away from the bushing.**

20. Position the tension strut in the spindle and install the bushing, the washer and a new nut. Tighten the nut to 41 ft. lbs. (55 Nm).

21. Position the rear wheel brake hose and install the bolt.

22. Install the stabilizer bar, if equipped. Tighten the bar to body bolts to 30 ft. lbs. (40 Nm) and the bar to link nuts to 71 inch lbs. (8 Nm).

23. Install the wheel and tire assembly.

24. Tighten the upper strut nuts to 22 ft. lbs. (30 Nm).

25. Install the parcel tray

OVERHAUL

See Figure 182.

❈❈ CAUTION

Do not remove the strut rod nut until the spring has been compressed until it comes away from the seat.

1. Remove the strut from the vehicle.

2. Compress the coil spring using a suitable spring compressor until the spring comes away from the seat.

3. Remove the large center nut and slowly release the spring compressor.

4. Remove the upper bearing from the strut assembly.

5. Remove the spring from the strut assembly.

6. Remove the lower spring insulator from the strut.

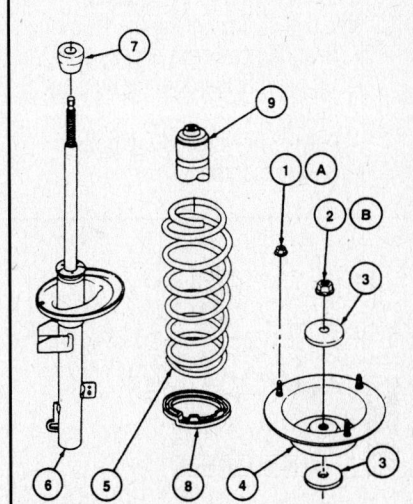

Item	Description
1	Nut (3 Req'd)
2	Nut
3	Washer (2 Req'd)
4	Rear Shock Absorber Bracket
5	Rear Spring
6	Shock Absorber
7	Rear Shock Absorber Jounce Bumper (Part of 18080)
8	Rear Spring Center Mounting Insulator (Part of 18080)
9	Dust Boot (Part of 18080)
A	Tighten to 25-34 N·m (19-25 Lb-Ft)
B	Tighten to 53-71 N·m (39-53 Lb-Ft)

Fig. 182 Rear strut components exploded view

To install:

7. If replacing the strut, transfer any necessary components from the old strut.

8. Install the lower spring insulator onto the strut.

9. Compress the spring and install it on the strut.

10. Install the lower washer and upper bearing assembly.

11. Install the upper washer and a new nut. Tighten the nut to 39–53 ft. lbs. (53–72 Nm) while holding the rod with a T-50 size Torx® socket.

12. Install the strut assembly in the vehicle.

SHOCK ABSORBER

REMOVAL & INSTALLATION

Wagons Only

See Figure 183.

1. Before servicing the vehicle, refer to the precautions section.

2. Remove the rear wheels and support the rear control arms on jackstands.

3. Remove or disconnect the following:
   • Rear compartment access panels
   • Upper shock mounting nuts and insulators
   • Lower shock mounting bolts
   • Shock absorbers

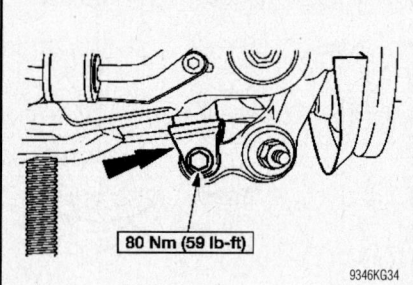

80 Nm (59 lb-ft)

9346KG34

Fig. 183 Shock absorber lower mounting bolt—Wagon

To install:

➡**Use new mounting fasteners and insulators.**

4. Install or connect the following:
   • Shock absorbers. Tighten the lower bolt to 50–68 ft. lbs. (68–92 Nm), and the upper nuts to 19–25 ft. lbs. (26–34 Nm).
   • Rear compartment access panels
   • Rear wheels

TESTING

The purpose of the shock absorber is simply to limit the motion of the spring during compression and rebound cycles. If the vehicle is not equipped with these motion dampers, the up and down motion would multiply until the vehicle was alternately trying to leap off the ground and to pound itself into the pavement.

Contrary to popular rumor, the shocks do not affect the ride height of the vehicle. This is controlled by other suspension components such as springs and tires. Worn shock absorbers can affect handling; if the front of the vehicle is rising or falling excessively, the "footprint" of the tires changes on the pavement and steering is affected.

The simplest test of the shock absorber is simply push down on one corner of the unladen vehicle and release it. Observe the motion of the body as it is released. In most cases, it will come up beyond it original rest position, dip back below it and settle quickly to rest. This shows that the damper is controlling the spring action. Any tendency to excessive pitch (up-and-down) motion or failure to return to rest within 2-3 cycles is a sign of poor function within the shock absorber. Oil-filled shocks may have a light film of oil around the seal, resulting from normal breathing and air exchange. This should NOT be taken as a sign of failure, but any sign of thick or running oil definitely indicates failure. Gas filled shocks may also show some film at the shaft; if the gas has leaked out, the shock will have almost no resistance to motion.

While each shock absorber can be replaced individually, it is recommended that they be changed as a pair (both front or both rear) to maintain equal response on both sides of the vehicle. Chances are quite good that if one has failed, its mate is weak also.

WHEEL BEARINGS

REMOVAL & INSTALLATION

1. Before servicing the vehicle, refer to the precautions section.

2. Remove or disconnect the following:
   • Rear wheel
   • Brake hose bracket
   • Brake caliper and rotor, if equipped with rear disc brakes
   • Brake drum, if equipped with rear drum brakes
   • Hub and bearing assembly grease cap and retaining nut
   • Hub and bearing assembly

To install:

➡**Use new retaining nuts and grease caps**

3. Install or connect the following:
   • Hub and bearing assembly and tighten the retaining nut to 221 ft. Lbs. (300 Nm).
   • Grease cap
   • Brake caliper and rotor, if equipped with rear disc brakes
   • Brake drum, if equipped with rear drum brakes
   • Brake hose bracket
   • Rear wheel

ADJUSTMENT

There is no adjustment for the rear wheel bearings due to the nature of their design. These bearings are permanently lubricated and require no periodic maintenance.

FORD, LINCOLN AND MERCURY

Diagnostic Trouble Codes

DIAGNOSTIC TROUBLE CODES

OBD II VEHICLE APPLICATIONS

FORD

Expedition
2005–2007
- 5.4L ....VIN 5

Excursion
2005
- 5.4L ....VIN L

Five Hundred
2005–2007
- 3.0L ....VIN 1

Focus
2005–2007
- 2.0L ....VIN N
- 2.3L ....VIN Z

Freestar
2005–2007
- 3.9L ....VIN 6
- 4.2L ....VIN 2

Freestyle
2005–2007
- 3.0L ....VIN 1

Fusion
2006–2007
- 2.0L ....VIN N
- 3.0L ....VIN 1

Mustang
2005–2007
- 4.0L ....VIN N
- 4.6L ....VIN H
- 5.4L ....VIN S

Ranger
2005–2007
- 2.3L ....VIN D
- 3.0L ....VIN V
- 4.0L ....VIN E

Taurus
2005–2007
- 3.0L ....VIN 2
- 3.0L ....VIN S
- 3.0L ....VIN U

LINCOLN

LS
2005–2006
- 3.0L ....VIN S
- 3.9L ....VIN A

MKZ
2007
- 3.5L ....VIN T

Navigator
2005–2007
- 5.4L ....VIN 5

Zephyr
2006
- 3.0L ....VIN 1

MERCURY

Milan
2006–2007
- 2.0L ....VIN N
- 3.0L ....VIN 1

Montego
2005–2007
- 3.0L ....VIN 1

Monterey
2005–2007
- 3.9L ....VIN 6
- 4.2L ....VIN 2

Sable
2006
- 3.0L ....VIN 2
- 3.0L ....VIN S
- 3.0L ....VIN U

INTRODUCTION

To use this information, first read and record all codes in memory along with any Freeze Frame data. *If the PCM reset function is done prior to recording any data, all codes and freeze frame data will be lost!* Look up the desired code by DTC number, Code Title and Conditions (enable criteria) that indicate why a code set, and how to drive the vehicle. **1T and 2T** indicate a 1-trip or 2-trip fault and the Monitor type.

Gas Engine OBD II Trouble Code List (P0xxx Codes)

DTC	Trouble Code Title, Conditions & Possible Causes
DTC: P0010 **2T CCM, MIL: Yes** **Years:** 2005, 2006, 2007 **Models:** All Models **Engines:** All **Transmissions:** All	**Variable Cam Timing Solenoid 'A' Circuit Malfunction** Key on or engine running; and the PCM detected an unexpected high voltage or low voltage condition on the Variable Cam Timing (VCT) Solenoid 'A' control circuit during testing. **Possible Causes:** • VCT 'A' solenoid connector is damaged, loose or shorted • VCT 'A' solenoid control circuit is open, shorted to ground or shorted to power • VCT 'A' solenoid is damaged or the PCM has failed
DTC: P0011 **2T CCM, MIL: Yes** **Years:** 2005, 2006, 2007 **Models:** All Models **Engines:** All **Transmissions:** All	**Variable Cam Timing Over Advanced (Bank 1)** Engine started; and the PCM detected the camshaft timing exceeded the maximum calibrated advance value, or the camshaft remained in an advanced position during the CCM test. **Possible Causes:** • Camshaft timing improperly set, or continuous oil flow to the VCT piston chamber • Camshaft advance mechanism (the VCT unit) is sticking or binding mechanically • VCT solenoid valve is stuck in open position
DTC: P0012 **2T CCM, MIL: Yes** **Years:** 2005, 2006, 2007 **Models:** All Models **Engines:** All **Transmissions:** All	**Variable Cam Timing Over Retarded (Bank 1)** Engine started; and the PCM detected the camshaft timing exceeded the maximum calibrated retard value, or the camshaft remained in a retarded position during the CCM test. **Possible Causes:** • Camshaft timing improperly set, or continuous oil flow to the VCT piston chamber • Camshaft advance mechanism (the VCT unit) is sticking or binding mechanically • VCT solenoid valve is stuck in open position
DTC: P0020 **2T CCM, MIL: Yes** **Years:** 2005, 2006, 2007 **Models:** All Models **Engines:** All **Transmissions:** All	**Variable Cam Timing Solenoid 'B' Circuit Malfunction** Key on or engine running; and the PCM detected an unexpected high or low voltage condition on the Variable Cam Timing (VCT) Solenoid 'B' control circuit during testing. **Possible Causes:** • VCT 'B' solenoid connector is damaged, loose or shorted • VCT 'B' solenoid control circuit is open, shorted to ground or shorted to power • VCT 'B' solenoid is damaged or the PCM has failed
DTC: P0020 **2T CCM, MIL: Yes** **Years:** 2005, 2006, 2007 **Models:** All Models **Engines:** All **Transmissions:** All	**Variable Cam Timing Over Advanced (Bank 2)** Engine started; and the PCM detected the camshaft timing exceeded the maximum calibrated advance value, or the camshaft remained in an advanced position during the CCM test. **Possible Causes:** • Camshaft timing improperly set, or continuous oil flow to the VCT piston chamber • Camshaft advance mechanism (the VCT unit) is sticking or binding mechanically • VCT solenoid valve is stuck in open position
DTC: P0022 **2T CCM, MIL: Yes** **Years:** 2005, 2006, 2007 **Models:** All Models **Engines:** All **Transmissions:** All	**Variable Cam Timing Over Retarded (Bank 2)** Engine started; and the PCM detected the camshaft timing exceeded the maximum calibrated retard value, or the camshaft remained in a retarded position during the CCM test. **Possible Causes:** • Camshaft timing improperly set, or continuous oil flow to the VCT piston chamber • Camshaft advance mechanism (the VCT unit) is sticking or binding mechanically • VCT solenoid valve is stuck in open position
DTC: P0102 **2T CCM, MIL: Yes** **Years:** 2005, 2006, 2007 **Models:** All Models **Engines:** All **Transmissions:** All	**MAF Sensor Circuit Low Input** DTC P0505 not set, engine started, and the PCM detected the MAF sensor signal was less than 0.23v during the CCM test period. **Possible Causes:** • Check for leaks at air outlet tube • Sensor power circuit open, sensor ground circuit open • Sensor signal circuit open (may be disconnected) • Check for loose tube clamps near the MAF sensor
DTC: P0103 **2T CCM, MIL: Yes** **Years:** 2005, 2006, 2007 **Models:** All Models **Engines:** All **Transmissions:** All	**MAF Sensor Circuit High Input** DTC P0505 not set, engine started, and the PCM detected the MAF sensor signal was more than 4.60v during the CCM test period. **Possible Causes:** • Check for a restricted inlet screen on the MAF sensor. • MAF sensor signal circuit is shorted to system power (B+) • MAF sensor is damaged or the PCM has failed

DTC	Trouble Code Title, Conditions & Possible Causes
DTC: P0106 2T CCM, MIL: Yes **Years:** 2005, 2006, 2007 **Models:** All Models **Engines:** All **Transmissions:** All	**Barometric Pressure Sensor Circuit Performance** Engine started, and the PCM detected the BARO sensor was out of range during the CCM test. The BARO sensor signal should be in a range of 4.0-6.0v. The Scan Tool displays the sensor reading as a frequency. **Note: The sensor VREF should be less than 6.0v at all times.** **Possible Causes:** • Sensor has deteriorated (response time too slow) or has failed • PCM has failed
DTC: P0107 2T CCM, MIL: Yes **Years:** 2005, 2006, 2007 **Models:** All Models **Engines:** All **Transmissions:** All	**Barometric Pressure Sensor Circuit Low Input** Engine started, and the PCM detected the BARO sensor indicated less than the minimum calibrated parameter. The BARO sensor is a variable capacitance unit used to detect altitude. **Possible Causes:** • BARO sensor signal circuit is shorted to ground • BARO sensor VREF circuit (5v) is open • BARO sensor is damaged or it has failed • PCM has failed
DTC: P0108 2T CCM, MIL: Yes **Years:** 2005, 2006, 2007 **Models:** All Models **Engines:** All **Transmissions:** All	**Barometric Sensor Circuit High Input** Engine started, and the PCM detected the BARO sensor signal was more than the maximum calibrated parameter of 5.0v. **Note: The sensor VREF should be 4.0v to 6.0v at all times.** **Possible Causes:** • BARO sensor connector is damaged, open or shorted • BARO sensor signal circuit is open or shorted to VREF (5v) • BARO sensor is damaged or it has failed • PCM has failed
DTC: P0109 2T CCM, MIL: Yes **Years:** 2005, 2006, 2007 **Models:** All Models **Engines:** All **Transmissions:** All	**Barometric Sensor Circuit Intermittent Input** Engine started, and the PCM detected the BARO sensor signal had an intermittent failure during normal engine operation. **Possible Causes:** • BARO sensor signal circuit is open or shorted to ground (intermittent) • BARO sensor VREF circuit (5v) is open • BARO sensor signal circuit is shorted to ground (Intermittent) • BARO sensor is damaged or it has failed
DTC: P0112 2T CCM, MIL: Yes **Years:** 2005, 2006, 2007 **Models:** All Models **Engines:** All **Transmissions:** All	**Intake Air Temperature Sensor Circuit Low Input** Key on or engine running; and the PCM detected the IAT sensor signal was less than the self-test minimum of 0.20v (Scan Tool reads over 250°F). This is a thermistor-type sensor with a variable resistance that changes when exposed to different temperatures. **Possible Causes:** • IAT sensor signal circuit is grounded (check wiring & connector) • IAT sensor is damaged or it has failed • PCM has failed
DTC: P0113 2T CCM, MIL: Yes **Years:** 2005, 2006, 2007 **Models:** All Models **Engines:** All **Transmissions:** All	**Intake Air Temperature Sensor Circuit High Input** Key on or engine running; and the PCM detected the IAT sensor signal was more than the self-test maximum 4.60v (Scan Tool reads under −46°F). This is a thermistor-type sensor with a variable resistance that changes when exposed to different temperatures. **Possible Causes:** • IAT sensor signal circuit is open (inspect wiring & connector) • IAT sensor signal circuit is shorted to VREF (5v) • IAT sensor is damaged or it has failed • PCM has failed
DTC: P0116 2T ECT, MIL: Yes **Years:** 2005, 2006, 2007 **Models:** All Models **Engines:** All **Transmissions:** All	**ECT Sensor / CHT Sensor Signal Range/Performance** Engine off for a calibrated period of time after an engine cold soak period over 6 hours, engine started, and the PCM detected the ECT sensor exceeded the IAT sensor by more than a calibrated value (e.g., 30°F), or the ECT sensor was more than a calibrated value of 225°F; the Catalyst, Fuel System, HO2S and Misfire Monitor did not complete, or the timer expired. **Possible Causes:** • Check for low coolant level or incorrect coolant mixture • CHT sensor is out-of-calibration or it has failed • ECT sensor is out-of-calibration or it has failed
DTC: P0117 2T CCM, MIL: Yes **Years:** 2005, 2006, 2007 **Models:** All Models **Engines:** All **Transmissions:** All	**ECT Sensor Circuit Low Input** Key on or engine running; and the PCM detected the ECT sensor signal was less than the self-test minimum of 0.20v (Scan Tool reads over 250°F). This is a thermistor-type sensor with a variable resistance that changes when exposed to different temperatures **Possible Causes:** • ECT sensor signal circuit is grounded in the wiring harness • ECT sensor is damaged or the PCM has failed

DTC	Trouble Code Title, Conditions & Possible Causes
DTC: P0118 **2T CCM, MIL: Yes** **Years:** 2005, 2006, 2007 **Models:** All Models **Engines:** All **Transmissions:** All	**ECT Sensor Circuit High Input** Key on or engine running; and the PCM detected the ECT sensor signal was more than the self-test maximum of 4.60v (Scan Tool reads under −46°F). This is a thermistor-type sensor with a variable resistance that changes when exposed to different temperatures **Possible Causes:** • ECT sensor signal circuit is open (inspect wiring & connector) • ECT sensor signal circuit is shorted to VREF (5v) • ECT sensor is damaged or it has failed • PCM has failed
DTC: P0121 **2T CCM, MIL: Yes** **Years:** 2005, 2006, 2007 **Models:** All Models Except Crown Victoria, Grand Marquis & Town Car **Engines:** All **Transmissions:** All	**TP Sensor Signal Range/Performance** Engine started; then immediately following a condition where the engine was running under at off-idle, the PCM detected the TP sensor signal indicated the throttle did not return to its previous closed position during the CCM Rationality test. **Possible Causes:** • Throttle plate is binding, dirty or sticking • TP sensor signal circuit open (inspect wiring & connector) • TP sensor ground circuit open (inspect wiring & connector) • TP Sensor is damaged or has failed
DTC: P0121 **2T CCM, MIL: Yes** **Years:** 2005, 2006, 2007 **Models:** Crown Victoria, Grand Marquis, Town Car **Engines:** 4.6L VIN V, W **Transmissions:** All	**ETC Throttle Position Sensor Signal Range/Performance** Key on or engine running; then immediately after the throttle is open or following a closed throttle (deceleration) event, the PCM detected the TP2 PID (TP Sensor 2) signal indicated more than 93% (4.65v) from its previous closed position during the CCM Rationality test. **Possible Causes:** • ECT TP sensor connector is damaged, loose or shorted • ETC TP sensor signal circuit is open • ETC TP sensor ground circuit is open • ETC TP sensor circuit VREF (5v) is open • ECT TP sensor is not seated properly, or it is sticking • ETC TP Sensor is damaged or it has failed
DTC: P0122 **2T CCM, MIL: Yes** **Years:** 2005, 2006, 2007 **Models:** All Models Except Crown Victoria, Grand Marquis & Town Car **Engines:** All **Transmissions:** All	**TP Sensor Circuit Low Input** Key on or engine running; and the PCM detected the TP sensor was less than 0.17v (Scan Tool TP PID reads under 3.42%) in the test. **Possible Causes:** • TP sensor signal circuit open (inspect wiring & connector) • TP sensor signal shorted to ground (inspect wiring & connector) • TP sensor VREF circuit is open (between the sensor and PCM) • TP sensor is damaged or has failed • PCM has failed
DTC: P0122 **2T CCM, MIL: Yes** **Years:** 2005, 2006, 2007 **Models:** Crown Victoria, Grand Marquis, Town Car **Engines:** 4.6L VIN V, W **Transmissions:** All	**ETC Throttle Position Sensor Circuit Low Input** Key on or engine running; and the PCM detected the Etc TP sensor was below the self-test minimum of 0.17v (Scan Tool below 3.42%). **Possible Causes:** • TP sensor signal circuit open (inspect wiring & connector) • TP sensor signal shorted to ground (inspect wiring & connector) • TP sensor VREF circuit is open (between the sensor and PCM) • TP sensor is damaged or has failed • PCM has failed
DTC: P0122 **2T CCM, MIL: Yes** **Years:** 2005, 2006, 2007 **Models:** Crown Victoria, Grand Marquis, Town Car **Engines:** 4.6L VIN V, W **Transmissions:** All	**ETC Throttle Position Sensor Circuit High Input** Key on or engine running; and the PCM detected the ETC TP sensor was less than the self-test maximum of 4.65v (Scan Tool TP PID reads more than 93%) during the CCM test. **Possible Causes:** • TP sensor connector is damaged, loose or shorted • TP sensor signal circuit is open or shorted to ground • TP sensor VREF circuit is open (between the sensor and PCM) • TP sensor is damaged or has failed • PCM has failed

DTC	Trouble Code Title, Conditions & Possible Causes
DTC: P0123 **2T CCM, MIL: Yes** **Years:** 2005, 2006, 2007 **Models:** All Models **Engines:** All **Transmissions:** All	**TP Sensor Circuit High Input** Engine started, and the PCM detected the TP sensor signal was more than the self-test maximum of 4.65v (equivalent to a Scan Tool TP PID of more than 93%) during testing. **Possible Causes:** • TP sensor not seated correctly in housing (may be damaged) • TP sensor signal is circuit shorted to VREF or system voltage • TP sensor ground circuit is open (check the wiring harness) • Perform a "sensor sweep test" and monitor for any glitches • PCM has failed
DTC: P0125 **2T ECT, MIL: Yes** **Years:** 2005, 2006, 2007 **Models:** All Models **Engines:** All **Transmissions:** All	**Insufficient Coolant Temperature For Closed Loop** Engine runtime at road load more than 6 minutes, and the PCM detected that the ECT sensor (or CHT sensor) signal did not indicate the required engine temperature value to enter closed loop within a specified amount of time. The amount of time is calculated from the point at which the engine is started, and depends upon the ECT or CHT sensor signal value at startup. **Possible Causes:** • Check the coolant mixture for an incorrect mixture • Check the operation of the thermostat (it may be stuck open) • ECT sensor (or the CHT sensor) has failed • Inspect for low coolant level
DTC: P0127 **2T CCM, MIL: Yes** **Years:** 2005, 2006, 2007 **Models:** All Models **Engines:** All **Transmissions:** All	**IAT Sensor 2 Circuit High Input** Engine started, engine running for a calibrated period of time, and the PCM detected the IAT Sensor 2 (PID IAT2) signal was too high. This code indicates a potential fault present in the Intercooler system (the Supercharger Boost is bypassed when this code is set). **Possible Causes:** • Blockage present in the Heat Exchangers • Low fluid level, or a fluid leak is present • Intercooler pump or relay has failed • Intercooler coolant lines may be crossed
DTC: P0128 **2T CCM, MIL: Yes** **Years:** 2005, 2006, 2007 **Models:** All Models **Engines:** All **Transmissions:** All	**Intake Air Temperature Sensor 2 Circuit High Input** Engine started, vehicle driven for over 10 minutes, and the PCM detected the engine did not reach an engine operating temperature of 160°F after an additional runtime of 2 minutes. **Possible Causes:** • Check the operation of the thermostat (it may be stuck open) • ECT sensor or CHT sensor is out-of-calibration, or has failed • Inspect for low coolant level or an incorrect coolant mixture
DTC: P0131 **2T CCM, MIL: Yes** **Years:** 2005, 2006, 2007 **Models:** All Models **Engines:** All **Transmissions:** All	**HO2S-11 (Bank 1 Sensor 1) Circuit Low Input** Engine running for more than 5 minutes, and the PCM detected the HO2S signal was in a negative voltage range referred to as "character shift downward". This code sets when the HO2S signal remains in a low state (usually less than 156 mv). In effect, it does not switch properly between 0.1v and 1.1v in closed loop operation. **Possible Causes:** • HO2S is contaminated (due to presence of silicone in fuel) • HO2S signal and ground circuit wires crossed in wiring harness • HO2S signal circuit is shorted to sensor or chassis ground • HO2S element has failed (internal short condition) • PCM has failed
DTC: P0132 **2T CCM, MIL: Yes** **Years:** 2005, 2006, 2007 **Models:** All Models **Engines:** All **Transmissions:** All	**HO2S-11 (Bank 1 Sensor 1) Circuit High Input** Engine running for more than 5 minutes, and the PCM detected the HO2S signal remained in a high state (i.e., more than 1.5v). **Note: The HO2S signal circuit may be shorted to the heater power circuit due to tracking inside of the HO2S connector. Remove the connector and visually inspect the connector for signs of oil or water.** **Possible Causes:** • HO2S signal shorted to heater power circuit inside connector • HO2S signal circuit shorted to VREF or to system voltage • PCM has failed
DTC: P0133 **2T O2S, MIL: Yes** **Years:** 2005, 2006, 2007 **Models:** All Models **Engines:** All **Transmissions:** All	**HO2S-11 (Bank 1 Sensor 1) Circuit Slow Response** Engine started, engine running in closed loop for over 5 minutes, and the PCM detected the HO2S amplitude and frequency were out of the normal range (e.g., the HO2S rich to lean switch time was more than 100 ms) during the HO2S Monitor test. **Possible Causes:** • HO2S is contaminated (due to presence of silicone in fuel) • HO2S signal circuit open • Leaks present in the exhaust manifold or exhaust pipes • HO2S is damaged or has failed • PCM has failed

DTC	Trouble Code Title, Conditions & Possible Causes
DTC: P0135 **2T O2HTR, MIL: Yes** **Years:** 2005, 2006, 2007 **Models:** All Models **Engines:** All **Transmissions:** All	**HO2S-11 (Bank 1 Sensor 1) Heater Circuit Malfunction** Engine started, engine running for 5 minutes, and the PCM detected an unexpected voltage condition, or it detected excessive current draw in the heater circuit during the CCM test. **Possible Causes:** • HO2S heater power circuit is open or heater ground circuit open • HO2S signal tracking (due to oil or moisture in the connector) • HO2S is damaged or has failed • PCM has failed
DTC: P0136 **2T O2S, MIL: Yes** **Years:** 2005, 2006, 2007 **Models:** All Models **Engines:** All **Transmissions:** All	**HO2S-12 (Bank 1 Sensor 1) Circuit No Activity** Engine started, engine running in closed loop for over 5 minutes, and the PCM detected the HO2S signal failed to meet the maximum or minimum voltage levels (i.e., it failed the voltage range check). **Possible Causes:** • Leaks present in the exhaust manifold or exhaust pipes • HO2S signal wire and ground wire crossed in connector • HO2S element is fuel contaminated or has failed • PCM has failed
DTC: P0138 **2T CCM, MIL: Yes** **Years:** 2005, 2006, 2007 **Models:** All Models **Engines:** All **Transmissions:** All	**HO2S-12 (Bank 1 Sensor 2) Circuit High Input** Engine running for more than 5 minutes, and the PCM detected the HO2S signal remained in a high state (i.e., more than 1.5v). Note: The HO2S signal circuit may be shorted to the heater power circuit due to tracking inside of the HO2S connector. Remove the connector and visually inspect the connector for signs of oil or water. **Possible Causes:** • HO2S signal shorted to heater power circuit in the connector • HO2S signal circuit shorted to VREF or to system voltage • PCM has failed
DTC: P0141 **2T O2HTR, MIL: Yes** **Years:** 2005, 2006, 2007 **Models:** All Models **Engines:** All **Transmissions:** All	**HO2S-12 (Bank 1 Sensor 2) Heater Circuit Malfunction** Engine running for 5 minutes, and the PCM detected an open or shorted condition, or excessive current draw in the heater circuit. **Possible Causes:** • HO2S heater power circuit is open or heater ground circuit open • HO2S signal tracking (due to oil or moisture in the connector) • HO2S is damaged or has failed • PCM has failed
DTC: P0148 **2T CCM, MIL: Yes** **Years:** 2005, 2006, 2007 **Models:** All Models **Engines:** All **Transmissions:** All	**Fuel Delivery Error** Engine started, engine running for a specified period of time in closed loop, then after at least one WOT event was recorded, the PCM detected a lean air/fuel condition in at least one engine bank during the wide-open throttle event. **Possible Causes:** • Severely restricted fuel filter • Severely pinched or restricted fuel delivery line
DTC: P0151 **2T CCM, MIL: Yes** **Years:** 2005, 2006, 2007 **Models:** All Models with a 4-Cyl, V6 or V8 engine **Engines:** All Except V10 **Transmissions:** All	**HO2S-21 (Bank 2 Sensor 1) Circuit Low Input** Engine started, engine running for over 5 minutes, and the PCM detected the HO2S signal was in a negative voltage range referred to as "character shift downward". This code sets when the HO2S signal remains in a low state (less than 156 mv). In effect, the sensor did not switch properly between 0.1v and 1.1v in closed loop. **Possible Causes:** • HO2S connector is damaged or shorted • HO2S signal and ground circuit wires crossed in wiring harness • HO2S signal circuit is shorted to sensor or chassis ground • HO2S element has failed (internal short condition) • PCM has failed
DTC: P0152 **2T CCM, MIL: Yes** **Years:** 2005, 2006, 2007 **Models:** All Models with a 4-Cyl, V6 or V8 engine **Engines:** All Except V10 **Transmissions:** All	**HO2S-21 (Bank 2 Sensor 1) Circuit High Input** Engine started, engine runtime over 5 minutes, and the PCM detected the HO2S signal remained in a high state (more than 1.5v). **Note: The HO2S signal circuit may be shorted to the heater power circuit due to tracking inside of the HO2S connector. Remove the connector and visually inspect the connector for signs of oil or water.** **Possible Causes:** • HO2S is contaminated (due to presence of silicone in fuel) • HO2S signal tracking (due to oil or moisture in the connector) • HO2S signal circuit is open or shorted to VREF • PCM has failed

DTC	Trouble Code Title, Conditions & Possible Causes
DTC: P0153 **2T O2S, MIL: Yes** **Years:** 2005, 2006, 2007 **Models:** All Models with a 4-Cyl, V6 or V8 engine **Engines:** All Except V10 **Transmissions:** All	**HO2S-21 (Bank 2 Sensor 1) Circuit Slow Response** Engine started, engine running in closed loop for over 5 minutes, and the PCM detected the HO2S amplitude and frequency were out of the normal range (e.g., the HO2S rich to lean switch time was more than 100 ms) during the HO2S Monitor test. **Possible Causes:** • HO2S is contaminated (due to presence of silicone in fuel) • Leaks present in the exhaust manifold or exhaust pipes • HO2S is damaged or has failed • PCM has failed
DTC: P0155 **2T O2HTR, MIL: Yes** **Years:** 2005, 2006, 2007 **Models:** All Models with a 4-Cyl, V6 or V8 engine **Engines:** All Except V10 **Transmissions:** All	**HO2S-21 (Bank 2 Sensor 1) Heater Circuit Malfunction** Engine running for 5 minutes, and the PCM detected an open or shorted condition, or excessive current draw in the heater circuit. **Possible Causes:** • HO2S heater power circuit is open • HO2S heater ground circuit is open • HO2S signal tracking (due to oil or moisture in the connector) • HO2S is damaged or has failed • PCM has failed
DTC: P0156 **2T O2S, MIL: Yes** **Years:** 2005, 2006, 2007 **Models:** All Models with a 4-Cyl, V6 or V8 engine **Engines:** All Except V10 **Transmissions:** All	**HO2S-22 (Bank 2 Sensor 2) Circuit No Activity** Engine running in closed loop for more than 5 minutes, and the PCM detected the HO2S signal failed to meet the maximum or minimum voltage (i.e., it failed the voltage check). **Possible Causes:** • Leaks present in the exhaust manifold or exhaust pipes • HO2S signal wire and ground wire crossed in connector • HO2S element is fuel contaminated or has failed • PCM has failed
DTC: P0158 **2T CCM, MIL: Yes** **Years:** 2005, 2006, 2007 **Models:** All Models with a 4-Cyl, V6 or V8 engine **Engines:** All Except V10 **Transmissions:** All	**HO2S-22 (Bank 2 Sensor 2) Circuit High Input** Engine running for more than 5 minutes, and the PCM detected the HO2S signal remained in a high state (i.e., more than 1.5v). **Note: The HO2S signal circuit may be shorted to the heater power circuit due to tracking inside of the HO2S connector. Remove the connector and visually inspect the connector for signs of oil or water.** **Possible Causes:** • HO2S signal shorted to the heater power circuit (due to oil or moisture in the connector) • HO2S signal circuit shorted to VREF or to system voltage • PCM has failed
DTC: P0161 **2T O2HTR, MIL: Yes** **Years:** 2005, 2006, 2007 **Models:** All Models with a 4-Cyl, V6 or V8 engine **Engines:** All Except V10 **Transmissions:** All	**HO2S-22 (Bank 2 Sensor 2) Heater Circuit Malfunction** Engine running for 5 minutes, and the PCM detected an open or shorted condition, or excessive current draw in the heater circuit. **Possible Causes:** • HO2S heater power circuit or the heater ground circuit is open • HO2S signal tracking (due to oil or moisture in the connector) • HO2S has failed, or the PCM has failed
DTC: P0171 **2T FUEL, MIL: Yes** **Years:** 2005, 2006, 2007 **Models:** All Models **Engines:** All **Transmissions:** All	**Fuel System Too Lean (Cylinder Bank 1)** Engine started, engine running at cruise speed for 3 to 4 minutes, and the PCM detected the Bank 1 Adaptive Fuel Control System reached its rich correction limit (a lean A/F condition). **Possible Causes:** • Air leaks after the MAF sensor, or leaks in the PCV system • Exhaust leaks before or near where the HO2S is mounted • Fuel injector(s) restricted or not supplying enough fuel • Fuel pump not supplying enough fuel during high fuel demand conditions • Leaking EGR gasket, or leaking EGR valve diaphragm • MAF sensor dirty (causes PCM to underestimate airflow) • Vehicle running out of fuel or engine oil dip stick not seated • TSB 01-20-5 contains a repair procedure for this trouble code

DTC	Trouble Code Title, Conditions & Possible Causes
DTC: P0172 **2T FUEL, MIL: Yes** **Years:** 2005, 2006, 2007 **Models:** All Models **Engines:** All **Transmissions:** All	**Fuel System Too Rich (Cylinder Bank 1)** Engine started, engine running at cruise speed for 3 to 4 minutes, and the PCM detected the Bank 1 Adaptive Fuel Control System reached its rich correction limit (a rich A/F condition). **Possible Causes:** • Camshaft timing is incorrect, or the engine has an oil overfill condition • EVAP vapor recovery system failure (may be pulling vacuum) • Fuel pressure regulator is damaged or leaking • HO2S element is contaminated with alcohol or water • MAF or MAP sensor values are incorrect or out-of-range • One of more fuel injectors is leaking
DTC: P0174 **2T FUEL, MIL: Yes** **Years:** 2005, 2006, 2007 **Models:** All Models With V6 Or V8 engine **Engines:** All V6, V8 **Transmissions:** All	**Fuel System Too Lean (Cylinder Bank 2)** Engine started, engine running at cruise speed for 3 to 4 minutes, and the PCM detected the Bank 2 Adaptive Fuel Control System reached its rich correction limit (a lean A/F condition). **Possible Causes:** • Air leaks after the MAF sensor, or leaks in the PCV system • Exhaust leaks before or near where the HO2S is mounted • Fuel injector(s) restricted or not supplying enough fuel • Fuel system not supplying enough fuel during high fuel demand conditions (e.g., the fuel pump may not supply enough fuel) • Leaking EGR gasket, or leaking EGR valve diaphragm • MAF sensor dirty (causes PCM to underestimate airflow) • Vehicle running out of fuel or engine oil dip stick not seated • TSB 1-20-5 contains a repair procedure for this trouble code
DTC: P0175 **2T FUEL, MIL: Yes** **Years:** 2005, 2006, 2007 **Models:** All Models With V6 Or V8 engine **Engines:** All V6, V8 **Transmissions:** All	**Fuel System Too Rich (Cylinder Bank 2)** Engine started, engine running at cruise speed for 3 to 4 minutes, and the PCM detected the Bank 2 Adaptive Fuel Control System reached its rich correction limit (a rich A/F condition). **Possible Causes:** • Camshaft timing is incorrect • Engine oil overfill condition • EVAP vapor recovery system failure (may be pulling vacuum) • Fuel pressure regulator is damaged or leaking • HO2S element is contaminated with alcohol or water • MAF or MAP sensor values are incorrect or out-of-range • One of more fuel injectors is leaking
DTC: P0180 **2T CCM, MIL: Yes** **Years:** 2005, 2006, 2007 **Models:** All Models **Engines:** All **Transmissions:** All	**Engine Fuel Temperature Sensor 'A' Circuit Malfunction** Engine runtime over 2 minutes, and the PCM detected the Engine Fuel Temperature (EFT) sensor 'A' signal was out-of-range (i.e., it was more than 4.54v [−46°F] or less than 0.21v [275°F]. **Note: Monitor the EFT PID value to identify an open or short circuit.** **Possible Causes:** • Engine operating under "low" ambient temperature conditions • EFT sensor signal circuit open or shorted in the wiring harness • EFT sensor is damaged or it has failed • PCM has failed
DTC: P0201 **2T CCM, MIL: Yes** **Years:** 2005, 2006, 2007 **Models:** All Models **Engines:** All **Transmissions:** All	**Cylinder 1 Injector Circuit Malfunction** Engine started, and the PCM detected the fuel injector "1" control circuit was in a high state when it should have been low, or in a low state when it should have been high (wiring harness & injector okay). **Note: Monitor the INJIF PID Fault "flags" with the Scan Tool. The appropriate INJF PID "flag" will read Yes when this code is set.** **Possible Causes:** • Injector 1 connector is damaged, open or shorted • Injector 1 control circuit is open, shorted to ground or to power • PCM has failed (the injector driver circuit may be damaged)
DTC: P0202 **2T CCM, MIL: Yes** **Years:** 2005, 2006, 2007 **Models:** All Models **Engines:** All **Transmissions:** All	**Cylinder 2 Injector Circuit Malfunction** Engine started, and the PCM detected the fuel injector "2" control circuit was in a high state when it should have been low, or in a low state when it should have been high (wiring harness & injector okay). **Note: Monitor the INJIF PID Fault "flags" with the Scan Tool. The appropriate INJF PID "flag" will read Yes when this code is set.** **Possible Causes:** • Injector 2 connector is damaged, open or shorted • Injector 2 control circuit is open, shorted to ground or to power • PCM has failed (the injector driver circuit may be damaged)

DTC	Trouble Code Title, Conditions & Possible Causes

DTC: P0203
2T CCM, MIL: Yes
Years: 2005, 2006, 2007
Models: All Models
Engines: All
Transmissions: All
	Cylinder 3 Injector Circuit Malfunction
	Engine started, and the PCM detected the fuel injector "3" control circuit was in a high state when it should have been low, or in a low state when it should have been high (wiring harness & injector okay).
	Note: Monitor the INJIF PID Fault "flags" with the Scan Tool. The appropriate INJF PID "flag" will read Yes when this code is set.
	Possible Causes:
	  • Injector 3 connector is damaged, open or shorted
	  • Injector 3 control circuit is open, shorted to ground or to power
	  • PCM has failed (the injector driver circuit may be damaged)

DTC: P0204
2T CCM, MIL: Yes
Years: 2005, 2006, 2007
Models: All Models
Engines: All
Transmissions: All
	Cylinder 4 Injector Circuit Malfunction
	Engine started, and the PCM detected the fuel injector "4" control circuit was in a high state when it should have been low, or in a low state when it should have been high (wiring harness & injector okay).
	Note: Monitor the INJIF PID Fault "flags" with the Scan Tool. The appropriate INJF PID "flag" will read Yes when this code is set.
	Possible Causes:
	  • Injector 4 connector is damaged, open or shorted
	  • Injector 4 control circuit is open, shorted to ground or to power
	  • PCM has failed (the injector driver circuit may be damaged)

DTC: P0205
2T CCM, MIL: Yes
Years: 2005, 2006, 2007
Models: All Models With V6, V8 or V10 Engine
Engines: All V6, V8, V10
Transmissions: All
	Cylinder 5 Injector Circuit Malfunction
	Engine started, and the PCM detected the fuel injector "5" control circuit was in a high state when it should have been low, or in a low state when it should have been high (wiring harness & injector okay).
	Note: Monitor the INJIF PID Fault "flags" with the Scan Tool. The appropriate INJF PID "flag" will read Yes when this code is set.
	Possible Causes:
	  • Injector 5 connector is damaged, open or shorted
	  • Injector 5 control circuit is open, shorted to ground or to power
	  • PCM has failed (the injector driver circuit may be damaged)

DTC: P0206
2T CCM, MIL: Yes
Years: 2005, 2006, 2007
Models: All Models With V6, V8 or V10 Engine
Engines: All V6, V8, V10
Transmissions: All
	Cylinder 6 Injector Circuit Malfunction
	Engine started, and the PCM detected the fuel injector control circuit was in a high state when it should have been low, or in a low state when it should have been high (wiring harness & injector okay).
	Note: Monitor the INJIF PID Fault "flags" with the Scan Tool. The appropriate INJF PID "flag" will read Yes when this code is set.
	Possible Causes:
	  • Injector 6 connector is damaged, open or shorted
	  • Injector 6 control circuit is open, shorted to ground or to power
	  • PCM has failed (the injector driver circuit may be damaged)

DTC: P0207
2T CCM, MIL: Yes
Years: 2005, 2006, 2007
Models: All Models With V8 or V10 Engine
Engines: All V8, V10
Transmissions: All
	Cylinder 7 Injector Circuit Malfunction
	Engine started, and the PCM detected the fuel injector "7" control circuit was in a high state when it should have been low, or in a low state when it should have been high (wiring harness & injector okay).
	Note: Monitor the INJIF PID Fault "flags" with the Scan Tool. The appropriate INJF PID "flag" will read Yes when this code is set.
	Possible Causes:
	  • Injector 7 connector is damaged, open or shorted
	  • Injector 7 control circuit is open, shorted to ground or to power
	  • PCM has failed (the injector driver circuit may be damaged)

DTC: P0208
2T CCM, MIL: Yes
Years: 2005, 2006, 2007
Models: All Models With V8 or V10 Engine
Engines: All V8, V10
Transmissions: All
	Cylinder 8 Injector Circuit Malfunction
	Engine started, and the PCM detected the fuel injector "8" control circuit was in a high state when it should have been low, or in a low state when it should have been high (wiring harness & injector okay).
	Note: Monitor the INJIF PID Fault "flags" with the Scan Tool. The appropriate INJF PID "flag" will read Yes when this code is set.
	Possible Causes:
	  • Injector 8 connector is damaged, open or shorted
	  • Injector 8 control circuit is open, shorted to ground or to power
	  • PCM has failed (the injector driver circuit may be damaged)

DTC	Trouble Code Title, Conditions & Possible Causes
DTC: P0209 **2T CCM, MIL: Yes** **Years:** 2005, 2006, 2007 **Models:** All Models With V10 Engine **Engines:** All V10 **Transmissions:** All	**Cylinder 9 Injector Circuit Malfunction** Engine started, and the PCM detected the fuel injector "9" control circuit was in a high state when it should have been low, or in a low state when it should have been high (wiring harness & injector okay). **Note: Monitor the INJIF PID Fault "flags" with the Scan Tool. The appropriate INJF PID "flag" will read Yes when this code is set.** **Possible Causes:** • Injector 9 connector is damaged, open or shorted • Injector 9 control circuit is open, shorted to ground or to power • PCM has failed (the injector driver circuit may be damaged)
DTC: P0210 **2T CCM, MIL: Yes** **Years:** 2005, 2006, 2007 **Models:** All Models With V10 Engine **Engines:** All V10 **Transmissions:** All	**Cylinder 10 Injector Circuit Malfunction** Engine started, and the PCM detected the fuel injector "10" control circuit was in a high state when it should have been low, or in a low state when it should have been high (wiring harness & injector okay). **Note: Monitor the INJIF PID Fault "flags" with the Scan Tool. The appropriate INJF PID "flag" will read Yes when this code is set.** **Possible Causes:** • Injector 10 connector is damaged, open or shorted • Injector 10 control circuit is open, shorted to ground or to power • PCM has failed (the injector driver circuit may be damaged)
DTC: P0219 **2T CCM, MIL: Yes** **Years:** 2005, 2006, 2007 **Models:** All Models **Engines:** All **Transmissions:** All	**Engine Over-Speed Condition** Engine started, and the PCM determined the vehicle had been driven in a manner that caused the engine to over-speed, and to exceed the engine speed calibration limit stored in memory. **Possible Causes:** • Engine operated in the wrong transmission gear position • Excessive engine speed with gear selector in Neutral position • Wheel slippage due to wet, muddy or snowing conditions
DTC: P0221 **2T CCM, MIL: Yes** **Years:** 2005, 2006 **Models:** LS **Engines:** 3.0L VIN S, 3.9L VIN A **Transmissions:** A/T	**Throttle Position Sensor 'B' Signal Performance** Engine started; and the PCM detected the TP Sensor 'B' circuit was out of its normal operating range during a condition with the throttle wide open, or with it completely closed. **Possible Causes:** • Throttle body is damaged • Throttle linkage is binding or sticking • ETC TP Sensor 'B' signal circuit to the PCM is open • ETC TP Sensor 'B' ground circuit is open • ETC TP Sensor 'B' is damaged or it has failed
DTC: P0222 **2T CCM, MIL: Yes** **Years:** 2005, 2006 **Models:** LS **Engines:** 3.0L VIN S, 3.9L VIN A **Transmissions:** A/T	**Throttle Position Sensor 'B' Circuit Low Input** Key on or engine running; and the PCM detected the TP Sensor 'B' indicated less than 0.17v (Scan Tool reads less than 3.42%). **Possible Causes:** • ETC TP Sensor 'B' connector is damaged or shorted • ETC TP Sensor 'B' signal circuit is shorted to ground • ETC TP Sensor 'B' is damaged or it has failed • PCM has failed
DTC: P0223 **2T CCM, MIL: Yes** **Years:** 2005, 2006 **Models:** LS **Engines:** 3.0L VIN S, 3.9L VIN A **Transmissions:** A/T	**Throttle Position Sensor 'B' Circuit High Input** Key on or engine running; and the PCM detected the TP Sensor 'B' indicated more than 4.65v (Scan Tool reads more than 93%) during the CCM test period. **Possible Causes:** • ETC TP Sensor 'B' connector is damaged or open • ETC TP Sensor 'B' signal circuit is open • ETC TP Sensor 'B' signal circuit is shorted to VREF (5v) • ETC TP Sensor 'B' is damaged or it has failed
DTC: P0230 **2T CCM, MIL: Yes** **Years:** 2005, 2006, 2007 **Models:** All Models **Engines:** All **Transmissions:** All	**Fuel Pump Primary Circuit Malfunction** Key on, and the PCM detected high current in fuel pump or fuel shutoff valve (FSV) circuit (NG only), or it detected voltage with the valve off, or it did not detect voltage on the circuit. The circuit is used to energize the fuel pump relay for 20 seconds at key on or while running. **Possible Causes:** • FP or FSV circuit is open or shorted • Fuel pump relay VPWR circuit open • Fuel pump relay is damaged or has failed • PCM has failed

DTC	Trouble Code Title, Conditions & Possible Causes
DTC: P0231 **2T CCM, MIL: Yes** **Years:** 2005, 2006, 2007 **Models:** All Models **Engines:** All **Transmissions:** All	**Fuel Pump Primary Circuit Low Input** Key on, and the PCM detected a lack of voltage on the FP Monitor circuit with the fuel pump commanded on. The fuel pump control circuit is used by the PCM to energize the fuel pump relay. At key on, the relay is energized for 20 seconds, and all the time the engine is running. **Possible Causes:** • FP or FSV circuit is open or shorted to ground • Fuel pump relay VPWR circuit open or fuel pump relay failed • PCM has failed
DTC: P0232 **2T CCM, MIL: Yes** **Years:** 2005, 2006, 2007 **Models:** All Models **Engines:** All **Transmissions:** All	**Fuel Pump Secondary Circuit High Input** Key on, and the PCM detected voltage on the FP Monitor circuit with fuel pump "off". The PCM uses the fuel pump control circuit to energize the fuel pump relay. At key on, the relay is "on" for 20 seconds or while running. This circuit is used to check voltage to the pump. **Possible Causes:** • Fuel pump relay contacts always closed • Fuel pump ground circuit has high resistance • Fuel pump secondary circuit is shorted to power • Low speed fuel pump relay damaged or related circuit problem
DTC: P0297 **2T CCM, MIL: Yes** **Years:** 2005, 2006, 2007 **Models:** All Models **Engines:** All **Transmissions:** All	**Vehicle Over-Speed Condition** Engine started, vehicle driven at a very high engine speed, and the PCM detected the vehicle speed exceeded the calibration limit, and then enabled the High Vehicle Speed Strategy to control the speed. **Possible Causes:** • The code indicates the vehicle was driven at very high engine speed (rpm) for too long. The PCM temporarily prohibits high engine speed by disabling the fuel injectors with this code set.
DTC: P0298 **2T CCM, MIL: Yes** **Years:** 2005, 2006 **Models:** LS **Engines:** 3.0L VIN S, 3.9L VIN A **Transmissions:** A/T	**Engine Oil Over-Temperature Condition** Engine started, engine running for several minutes, and the PCM detected an engine overheating condition, and then enabled the Engine Oil Temperature Protection Strategy (injectors off). **Possible Causes:** • Check for signs of base engine concern or engine overheating • EOP sensor or related circuit fault • Very high engine speed (rpm) for an extended period of time
DTC: P0300 **2T MISFIRE** **MIL: Yes** **Years:** 2005, 2006, 2007 **Models:** All Models **Engines:** All **Transmissions:** All	**Random Misfire Detected** DTC P0136, P0156, P0171, P0172, P0175, P1130 and P1150 not set, engine running under positive torque conditions, and the PCM detected a misfire in 1000 revolution (High Emissions) or the 200 revolution (Catalyst Damaging 1T) range in two or more cylinders. **Note: If the misfire is severe, the MIL will flash on/off on the 1st trip!** **Possible Causes:** • Base engine mechanical fault that affects two or more cylinders • Fuel metering fault that affects two or more cylinders • Fuel pressure too low or too high, fuel supply contaminated • EVAP system problem or the EVAP canister is fuel saturated • EGR valve is stuck open or the PCV system has a vacuum leak • Ignition system fault (coil, plug) affecting two or more cylinders • MAF sensor contamination (it can cause a very lean condition) • Vehicle driven while very low on fuel (less than 1/8 of a tank) • TSB 03-14-4 contains repair help for this code for COP ignition
DTC: P0301 **2T MISFIRE** **MIL: Yes** **Years:** 2005, 2006, 2007 **Models:** All Models **Engines:** All **Transmissions:** All	**Cylinder Number 1 Misfire Detected** DTC P0136, P0156, P0171, P0172, P0175, P1130 and P1150 not set, engine started, engine running under positive torque conditions, and the PCM detected a misfire a misfire in Cylinder 1 during the 200 revolution (Catalyst) or 1000 revolution (High Emissions) period. **Note: If the misfire is severe, the MIL will flash on/off on the 1st trip!** **Possible Causes:** • Air leak in the intake manifold, or in the EGR or PCM system • Base engine mechanical problem that affects only Cylinder 1 • Fuel delivery component problem that affects only Cylinder 1 (i.e., a contaminated, dirty or sticking fuel injector) • Ignition system problem (coil, plug) that affects only Cylinder 1 • TSB 02-16-2 contains repair help for this code (LS & T-Bird) • TSB 03-14-4 contains repair help for this code for COP ignition

DTC	Trouble Code Title, Conditions & Possible Causes
DTC: P0302 2T MISFIRE **MIL: Yes** **Years:** 2005, 2006, 2007 **Models:** All Models **Engines:** All **Transmissions:** All	**Cylinder Number 2 Misfire Detected** DTC P0136, P0156, P0171, P0172, P0175, P1130 and P1150 not set, engine started, engine running under positive torque conditions, and the PCM detected a misfire a misfire in Cylinder 2 during the 200 revolution (Catalyst) or 1000 revolution (High Emissions) period. **Note: If the misfire is severe, the MIL will flash on/off on the 1st trip!** **Possible Causes:** • Air leak in the intake manifold, or in the EGR or PCM system • Base engine mechanical problem that affects only Cylinder 2 • Fuel delivery component problem that affects only Cylinder 2 (i.e., a contaminated, dirty or sticking fuel injector) • Ignition system problem (coil, plug) that affects only Cylinder 2 • TSB 02-16-2 contains repair help for this code (LS & T-Bird) • TSB 03-14-4 contains repair help for this code for COP ignition
DTC: P0303 2T MISFIRE **MIL: Yes** **Years:** 2005, 2006, 2007 **Models:** All Models **Engines:** All **Transmissions:** All	**Cylinder Number 3 Misfire Detected** DTC P0136, P0156, P0171, P0172, P0175, P1130 and P1150 not set, engine started, engine running under positive torque conditions, and the PCM detected a misfire a misfire in Cylinder 3 during the 200 revolution (Catalyst) or 1000 revolution (High Emissions) period. **Note: If the misfire is severe, the MIL will flash on/off on the 1st trip!** **Possible Causes:** • Air leak in the intake manifold, or in the EGR or PCM system • Base engine mechanical problem that affects only Cylinder 3 • Fuel delivery component problem that affects only Cylinder 3 (i.e., a contaminated, dirty or sticking fuel injector) • Ignition system problem (coil, plug) that affects only Cylinder 3 • TSB 02-16-2 contains repair help for this code (LS & T-Bird) • TSB 03-14-4 contains repair help for this code for COP ignition
DTC: P0304 2T MISFIRE **MIL: Yes** **Years:** 2005, 2006, 2007 **Models:** All Models **Engines:** All **Transmissions:** All	**Cylinder Number 4 Misfire Detected** DTC P0136, P0156, P0171, P0172, P0175, P1130 and P1150 not set, engine started, engine running under positive torque conditions, and the PCM detected a misfire a misfire in Cylinder 4 during the 200 revolution (Catalyst) or 1000 revolution (High Emissions) period. **Note: If the misfire is severe, the MIL will flash on/off on the 1st trip!** **Possible Causes:** • Air leak in the intake manifold, or in the EGR or PCM system • Base engine mechanical problem that affects only Cylinder 4 • Fuel delivery component problem that affects only Cylinder 4 (i.e., a contaminated, dirty or sticking fuel injector) • Ignition system problem (coil, plug) that affects only Cylinder 4 • TSB 02-16-2 contains repair help for this code (LS & T-Bird) • TSB 03-14-4 contains repair help for this code for COP ignition
DTC: P0305 2T MISFIRE **MIL: Yes** **Years:** 2005, 2006, 2007 **Models:** All Models With V6, V8 or V10 Engine **Engines:** All V6, V8, V10 **Transmissions:** All	**Cylinder Number 5 Misfire Detected** DTC P0136, P0156, P0171, P0172, P0175, P1130 and P1150 not set, engine started, engine running under positive torque conditions, and the PCM detected a misfire a misfire in Cylinder 5 during the 200 revolution (Catalyst) or 1000 revolution (High Emissions) period. **Note: If the misfire is severe, the MIL will flash on/off on the 1st trip!** **Possible Causes:** • Air leak in the intake manifold, or in the EGR or PCM system • Base engine mechanical problem that affects only Cylinder 5 • Fuel delivery component problem that affects only Cylinder 5 (i.e., a contaminated, dirty or sticking fuel injector) • Ignition system problem (coil, plug) that affects only Cylinder 5 • TSB 02-16-2 contains repair help for this code (LS & T-Bird) • TSB 03-14-4 contains repair help for this code for COP ignition
DTC: P0306 2T MISFIRE **MIL: Yes** **Years:** 2005, 2006, 2007 **Models:** All Models With V6, V8 or V10 Engine **Engines:** All V6, V8, V10 **Transmissions:** All	**Cylinder Number 6 Misfire Detected** DTC P0136, P0156, P0171, P0172, P0175, P1130 and P1150 not set, engine started, engine running under positive torque conditions, and the PCM detected a misfire a misfire in Cylinder 6 during the 200 revolution (Catalyst) or 1000 revolution (High Emissions) period. **Note: If the misfire is severe, the MIL will flash on/off on the 1st trip!** **Possible Causes:** • Air leak in the intake manifold, or in the EGR or PCM system • Base engine mechanical problem that affects only Cylinder 6 • Fuel delivery component problem that affects only Cylinder 6 (i.e., a contaminated, dirty or sticking fuel injector) • Ignition system problem (coil, plug) that affects only Cylinder 6 • TSB 02-16-2 contains repair help for this code (LS & T-Bird) • TSB 03-14-4 contains repair help for this code for COP ignition

DTC	Trouble Code Title, Conditions & Possible Causes
DTC: P0307 2T MISFIRE **MIL: Yes** **Years:** 2005, 2006, 2007 **Models:** Models equipped with V8 or V10 engine **Engines:** All V8, V10 **Transmissions:** All	**Cylinder Number 7 Misfire Detected** DTC P0136, P0156, P0171, P0172, P0175, P1130 and P1150 not set, engine started, engine running under positive torque conditions, and the PCM detected a misfire a misfire in Cylinder 7 during the 200 revolution (Catalyst) or 1000 revolution (High Emissions) period. **Note: If the misfire is severe, the MIL will flash on/off on the 1st trip!** **Possible Causes:** • Air leak in the intake manifold, or in the EGR or PCM system • Base engine mechanical problem that affects only Cylinder 7 • Fuel delivery component problem that affects only Cylinder 7 (i.e., a contaminated, dirty or sticking fuel injector) • Ignition system problem (coil, plug) that affects only Cylinder 7 • TSB 02-16-2 contains repair help for this code (LS & T-Bird) • TSB 03-14-4 contains repair help for this code for COP ignition
DTC: P0308 2T MISFIRE **MIL: Yes** **Years:** 2005, 2006, 2007 **Models:** Models equipped with V8 or V10 engine **Engines:** All V8, V10 **Transmissions:** All	**Cylinder Number 8 Misfire Detected** DTC P0136, P0156, P0171, P0172, P0175, P1130 and P1150 not set, engine started, engine running under positive torque conditions, and the PCM detected a misfire a misfire in Cylinder 8 during the 200 revolution (Catalyst) or 1000 revolution (High Emissions) period. **Note: If the misfire is severe, the MIL will flash on/off on the 1st trip!** **Possible Causes:** • Air leak in the intake manifold, or in the EGR or PCM system • Base engine mechanical problem that affects only Cylinder 8 • Fuel delivery component problem that affects only Cylinder 8 (i.e., a contaminated, dirty or sticking fuel injector) • Ignition system problem (coil, plug) that affects only Cylinder 8 • TSB 02-16-2 contains repair help for this code (LS & T-Bird) • TSB 03-14-4 contains repair help for this code for COP ignition
DTC: P0309 2T MISFIRE **MIL: Yes** **Years:** 2005, 2006, 2007 **Models:** Models equipped with a V10 engine **Engines:** All V10 **Transmissions:** All	**Cylinder Number 9 Misfire Detected** DTC P0136, P0156, P0171, P0172, P0175, P1130 and P1150 not set, engine started, engine running under positive torque conditions, and the PCM detected a misfire a misfire in Cylinder 9 during the 200 revolution (Catalyst) or 1000 revolution (High Emissions) period. **Note: If the misfire is severe, the MIL will flash on/off on the 1st trip!** **Possible Causes:** • Air leak in the intake manifold, or in the EGR or PCM system • Base engine mechanical problem that affects only Cylinder 9 • Fuel delivery component problem that affects only Cylinder 9 (i.e., a contaminated, dirty or sticking fuel injector) • Ignition system problem (coil, plug) that affects only Cylinder 9 • TSB 03-14-4 contains repair help for this code for COP ignition
DTC: P0310 2T MISFIRE **MIL: Yes** **Years:** 2005, 2006, 2007 **Models:** Models equipped with a V10 engine **Engines:** All V10 **Transmissions:** All	**Cylinder Number 10 Misfire Detected** DTC P0136, P0156, P0171, P0172, P0175, P1130 and P1150 not set, engine started, engine running under positive torque conditions, and the PCM detected a misfire a misfire in Cylinder 10 during the 200 revolution (Catalyst) or 1000 revolution (High Emissions) period. **Note: If the misfire is severe, the MIL will flash on/off on the 1st trip!** **Possible Causes:** • Air leak in the intake manifold, or in the EGR or PCM system • Base engine mechanical problem that affects only Cylinder 10 • Fuel delivery component problem that affects only Cylinder 10 i.e., a contaminated, dirty or sticking fuel injector) • Ignition system problem (coil, plug) that affects only Cylinder 10 • TSB 03-14-4 contains repair help for this code for COP ignition
DTC: P0315 2T CCM, MIL: Yes **Years:** 2005, 2006, 2007 **Models:** All Models **Engines:** All **Transmissions:** All	**Unable to Learn Crankshaft Variation** Engine started, and the PCM determined that it was unable to correct for mechanical inaccuracies in the CKP wheel tooth spacing. **Note: The Misfire Monitor will be disabled.** **Possible Causes:** • Inspect the CKP sensor for damage • Inspect the CKP sensor for debris on the rotor • Inspect the crankshaft pulse wheel for damaged teeth • Inspect the crankshaft pulse wheel for wobble (loose condition)
DTC: P0316 2T MISFIRE **MIL: Yes** **Years:** 2005, 2006, 2007 **Models:** All Models **Engines:** All **Transmissions:** All	**Misfire in the First 1000 Revolutions** Engine started, and the PCM detected a severe misfire within the first 1000 engine revolutions. **Possible Causes:** • Check for CMC DTC P0136, P0156, P0171, P0172, P0175, P1130 and P1150. Repair these adaptive fuel and HO2S codes • Check for any other CMC in memory. Repair these codes first! • Ignore P1000 codes that set during KOEO and KOER Self-Test

DTC	Trouble Code Title, Conditions & Possible Causes
DTC: P0320 **2T CCM, MIL: Yes** **Years:** 2005, 2006, 2007 **Models:** All Models **Engines:** All **Transmissions:** All	**Ignition Engine Speed Input Circuit Malfunction** Engine started, and the PCM detected 2 or more successive erratic PIP signals during testing. **Possible Causes:** • Inspect for problems with an Aftermarket 2-way radio • Inspect for signs of "arcing" at one or more of the ignition coils • Inspect the Profile Ignition Pickup (PIP) unit inside distributor (check for damage or corrosion at the PIP sensor connector) • PIP sensor is damaged or it has failed (distributor models) • Ignition control module (ICM) has failed (Distributorless models)
DTC: P0325 **2T CCM, MIL: Yes** **Years:** 2005, 2006, 2007 **Models:** All Models **Engines:** All **Transmissions:** All	**Knock Sensor 1 Circuit Malfunction** Key on or engine running; and the PCM detected the knock Sensor 1 (KS1) signal was more than 0.5v at key on, engine off, or the KS1 signal was out of normal range (engine running). **Possible Causes:** • Knock sensor circuit is open • Knock sensor circuit is shorted to ground, or shorted to power • Knock sensor is damaged or it has failed • PCM has failed
DTC: P0326 **2T CCM, MIL: Yes** **Years:** 2005, 2006, 2007 **Models:** All Models **Engines:** All **Transmissions:** All	**Knock Sensor 1 Signal Range/Performance** Engine started, vehicle driven, and the PCM detected the Knock Sensor 1 (KS1) signal was more than the calibrated value. This code can set at key on, engine off, if the KS 1 signal is more than 0.5v. **Possible Causes:** • Knock sensor circuit is open • Knock sensor circuit is shorted to ground, or shorted to power • Knock sensor is damaged or it has failed • PCM has failed
DTC: P0330 **2T CCM, MIL: Yes** **Years:** 2005, 2006, 2007 **Models:** All Models **Engines:** All **Transmissions:** All	**Knock Sensor 2 Circuit Malfunction** Key on or engine running; and the PCM detected the knock Sensor 2 (KS2) signal was more than 0.5v at key on, engine off, or that the KS2 signal was out of the normal range with the engine running. **Possible Causes:** • Knock sensor circuit is open • Knock sensor circuit is shorted to ground, or shorted to power • Knock sensor is damaged or it has failed • PCM has failed
DTC: P0331 **2T CCM, MIL: Yes** **Years:** 2005, 2006, 2007 **Models:** All Models **Engines:** All **Transmissions:** All	**Knock Sensor 2 Signal Range/Performance** Engine started, vehicle driven, and the PCM detected that the Knock Sensor 2 (KS2) signal was more than the calibrated value. This code can set at key on, engine off, if the KS2 signal is more than 0.5v. **Possible Causes:** • Knock sensor circuit is open • Knock sensor circuit is shorted to ground, or shorted to power • Knock sensor is damaged or it has failed • PCM has failed
DTC: P0340 **2T CCM, MIL: Yes** **Years:** 2005, 2006, 2007 **Models:** All Models **Engines:** All **Transmissions:** All	**Camshaft Position Sensor Circuit Malfunction** Engine started, and the PCM detected the CMP sensor signal was missing or it was erratic. **Possible Causes:** • CMP sensor circuit is open or shorted to ground • CMP sensor circuit is shorted to power • CMP sensor ground (return) circuit is open • CMP sensor installation incorrect (Hall-effect type) • CMP sensor is damaged or CMP sensor shielding damaged • PCM has failed • TSB 02-22-1 contains repair information for this trouble code
DTC: P0350 **2T CCM, MIL: Yes** **Years:** 2005, 2006, 2007 **Models:** All Models **Engines:** All **Transmissions:** All	**Ignition Coil (Undetermined) Primary/Secondary Circuit Malfunction** Engine started, and the PCM did not receive valid IDM pulses from the ignition module. The PCM did not identify the coil with a problem. **Possible Causes:** • Ignition START/RUN circuit is open or shorted to ground • Ignition coil driver circuit is open or shorted to ground • Ignition coil circuit is shorted to power • Ignition coil damaged or it has failed • PCM has failed

DTC	Trouble Code Title, Conditions & Possible Causes
DTC: P0350 **2T CCM, MIL: Yes** **Years:** 2005, 2006, 2007 **Models:** Excursion, Five Hundred, Freestyle, LS, Montego **Engines:** 3.0L VIN S, 3.9L VIN A, 6.8L VIN S **Transmissions:** All	**Ignition Coil Primary/Secondary Circuit Malfunction** Engine started, and the PCM did not receive valid IDM pulses from the ignition module. The PCM did not identify the coil with a problem. **Possible Causes:** • Ignition START/RUN circuit is open or shorted to ground • Ignition coil driver circuit is open • Ignition coil driver circuit is shorted to ground • Ignition coil driver circuit is shorted to system power (B+) • Ignition coil damaged or it has failed • PCM has failed • TSB 01-1-6 contains a repair procedure for this trouble code
DTC: P0351-P0354 **2T CCM, MIL: Yes** **Years:** 2005, 2006, 2007 **Models:** Focus **Engines:** All With Coilpack **Transmissions:** All	**Ignition Coilpack 1-4 Primary/Secondary Circuit Malfunction** Engine started, and the PCM did not receive any valid IDM pulses from the ignition module for the Ignition Coilpack 1-4 primary circuit. **Possible Causes:** • Ignition START/RUN circuit is open or shorted to ground • Ignition coilpack 1-4 control circuit is open or shorted to ground • Ignition coilpack 1-4 control circuit is shorted to power • Ignition coilpack 1-4 is damaged or it has failed • PCM has failed
DTC: P0351-P0310 **2T CCM, MIL: Yes** **Years:** 2005, 2006, 2007 **Models:** **Engines:** All With Coil On Plug **Transmissions:** All	**Ignition Coil 1-10 Primary/Secondary Circuit Malfunction** Engine started, and the PCM did not receive any valid IDM pulses from the ignition module for the Ignition Coil 1-10 primary circuit. **Possible Causes:** • Ignition START/RUN circuit is open or shorted to ground • Ignition coil driver 1-10 circuit is open or shorted to ground • Ignition coil 1-10 circuit is shorted to power • Ignition coil -101 damaged or it has failed • PCM has failed
DTC: P0351-P0358 **2T CCM, MIL: Yes** **Years:** 2005, 2006, 2007 **Models:** Five Hundred, Freestyle, LS, Montego, Ranger **Engines:** All With Coil On Plug **Transmissions:** All	**Ignition Coil 1-8 Primary/Secondary Circuit Malfunction** Engine started, and the PCM did not receive any valid IDM pulses from the ignition module for the Ignition Coil 1-8 primary circuit. **Possible Causes:** • Ignition START/RUN circuit is open or shorted to ground • Ignition coil driver 1-8 circuit is open or shorted to ground • Ignition coil 1-8 circuit is shorted to power • Ignition coil 1-8 damaged or it has failed • PCM has failed
DTC: P0351-P0310 **2T CCM, MIL: Yes** **Years:** 2005, 2006, 2007 **Models:** Excursion **Engines:** 5.4L VIN L, 6.8L VIN S **Transmissions:** All	**Ignition Coil 1-10 Primary/Secondary Circuit Malfunction** Engine started, and the PCM did not receive any valid IDM pulses from the ignition module for the Ignition Coil 1-10 primary circuit. **Possible Causes:** • Ignition START/RUN circuit is open or shorted to ground • Ignition coilpack or COP 1-10 circuit is open or shorted to ground • Ignition coilpack or COP 1-10 circuit is shorted to power • Ignition coilpack or COP 1-10 damaged or it has failed • PCM has failed
DTC: P0351-P0358 **2T CCM, MIL: Yes** **Years:** 2005, 2006, 2007 **Models:** Excursion, Expedition, Navigator **Engines:** 5.4L VIN L With Coil On Plug **Transmissions:** All	**Ignition COP 1-8 Primary/Secondary Circuit Malfunction** Engine started, and the PCM did not detect a valid IDM pulse from the Ignition Module on the Ignition Coil on Plug 1 primary circuit. **Possible Causes:** • Ignition START/RUN circuit is open or shorted to ground • Ignition COP driver 1-8 circuit is open or shorted to ground • Ignition COP driver 1-8 circuit is shorted to power • Ignition COP 1-8 is damaged or it has failed • PCM has failed

DTC	Trouble Code Title, Conditions & Possible Causes
DTC: P0400 **2T EGR, MIL: Yes** **Years:** 2005, 2006, 2007 **Models:** Expedition, Focus, Mustang, Navigator, Sable, Taurus **Engines:** All **Transmissions:** All	**Exhaust EGR System Malfunction** DTC P0102, P0103, P0107, P0108, P1100 and P1101 not set, vehicle driven at over 48 mph at a steady speed in closed loop for 1 minute, and the PCM detected the EGR flow rate was less than or more than the calibrated flow rate limits during the EGR test period. **Possible Causes:** • DPFE EGR sensor connector is damaged, loose or shorted • EGR valve is sticking, damaged or it has failed • MAP sensor is damaged or out of calibration • PCM has failed • TSB 03-31-3 contains repair information for this trouble code
DTC: P0400 **2T EGR, MIL: Yes** **Years:** 2005, 2006, 2007 **Models:** Focus, Ranger **Engines:** 2.3L VIN D, 2.3L VIN Z **Transmissions:** All	**Electronic EGR System Malfunction** DTC P0102, P0103, P0107, P0108, P1100 and P1101 not set, engine started, vehicle driven at over 48 mph at a steady speed in closed loop for 1 minute, and the PCM detected the EGR flow rate was less than or more than the calibrated limits during the EGR test. **Possible Causes:** • EEGR valve connector is damaged, loose or shorted • EEGR valve is sticking, damaged or it has failed • MAP or TMAP sensor is damaged or not properly seated • PCM has failed
DTC: P0400 **2T EGR, MIL: Yes** **Years:** 2005, 2006, 2007 **Models:** Five Hundred, Freestyle, LS, Montego Models **Engines:** All **Transmissions:** All	**Exhaust EGR System Malfunction (ESM System)** DTC P0102, P0103, P0107, P0108, P1100 and P1101 not set, vehicle driven at over 48 mph at a steady speed in closed loop for 1 minute, and the PCM detected the EGR flow rate was less than or more than the calibrated flow rate limits during the EGR test period. **Possible Causes:** • DPFE EGR sensor connector is damaged, loose or shorted • EGR valve is sticking, damaged or it has failed • MAP sensor is damaged or out of calibration • PCM has failed
DTC: P0401 **2T EGR, MIL: Yes** **Years:** 2005, 2006, 2007 **Models:** All Models **Engines:** All **Transmissions:** All	**Insufficient EGR Flow Detected** Engine started, engine running in closed loop under steady cruise conditions, and the PCM detected the DPFE sensor input indicated insufficient EGR gas flow. Run the KOER Self-Test, and if DTC P1408 is present, the fault is currently present. **Possible Causes:** • DPFE sensor signal circuit is shorted to ground • DPFE sensor VREF circuit is open between sensor and PCM • DPFE sensor downstream hose off or plugged • DPFE sensor hoses both off, loose or damaged • DPFE sensor hoses connected wrong (reversed) • EGR orifice tube is damaged or restricted • TSB 03-31-3 contains repair information for this trouble code
DTC: P0401 **2T EGR, MIL: Yes** **Years:** 2005, 2006, 2007 **Models:** Excursion, Expedition, Focus, Mustang, Navigator, Ranger, Sable, Taurus **Engines:** All **Transmissions:** All	**Exhaust Gas Recirculation Malfunction** Engine started, engine running under at cruise speed in closed loop, and the PCM detected a problem in the EGR system. Run the KOER self-test. If DTC P1406 is set, test the EGR valve operation. **Possible Causes:** • DPFE EGR valve hoses are damaged, leaking or restricted • DPFE EGR valve hoses may be reversed at the sensor • EGR valve connector is damaged, loose or shorted • EGR valve is damaged or it has failed • PCM has failed • TSB 4-3-1 contains repair information for this trouble code
DTC: P0401 **2T EGR, MIL: Yes** **Years:** 2005, 2006, 2007 **Models:** Five Hundred, Freestyle, LS, Montego **Engines:** All **Transmissions:** All	**Exhaust Gas Recirculation Malfunction (ESM System)** Engine running under at cruise speed in closed loop, and the PCM detected a problem in the EGR ESM system. Run the KOER self-test. If DTC P1408 is present, inspect the EGR valve. **Possible Causes:** • DPFE EGR valve hoses are damaged, leaking or restricted • EGR valve connector is damaged, loose or shorted • EGR valve is damaged or it has failed • PCM has failed

DTC	Trouble Code Title, Conditions & Possible Causes
DTC: P0402 **2T EGR, MIL:** Yes **Years:** 2005, 2006, 2007 **Models:** All Models **Engines:** All **Transmissions:** All	**Excessive EGR Flow Detected** Engine started, engine running in hot idle speed, and the PCM detected the Actual DPFE sensor value indicated more than the KOEO DPFE sensor value stored in the PCM memory. **Possible Causes:** • DPFE EGR valve source hoses loose or connected wrong • DPFE sensor slow to respond or sluggish (it may have failed) • DPFE sensor signal circuit is open or shorted to ground • DPFE EGR sensor is damaged or the PCM has failed
DTC: P0402 **2T EGR, MIL:** Yes **Years:** 2005, 2006, 2007 **Models:** Five Hundred, Freestyle, LS, Montego **Engines:** All **Transmissions:** All	**EGR Flow At Idle Speed Detected (ESM System)** Engine started, engine running in hot idle speed, and the PCM detected the Actual DPFE sensor value indicated more than the KOEO DPFE sensor value stored in the memory. If DTC P1405 is set, repair the cause of that trouble code prior to repairing P0402. **Possible Causes:** • DPFE EGR sensor is damaged • DPFE EGR valve source hoses loose or connected wrong • DPFE sensor slow to respond or sluggish (it may have failed) • DPFE sensor signal circuit is open or shorted to ground • PCM has failed • TSB 03-31-3 contains repair information for this trouble code
DTC: P0402 **2T EGR, MIL:** Yes **Years:** 2005, 2006, 2007 **Models:** Excursion, Expedition, Focus, Mustang, Navigator, Ranger, Sable, Taurus **Engines:** All **Transmissions:** All	**EGR Flow At Idle Speed Detected (ESM System)** Engine started, engine running in hot idle speed, and the PCM detected the Actual DPFE sensor value indicated more than the KOEO DPFE sensor value stored in the memory. If DTC P1405 is set, repair the cause of that trouble code prior to repairing P0402. **Possible Causes:** • DPFE EGR sensor is damaged • DPFE EGR valve source hoses loose or connected wrong • DPFE sensor slow to respond or sluggish (it may have failed) • DPFE sensor signal circuit is open or shorted to ground • PCM has failed • TSB 03-31-3 contains repair information for this trouble code
DTC: P0403 **2T CCM, MIL:** Yes **Years:** 2005, 2006, 2007 **Models:** Ranger **Engines:** 2.3L VIN D **Transmissions:** All	**EGR Solenoid Circuit Malfunction** Engine started, and the PCM detected an unexpected "high" or "low" voltage condition on the EEGR solenoid control circuit at idle speed. **Possible Causes:** • EEGR solenoid control circuit is open, or shorted to ground • EEGR solenoid power circuit is open (check power to relay) • EEGR motor winding is open or shorted to power • EEGR solenoid connector not seated correctly or the EGR solenoid has failed • PCM has failed
DTC: P0403 **2T CCM, MIL:** Yes **Years:** 2005, 2006, 2007 **Models:** Five Hundred, Freestyle, LS, Montego **Engines:** All **Transmissions:** All	**EGR Solenoid Circuit Malfunction (ESM System)** Engine started, and the PCM detected an unexpected high or low voltage condition on the ESM EGR solenoid control circuit at idle. **Possible Causes:** • EGR solenoid connector is damaged, loose or shorted • EGR solenoid control circuit is open, or shorted to ground • EGR solenoid power circuit is open (check power to relay) • EGR solenoid is damaged or the PCM has failed
DTC: P0403 **2T CCM, MIL:** Yes **Years:** 2005, 2006, 2007 **Models:** Excursion, Expedition, Focus, Mustang, Navigator, Ranger, Sable, Taurus **Engines:** All **Transmissions:** All	**EGR Solenoid Circuit Malfunction** Engine started, and the PCM detected an unexpected high or low voltage condition on the EGR solenoid control circuit at idle speed. **Possible Causes:** • EGR solenoid connector is damaged, loose or shorted • EGR solenoid control circuit is open, or shorted to ground • EGR solenoid power circuit is open (check power to relay) • EGR motor winding is open or shorted to power • EGR solenoid is damaged or has failed • PCM has failed
DTC: P0405 **2T CCM, MIL:** Yes **Years:** 2005, 2006, 2007 **Models:** Five Hundred, Freestyle, LS, Montego **Engines:** All **Transmissions:** All	**DPFE Sensor Circuit Low Input (ESM System)** Engine started, and the PCM detected an unexpected low voltage condition (less than 0.20v) on the ESM DPFE sensor circuit. **Possible Causes:** • DPFE sensor connector is damaged or shorted • DPFE sensor power supply circuit is open or shorted to ground • DPFE sensor signal circuit is shorted to ground • DPFE sensor is damaged or the PCM has failed

DTC	Trouble Code Title, Conditions & Possible Causes
DTC: P0405 **2T CCM, MIL: Yes** **Years:** 2005, 2006, 2007 **Models:** Excursion, Expedition, Focus, Mustang, Navigator, Ranger, Sable, Taurus **Engines:** All **Transmissions:** All	**DPFE Sensor Circuit Low Input** Engine started, and the PCM detected an unexpected low voltage condition (less than 0.20v) on the ESM DPFE sensor circuit. **Possible Causes:** • DPFE sensor connector is damaged or shorted • DPFE sensor power supply circuit is open or shorted to ground • DPFE sensor signal circuit is shorted to ground • DPFE sensor is damaged or has failed • PCM has failed
DTC: P0406 **2T CCM, MIL: Yes** **Years:** 2005, 2006, 2007 **Models:** Five Hundred, Freestyle, LS, Montego **Engines:** All **Transmissions:** All	**DPFE Sensor Circuit High Input (ESM System)** Key on or engine running at idle speed, and the PCM detected an unexpected high voltage condition (more than 4.00v) on the ESM DPFE sensor circuit during the CCM test period. **Possible Causes:** • DPFE sensor connector is damaged or open • DPFE sensor signal circuit is open or it is shorted to VREF (5v) • DPFE sensor is damaged or has failed • PCM has failed
DTC: P0406 **2T CCM, MIL: Yes** **Years:** 2005, 2006, 2007 **Models:** Excursion, Expedition, Focus, Mustang, Navigator, Ranger, Sable, Taurus **Engines:** All **Transmissions:** All	**DPFE Sensor Circuit High Input** Key on or engine running at idle speed, and the PCM detected an unexpected high voltage condition (more than 4.00v) on the ESM DPFE sensor circuit during the CCM test period. **Possible Causes:** • DPFE sensor connector is damaged or open • DPFE sensor signal circuit is shorted to VREF (5v) • DPFE sensor signal circuit is open • DPFE sensor is damaged or has failed • PCM has failed
DTC: P0411 **2T AIR, MIL: Yes** **Years:** 2005, 2006, 2007 **Models:** All Models Except Sable & Taurus **Engines:** All **Transmissions:** All	**Secondary AIR System Incorrect Upstream Flow Detected** Engine started, engine running at idle speed in closed loop, and the PCM detected the secondary AIR pump airflow was not diverted correctly when requested during the self-test. **Possible Causes:** • Air pump output is blocked • AIR bypass solenoid leaking or blocked • AIR bypass solenoid is stuck open or stuck closed • Air injection pump hose(s) leaking • PCM has failed
DTC: P0411 **2T AIR, MIL: Yes** **Years:** 2005, 2006, 2007 **Models:** Sable, Taurus **Engines:** 3.0L VIN S **Transmissions:** All	**Secondary Air Injection System Upstream Flow Detected** Engine started, engine runtime from 20-120 seconds at any speed, and the PCM detected the Secondary AIR pump airflow was not diverted correctly when requested during the self-test. **Possible Causes:** • Air pump output is blocked or restricted • AIR bypass solenoid is leaking or it is restricted • AIR bypass solenoid is stuck open or stuck closed • Check valve (one or more) is damaged or leaking • Electric air injection pump hose(s) leaking • PCM has failed
DTC: P0412 **2T CCM, MIL: Yes** **Years:** 2005, 2006, 2007 **Models:** All Models Except Sable & Taurus **Engines:** All **Transmissions:** All	**Secondary Air Injection Solenoid Circuit Malfunction** Engine started, and the PCM detected an unexpected low or high voltage condition on the AIR solenoid control circuit during testing. **Possible Causes:** • AIR solenoid power circuit (B+) is open (check dedicated fuse) • AIR bypass solenoid control circuit is open or shorted to ground • AIR diverter solenoid control circuit open or shorted to ground • AIR pump control circuit is open or shorted to ground • Check valve (one or more) is damaged or leaking • Solid State relay is damaged or it has failed • PCM has failed

DTC	Trouble Code Title, Conditions & Possible Causes
DTC: P0412 **2T CCM, MIL: Yes** **Years:** 2005, 2006, 2007 **Models:** Sable, Taurus **Engines:** 3.0L VIN S **Transmissions:** All	**Secondary AIR Solenoid Control Circuit Malfunction** Engine started, and the PCM detected an unexpected low or high voltage condition on the AIR solenoid control circuit during testing. **Possible Causes:** • AIR solenoid power circuit (B+) is open (check dedicated fuse) • AIR bypass solenoid control circuit is open or shorted to ground • AIR diverter solenoid control circuit open or shorted to ground • Electric AIR pump control circuit is open or shorted to ground • PCM has failed
DTC: P0413 **2T CCM, MIL: Yes** **Years:** 2005, 2006, 2007 **Models:** All Models **Engines:** All **Transmissions:** All	**Secondary AIR System Switching Valve 'A' Circuit Malfunction** Engine started; Air Injection solenoid commanded "on", and the PCM detected an unexpected "high" voltage condition on the Secondary AIR control circuit during the CCM test. **Possible Causes:** • AIR solenoid control circuit is shorted to system power • AIR pump solenoid is damaged or has failed • PCM has failed
DTC: P0414 **2T CCM, MIL: Yes** **Years:** 2005, 2006, 2007 **Models:** All Models **Engines:** All **Transmissions:** All	**Secondary AIR System Switching Valve 'A' Circuit Malfunction** Engine started; AIR solenoid disabled, and the PCM detected an unexpected low voltage condition on the AIR Solenoid control circuit **Possible Causes:** • AIR solenoid control circuit is shorted to ground • AIR solenoid power circuit is open (no power to the solenoid) • AIR pump solenoid is damaged or has failed • Solid State relay is damaged or the PCM has failed
DTC: P0416 **2T CCM, MIL: Yes** **Years:** 2005, 2006, 2007 **Models:** All Models **Engines:** All **Transmissions:** All	**Secondary AIR System Switching Valve 'B' Circuit Fault** Engine started, AIR solenoid enabled, and the PCM detected an unexpected high voltage condition on AIR solenoid control circuit. **Possible Causes:** • AIR solenoid control circuit is open or it is shorted to system power • AIR pump is damaged or the Solid State relay is damaged or has failed • PCM has failed
DTC: P0417 **2T CCM, MIL: Yes** **Years:** 2005, 2006, 2007 **Models:** All Models **Engines:** All **Transmissions:** All	**Secondary AIR System Switching Valve 'B' Circuit Fault** Engine started; Air Injection solenoid commanded "on", and the PCM detected an unexpected "low" voltage condition on the AIR Solenoid control circuit during the CCM test. **Possible Causes:** • AIR solenoid control circuit is shorted to ground or there is no power to the circuit • AIR pump is damaged or the Solid State relay is damaged or has failed • PCM has failed
DTC: P0420 **2T CAT, MIL: Yes** **Years:** 2005, 2006, 2007 **Models:** All Models **Engines:** All **Transmissions:** All	**Catalyst System Efficiency Bank 1 Below Threshold** Vehicle driven at steady cruise speed for 5 minutes, and the PCM detected the switch rate of the rear HO2S-12 was close to the switch rate of front HO2S (it should be much slower). **Possible Causes:** • Air leaks at the exhaust manifold or in the exhaust pipes • Catalytic converter is damaged, contaminated or it has failed • ECT/CHT sensor has lost its calibration (the signal is incorrect) • Engine cylinders misfiring, or the ignition timing is over retarded • Engine oil is contaminated • Front HO2S or rear HO2S is contaminated with fuel or moisture • Front HO2S and/or the rear HO2S is loose in the mounting hole • Front HO2S much older than the rear HO2S (HO2S-11 is lazy) • Fuel system pressure is too high (check the pressure regulator) • Rear HO2S wires improperly connected or the HO2S has failed

DTC	Trouble Code Title, Conditions & Possible Causes
DTC: P0430 **2T CAT, MIL: Yes** **Years:** 2005, 2006, 2007 **Models:** All Models **Engines:** All **Transmissions:** All	**Catalyst System Efficiency Bank 2 Below Threshold** Vehicle driven at steady cruise speed for 5 minutes, and the PCM detected the switch rate of the rear HO2S-12 was close to the switch rate of front HO2S (it should be much slower). **Possible Causes:** • Air leaks at the exhaust manifold or in the exhaust pipes • Catalytic converter is damaged, contaminated or it has failed • ECT/CHT sensor has lost its calibration (the signal is incorrect) • Engine cylinders misfiring, or the ignition timing is over retarded • Engine oil is contaminated • Front HO2S or rear HO2S is contaminated with fuel or moisture • Front HO2S and/or the rear HO2S is loose in the mounting hole • Front HO2S much older than the rear HO2S (HO2S-11 is lazy) • Fuel system pressure is too high (check the pressure regulator) • Rear HO2S wires improperly connected or the HO2S has failed
DTC: P0442 **2T EVAP, MIL: Yes** **Years:** 2005, 2006, 2007 **Models:** All Models **Engines:** All **Transmissions:** All	**EVAP Control System Small Leak Detected** ECT sensor less than 90°F at startup (cold engine), engine running in closed loop at a steady cruise speed, and the PCM detected a leak in the EVAP system as small as 0.040" in the test. **Possible Causes:** • Aftermarket EVAP parts that do not conform to specifications • CV solenoid stays partially open when commanded to close • EVAP component seals leaking (i.e., leaks in the Purge valve, fuel vapor control valve tube assembly or fuel vapor vent valve) • Fuel filler cap damaged, cross-threaded or loosely installed • Loose fuel vapor hose/tube connections to EVAP components • Small holes or cuts in fuel vapor hoses or EVAP canister tubes
DTC: P0442 **2T EVAP, MIL: Yes** **Years:** 2005, 2006, 2007 **Models:** All Models **Engines:** All **Transmissions:** All	**EVAP Control System Small Leak (0.040") Detected** ECT sensor less than 90°F and within 10°F of the IAT sensor at startup (cold engine), engine started, the with the engine running in closed loop at a steady cruise speed, the PCM detected a leak in the EVAP system as small as 0.040" during the EVAP Monitor Test. **Possible Causes:** • Aftermarket EVAP parts that do not conform to specifications • CV solenoid remains partially open when commanded to close • EVAP component seals leaking (i.e., leaks in the Purge valve, fuel tank pressure sensor, canister vent solenoid, fuel vapor control valve tube assembly or fuel vapor vent valve). • Fuel filler cap damaged, cross-threaded or loosely installed • Loose fuel vapor hose/tube connections to EVAP components • Small holes or cuts in fuel vapor hoses or EVAP canister tubes • TSB 99-23-4, TSB 3-9-8 & TSB 3-20-3 contain a repair procedure for this trouble code
DTC: P0443 **2T CCM, MIL: Yes** **Years:** 2005, 2006, 2007 **Models:** All Models **Engines:** All **Transmissions:** All	**EVAP Canister Purge Solenoid Circuit Malfunction** Engine started, and the PCM detected an unexpected high or low voltage condition on the EVAP Purge solenoid control circuit when the device was cycled On/Off during testing. **Possible Causes:** • EVAP purge solenoid supply circuit is open • EVAP purge solenoid control circuit open, shorted to ground • EVAP purge solenoid control circuit is shorted to power (B+) • EVAP canister purge solenoid valve is damaged or it has failed • PCM has failed
DTC: P0446 **2T EVAP, MIL: Yes** **Years:** 2005, 2006, 2007 **Models:** All Models **Engines:** All **Transmissions:** All	**EVAP Canister Vent System Performance** ECT sensor less than 90°F, engine started, engine running at a steady cruise speed, and the PCM detected excessive vacuum was present in the EVAP system during the test period. **Possible Causes:** • Canister vent (CV) solenoid is stuck closed (partially or fully) • EVAP canister purge outlet tube blocked or kinked between the canister purge valve and the EVAP canister, or EVAP canister tube blocked between the fuel tank and canister • EVAP canister restricted, or plugged CV solenoid filter unit • Plugged or contaminated CV solenoid filter • EVAP canister purge valve stuck open • Fuel filler cap stuck closed (no vacuum relief) • FTP sensor VREF circuit open, or FTP sensor is damaged • Fuel vapor elbow at the EVAP canister contaminated

DTC	Trouble Code Title, Conditions & Possible Causes
DTC: P0446 **2T EVAP, MIL: Yes** **Years:** 2005, 2006, 2007 **Models:** All Models **Engines:** All **Transmissions:** All	**EVAP Canister Vent Solenoid Circuit Malfunction** Engine started, and the PCM detected an unexpected high or low voltage condition on the EVAP Canister Vent solenoid control circuit after the device was cycled On/Off in the test. **Possible Causes:** • Canister vent solenoid supply circuit is open • Canister vent solenoid control circuit open, shorted to ground • Canister vent solenoid control circuit is shorted to power (B+) • Canister vent solenoid valve is damaged or the PCM has failed
DTC: P0451 **2T CCM, MIL: Yes** **Years:** 2005, 2006, 2007 **Models:** All Models **Engines:** All **Transmissions:** All	**Fuel Tank Pressure Sensor Intermittent Signal** Engine started, and the PCM detected the FTP sensor signal changed from over +15" H2O to under −15" H2O within 100 ms. **Possible Causes:** • FTP sensor signal circuit has an intermittent open condition • FTP sensor signal circuit has an intermittent shorted condition • FTP sensor is damaged or it has failed
DTC: P0452 **2T CCM, MIL: Yes** **Years:** 2005, 2006, 2007 **Models:** All Models **Engines:** All **Transmissions:** All	**FTP Sensor Circuit Low Input** Key on or engine running; and the PCM detected the FTP sensor indicated less than the minimum calibrated limit of 0.22v in the test. **Possible Causes:** • FTP sensor connector has internal damage or contamination • FTP sensor signal circuit is shorted to chassis or signal ground • FTP sensor is damaged • PCM has failed
DTC: P0453 **2T CCM, MIL: Yes** **Years:** 2005, 2006, 2007 **Models:** All Models **Engines:** All **Transmissions:** All	**FTP Sensor Circuit High Input** Key on or engine running; and the PCM detected the FTP sensor indicated more than the maximum calibrated limit (4.50v) in the test. **Possible Causes:** • FTP sensor signal circuit is open or the ground circuit is open • FTP sensor signal circuit is shorted to VREF (5v) • FTP sensor is damaged or the PCM has failed
DTC: P0455 **2T EVAP, MIL: Yes** **Years:** 2005, 2006, 2007 **Models:** All Models **Engines:** All **Transmissions:** All	**EVAP Control System Large Leak Detected** ECT sensor less than 90°F at startup, engine running, and the PCM detected several small fuel vapor leaks or a large leak in the system. **Possible Causes:** • Aftermarket EVAP hardware non-conforming to specifications • Canister vent (CV) solenoid stuck open • EVAP canister purge valve stuck closed, or canister damaged • EVAP canister tube, EVAP canister purge outlet tube or EVAP return tube disconnected or cracked, or canister is damaged • Fuel filler cap missing, loose (not tightened) or the wrong part • Loose fuel vapor hose/tube connections to EVAP components • Purge sensor or FTP sensor is out of calibration or has failed
DTC: P0455 **2T EVAP, MIL: Yes** **Years:** 2005, 2006, 2007 **Models:** All Models **Engines:** All **Transmissions:** All	**EVAP Control System Large Leak (0.080") Detected** ECT sensor less than 90°F, engine running at a steady cruise speed, and the PCM detected multiple small fuel vapor leaks; or it detected a large leak in the system during the leak test. **Possible Causes:** • Aftermarket EVAP hardware non-conforming to specifications • EVAP canister tube, EVAP canister purge outlet tube or EVAP return tube disconnected or cracked, or canister is damaged • EVAP canister purge valve stuck closed, or canister damaged • Fuel filler cap missing, loose (not tightened) or the wrong part • Loose fuel vapor hose/tube connections to EVAP components • Canister vent (CV) solenoid stuck open • Fuel tank pressure (FTP) sensor has failed mechanically • TSB 99-23-4 contains a repair procedure for this trouble code • TSB 03-9-8 contains a repair procedure for this trouble code • TSB 3-20-3 contains a repair procedure for this trouble code

DTC	Trouble Code Title, Conditions & Possible Causes
DTC: P0456 **2T EVAP, MIL: Yes** **Years:** 2005, 2006, 2007 **Models:** All Models **Engines:** All **Transmissions:** All	**EVAP Control System Very Small Leak (0.020") Detected** ECT sensor less than 90°F (cold engine), engine started, engine running at a steady cruise speed, and the PCM detected a very small fuel vapor leak (0.020") during the leak test. **Possible Causes:** • Canister tube, EVAP canister purge outlet tube or return tube disconnected or cracked • EVAP canister purge valve stuck closed, or canister damaged • Fuel vapor hoses/tubes that have very small holes and/or cuts • Fuel vapor hose/tube connections are loose or damaged • EVAP component seals are leaking (i.e., Purge valve, fuel tank pressure sensor, canister vent solenoid, fuel vapor control valve tube assembly or fuel vapor vent valve assembly) • TSB 03-9-8 contains a repair procedure for this trouble code • TSB 3-20-3 contains a repair procedure for this trouble code
DTC: P0457 **2T EVAP, MIL: Yes** **Years:** 2005, 2006, 2007 **Models:** All Models **Engines:** All **Transmissions:** All	**EVAP Control System Leak Detected (Fuel Cap Missing)** ECT sensor less than 90°F at startup, engine running at a steady state cruise speed, and the PCM detected the fuel tank pressure changed more than minus (−) 7" H2O in 30 seconds, or excessive purge flow (over 0.06 pounds per minute) occurred in the EVAP Running Loss Monitor Test ("Check Fuel Cap" Lamp may be "on"). **Possible Causes:** • Fuel filler cap not installed after refueling (CMC P0457 is set) • Fuel filler cap missing, loose or cross-threaded • TSB 03-9-8 contains a repair procedure for this trouble code • TSB 3-20-3 contains a repair procedure for this trouble code
DTC: P0460 **2T CCM, MIL: Yes** **Years:** 2005, 2006, 2007 **Models:** All Models **Engines:** All **Transmissions:** All	**Fuel Level Sensor Signal Range/Performance** Engine started, and the PCM detected the FLI sensor did not match the fuel level (e.g., FLI V PID below 0.90v with FLI PID at 25%, or FLIV PID more than 2.45v with FLI PID at 75%). **Possible Causes:** • Fuel tank is empty • FP module is stuck open • Fuel gauge is incorrectly installed • Instrument cluster damaged • PCM Case ground circuit open • Fuel level indicator (FLI) circuit is shorted to power, or is open • Fuel tank has been overfilled, or fuel gauge is damaged • Fuel pump (FP) module is stuck closed, or is stuck open • Fuel level indicator circuit shorted to Case or to power ground • PCM Case ground shorted to VPWR (shorted to system power) • TSB 03-1-7 contains repair help for this code (LS & T-Bird)
DTC: P0462 **2T CCM, MIL: Yes** **Years:** 2005, 2006, 2007 **Models:** All Models **Engines:** All **Transmissions:** All	**Fuel Level Sensor Circuit Low Input** Key on or engine running; and the PCM detected the FLI sensor indicated less than 0.20v at any time during the CCM test period. **Possible Causes:** • Fuel tank is empty • FLI signal circuit is open • FLI signal circuit is shorted to case or chassis ground • PCM has failed
DTC: P0463 **2T CCM, MIL: Yes** **Years:** 2005, 2006, 2007 **Models:** All Models **Engines:** All **Transmissions:** All	**Fuel Level Sensor Circuit High Input** Key on or engine running; and the PCM detected that the FLI sensor indicated more than 4.50v at any time during the CCM test period. **Possible Causes:** • Fuel level sensor connector is damaged or shorted • Fuel tank has been over-filled • FLI signal circuit is shorted to VREF (5v or 12v) • PCM has failed
DTC: P0480 **2T CCM, MIL: Yes** **Years:** 2005, 2006, 2007 **Models:** Expedition, LS, Mustang, Navigator **Engines:** All With Vistronic Fan **Transmissions:** All	**Visctronic Drive Fan Primary Circuit Malfunction** Key on or engine running; and the PCM detected an unexpected high or low voltage condition on the Visctronic Drive Fan (VDF) primary circuit during the CCM test period. **Possible Causes:** • VDF variable control circuit is open • VDF variable control circuit is shorted to chassis ground • VDF variable control circuit shorted to Fan Speed Sensor circuit • VDF clutch power supply (VPWR) circuit is open • VDF clutch is damaged or it has failed • PCM has failed

DTC	Trouble Code Title, Conditions & Possible Causes
DTC: P0480 **2T CCM, MIL: Yes** **Years:** 2005, 2006, 2007 **Models:** Focus, Sable, Taurus, Ranger **Engines:** 2.3L VIN D, 2.3L VIN Z, 3.0L VIN 2, 3.0L VIN S, 3.0L VIN U, 4.0L VIN E **Transmissions:** All	**Fan Control Relay Circuit Malfunction** Key on or engine running; and the PCM detected an unexpected high or low voltage condition on the Fan Control relay control circuit. **Possible Causes:** • High/Low/Medium FC relay control circuit is open • High/Low/Medium FC relay control circuit is shorted to ground • High/Low/Medium FC relay VPWR circuit is open • High/Low/Medium FC relay direct battery (B+) circuit is open • High/Low/Medium FC relay is damaged or it has failed • PCM has failed
DTC: P0481 **2T CCM, MIL: Yes** **Years:** 2005, 2006, 2007 **Models:** Focus, Sable, Taurus, Ranger **Engines:** 2.3L VIN D, 2.3L VIN Z, 3.0L VIN 2, 3.0L VIN S, 3.0L VIN U, 4.0L VIN E **Transmissions:** All	**Fan Control Relay Circuit Malfunction** Key on or engine running; and the PCM detected an unexpected high or low voltage condition on the Fan Control relay control circuit. **Possible Causes:** • FC relay control circuit is open • FC relay control circuit is shorted to chassis ground • FC relay power supply (VPWR) circuit is open • FC relay direct battery (B+) circuit is open • FC relay is damaged or it has failed • PCM has failed
DTC: P0482 **2T CCM, MIL: Yes** **Years:** 2005, 2006, 2007 **Models:** Focus, Mustang, Ranger, Sable **Engines:** 2.3L VIN D, 2.3L VIN Z, 3.0L VIN 1, 3.0L VIN 2, 3.0L VIN S, 3.0L VIN U, 4.6L VIN H **Transmissions:** All	**Constant Control Relay Module Circuit Malfunction** Key on or engine running; and the PCM detected an unexpected high or low voltage condition on the High Fan Control (HFC) relay control circuit (located inside the CCRM) during the CCM test period. **Possible Causes:** • FC relay control circuit is open • FC relay control circuit is shorted to chassis ground • FC relay power supply (VPWR) circuit is open • FC relay direct battery (B+) circuit is open • PCM has failed
DTC: P0500 **2T CCM, MIL: Yes** **Years:** 2005, 2006, 2007 **Models:** All Models **Engines:** All **Transmissions:** All	**Vehicle Speed Sensor Malfunction** Engine running, then with the engine speed more than the TCC stall speed, the PCM detected a lack of vehicle speed data occurred. **Note: The PCM receives vehicle speed data from the VSS, TCSS, ABS module, CTM or GEM controller, depending up the application.** **Possible Causes:** • Modules connected to VSC/VSS harness circuits are damaged • Mechanical drive mechanism for the VSS or TCSS is damaged • VSS+ or VSS− harness circuit is open • TCSS signal or TCSS signal return harness circuit is open • VSS harness circuit, TCSS harness circuit is shorted to ground • VSS harness circuit, CSS harness circuit is shorted to power • VSS circuit open between the PCM and related control module • VSS or TCSS, or wheel speed sensors circuits are damaged • TSB 01-21-13 contains a repair procedure for this trouble code
DTC: P0500 **2T CCM, MIL: Yes** **Years:** 2005, 2006, 2007 **Models:** All Models **Engines:** All **Transmissions:** All	**Vehicle Speed Sensor Circuit Malfunction** Engine running, then with the engine speed more than the TCC stall speed, the PCM detected a lack of vehicle speed data occurred. **Note: The PCM receives vehicle speed data from the Vehicle Speed Sensor on these vehicle applications.** **Possible Causes:** • VSS signal circuit is open or shorted to ground • VSS ground circuit is open or VSS power circuit is open • VSS is damaged or it has failed • PSOM is damaged or it has failed (All Models) • PCM has failed
DTC: P0500 **2T CCM, MIL: Yes** **Years:** 2005, 2006, 2007 **Models:** Five Hundred, Freestyle, LS, Montego **Engines:** All **Transmissions:** All	**Vehicle Speed Sensor Circuit Malfunction** Engine running, then with the engine speed more than the TCC stall speed, the PCM detected a lack of vehicle speed data occurred. **Note: The PCM receives vehicle speed data from the ABS module.** **Possible Causes:** • The vehicle speed information on this vehicle application is provided to the PCM by the Antilock Brake System module. • Refer to the ABS diagnostics and trouble codes to diagnose this particular trouble code.

DTC	Trouble Code Title, Conditions & Possible Causes
DTC: P0500 **2T CCM, MIL: Yes** **Years:** 2005, 2006, 2007 **Models:** Expedition, Navigator With 4WD **Engines:** All **Transmissions:** All	**Vehicle Speed Sensor Circuit Malfunction** Engine running, then with the engine speed more than the TCC stall speed, the PCM detected a lack of vehicle speed data for a period of time. **Note: The PCM receives vehicle speed data from the Transfer Case Speed Sensor on these vehicle applications.** **Possible Causes:** • TCSS signal circuit is open or shorted to ground • TCSS ground circuit is open • TCSS is damaged or it has failed • PCM has failed
DTC: P0500 **2T CCM, MIL: Yes** **Years:** 2005, 2006, 2007 **Models:** Excursion, Ranger **Engines:** 3.0L VIN U, 5.4L VIN L, 6.8L VIN S **Transmissions:** All	**Vehicle Speed Sensor Circuit Malfunction** Engine started; then with the engine speed more than the TCC stall speed, the PCM detected a lack of vehicle speed data occurred. **Note: The PCM receives vehicle speed data from the Rear Wheel ABS (RABS) or 4-Wheel ABS (4WABS) on these applications.** **Possible Causes:** • VSC positive signal circuit is open or shorted to ground • VSC negative signal circuit is open • RABS or 4WABS control unit is damaged or has failed • One of the other modules (CTM or GEM) may be the cause of this trouble code. Diagnose other codes from these modules.
DTC: P0501 **1T CCM, MIL: Yes** **Years:** 2005, 2006, 2007 **Models:** All Models **Engines:** All **Transmissions:** All	**Vehicle Speed Sensor or PSOM Range/Performance** Engine started; engine speed above the TCC stall speed, and the PCM detected a loss of the VSS signal over a period of time. **Note: The PCM receives vehicle speed data from the VSS, TCSS, ABS module, CTM or GEM controller, depending up the application.** **Possible Causes:** • VSS+ or VSS− signal circuit is open or shorted to ground • TCSS signal or TCSS signal return harness circuit is open • VSS harness circuit, TCSS harness circuit is shorted to ground • VSS harness circuit, CSS harness circuit is shorted to power • VSS circuit open between the PCM and related control module • VSS or TCSS, or wheel speed sensors circuits are damaged • Modules connected to VSC/VSS harness circuits are damaged • Mechanical drive mechanism for the VSS or TCSS is damaged
DTC: P0501 **1T CCM, MIL: Yes** **Years:** 2005, 2006, 2007 **Models:** All Models **Engines:** All **Transmissions:** All	**Vehicle Speed Sensor Range/Performance** Engine started; then with the engine speed more than the TCC stall speed, the PCM detected a problem with the vehicle speed data. **Note: The PCM receives vehicle speed data from the Vehicle Speed Sensor on these vehicle applications.** **Possible Causes:** • VSS signal circuit is open or shorted to ground • VSS ground circuit is open • VSS power circuit (VPWR) is open • VSS is damaged or it has failed • PCM has failed
DTC: P0500 **2T CCM, MIL: Yes** **Years:** 2005, 2006, 2007 **Models:** Five Hundred, Freestyle, LS, Montego **Engines:** All **Transmissions:** All	**Vehicle Speed Sensor Signal Range/Performance** Engine started; then with the engine speed more than the TCC stall speed, the PCM detected a problem with the vehicle speed data. **Note: The PCM receives vehicle speed data from the ABS module.** **Possible Causes:** • The vehicle speed information on this vehicle application is provided to the PCM by the Antilock Brake System module. • Refer to the ABS diagnostics and trouble codes to diagnose this particular trouble code.
DTC: P0501 **2T CCM, MIL: Yes** **Years:** 2005 **Models:** Excursion **Engines:** 5.4L VIN L **Transmissions:** All	**Vehicle Speed Sensor Signal Range/Performance** Engine running, then with the engine speed more than the TCC stall speed, the PCM detected a problem with the vehicle speed data. **Note: The PCM receives vehicle speed data from the Transfer Case Speed Sensor on these vehicle applications.** **Possible Causes:** • TCSS signal circuit is open or shorted to ground • TCSS ground circuit is open • TCSS is damaged or it has failed • PCM has failed

DTC	Trouble Code Title, Conditions & Possible Causes
DTC: P0501 **2T CCM, MIL: Yes** **Years:** 2005, 2006, 2007 **Models:** Excursion, Ranger **Engines:** 3.0L VIN U, 5.4L VIN L, 6.8L VIN S **Transmissions:** All	**Vehicle Speed Sensor Signal Range/Performance** Engine running, then with the engine speed more than the TCC stall speed, the PCM detected a problem with the vehicle speed data. **Note: The PCM receives vehicle speed data from the Rear Wheel ABS (RABS) or 4-Wheel ABS (4WABS) on these applications.** **Possible Causes:** • VSC positive signal circuit is open or shorted to ground • VSC negative signal circuit is open • RABS or 4WABS control unit is damaged or has failed • One of the other modules (CTM or GEM) may be the cause of this trouble code. Diagnose other codes from these modules.
DTC: P0503 **2T CCM, MIL: Yes** **Years:** 2005, 2006, 2007 **Models:** All Models **Engines:** All **Transmissions:** A/T	**Vehicle Speed Sensor Signal Intermittent** Engine started, engine speed above the TCC stall speed, and the PCM detected the vehicle speed data was "noisy" or intermittent. **Note: The PCM receives vehicle speed data from the VSS, TCSS, ABS module, CTM or GEM controller, depending up the application.** **Possible Causes:** • Module or circuits connected to VSS/TCSS circuit are damaged • VSS/TCSS wiring harness or connector is damaged or loose • VSS/TCSS signal is "noisy" due to RFI or EMI interference from sources such as ignition components or charging system • VSS/TCSS gears are damaged or there is debris on the sensor
DTC: P0503 **2T CCM, MIL: Yes** **Years:** 2005 **Models:** Excursion **Engines:** 5.4L VIN L **Transmissions:** All	**Vehicle Speed Sensor Signal Intermittent** Engine started, engine speed above the TCC stall speed, and the PCM detected the vehicle speed data was "noisy" or intermittent. **Note: The PCM receives vehicle speed data from the VSS or TCSS.** **Possible Causes:** • TCSS or VSS signal circuit is open or shorted to ground • TCSS or VSS ground circuit is open (an intermittent problem) • TCSS or VSS power supply (VREF) circuit is open (intermittent) • TCSS or VSS is damaged or it has failed (intermittent problem) • PCM has failed
DTC: P0505 **2T CCM, MIL: Yes** **Years:** 2005, 2006, 2007 **Models:** All Models **Engines:** All **Transmissions:** All	**Idle Air Control System Malfunction** Engine started, engine running at hot idle speed, and the PCM detected the Actual Idle Speed was too low or too high when compared to the Target Idle Speed during the KOER self-test. Specification: The IAC valve resistance is 6-13 ohms at 68°F. **Possible Causes:** • Air inlet dirty, restricted or the air cleaner is severely restricted • IAC solenoid control circuit is open, shorted to ground or to B+ • IAC solenoid power circuit (VPWR) is open from the relay • IAC valve is damaged or has failed • PCM has failed • TSB 03-3-5 contains repair information for this trouble code
DTC: P0506 **2T CCM, MIL: Yes** **Years:** 2005, 2006, 2007 **Models:** All Models **Engines:** All **Transmissions:** All	**Idle Air Control System RPM Lower Than Expected** DTC P0402 not set, engine started, engine running in closed loop, and the PCM detected it could not control the idle speed correctly. **Possible Causes:** • Air inlet is plugged or the air filter element is severely clogged • IAC circuit is open or shorted to the VPWR circuit • IAC circuit VPWR circuit is open • IAC solenoid is damaged or has failed • PCM has failed • TSB 03-3-5 contains repair information for this trouble code
DTC: P0507 **2T CCM, MIL: Yes** **Years:** 2005, 2006, 2007 **Models:** All Models **Engines:** All **Transmissions:** All	**Idle Air Control System RPM Higher Than Expected** DTC P0402 not set, engine started, engine running in closed loop, and the PCM detected it could not control the idle speed correctly. **Possible Causes:** • Air intake leak located somewhere after the throttle body • IAC control circuit is shorted to chassis ground • IAC solenoid is damaged or has failed • PCM has failed • TSB 03-3-5 contains repair information for this trouble code

DTC	Trouble Code Title, Conditions & Possible Causes
DTC: P0511 **2T CCM, MIL: Yes** **Years:** 2005, 2006, 2007 **Models:** All Models **Engines:** All **Transmissions:** All	**Idle Air Control Valve Circuit Malfunction** DTC P0402 not set, engine started, engine running in closed loop, and the PCM detected it could not control the idle speed correctly. **Possible Causes:** • IAC control circuit is open • IAC control circuit is shorted to power (B+) • IAC power supply circuit (VPWR) is open • IAC solenoid is damaged or the PCM has failed
DTC: P0528 **2T CCM, MIL: Yes** **Years:** 2005, 2006, 2007 **Models:** Expedition, Five Hundred, Freestyle, LS, Montego, Mustang, Navigator **Engines:** All With Vistronic Fan **Transmissions:** All	**Visctronic Drive Fan Speed Sensor Circuit Malfunction** Engine started, Visctronic Drive Fan (VDF) commanded to a 100% duty cycle position, and the PCM detected the VDF Speed Sensor signal was less than a calibrated value in the test. **Possible Causes:** • VDF fan motor has a mechanical interference fault or is binding • VDF speed sensor circuit is open or shorted to ground • Vehicle Buffered Power (VBPWR) circuit is open or shorted • VDF speed sensor power ground circuit is open • VDF speed sensor is damaged or the PCM has failed
DTC: P0534 **2T CCM, MIL: Yes** **Years:** 2005, 2006, 2007 **Models:** All Models **Engines:** All **Transmissions:** All	**Low Air Conditioning Cycle Period** Engine started; A/C enabled, and the PCM detected frequent A/C compressor clutch cycling during the CCM test period. Note that this trouble code and test was designed to protect the transmission. In some cases, the PCM will unlock TCC operation. **Possible Causes:** • A/C cycling pressure switch signal to PCM open (intermittent) • A/C cycling pressure switch IGN (B+) circuit open (intermittent) • A/C mechanical problem (low A/C refrigerant charge or a damaged A/C cycling switch)
DTC: P0537 **2T CCM, MIL: Yes** **Years:** 2005, 2006, 2007 **Models:** All Models **Engines:** All **Transmissions:** All	**A/C Evaporator Temperature Circuit Sensor Low Input** Engine started; A/C enabled, and the PCM detected an unexpected low voltage condition on the A/C Evaporator Temperature (ACET) sensor circuit during the CCM test period. **Possible Causes:** • ACET sensor signal circuit shorted to sensor or chassis ground • ACET sensor is damaged or it has failed • PCM has failed
DTC: P0538 **2T CCM, MIL: Yes** **Years:** 2005, 2006, 2007 **Models:** All Models **Engines:** All **Transmissions:** All	**A/C Evaporator Temperature Sensor Circuit High Input** Engine started; A/C enabled, and the PCM detected an unexpected high voltage condition on the A/C Evaporator Temperature (ACET) sensor circuit during the CCM test period. **Possible Causes:** • ACET sensor signal circuit is open • ACET sensor signal circuit is shorted to VREF (5v) • ACET sensor ground circuit is open • ACET sensor is damaged or it has failed • PCM has failed
DTC: P0552 **2T CCM, MIL: Yes** **Years:** 2005, 2006, 2007 **Models:** All Models **Engines:** All **Transmissions:** All	**Power Steering Pressure Sensor Circuit Low Input** Engine started, and the PCM detected an unexpected low voltage condition on the Power Steering Pressure (PSP) sensor circuit. **Possible Causes:** • PSP sensor signal circuit is shorted to sensor ground • PSP sensor signal circuit is shorted to chassis ground • PSP sensor VREF (5v) circuit is open • PSP sensor is damaged or it has failed • PCM has failed
DTC: P0553 **2T CCM, MIL: Yes** **Years:** 2005, 2006, 2007 **Models:** All Models **Engines:** All **Transmissions:** All	**Power Steering Pressure Sensor Circuit High Input** Engine started, and the PCM detected an unexpected high voltage condition on the Power Steering Pressure (PSP) sensor circuit. **Possible Causes:** • PSP sensor ground circuit is open • PSP sensor ground circuit is shorted to VREF (5v) • PSP sensor signal circuit is shorted to VREF (5v) • PSP sensor is damaged or the PCM has failed

DTC	Trouble Code Title, Conditions & Possible Causes
DTC: P0597 **2T CCM, MIL: Yes** **Years:** 2005, 2006, 2007 **Models:** Ranger **Engines:** 2.3L VIN D **Transmissions:** All	**Thermostat Heater Control Circuit Malfunction** Engine started, and the PCM detected an unexpected low or high voltage condition on the Thermostat Heater Control (THTRC) circuit. **Possible Causes:** • THTRC circuit is open or shorted to ground • THTRC power (VPWR) circuit is open • Thermostat assembly is damaged or the PCM has failed
DTC: P0602 **1T PCM, MIL: Yes** **Years:** 2005, 2006, 2007 **Models:** All Models **Engines:** All **Transmissions:** All	**Control Module Programming Error** Key on, and the PCM detected a programming error in the VID block. This fault requires that the VID Block be reprogrammed, or that the EEPROM be re-flashed. **Possible Causes:** • During the VID reprogramming function, the Vehicle ID (VID) data block failed during reprogramming wit the Scan Tool.
DTC: P0603 **1T PCM, MIL: Yes** **Years:** 2005, 2006, 2007 **Models:** All Models **Engines:** All **Transmissions:** All	**PCM Keep Alive Memory Test Error** Key on, and the PCM detected an internal memory fault. This code will set if KAPWR to the PCM is interrupted (at the initial key on). **Possible Causes:** • Battery terminal corrosion, or loose battery connection • KAPWR to PCM interrupted, or the circuit has been opened • Reprogramming error has occurred • PCM has failed and needs replacement. Remember to check for Aftermarket Performance Products before replacing a PCM.
DTC: P0605 **1T PCM, MIL: Yes** **Years:** 2005, 2006, 2007 **Models:** All Models **Engines:** All **Transmissions:** All	**PCM Read Only Memory Test Error** Key on, and the PCM detected a ROM test error (ROM inside PCM is corrupted). The PCM is normally replaced if this code has set. **Possible Causes:** • An attempt was made to change the module calibration, or a Module programming error may have occurred • Clear the trouble codes and then check for this trouble code. If it resets, the PCM has failed and needs replacement. • Remember to check for signs of Aftermarket Performance Products installation before replacing the PCM.
DTC: P0606 **1T PCM, MIL: Yes** **Years:** 2005, 2006, 2007 **Models:** All Models **Engines:** All **Transmissions:** All	**PCM Internal Communication Error** Key on, and the PCM detected an internal communications register read back error during the initial key on check period. **Possible Causes:** • Clear the trouble codes and then check for this trouble code. If it resets, the PCM has failed and needs replacement. • Remember to check for signs of Aftermarket Performance Products installation before replacing the PCM.
DTC: P0622 **1T CCM, MIL: Yes** **Years:** 2005, 2006, 2007 **Models:** All Models **Engines:** All **Transmissions:** All	**Generator Regulator System Malfunction** Engine started; and the PCM detected an unexpected voltage condition on the Generator control circuit. **Possible Causes:** • Generator belt is loose or worn out • Generator or regulator is damaged or has failed • PCM has failed
DTC: P0645 **1T CCM, MIL: Yes** **Years:** 2005, 2006, 2007 **Models:** All Models **Engines:** All **Transmissions:** All	**Wide Open Throttle A/C Output Primary Circuit Malfunction** Key on or engine running; and the PCM detected an unexpected low or high voltage condition WAC output primary circuit during the test. **Possible Causes:** • WAC relay control circuit is open or shorted to ground • WAC relay power circuit (VPWR) is open • WAC relay is damaged or it has failed • PCM has failed
DTC: P0660 **1T CCM, MIL: Yes** **Years:** 2005, 2006, 2007 **Models:** Expedition, LS, Navigator, Sable, Taurus **Engines:** 3.0L VIN S, 5.4L VIN L **Transmissions:** All	**Intake Manifold Tuning Valve Circuit Malfunction** Key on or engine running; and the PCM detected an unexpected low or high voltage condition on the Intake Manifold Tuning Valve (ITMV) signal circuit during the CCM test. **Possible Causes:** • ITMV signal circuit is open • ITMV signal circuit is shorted to chassis ground • ITMV electric actuator assembly is damaged or failed • PCM has failed

DTC	Trouble Code Title, Conditions & Possible Causes
DTC: P0660 **1T CCM, MIL: Yes** **Years:** 2005, 2006, 2007 **Models:** Ranger **Engines:** 2.3L VIN D **Transmissions:** All	**Intake Manifold Swirl Control Actuator Circuit Malfunction** Key on or engine running; and the PCM detected an unexpected low or high voltage condition on the Intake Manifold Swirl Control (IMSC) signal circuit during the CCM test. **Possible Causes:** • IMSC signal circuit is open • IMSC signal circuit is shorted to chassis ground • IMSC actuator assembly is damaged or failed • PCM has failed
DTC: P0703 **2T CCM, MIL: Yes** **Years:** 2005, 2006, 2007 **Models:** LS Models **Engines:** All **Transmissions:** A/T	**Brake Switch Circuit Malfunction** Engine started, and the PCM did not detect any change in the Brake Pedal Position switch status, or with the vehicle running at Cruise speed, followed by a short deceleration periods, the PCM did not detect any change in the Brake Pedal Position switch status. **Possible Causes:** • BPA/ BPP switch circuit is open • BPA/ BPP switch is damaged or it is out of adjustment • BPA/ BPP switch power circuit is open (test switch inline fuse) • One or more of the Module(s) that connect to the BPA or the BPP switch circuits have a problem (e.g., Rear Electronic Module or the Vehicle Speed Control)
DTC: P0703 **2T CCM, MIL: Yes** **Years:** 2005, 2006, 2007 **Models:** All Except LS **Engines:** All **Transmissions:** A/T	**Brake Switch Circuit Malfunction** Engine started, and the PCM did not detect any change in the Brake Pedal Position (BPP) switch status, or with the vehicle at Cruise speed, followed by one or more short deceleration periods, the PCM did not detect any change in the Brake Pedal Position switch status. **Possible Causes:** • BPP switch circuit is open • BPP switch is damaged or it is out of adjustment • BPP switch power circuit is open (check the switch inline fuse)
DTC: P0704 **1T CCM, MIL: No** **Years:** 2005, 2006, 2007 **Models:** Five Hundred, Focus, Freestyle, LS, Montego Models **Engines:** All **Transmissions:** M/T	**Clutch Pedal Position Switch Circuit Malfunction** Engine running in gear, followed by several gearshift changes, and the PCM did not detect any change in the clutch switch status. **Note: The CCP PID should change (5v to 0v) with clutch depressed.** **Possible Causes:** • CPP switch signal circuit shorted to power • CPP switch ground (return) circuit is open • CPP switch is damaged or out of adjustment • PCM has failed
DTC: P0705 **2T CCM, MIL: Yes** **Years:** 2005, 2006, 2007 **Models:** All Models **Engines:** All **Transmissions:** A/T	**DTR Sensor / TR Sensor Circuit Malfunction** Key on or engine running; and the PCM detected that one or more of the Digital Transmission Range (DTR) or Transmission Range sensor (TR) signals (TR4, TR3, TR2 and TR1) were invalid (e.g., two TR or DR sensor signals received at the same time). **Possible Causes:** • DTR or TR sensor connector is damaged or shorted • DTR or TR sensor signal circuit is open or shorted to ground • DTR or TR sensor signal circuit is shorted to VREF (5v) • DTR or TR sensor damaged • PCM has failed
DTC: P0707 **2T CCM, MIL: Yes** **Years:** 2005, 2006, 2007 **Models:** All Models **Engines:** All **Transmissions:** A/T	**DTR Sensor / TR Sensor Circuit Low Input** Key on or engine running; and the PCM detected the Digital Transmission Range (DTR) or Transmission Range sensor (TR) signal was less than the self-test minimum value in the test. **Possible Causes:** • DTR or TR sensor connector is damaged or it is shorted • DTR or TR sensor signal circuit is shorted to sensor ground • DTR or TR sensor damaged • PCM has failed
DTC: P0708 **2T CCM, MIL: Yes** **Years:** 2005, 2006, 2007 **Models:** All Models **Engines:** All **Transmissions:** A/T	**DTR Sensor or TR Sensor Circuit High Input** Key on or engine running; and the PCM detected the Digital Transmission Range (DTR) or Transmission Range sensor (TR) input was more than the self-test maximum range in the test. **Possible Causes:** • DTR or TR sensor connector is damaged or open • DTR or TR sensor signal circuit is open • DTR or TR sensor is shorted to VREF (5v) • DTR or TR sensor is damaged or the PCM has failed

DTC	Trouble Code Title, Conditions & Possible Causes
DTC: P0711 **2T CCM, MIL: No** **Years:** 2005, 2006, 2007 **Models:** All Models **Engines:** All **Transmissions:** A/T	**TFT Sensor Signal Range/Performance** Engine started, KOER Self-Test enabled, engine running for over 10 minutes, and the PCM detected the Transmission Fluid Temperature (TFT) sensor value was not close its normal operating temperature. **Possible Causes:** • ATF is low, contaminated, dirty or burnt • TFT sensor signal circuit has a high resistance condition • TFT sensor is out-of-calibration ("skewed") or it has failed • PCM has failed
DTC: P0712 **2T CCM, MIL: No** **Years:** 2005, 2006, 2007 **Models:** All Models **Engines:** All **Transmissions:** A/T	**TFT Sensor Circuit Low Input** Key on or engine running; and the PCM detected the Transmission Fluid Temperature (TFT) sensor was less than its minimum self-test range (Scan Tool reads below −40°F) in the test. **Possible Causes:** • TFT sensor signal circuit is shorted to chassis ground • TFT sensor signal circuit is shorted to sensor ground • TFT sensor is damaged, or out-of-calibration, or has failed • PCM has failed
DTC: P0713 **2T CCM, MIL: No** **Years:** 2005, 2006, 2007 **Models:** All Models **Engines:** All **Transmissions:** A/T	**TFT Sensor Circuit High Input** Key on or engine running; and the PCM detected the Transmission Fluid Temperature (TFT) sensor was more than its maximum self-test range (Scan Tool reads over 315°F) in the test. **Possible Causes:** • TFT sensor signal circuit is open between the sensor and PCM • TFT sensor ground circuit is open between sensor and PCM • TFT sensor is damaged or has failed • PCM has failed
DTC: P0715 **2T CCM, MIL: No** **Years:** 2005, 2006, 2007 **Models:** All Models **Engines:** All **Transmissions:** A/T	**Transmission Speed Shaft Sensor Circuit Malfunction** Engine started, vehicle driven with the vehicle speed sensor indicating more than 1 mph, and the PCM detected the TSS signals were erratic, or that they were missing for a period of time. **Possible Causes:** • TSS signal circuit is open • TSS signal is shorted to chassis ground • TSS signal is shorted to sensor ground • TSS assembly is damaged or it has failed • PCM has failed
DTC: P0717 **2T CCM, MIL: No** **Years:** 2005, 2006, 2007 **Models:** All Models **Engines:** All **Transmissions:** A/T	**Transmission Speed Shaft Sensor Signal Intermittent** Engine started, vehicle speed sensor indicating over 1 mph, and the PCM detected an intermittent loss of TSS signals (i.e., the TSS signals were erratic, irregular or missing). **Possible Causes:** • TSS connector is damaged, loose or shorted • TSS signal circuit has an intermittent open condition • TSS signal circuit has an intermittent short to ground condition • TSS assembly is damaged or is has failed • PCM has failed
DTC: P0718 **2T CCM, MIL: No** **Years:** 2005, 2006, 2007 **Models:** All Models **Engines:** All **Transmissions:** A/T	**Transmission Speed Shaft Sensor Signal Noisy** Engine started, vehicle speed sensor signal over 1 mph, and the PCM detected the "noise" interference on the TSS signal circuit. **Possible Causes:** • TSS signal is "noisy" due to RFI or EMI interference from sources such as ignition components or charging system • TSS signal wiring is damaged or contacting other signal wiring • PCM has failed
DTC: P0718 **2T CCM, MIL: Yes** **Years:** 2005, 2006, 2007 **Models:** All Models **Engines:** All **Transmissions:** A/T	**A/T Output Shaft Speed Sensor Insufficient Input** Engine started, VSS signal more than 1 mph, and the PCM detected the Output Shaft Speed signal did not correlate to the incoming signals received from the VSS or TCSS devices or related modules. **Possible Causes:** • OSS sensor signal circuit is shorted to ground or • OSS sensor signal circuit is open • OSS sensor circuit is shorted to power • OSS sensor is damaged or it has failed • PCM has failed

DTC	Trouble Code Title, Conditions & Possible Causes
DTC: P0721 **2T CCM, MIL: No** **Years:** 2005, 2006, 2007 **Models:** All Models **Engines:** All **Transmissions:** A/T	**A/T Output Shaft Speed Sensor Noise Interference** Engine started, VSS signal more than 1 mph, and the PCM detected "noise" interference on the Output Shaft Speed (OSS) sensor circuit. **Possible Causes:** • After market add-on devices interfering with the OSS signal • OSS connector is damaged, loose or shorted, or the wiring is misrouted or it is damaged • OSS assembly is damaged or it has failed • PCM has failed
DTC: P0722 **2T CCM, MIL: No** **Years:** 2005, 2006, 2007 **Models:** All Models **Engines:** All **Transmissions:** A/T	**A/T Output Speed Sensor No Signal** Engine started, and the PCM did not detect any Output Shaft Speed (OSS) sensor signals upon initial vehicle movement. **Possible Causes:** • After market add-on devices interfering with the OSS signal • OSS sensor wiring is misrouted or damaged, or the OSS sensor is damaged • PCM has failed
DTC: P0723 **2T CCM, MIL: No** **Years:** 2005, 2006, 2007 **Models:** All Models **Engines:** All **Transmissions:** A/T	**A/T Output Speed Sensor Signal Intermittent** Engine started, and the PCM detected the Output Shaft Speed (OSS) sensor signal was interrupted or irregular during testing. **Possible Causes:** • OSS harness connector is damaged, loose or shorted, or the connector is not seated • OSS signal is open or it is shorted to ground (intermittent fault) • OSS assembly is damaged or it has failed
DTC: P0731 **2T CCM, MIL: No** **Years:** 2005, 2006, 2007 **Models:** All Models **Engines:** All **Transmissions:** A/T	**Incorrect First Gear Ratio** Engine started, vehicle operating with 1st Gear commanded "on", and the PCM detected an incorrect 1st gear ratio during the test. **Possible Causes:** • 1st Gear solenoid harness connector not properly seated • 1st Gear solenoid signal shorted to ground, or open • 1st Gear solenoid wiring harness connector is damaged • 1st Gear solenoid is damaged or not properly installed
DTC: P0732 **2T CCM, MIL: No** **Years:** 2005, 2006, 2007 **Models:** All Models **Engines:** All **Transmissions:** A/T	**Incorrect Second Gear Ratio** Engine started, vehicle operating with 2nd Gear commanded "on", and the PCM detected an incorrect 2nd gear ratio during the test. **Possible Causes:** • 2nd Gear solenoid harness connector not properly seated • 2nd Gear solenoid signal shorted to ground, or open • 2nd Gear solenoid wring harness connector is damaged • 2nd Gear solenoid is damaged or not properly installed
DTC: P0733 **2T CCM, MIL: No** **Years:** 2005, 2006, 2007 **Models:** All Models **Engines:** All **Transmissions:** A/T	**Incorrect Third Gear Ratio** Engine started, vehicle operating with 3rd Gear commanded "on", and the PCM detected an incorrect 3rd gear ratio during the test. **Possible Causes:** • 3rd Gear solenoid harness connector not properly seated • 3rd Gear solenoid signal shorted to ground, or open • 3rd Gear solenoid wiring harness connector is damaged • 3rd Gear solenoid is damaged or not properly installed
DTC: P0734 **2T CCM, MIL: No** **Years:** 2005, 2006, 2007 **Models:** All Models **Engines:** All **Transmissions:** A/T	**Incorrect Fourth Gear Ratio** Engine started, vehicle operating with 4th Gear commanded "on", and the PCM detected an incorrect 4th gear ratio during the test. **Possible Causes:** • 4th Gear solenoid harness connector not properly seated • 4th Gear solenoid signal shorted to ground, or open • 4th Gear solenoid wiring harness connector is damaged • 4th Gear solenoid is damaged or not properly installed
DTC: P0735 **2T CCM, MIL: No** **Years:** 2005, 2006, 2007 **Models:** All Models **Engines:** All **Transmissions:** A/T	**Incorrect Fifth Gear Ratio** Engine started, vehicle operating with 5th Gear commanded "on", and the PCM detected an incorrect 5th gear ratio during the test. **Possible Causes:** • 5th Gear solenoid harness connector not properly seated • 5th Gear solenoid signal shorted to ground, or open • 5th Gear solenoid wiring harness connector is damaged • 5th Gear solenoid is damaged or not properly installed

DTC	Trouble Code Title, Conditions & Possible Causes
DTC: P0736 **2T CCM, MIL: No** **Years:** 2005, 2006, 2007 **Models:** All Models **Engines:** All **Transmissions:** A/T	**Incorrect Reverse Gear Ratio** Engine started, vehicle operating with Reverse Gear commanded "on", and the PCM detected an incorrect reverse gear ratio occurred. **Possible Causes:** • Reverse Gear solenoid harness connector not properly seated • Reverse Gear solenoid signal shorted to ground, or open • Reverse Gear solenoid wiring harness connector is damaged • Reverse Gear solenoid is damaged or not properly installed
DTC: P0740 **2T CCM, MIL: No** **Years:** 2005, 2006, 2007 **Models:** All Models **Engines:** All **Transmissions:** A/T	**TCC Solenoid Circuit Malfunction** Engine started, KOER Self-Test enabled, vehicle driven at cruise speed, and the PCM did not detect any voltage drop across the TCC solenoid circuit during the test period. **Possible Causes:** • TCC solenoid control circuit is open or shorted to ground • TCC solenoid wiring harness connector is damaged • TCC solenoid is damaged or has failed • PCM has failed
DTC: P0741 **2T CCM, MIL: No** **Years:** 2005, 2006, 2007 **Models:** All Models **Engines:** All **Transmissions:** A/T	**TCC Mechanical System Range/Performance** Engine started, vehicle driven in gear with VSS signals received, and the PCM detected excessive slippage while in normal operation. **Possible Causes:** • TCC solenoid has a mechanical failure • TCC solenoid has a hydraulic failure • PCM has failed
DTC: P0743 **2T CCM, MIL: Yes** **Years:** 2005, 2006, 2007 **Models:** All Models **Engines:** All **Transmissions:** A/T	**TCC Solenoid Circuit Malfunction** Key on, KOEO Self-Test enabled and the PCM did not detect any voltage drop across the TCC solenoid circuit during the test period. **Possible Causes:** • TCC solenoid control circuit is open • TCC solenoid control circuit is shorted to ground • TCC solenoid wiring harness connector is damaged • TCC solenoid is damaged or it has failed • PCM has failed
DTC: P0746 **2T CCM, MIL: No** **Years:** 2005, 2006, 2007 **Models:** All Models **Engines:** All **Transmissions:** A/T	**A/T EPC Solenoid Circuit Malfunction** Key on, KOEO Self-Test enabled and the PCM did not detect any voltage drop across the EPC solenoid circuit during the test period. **Possible Causes:** • EPC solenoid control circuit is open • EPC solenoid control circuit is shorted to ground • EPC solenoid wiring harness connector is damaged • EPC solenoid is damaged or it has failed • PCM has failed
DTC: P0750 **2T CCM, MIL: Yes** **Years:** 2005, 2006, 2007 **Models:** All Models **Engines:** All **Transmissions:** A/T	**A/T Shift Solenoid 1/A Circuit Malfunction** Engine started, vehicle driven with the solenoid applied, and the PCM detected an unexpected voltage condition on the SS1/A solenoid circuit was incorrect during the test. **Possible Causes:** • SS1/A solenoid control circuit is open • SS1/A solenoid control circuit is shorted to ground • SS1/A solenoid wiring harness connector is damaged • SS1/A solenoid is damaged or has failed • PCM has failed
DTC: P0751 **2T CCM, MIL: No** **Years:** 2005, 2006, 2007 **Models:** All Models **Engines:** All **Transmissions:** A/T	**A/T Shift Solenoid 1/A Function Range/Performance** Engine started, vehicle driven with the solenoid applied, and the PCM detected a mechanical failure while operating the Shift Solenoid 1/A during the CCM test period. **Possible Causes:** • SS1/A solenoid is stuck in the "off" position • SS1/A solenoid has a mechanical failure • SS1/A solenoid has a hydraulic failure • PCM has failed

DTC	Trouble Code Title, Conditions & Possible Causes
DTC: P0752 **1T CCM, MIL: No** **Years:** 2005, 2006, 2007 **Models:** All Models **Engines:** All **Transmissions:** A/T	**A/T Shift Solenoid 1/A Function Range/Performance** Engine started, vehicle driven with the solenoid applied, and the PCM detected a mechanical failure while operating the Shift Solenoid 1/A during the CCM test period. **Possible Causes:** • SS1/A solenoid is stuck in the "on" position • SS1/A solenoid has a mechanical failure • SS1/A solenoid has a hydraulic failure • PCM has failed
DTC: P0753 **1T CCM, MIL: Yes** **Years:** 2005, 2006, 2007 **Models:** All Models **Engines:** All **Transmissions:** A/T	**A/T Shift Solenoid 1/A Circuit Malfunction** Engine started, vehicle driven with the solenoid applied, and the PCM detected an unexpected voltage condition on the SS1/A solenoid circuit was incorrect during the test. **Possible Causes:** • SS1/A solenoid control circuit is open • SS1/A solenoid control circuit is shorted to ground • SS1/A solenoid wiring harness connector is damaged • SS1/A solenoid is damaged or has failed • PCM has failed
DTC: P0755 **1T CCM, MIL: Yes** **Years:** 2005, 2006, 2007 **Models:** All Models **Engines:** All **Transmissions:** A/T	**A/T Shift Solenoid 2/B Circuit Malfunction** Engine started, vehicle driven with the solenoid applied, and the PCM detected an unexpected voltage condition on the SS2/B solenoid circuit was incorrect during the test. **Possible Causes:** • SS2/B solenoid control circuit is open • SS2/B solenoid control circuit is shorted to ground • SS2/B solenoid wiring harness connector is damaged • SS2/B solenoid is damaged or has failed • PCM has failed
DTC: P0756 **1T CCM, MIL: Yes** **Years:** 2005, 2006, 2007 **Models:** All Models **Engines:** All **Transmissions:** A/T	**A/T Shift Solenoid 2/B Function Range/Performance** Engine started, vehicle driven with the solenoid applied, and the PCM detected a mechanical failure while operating the Shift Solenoid 2/B during the CCM test period. **Possible Causes:** • SS2/B solenoid is stuck in the "on" position • SS2/B solenoid has a mechanical failure • SS2/B solenoid has a hydraulic failure • PCM has failed
DTC: P0752 **1T CCM, MIL: No** **Years:** **Models:** All Models **Engines:** **Transmissions:** A/T	**A/T Shift Solenoid 1/A Function Range/Performance** Engine started, vehicle driven with the solenoid applied, and the PCM detected a mechanical failure while operating the Shift Solenoid 1/A during the CCM test period. **Possible Causes:** • SS1/A solenoid is stuck in the "on" position • SS1/A solenoid has a mechanical failure • SS1/A solenoid has a hydraulic failure • PCM has failed
DTC: P0753 **1T CCM, MIL: Yes** **Years:** **Models:** All Models **Engines:** **Transmissions:** A/T	**A/T Shift Solenoid 1/A Circuit Malfunction** Engine started, vehicle driven with the solenoid applied, and the PCM detected an unexpected voltage condition on the SS1/A solenoid circuit was incorrect during the test. **Possible Causes:** • SS1/A solenoid control circuit is open • SS1/A solenoid control circuit is shorted to ground • SS1/A solenoid wiring harness connector is damaged • SS1/A solenoid is damaged or has failed • PCM has failed
DTC: P0755 **1T CCM, MIL: Yes** **Years:** **Models:** All Models **Engines:** **Transmissions:** A/T	**A/T Shift Solenoid 2/B Circuit Malfunction** Engine started, vehicle driven with the solenoid applied, and the PCM detected an unexpected voltage condition on the SS2/B solenoid circuit was incorrect during the test. **Possible Causes:** • SS2/B solenoid control circuit is open • SS2/B solenoid control circuit is shorted to ground • SS2/B solenoid wiring harness connector is damaged • SS2/B solenoid is damaged or has failed • PCM has failed

DTC	Trouble Code Title, Conditions & Possible Causes
DTC: P0756 **1T CCM, MIL: Yes** **Years:** **Models:** All Models **Engines:** **Transmissions:** A/T	**A/T Shift Solenoid 2/B Function Range/Performance** Engine started, vehicle driven with the solenoid applied, and the PCM detected a mechanical failure while operating the Shift Solenoid 2/B during the CCM test period. **Possible Causes:** • SS2/B solenoid is stuck in the "on" position • SS2/B solenoid has a mechanical failure • SS2/B solenoid has a hydraulic failure • PCM has failed
DTC: P0757 **1T CCM, MIL: Yes** **Years:** 2005, 2006, 2007 **Models:** All Models **Engines:** All **Transmissions:** A/T	**A/T Shift Solenoid 2/B Function Range/Performance** Engine started, vehicle driven with the solenoid applied, and the PCM detected a mechanical failure while operating the Shift Solenoid 2/B during the CCM test period. **Possible Causes:** • SS2/B solenoid is stuck in the "on" position • SS2/B solenoid has a mechanical failure • SS2/B solenoid has a hydraulic failure • PCM has failed
DTC: P0758 **1T CCM, MIL: Yes** **Years:** 2005, 2006, 2007 **Models:** All Models **Engines:** All **Transmissions:** A/T	**A/T Shift Solenoid 2/B Circuit Malfunction** Key on, KOEO Self-Test enabled, Shift Solenoid 2/B applied, and the PCM detected an unexpected voltage condition on the Shift Solenoid 2/B circuit during the CCM test period. **Possible Causes:** • Shift Solenoid 2/B connector is damaged, open or shorted • Shift Solenoid 2/B control circuit is open • Shift Solenoid 2/B control circuit is shorted to ground • Shift Solenoid 2/B is damaged or it has failed • PCM has failed
DTC: P0760 **1T CCM, MIL: Yes** **Years:** 2005, 2006, 2007 **Models:** All Models **Engines:** All **Transmissions:** A/T	**A/T Shift Solenoid 3/C Circuit Malfunction** Engine started, vehicle driven with Shift Solenoid 3/C applied, and the PCM detected an unexpected voltage condition on the Shift Solenoid 3/C circuit during the CCM test period. **Possible Causes:** • Shift Solenoid 3/C connector is damaged, open or shorted • Shift Solenoid 3/C control circuit is open • Shift Solenoid 3/C control circuit is shorted to ground • Shift Solenoid 3/C is damaged or it has failed • PCM has failed
DTC: P0761 **1T CCM, MIL: No** **Years:** 2005, 2006, 2007 **Models:** All Models **Engines:** All **Transmissions:** A/T	**A/T Shift Solenoid 3/C Function Range/Performance** Engine started, vehicle driven with Shift Solenoid 3/C applied, and the PCM detected a mechanical failure occurred (stuck "off") while operating Shift Solenoid 3/C during the test. **Possible Causes:** • SS3/C solenoid may be stuck "off" • SS3/C solenoid has a mechanical failure • SS3/C solenoid has a hydraulic failure • PCM has failed
DTC: P0762 **1T CCM, MIL: No** **Years:** 2005, 2006, 2007 **Models:** All Models **Engines:** All **Transmissions:** A/T	**A/T Shift Solenoid 3/C Function Range/Performance** Engine started, vehicle driven with Shift Solenoid 3/C applied, and the PCM detected a mechanical failure occurred (stuck "on") while operating Shift Solenoid 3/C during the test. **Possible Causes:** • SS3/C solenoid may be stuck "on" • SS3/C solenoid has a mechanical failure • SS3/C solenoid has a hydraulic failure • PCM has failed
DTC: P0765 **1T CCM, MIL: Yes** **Years:** 2005, 2006, 2007 **Models:** All Models **Engines:** All **Transmissions:** A/T	**A/T Shift Solenoid 4/D Circuit Malfunction** Engine started, vehicle driven with Shift Solenoid 4/D applied, and the PCM detected an unexpected voltage condition on Shift Solenoid 4/D circuit during the CCM continuous test. **Possible Causes:** • Shift Solenoid 4/D wiring harness or connector is damaged • Shift Solenoid 4/D control circuit is open or shorted to ground • Shift Solenoid 4/D is damaged or it has failed • PCM has failed

DTC	Trouble Code Title, Conditions & Possible Causes
DTC: P0781 **1T CCM, MIL: No** **Years:** 2005, 2006, 2007 **Models:** All Models **Engines:** All **Transmissions:** A/T	**A/T 1 to 2 Shift Error** Engine started, vehicle driven in gear with VSS signals received, and the PCM detected the engine speed (rpm) did not decrease properly (i.e., an incorrect 1-2 gear ratio was detected during a shift event). **Possible Causes:** • SS1/A solenoid may be stuck • SS1/A solenoid has a hydraulic problem • SS2/B solenoid may be stuck • SS2/B has a hydraulic problem • Transmission may have damaged friction material • Transmission has internal damage and needs replacement
DTC: P0782 **1T CCM, MIL: No** **Years:** 2005, 2006, 2007 **Models:** All Models **Engines:** All **Transmissions:** A/T	**A/T 2 to 3 Shift Error** Engine started, vehicle driven in gear with VSS signals received, and the PCM detected the engine speed (rpm) did not decrease properly (i.e., an incorrect 2-3 gear ratio was detected during a shift event). **Possible Causes:** • SS1/A solenoid may be stuck • SS1/A solenoid has a hydraulic problem • SS2/B solenoid may be stuck • SS2/B has a hydraulic problem • Transmission may have damaged friction material • Transmission has internal damage and needs replacement
DTC: P0783 **1T CCM, MIL: No** **Years:** 2005, 2006, 2007 **Models:** All Models **Engines:** All **Transmissions:** A/T	**A/T 3 to 4 Shift Error** Engine started, vehicle driven in gear with VSS signals received, and the PCM detected the engine speed (rpm) did not change properly (i.e., an incorrect 3-4 gear ratio was detected during the shift event). **Possible Causes:** • SS1/A solenoid may be stuck, or a hydraulic failure exists • SS2/B solenoid may be stuck, or a hydraulic failure exists • Transmission may have damaged friction material
DTC: P0784 **1T CCM, MIL: No** **Years:** 2005, 2006, 2007 **Models:** All Models **Engines:** All **Transmissions:** A/T	**A/T 4 to 5 Shift Error** Engine started, vehicle driven in gear with VSS signals received, and the PCM detected the engine speed (rpm) did not change properly (i.e., an incorrect 4-5 gear ratio was detected during a shift event). **Possible Causes:** • SS2/B solenoid may be stuck, or a hydraulic failure exists • SS3/C solenoid may be stuck, or a hydraulic failure exists • Transmission may have damaged friction material
DTC: P0812 **1T CCM, MIL: No** **Years:** 2005, 2006, 2007 **Models:** All Models **Engines:** All **Transmissions:** A/T	**A/T Reverse Switch Circuit Malfunction** Key on, engine off, KOEO Self Test enabled, and the PCM detected the reverse switch signal did not change as the selector was shifted in or out of reverse gear. **Note: The RS PID should change from ON to OFF while shifting.** **Possible Causes:** • Transmission shift not indicating neutral during the self-test • RS switch circuit shorted to VREF or VPWR • RS switch circuit is open or shorted to ground (signal return) • Reverse switch is damaged • PCM has failed
DTC: P0813 **1T CCM, MIL: Yes** **Years:** 2005, 2006, 2007 **Models:** All Models **Engines:** All **Transmissions:** A/T	**Transmission Control System Malfunction** Engine started, vehicle speed more than 1 in gear, and the PCM detected a problem in the Transmission Control System operation. **Possible Causes:** • Refer to the information in the Transmission Section of the appropriate Workshop Repair manual (i.e., the information for the particular vehicle that set this trouble code).
DTC: P0815 **1T CCM, MIL: Yes** **Years:** 2005, 2006, 2007 **Models:** All Models **Engines:** All **Transmissions:** A/T	**Transmission Control System Malfunction** Key on, engine off, KOEO Self Test enabled, and the PCM detected the reverse switch input did not change as the selector was shifted in or out of reverse (i.e., it was high when it should have been low). **Note: The RS PID should change from ON to OFF while shifting.** **Possible Causes:** • Refer to the information in the Transmission Section of the appropriate Workshop Repair manual (i.e., the information for the particular vehicle that set this trouble code).

Gas Engine OBD II Trouble Code List (P1xxx Codes)

DTC	Trouble Code Title, Conditions & Possible Causes
DTC: P1000 **1T PCM, MIL: No** **Years:** 2005, 2006, 2007 **Models:** All Models **Engines:** All **Transmissions:** All	**OBD II Monitor Testing Not Complete** Key on or engine running; and the PCM detected one the conditions shown under Possible Causes (i.e., this code cannot be cleared manually - it must clear itself after all of the OBD II Monitors complete). **Note: This code must be cleared to pass an Inspection/Maintenance Test required to register a vehicle in certain states.** **Possible Causes:** • Battery keep alive power (KAPWR) was removed to the PCM • One or more OBD II Monitors did not complete during an official OBD II Drive Cycle • PCM Reset step was performed with an OBD II Scan Tool
DTC: P1001 **1T CCM, MIL: No** **Years:** 2005, 2006, 2007 **Models:** All Models **Engines:** All **Transmissions:** All	**KOER Self-Test Not Completed, KOER Test Aborted** Key on, engine running self-test not completed during the normal allowable time period. **Possible Causes:** • Engine speed (rpm) out of specification during the KOER test • Incorrect Self-Test Procedure • Scan Tool has a communication problem • Unexpected response from Self-Test monitors
DTC: P1100 **2T CCM, MIL: Yes** **Years:** 2005, 2006, 2007 **Models:** All Models **Engines:** All **Transmissions:** All	**MAF Sensor Signal Intermittent** Engine started, engine running at idle or cruise speed, and the PCM detected the MAF sensor signal above or below the calibrated limit. **Possible Causes:** • MAF sensor continuity problems at the connector • MAF sensor continuity through the wiring harness • MAF sensor circuit intermittent open inside the sensor • PCM has failed
DTC: P1101 **2T CCM, MIL: Yes** **Years:** 2005, 2006, 2007 **Models:** All Models **Engines:** All **Transmissions:** All	**MAF Sensor Out Of Self-Test Range** Key on and engine off, and the PCM detected the MAF sensor was more than 0.27v, or with the engine running, the MAF sensor voltage was not within a normal range of 0.46v to 2.44v. **Possible Causes:** • Low battery charge • MAF sensor partially connected, or the sensor is contaminated • MAF sensor power ground circuit or sensor signal (return) open • MAF sensor is damaged or it has failed • PCM has failed
DTC: P1112 **2T CCM, MIL: Yes** **Years:** 2005, 2006, 2007 **Models:** All Models **Engines:** All **Transmissions:** All	**IAT Sensor Circuit Intermittent** Engine started, and the PCM detected an intermittent condition in the IAT sensor signal during the self-test. **Note: Select the IAT PID and monitor the signal for sudden changes.** **Possible Causes:** • IAT sensor wiring harness is damaged (wire may be open) • IAT sensor harness connector is damaged • IAT sensor is damaged or the PCM has failed
DTC: P1114 **2T CCM, MIL: Yes** **Years:** 2005, 2006, 2007 **Models:** All Models **Engines:** All **Transmissions:** All	**IAT Sensor Circuit Low Input** Engine started, and the PCM detected the IAT sensor signal was less than the self-test minimum of 0.20v (equivalent to 250°F). Monitor the IAT PID for very low signal. **Possible Causes:** • IAT sensor wiring harness is damaged (wire may be grounded) • IAT sensor harness connector is damaged (may be grounded) • IAT sensor is damaged or the PCM has failed
DTC: P1115 **2T CCM, MIL: Yes** **Years:** 2005, 2006, 2007 **Models:** All Models **Engines:** All **Transmissions:** All	**IAT Sensor 2 Circuit High Input** Engine started, and the PCM detected the IAT Sensor 2 signal was more than the self-test maximum of 4.60v (equivalent to 250°F). Monitor the IAT PID for very high signal. **Possible Causes:** • IAT sensor wiring harness or harness connector is damaged (wire may be open) • IAT sensor signal circuit is open, or the ground circuit is open • IAT sensor is damaged or has failed • PCM has failed

DTC	Trouble Code Title, Conditions & Possible Causes
DTC: P1116 **1T CCM, MIL: Yes** **Years:** 2005, 2006, 2007 **Models:** All Models **Engines:** All **Transmissions:** All	**CHT or ECT Sensor Out Of Self-Test Range** Key on, KOEO Self-Test enabled, and the PCM detected the ECT sensor was more than the expected range (50°F), or engine running, KOER Self-Test enabled, and the PCM detected the ECT senor signal was less than 180°F during the self test period. The ECT PID must be above 50°F in the KOEO test or above 180°F in the KOER self-test to pass these parameters. **Possible Causes:** • ECT sensor harness connector is damaged, loose or shorted • ECT sensor is damaged • KOER or KOER Self-Test performed with the engine "too cold"
DTC: P1117 **2T CCM, MIL: Yes** **Years:** 2005, 2006, 2007 **Models:** All Models **Engines:** All **Transmissions:** All	**CHT or ECT Sensor Signal Intermittent** Engine started, and the PCM detected an intermittent loss of the CHT or ECT sensor signal (it may have an open circuit condition). **Note: Select the CHT or IAT PID and monitor the signal for sudden changes while wiggling the CHT or IAT sensor connector. On the 5.4L V8, if the temperature exceeds 258°F, the PCM disables four fuel injectors at a time. It alternates which four fuel injectors are disabled every 32-engine cycles. The cylinders that are disabled do not inject fuel, so they act as air pumps to aid in cooling the engine. If the temperature exceeds 310°F, the PCM disables all of the fuel injectors until the engine temperature drops below 310°F.** **Possible Causes:** • ECT sensor harness connector is damaged, loose or shorted • ECT sensor is damaged or it has failed • Engine overheating condition present • Thermostat is faulty, or engine coolant level is low
DTC: P1120 **2T CCM, MIL: Yes** **Years:** 2005, 2006, 2007 **Models:** All Models **Engines:** All **Transmissions:** All	**TP Sensor Signal Out-of-Range Low** Key on or engine running; and the PCM detected the TP sensor signal was between 0.17-0.49v (3.42-9.85%) with the signal within the calibrated self-test range. **Possible Causes:** • ECT sensor harness connector is damaged • ECT sensor is damaged • Engine coolant level is low • PCM has failed
DTC: P1121 **2T CCM, MIL: Yes** **Years:** 2005, 2006, 2007 **Models:** All Models **Engines:** All **Transmissions:** All	**TP Sensor Inconsistent With MAF Sensor** Engine started; and the PCM detected the MAF and TP sensor signals were not consistent the calibrated values expected for these two sensors during the self-test. **Note: Drive the vehicle and monitor the TP PID in all gears. A TP PID of less than 0.24v (4.82%) with a LOAD PID over 55%, or a TP PID over 2.44v (49.05%) with a LOAD PID under 30% will set this code.** **Possible Causes:** • Air leak exists between MAF sensor and the throttle body • MAF sensor is damaged or it has failed • TP sensor is not seated properly • TP sensor is damaged
DTC: P1124 **1T CCM, MIL: Yes** **Years:** 2005, 2006, 2007 **Models:** All Models **Engines:** All **Transmissions:** All	**TP Sensor Out of Self-Test Range** Key on, KOEO Self-Test enabled, and the PCM detected the TP sensor signal was less than 0.66v (13.27%), or with the engine running, KOER Self-Test enabled, the PCM detected the TP sensor signal was approximately 1.17v (23.52%). **Note: A TP V PID less than 4.82 % (0.24 volt) with a LOAD PID more than 55%; or the TP V PID more than 49.05% (2.44 volts) with a LOAD PID less than 30% indicates a hard fault is present.** **Possible Causes:** • Throttle linkage is binding, or TP sensor is not seated properly • Throttle plate below closed throttle position • Throttle plate screw is misadjusted • TP sensor is damaged or it has failed • PCM has failed
DTC: P1125 **2T CCM, MIL: Yes** **Years:** 2005, 2006, 2007 **Models:** All Models **Engines:** All **Transmissions:** All	**TP Sensor Circuit Malfunction (Intermittent)** Engine started, and the PCM detected the TP sensor rotational angle changed beyond the minimum or maximum calibrated limit. **Note: Monitor the TP V PID, and tap lightly on the TP sensor housing and wiggle the wiring harness. Watch for the value to suddenly go below 0.49v or over 4.65v.** **Possible Causes:** • TP sensor wiring harness or connector has an intermittent open • TP sensor has an intermittent open or shorted condition

DTC	Trouble Code Title, Conditions & Possible Causes
DTC: P1127 **2T CCM, MIL: Yes** **Years:** 2005, 2006, 2007 **Models:** All Models **Engines:** All **Transmissions:** All	**Exhaust Not Warm, Downstream Sensor Not Tested** Engine started, KOER Self-Test enabled, and the PCM detected the inferred exhaust temperature was less than a minimum value. **Note: Monitor the HO2S Heater PID to determine their ON/OFF status (the heaters must work properly in order to pass this test).** **Possible Causes:** • Engine not operating long enough prior to the KOER Self-Test • Exhaust system temperature too cold to run the self-test
DTC: P1128 **2T CCM, MIL: Yes** **Years:** 2005, 2006, 2007 **Models:** All Models **Engines:** All **Transmissions:** All	**Upstream Oxygen Sensors Swapped From Bank-to-Bank** Engine started, KOER Self-Test enabled, and the PCM detected the HO2S signal response to a related fuel shift did not correspond to the correct engine cylinder bank (e.g., the HO2S-11 and the HO2S-21 wires were crossed) during the test period. **Possible Causes:** • Upstream HO2S-11, HO2S-21 wiring crossed at the connector • Upstream HO2S-11, HO2S-21 crossed in the wiring harness • Upstream HO2S-11, HO2S-21 crossed at PCM pin connector
DTC: P1129 **2T CCM, MIL: Yes** **Years:** 2005, 2006, 2007 **Models:** All Models **Engines:** All **Transmissions:** All	**Downstream Oxygen Sensors Swapped From Bank-to-Bank** Engine started, KOER Self-Test enabled, and the PCM detected the HO2S signal response to a related fuel shift did not correspond to the correct engine cylinder bank (e.g., the HO2S-12 and HO2S-22 wires were crossed) during the test period. **Possible Causes:** • Upstream HO2S-12, HO2S-21 wiring crossed at the connector • Upstream HO2S-12, HO2S-21 crossed in the wiring harness • Upstream HO2S-12, HO2S-21 crossed at PCM pin connector
DTC: P1130 **2T O2S, MIL: Yes** **Years:** 2005, 2006, 2007 **Models:** All Models **Engines:** All **Transmissions:** All	**Lack of HO2S-11 Switching, Fuel Trim at Rich/Lean Limit** DTC P0300-P0310 not set, engine running in closed loop, and the PCM detected the HO2S circuit was too lean or too rich, or that it could no longer change Fuel Trim because it was at its rich limit or its lean limit. **Possible Causes:** • Air intake system leaking, vacuum hoses leaking or damaged • Air leaks located after the MAF sensor mounting location • EGR valve sticking, EGR diaphragm leaking, or gasket leaking • EVAP vapor recovery system has failed • Excessive fuel pressure, leaking or contaminated fuel injectors • Exhaust leaks before or near the HO2S(s) mounting location • Fuel pressure regulator is leaking or damaged • HO2S circuits wet or oily, corroded, or poor terminal contact • HO2S is damaged or it has failed • HO2S signal circuit open, shorted to ground, shorted to power • Low fuel pressure or vehicle driven until it was out of fuel • Oil dipstick not seated or engine oil level too high (overfilled)
DTC: P1131 **2T O2S, MIL: Yes** **Years:** 2005, 2006, 2007 **Models:** All Models **Engines:** All **Transmissions:** All	**Lack of HO2S-11 Switching, HO2S Signal Low Input** DTC P0300-P0310 not set, engine started, engine running in closed loop, and the PCM detected the HO2S-11 was not switching (i.e., the HO2S-11 indicated a lean A/F mixture). **Possible Causes:** • Air intake system leaking, vacuum hoses leaking or damaged • Air leaks located after the MAF sensor mounting location • Base engine mechanical fault (i.e., compression, valve timing) • HO2S circuits wet or oily, corroded, or poor terminal contact • HO2S signal circuit open, shorted to ground, shorted to power, or the sensor has failed • Low fuel pressure or vehicle driven until it was out of fuel • Possible air leaks at the PCV valve or at the related hoses
DTC: P1132 **2T O2S, MIL: Yes** **Years:** 2005, 2006, 2007 **Models:** All Models **Engines:** All **Transmissions:** All	**Lack of HO2S-11 Switching, HO2S Signal High Input** DTC P0300-P0310 not set, engine started, engine running in closed loop, and the PCM detected the HO2S-11 was not switching (i.e., the HO2S-11 indicated a rich A/F mixture). **Possible Causes:** • Check air cleaner element and air cleaner housing for blockage • EVAP vapor recovery system has failed (canister full of fuel) • Fuel pressure too high, contaminated or leaking fuel injectors • HO2S is fuel contaminated, or coated with silicone or moisture

DTC	Trouble Code Title, Conditions & Possible Causes
DTC: P1137 **2T O2S, MIL: Yes** **Years:** 2005, 2006, 2007 **Models:** All Models **Engines:** All **Transmissions:** All	**Lack of HO2S-12 Switching, HO2S Signal Low Input** DTC P0300-P0310 not set, engine started, engine running in closed loop, and the PCM detected the HO2S-12 was not switching (i.e., the HO2S-12 indicated a lean A/F mixture). **Possible Causes:** • Air intake system leaking, vacuum hoses leaking or damaged • Air leaks located after the MAF sensor mounting location • Base engine mechanical fault (i.e., compression, valve timing) • HO2S circuits wet or oily, corroded, or poor terminal contact • HO2S is damaged or it has failed • HO2S signal circuit open, shorted to ground, shorted to power • Low fuel pressure or vehicle driven until it was out of fuel • Possible air leaks at the PCV valve or at the related hoses
DTC: P1138 **2T O2S, MIL: Yes** **Years:** 2005, 2006, 2007 **Models:** All Models **Engines:** All **Transmissions:** All	**Lack of HO2S-12 Switching, HO2S Signal High Input** DTC P0300-P0310 not set, engine started, engine running in closed loop, and the PCM detected the HO2S-12 was not switching (i.e., the HO2S-12 indicated a rich A/F mixture). **Possible Causes:** • Check air cleaner element and air cleaner housing for blockage • EVAP vapor recovery system has failed (canister full of fuel) • Fuel pressure too high, contaminated or leaking fuel injectors • HO2S is fuel contaminated, or coated with silicone or moisture
DTC: P1150 **2T O2S, MIL: Yes** **Years:** 2005, 2006, 2007 **Models:** All Models **Engines:** All **Transmissions:** All	**Lack of HO2S-21 Switching, Fuel Trim At Rich/Lean Limit** DTC P0300-P0310 not set, engine running in closed loop, and the PCM detected the HO2S circuit was too lean or too rich, or that it could no longer correct Fuel Trim (i.e., the Fuel Trim was at its calibrated rich limit or its calibrated lean limit). **Possible Causes:** • Air intake system leaking, vacuum hoses leaking or damaged • Air leaks located after the MAF sensor mounting location • EGR valve sticking, EGR diaphragm leaking, or gasket leaking • EVAP vapor recovery system has failed • Excessive fuel pressure, leaking or contaminated fuel injectors • Exhaust leaks before or near the HO2S(s) mounting location • Fuel pressure regulator is leaking or damaged • HO2S circuits wet or oily, corroded, or poor terminal contact • HO2S signal circuit open, shorted to ground, shorted to power, or the sensor has failed • Low fuel pressure or vehicle driven until it was out of fuel • Oil dipstick not seated or engine oil level too high (overfilled)
DTC: P1151 **2T O2S, MIL: Yes** **Years:** 2005, 2006, 2007 **Models:** All Models **Engines:** All **Transmissions:** All	**Lack of HO2S-21 Switching, HO2S Signal Low Input** DTC P0300-P0310 not set, engine started, engine running in closed loop, and the PCM detected the HO2S-21 was not switching (i.e., the HO2S-21 indicated a lean A/F mixture). **Possible Causes:** • Air intake system leaking, vacuum hoses leaking or damaged • Air leaks located after the MAF sensor mounting location or in the PCV system • Base engine mechanical fault (i.e., compression, valve timing) • HO2S circuits wet or oily, corroded, or poor terminal contact • HO2S signal circuit open, shorted to ground, shorted to power, or the sensor has failed • Low fuel pressure or vehicle driven until it was out of fuel
DTC: P1152 **2T O2S, MIL: Yes** **Years:** 2005, 2006, 2007 **Models:** All Models **Engines:** All **Transmissions:** All	**Lack of HO2S-21 Switching, HO2S Signal High Input** DTC P0300-P0310 not set, engine started, engine running in closed loop, and the PCM detected the HO2S-21 was not switching (i.e., the HO2S-21 indicated a rich A/F mixture). **Possible Causes:** • Check air cleaner element and air cleaner housing for blockage • EVAP vapor recovery system has failed (canister full of fuel) • Fuel pressure too high, contaminated or leaking fuel injectors • HO2S is fuel contaminated, or coated with silicone or moisture

DTC	Trouble Code Title, Conditions & Possible Causes
DTC: P1157 **2T O2S, MIL: Yes** **Years:** 2005, 2006, 2007 **Models:** All Models **Engines:** All **Transmissions:** All	**Lack of HO2S-22 Switching, HO2S Signal Low Input** DTC P0300-P0310 not set, engine started, engine running in closed loop, and the PCM detected the HO2S-22 was not switching (i.e., the HO2S-22 indicated a lean A/F mixture). **Possible Causes:** • Air intake system leaking, vacuum hoses leaking or damaged • Air leaks located after the MAF sensor mounting location • Base engine mechanical fault (i.e., compression, valve timing) • HO2S circuits wet or oily, corroded, or poor terminal contact • HO2S is damaged or it has failed • HO2S signal circuit open, shorted to ground, shorted to power • Low fuel pressure or vehicle driven until it was out of fuel • Possible air leaks at the PCV valve or at the related hoses
DTC: P1158 **2T O2S, MIL: Yes** **Years:** 2005, 2006, 2007 **Models:** All Models **Engines:** All **Transmissions:** All	**Lack of HO2S-22 Switching, HO2S Signal High Input** DTC P0300-P0310 not set, engine started, engine running in closed loop, and the PCM detected the HO2S-22 was not switching (i.e., the HO2S-22 indicated a rich A/F mixture). **Possible Causes:** • Check air cleaner element and air cleaner housing for blockage • EVAP vapor recovery system has failed (canister full of fuel) • Fuel pressure too high, contaminated or leaking fuel injectors • HO2S is fuel contaminated, or coated with silicone or moisture
DTC: P1183 **2T CCM, MIL: Yes** **Years:** 2005, 2006, 2007 **Models:** All Models **Engines:** All **Transmissions:** All	**Engine Oil Temperature Sensor Circuit Malfunction** Engine started, and the PCM detected the engine oil temperature (EOT) sensor circuit was open or shorted to ground (i.e., this fault is usually caused by an interruption of the signal - intermittent fault). **Possible Causes:** • EOT sensor circuit is open or shorted to ground • EOT sensor has failed • PCM has failed
DTC: P1184 **2T CCM, MIL: Yes** **Years:** 2005, 2006, 2007 **Models:** All Models **Engines:** All **Transmissions:** All	**Engine Oil Temperature Sensor Out Of Self-Test Range** Engine started, and the PCM detected the engine oil temperature (EOT) sensor circuit was open or shorted to ground (i.e., this fault can be caused by an intermittent loss of this signal). **Possible Causes:** • EOT sensor circuit is open or shorted to ground (intermittent) • EOT sensor is corroded, damaged or it has failed • PCM has failed
DTC: P1231 **1T CCM, MIL: No** **Years:** 2005, 2006, 2007 **Models:** All Models **Engines:** All **Transmissions:** All	**Fuel Pump Secondary Low, High Speed Pump On** Key on, KOEO Self-Test enabled; High Speed Fuel Pump (HFP) relay energized, fuel pump driver in VLCM off (to VLCM Pin 7) off, the PCM detected voltage on the FPM circuit. **Possible Causes:** • HFP relay circuit to battery power (B+) is open • HFP relay is damaged or it has failed • Power-To-Pump circuit between HFP relay and splice is open
DTC: P1232 **2T CCM, MIL: Yes** **Years:** 2005, 2006, 2007 **Models:** All Models **Engines:** All **Transmissions:** All	**Low Speed Fuel Pump Primary Circuit Malfunction** Engine started, Low Speed Fuel Pump (LFP) relay energized, the PCM detected excessive current on the LFP circuit; or with LFP commanded off it detected power on the LFP circuit. **Possible Causes:** • Low fuel pump (LFP) circuit open or shorted • Low speed fuel pump relay VPWR circuit open • Low speed fuel pump relay is damaged • PCM has failed
DTC: P1233 **2T CCM, MIL: Yes** **Years:** 2005, 2006, 2007 **Models:** All Models **Engines:** All **Transmissions:** All	**Fuel System Disabled Or Offline** Key on or engine running; and the PCM did not receive any diagnostic information (via duty cycle signals) from the FPDM. **Possible Causes:** • Inertia fuel shutoff (IFS) switch needs to be reset • FPDM ground circuit is open, or FPM circuit is open or shorted • Mark VIII: FPDM PWR circuit is open, the FPDM power supply relay VPWR circuit is opened or grounded, or power relay failed • Escort/Tracer: FPDM PWR circuit is open, or the CCRM pin 11 is open to power (B+), or the CCRM (relay) is damaged • Continental: FPDM circuit to VPWR is open, or the FPDM or the IFS is damaged • Refer to the GEM or REM controllers for related trouble codes

DTC	Trouble Code Title, Conditions & Possible Causes
DTC: P1234 **1T CCM, MIL: Yes** **Years:** 2005, 2006, 2007 **Models:** All Models **Engines:** All **Transmissions:** All	**Fuel System Disabled Or Offline** Key on, and the PCM did not receive any diagnostic information from the FPDM. **Possible Causes:** • Inertia fuel shutoff (IFS) switch needs to be reset or has failed • FPDM ground circuit is open, or FPM circuit is open or shorted • Mark VIII: FPDM PWR circuit is open, the FPDM power supply relay VPWR circuit is opened or grounded, or power relay failed • Escort/Tracer: FPDM PWR circuit is open, or the CCRM pin 11 is open to power (B+), or the CCRM (relay) is damaged • Continental: FPDM circuit to VPWR is open, or the FPDM or the IFS is damaged • LS6, LS8 **Models:** This code indicates the PCM is not receiving data about the fuel level on the SCP data line from the Rear Electronics Module (REM). Test the REM first! • PCM has failed
DTC: P1235 **2T CCM, MIL: Yes** **Years:** 2005, 2006, 2007 **Models:** All Models **Engines:** All **Transmissions:** All	**Fuel Pump Control Out Of Range** Key on or engine running; and the PCM received a signal from the FPM over the SCP bus that the FPDM had received an invalid or missing fuel pump command from the PCM. **Possible Causes:** • FP circuit is open or shorted • FPDM is damaged • PCM has failed
DTC: P1236 **2T CCM, MIL: No** **Years:** 2005, 2006, 2007 **Models:** All Models **Engines:** All **Transmissions:** All	**Fuel Pump Control Out Of Range** Key on or engine running; and the PCM received a signal (from the FPM over the SCP bus) that the FPDM had received an invalid or missing fuel pump command from the PCM. **Possible Causes:** • FP circuit is open or it is shorted • FPDM is damaged or the PCM has failed
DTC: P1237 **2T CCM, MIL: Yes** **Years:** 2005, 2006, 2007 **Models:** All Models **Engines:** All **Transmissions:** All	**Fuel Pump Secondary Circuit Malfunction** Key on or engine running; and the PCM received a signal from the FPDM that it had detected a fault in the fuel pump secondary circuit. **Possible Causes:** • FP PWR circuit is open or shorted • FPDM fuel pump return circuit is open • Fuel pump windings are open or shorted, or the rotor is locked • FPDM is damaged
DTC: P1238 **2T CCM, MIL: Yes** **Years:** 2005, 2006, 2007 **Models:** All Models **Engines:** All **Transmissions:** All	**Fuel Pump Secondary Circuit Malfunction** Key on or engine running; and the PCM received a signal from the FPDM that it had detected a fault in the fuel pump secondary circuit. **Possible Causes:** • FP PWR circuit is open or shorted • FPDM fuel pump return circuit is open • Fuel pump windings are open or shorted • Fuel pump rotor is locked • FPDM is damaged
DTC: P1244 **2T CCM, MIL: Yes** **Years:** 2005, 2006, 2007 **Models:** All Models **Engines:** All **Transmissions:** All	**Generator Load Circuit Low Input** Engine started, and the PCM detected the GLI signal was less than the calibrated limit for a calibrated amount of time. **Possible Causes:** • GLI circuit is open or shorted • Voltage regulator/generator is damaged • PCM has failed
DTC: P1245 **2T CCM, MIL: Yes** **Years:** 2005, 2006, 2007 **Models:** All Models **Engines:** All **Transmissions:** All	**Generator Load circuit High Input** Engine started, and the PCM detected the GLI signal was more than the calibrated limit for a calibrated amount of time. **Possible Causes:** • GLI circuit is open or shorted • Voltage regulator/generator is damaged • PCM has failed

DTC	Trouble Code Title, Conditions & Possible Causes
DTC: P1246 **2T CCM, MIL:** Yes **Years:** 2005, 2006, 2007 **Models:** All Models Except Crown Victoria, Grand Marquis & Town Car **Engines:** All **Transmissions:** All	**Generator Load Circuit Malfunction** Engine started, and the PCM detected the GLI was more than or less than a calibrated amount for too long a period of time. **Possible Causes:** • Generator circuit is open, shorted to ground or shorted to power • Generator drive mechanism has failed • Generator/regulator assembly is damaged or the PCM has failed
DTC: P1246 **2T CCM, MIL:** Yes **Years:** 2005, 2006, 2007 **Models:** Crown Victoria, Grand Marquis & Town Car **Engines:** 4.6L VIN V, W **Transmissions:** All	**Generator Load Circuit Malfunction** Engine started, and the PCM detected the GLI was more than or less than a calibrated amount for too long a period of time. **Possible Causes:** • Generator circuit is open, shorted to ground or shorted to power • Generator drive mechanism has failed • Generator/regulator assembly is damaged or the PCM has failed • TSB 03-14-2 contains repair information for this trouble code
DTC: P1260 **2T PCM, MIL:** Yes **Years:** 2005, 2006, 2007 **Models:** All Models **Engines:** All **Transmissions:** All	**Theft Detected, Vehicle Immobilized** Key on, and the PCM received a signal from the Anti-Theft System that a theft condition had occurred. The theft indicator on the dash will flash rapidly or remain on "solid" with the ignition switch in the "on" position. The engine may "start and stall", or may not crank if the vehicle is equipped with the PATS starter disable feature. **Possible Causes:** • A Previous theft condition has occurred • Anti-Theft System is damaged or has failed • TSB 01-6-2 (superseded from 76-65-4) contains an updated repair procedure
DTC: P1270 **1T CCM, MIL:** Yes **Years:** 2005, 2006, 2007 **Models:** All Models **Engines:** All **Transmissions:** All	**Engine Speed/Vehicle Speed Limiter Fault** Engine started, and after the PCM monitored the engine speed and VSS signals), it detected the vehicle was operated in a manner where the engine or vehicle speed to exceeded its limit. **Possible Causes:** • Excessive wheel slippage due to water, ice, mud and snow • Excessive engine speed (rpm) with the gearshift in Neutral • Vehicle driven at a high rate of speed
DTC: P1285 **2T CCM, MIL:** Yes **Years:** 2005, 2006, 2007 **Models:** All Models with CHT **Engines:** All With CHT **Transmissions:** All	**Cylinder Head Over-Temperature Sensed** Key on or engine running; and the PCM detected an engine overheat condition through inputs from the cylinder head temperature sensor. Engine started, and the PCM detected the CHT or ECT sensor signal was intermittent (it may have an intermittent open condition). **Note: Select the CHT or IAT PID and monitor the signal for sudden changes while wiggling the CHT or IAT sensor connector.** On the 5.4L V8, if the temperature exceeds 258°F, the PCM disables four fuel injectors at a time. It alternates which four fuel injectors are disabled every 32-engine cycles. The cylinders that are disabled do not inject fuel, so they act as air pumps to aid in cooling the engine. If the temperature exceeds 310°F, the PCM disables all of the fuel injectors until the engine temperature drops below 310°F. **Possible Causes:** • Base engine problems or related concerns • CHT sensor has deteriorated or it has failed • Engine coolant level is too low • Engine cooling system has a problem • TSB 10-29-1 contains repair help for this code (LS & T-Bird)
DTC: P1288 **2T CCM, MIL:** Yes **Years:** 2005, 2006, 2007 **Models:** All Models with CHT **Engines:** All With CHT **Transmissions:** All	**Cylinder Head Temperature Sensor Out of Self-Test Range** Key on and KOEO Self-Test enabled, or engine running with the KOER Self-Test enabled, and the PCM detected the CHT sensor was out of its self-test range (i.e., the engine was too hot or it did not warm to its normal operating temperature) during the test period. **Possible Causes:** • CHT sensor harness connector is damaged • CHT sensor is damaged • Engine coolant level is too low • Engine is cold, or the engine is overheated

DTC	Trouble Code Title, Conditions & Possible Causes
DTC: P1289 **2T CCM, MIL: Yes** **Years:** 2005, 2006, 2007 **Models:** All Models with CHT **Engines:** All With CHT **Transmissions:** All	**Cylinder Head Temperature Sensor Circuit High Input** Key on or engine running; and the PCM detected a Cylinder Head Temperature (CHT) sensor signal that was more than 4.60v. This code may be due to an intermittent fault. Wiggle the CHT sensor wiring and connector while monitoring the CHT PID for a sudden change in voltage. DTC P0118 may also be reported when this code is set, and either code will cause the PCM to activate the MIL. **Possible Causes:** • CHT sensor circuit is open in the wiring harness, or an open circuit exists in the CHT sensor circuit at the harness connector • CHT sensor is damaged or has failed • Engine coolant level is too low or the thermostat has failed • PCM has failed
DTC: P1290 **2T CCM, MIL: Yes** **Years:** 2005, 2006, 2007 **Models:** All Models with CHT **Engines:** All With CHT **Transmissions:** All	**Cylinder Head Temperature Sensor Circuit Low Input** Key on or engine running; and the PCM detected a Cylinder Head Temperature (CHT) sensor signal that was less than 0.2v. Note that this trouble code may be due to an intermittent type of fault. Wiggle the CHT sensor wiring and connector while monitoring the CHT V PID for signs of a sudden change in the voltage. DTC P0118 may also set along with this code (both codes will cause a MIL to be on). **Possible Causes:** • CHT sensor connector is damaged or a short circuit exists • CHT sensor signal circuit is shorted to sensor ground • CHT sensor is damaged or the PCM has failed
DTC: P1299 **2T CCM, MIL: Yes** **Years:** 2005, 2006, 2007 **Models:** All Models **Engines:** All **Transmissions:** All	**Cylinder Head Over-Temperature Protection Active** Engine started, and after a period of time with the engine running, the PCM detected the engine was in an overheated condition. **Note: The PCM enables the Fail-Safe Cooling whenever this code is set to cool the engine (a Failure Mode Effects Strategy or FMEM).** **Possible Causes:** • Cooling system has a problem • Engine coolant level is too low • A Base Engine problem may be present • TSB 10-29-1 contains repair help for this code (LS & T-Bird)
DTC: P1309 1T MISFIRE **MIL: Yes** **Years:** 2005, 2006, 2007 **Models:** All Models **Engines:** All **Transmissions:** All	**Misfire Monitor Disabled** DTC P0136, P0156, P0171, P0172, P0174, P0175, P1130 and P1150 not set, engine started, and the PCM disabled the Misfire Monitor in order to verify that the CMP sensor is synchronized. Note that this code can be caused by an incorrect input from the CMP sensor (i.e., it senses the passage of teeth from the CMP wheel). **Possible Causes:** • Camshaft position sensor is damaged or it has failed • CKP, ECT or MAF sensors may be out-of-calibration or failed • PCM has failed • TSB 02-22-1 contains repair information for this trouble code
DTC: P1336 **2T CCM, MIL: Yes** **Years:** 2005, 2006, 2007 **Models:** All Models **Engines:** All **Transmissions:** All	**CKP or CMP Signal Malfunction** Engine started, and the PCM detected an erratic signal from CKP sensor or the CMP sensor. It is possible for EMI/RFI interference to cause this code when they occur on these circuits. **Possible Causes:** • Base Engine problem or concern exists • CKP sensor or CMP signal circuit is open or shorted to ground • CKP sensor or CMP sensor is damaged or failed (check for EMI/RFI on this circuit). • PCM has failed • TSB 02-22-1 contains repair information for this trouble code
DTC: P1351 **2T CCM, MIL: Yes** **Years:** 2005, 2006, 2007 **Models:** All Models **Engines:** All **Transmissions:** All	**Ignition Diagnostic Monitor Circuit Malfunction** Engine started, and the PCM detected a loss of the IDM circuit from the ignition module in the distributor (the fault may be intermittent). **Note: If DTC P0350, P0351, P0352, P0353 or P0354 is set, repair these trouble codes and then recheck to see if DTC P1351 resets.** **Possible Causes:** • Camshaft position sensor may have failed • IDM signal circuit may be open or grounded • CKP, ECT or MAF sensors may be damaged or have failed • PCM has failed

DTC	Trouble Code Title, Conditions & Possible Causes
DTC: P1356 **1T CCM, MIL: No** **Years:** 2005, 2006, 2007 **Models:** All Models **Engines:** All **Transmissions:** All	**PIP Signals Present With Engine Off** Key on, and the PCM detected the presence of PIP signals, yet the Ignition Diagnostic Monitor (IDM) signals indicated the engine was not turning. **Possible Causes:** • Ignition Module has failed • PCM has failed
DTC: P1358 **2T CCM, MIL: Yes** **Years:** 2005, 2006, 2007 **Models:** All Models **Engines:** All **Transmissions:** All	**IDM Signals Out Of Self-Test Range** Engine started; and the PCM detected PIP signals that indicated that the Ignition Diagnostic Monitor signals were out of the self-test range under these operating conditions. **Possible Causes:** • Ignition Module has failed • PCM has failed
DTC: P1359 **2T CCM, MIL: Yes** **Years:** 2005, 2006, 2007 **Models:** All Models **Engines:** All **Transmissions:** All	**Spark Output Circuit Malfunction** Engine started, and the PCM did not detect any change in the Spark Output (SPOUT) signals during the test period. **Possible Causes:** • SPOUT signal circuit may be open (check the connector) • SPOUT signal circuit may be grounded • Ignition Module is damaged or has failed
DTC: P1380 **2T CCM, MIL: Yes** **Years:** 2005, 2006, 2007 **Models:** Focus, LS, Sable, Taurus **Engines:** 2.3L VIN Z, 3.0L VIN S, 3.9L VIN A **Transmissions:** All	**Variable Cam Timing Solenoid 'A' Circuit Malfunction (Bank 1)** Key on or engine running; and the PCM detected an unexpected voltage condition on the Variable Cam Timing signal circuit. Note that this code is due to an electrical fault (not a mechanical fault). **Possible Causes:** • VCT solenoid circuit is open or shorted • VCT solenoid is damaged or has failed • PCM has failed
DTC: P1381 **2T CCM, MIL: Yes** **Years:** 2005, 2006, 2007 **Models:** Focus, LS, Sable, Taurus **Engines:** 2.3L VIN Z, 3.0L VIN S, 3.9L VIN A **Transmissions:** All	**Variable Cam Timing Over-Advanced (Cylinder Bank 1)** Engine started, and the PCM detected the Variable Cam Timing position indicated the camshaft timing was over-advanced when compared to a maximum calibrated limit in an advanced position. **Note: This code is a mechanical problem - not an electrical problem. The engine may be hard to start or idle rough when this code is set.** **Possible Causes:** • Cam timing improperly set • No oil flow to VCT piston chamber, or low engine oil pressure • VCT solenoid valve stuck in closed position • Camshaft advance mechanism binding (inside the VCT unit)
DTC: P1383 **2T CCM, MIL: Yes** **Years:** 2005, 2006, 2007 **Models:** Focus, LS, Sable, Taurus **Engines:** 2.3L VIN Z, 3.0L VIN S, 3.9L VIN A **Transmissions:** All	**Variable Cam Timing Over-Retarded (Cylinder Bank 1)** Engine started, and the PCM detected the Variable Cam Timing position indicated the camshaft timing was over-retarded when compared to a maximum calibrated limit in a retarded position. Note that this code is a mechanical problem - not an electrical problem. The engine may be hard to start or idle rough when this code is set. **Possible Causes:** • Cam timing improperly set • Low oil pressure, VCT piston chamber not receiving any oil flow • VCT solenoid valve stuck in closed position • Camshaft advance mechanism binding (inside the VCT unit)
DTC: P1385 **2T CCM, MIL: Yes** **Years:** 2005, 2006, 2007 **Models:** LS **Engines:** 3.0L VIN S, 3.9L VIN A **Transmissions:** All	**Variable Cam Timing Solenoid 'A' Circuit Malfunction (Cylinder Bank 2)** Key on or engine running; and the PCM detected an unexpected voltage condition on the Variable Cam Timing signal circuit. Note that this code is due to an electrical fault (not a mechanical fault). **Possible Causes:** • VCT solenoid circuit is open or shorted • VCT solenoid is damaged or has failed • PCM has failed

DTC	Trouble Code Title, Conditions & Possible Causes
DTC: P1386 **2T CCM, MIL: Yes** **Years:** 2005, 2006, 2007 **Models:** LS **Engines:** 3.0L VIN S, 3.9L VIN A **Transmissions:** All	**Variable Cam Timing Over-Advanced (Cylinder Bank 2)** Engine started, and the PCM detected the Variable Cam Timing position indicated the camshaft timing was over-advanced when compared to a maximum calibrated limit in an advanced position. **Note: This code indicates the presence of a mechanical problem - not an electrical problem. The engine may be hard to start or idle rough when this code is set.** **Possible Causes:** • Cam timing improperly set • No oil flow to VCT piston chamber, or low engine oil pressure • VCT solenoid valve stuck in closed position • Camshaft advance mechanism binding (inside the VCT unit)
DTC: P1388 **2T CCM, MIL: Yes** **Years:** 2005, 2006, 2007 **Models:** LS **Engines:** 3.0L VIN S, 3.9L VIN A **Transmissions:** All	**Variable Cam Timing Over-Retarded (Cylinder Bank 2)** Engine started, and the PCM detected the Variable Cam Timing position indicated the camshaft timing was over-retarded when compared to a maximum calibrated limit in a retarded position. This code indicates a mechanical problem - not an electrical problem. The engine may be hard to start or idle rough when this code is set. **Possible Causes:** • Cam timing improperly set • Low oil pressure, VCT piston chamber not receiving any oil flow • VCT solenoid valve stuck in closed position • Camshaft advance mechanism binding (inside the VCT unit)
DTC: P1390 **1T CCM, MIL: No** **Years:** 2005, 2006, 2007 **Models:** All Models **Engines:** All **Transmissions:** All	**Octane Adjust Circuit Malfunction** Key on, KOEO Self-Test enabled, and with the octane adjust software activated, the PCM detected a malfunction in the OCT circuit. **Possible Causes:** • OCT shorting bar removed • OCT circuit open • PCM has failed
DTC: P1400 **2T CCM, MIL: Yes** **Years:** 2005, 2006, 2007 **Models:** All Models Except Five Hundred, Freestyle, LS, Montego **Engines:** All **Transmissions:** All	**DPFE Sensor Circuit Low Input** Key on, and the PCM detected the DPF EGR sensor signal was less than the minimum calibrated value of 0.2v. **Note: The DPF EGR PID will read less than 0.2v with this code set.** **Possible Causes:** • DPF EGR signal circuit shorted to ground • DPF EGR signal VREF circuit open • DPF EGR sensor is damaged or has failed • PCM has failed • TSB 4-3-1 contains repair information for this trouble code
DTC: P1400 **2T CCM, MIL: Yes** **Years:** 2005, 2006, 2007 **Models:** Five Hundred, Freestyle, LS, Montego **Engines:** All **Transmissions:** All	**DPFE Sensor Circuit Low Input** Engine started, and the PCM detected the DPF EGR sensor signal was less than the minimum calibrated value of 0.2v. The DPFE, EGR valve and EVR solenoid are integrated into the ESM assembly. **Possible Causes:** • DPFE sensor signal circuit is shorted to ground • DPFE sensor VREF circuit (5v) is open • DPFE sensor is damaged or it has failed • PCM has failed
DTC: P1401 **2T CCM, MIL: Yes** **Years:** 2005, 2006, 2007 **Models:** All Models Except Five Hundred, Freestyle, LS, Montego **Engines:** All **Transmissions:** All	**DPFE Sensor Circuit High Input** Key on; and the PCM detected the DPF EGR sensor signal was more than the maximum calibrated value of 4.5v. The DPF EGR PID will read more than 4.5v with this code set. **Possible Causes:** • DPF EGR signal circuit open, or sensor ground circuit open • DPF EGR signal shorted to VREF or to power • DPF EGR sensor is damaged or has failed • PCM has failed • TSB 4-3-1 contains repair information for this trouble code
DTC: P1401 **2T CCM, MIL: Yes** **Years:** 2005, 2006, 2007 **Models:** Five Hundred, Freestyle, LS, Montego **Engines:** All **Transmissions:** All	**DPFE Sensor Circuit High Input** Key on or engine running; and the PCM detected the DPF EGR sensor signal was more than the maximum calibrated value of 4.5v. On this vehicle application, the DPFE, EGR valve and EVR solenoid are integrated into the ESM assembly. **Possible Causes:** • DPFE sensor signal circuit is open • DPFE sensor ground circuit is open • DPFE sensor signal is shorted to VREF (5v) • DPFE sensor is damaged or it has failed • PCM has failed

DTC	Trouble Code Title, Conditions & Possible Causes
DTC: P1405 **2T CCM, MIL:** Yes **Years:** 2005, 2006, 2007 **Models:** All Models **Engines:** All **Transmissions:** All	**DPFE Sensor Upstream Hose Off Or Plugged** Engine started; and the PCM detected the DPF EGR sensor indicated EGR flow in a negative direction (a closed EGR valve). Check for signs of icing in the hose, or wrong hose routing. **Possible Causes:** • DPF EGR sensor upstream hose is disconnected • DPF EGR sensor upstream hose is plugged (ice) • EGR tube is plugged or damaged
DTC: P1406 **2T CCM, MIL:** Yes **Years:** 2005, 2006, 2007 **Models:** All Models Except Five Hundred, Freestyle, LS, Montego **Engines:** All **Transmissions:** All	**DPFE Sensor Downstream Hose Off Or Plugged** Engine started; and the PCM detected the DPF EGR sensor signal indicated EGR flow existed with the EGR valve commanded closed. **Possible Causes:** • Check for signs of icing in the hose, or for a restricted tube • DPF EGR sensor downstream hose is disconnected • DPF EGR sensor downstream hose is plugged (ice) • EGR tube is plugged or damaged
DTC: P1406 **2T CCM, MIL:** Yes **Years:** 2005, 2006, 2007 **Models:** Five Hundred, Freestyle, LS, Montego **Engines:** All **Transmissions:** All	**DPFE Sensor Downstream Hose Off Or Plugged** Engine started, and the PCM detected the DPFE sensor indicated that EGR flow was present with the EGR valve commanded closed. On this vehicle application, the DPFE, EGR valve and EVR solenoid are integrated into the ESM assembly. **Possible Causes:** • Check for signs of icing in the hose, or for a restricted tube • DPF EGR sensor downstream hose is disconnected • DPF EGR sensor downstream hose is plugged (ice) • EGR tube is plugged or damaged
DTC: P1408 **1T EGR, MIL:** Yes **Years:** 2005, 2006, 2007 **Models:** All Models Except Focus, Ranger **Engines:** All **Transmissions:** All	**EGR Flow Out Of Self-Test Range** KOER Self-Test enabled, and the PCM detected the EGR flow was out of the self-test range during the self-test with the engine running. **Possible Causes:** • EGR vacuum regulator solenoid vacuum supply problem • EVR valve stuck closed or iced up, or the flow path is restricted • EGR valve diaphragm leaking, hose is off, plugged or leaking • EGR VR solenoid open or the VPWR circuit is open • DPF EGR sensor pressure hoses connected wrong (reversed) • DPF EGR downstream hose connection leaking or plugged • EGR Orifice tube assembly is damaged • DPF EGR sensor or the EGR VR solenoid is damaged, or the PCM has failed
DTC: P1408 **1T EGR, MIL:** No **Years:** 2005, 2006, 2007 **Models:** Focus, Ranger **Engines:** 2.3L VIN D, 2.3L VIN Z **Transmissions:** All	**EGR Flow Out Of Self-Test Range** Engine started, KOER Self-Test enabled, and the PCM detected the EGR flow was out of the self-test range. There is no DPFE sensor or orifice tube assembly on this vehicle application. **Possible Causes:** • E-EGR valve connector is damaged, loose or shorted • E-EGR valve is sticking, damaged or it has failed • MAP or TMAP sensor is damaged or out of calibration • PCM has failed
DTC: P1408 **1T EGR, MIL:** No **Years:** 2005, 2006, 2007 **Models:** Five Hundred, Freestyle, LS, Montego **Engines:** All **Transmissions:** All	**EGR Flow Out Of Self-Test Range** Engine started, KOER Self-Test enabled, and the PCM detected the EGR flow was out of the self-test range during the self-test. On this vehicle application, the DPFE, EGR valve and EVR solenoid are integrated into the ESM assembly **Possible Causes:** • EGR vacuum regulator solenoid vacuum supply problem • EVR valve stuck closed or iced up, or the flow path is restricted • EGR valve diaphragm leaking, hose is off, plugged or leaking • EGR VR solenoid open or the VPWR circuit is open • DPF EGR sensor pressure hoses connected wrong (reversed) • DPF EGR sensor VREF circuit is open • DPF EGR downstream hose connection leaking or plugged • EGR Orifice tube assembly is damaged • DPF EGR sensor or the EGR VR solenoid is damaged • PCM has failed

DTC	Trouble Code Title, Conditions & Possible Causes
DTC: P1409 **2T CCM, MIL: Yes** **Years:** 2005, 2006, 2007 **Models:** All Models Except Five Hundred, Freestyle, LS, Montego **Engines:** All **Transmissions:** All	**EGR Vacuum Regulator Solenoid Circuit Malfunction** Engine started, and the PCM detected a fault in the EGR VR solenoid circuit (i.e., the VR circuit was too high or low when compared to the expected range with the solenoid enabled). **Possible Causes:** • EGR VR solenoid circuit is open, or shorted to ground • EGR VR circuit is shorted to power or the VPWR circuit is open • EGR vacuum regulator solenoid is damaged or the PCM has failed
DTC: P1409 **1T CCM, MIL: Yes** **Years:** 2005, 2006, 2007 **Models:** Five Hundred, Freestyle, LS, Montego **Engines:** All **Transmissions:** All	**EGR Vacuum Regulator Solenoid Circuit Malfunction** Engine started, and the PCM detected a fault in the EGR VR solenoid circuit (i.e., the VR circuit was too high or low when compared to its expected range with the solenoid enabled). **Possible Causes:** • EGR VR solenoid circuit is open, or shorted to ground • EGR VR circuit is shorted to power or the VPWR circuit is open • EGR vacuum regulator solenoid is damaged or the PCM has failed
DTC: P1411 **2T AIR, MIL: Yes** **Years:** 2005, 2006, 2007 **Models:** All Models **Engines:** All **Transmissions:** All	**Secondary Air Injection System Downstream Flow** Engine started, engine running with AIR system "on", and the PCM detected the HO2S signal did not go lean with the AIR system "on". **Possible Causes:** • Secondary AIR System Electric Pump is damaged • Secondary AIR System Mechanical Pump is damaged • Secondary AIR pump hose is leaking • Secondary AIR pump hose is blocked • Secondary AIR Bypass solenoid passage leaking or blocked • Secondary AIR Bypass solenoid stuck open or stuck closed
DTC: P1413 **2T CCM, MIL: Yes** **Years:** 2005, 2006, 2007 **Models:** All Models **Engines:** All **Transmissions:** All	**Secondary AIR System Monitor Circuit Low Input** Engine started, engine running with AIR system "off", and the PCM detected an unexpected "low" voltage condition on the Secondary AIR monitor during the CCM test. **Possible Causes:** • AIR solenoid control circuit is open or it is shorted to ground • AIR pump is damaged or it has failed • Solid State relay is damaged or it has failed • Solid State relay battery power circuit (B+) is open • PCM has failed
DTC: P1414 **2T CCM, MIL: Yes** **Years:** 2005, 2006, 2007 **Models:** All Models **Engines:** All **Transmissions:** All	**Secondary AIR System Monitor Circuit High Input** Engine started, AIR system not active, and the PCM detected a high voltage signal present on the Secondary AIR monitor signal circuit. **Possible Causes:** • AIR Monitor circuit from the pump to the PCM is open • AIR solenoid control circuit is shorted to power • Solid State relay is damaged or has failed • AIR pump ground circuit is open • AIR pump is damaged or has failed • PCM has failed
DTC: P1432 **1T CCM, MIL: Yes** **Years:** 2005, 2006, 2007 **Models:** All Models **Engines:** All **Transmissions:** All	**Thermostat Heater Control Circuit Malfunction** Engine started; and the PCM detected the Thermostat Heater Control circuit was less than or more than a calibrated limit for too long a period of time during the CCM self-test. **Possible Causes:** • Thermostat Heater Control (THTRC) circuit open or shorted • Thermostat Heater Control (THTRC) VPWR circuit open • Thermostat Heater assembly is damaged or has failed • PCM has failed
DTC: P1436 **2T CCM, MIL: Yes** **Years:** 2005, 2006, 2007 **Models:** All Models **Engines:** All **Transmissions:** All	**A/C Evaporator Temperature (ACET) Circuit Low Input** Key on or engine running; and the PCM detected the ACET signal was less than the self-test minimum amount of 0.13v in the self-test. **Possible Causes:** • ACET signal circuit shorted to sensor ground (return) • ACET signal circuit shorted to chassis ground • ACET sensor is damaged or has failed • PCM has failed

DTC	Trouble Code Title, Conditions & Possible Causes
DTC: P1437 **2T CCM, MIL: Yes** **Years:** 2005, 2006, 2007 **Models:** All Models **Engines:** All **Transmissions:** All	**A/C Evaporator Temperature (ACET) Circuit High Input** Key on or engine running; and the PCM detected the ACET signal was more than the self-test maximum amount of 4.5v in the self-test. **Possible Causes:** • ACET signal circuit is open, or the ground circuit is open • ACET signal is shorted to VREF • ACET sensor is damaged or has failed • PCM has failed
DTC: P1442 **2T EVAP, MIL: Yes** **Years:** 2005, 2006, 2007 **Models:** All Models **Engines:** All **Transmissions:** All	**EVAP System Small Leak (0.040") Detected** Cold startup requirement met, engine running at Cruise speed in closed loop for 2-3 minutes, and the PCM detected a leak (as small as 0.040") in the EVAP system. **Note: Inspect the CV solenoid for contamination (as contamination can hold the CV open set DTC P0442 and also plugs the port to atmosphere enough to keep system from being vented quickly).** **Possible Causes:** • Fuel filler cap damaged, cross-threaded or loosely installed • Aftermarket EVAP parts that do not conform to specifications • Small holes or cuts in fuel vapor hoses or EVAP canister tubes • CV solenoid stays partially open when commanded closed • Loose fuel vapor hose/tube connections to EVAP components • EVAP component seals leaking (i.e., leaks in the Purge valve, fuel tank pressure sensor, canister vent solenoid, fuel vapor control valve tube assembly or fuel vapor vent valve) • TSB 03-9-8 contains a repair procedure for this trouble code • TSB 3-20-3 contains a repair procedure for this trouble code
DTC: P1443 **2T EVAP, MIL: Yes** **Years:** 2005, 2006, 2007 **Models:** All Models **Engines:** All **Transmissions:** All	**EVAP Canister Purge System Malfunction** Engine started, engine warmup completed engine running at a steady cruise speed, and the PCM detected a leak or blockage was present somewhere in the vapor line between the intake manifold, EVAP purge valve and the charcoal canister during the Continuous self test. **Possible Causes:** • EVAP canister purge valve is damaged or has failed • PF sensor is out-of-calibration or it is "skewed" • PCM has failed
DTC: P1443 **2T EVAP, MIL: Yes** **Years:** 2005, 2006, 2007 **Models:** All Models **Engines:** All **Transmissions:** All	**Low Purge Flow Or No Purge Flow Condition Detected** ECT sensor less than 90°F at startup (cold engine), engine running at a steady cruise speed, and the PCM detected a fuel tank pressure change occurred of more than −7" H2O within 30 seconds with the purge flow less than 0.02 pounds per minute during testing. **Possible Causes:** • EVAP canister purge valve stuck closed (mechanically) • Fuel vapor hose blocked between EVAP purge valve and FTP sensor, or blocked between purge valve and intake manifold, or vacuum hose blocked between purge valve and intake manifold
DTC: P1444 **2T CCM, MIL: Yes** **Years:** 2005, 2006, 2007 **Models:** All Models **Engines:** All **Transmissions:** All	**Purge Flow Sensor Circuit Low Input** Key on or engine running; and the PCM detected the Purge Flow (PF) sensor signal was less than the minimum calibrated limit of 0.40v during the Continuous self test. **Possible Causes:** • PF sensor signal circuit is shorted to sensor or chassis ground • PF sensor is damaged or has failed • PCM has failed
DTC: P1445 **2T CCM, MIL: Yes** **Years:** 2005, 2006, 2007 **Models:** All Models **Engines:** All **Transmissions:** All	**Purge Flow Sensor Circuit High Input** Key on or engine running; and the PCM detected the Purge Flow (PF) sensor was more than the maximum calibrated limit of 4.80v. **Possible Causes:** • PF sensor signal circuit shorted to VREF or power (VPWR) • PF sensor signal circuit open or sensor ground circuit open • PF sensor is damaged or has failed • PCM has failed
DTC: P1450 **2T EVAP, MIL: Yes** **Years:** 2005, 2006, 2007 **Models:** All Models **Engines:** All **Transmissions:** All	**Unable to Bleed Up Fuel Tank Vacuum** ECT sensor less than 90°F at startup (cold engine), engine running at a steady cruise speed, and the PCM detected a high fuel tank vacuum condition was present during the EVAP test. **Possible Causes:** • CV solenoid is stuck partially or fully open or filter is plugged • EVAP canister tube or EVAP canister purge outlet tube blocked or kinked between fuel tank, purge valve and EVAP canister • Fuel filler cap stuck closed (vacuum relief cannot occur) • Contaminated fuel vapor elbow at the EVAP canister, or the EVAP canister is restricted or canister purge valve stuck open

DTC	Trouble Code Title, Conditions & Possible Causes
DTC: P1450 **2T EVAP, MIL: Yes** **Years:** 2005, 2006, 2007 **Models:** All Models **Engines:** All **Transmissions:** All	**Unable to Bleed Up Fuel Tank Vacuum** ECT sensor less than 90°F at startup (cold engine), engine running at a steady cruise speed, and the PCM detected a high fuel tank vacuum condition was present during the EVAP test. **Possible Causes:** • CV solenoid is stuck partially or fully open or filter is plugged • EVAP canister tube or EVAP canister purge outlet tube blocked or kinked between fuel tank, purge valve and EVAP canister • Fuel filler cap stuck closed (vacuum relief cannot occur) • Contaminated fuel vapor elbow at the EVAP canister, or the EVAP canister is restricted or canister purge valve stuck open • FTP sensor is damaged
DTC: P1451 **2T CCM, MIL: Yes** **Years:** 2005, 2006, 2007 **Models:** All Models **Engines:** All **Transmissions:** All	**EVAP System Canister Vent Solenoid Circuit Malfunction** Engine started, engine running at a steady cruise speed, canister vent solenoid enabled, and the PCM detected an unexpected voltage condition on the Canister Vent solenoid circuit. **Possible Causes:** • CV solenoid circuit is open, shorted to ground or system power • CV solenoid is damaged or has failed • PCM has failed
DTC: P1452 **2T CCM, MIL: Yes** **Years:** 2005, 2006, 2007 **Models:** All Models **Engines:** All **Transmissions:** All	**Fuel Tank Pressure Sensor Circuit Malfunction** Key on or engine running; and the PCM detected that the Fuel Tank Pressure (FTP) sensor signal was less than or more than the calibrated amount during the self-test. Note that the FTP V PID should read from 2.40-2.80 with the cap off. **Possible Causes:** • FTP sensor signal circuit is open or shorted to ground • FTP sensor ground return circuit is open • FTP sensor is damaged or has failed • PCM has failed
DTC: P1455 **2T EVAP, MIL: Yes** **Years:** 2005, 2006, 2007 **Models:** All Models **Engines:** All **Transmissions:** All	**EVAP System Gross Leak Detected** ECT sensor less than 90°F at startup (cold engine), engine running at a steady cruise speed for 2-3 minutes, and the PCM detected a gross leak in the EVAP system during the test. **Possible Causes:** • Fuel filler cap missing, loose (not tightened) or the wrong part • FTP sensor signal circuit open or sensor ground circuit open • FTP sensor ground circuit open • FTP sensor is damaged or has failed • PCM has failed
DTC: P1460 **1T CCM, MIL: Yes** **Years:** 2005, 2006, 2007 **Models:** All Models **Engines:** All **Transmissions:** All	**Wide Open Throttle A/C Cutout Relay Circuit Malfunction** Key on, and the PCM detected a malfunction in the A/C wide-open throttle (WOT) circuit during the test. **Note: If this code sets on vehicles without an A/C system, ignore this code.** **Possible Causes:** • WOT A/C Relay control circuit is open or shorted to ground • WOT A/C Relay VREF circuit is open • WOT A/C Relay is damaged or has failed • PCM has failed
DTC: P1461 **2T CCM, MIL: Yes** **Years:** 2005, 2006, 2007 **Models:** All Models **Engines:** All **Transmissions:** All	**A/C Pressure Sensor Circuit High Input** Engine started, and the PCM detected the A/C Pressure sensor signal was over the test limit. **Possible Causes:** • ACP sensor circuit shorted to VREF or to power (VPWR) • ACP sensor circuit is open, or the ground circuit is open • ACP sensor is damaged or has failed • PCM has failed
DTC: P1462 **2T CCM, MIL: Yes** **Years:** 2005, 2006, 2007 **Models:** All Models **Engines:** All **Transmissions:** All	**A/C Pressure Sensor Circuit Low Input** Engine started, and the PCM detected the A/C Pressure sensor signal was under the test limit. **Possible Causes:** • ACP sensor circuit shorted to VREF or to power (VPWR) • ACP sensor circuit is open, or the ground circuit is open • ACP sensor is damaged or has failed • PCM has failed

DTC	Trouble Code Title, Conditions & Possible Causes
DTC: P1463 **2T CCM, MIL:** Yes **Years:** 2005, 2006, 2007 **Models:** All Models **Engines:** All **Transmissions:** All	**A/C Pressure Sensor Insufficient Pressure Change** Engine started, and with the A/C compressor operating, the PCM detected the A/C refrigerant pressure did not change as the compressor cycled during the self-test period. **Possible Causes:** • A/C system mechanical failure, or A/C clutch always engaged • ACP sensor signal open, or sensor ground circuit open • A/C sensor is damaged or the PCM has failed
DTC: P1464 **1T CCM, MIL:** No **Years:** 2005, 2006, 2007 **Models:** All Models **Engines:** All **Transmissions:** All	**A/C Demand Out of Self-Test Range** Key on, KOEO Self-Test enabled, or with the engine running, KOER Self-Test enabled, and the PCM detected the A/C demand switch signal was high during the self-test period. **Possible Causes:** • A/C switch was left "on" during the KOER self-test • A/C PWR circuit is shorted to power (N/C WAC relay contacts) • ACCS circuit is shorted to power • A/C Demand Switch, WAC relay or CCRM is damaged
DTC: P1469 **2T CCM, MIL:** Yes **Years:** 2005, 2006, 2007 **Models:** All Models **Engines:** All **Transmissions:** All	**Low A/C Cycling Period** Engine started, and with the A/C selected, PCM detected frequent cycling of the A/C compressor clutch. This test was designed to protect the transmission. In some strategies, the PCM will unlock the torque converter during A/C clutch engagement. If a concern is present that results in frequent A/C clutch cycling, damage could occur if the torque converter was cycled at these intervals. This test will detect this condition, set the code and prevent the torque converter from excessive cycling. **Possible Causes:** • Cycling pressure switch circuit open between pin 41 (ACCS) and the PCM, or the IGN RUN circuit is open to the cycling pressure switch circuit (if applicable) • Mechanical A/C system concern (i.e., low refrigerant charge, damaged A/C switch)
DTC: P1473 **2T CCM, MIL:** Yes **Years:** 2005, 2006, 2007 **Models:** All Models **Engines:** All **Transmissions:** All	**Fan Secondary High with Fan(s) Off** Key on, KOEO Self-Test enabled, and the PCM detected an unexpected voltage condition on the Power-To-Cooling fan circuit **Possible Causes:** • Power-to-Cooling fan circuit open in the wiring harness • Power-to-Cooling fan circuit shorted to power in wiring harness • Cooling fan motor windings open, or fan ground circuit is open • VLCM is damaged or has failed
DTC: P1474 **2T CCM, MIL:** Yes **Years:** 2005, 2006, 2007 **Models:** LS **Engines:** 3.0L VIN S, 3.9L VIN A **Transmissions:** All	**Hydraulic Cooling Fan Primary Circuit Malfunction** Key on or engine running; hydraulic cooling fan "on", and the PCM detected an unexpected voltage (too high or too low) condition on the Hydraulic Cooling Fan (HFC) motor circuit. **Possible Causes:** • HCF control circuit is open or shorted to ground • HCF control circuit is shorted to power (VPWR) • HCF motor is damaged or has failed • PCM has failed
DTC: P1474 **2T CCM, MIL:** Yes **Years:** 2005, 2006, 2007 **Models:** All Models Except LS **Engines:** All **Transmissions:** All	**Hydraulic Cooling Fan Primary Circuit Malfunction** Key on or engine running; low cooling fan enabled, and the PCM detected the voltage to the Hydraulic Cooling Fan (HFC) motor was higher or lower than the expected range for the fan primary circuit. **Possible Causes:** • FC circuit is open or shorted to power • LFC circuit is open or shorted to power (CCRM models) • FC or LFC relay VPWR circuit is open (Start/Run on Probe)
DTC: P1477 **2T CCM, MIL:** Yes **Years:** 2005, 2006, 2007 **Models:** All Models **Engines:** All **Transmissions:** All	**Medium Fan Control Primary Circuit Malfunction** Key on, medium cooling fan (MFC) enabled; and the PCM detected excessive current draw in the circuit; or with the MFC disabled (off), it detected voltage present on the MFC circuit. **Possible Causes:** • MFC circuit is open • MFC relay circuit to IGN START/RUN is open • MFC relay is damaged or has failed • PCM has failed

DTC	Trouble Code Title, Conditions & Possible Causes
DTC: P1479 **2T CCM, MIL: Yes** **Years:** 2005, 2006, 2007 **Models:** All Models **Engines:** All **Transmissions:** All	**High Fan Control Primary Circuit Malfunction** Key on, high cooling fan (HFC) enabled, and the PCM detected excessive current draw in the circuit; or with the HFC commanded off, it detected voltage present on the HFC circuit. **Possible Causes:** • HFC circuit is open • HFC circuit is shorted to ground • HFC relay power circuit (VPWR) is open • High speed FC relay is damaged or it has failed • PCM has failed
DTC: P1481 **2T CCM, MIL: Yes** **Years:** 2005, 2006, 2007 **Models:** All Models **Engines:** All **Transmissions:** All	**Fan Secondary Low With High Fan On** Key on or engine running; high speed cooling fan enabled, and the PCM detected the fan secondary circuit was low with the High Speed cooling fan commanded "on" during testing. **Possible Causes:** • High speed cooling fan circuit is open • High speed cooling fan circuit is shorted to ground • High speed cooling fan relay power circuit (VPWR) is open • High speed FC relay is damaged or has failed • PCM has failed
DTC: P1483 **2T CCM, MIL: Yes** **Years:** 2005, 2006, 2007 **Models:** All Models **Engines:** All **Transmissions:** All	**Power To Fan Circuit Over-Current Detected** Key on or engine running; cooling fan enabled, and the PCM detected the current in the Fan PWR circuit exceeded the limit. **Possible Causes:** • Power-to-Cooling Fan circuit shorted to ground • Cooling fan motor is damaged or has failed • VLCM is damaged or has failed • PCM has failed
DTC: P1500 **2T CCM, MIL: Yes** **Years:** 2005, 2006, 2007 **Models:** All Models **Engines:** All **Transmissions:** All	**VSS Signal Or POSM Signal Intermittent** Engine running in gear with a VSS signal present, and the PCM detected that the VSS signal was intermittent **Note: The VSS signal is received from the VSS, transfer case speed sensor, ABS Control module, the GEM or the Central Timer module (CTM), depending upon the vehicle application.** **Possible Causes:** • VSS pins damaged, loose or pushed in at the connector • VSS circuit open or shorted in the wiring harness (insulation) • VSS wiring harness routing incorrect or VSS mounting incorrect • TSB 01-21-13 contains a repair procedure for this trouble code
DTC: P1501 **1T CCM, MIL: No** **Years:** 2005, 2006, 2007 **Models:** All Models **Engines:** All **Transmissions:** All	**VSS Signal Out Of Self-Test Range** Engine started, KOER Self-Test enabled, and the PCM detected a VSS signal during the self-test (i.e., with the vehicle not moving). **Possible Causes:** • VSS signal is noisy due to Radio Frequency Interference/ Electro-Magnetic Interference (RFI/EMI) from outside devices (ignition wires, charging circuit or aftermarket devices)
DTC: P1501 **1T CCM, MIL: Yes** **Years:** 2005, 2006, 2007 **Models:** All Models **Engines:** All **Transmissions:** All	**VSS Signal Intermittent** Engine started, and the PCM detected the VSS signal dropped out. The TCIL will flash on the first trip this code sets. The speed signal is received from the VSS, transfer case speed sensor, ABS Control module, GEM or the Central Timer module (depends upon the vehicle). **Possible Causes:** • VSS signal is noisy due to Radio Frequency Interference/ Electro-Magnetic Interference (RFI/EMI) from outside devices (ignition wires, charging circuit or aftermarket devices)
DTC: P1502 **1T CCM, MIL: Yes** **Years:** 2005, 2006, 2007 **Models:** All Models **Engines:** All **Transmissions:** All	**VSS Signal Intermittent** Engine started, and the PCM detected an intermittent VSS signal. The TCIL will flash on the first trip that this code is set. The VSS signal is received from the VSS, transfer case speed sensor, ABS Control module, GEM or the Central Timer module (depends upon the vehicle). **Possible Causes:** • VSS+ or VSS− harness circuit is open • TCSS signal or TCSS signal return harness circuit is open • VSS harness circuit, TCSS harness circuit is shorted to ground • VSS harness circuit, CSS harness circuit is shorted to power • VSS circuit open between the PCM and related control module • VSS or TCSS, or wheel speed sensors circuits are damaged • Modules connected to VSC/VSS harness circuits are damaged • Mechanical drive mechanism for the VSS or TCSS is damaged

DTC	Trouble Code Title, Conditions & Possible Causes
DTC: P1504 **2T CCM, MIL: Yes** **Years:** 2005, 2006, 2007 **Models:** All Models **Engines:** All **Transmissions:** All	**Idle Air Control Circuit Malfunction** Engine started, engine running for 1 minute, and the PCM detected an electrical load failure on the IAC motor circuit during the self-test. **Possible Causes:** • IAC circuit is open, shorted to ground or to the VPWR circuit • IAC solenoid VPWR circuit is open • IAC valve is damaged or has failed • PCM has failed
DTC: P1505 **2T CCM, MIL: Yes** **Years:** 2005, 2006, 2007 **Models:** All Models **Engines:** All **Transmissions:** All	**Idle Air Control System At Adaptive Clip** Engine running for over one minute, and the PCM detected the idle speed control had reached its "idle air trim limit" during the Continuous self test. **Possible Causes:** • Base engine air leaks are present • Air cleaner element is dirty, plugged or restricted • Throttle body/linkage is binding • IAC valve body is damaged or contaminated • Throttle body is damaged
DTC: P1506 **2T CCM, MIL: Yes** **Years:** 2005, 2006, 2007 **Models:** All Models **Engines:** All **Transmissions:** All	**Idle Air Control Overspeed Error** Engine started, engine running for 1 minute, and the PCM detected the idle speed was more than the desired engine Target Idle Speed. **Possible Causes:** • Base engine vacuum leaks present • EVAP system has a problem • IAC circuit shorted to ground • IAC valve is stuck open, or it is damaged • Throttle body or throttle plate is contaminated or very dirty
DTC: P1507 **2T CCM, MIL: Yes** **Years:** 2005, 2006, 2007 **Models:** All Models **Engines:** All **Transmissions:** All	**Idle Air Control Underspeed Error** Engine started, engine running for 1 minute, and the PCM detected the idle speed was less than the desired engine Target Idle Speed. **Possible Causes:** • Air inlet is plugged or the air filter element is severely clogged • IAC circuit is open, or shorted to the VPWR circuit • IAC circuit VPWR circuit is open • IAC solenoid is damaged or has failed • Throttle body or throttle plate is contaminated or very dirty
DTC: P1512 **2T CCM, MIL: Yes** **Years:** 2005, 2006, 2007 **Models:** All Models **Engines:** All **Transmissions:** All	**Intake Manifold Runner Control System Malfunction** Engine started, and the PCM detected the IMRC Monitor indicated that the IMRC was stuck closed during the Continuous self test. **Possible Causes:** • Leaky vacuum reservoir, vacuum lines loose or damaged • Vacuum solenoid or vacuum actuator is damaged • IMRC actuator cable/gears are seized, or the cables are improperly routed or seized • IMRC housing return springs are damaged or disconnected • Lever/shaft return stop may be obstructed or bent, or the lever/shaft wide open stop may be obstructed or bent, or the IMRC lever/shaft may be sticking, binding or disconnected • IMRC control circuit open, shorted or the VPWR circuit is open • PCM has failed
DTC: P1513 **2T CCM, MIL: Yes** **Years:** 2005, 2006, 2007 **Models:** All Models **Engines:** All **Transmissions:** All	**Intake Manifold Runner Control Malfunction (Bank 1)** Engine started, and the PCM detected the IMRC Monitor indicated the IMRC was not functioning correctly during the self-test period. **Possible Causes:** • IMRC actuator cable/gears are seized, or the cables are improperly routed or seized • IMRC control circuit open, shorted or the VPWR circuit is open • IMRC housing return springs are damaged or disconnected • Leaky vacuum reservoir, vacuum lines loose or damaged • Lever/shaft return stop may be obstructed or bent, or the lever/shaft wide open stop may be obstructed or bent, or the IMRC lever/shaft may be sticking, binding or disconnected • Vacuum solenoid or vacuum actuator is damaged • PCM has failed

DTC	Trouble Code Title, Conditions & Possible Causes

DTC: P1516
2T CCM, MIL: Yes
Years: 2005, 2006, 2007
Models: All Models
Engines: All
Transmissions: All
	Intake Manifold Runner Control Input Error (Bank 1)
	Key on or engine running; and the PCM detected the IMRC Monitor signal for Bank 1 was outside of its expected calibrated range during the Continuous self test.
	Possible Causes:
	  • IMRC mechanical fault - the linkage may be bound or seized
	  • Inspect for binding or improper routing. The cable core wire at the IMRC/IMSC housing attachment must have slack and lever must contact close plate stop screw

DTC: P1517
2T CCM, MIL: Yes
Years: 2005, 2006, 2007
Models: All Models
Engines: All
Transmissions: All
	Intake Manifold Runner Control Input Error (Bank 2)
	Key on or engine running; and the PCM detected the IMRC Monitor signal for Bank 2 was outside of its expected calibrated range during the Continuous self test.
	Possible Causes:
	  • IMRC mechanical fault - the linkage may be bound or seized
	  • Visually inspect for binding or improper routing. The cable core wire at the IMRC or IMSC housing attachment must have slack and lever must contact close plate stop screw

DTC: P1518
2T CCM, MIL: Yes
Years: 2005, 2006, 2007
Models: All Models
Engines: All
Transmissions: All
	Intake Manifold Runner Control Malfunction (Stuck Open)
	Engine started, and the PCM detected the IMRC Monitor signal was less than its expected calibrated range at closed throttle. An IMRCM PID of 1v at closed throttle indicates a fault.
	Possible Causes:
	  • IMRC monitor signal circuit shorted to power ground
	  • IMRC Monitor signal circuit shorted to signal ground (return)
	  • IMRC actuator is damaged or has failed
	  • PCM has failed

DTC: P1519
2T CCM, MIL: Yes
Years: 2005, 2006, 2007
Models: All Models
Engines: All
Transmissions: All
	Intake Manifold Runner Control Stuck Closed
	Key on, and the PCM detected the IMRC Monitor was more than the expected calibrated range at closed throttle.
	Note: An IMRCM PID of VREF at 3000 rpm may indicate a fault.
	Possible Causes:
	  • IMRC monitor signal circuit shorted to power ground
	  • IMRC Monitor signal circuit shorted to signal ground (return)
	  • IMRC actuator is damaged or has failed (e.g., there may be a small leak in the vacuum diaphragm of the actuator)
	  • PCM has failed

DTC: P1520
2T CCM, MIL: Yes
Years: 2005, 2006, 2007
Models: All Models
Engines: All
Transmissions: All
	Intake Manifold Runner Control Input Error
	Key on or engine running; and the PCM detected the IMRC Monitor signal for was outside of its expected calibrated range. Use the Active Command or Output State Control on a Generic Scan Tool to help determine if an electrical fault is present.
	Possible Causes:
	  • IMRC control circuit is open or shorted to ground
	  • IMRC Monitor VREF circuit is open
	  • IMRC is damaged or the PCM has failed

DTC: P1530
2T CCM, MIL: Yes
Years: 2005, 2006, 2007
Models: All Models
Engines: All
Transmissions: All
	Air Conditioning Clutch Circuit Malfunction
	Key on or engine running; and the PCM detected a circuit fault in the A/C Clutch power (Power To Clutch) circuit.
	Possible Causes:
	  • A/C Clutch power circuit open or shorted to VPWR in harness
	  • A/C clutch ground circuit is open
	  • A/C clutch is open
	  • VLCM is damaged or has failed

DTC: P1537
2T CCM, MIL: Yes
Years: 2005, 2006, 2007
Models: All Models
Engines: All
Transmissions: All
	Intake Manifold Runner Control Malfunction (Bank 1 Stuck Open)
	Key on or engine running; and the PCM detected the Bank 1 IMRC Monitor signal was less than its expected calibrated range at closed throttle (it may be stuck in open position). An IMRCM PID of 1v at closed throttle may indicate a fault is present.
	Possible Causes:
	  • IMRC monitor signal circuit shorted to power ground
	  • IMRC Monitor signal circuit shorted to signal ground (return)
	  • IMRC actuator is damaged or the PCM has failed

DTC: P1538
2T CCM, MIL: Yes
Years: 2005, 2006, 2007
Models: All Models
Engines: All
Transmissions: All
	Intake Manifold Runner Control Stuck Open (Bank 2)
	Key on or engine running; and the PCM detected the Bank 2 IMRC Monitor signal was more than its expected calibrated range at closed throttle (it may be stuck in open position). An IMRCM PID of VREF at 3000 rpm may indicate a fault is present.
	Possible Causes:
	  • IMRC monitor signal circuit shorted to power ground
	  • IMRC Monitor signal circuit shorted to signal ground (return)
	  • IMRC actuator is damaged or has failed
	  • PCM has failed

DTC	Trouble Code Title, Conditions & Possible Causes
DTC: P1539 **2T CCM, MIL: No** **Years:** 2005, 2006, 2007 **Models:** All Models **Engines:** All **Transmissions:** All	**Power To A/C Clutch Circuit Over-Current** Key on or engine running; and with the A/C switch "on", the PCM detected the current in the A/C Clutch power (PWR) circuit exceeded the normal current level during the self-test. **Possible Causes:** • A/C Clutch power circuit open or shorted to VPWR in harness • A/C clutch ground circuit is open • A/C clutch is open • VLCM is damaged or has failed
DTC: P1549 **1T CCM, MIL: No** **Years:** 2005, 2006, 2007 **Models:** Ranger **Engines:** 2.3L VIN D **Transmissions:** All	**Intake Manifold Tuning Valve Circuit Malfunction** Key on or engine running and the PCM detected an unexpected voltage on the Intake Manifold Tuning Valve (IMTV) during testing. An IMT valve (IMTVF) PID of YES status indicates a fault is present. **Possible Causes:** • IMTV circuit is open or shorted to ground • IMTV power circuit (VPWR) is open • IMTV assembly is damaged or it has failed • PCM has failed
DTC: P1549 **1T CCM, MIL: No** **Years:** 2005, 2006, 2007 **Models:** Excursion, LS, Sable, Taurus **Engines:** 3.0L VIN S, 5.4L VIN L, **Transmissions:** All	**Intake Manifold Runner Control Circuit Malfunction** Key on or engine running and the PCM detected an unexpected voltage on the Intake Manifold Runner Control (IMRC) during testing. An IMRC valve PID of YES status indicates a fault is present. **Possible Causes:** • IMRC circuit is open or shorted to ground • IMRC power circuit (VPWR) is open • IMRC assembly is damaged or it has failed • PCM has failed
DTC: P1549 **1T CCM, MIL: No** **Years:** 2005, 2006, 2007 **Models:** Ranger Models with a 2.3L VIN D engine **Engines:** **Transmissions:** All	**Intake Manifold Swirl Control Circuit Malfunction** Key on or engine running and the PCM detected an unexpected voltage on the Intake Manifold Swirl Control (IMSC) circuit. An IMSC valve PID of YES status indicates a fault. **Possible Causes:** • IMSC circuit is open or shorted to ground • IMSC power circuit (VPWR) is open • IMSC assembly is damaged or the PCM has failed
DTC: P1550 **1T CCM, MIL: No** **Years:** 2005, 2006, 2007 **Models:** All Models **Engines:** All **Transmissions:** All	**Power Steering Pressure Switch Circuit Malfunction** KOER Self-Test enabled, and the PCM detected the PSP switch signal did not change during the self-test. This code indicates the PSP input is out of its self-test range. **Possible Causes:** • PSP switch circuit open or shorted, or the ground circuit open • Steering wheel was not rotated during the KOER Self-Test • PCM has failed
DTC: P1572 **2T CCM, MIL: Yes** **Years:** 2005, 2006, 2007 **Models:** All Models **Engines:** All **Transmissions:** All	**Brake Pedal Switch Circuit Malfunction** Engine started, and the PCM detected the Brake Pedal switch and Brake Pressure switch inputs failed the Rationality test (i.e., one or both of these inputs did not change as expected). DTC P1572 is set when the PCM does not see the proper sequence of the brake pedal input signal from both the BPP and BPA when the brake pedal is pressed and released. **Possible Causes:** • BPP or BPA switches are out of adjustment (one or both) • Blown fuse to switch power circuit • BPP switch or BPA switch is damaged (one or both) • BPP or BPA switch circuit is open or shorted • PCM has failed
DTC: P1605 **1T PCM, MIL: Yes** **Years:** 2005, 2006, 2007 **Models:** All Models **Engines:** All **Transmissions:** All	**PCM Keep Alive Memory Test Error** Key on, and the PCM detected an internal memory fault. This code can be set if KAPWR to the PCM is interrupted. This trouble code will set at first key on if a battery circuit is opened. **Possible Causes:** • Battery terminals loose or corroded (high resistance in circuit) • Keep Alive Memory circuit to PCM interrupted or open • Reprogramming function not performed • PCM has failed

DTC	Trouble Code Title, Conditions & Possible Causes
DTC: P1633 **1T PCM, MIL: Yes** **Years:** 2005, 2006, 2007 **Models:** All Models **Engines:** All **Transmissions:** All	**PCM Keep Alive Memory Voltage Too Low** Key on, and the PCM detected that the KAM power circuit to the battery was interrupted. **Possible Causes:** • KAPWR circuit has been interrupted (this problem may be an intermittent condition) • PCM has failed
DTC: P1635 **1T PCM, MIL: Yes** **Years:** 2005, 2006, 2007 **Models:** All Models **Engines:** All **Transmissions:** All	**Tire Axle/Ratio Out Of Acceptable Range** Key on, and the PCM detected the tire and axle information in the VID Block does not match the vehicle hardware. **Note: This code indicates that the PCM needs to be reprogrammed.** **Possible Causes:** • Incorrect tire size or Incorrect axle ratio • Incorrect VID configuration parameters • PCM need to be reprogrammed • TSB 02-23-4 contains repair information for this trouble code
DTC: P1636 **1T PCM, MIL: Yes** **Years:** 2005, 2006, 2007 **Models:** All Models **Engines:** All **Transmissions:** All	**Inductive Signature Chip Communication Error** Key on, and the PCM determined it had lost communication with the Inductive Signature Chip. The PCM has internal damage when this trouble code is present. **Possible Causes:** • PCM has failed and needs to be replaced
DTC: P1639 **1T PCM, MIL: Yes** **Years:** 2005, 2006, 2007 **Models:** All Models **Engines:** All **Transmissions:** All	**Vehicle ID Block Not Programmed Or Is Corrupt** Key on, and the PCM determined the Vehicle ID Block information was incorrect. **Possible Causes:** • PCM may not be the correct application • PCM may need to be reprogrammed • VID configuration may not be correct • TSB 02-23-4 contains repair information for this trouble code
DTC: P1640 **1T PCM, MIL: Yes** **Years:** 2005, 2006, 2007 **Models:** All Models **Engines:** All **Transmissions:** All	**PCM Trouble Codes Available In Another Module** Engine started, and the PCM received a request from another module to turn on the MIL due to a fault that could affect emissions. **Note: Vehicles using a secondary Engine Control Module can request that the PCM turn on the Check Engine Light when a failure occurs that could affect emissions. Request PID 0946 to determine which module made the request. Then select that module to read the related trouble code(s).** **Possible Causes:** • Trouble codes are stored in a secondary module, which in turn, requested that the PCM turn on the MIL when this code is set.
DTC: P1650 **2T CCM, MIL: Yes** **Years:** 2005, 2006, 2007 **Models:** All Models **Engines:** All **Transmissions:** All	**Power Steering Pressure Switch Circuit Malfunction** Engine started, and the PCM detected the PSP switch signal did not change after a certain number of vehicle speed transitions. The PCM counts the number of times that the vehicle speed transitions from 0 mph to a calibrated speed. The PCM expects the PSP switch input to change after a certain number of transitions. **Possible Causes:** • Steering wheel must be turned during the KOER Self-Test • PSP switch/shorting bar is damaged • PSP signal circuit is open or shorted to ground • PSP switch ground (return) circuit is open • PCM has failed
DTC: P1651 **2T CCM, MIL: Yes** **Years:** 2005, 2006, 2007 **Models:** All Models **Engines:** All **Transmissions:** All	**Power Steering Pressure Switch Circuit Malfunction** Engine started, and the PCM detected the PSP switch signal did not change after a certain number of vehicle speed transitions. **Note: The PCM counts the number of times that the vehicle speed transitions from 0 mph to a calibrated speed. The PCM expects the PSP switch input to change after a certain number of transitions.** **Possible Causes:** • Steering wheel must be turned during the KOER Self-Test • PSP switch/shorting bar is damaged • PSP signal circuit is open or shorted to ground • PSP switch ground (return) circuit is open • PCM has failed

DTC	Trouble Code Title, Conditions & Possible Causes
DTC: P1700 **1T CCM, MIL: No** **Years:** 2005, 2006, 2007 **Models:** All Models **Engines:** All **Transmissions:** A/T	**Transaxle Mechanical Malfunction** Engine started, vehicle driven in gear, and the PCM detected a transmission mechanical fault. **Possible Causes:** • This code can set due to low transmission fluid level • Refer to the appropriate Transmission Repair Manual or information in electronic media to perform a complete diagnosis of the automatic transmission when this code is set
DTC: P1701 **1T CCM, MIL: No** **Years:** 2005, 2006, 2007 **Models:** All Models **Engines:** All **Transmissions:** A/T	**Reverse Engagement Error** Engine started, and the PCM detected a Transmission Range (TR) sensor signal that indicated a reverse engagement error. **Possible Causes:** • Refer to the appropriate Transmission Repair Manual or information in electronic media to perform a complete diagnosis of the automatic transmission when this code is set
DTC: P1702 **1T CCM, MIL: No** **Years:** 2005, 2006, 2007 **Models:** All Models **Engines:** All **Transmissions:** A/T	**TR Sensor Signal Intermittent** Key on or engine running; and the PCM detected the failure Trouble Code Conditions for DTC P0705 or P0708 were met intermittently. **Possible Causes:** • Refer to the appropriate Transmission Repair Manual or information in electronic media to perform a complete diagnosis of the automatic transmission when this code is set
DTC: P1703 **1T CCM, MIL: No** **Years:** 2005, 2006, 2007 **Models:** All Models **Engines:** All **Transmissions:** A/T	**Brake Switch Circuit Out of Self-Test Range** Key on, KOEO Self-Test enabled; and the PCM detected the brake switch signal was high, or with the KOER Self-Test enabled, the PCM detected the switch signal did not cycle On / Off. **Possible Causes:** • BPP switch circuit open or shorted • Brake Switch is misadjusted, damaged or has failed • Stop lamp circuits open or shorted • Malfunction in the module(s) connected to BPP circuit (i.e., the Rear Electronic Module on Windstar and LS, or the Lighting Control Module on the Continental and Town Car) • PCM has failed
DTC: P1704 **1T CCM, MIL: No** **Years:** 2005, 2006, 2007 **Models:** All Models **Engines:** All **Transmissions:** A/T	**Transmission Range Sensor Circuit Out Of Self-Test Range** Key on, KOEO Self Test enabled, and the PCM detected a Transmission Range (TR) sensor signal occurred in between gear positions. **Possible Causes:** • Digital TR sensor or shift cable misadjusted • Digital TR sensor circuit is open or shorted to ground • Digital TR sensor has failed
DTC: P1705 **1T CCM, MIL: No** **Years:** 2005, 2006, 2007 **Models:** All Models **Engines:** All **Transmissions:** A/T	**Transmission Range Sensor Out of Self-Test Range** Key on, KOEO Self Test enabled, and the PCM detected it did not receive a Transmission Range (TR) sensor signal in Park or Neutral position. **Possible Causes:** • Gear selector not in Park or Neutral during the self-test • Digital TR sensor circuit is open or shorted to ground • Digital TR sensor has failed • PCM has failed
DTC: P1708 **1T CCM, MIL: Yes** **Years:** 2005, 2006, 2007 **Models:** All Models **Engines:** All **Transmissions:** A/T	**Digital Transmission Range Sensor Circuit Malfunction** Engine started, and the PCM detected it did not receive a change in the Digital Transmission Range (TR) sensor signal after the vehicle was driven in gear. **Possible Causes:** • Digital TR sensor circuit open • Digital TR sensor ground circuit open • Digital TR sensor is damaged or has failed • PCM has failed
DTC: P1709 **1T CCM, MIL: No** **Years:** 2005, 2006, 2007 **Models:** All Models **Engines:** All **Transmissions:** A/T	**PNP Switch Out Of Self-Test Range** Key on, KOEO Self-Test enabled, and the PCM detected the PNP switch was high when is should have been low (wrong gearshift position). **Possible Causes:** • PNP switch ground circuit is open • PNP switch circuit short to power (VPWR) • PNP switch is damaged or has failed • PCM has failed

DTC	Trouble Code Title, Conditions & Possible Causes
DTC: P1710 **2T CCM, MIL: Yes** **Years:** 2005, 2006, 2007 **Models:** All Models **Engines:** All **Transmissions:** A/T	**TFT Sensor In-Range Circuit Malfunction** Engine started, vehicle driven to a speed over 1 mph, TFT sensor signal in-range, and the PCM did not detect any change in the TFT signal in the self-test. **Possible Causes:** • Refer to the appropriate Transmission Repair Manual or information in electronic media to perform a complete diagnosis of the automatic transmission when this code is set
DTC: P1711 **1T CCM, MIL: No** **Years:** 2005, 2006, 2007 **Models:** All Models **Engines:** All **Transmissions:** A/T	**TFT Sensor Out of Self-Test Range** Key on, KOER Self Test enabled; or engine running with the KOER Self Test enabled, and the PCM detected the Transmission Fluid Temperature (TFT) sensor was more than or less than the calibrated range (25°F to 240°F) during the self-test. **Possible Causes:** • Refer to the appropriate Transmission Repair Manual or information in electronic media to perform a complete diagnosis of the automatic transmission when this code is set
DTC: P1712 **1T CCM, MIL: No** **Years:** 2005, 2006, 2007 **Models:** All Models **Engines:** All **Transmissions:** A/T	**TFT Sensor Circuit Low Input** Engine started, and the PCM detected the TFT sensor signal was less than 0.2v (equivalent to a temperature of more than 357°F). **Possible Causes:** • Refer to the appropriate Transmission Repair Manual or information in electronic media to perform a complete diagnosis of the automatic transmission when this code is set
DTC: P1713 **1T CCM, MIL: No** **Years:** 2005, 2006, 2007 **Models:** All Models **Engines:** All **Transmissions:** A/T	**TFT Sensor No Activity or TFT Sensor Circuit Low Input** Engine started, VSS over 1 mph, and the PCM did not detect any change in the TFT low range circuit during the self-test. **Possible Causes:** • Refer to the appropriate Transmission Repair Manual or information in electronic media to perform a complete diagnosis of the automatic transmission when this code is set
DTC: P1714 **1T CCM, MIL: Yes** **Years:** 2005, 2006, 2007 **Models:** All Models **Engines:** All **Transmissions:** A/T	**Transmission Control System Malfunction** Engine started, VSS over 1 mph, and the PCM did not detect any change in the TFT low range circuit during the self-test. **Possible Causes:** • Refer to the appropriate Transmission Repair Manual or information in electronic media to perform a complete diagnosis of the automatic transmission when this code is set
DTC: P1715 **1T CCM, MIL: Yes** **Years:** 2005, 2006, 2007 **Models:** All Models **Engines:** All **Transmissions:** A/T	**Transmission Control System Malfunction** Engine started, VSS over 1 mph, and the PCM detected a mechanical problem in the Shift Solenoid 'B' (SSB) during the test. **Possible Causes:** • Refer to the appropriate Transmission Repair Manual or information in electronic media to perform a complete diagnosis of the automatic transmission when this code is set
DTC: P1716 **2T CCM, MIL: No** **Years:** 2005, 2006, 2007 **Models:** All Models **Engines:** All **Transmissions:** A/T	**Transmission Control System Malfunction** Engine started, VSS over 1 mph, and the PCM detected a problem in the Transmission Control system during the self-test. **Possible Causes:** • Refer to the appropriate Transmission Repair Manual or information in electronic media to perform a complete diagnosis of the automatic transmission when this code is set
DTC: P1717 **1T CCM, MIL: No** **Years:** 2005, 2006, 2007 **Models:** All Models **Engines:** All **Transmissions:** A/T	**Transmission Control System Malfunction** Engine started, VSS over 1 mph, and the PCM detected a problem in the Transmission Control system during the self-test. **Possible Causes:** • Refer to the appropriate Transmission Repair Manual or information in electronic media to perform a complete diagnosis of the automatic transmission when this code is set
DTC: P1718 **1T CCM, MIL: No** **Years:** 2005, 2006, 2007 **Models:** All Models **Engines:** All **Transmissions:** A/T	**TFT Sensor No Activity Or TFT Sensor Circuit High Input** Engine started, VSS over 1 mph, and the PCM did not detect any change in the TFT high range circuit during the self-test. **Possible Causes:** • Refer to the appropriate Transmission Repair Manual or information in electronic media to perform a complete diagnosis of the automatic transmission when this code is set

DTC	Trouble Code Title, Conditions & Possible Causes
DTC: P1719 **1T CCM, MIL: No** **Years:** 2005, 2006, 2007 **Models:** All Models **Engines:** All **Transmissions:** A/T	**Transmission Control System Malfunction** Engine started, VSS over 1 mph, and the PCM detected a problem in the Transmission Control system during the self-test. **Possible Causes:** • Refer to the appropriate Transmission Repair Manual or information in electronic media to perform a complete diagnosis of the automatic transmission when this code is set
DTC: P1727 **1T CCM, MIL: No** **Years:** 2005, 2006, 2007 **Models:** All Models **Engines:** All **Transmissions:** A/T	**Transmission Coast Clutch Solenoid Slip Malfunction** Engine started, VSS over 1 mph in gear, and the PCM detected a signal that indicated the coast clutch solenoid had a slippage fault. **Possible Causes:** • Refer to the appropriate Transmission Repair Manual or information in electronic media to perform a complete diagnosis of the automatic transmission when this code is set
DTC: P1728 **1T CCM, MIL: No** **Years:** 2005, 2006, 2007 **Models:** All Models **Engines:** All **Transmissions:** A/T	**Transmission Slip Malfunction** Engine started, VSS over 1 mph in gear, and the PCM detected a signal that indicated the transmission was slipping while in gear. **Possible Causes:** • Refer to the appropriate Transmission Repair Manual or information in electronic media to perform a complete diagnosis of the automatic transmission when this code is set
DTC: P1729 **1T CCM, MIL: No** **Years:** 2005, 2006, 2007 **Models:** All Models **Engines:** All **Transmissions:** A/T	**4 x 4 Low Switch Circuit Malfunction** Engine started and the PCM detected the 4x4 switch did not go low after the switch was on. **Possible Causes:** • Speedometer out of calibration • 4x4L wiring harness is open or shorted, 4x4L switch is damaged or has failed • Electronic Shift Control Module is damaged or has failed, or the PCM has failed
DTC: P1740 **1T CCM, MIL: Yes** **Years:** 2005, 2006, 2007 **Models:** All Models **Engines:** All **Transmissions:** A/T	**TCC Solenoid Mechanical Malfunction** Engine started, vehicle speed more than 20 mph, and the PCM detected that TCC lockup did not occur (the lockup event is inferred from other inputs). **Possible Causes:** • Refer to the appropriate Transmission Repair Manual or information in electronic media to perform a complete diagnosis of the automatic transmission when this code is set
DTC: P1741 **1T CCM, MIL: No** **Years:** 2005, 2006, 2007 **Models:** All Models **Engines:** All **Transmissions:** A/T	**TCC Engagement Error** Engine started, vehicle in gear at Cruise speed, and the PCM detected an error due to excessive TCC engagement. **Note: This problem can cause speed changes or vehicle surges.** **Possible Causes:** • Refer to the appropriate Transmission Repair Manual or information in electronic media to perform a complete diagnosis of the automatic transmission when this code is set
DTC: P1742 **1T CCM, MIL: Yes** **Years:** 2005, 2006, 2007 **Models:** All Models **Engines:** All **Transmissions:** A/T	**TCC Solenoid Failed On (Electrical Or Mechanical Fault)** Engine started, vehicle in gear at Cruise speed, and the PCM detected that the Torque Converter Clutch system had failed "on". **Possible Causes:** • Refer to the appropriate Transmission Repair Manual or information in electronic media to perform a complete diagnosis of the automatic transmission when this code is set.
DTC: P1744 **1T CCM, MIL: Yes** **Years:** 2005, 2006, 2007 **Models:** All Models **Engines:** All **Transmissions:** A/T	**TCC System Mechanically Stuck In Off Position** Engine started, vehicle in gear at Cruise speed, and the PCM detected the Torque Converter Clutch system had failed with the TCC in the mechanically "off" position. **Possible Causes:** • Refer to the appropriate Transmission Repair Manual or information in electronic media to perform a complete diagnosis of the automatic transmission when this code is set.
DTC: P1746 **1T CCM, MIL: No** **Years:** 2005, 2006, 2007 **Models:** All Models **Engines:** All **Transmissions:** A/T	**EPC Solenoid Circuit Malfunction** Engine started, vehicle in gear, and the PCM detected the Electronic Pressure Control (EPC) solenoid circuit indicated "open". This fault can cause harsh engagements and shifts. **Possible Causes:** • Refer to the appropriate Transmission Repair Manual or information in electronic media to perform a complete diagnosis of the automatic transmission when this code is set

DTC	Trouble Code Title, Conditions & Possible Causes
DTC: P1747 **1T CCM, MIL: No** **Years:** 2005, 2006, 2007 **Models:** All Models **Engines:** All **Transmissions:** A/T	**A/T EPC Solenoid Circuit Malfunction** Engine started, vehicle in gear at Cruise speed, and the PCM detected a shorted output driver or the TCC solenoid was shorted. **Possible Causes:** • Refer to the appropriate Transmission Repair Manual or information in electronic media to perform a complete diagnosis of the automatic transmission when this code is set.
DTC: P1749 **1T CCM, MIL: No** **Years:** 2005, 2006, 2007 **Models:** All Models **Engines:** All **Transmissions:** A/T	**A/T EPC Solenoid Failed Low** Engine started, vehicle in gear at Cruise speed, and the PCM detected the Torque Converter Clutch solenoid had failed "low". **Possible Causes:** • Refer to the appropriate Transmission Repair Manual or information in electronic media to perform a complete diagnosis of the automatic transmission when this code is set.
DTC: P1751 **1T CCM, MIL: No** **Years:** 2005, 2006, 2007 **Models:** All Models **Engines:** All **Transmissions:** A/T	**A/T Shift Solenoid 1 Performance** Engine started, vehicle in gear at Cruise speed, and the PCM detected a mechanical fault in the Shift Solenoid 1 (SS1) operation. **Possible Causes:** • Refer to the appropriate Transmission Repair Manual or information in electronic media to perform a complete diagnosis of the automatic transmission when this code is set.
DTC: P1754 **1T CCM, MIL: No** **Years:** 2005, 2006, 2007 **Models:** All Models **Engines:** All **Transmissions:** A/T	**A/T Coast Clutch Solenoid Circuit Malfunction** Engine started, vehicle in gear at Cruise speed, and the PCM detected an unexpected voltage condition on the Coast Clutch Solenoid (CCS) circuit during the CCM test period. **Possible Causes:** • Refer to the appropriate Transmission Repair Manual or information in electronic media to perform a complete diagnosis of the automatic transmission when this code is set.
DTC: P1756 **1T CCM, MIL: No** **Years:** 2005, 2006, 2007 **Models:** All Models **Engines:** All **Transmissions:** A/T	**A/T Shift Solenoid 2 Performance** Engine started, vehicle in gear at Cruise speed, and the PCM detected a mechanical fault in the Shift Solenoid 2 (SS2) operation. **Possible Causes:** • Refer to the appropriate Transmission Repair Manual or information in electronic media to perform a complete diagnosis of the automatic transmission when this code is set
DTC: P1760 **1T CCM, MIL: No** **Years:** 2005, 2006, 2007 **Models:** All Models **Engines:** All **Transmissions:** A/T	**A/T EPC Solenoid Circuit Malfunction** Engine started, vehicle in gear at Cruise speed, and the PCM detected a shorted output driver or the TCC solenoid was shorted. **Possible Causes:** • Refer to the appropriate Transmission Repair Manual or information in electronic media to perform a complete diagnosis of the automatic transmission when this code is set.
DTC: P1761 **1T CCM, MIL: No** **Years:** 2005, 2006, 2007 **Models:** All Models **Engines:** All **Transmissions:** A/T	**A/T Shift Solenoid 3 Performance** Engine started, vehicle in gear at Cruise speed, and the PCM detected a malfunction in the Shift Solenoid 3 (SS3) operation. **Possible Causes:** • Refer to the appropriate Transmission Repair Manual or information in electronic media to perform a complete diagnosis of the automatic transmission when this code is set.
DTC: P1762 **1T CCM, MIL: No** **Years:** 2005, 2006, 2007 **Models:** All Models **Engines:** All **Transmissions:** A/T	**Transmission System Malfunction** Engine started, vehicle in gear at Cruise speed, and the PCM detected a malfunction in the Transmission System operation. **Possible Causes:** • Refer to the appropriate Transmission Repair Manual or information in electronic media to perform a complete diagnosis of the automatic transmission when this code is set.
DTC: P1767 **1T CCM, MIL: No** **Years:** 2005, 2006, 2007 **Models:** All Models **Engines:** All **Transmissions:** A/T	**A/T Shift Solenoid Performance** Engine started, vehicle in gear at Cruise speed, and the PCM detected a malfunction in the Shift Solenoid operation. **Possible Causes:** • Refer to the appropriate Transmission Repair Manual or information in electronic media to perform a complete diagnosis of the automatic transmission when this code is set.

DTC	Trouble Code Title, Conditions & Possible Causes
DTC: P1780 **1T CCM, MIL: No** **Years:** 2005, 2006, 2007 **Models:** All Models **Engines:** All **Transmissions:** A/T	**Transmission Control Switch Out of Self-Test Range** Engine started, KOER Self-Test enabled, and the PCM detected the Transmission Control Switch (TCS) was out of range during the test. **Possible Causes:** • TCS circuit open or shorted in the wiring harness • TCS not cycled during the self-test • TCS is damaged, or the PCM has failed
DTC: P1781 **1T CCM, MIL: No** **Years:** 2005, 2006, 2007 **Models:** All Models with 4WD **Engines:** All **Transmissions:** All	**4X4 Low Switch Out Of Self-Test Range** Key on, KOEO Self-Test enabled, and the PCM detected the 4x4 switch input was not low with the switch engaged or "on". **Possible Causes:** • 4x4L switch circuit is open or shorted in the wiring harness • Electronic Shift Module is damaged or has failed • PCM has failed
DTC: P1783 **1T CCM, MIL: No** **Years:** 2005, 2006, 2007 **Models:** All Models **Engines:** All **Transmissions:** A/T	**Transmission Over-Temperature Malfunction** Engine started, engine runtime more than 5 minutes, vehicle in gear at Cruise speed, and the PCM detected the TFT sensor signal was more than 300°F during the CCM test period. **Possible Causes:** • Refer to the appropriate Transmission Repair Manual or information in electronic media to perform a complete diagnosis of the automatic transmission when this code is set.
DTC: P1784 **1T CCM, MIL: No** **Years:** 2005, 2006, 2007 **Models:** All Models **Engines:** All **Transmissions:** A/T	**Transmission System First Or Reverse Gear Malfunction** Engine started, vehicle speed over 1 mph in gear, shift command received for First or Reverse gear, and the PCM detected a problem in the Transmission Control system. **Possible Causes:** • Refer to the appropriate Transmission Repair Manual or information in electronic media to perform a complete diagnosis of the automatic transmission when this code is set.
DTC: P1785 **1T CCM, MIL: No** **Years:** 2005, 2006, 2007 **Models:** All Models **Engines:** All **Transmissions:** A/T	**Transmission System First Or Second Gear Malfunction** Engine started, vehicle speed over 1 mph in gear, shift command received for First or Second gear, and the PCM detected a problem in the Transmission Control system during the test. **Possible Causes:** • Refer to the appropriate Transmission Repair Manual or information in electronic media to perform a complete diagnosis of the automatic transmission when this code is set
DTC: P1786 **1T CCM, MIL: No** **Years:** 2005, 2006, 2007 **Models:** All Models **Engines:** All **Transmissions:** A/T	**Transmission System Second Or Third Gear Malfunction** Engine started, vehicle speed over 1 mph in gear, shift command received for Second or Third gear, and the PCM detected a problem in the Transmission Control system. **Possible Causes:** • Refer to the appropriate Transmission Repair Manual or information in electronic media to perform a complete diagnosis of the automatic transmission when this code is set.
DTC: P1787 **1T CCM, MIL: No** **Years:** 2005, 2006, 2007 **Models:** All Models **Engines:** All **Transmissions:** A/T	**Transmission System Third Or Fourth Gear Malfunction** Engine started, vehicle speed over 1 mph in gear, shift command received for Third or Fourth gear, and the PCM detected a problem in the Transmission Control system during the test. **Possible Causes:** • Refer to the appropriate Transmission Repair Manual or information in electronic media to perform a complete diagnosis of the automatic transmission when this code is set.
DTC: P1788 **1T CCM, MIL: No** **Years:** 2005, 2006, 2007 **Models:** All Models **Engines:** All **Transmissions:** A/T	**3-2 Timing/Coast Clutch Solenoid Signal High Input** Engine started, vehicle in gear at Cruise speed, and the PCM detected the malfunction 3-2 Timing or Coast Clutch solenoid circuit. **Possible Causes:** • 3-2 Timing or Coast Clutch solenoid circuit open or grounded, or the solenoid has failed • Coast Clutch solenoid is damaged or has failed
DTC: P1789 **1T CCM, MIL: No** **Years:** 2005, 2006, 2007 **Models:** All Models **Engines:** All **Transmissions:** A/T	**3-2 Timing/Coast Clutch Solenoid Signal Low Input** Engine started, vehicle in gear at Cruise speed, and the PCM detected the malfunction 3-2 Timing or Coast Clutch solenoid circuit. **Possible Causes:** • 3-2 Timing or Coast Clutch solenoid circuit is shorted • 3-2 Timing solenoid is damaged or has failed • Coast Clutch solenoid is damaged or has failed

DTC	Trouble Code Title, Conditions & Possible Causes
DTC: P1900 **1T CCM, MIL: No** **Years:** 2005, 2006, 2007 **Models:** All Models **Engines:** All **Transmissions:** A/T	**Transmission System Malfunction** Engine started, vehicle in gear at Cruise speed, and the PCM detected a malfunction in the Transmission System operation. **Possible Causes:** • Refer to the appropriate Transmission Repair Manual or information in electronic media to perform a complete diagnosis of the automatic transmission when this code is set
DTC: P1901 **1T CCM, MIL: No** **Years:** 2005, 2006, 2007 **Models:** All Models **Engines:** All **Transmissions:** A/T	**Transmission System Malfunction** Engine started, vehicle in gear at Cruise speed, and the PCM detected a malfunction in the Transmission System operation. **Possible Causes:** • Refer to the appropriate Transmission Repair Manual or information in electronic media to perform a complete diagnosis of the automatic transmission when this code is set.

Gas Engine OBD II Trouble Code List (P1xxx Codes)

DTC	Trouble Code Title, Conditions & Possible Causes
DTC: P2004 **1T CCM, MIL: No** **Years:** 2005, 2006, 2007 **Models:** Excursion, Five Hundred, Freestyle, LS, Montego, Mustang, Ranger **Engines:** 2.3L VIN D, 3.0L VIN S, 4.6L VIN H, 5.4L VIN L **Transmissions:** All	**Intake Air System Malfunction** Engine started, engine running at hot idle speed for one minute, and the PCM detected a problem in the Intake Air System operation. It should be noted that the throttle bore cannot be cleaned as any attempt to clean it will damage the throttle bore and plate. **Possible Causes:** • Test for a sticking Accelerator or speed control cable condition: Turn the key off and disconnect accelerator and speed control cable from the throttle body. Rotate the throttle body linkage to determine if it rotates freely (the throttle body may have failed). • Check the air cleaner and air inlet assembly for restrictions • Check the IAC motor response (it may be damaged or sticking) • Check the PCV system (valve and hoses) for leaks or plugging • Check for signs of vacuum leaks in the engine or components • Test TP sensor signal (due a sweep test at key on, engine off)
DTC: P2005 **1T CCM, MIL: No** **Years:** 2005, 2006, 2007 **Models:** Excursion, Five Hundred, Freestyle, LS, Montego, Mustang, Ranger **Engines:** 2.3L VIN D, 3.0L VIN S, 4.6L VIN H, 5.4L VIN L **Transmissions:** All	**Intake Air System Malfunction** Engine started, engine running at hot idle speed for one minute, and the PCM detected a problem in the Intake Air System operation. It should be noted that the throttle bore cannot be cleaned as any attempt to clean it will damage the throttle bore and plate. **Possible Causes:** • Test for a sticking Accelerator or speed control cable condition: Turn the key off and disconnect accelerator and speed control cable from the throttle body. Rotate the throttle body linkage to determine if it rotates freely (the throttle body may have failed). • Check the air cleaner and air inlet assembly for restrictions • Check the IAC motor response (it may be damaged or sticking) • Check the PCV system (valve and hoses) for leaks or plugging • Check for signs of vacuum leaks in the engine or components • Test TP sensor signal (due a sweep test at key on, engine off)
DTC: P2006 **1T CCM, MIL: No** **Years:** 2005, 2006, 2007 **Models:** Excursion, Five Hundred, Freestyle, LS, Montego, Mustang, Ranger **Engines:** 2.3L VIN D, 3.0L VIN S, 4.6L VIN H, 5.4L VIN L **Transmissions:** All	**Intake Air System Malfunction** Engine started, engine running at hot idle speed for one minute, and the PCM detected a problem in the Intake Air System operation. It should be noted that the throttle bore cannot be cleaned as any attempt to clean it will damage the throttle bore and plate. **Possible Causes:** • Test for a sticking Accelerator or speed control cable condition: Turn the key off and disconnect accelerator and speed control cable from the throttle body. Rotate the throttle body linkage to determine if it rotates freely (the throttle body may have failed). • Check the air cleaner and air inlet assembly for restrictions • Check the IAC motor response (it may be damaged or sticking) • Check the PCV system (valve and hoses) for leaks or plugging • Check for signs of vacuum leaks in the engine or components • Test TP sensor signal (due a sweep test at key on, engine off)

DTC	Trouble Code Title, Conditions & Possible Causes
DTC: P2008 **1T CCM, MIL: No** **Years:** 2005, 2006, 2007 **Models:** Excursion, Five Hundred, Freestyle, LS, Montego, Mustang, Ranger **Engines:** 2.3L VIN D, 3.0L VIN S, 4.6L VIN H, 5.4L VIN L **Transmissions:** All	**Intake Air System Malfunction** Engine started, engine running at hot idle speed for one minute, and the PCM detected a problem in the Intake Air System operation. It should be noted that the throttle bore cannot be cleaned as any attempt to clean it will damage the throttle bore and plate. **Possible Causes:** • Accelerator or speed control cable sticking or binding. To test for this condition, turn the key off. Then disconnect the accelerator and speed control cable from the throttle body. Then rotate the throttle body linkage to determine if it rotates freely. If it is sticking, the throttle body may need replacement. • Check the air cleaner and air inlet assembly for restrictions • Check the IAC motor response (it may be damaged or sticking) • Check the PCV system (valve and hoses) for leaks or plugging • Check for signs of vacuum leaks in the engine or components • Test TP sensor signal (due a sweep test at key on, engine off)
DTC: P2014 **1T CCM, MIL: No** **Years:** 2005, 2006, 2007 **Models:** Excursion, Five Hundred, Freestyle, LS, Montego, Mustang, Ranger **Engines:** 2.3L VIN D, 3.0L VIN S, 4.6L VIN H, 5.4L VIN L **Transmissions:** All	**Intake Air System Malfunction** Engine started, engine running at hot idle speed for one minute, and the PCM detected a problem in the Intake Air System operation. It should be noted that the throttle bore cannot be cleaned as any attempt to clean it will damage the throttle bore and plate. **Possible Causes:** • Accelerator or speed control cable sticking or binding. To test for this condition, turn the key off. Then disconnect the accelerator and speed control cable from the throttle body. Then rotate the throttle body linkage to determine if it rotates freely. If it is sticking, the throttle body may need replacement. • Check the air cleaner and air inlet assembly for restrictions • Check the IAC motor response (it may be damaged or sticking) • Check the PCV system (valve and hoses) for leaks or plugging • Check for signs of vacuum leaks in the engine or components • Test TP sensor signal (due a sweep test at key on, engine off)
DTC: P2019 **1T CCM, MIL: No** **Years:** 2005, 2006, 2007 **Models:** Excursion, Five Hundred, Freestyle, LS, Montego, Mustang, Ranger **Engines:** 2.3L VIN D, 3.0L VIN S, 4.6L VIN H, 5.4L VIN L **Transmissions:** All	**Intake Air System Malfunction** Engine started, engine running at hot idle speed for one minute, and the PCM detected a problem in the Intake Air System operation. It should be noted that the throttle bore cannot be cleaned as any attempt to clean it will damage the throttle bore and plate. **Possible Causes:** • Accelerator or speed control cable sticking or binding. To test these devices, turn the key off and disconnect the accelerator and speed control cable from the throttle body. Then rotate the throttle body linkage to determine if it rotates freely. • Check the air cleaner and air inlet assembly for restrictions • Check the IAC motor response (it may be damaged or sticking) • Check the PCV system (valve and hoses) for leaks or plugging • Check for signs of vacuum leaks in the engine or components • Test TP sensor signal (due a sweep test at key on, engine off)
DTC: P2070 **1T CCM, MIL: No** **Years:** 2005, 2006, 2007 **Models:** Ranger **Engines:** 2.3L VIN D **Transmissions:** All	**Intake Manifold Tuning Valve Malfunction (Stuck Open)** Key on or engine running; and the PCM detected an unexpected low voltage condition on the Intake Manifold Tuning Valve circuit during the CCM test period (i.e., the valve may be stuck open). **Possible Causes:** • IMTV signal circuit shorted to chassis ground • IMTV signal circuit shorted to sensor ground • IMTV actuator is damaged or has failed • PCM has failed
DTC: P2070 **2T CCM, MIL: No** **Years:** 2005, 2006, 2007 **Models:** Excursion **Engines:** 5.4L VIN L **Transmissions:** All	**Intake Manifold Runner Control Malfunction (Stuck Open)** Key on or engine running; and the PCM detected an unexpected low voltage condition on the Intake Manifold Runner Control circuit during the CCM test period (i.e., the valve may be stuck open). **Possible Causes:** • IMRC signal circuit shorted to chassis ground • IMRC signal circuit shorted to sensor ground • IMRC actuator is damaged or has failed • PCM has failed
DTC: P2070 **2T CCM, MIL: No** **Years:** 2005, 2006, 2007 **Models:** Ranger **Engines:** 2.3L VIN D **Transmissions:** All	**Intake Manifold Swirl Control Actuator Circuit Malfunction** Key on or engine running; and the PCM detected an unexpected low voltage condition on the Intake Manifold Swirl Control (IMSC) circuit (i.e., the valve may be stuck open). **Possible Causes:** • IMSC signal circuit is shorted to chassis ground • IMSC signal circuit is shorted to sensor ground • IMSC actuator assembly is damaged or failed • PCM has failed

DTC	Trouble Code Title, Conditions & Possible Causes
DTC: P2071 **2T CCM, MIL: No** **Years:** 2005, 2006, 2007 **Models:** Ranger **Engines:** 2.3L VIN D **Transmissions:** All	**Intake Manifold Tuning Valve Circuit Malfunction (Stuck Closed)** Key on or engine running; and the PCM detected an unexpected high voltage condition on the Intake Manifold Tuning Valve circuit during the CCM test period (i.e., the valve may be stuck closed). **Possible Causes:** • IMTV signal circuit is open • IMTV power circuit (VPWR) is open • IMTV actuator is damaged or has failed • PCM has failed
DTC: P2071 **2T CCM, MIL: No** **Years:** 2005, 2006, 2007 **Models:** Excursion, LS, Sable, Taurus **Engines:** 3.0L VIN S, 5.4L VIN L **Transmissions:** All	**Intake Manifold Runner Control Circuit Malfunction (Stuck Closed)** Key on or engine running; and the PCM detected an unexpected high voltage condition on the Intake Manifold Runner Control (IMRC) circuit during the CCM test (i.e., the valve may be stuck closed). **Possible Causes:** • IMRC monitor signal circuit is open • IMRC power circuit (VPWR) is open • IMRC actuator is damaged or has failed • PCM has failed
DTC: P2071 **2T CCM, MIL: No** **Years:** 2005, 2006, 2007 **Models:** Ranger **Engines:** 2.3L VIN D **Transmissions:** All	**Intake Manifold Swirl Control Circuit Malfunction (Stuck Closed)** Key on or engine running; and the PCM detected an unexpected high voltage condition on the Intake Manifold Swirl Control (IMSC) Monitor circuit (i.e., the valve is stuck closed). **Possible Causes:** • IMSC control (signal) circuit is open • IMSC power circuit (VPWR) is open • IMSC actuator assembly is damaged or failed • PCM has failed
DTC: P2075 **12T CCM, MIL: No** **Years:** 2005, 2006, 2007 **Models:** Ranger **Engines:** 2.3L VIN D **Transmissions:** All	**Intake Manifold Tuning Valve Monitor Circuit Malfunction** Key on or engine running; and the PCM detected an unexpected low or high voltage condition on the Intake Manifold Tuning Valve Monitor circuit during the CCM test period. **Possible Causes:** • IMTV monitor signal circuit is open • IMTV monitor signal circuit shorted to chassis ground • IMTV actuator is damaged or has failed • PCM has failed
DTC: P2075 **2T CCM, MIL: No** **Years:** 2005, 2006, 2007 **Models:** Excursion, LS, Sable, Taurus **Engines:** 3.0L VIN S, 5.4L VIN L **Transmissions:** All	**Intake Manifold Runner Control Monitor Circuit Malfunction** Key on or engine running; and the PCM detected an unexpected high voltage condition on the Intake Manifold Runner Control (IMRC) Monitor circuit during the CCM test period. **Possible Causes:** • IMRC monitor signal circuit is open • IMRC monitor signal circuit shorted to chassis ground • IMRC actuator is damaged or has failed • PCM has failed
DTC: P2075 **2T CCM, MIL: No** **Years:** 2005, 2006, 2007 **Models:** Ranger equipped with a 2.3L VIN D engine **Engines:** **Transmissions:** All	**Intake Manifold Swirl Control Monitor Circuit Malfunction** Key on or engine running; and the PCM detected an unexpected high voltage condition on the Intake Manifold Swirl Control (IMSC) Actuator monitor circuit during the CCM test period. **Possible Causes:** • IMSC monitor circuit is open • IMSC monitor circuit is shorted to chassis ground • IMSC actuator assembly is damaged or failed • PCM has failed
DTC: P2075 **2T PCM, MIL: No** **Years:** 2005, 2006 **Models:** LS **Engines:** All **Transmissions:** All	**Throttle Actuator Control Motor Circuit Malfunction (Open)** Key on or engine running; and the PCM detected an unexpected voltage condition on the Throttle Actuator Control Motor (TACM) circuit during the CCM test period. **Possible Causes:** • TACM wiring harness connector is damaged or open • TACM (motor) circuit is open • TACM assembly is damaged or it has failed (an open circuit) • PCM has failed

DTC	Trouble Code Title, Conditions & Possible Causes
DTC: P2101 **2T PCM, MIL: No** **Years:** 2005, 2006 **Models:** LS **Engines:** All **Transmissions:** All	**Throttle Actuator Control Motor Range/Performance** Key on or engine running; and the PCM detected an unexpected low or high voltage condition on the Throttle Actuator Control Motor (TACM) circuit during the CCM test. **Possible Causes:** • TACM wiring harness connector is damaged or open • TACM wiring may be crossed in the wire harness assembly • TACM (motor) circuit is open, or TACM assembly is damaged (possible open circuit) • PCM has failed
DTC: P2104 **2T PCM, MIL: No** **Years:** 2005, 2006 **Models:** LS **Engines:** All **Transmissions:** All	**Throttle Actuator Control System - Forced Idle Mode** Key on, and the PCM detected the Throttle Actuator Control Motor (TACM) system was in Forced Idle mode while operating in Failure Mode Effect Management (FMEM). **Possible Causes:** • PCM is damaged. Clear the codes (do a PCM reset), and if the same trouble code resets, the PCM will have to be replaced.
DTC: P2105 **2T PCM, MIL: No** **Years:** 2005, 2006 **Models:** LS **Engines:** All **Transmissions:** All	**Throttle Actuator Control System - Forced Engine Shutdown** Key on, and the PCM detected the Throttle Actuator Control Motor (TACM) system was in Forced Engine Shutdown mode while in Failure Mode Effect Management (FMEM). **Possible Causes:** • A total system failure has occurred • PCM is damaged. Clear the codes (do a PCM reset), and if the same trouble code resets, the PCM will have to be replaced.
DTC: P2106 **2T PCM, MIL: No** **Years:** 2005, 2006 **Models:** LS **Engines:** All **Transmissions:** All	Title: Throttle Actuator Control System - Forced Limited Power Trouble Code Conditions Key on, and the PCM detected the Throttle Actuator Control Motor (TACM) system was in Forced Limited Power mode while operating in Failure Mode Effect Management (FMEM). **Possible Causes:** • TACM (motor) wiring harness is disconnected or loose • TACM (motor) circuits are shorted to power • PCM may have failed. Clear the codes (do a PCM reset), and if the same code resets, the PCM will have to be replaced.
DTC: P2107 **2T PCM, MIL: No** **Years:** 2005, 2006 **Models:** LS **Engines:** All **Transmissions:** All	**Throttle Actuator Control Motor Processor Malfunction** Key on or engine running; and the PCM detected the Throttle Actuator Control Motor processor received an invalid command or the TACM processor did not execute a command. **Possible Causes:** • TACM (motor) wiring harness is shorted, or TACM signal wires are shorted together • TACM (motor) circuits are shorted to power • PCM is damaged. Clear the codes. If the same code resets, the PCM needs replacement.
DTC: P2110 **2T PCM, MIL: No** **Years:** 2005, 2006 **Models:** LS **Engines:** All **Transmissions:** All	**Throttle Actuator Control System - Forced Limited RPM** Key on or engine running; and the PCM detected the Throttle Actuator Control System was operating in Forced Limited RPM mode while in Failure Mode Effect Management (FMEM). **Possible Causes:** • PCM is damaged. Clear the codes. If the same code resets, the PCM needs replacement.
DTC: P2111 **2T PCM, MIL: No** **Years:** 2005, 2006 **Models:** LS **Engines:** All **Transmissions:** All	**Throttle Actuator Control System - Stuck Open** Key on or engine running; and the PCM detected the throttle plate angle (opening) was more the commanded amount during testing. **Possible Causes:** • PCM is damaged. Clear the codes. If the same code resets, the PCM needs replacement.
DTC: P2112 **2T PCM, MIL: No** **Years:** 2005, 2006 **Models:** LS **Engines:** All **Transmissions:** All	**Throttle Actuator Control System - Stuck Closed** Key on or engine running; and the PCM detected the throttle plate angle (opening) was less the commanded amount during testing. **Possible Causes:** • TACM wiring may be crossed in the wire harness assembly • Throttle body is binding - the throttle is stuck closed when these conditions are present • PCM has failed

DTC	Trouble Code Title, Conditions & Possible Causes
DTC: P2119 **2T PCM, MIL: No** **Years:** 2005, 2006 **Models:** LS **Engines:** All **Transmissions:** All	**Throttle Actuator Control Throttle Body Range/Performance** Key on or engine running; and the PCM detected a signal that indicated the throttle return spring was damaged or it had failed. **Possible Causes:** • Throttle body is binding or sticking • Throttle return spring is damaged or it is broken • PCM has failed
DTC: P2121 **2T PCM, MIL: No** **Years:** 2005, 2006 **Models:** LS **Engines:** All **Transmissions:** All	**Accelerator Pedal Position Sensor 'D' Signal Range/Performance** Key on or engine running; and the PCM detected the Accelerator Pedal Position Sensor 'D' signal circuit was out of the normal operating range during the CCM test. **Possible Causes:** • APP sensor signal circuits are shorted together • APP sensor is damaged or the PCM has failed
DTC: P2122 **2T PCM, MIL: No** **Years:** 2005, 2006 **Models:** LS **Engines:** All **Transmissions:** All	**Accelerator Pedal Position Sensor 'D' Circuit Low Input** Key on or engine running; and the PCM detected the Accelerator Pedal Position Sensor 'D' signal circuit was less than the normal range during the test period. **Possible Causes:** • APP sensor signal circuit is open • APP sensor signal circuit is shorted to ground • APP sensor is damaged or it has failed • PCM has failed
DTC: P2123 **2T PCM, MIL: No** **Years:** 2005, 2006 **Models:** LS **Engines:** All **Transmissions:** All	**Accelerator Pedal Position Sensor 'D' Circuit High Input** Key on or engine running; and the PCM detected the Accelerator Pedal Position Sensor 'D' signal circuit was more than the normal range during the test period. **Possible Causes:** • APP sensor connector is damaged or shorted • APP sensor signal circuit is shorted to VREF (5v) • APP sensor is damaged or it has failed • PCM has failed
DTC: P2126 **2T PCM, MIL: No** **Years:** 2005, 2006 **Models:** LS **Engines:** All **Transmissions:** All	**Accelerator Pedal Position Sensor 'E' Signal Range/Performance** Key on or engine running; and the PCM detected the Accelerator Pedal Position Sensor 'E' signal circuit was more than the normal range during the test period. **Possible Causes:** • APP sensor connector is damaged or shorted • APP sensor signal circuit is shorted to VREF (5v) • APP sensor is damaged or the PCM has failed
DTC: P212 **2T PCM, MIL: No** **Years:** 2005, 2006 **Models:** LS **Engines:** All **Transmissions:** All	**Accelerator Pedal Position Sensor 'E' Circuit Low Input** Key on or engine running; and the PCM detected the Accelerator Pedal Position Sensor 'D' signal circuit was less than the normal range during the test period. **Possible Causes:** • APP sensor signal circuit is open • APP sensor signal circuit is shorted to ground • APP sensor is damaged or the PCM has failed
DTC: P2128 **2T PCM, MIL: No** **Years:** 2005, 2006 **Models:** LS **Engines:** All **Transmissions:** All	**Accelerator Pedal Position Sensor 'E' Circuit High Input** Key on or engine running; and the PCM detected the Accelerator Pedal Position Sensor 'E' signal circuit was more than the normal range during the test period. **Possible Causes:** • APP sensor connector is damaged or shorted • APP sensor signal circuit is shorted to VREF (5v) • APP sensor is damaged or it has failed • PCM has failed
DTC: P2131 **2T PCM, MIL: No** **Years:** 2005, 2006 **Models:** LS **Engines:** All **Transmissions:** All	**Accelerator Pedal Position Sensor 'F' Signal Range/Performance** Key on or engine running; and the PCM detected the Accelerator Pedal Position Sensor 'F' signal circuit was more than the normal range during the test period. **Possible Causes:** • APP sensor connector is damaged or shorted • APP sensor signal circuit is shorted to VREF (5v) • APP sensor is damaged or it has failed • PCM has failed

DTC	Trouble Code Title, Conditions & Possible Causes
DTC: P2132 **2T PCM, MIL: No** **Years:** 2005, 2006 **Models:** LS **Engines:** All **Transmissions:** All	**Accelerator Pedal Position Sensor 'F' Circuit Low Input** Key on or engine running; and the PCM detected the Accelerator Pedal Position Sensor 'F' signal circuit was less than the normal range during the test period. **Possible Causes:** • APP sensor signal circuit is open • APP sensor signal circuit is shorted to ground • APP sensor is damaged or it has failed • PCM has failed
DTC: P2133 **2T PCM, MIL: No** **Years:** 2005, 2006 **Models:** LS **Engines:** All **Transmissions:** All	**Accelerator Pedal Position Sensor 'F' Circuit High Input** Key on or engine running; and the PCM detected the Accelerator Pedal Position Sensor 'F' signal circuit was more than the normal range during the test period. **Possible Causes:** • APP sensor connector is damaged or shorted • APP sensor signal circuit is shorted to VREF (5v) • APP sensor is damaged or it has failed • PCM has failed
DTC: P2135 **2T PCM, MIL: No** **Years:** 2005, 2006 **Models:** LS **Engines:** All **Transmissions:** All	**ETC Throttle Position Sensor A/B Voltage Correlation** Key on or engine running; and the PCM detected the Throttle Position 'A' (TPA) and Throttle Position 'B' (TPB) sensors disagreed, or that the TPA sensor should not be in its detected position, or that the TPB sensor should not be in its detected position during testing. **Possible Causes:** • ETC TP sensor connector is damaged or shorted • ETC TP sensor circuits shorted together in the wire harness • ETC TP sensor signal circuit is shorted to VREF (5v) • ETC TP sensor is damaged or the PCM has failed
DTC: P2195 **2T CCM, MIL: No** **Years:** 2005, 2006 **Models:** LS **Engines:** All **Transmissions:** All	**Lack of HO2S-11 Switching, Sensor Indicates Lean** DTC P0300-P0310 not set, engine running in closed loop, and the PCM detected the HO2S indicated a lean signal, or it could no longer control Fuel Trim because it was at lean limit. **Possible Causes:** • Base engine problems: engine oil level high, camshaft timing error, cylinder compression low, exhaust leaks in front of HO2S • EGR System problem: EGR valve is stuck open, the gasket is leaking, or the EVR diaphragm is leaking • Fuel System problem: damaged fuel pressure regulator or extremely low fuel pressure • HO2S problems: HO2S circuit is open or shorted in the wiring harness or the HO2S is damaged or it has failed • Induction System problems: air leaks after the MAF sensor, PCV system leaks, engine vacuum leaks or dip stick not seated
DTC: P2196 **2T CCM, MIL: No** **Years:** 2005, 2006 **Models:** LS **Engines:** All **Transmissions:** All	**Lack of HO2S-21 Switching, Sensor Indicates Rich** DTC P0300-P0310 not set, engine running in closed loop, and the PCM detected the HO2S indicated a rich signal, or it could no longer control Fuel Trim because it was at its rich limit. **Possible Causes:** • Base engine problems: engine oil level high, camshaft timing error, cylinder compression low, exhaust leaks in front of HO2S • Fuel System problem: excessive fuel pressure, leaking fuel injectors, fuel pressure regulator leaking • HO2S problems: HO2S circuit is open or shorted in the wiring harness, the HO2S signal circuit is contacting moisture in harness connector, or the HO2S is damaged or it has failed
DTC: P2197 **2T CCM, MIL: No** **Years:** 2005, 2006 **Models:** LS **Engines:** All **Transmissions:** All	**Lack of HO2S-21 Switching, Sensor Indicates Lean** DTC P0300-P0310 not set, engine running in closed loop, and the PCM detected the HO2S indicated a lean signal, or it could no longer control Fuel Trim because it was at lean limit. **Possible Causes:** • Base engine problems: engine oil level high, camshaft timing error, cylinder compression low, exhaust leaks in front of HO2S • EGR System problem: EGR valve is stuck open, the gasket is leaking, or the EVR diaphragm is leaking • Fuel System problem: damaged fuel pressure regulator or extremely low fuel pressure • HO2S problems: HO2S circuit is open or shorted in the wiring harness or the HO2S is damaged or it has failed • Induction System problems: air leaks after the MAF sensor, PCV system leaks, engine vacuum leaks or dip stick not seated

DTC	Trouble Code Title, Conditions & Possible Causes
DTC: P2198 **2T CCM, MIL: No** **Years:** 2005, 2006 **Models:** LS **Engines:** All **Transmissions:** All	**Lack of HO2S-21 Switching, Sensor Indicates Rich** DTC P0300-P0310 not set, engine running in closed loop, and the PCM detected the HO2S indicated a rich signal, or it could no longer control Fuel Trim because it was at its rich limit. **Possible Causes:** • Base engine problems: engine oil level high, camshaft timing error, cylinder compression low, exhaust leaks in front of HO2S • Fuel System problem: excessive fuel pressure, leaking fuel injectors, fuel pressure regulator leaking • HO2S problems: HO2S circuit is open or shorted in the wiring harness, the HO2S signal circuit is contacting moisture in harness connector, or the HO2S is damaged or it failed
DTC: P2270 **2T CCM, MIL: No** **Years:** 2005, 2006 **Models:** LS **Engines:** All **Transmissions:** All	**Lack of HO2S-12 Switching, Sensor Indicates Lean** DTC P0300-P0310 not set, engine running in closed loop, and the PCM detected the HO2S indicated a lean signal, or it could no longer control Fuel Trim because it was at lean limit. **Possible Causes:** • Base engine problems: engine oil level high, camshaft timing error, cylinder compression low, exhaust leaks in front of HO2S • EGR System problem: EGR valve is stuck open, the gasket is leaking, or the EVR diaphragm is leaking • Fuel System problem: damaged fuel pressure regulator or extremely low fuel pressure • HO2S problems: HO2S circuit is open or shorted in the wiring harness or the HO2S is damaged or it has failed • Induction System problems: air leaks after the MAF sensor, PCV system leaks, engine vacuum leaks or dip stick not seated
DTC: P2271 **2T CCM, MIL: No** **Years:** 2005, 2006 **Models:** LS **Engines:** All **Transmissions:** All	**Lack of HO2S-12 Switching, Sensor Indicates Rich** DTC P0300-P0310 not set, engine running in closed loop, and the PCM detected the HO2S indicated a rich signal, or it could no longer control Fuel Trim because it was at its rich limit. **Possible Causes:** • Base engine problems: engine oil level high, camshaft timing error, cylinder compression low, exhaust leaks in front of HO2S • Fuel System problem: excessive fuel pressure, leaking fuel injectors, fuel pressure regulator leaking • HO2S problems: HO2S circuit is open or shorted in the wiring harness, the HO2S signal circuit is contacting moisture in harness connector, or the HO2S is damaged or it failed
DTC: P2272 **2T CCM, MIL: No** **Years:** 2005, 2006 **Models:** LS **Engines:** All **Transmissions:** All	**Lack of HO2S-22 Switching, Sensor Indicates Lean** DTC P0300-P0310 not set, engine running in closed loop, and the PCM detected the HO2S indicated a lean signal, or it could no longer control Fuel Trim because it was at lean limit. **Possible Causes:** • Base engine problems: engine oil level high, camshaft timing error, cylinder compression low, exhaust leaks in front of HO2S • EGR System problem: EGR valve is stuck open, the gasket is leaking, or the EVR diaphragm is leaking • Fuel System problem: damaged fuel pressure regulator or extremely low fuel pressure • HO2S problems: HO2S circuit is open or shorted in the wiring harness or the HO2S is damaged or it has failed • Induction System problems: air leaks after the MAF sensor, PCV system leaks, engine vacuum leaks or dip stick not seated
DTC: P2273 **2T CCM, MIL: No** **Years:** 2005, 2006, 2007 **Models:** All Models **Engines:** All **Transmissions:** All	**Lack of HO2S-22 Switching, Sensor Indicates Rich** Trouble Code Conditions DTC P0300-P0310 not set, engine running in closed loop, and the PCM detected the HO2S indicated a rich signal, or it could no longer control Fuel Trim because it was at its rich limit. **Possible Causes:** • Base engine problems: engine oil level high, camshaft timing error, cylinder compression low, exhaust leaks in front of HO2S • Fuel System problem: excessive fuel pressure, leaking fuel injectors, fuel pressure regulator leaking • HO2S problems: HO2S circuit is open or shorted in the wiring harness, the HO2S signal circuit is contacting moisture in harness connector, or the HO2S is damaged or it failed

Gas Engine OBD II Trouble Code List (Uxxxx Codes)

DTC	Trouble Code Title, Conditions & Possible Causes
DTC: U1011 **1T PCM, MIL: No** **Years:** 2005, 2006, 2007 **Models:** All Models **Engines:** All **Transmissions:** All	**Data Circuit Message** Key on, and the PCM detected that invalid or Missing Data from the Engine Air Intake system was received on the SCP data bus. **Note: Network codes occur during module-to-module communication failures. Invalid and Missing data network faults are outlined below.** **Possible Causes:** • Invalid Data: Data transferred in normal inter-module messages with known invalid data. Transmitting module will set the code. • Missing Network Data: Missing message fault logged by a module upon failure to receive a message from another module within a defined retry period.
DTC: U1020 **1T PCM, MIL: No** **Years:** 2005, 2006, 2007 **Models:** All Models **Engines:** All **Transmissions:** All	**Data Circuit Message** Key on, and the PCM detected that invalid or Missing Data from the Air Conditioning system was received on the SCP data bus. **Note: Network codes occur during module-to-module communication failures. Invalid and Missing data network faults are outlined below.** **Possible Causes:** • Invalid Data: Data transferred in normal inter-module messages with known invalid data. Transmitting module will set the code. • Missing Network Data: Missing message fault logged by a module upon failure to receive a message from another module within a defined retry period.
DTC: U1021 **1T PCM, MIL: No** **Years:** 2005, 2006, 2007 **Models:** All Models **Engines:** All **Transmissions:** All	**Data Circuit Message** Key on, and the PCM detected that invalid or Missing Data from the Air Conditioning Clutch status was received on the SCP data bus. **Note: Network codes occur during module-to-module communication failures. Invalid and Missing data network faults are outlined below.** **Possible Causes:** • Invalid Data: Data transferred in normal inter-module messages with known invalid data. Transmitting module will set the code. • Missing Network Data: Missing message fault logged by a module upon failure to receive a message from another module within a defined retry period.
DTC: U1037 **1T PCM, MIL: No** **Years:** 2005, 2006, 2007 **Models:** All Models **Engines:** All **Transmissions:** All	**Data Circuit Message** Key on, and the PCM detected that invalid or Missing Data from the Telltale Lamp Module was received on the SCP data bus. **Note: Network codes occur during module-to-module communication failures. Invalid and Missing data network faults are outlined below.** **Possible Causes:** • Invalid Data: Data transferred in normal inter-module messages with known invalid data. Transmitting module will set the code. • Missing Network Data: Missing message fault logged by a module upon failure to receive a message from another module within a defined retry period.
DTC: U1039 **1T PCM, MIL: No** **Years:** 2005, 2006, 2007 **Models:** All Models **Engines:** All **Transmissions:** All	**Data Circuit Message** Key on, and the PCM detected that invalid or Missing Data from the Vehicle Speed Sensor was received on the SCP data bus. **Note: Network codes occur during module-to-module communication failures. Invalid and Missing data network faults are outlined below.** **Possible Causes:** • Invalid Data: Data transferred in normal inter-module messages with known invalid data. Transmitting module will set the code. • Missing Network Data: Missing message fault logged by a module upon failure to receive a message from another module within a defined retry period. • TSB 01-21-13 contains a repair procedure for this trouble code
DTC: U1041 **1T PCM, MIL: No** **Years:** 2005, 2006, 2007 **Models:** All Models **Engines:** All **Transmissions:** All	**Data Circuit Message** Key on, and the PCM detected that invalid or Missing Data from the Vehicle Speed Sensor was received on the SCP data bus. **Note: Network codes occur during module-to-module communication failures. Invalid and Missing data network faults are outlined below.** **Possible Causes:** • Invalid Data: Data transferred in normal inter-module messages with known invalid data. Transmitting module will set the code. • Missing Network Data: Missing message fault logged by a module upon failure to receive a message from another module within a defined retry period.

DTC	Trouble Code Title, Conditions & Possible Causes
DTC: U1051 **1T PCM, MIL: No** **Years:** 2005, 2006, 2007 **Models:** All Models **Engines:** All **Transmissions:** All	**Data Circuit Message** Key on, and the PCM detected that invalid or Missing Data from the Antilock Brake System was received on the SCP data bus. **Note: Network codes occur during module-to-module communication failures. Invalid and Missing data network faults are outlined below.** **Possible Causes:** • Invalid Data: Data transferred in normal inter-module messages with known invalid data. Transmitting module will set the code. • Missing Network Data: Missing message fault logged by a module upon failure to receive a message from another module within a defined retry period.
DTC: U1071 **1T PCM, MIL: No** **Years:** 2005, 2006, 2007 **Models:** All Models **Engines:** All **Transmissions:** All	**Data Circuit Message** Key on, and the PCM detected that invalid or Missing Data from the Engine Sensor was received on the SCP data bus. **Note: Network codes occur during module-to-module communication failures. Invalid and Missing data network faults are outlined below.** **Possible Causes:** • Invalid Data: Data transferred in normal inter-module messages with known invalid data. Transmitting module will set the code. • Missing Network Data: Missing message fault logged by a module upon failure to receive a message from another module within a defined retry period.
DTC: U1073 **1T PCM, MIL: No** **Years:** 2005, 2006, 2007 **Models:** All Models **Engines:** All **Transmissions:** All	**Data Circuit Message** Key on, and the PCM detected that invalid or Missing Data from the Engine Coolant Fan Status was received on the SCP data bus. **Note: Network codes occur during module-to-module communication failures. Invalid and Missing data network faults are outlined below.** **Possible Causes:** • Invalid Data: Data transferred in normal inter-module messages with known invalid data. Transmitting module will set the code. • Missing Network Data: Missing message fault logged by a module upon failure to receive a message from another module within a defined retry period.
DTC: U1089 **1T PCM, MIL: No** **Years:** 2005, 2006, 2007 **Models:** All Models **Engines:** All **Transmissions:** All	**Data Circuit Message** Key on, and the PCM detected that invalid or Missing Data from the Suspension System Module was received on the SCP data bus. **Note: Network codes occur during module-to-module communication failures. Invalid and Missing data network faults are outlined below.** **Possible Causes:** • Invalid Data: Data transferred in normal inter-module messages with known invalid data. Transmitting module will set the code. • Missing Network Data: Missing message fault logged by a module upon failure to receive a message from another module within a defined retry period.
DTC: U1098 **1T PCM, MIL: No** **Years:** 2005, 2006, 2007 **Models:** All Models **Engines:** All **Transmissions:** All	**Data Circuit Message** Key on, and the PCM detected that invalid or Missing Data from the Vehicle Speed Control Module was received on the SCP data bus. **Note: Network codes occur during module-to-module communication failures. Invalid and Missing data network faults are outlined below.** **Possible Causes:** • Invalid Data: Data transferred in normal inter-module messages with known invalid data. Transmitting module will set the code. • Missing Network Data: Missing message fault logged by a module upon failure to receive a message from another module within a defined retry period.
DTC: U1130 **1T PCM, MIL: No** **Years:** 2005, 2006, 2007 **Models:** All Models **Engines:** All **Transmissions:** All	**Data Circuit Message** Key on, and the PCM detected that invalid or Missing Data from the Fuel System was received on the SCP data bus. **Note: Network codes occur during module-to-module communication failures. Invalid and Missing data network faults are outlined below.** **Possible Causes:** • Invalid Data: Data transferred in normal inter-module messages with known invalid data. Transmitting module will set the code. • Missing Network Data: Missing message fault logged by a module upon failure to receive a message from another module within a defined retry period.

DTC	Trouble Code Title, Conditions & Possible Causes

DTC: U1131
1T PCM, MIL: No
Years: 2005, 2006, 2007
Models: All Models
Engines: All
Transmissions: All
	Data Circuit Message
	Key on, and the PCM detected that invalid or Missing Data from the Fuel System was received on the SCP data bus.
	Note: Network codes occur during module-to-module communication failures. Invalid and Missing data network faults are outlined below.
	Possible Causes:
	    • Invalid Data: Data transferred in normal inter-module messages with known invalid data. Transmitting module will set the code.
	    • Missing Network Data: Missing message fault logged by a module upon failure to receive a message from another module within a defined retry period.

DTC: U1135
1T PCM, MIL: No
Years: 2005, 2006, 2007
Models: All Models
Engines: All
Transmissions: All
	Data Circuit Message
	Key on, and the PCM detected that invalid or Missing Data from the Ignition Switch Signal was received on the SCP data bus.
	Note: Network codes occur during module-to-module communication failures. Invalid and Missing data network faults are outlined below.
	Possible Causes:
	    • Invalid Data: Data transferred in normal inter-module messages with known invalid data. Transmitting module will set the code.
	    • Missing Network Data: Missing message fault logged by a module upon failure to receive a message from another module within a defined retry period.

DTC: U1147
1T PCM, MIL: No
Years: 2005, 2006, 2007
Models: All Models
Engines: All
Transmissions: All
	Data Circuit Message
	Key on, and the PCM detected that invalid or Missing Data from the Vehicle Security System was received on the SCP data bus.
	Note: Network codes occur during module-to-module communication failures. Invalid and Missing data network faults are outlined below.
	Possible Causes:
	    • Invalid Data: Data transferred in normal inter-module messages with known invalid data. Transmitting module will set the code.
	    • Missing Network Data: Missing message fault logged by a module upon failure to receive a message from another module within a defined retry period.

DTC: U1243
1T PCM, MIL: No
Years: 2005, 2006, 2007
Models: All Models
Engines: All
Transmissions: All
	Data Circuit Message
	Key on, and the PCM detected that invalid or Missing Data from the Exterior Environment System was received on the SCP data bus.
	Note: Network codes occur during module-to-module communication failures. Invalid and Missing data network faults are outlined below.
	Possible Causes:
	    • Invalid Data: Data transferred in normal inter-module messages with known invalid data. Transmitting module will set the code.
	    • Missing Network Data: Missing message fault logged by a module upon failure to receive a message from another module within a defined retry period.

DTC: U1256
1T PCM, MIL: No
Years: 2005, 2006, 2007
Models: All Models
Engines: All
Transmissions: All
	Data Circuit Message
	Key on, and the PCM detected a signal indicating a communication error had occurred with another module over the SCP data bus.
	Note: Network codes occur during module-to-module communication failures. Invalid and Missing data network faults are outlined below.
	Possible Causes:
	    • Invalid Data: Data transferred in normal inter-module messages with known invalid data. Transmitting module will set the code.
	    • Missing Network Data: Missing message fault logged by a module upon failure to receive a message from another module within a defined retry period.

DTC: U1260
1T PCM, MIL: No
Years: 2005, 2006, 2007
Models: All Models
Engines: All
Transmissions: All
	Data Circuit Message
	Key on, and the PCM detected a signal that indicated an open or shorted condition was present in the SCP (+) bus circuit.
	Note: Network codes occur during module-to-module communication failures. Invalid and Missing data network faults are outlined below.
	Possible Causes:
	    • Invalid Data: Data transferred in normal inter-module messages with known invalid data. Transmitting module will set the code.
	    • Missing Network Data: Missing message fault logged by a module upon failure to receive a message from another module within a defined retry period.

DTC	Trouble Code Title, Conditions & Possible Causes
DTC: U1261 **1T PCM, MIL: No** **Years:** 2005, 2006, 2007 **Models:** All Models **Engines:** All **Transmissions:** All	**Data Circuit Message** Key on, and the PCM detected a signal that indicated an open or shorted condition was present in the SCP (-) bus circuit. **Note: Network codes occur during module-to-module communication failures. Invalid and Missing data network faults are outlined below.** **Possible Causes:** • Invalid Data: Data transferred in normal inter-module messages with known invalid data. Transmitting module will set the code. • Missing Network Data: Missing message fault logged by a module upon failure to receive a message from another module within a defined retry period.
DTC: U1262 **1T PCM, MIL: No** **Years:** 2005, 2006, 2007 **Models:** All Models **Engines:** All **Transmissions:** All	**Data Circuit Message** Key on, and the PCM detected a signal that indicated a fault was present in the SCP bus (perform the network communication tests). **Note: Network codes occur during module-to-module communication failures. Invalid and Missing data network faults are outlined below.** **Possible Causes:** • Invalid Data: Data transferred in normal inter-module messages with known invalid data. Transmitting module will set the code. • Missing Network Data: Missing message fault logged by a module upon failure to receive a message from another module within a defined retry period.
DTC: U1341 **1T PCM, MIL: No** **Years:** 2005, 2006, 2007 **Models:** All Models **Engines:** All **Transmissions:** All	**Data Circuit Message** Key on, and the PCM detected that invalid or Missing Data from the Function Read Vehicle Speed was received on the SCP data bus. **Note: Network codes occur during module-to-module communication failures. Invalid and Missing data network faults are outlined below.** **Possible Causes:** • Invalid Data: Data transferred in normal inter-module messages with known invalid data. Transmitting module will set the code. • Missing Network Data: Missing message fault logged by a module upon failure to receive a message from another module within a defined retry period.
DTC: U1451 **1T PCM, MIL: No** **Years:** 2005, 2006, 2007 **Models:** All Models **Engines:** All **Transmissions:** All	**Data Circuit Message** Key on, and the PCM detected that invalid or Missing Data from the Vehicle Antitheft Module was received on the SCP data bus. **Note: Network codes occur during module-to-module communication failures. Invalid and Missing data network faults are outlined below.** **Possible Causes:** • Invalid Data: Data transferred in normal inter-module messages with known invalid data. Transmitting module will set the code. • Missing Network Data: Missing message fault logged by a module upon failure to receive a message from another module within a defined retry period.
DTC: U2015 **1T PCM, MIL: No** **Years:** 2005, 2006, 2007 **Models:** All Models **Engines:** All **Transmissions:** All	**Data Circuit Message** Key on, and the PCM detected that invalid or Missing Data from the Function Read Vehicle Speed was received on the SCP data bus. **Note: Network codes occur during module-to-module communication failures. Invalid and Missing data network faults are outlined below.** **Possible Causes:** • Invalid Data: Data transferred in normal inter-module messages with known invalid data. Transmitting module will set the code. • Missing Network Data: Missing message fault logged by a module upon failure to receive a message from another module within a defined retry period.
DTC: U2195 **1T PCM, MIL: No** **Years:** 2005, 2006, 2007 **Models:** All Models **Engines:** All **Transmissions:** All	**Data Circuit Message** Key on, and the PCM detected an open or shorted condition in the Signal Link circuit (not on the SCP data bus circuits). **Note: Network codes occur during module-to-module communication failures. Invalid and Missing data network faults are outlined below.** **Possible Causes:** • Invalid Data: Data transferred in normal inter-module messages with known invalid data. Transmitting module will set the code. • Missing Network Data: Missing message fault logged by a module upon failure to receive a message from another module within a defined retry period.

DTC	Trouble Code Title, Conditions & Possible Causes
DTC: U2243 **1T PCM, MIL: No** **Years:** 2005, 2006, 2007 **Models:** All Models **Engines:** All **Transmissions:** All	**Data Circuit Message** Key on, and the PCM detected that invalid or Missing Data from the SCLM Status was received on the SCP data bus. **Note: Network codes occur during module-to-module communication failures. Invalid and Missing data network faults are outlined below.** **Possible Causes:** • Invalid Data: Data transferred in normal inter-module messages with known invalid data. Transmitting module will set the code. • Missing Network Data: Missing message fault logged by a module upon failure to receive a message from another module within a defined retry period.

GLOSSARY

ABS: Anti-lock braking system. An electro-mechanical braking system which is designed to minimize or prevent wheel lock-up during braking.

ABSOLUTE PRESSURE: Atmospheric (barometric) pressure plus the pressure gauge reading.

ACCELERATOR PUMP: A small pump located in the carburetor that feeds fuel into the air/fuel mixture during acceleration.

ACCUMULATOR: A device that controls shift quality by cushioning the shock of hydraulic oil pressure being applied to a clutch or band.

ACTUATING MECHANISM: The mechanical output devices of a hydraulic system, for example, clutch pistons and band servos.

ACTUATOR: The output component of a hydraulic or electronic system.

ADVANCE: Setting the ignition timing so that spark occurs earlier before the piston reaches top dead center (TDC).

ADAPTIVE MEMORY (ADAPTIVE STRATEGY): The learning ability of the TCM or PCM to redefine its decision-making process to provide optimum shift quality.

AFTER TOP DEAD CENTER (ATDC): The point after the piston reaches the top of its travel on the compression stroke.

AIR BAG: Device on the inside of the car designed to inflate on impact of crash, protecting the occupants of the car.

AIR CHARGE TEMPERATURE (ACT) SENSOR: The temperature of the airflow into the engine is measured by an ACT sensor, usually located in the lower intake manifold or air cleaner.

AIR CLEANER: An assembly consisting of a housing, filter and any connecting ductwork. The filter element is made up of a porous paper, sometimes with a wire mesh screening, and is designed to prevent airborne particles from entering the engine through the carburetor or throttle body.

AIR INJECTION: One method of reducing harmful exhaust emissions by injecting air into each of the exhaust ports of an engine. The fresh air entering the hot exhaust manifold causes any remaining fuel to be burned before it can exit the tailpipe.

AIR PUMP: An emission control device that supplies fresh air to the exhaust manifold to aid in more completely burning exhaust gases.

AIR/FUEL RATIO: The ratio of air-to-gasoline by weight in the fuel mixture drawn into the engine.

ALDL (assembly line diagnostic link): Electrical connector for scanning ECM/PCM/TCM input and output devices.

ALIGNMENT RACK: A special drive-on vehicle lift apparatus/measuring device used to adjust a vehicle's toe, caster and camber angles.

ALL WHEEL DRIVE: Term used to describe a full time four wheel drive system or any other vehicle drive system that continuously delivers power to all four wheels. This system is found primarily on station wagon vehicles and SUVs not utilized for significant off road use.

ALTERNATING CURRENT (AC): Electric current that flows first in one direction, then in the opposite direction, continually reversing flow.

ALTERNATOR: A device which produces AC (alternating current) which is converted to DC (direct current) to charge the car battery.

AMMETER: An instrument, calibrated in amperes, used to measure the flow of an electrical current in a circuit. Ammeters are always connected in series with the circuit being tested.

AMPERAGE: The total amount of current (amperes) flowing in a circuit.

AMPLIFIER: A device used in an electrical circuit to increase the voltage of an output signal.

AMP/HR. RATING (BATTERY): Measurement of the ability of a battery to deliver a stated amount of current for a stated period of time. The higher the amp/hr. rating, the better the battery.

AMPERE: The rate of flow of electrical current present when one volt of electrical pressure is applied against one ohm of electrical resistance.

ANALOG COMPUTER: Any microprocessor that uses similar (analogous) electrical signals to make its calculations.

ANODIZED: A special coating applied to the surface of aluminum valves for extended service life.

ANTIFREEZE: A substance (ethylene or propylene glycol) added to the coolant to prevent freezing in cold weather.

ANTI-FOAM AGENTS: Minimize fluid foaming from the whipping action encountered in the converter and planetary action.

ANTI-WEAR AGENTS: Zinc agents that control wear on the gears, bushings, and thrust washers.

ANTI-LOCK BRAKING SYSTEM: A supplementary system to the base hydraulic system that prevents sustained lock-up of the wheels during braking as well as automatically controlling wheel slip.

ANTI-ROLL BAR: See stabilizer bar.

ARC: A flow of electricity through the air between two electrodes or contact points that produces a spark.

ARMATURE: A laminated, soft iron core wrapped by a wire that converts electrical energy to mechanical energy as in a motor or relay. When rotated in a magnetic field, it changes mechanical energy into electrical energy as in a generator.

ATDC: After Top Dead Center.

ATF: Automatic transmission fluid.

ATMOSPHERIC PRESSURE: The pressure on the Earth's surface caused by the weight of the air in the atmosphere. At sea level, this pressure is 14.7 psi at 32°F (101 kPa at 0°C).

ATOMIZATION: The breaking down of a liquid into a fine mist that can be suspended in air.

AUXILIARY ADD-ON COOLER: A supplemental transmission fluid cooling device that is installed in series with the heat exchanger (cooler), located inside the radiator, to provide additional support to cool the hot fluid leaving the torque converter.

AUXILIARY PRESSURE: An added fluid pressure that is introduced into a regulator or balanced valve system to control valve movement. The auxiliary pressure itself can be either a fixed or a variable value. (See balanced valve; regulator valve.)

AWD: All wheel drive.

AXIAL FORCE: A side or end thrust force acting in or along the same plane as the power flow.

AXIAL PLAY: Movement parallel to a shaft or bearing bore.

AXLE CAPACITY: The maximum load-carrying capacity of the axle itself, as specified by the manufacturer. This is usually a higher number than the GAWR.

AXLE RATIO: This is a number (3.07:1, 4.56:1, for example) expressing the ratio between driveshaft revolutions and wheel revolutions. A low numerical ratio allows the engine to work easier because it doesn't have to turn as fast. A high numerical ratio means that the engine has to turn more rpm's to move the wheels through the same number of turns.

BACKFIRE: The sudden combustion of gases in the intake or exhaust system that results in a loud explosion.

BACKLASH: The clearance or play between two parts, such as meshed gears.

BACKPRESSURE: Restrictions in the exhaust system that slow the exit of exhaust gases from the combustion chamber.

BAKELITE®: A heat resistant, plastic insulator material commonly used in printed circuit boards and transistorized components.

BALANCED VALVE: A valve that is positioned by opposing auxiliary hydraulic pressures and/or spring force. Examples include mainline regulator, throttle, and governor valves. (See regulator valve.)

BAND: A flexible ring of steel with an inner lining of friction material. When tightened around the outside of a drum, a planetary member is held stationary to the transmission/transaxle case.

BALL BEARING: A bearing made up of hardened inner and outer races between which hardened steel balls roll.

BALL JOINT: A ball and matching socket connecting suspension components (steering knuckle to lower control arms). It permits rotating movement in any direction between the components that are joined.

BARO (BAROMETRIC PRESSURE SENSOR): Measures the change in the intake manifold pressure caused by changes in altitude.

BAROMETRIC MANIFOLD ABSOLUTE PRESSURE (BMAP) SENSOR: Operates similarly to a conventional MAP sensor; reads intake manifold pressure and is also responsible for determining altitude and barometric pressure prior to engine operation.

BAROMETRIC PRESSURE: (See atmospheric pressure.)

BALLAST RESISTOR: A resistor in the primary ignition circuit that lowers voltage after the engine is started to reduce wear on ignition components.

BATTERY: A direct current electrical storage unit, consisting of the basic active materials of lead and sulfuric acid, which converts chemical energy into electrical energy. Used to provide current for the operation of the starter as well as other equipment, such as the radio, lighting, etc.

BEAD: The portion of a tire that holds it on the rim.

BEARING: A friction reducing, supportive device usually located between a stationary part and a moving part.

BEFORE TOP DEAD CENTER (BTDC): The point just before the piston reaches the top of its travel on the compression stroke.

BELTED TIRE: Tire construction similar to bias-ply tires, but using two or more layers of reinforced belts between body plies and the tread.

BEZEL: Piece of metal surrounding radio, headlights, gauges or similar components; sometimes used to hold the glass face of a gauge in the dash.

BIAS-PLY TIRE: Tire construction, using body ply reinforcing cords which run at alternating angles to the center line of the tread.

BI-METAL TEMPERATURE SENSOR: Any sensor or switch made of two dissimilar types of metal that bend when heated or cooled due to the different expansion rates of the alloys. These types of sensors usually function as an on/off switch.

BLOCK: See Engine Block.

BLOW-BY: Combustion gases, composed of water vapor and unburned fuel, that leak past the piston rings into the crankcase during normal engine operation. These gases are removed by the PCV system to prevent the buildup of harmful acids in the crankcase.

BOOK TIME: See Labor Time.

BOOK VALUE: The average value of a car, widely used to determine trade-in and resale value.

BOOST VALVE: Used at the base of the regulator valve to increase mainline pressure.

BORE: Diameter of a cylinder.

BRAKE CALIPER: The housing that fits over the brake disc. The caliper holds the brake pads, which are pressed against the discs by the caliper pistons when the brake pedal is depressed.

BRAKE HORSEPOWER (BHP): The actual horsepower available at the engine flywheel as measured by a dynamometer.

BRAKE FADE: Loss of braking power, usually caused by excessive heat after repeated brake applications.

BRAKE HORSEPOWER: Usable horsepower of an engine measured at the crankshaft.

BRAKE PAD: A brake shoe and lining assembly used with disc brakes.

BRAKE PROPORTIONING VALVE: A valve on the master cylinder which restricts hydraulic brake pressure to the wheels to a specified amount, preventing wheel lock-up.

BREAKAWAY: Often used by Chrysler to identify first-gear operation in D and 2 ranges. In these ranges, first-gear operation depends on a one-way roller clutch that holds on acceleration and releases (breaks away) on deceleration, resulting in a freewheeling coast-down condition.

BRAKE SHOE: The backing for the brake lining. The term is, however, usually applied to the assembly of the brake backing and lining.

BREAKER POINTS: A set of points inside the distributor, operated by a cam, which make and break the ignition circuit.

BRINNELLING: A wear pattern identified by a series of indentations at regular intervals. This condition is caused by a lack of lube, overload situations, and/or vibrations.

BTDC: Before Top Dead Center.

BUMP: Sudden and forceful apply of a clutch or band.

BUSHING: A liner, usually removable, for a bearing; an anti-friction liner used in place of a bearing.

CALIFORNIA ENGINE: An engine certified by the EPA for use in California only; conforms to more stringent emission regulations than Federal engine.

CALIPER: A hydraulically activated device in a disc brake system, which is mounted straddling the brake rotor (disc). The caliper contains at least one piston and two brake pads. Hydraulic pressure on the piston(s) forces the pads against the rotor.

CAPACITY: The quantity of electricity that can be delivered from a unit, as from a battery in ampere-hours, or output, as from a generator.

CAMBER: One of the factors of wheel alignment. Viewed from the front of the car, it is the inward or outward tilt of the wheel. The top of the tire will lean outward (positive camber) or inward (negative camber).

CAMSHAFT: A shaft in the engine on which are the lobes (cams) which operate the valves. The camshaft is driven by the crankshaft, via a belt, chain or gears, at one half the crankshaft speed.

CAPACITOR: A device which stores an electrical charge.

CARBON MONOXIDE (CO): A colorless, odorless gas given off as a normal byproduct of combustion. It is poisonous and extremely dangerous in confined areas, building up slowly to toxic levels without warning if adequate ventilation is not available.

CARBURETOR: A device, usually mounted on the intake manifold of an engine, which mixes the air and fuel in the proper proportion to allow even combustion.

CASTER: The forward or rearward tilt of an imaginary line drawn through the upper ball joint and the center of the wheel. Viewed from the sides, positive caster (forward tilt) lends directional stability, while negative caster (rearward tilt) produces instability.

CATALYTIC CONVERTER: A device installed in the exhaust system, like a muffler, that converts harmful byproducts of combustion into carbon dioxide and water vapor by means of a heat-producing chemical reaction.

CENTRIFUGAL ADVANCE: A mechanical method of advancing the spark timing by using flyweights in the distributor that react to centrifugal force generated by the distributor shaft rotation.

CENTRIFUGAL FORCE: The outward pull of a revolving object, away from the center of revolution. Centrifugal force increases with the speed of rotation.

CETANE RATING: A measure of the ignition value of diesel fuel. The higher the cetane rating, the better the fuel. Diesel fuel cetane rating is roughly comparable to gasoline octane rating.

CHECK VALVE: Any one-way valve installed to permit the flow of air, fuel or vacuum in one direction only.

CHOKE: The valve/plate that restricts the amount of air entering an engine on the induction stroke, thereby enriching the air/fuel ratio.

CHUGGLE: Bucking or jerking condition that may be engine related and may be most noticeable when converter clutch is engaged; similar to the feel of towing a trailer.

CIRCLIP: A split steel snaring that fits into a groove to hold various parts in place.

CIRCUIT BREAKER: A switch which protects an electrical circuit from overload by opening the circuit when the current flow exceeds a pre-determined level. Some circuit breakers must be reset manually, while most reset automatically.

CIRCUIT: Any unbroken path through which an electrical current can flow. Also used to describe fuel flow in some instances.

CIRCUIT, BYPASS: Another circuit in parallel with the major circuit through which power is diverted.

CIRCUIT, CLOSED: An electrical circuit in which there is no interruption of current flow.

CIRCUIT, GROUND: The non-insulated portion of a complete circuit used as a common potential point. In automotive circuits, the ground is composed of metal parts, such as the engine, body sheet metal, and frame and is usually a negative potential.

CIRCUIT, HOT: That portion of a circuit not at ground potential. The hot circuit is usually insulated and is connected to the positive side of the battery.

CIRCUIT, OPEN: A break or lack of contact in an electrical circuit, either intentional (switch) or unintentional (bad connection or broken wire).

CIRCUIT, PARALLEL: A circuit having two or more paths for current flow with common positive and negative tie points. The same voltage is applied to each load device or parallel branch.

CIRCUIT, SERIES: An electrical system in which separate parts are connected end to end, using one wire, to form a single path for current to flow.

CIRCUIT, SHORT: A circuit that is accidentally completed in an electrical path for which it was not intended.

CLAMPING (ISOLATION) DIODES: Diodes positioned in a circuit to prevent self-induction from damaging electronic components.

CLEARCOAT: A transparent layer which, when sprayed over a vehicle's paint job, adds gloss and depth as well as an additional protective coating to the finish.

CLUTCH: Part of the power train used to connect/disconnect power to the rear wheels.

CLUTCH, FLUID: The same as a fluid coupling. A fluid clutch or coupling performs the same function as a friction clutch by utilizing fluid friction and inertia as opposed to solid friction used by a friction clutch. (See fluid coupling.)

CLUTCH, FRICTION: A coupling device that provides a means of smooth and positive engagement and disengagement of engine torque to the vehicle powertrain. Transmission of power through the clutch is accomplished by bringing one or more rotating drive members into contact with complementing driven members.

COAST: Vehicle deceleration caused by engine braking conditions.

COEFFICIENT OF FRICTION: The amount of surface tension between two contacting surfaces; identified by a scientifically calculated number.

COIL: Part of the ignition system that boosts the relatively low voltage supplied by the car's electrical system to the high voltage required to fire the spark plugs.

COMBINATION MANIFOLD: An assembly which includes both the intake and exhaust manifolds in one casting.

COMBINATION VALVE: A device used in some fuel systems that routes fuel vapors to a charcoal storage canister instead of venting them into the atmosphere. The valve relieves fuel tank pressure and allows fresh air into the tank as the fuel level drops to prevent a vapor lock situation.

COMBUSTION CHAMBER: The part of the engine in the cylinder head where combustion takes place.

COMPOUND GEAR: A gear consisting of two or more simple gears with a common shaft.

COMPOUND PLANETARY: A gearset that has more than the three elements found in a simple gearset and is constructed by combining members of two planetary gearsets to create additional gear ratio possibilities.

COMPRESSION CHECK: A test involving removing each spark plug and inserting a gauge. When the engine is cranked, the gauge will record a pressure reading in the individual cylinder. General operating condition can be determined from a compression check.

COMPRESSION RATIO: The ratio of the volume between the piston and cylinder head when the piston is at the bottom of its stroke (bottom dead center) and when the piston is at the top of its stroke (top dead center).

COMPUTER: An electronic control module that correlates input data according to prearranged engineered instructions; used for the management of an actuator system or systems.

CONDENSER: An electrical device which acts to store an electrical charge, preventing voltage surges.

2. A radiator-like device in the air conditioning system in which refrigerant gas condenses into a liquid, giving off heat.

CONDUCTOR: Any material through which an electrical current can be transmitted easily.

CONNECTING ROD: The connecting link between the crankshaft and piston.

CONSTANT VELOCITY JOINT: Type of universal joint in a halfshaft assembly in which the output shaft turns at a constant angular velocity without variation, provided that the speed of the input shaft is constant.

CONTINUITY: Continuous or complete circuit. Can be checked with an ohmmeter.

CONTROL ARM: The upper or lower suspension components which are mounted on the frame and support the ball joints and steering knuckles.

CONVENTIONAL IGNITION: Ignition system which uses breaker points.

CONVERTER: (See torque converter.)

CONVERTER LOCKUP: The switching from hydrodynamic to direct mechanical drive, usually through the application of a friction element called the converter clutch.

COOLANT: Mixture of water and anti-freeze circulated through the engine to carry off heat produced by the engine.

CORROSION INHIBITOR: An inhibitor in ATF that prevents corrosion of bushings, thrust washers, and oil cooler brazed joints.

COUNTERSHAFT: An intermediate shaft which is rotated by a mainshaft and transmits, in turn, that rotation to a working part.

COUPLING PHASE: Occurs when the torque converter is operating at its greatest hydraulic efficiency. The speed differential between the impeller and the turbine is at its minimum. At this point, the stator freewheels, and there is no torque multiplication.

CRANKCASE: The lower part of an engine in which the crankshaft and related parts operate.

CRANKSHAFT: Engine component (connected to pistons by connecting rods) which converts the reciprocating (up and down) motion of pistons to rotary motion used to turn the driveshaft.

CURB WEIGHT: The weight of a vehicle without passengers or payload, but including all fluids (oil, gas, coolant, etc.) and other equipment specified as standard.

CURRENT: The flow (or rate) of electrons moving through a circuit. Current is measured in amperes (amp).

CURRENT FLOW CONVENTIONAL: Current flows through a circuit from the positive terminal of the source to the negative terminal (plus to minus).

CURRENT FLOW, ELECTRON: Current or electrons flow from the negative terminal of the source, through the circuit, to the positive terminal (minus to plus).

CV-JOINT: Constant velocity joint.

CYCLIC VIBRATIONS: The off-center movement of a rotating object that is affected by its initial balance, speed of rotation, and working angles.

CYLINDER BLOCK: See engine block.

CYLINDER HEAD: The detachable portion of the engine, usually fastened to the top of the cylinder block and containing all or most of the combustion chambers. On overhead valve engines, it contains the valves and their operating parts. On overhead cam engines, it contains the camshaft as well.

CYLINDER: In an engine, the round hole in the engine block in which the piston(s) ride.

DATA LINK CONNECTOR (DLC): Current acronym/term applied to the federally mandated, diagnostic junction connector that is used to monitor ECM/PC/TCM inputs, processing strategies, and outputs including diagnostic trouble codes (DTCs).

DEAD CENTER: The extreme top or bottom of the piston stroke.

DECELERATION BUMP: When referring to a torque converter clutch in the applied position, a sudden release of the accelerator pedal causes a forceful reversal of power through the drivetrain (engine braking), just prior to the apply plate actually being released.

DELAYED (LATE OR EXTENDED): Condition where shift is expected but does not occur for a period of time, for example, where clutch or band engagement does not occur as quickly as expected during part throttle or wide open throttle apply of accelerator or when manually downshifting to a lower range.

DETENT: A spring-loaded plunger, pin, ball, or pawl used as a holding device on a ratchet wheel or shaft. In automatic transmissions, a detent mechanism is used for locking the manual valve in place.

DETENT DOWNSHIFT: (See kickdown.)

DETERGENT: An additive in engine oil to improve its operating characteristics.

DETONATION: An unwanted explosion of the air/fuel mixture in the combustion chamber caused by excess heat and compression, advanced timing, or an overly lean mixture. Also referred to as "ping".

DEXRON®: A brand of automatic transmission fluid.

DIAGNOSTIC TROUBLE CODES (DTCs): A digital display from the control module memory that identifies the input, processor, or output device circuit that is related to the powertrain emission/driveability malfunction detected. Diagnostic trouble codes can be read by the MIL to flash any codes or by using a handheld scanner.

DIAPHRAGM: A thin, flexible wall separating two cavities, such as in a vacuum advance unit.

DIESELING: The engine continues to run after the car is shut off; caused by fuel continuing to be burned in the combustion chamber.

DIFFERENTIAL: A geared assembly which allows the transmission of motion between drive axles, giving one axle the ability to rotate faster than the other, as in cornering.

DIFFERENTIAL AREAS: When opposing faces of a spool valve are acted upon by the same pressure but their areas differ in size, the face with the larger area produces the differential force and valve movement. (See spool valve.)

DIFFERENTIAL FORCE: (See differential areas)

DIGITAL READOUT: A display of numbers or a combination of numbers and letters.

DIGITAL VOLT OHMMETER: An electronic diagnostic tool used to measure voltage, ohms and amps as well as several other functions, with the readings displayed on a digital screen in tenths, hundredths and thousandths.

DIODE: An electrical device that will allow current to flow in one direction only.

DIRECT CURRENT (DC): Electrical current that flows in one direction only.

DIRECT DRIVE: The gear ratio is 1:1, with no change occurring in the torque and speed input/output relationship.

DISC BRAKE: A hydraulic braking assembly consisting of a brake disc, or rotor, mounted on an axle shaft, and a caliper assembly containing, usually two brake pads which are activated by hydraulic pressure. The pads are forced against the sides of the disc, creating friction which slows the vehicle.

DISPERSANTS: Suspend dirt and prevent sludge buildup in a liquid, such as engine oil.

DOUBLE BUMP (DOUBLE FEEL): Two sudden and forceful applies of a clutch or band.

DISPLACEMENT: The total volume of air that is displaced by all pistons as the engine turns through one complete revolution.

DISTRIBUTOR: A mechanically driven device on an engine which is responsible for electrically firing the spark plug at a pre-determined point of the piston stroke.

DOHC: Double overhead camshaft.

DOUBLE OVERHEAD CAMSHAFT: The engine utilizes two camshafts mounted in one cylinder head. One camshaft operates the exhaust valves, while the other operates the intake valves.

DOWEL PIN: A pin, inserted in mating holes in two different parts allowing those parts to maintain a fixed relationship.

DRIVELINE: The drive connection between the transmission and the drive wheels.

DRIVE TRAIN: The components that transmit the flow of power from the engine to the wheels. The components include the clutch, transmission, driveshafts (or axle shafts in front wheel drive), U-joints and differential.

DRUM BRAKE: A braking system which consists of two brake shoes and one or two wheel cylinders, mounted on a fixed backing plate, and a brake drum, mounted on an axle, which revolves around the assembly.

DRY CHARGED BATTERY: Battery to which electrolyte is added when the battery is placed in service.

DVOM: Digital volt ohmmeter

DWELL: The rate, measured in degrees of shaft rotation, at which an electrical circuit cycles on and off.

DYNAMIC: An application in which there is rotating or reciprocating motion between the parts.

EARLY: Condition where shift occurs before vehicle has reached proper speed, which tends to labor engine after upshift.

EBCM: See Electronic Control Unit (ECU).

ECM: See Electronic Control Unit (ECU).

ECU: Electronic control unit.

ELECTRODE: Conductor (positive or negative) of electric current.

ELECTROLYSIS: A surface etching or bonding of current conducting transmission/transaxle components that may occur when grounding straps are missing or in poor condition.

ELECTROLYTE: A solution of water and sulfuric acid used to activate the battery. Electrolyte is extremely corrosive.

ELECTROMAGNET: A coil that produces a magnetic field when current flows through its windings.

ELECTROMAGNETIC INDUCTION: A method to create (generate) current flow through the use of magnetism.

ELECTROMAGNETISM: The effects surrounding the relationship between electricity and magnetism.

ELECTROMOTIVE FORCE (EMF): The force or pressure (voltage) that causes current movement in an electrical circuit.

ELECTRONIC CONTROL UNIT: A digital computer that controls engine (and sometimes transmission, brake or other vehicle system) functions based on data received from various sensors. Examples used by some manufacturers include Electronic Brake Control Module (EBCM), Engine Control Module (ECM), Powertrain Control Module (PCM) or Vehicle Control Module (VCM).

ELECTRONIC IGNITION: A system in which the timing and firing of the spark plugs is controlled by an electronic control unit, usually called a module. These systems have no points or condenser.

ELECTRONIC PRESSURE CONTROL (EPC) SOLENOID: A specially designed solenoid containing a spool valve and spring assembly to control fluid mainline pressure. A variable current flow, controlled by the ECM/PCM, varies the internal force of the solenoid on the spool valve and resulting mainline pressure. (See variable force solenoid.)

ELECTRONICS: Miniaturized electrical circuits utilizing semiconductors, solid-state devices, and printed circuits. Electronic circuits utilize small amounts of power.

ELECTRONIFICATION: The application of electronic circuitry to a mechanical device. Regarding automatic transmissions, electrification is incorporated into converter clutch lockup, shift scheduling, and line pressure control systems.

ELECTROSTATIC DISCHARGE (ESD): An unwanted, high-voltage electrical current released by an individual who has taken on a static charge of electricity. Electronic components can be easily damaged by ESD.

ELEMENT: A device within a hydrodynamic drive unit designed with a set of blades to direct fluid flow.

ENAMEL: Type of paint that dries to a smooth, glossy finish.

END BUMP (END FEEL OR SLIP BUMP): Firmer feel at end of shift when compared with feel at start of shift.

END-PLAY: The clearance/gap between two components that allows for expansion of the parts as they warm up, to prevent binding and to allow space for lubrication.

ENERGY: The ability or capacity to do work.

ENGINE: The primary motor or power apparatus of a vehicle, which converts liquid or gas fuel into mechanical energy.

ENGINE BLOCK: The basic engine casting containing the cylinders, the crankshaft main bearings, as well as machined surfaces for the mounting of other components such as the cylinder head, oil pan, transmission, etc.

ENGINE BRAKING: Use of engine to slow vehicle by manually downshifting during zero-throttle coast down.

ENGINE CONTROL MODULE (ECM): Manages the engine and incorporates output control over the torque converter clutch solenoid. (Note: Current designation for the ECM in late model vehicles is PCM.)

ENGINE COOLANT TEMPERATURE (ECT) SENSOR: Prevents converter clutch engagement with a cold engine; also used for shift timing and shift quality.

EP LUBRICANT: EP (extreme pressure) lubricants are specially formulated for use with gears involving heavy loads (transmissions, differentials, etc.).

ETHYL: A substance added to gasoline to improve its resistance to knock, by slowing down the rate of combustion.

ETHYLENE GLYCOL: The base substance of antifreeze.

EXHAUST MANIFOLD: A set of cast passages or pipes which conduct exhaust gases from the engine.

FAIL-SAFE (BACKUP) CONTROL: A substitute value used by the PCM/TCM to replace a faulty signal from an input sensor. The temporary value allows the vehicle to continue to be operated.

FAST IDLE: The speed of the engine when the choke is on. Fast idle speeds engine warm-up.

FEDERAL ENGINE: An engine certified by the EPA for use in any of the 49 states (except California).

FEEDBACK: A circuit malfunction whereby current can find another path to feed load devices.

FEELER GAUGE: A blade, usually metal, of precisely predetermined thickness, used to measure the clearance between two parts.

FILAMENT: The part of a bulb that glows; the filament creates high resistance to current flow and actually glows from the resulting heat.

FINAL DRIVE: An essential part of the axle drive assembly where final gear reduction takes place in the powertrain. In RWD applications and north-south FWD applications, it must also change the power flow direction to the axle shaft by ninety degrees. (Also see axle ratio.)

FIRING ORDER: The order in which combustion occurs in the cylinders of an engine. Also the order in which spark is distributed to the plugs by the distributor.

FIRM: A noticeable quick apply of a clutch or band that is considered normal with medium to heavy throttle shift; should not be confused with harsh or rough.

FLAME FRONT: The term used to describe certain aspects of the fuel explosion in the cylinders. The flame front should move in a controlled pattern across the cylinder, rather than simply exploding immediately.

FLARE (SLIPPING): A quick increase in engine rpm accompanied by momentary loss of torque; generally occurs during shift.

FLAT ENGINE: Engine design in which the pistons are horizontally opposed. Porsche, Subaru and some old VW are common examples of flat engines.

FLAT RATE: A dealership term referring to the amount of money paid to a technician for a repair or diagnostic service based on that particular service versus dealership's labor time (NOT based on the actual time the technician spent on the job).

FLAT SPOT: A point during acceleration when the engine seems to lose power for an instant.

FLOODING: The presence of too much fuel in the intake manifold and combustion chamber which prevents the air/fuel mixture from firing, thereby causing a no-start situation.

FLUID: A fluid can be either liquid or gas. In hydraulics, a liquid is used for transmitting force or motion.

FLUID COUPLING: The simplest form of hydrodynamic drive, the fluid coupling consists of two look-alike members with straight radial varies referred to as the impeller (pump) and the turbine. Input torque is always equal to the output torque.

FLUID DRIVE: Either a fluid coupling or a fluid torque converter. (See hydrodynamic drive units.)

FLUID TORQUE CONVERTER: A hydrodynamic drive that has the ability to act both as a torque multiplier and fluid coupling. (See hydrodynamic drive units; torque converter.)

FLUID VISCOSITY: The resistance of a liquid to flow. A cold fluid (oil) has greater viscosity and flows more slowly than a hot fluid (oil).

FLYWHEEL: A heavy disc of metal attached to the rear of the crankshaft. It smoothes the firing impulses of the engine and keeps the crankshaft turning during periods when no firing takes place. The starter also engages the flywheel to start the engine.

FOOT POUND (ft. lbs., lbs. ft. or sometimes, ft. lb.): The amount of energy or work needed to raise an item weighing one pound, a distance of one foot.

FREEZE PLUG: A plug in the engine block which will be pushed out if the coolant freezes. Sometimes called expansion plugs, they protect the block from cracking should the coolant freeze.

FRICTION: The resistance that occurs between contacting surfaces. This relationship is expressed by a ratio called the coefficient of friction (CL).

FRICTION, COEFFICIENT OF: The amount of surface tension between two contacting surfaces; expressed by a scientifically calculated number.

FRONT END ALIGNMENT: A service to set caster, camber and toe-in to the correct specifications. This will ensure that the car steers and handles properly and that the tires wear properly.

FRICTION MODIFIER: Changes the coefficient of friction of the fluid between the mating steel and composition clutch/band surfaces during the engagement process and allows for a certain amount of intentional slipping for a good "shift-feel".

FRONTAL AREA: The total frontal area of a vehicle exposed to air flow.

FUEL FILTER: A component of the fuel system containing a porous paper element used to prevent any impurities from entering the engine through the fuel system. It usually takes the form of a canister-like housing, mounted in-line with the fuel hose, located anywhere on a vehicle between the fuel tank and engine.

FUEL INJECTION: A system replacing the carburetor that sprays fuel into the cylinder through nozzles. The amount of fuel can be more precisely controlled with fuel injection.

FULL FLOATING AXLE: An axle in which the axle housing extends through the wheel giving bearing support on the outside of the housing. The front axle of a four-wheel drive vehicle is usually a full floating axle, as are the rear axles of many larger (1 ton and over) pick-ups and vans.

FULL-TIME FOUR-WHEEL DRIVE: A four-wheel drive system that continuously delivers power to all four wheels. A differential between the front and rear driveshafts permits variations in axle speeds to control gear wind-up without damage.

FULL THROTTLE DETENT DOWNSHIFT: A quick apply of accelerator pedal to its full travel, forcing a downshift.

FUSE: A protective device in a circuit which prevents circuit overload by breaking the circuit when a specific amperage is present. The device is constructed around a strip or wire of a lower amperage rating than the circuit it is designed to protect. When an amperage higher than that stamped on the fuse is present in the circuit, the strip or wire melts, opening the circuit.

FUSIBLE LINK: A piece of wire in a wiring harness that performs the same job as a fuse. If overloaded, the fusible link will melt and interrupt the circuit.

FWD: Front wheel drive.

GAWR: (Gross axle weight rating) the total maximum weight an axle is designed to carry.

GCW: (Gross combined weight) total combined weight of a tow vehicle and trailer.

GARAGE SHIFT: initial engagement feel of transmission, neutral to reverse or neutral to a forward drive.

GARAGE SHIFT FEEL: A quick check of the engagement quality and responsiveness of reverse and forward gears. This test is done with the vehicle stationary.

GEAR: A toothed mechanical device that acts as a rotating lever to transmit power or turning effort from one shaft to another. (See gear ratio.)

GEAR RATIO: A ratio expressing the number of turns a smaller gear will make to turn a larger gear through one revolution. The ratio is found by dividing the number of teeth on the smaller gear into the number of teeth on the larger gear.

GEARBOX: Transmission

GEAR REDUCTION: Torque is multiplied and speed decreased by the factor of the gear ratio. For example, a 3:1 gear ratio changes an input torque of 180 ft. lbs. and an input speed of 2700 rpm to 540 Ft. lbs. and 900 rpm, respectively. (No account is taken of frictional losses, which are always present.)

GEARTRAIN: A succession of intermeshing gears that form an assembly and provide for one or more torque changes as the power input is transmitted to the power output.

GEL COAT: A thin coat of plastic resin covering fiberglass body panels.

GENERATOR: A device which produces direct current (DC) necessary to charge the battery.

GOVERNOR: A device that senses vehicle speed and generates a hydraulic oil pressure. As vehicle speed increases, governor oil pressure rises.

GROUND CIRCUIT: (See circuit, ground.)

GROUND SIDE SWITCHING: The electrical/electronic circuit control switch is located after the circuit load.

GVWR: (Gross vehicle weight rating) total maximum weight a vehicle is designed to carry including the weight of the vehicle, passengers, equipment, gas, oil, etc.

HALOGEN: A special type of lamp known for its quality of brilliant white light. Originally used for fog lights and driving lights.

HARD CODES: DTCs that are present at the time of testing; also called continuous or current codes.

HARSH(ROUGH): An apply of a clutch or band that is more noticeable than a firm one; considered undesirable at any throttle position.

HEADER TANK: An expansion tank for the radiator coolant. It can be located remotely or built into the radiator.

HEAT RANGE: A term used to describe the ability of a spark plug to carry away heat. Plugs with longer nosed insulators take longer to carry heat off effectively.

HEAT RISER: A flapper in the exhaust manifold that is closed when the engine is cold, causing hot exhaust gases to heat the intake manifold providing better cold engine operation. A thermostatic spring opens the flapper when the engine warms up.

HEAVY THROTTLE: Approximately three-fourths of accelerator pedal travel.

HEMI: A name given an engine using hemispherical combustion chambers.

HERTZ (HZ): The international unit of frequency equal to one cycle per second (10,000 Hertz equals 10,000 cycles per second).

HIGH-IMPEDANCE DVOM (DIGITAL VOLT-OHMMETER): This styled device provides a built-in resistance value and is capable of limiting circuit current flow to safe milliamp levels.

HIGH RESISTANCE: Often refers to a circuit where there is an excessive amount of opposition to normal current flow.

HORSEPOWER: A measurement of the amount of work; one horsepower is the amount of work necessary to lift 33,000 lbs. one foot in one minute. Brake horsepower (bhp) is the horsepower delivered by an engine on a dynamometer. Net horsepower is the power remaining (measured at the flywheel of the engine) that can be used to turn the wheels after power is consumed through friction and running the engine accessories (water pump, alternator, air pump, fan etc.)

HOT CIRCUIT: (See circuit, hot; hot lead.)

HOT LEAD: A wire or conductor in the power side of the circuit. (See circuit, hot.)

HOT SIDE SWITCHING: The electrical/electronic circuit control switch is located before the circuit load.

HUB: The center part of a wheel or gear.

HUNTING (BUSYNESS): Repeating quick series of up-shifts and downshifts that causes noticeable change in engine rpm, for example, as in a 4-3-4 shift pattern.

HYDRAULICS: The use of liquid under pressure to transfer force of motion.

HYDROCARBON (HC): Any chemical compound made up of hydrogen and carbon. A major pollutant formed by the engine as a by-product of combustion.

HYDRODYNAMIC DRIVE UNITS: Devices that transmit power solely by the action of a kinetic fluid flow in a closed recirculating path. An impeller energizes the fluid and discharges the high-speed jet stream into the turbine for power output.

HYDROMETER: An instrument used to measure the specific gravity of a solution.

HYDROPLANING: A phenomenon of driving when water builds up under the tire tread, causing it to lose contact with the road. Slowing down will usually restore normal tire contact with the road.

HYPOID GEARSET: The drive pinion gear may be placed below or above the centerline of the driven gear; often used as a final drive gearset.

IDLE MIXTURE: The mixture of air and fuel (usually about 14:1) being fed to the cylinders. The idle mixture screw(s) are sometimes adjusted as part of a tune-up.

IDLER ARM: Component of the steering linkage which is a geometric duplicate of the steering gear arm. It supports the right side of the center steering link.

IMPELLER: Often called a pump, the impeller is the power input (drive) member of a hydrodynamic drive. As part of the torque converter cover, it acts as a centrifugal pump and puts the fluid in motion.

INCH POUND (inch lbs.; sometimes in. lb. or in. lbs.): One twelfth of a foot pound.

INDUCTANCE: The force that produces voltage when a conductor is passed through a magnetic field.

INDUCTION: A means of transferring electrical energy in the form of a magnetic field. Principle used in the ignition coil to increase voltage.

INITIAL FEEL: A distinct firmer feel at start of shift when compared with feel at finish of shift.

INJECTOR: A device which receives metered fuel under relatively low pressure and is activated to inject the fuel into the engine under relatively high pressure at a predetermined time.

INPUT: In an automatic transmission, the source of power from the engine is absorbed by the torque converter, which provides the power input into the transmission. The turbine drives the input(turbine)shaft.

INPUT SHAFT: The shaft to which torque is applied, usually carrying the driving gear or gears.

INTAKE MANIFOLD: A casting of passages or pipes used to conduct air or a fuel/air mixture to the cylinders.

INTERNAL GEAR: The ring-like outer gear of a planetary gearset with the gear teeth cut on the inside of the ring to provide a mesh with the planet pinions.

ISOLATION (CLAMPING) DIODES: Diodes positioned in a circuit to prevent self-induction from damaging electronic components.

IX ROTARY GEAR PUMP: Contains two rotating members, one shaped with internal gear teeth and the other with external gear teeth. As the gears separate, the fluid fills the gaps between gear teeth, is pulled across a crescent-shaped divider, and then is forced to flow through the outlet as the gears mesh.

IX ROTARY LOBE PUMP: Sometimes referred to as a gerotor type pump. Two rotating members, one shaped with internal lobes and the other with external lobes, separate and then mesh to cause fluid to flow.

JOURNAL: The bearing surface within which a shaft operates.

JUMPER CABLES: Two heavy duty wires with large alligator clips used to provide power from a charged battery to a discharged battery mounted in a vehicle.

JUMPSTART: Utilizing the sufficiently charged battery of one vehicle to start the engine of another vehicle with a discharged battery by the use of jumper cables.

KEY: A small block usually fitted in a notch between a shaft and a hub to prevent slippage of the two parts.

KICKDOWN: Detent downshift system; either linkage, cable, or electrically controlled.

KILO: A prefix used in the metric system to indicate one thousand.

KNOCK: Noise which results from the spontaneous ignition of a portion of the air-fuel mixture in the engine cylinder caused by overly advanced ignition timing or use of incorrectly low octane fuel for that engine.

KNOCK SENSOR: An input device that responds to spark knock, caused by over advanced ignition timing.

LABOR TIME: A specific amount of time required to perform a certain repair or diagnostic service as defined by a vehicle or after-market manufacturer.

LACQUER: A quick-drying automotive paint.

LATE: Shift that occurs when engine is at higher than normal rpm for given amount of throttle.

LIGHT-EMITTING DIODE (LED): A semiconductor diode that emits light as electrical current flows through it; used in some electronic display devices to emit a red or other color light.

LIGHT THROTTLE: Approximately one-fourth of accelerator pedal travel.

LIMITED SLIP: A type of differential which transfers driving force to the wheel with the best traction.

LIMP-IN MODE: Electrical shutdown of the transmission/ transaxle output solenoids, allowing only forward and reverse gears that are hydraulically energized by the manual valve. This permits the vehicle to be driven to a service facility for repair.

LIP SEAL: Molded synthetic rubber seal designed with an outer sealing edge (lip) that points into the fluid containing area to be sealed. This type of seal is used where rotational and axial forces are present.

LITHIUM-BASE GREASE: Chassis and wheel bearing grease using lithium as a base. Not compatible with sodium-base grease.

LOAD DEVICE: A circuit's resistance that converts the electrical energy into light, sound, heat, or mechanical movement.

LOAD RANGE: Indicates the number of plies at which a tire is rated. Load range B equals four-ply rating; C equals six-ply rating; and, D equals an eight-ply rating.

LOAD TORQUE: The amount of output torque needed from the transmission/transaxle to overcome the vehicle load.

LOCKING HUBS: Accessories used on part-time four-wheel drive systems that allow the front wheels to be disengaged from the drive train when four-wheel drive is not being used. When four-wheel drive is desired, the hubs are engaged, locking the wheels to the drive train.

LOCKUP CONVERTER: A torque converter that operates hydraulically and mechanically. When an internal apply plate (lockup plate) clamps to the torque converter cover, hydraulic slippage is eliminated.

LOCK RING: See Circlip or Snapring

MAGNET: Any body with the property of attracting iron or steel.

MAGNETIC FIELD: The area surrounding the poles of a magnet that is affected by its attraction or repulsion forces.

MAIN LINE PRESSURE: Often called control pressure or line pressure, it refers to the pressure of the oil leaving the pump and is controlled by the pressure regulator valve.

MALFUNCTION INDICATOR LAMP (MIL): Previously known as a check engine light, the dash-mounted MIL illuminates and signals the driver that an emission or driveability problem with the powertrain has been detected by the ECM/PCM. When this occurs, at least one diagnostic trouble code (DTC) has been stored into the control module memory.

MANIFOLD ABSOLUTE PRESSURE (MAP) SENSOR: Reads the amount of air pressure (vacuum) in the engine's intake manifold system; its signal is used to analyze engine load conditions.

MANIFOLD VACUUM: Low pressure in an engine intake manifold formed just below the throttle plates. Manifold vacuum is highest at idle and drops under acceleration.

MANIFOLD: A casting of passages or set of pipes which connect the cylinders to an inlet or outlet source.

MANUAL LEVER POSITION SWITCH (MLPS): A mechanical switching unit that is typically mounted externally to the transmission/transaxle to inform the PCM/ECM which gear range the driver has selected.

MANUAL VALVE: Located inside the transmission/transaxle, it is directly connected to the driver's shift lever. The position of the manual valve determines which hydraulic circuits will be charged with oil pressure and the operating mode of the transmission.

MANUAL VALVE LEVER POSITION SENSOR (MVLPS): The input from this device tells the TCM what gear range was selected.

MASS AIR FLOW (MAF) SENSOR: Measures the airflow into the engine.

MASTER CYLINDER: The primary fluid pressurizing device in a hydraulic system. In automotive use, it is found in brake and hydraulic clutch systems and is pedal activated, either directly or, in a power brake system, through the power booster.

MacPherson STRUT: A suspension component combining a shock absorber and spring in one unit.

MEDIUM THROTTLE: Approximately one-half of accelerator pedal travel.

MEGA: A metric prefix indicating one million.

MEMBER: An independent component of a hydrodynamic unit such as an impeller, a stator, or a turbine. It may have one or more elements.

MERCON: A fluid developed by Ford Motor Company in 1988. It contains a friction modifier and closely resembles operating characteristics of Dexron.

METAL SEALING RINGS: Made from cast iron or aluminum, their primary application is with dynamic components involving pressure sealing circuits of rotating members. These rings are designed with either butt or hook lock end joints.

METER (ANALOG): A linear-style meter representing data as lengths; a needle-style instrument interfacing with logical numerical increments. This style of electrical meter uses relatively low impedance internal resistance and cannot be used for testing electronic circuitry.

METER (DIGITAL): Uses numbers as a direct readout to show values. Most meters of this style use high impedance internal resistance and must be used for testing low current electronic circuitry.

MICRO: A metric prefix indicating one-millionth (0.000001).

MILLI: A metric prefix indicating one-thousandth (0.001).

MINIMUM THROTTLE: The least amount of throttle opening required for upshift; normally close to zero throttle.

MISFIRE: Condition occurring when the fuel mixture in a cylinder fails to ignite, causing the engine to run roughly.

MODULE: Electronic control unit, amplifier or igniter of solid state or integrated design which controls the current flow in the ignition primary circuit based on input from the pick-up coil. When the module opens the primary circuit, high secondary voltage is induced in the coil.

MODULATED: In an electronic-hydraulic converter clutch system (or shift valve system), the term modulated refers to the pulsing of a solenoid, at a variable rate. This action controls the buildup of oil pressure in the hydraulic circuit to allow a controlled amount of clutch slippage.

MODULATED CONVERTER CLUTCH CONTROL (MCCC): A pulse width duty cycle valve that controls the converter lockup apply pressure and maximizes smoother transitions between lock and unlock conditions.

MODULATOR PRESSURE (THROTTLE PRESSURE): A hydraulic signal oil pressure relating to the amount of engine load, based on either the amount of throttle plate opening or engine vacuum.

MODULATOR VALVE: A regulator valve that is controlled by engine vacuum, providing a hydraulic pressure that varies in relation to engine torque. The hydraulic torque signal functions to delay the shift pattern and provide a line pressure boost. (See throttle valve.)

MOTOR: An electromagnetic device used to convert electrical energy into mechanical energy.

MULTIPLE-DISC CLUTCH: A grouping of steel and friction lined plates that, when compressed together by hydraulic pressure acting upon a piston, lock or unlock a planetary member.

MULTI-WEIGHT: Type of oil that provides adequate lubrication at both high and low temperatures.

needed to move one amp through a resistance of one ohm.

MUSHY: Same as soft; slow and drawn out clutch apply with very little shift feel.

MUTUAL INDUCTION: The generation of current from one wire circuit to another by movement of the magnetic field surrounding a current-carrying circuit as its ampere flow increases or decreases.

NEEDLE BEARING: A bearing which consists of a number (usually a large number) of long, thin rollers.

NITROGEN OXIDE (NOx): One of the three basic pollutants found in the exhaust emission of an internal combustion engine. The amount of NOx usually varies in an inverse proportion to the amount of HC and CO.

NONPOSITIVE SEALING: A sealing method that allows some minor leakage, which normally assists in lubrication.

O2 SENSOR: Located in the engine's exhaust system, it is an input device to the ECM/PCM for managing the fuel delivery and ignition system. A scanner can be used to observe the fluctuating voltage readings produced by an O2 sensor as the oxygen content of the exhaust is analyzed.

O-RING SEAL: Molded synthetic rubber seal designed with a circular cross-section. This type of seal is used primarily in static applications.

OBD II (ON-BOARD DIAGNOSTICS, SECOND GENERATION): Refers to the federal law mandating tighter control of 1996 and newer vehicle emissions, active monitoring of related devices, and standardization of terminology, data link connectors, and other technician concerns.

OCTANE RATING: A number, indicating the quality of gasoline based on its ability to resist knock. The higher the number, the better the quality. Higher compression engines require higher octane gas.

OEM: Original Equipment Manufactured. OEM equipment is that furnished standard by the manufacturer.

OFFSET: The distance between the vertical center of the wheel and the mounting surface at the lugs. Offset is positive if the center is outside the lug circle; negative offset puts the center line inside the lug circle.

OHM'S LAW: A law of electricity that states the relationship between voltage, current, and resistance. Volts = amperes x ohms

OHM: The unit used to measure the resistance of conductor-to-electrical flow. One ohm is the amount of resistance that limits current flow to one ampere in a circuit with one volt of pressure.

OHMMETER: An instrument used for measuring the resistance, in ohms, in an electrical circuit.

ONE-WAY CLUTCH: A mechanical clutch of roller or sprag design that resists torque or transmits power in one direction only. It is used to either hold or drive a planetary member.

ONE-WAY ROLLER CLUTCH: A mechanical device that transmits or holds torque in one direction only.

OPEN CIRCUIT: A break or lack of contact in an electrical circuit, either intentional (switch) or unintentional (bad connection or broken wire).

ORIFICE: Located in hydraulic oil circuits, it acts as a restriction. It slows down fluid flow to either create back pressure or delay pressure buildup downstream.

OSCILLOSCOPE: A piece of test equipment that shows electric impulses as a pattern on a screen. Engine performance can be analyzed by interpreting these patterns.

OUTPUT SHAFT: The shaft which transmits torque from a device, such as a transmission.

OUTPUT SPEED SENSOR (OSS): Identifies transmission/transaxle output shaft speed for shift timing and may be used to calculate TCC slip; often functions as the VSS (vehicle speed sensor).

OVERDRIVE: (1.) A device attached to or incorporated in a transmission/transaxle that allows the engine to turn less than one full revolution for every complete revolution of the wheels. The net effect is to reduce engine rpm, thereby using less fuel. A typical overdrive gear ratio would be .87:1, instead of the normal 1:1 in high gear. (2.) A gear assembly which produces more shaft revolutions than that transmitted to it.

OVERDRIVE PLANETARY GEARSET: A single planetary gearset designed to provide a direct drive and overdrive ratio. When coupled to a three-speed transmission/transaxle configuration, a four-speed/overdrive unit is present.

OVERHEAD CAMSHAFT (OHC): An engine configuration in which the camshaft is mounted on top of the cylinder head and operates the valve either directly or by means of rocker arms.

OVERHEAD VALVE (OHV): An engine configuration in which all of the valves are located in the cylinder head and the camshaft is located in the cylinder block. The camshaft operates the valves via lifters and pushrods.

OVERRUNCLUTCH: Another name for a one-way mechanical clutch. Applies to both roller and sprag designs.

OVERSTEER: The tendency of some vehicles, when steering into a turn, to over-respond or steer more than required, which could result in excessive slip of the rear wheels. Opposite of under-steer.

OXIDATION STABILIZERS: Absorb and dissipate heat. Automatic transmission fluid has high resistance to varnish and sludge buildup that occurs from excessive heat that is generated primarily in the torque converter. Local temperatures as high as 6000F (3150C) can occur at the clutch plates during engagement, and this heat must be absorbed and dissipated. If the fluid cannot withstand the heat, it burns or oxidizes, resulting in an almost immediate destruction of friction materials, clogged filter screen and hydraulic passages, and sticky valves.

OXIDES OF NITROGEN: See nitrogen oxide (NOx).

OXYGEN SENSOR: Used with a feedback system to sense the presence of oxygen in the exhaust gas and signal the computer which can use the voltage signal to determine engine operating efficiency and adjust the air/fuel ratio.

PARALLEL CIRCUIT: (See circuit, parallel.)

PARTS WASHER: A basin or tub, usually with a built-in pump mechanism and hose used for circulating chemical solvent for the purpose of cleaning greasy, oily and dirty components.

PART-TIME FOUR WHEEL DRIVE: A system that is normally in the two wheel drive mode and only runs in four-wheel drive when the system is manually engaged because more traction is desired. Two or four wheel drive is normally selected by a lever to engage the front axle, but if locking hubs are used, these must also be manually engaged in the Lock position. Otherwise, the front axle will not drive the front wheels.

PASSIVE RESTRAINT: Safety systems such as air bags or automatic seat belts which operate with no action required on the part of the driver or passenger. Mandated by Federal regulations on all vehicles sold in the U.S. after 1990.

PAYLOAD: The weight the vehicle is capable of carrying in addition to its own weight. Payload includes weight of the driver, passengers and cargo, but not coolant, fuel, lubricant, spare tire, etc.

PCM: Powertrain control module.

PCV VALVE: A valve usually located in the rocker cover that vents crankcase vapors back into the engine to be reburned.

PERCOLATION: A condition in which the fuel actually "boils," due to excessive heat. Percolation prevents proper atomization of the fuel causing rough running.

PICK-UP COIL: The coil in which voltage is induced in an electronic ignition.

PING: A metallic rattling sound produced by the engine during acceleration. It is usually due to incorrect ignition timing or a poor grade of gasoline.

PINION: The smaller of two gears. The rear axle pinion drives the ring gear which transmits motion to the axle shafts.

PINION GEAR: The smallest gear in a drive gear assembly.

PISTON: A disc or cup that fits in a cylinder bore and is free to move. In hydraulics, it provides the means of converting hydraulic pressure into a usable force. Examples of piston applications are found in servo, clutch, and accumulator units.

PISTON RING: An open-ended ring which fits into a groove on the outer diameter of the piston. Its chief function is to form a seal between the piston and cylinder wall. Most automotive pistons have three rings: two for compression sealing; one for oil sealing.

PITMAN ARM: A lever which transmits steering force from the steering gear to the steering linkage.

PLANET CARRIER: A basic member of a planetary gear assembly that carries the pinion gears.

PLANET PINIONS: Gears housed in a planet carrier that are in constant mesh with the sun gear and internal gear. Because they have their own independent rotating centers, the pinions are capable of rotating around the sun gear or the inside of the internal gear.

PLANETARY GEAR RATIO: The reduction or overdrive ratio developed by a planetary gearset.

PLANETARY GEARSET: In its simplest form, it is made up of a basic assembly group containing a sun gear, internal gear, and planet carrier. The gears are always in constant mesh and offer a wide range of gear ratio possibilities.

PLANETARY GEARSET (COMPOUND): Two planetary gearsets combined together.

PLANETARY GEARSET (SIMPLE): An assembly of gears in constant mesh consisting of a sun gear, several pinion gears mounted in a carrier, and a ring gear. It provides gear ratio and direction changes, in addition to a direct drive and a neutral.

PLY RATING: A. rating given a tire which indicates strength (but not necessarily actual plies). A two-ply/four-ply rating has only two plies, but the strength of a four-ply tire.

POLARITY: Indication (positive or negative) of the two poles of a battery.

PORT: An opening for fluid intake or exhaust.

POSITIVE SEALING: A sealing method that completely prevents leakage.

POTENTIAL: Electrical force measured in volts; sometimes used interchangeably with voltage.

POWER: The ability to do work per unit of time, as expressed in horsepower; one horsepower equals 33,000 ft. lbs. of work per minute, or 550 ft. lbs. of work per second.

POWER FLOW: The systematic flow or transmission of power through the gears, from the input shaft to the output shaft.

POWER-TO-WEIGHT RATIO: Ratio of horsepower to weight of car.

POWERTRAIN: See Drivetrain.

POWERTRAIN CONTROL MODULE (PCM): Current designation for the engine control module (ECM). In many cases, late model vehicle control units manage the engine as well as the transmission. In other settings, the PCM controls the engine and is interfaced with a TCM to control transmission functions.

Ppm: Parts per million; unit used to measure exhaust emissions.

PREIGNITION: Early ignition of fuel in the cylinder, sometimes due to glowing carbon deposits in the combustion chamber. Preignition can be damaging since combustion takes place prematurely.

PRELOAD: A predetermined load placed on a bearing during assembly or by adjustment.

PRESS FIT: The mating of two parts under pressure, due to the inner diameter of one being smaller than the outer diameter of the other, or vice versa; an interference fit.

PRESSURE: The amount of force exerted upon a surface area.

PRESSURE CONTROL SOLENOID (PCS): An output device that provides a boost oil pressure to the mainline regulator valve to control line pressure. Its operation is determined by the amount of current sent from the PCM.

PRESSURE GAUGE: An instrument used for measuring the fluid pressure in a hydraulic circuit.

PRESSURE REGULATOR VALVE: In automatic transmissions, its purpose is to regulate the pressure of the pump output and supply the basic fluid pressure necessary to operate the transmission. The regulated fluid pressure may be referred to as mainline pressure, line pressure, or control pressure.

PRESSURE SWITCH ASSEMBLY (PSA): Mounted inside the transmission, it is a grouping of oil pressure switches that inputs to the PCM when certain hydraulic passages are charged with oil pressure.

PRESSURE PLATE: A spring-loaded plate (part of the clutch) that transmits power to the driven (friction) plate when the clutch is engaged.

PRIMARY CIRCUIT: The low voltage side of the ignition system which consists of the ignition switch, ballast resistor or resistance wire, bypass, coil, electronic control unit and pick-up coil as well as the connecting wires and harnesses.

PROFILE: Term used for tire measurement (tire series), which is the ratio of tire height to tread width.

PROM (PROGRAMMABLE READ-ONLY MEMORY): The heart of the computer that compares input data and makes the engineered program or strategy decisions about when to trigger the appropriate output based on stored computer instructions.

PULSE GENERATOR: A two-wire pickup sensor used to produce a fluctuating electrical signal. This changing signal is read by the controller to determine the speed of the object and can be used to measure transmission/transaxle input speed, output speed, and vehicle speed.

PSI: Pounds per square inch; a measurement of pressure.

PULSE WIDTH DUTY CYCLE SOLENOID (PULSE WIDTH MODULATED SOLENOID): A computer-controlled solenoid that turns on and off at a variable rate producing a modulated oil pressure; often referred to as a pulse width modulated (PWM) solenoid. Employed in many electronic automatic transmissions and transaxles, these solenoids are used to manage shift control and converter clutch hydraulic circuits.

PUSHROD: A steel rod between the hydraulic valve lifter and the valve rocker arm in overhead valve (OHV) engines.

PUMP: A mechanical device designed to create fluid flow and pressure buildup in a hydraulic system.

QUARTER PANEL: General term used to refer to a rear fender. Quarter panel is the area from the rear door opening to the tail light area and from rear wheel well to the base of the trunk and roof-line.

RACE: The surface on the inner or outer ring of a bearing on which the balls, needles or rollers move.

RACK AND PINION: A type of automotive steering system using a pinion gear attached to the end of the steering shaft. The pinion meshes with a long rack attached to the steering linkage.

RADIAL TIRE: Tire design which uses body cords running at right angles to the center line of the tire. Two or more belts are used to give tread strength. Radials can be identified by their characteristic sidewall bulge.

RADIATOR: Part of the cooling system for a water-cooled engine, mounted in the front of the vehicle and connected to the engine with rubber hoses. Through the radiator, excess combustion heat is dissipated into the atmosphere through forced convection using a water and glycol based mixture that circulates through, and cools, the engine.

RANGE REFERENCE AND CLUTCH/BAND APPLY CHART: A guide that shows the application of clutches and bands for each gear, within the selector range positions. These charts are extremely useful for understanding how the unit operates and for diagnosing malfunctions.

RAVIGNEAUX GEARSET: A compound planetary gearset that features matched dual planetary pinions (sets of two) mounted in a single planet carrier. Two sun gears and one ring mesh with the carrier pinions.

REACTION MEMBER: The stationary planetary member, in a planetary gearset, that is grounded to the transmission/transaxle case through the use of friction and wedging devices known as bands, disc clutches, and one-way clutches.

REACTION PRESSURE: The fluid pressure that moves a spool valve against an opposing force or forces; the area on which the opposing force acts. The opposing force can be a spring or a combination of spring force and auxiliary hydraulic force.

REACTOR, TORQUE CONVERTER: The reaction member of a fluid torque converter, more commonly called a stator. (See stator.)

REAR MAIN OIL SEAL: A synthetic or rope-type seal that prevents oil from leaking out of the engine past the rear main crankshaft bearing.

RECIRCULATING BALL: Type of steering system in which recirculating steel balls occupy the area between the nut and worm wheel, causing a reduction in friction.

RECTIFIER: A device (used primarily in alternators) that permits electrical current to flow in one direction only.

REDUCTION: (See gear reduction.)

REGULATOR VALVE: A valve that changes the pressure of the oil in a hydraulic circuit as the oil passes through the valve by bleeding off (or exhausting) some of the volume of oil supplied to the valve.

REFRIGERANT 12 (R-12) or 134 (R-134): The generic name of the refrigerant used in automotive air conditioning systems.

REGULATOR: A device which maintains the amperage and/or voltage levels of a circuit at predetermined values.

RELAY: A switch which automatically opens and/or closes a circuit.

RELAY VALVE: A valve that directs flow and pressure. Relay valves simply connect or disconnect interrelated passages without restricting the fluid flow or changing the pressure.

RELIEF VALVE: A spring-loaded, pressure-operated valve that limits oil pressure buildup in a hydraulic circuit to a predetermined maximum value.

RELUCTOR: A wheel that rotates inside the distributor and triggers the release of voltage in an electronic ignition.

RESERVOIR: The storage area for fluid in a hydraulic system; often called a sump.

RESIN: A liquid plastic used in body work.

RESIDUAL MAGNETISM: The magnetic strength stored in a material after a magnetizing field has been removed.

RESISTANCE: The opposition to the flow of current through a circuit or electrical device, and is measured in ohms. Resistance is equal to the voltage divided by the amperage.

RESISTOR SPARK PLUG: A spark plug using a resistor to shorten the spark duration. This suppresses radio interference and lengthens plug life.

RESISTOR: A device, usually made of wire, which offers a preset amount of resistance in an electrical circuit.

RESULTANT FORCE: The single effective directional thrust of the fluid force on the turbine produced by the vortex and rotary forces acting in different planes.

RETARD: Set the ignition timing so that spark occurs later (fewer degrees before TDC).

RHEOSTAT: A device for regulating a current by means of a variable resistance.

RING GEAR: The name given to a ring-shaped gear attached to a differential case, or affixed to a flywheel or as part of a planetary gear set.

ROADLOAD: grade.

ROCKER ARM: A lever which rotates around a shaft pushing down (opening) the valve with an end when the other end is pushed up by the pushrod. Spring pressure will later close the valve.

ROCKER PANEL: The body panel below the doors between the wheel opening.

ROLLER BEARING: A bearing made up of hardened inner and outer races between which hardened steel rollers move.

ROLLER CLUTCH: A type of one-way clutch design using rollers and springs mounted within an inner and outer cam race assembly.

ROTARY FLOW: The path of the fluid trapped between the blades of the members as they revolve with the rotation of the torque converter cover (rotational inertia).

ROTOR: (1.) The disc-shaped part of a disc brake assembly, upon which the brake pads bear; also called, brake disc. (2.) The device mounted atop the distributor shaft, which passes current to the distributor cap tower contacts.

ROTARY ENGINE: See Wankel engine.

RPM: Revolutions per minute (usually indicates engine speed).

RTV: A gasket making compound that cures as it is exposed to the atmosphere. It is used between surfaces that are not perfectly machined to one another, leaving a slight gap that the RTV fills and in which it hardens. The letters RTV represent room temperature vulcanizing.

RUN-ON: Condition when the engine continues to run, even when the key is turned off. See dieseling.

SEALED BEAM: A automotive headlight. The lens, reflector and filament from a single unit.

SEATBELT INTERLOCK: A system whereby the car cannot be started unless the seatbelt is buckled.

SECONDARY CIRCUIT: The high voltage side of the ignition system, usually above 20,000 volts. The secondary includes the ignition coil, coil wire, distributor cap and rotor, spark plug wires and spark plugs.

SELF-INDUCTION: The generation of voltage in a current-carrying wire by changing the amount of current flowing within that wire.

SEMI-CONDUCTOR: A material (silicon or germanium) that is neither a good conductor nor an insulator; used in diodes and transistors.

SEMI-FLOATING AXLE: In this design, a wheel is attached to the axle shaft, which takes both drive and cornering loads. Almost all solid axle passenger cars and light trucks use this design.

SENDING UNIT: A mechanical, electrical, hydraulic or electromagnetic device which transmits information to a gauge.

SENSOR: Any device designed to measure engine operating conditions or ambient pressures and temperatures. Usually electronic in nature and designed to send a voltage signal to an on-board computer, some sensors may operate as a simple on/off switch or they may provide a variable voltage signal (like a potentiometer) as conditions or measured parameters change.

SERIES CIRCUIT: (See circuit, series.)

SERPENTINE BELT: An accessory drive belt, with small multiple v-ribs, routed around most or all of the engine-powered accessories such as the alternator and power steering pump. Usually both the front and the back side of the belt comes into contact with various pulleys.

SERVO: In an automatic transmission, it is a piston in a cylinder assembly that converts hydraulic pressure into mechanical force and movement; used for the application of the bands and clutches.

SHIFT BUSYNESS: When referring to a torque converter clutch, it is the frequent apply and release of the clutch plate due to uncommon driving conditions.

SHIFT VALVE: Classified as a relay valve, it triggers the automatic shift in response to a governor and a throttle signal by directing fluid to the appropriate band and clutch apply combination to cause the shift to occur.

SHIM: Spacers of precise, predetermined thickness used between parts to establish a proper working relationship.

SHIMMY: Vibration (sometimes violent) in the front end caused by misaligned front end, out of balance tires or worn suspension components.

SHORT CIRCUIT: An electrical malfunction where current takes the path of least resistance to ground (usually through damaged insulation). Current flow is excessive from low resistance resulting in a blown fuse.

SHUDDER: Repeated jerking or stick-slip sensation, similar to chuggle but more severe and rapid in nature, that may be most noticeable during certain ranges of vehicle speed; also used to define condition after converter clutch engagement.

SIMPSON GEARSET: A compound planetary gear train that integrates two simple planetary gearsets referred to as the front planetary and the rear planetary.

SINGLE OVERHEAD CAMSHAFT: See overhead camshaft.

SKIDPLATE: A metal plate attached to the underside of the body to protect the fuel tank, transfer case or other vulnerable parts from damage.

SLAVE CYLINDER: In automotive use, a device in the hydraulic clutch system which is activated by hydraulic force, disengaging the clutch.

SLIPPING: Noticeable increase in engine rpm without vehicle speed increase; usually occurs during or after initial clutch or band engagement.

SLUDGE: Thick, black deposits in engine formed from dirt, oil, water, etc. It is usually formed in engines when oil changes are neglected.

SNAP RING: A circular retaining clip used inside or outside a shaft or part to secure a shaft, such as a floating wrist pin.

SOFT: Slow, almost unnoticeable clutch apply with very little shift feel.

SOFTCODES: DTCs that have been set into the PCM memory but are not present at the time of testing; often referred to as history or intermittent codes.

SOHC: Single overhead camshaft.

SOLENOID: An electrically operated, magnetic switching device.

SPALLING: A wear pattern identified by metal chips flaking off the hardened surface. This condition is caused by foreign particles, overloading situations, and/or normal wear.

SPARK PLUG: A device screwed into the combustion chamber of a spark ignition engine. The basic construction is a conductive core inside of a ceramic insulator, mounted in an outer conductive base. An electrical charge from the spark plug wire travels along the conductive core and jumps a preset air gap to a grounding point or points at the end of the conductive base. The resultant spark ignites the fuel/air mixture in the combustion chamber.

SPECIFIC GRAVITY (BATTERY): The relative weight of liquid (battery electrolyte) as compared to the weight of an equal volume of water.

SPLINES: Ridges machined or cast onto the outer diameter of a shaft or inner diameter of a bore to enable parts to mate without rotation.

SPLIT TORQUE DRIVE: In a torque converter, it refers to parallel paths of torque transmission, one of which is mechanical and the other hydraulic.

SPONGY PEDAL: A soft or spongy feeling when the brake pedal is depressed. It is usually due to air in the brake lines.

SPOOLVALVE: A precision-machined, cylindrically shaped valve made up of lands and grooves. Depending on its position in the valve bore, various interconnecting hydraulic circuit passages are either opened or closed.

SPRAG CLUTCH: A type of one-way clutch design using cams or contoured-shaped sprags between inner and outer races. (See one-way clutch.)

SPRUNG WEIGHT: The weight of a car supported by the springs.

SQUARE-CUT SEAL: Molded synthetic rubber seal designed with a square- or rectangular-shaped cross-section. This type of seal is used for both dynamic and static applications.

SRS: Supplemental restraint system

STABILIZER (SWAY) BAR: A bar linking both sides of the suspension. It resists sway on turns by taking some of added load from one wheel and putting it on the other.

STAGE: The number of turbine sets separated by a stator. A turbine set may be made up of one or more turbine members. A three-element converter is classified as a single stage.

STALL: In fluid drive transmission/transaxle applications, stall refers to engine rpm with the transmission/transaxle engaged and the vehicle stationary; throttle valve can be in any position between closed and wide open.

STALL SPEED: In fluid drive transmission/transaxle applications, stall speed refers to the maximum engine rpm with the transmission/transaxle engaged and vehicle stationary, when the throttle valve is wide open. (See stall; stall test.)

STALL TEST: A procedure recommended by many manufacturers to help determine the integrity of an engine, the torque converter stator, and certain clutch and band combinations. With the shift lever in each of the forward and reverse positions and with the brakes firmly applied, the accelerator pedal is momentarily pressed to the wide open throttle (WOT) position. The engine rpm reading at full throttle can provide clues for diagnosing the condition of the items listed above.

STALL TORQUE: The maximum design or engineered torque ratio of a fluid torque converter, produced under stall speed conditions. (See stall speed.)

STARTER: A high-torque electric motor used for the purpose of starting the engine, typically through a high ratio geared drive connected to the flywheel ring gear.

STATIC: A sealing application in which the parts being sealed do not move in relation to each other.

STATOR (REACTOR): The reaction member of a fluid torque converter that changes the direction of the fluid as it leaves the turbine to enter the impeller vanes. During the torque multiplication phase, this action assists the impeller's rotary force and results in an increase in torque.

STEERING GEOMETRY: Combination of various angles of suspension components (caster, camber, toe-in); roughly equivalent to front end alignment.

STRAIGHT WEIGHT: Term designating motor oil as suitable for use within a narrow range of temperatures. Outside the narrow temperature range its flow characteristics will not adequately lubricate.

STROKE: The distance the piston travels from bottom dead center to top dead center.

SUBSTITUTION: Replacing one part suspected of a defect with a like part of known quality.

SUMP: The storage vessel or reservoir that provides a ready source of fluid to the pump. In an automatic transmission, the sump is the oil pan. All fluid eventually returns to the sump for recycling into the hydraulic system.

SUN GEAR: In a planetary gearset, it is the center gear that meshes with a cluster of planet pinions.

SUPERCHARGER: An air pump driven mechanically by the engine through belts, chains, shafts or gears from the crankshaft. Two general types of supercharger are the positive displacement and centrifugal type, which pump air in direct relationship to the speed of the engine.

SUPPLEMENTAL RESTRAINT SYSTEM: See air bag.

SURGE: Repeating engine-related feeling of acceleration and deceleration that is less intense than chuggle.

SWITCH: A device used to open, close, or redirect the current in an electrical circuit.

SYNCHROMESH: A manual transmission/transaxle that is equipped with devices (synchronizers) that match the gear speeds so that the transmission/transaxle can be downshifted without clashing gears.

SYNTHETIC OIL: Non-petroleum based oil.

TACHOMETER: A device used to measure the rotary speed of an engine, shaft, gear, etc., usually in rotations per minute.

TDC: Top dead center. The exact top of the piston's stroke.

TEFLON SEALING RINGS: Teflon is a soft, durable, plastic-like material that is resistant to heat and provides excellent sealing. These rings are designed with either scarf-cut joints or as one-piece rings. Teflon sealing rings have replaced many metal ring applications.

TERMINAL: A device attached to the end of a wire or cable to make an electrical connection.

TEST LIGHT, CIRCUIT-POWERED: Uses available circuit voltage to test circuit continuity.

TEST LIGHT, SELF-POWERED: Uses its own battery source to test circuit continuity.

THERMISTOR: A special resistor used to measure fluid temperature; it decreases its resistance with increases in temperature.

THERMOSTAT: A valve, located in the cooling system of an engine, which is closed when cold and opens gradually in response to engine heating, controlling the temperature of the coolant and rate of coolant flow.

THERMOSTATIC ELEMENT: A heat-sensitive, spring-type device that controls a drain port from the upper sump area to the lower sump. When the transaxle fluid reaches operating temperature, the port is closed and the upper sump fills, thus reducing the fluid level in the lower sump.

THROTTLE POSITION (TP) SENSOR: Reads the degree of throttle opening; its signal is used to analyze engine load conditions. The ECM/PCM decides to apply the TCC, or to disengage it for coast or load conditions that need a converter torque boost.

THROTTLE PRESSURE/MODULATOR PRESSURE: A hydraulic signal oil pressure relating to the amount of engine load, based on either the amount of throttle plate opening or engine vacuum.

THROTTLE VALVE: A regulating or balanced valve that is controlled mechanically by throttle linkage or engine vacuum. It sends a hydraulic signal to the shift valve body to control shift timing and shift quality. (See balanced valve; modulator valve.)

THROW-OUT BEARING: As the clutch pedal is depressed, the throwout bearing moves against the spring fingers of the pressure plate, forcing the pressure plate to disengage from the driven disc.

TIE ROD: A rod connecting the steering arms. Tie rods have threaded ends that are used to adjust toe-in.

TIE-UP: Condition where two opposing clutches are attempting to apply at same time, causing engine to labor with noticeable loss of engine rpm.

TIMING BELT: A square-toothed, reinforced rubber belt that is driven by the crankshaft and operates the camshaft.

TIMING CHAIN: A roller chain that is driven by the crankshaft and operates the camshaft.

TIRE ROTATION: Moving the tires from one position to another to make the tires wear evenly.

TOE-IN (OUT): A term comparing the extreme front and rear of the front tires. Closer together at the front is toe-in; farther apart at the front is toe-out.

TOP DEAD CENTER (TDC): The point at which the piston reaches the top of its travel on the compression stroke.

TORQUE: Measurement of turning or twisting force, expressed as foot-pounds or inch-pounds.

TORQUE CONVERTER: A turbine used to transmit power from a driving member to a driven member via hydraulic action, providing changes in drive ratio and torque. In automotive use, it links the driveplate at the rear of the engine to the automatic transmission.

TORQUE CONVERTER CLUTCH: The apply plate (lockup plate) assembly used for mechanical power flow through the converter.

TORQUE PHASE: Sometimes referred to as slip phase or stall phase, torque multiplication occurs when the turbine is turning at a slower speed than the impeller, and the stator is reactionary (stationary). This sequence generates a boost in output torque.

TORQUE RATING (STALL TORQUE): The maximum torque multiplication that occurs during stall conditions, with the engine at wide open throttle (WOT) and zero turbine speed.

TORQUE RATIO: An expression of the gear ratio factor on torque effect. A 3:1 gear ratio or 3:1 torque ratio increases the torque input by the ratio factor of 3. Input torque (100 ft. lbs.) x 3 = output torque (300 ft. lbs.)

TRACTION: The amount of usable tractive effort before the drive wheels slip on the road contact surface.

TORSION BAR SUSPENSION: Long rods of spring steel which take the place of springs. One end of the bar is anchored and the other arm (attached to the suspension) is free to twist. The bars' resistance to twisting causes springing action.

TRACK: Distance between the centers of the tires where they contact the ground.

TRACTION CONTROL: A control system that prevents the spinning of a vehicle's drive wheels when excess power is applied.

TRACTIVE EFFORT: The amount of force available to the drive wheels, to move the vehicle.

TRANSAXLE: A single housing containing the transmission and differential. Transaxles are usually found on front engine/front wheel drive or rear engine/rear wheel drive cars.

TRANSDUCER: A device that changes energy from one form to another. For example, a transducer in a microphone changes sound energy to electrical energy. In automotive air-conditioning controls used in automatic temperature systems, a transducer changes an electrical signal to a vacuum signal, which operates mechanical doors.

TRANSMISSION: A powertrain component designed to modify torque and speed developed by the engine; also provides direct drive, reverse, and neutral.

TRANSMISSION CONTROL MODULE (TCM): Manages transmission functions. These vary according to the manufacturer's product design but may include converter clutch operation, electronic shift scheduling, and mainline pressure.

TRANSMISSION FLUID TEMPERATURE (TFT) SENSOR: Originally called a transmission oil temperature (TOT) sensor, this input device to the ECM/PCM senses the fluid temperature and provides a resistance value. It operates on the thermistor principle.

TRANSMISSION INPUT SPEED (TIS) SENSOR: Measures turbine shaft (input shaft) rpm's and compares to engine rpm's to determine torque converter slip. When compared to the transmission output speed sensor or VSS, gear ratio and clutch engagement timing can be determined.

TRANSMISSION OIL TEMPERATURE (TOT) SENSOR: (See transmission fluid temperature (TFT) sensor.)

TRANSMISSION RANGE SELECTOR (TRS) SWITCH: Tells the module which gear shift position the driver has chosen.

TRANSFER CASE: A gearbox driven from the transmission that delivers power to both front and rear driveshafts in a four-wheel drive system. Transfer cases usually have a high and low range set of gears, used depending on how much pulling power is needed.

TRANSISTOR: A semi-conductor component which can be actuated by a small voltage to perform an electrical switching function.

TREAD WEAR INDICATOR: Bars molded into the tire at right angles to the tread that appear as horizontal bars when 1/16 in. of tread remains.

TREAD WEAR PATTERN: The pattern of wear on tires which can be "read" to diagnose problems in the front suspension.

TUNE-UP: A regular maintenance function, usually associated with the replacement and adjustment of parts and components in the electrical and fuel systems of a vehicle for the purpose of attaining optimum performance.

TURBINE: The output (driven) member of a fluid coupling or fluid torque converter. It is splined to the input (turbine) shaft of the transmission.

TURBOCHARGER: An exhaust driven pump which compresses intake air and forces it into the combustion chambers at higher than atmospheric pressures. The increased air pressure allows more fuel to be burned and results in increased horsepower being produced.

TURBULENCE: The interference of molecules of a fluid (or vapor) with each other in a fluid flow.

TYPE F: Transmission fluid developed and used by Ford Motor Company up to 1982. This fluid type provides a high coefficient of friction.

TYPE 7176: The preferred choice of transmission fluid for Chrysler automatic transmissions and transaxles. Developed in 1986, it closely resembles Dexron and Mercon. Type 7176 is the recommended service fill fluid for all Chrysler products utilizing a lockup torque converter dating back to 1978.

U-JOINT (UNIVERSAL JOINT): A flexible coupling in the drive train that allows the driveshafts or axle shafts to operate at different angles and still transmit rotary power.

UNDERSTEER: The tendency of a car to continue straight ahead while negotiating a turn.

UNIT BODY: Design in which the car body acts as the frame.

UNLEADED FUEL: Fuel which contains no lead (a common gasoline additive). The presence of lead in fuel will destroy the functioning elements of a catalytic converter, making it useless.

UNSPRUNG WEIGHT: The weight of car components not supported by the springs (wheels, tires, brakes, rear axle, control arms, etc.).

UPSHIFT: A shift that results in a decrease in torque ratio and an increase in speed.

VACUUM: A negative pressure; any pressure less than atmospheric pressure.

VACUUM ADVANCE: A device which advances the ignition timing in response to increased engine vacuum.

VACUUM GAUGE: An instrument used for measuring the existing vacuum in a vacuum circuit or chamber. The unit of measure is inches (of mercury in a barometer.

VACUUM MODULATOR: Generates a hydraulic oil pressure in response to the amount of engine vacuum.

VALVES: Devices that can open or close fluid passages in a hydraulic system and are used for directing fluid flow and controlling pressure.

VALVE BODY ASSEMBLY: The main hydraulic control assembly of the transmission/transaxle that contains numerous valves, check balls, and other components to control the distribution of pressurized oil throughout the transmission.

VALVE CLEARANCE: The measured gap between the end of the valve stem and the rocker arm, cam lobe or follower that activates the valve.

VALVE GUIDES: The guide through which the stem of the valve passes.

The guide is designed to keep the valve in proper alignment.

VALVE LASH (clearance): The operating clearance in the valve train.

VALVE TRAIN: The system that operates intake and exhaust valves, consisting of camshaft, valves and springs, lifters, pushrods and rocker arms.

VAPOR LOCK: Boiling of the fuel in the fuel lines due to excess heat. This will interfere with the flow of fuel in the lines and can completely stop the flow. Vapor lock normally only occurs in hot weather.

VARIABLE DISPLACEMENT (VARIABLE CAPACITY) VANE PUMP: Slipper-type vanes, mounted in a revolving rotor and contained within the bore of a movable slide, capture and then force fluid to flow. Movement of the slide to various positions changes the size of the vane chambers and the amount of fluid flow. **Note:** GM refers to this pump design as variable displacement, and Ford terms it variable capacity.

VARIABLE FORCE SOLENOID (VFS): Commonly referred to as the electronic pressure control (EPC) solenoid, it replaces the cable/linkage style of TV system control and is integrated with a spool valve and spring assembly to control pressure. A variable computer-controlled current flow varies the internal force of the solenoid on the spool valve and resulting control pressure.

VARIABLE ORIFICE THERMAL VALVE: Temperature-sensitive hydraulic oil control device that adjusts the size of a circuit path opening. By altering the size of the opening, the oil flow rate is adapted for cold to hot oil viscosity changes.

VARNISH: Term applied to the residue formed when gasoline gets old and stale.

VCM: See Electronic Control Unit (ECU).

VEHICLE SPEED SENSOR (VSS): Provides an electrical signal to the computer module, measuring vehicle speed, and affects the torque converter clutch engagement and release.

VESPEL SEALING RINGS: Hard plastic material that produces excellent sealing in dynamic settings. These rings are found in late versions of the 4T60 and in all 4T60-E and 4T80-E transaxles.

VISCOSITY: The ability of a fluid to flow. The lower the viscosity rating, the easier the fluid will flow. 10 weight motor oil will flow much easier than 40 weight motor oil.

VISCOSITY INDEX IMPROVERS: Keeps the viscosity nearly constant with changes in temperature. This is especially important at low temperatures, when the oil needs to be thin to aid in shifting and for cold-weather starting. Yet it must not be so thin that at high temperatures it will cause excessive hydraulic leakage so that pumps are unable to maintain the proper pressures.

VISCOUS CLUTCH: A specially designed torque converter clutch apply plate that, through the use of a silicon fluid, clamps smoothly and absorbs torsional vibrations.

VOLT: Unit used to measure the force or pressure of electricity. It is defined as the pressure needed to move one amp through the resistance of one ohm.

VOLTAGE: The electrical pressure that causes current to flow. Voltage is measured in volts (V).

VOLTAGE, APPLIED: The actual voltage read at a given point in a circuit. It equals the available voltage of the power supply minus the losses in the circuit up to that point.

VOLTAGE DROP: The voltage lost or used in a circuit by normal loads such as a motor or lamp or by abnormal loads such as a poor (high-resistance) lead or terminal connection.

VOLTAGE REGULATOR: A device that controls the current output of the alternator or generator.

VOLTMETER: An instrument used for measuring electrical force in units called volts. Voltmeters are always connected parallel with the circuit being tested.

VORTEX FLOW: The crosswise or circulatory flow of oil between the blades of the members caused by the centrifugal pumping action of the impeller.

WANKEL ENGINE: An engine which uses no pistons. In place of pistons, triangular-shaped rotors revolve in specially shaped housings.

WATER PUMP: A belt driven component of the cooling system that mounts on the engine, circulating the coolant under pressure.

WATT: The unit for measuring electrical power. One watt is the product of one ampere and one volt (watts equals amps times volts). Wattage is the horsepower of electricity (746 watts equal one horsepower).

WHEEL ALIGNMENT: Inclusive term to describe the front end geometry (caster, camber, toe-in/out).

WHEEL CYLINDER: Found in the automotive drum brake assembly, it is a device, actuated by hydraulic pressure, which, through internal pistons, pushes the brake shoes outward against the drums.

WHEEL WEIGHT: Small weights attached to the wheel to balance the wheel and tire assembly. Out-of-balance tires quickly wear out and also give erratic handling when installed on the front.

WHEELBASE: Distance between the center of front wheels and the center of rear wheels.

WIDE OPEN THROTTLE (WOT): Full travel of accelerator pedal.

WORK: The force exerted to move a mass or object. Work involves motion; if a force is exerted and no motion takes place, no work is done. Work per unit of time is called power. Work = force x distance = ft. lbs. 33,000 ft. lbs. in one minute = 1 horsepower

ZERO-THROTTLE COAST DOWN: A full release of accelerator pedal while vehicle is in motion and in drive range.

Commonly Used Abbreviations

2

2WD	Two Wheel Drive

4

4WD	Four Wheel Drive

A

A/C	Air Conditioning
ABDC	After Bottom Dead Center
ABS	Anti-lock Brakes
AC	Alternating Current
ACL	Air cleaner
ACT	Air Charge Temperature
AIR	Secondary Air Injection
ALCL	Assembly Line Communications Link
ALDL	Assembly Line Diagnostic Link
AT	Automatic Transaxle/Transmission
ATDC	After Top Dead Center
ATF	Automatic Transmission Fluid
ATS	Air Temperature Sensor
AWD	All Wheel Drive

B

BAP	Barometric Absolute Pressure
BARO	Barometric Pressure
BBDC	Before Bottom Dead Center
BCM	Body Control Module
BDC	Bottom Dead Center
BPT	Backpressure Transducer
BTDC	Before Top Dead Center
BVSV	Bimetallic Vacuum Switching Valve

C

CAC	Charge Air Cooler
CARB	California Air Resources Board
CAT	Catalytic Converter
CCC	Computer Command Control
CCCC	Computer Controlled Catalytic Converter
CCCI	Computer Controlled Coil Ignition
CCD	Computer Controlled Dwell
CDI	Capacitor Discharge Ignition
CEC	Computerized Engine Control
CFI	Continuous Fuel Injection
CIS	Continuous Injection System
CIS-E	Continuous Injection System - Electronic
CKP	Crankshaft Position
CL	Closed Loop
CMP	Camshaft Position
CPP	Clutch Pedal Position
CTOX	Continuous Trap Oxidizer System
CTP	Closed Throttle Position
CVC	Constant Vacuum Control
CYL	Cylinder

D

DBC	Dual Bed Catalyst
DC	Direct Current
DFI	Direct Fuel Injection
DIS	Distributorless Ignition System
DLC	Data Link Connector
DMM	Digital Multimeter
DOHC	Double Overhead Camshaft
DRB	Diagnostic Readout Box
DTC	Diagnostic Trouble Code
DTM	Diagnostic Test Mode
DVOM	Digital Volt/Ohmmeter

E

EBCM	Electronic Brake Control Module
ECM	Engine Control Module
ECT	Engine Coolant Temperature
ECU	Engine Control Unit or Electronic Control Unit
EDIS	Electronic Distributorless Ignition System
EEC	Electronic Engine Control
EEPROM	Electrically Erasable Programmable Read Only Memory
EFE	Early Fuel Evaporation
EGR	Exhaust Gas Recirculation
EGRT	Exhaust Gas Recirculation Temperature
EGRVC	EGR Valve Control
EPROM	Erasable Programmable Read Only Memory
EVAP	Evaporative Emissions
EVP	EGR Valve Position

F

FBC	Feedback Carburetor
FEEPROM	Flash Electrically Erasable Programmable Read Only Memory
FF	Flexible Fuel
FI	Fuel Injection
FT	Fuel Trim
FWD	Front Wheel Drive

G

GND	Ground

H

HAC	High Altitude Compensation
HEGO	Heated Exhaust Gas Oxygen sensor
HEI	High Energy Ignition
HO2 Sensor	Heated Oxygen Sensor

I

IAC	Idle Air Control
IAT	Intake Air Temperature
ICM	Ignition Control Module
IFI	Indirect Fuel Injection
IFS	Inertia Fuel Shutoff
ISC	Idle Speed Control
IVSV	Idle Vacuum Switching Valve

Commonly Used Abbreviations

K

KOEO	Key On, Engine Off
KOER	Key ON, Engine Running
KS	Knock Sensor

M

MAF	Mass Air Flow
MAP	Manifold Absolute Pressure
MAT	Manifold Air Temperature
MC	Mixture Control
MDP	Manifold Differential Pressure
MFI	Multiport Fuel Injection
MIL	Malfunction Indicator Lamp or Maintenance
MST	Manifold Surface Temperature
MVZ	Manifold Vacuum Zone

N

NVRAM	Nonvolatile Random Access Memory

O

O2 Sensor	Oxygen Sensor
OBD	On-Board Diagnostic
OC	Oxidation Catalyst
OHC	Overhead Camshaft
OL	Open Loop

P

P/S	Power Steering
PAIR	Pulsed Secondary Air Injection
PCM	Powertrain Control Module
PCS	Purge Control Solenoid
PCV	Positive Crankcase Ventilation
PIP	Profile Ignition Pick-up
PNP	Park/Neutral Position
PROM	Programmable Read Only Memory
PSP	Power Steering Pressure
PTO	Power Take-Off
PTOX	Periodic Trap Oxidizer System

R

RABS	Rear Anti-lock Brake System
RAM	Random Access Memory
ROM	Read Only Memory
RPM	Revolutions Per Minute
RWAL	Rear Wheel Anti-lock Brakes
RWD	Rear Wheel Drive

S

SBC	Single Bed Converter
SBEC	Single Board Engine Controller
SC	Supercharger
SCB	Supercharger Bypass
SFI	Sequential Multiport Fuel Injection
SIR	Supplemental Inflatable Restraint
SOHC	Single Overhead Camshaft
SPL	Smoke Puff Limiter
SPOUT	Spark Output
SRI	Service Reminder Indicator
SRS	Supplemental Restraint System
SRT	System Readiness Test
SSI	Solid State Ignition
ST	Scan Tool
STO	Self-Test Output

T

TAC	Thermostatic Air Cleaner
TBI	Throttle Body Fuel Injection
TC	Turbocharger
TCC	Torque Converter Clutch
TCM	Transmission Control Module
TDC	Top Dead Center
TFI	Thick Film Ignition
TP	Throttle Position
TR Sensor	Transaxle/Transmission Range Sensor
TVV	Thermal Vacuum Valve
TWC	Three-way Catalytic Converter

V

VAF	Volume Air Flow, or Vane Air Flow
VAPS	Variable Assist Power Steering
VRV	Vacuum Regulator Valve
VSS	Vehicle Speed Sensor
VSV	Vacuum Switching Valve

W

WOT	Wide Open Throttle
WU-TWC	Warm Up Three-way Catalytic Converter

ENGLISH TO METRIC CONVERSION: TORQUE

To convert foot-pounds (ft. lbs.) to Newton-meters (Nm), multiply the number of ft. lbs. by 1.36
To convert Newton-meters (Nm) to foot-pounds (ft. lbs.), multiply the number of Nm by 0.7376

ft. lbs.	Nm	ft. lbs.	Nm	ft. lbs.	Nm	ft. lbs.	Nm
0.1	0.1	34	46.2	76	103.4	118	160.5
0.2	0.3	35	47.6	77	104.7	119	161.8
0.3	0.4	36	49.0	78	106.1	120	163.2
0.4	0.5	37	50.3	79	107.4	121	164.6
0.5	0.7	38	51.7	80	108.8	122	165.9
0.6	0.8	39	53.0	81	110.2	123	167.3
0.7	1.0	40	54.4	82	111.5	124	168.6
0.8	1.1	41	55.8	83	112.9	125	170.0
0.9	1.2	42	57.1	84	114.2	126	171.4
1	1.4	43	58.5	85	115.6	127	172.7
2	2.7	44	59.8	86	117.0	128	174.1
3	4.1	45	61.2	87	118.3	129	175.4
4	5.4	46	62.6	88	119.7	130	176.8
5	6.8	47	63.9	89	121.0	131	178.2
6	8.2	48	65.3	90	122.4	132	179.5
7	9.5	49	66.6	91	123.8	133	180.9
8	10.9	50	68.0	92	125.1	134	182.2
9	12.2	51	69.4	93	126.5	135	183.6
10	13.6	52	70.7	94	127.8	136	185.0
11	15.0	53	72.1	95	129.2	137	186.3
12	16.3	54	73.4	96	130.6	138	187.7
13	17.7	55	74.8	97	131.9	139	189.0
14	19.0	56	76.2	98	133.3	140	190.4
15	20.4	57	77.5	99	134.6	141	191.8
16	21.8	58	78.9	100	136.0	142	193.1
17	23.1	59	80.2	101	137.4	143	194.5
18	24.5	60	81.6	102	138.7	144	195.8
19	25.8	61	83.0	103	140.1	145	197.2
20	27.2	62	84.3	104	141.4	146	198.6
21	28.6	63	85.7	105	142.8	147	199.9
22	29.9	64	87.0	106	144.2	148	201.3
23	31.3	65	88.4	107	145.5	149	202.6
24	32.6	66	89.8	108	146.9	150	204.0
25	34.0	67	91.1	109	148.2	151	205.4
26	35.4	68	92.5	110	149.6	152	206.7
27	36.7	69	93.8	111	151.0	153	208.1
28	38.1	70	95.2	112	152.3	154	209.4
29	39.4	71	96.6	113	153.7	155	210.8
30	40.8	72	97.9	114	155.0	156	212.2
31	42.2	73	99.3	115	156.4	157	213.5
32	43.5	74	100.6	116	157.8	158	214.9
33	44.9	75	102.0	117	159.1	159	216.2

METRIC TO ENGLISH CONVERSION: TORQUE

To convert foot-pounds (ft. lbs.) to Newton-meters (Nm), multiply the number of ft. lbs. by 1.36
To convert Newton-meters (Nm) to foot-pounds (ft. lbs.), multiply the number of Nm by 0.7376

Nm	ft. lbs.	Nm	ft. lbs.	Nm	ft. lbs.	Nm	ft. lbs.	Nm	ft. lbs.
0.1	0.1	34	25.0	76	55.9	118	86.8	160	117.6
0.2	0.1	35	25.7	77	56.6	119	87.5	161	118.4
0.3	0.2	36	26.5	78	57.4	120	88.2	162	119.1
0.4	0.3	37	27.2	79	58.1	121	89.0	163	119.9
0.5	0.4	38	27.9	80	58.8	122	89.7	164	120.6
0.6	0.4	39	28.7	81	59.6	123	90.4	165	121.3
0.7	0.5	40	29.4	82	60.3	124	91.2	166	122.1
0.8	0.6	41	30.1	83	61.0	125	91.9	167	122.8
0.9	0.7	42	30.9	84	61.8	126	92.6	168	123.5
1	0.7	43	31.6	85	62.5	127	93.4	169	124.3
2	1.5	44	32.4	86	63.2	128	94.1	170	125.0
3	2.2	45	33.1	87	64.0	129	94.9	171	125.7
4	2.9	46	33.8	88	64.7	130	95.6	172	126.5
5	3.7	47	34.6	89	65.4	131	96.3	173	127.2
6	4.4	48	35.3	90	66.2	132	97.1	174	127.9
7	5.1	49	36.0	91	66.9	133	97.8	175	128.7
8	5.9	50	36.8	92	67.6	134	98.5	176	129.4
9	6.6	51	37.5	93	68.4	135	99.3	177	130.1
10	7.4	52	38.2	94	69.1	136	100.0	178	130.9
11	8.1	53	39.0	95	69.9	137	100.7	179	131.6
12	8.8	54	39.7	96	70.6	138	101.5	180	132.4
13	9.6	55	40.4	97	71.3	139	102.2	181	133.1
14	10.3	56	41.2	98	72.1	140	102.9	182	133.8
15	11.0	57	41.9	99	72.8	141	103.7	183	134.6
16	11.8	58	42.6	100	73.5	142	104.4	184	135.3
17	12.5	59	43.4	101	74.3	143	105.1	185	136.0
18	13.2	60	44.1	102	75.0	144	105.9	186	136.8
19	14.0	61	44.9	103	75.7	145	106.6	187	137.5
20	14.7	62	45.6	104	76.5	146	107.4	188	138.2
21	15.4	63	46.3	105	77.2	147	108.1	189	139.0
22	16.2	64	47.1	106	77.9	148	108.8	190	139.7
23	16.9	65	47.8	107	78.7	149	109.6	191	140.4
24	17.6	66	48.5	108	79.4	150	110.3	192	141.2
25	18.4	67	49.3	109	80.1	151	111.0	193	141.9
26	19.1	68	50.0	110	80.9	152	111.8	194	142.6
27	19.9	69	50.7	111	81.6	153	112.5	195	143.4
28	20.6	70	51.5	112	82.4	154	113.2	196	144.1
29	21.3	71	52.2	113	83.1	155	114.0	197	144.9
30	22.1	72	52.9	114	83.8	156	114.7	198	145.6
31	22.8	73	53.7	115	84.6	157	115.4	199	146.3
32	23.5	74	54.4	116	85.3	158	116.2	200	147.1
33	24.3	75	55.1	117	86.0	159	116.9	201	147.8

ENGLISH/METRIC CONVERSION: TEMPERATURE

To convert Fahrenheit (F°) to Celsius (C°), take F° temperature and subtract 32, multiply the result by 5 and divide the result by 9

To convert Celsius (C°) to Fahrenheit (F°), take C° temperature and multiply it by 9, divide the result by 5 and add 32

F°	C°	F°	C°	C°	F°	C°	F°
-40	-40.0	150	65.6	-38	-36.4	46	114.8
-35	-37.2	155	68.3	-36	-32.8	48	118.4
-30	-34.4	160	71.1	-34	-29.2	50	122
-25	-31.7	165	73.9	-32	-25.6	52	125.6
-20	-28.9	170	76.7	-30	-22	54	129.2
-15	-26.1	175	79.4	-28	-18.4	56	132.8
-10	-23.3	180	82.2	-26	-14.8	58	136.4
-5	-20.6	185	85.0	-24	-11.2	60	140
0	-17.8	190	87.8	-22	-7.6	62	143.6
1	-17.2	195	90.6	-20	-4	64	147.2
2	-16.7	200	93.3	-18	-0.4	66	150.8
3	-16.1	205	96.1	-16	3.2	68	154.4
4	-15.6	210	98.9	-14	6.8	70	158
5	-15.0	212	100.0	-12	10.4	72	161.6
10	-12.2	215	101.7	-10	14	74	165.2
15	-9.4	220	104.4	-8	17.6	76	168.8
20	-6.7	225	107.2	-6	21.2	78	172.4
25	-3.9	230	110.0	-4	24.8	80	176
30	-1.1	235	112.8	-2	28.4	82	179.6
35	1.7	240	115.6	0	32	84	183.2
40	4.4	245	118.3	2	35.6	86	186.8
45	7.2	250	121.1	4	39.2	88	190.4
50	10.0	255	123.9	6	42.8	90	194
55	12.8	260	126.7	8	46.4	92	197.6
60	15.6	265	129.4	10	50	94	201.2
65	18.3	270	132.2	12	53.6	96	204.8
70	21.1	275	135.0	14	57.2	98	208.4
75	23.9	280	137.8	16	60.8	100	212
80	26.7	285	140.6	18	64.4	102	215.6
85	29.4	290	143.3	20	68	104	219.2
90	32.2	295	146.1	22	71.6	106	222.8
95	35.0	300	148.9	24	75.2	108	226.4
100	37.8	305	151.7	26	78.8	110	230
105	40.6	310	154.4	28	82.4	112	233.6
110	43.3	315	157.2	30	86	114	237.2
115	46.1	320	160.0	32	89.6	116	240.8
120	48.9	325	162.8	34	93.2	118	244.4
125	51.7	330	165.6	36	96.8	120	248
130	54.4	335	168.3	38	100.4	122	251.6
135	57.2	340	171.1	40	104	124	255.2
140	60.0	345	173.9	42	107.6	126	258.8
145	62.8	350	176.7	44	111.2	128	262.4

LENGTH CONVERSION

To convert inches (in.) to millimeters (mm), multiply the number of inches by 25.4
To convert millimeters (mm) to inches (in.), multiply the number of millimeters by 0.04

Inches	Millimeters	Inches	Millimeters	Inches	Millimeters	Inches	Millimeters
0.0001	0.00254	0.005	0.1270	0.09	2.286	4	101.6
0.0002	0.00508	0.006	0.1524	0.1	2.54	5	127.0
0.0003	0.00762	0.007	0.1778	0.2	5.08	6	152.4
0.0004	0.01016	0.008	0.2032	0.3	7.62	7	177.8
0.0005	0.01270	0.009	0.2286	0.4	10.16	8	203.2
0.0006	0.01524	0.01	0.254	0.5	12.70	9	228.6
0.0007	0.01778	0.02	0.508	0.6	15.24	10	254.0
0.0008	0.02032	0.03	0.762	0.7	17.78	11	279.4
0.0009	0.02286	0.04	1.016	0.8	20.32	12	304.8
0.001	0.0254	0.05	1.270	0.9	22.86	13	330.2
0.002	0.0508	0.06	1.524	1	25.4	14	355.6
0.003	0.0762	0.07	1.778	2	50.8	15	381.0
0.004	0.1016	0.08	2.032	3	76.2	16	406.4

ENGLISH/METRIC CONVERSION: LENGTH

To convert inches (in.) to millimeters (mm), multiply the number of inches by 25.4
To convert millimeters (mm) to inches (in.), multiply the number of millimeters by 0.04

Inches		Millimeters	Inches		Millimeters	Inches		Millimeters
Fraction	Decimal	Decimal	Fraction	Decimal	Decimal	Fraction	Decimal	Decimal
1/64	0.016	0.397	11/32	0.344	8.731	11/16	0.688	17.463
1/32	0.031	0.794	23/64	0.359	9.128	45/64	0.703	17.859
3/64	0.047	1.191	3/8	0.375	9.525	23/32	0.719	18.256
1/16	0.063	1.588	25/64	0.391	9.922	47/64	0.734	18.653
5/64	0.078	1.984	13/32	0.406	10.319	3/4	0.750	19.050
3/32	0.094	2.381	27/64	0.422	10.716	49/64	0.766	19.447
7/64	0.109	2.778	7/16	0.438	11.113	25/32	0.781	19.844
1/8	0.125	3.175	29/64	0.453	11.509	51/64	0.797	20.241
9/64	0.141	3.572	15/32	0.469	11.906	13/16	0.813	20.638
5/32	0.156	3.969	31/64	0.484	12.303	53/64	0.828	21.034
11/64	0.172	4.366	1/2	0.500	12.700	27/32	0.844	21.431
3/16	0.188	4.763	33/64	0.516	13.097	55/64	0.859	21.828
13/64	0.203	5.159	17/32	0.531	13.494	7/8	0.875	22.225
7/32	0.219	5.556	35/64	0.547	13.891	57/64	0.891	22.622
15/64	0.234	5.953	9/16	0.563	14.288	29/32	0.906	23.019
1/4	0.250	6.350	37/64	0.578	14.684	59/64	0.922	23.416
17/64	0.266	6.747	19/32	0.594	15.081	15/16	0.938	23.813
9/32	0.281	7.144	39/64	0.609	15.478	61/64	0.953	24.209
19/64	0.297	7.541	5/8	0.625	15.875	31/32	0.969	24.606
5/16	0.313	7.938	41/64	0.641	16.272	63/64	0.984	25.003
21/64	0.328	8.334	21/32	0.656	16.669	1/1	1.000	25.400
			43/64	0.672	17.066			

Manual Set ISBN 1-4180-6174-3/Part No. 136174

Benefits of Chilton Labor Data:
- hundreds of new labor operations, including maintenance services and electronic system diagnosis
- estimate with confidence using trusted Chilton labor times for 1981 through current domestic and imported vehicles that consider the real world environment in which technicians work
- reference any of three labor times: standard, severe, and warranty
- accepted by most insurance and extended warranty companies
- makes and models conform to current Automotive Aftermarket Industry Association (AAIA) Standard
- eliminate confusion by using standardized terms across different OEMs

Labor Guide Manual Benefits:
- save your wrists for wrenching and enjoy our perfectly sized, easy-to-handle manuals one for domestic vehicles, the other for imported vehicles
- find labor times faster with:
    - tabs that display contents by manufacturer and model
    - two indexes–labor operations and systems–in each model group
    - manufacturers arranged alphabetically, and page numbering that includes manufacturer code so you know where you are in the book

Hardcover Manuals are 8 1/2" x 11", ©2007

Labor Guide CD-ROM Benefits:
- save time with automatically calculated labor charges, taxes, and parts as total job estimates
- increase shop legitimacy with printable professional estimates for your customers and worksheets for your technicians
- keep track of customers, prior estimates, and your own parts or package jobs with less paperwork

CD ISBN 1-4180-6171-9/Part No. 136171
©2007

Previous Year Editions:
Chilton 2006 Labor Guide Manual, ISBN 1-4180-1688-8/Part No. 131688
Chilton 2006 Labor Guide CD-ROM, ISBN 1-4180-0605-X/Part No. 130605

Chilton 2008® Service Manuals include 12 manuals covering DaimlerChrysler, Ford, General Motors, Asian, and European vehicles. Users will be expertly provided with the most currently available information to assist in daily activities. These new, reliable, and comprehensive manuals provide essential information, allowing users to accurately and efficiently diagnose and repair. Step-by-step procedures and helpful illustrations provide easy references for jobs. These new service manuals cover 2006 and 2007 models, plus any available 2008 models.

Service Manual Benefits:

• twelve-volume manual set, organized by vehicle manufacturer, provides more than 2000 pages of expertly written content
• access new year, make, and model information without repeating previous edition's content
• comprehensive, technically detailed content—including exploded view illustrations, diagnostics and specification charts— arranged alphabetically by model group for quick, easy access

2008 Editions

Chilton 2008 DaimlerChrysler Service Manuals (2 volume set)—ISBN 1-4283-2204-3/Part No. 142204
Chilton 2008 Ford Service Manuals (2 volume set)—ISBN 1-4283-2208-6/Part No. 142208
Chilton 2008 General Motors Service Manuals (2 volume set)—ISBN 1-4283-2211-6/Part No. 142211
Chilton 2008 Asian Service Manuals (5 volume set)—ISBN 1-4283-2214-0/Part No. 142214
Chilton 2008 European Service Manual—ISBN 1-4283-2220-5/Part No. 142220

Domestic manuals available December 2007
Import manuals December 2008
Manuals are 8 1/2" x 11", ©2007

2006 Editions

Chilton 2006 DaimlerChrysler Mechanical Service Manual—ISBN 1-4180-0600-9/Part No. 130600
Chilton 2006 Ford Mechanical Service Manual—ISBN 1-4180-0601-7/Part No. 130601
Chilton 2006 General Motors Mechanical Service Manual—ISBN 1-4180-0602-5/Part No. 130602
Chilton 2006 Asian Mechanical Service Manual—Volume I—ISBN 1-4180-0947-4/Part No. 130947
Chilton 2006 Asian Mechanical Service Manual—Volume II—ISBN 1-4180-0948-2/Part No. 130948
Chilton 2006 Asian Mechanical Service Manual—Volume III—ISBN 1-4180-0949-0/Part No. 130949
Chilton 2006 Asian Mechanical Service Manual—3 Volume Set—ISBN 1-4180-0603-3/Part No. 130603
Chilton 2006 European Mechanical Service Manual—ISBN 1-4180-0604-1/Part No. 130604

Manuals are 8 1/2" x 11", ©2006

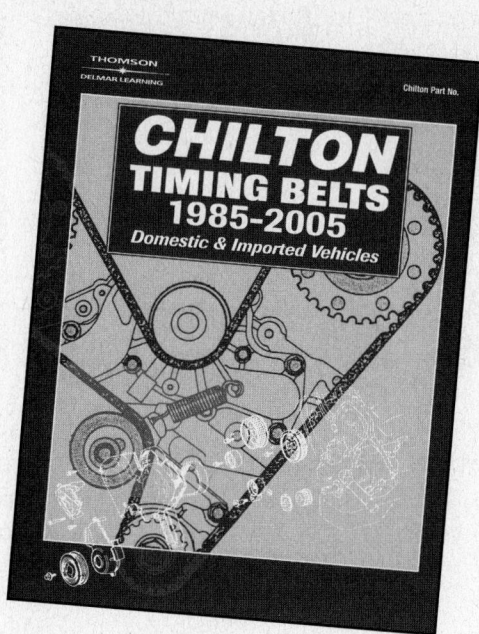

Chilton Timing Belts, 1985-2005

Chilton
ISBN 1-4018-9880-7/Part No. 129880

Timing belt procedures can represent increased profits for automotive repair shops and service stations, and this manual contains all the information automotive technicians need to properly service timing belts on domestic and imported cars, vans, and light trucks through 2005 models. Clear, straightforward procedures, illustrations, and specifications help to communicate 20 years of vehicle applications for fast, accurate inspection, replacement, and tensioning of timing belts. Readers will learn step-by-step how to perform key procedures both quickly and safely, while learning the correct labor time to charge for the service. OEM-recommended replacement intervals for proper maintenance of customer's vehicles are also featured.

Benefits

- detailed illustrations clearly demonstrate important concepts, such as how to correctly align camshaft and crankshaft timing marks, and how to simplify serpentine belt installation
- readers are made aware of potential hazards and time-wasting practices that can impede safe and profitable service procedures
- special tools are identified so that completing the service is as easy and quick as possible

544 pp, 8 1/2" x 11", softcover, ©2006

The *Chilton® Perennial Editions* contain repair and maintenance information for popular mechanical systems that may not be available elsewhere. They offer a wide range of repair information on cars, trucks, vans, and SUVs dating back to the early 1960s, and as current as 2002. Information for 1993 and later model years includes scheduled maintenance interval charts.

Benefits:

- covers the most common vehicle models found in the repair aftermarket today
- gain quick understanding of systems using exploded-view illustrations, diagrams, and charts
- simplify tough jobs with easy-to-follow removal and installation instructions for heater core and other components
- obtain complete coverage of repair procedures from drive train to chassis and associated components

Auto Repair Manual, 1998-2002, 1,426 pages
ISBN 0-8019-9362-8/Part No. 9362
Auto Repair Manual, 1993-1997, 2,064 pages
ISBN 0-8019-7919-6/Part No. 7919
Auto Repair Manual, 1988-1992, 1,284 pages
ISBN 0-8019-7906-4/Part No. 7906
Auto Repair Manual, 1980-1987, 1,344 pages
ISBN 0-8019-7670-7/Part No. 7670

Import Car Repair Manual, 1998-2002, 1,792 pps
ISBN 0-8019-9363-6/Part No. 9363
Import Car Repair Manual, 1993-1997, 2,080 pps
ISBN 0-8019-7920-X/Part No. 7920
Import Car Repair Manual, 1988-1992, 1,632 pages
ISBN 0-8019-7907-2/Part No. 7907
Import Car Repair Manual, 1980-1987, 1,488 pages
ISBN 0-8019-7672-3/Part No. 7672

Truck & Van Repair Manual, 1998-2002, 1,408 pages
ISBN 0-8019-9364-4/Part No. 9364
Truck & Van Repair Manual, 1993-1997, 2,096 pages
ISBN 0-8019-7921-8/Part No. 7921
Truck & Van Repair Manual, 1991-1995, 1,664 pages
ISBN 0-8019-7911-0/Part No. 7911
Truck & Van Repair Manual, 1986-1990, 1,536 pages
ISBN 0-8019-7902-1/Part No. 7902
Truck & Van Repair Manual, 1979-1986, 1,440 pages
ISBN 0-8019-7655-3/Part No. 7655

SUV Repair Manual, 1998-2002, 1,292 pages
ISBN 0-8019-9365-2/Part No. 9365

Hardcover manuals are 8 1/2" x 11".

Chilton Collector's Editions—*Reference Manuals for Vintage Vehicles*
Auto Repair Manual, 1964-1971, ISBN 0-8019-5974-8/Part No. 5974,
Truck & Van Repair Manual, 1961-1971, ISBN 0-8019-6198-X/Part No. 6198
Truck & Van Repair Manual, 1971-1978, ISBN 0-8019-7012-1/Part No. 7012

new editions!

ASE Test Preparation Series, 4E (A1-A8, L1, P2, X1, & C1)
ISBN 1-4180-3954-3
Part No. 133954

Each title in this popular series features the most up-to-date ASE task list available, along with practice test questions like those typically seen on an ASE certification exam to help users feel more comfortable and prepared to pass the actual test.

KEY FEATURES

- all ASE task lists are fully up-to-date, and completely current test preparation questions reflect the most recent ASE task changes for the broadest knowledge possible
- readers are given scores of opportunities to check their understanding of critical concepts through sample problems, refresher materials, and competency-specific test questions
- overviews of each task make an easy reference point for help in answering difficult ASE questions

Softcover manuals are 8½" x 11", SC, 1-Color, ©2006

(A1) Engine Repair, 4E
ISBN 1-4180-3878-4
Part No. 133878
The A1 manual covers the following topics: General Engine Diagnosis, Cylinder Head and Valve Train Diagnosis and Repair, Engine Block Diagnosis and Repair, Lubrication and Cooling Systems Diagnosis and Repair, Fuel, Electrical, Ignition and Exhaust Systems Inspection and Service.

(A2) Transmissions and Transaxles, 4E
ISBN 1-4180-3879-2
Part No. 133879
The A2 manual covers the following topics: General Transmission/ Transaxle Diagnosis (Mechanical/ Hydraulic Systems and Electronic Systems), Transmission/Transaxle Maintenance and Adjustment, In-Vehicle Transmission/ Transaxle Repair, Off-Vehicle Transmission/ Transaxle Repair.

(A3) Manual Drive Train and Axles, 4E
ISBN 1-4180-3880-6
Part No. 133880
The A3 manual covers the following topics: Clutch Diagnosis and Repair, Transmission Diagnosis and Repair, Transaxle Diagnosis and Repair, Drive Shaft/Half Shaft and Universal Joint/ Constant Velocity (CV) Joint Diagnosis and Repair (Front and Rear Wheel Drive), Rear Axle Diagnosis and Repair, Four Wheel Drive/All Wheel Drive Component Diagnosis and Repair.

(A4) Suspension and Steering, 4E
ISBN 1-4180-3881-4
Part No. 133881
The A4 manual covers the following topics: Steering Systems Diagnosis and Repair (Steering Columns and Manual Steering Gears, Power Assisted Steering Units, Steering Linkage), Suspension Systems Diagnosis and Repair (Front Suspensions, Rear Suspensions, Miscellaneous Services), Wheel Alignment Diagnosis, Adjustment and Repair, and Wheel and Tire Diagnosis and Repair.

(A5) Brakes, 4E
ISBN 1-4180-3882-2
Part No. 133882
The A5 manual covers the following topics: Hydraulic System Diagnosis and Repair, Drum Brake Diagnosis and Repair, Disc Brake Diagnosis and Repair, Power Assist Units Diagnosis and Repair, Miscellaneous Systems Diagnosis and Repair, Electronic Brake Control Systems, Antilock Brake Systems (ABS) Diagnosis and Repair.

(A6) Electrical-Electronic Systems, 4E
ISBN 1-4180-3883-0
Part No. 133883
The A6 manual covers the following topics: General Electrical/Electronic Systems Diagnosis, Battery Diagnosis and Service, Starting Systems Diagnosis and Repair, Charging Systems Diagnosis and Repair, Lighting Systems Diagnosis and Repair, Gauges, Warning Devices and Driver Information Systems Diagnosis and Repair, Horn and Wiper/ Washer Diagnosis and Repair, Accessories Diagnosis and Repair.

(A7) Heating and Air Conditioning, 4E
ISBN 1-4180-3884-9
Part No. 133884
The A7 manual covers the following topics: A/C System Service Diagnosis and Repair, Refrigeration System Component Diagnosis and Repair, Heating and Engine Cooling Systems Diagnosis and Repair, Operating Systems and Related Controls Diagnosis and Repair, Refrigerant Recovery, Recycling, Handling and Retrofit.

(A8) Engine Performance, 4E
ISBN 1-4180-3885-7
Part No. 133885
The A8 manual covers the following topics: General Engine Diagnosis, Ignition System Diagnosis and Repair, Fuel, Air Induction, and Exhaust Systems Diagnosis and Repair, Emissions Control Systems Diagnosis and Repair (Including OBDII), Computerized Engine controls Diagnosis and Repair (Including OBDII), Engine Electrical Systems diagnosis and Repair.

(L1) Advanced Engine Performance, 4E
ISBN 1-4180-3888-1
Part No. 133888
The L1 manual covers the following topics: General Powertrain Diagnosis, Computerized Powertrain Controls Diagnosis (Including OBDII), Ignition System Diagnosis, Fuel Systems and Air Induction Systems Diagnosis, Emission Control Systems Diagnosis, I/M Failure Diagnosis.

(X1) Exhaust Systems 4E
ISBN 1-4180-3886-5
Part No. 133886
The X1 manual covers the following topics: Exhaust Systems Inspection and Repair, Emissions Systems Diagnosis, Exhaust System Fabrication, Exhaust System Installation, Exhaust System Repair Regulations.

(P2) Automobile Parts Specialist, 4E
ISBN 1-4180-3887-3
Part No. 133887
The P2 manual covers the following topics: General Operations, Customer Relations and Sales Skills, Vehicle Systems Knowledge, Vehicle Identification, Cataloging Skills, Inventory Management, Merchandising.

(C1) Service Consultant, 4E
ISBN 1-4180-3889-X
Part No. 133889
The C1 manual covers the following topics: Communications, Product Knowledge, Sales Skills and Shop Operations.

Softcover Manuals are 8½" x 11", 1-Color, ©2006

ASE Test Preparation Series Español
(Complete Set Examenes A1-A8, L1, P2, X1)
ISBN 1-4018-1530-8
Part No. 21530

SPANISH AUTOMOTIVE SERIES
(A1) Reparación de Motores, 2a Edición
Part No. 21014
(10-Digit ISBN 1-4018-1014-4)
(A2) Transmission Automática/Eje de Transmission Automática, 2a Edición
Part No. 21015
(10-Digit ISBN 1-4018-1015-2)
(A3) Tren de y Mando Ejes Manuales, 2a Edición
Part No. 21016
(10-Digit ISBN 1-4018-1016-0)
(A4) Suspensión y Dirección, 2a Edición
Part No. 21017
(10-Digit ISBN 1-4018-1017-9)
(A5) Frenos, 2a Edición
Part No. 21018
(10-Digit ISBN 1-4018-1018-7)
(A6) Sistemas Eléctricos/ Electrónicos, 2a Edición
Part No. 21019
(10-Digit ISBN 1-4018-1019-5)
(A7) Calefacción y Aire Acondicionado, 2a Edición
Part No. 21020
(10-Digit ISBN 1-4018-1020-9)
(A8) Funcionamiento de Motores, 2a Edición
Part No. 21021
(10-Digit ISBN 1-4018-1021-7)
(L1) Especialista en el Funciommiato Avansado de Motores, 2a Edición
Part No. 21022
(10-Digit ISBN 1-4018-1022-5)
(P2) Especialista en Partes de Automovil, 2a Edición
Part No. 21023
(10-Digit ISBN 1-4018-1023-3)
(X1) Sistemas de Escape, 2a Edición
Part No. 21024
(10-Digit ISBN 1-4018-1024-1)

The ASE "Passing Lane" Package

(Complete Set A1-A8, L1, P2)
ISBN 0-7668-4338-6

The most comprehensive test preparation for Automotive Tests A1-A8, L1, and P2. Combining the most thorough ASE Test Preparation books with the latest in ASE videos, this package provides a comprehensive program of self-study for the automotive ASE Tests.

EACH BOOK IN THE SERIES FEATURES:
- test-taking strategies
- tasks lists and overview
- sample test questions
- ASE-style exams
- explanations to the answers
- glossary of terms

EACH VIDEO IN THE SERIES FEATURES:
- easy to follow videos emphasizing safety throughout
- major task areas and topics for each of the ASE exams
- Activity Sheets to help comprehend and retain information

(A1) Automotive Engine Repair Book/Video
ISBN 0-7668-4181-2
(A2) Automotive Transmissions and Transaxles Book/Video
ISBN 0-7668-4182-0
(A3) Automotive Manual Drive Trains and Axles Book/Video
ISBN 0-7668-4183-9
(A4) Automotive Suspension and Steering Book/Video
ISBN 0-7668-4184-7
(A5) Automotive Brakes Book/Video
ISBN 0-7668-4185-5
(A6) Automotive Electrical-Electronics Systems Book/Video
ISBN 0-7668-4186-3
(A7) Automotive Heating and Air Conditioning Book/Video
ISBN 0-7668-4187-1
(A8) Automotive Engine Performance Book/Video
ISBN 0-7668-4188-X
(L1) Automotive Advanced Engine Performance Book/Video
ISBN 0-7668-4189-8
(P2) Automobile Parts Specialist Book/Video
ISBN 0-7668-4190-1

ASE Test Preparation Series for Engine Machinist

(Complete Set M1-M3)
ISBN 0-7668-6283-6
Part No. 16283

These books are intended for automotive technicians who are preparing to take one or more of the Engine Machinist ASE examinations (for either gas or diesel engines). Each manual combines refresher materials with an abundance of sample test questions, as well as a wealth of information regarding test-taking strategies and the types of questions found in an ASE exam. In addition to the questions, thorough explanations are provided as to why each answer is correct or incorrect.

KEY FEATURES
- the History section explains why the exams are important to the industry
- test-taking strategies help prepare technicians for the environment they will encounter during the actual exam
- task lists and overviews help technicians focus their attention
- glossary of terms allows technicians to use the manual as a reference tool after they have passed the exam

(M1) Cylinder Head Specialist
ISBN 0-7668-6280-1
Part No. 16280

(M2) Cylinder Block Specialist
ISBN 0-7668-6281-X
Part No. 16281

(M3) Assembly Specialist
ISBN 0-7668-6282-8
Part No. 16282

Softcover manuals are 8½" x 11", 1-Color, ©2002

Automotive Technician Certification (ATC) Challenge CD-ROM Series

These exciting interactive CD-ROMs have been designed to prepare students and technicians for successful completion of the Collision or Automotive ASE task areas. This multimedia software assesses strengths and weaknesses by identifying topics needing further study while allowing users to review ASE task areas at their own pace. Not only are the *ATC Challenge 3.0* and *ATC Challenge for Collision Repair* the ultimate in test preparation, but they are also excellent learning tools!

KEY FEATURES
- explanation and hints for each answer aid in reader comprehension, critical thinking, and retention
- rationale for every answer, whether right or wrong
- "Notes" allow users to comment on any topic for future reference
- clear, detailed reports allow users to identify topics needing further review
- true ASE style questions
- LAN compatible

ATC Challenge 3.0 CD-ROM
ISBN 0-7668-2982-0
Part No. 12982
Covers tests A1 through A8, L1, P2, and X1. While all of the tests have been updated to the latest ASE task lists, particular attention has been paid to the L1 test and content on composite vehicles and related questions.
CD-ROM, ©2001

ATC Challenge for P2 CD-ROM
ISBN 0-7668-1827-6
CD-ROM, ©2000

ATC Challenge CD-ROM for Collision Repair
ISBN 0-7668-1511-0
Covers tests B2-B6.

Technician Test Preparation— Automotive Bilingual Series

Now both English and Spanish speaking technicians seeking ASE certification can access online test preparation material with ease! The *TTP-Automotive Bilingual* series for automotive training and certification provides up-to-date technology and content for tests A1-A8, L1, P2, X1, and C1. An easy-to-use format combined with helpful remediation addresses the unique needs of technicians by clearly demonstrating text-based theory for enhanced learning and retention. Not only is *TTP-Automotive Bilingual* the ultimate in test preparation, but it is also an excellent learning tool!

Technician Test Preparation Benefits:

- maps to the latest ASE task lists familiarize users with the actual work they should be able to do as technicians when taking the ASE tests
- well-illustrated remediation offered via digitized video clips, animations, and high impact graphics further explains key concepts for a more effective learning process
- practice questions provide helpful hints, insight into right and wrong answers, and links to further study specific task areas
- detailed reports provide accurate test results and instant feedback for selected test types so that users can pinpoint the task areas needing improvement
- switch between Spanish and English versions at the click of a button

Call Your Delmar Cengage Learning Sales Rep for Part Numbers & Pricing

Visit www.TechnicianTestPrep.com to see the latest modules and a free demo!

Automotive Technician Certification Test Preparation Manual, 3E
Don Knowles

ISBN 1-4180-4926-3
Part No. 134926

Filled with updated task list theory, practice tests, and abundant, demonstrative graphics, this revised edition provides all the latest information required to sufficiently prepare technicians to pass each of the A1-A8, and L1 ASE certification exams. Each chapter begins with a pretest that indicates the depth of preparation required to become familiar with the information in the chapter, followed by a description of each ASE task and the must-have information related to the task. ASE-type questions at the end of each chapter appear in the same format as on actual ASE tests to further prepare users to pass each exam.

KEY FEATURES

- current information provides practice questions which match the latest ASE task list
- answers to pretest questions and helpful analysis at the end of each chapter provide learners with faster access to accurate information
- supportive "Hints" throughout each chapter help users work through the process of determining the correct answers to the questions

CONTENTS

Engine Repair. Automatic Transmission/Transaxle. Manual Drive Train and Axles. Suspension and Steering. Brakes. Electrical/Electronic Systems. Heating, Ventilation, and Air Conditioning Systems. Engine Performance. Advanced Engine Performance.

656 pp, 8½" x 11", SC, 1-Color, ©2007

NATEF Standards Job Sheets
ISBN 0-7668-6375-1
(Complete Set: A1-A8)

Each of our eight *NATEF (National Automotive Technicians Education Foundation) Standards Job Sheets* workbooks has been thoughtfully designed to assist users in gaining valuable job preparedness skills and mastering specific technical competencies required for success as a professional automotive technician. The entire series is based on current NATEF standards.

Central to each manual are well-designed and easy-to-read job sheets, each of which contains specific, performance-based objectives, lists of required tools and materials, safety precautions, plus step-by-step procedures to lead users to completion of shop activities.

Key Features

- easy to use in any automotive education or training program in which NATEF coverage is desired
- completed Job Sheets may be kept as records, providing tangible evidence that instructors are addressing all NATEF tasks while paving the way for program certification

JOB SHEETS AVAILABLE FOR:

(A1) Automotive Engine Repair, 0-7668-6367-0
(A2) Automatic Transmissions and Transaxles, 0-7668-6368-9
(A3) Manual Drive Trains and Axles, 0-7668-6369-7
(A4) Automotive Suspension and Steering, 0-7668-6370-0
(A5) Automotive Brakes, 0-7668-6371-9
(A6) Automotive Electrical and Electronic Systems, 0-7668-6372-7
(A7) Automotive Heating and Air Conditioning, 0-7668-6373-5
(A8) Automotive Engine Performance, 0-7668-6374-3

All share the following information: 8½" x 11", softcover, ©2002

This pioneering eight-book series offers automotive service shop owners and those wanting to be shop owners the necessary business and customer service skills to run a successful automotive service facility.

The series covers three main topical areas: personnel management, business management, and sales and marketing. Each book provides a framework to help technicians make consistent, high-quality, and productive service a part of every day shop operations. According to the author, "Great performance coupled with increased customer loyalty, trust, and operational excellence will almost always result in increased profits."

Automotive Service Management Series Benefits:

- real-world approach reflects author's experience as a fourth generation technician, a repair & service company owner, and an automotive industry trainer
- all-inclusive coverage spans from designing an automotive repair facility floor plan through financial management techniques, customer/staff relations, and more
- length of each book makes it easy to incorporate this series into workshops, seminars, and training/education courses
- information is available "as is" or for customization

Total Customer Relationship Management
        ISBN 1-4018-2657-1/Part No. 22657
From Intent to Implementation
        ISBN 1-4018-2658-X/Part No. 22658
Operational Excellence
        ISBN 1-4018-2659-8/Part No. 22659
Building a Team
        ISBN 1-4018-2660-1/Part No. 22660
The High Performance Shop
        ISBN 1-4018-2661-X/Part No. 22661
Safety Communications
        ISBN 1-4018-2662-8/Part No. 22662
Managing Dollars with Sense
        ISBN 1-4018-2663-6/Part No. 22663
Operations Management
        ISBN 1-4018-2665-2/Part No. 22665
Entire Set of 8 Books
        ISBN 1-4018-2499-4/Part No. 2499

Softcover manuals are 8 1/2" x 11", ©2003

ABOUT THE AUTHOR

Mitch Schneider is a fourth generation mechanic/technician and is a frequent speaker at major conventions and meetings of automotive industry trade organizations. Schneider is also an award-winning journalist and is a regular contributor and senior contributing editor for *Motor Age* magazine. He provides commentary on the evolving relationship between service dealers, jobbers, warehouse directors and manufacturers.

Schneider has also appeared on the TNN cable show "Truckin' USA" where he hosted the "Tech Tips" segment. In addition to operating the award-winning Schneider's Automotive for 22 years in Simi Valley, CA, he is also the president and founder of Schneider's Future-Tech, a service company specializing in conducting management seminars for automotive service dealers, jobbers, warehouse distribution companies, and manufacturers.

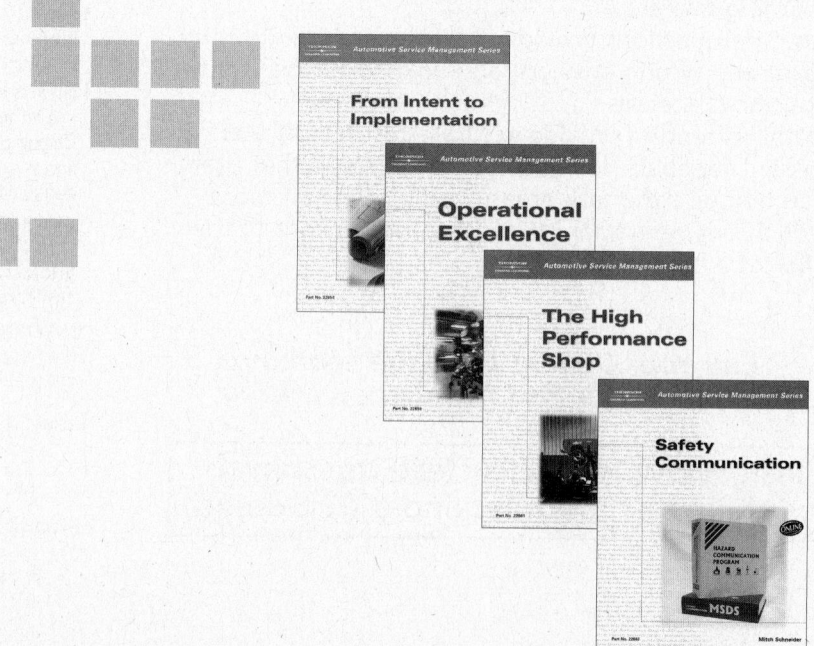

Introduction to OBDII
Roy Cox

ISBN 1-4180-1220-3/Part No. 131220

Here's an easy-to-understand, logical guide to the diagnosis and repair of today's complex and sophisticated automotive control systems! *Introduction to On-Board Diagnostics (OBD II)* readers will learn the fundamentals of how to perform diagnostic procedures, and be provided with valuable reference material for diagnosing and troubleshooting components and circuits. This book provides a simple, logical approach to explain the operation of the OBD II process and will teach the reader how to quickly spot problems and identify components that are not functioning correctly. In addition, the interrelationships between the fuel delivery, emission control, ignition, and accessory systems are clearly addressed and explained. This truly unique introduction to OBDII systems, and the troubleshooting of components and circuits, features an accompanying interactive diagnostic CD-ROM that leads readers through realistic trouble-code scenarios to reinforce its diagnostic and repair.

Benefits
- "quick hit" troubleshooting tricks teach readers how to diagnose problems when there is no stored OBDII trouble code, as well as how to handle situations where the trouble code is actually set by a basic mechanical problem rather than a failure of the indicated component
- information is useful for those who wish to expand their capabilities from more basic, mechanical repairs to complex electronics and drivability diagnosis and repair
- a substantial portion of the content focuses on logical troubleshooting that can be done without expensive, complicated test equipment and special tools
- also useful as a preparation manual for the ASE Certification exams

CONTENTS
Chapter 1- Introduction, Chapter 2- Evolution of OBD, Chapter 3- OBDII Terminology, Chapter 4- System Operating Protocols, Chapter 5- System Monitors, Chapter 6- Drive Cycles, Chapter 7- Diagnostic Trouble Codes (DTC's), Chapter 8- Diagnostic Routines

256 pp, 8 1/2" x 11", softcover, ©2006

SUPPLEMENTS
Diagnostic Tool CD-ROM 1-4180-1221-1/Part No. 131221
Instructor's Guide 1-4180-1222-X

TAKE YOUR TECHNICIAN TRAINING TO THE NEXT LEVEL

Comprehensive Skill Assessment Tool (CSAT) — Automotive

The online Comprehensive Skill Assessment Tool for Automotive helps instructors and trainers implement the necessary training programs for individual areas needing improvement over various key automotive topics. Within each key topic, strategic learning areas are measured to account for knowledge of theory, hands-on application, and diagnostics. Pre- and post-assessment phases assist with the identification of areas needing improvement. The combined phases of education and training, and post-assessment allow instructors to track skill level growth and target specific areas needing development and more teaching.

Benefits
- a low-cost solution benefiting trainers and students
- individual users can take tests online to identify areas of strength and areas needing improvement
- account set-up that enables instructors to assess and track the results of individual users

Call Your Delmar Cengage Learning Sales Rep for Part Numbers & Pricing

Visit **www.skillanalysis.com** to see the latest modules and a free demo!

CHILTON®PRO

ChiltonPRO is the new alternative for technicians who want a cost-effective electronic automotive repair system. It combines Chilton's famous automotive repair information into one solution covering more than 20 years of domestic and imported vehicles. The information is delivered online or on DVD-ROMs–your choice–updated regularly throughout the year.

Online Monthly Payment
Part No. 133002
13-Digit ISBN: 978-14180-3002-5
(10-Digit ISBN: 1-4180-3002-3)

DVD Monthly Payment
Part No. 133003
13-Digit ISBN: 978-1-4180-3003-2
(10-Digit ISBN: 1-4180-3003-1)

Online Annual Payment
Part No. 132876
13-Digit ISBN: 978-14180-2877-0
(10-Digit ISBN: 1-4180-2876-2)

DVD Annual Payment
Part No. 132877
13-Digit ISBN: 978-1-4180-2877-0
(10-Digit ISBN: 1-4180-2877-0)

Contact your sales representative for a free demo or visit www.chiltonpro.com

BENEFITS

- create better estimates using labor times developed with real-world factors
- save money by accurately identifying and solving engine performance problems
- save time with expert guidance through OBDII diagnostics
- increase efficiency by understanding system operation through detailed explanations and theory
- increase profits using Technical Service Bulletins to ensure that work is not going unperformed
- execute effective repairs by viewing cutaway diagrams and actual photos
- make better use of your time with information that can be found quicker using AAIA standards for year, make, and model
- increase confidence levels by always being able to print what you need
- eliminate guesswork with quick reference to critical specifications in helpful tables
- spend less on repair information

Automatically uploaded into online version or new DVD-ROM sets sent to customers. Initial content as follows:

- OEM recommended maintenance schedules, 1990–current
- trusted Chilton labor times, 1981–current
- step-by-step mechanical procedures, 1961–current
- diagnostics designed by instructors, 1990–current (Imported models through 2003)
- OEM Technical Service Bulletins, 1986–current

System Requirements:
Web browser

- Internet Explorer 5.0 or above (recommended)
- Firefox 1.5 or above
- High-speed internet connection
- Adobe Acrobat Reader 5.0 or above

DVD-ROMs:
The DVD versions of ChiltonPRO requires:

- Processor: Pentium II or equivalent
- Operating systems: Windows 2000, or Windows XP
- Memory: 128 RAM minimum
- Disk Space: 700 MB
- DVD-ROM drive
- Internet connection required for web authorization (product authorization also available via telephone)